Collectors' Information Bureau®
COLLECTIBLES
MARKET GUIDE & PRICE INDEX

Limited Edition: Plates • Figurines • Cottages • Bells • Graphics • Ornaments • Dolls • Steins

Fourteenth Edition

Your Complete Source for Information on Limited Edition Collectibles

Collectors' Information Bureau
Barrington, Illinois

Copyright© 1996 by Collectors' Information Bureau

All Right Reserved

Distributed by Wallace-Homestead,
a division of Chilton Book Company

No part of this book may be reproduced, transmitted or stored
in any form or by any means, electronic, or mechanical, without
prior written permission from the publisher.

Manufactured in the United States of America

Library of Congress Catalog Card Number: 95-71406

ISBN 0-930785-22-3 Collectors' Information Bureau

ISBN 0-87069-753-6 Wallace-Homestead

ISSN 1068-4808

—————— CREDITS ——————

Printing:
Wm. C. Brown Communications, Dubuque, Iowa

Book Design and Graphics:
Wright Design, Grand Rapids, Michigan

Original Photography (covers and color section):
Camacho & Assoc., Dundee, Illinois

Design of Cover Artwork:
Ad Design Inc., Grand Rapids, Michigan

Contributing Writers:
Catherine Bloom
Gail Cohen
Kim Fynewever
Jack McCarthy
Kelly Womer

Inquiries to the Collectors' Information Bureau should be mailed to:
5065 Shoreline Rd., Suite 200, Barrington, Illinois 60010
Phone (847) 842-2200

FORWARD

Dear Collector,

I am pleased to present you with the latest edition of the COLLECTIBLES MARKET GUIDE & PRICE INDEX. It represents the culmination of a year's efforts that began with in-depth interviews of industry experts, followed by exhaustive research on clubs, artists, and secondary market values. The result is an "encyclopedia of collectibles" that includes over 80 feature articles, profiles of 200 artists and secondary market prices for more than 50,000 limited edition collectibles.

In the 560 pages that follow, you'll learn about insuring your collectibles, as well as the fine points of buying and selling on the secondary market. You'll read about how to best care for your treasures so they maintain their beauty and value for years to come. And you'll look ahead with us as we share the insights of dozens of industry experts, who have helped us take a glimpse at where the future of collectibles is headed. You'll even learn to "talk collectibles" with the help of our extensive "Glossary of Terms," featuring the most commonly used words and phrases in the field of collectibles.

In the last 200 pages of this book, you'll find the most comprehensive Price Index to limited edition collectibles at your fingertips. Our prices are gathered by surveying over 300 secondary market dealers. These dealers report back to us the actual prices paid by collectors in recent purchases of limited edition collectibles that have been retired or closed. We know of no more up-to-date and thorough resource available to collectors that covers the categories of plates, dolls, figurines, cottages, bells, steins, ornaments and graphics. Its extensive use by the insurance industry is a testimony to its value.

We hope you'll enjoy the opportunity that this book —as well as the other Collectors' Information Bureau newsletters, directories and price guides — offers you to enhance your collecting hobby.

On behalf of the 83 companies who participate as members of the Collectors' Information Bureau and our staff of writers and researchers, I invite you to join us on a fascinating trip through the wonderful world of collectibles. We're glad you could join us!

Cordially,

Peggy Veltri

Peggy Veltri
Executive Director

A WORD OF THANKS...

A Special Thank You to the Staff of the Collectors' Information Bureau...
Joan Barcal, Sue Knappen, Lynda Stary, Carol Van Elderen, Debbie Wojtysiak and Cindy Zagumny

To the CIB Panel of Dealers...
Finally, we wish to thank the panel of over 300 limited edition retailers and secondary market experts whose knowledge and dedication have helped make our Price Index possible. We wish we could recognize each of them by name, but they have agreed that to be singled out in this manner might hinder their ability to maintain an unbiased view of the marketplace.

COLLECTORS' INFORMATION BUREAU
MEMBERSHIP ROSTER

Collectors' Information Bureau (CIB) is a not-for-profit business league whose mission is to serve and educate collectors, members and dealers, and to provide them with credible, comprehensive and authoritative information on limited edition collectibles and their current values.

Ace Product Management Group, Inc.

Kurt S. Adler, Inc.

Amaranth Productions

Amazze

Anheuser-Busch, Inc.

Annalee Mobilitee Dolls, Inc.

ANRI U.S.

Arcadian Pewter, Inc.

Giuseppe Armani Society

The Art of Glynda Turley

The Ashton-Drake Galleries

Attic Babies

Autom

BAND Creations

The Boyds Collection Ltd.

The Bradford Exchange

Brandywine Woodcrafts, Inc.

Byers' Choice Ltd.

Cardew Design

Carlton Cards
    A Division of American Greetings

Cast Art Industries, Inc.

Cavanagh Group International

Character Collectibles/
    Calabar Creations

Christopher Radko

Crystal World

Dear Artistic Sculpture

Department 56, Inc.

The Walt Disney Company

Duncan Royale

Enesco Corporation

Ertl Collectibles

FFSC, Inc./Charming Tails™

FJ Designs Inc./Makers of the
    Cat's Meow Village

The Fenton Art Glass Company

Flambro Imports

Forma Vitrum

The Franklin Mint

Margaret Furlong Designs

Ganz

Gartlan USA

Georgetown Collection

Goebel of North America

Great American Taylor
    Collectibles Corp.

The Greenwich Workshop

The Hamilton Collection*

Hand & Hammer Silversmiths

Harbour Lights

Harmony Kingdom

Hawthorne Village

Hudson Creek/ The Lance Corporation

M.I. Hummel Club*

Imperial Graphics, Ltd.

Ladie and Friends, Inc.

Ron Lee's World of Clowns

George Z. Lefton Co.

Legends/Starlite Originals, Inc.

Lenox Collections

Lilliput Lane

Lladró Society

Seymour Mann, Inc.

Maruri U.S.A.

Media Arts Group, Inc.

Michael's Limited

Midwest of Cannon Falls

Miss Martha Originals, Inc.

Old World Christmas

Pacific Rim Import Corp.

Possible Dreams

Precious Art Inc.

Pulaski Furniture Corporation

R.R. Creations, Inc.

Reco International Corp.*

Roman, Inc.*

Royal Copenhagen/Bing & Grondahl

Royal Doulton

Sarah's Attic

Shelia's Collectibles

Shube's Manufacturing

Swarovski America Limited

The Tudor Mint, Ltd.

United Design Corporation

WACO Products Corporation

Walnut Ridge Collectibles

*Charter Member

FRONT COVER

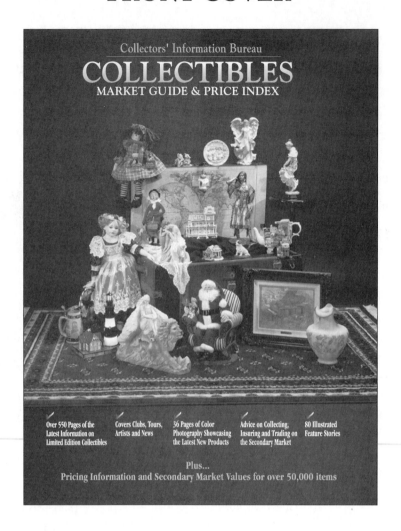

Collectors' Information Bureau

COLLECTIBLES
MARKET GUIDE & PRICE INDEX

Over 550 Pages of the Latest Information on Limited Edition Collectibles

Covers Clubs, Tours, Artists and News

36 Pages of Color Photography Showcasing the Latest New Products

Advice on Collecting, Insuring and Trading on the Secondary Market

80 Illustrated Feature Stories

Plus...
Pricing Information and Secondary Market Values for over 50,000 items

On top of the chest, from left to right: Attic Babies' "Savannah's 1st Rag Doll," Flambro's *Pocket Dragons* "Christmas Skates" & "De-pressing," Christopher Radko's "Frosty Weather," Enesco's *Cherished Teddies* "Mother's Day," and Roman Inc.'s Vanessa-"Heavenly Maiden" from the *Seraphim Classics™ Collection*. On the stand: Giuseppe Armani's "Allegra."

In the chest, from left to right: Byers' Choice Ltd.'s "Nanny," Lladró's "Lost in Dreams," Michael's Limited's "Angel of the Sea II" from Brian Baker's *Déjà Vu Collection*, Lilliput Lane's "Fill'er Up & Check the Oil" from the *Coca Cola Country Collection*, Pulaski Furniture Corp.'s "Curios Henry," Legends' *Gallery Editions* "Wind on Still Water," and Cardew's "'Lilliput Lane' Market Stall."

On the floor: Anheuser-Busch Inc.'s "Collectors Edition Official Centennial Olympic Games Stein," Forma Vitrum's "Fire Island, New York" from the *Coastal Heritage* series, Seymour Mann's "Cara" from the *Connossieur Doll Series*, United Design's "Angel, Lion and Fawn" from the *Angels Collection*, Amaranth Production's "Last Minute Details," Imperial Graphics' "Piano Sonata" from the *Celestial Symphony* series, and The Fenton Art Glass Company's "Queens Bird Burmese Vase" from the *1996 Connoisseur Collection*.

BACK COVER

Top, from left to right: Lightpost Publishing's "Stepping Stones" from the *Sweetheart Cottage Series*, Amazze's "Block Island" from the *Century Lights™ Century Classics* series.

In front of the chest, from left to right: Goebel of North America's "Abby Liz" from the *Bob Timberlake Signature Series*, Kurt S. Adler's *Polonaise Glass Ornament Collection* "Cinderella Boxed Set," Ron Lee's World of Clowns' "Merry Go Clown," Annalee Mobilitee Dolls' "Puppies for Christmas" Santa from the *Collector Edition Santa Series*, The Art of Glynda Turley's "Secret Garden II," and Lenox Collection's "Visitors from Afar."

PHOTO 1:

From left to right: Gartlan USA's "Ringo Starr" from the *All Starr Collection*, Miss Martha Originals' "Mary Mahoney" from the *All God's Children Historical Series*, Hawthorne's "McDonald's Classic" from the *McMemories Collection*, BAND Creations' *Best Friends* "Noah's Ark," Reco International's "Night Before Christmas" from the *Victorian Christmas Series*, and FJ Designs/The Cat's Meow "Grandmother's House," "Three Bears' House," "Seven Dwarfs' House" and "Gingerbread House" from the *Fairy Tale Series*.

PHOTO 2:

From left to right: WACO's "Candy Factory" from the *Melody In Motion* "I Love Lucy" series, Ace Product Management's "Road Trip" from the *Great Times Together Collection*, Maruri's "Waltz of the Dolphins," The George Z. Lefton Company's "Buffalo Lighthouse, Buffalo, NY" from the *Historic American Lighthouse Collection*, and "Benjamin and His Puppy" from The Ashton Drake Galleries' *Mommy Can I Keep It?* series.

PHOTO 3:

From left to right: Possible Dreams' "Christmas Stories" from the *Clothtique American Artist Collection*, Lance Corporation's "St. Nikkolo," Great American Taylor Collectibles' "Palmer Claus," Sarah's Attic's "Sunday Tillie," Ladie and Friends' "Sally Bowman, Second Edition" from the *Lizzie High Dolls* series and Duncan Royale's "Piano" from the *Jazzmen, Early American Ebony Collection*.

PHOTO 4:

From left to right: Harbour Lights' "Alcatraz," The Greenwich Workshop's "Levi Levitates the Stone Fish," Precious Art Inc.'s "Enough is Enough," from the *World of Krystonia*, Pacific Rim Imports' "Clear Sailing" from the *Birthday Bunny Toes Collection*, Character Collectibles/Calabar Creations' "Acapella & Alto" from the *Angelic Pigasus* series, Silvestri's "White Robed Angel with Heart," Midwest of Cannon Falls' "Creepy Castle" from the *Creepy Hollow* series, and Shelia's "Urfer House" from the *Victorian Springtime III* series.

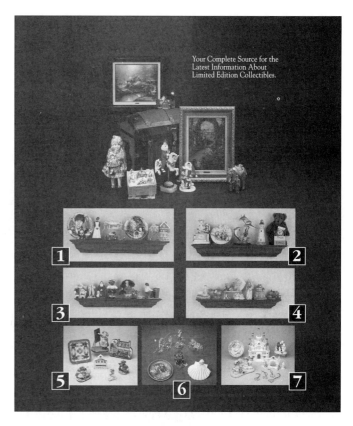

Your Complete Source for the Latest Information About Limited Edition Collectibles.

Photo 5:

Clockwise, from top left: The Bradford Exchange's "The Wedding Ring" from the *Cherished Traditions* series, ANRI Woodcarving's "Head of the Class" from the *School Days* series, Brandywine Collectibles' "Fire House" from the *Country Lane* series, Ganz' "Wooster & Schneider School Days" from the *Cottage Collectables* series, M.I. Hummel's "Blossom Time," R.R. Creations' "Drum Point Lighthouse, Solomons, MD" from *Lighthouse Series III*, and Autom's "Newborn Baby."

PHOTO 6:

Clockwise, from top left: Swarovski's Fabulous Creatures - "The Unicorn," Shube's "Majestic Unicorn" from the *Masterworks Fantasy Collection*, Crystal World's "Classic Motorcycle," Margaret Furlong Designs' "The Hope Angel" from the *Flora Angelica* series, The Tudor Mint's "Way Out Dragon" from the *Myth & Magic* series, and Bing & Grondahl's "1996 The Little Racer" from the *Children's Days* series.

Photo 7:

Clockwise, from top left: The Hamilton Collection's "Heaven's Little Helper" from the *Dreamsicles Special Friends* series, Department 56's "Snow Carnival Ice Palace" from the *Snow Village* series, Cavanagh Group International's "Refreshing Treat" from the *Coca Cola Heritage Collection*, Hand & Hammer Silversmiths' "Rose Window Ornament Set," and Cast Art Industries' "A Child is Born" from the *Dreamsicles* series.

TABLE OF CONTENTS

Background

Trends in Today's Marketplace ... 7
The Secondary Market ... 10
How to Care for Your Collectible Treasures ... 13
Insuring and Protecting Your Collectibles ... 15
Full-Color Collectibles Showcase ... 17

Features

Ace Product Management Group ... 53
Kurt S. Adler, Inc. ... 56
Amaranth Productions ... 59
Amazze ... 62
Anheuser-Busch, Inc. ... 65
Annalee Mobilitee Dolls, Inc. ... 68
ANRI U.S. ... 71
Arcadian Pewter, Inc. ... 74
G. Armani Society and Armani Collection ... 77
The Art of Glynda Turley ... 80
The Ashton-Drake Galleries ... 83
Attic Babies ... 86
Autom ... 89
BAND Creations ... 90
Bing & Grondahl ... 93
The Boyds Collection, Ltd. ... 96
The Bradford Exchange ... 99
Brandywine Woodcrafts, Inc. ... 102
Byers' Choice Ltd. ... 105
Calabar Creations ... 108
Cardew Design ... 111
Carlton Cards ... 114
Cast Art Industries, Inc. ... 117
Cavanagh Group International ... 120
Christopher Radko ... 123
Crystal World ... 126
Dear Artistic Sculpture ... 129
Department 56, Inc. ... 132
Walt Disney Classics Collection ... 135
Duncan Royale ... 138
Enesco Corporation ... 141
Ertl Collectibles ... 144
FFSC, Inc./Charming Tails ... 147
FJ Designs, Inc./Cat's Meow Village ... 150
Fenton Art Glass ... 153
Flambro Imports, Inc. ... 156
Forma Vitrum ... 159
The Franklin Mint ... 162
Margaret Furlong Designs ... 165
GANZ ... 168
Gartlan USA, Inc. ... 171
Georgetown Collection ... 174
Goebel of North America ... 177
Great American Taylor Collectibles Corp. ... 180

The Greenwich Workshop ... 183
The Hamilton Collection ... 186
Hand & Hammer Silversmiths ... 189
Harbour Lights ... 192
Harmony Kingdom ... 195
Hawthorne Architectural Register ... 198
M.I. Hummel Club ... 201
Imperial Graphics, Ltd. ... 204
Ladie and Friends, Inc. ... 207
The Lance Corporation ... 210
Ron Lee's World of Clowns ... 213
George Z. Lefton Co. ... 216
Legends ... 219
Lenox Collections ... 222
Lilliput Lane ... 225
Lladró ... 228
Seymour Mann, Inc. ... 231
Maruri, U.S.A. ... 234
Media Arts Group, Inc. ... 237
Michael's Limited ... 240
Midwest of Cannon Falls ... 243
Miss Martha Originals ... 246
Old World Christmas ... 249
Pacific Rim Import Corp. ... 252
Possible Dreams ... 255
Precious Art/Panton ... 258
Pulaski Furniture Corporation ... 261
R.R. Creations, Inc. ... 263
Reco International Corp. ... 266
Roman, Inc. ... 269
Royal Doulton ... 272
Sarah's Attic, Inc. ... 275
Shelia's Collectibles ... 278
Shube's Manufacturing ... 281
Swarovski ... 284
The Tudor Mint, Inc. ... 287
United Design ... 290
WACO Products Corporation ... 293
Walnut Ridge Collectibles ... 296

Reference Section

Meet the Artists ... 299
Books, Magazines and Newsletters ... 341
National Collectors' Clubs ... 342
Directory of Collectibles Manufacturers ... 346
National Association of Limited
    Edition Dealers (NALED) ... 350
Glossary ... 354
Price Index ... I-1
Index ... IN-1

TRENDS IN TODAY'S MARKETPLACE
Expert Observers Share Insights with Limited Edition Collectors

The popularity of "Angel of Sharing," and other plates from Sandra Kuck's Precious Angels *series, reflects collectors' renewed interest in faith and hope.*

"Buy only what you like"... "Secondary market potential should be the icing on the cake — not the main reason for selecting an item"... "Show off and enjoy your collectibles — don't store them in a closet or under a bed." Advice like this to collectors is as timeless as a blue-and-white Christmas plate. Yet from year to year and decade to decade there are meaningful changes in the marketplace — and many collectors like to stay abreast of these trends in order to make more informed choices for their personal holdings. That's why Collectors' Information Bureau has gathered a panel of experts to reveal some of the more important new directions in today's world of collecting. These "collectibles gurus" don't always agree, but you'll find their thoughts provocative, authoritative, and intriguing!

Figurines Lead All Other Collectibles in Popularity

Our first question to the experts centered on collectible art media. We wanted to know which media are most sought-after in today's market...and

why. The lion's share of our respondents replied with just one word: "Figurines." From the adorable and affordable *Enesco Cherished Teddies™* and Cast Art Industries' *Dreamsicles™*, to the sophistication of Lladró porcelain and Swarovski crystal, the figurine art market offers something for every taste and pocketbook. Yet for all the dominance of figurines as a "medium of choice," some of our experts offered a different viewpoint.

David MacMahan, president of Forma Vitrum, noted the strength of villages. These series of collectible cottages often carry a literary, historical or architectural theme. As MacMahan said, "Villages remain strong because they may be accessorized and changed with each new season for year-round display. Villages are an interactive collectible that allows collectors to design the scene and create the mood. They can build their own unique dreamlands and become a part of the scene."

The growth of Christmas collectibles as a year-round collecting theme was noted by Debra Mosier of Old World Christmas®. "The warmth and excitement surrounding the Christmas holidays are feelings people would like to keep all year long. Christmas ornaments and wooden collectibles provide them with a way to capture that magic," she said.

Collectibles Reflect Societal Change

When asked what general trends in society might affect collectors' choices, our respondents offered a wonderful range of ideas. For example, Marlene Marcus, product development manager at Reco International Corp., commented on the diversity of today's American culture. She observed, "As much as we see trends in society, such as environmentalism, return to basics, marriage and children, we also see a wealth of

differences. We have become an 'eclectic' society, and I believe this is very much reflected in the collectibles which are popular today.

"Just as some examples, people seem to appreciate wit and humor, as shown by the success of the 'Santa Paws' plate from The Franklin Mint. Collectibles featuring identifiable names, such as Coca-Cola®, STAR TREK®, and even McDonalds, familiar things that we have known for a long time, bring us comfort in a quickly changing world. Totally different is the interest in faith and the hope that someone really is looking out for us, as demonstrated by the overwhelming popularity of angels, such as the *Precious Angels* collection by Sandra Kuck."

Ms. Marcus continues, "One trend which cannot be denied, is the trend towards spending much more time at home. The availability to do shopping, banking and many other services electronically, the entertainment available through home theater and computer, the ability to work from one's home, is making the home the center of our lives."

Licensed products, such as "Sylvester's Holiday High Jinks" from Possible Dreams, continue to grow in diversity and prominence in today's world of collecting.

One collecting trend that appeals to home decorators focuses on cottages and villages. Collectors are displaying their village scenes all year 'round, often with seasonal accents. Here, an autumn setting enhances the charms of the lighted "Mayor's Mansion" from Forma Vitrum.

David Faas, the consumer services manager for Lladró USA, named three trends that he believes are most reflected in today's collectibles: family values, patriotism, and fantasy/whimsy/nostalgia. He says, "People have become more aware and drawn toward family. Figurines that capture family unity and devotion are strong. Collectibles that capture family occasions such as weddings, communions, new baby, anniversary and parents with children are growing in popularity.

"Love of country appears to be on the upswing. Recently Lladró introduced an astronaut with an American flag called 'The Apollo Landing' to very enthusiastic reviews. A new limited edition figurine called 'Abraham Lincoln' is quite popular with collectors.

"While life becomes increasingly hectic for many collectors, they long for items that can 'take them away' from today's fast-paced lifestyles. Many collectors collect items of fantasy or whimsy to remind them of simple

times, enchanting times," Faas concludes.

The vice president of marketing for Goebel of North America, William A. Belmont, Jr., reported succinctly that today's trends are "nature and environment, space limitation, and spiritualism." To illustrate, he noted the popularity of wildlife subjects in homage to nature, the enjoyment of miniatures which take up little space in the home, and the trend of collecting heavenly angels.

Peter Nourjian of Possible Dreams believes, "The biggest trends today seem to be entertainment driven. Naturally, licensed collectibles relating to the movie or personality spotlighted are going to have the biggest appeal. And with baby boomers coming into the collector's fold, quality will become more important to appeal to their more refined tastes."

Finally, Gideon Oberweger, vice president of Seymour Mann, takes a contrarion point of view to the discussion of trends. As he comments, "Trends in society do not affect collectibles as much as people may wish. Subjects dear to the heart which convey an emotion are always more popular than 'trendy' collectibles – this

A theme of religious faith and hope shines through in the Roman, Inc. Millenium™ series of annual Christmas plates and companion ornaments. Both the plate and ornament, shown here, are entitled "Cause of Our Joy."

Lladró's "Abraham Lincoln" figurine offers a fine example of the patriotic-theme figurines that have attracted collectors in recent years.

is why subjects such as birds, cats, bears and roses remain the best sellers."

Advice on Selecting Artists and Collectibles to Purchase

When asked who the "hottest" artists are today, many respondents cited the artists under contract to their own firms or studios. In addition, names like David Tate, Thomas Kinkade, Sandra Kuck, Sam Butcher, Priscilla Hillman, David Winter, and Christopher Radko came up often.

What's more, Sam Caggiula, manager of corporate communications for The Franklin Mint, had some specific advice on how to get started with a collection. We asked him what he would recommend to a collector with $500 to spend over the next year.

"First, decide what it is that you want to collect," suggests Caggiula. "This task sounds easy enough, but it does require some planning. There are simply too many 'things' that are or become collectibles. You've got to know – or at least have an idea – what type of collectible you want. It could be collector plates, porcelain dolls, die cast replicas, books, Christmas ornaments, or salt-n-pepper shakers, but it's helpful to have a type of collectible in mind before you begin collecting.

"If you can't quite decide, then take your research on the road. Visit museums, antique stores, craft shows, yard sales, and of course, collectible expos. The other alternative is to read a few of the many and varied collectible publications now available to the public."

The Year 2000...and Beyond

To round out our discussion, we asked our experts to look into their crystal balls and predict what collecting will be like circa 2005. Our respondent from Ganz predicts secondary market transactions on the Internet. Several individuals mentioned the continued strength of classic collectibles — items that have been popular for many decades and will continue to attract loyal buyers. Others commented that the market is saturated currently, and that only the "quality" artists, producers and marketers will survive.

Ronald T. Jedlinski, president of Roman, Inc., believes that the turn of the century itself will affect collecting. As he notes, "Millennium will have a big impact on what people will buy and read about. The coming of the end of the Millennium and the attendant uncertainty it generates has given rise to a surge in the return to the spiritual. Collectible producers are responding to this wave with collectibles reflecting images people associate with the Millennium."

To conclude on a more pragmatic note, Peter Nourjian of Possible Dreams believes that the future can be found in "Licensing, licensing, licensing. Big-budgeted Hollywood and TV-generated properties will rule!"

Collectors appreciate the wit and humor displayed in works of collectible art such as The Franklin Mint's "The Santa Paws Plate."

Advice from the Experts: Short Tips for Collectors

Here are a few quick hints from some of today's most knowledgeable collectibles producers and marketers:

To become a smart buyer:

- Obtain every bit of educational material possible about your collection. Go to antique shows — there are always lots of books available on just about any possible collectible. Ask your retailer to obtain as much information from the manufacturer as is available. — Nancy G. Fenton, The Fenton Art Glass Company

- Join the appropriate Collectors Society to be informed, entertained and educated about your favorite collectibles. — David Faas, Lladró USA

- Attend manufacturer-sponsored events and collectible expositions. Work with just one or two retailers exclusively, and choose them for their dedicated, knowledgeable staffs. — Claire Golata, Lilliput Lane

To better display and care for your collectibles:

- Create levels and layers on shelves and cabinets, to make collections more distinctive and easier to appreciate. Almost anything will do as "risers": books, covered boxes, or gift boxes wrapped in fabric or paper. — Linda Masterson, Enesco Corporation

- Invest in a good display case for your collectibles. You will be able to enjoy them while protecting them from dust, smoke, etc. Also, purchase insurance for your collection — better safe than sorry. — Gideon Oberweger, Seymour Mann Inc.

- Those little cordless keyboard vacuums are great for keeping collections dust free — and safe! — Linda Masterson, Enesco Corporation

- Keep an inventory of all items in the collection, including photos. Some insurance companies cover collectibles on homeowner insurance policies. — Debra Mosier, Old World Christmas

- Most boxes fold flat for storage and should be kept to increase the value of a retired piece. — Peter Nourjian, Possible Dreams

THE SECONDARY MARKET
A Basic Guide for Collectors on Buying and Selling
Sold-Out Limited Editions

They add sparkle and individuality to our home decor and provide daily enjoyment and inspiration to their owners. They make ideal conversation pieces for visitors, and coveted heirlooms to pass to the next generation. Even without considering their secondary market potential, limited edition collectibles reign among the most delightful of all possessions. In fact, many collectors are so enchanted by the sheer beauty of their holdings that they never even consider the possibility of price appreciation. Yet it is a wise collector who keeps abreast of the secondary market — and knows how to use it to their advantage if the opportunity or need should arise.

In this brief introduction, we'll provide an overview of the "how-tos" of market trading. Then, in our "ask the experts" section, you'll gain insights into some of the nuances of buying and selling collectibles on the aftermarket.

Limited Editions and the Law of Supply and Demand

The price of a limited edition collectible on the secondary market is a function of supply and demand. For example, an item that is in relatively limited supply and is experiencing

---

– ASK THE EXPERTS –
I'm a collector who is considering trading on the secondary market. What advice do you have for me?

OHI Exchange Division of Opa's Haus, Inc., New Braunfels, Texas; Ken Armke

"If selling, find a store or exchange service to sell for you on a commission basis — that is, unless you feel you have exceptional marketing skills. If buying, decide if you are buying strictly for pleasure or whether you are buying at least partially for 'investment.' If it's for pleasure, simply buy what you can afford and what pleases you. If it's for investment, then a) buy for a short-term return; today's collectibles have not been proven over a long term, and b) buy items you like, because you may 'get stuck' with them!"

Animation Fascination/Classic Endeavors, Joliet, Illinois; Dee Brandt

"Know who you are dealing with! Never mail payments to a post office box or answer a 'blind ad.' If not sure of your contact, use a referral service such as the Collectors' Information Bureau."

Collectible Exchange Inc., New Middletown, Ohio; Connie Eckman

"Manufacturer-sponsored collector clubs are one of the best sources for reliable information about a particular line. You can also ask the manufacturer if they recommend any secondary market services — many do."

Lighthouse Trading Company, Limerick, Pennsylvania; Matt Rothman

"First, understand that a secondary market trade takes time. Be patient and find out if the price you are asking is in line with the market. The more realistic the price, the faster the piece will sell."

Gift Music Book & Collectibles, Chicago Heights, Illinois; Joe Schulte

"Buy the oldest piece in a series that you can afford now, and fill in the middle of the collection later. First in a series almost always goes up faster than the rest."

Swan Seekers Network, Phoenix, Arizona; Maret Webb A.I.A.

"First, realistically assess the condition of your piece. Today's secondary market buyers demand perfection, and flawed merchandise is not tolerated. Scrutinize the item for damage or factory imperfections prior to offering it for sale. Buyers want the correct original packaging, and a realistic selling price may be compromised significantly without the box, certificate, sleeve, etc. A deduction of at least 10% for each missing element is not unreasonable. Pack well and ship fully insured. Require an adult signature for delivery of the parcel. Finally, understand how price guides work. The value printed in a price guide is what it may cost to buy the item. For a prospective buyer, this is good information to know when you go shopping for a collectible on the secondary market, as the price guide can give you a benchmark. A private seller generally will not be able to get 'book' price, but may receive 50% to 70% of the current retail value of an item."

great demand may appreciate in value. Similarly, if an item is part of a large edition that has not caught the attention and affection of a great number of collectors, it may not see any appreciation in price.

Some novice collectors assume that the lower the edition size, the most likely it is that an item will rise in price later. This may not necessarily be true, since an item must exist in sufficient quantity to "penetrate the market," in order for significant price appreciation to occur. People need to know about the item in order to build word of mouth and demand. Indeed, there have been collector plates limited by firing periods in which tens of thousands of a certain issue were made. Such items may well rise sharply in price if there is more demand than supply available once the edition closes.

Changes in supply and demand occur quite regularly. Over time, the supply of an item may diminish, particularly if the piece is fragile. Likewise, the demand for a particular piece may change as collectors' tastes and interests evolve. For example, a revival of interest in a "popular culture" subject such as a classic TV show or a renowned performer can result in an upturn in price for items inspired by that subject. Likewise, the death of a prominent artist may lead to a temporary surge in the price of his or her works.

As a result of these changes in supply and demand, collectors should realize that prices can and do fluctuate on the secondary market, sometimes quite dramatically. As prices rise, they may reach a level that collectors feel is unreasonable. As a result, demand falls. Once demand begins to fall, sellers may lower their price in order to make the sale. This may continue until collectors again feel that the value for the piece is reasonable and begin buying again. When that happens, demand may outpace supply and the cycle could begin again.

Going It Alone Vs. Using a Broker's Services

While some collectors believe they will save money by attempting to buy or sell on their own, the services of a knowledgeable broker are often well worth the cost of his or her commission. Brokers do the work for you: placing ads, making telephone contacts, ensuring that you are paid or that an item you purchase is delivered safely. In most cases, the seller pays the commission, which may vary from as low as 10% to 30% or more.

When comparing brokers and the prices they advertise, be aware that there are several possible listing methods. Some brokers list the price the buyer will pay, while others list the price the seller will receive. Shipping costs may or may not be included in these prices; if in doubt, ask for clarification.

Make sure you are aware of all surcharges and costs associated with working with a particular broker or buy-sell service. Some may require you to pay a subscription fee, a listing fee, or a surcharge for use of a credit card.

The Collectors' Information Bureau's *Directory to Secondary Market Retailers* features over 150 aftermarket brokers with full-page histories to help collectors learn more about each broker's business practices.

– ASK THE EXPERTS –

What should I look for in buying a new collectible if I am concerned about its future secondary market appreciation?

Gift Music Book & Collectibles, Chicago Heights, Illinois; Joe Schulte

"Strong name; history of appreciation; limited or exclusive availability (the less, the better); first in series; member, show, or mail-order-only promos; signed by a major artist; short production run (one year or less on the market); few discounters or 'gray market' able to sell them; and one that you like in case the market gets soft. Also, if the piece doesn't ship well (breaks easily), and you get one in mint condition, hold onto it for awhile: it'll go up."

Animation Fascination/Classic Endeavors, Joliet, Illinois; Dee Brandt

"Check the track record of the collection over the past six months. A steady climber is better than an overnight sensation. Only invest what you can afford — only buy what you like, and remember collectibles are at the top of the pyramid in high-risk investments."

Collectible Exchange Inc., New Middletown, Ohio; Connie Eckman

"Unless you can afford the risk, it's best not to speculate. If I could predict the secondary market, I wouldn't be working for a living, I would spend my time shopping!"

– ASK THE EXPERTS –

How should I choose a secondary market trading firm to assist me?

Crystal Reef, Foster City, California; Blaine Garfolo

"Look for an exchange that has collectors for employees as they tend to be more sensitive to the needs of collectors."

The Crystal Connection, Peoria, Illinois; Robin Yaw

"Check out their credentials — ask for references. What's the payment method — is there a waiting period before payment is made by the firm to the seller? Get a 'fact sheet' from the firm outlining all their procedures."

A Work of Art, Valhalla, New York; Joan Lewis

"Make sure that the secondary market firm has a strong knowledge of the collectible in which you are interested. I think it is also important to like the people you are dealing with. If they seem a little shifty or high pressure, or if they do not return your calls promptly or do not seem involved with what they're doing, they are probably not for you."

Gift Music Book & Collectibles, Chicago Heights, Illinois; Joe Schulte

"The five most important attributes of secondary market dealer are: 1) Service — we'll call fifty sources to find an item at the best price for our customers. 2) Flexibility — adapt to customer needs. 3) Takes credit cards — this covers everyone's liabilities. 4) Fair prices — not always highest or lowest. 5) Tenacious — we will call six months to a year later if the item a collector wanted shows up."

HOW TO CARE FOR YOUR COLLECTIBLE TREASURES

A Compendium of Do's and Don'ts To Help Keep Your Favorite Limited Editions in Excellent Condition

Figurines, bells, cottages, miniatures and other collectibles may be displayed safely in a handsome hardwood cabinet such as this one from Van Hygan & Smythe. Holding collectibles up to 5-3/4" high, the unit comes with appropriate hardware for hanging or it may also be set on a tabletop.

One of the wonderful qualities of limited edition collectibles is their permanence: most are durable works of art that can be handed down from generation to generation as an enduring legacy of love and distinction. Yet without proper care, these heirloom-quality pieces may lose their original beauty, brightness and appeal. Here are some simple tips that will enable you to keep your most precious treasures in prime condition for decades to come.

Collector Plates

The lion's share of collector plates are made of porcelain or china. These durable materials are highly resistant to chipping and breakage unless they are dropped on a hard surface. Because most plates have their decorations permanently fired on, they keep their bright good looks with a minimum of care. Most fired plates can be wiped with a damp cloth, or even washed gently by hand in a sink of lukewarm water with mild soap.

Porous, unglazed surfaces or hand-painted, unfired plates should never be immersed in water – dusting is the only safe way to freshen them. Also, if your plate has been hand-signed by the artist, it is best not to immerse it in water since the signature may not be adequately sealed.

There are plates made of crystal, wood, stoneware, resin, and many other substances. For care of unusual materials, seek the advice of the plate's manufacturer. If in doubt, treat your plate as you would any other item made of that material.

One final word to the wise: most collector plates are unsuitable for containing food due to the lead content of their decals or paints.

Figurines, Cottages, Bells and Steins

In general, three-dimensional works of art need more care in cleaning and handling than do collector plates. When handling, lift the piece by its base, handle or a sturdy part since delicate parts may snap under pressure. To clean, dust gently with a feather duster or a small shaving brush.

If your piece has been designated safe for washing by its manufacturer, line your double sink with towels and move the faucet out of the way. Fill one sink with a mild soap solution and the other with clear, lukewarm water. Use distilled water if your area has hard water. Dip the figurine carefully in the soapy water, and use a soft brush to clean nooks and crannies. Rinse in the second sink, using a plastic or paper cup to pour water over the piece. For a final rinse, fill a towel-lined sink with vinegar rinse (one-half cup vinegar to a gallon of water). Air dry the figurines, making sure not to place them on wooden surfaces until the unglazed bottoms are completely dry.

Dolls

The delicate porcelain faces, hands and other body parts of fine dolls should be dusted lightly to keep them fresh and pretty. It is best not to "play hairdresser" with a doll's hair – just smooth the hair back in place lightly with your fingers rather than trying to comb out and re-style. As for a doll's clothing, the main enemies of fine fabrics are dust and sunlight – so avoid both in displaying your treasures. If clothing becomes soiled, dry cleaning is the best option unless you are sure the fabric can be washed without damage or shrinking. Many avid collectors invest in handsome, glass and wood display boxes and cases that protect dolls from dirt and too much handling.

Christmas Ornaments

While some collectors now enjoy showing off their ornaments all year, many still pack them away after the holidays. Using the original packing material is wise – but if you no longer have it, you might purchase special ornament storage cases sold by closet/organizational stores and catalogs. For truly unique or heirloom ornaments, you might select an artifact storage box such as those used by museums.

Another option – suggested by a collector of Christopher Radko ornaments – is to use stackable, sealable rubber tray containers lined with bubble wrap. Individual ornaments then can be wrapped loosely in an acid-free paper such as Bounty® microwaveable paper towels. Add a humidity-absorbing packet in each tray and the ornaments are ready for storage.

Graphics

A museum-mounted, framed print behind glass is well protected, yet should still be hung out of direct sunlight and extreme temperatures to prevent fading and moisture build-up. Unframed prints lose beauty and value from overhandling, so invest in binders made especially for their storage within protective acetate sheets. There are also attractive wooden furniture pieces with shallow drawers meant to hold unframed prints in safety.

This broken Lladró figurine has been restored to its original beauty by experienced restorers at Old World Restorations, Inc., utilizing non-destructive methods and reversible materials to achieve restorations invisible to the naked eye.

COLLECTIBLES RESTORATION SERVICES

When a favorite collectible becomes damaged and it is scarce or has special sentimental value, collectors often prefer to have it restored rather than accept an insurance company settlement that requires turning over the broken pieces in exchange for its cash value. A qualified restorer can do wonders in repairing your treasures if damage or breakage occurs. A skillful restoration may recover 50% to 100% of an item's original issue price. The following restoration experts are recommended by the member companies of COLLECTORS' INFORMATION BUREAU. Services are listed in alphabetical order by state.

China & Crystal Clinic
1808 N. Scottsdale
Tempe, AZ 85281
1-800-658-9197

Attic Unlimited
22435 E. La Palma
Yorba Linda, CA 92686
(714) 692-2940

Foster Art Restoration
711 West 17th St., Suite C-12
Costa Mesa, CA 92627
1-800-824-6967

Geppetto's Restoration
31121 Via Colinas, Suite 1003
Westlake Village, CA 91362
(818) 889-0901

Delly Griffin (Harbour Lights and David Winter Cottages)
2626 Paxton Ave.
Palmdale, CA 93551
(805) 266-1328

Just Enterprises
2790 Sherwin Ave. #10
Ventura, CA 93003
(805) 644-5837

Restorations by Linda
1759 Hemlock St.
Fairfield, CA 94533
(707) 422-6497

Venerable Classics
645 Fourth St., Suite 208
Santa Rosa, CA 95404
(707) 575-3626

C.R.C. Workshop
16 Drumlin Hill
Groton, MA 01450
(508) 448-5252

Beth Haley
(Sebastian miniatures only)
16 Chestnut St.
P.O. Box 895
Marblehead, MA 01945
(617) 631-2267

Baer Specialty Shop
259 E. Browning Rd.
Bellmawr, NJ 08031
(609) 931-0696

Witherspoon Studios
17 Locke Court
W. Trenton, NJ 08628
1-800-883-2605

Ceramic Restoration of Westchester, Inc.
81 Water St.
Ossining, NY 10562
(914) 762-1719

China & Glass Repair Studios
282 Main St.
Eastchester, NY 10709
(914) 337-1977

Imperial China
27 and 24 North Park Ave.
Rockville Center, NY 11570
(516) 764-7311

Restoration Unlimited
3009 W. Genesee St.
Syracuse, NY 13219
(315) 488-7123

Old World Restorations
347 Stanley Ave.
Cincinnati, OH 45226
(513) 321-1911

Wiebold Studio, Inc.
413 Terrace Place
Terrace Park, OH 45174
(513) 831-2541

Attic Babies Doll Hospital
(Attic Babies only)
P.O. Box 912
Drumright, OK 74030
(918) 352-4414

Byers' Choice Ltd.
(Byers' Choice figurines only)
4355 County Line Rd.
Chalfont, PA 18914
(215) 822-6700

Lizzie High Doll Hospital
(Lizzie High dolls only)
220 North Main Street
Sellersville, PA 18960
1-800-76-DOLLS

Creart U.S.A.
(Creart sculptures only)
309 E. Ben White Blvd. #103
Austin, TX 78704
(512) 707-2699

June McKenna Collectibles, Inc.
(June McKenna collectibles only)
P.O. Box 1540-205 Haley Road
Ashland, VA 23005
(804) 798-2024

INSURING AND PROTECTING YOUR COLLECTIBLES

Ten Things That Every Collector Needs to Know to Guard Their Treasures from Loss

Not too long ago, a friend and avid plate collector called me, obviously upset, and told me a story that I never would have believed had I heard it from anyone else.

One evening, she and her husband returned to their suburban home to find some of her most valuable collector plates, which she had been proudly displaying on a plate rail in her living room, laying smashed on the floor.

There was no sign of forced entry, and nothing else in the house had been taken or vandalized. The "who" "how" and "why" of the broken plates remained a mystery, until a few heartbroken and worry-filled days later when my friend was first alarmed, then relieved, to see a field mouse, which had somehow made its way inside, scurrying across the now-empty plate rail.

Although the culprit was finally caught, the story does not have a

particularly happy ending. Because the plates were not covered at their replacement value by her homeowners' insurance policy, my friend's broken works of art — worth many hundreds of dollars — were insured for only a small fraction of their true price.

While most of us will never have to deal with rogue mice wreaking havoc among our treasures, the lesson to be learned from this story is "when it comes to protecting the things you love, be prepared for anything, because anything can happen — and not just to other people."

If you're like most people, the things you collect are highly personal reflections of your personality and your interests, and it would be difficult for any of us to put a price tag on the treasures we've lovingly acquired through the years. But the fact is, many collections also represent a sizable financial investment — one that may

have appreciated considerably in price since they were first purchased.

Should the unthinkable happen and your collection is lost through fire, flood, earthquake, storms, theft, or even intruding wildlife, your loss could easily exceed the amount that is specified by your insurance coverage, unless you act now to protect these highly-valued assets.

Ten Important Steps

Here are ten steps that every collector should take right now, to assure that your loss will be minimized should you be faced with a catastrophe.

1. Keep all receipts. Even if you purchase a collectible from a friend or a neighbor, make sure you get a receipt for each piece you acquire, and make sure that it clearly identifies the item bought and the price you paid for it.

2. Jot down crucial information on a piece of paper and staple it to the item's receipt:
- Item name or description
- Name of manufacturer
- Year of issue
- Artist's name
- Limited edition number
- Series number
- Special markings
- Cost at issue (if different than purchase price)
- Place of purchase
- Date of purchase
- Any other information you deem necessary

3. Augment this information with a visual record. All too often, collectors overlook this relatively simple, yet very effective, method of documenting their collections.

You can do this in a variety of ways. The simplest may be to save all brochures or catalogs which feature the items purchased. One drawback to this method is that such materials are not always readily available.

We recommend that you either

An effective method of documenting a collection, the use of a video camera allows collectors to visually record their collectibles as well as voice record all pertinent information about individual pieces.

photograph or videotape each item in your collection. If you choose to use still photography, be sure to take a shot of it as it is displayed in your home, and then close-up shots capturing any significant markings such as the back-stamp, artist signature, and/or limited edition number.

Video-taping is gaining in popularity as the method of choice to document entire collections. Video cameras are typically easy to use, and they give you the opportunity to voice record all pertinent information about the piece while you are taping. As with still photography, videotape each item as it is displayed, using close-ups to record all details which might contribute to the item's worth.

4. Get very rare or one-of-a-kind pieces appraised. Unlike collectibles which are issued in open or limited editions, it may be difficult or impossible to substantiate a claim for any unique items in your collection because there are no current market indicators to help determine the item's replacement cost.

Should your collection include a one-of-a-kind or other rare item, you may have to have it appraised in order to establish its worth. In this case, we recommend that you use a qualified appraiser. To find one, start by checking in your local yellow pages, or talk to a museum curator. Your insurance agent may also be able to offer suggestions of qualified individuals. Doing this now will be worth the time and cost if the appraised pieces are lost or destroyed. Note: Give high consideration to members of the American Society of Appraisers. They have passed rigorous certifying tests and are considered to be highly qualified. After you've decided on two or three appraisers, ask for references and check them. Use only appraisers for whom you have received high recommendations.

5. Keep all these records off site. You'll want to be sure that all your documentation — receipts, item information, appraisals, and photographs or videotape — is stored safely in a secured location away from your collection so you can easily retrieve it in the event of catastrophe. We recommend you maintain these records in the safety-deposit

or lock box where you keep your other vitally important papers.

6. Read your insurance policy carefully. This may seem obvious, yet every year, thousands of collectors are surprised after making a claim to find that their treasured belongings are uninsured or underinsured. And by then it is too late to do anything about it.

So take the time right now to review your homeowners' or renters' insurance policy to make sure your collectibles will be adequately covered in the event of a loss. Pay particular attention to whether yours is a cash-value policy or a replacement value policy. Typically, under the terms of a cash-value policy, the insured items are covered for their value at the time the items were purchased. Replacement value policies, on the other hand, usually cover your insured items for the amount it would take to replace them at the time you make a claim. In light of the fact that some collectibles escalate in value over time, you might want to make sure that yours is a "replacement value" policy.

7. If you have any questions, talk to your insurance agent. Make sure you ask him or her if special coverage is required to fully insure all your collectibles.

For many collectibles, a floater or rider will be required. This is a policy in which you "schedule" each piece individually for its replacement cost. Many companies have a fine arts or personal articles floater that covers collectibles for the full replacement cost of the item.

If your collection is of extremely high value, your insurer may require you to hold a special lines policy. This is a policy designed to cover unusual or relatively expensive items, and the premiums are typically very high.

Remember that in purchasing insurance coverage, you are always faced with a variety of options. Be certain that you discuss all your special concerns with your agent to make sure you have the coverage you want and need. And don't forget to ask such important questions as:
- Does the floater cover all risks, i.e., flood, fire, theft, etc.?
- Is there a deductible? If so, what is it?

- Does the policy cover breakage? If not, what is the additional cost?
- What constitutes breakage?
- Are the items covered if they are taken off-premises?

Before meeting with the agent, spend an evening or two jotting down any potential losses you think may arise and then ask your agent if the policies you are considering, cover you in each instance. If not, look for another policy.

8. Update your policy information regularly. In most cases, if your collection appreciates to a higher value than when it was scheduled, your insurance company is required to reimburse you for only the scheduled value. Because of this, you should be certain to reschedule your collectibles at least once a year, or whenever the collection experiences a drastic change in price. Also, don't forget to add newly acquired additions to your collection.

9. Should a loss occur, refer to the *Collectibles Market Guide and Price Index* to determine current values. This highly respected reference source is published by the Collectors' Information Bureau at the beginning of each year. Considered the industry standard, it is recognized by insurers as one of the most reliable and credible sources available. The price index section lists over 45,000 collectibles and their current market prices. An updated price index is available at mid-year in the *Collectibles Price Guide*. Make sure you refer to the most up-to-date price index to determine the most current value of your collectibles.

10. Exercise extra care in displaying and caring for your collectibles. By far, the most efficient and most desirable way to keep your collection intact is to keep it out of harm's way in the first place. Make sure your displays are well constructed and offer no threat to the collectibles themselves. Keep figurines away from the edge of shelves and tables, and check to see that wall items are firmly secured to the wall in their frames or hangers.

Take special care when dusting and cleaning all these items, and check the maker's recommendations for the safest, most effective cleaning procedures to follow.

All that glitters and shines...comes to life in a stunning group of collectible treasures. Top Row (left to right): Swarovski Silver Crystal *South Sea Series* "Dolphin" and *Sparkling Fruit Series* "Large Pineapple." Middle Row: Swarovski Silver Crystal *Endangered Species* "Mother Kangaroo with Baby" and *When We Were Young* "Rocking Horse." Bottom Row: *eggspressions!* "Eternity," Goebel of North America's Steinbach Crystal "American Indian Camp," and *eggspressions!* "Mother's Pride."

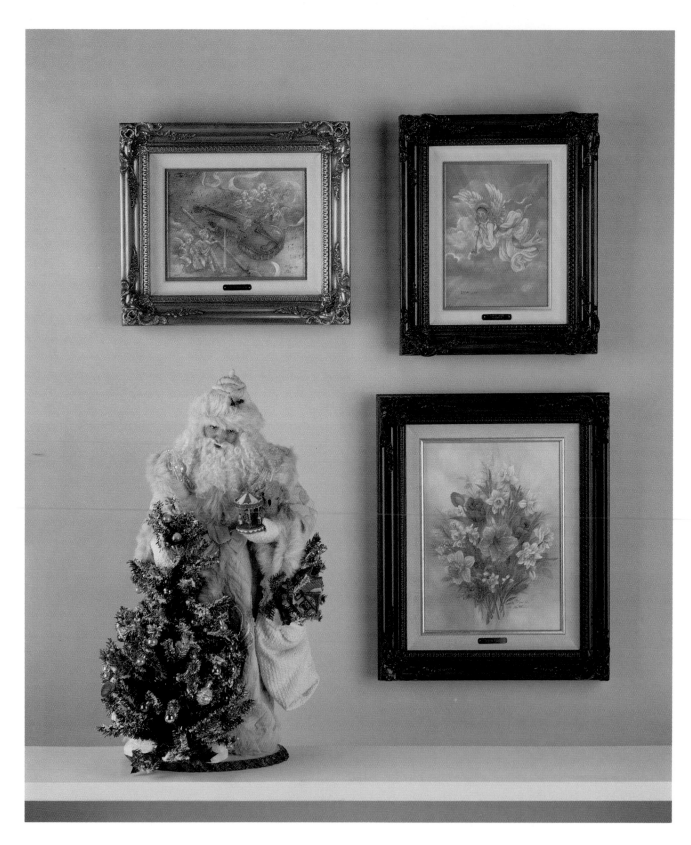

The grace and beauty of collectible treasures...make a wonderful addition to home and office decors. Top Row: (left to right) Imperial Graphics' "Violin Concerto" and "Angel with Trumpet." Bottom Row: Amaranth Productions' "Father Christmas" and Imperial Graphics' "Spring Bulbs."

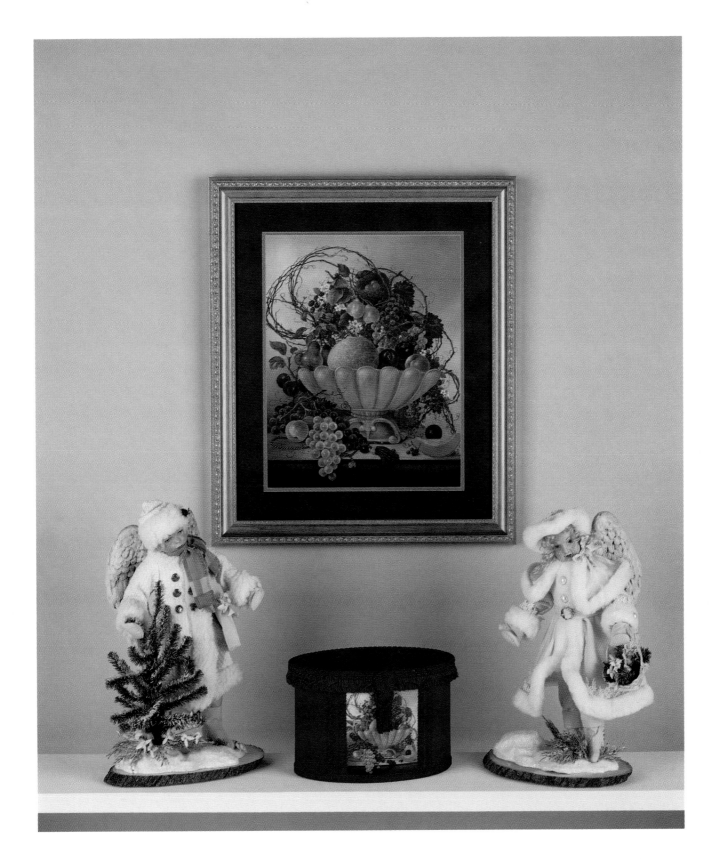

Top (center): The Art of Glynda Turley's "Abundance III." Bottom Row (left to right): Amaranth Productions' "Andre, The Victorian Winter Angel Baby," The Art of Glynda Turley's "Abundance III" Keepsake Box, and Amaranth Productions' "Anna, The Victorian Winter Angel Baby."

Some of our favorite places, faces and memories... are captured in an array of colorful collectibles. Top Row (left to right): From Amazze's *Century Lights Collection*: "Rose Island Lighthouse, RI," "Block Island (Southeast Lighthouse), RI," and "Split Rock Lighthouse, MN." Second Row: Harmony Kingdom's "Unbearables" and "Noah's Lark," and The Art of Glynda Turley's "Flowers for Mommy" figurine. Third Row: Cardew Design's "Teddy Bear's Picnic," Walnut Ridge Collectibles' "Snowy, Snowy Night" ornament and "Happy Christmas" figurine, and Cardew Design's "Green Betty-Gardening" from the *English Betty's* collection. Bottom Row: Gartlan USA's "Ringo Starr" large figurine, Dear Artistic Sculpture's "Black Bride and Groom" and Gartlan USA's "Leave It To Beaver" Jerry Mathers 10-1/4" plate.

Top Row (left to right): Ace Product Management's *Harley Davidson Holiday Figurines* "Skating Party," Arcadian Pewter's "Stake Side Truck," "Steam Boat Bank," and "Aeroplane Monocoupe." Second Row: Ace Product Management's *Harley Davidson Santa Figurines* "Suiting Up," Walnut Ridge Collectibles' "Holiday Sledding," Ace Product Management's *Harley Davidson Holiday Memories* series "Late Arrival," Cardew Design's "Golf Trolley," and Dear Artistic Sculpture's "Two Doves." Third Row: Ace Product Management's *Harley Davidson Holiday Memories* series "Late Arrival" stein, Dear Artistic Sculpture's "Tiger," and Shube's Manufacturing's "Night Song." Bottom Row: Shube's Manufacturing's "Victorious," "Old Enemies," and "Guardian of the Crystal."

The many faces of Santa...and other holiday characters are captured in collectibles that show the serious and silly sides of these universally loved figures. Top Row (left to right): United Design's "Getting Santa Ready," June McKenna Collectibles' "Light of Christmas", Cast Art Industries' "Santa's Kingdom," and Possible Dreams' "Jolly Traveller." Middle Row: Ladie and Friends' "The Little Ones at Christmas," Lladró's "A Christmas Wish," Christopher Radko's "Department Store Santa," Possible Dreams' "Giving Thanks," and ANRI U.S.'s "Checking It Twice." Bottom Row: Lance Corp.'s "Stars & Stripes Santa," Possible Dreams' "A Good Round," Christopher Radko's "Bishop," June McKenna Collectibles' "Peaceful Journey" and Annalee Mobilitee Dolls' " 'Puppies for Christmas' Santa."

Top Row (left to right): Duncan Royale's "Mongolian" Santa, Possible Dreams' "A Frisky Friend," Byers' Choice Ltd.'s "Working Santa," Possible Dreams' "Sounds of Christmas." Middle Row: June McKenna Collectibles' "Christmas Lullaby," Old World Christmas' "Merlin" and "Regal Father Christmas," Kurt S. Adler Inc.'s "Arm Chair Quarterback," Cavanagh Group International's "Santa at the Fireplace." Bottom Row: Byers' Choice Ltd.'s "Couple in Sleigh" and "Salvation Army Girl with 'War Cry'," and WACO Products' "Girl Caroler" and "Boy Caroler."

Time-honored traditions of the holidays...

are captured for generations to come in these sometimes whimsical and always wonderful Christmas collectibles. Top Row (left to right): Reco International's "Dear Santa," Hallmark Keepsake Ornaments' "Murray® Fire Truck," June McKenna Collectibles' "Finishing Touch," Roman Inc.'s *1920's Clothlike* "American Santas Through the Decades," Pacific Rim Import's *Bunny Toes* "Douglas-Frosty Friends," and Schmid's "Belsnickles' 9-inch Teal" Santa. Middle Row: Midwest of Cannon Falls' "Santa on Reindeer" Ornament, Christopher Radko's "Bubbly," Enesco's "T-Bird," Royal Copenhagen/Bing & Grondahl's "Christmas Around the World 1995," ANRI U.S.'s "First Christmas Stocking," and Christopher Radko's "My Favorite Chimp." Bottom Row: Old World Christmas' "Waldkirchen Father Christmas Nutcracker," Classic Collectables by Uniquely Yours' "Scrooge," "Children Carolers," and "Adult Carolers."

Top Row: (left to right) Christopher Radko's "On Top of the World," Old World Christmas' "Sugarplum Fairy Nutcracker," and Christopher Radko's "Little Prince." Bottom Row: Kurt S. Adler Inc.'s *Camelot Series'* "Queen Guenevere Steinbach Nutcracker," Great American Taylor Collectibles *Old World Santas* "Tomba Claus-South Africa," Royal Copenhagen's "Christmas Around the World Ornament" and Great American Taylor Collectibles *Old World Santas* "Lars Claus-Norway." On the Riser: Great American Taylor Collectibles *Old World Santas* "Raymond Claus-Galapagos Islands" and "Stach Claus-Poland."

Warm and wonderful memories...

of Christmas' gone by are evoked by a host of holiday collectibles. Top Row: (left to right) Department 56's *Winter Silhouette Christmas Concerto* "Cellist," "Harpist," and "Violinist," *eggspressions!* "Beary Pink Christmas" Band Creations' "River Song" and "Monthly Angels." Middle Row: Department 56's "We'll Plant the Starry Pines" and "Bringing Starry Pines," Cavanagh Group International's "Polar Bear Family," Ganz's *Little Cheesers* "Light of the World," Schmid's "Bah Humbug." Hanging Ornaments: Hand & Hammer Silversmiths' "Fabergé Egg" and "Joy," Hallmark Keepsake Ornaments' "Christmas Cardinal," and Hand & Hammer Silversmiths' "1995 Annual Star." Bottom Row: The Ashton Drake Galleries' "Beneath the Mistletoe," M.I. Hummel Club's "Ride Into Christmas," and United Design's "Into the Wind Victorian."

Top Row (left to right): Hand & Hammer Silversmiths' "The Night Before Christmas" (set of 4), Royal Copenhagen/Bing & Grondahl's "Jubilee Edition - The Capitol" and "Christmas Plate 1995," Pacific Rim Import Corp.'s *Bristol Township* "King's Gate School." Middle Row: George Z. Lefton Co's "Mundt Manor," Old World Christmas' "Santa in Sleigh," Department 56's "Hather Harness" and "Chelsea Market Curiosities Monger & Cart." Bottom Row: Forma Vitrum's "Community Chapel," Midwest of Cannon Falls' "Clara," Lilliput Lane's "Plum Cottage" Ornament, and Department 56's *Christmas in the City* "Heritage Museum of Art" and "Holiday Field Trip."

The mystery, magic and wonder of Angels...

and other religious themes are translated into an array of collectibles that inspire, comfort and amuse. Top Row (left to right): Cast Art Industries' *Dreamsicles* "Picture Perfect," *eggspressions!* "Angel of Hope," Margaret Furlong's "2-inch Wreath Angel", "3-inch Flower Garland Angel," "4-inch Flower Garland Angel" and "Faith Angel," Ganz's "Angelic Teachings," and *eggspressions!* "Oh, Holy Night." Middle Row: United Design's "The Gift '95," Roman Inc.'s *1995 Millenium Plate* "Cause of Our Joy" and *Seraphim Classics* "Seraphina-Heaven's Helper," ANRI U.S.'s "Angel of Kindness," Cast Art Industries' *Heavenly Classics* "On Wings of Love." Bottom Row: United Design's "A Little Closer to Heaven," Fenton Art Glass' "Radiant Angel," Georgetown Collection's "Arielle-The Spring Angel," and United Design's "Guardian Angel, Lion and Lamb, Light."

Top Row (left to right): VickiLane's "He Sets My Heart Free," Reco International's "Angel of Laughter," Band Creations' *Best Friends* "Noah's Ark." Middle Row: Roman Inc.'s Americana Collection "Noah & Friends" and Ladie and Friends, Inc.'s "The Little Angel." Bottom Row: Roman Inc.'s *Fontanini* "Heirloom Nativity," ANRI U.S.'s "Mary and Infant" from *The Vatican Library Collection* and Sarah's Attic's "Dignity Angel."

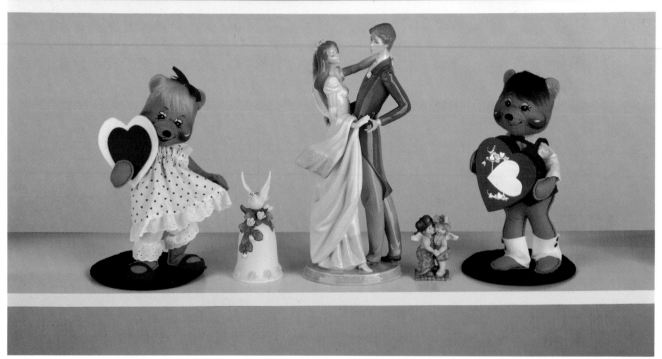

Love and marriage...are celebrated in a collection of serious and sweet collectibles. Top Row (left to right): Ganz's "Holy Mortrimony," Today's Creations' "With This Ring," Band Creations' *Best Wishes* "Anniversary," Today's Creations' "Slice of Life," VickiLane's "Wedding Bunnies," Today's Creations' "First Dance." Middle Row: Today's Creations' "Bride," Forma Vitrum's "Trinity Church," Duncan Royale's *Jubilee Dancers* "Bliss." Bottom Row: Annalee Mobilitee Dolls' "Valentine Girl Bear," Seymour Mann's "Dove Bell," Lladró's "I Love You Truly," Ganz's "Match Made in Heaven," Annalee Mobilitee Doll's "Valentine Boy Bear."

Garden delights...grace collectible plates and vases from some of America's premier collectibles manufacturers. Top Row (left to right): The Franklin Mint's "Imperial Hummingbird Plate," The Fenton Art Glass Company's "Hand-Painted Trellis Basket," Reco International's "Moments of Caring." Middle Row: Seymour Mann's "Hummingbird Duo Plate," Maruri U.S.A.'s "Violet Crowned Hummingbirds with Gentian," and Cavanagh Group International's "The Girl in Rose Arbor." Bottom Row: The Fenton Art Glass Company's "Victorian Art Glass Pitcher," "Favrene Ginger Jar" (base and lid not shown) and "Pansies on Cranberry 10-1/2" Pitcher."

The sweet innocence of childhood...is

reflected in a charming assortment of collectibles. Top Row (left to right): M.I. Hummel Club's "Honey Lover" and "Friend or Foe," PenDelfin's "Teddy," Miss Martha Originals' "Issie" and "Honey." Middle Row: Sarah's Attic's "Love & Hugs," M.I. Hummel Club's "Come Back Soon," ANRI U.S.'s "Tender Care," and Enesco's "Sharing the Common Thread of Love." Bottom Row: M.I. Hummel Club's "Strike Up The Band," Miss Martha Originals' "Gina," Calabar Creations' "Little Count" from *The Jazzy Five Collection*.

Mythical creatures and magical fairies...

work their spells in a myriad of collectible treasures. Top Row (left to right): Precious Art/Panton's "Moplos," "Escublar," and "Dubious Alliance," and Lance Corporation's "Have & Have Knot." Middle Row: The Tudor Mint's "The Visionary," "The Magical Encounter," and "The Unicorn of Justice," Precious Art/Panton's "Schnoogles," Flambro Imports' *Pocket Dragons* "Watson" and "Elementary My Dear." Bottom Row: The Tudor Mint's "The Great Earth Dragon," Rawcliffe's *Wish Fairies* "Love" and "Fun," "Fall" *Angel Fairy of the Seasons*, and Precious Art/Panton's "One Unhappy Ride."

Figures from literature and history...hold a special fascination for artists and collectors alike. Top row (left to right): Royal Doulton's "Charles Dickens," The Bradford Exchange's "Gettysburg," and Sarah's Attic's "Praise the Lord IV." Bottom Row: Lance Corp.'s "General Robert E. Lee, CSA," Miss Martha Originals' "Bessie Smith," Sarah's Attic's "Buffalo Soldier," and Midwest of Cannon Fall's "Paul Bunyan Nutcracker."

The fun and fascinating world of sports...

has long been an inspiration for collectible artists. Top Row (left to right): The Boyds Collections' "Sebastion's Prayer," Flambro's *The Negro Leagues™* Baseball Ornament "Brooklyn Royal Giants," VickiLane's *Golfer Bunny* "Fore You," and Cast Art Industries' *Cuddl'somes'* "Cubby." Middle Row: Miss Martha Originals' "William," The Bradford Exchange's "Joe Montana - King of Comebacks," Flambro's *The Negro Leagues* "Atlanta Black Crackers 1940" and "Homestead Grays 1938." Bottom Row: Ron Lee's World of Clowns' "Practice Swing," Calabar Creations' "Certain Tee" from *The Tee Club Collection* and "Strike So Sweet" from *Yesterday's Friends Collection* and Hallmark Keepsake Ornaments' "Shaquille O'Neal."

Animal antics take center stage...in a fanciful assortment of collectible treasures. Top Row (left to right): Anheuser-Busch Inc.'s "This Bud's For You" Plate, June McKenna Collectibles' "Christmas Down on the Farm," and Possible Dreams' "Clem Jingles." Middle Row: Calabar Creation's *Angelic Pigasus Collection's* "Angelo," Reco International's "You Quack Me Up," VickiLane's "Sunnydaze," Possible Dreams' "Buttercup." Bottom Row: Schmid's "Velveteen Rabbit," Anheuser-Busch Inc.'s "Horseplay," Cast Art Industries *Cuddl'somes* "Dress Up," and Cavanagh Group International's "Boy at the Well."

Top Row (left to right): The Boyds *Bears & Friends™ Bearstone* Collection's "Ms. Bruin & Bailey...The Lesson," "The Nurse," and "Celeste-The Angel Rabbit," Ganz's "Balderdash," and The Boyds Collections Ltd.'s "Bailey the Baker with Sweetie Pie." Middle Row: Enesco's *Cherished Teddies* "Our Hearts Belong to You," PenDelfin's "Jacky," "New Boy," and "Pepper," VickiLane's Blossom "Hopping Forward," and PenDelfin's "Mike." Bottom Row: Pacific Rim Imports' *Bunny Toes* "Charlotte-Best of the Bunch," The Hamilton Collections' "Jack and Jill," The Bradford Exchange's "Time for a Little Something," and Pacific Rim Import's *Bunny Toes* "Maggie-Joy of Giving."

Lifestyles of Native Americans...and the beauty found in nature provide the inspiration behind a great number of modern collectibles. Top Row (left to right): Legends' "Hunter's Quest," Maruri U.S.A.'s "Wild Wings," and Legends' "Rapture." Bottom Row: Legends' "Each, to the Other," Rick Cain Studios' "Winged Victor," and Legends' "Winds of Memory."

Top Row (left to right): Lance Corporation's "Warrior's Rescue," The Bradford Exchange's "Winter's Calm," The Tudor Mint's "Apache - Tonto Warrior." Middle Row: Anheuser-Busch Inc.'s "Golden Retreiver" Stein, The Hamilton Collection's "A Wolf's Pride," and Reco International's "Peace at Last." Bottom Row: Rick Cain Studios' "Family Tree," Anheuser-Busch Inc.'s "The Great Horned Owl" Stein, and Rick Cain Studios' "Arctic Heir."

The strength and beauty found in wildlife...

are captured for collectors to enjoy in a stirring array of figurines and steins. Top row (left to right): Rick Cain Studios' "Transcendental White Wolf" and "Fire & Ice," and Creart's "Moose." Bottom Row: Creart's "Grumbler" Cape Buffalo, Legends' "Scent in the Air," and Creart's "Over the Top" Puma.

Pop culture is preserved...in a variety of charming collectibles. Top Row (left to right): George Z. Lefton Co.'s "Pepsi Billboard," Hallmark Keepsake Ornament's "Space Shuttle," and George Z. Lefton Co.'s "Patriot's Diner." Middle Row: Schmid's "Pumbaa, Simba and Timon" Music Box, The Franklin Mint's "Sgt. Pepper's Lonely Hearts Club Band" Musical Bell Jar, Hallmark Keepsake Ornament's "Solo in the Spotlight" and Schmid's "Betty Boop as Scarlet." Bottom Row: Royal Doulton's "Captain Hook," The Franklin Mint's "Jukebox Jamboree Musical Sculpture," and Enesco's "Solo in the Spotlight."

Candy colored cottages...and other architectural beauties take us back to a simpler, more elegant time. Top Row (left to right): My Friends & Me "Boss House" and "91 East Bay St.," Michael's Limited's "River Belle Steamer." Middle Row: My Friends & Me "Cathedral of St. John the Baptist-1898," Shelia's "Eclectic Blue," "Edwardian Green," "Brandywine" and "Queen Rose." Bottom Row: Midwest of Cannon Falls' "Cottontail Lane Lighted Rosebud Manor," Michael's Limited's "Victorian Living" and "1905 Maple Lane."

Top Row (left to right): Michael's Limited's "Mountain Homestead," My Friends & Me "Pettingell House," "Owens Thomas House" and "The Herb House." Second Row: Band Creation's "Roseman Bridge," R.R. Creations' "Nathaniel Porter Inn," "Black Horse Inn," and "Herlong Mansion." Third Row: Brandywine Collectibles' "Country Lane General Store," "Hometown X Brick Church," "Hometown X Gift Shop," "Country Lane School" and "Hometown X Doll Shop." Bottom Row: Midwest of Cannon Falls' "Cannon Valley" Lighted Dairy Barn, The Cat's Meow Village "Creamery Bridge," "Becky Thatcher's House," "Sideshow" and "John Coffin House."

Decorating with collectibles…brings greater rewards to this growing hobby. Top Row (left to right): MAGI Entertainment Products' "To Elvis with Love." Middle Row: The Greenwich Workshop's "Into the Wilderness" Book and "Our Ladies of the Front Lawn." Bottom Row: The Greenwich Workshop's "Day Lilies" fine art poster and "Alphabet Soup" Book.

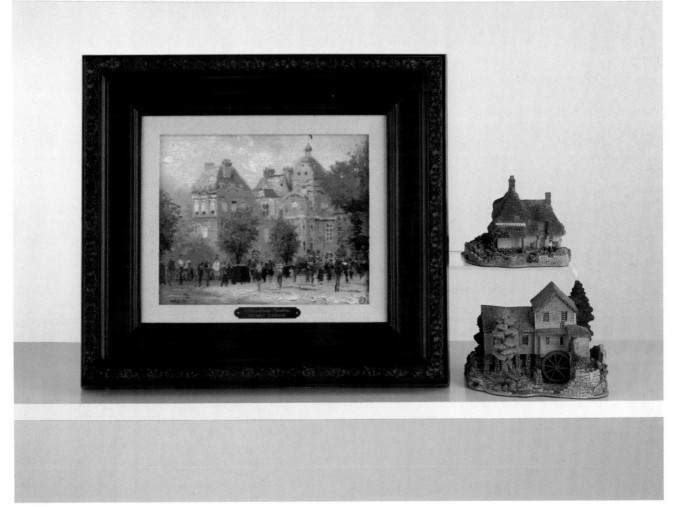

Top Row: (left to right) Lilliput Lane's "Chipping Coombe" and "Fountains Abbey." Bottom Row: Lightpost Publishing's "Luxembourg Gardens" by Thomas Kinkade, Lilliput Lane's "Gertrude's Garden" and "Harvest Mill."

The many faces of woman... Mother and friend, teacher and confidante are among the roles depicted in today's collectibles celebrating womanhood. Top Row (left to right): Lladró's "Spring Splendor," Royal Doulton's "When I was Young" and "Deborah," Lladró's "Ready to Learn." Bottom Row: Giuseppe Armani's "Diana," Royal Doulton's "Hello Daddy," Lladró's "Good Night" and Giuseppe Armani's "Minerva."

Giuseppe Armani's *Via Veneto* "Marina," "Nicole" and "Valentina."

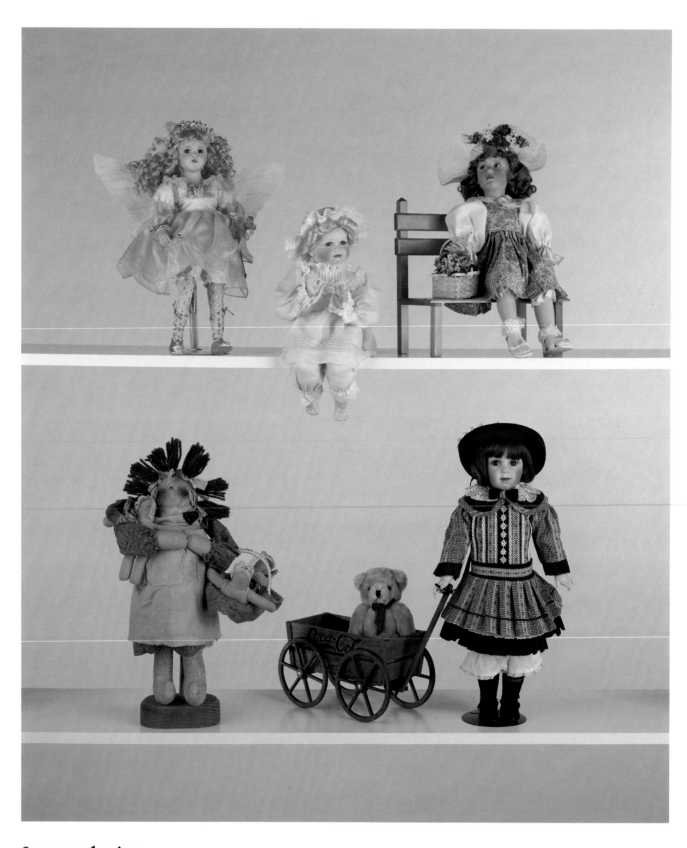

Sugar and spice...and everything nice is reflected in a sweet selection of limited edition collectible dolls and plates. Top Row (left to right): Seymour Mann's "Sugarplum Fairy for McRaes," The Ashton-Drake Galleries' "Now I Lay Me Down to Sleep," and Georgetown Collection's "Caroline." Bottom Row: Attic Babies' "Fertile Myrtle" and The Franklin Mint's "Coca Cola® Heirloom Collector Doll-Megan."

Top Row (left to right): The Hamilton Collection's "Chelsea" and "Love One Another," Enesco's "He Loves Me," Ladie and Friends' "Jillian Bowman." Bottom Row: Seymour Mann's "Carlotta" and The Ashton-Drake Galleries' "Elizabeth."

Amusing and adorable dolls...are created to reflect the childlike simplicity of days gone by. Top Row (left to right): Attic Babies' "Jessabell," Ladie and Friends' "Leona High" and "Regina Bowman." Bottom Row: Attic Babies' "Ruby Begonia," "Petunia Kay Alvertie" and "Old Raggedy Noah."

ACE PRODUCT MANAGEMENT GROUP

At Ace, Harley-Davidson® Collectibles
Move Faster Than Their Namesakes!

Perfect perspective sends collectors "Roaring into the 20's" on Ace's pewter issue. It's part of the Harley Decade Series. *Can't you hear those wheels skipping over the brick-covered streets? Notice the distinct border design!*

At the turn of the century, life picked up steam! Technology flourished while automation and communication changed lives. Everywhere we went, speed personified our nation's urge to go faster and further. The time was perfect for the invention of a new vehicle that was small, economical, spontaneous and impromptu. Enter the all-American Harley-Davidson motorcycle.

The year was 1903. William S. Harley, Arthur Davidson, Walter Davidson and William A. Davidson came up with the idea of an internal combustion engine fitted into a bicycle frame. Their prototype was a family affair: Aunt Janet applied the first pinstriping and logo by hand. As orders were taken and filled, founding fathers dubbed their first production run "Silent Gray Fellow."

The American public fell in love with Harley-Davidson and orders increased over time. A manufacturing facility, erected behind the Harley family home, sprang up in 1904. As the first decade of the new century progressed, V-twin engines came on the scene. Harley-Davidson entered, then won, its first sporting event. This landmark business was, "off and running." Today, the company looks forward to celebrating 100 years of excitement and innovation in 2003.

Ace Becomes Harley's "Partner-in-Time"

In 1947, World War II was over, and America was ready for a Renaissance. New enterprises sprang up from coast-to-coast. In Milwaukee, Wisconsin, the Ace Product Management Group entered into an agreement with Harley-Davidson as the motorcycle company began its 44th year of business. Ace would distribute apparel and accessories bearing the Harley-Davidson Motor Company insignia to its growing dealership network.

The 50-year-long relationship between Harley-Davidson and Ace continues to flourish, and growth has been remarkable. Ace's 1,000 square foot factory (from which the popular apparel was distributed) is now a 160,000 square foot warehouse. Product offerings have expanded well beyond apparel. In 1981, Ace became the source for Genuine Harley-Davidson collectibles and giftware items – a product line which quickly grew through the demands of a waiting audience of "bike enthusiasts" across the U.S. Each gift and limited edition collectible produced by Ace is distinct and bears the imprint of Harley-Davidson, but unlike licensed art, Ace issues are included as part of the motorcycle giant's *Genuine* line, known as *Genuine MotorClothes® & Collectibles.* Harley-Davidson fans can find this gathering of seasonal and non-seasonal delights only at authorized Harley-Davidson dealerships.

Today, Ace executives are committed to growth, innovation and excitement. From Ace's Product Center, an amazing variety of art emerges each year, all of it dedicated to enhancing the pleasure and lifestyle of the Harley-Davidson enthusiast. When a collector acquires a piece of art from Ace, he or she is assured of an "off-road Harley experience" that won't be duplicated. To make sure everything emerging from Ace's Product Center is on target, five designers work tirelessly to develop new ideas. Research is painstaking. Whether a figurine, collector plate, holiday ornament or personal accessory, collectors can be sure they've purchased a genuine Harley treasure.

Dynamic engine at his feet, Santa's packed and ready for a ride! This hand-painted figurine, "Something for Everyone," follows in the tradition of Ace's 1994 piece "The Old Toymaker."

Holiday Collectibles: At Ace, It's on the Fast Track

It's common knowledge. Santa rides a Harley-Davidson during the "off season." This should come as no surprise to Harley fans, since Santa's no fool when it comes to prestige, and time is precious in his line of work. Given Santa's passion for his bike, it's no wonder some of Ace's greatest collectible successes are holiday Harley issues; ornaments, collector plates, snow domes (water globes), figurines and personal accessories. Past issues of the company's annual Christmas plate and ornament have sold out and appreciated significantly.

The cornerstone of the Ace holiday library is the *Holiday Memories* series. Each year's grouping consists of a collector plate, glass ornament, music box and German-crafted stein. The annual theme is illustrated by celebrated Midwest artist Ben Otero. His illustrations are eagerly awaited. In 1998, *Holiday Memories* will conclude its successful five-year run with special 95th Anniversary art sure to excite the most seasoned Harley-Davidson collector.

Because collectors insist upon stringent limits to assure exclusivity, Ace has chosen to individually number most issues. The most highly prized Harley limited edition, the annual collector plate, is produced in limits not exceeding 15,000. The first issue in the *Holiday Memories* series was "Under the Mistletoe," depicting a lovestruck couple beside his sleek, vintage Harley in the winter snow. Original water-colors add sparkle and life to the setting which is transferred to a fine porcelain plate, then trimmed with a 24K gold border.

Given the nostalgia and charm of this image, it's easy to understand why "Under the Mistletoe" was so popular when it was introduced in 1994 as a plate, wood music box (playing "On the Street Where You Live"), pearlescent glass ornament and German stein. Only 7,500 music boxes and steins were made, to the delight of Harley collectors.

In 1995, Ace introduced a new

Ace's 1996 holiday plate, "After the Pageant," is filled with color, rimmed in gold and showcases a vintage Harley, with sidecar, on a snowy Christmas day.

success story to the popular series titled "Late Arrival." The following year (1996), "After the Pageant" debuted. Each work features gatherings of Yuletide merrymakers surrounding the "stars" of the series: vintage Harley-Davidson motorcycles. A heartwarming tale comes with each collectible in the *Holiday Memories* series, too.

Figurine lovers won't be disappointed when Christmas rolls around. Ace has developed several complex, annual figurines, such as "Twenty-Nine Days 'Til Christmas," limited to only 3,000 numbered pieces. This sculpture, based on the 1989 Christmas plate, shows four figures admiring a shiny Harley-Davidson in a showroom window.

When It Comes to Harley Collectibles, There's No Place Like Ace for Innovation!

While many of Ace's limited edition collectible designs fall into what we would consider a "traditional collectible category," there are also unusual items for the Harley collector, such as Ace's limited edition belt buckles. Distinguished by bold designs and

fashioned of fine brass and pewter, *The Engine Buckle* series depicts famous V-twin engines used to power Harley-Davidson motorcycles over time. First introduced in 1994, this buckle collection ends with "1st V-twin Engine," set to debut in 1997. Cast in fine pewter with brass accents, only 5,000 each of these annual belt buckles are made.

For the "serious buckle collector," Ace debuted the *Decade Series Buckles*, each featuring an accurately-sculpted scene from Harley-Davidson history. Nearly four inches wide and three inches high, the *Decade* collection is typified by its "1930's — Growing Stronger through Hard Times" buckle which depicts a Harley in use during the Great Depression.

Each of the belt buckles in this collection is part of a larger library of collectible art called the *Harley-Davidson Decade Series*. You'll find such accessories as pewter-cast collector plates, shot glasses and German-crafted steins in this series, each thematically designed to highlight Harley-Davidson's place in history over time.

While Ace prides itself on producing Harley-Davidson collectibles that are priced and sized for everyone's pleasure, "high rollers" haven't been forgotten! Ace developed an impressive Harley-Davidson Collector's Chess Set that's not only beautiful, it's limited to

Lavish detail, distinct imagery and impressive size make this "Panhead" belt buckle from Ace's Engine series a must-have for all Harley-Davidson collectors.

just 3,000 sets! The Harley chess set includes customized, hand-sculpted pieces cast in zinc and plated in chrome and 24K gold. Glittering eagles, engines and Harley logos serve as the playing pieces for this marvelous game. A handcrafted maple and walnut board, with laser engraved Harley designs on either side, provides the perfect game surface. Pieces are stored in a felt-lined drawer beneath the board embellished with a sculpted eagle drawer pull!

Not a fan of chess because you're too busy buzzing around on the back of your favorite cycle? Not to worry! Ace has created collectible gems sure to find a place in your heart. Consider *Young Rider* figurines – the ideal limited edition figurine collection to share with your child. Each sculpture represents youngsters seeking to make their dream of riding a Harley, just like Dad and Mom, come true!

If figurines are not your art choice, how about the *Harley Collectible Lighter Collection*? These refillable lighters have found a huge audience appreciative of their themes, sleek designs and usefulness. Big sellers include a replica of the lighter used by World War I pilots called "The Harley-Davidson Trench Lighter," "The Casablanca Lighter" (modeled after a "spy lighter"), and a World War II version identical to one used in the early 40's.

Harley-Davidson lighter collectors without a penchant for war themes can choose from a leather-encased lighter with a true "biker look," or a full line of traditional Zippo® lighters emblazoned with logo designs (both medallion styles and silk-screened). Like all official Harley-Davidson collectibles created by Ace, each of these lighter styles is available only from authorized dealerships.

Ace Remembers the Ladies with Something Special

Catering to Harley-Davidson enthusiasts has been Ace's full-time job for nearly 50 years. During that time, most every Harley audience member has been recognized – even the ladies! The growing female motorcycle rider population is now showcased with the first Harley-Davidson limited figurine celebrating women who love to ride!

Noted sculptor Mark Patrick created many of Ace's earlier sensations, including "The Reunion," limited to just 2,500 figures, plus "Milwaukee Ride" and "The Old Soldier," limited to only 1,500 pieces each. He was commissioned to design this fifth sculpture titled "Daytona Bound." The sculpture portrays a woman biker en route to the fun and sun of Daytona Beach, Florida's annual Bike Week.

Like "The Reunion," "Milwaukee Ride" and "The Old Soldier," "Daytona Bound" is sculpted in clay and wax to Patrick's exacting standards. Once satisfied with every detail, Ace sees to the edition's manufacture, from hand-casting in hydrastone to mounting each of the 1,500 sculptures onto its fine wood base. Individually numbered, "Daytona Bound" has already become a hot seller.

It's hard to imagine what the four founding fathers of the Harley-Davidson Motorcycle Company might say today if they had an opportunity to look through the impressive library of Harley-Davidson collectibles that have come from Ace. Would they find it hard to believe that cycle riders have fallen so in love with the freedom and fun of their machines that they find art associated with their Harleys irresistible? Probably not. After all, they know their audience. So do the folks at Ace. Based upon that assumption, Harley-Davidson fans will be eagerly awaiting the surprises Ace Product Management Group has in store for them in the decades ahead!

Harley-Davidson and Harley are registered trademarks of the Harley-Davidson Motor Company.

Ace Product Management Group
9053 North Deerbrook Trail
Brown Deer, WI 53223
Phone: (414) 365-5400
Fax: (414) 365-5410

KURT S. ADLER, INC.
The World's Leading Resource for
Christmas Accessories and Collectibles

Kurt S. Adler, Inc. presents "Toys for Good Boys and Girls," a Fabriché™ Santa figurine that features a design recreated from the Smithsonian Museum Archives.

Christmas may only come once a year, but at Kurt S. Adler, Inc., it always looks like Christmas. In fact, over the years Kurt S. Adler, Inc. has become almost synonymous with the great holiday of Christmas. Nearly 50 years ago, Kurt S. Adler virtually founded the Christmas decorating industry when he established Kurt S. Adler, Inc./Santa's World. Mr. Adler, a soft-spoken, charming businessman, brought a European flavor and sense of fashion and integrated it with American tastes, bringing a new look to Christmas in the United States. These efforts built the foundation for the company's success today with its current position as the world's leading resource for holiday decorative accessories and as a leader in the collectibles world.

Mr. Adler enjoys reminiscing about his nearly half-century of bringing Yuletide joy to so many people. He traveled the world over in search of unique decorative accessories that would capture the imagination of post-war America. When he wasn't buying and designing new products, Mr. Adler traveled all over the U.S. selling merchandise out of his case of samples. Gifted with the talent for knowing his market and a keen eye for appealing designs and colors, he carried prototypes of his ideas overseas. There, he worked with factories to develop the finest products, using the best materials at the most affordable prices. He quickly learned that the American consumer was quality-conscious and that his products would have to meet stringent standards for his company to succeed in the marketplace.

During its history, the firm has been recognized for many breakthroughs and significant achievements. Ornaments have always been one of the mainstays of the line. Kurt S. Adler, Inc. was the first to design, develop, import and distribute ornaments that were crafted of high-quality materials including better woods, ceramic, stained glass, resin, higher quality plastics, and capiz shell, a byproduct of mother-of-pearl. The firm also introduced the Old World art of wood-turned ornaments to the Orient. In the mid-1950s and well into the 1960s, Kurt S. Adler, Inc. imported the first "quality-made" snowglobes from West Germany. These snowglobes, also called snowdomes, featured Christmas scenes with Santa and other holiday characters. Many of these ornaments and accessories were saved and collected by Americans throughout the years. These consumers have become familiar with the company's products and learned to trust the Kurt S. Adler, Inc. name.

In the early 1970s, utilizing the unique talents of its veteran holiday accessory designer Marjorie Grace Rothenberg, Kurt S. Adler, Inc. introduced cornhusk ornaments. These items include the famous cornhusk mice and angels which depict human characters in fabric and lace costumes. Today, cornhusk mice ornaments are designed for every season and are still highly sought-after by collectors. Marjorie creates collectibles in her country studio at the foothills of the Berkshire Mountains, where she continues to design cornhusk mice ornaments, Fabriché™ figurines and ornaments that depict Santa and Mrs. Claus wearing their trademark gold wedding bands.

During the 1980s, Kurt S. Adler, Inc. introduced The *Louis Nichole Heirloom Collection*, one of the most elegant ornament lines ever produced. This group, which was designed by renowned home furnishings designer Louis Nichole, featured Victorian styled doll ornaments dressed in elaborate fabric and lace costumes with stunning colors. These collectibles reinforced the firm's position in the high fashion end of the Christmas market.

In the 1980s, Kurt S. Adler, Inc. introduced *The Smithsonian Carousel Series*, which features ornaments that represent small replicas of antique carousel animal figures found on merry-go-rounds in the Smithsonian Museum Archives. These museum-quality reproductions feature hand-painted designs and the exact detailing of original, turn-of-the-century carousel animal figures.

Kurt S. Adler, Inc. retains the largest team of first-class, exclusive designers "under one roof" that creates collectible holiday ornaments and accessories in a broad variety of looks and styles. Kurt S. Adler, Inc. is credited for designing the first ornaments and figurines featuring African-American Santas and Santas designed in a variety of unique and whimsical settings.

Charter members of The Steinbach Collectors Club will receive the exclusive opportunity to purchase "King Wenceslaus," an 18" members-only nutcracker. This handsome nutcracker features the good king in his regal attire, hand-painted and hand-turned in the Steinbach Factory.

Steinbach Nutcrackers and Smokers Widely Recognized for Tremendous Demand and Soaring Values

Since it began marketing collectible nutcrackers just a few years ago, Kurt S. Adler, Inc. has enjoyed a tremendous response to the line. Kurt S. Adler, Inc. is sponsoring the Steinbach Collectors Club, which provides free gifts, newsletters and brochures, and offers Charter Members the opportunity to purchase the members-only "King Wenceslaus" Nutcracker.

Kurt S. Adler, Inc. markets and distributes limited edition nutcrackers and smoking figures from the famous Steinbach factory, located in Hohenhameln in the northern region of Germany. For six generations, the Steinbachs have been handcrafting fine nutcrackers and smokers and today are world-renowned for quality and craftsmanship. One of the first limited edition nutcrackers was "Merlin

The Magician," which recently sold for over $2,000 on the secondary market after its 1991 release at a retail price of $185.

The *Steinbach Limited Edition Nutcracker Collection* is quite extensive. The *Camelot Series* includes "Queen Guinevere," "Sir Galahad," "Sir Lancelot," "King Arthur" and "Merlin The Magician." The *Tales of Sherwood Forest Series* includes "Friar Tuck" and "Robin Hood," while *The Famous Chieftains* features "Chief Black Hawk," "Chief Red Cloud" and "Chief Sitting Bull." The *Christmas Legends Series* offers the "1930 Santa," "St. Nicholas" and "Father Christmas." The *American Presidents Series* includes "Teddy Roosevelt," "Abraham Lincoln" and "George Washington," while "Benjamin Franklin" is the first issue in *The Great Inventors Series*.

Award-Winning Polonaise™ Collection

The tremendous popularity and recognition for *The Polonaise™ Christmas Collection* was evidenced in the spring of 1995 when it received the "Best Glass Ornament Collection" at the Collectors Jubilee in Tulsa, Oklahoma. Molded glass ornaments are handcrafted in Poland in the age-old tradition of European master glassblowers. The ornaments feature hand-workmanship that is very involved, performed by Europe's most highly skilled and well-trained artisans who create forms and fashion shapes by hand-blowing glass. Boxed sets include a limited edition "Wizard of Oz" set, "Ancient Egyptians," "Antique Trains," "Roman Empire," "Holy Family" and more.

Rosemary Volpi's Timeless Treasures

Rosemary Volpi is a gifted doll artist who is well-known for her sensitive Christmas figures. She recently created *The Timeless Treasures Collection,* which includes "Neapolitan Angels,"

that range in size from 7" to 12" and are reproduced from her originals. She also designed the "Woodland Santa" and other holiday figures.

Jocelyn Mostrom's Doll Ornaments

Nationally recognized in the doll world as the woman who raised the American craft of cornhusk doll making into a fine art, Jocelyn Mostrom has contributed to The *KSA Storybook Collection* with humorous renditions and romantic interpretations from classic nursery rhymes and fairytales. She also created *The Small Wonders of the World,* an international collection featuring brother and sister pairs of porcelain dolls dressed in traditional folk costumes crafted of paper twist. Her turn-of-the-century collection includes Victorian styled musicians and snow children. Jocelyn's dolls stand approximately 5" to 6" in height and can be displayed or used as tree ornaments.

Christmas Legends by Paul Bolinger

Paul F. Bolinger, the famed Californian woodcarver, combines both fine art and folkart techniques in his stylized

The limited edition "Wizard of Oz" six-piece set is from Kurt S. Adler, Inc.'s award-winning Polonaise™ Collection. The boxed set features hand-blown glass ornaments depicting Dorothy, The Tin Man, The Scarecrow, The Cowardly Lion, The Wizard and The Wizard of Oz ball ornament.

"Bountiful" is a unique 18" figurine designed exclusively by famed woodcarver Paul F. Bolinger for the Christmas Legends *series in the KSA Collectibles line from Kurt S. Adler, Inc.*

Christmas Legends series of figurines and ornaments. Cast in wood resin directly from originals and hand-painted by skilled artisans, these gift-giver legends are shown with distinctive looks and personalities. Many are inspired from old German and Celtic lore.

Adorable *Holly Bearies*

Holly Bearies features ornaments and figurines depicting bears that are "Looking for a Home in Your Heart." Each bear is distinguished by its own playful character and personality and is designed by veteran artist and avid teddy bear collector Holly Adler. These resin and wooden bears are offered in a broad variety of themes, from sports and professional settings to traditional Christmas motifs.

Whimsical Fabriché™ Sculptures

Fabriché™ sculptures are guaranteed for unparalleled design, superior quality and skillful workmanship. They feature a mixed media technique based on the Old World art of papier maché combined with modern methods and materials. The *Fabriché™ Collection* features the designs of Marjorie Grace Rothenberg, the KSA Design Team and reproductions of original designs found in the Smithsonian Museum Archives. Fabriché™ figurines and ornaments include exquisite angels and Santa and Mrs. Claus, designed in many whimsical professional, transportation and sports settings.

Whimsical *Hole-In-The-Wall Gang*

The *Hole-In-The-Wall Gang,* designed by Kandy Schlesinger, is a collection of whimsical mice living in their own city, beyond that mouse hole in the wall. These ornaments depict mice scurrying about performing daily routines in a humorous fashion.

Kurt S. Adler, Inc.
1107 Broadway
New York, NY 10010
(212) 924-0900
Fax (212) 807-0575

COLLECTORS' CLUB

The Steinbach Collectors Club
Kurt S. Adler, Inc.
1107 Broadway
New York, NY 10010
(800) 243-9627

Annual Dues: $40.00
Club Year: Anniversary of Sign-Up Date

Benefits:
• Membership Gift: 7" Nutcracker
• Redemption Certificate for Members-Only Nutcracker
• Newsletter
• Club Portfolio
• Membership Card and Certificate
• Special Edition Pin
• Color Brochures

AMARANTH PRODUCTIONS
Creator of Fine American Collectibles

This "Old World Santa" by Lynn West is eighth in a series that has become one of West's trademarks since the 1980s. Emerging from an enchanted winter forest, the musical "Old World Santa" carries a snow-laden fresh pine tree and golden branches, as well as a traditional pack loaded with evergreens, berries and roses on his back.

"The truly unique quality of Amaranth Productions," says owner Michela Engle, "is our commitment to our artists and their original creations. A dedication to quality guides our painstaking efforts to recreate designs to exacting detail because we appreciate the investment of time and inspiration that goes into each character our artists devise."

Under Engle's leadership, Amaranth Productions is dedicated to presenting limited edition collectibles of the highest artistic quality for the discriminating collector. Each creation, handcrafted in the U.S.A., exults the workmanship of American artisans.

The company's headquarters in Huntington Beach, California, provides a workshop environment where a team of artisans recreate the work of two designers: Lynn West and Linda Gill. *Lynn West Designs* exhibit classic elegance and timeless appeal, while the *Home-Bred Folks* by Linda Gill are country characters who serve up a slice of rural Americana.

Only hand techniques and detailed processes can replicate the intricate designs of the artists' originals. Experienced artisans pour the resin molds, hand-paint the faces, sew the opulent fabrics into enchanting costumes, style the wool used for the hair, and dress each work of art. This respect for the original design and commitment to artistic quality truly sets Amaranth apart.

Greek Mythology Inspires the Amaranth Name

Michela Engle is uniquely qualified for her role as President of Amaranth's whimsical workshop. Before founding the company, she was Director of Manufacturing for Lasting Endearments. It was there that she first worked with the designs of Lynn West. In 1988, the doors closed on Lasting Endearments, but Engle wanted to continue utilizing her unique experience, transforming artists' originals into limited edition collectibles. She established Amaranth Productions with Lynn West as her first art partner. In 1995, the company added Linda Gill to its artist roster.

The name "Amaranth" was chosen by Engle to express the company's creative concept. The name comes from Greek mythology and describes an imaginary flower that never fades, is ongoing and continuous...descriptive of the beauty and quality of the company's limited editions. A nine-year history of creating collectibles of everlasting value has proven that the name "Amaranth" was well chosen.

Collectibles "Handmade in the U.S.A."

Amaranth Productions proudly states that their creations are "handmade in the U.S.A." by American artisans. Amaranth's employees are a typical melting pot of nationalities with ages that range from no younger than 18 up to 74. Because Amaranth is a small company, they only produce limited edition sizes of 350 or less, which helps maintain the high standards of American craftsmanship.

A great deal of time is spent researching and gathering the finest available materials and accessories before Amaranth's artists even begin to design a new piece. Each exquisitely detailed collectible takes many hours to create and utilizes only the highest quality fabrics and components. This painstaking effort assures collectors that when they purchase an Amaranth Productions' American-made creation, they get only the best!

The Secrets of Amaranth's Production Process

Have you ever wondered how an artist's original creation is transformed into a collectible that will last from generation to generation? How do artisans take vulnerable material such as bread dough and make it into a doll that will not be attacked by pesky flour bugs?

The answer for Amaranth stems from the latest technology and materials, used to accurately reproduce the textures and nuances of each individual piece. Molds are made by placing the pieces sculpted by the artist into a cardboard box. A liquid material is poured into the box to harden overnight. By morning, the mold has formed, and it can be used to make the pieces of that edition.

Next, resin material is poured into the mold, creating a longer-lasting base.

The artisans use a multi-step process of painting and finishing techniques to create the Old World antique look of a Lynn West piece, and to bring to life the wonderful, expressive faces of Linda Gill's country characters.

A Vivid Imagination Sparks Lynn West's Artistic Vision

During our childhood, our minds are capable of creating fabulous images in intricate detail, where anything is possible. Lynn West envisioned mystical lands of sparkling wonder, where faeries fly, lords rule, and angels protect in splendor. West's unique creations are born out of the rich and wonderful fantasy life she enjoyed as a child.

When she reached adolescence, she began to wonder what had happened to the magic of her childhood Christmases. It was at this point in her life that she decided her gift to the world would be the rekindling of the joy of Christmas for generations to come.

Through her classic heirloom creations, Lynn West brings back the pleasure and warm memories of holidays past through the richly textured, deeply expressive Father Christmas designs that have made her an internationally known collectibles artist.

For over 16 years, West has been combining her talents for sculpture, painting, sewing and engineering design to bring to life the inhabitants of her imagination's magical realm. Her *Old World Santa* series, whimsical faeries and elves, *Victorian Santas*, caroling angels, and traditional Santas have long enchanted collectors.

Amaranth's 1996 Faerie Line, designed by Lynn West, comes with stands made especially for them. Pictured from left to right are: "Dreamweaver," "Jubilee," "Gardino" and "Gumdrop" Faeries.

Santas, Elves and Faeries from Lynn West

Lynn West's nostalgic *Old World Santas* carry on a tradition that began over 15 years ago and have become one of West's trademarks since the 1980s. Her latest creation — eighth in the series — is a musical Father Christmas. Standing 22" high, this regal old gentleman wears a free-flowing white brocade robe inspired by Victorian times.

The Christmas wrapping duo of "Jolly Holiday" and his companion elf, "Krister," are two limited edition creations by Lynn West. The 33" tall "Jolly Holiday," limited to 200, holds Christmas paper and ribbons, as he completes his wrapping assignments. The very helpful "Krister," limited to 250, is seated on a red velvet cushion and holds another package decorated with flowing ribbons. This pair is perfect for any seasonal tabletop or holiday mantle display.

Four new faeries from Lynn West debuted during 1996, with a unique twist: these were the first Amaranth faeries to come with bases created especially for them. Each faerie flies through a magical land on pearlized gossamer wings. Full foam bodies

Lynn West's Yuletide Winter Series encompasses the rich and wonderful traditional holiday colors of Christmases past with two caroling angels and the musical "Yuletide St. Nick."

allow the collector to pose each piece so that it can sit or be poised to fly when the urge strikes. Beautiful white wool beards accent the whimsical resin faces that are hand-painted by Amaranth's artisans.

To enhance our belief that all wishes do come true, "Dreamweaver Faerie" holds a magical acrylic moon and stars, and stands on a black base with silver accents. Preparing to blow his horn in celebration is "Jubilee Faerie." Dressed in green velvet and shiny brocade, he is trimmed in jewel tone beads and stands on a black base with gold trim. "Gardino Faerie" is happiest flying through your garden, watering and collecting fresh flowers. He stands on a gold base. "Gumdrop Faerie's" sugar-coated goodies accent his seasonal attire. A base of white with gold trim is Gumdrop's favorite!

Returning to a time of classic Old World elegance, Lynn West has designed two nostalgic Victorian-era winter scenes. The *Victorian Winter Series* was introduced in 1995 with the exquisitely dressed "Victorian Winter Father Christmas" and two beautiful child angels, "Anna" and "Andre." In 1996, the *Yuletide Winter Series* featured a musical "Yuletide St. Nick" and the caroling angels, "Katherine" and "Nathanael."

Designed by Linda Gill for Amaranth Productions, "Belle, the Home-Bred Angel" happily plies her trade. She's the one who checks to make sure a bell chimes whenever an angel gets her wings!

American Country Art Masters Influence Linda Gill

Imagine a little town, nestled in a green valley, surrounded on the north by a forest and to the south by rolling farmlands. Keep traveling back to the days when screen doors slammed, ice cream was homemade, and neighbors gossiped over white picket fences, while their pies cooled on the window sill. Welcome to the enchanting village of Gillwell Corners, a quaint small town somewhere in America, populated by Linda Gill's *Home-Bred Folks*.

Fifteen years ago, Gill attended her first crafts fair and decided to replace an apple head on a doll with one made out of bread dough. Inspired by American artists Charles Wysocki and Norman Rockwell, she began creating bread dough characters who lived in a time when life was simple

and unhurried. In those days, pride in one's country and love of family were important to all — and these characteristics are inherent in each of Linda Gill's designs.

To create the *Home-Bred Folks* for Amaranth Productions, Gill originally molds her characters' unique faces from bread dough. Amaranth's artisans then create a mold, reproduce the distinctive faces from resin, and hand-paint each detail to bring the endearing characters to life.

One of the most delightful *Home-Bred Folks* is "Belle, the Home-Bred Angel," who has a most essential divine assignment in her heavenly home. As the Quality Control Supervisor in the Wings Department, "Belle" is the chosen one who checks to make sure a bell chimes whenever an angel gets her wings. Belle's serenely happy countenance will surely warm collectors hearts and remind them of someone they have loved before. Standing 19" high, "Belle" wears her feather wings with pride. A gold halo, resting above her curly white wool hair, complements the gold bell she rings at that special moment in Wingdom.

Communicating With Collectors: An Amaranth Specialty

Amaranth Productions has pledged to its collectors to create only the very best American-made limited edition collectibles. The company's masterful attention to detail and tradition bring

back warm and happy memories of times past. This dedication is communicated through each Amaranth creation — and also through the company's newsletter, "The Legacy."

Each bi-annual edition features articles on the artists, the production process, new introductions, and spotlights on several pieces from the current line. The company also participates in collectible and doll shows open to the public to enable Amaranth collectors to get a first-hand look at their favorite creations.

By purchasing an Amaranth Productions limited edition, all collectors automatically become members of the company's Collector's Club. Each member receives a free subscription to "The Legacy," as well as catalog mailings and a list of authorized dealers. A drawing for one of Amaranth's Christmas pieces is held yearly for collectors, as well.

All Amaranth Productions pieces are limited editions, handmade in the U.S.A. What's more, each recreates a design of high artistic value that celebrates the workmanship of American artists and designers.

Amaranth Productions
P.O. Box 3505
Huntington Beach, CA 92605-3505
(714) 841-9972
Fax: (714) 847-1090

AMAZZE

Landmark Lighthouses and Architectural Treasures... Captured Through the Fine Art of Stained Glass

"Block Island (Southeast), Rhode Island" is a brilliant example of the art of stained glass in the classic Tiffany tradition. Introduced by Century Lights *in an edition limited to 4,896 numbered, signed and dated lighthouse replicas, it is crafted of 315 pieces of stained glass. The retail price is $86.00.*

"Our objective is to provide distinctive, affordable examples of stained glass art which can be appreciated by serious collectors and casual buyers alike," says Jack Mazze, President of Amazze of Vermilion, Ohio. Noting that stained glass is one of the fastest growing categories in today's collectibles market, Mazze asserts his determination to "offer collectors outstanding items which will produce solid value now, and increasing value over the years to come."

To achieve this goal, Amazze first allied itself with one of the world's most honored stained glass artists, S. N. Meyers. As the creator of Amazze's *Century Classics™* collection including *Centuryville™, Evergreen Village™* and *Century Lights™*, Meyers has channeled his genius into recapturing 19th century America with elegance and painstaking detail. More recently, Amazze forged a bond with another stained glass master, George C. Innes, for The *CHOCOLATE TOWN, U.S.A.!* ™ Collection.

A Far Eastern Trip Sets the Stage for Amazze

It was 1993 when Jack Mazze met stained glass artist S. N. Meyers in Meyers' adopted home of Hong Kong. Meyers was in the final stages of perfecting his process to manufacture stained glass replica structures of remarkable quality, craftsmanship and affordability.

Born and raised in St. Louis, Missouri, S. N. Meyers exhibited outstanding art talent at an early age, along with an ability to create distinctive designs. After graduating from the University of Kansas where he studied architecture and design, Meyers moved to the Far East. It was there that he began refining his creative skills and expressing his artistic talent in stained glass.

After his fortuitous meeting with Jack Mazze, Meyers embarked on a serious quest for knowledge about 19th century America, doing what he calls both "learning and living" the culture of that time. This work was aimed at enabling the artist to fully capture the essential character of this period in the *Century Classics* designs.

A Visit to *Centuryville*

Amazze's first offering was *Centuryville*, a series of homes, business facilities and other structures comprising a typical 19th-century American community. The collection is a brilliant example of the art of stained glass.

To create each piece, large sheets of U.S.-made stained glass are individually cut and polished, copperfoiled, soldered, and followed with a hand-applied patina. Louis Comfort Tiffany, renowned American stained glass artist, first used this same creative process over 100 years ago.

Each *Centuryville* creation requires many individual pieces of stained glass, lovingly assembled to capture every detail of the Meyers original. The house of town eccentric Lawrence Keith, for example, has 144 pieces, while the "Centuryville Fire Station" boasts 95 pieces. Each building comes complete with its own internal light and cord, assuring that it will radiate a warm glow. What's more, the translucence and luminous color of the stained glass provides exceptional decorative impact to any setting, all year long.

Centuryville offers a charming mix of buildings, including town institutions like the "Centuryville Cathedral," "B&O Railroad Station," "Village Church," "Fire Station" and "Schoolhouse." There are many private homes represented as well, including those of the local grocer, librarian, teacher, hardware store owner, town eccentric, and founding family. Foreshadowing his highly successful *Century Lights*, Meyers also designed the "Cranes Eye Point Lighthouse," "Ship Island Miss Lighthouse" and "Foggy Point Lighthouse" for *Centuryville*. All of the pieces are limited editions with Certificates of Authenticity.

The Cozy Charm of *Evergreen Village*

On the outskirts of *Centuryville*, according to S. N. Meyers and Amazze, stands a semi-rural community of cottages called *Evergreen Village*. Here, several of the town merchants and craftsmen reside in order to escape the hustle and bustle of the city.

The townspeople have their own "Village Church" and "Cottage Point Lighthouse," as well as four handsome little abodes: "Train Conductor's Cottage," "Cobbler's Cottage," "Carpenter's Cottage" and "Candymaker's Cottage."

To enhance both *Centuryville* and *Evergreen Village*, Amazze offers a wonderful selection of accessories.

Most imposing of these are the 4" tall "Stained Glass Tree" and the 3" tall "Stained Glass Gazebo." There are also pieces such as the park clock, street lights, mail boxes, Victorian fences, fire hydrants, park benches, street signs, figurines of people and snowmen, pine trees, and house signs to add a lively touch of realism to either village in a home display.

Amazze Presents the Original Stained Glass Landmark Lighthouse Replicas

The most complete and extensive stained glass landmark lighthouse collectibles available, *Century Lights* also represents the very first series of its kind. This grouping of originals by S. N. Meyers and Amazze reigns today as the best-selling and most popular glass landmark lighthouses.

The 47 *Century Lights* lighthouses introduced to date represent a host of recognizable landmarks that grace America's shores. Each illuminated collectible comes with two lights: one for the lighthouse beacon and one for the base. Every part of North America is represented, with Western, Southern, Eastern, Canadian and Great Lakes land-

"Split Rock, Minnesota" is considered one of the most picturesque lighthouses of the Great Lakes. Now it has inspired stained glass designer and craftsman S. N. Meyers to create this 7" replica, containing 162 pieces of fine American-made stained glass. The retail price is $66.00.

marks selected especially to capture the hearts of collectors who appreciate our nation's seafaring heritage.

Each lighthouse is crafted according to the same painstaking process as the *Centuryville* and *Evergreen Village* pieces, in the tradition established over a century ago by Louis Comfort Tiffany. The lighthouses' standard size is approximately 8" tall. A special limited series of six lighthouses also is available, each standing 24" in height.

"Our lighthouse series is a natural," says partner Don Olson. "People are endlessly fascinated with the colorful, romantic history of 19th century seafaring America. Our lighthouses serve as ideal mementos of this era."

The architecture of the lighthouses has been captured with great fidelity by Meyers, portraying the diversity of styles within each section of the country. For instance, the Western series includes both the squared off, vertical style of "Diamond Head, Hawaii" and the look of "Admiralty Head, Washington," which encompasses both a lighthouse and a welcoming farmhouse-style structure.

"Big Red, Michigan" features a barn-like structure, while another Great Lakes lighthouse, "Marblehead, Ohio" rises almost to a point from a larger, rounded base. "Cape Hatteras, North Carolina" boasts a barber pole-style striped effect, while another Southern lighthouse, "Hilton Head, South Carolina," sports horizontal red and white stripes. In the Eastern series, "Block Island, Rhode Island" has the look of a country inn, while the contrasting "Nauset Beach, Massachusetts" is all functional simplicity in a cylindrical, vertical shape.

The *CHOCOLATE TOWN, U.S.A.!*™ Collection

Amazze's newest collection is The *CHOCOLATE TOWN, U.S.A.!*™ Collection, a limited edition stained class cottage/architectural art collection. The *CHOCOLATE TOWN, U.S.A.!* Collection is a flavorful tribute to candymaker Milton S. Hershey's beloved hometown – Hershey, Pennsylvania – as it existed a century ago.

Located on the Southwest point of Rhode Island, "Rose Island Light" was built in 1870 and actively guarded vessels from the dangerous shoals of Newport Harbor for more than 100 years. Now replicated as a 7-1/2"-tall stained glass lighthouse, it sells for $68.00.

You need not be a chocolate lover to recognize and appreciate the small town charm and nostalgia of The *CHOCOLATE TOWN, U.S.A.!* Collection. Designer George C. Innes and stained glass artist S.N. Meyers, commissioned by Amazze, have made The *CHOCOLATE TOWN, U.S.A.!* Collection truly unique and innovative in the stained glass collectible cottage product category. Every detail in architecture and color is true to the turn-of-the-century period. And everywhere you look, you see recreations of genuine HERSHEY'S™ signage – all authenticated and authorized by Hershey Foods Corporation.

Peek inside "HERSHEY'S™ CHOCOLATE SHOPPE" to see authentic miniature displays of HERSHEY'S KISSES® chocolates, HERSHEY'S® chocolates, and HERSHEY'S™ posters. Stroll by the "CHOCOLATE TOWN™ CINEMA" to see what is now showing. Notice the streetlights shaped like HERSHEY'S KISSES chocolates and the famous corner street sign "CHOCOLATE AVENUE - COCOA AVENUE."

The first series of The *CHOCOLATE TOWN, U.S.A.!* Collection, released in September 1996, consists of "HERSHEY'S™ CHOCOLATE SHOPPE,"

"CHOCOLATE TOWN™ POST OFFICE," "HERSHEY'S™ 5 AND 10 CENT STORE," "CHOCOLATE TOWN™ CINEMA," "HERSHEY'S™ GALLERY" and the "MR. GOODBAR™ CAFE." All of the pieces are brilliantly illuminated from within, radiating a warm glow. The *CHOCOLATE TOWN, U.S.A.!* Collection is officially authorized by Hershey Foods Corporation, and each limited edition handcrafted piece bears a Certificate of Authenticity with a reproduction of the famous HERSHEY'S™ logo.

An Unlimited Horizon in Stained Glass Artistry

What does the future hold for Amazze and its stained glass treasures? "It's hard to say," Mazze and Olson respond. "Our future collections are limited only by the talent and imagination of S.N. Meyers, George Innes and other stained glass masters...which means there are no limits at all."

Mazze and Olson predict that Amazze will continue to pioneer the medium of stained glass in the gifts and collectibles industry. They foresee pieces inspired by still more famous landmarks, and perhaps an additional venture or two in licensing. Most important of all, Amazze will strive to continue its legacy as the collector's choice for exceptional quality, uncompromising craftsmanship, and affordability.

Amazze
1030 Sunnyside Road
Vermilion, OH 44089
(800) 543-6759
Fax (216) 967-5199

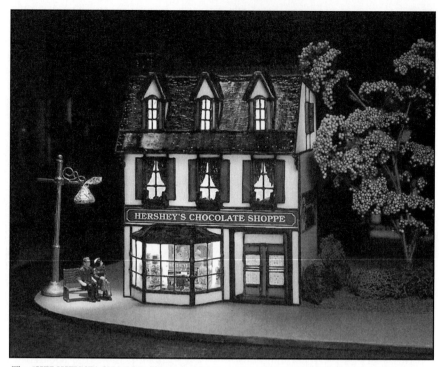

The "HERSHEY'S™ CHOCOLATE SHOPPE," from The CHOCOLATE TOWN, U.S.A.!™ *Collection, captures all the architectural details of the turn-of-the-century period. Designed by George Innes, this work of art features recreations of genuine HERSHEY'S™ signage and miniature products. Introduced in an edition of 9,988, it sells for $76.00 and is handcrafted in the traditional Tiffany stained glass style.*

ANHEUSER-BUSCH, INC.

Collectors Express Their Love for the "King of Beers®" and Their Appreciation of a 500-Year-Old Craft with Anheuser-Busch Steins

Beer making is a form of true artistry to a master brewer — and for centuries, handsome beer steins have been created to contain and protect the delicious results of this careful blending of hops, malt and grain. While the earliest steins were mainly functional, the past 100 years have seen the creation of true works of art. German firms like Villeroy & Boch and Gerz offered steins in the 1800s that today can bring hundreds of thousands of dollars on the auction market. And while these collectible steins may be out of financial reach for many of us, since 1975 Anheuser-Busch's remarkable *Collector Series* has captured the glories of 19th-century steins at affordable prices.

All Anheuser-Busch steins are crafted with the same dedication to perfection that makes Budweiser® and the firm's other beers so honored and renowned. Some feature classic themes, while others boast contemporary topics. The steins of character and celebration are ready for actual use, or they can be preserved in "mint condition" as cherished display pieces.

The Leading Brewer Also Sets the Pace in Stein Artistry

Anheuser-Busch has reigned as the world's larg-est brewer for nearly four decades with record annual sales of 88.5 million barrels of beer in 1994. Founded in St. Louis, Missouri, in 1852, the firm forged an association with several renowned stein manufacturers in the mid-1970s to create its own fine steins. Collaborators included the Ceramarte stein factory in Brazil and classic German stein makers including Gerz, Thewalt and Rastal — making it possible for Anheuser-Busch to offer a greater variety of steins with each passing year.

At first, the concept was to create commemorative pieces and rewards for Anheuser-Busch beer wholesalers. But the steins were so attractive to collectors that Anheuser-Busch was inspired to test the retail sale of steins in 1980. Results were astounding: in the first year alone, 50,000 *Holiday* steins were sold. By 1990, annual sales of the *Holiday* stein had topped the 1,000,000 unit mark!

Anheuser-Busch "Breweriana" Also Intrigues Stein Collectors

Anheuser-Busch steins have proven so attractive to collectors that some aficionados boast ownership of almost every piece introduced since 1975. In addition to steins, many of these enthusiasts also collect what is known as "breweriana" — such stein accouterments as bottles, cans, labels and signs.

While many Anheuser-Busch steins focus on brewery heritage for their

A whimsical baseball mitt stein entitled "Play Ball" features a baseball emblazoned with the red Budweiser bowtie logo.

subject matter, others showcase holiday celebrations, or non-profit organizations supported by Anheuser-Busch. The firm also commissions local and national artists based upon their specialties to create "theme" steins.

Gerz and Anheuser-Busch Join Forces

Anheuser-Busch works in an exclusive joint venture with S.P. Gerz GMBH and Gerz Inc., the largest manufacturer of handcrafted steins in Germany, and its U.S. subsidiaries. Gerz, founded in 1897, is well known among collectors for its high-quality, handcrafted steins. This landmark association makes Anheuser-Busch — already the world's largest marketer of collectible steins — the exclusive North American distributor and marketing agent of a line of steins designed and produced by Gerz: the *Gerz Meisterwerke Collection*.

The first in the series of limited edition steins, titled "Santa's Mail Bag," captures the warmth and spirit of giving presents during the holiday season. This premier stein was issued in an edition of 5,000 pieces, and is part of *The Saturday Evening Post Christmas Collection*, featuring designs by

"Budweiser Salutes the Navy" is the name of this handsome stein combining images of air and sea operations as well as an anchor chain sculptured handle and harmonizing chain-motif trim. The Budweiser logo with Navy mascot completes this impressive work of art.

Norman Rockwell. The second in the series is entitled "Santa's Helper," and it portrays a beloved Post cover by famed illustrator J. C. Leyendecker. Third in the collection is "All I Want for Christmas," another Leyendecker favorite.

Several other recent introductions have been made possible through the Gerz/Anheuser-Busch alliance. For example, the "Rosie the Riveter" stein honors all the women who answered the wartime call to keep America's factories working in the 1940s. Representing the *Portrait of America* series, it portrays a Norman Rockwell Post cover illustration. A Rockwell "Triple Self-Portrait" stein honors the 100th anniversary of Norman Rockwell's birth. Also by Rockwell and created by Gerz and Anheuser-Busch is "The Dugout" stein, featuring the September 4, 1948 cover illustration from the *Post*; a portrait of the disconsolate Chicago dugout in the midst of a disastrous season.

Showing the range of the Gerz/Anheuser-Busch collaboration are four additional steins. "Mallard" is a special, full-dimensional deep relief ceramic stein portraying a richly colored mallard duck. "Giant Panda" shows a playful giant panda that appears to be

reaching out of the stein for a bamboo shoot. The "Winchester 'Model 94' Centennial" stein honors the most famous of all lever-action rifles, and comes topped with a pewter lid-top figurine of the signature Winchester horse and rider. Finally, the "John F. Kennedy" stein — first in the *American Heritage* series — presents a presidential portrait.

Anheuser-Busch's "A&Eagle Trademark" stein offers historic images from the company's proud tradition as the makers of Budweiser. Company trademarks from the 1890s-1900s, 1910s and 1930s are depicted, with alternating panels of the Bevo Fox.

Birds of Prey Offers Final Issue While Anheuser-Busch Figurines Debut

The "Great Horned Owl" stein — fourth and final edition in Anheuser-Busch's celebrated *Birds of Prey* series — showcases this formidable hunter in all his majesty and grace. The bird's deep-forest habitat, finely feathered body and sharp-eyed face area are beautifully illustrated in detailed ceramic relief — surely a fitting choice to conclude the *Birds of Prey* collection.

Meanwhile, Anheuser-Busch unveils a new series of handsome, hand-painted figurines with two recent issues: "Buddies," and "Horseplay." "Buddies" captures the bright-eyed curiosity of two playful golden retriever puppies in porcelain bisque. The sculpture is inspired by an illustration by nature artist Marlowe Urdahl. The second-edition "Horseplay" depicts three Dalmatian puppies mischievously tugging away at one of the Clydesdales' harnesses. It was inspired by an illustration by Paul Radtke.

Hunter's Companion and A&Eagle Steins Win Collectors' Attention

A series of noble canines in the field star in Anheuser-Busch's *Hunter's Companion* collection, which debuted with "The Labrador." Handcrafted by Ceramarte in Brazil, each ceramic relief stein in the series stands 8-1/4" tall and features a pewter lid topped by a unique canine figurine. The second *Hunter's Companion* is "Golden

Retriever." Each stein in this limited edition is individually gift boxed and numbered with a Certificate of Authenticity.

The "A&Eagle Trademark Stein" premiered Anheuser-Busch's historical *A&Eagle* series, featuring three early versions of the famous A& Eagle trademark dating from 1872 to 1885. The third stein in the series, introduced in 1995, is called "A&Eagle Trademark III" stein. It features an antique design by artist Don Langeneckert as well as trademarks spanning the 1890s to the 1930s. There will be four steins in all in this collection, each handcrafted by Ceramarte of Brazil, gift-boxed, individually numbered, and accompanied by a Certificate of Authenticity.

A Cordial Invitation to Join the Anheuser-Busch Collectors Club

The Anheuser-Busch Collectors Club made its debut on January 1, 1995, with two unique collectible steins as enticements for charter members. The old-world flavor of the Budweiser Clydesdales and the Anheuser-Busch Brew House Clock Tower is captured exquisitely on two steins, both handcrafted by Ceramarte of Brazil and available to members only.

From the Hunter's Companion *series, this is "Golden Retriever," a stein paying tribute to this noble breed both with bas-relief artistry and a handsome, ceramic figurine on its pewter-rimmed lid.*

The "Budweiser Clydesdales at the Bauernhof" stein is part of the Anheuser-Busch Collectors Club membership kit, available at Authorized Collectors Club Dealers. It depicts the regal eight-horse Budweiser Clydesdale hitch pulling an antique beer wagon emerging from the European-inspired Bauernhof Courtyard in St. Louis. Club members may order the "Brew House Clock Tower" stein, introduced in June 1995. It features a stunning design modeled after a century-old six-story building, and is the first Anheuser-Busch stein with a working clock.

The charter membership fee of $35.00 provides new members with many benefits including: the "Clydesdales" stein already mentioned, valued at $60.00; a history and information-filled binder; a one-year subscription to the club's quarterly magazine, *First Draft*; a personalized membership card; and a redemption certificate for the exclusive "Brew House Clock Tower" stein. For information on how to join, collectors may call the club at 1-800-305-2582.

A great deal of the fun of owning Anheuser-Busch steins resides in the enjoyment of showing them off. Secondary market price rises after prompt sell-outs for many steins bode well for continued growth in the Anheuser-Busch stein market. And with expansion ongoing in collector plates, ornaments and figurines, the firm continues to unveil new designs and styles — all aimed at continuing the stein-making quality and tradition established by Anheuser-Busch more than 20 years ago.

Anheuser-Busch, Inc.
Retail Sales Department
2700 South Broadway
St. Louis, MO 63118
(800) 325-1154
Fax (314) 577-9656

COLLECTORS' CLUB

The Anheuser-Busch Collectors Club
2700 South Broadway
St. Louis, MO 63118
(800) 305-2582

Annual Dues: $35.00
Club Year: Anniversary of Sign-Up Date

Benefits:
• Membership Gift: Stein
• Redemption Certificate for Members-Only Stein
• Quarterly Magazine, *First Draft*
• Personalized Membership Card
• Binder Which Includes Information on the History of Anheuser-Busch, Inc. and the Manufacturing of Steins

ANNALEE MOBILITEE DOLLS

Annalee Demonstrates New England Charm at
Annual Annalee Doll Society Auction Extravaganza

One of the charming additions to the Annalee Doll line for 1995-96 is the 10" "Red Treetop Angel" (Item No. 7274). Its suggested retail price is $37.50.

A visit to an Annalee Doll Society* Auction Weekend is enough to restore anyone's faith in good old American values. While relaxing in the sunshine with friends, visitors enjoy historical costumes and crazy getups, wonderful food and drink under festive tents, and the drama of skyrocketing auction prices on the rarest and most coveted of Annalee's* collectible dolls, from '50s classics to today's one-of-a-kind "Artist's Proofs."

Annalee Thorndike presides over the event, her ready smile a warm welcome to collectors nationwide who converge on Meredith, New Hampshire. And as always, Annalee's husband Chip — joined by sons Townsend (Town) and Chuck — is present to make sure all their guests are having the time of their lives.

To the uninitiated, this auction can provide a real awakening. One-of-a-kind pieces may sell for hundreds or thousands of dollars, and Annalee designs from the early years attract furious

bidding. The all-time record-breaker, a "Halloween Girl" doll from the '50s, brought $6,600 at the 1995 auction. That same day, a 20" Santa Claus from the same period sold for $3,300. Another highlight of the Summer Auction is the unveiling of the Doll Society's exclusive "Folk Hero™" doll and the auction of its Artist's Proof — one of several one-of-a-kind Proof dolls auctioned yearly for charitable purposes.

Prices are only part of the excitement, however. Collectors can choose from a wide range of designs and special products each year, at prices from $5.95 and up. The most recent Annalee catalog and *Collector* magazine features limited-edition pieces based on themes like sports, careers, diverse cultures and more. The rest of the line is drawn largely from seasonal and holiday themes.

Brought to life in the form of flowers, human figures, holiday characters, and animals, the line varies widely. All, however, share the same sense of timeless whimsy and — naturally — the same sunny, crinkly-eyed smile that lights up the face of Annalee Thorndike herself!

Where It All Began

Annalee and Chip Thorndike never suspected that Annalee's whimsical dolls would captivate collectors worldwide. In fact, doll making began as a hobby for a teenage Annalee, who first made them in the 1930s, "just for fun." When friends saw how special her characters could be, they asked Annalee to create designs for them, too.

Eventually, she began selling her pieces through the League of New Hampshire Craftsmen, to merchants for their holiday displays, and to family and friends. When she married Chip in 1941, however, she was content to join him on his chicken farm and start a

family. The Harvard-educated Chip wanted nothing more than to enjoy the farmer's simple life. Indeed, it was not until 1953, after the chicken industry moved southward, that the Thorndikes "phased out" the chickens and officially transferred their energies to the establishment of Annalee Mobilitee Dolls*, Incorporated.

Despite outside jobs and hard work on the farm, the Thorndikes had realized that providing for their family would require a change, and they decided to commit themselves to doll making, hoping that the public's love of her happy little characters could support them. The young family pitched in, determined to try. The public became entranced by Annalee's dolls, and soon word spread far beyond New Hampshire. Chuck and Town recall that their childhood years were surrounded by their mother's designs. In the early days of Annalee Mobilitee™ Dolls, the family farmhouse *was* their "Factory in the Woods," and every available space

The "Goin' Fishin' Logo Kid" is the 1995-96 Logo doll for Annalee Doll Society members. This charming doll has a retail value of $50, but it is one of the many benefits of annual membership in the Doll Society, which is just $29.95.

was piled with dolls in various stages of completion. Doll fever seems to have stayed with the Thorndike boys, since today Chuck is CEO and President, and Town is Director of Development for the company.

In the early days, Annalee wondered if she could continue to create new designs, but her innovative spirit has never waned. Now, with Chuck and Town involved in the creative process, it seems that the possibilities remain unlimited. Yet no matter how many dolls they create, the Thorndikes remain devoted to the same careful craftsmanshp that has served them well since the 1950s.

Each doll begins with a conceptual drawing, which is fine-tuned until it meets with Annalee's approval. Then, a manual for each new doll's design is prepared to ensure that every department performs every detail correctly. Annalee passes judgment on the positioning of every doll that leaves the studio — each is equipped with a flexible frame that allows the utmost in "poseability." Chip continues to design accessories — from the wooden skis of the early days to wooden boats for the recently released fishing dolls.

The Thorndike family has chosen to keep the dolls as handcrafted as possible, and make each an individual, with a variety of facial expressions for each "character." To keep the line fresh, the Thorndikes retire dolls and add new dolls or variations yearly. When a doll retires it may eventually join the ranks of the "auction successes" that are so actively pursued by collector/investors.

The Annalee Doll Society: Join The Club

Ever since the Annalee Doll Society was initiated in 1983 to meet the needs of Annalee collectors, it has provided fun and opportunity for these enthusiasts. With a membership in the tens of thousands and growing, the Society offers many benefits. The Membership Kit includes a yearly 7" Logo Kid doll, annual pin and membership card, a special-edition Annalee Felt Pin, and a subscription to *The Collector*, a full-color quarterly magazine devoted to Annalee's dolls and collectors, including a doll listing of valuable dolls available through Annalee's Antique and Collectible Doll Shop. Other benefits include admission to Doll Society events and eligibility to purchase exclusive, signed and numbered dolls available only to Doll Society members.

While the value of the current Logo Kid alone is $50.00, the Kid and all other benefits are available to Doll Society members for only $29.95 annually. For more information or to join the Doll Society, contact any Doll Society Sponsor Store or call 1-800-43-DOLLS.

Reaching Out

The Thorndikes participate enthusiastically in philanthropy today as they have all their lives. They believe in using their success to better society — and not simply by making donations. This family gets involved.

The Thorndikes often use the popularity of their dolls to support a variety of causes. By featuring the logo or theme of the group they wish to benefit on an original Annalee creation, the Thorndikes draw attention to that group's needs. By donating the price paid for the Artist's Proof at auction and setting aside a percentage of the total proceeds from the sales of that item, they are able to address these needs. The dolls are often marketed through the Doll Society, whose members appreciate the value of these extremely limited-run items.

During each annual Annalee Doll Society Auction Weekend, Annalee's auctions several of their Artist Proofs and donates the proceeds to favorite causes including health, education (Annalee's sponsors the Thorndike Scholarship Fund, dedicated to assisting Annalee employees and their families), conservation, homelessness, and the arts. To demonstrate their commitment to the environment, Annalee created the "Two-in-a-Tent" mouse, featuring two mice snuggling in a pup tent. Proceeds from this work of art have benefitted the New Hampshire Land Trust.

During Operation Desert Storm in 1991, the Thorndikes met with the Chairman of the Joint Chiefs of Staff General Colin Powell and White House Chief of Staff John Sununu, presenting General Powell with the first 7" "Desert Storm Mouse." Annalee's donation of 500 of the mice and 1,500 special "Desert Mouse Head" pins were delivered to American troops in the Gulf. In addition, ten percent of the proceeds from the sale of every "Desert Mouse" and "Desert Mouse Head" pin was donated to the American Red Cross. More recently, the "Mississippi Levee Mouse" and "California Mud Slide Mouse" were created to raise funds for flood relief in the wake of the flooding of 1993 and 1995. Ten percent of its proceeds will be donated to flood relief efforts.

Meet The Artist

While the Annual Auction Weekend draws capacity crowds to Meredith, New Hampshire, the Thorndikes are always delighted to welcome visitors. The Annalee Doll Museum and Town

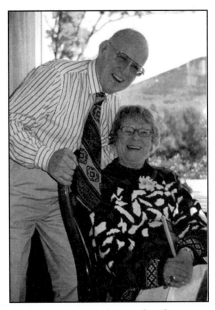

Always energetic, upbeat and smiling, Annalee and Chip Thorndike are a familiar sight to visitors at the Factory in the Woods in Meredith, New Hampshire. Chip often creates charming accessories to enhance the dolls designed by his gifted wife, Annalee.

Thorndike's Antique and Classic Car Collection are within walking distance of one another, and convenient to Lake Winnipesaukee's many attractions. But for those who can't make the trek to New Hampshire, Annalee and the family provide another way to "meet the artist" — they travel throughout the country, not only visiting collectible shows, but dropping in on Doll Society Sponsor Stores as well. A visit to one of these nearly 300 sponsors brings out crowds of Annalee admirers and collectors, eager for the chance to meet Annalee or Chuck, talk with them, and have them sign autograph cards or personal items.

Similarly, the realization that many collectors are unable to get all the way to New Hampshire led Annalee's to move the Fall Auction to Williamsburg, Virginia, in 1994, and to Nashville, Tennessee, in 1995. This allowed Southern and Midwestern collectors a chance to share in the Annalee auction experience.

Always cheery and upbeat herself, Annalee Thorndike proclaims her goal as a simple one: she simply wants to "make people smile." With the happy expressions on her dolls' faces to cheer every admirer, this artist meets her goal with grace and enthusiasm. From "Thorndikes' Eggs and Auto Parts" to the delightful world of Annalee Mobilitee Dolls, the Thorndikes' success story warms the hearts of all who experience the joy of Annalee, her family, and her appealing Annalee dolls.

Annalee Mobilitee Dolls, Inc.
P.O. Box 1137
Reservoir Road
Meredith, NH 03253-1137
(800) 433-6557
Fax (603) 279-6659

COLLECTORS' CLUB/MUSEUM

Annalee Doll Society
P.O. Box 1137
Meredith, NH 03253-1137
1-800-43-DOLLS

Annual Dues: $29.95
Club Year: Anniversary of Sign-Up Date

Benefits:
• Membership Gift: 7" Doll, Membership Pin and Card
• Opportunity to Purchase Members-Only Folk Hero Doll
• Quarterly Magazine, *The Collector*
• Buy/Sell Matching Service
• Members-Only Auctions
• Special Members-Only Event Pieces

Annalee Doll Museum
50 Reservoir Road
Meredith, NH 03253
(603) 279-3333

The Annalee Doll Museum features rare and older Annalee Dolls, as well as a videotaped presentation featuring the history of the company and interviews with Annalee. A Gift Shop is also open to visitors.

Hours: Daily from 9 a.m. - 5 p.m. Closed during the winter months.
Admission Fee: None

ANRI U.S.

Sculptures in Wood Carve Out Old Traditions and New Collectors

From the Vatican Library Collection, *Mary and the Infant Jesus are part of the "Holy Land" nativity authorized by the Biblioteca Apostolica Vaticana. The nativity is accompanied by a signed certificate noting ANRI's collaboration with the Vatican Library for this exclusive collection introduced in 1995.*

In an age of automated machines, assembly lines and computers, there's still a small workshop nestled in the Dolomite Mountains of Northern Italy where time-honored traditions remain untouched by modern technology.

Since 1912, ANRI has been creating beautiful wood sculptures that combine traditional craftsmanship with a continuous search for new expressions. From religious figurines and nativities to those portraying playful children, the limited edition woodcarvings have become family heirlooms. No matter what artist, style or figurine a collector chooses, each woodcarving has very low edition sizes of only 250, 500 or, at the most, 1,000 pieces.

ANRI woodcarvings are among the few collectibles in the world that are truly handcrafted works of art. Each sculpture is carved by skilled artisans from a single block of aged, alpine maple and then delicately painted in oils. No two collectible wood sculptures are alike.

With the continued popularity and appreciation for these sculptures, ANRI of Italy launched a new company in 1995 to distribute its collectibles in the United States. ANRI U.S., based in the Dallas area, helps new collectors turn today's wood sculptures into tomorrow's memories.

The History of ANRI's Woodcarved Nativities

During the 15th century, a unique transformation was taking place in the Groden Valley of Italy, where ANRI makes its home. Grodeners, already known for their fine lace and cloth, were turning their talents to the art of woodcarving. They especially focused on wooden nativity figures that recreated the first Christmas and captured the hearts of Europeans.

Grodeners left a permanent mark on the history of nativities. They were the first to add snow to the Bethlehem scene. This feature, coupled with the intricate detail of their carvings, quickly endeared Groden nativities to churches and collectors throughout Europe. By the 18th century, the Groden Valley became one of the world's primary sources of handcarved nativities. By 1800, two-thirds of the valley's population made their living from woodcarving. Unfortunately, competition led to undercutting on price, and quality began to suffer. So during the late 1800s, Luis Riffeser and

later his son, Anton, set out to create woodcarvings that would meet the highest standards of artistry and quality. Anton Riffeser founded The House of ANRI (taken from the first two letters of his first and last name), where he brought together the valley's finest woodcarvers under one roof. Today, four generations of Riffesers later, ANRI is still home to world-famous artists, Groden master woodcarvers and painters. And faithful to the philosophy of its founder, ANRI proudly continues the tradition of nativity woodcarvings begun by their ancestors more than 300 years ago.

Sculptors Carry on the ANRI Tradition of Excellence

Collectors can choose from a wide variety of nativities and sculptures created exclusively for ANRI by a team of artists and designers who bring their

Created by Juan Ferrandiz, "Tender Care" portrays a shepherdess kneeling beside her lamb. As with the artist's other works, the 6-inch figurine captures childhood delight and love.

Introduced in 1995, the Heavenly Angels *collection is the first ANRI creation by American artist Charlotte Hallett. In "Angel of Peace," the cherub stands on a pillar and wears a golden halo. The woodcarving is limited to 250 pieces and is available in a painted or natural finish.*

personal styles and talents to each piece. A native of Groden Valley, Ulrich Bernardi has made a life of modelling and designing religious figurines, cherubs and other figures in the spirit of European folklore. Simple attire and innocent expressions characterize his work, which has graced the ANRI studio for more than three decades. He also created the Florentine crèche, which is more ornate and captures the glory of Italy's most fabled city of Renaissance art.

Professor Karl Kuolt, who passed away in 1937, was a student at the Munich School of Art and the Munich Academy. Besides a large number of well-known monuments and memorial chapels throughout Southern Germany, he also created countless smaller works which are now housed in museums and private collections. ANRI's world-famous nativity figurines bear his name and artistry. ANRI has also made additions to the Kuolt crèches with animals and shepherds. New or traditional, each Kuolt piece spreads a message of peace.

Walter Bacher apprenticed to a well-known sculptor at the age of 14. Then he attended two years of art school in

Munich and four additional years at the Academy of Art. His works are displayed in churches and museums in Europe and overseas, and one of his most famous creations is an ANRI nativity.

Childhood Innocence Through the Artistry of Juan Ferrandiz and Sarah Kay

For more than 25 years, Spanish artist Juan Ferrandiz has shared his talent with ANRI collectors. Through his artwork, Ferrandiz seeks to create a world of love, unity and compassion. His drawings are translated into three-dimensional collectible woodcarvings, including the Holy Family, traditional nativity characters and animals. The nativity scenes celebrate the innocence of children and animals, both of which bear gentle expressions of happiness.

For more than a decade, Australian artist Sarah Kay has enjoyed worldwide recognition for her interpretations of childhood pastimes. Her association with ANRI began in 1983, when her drawings were first transformed into hand-carved figurines. Her sweet-faced children can be found doing everything from hanging Christmas stockings to heading to the river bank to go fishing. Sarah Kay has also created miniatures and a wonderful Santa Claus figurine series.

Heavenly Angels Descend on ANRI

Created by American artists William and Charlotte Hallett, the *Heavenly Angels* collection was introduced in 1995 as a series of four limited edition pieces. The first in the series, "Angel of Peace" features an angel standing atop a column and wearing a flowing robe. Her face is framed by a halo applied in gold leaf. "Angel of Kindness" portrays a haloed angel with a tiny bird perched on her hand. Each woodcarving is limited to 250 pieces and is available in a painted or natural finish. The Halletts work in their Massachusetts studio, where they have created some privately commissioned pieces for churches throughout the United States.

ANRI Announces *Vatican Library* Collection

Inspired by artwork in the Vatican Library, ANRI proudly introduced another nativity series in 1995. The Biblioteca Apostolica Vaticana authorized ANRI to exclusively reproduce some of its treasures in wood in *The Vatican Library Collection*. The first introduction included a two-piece Holy Family in both the 4-inch and 6-inch sizes. An ox and donkey also joined the set with figurines of kings, shepherds and sheep to be added in upcoming years. The "Holy Land" nativity is accompanied by a signed certificate ensuring outstanding craftsmanship and guaranteeing the collaboration between ANRI and the Vatican Library.

The Making of an ANRI Sculpture Requires Patience and Skill

Each ANRI figurine — whether carved by Bernardi or recreated from the artwork of Ferrandiz — begins with wood from hand-picked Alpine maple trees available only in Austria. The maples are chopped down during the winter, then cut into boards which are left standing for two to three years so the sap will be completely drained. Only unblemished sections of the tree are used.

Frequent inspections of the wood

As an addition to the nativity by Ulrich Bernardi, this shepherd boy and his cat greet the Holy Family. The figurine is available in three sizes — 4, 6 or 8 inches.

Designed by Australian artist Sarah Kay, "I Know, I Know" portrays a school girl anxiously raising her hand to answer a teacher's question. The wood sculpture is available in a 4" edition limited to 500 pieces and a 6" edition limited to 250 pieces.

ensure that flaws in texture, shape, grain or any number of other elements are detected. Control is so tight that only 20 percent of the wood originally cut ever reaches the carver's table.

Once the rough cut is completed by lathe, the sculptor then uses progressively smaller and finer tools to gradu-ally work his way toward the extremely detailed carving. At this stage of the process, any slip destroys the sculpture. When the carving is completed, the piece arrives in the hands of painters, who use special transparent oils to adorn the figurine.

The entire process, from the raw piece of wood to the copyrighted work of art, is continuously monitored for quality control, thus exemplifying the skill handed down from generations.

ANRI U.S. Establishes Increased Presence in America

ANRI Woodcarvings were introduced to American collectors in 1936. But to enhance the company's presence in America, the sales, marketing and distribution of ANRI's collectibles in the United States is now under the management of the new ANRI U.S. "Our network of loyal retailers convinced us that we needed to invest in the future of ANRI's role within the American marketplace," said Ernst Riffeser, the fourth generation of the family who has brought the figurines to collectors for more than a century. "I am fully committed to the U.S. market and the thousands of collectors who appreciate ANRI's creations."

ANRI Introduces Collector's Society

Along with the opening of ANRI U.S. in 1995, the ANRI Collector's Society was launched for collectors to enjoy the handcarved wood sculptures even more. Benefits include full-color newsletters, an authorized ANRI Collector's Society Retailer listing, color catalog featuring all the current pieces, membership certificate, exclusive Society woodcarvings and the opportunity to benefit from the available resources of the ANRI research department to identify older sculptures. Charter Year members also received a wristwatch.

The first exclusive woodcarving offered to members was "On My Own," designed by Sarah Kay. The sculpture portrays a toddler with outstretched arms taking her first important step in life. The annual membership fee is $40. For information, call (800) 763-ANRI or write to the ANRI Collector's Society, P.O. Box 2087, Quincy, MA 02269-2087.

ANRI U.S.
P.O. Box 380760
1126 So. Cedar Ridge, Ste. 111
Duncanville, TX 75138
(800) 730-ANRI
Fax (214) 283-3522

COLLECTORS' CLUB/TOUR

ANRI Collector's Society	Benefits:
P.O. Box 2087	• Membership Gift
Quincy, MA 02269-2087	• Reservation Card to Acquire Members-Only Figurine
(800) 763-ANRI (2674)	• Newsletter Published Three Times Yearly
	• Membership Card
Annual Dues: $40.00	• Buy/Sell Matching Service through Newsletter
Club Year: Society Year–January-December	• Full Color ANRI Catalog
Collector's Year–Anniversary of Sign-Up Date	• Authorized Retailer Listing
	• In-House Research Department
	• In-Store ANRI Master Carver Events
	• Travel Opportunities to ANRI Workshop in Italy

ANRI Woodcarvings Tour	**Admission:** Only for Members of ANRI Collector's Society
Groden Valley	
Italy	Club members visiting the ANRI Workshop receive a guided tour of the facility including the painting and carving studios.
Hours: By advance reservation through ANRI Collector's Society, P.O. Box 2087, Quincy, MA 02269, (800) 763-ANRI	

ARCADIAN PEWTER, INC.

Vintage Pewter Toys From Arcadian Pewter
Weave a Beautiful Ribbon Between Yesterday and Today

Heads must have turned when this "Sedan," "A-Express Truck" and "Fire Engine" hit the streets at the turn-of-the-century. Arcadian's replicas are limited to just 10,000 each.

Like most of our country's idealistic entrepreneurial efforts, the Arcade Manufacturing Company, of Freeport, Illinois, was a true pioneer. Before the turn of the century, Arcade made wrought iron doll strollers, swings and beds using the same materials and methods as our nation's first blacksmiths.

When cast-iron became available, Arcade used this material to make banks, irons and coffee mills. But the company's destiny was shaped in 1903 when it began to produce its first toys at what could be called the beginning of America's cast-iron toy era. These unique designs quickly dominated all others on the market and were sold across the United States. Using aggressive marketing techniques and innovative catalogs, the Arcade Manufacturing Company soon boasted offices in Manhattan, New York, and in the Chicago Merchandise Mart.

Over 300 toys were introduced by Arcade during its early manufacturing days. Among the subjects beloved by children receiving these delights were horse-drawn fire wagons, farm machinery, circus wagons, cars, trucks, buses and "aeroplanes." Each was marketed under Arcade's timely slogan: "They look real, and they are built to last."

After being painted with high quality enamels, Arcade toys looked exactly like the machines they represented. Many were fashioned as tributes to important companies. A copy of the famous Yellow Cab of Chicago debuted in 1921 as the company's first "promotional toy." It was followed by an Andy Gump car modeled after the popular cartoon character. Pricing also made Arcade toys perennial favorites. The company sold its goods for under $1.00 each (many cost just a quarter) during the 20's and 30's. Given these prices, it's easy to see why the sale of an original Arcade Checkered Cab in 1994 for $68,000 impressed collectors of vintage replicas.

Arcade was fortunate to have successfully taken its 600 employees through the Great Depression and World War II, but radical post-war economic changes impacted many industries, including Arcade. In 1946, the foundry was purchased by Rockwell Standard, and the toymaking dynasty came to an end in 1953. When Arcade shut its doors that year, its fate seemed sealed. But the company's spirit re-emerged 36 years later, thanks to Illinois businessmen Neal Lindblade and Art Gipson, founders of Valu-Cast Products. Their company, housed in Lindblade's 1-1/2 car garage, was established in 1982 with equipment purchased from a casting company in Oregon.

The men managed their regular jobs by day and gave Valu-Cast their evenings and weekends. They were so successful, Lindblade was able to leave his full-time job at a local manufacturing company in 1983. But Art Gipson decided he could not leave his career. The partnership was dissolved, and the men parted business company, though their friendship has remained as strong as ever. They still get together as often as possible to go fishing, so they'll have plenty of time to reminisce about the casting company that accidentally became one of America's top makers of fine pewter replica toys.

From these modest beginnings, grew a company rich in tradition and size. Today, the successor to the Arcade Manufacturing Company, Lindblade's Arcadian Pewter, Inc., boasts about eight million castings and a plant of approximately 10,000 square feet. From within its walls, Lindblade likes the feeling of "making memories," each time one of his remarkable toy replicas leaves his building.

The Gift of Love: An Unforgettable 20th Anniversary

In 1989, while trying to come up with an idea for a 20th Anniversary gift for his wife, Neal Lindblade decided to produce an Arcade toy farm wagon in a new material. He already owned the original cast-iron Arcade toy farm wagon used as his model and was anxious to try casting the design in pewter.

"The pewter wagon turned out great," he recalls. "I filled it with little straw flowers and gave it to my wife. She loved it, but then so did everyone else who saw it. For Christmas that year, I made five more toy farm wagons for my mother, mother-in-law and three friends."

After seeing their reactions, Neal realized he was onto something big. Arcadian moved into the production of pewter replica toys.

Lindblade began searching auctions and other secondary market sources in hopes of finding more original Arcade toys as models for his emerging business. Then, he moved further toward associating his venture with the prestigious old Arcade Toy Company by acquiring their original logo as his trademark in 1993. Soon, Neal's library of original Arcade toys was complete enough to jump-start his first series: the *Pewter Replica Collection*. It consisted of cars, trucks, fire engines, an airplane, bank and a coaster wagon. Retailers took one look at Neal's first reproductions and knew they would be fast sellers. In just three months, Lindblade sold over 1,000 pewter replicas, and collectors stood in line up to two hours to have Neal personally sign their treasures.

No Corners Cut in Search of Perfection

Because authenticity is critical to the manufacture of quality vintage toys, Arcade Pewter Replicas are crafted by hand, using the best materials available. The process begins when Neal selects an original toy for replication, disassembles it and removes its finish, creating a "pattern" from which a rubber mold is made. This process is painstaking because each detail of the toy must be retained (this includes any imperfections found in the original).

High-grade, lead-free pewter is used in all Arcadian Pewter castings. The

molten metal is poured into a spinning mold and is evenly distributed by centrifugal force. After cooling, the castings are de-burred and de-flashed before they are dipped into an oxidizing agent which turns them black. A brushing lathe polishes raised surfaces, revealing the shining pewter finish we all recognize. This silvery color creates a marked contrast between "buffed" and dark, recessed areas. The replica toy now is ready to be re-assembled by hand "the old-fashioned way." A clean-up brushing and clear acrylic lacquer coating complete the process.

"We worry about pewter casters who don't feel they should eliminate lead, a potentially dangerous metal, from their molding mix," Neal confesses when discussing the pewter he uses to craft his toys. Owners of his reproductions are thrilled about his cautionary attitude, because Arcade Toys are ideal heirlooms for children. Knowing their legacy is lead-free makes collectors feel doubly secure.

Arcadian replicas are produced in limits of 10,000 each, with the exception of a select number of stand-alone issues limited to only 2,500 of each. Considering the limits, complexity of production and finishing process, collectors find the prices of Arcade issues to be surprisingly low, ranging from $30 to $60 each.

Pewter Toys Are Now Affordable For Everyone

Neal Lindblade discovered, during his journey toward becoming a replica toymaker, Americans are fond of cast-iron toys but may be frightened away by high prices and the scarcity of originals. Some people, he learned, are afraid to display their original Arcade toys for

This "Motorcycle Policeman" paces a gallant "Prancing Horse Bank." Each fine pewter toy replica is limited to just 10,000 before production is stopped forever.

fear of loss. Consequently, Neal always gets a thrill when he sees the look on the face of a new collector each time they realize these concerns have been eliminated by his contemporary replicas.

In addition to giving collectors peace of mind, Neal and the folks at Arcadian Pewter, Inc. pride themselves on their patriotic business ethic. "True Americana can only be made by Americans," he insists, "so our replicas, components and packaging all originate in the U.S. I believe American manufacturers have a responsibility to employ American workers before anyone else. Since Arcade originals were made in America, shouldn't the replicas be made here, by Americans?" With this virtuous attitude, it's easy to see why collectors appreciate both Neal's philosophy and his product.

A Personal Mission: Toy Reproductions to Please the Eye and Heart

In 1995, the Arcadian Pewter staff took its already-popular collectible toys plus six new introductions (a car with rumble seat, a bus, bank, coffee mill, farm tractor and horse-drawn fire wagon) to The Collectors' Jubilee. A surprise awaited them at the end of the show: Arcade won the show's "Best Die Cast Toy" award, beating out power-

Save up for more toy replicas with Arcadian's "Cottage Bank." It's shown with a tiny pewter "Rocking Chair," the perfect gift for new grandmas and all collectors!

Study this "Two-Man Racer" and "Row Crop Tractor" and you'll understand the precise workmanship associated with each Arcadian Pewter issue. After all, molds creating each originate with real Arcade toys!

house companies like Ertl, Fort, Winross and Hallmark. What a proud moment! The company was also nominated for this prize in 1996.

"You may get the impression that a lot of what we're doing is a very personal thing for us," Neal states. "That's because it is. It's been a personal 'mission' ever since the day I made that anniversary gift for my wife. Now, it's a matter of making gifts for people who have come to love our replica toys." To reinforce his personal commitment, Neal selected a photo showing his stepdad and aunt as children for Arcadian Pewter Replicas' first national advertisement. Lindblade likes to think his late stepdad is keeping a watchful eye on his growing business because he had such a strong influence on Neal's life. He follows his stepfather's credo, "If it's worth doing, it's worth doing well."

"Meeting collectors at in-store events is one of the highlights of this job," Neal concludes. "When I sign their certificates or replicas, I like to hear what they have to say. Their insights help me get through the demands our growing business makes on my time and energy. I talk with collectors and realize all the hard work is worth it!"

"Watching the response of a shopper when he spins the wheels on the car he or she is holding really affects me," Lindblade adds. "Collectors get lost in their memories, and I'm there to witness that. Their thoughts go back to their childhoods, to a grandparent or parent. To be honest, I never realized what a compliment it is to have someone buy one's product until I began meeting collectors. I see how much our limited editions mean to them when I look at their faces. One elderly lady at an in-store event had tears in her eyes. She bought the entire collection for her son. This is an awesome responsibility."

Arcadian Pewter
1802 Broadway, Suite 200
Rockford, IL 61104
(815) 395-8670
Fax (815) 395-9523

G. ARMANI SOCIETY AND ARMANI COLLECTION
Italian Artist Brings About a Renaissance
in Hand-Made Sculptures

As one of Italy's most famous sculptors, Giuseppe Armani spends many hours in his home studio, where he creates his original works of art. Armani's renowned and elegant styles reflect the glorious artistic legacy of Tuscany, birthplace of the Renaissance.

Residing and working in the heart of Tuscany, Giuseppe Armani is surrounded by the works of artistic giants. Michelangelo Buonarroti and Leonardo da Vinci, Renaissance legends both, are his inspiration. In his studio, Armani today sculpts to the same ancient rhythms that resounded in the studios of the 15th century Maestros. The legacy of those geniuses inspire Armani to sculpt modern masterpieces.

Even though his work is acclaimed throughout the world, Giuseppe Armani still strives to expand his sculptural horizons. Currently while working on commissions from Disney, Armani is creating a glorious group of religious figurines.

Giuseppe Armani was born in Calci, a quaint little town not far from Pisa. Like children all over the world, young Giuseppe (known as "Beppe" to his many friends) loved to play. But for Beppe, the only game in town he thought worth playing was "drawing pictures." On walls or on any other flat surface, Armani sketched animals, trees and fairy-tale characters. Giuseppe and his family moved to Pisa when he was 14 because Calci lacked inspirational material suitable for an aspiring artist. He mined the artistic treasures of two other renowned Renaissance cities: Siena and Florence. Over the next ten years, Armani taught himself Art and Anatomy. He assiduously immersed himself in the techniques, textures and styles of Michelangelo, da Vinci, Donatello and Pisano. Eventually, he apprenticed himself to a master-sculptor.

Following an Artistic Heritage

Tuscany, the birthplace of the Italian Renaissance, enjoys a recognized cultural tradition in figurative art. Similar to other art forms, sculpture faithfully records the human experience. In Tuscany, the art of sculpture has been handed down from generation to generation since the Etruscans. Michelangelo and da Vinci, who were both capable of sculpting as well as painting, debated throughout their lives about which form of art best and most faithfully represented reality. While Michelangelo asserted that only the multi-sided shapes of sculpture could achieve this purpose, da Vinci argued that only painting, even though created on a flat surface, had the elements of perspective and color, without which, any attempt at representing reality would fail. Particularly in Italy, the art of creating sculpture became an accepted way of expression. People yearned to own and enjoy extraordinary three-dimensional art — in the privacy of their own homes.

Although Armani disciplined himself to study painting and other two-dimensional art, only sculpture resonated in consonance with his uniquely artistic soul. His professional career soon began in Pisa, where he sculpted in the oblique shadows of the Leaning Tower.

Florence Sculture d'Arte Studios Brings Armani's Works to Collectors

In 1975, Armani and Florence Sculture d'Arte began an inspired, exclusive and extraordinarily successful relationship. The factory of Florence Sculture d'Arte is located in the heart of Tuscany where Florence, Siena, Volterra and San Gimignano nestle among lush, rolling hills. The primary ambition of the founders of the Florence factory was to create an environment in which the best Italian sculptors and painters could flourish.

No one living or visiting Tuscany is immune to the pervading artistic atmosphere created by the Renaissance Masters. In this environment, Florence Sculture d'Arte, with its superior sculptors and the natural skills of its fine Tuscan craftsmen, has produced exemplary Armani figurines for more than two decades.

A Work of Art From Start to Finish

At Florence Sculture d'Arte, the sculpture process begins when Armani creates an original piece in clay. Although the artist began his career chiseling in the classic medium of marble, he considers clay a magical material that allows him to massage and manipulate it into incredibly life-like works of art. About three weeks is required for the artist to sculpt a new figurine. Once the original is completed, it is fired in a kiln at very high temperatures and then smoothed. From this piece, a flexible mold is made using a special technique that allows faithful replication of the original. The mold is then filled with a liquid compound, which hardens in several hours. The figurine is taken out of the mold and hand polished with extreme care. Intricate pieces are cast separately and mounted to form a solid piece. Finally, each sculpture is hand-painted according to the original model conceived by Armani.

"People often ask me how I am able to create new sculptures," Armani once said. "Sculpting comes naturally to me, but the process is not easy to explain. Think about what relaxes you the most. Perhaps you enjoy cooking. When you are chopping vegetables, or measuring ingredients, your mind is clear except for the task at hand. You become totally focused on the food: its texture, and smell — the art of cooking. When you finally present the meal, and it's a success, you get a wonderful feeling inside. And so it is for me with sculpting."

Created exclusively for the 1995 Disneyana convention in Orlando, Florida, "Beauty and the Beast" captures the warmth and magic of the classic fairy tale. In this scene, Belle and the almost human Beast, having found true love, are tenderly holding hands.

Mythology Comes to Life

Two of Giuseppe Armani's newest sculptures are "Diana" and "Minerva." Diana, child of the great god Jupiter, is the goddess of The Hunt. When she was a very little child, Jupiter sat her on his enormous knee and magnanimously asked his precocious girl what gifts she wanted him to give her. She rapidly reeled off a list of things which included a flowing hunting tunic; a bow and arrow like Apollo's (her twin brother); eternal virginity; 60 young nymphs as her companions and all the mountains in the world in which to live and roam.

Minerva, though gentler than Diana, shared many of her traits. She was the goddess of Skilled Art. Minerva invented the flute, trumpet, earthenware pot, ox yoke, chariot and ships. She was the first to teach mathematics and all of the domestic arts such as: cooking, weaving and spinning.

Armani has sculpted Diana as a chaste beauty who roams mountain ranges seeking to protect children in danger. It is the wise and gentle side of Minerva that Armani chose to sculpt. The doves that flutter around her show her preference for peace, even though she possesses the terrible power to wage devastating wars.

Since both "Diana" and "Minerva" are classic mythological figures, Armani has sculpted them in the classic style of the Renaissance masters.

Inspiration from Childhood Trips to Rome

When Armani was a very small boy, his parents took him to Rome once a year. For a child from a tiny town outside Pisa, Rome was in a wholly different solar system — big, bustling and filled with noise and excitement. Armani has recently successfully captured the cosmopolitan nature of Via Veneto, a famous tree-lined street in Rome where fashion, fettucini and film meet. Via Veneto is home to some of the world's most fashionable shops, hotels and cafes. Giuseppe Armani's

"Diana" — the daughter of Jupiter — always carries her bow and arrow as she roams the mountains protecting children. The sculpture shows the intricate details and expressions beautifully captured by Giuseppe Armani.

poised, beautiful and thoroughly modern models are dressed for today. Armani has even dared to put one flamboyant figurine called "Marina" in slacks — quite a departure from ancient Greek tunics!

Armani Participates in Disneyana Convention

Giuseppe Armani enjoys meeting with collectors, who admire his work; it was with great pride and happy anticipation that Armani once again decided to accept an invitation to participate in and make a personal appearance at the 1995 Disneyana Convention in Orlando, Florida. Exclusively for the 1995 convention, Armani sculpted a captivating "Beauty and the Beast." It takes the genius of Giuseppe Armani to breathe life into statues. "Beauty and the Beast" depicts the compelling drama of beautiful Belle's search for true love and the Beast's redemption through her love.

G. Armani Society Unites Collectors

The Society was launched for collectors to: learn more about the artist himself, meet fellow collectors, go "behind the scenes" of the studio, find out about new introductions, have the opportunity to acquire exclusive merchandise and participate in members-only activities. Dues are $40.00 for the first year, with renewal memberships at $27.50 per year. Members-only figurines include some of Armani's most inspired works, as unveiled in the quarterly Society publication, "The Review."

Armani is an artist on a double mission: dedicated to his collectors and impelled to bring beauty into their lives. It is for the collector that Armani creates art for today, and it is for the Armani collector that he continues to sculpt wondrous and compelling figurines out of space, air and imagination.

Giuseppe Armani Society
Miller Import Corp.
300 Mac Lane
Keasbey, NJ 08832
(800) 3-ARMANI
Fax: (908) 417-0031

Giuseppe Armani rekindles mythological characters and stories with this introduction named "Minerva," the goddess of Skilled Art. A pair of doves flock around the beautiful woman, showing her gentle side and devotion to peace.

COLLECTORS' CLUB

Giuseppe Armani Society
300 Mac Lane
Keasbey, NJ 08832
(800) 3-ARMANI

Annual Dues: $40.00 - Renewal: $27.50
Club Year: January-December

Benefits:
- Membership Gift: Armani Figurine
- Opportunity to Purchase Members-Only Figurines
- Quarterly Magazine, *The Review*
- Membership Card
- Special "Members Events" Throughout the Year

THE ART OF GLYNDA TURLEY
Prints, Collectibles and Decorative Accessories
that Share Romance and Nostalgia

Released in 1994, "A Summer Stroll" was the fastest selling print ever produced by Glynda Turley. The print depicts Villa Marre, a Victorian home located in Little Rock, Arkansas, that was made famous on the television series "Designing Women."

At her home nestled in the beautiful Ozark Mountains of Arkansas, Glynda Turley finds the quiet inspiration for her exquisite oil paintings that have won her international acclaim. As president and sole artist of her company, The Art of Glynda Turley, she has turned her creative talents into a thriving family business that invites collectors to enjoy the simpler pleasures of life. Her artwork reflects the vibrant colors of a springtime garden, the country charm of beloved antiques or the playful afternoon pastimes of children.

"I strive to take the viewer into a time and place of beauty, peace and harmony — where time seems to stand still," Glynda says. "I suppose my style of work could be described as romantic." It is this captivating combination of romance and nostalgia that has blossomed The Art of Glynda Turley into a successful print and collectibles

company. Collectors can now find Glynda's artwork adorning everything from limited edition prints to hand-painted figurines and tapestry pillows.

"I love my work," Glynda says. "My paintings are the way I share that magical place or old-fashioned bouquet that represents the way I see things and the way I feel inside. It is a very rewarding thing to know you have helped someone to smile."

Inspired Beginnings
for a Self-Taught Artist

Glynda's artistic style has evolved since her childhood. She had no formal art training but can't recall a time when she wasn't filling blank pieces of paper or canvases with the images in her mind and heart.

"My grandmother was probably my very first influence," she recalls. "She

inspired me to be creative by her constant creativity. She was always making beautiful gifts. She never had the opportunity to paint, but I have no doubt that she could have been a great artist."

Even though this self-taught artist loved to sketch, Glynda didn't begin to paint until the mid-1970s, when as a young mother and housewife, she was introduced to oil paints. Ozark Mountain scenes and barnyard animals were among her first subjects. She sold some of her paintings at arts and crafts fairs throughout the state. During this time, she also started teaching art lessons to neighborhood children and adults in her kitchen, as well as a local beauty shop and school gymnasium. In 1977, she opened an art supplies store in Heber Springs, Arkansas. A few years later, Glynda's first two prints were published. Soon, she was winning awards and receiving many requests for her work from galleries, gift shops and collectors.

In 1985, she founded The Art of Glynda Turley to market her prints. Since then, the number of outlets and mediums for her work has grown by leaps and bounds. Glynda's work is sold in more than 7,000 stores nationwide and in several foreign countries. Glynda is even the exclusive artist at the Grand Palace in Branson, Missouri. More than 100 prints and several originals hang in the 4,000-seat country music theater, where there is a "Glynda Turley Gallery" in the lobby.

Collectors line up at the Palace Gift Shop to purchase her new prints. J.C. Penney is adding Glynda Turley boutiques to some of its stores, where prints are displayed along with her full range of home accessories. The first company-owned retail store opened in April 1996 in Branson to carry the extensive line of every Glynda Turley product, including licensed products.

To keep up with the demand,

"In Full Bloom III" is the third in a series of prints that feature a beautiful arrangement of roses.

Glynda now employs about 75 people, including 14 family members. But the company and collectors are truly her extended family. In 1992, when a fire destroyed her manufacturing plant and 83 of her original oil paintings, her employees, suppliers, retailers and collectors came to the rescue. They gave a helping hand and encouraging words to rebuild the business and plant located in Heber Springs, Arkansas, a picturesque resort area 80 miles north of Little Rock.

"We have a wonderful team that pulled together," Glynda says. "There's a real family bond." In recent years, Glynda has expanded the scope of her products through licensing agreements. Her designs appear on many different kinds of home-decor items and gifts, including soaps, candles, journals, desk calendars, pillows, throws, wallpaper borders, clothing, needlepoint kits, wreaths and gift bags. Other items are always in the works. "Nothing is more exciting than to see one's artwork adapted to other products," she says.

Prints Capture Everything from Florals to Family

Although her artwork is being adapted to a variety of products, Glynda is still most renowned for her prints — especially those featuring beautiful florals. "Florals are my true love," Glynda reveals. "Flowers are so short-lived that if I can capture them on canvas, they can be enjoyed forever."

At her cottage-style home, Glynda enjoys working in her gardens, which grow among a backdrop of picket fences and are filled with multi-colored roses, delphiniums and foxgloves, among others. "I only have to look out my window for inspiration," she says.

But some of her ideas don't just come from her backyard. Her family also appears in many of her works. The 1996 release "Secret Garden III," for example, shows two of her grandchildren — Jordan and Crystal — sitting on the wisteria-covered arbor in her yard.

On her extensive travels, she always packs her camera and many rolls of film. In 1994, she went to England for the first time and saw Anne Hathaway's cottage and gardens. The trip inspired the 1995 print release titled "Hollyhocks III," the third in a series of Hollyhocks prints. From a visit to Victoria, British Columbia, Glynda painted a quaint Victorian house with its black iron gate and rose-covered arched walkway. The painting became "Summer In Victoria."

Another print titled "Summer Stroll" features Villa Marre, a Victorian home in a historic neighborhood of Little Rock, Arkansas. The house is best known as the home of the Sugarbaker Design Firm in the television series "Designing Women." Another recent release, "Little Red River," depicts fishermen on the famous Arkansas trout stream. A portion of the sales from the limited edition print will be donated to "Friends of the Little Red River," an organization devoted to the preservation and enhancement of the stream.

"My inspiration today comes from my environment," she says. "I live in one of the most beautiful places in the world, so I only have to look around me for the inspiration to create. My head is full of ideas for paintings, many of which come from the extensive amount of traveling that I do throughout the year."

Glynda's limited edition prints include more than 100 titles with many selling out within a matter of months. The company also offers custom framing, and some sold-out limited edition prints are available in smaller sizes in an open edition.

Figurines Add New Dimension to Artwork

Glynda's artwork has also been transformed into limited edition figurines that are carefully sculpted to capture all the detail of the original paintings. The line of collectible figurines recreates Glynda's most popular paintings, including "Secret Garden II," "Flowers

"Hollyhocks III," the third print in a series, was inspired by Glynda Turley's trip to England in 1994. The print features the Anne Hathaway cottage in England and was nominated for a 1996 "Award of Excellence" from Collector Editions *magazine.*

"The Courtyard II" is a replica of one of Glynda Turley's most popular prints of the same name. This hand-painted resin figurine is limited in edition to 4,800 pieces and comes with a Certificate of Authenticity.

For Mommy" and "Circle of Friends" — all of which feature her grandchildren or children. Also included in the collection are: "The Courtyard II," "Playing Hookie" and "Past Times."

"Bringing the prints to life in the form of six new figurines has been one of the most enjoyable projects we've developed, especially since three of those figurines feature members of my family," she says.

The poly-resin figurines are mounted on a wooden base with a brass-colored plaque bearing the name of the design. The figurines, which are each limited to 4,800 pieces, also come with a Certificate of Authenticity.

Plans for Expanding into New Markets

In the future, Glynda hopes to add more items to her range of home decor designs that will complement her prints, figurines and other collectibles. The line recently expanded to include plates, eggs and ornaments. "The company goals are to keep the same quality standards and ethics that have

made us successful," says Glynda, whose company was named a finalist for the Arkansas Business of the Year, as well as a nominee for Wall Decor Company of the Year in 1996 by the Dallas Market Center.

"My personal goals as an artist are to recreate the wonderful things that I have had the privilege or opportunity to see, whether they are found in my travels, at home or in my imagination. I wish to record with my paintings some of the beauty of the past." Today's lovely Glynda Turley prints, decorative accessories and collectibles will surely be the heirlooms of tomorrow. Whether in the Ozark Mountains or traveling around the world, Glynda is always working on new ideas and expanding her collection for more collectors to enjoy.

The Art of Glynda Turley
P.O. Box 112
74 Cleburne Park Road
Heber Springs, Arkansas 72543
(800) 203-7620
Fax (501) 362-5020

ASHTON-DRAKE GALLERIES

In Just Ten Years, The Ashton-Drake Galleries Has Become America's Top Doll Company! Everyone Wants to Know: What's Their Secret?

When The Ashton-Drake Galleries opened in 1985, collectors wondered what this new company was all about. At the time, collector plates were "king" and interest in limited edition figurines was growing, but dolls? Too expensive, even non-collectors said. But, producing a quality doll with personality and affordability built-in was the goal of Ashton-Drake, an offshoot of The Bradford Exchange. Challenge in place, they began to work toward what many thought an impossible goal. Who could have imagined so extraordinary an outcome from so simple a beginning as this...

His name was "Jason." Her name was "Heather." They first met at a bustling office in a Chicago suburb ten years ago. He looked dashing in his powder blue clown suit. Her peach dress, bare toes, pillow and white bonnet charmed everyone who saw her.

"What a doll!" collectors said when

Babe Ruth was never more eloquently immortalized. Award-winning sculptor Titus Tomescu bats a thousand with his realistic, limited edition offering, "The 60th Home Run." A sandy base with solid brass plate bears an impression of The Babe's signature!

"Jason," then "Heather," debuted at collector shows across the U.S. Who could argue with rave reviews? Today, "Jason" and "Heather" are the revered "first-borns" of The Ashton-Drake Galleries. They now boast lots of brothers and sisters as Ashton-Drake continues to introduce additional, exclusive editions for doll lovers around the world.

How did Ashton-Drake become the recognized leader in the design, manufacture and marketing of high quality collectible dolls in ten short years? The answer is no mystery: Lifelike, beautifully designed dolls at affordable prices. Many say Ashton-Drake literally "reinvented" the collectible doll industry...a statement few can argue.

A Simple Philosophy Behind the Name

Behind the simple philosophy of "lifelike dolls at affordable prices" stands an army of creative minds devoted to picking talented doll artists (some well known...others stars-in-the-making) and embracing new materials, styles and looks. Their efforts show! Ashton-Drake makes dolls that appeal to collectors of every age and interest.

Among the recent ideas explored by Ashton-Drake are personalized babies, dolls scented to excite the senses, mini-dolls, dolls that talk, and moveable, musical dolls. Whether porcelain or vinyl, all Ashton-Drake dolls have a common denominator: each creation is the epitome of personality-filled art, a goal that's at the very heart of Ashton-Drake.

Many founding members of Ashton-Drake have stayed around to shepherd this decade's innovations and its growing family of artists and designers. If you're already an Ashton-Drake fan, you've seen the results of experience and flair. If you're not currently an observer of this dynamic company's

efforts, you're in for a treat. Read on to discover why Ashton-Drake Galleries has set a standard for excellence that's become the industry benchmark!

The Start of the Dream Team...

With an eye to the future, the Ashton-Drake start-up team used visionary talent scouts to find doll artists willing to take a chance on the fledgling company. If Ashton-Drake grew, artists were assured their designs would reach collectors across America. The search had hardly begun when Yolanda Bello was discovered. Her work seemed the ideal starting-point for Ashton-Drake. Her dolls were lifelike and endearing. They had the perfect "look" for the new company's launch.

Happily, Bello shared the dream. She longed to expand her audience beyond the local following she already enjoyed. A passionate crusader for peace, love and spirituality, Bello saw her dolls as tiny missionaries and welcomed the chance to spread her philosophy through her art. Working tirelessly through the first days of her association with Ashton-Drake, Yolanda's premier doll, "Jason," was born. This blue-suited, now-pricey premier doll is a near-legend.

Today, Yolanda Bello carefully balances her successes of yesterday with the wishes of contemporary collectors. Fashioning small versions of her best selling dolls (including the landmark "Jason" and "Heather"), miniature *Picture Perfect Babies*®, filled with nostalgia, now greet her adoring public. But Yolanda didn't stop with her miniatures, she also pioneered Ashton-Drake's *Heirloom Ornaments*.

These tiny classics are petite sensations. "Jason," "Heather," "Matthew," "Sarah," "Michael"...indeed, every member of the original *Picture Perfect Babies* gang is now an ornament. These perennial delights make ideal shelf

These babies are legends in their own time! Authentic recreations of first Yolanda Bello designs, award-winning Picture Perfect Babies® miniatures keep Ashton-Drake Galleries at the forefront of doll innovation!

and mantle decorations when they're not enhancing Christmas trees in December. Additional ornaments are "waiting in the wings." Collectors can expect surprises in the year ahead as the Ashton-Drake ornament collection expands.

If you think Ashton-Drake's launch of *Picture Perfect Babies* ornaments

Winner of awards...and hearts..."Cute as a Button" is everything little porcelain girls are made of! Sculptor Titus Tomescu's "first-born" launched Ashton-Drake's popular Barely Yours *collection.*

completes the list of new Yolanda Bello ideas, think again. Collectors enamored with her award-winning, porcelain "Meagan Rose" doll wrote to say how much they wished their children could own a less fragile version of this precious doll. Voila! A vinyl "Meagan Rose" now delights doll fans of all ages. She looks exactly like her namesake. A quilted blanket and pillow complete every little girl's dream. Bello fans wonder what she'll think of next!

The Galleries' Award-Winning Artist Family Grows

With Yolanda Bello firmly entrenched as grand matriarch of dolls for The Ashton-Drake Galleries, other artisans were carefully scouted to join the elite family. One star is sculptor Titus Tomescu. Titus looks much too young to be "the dad" of the lifelike babies he designs for Ashton-Drake, but talent sometimes blooms early, and awards for Titus' "Cute as a Button" confirm his genius.

Collectors confess they can't decide what to look at first when they see Tomescu's "Cute as a Button." The T-shirt with embroidered applique? The signature button in baby's realistic hair? Ruffled panties? Many insist her "poseability" makes "Cute as a Button" a winner! Whatever it is, that secret is propelling Titus Tomescu into stardom.

And lest you conclude that his designs appeal only to the maternal side of our collecting senses, take a peek at the lifelike "Babe Ruth" Titus sculpted to commemorate the sports legend! "The 60th Home Run" has such realistic detail, you can almost hear the pop of the bat!

Turning away from the roar of the ball park, we enter a world that's filled with wonder. Lights dim! A curtain opens. From the wings, a tiny ballerina emerges. She's "My Little Ballerina," a rising star in the doll world. Not only is "My Little Ballerina" deliciously poseable, she also comes with her own costume and accessory-filled trunk!

"My Little Ballerina," the brainchild of award-winning sculptor/doll designer Kathy Barry-Hippensteel, is a perfect example of the kind of

The "My Little Ballerina" collection is crafted in a hand-numbered edition ending forever in 1995! She is 16" tall and comes all dressed for her performance. Collectors may acquire additional costumes in a darling, pink trunk filled with surprises.

diversity that continues to fuel Ashton-Drake's mission and the sort of concept that has jump-started in-house design innovations like *Calendar Babies.* This unique concept combines practicality with collector passion for surrounding themselves with dolls year-round.

Collectors subscribing to *Calendar Babies* receive a 25" x 11" master calendar of fine wood with a complete set of date and month tiles. A shadowbox showcases a darling array of "dolls of the month"...each dressed to celebrate a special occasion. There's calendar fun for everyone with this one-of-a-kind collection.

Another perennial Ashton-Drake favorite, Cindy McClure, continues to shine as the distinguished winner of many "Doll of the Year" awards. Her newest originals are recreations of her favorite era: the days of Victoriana. Cindy's flair for dramatic costume design makes her sweet collectible tots a category unto themselves. *Victorian Nursery Heirloom Collection* dolls and the *Cross-Stitch* collection exemplify a sensitive style that's beloved by collectors across the country.

Joyce Wolf's *Nursery Newborns*

A doll collector's dream! Keep track of every year, for years to come, with this perpetual calendar starring tiny dolls dressed to celebrate each month. This mini-collection will be noticed and admired!

double the thrill of doll ownership by combining the look of tiny infants with innovative, real-life twists. Collectors can "adopt" their favorite infant by gender, then dress him or her for a first outing...in the most adorable Christmas

outfit anyone could imagine...or in a pristine christening outfit marking this sacred occasion.

Renowned doll creator Wendy Lawton brings her genius to Ashton-Drake with a trail of awards and a national following. A gifted clothing designer, Wendy's dolls win awards for their wonderful faces and the sophisticated clothing they wear; a hallmark of her talent. Thorough research and a passion for historical detail distinguish her work from all others and bring to the Ashton-Drake family of artists and designers a recognized leader.

Inspiring Visions Continue the Legacy

When Julie Good-Krüger first approached Ashton-Drake with her idea for crafting the Holy Family as a limited edition doll collection, she couldn't have picked a better time. Ashton-Drake's strong move into the world of inspirational dolls was already making headlines and her new collection would be the perfect addition. Today, Julie's *Oh, Holy Night* dolls include three adorable wise men, a shepherd boy and a Gloria Angel!

Based on another beloved Christmas story, "The Little Drummer Boy" is moveable and musical. He literally takes collectors back in time to the birth of Baby Jesus as he beats his drum to the accompaniment of the beloved "Little Drummer Boy" tune. Big brown eyes

gazing upward, "Little Drummer Boy" looks for divine guidance as he slowly approaches the stable with his gift of song.

Given the early popularity of "Little Drummer Boy," and country-wide excitement of Julie Good-Krüger's *Oh, Holy Night* collection, Ashton-Drake's award-winning artist Titus Tomescu sculpted a highly unusual doll series of scenes depicting the life of Jesus as an adult. Already well-known for his realistic *Barely Yours* collection, debuting with "Cute as a Button," Titus was given the go-ahead to develop this sacred series.

Messages of Hope introduced "Little Children Come to Me" to a ready-made audience of appreciative collectors. Even seasoned Ashton-Drake staffers were impressed and concluded that with such artists as Yolanda Bello, Cindy McClure, Joyce Wolf, Kathy Barry-Hippensteel, Titus Tomescu, Julie Good-Krüger, Wendy Lawton, Dianna Effner and others, the next ten years will be a rocket ride to the stars...a ride doll collectors will be queued up to join!

The Ashton-Drake Galleries
9200 N. Maryland Avenue
Niles, IL 60714
(800) 634-5164
Fax (708) 966-3026

ATTIC BABIES
Rediscovering the Simple Joys of Childhood

Realtor (and ostrich) "Elmira Truelove" is 28" tall and comes with her own birdhouse.

"Even though growing up can sometimes make us tuck away the very best in all of us – the hopes, the dreams, the sense of possibility – the child is alive and well in all of us. And rediscovering that is one of life's greatest joys."

This, to Attic Babies™ founder and designer Marty Maschino-Walker, is the voice of experience. It has also been her inspiration throughout her life, and especially in the nine years that her company has been in existence – the inspiration that has brought hundreds of whimsical rag dolls and teddy bear creations into our lives – and that has helped her thousands of collectors rediscover the simple joys of childhoods past. This special understanding of Marty's that everyone, someday, returns to their own "attic" is in large part what makes her designs so irresistible.

From Home-Based Business to Award-Winning Company

Attic Babies began as a home-based business in 1987. Marty was pregnant at the time – and she'd found that the rag dolls and teddy bears that she'd been exhibiting at arts and crafts shows were exceptionally popular – not to mention the fact that they were much easier to carry around for the pregnant artist!

Based on her local success, Marty decided in 1987 to invest in exhibiting at the Dallas Gift Market, and sent 16 designs to the show. Interest from the retail trade was exceptional, and orders came in by the droves. Once the show was over, she realized that, while she worked very well under pressure, she just couldn't handle this new level of demand by herself.

So Marty hired some local women who liked the idea of being able to sew at home, watch kids if they needed to, and earn some money while they were at it. True to her instincts, success continued to follow, and to make a long but wonderful story short – what has become Attic Babies today, continued to grow over the next two years – and in the process Marty found her first building to house production. She's now re-located three times, each time to larger facilities. The company now resides in Drumright, Oklahoma – halfway between Tulsa and Oklahoma City. Marty now designs Attic Babies in a 15,000 square foot facility where almost 100 employees bring her designs to life every day. The office and factory are open Monday through Thursday, and factory tours can be arranged Monday through Thursday, from 9:30 a.m. until 2:30 p.m.

Aside from what is to Marty the privilege of having brought hundreds of designs to life, it has been a special thrill in the last nine years to have been: chosen in 1990 as Oklahoma's Small

Business Person of the Year; invited to Washington, D.C. to present Mrs. Bush with a special rendition of the First Lady entitled "Grammy Bar;" and invited to the National Governor's Convention in 1993, to present specially designed dolls which commemorated Native Oklahoma to all of the Governors' spouses.

It's been pretty exciting, to say the least. And so, you just have to ask – what does the future hold for Attic Babies? "That's a tough question. One day at a time is just about as much excitement as anyone can stand around here!" quips Marty. Whatever shape it all takes, she is living proof of the adage "do what you love, the money will follow" – so we'd say the future looks very bright indeed.

Available only to Attic Babies™ Club Members is "Tricia Kay Yumyum," the 1995 Club Doll.

Distinct Personalities and Original Names Make Attic Babies Unique

If there is such a thing, your average Attic Baby is an extremely cuddly rag doll or teddy bear — and no two are ever exactly alike. But there's much, much more variety in the products — especially the hilarious parodies that come to life from Marty's visions of the "ultimate professional" — whether doctor, lawyer, sports figure, or even her favorite members of the animal kingdom.

One thing is for certain — each design has its own distinctive personality, and a hysterical name to match. Part of the charisma of Attic Babies is wrapped up in those names which Marty develops — names like "Fertile Mertle," "Virtuous Vergie," "Luscious Lulu" and "Fatty Matty" to name a very few. Most of the designs and names alike are influenced by friends and family in Marty's own charmed life — inspired by both childhood and recent memories.

Attic Babies are not developed as collections or series, although there are common threads which are sustained

"Ms. Kizzie Tiddle E. Winks" is a bear whose not-so-secret desire is to be a bunny. At 18" tall, she is available in country colors.

from one design season to the next — Marty designs twice a year — which make for wonderful collections. Each has its own personality, and while they are all limited in production — each "living their lives with great service and loyalty" as Marty would say — many are number-limited in small editions, or are limited by year of production, as are all of Marty's heartwarming Santas.

Almost without exception, though, every Attic Baby can be customized to make it very much a collector's very own one-of-a-kind — from your choice of fabric color, to personalization of accessories, to choice of size and the degree of choice which makes each design a unique character that forms an indelible bond between doll and collector.

Imagination, Experience and Common Sense Go Into Each Attic Babies Design

Attic Babies are the original tea-stained muslin dolls of their kind — and everything in the way that they're made adds charm and whimsy to the delightful concepts which their designer develops.

From Marty's initial prototype, the ingenuity, imagination and experience of her production staff takes over in all the areas which she believes are so critically important to making an Attic Baby a very high-touch collectible. This includes sourcing the right fabric, layering and cutting it just right, developing the accessories, making sure that the facial expressions in production match the prototype, and insuring that Attic Babies are as affordable as they are cute.

"The whole process hasn't really changed significantly in nine years. Just a few more hands out there," says Marty. As with nature, there is a beauty in the simple elegance and common sense that goes into making each and every Attic Baby.

Between design seasons, when Marty can schedule a block of time

An impromptu gathering of Attic Babies includes "Mary Jane Hackensack," a little girl with her wagon full of blocks; "Scruffy Gilhooley," a little boy bear with tricycle who's looking for Poo; "Epple Moneyworth," a felt bunny with wheelbarrow, ready for gardening; and "Albert P. Thigpen," a froggle going a-courtin' with bouquet and trusty fiddle in hand.

away from the family she loves very much, she goes on signing tours that take her from coast to coast, with dozens of stops in just a few weeks. It keeps her in touch not only with her retail stores, but more importantly — her thousands of collectors. Says Marty, "They are a constant, heaven-sent source of humility to me. After nine years, their connection to what I do is not only gratifying, it's downright perplexing!"

Collectors Club Continues to Grow

Attic Babies Collectors' Club began in 1992, and membership has almost doubled every year since. Many Club Members have become great friends with Attic Babies staff over the years — and Club Members are constantly calling each other to keep in touch with the latest news. They've even established their own contact network on Prodigy!

One way or another, Club Members get all the information. A quarterly newsletter is both informative and whimsically humorous in a true-to-form way. Members also receive regular mailings with details on signings, appearances at major collectibles shows, and updates on both new designs and retiring dolls. Special offers are often made to Club Members only — everything from T-shirts, buttons, and mugs to an annual Club Doll which is numbered and hand-signed by Marty.

Initial membership is $30.00, and renewals thereafter are $20.00. Marty and all the office staff at Attic Babies believe their Club is truly special. "Our Club Members know our names, and we know theirs. It's really turned into a mutual admiration society. We're truly blessed."

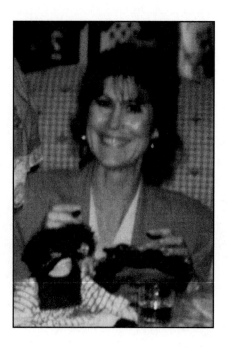

Marty Maschino-Walker is the designer of Attic Babies — the whimsical, tea-stained rag dolls that are a tribute to a rediscovered childhood.

Attic Babies
P.O. Box 912
Drumright, OK 74030
(918) 352-4414
Fax (918) 352-4767

COLLECTORS' CLUB/TOUR

Attic Babies Collectors' Club
P.O. Box 912
Drumright, OK 74030
(918) 352-4414

Annual Dues: $30.00 - Renewal: $20.00
Club Year: Anniversary of Sign-Up Date

Benefits:
• Membership Gift: T-Shirt and Button
• Opportunity to Purchase Members-Only Doll
• Quarterly Newsletter, "News From The Attic"
• Membership Card
• Buy/Sell Matching Service

Attic Babies Factory Tour
Rt. 1 Box 487
Drumright, OK 74030
(918) 352-4414

Hours: Monday through Thursday, 9:30 a.m. - 2:30 p.m.
Admission Fee: None

Visitors can tour the 15,000 square foot Attic Babies Factory and see how the delightful Attic Babies rag dolls "come to life."

AUTOM

Exclusive United States Distributor
of Dolfi Hand-Carved Wood Figurines

Quality craftsmanship and meticulous detailing make each Matteo *Nativity a work of art. Crafted by Dolfi artisans and distributed in the United States by Autom, there are 28 pieces now available in the* Matteo *Nativity line.*

The Dolfi Company was founded in 1892 by Franz Comploi who, by himself, carved and painted the first solid wood Tyrolean figurines. The company, located in Northern Italy, still operates in the century-old tradition which makes Dolfi what it is today — one of the world's largest producers of hand-carved wood figurines.

Dolfi Artists Carry On the Tradition of Woodcarving

In today's era of high technology and mass production, the Dolfi Studios still offer hand-carved and hand-painted, one-of-a-kind collectibles that retain their value throughout the years. Dolfi's artists and carvers breathe life into seasoned wood, keeping the lost art of woodcarving alive and respected.

Over the years, Dolfi's carvers have learned how technology can enhance their detailed figurines. Today's modern technology, in the hand's of skilled artisans, has resulted in Dolfi's finest carvings. Dolfi's time-tested procedures have reaped the benefit of years of experience from devoted artisans and proven methods.

Dolfi Nativities Distributed in the U.S. by Autom

Dolfi's heirloom-quality Nativity sets are produced in numerous sizes, as well as from many different types of materials, such as poly-resin, fiberglass and hand-carved wood. Sizes range from 3-inch figurines in poly-resin to beautiful four-foot statues made of molded fiberglass.

Autom, Dolfi's United States partner, has been serving customers since 1948, from its home in Phoenix, Arizona. Autom is proud to be Dolfi's exclusive United States distributor and to introduce Dolfi's premier Nativity line, *Matteo*, to retailers and collectors everywhere.

The *Matteo* Nativity line was introduced in the United States in 1995. Each year, Autom will be adding new pieces to the collection, including limited edition pieces. *Matteo* Nativities are available in genuine hand-carved wood, as well as hand-painted resin. The hand-painting, quality craftsmanship and attention to detail make each Nativity a work of art. Both the wood and resin lines are manufactured by Dolfi in the same century-old tradition that has made the company world renowned.

Autom
5226 S. 31st Place
Phoenix, AZ 85040
(800) 572-1172
Fax (800) 582-1166

BAND CREATIONS
BAND Creations Incorporates Friendship, Romance and History into Collectible Figurines

Since BAND Creations was established in 1988 by Dennis Sowka, it has distributed numerous lines of giftware items by different artists to the collectible world. Sowka's 17 years of experience with inspirational, Christmas and collectible items prior to starting BAND Creations provides him with a knowledge of the artists and pieces that are most admired by collectors.

Currently, BAND Creations exclusively distributes the popular *Best Friends* figurines created by talented artists Jeanette Richards and Sandra Penfield. BAND is also creating excitement in the collectibles field with the introduction of its new collectible lines – *America's Covered Bridges*.

Own A Piece of American History

In 1994, BAND introduced the *America's Covered Bridges* series to its vast and impressive lines of giftware items. The collection of 22 bridges features replicas of historical American bridges built during the mid 1800s and early 1900s at various sites across the U.S., which have been carefully selected and researched prior to creation.

The bridges capture the history and romance of the structures that have linked farmlands with generations of memories. A few of the famous bridges included in the *America's Covered Bridges* series are the well-known tourist attraction, "Narrows Covered Bridge," in Parke County, Indiana; the oldest covered bridge in the West, "Wawona Covered Bridge," within Yosemite National Park; and the "Roseman Covered Bridge" in Madison County, Iowa, the inspiration for the romantic novel. Each of the replicas comes with its own history card detailing such information as the story and date of the bridges construction, the bridges location, world guide number, and a few interesting anecdotes.

BAND Creations unique covered bridges collectibles are handcrafted of poly resin and carefully hand-painted to capture the bridges' individual design and character. The *America's Covered Bridges* feature great attention to detail in everything from the color and texture of the external constructions to the interior truss designs. The bridges come with an attractive wood base and a metal plaque. They range in size from 6" to 10" long and retail for $29.95 to $39.95.

BAND Creations is already selecting and researching additional bridges to be included in the *America's Covered Bridges* series in the future.

Quiet Country Life Is Represented in BAND's New *Best Friends* "RiverSong" Collection

BAND Creations, Jeanette Richards and Sandra Penfield have again combined their creative talents in the artists new *Best Friends* "RiverSong" collection, which reflects the quiet majesty of a small village on the St. Croix River. The quaint village homes and townspeople are the newest addition to Richard's and Penfield's *Best Friends* lines of adorable miniatures. Each of the collectible "RiverSong" buildings is decorated to capture the festive and warm feelings of small-town life. The miniatures also double as candle votives. Richards says, "We based 'RiverSong' on the small river town where we live. It's here that we enjoy the simple pleasures of country living and the various activities of our children."

The new miniature village collection, which is hand-painted and constructed of poly resin, ranges in size from 2" for the citizens to 7" for the houses. They are available for the suggested retail prices of $14.00 to $30.00, or $255.40 for the complete 28-piece set.

Spanning waterways, farmlands and generations of cherished memories, BAND Creations brings unique charm and character to the "Knox Covered Bridge" in Chester County, Pennsylvania, as part of the America's Covered Bridge *series.*

BAND Creations Adds the New "Noah's Ark" to Its Popular Line of *Best Friends* Miniatures

He gathered the animals two by two.
Noah and his wife,
they made quite a crew.

The animals were housed both fore
and aft, while two less popular
rode on the raft.

The rain came down,
forty nights 'til at last appeared land,
the most beautiful of sights.

They all rejoiced as the ark
came to shore. The rainbow,
His promise to flood nevermore.

Jeanette Richards and Sandra Penfield bring their poem to life in their new Noah's Ark creation for BAND Creations. The artists biblical boat figurine is the latest addition to their *Best Friends* line.

Noah's Ark features Noah and his wife sailing happily along in the main ark, surrounded by a variety of their animal friends including monkeys and colorful parrots. In addition,

"RiverSong," the make believe town on the banks of the St. Croix River, becomes a winter playland for BAND Creations' Best Friends series.

an attached raft is the form of transportation for two adorable skunks.

Richards and Penfield have designed their new 7" tall Noah's Ark out of durable poly resin material and have carefully hand-painted each piece in bright colors. Everything from the

straw roof on the ark's cabin, to the bananas on the palm tree and Noah's and his wife's smiling faces, feature the artists attention to detail.

The complete 10-piece set of the *Best Friends* "Noah's Ark" is available now for the suggested retail price of $62.00. In addition, collectors can purchase the decorative ark separately for the suggested retail price of $42.00 and the animals separately for $20.00.

Meet the BAND Creations Artists

The creators of BAND Creations *Best Friends* collections, Jeanette Richards and Sandra Penfield have discovered the excitement of creating a world of clay miniatures. Combining their varied talents, creative abilities and formal education, they have succeeded in capturing the simplicity of the American spirit.

Jeanette, from Rocky River, Ohio, studied art in Washington, D.C. and received her B.A. in English and Art from the University of Dayton, Ohio. Growing up in a family of artists, illustration was her first love.

Sandra grew up in Detroit Lakes, Minnesota, and received a B.S. in Art from the University of North Dakota. She taught art and shared her talents

BAND Creations' replica of "The Humpback Covered Bridge," located in Allegheny County, Virginia, captures the history and romance of this unique structure built in 1835. This bridge, with no middle supports, is believed to be the only one of its design in the United States.

through her woodcut prints.

Their mutual interest in art brought Richards and Penfield together in Hudson, Wisconsin, where they became partners in a graphic design business in 1984. Always experimenting with new ideas, they created their first Christmas Angel in October 1990. Using the limitless boundaries of clay, their designs soon evolved to encompass all the facets of friendship and family life. Their collections for BAND Creations include *Best Friends* "O Joyful Night" nativity set, "First Friends Begin at Childhood," "Monthly Angels," "RiverSong," "Winter Wonderland," "Angel Wishes," "A Star is Born," "Noah's Ark" and the popular Angel Pin Cards.

He gathered the animals two by two... Artists Jeanette Richards and Sandra Penfield's "Noah's Ark" is surrounded by a joyful crew!

BAND Creations
28427 N. Ballard
Lake Forest, IL 60045
(800) 535-3242
Fax (708) 816-3695

BING & GRONDAHL

One Hundred Years of Beloved Artistry:
Bing & Grondahl, The Company That Pioneered Plate Collecting

The plate that started a tradition! "Behind the Frozen Window" is the first collector plate ever made, limited to 400! Today, F.A. Hallin's design is coveted by collectors and sells for up to $8,000 on the secondary market!

The year was 1895. Denmark prepared for a festive Yuletide season, readying presents to usher in the season of Jesus' birth. As was the custom, generous Danes prepared gifts of candy, cake and fruits to thank members of their household staff for their loyalty and hard work. Treats were elaborately presented on plates made of metal or wood. No one's quite sure when or how this delightful custom began, but it would be hard to say who enjoyed it more: the grateful giver or happy receiver!

As fate would have it, Harald Bing, one of the founders of Bing & Grondahl (producer of fine dinnerware and other renowned pottery) became intrigued by the presentation of holiday plates. He wondered if the custom could be expanded to all Danish society. Determined to test the idea during the 1895 Christmas season, Bing & Grondahl issued an elegant porcelain plate commissioned of artist F. A. Hallin. Called "Behind the Frozen Window," this hand-painted limited edition showcased the Copenhagen skyline as seen through a frosty window pane. Drenched in signature blue and white, the message "Jule Aften" (Christmas Eve) was gently scrolled around the bottom of the plate.

Bing's idea was embraced by the Danish public with enthusiasm and "Behind the Frozen Window" became a legendary work of art. Made in an edition size of just 400, all plates sold out in quick order, despite a 'hefty' price tag of 50¢ per plate! Today, these rare finds continue to be called the most valuable collector plates ever, commanding an average of $8,000.00 on today's secondary market!

A Company Dedicated to Preserving Memories

To appreciate Bing & Grondahl's pioneering collector plate, some background history is helpful. In 1853, 42 years before "Behind the Frozen Window" was made, artist Frederick Grondahl, with brothers Meyer and Jacob Bing, shared a vision: the continuation of an art style pioneered by the legendary Danish sculptor Thorvaldsen. Hoping Thorvaldsen's style would have country-wide appeal, the three men merged their resources, energy and ideas to open a factory dedicated to crafting replicas of the sculptor's work.

Initially, Bing & Grondahl manufactured and sold figurines, but the popularity of these sculptures was so significant, Danish consumers clamored for more variety. Elated, Bing & Grondahl produced elegant dinnerware and coffee services. This remarkable collection rapidly became a benchmark of tabletop fashion across Denmark.

By 1889, the company's distinguished evolution came into the spotlight at the Paris World's Fair. There, a dinner service called *Heron*, by Bing & Grondahl artistic director Pietro Krohn, was unveiled to an adoring public. Visitors from around the world admired *Heron's* bold design and the unique decorating technique used to finish each piece. That same look and finish was selected just six years later, when Harald Bing brought his idea for making a "holiday plate" in the now highly-recognized cobalt glazed finish, to the company. "Behind the Frozen Window" was the result...a history of plate art had begun.

The Idea of "Collecting" Cobalt Plates Spreads Like Wildfire!

Bing & Grondahl's idea for producing limited edition Christmas plates spread beyond the border of Denmark rapidly. Holiday plates fast became a continental passion. Despite unrest and political upheaval, plates continued to be made at Bing & Grondahl's factory through the first World War, the Depression and even during the Nazi occupation. Somehow, materials, desire and resolution kept the tradition alive.

With each Christmas season during these troubled times, a new artistic reflection of the year's events poured from the hands and hearts of the Bing & Grondahl artisans. Fishing boats, quaint homes, gentle animals, Danish landmark buildings, people of all ages and holy symbols graced plates fabricated during the first World War and Depression. Pastoral art featuring horses, churches, a farm and Danish landmarks soothed spirits during World War II, and ushered in the long-awaited peace. Reverently, Bing & Grondahl issued artist Margrethe Hyldal's "Commemoration Cross in Honor of Danish Sailors Who Lost Their Lives During World War II" as its 1946 plate.

It was inevitable that American servicemen, stationed in Europe, would notice and admire Bing & Grondahl's distinct plates. Soldiers and sailors purchased them to bring home to family and friends, and, of course, Americans with an eye for fine detail and old world charm fell in love! Before long, America joined the now-impressive list of over 70 countries awaiting annual Christmas editions as eagerly as the Danes each year.

How Bing & Grondahl Treasures Are Made

The process of creating a fine Bing & Grondahl collector plate has remained virtually unchanged for 100 years! First, years of drawing, planning and subject evaluation are undertaken by the staff to pick the ideal art. When everyone has agreed on the design, a master sculptor crafts a bas-relief model.

Painstakingly, a plaster of Paris copy is sculpted. This will determine the all-important master mold, so it must be perfection. Finally, a cast bronze image becomes central to the production process, acting as the permanent master. From it, plaster molds are recreated and only 20 plates are made from each before the plaster is destroyed. This is a demanding production method, but one that must be followed to meet stringent quality control standards.

Plates are now ready for firing and decorating in the world-famous "underglaze technique" that has made

Bringing to mind Bing & Grondahl's first Christmas plate, "The Towers of Copenhagen" visually escorts collectors through the famous gates of Tivoli Gardens, bordered by frozen swirls and a star of wonder.

Bing & Grondahl famous. Colors are applied carefully by artisans receiving special training. Because exact shades of blue don't emerge until the final firing has taken place, craftsmen must know how to adjust the intensity of their colors to attain a perfect finished product.

Before the final firing, the authentification process must be completed. The date and artist's initials are placed on the backstamp. Finally, the distinguished Bing & Grondahl logo is applied. Each plate is carefully dipped into glaze, then fired. In the kiln, kaolin, quartz and feldspar meld into a hard paste over a 48 hour period. The precise 2700 degree Fahrenheit temperature melts the glaze and creates an everlasting, glass-like surface of shimmering "Copenhagen Cobalt Blue."

If an issue is examined and found undesirable for a reason determined by the quality control team, the plate is destroyed. Since production of all Bing & Grondahl plates are strictly limited by year, this examination process is particularly critical. Of course, all molds are destroyed at the end of a year's production.

An Expanded Library and Distinguished Designers

The very first Christmas plate introduced by Harald Bing debuted just eight years after Orville and Wilber Wright invented the airplane. Since that time, Bing & Grondahl has offered collectors an ever-growing library of delights, such as Mother's Day plates, annual bells, thimbles, Christmas bells and a figurine of the year.

Bing & Grondahl works hard to expand its collection of offerings to include the perfect gifts for newlyweds, anniversary and birthday celebrants and just about every gift-giving occasion Americans can dream up. The idea of a dated collectible to celebrate a special occasion is becoming increasingly more popular. In fact, many collections begin with the birth of a child, marriage or to honor the year of a child's special event, such

Parent company Royal Copenhagen's 88th Christmas annual edition is the splendid "Christmas at the Manor House." Gift boxed, "Christmas at the Manor House" is also issued as an ornament, bell and collectible cup, saucer and 24K, gold-plated spoon!

as a first communion, graduation or confirmation.

Regardless of the event it commemorates, every stunning new issue created at the Bing & Grondahl design studios comes from the hands and hearts of a brilliant family of artists. Past masters include Friis, Larsen, Bonfils, Thelander, Hallin, Hyldahl and other greats. More recently, Jorgen Nielsen and Sven Vestergaard have shown their distinct creative spirits on Bing and Grondahl collectible art.

Each of these artists has contributed mightily to the Bing & Grondahl success story and will forever be an honored member of its artistic family. Today, over 350 figurines and hundreds of 'Blue and White' classics form the base of the Bing & Grondahl library. From this eclectic mix, colorful annual eggs, delicate porcelain spring flower plates, annual animal figurines, new Christmas plate series and fabulous ornaments are introduced each year to the delight of an adoring public.

The Celebration That's Lasted One Hundred Years

As a tribute to the tradition that started a century ago, Bing & Grondahl marks this centennial with several

Intertwined spruce twigs, pine cones and glowing candles graciously circle the first-ever Bing & Grondahl "Centennial Platter." Only 7,500 of these 13" masterpieces will be made and sold world-wide.

landmark issues. The first, a series of five limited editions, replicate the most popular motifs from that past 100 years. Each six-inch plate features a hand-applied, 24K gold rim. The first in this exquisite retro plate collection debuted in 1991. Called "Crows Enjoying Christmas," this recreated 1899 plate was snapped up by collectors. In 1995, the series culminated

with the re-issuing of a 24K gold-banded "Behind the Frozen Window."

Unveiled in 1995, the magnificent "Centennial Platter" bears the image of the 101st Christmas plate art. Amply sized at 13", collectors can recreate days of Christmas past in Denmark by serving sweets on this commemorative platter before putting it on display. The "Centennial Platter" features a unique, 2-1/2" border lavished with spruce twigs, pine cones and candles. Limited to just 7,500 pieces, this platter marks the only time a Christmas Jubilee Edition has been designed as anything other than a plate!

For Bing & Grondahl, a 100th anniversary celebration could literally be called "icing on the cake." Awards, recognition and spectacular attention has come to the company that pioneered collector plate art.

Before and since becoming part of the Royal Copenhagen group of companies, world-wide recognition has abounded. Royal courts in Denmark, Sweden and the United Kingdom have saluted Bing & Grondahl's considerable contribution to art collecting and major museums count outstanding examples of Bing & Grondahl art

among their collections.

But accepting laudits is only part of this legendary company's history. Bing & Grondahl has also presented commemorative gifts to other nations as tributes of friendship. A good example is the Bicentennial Eagle, limited to just 100 figures, crafted in honor of the 200th anniversary of the United States. "Eagle #1" was presented to the White House — the meaningful gift from one friend to another — in much the same way a neighbor might have given a plate of home-baked cookies to a good friend in Denmark one hundred years ago.

Become a part of history and start your own tradition today with a fine collectible treasure from Bing and Grondahl!

Royal Copenhagen/Bing & Grondahl
27 Holland Avenue
White Plains, NY 10603
(914) 428-8222
Fax (914) 428-8251

THE BOYDS COLLECTION, LTD.
Bears...Hares...Tabbies and a Zoo-Full of Offbeat Critters
Give Collectors New Reasons to Laugh Out Loud

Collectors with a taste for whimsy, an eye for quality, and a heart for nostalgia have made a great discovery called the Boyds Collection, Ltd. This zoo-full of plush and sculptured animals resides, in perfect harmony, somewhere between the heartstrings and funny bone.

The Boyds Collection isn't your average animal menagerie. It's the wackiest collection of party animals you've ever met! Hunting for their stomping grounds? Look about ten miles west of the hills and battlefields of Gettysburg in McSherrystown, Pennsylvania. Here, Gary Lowenthal and his wife Tina spend their days happily conversing with bears, cats, hares and moose — make that meese.

Given the "beastly nature" of the Lowenthal business, most folks wonder how it got so formal a name as The Boyds Collection, Ltd. Fact is, the Lowenthals ran a thriving antique business in Boyds, Maryland, for years. When they launched their collectibles business, it didn't seem right to tamper with success, so the name stayed.

The Boyds Collection began with a successful library of duck decoys. These jewels, sized from nine inches to three feet, kept Gary busy from dawn to dusk. He painted, antiqued, packaged, sold and shipped his decoy designs, while Tina handled business operations. It was inevitable that their home-based industry would grow "like wild."

By 1982, they moved from their 1880s home to a "newer" building (circa 1890). A thriving industry crafting precious replicas of whimsical, old-fashioned critters was, say the hares, off and running.

Old Fashioned Philosophy...New Fangled Success

When a collector acquires a huggable teddy, tabby, hare or other furry member of the Boyds menagerie, they get more than a plush animal. They also get a big slice of philosophy, detailed inside the hang-tag suspended from each Boyds original. It's "stamped" for authenticity by one of the official Boyds bears hired for the job (rumor has it he works for peanuts). Read the inside of the tag and discover a mix of fun, sincerity and facts about how, and why, each critter is made. Collectors learn the Boyds Collection has been around since 1979, that the cast resin *Bearstone Collection™* launched a popular second division, and that their formula for dreaming up new characters keeps things hopping creatively.

While there's no standard formula for coming up with new designs for plush animals, the process usually begins with Gary Lowenthal's sketches. A stickler for perfection, there are sometimes 20 or 30 refinements made to the original before it starts the production circuit. Depending upon complexity, seamstresses cut patterns by hand or machine, embroiderers make their magic and bears are hand-brushed and inspected three times. It's a long, exacting process, but well worth the wait!

In the case of cast resin collectibles, Gary's conceptual sketch is translated into clay, studied, revised and re-worked. When everyone agrees that the look is perfect, it's cast as "White Wear," then handed to a master painter to select a color pallet. Only then is the issue ready to be produced in accordance with the colors and detail of the original.

By-the-way, before a cast resin critter is "born," the official Boyds Pawprint is painted or embossed onto the new-

Some say Boyds Collection Bearware *Pins are "crittercal" fashion statements. Get ready to collect 'em all: "Bailey," "M. Harrison," Santa, some Incognito Cows, plus a single Moose looking for love. They're sensational on sweaters and shirts!*

comer. This Symbol of Authenticity promises perfection!

Meet A Few of the Boyds' Boyz (and the Ladies, too)

Describing Boyds Collection animals is like trying to describe your own kids. Each one is precious, unique, irresistible in his or her own way. There are currently more than 350 plush bears, hares, moose and assorted critters in Boyds' growing library of delights. They're showcased, to perfection, in a delightful collector catalog.

Open the cover and you'll first encounter 15 *Board of Directors™*, bean bag bears with funny names like "Binkie," "Dufus" and "Otis." Ten flop-eared hares and ten tabbies, all of plush, pose for the cameras on pages three and four. There's even a litter of five *Mitten Kittens™*, part of *The Archive Series™*, named for British poets "Browning," "Byron," "Tennyson," "Keats" and "Shelly," to be specific. *Mitten Kittens* are fully jointed and fashioned with over 30 separate pieces!

If domestic animals aren't your bag, the Boyds folks have something special for you: wild and woolly farm creatures and exotic animals you're more likely to see in a circus than in the wild. Collectors of the *Farmyard Series™* may choose from cows, pigs and ewes with funny names ranging in size from 7" to a grand 16". Lions, elephants and monkeys in the *Circus™* grouping are anything but ferocious-looking!

Boyds has experimented with various materials outside of plush and come up with some winning combinations. *Bean Curlies™*, unique bean bag bears and hares of soft sherpa fleece, and *The Chenille Group™*, "soft and squooshie" critters sewn from what might be the most comforting material on the planet, are particular favorites.

What collection would be complete without an adorable gathering of Christmas animals? As always, Boyds has the holiday covered. *T.J.'s Best Dressed™...Let it Snow™*, boasts Santa bears, moose and mice all dressed up in red robes with holiday trim. The Christmas party continues with *Northern Lights™*, whimsical, fully-jointed bears and moose featuring hand-embroidered detailing. To be sure

Bailey Bear helps Simone after a tumble on "Thin Ice." If you've ever had a good friend help you out (especially when they were right and you were wrong!), this collectible confection is the perfect "Thanks," "I'm glad we're friends" or "Bless you!" gift.

Talk about a harey twist on life! "Myrtle Believe" could be mistaken for a TV antennae since she's getting such great reception from collectors.

no Boyds collector's tree goes "undressed," there's even a gathering of small 4-1/2" to 7-1/2" animals, mini-dolls and angels.

There's more...but you'll want to get your paws on a catalog to see every adorable Boyds bean bag delight for yourself. If you can't locate a plush catalog at your local Boyds' dealer, please send $2.50 to the Boyds Collection Ltd., Somethin' Ta Say Dept. C.I.B., Gettysburg, PA 17325-4385.

Vintage and New Bears & Hares Are Today's Big Stars

The folks at Boyds are the proud parents of a collection of resin sculptures called *The Folkstone Collection™*. Part of the *Boyds Bears & Friends Collection™*, The Folkstones are one-of-a-kind original sculptures made of cast resin and designed to melt collector hearts.

Among the *Folkstone* family, collectors will meet up with an unlikely gathering of the "N.Q.G.A.'s" (That's "Not Quite Guardian Angels"), farmer cows, bunnies with ears reaching almost to the clouds and a group of the most outrageous snowmen you'll ever see. Add a moose with a fascination

for bells and a few versions of Santa guaranteed to tickle the funny bone, and you've got yourself a mighty popular collection of resin pencil figures.

Then there's the *The Bearstone Collection™*. Don't count on seeing only bears in this series. A select group of bunnies, moose and a cow snuck in and weren't discovered until after the *Bearstone* catalog had gone to press! One glimpse at the cast resin *Bearstone Collection* tends to start a chuckle. Discover sports heroes, holiday dudes (like angels and Santas), some dainty dressers and an entrepreneur or two. Retired members of *The Bearstone Collection* hold lofty positions and are now available only on the secondary market.

Folkstones and *Bearstones* reflect the true benchmarks of collectibility. Based on traditional folk art themes, they're hand-painted, individually numbered, gift boxed, and of course, each comes with a Certificate of Authenticity.

The Dreams and Dreamers Who "Make It All Happen"

Behind the curly chenille...behind the hand-stitched noses and precious poses...an army of creative spirits back the Lowenthal success story. Of particular note, licensed artists lend their names and talents to some of the most remarkable plush and resin personalities collectors have ever seen. To understand how everyone came together, you'll want to acquaint yourself with the leader of all this madness: Gary M. Lowenthal.

Lowenthal likes to refer to himself as the "Head Bean." You'll likely find the nom de plume dotting his publications, chatty newsletters and hang tags. Actually, wherever the spirit moves him, Gary's alter ego, "Head Bean," appears. A child of the raging 60's, Lowenthal survived a New York City upbringing with his offbeat humor intact. Thus, no one was surprised when he earned a masters degree in biology before heading to the Fiji Islands in the South Pacific, courtesy of the Peace Corps. This, quite naturally, led to a great longing for civilization

"Smith Witter II" is Boyds' ultimate yuppie bear. A 17", jointed beanbag bear made of ultra long, curly chenille, he sports paw pads and a bow of material Bearberry's of London would be proud to use.

and all of its hedonistic trappings. Deciding the most logical place to work out these rediscovered sentiments would be the wilds of Bloomingdale's, Gary set off on an exotic, new adventure in retailing.

Following seven years in purchasing, design and merchandising in the Big Apple, Lowenthal did what anyone with a zest for life would do: he bid adieu to Bloomingdale's and started the antique shop of his dreams, described at the beginning of this story. The rest, he might say, is harestory.

Understanding the mind set of shoppers from his rich (if not harey)

Bloomingdale's days, Gary Lowenthal recognized early-on that talent keeps a growing company at the forefront of innovation. He enthusiastically sought artisans who might not otherwise have an opportunity to break into the national giftware limelight. Talented Gae Sharp brought her bean bag creations to Boyds, and soon other designers were on board. This happy mix has resulted in new introductions that have made a lot of people (bears, hares and moose) happy.

Inevitably, all this talent and enthusiasm resulted in national recognition and awards for the Boyds Collection. This started Gary thinking about how to better reach his audience. Because Boyds does not sell directly to collectors, a two-faceted plan was devised to reach both shop keepers and collectors. Toward that end, colorful brochures, the enticing catalog mentioned, even a newspaper publication, full of fun reading, are being published. These days, merchants and collectors feel very connected to Boyds via such lively publications.

If you pick up a copy of the *Boyds Bear Retail Inquirer*, prepare for anything! There could be a biography of a new designer, the inside story on a new series of collectible flags, retirement bulletins, updates on Boyds limited editions nominated for awards — even a

classified section. Boyds fans from across the country looking for hard-to-find bears and hares hope to locate kindred souls willing to part with a special collectible; but something tells us this doesn't happen often.

In sum, it's a comfort to know that a company like The Boyds Collection exists in 1995. As today's world races quickly along, everyone has too much to do — and too little time to do it in! But at the center of the whirlwind, how delightful it is to know that somewhere, not far from Gettysburg, a family of folks dedicated to bringing a huge helping of yesterday into our world, exists.

They're the kind of people who take time to put a young artist's profile on the inside of their catalog...who make a point of calling their flags "big hummers" so no one mistakes their size...who quote Susan Powter's *Stop the Insanity* in their headlines...and who still believe a good bear is better than all the tranquilizers in the world.

The Boyds Collection Ltd.
Somethin' Ta Say Dept.
Gettysburg, PA 17325-4385

THE BRADFORD EXCHANGE
New Plate Artist Hall of Fame Marks
the 100th Anniversary of Plate Collecting

For more than 20 years, The Bradford Exchange has played a unique dual role in the limited edition plate market, serving collectors interested in acquiring both new releases and back-issue plates. Just as significant, the firm displays almost 800 historic issues spanning 100 years at the Bradford Museum of Collector's Plates. Now – in celebration of the centennial of plate collecting – the Exchange has unveiled a special exhibit to be permanently housed at the Museum: the Plate Artist Hall of Fame.

Since its founding in 1973, The Bradford Exchange has become one of the world's most successful marketers of new collector's plates. Over the years, it has introduced many innovative series, continually expanding the boundaries of plate collecting in the process.

The marketing of newly issued, or primary market plates, however, is only one aspect of the services provided by the Exchange. The company also operates an organized, orderly secondary market where collectors can buy and sell back-issue plates. To eliminate the risk of buying and selling plates long-distance, The Bradford Exchange guarantees both ends of the trades it brokers. Only Bradford-recommended plates are eligible for trading on the Exchange.

Celebrating a Century of Collector's Plates

The year 1995 marked the 100th anniversary of limited edition collector's plates: an event commemorated by the Exchange with the introduction of a special Bradford Museum exhibit, "Collector's Plates: The First 100 Years." Located at museum headquarters in Niles, Illinois, the centennial retrospective, which is the first of its kind anywhere in the world, includes "Behind the Frozen Window" – the premier

collector's plate issued in 1895 by the famed Danish porcelain house of Bing & Grøndahl.

On permanent exhibit at the Bradford Museum of Collector's Plates is the Plate Artist Hall of Fame, which debuted during the grand opening of the centennial exhibit in May 1995. In recognition of their outstanding contributions to the art of collector's plates, five individuals were named inaugural inductees. Honored artists Thomas Kinkade, Sandra Kuck and Lena Liu attended the grand opening along with Thomas Rockwell, representing his late father, Norman Rockwell. The fifth honoree was Charles Fracé.

Charles Fracé Wins Honors for Wildlife Art

Hall of Fame inductee Charles Fracé strives to find the soul in the animals he paints. "Each animal has an inner spiritual quality that makes it unique," Fracé says. "I try to portray that sense of personality, as well as the beauty of the animal."

Driven by reverence for the subjects he paints and enormous artistic talent, Fracé has attracted a large and devoted following among plate collectors since the 1990 release of his series for The Bradford Exchange entitled *Nature's Lovables.* Enthusiastic response to this and seven subsequent series – including *The World's Most Magnificent Cats, Soaring Majesty* and *Nature's Playmates* – has prompted his Hall of Fame selection.

What makes Fracé's work stand out from the rest? Says one admirer: "The fur is so lifelike you could fluff it." Says another, "When you look at a Fracé, it looks like the animal is going to walk right out of the print."

Since the earliest years of his wildlife art career, Fracé has been an active supporter of conservationist causes. In 1987, he established the Fracé Fund for

Master wildlife artist Charles Fracé is especially known for his portrayals of big cats, such as the jaguar in "Mystic Realm."

Wildlife Preservation, which annually awards major grants to conservation organizations large and small, including wildlife parks and zoos. It is Fracé's hope that his art might also serve to prolong the existence of endangered animals by bringing people closer to the awesome – but fragile – beauty of nature. As the artist says, "I think I just try to paint what I feel, and hope that people feel the same thing I do when they view my work."

The "Painter of Light" Earns His Place in the Hall of Fame

A unifying element infuses all of the art of Thomas Kinkade: the luminous glow of light. His mastery of painting light – whether recreated on collector's plates, canvas lithographs or limited edition prints on paper – has earned him the title of the "Painter of Light." A student of the 19th century school of painters known as "Luminists," Kinkade has developed his own variations – what he thinks of as "more of a Romantic Realism, using light."

Kinkade's first collector's plate, issued in 1991, was the award-winning "Chandler's Cottage," part of the

An oval shape and a delicate filigree border add to the charm of "Lamplight Brooke" by Thomas Kinkade.

"Moments of Caring" is a recent example of Sandra Kuck's talent for creating romantic portraits of children that recall Victorian times.

Lena Liu's delicate, pastel-hued paintings of flowers, birds and butterflies have been recreated on plates such as "Circle of Love."

Garden Cottages of England series. Since then, his artwork has been featured on ten more plate series for The Bradford Exchange — including *Home for the Holidays*, *Home Is Where the Heart Is*, and *Thomas Kinkade's Lamplight Village* — winning additional awards along the way.

Kinkade's work is so captivating that, in just four short years, his plates have become some of the most popular and sought-after on the market. In recognition of his achievements, he has been named as one of the first Hall of Fame artists.

Another Award for the Much-Honored Sandra Kuck

One of the most popular artists in the collectibles field, Sandra Kuck adds Plate Artist Hall of Fame honors to her countless awards for limited edition plates, prints and dolls. Kuck celebrates childhood, family and friends in her warmly nostalgic works — presenting dreamy, yet realistic depictions of women and children that summon tender memories of childhood.

"Me First," Kuck's first plate, was issued in 1979. But it wasn't until the 1983 release of "Sunday Best" that she began to attract a large and devoted following among plate collectors worldwide. Since then, she has produced a succession of widely acclaimed and sought-after plate series, including *Sugar and Spice*, *Precious Angels*, and *Moments at Home*.

"My fantasy is to have lived at the turn of the century, and that's what I paint," Sandra Kuck confides. By her own definition, she is "hard working, disciplined, and compassionate." As she explains, "I try to put a single positive thought into each work I do, a message that reaffirms our culture's shared love of beauty and family."

Nature Inspires the Gentle Art of "Hall of Famer" Lena Liu

Lena Liu's delicate, pastel-hued scenes of flowers, birds and butterflies have captivated plate collectors since the debut of her first series for The Bradford Exchange, *On Gossamer Wings*, in 1988. Her distinctive style is the result of her personal experience with both Eastern and Western cultures. An intriguing mix of romance and realism, it brought a new look to nature-themed collector's plates, combining highly detailed subjects with softly colored backgrounds.

Eight subsequent collections showcasing her work have been introduced in the past seven years, including *Floral Greetings from Lena Liu* and *Lena Liu's Hummingbird Treasury*. Along the way, she has earned legions of fans and numerous honors, including "Artist of the Year" in both the U.S. and Canada, and "Plate of the Year" in the U.S. These achievements gain full recognition through her induction into the Plate Artist Hall of Fame.

Raised in Taiwan, Liu was trained from a young age in traditional Oriental painting by Chinese masters. A United States resident since 1972, Liu found new inspiration for her work in the flora and fauna of North America. Even while painting Western subjects, however, she continues to employ many of the tools of conventional Chinese art — much to the delight of collectors.

America's Favorite Artist Is Inducted Posthumously

On the 100th anniversary of his birth in 1994, Norman Rockwell still reigned as both the best-known and best-liked American artist, according to a survey. If Rockwell were alive, according to his son, Thomas, the unassuming illustrator would have been surprised by his continued popularity. "My father certainly didn't realize that there would be this amount of interest in his work years after he had done it. He painted for an immediate use — magazine covers and illustrations — and nobody thought there would be all of these secondary uses."

But there have been scores of such uses in recent decades, with Rockwell's famous magazine covers, advertising art and calendar illustrations inspiring hundreds of collector's plates and other limited editions. Norman Rockwell loved people. He was inspired by them, and it showed. So it's no wonder that people in turn love

Norman Rockwell's lively sense of humor is obvious in "Triple Self-Portrait," part of a series issued to commemorate the centennial of the artist's birth.

Norman Rockwell, earning him the first posthumous induction into the Plate Artist Hall of Fame.

Bradford Museum Invites Collectors' Visits

Almost 800 plates spanning the 100-year history of collector's plates beckon visitors to the Bradford Museum of Collector's Plates in Niles, Illinois. Open from 9 a.m. to 5 p.m. Monday through Friday and 10 a.m. to 4 p.m. Saturday and Sunday, the museum is closed for major holidays. Admission charge is $2.00 for adults, $1.00 for senior citizens, and free for children under 12.

As museum visitors, collectors will have the opportunity to review the rich history of 100 years of plate collecting, and enjoy tributes to the wonderful painters whose creations have earned them a place in the Plate Artist Hall of Fame.

The Bradford Exchange
9333 Milwaukee Avenue
Niles, IL 60714
(800) 323-5577

COLLECTORS' MUSEUM

The Bradford Museum of Collector's Plates
9333 Milwaukee Avenue
Niles, IL 60714
(708) 966-2770

Hours: Monday through Friday, 9 a.m. - 5 p.m.;
Saturday and Sunday, 10 am. - 4 p.m.

Admission Fee: $2.00 for adults; $1.00 for Senior Citizens;
Free for Children under 12 Years of Age.

The Bradford Museum of Collector's Plates houses almost 800 plates, spanning the 100-year history of collector's plates.

BRANDYWINE WOODCRAFTS, INC.
Captures the Heart of America

Collectors of miniature buildings from Brandywine Woodcrafts Inc. can expect a few twists to inspire their imaginations, rekindle their memories...and capture their hearts.

For starters there will be additions to Brandywine's *Country Lane* collection, created in 1995. *Country Lane* combines flat, wooden, detailed print backgrounds with cast resin hand-painted accents on the foregrounds to achieve a three-dimensional effect. At approximately 6.5" x 6.5", *Country Lane* houses are slightly larger than those in other Brandywine collections. They're complemented by Brandywine's line of accessories.

The initial installment of *Country Lane* featured the "Dairy Farm" with barn doors, haystack and pitchfork; the "Farm House," a traditional southern home with shady porch and clothesline laden with quilts for sale; the "Country School," based on a rural Virginia elementary school including its own school bus; the "Berry Farm," with "berry special crafts;" and the "General Store," offering cider, jelly, flour and farm supplies.

Designs for new *Country Lane* houses are kept secret until release time, but collectors can expect them to retain the collection's focus on the nos-talgic sights and activities from the old-time farm communities that still dot the American landscape.

Another Brandywine focus is the company's personalization service, which allows collectors to add a unique touch to buildings that hold special meaning for them. Although Brandywine has been offering personalization for several years, some collectors aren't aware of how they can take advantage of it to build value and diversity for their own collections, or to add a special touch to gifts.

Any buildings from Brandywine's *Country Lane, Hometown* and *Downtown USA* collections can be personalized to reflect family names and interests, historic places and events, and even whimsy. For example, the *Country Lane* "General Store" might be personalized to recall the store down the road from Grandma's Farm. The *Hometown* "Antiques Shop" can be customized to carry the name of a collector's favorite shopping spot.

The "Hometown School" is one of more than 50 creations in Brandywine's Hometown *collection.*

And the *Downtown USA* "Train Station" might bear the name of a station remembered from a childhood hometown.

Personalization is done by hand with brush and acrylic paint. Many dealers personalize Brandywine products in their shops, while others prefer to have it accomplished at the company's manufacturing facility.

1996 promises to be the year that Brandywine collectors in the Midwest and West see the results of their requests for increased product availability, as the company continues to add shops to its roster of dealers. Additionally, the company is building a computerized database of collectors to help determine other means of serving its customers.

"We Can Make It Ourselves"

Marlene Dragar Whiting of York-town, Virginia, Brandywine's founder, continues to design and handpaint the

"Mercy Drive," from Brandywine's Downtown USA *collection, honors people in the medical professions.*

originals from which all Brandywine products are made. Hers is an eye for detail that's rarely matched in Americana.

"We can make it ourselves," was the motto in the Dragar household in Pittsburgh, Pennsylvania, when Marlene was growing up. Her mother Sophie taught her to sew, knit and crochet, and, assuming that anyone could accomplish intricate handwork, Marlene studied organic chemistry and English in college.

It was only after marrying Air Force pilot Truman C. Whiting Jr. and finding herself coping with frequent moves and separations that Marlene became hooked on tole painting. To afford classes, she designed appliqued infant quilts, seat covers, burp cloths and bibs in Phoenix, Arizona.

When Truman later served in Iran, quilt supplies weren't available in local bazaars, so Marlene designed gingerbread house kits and macramé items handcrafted with local supplies. The Shah was expelled in 1979, and with him the Whitings and their young son and daughter. It was back to Phoenix and a job teaching tole painting, and then to Yorktown, where the humid climate foiled an attempt at oil painting.

To solve this problem, Marlene invested $50.00 in acrylics and brushes and painted wooden cutouts of cows, ducks and hearts. Miniature buildings were soon to follow.

Brandywine's "Halloween House," from the Treasured Times collection, is one of several miniature houses that celebrates the occasions close to the heart.

"I've always been fascinated with the little shops, businesses and homes that small towns have in common," Marlene says. "From my childhood I remember how the shops were operated by friends and family. These memories stick with you forever, and they're the ones I incorporate into our buildings."

Handmade, from the Beginning

Brandywine began on a kitchen table. It was 1981 when Marlene took a basketfull of her homemade folk art to a gift shop in historic Hilton Village, Virginia. These were the wooden hearts and such that Truman had cut with a band saw and that she hand-painted.

The owner was busy, so Marlene left the basket on the floor while she browsed. Moments later, the owner ran up. Customers had seen the basket and wanted to buy everything in it.

Soon, Marlene was commissioned to make miniature buildings based on those in Hilton Village. Another order came from Colonial Williamsburg (today Brandywine is their official miniature house builder), and Brandywine Woodcrafts Inc. was off and running.

The company is still based in Yorktown, but it has outgrown the kitchen table – and the house, and the garage, and its first manufacturing facility. In 14 years, Brandywine has gone from two to 20 employees and from one to 22 home-based artisans. Sales have doubled every year since 1992, and in 1994 the company moved into a new 9,400 square foot facility.

Over the years, one thing hasn't changed: the company's family outlook. Truman was appointed president/CEO of Brandywine in 1994, after a 30-year aviation career.

Something for Every Collector

Brandywine Woodcrafts Inc. has two

The "Dairy Farm" and other three-dimensional miniature houses from Brandywine's new Country Lane collection are quickly becoming collector favorites.

divisions: Brandywine Collectibles and Brandywine Woodcrafts.

The Brandywine Collectibles Division produces cast resin hand-painted buildings and accessories. Marlene sculpts the original of every cast piece from clay. After the original has been baked, a mold is made from it and cast in virtually indestructible resin. Each is then sanded and painted completely by hand. No silk-screening is involved.

Brandywine Collectibles are historic, generic and whimsical in nature.

Historic collections include Williamsburg and Yorktown, Virginia; Old Salem, North Carolina; Seymour, Indiana; and Barnesville, Ohio, as well as Patriots and Custom renditions. On the back of these buildings, collectors find labels providing historic information.

Generic buildings are in two collections, Treasured Times and Hometown.

Treasured Times celebrates the happy moments with such buildings as the "Birthday Houses," "New Baby Houses," "Mother's Day Houses," "Happy Valentine's Day House" and the "Halloween House." Each is a collectible, as designs are limited to production of 750 pieces.

Hometown is perhaps the most popular of the cast resin lines. The Hometown series includes nostalgic representations of buildings from small towns across our country, from the "General Store" to the "Fire Company" to the "Dress Shop" to the "Brick Church" — more than 50 so far. Brandywine introduces a new *Hometown* series every six months to coincide with major gift show cycles, and retires each *Hometown* series after two years on the market.

In the way of whimsy, Brandywine offers the *North Pole* collection, replete with the "Claus Haus," "Candy Cane Factory," "Sugarplum Bakery," "Elf Club" and a dozen other visions from everyone's favorite northern locale.

Miniature buildings in the *Treasured Times* and *Hometown* collections are individually numbered in sequence and hand-signed by Marlene. All cast

Williamsburg and other picturesque locales are represented in Brandywine's various historic collections.

pieces are shipped in distinctive tote boxes and come with a postcard that collectors can send, in order to receive a free Certificate of Authenticity and register their purchase.

To accompany these buildings, Brandywine offers some 20 accessories, such as trees, carts, wagons and even a snowman.

Handpainted Look, Not Price

The Brandywine Woodcrafts Division produces wooden miniature buildings in a group called *Downtown USA. Downtown USA* pieces are flat, and each is made by affixing a highly-detailed print of Marlene's original painting to the wood. Before cutting and finishing, each print is covered with a clear "environmentally-friendly mystery substance," which protects it. The result is a hand-painted look without a hand-painted price.

Downtown USA includes more than 70 designs, available in individual pieces or linked together in 16 street scenes, each containing four buildings and a street sign on a single piece of wood. Brandywine will even build a unique street scene using a customer's favorite four buildings and street sign, personalized as requested.

Mercy Drive, one of the newest street scenes, honors

those in the medical professions, with the "Optical Shop," "Family Practice," "General Hospital" and "Dentistry." *Second Street*, another recent addition, features the "Police Station," "Car Care Garage" and "Diner."

Downtown USA pieces are rapidly becoming favorites for their attractive pricing, tremendous detail and personalized signs.

Custom Work Recreates History

Brandywine recently completed special designs of The Ryman Auditorium in Nashville, Tennessee; the famous Lynchburg, Tennessee, Hardware & General Store; the Abingdon, Virginia, Barter Theatre; and the Maryland Statehouse, among others. Collectors can call Brandywine to find out how to purchase those special pieces.

Brandywine Woodcrafts
104 Greene Drive
Yorktown, VA 23692-4800
(804) 898-5031
Fax (804) 898-6895

BYERS' CHOICE LTD.

Carolers Share the Christmas Spirit for All Seasons

Collectors are welcome to visit the Byers' Choice Christmas Gallery in Bucks County, Pennsylvania, where visitors can enjoy seeing the first figurines, production process and displays of more than 400 Carolers in beautiful winter settings. At the center's grand opening in 1994, it was a dream come true for (left to right) Jeff Byers, Bob Byers, Sr., Joyce Byers and Bob Byers, Jr.

In Bucks County, Pennsylvania, Joyce and Bob Byers celebrate Christmas all year round. There's lampposts flickering on cobblestone streets, shop windows brimming with toys, and musicians performing on one street corner and a Salvation Army band on the other. There's a postman delivering holiday cards, students walking to their school house, a children's Nativity pageant at a country church, skaters sliding across a frozen mill pond, and Santa's workshop filled ceiling high with toys.

From the beloved Charles Dickens' novel *A Christmas Carol*, there's the Cratchit family in their humble home, while Scrooge wanders throughout the village. Of course, Carolers are singing everywhere you look.

These winter wonderland scenes greet Joyce and Bob as they go to work every day at Byers' Choice Ltd., which they built on the spirit of Christmas. For nearly two decades, the Byers have been creating a joyous choir of limited edition Caroler figurines that rekindle days gone by and the gentle beauty of the holiday season. From a Victorian Mrs. Claus to a man roasting chestnuts, each has its own personality and story to share.

Located in the company's Chalfont, Pennsylvania, production facility is the Byers' Choice Christmas Gallery, which opened in 1994 to display more than 400 figurines in various winter vignettes. Collectors are invited to stop by the gallery, where they learn the history of the Carolers and see firsthand the reason why these singing characters have found a special place in the hearts of collectors around the world.

Charles Dickens and Christmas Inspire First Caroler Figurines

During a trip to London in the 1960s, Joyce and Bob were browsing in an antique shop when they spotted a unique series of porcelain figures that appeared to step right from the pages of a Charles Dickens' tale. The timeless pieces captured the warm, traditional flavor of 19th century England.

When she returned home, Joyce came across a set of papier-maché choir figures that reminded her of the spirit of Christmas. While debating whether or not to purchase these as gifts, she was suddenly struck by a clever idea. She could create caroling figures that combine the feeling of 19th century England and Christmas.

An amateur artist with a degree in fashion design, Joyce began working on the project using materials she had at home: plaster, papier-maché, wire, paint and stacks of assorted fabrics. She was already adept at making crafts, which she enjoyed seeing come to life right before her eyes. Dressed in wintertime attire, each figurine opened its rounded mouth to sing favorite Christmas songs — just like carolers who go door to door during the holiday season. Joyce's first figurines reminded her of the classic characters from *A Christmas Carol*, so she simply called them The Carolers.

Byers' Choice Reaches New Markets

Family members adored The Carolers. Christmas shopping for Joyce soon became much easier, as many of the Byers' friends and relatives began asking for the figurines as gifts. A neighbor suggested taking the figurines to craft and antique shows, where they sold out quickly and word spread about Joyce's delightful creations. At one show, a New York display

This traditional grouping of Carolers shows the Victorian beauty and harmony of the Byers' Choice Ltd. line. Led by a matronly conductor, each child and adult figurine looks upward and sings out with joy.

All bundled up for a wintry day, this caroling couple happily sings from their wooden sleigh. They're ready to deliver the holiday spirit and a basket of gifts.

company official told Bob that his firm would be interested in buying figurines if they could be enlarged and altered according to the needs of its customers. Joyce rose to the challenge, thus sealing the fate of Byers' Choice Ltd.

Over the next years, Joyce, Bob and their two sons spent much of each autumn making figurines for friends, craft fairs, a few stores and the display company. As the demand grew, the family became busier in other seasons. After The Carolers began overtaking the Byers' dining room, they converted their garage to a workshop. In 1981, with the addition of full-time helpers, the family hobby was incorporated with Bob and Joyce officially casting their lot with the Carolers.

A Collectible Business That's All in the Family

Today, Byers' Choice Ltd. is still a family business that hires skilled hand-crafters and professionally trained artists. In order to keep up with all the orders, the Byers had to make some changes in both the manufacturing process and, to a limited extent, the appearance of the figurines. While today's Carolers are very different from those produced in the early years, almost everyone agrees that the current look captures the Dickensian Christmas spirit even better.

Joyce still sculpts all of the faces and designs most of the clothing for each Caroler. Meanwhile, Bob tends to the financial and administrative side of the business. He also directs the company's extensive charitable giving to a host of local, national and international concerns. In 1987, son Robert took on the job of overseeing the figurine production process. Son Jeffrey joined the family business in 1990 as marketing manager. The company and its 150 employees moved into a larger facility in 1994. With a lot of hard work and imagination, Bob and Joyce have watched their hobby grow into a successful family business dedicated to serving the customer and, through their philanthropy, the community.

A Family Album of Carolers

The family of Caroler figurines gets better each year and many of the older ones have become valuable collectors' items. Within the collection, there are various series and styles for everyone to enjoy. The *Traditional Carolers* portray men and women, boys and girls, and grandmothers and grandfathers dressed in wools, felts and plaids. They hold everything from scrolls and wreaths to muffs and snowballs. Each of the figurines is designed with a matching partner and is produced in an edition of 100 pieces.

The *Victorian Carolers* wear elegant satins, velvets, lace and furs. These are also produced in pairs limited to 100 of each design. *Victorian Mothers* pushing prams or helping their toddlers learn to walk have also been created.

In 1992, Joyce created the first *Salvation Army* figurine to celebrate the season of giving. A new piece is introduced annually with a portion of the proceeds benefiting the work of the agency.

In 1983, Joyce began working on a series of Caroler figurines based on *A Christmas Carol.* "Scrooge" in his nightgown was the first piece and one or two figures were added each year for the next decade. First and second editions were produced. Now the cast of characters — from the "Fezziwigs" to "Marley's Ghost" — is complete. All but a few second edition pieces have been retired. With the close of the *Christmas Carol,* Joyce then began work on *The Nutcracker Suite* series in 1993. The figurines, which began with "Marie," are based on the German tale written by E.T.A. Hoffman that inspired Tchaikovsky to write his magical Christmas ballet.

The *Cries of London* series recreates the 19th century street vendors who often chanted catchy songs to get their customers' attention. Each year, Joyce designs a new figurine in the series, and the previous year's piece is retired.

In addition to a variety of Santas from around the world, Mrs. Claus and other holiday characters, Byers' Choice also offers specialty figurines, including choir directors, postmen, parsons and school children.

These two Carolers celebrate the season of sharing and caring as well as the dedicated work of the Salvation Army and its volunteers. Since 1992, Byers' Choice has introduced an annual Salvation Army *figurine with part of the proceeds benefitting the agency.*

Sitting down at a piano, "Louise" leads children in a chorus of Christmas songs. "Marie," the first in The Nutcracker Suite *series, holds a wooden nutcracker while "Fritz" rides a stick horse. The figurines are inspired by the magical Christmas ballet based on E.T.A. Hoffman's book.*

A rotating selection of 200 Carolers, as well as other Christmas-related gifts, are sold at the Emporium. As one Caroler fan said: "It is indeed Christmas 365 days a year at Byers' Choice." The gallery is open to the public Monday through Saturday from 10 a.m. to 4 p.m. It is closed holidays and for the month of January. For information and directions, call (215) 822-0150.

"Caroler Chronicle" Keeps Collectors Up To Date

From the beginning, Byers' Choice has received wonderful letters from fans telling how much the Caroler figurines mean to them. An overwhelming number of questions prompted the company to publish the "Caroler Chronicle," a color newsletter published three times a year. The "Caroler Chronicle" highlights stories behind various figurines, upcoming special events or introductions, and a chronological index of characters and the years of production.

Byers' Choice Ltd.
P.O. Box 158
Chalfont, PA 18914
(215) 822-6700
Fax (215) 822-3847

Gallery Welcomes Collectors to Christmas at Byers' Choice

The Byers' Choice Christmas Gallery displays many Carolers from the past and present. Joyce and Bob always received many requests from collectors to tour the place where The Carolers are made, but the old facility wasn't set up to handle this activity. When the blueprints were drawn for the new Byers' Choice building, a special wing was conceived and dedicated to collectors. This visitors' center features scenes where collectors and Christmas aficionados can view The Carolers strolling among the streets of a London-like city, acting out roles in *A Christmas Carol* and much more.

Visitors can also see Joyce's very first Carolers, retired pieces, a video of the company's history, and an observation deck overlooking the production floor.

COLLECTORS' MUSEUM

Byers' Choice Christmas Gallery & Emporium
4355 County Line Rd.
Chalfont, PA 18914
(215) 822-0150

Hours: Monday through Saturday, 10 a.m.-4 p.m. Closed Sundays, Holidays and in January.

Admission Fee: None

Visitors to the Byers' Choice Christmas Gallery enjoy a self-guided tour through the museum which displays old and new Caroler® figurines. They can also see a video of the company's history and view the production floor from an observation deck. Selected gifts and caroling figures are sold at the Emporium.

CALABAR CREATIONS
Limited Edition Collectibles Celebrate a Colorful World Between Dreams and Reality

Tony Van and his company Character Collectibles were already well-established in the giftware industry when he met artist Pete Apsit. But it was a meeting that would put a new face — and eventually a new name — on Van's company.

The pair teamed up to introduce Pete's "critters" made out of a material known as hydrostone, which gave the animals a warm, country charm. Three years later, Character Collectibles had tripled the number of items in its line that quickly extended far beyond the company's original country themes. The designs, which ranged from humorous pigs to whimsical cows, established a different direction for Character Collectibles, signaling the time to branch out and expand its

horizons. Calabar Creations was born. As its motto says: In the Land of Calabar Colorful Art Life And Beauty Are Raised.

Creations from the Heart and Hands of Pete Apsit

With a collectibles career spanning 25 years and a host of admiring collectors, Pete Apsit is one of today's most renowned sculptors. His new era of figurines for Calabar Creations dawns with what he and Tony Van call "a tribute to all American children." Each figurine recognizes the fact that children and animals hold a special place in everyone's heart.

Apsit's creations reflect his California attitude — the belief that life is a gift to be enjoyed. Apsit believes that through the eyes of children he can bring home a message that little ones allow us to see life unblemished by stress and complications.

Apsit's children are not "sweet little sophisticated darlings" impeccably dressed and well-mannered. Instead, they belong to a fresh, free "kid society" where innocence prevails, but misbehavior inevitably occurs. It's a place where old clothes sure feel better than Sunday best and where friends, including animals, are the most precious gifts on earth. Apsit's children are unencumbered by class barriers, racial prejudice and adult inhibitions. With Apsit's careful workmanship, the expressions on each figurine tell a story without saying a word. "If it's a cute type of thing with expression in its face and it's telling a story, people will collect it," says Apsit, who finds inspiration from his children and grandchildren. "When children do something really well, they get such a proud look on their faces. That's why expression is the most important part

All aboard the "Pigmobile" for a trip filled with fun and adventure. From the Pig Hollow™ *series created by artist Pete Apsit, this 3" figurine takes the whimsical pigs off the farm and into town.*

of a piece. If it doesn't have expression, you've missed it."

Working in a studio near his home in Bakersfield, California, Apsit sculpts next to a big window listening to talk radio or classical music. "I work quite fast. I sit down, and within five minutes I have an idea," he says. "I don't know what a piece will look like until I'm done."

New Series Welcome Children and Animals

Apsit's *Little Farmers*, which shows the joy of rural life on a farm, was the first series that established Calabar Creations in the limited edition market. Today, Apsit is constantly designing new series, each with its own fine details, meaning, innocence, humor or memories.

Angelic Pigasus™ features golden winged pigs limited in time not quantity. The first retirement was "Anna" in June 1995. Every six months thereafter, one more cold-cast porcelain pig will be retired to make room in the line for more introductions.

From childhood photographs snapped by the father of Art Director Danielle Aphessetche, the Daddy's Girl™ *series captures an innocent picture of youth. "Spring Harvest" features Danielle proudly holding a freshly cut bouquet of flowers.*

The *Little Professionals™* series shows children trying different occupations on for size. There's "Little Red" struggling with a firehose, "Little Florence" wrapping bandages around her friend, "Little Miss Market" selling lemonade and "Little Angelo" painting with her palette and brush.

Junior Murphy's Law™ is a comical look into the tried-and-true philosophy of, "If something can go wrong, it will." The figurines, which are limited to 5,000 pieces, portray hard-luck kids doing everything from tossing pizza dough on their heads to watching a puppy steal hot dog links.

Days of Innocence™ launched with three figurines that portray the tender moments of childhood. "To Grandma's," "A Letter From Grandma" and "Dear God" are each limited in edition to 5,000. *Kiti Kondo™* is a special home for kittens who happily sit for an afternoon tea.

Introductions Added to Favorite Series

Known as the landmark collection of

It's off to grandmother's house for this little girl, who has her overstuffed suitcase, teddy bear and a special gift ready for the trip. "To Grandma's" is a heartwarming introduction to the Days of Innocence™ series that shows the softer side of childhood.

Calabar Creations, the *Yesterday's Friends™* series continues adding to its wonderful troupe of happy youngsters. In 1995, an all-star team of three boys joined the collection in the figurines titled "Fly High," "Pop Up!" and "Out!" The boys enjoy America's favorite pastime – caring more about having fun than winning or losing the game. The line also includes the friends reading books, playing basketball, dressing up like an Indian chief, washing a pig and gliding along on a soap box scooter.

The ever popular *Angelic Pigasus* series welcomes two new additions, a charming signature piece and "Allegria," with arms spread wide and a heavenly glance. This figurine would make believers of anyone that pigs can fly!

Listen closely and imagine soulful, spirited music melting through the air. The *Jazzy Kids* have arrived to join the *Little Professionals* series. Coaxed from clay by the skilled hands of Pete Apsit, this joyful Dixieland quintet exists to serenade you with all their heart and soul. "Little Count" sets melody, "Little Gypsy" keeps time on the tambourine, "Little Desi" beats the bongos, "Little Ringo" plays his drum, and "Little Louis" blares away on trumpet.

Calabar's newest series is the *Grandpions™*, the grand champions of "have beens" and "wannabes." This humorous collection of dwarfed professionals, sportsmen and hobbyists are sure to unwrinkle many grumpy faces. From the faithful fireman "Old Red" to the doughnut-eating police officer "The Finest," everyone knows someone who looks and acts like a *Grandpion!*

Apsit also created *Daddy's Girl*, which is inspired by old photographs found in the family albums of Calabar Creations Art Director Danielle Aphessetche. As an avid photographer, Danielle's father used his hobby to capture the precious moments of his daughter's childhood. Now Apsit has turned these photographic memories into three-dimensional figurines for all to recall special days gone by. Recent

Listen closely and imagine soulful, spirited music melting through the air ... the Jazzy Kids have arrived! Coaxed from clay by the skilled hands of Pete Apsit, this joyful Dixieland quintet exists to serenade you with all their heart and soul.

introductions include "Spring Harvest" with Danielle holding a bunch of colorful flowers and "Summer" finding Danielle sitting on a fence post. In "Peek-a-Boo," the little girl looks at the world from upside down.

In keeping with his fascination for swines, Apsit has added more to the fun-loving family of *Pig Hollow*. The pigs are now off the farm and heading on a camping trip in their "Pigmobile." "Pendelton" is pitching the tent, "Pot Belly" is cooking dinner over the fire, "Pepin" is eating watermelon and "Pilar" is scrubbing the clothes on a washboard. The pigs also found a new home in a beautiful castle, which is bustling with activity. "Prude" watches television in the living room, "Pristine Pig" makes sure everything is spotless in the bathroom, "Prof" reads a book to "Plopsy," and "Pig Kahuna" lounges on the sofa.

Classic Series Still Charm Collectors

Although some lines don't have any new introductions, they are still available for collectors to enjoy and complete their collections. Undoubtedly inspired by Apsit's first bad encounter with the serious game of golf, *Tee Club™* hits the course with a group of grouchy old men showing those true-to-life expressions on the

From the Angelic Pigasus *series created by sculptor Pete Apsit, "Allegria" with arms spread wide and a heavenly glance would make believers of anyone that pigs can fly!*

green. There's golfers like "TEEd-off" who broke his club and "Prac-TEEs" with a pail of golf balls.

As a seasonal greeting, Apsit created *Santa Venture™*, which shows another side of St. Nick. Santa personally tests the toys, makes sure even the smallest animals receive a Christmas gift, takes a rest along his delivery route and hitches up a donkey when his reindeer go on strike. These moments and others open everyone's eyes to Santa's colorful personality and adventures.

Red Moon Children™, created by western artist Richard Myer, centers on memories of when the West was still open, and young Americans of the frontier were blessed with an unclouded view of the world. Each limited edition figurine, which comes with a miniature book, reflects an

atmosphere of peace, calm and simplicity.

Personal Attention to Detail

Each Calabar Creations work begins as a clay original designed by the artist. The company's art department then uses this piece as a master for producing a mold. The master is poured from a hard-cast material able to withstand the rigors of many mold formings. Several masters are created because a production mold rapidly loses its ability to reproduce intricate details and variety in texture — both of which are Calabar Creation trademarks.

At this stage, unpainted samples called "whites" are sent to Danielle Aphessetche, the company's art director and colorist. She chooses the colors for the piece and paints the "white" prototype. The artisans in the factory pour and cure the figurines, which are then meticulously cleaned and polished. The painter duplicates the original color scheme. After inspection, each piece receives its brass registration plaque. Finally, the figurine is ready to be gift boxed and shipped to stores for collectors.

A Commitment to Excellence and Beauty

The commitment of Calabar Creations is to offer figurines that will give pleasure both to the eyes and the soul; works of art that will touch a child's curiosity and awaken the sleeping child in all adults. Calabar Creations strives to portray a world between

Meet "Old Red" from The Grandpions, *a new collection by Calabar Creations. This faithful fighter of fires is just one of 20 in the lovable collection sculpted by Pete Apsit. This humorous collection of dwarfed professionals, sportsmen and hobbyists are sure to unwrinkle many grumpy faces.*

dreamland and reality...a land where children are wise and adults are allowed to dream...a special corner of the world filled with laughter and rainbows. After all, in the land of CALABAR: Colorful Art Life And Beauty Are Raised.

Calabar Creations
1941 S. Vineyard
Ontario, CA 91761
(909) 930-9978
Fax (909) 930-9928

CARDEW DESIGN
Collectible Teapots Brim with Tradition and Creativity

When Paul Cardew arrives at work each morning, he performs the most important job of the day: putting the kettle on the stove for the first cup of tea. After taking a sip, everything else seems to fall perfectly into place.

"This ritual is essential for getting the inner man going but also gives me time to allow the day-to-come a considered moment of reflection, putting my thoughts and priorities in order before the rush starts," Cardew says.

The rush these days is designing and creating teapots that have found a warm reception from collectors all over the world. Since 1991, Cardew Design has been bringing back the fine art of teapots and adding its own sense of whimsy and style to brew one of the hottest collectibles on today's market. From the company's two British pottery factories, teapots in all shapes and sizes delight collectors with their creativity. Everyday objects such as stoves, desks, toy boxes and sewing machines are transformed into teapots and embellished with miniature treasures that make each piece a fascinating vignette.

The Beginnings of a Successful Business

Paul Cardew always intended to be an architect, but the courses didn't live up to his expectations. So with his grandmother's prodding, he entered Plymouth College for Art and Design in England. He took a ceramics class and within 10 minutes was in love. "I think it's the fact that you're working in 3-D just like architecture, only all the control and decision making is right there in your own hands," Cardew says. "This was the medium for me!"

To hone his skills, he then attended Loughborough University, where he met his wife, Karen, also a ceramics designer. She decided to try her hand at making brooches and earrings for a local college craft fair. For no particular reason, she made some of the jewelry in the shape of miniature teapots. They sold out, and she soon got an order for 5,000 more brooches. After a year, their newly formed company, Sunshine Ceramics, grew from two to 12 staff members. More orders kept flooding in, including one from the British Tea Council.

Overwhelmed with their success, they decided to focus more and more on teapots. During this time, Peter Kirvan, a close friend of Cardew, had been running his own London advertising agency but was looking for a new challenge. With Kirvan's experience in managing the creative process and Cardew's design talents, they joined forces in 1991 to form Cardew Design.

Together, they studied the fine tradition of teapots and tea drinking, which began in China more than 4,000 years ago. Tea came to Europe in the early 1600s. And, of course, with tea came teapots. Thanks to new technologies, mediums and ideas, master potters and craftsmen shared endless opportunities for teapot designs. Today, Cardew Design takes advantage of this same concept. "As a three-dimensional item, the teapot's potential for great design, and a lot of fun, is almost limitless," Cardew says.

The Making of a Cardew Teapot

Tea for two may be an afternoon pastime, but creating a Cardew teapot is an around-the-clock process. The seven-member design team, including

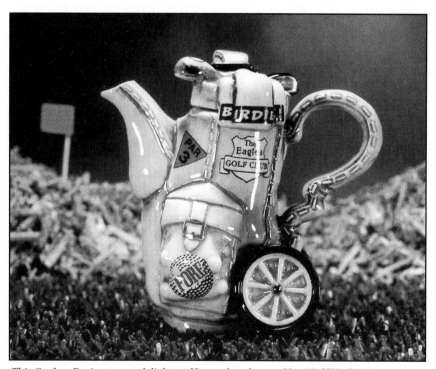

This Cardew Design teapot delights golfers and tea lovers alike. "Golf Trolley," a one-cup teapot, features decals that say "Fore," "Birdie," and other terms recognized by golfers everywhere.

111

Cardew, comes up with all the new teapot concepts, handcrafts all the prototypes, creates master molds, determines production schedules and ensures the highest quality.

Each day, the designers gather around a table to brainstorm different ideas and write down suggestions. "Then, one by one, we challenge them to see if the idea really has what it takes to make an outstanding teapot," Cardew says. "There has to be a little piece of magic that sets the imagination racing and makes the whole idea work. The secret ingredient that you as a collector look at afterwards and say to yourself: `Yes, that's Cardew all right; trust them to think of that!'"

In deciding what ideas should be turned into three-dimensional teapots, the designers go through a standard checklist: Does the idea have magic factor X?; Can it actually function as a teapot?; Will the teapot be able to be produced with quality and at an affordable price?; and Is it something collectors will really enjoy?

From sketches and ideas in their mind, the sculptors work with clay to bring the teapots to life. A master mold is created from plaster of paris. All the pots are then fired in electric kilns to carefully regulate the temperature for the best results. All Cardew teapots receive three separate firings at different temperatures. The first at 1010 degrees Centigrade turns the clay into porous biscuit. The second is hotter to turn the glazed biscuit into a glazed pot. A final gentler firing fuses onto the pot surface the decorations, such as precious metal lustres and picture transfers. Final delicate miniatures, which have been separately cast and decorated, are then bonded directly to the pot surface. As the last step before shipping, each teapot is thoroughly inspected, even though every craftsperson had already checked his or her own work at every stage. "Like many an enterprise, we would be nothing without the skilled, hardworking and dedicated team that's come together now," Cardew says.

The main design studio sits on about nine acres on Woodmanton Farm, located in Devon County with its rolling green hills and meadows. The farmhouse and out-buildings have been trans-formed into a pottery factory. Cardew works from the old farmhouse kitchen. The second pot-tery at Bovey Tracey lies near Dartmoor. Bovey, unlike Woodmanton, has the space to offer factory tours. During normal busi-ness hours in the week, Cardew Design invites all visitors for a free tour to see the world's most collectible teapots being made.

Cardew Offers Four Different Teapot Sizes

Cardew Design started by making larger teapots that could hold six to eight cups. The Cardew full-size pots are all designed according to the rules of functional teapots, so that handles and spouts are in the right places and the position of the main body encloses an appropriate volume for brewing tea. News from retailers indicates that pots on the secondary market, such as the "Liquorice Allsort" and "Cactus," are trading well over their original price. To further enhance the value, these designs, beginning in 1996, are only being produced as a limited edition. Each piece is clearly marked in the tradition of English fine art with its own unique identity number within the run. Once the 5,000 edition limit has been reached, the designs will come out of the catalog and the production molds destroyed.

Cardew also offers high-quality designs in three other sizes to satisfy a collector's price range and space limitations. The company began pro-ducing "One-Cup" teapots in 1994 and "Tiny" teapots last year. "These not only allow a sizable collection to be gathered without moving house and home, but also follow an old pottery

A curious cat quietly watches a mouse on the face of "Grandfather Clock," a one-cup teapot design. Practical and collectible, the teapot features the intricate detail found in all Cardew creations.

tradition in that every major pottery used to produce miniature replicas of their ranges," Cardew says.

In 1995, Cardew also developed a teapot that was practical to use for an everyday cup of tea but also collectible and fun. The result was the "Brown Betty" line of full-size teapots, which are dishwasher safe. The classic round teapot is fired in brownware but a little more detailed than the traditional original. In fact, the colors of the teapot base range from dark green to bright yellow to complement the highly decorated lid, which is the only area that can carry miniature ceramic designs and decorations. In 1996, Cardew added more than 50 new teapot designs to his line. Cardew teapots are exclusively distributed in the United States by the S.P. Skinner Co., Inc.

Cardew Adds Special Touch to Teapots

Some collectors have discovered the lighter side and humor of Cardew's

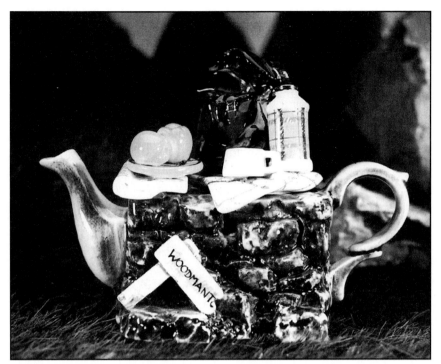

"Hiker's Rest" invites collectors to relax at a cobblestone wall, where a backpack is emptied of its apples, thermos and, of course, a teacup! Collectors will also notice a broken sign that says "Woodmanton," the name of Cardew Design's farm and pottery factory.

pots in the *Market Stall* series contain the company's postcode in the decorations as well as reproductions of authentic shoe company posters. A signed photograph of Marilyn Monroe on "Crime-writer's Desk" is addressed to Paul. The scrunched up newspapers in the "Moving Day" special edition features tiny reproductions of articles written about Cardew Design. Look closely and you'll also see a reproduction of Cardew's wedding portrait. This combination of ceramic art and entertaining designs has become Cardew's trademark. The designers have just as much fun creating the riddles as collectors do finding them. For several years, collectors had been asking Cardew about the possibility of launching a club just for lovers of the teapots. At the end of 1995, the Cardew Collectors' Club was formed to satisfy this request and the curiosity of others who fell in love with the teapots. Members receive the latest news on the collection, as well as an exclusive collectors' club teapot.

designs. Many of the teapots tuck away whimsical and personal touches. On the "Fridge" one-cup, for example, sits kitchen clutter, including a carton of cornflakes. It's not just any old box of cornflakes; these are Kirvan's, referring to Cardew's partner. The box

informs careful readers that "people who know him say he's a bit flaky." The slightly-opened refrigerator door also reveals Cardew's phone number and the offer of a free teapot to the first person to call. (This didn't take long for a collector to win.) Some of the

Cardew Design
c/o S.P. Skinner Co., Inc.
91 Great Hill Rd.
Naugatuck, CT 06770
(203) 723-1471
Fax (203) 723-5867

COLLECTORS' CLUB/TOUR

The Cardew Collectors' Club	**Annual Dues:** $30.00
Cardew Design	**Club Year:** Anniversary of Sign-Up Date
Woodmanton Farm	**Benefits:**
Woodbury NR. Exeter	• Tiny Teapot Membership Gift
Devon EX5 1HQ England	• Opportunity to Purchase Members-Only Teapot
01144 1395 233633	• Quarterly Newsletter, "Teapot Times"
Fax: 01144 1395 233470	• Membership Card
	• The Cardew Teapot Collection Catalog

The Cardew Teapot Pottery Tour	**Hours:** Tours Monday through Friday, 9:30 a.m. - 5:30 p.m.
Cardew Design	Tea Shop and Gift Shop open 7 days a week, 9:30 a.m. - 5:30 p.m.,
Bovey Tracey Pottery	excluding Bank Holidays.
Newton Road	**Admission Fee:** None
Bovey Tracey TQ13 9DX England	Visit the Cardew Teapot Pottery and see the world's most collectible
01144 1626 834441	teapots actually being made.

CARLTON CARDS

Heirloom Collection™ Ornaments
Become Collector Favorites For All Seasons

The second issue in a series, "Elvis" sings the Christmas classic "Santa Bring My Baby Back (To Me)" when you press a button on this dated 1996 ornament. It will have everyone rockin' around the Christmas tree.
©*1996 Elvis Presley Enterprises, Inc.*

It's a holiday tradition that captures the spirit of the season with nostalgia and beauty, warmth and whimsy. The *Heirloom Collection* ornaments from Carlton Cards are collectibles that have become a favorite part of the holidays that can be enjoyed throughout the year.

Since its debut in 1988, the *Heirloom Collection* has grown with hundreds of ornaments for everyone and every occasion. They celebrate firsts: Baby's first Christmas, a first Christmas together, a first home. They recognize special people and professions: Mom, Dad, godmothers, grandparents, brothers, sisters, teachers and nurses. They cheer for your favorite pastimes: bowling, bicycling, golfing, sewing, dancing, football. They commemorate the true meaning of Christmas, delight the imagination and capture familiar characters. The *Heirloom Collection* starts new

traditions, and the *Collector's Series* encourages new collectors. It just doesn't seem like the holidays without them.

The Beginnings of the *Heirloom Collection*

The *Heirloom Collection* traces its history to 1988 when the Summit Corporation, an American Greetings subsidiary, introduced 41 ornaments. The ornaments were sold under the Summit logo in various stores throughout the United States and Canada. One of the most popular ornaments in the first *Heirloom Collection* was the dated "Mouse on an Ice Cube," which remains popular on the secondary market.

In 1989, Summit expanded its line to 44 ornaments. Carlton Cards, an American Greetings division, made its grand entrance into the ornament industry by offering 40 Summit-designed ornaments under the Carlton logo. "From the beginning, we knew that we had a talented group of artists and the know-how and desire to create three-dimensional products," says Suzi Cipra, senior product developer/ creative planner for American Greetings, who has been working with the collection since 1989. "We were just getting our feet wet."

In 1990, Summit again expanded with 72 more ornaments, while Carlton offered 50 of the designs. It also marked the beginning of the popular *Collector's Series* ornaments with "Santa's Roommate," "Christmas Hello," "A Little Bit of Christmas," "Christmas Go-Round" and "Christmas Express."

Summit and Carlton ornaments were exclusively offered under the Carlton logo in 1991. The assortment included 72 ornaments and the continuation of the *Collector's Series*. For 1992, Carlton expanded to 90 ornament designs in the *Heirloom Collection*. In 1993, 135 designs were

introduced, along with two new series: *Book of Carols* and *Tiny Toymaker*.

Three new ornament series started in 1994: *Big Fun, Snug In Their Beds* and *Santa's Toy Shop*.

In 1995, the *Heirloom Collection*, which is available exclusively at Carlton retailers, debuted 135 designs, with "Elvis" ranking among collectors' favorites.

Innovation Becomes an *Heirloom Collection* Tradition

For 1996, the *Heirloom Collection* focused on traditional themes but also used the latest technology to delight collectors with lights, motion and music. "We feel that innovations like moving parts add magic to the ornament," Cipra says. "My idea of a successful ornament is when you look at it, you can't help but say 'ahhh.' It grabs you as if you walked into a

"Marilyn" makes her star-studded debut with the Heirloom Collection *in this stunning ornament. The exclusive design retails for about $18.*
©*1996 The Estate of Marilyn Monroe*

Santa and his reindeer spin 'round and 'round in this ornament that features incredible details from the mirrored post to shimmering rhinestones. "Christmas All Around" also plays a festive tune. ©1996 AGC, Inc.

situation and there is a story already going on."

Among the *Heirloom Collection's* 135 designs in 1996, "Christmas All Around" features a Santa riding a carousel with reindeer that go 'round and 'round to a festive tune. Look closely and you'll see the center post is metalized to look like a mirror, which reflects the holiday scene. "I like things that come to life with sparkle," Cipra says.

Besides the merry and whimsical, some ornaments also have a serious side. "We're seeing that people want more than just cute, so we've balanced our line to reflect this desire," Cipra says.

"Wonderland Express" features an authentic train engine from the gears to the other gadgets that keep it right on track. Carlton found an expert to research the trains and create a life-like drawing for the ornament. Following a demand for religious-themed ornaments, "O Holy Night" recreates the First Christmas, complete with an insert to hold a light that makes the stars sparkle above the Nativity scene. The *Heirloom Collection* also

emphasizes quality and fine craftsmanship in every detail. "Joy Is In The Air," the first in a series of flying machine ornaments, portrays a nostalgic, roaring '20s Victorian look with bows, rhinestones and a couple sitting side by side in the zeppelin. "It features lots of details," Cipra says.

New Faces, New Series, New Traditions

The 1996 collection brought collectors the second Elvis series issue which plays "Santa Bring My Baby Back (To Me)." Another recognizable face, Marilyn Monroe, also joined the collection.

The new *Collector's Series* included "Joy Is In the Air," "Merry Mischief," "O Holy Night," "Jolly Old St. Nick" and "Wonderland Express." Also premiering in 1996 were five holiday collections, each featuring three coordinated ornaments. But collectors don't have to wait three years to complete the set. The trios of ornaments are available the same year, so collectors can purchase one or all three at a time. They include the *Angels* collection with "Song of Peace," "Song of Hope" and "Song of Joy." The *Antique Toys* collection includes "Holiday Recollections," "Christmas Tidings" and "Holiday Fun." The *Candy Buildings* collection, features "Candy Cane Cabin," "Sugarplum Chapel" and "Gingerbread Farm." The *Farm Animals* collection teams with favorites like "Country Cow," "Perky Pig" and "Prancing Pony." The *Whimsical* collection includes "Joy," "Merry" and "Love."

Collection Expands With Licensed Ornaments

The more things change in society, the more people long for familiar treasures and times. The *Heirloom Collection* is bringing back memories and collectors' favorite things with licensed ornaments from some of the most recognizable and popular brands. "People seem to be looking for things that are more nostalgic," Cipra says. "We're featuring many licensed nostalgic ornaments with designs that

were perhaps their favorite foods, old-fashioned toys or cartoon characters. They tug at your heart and make you want to share those memories with your children. People want to introduce their children to some of the lovely things from their past."

Some of the licenses for 1996 include Play-Doh, Volkswagen, Campbell's® Soup, Hershey's™ and Radio Flyer®. "I remember finding a Radio Flyer wagon underneath my tree one Christmas," Cipra says. "It was overflowing with toys and beautiful packages. Suddenly, a lid popped open, and a new puppy poked his head out. It was love at first sight! Daisy and I spent a lot of time together in that wonderful wagon."

Other licenses feature Opus 'n Bill™, Rocky and Bullwinkle and Friends™, Care Bears™, Paddington Bear™, Nintendo™ and characters from Nickelodeon children's shows, "Rugrats" and "Ren & Stimpy."

The Making of an *Heirloom Collection* Ornament

Like any collectible, an *Heirloom Collection* ornament begins with an idea. The collection's research and design team works throughout the year trying to find new inspirations and creative concepts for the next ornament. Sometimes ideas for the ornaments come from a popular greeting card or

A train buff researched and designed "Wonderland Express" to make every detail as authentic as possible. The dated ornament is first in a series of trains. ©1996 AGC, Inc.

"O Holy Night" celebrates the beloved Nativity scene that is illuminated by a light that makes the background stars sparkle. The dated ornament, which is first in a series, can be open or closed.
©1996 AGC, Inc.

Christmas ornament," Cipra says. "I knew from then that there would be ornaments in my future. I think I've got the best job in the company!"

After an ornament design has been completed and approved, specifications are sent to sculptors in the Orient. They develop a prototype ornament according to the designs from the shape, size and color right down to the sparkle in Santa's eyes. Using the prototype as a model, artisans hand-sculpt all the individual components of the ornament into a steel die. The die is then placed in a hydraulic press, and heated plastic is forced into the mold through an injection process.

After the pieces have cooled, they are carefully checked by hand for accuracy against the original line drawing and the prototype ornament. "We have a dedicated team from beginning to end, so there is always continuity," Cipra says. The team, for example, makes sure that a certain expression on a face doesn't get lost from the first drawing to the final production.

Each ornament has a specific color palette that may contain up to 56 different colors. Artisans separately hand spray each color. As the ornament moves throughout the process, more colors are added. When all the pieces are painted, each ornament is assembled by hand. Using a strong bonding agent, the workers melt each of the individual pieces together for durability. The final result is a beautiful collectible ornament that will be cherished for years to come.

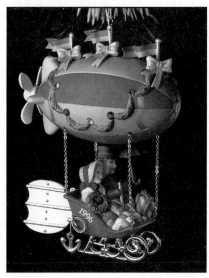

Up, up and away in this zeppelin built for two! "Joy Is In The Air," first in a series of traveling machines, features a Victorian flair and embellishments from pink bows to boughs of greenery.
©1996 AGC, Inc.

gift wrap. Other ideas, which may take up to three years to formulate, stem from the latest paint finish or technological advance, such as a new sound chip that could be placed inside an ornament. Designers also visit gift and toy shows searching for inspiration. "We're not looking for gimmicks," Cipra says. "New innovations are only added if they enhance our line."

Most importantly, the design team and artists understand what collectors are looking for. "I became a collector back in 1972, when my sister gave me a

Carlton Cards
A Division of American Greetings
One American Road
Cleveland, Ohio 44144
(216) 252-7300
FAX (216) 252-6751

CAST ART INDUSTRIES, INC.
Bringing Figurines to Collectors from a Variety of Artists

Picture Perfect" is one of the limited edition Dreamsicles. *So far, all of the retired limited editions have increased in value on the secondary market.*

Just over four years ago, California-based Cast Art Industries took the collectible gift market by storm with the introduction of the now-popular *Dreamsicles®* collection. Since that time, the company has produced the works of additional talented artists representing a wide range of styles and subjects. The result is an exciting array of collectible figurines certain to please any collector.

Cast Art Industries was founded in December 1990 by Scott Sherman, Frank Colapinto and Gary Barsellotti, three friends with more than 50 years of combined experience in the gift industry. Sherman was formerly a Florida corporate president, who, despite his youth, had substantial experience in administration and marketing. Colapinto, a long time resident of California, has spent most of his career building a national sales force in the gift industry. Barsellotti, Italian-born and trained, is an expert in the manufacturing of fine quality figurines.

The company began as a manufacturer, securing contracts to produce decorative boxes, figurines, lamps and souvenir items for other companies. Within a few months, Cast Art signed exclusive contracts with independent artists and was producing and selling its own product lines. The success of the designs, and the consistent high quality of the reproductions, quickly caused the collecting world to take notice and made Cast Art one of the fastest-growing companies in the industry.

The *Dreamsicles®* Phenomenon

In March 1991, Cast Art introduced *Dreamsicles®*, a group of 31 adorable cherub and animal figurines designed by artist Kristin Haynes. Kristin's fresh approach to a timeless subject was an instant hit with the gift-buying public, and *Dreamsicles* rapidly became one of the most popular new lines in the world of collectibles.

The collection now numbers over 250 designs and includes animals, holiday pieces, Christmas ornaments, and a birthday collection in addition to a growing variety of cherubs. All are hand-cast and hand-painted, then decorated with dried flowers to assure that no two are ever exactly alike.

Within one year, the *Dreamsicles* line received national recognition as the Best Selling New Category at the Gift Creations Concepts (GCC) industry show in Minneapolis. In addition, *Dreamsicles* has been recognized as the #1 selling general gift line, and Kristin has received numerous industry awards.

In a relatively short time, *Dreamsicles* have gained recognition in the collectibles category with collector pieces. *Giftbeat Newsletter* recently ranked *Dreamsicles* as the country's #2 collectible line, after *Precious Moments* and ahead of *Heritage Village* and *Cherished Teddies.* Each of the limited edition *Dreamsicles* cherubs, consisting of 10,000 pieces signed and numbered by the artist, sold out in a few months and became a valued

"Three Cheers," by Kristin Haynes, celebrates the third year of growth and fun for the Dreamsicles® Collectors Club. The 4-3/8" figurine is free to Club members as the "Symbol of Membership" for 1995.

collectors' piece.

This success is highly unusual, since most items of this type are not recognized as true collectibles until several years after release. Virtually all designs in the line have attained a collectible status, and many of the retired figurines have already shown substantial price increases in the secondary market.

In response to public demand, Cast Art is actively engaged in a licensing program which offers leading manufacturers of a variety of products the use of the *Dreamsicles* designs and logo. These delightful cherubs are appearing on such items as collector plates, candles, garden accessories, rubber stamps, counted cross-stitch patterns, plush toys and a variety of stationery products.

In addition, Cast Art has introduced a *Dreamsicles Gift Collection* which features beautifully decorated porcelain and ceramic items including collectors bells, decorated boxes, coffee mugs, tea sets, picture frames, gift bags and more, all adorned with colorful artwork depicting the popular cherubs.

Cuddl'somes™ Delight Bear Lovers

When Cast Art recently introduced its *Cuddl'somes™* line, the initial response was far greater than they had anticipated, exceeding even the successful *Dreamsicles*. It was Cast Art's first indication that they might have not one, but two collectible lines destined for success. This collection of 52 teddy bears and other adorable animal figurines is based on several original designs by Kristin Haynes, as interpreted and expanded by the in-house design team of Steve and Gigi Hackett.

Each figurine in the *Cuddl'somes* collection is intricately detailed and hand-painted to perfection. In addition, these adorable figurines are competitively priced, starting at under $10.00.

Cuddl'somes feature fanciful characters including teddy bear pirates, cowboys, firemen and sports figures, as well as delightful cows, pigs and more. This unique collection of precious teddy bears and their adorable animal friends is designed right and priced

Cast Arts Cuddl'somes™ *line is a collection of unique teddy bears and other animals that have captured the hearts of bear lovers everywhere.*

right, making the collection an instant winner.

In fact, two *Cuddl'somes* figurines were nominated for the sixth annual TOBY® awards in the category of "Figurine Bear-Manufacturer." The popularity of this line has led to Cast Art's introduction of *Cuddl'somes* water globes and Christmas ornaments.

Other Creative Product Lines

As part of its goal to create figurines for every collector, Cast Art uses different artists who develop a variety of designs.

In addition to *Cuddl'somes*, the husband and wife team of Steve and Gigi Hackett have created *Animal*

Attraction™, a group of offbeat animal characters. The line includes dancing bears, "flasher" cows, and a variety of hilarious pigs in bikinis, aerobics outfits, "punker" attire and other poses. The tongue-in-cheek, slightly off-color attitudes of the collection represent a substantial departure from Cast Art's other lines, and make *Animal Attraction* popular with youthful collectors.

The success of their collaboration is further evidenced by *Story Time Treasures™*. This grouping depicts a new approach to six timeless children's classics, from *Peter Rabbit to The Frog Prince*. Each sculpture consists of the title character reading the bedtime story to his youngster, and reminds us of the joys of sharing a special moment and a good book with a child.

For those who enjoy the humorous side of life, there are few collections which compare to the whimsical *Cuckoo Corners™*, a mythical place populated by a growing collection of offbeat characters who remind us of people we know and love. Introduced in 1993, these lighthearted designs by the multi-talented Kristen Haynes have rapidly become favorites with collectors everywhere. From screaming babies to silly seniors, they remind us of our own friends and relatives in their best and worst moods. The collection of 59 pieces portrays a wide range of emotions, some subtle, some outrageous, yet all with a keen empathy for the human spirit which sets Kristin apart from other artists.

Wildlife™, a humorous assortment of porcelain animals from the "wild," was introduced by Cast Art in 1994. Designed by Barbara and Bob Sullivan,

these whimsical figurines feature a variety of animals, everything from penguins to camels to puppy dogs. Each *Wildlife* figurine is carefully fired at 2350 degrees Fahrenheit, giving the clay a translucent quality, and turning the glaze into glass which creates the distinctive look of china.

Dreamsicles Collectors Club

The Dreamsicles Collectors' Club, formed in 1993, continues to be one of the nation's fastest growing collector organizations. The Club offers members the opportunity to share their appreciation of the charm and beauty of Kristin Haynes' adorable cherubs and animals. They have the chance to purchase Members-Only figurines, many of which have already become highly collectible. Figurines such as "Daydream Believer" and "Makin' A List" are among the unique designs that

only Club members have been able to purchase. Other benefits including a free "Symbol of Membership" figurine, a Club binder and printed photo guide to the collection, an embossed personalized membership card, and a subscription to the colorful "Club-House" newsletter. The newsletter allows members to be the first to learn about new product introductions, retirements and much more. Annual membership dues are $27.50.

Cast Art Industries, Inc.
1120 California Ave.
Corona, CA 91719
(800) 932-3020
Fax (909) 270-2852

COLLECTORS' CLUB

Dreamsicles Collectors' Club
1120 California Ave.
Corona, CA 91719
(800) 437-5818

Annual Dues: $27.50 - Renewal: $23.50
Club Year: Anniversary of Sign-Up Date

Benefits:
• Membership Gift: Cherub Figurine
• Opportunity to Purchase Members-Only Cherub Figurine
• Quarterly "ClubHouse Newsletter"
• Three Ring Binder
• Personalized, Embossed Membership Card
• Buy/Sell "Wish List" in Newsletter
• "Guide To The Dreamsicles" Photo Book

CAVANAGH GROUP INTERNATIONAL
It's the Real Thing! The Story Behind Cavanagh Group International's Refreshing Collectible Delights

It's hard to recall a time when Coca-Cola® wasn't our favorite national drink! From coast-to-coast, the "Coke" logo fanned across billboards and magazines from April to September, even before the turn-of-the-century. In 1931, folks at Coca-Cola's corporate headquarters realized they needed to change our nation's seasonal mindset about their drink. After all, Coca-Cola tastes just as good in the winter as it does in the summer. They set out to make their point with a revolutionary ad campaign.

Commissioning highly regarded illustrator Haddon Sundblom to paint Santa Claus, plans were made to introduce America's favorite drink to America's holiday hero. The marriage was a happy success. Sundblom's burly, fun-loving Santa debuted on the pages of *The Saturday Evening Post* magazine in 1931. Just about everyone in America read the *Post*, so the Coca-Cola Santa quickly became America's most

Inspired by a 1917 calendar produced by Coca-Cola, "Calendar Girl Swinging" is part of the Calendar Girls Series *within the* Coca-Cola Heritage Collection. *Only resin crafting and hand-painting can create such delicate ruffles, buds and other realistic touches on this figurine.*

recognized St. Nick!

Happily, that still holds true today...thanks to Cavanagh Group International. Established in 1990, Cavanagh has made the Coca-Cola Santa Claus image a flagship of collectible art, carrying the heritage of this heartwarming symbol toward the new millennium with designs collectors from coast-to-coast collect and adore year 'round.

A Heritage of Art Meets a Group of Funny Polar Bears

From the first day it began advertising, the Coca-Cola Bottling Company put its heart and soul into its ads and set records for the numbers of "giveaways" presented to Coke drinkers across America. There were glasses and calendars. Serving trays and wallets. Post cards. Blotters. Cards. Match books. Even sheet music! Some of this art, much from the turn-of-the-century, was selected to be placed on items made for *The Coca-Cola Heritage Collection.*

For Coca-Cola collectors with a passion for "the real thing," Santa Claus figurines, musicals and snowglobes based on Haddon Sundblom's 1951 "Good Boys and Girls" illustration fill the bill. Each hand-painted resin delight is impressively sized and authentically detailed. A classic, bordered collector plate is included in this library. As always, a die-struck medallion attests to each piece's authenticity.

Far removed from classic Sundblom Santa figurines, musicals and snowglobes, are everyone's favorite contemporary television stars: members of the *Coca-Cola Polar Bear Collection.* You've seen these guys and laughed at their antics: each is roly-poly and sugar white! Fans can now have their polar bears in a snowglobe. On a musical base. As a figurine. Or in a whimsical group, posing for a 'family' portrait!

When you're hot, you're hot—even when you're cold! Behold the world-renowned Coca-Cola Polar Bear in signature muffler frolicking on the ice with feisty offspring and a Coke to make the day perfect! The "Polar Bear Family Figurine Musical," from the Always Coca-Cola *series, is made of resin, hand-painted and embellished with a Coca-Cola seal in its base.*

Each is made of hand-painted resin with an official die-struck medallion.

For 1995, the bears appeared as two limited edition ornaments. One is shown on a bottle opener, the other on a snowboard. These two join the 1994 bears who skate, sled, deliver Coke and, of course, sneak an ice cold bottle of their favorite drink from a nearby vending machine. Also new for 1995: four bear ornaments dressed in adorable outfits, wearing ear muffs, stocking hats and formal bow ties. "Cousins" of this happy group unveiled in 1995: enchanting, miniature plush polar bear ornaments.

Coca-Cola Landmark Designs Distinguish the '95 Collection

In addition to the lavishly made collectible art described above, 1995

Coca-Cola introductions gave collectors plenty to cheer about. Four high-quality porcelain buildings are slated for construction in the *Coca-Cola Town Square Collection*. Each rekindles the spirit and memories of days-gone-by, when life was gentle and simple. Merchants welcome these new businesses to *Coca-Cola's Town Square* in '95: "Light House Point Snack Bar," "Grist Mill Restaurant," the "Sweete Shoppe" and the "Bottling Works." Each new building bears a special decal indicating year of release. Now a community of 21 buildings, *Coca-Cola Town Square* has the distinction of having retired nine buildings, three on Christmas, 1994. Many are selling on the secondary market for several times their original price.

Of course, no town would be complete without realistic accessories, so Cavanagh introduces four new pieces to display with *Coca-Cola Town Square*. There's a young couple sitting together on a park bench, rambunctious boys throwing snowballs, a couple of skiers relaxing on the slopes and a horse pulling a lunch wagon filled with all the delights a hungry villager could wish for.

Down the road, stop at the *Coca-Cola North-Pole Bottling Works*. Building on the success of an ornament series of the same theme, Cavanagh debuts ten sculptures for 1995 depicting Santa's elves running a Coca-Cola bottling plant when they're not making or delivering gifts. Three "corner buildings" show both sides of each structure in detail, and seven figures give collectors a peek at the three operations the busy elves run during "the off season." New facades, introduced over the next three years, will complete the series.

Finally, a shimmering new collection of silk on glass Christmas ornaments astonishes collectors of all ages! Called *Santa on Silk*, this elegant series combines European lithographed silk over fine glass balls. Assembled in the United States, these six exquisite holiday ornaments feature the Coca-Cola Santa based on ad designs beginning in 1931. As is Cavanagh's practice, some of the 1995 *Santa on Silk* ornaments will be retired at the end of 1995. These retirements make select Coca-Cola collectibles the rarest limited editions of all!

It's Christmas Every Day For Cavanagh's Coca-Cola Club

The portrait is dignified. The message is clear: "Go ahead and sign up." This invitation, offered by a smiling Coca-Cola Santa toasting with an old-fashioned fountain glass of Coke, is the first thing a shopper sees on a brochure for Cavanagh's Coca-Cola Christmas Collectors Society. The Society is old-fashioned fun. Members are invited to celebrate Christmas twelve months a year as Cavanagh makes sure Club perks are value-packed, educational and festive.

From the moment a new member's application reaches the Cavanagh offices, special treatment is afforded the Coca-Cola art collector. A membership kit speeds its way via the U.S. Mail—no reindeer involved here! Inside, a personalized membership card in signature red with white snowflakes awaits. There's a red-bordered membership certificate, ready for framing, and a quarterly subscription to the Christmas Collector Society's information-packed newsletter. Every three months, this publication arrives filled with announcements of new art, retirements, facts behind the design and manufacture of Coca-Cola collectibles, trends and much, much more.

A unique gift, crafted exclusively for members, is also sent to Society members when they join. This authentic collectible is drawn from the archives of the Coca-Cola Company. For 1995, the membership gift is a delightful Santa ornament circled with a halo of evergreen and perfect for illuminating when hung in front of a Christmas tree light.

Members covet invitations to purchase special limited edition art not offered to non-members. The 1995 Members-Only exclusive is the extraordinary First Edition Collectors Lithograph, "It Will Refresh You Too," inspired by Haddon Sundblom's original illustration. Embossed with the Society seal, this impressive 22" x 28"" lithograph is ready-to-frame and hang. There's more! Browse the Society Members-Only Catalog and you know this is no ordinary collectors club. Members can purchase shirts, tote bags, mugs, a binder and other delights to show the world that their membership in Cavanagh's Coca-Cola Christmas Collectors Society is a joy all year long.

Keys to the Realm of Joy, Tradition and Fun

"We've been given the keys to the Coca-Cola Company archives," says John F. Cavanagh, president of the Cavanagh Group International, "and we're creating a line of high-quality, authentic collectibles. It's a wonderful opportunity for collectors to discover and enjoy a wealth of Coca-Cola art and advertising images by such renowned artists as Haddon Sundblom, N.C. Wyeth and Norman Rockwell." These words sum up the goals and promises of a young company committed to sharing, with millions of Americans, the rich heritage of Coca-Cola art. The

The musical "Santa on the Steps" prepares to deliver gifts and memories! Artist Haddon Sundblom created an original Coca-Cola ad in 1931 that lives on as this extraordinary sculpture. Fashioned of resin and hand-painted in a rainbow of shimmering colors, this impressive figure is part of the Coca-Cola Heritage Collection.

current Cavanagh Collection shows these goals are being met with remarkable vision. This year's variety is breathtaking in size and scope.

The Coca-Cola Heritage Collection, mentioned earlier in this article when we spotlighted the 1995 introductions, includes ornaments, figurines, musicals, polar bears and snowglobes. Within this popular category, *The Coca Cola North Pole Bottling Works* introduces a new collection of corner buildings and accessories sure to charm collectors the moment they discover these magnificently detailed collectible buildings and the helpers who inhabit and visit them.

An astonishing array of other Coca-Cola treats awaits collector pleasure, as well. There are elaborate sculptures of Santa sold as *Major Musical* collectibles. *Miniature Musicals* follow Santa, elves and the Coca-Cola Polar Bear on their Christmas adventures. Crystal-clear *Coca-Cola Santa Snowglobes* shower Santa and the Coke Polar Bear with white flakes as they show up in the most unlikely places. The *Santa Claus Trim-a-Tree* galaxy is a sight to behold,

Norman Rockwell's signature look distinguished this 1933 portrait of a young boy enjoying a Coke as he patiently awaits a bite on his line! Now a gloriously bordered limited edition collector plate, "Boy Fishing" bears the official seal of Coca-Cola authorized art. This Rockwell delight is also part of the Coca-Cola Heritage Collection.

as well. Dozens of ornaments, each inspired by a vintage illustration, swing happily from branches. Collectors may purchase these ornaments individually

or as sets. Many have been retired!

"From our initial offering of four ornaments in 1990 to our present collection of more than 150 individual pieces, we've been able to respond to the strong desires of collectors who can't get enough Coca-Cola collectible art," John Cavanagh smiles. He sits back and reviews the past five years with an observation that sums up Cavanagh's promise to the fans enriching their lives with Coca-Cola collectibles. "We're committed to continually expanding the breadth and depth of our Coca-Cola treasures. Our collectors can count on us for spectacular, heartwarming art crafted so expertly, these vintage collectibles will become the heirlooms of tomorrow."

Cavanagh Group International
1000 Holcomb Woods Pkwy.
#440-B
Roswell, GA 30078
(800) 895-8100
Fax (404) 643-1172

COLLECTORS' CLUB

Cavanagh's Coca-Cola Christmas Collectors Society
P.O. Box 420157
Atlanta, GA 30342
(800) 653-1221

Annual Dues: $25.00
Club Year: January-December

Benefits:
• Membership Gift: Authentic Collectible Drawn from the Archives of the Coca-Cola Company
• Opportunity to Purchase Members-Only Collectible
• Quarterly Newsletter
• Membership Certificate, Suitable for Framing
• Personalized Membership Card
• Periodic Offers on Special Items Reserved for Society Members

CHRISTOPHER RADKO
Celebrating a Decade of Holiday Memories and Traditions

In 1995, members of the Christopher Radko Starlight Family of Collectors had the opportunity to purchase "Dash Away All." The members-only ornament is part of a wide range of exclusive benefits awaiting collectors who enjoy the fine quality, craftsmanship and nostalgia of the collection.

For Christopher Radko, what appeared to be his family's loss has turned into a colorful and nostalgic gain for collectors around the world. It all began in 1984 when the holiday season was unfolding according to the Radko family tradition. While Christopher was growing up in Scarsdale, New York, the highlight of his family's Christmas was decorating the tree with their astonishing collection of blown-glass ornaments. Three generations of Radkos had collected more than 2,000 of the handcrafted treasures. As a boy, Christopher loved to slide under the fresh pine tree's lowest branches, where he was mesmerized by the reflection of the bubble lights, twinkling stars and shimmering spheres.

But in 1984, as Christopher was performing his annual chore of removing sap and needles from the old tree stand, he decided that a new one was needed. After shopping around, he bought a stand guaranteed to hold up an 18-foot tree — a good 4 feet taller than the Radko's own tree. With the new stand, the old traditions still continued as family members trimmed the tree.

One cold December morning, however, a loud crash suddenly changed the idyllic scene. Despite its guarantee, the stand buckled and the tree fell to the floor, shattering more than half of the fragile decorations.

"I was absolutely heartbroken because those ornaments were our family's direct link to the traditions and memories of four generations of Christmas celebrations," Christopher recalls. "Even though I knew there was no way I could replace the ornaments my great-grandmother and grandmother had handed down, I thought that the least I could do was buy some substitutes so our tree wouldn't look so forlorn."

He searched in the stores near his hometown and shopped the major department stores all over New York City. Sadly, he discovered that most ornaments were being made from plastic and other mysterious materials. The few glass ornaments that he found were poorly crafted, and the painted details were frightful. Needless to say, it was a depressing Christmas for the Radko family.

Reviving a Turn-of-the-Century Technique

The following spring, while Christopher was visiting relatives in Poland, a cousin introduced him to a farmer who once made blown-glass ornaments. He said he might be able to make several new ones. There was only

one catch: Christopher had to supply him with detailed drawings of the kinds of ornaments he wanted. Upon seeing the designs, the glassblower said that they were just like the ornaments that his father and grandfather had made before World War II and that although he had never made such complicated pieces, he would be happy to try.

After Christopher returned to the United States with his newly crafted glass ornaments, family members and friends clamored for glorious glass ornaments of their own. At that point, he realized that he had discovered not only a need but his own niche for fulfilling the demand.

Today, a decade later, Christopher engages the services of nearly 800 Polish, German, Czech and Italian glassblowers who masterfully create limited editions of his ornaments. The 1995 line features more than 750 dazzling designs with ideas coming from memories of his family's antique ornaments as well as his other inspirations: architecture, fabrics, films and museum collections. It takes about a week to make each ornament, which is blown, silvered, lacquered, painted and glittered entirely by hand. Designs range from the traditional Santa Claus to a pipe-smoking monkey and rabbits to Persian peacocks.

"My company's success has allowed me to revive Christmas crafts and techniques that were all but lost," Christopher says. "As a Christmas artist with my annual collection of new designs, I am reviving a tradition of designing that had its heyday at the turn of the century. My glassblowers are uncovering old molds and relearning skills that their cottage industry hasn't used in 70 years. Now, even young apprentice glassblowers are being trained in the traditions of their great-grandfathers, ensuring that fine glass ornament making will continue

Created to benefit AIDS-related organizations and raise awareness about the disease, "On Wings of Hope" features an angel with shimmering details and vibrant colors. Each year, Christopher Radko divides the proceeds from the ornament among different agencies that serve those with AIDS.

into the next century. That's something to celebrate!"

Collection Marks Its 10th Anniversary

The collection of glass ornaments also had something to celebrate: its 10th anniversary throughout 1995. In honor of the occasion, Christopher introduced "On Top of the World" as his special Santa Claus for the year.

For collectors to always remember the occasion and enjoy all the ornaments offered to date, Christopher published a 10th anniversary book. The 200-plus-page volume pictures all the ornaments along with articles on the traditions, manufacturing and creative uses of Christopher's ornaments. The book is available in two versions: the 10th anniversary commemorative book limited in edition to 2,500 pieces and bound in leather with a slip case, and the standard version with a hardcover and dust protector.

For the first time, Christopher also introduced the *Boutique Collection* featuring a silk scarf in four color selections, three different tie styles, unisex boxer shorts, a 500-piece jigsaw puzzle, shopping bags and wrapping paper — all of which showcase his renowned ornaments.

New Ornaments Offer Something For Everyone

Because half of the ornaments in the line are retired or changed in some way each year, Christopher's ornaments become highly collectible. For 1995, following the success of "A Partridge in a Pear Tree" and "Two Turtle Doves," another ornament has been added to the *Twelve Days of Christmas* series. Like previous introductions, "Three French Hens" was inspired by the holiday song and is limited to 10,000 pieces with a hand-numbered tag.

For 1995, Snow White has also joined the collection. "And Snowy Makes Eight" is a numbered and pre-packed introduction that includes all seven dwarfs and Snow White straight from the popular children's story. Christopher also introduced two three-year limited series sets. The "Three Wise Men" is limited to 15,000 sets with hand-numbered tags. This is the first part of the company's three-year Nativity set. *The Nutcracker Suite* features the 1995 debuts of "Clara," "Toy Soldier" and "Herr Drosselmeier," each hand-numbered and limited to 15,000 sets.

The 1995 event piece — only available during Christopher Radko presentations nationwide — is "Forever Lucy." Continuing his tradition of raising funds to spread awareness and support the fight against AIDS and pediatric cancer, Christopher has introduced several new ornaments to help others. "On Wings of Hope" will benefit various AIDS-related organizations while "Christmas Puppy Love" will go toward pediatric cancer agencies. Christopher is also proud of the fact that organizations such as World Wildlife Fund, the Smithsonian Institution and the Metropolitan Museum of Art have commissioned

limited editions of his ornaments. His ornaments are also bought year-round as gifts for birthdays, anniversaries, housewarming parties and bridal or baby showers.

Starlight Club Welcomes Ornament Collectors

All collectors seem to find something captivating and comforting in the ornaments. Even Vice President Al Gore, Elton John, Katharine Hepburn, Bruce Springsteen, Dolly Parton, Mikhail Barishnikov and Hillary Rodham Clinton are numbered among the devoted Christopher Radko collectors.

Many other fans around the world have joined the Christopher Radko Starlight Family of Collectors. Launched in 1993, this collectors' club offers members exclusive pieces and keeps them up to date on the latest introductions. For 1995, a $50.00 membership included the gift ornament "Purrfect Present," personalized and embossed membership card, an annual

Christopher Radko strongly believes in giving something back to others — and he is an ardent supporter of pediatric cancer agencies. Proceeds from "Christmas Puppy Love," which features a dog in a Christmas stocking, will benefit that cause.

"Three French Hens," the 1995 introduction to the Twelve Days of Christmas *series, follows in the popular tradition of the holiday song. The ornament is limited to 10,000 pieces with a hand-numbered tag.*

ornament button, the 10th anniversary cloisonne collector's pin, 10th anniversary Collector's Catalogue, subscription to the quarterly *Starlight* publication, and a linen bound *Starlight* and Collector's Catalogue storage folio. Members also received a voucher entitling them to purchase the members-only figurine, which for 1995 was titled "Dash Away All."

"I am supported by thousands of loyal collectors who recognize the care and extraordinary quality each ornament represents," Christopher said.

And now, thanks to Christopher Radko and the holiday mishap at his family's home more than 10 years ago, any collector can trim a tree with old-fashioned, blown-glass ornaments without going to Europe to find them.

Christopher Radko
P.O. Box 238
Dobbs Ferry, NY 10522
(800) 71-RADKO
Fax: (914) 693-3770

COLLECTORS' CLUB

Starlight Family of Collectors
P.O. Box 238
Dobbs Ferry, NY 10522
(800) 71-RADKO

Annual Dues: $50.00 - Renewal: $45.00
Club Year: January-December

Benefits:
• Membership Gift: Ornament
• Opportunity to Purchase Members-Only Ornament
• Quarterly Magazine, *Starlight*
• *Starlight* Folio
• Personalized Membership Card
• Annual Ornament Button
• Exclusive Christopher Radko Pin
• Tenth Anniversary Catalogue

CRYSTAL WORLD

America's Largest Producer of Full-Lead Crystal Figurines Offers Collectors a Wealth of Intriguing Designs

Crystal Worlds' new, miniature "Classic Motorcycle" measures only 3-3/4" front to back, rests on its own tiny crystal kick-stand and features movable front-wheel forks. A replica of the enormously popular, limited edition "Classic Motorcycle," this smaller model, in an open edition, retails for a suggested $210.

Architecture, whimsy, animals, fantasy, floral, holiday, seashore and more — the themes that make up the amazing array of figurines produced by Crystal World are varied indeed. In 1983, the firm began operations out of a small warehouse in Queens, New York. Today, it's located at much larger quarters in Lincoln Park, a New Jersey suburb. The years between have seen Crystal World grow by leaps and bounds to become the largest producer of crystal collectibles in the United States.

"The reason for this," notes Crystal World's founder and leading designer Ryuju Nakai, "is our consistent commitment to innovation and quality. Rather than simply reproducing the kind of figurines other companies offer, we like to pioneer new designs." And pioneer they do. It was Crystal World, in fact, that copyrighted *The Original Rainbow Castle Collection*® back in 1987, producing the first rainbow colored crystal castles to reach the marketplace.

Architectural Themes Appeal to Collectors and Tourists Alike

The company's famous architectural-themed pieces are another "first." From the Eiffel Tower to the Taj Mahal, from New York's Empire State Building and Chicago's Water Tower to the U.S. Capitol in Washington, D.C., Crystal World has crafted in crystal some of the world's most sought-after structures. These have proven popular not only with collectors but with visitors to the cities that are home to these architectural wonders.

Crystal World also pioneered another idea that has captivated collectors, even though collectors may not be aware of its existence. This is the concept of what Crystal World designers call "give and take." "What we're doing," explains Nakai, "is telling a story by using two characters in one figurine." A prime example of this technique is found in the company's "Curious Cat," the figurine that won a *Collector Editions* magazine "Award of Excellence" in 1990. Here, a tiny crystal cat peers over the rim of a fish bowl as a fish swims by. Is the cat simply watching the fish or eyeing his next meal? The collector must decide, and it's this bit of drama between the cat, the fish and the viewer that provides that extra "kick" which makes so many of Crystal World's figurines different and much more interesting.

The company's Teddy Bear line, titled *Once Upon a Time in Teddyland*, offers plenty of this "give and take," as well. Figurines such as "Blackjack Teddies" engaged in a game of Blackjack; "Ice Cream Teddies" enjoying a sundae treat; or "Teddies at Eight" having dinner in an elegant art deco setting, all offer situation, interaction and the beginning of a story — which

collectors can then use their own imagination to complete. It's not even necessary to have a second character in order for this give and take to work, points out Crystal World's Vice President Joseph J. Art. "Look at our 'Frisky Fido,' for instance. This 1995 piece features an adorable little clear crystal puppy at play with his master's (or mistress') frosted crystal shoe. While there is only a single character, there's plenty of situation and action."

"Pay Attention to Detail, then Trust Your Instincts"

Attention to detail in the design and production, as well as in each situation, is another Crystal World feature that collectors love. This, notes Mr. Nakai, is extremely important to the firm's architectural pieces. "Although you cannot duplicate each detail in the Eiffel Tower or the Empire State Building, you must still research very carefully every building you reproduce, taking note of all the statistics. Then you must trust your own instincts regarding design and proportion." No matter how correct the proportion, the finished piece must still please the eye of the collector, and the human eye is very good at playing tricks. For this reason, Crystal World's designers usually pay special attention to whatever feature of the building or object is most important.

"Take the 'Taj Majal,' " explains Mr. Nakai. "Most people remember the large middle section of that building, so we made that section most prominent in our design." This approach works well, it seems, since the "Taj Mahal" has been a consistently popular collectible in all its various sizes and price ranges.

Attention to detail pays off with themes other than architecture, too. Crystal World's version of the U.S. Space Shuttle is of such high standards that its reproductions are sold in the

Kennedy Space Center Museum Gift Shop in Florida. The firm's popular line of beautifully designed ships is grounded in a firm sense of detail and reality, as well.

Interestingly, this insistence on proper research and finished details is used as much in Crystal World's Fantasy Castle line as in its realistic pieces. Before Ryuju Nakai fashioned his first castle, he twice traveled to Germany to visit the world-famous Neuschwanstein Castle. "I needed to see it with my own eyes and to experience the wonder of its exteriors and interiors," he recalls. "And although my castles are more rounded than Neuschwanstein, which is long and rectangular, I could not have done as good a job without actually visiting the real castle first!"

Another Crystal World designer, Nicolo Mulargia, often travels around the country prior to designing his crystal pieces. Mulargia's popular "Victorian House" came out of the artist's trips to locations as diverse as the Victorian homes found in Springfield, Massachusetts, as well as those in San Francisco. Mulargia's creations run the gamut from Victoriana to an amazing "Riverboat," complete

Exquisite is the word for this "Merry-Go-Round" from Crystal World, which is limited to an edition of 750 and priced at $275 suggested retail. Only 4-3/8" high, the colorful new figurine was designed by award-winning artist Nicolo Mulargia.

with paddle wheel, to a tiny version of The White House.

From Century-Old Traditions to Modern Classics

While riverboats and Victorian houses hark back to a century past, Crystal World also offers more modern "classics" from which collectors can choose. 1995 saw the production of the firm's signed and numbered "Classic Motorcycle," which is limited to 950 worldwide and retails for a suggested $410. This unusual collectible, designed by Crystal World artist Tom Suzuki, offers an amazing array of faceted, full-lead crystal in enormous detail. The 4-1/8"-long cycle also features movable front-wheel forks and a tiny crystal kick stand. None other than famous movie star/body builder Arnold Schwarzenegger is the proud owner of one of these "Classic Motorcycles," which was given to him as a recent birthday gift.

Not every collector, of course, has the budget of a Schwarzenegger, or, for that matter, of the Sultan of Brunei, considered by some to be the world's richest man. Back in 1995, the Sultan bought two large Crystal World "Taj Mahals." Limited to an edition size of 1,000, the large "Taj Mahal" stands 6" high and retails for a suggested $2,300. So the company has now produced a smaller version of the popular motorcycle in an open edition, which stands 3-3/4" long and retails for a suggested $210. Crystal World has also produced a medium and a small version of its "Taj Mahal," priced at $785 and $210 respectively. All three figurines have been very well received by collectors, notes Joseph Art.

Years of Training Go into Each New Design

All Crystal World figurines are made with the finest full-lead crystal available today. Crystal World artisans, who have years of training in their various skills, then cut, grind and polish the raw crystal and then assemble the individual figurines. Over the past few years, the firm has developed its technology

Put another nickel in and play your favorite song! Crystal World's new "Fabulous Fifties Jukebox" replicates those wonderful music machines of decades past. Standing only 2-1/8" high, this colorful creation is priced at $80.00 suggested retail.

to the point where it can now work with larger blocks and shapes of crystal, from which can come many more unusual and different designs. Some of the largest designs, such as the company's enormous crystal Pagoda which weighs 35 pounds, retail for as much as $50,000, while the most reasonably priced figurines are as little as $12.00. Most designs, however, range between $50.00 and $75.00.

Where does Crystal World find its inspiration to create so many different themes? "We just look around at the world in front of us and try to recreate what we see," says Mr. Nakai. "Our inspiration comes from daily life, whether it's in the city, with our skyscrapers, or the country, with a grist mill or barn." It was nearby Atlantic City that inspired the firm's popular crystal slot machines and dice; while a simple walk around the block can lead to the pair of birds that sit in a frosted crystal tree, or the hummingbirds sucking honey from a flower with their long, pointed beaks. "A wedding we attended inspired our popular bride and groom which has become one of our perennial best-sellers and is now available in three different sizes," notes Joseph Art. "Spring and Summer offer up many flowers, and with Winter come snowmen and Christmas trees."

At the Forefront of Today's Trends

Crystal World often finds itself in the forefront of trends, too. More than a year before the Academy Award nominated film "Babe" made pig-lovers of moviegoers throughout the world, Nakai and his crew offered collectors a delightful little pig named "Wilbur." The following year, "Wilbur" appeared again, this time with a female companion in the figurine titled "Wilbur in Love."

Enthusiasts of trains, planes, fire engines and cable cars will discover a Crystal World figurine to suit their taste, too. So will music lovers, who can find much to delight in via the company's crystal violin, guitar, or amazing grand piano. The latter is a mere 2-3/4" and is even available with its own tiny 3/4" piano bench!

Indeed, Crystal World's array of figurines is so vast and so special that there is quite literally something for everyone. 1996 saw the production of a sparkling and intricate "Merry-Go-Round" designed by Nicolo Mulargia. Limited to an edition size of 750 and priced at $280, this enchanting and colorful carousel stands just 4-3/8" high. Other new selections for 1996 included everything from frogs to flowers, pelicans to pineapples, clowns, teddy bears, a "Fabulous Fifties Jukebox" and, as a perfect gift for the couple who's just had a baby, a crystal pacifier complete with pink or blue ribbon.

Selections for 1997 include a small version of the 1996 "Merry-Go-Round" in an open edition; the very first "Eagle" ever produced by Crystal World; new teddy bears, cats and other animals; and lots of new surprises, too.

With all this to choose from, no wonder collectors around the world eagerly anticipate each new Crystal World collectible.

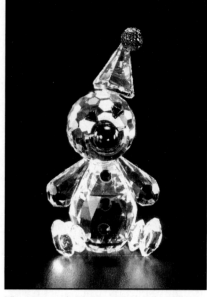

The circus is back in town and Crystal World's new "Bo-Bo the Clown" is sure to become a favorite of circus lovers everywhere. Priced at $50.00 suggested retail, this little crystal charmer sits 2-1/8" high.

Crystal World
3 Borinski Drive
Lincoln Park, NJ 07035
(201) 633-0707
Fax (201) 633-0102

DEAR ARTISTIC SCULPTURE, INC.
Sculptures Share the Historic Beauty and Tradition of the Tuscany Region

Created by Master Sculptor Auro Belcari, "Bald Eagle" sits atop a rocky crag, scanning the horizon with its piercing eyes and natural beauty. The cold cast porcelain figurine showcases the amazing attention to detail found in all Dear sculptures. "Bald Eagle" stands 12" tall and is an open edition.

The natural, cultural and culinary endowments of the Tuscany region in Italy are legendary. It is infused with good fortune: rolling hills blanketed with vineyards and olive groves, a generously temperate climate, and an untold wealth of artistic treasures showcased in opulent museums in Florence and tucked away in often unexpected places in quaint towns and villages. All of this, combined with a profound and influential intellectual history and tradition, have molded the Tuscany of today.

Nestled in the beautiful hills of Tuscany, you will find the Dear Studios, where master sculptors work their magic creating art with astonishing detail and realism. The studio is located between the famous cities of Florence and Siena, with their narrow streets winding among towering cathedrals, timeless museums and finely preserved Gothic buildings. It is in this magnificent setting that the sculptors make their masterpieces — a collection of animals, birds and human figures meticulously hand-made in cold cast porcelain. Dear's *Art Gallery Collection* features limited edition sculptures in a grander scale with soaring eagles, horses with flowing manes and a noble pair of swans, among others. But no matter what the subject, all the sculptures are created in the fine tradition of Tuscany, the legendary home of Renaissance art.

Sculptures Find Home with American Collectors

To share these works of art with American collectors, Dear Artistic Sculpture was created in January 1996. The Oaks, Pennsylvania-based company has become the sole marketer and distributor of Dear sculptures in the United States, opening a new market and audience for these beloved pieces.

"I was impressed by the quality and uniqueness of these sculptures," explains Allen Goeldner, president of Dear Artistic Sculpture. "That caused me to take an active role in introducing this line in the United States. They remind me of some of the great pieces that were created by some of the major china and porcelain houses years ago. From the bald eagle and regal peacock to the horse head and fantasy-inspired unicorn, collectors will appreciate these limited edition works of art that are painstakingly created for their pure beauty and form."

The History of Dear Studios

The art of sculpting has fascinated humankind since the beginning of time. Objects made of clay, worked and modelled by hand, have attracted not only artists but admirers. Creating masterpieces from simple materials has inspired such greats as Michelangelo, Cellini and Donatello, as well as the Etruscans — an ancient people who lived in central Italy.

The Etruscans have handed down culture and sculpture that even today can captivate us with the striking beauty of their form and color. In 1710 around Naples, the Capodimonte art was born — so named because the factory sat atop a mountain. This beautiful porcelain was made and decorated completely by hand. A statue from that

With such lifelike detail, you can almost hear the doves cooing in this sculpture created by artist Ermanno Farina. "Group of Doves" is limited in edition to 2,000 pieces worldwide.

period is now priceless. But more recently, this art has been brought back into vogue. Dear Studios is among the leaders in marking the return of this art form.

Since 1978, the Dear Studios in Italy has been the home of famous artists like Auro Belcari and Ermanno Farina. Through Dear, these masters produce sculptures reflecting realism, richness of detail, and natural movement and color.

All products from the studio are greatly appreciated for their high quality, wide variety and limited editions. Once the limited number of pieces is reached, the original molds are broken. Dear's remarkable standard of quality is also evident in the care provided to the smallest detail of the sculpture, from the colorful feathers on a peacock to the puzzle-like pattern of a giraffe's skin. This attention to detail has made Dear a leading producer not only in Italy but around the world.

The Making of a Dear Sculpture

Italy has a long-standing tradition of

From the Art Gallery Collection *of limited edition sculptures, "The Stag" shows the unspoken gentleness, yet amazing power, of the animal. Artist Auro Belcari created the sculpture, which stands an impressive 22" tall and is limited in edition to 1,000 pieces.*

molding very different materials into works of art – a tradition that goes back to the very early civilization of Etruria, now Tuscany. From these ancient times, sculpting has been handed down from craftsmen to modern artists like Belcari and Farina, who create most of the Dear collection. They preserve the skill of turning a lump of clay into a precious and real-looking figurine.

Dear relies on the experience of renowned artists who have been working in the field and with the company for many years. These artists sculpt the original subject with clay. A mold is then made from this original sculpture and perfected by the artist. A special cold cast porcelain mixture consisting of kaolin powder and resin is then poured into the molds and dried in a cold vacuum-like surrounding.

Once removed from the mold, the figurine is carefully cleaned and ready for decorative, yet realistic, touches. This is one of the most important steps, as the piece is entirely hand-painted and embellished under the close supervision of the artist who created the original sculpture. The artist wants to ensure that the final product remains true to his vision and clay sculpture. Once checked and carefully packaged, the sculpture is ready to be shipped to collectors worldwide.

Sculptures Created with the Collector in Mind

Dear offers something for every collector. For women, there is the Capodimonte classic-style figurines. Men will find the collection teeming with wildlife and birds. For all collectors, there are many world-class limited edition pieces that would be a welcome addition and investment. The sculptures range in price from

With an arched back and intense green eyes, "Tiger" is on the prowl as it descends from a rock. The open edition figurine by Auro Belcari is 15" tall and comes on a wooden base with the artist's name inscribed on a gold plate.

$200 to $1,500.

Some of the most treasured pieces are from the *Art Gallery Collection* of limited edition sculptures, most notably by Auro Belcari. Born in Tuscany, Belcari was trained in the artisan shops where he worked with simple materials. He studied and achieved a master's diploma in art and a fine reputation for his work. Through his work with Dear, Belcari has had the opportunity to express himself by creating pieces of art from formless clay and rendering them noble. The humility of the artist is manifested through all his works. The *Art Gallery Collection* showcases his talents in wildlife and bird sculptures that feature sea gulls, geese, eagles, horses, flamingos and giraffes. He has also created human figures of women riding horses, sitting on a tree swing or posed like an ancient goddess.

Another popular Dear sculptor is Ermanno Farina, who was born in Milan. Ever since childhood, he expressed his special artistic ability and eye for beauty. His initial artwork and studies demonstrate a preference for nature. In the years that followed, he became the pupil of a master sculptor who inspired him to pursue art as a profession. In 1975, he started his career as a ceramic sculptor and soon received worldwide recognition. His collaboration with Dear Studios allowed him to further express his inner self and talents. Today, his works still focus on nature, with particular attention given to the many species of birds.

Dear Artistic Sculpture, Inc.
P.O. Box 860
Oaks, PA 19456-0860
(610) 666-1650
Fax (610) 666-1379

Master sculptor Auro Belcari captured the pure beauty and form of a "Swan" in this elegant 15" sculptor.

Seemingly frozen in time, "The Classic Horse Head" captures the beautiful animal in a moment that is left to the collector's imagination. The sculpture from the Art Gallery Collection of limited edition pieces was designed by Auro Belcari, who carefully included everything from the wind-swept mane to the wide black eyes. The figurine stands 20" tall.

DEPARTMENT 56®, INC.
Just Imagine . . . Snow-Laden Trees, Wreaths at the Windows, and Welcome Mats Out . . . The Tradition Begins

From the Dickens' Village *series comes these quaint pieces entitled "Portobello Road Thatched Cottages."*

"Department 56" may seem a curious name for a firm that designs and manufactures nostalgic, collectible villages. How the name originated is a story that intrigues the firm's many loyal collectors.

Before Department 56, Inc. became an independent corporation, it was part of a large parent company that used a numbering system to identify each of its departments. While Department 21 was administration and Department 54 was the gift warehouse, the name assigned to wholesale gift imports was "Department 56."

Department 56, Inc. originally began by importing fine Italian basketry. However, a new product line introduced in 1977 set the groundwork for the collectible products of today. Little did the company's staff realize that their appealing group of four lighted houses and two churches would pave the way for one of the late-20th century's most popular collectibles.

These miniature buildings were the beginning of *The Original Snow Village*. Each design was handcrafted of ceramic, and hand-painted to create all the charming details of an "olden day" village. To create the glow from the windows, a switched cord and bulb assembly was included with each individually boxed piece.

Collectors could see the little lighted buildings as holiday decorations under a Christmas tree or on the mantel. Glowing lights gave the impression of cozy homes and neighborhood buildings with happy, bustling townsfolk in a wintry setting. Sales were encouraging, so Department 56, Inc. decided to develop more *Snow Village* pieces to add to their 1978 line.

Word of mouth and consumer interest helped Department 56 realize *The Original Snow Village* collection would continue. Already there were reports of collectors striving to own each new piece as it was introduced.

By 1979, the Department 56, Inc. staff made an important operational decision. In order to keep *The Original Snow Village* at a reasonable size, buildings would have to be retired from production each year to make room for new designs. Being new to the world of collectibles, they did not realize the full impact of this decision. Collectors who had not yet obtained a retired model would attempt to seek out that piece on the secondary market. This phenomenon has led to reports that early *Snow Village* pieces may be valued at considerably more than their original issue price.

Today, as in the past, the Department 56 architects continue to keep the Village alive by bringing collectors new techniques and new materials, all of which result in an exciting array of buildings and charming accessories.

The Heritage Village Collection®
From Department 56, Inc.

Love of holiday traditions sparked the original concept of *The Heritage Village Collection*. When decorating our homes, we are often drawn to objects reminiscent of an earlier time. Holiday memories wait, hidden in a bit of wrinkled tissue or a dusty box, until that time each year, when rediscovered, we unpack our treasures and are magically transported to a beloved time and place.

The first *Heritage Village* grouping was *The Dickens' Village® Series* introduced in 1984. Extensive research, charming details and the fine hand-painting of the seven original porcelain shops and "Village Church" established them as favorites among collectors.

Other series followed with the introduction of *The New England Village®*, *The Alpine Village©*, *Christmas In The City®*, *The Little Town of Bethlehem©*, *The North Pole©*, and in 1994, *The Disney Parks Village Series*. Each of these ongoing collectible series has been researched for authenticity and has the same attention to detail as the original Dickens' Village.

As each of the villages began to grow, limited edition pieces were added, along with trees, street lamps, and accessory groupings to complete the nostalgic charm of each collection. Each lighted piece is stamped in the bottom with its designated series name, title, year of introduction, and Department 56, Inc. logo to assure authenticity.

Each model is packed in its own individual styrofoam storage carton and illustrated sleeve. A special compartment in the boxing of all lighted pieces holds a UL-approved switched cord and bulb. This method not only protects the pieces during shipping, but also provides a convenient way of repacking and storing the collection for many years.

Each grouping within *The Heritage Village Collection* captures the holiday spirit of a bygone era. *Dickens' Village*, for instance, portrays the bustling, hearty and joyous atmosphere of the holidays in Victorian England. *New England Village* brings back memories of "over the river and through the woods," with a journey through the countryside.

The *Alpine Village* recreates the charm of a quaint mountain town, where glistening snow and clear lakes fed by icy streams dot the landscape. *Christmas In The City* evokes memories of busy sidewalks, street corner Santas, friendly traffic cops and bustling crowds amid cheery shops, townhouses and theaters.

In 1987, Department 56, Inc. introduced *The Little Town of Bethlehem*. The unique 12-piece set reproduces the essence of the birthplace of Jesus. This complete village scene continues to inspire and hearten those who celebrate Christmas everywhere.

In 1991, Department 56, Inc. presented *The North Pole Series*. The brightly lit *North Pole* buildings and

Santa and his reindeer are charmingly portrayed in these whimsical figurines, "To His Team He Gave a Whistle" and " Sleigh Full of Toys and St. Nicholas Too," from the All Through The House *series.*

accompanying accessories depict the wonderful Santa Claus legend with charm and details that bring childhood dreams to life for the young and the young-at-heart.

In 1994, *The Disney Parks Village Series* became the newest addition to *The Heritage Village Collection*. Replicas of Disney theme park buildings are accompanied by Mickey and Minnie Mouse, along with other coordinated accessories. This new line has caught the eye of Department 56 collectors and Disney fans alike.

Celebrate *Snowbabies*® and Other Department 56 Favorites

Another collectible series from Department 56, Inc. is *Snowbabies©*. These adorable, whimsical figurines have bright blue eyes and creamy white snowsuits covered by flakes of new-fallen snow. They sled, make snowballs, ride polar bears and frolic with their friends. Since their introduction, *Snowbabies* have enchanted collectors around the country and have brightened the imagination of all of us who celebrate the gentle play of youthful innocence.

Each of the finely detailed bisque porcelain collectibles, with hand-

painted faces and hand-applied frosty bisque snow crystals, is complete in its own gold foil stamped storybook box.

In 1989, a line of pewter miniature *Snowbabies* was introduced, to the great delight of collectors of miniatures. These tiny treasures are made from many of the same designs as their bisque counterparts, and come packaged in little white gift boxes sprinkled with gold stars.

Every year, new *Snowbaby* friends are introduced in these very special collections.

In addition to *Snowbabies* and the Villages, several other series have caught the loyal Department 56 collectors' fancy.

Winter Silhouette™ is a collection of highly detailed white porcelain figurines, many with pewter, silver, gold or red accents. *Winter Silhouette* has an elegant simplicity that brings back Christmas visions of family pleasures in a bygone era.

Introduced in 1991, *Merry Makers*® are chubby little monks dressed in dark green robes. Standing just under four inches tall, each of these delightful friars is handcrafted of porcelain, and hand-painted. They work, play and sing together in happy harmony.

The year 1991 also saw the beginning of another new series, *All Through The House*®. Featuring backdrops and furniture, as well as figurines, these highly detailed pieces

"Lift me Higher, I Can't Reach" (left) and "Stringing Fallen Stars" represent the Snowbabies *collection of finely detailed bisque porcelain collectibles with hand-painted faces and hand-applied frosty bisque crystals.*

The proper Edwardian Bears, "Nanny Maybold & Baby Arthur," are part of the delightful Upstairs, Downstairs Bears *series.*

offer warm, nostalgic memories inspired by the activities they portray. Made of cold cast porcelain and beautifully hand-painted, this charming collection celebrates family traditions *All Through The House.*

In 1994, a new collectible series was introduced called *The Upstairs, Downstairs Bears™*. Once upon a time...there was a household of proper Edwardian Bears. They resided in a large stately townhouse at Number 49 Theodore Square. Some of the bears lived Upstairs and some of the bears lived Downstairs. From the original designs by Carol Lawson, the well-known English illustrator and author, each of these enchanting, hand-painted resin bears are presented on mahogany bases with porcelain bottom stamps.

Snowbunnies™ are the latest introductions from Department 56, Inc. *Snowbunnies* collectibles are made of creamy bisque porcelain with delicate touches of pink on their ears and on the springtime bows tied around their necks. Their little bunny suits are covered with tiny bisque crystals, and their small cheerful faces are hand-painted with care. *Snowbunnies* are sure to hop into the springtime hearts of collectors everywhere.

Collectors Discover the Wide Range of Department 56, Inc. Creations

In addition to the popular collectibles already mentioned, Department 56, Inc. continues to develop colorful and innovative giftware, as well as ongoing lines for Spring and Easter, Christmas Trim, and many beautiful Christmas ornaments.

Seldom does a firm win the attention and loyalty of collectors as quickly as Department 56, Inc. has done since its first *Original Snow Village* buildings debuted in 1977. As one enthusiast stated, "A company can't make an item collectible. People have to make it collectible, and the people have discovered Department 56."

Department 56, Inc.
P.O. Box 44456
Eden Prairie, MN 55344-1456
(800) 548-8696

COLLECTORS' TOUR

One Village Place Showroom Tour
6436 City West Parkway
Eden Prairie, MN 55344
(800) LIT-TOWN (548-8696)

Reservations required. Call for further information.

Admission Fee: None

Collectors are greeted by staff members and are guided through historical displays of *The Original Snow Village, The Heritage Village Collection* and *Snowbabies,* plus a look at all the current giftware produced by Department 56, Inc.

WALT DISNEY CLASSICS COLLECTION
The Magic of Disney Welcomes
the *Enchanted Places* Series

For more than 60 years, generations of moviegoers have grown up with a host of memorable Disney characters that seem a part of life. Everyone can recall the innocence and wonder of Bambi and his woodland friends. There's the artistic brilliance of *Fantasia*, with its Cupids, Centaurettes and Mushroom Dancers filling the screen. Cinderella found her Prince Charming and lived happily ever after. Audiences soared with Peter Pan on his adventures with the villain Captain Hook and the tick-tocking crocodile. And, of course, Mickey Mouse always makes everyone smile.

The *Walt Disney Classics Collection* brings a new dimension to these beloved characters, places and scenes that have warmed the hearts of children and adults. First introduced in 1992, the award-winning collection has its roots in animation with its more than 40 fine sculptures based on animated Disney films. With the Collection, Disney's cast of characters

"White Rabbit's House," an animation art sculpture from Disney's Enchanted Places, *perfectly duplicates the unique color combinations, asymmetrical lines and flamboyant detail of the famous scene from* Alice in Wonderland. *The suggested retail price is $175.*

has gone from the big screen and into the homes of collectors around the world.

"Moments are what a film is essentially made of," said Roy E. Disney, vice-chairman of the board for The Walt Disney Company. "The notion that you can recreate some of those as a sculpture is pretty spectacular. The *Walt Disney Classics Collection* does this so well that the lifelikeness and believability of these pieces will catch your imagination and earn your affection like the original screen versions."

Disney Launches
Enchanted Places Series

While millions have been touched by the warmth and charm of the Disney characters, many have also been intrigued by the imaginary worlds in which they live — worlds that were brought to life through the beautiful background art found only in Disney animation.

For the first time, these unforgettable film settings have been captured in a unique collection of fine animation art sculptures called *Disney's Enchanted Places*. Each handpainted sculpture is a work of art, replicating the look, mood and style of the original background art used in the film.

The design and use of backgrounds have changed dramatically over the years. They have gone from flat, simple layouts to elaborate scenes of make-believe places such as the zany White Rabbit's House in *Alice In Wonderland*, Gepetto's Toy Shop in *Pinocchio* or the ominous Cave of Wonders in *Aladdin*.

The first three *Enchanted Places* sculptures, released in the summer of 1995, were "The Seven Dwarfs'

Cottage" from *Snow White and the Seven Dwarfs*, "White Rabbit's House" from *Alice in Wonderland*, and "Woodcutter's Cottage" from *Sleeping Beauty*. Collectors are invited to register their sculptures to receive an official "property deed" signed by the animated owners.

"It's really quite astonishing that all the wonderment of these beautiful film settings has been recreated on such a small scale with the *Enchanted Places* collection," said John Hench, Disney artist and guiding spirit behind the creation of the series. "The richness of detail in the three-dimensional sculptures could never be replicated in the two dimensions of a picture."

Turning Two-Dimensional
Artwork Into Three-Dimensional
Works of Art

Walt Disney himself felt the use of backgrounds was key to the storytelling process. He brought a variety of classically trained artists to the studio and challenged them to develop film settings that would enhance the dramatic quality of the film. They sought this inspiration from a variety of resources including countless books, illustrations, architectural designs and locations worldwide.

To fully capture the rich detail found in these style-setting backgrounds, *Enchanted Places* artists study original layout drawings, paintings and the films themselves. They must also understand proper scale and envision unseen angles and viewpoints like the back of the "Seven Dwarfs' Cottage." It's this type of in-depth research and knowledge that enables Disney artists to transform these two-dimensional masterpieces into three-dimensional works of art.

Each *Enchanted Places* sculpture is originally sculpted in clay, then cast in a mixture of alabaster, marble and resin,

The Walt Disney Classics Collection introduces Disney's Enchanted Places, recapturing the charm and magic of original film settings. "Woodcutter's Cottage," from Sleeping Beauty *features detailed painting techniques that convey textures as varied as weathered wood and damp moss. The suggested retail price is $170.*

which is specially formulated to capture even the most minute detail. Small props such as the Dwarfs' picks, axes and shovels are cast individually in fine pewter then carefully hand-painted to enhance each sculpture, giving it that extra Disney touch.

Painting is one of the most complex and challenging parts of the creative process. Artists must treat each sculpture as a three-dimensional painting, using both oil and water colors and blending and shading to create the illusion of light, shadow and special textures such as weathered wood or old brick.

Because of this unique painting process, no two sculptures are exactly alike, which is why each piece is hand-numbered. They can evoke fond childhood memories and give everyone the chance to revisit some of the most magical places that until now only existed in fairy tales.

Walt Disney *Classics Collection* Recreates Disney Favorites with Perfection

Just as Disney artists painstakingly ensure perfection in the *Enchanted Places* series, each exquisite piece in the entire *Walt Disney Classics Collection* goes through several challenging processes to create a new genre — the animation art sculpture.

"It's a frozen moment in the duration of a Disney film," said Andreas Deja, a Disney animator. "We probably all experience scenes in these films we wish could go on longer, but of course they don't because they're telling a story and they have to move onto the next story point. That's the language of the film. What the *Classics Collection* does is hold it for you. If you have one of those moments in front of you interpreted in three dimensions as a sculpture, it is a whole new experience, and you come to appreciate the beautiful design, color and life of these characters."

Artists begin by going back to the original animation and studying original film references, sketches, painted cels, production drawings and video prints. From these, they select which

magical storytelling moments to recreate such as Bambi meeting the little skunk named Flower or Donald Duck admiring Daisy's photograph. Through the use of Disney animators, each piece features specific designs to help convey the character's personality whether it's Goofy's flying ears and off-balance stance from *Symphony Hour* or the dancing pigs from *Three Little Pigs*. The sculptures are then painted using the same color palette as the original film. Captain Hook's vibrant appearance as he lunges for Peter Pan requires 30 colors and multiple kiln firings to make the original film hues.

Finally, animators always stretch to add that extra touch for believability — known at Disney as "plussing." The *Classics Collection* continues that tradition by uniquely combining the porcelain with materials such as blown glass, crystal or platinum to further the Disney "illusion of life."

"We learned as we began developing the *Walt Disney Classics Collection* that Disney really could bring magic to porcelain by applying the same principles we apply to animation, to our theme parks, to all the other things that Disney is known and loved for," said Susanne Lee, vice president of

Created by Disney artists with the utmost attention to detail and authenticity, "Snow White and the Seven Dwarfs" is among the memorable scenes from the Walt Disney Classics Collection.

The second in the American Folk Heroes *series created exclusively for Walt Disney Collectors Society members, "Slue Foot Sue" twirls her lasso as she rides a giant catfish down the river. The scene recreates the moment Pecos Bill first laid eyes on her. The suggested retail price is $695.*

Disney Collectibles.

The backstamp on each sculpture includes Walt Disney's signature logo, the name of the film and a special symbol to denote the year in which the piece was produced. Each piece also comes with a special Certificate of Authenticity signed by Roy E. Disney.

Limited Edition Collectibles Bring Back Memories

Within the Collection are special hand-numbered limited editions, annual editions and anniversary commemoratives that have become sought after by collectors. Among the most popular limited edition sculptures are "He Can Call Me A Flower If He Wants To" from the *Bambi* scene, "A Lovely Dress For Cinderelly" from the *Cinderella* scene, "Who's Afraid of the Big Bad Wolf?" from the *Three Little Pigs* scene and "A Firefly, A Pixie! Amazing!" from the *Peter Pan* scene.

The collection also features many scenes and characters that have never been portrayed in three dimensions, including Clarabelle Cow and Horace Horsecollar from *Symphony Hour* and Mickey and Minnie in the "rubber hose" animation style from the early black-and-white cartoon short *The Delivery Boy*.

Sharing the Magic with the Walt Disney Collectors Society

In 1993, the Walt Disney Collectors Society was launched to further celebrate the beauty of these animated sculptures and support the Collection. It's the first Disney-sponsored membership organization for collectors and Disney enthusiasts.

Members receive many benefits including a membership gift, which in past years has featured sculptures of Jiminy Cricket, the Cheshire Cat and Dumbo. Society members also have the special opportunity to acquire exclusive pieces, including those in the *Holiday Ornament, Animator's Choice* and *American Folk Heroes* series.

The third annual *Animator's Choice* sculpture brought back Cruella De Vil, everyone's favorite villainess from *101 Dalmatians*. Past characters in the series have included Donald Duck as "Admiral Duck" in *Sea Scouts*, and Mickey Mouse as "The Brave Little Tailor."

The second in the *American Folk Heroes* series was "Slue Foot Sue," the one true love of Pecos Bill, which was the debut sculpture. In 1995, the Society announced its first offering from the *Holiday Ornament* series. The ornament portrays Dumbo as he splashes in his first bath.

To join the Walt Disney Collectors Society, collectors can visit a Walt Disney Classics Collection dealer or call (800) WD-CLSIX.

The Walt Disney Company
500 South Buena Vista Street
Burbank, CA 91521-6876
(800) WD-CLSIX (678-6528)
Fax (818) 842-6039

COLLECTORS' CLUB

Walt Disney Collectors Society
P.O. Box 11090
Des Moines, IA 50336-1090
(800) 678-6528

Annual Dues: 1 Year – $55.00 for 1 Year; 2 Years – $99.00
Club Year: January-December

Benefits:
- Membership Gift: Disney Sculpture
- Redemption Certificate for Members-Only Figurine and Ornament
- Quarterly Magazine, *Sketches*
- Hard-bound Folio
- Personalized Membership Card
- Cloisonne Membership Pin
- "Newsflashes," Mailed to Members Announcing Special Events or Figurines

DUNCAN ROYALE

Bringing Santa Claus and a World of Fine Collectibles into the Hearts of Collectors

Back in 1983, Duncan Royale re-introduced Santa Claus to the world. But it wasn't simply the familiar jolly St. Nick with a flowing white beard, round belly, rosy cheeks, red coat and a team of reindeer waiting for the Christmas Eve adventure. The company's *History of Santa Claus Collection* retraced the origins, personalities and folklore surrounding this famous symbol of the holidays and good will.

For Duncan Royale, the rest is also history. The popular collection took the collectible market by storm and prepared the way for the company to launch other lines. Today, Duncan Royale offers hundreds of collectible pieces portraying everything from angels to "Little Rascals" characters and jazz musicians to clowns.

Under the leadership of Catherine Duncan, the company promises to con-tinue its growth while still celebrating the many faces of Santa Claus and the holiday season.

Santa Series Delivers Magic for Duncan Royale

For more than a decade, Duncan Royale has been manufacturing limited edition cold cast porcelain figurines. It began with the *Santa I Collection*, which included 12 different Santas from around the world. Through extensive research, artists uncovered literature, history and mythology regarding Santa Claus, all of which influenced the present-day notion of St. Nick.

This research appears in a beautiful hard-cover book with the history of each Santa figurine for everyone to read about. The full-color book was so popular that it went to many printings, even after the collection was retired and sold out. The collectors of *Santa I* have enjoyed an average increase as high as any on the secondary market. The Nast Santa has sold for more than $5,000 yet originally retailed for only $90.00.

The Duncan Royale line now boasts *Santa II and III, Christmas Images, The History of Classic Entertainers* (retired with limited availability), *Masks of the Clown* (retired with limited availability), *The Early Americans, Ebony* collection, *Jazz Man, Buckwheat Collection, Jubilee Dancers, Ebony Angel, Greatest Gift ... Love, Family & Friends, Calendar Secrets* (retired with limited availability), and *Woodland Fairies*. Many lines are available in 18", 12" and 6" sizes while others appear on full-size and 3 1/2" mini plates. *Santa I and II* have been produced as Christmas ornaments.

Diverse Lines Join Santa Claus

In 1987, Duncan Royale introduced the *History of Classic Clowns and*

"Auguste" is known to be a fun-loving, whiteface clown. In the History of Classic Clowns and Entertainers *collection, the comical character shows exactly why he found a target for his pranks and often became a scene stealer.*

Entertainers. This 24-piece collection chronicles the evolution of clowns and entertainers during the past 4,000 years — from Greco-Roman times through the 20th century with Bob Hope. A beautifully illustrated, hard-cover collector's book, *History of Classic Clowns and Entertainers*, puts in writing the memorable stories of these endearing champions of comedy who made everyone laugh.

One of the most delightful Duncan Royale inventions in the late 1980s was the *Woodland Fairies* series: a group of delightful characters capturing the antics of magical forest folk. Each character bears the name of a favorite tree or flower, including "Cherry," "Mulberry," "Apple," "Sycamore" and "Almond Blossom."

Calendar Secrets depicts the celebrations, traditions and legends of the 12 months of the year. They also illustrate the history of each month of the Roman calendar as the secrets unfold. To complement this magnificent col-

In Greece, St. Basil's Day — also known as New Year's Day — is the time for exchanging gifts. Highly honored by the Greeks, "St. Basil" is considered the gift bringer and now appears in the Santa III *collection.*

lection, Duncan Royale has introduced a *Calendar Secrets* book, colorfully illustrated and filled with historical information and the lore behind how our calendar was formed and how the months were named. The collection is now retired, but some figurines are still available at stores nationwide.

America is a "new" country at just over 200 years of age. Since today's professionals enjoy learning about their counterparts of the past, Duncan Royale captured the essence of colonial careers in *The Early Americans*. Each individual honored in a limited edition figurine was selected for outstanding skills, as well as the ability to use imagination and humor to pave the way for others. The occupations include fireman, salesman, doctor, storekeeper, secretary and lawyer.

Inspired by the "Little Rascals" character from the famous "Our Gang" comedies, the *Buckwheat Collection* shows the renowned youngsters in a variety of popular poses and activities. Crafted by hand and painted in many bright colors, the figurine scenes show *Buckwheat* making a mess of his painting chore, smiling for the camera, and sitting beside his dog with the trademark bull's-eye marking.

Collections Celebrate African-American Culture

The *Ebony* collection was created in tribute to African-American life, accomplishments and culture. This heritage has become one of the strongest building blocks of American society as we know it today. The musical forerunners of Soul, Gospel, Rock n' Roll, Blues and Jazz are deeply imbedded in Black American culture. The *Ebony* collection highlights numerous compelling personalities from these diverse musical "roots." Each figurine is individually numbered with an edition limited to 5,000 pieces. These endearing characters are sure to be treasured by collectors for years to come.

Another African-American collection is *Jubilee Dancers*. The collection spotlights energetic African dancers in colorful, traditional garb. Among the most recent introductions is "Bliss," a wedding couple celebrating the joyous bond of marriage. Limited to 5,000 pieces, "Bliss" is hand-painted and individually numbered. The other five figurines in the grouping are: "Lottie," "Lamar," "Fallana," "Keshia" and "Wilfred."

Family and Friends is the latest addition to the ongoing Ebony collection. Premiering the *Family and Friends* collection are five delightful figurines which depict a family on a picnic. "Millie" and "Agnes" are two friends sharing a lively conversation. In "Daddy," a father holds up a baby, while "Mommy and Me" shows a mother and daughter playing ring-around-the-rosie. A darling baby and his best friend, a large shaggy dog, look into a picnic basket in "Lunchtime." Each figurine in the series, created from an original sculpture by talented artist Shelley Tincher Buonaiuto, is hand-painted, individually numbered and limited to an edition of 5,000 pieces.

From the Jubilee Dancers *collection, "Lottie" shows off her traditional African-American dress and a wide smile. The highly detailed and colorful figurine stands about 12" tall.*

New Production Process Developed For Duncan Royale Figurines

A new process for creating the cold cast porcelain figurines has been invented by Duncan Royale's director of artists, Donna Pemberton. A patent is pending on this vibrant breakthrough. Donna has been experimenting with hundreds of formulas during her tenure with Duncan Royale, and now all new lines will incorporate Donna's molds and formulas.

Each Duncan Royale collection emerges as a result of hours of painstaking research and creative production. After the theme for a collection is developed, artists sketch renderings that exemplify the theme, tradition and history of each personality. When final drawings and colors are selected, the sculptor breathes dimension and "stop-frame action" into each character, adding detail and depth as directed by Catherine Duncan.

Molds are cast from the original clay sculpture, and the porcelain figurines are produced by a cold cast process which captures minute and intricate details. Precision hand-paint-

According to Danish folklore, "Julenisse" would always leave gifts on Christmas Eve. From storybooks and traditional tales, this kind-hearted gnome is now remembered in the Santa III *collection.*

ing strokes each piece with vivid, vibrant color. On some pieces, 40 colors and shades may be used to obtain the desired hues. Each piece receives a limited edition number and its own mini book that tells a brief story about the figure. All Duncan Royale collectibles are security-packed in their own handsome gift boxes.

New Artists Add Creative Touch

Catherine Duncan recently announced the commissioning of several new artists, including Michael and Shelley Tincher Buonaiuto. The artists will each develop their own unique line of products for Duncan Royale for introduction in 1996. Catherine has worked very closely with the in-house artists and commissioned artists throughout Duncan Royale's history. She has helped create the most popular items in Duncan Royale's wide range of collectibles.

Overseeing all in-house and commissioned artists is Donna Pemberton. At the tender age of four, Donna decided to devote her life to art — which has progressed from fingerpainting to ceramics, to painting and sculpting in all mediums. Donna's original work has been commissioned and purchased by such art collectors as John DuPont, Dick Clark and Herb Albert, just to name a few.

The sculptures of Michael and Shelley Buonaiuto use an unusual combination of various clays, porcelain and stoneware in a single work of

From the new Family and Friends *collection, "Agnes" and "Millie" share the latest news and gossip during a family picnic. The figurines are created from original sculptures by artist Shelley Tincher Buonaiuto and are limited to an edition of 5,000.*

art. Collectors are drawn to this pair's work not only for the technical achievement but also the highly personal quality that gives each piece a unique life and expression.

Invitation to Join the Duncan Royale Collectors Club

For those interested in learning more about these popular artists and lines, a membership in the Duncan Royale Collectors Club will answer any questions, preview upcoming introductions and provide exclusive opportunities. Members are invited to acquire special members-only pieces

and to buy or sell Duncan Royale back issues on the exclusive Royale Exchange.

The "Royal Courier" is an informative and exciting newsletter that gives collectors news about product releases, company history, special offerings and more. Much-anticipated retirements are also announced in the newsletter.

Duncan Royale
1141 S. Acacia Ave.
Fullerton, CA 92631
(714) 879-1360
Fax: (714) 879-4611

COLLECTORS' CLUB

Duncan Royale Collectors Club
1141 S. Acacia Ave.
Fullerton, CA 92631
(714) 879-1360

Annual Dues: $30.00
Club Year: Anniversary of Sign-Up Date

Benefits:
• Membership Gift: Porcelain Bell Ornament
• Opportunity to Purchase Members-Only Figurines
• Quarterly Newsletter, "Royale Courier"
• Elegant Binder
• Membership Card
• Membership Certificate
• Catalog of Duncan Royale Limited Editions
• Free Regisration of Members' Collection

ENESCO CORPORATION
Collectibles for Every Collector

Enesco Corporation, one of the most respected names in the giftware industry, has been regarded as a leader in its field for thirty-six years. Credited with being among the most innovative and trend-setting designers and producers of fine gifts and collectibles, Enesco continues its steady growth and prominence worldwide.

The introduction of the now-famous Enesco *Precious Moments®* Collection catapulted Enesco from being a gift designer to its expanded role as a leading collectibles producer. Today Enesco has an international following of collectors with such award-winning collections as *Cherished Teddies®, Memories of Yesterday®, Small World of Music™, Treasury of Christmas Ornaments®* and many others.

Love, Caring and Sharing with the *Precious Moments* Collection

It was in 1978 that simple drawings of teardrop-eyed children evolved into The Enesco *Precious Moments* Collection. Under the guidance of Enesco President Eugene Freedman, the children with soulful expressions and inspirational titles soon became a phenomenon in the collectibles industry and are now the number one collectible in the country.

Adapted from the work of artist Sam Butcher, the *Precious Moments* Collection of porcelain bisque figurines has touched collectors with messages of love, caring and sharing. Even with his remarkable vision for the Collection, Freedman could not have foreseen the deep attachment collectors have for these teardrop-eyed figurines.

In June of 1995, Enesco launched the Century Circle Retailer program for 35 of its *Precious Moments* retailers. The new program gives consumers the opportunity to purchase exclusive, limited edition porcelain bisque figur-

ines and product from these retailers. Century Circle Retailers are chosen for their commitment to support and maintain the integrity of the Collection. They have also shown extraordinary support to the hundreds of thousands of *Precious Moments* collectors and Club members throughout the country.

For collectors to communicate, exchange information and learn more about the Collection, Enesco sponsored the Precious Moments Collectors' Club in 1981. By the end of the charter year, tens of thousands had joined. Today the Enesco Precious Moments Collectors' Club is the largest club of its kind in the world and has been honored several times as the Collectors' Club of the Year by the National Association of Limited Edition Dealers (NALED), including the 1995 Collectors' Club of the Year. The Enesco Precious Moments Birthday Club was formed in 1985 to introduce children to collectibles and is celebrating its Tenth Anniversary

As a first-time introduction, Enesco Corporation is offering two personalized figurines as part of the Precious Moments® Collection. *The figurine of a stork with a baby bear is designed to include baby's name, birth date, weight and height in pink writing for girls and blue writing for boys. The girl with birthday cake figurine can be personalized by having a name imprinted on the cake.*

during 1996. Both clubs have more than 500,000 members.

Memories of Yesterday Collection Develops Strong Following

While the *Precious Moments* Collection has flourished for more than fifteen years, other Enesco collectible lines have gained an enthusiastic collector following. Introduced in 1988, the *Memories of Yesterday* Collection is based on the work of famed British artist Mabel Lucie Attwell (1879-1965), regarded at the foremost illustrator of children in England this century.

The Collection portrays chubby-legged children of the '20s and '30s and is ranked among the country's top ten collectibles. In support of the collection, Enesco established the Memories of Yesterday Collector's Society, which officially began in 1991. In November of 1995, the Memories of Yesterday Collectors' Society celebrated its Fifth Anniversary with a Society Social.

Music, Magic and Motion with the *Small World of Music* Collection

The Enesco Musical Society also began its charter year in 1991 and supports the Enesco *Small World of Music* Collection of deluxe action musicals. More than 12 years ago, Enesco introduced the first of its action musicals by combining creativity, new technology, ambitious engineering and fine craftsmanship.

Subjects for the action musicals range from mice dancing on a grand piano to dalmatians frolicking in a fire truck, to "The Majestic," an old fashioned ferris wheel with flickering lights, motion and its own cassette deck that plays a tape of calliope music. These action musicals have earned numerous international awards and are highly sought-after throughout the world.

The Enesco Cherished Teddies® *Collection celebrates autumn with "Falling for You," a 3-1/2" figurine which features a bear sitting inside a bushel basket of leaves, holding a pin-wheel*

Cherished Teddies **Wins Worldwide Recognition**

Only introduced in 1992, the *Cherished Teddies* Collection has received international recognition from collectors and the collectibles industry. The adorable teddy bear figurines have found a special place in the hearts of collectors with their warm expressions and universal appeal.

Designed by artist and children's author Priscilla Hillman, each cold cast figurine comes with a Certificate of Adoption and its own name so collectors can "adopt" the teddy bear. Hillman's illustrations have also been recreated in the *Calico Kittens™* Collection, featuring cats and messages of love and friendship, and the *Priscilla's Mouse Tales™* Collection, which is based on well-known nursery rhymes.

On July 29, 1995, the first-ever nationwide *Cherished Teddies* Founder's Day event was held in honor of the Enesco *Cherished Teddies* Collection, the Cherished Teddies Club and the 100th Anniversary of Cherished Teddies Town, which is the imaginary town where the club bears reside.

The Enesco Cherished Teddies Club was formed on January 1, 1995, and currently has over 80,000 mem"bears" and has become one of Enesco's fastest growing clubs.

Enesco *Treasury of Christmas Ornaments* **Sponsors Collectors' Club**

With Christmas ornaments continuing as one of the fastest growing collectibles, the Enesco *Treasury of Christmas Ornaments* Collection has become a year-round collector favorite. Subjects for the extensive Collection include classic characters such as Mickey Mouse and GARFIELD as well as recognized licenses, including Disney, Parker Brothers, General Mills, McDonald's and Coca-Cola. Intricate detail, creativity and the use of familiar objects such as eyeglasses, teacups and utensils also characterize the Collection.

The popularity of the Collection resulted in the formation of the Treasury of Christmas Ornaments Collectors' Club, which began its Charter Year on July 1, 1993.

Enesco Forms Third Corporate Division — International Collections

In late 1994, Enesco formed the International Collections division as a marketing group to oversee the recent acquisitions of Lilliput Group PLC, Border Fine Arts, Otagiri Co. and Via Vermont. The division has since grown

The "Solo In The Spotlight, 1960" musical figurine recently introduced by Enesco Corporation portrays Barbie as a brunette. Limited to 2,500 pieces, this popular porcelain musical is part of the From Barbie™ With Love *collection and plays the tune "Turn Around."*

to include Calik's Artistry, Winterthur and the Elisa Collection.

Collectibles include Lilliput Lane, a collection of miniature cottages, buildings and villages, Border Fine Arts, a collection of high-quality collectible animal sculptures, and the Elisa Collection of limited edition, contemporary ceramic sculptures based on the art work of Spanish sculptor Montserrat Ribes. Via Vermont, a producer of fine art glass giftware, and Calik's Artistry, a collection of hand-blown glass ornaments, are also produced as collectible lines. Otagiri is the producer of fine giftware and home accent products, and the Winterthur Collection is home decorative accessories based on antiques in Francis du Pont's Winterthur home.

The International Collections division adds diversification to Enesco by providing a solid foundation in the home decor and home accents market.

Lucy & Me **and Other Enesco Collectibles**

The year Sam Butcher's drawings were transformed into the *Precious Moments* Collection, Enesco discovered another artist. Lucy Rigg had been making teddy bears out of baker's clay for almost ten years when Freedman decided to turn her creations into porcelain bisque figurines in 1978. The *Lucy & Me®* Collection features teddy bears dressed up as familiar subjects and objects from flowers to pizza. The charming and whimsical appeal of these teddy bears has kept the collection growing in size and popularity over the past 15 years.

Enesco began a business relationship with Disney in 1989 as a licensee for Mickey & Co. giftware. To further enhance their relationship, Enesco acquired the rights, in 1995, to produce merchandise based on the Disney movie *Pocahontas*, making this new line Enesco's largest Disney collection. Merchandise includes ceramic and resin figurines, musicals, ornaments, banks, photo frames and waterballs based on the main human characters in the story. Enesco also recently acquired the license to produce giftware based on Disney's 34th full-length animated movie, *The Hunchback of Notre Dame*, to be released in June of 1996.

Enesco's *From Barbie™, With Love* Collection features authentically reproduced nostalgic and modern Barbie porcelain plates, musicals and accessory items. The Collection includes many limited edition pieces that capture the doll's glamour, beauty, style and careers over a period of 35 years.

In addition to a talented staff of nearly 60 artists and designers, Enesco also has collectibles from such well-known artists as Karen Hahn (*Laura's Attic™*), Mary Rhyner-Nadig (*Mary's Moo Moos, This Little Piggy, Mary's Hen House*), Ellen Williams (*Sisters and Best Friends*), Walt Disney (*Mickey & Co.*), Lesley Anne Ivory (*Ivory Cats*), Kathy Wise, Ed Van Rosemalen, Warren Kimble, Carol Endres, Bush Prisby, June Somerford (*Melly & Friends*), Peter Fagan (*Pennywhistle Lane/Centimental Bears*) and Klaus Wickl (*Gnomes*).

As collectors discriminately seek new collections for lasting appeal and interest, Enesco always discovers classics and new art to meet the demand. Based on its success with the *Precious Moments* Collection and its other popular collections, Enesco will certainly be a driving force in collectibles in the 1990s and beyond.

Enesco Corporation
225 Windsor Dr.
Itasca, IL 60143
(708) 875-5300
Fax (708) 875-5858

COLLECTORS' CLUBS

Enesco Cherished Teddies Club
P.O. Box 91796
Elk Grove Village, IL 60009-9179
(708) 875-5422

Annual Dues: $17.50
Club Year: January 1-December 31

Benefits:
• Membership Gift: Symbol of Membearship Figurine
• Opportunity to Purchase Two Membears Only Figurines
• Newspaper, *The Town Tattler*
• Key to Cherished Teddies Town Lapel Pin
• Membearship Certificate
• Decorative Easel

Enesco Precious Moments Birthday Club
P.O. Box 689
Itasca, IL 60143-0689
(708) 875-5411

Annual Dues: $20.00 for One Year — $38.00 for Two Years
Club Year: July 1-June 30

Benefits:
• Membership Gift: Symbol of Membership Figurine
• Opportunity to Purchase Members Only Porcelain Bisque Collectibles
• Newsletter, "Good News Parade"
• Personalized, Ready-To-Frame Certificate of Membership
• Personal Happy Birthday Card

Enesco Precious Moments Collectors' Club
P.O. Box 1466
Elk Grove Village, IL 60009-1466
(708) 875-5411

Annual Dues: $27.00
Club Year: January 1-December 31

Benefits:
• Membership Gift: Symbol of Membership Figurine
• Opportunity to Purchase Members-Only Figurines
• Newsletter, "The GOODNEWSLETTER"
• Official Binder   • Membership Card
• Official Gift Registry   • Special Mailings
• Full Color Pocket Guide to The Enesco *Precious Moments* Collection
• Precious Moments Collectors' Club Cookie Cutter
• Invitations to Local and Regional Chapter Conventions

Enesco Treasury of Christmas Ornaments Collectors' Club
P.O. Box 773
Elk Grove Village, IL 60009-0773
(708) 875-5404

Annual Dues: $20.00
Club Year: January 1-December 31

Benefits:
• Membership Gift: Symbol of Membership Ornament
• Opportunity to Purchase Members-Only Ornaments
• Newsletter, "Treasured Times"
• Personalized Membership Card
• Collectors' Guide to the Treasury Collection
• Complimentary Lapel Pin for Renewing Members

Memories of Yesterday Collectors' Society
P.O. Box 245
Elk Grove Village, IL 60009-0245
(708) 875-5799

Annual Dues: $22.50
Club Year: January 1-December 31

Benefits:
• Membership Gift: Symbol of Membership Figurine
• Opportunity to Purchase Members-Only Offerings
• Quarterly Newsletter, "Sharing Memories..."
• Personalized Membership Card   • Gift Registry
• Set of Exclusvie Stationery
• Exclusive Brooch for Renewing Members

ERTL COLLECTIBLES

World-Renowned Collectible Manufacturer
Has Its Roots in the Family Basement

Fred Ertl, Sr. was an out-of-work journeyman molder who turned a hobby into a way of life. The Dubuque, Iowa, native enjoyed making toy tractors in the basement furnace for his children. In 1945, Fred secured the rights from a few farm equipment manufacturers to produce die cast metal replicas of their tractors. Fred formed the tractors from molten war surplus metal in crude sand molds. His wife, Gertrude, painted them, and their children put them together. Ertl's hard work earned him a reputation as a skilled craftsman of quality products, as well as more clients. When the production load became too large for the family basement, Ertl purchased a manufacturing plant in his hometown, which he soon outgrew. In 1959, Fred Ertl, Sr. moved production to a newly built facility 30 miles west in Dyersville, Iowa, where the company continues to prosper.

Today, The Ertl Company has grown far beyond the confines of the Ertl family basement. Headquartered in Dyersville, Iowa, Ertl now occupies administrative and production facilities of nearly a half million square feet. Ertl is an international firm with manufacturing plants in Mexico and the people's Republic of China, sales offices in Canada and the United Kingdom, and a Far East procurement office in Hong Kong. The Ertl Company spans the globe, utilizing modern facilities and high-tech equipment, making them the unchallenged, world-leading manufacturer of die cast collectibles.

Renowned Rural-Life Artist Finds His Roots as an Inspiration

At the same time that Fred Ertl, Sr. was starting his fledgling company, Lowell Davis was discovering that he had a gift as an artist. Under his grandfather's guidance, Lowell began to draw, and under the guidance of Red

Oak, Missouri's old-timers, he began to whittle on the porch of the family's general store. The little town began to fade away like so many other "Red Oaks" in America, and Lowell joined the hordes looking for the good life outside the imagined walls of their town. He spent some time in the Air Force, then at Kansas State University at Pittsburgh, and then 13 years at an ad agency in Dallas, Texas, but nothing felt like home. So he and his wife, Charlotte (Charlie), headed back to the open skies of country life, but he found that his beloved Red Oak was a mere image of its former self.

With part of their savings, the Davis' bought a run-down, four-acre farm some 20 miles down the road from Lowell's hometown. They also purchased an old feed store that they

moved to their farm and restored. As Lowell stared out at his field one day, it hit him — his farm was a blank canvas. Each time he made a little money from selling his paintings or sculptures, he would buy a few acres, or some livestock, or a building from his old hometown. After Lowell acquired his uncle's general store, his grandfather's blacksmith shop, and the gas station that sat on Route 66 at the turn to Red Oak, he realized he was reconstructing his hometown on his now 60-acre farm. The canvas was coming to life as Red Oak II, and so was Lowell's dream of returning home! Lowell Davis' Red Oak II now serves as an inspiration for his paintings and sculptures, and as an art gallery that displays real life from a time too quickly forgotten.

Just as the kitchen is the place for humans to gather, the barn is where the animals on the farm gather. Lowell Davis' "The Barn," from the Farm Country Chirstmas™ *series, is a wonderful example of Lowell's warm, whimsical style.*

This unique sculpture, from the Farm Country Christmas™ *series, depicts a fanciful turn of the pecking order. What began as a way to keep the dogs out of the cats' food, has turned into an uncommon bond between the feathered and the furry. In "Cat & Bird House," a sweet moment is captured by Lowell's keen eye.*

Ertl Collectibles and Lowell Davis: Leaders of Rural-Inspired Collectibles

Ertl Collectibles and Lowell Davis have teamed their talents to produce a vast array of rural-inspired collectibles. Lowell's unique, "home-spun" style, plus the Ertl Company's production capabilities and respected reputation as a leading manufacturer of die cast replicas, equals highly detailed, finely crafted collectibles. The rural-inspired sculptures of the inhabitants and structures that make up country life are produced in a mixed medium of die cast metal and cold-cast porcelain from the artist's originals and are masterfully hand-painted.

Return Home to a *Farm Country Christmas™*

The Holiday Season is the time to return to simpler times and appreciate the priceless little things in life; things that too often go unnoticed in the hustle-bustle world today. Rural artist and country chronicler Lowell Davis invites everyone to return home for a *Farm Country Christmas™*.

This collection of sculptured scenes portrays universally delightful slices of country life. Whether it's the fox, Ragweed, poised outside the "Silo" waiting for an unsuspecting barn mouse, Grandma down in the "Smokehouse" root cellar gathering preserves for Christmas dinner, or the horses coming to the "Barn" to feed on a freshly dropped bale of hay, each sculpture tells a story.

There are seven *Farm Country Christmas* scenes in the first series: "Silo," "Smokehouse," "Barn," "Farmhouse," "Cat & Bird House," "Dinnerbell" and "Mailbox." Each cold-cast porcelain sculpture is inspired by Lowell's FoxFire Farm™ surroundings, and his rustic irresistible style is evident in each artistic rendition. The "Farmhouse" and "Barn" scenes illuminate, warming the landscape on a chilly Christmas morning.

Collectors may display each sculpture individually, or collect all seven. Their unique base design allows the sculptures to be joined into a larger rural setting that conveys the home-for-the-holidays spirit of a *Farm Country Christmas*.

Sparrowsville™ Ornament Collection Spruces Up the Holiday Tree

Imagine snow crunching beneath your feet as you approach the 19th Century Missouri farmhouse. Through the frosty glass of Lowell Davis' window you can see a Christmas tree filled with miniature birdhouses and their resident sparrows. Lowell smokes his corncob pipe and upon seeing you in the window, leans forward in his rocking chair to beckon you in.

Accept your personal invitation to A Lowell Davis Christmas with the artist's *Sparrowsville™* Ornament Collection. Holding his winged friends in high esteem, Lowell has captured their beauty and good cheer in a collection of nine whimsical birdhouse ornaments. Among the many wonders, you'll find the red barnhouse with a stone silo in "The Hayloft" and the comfy confines of an old leather boot in "Leather Nest." The other seven in the series include: "Snowbirds," "The Smith's," "Winter Retreat," "Love Nest," "Bachelor Pad," "Home Sweet Home" and "Hearthside Manor." Each ornament features a sparrow perched upon its rustic home.

Preserving America's Rural Heritage

Ravaged by weather and neglected by time, barns across our great land have begun to decay and fall into disrepair. But through the efforts of Ertl Collectibles, *Successful Farming* magazine, and the National Trust for Historic Preservation's Barn Again! program, collectors have the opportunity to help preserve the American barn and ensure its rightful place on the American horizon.

The Ertl Collectibles *American Country Barn Series™* honors the grand cathedrals of the prairie in miniature. This significant portrayal of the American country barn is

These two beautiful ornaments, "Leather Nest" and "The Hayloft," from the Sparrowsville™ *collection, feature Lowell's favorite winged friends, the sparrow. Each piece in this series is meticulously crafted, cold cast in porcelain, and masterfully hand-painted.*

unequaled. Lowell Davis has faithfully reproduced these replicas from actual Barn Again! Merit Award winners. Four barns were released this year, with 12 tentatively slated in the series. All the barns represent regional and architectural styles nestled in the American countryside. The "Gambrel-Roofed Bank Barn" is the first issue. The actual barn, built in the 1870s, is a Barn Again! benchmark for functional renovation and restoration. The second release is the "Western Log Barn." The actual rough-hewn barn has withstood three generations of harsh Wyoming weather and hard use; a testament to the craftsmanship of yesteryear. The third release, "Victorian Barn," is a sculpture of a fourth generation dairy barn found in Illinois. Finally, the "Round Barn" is a unique replica of a barn found in Ohio. This barn is a perfect example of restoring an older farm building for new farming purposes, while sustaining its historical importance.

For each barn purchased, a portion of the profits is dedicated in support of Barn Again! efforts to ensure the future of the American barn.

Life on FoxFire Farm™

Chores must be done, yarns must be spun, and the legacy passed down on FoxFire Farm™ just like any other farm. The *FoxFire Farm™ Collectible Figurines* portray these same truths sculpted in 1/16th scale. The figurines are scrupulous sculptures of friends, family, and neighbors that have had an influence on Lowell's life.

There are four life-like figurines sculpted to either stand on their own or seated for placement on 1/16th scale Ertl die cast tractors. "Frank," one of Lowell's fondest heroes, taught the young artist how to whittle on the porch of his family's store. "Eva" is a farm wife whom Lowell feels deserves a place of honor for being a marvelous wife, mother and farmer. "Mac," the mechanic, is the epitome of the farmer; a jack of all trades. "Henry & Jimmie" are a father and son team who depict the tradition and honor of preparing the future farmer for his or her inheritance.

The *FoxFire Farm Collectible Figurines* collection also features three finely crafted figurines that come seated on specific 1/16th scale, die cast Ertl tractors. Lowell fondly remembers hearing the pop-pop of his neighbor's Johnny Popper: "Red" comes with a John Deere Model A replica. Lowell's wife had never been on a farm before they were married, let alone a tractor, but she loves to relax by working the fields: "Miss Charlotte" comes seated on a 1/16th scale Farmall 826, her favorite. Lowell has a neighbor who has sheds and sheds of tractors and is more than willing to talk about them: "Jim" comes with a replica of his pride and joy – a Ford 901.

All figurines are sold separately, and each comes with a whimsical storycard, written by Lowell, that tells why each is so dear to his heart. Their unique personalities make each sculpture in the *FoxFire Farm Figurines* collection come to life.

This is just the beginning for the two founding fathers of rural-inspired collectibles. The creative collaboration between Lowell Davis and Ertl Collectibles will continue to grow, as they bring together over 100 years of experience in the world of collectibles.

Ertl Collectibles
Highways 136 & 20
P.O. Box 500
Dyersville, IA 52040
(800) 553-4886
Fax (319) 875-5603

FFSC, INC.
The Charming Tale of *Charming Tails™*

It's all in the fun of a day in the sun as these two Charming Tails™ *characters enjoy* "The Waterslide." *The 3-3/4" tall figurine has a suggested retail price of $20.00.*

Charming Tails Characters Come to Life in a Magical World

The woodland creatures inhabiting the magical world of this collection are often found in human situations, but can never be mistaken for cartoon animals — they appear very much as they would in their forest homes. By adding equal parts of magic, mischief and innocence, Dean succeeds in giving his collectors a lovely link back to the natural ties many of us have forgotten. Mice, bunnies, raccoons, butterflies and skunks, to name a few, have come to life to tell the charming tale. A recently introduced character, Chauncey, is a charming chipmunk with just the right touch of the theater in him. It is no surprise Chauncey is currently Dean's favorite!

The creations of Dean Griff have the knack of spurring memories long forgotten and evoking emotions unique to each piece. The consideration of those qualities is key to his design process. Dean feels the true essence of "collectibility" has less to do with the mechanics of availability, but much more with the feelings the items bring to their collectors. It is his wish for people to collect the things meaningful to them, and he thanks the fans of *Charming Tails* for making the group collectible!

The Early Years of *Charming Tails*

The *Charming Tails* collection was introduced as a line of seasonal decorative products with a heavy emphasis on Autumn and Christmas themes. Mackenzie Mouse debuted as the first named character of the group. Many of the early designs were functional. Wreathes and baskets of woven grapevine became "playgrounds" for some of the collection's critters. Candleholders were also available.

Dean Griff, creator of the *Charming Tails™* collection, was the fourth of six children born to owners of a 500 acre farm in rural Oneida, New York. There could not have been a better setting for Dean to develop a lifelong fascination with and love for the natural world. While growing up, he took long walks through the nearby woods and observed with keen interest the animals who made their home there.

During his years at Stockbridge Valley Central School, a growing interest in drawing led Dean to study art rather than enroll in agricultural classes with his siblings. In 1983, at 23, he left the family farm to take a job as Assistant to the Curator of the Syracuse University Art Collection. Entries and awards for his wildlife paintings in university art shows followed, as did a small business in hand-painted, hanging ornaments, which Dean originally gave as gifts to his friends.

In 1989, Dean moved from New York to Florida to work as a set decorator for television programs and commercials. After Dean submitted a dozen introductory designs to FFSC, Inc. for consideration, more were requested — and *Charming Tails* was born.

Maxine and Mackenzie are never quite sure what will happen next, but they do know that "We'll Weather the Storm Together" in this adorable Charming Tails™ *figurine which retails for $15.00.*

Originally, the *Charming Tails* collection was divided into seasonal categories — "Easter Basket," "Spring Has Sprung," "Trick-or-Treat," "Autumn Harvest," "Deck the Halls" and "Squashville." Dimensional Greetings, originally a separate line of figurines with "greeting card" type messages and not attributed to *Charming Tails*, was introduced and sold through wider channels of distribution. The current evolution of the group has narrowed the offering to five major classifications. The *Charming Tails* group includes non-seasonal pieces and incorporates the original Dimensional Greetings line which is now distributed through the same limited channel of dealers as the rest of the collectibles. It is interesting to note that more pieces of "Greetings" will be added soon, due to the many requests received. "Easter Basket" covers the Spring season. "Autumn Harvest" captures the best of the Fall with Halloween, harvest and Thanksgiving themes. "Squashville" continues with figurines, as well as a lighted village group, and "Deck-The-Halls" rounds out the collection with unforgettable Christmas and Winter themes.

Shortly thereafter, a transition to a more traditionally collectible line began. The functional accessories were discontinued, and the first dated piece appeared in 1994 with "A Mackenzie Snowball," the annual ornament for that year. Since then, a dated annual ornament has been offered each year. Annual ornaments celebrating "First Christmas Together" and "Baby's First Christmas" are now also available.

The Collection Evolves with Exciting New Introductions

Already, many of the molds for these high-quality resin pieces have been retired. Care is being taken to keep the collection fresh and exciting. In 1996, the first pieces with specific production runs were introduced. These two pieces, "Mackenzie Building a Snowmouse" and "Sleigh Ride," sold out immediately. This year, the first numbered pieces were added to the collection. One of these is in the form of a new addition to the

"Squashville" lighted village. To add to all of this interest, a formalized Artist Appearance Program has been finalized. In addition to the trade shows, Dean will be appearing in nearly 30 retail stores for signing events.

A Bright Future for *Charming Tails*

Many things, exciting and meaning-

Mackenzie drives the "Charming Choo Choo," while Stewart enjoys his "Choo Choo Ride," and Binkey brings up the end in his adorable "Caboose" car.

ful, are planned for *Charming Tails* in the months and years to follow. The news of the introduction of a Collector's Club has already prompted hundreds of requests for additional information. The Club will be launched in January 1997 and will serve as a two-way conduit for information and ideas.

New line extensions will include *Charming Tails* pins, as well as subgroups to the classifications listed above. For instance, the *Charming Tails* group will include the new *Lazy Days of Summer* collection — one of the cutest categories ever! Over time other small groups will follow.

The long-term direction for the distribution of *Charming Tails* pivots around the retailer as much as the collector. Programs will continue to be developed and introduced to assist the retailer in anyway possible, creating a partnership of great benefit. Work continues on expanding the advertising and marketing tool package for dealers. Dean travels extensively throughout the United States, and recently Toronto, Canada, attending signing events. These events continue to astound both retailers and collectors alike with the incredible turnout of collectors and enhanced business. The sense of occasion which accompanies them provides an intimate and friendly atmosphere for the established collector and an exciting place for a new collector to become acquainted with the world of *Charming Tails.*

Whether by walking through "Squashville," or taking a ride on the "Charming Choo Choo," or just by enjoying the many everyday moments of the *Charming Tails* family, Dean Griff and FFSC, Inc. want to thank collectors again for sharing in the magic!

This delightful character can "Reach for the Stars" in the playful world of Charming Tails™, *where there's fun both day and night.*

Listen closely and you can almost hear the band playing. Hear comes the Squashville™ Christmas Parade with "Chauncey's Noisemakers."

FFSC, Inc.
13111 N. Central Expressway
Dallas, TX 75243
(214) 918-0098
Fax (214) 454-1208

FJ DESIGNS, INC./THE CAT'S MEOW VILLAGE
America's Heritage Handcrafted in Miniature

Faline Fry Jones: creator of The Cat's Meow Village™.

With her bright smile and lively personality, Faline Fry Jones makes a wonderful "art ambassador" for her own delightful *The Cat's Meow Village*™. Created by Ms. Jones, these miniature, handcrafted buildings have delighted collectors for 13 years. What's more, Faline's marvelous accessories — everything from classic "Burma Shave Signs" to a "Rubbermaid Train Car" — add historical significance and warmhearted charm to each *Village* collection.

Faline's designs were in demand from the earliest days of her business — when she developed her concept of architectural reproductions of America's past while working in the basement of her home. Local Ohio gift shops sold the collectibles as fast as she could create them! When she entered the Columbus Gift Mart, the onslaught of orders was remarkable. By the Spring of 1984, 800 dealers were carrying *The Cat's Meow Village*™ and Faline had hired 19 employees.

At first, the artist designed only fictitious buildings, but her initial attempts at creating replicas of actual buildings and historical landmarks earned great collector enthusiasm. In 1989, a new facility opened to house Faline's 130-member team of employees. Retirement of the first *Village* collectibles and the formation of the national Cat's Meow Collector's Club during that same period catapulted the *Village* into the national and international arena.

Another landmark event took place on August 9, 1993: the first-ever Cat's Meow Convention in Wooster, Ohio. Nearly 4,000 avid collectors gathered at the Wayne County Fair Grounds to celebrate the 10th anniversary of *The Cat's Meow Village*™. They viewed displays, enjoyed the Village museum, shopped in the company store, and chatted with Faline in her autograph tent, and through an auction helped raise over $9,000 for the Children's Defense Fund.

A Thriving Business Retains the "Family Touch"

As they did from the beginning, Faline Fry Jones' family members play an important part in the creation of her unique collectibles. In addition, more than 300 people are involved in producing Faline's irresistible buildings and accessories. Faline prides herself on providing opportunities for women, including numerous leadership roles, as well as opportunities to complete work at home or on "flex-time."

Even while her company grows and flourishes, Faline remains the driving force behind each design. Her camera is a constant companion when traveling, and she continues to take leads from her faithful collectors. She thrives on researching U.S. history and selects all the items in the regular product line. Casper, the famous *Village* black cat and trademark of an original Cat's Meow, appears on every piece along with Faline's signature.

Each *Village* piece travels through a painstaking, seven-stage production process which includes hand-tracing of pattern, hand-cutting, screen printing, and individual hand-finishing. Products are made from a wood medium, which proves ideal both for cutting and screen printing, and for long-term durability in display.

A Corporate Commitment to Community Service

An annual portion of the profits from the sale of *The Cat's Meow Village*™ goes to the National Arbor Day Foundation. In addition, each year Faline selects different series and donates a portion of the first year's sales to other, established charitable organizations such as the American Red Cross, Salvation Army, United Negro College Fund, National Sudden Infant Death Syndrome Foundation, and the Children's Defense Fund.

This commitment to the larger community fits with the company's corporate values, which center on a positive work environment, mutual cooperation and support, friendliness, honesty, efficiency, clarity and partnership.

Historic Buildings Highlight Recent *Village* Introductions

Architectural gems from coast to coast inspired Faline's introductions for 1995. Her *California Mission Series* will retire at the end of the year 2000 and includes the renowned church buildings: "Mission San Luis Rey," "Mission San Buenaventura," "Mission Dolores" and "Mission San Juan Bautista."

The *Mt. Rushmore Presidential Series*, the 1995 Collectors Club Edition, covers four renowned edifices: "Tuckahoe Plantation," "Theodore

Roosevelt Birthplace," "Metamora Courthouse," and "George Washington Birthplace." In addition, the Club Gift House for 1995 is "Eleanor Roosevelt House."

Series XIII of the Village pieces was one Faline was ready to skip for superstitious reasons, until she realized she could simply place two images of Casper on each piece. "You've heard the saying 'two negatives equal a positive,'" she relates, referring to the so-called "bad luck" a black cat like Casper could bring. Included in this series are replicas of eight charming "vintage" buildings from around the nation including "Hospital," "Alvanas & Coe Barbers," "Schneider's Bakery," "YMCA," "Cedar School," "Public Library," "Needleworker" and "Susquehanna Antiques." All of these items are set to retire on December 31, 2000.

Also unveiled during 1995 was an appealing *Annual Edition Collection* – each with a special paw print mark added to the building. These pieces are limited in production to the year of introduction only. They include: "Becky Thatcher House," first of four in the

Mark Twain's Hannibal Series; "Creamery Bridge," first of four in the *Covered Bridge Series;* "Sideshow," first of four in the *Circus Series;* and John Coffin House, first of four in the *Martha's Vineyard Series.*

Wonderful Victorian homes in the *Daughters of the Painted Ladies Series* were introduced April 1, 1995 to retire at the end of the year 2000. They include: "Barber Cottage," "Hall Cottage," "The Painted Lady" and "The Fan House." From the *Historic Nauvoo Series* – focused on the restored village of Nauvoo, Illinois – come these Village beauties: "Cultural Hall," "J. Browning Gunsmith," "Printing Office," and "Stoddard Home & Tinsmith." Introduced June 1, 1995, these four pieces also will retire on December 31, 2000.

The *Shaker Village Series* offers the "Great Stone Dwelling," "Meetinghouse," "Trustees Office" and "Round Barn," while the *Bed and Breakfast Series* combines "Kinter House Inn," "Southmoreland," "Victorian Mansion" and "Glen Iris." All will be available until retirement at the end of the year 2000.

A *New York Christmas Series* – available only from June 1, 1995 until December 31 of the same year – includes "Clement C. Moore House," "Fulton Market," "St. Marks-In-The-Bowery," and "Fraunces Tavern." Also on the Christmas theme are a series of ornaments available during that same limited time period in 1995: "Yaquina Bay Light," "Holly Hill Farmhouse," "Carnegie Library," "Unitarian Church," "St. James General Store," and "North Central School."

New accessory pieces introduced at various points throughout 1995 all are slated to retire on December 31, 2000. They add a great deal of ambiance and charm to a home display of *Village* pieces, and they include everything from trees, railroad cars and mission bells, to fences, signs and ball players.

A "surprise" release in mid-1995, the *New Life Celebration Series*, offers collectors the added attraction of personalization for certain *Village* pieces. In addition, many popular *Village* issues introduced since 1990 are still available from dealers or are only recently retired.

Collectors Are Warmly Invited to "Join the Club"

The Cat's Meow Collectors Club is one of the fastest growing collectors clubs in the country with more than 35,000 members in the first five years of its existence. Its exclusive Club pieces already have exhibited strong secondary market growth as well. Weekly, Club personnel receive approximately 500 letters and answer about 100 phone calls from members across the country.

New members pay an enrollment fee of $25.00, for which they receive a Free Club Gift House, Free Club Logo Gift, a Membership Card, Club Notebook with color product sheets for the year, a subscription to "The Mews" Club Newsletter, a subscription to the "Village Exchange" with secondary market information, and access to the Custom Search program featuring custom designs. Renewing members pay $22.00 per year for the same benefits. Canadians and individuals

Series XIII of The Cat's Meow Village™ features two black Caspers (the Cat's Meow trademark cat) on each building. Introduced in 1995, these pieces will retire at the end of the year 2000. They include: (top row, left to right) "Cedar School," "Schneider's Bakery," "Needleworker," "YMCA," and (bottom row, left to right) "Hospital," "Susquehanna Antiques," "Public Library" and "Alvanas & Coe Barbers."

outside the U.S. pay $5.00 additional (American dollars only).

Cat's Meow enthusiasts enjoy a standing invitation to visit Club headquarters in Wooster, Ohio, and tour the production facilities for the *Village* collections. Tours take place each weekday Monday through Friday at 10:00 a.m. and 1:00 p.m.

A Future With International Flair

While the *Village* first won popularity in Ohio and Pennsylvania, each year brings more and more geographic diversity to *The Cat's Meow Village*™ collector family. Expansion into the West Coast is enhanced by Faline's development of buildings and accessories highlighting the West and Southwest. The firm has entered the international market, which will help boost the firm's dealer roster from the present 2,900 to nearly 4,000.

The *Village* will have new, special, one-year editions while reviving a long-time favorite: Christmas ornaments. More and more buildings featuring American heritage are in the works, and there will be future Conventions to celebrate milestones. Whatever surprises are in store for collectors, how-

The birth of Faline's daughter, Grace Elizabeth, in 1993 inspired her to create this Nursery Rhyme series, including: (top row, left to right) "House That Jack Built," "Cat & The Fiddle," "Crooked House;" and (bottom row, left to right) "Street Lamp," "Old Woman In The Shoe" and "Peter, Peter Pumpkin Eater."

ever, Faline Fry Jones and her crew promise that the charm and craftsmanship which have established *The Cat's Meow Village* will remain at the center of each new venture.

FJ Designs, Inc.
Makers of Cat's Meow Village
2163 Great Trails Drive
Wooster, OH 44691-3738
(216) 264-1377
Fax (216) 263-0219

COLLECTORS' CLUB/TOUR

Cat's Meow Collectors Club
Box 635
Wooster, OH 44691-0635
(216) 264-1377 Ext. 225

Annual Dues: $25.00 - Renewal: $22.00
Club Year: Anniversary of Sign-Up Date

Benefits:
• Membership Gift: Choice of Club Logo Umbrella or Collectors Club Accessory, "Westtown Water Tower"
• Opportunity to Purchase Members-Only Piece
• Quarterly Newsletter, "Mews"
• Subscription to the "Village Exchange"
• Membership Card
• Club Notebook
• Custom Search Program for Dealer Exclusives

FJ Designs, "The Cat's Meow" Factory Tour
2163 Great Trails Drive
Wooster, OH 44691
(216) 264-1377 Ext. 200

Hours: Monday through Friday, 10 a.m. and 1 p.m.
Closed major holidays.

Admission Fee: None

The tour of the production facilities at FJ Designs takes approximately 30 minutes. Visitors are able to watch skilled artisans produce the handcrafted *Cat's Meow Village*™ collections.

FENTON ART GLASS
A Continuing Celebration in Fine Glass

The year: 2005. The event: an extravaganza to mark the 100th anniversary of Fenton Art Glass. Today — with less than 10 years to go before this remarkable milestone — Fenton family members and artists work in a concerted effort to continue their company's rise as one of America's leading creators of collector's items.

Each year Fenton introduces new collectibles in the spirit of the company's long-standing philosophy: the production of unique glass treatments featuring the age-old techniques of handcraftsmanship, conveyed from generation to generation.

A Family of Innovative Glass Artists

The Fenton Art Glass Company was founded in 1905 by Frank L. Fenton and his brother John, in an old glass factory building in Martins Ferry, Ohio. Here, they painted decorations on glass blanks made by other firms. The Fentons had trouble getting the glass they wanted when they wanted it, and soon decided to produce their own. The first glass from the Fenton factory in Williamstown, West Virginia, was made on January 2, 1907.

One of the first colors produced by the new company was called Chocolate Glass, and in late 1907, Fenton introduced iridescent pressed glass. (Fifty years later this glass was called Carnival Glass.) Iridescent glass was still selling in the 1920s, but it was made in delicate pastel colors with very little pattern in a treatment called "stretch glass." High quality Carnival Glass now sells for as much as $600 to $4,500 a piece. Recently, a rare piece sold for $22,500.

A Perfume Bottle Brightens the Depression for Fenton

During the 1930s and 1940s, Fenton Art Glass struggled to survive the Depression and war shortages. Fenton included production of mixing bowls and orange juice reamers to keep people working, but did not hold back on developing beautiful new colors. Jade, Mandarin Red, Mulberry and Peach Blow from this period are eagerly sought by Fenton collectors today.

Fenton recovered after the Depression with the help of a little hobnail perfume bottle designed at the behest of the Allen B. Wrisley Company. The bottle business made Fenton well again and also opened new business for hobnail glass and antique reproductions of Victorian glass.

Frank and Bill Fenton Assume Leadership Roles

Between 1948 and 1949, the top three members of Fenton's original management died, and brothers Frank M. Fenton, age 33, and Bill Fenton, age 25, took over as President and Vice-President of Sales respectively. The next five years were rough ones, but then milk glass began to sell beautifully all over the country. Fenton's hobnail milk glass became the company's bread-and-butter line.

The team of Frank and Bill Fenton led the factory through significant growth for the next 30-plus years. Together they continued to develop new designs based on the flexibility and character of handmade glass.

A Third Generation of Leadership

In February, 1986, the leadership of Fenton Art Glass passed to the third generation when George W. Fenton became President. Bill Fenton is Chairman of the Board and Frank is retired, but both are at work every day as advisors. Today there are 11 family members working in the management of The Fenton Art Glass Company. With 450 employees, the company is now the largest producer of handmade colored glass giftware in the United States.

While a number of hand glass companies have closed their doors over the past 15 years, Fenton has survived and grown by continuing to be flexible, and by offering a constant stream of new products to the market.

An Array of Jewel-Like Fenton Glass Creations

Fenton Art Glass is renowned for creating beautiful and unique colors in glass. These include exotic glass varieties in rich shades such as Cranberry,

This bell, vase and basket — introduced as part of Fenton's 90th Anniversary Collection for a one-year period — combine a classic coloration called Celeste Blue with hand-painted Coralene Floral. Celeste Blue was first developed in 1921 and has not been offered in the Fenton line since the mid-1920s. The raised "Coralene" texture is achieved with ground-up glass and adds texture and dimension to each piece.

Mulberry, Opalescent and Burmese. Fenton's iridescent "Carnival" glass enjoys a history extending back to 1907, and fiery Opalescent gleams in transparent colored glass that shades to opaque white. With an appreciation of the past and an eye to the future, Fenton brings back the rare collectible treatments of bygone eras while continually developing new and exciting colors to coordinate with new decorating trends.

At Fenton, each piece of glassware is an individual creation from a skilled hand glassworker. As seasoned collectors know, only an unfeeling machine can produce "glass armies" of unvarying detail. Much of the charm of true Fenton Art Glass comes from its stretched and fluted shapes that can only be created by hand.

Like most experts, the master glassworker makes this craft appear simple. Even so, if you watch the people making Fenton glass, you will see the hundreds of appraising glances that carefully assay each piece as it passes from hand to hand. Many of the looks say proudly, "That's mine, I created it."

Fenton has its own mould shop, which enhances the company's ability to develop and introduce new designs. Patterns and designs are chipped into the cast iron moulds by hand. Many Fenton creations are painted by hand by individual artists who proudly sign each piece.

Special Fenton Offerings Intrigue Collectors

Each year, Fenton Art Glass produces new editions for several popular series which are strictly limited editions. These include the *Family Signature* series, *Historical Collection*, *Connoisseur Collection*, *Collectible Eggs*, and *Christmas*, *Valentines* and *Easter* limited editions.

The *Family Signature* series includes a few select pieces which represent the glass worker's and decorator's finest creations. Classic moulds from the past inspire the *Historical Collection* pieces, all made in unique colors and treatments. The *Connoisseur Collection* features a small grouping of art objects

made in exotic glass treatments.

For Christmas, Fenton produces an annual limited edition collection including a plate, bell, fairy light and lamp — all entirely hand-painted. For Valentines, Fenton introduces new items each year in a Cranberry Opalescent Heart pattern, as well as one to three items in the Mary Gregory style of painting. Mouthblown eggs and hand-pressed collectible eggs are showcased in Fenton's Easter offerings.

What's more, Fenton Showcase Dealers now may offer two exclusive Fenton special items each year. In 1995, the Showcase Dealer exclusives were: one additional *Family Signature* series item in Cranberry Opalescent, signed by President George Fenton; and one exclusive Burmese piece from the special *90th Anniversary* collection.

Fenton Collectors Benefit by Knowledge of Glass Markings

The Handler's Mark, Decorator's Signature, and Fenton Logo represent three markings that "savvy" Fenton collectors should know. A "Handler's Mark" — different for each craftsman — is applied to each Fenton basket by the highly skilled person who attaches the handle. The "Decorator's Signature" appears on the bottom of each hand-painted piece, and the "Fenton Logo" is placed on each piece of glass to permanently mark it as authentically Fenton.

Fenton logos vary slightly depending upon when the piece was made and what type of glass it represents. These markings help collectors to authenticate their holdings and evaluate possible purchases on the secondary market.

Clubs and Tours Enhance Fenton Collecting

Fenton invites collectors to join one or both of the national organizations formed in celebration of Fenton Art Glass. The Fenton Art Glass Collectors of America (FAGCA) was chartered in 1977. With 20 local chapters, the organization has over 5,000 current members. The National Fenton Glass Society was formed in 1990 and incorporated in Ohio in 1991.

Regular 45-minute tours of the Fenton Art Glass factory and museum take place Monday through Friday. Collectors are invited to call the Fenton Gift Shop at (304) 375-7772 for specifics on the free tours of the Williamstown, West Virginia facility.

The Fenton Tradition: Born of a Proud Glassmaking History

For three millennia, glass has delighted and served people in their homes, their industries, and their places of worship. The first industry in the American colonies was a hand glass shop started at Jamestown, Virginia, in 1608. In America, glassware reached a new zenith during the last half of the 1800s, as a newly united nation grew to its full destiny.

It is this tradition of the glassmaker's art which is painstakingly recreated in Fenton Art Glass. Now, as they approach their Centennial as a family-owned company, the Fentons take pride in the fact that Fenton glass has itself become a modern American tradition. To every beholder, Fenton handmade glass gives back a little store

Don Fenton's signature appears on this Spruce Green "Hex Vase," which features hand-painted flowers and a butterfly. Pieces like this from the Fenton Family Signature series are available for a limited time each year.

of the affection that went into its making. No gift seems quite as intimate in its ability to convey this care and regard. And to those who collect, display and use Fenton Art Glass pieces, this may be the greatest gift of all.

The Fenton Art Glass Company
700 Elizabeth Street
Williamstown, WV 26187
(304) 375-6122
Fax (304) 375-6459

The "Burmese Hummingbird Vase," part of Fenton's 90th Anniversary Special Burmese Offering, is hand-painted with gold accents, and signed by its artist. It is limited to 790 pieces.

COLLECTORS' CLUBS/MUSEUM/TOUR

Fenton Art Glass Collectors of America (FAGCA)
P.O. Box 384
Williamstown, WV 26187
(304) 375-6196

Annual Dues: $15.00 - Associate Membership: $2.00
Club Year: Anniversary of Sign-Up Date

Benefits:
• Opportunity to Purchase Members-Only Glass Piece
• Bi-monthly Newsletter, "The Butterfly Net"
• Buy/Sell Matching Service through Newsletter
• Annual Convention
• Local Club Chapters

National Fenton Glass Society (NFGS)
P.O. Box 4008
Marietta, OH 45750

Annual Dues: $15.00 - Associate Membership: $2.00
Club Year: Anniversary of Sign-Up Date

Benefits:
• Opportunity to Purchase Members-Only Glass Pieces
• Bi-monthly Newsletter, "The Fenton Flyer"
• Buy/Sell Matching Service
• Annual Convention and Auctions
• Local Club Chapters

Fenton Art Glass Company Museum & Tour
420 Caroline Ave.
Williamstown, WV 26187
(304) 375-7772

Hours: Monday through Saturday, 8:30 a.m. - 4:30 p.m.
Closed on major holidays and the first two weeks in July.
Admission Fee: Museum: $1.00 Adults: $.50 Children
                             Tour: Free

The Fenton Art Glass Museum offers examples of Ohio Valley glass with major emphasis on Fenton glass made from 1905 to 1955. A 30-minute movie on the making of Fenton glass is shown throughout the day.

The 40-minute factory tour allows visitors to watch highly skilled craftsmen create handmade glass from its moulten state to the finished product. A gift shop is also located on the premises.

FLAMBRO IMPORTS, INC.
Emmett Kelly, Jr. Was Just the Beginning...Many Collectibles Now Carry the Line "Exclusively Flambro"

When Louis and Stanley Flamm started Flambro Imports, Inc. in 1965, they had no idea how successful their business would become! Farsightedness, savvy business 'know-how' and creative thinking turned out to be the "right stuff" for Flambro, whose name has become synonymous with the word 'collectible.' Thirty years later, this company, which took off by promoting 'America's Favorite Clown' - Emmett Kelly, Jr., has expanded to include many "Exclusively Flambro" lines, and is growing internationally as well!

Flambro's Remarkable History

Initially, the Flamm brothers sold promotional merchandise used as give-aways and door-busters (loss-leaders to entice new customers into stores). At that time, many ceramic products in the U.S. were made in Japan, and of low quality. Business proved so successful, Flambro, who had been buying from other importers, decided to join the importing business themselves. They continued importing inexpensive promotional items until the 1970s when they began importing better-quality giftware from Taiwan.

During the '70s, many less expensive ceramic factories turned to Taiwan, not Japan, since the labor market could support a low-cost, high-quality product. In those days, many key employees joined other competitors or started their own factories. Instigated via a friendship between Louis Flamm and one of the top porcelain manufacturers, ten leading porcelain producers banded together to form the TTTMA (Taiwan Tao Tsu - Ceramics - Manufacturers Association) in 1978, when industry control was greatly needed. TTTMA's purpose was to cooperate in the purchase of raw materials, share technology and information and stop corporate espionage. Each factory who joined produced a different item.

Flambro was named U.S. representative of the group, and in 1980, ten additional factories joined the association.

In 1972, Allan Flamm joined his father, Louis, as a Flambro Sales Executive. In 1975, Allan was promoted to Vice President of Sales, then to Company President when Louis retired in 1982. Stanley Flamm, Allan's uncle, died in 1975. In January of 1995, Louis died, but not before seeing Flambro enter its 30th year of business.

In 1994, Flambro, under Allan's leadership, joined forces with Collectible World Studios of Stoke-On-Trent, England. This collectible firm, run by President Bill Dodd, named Flambro its sole USA distributor for their highly successful collectible lines, *Pocket Dragons* and *Piggin'*. With sales and collector club memberships growing rapidly and internationally, this alliance is proving to be a major success.

Flambro's Philosophy and a Peek at the Future

Flambro's company philosophy is to keep their collectors happy! Today, happy means knowing the collectors' ideals of high quality and reasonable price in a desirable piece of merchandise. As collector demands grow, so do Flambro's efforts to provide excellent product, promotions, sales, service and customer satisfaction. Company growth is rapid with sales up, current lines expanding and new collectibles being introduced. Many new lines are labeled "Exclusively Flambro" - another 'self-promotion' in terms of retailer and consumer recognition.

Flambro's strength has always rested with its limited edition collectibles, especially since signing its first licensing agreement with Emmett Kelly, Jr. in 1980. Today, they carry a full range of collectible merchandise. 1996 will see the addition of *Peanuts* character items and the National Hockey League.

Flambro's goal is to carry products to make and keep every collector happy!

Inspired Product Lines Attract Fans of All Ages

The *Emmett Kelly, Jr.* series, begun in 1980, was Flambro's first claim to fame! Its phenomenal success has helped early limited edition pieces soar in value on the secondary market - now worth many times their original retail price. Emmett Kelly, Jr. collectibles have expanded from the first porcelain lines and annual limited edition pieces to include newer resin series: *Real Rags*, fashioned after EKJ's famous tattered suits; *Images of Emmett*, displaying a distinct likeness to EKJ's facial features; and the *Little Emmett* line, created in celebration of EKJ's 70th birthday in 1994.

Little Emmett, a reflection of Emmett's childhood, is an adorable line that brings out the 'kid' in collectors of

"35 Years of Clowning" (left) depicts Emmett in full makeup on a regal elephant standing atop a fine wood base with brass nameplate. On the right, "Emmett Kelly Jr.'s All-Star Circus 20th Anniversary" sculpture is a masterpiece of complexity and color. Both are 1995 limited editions.

all ages. It provides a positive image for children, is of interest to parents and grandparents, and features birthday figurines from ages one to ten, musicals, bookends, vignette figurines and more. New pieces are added annually.

Pocket Dragons, part of Flambro's alliance with Collectible World Studios, is proving to be a highly-successful line. Created by nationally-known artist/sculptor, Real Musgrave, these collectibles originated from his childhood love of dragons and an interest in bringing "magic" to life. *Pocket Dragons* are mischievous and playful, with a keen desire to hide in cozy corners and collectors' pockets. Real's love for his creations is of special interest to collectors. New *Pocket Dragons* are introduced annually.

Piggin', another line Flambro distributes nationally for CWS, is a comical pig line created by English artist David Corbridge. A self-proclaimed pig lover, David designs his collection with English humor. New pieces appear annually.

Flambro Products — Something For Every Collector

From Joan Berg Victor's imagination comes the collectible Christmas villages, *Pleasantville* and *Santaville*, created exclusively for Flambro. Based on the book, *Pleasantville 1893*, this town captures the simplicity of small-town, turn-of-the-century America, inviting the collector to step back in time, meet the make-believe townfolk and enjoy their easy way of life. The village consists of vignettes: Main Street, Orchard Street, Elm Street, River Road and Balcomb's Farm, each adding to *Pleasantville's* charm.

Santaville - The Christmas That Almost Never Was, offers an enchanting look at the North Pole. This unique village, based on a poem written by Stanley Wiklinski with creative concept by Joan, takes the collector inside the working world of Santa, his elfin helpers and their critter assistants. Many pieces are created from a tree, and the buildings offer a cut-out back view of what's going on inside. "Father Christmas' Ice Castle" and the "Baby's

Toy Shoppe" are two of *Santaville's* fascinating pieces.

In 1994, Flambro created baseball collectibles, with official licensing by Major League Baseball Properties. *Major League Baseball Santa* ornaments, superbly detailed and painted, are dressed in uniforms of today's favorite teams. *The Cooperstown Collection* recreates fond memories of a bygone baseball era, and includes action-posed Santa figurines and ornaments in uniforms of yesterday's great teams, and musical waterglobes with detailed bases that play "Take Me Out to the Ball Game." Both baseball lines grow on a yearly basis, with the addition of more teams to the lists.

Great African-American baseball players, and the teams that nurtured their dreams, receive Flambro's MVP Award as The Negro Leagues *opened the 1995 season. The series includes: collectible figurines sporting authentic logos of legendary teams, ornaments, coffee mugs, baseball ornaments, magnets, lapel pins and a collector's plate.*

1995 introduced *The Negro Leagues*, a tribute to the professional African-American teams of yesterday. This series, honoring the achievements of great teams and players, includes figurines, Santa ornaments, baseball ornaments, lapel pins, magnets, coffee mugs and a multi-logo collector plate.

Fascinating new resin technology is behind Flambro's whimsical pen line, *The Pen Station*. Created by Systems

Technologies of New York, who chose Flambro as its sole sales/marketing partner in this exciting venture, the line presently includes pens and bases with Christmas, cat, zodiac, fruit, vegetable and sports designs. Patents are pending on the process alone, so more is sure to follow.

Meet Flambro's "Star Performers"

Emmett Kelly, Jr.'s earliest memories are of the circus and performing! Born in November 1924, to two circus aerialists, Emmett Kelly, Sr. and wife Eva, Emmett spent his early years traveling with his parents and the circus. As a young man, he joined the Navy. He served during World War II in the Pacific, participating in three invasions, including Okinawa and Iwo Jima.

His life as a clown began in the mid-60s. His dad decided that Emmett, Jr. should carry on the Weary Willie character he had created during the Depression. Emmett altered Weary Willie a little, added a crownless hat, and became Emmett Kelly, Jr! For many years, EKJ has provided a special joy for fans who throng to get his autograph and peek at 'America's Favorite Clown.'

Joan Berg Victor's diversified background has played a part in her creative work with Flambro. Raised in the Midwest, she earned degrees from Newcomb College, the Women's College of Tulane University and Yale University. Over the years, Joan has written and illustrated over two dozen books, many created for children. As her own children grew older, she adapted her books to their interest level. Joan's favorite book is the one on which the *Pleasantville* village is based. Her drawings and paintings can be found in private and museum collections across the country, and she has been featured in *Fortune* magazine and *The Wall Street Journal*.

Real Musgrave has always been an artist. While young, he took private art lessons. Throughout his school years, he came to realize the creative world he could produce might bring him great joy, fame and fortune. Later, he graduated with a BFA in drawing, painting and printmaking from Texas

The 1995 Pocket Dragons. *These precious tricksters are individual delights - displayed as a group, they're sheer magic.*

Tech University where he also studied sociology and anthropology. This unusual combination of science and fine art led Real to see everyday events in a "magical," whimsical way.

Real and his wife Muff developed

and marketed limited edition etchings and prints featuring the *Pocket Dragons*, wizards and gargoyles. In 1978, Muff quit her job to become Real's full-time creative partner. Real has won awards and licensed his art for greeting cards, posters, etc. His whimsical style attracted Bill Dodd, President of Collectible World Studios in England. Soon, *The Whimsical World of Pocket Dragons* was launched, with production of the *Pocket Dragon* figurines.

As creator of *Piggin'*, David Corbridge combines interests in wildlife, painting, drawing, illustrating, sculpting — and pigs! Having lived on an English farm for years, he developed a keen understanding of pigs, their personalities and idiosyncratic ways. David fondly states, "To know pigs is to love them." The dominant appeal of *Piggin'* collectibles is David's English sense of humor, displayed not only on each pig's face, but in their names as well.

Important Information About Popular Flambro Collector Clubs

Flambro sponsors several fun-filled collector clubs. The Emmett Kelly, Jr. Collectors' Society is a select group of collectors who share affection and admiration for America's favorite clown. The Little Emmett Collectors' Club — a club with the focus on children, but open to collectors of all ages — is a way to spark childrens' interest in the art of collecting. Parents and grandparents are especially welcome.

Pleasantville 1893 Historical Preservation Society is a must for true collectors of the *Pleasantville 1893 Storybook Village*, and the Pocket Dragons and Friends Collectors Club is a necessity for all lovers of these magical green characters.

Flambro Imports
1530 Ellsworth Industrial Drive
Atlanta, GA 30318
(404) 352-1381
Fax (404) 352-2150

COLLECTORS' CLUBS

EKJ Collectors' Society
P.O. Box 93507, Atlanta, GA 30377-0507
(800) EKJ-CLUB
Annual Dues: $30.00
Renewal: $15.00 for One Year
$50.00 for Four Years
Club Year: January-December
Collectors' Year: Anniversary of Sign-Up Date

Benefits:
• Membership Gift: Collectors' Plaque
• Redemption Coupon for Members-Only Figurine
• Quarterly Newsletter, "EKJournal"
• Binder
• Membership Card
• EKJ Catalog
• Toll Free Collectors' Hotline
• EKJ Lapel Pin
• Free Registration of Figurines
• Annual Collector Registry Listing
• Special Club-Sponsored Events

Little Emmett Collectors' Society
P.O. Box 93507, Atlanta, GA 30377-0507
(800) EKJ-CLUB
Annual Dues: $10.00
Club Year: Anniversary of Sign-Up Date

Benefits:
• Personalized Membership Card
• Quarterly Newsletter, "What's News with Little Emmett"
• Bookmark
• Cut-Out Color Mask
• Collectors' Catalog
• Little Emmett Activity Book
• Little Emmett Puzzle
• Toll Free Collectors' Hotline

Pleasantville 1893 Historical Preservation Society
P.O. Box 93507, Atlanta, GA 30377-0507, (800) 355-CLUB
Annual Dues: $30.00
Renewal: $15.00
Club Year: January-December
Collectors' Year: Anniversary of Sign-Up Date

Benefits:
• Membership Gift: Lighted "Pleasantville Gazette" Building
• Quarterly Newsletter, "The Pleasantville Gazette"
• Membership Card
• Collectors' Catalog
• Lapel Pin
• Toll Free Collectors Hotline
• Bisque Porcelain Christmas Ornament from the Pleasantville Coll.

Pocket Dragons and Friends Collectors Club
P.O. Box 93507, Atlanta, GA 30377-0507
(800) 355-CLUB
Annual Dues: $29.50
Two Year Enrollment: $54.00
Club Year: June 1 - May 30
Collectors' Year: Anniversary of Sign-Up Date

Benefits:
• Membership Gift: Pocket Dragons Figurine
• Redemption Coupon for Members-Only Figurine
• Quarterly Magazine, *Pocket Dragons Gazette*
• Membership Card
• Collectors' Catalog
• Lapel Pin
• Toll Free Collectors Hotline
• Invitations to Special Appearances by Real Musgrave
• Travel Opportunities to Tour Collectible World Studios in England

FORMA VITRUM

Bill Job and Forma Vitrum Give New Meaning to the Words "Beautiful Glass"

Stained glass is an elegant, timeless art form with roots in 19th century America. Brought to prominence by Louis C. Tiffany, his pioneering techniques are world renowned. From Tiffany's glass cutting methods to precise assembly techniques and wrapped-copper soldering processes, Tiffany art has delighted collectors for over one hundred years. Inspired by Tiffany and other glass craftsmen, artist Bill Job carries on their time-honored traditions. Some say he has single-handedly turned stained glass art from a "studio craft" into a contemporary collectible category.

A Tennessee native, Bill's interest in houses began as a child, spurred by his brother's architectural studies. Later, Victorian dwellings in San Francisco and Portland, Oregon, inspired him. Bill studied post and beam construction, hoping to use it to build a dream home of his own some day. His studies helped him do just that: build dream homes – thousands of them. Each is a unique and wonderful construction of stained glass, now available, and affordable for collectors around the world.

The Journey That Dreams Built

When Bill Job realized people shared his love of stained glass but few could afford it, he decided to change that. He turned to mainland China for the skilled hands and patience needed to craft affordable stained glass. Bill's studies in philosophy had already introduced him to Chinese culture, and his family was delighted at the prospect of moving abroad. As soon as he was granted permission by the Chinese government, Bill became one of the first Americans to own a company on the mainland.

By 1989, Bill's stained glass rivaled the quality and grace of Tiffany. He designed, instructed and oversaw the crafting of his ideas using American

stained glass. Believing it to be the finest in the world, Bill learned new methods of scoring, cutting and wrapping individual pieces in copper foil tape before soldering sections together. He became adroit at applying the patina required to oxidize a solder (this gives stained glass creations a look of antiquity), then applying silicon oil to seal the solder and stop the oxidation process.

Initially, Tiffany reproduction lamp shades were the company's mainstay, but Bill expanded his offerings to sun catchers, art panels and detailed little houses lit from within by a bulb or candle. The houses were favorites of Bill's family. They convinced him to test them in America. Always ready for new adventures, Bill packed his samples, rented a booth at a trade show and left China for California.

A Fortuitous Meeting with David MacMahan

At the January, 1993 Los Angeles Gift Show, interest in Bill's stained glass was keen, but not overwhelming. During a break, Bill struck up a conversation with gadget and toy promoter David MacMahan. MacMahan, an inventor of gifts that make people laugh and cope with stress, was curious about Job's creations. The moment he saw the houses, David recognized the enormous potential of Bill's designs.

The two quickly realized their business and personal outlooks were compatible, too. By show's end, a partnership was launched with a handshake. Bill would design and create. David would promote and market. The business was born when the two

picked the Latin words "forma" (beautiful) and "vitrum," (glass) as the new firm's name. Next, designs were divided into two collections: *The Vitreville Collection*, a series of structures with a "small, home-town feeling," and the *Woodland Village*, a whimsical village of houses named for animals. That accomplished, Bill returned to China with exciting news of the company's formation.

Building a Town: See How It Grows

Bill and David decided the town of *Vitreville* would be built the way small towns grew in America, beginning with homes for residents. Each structure was designed in a traditional style, reflective of people who built houses to last generations. Then, every house was named for the profession of its resident. Next, churches, lighthouses and other buildings were added. Before long, these first issues began to sell briskly! Two *Vitreville* collection

Shingled walls of 373 pieces of glass and pewter invite the world to spend a tranquil weekend at "Brookview Bed and Breakfast." Stone fireplaces, made of fused glass, look just like river rock. Only 1,250 buildings were created for worldwide distribution. This outstanding issue was sold out before the first one reached store shelves!

An Award of Excellence nominee by Collector Editions *magazine, "Thompson's Drug," created from 219 pieces of glass and pewter, features an arched entry awning and hand-numbered brass artist signature plate. Issued for worldwide distribution in limits of just 5,000, "Thompson's Drug" sold out in one year!*

designs reached landmark status a year later. In January 1994, "The Bavarian Chapel" and "Pillars of Faith" were retired after approximately 2,400 of each was produced. By March of 1994, they were completely sold out.

These days, collectors may add "Maplewood Elementary," the "Vitreville Post Office," the "Breadman's Bakery" and the award-nominated "Thompson's Drug" to their collections. *Collector Editions* magazine and the National Association of Limited Edition Dealers selected "Thompson's Drug" as a 1994 award nominee. In addition, "Brookview Bed and Breakfast," Bill's most complex work, has become a highly sought after favorite. Inspired by a house built in Oregon, circa 1892, 1,250 of these limited editions were officially sold out before the first piece shipped.

Finally, every small town in America prides itself on its houses of worship. *Vitreville* collectors may choose from "Country Church," "Community Chapel," "Tiny Town Church," "Trinity Church," and the retired "Bavarian Church" and "Pillars of Faith" to enhance collections.

Forma Vitrum Launches Two Lighthouse Collections

Americans have strong ties to our seacoasts, so Bill's next challenge was designing romantic lighthouses. The Forma Vitrum *Coastal Classics* collection includes six. "Carolina," "Michigan" and "Maine," range in complexity from 41 to 74 pieces of glass. "Sailor's Knoll Lighthouse," "Lookout Point Lighthouse" and "Patriot's Point Lighthouse" round out the current series, each constructed of finely cut sections of American stained glass.

1995 debuted Forma Vitrum's newest innovative replica lighthouse collection: *Coastal Heritage*. This limited edition series was developed under the guidance and sponsorship of the U.S. Lighthouse Society. Only 1,995 of each of the first introductions will be produced to commemorate the year this series was introduced. Every piece comes with a history of the actual lighthouse, and a 50¢ donation will be given to the Society to help with its lighthouse preservation efforts.

Bill Job's *Coastal Heritage* is a true wonder. Using techniques developed after two years of research and experimentation, the result is astonishing. No artist has ever merged so many mediums to create such exacting replicas. American glass is hand-cut and soldered with blown, slumped and fused stained glass and spin cast metals. Many of the towers are blown cylinders of glass to replicate authentic shaping and dimension. Diamond drills cut door and window openings. The incorporation of fiber optics replicates a true beacon shining from each lighthouse!

Debuting the *Coastal Heritage* collection is "Sandy Hook, New Jersey," the oldest lighthouse in the U.S. This 10" tall masterwork is limited to a worldwide edition of 3,759 (1,995 plus 1,764 symbolizing the year the real lighthouse was built). Collectors can expect yearly additions, each crafted using Bill Job's revolutionary new glass techniques!

Extra Special Touches that Make Forma Vitrum Unique

Bill tries to remain impartial about his designs, but pin him down, and he'll confess *Woodland Village* is his personal favorite. Perhaps it's because the buildings are fashioned of curvy glass, more difficult to cut than straight pieces. Maybe it's memories of designing the series with his 12-year-old daughter beside him. Whatever the reason, collectors still 'flock' to *Woodland Village*, with its quaint, animal-named houses: "The Owl House," "The Raccoon House," "The Chipmunk House," "The Rabbit House" and "The Badger House."

Woodland Village is inspired by an imaginary community of tiny people who live peacefully in a forest, free from illness and crime. Their appreciation for nature inspires dwelling names, and according to the *Woodland Village* legend, each house is so beautifully lit, villagers nap by day so they can enjoy the glow coming

Revolutionary design methods make "Sandy Hook, New Jersey," a replica of the oldest lighthouse in the U.S., one-of-a-kind. Limited to a worldwide edition of 3,759 (1,995 plus 1,764 symbolizing the year the real lighthouse was built), fiber optics help create a glowing tribute to innovation and beauty.

from their homes after dark.

Enjoy Your Collection Year-Round

Forma Vitrum collectors prize selecting lifelike accessories to compliment their villages year-round, so realistic accent pieces are a major development focus for the company. Home displays are enhanced by trees, flowers, *Vitreville* residents and 'everyday' touches like signs, benches, fences and lamp posts. Each is perfectly scaled to help collectors personalize their realistic displays.

Authentification is also important to Forma Vitrum. Before each structure is boxed, a number is inscribed by hand and Bill Job's artist signature plate is attached. Additionally, all Forma Vitrum collectibles may be registered with the company by using the form included with each design.

A Future as Bright as the Town Itself

To make sure collectors have everything they want (including the formation of the Forma Vitrum Collectors' Club in the near future and lots of opportunities to meet the artist), Bill communicates regularly with them. A quarterly newsletter, "The Vitreville Voice," broadcasts all the latest product news, and Bill puts as much enthusiasm

into his tours as he does his writings. In 1995, his appearances included California, Texas, Minnesota, Wisconsin, Iowa, North Dakota, Arizona, Oklahoma, Indiana and everywhere else he can fit into his schedule.

Whether it's the annual International Collectible Expositions or visits to some of the 2,500 shops selling Forma Vitrum art in Canada, Japan, Australia or the U.S., Bill is one of America's foremost hands-on artists, enjoying standing-room-only at personal appearances. One of the reasons Bill can be here...there...and everywhere...is the faithful hand of Forma Vitrum president David MacMahan and an energetic staff in China and stateside. Bill knows his dream is in able hands when he's out and about. The partnership he and David share is just one good reason the future looks bright.

The remainder of the credit goes to Bill's family. Cheerfully exploring a new country and culture with as much enthusiasm as the man who brought them to China, wife Kitty and daughters Patti and Christy have had the opportunity to do what few families have. They've not only witnessed a dream come true — they also helped

Knowing his vision and energy has helped make stained glass collectible art affordable for people across America is truly Bill Job's greatest joy.

make that wish a reality for someone they love and respect.

Forma Vitrum
20414 N. Main Street
Cornelius, NC 28031
(800) 596-9963
Fax (704) 892-5438

THE FRANKLIN MINT

The Franklin Mint: Excellence in Artistic Mastery Delights and Surprises Collectors with an Eye for Perfection and a Heart for Tradition

Historians have a passion for exploring the habits and passions of societies here and abroad. Their languages. Various foods. Mysterious traditions. Exotic clothing. But perhaps the most fascinating subject of all is a culture's rich artistic base. Even today, nothing fascinates social scientists more than the artifacts primitive and advanced societies covet.

Consider the wealth of treasures emerging from the past. Cave drawings. Arrowheads. Bits of carved clay mined from an earth now covered by centuries of time. Whether a shiny crystal plucked from a riverbed or the whittled symbol of luck and fortune, who can resist gathering treasures and keeping them as reminders of special places and unforgettable moments?

Our propensity for gathering and saving helps mark the stepping stones of our growth as distinct societies. Those changes are wonderfully reflected in the evolution of the artifacts we revere: Pre-Columbian carvings. Native folk art. Classic oil paintings. A heritage of decorated eggs commissioned of the famous Peter Carl Fabergé.

In every culture, collectible art has taken its rightful place — been given as gifts and beloved as keepsakes. Styles

Sixty years after it debuted, this American icon still symbolizes the wild, defiant spirit of America! Recreated in 1:24 scale, this beauty is hand-assembled, incredibly detailed, painted by hand and loaded with real moving parts! This 1032 V-8 Coupe is authorized by the Ford Motor Company and sells for an astonishing $90.

have emerged and new artisans have brought their own talents to changing and enhancing these treasures. Whether we live in a house, a hut, a tent or a castle, each memento picked for its subject matter, elegance, rarity or memory, ultimately finds a home in our heart.

A legacy for collecting memories established, let us visit a fine art studio flourishing for the past three decades called The Franklin Mint. This haven of innovation and artistry provides incomparable works of historic significance destined to become the prized heirlooms of tomorrow. The award-winning artists of The Franklin Mint use the skills of their hands and the love in their hearts to create treasures of timeless beauty . . . and endless fascination.

As the millennium approaches, these gifted artisans commit themselves to providing the world with the most extraordinary personal luxury items for today...tomorrow...and forever.

Collector Wishes Are Answered, with a Flourish, Each Time New Franklin Mint Art Debuts

The Franklin Mint is a place where dreams begin. Located deep in the heart of the historic Brandywine River Valley, The Franklin Mint is the home of some of the most talented people in the world. Artists in every discipline, designers, sculptors, jewelers, engravers, medallists, doll and model makers, work together in an environment of unlimited creative freedom and endless inspiration.

In their quest for perfection, these individuals create works of art to which few can compare. Extraordinary sculpture in porcelain, pewter, crystal and bronze. The world's finest commemorative coins and stamps. Authentic replicas of historic masterpieces. Award-winning heirloom collector

dolls. Books handcrafted in old-world tradition. Collector plates of universal appeal. Furnishings of uncompromising quality and craftsmanship for the home. The ultimate in die-cast automotive classics. Jewelry ablaze with the most precious of gems, gleaming with the richness of gold and silver. Miniature sculptures preserved under a crystal-clear dome. Classic games the whole family can share and enjoy. Acquisitions of taste, beauty and supreme artistry. Personal treasures destined to command attention and admiration.

Prestigious Organizations... Worldwide...Benefit from The Franklin Mint's Galaxy of Renowned Artists

The achievements of great artists, distinguished organizations and master craftspeople are shared with collectors around the world through the resources of The Franklin Mint. Beautiful showpieces include those from The Vatican in Rome, and masterworks from renowned art museums like the Louvre in Paris and the Victoria and Albert in London. Franklin collectors also share in the majesty of time-honored institutions with the House of Fabergé, The House of Coppini, and The Princess Grace Foundation.

In 1995, The Franklin Mint and Royal Doulton signed an agreement providing the Mint the rights to market Royal Doulton and Minton collector plates throughout the world.

Models authorized by Rolls-Royce, Mercedes-Benz, General Motors, Lamborghini and Ferrari grace The Franklin Mint list of offerings, as do works created in collaboration with important environmental causes like the World Wildlife Fund, the Humane Society and Conservation International.

Fabulous fashion classics from

Coca-Cola art...prized by collectors worldwide...created by renowned artist Haddon Sundblom. Santa and his elves sparkle beneath a 5-1/2" crystal dome which is the first of its kind, authorized by the Coca-Cola Company and available for only $37.50.

Franklin emerge in creative coalition with Bill Blass, Adolpho, Givenchy, Bob Mackie, Hanae Mori and Mary McFadden. The Franklin Mint classics of literature include famed works of award-winning authors like Norman Mailer, E.L. Doctrow, Michael Crichton and John Updike. And inspiring master-pieces, from world-renowned artists including Norman Rockwell, Andrew Wyeth, Erte and Peter Max, also intrigue Franklin collectors.

Museums and Governments Rely Upon The Franklin Mint for Commemorative Art to Celebrate Heritage and Pride

Much of The Franklin Mint's finest work involves the creation of com-memorative art — for governments, major museums, and prestigious or-ganizations on all seven continents. Commemorative partners include the United Nations, the International Olympic Committee, the Royal Geographic Society and the World Wildlife Fund.

Franklin Mint originals honor those who share the spirit of heritage and pride such as The White House Historical Association, the National Historical Society and the Western Heritage Museum. Franklin also shares in the concerns of distinguished

cultural organizations as The Kabuki National Theater, La Scala in Milan and the Royal Shakespeare Theatre.

In search of treasures from the Far East and the Wild West...from the frozen North to the deep South...from the Caribbean to the Gold Coast and from enchanted fairy tale kingdoms to the realms of royalty, The Franklin Mint scans the globe to create works of art to touch the innermost places of the heart.

The Franklin Mint Brings Alive the Forgotten Treasures of Exotic Societies for All Collectors

The Franklin Mint has never forgot-ten that the traditions of the past inspire the creations of today...and the treasures of tomorrow. Thus, from the ancient civilizations of the Egyptians and Etruscans, come new works to rival those buried for thousands of years.

From the depths of Atlantis to the gods of ancient Greece and Rome come new masterpieces of sculpture to rival those found only in the world's most prestigious museums and private col-lections. From the dynasties of the Ming to priceless works created for the Czars of Imperial Russia come porcelains of incomparable beauty and splendor.

From the masters of the Renaissance

Futuristic magic! Precision cast pieces of sterling silver and 24K gold go "Where no man has gone before," aboard the U.S.S. Enterprise for the ultimate chess chal-lenge. Paramount Pictures' authorization and authentication make this game of the future unmatched at $195.

to sparkling reflections of the New Age come treasures that speak of power, and individual achievement. From Asia's mighty warriors to America's legendary heroes come works of history, heritage and pride.

Gallery Stores Take Collector Delight to New Heights

For those collectors who prefer to see and touch things before they buy, like the Mint's beautiful "Scarlett O'Hara" or "Marilyn Monroe" dolls, The Franklin Mint has expanded its retail locations to more than 50 sites in 1995. Its retail operations allow collectors to view and hold the products they will enjoy for many, many years.

The Franklin Mint Gallery Stores were designed by renowned retail space designer Harvey Bernstein, who created a museum-style environment befitting The Franklin Mint's product line — with marble pedestals, pin-point lighting and an open floor plan.

Franklin Mint's Distinguished Collection Earns Awards... Laudits...and a Reputation for Incomparable Quality

Since its founding, The Franklin Mint has brought pleasure and enjoy-ment to millions of collectors the world over, with works of art that bring to life memorable characters that have

Doll master Maryse Nicole's first bride doll combines lush romance with splendor. "Vanessa's" bisque porcelain body is fully jointed; sapphire crystal eyes sparkle be-neath natural lashes. Gowned and veiled in shimmering white taffeta, iridescent lace, silk blooms, tulle and pearls, "Vanessa" car-ries ribbon roses and is available for $750.

touched our hearts.

These include the legendary Scarlett O'Hara and the dashing Rhett Butler from the most romantic love story of all time - *Gone With The Wind*, and Dorothy and Toto, the Tin Man, Scarecrow and the Cowardly Lion from the unforgettable *Wizard of Oz*. The Franklin Mint is also proud to offer the world-famous illustrations of Charles Dana Gibson, whose legendary Gibson Girl art set the standard of beauty at the turn-of-the-century.

Franklin also works exclusively with one of America's favorite doll artists, the beloved "Sparkle Queen," Maryse Nicole, and with some of Europe's most famous doll artists, including Sylvia Natterer and Gerda Neubacher.

Collectors enjoy timeless tributes to legends of the silver screen like The Duke, John Wayne, and with portraits that recapture the glamour of the one - the only - Marilyn Monroe. All in all,

Following the signing of their agreement, Stuart Lyon, Chief Executive of Royal Doulton and Lynda Resnick, Vice Chairman of The Franklin Mint, view historic pattern styles at Royal Doulton headquarters in Stoke-on-Trent, England and discuss joint, future projects.

a collection of works of art with a precious heritage and a never-ending future of beauty.

Nothing But the Best For Adventurous Collectors

For those driven to new heights of excitement and new levels of achievement, Franklin Mint Precision Models are simply miles ahead. These fine die-cast automotive replicas include classics from the past, like the Rolls-Royce Silver Ghost, the Mercedes Gullwing, the Ford Model-T, the Duesenberg Twenty Grand, and all-American legends like Harley-Davidson, the Petty Nascar, the Cadillac Eldorado and the Chevrolet Bel Air.

Franklin also presents Europe's elite dream machines: the fabulous Ferrari, the Porsche 911 and the Bugatti Royale. Collectors get on the fast track with The Southern Crescent, fly high with Shoo-Shoo Baby and put out fires with the Ahrens-Fox Fire Engine. In addition, there are daring innovations like the Lamborghini Countach, and America's hottest sports car, the Corvette Sting Ray.

Cartoon Legends Find Homes in the Hearts of Americans of Every Age Thanks to The Franklin Mint

The Franklin Mint works together with those at the forefront of the entertainment industry: Paramount Pictures, Twentieth Century Fox and Turner Home Entertainment. Franklin also shares a partnership with great "families" like Warner Brothers and Parker Brothers to bring to life some of the most lovable characters of all

time: The Jetsons, The Flintstones, the Road Runner, and Bugs Bunny, just to name a few.

Franklin creates classic games the whole family will share and enjoy such as the Collector's Edition of "The Looney Tunes Chess Set," and with all-time favorites like Scrabble and Monopoly.

Creating magic with the one and only Walt Disney Company, Franklin had paid tribute to Walt Disney's genius with sculpture and dolls of sheer enchantment like Mickey and Minnie Mouse, the beautiful Snow White and the unforgettable Cinderella.

Leading The Franklin Mint Family Into the Future, Stewart and Lynda Rae Resnick's Vision Continues

The Franklin Mint is guided by Lynda and Stewart Resnick, who serve as Vice Chairman and Chairman. As such, they are committed to preserving and honoring the great artistic and historical traditions of the past - and to creating new works of art for today's collector. They are also community and civic leaders, lending their talents, support and expertise to institutions including The National Gallery of Art, The Metropolitan Museum of Art and The Los Angeles County Museum of Art. As the 21st century approaches, Mr. and Mrs. Resnick lead The Franklin Mint into a future destined for glorious achievement in the fine art field.

The Franklin Mint
Franklin Center, PA 19091
(800) 225-5836
Fax (610) 459-6880

COLLECTORS' MUSEUM

The Franklin Mint Museum
U.S. Route 1
Media, PA 19091
(610) 459-6881

Hours: Monday through Saturday, 9:30 a.m.-4:30 p.m.; Sunday, 1 p.m.-4:30 p.m. Closed Major Holidays.

Admission Fee: None

Exhibits at The Franklin Mint Museum include sculpture, dolls, books, die-cast models, stamps and other collectibles. In one wing of the museum, a new exhibit is opened every two months. Special events are scheduled throughout the year, and exclusive Franklin Mint products are available at the Gallery Store, located within the museum.

MARGARET FURLONG DESIGNS
America's Favorite Angel Design
Receives Her Inspiration from Heaven and Earth

If you have a chance to meet Margaret Furlong, don't turn it down! This dynamo of energy and high-powered talent is sure to enchant you. If *she* doesn't, her work will. Ask Margaret what drives her spirit and she will list God, her family and the beauty of nature. Splendid angels are the gifts she gives, joyfully, to our world of limited edition collectible art.

Furlong's road to so lofty a place as angel designer was filled with twists, turns and a series of equilibrium-jarring moves. On one occasion, a thousand white angels emerged from her kiln a rosy pink (and yes, she had the courage to break them), testing her patience and sense of humor. This is just one memory Margaret Furlong has of the early days when her business grew so fast, it surprised even Furlong. But, Margaret managed to master each challenge, emerging wiser and more committed to her art.

Armed with a Masters Degree in Fine Arts from the University of Nebraska, Margaret taught briefly, then retired from shepherding students to establish her first studio. There, Furlong pioneered "Midwest Snowscapes" in her signature color: white. Today, her work is a hundred light years from her snowscape era. A fortuitous experiment, making angels from seashells left over from a commissioned project, propelled her to fame in the collectible art industry.

Starting a Company with Dreams and Faith

When Margaret Furlong studied the array of "leftover" shells lying about her studio in 1979, she realized these gracefully-shaped wonders looked like natural angels. By sculpting clay faces and delicate embellishments, a personality emerged from each shell. When her initial batch of angels was finished and displayed, Furlong knew this avenue of

design was God's plan for her. "I began my business with a commitment to share, in all of my designs, the things I held dear to my heart..." Margaret recalls. "My first angel was also a tribute to my recent personal commitment to Christianity."

Margaret recalls her first year as being "rather slow and laborious." Much time was spent learning production techniques and marketing. With no one to represent her designs, it was up to her to do it, so this one-woman-band managed to juggle every role with grace. Somehow, she even managed to fall in love and plan a wedding. Happily, Jerry Alexander was a supportive soul who encouraged his wife's dream. All he asked was that she move her dream west — to Seattle!

Relocating to the Northwest from Nebraska meant a disruption of major proportions. A new city. New neighbors. New lifestyle! Settling into the basement garage of a condominium in suburban Seattle, Margaret stoically recalls how she "started over." This move proved to be a blessing in disguise. This would be the year Furlong would stretch her wings and fly...just like the angels she creates.

Taking Margaret Furlong Designs National

Soon after moving to Seattle, Margaret declared she was ready to go national. She set up a more elaborate marketing plan, recruited sales representatives and printed materials showcasing her designs. The business was flourishing when another geographic jog, just down the road to Salem, Oregon, made Margaret realize Furlong Designs had grown beyond her ability to handle it alone. Husband Jerry

Margaret Furlong's premier limited edition angel celebrates her first venture into collectibles. The first of five angels in the Musical *series, "The Caroler Angel" helped start today's mega-trend in angel collecting!*

Alexander agreed. He gave up his job to become a full-time partner, bringing considerable fiscal and administrative skills to the company.

Since the move to Oregon, it's been non-stop growth for the business, and not just the kind of 'mundane' growth you might imagine.

Margaret Furlong's angels caught the eye of President and Mrs. Ronald Reagan. A selection of Furlong creations was requested to decorate the Reagan's personal tree at the White House in 1981. Each angel hung proudly, surrounded by family heirlooms.

Given this remarkable exposure, it wasn't long before the media took notice. America's top publications featured Margaret's work in their holiday issues. *Victoria, Victorian Homes, Country Home, Traditional Home, Country Living, Gourmet, Redbook, Good Housekeeping* and *Ladies Home Journal* are just a few of the magazines spreading the joy of Furlong angels to

Peek at the face of the infant cradled in this beautiful angel's arms and you'll glimpse Margaret Furlong's sheer joy at having given birth to her daughter Caitlin! "The Messiah Angel," issued in 1994, is the last of the five Joyeux Noel *angels.*

millions of readers.

In 1983, Margaret produced her most distinguished work of art, Caitlin Alexander. The birth of a daughter spurred Margaret's artistic spirit to new heights. Now, she had an angel of her very own to treasure!

First Margaret Furlong Limited Editions Take Flight

Margaret Furlong's *Musical* series, launched in 1980, was her first limited edition series. For five consecutive years, Margaret's definition of the "true meaning of Christmas," was given to the world. The first, "Caroler Angel," depicts an angel holding a hymnal and singing a song of joy. Only 3,000 were made. The following year, "The Lyrist Angel" made her appearance holding a lyre. This angel melted hearts and sold fast. In 1982, "The Lutist Angel," fashioned in the style of the Renaissance masters and limited to 3,000, debuted.

By the time "The Concertinist Angel" was unveiled for the 1983 Christmas season, Margaret Furlong's audience had grown to huge proportions. They eagerly awaited her surprises and were not disappointed when they saw the dainty halo, holly and berry accents

and delicate folds of her concertina. When the series concluded, in 1984, fans were reluctant to see it end but agreed the final issue, "The Herald Angel," was a spectacular finale. Crowned with roses and olive branches, "The Herald Angel" proved the perfect conclusion to an outstanding collection.

In 1985, Furlong debuted her next series: *Gifts From God*, also limited to 3,000 of each design. The new series captivated collectors with lavish touches: tiny shells, a cross, primrose, tulips, crocus, the sun and stars and other glorious gifts of nature reflecting the miracle of Jesus' birth, His life on earth and glorious resurrection. The *Gifts From God* collection includes "The Charis Angel" (Charis means grace gift from God), "Hallelujah Angel," "Angel of Light," "The Celestial Angel" and "The Coronation Angel."

Heralding Margaret's Newest Designs and First Retirements

The last decade of the century was reason for celebration. 1990 saw the introduction of the *Joyeux Noel* collection, a five-year series of angels limited to 10,000 of each design. Every figure has a fanciful name. "Celebration Angel," "Thanks-giving Angel," "Joyeux Noel Angel," "Star of Bethlehem Angel" and "Messiah Angel." Each design showcases Margaret's growth and working relationship with God.

"Messiah Angel," the final piece in the *Joyeux Noel* series, is particularly memorable. Sketches of Caitlin, Margaret's daughter, inspired the face of the child on this final figure in the collection. This highly personal design, celebrating both Jesus' birth and the miracle of motherhood, may be the most popular of Margaret's angels to date. Collectors seem to see in it a bit of the divine influence that guides Margaret

Furlong's hands.

With the completion of *Joyeux Noel*, a new series, *Flora Angelica*, was prepared for its 1995 unveiling. *Flora Angelica* combines the radiance of angels with the symbolism of flowers. This series is limited to just 10,000 of each annual angel, beginning with the "Faith Angel." A tribute to belief and love, "Faith Angel" holds a delicate bouquet of roses and is crowned with a dainty headdress of roses and leaves. Each angel in this five-year collection will share God's floral delights with the world. Toward this end, Margaret has also introduced new 2", 3" and 4" angels with a botanical theme for 1995.

In the tradition of fine collectible art, retirements are an important part of Margaret Furlong's commitment to give collectors true limited editions. 1995 marks the retirement of both the 3" and 4" "Dove" angels, created in 1984 to celebrate Caitlin's birth. The "Dove" joins the "Star" angel and the "Trumpeter" angel, both of which were retired in 1994.

The Sky's the Limit for Margaret Furlong Designs

Visually wander through one of Margaret Furlong's new catalogs, and

Margaret Furlong's introduction of the new Flora Angelica *series showcases her love of flowers and God's bountiful gifts of nature. "The Faith Angel," introduced in 1995, is limited to just 10,000 angels.*

you'll understand how far her gift for design has blossomed: Discover delicate morning stars, charming hearts, fragile snowflakes, spiraling icicles, elegant tassels and whimsical shell fish — all inspired by enchanting gifts from the sea. Each of Margaret Furlong's unique designs is proudly made in the United States using the exacting techniques and standards she pioneered back in Nebraska.

Today, Margaret Furlong's dreams and creations have come full circle. Each is a reflection of her personal commitment to quality, value and good design. Toward that end, Margaret uses a meticulous production process that moves her creations from prototype to first modeling, from carving to a master mold, all with methodical care. Each

step of the crafting and finishing process is overseen by Margaret and her growing staff of artisans and crafters, now numbering more than 85!

With all this excitement, growth and responsibility, it's hard to imagine Margaret has a spare moment, yet she makes herself available to her faithful collectors with tours of her soon-to-be-expanded studios and production facility in Salem, Oregon, and as many personal appearances as she can fit into her schedule.

Margaret Furlong fans may already have heard the rumor that a collector club is in the stars, and you've not finished reading about the other exciting changes planned for Margaret Furlong Designs in the coming years. But you can be sure that the future promises

many new challenges and more blessings. With God's help, her family's encouragement and collector support, the sky's the limit...and that's exactly where this popular collectible artist is headed.

Margaret Furlong Designs
210 State Street
Salem, OR 97301
(503) 363-6004
Fax (503) 371-0676

COLLECTORS' TOUR

Margaret Furlong Designs Studio Tour
210 State Street
Salem, OR 97301
(503) 363-6004

Hours: Monday through Friday, 8 a.m.-5 p.m. Please phone for an appointment.

Admission Fee: None

Visitors can tour the production area at Margaret Furlong Designs Studio where skilled craftspeople make each porcelain design by hand.

GANZ

Little Cheesers Leads to Big Success and More Collectibles to Squeak About

Join the Little Cheesers *for a hummin', strummin', foot-tapping day in Cheeserville! From the piano to the banjo, this band of mice plays some down-home tunes in* A Little Country Music *series from the popular collection.*

Ganz began in 1950 as a small, family-owned and operated company that originally produced stuffed teddy bears. The business gave a new start to the Ganz family, who fled to Austria, Germany, and ultimately to Canada after the Nazi army invaded their native Rumania. With $100 of the family's own money and lots of hard work, Ganz (known then as Ganz Bros. Toys Limited) grew steadily and crossed the border into the United States, where the company became recognized for its fine quality plush animals.

But in 1991, company President Howard Ganz made a conscious decision to expand its product line beyond toys to include figurines, mugs, novelties, frames and other gifts. The savvy move welcomed the birth of the *Little Cheesers*, an adorable line of collectible mouse figurines that became an instant hit at its 1991 debut and has since paved a new path of success for Ganz. Today, *Little Cheesers* heads the

company's continued growth and prominence in the collectibles industry. Besides the community of old-fashioned mice from Cheeserville, Ganz has introduced collectors to a gallery of collectibles ranging from cows and pigs to teddy bears and angels.

Little Cheesers Opens a New World of Adventures

"A long time ago," starts a page in the book called *The Historical Chronicle of Cheeserville*, "the *Little Cheesers* lived in the Old World. They made their homes in tree stumps, toadstools and burrows. Very cleverly, they used leaves for umbrellas, blossoms for drinking cups and spider webs for fishing nets. Then one day, some of the *Little Cheesers* made a courageous voyage across the Billowing Sea to the New World where they settled and built a new way of life. Instead of living in tree trunks, they learned to make cozy cottages from clapboards and shingles."

Little Cheesers share their new way of life through more than 200 miniature figurines, each bearing a name, story and charming personality that has warmed the hearts of collectors around the world. The *Little Cheesers* population keeps growing around various themes: a picnic, wedding, Christmas celebration, family traditions, springtime and fall holidays.

Although Frowzy Roquefort III spins a fictional tale about the *Little Cheesers* in the fully illustrated book, *The Historical Chronicles of Cheeserville*, the collection's real story began in 1990 when gift industry veteran William R. Dawson traveled to the Far East. There

he discovered a special line of mice figurines, which he named *Little Cheesers* and introduced in January 1991. In July of that year, Ganz made special arrangements to purchase *Little Cheesers*.

Christine Thammavongsa, product designer and director of the Ganz Collectibles division, is the on-going creative force behind the collection. Besides sketching each mouse, Christine names the characters and develops all the delightful stories of their lives and pastimes. Since the *Little Cheesers* care about the environment and their neighbors, Christine's designs also capture the tender spirit of family togetherness and love.

Christine recently completed a hardcover *Little Cheesers* storybook called *More Precious Than Gold* that tells a tale of the Woodsworth twins, Little Truffle and Sweet Cicely. These mice

Christine Thammavongsa created Grandma's Attic to rekindle warm memories of old-fashioned and well-worn teddy bears that seem real to children. Balderdash, Tootoo, Crumples & Creampuff and Bumblebeary (clockwise from the top) are among the bears that play make-believe games in the attic. The figurines stand about two to three inches tall.

learn the valuable lessons of sharing, caring for Mother Nature, helping each other and understanding that one child is more precious than gold, silver or even diamonds. Christine is the ghost writer for Frowsy Roquefort III, the "author" of the storybook.

Special *Little Cheesers* Retirements and Additions

Each year, Ganz announces the retirement of selected *Little Cheesers* figurines to make way for new introductions. Once a piece is retired, it may be acquired through retailers until their stock is sold out. The first ten pieces were retired in 1991 and sold out within four months. Ganz now announces retirements twice a year in July and December.

In 1993, Ganz also introduced the first limited edition *Little Cheesers* figurines, including Frowzy Roquefort III reading from a book, Blossom Thistledown and Hickory Harvestmouse rowing a boat in "Gently Down the Stream" and the festive "Santa's Sleigh."

Other forest friends have also joined the *Little Cheesers*. *The Silverwoods* — close relatives of the

Life is wonderful in Pigsville, *where the days are long and lazy and the townsfolk are friendly, playful pigs! Designed by Christine Thammavongsa, the humorous figurines include "Bakin' at the Beach," "True Love," "Tipsy," "Wee Little Piggy" and a pig pen of other favorites.*

Fun is easy to round up in Cowtown, *an udderly cool collectible introduced in 1993. Pictured from left to right are: "Bull Rogers," "Cowlamity Jane," "Buffalo Bull Cody," "Moo West," "Old MooDonald" and "Gloria Bovine & Rudolph Bullentino." They join a herd of other cow figurines that rank among the most popular lines at Ganz.*

Little Cheesers — make an annual Christmas pilgrimage across the Billowing Sea. They have grey fur to add a new dimension and personality to anyone's collection. In Cloverdale Clearing, just a hop away from Gooseberry Grove on the Cheeserville map, a group of adorable bunnies shares their favorite activities. *Little Hoppers* are the long-eared friends of the *Little Cheesers*.

Collectors' Club Celebrates *Little Cheesers*

To share the joys, adventures and latest news around Cheeserville, Ganz introduced the Little Cheesers Collectors' Club in 1993. Members receive a membership figurine, membership card, club binder, "Cheeserville Gazette" newsletter and redemption certificates for special member's only pieces throughout the year. The colorful newsletter previews upcoming introductions, answers collectors' questions, sponsors contests, offers display tips, announces retirements and tells interesting insider facts about the collection.

Quality Craftsmanship Goes Into Each Collectible

Whether its a figurine for Club members or the latest addition to the picnic scene, Christine's process for creating each *Little Cheesers* piece requires

many careful and time-consuming steps. To begin, Christine sketches the characters she has in mind and then presents them to a sculptor in the Far East who brings her work to life in three dimensions. Christine and the sculptor work together to perfect each detail before an original model is produced. A mixture of finely ground porcelain, resin and other ingredients are poured in the molds. *Little Cheesers* figurines are handcrafted in cold cast resin which allows for exceptional detail, durability, texture and color.

The *Little Cheesers* figurines are then hand-painted with water-based paints, producing a striking finish to complement their personalities. The process is repeated in Christine's other creations that reflect the same attention to detail.

A Barn Yard Of Collectible Friends

The *Cowtown* collection, released in 1993, was an original Ganz creation inspired by Christine's childhood memories and visits to her grandparents' farms. The herd of whimsical cow figurines include "Ma & Pa Cattle," "Pocowhantis," "King Cowmooamooa," "Sheriff Bull Masterson," "Cowlamity Jane" and "Buffalo Bull Cody." Wonderful experiences on the farm also influenced Christine's *Pigsville* collection, introduced in 1993. The

"All at once the precious Angels went tumbling down through space and now they are all searching for a perfect little place." This 1995 line of cherubic figurines represents the little angels in everyone's life. A Perfect Little Place features angels enjoying favorite childhood pastimes.

carefree pigs enjoy relaxing days from the barn to the beach as they strike humorous poses. The collections also include ornaments, plush, mugs and other accessories. In keeping with the barnyard theme, Christine also created *Cock-A-Doodle Corners* featuring "home-grown" chickens.

More Creations from the Studio of Christine Thammavongsa

Christine's pencils, paintbrushes and imagination have brought to life old-fashioned teddy bears that play make-believe games in *Grandma's Attic,*

which premiered in 1995. The story accompanying the collection tells about a 5-year-old girl whose grandmother led her to the corner of the attic, where a well-worn toy chest was hidden under piles of clothes and books. "She gently placed a tiny brass key in the palm of my hand and shared a special secret with me, a secret she had shared with my mother many years before," the story reads. Inside the trunk were vintage teddy bears that the girl's great-grandmother patiently stitched by hand. With names like Dumblekin, Bumblebeary and Balderdash, the anything - but - ordinary bears invite the girl to join in their afternoon games.

Collectors can also discover the charming world of a *Perfect Little Place* as envisioned by Howard Ganz and Christine Thammavongsa. Introduced in 1995, the hand-painted resin figurines feature cherubic and child-like angels that are searching for a wonderful home on earth. Christine has also created *Watching Over You*, a line of classical angel figurines expressing the feelings of motherhood that she has experienced since the birth of her daughter.

Street Scenes and Trains Find a Home With Collectors

Christine also oversees the development of other lines. Introduced in 1995, *Just Around The Corner* is designed for collectors to create their

own towns from an authentic selection of shops, restaurants, businesses and apartments that can be joined together to construct endless combinations of winding historic streets. Created by Ganz artist Lisa Sunarth, the first series features an Old Boston flavor with brick buildings, arched doorways and charming storefronts. The buildings in the second series capture the rugged and pioneering spirit of the Old West and life in Tombstone.

Trains Gone By, launched in 1995, features highly detailed resin figurines that recreate famous trains dating back to the mid-1800s. The 10" trains are limited in edition to 5,000, with 1,000 of those pieces also designed to make authentic sound effects. The first five introductions include locomotives from the nation's most recognized railroads: Pennsylvania, Western & Atlantic, Santa Fe, New York Central and Central Pacific. With its continued success in the collectibles industry, Ganz plans to stay right on track by introducing and developing other lines. Of course, Cheeserville will also keep growing with a delightful cast of characters that has collectors around the world following all the adventures and excitement.

Ganz
908 Niagara Falls Blvd.
North Tonawanda, NY 14120-2060
(800) 724-5902
(905) 851-6669

COLLECTORS' CLUB

GARTLAN USA, INC.
First Good Sports, Now Great Entertainers, Too

Ringo Starr, right, points the way for Gartlan USA's new direction to R.H. Gartlan, President, Gartlan USA, Inc.

It's easy to make too much of it; hard to make light of it.

Encounters with famous entertainers and athletic luminaries were commonplace to five of the seven pacing the Chopin Room at Los Angeles' Belage Hotel, just off Sunset Blvd. on April 25, 1996.

For more than 11 years, the core team of Gartlan USA signing specialists and executives has created keepsakes that include the hand autographed approvals of the world's most famous athletes...Joe DiMaggio, legendary UCLA coach John Wooden, Magic Johnson, Wayne Gretzky, Ted Williams, Olympian Kristi Yamaguchi and more than 36 others.

But cultural icons are different. And for boomers and near boomers, there are no bigger icons. At precisely noon, the short, wispy-haired English-man entered the room. With a secure bounce in his step, he circled the large conference table — draped with pristine white table clothes — and introduced himself to the gathered.

An immediate familiarity swept the room. So did several moments of

memory loss as the immediate embraced the impossible.

The group, each, had just shaken hands with Ringo Starr.

Ringo Starr of the Beatles. *The* Ringo Starr.

No musical group, no cultural force has had the impact the Beatles has had on a single generation. And as society poises for the next millennium, the fabric of their legacy remains one of the great possibilities for generations yet born.

So, the back beat for a musical monolith — melodic, harmonic and lyrical geniuses — sat and reviewed production samples of the Gartlan USA figurines capturing him at the beginning and end of his Beatle tenure. "I look a bit goofy don't I?" Ringo quipped, referring to a six-inch drumming figurine portraying that moment in 1964 when America collectively stopped to peer into the stark black and white pictures of its televisions and ushered in a new era. Shrills from several hundred adolescents, on the "Ed Sullivan Show," sounded a cacophony, drowning the music itself. "I never pictured myself, in my mind's eye, looking the way I did," he says to a room full of good-natured giggling.

A History-Making Event

After reviewing the pieces before him and raving a profound approval for a new Christmas ornament which he had not seen before, Ringo began the task at hand: signing 1,000 collector plates and 250 Artist Proof plates. Each plate was created from original artwork by Michael J. Taylor, Gartlan USA's most noted portraitist.

Gartlan USA was launched in 1985 by R.H. Gartlan, and for more than 11 years, focused exclusively on the autographs, likenesses and collectibles featuring the world's foremost athletes.

The signing session was no cure for

cancer; nor space exploration; nor brain surgery; but for millions of Beatles fans and disciples of musical sermons preaching peace and love, it was history. No autographed collection of limited edition collectibles had ever been produced or brought to market, until now. (George Harrison had signed copies of his book, *I, Me, Mine.*)

So, why now? Bruce Grakal, Ringo's attorney, answered, "For 30 years most everything out there has been bootleg. Ringo, as well as the others to varying degrees, wants to see more control...develop more quality...and provide something for the fans."

So, why Gartlan? Bob Gartlan had been escorted to Ringo and his All-Starr Band's August 1995 Los Angeles concert by executives at Sony Signatures, the Beatles' current licensing care-taker, Grakal recalls. "He met with me and Ringo's confidant, Hillary. Bob shared his background in the

The Ringo Starr figurine, limited to 1,000 pieces worldwide and personally autographed by Ringo Starr, is one of the few items ever autographed by a Beatle.

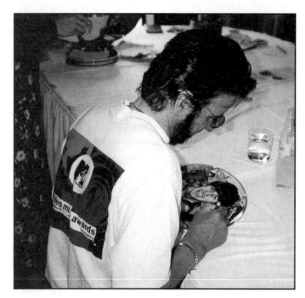

Ringo finds his rhythm during plate signing session. The former Beatle and solo artist autographed 1,000 collector plates featured in the Gartlan USA collection.

collectibles field, had brought prototypes of the figurines and greatly impressed Hillary.

"I took the product in for Ringo to see (and) shared Hillary's positive impressions. He evaluated the product, absorbed the input and said simply, 'Let's do it,'" Grakal says.

Having signed the figurines in Monte Carlo in December 1995, it had come to this. The plates had been decorated, fired and cooled for the drummer's signature. The marketing was finished, and the product sold out in record time for any Gartlan USA project.

Each of the plates is hand-banded in 24K gold; sequentially numbered to the edition of 1,000 signed plates and an additional 250 autographed Artist Proof plates. Taylor also signed the A.P. plates.

Up Close and Personal with Ringo

Ringo began the task at hand, occasionally — and ironically — commenting, "I can't find me rhythm," alluding to his personal, albeit minor, frustration in not being able to

expedite the process.

The banter was sparse at first, but the group found its own rhythm of conversation with the man whose life the working party could never comprehend. There was talk of Ringo's impending anniversary, his 15th, and each person in the room shared their matrimonial longevity. The stick-to-itiveness impressed the drummer. "I don't think people today understand the work and effort it takes to make a marriage work," he said.

Asked about his own collecting habits, he shared his affinity for early pirates, owls, and dragons – "European, only," he said.

Of the success of the newly released anthologies: "People know me now," he offered, self-deprecatingly, adding that when he doesn't feel like signing autographs, he'll tell would-be suitors, "I don't sign when I'm walking." He added, seriously, that he won't sign when he's eating, at the movies or in the toilet.

And of course the conversation turned to music. "When will you tour next?" the marketing exec asked. "Maybe again next year," Ringo said. "I only like to go out, at best, every other year. I don't have that many songs, you know. I mean how many times can you hear 'Yellow Submarine?'"

"How often do you talk to George and Paul?" Taylor queried. "About once a week...although I think George is in India," Ringo said.

Taylor, a Beatles trivia expert, was hitting his stride and talk turned to the Paul McCartney death hoax, where a disc jockey

turned up "evidence" that Paul had died and substantiated it with several "clear references" in music and collateral.

Referring specifically to the various funeral participants on the Abbey Road cover (also the image used for Ringo's series of figurines) — each Beatle emblematic by the attire he wore on that August day in 1969 — Taylor wondered if the four lads didn't play into the fanciful whimsy of the rumors. "We did some crazy stuff on the albums and in the studio, but nothing related to that whole bit...it wasn't like we called each other up that morning and discussed what we were going to wear," Ringo said.

And then he interrupted the dialogue with a "bummer," and one of the plates would be removed from the table and cleaned. Ringo wasn't pleased with the clarity of his signature.

This went on for more than three hours. Once he stopped and sketched a design for another ornament on the table cloth. In another moment, he explained that he's wearing fewer rings, particularly in public. "I'm trying to draw less attention to myself," he says.

Occasionally he would rest, stepping

An 8-1/4" unautographed plate featuring Ringo Starr is the gift to members in the 1996 Gartlan USA "New" Collectors' League.

onto the room's balcony and soaking up the afternoon L.A. sunshine; once an impromptu shoulder rub eased the tentative cramping in his arm and wrist.

Ringo — A Gartlan USA Collector, Too

It was during one such break that he asked if he couldn't get six sets of the product for himself. He asked for specific numbers, and Bob Gartlan assured him that it could be accomplished.

And as he began to sign the last 100 plates, he announced he would not sign any personal items. He didn't personalize any of the plates either. "It's hard enough signing my own name," he said jokingly. Beyond the 10-1/4" plates, the only other item Ringo autographed was an 8-1/2" plate — these are unsigned in a production of 10,000 pieces worldwide — for a Sony employee.

And then he was done. As quickly as he bounced into the room, he put on his black sports coat, over a white tee shirt, and slipped out of the room in an instant.

It was over. The signing had gone relatively well — a factory production problem yielded only 909 of the 1,000 numbered plates, yet another session was hoped to be arranged. Now the plates and figurines would begin shipping to various, yet selective, retailers around the country.

Gartlan USA's Collectors' League Offers Great Benefits

Because the demand for the signed items has been so intense, collectors who wish to get advanced information regarding such signing sessions and availablity will want to join Gartlan USA's Collectors' League. The Collectors' League was founded in 1989 and issues members-only products and exclusive gifts each year.

The 1996 members-only gift, free with membership, is an 8-1/4" collectors' plate with a distinctive backstamp marking the exclusivity of the plate. Only 1,000 of such plates were created and were excerpted from the open edition of 10,000 unsigned plates.

Meanwhile, for the seven attending the signing session, the stories would be retold in bad English accents well into the weekend...and the music will now evoke even more memories than just those of adolescent fancy.

Gartlan USA, the leading manufacturer of limited-edition sports collectibles for the past 11 years, features collections commemorating such sports luminaries as Joe Montana, above.

Gartlan USA, Inc.
575 Route 73 North, Suite A-6
West Berlin, NJ 08091
(609) 753-9229
Fax (609) 753-9280

COLLECTORS' CLUB

Gartlan USA's "New" Collectors' League
575 Rt. 73 N., Suite A-6
West Berlin, NJ 08091
(609) 753-9229

Annual Dues: $30.00
Renewal: $20.00
Club Year: Anniversary of Sign-Up Date

Benefits:
- Membership Gift: 8-1/4" Ringo Starr Collectors' Plate
- Opportunity to Purchase Remarqued Plaques
- Quarterly Newsletter
- Membership Card
- Buy/Sell Matching Service
- Opportunity to Join Club Cruise in 1997
- Advance Notice of New Releases
- Free Gifts at Special Events

GEORGETOWN COLLECTION
The Studio That Puts the Doll Artist "In Charge"

Multi-award-winning artist Linda Mason's "Lavender Dreams," standing 15-1/2" tall and retailing for $150, comes complete with her own upholstered chair and miniature book.

The artists who create the dolls that bring such joy to collectors are an amazing group: talented, intuitive and possessed of a truly astonishing understanding of children and their world. Without these gifted virtuosos, the doll realm would be a poorer place indeed.

All of which accounts for why Georgetown Collection, from its studios in Portland, Maine, always insists that the doll artists must have creative control over each doll they design. The result? The finest collectible dolls for today — and tomorrow — in the tradition of the priceless heirloom dolls of yesterday.

Each doll produced by Georgetown, in fact, is an *Artist's Edition®*, the collector's guarantee that the doll is crafted, finished and painted by hand — with every stage subject to the total control and approval of the artist who created that doll. This unusual commitment to excellence is available only to the dolls created for the Georgetown Collection.

Top-Notch Artistic Talents Make Creative Decisions

"We do things differently here," explains Jeff McKinnon, Georgetown's President and founder. "To begin with, we give our artists total artistic control over their dolls. They do what *they* feel is right, so the end product is *their* design rather than some 'composite idea' by an anonymous group."

Because artistic control rests in the hands of the artists, notes McKinnon, Georgetown is able to attract such superb talent — and produce dolls that are among the most popular with collectors.

As an example, McKinnon points out Georgetown's current crop of talent, a list that sounds like a "Who's Who" among leading doll artists: Linda Mason, Ann Timmerman, Carol Theroux and Sissel Skille, as well as talented newcomers to the field such as Pamela Phillips, Joyce Reavey, Anne DiMartino, Jutta Kissling, Barbara Prusseit and Marlene Sirko. Further proof of this studio's achievements is provided by the industry press: feature-length articles on the company and/ or its artists have appeared in *Contemporary Doll*, *Dolls* and *Doll Reader* magazines. And then there are the awards: over the past several years, the dolls produced for Georgetown Collection have garnered a total of 17 nominations and six awards!

Extraordinary Quality Control; Responsive Customer Service

As partner and supporter of great doll artists, McKinnon explains, Georgetown also insists that only top quality components be used in the making of its dolls. "Among the tradespeople who produce our porcelain, wigs and the material for our costuming, we have a reputation for accepting only the very best quality. So that's what we get — consistently."

Responsive customer service is another important reason for the firm's continued success. "This," says McKinnon, "comes down to simply working harder. At Georgetown, we treat all our customers as individuals, and we listen to what they tell us. The success of our program is proven by how many of our collectors come back to us again and again." And it's not just the customers who remain faithful to Georgetown: "Since our company first began," notes McKinnon, "we've had very little turnover in our employees, our artists or our suppliers."

A Popular, New Georgetown Newsletter

All this fruitful give-and-take between the company, its artists, employees, suppliers, and its customers, has resulted in the creation of something new and extremely useful for collectors. This is the quarterly newsletter entitled "News from Georgetown" that keeps collectors abreast of the latest information on doll artists, their work, personal appearances and awards, as well as on various Georgetown employees — customer service representatives, for instance — whom customers talk with and might enjoy learning more about.

"We knew there was a need for something like this newsletter," notes McKinnon, "but we never expected such an enormous response. We've

Pamela Phillips' new doll for Georgetown Collection, "Madeleine & Harry" – standing 18" high and retailing for $140 – offers collectors not only an adorable little girl, but a fluffy white puppy, as well.

always considered our employees, artists, suppliers and customers to be a kind of large, extended family, so it's very gratifying to learn that our customers feel this way, too." Collectors interested in receiving an initial copy of "News from Georgetown" can write to Georgetown Collection, P.O. Box 9730, Portland, ME 04104-5030. The initial copy is free, and a further subscription costs only $4.95 – "just to pay for postage and handling," explains McKinnon.

Honors for Georgetown Artists Linda Mason and Pamela Phillips

One of the topics about which the newsletter keeps collectors informed is the latest awards to be handed out to Georgetown artists. And there are always plenty of these! Among the many honors Georgetown artist Linda Mason has won, for instance, is the *Dolls* magazine "Award of Excellence" for an unprecedented three years in a row. Mason, who says she has always loved dolls, as well as the romance of things Victorian, has just created "Lavender Dreams," her first doll in Georgetown's *Victorian Fantasies™* collection.

Pamela Phillips, a relative newcomer to Georgetown, won her *Dolls* magazine "Award of Excellence" in 1994 and has three of her dolls nominated for *Doll Reader's* "Doll of the Year" award in 1995. Portraiture has always been Pamela's first love, and her enormous skill at creating faces as true-to-life as they are beautiful is apparent in her latest work for Georgetown – "Madeleine and Harry." This unique work features a little girl dressed in red, white and blue, together with her adorable dog, a fluffy white West Highland Terrier.

Awards to Ann Timmerman, Joyce Reavey and Marlene Sirko

Popular artist Ann Tim-merman has won an International Doll Exhibition (IDEX) award, as well as receiving two recent nominations from *Doll Reader* for her cherubic angels in Georgetown's *Little Bit of Heaven™* series. Likewise, Marlene Sirko – whose first Georgetown doll "Amanda" sports her own set of ice skates – was previously honored with a *Doll Reader* "Doll of the Year" award.

Another Georgetown artist Joyce Reavey, whose spunky children are becoming a staple of doll collectors, is also the recipient of a *Dolls* magazine "Award of Excellence." All five of the above doll artists – plus European baby doll artist Barbara Prusseit – are discussed in greater detail in the *Artists Profile* section later in this book.

In addition to the six doll-makers just mentioned, the Georgetown Collection also works with several other popular doll artists, whose creations have brought joy and delight to collectors worldwide.

Carol Theroux's *Buffalo Clan* and the *Faraway Friends* of Sissel Skille

Georgetown artist Carol Theroux is considered one of the finest artists now painting Native American subjects, and she has been an honored exhibitor at America's most prestigious invitational Western art shows. Drawing from her own Native American ancestry, Carol has created several beautifully crafted dolls, each of which the artist researches carefully for authenticity and accuracy.

What this means to the collector is that every detail – from necklace to moccasins – has been perfected to the artist's satisfaction. Carol Theroux's dolls for Georgetown now include "Winter Baby" in her traditional blanket-like coat, called a capote, the sister and brother team of "Buffalo Child" and "Buffalo Boy," "Golden Flower" and "Little Fawn's Papoose."

When the very first word a young girl speaks aloud is "doll," is it any wonder she would go on to create dolls of her own? Such is the case with Norwegian artist Sissel Skille, whose *Faraway Friends™* collection for Georgetown includes the enchanting little Norwegian girl "Kristin," "Mariama" from Senegal and "Dara," a delightful kite flyer from Thailand. The dolls in this series celebrate the special friendship shared by young pen pals.

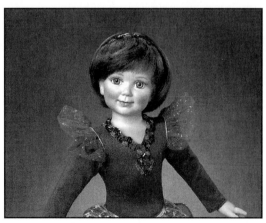

Skating up a storm is Marlene Sirko's "Amanda," a new doll for Georgetown Collection that is brimming with vitality. "Amanda" stands 15-1/2" high and retails for $120.

Soft as moonlight, Ann Timmerman's "Sweetdreams and Moonbeams" for Georgetown Collection is alive with enchantment. With its soft sculpture moon included, the doll is 10" seated and retails for $130.

Sissel, who has always loved children, expresses that love not only in doll making but in teaching in a Norwegian school system, where she can watch her charges progress from tiny tots into young adults. While her original dolls were all one-of-a-kind and very expensive, Sissel is now reaching a much wider audience via her creations for Georgetown.

The *Class Portraits* of Jutta Kissling and Anne DiMartino's *Little Dreamers*

For years Jutta Kissling worked in public relations, helping entrepreneurs bring their creative work to the public eye. As a long-time doll lover, Jutta at last decided to try her hand at doll making. Completely self-taught, she mastered the technique of porcelain doll making and eventually her dolls became known throughout Europe.

Now, Jutta has completed her first creation for Georgetown: "Anna," a lovely European schoolgirl in the *Class Portraits*™ collection. This is the first of Jutta's dolls to be made available to American collectors, and quite a prize she is! Complete with schoolbooks and a bouquet of tulips, "Anna" expresses both excitement and uncertainty, as her first class picture is about to be taken.

"Strong feelings are an important part of life," says Anne DiMartino, and this sculptor-turned-doll maker has discovered that dolls are wonderful creations through which to express these feelings. In her Georgetown collection called *Little Dreamers*™, Anne has brought to life two exquisite dolls: "Beautiful Buttercup" and "Julie," both of which demonstrate the beauty that can be found in real-life emotions.

"What I love most about children," notes Anne, "is the freedom they feel to show their emotions. Their faces reflect everything in their hearts — love, sadness, excitement, glee — and it's all there for us to see and to share with them." And those amazing emotions, so difficult to achieve, are exactly what Anne has brought to each of her dolls.

A Continuing Commitment to Excellence

Over the past decade, the Georgetown Collection has built a strong reputation for award-winning doll art, as well as a growing coterie of enthusiastic collectors. In the decade ahead, Georgetown will continue this devotion to excellence. And it will work, as always, with a small cadre of the world's most honored doll artists — whose complete creative control promises collectors an array of dolls that will exceed their very highest expectations.

Georgetown Collection
866 Spring Street
Portland, ME 04104-5030
(800) 626-3330
Fax (207) 775-6457

GOEBEL OF NORTH AMERICA

M.I. Hummel® Artworks Lead a Host of Fine Collectibles and Distinctive Licensed Products

With a wistful wave of his hankie, a young boy bids adieu to a 25-year collection tradition. "Come Back Soon" is the final edition of the beloved M.I. Hummel Annual Plate Series. A matching figurine is also available.

It was 125 years ago that Franz Detleff Goebel and his son, William, founded F. & W. Goebel in Coburg, Germany. Since then, five generations of the family have stood at the helm, directing a company whose diversified line now includes handcrafted figurines, porcelain and crystal collectibles, and decorative accessories — all distinctive products prized for high-quality workmanship and design.

Goebel already had earned a fine reputation for product innovation when the firm introduced the famed *M.I. Hummel* figurines in 1935. After World War II, the popularity of the *M.I. Hummel* figurines grew rapidly in the United States, prompting Goebel to establish its first distribution company there in 1968.

Today, the United States represents Goebel's largest single "international" market. Renamed Goebel of North America in 1994, the company currently handles over a dozen distinct lines of gifts and collectible products.

The Latest Creations Inspired by Sister Maria Innocentia Hummel's Art

Franz Goebel, the Goebel founder's great-grandson and fourth-generation owner of the firm, is credited with striking a unique product development arrangement with Sister Maria Innocentia Hummel and the Convent of Siessen. This provided Goebel with the worldwide exclusive rights to transform the artist's drawings into three-dimensional products. The pact remains in force today, as evidenced by a host of appealing new *M.I. Hummel* products introduced recently.

The newcomers to the *M.I. Hummel* collection continue to capture the wide-eyed innocence and tender charm of childhood. Handcrafted and hand-painted by artisans at the Goebel factory in Germany, each new figurine, plate, and bell bears the Goebel backstamp and the signature of the late Sister Maria Innocentia Hummel.

A Wide-Ranging Collection of M.I. Hummel Treasures

The year 1995 marked the 60th anniversary of *M.I. Hummel* figurines. In honor of the occasion, W. Goebel Porzellanfabrik of Germany has produced a special edition "Puppy Love Plaque." Offered for one year only, this delightful display plaque features the endearing "Puppy Love" motif, the very first *M.I. Hummel* figurine created in 1935 and retired in 1988.

The new collection is an eclectic one, with something to appeal to every taste. Those who are partial to little girls will say "thank heavens" when they see the nimble knitter, "To Keep You Warm," and "Pixie," a saucy pigtailed imp. Another darling child, "Ooh, My Tooth," is a winsome reminder of one of the more painful passages of youth. This figurine boasts a first-issue and special event backstamp and was available only in the United States and Canada at certain in-store events during 1995.

Boys will be boys, any time, any place. "The Angler" recalls the pride and pleasure every young fisherman feels when he lands his first catch. "Just Dozing" captures the sweet serenity of a wee one at rest. Add a note of merriment to any room with "Strike Up the Band," the tenth release in the *Century Collection* category. This lively quartet of rosy-cheeked music-makers will be produced for only one year and is accompanied by a Certificate of Authenticity.

Ring in the holidays with the annual dated "*Christmas Bell*" and its matching hanging ornament, figurine, and dated plate. Titled "Festival Harmony with Flute," this adorable band of musical cherubs is the third in a series of four annual groupings. The miniature dated plate made a special debut in 1995. It is finished in soft tones of gold and green and features the same coloration and motif as the yule figurine, ornament and bell.

Plate fanciers will welcome "Come Back Soon," the final edition of the

The year 1995 marked the 60th anniversary of M.I. Hummel figurines. To mark the occasion and celebrate, this special edition "Puppy Love Plaque" made its debut.

renowned *M.I. Hummel Annual Plate Series* of 25 that began in 1971. The cheerful fellow extending his hand to bid farewell is also available in a matching figurine. Rounding out the new plate issues is the final edition of the *Friends Forever* series. Titled "Surprise," this plate depicts two buddies in a field of flowers who are

The M.I. Hummel Anniversary Clock, *"Goose Girl," was made in Germany and features a ceramic, bas-relief rendering of the famous portrait of girl and geese. The clock itself is flanked by pillars of polished brass and enclosed in a crystal dome. The 12"-high time piece is battery powered for quiet, efficient, virtually maintenance-free operation and comes with a one-year warranty.*

startled by a buzzing bumblebee.

Because Sister Maria Innocentia Hummel produced such a wealth of artwork during her lifetime, there are enough images available to provide wonderful new subjects for many years to come. The Convent of Siessen, where she lived and worked, continues to receive royalties from Goebel to endow charities and benevolent programs throughout the world.

Produced by W. Goebel Porzellanfabrik of Germany, each of these hand-made pieces features the famous incised *M.I. Hummel* signature on the

base of the figurine to indicate its authenticity. Production time varies according to the size and complexity of each piece. For example, a six-inch *M. I. Hummel* figurine can require as many as 700 hand operations and can take as long as several weeks to complete. Such pieces are created by highly skilled artisans who have been trained by Goebel, beginning with a three-year apprenticeship program.

Bette Ball and Karen Kennedy Keep Yesterday's Memories Alive

Goebel's gifted doll designers, Bette Ball and Karen Kennedy, have not forgotten their childhood memories. In fact, they cherish the innocence and delight so much that they have made it the basis of their careers — sharing visions of gentle days gone by in a marvelous array of limited edition porcelain dolls, many of which are musical.

Each creation, whether it be from the *Victoria Ashlea Originals®, Dolly Dingle®, Betty Jane Carter®, Carol Anne®, Goebel Angels®* or *Charlot Byj®* series, is a masterpiece of fine detailing, craftsmanship and tasteful design. The goal of Ms. Ball and Ms. Kennedy is to capture the imagination and love of discerning collectors today and for many generations to come.

The Success of *Dolly Dingle*

In 1983, Bette Ball and her daughter Ashlea were browsing through an antique shop and happened upon a box of old *Dolly Dingle* cut-outs. Ms. Ball recalls, "As a child, I made an army of paper dolls and supplied them with enormous wardrobes." The cut-out character of *Dolly Dingle* was destined to win her heart. Goebel bought the rights to this early twentieth-century cut-out doll originally owned by Grace Drayton.

By 1985, *Dolly Dingle* had become "America's Sweetheart" in the form of lifelike, three-dimensional dolls created by Bette Ball. That year, Ms. Ball earned the prestigious "Doll of the Year" (DOTY) Award for her creation of a sixteen-inch *Dolly Dingle* musical

Bette Ball designed this wonderful collection of Dolly Dingle *dolls for Goebel. Ms. Ball gained the rights to the original cut-out doll designs of Grace Drayton, and created these three-dimensional "Dollies" in a variety of sizes, themes, and costumes.*

doll. Today, the *Dolly Dingle* line continues to win admirers all over the world. Indeed, you can see Ms. Ball's creations in over 50 museums across the globe. *Dolly Dingle's* family tree grows new members each year. The branches include the Sweeties, the Blossoms, the Twinkles, the Snooks, the Tingles, the Dumplings, the Bumps, and many others.

Goebel Presents Masterpieces in Miniature

Working in harmony with gifted contemporary artists like Peter Yenawine and Douglas Norrgard, Goebel offers a remarkable array of miniature figurines. Yenawine's *Nature's Moments* sculptures in crystal and precious metals feature graceful birds, fish and animals in their favorite habitats — be they mountain summits, coral reefs, arctic islands or backyard baths. Norrgard combines his accomplished artistry with a gift for storytelling, presenting "Once Upon a Winter's Day" — Vignette to recall a childhood memory.

Also in miniature, Goebel offers the tiny novelty clocks of Paul Larsen, created in collaboration with Gordon Converse. What's more, Norman Rockwell's classic *Portraits of America* now are available as handsome miniatures — a series of cameos and vignettes based on some of America's most popular paintings.

A Diverse Array of Artists and Media — All From Goebel

Rockwell's *Portraits of America* not only inspire Goebel Miniatures, but also a wonderful series of regular size plates and figurines. Goebel Crystal — which is 24% full lead crystal made in Germany — offers a dazzling selection of animals, Disney characters, and classic cars.

Goebel's Steinbach designs combine crystal and molten glass to offer marvelously detailed, engraved designs, presented on bold geometric shapes. Goebel Gifts include pieces for Easter and Christmas presentation, as well as precious *Snowbirds* that make a fine gift for any occasion. The *Christmas Treasures* designed by Goebel include colorful, intricately painted angels, Santas, nativity scenes, and other holiday delights.

The Goebel family of products continues to grow with works in porcelain, crystal, and other fine media from talented artists of the past and present. Ranging in appeal from contemporary tastes to traditional Americana, each line is identified by the highly regarded "Goebel" brand, or one of several distinctive licenses. What's more, each is intended to bring lasting pleasure to its purchaser or gift recipient — a five-generation Goebel tradition since 1871.

Goebel of North America
Goebel Plaza
P.O. Box 10, Rte. 31
Pennington, NJ 08534-0010
(609) 737-8700
Fax (609) 737-1545

The "Once Upon a Winter's Day" — Vignette by Douglas Norrgard is one of Goebel's Masterpieces in Miniature. The vignette includes seven hand-painted bronze sculptures, and relates a childhood memory with great visual eloquence.

THE GREAT AMERICAN® TAYLOR COLLECTIBLES CORP.

A World of Collecting from Teddy Bears to Santa Claus

These adorable members of The Taylor Bear Family *were among the first works of art from The Great American Taylor Collectibles Corp. They include grandparents "Glyn" and "Marcie," their daughter "Elizabeth" and her husband "Beauregard," and the grandchildren "Suzy" and "Sidney."*

With their soulful, shoe-button eyes and cuddly good looks, the *Taylor Bears*™ of The Great American® Taylor Collectibles Corp. were born to win collectors' hearts. Indeed, these wonderful folk art bear characters established Great American as an important new force in the world of collecting – soon after the North Carolina company's founding in 1980 by its namesake, Jack Taylor.

More than 100 different designs in *The Taylor Bear Family*™ have introduced a marvelous clan of bears dressed in bright clothing and ready for fun and adventure. Favorite characters include "Glyn" and "Marcie," their daughter "Elizabeth," her husband "Beauregard" and the grandchildren "Suzy" and "Sidney."

Although they are cold cast before hand-painting, these adorable bears boast a hand-carved look reminiscent of the great, classic folk arts of their Carolina roots. The original *Taylor Bear Family* retired in 1989, but they were succeeded by another marvelous collection, *The Taylor Bear Professionals*™. Most of these doctors, firefighters, teachers, nurses and other "hard-working" bears are still available today. Sadly, their creator, Glyn Snow, died in 1989: a tragedy for all those who love the *Taylor Bears*.

Old World Santas Find New Collectors

While the bears hold a special place in people's hearts, perhaps Great American's most beloved line of all is Lancy Smith's *Old World Santas*, which were introduced in 1988. Each year, five new originals are carved in wood and five from the past are retired. Each year's set "lives" three years before retirement. All are serially numbered, gift boxed and – as is traditional with Great American collectibles – come with rights to full-color personalized Certificates of Ownership. All the collector needs to do is mail the blue request card enclosed with each figurine to acquire this attractive certificate with its gold seal: a personalized document handsome enough for framing.

Each of the *Old World Santas* is completely made in the United States from an oak-like, cold cast material, then hand-painted to perfection by skilled artists in North Carolina's Sandhills. Pieces range in height from 6" to 8" and the issue price for active editions is $29.00 each.

The first 20 *Old World Santas* already have been retired, with secondary market trading well underway for most pieces.

The 1993 collection, which retired at the end of 1995, featured "Franz" of Switzerland, "Otto" of Germany, "Vito" of Italy, "Bjorn" of Sweden and "Ryan" of Canada. The pieces also come with interesting and personal stories, as if they were real people. "Otto," for example lives in Wiesbaden, Germany. His great-grandfather was a Prussian general who loved to have his men march to drums. Every Christmas, "Otto" marches along the Rhine River, beating his drums and distributing toys to the

Among the most popular Great American lines is Lancy Smith's Old World Santas, *which were introduced in 1988. The 1995 introductions include (from left to right): "Lars" of Norway, "Tomba" of South Africa, "Butch" of the United States, "Raymond" of the Galapagos Islands and "Stach" of Poland.*

Collectors can join the Great American Collectors' Guild by simply purchasing one of the company's special Collectors Club pieces, including "Winston" and "Timothy." In addition to enjoying these finely crafted pieces, collectors will receive a free one-year membership and receive three issues of the Club newsletter.

delight of girls and boys.

Retired at the end of 1994 were the Santas first unveiled in 1992. They are: "Jacques" of France, "Mickey" of Ireland, "Terry" of Denmark, "Jose" of Spain and "Stu" from Poland. "Stu" even has his own special story. It seems he's from Warsaw and can't stand clutter or dust. So he carries his straw broom everywhere to keep everything tidy. The pieces, retired in 1994, are already selling on the secondary market for between $36.00 and $50.00.

First introduced in 1994 and available through 1996 are these wonderful Santas: "Ivan" of Russia, "Desmond" of England, "Gord" of Canada, "Wilhelm" of Holland, and "Angus" of Scotland. "Angus" hails from Aberdeen, Scotland, where he and his pet Scotty dog, McNeil, raise Aberdeen Angus cattle on a nearby ranch. "Angus" plays checkers with the Lord Mayor of Aberdeen every Tuesday night, and McNeil entertains them by dancing on his hind legs when he hears the Lord Mayor's bagpipes played on his CD.

Introduced in 1995 are "Lars" of Lillihammer, Norway, who is so glad that the Olympics are over so he can get back to his serious salmon fishing; "Tomba" of South Africa; "Butch" of the United States, who is a fireman when

not playing Santa Claus; "Raymond" of the Galapagos Islands; and "Stach" of Poland.

Collectors can also join the Great American Collectors' Guild for free by purchasing one of the company's special Collectors Club pieces. Collectors will receive a free one-year membership and receive three issues of the Club newsletter. The current special Club pieces are "Winston" and "Timothy," who lives on the River Shannon in Limerick with his favorite leprechaun named Shenanigan. "Winston" retires in 1995 and "Timothy" in 1996. "William," the first edition piece, retired in 1994

Each year, five new pieces join the Jim Clement Santas collection and the same number of pieces are retired. The figurines that retired in 1995 were (top row from left to right): "Down the Chimney," "The Day After Christmas," "Mr. Egg," "Santa With Hobby Horse" and "Golfer Santa." Retiring in 1996 are (second row from left to right): "Tennis Santa," "Night After Christmas," "Noah," "Bald Santa With Rover," "Big Santa With Toys." The third row contains the 1997 retirees: "Doe A Deer," "Ho! Ho! Ho! Stuck in the Chimney," "Silent Night," "Mountain Dream." "Visions of Sugar Plums" is on the bottom row along with "Kris Jingle," the first edition Collectors' Guild piece that retires in 1996.

The Ruskins™ are here to share words of conservative wisdom and wit! Designed by artist Kevin Cagle and Jack Taylor, the line features these little devils that offer their insights on everything from family values to the value of good cigars.

and has appreciated in value on the secondary market.

Jim Clement's Santas Carve a New Niche

Jim Clement's 15 wood carving Santas were introduced in 1994 and have become extremely popular. As a master artisan from Ellijay, Georgia, Jim carves five new pieces each year and five are retired to ensure the line continues to contain only 15 subjects. Jim added "Kris Jingle" in 1995, his first edition Collectors' Club piece which is available both as a figurine and as a handsome lamp with a rich burgundy shade.

His other 1995 lamps, which are all serially numbered, include "Clementine Cat," "Uncle Sam," "Toy Soldier" and "Roosevelt Rooster." The figurines that retired in 1995 were: "Down the Chimney," "The Day After Christmas," "Mr. Egg," "Santa With Hobby Horse" and "Golfer Santa." Retiring in 1996 are: "Tennis Santa," "Night After Christmas," "Noah," "Bald Santa With Rover," "Big Santa With Toys" and "Kris Jingle." The 1997 retirees will be "Doe A Deer," "Ho! Ho! Ho! Stuck in the Chimney," "Silent Night," "Mountain Dream" and "Visions of Sugar Plums." They range in price from $13.75 to $70.00 each.

Ruskins™ Share Words of Wisdom

Another promising artist is Kevin Cagle from the Sandhills of North

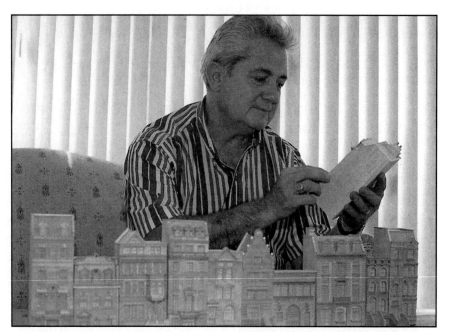

Great American's newest collectible line is New York Townhouses *crafted by award-winning architect Richard Banks. These turn-of-the-century designs recreate some of the finest townhouses owned by New York City's elite. Richard has researched and handcrafted in wood the originals of these townhouses on a 1/8" scale.*

angel and a devil, and will retire in 1998. The *Ruskins*, which sell for about $20.00 each, are gift boxed and serially numbered.

New York Townhouses Bring Back Memories

To combine his love of architecture, art and history, Richard Banks has created miniature historical town-houses built for the wealthy movers and shakers of 19th century New York. With more than 25 years of profes-sional experience, Richard has been a university teacher, president of an international architecture and plan-ning firm, head of his own design and real estate development group and construction management consultant to the Mayor of New York City on large-scale projects. Now he's building *New York Townhouses* — on a small scale.

From Fifth Avenue to 82nd Street, Richard has meticulously researched and handcrafted in wood the originals of these elite townhouses on a 1/8" scale.

Carolina. Kevin and Jack Taylor designed a line of *Ruskin™* figurines — conservative little devils who know the truth and have true courage to speak it ... with a smile. Each *Ruskin* comes with a special story. "Ruskin #1," which retired at the end of 1995, gives wis-dom on the family: "Folks, we need to return this country to its traditional family values..."

"Ruskin #2," retiring in December 1996, offers wisdom on our national wealth: "Folks, our national wealth is not a fixed amount of money that can be divided, but is a dynamic that depends for its continuation and growth on liberty and individual initia-tive, things that as a country we should nurture carefully." "Ruskin #3" talks about hard work and good cigars while "Ruskin #4," wearing a red jacket, promotes speaking the truth. Both will retire at the end of 1997. "Ruskin #5" and "Ruskin #6" are dressed as an

Great American Taylor Collectible Corp.
Dept. BIC Box 428
Aberdeen, NC 28388
(910) 944-7447
Fax (910) 944-7449

COLLECTORS' CLUB

The Great American Collectors' Guild
P.O. Box 428
Aberdeen, NC 28315
(910) 944-7447

Annual Dues: Free with purchase of Club Piece
Club Year: January-December

Benefits:
• Newsletter Published Three Times Yearly
• Buy/Sell Matching Service
• Tour of Factory Available

THE GREENWICH WORKSHOP

Bringing "Art as Entertainment" into People's Lives Is The Greenwich Workshop's Mission

As the leading North American publisher of art and art-inspired products, including limited edition fine art prints, art books, videos, art furniture and figurines, as well as an innovator in the art entertainment industry, The Greenwich Workshop sees its mission as bringing art into our lives to enhance everyday entertainment and enjoyment. And The Greenwich Workshop believes that there is more than just one way to do it. The art, artists and offerings of the Workshop are as varied as the people who collect them. Be it a limited edition fine art print, a book, an art furnishings frame, porcelain figurine, silk neck tie with a favorite artist's image or an entertaining video, the works of The Greenwich Workshop and their family of artists can take you into the realms of the imagination, preserve a favorite experience in the wilderness, explore new lands, commemorate our history and cultural heritage, or quite simply create a beautiful impression.

"Everyone enjoys art regardless of their level of knowledge and personal taste. Although few of us are fortunate enough to have access to original works of art by outstanding artists," says David Usher, co-founder and chairman of The Greenwich Workshop,

Journey into the wilderness to witness one of our planet's most magnificent animals in his natural habitat. "Golden Silhouette" is from Simon Combes' exciting The Great Cats Adventure *series.*

"many of us can enjoy them in the form of limited edition fine art prints, posters, books, or a high-quality porcelain figurine in our homes."

Greenwich's Window on the World Is Opened by Today's Most Accomplished Artists

The Greenwich Workshop is proud to offer wildlife artist Simon Combes' one-of-a-kind collection: *The Great Cats Adventure.* Prints in this series capture and preserve, on canvas and print, and bring to our attention the tenuous status of endangered feline predators as they have never before been seen. Collectors discover in Combes' detailed works a sensitivity and eye for color that makes *The Great Cats Adventure* a popular contemporary series. Look for a picture of "Golden Silhouette" in this article! It gives you a sample of the power and grace of Combes' magnificent animal art.

For fans of Native American art, painter Howard Terpning's sensitive studies are unrivaled. Terpning's reputation for authentic art depicting our indigenous peoples is so remarkable, he's been called "The Storyteller of the Native American People." Current Greenwich Workshop prints by Terpning are in great demand from coast-to-coast.

Few contemporary artists have known the adulation, awards and success of Bev Doolittle. The Greenwich Workshop counts her western spiritual works among its current best sellers. Doolittle has sold more prints than any other artist worldwide; some say her "Prayer for the Wild Things" will remain a benchmark for every artist wishing to infuse their paintings with spiritual reminders of nature's majesty.

Reknowned for his best-selling, groundbreaking book Dinotopia®, *artist James Gurney again ventures into a world of fantasy in his new book* The World Beneath. *"Exhultation" is the dynamic art created to grace the book's cover.*

Fantasy...History...Folk Art and Fairy Tales

Because American collectors have eclectic tastes and enjoy variety, The Greenwich Workshop represents the work of today's most innovative artists. Who hasn't heard of James Gurney, creator of the international best-seller *Dinotopia?* Images of Gurney's land, where dinosaurs and people live in harmony, are available as fine art prints from Greenwich. By the way, if you're a fantasy buff and love lots of bright color and imaginative detail in your prints, James Christensen's work is right up your alley. His charming works (self-described as 'a little left of reality') are eagerly collected by art fans of every age.

Just down the sky a piece from Gurney and Christensen, the adventurous world of aviation history awaits. William S. Phillips' sold out print, "The Giant Begins to Stir," artfully depicts the flight of the Doolittle Raiders when they dominated the skies over 50 years ago during World War II. The historic value of this print doesn't rest with the art alone; collectors will discover counter-signatures of Doolittle and the surviving crew members of the 16-aircraft armada featured in this exciting print.

The Greenwich Workshop recently published two highly notable works which commemorate aviation history: The flights of the Enola Gay ("Dawn, the World Forever Changed," also by Phillips), and Bock's Car (Craig Kodera's "Lonely Flight to Destiny"). Each pays tribute to our bravest men and their daring missions which many believed helped to bring an end to the war in the Pacific.

Countersignatures of ten crewman (including General Paul Tibbets, command pilot of the Enola Gay) appear on these dynamic prints. As an added note, when these legendary heroes were assembled to sign the prints, the idea for a documentary took shape. "The Men Who Brought The Dawn," produced by The Greenwich Workshop, debuted this fall.

From the dangerous skies over the Pacific to the more idyllic places of the heart in America, The Greenwich Workshop also offers a superior variety of popular subjects to suit every taste. Popular folk artist John Simpkins' bold colors and simple lines have captured hearts of every age. Both adults and children flock to Scott Gustafson's fanciful fairy tales and nursery rhymes, done in his opulent painting style. Finally, discover the soft light twinkling from the windows in artist Paul Landry's "Morning Mist," featured in this article.

Windows reflect light everywhere after a drenching rain! Paul Landry's "Morning Mist" exemplifies his masterful ability to make us feel we're standing on this street.

Music to Soothe the Spirit...Art to Warm the Soul

As an innovator in today's art entertainment arena, The Greenwich Workshop is exploring a variety of media to bring art into every facet of our lives. A prime example is "Art in Concert™," an entertainment combining visual and audio elements. Developed exclusively by The Greenwich Workshop, "Art in Concert" brings together legendary musicians, composers, artists and painters.

The premier "Art in Concert" production, which was awarded a Grammy this year, pairs two legends: Grammy award-winning musician/composer Paul Winter and the inspired art of Bev Doolittle. This marriage of sights and sounds meshes Paul Winter's composition "Prayer For the Wild Things" with Bev's best-selling, award-winning artwork of the same title. Viewers are treated to a sensory celebration when they see and hear these glorious works. A second "Art in Concert" matches James Christensen's wonderful "Evening Angels" image with a new composition by the Emmy-award winning composer Kurt Bestor. Stay tuned!

Four years ago, The Greenwich Workshop pioneered a film and video project presenting art as 'a living experience.' This innovative program, called "The Living Canvas," takes viewers into a work of art to examine the people, events, emotions and stories that emerge from the heart and hand of the artist. Among the stories presented in "The Living Canvas" are "Memories of War," a documentary that details the surprise attack at Clark Field on Pearl Harbor in December 1941.

It was the first ever documentary picked for airing on a Pay-Per-View channel. Based on its success, The Greenwich Workshop took "The Living Canvas," hosted by actor Billy Dee Williams, to Public Television, where it aired initially on WNET, New York. Subsequently, over 300 more stations around the country broadcast this program.

Stephen Lyman's "Cathedral Snow" exemplifies the artist's sensitive view of nature. Lyman's prints are best-sellers. His new book, Into the Wilderness, was released in the fall of 1995.

Keeping Company with Some of America's Giants

Though The Greenwich Workshop is just 23 years old, it has had a remarkable evolution. Beginning as a publisher of limited edition fine art prints, Greenwich has expanded its scope to include licensing, art furnishings, porcelain figurines and book publishing. Distinguished among its first offerings was the best selling book, *Dinotopia*, which has sold over one million copies. Now, over 16 titles are in print, including *The World Beneath* (James Gurney's newest book, slated for publication in Fall, 1995) and Bev Doolittle's *New Magic*, also a Fall, 1995, release.

Perennial favorite Stephen Lyman's new book, *Into the Wilderness*, combines his "light in the wilderness" painting style and photography with an inspiring text. Lyman shows readers the natural wonders of Yosemite and the American Northwest as they've never before been seen. A classic example of Stephen Lyman's gentle eye for nature's magic can be found in this article!

In addition to publishing, The Greenwich Workshop debuts a new collection of three-dimensional figurines from world-famous artists James Christensen, Scott Gustafson and Will Bullas. Called *The Greenwich Workshop Collection*, each delightful figure in this new library is highly detailed, hand-painted and beautifully colored. Because each artist supervises

James Christensen's imaginative "Mother Goose" and her trusty transportation are about to take collectors on a magical journey into the imagination. This sculpture, a premier Greenwich Workshop Collection figurine, inaugurates this new venture into three-dimensional art.

the creation of his work...to be sure each is exactly as he imagined them...collectors are guaranteed something out-of-the-ordinary. Be sure to ask your favorite authorized Greenwich dealer to advise you as soon as The Greenwich Workshop Collection debuts!

Finally, partnerships with some of this nation's most dynamic multi-media companies are also being forged. The Greenwich Workshop has formed alliances with Universal, Columbia Pictures, Turner Publishing, Hallmark Cards, Inc., Bruce McGaw Publishing, Barnes and Noble, Random House, Mattel and Lenox. You can look forward to an exciting array of art, books, music, entertainment, giftware and collectible introductions as the new millennium approaches!

Stretching the Boundries While Remembering the Planet

When Greenwich Workshop was first established in 1972, no one could predict its meteoric success. But a combination of business savvy, foresight and a feel for America's eclectic taste in art and entertainment has given The Greenwich Workshop invaluable insight into the future. Without self-imposed limits, this young company can soar in new directions and find homes for its new introductions all over the world.

At present, the company distributes its limited edition fine art prints and other art-inspired offerings through a network of authorized dealers across the United States, Canada and the United Kingdom. To efficiently serve the Canadian and British markets, Greenwich U.S. oversees The Greenwich Workshop, Ltd. of Scarborough, Ontario, Canada and Greenwich Workshop Europe, located in Upton-upon-Severn, England.

The Greenwich Workshop also operates a select number of retail galleries specializing in original art. Named "Big Horn Galleries," these are located in Fairfield, Connecticut; Cody, Wyoming; Aspen, Colorado and Carmel, California.

Though growing by leaps and bounds in terms of international recognition and the scope of art it develops, The Greenwich Gallery continues to stay focused on its corporate mission. Toward that end, a never-ending search for new talent continues. Once an artist becomes a member of the Greenwich family, he or she is welcomed into a supportive environment of creative freedom. Importantly, artists associated with Greenwich share a concern for our fragile planet and our cultural heritage.

Throughout its existence, The Greenwich Workshop is proud to have made donations valued at more than three million dollars to various not-for-profit organizations related to health, the environment, public service, history and cultural preservation. This legacy will continue for as long as The Greenwich Workshop is privileged

The Greenwich Workshop
One Greenwich Place
Shelton, CT 06484
(800) 243-4246
Fax (203) 925-0262

THE HAMILTON COLLECTION
Renowned Artists and New Initiatives Keep Hamilton a Step Ahead in the World of Limited Edition Collectibles

The year: 1978. The plate: "Clara and Nutcracker." For the first time, The Hamilton Collection introduced a major limited edition collector plate — and the response was extraordinary! Winner of multiple honors and a strong performer on the secondary market, Shell Fisher's ballet-theme "Clara" set the stage for Hamilton's emergence as a leading direct response marketer of collectibles. Since then, the Jacksonville, Florida-based firm has won scores of honors — and set numerous sales records — with its collectible dolls, plates and figurines. What's more, Hamilton continues its innovative ways with planned introductions of miniature cottages, plaques and ornaments.

Over the last year or two, Hamilton's top performers included *Precious Moments*⁸ and *Dreamsicles*⁸ plates, as well as the adorable *Cherished Teddies*⁸ figurine collection. *STAR TREK™* plates — long a favorite of Hamilton collectors — continue their run of popularity, while Victorian and wildlife themes by top artists also intrigue art lovers. What's more, Hamilton continues to forge fruitful associations with some of today's most gifted doll designers, including Connie Walser Derek, Connie Johnston and Virginia Turner.

Heavenly *Dreamsicles* Make Their Plate Debut

Month after month, dealer polls reveal that the charming little *Dreamsicles* cherubs reign as one of today's most popular giftware figurines. Created by artist Kristin Haynes, the *Dreamsicles* began their life in three dimensions. Now — thanks to an exclusive association with The Hamilton Collection — these roly-poly cherubs star in their own plate collection as well — a *Dreamsicles* first.

The premiere plate, "The Flying Lesson," features a central scene of an apprehensive cherub and his two "flying tutors." The little angel is proud of his brand-new wings, but now he has to "take the plunge and give 'em a try!" Each heavenly cherub boasts his own heartwarming personality and expression. One tutor boldly claps his pupil on the back, urging the little hero to "go for it," while the other...soft-eyed and gentle...reads step-by-step directions from the "How to Fly" book. Meanwhile in the background, a brand-new flyer steadies herself for her first "solo spin."

The original *Dreamsicles* progressed from a series of pieces artist Haynes perfected while living in California. Some were crafted of cement in large sizes — as lawn ornaments — while others were smaller and cast in materials better suited for indoor display. The characteristic dried flower "halos" worn by *Dreamsicles* cherubs came about by experimentation. "Dried flowers are so popular, I just popped a little wreath on the cherub's head," Ms. Haynes recalls of a whim she followed one day. "It added so much — such a neat touch!"

Priscilla Hillman Presents *Monthly Friends to Cherish*

Bursting with irresistible charm and personality, the award-winning *Cherished Teddies* collection from Enesco has won the hearts of collectors all over the country. Now, The Hamilton Collection has joined forces with Enesco Corporation to present the *Monthly Friends to Cherish* figurine collection, featuring 12 irresistible teddy bears, one to help collectors celebrate each month of the year.

"Oscar" the October Bear visits neighbors and friends to enjoy lots of tricks and treats. The December bear's festive holiday attire shows her love for Christmas, from the holly on her Santa cap to the candy cane on the present she's holding. Each of the other 10 teddies boasts just such seasonal adornments and touches, and all are expertly crafted and hand-painted.

With *Cherished Teddies* recently voted the best-selling figurine in the nation's heartland according to *Collector's Mart* magazine, it's clear their admirers consider these much more than "bear necessities." In fact, teddy bear lovers everywhere have pronounced the *Monthly Friends to Cherish* a true "honey" of a collection!

An Encounter With...The Borg

Considering the continuing fascination for the original *STAR TREK* plate collection and the many collectible series and special editions that have followed the Starship Enterprise crew, it comes as no surprise that *STAR TREK: The Next Generation™* also has

"The Flying Lesson" by Kristin Haynes premieres The Hamilton Collection's Dreamsicles™ *plate collection.*

"A Wolf's Pride" by David Geenty represents the first issue in a Hamilton sculpture collection titled Wolves of the Wilderness.

inspired a host of popular Hamilton collectibles. Among the most recent is "The Best of Both Worlds," a fine porcelain plate that premiers a series entitled *STAR TREK: The Next Generation™ — The Episodes.*

In this work of art by renowned cinematic painter Keith Birdsong, a cataclysmic, all-consuming spiral of events thrusts the entire crew of the Starship Enterprise into a confrontation with their great adversary, the Borg. This is an alien species whose very existence knows but one command — to assimilate all other life forms. Now the Borg seeks to annihilate humankind, and the crew must stop them.

This stunning drama so astounded the television industry that "The Best of Both Worlds" was honored with four Emmy nominations. Now it premieres a dazzling plate series of montage scenes from the series' most exciting and provocative shows.

Love's Messengers Capture the Glories of Victoriana

Artist and designer John Grossman is considered one of the world's leading authorities on Victorian paper keepsakes. Twenty years ago, this California painter happened into an antique shop, a visit that changed his

life forever. Fascinated with the Victorian antique paper mementos, he found them to be an unending source of inspiration and the foundation for a passion that has grown into a distinguished collectibles career.

Over the years, Grossman has acquired a treasury of exquisite paper memorabilia, which he fashions into wonderfully touching collages such as the one which appears on "To My Love" — premiere issue in the *Love's Messengers* plate collection.

Like previous Grossman plate series featuring Victorian children and holiday themes, "To My Love" displays a wonderful, central image: in this case an adorable cupid holding a beautiful floral wreath — the universal symbol of affection. Surrounding this vision of romantic love are all manner of roses, lace, forget-me-nots and trinkets: the perfect expression of Victorian style.

Nature's Beautiful Creatures...Captured in Three Dimension

Two recent series of hand-painted sculptures from The Hamilton Collection pay tribute to beloved creatures of the wild. *Little Friends of the Arctic* premieres with "The Young Prince," while *Wolves of the Wilderness* unveils "A Wolf's Pride."

"The Young Prince" — an adorable polar bear baby — is as cute and playful as he can be. One day he will grow up to be ruler of his snow-bound kingdom. But for now, he seems content to rest on his crystal ice throne, dreaming of his next adventure. Handcrafted of fine porcelain and painted by hand, "The Young Prince" comes complete with a handsome, lead crystal base. Other pieces in the collection will present additional charming baby animals of the polar region.

"A Wolf's Pride" is the creation of British artist David Geenty, who spent much of his childhood on his parents' ranch in Southeast Africa. There his

love of nature was nurtured, while his father led photographers and other lovers of nature on safaris through the bush. According to Geenty, *Wolves of the Wilderness* is intended "to draw attention to the importance of preserving America's rich natural history, as represented by its indigenous wolf population."

This first issue focuses on three handsome, curious pups, nestled against their mother for safety and warmth. Meticulously crafted and hand-painted, it lets viewers admire an animal that is highly intelligent and remarkably skilled as a hunter, caring for its young with tenderness and pride.

A Trio of Enchanting Dolls Showcase Three Designers' Gifts

The Hamilton Collection has become a major force in the contemporary doll market over the last decade, with collectors offering kudos for the firm's ability to "team up" with some of the world's most honored doll designers. Foremost among these is Connie Walser Derek, who brings a unique and lovable personality to each of her doll creations.

Take "Chelsea" for example — who is becoming such a big girl and quite a pro at sitting up. In this newly mastered position, she's discovering so many exciting things around her...like her shoelaces which are sure to keep her busy for hours! So marvelously true-to-life as she reaches for her laces, "Chelsea" is crafted of fine, bisque porcelain, painted by hand and inscribed with Connie Walser Derek's signature. In her lavender and rose floral playsuit, "Chelsea" is dressed for a day of fun and discovery!

Next, you're invited to meet "Savannah" by the gifted new artist Connie Johnston. "Savannah" is a sweet little cowgirl from the wide open prairie, and her cornflower blue eyes and sun-kissed charm are sure to steal your heart! All dressed up in her toe-tapping best, "Savannah" proudly shows off her new boots she'll wear to tonight's rodeo. Her Western-style outfit is cheery and wholesome as the

Dressed in her Western best, lovely "Savannah" is the creation of gifted doll designer Connie Johnston.

sky is big and blue. And her pretty hand is accented by a delicate, heart-shaped silver-tone ring.

Don't forget lovely "Amelia," the creation of award-winning doll artist Virginia Turner. All dressed up in a beautiful gown, she presents a timeless portrait of innocence and friendship. "Amelia" wears her hair upswept with a lacy, silk flower-trimmed bow, and her lace-trimmed slip and bloomers coordinate with her matching socks. Pretty shoes with satin ribbon, floral accents and faux pearls complete this sweet child's attire — and she holds an adorable plush teddy named "Cinnamon!"

Never content to rest on their laurels, Hamilton Collection officials constantly draw upon their worldwide resources to develop even more delightful collector plates, figurines and dolls for the future. What's more, with works in innovative new media like miniature cottages, plaques and ornaments under development, the future for Hamilton collectors remains full of bright anticipation.

The Hamilton Collection
4810 Executive Park Court
Jacksonville, FL 32216-6069
(800) 228-2945
Fax (904) 279-1339

188

HAND & HAMMER SILVERSMITHS

A Renowned Family of Silversmiths Makes Its Mark with Handcrafted Collectibles and a Traditional Craft

Chip deMatteo (left) and Philip Thorp founded Hand & Hammer Silversmiths and today lead a team of talented artisans from the company's studio in Woodbridge, Virginia. Both learned and perfected their trade from Chip's father, Bill deMatteo, Jr.

During the bustling 1920s in New York City, William deMatteo, Sr. began perfecting a craft that would inspire three generations of his family and reach audiences around the world from presidents to royalty. As a 16-year-old Italian immigrant, deMatteo transformed silver into beautiful, shimmering works of art. He became a premier silversmith — sharing the mysteries and secrets of his trade with his son, William (Bill) deMatteo, Jr., who in 1979 founded Hand & Hammer Silversmiths.

Today, the thriving business is guided by Bill's son, Chip deMatteo, and his partner Philip Thorp. They follow in the same time-worn traditions as the elder deMatteo, who set the family on a course to become world renowned for their silver collectible ornaments and jewelry.

The company's creations have graced rooms at the White House.

American presidents have commissioned gifts for Queen Elizabeth II, Anwar Sadat, Menacham Begin and Winston Churchill. Leading companies call upon Hand & Hammer Silversmiths to design exclusive gifts for their customers. But whether presented to a dignitary or cherished by collectors nationwide, each piece reflects the deMatteo's legacy and the rich heritage of silversmithing.

A Legacy of Excellence Follows Three Generations

Bill deMatteo, Jr. settled his young family in Colonial Williamsburg, where he became a master silversmith during the 1950s and directed a workshop of more than 100 craftsmen. His designs were recognized beyond the historic streets of Williamsburg. John F. Kennedy selected a pair of solid silver lanterns for the Oval Office. Richard Nixon commissioned a silver globe, and Gerald Ford was presented with a miniature Liberty Bell.

The deMatteos also strongly advocated preserving the integrity and tradition of their craft, which Bill taught to hundreds of apprentices and journeymen. His two most talented pupils were Philip Thorp and Chip deMatteo.

By the time he was 10 years old, Chip started doing chores around the shop and showing a remarkable talent for silversmithing. After college, Chip moved to Washington D.C., where he played the "starving artist" role for several years. During that time, Chip supplemented his income doing silver work for his father and Philip, who was then Bill's foremost journeyman silversmith.

Along with several other silversmiths from Williamsburg, Bill, Phil and Chip moved to Alexandria, Virginia, in

the late 1970s to set up their own shop at Hand & Hammer Silversmiths. The unique designs that are the hallmark of Hand & Hammer's work began to shine. As the studio attracted more craftsmen, the small shop in Old Town Alexandria was bursting at the seams. To meet the demands of growth, Hand & Hammer and its centuries-old craft jumped into the 21st century with a spacious, high-tech, custom-designed shop in Woodbridge, Virginia. It is from here that all the beautiful Hand & Hammer pieces are created today.

The Creation of a Hand & Hammer Design

Silversmithing is an art that predates written history. Bright white and lustrous in its natural state, silver is the most reflective material on the earth and the best conductor of heat and electricity. An ancient treatise on metals proclaimed: "He who wished to be acclaimed a master silversmith must be a good universal master in many arts, for the kind of work which comes to his hand are infinite. Those who work in silver must outdistance all other craftsmen in learning and achievement to the same degree that their materials outdistance other metals in nobility."

Each Hand & Hammer design comes from the mastery, heart and hands of Chip deMatteo. From his drawing table, he turns his quick sketches into complete, scaled pictures. From there, they become actual patterns sculpted by hand in either wax or metal. Making the pattern is an exacting process, often taking many weeks to complete.

Attention to detail at this stage is critical to the successful outcome of the prototype, from which molds for the casting process will be made. Hand & Hammer's ornaments are cast using the age-old "lost wax" method in which a casting model is made and then destroyed as part of the difficult, time-

As intricate and timeless as its jeweled counterpart, this "Fabergé Egg" sterling silver ornament captures the intricate beauty and elegance found in all works by Hand & Hammer Silversmiths. The ornament measures 2-3/4".

consuming process. Lost wax casting is much preferred over machine stamping because it yields a piece with greater detail and allows the designer more creativity in terms of overall form, shape or size.

After it is cast, each piece must be "finished" in the Woodbridge shop. This is accomplished through a series of abrasives. The first step is tumbling, a procedure in which pieces are placed with abrasives in a rotating barrel for an entire day. The next steps involve progressive hand-polishing with a succession of finer and finer abrasives until the piece's silver surface resembles a shiny mirror. Hand & Hammer's polishers, Tim, Cherie, Bill and Art, have been with the company for a long time, as it takes many years to develop the skills needed to make the pieces of raw silver come to life.

The shop is supervised by Gene Sutton, who like Phil Thorp and Chip deMatteo, was trained by Bill deMatteo in Williamsburg. The pieces are all held to a rigorous quality check at each stage of finishing, so only the finest works of art leave the shop. Of course, there is still more to be done. Washing, wrap-ping and packaging takes time and careful effort. Employees Pam, Kathy and Phyllis ensure everything that goes out to stores nationwide is first-rate.

A Tradition of Contemporary Designs and Childhood Favorites

Chip deMatteo is always asked: "Where do you get the ideas for your wonderful designs?" According to him, it's one of the hardest questions to answer. "I've always been creative," he explains. "When I was little, the most fun to me was figuring out how to make something or to find out how something worked. I got into trouble for taking apart the seat of a school bus to see how it was put together.

"But I can have an idea buzzing around in my head for a long time before I figure out how I want it to look as an ornament or piece of jewelry. Sometimes I'll agonize over a design and sometimes it comes out just right on the first try. It's a whole new process each time. That's why it's always interesting," he says with a smile.

While original designs take most of Chip's time, he also enjoys working from old and famous drawings. The *Alice In Wonderland* set of four ornaments was designed using the original John Tenniel drawings for Lewis Carroll's classic story. "Those were fun to do," says Chip.

"Tenniel's drawings are what everyone refers to when they talk about *Alice In Wonderland*, and I think ours turned out very well. By contrast, look at our *Christmas Carol* set of four ornaments. I wanted to illustrate the Charles Dickens book in my own way, and I'm pleased with the result." In 1995, Hand & Hammer introduced a set of four ornaments illustrating Clement Moore's beloved poem *'Twas the Night Before Christmas*.

In recent years, Chip has enjoyed designing sterling silver charms for bracelets. He did a set of charms portraying *Alice in Wonderland*, The *Wizard of Oz* and *Mother Goose*, as well as a full line of Beatrix Potter's delightful creatures in miniature. "The Beatrix Potter pieces are wonderful and working from her original drawings in England was a real thrill for me," Chip says. "People have a wonderful nostalgic response to her little animals." Each year, Hand & Hammer adds another piece to the Peter Rabbit line.

Hand & Hammer Silversmiths also continues existing lines with its "1995 Silver Bells," "1995 Star" and the "Three French Hens" from the *12 Days of Christmas*.

Custom Designs for Companies and Collectors Nationwide

Over the years, Chip has designed more than 500 ornaments with some in collaboration with his father. Many of these also have been sold through finer department and gift stores. In addition, some of Hand & Hammer's most collectible designs are series produced exclusively for the world's most honored institutions, museums and private companies.

Since 1963, Shreve, Crump & Low of Boston has commissioned Hand & Hammer to create exclusive ornaments, including two notable series, *Boston Landmarks* and *Landmarks of America*. Also in Boston, the Museum

A perfect addition to any Christmas tree, "Heralding Angel" proclaims the holiday season in this sterling silver ornament, which measures 2".

Each year, Hand & Hammer Silversmiths introduces a dated sterling silver star. Limited to the year of issue, "1995 Star" is a six-pointed creation by Chip deMatteo.

of Fine Arts has commissioned Hand & Hammer's ornaments for its Christmas catalog since 1979. The museum's series have included an annual snowflake and pieces based on a Kate Greenaway collection. Other special subjects include an annual angel for the Smithsonian catalog and San Francisco Scenes for Shreve & Co.

Keeping Collectors Up To Date with the Latest Creations

With the tremendous growth of the company and its continuous introduction of new designs, Hand & Hammer collectors often ask for a complete list of collectibles from their favorite studio. This request inspired the 1979 introduction of "Silver Tidings," the newsletter of the Hand & Hammer Collectors' Club. The entire list is updated and published annually, along with occasional newsletters that mention the latest collectibles and where to find them.

Hand & Hammer's Collectors' Club membership is free, and the Club sponsors store and show appearances by Chip deMatteo and Philip Thorp. Collectors may sign up for the Club through participating Collectors' Club retailers or by calling Hand & Hammer at 1-800-SILVERY.

Despite all the new pieces coming out of the Hand & Hammer workshop, Chip says he still has many more ideas in his head — and never grows tired of creating new designs. "I have so much to keep me interested," he says. "I work with people I like and I make beautiful things. That's what keeps me going."

Three generations of silversmiths and a tradition of excellence will also keep Hand & Hammer going for a long, long time.

Hand & Hammer Silversmiths
2610 Morse Lane
Woodbridge, VA 22192
(800) SILVERY
Fax (703) 491-2031

COLLECTORS' CLUB

Hand & Hammer Collectors' Club
2610 Morse Lane
Woodbridge, VA 22192
(800) SILVERY

Annual Dues: None
Club Year: January 1-December 31

Benefits:
• Newsletter, "Silver Tidings"
• Complete List of Hand & Hammer Ornaments, Updated Annually
• Club Sponsored Artist Events

HARBOUR LIGHTS
Collectible Lighthouses of the World

Nothing indicates the prosperity or intelligence of a nation more clearly than the facilities which it affords for the safe approach of the mariner to the shore.

—Report of the Lighthouse Board, 1868

Since the earliest days of man, when fires were lit atop hills to guide fishermen safely into port, mariners have struggled to develop nighttime navigational aids. The oldest known lighthouse, dating back to 300 B.C., was built by the Egyptians on the island of Pharos, at the entrance to the harbor of Alexandria. As time went by, lamps and reflectors replaced fires, and lighthouses became a commonplace sight throughout the European continent, America, and beyond.

Bill Younger's Dream Becomes Reality

Lighthouses have always symbolized strength and hope in the face of adversity. When Bill Younger, the founder of Harbour Lights, was just a small boy, his uncle would often take him fishing on the Chesapeake Bay. At night, as he watched the flickering lights of the distant lighthouses, he was reminded of an earlier time, when the diligence of a light keeper was the only thing to prevent a ship from being dashed to pieces on dangerous shoals.

A natural storyteller, Bill has always had a deep and abiding appreciation of history. Growing up in the nation's capitol gave him ample opportunity to visit museums and historical sites. His love for old buildings, and architecture in general, planted the seeds that would eventually become Harbour Lights. Bill believes that any study of American history would be incomplete without examining the role that lighthouses have played in shaping our destiny.

The idea for Harbour Lights began to

form in 1989, when the Postal Service issued a collection of stamps in honor of our nation's lighthouses. Bill felt inspired to create a line of lighthouse sculptures that would accurately depict American architecture. With a solid background in collectible buildings behind him - Younger was the first representative in the United States to market David Winter Cottages - he set about to transform his ideas into a three-dimensional form.

Working closely with his family, Bill's dream became a reality, when in the spring of 1991, Harbour Lights was introduced to the general public. Rather than developing a single artist, he decided to work with a small team of staff sculptors. The reasons are two-fold. For one thing, our coastal lighthouses were built by many different individuals, and are quite unique in their own right. Also, Bill felt that the underlying goal of Harbour Lights was to promote maritime history and architecture, rather than a particular artist. In each recreation, he wants to achieve a rendering that is so accurate, it is unmistakable for the real thing. At the same time, he has made a sincere effort not to stifle the creativity of the artists.

The original collection consisted of 17 pieces, including two of America's most famous lighthouses, Boston Harbor and Cape Hatteras. Boston Harbor Light has a particularly special meaning to Bill. It was the first lighthouse to be erected in the American colonies in 1713. Destroyed by the British just prior to the signing of the Declaration of Independence, the original tower was not replaced until 1783. The newly erected tower has endured and protected mariners to this day, and has remained a symbol of our nation's nautical tradition. Although automation has made the need for light keepers all but unnecessary, the Coast Guard has determined

"Fire Island, NY" was erected on the southern shore of Long Island in 1857. Through local preservation efforts, this beautiful light is being restored to its original splendor. "Fire Island" Light measures 9" x 7", is limited to 9,500 hand-numbered pieces and retails for a suggested $70.00.

that Boston Light will be our last manned lighthouse.

A Thriving Family Business

Like many great ideas, Harbour Lights is a family affair. The first 17 pieces were chosen by Bill, his wife Nancy, daughters Kim and Tori Dawn, and Tori's husband, Harry Hine. Since then, the pieces have been chosen through popular request by consumers. The current collection consists of more than 50 pieces from all regions of the country and will soon expand to include lighthouses from Canada and other parts of the world.

Much of the original research was carried out by Bill's daughter, Kim Andrews. Kim currently serves as

Managing Director and is responsible for the day-to-day operations of the company, as well as direction of the staff artists. Since retiring from work with John Hine Ltd., Bill Younger is devoting full time to research and promotion of Harbour Lights. He has personally visited dozens of lighthouses in the United States and other countries, often in quite remote settings. To understand what life may have been like growing up in a real lighthouse setting, Bill has also made an effort to interview children of light keepers.

Harbour Lights collectibles are cast from several durable substances, including hydrostone (a gypsum material) and cold-cast porcelain. Both materials are renowned for their strength and hardness. These are made into a pouring mixture and cast, capturing extremely fine detail in every figure. Before a new piece is considered "ready" for production and release, an enormous amount of time is spent on review and inspection.

Earlier editions were generally limited to productions of 5,500 hand-numbered pieces, and then ceremoniously retired. Most of the original 17 are currently sold out and can only be obtained on the secondary market. To accomodate an ever-expanding collector base, future releases may number up to 9,500 pieces. Upon retirement, the original molds are completely destroyed, never to be used again.

Tori Dawn Younger Hine is the origination painter for Harbour Lights. She is well known as the first promotional painting artist in the U. S. for David Winter Cottages. A talented artist who began honing her skills at the tender age of eight, she accepts her responsibilities seriously, sometimes working around the clock to complete an assignment. Capturing beauty and emotion in a miniature sculpture is no easy task. Tori Dawn uses a combination of oil-based paints, as well as acrylic to achieve the desired effect. If you look carefully at each of her lighthouse reproductions, you can feel a part of our history coming through, from the weathered brick and stone towers to the sun-worn roofs of the keeper's cottages.

Award-Winning Lighthouses

The United States is blessed with some of the finest shoreline in the world and has a rich maritime history. Since the early 1700s, our forefathers have taken prudent steps to provide lighted navigational aids for our brave mariners. To honor these important sentinels, Harbour Lights has created lighthouse series from the Northeast, Great Lakes, Southeast, Western and Gulf Coast regions.

Each limited edition collectible created by Harbour Lights is carefully hand-painted and hand-numbered. It comes complete with its own history, Certificate of Authenticity, and registration card. Late in 1994, Harbour Lights introduced its first open edition piece, "Cape Hatteras, NC" as part of the *Great Lighthouses of the World* collection. This important series will feature select famous lighthouses from all over the world. While generally smaller than the limited edition series, the open edition collection will be subject to the same exacting standards of quality that have made Harbour Lights so popular among collectors.

The reception to Harbour Lights has been overwhelming. In four short years, they have become the collectors' choice for serious lighthouse afficionados. Wayne Wheeler, President of the U. S. Lighthouse Society, has spoken of Harbour Lights as "quite simply the best quality lighthouse collectible available." In fact, it is the only lighthouse line to be honored with national awards. In 1994, "St. Simon's Light" received the prestigious "Award of Excellence" from *Collector Editions* magazine, while "Cape Hatteras" was presented with a meritorious "Achievement Award" by The National Association of Limited Edition Dealers (NALED). The following year, "Cape Neddick" was named a finalist for the "Award of Exellence," and NALED named Harbour Lights as one of five finalists for the industry's top honor, "Collectible of the Year." This past Spring, at the Collectors Jubilee in Tulsa, Harbour Lights received the prestigious "1996 Collector's Choice Award for Best Unlighted House."

Harbour Lights Collector's Society

In April of 1995, Harbour Lights achieved a major milestone, with the introduction of the Harbour Lights Collector's Society. With the founding of the society, members will have an opportunity to share with fellow enthusiasts the joys of collecting and

Harbour Lights is proud to present a limited edition series, honoring the heroism of the ladies that kept our nation's lighthouses. Shown here from the top, clockwise are: "Matinicus, ME" kept by Abbie Burgess, "Point Piños, CA" kept by Emily Fish, "Saugerties, NY" kept by Kate Crowley, "Lime Rock, RI" kept by Ida Lewis and "Chatham Light" kept by Angeline Nickerson.

expand their knowledge of lighthouses and maritime history. Memberships are renewable on an annual basis and cost just $30.00 per year.

Response to the Collector's Society during the Charter Year was absolutely tremendous. The 1996 - 1997 Membership Period offers even more exciting benefits. Privileges include:

- An exclusive member gift: 4-Piece "Spyglass" Mini Lighthouse collection, gift boxed.
- Each member will also receive a beautiful cloisonné "Stonington Harbor" pin.
- Quarterly Subscription to the "Lighthouse Legacy," including a handsome binder for new members.
- Renewing Members will receive a Limited Edition, matted watercolor print of "Stonington Harbor." Each museum quality print will be signed and numbered by artist Mark Sherman.
- A Redemption Letter for the exclusive annual piece, "Stonington Harbor, CT." This historic sentinel was Connecticut's first lighthouse.
- A Certificate suitable for framing for each new member.
- A personal Membership Card.

The Future

Harbour Lights will continue to expand its collection in the coming months. Sculptors are currently working on foreign lighthouses, and the *Great Lighthouses of the World* will soon become a reality. In the course of his travel and research, Bill Younger has visited lighthouses in China, England, Russia and Finland.

"Lighthouses are just beginning to touch the imagination of the public," says Younger. "People are coming to appreciate their historical importance." He loves to speak at gatherings of collectors and lighthouse enthusiasts, entertaining audiences with nautical lore. Before finishing a presentation, he encourages everyone present to join a lighthouse preservation group.

The days of lighthouse keepers climbing tower steps to keep an oil lantern burning are long past, but their memory is not forgotten. Lighthouses and the courageous men and women who accepted the call as keepers of the light, will always remain an important part of our heritage. It is to them and their legacy that Harbour Lights dedicates these fine works of art.

"Thomas Point Shoal Light, MD" stands proudly after more than a century. It is the last remaining, active screw-pile light on the Chesapeake Bay. Limited to 9,500 pieces, this beautiful sculpture is a remarkable technical and artistic achievement.

Harbour Lights
1000 N. Johnson Avenue
El Cajon, CA 92020
(800) 365-1219
Fax (619) 579-1911

COLLECTORS' CLUB

Harbour Lights Collector's Society
1000 N. Johnson Avenue
El Cajon, CA 92020
(800) 365-1219

Annual Dues: $30.00
Club Year: Anniversary of Sign-Up Date

Benefits:
- Free Annual Membership Gift
- Redemption Letter for Members' Only Exclusive annual piece
- Membership Certificate Suitable for Framing for each new Member
- Quarterly Newsletter, "Lighthouse Legacy"
- Specialty Binder for new Members
- Cloisonné Pin

HARMONY KINGDOM®

Discover the Hidden Secrets of Harmony Kingdom...
Handmade Boxes from Great Britain

Martin Perry, moldmaker and chief designer for the Harmony Kingdom Collection.

"I have never regarded myself as an artist and never really made anything until I was in my early thirties," confesses Martin Perry, moldmaker and chief designer for the Harmony Kingdom Collection. "I think it would be more appropriate to describe me as an artisan/designer or perhaps — now that we are accumulating a stable of artists — as an artistic director. I have an image in my mind of what Harmony Kingdom should look like and am steering the origination of new pieces in this direction."

That direction already has proven most pleasing to collectors and dealers alike. Indeed, from the moment The Harmony Ball Company introduced Harmony Kingdom's first series, *Treasure Jest®*, the response was immediate, affectionate and overwhelming. The unveiling took place

at the International Collectible Exposition in Long Beach, California, in April 1995. All in attendance agreed that these handmade animal boxes from England were something unusual and special.

Several of the *Treasure Jest* animals made an earlier debut as lovely marble/resin jewelry boxes to house Harmony Ball™ chiming spheres and other favorite keepsakes. It soon became apparent, however, that the boxes themselves were stand-alone *objets d'art*. A growing group of figurine collectors were requesting information on a collector's club, anxiously awaiting the introduction of new pieces, and eager to learn more about the production process and artists involved in creating their new treasured collectibles.

It was at this juncture that Harmony Ball Company President Noel Wiggins and Designer Martin Perry decided to organize their efforts to present these unique boxes as fine collectibles. It was clear that in the minds of international art lovers, the boxes combined both the appeal of handmade English collectibles and the charm and function of classic French Limoges boxes.

Perry's Dramatic Past Sows the Seeds for Harmony Kingdom

How does a range of such desirable collectible objects spring into existence? Martin Perry admits, "The Harmony Kingdom has a genuinely unorthodox history. Looking back now, it is easy to sense the thread of destiny unfolding." Between 1969 and 1971, he worked as a shepherd in the Snowdonia Mountains of North Wales. "I had a stewardship of 5,000 of the bleakest, wettest, most windswept acres in the British Isles, and my task was to grow as many sheep as possible, or perhaps merely to keep as many

sheep as possible alive.

"If you cut yourself off from your fellow man for a long period of time and your only real relationships are with sheep, dogs, cattle, foxes, badgers, weasels, frogs, ravens, buzzards, rocks, heather and extreme weather conditions, then a picture of 'nature' emerges." Perry's appreciation for the dignity and nobility of animals shines through now in his artistic creations.

"When shepherding ceased," Perry continues, "I was offered a job by a friend of my wife's, packing parcels for a small company that made replicas for museums. This was my first experience with making things. I can remember the first thing I ever made, a replica of an ivory Japanese netsuke, a rabbit, for the Birmingham Museum. Over the next ten years, I taught myself how to make all sorts of things and how to replicate all sorts of materials. I have produced replicas for the Metropolitan Museum of Art in New York, The British Museum, The Victoria and Albert Museum, the Royal Academy of Arts and numerous smaller museums.

"Learning by copying can go only so far. By 1989, I was becoming bored and decided to become a one-man business, producing my own work. I started by carving ducks but quickly realized that carving and reproducing were two distinctly different activities. I asked a well-known animal sculptor to come and see me. He brought a friend with him, to keep him company on the journey, and the three of us spent several hours at my kitchen table while I tried to explain what I wanted. In the end, we decided that we didn't want to work together, and as they were leaving, the friend turned to me and asked if he might have a go at the carving — although he'd never done any before. This person turned out to be Peter Calvesbert." For the next four years, until they joined forces with

Harmony Ball, Calvesbert and Perry produced boxes as partners.

The Evolution of Harmony Kingdom

The distinctly recognizable style of the Harmony Kingdom box developed over time, as Perry explains. "Originally, we were trying to capture the elegance and quirkiness of Japanese netsuke. Then we wanted to make our own statements about how we saw nature and not how it is generally depicted. We had to retain the charm and magic, but avoid the sentimentality.

"Another chance event occurred in March 1994. I met Noel Wiggins and Lisa Yashon, who own the Harmony Ball Company. What had fallen into place was the missing piece in the circle: the creation, the manufacturing and now the wide distribution of a very desirable object. But more than that, Noel and Lisa have become close friends, and we all now contribute to the creation of the boxes. The energy and enthusiasm that is generated by being successful is now turning into a whole new generation of products and ideas.

"The future looks very exciting indeed. Peter has a list of designs that stretches away into the next millennium. Also, I have been working with our newest artist, David Lawrence, in the creation of Harmony

Hoping to turn into the proverbial handsome prince is the frog in "Awaiting a Kiss" by Peter Calvesbert from the Harmony Kingdom Treasure Jest *series of treasure boxes. Issue price: $55.00.*

Kingdom's second series of boxes, the *Harmony Circus™*. I don't know where all this is leading, but for the moment it seems unstoppable."

Corinna Perry Adds Her Contribution in the Cottage Industry Tradition

The creation of each Harmony Kingdom box begins when the original work from the sculptor is molded using silicone rubber. This original is then used to create production molds for the casting department. Castings are created in the mold using crushed marble. The casting is then fettled (cleaned up) and made ready for staining. The stain itself has been formulated by Martin Perry and is regarded as a trade secret. The piece is then polished back to remove most of the stain prior to being sent out into the countryside for painting.

The wonderfully subtle tinting and hand-painting of all the Harmony Kingdom boxes is in the care of Martin Perry's wife, Corinna. In explaining her contribution, she notes, "The early boxes were entirely Martin's painting plan and execution. Understanding the properties and interactions of the materials he was using, he combined experience and experimentation to achieve the patina and tinting.

"When it became clear that he could no longer make and finish every box single-handed, I left my teaching career to help him. He showed me his technique, the reasons for the different stages in the process, and in the early days, got me out of many a difficulty. Having gained in expertise, I gained in confidence, and dared to make suggestions for future coloring. Whenever a new box arrives, we are eager to get our hands on it and start playing with the tinting.

"It soon became clear that I could not cope without future help, and I enlisted some women friends. We would sit around my kitchen table, children playing on the floor, as I initiated them into the secrets of the tinting. We were carrying on the cottage industry tradition of the valley we live in. Many of the cottages were

A fascinating host of turtles combine in Peter Calvesbert's "Primordial Soup" from the Treasure Jest *series, which carries a retail price of $150.*

home and workplace to the weaving community which thrived during the 19th century. Our daily painting sessions were very satisfying and fulfilling; we felt artistic pride in our work, were earning our living, and we were able to set the world to rights in between gossip and laughter.

"Soon my warm kitchen was bulging at the seams as more painters joined us, and some of my friends volunteered to open up their homes to new painters and to train them. And so the painting guild grew. Some work in groups, others alone. It offers opportunities and flexibility for people, particularly women, who want or need to work but are unable to leave the home. Although we have had to centralize some aspects of the business, it is still a cottage industry in the true sense of the word.

"We follow a painting and quality specification, but many factors can alter the finished look: room temperature, base color, dilution of the tints, or just the mood of the day. So if you find one animal is looking particularly pleased with itself, remember it is handcrafted and individual!"

The Inauguration of The Harmony Kingdom Royal Watch™ Society

Harmony Kingdom launched their

new collectors club, The Royal Watch Society, in early 1996. To invite Harmony Kingdom collectors to join the Royal Watch Society, the firm has unveiled "Big Blue," a graceful pod of whales, as the special edition exclusively for Society members. Membership entitles collectors to a subscription to the quarterly newsletter, "The Queen's Courier™," and "The Big Day," a free club gift by Peter Calvesbert. There is also a bonus inaugural piece, "Purrfect Fit," by David Lawrence.

From Humble Beginnings to an Unlimited Future

When asked for his vision of the future of Harmony Kingdom, Martin Perry responds without hesitation. "Henry Doulton started Royal Doulton in a shed 208 years ago, so we both started at the same place. It is the people I now have around me that make me feel that this is more than mere presumption. It has been illuminating for me to see the energy that can be generated when a group of people come together in a common cause. That cause is to make a collectible range of goods better than it's ever been done before. And if we fail, then we'll all have had a lot of fun trying!"

Harmony Kingdom
232 Neilston St.
Columbus, OH 43215
(614) 469-0600
Fax (614) 469-0140

David Lawrence's Harmony Circus *series includes the whimsical "Henry the Human Cannonball," issued at $35.00.*

COLLECTORS' CLUB

The Royal Watch Society
c/o Harmony Kingdom
232 Neilston St.
Columbus, OH 43215
(800) 783-5683

Annual Dues: $35.00
Club Year: Anniversary of Sign-Up Date

Benefits:
• Membership Gifts
• Redemption Voucher for Members-Only Piece
• Quarterly Newsletter, "The Queen's Courier™"
• Referral Service
• Club Sponsored Contests

HAWTHORNE ARCHITECTURAL REGISTER

A Host of Handsome Miniature Buildings Inspired by Art Masters Thomas Kinkade, Charles Wysocki, M.I. Hummel, and Norman Rockwell

Anyone who reads the business pages knows that housing starts have been down for some time, and the real estate market is sluggish — especially compared to the "boom years" of the 1980s. But the 1990s are developing a housing sales boom of their own, at least in one segment: miniature buildings and villages based on the works of world-renowned artists.

Leading the way in this housing market upswing is Hawthorne Architectural Register: a top marketer of highly detailed architectural sculptures. Although these pieces range from just three to eight inches tall, they beautifully capture every aspect of emotion, style and detail found in the artist's paintings. Hawthorne's cottages bring the artist's paintings to life.

Hawthorne's "listings" include houses in styles ranging from 18th-century native stone cottages to antebellum mansions to Victorian. However, no matter what style they are, all Hawthorne buildings must meet standards of excellence which the company

has established in the following areas: faithful representation of the artist's work and intentions; quality of sculptural detail at scale; authenticity of architectural detail; authenticity of environmental details; and statement of edition and required documentation.

Recent issues from Hawthorne call upon the talent and inspiration of some of the most gifted art masters of the present, including Thomas Kinkade and Charles Wysocki; and the past, including M.I. Hummel and Norman Rockwell. In addition to sculptures of buildings, Hawthorne also draws upon these artists' works to create a wide range of accessories and figurines to increase the fantasy aspects and emotional involvement of the buildings.

"Olde Porterfield Gift Shoppe" represents one issue in Thomas Kinkade's Christmas Memories, *a collection of quaint holiday cottages from the world-renowned Painter of Light™.*

series of vivid oil paintings, Kinkade recreated the charm and beauty of these small country villages of England. And now Hawthorne has captured the emotion of Kinkade's paintings in several remarkable collections of handcrafted cottage sculptures.

Thomas Kinkade's Candlelight Cottages collection of eight pieces begins with "Olde Porterfield Tea Room," the very first recreation of one of Mr. Kinkade's famous canvases for the three-dimensional cottage sculpture medium. Hawthorne's marvelous sculpture allows the artist's legions of admirers to rediscover all the charm and detail of this original art, now brought to life with meticulous sculpting, and careful hand-painting.

Another Hawthorne collection of Kinkade's works begins with "McKenna's Cottage." Entitled *Thomas Kinkade's Enchanted Cottages*, this series welcomes admirers to a world of peace and enchantment. Every detail is beautifully handcrafted, from the straw of the thatched roofs, to the landscaping which provides the perfect setting for each architectural gem.

The Renowned Painter of Light™ Joins Forces With Hawthorne

For more than a decade, Thomas Kinkade has been creating remarkable landscape paintings and collectible prints. Winner of numerous awards, he travels the world to research and sketch ideas for his work. Honored with the title Painter of Light™, Kinkade delights his admirers with works that seem to glow with a unique radiance.

When Kinkade first visited the English countryside, he fell in love with its cozy cottages, verdant fields and rolling hills. In a magnificent

From the series entitled Thomas Kinkade's Enchanted Cottages *comes "McKenna's Cottage" — cozy, warm, and delightfully whimsical.*

Share the Joy of Thomas Kinkade's Old-Fashioned Christmas

The Christmas we love to remember was a gentle time of warmth, wonder and love. And now Hawthorne's *Thomas Kinkade's Christmas Memories* collection brings life to a joyous Christmas celebration in a lovely and inviting place. Quaint little curiosity shops like "Olde Porterfield Gift Shoppe" are part of the tiny, tucked-away villages that dot the English countryside. From the signpost that stands at the edge of the walk, to the snow that blankets the roof, trees, and walk, the "Olde Porterfield Gift Shoppe" has been meticulously crafted and hand-painted to Thomas Kinkade's exacting standards — the ideal premiere for this collection of eight holiday landscapes.

Charles Wysocki Welcomes Collectors to *Peppercricket Grove*

Master of Americana Charles Wysocki has created a special place where handsewn quilts, horsedrawn wagons and homemade joy add comfort to a wonderful way of life. He invites collectors to take a leisurely stroll through charming and peaceful *Peppercricket Grove* — and in doing so

Popular artist Charles Wysocki recently introduced his first-ever sculpture, "Peppercricket Farms," through Hawthorne Architectural Register. It marks the premiere of the Peppercricket Grove sculptured cottage collection.

to discover this much-honored painter's very first sculpture.

"Peppercricket Farms" premieres *Wysocki's Peppercricket Grove* sculptured cottage collection. Inspired by the famous painting of the same name, it captures all the whimsy and wonder of Wysocki's world — now in three dimensions. For the first time ever, Wysocki's admirers can see the back of "Peppercricket Farms" — a unique, new perspective created exclusively for this sculpture with Charles Wysocki's personal involvement. What's more, each sculpture is carefully painted and decorated by hand to capture the beauty and detail of Wysocki's original art.

Bring the Charms of *M.I. Hummel's* Bavarian Village to Your Home

Imagine a quaint Bavarian village at Christmastime, full of charm and spirit. Magic is everywhere...the sweet aroma of holiday pastries...carefree sounds of rosy-cheeked children at play...the children so dear and special to M.I. Hummel. This beloved artist's children recall timeless images of innocence and hope. And now, in "Angels Duet" and "Village Bakery," their world is recaptured in lighted sculptures that feature some of M.I. Hummel's own most beloved images. "Angel's Duet" portrays a Bavarian village church featuring the Hummel cherubs known as "Angel's Duet" and "Candle Light." "Village Bakery" showcases a reproduction of M.I. Hummel's classic little baker carrying a mouth-watering goody fresh from the oven.

Introduced by Hawthorne Porchlight Collections™, each issue in the *Bavarian Village* collection combines

"Angels Duet" is the first-ever lighted ceramic cottage sculpture to depict the beloved art of M.I. Hummel. It is issued exclusively through Hawthorne Porchlight Collections™.

handcraftsmanship with meticulous hand-painting to reproduce the distinctive tones and hues of an *M.I. Hummel* figurine. The *Hummel* images themselves glow with the light inside their pretty buildings — and they emerge in rich detail through a carefully-controlled, 18-color process involving three separate porcelain firings.

Come Home for a Rockwell Christmas

"Welcome to Stockbridge," reads the sign outside Norman Rockwell's famous Massachusetts home town, and now Rockwell's family invites us all to join them there for *Rockwell's Christmas in Stockbridge*. Based on Rockwell's famous painting "Mainstreet, Stockbridge," Hawthorne Porchlight Collections™ introduced this series as the first lighted village ever authorized by The Norman Rockwell Family Trust — an official Centennial Edition issued in honor of the 100th anniversary of the artist's birth.

Each sculpture beckons with its bright lights, and we are drawn to relive the small-town Christmas that "America's Favorite Illustrator" himself held so dear. From Rockwell's own studio to the town bank, country store, insurance agency and other Main Street fixtures, Stockbridge comes alive as an enchanting village. Each sculpture is hand-painted, and each glows with soft light shining through its windows on all four sides.

Hawthorne Miniatures Add Vitality to Your Sculpture Collection

Hawthorne's Stockbridge or any other Christmas village gains even more life and realism with the addition of the Hawthorne Miniatures — an inspired selection of people, trees, vehicles and accessories that complete the scene of a bustling and happy home town. Sets featuring people include:

"The Skating Pond," "Decorating the Tree," "Shopkeeper and Travelers," "Bringing Home the Tree," "Christmas Shopping," "Slipping and Sliding," "Greetings and Games," and "Norman Rockwell and a Trio of Merry Carolers."

To enhance a village even further, there are automobile sets including "Village Vehicles," "Vintage V-8s," and "Roaring Roadsters." More atmosphere can be added with the "Snow-covered Evergreen Tree Set" and the "Old-fashioned Streetlight Set."

With a selection from Hawthorne,

Charming figurines and accessories from Hawthorne Miniatures make a collector's Christmas village come alive. Available pieces — all created to scale with the village buildings — include vehicles, evergreen trees, streetlights, a skating pond, and townspeople in various groupings.

collectors enjoy the opportunity to become "real estate moguls" while they rediscover the gentle joys of everyday life through the eyes of some of today's most honored artists. From the English countryside of Thomas Kinkade, to the sleepy Bavarian village of M.I. Hummel to the "small-town U.S.A." of Charles Wysocki and Norman Rockwell, these marvelous, architecturally significant buildings captivate and charm us all.

Now collectors can experience the New England charms of Rockwell's Christmas in Stockbridge with this collection of enchanting, lighted sculptures depicting the town where "America's Favorite Illustrator" lived and worked. The series is authorized by the artist's family through The Norman Rockwell Family Trust.

Hawthorne Architectural Register
9210 N. Maryland Avenue
Niles, IL 60714
Customer Service (800) 772-4277
Ordering Number (800) 327-0327

M. I. HUMMEL CLUB®

Loyal Club Members and Collectors Celebrate
the Enduring Spirit of Sister M. I. Hummel

"I Brought You a Gift" (HUM 479) is the new member gift provided to each individual who joins the M. I. Hummel Club for the first time. She is retiring as of May 31, 1996. Crafted with care in Germany, this charming figurine carries on the enduring tradition of Sister M. I. Hummel and her art. It has a retail value of $85 U.S. and $105 Canadian, but it is provided to new Club members for free.

She drew and painted them practically from the time she could first hold a pencil: the rosy-cheeked, bright-eyed youngsters who surrounded her during her happy German childhood. Sister Maria Innocentia Hummel delighted in the energy and optimism of little ones — and she captured their charm in hundreds of drawings that brought cheer to all at the Convent of Siessen. As a member of the Sisters of the Third Order of St. Francis, Sister M. I. Hummel came to understand that her finest service to the Lord would be to share her talent for art. But little did she know that this marvelous gift would provide pleasure to collectors all over the world for generations after her death.

The brilliance of this shy German nun might never have been known outside the convent community had it not been for the vision of Franz Goebel. As the fourth-generation family member to head the company bearing his name, Goebel was always on the lookout for promising new artists. In 1879, the Duke of Saxe-Coburg-Gotha first granted permission for the Goebel Company to create kiln-fired porcelain figurines. Originally founded in 1871 to manufacture marbles, slates and slate pencils, Goebel artisans already had spent four decades earning an international reputation for porcelain craftsmanship when Franz Goebel discovered Sister M. I. Hummel in 1934.

While strolling through gift shops in Munich, Goebel happened upon a little store that specialized in religious images. A display of greeting cards captivated him: it was the art of Sister M. I. Hummel! Simple and touching in their innocence, the drawings spoke to Goebel like nothing else he had seen in Munich. It struck him that this would be the perfect basis for a new line of figurines.

Franz Goebel wrote to Sister Hummel, proposing that his artists translate her two-dimensional drawings into three-dimensional figurines. At first, the gentle nun hesitated. But when Goebel arranged a meeting among himself, Sister Hummel, and the Mother Superior of the convent, a historic agreement was reached. Goebel assured the sisters that the figurines would be completely true to the original artwork. He promised that they would be handcrafted to meet the highest quality standards. He gave Sister Hummel and the Convent of Siessen final artistic control. Indeed, he stated that once she approved an original figurine, her signature would be incised on the base of each piece. What's more, beginning then and to this very day, part of the proceeds of each figurine is provided to the convent and then sent to charitable organizations throughout the world.

The first *M. I. Hummel* figurines were unveiled at the 1935 Leipzig Fair, where buyers from all over Europe expressed their excitement at the art's uniqueness and fresh charm. The figurines were a tremendous success, and everyone looked forward to long years of happy productivity from the gifted nun of Siessen.

Alas, the hardships of World War II took their toll on the convent and on Sister M. I. Hummel herself. She fell ill and died in 1946 at the age of 37. Ironically, her fame was spreading quickly across the Atlantic at the time of her death. American GIs were bringing the adorable child-subject figurines home to America as special gifts for family and friends. When they got the news about the popularity of the "Hummels," American gift sellers and department stores flocked to order them and to share them with a wider audience. And since Sister M. I. Hummel had been prolific in her short life, there were still many drawings to serve as inspiration.

How an *M.I. Hummel* Drawing Becomes a Hand-Painted Figurine

Today, collectors all over the world await each new *M. I. Hummel* presentation, brought to life by the gifted artisans of Goebel. The process of creating an *M. I. Hummel* figurine is long and involved, performed by a team of dedicated masters. Each new artist must serve a three-year apprenticeship under the watchful eye of senior Goebel craftspeople before joining the prestigious ranks of the *M. I. Hummel* "team." This long apprenticeship is necessary because of the exacting, ten-step process required to craft each *M. I. Hummel* work of art. The ten steps are: sculpting, model-cutting, moldmaking, casting, assembling, bisque firing, glazing, glaze firing, decorating, and decor firing(s).

To begin, the sculptor creates a clay model using Sister M. I. Hummel's original art as the basis. The Convent of Siessen must approve each model before prototypes are crafted for mold-making. A single figurine may require as many as 40 individual mold pieces! To make the molds, individual parts are embedded in clay. Then plaster of paris is poured over them to make the master mold. The working model is made of acrylic resin, and then a series of working molds are devised — again using plaster of paris. More than one working mold is required because each mold must be rejected as soon as it loses its exactness of detail.

In casting, liquid porcelain "slip" is poured into the working mold. Excess slip is poured out after about 20 minutes, leaving the shell of the figurine. Next, individual pieces of the figurine are assembled, using more slip to join them. After smoothing to remove seams, the assembled figurines dry at room temperature for about one week. Bisque firing at approximately 2100°F follows, during which each figurine shrinks in size and emerges with a powdery white finish. Glaze firing at 1870°F comes next, after figurines are hand-dipped and sprayed with a tinted liquid glaze. At this stage, the Goebel

Collectors who are celebrating fifteen years of membership in the M. I. Hummel Club are privileged to acquire "Honey Lover" (HUM 312), an exclusive figurine created to mark this special anniversary.

trademark also is fired onto the base.

For decorating, thousands of individual colors have been developed in Goebel's own laboratories. The goal is to approximate the varied palette used by Sister M. I. Hummel herself. To produce an edition of figurines, highly skilled painters follow a decorated sample which has been approved by the Convent of Siessen. The initials under the base of each figurine indicate a final decorating check before decor firing commences at approximately 1100°F. As many as three decor firings may be necessary to fuse the colors permanently to each porcelain figurine. All in all, an *M. I. Hummel* figurine requires many weeks to produce, including a total of over 700 detailed hand operations. This painstaking process has been the standard of excellence for Goebel ever since the first *M. I. Hummel* figurines were produced 60 years ago.

Members Enjoy the Many Benefits of the M. I. Hummel Club®

Ever since 1977, collectors of *M. I. Hummel* figurines have relished the friendship, the fun, and the special privileges that come with membership in the M. I. Hummel Club. For the affordable annual fee of $45 (U.S.) and $60 (Canadian), a new member may join the oldest collectors' club of its kind. Renewing members pay a smaller fee: currently $35 (U.S) and $47.50 (Canadian). Each new member receives a special welcome gift, currently a charming *M. I. Hummel* figurine called "I Brought You a Gift." Interested members need to act quickly because she'll be retiring as of May 31, 1996. Renewing members also are sent a yearly token of appreciation, such as the 1994-95 piece, "From Me to You." Each of these figurines carries a retail value of $85 U.S. or $105 Canadian — at least double the membership or renewal fee.

Members of the Club are privileged also to acquire other special *M. I. Hummel* works of art created with their pleasure in mind. There is an annual exclusive figurine, available only to Club members. Most recent of these issues is the adorable "Country

Suitor." There is also a Preview Edition called "Strum Along," available only to Club members for two years. This piece bears a special M. I. Hummel Club backstamp, but after the preview period ends, it may become an open edition available to everyone — then bearing the non-exclusive regular Goebel backstamp. What's more, the Club celebrates its long-time members by offering them the opportunity to purchase figurines to mark their personal anniversaries as Club members. Five-year Club members are provided with special redemption certificates for "Flower Girl," while ten-year members may acquire "The Little Pair," and fifteen-year veterans are eligible for "Honey Lover."

As one of the most comprehensive collectors' clubs in the world, the M. I. Hummel Club offers a wide range of services and special opportunities to members. These include Collectors' Market, Research Service, Annual Essay Contests, Travel Opportunities, and Local Chapters. Collectors' Market is a free service to M. I. Hummel Club members who wish to buy and or sell any Goebel collectible. The Club endeavors to match potential buyers with individuals who wish to sell the same item. Then the buyer contacts the potential seller to negotiate a price. Research Service is available to members who wish to authenticate older Goebel pieces they may own. When the Club is sent a clear photograph or drawing of the piece's markings, mold numbers and trademarks, as well as a photograph of the entire piece, such facts as authenticity, identity, age, background and production history can often be provided.

The M. I. Hummel Club sponsors an Annual Essay Contest for members. The recent "Say It With Song" contest asked members to compose original song lyrics which expressed the way they felt about *M. I. Hummel* figurines set to the tune of a well-known song of their choice. Winning entries earned *M. I. Hummel* figurine awards ranging in retail value from $300 to $1,200.

An annual range of Travel Opportunities afford Club members the opportunity to see the world,

The adorable figurine, "Country Suitor" (HUM 760), is the M. I. Hummel Club's Exclusive Edition for 1995-96.

spend time with their fellow *M.I. Hummel* collectors, and tour the legendary W. Goebel Porzellanfabrik. There are tours offering a variety of destinations throughout Europe, and — of course — Sister M. I. Hummel's homeland of Germany.

Members say that one of the most personal pleasures of Club membership is the chance to become active in one of the over 140 Local Club Chapters throughout North America. At no additional cost, Club membership brings each individual a subscription to a Local Chapter newsletter, a Local Chapter patch and membership card sticker, and invitations to Regional Conferences. If there is no Local Chapter in a collector's home area, he or she is invited to start one with the help of the Club's Local Chapter Services division.

In addition to all of these benefits, Club members also receive: a subscription to *Insights*, the Club's colorful and informative quarterly magazine; a Membership Card; and a handsome binder filled with a collector's log, price list and facts about *M. I. Hummel* history and production.

Surely the gentle young Sister M. I. Hummel could never have dreamed that her charming drawings would continue to captivate millions for decades after her death. But today, the delightful and varied *M. I. Hummel* figurines are considered among the world's most cherished collectibles. And members of the M. I. Hummel Club enjoy the best opportunities of all to share in the delights of Sister Hummel's art and the warm friendship of fellow collectors!

M.I. Hummel Club
Goebel Plaza
P.O. Box 11
Pennington, NJ 08534-0011
(800) 666-2582
Fax (609) 737-1545

COLLECTORS' CLUB/MUSEUM

M.I. Hummel Club
Goebel Plaza
P.O. Box 11
Pennington, NJ 08534-0011
(800) 666-CLUB

Annual Dues: $45.00 - Renewal: $35.00
          Canada: $60.00 - Renewal: $47.50
Club Year: June 1 to May 31

Benefits:
• Membership Gift: *M.I. Hummel* Figurine. Renewing Members Receive a Yearly Token of Appreciation Figurine.
• Opportunity to Purchase Members-Only Figurine and Preview Editions
• Quarterly Magazine, *Insights*
• Buy/sell Matching Service through Collectors' Market
• Research Service
• Annual Essay Contests
• Travel Opportunities
• Local Club Chapters
• Membership Card
• Binder Includes Collector's Log, Price List and *M.I. Hummel* History and Production Facts

The Hummel Museum
199 Main Plaza
New Braunfels, TX 78130
(210) 625-5636

Hours: Monday through Saturday, 10 am. - 5p.m., Sunday, noon-5p.m.
Admission Fee: $5.00 Adults; $4.50 Seniors; $3.00 Students

The Hummel Museum displays the world's largest collection of Sister Maria Innocentia Hummel's original art. This one-of-a-kind museum offers guided tours, video presentations, historical vignette rooms of Sister Hummel's personal items, extensive display of rare *M.I. Hummel* figurines with over 1,100 on exhibit. The Museum Gift Shop offers a great variety of Hummel collectibles.

IMPERIAL GRAPHICS, LTD.

Artist Lena Liu Achieves
Tranquility and Beauty Through Floral Artistry

"The Music Room IV — Swan Melody" is a painting within a painting, as a beautiful dance from Swan Lake *is portrayed along with a bouquet of soft white magnolias. The portrait is part of the annual* Music Room Series. *"Swan Melody" is limited to 6,500 signed and numbered prints and 300 canvases.*

Imagine a quiet corner of the world where sweet strawberries overflow from a woven basket, colorful spring blossoms encircle a country wreath, a wooded glen welcomes visitors with magnolias, day lilies and hydrangeas. It's a place where musical instruments play favorite symphonies in perfect harmony, and white doves flutter above angels. It's the world of Lena Liu, an award-winning artist who captures nature's beauty at its best.

From its studios in Potomac, Maryland, Imperial Graphics, Ltd. introduces and distributes works by Lena Liu, an artist of unparalleled popularity in today's collectibles market. Since Lena and her husband, Bill, founded their firm in 1984, Imperial Graphics has become renowned for its versatile subjects and highly detailed compositions.

Art lovers all over the world enjoy the universal, yet personal, character of Lena's paintings that include every-

thing from landscapes to musical still lifes, and breathtaking floral gardens to elegant birds. "I strive to create a sense of poetry and music in my painting like a beautiful song or poem, with that sense of romance," Lena says. "Emotion, love and nature will never change. I try to capture that in my art — in painting the human interpretation of nature, I let what touches my heart pass through my fingers. I hope you and I can keep sharing this love of nature s beauty, and continue to delight in the splendor of the world that surrounds us."

Oriental Brushwork
Influences Artistic Style

Lena was born in Tokyo of a military Chinese family and raised and educated in Taiwan. Her parents discovered her painting talent at a very young age and sent her to private tutors, with whom she began to learn and apply traditional Chinese brushwork. She took

her first painting lessons in Taiwan under the guidance of renowned painters, Professors Sun Chia-Chin and Huang Chun-Pi. Through the years, she also combined traditional Oriental brushwork with Western painting techniques, which can be seen in many of her works today.

As a young woman, Lena moved to the United States as a college sopho-more in 1970 to study architecture at the State University of Buffalo. She then pursued a graduate degree at UCLA, but true love won out after her first year, as she returned to the East Coast to marry Bill.

Having worked for an architectural firm for two years, Lena made the decision in 1976 to devote herself full time to art. She began selling her art-work locally, developing her own style along the way. Eventually she was approached by a firm, who began marketing her work in open editions. It was soon discovered that Lena's artwork had broad appeal and her popularity began to soar. So Lena and Bill launched Imperial Graphics, Ltd., with the express purpose of marketing her limited edition artwork. Subjects ranged from birds and butterflies to flowers and landscapes. The company grew and thrived. Over the years, Lena's Chinese style evolved into her own unique blend of the past and pre-sent, where beauty and tranquility are experienced by all who collect Lena's artwork, whether as a print or canvas.

Lena's limited editions are printed on high-quality archival acid-free paper to ensure their long-lasting beauty. Her canvases are now stamped as "Archival, Museum Quality" artwork. The stamp, which is located on the back of the stretcher bar, guarantees that collectors are receiving a museum-quality piece that is certified Ph balanced, ultra-violet ray protected, fade resistant, and meets the needs of the custom framer. These benefits assure collectors that they are making a sound investment when purchasing Lena's limited edition canvases.

New Subjects Share Artist's Inspirations

Lena is perhaps best known for her floral artistry that brings the outdoors inside the homes of many collectors. Through a soft palette of colors, she celebrates the delicate beauty of flowers — whether peonies, lilacs, day lilies or white daisies. Some look as if they were just snipped from a well-tended garden and carefully placed in a favorite vase. Others are planted in terra cotta pots or freely blooming along a landscaped path. No matter what the setting, Lena has a special talent for floral designs that reveal the wonder of nature.

Lena's beloved floral still lifes show her attention to the smallest details. In a recent print titled "Sweet Bounty," for example, Lena contrasts the elegance of freshly cut roses with the rustic appearance of a water pail, conveying the message that nature can bring beauty to even the simplest setting. A

In "Sweet Bounty," Lena Liu contrasts the elegance of freshly cut roses with the rustic appearance of a water pail, while plump strawberries and sweet peas add to the beauty of the still life. The print is limited to 5,500 signed and numbered pieces with the artist's canvas limited to only 300.

"Guardian Angel," the centerpiece of Lena Liu's triptych, shows the powerful, unspoken beauty of these heavenly messengers. The print is limited to 5,500 signed and numbered pieces. The canvas is limited to 300 portraits.

crisp white linen draped beneath the bouquet suggests a gardenside picnic, complete with a woven basket of hand-picked strawberries.

Adding to Lena's renowned nature and floral portraits, Imperial Graphics has also debuted other subjects such as angels and musical instruments. Long inspired by celestial messengers, Lena recently created "The Guardian Angel" in an elaborate triptych. "Angels hold profound meaning for people of all ages and from all walks of life," reflects Lena. "In art, angels are often depicted in human form, with wings, signifying their role as heavenly messengers. Once my thoughts on all of the various artistic components matured, I was ready to begin my triptych — the story of the guardian angel."

Lena painted the triptych on silk to achieve the intricate detailing. Silk tends to bleach colors so Lena spent many hours applying layer after layer of color to achieve the degree of intensity desired. The angel triptych is limited to 5,500 signed and numbered prints. "The Guardian Angel" canvas is limited to 300 pieces.

Music has also inspired Lena, whose

work epitomizes the Chinese word "tien-lai" which describes music so beautiful that it is considered to be from heaven. Since its inception in 1991, the *Music Room Series* has proven to be a favorite among collectors with a new piece added annually. All of these music pieces are now selling on the secondary market well above their issue prices and are extremely difficult to locate. The 1995 addition, "Music Room IV — Swan Melody," combines music with dance to create a romantic theme. The piece includes a painting within a painting, as the beautiful dance from *Swan Lake* is depicted on the wall, where an ethereal swan sets the mood for the dreamy ballet. In the foreground, a bouquet of soft white magnolias mirrors the swan's beauty, each petal gracefully curved like the tulled skirts of the ballerinas.

To complement the *Music Room Series*, Lena also introduced *Celestial Symphony*, a four-piece collection to celebrate the instruments responsible for such beautiful harmonies. The pieces include "Flute Interlude," "Violin Concerto," "Piano Sonata" and "French Horn Melody."

Artwork Transformed to Collector Plates and Other Collectibles

Upon seeing her work, The Bradford Exchange, one of the world's most successful marketers of collector plates, contacted Imperial Graphics to represent Lena in the plate field. In 1988, Lena's first plates debuted with the *On Gossamer Wings* series, featuring a collection of breathtaking butterflies. The series was an instant success, with collectors eagerly anticipating each and every Lena Liu plate series. Today, The Bradford Exchange continues marketing Lena's plates, along with other innovative products designed by this talented artist, including ornaments, music boxes and, most recently, an elegant tea service collection. The Bradford Exchange recently honored Lena by making her one of the first inductees to its "Plate Hall of Fame" at the company's headquarters in Niles, Illinois. She was part of the ceremony that celebrated the 100th year of collector's plates. Opportunities to expand into other categories continue. The Danbury Mint introduced a figurine program in 1996 featuring Lena's exquisite Oriental maiden sculptures. Avid collectors can also enjoy her work on cards and calendars.

Awards Recognize Artistic Talent and Success

For quality, creativity and a style that

As part of a landscape triptych, "Magnolia Path" takes collectors to a peaceful garden and into their own imagination. A magnolia tree bursts with saucer-shaped blossoms, signifying the beginning of summer. The print is limited to 5,500 signed and numbered pieces. The canvas is available in an edition of 300.

has won the hearts of collectors, Imperial Graphics and the artist continue to win prestigious industry awards, including Lena's recent recognition as "Artist of the Year" in both the United States and Canada. She also received "Plate of the Year" honors from the National Association of Limited Edition Dealers (NALED). Lena travels to collector conventions and galleries as time permits from her hectic and demanding painting schedule. She enjoys meeting collectors and sharing her love of art with those who have come to know her and find special meaning in her portraits.

Imperial Graphics also believes strongly in giving back to the community. The company, located in a suburb of Washington, D.C., supports its local chapter of the American Red Cross and area schools.

Lena Liu Shares the Comforts of Home

In the midst of her hectic schedule, Lena finds peace and renewal in the comforts of home. Lena only has to look around her home and backyard in Maryland for many of the subjects that fill her artworks. Lena and Bill specially designed their home to accommodate their joint love of art, music and nature. As often as she has the chance, Lena spends time in her garden, where the inspiration blooms for many of her paintings. She also loves to watch the birds that live near her home and studio. "I surround myself with what I love," says Lena. "It's inspiring to me."

Imperial Graphics
11516 Lake Potomac Dr.
Potomac, MD 20854
(800) 541-7696
Fax (301) 299-4837

LADIE AND FRIENDS, INC.

Celebrating Ten Years of *Lizzie High*® Dolls

Just about a decade ago, the creators of the *Lizzie High*® line of dolls tapped into an idea rooted in the simplicity of childhood memories. It began in a moment of wonder when founder Barbara Wisber picked up a small wooden ball and started rolling it around in her fingers. "I wonder...what can I make with this?" she asked herself.

A simple question evolved into a simple solution. In an inspired moment, she took a paint brush, dabbed two tiny dots on the ball of wood, and invented a well-known trademark in the collectible doll world. It flowered into a cottage industry that has since outgrown the cottage.

Lizzie High Dolls Retain Their Original Sense of Simplicity

The evolution of *Lizzie High* through the past decade has seen a series of wooden dolls develop from primitive beginnings to a level of sophistication that still retains that original sense of simplicity. Enlisting the artistic talents and moral support of her husband Peter, Barbara dove into her childhood and came up with ideas for dolls that are tied to universal delights: games to be played, friends to be made, wonderlands to be explored, adventures to be lived, lessons to be learned. She suggests these ideas through short phrases on the tags tied to each doll that hint at whole worlds where children keep their childhood intact, where pets frolic in harmless mischief, and where the good humor of life's little pleasures shine through two well-placed child's eyes on a wooden ball.

Dolls' Names Inspired from Peter Wisber's Family Tree

The first nine dolls created for introduction at the January 1985 giftware

Early Lizzie High® *dolls had names borrowed directly from Peter Wisber's family tree. From left to right are: "Flossie High" (Peter's great grandmother); "Lizzie High" (Peter's great-great grandmother); "Johanna Valentine" (Peter's mother) and "Mary Valentine" (Peter's grandmother).*

shows were very simple indeed. Six little girls wore simple muslin frocks with a variety of shawls and kerchiefs in country plaids, and three young boys in painted overalls sported checkered neckerchiefs. The tales that accompanied these dolls could have been from simpler times a hundred years ago, or from gentler times a childhood ago. These characters care for a pet goose, a prize-winning pig and a baby brother. They jump rope, make wreaths, and love to dress up in their Sunday best. They love picnics, gathering fruit for mom's pies and jams, and gathering eggs to earn money for dance lessons and candy.

The dolls' names are as inspired as their beginnings were humble. Most names spring from Peter's family Bible and history. His family had extensive genealogical studies made and can trace their roots back through a tree

blossoming with names filled with history and charm. "Lizzie High" was the first character, and most of the next eight names came naturally from great-great grandmother Lizzie's Good Book: Sabina Valentine, Emma High, Rebecca Bowman, Mary Valentine, Wendel Bowman and Luther Bowman. Since those early beginnings, there have been over 200 characters, each with its own name, a distinct personality, and a message that suggests a story that could go on forever. Most of the original dolls have been retired. Many have been brought back in a new form. Even "Lizzie High" is in her Second Edition as she goes into her second decade. Generally, the newer editions display more detail and animation than the original editions. They appear to embrace a larger world than they previously did. Part of the reason for this is the inclusion of more extensive complementary accessories such as tiny books, animals, wagons, buttons, bows and hats.

The animals in particular add clever moments of humor to each doll's story. Peter sculpts them in clay, then they're cast in a resin that holds not only their shapes, but also their character. Tiny kittens bat at each other, geese strut to some whimsical unheard tune, bunnies flop over their own ears, and they all look as if they absolutely belong with the doll they're with.

Other developments over the last ten years include the creation of "event pieces." Each piece is a miniature version of a full-size character, and each piece is only available for one year at sanctioned *Lizzie High* dealer parties.

The Little Ones Grow in Popularity

Barbara and Peter have found that their line of *The Little Ones*, the smaller-sized dolls, are becoming as popular as the full-sized dolls. *The Little Ones* are not given a particular name, they're universal children expressing a moment each of us might recognize as a childhood memory, rich in detail and evoking an expression of "Oh, yes, I remember when...." Some of these are seasonal — children with a sled and with a snowman, wearing a Halloween mask and carrying a trick-or-treat bag, waving their pinwheels at the Independence Day parade, or gathered 'round a Christmas tree. Barbara and Peter believe that as many people are choosing to live in smaller homes, they'll always have room for *The Little Ones*.

Lizzie High Society News Covered in the "Lizzie High Notebook"

In order to provide *Lizzie High* fans with the literature and information they were requesting, the Wisbers began The Lizzie High Society™ in 1992. Membership includes a subscription to the semi-annual publication called the "Lizzie High Notebook"™. The Notebook is designed as a black and white marble-patterned composi-

tion book most of us are familiar with from our school days. It's divided into sections such as "Arithmetic" where news of the dolls that are being added and subtracted from the collection can be found, along with collectors' wishlists for hard-to-find dolls and listings of collectors' dolls that are available for purchase. "Art" might include pictures sent in from collectors who have clever ways of displaying their dolls. "History" recalls tidbits of *Lizzie High* doll history and sometimes family history uncovered in the genealogical research. "Reading" is often a fascinating little story sent in by fans, like the principal from a Central Pennsylvania elementary school who displays her dolls in her office, and her kids love it.

A new feature will be appearing in future Notebooks – "Lizzie's Diary" will translate the brief suggestions of life found on each doll's tag into whole story lines, with dolls interacting with other dolls, and where each stays in character and develops a life beyond what was intended at the original inception of their accompanying tale. Most of the stories will come from suggestions sent in by collectors. Take *Lizzie High's* own tale that reads, "Lizzie High...walks her goose Lily to the pond every day before school...she's always late...." That might evolve into a story of a little girl who dawdles and dawdles, running on her own clock, frustrating teachers, parents and friends, yet experiencing a rich and wonderful world of discovery at her own speed.

Another of the benefits that comes with membership in the Lizzie High Society is a series of pewter ornaments that depict each of the first nine dolls introduced in 1985. This series started in the term that coincided with the Tenth Anniversary of the dolls. The first character cast as a 4" ornament was "Lizzie High." Number two in the series is "Rebecca Bowman." Each character is only available to club members during one term, and these are becoming treasured collectibles in their own right.

"Little Lizzie High," the first Special Event Edition, is available during the Tenth Anniversary year of Lizzie High® *dolls.*

Dolls Develop from Happy Childhood Memories

The evolution of any particular *Lizzie High* doll isn't always a planned event, and it's never the result of an extensive corporate study, research of marketing trends, or the product of some task force assigned to match a doll's form to a desired bottom-line-profit figure. It begins with memory — from Barbara's memory. There is no drawing to work from, nor plan to develop. Just as she did when she turned that ball of wood over in her hands, each new doll comes to her as a result of playing with little bits of stuff. Perhaps Barbara will find a piece of fabric she likes in a store one day. She'll purchase a small sample of it, take it to her studio, and somewhere in its tiny folds she'll find an idea, a starting point. Barbara will see a button here, an accessory there, and she'll play with wood and miniature toys. She ties it all together with a memory from her childhood, or from the happy childhoods of her children, and eventually a rough prototype will appear. Somewhere along the line, she'll ask Peter, "What do you think?" and together they will shape the animals and accessories needed to complete the

"Lizzie High, Second Edition" represents the "new" look in Lizzie High® *dolls.*

picture, although it's more like a sculpture. Barbara and Peter discuss shapes, patterns, colors, and poses, and then names and tag lines, and all the other bits and pieces that form these remarkable dolls. They involve carpenters, painters and detailers, seamstresses, and assemblers to put all the whimsy together, and quality inspectors to ensure each doll meets the standards *Lizzie High* collectors have come to expect.

While the dolls have evolved a great deal from the simple characters of a decade ago, and the popularity of the collection has grown far beyond what Barbara and Peter could have imagined ten years back, it's still their intention to evoke the fondest of life's little pleasures as seen through the eyes of the child within each collector.

Ladie and Friends, Inc.
220 North Main Street
Sellersville, PA 18960
(800) 76-DOLLS
Fax (215) 453-8155

COLLECTORS' CLUB/MUSEUM

The Lizzie High Society
220 North Main Street
Sellersville, PA 18960
(800) 76-DOLLS

Annual Dues: $25 - Renewal: $15.00
Club Year: January-December

Benefits:
- Membership Gift: Pewter Lapel Pin of Lizzie High Logo
- Opportunity to Purchase Members-Only Doll
- Bi-annual Newsletter, "Lizzie High Notebook"
- Complete Color Catalog in Leather-grained Binder
- Membership Card
- 4" Pewter Ornament Depicting One of the First Nine Dolls from 1985
- Buy/Sell Matching Service

Lizzie High Museum
A Country Gift Shoppe
Rt. 313, Dublin Pike
Dublin, PA 18917
(215) 249-9877

Hours: Monday through Saturday, 10 a.m. - 5p.m., Extended Holiday Hours

Admission Fee: None

All retired *Lizzie High* Dolls are on display in the museum, and current dolls are available in the gift shop.

THE LANCE CORPORATION
Fine Metal and Porcelain Sculpture Produced in New England for Over Twenty-five Years

"The Rainmaker" – 1994-95 Chilmark American West *Redemption Special by Michael Boyett.*

The Lance Corporation has begun its second quarter-century in the art metal sculpture field. Grounded in American history and culture, Lance nonetheless prides itself on innovation—both in sculptural subjects and in fine art techniques. Indeed, since 1968, Lance has been recognized as a pacesetter in the field of fine art sculpture.

From its picturesque hometown of Hudson, Massachusetts, Lance offers renowned lines of fine art sculpture—each with its own personaltiy and following. Some pieces are crafted in fine pewter, others are handpainted over pewter, while still others are hand-painted over cast porcelain. Yet all the works of Chilmark, Hudson Pewter and Sebastian Miniatures meet Lance's high standards of quality, historical accuracy and detail in every stage of creation and production.

Don Polland and the Chilmark Polland Collectors Society Enter a New Era

Like the characters of the Old West he depicts in his work, Chilmark artist Don Polland is a true pioneer. While we may never know if he was the first to sculpt scenes of the American West in miniature scale, he certainly has become the most prolific. With well over 100 individual designs to his credit—in bronze, fine pewter and porcelain—Don has earned his place next to Remington, Russell and Fraser, and contemporary artists such as McCarthy and Beeler. Don Polland has invested over 25 years of his life to an art form and a body of work that has integrity and permanence.

The 22-year association between sculptor Don Polland and The Lance Corporation enters a new phase as Polland has "handed over the reins" of the Polland Collectors Society to Ron Larson, president of Lance.

"We are delighted that Don has chosen us to operate the Collectors Society. Don has many loyal collectors, a number of whom have been with him since we first began producing his miniature pewters in 1973. Some have been members of his Society from its inception in 1987; they are old friends of Chilmark, too".

For his part, Polland is extremely happy that the move has been made. "With Chilmark and Lance taking over the management of the Polland Collectors Society, I hope to have the time to do more sculpting."

The Polland Collectors Society was started and has been run by the Polland Studios since 1987. Chilmark now assumes operation of the Collectors Society and will continue to provide the high level of product and service expected by collectors and society members.

Chilmark Awarding Winning Sculpture — *American West, Civil War, Mickey & Co.*

In addition to the work of Don Polland, the Chilmark line has expanded over the years to include the *Civil War* sculptures of Francis J. Barnum, *American West* studies by Michael Boyett, Joe Slockbower and Anne McGrory and Lowell Davis' *Americana* subjects. The most rapidly expanding category over the past few years has been the *Mickey & Co.* designs, which find Mickey and his pals revolutionizing the world of art metal sculpture.

The body of Chilmark sculpture currently available has captured the attention of the collectibles industry, and since 1990, 12 different designs, by six different artists, have been nominated for awards. Eight of these nominees have won awards from prestigious organizations such as *Collector Editions* magazine, the National Association of Limited Edition Dealers and The Walt Disney Company.

"The Children's Nativity Pageant" from Hudson Pewter Villagers Collection

"Christ Kindle, Switzerland" from Hudson's Père Nöel Collection is a limited edition of 3,500.

Hudson - Old Favorites and Exciting New Collections

As Mickey Mouse continues to transcend time and age groups, The Lance Corporation offers Fine Pewter *Mickey & Co.* gift items in addition to the limited editions. The World of Mickey (and Minnie!) continues to find favor with collectors of Disneyana and gift-givers alike. The *Mickey and Co.* Birthday and Music Trains, Barnyard Symphony and Carousel, along with keychains and ormanents, offer something for everyone.

Hudson Pewter Villagers - A Nostalgic Winter Wonderland

While there are many village scenes in today's collectibles market, the *Hudson Villagers* collection is unique because the focus is on the people—the heartbeat of any community—rather than a town's buildings. Crisply detailed nostalgic turn-of-the-century characters combine with props and accessories that let collectors create a delightful small town winter wonderland. Each of the pewter pieces is enhanced by bright, hand-painted touches that make the shimmering metal seem all the more beautiful.

Villagers pieces celebrate the joys of hometown Christmas, complete with sliding hill and skating pond at the Town Common, Christmas tree stand, a quaint country church and the children's homemade stable for the annual Christmas pageant. The *Villagers* offer Hudson collectors the opportunity to build a fine art collection in pewter with a combination of open, annual editions and limited edition offerings that provide year-round enjoyment.

A New Twist on Old Favorite

One of the most popular collections in the Hudson line, since its introduction in the early 1980s, continues to be the *Noah's Ark* collection. Over the years, Lance has added more than one hundred different members of the animal family as well as "Noah" and "Mrs. Noah," of course. It is the longest running Hudson Pewter collection to date.

In 1995, Hudson's oldest collection spurred a great idea for the newest and youngest grouping, *Ark Babies.* Young animals adorned with pink and blue bows take the story of Noah's Ark to the younger set. Complete with the beautiful wicker bassinet "ark," the collection has already begun to attract collectors attention — not only the young but the young at heart.

The *Père Nöel Collection*

Hudson's *Père Nöel Collection* is a medley of the many faces of Santa. Every nation and nationality has recognized its own version of Santa Claus — "Père Nöel" in France, "St. Nikkolo" in Austria, "Father Christmas" in England and "Christ Kindle" of Switzerland. Although his garments changed from decade to decade and his name has varied from country to country, the generosity and spirit of old St. Nicholas has survived through legend and fable.

Cindy Smith, *Père Nöel* artist, has been designing and producing handmade, limited edition sculptures for over 12 years. Her first collection for The Lance Corporation was a collection of woodland fairies and folks called Shirelings who dwell in a land known as *cp smithshire.*

The faces and personalities of each and every one of her figures are unique and sculpted directly from the images seen in Cindy's own mind's eye. She carefully researches costuming and has a gift for small details which may be overlooked by others. The color schemes for each limited edition sculpture are developed by Cindy and her palette evokes warm, down-to-earth feelings.

Sebastian Miniatures - Still Young at Heart at Fifty-Eight

America's longest continually produced collectible line, Sebastian Miniatures have been hand cast and hand-painted in New England since 1938. The figures exhibit pure American flavor, depicting themes including historic, nostalgic, and "ordinary people doing ordinary things." The feeling is one of reminiscence and a stirring of memories of days gone by.

In the 1950s, Baston developed a "story-series plan," selling his Sebastian Miniatures as themed groupings. Baston's Sebastian Miniatures were seen as collectible 20 years before the huge collectibles boom of the 1970s.

In 1976, The Lance Corporation took over production and national distribu-

"California or Bust!" from the Chilmark Mickey & Co. collection is available in a Fine Pewter Edition of 250 and a Bronze Edition of 25.

tion of Sebastian Miniatures. As the company was inundated with requests for information from people who had old miniatures, it was obvious that Mr. Baston's sales approach had indeed spurred thousands of long time Sebastian collectors. The result was The Sebastian Miniatures Collectors Society. Today after 15-plus years as an organized information center, it is one of the oldest, active collectors clubs in the country.

The Sebastian Miniature Legacy

Baston's son "Woody" worked in the Sebastian Studio throughout his youth and later went on to earn a bachelor's degree in sculpture. Under his father's tutelage, Woody designed his first miniature for the line in 1981. Since his father's death in 1984, Woody has been the sole creative force in the continuation of Sebastian Miniatures.

Lance Corporation
321 Central Street
Hudson, MA 01749
(508) 568-1401
Fax (508) 568-8741

COLLECTORS' CLUBS/MUSEUM

The Chilmark Polland Collectors Society
The Lance Corporation
321 Central St.
Hudson, MA 01749
(508) 568-1401
Annual Dues: $45.00
Club Year: Anniversary of Sign-Up Date

Benefits:
• Membership Gift: Pewter Figurine
• Opportunity to Purchase Members-Only Sculpture
• Bi-annual Newsletter, "Collector's Review"
• Membership Card
• Tours Upon Request

The Chilmark Registry
The Lance Corporation
321 Central St.
Hudson, MA 01749
(508) 568-1401
Annual Dues: Free Upon Registration of a Chilmark Sculpture
Club Year: Up to 5-Year Free Membership

Benefits:
• Two Annual Redemption Certificates for Members-Only Sculptures
• Quarterly Newsletter, "Chilmark Report"
• Tours Upon Request   • Buy/Sell Matching Service
• Annual Price Guide Updates   • Listing of Showcase Dealers
• Color Brochures on New Introductions
• Invitations to Special Events

The Pangaean Society
Official Collectors Club of cp smithshire™
The Lance Corporation
321 Central St., Hudson, MA 01749
(508) 568-1401
Annual Dues: $25.00
Club Year: Anniversary of Sign-Up Date

Benefits:
• Membership Gift: Sculpture
• Opportunity to Purchase Members-Only Sculpture
• Bi-annual Newsletter, "Shirespeak"
• Membership Card   • Enameled "Merlin" Pin
• Buy/Sell Matching Service
• Tours Upon Request   • Invitations to Special Events

Sebastian Miniatures Collectors Society
The Lance Corporation
321 Central St.
Hudson, MA 01749
(508) 568-1401
Annual Dues: $29.50
Club Year: Anniversary of Sign-Up Date

Benefits:
• Membership Gift: Figurine   • Buy/Sell Matching Service
• Membership Card   • Annual Value Register and Updates
• Opportunity to Purchase Members-Only Figurine
• Newsletter, "Sebastian Collectors Society News/Sebastian Exchange"
• Invitations to Special Events Including Stacy's Sebastian
  Festival and Midwest Fair   • Tours Upon Request

Official Sebastian Miniatures Museum
Stacy's Gifts and Collectibles
Walpole Mall
E. Walpole, MA 02032
(800) STACYS1
Hours: Monday through Saturday, 10 a.m.-9:30 p.m.,
Sunday, 1 p.m.-6 p.m.

Admission Fee: None

The Official Sebastian Miniatures Museum houses the largest public display of Sebastian Miniatures Figurines spanning "America's oldest continually produced collectible lines" from 1938 to the present.

RON LEE'S WORLD OF CLOWNS
Bringing Collectors Smiles, Magic and Childhood Dreams

As the last vestige of sun slips behind the trees, its final glow filters through the windows to focus on a huge room abundantly decorated with every conceivable clown artifact. Like a spotlight capturing an entertainer, the elongated rays pinpoint an artist intently at work. As the artist concentrates on the mass of clay in one hand and the small tool in the other, a new clown creation soon emerges from the creative mind and talented fingers of Ron Lee.

In a household filled with active sounds of his family, "Hobo Joe" was born. So were "Puppy Love," "Snowdrifter," "Heartbroken Harry" and countless other clown characters. Thriving in a room bursting with his energy as well as that of his wife and four children, Ron diligently follows an arduous daily routine that could easily include sculpting a new figurine, sketching a life-size carousel animal, writing a newsletter for his Collectors Club, making a personal appearance at a collectible shop or helping raise money for charity.

His non-stop energy and outgoing personality are apparent as four, five or even six new ideas could be hatching at the same time. While his highly competent staff often has difficulty keeping up with such a busy schedule, Ron avows it's "the only way to go." If you ask Ron Lee why he chose sculpting instead of other forms of art, he will simply tell you: "I need to be able to touch, to feel, to turn, to lift, to know it has dimension, a sense of reality. Even though the figurines I create are, what would you say, fanciful, if I could hold them in my hands, to me they suddenly become alive. They take on life and seem real, almost like children to be cherished and cared for."

Clowns, Clowns and More Clowns From Ron Lee

Recently establishing himself as the foremost sculptor of classic cartoon character limited edition sculptures, Ron returned to the basics in 1993. That year, he introduced more than 50 new clowns, focusing on the traditional antics of the circus and adventures under the big top. "Although I enjoy creating all these wonderful cartoon characters in three dimensions and in complete scenes, I really felt a need to get back to my 'clowning around' roots," he candidly admitted.

Presented in a broad spectrum of primary and pastel colors, the clowns range in height from 5 to 18 inches. There are clowns with cars, clowns with boats, clowns with trains, clowns with planes, and just clowns being clowns. Lollipop-colored favorites catch everyone's eyes as balloons and umbrellas often fly high above the scene.

A Dream of a Lifetime Comes True

As 1994 drew to a close, Ron and his wife, Jill — whose immense job is to ensure all the design and production of the pieces come together — realized a lifelong dream. They moved their complete factory to Henderson, Nevada, located just outside Las Vegas. Not only did they completely move everything, but they created a tourist attraction that draws hundreds of visitors daily. Within the 30,000 sq. ft. facility, guests discover a museum of circus and clown memorabilia, the famed Jitters Gourmet Cafe, Ron's personal archives, the Ron Lee Gallery and the company's very own clown who leads everyone through a self-guided tour of the making of a clown or animation sculpture from start to finish.

To top off this magnificent attraction, children of all ages can ride the full-size, $250,000 Carousel. Within these confines, one can do it all: learn about the history of the clown, view Ron's artistry since his youth, eat lunch,

As the breathtaking centerpiece of Ron Lee's factory and museum in Henderson, Nevada, this grand Carousel takes visitors on a trip back to their childhood. The $250,000 Carousel spins with lights, music, animals and action.

213

browse or shop at the Gallery, and, of course, go 'round and 'round to the exhilarating music of the glorious Carousel.

New Clown Sculptures and a Life-like Mural Delight Collectors

In the summer of 1995, Ron introduced a special series of limited edition sculptures — all dozen of which were highly detailed, exquisitely painted and featured a variety of clowns in unique scenes. These clowns are in the smaller size category, but each character is so clearly defined that its appearance is magnificent to behold. There's a clown wedding cake as well as a clown bathing, snoozing, painting and sitting in a doghouse, just to name a few.

Ron also created larger-than-life clowns. Covering a 53-foot wall at the Henderson facility, a hand-painted and original mural depicts a parade of clowns. Ron chose a small portion of this mural and created two delightful clown scenes entitled "Leading the

Ron Lee makes everyone smile with his fun-loving clowns. In these sculptures, the clown dresses up like a fireman with his trusty Dalmatian, gives flowers to his sweetheart, and takes a snooze on the chair.

Way" and "Want to Ride." Based on the mural, each vignette includes several characters and circus animals. These two new sculpture collections have a very low edition size of only 750. Throughout the year, Ron will be designing other clown scenes from this very astonishing mural. All of Ron Lee's

sculptures are individually hand-painted by a staff of talented artists and are limited to low edition sizes.

Ron Lee Heads West With Favorite Looney Tunes Characters

In 1995, Ron also created and designed an extraordinary collection of Looney Tunes sculptures with the popular cartoon characters stirring up trouble along their trail to settle the Old West. There's Tweety branding Sylvester, while Penelope serenades Pepe saloon style. Sheriff Bugs guards the General Store and the Tasmanian Devil is the consummate "Heap Big Chief." These are just four of the eight sculptures in the collection, which features low edition sizes to enhance collectibility. The pieces are also meticulously hand-painted, manufactured in the finest pewter and metal, and 24-K gold plated.

Ron Lee Expands His World to Include Limited Edition Plates

Ron Lee — recognized sculptor of heirloom quality cartoon characters and clown and circus-theme collectibles — recently ventured into another area. He introduced his own series of collector plates focusing on his famous "Hobo Joe" clown character.

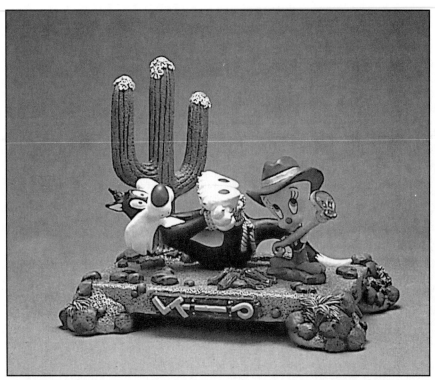

Sylvester is in for a rough time as he and his sidekick Tweety roam the range in the Looney Tunes collection by Ron Lee. Wearing a cowboy hat, Tweety tries to brand Sylvester with an iron portraying a picture of himself! There are eight different sculptures in the collection.

"I waited to present this series because I wanted to convey a special feeling in the designs," he said. "Whenever I create art, whether a single sculpture or a scene featuring numerous characters, I strive to evoke emotion that will translate to all the viewers of my work."

These plates have evolved into vividly colored, gold accented trimmed works of art portraying complete scenes featuring the antics of that lovable hero of the downtrodden, "Hobo Joe." Working to deliver the utmost quality in collectible plates, Ron Lee proudly presented a total of five irresistible designs that certainly complement his collectible "Hobo Joe" clown sculptures.

"Holy Cow, Batman! It's Ron Lee!"

Commemorating the hit movie and crime-fighting pair of Gotham City, Ron Lee designed a "Batman and Robin" sculpture that is so lifelike, they all but leap off the top of the building that they're standing on. With the characters in their full and familiar costumes, the sculptures convey the duo's power and personality. Ron's tireless energy is always apparent as his creativity covers all the bases. From the clowns that have captivated young and old alike for centuries to the latest popular characters on television and the big screen, Ron shares his artistry with everyone.

Ron Lee's World of Clowns
330 Carousel Parkway
Henderson, NV 89014
(702) 434-1700

One of Ron Lee's most popular characters, "Hobo Joe," can also be enjoyed in a five-issue plate series. The first in the series is "No Vacancy" produced in the finest quality porcelain, gold banded, and individually numbered and certified.

COLLECTORS' CLUB/TOUR

Ron Lee's Collectors Club
330 Carousel Parkway
Henderson, NV 89014
(702) 434-1700

Annual Dues: $28.50
Club Year: Anniversary of Sign-Up Date

BENEFITS:
• Membership Gift: New Clown Sculpture Each Year
• Quarterly Newsletter
• Annual Convention
• Brochures on New Products
• Members-Only Pieces

Ron Lee's World of Clowns
330 Carousel Parkway
Henderson, NV 89014
(702) 434-1700

Hours: Daily, 9 a.m.-6 p.m.
Admission: Free; $1 for carousel ride.

Visitors enjoy a self-guided tour featuring a start-to-finish demonstration of how a clown sculpture is developed and produced. Curious clown-lovers can view the gallery, archives and circus memorabilia.

GEORGE Z. LEFTON CO.
Villages Capture the Magic of American Traditions

Join us today on a journey back in time to a *Colonial Village* where the pace is slower, neighbors are friendlier, and everyone understands the joy of caring and sharing! This ideal vision of "small town USA" comes alive in Lefton's beloved *Colonial Village Collection* – a group of buildings and wonderful accessories that has been winning a place in the hearts and homes of collectors since 1987.

Now approaching its 10th-anniversary year, the *Colonial Village Collection* has grown from just a few buildings and citizens, to a prospering community of more than 100 buildings and countless neighbors. What's more, each addition has been artfully conceived and crafted with ultimate care. And if the buildings are the heart of the Collection, its accessories and people are surely its soul.

Each building in the Collection is hand-painted and handcrafted of fine ceramic, with vibrant color and detail. Each comes with a Deed of Title that explains the history of the building and symbolizes "ownership" of that particular piece of "real estate."

Among the most impressive recent introductions is the Collection's fifth limited edition building, the "Wycoff Manor." This stately home for senior citizens adds a wonderful new dimension of caring and compassion to the town. The edition is strictly limited to 5,500 pieces.

A Colorful Treat: *The Illustrated Collector's Guide & History*

To complement Lefton's *Colonial Village Collection* – and light the way for the future – company Chairman George Z. Lefton introduced a handsome book: the *Illustrated Collector's Guide & History*. Beautifully rendered in full color, the book includes every building and accessory introduced to date in the Collection – including

The inviting lights inside the "Colonial Savings & Loan" (Item #01321) let the folks of the Colonial Village know that Banker Arthur Pemberton is ready to help them out with loans and financial advice. This hand-painted work of art is typical of the charm and quality of Lefton's Colonial Village Collection.

retired pieces, limited editions, special editions, and suspended pieces. Now in its fifth edition, the book contains a wonderful tale that narrates beautiful photos of detailed *Colonial Village* vignettes.

The story, "Searching for Rover," introduces a canine hero and then tells of the frightful day when Rover's family awoke to find that their beloved dog had disappeared. The search for Rover takes readers on a trip through the Village, where its buildings, businesses and people come to life. Young Lenny Mullen, Rover's frantic owner, asks everyone he meets to keep a lookout for Rover – and so they do. After many adventures and near-misses, Lenny finally finds his beloved Rover at "Rainy Days Barn" – helping to watch over his

new canine family of six adorable puppies and their mother, a dog named Spot.

This eventful tour of *Colonial Village* enables its readers to meet the citizens, explore the architecture, and enjoy a delightful journey through the town that a host of collectors have grown to love. *The Illustrated Collector's Guide & History* book is available from Lefton's Collectors' Service Bureau, attention Guide & History, Post Office Box 09178, Chicago, Illinois 60609-9970.

Collectors' Service Bureau Keeps *Colonial Village* Enthusiasts Informed

While the *Colonial Village Collection* does not have a collectors club, it does have a quarterly newsletter to which thousands of readers subscribe. Subscribers of the "Colonial Village News" get first-hand, "hot-off-the-presses" news about the goings-on in the

The "Colonial Village News," issued quarterly, can be acquired in yearly subscriptions for just $2.00 to cover postage and handling. An Official Deed of Ownership accompanies each Colonial Village Collection building. In addition, missing deeds may be acquired through Lefton's Collectors' Service Bureau in Chicago.

Village. They are the first to know of upcoming product retirements, new introductions to the Collection, events locations, and collectible show information.

The "News" is free with just a $2.00 annual fee for shipping and handling of the four yearly issues. Collectors may call Lefton at 1-800-628-8492 to begin subscribing.

That same number serves as the Lefton Consumer Hotline, where collectors may call to locate a stocking retailer near them – a dealer that carries all of Lefton's collectible lines. In addition to newsletter subscriptions, the Hotline handles orders for replacement Deeds of Ownership, provides product brochures and catalogs, offers up-to-date retirement announcement information and new product introductions, and sells the *Guide & History* book.

In 1995, the first formal events program for *Colonial Village* collectors began, centered around an events-only building entitled the "Bayside Inn." This exclusive building is available only through retailers who hosted *Colonial Village* events during 1995.

Lefton's *Historic American Lighthouse Collection*

The majesty and mystery of the sea can belong to collectors – right in their own homes – when they acquire the *Historic American Lighthouses* from Lefton. First introduced in 1992, these fully illuminated beacons of light have been carefully researched for authenticity, then handcrafted and hand-painted to reflect the care and quality that is so much a part of each original structure.

Lighthouses depicted in this collection are located throughout the country, from east to west coast and the lakes in-between. The series has subsets distinguished by their geography, including "Atlantic," "Southern," "Great Lakes," and "Pacific Coast." In the case where an important lighthouse is no longer standing, Lefton has created the mold for its work of art from renderings in historical archives.

In addition to the larger "lights,"

"Toledo Harbor" (Item #01331) from Lefton's Historic American Lighthouse Collection *depicts the famous 1904 Great Lakes lighthouse located on a concrete pier in Maumee Bay. Its issue price is $47.00.*

which range up to 11" in height proportional to the original building, Lefton also offers a charming collection of *Little Lighthouses*. As carefully detailed as the full-size originals, each lighthouse in this collection stands about 6" tall. They are not lighted like the full-size replicas, but still are shining examples of high-quality ceramic collectibles.

To honor America's great and long history of lighthouses, a portion of the proceeds from each lighthouse is donated to the United States Lighthouse Society, a non-profit organization dedicated to the restoration and preservation of these national treasures.

Each of the over 40 full-size lighthouse replicas now available comes complete with an embossed hangtag detailing its construction, location, and the history of the original, plus a UL-listed cord and bulb with on/off switch. There are over 36 *Little Lighthouses* available, as well.

To receive a colorful catalog that pictures the entire *Historic American Lighthouse Collection*, plus miniatures, musicals and lighthouse ornaments,

collectors may call Lefton's Collectors' Service Bureau at the number quoted earlier. The cost of the catalog is $4.00, and it also may be acquired from Lefton's stocking retailers.

Take a Trip Down Memory Lane with Lefton's *Roadside USA Collection*

With six colorful series of nostalgic collectibles, Lefton's *Roadside USA Collection* captures the charm of an earlier American era with its landmark eateries, billboards, transportation modes, and firefighters.

The *Great American Diner* series was first introduced in 1994 with eight styles of classic roadside eating establishments in the premier edition. Fondly known as the "Spectacular Vernaculars," Lefton's *Roadside Delites* continues the Diner series with ten incredible places to stop for "eats": "The Coffee Pot," "Airplane Cafe," "Zep Diner," "The Dog House," "Kone Inn," and five more. Each of these diners – created by award-winning artist/ designer David Stravitz, is shaped likes the item it names – wonderfully quirky!

To complement the diners along a collector's personal roadside display, Lefton offers *Billboards of Yesteryear*, a dozen handsome, richly colored signs recreating famous American advertising motifs and billboard foundations from decades past. Products and concepts promoted on the licensed

Lefton's Great American Diners – from the Roadside USA Collection – *includes this wonderful old diner known as "The Star Light" (Item #01178) – a uniquely American culinary and architectural statement.*

billboards include: World War II images like "Work for Victory" and "Women at Work;" Smokey the Bear's messages such as "Remember, Only You Can Prevent Forest Fires!" and "Smokey's Friends Don't Play With Matches;" and product promotions for "Kew-Bee Bread," Pepsi-Cola's "More Bounce to the Ounce," and Campbell's Soups' "Eat Soup — And Keep Well." There are also a couple of renowned Ford billboard images — for the Model T and for 1950's "Quiet as a Ford."

Where transportation modes are concerned, Lefton portrays both *Railroad Depots and Trolleys*. The railroad's "Sentimental Journey" includes famous stations from the Atchison, Topeka & Santa Fe line as well as the Erie, B&O, Western Maryland and Wisconsin Central railroads. The "trib-ute to trolleys and cable cars" features beloved models including the historic San Francisco Cable Cars from "Market Street" and "City Hall 6," Cleveland's "Payne Avenue" railway, and old-fashioned cars from North Chicago, Sioux City, and Baltimore.

Lefton's *Firehouses* — affectionately known as the "Great Halls of Fire," include images of architectural marvels originally built in brick, concrete and steel, stone, wood, and clapboard. They proudly watched over towns in Colorado, New Jersey, New York, New England, Chicago, and Seattle — and they have been lovingly recreated down to the last brick, fire engine and flagpole waving "Old Glory."

From the small-town America of the *Colonial Village Collection* to the legacy of *Historic Lighthouses* and the nos-talgia of *Roadside USA*, Lefton recreates a warmhearted world for collectors to explore. And with the services of the firm's Collectors' Service Bureau, each owner of Lefton's "real estate" can maximize their enjoyment in acquisition and display.

George Z. Lefton Co.
3622 S. Morgan St.
Chicago, IL 60609
(800) 628-8492

LEGENDS

Bronze and Pewter Combine With Vermeil of Brass and 24K Gold in Brilliant Mixed Media® Creations

When a team of four brothers launched Legends® in 1986, they were already renowned for their fine art sculptures for giftware-related companies like American Express and Walt Disney Productions. Since then, Legends has dramatically impacted the world of collectibles with works ranging from small-scale issues to full-sized gallery sculptures.

The company's subject matter is remarkably broad as well: encompassing authentic Native American figures, Western and Civil War history, and endangered wildlife. Through the everlasting medium of sculpture, Legends fine art sculpture proudly represents and preserves the inspiring heritage of the Native American Indian, as well as many other significant American heroes, leaders and legends who grace the annals of our nation's history.

Committed to environmental and wildlife conservation, Legends actively supports the work of various non-profit organizations, such as Defenders of Wildlife, the Grounded Eagle Foundation, and the World Wildlife Fund. Additionally, Legends maintains its commitment to the preservation and advancement of today's Native Americans through significant donations that support vital organizations such as the Native American Rights Fund (NARF), Red Cloud Indian School in South Dakota, and the American Indian Dance Theatre.

The Latest Releases from Legends

From the warrior hunters of Michael Boyett's *The Animal Dreamer Collection* to the legendary dancer of Willy Whitten's "Rapture," the artists of Legends capture the drama and dignity of Native American life — and the glories of the wildlife of their western homelands.

Michael Boyett has been specially commissioned to create a stunning

"He Hunts With the Eagle Medicine" by Michael Boyett premieres The Animal Dreamer Collection *for Legends. The 10"-high sculpture has been issued in a certified limited edition of 950 pieces.*

five-piece series, *The Animal Dreamer Collection*, exclusively for Legends. Each sculpture reflects the interdependent relationship that existed between the warrior hunter and the wild creatures which roamed the untamed frontier.

The collection's first release, "He Hunts With the Eagle Medicine," presents a warrior using the swiftness and cunning of an eagle to lead him in the hunt. The second introduction, "Buffalo Runner," offers Boyett's presentation of the supreme cunning and courage exhibited by the buffalo hunters of days past.

David Lemon's "Winds of Memory," the second release from the five-piece *Western Memories Premiere Edition*, depicts the legendary Sacajawea in her later years. She remembers wearing the same blanket she wears now, one she had as a young girl with the Lewis and Clark Expedition, sitting on the banks of a river looking down into the face of her newborn son.

"Each, to the Other" offers artist

Christopher Pardell's romantic tribute to the transformative power of love and marriage. This poignant piece — second in Pardell's *Culture Covenant Premier Edition* for Legends — features a young Native American couple reflecting upon the powerful change wrought by the tribal ceremony of marriage.

David Lemon's "Winds of Memory" sculpture captures Sacajawea as an older woman, remembering her days as part of the Lewis and Clark Expedition with her infant son as her companion.

With "Scent in the Air," Kitty Cantrell has once again captured the wolf as one of the most majestic examples of wild America. In this specially commissioned sculpture for Legends, the wolf has caught a scent in the air and wrinkles his nose slightly to track its origin. Meanwhile, the wind ruffles his beautiful fur.

"Rapture" by Willy Whitten represents a stunning, specially commissioned sculpture which artfully depicts a moment in the Native American Ghost Dance. At the moment this sculpture portrays, the dancer's costume still stands in its pose, while the dancer has just vanished into the sky.

The Ghost Dancer has just ascended to the sky, leaving his costume still in dance position, in this mystical work of art entitled "Rapture." It is the creation of sculptor Willy Whitten, exclusively for Legends.

A Host of Gifted Sculptors Contribute Their Talents to Legends

Because of their complete dedication to quality and integrity in the creation of fine art sculpture, Legends has attracted some of America's most honored sculptors of Native American and wildlife subjects. The firm's current endeavors include associations with Christopher Pardell, Kitty Cantrell, Willy Whitten, Dan Medina, David Lemon, and Michael Boyett.

Christopher A. Pardell was one of the first artists to join the Legends family. "My work is about more than just excitement and motion and fear," he says. "It's about the bittersweet mixture of joy and sorrow that we all know, we all feel. When they poured the slab for my studio, I carved a motto into the concrete as it hardened. It says, 'Life is a performance artwork, make yours beautiful.'"

Kitty D. Cantrell is known for her striking sculptures of North American wildlife, with wolves, eagles and humpback whales among her favorite subjects. A member of a half-dozen environmental associations, Ms. Cantrell donates a portion of the proceeds from her art to the Nature Conservancy, the World Wildlife Fund and the Grounded Eagle Foundation.

Willy Whitten is a self-taught artist, yet acknowledged as a master craftsman. Fluent in an extensive variety of media and techniques, Whitten finds fascination with the beauty and variety of Native American costume and its wealth of symbolism.

Dan Medina's artistic genius shines through in his award-winning works. Research is essential to his craft, but his true inspiration springs from within. As he says, "To portray emotion and form in metal — that is the essence of art. It all starts in the mind."

David Lemon, a member of the prestigious American Indian and Cowboy Artists Association, is a mesmerizing storyteller as well as an inspired sculptor. "You have to be thick-skinned to be an artist," Lemon says. "Your art is your soul — those are my thoughts and feelings out there on the table for people to comment on or criticize. Or worst of all, ignore."

Michael Boyett's moving style was born of his interest in heroic and historic America, coupled with a strength in realism. Wounded in battle during an enemy ambush, his experience as an infantryman during the years of the Vietnam War burned a deep sensitivity into his nature which carries over into his works of art.

The Mixed Media® Creative Process

Legends has always remained in the forefront of new concepts and innovations in the collectibles and fine art markets — most notably in the conception and creation of Mixed Media®. This significant and valuable contribution to the world of limited edition fine art sculpture combines multiple brilliant media, including Legends Bronze, Fine Pewter, Brass Vermeil, 24K Gold Vermeil, Lucite®, and many other vibrant metals and hot torched-acid patinas. Also used periodically are Black Nickel, Rose Copper Vermeil, Sunrise Gold Copper Vermeil and Flame Copper Vermeil.

When Legends unveiled their first Mixed Media™ work in 1987, collectors immediately recognized the uniqueness of this stunning new concept in

fine art sculpture. And while imitators have surfaced over the years, Legends remains the only studio to create each of its works using the authentic colors of the actual metals to create color on the sculpture — never paints or dyes.

The step-by-step crafting process for a Legends sculpture begins when a Legends artist creates an original work. This sculptural original may require many months — sometimes years — of sculpting and re-sculpting soft clay before the original is finalized in the form of plastiline. From these masters, working models are created.

Each piece is sectioned into many tiny component parts to help Legends create the intricate detail found in all of their sculptures. They are then placed into molds for the creation of individual cavities. Hot molten metal is poured into these cavities and is left until it cools down to room temperature.

Each component part is tirelessly hand-cleaned and refitted by foundry artisans with over two decades of experience. Handwork with fine stainless steel tools recovers detail lost in the soldering process. The finished Mixed Media work is oxidized to a deep black patina and then relieved by hand with steel wool and sand to bring back highlights of the original metals. Only then is the piece appointed with the unique characteristics that make Legends

Kitty Cantrell portrays a stunning wolf in this 11-1/2"-high sculpture from Legends, entitled "Scent in the Air."

sculptures the leaders in today's fine art marketplace.

Starlite Collector's Society Boasts Free Membership

Legends supports its collectors through the Starlite Collector's Society (SCS) – formerly Legends Collectors Society – an exclusive, free membership program that collectors receive upon the purchase of any Legends limited edition sculpture. As members, collectors acquire a personalized SCS membership i.d. number which provides access to a wide range of services and opportunities, as well as many other valuable and exclusive benefits.

Among the most coveted of these benefits is the opportunity for collectors to acquire new sculptures before the open market release. Also important is *Starlite*, the quarterly full-color magazine featuring all new releases. In addition, the SCS records sculpture titles, insurance, and secondary market activity for safekeeping as a service to Starlite Collector's Society members,

and provides assistance in sculpture appraisal.

It has been only a few short years since Legends developed the masterful innovation of Mixed Media and began creating sculptures using that exquisite media. Since then, this California-based firm has earned a strong – and growing – reputation for integrity, sculptural excellence and innovation. Considering these factors – and the company's commitment to historical accuracy and old-world craftsmanship in fine metal – the "Legends tradition" stands to flourish and grow for generations to come.

Legends
2665D Park Center Drive
Simi Valley, CA 93065
(800) 726-9660
Fax (805) 520-9670

Christopher Pardell's "Each to the Other" represents the second release in the Culture Covenant Premier Edition *from* Legends. *The sculpture offers a romantic tribute to the transformative power of love and marriage, featuring a young Native American couple.*

COLLECTORS' CLUB

Starlite Collector's Society
2665-D Park Center Drive
Simi Valley, CA 93065
(800) 726-9660

Annual Dues: Free Upon Purchase of a Legends' Sculpture
Club Year: Anniversary of Sign-Up Date

Benefits:
• Quarterly Full-Color Magazine, *Starlite*
• Personalized SCS I.D. Number
• Opportunity to Acquire New Sculptures Before the Open Market Release
• Special Event Pieces Available
• Record Keeping Services
• Appraisal Service

LENOX COLLECTIONS

"The Lenox Difference" Is a 100-Year-Old Tradition of Excellence Carried Forward in Every Work of Art

It began in 1889. A young artist-potter named Walter Scott Lenox founded a company dedicated to the daring proposition that an American firm could create the finest china in the world. He possessed a zeal for *perfection* that he applied to the relentless pursuit of his artistic goals.

In the years that followed, Lenox china became the first American chinaware ever exhibited at the National Museum of Ceramics, in Sevres, France. In 1918, Lenox received the singular honor of being the first American company to create the official state table service for The White House.

Lenox China has been in use at The White House ever since, commissioned by Presidents and First Ladies of four different eras. Works of Lenox may also be found in more than half our Governors' mansions. They are in United States embassies around the world, and they have been specially commissioned for gifts of state.

Today, in every work of art created by Lenox Collections, the traditions begun by Walter Scott Lenox are carried forward.

The Lenox Tradition

On one occasion in the struggling early days of the firm, Walter Scott Lenox took an eminent guest on a tour through the new workshops. They stopped before a kiln and watched as craftsmen removed chinaware representing an investment of $2,000 (quite a large sum in those days). Lenox looked at the pieces with his usual piercing scrutiny and noticed a tiny flaw in every one, possibly visible only to him. Before Lenox could voice his dismay, the enthusiastic visitor cried out, "This is exhilarating. Such excitement!" "Yes," Lenox replied. Without hesitation, he then ordered everything that had just come out of

the kiln to be destroyed.

The Lenox Difference

Lenox Collections today creates works in many mediums. In every case, it maintains an unbending position regarding *quality*. The collector will see this difference in the detail of each Lenox hand-painted porcelain sculpture...in the fiery, hand-polished luster of each Lenox crystal bowl, sculpture or vase...and, of course, in the flawless finish of every piece of Lenox china.

This quest for excellence in artistry has earned Lenox the privilege of creating authorized works for famed organizations throughout the world, from the Smithsonian Institution in Washington, D.C. to the famed Palace Museum in Peking's Forbidden City.

Lenox Craftsmanship

From the company's very beginning, Walter Scott Lenox stopped at nothing to locate the most gifted craftsmen both in America and abroad. When he set out to reproduce a special, pearlescent china, nothing would do but to send to Ireland for those potters who knew the craft best. Having served as an apprentice himself, Lenox realized that craftsmanship is what bridges the gulf between dream and reality.

Now, in our own time, Lenox Collections literally searches the world to find the craftsmen most particularly skilled in producing each special work.

And these craftsmen are then challenged to surpass themselves – to apply their gifts to a standard of excellence that is *unique* in all the world.

Lenox Beauty...To Endure Forever

On the subject of beauty, Walter Scott Lenox schooled his company to satisfy only one critic — posterity. His goal was to create art that would live forever.

Today, this goal remains unchanged. Every work of art Lenox Collections creates is a message to collectors, and to the world, about the company's firm

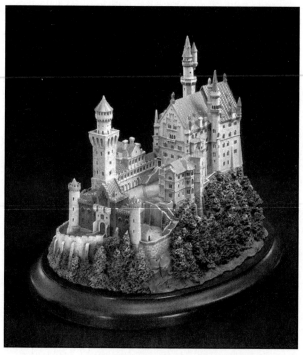

"Neuschwanstein" is the remarkable re-creation of a king's fantasy. The castle's four buildings, two courtyards, seven towers and 293 windows are portrayed with breathtaking detail by master miniaturist Ron Spicer. The sculpture is handcrafted in an artist's blend of resin porcelain and painted entirely by hand. "Neuschwanstein" is 8" long by 6" high, including base.

commitment to uphold its founder's mission. Lenox works are created today to endure for generations and to be treasured by collectors a hundred years from now.

Lenox and Its Collectors

Throughout its history, Lenox has attracted some of the most exacting customers in the world...from the royal patron who commissioned a service of the most elegant china to set a table for 1,000 guests...to heads of state and dignitaries from countries throughout the world. From United States Presidents Wilson and Roosevelt to Truman and Reagan, each has turned to Lenox, confident of receiving the very best.

Today, Lenox Collections conducts an ongoing search for great talent and has extended its patronage to gifted artists of many different lands. To earn the Lenox hallmark, the highest standards must be met. Every nature subject must be shown completely true to life. Each historical piece must be authentic in every detail, and all works must be infused with the fire of imagination.

The Lenox Pledge of Satisfaction

Lenox Collections takes pride in offering works of uncompromisingly high standards of quality, crafted with care and dedication by skilled artisans. The Lenox goal, in every case, is to meet the highest expectations of artistry and fine workmanship. Therefore, if a collector is ever less than completely satisfied, Lenox will either replace the work or refund the purchase price.

Similarly, if a work is ever broken or damaged, Lenox will strive to satisfy the collector as well. If the edition is still open and a replacement is available, Lenox will send it to the owner at only one-half the current price of the work.

Lenox Collections invites collectors to share in the Lenox heritage of excel-

"Golden Splendor" is the first collector plate by the outstanding nature artist Catherine McClung. This award-winning artist portrays beautiful birds in their glorious natural setting. The 8-1/4" plate is crafted of Lenox ivory china to the quality standard that has made Lenox collector plates prized for generations.

lence. And the company pledges to make today's collectors as satisfied as the Presidents, First Ladies and royalty who have gone before.

The Tradition Continues with Lenox Collector Plates

Lenox entered the collectible plate market in 1902 by introducing bone china dinnerware with special-order decorations. It was William Morley, perhaps the most celebrated artist in the company's early history, who set the standard for superior artistry with these original custom-order plates. Orchids, first requested in 1906, were among Morley's best subjects. A set of 18 portrait plates that were created at this time were auctioned in 1979 for $14,000.

Today, Lenox Collections offers fine art plates by some of today's most highly regarded artists.

Catherine McClung, nationally recognized for her paintings of birds, has been awarded Best of Show at the Chicago Art Exhibition, and featured in

the Birds in Art Exhibition at the prestigious Leigh Yawky Woodson Museum. *Nature's Collage* is the artist's first plate collection.

Lynn Bywaters creates Santas robed in regal splendor, adorned in snowy ermine, embroidered in silver and gold. Collectors can acquire *The Magic of Christmas*, a collection of Lynn Bywater's Santas, directly from Lenox Collections.

There are few artists today who enjoy as much critical and collector acclaim as folk artist Warren Kimble. His work is featured in prestigious collections all over the world. Now, collectors can acquire some of Warren Kimble's most sought-after art in his first-ever Lenox plate collection – *The Warren Kimble Barnyard Animals*.

Lenox Supports Conservation Efforts

Because of illegal poaching and shrinking habitats, many of the worlds' magnificent animals face extinction. To raise awareness of their plight, the artists of Lenox work with wildlife organizations such as the Smithsonian Institution's National Zoological Park in Washington, D.C., the National Foundation to Protect America's Eagles™ and the Rainforest Alliance. Together, Lenox Collections and the specialists of these organizations create works of art to serve as constant reminders that our animals, and their natural habitats, must be preserved to prevent their extinction.

Lenox Porcelain and Crystal

The difference that Lenox demands in quality of workmanship, artistry and imagination may be observed in every one of today's classic porcelain and crystal sculptures.

One stunning example of Lenox hand-painted porcelain wildlife sculpture is the "African Elephant Calf." This work has been sculpted under the supervision of specialists at the

Smithsonian Institution's National Zoological Park in Washington, D.C.

With "Prim & Proper," the artists of Lenox have captured feline grace in Lenox Crystal. This elegant pair of crystal cats — one clear, one frosted — can stand alone, or they can nestle together producing an interplay of contours and contrasts.

The grace of the dolphin is portrayed in a work of art in pure white bone china glistening with a touch of gold. Dramatic and elegant, "Dance of the Dolphins" is a true showpiece.

These are but a few of today's best-known Lenox sculptures.

Lenox Looks to the Future

Never a company to rest on its laurels, Lenox Collections actively seeks opportunities to collaborate with prestigious organizations to bring today's collectors fascinating new works of art.

Collectors can watch for exciting creations, authorized by Turner Entertainment, which celebrate the drama and passion of *Gone With the Wind*. And car enthusiasts will be pleased to hear that Lenox Collections,

in association with the Chevrolet Motor Division, will be crafting new works to "rev" the engine of the most dedicated collector.

The Tradition Lives On

Walter Scott Lenox died in 1920 at the age of 60, but his dream lives on in the work of today's talented Lenox artists, designers and craftsmen. And in the remarkable works of art that are cherished, treasured and enjoyed by generations of collectors across America and around the world.

Lenox Collections
1170 Wheeler Way
Langhorne, PA 19047
(800) 225-1779
Fax (215) 750-7362

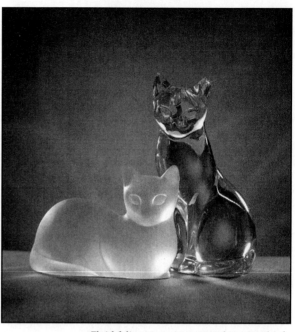

Fluid feline grace is captured in a work of art that combines the clarity of polished crystal with the luster of frosted crystal. A sleek and sophisticated pair, "Prim and Proper" are etched with the Lenox hallmark, symbol of incomparable quality.

LILLIPUT LANE

There's a Place Known as Lilliput Lane...Somewhere Between England...Artist David Tate's Dreams...and Collector Fantasies

"Jones the Butcher" boasts the freshest mutton. And stop at the "The Greengrocers," too. Tots will be angelic after a visit to "The Toy Shop," but if their behavior isn't perfect, a treat from "Penny Sweets" will suffice. Find every enchantment in this delightful mini-series!

Americans who have never visited the United Kingdom tend to think of England in legendary, symbolic terms. Crown jewels. Big Ben. A civilized cup of tea.

Americans who *have* walked the streets of London, Bradford, Bath, Penzance and England's other charming hamlets and cities, know that clocks and kings are but a sampling of a culture steeped in tradition. Some say, "if you wish to know England, you must first understand her architecture." If that's true, you'll want to meet David Tate and hear about his efforts to preserve the rich architectural heritage of the British Isles. As founder of Lilliput Lane, Tate has managed to pack centuries of structural wonders into the burgeoning library of collectible treasures he designs and markets all over the globe.

Today, Tate's mission to preserve British architecture has taken him beyond the English Channel. The architectural styles of continental Europe have become a passion, too. The now-International Lilliput collection includes charming German structures, cozy dwellings from the Netherlands, French country houses – even Americana!

To find out how David Tate accomplished his vision, read on. Sample the gardens. Peek in windows! But be forewarned – once you visit this idyllic world, you might not want to leave Lilliput Lane.

A "Cottage Industry" Becomes a Cottage Phenomenon

Born in 1945 in the Yorkshire district of England, David Tate was the only son of a small, close-knit family. A creative child, he showed a remarkable aptitude for drawing, earning an art scholarship at the age of ten. Just five years later, Tate's artistic education was halted when family obligations required a job to help with expenses. Putting his art ambition on hold, he pursued an eclectic variety of work as a salesman, photographer, British fiberglass industry executive and public relations expert.

Fortuitously, Tate's public relations experience was in the ceramics industry. When he decided to resurrect his life's ambition to be an artist, his knowledge of ceramics would serve him well. Tate and his wife moved to Penrith, in northern England's Lake District. Not far from the Scottish border and his village of birth, he restored an old farm house, creating living quarters and a studio.

All that was left to be done before the work began was to bestow a name on his new venture. Given Tate's love of English literature, he fondly recalled Jonathan Swift's classic *Gulliver's Travels*, picking the name Lilliput Lane. Now his adventure was about to begin.

Tate's Philosophy: Be Fanciful... Be Professional!

Personally supervising the search for new subjects to sculpt, David Tate is a stickler for authenticity and detail – qualities that make his cottages stand out. He has been known to study mountains of books and to rummage through crates of photographs, looking for a single cottage of a particular vernacular styling. For the uninitiated, "vernacular" describes a distinct type of building found only in one area. Thus, both adobe structures in the Southwest and the brownstones of New York City could be called "vernacular." Each is unique to its region and the culture of the area.

Once a vernacular style had been selected for the Lilliput Lane collection, 20th century embellishments, added to the building since its construction, are eliminated as the first model is shaped. This assures collectors the finished piece will be completely representative of its original era. When the model is complete, a silicone mold is made.

Cottages are then fashioned of "amorphite," a material lauded for its fine detailing and undercuts. After

Town and villages are proud of their local tea rooms! The biscuits are hot and fresh and the sweet aroma of tea comforts the soul! Step into one of Lilliput Lane's new tea rooms and you're bound to want to sit awhile and reminisce.

unmolding, sculptures are "fettled" (cleaned) to remove excess material, dipped in sealant and dried.

The fabrication of every limited edition collectible made by Lilliput Lane is predicated upon quality. Tate urges his staff to think professionally at all times. Whether a member of the studio art staff, a customer service representative, or a Lilliput Lane Club staff member, all employees are in accord with the company's founder: "Lilliput Lane's business policy is built on quality. We strive to do everything professionally. Whether it's painting a flower garden or answering collector questions, we'll always put our most professional foot forward!"

At "Langdale Cottage," the wassail bowl greets visitors and the smell of pine boughs strung throughout the little house is the stuff of which Christmas dreams are made!

Lilliput Lane Comes to America - A Club Is Launched

Lilliput Lane's subsidiary, Gift Link, Inc., launched the United States distribution of cottages in 1988. By 1993, the bond between the parent British corporation and American group had become so strong, a unanimous decision to re-name the American company "Lilliput, Incorporated" was reached.

Meanwhile, in England, Lilliput Lane was experiencing its own phenomenon: record growth...far beyond original projections. A decision to put the Lilliput Group plc, the parent company of Lilliput Lane Ltd., on the London Stock Exchange was reached! This move, in November, 1993, was just the first of many advancements. Less than a year later, in October 1994, Lilliput Group plc was acquired by Stanhome, Inc., making Lilliput Lane the newest family member of the prestigious Enesco Corporation.

Corporate changes in place, Lilliput could now put its creative energies into projects and programs beloved by collectors. At the top of the list was the Lilliput Lane Collectors' Club, originally formed in 1986. Now an astonishing 70,000 strong, worldwide Club membership continues to grow at a remarkable rate.

Each year, members eagerly anticipate a Members-Only gift cottage ("Thimble Cottage" is the 1995/96 exclusive); a new color catalog; a subscription to the Club's quarterly magazine, *Gulliver's World*; and a card that allows members to reserve the newest Members-Only Redemption piece. Lilliput proudly presents "Porlock Down" to 1995/96 members, and always looks forward to hearing about the thrill collectors experience upon seeing their Club Special Redemption cottage for the first time.

Awards...Rewards...the New Art That Makes Lilliput Unique

Each year, attempting to write about Lilliput Lane's awards, retirements, new issues and distinguishing achievements becomes harder, for the list grows so rapidly. At present, just over 200 cottages have been retired while 210 structures are now available to collectors! These numbers are precedent-setting.

Of the numerous awards won by David Tate designs, "Convent in the Woods," picked "Best Collectible of Show" at the 1990 South Bend Exposition the same year *Collector Editions* "Award of Excellence" went to "Periwinkle Cottage" are particular favorites. But awards tell only part of the story. The heart of this company's success is found in the diversity that makes new issues "winners" from the moment they debut. Consider the delights collectors may choose this year:

The snow-covered steps at "Rydal Cottage" have been swept clean in anticipation of your visit! Inside, a fire burns merrily as children peek from icy windows to share their Christmas joy.

• *THE VILLAGE SHOP COLLECTION:*
Come visit Midland villages and towns in England and see country shops in miniature! There's "Penny Sweets," "The Greengrocers," "The Toy Shop," "Jones the Butcher," "The China Shop" and "The Bakery." But, don't be surprised if you smell fresh-baked scones when you see this collection in person!

• *THE ENGLISH TEA ROOM COLLECTION*
Every town, and most villages in England, has at least one tea room. It's a mecca for news-sharing, chatting and taking a moment to reflect on the day's events. Lilliput Lane's *English Tea Room Collection* highlights the exquisite differences in tea rooms across Britain. Though "Grandma Batty's Tea Room" and "Bargate Cottage Tea Room," are located at opposite ends of England, both are charming examples of romantic English tea rooms beloved by the people of Britain.

• *HISTORIC CASTLES OF BRITAIN*
Britain would not be Britain without her fabulous castles. Splendid monuments to days-gone-by, British castles have never been more eloquently rendered than in this intricate collection of miniatures. Collectors will be enthralled by tiny details: classic, medieval fortifications and foreboding towers. Traditional moats make these 19th century castles impenetrable to all

but the bravest knights!
• *CHRISTMAS AT LILLIPUT LANE*

If Father Christmas chose to copy Santa Claus and climb down rooftops, he'd surely love the chimneys and roofs atop these 12 miniature marvels! Designed with the festive Yuletide season in mind, *Christmas at Lilliput Lane* is a wonderland of snow-covered dwellings. The *Christmas at Lilliput Lane* collection also includes an annual ornament, strictly limited to its year of issue!

The Journey Down Lilliput Lane Continues

Could David Tate have foreseen the heights his company would reach on

Who's that waiting in the entryway of "Patterdale Cottage?" This elegant cottage is decorated from top to bottom in anticipation of the gala Christmas homecoming welcoming the entire family!

the fateful day he chose to leave the security of his job to jumpstart his business in 1982? Probably not. Artistic visionaries tend to be focused on the intriguing mysteries of creating "something from nothing" rather than wondering about the future.

In the years bridging today and his move to Penrith, much attention has come to David Tate. In 1988, his name was placed on an Honors List compiled by British citizens saluting those who have made outstanding contributions to England's prestige and economy. Soon after, he was invested as an M.B.E. by Queen Elizabeth II. As a Member of the Order of the Royal Empire, many wondered if the dizzying parade of laudits had reached its pinnacle. But David Tate's Lilliput Lane collectibles continued to flourish. The company was twice named one of England's Five Top Companies by the Confederation of British Industry and Tate also accepted the Queen's Award for Export from former Prime Minister Margaret Thatcher. David Tate was also the recipient of the 1995 International Collectible Artist Award.

At age 15, David Tate came to terms with the fact that his dream would have to be put on hold for a while. That's exactly what he did...put it on hold. What's to be learned from the philosophy David Tate adopted at so early an age? Perhaps its that putting a dream on hold tends to makes it doubly sweet when it's realized...at last.

Behold the architectural wonders of bygone days! These castles are historic monuments accurately rendered in exquisite detail. Beloved by noble families...and the sites of exquisite balls...each castle is a tribute to the combined talent of the Lilliput Lane family!

Lilliput Lane
P.O. Box 665
Elk Grove Village, IL 60009-0665
(800) 545-5478
Fax (708) 875-5360

COLLECTORS' CLUB

Lilliput Lane Collectors' Club
P.O. Box 665
Elk Grove Village, IL 60009-0665
(800) -LILLIPUT

Annual Dues: One Year: $40.00 - **Two Years:** $65.00
Club Year: May 1-April 30
Collector's Year – Anniversary of Sign-Up Date

Benefits:
• Membership Gift
• Card to Reserve Members-Only Redemption piece
• Quarterly Newsletter, "Gulliver's World"
• Binder (Optional Purchase)
• Membership Card
• Special Selections Catalog
• Buy/Sell Matching Service (Referrals Only)
• Travel Opportunities to Tour the Lilliput Lane Studios in Penrith, England
• Painter's Demonstrations & "Paint Your Own" Cottage Events

LLADRÓ
Journey into a World of Beauty and Romance

The year was 1951 when three brothers, Juan, José and Vicente, pooled their talents and finances to start a ceramic-making operation in Almacera, Spain. The kiln built by the brothers on the family patio that year was a meager one capable only of firing ceramics. However, the products that issued forth from that furnace set in motion several decades of growth and development that has made the name Lladró synonymous with quality collectible porcelain.

There are few, if any, historical parallels to the notable success of this company which, from the start, concentrated almost exclusively on its production of ceramic figurines at the expense of the utilitarian wares which normally provide the backbone of a ceramic studio's prosperity. This emphasis reflects the predominantly sculptural sympathies of the brothers. Their ability to parlay their artistic preferences into a vast collection of internationally renown porcelain, however, is due to none other than their artistic talents, business acumen and foresight.

Laying the Cornerstone for Success

Born to the luscious agricultural lands of southern Spain, Juan, José and Vicente are the sons of Juan Lladró Cortina and Rosa Dolz Pastor. Their father was a day laborer who taught his sons to appreciate the land for its qualities as a malleable material, which could be shaped into porcelain. Their mother, as uncomplicated as she was intelligent, imbued her sons with a sensitivity for small things while setting their sights on a successful and financially rewarding future.

The brothers became laborers themselves while very young, toiling in the family fields while pursuing their formal training. On his own time, each brother attended the Escuela de Artes y Oficios de San Carlos where Juan and José focused on painting and Vicente on sculpting. Apprenticeships further enhanced their training and bolstered their confidence, leading them to the construction of their kiln. They began to investigate new procedures for glazing and firing. The diminutive flowers that were their first production pieces attracted unexpected numbers of customers and from these sales blossomed new economic possibilities and plans.

Today, finely detailed and delicate flowers still play an important role in the decoration of Lladró porcelain with their constant and fragile presence.

The year 1953 was a turning point for the Lladró brothers. As masters of making-do, they built a kiln with discarded bricks from the Altos Hornos (High Kilns) at Sagunto. Although still rather rudimentary, this kiln could produce the temperatures necessary to vitrify porcelain. And from the moment they first handled porcelain, they have explored its many possibilities. In 1955, the brothers opened a shop in Valencia and in 1958 laid the foundation for their first factory in the neighboring town of Tavernes Blanques. Their highly specialized endeavors attracted teams of workers with experience in the field of porcelain artistry and manufacturing, laying the cornerstone for Lladró's success.

From the early years, when they modeled their vases in the style of Dresden or Sevres, to the stylizations of flowers, animals and figures of the present, the Lladró brothers have shared their special visions of the world of everyday through the medium of porcelain. Their subjects are diverse, including those already explored in the arts of ancient Greece and Rome, as well as juvenile, religious and literary figurines.

After nearly forty years, Lladró's studies in color, form and posture continue to represent a never-ending

"Ten and Growing," the Lladró Society's tenth anniversary figurine, available in 1995 to members only.

fountain of invention, a constant merging of technical expertise and supreme artistry. Lladró truly is "Art in fine porcelain."

Celebrating the Lladró Society's 10th Anniversary

When the famed Spanish porcelain firm first announced plans for an international collectors society in 1985, few could have predicted the worldwide impact. Today, the Lladró Society looks back on a decade of successes in providing inspiration, information and enjoyment to Lladró aficionados around the world.

In 1995 the Society celebrated its tenth anniversary in grand Lladró style with elegant receptions for members attended by members of the Lladró family, exclusive Society figurines for members only, and a deluxe 54-page edition of *Expressions* magazine.

"Ten and Growing," was created for members-only with a tenth anniversary backstamp on its base. The charming figurine recalls a special time and a

228

special moment – first love, first kiss. Like the Society, the two children so enchantingly portrayed are "Ten and Growing."

As a special tribute, charter members of the Lladró Society were honored with a figurine, "Now and Forever." They alone were eligible to redeem this figurine in its introductory year. Each "Now and Forever" redeemed by a charter member featured a personalized backstamp reading "Charter Member, 1985-1995." Thereafter, the figurine will be available to all members who celebrate their personal tenth anniversary with the Lladró Society.

Gala anniversary receptions were held in Chicago, Los Angeles and New York City. Society members were invited to socialize with members of the Lladró family, dine, reminisce and hear plans for their Society's future.

Leading the Society into the Future

In 1995 Rosa María Lladró assumed the new position of Lladró Society President, thereby assuring a close involvement by the Lladró family with Society planning worldwide. Margarita

In 1995 "Now and Forever" was introduced for Lladró Society Charter Members only. Thereafter it will become available to members as they celebrate their personal tenth anniversary with the Society.

Arriagada became Lladró Society Director for the U.S. replacing the retiring founding Director Hugh Robinson.

Rosa María Lladró grew up with close ties to the family business. She absorbed the artistic atmosphere of the Lladró Studios which were situated next to her parent's home. As youngsters she and her siblings and cousins played in the studios, drawing, painting and sculpting alongside the artisans who were crafting the world-famous figurines. Besides her playful childhood experiences, Rosa María has impressive academic credentials in law and business. She joins her sister Mari Carmen, and her cousins, Rosa and Juan Vicente, to represent the second generation on the Lladró family council which also includes the three founding brothers.

Margarita Arriagada, Lladró USA Sales Director for the Western United States, has had a lengthy relationship with and admiration for Lladró. Speaking about her new position, Margarita commented, "Lladró represents many things to me, from fine, handcrafted product to an organization built on human values, integrity and quality. In this spirit of pride and joy, I will continue to advance the Society's mission to inform and entertain its members."

Lladró Enhances Membership Benefits

The Lladró Society New Member Package welcomes members to "journey into a world of beauty and romance." The Package overflows with gifts: a high quality Lladró leather key case featuring a small porcelain Lladró logo on the snap, the Society's official porcelain plaque bearing the signatures of the three Lladró brothers, an introductory issue of *Expressions* and a registration form to activate the membership. The New Member Package box serves as a hard-cover binder for *Expressions*, the Society's quarterly magazine.

A special Lladró videotape makes an additional benefit for new members. This fascinating video dramatically highlights the intricate

"Three Sisters" series of annual Society figurines began with "Basket of Love," in 1994, followed by "Afternoon Promenade," shown above, in 1995.

process required to create a beautiful figurine by Lladró. It will be mailed on receipt of each new member's registration form.

For New and Renewing Members – A Host of Benefits and Services

High on the list of membership benefits is the opportunity to acquire exclusive figurines which are introduced annually and made available to Society members only. In 1985, the first of these charming figurines, "Little Pals" made its debut at an original price of $95. At recent Lladró auctions "Little Pals" has commanded from $3,000 to $4,000 in intense bidding battles. The second annual figurine to be introduced, "Little Traveler," has garnered $1,500 to $2,000. Indeed, every retiring members-only figurine has attracted strong secondary market trading as new Society members seek to complete their collections with previous years' issues. Yet for most Lladró connoisseurs, the demonstrated investment potential of their beloved figurines plays only a minor part in their enjoyment of collecting.

In 1994 the Society introduced the first figurine in a Lladró first-time members-only series of three. "Three Sisters" were to arrive one annually through 1996. Beginning with "Basket of Love," followed by "Afternoon Promenade," the sisters rapidly won hearts. The Sisters were the latest in the Society's widely admired members-only collection of fine figurines.

All Society members are entitled to VIP services, as well as privileges and benefits not available to the general public. Among them are: a resident archivist to aid in identifying figurines and to report prices from public auctions (not affiliated with Lladró) for retired figurines and sold-out editions. General information includes the care of figurines, the location of Authorized Lladró Dealers, and information on replacement parts or restoration services for damaged pieces. (Lladró offers a unique Lladró Assurance Program that covers all figurines purchased through an Authorized Lladró Dealer in the U.S.).

The "Lladró Antique News" is an informative newsletter that provides an update on activity by Lladró in the sec-

The Lladró Society New Member Package. Each Package includes a porcelain plaque, leather key case, Expressions *magazine and handsome blue binder.*

ondary market. Compiled by an independent consultant, "Lladró Antique News" is published twice a year and mailed to members along with *Expressions.*

Lladró's award-winning publication, *Expressions* features articles and

stories of special interest to people who love fine porcelain figurines. Readers are kept informed of special appearances by Juan, José and Vicente Lladró, as well as other members of the Lladró family and Society Director for the U.S., Margarita Arriagada.

The Society sponsors popular events such as signing tours by Lladró family members and trips to Spain that conclude with a tour of the famed Lladró facilities. Members also receive a member card identifying them as an Associate Member of the showcase Lladró Museum in New York City, where the world's largest collection of retired and one-of-a-kind Lladró porcelain is on display.

For more information contact the Lladró Society, One Lladró Drive, Moonachie, NJ 07074, (800)634-9088.

Lladro Society
1 Lladro Drive
Moonachie, NJ 07074
(800) 634-9088
Fax (201) 807-1168

COLLECTORS' CLUB/MUSEUM

Lladro Society
1 Lladro Drive
Moonachie, NJ 07074
(800) 634-9088

Annual Dues: $40.00 - Renewal: $27.50
Club Year: Anniversary of Sign-Up Date

Benefits:
• Membership Gift: Porcelain Plaque and Leather Key Case
• Opportunity to Purchase Members-Only Figurine
• Quarterly Magazine, *Expressions*
• Membership Card
• Binder
• Lladro Video
• Associate Membership to the Lladro Museum in New York City
• Renewal Gift
• Figurine Research Service
• Society-sponsored Trips to Spain
• Members-Only Signing Events

Lladro Museum and Galleries
43 West 57th St.
New York, NY 10019
(212) 838-9341

Hours: Tuesday through Saturday, 10 a.m. - 5:30 p.m.
Admission Fee: None

The Lladro Museum includes the largest collection of retired Lladro porcelains — over 1,000 pieces occupy three floors of the building.

SEYMOUR MANN, INC.

Innovative Design and Accessible Pricing Are the Hallmark of Leading Marketer of Collectible Porcelain Dolls

Currently celebrating its 25th anniversary in the collectibles arena, Seymour Mann, Inc. is using the opportunity to undertake the most significant year of expansion in its history. Introduction of new dolls is at a record high, and the addition of several new artists brings the number of doll designers in the Seymour Mann Gallery to a total of 15. In addition, the company has just increased its New York headquarters space by 33%, opened a new showroom in Los Angeles and completely renovated its showroom in Atlanta.

As the company enters its second quarter-century, it will continue to play a leadership role in the ever-changing doll industry. Many of the recent turns of events in the collectible doll arena are fueled by the discerning collector's growing reluctance to accept "generic" doll heads and inferior costuming. In the tradition the company established when it first opened its doors, Seymour Mann will continue to use doll artists who specialize in unique, distinctive, "human" faces and who pride themselves on using only the most extraordinary fabrics and trim for their costumes.

Founder and President Seymour Mann continues his mandate that every collectible from his company must be above all else a work of art. And with each new award and product honor he receives, this credo is justified by critics and connoisseurs, by professional journals and societies, and by consumer response.

In 1995 alone, the company received eight coveted honors for design of collectible dolls from the three most prestigious award-giving institutions in the collectible field. The Collectors' Society of America named "Sparkle, the Sugar Plum Faerie," by Edna Dali, its third-place winner for Outstanding Doll produced during 1994. *Dolls* magazine named six Seymour Mann creations

as nominees for the journal's 1995 Awards of Excellence: "Princess and the Frog" and "Dulcie," both by Carolyn Wang; "Lady Windemere" by Gwen McNeil and "Cara" by Eda Mann. Award of Excellence winners were "Hope" by Eda Mann and "Guinevere" by Pamela Phillips, which also received a DOTY (Doll of the Year) Award from *Doll Reader* magazine. These nominations brought to a total of 15 the number of awards for which Seymour Mann dolls had been nominated in the previous 12-month period.

Seymour and Eda Mann
A Family of Artists

Artist Eda Mann has been a designer for her husband's company since the very beginning – 1965. Eda was born in London and spent her youth studying art under the tutelage of her father and two uncles, all three professional artists. When Eda was 16, the family emigrated to the United States, where her father became a well-known society artist during the 1930s and 1940s. He also created many movie posters for such studios as MGM and Columbia Pictures.

Eda studied art at the National Academy of Design in New York, where she won many awards for her sculpture and paintings. She also worked as a fashion designer, a talent that is still on display in her costume designs for Seymour Mann dolls. Over the years, her works have been acquired by such institutions as the Metropolitan Museum of Art in New York and the National Academy of Design.

Seymour met Eda while he was working as a professional musician and band leader in the '30s. After their courtship and marriage, the Manns combined their talents to form a partnership: Eda designed figurines and other decorative accessories, and Seymour marketed her creations. They

"Cara," a collectible porcelain doll by Edna Dali for Seymour Mann, Inc., received a 1995 Award of Excellence nomination from Dolls *magazine and is featured on the cover of the company's new catalog.*

carried her design talent and his marketing genius into the tabletop, giftware and collectible fields, and Seymour Mann, Inc. soon grew to be a leader in those arenas.

In the meantime, Eda had begun to create dolls for her daughters – and later her granddaughters – and it occurred to her husband that these delightful creations might also be added to their company's assets. By the late 1970s, Seymour Mann, Inc. began to transform Eda's "hobby" into a treasury of collectibles. Since then the Seymour Mann line of collectible dolls has grown to include many hundreds of dolls, and the company has become renowned worldwide as a leading resource of collectible dolls that are works of art at affordable prices.

The Seymour Mann *Connoisseur Collection* and *Signature Series*

By the 1990s, Seymour Mann, Inc. had evolved into a doll artists' company, whose member artists were becoming as well known as the name Seymour Mann. In addition to Eda Mann herself, the company's *Connoisseur Collection* featured works by such top names as Paulette Aprile, June Amos Grammer, Hanna Hyland, Pat Kolesar, Hal Payne and Michelle Severino.

The *Connoisseur Collection* was solidly established as a premiere resource for collectible dolls in the under-$150 retail price range, and Seymour felt strongly committed to providing top-quality collectible dolls at such moderate prices. At the same time, however, he heard the beginnings of a groundswell demand for something never seen before in this market — artists' dolls at prices so favorable that even novice collectors could begin to acquire them. Thus was born the Seymour Mann *Signature Series*.

It was Seymour's idea that the *Signature Series* would give doll artists an opportunity to reach a wider audience by producing larger editions at lower prices. The series debuted at the

"Lady Windemere" by Gwen McNeill, is one of several collectible porcelain dolls from Seymour Mann, Inc. to be honored by a Dolls *magazine 1995 Award of Excellence nomination.*

1992 International Toy Fair and was an immediate success. Today, both the *Connoisseur Collection* and the *Signature Series* occupy enviable positions of leadership in the moderate-priced categories of collectible porcelain dolls.

Noted doll designer Paulette Aprile explains the unique niche occupied by Seymour Mann, Inc.: "As an artist, I can produce only a very limited number of dolls, and therefore, my dolls are available to only a few collectors. By working with Seymour Mann, I can offer comparable quality at a much more affordable price to a broader range of collectors. Since Seymour is married to a well-known artist, his company is especially attuned to working with designers and very sensitive to our needs and wishes."

The Seymour Mann Gallery

Today, Seymour Mann's "stable" of doll artists has evolved into a true "studio"–a creative environment where artists can give expression to the full range of their talents and, at the same time, effectively reach audiences with differing budgets for the acquisition of collectible dolls. Known as the Seymour Mann Gallery, this modern "atelier" includes not only the artists whose works form the *Connoisseur Collection* and the *Signature Series*, but also newer talents like Sandra Bilato, Margie Costa, Edna Dali, Gwen McNeil, Pamela Phillips, Valerie Pike, Lynne Randolph, C.K. Wang and Catherine Wang.

CEO Gideon S. Oberweger is a guiding influence on the artists in the Seymour Mann Gallery and on the direction of the company itself. A founding member of the company's management team, Gideon uses his marketing and sourcing expertise to identify and select overseas manufacturers that can best capture the essence of each artist's distinctive work.

"Each artist brings a new set of challenges," Gideon observes. "We don't want artists' work to compete with one another, so we have to be very selective in granting commissions. In addition, when an artist works in

Whimsical ceramic teapots are among the most popular items in the wide range of collectible decorative accessories available from Seymour Mann, Inc.

another medium, it doesn't always translate easily into porcelain.

"It's critical to our success," he continues, "to select manufacturers that can provide the best reproductions of each artist's dolls. We closely supervise the manufacture of each doll in order to transform the original into a first-rate collectible work. Some adjustments have to be made to accommodate cost and production objectives, but these decisions are always made with the full participation of the artist and are never made by the manufacturer alone."

Asked to name his favorite doll, Gideon answers: "That's easy–'Hope.' Eda, who is several times a grandmother, was distressed by the effect of world events on children, from Bosnia to Rwanda. So she created a guardian angel holding three children, one Black, one White, one Asian. Eda doesn't see 'Hope' as a political statement–she doesn't believe in politicizing art–but as an emotional plea to save children, who are our hope for the future."

Collectible Giftware and Decorative Accessories

While dolls have made Seymour

Mann a household name, the company continues its commitment to its other lines of collectible porcelains — giftware, tabletop, Christmas items and decorative accessories. In these fields also, the company has staked a reputation for itself on the strength of the design talent it has discovered and employed.

Just this year, the company's limited edition bisque porcelain "Hummingbird Bell," by Mario Bernini, received *Collector Editions* magazine's Award of Excellence. The entire Bernini series includes a bell, music box and three-dimensional plate, each depicting one of six native American birds surrounded by flowers.

In past years, the company has received similar accolades for such products as "Reindeer Stable" by Lorraine Sciola; "Gingerbread Dreams" by Janet Sauerby; "Shoebox Elf" by Mary Alice Byerly; and "Christmas Cat" by Kenji.

Seymour Mann, Inc. also offers a complete line of collectible ceramic teapots in a variety of distinct designs, from Oriental elephants and cats to art deco triangles to fruit and vegetable motifs.

Asked to comment on the future, Gideon Oberweger stresses the company's efforts to hold down prices. "We've begun to see a market backlash against high-priced collectibles from unknown designers. Our challenge is to keep our work — be it a doll, a teapot or a limited edition plate — truly exquisite — and therefore desirable to the collector, but also affordable."

And what drives and inspires his artists and his management team, including himself? "Collectibles are a wonderful, rewarding business. Each day we get letters and pictures from collectors who share the joy our creations have brought into their lives. Who could ask for more?"

Seymour Mann, Inc.
225 Fifth Avenue
Showroom #102
New York, NY 10010
(212) 683-7262
Fax (212) 213-4920

"Sparkle the Sugar Plum Faerie," designed by Edna Dali for Seymour Mann, Inc., was named third-place winner for Outstanding Doll of 1994 by the Collectors' Society of America.

COLLECTORS' CLUB

Seymour Mann, Inc. Doll Club
230 Fifth Avenue, Suite 1500
New York, NY 10001
(212) 683-7262

Annual Dues: $17.50
Club Year: January-December

Benefits:
• Membership Gift: Poster
• Newsletter
• Membership Card
• Buy/Sell Matching Service
• Special Members-Only Dolls

MARURI U.S.A.

Making the Ancient Art of Priceless Porcelain Today's Collectible Sensations

The art of creating exquisite porcelain sculptures requires two things above all else: talented art masters and a total commitment to quality. In the entire world, there are no more than a score of studios achieving true excellence in porcelain. You're probably familiar with some of their names. The European houses of Royal Worcester and Meissen earned their reputations centuries ago. American producers Cybis and Boehm are always counted among the finest in the world. But when it comes to contemporary mastery, few can compare to the dynamic company that took its place among the world's best gift and collectible producers just ten short years ago: Maruri.

Maruri is a Japanese company with roots firmly planted in Seto, Japan. There, highly skilled artisans produce the world's most respected and collected porcelain giftware and collectibles. This legacy began centuries ago and continues today. Maruri's entry into the American market just ten years ago has attracted the attention of collectors, gift shop owners and the media. In sum, Maruri has, in a short amount of time, proven itself a powerful force in today's giftware and limited edition collectibles industries.

A Family Business Flourishes in Central Japan

Long before America discovered the magic of porcelain art, Japan's ceramics industry flourished in the fabled ceramic capital of Seto. Located in central Japan, near the exotic, old-world capital of Nagoya, this region boasted the finest family-oriented workshops in the land. One particularly successful enterprise was started by the Mizuno brothers who carefully selected the name "Maruri" for their design studio. The "ri" means "benefits." "Maru" is a time-honored symbol for a circle symbolizing the never-end-

ing nature of classic, fine art.

With such an appropriate name, how could the company help but flourish? The studio quickly earned a distinguished reputation for excellent bone china, delicate figurines and true-to-nature bird and animal sculptures. When at last the name "Maruri" became established in the United States, a remarkable thing happened. Collectors began to use Maruri as a benchmark of comparison for all other wildlife sculptures on the market.

Standards of Excellence Set Maruri Apart from All Others

Today, Maruri prides itself on upholding the "studied approach" in the creation of its limited edition sculptures. Every flower, eagle, bird and animal takes many days to complete using a multi-step process that has been followed faithfully over the years.

Artisans begin by crafting multiple molds for a single piece. By making individual molds, every detail is captured to perfection. Once the molds are approved, creamy feldspar mixture in the form of liquid slip is carefully poured. This Grand Feu formula is the same one used in ancient times. It continues to be the preferred ceramic material today, prized for its excellent finished look and feel.

Molds are filled to a specific thickness, then allowed to dry very slowly to meet Maruri's stringent specifications. Only when a proper degree of hardness is reached are pieces carefully removed from their molds and placed together. Seam lines and points of juncture are smoothed and refined. Everything is done by hand to ensure a seamless work of art guaranteed to delight collectors everywhere.

Sculptures are next placed in a temperature-controlled drying room, carefully braced between support molds because the hardening process

This American bald eagle figurine is from Maruri's American Eagle Gallery. These soaring eagles are 8-3/4" high and sell for $110. Like all Maruri eagles, this powerful pair is hand-painted and comes with a wood base and Certificate of Authenticity.

will continue for several days. When sufficiently dry, a sculpture is placed in a kiln and fired for 16 hours. During this critical period, temperatures in the kiln are brought to an ideal degree of heat. Then the kiln is subtly cooled to complete the firing process.

Maruri artisans carefully inspect sculptures as soon as they are removed from their kilns. As many as 35% to 40% may be eliminated as 'less than perfect.' Those passing inspection are sandblasted to a brilliant, strong finish. At last, highly trained artists paint every sculpture by hand in subtle tones chosen by color experts. Finally, the sculpture is ready to be wrapped and shipped to fine shops across the world.

The Maruri Studios Proudly Present "Independent Spirit," and Other Aviary Delights

From time to time, Maruri introduces a complex and distinguished work of art featuring several figures as

Detail so realistic, collectors can hear the cry of these eagles! The newest Maruri Studio Collection sculpture is "Independent Spirit." Sequentially numbered and stringently limited to 3,500, this fine porcelain and bronze limited edition has a handsome wood base and comes with a Certificate of Authenticity.

Maruri's exquisite hummingbird family competes with nature for realism! Part of a 16-piece collection that ranges in price from $95 to $150, this mother feeding her babies is an excellent example of Maruri's attention to the smallest detail.

a single work of art. "Independent Spirit" is such a piece. A gathering of sturdy bronze tree branches reach up to support two American bald eagles fiercely battling for dominance of the sky. Their expressive faces are powerful and bold. Wings flare out to reveal astonishing detail. A pallet of realistic colors stroke every inch of this porcelain masterwork.

To create such a complex figure, eagles, wings, tree branches and trunks must all be created independently of one another. Fusing of the individual pieces takes place as it's molded, assembled and painted. It's an arduous process, but well worth the time it takes.

Individually numbered and limited to just 3,500 pieces for world-wide distribution, "Independent Spirit" is a remarkable 14" high on its wood base. A Certificate of Authenticity accompanies this new sculpture, priced at just $395.

Because birds are so popular, Maruri's "Delicate Motion" was designed and produced for collectors of fine aviary art. This sculpture features three violet-crowned hummingbirds circling a bright spray of morning glories. Like "Independent Spirit," "Delicate Motion" is sequentially numbered and limited to 3,500 pieces, world-wide. This remarkable porcelain and bronze figure comes on a wood base and includes a Certificate of Authenticity. Its issue price is $325.

Happily, "Delicate Motion" is but one of Maruri's hummingbird offerings. *The Maruri Hummingbird Collection* also showcases this elusive winged creature. And, for collectors of other types of birds, *Eyes of the Night*, an exotic owl series and a fragile pair of snow-white doves called "Wings of Love" may also be found in Maruri's porcelain aviary.

Savvy collectors are well-aware that Maruri collectible bird sculptures are known for their secondary market performance. Consider, for example, artist W.D. Gaither's "American Bald Eagle I." Introduced by Maruri in 1981 at $165, the figure commanded $600 on the secondary market one year later...$1,750 by 1995! This stunning increase exemplifies Maruri's commitment to producing art rich in detail that also may have great after-market potential.

A Polar Expedition Unlike Any You've Seen Before

Few of us will ever have the privilege of seeing polar bears, harp seals, arctic foxes and penguins in their natural environments, so Maruri brings these magnificent animals and birds to you in the *Polar Expedition* collection. Each replica of its real-life cousin is hand-painted in natural colors and so real, you can almost feel the cold!

From the mighty "Polar Bear" to the delightful "Baby Seal," from a formally dressed "Emperor Penguin" to an "Arctic Fox" so real you'll swear you can imagine him scampering behind a bluff, discover a wonderland of gentle faces and soft shapes in the *Polar Expedition* collection. If you haven't yet seen the figures in this series, we invite you to take a peek at "Baby Harp Seals," depicted in this article.

As always, each sculpture in the *Polar Expedition* library comes with Maruri's Certificate of Authenticity. It's your assurance that each member of the *Polar Expedition* family has been made with all the quality and care for which Maruri is known worldwide.

Maruri Travels to Africa to Preserve Magnificent Animals

Maruri artisans transported their talent and vision from the icy Arctic to the plains and savannas of exotic Africa when they announced the debut of *Gentle Giants*, a stunning collection of African elephant sculptures. In this series, five African elephants are fashioned of fine porcelain and detailed so exquisitely, every wrinkle shows!

Gentle Giants collectors may choose from a single, standing baby elephant...a sitting baby elephant...or a playful pair of youngsters!

Everyone's favorite subject, a mother and child, is also included, as well as a beautiful pair of adult elephants. A fine wood base showcases these limited editions, and a Certificate of Authenticity is included.

Fortunately, *Gentle Giants* isn't the only African collection Maruri has developed. A signature collection, designed by noted artist W.D. Gaither and called *African Safari*, shares

These dark-eyed "Baby Harp Seals" are among the delights collectors find in Maruri's Polar Expedition sculpture collection. Also featured are realistic "Arctic Fox," "Emperor Penguin" and other wonders.

Gaither's actual experiences in Zululand, South Africa, with collectors. Every sight provided new vistas. The artist sketched and photographed elephants, rhinos, buffalo, lions, leopards, kudus, impalas and other great beasts. Each served as inspiration for his true-to-life *African Safari* animal series.

Maruri Presents Horses from Around the World

Relatively new to the Maruri library is a bold collection of equines entitled *Horses of the World.* From a common prehistoric ancestor, horse breeds have developed independently. Today, each has its own distinct look, behavior and style. Some are strong. Others are fast. Some breeds are known for their endurance; others for their beauty.

Maruri designers recognize certain breeds as standard-bearers, the best of breeds. Each of the following is represented in the *Horses of the World* collection, attractively priced from $145 to $175:

• The dignified "Clydesdale," known for its sweet disposition and strength, has historically been used for farm work and transporting coal from Scottish mines.

• The sleek "Thoroughbred," originating in England, is now most often found streaking across race courses at lightening speed! They are also considered one of the most beautiful breeds on earth.

• The gentle "American Quarter Horse" is beloved by horse fans for its agility, intelligence and good temper. The Quarter Horse is a favorite of those just learning to ride.

• In France, the "Camargue" is known as the 'White Horse of the Sea' despite having a sleek, dark coat at birth! By the time they reach adulthood, Camargues have turned snowy-white.

• The distinct "Paint" was everyone's favorite mount in the Old West. Its broken color patterns provided good camouflage as "cowboys and Indians" chased each other across the Badlands of America.

• Finally, the magnificent "Arabian" is the oldest purebred in the world. Arabians are known for their great stamina, intelligence and gentle love of human companions.

As Maruri broadens and extends its creative wings, its future is limitless. Age-old methods and award-winning sculptors with a boost from the newest porcelain technology promise lasting works of fine art, generation after generation. Today, Maruri continues its time-honored tradition of providing enduring tributes to some of the world's most enchanting creatures.

Maruri U.S.A.
7541 Woodman Place
Van Nuys, CA 91405
(800) 5-MARURI
Fax (818) 780-9871

MEDIA ARTS GROUP INC.
A Growing Member of the Collectibles Community

There is a "new kid on the block" in the collectibles industry: Media Arts Group Inc. MAGI, as it is more familiarly called, is the corporate umbrella that includes Lightpost Publishing Inc., John Hine Studios and the newest member of the family, MAGI Entertainment Products. Together, these businesses represent fresh, exciting, innovative collectibles for a wide range of today's collectors.

The company was founded in 1990 to publish the limited edition lithographs of award-winning artist Thomas Kinkade. Its growth has been phenomenal, and, in August 1994, Media Arts Group Inc. became a public corporation listed on NASDAQ (ARTS).

Thomas Kinkade — Painter of Light™

The consistent growth of Lightpost Publishing can be attributed to the remarkable artwork of Thomas Kinkade. Regarded as one of America's most popular artists, Kinkade's limited edition canvas and paper lithographs have become the standard in the art publishing industry. Using an exclusive process, Lightpost is able to authentically replicate the quality and color of each Thomas Kinkade painting. Renowned as the *Painter of Light™*, Kinkade imparts "light" into each of his works – in the style of the 19th century luminists – and Lightpost has developed a method of capturing that light in its canvas lithographs, making them unique.

Thomas Kinkade has received numerous honors, been profiled in a number of leading publications and made many appearances on national radio and television programs. Kinkade was honored by NALED in 1993, 1994 and 1995 with the prestigious "Lithograph of the Year Award," receiving four of five nominations in the 1995 award. He received the prestigious 1995 NALED "Artist of the Year Award." He received a 1993 and 1994 *Collector Editions* "Award of Excellence" for Lithographs over $100. *US Art Magazine* named Kinkade an "Artist To Watch In 1995" and Kinkade was named "Artist of the Year" at the 1995 Collectors Jubilee.

The Thomas Kinkade Collection is supported by the Thomas Kinkade Collectors' Society, which was organized in 1993. As part of their benefits, members receive an exclusive Membership Lithograph and the opportunity to purchase a limited edition Members Only Lithograph, especially created by the artist. Worldwide membership in 1995 was close to 20,000 members.

The newest introduction by British sculptor David Winter is a portrayal of his family retreat in Ireland. Limited to 4,500 pieces worldwide, "Newton Millhouse" comes with a special David Winter video and scrapbook, which give collectors a very personal glimpse into the private life of this distinguished artist.

John Hine Studios Joins the MAGI Family

In 1993, John Hine Studios became a wholly owned business, bringing its world-famous *David Winter Cottages Collection* into the MAGI family of collectibles. English sculptor David Winter is regarded as one of the foremost creators of miniature architectural structures. His whimsical, nostalgic cottages of British lifestyle have been an award-winning line since it was introduced to U.S. collectors in the early 1980s.

The Collection was named "Collectible of the Year" by NALED in both 1987 and 1988, and David Winter was named "Artist of the Year" in 1991. He has earned numerous other awards over the years. The Studios and Workshops of John Hine Limited are located at Eggars Hill, Hampshire, England, and the Collection continues to be created and produced in the U.K.

The David Winter Cottages Collectors' Guild began in 1986 and has more than 45,000 members world-

Second in the new Hometown Memories *series, "Hometown Chapel," has been introduced by Lightpost Publishing. This enchanting country church first appeared in the background of "Hometown Memories" and now forms the subject of Thomas Kinkade's latest issue.*

Alpine Christmas, *the unique new lighted village from* Illuminations *by John Hine Studios, includes six independent structures, plus a park with pond. The "Clock Tower" has a working clock in it, and using patented technology, this beautifully sculpted architectural structure can be illuminated individually now and added to later.*

wide. Member benefits include a variety of items, including an exclusive Membership Cottage. During the membership year, members have the opportunity to purchase at least two Members Only Cottages sculpted exclusively for the Guild. In addition to the International Guild, there are a number of regional and local collector groups that are dedicated to *David Winter Cottages,* including England and Australia.

In addition to David Winter, John Hine Studios is home to several other collectible lines. *Father Time Clocks* and *The Shoemaker's Dream* collections are created by sculptor Jon Herbert, who began his career at the Studios as a mouldmaker for *David Winter Cottages.* His two collectible lines continue to win collector support.

New Lines and Artists Add Breadth and Depth to MAGI

A roster of new lines and artists were added to John Hine Studios in

1995. These include artists Gary Patterson, Ted Slack, Gavin Fifield and Matt Danko.

Illuminations by John Hine Studios is a lighted village collection with self-contained electrical system, for which the company is in the process of obtaining a patent. The highly detailed, miniature architectural structures will portray houses and buildings synonymous with different cities or attractions around the world. Sculpting of the unique line will be undertaken by different artisans, based on expertise and interests.

The first two introductions are *Alpine Christmas,* a snow-covered collection of structures surrounding a miniature skating pond; and *London By Gaslight,* a completely resculpted collection of English buildings portraying Victorian England's most famous city. Utilizing new technology, *Illuminations* provides collectors with a safe, colorful, illuminated display that will enhance enjoyment for the entire family.

Artist Gary Patterson has been called "creator of smiles" because of his ability to take serious situations and artistically make people laugh at themselves. He has used sports as a primary subject for his intricate, richly detailed artwork, which has earned him international acclaim. It is estimated that Gary Patterson's art is owned or recognized by more than 250 million people worldwide.

The *Gary Patterson Collec-tions* initially include a collection of figurines and trophies based on characters in his artwork, as well as a line of limited edition, signed and numbered, framed and matted lithographs of his art. There will also be smaller, unframed, open edition prints.

British sculptor Ted Slack has created a whimsical collection of treehouses called *Woodly Wise,* a mythical land inhabited by elusive keepers of the land called Twiggs. Slack is recognized for his highly detailed, miniature structures, which he has created over the past decade. This newest collection combines a lifelong

love of nature with his interest in unusual architectural structures.

Another English sculptor, Gavin Fifield, has been introduced to the United States with a fanciful collection of beautiful lighted fairytale-inspired cottages. The *Gavin Fifield Collection* is his first U.S. collectible. It will debut in 1996.

Artist Matthew Danko has worked in the U.S. collectibles industry for the past 25 years, creating everything from memorable greeting cards to dolls and folk art. His new line is the *Once Upon A Story Collection,* a unique storybook-doll collectible. The collection utilizes mixed-media to create movable *StoryScenes™* that each include a named doll that is the subject of the individual storybook, which comes with every vignette. The dolls are handmade, hand-painted and fully dressed. Each *StoryScene* is comprised of freestanding items that can be moved about, rearranged and placed wherever the collector chooses.

MAGI Entertainment Focuses on Entertainment-Based Licensed Products

The newest subsidiary in Media Arts Group is MAGI Entertainment Products, which recently signed a two-year, multi-film agreement with MCA/Universal Studios to produce and market limited edition art and collectible products based on selected films. A completely new collectible

Artist Gary Patterson depicts the ultimate golf setting in this highly detailed lithograph from Lightpost Publishing entitled "World of Golf."

Limited to 2,950 pieces, "Wendy House" is the first limited edition in the Woodly Wise *collection of intricate treehouse sculptures created by British sculptor Ted Slack.*

movie memorabilia product called *CinemaClips™,* has been introduced by MAGI Entertainment and features a 35mm film clip on an oversized movie ticket with artwork from the film. The first product launched was based on three 1995 Universal films: *Casper, Apollo 13* and *Waterworld.* MAGI Entertainment is also marketing limited edition art and three-dimensional products under the banner of Universal Studios Art Editions by MAGI.

In addition to motion picture-related licensed product, MAGI Entertainment Products will create and market collectible memorabilia for sports, music, theatre and familiar personalities. *Recollections* by *Lightpost Classic Clips™,* a nostalgic collection of historic and cultural art and memorabilia, has introduced new licenses and new product concepts for such familiar faces as Elvis, the Cowardly Lion and

Rhett Butler. They will be joined later by a star-studded cast for the enjoyment of collectors.

Media Arts Group Inc. is headquartered in San Jose, California, with production and distribution facilities in San Jose, Houston and the United Kingdom. The company also exhibits at major gift and collectible shows and maintains showrooms in major markets.

Media Arts Group
Ten Almaden Blvd. 9th Floor
San Jose, CA 95113
(800) 544-4890
Fax (408) 947-4640

COLLECTORS' CLUBS

Thomas Kinkade Collectors' Society P.O. Box 90267 San Jose, CA 95109 (800) 366-3733 **Annual Dues:** $45.00 – 2-Year: $75.00 **Club Year:** January-December **Collector's Year:** Anniversary of Sign-Up Date	**Benefits:** • Membership Gift: Pencil Sketch Lithograph • Opportunity to Purchase Members-Only Canvas and Paper Lithograph • Special Collector Benefit Certificates for Free Frame with Purchase of Members-Only Canvas Lithograph • Quarterly Newsletter, "The Beacon" • Membership Card • National and Regional Special Events
David Winter Cottages Collectors' Guild P.O. Box 90038 San Jose, CA 95109-3038 (800) 366-3733 **Annual Dues:** $40.00 – 2-Year: $75.00 **Club Year:** Anniversary of Sign-Up Date	**Benefits:** • Membership Gift: Membership Cottage • Opportunity to Purchase Members-Only Cottages • Quarterly Newsletter, "Cottage Country" • Membership Card and Certificate • National and Regional special Events and Tour Signings • Advance Mailings

MICHAEL'S LIMITED

Brian Baker's Déjà Vu Collection Welcomes Memories
Through Architectural Wall Sculptures

Michael's Limited began with a block of clay that has turned into neighborhood blocks that may look like your hometown. There's "Old White Church," "Main Street Cafe," "County Bridge," "Dinard Mansion," "Victorian Tower House" and other houses and buildings inspired by architecture around the world. It's also the world of *Brian Baker's Déjà Vu Collection*, where beautiful sculptures bring back warm memories and let everyone explore familiar places. "We believe when you study one of these works of art, you get the feeling you've been there before," says Michael O'Connell, president of Michael's Limited.

From the Imagination and Creativity of Artisans

Michael O'Connell began his career with Walt Disney Productions working for the company's Imagineering department, which designs and brings to life the famous theme parks. In 1976, Michael left Walt Disney Productions to pursue other interests, including model railroading. As a result, he developed Chooch Enterprises, Inc., a leading manufacturer of model railroad hobby products. By 1980, Chooch Enterprises, Inc. moved to Seattle, where the company continues serving the hobby industry.

For several years, Michael was also interested in creating architectural wall decor. However, it wasn't until 1987 that Brian Baker, an employee of Chooch Enterprises, Inc., made the dream into a reality. It all started with Brian's simple request for a block of clay so that he could make a Christmas present for a friend. Brian's sculpture not only inspired Michael, but is also inspired an idea. Brian had sculpted the first "Hotel Couronne," launching his career and the creation of Michael's Limited. Today *Brian Baker's Déjà Vu*

Members of the Brian Baker's Collector's Club had the opportunity to add "Welcome Home" to their collection in 1995. The members-only redemption sculpture features a small, inviting cottage complete with heart cut outs on the shutters to potted plants on the front door step. Brian created the piece based on the Carpenter's Gothic style.

Collection is one of the most exciting collectibles and decorative accessories in the gift industry.

World Travels Inspire Collection

From Europe to Mexico and Thailand to America, Brian Baker's zest for life comes from his fascination for history and the arts. When he isn't busy creating new sculptures, Brian can be found exploring the Pacific Northwest or searching for adventure in a distant land. The culture and architecture of the world inspire him to share his experiences through the collection.

Born in 1962, Brian was raised in Seattle's Puget Sound area. In 1981, he started working for a gift company specializing in framed plaques featuring calligraphy and strips of decorative European braid. In just five years, Brian advanced quickly within the company,

acquiring valuable gift industry knowledge and developing his craft.

But Brian embarked on his most ambitious adventure in 1986 when he began a solo trip around the world. He toured throughout Asia and then parts of Europe. In Paris, Brian was enchanted by paintings that captured the character and personality of the charming buildings. This inspired him to delve into the wonderful European heritage. His keen interest quickly spread to a love for the varied styles of American architecture.

Over the years, Brian's travels have taken him to more than 40 countries from the Far East and Middle East to Europe and the South Pacific. And he has stories to tell from each destination. Brian has found beautiful architecture and friendly people throughout the world. He likes Bali for its fascinating culture and Germany for its medieval

Brian Baker first remembers visiting Philadelphia when he was only three years old. When he returned as an adult, he rediscovered a place rich in history with colonial brick rowhouses. He recreated his impressions in "Philadelphia," which he dedicated to two late friends. You'll find a red umbrella by the door, representing the gift given to him by one of those friends.

castles and lush landscapes. He often visits friends in Mexico and explores remnants of the country's ancient civilizations. In Sweden, Brian has nearly 100 distant relatives. He has visited the Scandinavian country three times.

After his travels around the world, Brian returned home to Redmond, Washington, in 1986. At this time, he began working for Michael O'Connell. After he made his first wall hanging sculpture, Michael suggested he create a few more. The finished sculptures were shown at the San Francisco Gift Show. The rest, as they say, is history.

Building a *Déjà Vu Collection* Sculpture

Brian crafts each new building similar to the way each is actually constructed, including additions and remodeling. He lets the building "create itself." Brian's clay sculpting talents represent the first in a series of important and often difficult steps leading to the finished work. The second step involves forming a mold for

casting. All of the designs are hand cast in fine bonded stone. Brian then carefully develops a color scheme suitable for the building and its place in the overall collection. His first proof is reproduced to establish a sample for an excellent team of artisans, who carefully completes dozens of designs — each one faithful to Brian's original.

Brian's trademark in the collection is an umbrella. Although not every building has one, there is often an umbrella hidden in the shadows or quietly tucked away in a corner. Some people think the umbrellas represent the well-known rainy days in Seattle, but Brian tells a different story. "On my first building — #1000, the original "Hotel Couronne" — I wanted a hungry French cat sitting by the door," Brian explains. "I could not seem to design a cat that pleased me, so I left the cat's tail as the handle and made the body into an umbrella. This result became a souvenir of the rainy day when I first saw the building in Rouen."

This same detail-oriented creativity goes into every sculpture. At his sculpt-

ing table, he takes great care and pride in creating each house. Brian tries to become a resident of the building, imagining the people who would live or work there. This is just his way of bringing history to life and making one feel like Déjà Vu — you've been there before.

An Open Door to Brian Baker's Déjà Vu Collectors' Club

With the tremendous response to the collection, the Brian Baker's Déjà Vu Collectors' Club was founded in 1993. Each year, the club unveils a membership piece and an exclusive building that only members have the opportunity to acquire. For 1995, "Marie's Cottage" was the symbol of membership sculpture, inspired by a small home located on an island in Casco Bay, just north of Portland, Maine. The cottage belongs to the Mead family and is a tribute to Marie Mead, a recently retired and pioneering Michael's Limited sales representative in New Jersey. "Welcome Home," the members-only redemption sculpture for 1995 is based on a house in a restored Toronto neighborhood called Cabbagetown. The small cottage represents the Carpenter's Gothic style.

Limited Editions Make Places More Special

"Amsterdam Canal" is the only limited edition sculpture to be signed and numbered by Brian. The beautiful piece reflects another one of Brian's favorite places. He was impressed by Amsterdam's 6,700 houses and buildings under the care of the National Trust, which makes it the largest historical city in Europe. During the 17th century, the city reached its golden age with canals dug around medieval walls and powerful merchants constructing richly decorated buildings to flaunt their wealth. Today, more than 1,000 bridges cross the city's 160 canals, and the best way of getting around is still by boat. Limited to only 1,000 pieces, "Amsterdam Canal" sold out in 1993.

"Southern Mansion," the first sculp-

Among the most popular pieces in Brian Baker's Déjà Vu Collection, *"Cottage House" was created in two versions: blue and white. This white home was first introduced in 1987 and retired in December 1994. The cozy home represents the bungalow, where Americans settled down after World War II to start a family.*

Adding to the Collection and Retiring All-Time Favorites

For the first time, accessories to the collection were released in 1995. From a weeping willow to a dog house, the 17 sculptures bring a welcome addition to the collection and complement the nostalgic buildings. For 1996, the collection introduced a "Japanese Tea House" and "Japanese Pine" accessory set, "Country Christmas" and "Village Pharmacy."

To make room in the collection for more handcrafted introductions, a sculpture may be retired, thus no longer be produced. "Cottage House," the famous post-World War II bungalow, was among the earliest sculptures created and the first to be retired. "Cottage House" was the small home where America "began again" and settled down after the war. This little house also represents the baby boom, the cozy place where the family rebuilt its faith in America and a hope for a better world. The sculpture was released in two colors: blue (#1531) and white (#1530). In June 1988, the blue version was retired, followed in December 1994 by the best-selling white cottage.

ture from the collection to be limited to the year of production, was released in February 1995. "Philadelphia," a 1995 numbered limited edition of 1,500 sculptures, was inspired by Brian's collector friends in Louisville, Kentucky. They gave him a red umbrella during the 1993 Christmas season. On the umbrella were many signatures and drawings of Brian's first house and the Old Kentucky Home, which were sketched by the late Kelly Ostrander. That fall, while Brian was in Philadelphia, a close friend named Raleigh Pettaway passed away. So Brian dedicated "Philadelphia" to Kelly and Raleigh. You'll find Kelly's red umbrella at the door.

Michael's Limited
P.O. Box 217
Redmond, WA 98052-0217
(800) 835-0181
Fax (206) 861-0608

COLLECTORS' CLUB

Brian Baker's Déjà Vu Collectors' Club
PRDV
P.O. Box 217
Redmond, WA 98052-0217
(800) 835-0181

Annual Dues: $35.00
Club Year: March1 to March 1

Benefits:
• Membership Gift: Symbol of Membership Sculpture
• Opportunity to Purchase Members-Only Redemption Sculpture
• Bi-annual Newsletter, "Brian's Backyard"
• Membership Card
• Artist Appearances

MIDWEST OF CANNON FALLS
Designed in the Heartland, Crafted Around the World

In a scenic river valley in southern Minnesota - just 30 minutes from the Twin Cities, the small town of Cannon Falls has an unmistakable midwestern charm. With its down-to-earth hospitality and naturally inspiring environment, there's no better home for one of the country's leading designers of collectibles and giftware.

Welcome to Midwest of Cannon Falls!

Midwest of Cannon Falls was founded in 1955 by Kenneth W. Althoff as a small, family-owned business specializing in importing European products. Over the years, Midwest has grown to be an industry leader in designing collectibles and giftware. Since 1985, Kathleen Brekken, daughter of Mr. Althoff, has served as President and CEO, guiding the company into its present position of unparalleled success.

Today, Midwest's line features more than 5,000 products including seasonal giftware, exclusive collectibles and distinctive home decor. While the company continues to import fine collectibles from the Erzgebirge region in Germany, the majority of its line is now exclusively designed by Midwest and crafted around the world.

Distinctive Lighted Houses and Figurines

With its talented team of designers, Midwest has created several collections of popular lighted houses and figurines.

Recreate touching stories of America's heartland with the lifelike accessories and porcelain lighted houses of *Cannon Valley*™. From the neighborly "Ace's Garage" and "Church" to the authentic "Four Square Farmhouse" and "Grain Elevator," *Cannon Valley* continues to rekindle memories of small town living. In 1995, this celebra-

tion of American tradition has grown to ten porcelain lighted houses including the new "Dairy Barn," limited to 5,000 pieces. Choose from over 50 true-to-life accessories from the "Farm Cat" and "Dog" to "Parking Meters" and "Telephone Poles." Authentically sculpted and hand-painted, every collectible evokes a wonderful feeling of a simpler place and time. Come home to this nostalgic collection, and feel the warm sunshine of the countryside every day of the year.

Bring Halloween to life with the wickedly amusing characters and lighted porcelain houses of *Creepy Hollow*™. As the leading line of Halloween collectibles, *Creepy Hollow* is the first to provide collectors with both the sights and sounds of the season. Lighted from within, the eerie estates cast ghostly shadows to fill your home with the holiday spirit. In 1995, treat yourself to the "Skeleton Cinema" - the collection's first limited edition lighted house. Or if collectors are superstitious, they can collect all 13 of *Creepy Hollow's* hauntingly memorable houses. From the battery-operated "Pumpkin Street Lamps" to the light-activated blinking eyes and spooky musical sounds of the "Hinged Tomb With Ghoul," *Creepy Hollow* offers over 40 accessories to make decorating for Halloween really a scream!

Invite the charming bunnies and lighted cottages of *Cottontail Lane*™ into your home. Follow the lights of "Town Hall," and meet all the residents

"Skeleton Cinema," limited to 5,000 pieces, is one of 13 hauntingly memorable houses in the Creepy Hollow *collection. Lighted from within, each eerie estate casts ghostly shadows to fill any room with the holiday spirit.*

in this enchanting springtime village. Visit the "Rosebud Manor," where pastel flowers brightly bloom. Down at the local "Boutique," every bunny becomes a spring beauty. In 1995, Midwest has added four porcelain lighted houses including the limited edition "Rosebud Manor." The current collection features 15 porcelain lighted houses and over 50 accessories. You'll even find a cobblestone road and street lights that actually illuminate this adorable city! Each collectible is sculpted in precious detail and delicately hand-painted. With *Cottontail Lane* beautifully displayed in their homes, collectors can celebrate the wonderful feeling of spring anytime.

Enjoy an endless adventure of fun

Absolutely entrancing, Lou Schifferl's images have an heirloom quality that touches the hearts of collectors everywhere. "Bearing Gifts" is just one of the extraordinary pieces featured in Midwest's Folk Art Gallery Collection.

and friendship. *MouseKins™ Tales of Town & Country* shares the heartfelt stories between two tiny mice families. Although distanced by many miles and different lifestyles, they are forever bonded by a very special relationship. The complete collection features over 50 ornaments and figurines that celebrate every season from Valentine's Day and Easter to Halloween and Christmas.

Extraordinary Folk Art

In addition to its collectible lighted houses and figurines, Midwest develops partnerships with exceptional artists creating exclusive collections that feature unique works of art.

Discover the legends and lore of limited edition folk art collectibles from the *Leo R. Smith III Collection*. Every year, Midwest introduces new limited edition folk art collectibles from this nationally-recognized woodcarver. With his remarkable carving and rare insight, Leo R. Smith III brings the legends of the Mississippi River Valley to life. The complete collection features over 35 seasonal ornaments and figurines, as well as year-round images that appear beautifully in the home any day of the year. Hand-cast in

resin, each piece is a precise reproduction of Mr. Smith's original woodcarving. Hand-painted and numbered, every collectible includes a legend card and Certificate of Authenticity.

Create conversation with the original designs featured in *Folk Art Gallery Collection™*. The first of its kind in the collectibles industry, this extraordinary collection features an exciting group of American folk artists. Inscribed with the artist's signature, each piece is a faithful reproduction of the original design. From traditional to contemporary, every artist specializes in different mediums. No other collection combines this diversity and originality to benefit both folk art enthusiasts and the artists. In 1995, you'll find a complete selection of over 60 seasonal and year-round ornaments and figurines.

Exquisite German Collectibles

For over 50 years, Midwest has been sharing handcrafted German treasures with collectors. Today, the company's line features over 250 nutcrackers, as well as smokers, pyramids, blown glass ornaments and wood-turned figures.

Experience the "best of the Erzgebirge" nutcrackers with the *Ore Mountain Collection™*. As the

largest U.S. importer of these handcrafted treasures, Midwest unveiled this extraordinary collector's series in 1994. Every wooden figure is imported from the nutcracker's 17th century birthplace in the Erzgebirge region of Germany. Each one is crafted with virtually the identical workmanship that made the nutcracker famous over 250 years ago. From traditional images like soldiers and Santas to contemporary figures like cowboys and golfers, Midwest has carefully preserved the tradition of the Erzgebirge in every *Ore Mountain* nutcracker. In addition to over 70 nutcrackers, the *Ore Mountain Collection* features two limited edition series - *Nutcracker Fantasy* and *A Christmas Carol*.

See how the legend of the nutcracker lives on through the exquisite German craftsmanship of *Christian Ulbricht Nutcrackers*. A world-renowned master in the art of German woodcrafting, Christian Ulbricht creates nutcrackers with exceptional warmth and personality. Each one

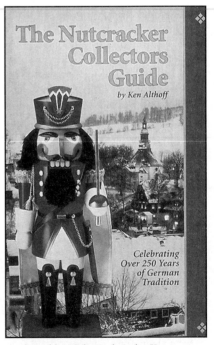

Authored by Midwest founder Ken Althoff, The Nutcracker Collector's Guide *features everything from the history of Germany's Erzgebirge region and how nutcrackers are made to the basics of starting a collection.*

Only a whisper is heard as Santa glides through the starry night on his snowy-white reindeer. Exclusively from Midwest of Cannon Falls, "Santa on Reindeer" is the second issue in the limited edition ornament series from Leo R. Smith III.

in the Erzgebirge for generations. Of all the family workshops, *Wendt & Kühn* is recognized as one of the finest. Founded in 1915, the company continues to thrive over 80 years later under family ownership by reproducing the founders' original designs. Midwest is the exclusive distributor of this collection in the U.S. and Canada. With their limited availability, these wood-turned figurines are cherished by collectors around the world. In addition to figurines, Midwest's collection of over 80 *Wendt & Kühn* designs includes ornaments, music boxes and candleholders.

Available at specialty gift shops and department stores across the U.S. and Canada, Midwest continues to offer an extensive variety of exclusive collectibles that appeal to the distinctive taste and personality of every individual. Call 1-800-377-3335 to locate your nearest retailer.

features the highest detail imaginable - a tradition for perfection passed down through the Ulbricht family since 1709. Even today, every Ulbricht nutcracker is created entirely with German parts and labor. In 1995, Midwest remains the largest U.S. distributor of *Christian Ulbricht* with over 40 nutcrackers including 25 exclusive designs and two limited edition series - *Traditional Santas* and *American Folk Heroes*.

Discover the collectible figurines of *Wendt & Kühn*. Truly an art form, wood-turned figures have been created

Midwest of Cannon Falls
32057 64th Avenue
P.O. Box 20
Cannon Falls, MN 55009-0020
(800) 377-3335
Fax (507) 263-7752

MISS MARTHA ORIGINALS

All God's Children Figurines Capture the Essence of Childhood and Memories of "Way Back When"

From the Miss Martha Originals Historical Series, *"Bessie Smith" was known to many as the "Empress of the Blues" because of her incredible musical talent. In 1923 her record "Downhearted Blues/Gulf Coast Blues" was the first recording by a black singer to sell over a million copies. She holds an honored place as one of the most important women in the history of American music.*
"Bessie Smith" is 10" high, crafted of a resin and pecan shell flour mixture, and retails for $70.00.

Without a doubt it was the carefree summer days spent on her grandmother's farm that most influenced Martha Holcombe as a child. Those delightful days of long ago still rest warmly in her heart and translate often into the beautiful children that she sculpts today. Summers spent in the Appalachian foothills of Northeast Alabama were filled with days of swimming, fishing, picking cotton and riding the old mule; along with raiding grandmother's watermelon patch.

Ms. Holcombe is a self-taught artist and never stops looking for inspiration for her artwork. Collectors of the *All God's Children* line of figurines keep her supplied with photographs of their loved ones which often inspire Martha Holcombe's art, as well as the names she gives each figurine. Yet, it is God that she credits for her artistic gifts, and it is His love for all His children that is the message of her work.

A native of Alabama, Ms. Holcombe is the mother of three children: Lisa, Keith and Kim. She holds a degree in Mental Health Technology with professional certificates in Counseling, Bible and Christian Education. She is the proud grandmother of Garrett and Alexandria, both of whom are represented by Members-Only club pieces.

How It All Began For Miss Martha

Miss Martha Originals, Inc. began in 1980 with a simple doll pattern design. In order to meet a pledge for a new roof for her church, Gadsden First Church of the Nazarene, she created a soft-sculpture doll that she sold at the church bazaar. Later that initial doll pattern was sold by mail, with proceeds given to the church. It was from the children in her Sunday School class that she was given the name, Miss Martha. It stuck and seemed like just the right name for her company, since it was the needs of the church that gave her the impetus to enter the business world.

The one doll pattern grew to a box of patterns and then enough to fill her garage. Eventually it was necessary to move to a vacant store building, then two store buildings, then in 1985 to a brand-new facility in the Gadsden Industrial Park. The new facility soon became too small, and after continued expansion, it became apparent that a second facility was needed. In 1992 Miss Martha Originals purchased the Coca-Cola plant in Gadsden and moved all administrative offices, the showroom, and the warehouse to that location, giving the original facility increased production capabilities.

It was not the doll patterns that created this sensational growth but the introduction of eight figurines that Miss Martha sculpted and introduced in 1985 that started the company on its dynamic growth spurt. In search of a name for her adorable sculpted children, she simply drew from a favorite Bible verse: "See how much the Father has loved us! His love is so great that we are called God's Children" (1 John 3:1). Thus the name, *All God's Children* was given to the beautiful sculptures by Miss Martha.

At its inception, Miss Martha Originals worked with many United States companies to produce the pecan shell/resin castings from Martha Holcombe's original sculptures. But after the first year the quality did not meet with the artist's high standards, so the decision was made to learn to do the entire process at the plant in Gadsden. The *All God's Children* line is crafted with pride in the U.S.A., at the Gadsden, Alabama, factory.

All God's Children Collectors Celebrate the Precious Memories of Childhood

Each summer for the past five years, collectors have traveled from far and wide to attend the annual All God's Children Family Reunion in Gadsden, Alabama. The 1995 reunion was the biggest yet with over 3,000 collectors coming to meet Miss Martha, and enjoying a day of fellowship, fun, and home-spun love with other collectors and their families.

The reunion is definitely a highlight for collectors from across the land, as they get together for a day of food, friendship, meeting Miss Martha and getting pieces signed, as well as buying and trading at the swap meet. And into all of the above is a jammed-packed day of entertainment and fun.

In 1995 the *All God's Children* line celebrated its tenth anniversary and through the years has won the hearts of its enthusiastic collectors. For some, it is the warm nostalgic vision of times "way back when" that Miss Martha creates in her three-dimensional portraits of African-American children. Yet for others, it is the face of each child which seems to reflect the heart of childhood in all its innocence, tenderness and beauty. In a letter to Miss Martha, Karen Berry of Portland, Oregon, says, "I believe AGC's universal appeal lies in your unique talent for capturing an instant in childhood, and making it last forever."

"William," a 1995 introduction, is every mother's precious child. From the hole in the knee of his pants to the dream he holds in his heart, M. Holcombe's sculpture has again captured the essence of childhood in this delightful, everyday situation. While his clothes are a little rumpled after hours of practice, his face reflects the hope of the future - possibly a home run! "William" is 6" high and retails for $38.00.

Laurie Dudenhoefer of New Brighton, Pennsylvania, says, "I love the manner in which you have captured and honored black children with your God-given talent. "

Collector's Club Continues to Delight Collectors

Thousands of other collectors of Miss Martha Originals also have discovered the fun, sharing and touch of family that comes with membership in the *All God's Children* Collector's Club. The annual fee of just $20.00 entitles members to the following benefits: a free figurine, a membership card, free subscription to a quarterly magazine, announcements of special appearances by Martha Holcombe, exclusive invitations to special events such as the annual reunion, opportunity to buy the exclusive "members only" figurine, and a personal checklist to keep accurate records of the collection.

Martha Holcombe keeps a busy schedule dividing her time between sculpting and personal appearances across the country. The Collector's Club magazine keeps collectors notified of upcoming signings, and they are among the first in line to meet the gentle-mannered artist and have their collectibles signed.

Miss Martha Originals and the All God's Children Collector's Club has widespread appeal because there is a little bit of child still left in each of our hearts. These delightfully sculpted children help us to reach back and touch a time when our lives were filled with a sense of awesome wonder.

Richard Gass of Bowen and Associates explained that "The beautiful faces seem to fascinate and capture the viewer's heart immediately." He further added, "that one of the statements I hear most often from collectors and dealers alike is that they truly feel the *All God's Children* collection is one of the most affordable collectible lines in the marketplace." With open edition figurines starting as low as $24.00, these adorable sculptures certainly are a joy to own as well as a good value.

Historical Series Premiered in 1989

While the nostalgic children figurines were being embraced by collectors across the country, Martha began in 1989 to turn her thoughts toward African-American history. She does all of her own research before sculpting each original figurine in the series. This has enriched and challenged her own daily life, as she encounters the determination, vision, and courage that men and women in Black history have unselfishly given as a legacy to the generations that followed.

Her first introduction in 1989 was "Harriet Tubman," who played an influential part in the Underground Railroad, as she bravely faced all odds while securing safety for those yearning for freedom. The "Harriet Tubman" sculpture retired in 1994 but is still a much loved and sought after figurine.

The series includes men and women whose lives have impacted and enriched this nation. The series proudly includes other great historical figures such as "Frederick Douglass," "Ida B. Wells," "Mary Bethune," "George Washington Carver," and the newest introduction "Mary Mahoney" — the first black registered nurse in the United States.

Don Neal, a collector for many years and president of the local New Jersey All God's Children Collector's Club says, "Harriet Tubman was the first piece I purchased." He adds that because "Martha sculpts her own line, you can feel the love she puts into each piece — somehow it just seems to come through. She puts herself into the artwork which gives a truth to it — a genuineness. There is a dignity to the line that is captivating and reflects that she views her art as a ministry."

Miss Martha Originals Created in the U.S.A.

The development of each Miss Martha Original figurine requires an intense period of research, sculpting, and painstaking production. The process begins when Martha Holcombe sculpts the original figurine using soft clay. In the mold room,

"Issie," premiered in the spring of 1995 with five other ragdolls in the latest series by sculptress M. Holcombe named, All God's Children Ragbabies. Cute and a bit whimsical, each ragbaby in the series has its name and a special message stamped on the bottom of the figurine. "Issie," putting on an old pair of shoes with a hole in the sole, carries the message - 'Bless my sole!' At 2-3/4" high, "Issie" retails for $33.00.

silicone rubber is then poured over the original sculpture making the first master.

Next, the master prototypes are cast, and the first castings are sent back to

Martha for approval. Production molds are then made, and each separate mold is marked with a number which appears on each figurine crafted with that mold. Any one mold can be used only 50 to 75 times before it is destroyed to avoid loss of detail.

Figurines are cast using a special blend of resins and pecan shell flour, washed in a special solution, and then the bottoms of the figurine are sanded. Mold seams are removed and each piece is inspected for quality.

Figurines are painted by skilled craftspeople, with the quality control department inspecting the painting, doing necessary touch-ups and painting of facial features. Antiquing stain is applied next, followed by finishing touches such as hairbows. After a final quality control inspection, figurines are boxed for shipment.

To authenticate each figurine, the signature of M. Holcombe, the name of the piece, copyright line, the phrase "God is Love," and the mold number are etched in. A Certificate of Authenticity is provided with each figurine at the time of purchase. Each collector is invited to establish a personal number

for the *All God's Children* pieces through their retailer. As figurines retire, they are then available only on the secondary market.

Additional Collections Sculpted by Miss Martha

In the spring of 1995, Miss Martha introduced a new series called *All God's Children Ragbabies*. With nine pieces in the collection at the present time, these whimsical, ragdoll cuties add still another dimension to the collection sculpted by M. Holcombe. "Issie" has already been singled out by many collectors as a favorite.

Two other collections created by the artist were the *Miss Martha Collection* in which all pieces are now retired; and the *Endearing Memories Series*. Both of these series are more intricate in detail and of a slightly smaller stature, but beautifully capture the tenderness and dignity that is a reflection of Martha Holcombe's goal in creating her art: "I sculpt only with the desire that Jesus Christ will be honored through my work."

Miss Martha Originals, Inc.
P.O. Box 5038
Glencoe, AL 35905
(205) 492-0221
Fax (205) 492-0261

COLLECTORS' CLUB/SHOWROOM

All God's Children Collector's Club
P.O Box 5038
Glencoe, AL 35905
(205) 492-0221

Annual Dues: $20.00
Club Year: June 1-May 31
Collector Year: Anniversary of Sign-Up Date

Benefits:
• Membership Gift: Figurine
• Opportunity to Purchase Members-Only Figurine
• Quarterly Magazine
• Membership Card
• Invitation to Annual "Family Reunion"
• Personal Checklist to Keep Accurate Records of Collection
• Local Club Chapters

Miss Martha Originals, Inc. Showroom
P.O. Box 5038
Glencoe, AL 35905
(205) 492-0221

Hours: Monday through Thursday, 8 a.m.-5 p.m.; Friday, 8 a.m.-Noon
Admission Fee: None

Located at 1119 Chastain Blvd. in Gadsden, Alabama, the showroom displays every figurine sculpted by Martha Holcombe including *All God's Children, Miss Martha Collection, Endearing Memories Collection* and *Ragbabies.*

OLD WORLD CHRISTMAS
Creating Tomorrow's Heirlooms Today

1995 marked Old World Christmas' celebration of their 20th anniversary. It was back in 1975 that Tim and Beth Merck, owners of Old World Christmas, decided to branch out from their locally-owned antique business into the fledgling market of collectible-quality tree ornaments. With their creative talent and hard work Old World Christmas has flourished, and millions of homes throughout the country will be trimmed with the Mercks' exclusive decorations this Christmas.

Old World Christmas began more or less by accident. The Mercks owned a retail store in Spokane, Washington, in which they sold antiques they imported directly from Europe. During a buying trip in Europe, they purchased a large assortment of German Christmas decorations, inspired by the heirloom ornaments Beth's grandmother had put on her Christmas trees. This new venture proved to be extremely successful, and before long, Beth and Tim were not only selling to retail customers, but were wholesaling their decorations to local merchants as well. Soon they phased out their antiques business to pursue Christmas in

The Bells, Stars and Stripes and Santas from Old World Christmas' Patriotic Ornament Series celebrate our nation's freedom and the spirit of Christmas.

earnest. As Tim Merck says with a chuckle, "Handling ornaments is much easier than moving pianos, armoires and sideboards!" Shortly thereafter, they commissioned a family workshop in Germany and began working directly with the manufacturers.

Beth eventually became very involved in developing both color schemes and original designs, and soon the business began to flourish. Since the very beginning, the company has held the philosophy that it is creating tomorrow's heirlooms today. As they use only the finest of raw materials, creating each piece individually to the most exacting of standards, heirloom quality is guaranteed. Old World Christmas will settle for nothing less.

Patriotic Theme Featured in New Series

Beth Merck's most recent additions to the Old World Christmas product lines include a patriotic ornament series, a 10th addition to the series of Santa Lights, first introduced in 1985, and, exclusive to Old World Christmas, the *E.M. Merck Signature Series* of nutcrackers.

Old World Christmas is proud to introduce its patriotic ornament collection commemorating the 50th anniversary of World War II's end and honoring our brave veterans who fought for our freedom and peace. We can reflect and be thankful that today's Christmas celebrations are free from the pain, suffering and blight clouding the Christmases in Europe and the world during the war.

Uncle Sam is the epitome of American patriotism. As reflected in E.M. Merck's most recent addition to Old World Christmas's line of unique and distinctive nutcrackers, this "Uncle Sam" nutcracker is destined to inspire pride and respect in the youngest of

hearts during the Christmas season. From his jaunty hat to his patriotic attire, this magnificent nutcracker is destined to be a cherished collector's piece as it inspires collectors to recall the dedication and patriotism of our war heroes, as well as their desire to be home for the Christmas holidays and in the presence of loved ones.

Also, mouth-blown and intricately hand-painted with the care and quality that has become the trademark of Old World Christmas, their bright and colorful glass patriotic ornament theme will enliven and enrich any tree. Made from antique molds, the cheerful ornaments celebrate the freedom and joy the heart of our nation shares with the spirit of Christmas. Bells, Stars and Stripes, Santas and many more ornament patterns shine in tribute to the peace and liberty of Christmas and America. The reds, whites and blues sparkling with Christmas cheer will be proud additions to Christmas trees "from sea to shining sea."

Ten-Year Tradition of *Santa Lights* Continues

Old World Christmas' "Santa in Sleigh" is the tenth anniversary edition in the *Santa Light* series. Since its first Santa Light in 1985, these annual introductions have become collectible additions to holiday celebrations throughout the country. The excitement surrounding these pieces is overwhelming! Each year, before the design for the new Santa Light has been announced, Old World Christmas receives several calls each day requesting information on the forthcoming light.

E.M. Merck fashions each finely crafted glass light after a lovable, familiar Santa figure. The *Santa Lights* come complete with a wood base, U.L. approved cord with switch, and light bulb. Each piece is presented in a glossy red box featuring a full-color picture of the *Santa Light*. A brass "Ten Year Anniversary Edition" commemorative plaque is included with each "Santa in Sleigh" Light and may, at the option of the owner, be applied to the wooden base.

To ensure their continuing importance as collectibles and to make room for new introductions, each design is retired after three years. The earliest designs are now coveted collectibles sought after by Christmas enthusiasts everywhere.

Meet E.M. Merck

A common thread throughout the successes of Old World Christmas lies in the acclaimed talents of its artist, E.M. Merck. Old World Christmas is sure that all avid collectors of their ornaments and collectibles are more than curious about who is the design genius behind the fabulous products that grace their trees, wreaths, garlands and showcases. Well, today you, the reader, are in for a treat as Old World Christmas would like you to meet its talented artist and premier designer, E.M. Merck.

Beth, as she likes to be called, began designing for Old World Christmas ten years ago. It was at this time that she and her husband, Tim Merck, joined forces with the German family workshop, Inge-Glas, to produce mouth-

"Santa in Sleigh" Light commemorates the Tenth Anniversary of the Santa Light Series *from Old World Christmas.*

Talented artist and premier designer, E.M. Merck, is the creative force behind Old World Christmas' successful line of ornaments and collectibles.

blown glass ornaments for importation into the United States.

Skilled glassblowers from the tiny village of Neustadt, Germany, use actual antique molds to produce the majority of the ornaments, and Beth creates all of the painting designs. Her attention to detail, exceptional eye for color and intuition about collectibles has helped to create a tremendous demand for Old World Christmas products. Her talents were nurtured by her many years of studying fine arts, art history, and German cultural traditions at Pomona College, Gonzaga University and Eastern Washington University.

In addition to her glass ornament designs, Beth is also the creative genius behind all of the Old World Christmas light covers, *Santa Lights*, and exclusive nutcracker designs. Where does she receive her design inspiration? Beth was quoted in the October 1992 issue of *Collector's Mart* magazine as approaching new projects "with the idea in mind of what a child would think seeing this for the first time. I want the child to have feelings of awe, amazement, warmth." This sentiment is certainly clearly depicted and brought to life in all of Beth's work.

The most recent additions to Beth's extensive design portfolio are exclusive nutcrackers that are produced by a

German wood workshop. These unique designs have won the hearts of collectors and dealers alike. E.M. Merck's new designs in 1995 include, among others, the Uncle Sam nutcracker, a Cowboy nutcracker, a Panda, a Pharmacist, an Attorney, and also a Sugar Plum Fairy nutcracker. This "Sugar Plum Fairy" is very special, not only because it is hand-produced with Old World Christmas's trademark standards of quality and attention to detail, but because when one purchases this unique collectible, Old World Christmas donates a portion of the proceeds to the Juvenile Diabetes Foundation. All of Beth's designs possess incredible detail, whimsy and charm, and all in this new series are signed by the artist herself.

Creating Ornaments in the Old World Tradition

The steps involved in creating tomorrow's heirlooms are numerous. Several times each year, Tim and Beth Merck travel to Germany, where they monitor the multitude of steps and tremendous amount of tedious details involved in making each piece. A large number of their ornaments are still blown in cottages nestled in small towns in northern Bavaria, but whether they are produced in the cottages or in the family-owned factory, the process Inge-Glas follows is exactly as it was one hundred years ago.

Each ornament is made from a "blank" which is a small hollow ball of glass with a 6" hollow stem. The glassblower heats the ball of glass over a Bunsen burner until it is red hot. He then sets that portion of the blank into the bottom half of the mold, covers it with the top half and blows on the stem until the molten glass conforms to the shape of the mold. He then removes the ornament from the mold, reheats it a second time and gives it one last puff. This extra step tempers the ornament, preventing stress cracks. Many of these molds were lost for years when German products were out of favor due to wars or changes in decorating styles. Thousands of molds disappeared forever during this time because they were

The 9" "Sugar Plum Fairy" from the E.M. Merck Signature Collection retails for $55.00. Old World Christmas donates a portion of the sales from this charming nutcracker to the Juvenile Diabetes Foundation.

converted into cobblestones for streets and building materials for homes.

Silvering the ornament is the next step. A mixture of silver nitrate, ammonia and distilled water is poured into the ornament, followed by a few drops of a combination of saltpeter, sugar and distilled water. The solution is an unappealing brown until the ornament is dipped into a hot water bath where it magically turns into silver. This process gives the ornament its mirror-like interior and greatly enhances its reflectivity. Next it is dipped into an iron chloride solution, rinsed in clear water, and is then placed upside down on a nail and placed in a drying oven. Each one of Old World Christmas's ornaments goes through all of these silvering steps regardless of its final color.

When the ornament is dry, a painter hand-dips it into the appropriate background paint. It is then put back to dry. From there it is taken to an artist's table for painting. Applying each color is a separate step and the ornament is set aside to dry before the next color may be added.

Next, glitter is applied where needed, the stem is broken off, and the trademark star cap is put in place. It is difficult to estimate how much time is involved in making each ornament as each mold is different, but obviously a tremendous amount of labor is required. The steps are numerous, and the quality of the final product is unsurpassed.

Collectors' Club Offers Many Benefits

As these items inspire collectibility, naturally Old World Christmas has begun a Collectors' Club. Formed three years ago, the Club was designed in response to tremendous demand from avid collectors across the country to obtain more information about Old World Christmas and its history, as well as gain access to information on limited edition pieces, exclusively for Club members only. The benefits of the Club are numerous. For a $30.00 annual membership fee, Club members receive a 100-page full-color guide featuring beautiful pictures of all the items currently available in Old World Christmas' line. Club members also receive informative newsletters containing articles on new and retiring products, and stories, perhaps on the making of the wooden nutcrackers or the history behind the trademark star cap.

Another valuable benefit to becoming a Club member is the opportunity to purchase special members-only pieces. Every year Old World Christmas introduces new products, designed by their artist only for members of the Club, and every year they retire the previous years' pieces, thus guaranteeing their collectibility. For 1995 the Collectors' Club featured a glass ornament called the "Large Christmas Carousel" and a special member of the *EM Merck Signature Series* of nutcrackers, the "Konigsee King." Both of these valuable pieces are handcrafted and imported from Germany, and are available to Club members through their favorite Old World Christmas retailer.

And, in addition to all this, members also receive a complimentary gift upon joining or renewing their Club membership. Free to Club members is another exclusive German collectible entitled "A Heavenly Gift." Having a retail value of $32.50, this carefully painted angel reflector ornament adorned with spun glass and a delicate wire wrap is destined to become a treasured family heirloom.

The Club is a fun and informative way to communicate valuable information to Old World Christmas' most avid and dedicated supporters – the private collector. Hopefully with the continued success of the Collectors' Club and with Beth's artistic genius and inspiration, Old World Christmas will continue to spark magic and joy in the hearts of Christmas enthusiasts everywhere, remaining a vital force in the collectibles market for many years to come.

Old World Christmas
P.O. Box 8000
Spokane, WA 99203
(509) 534-9000
Fax (509) 534-9098

COLLECTORS' CLUB

Old World Christmas Collectors' Club
P.O. Box 8000 – Department C
Spokane, WA 99203
(800) 962-7669

Annual Dues: $30.00
Club Year: Anniversary of Sign-Up Date

Benefits:
- Membership Gift: "Angel Reflector"
- Opportunity to Purchase Members-Only Pieces
- Quarterly Newsletter, "Old World Christmas Star"
- Buy/Sell Matching Service through Newsletter
- 100-Page, Full-Color, Collectors' Guide Detailing Complete Current Product Line
- Local Retailer Listings

PACIFIC RIM IMPORT CORP.
Bristol Township and *Waterfront Collections*
Set Sail With English Charm

With its winding exterior stairway, the "Bristol Channel Lighthouse" shines its blinking light to passing ships. Introduced in 1995, the third porcelain lighthouse to the Bristol Waterfront *line stands 8-1/2" tall and sells for about $30.00.*

Nestled along the Avon and Fromme Rivers in England, there's a quaint waterfront village that was once known around the world for its bustling trading port. For two centuries, Bristol claimed the country's second most important shipping center. With a harbor in the heart of the city, the Bristol skyline reflected an interesting mix of ship masts and church spires. But during World War II, nearly half of the city was destroyed.

Today, Bristol is experiencing a revival – not only along its old cobblestone streets but through a porcelain village collection by Pacific Rim Import Corporation. Known as the *Bristol Township Collection*, the collectibles have built a new niche for the company and put a new twist on the popularity of cottages. *Bristol Township*, intro-

duced in the spring of 1990 with seven pieces, and followed quickly by six more, was the company's first venture into a line of collectibles. A few years later, the *Bristol Waterfront* line brought back the city's nautical roots. Pacific Rim Import Corp. has since dedicated itself to other collectible lines while turning *Bristol Township* into a very unique village.

The Founding of
Bristol Township

Bristol Township Collection wasn't initially envisioned or created from its namesake British city. Instead, artist Pat Sebern was asked to draw a half dozen designs of porcelain buildings for Pacific Rim, which wanted to explore new avenues. She came up with a tiny village of charming Victorian buildings, including a manor, cottage and livery stable. When it came time to name the new collection, Sebern proposed "Bristol," which seemed to add an Olde English flavor to the buildings while distinguishing it from other cottages on the market.

But with the name, Sebern became more interested in the story behind Bristol and its harbor. Inspired by this, Sebern submitted drawings in 1991 for a waterfront version of *Bristol Township*. She traveled to Britain, where she studied the Victorian architecture, read about Bristol's past, and experienced firsthand the city's waterfront views. She was particularly intrigued by the harbor areas of western England, where she took photos and made sketches of small but important details. She traveled from London to Bristol where history books chronicled the major damage that the city suffered during World War II. Many wonderful buildings were ultimately replaced by new ones. Fortunately, Sebern spent time in the archives of the city's main library to study line

drawings, descriptions and a few photographs of old Bristol buildings and landmarks as they appeared before the war.

Sebern also visited several coastal cities with waterfront architecture. Original stone work remained on many towers and bridges, and every neighborhood seemed to boast a major church. Numerous coaching inns and pubs lined the streets, many with their founding dates etched in stone. Hanging signs made of wood and resembling book illustrations adorned most buildings. These displayed the owner's or business' name with great flair, and gave information about each shop to villagers passing by.

Innovative Yet Traditional
Designs Reflect Bristol's
Olde World Charm

Returning to Pacific Rim headquarters in Seattle, Sebern began working these ideas into new designs. The *Waterfront* buildings were creatively designed to appear suspended above water. To achieve this effect, Sebern undercut the bottom edge and added boardwalks and pilings. Small hanging signs were developed on wire brackets to fit into small holes in the porcelain buildings. Mounted at the corners or near the doors of these pieces, the signs help recreate the traditional rustic street scenes with most shops and inns bearing two or three. The signs identify the "Customs House" and "Admiralty Shipping." They tell that the "Rusty Knight Inn" provides extra moorage for travelers' boats. To further add to the realistic scenes, a felt ground cover depicting cobblestones and brick roads was developed to properly display the collector villages. The designs are screen printed on felt with various color backgrounds. This creates the look of stony roads, courtyards and narrow lanes often seen in the English

This porcelain light cover ornament portraying the popular "Portshead Lighthouse" was the first in a dated series. The lighthouse, which measures 4-1/2" and retails for about $10.00, captures the quaint waterfront architecture.

countryside and older parts of cities. The product can be cut into individual lanes or be placed down like a blanket with the buildings arranged on top.

Another unusual feature is the light, which is mounted in the bottom of each building. All four sides of the building are illuminated, allowing collectors to set up the scenes from any angle, as the light bulb is hidden from view. The cords can then run down through the felt to create a neighborhood of cobblestone or brick lanes instead of a maze of electrical wiring. The introduction of the *Waterfront* also created a wave of collector demand for a product that resembled water. In response, Pacific Rim packaged Bristol Bay Reflective Film. When used over a smooth cardboard or foam board, the product puts the buildings exactly where they should be: on the waterfront.

Additions Keep *Bristol's* Population and Popularity Growing

Pacific Rim, which was founded

about 40 years ago, had its first group of collectibles, *Bristol Township*, produced in Taiwan. While experimenting with different ideas, a few goals remained constant: striving for the highest quality and compatibility with other cottages on the market. Production on all *Bristol Township* pieces was eventually moved to China in 1992. Shortly thereafter, the *Waterfront* pieces were introduced and appeared in stores in time for the 1992 holiday season. At this time, the first lighthouse was also approved for production with its unique two-light design. It features an old stone and timber building with a pier at one end. Its stone tower has a second light that extends up inside and blinks through the cut out windows. In 1994, a second light house, "Portshead Lighthouse," was added. In 1995, a third lighthouse, "Bristol Channel Lighthouse," joined the collection.

In 1993, six pieces were retired, most of which are available now only on the secondary market. The most popular of these was the "Iron Horse Livery," an interesting building that has four hanging signs.

Artist Builds New Cottages Through a Labor of Love

Sebern continues researching new ideas for future introductions to the *Bristol Township Collection*. Sebern, a self-taught artist, began her career as a fashion illustrator and then spent several years involved in Western fine art. When she first joined Pacific Rim Import Corporation in the late 1980s, she did floral design and window display. But a new direction was taken when the opportunity arose to design porcelain houses and establish a collectible group for the company. With each cottage, Sebern carefully researches the architecture and style of the buildings to ensure accuracy.

In 1994, four new buildings were added to the collection. *Bristol Township* (the non-waterfront group) was joined by the "Shotwick Inn and Surgery," a colorful inn where the local doctor also hangs his shingle; and "Surrey Road Church" with its stone

arched windows and cross on top. The *Waterfront* line was increased by the "Portshead Lighthouse" with a blinking tower light and no Christmas decor; and the "Tattler Foghorn Inn" combination that includes a newspaper, print shop and inn all rolled into one.

Also introduced were four sets of very small resin figures that inhabit the township: a set of eight caroler musicians, two smaller sets of villagers and an additional group of popular waterfront characters. In 1995, the third lighthouse with its exterior stairway and blinking light was joined by a much requested school. As part of the original *Bristol Township*, "King's Gate School" features four brick chimneys and a coal bin. A porcelain light cover ornament portraying the popular "Portshead Lighthouse" was also introduced in 1995 and is the first in a dated ornament series. The *Bristol Township* and *Waterfront* continue to attract additional admirers with prices ranging from $25.00 to $45.00.

Bunny Toes and *Birthday Bunnies* Celebrate Life's Special Moments

With the popularity of the *Bristol Township Collection*, Pacific Rim introduced a second group of collectibles in

Designed by artist Pat Seburn, "Beth – Back to School" marks that memorable time in September. The adorable bunny walks to school carrying her books, chalkboard and an apple for the teacher.

"Pieter – Higher Education" portrays an adventurous bunny climbing a fence on his way home from school. The Birthday Bunnies *collection by artist Pat Sebern features figurines representing memorable scenes from every month of the year.*

the spring of 1994. *Bunny Toes* debuted with "Tillie and Timothy" in their spring gardens while "Winifred and Wendell" scooped up arms full of tulips. These adorable characters stand about 3" tall and are created in cold cast resin. Delicate watercolor details grace each piece and give the bunnies a heartwarming appeal.

The original *Bunny Toes* group carries a springtime theme and includes a flowered gazebo and garden trellis accessories. A large light-up piece of "Willis and Winifred" is also available. With the summer of 1995, *Birthday Bunnies* came bounding onto the scene. Designed by Sebern, this group of bunnies is leaping into every season as they commemorate birthdays, childhood and all the simple pleasures of growing up. There are 24 figurines as two bunnies represent each month of the year. "Molly" and

"Chester" can be found in February while "Anabell" and "Nicholas" romp through July. Wearing the charming country attire of pinafores and overalls, these bunnies portray typical childhood activities. They tell stories of sand castles, snowmen, wishing wells and kites. *Bunny Toes* and *Birthday Bunnies* are affordably priced between $13.00 and $20.00. With its product line of thousands of items, Pacific Rim truly lives up to its motto of a "Company For All Seasons."

Pacific Rim Import Corp.
5930 4th Avenue South
Seattle, WA 98108
(800) 425-5932
Fax (206) 767-9179

POSSIBLE DREAMS® LTD.

Clothtique® Originals Open Up World of Possibilities

Recreated from a Dec. 4, 1920, Saturday Evening Post *cover portrait, this Clothtique Santa reviews his holiday finances in "Balancing the Budget." The 11" figurine features the popular Clothtique blend of stiffened cloth, resin and porcelain for a unique look.*

It has been said that creativity lies in the eyes of those who look at the same old thing and see something brand new. Leni Miler and Warren Stanley took that philosophy to heart when they founded Possible Dreams Ltd. Teaming up in a small business that focused on designing, modeling and producing porcelain inspirational products, the pair began to look beyond the religious giftware market to find a need for high quality porcelain in the general collectibles area.

In 1983, Possible Dreams launched a line of figurines, including clowns and carousel horses. The response was discouraging: too much competition matched by too little experience. But there was a flicker of encouragement that came in the form of a limited edition Santa dropped into the line at the last minute. Its overwhelming success set a new course for Possible

Dreams, and the search began for more items to build the company into a Christmas specialty house.

In 1984, Stanley discovered a wonderful line of stiffened cloth angels and Santas, which would soon become the flagship of the Possible Dreams line. At first, production problems curtailed the success of the Santas, but the angels were an instant hit. Several names were suggested to describe the new product line including Clothtique – which was added to the gift market vocabulary and has since added Possible Dreams as a collectibles leader.

Clothtique Originals Builds a Firm Foundation

For the company that took an unknown process for stiffening cloth and nurtured it into one of the country's leading giftware lines, every day is a holiday. The company's collectibles go beyond the Christmas season. Now after more than a decade, Clothtique Originals from Possible Dreams has grown from a few angels and a handful of Santas to a broad offering of elegant collectibles. Providing inspiration are some of America's most renowned artists: Tom Browning, Judith Ann Griffith, Lynn Bywaters, Jan Brett, Judi Vaillancourt and Thomas Blackshear, to name a few. Pepsi-Cola®, *The Saturday Evening Post* covers by Norman Rockwell and J.C. Leyendecker, Warner Bros.®, and most recently, Garfield® have also joined the Clothtique family.

Creation of a Clothtique Original

Centuries ago, a process much like Clothtique originated in Southern Europe. Yet for most of today's art masters, the concept was completely new. The artists and designers at Possible Dreams perfected the technique. The resulting medium combines charm,

beauty and a special, life-like "feel" that is unique to Clothtique Originals by Possible Dreams.

This blend of old-world artistry and modern technology, as well as the mixture of porcelain, resin and cloth makes Clothtique figurines look realistic. The textures of fur, rich fabrics, embroidered tapestry and soft folds of a robe come alive in each piece.

Clothtique Santas and Other Figurines Deliver Originality and Memories

Santas remain the most popular Clothtique figurines, with new introductions that let collectors share the Christmas spirit all year. Sometimes — as in "Homespun Holiday" featuring an African-American Santa — the legendary character is portrayed in his traditional role and red garb to make his delivery for December 25.

Other times, a special friend joins Santa. In "Frisky Friend," Santa has an overzealous puppy. "Special Treat" features Santa holding an adorable baby deer along with his traditional bag of toys. Some Clothtique Santas also feature exquisite European Victorians dressed in luxurious greens, blues and whites with tapestry and fur trim. Their faces reflect an Old World nobility from vibrant eyes to beards rich with a sculptured integrity.

The *American Artists Collection* showcases the talents of artists, who bring their own touch to Santas and the Clothtique process. Among the introductions is "Santa Fe Santa" by Virginia Wiseman, who captures the familiar Southwest feeling of blue jeans, peasant shirts and a string of hot chili peppers. Lisa Nilsson's "Riding High" shows St. Nick in a fur-trimmed Old World outfit, wheeling around on a tricycle with a basket of goodies.

From Warner Bros., Possible Dreams is making show-biz history by dressing

Bugs Bunny in a Clothtique Santa suit. Yosemite Sam, Sylvester and Tweety are also part of the *Looney Tunes Collection*, a classic cast of superstars with a universal appeal to all ages.

But Santas are just part of the year round selection of figures. Londonshire is a fantasy isle complete with clothtique animal citizenry, while the *Lifestyle Collection* features every day professionals dressed in smart Clothtique wardrobes ranging from doctors to firefighters.

The Santa Claus Network

Collectors who find themselves caught up in the magic of the Clothtique Santas may want to join The Santa Claus Network from Possible Dreams. Each member receives many benefits including a free Clothtique Santa, available exclusively to SCN members. Membership offers the

From the Crinkle Claus *collection, Santa climbs down a snow-covered chimney. The collection gets its distinctive name from the elaborate texture, wrinkly puckers and pleats that give each figurine an animated quality.*

opportunity to purchase another exclusive Santa each year, as well as a subscription to a colorful, quarterly newsletter, a complete directory of Clothtique Santas in the *Collectors Guide Book*, and a personal membership card. All this is available for $25.00 annually. (Add $5.00 more for memberships outside the continental United States.) Write to address listed.

More Holiday Magic

Beyond the Clothtique realm are many other holiday gifts and collectibles that capture traditional themes and the season of giving in a whole new light. *Candy Colored Christmas®* borrows coloration from 1950s ribbon-candy to create a dazzling surface on ceramic and porcelain. From stocking holders to ornaments, this line catches the attention of those who want something original and unique.

Crinkle Claus® is a clan of cold cast characters finished in a wrinkly, puckered texture that proved a big winner in 1995. Borrowing the same idea and procedure, *Crinkle Crackers* are zany officers elaborately dressed in military garb reminiscent of Gilbert & Sullivan. *Santa Go Round™* are roly poly originals, sculpted in cold cast and hand-painted to capture a detailed expression of Christmas fun and delight.

From the renowned studios of Vaillancourt Folk Art comes another relic of Christmas past. Like all the wonderful Santa designs and antique candy mold creations that Judi Vaillancourt has created for Possible Dreams, *Vaillancourt Cats* combine nostalgia and innovation. Wide-eyed stares full of curiosity and realistic fur coloration make this ceramic collection perfect for feline fanciers.

Santa hops aboard a tricycle filled with a basket of gifts in "Riding High" from the American Artists Collection. *Designed by artist Lisa Nilsson, the Clothtique Santa wears a fur-trimmed outfit as he pedals his bike and rings a bell to announce his arrival.*

Artist David Wenzel catches Santas in the midst of sledding, skiing, fishing and other outdoor activities. *Santa Antics* is crafted in cold cast for exquisite detailing in the faces and wardrobe. *Baby's First Christmas* celebrates a new addition to the family with a collection of delicate, handcrafted ornaments.

Possible Dreams technicians are always experimenting with new materials to give the products a new — or old — look. Santas and angels in the *Artiva™* collection are crafted from an innovative process that makes Santas and angels appear as though they were discovered in an old dusty attic. Despite its crackled surface and yellowing of age, *Artiva* pieces are lightweight and soft to the touch.

Other Possible Dreams' products include waterdomes, hinged hanging ornaments that open to cherished scenes, and tins to hold gifts the old-fashioned way.

Year-Round Collectibles

Besides the holiday collectibles, Possible Dreams has created lines that extend past the holidays. Mache Mystique®, a technique using hand-pulped Abaca and rice straw paper delicately shaped and bound, hand-dyed and painted, brings the *People of the World*™ collection to life. Researched and authenticated to determine the look that best expresses a cultural identity, the collection portrays American Indians, Africans, Kabuki Actors and Samurai Warriors. *Kidoughs*™ show off adorable little girls in Shirley Temple dresses and curly-locks hair. The figurines are made of a soft resin and painted in pastels. The girls' tiny hands clutch either dolls, bears, teapots or other favorite childhood toys.

In *The Thickets at Sweetbriar*™, never before has such artistry and diligence to detail been applied to a realm of endearing characters. Each personality from the collection seems to have popped out of the dusty pages of a Victorian classic, elegantly dressed in authentic period costumes accentuated by full-color blossoms.

Creativity lies in the eyes of those who look at the same old thing and see something brand new. From outside resources and an in-house creative staff come a steady flow of new ideas to rekindle memories of the past. For at Possible Dreams, illuminating the past in a new light is what keeps the fire lit under its business.

"Parsley Divine" and "Clem Jingles" sing a few carols together in their classic Victorian finery. The figurines are part of The Thickets of Sweetbriar *collection that features a cast of endearing characters.*

Possible Dreams
6 Perry Drive
Foxboro, MA 02035
(508) 543-5412
Fax (508) 543-4255

COLLECTORS' CLUB

Santa Claus Network®
c/o Possible Dreams
6 Perry Drive
Foxboro, MA 02035
(508) 543-6667

Annual Dues: $25.00 ($30.00 Outside Continental U.S.)
Club Year: Anniversary of Sign-Up Date

Benefits:
• Membership Gift: Clothtique Santa
• Opportunity to Purchase Members-Only Santa
• Quarterly Newsletter
• Embossed Membership Card
• Collectors Guide Book – Directory of Clothtique Santas
• Buy/Sell Matching Service Through Newsletter

PRECIOUS ART/PANTON
A World of Collecting from Fantasy to Fun

From the Krystonia collection, "Barlow" has stumbled across "Okinawathe" and his mate "Tinchachuik." These creatures are as mystified at what to do with "Barlow" as he is afraid of them!

When Precious Art/Panton first began in 1980, the company's new line of products reflected an ancient tradition. Pictures, music boxes and other accessories captured the distinctive look of Chokin art, a beautiful 13th century Japanese technique that features engraved designs on copper, gold and silver plates. These engravings used by Samurai warriors marked the beginning of a long and creative list of products that would find its way to America.

Since many of the Chokin items were musicals, Precious Art soon found a niche in this area. At one time, 90 percent of its introductions were musicals with other items including beveled and etched glass boxes along with redwood and oak jewelry boxes. The success of the company's musicals led to the creation of the first up-and-down movement carousel. These limited edition pieces brought Precious Art into the collectibles market and paved a path for the company's most popular collection – *Krystonia*.

In 1987, Precious Art opened the door to the *World of Krystonia* – a whimsical place filled with mysterious, magical adventures. This mystical land of expansive deserts, towering mountains and lush valleys boasts an assortment of inhabitants that come to life as hand-painted figurines. But *Krystonia* also has put a new twist on collecting. Corresponding storybooks tell the tale of this make-believe kingdom, with the fourth book published in 1995.

The fascinating books give collectors an opportunity to not only further enjoy their quality figurines but to also follow the storylines of their favorite characters from "Grumblypeg Grunch" to "Kephren." It's an up-close and personal approach that sparks the imagination and has led to great success for Precious Art/Panton.

A Land of New Beginnings That Has No End

Since its inception in 1987 with 19 figurines, *Krystonia* has delighted collectors of all ages with its continuing introductions and stories filled with humorous anecdotes, colorful personalities and struggles of good versus evil. The four *Krystonia* books reveal the magic found throughout the wonderful land, where the search is always on for magical krystals. Whoever controls the krystals rules all of *Krystonia*.

The evil "N'Borg" dreams of the day he will sit at the top. Under his power, *Krystonia* would become a bleak and barren wasteland, a winter with no end. With his henchdragon "N'Grall"

and his legion of snords, "N'Borg" won't rest until his conquest of *Krystonia* is complete. From his menacing castle "Krak N'Borg," he waits for the day he will cast the darkest of spells and crush the Council of Wizards. He also has a score to settle with "Klip" for taking away his beautiful "N'Leila."

The Council of Wizards looks out for the best interests of *Krystonia*, wanting the land to be filled with peace and harmony. Working from the Obelisk, the Council has successfully thwarted all of "N'Borg's" conniving plans. Since the day "Azael" first founded the Council, the members have joined to strengthen and improve *Krystonia*. Their diverse spell-casting abilities make them a formidable foe. By whispering their charm words through the krystals, the wizards have cast the most wonderful spells – while showing they're an interesting cast of characters. If you need rest, call on "Turfen" – a change in the weather, there's "Shepf." For utter confusion, look to "Haaph." "Rueggan," the tinkerer, spends his time bringing ancient machines back to life – often with hilarious results.

"Poffles" and "Trumph" jump from the pages of storybooks that tell the magical tales of a land called Krystonia. These fun-loving characters – along with many collectors worldwide – delight in the adventures found in this make-believe kingdom.

In this figurine, little "Shadra" is daydreaming about "Escublar the Emperor Dragon," a hero in Krystonia *for saving the land from evil. She's imagining what the emperor looks like — dressed in a purple robe and jewels with a noble expression.*

"Graffyn" may have the toughest job of all the wizards. He negotiates the transportation contracts with the dragon's leader "Grumblypeg Grunch." Nowhere is there a more zany bunch than The Dragon Society of Carin Tor. "Zanzibar" is always looking for adventure even if he has to make it up. "Jumbly" can't stop juggling, and "Stoope the Stupendous" can't wait to show off his latest magic trick. Maybe he will make himself disappear.

The *Krystonia* stories also tell about the trolls, "Maj-Drons" and the dreaded "Hagga-Beast." Remember you are safe in the comfort of the words of "Kephren." Who is "Kephren" you say? He is the teller of tales and translator of scrolls that arrive daily by dragon transport. From these scrolls, he recounts the exciting stories for the *Krystonia* books. Do not be deceived by his comfortable position, for since the arrival of the mysterious Root, his life has been disrupted more than he would care.

Never a Day Without a New Collector

The Krystonia Collectors Club lets everyone enjoy these magical stories and characters even more. The troll "Twingnuk" is the members-only figurine for 1995. His cart, which he uses to mine for krystals in the mountains of Kappah, is a free gift for members. The concept of having a related gift and members-only figurine was started in the club's third year and has been very popular. Members also receive a quarterly newsletter, in which the introduction is narrated by a *Krystonia* character. With 1996 marking the 10th anniversary of *Krystonia*, special surprises are planned. A one-year membership in the club is $25.00. For information, write the Krystonia Collectors Club, 110 E. Ellsworth, Ann Arbor, MI 48108.

The Founding of *Krystonia* and Its Wonderful Tales

Krystonia started in a tiny factory in England, where its creators tapped into the British tradition of excellence and generations of skilled artisans. Although Precious Art's original product lines were produced in the Far East, company officials decided to change locations, knowing the collection needed special care in combining high-quality collectibles with enjoyable stories. *Krystonia* quickly outgrew its original studios and a modern facility was built in Chesterton, England, where all of Precious Art's English products are now produced. Using cold-cast porcelain, the hand-painted figurines and every sculpted detail are carefully monitored throughout the production process. Of course, each character must have its own sparkling krystal adornment for the finishing touch.

While *Krystonia* is made in England, the collection was born from the hearts and minds of David Lee Woodard and Pat Chandok. They spend countless hours making sure that no two characters are the same, while leading a creative team of artists who breath life into every *Krystonia* resident. Without just the right design and color, each figurine may never make it to the production stage. Once it is ready for production, the hardest part follows: deciding on a name. This could take weeks. After all, you must remember that there are no "Bob" the dragons in *Krystonia*.

Storylines for the books come from Dave, Pat and Mark Scott. They collaborate to bring to life all the different characters and adventures. After one book is completed, they start planning the next — which is sure to be filled with pages of fantasy and fun.

New Lines Celebrate the Beauty of Nature

Always looking to develop new products, Precious Art/Panton introduced two lines in 1995. While different in appearance, *Rainforest Children* and *Funny Galore* both reflect an ecological theme. *Rainforest Children* symbolizes the bond among children, wildlife and nature. With their homes being destroyed, the *Rainforest Children* seek help to save the planet with their animal kingdom friends, which are portrayed as endangered and unprotected species. *Rainforest Children* was created to show the inevitability of extinction if no one shows concern for the environment. A portion of the sales of this new line is donated to

Created by Mary Ann Orr, a South African artist, the Funny Galore *collection celebrates the humor, color and beauty of nature. There's* Funny Birds, Funny Frogs *and* Funny Cats *to make everyone laugh. Each figurine is brightly painted for a whimsical look.*

Rainforest Children *shows the special, unspoken bond between children and nature. In this figurine, a child nestles up against a tiger, just one of several endangered or unprotected species that the* Rainforest Children *want to help save. A portion of the sales of this collection is donated to Conservation International.*

Conservation International.

Funny Galore is the creation of Mary Ann Orr, a South African artist. After Mary Ann and her family found themselves caught up in the trappings of a young Yuppie lifestyle, they sold everything and escaped to an idyllic forest on the coast. Returning to the very roots of nature, they decided to make a living in the pottery business. In order to tempt her dormant artistic soul out of hibernation, Mary Ann used clay to reveal her feelings about the relationship between man and nature.

She found herself fascinated by "how enormous the controversy of issues such as water pollution, air pollution and over population of man had affected our little creatures."

She may not be an authority on ecological issues, but she realizes many feel powerless and watch helplessly as scientists, biologists and politicians shape the future of the planet. Without wanting to ponder the "doom and disaster" of these issues, she chose instead to highlight the adaptability and pristine beauty of nature, which

comes across in her colorful work.

Mary Ann's brightly painted animals are bound to make anyone smile. Her *Funny Birds* result from a mixture of feathered friends. *Funny Cats* find their names from *Puss In Boots* and *Funny Frogs* get their names from the silly noises that they make. This is only the start of Mary Ann's work for Precious Art.

Besides these new collections and *Krystonia*, Precious Art/Panton also features several other lines. The *Safari Kingdom* and *Mischievous Mice* were introduced in 1989. *Safari Kingdom* features African and American animals in their natural habitats and often in mother and baby poses. The *Mischievous Mice* cold cast figurines eat fruit, climb on old books or live humbly and happily in an old can. What's next? The future looks bright not only in the land of *Krystonia* but throughout the company, which will continue growing with more introductions and stories from a far-away magical land.

Precious Art/Panton
110 E. Ellsworth Road
Ann Arbor, MI 48108
(313) 677-3510
Fax (313) 677-3412

COLLECTORS' CLUB

Krystonia Collectors Club
110 E. Ellsworth Road
Ann Arbor, MI 48108
(313) 677-3510

Annual Dues: $25.00
Club Year: February 1-January 31

Benefits:
• Membership Gift: Figurine
• Opportunity to Purchase Members-Only Figurine
• Quarterly Newsletter, "Phargol-Horn"
• Membership Card
• Store Events/Artist Signings

PULASKI FURNITURE CORPORATION

Displaying Your Favorite Collectibles
with Style and Care

Collectors across the country have found a special place in their hearts for figurines, plates, dolls, ornaments, bells, crystal, cottages and teddy bears. But where can you keep your prized possessions safely and beautifully displayed for all to enjoy?

Pulaski Furniture Corporation, America's largest producer of curio cabinets, helps collectibles find a home they deserve. The company's Collectors Curios feature a variety of styles and finishes featuring mirrored backs and canister lighting that create the ultimate showcase for a few of your favorite things. Are your collectibles collecting dust? Are they packed away in the attic, basement or closet? Are they lined up on shelves that are either too high or low to see? PFC Collectors Curios give figurines a stage, dolls a house, bears a den and cottages a neighborhood, where they can be admired by friends, family and guests.

Pulaski Furniture Corporation is dedicated to crafting quality furniture that fits any room and budget. The company is also dedicated to providing collectors with curio cabinets that let treasures move into their own little corner of the world.

PFC Collectors Curios Continue Tradition of Fine Furniture

Founded in Pulaski, Virginia, in 1955, Pulaski Furniture Corporation is one of the country's largest furniture producers with domestic and export sales exceeding $175 million annually. Pulaski dominates the curio cabinet market with 62 percent of all sales in the United States.

In 1996, Pulaski repackaged its curio program under the PFC Collectors Curio umbrella to better target this $7.5 billion market. The company manufactures hundreds of design and finish combinations in its curio line, offering collectors a wide variety to choose from, complementing any decor. PFC Collectors Curios advertisements can be seen in several leading collectible magazines, promoting the furniture as offering the perfect place for everything from porcelain figurines to wooden nutcrackers. More and more collectors nationwide are educating themselves on caring for and displaying their cherished collectibles. In doing so, they are turning to Pulaski for the answer.

The company plans to continue serving collectors with its broad line of curio cabinets and curio clocks. Ridgeway Curio Clocks, a division of Pulaski Furniture Corp., features a grandfather clock surrounded by shelves for collectibles, making anyone's treasures even more timeless.

PFC Collectors Club Welcomes Charter Members

To establish stronger ties and get to know its curio customers, Pulaski launched the PFC Collectors Club in the summer of 1996. Charter members receive the company's first limited edition figurine, "Curios Henry," an adorable and popular Jack Russell Terrier. The hand-painted polymer figurine is available free to collectors who join the Club — and can be displayed in the company's curio cabinets. An annual membership is $29.95.

"Curios Henry will become a very cherished collectible," says Randy Chrisley, Pulaski's vice president of sales. "And because of its limited distribution, we expect the series to eventually do quite well on the secondary market." For more information on the Club, please write to Pulaski Furniture Corporation, Attention: Collectors Club, P.O. Box 1371, Pulaski, VA 24301.

Pulaski Furniture Corporation offers a complete line of Collectors Curios in a variety of styles and finish to suit any decor. Curios feature mirrored backs and canister lighting, creating a beautiful showcase for collectibles.

For the first time, Pulaski Furniture Corporation has launched a club especially for collectors. Charter members of the PFC Collectors Club can receive "Curios Henry," a limited edition figurine that comes free with the $29.95 annual Club fee. The figurine features a popular and adorable Jack Russell Terrier.

HomeTrack Collection, a line of curios, clocks, hall trees, consoles, tables and recliners that target racing fans. The collection is sold exclusively through the large furniture chain Heilig-Meyers. Over the years, Pulaski has been recognized for its creative furniture, most of which can be attributed to its renowned designer Leonard Eisen. Pulaski furniture, curios, clocks and accessories can be found at thousands of independent furniture stores, department stores and major furniture chains nationwide.

A Full Line of Furniture

Curios are part of Pulaski's accessories division, which also includes hall trees, tables and consoles. Other business segments of the corporation include Ridgeway Clocks' grandfather, wall and mantel clocks; casegoods for bedrooms, dining rooms and living rooms; Accentrics, occasional furniture with a European accent; and Accents-To-Go, a furniture line that can fold down to fit in cars.

Pulaski also owns Craftique Furniture, a Mebane, North Carolina-based manufacturer of high-end 18th and 19th century mahogany reproductions.

In 1996, Pulaski launched the

The HomeTrack recliner is part of a racing-inspired furniture collection by Pulaski Furniture Corporation. The HomeTrack Collection, which also includes curios, clocks, hall trees, consoles and tables, is available exclusively at Heilig-Meyers furniture stores.

Ridgeway Clocks, a division of Pulaski Furniture Corporation, presents a line of curio clocks that make timeless keepsakes. Available in a selection of designs and finishes, Ridgeway Curio Clocks offer collectors another opportunity to display any collection.

Pulaski Furniture Corporation
One Pulaski Square
Pulaski, VA 24301
(800) 287-4625

COLLECTORS' CLUB

PFC Collectors Club
P.O. Box 1371
Pulaski, VA 24301
(540) 980-7330

Annual Dues: $29.95
Renewal: $24.95
Club Year: Anniversary of Sign-Up Date

Benefits:
• Membership Kit: "Curios Henry," limited edition Jack Russell Terrier figurine, and other special members-only gifts
• Quarterly Newsletter, "The Yapper"
• Membership Card
• Special Sneak Previews and Member Incentives for Purchase of Pulaski Furniture

R.R. CREATIONS, INC.
Over One Million 'Windows on the World' Now Open Nationwide

What began as 'an open window of opportunity' became Doreen and Dave Ross' dream! Starting from a modest garage in Pratt, Kansas, R.R. Creations, under the Ross' guidance, has become one of the state's most distinguished small businesses.

Real estate. More than stocks, bonds or money markets, real estate has always been America's favorite investment! Buy a house and treasure it because it's uniquely yours. As a bonus, the longer you live there, the more valuable the property becomes.

R.R. Creations, a dynamic, young Midwest company with a passion for real estate, couldn't agree with this philosophy more. They've made one million buildings...and it's likely they'll make 200,000 more in the year ahead! Amazingly, not one required a plot of land or a building permit, because these distinct structures are finely crafted wood miniatures, styled and manufactured exclusively for the collectibles market.

Dave and Doreen Ross, owners of R.R. Creations, have single-handedly put miniature wood houses on the collectibles map. Each time they place their trademark logo, an open window, on a finished piece, they move one step

closer to a shared dream. "The open window symbolizes something we both believe in," explains Doreen. "When God closes a door, He opens a window."

Doreen and husband Dave not only believe this inspired saying, they live it. Recalling the job loss that might have taken them away from the town they loved, both Rosses realized the choice was up to them.

If they stayed, they would need a way to earn a living, so Doreen asked Dave what he thought about making and selling wood miniature buildings, showcasing the distinct architectural styles of the Midwest. After much prayer and considerable research, the couple sprung into action. "We set up a carpentry shop in the family garage," Doreen recalls fondly. "We started without even knowing what a silk screen looked like!"

History Repeats Itself All Over America

When the Rosses begin creating a new design, they carefully select structures for their historic and aesthetic appeal. Their first creation, the "Pratt County Courthouse," established their signature style. Since then, an exciting array of landmark buildings have come from the busy workshops of R.R. Creations. Recent examples are typical of the range and scope of the company's offerings: Susan B. Anthony's residence, Betsy Ross' home and the houses of John F. Kennedy, Mark Twain and Harriet Beecher Stowe.

In addition to creating the homesteads of "the rich and the famous," the Rosses also craft custom-made 'memories to order.' Collectors provide a photograph of a beloved home, school, courthouse or other special place. The Rosses will then make as few as 12 for them at a reasonable $10.00 to

$20.00 each. "Whether or not we like the building a customer asks us to recreate is never an issue. We just want to make it as accurately as possible," Doreen Ross assures us. "The people just love them because it's their special memory. Each time we make and paint a building, we try to see it through their eyes."

By the way, houses, schools and other typical requests are occasionally interspersed with a challenge to make something that's never been done before. Dave and Doreen fondly recall some of the more unusual requests coming their way, such as the high school band seeking replicas of their equipment truck as a fund raiser, an order for the creation of football stadiums and an unforgettable request for ten-seated outhouses!

Doreen believes the possibilities for such creations are endless. "There are so many opportunities to do different buildings, many of which no longer exist. Even a small town can afford to have our miniature wood buildings done affordably, capturing forever a beloved memory. We all know people who collect a single subject, like a firehouse because their grandfather or dad

A simple piece of wood and a set of detailed sketches eventually became a brightly colored collection of buildings in an amazing variety of architectural styles. Over one million have been sold...and R.R. Creations is only nine years old!

Collectors look for the benchmark 'open window' on every R.R. Creations building. It's applied by silk screening carefully cut wood to ensure a perfectly detailed and affordable limited edition treasure.

was a fireman. These are the kinds of 'unforgettable memories' we recreate every day," she adds.

The Crafting of a Typical Open Window Treasure

The Rosses love to innovate, but when it comes to the process they use to craft their buildings, there are no experiments or short cuts.

In the beginning, absolute quality was assured because Doreen and Dave performed every step in the production process themselves. They did the research, cut the wood, hand-painted the finished product and marketed it. Happily, growth has forced an expansion. Though Dave and Doreen are still hands-on owners, a skilled staff of Pratt residents now help the company enjoy its meteoric growth.

The division of labor takes advantage of Dave and Doreen's unique talents. Dave and his crew handle the actual production of each piece. Doreen and her staff then guide the cut wood through a computer-based drafting and design system that allows everyone to see exactly how the trim, color and embellishments will appear on the building, even before the silk screen is produced. Color separations are done on site. Screening takes place only after background colors and edges are hand-painted onto the cut forms.

Only when each structure has been dried, sealed, inspected and declared perfect do the Rosses add their signature, certifying it a true R.R. Creation.

By the way, early versions of their window logo were burned into the bottom of each piece, but contemporary buildings display a silk-screened logo on the reverse side, adjacent to the historical fact sheet applied to the back of every structure.

From the Heartland to Harrod's to Hollywood!

Not long ago, millions of people shopping at London's famous store, Harrod's, had a chance to see an assortment of R.R. Creations' charming Midwest buildings. This appearance was the happy result of the state of Kansas' search for the best examples of Midwest craftsmanship for an "American Frontier" promotion.

During the preliminary search, the competition seemed formidable! "There were 500 booths set up at the Harrod's market in Wichita," Doreen recalls. "Everyone wanted to show their best wares and many booths showcased more than one line, so you can imagine how many products from Kansas were represented!" Happily, the Rosses learned their buildings were among only six companies selected to make the journey across the Atlantic.

"We were so fortunate to have been picked," Doreen says, recalling the 16 R.R. Creations on display at Harrod's. The experience inspired both Rosses to think about spreading their geographic wings. No sooner were those hopeful thoughts exchanged than the Rosses heard of another trade show in Wichita sponsored by America's Shopping Channel, QVC.

Again competing this time with 250 other companies for the few slots QVC hoped to fill, the Rosses talked with network representatives about their *Amish Collection*. The ten minute chat was less than memorable, and the Rosses went home vowing they'd be on QVC one day. Imagine their shock when a phone call from the

network came just two days later requesting an immediate shipment of 1,000 complete sets — that's 5,000 pieces — of the Amish village!

The rest, as they say, is history. Soon, Doreen and her Amish village were being beamed to 50 million homes across the United States plus an additional 17 million homes in England and Mexico.

Special Limited Editions Promise Exclusivity

When the Rosses sat down to begin their long-term planning in 1993, they decided the time had come to give collectors 'true limited edition works of art.' Beginning in 1994, every R.R. Creations structure was numbered, and all series were stringently limited to just 2,500.

The "limited edition decision" proved a popular one. Shops selling their buildings were thrilled. So were collectors, who could now look forward to all-important retirements such as these 1993 series, now no longer in production: the *Historical Collection II, Williamsburg Collection II, In the Country Series II* and *Christmas Memories Series II*. These collections join *Grandpas Farm Collection Series II, On the Square Series II* and *Amish Collection Series II* as prime candidates for strong secondary market activity in the years ahead.

Members of the Open Window Club House delight in all the information they receive about their personal real estate! Historical data is plentiful and members have the unique opportunity to choose their own gift from R.R. Creations comprehensive catalog of delights.

QVC, the popular television shopping network, knew their customers when they selected this example of true Americana, the Amish Collection, *to show to the nation. The Rosses were thrilled to have received an initial order for 5,000 pieces just two days after the series was previewed.*

R.R. Creations Celebrates Its Growing Collectors Club

Countrywide fans of R.R. Creations' miniatures have taken their passion one step further: they've joined the Open Window Club House Collectors Club. Even the name is like a fresh, spring breeze, and benefits for members are plentiful.

New and renewing members receive something out-of-the-ordinary: their choice of a free, hand-signed building from the company's current collection. Unlike collector clubs offering a single gift of the same style to everyone, the Open Window Club House encourages individual choice. The only proviso: the style must be in production.

Each year, a special "Members-Only" piece is created exclusively for Club Members. These are the rarest collectible offerings of all. 1995 members are given a chance to acquire a lovely handcrafted mill in a barnwood stain. Open Window Club Members also look forward to receiving a hard-bound catalog of all available designs that's updated twice yearly.

An official newsletter, "Club House News," is packed with information, published bi-annually and eagerly awaited. Fees are $22.50 initially; members renew each year for $19.50.

In addition to these terrific membership perks, a multi-purchase gratitude rebate program is now in place to reward loyal collectors.

As a service to those seeking to track and evaluate their collections, the Rosses have established a toll-free telephone line. You are invited to call 1-800-779-3610 to get information about any building ever crafted by the Rosses or call 1-800-779-3610 to book a fascinating tour of R.R. Creations, if you happen to be coming through Kansas. Advance notice is required, but the stop is both fun and educational...well worth the trip!

Those who wish information by mail may write to Debi Gaston at R.R. Creations, Inc., P.O. Box 8707, Pratt, Kansas 67124. You can be sure there will be a friendly voice at the end of the phone line or a cheery smile on the face of the person opening your letter. After all, the reason the Rosses started their company was as simple as not wanting to leave the small town they had grown to love with its friendly hearts and talented hands!

R. R. Creations
P.O. Box 8707
Pratt, KS 67124
(800) 779-3610
Fax (316) 672-5850

COLLECTORS' CLUB/TOUR

Open Window Club House Collectors Club P.O. Box 8707 Dept. Club Pratt, KS 67124 (800) 779-3610 **Annual Dues:** $22.50 - Renewal: $19.50 **Club Year:** Anniversary of Sign-Up Date	**Benefits:** • Membership Gift: Choice of Hand-Signed Building from Current Line • Opportunity to Purchase Members-Only Piece • Bi-annual Newsletter, "Club House News" • Hard-Bound Catalog with Binder • Personalized Membership Card • Buy/Sell Matching Service
Open Window Video Tour P.O. Box 8707 Pratt, KS 67124 (800) 779-3610 **Hours:** Tour is limited to groups only and must be scheduled in advance. **Admission Fee:** None	The tour includes a history of R.R. Creations, tour of the showroom, drafting demonstration and a video tour of the manufacturing facilities.

RECO INTERNATIONAL CORP.

Committed Leadership and Award-Winning Artists Keep Reco at the Pinnacle of Collectibles Excellence for Nearly Three Decades

Sandra Kuck's "Moments of Caring" warms our hearts as a sweet little girl – surrounded by real and stuffed animal friends – waters her pretty flowers. The open window and the graceful vines make this a welcoming image, and the child's lovely face and glowing complexion provide each viewer with a sense of happy well-being.

When Heio Reich founded Reco International Corp. in 1967, his goal was to provide American collectors with a panorama of world-class collectibles in a host of fine art media. As a native of Berlin, Germany, Reich enjoyed a great many contacts with European art studios. Thus Reco gained fame by introducing plates from some of Europe's most celebrated makers, including Fuerstenberg, Royale, Dresden, Royal Germania, Crystal, King's and Moser.

Many of the plates Reco imported to the United States have risen substantially in price since their introduction in the late 1960s and early 1970s. But Reich sensed a golden opportunity in 1977, and he steered his business in a whole new direction. Since then, Reco International has reigned as one of the nation's top producers of limited edition plates by renowned American painters like Sandra Kuck, John McClelland and Jody Bergsma.

While some studios specialize in only one area such as child-subject art or wildlife, Reco seeks out artists of excellence in many different subjects and styles. Sandra Kuck's Victorian children and the fantasy visions of Jody Bergsma take center stage in the current Reco line-up. Retired from the active plate market, John McClelland nonetheless remains an all-time collector favorite for his paintings of adorable children. In the past, Dot and Sy Barlowe created vivid portraits of wildlife and nature for Reco, while Clemente Micarelli painted homages to the ballet, religious events and weddings. Subjects as diverse as Edwardian bears and military art also may be found in the Reco archives.

A Pledge to Collectors: Only the Very Best

While Reco's productions represent a panorama of art styles, media and subjects, Heio Reich's company philosophy unites all Reco creations with a shared vision of excellence. Reich's goal for Reco is that the company creates objects to bring enjoyment, a life-long interest and hobby to collectors, meanwhile providing beautiful products for the public. Reco's commitment to produce only the very best art on plates and in other media will continue into the future – just as it has since 1967.

Reich and his artists have never sought personal glory or awards – indeed, they consider their finest accolade the gleam in a happy collector's eyes. Even so, Heio Reich has been the recipient of most every prestigious honor available to a collectibles marketer or producer. These include "Vendor of the Year," "Producer of the Year," the "Lee Benson Memorial Award," the "International Collectible Achievement Award" and the "Silver Chalice Award" for selected plates.

Reich has long been an active member and leader in the National Association of Limited Edition Dealers (NALED) and the Plate Makers Guild, and he was a charter member of the Board of Directors of Collectors' Information Bureau.

What's more, John McClelland and Sandra Kuck have been lauded at scores of conventions and collectors' gatherings with "Plate of the Year," "Artist of the Year," and many other honors. Indeed, Ms. Kuck is acknowledged as the most honored collectibles artist of all time – including an unprecedented six consecutive "Artist of the Year" awards from the National Association of Limited Edition Dealers. Heio Reich is particularly proud that Reco International Corp. has exhibited at every South Bend Collectibles Exposition since the famous show's inception over 20 years ago.

"Peace at Last" by Jody Bergsma explores the natural relationship of Native American peoples with the wildlife that grace their glorious lands. A proud eagle forms the backdrop for a full-body portrait of an Indian brave with his horse, celebrating a victory that will bring peace to his people. This work of art is the second issue in Ms. Bergsma's Totems of the West plate collection.

The Renowned Plate Maker Offers Works in Other Popular Media

Although Reco's fame stems primarily from works of art in fine porcelain, the firm has marketed and manufactured pieces in many other materials and media over the years. The early King's plates, for example, featured delicate, bas-relief floral motifs, and the Royale Germania plates were crafted of gleaming crystal.

Say the name "Reco" to a contemporary collector, however, and he or she is most likely to think of porcelain plates with art by Kuck, McClelland and Bergsma. Another important concentration for Reco in the porcelain plate realm is what Heio Reich likes to call "Special Occasions" plates. The firm's early European-made series often focused on Christmas, Mother's Day, Father's Day and Easter. Sandra Kuck's Christmas series — showing little ones in holiday scenes — have won many a collector's heart. Ms. Kuck also has created original art to honor Mother's Day, christenings, weddings, and other memorable days.

Reco crafts figurines both in shimmering porcelain and using the cold-cast method: a medium which is growing in popularity because of the intricate detail it can capture. John McClelland's silky white angels helped establish Reco as an important maker of three-dimensional art. Now Jody Bergsma enhances this well-earned reputation with the adorable animals in her *Laughables* line.

Sandra Kuck's precious children seemed destined to come alive as elegant, collectible dolls — and Reco was up to the challenge of creating heirloom-quality bisque beauties. Ms. Kuck's lovely characters are captured in fine porcelain and painted to enhance the delicate blush of a cheek...the grace of a child's tiny fingers and hands. The dolls' costumes faithfully portray Ms. Kuck's love for Victoriana and whimsy — with flowing frocks, charming accessories, and marvelous trimmings in ribbon and lace. What's more, each Sandra Kuck doll tells a story — in fact, the doll *herself* is sharing a story in a recent Kuck introduction, "Reading with Teddy."

Using Proverbs 22:17 — "A cheerful heart is good medicine" — as inspiration, Jody Bergsma created these adorable figurines called Laughables. *They are, clockwise from center top: "Whiskers & Willie," "Sunny," "Daisy & Jeremiah," "Annie, George & Harry," "Millie & Mittens" and "Patches & Pokey." Each comes complete with its own humorous saying for life's ups and downs.*

Ever on the alert for new ways to share the art of favorite painters with collector friends, Reco has diversified its offerings to include music boxes and keepsake boxes, each enhanced by beloved artwork. Some of the boxes are handcrafted of walnut and mahogany, while others are made of shimmering porcelain.

Reco Nurtures An Extended Family of Artists

Reco International remains a family-owned business, and the firm cultivates a warm and friendly atmosphere: both in its internal operations and in its relationships with artists. Each Reco employee takes a personal interest in the products they help create, and in the artists whose work inspires each new edition.

Although John McClelland now is retired from the creation of collector plate art, many of his works are still available on the primary and secondary markets. Later series may be acquired at issue price through many dealers, while earlier McClelland favorites are available only at auctions and through exchanges of various types. Reco

International continues to receive scores of letters from McClelland fans and collectors, and it is clear that the personable artist remains a favorite for many.

Sandra Kuck has charmed Reco collectors with her romantic and nostalgic portraits for more than 15 years. Ever since her "Sunday Best" plate was introduced in 1983, Ms. Kuck has reigned as the "sweetheart" of collectors throughout North America and beyond. She enjoys a remarkable gift for intricate detail work, as well as a deep love for "all things Victorian." Combine this with her ability to capture the fresh-faced innocence of little ones, and it is easy to understand why collectors are so devoted to Ms. Kuck and her creations.

Jody Bergsma has a whimsical and joyous heart, which she displays in all her fantasy art. Her unicorns and dragons combine mystery with beauty, and her "Little People" and animals are equally endearing. Ms. Bergsma recently has expanded her repertoire beyond watercolor prints and collectors plates to include the *Laughables* figurines — a lighthearted group of animal portraits that are sure to bring a smile to each

Lucky Teddy! His owner — a beautiful little girl with a lacy Victorian frock, silky slippers, and a flower-trimmed hat — has decided to read him a book called Teddy's Adventures! *For the occasion, this cuddly stuffed bear has donned his own wire-rimmed glasses. This whimsical doll charmer was designed by Sandra Kuck and is entitled "Reading with Teddy."*

recipient. What's more, the artist shows her contemplative side in a plate series entitled *Totems of the West.* To create this dramatic collection, Ms. Bergsma traveled extensively and studied the spiritual forces that Native American tribes consider sacred.

Sandra Kuck Collectors Enjoy the Kuck Newsletter

Reco International Corp. publishes a bi-annual newsletter to keep collectors informed about Sandra Kuck and the wonderful artwork she creates. The newsletter provides an "up-close and personal" glimpse into the world of this lovely, warm lady and her world of "updated Victoriana." It also offers Kuck collectors news about upcoming products and their availability.

To add your name to the mailing list and receive the Sandra Kuck Newsletter at no charge, simply send your name and address to: Sandra Kuck Newsletter, c/o Reco International Corp., P.O. Box 951, Port Washington, New York 11050.

Reco International Corp.
150 Haven Avenue
Port Washington, NY 11050
(516) 767-2400
Fax (516) 767-2409

ROMAN, INC.
Premier Collectible Producer Meets Demand for Angels for All Reasons, All Seasons with Magnificent Works by American, European Artists

"Alyssa—Nature's Angel" is the first in a series of limited edition figurines for Roman, Inc.'s popular Seraphim Classics™ *collection.*

With a 32-year history of successfully responding to collector angel needs, Roman, Inc. finds itself in the unique position of being perfectly equipped with a variety of breathtaking masterpieces for the current upsurge in angel collectibles interest. The company lists more than 400 kinds and 16 collections of angels in a virtual kaleidoscope of sizes, shapes and mediums. They range from porcelain bisque, resin and papier maché to sinamay, acrylic, brass, fabric and glass.

Seraphim Classics™ by Seraphim Studio Rank as Top U.S. Angels

Currently, Roman, Inc. is the nation's leading angel resource with collections featuring celestial messengers that have captured collectors' hearts and minds. Whether you've browsed casually or you are an avid fan of angels, you have heard of or seen the *Seraphim*

Classics™ angels from Roman, Inc. that are currently ranked as the most popular in the United States. Ethereal beauties with graceful flowing robes and tresses featuring gloriously sculpted wings, they embody the romantic classical style reminiscent of Michelangelo and subsequent fine art of the 1700s and 1800s. The seemingly translucent resin figurines by Roman's Seraphim Studio are being unanimously hailed by collectors as heavenly masterpieces.

Seraphim Studio artists created original art in 1995 for the exquisite first *Seraphim Classics* limited edition figure, "Alyssa - Nature's Angel," who rapidly found her home in prized collections. Spring '95 introductions included a collection of 4" miniature figures, postcards and a full color journal, all featuring the complete set of 12 angels. Collectors eagerly anticipate 1996 when the Seraphim Studio debuts six new figures, four ornaments, a pin and a nativity.

Fontanini Heirloom Nativity Angels by Simonetti Set Standards

"We've always held prominence in this area because of our long-standing relationship with Italy's famous House of Fontanini® and their master sculptor Elio Simonetti," explains owner and Chief Executive Officer Ronald T. Jedlinski. "The Fontanini angels and cherubs are so breathtaking that Simonetti's designs have become a standard many try to emulate. That is why Fontanini instituted worldwide copyrights that Roman, Inc. diligently defends as the exclusive Fontanini source in North America."

Simonetti has created over 200 master sculptures for angels and cherubs during his 40-year career with the Fontanini family. Many collectors hail the magnificent life-sized Heirloom Nativity that is featured in the hit

movie *Home Alone* and graces the Pope's private quarters in the Vatican as Simonetti and Fontanini's crowning achievement. These 50" tall masterpieces exhibit the full scope of the gifted Simonetti's sculpting and the Fontanini dedication to their almost 90-year tradition of excellence in artistry and crafting.

Speaking of the most recent character he has created for this famous set, Simonetti has long believed the angel is a very important element in his celebration of the birth of Christ, and had always planned to add it to the life-sized Nativity. It is fortuitous that his inspiration to shape this figure with his gifted hands came at a time when all attention is focused so strongly on angels.

The history of the House of Fontanini is one steeped in tradition and family values. In 1908, the family

One of a host of celestial messengers ranked as the top angel collection in the nation, the Seraphim Classics™ *collection embodies ethereal beauty with unequaled grace and elegance. "Seraphina—Heaven's Keeper" portrays a graceful angel ministering to a babe in her arms.*

The best-seller Millenium™ *Series of limited edition plates and companion ornaments will issue editions annually until the year 2000.*

patriarch, Emanuele Fontanini, launched the company when he began working with the finest sculptors and painters in Tuscany, Italy, to craft figures and decorations of heirloom quality in a one-room workshop. His sons joined him and, in turn, passed their tradition of superior craftsmanship to their sons. Today, the humble workshop has given way to spacious facilities 60 miles from Florence, in Bagni di Lucca, a region steeped in the rich heritage of the glorious Renaissance period.

The creation of the Fontanini figures is truly a family affair from concept to completion. The exquisite sculptures begin in the skilled hands of Simonetti. A meticulous molding process follows under vigilant Fontanini supervision. Finally, each figure is painstakingly painted by hand by artisans utilizing skills passed from generation to generation in their families.

During his four decades with the House of Fontanini, Simonetti has fine-tuned his already superlative artistry with his current work reflecting the maturing of his perceptions and talents. He explores new and unique areas of design in the crafting of a duo

of 12" celestial musicians. Divine in detail with golden flowered accents on the front of their flowing gowns, these sophisticated, stylized angels can stand alone or with the 12" *Heirloom Nativity Collection.*

In 1991, the master sculptor pledged to resculpt all the original 5" Nativity figures he created at the outset of his career with Fontanini. As he resculpts the new concepts, the originals are retired. Simonetti resculpted the 5" standing and kneeling angels that were retired the previous year. Since 1991, 11 five-inch Nativity figures have been retired.

Plate, Ornament *Seraphim™ Collection* and *Millenium™ Series* Earn Laurels

FARO Studios of Italy is the font of creativity that brings international limited edition plates of incomparable beauty to aficionados of this medium. Beginning with the *Millenium™ Series* in 1992 and continuing until the year 2000, FARO's designer Ennio Morcaldo has drafted art that sculptor Alfonso Lucchesi fashions into bas relief plates of infinite grace. Themes center around the birth of the Blessed Child focusing on the Madonna and always featuring angels in either central roles as in "The Annunciation" or supportive as in "Peace on Earth." These tremendously popular plates of pristine white oxolyte also have companion ornaments reflecting the grace and flow of the sculpting in miniature. Oxolyte is a blending of polymer resin and powdered alabaster. When polished, the plates and ornaments resemble marble.

"Rosalyn - Rarest of Heaven" — the first limited edition in the *Seraphim Collection* from FARO has proven rare, indeed, by garnering the *Collector Editions* 1995 "Award of Excellence" honor in its category. The 1995 issue in this plate collection featuring angels is "Helena - Heaven's Herald" — a portrayal of an angel with gloriously sculpted wings full spread with a dove perched on her hand. *Seraphim Collection*

companion ornaments again mirror Rosalyn and Helena in exquisitely detailed mini-form.

Angela Tripi Creates Museum Gallery Messengers

Sicilian sculptor Angela Tripi has forged a reputation for distinctive renderings of historical and biblical subjects. Her talent for instilling character into her unique sculptures has earned Tripi "Collectible Sculpture of Show" at the California International Collectibles Exposition in 1991. First, Tripi shapes and molds the clay, her preferred medium, into sculptures whose features reflect her years of studying the people of her homeland. Her figures are then costumed in garments of fabric, dramatically draped and fixed to a hard finish using a secret family formula. Tripi then hand paints each character, even the patterns on the cloth. Roman translates her originals into durable resin, faithfully preserving every nuance.

First, Tripi created angels for her religious nativities that have earned acclaim and best sculpture honors in Palermo and Sorrento. Next, Tripi explored heaven's creatures further with limited editions figures and ornaments including "Serenade," "Rhapsody" and "Sonata" figurines and annual ornaments.

Home-Grown Jauquet Contributes Americana Winged Creatures

With exhibits in the Smithsonian Institute and top U.S. galleries and features in magazines, word is spreading on the country charm of Bill Jauquet's woodcarvings. His sculpts in aged white cedar preserve a vanishing, more relaxed way of life in America. His deceptively simple renderings of life in rural America, including Amish, farm and Native American themes, are also giving him a successful entry into the collectibles world.

Jauquet's Midwestern charm surfaces in his *Americana Collection*, which provides a whimsical look into rural America, complete with barnyard animals and folksy characters. The collection expanded into Christmas with the addition of Santa Claus figures, ornaments and a limited edition plate. In 1996, Jauquet will introduce a collection of angels. Jauquet took his imagination to another level when he debuted *Molly's World* in 1995. A loving gift to his baby granddaughter, *Molly's World* is a collection of whimsical animals that mirror the wondrous active imaginations of small children.

Why Angels?

The reasons behind the ongoing popularity of angels are as infinite as the heavens are high. Some collectors cite the sense of hope and protection that angels offer; others value the spirituality angels provide in difficult times. Perhaps the world's most prolific angel collector (and a member of the Fontanini Collectors' Club), Joyce Berg of Beloit, Wisconsin, boasts more than 10,000 angels in her collection. Like the majority of angel collectors, she began

collecting long before it became in vogue, when traveling through Florida in 1976. Joyce happened upon an antique store with cherubs in the window. The rest, as they say, is angel history. Her Fontanini figures are among the most cherished in her collection. Joyce's devotion to angels has sparked a group of women in Beloit to create an angel museum, paying tribute to a variety of celestial messengers.

Avid collectors such as these are the reason Roman, Inc. will continue to offer "the most angels this side of heaven," as well as a wide variety of distinctive collectibles.

"Rosalyn–Rarest of Heaven" is a Collector Editions *award-winning plate from the* FARO Studios Seraphim Collection.™

Roman, Inc.
555 Lawrence Avenue
Roselle, IL 60172-1599
(708) 529-3000
Fax (708) 529-1121

COLLECTORS' CLUB/TOUR

Fontanini Collectors' Club[SM]
555 Lawrence Avenue
Roselle, IL 60172
(800) 729-7662

Annual Dues: $19.50 - Renewal: $17.50
Club Year: Anniversary of Sign-Up Date

Benefits:
• Membership-Gift: Symbol-of-Membership Figure
• Opportunity to Purchase Members-Only Figure
• Quarterly Newsletter, "The Fontanini Collector"
• Binder with Club Logo
• Personalized Membership Card
• Club Pin
• Fontanini Registry Guide
• Research Service
• Advance Notice of Tour Appearances by Fontanini Family Members
• Travel Opportunities
• Contests

House of Fontanini Studio Tour in Italy
c/o The Fontanini Collectors' Club
555 Lawrence Avenue
Roselle, IL 60172
(800) 729-7662

Hours: Advance Reservations through the Fontanini Collectors' Club
Admission Fee: None

For collectors planning a trip to Italy, the House of Fontanini offers tours of their facilities in Bagni di Luca, Italy.

ROYAL DOULTON
Child Figures and a Family of Collectibles
Continue a Tradition of Excellence

Generations of collectors have treasured the figurines from the famed British firm of Royal Doulton. Whether historical legends, childhood story-book favorites, 17th century women or images of nature, the three-dimensional works of art open the doors to a world of discovery. It is a world that has attracted many thousands of collectors, most of whom started off with a solitary figurine but were drawn back again and again to the memories and passion found in every piece.

Each character tells its own story through the captivating expressions, fine detail, remarkable design and painstaking craftsmanship that are international hallmarks of Royal Doulton. Many figurines have become heirlooms, passed down for children and future generations to enjoy. Fittingly, children have always held an important place in the collection.

Bringing Back Childhood Memories

Introduced in 1913, the first child figurine ever produced by Royal Doulton was titled "Darling." Inspired by poems by A.A. Milne and Robert Louis Stevenson, the figurine received its name after Queen Mary picked it out during a visit to the Royal Doulton factory and exclaimed, "Isn't he a darling!" She — and many other collectors — immediately fell in love with the small child dressed in a white nightgown. A version of this figurine still exists in the current product line.

Since then, many other childhood subjects have been produced over the years, including such favorites as "This Little Pig," "Bo Peep" and "Dinky Do."

In the past several years, Royal Doulton has focused on creating more figures to evoke a certain nostalgia for childhood days gone by. A range of figures which shows a little girl with a dog in several poses has been a most sought

after group from Royal Doulton. These figures include "Sit," "Buddies," "Reward" and "Let's Play."

Still a popular theme with collectors, childhood offers continuing inspiration to Royal Doulton's artists. In keeping with this tradition and the popularity of these childhood subjects, several figurines were introduced in 1994: "Flowers For Mother," "Young Melody," "First Recital," "Mother's Helper," "A Posy for You" and "Special Friend," the first boy figurine in recent years.

Also introduced was "Hello Daddy" which portrays a little girl greeting her father over an old-fashioned, metal telephone. The figurines were designed to celebrate memorable family moments, such as "First Recital" and "Young Melody" to mark musical achievements while "Mother's Helper" and "Hello Daddy" pay tribute to the special relationship between parent and child.

In the spring of 1995, another range of three child figures premiered to the delight of collectors. "Hometime" portrays a little girl carrying her book-bag home from school while her dog trails alongside. "What's the Matter?" features another girl nursing her sick teddy bear back to health. A girl in her red dress carefully holds her lollipop in "Special Treat."

Royal Doulton has also introduced additions to previous series that bring back the joys of youth. "Dinnertime" shows a little girl holding a supper bowl while her grey poodle anxiously awaits his meal. Pets and children are familiar combinations in other subjects. "Home At Last" features a little girl lovingly cradling her cat, and "Faithful Friend" features another girl holding her spaniel. "Storytime" finds a little girl sitting on a bench reading her favorite nursery rhyme — the title of which actually appears in the book.

Royal Doulton is always planning

The warm bond between a father and daughter inspired this china figurine titled "Hello Daddy." A little girl calls up her father using an old-fashioned telephone, which adds a special touch to the piece. Modelled by artist Nada Pedley, the figurine was introduced in the fall of 1994.

more child figures, including a follow-up ballerina to the existing "Ballet Shoes" and "Little Ballerina," as well as other little boys.

Bunnykins Continues a Rich Tradition

Children and adults have also enjoyed other series that bring animals to life. *Bunnykins* was created by Royal Doulton in 1934 and has since become the delight of three generations. The lovable characters help celebrate the many happy moments in family life. Whether the rabbits are getting ready for bedtime or playing in the snow, each piece is designed to treasure today and tomorrow as even more new generations discover the adventures of *Bunnykins*. The most recent introductions include "Goodnight," "New Baby," "Girl Skater" and "Boy Skater."

Children always seem to find special friends in pets. In "Dinnertime," "Faithful Friend" and "Home At Last" (from left to right), Royal Doulton shows little girls giving tender loving care to their poodle, spaniel and cat. In "Storytime," another girl reads her favorite nursery rhyme.

Beatrix Potter's Famous Characters

Lifted from the pages of *The Tales of Peter Rabbit*, Royal Doulton has introduced the beloved characters from Beatrix Potter's timeless books. Among the most recent additions, "Mr. McGregor" has the distinction of being the only human figure in the collection. "Peter Ate A Radish" shows the rabbit's antics, that always seem to get him into trouble, and is perhaps the most popular image of the mischievous character. All of the pieces in this popular Beatrix Potter collection are faithful to the gentle nature of the original illustrations.

Royal Doulton Relives History and Romance

The *Royal Doulton Figure Collection* is now more varied and extensive than ever, with hundreds of different subjects. Besides the child figures, Royal Doulton is renowned for its pretty ladies dressed in the most fashionable attire of their day. Characters from literature and legend are portrayed in china and resin. Recent additions include "Sherlock Holmes," "Gulliver" and "Richard the Lionheart."

The first large-scale prestige sculpture in 15 years, "Charge of the Light Brigade" commemorates a glorious defeat in 1854 when 673 gallant British cavalry men faced the mighty mass of Russian guns during the Crimean War. Introduced in 1995, the magnificent work of art is made in bone china and features a soldier holding leather reins and a metal lance, rifle and sword. Because of the intricate detail and complexity of the piece, each figure takes months to make and must be special ordered.

Many famous characters have also been immortalized on the limited edition character and toby jugs: Cyrano de Bergerac, Robin Hood, Confucius, Captain Bligh, Abraham Lincoln, George Washington, Charles Dickens and Alfred Hitchcock, just to name a few. Collectors can also join the Royal Doulton International Collectors Club to acquire exclusive figurines and stay up to date on the latest introductions.

A Historical View of Royal Doulton

As the world's largest manufacturer and distributor in the premium ceramic tableware and giftware market, Royal Doulton has come a long way from its humble beginnings. In 1815, John Doulton invested in a small pottery plant in London that produced practical and decorative stoneware. His son, Sir Henry Doulton, extended the product range to include sanitary ware, drain pipes and other related items, thereby establishing the business at the forefront of the ceramics industry. In 1877, the business acquired an interest in a factory in Stoke-on-Trent and later began producing bone china tableware at that site.

In 1901, H.M. King Edward VII authorized Doulton to use the word "Royal" to describe its products. Production expanded in the 1930s to include figurines and other giftware items. In 1966, Royal Doulton was the first china manufacturer to be awarded The Queen's Award for Technological Advancement. The company's brands now include Royal Crown Derby, Minton, Royal Albert and Royal Doulton.

Attention to Detail and Tradition

Royal Doulton artists who paint the colorful costumes, facial expressions and subtle skin tones of the *Figure Collection* follow in a tradition that dates back to the 19th century. During the 1890s, one of the company's most

Many little girls around the world dream of dancing on stage in a famous ballet. And their dreams all begin in the dance studio, as they lace up their slippers and put on their pink tutus. In this heartwarming figurine titled "Ballet Shoes," a girl takes a step toward her aspirations in the spotlight.

A popular theme for collectors, childhood inspired these three 1995 bone china figures titled (from left to right) "Hometime," "What's the Matter?" and "Special Treat." A girl strides out purposely clutching her school bag as she's followed by her puppy in "Hometime." "What's the Matter?" is a question posed by a concerned girl cradling her teddy bear, who she suspects is ill. "Special Treat" is the reward of a big yellow lollipop for a good girl.

distinguished art directors, Charles Noke, modeled the earliest examples, "Cardinal Wolsey" and "Queen Catherine." By 1909, Noke wanted to revive the genre of Staffordshire figures and the first productions, based on classical and literary themes, caused quite a stir among critics.

More extensive production of the figure series began in 1920 after Doulton received rave reviews at the British Industries Fair. Since then, new additions have constantly been designed and more than 1,000 different figures have been created.

Royal Doulton has its own in-house design team, combining artistic talent and technical expertise. Giftware ranges have also increasingly been

designed to incorporate new working practices and decorating techniques, such as spray painting, the use of color clay, and the use of lithographic transfers for fine detail. These changes have resulted in greater consistency in quality, greater productivity, and the reduction of various decorating costs. Of course, a high level of hand work will always be maintained.

Royal Doulton
701 Cottontail Lane
Somerset, NJ 08873
(800) 68-CHINA
Fax (908) 356-9467

COLLECTORS' CLUB/TOURS

Royal Doulton International Collectors Club
701 Cottontail Lane
Somerset, NJ 08873
(800) 582-2102

Annual Dues: $25.00
Club Year: Anniversary of Sign-Up Date

Benefits:
• Opportunity to Purchase Members-Only Figurines
• Quarterly Magazine
• National Newsletter
• Advance Information on Introductions
• Historical Enquiry Service
• Invitations to Michael Doulton Events and Childsworld Artisan Events

Royal Doulton Factory Tours
Nile Street
Burslem Stoke-on-Trent Staffs ST6 2AJ
England
01144 1782 292292

Hours: Monday through Friday, 10:30 a.m. and 2 p.m.

Admission Fee: Nominal charge. For safety reasons the tour is not available for babies or children under ten years of age.

The Royal Doulton Factory Tour takes you behind the scenes at the world's leading fine china company. The tour also includes the Sir Henry Doulton Gallery, displaying examples of Royal Doulton products spanning over 170 years, and a factory gift shop.

Beswick Factory Tours
Gold Street
Longton Stoke-on-Trent ST3 2JP
England
01144 1782 292292
Hours: Monday through Friday, 10:15 a.m. and 2 p.m.
Admission Fee: Nominal charge. For safety reasons the tour is not available for babies or children under ten years of age.

The guided tour of the Beswick Factory allows visitors to see most stages of production of the Royal Doulton Character Jugs, animal models, studies of Beatrix Potter characters and *Bunnykins*. The Beswick Museum is open immediately before tours commence, and the Factory Gift Shop offers a wide selection of items from the John Beswick Studios.

SARAH'S ATTIC, INC.

The Journey to a Dream

"The Tuskegee Airman," a product of World War II was released by Sarah's Attic in June, 1995 (from the Sarah's Attic Historical Collection).

Sarah Johnston Schultz first graced this earth on a cold winter's day in the picturesque little village of Chesaning, Michigan. Sarah still calls this little town home. The influence of a small-town childhood coupled with the various experiences of running a nationwide business have helped Sarah to form her personal philosophy and thus the company philosophy of **Love**, **Respect** and **Dignity**. The purpose for and the effectiveness of each piece is carefully weighed before its debut. If it does not portray the qualities of Love, Respect and Dignity, the project is scuttled. Thus Sarah Schultz and Sarah's Attic, Inc. are as one.

Dreams Begin in Childhood

Sarah Johnston Schultz, daughter of William and Louise Johnston, was born

in Chesaning, Michigan on February 23, 1943. She was "forever creative" and "ready for action." Little Sarah was the village's first paper girl. When she was not peddling papers or doing other chores, she was scooting about town on her bike, stopping to chat with friends both old and new.

Sarah and her father loved to fish, and when the time could be spared, the two could be found with fishing poles, wading the waters near the dam of the Shiawassee River. The father-daughter closeness is evident in many of Sarah's creations including "Contentment" which sold out in 1992. This endearing figurine portrays Sarah and her beloved father enjoying their very favorite pastime and captures those profound feelings of Love, Respect and Dignity that they had for each other.

Sarah graduated from Our Lady of Perpetual Help High School, and later married her childhood sweetheart, Jack "Jackboy" Schultz. While Sarah worked at Michigan Bell Telephone Company, Jack attended college and received his degree in pharmacy. After graduation, Jack went to work in his father's pharmacy, which he and Sarah eventually purchased, and Sarah developed a thriving gift department in the store. During these lean years, Sarah had five children: Mark, Tim, Tom, Julie and Mike. Tim and Julie have joined their mother in her business, while Mark and Tom have pursued other careers, but still help out when needed. Mike is currently attending Michigan State University.

The Dream Begins

Sarah's hectic life became even busier when she discovered that the best-selling gift items in the Schultz Country Pharmacy were her own creations. Items such as her stenciled slates, boards, pictures and sweet-faced dolls were in much demand. A sales

representative suggested that she market her own creations, and after careful consideration, she decided, "Why not?" Demands on her time were already great, but since she was "itching" for some of her creativity to emerge, she began to create in earnest.

Sarah's business rapidly expanded from the dining room table, to a 5' by 20' room in the back of the very cramped pharmacy. In 1984, no longer able to "fit" everything and everybody into the available space, Sarah and company moved to the "Attic" which consisted of 1,200 square feet of floor space located above the pharmacy.

In 1986, pecan resin figurines replaced stenciled rulers and slates as the company's top sellers. The members of *Sarah's Gang*, "Tillie," "Willie," "Cupcake," "Twinkie," "Katie," "Whimpy" and baby "Rachael," became best sellers. Even though their poses and locales have changed through the years, they remain a mainstay of Sarah's Attic, Inc.

As the business grew, so did the need for more room. After much soul-searching and worry, Sarah purchased and remodeled a 10,000 square-foot grocery store on the Shiawassee River near the dam and close to the spot where she and her father had fished years earlier. It was the right decision, and today the production operations are located in this building. The art room, mail room and business offices remain in the "Attic" above the pharmacy. Despite all of the moves and growth in the company, Love, Respect and Dignity remain as the solid foundation for each collectible produced by Sarah's Attic.

Specializing in Dreams

Each of the collections created by Sarah and Sarah's Attic reflects a personal experience from the past or the present. For example, Sarah became

The Tender Moments-From Our Heart to Yours Collection *was created to promote aware-ness for special needs people. Sarah's Attic donates a portion of the proceeds from the sale of these figurines to two charities that help special children and adults, The Starlight Foundation and Hear Now.*

seriously ill with rheumatic fever when she was a child. Her father was very concerned and often brought angel figurines to her. To honor that special memory, the *Angels in the Attic Collection* was created.

In the past, it appeared that African-Americans were being ignored in the collectibles industry. Sarah saw the need for tasteful figurines to be created in their honor. Sarah's Attic filled that void by creating realistic black fig-urines that have become an important part of the company and of the col-lectibles industry. Sarah recalled the black family she grew up with in Chesaning, and from this enjoyable time in her life, the *Black Heritage Collection* was created.

The *Daisy Petals* series from the *Cherished Memories Collection* depicts Sarah's beloved children in their formative years. Thus "Spike" (Mark), "Sparky" (Tim), "Bomber" (Tom), "Jewel" (Julie) and "Stretch" (Mike) were born. To complete the family, "Sally Booba" (Sarah) and "Jack Boy" (Jack) came into existence. The *Cookie Kids & Friends©* also has mem-orable ties to the early days of the Schultz family. The growing business of Sarah's Attic allowed Sarah less time with her children. Years later, these "guilty feelings" led to the creation of the *Cookie Kids & Friends Collection.*

During the long illness of her mother Louise, Sarah searched for little pick-me ups to take to her. Sarah looked for mementos that would remind her mother of the pleasant chores and delightful activities that she cherished when she and her late husband, Willie Bill, were younger, healthy and raising their family. This was an impossible task because nothing was available. That difficult time in Sarah's life was the inspiration for the *Labor of Love Collection* which is currently in pro-duction. Although "Angel Willie Bill" and "Angel Louise" have departed this earth, they remain an influence on all that is created at Sarah's Attic.

The company continues to appreci-ate the efforts of the courageous patriots that have made America great. The *Spirit of America* and the *Black Heritage Collections* continue to feature pioneers that practiced a philosophy very similar to that of Sarah's Attic — Love, Respect and Dignity. Each one of these noble patri-ots has carved their niche in the history of the United States of America.

The *Tender Moments-From Our Heart to Yours Collection*, portraying children in wheelchairs, as well as the "Love and Hugs" figurine showing a child "signing" love and hugs, were created to promote awareness for people with special needs. A portion

of the proceeds from the sale of these figurines is contributed to several charities.

The Dream Continues

The company continues to adapt to today's changing society. In 1994, Sarah's Attic was granted permission by the Martin Luther King, Jr. Estate to create figurines portraying Dr. King, his family and his world. This collection has proven very popular, and pieces are continually being added to it. Sarah's Attic has been given permission by Rosa Parks to create a figurine in her honor. This amazing likeness, which was recently released, has also been a great success.

Keeping abreast of today's trends, Sarah's Attic has granted licensing to several companies to produce compa-ny-related items including afghans and glitter domes.

The Sarah's Attic Forever Friends Collector's Club is a very important part of the company. The fifth club year began June 1, 1995 and continues through May 31, 1996. The free mem-bership piece is entitled "Friends Forever" and features a lovable little African-American angel girl and a

To honor the memory of Dr. Martin Luther King, Jr., Sarah's Attic introduced the "Martin Luther King, Jr." figurine and sign and the "Coretta Scott King" figurine. These first three pieces in the Martin Luther King, Jr. Collection *are limited in production to December 31, 1996.*
* Licensed by the Estate of Martin Luther King, Jr., 1994

Those joining the Sarah's Attic Forever Friends Collector's Club in 1995-96 receive the free membership figurine entitled, "Friends Forever."

Caucasian angel boy perched on a crescent moon atop a cloud of friendship. The Members-Only Redemption pieces are titled "Playtime Pals" and "Horsin' Around." In "Playtime Pals" an Afro-American angel boy and girl frolic with their rocking horse and favorite toys. "Horsin' Around" finds an adorable Caucasian angel boy and girl cavorting with their rocking horse and toys. These special pieces, along with additional club benefits and the tender loving care that members receive during the year, make the Sarah's Attic Forever Friends Collector's Club very unique. Both club pieces are additions to the *Labor of Love Collection*. The piece, "Flags in Heaven," offered only at promotional events, is also part of the *Labor of Love Collection*.

Many accolades have come to Sarah and Sarah's Attic, Inc. over the years. Each one has a special place in Sarah's heart. One of the highlights was receiving the 1992 Michigan Wholesale/Retail Entrepreneur of the Year award. This was a magnificent tribute to Sarah and the company that had come so far, overcoming many obstacles, in nine short years. From Chesaning's little paper girl to Michigan's Entrepreneur of the Year is a giant step. Only in America and only with the help of good people and Sarah's philosophy of Love, Respect and Dignity could the dream come true.

Speaking of dreams — Sarah has in her dreams a theme park promoting Love, Respect and Dignity, as well as Sarah's Attic shelters for the homeless. Those who know Sarah realize that her dreams are very likely to come true.

Sarah's Attic, Inc.
126-1/2 West Broad
P.O. Box 448
Chesaning, MI 48616
(800) 4-FRIEND
Fax (517) 845-3477

COLLECTORS' CLUBS

Sarah's Attic Forever Friends Collector's Club
P.O. Box 448
Chesaning, MI 48616
(800) 4-FRIEND

Annual Dues: $32.50
Club Year: June 1-May 31

Benefits:
• Membership Gift: "Forever Friends" Figurine
• Opportunity to Purchase Members-Only Figurines
• Newsletter, "Attic Updates"
• Folder to Hold Newsletters
• Catalogs
• Special Mailings
• Local Club Chapters

SHELIA'S COLLECTIBLES
Tour the Country as History Repeats Itself — in Miniature Buildings

As a young girl growing up in the South in the 1940s and 1950s, Shelia Thompson was raised in true Southern fashion — young women were not expected to further their education beyond high school, let alone aspire to own their own companies! Like most Southern women, Shelia's own grandmother believed that a woman's role as a good mother and good wife was the best that life could offer — a true measure of success. It was in this atmosphere that Shelia Thompson, who always excelled artistically, was never encouraged to pursue her talents, except as they related to being a wife and mother.

So how did Shelia's Collectibles get its start and continue to expand to its present success? How did Shelia Thompson become known as the "woman who makes history every day?" And how is it that Shelia Thompson, both wife and mother, presents seminars to women's groups today about the secret of success as a self-taught artist: "Don't impose limitations! Are credentials important? They may open doors faster, but it is your drive, determination and desire, and being in the right place at the right time, that makes all the difference in the world."

Early Beginnings

During her childhood, Shelia Thompson loved anything related to art. "As a child, you assume that if you can do it, everyone else can too," explains Shelia. "It wasn't until later that I discovered my artistic talent was a gift, a part of me that couldn't be denied. At four or five, I used to carefully remove the family portraits from the wall and trace the outline of my ancestors' faces and try to draw their eyes and lips. I would then take these masterpieces to my grandmother, but never did tell her how I composed my pictures!"

Thompson's artistic endeavors continued in high school. Anytime there was an art project in high school, she headed the committee, whether it was making posters or creating backdrops for the school plays. Years later, Thompson's love of art turned into a hobby, as she cared for her two young daughters and experimented with various materials and media.

Many collectible companies were started by women who sought innovative ways to add income to meet their families' needs, and Shelia is no exception. This talented artist was looking for a way to raise some extra cash for the holidays in 1978 and decided to make wall-mounted Mallard ducks to sell at the famed Charleston Market. These ducks were a hit, Shelia caught the entrepreneurial bug, and Shelia's Collectibles was launched!

With the Charleston Market at her fingertips, Shelia observed thousands of tourists passing through this historic market looking for something to take home as a remembrance. Shelia's love for old houses, combined with numerous requests from customers asking for historic buildings, made it a natural for her to begin creating miniature wooden replicas of historic houses and public buildings. Shelia began this venture by creating the *Charleston* series, and today, Shelia's Collectibles' series span the nation.

Shelia has always taken great pride in developing concepts that are uniquely and distinctively hers. With this goal in mind, she researched the market and thus created an interpretation with an exciting new look: the layered facade house. "I wanted each miniature replica to look as if you could actually walk into the building," explains Shelia. Instead of creating designs on both

"This house oozes Southern," according to Shelia Thompson. She is, of course, referring to "Tara," from the popular Gone With The Wind *series.*

sides of the structures, Shelia felt collectors would appreciate learning some of the history of the locales; therefore, the backs of all pieces contain pertinent facts about the residences, the people who built them and other fascinating information. For example, "Ivy Green," Helen Keller's birthplace, featured a message in braille on the back of this Collector Society piece, and members received the written transcription in their Society notebooks.

Today, the Shelia's Collectibles manufacturing facility hums with activity, as each house designed by Shelia begins as a block of wood, which is first sanded. The wood is then cut to design specifications and sprayed with its base color of paint. The house begins to take shape, as artisans print the designated design on each wood form. Roofs are hand-painted, in addition to the beautiful bushes, flowers and trees which grace each structure: a trademark of Shelia's attractive houses. The layers of the houses are then assembled, forming complete pieces. "We're always improving our quality," explains Shelia. "We experiment with raw materials such as wood and paint. We try different color combinations and locate different ways to create sharper details, such as our laser cutting methods."

Backed By History

Shelia's deep appreciation of history is apparent upon examining the company's product line. "What started out as my love of old houses and customers' requests for historic buildings, has evolved into our mission of acting as ambassadors to help people appreciate the history of the United States," relates Shelia. "Our country is so diversified, whether you're studying the South and the effects of the Civil War or the beautiful plantations, or the North, where you can appreciate the significance of our forefathers responsible for signing the Declaration of Independence and what they contributed to history – the buildings they built, the homes in which they lived and the meetings that took place. Of course, we can't forget the western expansion to California, the famous Gold Rush and the architectural styles unique to this region. Now that I have grandchildren, I understand the importance of preserving the past. We hope to encourage people to appreciate their heritage by saving it for their grandchildren and, in turn, their grandchildren."

How does an artist go about selecting her subject matter? For Shelia Thompson, the ideas came naturally.

A new category for Shelia's collectibles, nine painted metal ornaments debut this stunning collection, which includes the "Drayton House." Located in Charleston, this house is nicknamed the 'Chinese Chippendale' because of the Medieval European and Chinese architectural influences.

Once she introduced the *Charleston* series and observed collectors' enthusiasm for historic areas, Shelia proceeded to research and select sites around the country to launch other historic series. Although Shelia and her husband and business partner Jim, travel extensively to locate buildings for their historical miniature house series, they rely on recommendations from collectors and retailers, who send postcards, photographs and news clippings to share their recommendations. Most of Shelia's series are ongoing, as she selects historic cities that according to the artist, "include so many wonderful buildings that I could add to them my entire lifetime and never run out of sites!" Some of these ongoing series include *Savannah, Williamsburg, Martha's Vineyard, Key West, West Coast Lighthouses, American Barns, Jazzy New Orleans, Plantations, Amish Village, Atlanta* and *San Francisco.*

Innovations that Shape Shelia's

Although Shelia creates miniature homes in various architectural styles, she is best known for her lovely Victorian homes, which collectors admire for their intricate gingerbread motifs, expansive entrances, turrets, and lace curtains at the windows. The *Victorian Springtime* series features a Victorian home from every state, complete with springtime flowers in bloom to commemorate this lovely season. On the back of each piece is the history of the house, along with the State bird, tree, flower, motto and nickname. Five homes will be added to this series each year until all 50 states are represented.

One of Shelia's favorite annual introductions is what the company calls the *Artist's Choice* series. Shelia describes this strictly limited edition series as "the freedom to have the ability to explore those things no one is asking for and to offer them as part of my line!" Prior releases have included such innovations as the "Mail-Order

Part of the West Coast Lighthouse *series, "East Brother Light" is one of seven lighthouses located in the San Francisco Bay area. This structure more closely resembles a home than a lighthouse.*

Victorians," four striking Victorian homes from George F. Barber's catalog of home plans dating back to the 1800s.

Always interested in experimenting with various techniques, Shelia achieved a glow-in-the-dark look in her *Ghost Houses* series. Collectors beware, because this series includes all real, documented ghost houses, with folklore included on the back of each piece! Stemming from a fascination with ghosts, Shelia also studied the various moon phases and introduced two houses per year featuring a moon phase, which glows in the dark.

Another 'first' for Shelia's Collectibles is their venture into licensing, and the firm began in grand style with the introduction of everyone's favorite, *Gone With The Wind*. "Collectors' enthusiasm for memorabilia and items related to this epic novel and movie were so overwhelming," reminisces Shelia, "that we obtained a license through Turner Entertainment to create favorite landmarks such as 'Tara,' and 'Twelve Oaks.'" The designs were all approved by the licensing firm, and each piece bears the Turner trademark and licensing information.

Just when Shelia thought her miniature replicas couldn't get any smaller, a large firm known for their metalwork ornaments, contacted the artist regarding the creation of painted metal ornaments. Prototypes were created,

From the San Francisco *series comes "Eclectic Blue," aptly named for its shades of blue and somewhat unconventional style, with all of the "swirls and turns," as Shelia describes.*

and much to Shelia's delight, they were historically accurate, right down to the coloration of each original structure. Nine ornaments debuted the collection, carefully selected by Shelia from her existing series. Lighthouses, Victorian homes and a cottage from the *Martha's Vineyard* series were painstakingly created, and each includes a 'romance card' featuring historical facts.

Looking to the Future

Shelia's Collectibles is certainly a company on the move, as the firm is constantly seeking exciting projects to parlay into wonderful collector series. Plans include more licensing opportunities like the *Gone With The Wind* series, in addition to locating ways to use Shelia's images on other materials, as they did with the Christmas ornaments. Collectors can keep current on news about the company through membership in the Collectors Society, with benefits including the chance to obtain exclusive Society pieces, and information about Shelia and her latest introductions and travels. Collectors will be particularly interested in hearing that Shelia's Collectibles has ventured into television, with appearances on "Start to Finish" on the Discovery Channel and "The Contemporary Collectibles Show," the first industry-wide television show for collectors.

Shelia Thompson is a Southern woman, proud of her heritage, who followed her dreams like other artists, to create artwork for collectors' enjoyment. "I strive for quality and a sense of color and design. When I create a piece of artwork, I'm saying something about myself and the way I interpret life. Anytime you buy an artist's work, you're truly buying a piece of that artist who has put his or her heart and soul into the project. But above all, what makes my job so rewarding is the collectors that I meet while traveling and the letters I receive. It's a real honor to recreate historical buildings and to put them on the real estate market, an honor I will enjoy for many years to come!"

Shelia's Collectibles
P.O. Box 31028
Charleston, SC 29417
(800) 227-6564
Fax (803) 556-0040

COLLECTORS' CLUB/TOUR

Shelia's Collectors Society
1856 Belgrade Avenue, Bldg. C
Charleston, SC 29407
(803) 766-0485 or (800) 227-6564

Annual Dues: $25.00 - Renewal: $20.00
Club Year: Anniversary of Sign-Up Date

Benefits:
- Special Society Gift
- Opportunity to Purchase Members-Only House
- Quarterly Newsletter
- Binder
- Personalized Membership Card Issued Annually
- Members-Only Tour of Shelia's Collectibles

Shelia's Collectibles Tour
1856 Belgrade Avenue
Charleston, SC 29407
(803) 766-0485 or (800) 227-6564

Hours: Monday through Friday by Appointment Only
Admission: For Shelia's Collectors Society Members Only

Members of Shelia's Collectors Society are welcome to tour the art studio and manufacturing facility of Shelia's Collectibles.

SHUBE'S MANUFACTURING, INC.
Masterworks® Fine Pewter and Collectibles
Shine with Success

Playfully sculpted by artist Michelle Phelps, "Karlie" is just one of the beautifully diamond-cut pieces in the Masterworks *fantasy line. This cheerful and mischievous fairy, which stands 4-1/2" tall, will spark any collector's imagination.*

A native of the American Southwest, Ric Shube was always attracted to the region's jewelry and crafts. In his eyes, they seemed to magically combine the Old West, rugged landscape, rich ancestry, timeless traditions and natural beauty of the land he called home.

So Ric began producing Southwest jewelry out of his home in 1974 and quickly discovered that many other people also shared his taste and appreciation for the Southwest styles. Within a year, he was running a shop of more than 20 artisans and craftsmen. More than two decades later, Ric heads one of the leading silver jewelry manufacturers, producing not only a line of Southwest American designs but some of the best known and best-selling fashion jewelry pieces on today's market.

Shube's Manufacturing, Inc. has also made its mark in the collectibles industry with pewter figurines that bring back this art form with magnificent workmanship and quality. The *Masterworks® Fine Pewter* line follows a simple philosophy: to offer the best value in fine art sculptures. With the popularity of its pewter designs, the company recently expanded its line to include cold-cast figurines. Back in the mid-1970s, Ric never imagined his one-man jewelry company would turn into one of the world's most successful manufacturers of pewter figurines.

Discovering the Beauty of Pewter

The work with pewter started almost by accident when Shube's commissioned another company to create some pewter pieces. Afterward, Shube's artisans realized that they could have done the work themselves just as well or even better. In 1982, having mastered and established the company's leadership in the production of jewelry by both the lost-wax and centrifugal casting methods, Ric decided to redirect some of the company's efforts to pewter figurines. Although pewter was commonplace on the market, most of it was made primarily out of lead. Ric saw a market for high-quality pewter. Since that time, Shube's has worked to produce a line of pewter figurines unsurpassed in craftsmanship, quality and detail.

The first line of pewter was miniatures titled *Cuter! Pewter®*, which immediately found its niche. By 1988, Shube's steadily expanded the miniature figurine offerings and began to branch out with larger and more innovative works, including lines with themes of fantasy, wildlife, Native Americans, Civil War and sea life. Some were produced as limited edition pieces.

In 1990, having outgrown the *Cuter! Pewter* name, Shube's adopted the title of *Masterworks Fine Pewter* to better describe the variety and excellence of the line. Today, *Masterworks* has nearly 600 pieces sold in stores throughout the United States and abroad.

Using skills developed and honed during two decades as a jewelry manufacturer, Shube's was the first company to offer a line of diamond-cut pewter figurines. With its FusionART™ process — combining fine pewter with copper tint, bronze accessories, fully-leaded Austrian Crystal, colorful pastels and other elements — *Masterworks* has brought a new level of quality and originality to the fine art figurine market. In addition, *Masterworks* has added a new line of ArtStone cold-cast figurines and continues to produce new works to delight the senses.

Fine Art Sculptures
Capture Beauty of Life

Masterworks takes collectors back in time and lets them discover adventures through its creative designs. The *Native American Collection* — with its innovative blend of pewter and FusionART — celebrates the richness of this culture

281

and remains one of the best-selling pewter lines. The *Wildlife Collection* includes both American and African wildlife with a diverse assortment of sea life, including dolphins, angel fish and others. The *Fantasy Collection* offers a wide variety of eye-catching figurines, including unicorns, wizards, glimmering castles and colorful fairies – all designed to capture the imagination. Another collection brings back scenes from the Civil War with Confederate and Union soldiers along with General Grant and General Lee.

Limited edition pieces are created by some of the top sculptors, including Peter C. Sedlow, Michelle G. Phelps and Dick Wimberly. Sedlow has been the primary artist on most of the *Native American Collection* as well as the striking limited editions of "Sitting Bull," "White Water Rush" and "Saga on the Plains."

Phelps sculpted most of the *Fairy Collection,* along with the limited edition pieces "Traditional Dancer," "Pueblo Dancer" and "Old Enemies."

Peter Sedlow's sculptures are distinctive in detail and vitality. From the Masterworks *Great Leaders and Chiefs Collection, "Quanah Parker," "Sitting Bull" and "Chief Joseph" showcase the pride and power of these famous Native American leaders, all painstakingly sculpted and historically accurate.*

Wimberly designed and sculpted the sold-out "American Eagle" and best-selling fantasy piece, "Guardian of the Crystal." Another up-and-coming artist is Alexander Scherback. A native of the Ukraine, he learned his sculpting craft there from his father.

The Creation of a *Masterworks* Work of Art

Shube's has more than 11 full-time staff members devoted to developing new products. Most *Masterworks* pieces begin as drawings or three-dimensional mock-ups, which are then reviewed by the artists. Promising designs are given the go-ahead, and a final sculpture is created. Working from the final sculpture, molds are made for the figurine and any accessories for the piece such as spears or shields. From these molds, production copies are made. Each piece is meticulously cleaned, buffed, soldered, painted and accented – all by hand.

Shube's has enlisted the services of renowned sculptors, pioneered innovative sculpting techniques and created an impressive array of products. The craftsmen follow the traditional composition of the pewter alloy developed by English artisans in the 18th century. This delicate combination of tin and antimony, with a touch of sterling silver, explains the metal's shine and durability. The earlier alloy for pewter included a high lead content that tended to dull with age. *Masterworks* pewter contains no lead and retains its lustre with little care. *Masterworks* has also preserved the artistic tradition of handcrafted metallurgy, a tradition that has made pewter a highly prized commodity since the beginning of the Bronze Age.

Cold Cast Figurines Add New Medium to Shube's Lines

With its position as one of the nation's top manufacturers of pewter

The majestic eagle gracefully glides through the sky in Dick Wimberly's breathtaking "Soaring Spirit." This beautiful limited edition piece, which stretches 15" high, is available in classic pewter as well as in FusionART .

figurines, Shube's decided to explore producing collectibles in other mediums that offered more artistic possibilities. In 1995, Shube's created its first line of cold cast figurines called *Snowflake Angels™* – childlike characters that share blessings from above. Handcrafted in ArtStone by designer Dick Wimberly and sculptor Alexander Scherback, each angel sits atop a snowflake and is hand-painted to showcase its delicate details, from the plump arms and legs, to the glistening wings and tiny toes. Each figurine comes with an inspirational story card.

In 1996, Shube's again expanded its cold cast figurine line with the innovative *Children of the Earth™* series and a licensed series called *Angel Academy®* based on the popular children's books of the same name by author Misty Taggart.

The characters from author Misty Taggart's successful children's book series, The Angel Academy®, *have been recreated into cold cast figurines from Shube's. The figurines feature the five lead characters, who are young angels in training.*

The *Angel Academy* features cold cast figurines from the series of books that provide wholesome entertainment for kids and have been well-received by parents and children nationwide. The figurines recreate the books' five lead characters who are young angels in training. These successful children's books have already spawned a large secondary market with different licensed products. Shube's received an exclusive license to produce the figurines.

The *Children of the Earth* will delight collectors of all ages with charming, green-thumbed creatures that help Mother Earth plant seeds and tend the flowers. The small character's green thumbs ensure that each garden will be blessed with beauty and a bountiful harvest, while their sparkling green eyes give a hint of harmless mischief. Mother Nature has given each little sprite a special job in the garden, and the details in the figurines convey their special duties and personalities. The *Children of the Earth* series is a reminder to cherish life, nurture what is important and enjoy the changing seasons.

Collectors Invited to Join Masterworks Club

The Masterworks Collectors' Club, established in 1995, allows collectors to further enjoy the beauty of the fine art pewter sculptures. As part of the charter year membership, collectors receive their choice of an exclusive gift — the Native American piece titled "Defiance" or the fantasy figurine "Enchanted Castle." Both figurines, which were designed by Peter Sedlow, come with an artist-signed Certificate of Authenticity. With a membership of $49.95, collectors also receive a newsletter that keeps them informed about upcoming introductions.

Shube's Manufacturing, Inc.
600 Moon St. S.E.
Albuquerque, NM 87123
(800) 545-5082
Fax (505) 275-8182

COLLECTORS' CLUB

Masterworks Collectors' Club 600 Moon St. S.E. Albuquerque, NM 87123 (800) 867-9173 **Annual Dues:** $49.95 **Club Year:** Anniversary of Sign-Up Date	**Benefits:** • Membership Gift: Choice of Native American piece or Fantasy Figurine • Bi-Annual Newsletter • Membership Card
The Angel Academy Alumni Society P.O. Box 39480 Phoenix, AZ 85069-9480 (602) 906-0328 **Annual Dues:** 1 Year - $25.00; 2 Years - $45.00 **Club Year:** January-December	**Benefits:** • Membership Gift • Quarterly Newsletter, "Cloud Play" • Binder • Personalized Membership Card • Membership Certificate, Suitable for Framing • Special Events • Notification of Release and Retirement Dates, Collectible Pieces and Personal Appearances by Misty Taggart • Reservation Card to Use at Local *Angel Academy* Retailers

SWAROVSKI
One Hundred Years of Crystal Perfection

In 1895, together with his family, 33 year old Daniel Swarovski left Georgenthal in northern Bohemia and headed for the tiny village of Wattens in the Austrian Tyrol to set up his own company. Even as an adolescent, this son of a glass cutter had made exploratory attempts to improve the manual cutting of crystal jewelry stones. Not long after, Daniel Swarovski had a vision of making affordable high-quality jewelry stones available throughout the world. Then, during a visit to the International Electricity Exhibition in Vienna, he saw the inventions of Edison, Siemens and Schuckert and decided to develop a machine that would cut crystal jewelry stones with previously unknown perfection and precision. Having done so, he decided to leave his birthplace, which had been a major center for the manufacture of crystal jewelry stones since the 17th century, and settle in Tyrol, which offered him the hydroelectric power he needed for his machines.

By the end of the century, Swarovski's crystal stones were synonymous with perfectly cut crystal jewelry stones in the world's major fashion centers.

In 1911, Swarovski and his three sons, Wilhelm, Friedrich and Alfred, set up a laboratory and found a way of producing their own raw material, pure crystal. In their striving for ever-higher quality and independence, they established principles that are still central to the company success to this day.

Still headquartered in Wattens in the Austrian Tyrol, Swarovski is the world's leading manufacturer of full cut crystal and is still run by the descendants of its founder, Daniel Swarovski, now in the fourth generation.

Today, Swarovski products range from jewelry stones used by the fashion, jewelry, lighting and cosmetic packaging industries to gift items, collectibles, decorative objects and their own fashion accessories and jewelry lines. Other product lines include precision optical instruments, grinding tools and abrasives, and other industrial items.

Swarovski Celebrates 100th Anniversary in 1995

In 1995, Swarovski, celebrated its centennial. The company's success is still very much based on the principle set by its founder generations ago: the constant striving for perfection, a belief in the importance of innovation and a corporate culture in which a sense of responsibility towards the company and its employees are of central importance.

Swarovski Silver Crystal introduced the "Centenary Swan" available only in 1995. Included was a decorative column display, a perfect way to display the exquisitely cut swan. A "maxi" swan was also introduced and is available indefinitely. Both were designed by Swarovski designer, Anton Hirzinger.

The Swarovski Collectors Society organized special events and activities to commemorate this special occasion, including 10-day centenary tours. Following the footsteps of Daniel Swarovski, the tour started in Prague where Swarovski patented his first invention, then went on to Vienna where he visited the First International Electricity Exhibition in 1883. The

Founded in 1895 by Daniel Swarovski, the Swarovski factory is still headquartered in Wattens in the beautiful Austrian Tyrol.

climax of the tour was a visit to the Austrian Tyrol, home to Swarovski since 1895.

The Swarovski Collectors Society renewal gift for 1995 was a miniature swan, the smallest in the series of swans designed for the centenary year. Also available exclusively for members was a crystal-studded swan brooch, and a centenary coin for members visiting Wattens in 1995. Members could stamp their own coins at the ancient mint in the historic town of Hall in the Tyrol or obtain it from the Swarovski Crystal Shop in Wattens.

The highlight of the centenary year was the opening of the "Swarovski

Crystal Worlds" in Wattens. Designed by the internationally renowned multi-media artist Andre Heller, it is a half-underground, half-aboveground structure with an internal volume of 600,000 cubic feet. Inside the structure is a series of rooms and halls that highlight the aesthetic qualities of crystal. For instance, one room is actually a dome made of 590 mirrors that gives those inside the feeling of being inside a crystal. Located adjacent to the company's factory in Wattens, Austria, "Swarovski Crystal Worlds" also features the work of important contemporary artists including Salvador Dali and Keith Haring. Also included are a

cafeteria, a lounge for SCS members and a retail shop.

Swarovski Silver Crystal

A tiny crystal mouse introduced in 1976 marked the beginning of a new era for Swarovski. The mouse was the first item in the Swarovski Silver Crystal line, which today consists of over 120 gift items and collectibles featuring 20 theme groups, including *Our Woodland Friends*, *South Sea*, and *When We Were Young*. The brilliant, full cut crystal designs of animals, fruits and other decorative objects, are available at more than 13,000 selected retailers worldwide.

Newer introductions in the Silver Crystal line include the "Angel" and "Sir Penguin" by Adi Stocker, and a 4-piece "miniature" train set designed by Gabriele Stamey.

First Swarovski Silver Crystal Limited Edition

For the first time ever, Swarovski Silver Crystal introduced its first limited edition, "The Eagle," early in 1995. Created by Adi Stocker, one of the company's best known designers, it admirably captures the power and grace of a Golden eagle about to launch into flight. Society members were offered this masterpiece on a "first come–first serve" basis, and only 2,900 U.S. Society members were lucky enough to acquire this special edition. Each piece is unique, due to its individual number indelibly lasered into the base of the artwork. It rests on a hand-crafted mahogany base bearing the signature of Adi Stocker and the year of introduction.

"The Eagle's" bill and talons are crafted of solid sterling silver and the piece was accompanied by a Certificate of Authenticity signed by Helmut Swarovski and Adi Stocker.

Will Swarovski Silver Crystal introduce other limited editions in the future? We'll just have to wait and see.

Swarovski Collectors Society

The success and popularity of

Available only in 1995, the "Centenary Swan" was intoduced by Swarovski Silver Crystal to celebrate its 100th Anniversary. A decorative column was included to display this exquisitely cut swan.

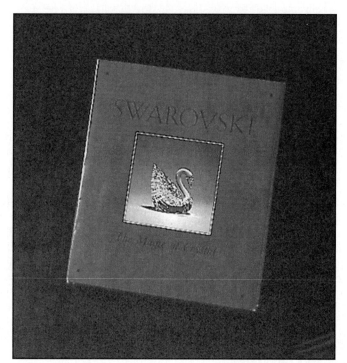

Swarovski: The Magic of Crystal, *written by jewelry historian Vivienne Becker, documents the history of Swarovski from its foundation in 1895 until today.*

invitations to special events, exhibitions, and seminars; and organized visits to Wattens, the home of Swarovski. The membership fee is $35 – renewal: $25.

Swarovski: *The Magic of Crystal*

A lavishly illustrated, 160-page book telling the story of Swarovski has been published in six languages: English, German, Italian, French, Spanish and Dutch. Written by Vivienne Becker, jewelry historian, *Swarovski: The Magic of Crystal* documents the history of the traditional family firm from its foundation in 1895 on to the present day, with the main emphasis on the Swarovski Silver Crystal figurines first launched in 1976. Anyone interested in reading more about Swarovski's history is able to obtain the book at Swarovski Silver Crystal retail outlets and distinguished book stores worldwide.

Swarovski Silver Crystal, together with the fact that it has so many devoted followers, led to the foundation of the Swarovski Collectors Society (SCS) in 1987. Today, SCS boasts more than 200,000 members in 25 countries.

Membership benefits include special limited editions created exclusively for SCS members, a bi-annual full color magazine; membership renewal gifts;

Swarovski America Limited
2 Slater Road
Cranston, RI 02920
(800) 426-3088
Fax (401) 463-8459

COLLECTORS' CLUB/VISITOR CENTER

Swarovski Collectors Society
2 Slater Road
Cranston, RI 02920
(800) 426-3088

Annual Dues: $35.00 - Renewal: $25.00
Club Year: Anniversary of Sign-Up Date

Benefits:
• Opportunity to Purchase SCS Annual Edition Figurine
• Membership Certificate: 40mm Swarovski Paperweight
• Complimentary Renewal Gift
• Bi-annual Magazine, *Swarovski Collector*
• Bi-annual Newsletter
• Travel Opportunities
• Designer Signature Sessions, Special Events, Exhibitions, Seminars

The Swarovski Crystal Shop & Visitor Center
A-6112 Wattens
Innstrasse 1
Austria
(43-5224-5886)

Hours: May to September – Monday through Saturday, 8 a.m. - 6 p.m., Sunday, 8 a.m. - Noon
October to April – Monday through Friday, 8 a.m. - 6 p.m., Saturday, 8 a.m. - Noon

Admission Fee: None

The Swarovski Crystal Shop & Visitor Center displays all Swarovski crystal brands, as well as unique articles from other leading manufactures. Members of Swarovski Collectors Society are given a special welcome in the lounge. Exhibits highlight engraving, various glass techniques and gem cutting.

THE TUDOR MINT INC.

A Fantasy World of *Myth and Magic* Portrayed in Shimmering Figurines With Brilliant Crystals

Houston, Texas, marks the new American home of The Tudor Mint Inc. – and a cause for celebration among all those who love the fantasy world of *Myth and Magic.* This new company has been created especially to serve the interests of Myth & Magic Collectors' Club members who reside in the United States. It is also the route through which The Tudor Mint's figurines now enter America for distribution to shops throughout the country.

The principal persons in the company are: President Graham Hughes (United Kingdom); Vice-President and USA Manager Bruce Kollath; Secretary Richard Power (United Kingdom); Treasurer Louis DeCou; and Operations Manager Chuck Smith. American collectors first enjoyed the opportunity to meet club officials and see Tudor Mint collections at the Long Beach and South Bend collectibles shows during 1995.

The British Origins of The Tudor Mint Inc.

Birmingham, at the heart of the English Midlands, once was the home of many jewelers who lived and worked there for generations, producing fine-quality, detailed work. One such craftsman was Walter Archibald Parker Watson.

In 1915, Watson sold his business to A.H. Power and C. Flint, who kept his name when they established their new company – W.A.P. Watson Limited – presumably to retain the reputation he had established over a number of years. Power and Flint originally produced costume jewelry under the trade name of *Exquisite Jewellery.* The business did well and by 1935, products included souvenirs such as ashtrays, sweet dishes, condiment sets, cake stands, letter openers and keepsake spoons.

During World War II, the company's workshops were turned over to essential war production, making small, precise components. In 1945, after the war, W.A.P. Watson resumed its costume jewelry and souvenir business. In 1954, the company moved out of the jewelry quarter to a three-acre site in Solihull, England, where it still remains today. With room to expand, W.A.P. Watson became the second largest manufacturer of costume jewelry in the United Kingdom.

Graham Hughes joined W.A.P. Watson on November 1, 1970 as company secretary – at a time when business was thriving. In the late 1970s, though, the arrival of "cheap products" in costume jewelry brought large declines in the firm's jewelry sales. As a result, new product ideas were being developed by Mr. Hughes. All of these new product ideas were created and tested under the name "Tudor Mint" in order to create a quality base upon which to establish the giftware side of the business.

Graham Hughes went on to become the Managing Director of The Tudor Mint Ltd. Changes were also made within the company structure: The Watson Group Limited was created as the holding company, with W.A.P. Watson Limited being the trading company (hence the "WAPW" nameplate on all Tudor Mint products).

A range of silver and gilt-plated animals, each incorporating a crystal, was developed and named *Crystalflame.* This was a successful line for The Tudor Mint until 1988, when sales had peaked and were beginning to drop. Graham Hughes realized that a new giftware line was needed to take its place. *Myth and Magic* was this collection.

At over 9" in height, "The Power of Crystal" serves as the most intricate and largest study in the Myth and Magic *collection.*

The International Debut of *Myth and Magic*

The Tudor Mint's chief designer was invited to submit drawings for a collection of dragons, wizards, castles and mythical creatures, to be manufactured incorporating crystals. She presented 25 original designs, from which 12 were sculpted and first shown at a trade show in Birmingham. As soon as the collection became available in stores, it was an instant success. The same was true when *Myth and Magic* debuted in the United States in February 1989.

The Myth and Magic Collectors' Club was founded in the United Kingdom in 1990 because the products already had earned an incredible following. By the end of July 1990, 3,000 members had been enrolled. The popularity of the club continued to increase, and the United States division opened May 1, 1991 through Fantasy Creations of New York City. In 1991, a distributorship was opened in Canada: SAMACO Trading Limited. SAMACO then launched a

Genuine crystals sparkle and boast a whole rainbow of colors in "The Earth Dragon" from the Myth and Magic *collection.*

Canadian division of the Collectors' Club in May, 1992.

In early 1994, W.A.P. Watson Limited and Graham Hughes realized that in order to reach full market potential in the United States, it would be necessary for The Tudor Mint to have a physical presence in North America. The central United States location and the availability of experienced management personnel, trained staff, and an expert collectibles sales force gave rise to the decision to locate this fully owned subsidiary in Houston.

The Tudor Mint Inc. became the official and exclusive distributor for all Tudor Mint products and the headquarters for the United States division of the Myth and Magic Collectors' Club on January 1, 1995. This offered a fresh beginning for Tudor Mint products, which now are sold mostly through retail shops instead of through other distributors or directly to the public. The company's main goals include re-establishing its line to increase its collectibility, and increasing visibility in the marketplace.

The Tudor Mint: Product Information

New releases from The Tudor Mint are launched each January and July, with retirements announced each July for December 31 implementation. Annual "One Year Only Studies" are released in January and retire on December 31 of the same year. "Extravaganza Studies" debut at the annual Collector "Extravaganza" hosted by The Tudor Mint Ltd. in England. The Extravaganza is a special show for Tudor Mint collectors only, with about 800 - 1,000 attendees annually. All Tudor Mint artists are in attendance, and collectors also enjoy entertainment and contests. The "Extravaganza Studies" are available only on the day of this event. "Exhibition Only Studies" are sculpted for the purpose of small exhibitions or events, and again are available for purchase only on the day of the event.

Myth and Magic remains the showpiece of The Tudor Mint Ltd. product line which consists of wizards, dragons, unicorns, pegasus, and other fantasy figurines. From 1" miniature studies with one crystal, to 9" extra large studies with more than five crystals, this varied line serves as the focus of the collectors' club. In addition to figurines of various sizes and prices, there are *Myth and Magic* jewelry, memorabilia and miscellaneous items like key rings, trinket boxes and letter openers, a chess set, and "club studies" released specifically for club members.

The *Arthurian Legend* Collection was a direct result of the widespread interest in *Myth and Magic*. All figurines are based on reading done by Chief Designer Sharon Riley, from sources such as Mallory's *Le Morte d' Arthur*, and John Boorman's film *Excalibur*.

The *J.R. Tolkien Collection* was created in response to requests by collectors, and all figurines are based on the stories of Tolkien including *The Hobbit* and *Lord of the Rings*.

Dark Secrets, launched in January, 1994, is kept separate from *Myth and Magic* because the subject matter consists of skulls, skeletons and demons. Introduced in 1993 as an "experiment," "The Keeper of the Skulls," sold 25,000 pieces in the first year alone. As a direct result, the *Dark Secrets* collection and its three chambers, for Skulls, Demons and Skeletons, were born.

Launched in 1995 in the United States the *Native American Collection* features 12 subjects depicting the life of certain tribes in the 1800s. Tribes featured include Apache, Comanche, Arapaho, Sioux and others. Each of the 12 figurines is available in silver or bronze finish.

Fine Designs and Careful Craftsmanship Bring Tudor Mint Products to Life

Tudor Mint products are not made of pewter, but rather their manufacturing process allows for figurines with more definition than pewter can achieve. The pieces, called "antique, silver plate figurines," have varied tones of gray rather than appearing to be all of one color, and they are highly detailed in their sculpture. What's

"The Unicorn" was one of the first Myth and Magic *studies ever introduced. Its simple elegance illustrates the beauty and grace of a unicorn.*

"Reflections," introduced in July 1995, is a unique study. If you look closely, you can see the dragon's reflection in the crystal!

more, these pieces are truly collectibles rather than giftware: each has its own individual name and the number of images is limited to provide the proper drama and distinctiveness for each.

Most figurines from The Tudor Mint have one designer and one model maker. Each designer and model maker works on various models within each collection. The very first designer (now Chief Designer) is Sharon Riley, and the first model maker (now Chief Model Maker) is Roger Gibbons. Other designers for The Tudor Mint include Jessica Watson and Helen Coventry, while other model makers include Mark Locker, Anthony Slocombe and Steve Darnley.

The manufacturing process is a unique one that includes many steps: from drawing to design to model sculpting, master mould making, production, antiquing, burnishing, and the addition of crystals. Finally, each new study must survive The Drop Test! It is boxed and shrink wrapped, then dropped from shoulder height eight times — onto each face and corner. Only when it has successfully passed this final test is it ready for shipment.

Club Members Enjoy Special Benefits

The Myth and Magic Collectors' Club is the only United States club of its kind for collectors of fantasy figurines. With about 20,000 members worldwide, the club focuses attention on *Myth and Magic* products — all of which feature genuine, beautifully cut crystals and an exceptional value. For a $37.50 annual fee, members receive a free yearly presentation piece, a club membership card, a catalog of the current collection and updates, two issues of the popular "Methtintdour Times" newsletter, special purchase opportunities, and opportunities to win valuable prizes.

Collectors may correspond with The Myth and Magic Collectors' Club at The Tudor Mint Inc., P.O. Box 431729, Houston, Texas 77243-1729. The phone number is (713) 462-0076.

The Tudor Mint
P.O. Box 431729
Houston, TX 77243-1729
(713) 462-0076
Fax (713) 462-0170

COLLECTORS' CLUB

Myth and Magic Collectors' Club
c/o The Tudor Mint
P.O. Box 431729
Houston, TX 77243-1729
(713) 462-0076

Annual Dues: $37.50
Club Year: July 1 - June 30

Benefits:
• Membership Gift: Figurine
• Renewal Gift
• Redemption Cards for Members-Only Figurines
• Bi-annual Newsletter, "Methtintdour Times"
• Membership Card
• Invitation to Attend "Extravaganza," held in England
• Current Catalog, Plus Updates

UNITED DESIGN

Capturing Nature's Beauty and Life's Simple Pleasures With Creativity and Hands-On Craftsmanship

Gary and Jeanie Clinton, founders of United Design, have worked hand-in-hand to build their Oklahoma-based company that also includes a gift shop. Figurines from the White Christmas *collection are among the thousands on display and for sale.*

When Gary and Jeanie Clinton first started their pottery business, they worked side by side in a tiny chicken coop. Today, they have a zoo of creations that has turned their backyard hobby into a thriving multi-national company. United Design currently offers 16 product catalogs with more than 3,000 different items that capture nature's beauty, diversity and mystery. As noted in its mission statement, the Oklahoma-based company is "inspired by the joy and wonder of the world around us."

People ask, "Did you ever think you'd get to this point,'" says Jeanie. "But consciously, we did dream that it would happen." The Clintons launched their business in 1973, building it around a love of animals and an uncanny talent that would eventually turn the animal kingdom into a host of highly successful product lines. "We had been art students at the University of Oklahoma," explains Jeanie. "I'd been making pottery and started selling it on weekends at craft fairs. Then I started making it full time. That sort of just grew."

Gary received his master of fine arts degree in 1975. "But I was enjoying making things more than I thought I'd enjoy teaching," Gary says. The next couple of years found Gary and Jeanie making pottery in their back yard studio and setting up booths at craft shows. They made $300 at their first fair to put a down payment on two pottery kilns. With the growing demand for their handmade items, the Clintons hired their first employee in 1976. "We began getting more and more business, so we hired another person," recalls Gary. With this extra helping hand, Gary and Jeanie created more products — and more customers — that fit in with their goals for the business. Things haven't stopped since.

Over 700 employees in its Noble, Purcell and Wekoka, Oklahoma, locations now produce the detailed figurines ranging from teddy bears and Dalmatians to Santa Claus and angels. A sister facility in Norwich, Ontario, produces some of the product lines for distribution in Canada, and a European sales and distribution company is headquartered in Nottingham, England.

Like their employees, the Clintons work as a team, dividing their business responsibilities according to their personal strengths. Jeanie is in manufacturing and operations while Gary is in charge of the various stages of product development. "If I had been on my own, I'd still just have my little studio," Gary confides. "Jeanie is good at working on day-to-day projects. She's very pragmatic and practical. She's the heartbeat of our operation. I'm more of a dreamer, and the combination works really well." Their dreams, ideas and hard work go into all the new and continuing lines that have made United Design a resounding success.

Winging Their Way To United Design . . . *Teddy Angels*

Divinely down-to-earth characters have descended on United Design. The *Teddy Angels* collection, which features lovable teddy bears with wings, was inspired by antique and contemporary teddies. Created by sculptor Penni Jo Jonas, each *Teddy Angels* character has something very special to share through uplifting sentiments and messages that address everyday situations. There's "Cowboy Murray" dressed in boots to say "Have a doo-da day." "Old Bear" carries his well-traveled suitcase to proclaim: "Always remember your way home." Each figurine also comes with a *Teddy Angels* story booklet describing the collection's origin and mission.

Santa Claus and Angels Continue To Delight Collectors

No legend is more filled with wonder and magic than Santa Claus. Introduced in 1986, *The Legend of Santa Claus* collection has become a beloved limited edition collectible and year-round tradition for many families. The hand-cast, hand-painted figurines designed by the company's creative artisans make the collection a tremendous hit with Santa collectors worldwide.

The *Angels Collection* sends messengers and messages of good tidings. The limited edition collectibles have spurred a tremendous response since debuting in 1991. One very special figurine in the collection is titled "The Gift." Designed exclusively to support the work of The Starlight Foundation, the highly detailed figurine symbolizes the dreams and wishes that can come true for chronically and terminally ill children. A new figurine is designed each year to benefit this worthy cause.

A Menagerie of Stone Critters

Dalmatians, turtles, frogs, owls, eagles, otters, bears, bunnies, pigs and cows! What more could a collector ask for? United Design's *Stone Critters The Animal Collection* offers those and more than 400 creatures that have become America's most popular collectible animal figurine. Every phase of a *Stone Critters* creation – from the heartwarming poses and expressions to the sculptured detail, to the hand-painting and finishing – achieves a natural look. Realistic eyes are also added, which seem to magically bring the *Stone Critters* to life. Whether a collector is just beginning or looking for a special piece to add to a collection, the *Stone Critters* line is a great place to start and end.

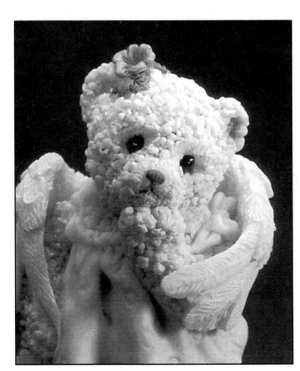

"Sweetie" is among the heavenly characters in the Teddy Angels *collection. Each piece is inscribed with its own special sentiment and sculpted by Penni Jo Jonas.*

Eggstra! Eggstra! Bunnies Are A Hopping Success

The normally quiet Cottontail Valley just north of United Design is abuzz with a flurry of furry activity. Creating the commotion are designs hopping down the bunny trail in the *Easter Bunny Family Collection*. The collection started in 1988 when sculptor Donna Kennicutt created the first seven designs. Since then, this popular collectible has continued to multiply to the delight of many Easter Bunny enthusiasts. In 1993, *Easter Bunny Family Miniatures*, a co-creation of Penni Jo Jonas and Dianna Newburn, were added to the collection. Kennicutt designed the adorable *Easter Bunny Family Babies* in 1994. Though not limited in edition, the collection has several designs that are retired each year and replaced by new creations. The seven original designs were retired in 1991.

Communicating With Collectors

Collectors of the *Easter Bunny Family* and the limited edition Santas and Angels have the opportunity to receive the annual "The Legend of Santa Claus," "Angels Collection" and "Eggspress" newsletters. These publications inform collectors about new releases and retirements, provide a checklist of available pieces, and often give a sneak peek at upcoming introductions that sculptors are working on. Collectors are also invited to visit and tour United Design's Oklahoma facility, where they can get a fascinating and first-hand glimpse at the manufacturing process. A showroom also displays thousands of the company's figurines.

A Masterful Attention To Detail

Most United Design products are

Created to benefit The Starlight Foundation, this 1994 figurine titled "The Gift" was limited to 5,000 pieces and sculpted by Dianna Newburn. From its Angels Collection, *United Design creates an annual piece for the non-profit organization.*

made in the heart of America: Noble, Oklahoma. Each design begins as a simple idea in someone's imagination – the Clintons, a sculptor or even collectors who submit concepts. United Design's team of talented sculptors include Ken Memoli, Larry Miller, Dianna Newburn, Donna Kennicutt, Suzan Bradford, Penni Jo Jonas, Midge Ramsey and Terri Russell.

The figurine production starts in the studio of one of United Design's gifted artists. Using their hands and a variety of tools, the sculptors capture the idea in a three-dimensional clay design.

Once the clay sculpture is complete, a master mold is made by applying latex or silicone over the original, layer by layer. The first hard cast model from the mold is called a "master." The master is returned to the sculptor to be reworked for exact detail. Production molds are then created. Two raw materials are used for casting the majority of United Design's products: a bonded porcelain and Hydrostone, which is mined in Oklahoma. Each material allows for great surface detail.

Casting is actually done by hand by mixing the material, which is poured into molds. When set, the mold is removed – like taking off a glove from your hand — and what results is a near-perfect replica of the original sculpture. From the pouring room, each item makes its way to what is called a "fettling" area. Here, precision drills are used to remove any extra or unwanted material which may be on the cast piece. This clean-up operation prepares each piece for the hand-painting process.

The painting is done using both regular brushes and airbrush techniques depending on the desired effect. Because of the hand-painting process, it can truly be said that no two pieces are exactly alike. Every item is an original! Supplementing the artisans at United Design is a "cottage industry" — or a group of home painters. These independent workers check out the pieces to paint and return them when finished. The cottage industry phenomenon has been an exciting part of the growth at United Design.

Near the end of the production cycle, United Design adds those trademark eyes, either glass or plastic depending on which gives the most life-like appearance. A final inspection is done before the item is carefully packed and ready to find a new home.

Dedication To Quality Guides United Design

Though the days of the backyard chicken coop are long gone, Gary and Jeanie are still active in the daily activities of the company. This husband-and-wife team strives to retain the down-home values, family atmosphere and team cooperation that has guided the company for more than 20 years. Devotion to creativity, quality and hands-on craftsmanship have distinguished United Design from the rest.

Two enthusiastic collectors of the Easter Bunny Family *suggested the adorable idea for this 1995 addition titled "Easter Cookies." Artist Donna Kennicutt created the collection in 1988.*

United Design Corporation
P.O. Box 1200
Noble, OK 73068
(800) 527-4883
Fax (405) 360-4442

COLLECTORS' TOUR

United Design Gift Shop & Factory Tour
1600 N. Main
Noble, OK 73068
(800) 527-4883

Hours: Tours — Monday through Friday at 10 a.m. and 1 p.m.
Gift Shop — Monday through Friday, 8 a.m. - 6 p.m.; Saturdays in November and December, 10 a.m. - 4 p.m. (Open First Saturday of the Month During the Rest of the Year, 10 a.m. - 4 p.m.).

Admission Fee: None

The tour of the United Design factory, which lasts about 25 minutes, shows visitors how figurines are made, beginning with a clay sculpture, through molding, casting, hand-painting and finishing.

WACO PRODUCTS CORPORATION
Melody In Motion Moves Toward More Success and Magic

With music, motion and magic, WACO Products Corporation has found a winning combination that hits all the right notes. For the past 10 years, WACO has brought together fine art and advanced technology to create a line of delightful *Melody In Motion* figurines, which have found a home with collectors all over the world.

These creations are prized for their fine porcelain sculptures, beautiful studio-recorded music and complex, life-like movements. From a lovable hobo named "Willie" to classic holiday scenes featuring Santa Claus, *Melody In Motion* musicals truly bring magic to life. Each has a special story that's waiting to be told.

Time, Technology, Quality and Excellence Make Musical Masterpieces

Before the musicals entertain collectors, each piece undergoes a lengthy production process.

The *Melody In Motion* porcelain

Fore! Willie tries his hand at golfing in "The Longest Drive" — an ironic title since the ball simply falls off the tee. The musical plays "Blue Skies" as Willie moves from side to side.

figurines are molded from sculptures created by the award-winning Japanese master sculptor Seiji Nakane. Hand-crafted in Seto — the porcelain capital of Japan — each figurine is faithfully reproduced by highly skilled artisans to match Nakane's original sculptures.

Crafted from pure clay found only in Seto, the figurines are then fired to a bisque finish before trained artisans put on the final touch by hand-painting each detail. The figurines are fired for a second time and thoroughly inspected to ensure that every piece meets the exact specifications of the original artwork.

State-of-the-art technology and solid state sound reproduction inside every *Melody In Motion* figurine create an electro-mechanical device that activates the music and graceful movements. This makes every *Melody In Motion* figurine unique. A high-quality precision motor drives a gear train that activates a maze of cams and levers to set in motion the realistic movements in each figurine. Each part of the mechanical device is custom made for that style figurine, with each mechanism designed and engineered to achieve a specific movement. This advanced technology is truly exceptional, and is comparable to that found in high-quality appliances and camcorders.

Adding music to complete the story of each figurine is achieved by selecting the appropriate tune and musical instrument. The selected song is then recorded in a sound studio by professional musicians. The music's high quality is evident in everything from the Tchaikovsky theme played by a professional concert cellist to the carousel music recorded from working carousel band organs from around the world.

Combining the art of porcelain with precision technology, each figurine is presented as a tableau that tells a story

It's Willie's lucky day! The hobo that has become one of the most popular Melody In Motion *characters collects his winnings in "Jackpot Willie." The musical plays "We're In The Money" as Willie moves his head back and forth.*

to spark a collector's imagination. *Melody In Motion* figurines, which can only be produced in limited quantities due to their complex design and painstaking craftsmanship, are exceptional both in beauty and technology.

A Musical Legacy and History of "Automata"

Although the *Melody in Motion* figurines are unique in today's collectible market, the concept of moving figures and mankind's fascination with "automata" can be traced to centuries-old traditions. As early as the 3rd century B.C., during the Han dynasty in China, a mechanical orchestra was handcrafted for the Emperor. In those days, these entertaining devices were powered by water movement or air pressure. By the mid-15th century, wind-up spring mechanisms were introduced and they became a portable power source for automata. By the end of the 1700s, very intricate automatons in human form were created by master artisans — who were only able to produce a few pieces in their lifetime. All were made for wealthy persons and only a handful of those works survive. Today, they can only be found in museums or private collections. *Melody In Motion* follows in this rich legacy with figurines that delight collectors of all ages.

Melody In Motion: The Willie Collection

The character of "Willie" is at the heart of *Melody in Motion* — and warms the hearts of collectors. The hobo brings back special memories and timeless stories about friendship, happiness and life with new introductions each year that chronicle his adventures. To celebrate *Melody In Motion*'s 10th anniversary, Willie brings together his feathered friends and conducts an imaginary orchestra to play "When You're Smiling." As he sways, the chirping doves turn the already happy moment into a celebration. "Jackpot Willie" drops a quarter in the slot to come out a winner! As his head moves back and forth in amazement of his luck, the red light flashes to announce Willie's success. He whistles "We're In The Money" as he scrambles to fit all his

In "Chattanooga Choo Choo," Willie whistles the song of the same name while he waits for the train. He's ready to climb aboard as his head moves up and down to look at the track.

winnings into his overworked hat. In "Chattanooga Choo Choo," Willie finds himself on the move again, this time waiting to hitch a ride on his favorite box car. With his bags ready to toss on board, he looks up and down the tracks as he whistles "Chattanooga Choo Choo." In "The Longest Drive," Willie thinks he hit the golf ball far down the fairway. But the ball simply fell off the tee, where it sits as Willie moves his head to the tune "Blue Skies." "Willie The Yodeler" rolls out a barrel of fun and a few oom-pahs! The musical plays "German Folksong/Yodeling."

Melody In Motion: The Carousel Collection

The "Grand Carousel" is the show piece of the *Melody In Motion* line. Standing 22-1/2" tall and weighing 25 pounds, it is a wonder of animation and music. The pre-production process took Seiji Nakane more than a year, and the completion of the first Carousel was a two-year project. This combination of "beauty" (porcelain) and "beast" (motors, gears and audio system) has emerged as one of the masterworks in the contemporary collectibles field. It is as magnificent in appearance as it is in technological achievement. With flashing lights, two levels of moving animals, intricate details and brilliant colors, the carousel is a childhood fantasy crowded with golden lions, purple elephants and legendary griffins. The carousel comes with two audio tapes of authentic band music. The audio tape player, which is built into the base, also plays standard cassette tapes.

The *Melody In Motion* collection also boasts three additional carousels of various sizes and features. The "Blue Danube Carousel" features colorful horses moving gracefully up and down their shiny gold poles to the popular tune "Blue Danube Waltz." "Victoria Park Carousel" is sculpted in exquisite detail and delicately painted in soft pastels. This grand carousel plays the glorious melody "Under the Double Eagle." The "King of Clowns Carousel" displays two exquisitely sculpted reliefs crowned with a scallop-shaped edge.

As much of a tradition as holiday gatherings, WACO introduces a Santa Claus figurine each year. For 1995, Santa relaxes in his chair to read a stack of children's letters while an old-time radio plays "Deck The Halls."

The artisan's touch can be seen from the extravagant flourishes and energetic clowns to the lively and nostalgic organ music.

Melody In Motion: The Clock Collection

"Willie" and other characters star in the *Melody In Motion* clocks that keep everyone on time. The collection features eight hand-made and hand-painted porcelain figurines complete with beautiful, built-in clocks. Of course, each piece also has music and movement. There's "Low Pressure Job," "Day's End," "Willie The Golfer," "The Artist," "Wall St. Willie" and "Clockpost Willie" — all portraying the collection's signature character.

In addition, "Grandfather Clock" shows a distinguished gentleman in his rocking chair as he smokes his pipe and rocks back and forth to the rhythmic tune of "The Syncopated Clock." Finally, "Golden Mountain Clock" portrays three gnomes pushing ore cars through a tunnel, while two others work their pick axes into the gold mine walls to the tune "Viennese Musical Clock."

Melody In Motion: The Santa Collection and Retired Pieces

Each year since 1986, WACO has introduced an annual Santa. And each year, these appealing "St. Nick" sculptures have sold out and retired. For 1995, the official *Melody In Motion* Santa relaxes in his favorite chair to read letters from children throughout the world. His favorite song "Deck The Halls" plays on an old-time radio while Santa's head turns to and fro as he swings his foot.

In addition, there are more than 30 limited edition *Melody In Motion* figurines that have been retired or will soon receive that honor. The success and popularity of the line is evident in the strong interest of collectors for these older additions.

Classic Scenes Come To Life with *Melody In Motion*

Even the 1930s "Coca-Cola" calendars created by Norman Rockwell

This Coca-Cola brand musical figurine is based on Norman Rockwell's painting "Gone Fishin'" when a country boy spends a lazy summer day at the fishing hole.

become more nostalgic when put with music and motion. The Coca-Cola® brand musical figurine based on the artist's drawing "Gone Fishin'" takes a look back to simpler days, country life and the lazy summer days of youth. It was a time when nothing could be better than a trip down to the fishing hole on a hot summer's day. The musical plays the tune "Thank God I'm A Country Boy."

Share In The Magic with the Melody In Motion Collectors Society

To support the collection of fine musicals, WACO invites collectors to experience the magic first hand by joining the Melody In Motion Collectors Society. Dues are $27.50 for the first year or $50.00 for a two-year membership. Collectors also have the opportunity to purchase gift memberships for family and friends.

As members, collectors receive the exclusive figurine titled "Best Friends" which is a special gift from sculptor Seiji Nakane. If "Best Friends" were available in stores, it would sell for $45.00 or more. Members also receive a personal Membership Card, complimentary annual subscription to the "Melody Notes" newsletter, the latest *Melody In Motion* catalog and a $10.00 member coupon which can be applied to the purchase of any figurine except the Members' Only issue.

Members will also receive a Personal Redemption Certificate entitling them to purchase the Society's limited edition figurine created exclusively for

To celebrate Melody In Motion's *10th anniversary, Willie leads a choir of his feathered friends to the tune "When You're Smiling." Titled "Willie The Conductor," the clown sways with the music.*

members. "Willie The Collector," a 9-3/4" work of art, has assembled his own miniature collection. His head moves as he whistles "When The Saints Go Marching In." The same tune is heard in the background as if it were played by the miniature "Willie The Trumpeter" that he holds.

WACO Products Corp.
I-80 & New Maple Avenue
P.O. Box 898
Pine Brook NJ 07058-0898
(201) 882-1820
Fax (201) 882-3661

COLLECTORS' CLUB

Melody In Motion Collectors Club
WACO Products Corporation
I-80 & New Maple Avenue
P.O. Box 898
Pine Brook, NJ 07058-0898
(201) 882-1820

Annual Dues: $27.50
Club Year: Anniversary of Sign-Up Date

Benefits:
• Membership Gift: Porcelain Bisque Figurine
• Redemption Certificate for Members-Only Figurine
• Bi-annual Newsletter, "Melody Notes"
• Membership Card & Certificate
• Two Members "Savings" Coupons
• Melody In Motion Catalog
• Personal Purchasing Record
• Retired Edition Summary
• List of Collectors' Centers

WALNUT RIDGE COLLECTIBLES

Kathi Lorance Bejma's Collection of Antique Chocolate Molds Inspires Her Whimsical Chalkware Creations

Proceeds of Kathi Bejma's "Glimmer of Hope" ornament will benefit the Michael Bolton Foundation and Cities In Schools: charities that support women and children at risk. This ornament's retirement date is December 31, 1996.

To moneyed Europeans of the 19th century, chocolate became much more than a mere confectionery treat. When cast in the marvelously intricate molds made by Maison Létang Fils of France or Anton Reiche of Germany, the rich, dark candy was transformed into a true work of art! Today those "in the know" offer strong bids for classic chocolate molds at antique auctions and shows. And among these chocolate mold enthusiasts, Walnut Ridge President and Designer Kathi Lorance Bejma reigns supreme. She buys hundreds of molds from her favorite antique dealer, and uses her treasures as inspiration for her appealing chalkware figures for Walnut Ridge Collectibles.

Kathi has found fascination in both antiques and history since her childhood. As an adult, she began collecting Father Christmases and exhibiting at craft shows, where she sold items made of clay, wood and soft sculpture. At about the time her Father Christmas collection numbered 400, she discovered an antique chocolate mold in Santa's kindly image. She purchased it and put it on display that Christmas. Then as she was re-packing her collectibles after the holiday season, it occurred to her that the Father Christmas antique chocolate mold might make a wonderful image in chalkware. She experimented, with outstanding results: the chalkware Santa became an overnight favorite with her collectors!

That first chalkware creation launched Kathi's tireless quest for wonderful antique chocolate molds — of which she now has nearly 4,000 examples. "I ended up with 700-800 different types of Father Christmas (molds)," she says with a smile. Just as significant, "Father Christmas" inspired Kathi to found her thriving business, Walnut Ridge Collectibles. Subjects to date include Father Christmases, rabbits, cats, a wide range of ornaments, Santas, snowmen, angels, Halloween and fall lines, and many home decor items including lamps — all using intricate chocolate molds from their designer's collection.

Kathi Bejma Invents Her Own Ingenious Chalkware Formula

For years, Kathi had admired antique chalkware figures, but she was amazed at the high prices antique pieces commanded: anywhere from $700 to $10,000 each! "Chalkware is a folk art that originated in the 1700s," she explains. "It was the first official decorative item that came to the (American) colonies." It occurred to Kathi that she could develop her own chalkware formula. "I came up with my own composition that was much more durable than the antique chalkware, but still looked authentic," she says. The exploration process took considerable time and about 20 preliminary formulations. "I was striving for an old-world patina, so I just kept trying until I came up with something I liked."

At first, the artist did all the chalkware production herself: mixing, molding, painting and promoting. "I would sell out at a craft show, run home to make some more, then sell them the next week," she recounts. Strong response encouraged Kathi to seek a wider market for her creations, with gratifying results. She wrote $26,000 in dealer orders on the first day in 1988 that she unveiled her line at the wholesale market in Valley Forge, Pennsylvania!

Today, Kathi's chalkware composition is still mixed by hand, but the work takes place in her spacious new manufacturing facility — 15,000 square feet in Westland, Michigan. Then each piece is individually hand-poured, allowed to set, and finally unmolded. Once the seams are cleaned, the newly formed products are moved to a special room, where temperatures remain at 90 to 100 degrees F. Fans eliminate humidity while the chalkware pieces dry.

A pool of 90 painters decorate the dried pieces with their basic colors, and finally a staff of 20 skilled painters add the final touches, including faces and detail work. Products are then antiqued — and some are "diamond dusted" — before they are prominently tagged "Made in the U.S.A." "We're very proud to let everyone know that our products are totally handmade in the U.S.," Kathi Bejma explains.

"Snow Children" Molds Make Whimsical Chalkware Charmers

A recent chocolate mold discovery sparked the idea for one of Kathi Bejma's latest creations – a set of two chalkware "Snow Children" inspired by a pair of Anton Reiche molds from the early 1900s. The little boy and girl images captured Kathi's heart, both for their innocent appeal and their significance as classics from chocolate's "golden age."

"Snow children were very popular during the Victorian Era," Kathi reveals. "You would see a lot of greeting cards depicting these little ones, but they're not real common in the chocolate mold field. I happened to stumble upon these last year, and I bought them at an antique show. The boy and girl molds are each 3" tall, and they're fine examples of German moldmaker Anton Reiche's handiwork.

"The boy is all white...completely coated with my sparkly 'diamond dust,'" Kathi describes. His suit is completely covered with snow, and he's holding a package with a sprig of holly. Great for the holidays!" The little girl continues the snow-white theme, as Kathi notes. "She has a little white dress with a big white muff in

Kathi Bejma used a set of classic German Anton Reiche chocolate molds to create her adorable chalkware "Snow Children," then added colorful touches to bring the little ones' personalities alive.

front, and her little leggings and hat are white. She has a holly wreath around her hat for color." The chalkware "Snow Children" are sold in a set of two: one boy and one girl. They carry an open edition limit and an issue price of $48.00. They are completely handmade and hand-painted in the U.S.A.

Angels and Santas Star in Kathi Bejma's Porcelain Ornaments

Ever since Kathi Bejma founded Walnut Ridge Collectibles in 1988, she dreamed of creating a special collectible series, with proceeds helping victims of child abuse. "I feel very fortunate with my life," she relates, "and where I'm at, and wish to give something back. You hear of so many children who are abused and lead such horrible lives. Anything we can do to make their lives better, or to make an impact in this area, should be attempted."

To fulfill her goal, Bejma has created an annual series of angel ornaments premiering with "Glimmer of Hope." As she explains, "All of our proceeds from the ornament are being contributed to charities that fund women and children at risk, including the Michael Bolton Foundation and Cities In Schools, a national organization that has facilities in all 50 states. Cities In Schools takes children who are in abusive situations and teaches them a vocation so that they can live a viable life. We're really excited about that."

"Glimmer of Hope" depicts a white angel with "diamond dusted" wings, sitting on top of the world, surrounded by clouds. One arm is crooked, as she holds a beautiful bouquet of roses, while she joyfully throws a rose onto the world with her other arm. The world looks very peaceful, with shades of dark blue sky aglow. Created in porcelain, "Glimmer of Hope" measures 4" in height and 4" wide and has a retirement date of December 31, 1996. It can be hung, or placed on a base and enjoyed as a figurine. The issue price is $40.00. The 1997 annual ornament also will depict an angel.

For her ongoing *Limited Edition*

The Walnut Ridge Halloween Haven collection features the witch, "Bewitching Halloween" as well as assorted ghosts, a black cat, and other brightly decorated Halloween figures.

Christmas series, Kathi Bejma's 1996 creation is the first ornament in the collection: "Snowy, Snowy Night." The Santa ornament represents a porcelain adaptation of a design Kathi once admired in an antique book. The old world Santa wears a midnight blue coat, adorned with a border of delicate snow-laden pine trees, and red mittens. His long white beard keeps his kind and gentle face warm during this wintry season. He carries a miniature tree tucked in his left arm, while he treks through the snowy woods beneath a dark starlit sky. The diamond-dusted "Snowy, Snowy Night" measures 5" in height and carries an issue price of $56.00. Its retirement date is December 31, 1996.

Bunnies and Halloween Characters Charm Walnut Ridge Collectors

In addition to her holiday and wintry creations, Kathi Bejma has spread her artistic wings to develop a

"Christkindl" is one of Kathi Bejma's latest Father Christmas creations. Crafted from a rare German chocolate mold in her own secret chalkware formula, this enchanting piece is hand-painted and "diamond dusted" for an elegant holiday appearance.

wonderful series of popular chalkware bunnies, as well as a new grouping entitled *Halloween Haven.* The latest bunny is called "Robin Tracks," and features both a bunny and a robin popping out of an egg that has cracked open. Limited to an edition of 1,000, the 5" x 4" piece carries an issue price of $48.00.

The *Halloween Haven* series is offered in an open edition so that Halloween enthusiasts may add to their collections in the coming year as well. The lead character is entitled "Bewitching Halloween," and she's a chalkware witch with a pumpkin and broom as accessories. Also included in the grouping are a black cat, some appealing "pumpkin people," a ghost, some jack-o-lanterns, an owl, and two more witches.

News for 1997 from Walnut Ridge

Many Walnut Ridge collectors have asked Kathi Bejma to develop a club for their enjoyment, and she is delighted to announce that the Walnut Ridge Collector's Club will debut in 1997. It will feature a host of benefits, and share more information on Kathi's wonderful chocolate mold collection and the stories behind these cherished antiques.

What's more, Walnut Ridge has plans for a whole new line of fruits and flowers to complement the firm's popular chocolate mold designs. These decorative home accessories will include miniature topiaries with fruits and flowers, a cornucopia with fruits and vegetables, and baskets with individual flowers including roses, day lilies, tulips and many others. These pieces will be crafted from antique ice cream molds — another of Kathi Bejma's passions.

Although it has been nearly a decade since Kathi Bejma invented her chalkware formula and charmed collectors with "Father Christmas," she still retains an attitude of delight and wonder at her collectibles' success. Yet she's crystal clear in her explanation of how it all came about. As the artist explains with a smile, "You have to make a decision, and jump in with both feet!"

Walnut Ridge Collectibles
39048 Webb Dr.
Westland, MI 48185
(313) 728-3300
Fax (313) 728-5950

MEET THE ARTISTS

Biographies of Some of Today's Most Popular and Talented Artists in the Field of Limited Edition Collectibles

Some of the best-known artists in today's world of limited edition collectibles are showcased in the following articles. This listing provides an introduction to many of these talented men and women whose works bring pleasure to collectors world-wide.

HOLLY ADLER

Collectors, friends and neighbors await the works of Holly Adler with delight and anticipation. Her sun-drenched studio in Andover, Minnesota, is a menagerie of sketches, wood carvings, prototypes, books, paint brushes and fabrics — reminders of a dedicated, hard-working artist.

As a designer for Kurt S. Adler, Inc. for the past decade, Holly has developed new major themes featuring Christmas ornaments and decorative accessories and designs for Christmas products for leading licensors. Holly designs Christmas accessories and collectibles in wood, resins and fabrics.

Having accumulated more than 300 teddy bears, some of which she designed herself, Holly decided to introduce her very special bears to the world. In 1995, Holly created the *Holly Bearies Collection*, which features collectible ornaments and figurines depicting teddy bears — each with its own playful character and personality — that are "Looking for a Home in Your Heart."

Holly believes that the hand-made decorations and collectibles she creates today are destined to become the treasured keepsakes and heirlooms of tomorrow.

MARTYN ALCOCK

Martyn Alcock became a modeller for Royal Doulton at the John Beswick studio in 1986. He began work on several figure subjects for *Bunnykins*, including "Policeman" and "Schoolboy" (1988). Since then, he has modelled numerous additions to the *Bunnykins*, culminating in 1994's *Sixtieth Anniversary Bunnykins*.

Martyn has contributed several studies of Beatrix Potter characters to the *Royal Albert* figure collection, including "Peter and the Red Handkerchief" and "Christmas Stocking." He also recreated several of the most popular Beatrix Potter subjects in a large size.

Like all the modellers in the Beswick studio, Martyn has been encouraged to show his versatility, and more recently has turned his hand to character jugs. His first character jug, "Captain Hook," was selected to be Royal Doulton's *Character Jug of the Year* for 1994. He also modelled the charming miniature "Snowman" character jug.

Away from the studio, Martyn spends time with his family and still finds time to play goalkeeper for Royal Doulton's Nile Street soccer team.

As Martyn says, "To know that people enjoy and appreciate my work is the most rewarding part of my job."

DANIELLE A. APHESSETCHE

As art director at Calabar Creations, Danielle's warm spirit and optimistic outlook is mirrored on each new design and collection. Danielle's cheerful book-lined studio is a testament to the thoughtful and creative research she puts into each design. She is valued for the coloration, names and stories of all Calabar figurines.

A native of France, Danielle earned a diploma for ceramic art and sculpture and another for drawing and design from the State School of Applied Art, and her teaching credentials from the Ecole Normale D'Instituteurs. Later she earned her master of arts degree in design from the University of Bordeaux and a second master of arts from California State University at Fullerton.

She traveled extensively in Europe and won several of the highest awards from the French School of Beaux Art. Danielle taught art before her marriage but later immigrated to the United States. She enjoys working in her beautiful and bountiful garden and spending time with her husband and three grown children.

PETE APSIT

Born in Los Angeles, Pete Apsit majored in art at the University of Southern California. He enjoys working from his Bakersfield studio where he can be near his wife and children.

One Christmas, Pete was short of money and chose to sculpt a whale for his brother. Impressed with the statue's rugged artistry, his brother convinced Pete to quit his job and form the

Apsit Brothers of California Co., which manufactured and sold statuary. In 1977, Pete separated from his brother and created California Originals, a company offering free-lance designs.

For Calabar Creations, Pete created the limited edition series *Little Farmers*, *Yesterday's Friends* and *Daddy's Girl* in tribute to America's children.

A jovial, life-loving person, Pete has created many collections that fit his bubbly personality, such as *SantaVenture*, *Tee Club*, and *The Grandpions*. His humorous Santas reveal the "other side" of Santa Claus. His golfers' facial expressions depict with humor and empathy the strong emotions hidden in the seemingly peaceful game of golf. *The Grandpions* are collections of dwarfed professionals, sportsmen and hobbyists that are sure to unwrinkle many grumpy faces.

GIUSEPPE ARMANI

Born in Calci, a quaint little town not far from Pisa, Italy, Giuseppe Armani found it lacking in inspirational material suitable for a young and avid artist. As an adolescent, he felt impelled to seek his future elsewhere. He set out to mine the artistic treasures of the great triumvirate of quintessential renaissance cities – Pisa, Siena and Florence – and he struck gold!

Beginning his professional career in Pisa, Armani worked in the workshop of a gallery located directly opposite The Leaning Tower. In 1975, Florence Sculture d'Arte and Armani began an inspired, exclusive and extraordinarily successful relationship. Armani and Florence Sculture d' Arte are currently forming a workshop in the tradition of the renowned Renaissance workshops, enabling the world's most talented sculptors to work with and learn from the master sculptor himself, Giuseppe Armani.

Armani's mythic, almost mystical, ability to put character and "soul" into his sculptures continues to amaze, astound and intrigue. The geniuses of the Renaissance have inspired Armani to sculpt modern masterpieces. Giuseppe Armani Creates Art For Today!

MABEL LUCIE ATTWELL

British artist Mabel Lucie Attwell sold her first drawing before she was 16 to a London publisher. From there, Attwell worked as an artist to pay for art school.

Attwell married illustrator Harold Earnshaw. They had two sons and a daughter, Peggy, who became the "Attwell child," the toddler with large eyes, a winsome expression and often a large bow in her hair.

Attwell's earliest published illustrations for gift books, children's books and fairy tales appeared in 1905. Her distinctive treatment of children as cherubic, chubby-legged and winsome was established early in her career. Throughout her career, her art was always in demand – even by the Royal Family. As a toddler, Prince Charles was presented with a set of nursery china bearing Attwell's illustrations, and Princess Margaret chose Attwell's artwork for personal Christmas cards.

After Attwell's death in 1964, Enesco licensed the rights to translate her artwork into porcelain bisque figurines for the *Enesco Memories of Yesterday®* collection, which premiered in 1988.

BRIAN BAKER

Brian Baker's fascination for history, art and architecture has taken him to over 40 countries, from Europe to Mexico. Brian's discoveries have inspired him to share those experiences with others through the creation of the *Déjà Vu Collection* from Michael's Limited.

Brian believes each building creates itself, but really it's the charming way he sculpts and his attention to detail. He hand-casts the designs in fine bonded stone and carefully develops a color scheme for each building.

Brian's trademark is an umbrella. Watch for one hidden in the shadows or tucked away in a corner of many of his sculptures. Brian explains, "On my first building, I wanted a hungry French cat sitting by the door. I couldn't seem to design a cat that pleased me, so I left the cat's tail as the handle and made the body into an umbrella."

The *Déjà Vu Collection* is Brian Baker's way of bringing history to life and making you feel like you've been there before.

BETTE BALL

As director of doll design for Goebel of North America, Bette Ball is the award-winning designer of the highly acclaimed *Betty Jane Carter®*, *Goebel Angel Dolls®* and *Victoria Ashlea Originals®* porcelain dolls. She is known and appreciated by doll collectors for her uncompromising quality of design.

Bette double majored in Fine Arts and Costume Design in art school. Her paintings hang in many private collections around the world, and she enjoys an international reputation for her design in fine china and giftware.

She is a recipient of the prestigious DOTY award and NALED "Doll of the Year" awards. Bette's dolls have been honored by acceptance in more than 50 museums worldwide.

Bette has endeared herself to countless admirers through personal and television appearances, where she lends her vibrant personality to discussions on designing and collecting dolls.

DOT AND SY BARLOWE

Collaborating as fellow artists at New York's Museum of Natural History in the 1940s, Dot and Sy Barlowe have been illustrating since then — together and separately — and earning national recognition for their historic and naturalist art.

The Barlowes have illustrated nature books such as *Seashores*, *Trees of America* and *Amphibians of North America* for some of the largest publishing houses in America.

In addition, the Barlowes have contributed illustrations to Audubon Society guides and to *The Audubon Society Encyclopedia of North American Birds*. They also teach nature illustration and botany at the Parsons School of Design in New York. Their works have been honored with numerous awards and exhibitions at the Society of Illustrators in New York and Expo '67 in Montreal.

Reco International Corp. has presented an eight-plate *Vanishing Animal Kingdoms* collection by Sy and a *Gardens of Beauty* plate collection by Dot, as well as a series of animal figurines by both artists. Other recent introductions include *Town & Country Dogs* and *Our Cherished Seas* plate series.

FRANCIS J. BARNUM

Born and raised in Ohio's Cuyahoga River Valley, Francis J. Barnum joined the Chilmark Gallery in the midst of a 35 year career as a designer, modelmaker and sculptor. Barnum has now made a name for himself as a historian and prominent artist in the realm of Civil War sculpture.

Barnum has designed the *Civil War* collection commemorating America's most remembered war through depictions of well-known leaders, as well as anonymous heroes, in fine pewter, MetalART™ and bronze. Painstaking research and attention to the smallest details are obvious in Barnum's work. In addition to bringing a sense of high drama to his scenes, he captures the very emotions of his characters.

Numbering over 75 pieces in 1995, the Barnum *Civil War* collection takes us from Gettysburg to Shiloh to Antietam and runs the gamut of emotions from victory to defeat.

KATHY BARRY-HIPPENSTEEL

Kathy Barry-Hippensteel, a sculptor of child and baby dolls, has received widespread acclaim for their lifelike quality and has been bestowed with many awards.

"Chen" was nominated for a *Dolls* magazine 1989 "Award of Excellence" and received the National Association of Limited Edition Dealers' 1990 "Achievement Award." In 1992,

"Patricia, My First Tooth" doll, from the *Happiness Is...* collection, was nominated for *Dolls'* "Award of Excellence" and *Doll Reader's* "Doll of the Year" award. In 1993, "Tickles" — the first issue in the *Joys of Summer* collection and one of her most sought-after dolls — was nominated for the same two awards.

In 1994, the International Doll Exposition (IDEX) recognized Kathy, giving her international acclaim. She displays art in France and the U.S., while both her "Tickles" and "Elizabeth's Homecoming" dolls have received prestigious "Canadian Collectibles of the Year Award" from *Collectibles Canada*.

Kathy hopes "to bring a smile to people's faces. If I can make something that hugs somebody's heart and makes them smile, then I've done what I set out to do."

PRESCOTT "WOODY" BASTON, JR.

In 1938, Prescott Baston was asked by a friend to sculpt a pair of figures for her to sell at her restaurant. From this modest beginning came *Sebastian Miniatures*. Over a 46 year period, Baston sculpted more than 1,200 designs and variations, many of which are highly collectible today.

Baston's son, Prescott Jr. or "Woody," worked in the Sebastian Studio throughout his youth and later earned a bachelor's degree in sculpture from Boston University. Under his father's tutelage, Woody designed his first miniature, "First Kite," in 1981. Since Baston, Sr.'s death in 1984, Woody has been the sole creative force behind *Sebastian Miniatures*, America's oldest continually produced collectible line.

Woody has sculpted over 300 miniatures including figures in both cold cast porcelain and pewter, as well as Christmas ornaments. Currently offered series include *Santa's World*, *Sunday Afternoon in the Park*, *The Sebastian Firefighter Collection* and *Lighthouses*.

KATHI BEJMA

From the time she was a young girl, Kathi Lorance Bejma was fascinated by both antiques and history. As an adult, she began collecting Father Christmases and exhibiting at craft shows, where she sold items made of clay, wood and soft sculpture.

At about the time her Father Christmas collection numbered 400, Bejma discovered an antique chocolate mold to add to her collection. She experimented with the mold, creating a piece of chalkware. This design was so popular with her customers that she began collecting these fascinating antique molds, which now number nearly 4,000, and founded a thriving business. Through her company, Walnut Ridge Collectibles, Bejma creates numerous chalkware and porcelain designs for both the giftware and limited edition collectibles industries. Subjects include Santas, angels, snowmen, rabbits, cats, trees, and many others.

Walnut Ridge Collectibles maintains a spacious facility in Westland, Michigan, a suburb of Detroit. It is there that Bejma oversees her entire operation, where all products are tagged 'Made in the USA.' "We're very proud to let everyone know that our products are totally handmade in the U.S.," says Bejma.

AURO BELCARI

Tuscany, with its natural, cultural and culinary endowments, is the birthplace of Renaissance Art. It is also the birthplace of Master Sculptor Auro Belcari.

Belcari was trained in the artisan shops, where he worked with simple materials. He studied diligently and achieved a master's diploma in art.

Since 1978, Belcari has worked for the Dear Studio in Italy, creating masterpieces from shapeless lumps of clay. His abundant talent is showcased in wildlife and bird sculptures that feature eagles, horses, sea gulls, geese, flamingos and giraffes. He has also created magnificent human figures. The artist's humility is manifested in all his works, which are valued throughout the world by discriminating collectors.

YOLANDA BELLO

In 1995, doll artist Yolanda Bello celebrated her tenth anniversary at The Ashton-Drake Galleries.

As a child in Venezuela, Bello "restyled" her dolls into new and exciting characters. At age 14, Bello moved to Chicago, Illinois, where she worked as a figurine sculptor and pursued doll design and sculpture in her spare time. In 1981, Bello created a pair of porcelain Spanish girl dolls, which turned doll making into a full-time profession.

Since then, Bello has earned more than 60 awards, including a "Doll of the Year®" award in 1985 for one of her studio dolls, and in 1993, for her Ashton-Drake doll, "Meagan Rose."

Bello's designs range from dolls portraying characters in the opera *Carmen*, to her most sought-after limited edition dolls, such as *Yolanda's Picture-Perfect Babies®*, her first dolls for Ashton-Drake. They sold out years ago but are available again, in the brand-new forms of porcelain mini-dolls and ornaments.

Bello is still best-known for her Ashton-Drake dolls, including *Yolanda's Lullaby Babies®*, *Yolanda's Heaven-Scent* collection, and *Yolanda's Rainbow of Love* collection, featuring babies of many ethnic origins.

JODY BERGSMA

Attending a small college in Vancouver, Canada, Jody Bergsma was influenced by the Canadian impressionists called the "Group of Seven." In 1978, she travelled to Europe and painted in southern France, Venice and Florence, ending her studies in Athens and the Greek Islands. Returning home, Bergsma withdrew from

her engineering studies and became a serious, full-time artist.

Along with many one-woman shows of her abstract water-colors, Jody has released over 300 different "Little People" prints through the Jody Bergsma Gallery. She teamed up with Reco International to produce her first plate series, *Guardians of the Kingdom*. Since then, they have produced a Mother's Day series, two Christmas Series, *The Castles and Dreams* series and her newest, *Magic Companions*. Her recent trip to the Queen Charlotte Islands inspired many new prints based on the rich heritage and customs of the natives and a plate series entitled *Totems of the West*.

Inspired by the proverb, "A Cheerful Heart Is Good Medicine," Jody designed the *Laughables*, a line of figurines, bringing a joyful chuckle to all who receive them.

ULRICH BERNARDI

Born in the Groden Valley of Northern Italy's Dolomite Mountains, Ulrich Bernardi dreamed of becoming a woodcarver. There, woodcarving has been passed from generation to generation for more than 300 years.

Bernardi's grandfather, an altar builder, and grandmother, an ornamental wood sculptress, inspired him and shared their knowledge and skills with him. During World War II, Bernardi, a deeply religious man, applied those skills by carving madonnas and crucifixes which he gave as symbols of hope to soldiers heading to the battlefields.

Bernardi earned a master of art degree at the Academy of Art in St. Ulrich and served a four-year apprenticeship with a master woodcarver. At age 30, his sculpture of a madonna earned him the rank of master woodcarver.

Working with the House of ANRI for more than 35 years, Bernardi's religious woodcarvings, including the Florentine Nativity presented to Pope John Paul II, and his woodcarvings of Australian artist Sarah Kay have earned him a worldwide reputation for finely detailed, inspirational art.

KEITH BIRDSONG

Keith Birdsong may not be a space traveler, but as a former parachutist, he knows the breathtaking excitement of hurtling through space — and that's an experience he's drawn upon to create some of the most thrilling *STAR TREK®* illustrations ever seen.

Avid "trekkies" know him as the gifted illustrator of every issue of Pocket Books' fantastically successful *STAR TREK* paperback series for the past four years. Now, collectors can enjoy the talents of this self-taught artist from Oklahoma through his stellar plate painting of the "U.S.S. Enterprise™ NCC-1701" as the premier issue in a new collection for The Hamilton Collection entitled *STAR TREK: The Voyagers*. This collection is dedicated to the most famous spaceships seen in the *STAR TREK* series.

PAUL BOLINGER

Debuting for Kurt S. Adler, Inc. in 1994, Paul Bolinger specializes in distinctive stylized Old World Santas. Ever since receiving a chisel from a friend for Christmas, he has taught himself the art of woodcarving, from relief carving to carving in the round. He creates holiday legends from his "Three Bears Cottage" studio in the Santa Cruz Mountains in California.

Selected as one of the top 200 American craftsmen by *Early American Life* magazine, Paul combines both fine art and folk art techniques to hand-carve each of his Santas.

His *Christmas Legends* collection, designed exclusively for KSA Collectibles from Kurt S. Adler, Inc., includes hand-painted Santas cast in wood resin directly from his originals. New collectibles feature Corn Cob Pipe and North Pole sign ornaments, candle holders and novelty ornaments. "Bountiful," an elegant, large Santa, is featured in the *Christmas Legends* series, along with "Cookie Claus" and "No Hair Day Santa." Each of Paul's characters, whether they're inspired from old German and Celtic lore or are just whimsical creations, are based on an original humorous tale that he created.

MICHAEL BOYETT

Michael Boyett is recognized as one of the most important sculptors of the American West. His works are exhibited in Western galleries and museums throughout the United States, including exhibitions at the inauguration of President Carter, The George Phippen Memorial Art Show, Texas Rangers Hall of Fame, and the Texas Art Classic.

Born in Boise, Idaho, Boyett's childhood passion for drawing and carving propelled him into a career in fine arts. After serving in the Vietnam War, he received bachelor's and master's degrees in Fine Arts from Stephen F. Austin State University.

Boyett worked exclusively in bronze until 1979, when The Lance Corporation began casting his miniature scale sculptures in pewter. His works for Chilmark include the *Legacy of Courage* Indian series, *Flat Out for Red River Station* and *He Who Taunts the Enemy*.

His work for Legends® represents the interdependent relationship that existed between the Native American warrior hunter and wild creatures. Creating each detailed sculpture with a sense of movement, Michael hopes that "each of my pieces will give viewers the impression that they have actually witnessed the event portrayed."

SUZAN BRADFORD

Suzan Bradford's background, education and own natural talent have combined to provide us with the inspired figurine sculptor Suzan is today. Her freelance and commissioned artworks are in private collections across the country.

Suzan defines herself as primarily a self-taught artist. Always adventuresome, Suzan explores the mediums of drawing, oil painting, watercolor, bronzes and lithographs as she does sculpture.

Suzan, who joined United Design in 1985, has been instrumental in making *The Legend of Santa Claus*™ one of the most sought-after Santa collections available. She is also responsible for creating the first design in the *Angels Collection* and the *Fancy Frames*™ offering.

In Suzan's free time, she has turned her talents to renovating her pre-statehood Norman, Oklahoma, home.

RICK BROWN

With a combined passion for drawing, painting and football, Omaha native Rick Brown knew he could be happy with only one career – as a sports artist.

After college at the University of Nebraska-Omaha, Rick moved to California where he studied at the Art Center College of Design in Pasadena, and at Long Beach State. Afterwards, he landed a position with a major California studio working with noted illustrators.

In 1984, Rick began freelancing with an impressive client list that includes Disney, Universal Studios, Milton Bradley, Pro-Line and Pro-Set trading cards, and NFL Properties.

His skill and success in combining acrylics, airbrush and brush painting brought him to the attention of The Bradford Exchange, which recently released the first series of collector's plates to feature his vibrant art, *The Great Super Bowl Quarterbacks*.

TOM BROWNING

Tom Browning found that art was an important part of his childhood, and what he wanted to do with his life. Today, he is one of America's leading artists. His work is displayed at galleries throughout the West and Northwest including Settlers West in Tucson and Wadles Gallery in Santa Fe. He is a member of the Northwest Rendezvous Group (NWR) in Helena, Montana.

In addition to painting full time, Browning and his wife Joyce own and operate Arbor Green Publishers, where they publish and distribute the popular

Santa's Time Off™ greeting cards and prints.

Tom Browning's work is also featured in the *American Artist Collection*® and the *Santa's Time Off*™ porcelain collection from Possible Dreams.

Browning describes himself as a quiet, sensitive person who produces "a picture that is simple and straightforward."

MICHAEL AND SHELLEY TINCHER BUONAIUTO

The sculptures of Michael and Shelley Buonaiuto use an unusual combination of various clays, porcelain and stoneware in a single work. Collectors are drawn to their work not only for the technical achievement but also for the highly personal quality that gives each piece a unique life and expression.

At the University of Massachusetts, Shelley studied painting and etching, and Michael studied architecture and sculpture. Unable to find a direction in art, Shelley studied flute and music theory at The New England Conservatory in Boston. Later in New York, Shelley studied and taught sacred dance, and began working in pottery to capture the tranquility of ancient Asian Buddhas and DaVinci's madonnas. Her work is also influenced by her love for music and dance.

Feeling a need for change and fresh inspiration, Michael and Shelley sold their house and moved to Santa Fe via South America.

Michael began working in pottery in 1975. Although his figures are fairly realistic, he is influenced by the art objects and ceremonies of primitive cultures. He finds inspiration by watching the earth and clouds out of an airplane window, from dream imagery or even by walking through a fish market.

In their spare time, Michael improves his Haitian drumming and Shelley is pursuing a degree in art therapy, as well as beginning a new series of art pieces to be cast in bronze. They are under commission from Duncan Royale.

FRANCES BURTON

Frances Elaine Montgomery Burton has always loved art. After completing the Famous Artist Course, she began her training as a Fenton decorator in 1973. For the next ten years, she balanced work with raising her children. Later returning to Fenton full-time, she quickly progressed from decorator to trainer, designer, head designer and finally department supervisor.

In her spare time, Frances likes walking, sewing and growing the beautiful flowers she later brings to life on glass. Her delicate floral Vining Garden design enhanced the beauty of Fenton's Transparent Seamist Green Glass.

Romance novels and old movies also capture her interest. She is content when curled by the fire with a good book, her three cats, and Nikki, the dog. Frances and Lanny, her husband of 25 years, love to escape to Vermillion on Lake Erie where they fish, share the quiet beauty and their dream of residing there someday.

SAM BUTCHER

Sam Butcher began his artistic career creating the teardrop-eyed children with inspirational messages for use on greeting cards and posters. In 1978, Enesco President and CEO, Eugene Freedman, transformed Butcher's two-dimensional art into the popular three-dimensional *Precious Moments*® Collection.

Butcher creates all artwork for the Collection and coordinates with Enesco and the Precious Moments Design Studio in Japan to create dozens of new subjects each year, all inspired by personal events and collector requests. Butcher also creates contemporary art, depicting men, women and children.

Butcher's faith and art led to the construction of the Precious Moments Chapel in Carthage, Missouri, which houses a myriad of artwork, stained glass windows and a painted ceiling, all featuring *Precious Moments* children.

Butcher has been honored with a multitude of awards within the collectibles industry including the 1988 "Special Recognition Award," 1992 "Artist and Collectible of the Year," and 1994 "Figurine and Ornament of the Year," all by the National Association of Limited Edition Dealers.

The father of seven children and grandfather of 13, Butcher divides his time between his home on the Chapel grounds, his residence near Chicago and the overseas studio.

JOYCE F. BYERS

Joyce Fritz Byers' artistic curiosity at age 12 had expanded from sewing doll costumes to include sculpture and oil painting. She earned a degree in Home Economics at Drexel University and after graduation, took a position designing children's clothing.

By the late 1960s, Joyce had married Bob Byers and lived with their two sons in Bucks County, Pennsylvania.

Joyce began making caroling Christmas figures, first for herself, and then as gifts for her family and friends. For about ten years, Joyce perfected the construction methods and refined her sculpting skills.

In the late 1970s, the demand for the Carolers® became so great that with Bob's assistance, they turned a hobby into a business.

Joyce sculpts each original face in clay and designs the costumes. She teaches artisans the skills necessary for quantity production of the hand-made Byers' Choice figurines. This handwork imparts each figurine with the delightful personality sought by nearly 150,000 collectors.

The incredible success of Byers' Choice figurines has enabled Bob and Joyce to share the joy of giving in Christmas' true spirit.

Each year, they give a substantial amount of their company's profits to charities.

PETER CALVESBERT

Born in Hereford, England, in 1960, Master Sculptor Peter Calvesbert first picked up a piece of modeling clay at the age of three. A full and active school life kept him occupied until 1976, when he took a job as a trainee ceramic artist at Boehms of Malvern.

Six years later, Peter thought it was time for a change. He traveled throughout England and to and from the continent, dabbling in a variety of occupations such as computer programming, brick laying, plumbing, journalism and giftware management. One day while watching a friend sculpt, he remembered those long-ago days as a ceramics trainee and said, "I could do that." And he did!

Once word spread of his sculpting skills, commissions poured in, including a request from the Queen's courier to sculpt the royal pets. Through a chance meeting, Peter teamed up with Martin Perry, the chief designer and moldmaker for the Harmony Kingdom. Peter now concentrates on humorous work, adding his own special twists to Harmony Kingdom's *Treasure Jest* boxes. He has a list of designs that stretches well into the next millennium, and he hopes that "I'm still doing this when I'm 100."

KITTY D. CANTRELL

Award-winning artist and environmentalist Kitty Cantrell is known for her striking sculptures of North American wildlife. Intricately designed and detailed, her Mixed Media® sculptures capture expressions of animals that have never known human touch such as wolves, eagles and humpback whales. Through her sculptures, people can better understand the earth's wild creatures. "If my sculptures can make people think about wildlife and appreciate the importance of wildlife, then maybe they will feel compelled to help protect it."

After researching an animal, Cantrell produces a rough sculpture out of soft clay to check for composition and form. She then forms a master sculpture – authentic to scale and anatomically accurate – and coats it with silicone rubber and plaster casting. When the mold is ready, she sends it to the Legends® foundry where a resin cast is made. Pewter is used as a base for the sculptures which are covered with various metals – bronze, copper and 24K gold. Using actual hot-torched acid patinas, not paints or dyes, the metals are beautifully colored to bring the sculptures to life.

For her work including bronzes and pastels, Cantrell has received several awards. She resides in Southern California with her husband, sculptor Erik Fredsti, and their many animals.

PAUL CARDEW

Design phenomenon Paul Cardew is the award-winning artist acknowledged worldwide as the most talented and prolific creator of collectible teapots.

An honors graduate of Loughborough Art College, later to become head of his department at Exeter Art College, Cardew was the first designer to concentrate on collectible teapots. His innovative work over the past 20 years has won wide recognition in exhibitions and from museums, such as the Victoria & Albert, as well as from collectors around the world.

Together with long-time friend and partner, Peter Kirvan, Cardew established Cardew Design in 1991. Since then, the company has produced more than 45,000 highly collectible, whimsical and functional teapots which are sold in 20 countries. Cardew teapots are imported and distributed in the United States by the S.P. Skinner Co.

PAT CHANDOK AND DAVID LEE WOODARD

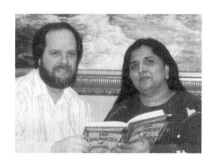

The art of collaboration is alive and well at Precious Art's *World of Krystonia* with Pat Chandok and David Woodard heading a creative team. They have worked together to produce some of the gift industry's most innovative products – from carousel ponies to fantasy figurines and music boxes.

A native of Bombay, India, Pat Chandok brings a sphere of Asian influence. After finishing her schooling, she married and moved to the U.S., where her love of business and fine art directed her into the giftware industry.

In 1975, Dave, already a friend, joined Pat, bringing with him an impressive array of marketing, merchandising and sales skills. In 1980, the pair began importing and distributing their own giftware, which became so successful that they closed their retail shops.

Pat and Dave's early success in oriental designs led into musical items, including the market's first up-and-down carousel. In 1987, they premiered the award-winning *World of Krystonia*, a whimsical make-believe kingdom. With three books on the market and a fourth in the making, collectors can read about their favorite characters. Creating new figurines for their stories is one of Pat and Dave's most rewarding tasks. Whatever the results, the collector is always the first in the minds and hearts of this creative pair.

JAMES C. CHRISTENSEN

James Christensen fills his art with wonderful people, places and things as real as your adult dreams and as beloved as your childhood memories. He has created a unique kinetic kingdom, "a land a little left of reality," where human emotions are often manifested as fish or fowl, utilizing the viewer's own imagination.

His art-inspired offerings from The Greenwich Workshop include porcelain figurines; Art Furnishings; unique Bookcase Puzzles; *Evening Angels*, an Art in Concert™ art and music collaboration with composer Kurt Bestor; and, from The Greenwich Workshop Press, *A Journey of Imagination.*

After studying painting at the University of California and Brigham Young University, Christensen has had one-man shows in the West and the Northeast. His work is prized in America and Europe, and has been included in the *New York Society of Illustrators Annual* and Japan's *Outstanding American Illustrators* book.

Christensen is now a professor of art at Brigham Young University. He has been part of The Greenwich Workshop family of artists since 1985.

JOYCE CLEVELAND

Animals, nature and children are the focus of Joyce Cleveland's art-work. By the time she graduated from Syracuse University, top greeting card companies were already interested in her creations. She immediately began designing party goods and three-dimensional items. Often traveling to Japan, Taiwan and Hong Kong on design trips, she later went back and lived in Taiwan to get a better understanding of factory capabilities.

In 1973, Joyce formed her own company, J. Cleveland Design Inc. Her work ranged from creating textile designs to children's products and packaging, yet she found time to illustrate three children's books.

Joyce enjoys doing a wide variety of designs, from humorous to cute, to realistic wildlife. "I like to make people smile, laugh and have fun with life as well as appreciate the beauty of nature."

Joyce Cleveland is currently designing for Possible Dreams.

LAURA COBABE

To be a great doll designer, two qualities are particularly important — exceptional artistic ability and a deep, abiding love of children. This unique combination can be found in Laura Cobabe, who creates wonderfully animated collector dolls.

The very first doll Laura entered in competition, "Dustin," won a blue ribbon. Today, her dolls continue to win awards, including the coveted "Rolf Ericson Award for Outstanding Doll Sculpture" for "Amber," and back-to-back "Doll of the Year" awards for "Brianna" in 1992

and "Tamika" in 1993. And her adorable trick-or-treater doll, "Lil' Punkin," was nominated for a 1994 DOTY award. Her most recent creation is "Nica" for The Hamilton Collection.

Laura spends so much of her time making her dolls look authentic — from their decorative costumes to their realistic child features — that she only makes five dolls a year. A percentage of the money these dolls draw is donated to the Adam Walsh Children's Fund to give children a chance for a better future.

DAVID CORBRIDGE

A uniquely talented person, David Corbridge combines passionate interests in conservation, wildlife, drawing, painting, illustrating, sculpting, education...and pigs! Living on an English farm in a remote part of County Durham where there is abundant wildlife, Corbridge has developed a keen understanding of pigs by closely watching their personalities and idiosyncratic ways. As he fondly says, "To know pigs is to love them!"

Corbridge is a much sought-after lecturer and exhibiting artist who spends his time studying wildlife and expressing his feelings through writing, sculpture, painting and drawing. He enjoys sharing his love of nature with others, especially collectors who have fallen in love with the *Piggin'* line. His English sense of humor is a dominant reason for the appeal of this collectible series produced by Collectible World Studios in England and exclusively distributed in the U.S. by Flambro Imports.

HELEN COVENTRY

Helen Coventry joined W.A.P. Watson Ltd. in 1991 (parent company to The Tudor Mint), and has worked on designs for jewelry, display stands and packaging, including the new *Myth and Magic* box design for 1995.

Helen's first *Myth and Magic* figurine was "The Rising of the Phoenix" and since then she has designed "The Wizard of the Skies" and most of the "Demon" studies from the *Dark Secrets* line. Many of the exciting 1995 introductions have been designed by Helen.

Despite being involved in creating original artwork these days, Helen actually specialized in photography for her degree in design at North Staffordshire Polytechnic.

EDNA DALI

A graduate of Ben-Gurion University in Israel, Edna Dali immigrated to Nottingham, England, in 1977, where she studied painting and sculpting. She and her family later moved to the United States. She continued her art studies in Massachusetts, where she first became interested in doll sculpture. This interest has won her a "Public's Favorite Award" at IDEX and two "Awards of Excellence" from *Dolls* magazine.

Edna creates a few one-of-a-kind dolls, much prized by high-end collectors, as well as limited edition dolls that are more accessible to the amateur collector. She makes her home in Ra'Anna, Israel, with her husband Avi and their three children, Tamir, Assaf and Ma'ayan. Her recent creations for the Seymour Mann Gallery include "Patricia," "Stacy" and "Cara," nominee for *Dolls* magazine's 1995 "Award of Excellence."

STEVE DARNLEY

Born in 1962, Steve Darnley worked for W.A.P. Watson Ltd. (parent of The Tudor Mint) for three years in casting and mold making, then left for nearly five years before returning as a model maker in 1991. Although always interested in model making, he has never had any formal training and joined the company on the merits of his self-taught skills gained using tools handmade by his father. As a new model maker, he tended to work initially on souvenirs but now is much more involved with *Myth and Magic*. His first study was "Banishing the Dragon." He also sculpted "The Armoured Dragon" (a favorite of his), "The Hatchlings" and a number of *Dark Secrets'* studies. He prides himself on trying to make the back side of his studies as interesting as the front side, this part not being covered by the original design drawings which allows for greater creativity.

LOWELL DAVIS

Born in Red Oak, Missouri, Lowell's life-long artistic interest in animals and rural settings was nurtured by the family and friends that gathered at the general store to tell stories and whittle. After spending some time in the Air Force, in college, and as an art director in a Dallas advertising agency for 13 years, Davis realized that he greatly missed the freedom of his hometown, so he headed back to Missouri to pursue art and the open skies.

Now, Lowell Davis has paired his talents with Ertl Collectibles™, a leading manufacturer of die cast replicas. He is sculpting miniature members of his rural community to accompany the company's die cast tractor line. Lowell is also creating a series of barn sculptures, called the Ertl Collectibles *American Country Barn Series™*, a new line of Christmas ornaments, entitled *Sparrowsville™*, and the *Farm Country Christmas™* collection of country scenes.

Through the years, Lowell has virtually reconstructed his old hometown, buying homes and businesses and restoring them to their original grandeur. Now known as Red Oak II™, Lowell considers it and his 60-acre FoxFire Farm™ as living works-of-art.

RAY DAY

Since 1973, Ray Day has painted America's rural landscape in water-color and published limited edition originals. From 1986, Ray's watercolors have been published on limited edition porce-

lain plates. Ray's watercolors bring enjoyment to collectors who find pleasure in the nostalgic and historic. He finds inspiration all over America...from coast to coast... from noted landmarks to hidden treasures.

At the invitation of Lilliput Lane, Ray has created the *American Landmarks* collection. He sculpts each building based on actual locations in wax, then sends it to the Lilliput Lane Studios in Penrith, England, where molding, casting and painting takes place.

Ray has spent 33 years teaching high school art and theater. In addition, he and his wife Eileen continue to publish his watercolors from their southern Indiana home.

Ray serves on the Rural Landmarks Council of the Historic Landmarks Foundation in Indiana. He encourages collectors to join protective societies in order "to be informed of preservation needs and efforts throughout the country."

CHIP DEMATTEO

Growing up in a restored home in Colonial Williamsburg, Chip deMatteo watched his father, William, set off for his silversmith's shop. As a child, he enjoyed spending time in his father's shop, and by age ten, he was actually doing small jobs.

Eventually, Chip studied art in college and then spent a few years as a "starving artist" in Washington, D.C. Meanwhile, he supplemented his income with silver work for his father.

In the late 1970s, Chip, his father and a partner Philip Thorp formed Hand & Hammer Silversmiths in Alexandria, Virginia. Since 1981, Chip has been the sole designer for Hand & Hammer, creating more than 400 ornament designs.

Using the "lost-wax" technique, Chip has designed a number of highly sought-after series. Especially popular are the *Bell, Star,* and *Twelve Days of Christmas* series, in addition to the *Beatrix Potter, Night Before Christmas* and *Alice in Wonderland* collections.

BEV DOOLITTLE

Bev Doolittle has set the world's record for the number of commissioned limited edition prints sold, and the book *The Art of Bev Doolittle* has more than 350,000 copies in print.

Following the announcement of a "hiatus for creative exploration," the anticipation was great for her 1995 fine art print "Two More Indian Horses," and her book *New Magic*, which is offered in a Collector's Edition with a new signed and numbered limited edition print.

After graduating from the Art Center College of Design in Los Angeles, Bev became involved in advertising art and television commercial production with her husband, Jay. However, she had a strong desire to create her own art and be close to nature.

Now with both goals accomplished, Bev's talents in the medium of transparent watercolor have won her a worldwide following. Often referred to as a 'camouflage' artist, Bev thinks of herself as a 'concept painter' who uses camouflage to get her story across. "For me, camouflage is a means to an end, not an end in itself. My meaning and message are never hidden."

ERMANNO FARINA

Ermanno Farina was born in Milan in 1951. Ever since childhood, he has exhibited a special artistic ability and an eye for beauty. In his initial artwork, he demonstrated his preference for nature. Farina studied with the great master sculptor G. Tagliariol-Tay, who inspired him to pursue art as a profession.

In 1975, Farina started his career as a ceramic sculptor, dedicating himself to his art and always striving for improvement. His work soon received worldwide recognition, and through his collaboration with the Dear Studio, he has been able to further express his talents.

Today, Farina's work still focuses on nature, and he is especially inspired by the numerous species of birds that abound in nature. His sculptures are rich in detail and possess a natural feeling of movement and color that makes his creations true to life.

DECLAN FEARON

A standard of Irish folklore for centuries, the Blarney Stone is believed to bestow the gifts of good luck and eloquence upon all who kiss it. People have traveled long distances for this opportunity.

Thanks to Declan Fearon, a journey to your local collectible store is all that's necessary to share in the enchantment through *Declan's Finnians: Guardians of the Blarney Stone*. These colorful, hand-crafted characters with tales on Story Cards bear a stone chip from the same quarry that was the source for the historic Blarney Castle. Fearon and his wife, Camilla, collaborated on the Finnians' concept and design.

Fearon personally brought a bit of Ireland to the Fightin' Irish in 1994 by presenting a piece of quarry stone to University of Notre Dame's Head Football Coach, Lou Holtz.

A successful businessman for over 30 years, Fearon is a native of the capital of Ireland and studied at the University of Dublin.

PAT FORD

Pat Ford is influenced by all the roles that have fulfilled her unique life — that of mother, wife, and consummate artist. Her development as a naturalist artist came out of her own experience. "I married an outdoorsman. Instead of going to the opera or ballet, we went camping, raised horses and cattle...the boys were interested in wildlife and we took care of injured animals

and birds."

Of her art she says, "I'm doing what I do best and what I enjoy most." Ford not only brings her tremendous talent into each painting, but also does textbook and field research on each animal she paints. Her dedication to factual detail takes her art one step beyond photorealism.

Each painting takes about three weeks. Sometimes she will paint 18 hours a day, seven days a week. The rest of her time is spent in wildlife refuges, or dedicating time and her artwork to raise funds for Ducks Unlimited®. Anheuser-Busch features her art on limited edition steins and collectibles.

CHARLES FRACÉ

Although especially known for his paintings of big cats, Charles Fracé is captivated by all wildlife subjects, ranging from wolves and grizzly bears to mountain goats and harp seals. "Every time I sit down to paint, I get excited about the painting, the animal and the exploration ahead," says Fracé.

Believing that nothing substitutes for seeing animals firsthand, Fracé has traveled the globe to conduct field studies and to observe animals at zoos and private breeding compounds throughout the U.S.

Featured in more than 300 one-man shows throughout the U.S. and Canada, Fracé has been honored by a number of museums, including the Smithsonian's National Museum of Natural History, the Leigh Yawkey Woodson Art Museum and the Denver Museum of Natural History. Most recently, he was one of the first five artists inducted into The Bradford Exchange Plate Artist Hall of Fame.

Fracé's paintings have been reproduced on eight plate series available from The Bradford Exchange, including *The World's Most Magnificent Cats* and *Kingdom of Great Cats: The Gold Signature Collection*.

TOBIN FRALEY

Renowned carousel restorer and author Tobin Fraley, whose fascination with carousels goes back to his childhood experiences at his grandfather's amusement park, has been involved with carousel restoration for more than three decades. Recently Fraley signed on with George Zoltan Lefton Company to design an exclusive collection of colorful, hand-painted carousel figures.

Under his own publishing company, Zephyr Press, he has published more than 100 wall calendars and a coffee table book, *The Carousel Animal*, which traces the rich history of the carousel from its beginnings to the early 20th century. As a gift designer for Hallmark Galleries and Willitts Designs, Fraley has created original carousel collections and ornaments.

Of his association with Lefton and the new carousel collection, Fraley comments: "I believe carousels are an artistic category that will never die. The carousel is something that everyone has experienced — it has universal appeal."

MARGARET FURLONG

Margaret Furlong Alexander combines her "commitment to personal and spiritual values" with her artistic gifts in producing the beautiful white porcelain angels, stars and other designs for her company, Margaret Furlong Designs.

Margaret's love affair with white began when she started sculpting abstract snowscapes in Nebraska in the '70s. Her first angel ornament appeared in 1979, after she combined several shell forms, a molded face, a textured coil and a tapered trumpet into a "shell angel" from unshaded and unglazed porcelain.

Since then she has married, moved to Seattle and then to Salem, Oregon, where her business is thriving and she and her husband Jerry are raising their daughter Caitlin.

Margaret divides her time between her family, home studio and the Carriage House Studio. Her staff of more than 90 produces over 120 different designs, which are sold throughout the country.

Margaret views each new design as a gift from God that she can share with all her collectors. And her genuineness, wisdom and joy are worth sharing, both as visions of pure white angels and as an example for others.

W.D. GAITHER

W.D. "Bill" Gaither is a multi-faceted artist with thousands of paintings and prints on display in galleries and private collections all over America.

As a sculptor and painter, Gaither's special gift stems from his immersion in the world of wildlife with his involvement in several environmental and wildlife conservation organizations. His workshops hold books on a myriad of subjects, mounted specimens, dozens of sketches and partially completed sculptures.

Gaither creates works which are active, fluid and alive — never static or frozen. His wildlife studies reflect a living moment in the animal's life in the wild — feeding, running, attacking, playing, leaping, soaring or charging.

Gaither's first sculpture in association with the Maruri Studio premiered in 1982. Since then, wildlife art connoisseurs eagerly await each Maruri introduction — many of which sell out immediately and begin rising in value.

ROGER GIBBONS

Born in 1954, Roger Gibbons started his career as a precious stones salesman in Birmingham's Jewelry Quarter before gaining an apprenticeship in W.A.P. Watson Ltd.'s Model Making Department (parent of The Tudor Mint). Part of his training involved a three-year jewelry course at Mid-Warwickshire College of Higher Education under Rex Billingham. Since then, he has worked on fashion jewelry, souvenirs, giftware, Crystalflame and Victorian scenes that launched The Tudor Mint name. Roger modeled the first *Myth and Magic* figurines from Sharon Riley's designs and has worked on a great number since. However, as Chief Model Maker, he also has administrative duties to consider and doesn't sculpt quite as much as he has done in the past. In 1994, he celebrated 20 years with the company.

LINDA GILL

Fifteen years ago, Linda Gill attended her first crafts fair and decided to replace an apple head on a doll with one made out of bread dough. Inspired by American artists Charles Wysocki and Norman Rockwell, Linda began creating bread dough characters who lived in a time when life was simple and unhurried, where pride in one's country and love of family were important to all — characteristics inherent in each of her designs. For the next 15 years, Linda worked on perfecting her uniquely distinctive faces out of bread dough before joining forces with Amaranth Productions.

To create the *Home-Bred Folks* line for Amaranth Productions, Linda originally molds her character's distinctive faces from bread dough. Amaranth's artisans then create a mold, reproduce the distinctive faces from resin, then hand-paint each detail to bring the endearing characters to life. Linda's *Home-Bred Folks* enable all collectors to enjoy a slice of Americana, served up in each of her creations.

NATE GIORGIO

Even before his 1991 debut as a limited edition plate artist, Nate Giorgio had already made a name for himself in the arts. He has created commissioned artwork of several famous celebrities, including Michael Jackson, Quincy Jones, Madonna, Prince and Johnny Cash.

Giorgio's world-tour program cover and 1989 calendar for Michael Jackson was enthusiastically received, leading him to create not only many movie posters and entertainment companies' logos but also numerous pieces for collectors throughout the United States and England.

Working in mixed media, including oils, pastels and watercolors, Giorgio explores and celebrates the spirit of the entertainer. "It's not photographic or realistic. I try to really capture their personalities," says Giorgio.

His four plate series available from The Bradford Exchange – *The Beatles Collection*, *Elvis Presley Hit Parade*, *Superstars of Country Music* and *Remembering the King* – have also captured some of music's legendary entertainers.

JULIE GOOD-KRÜGER

For Julie Good-Krüger, life as a doll artist includes living and working in Amish country's Strasburg, Pennsylvania, where she, her husband and daughter live in a stone grist mill. The influence of the Amish inspired her to create the *Amish Blessings* doll collection for The Ashton-Drake Galleries.

In high school, Julie enjoyed reading doll magazines and creating small sculptures on plaques. Her interest in dolls waned in college until the late 1970s when she began experimenting with doll making to earn extra money for graduate school.

Perfecting her craft for three years, Julie finally introduced her first original child dolls to the public. Since then, her dolls have won numerous awards, including 1988 and 1989 "Doll of the Year" award nominations, and in 1995, a "Doll of the Year" award nomination for "I Wish You Love."

Since *Amish Blessings*, Julie has created three other collections for Ashton-Drake: the *Oh Holy Night* nativity collection, the *Baby Talk* collection, and the *All I Wish for You* collection of baby angels, of which the DOTY® award nominee doll, "I Wish You Love," is the first issue.

DEAN GRIFF

Dean Griff, creator of the *Charming Tails*™ collection, was born on a 500-acre farm in rural Oneida, New York. From an early age, Dean took long walks through the nearby woods, where he watched with keen interest the animals who made their home there.

During his school years, a developing interest in drawing led Dean to study art rather than enroll in agriculture classes with his siblings. At age 23, he left the family farm to take a job as Assistant to the Curator of the Syracuse University Art Collection. Entries and awards for his wildlife paintings in university art shows followed, as did a small business in hand-painted hanging ornaments.

In 1989, Dean moved from New York to Florida to work as a set decorator for television programs and commercials. After Dean submitted a dozen introductory designs to FFSC, Inc. for consideration, more were requested, and the *Charming Tails*™ collection was born. Now, over 200 of his designs for delightful figurines, hanging ornaments, waterglobes and lighted houses have been produced.

JAMES GRIFFIN

Born in Ontario, Canada, James Griffin came to the U.S. with his family at age five. Earning a bachelor's degree from Pratt Institute, he has exhibited at numerous locations from New York and the Midwest to South America.

His illustrations have appeared in publications, ranging from *Good Housekeeping* to *The Wall Street Journal*. Listed in *Who's Who in American Art*, he has also illustrated for such publishing and media giants as Harcourt Brace Jovanovich, Random House, Doubleday, NBC and Warner Communications.

He cites the great illustrators of the past – including Norman Rockwell and N.C. Wyeth – as important influences on his artwork, along with Japanese prints, Mughal miniatures and Gustav Klimt.

A seasoned world traveler who draws on other cultures for inspiration, Griffin has toured France, Italy, Japan, Mexico, Turkey, Morocco, India and Nepal. He has lived in England, Peru and Brazil. He currently resides in New York's Hudson Valley with his wife Tabita and their cat Pushkin.

Griffin's work has appeared in three plate series available from The Bradford Exchange – *Casablanca*, *World War II: A Remembrance*, and *Battles of the American Civil War*.

JUDITH ANN GRIFFITH

Growing up in rural Pennsylvania, it was natural for Judith Ann Griffith to start drawing pictures of birds and animals at an early age. Later she attended an art college in Philadelphia and, after graduation, worked for a large greeting card company. There, her artistic style naturally continued to grow.

Today, Judith lives in the Ozark Mountains of Arkansas, a wooded setting she discovered while on a vacation. She finds inspiration surrounded by vast natural areas. "I've spent most of my life in the woods of Pennsylvania and Arkansas. When I'm not painting, I hike or garden, and have learned much from nature, especially from the great sentient forests."

Judith's artwork celebrates a deep reverence for life, and for the beauty and peace which truly exist on earth. She hopes that her art is an inspiration for others to work in love and harmony for the well-being of life on this planet.

Judith Ann Griffith has designed figurines for the *American Artist Collection®* from Possible Dreams.

JOHN GROSSMAN

"I feel a tremendous responsibility to conserve and preserve these old images," artist John Grossman says of his 200,000-piece collection of Victorian paper keepsakes. "But as an artist, I also love taking an old design and transforming it into something new."

After attending the Minneapolis School of Art, Grossman honed his skills at the Cours de la Civilization Francais at the Sorbonne in Paris.

With his gift for art and his natural appreciation for "all things Victorian," Grossman has been able to assemble and share his remarkable collection of antique Victorian keepsakes and mementos in the form of appealing collages. These Victorian keepsake collages are now available to collectors in the form of a limited edition plate series entitled *Romantic Victorian Keepsakes* under the commission of The Hamilton Collection.

In celebration of a festive Victorian Christmas, Grossman created another plate series of porcelain collages entitled *Victorian Christmas Memories*, beginning with "A Visit From St. Nicholas."

JAMES GURNEY

James Gurney's ability to recreate moments of history with scientific accuracy and to imagine fantastic realms in a wealth of detail has resulted in the creation of *Dinotopia®*, a place where humans and dinosaurs live in peaceful interdependence. Selling more than a million copies, *Dinotopia* (1992) has won numerous awards. The next *Dinotopia* adventure, *The World Beneath* (1995), features more than 160 full color illustrations.

To develop this new land, Gurney consulted experts at several museums, including The Smithsonian. Wanting to make things "as believable as possible," Gurney has done extensive work with historic realism. While pursuing anthropology at the University of California at Berkeley, he assisted at the Lowie Museum of Anthropology. He continued at the Pasadena Art Center College of Design and then traveled across America armed with sketchbook and tape recorder for two years.

Gurney's paintings have been exhibited by the New York Society of Illustrators, the Cleveland Museum of Natural History and the National Geographic Society.

SCOTT GUSTAFSON

Scott Gustafson's interpretations of classic fairy tales and stories show his love for stories. "My work creates an opportunity to revisit and reacquaint people with stories and make them accessible, so you might feel like you're visiting old friends."

Gustafson was first introduced to The Greenwich Workshop in 1992, and in less than a year, he became one of the most popular artists in the realm of limited edition prints, which include *Touched by Magic* (depicting Cinderella), *Goldilocks*

and the Three Bears, Little Red Riding Hood, The Frog Prince, Snow White and the Seven Dwarfs, Humpty Dumpty, Pat-a-Cake, The Alice in Wonderland Suite, and Jack and the Beanstalk.

His classic, opulent style has appeared in such magazines as *The Saturday Evening Post* and *Playboy*. Gustafson has illustrated anew such classics as *The Night Before Christmas*, *The Nutcracker* and *Peter Pan* and created new stories with *Alphabet Soup* and *The Animal Orchestra*.

Scott's artwork has been interpreted in three dimensional works included in the recently introduced figurine collectibles line called *The Greenwich Workshop Collection.*

STEVE AND GIGI HACKETT

Steve and Gigi Hackett are a talented husband and wife team whose figurines have been produced by Cast Art Industries since 1993.

Steve apprenticed with the Disney organizations and left to undertake freelance commissions, including one-of-a-kind sculptures for the rich and famous. Together with his wife Gigi, a unique team approach and wry sense of humor have made vital contributions to several delightful collectible series.

Animal Attractions™ is an assortment of humorous portrayals of favorite pigs and dancing bears. *Story Time Treasures*™ are representations of beloved children's stories, from *The Three Pigs* to *The Frog Prince*, each depicting a parent animal reading to his youngster. The Hacketts and artist Kristin Haynes have also developed *Cuddl'somes*™, a line of teddy bears and other animal figurines.

These wonderful collectible figurines, like all Cast Art products, are painstakingly hand-cast and hand-painted, and are sold in fine gift and collectibles stores.

HANS HENRIK HANSEN

Born in 1952, Hans Henrik Hansen graduated from the Academy of Applied Art in Copenhagen with an emphasis on graphic design.

For 12 years, he was the principal decorator at the retail store for the Royal Copenhagen Porcelain Manufactory, where his window decorations were the rage of fashionable Copenhagen.

Since 1987, Hansen has been devoted almost exclusively to creating designs and illustrations for the porcelain manufactory. His first Christmas series, *Jingle Bells*, was very successful.

With the introduction of the *Santa Claus* collection in 1989, Hansen became the first artist since 1895 to create a colorful Christmas plate for Bing & Grondahl.

For the first time since 1908, Royal Copenhagen issued a series of six annual Christmas plates and coordinating ornaments titled *Christmas in Denmark*. The original art for this epoch-making series was created by Hans Henrik Hansen.

KRISTIN HAYNES

Raised in Utah, Kristin Haynes is the product of an extremely artistic family. She majored in fine arts at the University of Utah and then moved with husband Scott to California in 1978 to pursue their careers — his in music, hers in sculpture. Kristin began creating a group of cherubs, animals, and other storybook characters which became popular with fans throughout southern California. Demand grew so great that Kristin began searching for a partner to help make reproductions in commercial quantities.

After showing her samples to Cast Art Industries, a gift manufacturing company, they agreed that the line must maintain its unique characteristics — manufactured from natural gypsum materials, handcrafted, and offered at an affordable price. The line, named *Dreamsicles®*, became one of the fastest growing in collectibles history.

Kristin's *Dreamsicles* now include more than 250 cherubs and animals, and she continues to create new designs from her farmhouse studio. In addition, *Cuckoo Corners™*, a collection of humorous characters, and several *Cuddl'somes™* teddy bears continue to be collectors' favorites.

JON HERBERT

Jon Herbert, a talented British sculptor, has been known to American collectors for years but made his first United States collector appearance in 1995 for John Hine Studios.

Herbert's works first came to the United States in 1988 with the *The Shoemaker's Dream*, a collection of cottages sculpted in the shape of a variety of shoes and boots. A special "Military Boot" was crafted by Herbert in 1995 exclusively for military personnel, to commemorate the 50th anniversary of the end of World War II.

Herbert also sculpted and designed *The Father Time Clocks* collection, which premiered in 1991, and a collection of miniature clock sculptures in 1995.

Herbert began his career with John Hine Studios as a mould-maker, making the intricate moulds for David Winter Cottages. His work begins with drawings, which cover a wide gamut of fantasy subjects, and from there, he proceeds to sculpt his original creations. Since joining John Hine Limited in 1987, his talents and his collections have attracted collectors around the world.

PEGGY HERRICK

Already a talented designer, Peggy Herrick discovered woodcarving over ten years ago. Through the carving of smiling animals, Peggy realized that she had found an artistic home.

Peggy's husband, a life-long woodworker, introduced her to an air-powered die grinder. With this tool, Peggy could further express her creativity and keep up with the demand for her

unique and extraordinary pieces. After applying her whimsically hand-painted final touches, Peggy introduces another member to her enchanting animal kingdom — creating a smile on the original piece, as well as on the faces of everyone who sees it.

Midwest of Cannon Falls is pleased to present an exclusively-designed collection of precise reproductions of folk art pieces by Peggy Herrick. Her original ornaments and figures are certain to generate smiles on the faces of collectors and folk art enthusiasts alike.

PRISCILLA HILLMAN

Childhood memories of sketching at the kitchen table with her twin sister, Greta, influenced Priscilla Hillman's charming illustrations and uplifting children's books that have touched the hearts of collectors worldwide.

After writing and illustrating the children's books *Tumpy Rumple* and *Squeaky Nibble*, Western Publishing saw her work and asked her to illustrate several of its books. From there, she illustrated and wrote nine *Merry Mouse* books for Doubleday. In 1995, Enesco Corporation transformed her drawings of *Merry Mouse* into a giftware collection of figurines, titled *Mouse Tales*.

After recovering from a serious back problem in the late 1980s, Priscilla sent sketches of teddy bears to Enesco President and CEO, Eugene Freedman, who transformed them into the *Cherished Teddies® Collection* in 1992. Since its debut, the Collection has been honored with several awards, including "Collectible of the Year" and "Figurine of the Year" by NALED. Priscilla was recognized in 1994 as the "Artist of the Year."

Priscilla also designed the *Enesco Calico Kittens™ Collection*, based on messages of friendship and love in 1994, and recently created a new bunny giftware line titled *My Blushing Bunnies*.

TORI DAWN YOUNGER HINE

As a child, Tori Dawn Hine exhibited natural artistic talent. At eight years old, she was submitting drawings to national publications, and at nine, she undertook formal training in the use of oils, acrylics and pastels.

In 1985, Tori Dawn's father, Bill Younger, introduced David Winter Cottages in the United States. The following year, his gifted daughter traveled to England to study cottage painting and became the first American painting artist for John Hine Studios.

During one of her visits to England, Tori Dawn met Harry Hine, whom she married in 1990. They currently live in San Diego where Tori Dawn keeps busy with her two boys and an active painting schedule.

When her father and sister Kim, founded Harbour Lights in 1991, Tori Dawn extended her cottage painting skills to lighthouse miniatures. As origination painter for Harbour Lights, she has earned accolades from collectors for her ability to capture romance and drama in each new release.

GERNOT HIRSCH

From a family of porcelain painters, Gernot Hirsch, production manager and a master painter, began his career with W. Goebel Porzellanfabrik (producer of *M.I. Hummel* figurines) in 1957.

After completing the three-year apprenticeship program and passing the porcelain painting exam given by the Chamber of Commerce and Industry in Coburg, Gernot developed his professional skills in various painting departments at Goebel. In 1962 he was promoted to Painting Supervisor.

Continuing to train and participate in special courses, Gernot became a Master of Industrial Arts in 1973. For many years, he served as Project Leader of special tasks in the Time and Motion Studies Department.

In 1986, Gernot was awarded, and maintains today, the position of head of Goebel's plant in Teuschnitz, where he supervises all aspects of operations including training the many new and talented painters. In addition, Gernot has participated in promotions in Japan, Australia, Germany and other European countries.

Married and living in Roedental, Gernot enjoys chess, choir singing, hiking and painting with water colors in his spare time.

ANTON HIRZINGER

Anton Hirzinger has lived in Kramsach, Tyrol, home of the famous Technical School for Glass Craft and Design, since he was born in 1955. "Even as a child, I was fascinated by glass production and knew at a very early age that when I grew up I wanted to make it my career," says Anton, who studied at his "hometown school." He initially worked as a hollow glass craftsman at a small company.

Now, Anton has been working for Swarovski for more than eight years. He initially started work in the Swarovski Crystal Shop in Wattens, providing countless visitors from all over the world a closer insight to glass and crystal craftmanship. Transferring to the Design Center in 1991, Anton created the Swarovski Silver Crystal "Pelican" and "Owlet." His greatest achievement so far is the "Centenary Swan" design, a commemorative edition for the company's 100th anniversary in 1995.

In his spare time, Anton and his family walk through Tyrol's beautiful countryside and ski in winter.

JOSEPH HOFFMAN

Joseph Hoffman, originally from Harrisburg, Pennsylvania, has always loved sculpting. An accomplished art student, he studied many media, and by age 14, the three-dimensions of sculpting overshadowed any inclination he may have had in academia's three R's. His sculptures were featured in exhibitions at several galleries, and at 18, he was commissioned to create a portrait of Pennsylvania's governor. Presented during a special ceremony, the image and the event were reported statewide.

Today, Joseph makes his home in the village of Vicksburg, Pennsylvania, where he and his wife Sheryl are restoring their Victorian home and furnishing it with antiques which Joseph also restores.

In 1980, Joseph and Sheryl launched Hoffman Dolls and Designs, originally creating portrait dolls. Soon, they were designing dolls for such companies as Hershey Foods, recreating many images from Hershey's vintage advertising.

Beyond their own unique and popular creations, Hoffman most recently contributed to the continuing Gartlan USA legacy with one of 1996's most popular figurines – Ringo Starr. He sculpted images of the Beatles' drummer at his drum set during the Fab Four's 1964 "Ed Sullivan Show" appearance, as well as a strolling pose from the Abbey Road album fame.

Joseph and Sheryl share their time and creative endeavors with their children Joseph, Eric and Christina.

MARTHA HOLCOMBE

Martha Holcombe creates sculptures of children whose expressions and situations reflect the tenderness, innocence and love of childhood. For Martha, each year is marked by the children "born" in that year, such as "Booker T." in 1985 and "Betsy and Bean" in 1988. In 1995 she introduced a new series called *All God's Children Ragbabies* that are adorable, whimsical and tickle the heart with their charming situations and sayings.

Known to many as Miss Martha, she creates from her heart and deep personal faith. Martha's childhood memories of growing up in the Appalachian foothills of northeast Alabama have inspired her sculptured art and have made her one of America's foremost artisans.

Her handcrafted cold-cast figures depict African-American children in delightful situations. Each piece, sculpted by Martha, is made entirely in the USA at Miss Martha Originals, located in Gadsden, Alabama.

Martha is pleased and humbled that her "children" have been so lovingly embraced by collectors across the country. For her, the high point of sculpting is the loving response and encouragement that collectors share with her.

FRANCES HOOK

The collectibles, art and publishing business communities saluted the inimitable artistry and spirit of the late Frances Hook by establishing a foundation in her name to foster young artists' studies. Since its inception following Hook's death in 1983, the Frances Hook Scholarship Fund currently awards over $55,000 in awards and scholarships to art students from first grade to college undergraduates.

A scholarship to the Pennsylvania Museum of Art led to the development of Hook's style in pastel and her unique manner of capturing the spirit and vitality of children. Her talent is evident in her renderings of famous 1960s Northern Tissue children.

Having illustrated children's books, Hook joined her husband Richard to successfully illustrate *The Living Bible* by Tyndale House Publishers.

Through her association with Roman, Inc., Hook's illustrations are reproduced in the form of limited edition figurines, plates and prints.

Much of Frances Hook's work can be seen today in the Frances Hook Museum and Gallery located in the Old School of Mishicot, Wisconsin.

SISTER MARIA INNOCENTIA HUMMEL

Sister Maria Innocentia Hummel created hundreds of colorful and charming sketches, drawings and paintings of children. Her work is the basis for scores of appealing, hand-painted fine earthenware figurines, as well as limited edition plates and bells, created and offered exclusively by W. Goebel Porzellanfabrik of Germany.

Born Berta Hummel in Bavaria in 1909, she had inclinations toward art from an early age. She graduated from the Munich Academy of Applied Art, meanwhile devoting much of her energy toward her religion.

After graduation, Berta entered a convent, taking the name Sister Maria Innocentia. Because the convent of Siessen, a teaching order, was quite poor, she sold some of her artwork in the form of postcards to raise money. In 1934, Franz Goebel, the fourth-generation head of the porcelain-producing firm, discovered her art.

The first *M.I. Hummel* figurines debuted at the Leipzig Fair in 1935, and since then have been popular with collectors around the world. Sadly, Sister M.I. Hummel died in 1946 at the age of 37, not yet aware of her full triumph as an artist.

GEORGE C. INNES

George C. Innes was born in Elyria, Ohio, in 1923. He received his formal art training at The Cleveland School of Art and John Huntington Polytechnic Institute. His long and varied career has encompassed many art forms, including painting, sculpting,

advertising art, and product and industrial design. Much of this work is housed in private collections throughout the United States and Europe. An experimenter and explorer, his current works are devoted to designs in the stained glass medium.

In late 1995, Innes was commissioned by Amazze, in a licensing arrangement with Hershey Foods Corporation, to design *The CHOCO-LATE TOWN USA!™ Collection,* a limited edition stained glass cottage collection. This unique and innovative collection is a flavorful tribute to candymaker Milton S. Hershey's beloved hometown a century ago — Hershey, Pennsylvania. Every detail in architecture and color are true to the turn-of-the-century. And everywhere you look, you see recreations of genuine HERSHEY'S™ signage and miniature displays — all authenticated and authorized by Hershey Foods Corporation.

CLIFF JACKSON

Cliff Jackson started his career as an artist while a youngster in Georgia, filling sketchbooks with the faces and places in his small hometown.

Later, winning a scholarship to the School of Visual Arts in New York City, Jackson honed his talents for illustration and design, graduating with a degree in fine arts and an appreciation for the dual roles of artist and educator. Jackson has taught drawing to schoolchildren and practices his art as an independent illustrator, designer and sculptor for corporate and private clients across America. His combined works include book jackets, magazine illustrations and sculptures.

Five three-dimensional plate series for The Bradford Exchange have featured his work: *Egypt: Splendors of an Ancient World, Field Pup Follies, Immortals of the Diamond, A Visit from St. Nick, Native Legends: Chiefs of Destiny* and *Winnie the Pooh and Friends.*

"I want the image to look alive and soft," Jackson says, "which is hard to do on clay. I try to make the plates as high relief as possible, bringing more depth."

BILL JAUQUET

Bill Jauquet's wood carvings chronicle a lifestyle little changed from American history's early years. Whimsical portraits spring from Jauquet's appreciation of the humor inherent in working with unpredictable livestock and weather. His impishness also surfaces in a holiday theme that embraces two styles of Santas — solemnly slender and playfully plump.

The *Bill Jauquet Americana Collection,* exclusive to Roman, Inc., features resin reproductions faithfully capturing the hand-wrought look, natural charm and power of each Jauquet original wood sculpture. The Wisconsin artist's carvings are worked directly from his mind's vision. Using aged cedar, Bill first roughs out the log with power tools. Then he planes and rasps the wood to achieve the desired form. After sanding and sealing, he applies stain or paint to achieve an antiqued look.

Jauquet's 1979 sculpture of a swan for his wife's antiques/folk art shop started him on the pursuit of art full-time. Now Jauquet's work appears in fine galleries nationwide and has been acquired by the Smithsonian Institute, corporations and celebrities.

BILL JOB

Raised in the Tennessee mountains, Bill Job learned to appreciate the local craftsmen's skills. First working with wood and then glass, Bill began reproducing the famous Tiffany lamp shades. Pursuing his interest in traveling, Bill eventually settled with his family on mainland China's east coast in 1987. Combining his love of the natives with western management practices, he built a large studio to create glass treasures. Bill immediately gained recognition for his beautiful Tiffany style lamps, and as a pioneer in business, he became one of the first Americans granted permission for sole proprietorship of his own company in China.

Bill's latest collection for Forma Vitrum, *Coastal Heritage*, is a series of limited edition lighthouse replicas which are sponsored by the U.S. Lighthouse Society. The original Bill Job stained glass collectible villages – *Vitreville, Woodland Village* and *Coastal Classics* – are handcrafted from the highest quality American stained glass. When completed, each piece is truly an individual work of art with its own color and cut variations, but all reflect the style, detail and quality of his design.

PENNI JO JONAS

Penni Jo Jonas made her first figurines in her kitchen and sold them at craft shows. The miniature teddy bear she made for her daughter's doll house was the inspiration for a series of similar bears. Using colored clays, a food processor, and a toaster oven, Penni Jo created miniature teddy bears that propelled her into the national spotlight among collectible figurine artists.

Penni Jo still uses the toaster oven, along with many other innovative tools, to create just the right detail needed in her sculptures.

Having joined United Design in 1989, Penni Jo designs and sculpts several other collectible figurine editions, including *Itty Bitty Critters™* and the small and miniature angels in the *Angels Collection*.

These days, Penni Jo is keeping busy creating some exciting new works, including a brand new collection of teddy bear angels called *Teddy Angels™*.

FALINE FRY JONES

Faline Fry Jones developed her concept of architectural reproductions of America's past in the basement of her home in 1982. She patterned her designs after actual buildings and historic landmarks no longer in existence, naming them *The Cat's Meow Village™*.

By 1989, a new facility was built for the 130 member-team of employees, and the firm's name was changed to FJ Designs. Today, FJ Designs is a highly successful multi-million dollar international company.

Faline has won several awards for her business and artistic efforts, including the Small Business of the Year and Entrepreneur of the Year from the Wooster Area Chamber of Commerce in 1989 and Business of the Year from the North Central Business Journal in 1994.

In addition to FJ Designs and motherhood, Faline is active in several local and national organizations and serves on the board of directors at Junior Achievement and the Wooster Area Chamber of Commerce.

RU KATO

Wearing many hats at a time, Ru Kato's talents, as a producer, ex-musician, creative officer and President of WACO Products, served him well on orchestrating the *Melody In Motion (MIM)* development team including Seiji Nakane, Chief Sculptor.

In 1972, WACO Japan introduced "Whistling Hobo," a painted resin figurine equipped with a mechanical whistling device, but his whistling was not entertaining. Going back to the drawing board, MIM's research and development team introduced the first porcelain figurines with motion and music – "Willie The Trumpeter," "Willie The Hobo" and "Willie The Whistler" in 1985.

Although Ru calls America his home, he frequently travels to Japan to work with those involved in *Melody In Motion's* production.

A quiet man, Ru Kato prefers a background role when it comes to the promotion of MIM. As *Melody In Motion* celebrates its 10th Anniversary, Ru is pleased that so many enjoy what took so many years to create. He still lives by the same motto that he had in 1972..."Never Give Up."

GARRI KATZ

As a child in the Soviet Union, Garri Katz drew and painted to calm his fears during World War II. After the war, Katz studied at the Odessa Institute of Fine Arts, before launching his career as a painter and illustrator.

In 1973, having immigrated to Israel, Katz painted religious and historic subjects and his celebrations of everyday life in Israel, which he displayed in many one-man shows in Israel. Then in 1984, Katz began a series of shows in the U.S. sponsored by patrons who discovered his genius on trips to Israel. Today, art connoisseurs from all over purchase Katz' paintings and watercolors for as high as $12,000 each. His works are on display in Israel, Belgium, Germany, Canada and the U.S. Katz resides in Florida.

Katz's first limited edition collector plate series, *Great Stories from the Bible* — eight plates which portray a memorable moment from a beloved Bible story — represents a commission from Reco International Corp.

EMMETT KELLY, JR.

Emmett Kelly, Jr.'s earliest childhood memories are of the circus and performing. Born in November 1924 to Emmett and Eva Kelly, Sr., circus performers, Emmett spent his early years traveling with his parents. During his school years, he lived with relatives and later joined the Navy. Emmett served during World War II in the Pacific and participated in three invasions, including Okinawa and Iwo Jima.

In the mid-60's, Emmett's life as a clown began. Although alienated from his father for many years, they put aside their differences when both agreed that Emmett would continue the Weary Willie character that his father created during the Depression. Emmett changed the Weary Willie image somewhat, putting on a crownless hat and billing himself as Emmett Kelly, Jr.

Throughout his many years of clowning, "America's Favorite Clown" has given a special joy to clown lovers everywhere.

BUD KEMPER

Although Bud Kemper's childhood interest was in music, his high school music teacher persuaded him to submit his paintings to the local college. Bud was awarded a scholarship to Washington University, where he obtained a Bachelor of Fine Arts in Illustration. After serving in the military, he received a Master of Fine Arts in Painting from the University of Kansas. Bud is a member of the New York Society of Illustrators and the American Society of Portrait Artists.

Bud has consistently received prestigious awards in his field, including seven Society of Illustration Awards, Communication Art Annuals, and numerous awards from local and regional shows.

Bud's style of painting has been developed from raw talent, formal education and 37 years of practice and teaching painting.

Bud, a master painter, can paint any subject in a unique way. "I do portraits because I like people and enjoy working with them. I also like to paint wildlife and landscapes. I guess I don't like to paint just one thing all the time."

Bud's artwork is also featured on Anheuser-Busch steins.

KAREN KENNEDY

A love affair with fashion design and dolls began at an early age for Goebel's talented doll designer Karen Kennedy. In the artisitc atmosphere of Goebel's atelier, she is free to combine both loves by creating exclusive costumes for *Victoria Ashlea Originals®*, *Carol Anna®* and *Charlot Byj®* doll lines.

Three of Karen's designs were accepted into museums: Victorian Doll Museum in North Chili, New York, Hobby City Doll and Toy Museum in Anaheim, California, and Mary Stolz Doll and Toy Museum in East Stroudsburg, Pennsylvania.

Karen loves to meet with collectors personally to share her knowledge and thoughts on collecting and has appeared on television many times to promote her appearances.

Karen is a quickly rising young star for Goebel of North America.

DONNA KENNICUTT

Primarily self taught, Donna Kennicutt says she loved art during her high school years but never pursued it as a career until her children were grown. Even then, her painting and sculpting began as a hobby. Her talent, however, won her wide recognition, as she was soon voted one of the state's outstanding women artists.

Donna's subjects for her cast bronze pieces were primarily animals, which gave her an ideal background for creating the originals for the animal figurines produced by United Design. They are now in private collections across the United States and in several foreign countries.

One of the most popular collectible editions Donna has created and sculpted since coming to United Design is the *Easter Bunny Family™* collection. She is also responsible for *Children's Garden of Critters™* and many of the *Stone Critters™* and *Animal Magnetism®* designs.

THOMAS KINKADE

Thomas Kinkade is renowned for infusing light into his canvas lithographs, which are published by Lightpost Publishing in San Jose, California. A modern day impressionist, Kinkade has received numerous national awards, including the 1994 "Lithograph of the Year Award" from the National Association of Limited Edition Dealers and the 1995 *Collector Editions* "Award of Excellence." He was honored as a charter inductee into The Bradford International Hall of Fame for plate artists.

Though his family did not have wealth, Kinkade often says they were "rich in the greatest form of wealth — a nurturing and affirming love."

Kinkade studied art at the University of California at Berkeley and at the Art Center College of Design in Pasadena.

While writing *The Artist's Guide to Sketching* with James Gurney, Kinkade painted some 600 scenic backgrounds for the animated motion picture, *Fire and Ice* in a two-year period.

A devout Christian and family-oriented individual, Thomas Kinkade draws on personal experience for much of his artistic inspiration. Many of his scenes of peace, tranquility and nostalgia are based on family travels and memories.

PAT KOLESAR

As an avid doll collector, Pat Kolesar complained that all dolls look the same, and in 1979, she decided to take matters into her own hands. Today, she is well known for dolls whose faces reveal the varied and unpredictable moods of children. Her realistic dolls show on the outside what people feel on the inside.

Pat has won more than 40 blue ribbons at regional and national UFDC conventions. She has also received eight "Dolls of Excellence" nominations from *Dolls* magazine, including one each for "Enoc the Eskimo Boy," "Baby Cakes" and "Baby Cake Crumbs," all for the Seymour Mann Gallery. In addition, she has designed several of Seymour Mann's most popular dolls, including "Clair Mann," "Enid," "Sparkle," "Kissing Kyle," "Kissing Kelly" and "Kissing Casey."

A former student of artist Nat Ramer, Pat is an accomplished painter and sculptor. Among her commissions are a portrait doll of former Treasury Secretary William Simon. Several of her dolls are on display in museums across the country.

SANDRA KUCK

Sandra Kuck, a talented artist, echoes her strong sense of family and appreciation for beauty in all of her works.

While attending UCLA and The Art Student's League in New York, Sandra realized her love for painting children. Her husband, John, encouraged her to pursue her dream. But Sandra did not begin to devote much time to her work until their two children were in school.

In 1979, Heio Reich, President of Reco International Corp., discovered her paintings of children in a Long Island gallery. Sandra's career skyrocketed with the creation of the plate "Sunday Best" in 1983. Since then, NALED honored her with many awards, including an unprecedented six-time honor as "Artist of the Year."

Constantly working, Sandra's recent works include the *Moments at Home* plate series, a new Mother's Day collection debuting with "Home Is Where the Heart Is," the *Victorian*

Christmas series introduced with "Dear Santa," and "God's Gift," a portrait of a mother and infant, released as a Christening Plate. She also released the third doll in the *Childhood Doll Collection*, "Reading With Teddy," along with a collection of *Angel Ornaments*.

PAUL LANDRY

Paul Landry's prints portray halcyon days of the sea and shore in bright, airy and lush colors which are worth treasuring.

A native of Nova Scotia and the grandson of two sea captains, Landry naturally took to the sea for amusement and occupation. Developing his artistic talent, he brought his sketchbook along while pulling up nets and traps with local fishermen.

At 17, Landry became an apprentice photo-engraver. He then attended the Nova Scotia College of Art and the Art Students League in New York City. He traveled from Canada to the Midwest, plying his photo-engraving trade and pursuing his interest in commercial art.

Finally he settled in Connecticut, where he taught at Westport's Famous Artists School, wrote the popular textbook *On Drawing and Painting*, and continued to paint seaside villages and American towns.

Landry's paintings attract a growing audience, thanks to their beauty and romantic, stirring nostalgia. In 1984, The Greenwich Workshop published the first of its many Paul Landry fine art prints.

PAUL LARSEN

Native Californian Paul Larsen came to Goebel Miniatures with his own wealth of experience, having completed over 700 wax and clay masters for the manufacture of buckles, coins, plaques and statuary work. But, as a protege of the renowned Bob Olszewski, he became a master of miniatures himself. "I love detail," Larsen says, "And that's what miniatures are about."

Larsen's virtuosity and expertise are evident in everything from classic period pieces to cartoon characters and miniature clocks. His new collection of *Classic Timepieces* made its public debut in 1995 at the International Collectible Exposition in Long Beach. The *M.I. Hummel* "Honey Lover" pendant is Paul's work, and his "Mickey's Self-Portrait" was a sell-out at last year's Disneyana convention.

DAVID LAWRENCE

As an academically-trained artist for many years, David Lawrence sat at his easel, palette and brush in hand, creating masterpieces for the advertising trade — sausages painted in the style of Rembrandt, margarine in the style of Monet. "It may have been painting, but it was not art," says David.

David's thoughts turned to creating something less ephemeral, something which people actually wanted. He took to thumbing through his old two-dimensional notebooks (packed full of rabid imaginings, scribbles, strange rambling observations and half-remembered, delirious dreams) looking for a new direction. At about the same time, he met Martin Perry who, with the Harmony Kingdom, suggested he enter the three dimensional world and turn his thoughts into reality. Suddenly, he had a new direction for his energies, and the creation of the Harmony Kingdom's new series, *The Harmony Circus*, poured forth.

When he is not engaged in his 'Ring Master's' duties, David can be found around his village sampling the locally made, near lethal, cider called 'scrumpy.' Or he may be celebrating life and the equinox or solstice by practicing the ancient art of Morris dancing, be it at dawn or dusk, rain or shine.

DAVID LEMON

David Lemon, a member of the American Indian and Cowboy Artists Association (A.I.C.A.), traces his artistic yearnings as far back as kindergarten, when he impressed the girls by drawing their portraits.

Through his father's and grandparents' stories, David developed an interest in the Old West. His parents encouraged him in his art, despite calls from his fifth grade teacher that he spent his time drawing cowboys and Indians.

In his senior year of high school, David signed up for a ceramics class where his teacher suggested he sculpt using terra-cotta clay. His efforts earned him three scholarships. After serving 12 years in the U.S. Navy, David finally went beyond sculpture as a hobby when he won first place in the Utah State Fair of 1977.

"You have to be thick-skinned to be an artist," Lemon said. "Your art is your soul." The bountiful accolades Lemon has received for his work through the years are sufficient to dispel his fears of being ignored. Currently a resident of Montana, David creates sculptures for Legends® that speak of the people who toiled and sacrificed to build a new nation.

ANTHONY LEON

Illustrator Anthony Leon knew early on that painting was going to be more than a hobby.

After 12 years and hundreds of illustrations for dozens of major corporations, Leon, who relies on a hand-held brush and the added versatility of an airbrush, is now one of the artists commissioned by Anheuser-Busch, Inc.

Leon was influenced by N.C. Wyeth's use of atmosphere in his mood-setting scenes of knights and castles which illustrate *Treasure Island* and *Robin Hood*. Leon's

depiction of the World Famous Clydesdales in the exceptional Charter Member Issue Stein for the Anheuser-Busch Collectors Club is an outstanding example of his own use of this technique. Leon beautifully depicted the majestic eight-horse hitch pulling an antique beer wagon from the European-inspired Bauernhof Courtyard at Grant's Farm on this handcrafted stein in genuine ceramic relief.

Two oval vignettes — one showcasing the elaborate harnessware and festive braided mane, and the second illustrating the Dalamatian trained to protect the horses and guard the wagon — frame the central image of the stein.

NEAL LINDBLADE

In 1982, Neal Lindblade, president of Arcadian Pewter, Inc., and a friend started their first company, a custom spin casting business, in 1-1/2-car garage behind Lindblade's home in Rockford, Illinois. Several years later, Neal, who was now the sole owner of the company, wanted a unique gift to give to his wife for their 20th wedding anniversary. Combining his long-time interest in antique toys with his casting experience, he crafted a pewter replica of a toy farm wagon and filled it with tiny straw flowers. His wife loved it, and so did everyone else who saw it, prompting Neal to produce other cast-iron toys in pewter.

At auctions and other secondary markets, Neal sought out more antique toys originally made by the Arcade Manufacturing Co. over 50 years ago. By 1994, he had acquired a large enough assortment to produce the first *Arcade Toys Fine Pewter Replica Collection*.

The name of the company has since been changed to Arcadian Pewter, Inc. and is now located in a 10,000 square foot facility with several employees. All Arcade Toys Fine Pewter Replicas, components and packaging are made in the U.S. by American workers, just like the originals.

LENA LIU

Lena Liu is an artist of unparalleled popularity in today's collectibles market — art lovers the world over enjoy the universal yet personal character of her paintings. Beautiful birds, tranquil landscapes, and breathtaking floral and musical still lifes are among her collectors' favorites.

Lena had her first painting lessons as a child in Taiwan and came to the United States in 1970 to study architecture at the State University of Buffalo. She later did graduate work at the School of Architecture at U.C.L.A. However, her true passion for painting never left her, and in 1977, she began to paint full time.

Today, her work is enjoyed in various media, including limited edition prints, porcelain collector's plates, music boxes, figurines, ornaments, cards and calendars. Lena has achieved recognition at national shows and exhibits, but she is most proud of the titles she received in 1993 when she was honored as the "Artist of the Year" and her collector plate was awarded "Plate of the Year" by the National Association of Limited Edition Dealers (NALED). She was also named the "Artist of the Year" at the Canadian Collectible of the Year Awards.

Lena and her husband Bill live in Maryland, in the home she designed to accommodate their joint love of art, music and nature. As often as she has the chance, Lena spends time in her garden where she attains inspiration for many of her paintings.

MARK LOCKER

Model making has always interested Mark Locker ever since his grandfather taught him to carve wood as a boy. As one of W.A.P. Watson's (parent of The Tudor Mint) two solderers nine years ago (now there are twelve), he pestered Roger Gibbons to teach him the craft's finer skills. Eventually, Roger said, "Come and find out for yourself" – and Mark was thrown in at the deep end as a full-time model maker.

Just prior to the beginning of the *Myth and Magic* line, Mark worked on the Victorian scenes before becoming "Mister Fantasy and Legend" to Roger's "Mister Myth and Magic." But Fantasy and Legend did not work out, and Mark has since sculpted a number of *Myth and Magic* studies, as well as turning his hand to other requirements. His favorite study is "The Tortured Skull" (*Dark Secrets*), as he worked hard to get the anatomy just right. He also admires Anthony Slocombe's work on "The Dragon of Darkness."

G.M. LOWENTHAL

Raised on Manhattan Island, G.M. Lowenthal, Chief Designer and President of The Boyds Collection Ltd., received a B.S. and M.S. in Biology from Alfred University. Then, as a "Child of the Sixties," he left for the Fiji Islands and the Peace Corps.

Later, G.M. returned to New York City and began purchasing, designing and merchandising at Bloomingdales. Taking a bold step, G.M. moved to rural Boyds, Maryland, to start The Boyds Collection Ltd., an out-of-the-way antique shop. In a restored 1800's farmhouse, G.M. built his business, designing the miniature ceramic "Gnome Homes" and hand-carved wood duck decoys.

Moving his business and growing family to Gettysburg, Pennsylvania, in 1987, G.M. teamed up with Gae Sharp and began designing a line of award-winning collectible plush animals called *Boyds Bears*. In 1992, G.M. introduced the *Boyds Bears and Friends Collection*™. In 1993, the *Folkstones*, whimsical folk art figurines, were introduced, and in August of 1995, the new line of *Yesterday's Child...the Dollstone Collection*™ was unveiled, adding to the growing line of Boyds Collectibles.

STEPHEN LYMAN

Stephen Lyman is an explorer who paints elusive moments in nature. Lyman enrolled at Pasadena's Art Center School of Design to learn more about the commercial art field and then began a commercial illustration career in Los Angeles. Later he returned to Idaho to explore and develop his own painting style.

Lyman has been sharing the wonders of the natural world with collectors since 1983, when his first limited edition print was published by The Greenwich Workshop. He has been a frequent participant in the prestigious international "Birds in Art" show at the Leigh Yawkey Woodson Art Museum and was invited to be "Artist of the Year" at the 1991 Pacific Rim Wildlife Art Show.

The latest image from Lyman's "firelight" works is titled "Midnight Fire," and his most recent limited edition fine art print is "Cathedral Snow." Recently released, Lyman's book, *Into the Wilderness*, features his wilderness and wildlife artwork and photography. A limited edition fine art print, "Evening Star" will accompany the Collector's Edition of the book.

MARTY MASCHINO-WALKER

Marty Maschino-Walker is president, founder and designer of *Attic Babies*™, a rag doll manufacturing company in Drumright, Oklahoma. A talent for design and a love for dolls found Marty exhibiting her creations at local craft shows for many years and led to her first home-based business in 1986. But her success in 1987 at the Dallas Gift Market and continued success has forced her to move the business three times to larger facilities, where she now employs approximately 100 people.

Along the way, special honors have come her way. In 1990, she was chosen as Oklahoma's Small Business Person of the Year, and also presented Mrs. Bush with "Grammy Bar," a special characterization of the First Lady. In 1993, she designed special dolls commemorating Native Oklahoma for each Governor's spouse attending the National Governors' Convention. And in 1995, collectors from across the country awarded Attic Babies the "Best Dolls Under $100" at the 2nd Annual Collectors' Jubilee.

Marty's whimsical babies shine with her own carefree and charismatic charm. While many of Marty's designs are signed and numbered limited editions, none of her Babies retires until "it has lived its life with great service."

LINDA MASON

Few doll artists have been more often honored than Linda Mason, who has been on the high road ever since creating her first doll. In an unprecedented achievement, Mason won *Dolls* magazine's "Award of Excellence" three years in a row – in 1991, for "Bridget Quinn;" in 1992, for "Many Stars;" and in 1993, for "Tulu" – all from Georgetown's *American Diary Doll*™ series. Not surprisingly, her doll "Lian Ying," newest in this series, has been nominated for a 1995 "Award of Excellence."

All told, this popular artist is a six-time winner of that award, as well as a winner of *Doll Reader's* prestigious "Doll of the Year" award. And Mason's entire *American Diary Doll™* series was nominated for the *Doll Reader* special award for "Concept of the Year."

Never one to allow success to alter her work habits, Mason continues to work carefully and slowly, sculpting only a few new designs each year, with "Lavender Dreams" from Georgetown's *Victorian Fantasies™* collection as her latest.

JOHN MCCLELLAND

Some years back, John McClelland created a life-sized portrait of his daughter Susan. The portrait was used for an ad in a trade magazine, and Miles Kimball, the mail order company, spotted it and asked McClelland to do a Christmas cover for their catalog. That was the beginning of an association which continues today.

In the mid-1970s, Reco International arranged for the artist to create limited edition plates. McClelland today is one of the field's most celebrated artists with numerous "Plate of the Year" and "Artist of the Year" awards. He also has designed several figurine series and a number of limited edition lithographs.

McClelland is a portraitist and has taught both intermediate and advanced classes in portrait painting. Scores of his illustrations have appeared in *The Saturday Evening Post, Redbook, American* and *Readers Digest,* and he has written two "how to" books for artists.

Among his works for Reco are T*he Treasured Songs of Childhood, The Wonder of Christmas* and *A Children's Garden* plate series, as well as *The Children's Circus Doll Collection,* based upon the popular Reco plate series.

CINDY M. MCCLURE

Cindy McClure is one of a few artists in the world to win the prestigious "Doll of the Year" award (DOTY) from the International Doll Academy in 1986 and 1987. Most recently, she won *Dolls* "Award of Excellence" for her original wax-over-porcelain issue named *Cross-Stitch* — an exclusive porcelain edition by The Ashton-Drake Galleries. Her Ashton-Drake doll "Victorian Lullaby" has been nominated for the 1995 *Dolls* "Award of Excellence." In all, Cindy has captured more than 20 awards.

Today, Cindy's dolls are eagerly sought by collectors because her originals and some of her Ashton-Drake issues have appreciated considerably on the secondary market.

Most collectors, however, are attracted to her dolls for her ability to capture the sensitive and appealing portraits of children. And her flair for costume design has resulted in the creation of two new Ashton-Drake collections — *Victorian Nursery Heirloom* and *Cross-Stitch* — portraying McClure's love for the Victorian era.

ANNE TRANSUE MCGRORY

Anne McGrory has always been interested in wildlife and nature. She received her bachelor's degree with an emphasis in wildlife art illustration from the Rhode Island School of Design in 1981. After graduation, she did illustrations for the Massachusetts Audubon Society and for the next three years designed jewelry for a manufacturer in Belmont, Massachusetts. From this experience, Anne developed an interest in three-dimensional art.

McGrory began sculpting for The Lance Corporation in 1985, where she helped in several product innovations, including three-dimensional art based on the paintings of Frederic Remington and the concept of "hidden image" sculpture.

Her collections in Chilmark Pewter and MetalART™ include *The OffCanvas™ Collection, The Seekers* and *Kindred Spirits.* Two of McGrory's Chilmark sculptures, "Buffalo Vision" and "Brother Wolf" have been honored in being nominated for *Collector Editions* "Award of Excellence."

GWEN MCNEILL

In a career only ten years old, Gwen McNeill has become one of the leading doll artists in Australia. She began by making reproduction porcelain dolls but felt limited by the painting and finishing techniques. After perfecting her own methods, she began to design and sell her own dolls. In addition to creating dolls, she now teaches painting and sculpture in Australia and serves as an expert judge in doll competitions around the world.

Gwen first came to the New York Toy Fair in 1993. Since then she has become a leading doll artist among U.S. collectors. While Gwen's specialty is modern dolls, she is equally at home working with period costumes.

Her fanciful "Lady Windemere" for Seymour Mann received a 1995 nomination for an "Award of Excellence" from *Dolls* magazine. Another McNeill favorite for Seymour Mann is "Chelsea."

DAN MEDINA

A self-taught illustrator, painter and sculptor, Dan Medina's award-winning artistic genius has proven that he possesses genuine God-given talents.

Early on in his career, Dan realized that he would only be able "to see as far as my eyes would allow me to." This realization led Dan to sculpting — a world balanced in logic, spirit, and creativity, and influenced by Renaissance artists Michelangelo and Leonardo daVinci.

Before creating, Dan researches his subject to ensure its authenticity and sense of motion. "To portray emotion and form in metal — that is the essence of art," says Medina. "It all starts in the mind." He begins to sculpt only when he is satisfied with the two-dimensional image.

Through his work, Dan sees the world with his heart, using his hands and eyes as the conduits to express the human experience. "The kinetics and emotions of the human body, along with the pure beauty of nature, flourish through art."

As Legends' Art Director, Dan expresses that working within the organization has allowed him to find a balance between science and art.

KEN MEMOLI

Ken Memoli was surrounded from an early age by the cultural riches of New England, which included artists such as Calder, Rockwell and D.C. French. With an inspired interest in nature and the arts, Ken studied sculpture at the University of Hartford Art School, melding his experience into a line of outdoor animal statuary.

Ken's talent in sculpting animals brought him to the attention of United Design, where he now works sculpting many of the company's large life-like *Animal Classics™* figurines and animal statuary for the *Stone Garden™* line.

As well as the intricately detailed wildlife and domestic animals Ken creates, he also sculpts figurines for the company's limited edition series *The Legend of Santa Claus™*. The *Angels Collection* features many of Ken's inspired designs, too.

In addition to his sculpture, which he works on daily in his studio, Ken enjoys photography and playing the guitar.

E.M. MERCK

E.M. Merck's success as a bright and popular artist is well represented by her ever-growing series of ornament designs and her *Signature Collection* of nutcrackers for Old World Christmas. Merck's attention to detail, eye for color and intuition about collectibles has furthered the demand for Old World Christmas' heirloom quality mouth-blown ornaments, which are produced by skilled glassblowers in Germany.

E.M. Merck studied fine arts, art history and German cultural traditions at Pomona College, Gonzaga University and Eastern Washington University. Her ornament and nutcracker designs have been nominated for *Collector Editions* "Award of Excellence," and her talents have been showcased in newspaper articles and on radio talk shows. However, her true gratification and feeling of Christmas comes from watching children enjoy the treasures she creates and carrying on Old World Christmas' tradition of bringing affordable, high-quality collectibles to consumers.

RICHARD MEYER

Richard Meyer has an insatiable desire to create three-dimensional art. He finds reality and art a challenge.

Sculpting for over 20 years, his formal training began at Brigham Young University and moved on to the Art Student League and the Sculpture Center. He works from his California home and is a member of the American Indian and Cowboy Artists. He is inspired by themes from the Great West, and his well known bronze sculptures grace the collections of such notables as Roy Rogers and Gene Autry.

Meyer's latest creations for Calabar Creations take us on a journey to the Western Frontier where the modern cowboy works and plays in contem-porary settings and dignified Native Americans in traditional attire inspire reverence. He hopes collectors will enjoy sharing this journey and see each piece as an artistic reality.

S. N. MEYERS

S. N. Meyers was born and raised in St. Louis, Missouri. At an early age, Meyers was recognized for his talent with his hands and his ability to create distinctive images.

After graduating from the University of Kansas where he studied architecture and design, Meyers moved to the Orient. It was there that he began refining his creative skills and expressing his artistic talent in stained glass.

Meyers is best known for his *Century Lights™* designs. *Century Lights* is the original and most extensive collection of stained glass landmark lighthouse replicas available today.

All 47 of these superbly handcrafted collectibles have been created by Meyers in the classic Tiffany tradition using the highest quality stained glass made in the United States. Every landmark lighthouse replica has two sources of illumination, one in the beacon and one in the base. Each piece, upon passing a 17-point personal inspection, is awarded a signature plate which is signed, dated and numbered by S. N. Meyers.

CLEMENTE MICARELLI

Clemente Micarelli studied art at both the Pratt Institute and The Art Students League in New York and the Rhode Island School of Design.

His paintings have been exhibited in numerous shows and have won many awards. Represented nationally by Portraits, Inc. and C.C. Price Gallery in New York, Micarelli has painted the portraits of prominent personalities throughout the United States and Europe.

The artist has done fashion illustrations for many leading department stores and has taught at the Rhode Island School of Design, the Art Institute of Boston and the Scituate Arts Association and South Shore Art Center.

For Reco International, Micarelli has created *The Nutcracker Ballet* plate series, a *Wedding Series* of plates and bells and *The Glory of Christ Collection,* a plate series depicting revered events in the life of Jesus Christ.

LARRY MILLER

Larry Miller's love for the work he does is evident in the charming humor and rich detail he sculpts into his designs.

Larry graduated from the University of Oklahoma with a Bachelor of Fine Arts in Design, yet he credits an art professor at the former Oklahoma College of Liberal Arts in Chickasha as the person who inspired his career in art and design.

After working in graphic arts, Larry came to United Design in 1981 because of the opportunity to work in three dimensional art. Larry had always loved the feel and texture of sculpture, so working independently, he developed his technique by sculpting western bronzes.

Larry is credited with creating several of *The Legend of Santa Claus™* limited edition figurines, many of the *Animal Classics™* − a series of large, exceptionally life-like animals − and many designs in the *Stone Garden™* line.

MARY MONTEIRO

Unlike many artists, Mary Monteiro wasn't drawn to art as a child. Her first introduction came when she entered a university program. After only two years of study, it became evident that the program wasn't moving fast enough for her. For the next four years, she immersed herself in private studies with artist Eugene Tonoff where she focused on portraiture and oil painting. She then built a successful commercial and fine arts career. Despite this success, she still longed "to get in touch with the spiritual part of myself."

After five years of studying and experiencing Eastern Religion, Mary re-entered the field of commercial art, this time to search for a style that was uniquely her own. She thought that, "it was time to paint and draw what was inside of me."

Inside she found kittens, toys, teddy bears and Christmas wreaths which soon became greeting cards. She also found angels and children which were transformed into fine porcelain figurines from Possible Dreams. Today, these designs provide her with "a way to share my feelings and thoughts with others."

JOCELYN MOSTROM

Jocelyn Mostrom first came to national recognition as the woman who raised the American craft of cornhusk doll making into a fine art. She utilized a primitive folk art to design wonder-

ful porcelain dolls, which took up to 60 hours to make.

Aiming to give each doll a sense of timelessness and universal appeal, she captures the lifestyles of favorite historical periods and transforms them into exquisite doll designs. Known for creating dolls with unique personalities, she depicts them with open-mouths, outstretched arms and bodies-in-motion.

Recently Jocelyn created 5" dolls that also double as Christmas ornaments for the *KSA Storybook Collection,* which include "Bo Peep," "Alice in Wonderland," "Red Riding Hood," "Boy Blue" and "Cinderella." In addition, she has created the *When I Grow Up* series of children playing dress-up as a doctor, nurse, firefighter, teacher and golfer. Jocelyn also expanded her current collections, portraying Kwanza, an American cowboy and cowgirl, children from Ireland and Mexico for *Small Wonders of the World,* and also musicians and snow children for the *Royal Heritage Collection.*

NICOLO MULARGIA

A native of the island of Sardinia, off the coast of Italy in the Mediterranean Sea, Nicolo Mulargia brings the warmth and vitality of his birthplace to his designs for Crystal World. A lover of all things joyful and spirited, Mulargia is the principal artist behind Crystal World's famous *Teddyland* collection, which offers some of the most popular crystal Teddy Bear figurines ever made, including the "Teddies at Eight," "Beach Teddies" and the computer-inspired "CompuBear."

Several of his figurines have been nominated for *Collector Editions* magazine's "Award of Excellence," including "Small Riverboat" and "Small White House." Mulargia's enormous range of talent can be seen in figurines as different as his whimsical animals and his highly detailed "Victorian House" and "Waterfront Village."

The artist currently resides in suburban New Jersey with his wife and four children.

REAL MUSGRAVE

Real Musgrave is an artist who follows a whimsical muse. The *Pocket Dragons,* wizards and other creatures that Real sculpts spring to life from the complex and wonderful world he has created in drawings and paintings for over 20 years. Those finely detailed drawings bespeak the heritage of beautifully illustrated children's books from the turn of the century, but to everything he adds a vision of gentleness and humor which is uniquely his own.

(Sampsel/Preston Photographic Design)

Together Real and his wife Muff developed and marketed a line of limited edition etchings and prints featuring the *Pocket Dragons*, wizards, gargoyles and friends. In 1978, Muff quit her job to become Real's full-time creative partner.

Real's work has won awards and been exhibited in shows at major museums, art institutes and galleries. Today, Real is recognized as one of the foremost fantasy artists in the world. The *Pocket Dragons* appear on greeting cards, posters, and other products, as well as the delightful sculptures produced by Collectible World Studios in England and exclusively distributed in the U.S. by Flambro Imports, Inc.

ALLYSON NAGEL

The name of Allyson Nagel's company, A.N. Original, reflects her passion for perfection, resulting in authentic art with fascinating personality. In her South Dakota studio, she creates whimsical egg characters, stars with personality and unique dolls entirely by hand, using no molds. Her labor-intensive art form requires hand sculpting distinctive faces full of character, firing to a bisque in her kiln and meticulous hand-painting.

Reflecting on her success garnering recognition and coveted "Judge's Choice" awards, Nagel says, "I started out in portraiture. My turn to crafting dolls began when the noted doll maker Faith Wick viewed my work and asked me if I would make faces for dolls."

Nagel turned her attention to designing porcelain eggs with personalities...even dressing them! This new idea turned into a successful, intriguing new egg collection, *Sunny Side Up*™, for Roman, Inc.

For her encore, Nagel's *Home Gnomes*™ dolls, *Starlight Starbright* and *Soul Sisters* collections are charming America.

RYUJU NAKAI

As the founding artist and leading designer for Crystal World, Ryuju Nakai created the award-winning *Original Rainbow Castle Collection*®. He also designed the company's most popular architectural sculptures, such as the "Empire State Building" and "Independence Hall." Other creations feature animals such as the "Tea Mouse" and the panda "Ling Ling," "Crystal Sailboat" and "Tall Ship" and the unusual "Happy Birthday Cake."

Nakai's mastery of detail and commitment to uncompromising quality is reflected in all his designs, including the "Enchanted Castle," which won an "Award of Excellence" from *Collector Editions* magazine. For the past dozen years, he has led Crystal World to its present standing as the United States' largest manufacturer of crystal collectibles.

Ryuju Nakai lives in New Jersey, near the Crystal World headquarters, with his wife and three children.

SEIJI NAKANE

Born in Tajimi, Gifu prefecture of Japan in 1938, Seiji Nakane, award-winning master sculptor, graduated from Tajii Art and Industrial School and studied art in Asia and Europe. Fascinated by the porcelain-making industry in Seto, he began working in clay at age 18, which he continued in addition to painting in oil and watercolor.

Captivated by Seiji's figurines, which seem almost alive with personality, WACO Products Corporation used a selection of his figurines as prototypes for the first *Melody In Motion* introductions.

Billed as "the only porcelain, moving, animated sound musical collectible," the *Melody In Motion* figurines have set collectors' hearts singing.

Merging art and technology, each meticulously hand-painted and assembled figurine is fitted with gears, cams, motor, amplifier and speaker. Taking four weeks to create, the lifelike figurines move and sing. Established in 1992, the *Melody In Motion* Collectors Society teaches collectors about this fascinating process and the artist who inspired it all.

DIANNA NEWBURN

Dianna Newburn has always enjoyed doing creative works, and when her children were small, she taught decorative painting. Dianna would take some of her own works to craft fairs, but her real talent and love of sculpture was discovered as she experimented with making miniature clay dolls. Dianna says, "Part of the reason I love doing this so much is because I have three sons and no daughters. Now I have my dolls to dress up."

In 1990, Dianna's work had become so popular, she was exhausted from trying to keep up with the demand. That was when she joined the staff of United Design, where she continues to create dolls and figurines for many different collections.

Currently, Dianna is sculpting figurines for the *Angels Collection*. She has created several designs for the limited edition series and the small angels. Dianna is also kept busy working on *Angel Babies*™ and *Itty Bitty Critters*™.

MARYSE NICOLE

Born in the French wine country, Maryse Nicole's father, a guitarist, and mother, a ballroom dancer, introduced her to show business. As a child, Maryse travelled all over Europe, Venezuela, Chicago and finally to California, and became fluent in French, English, Spanish and Italian.

Wherever she is, Maryse is always looking for joyful and artistic ways to express her own unique personality and style. Originally a professional singer, Maryse created dolls as a hobby. She carried her trademark, a dazzling, beaded costume that sparkled on stage, to TV when she began selling her dolls through television, and collector's nicknamed her the "Sparkle Queen."

Today, singing is a hobby to her doll designing. As Executive Director of The Franklin Mint Heirloom Dolls in Los Angeles, Maryse personally sculpts each original porcelain doll, oversees the intricate hand-painting and carefully selects each fabric, trim and accessory for her dolls.

"When I am with collectors, it's like seeing an old friend," says Maryse. "Their friendship and love for my dolls makes it all worthwhile."

JORGEN NIELSEN

Jorgen Nielsen joined the artists and manufacturers at Royal Copenhagen Porcelain Manufactory in 1959. Since then he has ambitiously pursued various types of artistry at Royal Copenhagen and abroad.

Although he was originally trained as an onglaze painter, Nielsen began working in 1965 as a painter of unique underglaze vases. After a two-year study tour to Japan, he returned to onglaze painting for a few years.

From 1976 to 1986, Nielsen worked under the tutelage of ceramist Nils Thorsson, using the media of faience, porcelain and stoneware.

Currently, Jorgen Nielsen works on a freelance basis for Royal Copenhagen and manages his own painting studio.

DOUGLAS NORRGARD

Douglas Norrgard is more than an accomplished artist — he is a skilled storyteller. His newly introduced Goebel Miniatures "Once Upon a Winter's Day" relates a childhood memory with such visual eloquence that no words are needed.

Trained as a painter both here and abroad, Douglas didn't realize until later in his career that sculpture was his true calling. On a trip to Japan in 1985, he watched a sculptor turn a lifeless lump of clay into a figurine that seemed to come alive in his hands. The classically trained painter became a self-taught sculptor.

"What I strive for," Douglas explains, "is the feeling beyond the form. I want people to be able to relate to my work with their hearts as well as their eyes."

Collector reponse to his first commission for Goebel Miniatures indicates he has achieved that goal.

BEN OTERO

Heartwarming impressions from pictures by Ben Otero speak of this artist's ability to create mood, atmosphere, excitement and

unique images. With the necessary research, craftsmanship and devotion to his work, Otero brings life to his story-telling illustrations.

This talented painter and illustrator has been creating pictures for over 35 years. His paintings hang in galleries across the United States, and he has also worked extensively as a commercial illustrator. Harley-Davidson® celebrates the work of Ben Otero in a limited edition, five-year series of holiday collectibles entitled *Holiday Memories*. In addition to a holiday plate, the collection includes a music box, bulb ornament and holiday stein.

Otero currently lives and works as a freelance artist in Shorewood, Wisconsin. He shares his work and his life with his wife and four sons.

CHRISTOPHER PARDELL

Christopher Pardell, one of Legends® first artists, began sculpting at age four. After pursuing a university art education, he left after two years frustrated with the "narrow viewpoints."

At 21, Christopher apprenticed as a moldmaker for a commercial statuary company owned and operated by Italian immigrants trained in the Old World style. He rapidly learned the skills to excel as an artist and a sculptor.

Never sketching his designs on paper, Christopher composes all of his work in three dimensional maquette, which explains the beauty of line and sense of action that is his trademark.

Christopher is drawn to the aesthetic of the human figure and strives to capture the tragedy and nobility of the human endeavor. For him, the history of Native Americans, defiantly holding to their traditions and beliefs in the face of opposition, exemplifies the human condition. In sculpting, Christopher strives to shape his feelings for humanity, so that we can see how much of ourselves exist in each other.

In his wish to pass on his realizations, Christopher formed an apprenticeship program that gives young artists Old World training.

GARY PATTERSON

Artist/humorist Gary Patterson made his first venture into gifts and collectibles with Media Arts Group Inc. in 1995, with a series of three-dimensional figurines, limited edition and open lithographs of his famous illustrations.

Widely known by an estimated 250 million people as the "creator of smiles" for his highly detailed, richly insightful — yet witty and humorous — portraits of life through sports scenes, Gary Patterson has earned many accolades over the years, including induction into the Basketball Hall of Fame, Sports Artist of the Year and Art Director for an Academy Award-winning film. However, Gary has not limited his talent to sports. Among his most famous paintings are his unique, whimsical and appealing cats and a charming little mouse he calls "Boo."

He is often described as having "put a mirror in front of all of us and has shown that in smiling through our tears, the unbearable can become bearable and even laughable." His world-famous works are exhibited in the Los Angeles County Museum of Art and have been enjoyed on television and in newspapers and magazines over the past 25 years.

DONNA PEMBERTON

Donna Pemberton, the vibrant Director of Artists for Duncan Royale, showed a remarkable talent for drawing at the early age of four. Her art progressed from finger painting to ceramics, sculpting, and graphic arts. Donna received her formal training at U.C.L.B., where she was one of the few students elected for the coveted ceramic program. Since graduating at the top of her class, Donna works with some of the world's best known and highly qualified artists in various disciplines.

Donna's original work, which she creates in her own studio in Orange County, California, has been commissioned and purchased by such well-known art collectors as John Dupont, Dick Clark and Herb Albert, to name a few.

At Duncan Royale, Donna's wide range of responsibilities include assisting with the development of new products and color schemes, working with staff and commissioned artists, supervising the development of catalogs and brochures, assisting with figurine repair and communicating with collectors.

MICHELLE G. PHELPS

Michelle G. Phelps was born in California and currently resides with her family in the Blue Ridge Mountains. She has been sculpting professionally for about 11 years.

Her main interests are in Native American art, the outdoors and horses. Most of her inspirations are derived from these interests, as seen in her pewter sculptures for the Masterworks® line from Shube's Manufacturing, Inc.

Michelle sculpted most of the Masterworks *Fairy Collection*, and the striking limited edition pieces, "Traditional Dancer," "Pueblo Dancer" and "Old Enemies" from the *Native American Collection*.

PAMELA PHILLIPS

A creative painter and portrait artist since childhood, Pamela Phillips recently began designing dolls. As she explains, "I saw a

face so compelling it could only be expressed in sculpture. After much trial, but mostly error, I made my first doll."

Although a newcomer to the doll field, Phillips' work has already been graced with major nominations and awards. In 1994, she received three nominations for *Dolls* magazine's "Award of Excellence," one of which, the 26-inch "Anna," won. Now, two of her dolls have been nominated for *Doll Reader's* "Doll of the Year" award for 1995: "Mary Elizabeth and her Jumeau," first in the *Yesterday's Dream™* collection from the Georgetown Collection and "Caroline" for Georgetown's elegant *Sweethearts of Summer™* collection.

Pamela created some of her first dolls for the Seymour Mann Gallery; these dolls — "Alyssa" and "Nizhoni" — both received a 1993 *Dolls* magazine nomination for "Awards of Excellence" as well as being nominated for a DOTY. In addition, her doll for Seymour Mann, "Guinevere," received both an "Award of Excellence" nomination and a DOTY nomination from *Doll Reader* magazine.

VALERIE PIKE

A resident of Australia's Gold Coast, Valerie Pike's first artistic efforts were in oil portraits. Later she turned to hand-painted clothing and soft sculpture, which she regards as a natural progression toward doll sculpting. The people she sees around her inspire her lifelike creations, which have won many enthusiasts in the South Pacific.

Valerie sculpts her dolls from a water-based clay, from which she makes a mold for the porcelain head, shoulder plate, hands and feet. She designs her own body patterns and often makes her own wigs from mohair.

Until recently Valerie's dolls were produced only in limited editions of ten to twenty-five. By joining the Seymour Mann Studios, she now makes her works available in editions of 5,000 each. Her first Seymour Mann doll will be introduced at Toy Fair in 1996.

DON POLLAND

Don Polland describes himself as a "self-taught experimenter." He cannot remember a time when he was not making figures, even as a boy. In 1966, he began a new hobby — sculpting miniatures of the American West.

In 1973, a series of miniature sculptures of Bicentennial events by Robert Sullivan caught Polland's eye. They were cast in pewter, not bronze, for Royal Worcester by The Lance Corporation. "The thing that interested me," remembers Polland, "was how quickly you could read the detail in the pieces — the eyes, the folds of the clothing, the buttons on the shirt."

Polland asked Lance if they would cast his miniatures, and they introduced three *American West* pewter sculptures in 1974. Today, over 20 years later, Polland and Chilmark have created an innovative and immense body of art owned and appreciated by more than 50,000 people around the world.

BARBARA PRUSSEIT

Those tiny hands...that little cooing voice...the fresh-as-a-snowflake smell.... That's right: It's baby time at Georgetown Collection, and the creator of all this delight is a new artist – Barbara Prusseit. Barbara hails from the German region of Bavaria, and, until recently, only Europeans knew and loved her baby dolls. Now, she's creating them for Georgetown, and the first arrival is "Good as Gold," the premier issue in the *Gifts from Heaven™* collection.

This tiny treasure, a mere 13 inches, sleeps in a pose that's sheer perfection, with a secret smile that says "Somebody loves me" and hands and toes so lifelike they might start wiggling at any moment. Barbara explains that her husband, a physician, has helped her learn the art of anatomy. Everything else – from the pose to the clothes – is the design of this talented artist.

CHRISTOPHER RADKO

When Christopher Radko began designing his collection of fine glass Christmas ornaments ten years ago, there were only 50 styles in the collection. Today, there are over 750 fabulous designs – a crowning achievement of a decade of Christopher's personal design, development and plain hard work.

Growing up with diverse traditions handed down from relatives in Poland, Austria and France, Christopher remembers that, "Christmas was like being at the United Nations. We had carols, food and ornaments from all over Europe."

In an effort to replace his family's lost ornament collection – caused by their Christmas tree falling over – Christopher started designing and creating ornaments "with the quality of the old days."

His desire to create exquisitely blown and intricately decorated ornaments leads Christopher to select only expert craftsmen in Italy, the Czech Republic, Germany and Poland. He visits the cottage factories and retrains glass blowers and decorators in the art perfected by their own great-grandparents. Through his designs, Christopher has put both quality and magic back into Christmas.

LYNNE RANDOLPH

An avid sketch artist and painter since childhood, Lynne Randolph turned to calligraphy after the birth of her second child. From there she progressed to sculpting, a phase she describes as "a classic plaster-all-over-the-kitchen-floor story." While on vacation in 1990, she visited a doll shop in Maine, where she admired some porcelain baby dolls. "I was instantly fascinated," she remembers, "and I said to my husband 'I have to learn to do this.'" Soon afterwards she created her first original

doll, "Rachel Beth," using her own daughter as a model.

Her many awards include a DOTY nomination from *Doll Reader*. Her favorite dolls for the Seymour Mann Gallery include "Tiffany," "Meredith" and "Ginnie." Speaking of her dolls, she says, "They are a gentle reminder that children are ours to protect, nurture and love."

JOYCE REAVEY

What artist could create both the charm and innocence of "Clarissa Comes Calling" (Georgetown's *Pictures of Innocence™* series) and the delightfully mud-splattered "Mr. Mischief" (first in the *Boys Will Be Boys™* collection)? It should come as no surprise that Joyce Reavey, the mother of three, portrays the cheer and challenge of parenting with love and a good-natured sense of humor. "My inspiration," she laughs, "comes from seeing my own kids tromping into the house every day, bringing mud and wildlife adventures to share."

Reavey has an eye for the opulence of Victoriana, too, as witnessed by "Catherine," the new doll in the *Age of Romance™* collection. Every detail of this ravishing beauty's wedding gown – from its rich fabric and lace to the floral headpiece – bespeaks Victorian style. Reavey is yet another Georgetown Collection artist who has been honored with a *Dolls* magazine "Award of Excellence" nomination.

MARTHA REYNOLDS

Vibrant – a wonderful word that describes both Martha Reynolds and her art.

A Fenton designer for over four years, Martha constantly experiments with new materials and styles, creating designs that range from simple and contemporary to the ornate and richly embellished look of Victorian glass.

Martha has frequently been honored with design awards since graduating cum laude from Shepherd College. Her "Best of Show" awards cover a variety of media including sculpture, water-color and woodcuts. In 1993, the Society for Glass and Ceramic Decorators honored her with their prestigious Vandenoever Award.

Few artists choose to paint on glass because it is difficult to adjust to the different background colors, shapes and the non-absorbent slick surfaces. Martha welcomes these challenges and her ringing laughter lifts everyone's spirits when deadlines are short.

Look for more of Martha's glass painting in the *90th Anniversary* and *Connoisseur* collections from Fenton Art Glass.

MARY RHYNER-NADIG

As a teenager, Mary Rhyner-Nadig considered being a veterinarian but planned to enjoy art as a hobby. But when she showed a sketch to a friend's father, he told her she could make a living with art.

Mary, who has been with the Enesco Corporation since 1990 and is a Senior Product Designer, studied at the American Academy of Art in Chicago. Enesco has honored Mary with the "Division Designer of the Year" and "Associate of the Month" awards, and the "Stanhome Achievement Award" from Stanhome, Enesco's parent company.

Mary designs her figurines in watercolors and colored pencils, and she gets her inspiration from antique stores, flea markets and other shops, as well as from magazines and catalogs. Mary's most recent Enesco lines, *This Little Piggy* and *Santa's Special Deerlivery™*, together with *Mary's Moo Moos, Cute As A Button™, Cream & Cocoa* and *Partners in Crime™* have become the talk of the industry.

Mary says, "When I walk into a store and I see the product I worked on, I'm in disbelief. I'll ask myself, 'Did I really do that?'"

JEANETTE RICHARDS AND SANDRA PENFIELD

The artists of the *Best Friends* collection, Jeanette Richards and Sandra Penfield, have discovered the excitement of creating a world of clay miniatures that capture the true essence of friendship.

Jeanette, from Rocky River, Ohio, studied art in Washington, D.C. and received a B.A. in English and Art from the University of Dayton, Ohio. Growing up in a family of artists, her first love was illustration.

Sandra, from Detroit Lakes, Minnesota, received a B.S. in Art from the University of North Dakota. She taught art and shared it through her woodcut prints.

The pair's mutual interest in art brought them together in Hudson, Wisconsin, where they became partners in a graphic design business in 1984.

In 1990, Jeanette and Sandra created the first figure in the *Best Friends* series for BAND Creations, recreating their experiences along the St. Croix River. These designs soon evolved to include all the facets of friendship and family life. The line includes *Monthly Angels, Angel Wishes, Noah's Ark, First Friends Begin at Childhood, Winter Wonderland, O Joyful Night* and the *Town of RiverSong*.

LUCY RIGG

Lucy Rigg began making baker's clay teddy bear figurines in 1969 while awaiting the birth of her daughter, Noelle. She decorated the nursery with her first teddy bears, but friends and family were so enchanted with the original creations that Lucy began

making them for others.

Teddy bear collectors bought her hand-painted clay dough bears, known as "Rigglets," at street fairs. To keep up with the growing demand, she imposed a quota on herself to make 100 teddy bears per day.

As her teddy bears became more popular, Lucy formed her own company. In the late 1970s, Enesco Corporation President Eugene Freedman approached Lucy and proposed turning her hand-made teddy bears into a line of porcelain bisque figurines and accessories. Since Enesco introduced the *Lucy & Me®* Collection in 1978, it has enjoyed steady support from collectors and teddy bear lovers.

Lucy continues to operate Lucy & Company, designing diaries, baby announcements, calendars and her "teddy bear" version of popular children's books.

SHARON RILEY

Sharon Riley joined W.A.P. Watson Ltd. (parent of The Tudor Mint) as a designer in 1983 and apart from an 'O' level in Art, is an entirely self-taught artist. In the past decade, she has worked on all aspects of the company's products and was responsible for the first 12 *Myth and Magic* designs launched in 1989. As Chief Designer for The Tudor Mint, she has generated more ideas for studies than any other designer. Her favorite models are "The Dragon of the Underworld" and "Dactrius." She likes the effect of dragons coiling themselves around objects. Sharon's son, Daniel, was born around the same time she designed the Collectors' Club study "Playmates" — hence the little cherub on the piece.

SUSAN RIOS

At age 13, Susan Rios' artistic talent became apparent in her pen and ink explorations which led to a summer scholarship at Cal State Northridge. Her artistic ventures, however, led her to abandon her college classes to explore the worlds of graphic design and flower arrangement.

After her daughter's birth, Susan decided to evolve her artwork from avocation to vocation. Since then, she has balanced her busy schedule of painter and homemaker.

A self-taught painter, Susan derived her influences from Matisse and Monet. Whether they depict lush gardens, floral sanctuaries or intimate corners furnished in wicker chairs and overstuffed love seats, her acrylic paintings offer a feeling of coziness, peace-fulness and a sense of familiarity.

Relying on her inborn gifts of tenacity and discipline to

struggle through a painting's beginning stages, Susan relishes the distinct moment when she can step back and begin to feel the "harmony and wholeness" of her artwork. Her works are published by Lightpost.

NORMAN ROCKWELL

© Copyright Louie Lamone

The most popular American artist and illustrator of the 20th century, Norman Rockwell, sold his first cover illustration to *The Saturday Evening Post* in 1916. By 1920, he was the *Post's* top illustrator. His trademark style, a realistic technique highlighted by a warm and whimsical sense of humor, is best summed up by him: "I paint life as I would like it to be."

Through the years, Rockwell created classic illustrations for *Life, McCall's* and *Boy's Life*, and for many advertisers. Among his best works, "The Four Freedoms" raised more than $130 million in war bonds during World War II, and the *American Family* series, portrayed in more than 70 sketches for the Massachusetts Mutual Life Insurance Company, is on display in The Norman Rockwell Museum.

In the 1970s, Rockwell's illustrations became some of the most sought-after subjects for limited edition collectibles. The Norman Rockwell Gallery offers only those collectibles bearing The Norman Rockwell Family Trust's official authorization seal. Also, Hawthorne Architectural Register distributes three-dimensional cottage sculptures based on his original artwork.

Rockwell continued as an artist and illustrator in his Stockbridge, Massachusetts, studio until his death in 1978.

CINDY MARSCHNER ROLFE

Noted artist Cindy Marschner Rolfe has taken the doll collecting world by storm with her innovative creations and their adorable, lifelike expressions.

"I make my dolls as lifelike and appealing as possible so that, hopefully, they will remind collectors of their own children and grandchildren," Cindy says.

She credits her father for recognizing and developing her talent. When she was young, she watched for hours while he sketched and carved wood products. That initial interest in art prompted her many years later to teach herself to sculpt. The resulting clay babies were so much admired by neighbors and family members that Cindy developed her talent further, finally agreeing to sell her dolls to the public.

"Shannon," a doll created for The Hamilton Collection, was inspired by Cindy's young daughter, who loves to pose for pictures and served as a wonderful model for the irresistible doll.

BRONWEN ROSS

Creator of *The Thickets At Sweet-briar*™, internationally renowned artist Bronwen Ross has always been captivated by the beauty of flora and fauna. A self-taught artist with no formal train-

ing, Bronwen began drawing at an early age, often creating stories as she went along.

Bronwen has a precise eye for detail and a colorful imagination. When working on new artwork, she never does a preliminary sketch. Instead, she visualizes what she'll paint, seeing the artwork on blank paper before she even picks up a brush.

Bronwen's creations for Possible Dreams entwine the detailed intricacies of nature with the romantic renderings of a bygone era. *The Thickets At Sweetbriar* collection includes charming cats, bunnies and mice dressed in Victorian costume and accented with beautiful flowers, feathers and butterflies.

Living in rural Missouri, Bronwen is inspired by the nature around her. She enjoys pressing flowers and using her garden florals as models. Her work has been reproduced on greeting cards, stationery and limited edition prints and has been shown in *Good Housekeeping* magazine.

DOREEN M. ROSS

Doreen Ross is always on the lookout for new and interesting buildings or ways to make a process better at the company she and her husband, David started — R.R. Creations.

As a very craft-oriented person, Doreen is always renewing or redecorating something at home or at the office. Working hard has paid off, as R.R. Creations recently emerged into the foreign market by producing buildings from Denmark, and several of R.R.'s collectibles have been highlighted at Harrod's of London. Doreen hopes to double the number of shops that carry the *Open Window* collection in the next year.

For a person who thinks of herself as the "Queen of QVC," Doreen fulfilled her dream in 1995 by having a collection of three buildings and two accessories represented on the QVC shopping network.

A few on her office staff have made the statement that she is one to "jump into the fire" with new ideas and challenges. But her philosophy is that "anything is possible with the Lord." She enjoys a challenge, even friendly competition, because the pressure has a profound effect on creativity.

MARJORIE GRACE ROTHENBERG

Marjorie Grace Rothenberg, also known affectionately as MGR, received her first commissions to illustrate children's books and magazine and advertising art while in high school.

In 1970, MGR became art director at Kurt S. Adler, Inc. For 20 years, she frequently travelled abroad to work with talented artisans. Along with Mr. Kurt S. Adler, MGR is one of the early

328

pioneers of the Christmas trade. Under their guidance, she taught a Far East cottage craft industry the fine art of Christmas design.

Now a grandmother, MGR works mostly in her studio in the Berkshires' foothills. "It is here," says Marjorie, "that I draw constant inspiration..." and create "little people." Starting with a detailed drawing, Marjorie then oversees the sculpting, painting, sewing and trimming of each figure to her standards.

Designing exclusively for Kurt S. Adler, Inc., MGR is well-known for the cornhusk mice ornaments, depicting human characters and created for Christmas and Easter holidays. Recently, she designed many new Fabriché™ figurines and ornaments in fine fabric maché, featuring Santa, Mrs. Claus, elves and other holiday characters. Look for MGR's signature trademark, a gold wedding band, on all her Fabriché Santas and Mrs. Claus.

SUSAN RYAN

Susan Ryan's dream of going to art school was delayed by marriage and five children. In 1990 when the last child graduated from high school, Ryan graduated from Madison Area Technical College with a degree in commercial art.

Although Ryan has painted outdoor scenes, flowers, people and animals, the majority of her commissioned work is animals.

She has painted a long list of field trial labrador and golden retrievers. The most famous, "Lottie of Candlewood Kennels," is the only three-time National Field Champion in history

Ryan's experience in painting hunting dog breeds led to a referral to Anheuser-Busch. She has designed and painted the Setters, Golden Retrievers and Beagle Steins in the *Hunters Companion* collectibles series.

Susan Ryan continues to work out of her home studio located in Madison, Wisconsin, painting subjects for future prints and commission portraits.

BARBI SARGENT

Barbi Sargent is known as "one of the most reproduced artists in the world" because of her thousands of greeting card designs exchanged around the world since 1966. Today her renderings weave into the tapestry of American gifts and collectibles, surfacing as popular greeting cards, collections, dolls, books and prints.

Drawing since age two, Sargent later earned a scholarship to the Cooper School of Commercial Art. She began creating greeting cards at age 18 leading to the creation of characters like "Gretchen" and "Poppyseed" which achieved her national fame.

Years later, an inspirational meeting with renowned artist Edna Hibel encouraged Sargent to form Barbie Sargent and Company, Inc. in 1989 to produce greeting cards, fine art prints and licensed designs.

Sargent's volunteer work with youngsters at the Cleveland Clinic Foundation inspired her *Tender Expressions™* character, "Sunshine," for Roman, Inc. Sargent donates all royalties from two pledge figurines to the Tender Expressions Endowment Fund for vital programs at The Cleveland Clinic Foundation Children's Hospital. Roman contributes a matching donation.

ALEXANDER SCHERBACK

Currently residing in Colorado, Alexander Scherback was born in 1959 in Lvov, in the Western Ukraine. Alexander regularly visited the great museums in St. Petersburg, Moscow and Kiev, and was inspired by Renaissance artists such as Leonardo da Vinci and Michelangelo.

Alexander started sculpting historical figures and knights wearing armor at the age of five. At age 14, he was sculpting Napoleonic soldiers out of tin. Many of Alexander's technical skills were taught to him by his father, who was a painter, sculptor, jeweler and model ship builder, in addition to his career as a medical doctor.

Alexander has exhibited his work throughout Russia, including sculptures depicting the history and development of Russian weapons and uniforms from ancient times up to the Russian Revolution.

Although he is a professional geologist, Alexander's interests have branched out in numerous other directions since his arrival in the United States in 1991. He now makes his living as a professional sculptor. For the Masterworks® line from Shube's Manufacturing, Inc., Alexander Scherback sculpted the *Civil War Collection*.

LOU AND PAM SCHIFFERL

Growing up in a family that nurtured creativity, Lou Schifferl spent hours watching his father's skillful woodcrafting. And then in turn, Lou inspired his daughter Pam.

A treasured woodcrafting tradition passed down through three generations continues through the father-daughter artistic team of Lou and Pam Schifferl. Combining their shared love for woodcarving and their distinctive styles, they create folk art that excites the imagination. The Schifferls' images of Christmas have a remarkably nostalgic appearance — an heirloom quality that touches the heart.

Midwest of Cannon Falls proudly offers exclusive reproductions of the Schifferls' imaginative folk art pieces. Folk art lovers and collectors alike will want to include these delightful ornaments and figures among their holiday treasures.

KANDY SCHLESINGER

"It's impossible to grow up and live in the Blue Ridge Mountains and not be touched by the mystical beauty and folklore," says folk artist Kandy Schlesinger. "These mountains reflect a spirit, strength and simplicity that has been an inspiration for much of my work and is inherent to all that I am."

Kandy employs many mediums to give life to her incredible array of Santas, wizards, animals, witches and other whimsical creatures in her art. She is equally comfortable working with clay, wood, fabric or paint.

Kandy is a whirlwind of energy and emits a tremendous sense of excitement in each project she does for Kurt S. Adler, Inc. Her inspiration can be sparked by a scrap of material, the flash of a mental image or piece of oddly shaped wood. Each work reflects the best of American country art. She has designed the *Kandy's Folkart* and *Hole-in-the-Wall Gang* collections, both exclusively available from Kurt S. Adler, Inc.

SARAH SCHULTZ

While working in her husband's pharmacy managing the gift department in 1983, Sarah Schultz observed that the best selling products were her original creations – stenciled slates, boards, pictures and dolls.

Many of Sarah's creations come from her memories. For example, when Sarah developed rheumatic fever as a child, her father began an angel collection for her. Through prayers, her father's faith and the angels, she recovered. Later, in dedication to her father who passed away, and to everyone who has lost a loved one, Sarah created the collection, *Angels in the Attic.*

While delivering the daily paper as a child to an African-American family living nearby, Sarah developed a loving friendship with them which inspired her to create the *Black Heritage Collection.*

As a firm believer in love, respect and dignity, Sarah paints a heart on each piece to symbolize these words. The signature heart also guarantees the product's unmatched quality and originality. This guarantee assures collectors that much love and pride were put into creating, painting and shipping the product.

PETER C. SEDLOW

Peter C. Sedlow has been sculpting for many years. The subject matter of his art is widely varied, from Native American themes to wildlife and fantasy.

From his hilltop studio, surrounded by the natural scenic beauty of the mountains of the Pacific Northwest, Peter researches every piece he sculpts, drawing from a vast amount of materials he has collected over many years for his personal reference library. From this extensive research, he is able to literally breathe life into his sculptures.

Peter has been the primary artist for most of the Masterworks® *Native American Collection* produced by Shube's Manufacturing, Inc. Among his creations are the striking 13-1/2" tall "Sitting Bull"

sculpture and the popular limited edition Native American pieces, "Saga On The Plains" and "White Water Rush," as well as dozens of other Masterworks pieces.

MARK SHERMAN

Studying at New York's Art Student's League and in California with Rex Brandt and Joseph Mugnaini, Mark Sherman's paintings have appeared in juried exhibitions and are included in many private and corporate collections. His creations in pastels, oil and watercolors reveal his wide range of interests and talents.

Currently a professor in San Diego, Mark instructs a studio art class for the humanities program. Travels with his family in North America and Europe have inspired many of his transparent watercolors. A long time admirer of our nations' lighthouses, Mark naturally chose "Old Point Loma," only a few miles from his home, as the subject of his first lighthouse watercolor.

Beginning with the 1995 *Harbour Lights Calendar*, Mark has been commissioned to offer 12 original lighthouse watercolors for the annual publication. He also created a beautiful watercolor rendering of "Point Fermin Lighthouse, CA" to launch the Harbour Lights Collectors Society. Signed and numbered museum-quality prints of "Point Fermin" will be framed and given as gifts to Charter Society Members.

ELIO SIMONETTI

Creating the life-sized Fontanini® Heirloom Nativity sculptures is a crowning achievement of Elio Simonetti's distinguished artistic career with the renowned House of Fontanini. Receiving the Fontanini family gift of a 50" nativity, Pope John Paul II said of Simonetti's breathtaking masterpiece, "I hope God grants him a long life to continue his fantastic sculpting."

Countless people worldwide share this appreciation for Simonetti's talent and the fine Fontanini craftsmanship when viewing life-sized nativities in American movies like *Home Alone*, famous European cathedrals and parades.

Working with the Fontaninis for 40 years, Master Sculptor Simonetti pledged to resculpt all his early 5" subjects bringing to them the maturing of his perception and skills.

Born in Lucca in 1942, Simonetti attended the Liceo for art for a few years but abandoned his studies for full-time work to help support his large family.

Recently, Simonetti has turned his magical touch to exploration of one of his favorite themes – angels.

MARLENE SIRKO

Vitality is the key to Marlene Sirko's creations. When this doll artist was young, her relatives and friends noticed that Marlene had a gift for painting. Today, the artist still recalls the thrill when, at age 16, she received her first oil paints set. Her studies at the Pennsylvania Academy of the Fine Arts led her to sculpting, which in turn led her to the creation of dolls – one of which won a *Doll Reader* magazine "Doll of the Year" award.

Marlene loves to portray the incredible natural talent of children – often using her own two as inspiration. "Every child is gifted in some way," she says, "whether it's in painting, playing a musical instrument or throwing a baseball." Her creations for Georgetown Collection include a doll based on one of her childhood dreams – skating. Named "Amanda," this 15-1/2" beauty is poseable, so collectors can display her in their favorite skating poses!

GERHARD SKROBEK

Gerhard Skrobek, a master sculptor of the Goebel company, was born in Silesia, the northernmost part of Germany, subsequently moving with his family to Berlin. There, surrounded by museum art treasures and encouraged by his artist mother, Skrobek became immersed in the artistic tradition. From early childhood, he was fascinated with sculpture and its many artistic forms. He studied at the Reimannschule in Berlin, a renowned private academy of arts, and continued his studies in Coburg. Through a professor, he was introduced to porcelain sculpture at W. Goebel Porzellanfabrik.

Skrobek joined Goebel in 1951, becoming one of its leading sculptors and eventually the predominant interpreter of Sister Maria Innocentia Hummel's drawings into three-dimensional form.

According to his interpretation, Skrobek is able to capture the life and vitality of two-dimensional art through the use of a textured surface in the sculpting process. Skrobek is articulate and personable, and a delight to meet and talk with about *M.I. Hummel* figurines.

TED SLACK

British sculptor, Ted Slack finds that combining his love of nature with a long-time fascination for the unusual has resulted in his ability to create the unique. In his newest achievement, *Woodly Wise* for John Hine Studios, Ted Slack demonstrates his artistic talent and his penchant for incorporating whimsy, architecture and natural beauty in these remarkably miniature treehouses.

As a budding artist, Slack found old churches, windmills, buildings and boats along river banks as interesting drawing subjects. But his main interest was in the dilapidation and decay of castle ruins, old buildings and quaint cottages.

At 16, he was accepted at an art school in Cambridge and later completed his diploma in Art and Design at Sunderland.

Returning to England, Slack took a position with a master craftsman working on the renovation of buildings and discovered he enjoyed sculpting in miniature. This led to his joining Lilliput Lane Ltd., where he devoted himself full-time to the sculpting of miniature architectural structures and cottages.

In his home studio, Slack now combines his many years of sculpting, traveling, research and architecture to create his treehouses. His three sons contribute, each in his own way, to the creation of *Woodly Wise*.

JOSEPH SLOCKBOWER

Indians have always held a special fascination for Joseph Slockbower, who studied drawing and sculpting at California State University, Long Beach in the late 1970s. He started researching the Indian culture, customs, beliefs and costuming, striving to capture physical features, as well as the right expression and the true spirit of each subject. Joe believes that, "Just as every detail on the person or subject is critical to the finished piece, so is the soul or spiritual aspect of the subject."

Joe joined forces with The Lance Corporation in 1991. His striking collections for the Chilmark Pewter line include *The Great Chiefs*, *Guardians of the Plains* and *Legends of the Wild West: The Lawman*. His "Chief Joseph," MetalART™ bust from *The Great Chiefs* collection was awarded the 1992 *Collector Editions* "Award of Excellence."

ANTHONY SLOCOMBE

Like Roger Gibbons, Anthony Slocombe studied under Rex Billingham at Mid-Warwickshire College for Further Education. After an initial three-year stint with W.A.P. Watson (parent of The Tudor Mint), he left but returned four years later. During his time away, Anthony worked for Citadel Miniatures, sculpting fantasy figurines, which helped him when he later found himself immersed in creating *Myth and Magic*. His first model was "Le Morte D'Arthur." Anthony likes to give his pieces a hard edge, especially the dragons, and "The Dragon of Darkness" is a favorite of his. His son (age 8) has been immortalized on more than one study: his initials (JOS) can be seen on "The Well of Aspirations" and the name "Jack" appears on "The Chamber of the Skulls."

Anthony was born in Hall Green, Birmingham, in 1962 and after moving all around Britain, now finds himself back in Hall Green.

CINDY SMITH

Born and raised in Irwin, Pennsylva-nia, Cindy Smith has been designing and producing handmade, limited edition clay sculptures for nearly 12 years. Her works have been eagerly sought by collectors, some of whom have waited up to a year for a single piece.

Her choice of subject matter – traditional and whimsical Santas, woodland fairies and folk art – all come from a special place in her heart.

The faces and personalities of every figure are unique and sculpted directly from the images in Cindy's mind. She carefully researches costuming and has a gift for small details which may be overlooked by others. The color schemes for each sculpture are developed by Cindy and her palette evokes warm, down-to-earth feelings. Her *cp smithshire*™ and *Pére Nöel* collections for The Lance Corporation embody all of the varied talents of this skilled American artist.

LEO R. SMITH III

Woodcarver Leo R. Smith III believes "the artist is a reflection of the environment." His choice of inspirational atmosphere is the picturesque town of Fountain City, Wisconsin. This Mississippi River town and its surrounding woodlands are a rich source of legends and folklore captured in Leo's folk art pieces.

Largely self-taught, Leo creates his original carvings in the studio adjacent to his home. After sculpting a clay model of his design, Leo begins handcarving the wood sculpture – a process that often requires months. Leo and his wife Marilyn then develop a color scheme and bring the character to life through hand-painting.

Midwest of Cannon Falls offers an exclusive collection of resin reproductions of Smith's carvings. Richly detailed and individually numbered for authenticity, these limited edition figures and ornaments bring the legends of the Mississippi River Valley to collectors and folk art lovers alike.

IRENE SPENCER

Irene Spencer, a pillar of the collectibles world and one of America's most beloved artists, became the first female to design a limited edition plate in 1972. Today, Spencer ranks as one of the industry's most popular artists. She has received many honors, including "Litho and Plate of the Year," "Silver Chalice Award," "Artist of the Year" and the NALED "Award of Devotion."

The talented artist credits her adherence to her life's philosophy for much of her success: "My intention in creating is to express, with my best technical ability, a depth of feeling that defies verbal description." Her moving portrayals of that loving and endearing bond between mother and child attest to Spencer's superb artistry.

Powerful emotions are aroused by Spencer's many collectibles,

including plates, sculptures and ornaments based on her celebrated themes of love, as well as her penchant for cats' mischievous antics.

GABRIELE STAMEY

Born in the small Tyrolean town, Worgl, Gabriele Stamey began her professional career designing aesthetic, hand-blown stemware after studying at the Technical School of Glassmaking and Design of Kramsach/Tyrol.

In 1986, Gabriele accepted a full-time design position with Swarovski Silver Crystal. Her professional skills and lively imagination were immediately evident in her first designs comprising a whimsical "Miniature-Cockerel," a "Miniature-Hen" and three "Miniature-Chicks" in fine cut crystal.

Inspired by her two sons, she created the new theme group, "When We Were Young," which brings back childhood memories. One design in this series, "Silver Crystal Express" – a cut crystal train complete with "Locomotive," "Tender" and three "Wagons" – is dedicated to man's fascination with flight and travel. Another piece, the "Santa Maria," is the flagship which Gabriele designed especially for the "Columbus Quincentennial."

To balance her demanding job, Gabriele relaxes with her family and her hobbies, such as hiking, swimming, art and music.

MICHAEL STAMEY

Born in Munich, West Germany, in 1951, Michael Stamey now lives and works in the Austrian Tyrol, where he studied at the College of Glassmaking and Design.

In 1977, he began designing for Swarovski Silver Crystal. Among his designs are the "Rose," and most figurines in the "South Sea" theme, including "Dolphin" and "Maritime Trio." An avid snorkeler, Stamey loves to watch the light change underwater and witness the abundant sea life when vacationing on the Mediterranean.

Stamey also created the Annual Edition pieces, "Lead Me" - The Dolphins, "Save Me" - The Seals, and "Care For Me" - The Whales for the Swarovski Collectors Society series, *Mother and Child*, and the "Kudu" in the *Inspiration Africa* series.

The most important thing in his life and his artistic work is nature. "If you just look at something beautiful or complex long enough, parallels to Nature become obvious," says Stamey.

SCOTT STEARMAN

Born in 1953, Scott Stearman was raised the son of a minister and spent most of his childhood in the Midwest. Beginning to sculpt in the early 1980s, his fascination with three-dimensional art had become a full time career by 1985. He built his studio and log home in the Colorado Rockies above Colorado Springs where he lives with his wife Hermine.

Scott has accepted commissions from corporations, organizations and individuals. While many of his sculptures are in private collections, his life-size and larger works have been placed in public locations.

As a sculptor, he has pursued the classical tradition of realism. "It seems to me that the best way to communicate ideas is to use language that is understood by everyone. My desire is that when someone looks at the work I have created over my lifetime, they will see a sincere body of work that reflects the dignity of the human spirit, the glory of God in creation, and the wonder of life."

HERR CHRISTIAN & KARLA STEINBACH

Herr Christian and Karla Steinbach are the current President and Vice President of the Stein-bach Factory, the world-famous producer of nutcrackers and smoking figures in Germany. Together they oversee product development and manufacturing of limited edition collectibles for Kurt S. Adler, Inc.

Christian, especially known for his own "Old World Charm," captivates collectors with insights and lore, signs nutcrackers and smokers, and has been known to perform impromptu repair work.

Born November 1957 in the town of Schneeberg in the Erzgebirge Mountains in Germany, Karla is destined to become the sixth generation to head the company when Herr Christian retires.

Founded in 1832, the Steinbach company continues to manufacture nutcrackers, smoking figures, ornaments and music boxes in the Old World tradition. Each piece is handcrafted and hand-painted from the finest northern European wood and represents the best examples of the medieval art of wood turning.

ADI STOCKER

Born in St. Johann in Tyrol, Austria, Adi Stocker studied at the College of Glassmaking and Design. After graduating in 1977, he worked in a glass studio in New Hampshire for four years. Then he traveled around the world for a year, visiting Japan, China, Thailand, Nepal and India. Upon his return, he began working for Swarovski.

In 1992, Adi and his wife moved into their newly built home in St. Ulrich am Pillersee. From his atelier there he creates his newest figures but maintains contact with his colleagues in Wattens. Since his son's birth in 1993, he enjoys the contentment of family life.

His Swarovski Silver Crystal designs include the limited edition "Eagle" and "Polar Bear." His creation, the "Lion," rounded off the *Inspiration Africa* trilogy for the Swarvoski Collectors Society

as the 1995 Annual Edition. Designer objects such as jewelry boxes and pen holders designed for Swarovski Selection in 1992, testify to Adi's highly diversified talent. He also developed various miniatures in the *Swarovski Crystal Memories* line.

DAVID STRAVITZ

David Stravitz owns one of America's most important collections of New York architectural photographs and has donated a portion to the Library of Congress. His fascination for architecture and the design and beauty of diners of the 20's, 30's and 40's led him to create the *Roadside USA Collection* for George Z. Lefton Co. in order to preserve a piece of Americana.

As Stravitz explains, "This [project] was for the pure enjoyment of recreating some of America's best! I brought back to life the color and designs of diners often left unattended for years and in ruin...recreating each feature to perfection!" Since then, he has created five additional series as part of *Roadside USA* – *Billboards of Yesteryear*, *Firehouses*, *Cable and Trolley Cars*, *Railroad Depots*, and *Roadside Delites*.

David has been awarded over 100 patents, copyrights and trademarks. He has designed, developed and manufactured products for numerous clients including *Readers Digest*, *Business Week*, RCA, CBS, Danbury Mint, Lenox, Time-Life and others.

TOM SUZUKI

As versatile as he is talented, Tom Suzuki is the artist responsible for one of Crystal World's most popular figurines, "Curious Cat," which won an "Award of Excellence" from *Collector Editions* magazine in the year it was first produced. Other creations by Suzuki include the company's famous "Taj Mahal" and "Eiffel Tower," as well as such whimsical delights as "Peek-a-Boo Kitties," "Hush Puppy," "Mozart," "Fido" and "Wilbur the Pig."

These very special animal designs portray a unique perspective on the animal kingdom, while demonstrating the artist's adept sense of proportion and attention to the smallest detail. One of Suzuki's newer designs, the now famous "Classic Motorcycle," showcases his skill and originality in the medium of faceted, full-lead crystal.

Suzuki resides in suburban New Jersey with his wife and child.

MISTY TAGGART

Misty Taggart, mother of three and grandmother of five, began her writing career at the age of eight, writing and putting on plays for her neighborhood friends.

Over the years, Misty expanded her writing career and scripted hundreds of cartoon shows, as well as drama and comedy programs for live action television. She was a staff writer for the NBC daytime drama, "Another World," and wrote scripts for many other TV shows. For her film work, Misty has won awards from both the US Film Festival and the USA Film Festival. She has also written two stage plays, "Almost Paradise" and "The Calling," produced in 1985 and 1988 respectively.

Together with her husband, actor Joseph Taggart, Misty formed her own production company, Estee Productions, Inc. Out of this collaboration, her popular children's book series, *The Angel Academy*, was born. The books' five lead characters, who are young angels-in-training, have been recreated as cold-cast figurines, through an exclusive license with Shube's Manufacturing, Inc.

Misty and her husband reside in Phoenix, Arizona, where she continues to write children's books and develop products for other companies.

ROBERT TANENBAUM

Renowned as a gifted entertainment-theme artist, Robert Tanenbaum has been commissioned to create numerous portraits of America's most famous personalities, as well as movie posters for many top films.

Tanenbaum established himself as a superbly talented portrait artist in 1977 when his portrait of Howard Hughes for Hughes Aircraft astounded them with its realism, though only a few photographs existed of the eccentric genius at age 33. Word of the artist's remarkable abilities spread quickly, and other coveted Hollywood commissions soon followed.

Although Tanenbaum had little formal artistic training prior to college, he won the All-College Self-Portrait contest in his freshman year at Washington University in St. Louis. Since then, the artist has earned a number of honors, which include becoming one of 22 artists nationwide certified by the American Portrait Society.

Tanenbaum entered a new phase of his prolific career with his series of collector plate portraits for The Hamilton Collection, entitled *The Best of Baseball*, beginning with "The Legendary Mickey Mantle," and the new plate series, entitled the *Drivers of Victory Lane*, beginning with "Bill Elliott."

DAVID TATE

David Tate formed Lilliput Lane in 1982 with family and friends, which has become the United Kingdom's leading producer of miniature cottages. Their friendliness and open style of management has brought David and the company many accolades, such as the Queen investing David as a Member of the Order of the British Empire (M.B.E.).

David had no formal art training but has successfully painted in oils and watercolors and worked with some great sculptors. With Robert Glen, a Kenyan sculptor, he helped create the "Los Colinas

Mustangs" near Fort Worth in Dallas.

Having acquired specialist skills in the fiberglass industry, David created unique and complex models of England's architectural history. Many of Lilliput Lane's systems still in use today were his inventions. He now spends most of his time with his creative team at Penrith, England, as the technical and art director. When not in his studio, he takes photographs of original medieval cottages either as inspiration for new Lilliput models or to include in his evocative and inspiring audio-visual shows, which he presents around the world with his wife Sandra.

RANDY TATE

Inspired by the whimsy of everyday life, Randy D. Tate of Sycamore, Illinois, creates a refreshing variety of light-hearted woodcarvings.

Each with its own colorful personality, his folk art pieces vary from spirited birdhouses and lively gameboards to festive holiday ornaments. With every new design, Randy combines his precise hand-carving techniques with a witty perspective to distinguish his specialities from other folk artists.

Midwest of Cannon Falls is pleased to offer folk art enthusiasts and avid collectors exclusive reproductions of Randy Tate's imaginative carvings. This folk art will fill the home with holiday cheer and inspire the spirit of giving throughout the year.

MICHAEL J. TAYLOR

Influenced by an artistic correspondence course during his collegiate days, Gartlan USA artist Michael J. Taylor has spent more than a dozen years doing commercial and advertising illustrations.

In his spare time, Taylor created drawings and paintings for local art shows in his native state of Michigan. With a passion for sports, his moonlighting efforts featured many local heroes, and he was often asked by parents to draw a portrait of their son or daughter athlete.

In 1984, Taylor began creating original portraits of renowned athletes and worked to get those works autographed. Taylor's enthusiasm for sports and artistic talent attracted the critical eye of Gartlan USA, a leader in limited edition sports and entertainment collectibles. Subsequently, Taylor has created original art for Gartlan USA featuring Kareem Abdul-Jabar, Joe Montana, John Wooden, Yogi Berra, Whitey Ford, Kristi Yamaguchi, Sam Snead, Bob Cousy, Rod Carew, and Brett and Bobby Hull.

Recently, Taylor produced the original artwork featured on the *Leave It to Beaver* and *Ringo Starr* series of collectors' plates for Gartlan USA.

CHRISTINE THAMMAVONGSA

Born in rural Ontario, Christine Thammavongsa has always kept close to nature and simple country ways. By age 12, Christine was determined to pursue art as a career despite her teacher's advice to follow her interests in literature and natural sciences. However, Christine has combined her interests in writing and nature with her Ganz creations, most notably as author and illustrator of *More Precious Than Gold*.

As both product designer and director of Ganz Collectibles, Christine's attention to detail and creativity have put their mark on several successful lines. Howard Ganz, company President, selected her to design the *Little Cheesers®* line in mid-1991. The 1993 *Cowtown®* collection was inspired by memories of visits to her grandparents' farms. Farm experiences also influence her sketches for the *Pigsville®* collection.

For 1995, Christine created old-fashioned teddy bears who play make-believe in *Grandma's Attic™* and cherubic angels who search for a *Perfect Little Place™* on earth. *Watching Over You™*, which initially consists of three classical angels, expresses the motherly feelings Christine experienced over the birth of her daughter Tanisha in 1993.

SHELIA THOMPSON

As a young girl growing up in the South, Shelia Thompson showed an aptitude for art by removing the family portraits off the wall to study and then hone her talents. In high school, Shelia headed up numerous committees, creating posters and play backdrops.

Shelia's Collectibles was founded in 1978 when this self-taught artist discovered a creative way to increase her family's income by making wooden replicas of historic houses to sell at the Charleston City Market.

Shelia's work can be best recognized by the layered facade interpretation she gives each building, with colorful foliage and a fascinating history on the back. She is most well known for, but not limited to, her creations of Victorian-style houses.

Shelia is highly creative and imaginative, as shown by her designs, including the *Ghost House* series which glows in the dark; her first licensed series, *Gone With The Wind*; and a new category: painted metal ornaments. Shelia was the recipient of the 1995 Collectors' Jubilee award for the "Best Unlighted House."

ANNALEE THORNDIKE

Annalee Davis Thorndike was destined for doll-making fame almost in spite of herself. Coming from an artistic family, Annalee loved to watch her mother sew, and they made doll clothes together. "I never played 'house' with dolls," says Annalee, "I just made clothes."

After graduating from high school, in order to "cough up some

money to help at home," Annalee began making dolls, selling them through the League of New Hampshire Craftsmen.

In 1941, Annalee married Charles "Chip" Thorndike, son of a distinguished Boston surgeon. Chip, a free-spirited individual, preferred poultry farming. When the poultry business in New Hampshire went south, their farm became the "Factory in the Woods" for Annalee's doll hobby turned business. By the 1960s, an entire work force was involved in meeting the demand for Annalee dolls. With a work force of 400, Annalee's has become a leader in the Christmas and gift industry.

CHUCK THORNDIKE

Chuck Thorndike inherited the family's artistic talents and serves as CEO and President of Annalee Dolls.

Born March 17, 1945, Chuck attended Meredith schools, Paul Smith College, the University of New Hampshire, and is a Vietnam veteran. Chuck, also an inventor, designed and patented a device for lifting logs and stones, and has made many improvements to doll-making tools and its assembly process. His wife Karen established the Annalee Gift Shop, which opened over 20 years ago in Meredith. They have two sons and a daughter.

Chuck's hobbies have centered around seasonal sports activities found in New Hampshire's lakes and mountains, which inspire ideas for dolls.

Chuck recalls growing up in a household where, at one time, Rhode Island Red hens roamed the premises of the Thorndike poultry farm, and where Annalee Dolls covered the tables and beds, and a squadron of doll makers worked around the dining room table. "My brother and I both agree it was an enchanted childhood," he says.

ANN TIMMERMAN

When she began creating dolls as a child in Alabama, Ann Timmerman used any material available, from clay to corn husks. Now, as one of Georgetown Collection's premier doll artists, she works with the best materials available to produce the company's famous *Artist's Editions®*. Timmerman is known for her ability to portray the essence of each particular character in the face of the doll she creates.

Awards and honors are starting to pile at her feet. At the 1993 International Doll Exhibition (IDEX), "Sweet Strawberry" from the *Portraits of Perfection™* series was voted an IDEX award in the category of porcelain dolls available for under $500. In her popular *Portraits of Perfection™* series, new dolls include "Apple Dumpling" and "Blackberry Blossom." Her most recent dolls for Georgetown — "Noelle the Christmas Angel" and "Arielle the Spring Angel," from the *Little Bit of Heaven™* collection, were both honored with 1995 award nominations from *Doll Reader* magazine.

TITUS TOMESCU

A renowned artist and sculptor even before he created his first fine-porcelain doll, "Cute as a Button," Titus Tomescu is today one of the leading names in the doll collecting world. His dolls have been praised for the lifelike realism and intricate detailing that captures each doll's distinctive personality.

Among his most recent achievements are the "Babe Ruth" doll, and the "I Am the Good Shepherd" doll, an original issue in the *Messages of Hope* collection and recipient of a prestigious nomination for *Doll Reader* magazine's 1995 "Doll of the Year" award. Tomescu is the creator of the now-legendary *Snow-Babies™* dolls. The first issue, "Beneath the Mistletoe," received a prized nomination for 1995 *Dolls* magazine's "Award of Excellence." Tomescu's "Cute as a Button" doll continues to be one of the most sought-after all-porcelain dolls, receiving both 1994 "Doll Award of Excellence" and "Doll of the Year" awards.

ANGELA TRIPI

Determination and a lifelong dream have brought Italy's Angela Tripi to her current status as a world-class artist. This gifted sculptor has come far since the days she abandoned formal art study to help with family finances.

Born in 1941, Tripi showed early signs of talent — first painting; then sculpting in terra cotta. She fired her initial primitive figures in a makeshift oven. For 15 years, Tripi worked in an office by day and devoted all her spare time to shaping clay into figures reflecting the Sicilian peasants she knows so well.

Before her discovery by Roman, Inc. President Ron Jedlinski, Tripi achieved recognition with exhibitions in Italy, France and Japan. Her nativities in Palermo's Villa Niscemi and Sorrento have earned best sculpture honors.

Today, Tripi creates masterpieces in her Palermo workshop for *The Museum Collection of Angela Tripi*, a distinctive gallery of limited edition sculptures for Roman, Inc., which earned her the 1991 "Collectible of Show," sculpting category, at the Long Beach Collectible Show.

GLYNDA TURLEY

From her home in the beautiful Ozark Mountains of Arkansas, internationally acclaimed artist Glynda Turley creates exquisite oil paintings from which she derives many of her prints. Glynda's romantic, nostalgic style of painting has evolved over the years.

The self-taught artist has always loved to sketch, but did not begin to paint until the mid-1970s.

Glynda is the president and sole artist of her company, The Art of Glynda Turley. Since its beginning in 1985, Glynda's family-owned company has grown considerably each year. Glynda's limited edition prints include over 100 titles, with many selling out within months of their release. Her collectible line has expanded to include plates, eggs, ornaments and a new line of hand-painted figurines. Glynda's prints and other home accessories are now sold throughout the United States and in several foreign countries.

Glynda is continually working on new ideas and expanding *The Glynda Turley Collection* of decorative and collectible products for the home, as well as painting the pictures her collectors love so much.

VIRGINIA EHRLICH TURNER

Virginia Ehrlich Turner remembers her mother, father and other family members gently trying to dissuade her from becoming an artist when she grew up — no one believed she had enough "imagination" to accomplish this lifelong dream.

But today after much success, Virginia says that it is probably this "non-imaginative" approach to her craft that has made her little "characters" so popular with collectors. She describes her dolls as "characters" because she doesn't care for the "pretty baby-type" dolls but rather real children with real personalities. Virginia's rare ability to capture children's expressions has become the unmistakable trademark of Turner Dolls, which she began in 1982 when a retired ceramics teacher gave her his kiln. At that time, Turner Dolls was one of just three companies in the U.S. producing entirely handcrafted dolls.

In 1991, Virginia's doll "Hannah" was chosen for an "Award of Excellence" by *Dolls* magazine. And "Michelle" was the first doll she created for The Hamilton Collection.

CHRISTIAN ULBRICHT

The legend of the nutcracker lives on through the finely handcrafted and lovingly detailed works of Christian Ulbricht. His delightful nutcrackers and smoking men are the culmination of a woodcrafting tradition born deep in Germany's Erzgebirge region.

The Ulbricht family began woodcrafting in 1705. Today, the tradition continues with Christian Ulbricht's company, *Messrs. Holzhunst Christian Ulbricht*, located in the Bavarian town of Lauingen. Together with his wife Inge, daughter Ines and son

Gunther, Ulbricht has built a successful business creating original designs renowned for their attention to detail and unique sense of whimsy. The Ulbrichts pride themselves on developing only products that are made with 100% German materials and labor.

For more than 20 years, Midwest of Cannon Falls has been bringing the art of Christian Ulbricht to America. To both collectors and admirers, his works are German treasures destined to delight generations to come.

JUDI VAILLANCOURT

Judi Vaillancourt has an uncanny ability to adapt old designs and blend them into contemporary works. The creative force behind Vaillancourt Folk Art, she has been an artistic talent since her youth. Over the years, she has designed and created various pieces of colonial furniture; developed a line of antique-style clocks; painted various scenes and portraits; and designed and constructed custom fireplace mantels. Judi became interested in antiques as a teenager.

In 1984, Judi began experimenting with antique chocolate molds by filling them with chalkware, a plaster-like substance, and hand-painting each piece. By chance, she was invited to display one of her pieces at a local folk art show where she received orders for 30 more. A hobby soon became a business, and Vaillancourt Folk Art was born.

Today, Judi Vaillancourt is best known for her ability to bring an historical perspective, along with a personal warmth, to all her creations, including her Clothtique® Santas for Possible Dreams.

SVEN VESTERGAARD

Sven Vestergaard became an apprentice at the Royal Copenhagen Porcelain Manufactory at the age of 16. Four years later, he was given the highest award — the Silver Medal — and remained at the factory as an overglaze painter until 1959.

He then worked as a designer at Denmark's oldest newspaper, *Berlinske Tidenade*, as well as at various advertising agencies. In 1965, he returned to the factory as a draftsman and became the head of Royal Copenhagen's drawing office in 1976.

Vestergaard has become well known and respected throughout the world for his designs for Royal Copenhagen's *Christmas, Olympic, Hans Christian Andersen, National Parks of America* and *Mother's Day* plates and *Children's Day* series.

Vestergaard lives 30 miles south of Copenhagen on an estate originally owned by nobility, where he creates the many themes for Royal Copenhagen plates and his oil paintings of peaceful Danish landscapes, animals and nature.

JOAN BERG VICTOR

Joan Berg Victor, renowned artist, designer and author, has created *Pleasantville 1893* exclusively for Flambro Imports.

Born and raised in the Midwest, Victor earned her undergraduate degree with honors from Newcomb College, the Women's College of Tulane University, where she not only received academic honors, but was elected Miss Tulane. At Yale University, Victor was awarded a Master of Fine Arts degree with honors.

A highly regarded draftsman, her drawings and paintings can be found in private and museum collections. Her subjects have appeared in *Fortune* magazine, *The New York Times* and *The Wall Street Journal*.

Through the years, Victor has written and illustrated over two dozen books for both young children and adults. Her favorite book, of course, is *Pleasantville 1893*.

Her newest venture is a wonderful collectible Christmas village entitled *Santaville — The Christmas That Almost Never Was*. Based on an endearing poem, conceived and illustrated by Victor and written by Stanley Wiklinski, *Santaville* was created exclusively for Flambro Imports. The village invites the collector to get a first-hand peek at the working world of Santa and all his helpers.

JESSICA WATSON

Jessica Watson studied at Birmingham University and gained a first class BA degree in Fine Arts. She originally joined The Tudor Mint in 1987 and among other things, worked on designs for bookmarks and Crystalflame. During the next two years, she took time off to obtain a Post Graduate Certificate of Education.

When Jessica returned in 1990, *Myth and Magic* was already in full swing, and she recalls enjoying the challenge of working on a project requiring such a great deal of imagination. In college, she specialized in painting and drawing, and her color work can be seen in the illustrations for Allan Frost's *The Stracyl of Unity*. Among Jessica's favorite studies are "The Dark Dragon" and "The Dragon of Darkness." She also admires in particular some of Sharon Riley's larger designs, such as "The VII Seekers of Knowledge" and "The Dragon Master."

WENDT & KÜHN

More than 80 years have passed since Grete Wendt and her friend Grete Kühn first created their little hand-turned wood figurines in the German village of Grünhainichen.

Among the best-loved Wendt & Kühn figures are the delightful little angel musicians with the trademarked eleven dots on green wings — a statement of authenticity for collectors.

Uniquely-crafted Santas and charming village children add to this wonderful collection. Each piece is beautifully hand-painted and hand-finished by craftsmen who honor the design and workmanship originated by Wendt & Kühn in 1915. Today, under the leadership of Grete's nephew, Hans Wendt, the tradition of quality and craftsmanship continues in the Erzgebirge region of Germany.

In the *Wendt & Kühn Collection*, the designs available to collectors are reproductions of the originals created over 80 years ago. Midwest of Cannon Falls is proud to be the exclusive U.S. distributor of these treasured collectibles.

LYNN WEST

Lynn West's unique creations are born out of the rich and wonderful fantasy life she enjoyed as a child. When she reached adolescence, Lynn became determined not to lose the magic of her childhood Christmases and decided that her gift to the world would be to rekindle the magic of the holiday season. Through her classic heirloom creations, Lynn brings back the pleasures and warm memories of holidays past through the richly textured, deeply expressive Father Christmas designs that have made her an internationally-known collectibles artist.

For over 16 years, Lynn has been combining her talents of sculpting, painting, sewing and engineering design to bring the inhabitants from the magical realm of her imagination to life. Lynn West's designs were originally recreated by Lasting Endearments, a company dedicated to a measure of quality that is now being continued by Amaranth Productions.

Lynn West, one of America's premier Santa artists, grew up near the most magical of kingdoms, Disneyland, and currently resides in Irvine, California.

MARLENE WHITING

Marlene Whiting of Yorktown, Virginia, is well-known among collectors of miniature buildings for her ability to capture the spirit and charm that define Americana.

The founder of Brandywine Woodcrafts Inc. grew up in Pittsburgh in the late 1940s and 1950s, fascinated by the color and diversity of the small shops, businesses and homes of the city's neighborhoods. It's these memories, along with her love of architecture, literature and gardening, that she's incorporated into her nostalgic, historic and whimsical collections since Brandywine's beginning in 1981.

Though Brandywine has grown from a kitchen-table pastime to a full-fledged manufacturing operation, Marlene has insisted that the company never lose sight of its family orientation. Indeed, she still designs, sculpts and handpaints the original of every Brandywine creation. Her husband Tru serves as the company's president, while her mother, son and daughter participate in manufacturing and promotional activities.

WILLY WHITTEN

Skilled in a variety of media and techniques, Willy Whitten is a self-taught artist who is now a master craftsman. His interest in art began at a young age, but an exhibition he viewed at the Museum of Art in Los Angeles in his late twenties made him realize he wanted to sculpt for a living.

Gifted with natural talent and unique vision, Willy acquired extensive modeling and design experience in the field of cinematic special effects. In the last decade, he has been a creative artist on more than two dozen films, including *Ghostbusters* and *The Terminator*. His sets and animatronic characters can be found in theme parks such as Universal Tours and Disneyland.

Willy's greatest artistic love, and his most renowned, is sculpting miniatures. To all his work Willy brings an expressiveness and realism, demonstrating the ability to capture the sense of a person's character and inner identity. He realized his dream of seeing that work "come alive in the brilliant dimension of metal," when he began working with Legends®.

Originally from Indiana, Willy now resides in southern California with his wife Linda.

KLAUS WICKL

A native of Salzburg, Austria, sculptor-designer Klaus Wickl loves nature and rural life and says he immigrated to America in 1984 because he was attracted by "America's free pioneer spirit, its love of the land and its survival."

Fascinated by Rien Poortvliet's illustrations of Gnomes, Wickl made three-dimensional sculptures and traveled to The Netherlands to meet with the artist. After several trips for advice and approvals, Klaus Wickl Studios introduced the first Gnomes figurines in 1988.

Wickl says he designed and sculpted the Gnomes to "share the message of living in a more perfect society in harmony with both nature and each other." The sculptor sees the Gnomes as a means of stimulating environmental and ecological awareness. Wickl created a storyland where each of the Gnomes has a purpose and a place in his natural setting.

In joining with Enesco in this venture, Wickl hopes to broaden the influence of the Gnomes and to spread their message to new and appreciative audiences worldwide.

PRESTON WILLINGHAM

In the past 14 years, Preston Willingham has completed nine commissions of public sculpture on permanent display, two war memorials for public parks and 12 private commissions for offices and homes in marble, bronze, glass and aluminum. One of the public sculptures has been named a historic monument by the Governor and Cabinet of the State of Florida. Another resides in a library of a former President of the United States.

Of his pieces, nothing has been more emotionally moving than "From a Child's Heart" – the first of a new series which features porcelain figurines with *inspirational messages* from the hearts of children – since this represents the relationship and emotions Preston shares with his son Noah. These exquisite sculptures are distributed by WACO Products.

DICK WIMBERLY

One of Dick Wimberly's earliest memories includes picking up clay from the middle of a dirt road in Texas and sculpting a human head. His artistic ability was recognized because of episodes like this, and formal art training began early. His formal art education culminated in a degree in art from Eastern New Mexico University.

Shortly after graduation, Wimberly began working on sculptures in Santa Fe, New Mexico. An award-winning artist in various media, he has worked and grown with the Masterworks® line from Shube's Manufacturing, Inc.

For Masterworks, Wimberly designed and sculpted the best-selling "American Eagle," a sold-out edition, and the fantasy piece "Guardian Of The Crystal."

DAVID WINTER

Gifted British sculptor David Winter has gained worldwide acclaim for his unique miniature cottages, with their remarkable detail and whimsical touches – including the illusive Mouse. Winter tries to convey the feeling of life in the past, by recreating the buildings in which people lived and worked in days gone by.

Born in Catterick, Yorkshire, David, the son of an army colonel and famed sculptor Faith Winter, created his own clay sculptures as his mother worked. In 1979, John Hine approached Faith to work on a dimensional heraldic plaque project, and she recommended her son.

Following the failure of the plaque venture, David sculpted his first miniature cottage, "Mill House." The sculpture was taken to a local gift shop, where it sold the same afternoon. Soon, David Winter Cottages were available in several shops and soon spread worldwide. From a single painter, an entire "cottage industry" was born.

David won the coveted "Collectible of the Year Award" from NALED in 1987 and 1988 and "Artist of the Year" in 1991, among other awards over the years.

BARBARA AND PETER WISBER

Barbara and Peter Wisber have been bringing *The Family* and *Friends of Lizzie High*® as a collaborative effort and labor of love to delighted collectors since 1985.

When Barbara decided to add dolls to their already popular folk art line, she took her ideas to Peter who turned her sketch

into a doll cut out of pine and standing on two egg-shaped feet. Each doll was given an old-fashioned name borrowed from Peter's family tree and an accompanying "tale" to enhance their charm.

Married in 1971, they first lived on a large working farm and later moved to a farmhouse in Bucks County when they started a family. Happy childhood memories and the joys of raising their two children shine forth in additions to the *Lizzie High* collection. Peter's talents also extend to sculpting an array of adorable little animals added to many *Lizzie High* characters.

Barbara and Peter have parlayed the joys of their partnership into a successful line of lovingly crafted dolls that bring joy to the hearts and homes of an ever-growing number of collectors.

CHARLES WYSOCKI

Charles Wysocki, a Detroit native who now lives in Joshua Tree and Lake Arrowhead, California, is a painter who is a lot like his art. Looking into Wysocki's laughing eyes sparks the same feelings as one of his paintings – charming.

His homey, vividly-colored scenes of New England set in the 1700s and 1800s reveal intricate details and whimsical touches that provide insights into the lives of early Americans. Sold as limited edition prints through The Greenwich Workshop, Wysocki's paintings have steadily gained popularity since 1979.

Today, his limited edition prints are carried by more than 1,000 galleries, and his collector's plates have taken the market by storm. Now he brings his unique vision to the sculpture medium for the first time with the *Peppercricket Grove* cottage collection from Hawthorne Architectural Register.

MANUELLA YATES

Many children have read the wonderful tales written by Beatrix Potter and therefore have become familiar with the adventures of characters such as Jemima Puddleduck, Peter Rabbit and Tom Kitten. After 16 years Manuella Yates, a ceramic artisan at the Royal Doulton Design Studios in the United Kingdom, has mastered the expertise required in hand-painting the various subjects of Beatrix Potter, *Bunnykins* and *Brambly Hedge*.

She has worked in other areas of ceramic manufacturing for over 25 years. Among her favorite figures to paint are "Lady Mouse" and "Peter Rabbit." Some of Yates work includes "Bedtime Bunnykins," "Be Prepared," "Benjamin Bunny Wakes Up" and the ever popular "Peter Rabbit" figurines. With her considerable expertise, Yates produces intricately hand-painted pieces.

Yates enjoys talking about her work, the techniques and the folk legends surrounding the Royal Doulton family of figurines. Her knowledge of Royal Doulton products and their history fascinate many, and the signing of her name to a figurine selection is a very special and rare opportunity for long-time collectors and first-time purchasers alike.

BILL YOUNGER

If Bill Younger could have his way, all lighthouses would be open to the public. As a child, he would often observe lighthouses during fishing expeditions on the Chesapeake Bay. Those memories and his love for history, old buildings and architecture, provided fertile ground for the dream that has become Harbour Lights.

As founder and conceptual artist, Bill feels that Harbour Lights' purpose is to promote history and maritime tradition. In each lighthouse miniature, he hopes to achieve a rendering that is not only aesthetically pleasing, but also as accurate as the real thing.

To research new lighthouse editions, Bill often travels to deserted locations far off the beaten path. On some of these trips, he has had to walk for several hours, sometimes through water. "When I finally arrive at the lighthouse, I forget all of the difficulties. I'm immediately taken into the past and reminded of the families that worked and played there."

MARTIN ZENDRON

Born in the medieval town of Hall in Tyrol, Austria, Martin Zendron now lives and works only a few miles away in Wattens, the home of Swarovski.

In his late teens, Martin attended the College of Glassmaking and Design of Kramsach/Tyrol, where he studied glass design with a special course in cutting and engraving. After graduation, he worked for a well-known Tyrolean retailer specializing in glass objects. There his work came to Swarovski's attention, where he became a designer in 1988.

His first creations for Swarovski were the "Harp" and the "Lute," followed by the "Grand Piano," which all reveal a rare artistic talent and craftsmanship. He also created the first piece in the *Inspiration Africa* series, the "Elephant," for the Swarovski Collectors Society.

Although Martin spends much of his spare time in the mountains, his real passion is deep-sea diving. For him, it is a wonderful way of relaxing from the precision and concentration required for his work with Swarovski.

BOOKS, MAGAZINES AND NEWSLETTERS

The following publications are designed to keep you current on the latest news about limited edition collectibles. In addition, many manufacturers and collector clubs publish newsletters that will help you enjoy your hobby to the fullest. See the club listing on page 336 for information about club publications.

— BOOKS —

A COLLECTORS GUIDE TO
MYTH AND MAGIC
by John Hughes and Chris
Wotton. Collectables
Publishing Limited.

AMERICAN TEDDY BEAR
ENCYCLOPEDIA
by Linda Mullins.
Hobby House Press.

THE CHILMARK COLLECTION
by Glenn S. Johnson and
James E. Secky.
Commonwealth Press,
Worcester, Massachusetts.

CHRISTMAS THROUGH
THE DECADES
by Robert Brenner.
Schiffer Publishing.

DECK THE HALLS
by Robert Merck.
Abbeville Press.

DIRECTORY TO LIMITED
EDITION COLLECTIBLE
STORES
by Diane Carnevale Jones.
Collectors' Information
Bureau, Barrington, Illinois.

DIRECTORY TO SECONDARY
MARKET RETAILERS
by Collectors' Information
Bureau.

FENTON GLASS, THE FIRST
TWENTY-FIVE YEARS
(1905-1930)
by William Heacock.
Richardson Printing.

FENTON GLASS, THE
SECOND TWENTY-FIVE
YEARS (1931-1955)
by William Heacock.
Richardson Printing.

FENTON GLASS, THE THIRD
TWENTY-FIVE YEARS
(1956-1980)
by William Heacock.
Richardson Printing.

LLADRÓ – THE MAGIC
WORLD OF PORCELAIN
by Several. Salvat.

MORE PRECIOUS THAN GOLD
(A CHEESERVILLE TALE)
by Christine Thammavongsa.
GANZ.

NUMBER ONE PRICE GUIDE
TO M.I. HUMMEL FIGURINES,
PLATES, MINIATURES
AND MORE
by Robert Miller.
Portfolio Press.

THE OFFICIAL LLADRÓ
COLLECTION
IDENTIFICATION CATALOG
AND PRICE GUIDE
by Glenn S. Johnson.
Lladró Collectors Society.

THE OFFICIAL MSA IDENTIFI-
CATION AND PRICE GUIDE
TO THE CHILMARK
COLLECTION
by Glenn S. Johnson and
Ann Hagenstein. Grafacon,
Hudson, Massachusetts.

THE SEBASTIAN MINIATURE
COLLECTION
by Glenn S. Johnson.
Commonwealth Press,
Worcester, Massachusetts.

THE STRACYL OF UNITY
by Allan Frost.
AJF Desk Top Publishing.

SWAROVSKI: THE MAGIC
OF CRYSTAL
by Vivienne Becker.
Abrams, New York.

VALUE REGISTER
HANDBOOK FOR SEBASTIAN
MINIATURES
by Paul J. Sebastian.
The Sebastian Exchange,
Lancaster, Pennsylvania.

— MAGAZINES/NEWSLETTERS —

AMERICAN ARTIST
1515 Broadway
New York, NY 10036
(212)536-5178

ANTIQUES & COLLECTING
1006 S. Michigan Avenue
Chicago, IL 60605
(312)939-4767

THE ANTIQUE TRADER
P.O. Box 1050
Dubuque, IA 52004
(800)334-7165

CIB REPORT & SHOWCASE
5065 Shoreline Road,
Suite 200
Barrington, IL 60010
(708)842-2200

COLLECTOR EDITIONS
170 Fifth Avenue
New York, NY 10010
(800)347-6969

COLLECTOR'S MART
700 E. State Street
Iola, WI 54990
(715)445-2214

COLLECTORS NEWS
P.O. Box 156
Grundy City, IA 50638
(319)824-6981

CONTEMPORARY DOLL
COLLECTOR
30595 8 Mile
Livonia, MI 48152-1798
(810)477-6650

DOLLS MAGAZINE
170 Fifth Avenue, 12th Floor
New York, NY 10010
(800)347-6969

THE DOLL READER
6405 Flank Drive
Harrisburg, PA 17112
(717)657-9555

DOLL WORLD
P.O. Box 420077
Palm Coast, FL 32142-9895

FIGURINES & COLLECTIBLES
6405 Flank Drive
Harrisburg, PA 17112
(717)657-9555

KOVELS ON ANTIQUES &
COLLECTIBLES
P.O. Box 420347
Palm Coast, FL 32142-0347
(800)829-9158

KOVELS SPORTS
COLLECTIBLES
P.O. Box 420026
Palm Coast, FL 32142-0026
(800)829-9158

MINIATURE COLLECTOR
30595 8 Mile
Livonia, MI 48152-1798
(810) 477-6650

SOUTHWEST ART
P.O. Box 460535
Houston, TX 77056
(713)850-0990

TEDDY BEAR AND FRIENDS
6405 Flank Drive
Harrisburg, PA 17112
(717)657-9555

TEDDY BEAR REVIEW
170 Fifth Avenue, 12th Floor
New York, NY 10010
(800)347-6969

U.S. ART COLLECTIBLES
220 S. 6th Street, Suite 500
Minneapolis, MN 55402
(612)339-7571

WILDLIFE ART NEWS
4725 Highway 7
St. Louis Park, MN 55416
(612)927-9056

NATIONAL COLLECTORS' CLUBS

Club	Annual Dues/Renewals	Club Year	Membership Gift	Members-Only Piece	Club Publication	Binder	Membership Card	Buy-Sell Matching Service	Local Chapters	Tours/Special Events	Other Benefits
All God's Children Collector's Club* / Miss Martha Originals, P.O. Box 5038, Glencoe, AL 35905, (205) 492-0221	$20.	June 1-May 31	●	●	4/yr.	●			●	●	Personal Checklist
The Angel Academy Alumni Society* / Shube's Manufacturing, P.O. Box 39480, Phoenix, AZ 85069-9480, (602) 906-0328	25.-1 yr. / 45.-2 yrs.	Jan.-Dec.	●		4/yr.	●	●			●	Membership Certificate; Special Mailings
The Anheuser-Busch Collectors Club*, 2700 South Broadway, St. Louis, MO 63118, (800) 305-2582	35.	Anniv. of Sign-Up Date	●	●	4/yr.	●					
Annalee Doll Society*, P.O. Box 1137, Meredith, NH 03253-1137, (800) 43-DOLLS	29.95	Anniv. of Sign-Up Date	●	●	4/yr.	●	●			●	Membership Pin; Members-Only Event Pieces
ANRI Collector's Society*, P.O. Box 2087, Quincy, MA 02269-2087, (800) 763-ANRI (2674)	40.	Jan.-Dec.	●	●	3/yr.	●				●	ANRI Catalog; Research Dept.; Authorized Retailer Listing
G. Armani Society*, 300 Mac Lane, Keasbey, NJ 08832, (800) 3-ARMANI	40./27.50	Jan.-Dec.	●	●	4/yr.	●				●	
Attic Babies Collectors' Club*, P.O. Box 912, Drumright, OK 74030, (918) 352-4414	30./20.	Anniv. of Sign-Up Date	●	●	4/yr.	●	●			●	
Brian Baker's Déjà Vu Collectors' Club* / Michael's Ltd., PRDV, P.O. Box 217, Redmond, WA 98052-0217, (800) 835-0181	35.	Mar. 1-Mar. 1	●	●	2/yr.	●				●	
The Belleek Collectors International Society, 9893 Georgetown Pike, Suite 525, Great Falls, VA 22066, (800)-BELLEEK	35.	Anniv. of Sign-Up Date	●	●	3/yr.	●			●	●	Membership Certificate
Boehm Porcelain Society, 25 Fairfacts Street, Trenton, NJ 08638, (800) 257-9410	15.	Jan.-Dec.		●	1/yr.		●			●	Catalogs
Caithness Collectors' Club - Caithness Glass Inc., 141 Lanza Ave., Bldg. 12, Garfield, NJ 07026, (201) 340-3330	35.	Anniv. of Sign-Up Date	●	●	●	●				●	
The Cardew Collectors' Club* / Cardew Design, Woodmanton Farm, Woodbury NR. Exeter, Devon EX5 1HQ England, 01144 1395 233633	30.	Anniv. of Sign-Up Date	●	●	4/yr.	●				●	Cardew Teapot Collection Catalog
Cat's Meow Collectors Club*, Box 635, Wooster, OH 44691-0635, (330) 264-1377 Ext. 225	25./22.	Anniv. of Sign-Up Date	●	●	4/yr.	●					Club Notebook; Custom Search Program
Cavanagh's Coca-Cola Christmas Collectors Society*, P.O. Box 420157, Atlanta, GA 30342, (800) 653-1221	25.	Jan.-Dec.	●	●	4/yr.	●					Membership Certificate; Special Items Offer
The Chilmark Polland Collectors Society* / The Lance Corporation, 321 Central Street, Hudson, MA 01749, (508) 568-1401	45.	Anniv. of Sign-Up Date	●	●	2/yr.	●				●	
The Chilmark Registry* - The Lance Corporation, 321 Central Street, Hudson, MA 01749, (508) 568-1401	None	Up to 5 yrs. Free		●	4/yr.		●			●	Free Upon Registration of Chilmark Sculpture. Price Guide Updates
Lowell Davis Farm Club, P.O. Box 636, Carthage, MO 64836, (800) 989-0103	25./20.	Anniv. of Sign-Up Date	●	●	4/yr.	●		●	●	●	Collector's Guide, Cap, Coloring Book
Walt Disney Collectors Society*, P.O. Box 11090, Des Moines, IA 50336-1090, (800) 678-6528	55.-1yr. / 99.-2 yrs.	Jan.-Dec.	●	●	4/yr.	●				●	Cloisonné Pin, "Newsflashes"

* For more information, see company feature articles (pp. 53 - 298).

NATIONAL COLLECTORS' CLUBS

	Annual Dues/Renewals	Club Year	Membership Gift	Members-Only Piece	Club Publication	Binder	Membership Card	Buy-Sell Matching Service	Local Chapters	Tours/Special Events	Other Benefits
Dreamsicles Collectors' Club* - Cast Art 1120 California Avenue, Corona, CA 91719 (800) 437-5818	27.50/ 23.50	Anniv. of Sign-Up Date	●	●	4/yr.	●	●	●			Photo Book
Duncan Royale Collectors Club* 1141 S. Acacia Ave., Fullerton, CA 92631 (714) 879-1360	$ 30.	Anniv. of Sign-Up Date	●	●	4/yr.	●	●			●	Certificate, Catalog, Free Figurine Registration
EKJ Collectors' Society* - Flambro Imports P.O. Box 93507, Atlanta, GA 30377-0507 (800) EKJ-CLUB	30./15.	Jan.-Dec.	●	●	4/yr.	●	●			●	EKJ Pin and Catalog Free Figurine Registration Collector Registry Listing
Enchantica Collectors Club P.O. Box 200, Waterville, OH 43566 (419) 878-0034	27.50	Jan.-Dec.	●	●	2/yr.		●			●	
Enesco Cherished Teddies Club* P.O. Box 91796, Elk Grove Village, IL 60009-9179 (630) 875-5422	17.50	Jan. 1-Dec. 31	●	●	●						Lapel Pin, Easel, Certificate
Enesco Precious Moments Birthday Club* P.O. Box 689, Itasca, IL 60143-0689 (630) 875-5411	20.-1yr. 38.-2yrs.	July 1-June 30	●	●	●						Certificate, Happy Birthday Card
Enesco Precious Moments Collectors' Club* P.O. Box 1466, Elk Grove Village, IL 60009-1466 (630) 875-5411	27.	Jan. 1-Dec. 31	●	●	●	●	●			●	Gift Registry, Pocket Guide, Cookie Cutter Special Mailings
Enesco Treasury of Christmas Ornaments Collectors' Club* P.O. Box 773, Elk Grove Village, IL 60009-0773 (630) 875-5404	20.	Jan. 1-Dec. 31	●	●	●		●				Lapel Pin, Collectors' Guide
Fenton Art Glass Collectors of America (FAGCA)* P.O. Box 384, Williamstown, WV 26187 (304) 375-6196	15.	Anniv. of Sign-Up Date		●	6/yr.			●	●	●	
National Fenton Glass Society (NFGS)* P.O. Box 4008, Marietta, OH 45750	15.	Anniv. of Sign-Up		●	6/yr.			●	●	●	
Fontanini Collectors' Club* - Roman, Inc. 555 Lawrence Avenue, Roselle, IL 60172 (800) 729-7662	19.50/ 17.50	Anniv. of Sign-Up Date	●	●	4/yr.	●	●			●	Registry Guide, Pin, Research Service, Contests
Gartlan USA's "New" Collectors' League* 575 Rt. 73 N., Ste. A-6, West Berlin, NJ 08091 (609) 753-9229	30./20.	Anniv. of Sign-Up Date	●	●	4/yr.		●	●		●	Advance Notification of New Issues
The Great American Collectors' Club* P.O. Box 428, Aberdeen, NC 28315 (910) 944-7447	None	Jan.-Dec.		●	3/yr.		●			●	Membership Free with Purchase of Club Piece
Jan Hagara Collectors' Club 40114 Industrial Park, Georgetown, TX 78626 (512) 863-9499	44./39.	July 1-June 30	●	●	4/yr.	●	●	●	●	●	Cloisonne Pin, Contest, Drawings, Savings on Products
Hallmark Keepsake Ornament Collector's Club P.O. Box 419034, Kansas City, MO 64141-6034	20.	Jan.-Dec.	●	●	4/yr.		●	●	●	●	Early Mailing of *Dreambook*
Hand & Hammer Collectors' Club* 2610 Morse Lane, Woodbridge, VA 22192 (800) SILVERY	None	Jan. 1-Dec. 31			●					●	Updated List of Ornaments
Harbour Lights Collectors Society* 1000 N. Johnson Ave., El Cajun, CA 92020 (800) 365-1219	30.	Anniv. of Sign-Up Date	●	●	4/yr.	●	●				Cloissone Pin Membership Certificate
Edna Hibel Society P.O. Box 9721, Coral Springs, FL 33075 (407) 848-9663	20.-1yr. 35.-2yrs.	Anniv. of Sign-Up Date	●	●	4/yr.		●		●	●	Previews of Hibel Artworks
Mark Hopkins Bronze Guild 21 Shorter Industrial Blvd., Rome, GA 30165-1838 (800) 678-6564	None				2/yr.			●			
M.I. Hummel Club* Goebel Plaza, P.O. Box 11 Pennington, NJ 08534-0011 (800) 666-CLUB	45./35.	June 1-May 31	●	●	4/yr.	●	●	●	●	●	Research Service Essay Contests

* For more information, see company feature articles (pp. 53 - 298).

343

	Annual Dues/Renewals	Club Year	Membership Gift	Members-Only Piece	Club Publication	Binder	Membership Card	Buy-Sell Matching Service	Local Chapters	Tours/Special Events	Other Benefits
Thomas Kinkade Collectors' Society* Media Arts Group Inc. P.O. Box 90267, San Jose, CA 95109 (800) 366-3733	$45.-1yr. 75.-2yrs.	Jan.-Dec.	●	●	4/yr.		●			●	Free Frame with Purchase of Members-Only Canvas Lithograph
Krystonia Collectors Club* Precious Art 738 Airport Blvd., Suite 5, Ann Arbor, MI 48108 (313) 663-1885	25.	Feb. 1-Jan. 31	●	●	4/yr.		●			●	
Lilliput Lane Collectors' Club* 225 Windsor Dr., Itasca, IL 60143 (800)-LILLIPUT	40.-1yr. 65.-2yrs.	May 1-Apr. 30	●	●	4/yr.	●	●	●		●	Catalog
Little Cheesers Collectors' Club* - GANZ 908 Niagara Falls Blvd., North Tonawanda, NY 141201-2060 (800) 724-5902	27./24.	Anniv. of Sign-Up Date	●	●	2/yr.	●	●	●			Item Checklist, Contests, Birthday Cards, Special Mailings
Little Emmett Collectors' Society* Flambro Imports P.O. Box 93507, Atlanta, GA 30377-0507 (800) EKJ-CLUB	10.	Anniv. of Sign-Up Date			4/yr.		●				Bookmark, Mask, Activity Book, Puzzle, Catalog
The Lizzie High Society* - Ladie and Friends 220 North Main Street, Sellersville, PA 18960 (800) 76-DOLLS	25./15.	Jan.-Dec.	●	●	2/yr.	●	●			●	Pewter Ornament
Lladró Society* 1 Lladró Drive, Moonachie, NJ 07074 (800) 634-9088	40./27.50	Anniv. of Sign-Up Date	●	●	4/yr.	●	●			●	Video, Research Service Assoc. Membership to Lladró Museum
Seymour Mann, Inc. Doll Club* 230 Fifth Avenue, Suite 1500, New York, NY 10001 (212) 683-7262	17.50	Anniv. of Sign-Up Date	●	●	●		●	●			
Masterworks Collectors Club* Shube's Manufacturing 600 Moon St. S.E., Albuquerque, NM 87123 (800) 867-9173	49.95	Anniv. of Sign-Up Date	●		2/yr.		●				
Melody In Motion Collectors Club* WACO Products Corporation I-80 & New Maple Avenue, P.O. Box 898 Pine Brook, NJ 07058-0898 (201) 882-1820	27.50	Anniv. of Sign-Up Date	●	●	2/yr.		●				Catalog, "Savings" Coupons, Personal Purchasing Record, Retired Edition Summary List of Collectors' Centers
Memories of Yesterday Collectors' Society* Enesco Corporation P.O. Box 245, Elk Grove Village, IL 60009-0245 (630) 875-5799	22.50	Jan. 1-Dec. 31	●	●	4/yr.		●				Gift Registry, Brooch, Stationery
Myth and Magic Collectors' Club* - The Tudor Mint P.O. Box 431729, Houston, TX 77243-1729 (713) 462-0076	37.50	July 1-June 30	●	●	2/yr.		●		●		Catalog and Updates
Old World Christmas Collectors' Club* P.O. Box 8000 — Department C, Spokane, WA 99203 (800) 962-7669	30.	Anniv. of Sign-Up Date	●	●	4/yr.			●			Collectors' Guide Local Retailer Listings
Open Window ClubHouse Collectors Club* R.R. Creations P.O. Box 8707, Dept. Club, Pratt, KS 67124 (800) 779-3610	22.50/19.50	Anniv. of Sign-Up Date	●	●	2/yr.	●	●		●		
The Pangaean Society* Official Collectors Club of cp smithshire The Lance Corporation 321 Central Street, Hudson, MA 01749 (508) 568-1401	25.	Anniv. of Sign-Up Date	●	●	2/yr.		●	●		●	Pin
PenDelfin Family Circle - Miller Import Corp. 230 Spring Street N.W., Atlanta Gift Mart, Suite 1238 Atlanta, GA 30303 (404) 523-3380 or (800) 872-4876	30.	Jan.-Dec.	●	●	4/yr.		●	●	●	●	Membership Certificate
Pennibears Collectors Club 1413 N.E. Lincoln Avenue, Moore, OK 73160 (405) 799-0006	5.	Anniv. of Sign-Up Date		●	4/yr.		●				

* For more information, see company feature articles (pp. 53 - 298).

NATIONAL COLLECTORS' CLUBS

	Annual Dues/Renewals	Club Year	Membership Gift	Members-Only Piece	Club Publication	Binder	Membership Card	Buy-Sell Matching Service	Local Chapters	Tours/Special Events	Other Benefits
PFC Collectors Club* **Pulaski Furniture Corporation** P.O. Box 1371, Pulaski, VA 24301 (540) 980-7330	29.95/ 24.95	Anniv. of Sign-Up Date	●		4/yr.		●				Sneak Previews Member Incentives for Purchase of Pulaski Furniture
Pleasantville 1893 Historical Preservation Society* **Flambro Imports** P.O. Box 93507, Atlanta, GA 30377-0507 (800) 355-CLUB	30./15.	Jan.-Dec.	●		4/yr.		●				Pin, Catalog, Christmas Ornament
Pocket Dragons and Friends Collectors Club* **Flambro Imports** P.O. Box 93507, Atlanta, GA 30377-0507 (800) 355-CLUB	29.50- 1yr. 54.-2yrs.	June 1- May 30	●	●	4/yr.		●			●	Pin, Catalog
Red Mill Collectors Society One Hunters Ridge, Summersville, WV 26651 (304) 872-5237	15.	Mar. 31 and Sept. 30			4/yr.		●	●			
Royal Doulton International Collectors Club* 701 Cottontail Lane, Somerset, NJ 08873 (800) 582-2102	25.	Anniv. of Sign-Up Date		●	4/yr.					●	Historical Enquiry Services Advance Mailings
The Royal Watch™ Society* **Harmony Kingdom** 232 Neilston St., Columbus, OH 43215 (800) 783-5683	35.	Anniv. of Sign-Up Date	●	●	4/yr.						Contests Referral Service
Sandicast Collectors Guild P.O. Box 910079, San Diego, CA 92191 (800) 722-3316	25.	Anniv. of Sign-Up Date	●		2/yr.		●			●	
Sarah's Attic Forever Friends Collector's Club* P.O. Box 448, Chesaning, MI 48616 (800) 4-FRIEND	32.50	June 1- May 31	●	●	●	●			●		Catalogs, Special Mailings
Santa Claus Network* **Possible Dreams** 6 Perry Drive, Foxboro, MA 02035 (508) 543-6667	25.	Anniv. of Sign-Up Date	●	●	4/yr.		●	●			Collectors Guide Book
Sebastian Miniatures Collectors Society* **The Lance Corporation** 321 Central Street, Hudson, MA 01749 (508) 568-1401	29.50	Anniv. of Sign-Up Date	●	●	●		●	●		●	Annual Value Register and Updates
Shelia's Collectors Society* 1856 Belgrade Avenue, Bldg. C Charleston, SC 29407 (803) 766-0485 or (800) 227-6564	25./20.	Anniv. of Sign-Up Date	●	●	4/yr.	●	●			●	
Starlight Family of Collectors* **Christopher Radko** P.O. Box 238, Dobbs Ferry, NY 10522 (800) 71-RADKO	50./45.	Jan.-Dec.	●	●	4/yr.	●	●				Button, Pin, Catalog
Starlite Collector's Society* **Legends** 2665-D Park Center Drive, Simi Valley, CA 93065 (800) 726-9660	None				4/yr.						Record-Keeping Services Appraisal Service, Advance Notice of New Sculptures
The Steinbach Collectors Club* **Kurt S. Adler, Inc.** 1107 Broadway, New York, NY 10010 (800) 243-9627	40.		●	●	●		●				Portfolio, Pin, Brochures
Swarovski Collectors Society* 2 Slater Road, Cranston, RI 02920 (800) 426-3088	35./25.	Anniv. of Sign-Up Date	●	●	2/yr.					●	
VickiLane Collectors' Club 3233 NE Cadet Avenue, Portand, OR 97220 (800) 456-4259	28.	Anniv. of Sign-Up Date	●		3/yr.		●				Club Button
David Winter Cottages Collectors' Guild* **Media Arts Group, Inc.** P.O. Box 90038, San Jose, CA 95109-3038 (800) 366-3733	40.-1yr. 75.-2yrs.	Anniv. of Sign-Up Date	●	●	4/yr.		●			●	Advance Mailings Membership Certificate

* For more information, see company feature articles (pp. 53 - 298).

DIRECTORY OF COLLECTIBLES MANUFACTURERS
"Who's Who" in Limited Edition Collectibles

This directory provides information about many companies actively involved in the field of limited edition collectibles. Collectors will find this listing helpful when inquiring about a firm's products and services.

Ace Product Management Group
9053 N. Deerbrook Trail
Brown Deer, WI 53223
(414) 365-5400
Fax: (414) 365-5410
Specialty: See article on page 53

Kurt S. Adler, Inc.
1107 Broadway
New York, NY 10010
(212) 924-0900
Fax: (212) 807-0575
Specialty: See article on page 56

Amaranth Productions
P.O. Box 3505
Huntington Beach, CA
92605-3505
(714) 841-9972
Fax: (714) 847-1090
Specialty: See article on page 59

Amazze
1030 Sunnyside Road
Vermilion, OH 44089
(800) 543-6759
Fax: (216) 967-5199
Specialty: See article on page 62

American Artists
66 Poppasquash Road
Bristol, RI 02809
(401) 254-1191
Fax: (401) 254-8881
Specialty: Lithos and plates

American Artist Portfolio, Inc.
9625 Tetley Drive
Somerset, VA 22972
(703) 672-0400
Fax: (703) 672-0286
Specialty: Graphics

Anheuser Busch, Inc.
2700 South Broadway
St. Louis, MO 63118
(800) 325-1154
Fax: (314) 577-9656
Specialty: See article on page 65

Anna-Perenna Inc.
35 River Street
New Rochelle, NY 10801
(914) 633-3777
Fax: (914) 633-8727
Specialty: Figurines,
ornaments and plates

Annalee Mobilitee Dolls, Inc.
P.O. Box 1137
Meredith, NH 03253-1137
(800) 433-6557
Fax: (603) 279-6659
Specialty: See article on page 68

ANRI U.S.
P.O. Box 380760
1126 So. Cedar Ridge, Ste. 111
Duncanville, TX 75138
(800) 730-ANRI
Fax: (214) 283-3522
Specialty: See article on page 71

Arcadian Pewter
1802 Broadway, Suite 200
Rockford, IL 61104
(815) 395-8670
Fax: (815) 395-9523
Specialty: See article on page 74

**G. Armani Society/
Miller Import Corp.**
300 Mac Lane
Keasbey, NJ 08832
(800) 3-ARMANI
Fax: (908) 417-0031
Specialty: See article on page 77

The Art of Glynda Turley
P.O. Box 112
Heber Springs, AR 72543
(800) 633-7931
Fax: (501) 362-5020
Specialty: See article on page 80

Artists of the World
2915 N. 67th Place
Scottsdale, AZ 85251
(602) 946-6361
Fax (602) 941-8918
Specialty: DeGrazia plates and
figurines

The Ashton-Drake Galleries
9200 N. Maryland Avenue
Niles, IL 60714
(800) 634-5164
Fax: (847) 966-3026
Specialty: See article on page 83

Attic Babies
P.O. Box 912
Drumright, OK 74030
(918) 352-4414
Fax: (918) 352-4767
Specialty: See article on page 86

Autom
5226 S. 31st Place
Phoenix, AZ 85040
(800) 572-1172
Fax: (800) 582-1166
Specialty: See article on page 89

The B & J Company
P.O. Box 67
Georgetown, TX 78626
(512) 863-8318
Fax: (512) 863-0833
Specialty: Dolls, figurines,
miniatures and plates

BAND Creations
24801 N. Ballard
Lake Forest, IL 60045
(800) 535-3242
Fax: (847) 816-3695
Specialty: See article on page 90

Marty Bell Fine Art
9550 Owens Mouth Ave.
Chatsworth, CA 91311
(800) 637-4537
Fax: (818) 709-7668
Specialty: Graphics

Belleek Collector International
Society
9893 Georgetown Pike
Great Falls, VA 22066
(800) - BELLEEK
Fax: (703) 847-6201
Specialty: Belleek china
and plates

Jody Bergsma Galleries
1344 King Street
Bellingham, WA 98226
(800) BERGSMA
Fax: (206) 647-2758
Specialty: Graphics and plates

Boehm Porcelain Studio
25 Fairfacts Street
Trenton, NJ 08638
(800) 257-9410
Fax: (609) 392-1437
Specialty: Dolls, figurines and
plates

The Boyds Collection Ltd.
Somethin' Ta Say Dept.
Gettysburg, PA 17325-4385
Specialty: See article on page 96

Michael Boyett Studio
P.O. Box 632012
Nacogdoches, TX 75963
(409) 560-4477
Specialty: Figurines and graphics

The Bradford Exchange
9333 Milwaukee Avenue
Niles, IL 60714
(800) 323-5577
Specialty: See article on page 99

Bradley Doll
1400 N. Spring Street
Los Angeles, CA 90012
(213) 221-4162
Fax: (213) 221-8272
Specialty: Dolls

Brandywine Collectibles
104 Greene Dr.
Yorktown, VA 23692
(804) 898-5031
Fax: (804) 898-6895
Specialty: See article on page 102

Briant & Sons
5250 SW Tomahawk
Redmond, OR 97756
(503) 923-1473
Fax: (503) 923-7403
Specialty: Plate hangers and
accessories

Buccellati Silver Ltd.
P.O. Box 360
East Longmeadow, MA 01028
(413) 525-4800
Fax: (413) 525-8877
Specialty: Ornaments

Byers' Choice Ltd.
P.O. Box 158
Chalfont, PA 18914
(215) 822-6700
Fax: (215) 822-3847
Specialty: See article on page 105

Rick Cain Studios
619 S. Main Street
Gainesville, FL 32601
(800) 535-3949
Fax: (904) 377-7038
Specialty: Wildlife sculptures

Cairn Studio
P.O. Box 489
Davidson, NC 28036
(704) 892-3581
Specialty: Figurines

Caithness Glass Inc.
141 Lanza Avenue, Bldg. 12
Garfield, NJ 07026
(201) 340-3330
Fax: (201) 340-9415
Specialty: Glass paperweights

Cameo Guild Studios
5217 Verdugo Way, Suite D
Camarillo, CA 93012
(805) 388-1223
Specialty: California missions,
miniatures and plates

L.M. Cape Craftsmen, Inc.
415 Peanut Road
Elizabethtown, NC 28337
(800) 262-5447
Fax: (949) 862-4611
Specialty: Figurines

Cardew Design
c/o S.P. Skinner Co.
91 Great Hill Road
P.O. Box 5
Naugatuck, CT 06770
(203) 723-1471
Specialty: See article on page 111

Carlton Cards... A Division of
American Greetings Corp.
One American Road
Cleveland, OH 44144
(216) 252-7300
Fax: (216) 252-6751
Specialty: See article on page 114

Cast Art Industries, Inc.
1120 California Avenue
Corona, CA 91719
(800) 932-3020
Fax: (909) 270-2852
Specialty: See article on page 117

Cavanagh Group International
1000 Holcomb Woods Pkwy.
#440-B
Roswell, GA 30078
(800) 895-8100
Fax: (404) 643-1172
Specialty: See article on page 120

Cazenovia Abroad
67 Albany Street
Cazenovia, NY 13035
(315) 655-3433
Fax: (315) 655-4249
Specialty: Sterling silver
figurines and ornaments

**Character Collectibles/
Calabar Creations**
10861 Business Drive
Fontana, CA 92337
(909) 822-9999
Fax: (909) 823-6666
Specialty: See article on page 108

Chimera Studios
3708 E. Hubbard
Mineral Wells, TX 76067
(800) 843-4647
Specialty: Figurines

Christopher Radko
P.O. Box 238
Dobbs Ferry, NY 10522
(800) 71-RADKO
Fax: (914) 693-3770
Specialty: See article on page 123

Classic Collectables by
Uniquely Yours
P.O. Box 16861
Philadelphia, PA 19142
(610) 586-6266
Fax: (610) 522-2259
Specialty: Figurines

346

Clay Art
239 Utah Avenue
So. San Francisco, CA 94080
(415) 244-4970
Fax: (415) 244-4979
Specialty: Masks

Sandy Clough Studio
25 Trail Road
Marietta, GA 30064-1535
(404) 428-9406
Specialty: Limited edition prints

The Constance Collection
Rt.1, Box 538
Midland, VA 22728
(703) 788-4500
Fax: (703) 788-4100
Specialty: Figurines

M. Cornell Importers, Inc.
1462-18th St. N.W.
St. Paul, MN 55112
(612) 633-8690
Fax: (612) 636-3568
Specialty: Steins and teapots

Country Artists USA
9515 Gerwig Lane, Ste. 112
Columbia, MD 21046
(410) 290-8990
Fax: (410) 290-5480
Specialty: Figurines

Creart
209 E. Ben White, Suite 103
Austin, TX 78704
(800) 343-1505
Fax: (512) 707-9918
Specialty: Wildlife sculptures

Cross Gallery, Inc.
180 N. Center
(Mail: P.O. Box 4181)
Jackson Hole, WY 83001
(307) 733-2200
Fax: (307) 733-1414
Specialty: Graphics,
ornaments and plates

Crystal World
3 Borinski Road, Suite B
Lincoln Park, NJ 07035
(201) 633-0707
Fax: (201) 633-0102
Specialty: See article on page 126

Cybis
65 Norman Avenue
Trenton, NJ 08618
(609) 392-6074
Specialty: Figurines and
ornaments

Daddy's Long Legs
c/o KVK INC.
300 Bank Street
Southlake, TX 76092
(817) 488-4644
Specialty: Dolls

Andrew D. Darvas Inc.
2165 Dwight Way
Berkeley, CA 94704
(510) 843-7838
Fax: (510) 843-1815
Specialty: Bossoms
characters and wall masks

Dear Artistic Sculpture
P.O. Box 860
Oaks, PA 19456-0860
(610) 666-1650
Fax: (610) 666-1379
Specialty: See article on page 129

Department 56, Inc.
P.O. Box 44456
Eden Prairie, MN 55344-1456
(800) 548-8696
Specialty: See article on page 132

The Walt Disney Company
500 South Buena Vista Street
Burbank, CA 91521-6876
(800) WD-CLSIX
Specialty: See article on page 135

Donjo Studios Inc.
31149 Via Colinas Suite 609
Westlake Village, CA 91362
(818) 865-2390
Fax: (818) 865-0996
Specialty: Crystal figurines and
miniatures

Dram Tree/C.U.I.
1502 N. 23rd Street
Wilmington, NC 28405
(910) 251-1110
Specialty: Steins

Duncan Royale
1141 S. Acacia Avenue
Fullerton, CA 92631
(714) 879-1360
Fax: (714) 879-4611
Specialty: See article on page 138

Ebeling & Reuss Co.
P.O. Box 1289
Allentown, PA 18105-1289
(610) 366-8304
Fax: (610) 366-8307
Specialty: Figurines and teacups

Egg Fantasy
4040 Schiff Drive
Las Vegas, NV 89103
(702) 368-7747
Specialty: Egg creations

eggspressions! inc.
1635 Deadwood Avenue
Rapid City, SD 57702
(800) 551-9138
Fax: (605) 342-8699
Specialty: Collectible eggs

Eklund's Ltd.
1701 W. St. Germain
St. Cloud, MN 56301
(612) 252-1318
Specialty: Plates; horse and
wildlife

Enesco Corporation
225 Windsor Drive
Itasca, IL 60143
(630) 875-5300
Specialty: See article on page 141

Ertl Collectibles
P.O. Box 500
Dyersville, IA 52040
(800) 553-4886
Fax: (319) 875-5603
Specialty: See article on page 144

Federica Doll Company
4501 W. Highland Road
Milford, MI 48380
(810) 887-9575
Fax: (810) 887-9575
Specialty: Dolls

The Fenton Art Glass Company
700 Elizabeth Street
Williamstown, WV 26187
(304) 375-6122
Fax: (304) 375-6459
Specialty: See article on page 153

FFSC, Inc./Charming Tails™
13111 N. Central Expressway
Dallas, TX 75243
(214) 918-0098
Fax: (214) 454-1208
Specialty: See article on page 147

Figaro Import Corporation
325 South Flores Street
San Antonio, TX 78204-1178
(210) 225-1167
Specialty: Figurines

Figi Graphics
3636 Gateway Center
San Diego, CA 92102
(619) 262-8811
Fax: (619) 264-7781
Specialty: Figurines

FJ Designs, Inc.
Makers of Cat's Meow Village
2163 Great Trails Drive
Wooster, OH 44691-3738
(330) 264-1377
Fax: (330) 263-0219
Specialty: See article on page 150

Flambro Imports
1530 Ellsworth Industrial Dr.
Atlanta, GA 30318
(404) 352-1381
Fax: (404) 352-2150
Specialty: See article on page 156

Forma Vitrum
20414 N. Main Street
Cornelius, NC 28031
(800) 596-9963
Fax: (704) 892-5438
Specialty: See article on page 159

The Franklin Mint
Franklin Center, PA 19091
(800) 225-5836
Fax: (610) 459-6880
Specialty: See article on page 162

Fraser International
5990 N. Belt East, Unit 606
Humble, TX 77396
(800) 878-5448
Fax: (713) 441-7707
Specialty: Miniature historical
buildings

Margaret Furlong Designs
210 State Street
Salem, OR 97301
(503) 363-6004
Fax: (503) 371-0676
Specialty: See article on page 165

Ganz
908 Niagara Falls Blvd.
North Tonawanda, NY
14120-2060
(800) 724-5902
Fax: (905) 851-6669
Specialty: See article on page 168

Michael Garman Productions,
Inc.
2418 W. Colorado Avenue
Colorado Springs, CO 80904
(800) 874-7144
Fax: (719) 471-3659
Specialty: Figurines

Gartlan USA
575 Rt. 73 North, Suite A-6
West Berlin, NJ 08091
(609) 753-9229
Fax: (609) 753-9280
Specialty: See article on page 171

Georgetown Collection
P.O. Box 9730
Portland, ME 04104
(800) 626-3330
Fax: (207) 775-6457
Specialty: See article on page 174

Goebel of North America
Goebel Plaza
P.O. Box 10, Rte. 31
Pennington, NJ 08534-0010
(609) 737-8700
Fax: (609) 737-1545
Specialty: See article on page 177

Good-Krüger Dolls
1842 William Penn Way, Ste.A
Lancaster, PA 17601
(717) 399-3602
Specialty: Dolls

Great American Doll Co.
438 E. Katella Avenue #226
Orange, CA 92667
(800) VIP-DOLL
Specialty: Dolls

Great American Taylor
Collectiblles Corp.
Dept. BIC, P.O. Box 428
Aberdeen, NC 28315
(910) 944-7447
Fax: (910) 944-7449
Specialty: See article on page 180

The Greenwich Workshop
One Greenwich Place
Shelton, CT 06484
(800) 243-4246
Fax: (203) 925-0262
Specialty: See article on page 183

Dave Grossman Creations
1608 N. Warson Road
St. Louis, MO 63132
(800) 325-1655
Fax: (314) 423-7620
Specialty: Figurines and plates

Gund Inc.
1 Runyons Lane, P.O. Box H
Edison, NJ 08818
(908) 248-1500
Specialty: Bears; stuffed toys

H & G Studios Inc.
5660 Corporate Way
West Palm Beach, FL 33407
(407) 615-9900
Fax: (407) 615-8400
Specialty: Decorative and music
boxes, graphics and plates

Hadley House
11001 Hampshire Avenue S.
Bloomington, MN 55438
(800) 927-0880
Fax: (612) 943-8098
Specialty: Cottages, graphics,
ornaments, plates, steins

Jan Hagara Collectables, Inc.
40114 Industrial Park Circle
Georgetown, TX 78626
(512) 863-3072
Fax: (512) 869-2093
Specialty: Dolls, miniature
figurines and plates

Hallmark Cards, Inc.
Keepsake Ornament Collectors
Club #161
P.O. Box 412734
Kansas City, MO 64141-2734
Specialty: Ornaments and
figurines

The Hamilton Collection
4810 Executive Park Court
Jacksonville, FL 32216-6069
(800) 228-2945
Specialty: See article on page 186

Hand & Hammer Silversmiths
2610 Morse Lane
Woodbridge, VA 22192
(800) SILVERY
Fax: (703) 491-2031
Specialty: See article on page 189

Harbour Lights
1000 N. Johnson Ave.
El Cajun, CA 92020
(800) 365-1219
Fax: (619) 579-1911
Specialty: See article on page 192

Harmony Kingdom
232 Neilston St.
Columbus, OH 43215
(614) 469-0600
Fax: (614) 469-0140
Specialty: See article on page 195

Hawthorne Village
9210 N. Maryland Avenue
Niles, IL 60714
(800) 772-4277 customer service
(800) 327-0327 ordering
Specialty: See article on page 198

Heirloom Editions Ltd.
25100-B So. Normandie Ave.
Harbor City, CA 90710
(310) 539-5587
Fax: (310) 539-8891
Specialty: Bells, Staffordshire
dogs & teapots, and thimbles

Heirloom Ltd.
4330 Margaret Circle
Mound, MN 55364
(612) 474-2402
Specialty: Dolls and lithos

The Heritage Collections, Ltd.
6647 Kerns Road
Falls Church, VA 22042-4231
(703) 533-7800
Fax: (703) 533-7801
Specialty: Music boxes,
ornaments, paperweights

Edna Hibel Studio
P.O. Box 9967
Riviera Beach, FL 33419
(407) 848-9633
Fax: (407) 848-9640
Specialty: Bells, crystal, dolls,
figurines, graphics (original
lithographs and serigraphs,
limited edition reproductions),
ornaments and plates

Mark Hopkins Sculptures
21 Shorter Industrial Blvd.
Rome, GA 30165-1838
(800) 678-6564
Fax: (706) 235-2814
Specialty: Sculptures

**Hudson Creek/
The Lance Corporation**
321 Central Street
Hudson, MA 01749
(508) 568-1401
Fax: (508) 568-8741
Specialty: See article on page 210

M.I. Hummel Club
Division of Goebel Art GmbH,
Goebel Plaza
P.O. Box 11
Pennington, NJ 08534-0011
(800) 666-2582
Fax: (609) 737-1545
Specialty: See article on page 201

Imperial Graphics, Ltd.
11516 Lake Potomac Dr.
Potomac, MD 20854
(800) 541-7696
Fax: (301) 299-4837
Specialty: See article on page 204

Incolay Studios Inc.
445 N. Fox Street
San Fernando, CA 91340
(818) 365-2521
Specialty: Plates

Iris Arc Crystal
114 East Haley Street
Santa Barbara, CA 93101
(805) 963-3661
Fax: (805) 965-2458
Specialty: Crystal and
figurines

Janco Studio
P.O. Box 30012
Lincoln, NE 68503
(800) 490-1430
Fax: (402) 435-1430
Specialty: Figurines,
miniatures and ornaments

Kaiser Porcelain (US)
2045 Niagara Falls Blvd.
Niagara Falls, NY 14304
(800) 287-0077
Fax: (716) 297-2749
Specialty: Figurines and plates

Mark Klaus LTD
P.O. Box 470758
Broadview Heights, OH
44147-0758
(216) 582-5003
Specialty: Figurines

Ladie and Friends, Inc.
220 North Main Street
Sellersville, PA 18960
(800) 76DOLLS
Fax: (215) 453-8155
Specialty: See article on page 207

Lalique
400 Veterans Blvd.
Carlstadt, NJ 07072
(800) CRISTAL
Specialty: Crystal and plates

The Lawton Doll Company
548 North First
Turlock, CA 95380
(209) 632-3655
Fax: (209) 632-6788
Specialty: Dolls

Ron Lee's World of Clowns
330 Carousel Pkwy.
Henderson, NV 89014
(800) 829-3928
Fax: (702) 434-4310
Specialty: See article on page 213

George Z. Lefton Co.
3622 S. Morgan St.
Chicago, IL 60609
(800) 628-8492
Specialty: See article on page 216

Legacy Works
4020 Will Rogers Parkway,
Suite 700
Oklahoma City, OK 73108
(800) 460-3661
Fax: (405) 948-1784
Specialty: Figurines

Legends/Starlite Originals
2665D Park Center Drive
Simi Valley, CA 93065
(800) 726-9660
Fax: (805) 520-9670
Specialty: See article on page 219

Lemax, Inc.
25 Pequot Way
Canton, MA 02021
(617) 821-4555
Fax: (617) 821-4455
Specialty: Christmas village
collectibles and accessories

Lenox Collections
1170 Wheeler Way
Langhorne, PA 19047
(800) 225-1779
Fax: (215) 750-7362
Specialty: See article on page 222

Lilliput Lane
225 Windsor Ave.
Itasca, IL 60143
(800) 545-5478
Specialty: See article on page 225

Lladro Society
1 Lladro Drive
Moonachie, NJ 07074
(800) 634-9088
Fax: (201) 807-1168
Specialty: See article on page 228

Lynette Decor Products
1559 W. Embassy Street
Anaheim, CA 92802
(800) 223-8623
Fax: (714) 956-0653
Specialty: Collectible
displays and accessories

Magus Fine Arts &
Collectibles, Inc.
9437 Kilimanjaro Rd.
Columbia, MD 21045
(301) 596-6156
Specialty: Dolls

Seymour Mann, Inc.
225 Fifth Avenue
Showroom #102
New York, NY 10010
(212) 683-7262
Fax: (212) 213-4920
Specialty: See article on page 231

M C K Gifts Inc.
P.O. Box 621848
Littleton, CO 80162-1814
(303) 789-9394
Specialty: Figurines

Marty Sculpture, Inc.
P.O. Box 15067
Wilmington, NC 28408
(800) 654-0478
Specialty: Figurines

Maruri, U.S.A.
7541 Woodman Place
Van Nuys, CA 91405
(800) 5-MARURI
Fax: (818) 780-9871
Specialty: See article on page 234

June McKenna Collectibles, Inc.
P.O. Box 846
Ashland, VA 23005
(804) 798-2024
Fax: (804) 798-2618
Specialty: Figurines

Media Arts Group
Ten Almaden Blvd. 9th floor
San Jose, CA 95113
(800) 544-4890
Fax: (408) 947-4640
Specialty: See article on page 237

Michael's Limited
P.O. Box 217
Redmond, WA 98052-0217
(800) 835-0181
Fax: (206) 861-0608
Specialty: See article on page 240

Midwest of Cannon Falls
32057 64th Avenue
P.O. Box 20
Cannon Falls, MN 55009-0020
(800) 377-3335
Fax: (507) 263-7752
Specialty: See article on page 243

Miss Martha Originals, Inc.
P.O. Box 5038
Glencoe, AL 35905
(205) 492-0221
Fax: (205) 492-0261
Specialty: See article on page 246

The Moss Portfolio
1 Poplar Grove Lane
Mathews, VA 23109
(804) 725-7378
Specialty: Graphics

Munro Enterprises, Inc.
P.O. Box 200
Waterville, OH 43566
(419) 878-0034
Fax: (419) 878-2535
Specialty: Bronzes, figurines and
graphics

My Friends and Me
P.O. Box 2274
Hudson, OH 44236
(216) 650-6157
Fax: (216) 650-2342
Specialty: Miniature buildings

Napoleon
P.O. Box 860
Oakes, PA 19456
(610) 666-1650
Fax: (610) 666-1379
Specialty: Capidimonte
figurines

New Masters Publishing Co., Inc.
2301 14th Street, Ste. 105
Gulfport, MS 39501
(601) 863-5145
Fax: (601) 863-5145
Specialty: Bronzes and graphics

North American Bear Co.
401 North Wabash, Suite 500
Chicago, IL 60611
(312) 329-0020
Fax: (312) 329-1417
Specialty: Teddy Bears

Oldenburg Originals
W5061 Pheasant Valley Road
Waldo, WI 53093
(414) 528-7127
Fax: (414) 528-7127
Specialty: Limited edition and
porcelain original dolls

Old World Christmas
P.O. Box 8000
Spokane, WA 99203
(509) 534-9000
Fax: (509) 534-9098
Specialty: See article on page 249

Olszewski Studios
355 N. Lantana, Suite 500
Camarillo, CA 93010
(805) 374-9990
Fax: (805) 484-4993
Specialty: Miniature figurines

Opa's Haus, Inc.
1600 River Road
New Braunfels, TX 78132
(210) 629-1191
Fax: (210) 629-0153
Specialty: Steins

Orrefors of Sweden
140 Bradford Drive
Berlin, NJ 08009
(609) 768-5400
Fax: (609) 768-9726
Specialty: Figurines and
ornaments

Pacific Rim Import Corp.
5390 4th Avenue South
Seattle, WA 98108
(800) 425-5932
Fax: (206) 767-9179
Specialty: See article on page 252

Past Impressions
P.O. Box 188
Belvedere, CA 94920
(415) 358-9075
Fax: (415) 358-8676
Specialty: Graphics

PenDelfin Studios
c/o Miller Import Corp.
300 Mac Lane
Keasbey, NJ 08832
(800) 547-2006
Fax: (908) 417-0031
Specialty: Figurines

Penni Jo's Originals Ltd.
1413 N.E. Lincoln Ave.
Moore, OK 73160
(405) 799-0006
Specialty: Figurines

Pickard Inc.
782 Pickard Ave.
Antioch, IL 60002
(708) 395-3800
Specialty: Plates

Polland Studios
P.O. Box 1146
Prescott, AZ 86301-1146
(520) 778-1900
Fax: (520) 778-4034
Specialty: Pewter figurines

Porsgrunds Porselaensfabrik
A/S – P.O. Box 100
N-3907 Porsgrunn/Norway
+4735550040
Fax: +4735559110
Specialty: Christmas plates

Porterfield's
5020 Yaple Avenue
Santa Barbara, CA 93111
(805) 964-1824
Fax: (805) 964-1862
Specialty: Plates

Possible Dreams
6 Perry Drive
Foxboro, MA 02035
(508) 543-6667
Fax: (508) 543-4255
Specialty: See article on page 255

Precious Art/Panton
738 Airport Blvd., Suite 5
Ann Arbor, MI 48108
(313) 663-1885
Fax: (313) 663-2343
Specialty: See article on page 258

Pulaski Furniture Corporation
One Pulaski Square
Pulaski, VA 24301
(800) 287-4625
Specialty: See article on page 261

R.R. Creations
P.O. Box 8707
Pratt, KS 67124
(800) 779-3610
Fax: (316) 672-5850
Specialty: See article on page 263

Rawcliffe Corporation
155 Public Street
Providence, RI 02903
(800) 343-1811
Fax: (401) 751-8545
Specialty: Figurines

Reco International
150 Haven Avenue
Port Washington, NY 11050
(516) 767-2400
Fax: (516) 767-2409
Specialty: See article on page 266

Red Mill Mfg., Inc.
1023 Arbuckle Road
Summersville, WV 26651
(304) 872-5231
Fax: (304) 872-5234
Specialty: Character and wildlife
figurines

Harold Rigsby Graphics
4108 Scottsville Rd.
Glasgow, KY 42141
(800) 892-4984
Specialty: Graphics

Roman, Inc.
555 Lawrence Avenue
Roselle, IL 60172-1599
(630) 529-3000
Fax: (630) 529-1121
Specialty: See article on page 269

**Royal Copenhagen/
Bing & Grondahl**
27 Holland Avenue
White Plains, NY 10603
(914) 428-8222
Fax: (914) 428-8251
Specialty: See artictle on page 93

Royal Doulton
701 Cottontail Lane
Somerset, NJ 08873
(800) 68-CHINA
Fax: (908) 356-9467
Specialty: See article on page 272

Royal Worcester
Severn Street
Worcester, England
(01905) 23221
Fax: (01905) 23601
Specialty: Figurines,
ornaments and plates

Helen Sabatte Designs, Inc.
6041 Acacia Avenue
Oakland, CA 94618
(510) 653-4616
Fax: (510) 547-5806
Specialty: Figurines

Saint-Alexis Santons
P.O. Box 307
Searsport, ME 04974
(800) 829-0243
Fax: (207) 548-0244
Specialty: Figurines and villages

Salvino, Inc.
1379 Pico Street, Ste. 103
Corona, CA 91719
(909) 273-7850
Fax: (909) 279-3409
Specialty: Sports figurines

Sandicast, Inc.
8480 Miralani Drive
San Diego, CA 92126
(800) 722-3316
Fax: (619) 695-061
Specialty: Cast stone animal
figurines

Sarah's Attic
126-1/2 West Broad
P.O. Box 448
Chesaning, MI 48616
(800) 4-FRIEND
Fax: (517) 845-3477
Specialty: See article on page 275

Sculpture Workshop Designs
510 School Rd. P.O. Box 420
Blue Bell, PA 19422
(215) 643-7447
Fax: (215) 643-7447
Specialty: Sterling silver
ornaments

Second Nature Design
110 S. Southgate Bldg. C-4, #2
Chandler, AZ 85226
(602) 961-3963
Specialty: Figurines

Shade Tree Creations
6210 NW 124th Place
Gainesville, FL 32653
(904) 462-1830
Fax: (904) 462-1799
Specialty: Figurines

Shelia's Inc.
P.O. Box 31028
Charleston, SC 29417
(800) 227-6564
Fax: (803) 556-0040
Specialty: See article on page 278

**Shenandoah Designs
International**
P.O. Box 911
Rural Retreat, VA 24368
(800) 338-7644
Specialty: Figurines

Shube's Manufacturing
600 Moon St. S.E.
Albuquerque, NM 87123
(800) 545-5082
Fax: (505) 275-8182
Specialty: See article on page 281

Silver Deer Ltd.
963 Transport Way
Petaluma, CA 94954
(800) 729-3337
Fax: (303) 449-0653
Specialty: Figurines

Spencer Collin Lighthouses
2 Government Street
Kittery, ME 03904
(207) 439-6016
Fax: (204) 439-5787
Specialty: Lighthouses

Steiff USA
200 Fifth Avenue Ste. 1205
New York, NY 10010
(212) 675-2727
Fax: 212 779-2594
Specialty: Plush bears

Studio Collection
69 Thomas Lane
Falmouth, MA 02540
(800) 314-7748
Fax: (508) 548-8829
Specialty: Figurines and
ornaments

Swarovski America Limited
2 Slater Road
Cranston, RI 02920
(800) 426-3088
Fax: (401) 463-8459
Specialty: See article on page 284

Talsco of Florida
5427 Crafts Street
New Port Richey, FL 34652
(813) 847-6370
Fax: (813) 847-6786
Specialty: Collectible
accessories, glass displays and
plate frames

Jack Terry Fine Art Publishing
25251 Freedom Trail
Kerrville, TX 78028
(210) 367-4242
Fax: (210) 367-4243
Specialty: Limited edition prints
and sculptures

Texas Stamps
P.O. Box 42388
Houston, TX 77242-2388
(800) 779-4100
Fax: (713) 266-7706
Specialty: Stamps-individual and
collections

Angela Trotta Thomas
1107 E. Longwood Drive
Clarks Summit, PA 18411
(717) 586-0774
Fax: (717) 586-0774
Specialty: Nostalgic water color
painting

Timeless Creations
333 Continental Blvd.
El Segundo, CA 90245-5012
(310) 524-2000
Specialty: Dolls

Towle Silversmiths
144 Addison Street
Boston, MA 02128
(617) 568-1300
Fax: (617) 568-9185
Specialty: Bells and ornaments

The Tudor Mint
P.O. Box 431729
Houston, TX 77243-1729
(713) 462-0076
Fax: (713) 462-0170
Specialty: See article on page 287

United Design
P.O. Box 1200
Noble, OK 73068
(800) 527-4883
Fax: (405) 360-4442
Specialty: See article on page 290

Vaillancourt Folk Art
145 Armsby Road
Sutton, MA 01590
(508) 865-9183
Fax: (508) 865-4140
Specialty: Figurines

Bill Vernon Studios
6210 NW 124th Place
Gainesville, FL 32653
(904) 462-1830
Fax: (904) 462-1799
Specialty: Figurines

VF Fine Arts
11191 Westheimer #202
Houston, TX 77042
(713) 461-1944
Specialty: Graphics

VickiLane
3233 NE Cadet Avenue
Portland, OR 97220
(800) 678-4254
Fax: (503) 251-5916
Specialty: Figurines

Viking Import House
690 NE 13th Street
Ft. Lauderdale, FL 33304
(800) 327-2297
Specialty: Bells, dolls, steins,
figurines, ornaments and plates

Viletta China Company
10130 Mula Road
Stafford, TX 77477
(713) 564-2400
Fax: (713) 564-3882
Specialty: Plates

WACO Products Corp.
I-80 & New Maple Avenue
P.O. Box 898
Pine Brook, NJ 07058-0898
(201) 882-1820
Fax: (201) 882-3661
Specialty: See article on page 293

The Susan Wakeen Doll Company
425 Bantam Road
Litchfield, CT 06759
P.O. Box 1321
(203) 567-0007
Fax: (203) 567-4636
Specialty: Dolls

Wallace Silversmiths
175 McClellan Highway
E. Boston, MA 02128-9114
(617) 561-2200
Fax: (617) 568-9185
Specialty: Bells and
ornaments

Walnut Ridge Collectibles
39048 Webb Dr.
Westland, MI 48185
(313) 728-3300
Fax: (313) 728-5950
Specialty: See article on page 296

Waterford Crystal
1330 Campus Parkway
Wall, NJ 07719
(908) 938-5800
Specialty: Crystal

Wedgwood
1330 Campus Parkway
Wall, NJ 07719
(908) 938-5800
Specialty: Ornaments and plates

Wild Wings
South Highway 61
Lake City, MN 55041
(800) 445-4833
Specialty: Plates and prints

Willitts Designs
1129 Industrial Avenue
Petaluma, CA 94952
(800) 358-9184
Fax: (707) 769-0304
Specialty: Figurines, graphics,
ornaments and plates

W.T. Wilson Limited Editions
185 York Avenue
Pawtucket, RI 02860
(800) 722-0485
Specialty: Bells and figurines

The Wimbledon Collection
P.O. Box 21948
Lexington, KY 40522
(606) 277-8531
Fax: (606)277-9231
Specialty: Dolls

Windstone Editions
13012 Saticoy Street #3
North Hollywood, CA 91605
(800) 982-4464
Fax: (818) 982-4674
Specialty: Figurines

Winston Roland Ltd.
1909 Oxford Street E.
Unit 17
London, Ont. CAN N5V 2Z7
(519) 659-6601
Fax: (519) 659-2923
Specialty: Graphics and plates

R. John Wright Dolls
15 West Main Street
Cambridge, NY 12816
(518) 677-8566
Specialty: Bears and dolls

Donald Zolan Studio
29 Cambridge Drive
Hershey, PA 17033
(717) 534-2446
Specialty: Bells and plates

Johannes Zook Originals
P.O. Box 256
Midland, MI 48640
(517) 835-9388
Specialty: Dolls

NALED
National Association of Limited Edition Dealers

Formed in 1976, NALED is a national group of retail and wholesale merchants who are in the specialized market of selling limited edition collectibles. The National Headquarters for NALED is located at 5235 Monticello Street, Dallas, Texas 75206, (800) HI-NALED.

ALABAMA
COLLECTIBLE COTTAGE, Gardendale, AL, 205-631-2413
COLLECTIBLE COTTAGE, Birmingham, AL, 205-988-8551
MARGO COLLECTIBLES, Cullman, AL, 205-734-1452
OLD COUNTRY STORE, Gadsen, AL, 205-492-7659
OLDE POST OFFICE, Trussville, AL, 205-655-7292
TOMORROW'S TREASURES, Birmingham, AL, 205-838-1887
TRADITIONS GIFT SHOP, Albertville AL, 205-891-2903

ARIZONA
ANNIE'S HALLMARK, Tucson, AZ, 602-790-7430
ARTISAN COLLECTORS GALLERY, THE, Mesa, AZ, 602-833-0495
BONA'S CHRISTMAS ETC, Tucson, AZ, 602-885-3755
FOX'S GIFTS & COLLECTABLES, Scottsdale, AZ, 602-947-0560
LAWTON'S GIFTS & COLLECTIBLES, Chandler, AZ, 602-899-7977
MARYLYN'S COLLECTIBLES, Tucson, AZ, 602-293-4603
MILLIE'S HALLMARK, Phoenix AZ, 602-893-3777
RUTH'S HALLMARK SHOP, Cottonwood, AZ, 602-634-8050

CALIFORNIA
ALLOVIO GALLERY, THE, Roseville, CA, 916-782-5330
BLEVINS PLATES 'N THINGS, Vallejo, CA, 707-642-7505
BUNNY HUTCH, THE, Fair Oaks, CA, 916-967-7044
CAMEO GIFTS & COLLECTIBLES, Temecula, CA, 909-676-1635
CAPRICE, Northridge, CA, 818-363-0796
CARDTOWNE HALLMARK, Garden Grove, CA, 714-537-5240
CAROL'S GIFT SHOP *, Artesia, CA, 310-924-6335
COLLECTIBLE CORNER, Placentia, CA, 714-528-3079
COLLECTIBLES UNLIMITED, Woodland Hills, CA, 818-703-6173
COLLECTOR'S WORLD, Montrose, CA, 818-248-9451
CRYSTAL AERIE, Fremont, CA, 510-791-0298
DANA DRUG STORE, Burbank, CA, 818-562-1177
DODIE'S FINE GIFTS & COLLECTIBLES, Woodland, CA, 916-668-1909
DOLLS GIFTS & MORE, Danville, CA, 510-831-8981
DOLLS GIFTS & MORE, San Ramon, CA, 510-830-9546
EASTERN ART, Victorville, CA, 619-241-0166
EASTLAND HALLMARK & STATIONERS, Ojai, CA, 805-646-8963
ENCORE CARDS & GIFTS, Cypress, CA, 714-761-1266
EVA MARIE DRY GROCER, Redondo Beach, CA, 310-375-8422
FRAME GALLERY, THE, Chula Vista, CA, 619-422-1700
FRAN'S HALLMARK, Red Bluff, CA, 916-527-6789
FRIENDS COLLECTIBLES, Canyon Country, CA, 805-298-2232
GALLERIA GIFTS, Reedley, CA, 209-638-4060
GALLERY DECOR, Arcadia, CA, 818-445-7679
GIFT GALLERY NORTHRIDGE PHARMACY, Northridge, CA, 818-349-7000

HEIRLOOMS OF TOMORROW, Fullerton, CA, 714-525-1522
HIDDEN COTTAGE, THE, Simi Valley, CA, 805-584-2252
KENNEDY'S COLLECTIBLES & GIFTS, Sacramento, CA, 916-973-8754
LENA'S GIFT GALLERY *, San Mateo, CA, 415-342-1304
LESLIE'S HALLMARK SHOP, Ventura, CA, 805-644-2331
LOUISE MARIE'S FINE GIFTS, Livermore, CA, 510-449-5757
MARGIE'S GIFTS & COLLECTIBLES, Torrance, CA, 310-378-2526
MARY ANN'S CARDS, GIFTS & COL, Yorba Linda, CA, 714-777-0999
MC CURRY'S HALLMARK, Citrus Heights, CA, 916-969-9452
MC CURRY'S HALLMARK, Sacramento, CA, 916-925-6485
MC CURRY'S HALLMARK, Sacramento, CA, 916-567-9952
MUSICAL MOMENTS & COLLECTIBLES, Shingle Spgs, CA, 916-677-2221
NORTHERN LIGHTS, San Rafael, CA, 415-457-2884
NYBORG CASTLE, Martinez, CA, 510-930-0200
P M COLLECTABLES, Cupertino, CA, 408-725-8858
PARDINI'S GIFTS & COLLECTIBLES, Stockton, CA, 209-957-2414
RUG RAT COLLECTABLES, Monterey, CA, 408-657-1055
RUMMEL'S VILLAGE GUILD, Montebello, CA, 213-722-2691
RYSTAD'S LIMITED EDITIONS, San Jose, CA, 408-279-1960
SUGARBUSH GIFT GALLERY, San Marcos, CA, 619-599-9945
SUTTER STREET EMPORIUM, Folsom, CA, 916-985-4647
TOMORROW'S TREASURES, Riverside, CA, 909-354-5731
VICTORIA'S COTTAGE, Newhall, CA, 805-287-9387
VILLAGE PEDDLER, La Habra, CA, 310-694-6111
WEE HOUSE FINE GIFTS & COLLECTIBLES, Irvine, CA, 714-552-3228
WILSON GALLERIES, Fresno, CA, 209-224-2223
WONDERLAND COLLECTIBLES, Fresno, CA, 209-435-1002

COLORADO
GIFT HOUSE, THE, Lakewood, CO, 303-922-7279
GRECO COLLECTIBLES, Aurora CO, 303-755-6048
KATHIE'S IMPORT CHALET, Englewood, CO, 303-761-1740
KENT COLLECTION, THE, Englewood, CO, 303-761-0059
KING'S GALLERY OF COLLECTABLES, Colorado Springs, CO, 719-636-2228
NOEL - THE CHRISTMAS SHOP, Vail, CO, 303-476-6544
PLATES ETC, Arvada, CO, 303-420-0752
QUALITY GIFTS & COLLECTIBLES, Colorado Springs, CO, 719-599-0051
SWISS MISS SHOP, Cascade, CO, 719-684-9679
TOBACCO LEAF, Lakewood, CO, 303-274-8720

CONNECTICUT
COLLECTIBLES, Hawleyville, CT, 203-790-1011
MAURICE NASSER *, New London, CT, 203-443-6523
NEW ENGLAND HOUSE OF COLLECTIBLES, Meriden, CT, 203-634-7509
PERIWINKLE, Vernon, CT, 203-872-2904

REVAY'S GARDENS & GIFT SHOP, East Windsor, CT, 203-623-9068
TAYLOR'D TOUCH, THE, Marlborough, CT, 203-295-9377
UTOPIA COLLECTABLES & FINE GIFTS, Oxford, CT, 203-888-0233
WINDSOR SHOPPE, North Haven, CT, 203-239-4644

DELAWARE
GIFT DESIGN GALLERIES, Dover, DE, 302-734-3002
HOBBY HOUSE OF GIFTS, Townsend, DE, 302-378-1408
PEREGOY'S GIFTS, Wilmington, DE, 302-999-1155
TULL BROTHERS, Seaford, DE, 302-629-3071
WASHINGTON SQUARE LIMITED, Newark, DE, 302-453-1776

FLORIDA
CARDS N' GIFTS GALORE, Daytona Beach, FL, 904-255-6624
CAROL'S HALLMARK SHOP, Tampa, FL, 813-960-8807
CHRISTMAS COLLECTION, Altamonte Springs, FL, 407-862-5383
CHRISTMAS PALACE, THE, Hialea Gardens, FL, 305-558-5352
CHRISTMAS SHOPPE, THE, Tallahassee, FL, 904-422-8990
CHRISTMAS SHOPPE, Miami, FL, 305-255-5414
CLASSIC CARGO, Destin, FL, 904-837-8171
CORNER GIFTS, Pembroke Pines, FL, 305-432-3739
ENTERTAINER, THE, Jacksonville, FL, 904-725-1166
GALLERY OF ANTIQUES & COLLECTIBLES, Jacksonville, FL, 904-783-6787
GIFT GALLERY, THE, Palm Harbor, FL, 813-786-1984
GIFTS UNLIMITED, Miami, FL, 305-253-0146
HEIRLOOM COLLECTIBLES, Clearwater FL, (813)797-8007
HEIRLOOMS OF TOMORROW, North Miami, FL, 305-899-0920
HUNT'S COLLECTIBLES, Satellite Beach, FL, 407-777-1313
JOHNSTONS HALLMARK, Tampa, FL, 813-968-2625
METHODIST FOUNDATION GIFT SHOPS, Jacksonville, FL, 904-798-8210
PAPER MOON, West Palm Beach, FL, 407-684-2668
PARK AVENUE GALLERY, Winter Park, FL, 407-644-1545
SUN ROSE GIFTS, Indian Harbor Beach, FL, 407-773-0550
VILLAGE PLATE COLLECTOR *, Cocoa, FL, 407-636-6914

GEORGIA
BECKY'S SMALL WONDERS, Helen, GA, 706-878-3108
CHAMBERHOUSE, Canton, GA, 404-479-9115
COTTAGE GARDEN, Macon, GA, 912-743-9897
CREATIVE GIFTS, Augusta, GA, 706-796-8794
GALLERY II, Atlanta, GA, 404-458-5858
GLASS ETC, Atlanta, GA, 404-493-7936
HEART OF COUNTRY, Fayetteville, GA, 404-460-0337
IMPRESSIONS, Brunswick, GA, 912-265-1624
MTN CHRISTMAS-MTN MEMORIES, Dahlonega, GA, 706-864-9115
PAM'S HALLMARK SHOP, Fayetteville, GA, 404-461-3041

PLUM TREE, Tucker, GA, 404-491-9433
SACKS ROUTE 1, Warm Springs, GA, 706-655-9093
SWAN GALLERIES, Stone Mountain, GA, 404-498-1324
WESSON'S, Helen, GA, 706-878-3544
WHIMSEY MANOR, Warner Robins, GA, 912-328-2500

HAWAII
OUR HOUSE COLLECTIBLE GIFT GALLERY, Honolulu,
  HI, 808-593-1999

IDAHO
CINNAMON TREE GIFT & COL. GALLERY, Pocatello, ID,
  208-232-6371

ILLINOIS
BITS OF GOLD JEWELRY & GIFTS, Nashville, IL,
  618-327-4261
C A JENSEN, LaSalle, IL, 815-223-0377
CHRYSLER BOUTIQUE, Effingham, IL, 217-342-4864
CLASS ACT, LAKE ZURICH, IL, 708-540-7700
COLLECTOR'S PARADISE, Monmouth, IL, 309-734-3690
CONTINENTAL GIFTS, Wheaton, IL, 708-653-3055
COUNTRY OAK COLLECTABLES, Schaumburg, IL,
  708-529-0290
CROWN CARD & GIFT SHOP, Chicago, IL, 312-282-6771
DORIS COLLECTIBLES, St Peter, IL, 618-349-8780
EUROPEAN IMPORTS & GIFTS, Niles, IL, 708-967-5253
FINE & FANCY, Aurora, IL, 708-898-1130
GATZ COLLECTABLES, Wheeling, IL, 708-541-4033
GIFTIQUE OF LONG GROVE, Long Grove, IL, 708-634-9171
GLORY B!, Carthage, IL, 217-357-2599
GRIMM'S HALLMARK - WEST, St Charles, IL, 708-513-7008
GUZZARDO'S HALLMARK, Kewanee, IL, 309-852-5621
HALL JEWELERS & GIFTS LTD, Moweaqua, IL, 217-768-4990
HAWK HOLLOW, Galena, IL, 815-777-3616
HUMMEL KORNER & GIFTS, Wheeling, IL, 708-215-2908
JBJ THE COLLECTORS SHOP, Champaign, IL, 217-352-9610
KIEFER'S GALLERIES LTD, LaGrange, IL, 708-354-1888
KIEFER'S GALLERY OF C HILL, Plainfield, IL, 815-436-5444
KRIS KRINGLE HAUS, Geneva, IL, 708-208-0400
LYNN'S & COMPANY, Arlington Heights, IL, 708-870-1188
MAY HALLMARK SHOP, Woodridge, IL, 708-985-1008
MC HUGH'S GIFTS & COLLECTIBLES, Rock Island, IL,
  309-788-9525
PAINTED PLATE LTD EDITION, O'Fallon IL, 618-624-6987
PEGGY'S HALLMARK SHOP, Bloomington, IL, 309-663-1977
PEGGY'S HALLMARK SHOP, Normal, IL, 309-452-5831
POTPOURRI CARD & GIFT, Bolingbrook, IL, 708-759-8222
POTPOURRI CARD & GIFT, Westchester, IL, 708-562-1440
RANDALL DRUG & GIFTS, Aurora, IL, 708-907-8700
ROYALE IMPORTS, Lisle, IL, 708-357-7002
RUTH'S HALLMARK, Bloomingdale, IL, 708-894-7890
SANDY'S DOLLS & COLLECTABLES INC, Palos Heights,
  IL, 708-423-0070
SOMETHING SO SPECIAL, Rockford, IL, 815-226-1331
STONE'S HALLMARK SHOPS, Rockford, IL, 815-399-4481
STRAWBERRY HOUSE, Libertyville, IL, 708-816-6129
STROHL'S LIMITED EDITIONS, Shelbyville, IL, 217-774-5222
TICK TOCK GIFT SHOP, Aurora, IL, 708-851-7767
TRICIA'S TREASURES, Fairview Hgts, IL, 618-624-6334
WHYDE'S HAUS, Canton, IL, 309-647-8823

INDIANA
ANGEL LIGHT, Mishawaka, IN, 219-256-9403
ART & CRAFT GALLERY, Corydon, IN, 812-738-4147
BEA'S HALLMARK, Indianapolis, IN, 317-888-8408
CARD & GIFT GALLERY, Indianapolis, IN, 317-783-1555
CAROL'S CRAFTS, Nashville, IN, 812-988-6388

CURIO SHOPPE, Greensburg, IN, 812-663-6914
DEARLY YOURS, Noblesville, IN, 317-773-3098
GIFT BOX, THE, Logansport, IN, 219-753-8442
HILBISH DRUG, La Porte, IN, 219-362-2247
JORGENSENS, Fort Wayne, IN, 219-432-5519
LANDMARK GIFTS & ANTIQUES, Kokomo, IN,
  317-456-3488
LOUISE'S HALLMARK, St John, IN, 219-365-3837
NANA'S, Butler, IN, 219-868-5634
ROSE MARIE'S, Evansville, IN, 812-423-7557
ROSIE'S CARD & GIFT SHOP, Newburgh, IN, 812-853-3059
SMUCKER DRUGS, Middlebury, IN, 219-825-2485
TEMPTATIONS GIFTS, Valparaiso, IN, 219-462-1000
TOMORROW'S TREASURES, Muncie, IN, 317-284-6355
WALTER'S COLLECTIBLES, Princeton, IN, 812-386-3992
WATSON'S *, New Carlisle, IN, 219-654-8600

IOWA
COLLECTION CONNECTION, Des Moines, IA,
  515-276-7766
DAVE & JANELLE'S, Mason City, IA, 515-423-6377
DAVIS COLLECTIBLES, Waterloo, IA, 319-232-0050
HAWK HOLLOW, Bellevue, IA, 319-872-5467
JAKOBSON DRUG & HALLMARK SHOP, Osage, IA,
  515-732-5452
VAN DEN BERG'S, Pella, IA, 515-628-2533

KANSAS
CAROL'S DECOR, Salina, KS, 913-823-1739 Ext 186

KENTUCKY
ANN'S HALLMARK, Lexington, KY, 606-266-9101
ANN'S HALLMARK, Florence, KY, 606-342-7595
BETSY'S HALLMARK, Benton, KY, 502-527-1848
KAREN'S GIFTS, Louisville, KY, 502-425-3310
STORY BOOK KIDS, Florence, KY, 606-525-7743

LOUISANA
AD LIB GIFTS, Metairie, LA, 504-835-8755
GALILEAN, THE, Leesville, LA, 318-239-6248
LA TIENDA, Lafayette, LA, 318-984-5920
PARTRIDGE CHRISTMAS SHOPS, Covington, LA,
  504-892-4477
PLATES AND THINGS, Baton Rouge, LA, 504-753-2885
PLUM TREE, Lake Charles, LA, 318-439-9526
PONTALBA COLLECTIBLES, New Orleans, LA,
  504-524-8068
SANTA'S QUARTERS, New Orleans, LA, 504-581-5820

MAINE
CHRISTMAS SHOPPE, THE, East Holden, ME, 207-989-4887
GIMBEL & SONS COUNTRY STORE, Boothbay Harbor,
  ME, 207-633-5088
HERITAGE GIFTS, Oakland, ME, 207-465-3910

MARYLAND
BODZER'S COLLECTIBLES, Baltimore, MD, 410-931-9222
CALICO MOUSE, Glen Burnie, MD, 410-760-2757
CALICO MOUSE, Annapolis, MD, 410-266-7204
CALICO MOUSE, Annapolis, MD, 301-261-2441
CHERRY TREE CARDS & GIFTS, Laurel, MD, 301-498-8528
EDWARDS STORES, Ocean City, MD, 410-289-7000
ELLEN'S HALLMARK, Bel Air, MD, 410-838-0284
HANDS OF TIME CLOCKS & COLLECTIBLES, Savage,
  MD, 301-206-3281
KEEPSAKES & COLLECTIBLES, Owings Mill, MD,
  410-356-3578
MUSIC BOX, THE, Baltimore, MD, 410-727-0444

PENN DEN, Bowie, MD, 301-262-2430
PRECIOUS GIFTS, Ellicott City, MD, 410-461-6813
TIARA GIFTS, Wheaton, MD, 301-949-0210
TOMORROW'S TREASURES, Bel Air, MD, 410-893-7965
WANG'S GIFTS & COLLECTIBLE, Bel Air, MD, 410-838-2626
WANG'S GIFTS & COLLECTIBLES, White Marsh, MD,
  410-931-7388

MASSACHUSETTS
GIFT GALLERY, Webster, MA, 508-943-4402
HONEYCOMB GIFT SHOPPE, Wakefield, MA, 617-245-2448
KAY'S HALLMARK, Tewksbury, MA, 508-851-7790
LEONARD GALLERY, Springfield, MA, 413-733-9492
MERRY CHRISTMAS SHOPPE, Whitman, MA, 617-447-6677
PAPER STORE, THE, Bedford, MA, 617-275-3232
PAPER STORE, THE, Maynard, MA, 508-897-3338
SAVAS LIMITED, Hanson, MA, 617-294-0177
SHROPSHIRE CURIOSITY SHOP II, Shrewsbury, MA,
  508-799-7200
SHROPSHIRE CURIOSITY SHOP II, Shrewsbury, MA,
  508-842-5001
SHROPSHIRE CURIOSITY SHOP I, Shrewsbury, MA,
  508-842-4202
STACY'S GIFTS & COLLECTIBLES, East Walpole, MA,
  508-668-4212
WARD'S, Burlington, MA, 617-229-0068
WARD'S, Medford, MA, 617-395-4099
WAYSIDE COUNTRY STORE, Marlboro, MA, 508-481-3458

MICHIGAN
1/2 OFF CARD SHOP, Bay City, MI, 517-686-9820
1/2 OFF CARD SHOPS, Southfield, MI, 810-851-4358
1/2 OFF CARD SHOP, Taylor, MI, 313-374-2450
AFTER EFFECTS, Clinton Twp, MI, 810-791-2265
CARAVAN GIFTS & COLLECTIBLES, Fenton, MI,
  810-629-4212
CINDY'S HALLMARK, Sturgis, MI, 616-651-1424
DEE'S HALLMARK, Clinton Twp, MI, 810-792-5510
DOLL LEE GIFTS & COLLECTIBLES, Roseville, MI,
  810-771-4438
ELLE STEVENS JEWELERS, Ironwood, MI, 906-932-5679
ELSIE'S HALLMARK SHOP, Petoskey, MI, 616-347-5270
EMILY'S GIFTS, DOLLS, COLLECTIBLES, St Clair Shores,
  MI, 810-777-5250
FRITZ GIFTS & COLLECTIBLES, Monroe, MI, 313-241-6760
GEORGIA'S GIFT GALLERY, Plymouth, MI, 313-453-7733
HARPOLD'S, South Haven, MI, 616-637-3522
HOUSE OF CARDS & GIFTS, Sturgis, MI, 616-651-6011
HOUSE OF CARDS & COLLECTIBLES, Macomb, MI,
  313-247-2000
JACQUELYNS GIFTS, Warren, MI, 810-296-9211
KEEPSAKE GIFTS, Kimball, MI, 810-985-5855
KNIBLOE GIFT CORNER, Jackson, MI, 517-782-6846
LAKEVIEW CARD & GIFT SHOP, Battle Creek, MI,
  616-962-0650
MILLER'S UNIQUE GIFTS, Tecumseh, MI, 517-423-3848
MOMBER PHARMACY & GIFTS, Sparta, MI, 616-887-7323
PEWTER CLASSICS, Grand Rapids, MI, 616-942-8822
PINOCCHIO'S INC, Frankenmuth, MI, 517-652-2751
PLATE LADY, Livonia, MI, 313-261-5220
ROBINETTE'S GIFT BARN, Grand Rapids, MI, 616-361-7180
SCHULTZ GIFT GALLERY, Pinconning, MI, 517-879-3110
SPECIAL THINGS, Sterling Heights, MI, 810-739-4030
TOUCH OF COUNTRY, Howell, MI, 517-546-5995
TROY STAMP & COIN EXCHANGE, Troy, MI, 810-528-1181
VEENA'S CARDS & COLLECTIBLES, Farmington Hills,
  MI, 810-489-4060

MINNESOTA

ANDERSEN HALLMARK, Albert Lea, MN, 507-373-0996
BJORNSON IMPORTS, Mound, MN, 612-474-3957
COLLECTIBLES SHOWCASE, Bloomington, MN,
    612-854-1553
GUSTAF'S, Lindstrom, MN, 612-257-6688
HELGA'S HALLMARK, Cambridge, MN, 612-689-5000
HUNT HALLMARK CARD & GIFT, Rochester, MN,
    507-289-5152
HUNT SILVER LAKE DRUG & GIFT, Rochester, MN,
    507-289-0749
MARY D'S DOLLS & BEARS & SUCH, Minneapolis, MN,
    612-424-4375
ODYSSEY, Rochester, MN, 507-288-6629
ODYSSEY, Mankato, MN, 507-388-2006
ODYSSEY GIFTS, Mankato, MN, 507-388-2004
SEEFELDT'S GALLERY, Roseville, MN, 612-631-1397

MISSOURI

DICKENS GIFT SHOPPE, Branson, MO, 417-334-2992
ELLY'S, Kimmswick, MO, 314-467-5019
EMILY'S HALLMARK, Chesterfield, MO, 314-391-8755
FIRST CAPITOL TRADING POST, St Charles, MO,
    314-946-2883
HELEN'S GIFTS & ACCESSORIES, Rolla, MO, 314-341-2300
K C COLLECTIBLES & GIFTS, Kansas City, MO,
    816-741-2448
OAK LEAF GIFTS, Osage Beach, MO, 314-348-0190
TOBACCO LANE, Cape Girardeau, MO, 314-651-3414
TRA-ART LTD, Jefferson City, MO, 314-635-8278
UNIQUE GIFT SHOPPE, Springfield, MO, 417-887-5476

MONTANA

TRADITIONS, Missoula, MT, 406-543-3177

NEBRASKA

L & L GIFTS, Fremont, NE, 402-727-7275
MANGELSEN'S, Omaha, NE, 402-339-3922
MARIANNE K FESTERSEN *, Omaha, NE, 402-393-4454
SHARRON SHOP, Omaha, NE, 402-393-8311
WOOD 'N DOLL, North Platte, NE, 308-534-3618

NEW HAMPSHIRE

STRAW CELLAR, THE, Wolfeboro, NH, 603-569-1516

NEW JERSEY

CHINA ROYALE INC, Englewood, NJ, 201-568-1005
CHRISTMAS CAROL, Flemington, NJ, 908-782-0700
CLASSIC COLLECTIONS, Livingston, NJ, 201-992-8605
COLLECTORS CELLAR, Pine Beach, NJ, 908-341-4107
COLLECTORS EMPORIUM, Secaucus, NJ, 201-863-2977
CRAFT EMPORIUM, Waldwick, NJ, 201-670-0022
EMJAY SHOP, Stone Harbor, NJ, 609-368-1227
EXTRA SPECIAL TOUCH INC, Pompton Lakes, NJ,
    201-835-5441
GIFT CARAVAN, North Arlington, NJ, 201-997-1055
GIFT GALLERY, Paramus, NJ, 201-845-0940
GIFT GALLERY, Edison, NJ, 908-494-3939
GIFT WORLD, Maple Shade, NJ, 609-321-1500
J C'S HALLMARK, Old Bridge, NJ, 908-826-8208
JIANA INC, Union, NJ, 201-492-1728
KATIE'S KACHE, Red Bank, NJ, 908-576-1777
LA MAISON CAPRI, Atlantic City, NJ, 609-345-4305
LITTLE TREASURES, Rutherford, NJ, 201-460-9353
MEYER HOUSE GIFT SHOP, Newfoundland, NJ,
    201-697-7122

MOLK BROTHERS, Elmwood Park, NJ, 201-796-8377
NOTES-A-PLENTY GIFT SHOPPE, Flemington, NJ,
    908-782-0700
OAKWOOD CARD & GIFT SHOP, Edison, NJ, 908-549-9494
OLD WAGON GIFTS, Colts Neck, NJ, 908-780-6656
SOMEONE SPECIAL, Cherry Hill, NJ, 609-424-1914
SOMEONE SPECIAL, W Berlin, NJ, 609-768-7171
TOM'S GARDEN WORLD, McKee City, NJ, 609-641-4522
WESTON'S LIMITED EDITIONS, Eatontown, NJ,
    908-935-0301
ZASLOW'S FINE COLLECTIBLES *, Matawan, NJ,
    908-583-1499
ZASLOW'S FINE COLLECTIBLES, Middletown, NJ,
    908-957-9560

NEW MEXICO

COVERED WAGON GIFTS & COLLECTIBLES, Rudioso,
    NM, 505-257-4591
LORRIE'S COLLECTIBLES, Albuquerque, NM, 505-292-0020

NEW YORK

ANDREW'S COLLECTIBLES, Buffalo, NY, 716-823-4131
ANN'S HALLMARK CARDS & GIFTS, Newburgh, NY,
    914-564-5585
ANN'S HALLMARK SHOPPE, Newburgh, NY, 914-562-3149
CANAL TOWN COUNTRY STORE, Rochester, NY,
    716-424-4120
CANAL TOWN COUNTRY STORE, Rochester, NY,
    716-225-5070
CANAL TOWN COUNTRY STORE, Irondequoit, NY,
    716-338-3670
CERAMICA GIFT GALLERY, New York, NY, 212-354-9216
CLASSIC GIFT GALLERY, Centereach, NY, 516-467-4813
CLIFTON PARK COUNTRY STORE, Clifton Park, NY,
    518-371-0585
CLOCK MAN GALLERY, Poughkeepsie, NY, 914-473-9055
COLLECTIBLES, Poughkeepsie, NY, 914-298-0226
COLLECTIBLY YOURS, Spring Valley, NY, 914-425-9244
CORNER COLLECTIONS, Hunter, NY, 518-263-4141
COUNTRY GALLERY, Fishkill, NY, 914-897-2008
COW HARBOR FINE GIFTS & COLLECTIBLES, Northport,
    NY, 516-261-7907
CROWN SHOPPE, Rockville Centre, NY, 516-536-2712
CRYSTAL CAVE, THE, Woodhaven, NY, 718-441-0144
DAYDREAMS, Latham, NY, 518-783-7513
ELLIE'S LTD ED & COLLECTIBLES, Selden, NY,
    516-698-3467
ELLIE'S LTD ED & COLLECTIBLES, Miller Place, NY,
    516-698-3467
FLOWERS & MORE, Clarence, NY, 716-759-2988
FOREVER CHRISTMAS, Hyde Park, NY, 914-229-2969
GRANDMA'S COUNTRY CORNERS, Albany, NY,
    518-459-1209
ISLAND TREASURES, Staten Island, NY, 718-698-1234
LIL' SUSIES KEEPSAKES & COLLECTIBLES, Shirley, NY,
    516-281-9481
LIMITED COLLECTOR, Corning, NY, 607-936-6195
LIMITED EDITION, THE *, Merrick, NY, 516-623-4400
LYN GIFT SHOP, Lynbrook, NY, 516-593-6500
MARESA'S CANDELIGHT GIFT SHOPPE, Port Jefferson,
    NY, 516-331-6245
PAUL'S ECONOMY PHARMACY, Staten Island, NY,
    718-442-2924
PLATE COTTAGE, St James, NY, 516-862-7171
PRECIOUS GIFT GALLERY, Levittown, NY, 516-579-3562
PREMIO, Massapequa, NY, 516-795-3050
SIX SIXTEEN GIFT SHOPS, Bellmore, NY, 516-221-5829

VILLAGE GIFT SHOP, Tonawanda, NY, 716-695-6589

NEVADA

CARLAN'S FINE GIFTS, Las Vegas, NV, 702-734-6003
JAN'S HALLMARK, Reno, NV, 702-825-2205
OOH'S AND AH'S, Las Vegas, NV, 702-870-2078

NORTH CAROLINA

AUNT EDYE'S COLLECTIBLES, Charlotte, NC, 704-545-2658
BUSH STATIONERS & GIFTS, Charlotte, NC, 704-333-4438
GIFT ATTIC, Raleigh, NC, 919-781-1822
GIFT ATTIC, Raleigh, NC, 919-781-1822
MC NAMARA'S *, Highlands, NC, 704-526-5551
OLDE WORLD CHRISTMAS SHOPPE, Asheville, NC,
    704-274-4819
PLEASURES & TREASURES, Greensboro, NC, 910-855-1301
PLEASURES & TREASURES, High Point, NC, 910-855-1301
TINDER BOX, Charlotte, NC, 704-366-5164
TINDER BOX, Charlotte, NC, 704-568-8798
TINDER BOX, Pineville, NC, 704-542-6115
TINDER BOX OF WINSTON-SALEM, Winston-Salem, NC,
    919-765-9511

NORTH DAKOTA

BJORNSON IMPORTS, Grand Forks, ND, 701-775-2618
FRAMEMAKER, Grand Forks, ND, 701-775-9675
JUNIQUE'S, Bismarck, ND, 701-258-3542

OHIO

ALADDIN LAMP, Lima, OH, 419-224-5612
ARTIST'S TOUCH, THE, New Bremen, OH, 419-629-3815
BELLFAIR COUNTRY STORES, Dayton, OH, 513-426-3921
BETTY'S HALLMARK, Twinsburg, OH, 216-425-1661
CABBAGES & KINGS, Grand Rapids, OH, 419-832-2709
CELLAR CACHE, Put-in-Bay, OH, 419-285-2738
CHRISTMAS TREASURE CHEST, Ashland, OH, 419-289-2831
COLLECTION CONNECTION, Piqua, OH, 513-778-9909
COLLECTOR'S GALLERY, Marion, OH, 614-387-0602
COLLECTOR'S OUTLET, Mentor On The Lake, OH,
    216-257-1141
COMSTOCK'S COLLECTIBLES, Medina, OH, 216-725-4656
CURIO CABINET, Worthington, OH, 614-885-1986
EASTERN ART, Parma, OH, 216-888-6277
EMPORIUM, THE, Bucyrus, OH, 419-562-1943
EXCALIBUR GIFTS, Sandusky, OH, 419-626-3539
GIFT GARDEN, No Olmsted, OH, 216-777-0116
GINGERBREAD HOUSE GIFTS & COL, West Milton, OH,
    513-698-3477
HIDDEN TREASURES, Huron, OH, 419-433-2585
HOUSE OF TRADITION, Perrysburg, OH, 419-874-1151
KATHRYN'S GALLERY OF GIFTS, Solon, OH, 216-498-0234
LAKE CABLE GIFTS & COLLECTIBLES, Canton, OH,
    216-494-4173
LAKESHORE LTD, Huron, OH, 419-433-6168
LITTLE RED GIFT HOUSE, Birmingham, OH, 216-965-5420
LITTLE SHOP ON THE PORTAGE, Woodville, OH,
    419-849-3742
LOLA & DALE GIFTS & COLLECTIBLES, Parma Heights,
    OH, 216-885-0444
MUSIK BOX HAUS, Vermilion, OH, 216-967-4744
NORTH HILL GIFT SHOP, Akron, OH, 216-535-4811
OLDE TYME CLOCKS, Cincinnati, OH, 513-741-9188
PORCELLANA LTD, Hamilton, OH, 513-868-1511
ROCHELLE'S FINE GIFTS, Toledo, OH, 419-472-7673
SAXONY IMPORTS, Cincinnati, OH, 513-621-7800
SCHUMM PHARMACY HALLMARK & GIFTS, Rockford,
    OH, 419-363-3630

SETTLER'S COLLECTIONS, Middlefield, OH, 216-632-1009
STORY BOOK KIDS, Cincinnati, OH, 513-769-5437
STRAWBERRY PATCH, Brunswick, OH, 216-225-7796
STRUBLES OF SHELBY, Shelby, OH, 419-342-2136
STUHLDREHER FLORAL CO, Mansfield, OH, 419-524-5911
TOWNE CENTRE SHOPPE, Streetsboro, OH, 216-626-3106
UP-TOWNE FLOWER & GIFT SHOPPE, Worthington,
    OH, 614-889-1001

OKLAHOMA
COLONIAL FLORISTS, Stillwater, OK, 405-372-9166
CURIOSITY SHOP, THE, Ada, OK, 405-332-5355
DODY'S HALLMARK, Lawton, OK, 405-353-8379
EARL'S JEWELERS, Cushing, OK, 918-225-1685
EMPORIUM - THE GIFT SHOPPE, THE, Ponca City, OK,
    405-762-5345
NORTH POLE CITY, Oklahoma City, OK, 405-685-6635
PERFECT TOUCH, Tulsa, OK, 918-496-8118
SHIRLEY'S GIFTS, Ardmore, OK, 405-223-2116
SUZANNE'S COLLECTORS GALLERY *, Miami, OK,
    918-542-3808
W D GIFTS, Okmulgee, OK, 918-756-2229

OREGON
CROWN SHOWCASE, Portland, OR, 503-280-0669
DAS HAUS-AM-BERG, Salem, OR, 503-363-0669
KESSEL'S COLLECTIBLES & GIFT SHOPPEE, Salem, OR,
    503-362-5342
MANCKE'S COLLECTIBLES, Salem, OR, 503-371-3157
PRESENT PEDDLER, Beaverton, OR, 503-641-6364
TICKLED PINK, Portland, OR, 503-297-4102
TREASURE CHEST GIFT SHOP, Gresham, OR, 503-667-2999

PENNSYLVANIA
BOB'S CARDS & GIFTS, Southampton. PA, 215-364-2872
COLLECTOR'S CHOICE, Pittsburgh, PA, 412-366-4477
COLLECTOR'S MARKETPLACE, Montrose, PA, 717-278-4094
DEN, THE, Lahaska, PA, 215-794-8493
DIGBY'S SIDE DOOR, Mc Murray PA, 412-941-3750
DUTCH INDOOR VILLGE, Lancaster, PA, 717-299-2348
EMPORIUM COLLECTIBLES GALLERY, Erie, PA, 814-833-
    2895
EUROPEAN TREASURES, Pittsburgh, PA, 412-421-8660
GIFT DESIGN GALLERIES, Wilkes-Barre, PA, 717-822-6704
GIFT DESIGN GALLERIES, Whitehall, PA, 610-266-1266
GILLESPIE JEWELER COLLECTORS GALLERY *,
    Northampton, PA, 215-261-0882
GOLDCRAFTERS, Springfield, PA, 610-544-9521
JAMIE'S COLLECTABLES, Reading, PA, 610-373-4270
KRINGLE'S CHRISTMAS BARN & COTTAGE, Scotrun,
    PA, 717-629-3122
LAUCHNOR'S GIFTS & COLLECTABLES, Trexlertown,
    PA, 610-398-3008
LIMITED EDITIONS, Forty Fort, PA, 717-288-0940
LIMITED PLATES & COLLECTIBLES, Collegeville, PA,
    610-489-7799
MARIE'S GIFT SHOP, Tafton, PA, 717-226-3345
MOLE HOLE OF PEDDLERS VILLAGE, THE, Lahaska, PA,
    215-794-7572
NEWTOWN SQUARE GLASS & CHINA, Newtown Square,
    PA, 610-353-7726
PICCADILLY CENTRE, Duncansville, PA, 814-695-8383
SAVILLE'S LIMITED EDITIONS, Pittsburgh, PA,
    412-366-5458
SHAKER TREE STUDIO, Hermitage, PA, 412-347-4141
SOMEONE SPECIAL, Bensalem, PA, 215-245-0919
SPECIAL ATTRACTIONS, Sayre, PA, 717-888-9433
THINGS COLLECTIBLE, Feasterville, PA, 215-355-4733

TODAY'S TREASURES, Pittsburgh, PA, 412-341-5233
WISHING WELL, Reading, PA, 610-921-2566
YEAGLE'S, Lahaska, PA, 215-794-7756

RHODE ISLAND
GOLDEN GOOSE, Smithfield, RI, 401-949-9940

SOUTH CAROLINA
ABRAMS DOLLS & COLLECTIBLES, Conway, SC,
    803-248-9198
CHRISTMAS CELEBRATION, Greenville, SC, 803-242-1804
CHRISTMAS CELEBRATION, Mauldin, SC, 803-277-7373
CHRISTY'S CHRISTMAS, Cayce, SC, 803-794-5152
CURIOSITY SHOPPE, THE, Darlington, SC, 803-665-8686
DUANE'S HALLMARK CARD & GIFT SHOP, Columbia,
    SC, 803-772-2624
TINDER BOX, Myrtle Beach, SC, 803-272-2336
TINDER BOX, Myrtle Beach, SC, 803-626-2654

SOUTH DAKOTA
AKERS GIFTS & COLLECTIBLES, Sioux Falls, SD,
    605-339-1325
GIFT GALLERY, Brookings, SD, 605-692-9405

TENNESSEE
CALICO BUTTERFLY, Memphis, TN, 901-362-8121
COX'S HALLMARK SHOP, Maryville, TN, 615-982-0421
GIFTS UNIQUE, Lenoir City, TN, 615-986-1211
HOUR GLASS II, Chattanooga, TN, 615-877-2328
ORANGE BLOSSOM, Martin, TN, 901-587-5091
PAPILLON INC, Chatanooga, TN, 615-499-2997
PATTY'S HALLMARK, Murfreesboro, TN, 615-890-8310
STAGE CROSSING GIFTS & COLLECTIBLES, Bartlett,
    TN, 901-372-4438

TEXAS
BETTY'S COLLECTABLES LTD *, Harlingen, TX,
    210-423-8234
CHRISTMAS TREASURES, Baytown, TX, 713-421-1581
COLLECTIBLE HEIRLOOMS, Friendswood, TX,
    713-486-5023
ELOISE'S COLLECTIBLES, Katy, TX, 713-578-6655
ELOISE'S COLLECTIBLES, Houston, TX, 713-783-3611
ELOISE'S GIFTS & ANTIQUES, Rockwall, TX, 214-771-6371
GALAXY HALLMARK SHOP, Houston, TX, 713-335-1211
GIFTS CARTOONS COLLECTIBLES, Hurst, TX,
    817-590-0324
HOLIDAY HOUSE, Huntsville, TX, 409-295-7338
KEEPSAKES & KOLLECTIBLES, Spring, TX, 713-353-9233
LACEY'S HALLMARK, Pasadena, TX, 713-998-7171
LOUJON'S GIFTS, Sugar Land, TX, 713-980-1245
MR C COLLECTIBLE CENTER, Carrollton, TX,
    214-242-5100
OPA'S HAUS, New Braunfels, TX, 210-629-1191
SHEPHERD'S SHOPPE, THE, San Antonio, TX,
    210-342-4811
SUNSHINE HOUSE GALLERY, Plano, TX, 214-424-5015
TIMES & CHIMES, Friendswood, TX, 713-488-1574

UTAH
RIVERTON DRUG & GIFT, Riverton, UT, 801-254-7407

VIRGINIA
CREEKSIDE COLLECTIBLES & GIFTS, Winchester, VA,
    703-662-0270
GAZEBO GIFTS, Newport News, VA, 804-591-8387
PLATE SHOPPE, THE, Alexandria, VA, 703-360-1708

WASHINGTON
CHALET, THE, Tacoma, WA, 206-564-0326
GOLD SHOPPE'S COLLECTORS GALLERY, Tacoma, WA,
    206-473-4653
LORETTA'S GIFTS & COLLECTIBLES, Poulsbo, WA,
    360-779-7171
NATALIA'S COLLECTIBLES, Woodinville, WA, 206-481-4575
SERENDIPITY GIFTS & COLLECTIBLES, Puyallup, WA,
    206-770-1990
STEFAN'S EUROPEAN GIFTS, Yakima, WA, 509-457-5503
TANNENBAUM SHOPPE, Leavenworth, WA, 509-548-7014

WEST VIRGINIA
ARACOMA DRUG GIFT GALLERY, Logan, WV, 304-752-3812
FENTON GIFT SHOP, Williamstown, WV, 304-375-7772

WISCONSIN
A COUNTRY MOUSE, Milwaukee, WI, 414-281-4210
BEAUCHENE'S LTD ED, Thiensville, WI, 414-242-0170
CENTURY COIN SERVICE, Green Bay, WI, 414-494-2719
COLLECTIBLES ETC INC, Port Washington, WI,
    414-355-4545
GREEN TREE GIFTS & COLLECTIBLES, Manitowoc, WI,
    414-684-4300
JAN'S HALLMARK & GIFT GALLERY, Delavan, WI,
    414-728-8447
JANE'S COUNTRY COLLECTIBLES, Random Lake, WI,
    414-994-4747
KRISTMAS KRINGLE SHOPPE, Fond Du Lac, WI,
    414-922-3900
P J'S COLLECTIBLES, Green Bay, WI, 414-437-3443
P J'S HALLMARK SHOP, Marinette, WI, 715-735-3940
SPIRIT OF CHRISTMAS, Mayville, WI, 414-387-4648
TIVOLI IMPORTS, Milwaukee, WI, 414-774-7590

INTERNATIONAL MEMBERS

AUSTRALIA
LIBERTY LANE, Sydney, NSW Aust, 011-61-2-261-3595

CANADA
BAKEROSA COLLECTIBLES & BOOKS, London,
    Ont CAN, 519-472-0827
CHORNYJS-HADKE, Sault Ste Marie, Ont CAN,
    705-253-0315
DURAND'S LTD ED, Calgary, Alberta CAN, 403-277-0008
OVER THE RAINBOW COLLECTABLES, Islington,
    Ont CAN, 416-622-6835
PLATEFINDERS, Edmonton, Alberta CAN, 403-435-3603
TOMORROW'S TREASURES, Bobcaygeon, Ont CAN,
    705-738-2147

ENGLAND
CASTLE CHINA GROUP, Warwick, ENG, 44-1926-419102

GLOSSARY

Some Terms Commonly Used by Collectors and Dealers
to Describe Limited Edition Collectibles

Acid-free. A description of paper and materials treated to remove the acids that cause deterioration.

Alabaster. A fine-textured gypsum which is usually white and translucent. Some collectors' plates are made of a material called ivory alabaster which is not translucent, but has the look and patina of old ivory.

Allotment. The number within a limited edition which a manufacturer allows to a given dealer, direct marketer or collector.

Annual. The term is used to describe a plate or other limited edition which is issued yearly. Many annual plates commemorate holidays or anniversaries, and they are commonly named by that special date, i.e. the Annual Bing & Grondahl Christmas plate.

Artist/gallery/publishers' proofs. Originally, the first few prints in an edition of lithographs were used to test colors and then given to the artist. They were not numbered but were signed. Artist's proofs are not considered part of the edition. Gallery and publishers' proofs are used as a means of increasing the number of prints in an edition.

Baby doll. A doll with the proportions of a baby; with a short-limbed body and lips parted to take a nipple.

Back issue. An issue in a series other than the issue that is currently being produced. It can be either open or closed and may or may not be available.

Backstamp. The information on the back of a plate or other limited edition which documents it as part of a limited edition. This information may be hand-painted onto the plate, or it may be incised, or applied as a transfer (decal). Information which typically appears on the backstamp includes the name of the series, name of the item, year of issue, some information about the subject, the artist's name and/or signature, the edition limit, the item's number within that edition, initials of the firing master or production supervisor, etc.

Band. Also known as a rim, as in "24K gold banded, or rimmed." A popular finishing technique is to band plates and bells with gold, platinum or silver which is then adhered to the plate through the firing process. Details from the primary artwork may also be adapted to form a decorative rim.

Bas-relief. A technique in which the collectible has a raised design. This design may be achieved by pouring liquid material into a mold before firing, or by applying a three-dimensional design element to the flat surface of a plate, figurine or other "blank" piece.

Bavaria. A section of Germany that is one of the world's richest sources of kaolin clay, an essential component of fine porcelain. The region is home to a number of renowned porcelain factories.

Bisque or biscuit. A fired ware which has neither a glaze nor enamel applied to it. Bisque may be white or colored. The name comes from its biscuit-like, matte texture.

Body. The basic form of a plate, figurine, bell or other collectible, or its component materials.

Bone ash. Fire is used to reduce animal bones to calcium phosphate, a powder which is an ingredient of bone china or porcelain.

Bone china/bone porcelain. Bone porcelain is similar to hard porcelain in its ingredients, except that bone ash is the main component of the mix and is the primary contributor to the vitrification and translucency. Bone clay allows for extreme thinness and translucency without sacrificing strength or durability.

Bottomstamp. The same as a backstamp, but usually refers to documentation material found on the bottom of a figurine or the inside of a bell.

Bye-lo-baby. Grace Storey Putman copyrighted this life-sized baby doll (three days old) in 1922. This style of baby doll is a favorite among limited edition collectors.

Cameo. Relief decoration with a flat surface around it similar to the look of a jeweler's cameo. A technique used by Wedgwood, Incolay, Avondale and others.

Cancelled plate. A plate that was planned as part of a series, but never produced because of technical problems or lack of interest in early issues.

Canvas transfer process. A lithograph is treated with a latex emulsion. The paper is removed and the image on the latex emulsion is placed on a cotton duck canvas. It is then topcoated, retouched and highlighted by hand before being hand-numbered.

Capodimonte. Originally a fine porcelain produced at a "castle on the mountain" overlooking Naples, the term currently describes a highly ornate style rather than an actual product. Frequently features flowers, fruits and courtly or native figures.

Cast. The process of creating a copy of an original model by pouring liquid clay or slip into a mold.

Ceramic. The generic term for a piece which is made of some form of clay and finished by firing at high temperatures.

Certificate/Certificate of Authenticity. A document which accompanies a limited edition item to establish its place within the edition. Certificates may include information such as the series name, item title, artist's name and/or signature, brief description of the item and its subject, signatures of sponsoring and marketing organizations' representatives, and other documentation material along with the item's individual number or a statement of the edition limit.

Character dolls. These dolls are often created to resemble actors or celebrities. Character dolls also include fairytale images, folk heroes and cartoon characters.

Chasing. A sculpting process in which tiny hammers and punches are used to create decorative details on ornaments.

China. Originally "china" referred to all wares which came from China. Now the term means products which are fired at a high temperature. China usually consists of varying percentages of kaolin clay, feldspar and quartz. Also see "porcelain".

Cinnabar. A red mineral found in volcanic regions, and an ingredient in mercury. It is used to create collectors' items.

Cire perdue. See lost wax.

Clay. A general term for materials used to make ceramic items. Pliable when moist, clay becomes hard and strong when fired. It may be composed of any number of earthen materials.

Cloissone. An enameling process in which thin metal strips are soldered on the base of a piece to create a pattern. Then, various enamels are poured in to provide the color.

Closed edition. A limited edition that is no longer being issued because it has reached the designated limit, or no longer has market appeal.

Closed end edition. A series with a predetermined, and usually pre-announced, number of issues.

Cobalt blue. Also known as Copenhagen blue, this rich color was an early favorite because it was the only color that could withstand high firing temperatures needed for glazing. Cobalt oxide is a black powder when applied, but fires to a deep blue.

Cold cast. A relatively new process which combines polyester resins and a variety of materials (metal powders, ground porcelain, wood shavings and other natural materials). The combination is forced into a mold or die under high pressure and a forging process occurs. Allows for exceptional detailing which can be easily hand-painted.

Collector plate. A limited edition plate which is created to be collected for its decorative appearance.

Commemorative. An item created to mark a special date, holiday or event.

Dealer. An individual or store where collectors can purchase collectibles at retail prices.

Decal. Also known as a transfer, this is a lithographic or silkscreen rendering of a piece of artwork, which is applied to ceramic or other materials and then fired on to fuse it to the surface.

Delftware. Heavy earthenware coated with an opaque white glaze that contains tin oxide. First developed in Delft, Holland in the 16th century.

Drafting. Process for shaping metal into hollowware.

Earthenware. A non-vitrified ceramic made of ball clay, kaolin and pegmatite. Remains porous until glazed and fired at a low temperature.

Edition. A term referring to the number of items created with the same name and decorations.

Embossing. A process of producing an image in relief by using dies or punches on a surface.

Engraving. An intaglio process in which an image is cut into the surface. Term also used to describe a print made by an engraving process.

Etched design. Decoration produced by cutting into a surface with acid. An acid-resistant paint or wax is applied and the design is inscribed through this coating. When immersed in acid, the acid etches the surface to form the design.

Faience. Named after an Italian town, Faenza, faience is similar to Delftware and Majolica because it is earthenware coated with a glaze that contains tin oxide.

Feldspar. When decomposed, this mineral becomes kaolin, which is the essential ingredient in china and porcelain. Left in its undercomposed form, feldspar adds hardness to a ware.

Fire. To heat, and thus harden, a ceramic ware in a kiln.

Firing period. A time period—usually 10-to-75 days, which serves to limit an edition, usually of plates. The number of items is limited to the capacity of the manufacturer over that 10-to-75 days.

First issue. The premiere item in a series, whether closed-ended or open-ended.

French bronze. Also known as "spelter," this is zinc refined to 99.97% purity. It has been used as an alternative to bronze for casting for more than a century.

Glaze. The liquid material which is applied to a ware for various purposes. Cosmetically, it provides shine and decorative value. It also makes the item more durable. Decorations may be applied before or after glaze is applied.

Graphic. A print produced by one of the "original" print processes such as etching, engraving, woodblocks, lithographs and serigraphs. This term is frequently used interchangeably with "print".

Greenware. Undecorated ceramic before it is fired.

Hallmark. The mark or logo of the manufacturer of an item.

Hard paste porcelain. The hardest porcelain made, this material uses feldspar to enhance vitrification and translucency, and is fired at about 2642 degrees Fahrenheit.

Hydro-stone. The hardest form of gypsum cement from which many limited edition collectibles are produced. A registered trademark of the United States Gypsum Co.

Incised. Writing or design which is etched or inscribed into a piece to provide a backstamp or decorative design.

Incolay stone. A man-made material combining minerals including carnelian and crystal quartz. Used by Incolay Studios to make cameo-style collectibles.

Inlay. To fill an etched or incised design with another material such as enamel, metal or jewels.

In stock. A term used to refer to an item of a given edition still available from the producers' inventory.

Issue. As a verb, to introduce. As a noun, the term means an item within a series.

Issue Price. The price established by the manufacturer or principal marketer when a collectible is introduced.

Jasper ware. Josiah Wedgwood's unglazed stoneware material, first introduced in the 1770s. Although jasper is white in its original form, it can be stained a medium blue called "Wedgwood Blue," or a darker blue, black, green, lilac, yellow, brown and gray. Colored Wedgwood "bodies" are often decorated with white bas-relief, or vice/versa.

Kaolin. The essential ingredient in china and porcelain, this special clay is found in several spots throughout the world. Many famous porcelain factories are located near these deposits.

Lead crystal. Lead oxide is added to glass to give it weight, brilliance and a clear ring. Lead crystal has a lead oxide content of 24%, while "full" lead crystal contains more than 30%.

Limited edition. An item produced only in a certain quantity or only during a certain time period. Collectible editions are limited by: specific numbers, years, specific time periods or firing periods.

Limoges. A town in France with rich deposits of kaolin clay and other essential ingredients for making china and porcelain. Home of a number of famed porcelain manufacturers.

Lost wax. An ancient method used by sculptors to create a detailed wax "positive" which is then used to form a ceramic "negative" shell. This shell becomes the original mold used in the creation of finely carved three-dimensional pieces.

Majolica. Similar to Delftware and Faience, this glazed earthenware was first produced on the Spanish island, Majorca.

Market. The organized buy-sell medium for collectibles.

Marks or markings. The logo or insignia which certifies that an item was made by a particular firm.

Miniatures. Collectibles, including figurines, plates, graphics, dolls, ornaments and bells, which are very small originals or smaller versions of larger pieces. Usually finely detailed, many figurine miniatures are created using the lost wax process.

Mint condition. The term originated in coin collecting. In limited edition collectibles, it means that an item is still in its original, like-new condition, with all accompanying documents.

Mold. The form that supplies the shape of a plate, bell, figurine or other items.

Open edition. A reproduction of an original with no limit on time of production or the number of pieces produced, and no announcement of edition size.

Open-ended series. A collection of plates or other limited editions which appear at intervals, usually annually, with no limit as to the number of years it will be produced.

Overglaze. A decoration which is applied to an item after its original glazing and firing.

Paste. The raw material of porcelain before shaping and firing. See "slip."

Pewter. An alloy containing at least 85% tin.

Polyester resin. A bonding compound mixed with powdered, ground or chipped materials (pulverized porcelain, wood, shells and other materials) to form cold-cast products. Cold-cast porcelain is made by mixing resin with porcelain dust; cold-cast bronze is made by blending resin with ground bronze.

Porcelain. Made of kaolin, quartz and feldspar, porcelain is fired at up to 1450 degrees centigrade. Porcelain is noted for its translucency and its true ring. Also called "china".

Pottery. Ceramic ware, more specifically that which is earthenware or non-vitrified. Also a term for manufacturing plants where such objects are made and fired.

Primary market. The first buy-sell market used by manufacturers to reach collectors. Sold at issue price, collectibles are offered to the public through retailers, direct mail and home shopping networks.

Print. A photomechanical reproduction process such as offset, lithography, collotypes and letterpress.

Printed remarque. A hand drawn image by the artist that is photomechanically reproduced in the margin of a print.

Queen's ware. Cream-colored earthenware developed by Josiah Wedgwood; now used as a generic term for similar materials.

Quote. The average selling price of a collectible at any given time. It may be the issue price, or above or below.

Release price. The price for which each print in the edition is sold until the edition is sold out and a secondary market is established.

Relief. A raised design in various levels above a background.

Remarque. A hand-drawn original image by the artist, either in pencil, pen and ink, watercolor or oil that is sketched in the margin of a limited edition print.

Resin. See polyester resin.

Retired. No longer available from the producer, and none of the pieces will ever be produced again.

Sculpted crystal. A general term for products made by assembling faceted Austrian crystal prisms with a 32 % lead content

Second. An item which is not first quality and should not be included in the limited edition. Normally, such items are destroyed or at least marked on the backstamp or bottomstamp to indicate they are not first quality.

Secondary market. Once the original edition has been sold out, the buying and selling among collectors, through dealers or exchanges, takes place on the "secondary" market.

Secondary market price. The price a customer is willing to sell or buy an item for once it is no longer available on the primary market. These prices will vary from one part of the country to another, depending on the supply and demand for the collectible.

Serigraphy. A direct printing process used by artists to design, make and print their own stencils. A serigraph differs from other prints in that its images are created with paint films instead of printing inks.

Signed and numbered. Each print is signed and consecutively numbered by the artist, in pencil, either in the image area or in the margin. Edition size is limited.

Signed in the plate. The only signature on the artwork is reproduced from the artist's original signature. Not necessarily limited in edition size.

Signed only. Usually refers to a print that is signed without consecutive numbers. May not be limited in edition size.

Silver crystal. Faceted Austrian crystal prisms with a 32% lead content used to produce sculpted crystal. The name is registered by Swarovski.

Silverplate. A process of manufacturing ornaments in which pure silver is electroplated onto a base metal, usually brass or pewter.

Slip. A creamy material used to fill the molds in making greenware. Formulas for slip are closely guarded secrets.

Soft paste. A mixture of clay and ground glass first used in Europe to produce china. The vitrification point of soft paste is too low to produce the hardness required for true porcelain.

Sold out. The classification given to an edition which has been 100% sold out by the producer.

Spin casting. A process of casting multiple ornaments from rubber molds; commonly used for low-temperature metals such as pewter.

Sterling silver. An alloy of 92-1/2% pure silver and 7-1/2% copper.

Stoneware. A vitrified ceramic material, usually a silicate clay that is very hard, heavy and impervious to liquids and most stains.

Suspended. Not currently available from the producer — production has ceased but may be resumed at a later date.

Terra cotta. A reddish earthenware or a general term for any fired clay.

Tin glaze. The glaze on Delftware, Faience or Majolica. This material results in a heavy white and opaque surface after firing.

Transfer. See decal.

Translucency. Allowing light to shine through a nontransparent object. A positive quality of fine china or porcelain.

Triptych. A three-panel art piece, often of religious significance.

Underglaze. A decoration which is applied before the final glazing and firing of an item. Most often, such decorations are painted by hand.

Vinyl. A relatively new synthetic material developed with the special properties of color, durability and skin-like texture which is molded into collectible dolls.

Vitrification. The process by which ceramic artwork becomes vitrified or totally nonporous at high temperatures.

Collectors' Information Bureau
PRICE INDEX 1997

Limited Edition
Plates • Figurines • Cottages • Bells • Graphics • Ornaments • Dolls • Steins

This index includes thousands of the most widely traded limited editions in today's collectibles market. It is based on surveys and interviews with several hundred of the most experienced and informed limited edition dealers in the United States, as well as many independent market advisors.

HOW TO USE THIS INDEX

Listings are set up using the following format:

| Enesco Corporation ❶ |

Precious Moments Figurines ❷ — S. Butcher ❸

❹ ❺ ❻ ❼ ❽ ❾
1979   Praise the Lord Anyhow-E1374B   Retrd.   1982   8.00   95-130

---

❶ Enesco Corporation = Company Name

❷ Precious Moments Figurines = Series Name

❸ S. Butcher = Artist's Name. The word "Various" may also be indicated, meaning that several artists have created pieces within the series. The artist name then appears after the title of the collectible. In some cases, the artist's name will be indicated after the series name "with exceptions noted."

❹ 1979 = Year of Issue

❺ Praise the Lord Anyhow-E1374B = Title of the collectible. Many titles also include the model number for further identification purposes.

❻ Retrd. = Edition Limit. In this case, the collectible is no longer available from the producer. The edition limit category generally refers to the number of items created with the same name and decoration. Edition limits may indicate a specific number (i.e. 10,000) or the number of firing days for plates (i.e. 100-day, the capacity of the manufacturer to produce collectibles during a given firing period). Refer to "Open," "Suspd.," "Annual," and "Yr. Iss." under "Terms and Abbreviations" below.

❼ 1982 = Year of Retirement. May also indicate the year the manufacturer ceased production of the collectible. If N/A appears in this column, it indicates the information is not available at this time, but research is continuing.
Note: In the plate section, the year of retirement may not be indicated because many plates are limited to firing days and not years.

❽ 8.00 = Original Issue Price in U.S. Dollars

❾ 95-130 = Current Quote Price listed may show a price or price range. Quotes are based on interviews with retailers across the country, who provide their actual sales transactions. Quotes have been rounded up to the nearest dollar. Quote may also reflect a price increase or decrease for pieces that are not retired or closed.

A Special Note to Beatrix Potter, Boyds Bears, Cherished Teddies, Disney Classics, Goebel Miniatures, M.I. Hummel and Precious Moments Collectors: *These collectibles are engraved with a special annual mark. This emblem changes with each production year. The secondary market value for each piece varies because of these distinctive yearly markings. Our pricing reflects an average for all years.*

A Special Note to Hallmark Keepsake Ornament Collectors: *All quotes in this section are for ornaments in mint condition in their original box.*

A Special Note to Department 56 Collectors: *Year of Introduction indicates the year in which the piece was designed, sculpted and copyrighted. It is possible these pieces may not be available to the collectors until the following calendar year.*

A Special Note to Lilliput Lane Collectors: *Prices in the quote column may reflect a primary market price increase <u>or</u> decrease as compared with the original issue price. These changes have occured over a period of years.*

TERMS AND ABBREVIATIONS

Annual = Issued once a year.
A/P = Artist Proof.
Closed = An item or series no longer in production.
G/P = Gallery Proof.
N/A = Not available at this time.
Open = Not limited by number or time, available until manufacturer stops production, "retires" or "closes" the item or series.

P/P = Publisher's Proof
Retrd. = Retired. No longer available from the producer. None of the pieces will ever be produced again.
R/P = Retouched Proof.
Set = Refers to two or more items issued together for a single price.
S/N = Signed and Numbered.

S/O = Sold Out.
S/P = Studio Proof.
Suspd. = Suspended. Not currently being produced: may be produced in the future.
Unkn. = Unknown.
Yr. Iss. = Year of issue (limited to a calendar year).
28-day, 10-day, etc. = Limited to this many production (or firing) days, usually not consecutive.

BELLS

Ace Product Management Group, Inc.

Harley-Davidson Crystal Christmas Bells - Ace

YEAR ISSUE		EDITION LIMIT	YEAR RETD.	ISSUE PRICE	*QUOTE U.S.$
1988	Crystal Bell 99212-89V	Yr.Iss.	1988	29.95	30
1989	Crystal Bell 99212-90V	Yr.Iss.	1989	29.95	30
1990	Crystal Bell 99212-91V	Yr.Iss.	1990	29.95	30
1991	Crystal Bell 99212-92V	Yr.Iss.	1991	32.95	33
1992	Crystal Bell 99212-93Z	Yr.Iss.	1992	38.00	38

Harley-Davidson Porcelain Holiday Bells - Ace

1993	Checking It Twice 99411-94Z	Yr.Iss.	1993	25.00	25
1994	Santa's Predicament 99439-95Z	Yr.Iss.	1994	25.00	25
1995	Finding The Way 99449-96Z	Yr.Iss.	1995	25.00	25

Artists of the World

DeGrazia Bells - T. DeGrazia

1980	Festival of Lights	5,000	N/A	40.00	85-100
1980	Los Ninos	7,500	N/A	40.00	75-100
1980	Los Ninos (signed)	500	N/A	80.00	200-250

Belleek

Belleek Bells - Belleek

1988	Bell, 1st Ed.	Yr.Iss.		38.00	38
1989	Tower, 2nd Ed.	Yr.Iss.		35.00	35
1990	Leprechaun, 3rd Ed.	Yr.Iss.		30.00	30
1991	Church, 4th Ed.	Yr.Iss.		32.00	32
1992	Cottage, 5th Ed.	Yr.Iss.		30.00	30
1993	Pub, 6th Ed.	Yr.Iss.		30.00	30
1994	Castle, 7th Ed.	Yr.Iss.		30.00	30
1995	Georgian House, 8th Ed.	Yr.Iss.		30.00	30
1996	Cathedral, 9th Ed.	Yr.Iss.		30.00	30

Twelve Days of Christmas - Belleek

1991	A Partridge in a Pear Tree	Yr.Iss.		30.00	30
1992	Two Turtle Doves	Yr.Iss.		30.00	30
1993	Three French Hens	Yr.Iss.		30.00	30
1994	Four Calling Birds	Yr.Iss.		30.00	30
1995	Five Golden Rings	Yr.Iss.		30.00	30

Dave Grossman Designs

Norman Rockwell Collection - Rockwell-Inspired

1975	Faces of Christmas NRB-75	Retrd.	N/A	12.50	35
1976	Drum for Tommy NRB-76	Retrd.	N/A	12.00	30
1976	Ben Franklin (Bicentennial)	Retrd.	N/A	12.50	25
1980	Leapfrog NRB-80	Retrd.	N/A	50.00	60

Enesco Corporation

Cherished Teddies - P. Hillman

1992	Angel Bell-906530	Suspd.		20.00	45-70

Memories of Yesterday Bell - M. Attwell

1990	Here Comes the Bride-God Bless Her-523100	Suspd.		25.00	25
1994	Time For Bed-525243	Open		25.00	25

Precious Moments Annual Bells - S. Butcher

1981	Let the Heavens Rejoice-E-5622-	Yr.Iss.	1981	15.00	175-240
1982	I'll Play My Drum for Him-E-2358	Yr.Iss.	1982	17.00	65-75
1983	Surrounded With Joy-E-0522	Yr.Iss.	1983	18.00	40-65
1984	Wishing You a Merry Christmas-E-5393	Yr.Iss.	1984	19.00	45
1985	God Sent His Love-15873	Yr.Iss.	1985	19.00	40-50
1986	Wishing You a Cozy Christmas-102318	Yr.Iss.	1986	20.00	40
1987	Love is the Best Gift of All-109835	Yr.Iss.	1987	22.50	40
1988	Time To Wish You a Merry Christmas -115304	Yr.Iss.	1988	25.00	43
1989	Oh Holy Night-522821	Yr.Iss.	1989	25.00	35
1990	Once Upon A Holy Night-523828	Yr.Iss.	1990	25.00	35
1991	May Your Christmas Be Merry-524182	Yr.Iss.	1991	25.00	25-35
1992	But The Greatest Of These Is Love-527726	Yr.Iss.	1992	25.00	25-40
1993	Wishing You The Sweetest Christmas-530174	Yr.Iss.	1993	25.00	30-45
1994	Your're As Pretty as a Christmas Tree-604216	Yr.Iss.	1994	27.50	28-40

Precious Moments Various Bells - S. Butcher

1981	Jesus Loves Me (B)-E-5208	Suspd.		15.00	40-50
1981	Jesus Loves Me (G)-E-5209	Suspd.		15.00	50
1981	Prayer Changes Things-E-5210	Suspd.		15.00	55-60
1981	God Understands-E-5211	Retrd.	N/A	15.00	40-60
1981	We Have Seen His Star-E-5620	Suspd.		15.00	50-60
1981	Jesus Is Born-E-5623	Suspd.		15.00	50-65
1982	The Lord Bless You and Keep You-E-7175	Suspd.		17.00	40-50
1982	The Lord Bless You and Keep You-E-7176	Suspd.		17.00	55-65
1982	The Lord Bless You and Keep You-E-7179	Suspd.		22.50	65-85
1982	Mother Sew Dear-E-7181	Suspd.		17.00	35-45
1982	The Purr-fect Grandma-E-7183	Suspd.		17.00	50-60

Fenton Art Glass Company

American Classic Series - M. Dickinson

1986	Jupiter Train, 6 1/2" on Opal Satin	5,000	1986	50.00	50
1986	Studebaker-Garford Car, 6 1/2" on Opal Satin	5,000	1986	50.00	50

Artist Series - Various

1982	After The Snow - D. Johnson	15,000	1982	14.50	15
1983	Winter Chapel - D. Johnson	15,000	1984	15.00	15
1985	Flying Geese - D. Johnson	15,000	1985	15.00	15
1986	The Hummingbird - D. Johnson	15,000	1986	15.00	15
1987	Out in the Country - L. Everson	15,000	1987	15.00	15
1988	Serenity - F. Burton	5,000	1988	16.50	17
1989	Househunting - D. Barbour	5,000	1989	16.50	17

Childhood Treasurers Series - Various

1983	Teddy Bear, 4 1/2" - D. Johnson	15,000	1983	15.00	15
1984	Hobby Horse, 4 1/2" - L. Everson	15,000	1984	15.00	15
1985	Clown, 4 1/2" - L. Everson	15,000	1985	17.50	18
1986	Playful Kitten, 4 1/2" - L. Everson	15,000	1986	15.00	15
1987	Frisky Pup, 4 1/2" - D. Barbour	15,000	1987	15.00	15
1988	Castles in the Air, 4 1/2" - D. Barbour	5,000	1988	16.50	17
1989	A Child's Cuddly Friend, 4 1/2" - D. Johnson	5,000	1989	16.50	17

Christmas - Various

1978	Christmas Morn - M. Dickinson	Yr.Iss.	1978	25.00	25
1979	Nature's Christmas - K. Cunningham	Yr.Iss.	1979	30.00	30
1980	Going Home - D. Johnson	Yr.Iss.	1980	32.50	33
1981	All Is Calm - D. Johnson	Yr.Iss.	1981	35.00	35
1982	Country Christmas - R. Spindler	Yr.Iss.	1982	35.00	35
1983	Anticipation - D. Johnson	7,500	1983	35.00	35
1984	Expectation - D. Johnson	7,500	1984	37.50	38
1985	Heart's Desire - D. Johnson	7,500	1986	37.50	38
1987	Sharing The Spirit - L. Everson	Yr.Iss.	1987	37.50	38
1987	Cardinal in the Churchyard - D. Johnson	4,500	1987	29.50	30
1988	A Chickadee Ballet - D. Johnson	4,500	1988	29.50	30
1989	Downy Pecker - Chiseled Song - D. Johnson	4,500	1989	29.50	30
1990	A Blue Bird in Snowfall - D. Johnson	4,500	1990	29.50	30
1990	Sleigh Ride - F. Burton	3,500	1990	39.00	39
1991	Christmas Eve - F. Burton	3,500	1991	35.00	35
1992	Family Tradition - F. Burton	3,500	1992	39.00	39
1993	Family Holiday - F. Burton	3,500	1993	39.50	40
1994	Silent Night - F. Burton	2,500	1994	45.00	45
1995	Our Home Is Blessed - F. Burton	2,500	1995	45.00	45
1996	Star of Wonder - F. Burton	2,500		48.00	48

Christmas Limited Edition - M. Reynolds, unless otherwise noted

1992	Winter on Twilight Blue, 6 1/2"	2,500	1992	29.50	30
1993	Manager Scene on Ruby, 6 1/2"	2,500	1993	39.50	40
1993	Reindeer on Blue, 6 1/2"	2,500	1993	30.00	30
1993	Floral on Green-Musical, 6 1/2"	2,500	1993	39.50	40
1994	Magnolia on Gold, 6 1/2"	1,000	1994	35.00	35
1994	Angel on Ivory, 6 1/2"	1,000	1994	39.50	40
1994	Partridge on Ruby-Musical, 6 1/2"	1,000	1994	48.50	49
1995	Bow & Holly on Ivory, 6 1/2"	900	1995	39.50	40
1995	Chickadee on Gold, 6 1/2"	900	1995	39.50	40
1995	Iced Poinsettia on Ruby, 5 1/2"	900	1995	45.00	45
1995	Angel, Heavenly Bell, 5 3/4" - R. Spindler	1,900	1995	35.00	35
1996	Holly Berries on Gold, 6 1/2"	1,500		39.50	40
1996	Golden Partridge on Spruce, 6 1/2"	1,500		35.00	35
1996	Moonlit Meadow on Ruby, 6 1/2" - R. Spindler	1,500		45.00	45
1996	Nativity Scene on Ivory, 6 1/2" - R. Spindler	1,500		49.00	49
1996	Golden Winged Angel, Hndpt. 6 1/2"	1,500		39.50	40
1996	Golden Winged Angel, 6"	2,500		39.50	40

Connoisseur Bell - Various

1983	Bell, Burmese Handpainted - L. Everson	2,000	1983	50.00	95
1983	Craftsman Bell, White Satin Carnival - Fenton	3,500	1983	25.00	50
1984	Bell, Famous Women's Ruby Satin Irid. - Fenton	3,500	1984	50.00	50
1985	Bell, 6 1/2" Burmese, Hndpt. - L. Everson	2,500	1985	55.00	95
1986	Bell, Burmese-Shells, Hndpt. - D. Barbour	2,500	1986	60.00	100
1988	Bell, 7" Wisteria, Hndpt. - L. Everson	4,000	1988	45.00	85
1989	Bell, 7" Handpainted Rosalene Satin - L. Everson	3,500	1989	50.00	75
1991	Bell, 7" Roses on Rosalene, Hndpt. - M. Reynolds	2,000	1991	50.00	60

Designer Bells - Various

1996	Floral Medallion, 6" - M. Reynolds	2,500	1996	60.00	60
1996	Gardenia, 7" - R. Spindler	2,500	1996	55.00	55
1996	Gilded Berry, 6 1/2" - F. Burton	2,500	1996	60.00	60
1996	Wild Rose, 5 1/2" - K. Plauche	2,500	1996	50.00	50

Designer Series - Various

1983	Lighthouse Point, 6" - M. Dickinson	1,000	1983	55.00	55
1983	Down Home, 6" - G. Finn	1,000	1983	55.00	55

1984	Smoke 'N Cinders, 6" - M. Dickinson	1,250	1984	55.00	55
1984	Majestic Flight, 6" - B. Cumberledge	1,250	1984	55.00	55
1985	In Season, 6" - M. Dickinson	1,250	1985	55.00	55
1985	Nature's Grace, 6" - B. Cumberland	1,250	1985	55.00	55
1985	Statue of Liberty, 6" - S. Bryan	1,250	1985	55.00	55
1986	Statue of Liberty, 6" - S. Bryan	1,250	1986	55.00	55

Mary Gregory - M. Reynolds

1993	Bell, 6" Ruby	Closed	1993	49.00	49
1994	Bell, 6" Ruby - Loves Me, Loves Me Not	Closed	1994	49.00	49
1995	Bell, 6 1/2"	Closed	1995	49.00	49

Mother's Day Series - Various

1980	New Born - L. Everson	Closed	1980	25.00	25
1981	Gentle Fawn - L. Everson	Closed	1981	27.50	28
1982	Nature's Awakening - L. Everson	Closed	1982	28.50	29
1983	Where's Mom - L. Everson	Closed	1983	28.50	29
1984	Precious Panda - L. Everson	Closed	1984	28.50	29
1985	Mother's Little Lamb - L. Everson	Closed	1985	35.00	35
1990	White Swan - L. Everson	Closed	1990	35.00	35
1990	White Swan (Musical) - L. Everson	Closed	1990	45.00	45
1991	Mother's Watchful Eye - M. Reynolds	Closed	1991	35.00	35
1992	Let's Play With Mom - M. Reynolds	Closed	1992	37.50	38
1993	Mother Deer - M. Reynolds	Closed	1993	39.50	40
1994	Loving Puppy - M. Reynolds	Closed	1994	39.50	40

Valentine's Day Series - M. Reynolds

1992	Bell, 6" Vining Hearts Hndpt. Opal Irid.	Closed	1992	35.00	35

Goebel/M.I. Hummel

M.I. Hummel Collectibles Annual Bells - M. I. Hummel

1978	Let's Sing 700	Closed	N/A	50.00	75-100
1979	Farewell 701	Closed	N/A	70.00	75
1980	Thoughtful 702	Closed	N/A	85.00	75
1981	In Tune 703	Closed	N/A	85.00	85-100
1982	She Loves Me, She Loves Me Not 704	Closed	N/A	90.00	125
1983	Knit One 705	Closed	N/A	90.00	125
1984	Mountaineer 706	Closed	N/A	90.00	125
1985	Sweet Song 707	Closed	N/A	90.00	125
1986	Sing Along 708	Closed	N/A	100.00	150-200
1987	With Loving Greetings 709	Closed	N/A	110.00	175-200
1988	Busy Student 710	Closed	N/A	120.00	130-175
1989	Latest News 711	Closed	N/A	135.00	175-200
1990	What's New? 712	Closed	N/A	140.00	200
1991	Favorite Pet 713	Closed	N/A	150.00	150-200
1992	Whistler's Duet 714	Closed	N/A	160.00	175-225

Gorham

Currier & Ives - Mini Bells - Currier & Ives

1976	Christmas Sleigh Ride	Annual	1976	9.95	35
1977	American Homestead	Annual	1977	9.95	25
1978	Yule Logs	Annual	1978	12.95	20
1979	Sleigh Ride	Annual	1979	14.95	20
1980	Christmas in the Country	Annual	1980	14.95	20
1981	Christmas Tree	Annual	1981	14.95	18
1982	Christmas Visitation	Annual	1982	16.50	18
1983	Winter Wonderland	Annual	1983	16.50	18
1984	Hitching Up	Annual	1984	16.50	18
1985	Skaters Holiday	Annual	1985	17.50	18
1986	Central Park in Winter	Annual	1986	17.50	18
1987	Early Winter	Annual	1987	19.00	19

Mini Bells - N. Rockwell

1981	Tiny Tim	Annual	1981	19.75	20
1982	Planning Christmas Visit	Annual	1982	20.00	20

Various - N. Rockwell

1975	Sweet Song So Young	Annual	1975	19.50	50
1975	Santa's Helpers	Annual	1975	19.50	50
1975	Tavern Sign Painter	Annual	1975	19.50	30
1976	Flowers in Tender Bloom	Annual	1976	19.50	40
1976	Snow Sculpture	Annual	1976	19.50	45
1977	Fondly Do We Remember	Annual	1977	19.50	55
1977	Chilling Chore (Christmas)	Annual	1977	19.50	35
1978	Gaily Sharing Vintage Times	Annual	1978	22.50	23
1978	Gay Blades (Christmas)	Annual	1978	22.50	23
1979	Beguiling Buttercup	Annual	1979	24.50	45
1979	A Boy Meets His Dog (Christmas)	Annual	1979	24.50	50
1980	Flying High	Annual	1980	27.50	28
1980	Chilly Reception (Christmas)	Annual	1980	27.50	28
1981	Sweet Serenade	Annual	1981	27.50	45
1981	Ski Skills (Christmas)	Annual	1981	27.50	45
1982	Young Mans Fancy	Annual	1982	29.50	30
1982	Coal Season's Coming	Annual	1982	29.50	30
1983	Christmas Medley	Annual	1983	29.50	30
1983	The Milkmaid	Annual	1983	29.50	50
1984	Tiny Tim	Annual	1984	29.50	50
1984	Young Love	Annual	1984	29.50	50
1984	Marriage License	Annual	1984	32.50	33
1984	Yarn Spinner	5,000	1984	32.50	33
1985	Yuletide Reflections	5,000	1985	32.50	50
1986	Home For The Holidays	5,000	1986	32.50	33

YEAR ISSUE		EDITION LIMIT	YEAR RETD.	ISSUE PRICE	*QUOTE U.S. $
1986	On Top of the World	5,000	1986	32.50	45
1987	Merry Christmas Grandma	5,000	1987	32.50	33
1987	The Artist	5,000	1987	32.50	33
1988	The Homecoming	15,000	1988	37.50	38

Kirk Stieff

Bell - Kirk Stieff
1992	Santa's Workshop	3,000		40.00	40
1993	Santa's Reindeer	Closed	N/A	30.00	30

Musical Bells - Kirk Stieff
1977	Annual Bell 1977	Closed	N/A	17.95	90-125
1978	Annual Bell 1978	Closed	N/A	17.95	80-100
1979	Annual Bell 1979	Closed	N/A	17.95	50
1980	Annual Bell 1980	Closed	N/A	19.95	55
1981	Annual Bell 1981	Closed	N/A	19.95	80
1982	Annual Bell 1982	Closed	N/A	19.95	65-95
1983	Annual Bell 1983	Closed	N/A	19.95	55-65
1984	Annual Bell 1984	Closed	N/A	19.95	40
1985	Annual Bell 1985	Closed	N/A	19.95	50
1986	Annual Bell 1986	Closed	N/A	19.95	60
1987	Annual Bell 1987	Closed	N/A	19.95	45
1988	Annual Bell 1988	Closed	N/A	22.50	40-50
1989	Annual Bell 1989	Closed	N/A	25.00	35
1990	Annual Bell 1990	Closed	N/A	27.00	35
1991	Annual Bell 1991	Closed	N/A	28.00	35
1992	Annual Bell 1992	Closed	N/A	30.00	30
1993	Annual Bell 1993	Closed	N/A	30.00	30
1994	Annual Bell 1994	Open	N/A	30.00	30

Lance Corporation

Hudson Pewter Bicentennial Bells - P.W. Baston
1974	Benjamin Franklin	Closed	1977	Unkn.	70-80
1974	George Washington	Closed	1977	Unkn.	30-40
1974	James Madison	Closed	1977	Unkn.	30-40
1974	John Adams	Closed	1977	Unkn.	100-125
1974	Thomas Jefferson	Closed	1977	Unkn.	40-50

Lenox China

Songs of Christmas - Unknown
1991	We Wish You a Merry Christmas	Yr.Iss.	1992	49.00	49
1992	Deck the Halls	Yr.Iss.	1993	53.00	53
1993	Jingle Bells	Yr.Iss.	1994	57.00	57
1994	Silver Bells	Yr.Iss.	1995	62.00	62
1995	Hark The Herald Angels Sing	Yr.Iss.	1996	62.50	63

Lenox Collections

Bird Bells - Unknown
1991	Bluebird	Open		57.00	57
1991	Chickadee	Open		57.00	57
1991	Hummingbird	Open		57.00	57
1992	Robin Bell	Open		57.00	57

Carousel Bell - Unknown
1992	Carousel Horse	Open		45.00	45

Crystal Christmas Bell - Lenox
1981	Partridge in a Pear Tree	15,000	1981	55.00	55
1982	Holy Family Bell	15,000	1982	55.00	55
1983	Three Wise Men	15,000	1983	55.00	55
1984	Dove Bell	15,000	1984	57.00	57
1985	Santa Claus Bell	15,000	1985	57.00	57
1986	Dashing Through the Snow Bell	15,000	1986	64.00	64
1987	Heralding Angel Bell	15,000	1987	76.00	76
1991	Celestial Harpist	15,000	1991	75.00	75

Lenox Crystal

Annual Bell Series - Lenox
1987	Partridge Bell	Yr.Iss.	1990	45.00	45
1988	Angel Bell	Open	1991	45.00	45
1989	St. Nicholas Bell	Open	1991	45.00	45
1990	Christmas Tree Bell	Open	1993	49.00	49
1991	Teddy Bear Bell	Yr.Iss.	1992	49.00	49
1992	Snowman Bell	Yr.Iss.	1993	49.00	49
1993	Nutcracker Bell	Yr.Iss.	1994	49.00	49
1994	Candle Bell	Yr.Iss.	1995	49.00	49
1995	Bell	Yr.Iss.	1996	49.50	50

Lladró

Lladró Bell - Lladró
XX	Crystal Wedding Bell L4500	Closed	N/A	N/A	195

Lladró Christmas Bell - Lladró
1987	Christmas Bell - L5458M	Annual	1987	29.50	70-85
1988	Christmas Bell - L5525M	Annual	1988	32.50	35-45
1989	Christmas Bell - L5616M	Annual	1989	32.50	100-125
1990	Christmas Bell - L5641M	Annual	1990	34.50	60
1991	Christmas Bell - L5803M	Annual	1991	37.50	45
1992	Christmas Bell - L5913M	Annual	1992	37.50	45
1993	Christmas Bell - L6010M	Annual	1993	37.50	50
1994	Christmas Bell - L6139M	Annual	1994	39.50	45-65
1995	Christmas Bell - L6206M	Annual	1995	39.50	45-55

YEAR ISSUE		EDITION LIMIT	YEAR RETD.	ISSUE PRICE	*QUOTE U.S. $
1996	Christmas Bell - L6297M	Annual		39.50	40

Lladró Limited Edition Bell - Lladró
1994	Eternal Love 7542M	Annual	1994	95.00	95

Lowell Davis Farm Club

RFD Bell - L. Davis
1979	Blossom	Closed	1983	65.00	400
1979	Kate	Closed	1983	65.00	375-400
1979	Willy	Closed	1983	65.00	375-400
1979	Caruso	Closed	1983	65.00	275-400
1979	Wilbur	Closed	1983	65.00	375-400
1979	Old Blue Lead	Closed	1983	65.00	275-400
1993	Cow Bell "Blossom"	Closed	1994	65.00	75-90
1993	Mule Bell "Kate"	Closed	1994	65.00	75-90
1993	Goat Bell "Willy"	Closed	1994	65.00	75-90
1993	Rooster Bell "Caruso"	Closed	1994	65.00	75-90
1993	Pig Bell "Wilbur"	Closed	1994	65.00	75-90
1993	Dog Bell "Old Blue and Lead"	Closed	1994	65.00	75-90

Old World Christmas

Porcelain Christmas - E.M. Merck
1988	1st Edition Santa Bell	Retrd.	1988	10.00	10
1989	2nd Edition Santa Bell	Retrd.	1989	10.00	10

Reed & Barton

Noel Musical Bells - Reed & Barton
1980	Bell 1980	Closed	1980	20.00	55-70
1981	Bell 1981	Closed	1981	22.50	50-60
1982	Bell 1982	Closed	1982	22.50	35-50
1983	Bell 1983	Closed	1983	22.50	35-50
1984	Bell 1984	Closed	1984	22.50	40-60
1985	Bell 1985	Closed	1985	25.00	30-55
1986	Bell 1986	Closed	1986	25.00	50-60
1987	Bell 1987	Closed	1987	25.00	25-55
1988	Bell 1988	Closed	1988	25.00	35-60
1989	Bell 1989	Closed	1989	25.00	45-60
1990	Bell 1990	Closed	1990	27.50	35
1991	Bell 1991	Closed	1991	30.00	35
1992	Bell 1992	Closed	1992	30.00	35-45
1993	Bell 1993	Yr.Iss.	1993	30.00	30-40
1994	Bell 1994	Yr.Iss.	1994	30.00	35-45
1995	Bell 1995	Yr.Iss.	1995	30.00	30
1996	Bell 1996	Yr.Iss.		30.00	30

Yuletide Bell - Reed & Barton
1981	Yuletide Holiday	Closed	1981	14.00	25
1982	Little Shepherd	Closed	1982	14.00	25
1983	Perfect Angel	Closed	1983	15.00	25
1984	Drummer Boy	Closed	1984	15.00	25
1985	Caroler	Closed	1985	16.50	25
1986	Night Before Christmas	Closed	1986	16.50	25
1987	Jolly St. Nick	Closed	1987	16.50	25
1988	Christmas Morning	Closed	1988	16.50	25
1989	The Bell Ringer	Closed	1989	16.50	25
1990	The Wreath Bearer	Closed	1990	18.50	20
1991	A Special Gift	Closed	1991	22.50	25
1992	My Special Friend	Closed	1992	22.50	25
1993	My Christmas Present	Yr.Iss.	1993	22.50	25
1994	Holiday Wishes	Yr.Iss.	1994	22.50	25
1995	Christmas Puppy	Yr.Iss.	1995	20.00	20
1996	Yuletide Bell	Yr.Iss.		22.50	23

River Shore

Norman Rockwell Single Issues - N. Rockwell
1981	Grandpa's Guardian	7,000		45.00	45
1981	Looking Out to Sea	7,000		45.00	95
1981	Spring Flowers	347		175.00	175

Rockwell Children Series I - N. Rockwell
1977	First Day of School	7,500		30.00	75
1977	Flowers for Mother	7,500		30.00	60
1977	Football Hero	7,500		30.00	75
1977	School Play	7,500		30.00	75

Rockwell Children Series II - N. Rockwell
1978	Dressing Up	15,000		35.00	50
1978	Five Cents A Glass	15,000		35.00	40
1978	Future All American	15,000		35.00	52
1978	Garden Girl	15,000		35.00	40

Roman, Inc.

Annual Nativity Bell - I. Spencer
1990	Nativity	Closed	N/A	15.00	15
1991	Flight Into Egypt	Closed	N/A	15.00	15
1992	Gloria in Excelsis Deo	Closed	N/A	15.00	15
1993	Three Kings of Orient	Closed	N/A	15.00	15

F. Hook Bells - F. Hook
1985	Beach Buddies	15,000		25.00	28
1986	Sounds of the Sea	15,000		25.00	28
1987	Bear Hug	15,000		25.00	28

YEAR ISSUE		EDITION LIMIT	YEAR RETD.	ISSUE PRICE	* QUOTE U.S. $

The Masterpiece Collection - Various
1979	Adoration - F. Lippe	Open		20.00	20
1980	Madonna with Grapes - P. Mignard	Open		25.00	25
1981	The Holy Family - G. Notti	Open		25.00	25
1982	Madonna of the Streets - R. Ferruzzi	Open		25.00	25

Seymour Mann, Inc.

Connoisseur Christmas Collection - M. Bernini
1996	Cardinal CLT-312	Open		15.00	15
1996	Chickadee CLT-302	Open		15.00	15
1996	Dove CLT-307	Open		15.00	15

Connoisseur Collection - M. Bernini
1995	Bluebird CLT-15	Open		15.00	15
1995	Canary CLT-12	Open		15.00	15
1995	Cardinal CLT-9	Open		15.00	15
1995	Dove CLT-3	Open		15.00	15
1995	Hummingbird CLT-6	Open		15.00	15
1995	Pink Rose CLT-72	Open		15.00	15
1995	Robin CLT-18	Open		15.00	15
1995	Swan CLT-52	Open		15.00	15
1996	Magnolia CLT-78	Open		15.00	15

DOLLS

All God's Children

All God's Children - M. Root
1996	Anika - 2600	5,000		N/A	N/A

Annalee Mobilitee Dolls, Inc.

Doll Society-Animals - A. Thorndike
1985	10" Penguin and Chick	3,000	N/A	29.95	225
1986	10" Unicorn	3,000	N/A	36.95	350
1987	7" Kangaroo	3,000	N/A	37.45	450
1988	5" Owl	3,000	N/A	37.45	300
1989	7" Polar Bear	3,000	N/A	37.50	300
1990	10" Thorndike Chicken	3,000	N/A	37.50	275

Doll Society-Folk Heroes - A. Thorndike
1984	10" Johnny Appleseed	1,500	N/A	80.00	1000
1984	10" Robin Hood	1,500	N/A	90.00	850
1985	10" Annie Oakley	1,500	N/A	95.00	700
1986	10" Mark Twain	2,500	N/A	117.50	500
1987	10" Ben Franklin	2,500	N/A	119.50	525
1988	10" Sherlock Holmes	2,500	N/A	119.50	500
1989	10" Abraham Lincoln	2,500	N/A	119.50	500
1990	10" Betsy Ross	2,500	N/A	119.50	450
1991	10" Christopher Columbus	1,132	N/A	119.50	300
1992	10" Uncle Sam	1,034	N/A	87.50	N/A
1993	10" Pony Express Rider	Yr.Iss.	N/A	97.50	N/A
1994	10" Bean Nose Santa	Yr.Iss.	1994	119.50	N/A
1995	10" Pocahontas	Yr.Iss.	1995	87.50	88
1996	10" Fabulous 50's Couple	Yr.Iss.		150.00	150

Doll Society-Logo Kids - A. Thorndike
1985	Christmas Logo w/Cookie	3,562	1986	N/A	675
1986	Sweetheart Logo	6,271	1987	N/A	275
1987	Naughty Logo	1,100	1988	N/A	425
1988	Raincoat Logo	13,646	1989	N/A	200
1989	Christmas Morning Logo	16,641	1990	N/A	150
1990	Clown Logo	20,049	1991	N/A	150
1991	Reading Logo	26,516	1992	N/A	125
1992	Back to School Logo	17,524	1993	N/A	90
1993	Ice Cream Logo	Yr.Iss.	1994	N/A	N/A
1994	Dress Up Santa Logo	Yr.Iss	1995	N/A	N/A
1995	Goin' Fishin' Logo	Yr.Iss	1995	29.95	30
1996	7" Little Mae Flower Logo	Yr.Iss		29.95	30

Assorted Dolls - A. Thorndike
1987	3" Baby Witch	3,645	1987	13.95	275
1987	3" Bride and Groom	1,053	1987	38.95	375
1983	3" PJ Kid (designer series)	2,360	1983	10.95	200
1971	3" Reindeer Head	N/A	1976	1.00	200
1991	3" Water Baby in Pond Lily	3,720	1991	14.95	175
1984	5" E.P. Boy Bunny	2,583	1984	11.95	200
1984	5" E.P. Girl Bunny	2,790	1984	11.95	200
1983	5" Easter Parade Girl Bunny w/ Music Box	1,167	1983	29.95	400
1963	5" Elf (Lilac)	N/A	1963	2.50	325
1959	5" Man (Special Order)	N/A	1959	N/A	1525
1956	5" Miniature Girl	N/A	1956	N/A	1000
1956	5" Miniature Man	N/A	1956	N/A	1600
1960	5" Wee Skis	N/A	N/A	3.95	325
1978	7" Airplane Pilot Mouse	2,308	1981	6.95	425
1964	7" Angel in a Blanket	N/A	1964	2.45	325
1984	7" Angel on Star	772	1984	32.95	475
1983	7" Angel w/Musical Instrument on Music Box	N/A	1983	29.95	425
1960	7" Angel w/Paper Wings	N/A	1966	N/A	400
1970	7" Artist Mouse	298	1974	3.95	400
1950	7" Baby Angel	N/A	1950	2.45	1650
1960	7" Baby Angel (yellow feather hair)	N/A	1962	N/A	350
1964	7" Baby Angel Flying w/Halo	N/A	1964	2.45	450
1962	7" Baby Angel on Cloud	N/A	1963	2.45	500-700
1962	7" Baby Angel w/Star	N/A	1962	2.00	325

YEAR ISSUE		EDITION LIMIT	YEAR RETD.	ISSUE PRICE	*QUOTE U.S.$
1980	7" Baby in Bassinet	12,215	1983	13.95	275
1968	7" Baby in Christmas Bag	N/A	1968	2.95	350
1968	7" Baby in Santa's Hat	N/A	1969	2.95	500
1975	7" Baby Mouse	N/A	1975	5.50	150
1971	7" Baby w/Bottle	N/A	1971	N/A	300
1965	7" Baby w/Bow	N/A	1965	N/A	325
1979	7" Ballerina	4,700	1979	7.45	275
1967	7" Ballerina Mouse	N/A	1968	3.95	450
1980	7" Ballooning Santa	N/A	1983	49.95	350
1970	7" Bartender Mouse	289	1973	3.95	400
1971	7" Baseball Player Mouse	1,085	1975	5.50	175
1969	7" Bather-Boy	N/A	1969	N/A	475
1969	7" Bather-Girl	N/A	1969	5.95	800
1987	7" BBQ Mouse	1,798	1987	17.95	300
1975	7" Beautician Mouse	1,349	1975	5.50	600
1974	7" Black Santa w/ Oversized Bag	1,638	1975	5.45	550
1977	7" Boating Mouse	1,186	1977	5.95	175
1964	7" Boudoir Puff Baby Angel	N/A	1965	3.95	400
1984	7" Boy w/ Firecracker	1,893	1984	19.95	400
1966	7" Bride & Groom Mice	N/A	1966	3.95	600
1979	7" Bunny	3,125	1979	6.95	175
1970	7" Bunny (yellow)	3,215	1973	3.95	375
1987	7" Bunny in 10" Carrot Balloon	624	1987	49.95	375
1974	7" Camper in Tent Mouse	468	1974	5.45	325
1976	7" Card Playing Girl Mouse	2,878	1977	5.50	275
1968	7" Caroller Boy Mouse w/ Music	N/A	1969	4.45	400
1978	7" Carpenter Mouse	1,494	1978	6.95	350
1974	7" Carpenter Mouse	2,687	1978	5.45	275
1983	7" Cheerleader Mouse	N/A	1983	11.95	450
1970	7" Christmas Baby on Hat Box	1,894	1971	2.95	350
1965	7" Christmas Dumb Bunny	N/A	1965	3.95	775
1975	7" Christmas Mouse in Santa Mitten	3,959	1976	5.45	375
1977	7" Christmas Mouse in Santa's Mitten	15,916	1979	7.95	175
1975	7" Colonial Boy Mouse	12,739	1976	5.45	350
1975	7" Colonial Girl Mouse	9,338	1976	5.45	350
1965	7" Colored Mouse (Peek)	N/A	1965	3.95	550
1982	7" Cowboy Mouse	3,776	1983	12.95	300
1982	7" Cowgirl Mouse	3,116	1983	12.95	300
1984	7" Cupid in Hanging Heart	2,445	1985	32.95	375
1984	7" Dentist Mouse	2,362	1985	14.95	400
1976	7" Diet Time Mouse	3,399	1977	6.00	200
1992	7" Disney Kid	300	1992	59.95	400
1985	7" Dress-Up Boy	1,174	1985	18.95	225
1985	7" Dress-Up Girl	1,536	1985	18.95	225
1993	7" Eric & Shane Boating in Hawaii	100	1993	105.00	750
1979	7" Fishing Mouse	N/A	1979	7.95	275
1972	7" Football Mouse	744	1974	3.95	300
1991	7" Fun in the Sun Kid	300	1991	80.00	300
1962	7" Furcapped Baby	N/A	1962	2.45	400
1967	7" Garden Club Baby	N/A	1969	2.95	800
1979	7" Gardener Mouse	1,939	1980	7.95	325
1969	7" Gardener Mouse	N/A	1973	4.45	300
1974	7" Gardener Mouse	485	1980	5.45	400
1992	7" Gnome w/ Mushroom	1,691	1992	35.95	350
1967	7" Gnome w/ Pajama Suit	N/A	1970	2.95	375
1965	7" Gnome w/ Vest	N/A	1965	2.45	675
1965	7" Hangover Mouse	N/A	1987	3.95	375
1987	7" Hangover Mouse	1,548	1987	13.95	175
1977	7" Hobo Mouse	1,004	1977	5.95	275
1980	7" Hockey Mouse	2,477	1981	9.95	250
1985	7" Hockey Player Kid	1,578	1985	18.95	400
1974	7" Hunter Mouse w/ Bird	690	1975	5.45	325
1981	7" I'm Late Bunny	100	1981	N/A	475
1985	7" Kid w/ Kite	1,084	1985	17.95	300
1965	7" Lawyer Mouse	N/A	1965	3.95	350
1966	7" M/M Indoor Santa	N/A	1966	5.95	450
1970	7" M/M Santa on Ski Bob	N/A	1970	5.95	600
1983	7" M/M Santa w/ Basket	5,105	1983	25.95	300
1980	7" M/M Santa w/ Pot Belly Stove	6,552	1980	20.94	325
1970	7" M/M Tuckered Santa w/ Hot Water Bottle	1,761	1971	6.45	200
1959	7" Man (special order)	N/A	1959	N/A	1200
1993	7" Mississippi Levee Mouse	341	1993	N/A	400
1973	7" Monkey (Boy)	370	1973	4.50	850
1973	7" Monkey (Girl)	370	1973	4.50	600
1982	7" Mouse w/ Strawberry	10,267	1985	12.95	175
1982	7" Mr. A.M. Mouse	3,724	1983	11.95	150
1970	7" Mr. Holly Mouse	1,726	1970	3.95	225
1977	7" Mr. Santa Mouse	7,197	1979	6.00	300
1967	7" Mrs. Holly Mouse	N/A	1970	3.95	350
1967	7" Mrs. Santa w/ Fur-Trimmed Cape	N/A	1973	2.95	450
1971	7" Naughty Angel	12,359	1971	10.95	275
1976	7" Needlework Mouse	3,566	1978	6.95	400
1964	7" Nude Angel Bath Puff	N/A	1965	3.95	275
1970	7" Painter Mouse	349	1970	3.95	400
1968	7" Patches Pam	N/A	1968	2.95	850
1979	7" Quilting Mouse	213	1979	N/A	375
1991	7" Santa in Tub w/ Rubber Duckie	5,373	1991	33.95	200
1971	7" Santa Mailman	8,296	1974	5.50	375
1972	7" Santa on Ski-Bob w/ Oversized Bag	7,590	1974	7.95	400
1978	7" Santa w/ 10" Reindeer Trimming Christmas Tree	1,621	1978	18.45	425
1981	7" Santa w/ 18" Moon	N/A	1981	6.95	200
1963	7" Santa w/ Fur Trimmed Suit	N/A	1967	2.95	400
1969	7" Santa w/ Oversized Bag	N/A	1969	3.95	350
1979	7" Santa w/ Pot Belly Stove	11,551	1979	7.95	375
1971	7" Santa w/ Skis and Poles	N/A	1978	5.45	300
1989	7" Science Center Mouse	500	1989	75.00	525

YEAR ISSUE		EDITION LIMIT	YEAR RETD.	ISSUE PRICE	*QUOTE U.S.$
1972	7" Secretary Mouse	727	1974	3.95	500
1970	7" Secretary Mouse	727	1972	3.95	150
1970	7" Sherriff Mouse	11	1970	3.95	650
1991	7" Sherriff Mouse #92	1,191	1992	49.50	700
1965	7" Singing Mouse	N/A	1965	3.95	600
1978	7" Skateboard Mouse	3,733	1979	7.00	200
1979	7" Skateboard Mouse	1,821	1979	7.95	275
1976	7" Ski Mouse	10,375	1981	6.95	225
1974	7" Ski Mouse	1,603	1974	5.45	225
1954	7" Sloppy Painter Boy	N/A	1954	N/A	900
1974	7" Sloppy Painter Mouse	349	1974	5.45	550
1971	7" Swimmer Mouse w/ Inner Tube	267	1971	3.95	325
1967	7" Tuckered Mr. & Mrs. Santa Water Bottle	N/A	1969	5.95	400
1973	7" Vacationer Girl Mouse	1,017	1974	4.45	325
1986	7" Witch Mouse w/ Pumpkin Balloon	868	1987	59.95	300
1982	7" Wood Chopper Mouse	1,910	1982	11.95	375
1992	7" Workshop Mouse	6,618	1992	21.95	275
1971	7" Yachtsman Mouse w/ Binnacle	249	1974	3.95	400
1966	7" Yum Yum Bunny	N/A	1966	3.95	600
1968	8" Elephant (Tubby)	N/A	1969	4.95	450
1980	8" Girl BBQ Pig	3,854	1981	9.95	175
1975	8" Lamb	234	1975	8.95	450
1977	8" Rooster	1,642	1977	5.95	350
1959	10" 4th of July Doll	N/A	1959	N/A	1525
1982	10" Annalee Artist	160	1982	295.00	1100
1959	10" Architect	N/A	1959	19.95	1250
1991	10" Aviator Frog w/ Flag	2,110	1991	19.95	425
1957	10" Baby Angel	N/A	1958	8.95	525
1963	10" Ballerina	N/A	1963	5.95	1350
1980	10" Balloon w/ Two 10" Frogs	837	1980	49.95	850
1968	10" Bather (Skinny Minnie w/ Towel)	N/A	1968	5.95	950
1966	10" Bathersome Chick w/ Flippers	N/A	1966	5.95	650
1959	10" Bathing Boy	N/A	1959	5.75	1800
1959	10" Bathing Girl	N/A	1959	7.95	2800
1957	10" Bathing Girl	N/A	1957	N/A	1300
1989	10" BBQ Pig	2,471	1989	27.95	325
1964	10" Black (Monk)	N/A	1965	2.95	375
1994	10" Boston Bruins Hockey Player (Signed by team)	2	1994	N/A	500
1966	10" Boy & Girl on Tandem Bike	N/A	1966	20.95	1350
1960	10" Boy Building Boat	N/A	1968	12.95	1600
1956	10" Boy Building Boat	N/A	1969	N/A	1550
1950	10" Boy Building Boat	N/A	1950	9.95	1200
1976	10" Boy in Tire Swing	358	1976	6.95	350
1965	10" Boy on Bike	N/A	1965	N/A	600
1980	10" Boy on Raft	1,087	1981	28.95	325
1955	10" Boy Skier	N/A	1956	10.95	2750
1969	10" Bride & Groom Set	N/A	1969	11.95	800
1967	10" Brown Nun	N/A	1967	2.95	375
1950	10" Calypso Dancer	N/A	1950	N/A	1350
1967	10" Carnaby Street Boy	N/A	1967	3.95	400
1960	10" Carpenter	N/A	1965	N/A	575
1987	10" Carrot Balloon w / 7" Bunny in Basket	624	1987	49.95	500
1970	10" Casualty Ski Elf w/ Crutch & Leg in Cast	2,818	1972	4.50	600
1959	10" Catcher	N/A	1959	N/A	1900
1967	10" Choir Boy (set/3)	N/A	1967	2.95	725
1950	10" Christmas Girl	N/A	1957	N/A	2350
1970	10" Christmas Mushroom w/ 7" Mouse	198	1970	7.95	400
1987	10" Clown	2,699	1987	17.95	450
1981	10" Clown	6,479	1981	9.95	200
1971	10" Clown (black & white)	N/A	1971	2.00	300
1969	10" Clown (bright stripes)	N/A	1971	3.95	350
1969	10" Clown (pink w/green polka dots)	N/A	1969	3.95	525
1971	10" Clown w/ Mushroom	45	1971	7.95	850
1975	10" Colonial Drummer Boy	1,846	1976	5.95	375
1989	10" Country Boy Pig	2,566	1989	25.95	175
1989	10" Country Girl Pig	2,367	1989	25.95	175
1968	10" Cross Country Skier	N/A	1968	7.95	700
1982	10" Cyrano de Bergerac	35	1982	N/A	2300
1961	10" Dalmation	N/A	1961	N/A	1500
1972	10" Democratic Donkey	861	1972	3.95	450
1960	10" Elf	N/A	1966	N/A	400
1950	10" Elf	N/A	N/A	N/A	900
1963	10" Elf	N/A	1963	N/A	350
1954	10" Elf w/ Cap	N/A	1954	N/A	1150
1978	10" Elf w/ Planter	1,978	1978	6.95	275
1967	10" Elf w/ Skis and Poles	48	1971	2.95	425-900
1988	10" Fall Elf	3,183	1988	13.95	125
1959	10" Fisherman & Girl in Boat	N/A	1959	N/A	2550
1963	10" Friar	N/A	1963	2.95	500
1959	10" Girl	N/A	1959	N/A	1000
1959	10" Girl and Boy on Tandem Bike	N/A	1959	20.95	2200
1965	10" Girl on Bike	N/A	1965	N/A	600
1955	10" Girl Skier	N/A	1956	10.95	2750
1967	10" Go-Go Boy	N/A	1967	3.95	450
1967	10" Golfer Boy	N/A	1968	5.95	925
1965	10" Golfer Boy Doll	N/A	1968	5.95	700
1966	10" Golfer-Girl Putter	N/A	1968	5.95	925
1957	10" Halloween Girl	N/A	1968	9.95	3200
1965	10" Hiking Doll	N/A	1968	9.95	750
1957	10" Holly Elf	N/A	1957	N/A	1600
1987	10" Huck Finn (#62)	800	1988	102.95	700
1991	10" Husky w/ 5" Puppy in Dog Sled	2,860	1991	54.95	350
1960	10" Impski	N/A	1966	3.95	500

YEAR ISSUE		EDITION LIMIT	YEAR RETD.	ISSUE PRICE	*QUOTE U.S.$
1960	10" Impski (red)	N/A	1966	3.95	325
1960	10" Impski (white)	N/A	1966	3.95	350
1977	10" Jack Frost Elf	5,580	1977	6.00	225
1982	10" Jack Frost Elf w/ 10" Snowflake	N/A	1982	13.50	150
1981	10" Jack Frost Elf w/ 5" Snowflake	5,950	1981	31.95	325
1959	10" Lawyer	N/A	1959	N/A	3000
1974	10" Leprechaun w/ Sack	8,834	1974	5.45	350
1956	10" Man	N/A	1956	N/A	3000
1959	10" Man (special order)	N/A	1959	N/A	1400
1967	10" Man w/Guitar	N/A	1967	N/A	1000
1964	10" Monk (red robe)	N/A	1965	2.95	800
1965	10" Monk w/ Christmas Tree Planting	N/A	1967	2.95	450
1967	10" Monk w/ Jug	N/A	1969	2.95	375
1970	10" Monk w/ Skis and Poles	1,386	1972	3.95	350
1970	10" Mushroom w/ 7" Santa	1,535	1971	7.95	250
1967	10" Nun (green)	N/A	1967	42.95	700
1967	10" Nun w/Basket	N/A	1967	2.95	600
1994	10" Piper Bear	200	1994	130.00	650
1974	10" Polly Frog Spring Cleaning	580	1974	5.50	325
1965	10" Reindeer	N/A	1965	4.95	425
1975	10" Reindeer w/ 7" Santa	2,429	1976	10.50	400
1964	10" Robin Hood Elf	N/A	1965	2.50	500
1988	10" Scrooge Head	N/A	1988	N/A	325
1984	10" Shriner (special order)	1,000	1984	N/A	875
1987	10" Sitting Frog w/Instrument	2,162	1987	19.95	525
1971	10" Ski Elf	1,262	1971	3.95	275
1987	10" Ski Elf	N/A	1987	19.95	350
1985	10" Skier (Cross Country)	1,076	1985	33.50	225
1956	10" Skier Girl w/ Broken Leg in Cast	N/A	1957	14.95	1550
1954	10" Sloppy Painter Boy	N/A	1954	N/A	900
1990	10" Spirit of '76	1,080	1990	175.00	550
1992	10" Spring Chicken w/ Boa	N/A	1992	34.95	150
1965	10" Spring Elf	N/A	1965	2.50	375
1954	10" Spring Girl	N/A	1954	N/A	2350
1957	10" Square Dancer (Girl)	N/A	1959	9.95	900
1950	10" Square Dancers (Boy & Girl)	N/A	1959	9.95	2100
1956	10" Square Dancers (set/8)	N/A	1956	59.95	5200
1987	10" State Trooper (#642)	511	1988	134.00	500
1991	10" Summer Santa #1663	1,926	1991	59.95	425
1967	10" Surfer Boy	N/A	1968	5.95	525
1967	10" Surfer Girl	N/A	1968	5.95	625
1989	10" Three Bunnies w/ Maypole	647	1989	190.00	600
1959	10" Two Painters on Scaffold	N/A	1959	39.95	3400
1976	10" Uncle Sam	1,095	1976	5.95	500
1957	10" Valentine Doll	N/A	1957	9.95	1800
1991	10" Victory Ski Doll	1,192	1991	49.50	350
1956	10" Woman	N/A	1956	N/A	2600
1959	10" Woman in Red	N/A	1959	5.75	2200
1959	10" Woman's Head	N/A	1959	N/A	500
1959	10" Wood Sprite	N/A	1967	N/A	750
1966	10" Workshop Elf	N/A	1966	N/A	425
1976	12" Angel	13,338	1979	10.95	350
1960	12" Baby in Green	N/A	1960	N/A	550
1992	12" Bat	2,107	1992	31.95	225
1965	12" Christmas Bonnet Lady Mouse	N/A	1965	9.95	400
1967	12" Country Cousin Boy Mouse	N/A	1967	9.95	500
1990	12" Easter Parade Duck w/ Watering Can	2,891	1990	49.95	300
1967	12" Fancy Nancy Cat	N/A	1967	6.95	1950
1968	12" Gnome w/ Gay Apron	N/A	1968	5.95	900
1968	12" Laura May Cat	N/A	1971	7.95	900
1967	12" Laura May Cat	N/A	1967	6.95	1000
1981	12" Monkey Boy w/ Banana	N/A	1971	23.95	225
1970	12" Mr. Santa Mouse w/ Toybag	N/A	1971	10.95	525
1967	12" Mrs. Santa w/ Muff	N/A	1969	9.95	550
1969	12" Myrtle Turtle	N/A	1969	6.95	800
1968	12" Myrtle Turtle	N/A	1969	6.95	2600
1969	12" Nightshirt Boy Mouse	N/A	1976	9.95	550
1957	12" Santa	N/A	1957	N/A	925
1954	12" Santa (Bean Nose)	N/A	1957	19.95	1000
1990	12" Santa Duck	506	1991	49.95	300
1981	12" Santa Monkey	1,800	1981	23.95	600
1982	12" Skunk Boy	935	1982	27.95	225
1982	12" Skunk Girl	936	1982	27.95	225
1967	12" Sneaky Peaky Boy Cat	N/A	1967	6.95	375
1992	12" Spider	3,461	1992	38.95	200
1967	12" Yum-Yum Bunny	N/A	1968	9.95	850
1980	14" Dragon w/ Bush Boy	2,130	1982	32.95	300
1955	14" Fireman	N/A	1955	N/A	4750
1955	15" Christmas Dragon	448	1990	49.95	400
1970	16" Christmas Wreath w/ Santa Head	1,662	1974	9.95	375
1972	16" Democratic Donkey	219	1972	12.95	1600
1972	16" Elephant (Republican)	230	1972	12.95	800
1984	18" Aerobic Doll	622	1984	35.95	375
1988	18" Americana Couple #82	7,258	1988	169.95	700
1990	18" Angel w/ Instrument	398	1990	51.95	325
1978	18" Artist Bunny w/ Brush & Palette	2,023	1979	14.00	300
1985	18" Ballerina Bear	918	1985	39.95	275
1980	18" Ballerina Bunny	7,069	1982	27.95	425
1979	18" Ballerina Bunny	2,315	1982	15.95	450
1984	18" Bear w/ Brush	1,392	1984	39.95	250
1985	18" Bear w/ Honey Pot & Bee	2,032	1986	41.50	600
1974	18" Bell Hop (special order)	3	1974	N/A	1000
1974	18" Bob Cratchet w/ 7" Tiny Tim	984	1974	11.95	425
1977	18" Boy Bunny w/Carrot	1,159	1977	13.50	250
1979	18" Boy Frog	3,524	1981	22.95	175
1977	18" Bunny w/Egg	1,172	1977	13.50	250

YEAR ISSUE		EDITION LIMIT	YEAR RETD.	ISSUE PRICE	*QUOTE U.S.$
1981	18" Butterfly w/ 10" Elf	2,507	1982	27.95	500
1972	18" Candy Kid Boy	4,350	1973	11.95	775
1972	18" Candy Kid Girl	4,350	1973	11.95	775
1975	18" Caroller Boy	1,024	1975	12.00	400
1963	18" Choir Boy	1,470	1963	7.45	550
1973	18" Christmas Panda	437	1973	10.50	600
1975	18" Clown	166	1975	N/A	450
1983	18" Country Girl Bunny w/ Basket	2,905	1983	29.95	400
1984	18" E.P. Girl Bunny	2,952	1984	35.95	350
1976	18" Elephant "Vote '76"	806	1976	8.50	500
1981	18" Escort Fox	657	1981	28.50	650
1984	18" Fawn w/ Wreath	2,080	1984	32.95	375
1979	18" Girl Frog	3,677	1981	22.95	175
1979	18" Gnome	15,851	1980	19.95	350
1976	18" Gnome	N/A	1976	9.95	750
1975	18" Horse	221	1976	16.95	375
1975	18" Jockey w/18" Horse	84	1975	30.00	1700
1981	18" Lady Fox	643	1981	28.50	650
1974	18" Martha Cratchet	1,043	1974	11.95	425
1982	18" Monk w/Jug	3,024	1982	26.45	525
1970	18" Mr. & Mrs. Fireside Couple	N/A	1971	7.45	300
1968	18" Mrs. Santa w/ Boudoir Cap & Apron	N/A	1968	7.45	250
1968	18" Mrs. Santa w/ Hot Water Bottle	N/A	1968	7.45	525
1990	18" Naughty Kid	1,454	1991	69.95	525
1970	18" Patchwork Kid	496	1970	7.45	450
1978	18" Pilgrim Boy	1,213	1978	14.95	275
1964	18" PJ Kid	N/A	1964	6.95	500
1980	18" Santa Frog w/ Toybag	2,126	1980	24.95	450
1971	18" Santa Fur Kid	1,191	1972	7.45	250
1964	18" Santa Kid	N/A	1965	6.95	450
1990	18" Santa Playing w/ Electric Train	168	1990	119.00	350
1987	18" Special Mrs. Santa (special order)	341	1987	N/A	400
1976	18" Uncle Sam	345	1976	16.95	500
1985	18" Valentine Bear	2,439	1986	41.50	275
1987	18" Workshop Santa (special order)	1,001	1987	N/A	450
1975	18" Yankee Doodle Dandy w/ 18" Horse	437	1976	28.95	900
1968	18" Yum Yum Bunny	N/A	1968	14.95	1000
1981	22" Christmas Giraffe w/ 10" Elf	1,377	1982	36.95	500
1974	22" Christmas Stocking	8,536	1974	4.95	150
1973	22" Holly Hobby	N/A	1973	N/A	1000
1974	22" Leprechaun	199	1974	11.45	650
1970	22" Monkey (chartreuse)	70	1970	10.95	725
1990	22" Spring Elf (yellow)	1,636	1990	34.95	325
1981	22" Sun Mobile	3,003	1985	36.95	475
1963	24" Bellhop	N/A	1963	13.95	1750
1975	25" Lad w/ Kite	95	1975	28.95	400
1975	25" Lass w/ Flowers	92	1975	28.95	450
1954	26" Elf	N/A	1956	9.95	550
1963	26" Friar	N/A	1963	14.95	2500
1955	26" Woman	N/A	1955	N/A	6500
1979	29" Artist Bunny w/ Brush & Palette	179	1979	42.95	350
1974	29" Bell Hop (special order)	3	1974	29.00	1200
1970	29" Boy Bunny	N/A	1970	24.95	600
1978	29" Caroller Mouse	658	1978	49.95	475
1976	29" Clown (blue w/ white polka dots)	466	1976	29.95	925
1981	29" Dragon w/ 12 Bush Boy	151	1982	69.95	700
1960	29" Fur Trim Santa	N/A	1979	N/A	1000
1971	29" M/M Tuckered w/ 2 18" Kids	811	1972	51.95	800
1974	29" Motorized See-Saw Bunny Set	43	1975	250.00	1600
1977	29" Mr. Santa Mouse w/ Sack	704	1977	49.95	800
1968	29" Mrs. Indoor Santa	N/A	1968	16.95	475
1977	29" Mrs. Santa Mouse w/ Muff	571	1977	49.95	800
1969	29" Mrs. Santa w/ Wired Cardholder Skirt	N/A	1969	18.95	250
1972	29" Mrs. Snow Woman w/ Cardholder Skirt	331	1972	19.95	700
1990	30" Clown	530	1990	99.95	350
1984	30" Santa in Chair w/ 2 18" Kids	940	1984	169.95	1200
1984	30" Snowgirl w/ Muff	685	1984	79.50	1000
1984	32" Monk w/ Grapes	416	1984	78.50	450
1959	33" Boy & Girl on Tandem Bike	N/A	1959	N/A	4500
1960	36" PJ Kid	N/A	1960	N/A	1200
1980	42" Clown	224	1980	74.95	700
1977	42" Scarecrow	365	1978	61.95	2050
1978	48" Mrs. Santa	151	1978	150.00	1450
1978	48" Santa	200	1978	150.00	1450
1986	48" Velour Santa	410	1988	269.95	750
1963	Baby Angel Head w/ Santa Hat	N/A	1963	1.00	350
1965	The Bang Hat (red)	N/A	1965	N/A	175
1963	Bath Puff (yellow)	N/A	1965	1.95	325
1968	Bunny Head Pin On	N/A	1968	1.00	400
1950	Cellist	N/A	N/A	N/A	5250
1976	Colonial Boy Head Pin On	N/A	1976	1.50	275
1976	Colonial Girl Head Pin On	N/A	1976	1.50	275
1972	Donkey Head Pin On	1,371	1972	1.00	300
1972	Elephant Head Pin On	1,384	1972	1.00	325
1962	Fur-Capped Baby on Cloud	N/A	1962	N/A	350
1961	Fur-Capped Head Pin-On	N/A	1962	1.00	225
1960	Head Pin On	N/A	N/A	N/A	200
1968	Hippy Head (Boy)	N/A	1969	1.00	350
1968	Hippy Head (Girl)	N/A	1969	1.00	350
1960	Man Head Pin-on	N/A	N/A	N/A	800
1970	Monkey Head Pin-on (boy)	153	1973	1.00	275
1970	Monkey Head Pin-on (girl)	153	1973	1.00	275
1971	Monkey Head Pin-on (hot pink)	N/A	1973	1.00	450
1960	Mouse Head Pin-On	N/A	1976	1.00	250

YEAR ISSUE		EDITION LIMIT	YEAR RETD.	ISSUE PRICE	*QUOTE U.S.$
1970	Mouse Pin	N/A	1970	1.45	150
1971	Snowman Head Pin-on	4,040	1972	1.00	200
1971	Snowman Kid	1,374	1971	3.95	450
1985	Tree Skirt	1,332	1985	24.95	350
1989	Two Bunnies on Flexible Flyer Sled	4,104	1990	52.95	325

ANRI

Disney Dolls - Disney Studios

1990	Daisy Duck, 14"	2,500	1991	895.00	1250
1990	Donald Duck, 14"	2,500	1991	895.00	1250
1989	Mickey Mouse, 14"	2,500	1991	850.00	1000
1989	Minnie Mouse, 14"	2,500	1991	850.00	1000
1989	Pinocchio, 14"	2,500	1991	850.00	895

Ferrandiz Dolls - J. Ferrandiz

1991	Carmen, 14"	1,000	1992	730.00	730
1991	Fernando, 14"	1,000	1992	730.00	730
1989	Gabriel, 14"	1,000	1991	550.00	575
1991	Juanita, 7"	1,500	1992	300.00	300
1990	Margarite, 14"	1,000	1992	575.00	730
1989	Maria, 14"	1,000	1991	550.00	575
1991	Miguel, 7"	1,500	1992	300.00	300
1990	Philipe, 14"	1,000	1992	575.00	680

Sarah Kay Dolls - S. Kay

1991	Annie, 7"	1,500	1993	300.00	300
1989	Bride to Love And To Cherish	750	1992	750.00	790
1989	Charlotte (Blue)	1,000	1993	550.00	575
1990	Christina, 14"	1,000	1993	575.00	730
1989	Eleanor (Floral)	1,000	1993	550.00	575
1989	Elizabeth (Patchwork)	1,000	1993	550.00	575
1988	Emily, 14"	Closed	1989	500.00	500
1990	Faith, 14"	1,000	1993	575.00	685
1989	Groom With This Ring Doll, 14"	750	1992	550.00	730
1989	Helen (Brown), 14"	1,000	1991	550.00	575
1989	Henry, 14"	1,000	1991	550.00	575
1991	Janine, 14"	1,000	1993	750.00	750
1988	Jennifer, 14"	Closed	1989	500.00	500
1991	Jessica, 7"	1,500	1993	300.00	300
1991	Julie, 7"	1,500	1993	300.00	300
1988	Katherine, 14"	Closed	1989	500.00	500
1988	Martha, 14"	Closed	1989	500.00	500
1989	Mary (Red)	1,000	1991	550.00	575
1991	Michelle, 7"	1,500	1993	300.00	300
1991	Patricia, 14"	1,000	1993	730.00	730
1991	Peggy, 7"	1,500	1993	300.00	300
1990	Polly, 14"	1,000	1993	575.00	680
1988	Rachael, 14"	Closed	1989	500.00	500
1988	Rebecca, 14"	Closed	1989	500.00	500
1988	Sarah, 14"	Closed	1989	500.00	500
1990	Sophie, 14"	1,000	1993	575.00	660
1991	Susan, 7"	1,500	1993	300.00	300
1988	Victoria, 14"	Closed	1989	500.00	500

Ashton-Drake Galleries

All I Wish For You - Good-Kruger

1994	I Wish You Love	Closed	1995	49.95	50
1995	I Wish You Faith	12/98		49.95	50
1995	I Wish You Happiness	12/98		49.95	50
1995	I Wish You Wisdom	12/98		49.95	50
1996	I Wish You Charity	12/99		49.95	50
1996	I Wish You Luck	12/99		49.95	50

America the Beautiful - Y. Bello

1995	Billy	12/96		49.95	50
1995	Bobby	12/96		49.95	50

The American Dream - J. Kovacik

1994	Patience	Closed	1995	79.95	80
1994	Hope	Closed	1995	79.95	80

Amish Blessings - J. Good-Kruger

1990	Rebeccah	Closed	1993	68.00	125
1991	Rachel	Closed	1993	69.00	125
1991	Adam	Closed	1993	75.00	125-150
1992	Ruth	Closed	1993	75.00	125
1992	Eli	Closed	1993	79.95	125
1993	Sarah	Closed	1994	79.95	125

Amish Inspirations - J. Ibarolle

1994	Ethan	Closed	1995	69.95	70
1994	Mary	Closed	1995	69.95	70
1995	Seth	12/96		74.95	75
1995	Anna	12/96		74.95	75

Anne of Green Gables - J. Kovacik

1995	Anne	12/98		69.95	70
1996	Diana Barry	12/99		69.95	70

As Cute As Can Be - D. Effner

1993	Sugar Plum	Closed	1994	49.95	75-95
1994	Puppy Love	Closed	1995	49.95	75
1995	Angel Face	Closed	1995	49.95	50
1995	Patty Cake	12/98		49.95	50

Babies World of Wonder - K. Barry-Hippensteel

1996	Andrew	12/99		59.95	60

YEAR ISSUE		EDITION LIMIT	YEAR RETD.	ISSUE PRICE	* QUOTE U.S.$

Baby Book Treasures - K. Barry-Hippensteel

1990	Elizabeth's Homecoming	Closed	1993	58.00	58
1991	Catherine's Christening	Closed	1994	58.00	58
1991	Christopher's First Smile	Closed	1992	63.00	63

Baby Talk - Good-Kruger

1994	All Gone	Closed	1995	49.95	75-95
1994	Bye-Bye	Closed	1995	49.95	50
1994	Night, Night	Closed	1995	49.95	50

Barely Yours - T. Tomescu

1994	Cute as a Button	Closed	1994	69.95	70
1994	Snug as a Bug in a Rug	Closed	1995	75.00	75
1995	Clean as a Whistle	12/96		75.00	75
1995	Pretty as a Picture	12/96		75.00	75
1995	Good as Gold	12/96		75.00	75
1996	Cool As A Cucumber	12/99		75.00	75

Beautiful Dreamers - G. Rademann

1992	Katrina	Closed	1993	89.00	95-125
1992	Nicolette	Closed	1994	89.95	95
1993	Brigitte	Closed	1994	94.00	94
1993	Isabella	Closed	1994	94.00	94
1993	Gabrielle	Closed	1994	94.00	94

Blessed Are The Children - B. Deval

1996	Blessed Are The Peacemakers	12/99		69.95	70

Born To Be Famous - K. Barry-Hippensteel

1989	Little Sherlock	Closed	1991	87.00	87
1990	Little Florence Nightingale	Closed	1991	87.00	87
1991	Little Davey Crockett	Closed	1994	92.00	92
1992	Little Christopher Columbus	Closed	1993	95.00	95

Calendar Babies - Ashton-Drake

1995	New Year	Open		24.95	25
1995	Cupid	Open		24.95	25
1995	Leprechaun	Open		24.95	25
1995	April Showers	Open		24.95	25
1995	May Flowers	Open		24.95	25
1995	June Bride	Open		24.95	25
1995	Uncle Sam	Open		24.95	25
1995	Sun & Fun	Open		24.95	25
1995	Back to School	Open		24.95	25
1995	Happy Haunting	Open		24.95	25
1995	Thanksgiving Turkey	Open		24.95	25
1995	Jolly Santa	Open		24.95	25

Caught In The Act - M. Tretter

1992	Stevie, Catch Me If You Can	Closed	1994	49.95	125-145
1993	Kelly, Don't I Look Pretty?	Closed	1994	49.95	95
1994	Mikey (Look It Floats)	Closed	1994	55.00	55
1994	Nickie (Cookie Jar)	Closed	1995	59.95	60
1994	Becky (Kleenex Box)	Closed	1995	59.95	60
1994	Sandy	Closed	1995	59.95	60

Children of Christmas - M. Sirko

1994	The Little Drummer Boy	Closed	1995	79.95	80
1994	The Littlest Angel	Closed	1995	79.95	80
1995	O Christmas Tree	12/98		79.95	80
1995	Sugar Plum Fairy	12/98		79.95	80

Children of Mother Goose - Y. Bello

1987	Little Bo Peep	Closed	1988	58.00	125-135
1987	Mary Had a Little Lamb	Closed	1989	58.00	125
1988	Little Jack Horner	Closed	1989	63.00	95
1989	Miss Muffet	Closed	1991	63.00	63

Children Of The Sun - M. Severino

1993	Little Flower	Closed	1994	69.95	70
1993	Desert Star	Closed	1995	69.95	70

A Children's Circus - J. McClelland

1990	Tommy The Clown	Closed	1993	78.00	78
1991	Katie The Tightrope Walker	Closed	1993	78.00	78
1991	Johnnie The Strongman	Closed	1994	83.00	83
1992	Maggie The Animal Trainer	Closed	1994	83.00	83

Christmas Memories - Y. Bello

1994	Christopher	Closed	1995	59.95	60
1994	Joshua	Closed	1995	59.95	60
1994	Stephanie	Closed	1995	59.95	60

Cindy's Playhouse Pals - C. McClure

1989	Meagan	Closed	1990	87.00	87
1989	Shelly	Closed	1993	87.00	87
1990	Ryan	Closed	1993	89.00	89
1991	Samantha	Closed	1993	89.00	89

Classic Brides of The Century - E. Williams

1990	Flora, The 1900s Bride	Closed	1993	145.00	145
1991	Jennifer, The 1980s Bride	Closed	1992	149.00	149
1993	Kathleen, The 1930s Bride	Closed	1993	149.95	150

Classic Collection - D. Effner

1995	Hilary	12/98		79.95	80
1996	Willow	12/99		79.95	80

Cuddle Chums - K. Barry-Hippensteel

1995	Heather	12/98		59.95	60

YEAR ISSUE		EDITION LIMIT RETD.	ISSUE PRICE	*QUOTE U.S.$
1995	Jeffrey	12/98	59.95	60

Days of the Week - K. Barry-Hippensteel
1994	Monday	Closed 1995	49.95	50
1995	Tuesday	12/96	49.95	50
1995	Wednesday	12/96	49.95	50
1995	Thursday	12/96	49.95	50
1995	Friday	12/96	49.95	50
1995	Saturday	12/96	49.95	50
1995	Sunday	12/96	49.95	50

Dianna Effner's Mother Goose - D. Effner
1990	Mary, Mary, Quite Contrary	Closed 1992	78.00	200
1991	The Little Girl With The Curl (Horrid)	Closed 1992	79.00	150-195
1991	The Little Girl With The Curl (Good)	Closed 1993	79.00	95-125
1992	Little Boy Blue	Closed 1993	85.00	85
1993	Snips & Snails	Closed 1994	85.00	125-145
1993	Sugar & Spice	Closed 1994	89.95	125
1993	Curly Locks	Closed 1995	89.95	95

Down The Garden Path - P. Coffer
1991	Rosemary	Closed 1994	79.00	79
1991	Angelica	Closed 1994	85.00	85

Elvis: Lifetime Of A Legend - L. Di Leo
1992	'68 Comeback Special	Closed 1994	99.95	100
1994	King of Las Vegas	Closed 1994	99.95	100

European Fairytales - G. Rademann
1994	Little Red Riding Hood	Closed 1996	79.95	80
1995	Snow White	12/96	79.95	80

Family Ties - M. Tretter
1994	Welcome Home Baby Brother	Closed 1995	79.95	80
1995	Kiss and Make it Better	12/96	89.95	90
1995	Happily Ever Better	12/96	89.95	90

Father's Touch - L. Di Leo
1993	2 A.M. Feeding	Closed 1994	99.95	100

From The Heart - T. Menzenbach
1992	Carolin	Closed 1994	79.95	80
1992	Erik	Closed 1994	79.95	80

From This Day Forward - P. Tumminio
1994	Elizabeth	Closed 1995	89.95	90
1995	Betty	12/96	89.95	90
1995	Beth	12/96	89.95	90
1995	Lisa	12/96	89.95	90

Garden of Inspirations - B. Hanson
1994	Gathering Violets	Closed 1995	69.95	70
1994	Daisy Chain	Closed 1995	69.95	70
1995	Heart's Bouquet	12/96	74.95	75
1995	Garden Prayer	12/96	74.95	75

Gene - M. Odom
1995	Premiere	12/96	69.95	70
1995	Red Venus	12/96	69.95	70
1995	Monaco	12/96	69.95	70

Gingham & Bows - S. Freeman
1995	Gwendolyn	12/98	69.95	70
1996	Mallory	12/99	69.95	70

God Hears the Children - B. Conner
1995	Now I Lay Me Down	12/98	79.95	80
1996	God Is Great, God Is Good	12/99	79.95	80
1996	We Give Thanks For Things We Have	12/99	79.95	80

Growing Up Like Wildflowers - B. Madeja
1996	Annie	12/99	49.95	50

Growing Young Minds - K. Barry-Hippensteel
1991	Alex	Closed 1992	79.00	80

Happiness Is... - K. Barry-Hippensteel
1991	Patricia (My First Tooth)	Closed 1993	69.00	95-125
1992	Crystal (Feeding Myself)	Closed 1994	69.95	100
1993	Brittany (Blowing Kisses)	Closed 1993	69.95	100
1993	Joy (My First Christmas)	Closed 1994	69.95	70
1994	Candy Cane (Holly)	Closed 1994	69.95	70
1994	Patrick (My First Playmate)	Closed 1994	69.95	70

Happy Thoughts - K. Barry-Hippensteel
1994	Laughter is the Best Medicine	Closed 1995	59.95	60

Heavenly Inspirations - C. McClure
1992	Every Cloud Has a Silver Lining	Closed 1994	59.95	75-95
1993	Wish Upon A Star	Closed 1994	59.95	60
1994	Sweet Dreams	Closed 1994	65.00	65
1994	Luck at the End of Rainbow	Closed 1994	65.00	65
1994	Sunshine	Closed 1994	69.95	70
1994	Pennies From Heaven	Closed 1995	69.95	70

Heritage of American Quilting - J. Lundy
1994	Eleanor	Closed 1995	79.95	80
1995	Abigail	12/96	79.95	80

1995	Louisa	12/96	84.95	85
1995	Ruth Anne	12/96	84.95	85

Heroines from the Fairy Tale Forests - D. Effner
1988	Little Red Riding Hood	Closed 1990	68.00	200
1989	Goldilocks	Closed 1991	68.00	75
1990	Snow White	Closed 1992	73.00	175
1991	Rapunzel	Closed 1993	79.00	150-175
1992	Cinderella	Closed 1993	79.00	150-200
1993	Cinderella (Ballgown)	Closed 1994	79.95	150-200

How Little Was I? - S. Bryer
1995	Brittany	12/96	59.95	60
1995	Claire	12/96	59.95	60

I Want Mommy - K. Barry-Hippensteel
1993	Timmy (Mommy I'm Sleepy)	Closed 1994	59.95	145
1993	Tommy (Mommy I'm Sorry)	Closed 1994	59.95	125
1994	Up Mommy (Tammy)	Closed 1994	65.00	95

I'm Just Little - K. Barry-Hippensteel
1995	I'm a Little Angel	12/96	49.95	50
1995	I'm a Little Devil	12/96	49.95	50
1996	I'm a Little Cutie	12/99	49.95	50

International Festival of Toys and Tots - K. Barry-Hippensteel
1989	Chen, a Little Boy of China	Closed 1990	78.00	85-125
1989	Natasha	Closed 1992	78.00	78
1990	Molly	Closed 1993	83.00	83
1991	Hans	Closed 1993	88.00	88
1992	Miki, Eskimo	Closed 1994	88.00	88

Joys of Summer - K. Barry-Hippensteel
1993	Tickles	Closed 1994	49.95	110
1993	Little Squirt	Closed 1994	49.95	65
1994	Yummy	Closed 1994	55.00	65
1994	Havin' A Ball	Closed 1994	55.00	65
1994	Lil' Scoop	Closed 1994	55.00	65

Just Caught Napping - A. Brown
1996	Asleep in the Saddle	12/99	69.95	70

The King & I - P. Ryan Brooks
1991	Shall We Dance?	Closed 1992	175.00	395

Lasting Traditions - W. Hanson
1993	Something Old	Closed 1993	69.95	70
1994	Finishing Touch	Closed 1994	69.95	70
1994	Mother's Pearls	Closed 1994	85.00	85
1994	Her Traditional Garter	Closed 1995	85.00	85

Lawton's Nursery Rhymes - W. Lawton
1994	Little Bo Peep	Closed 1995	79.95	80
1994	Little Miss Muffet	Closed 1995	79.95	80
1994	Mary, Mary	Closed 1995	85.00	85
1994	Mary/Lamb	Closed 1995	85.00	85

The Legends of Baseball - Various
1994	Babe Ruth - T. Tomescu	Closed 1995	79.95	80
1994	Lou Gehrig - T. Tomescu	Closed 1995	79.95	80
1995	Ty Cobb - E. Shelton	12/96	79.95	80

Let's Play Mother Goose - K. Barry-Hippensteel
1994	Cow Jumped Over the Moon	Closed 1995	69.95	70
1994	Hickory, Dickory, Dock	Closed 1995	69.95	95

Little Bits - G. Rademan
1993	Lil Bit of Sunshine	Closed 1993	39.95	40
1993	Lil Bit of Love	Closed 1994	39.95	40
1994	Lil Bit of Tenderness	Closed 1994	39.95	40
1994	Lil Bit of Innocence	Closed 1994	39.95	40

Little Girls of Classic Literature - W. Lawton
1995	Pollyanna	12/98	79.95	80
1996	Laura Ingalls	12/99	79.95	80
1996	Rebecca of Sunnybrook Farm	12/99	79.95	80

Little Gymnast - K. Barry-Hippensteel
1996	Little Gymnast	12/99	59.95	60

Little Handfuls - M. Severino
1993	Ricky	Closed 1994	39.95	40
1993	Abby	Closed 1995	39.95	40
1993	Josie	Closed 1994	39.95	40

Little House On The Prairie - J. Ibarolle
1992	Laura	Closed 1993	79.95	80-90
1993	Mary Ingalls	Closed 1993	79.95	300-395
1993	Nellie Olson	Closed 1994	85.00	85
1993	Almanzo	Closed 1994	85.00	85
1994	Carrie	Closed 1994	85.00	85
1994	Ma Ingalls	Closed 1995	85.00	85
1994	Pa Ingalls	Closed 1995	85.00	85
1995	Baby Grace	12/96	69.95	70

Little Women - W. Lawton
1994	Jo	Closed 1995	59.95	60
1994	Meg	Closed 1995	59.95	60
1994	Beth	12/96	59.95	60
1994	Amy	12/96	59.95	60

1995	Marmie	12/96	59.95	60

The Littlest Clowns - M. Tretter
1991	Sparkles	Closed 1992	63.00	63
1991	Bubbles	Closed 1992	65.00	65
1991	Smooch	Closed 1992	69.00	69
1992	Daisy	Closed 1993	69.95	70

Look At Me - L. Di Leo
1993	Rose Marie	Closed 1994	49.95	50
1994	Ann Marie	Closed 1994	49.95	50
1994	Lisa Marie	Closed 1995	55.00	55

Lots Of Love - T. Menzenbach
1993	Hannah Needs a Hug	Closed 1994	49.95	95
1993	Kaitlyn	Closed 1994	49.95	95
1994	Nicole	Closed 1994	55.00	55
1995	Felicia	12/98	55.00	55

Lucky Charmers - C. McClure
1995	Lucky Star	12/98	69.95	70

Madonna & Child - B. Deval
1996	Madonna & Child	12/99	99.95	100

Magic Moments - K. Barry-Hippensteel
1996	Birthday Boy	12/99	69.95	70

Magical Moments of Summer - Y. Bello
1995	Whitney	12/98	59.95	60
1996	Zoe	12/99	59.95	60

Mainstreet Saturday Morning - M. Tretter
1994	Kenny	Closed 1995	69.95	70
1995	Betty	12/96	69.95	70
1995	Donny	12/96	69.95	70

Me And My Dolly - M. Girard-Kassis
1996	Lauren	12/99	59.95	60

Memories of Yesterday - M. Attwell
1994	A Friend in Need	12/96	59.95	60
1994	Tomorrow is Another Day	Closed 1995	59.95	60
1995	Beauty is in the Eye of the Beholder	12/96	59.95	60

Messages of Hope - T. Tomescu
1994	Let the Little Children Come to Me	Closed 1995	129.95	130
1995	Good Shepherd	12/96	129.95	130
1995	I Stand at the Door	12/96	129.95	130
1996	Our Father	12/99	129.95	130

Miracle of Life - Y. Bello
1996	Beautiful Newborn	12/99	49.95	50

Moments To Remember - Y. Bello
1991	Justin	Closed 1994	75.00	75
1992	Jill	Closed 1993	75.00	75
1993	Brandon (Ring Bearer)	Closed 1994	79.95	80
1993	Suzanne (Flower Girl)	Closed 1994	79.95	80

A Mother's Work Is Never Done - T. Menzenbach
1995	Don't Forget To Wash Behind Your Ears	12/98	59.95	60
1996	A Kiss Will Make It Better	12/99	59.95	60
1996	Who Made This Mess	12/99	59.95	60

My Closest Friend - J. Goodyear
1991	Boo Bear 'N Me	Closed 1992	78.00	125-150
1991	Me and My Blankie	Closed 1993	79.00	95
1992	My Secret Pal (Robbie)	Closed 1993	85.00	85
1992	My Beary Best Friend	Closed 1993	79.95	80

My Fair Lady - P. Ryan Brooks
1991	Eliza at Ascot	Closed 1992	125.00	395

My Heart Belongs To Daddy - J. Singer
1992	Peanut	Closed 1994	49.95	95
1992	Pumpkin	Closed 1994	49.95	60
1994	Princess	Closed 1994	59.95	60

My Little Ballerina - K. Barry-Hippensteel
1994	My Little Ballerina	Closed 1995	59.95	60

Nursery Newborns - J. Wolf
1994	It's A Boy	Closed 1995	79.95	80
1994	It's A Girl	Closed 1995	79.95	80

Oh Holy Night - Good-Krüger
1994	The Holy Family (Jesus, Mary, Joseph)	Closed 1995	129.95	130
1995	The Kneeling King	Closed 1995	59.95	60
1995	The Purple King	Closed 1995	59.95	60
1995	The Blue King	Closed 1995	59.95	60
1995	Shepherd with Pipes	Closed 1995	59.95	60
1995	Shepherd with Lamb	Closed 1995	59.95	60
1995	Angel	Closed 1995	59.95	60

Only At Grandma and Grandpa's - Y. Bello
1996	I'll Finish The Story	12/99	89.95	90

YEAR ISSUE	EDITION LIMIT	YEAR RETD.	ISSUE PRICE	*QUOTE U.S.$

Our Own Ballet Recital - P. Bomar
1996	Chloe		12/99	69.95	70

Parade of American Fashion - Stevens/Siegel
1987	The Glamour of the Gibson Girl	Closed	1989	77.00	100
1988	The Southern Belle	Closed	1989	77.00	100
1990	Victorian Lady	Closed	1993	82.00	82
1991	Romantic Lady	Closed	1993	85.00	85

Passports to Friendship - J. Ibarolle
1995	Serena	12/98		79.95	80
1996	Kali	12/99		79.95	80
1996	Asha	12/99		79.95	80

Patchwork of Love - Good-Krüger
1995	Warmth of the Heart	12/98		59.95	60
1996	Love One Another	12/99		59.95	60
1996	Family Price	12/99		59.95	60
1996	Simplicity Is Best	12/99		59.95	60
1996	Fondest Memory	12/99		59.95	60
1996	Hard Work Pays	12/99		59.95	60

Perfect Pairs - B. Bambina
1995	Amber	12/96		59.95	60
1995	Tiffany	12/96		59.95	60
1995	Carmen	12/96		59.95	60
1996	Susie	12/99		59.95	60

Petting Zoo - Y. Bello
1995	Andy	12/96		59.95	60
1995	Kendra	12/96		59.95	60
1995	Cory	12/96		59.95	60
1995	Maddie	12/96		59.95	60

Polly's Tea Party - S. Krey
1990	Polly	Closed	1992	78.00	125
1991	Lizzie	Closed	1993	79.00	79
1992	Annie	Closed	1993	83.00	83

Potpourri Babies - A. Brown
1995	Bubble Trouble	12/98		79.95	80

Precious Memories of Motherhood - S. Kuck
1989	Loving Steps	Closed	1991	125.00	125-150
1990	Lullaby	Closed	1993	125.00	125
1991	Expectant Moments	Closed	1993	149.00	195
1992	Bedtime	Closed	1993	150.00	150

Precious Papooses - S. Housely
1995	Sleeping Bear	12/98		79.95	80
1996	Bright Feather	12/99		79.95	80

Pretty in Pastels - J. Goodyear
1994	Precious in Pink	Closed	1995	79.95	80

Rainbow of Love - Y. Bello
1994	Blue Sky	Closed	1995	59.95	60
1994	Yellow Sunshine	Closed	1995	59.95	60
1994	Green Earth	Closed	1995	59.95	60
1994	Pink Flower	12/96		59.95	60
1994	Purple Mountain	12/96		59.95	60
1994	Orange Sunset	12/96		59.95	60

Rockwell Christmas - Rockwell-Inspired
1990	Scotty Plays Santa	Closed	1991	48.00	48
1991	Scotty Gets His Tree	Closed	1992	59.00	59
1993	Merry Christmas Grandma	Closed	1993	59.95	60

Romantic Flower Maidens - M. Roderick
1988	Rose, Who is Love	Closed	1990	87.00	87
1989	Daisy	Closed	1993	87.00	87
1990	Violet	Closed	1993	92.00	92
1990	Lily	Closed	1991	92.00	92

Season of Dreams - G. Rademann
1994	Autumn Breeze	Closed	1995	79.95	80

Secret Garden - J. Kovacik
1994	Mary	Closed	1995	69.95	70
1995	Colin	12/96		69.95	70
1995	Martha	12/96		69.95	70
1995	Dickon	12/96		69.95	70

A Sense of Discovery - K. Barry-Hippensteel
1993	Sweetie (Sense of Discovery)	Closed	1994	59.95	60

Siblings Through Time - C. McClure
1995	Alexandra	12/96		69.95	70
1995	Gracie	12/96		59.95	60

Simple Pleasures, Special Days - J. Lundy
1996	Gretchen	12/99		79.95	80
1996	Molly	12/99		79.95	80

Snow Babies - T. Tomescu
1995	Beneath the Mistletoe	Closed	1995	69.95	70
1995	Follow the Leader	12/96		75.00	75
1995	Snow Baby Express	12/96		75.00	75

Someone to Watch Over Me - K. Barry-Hippensteel
1994	Sweet Dreams	Closed	1995	69.95	70
1995	Night-Night Angel	Closed	1995	24.95	25
1995	Lullaby Angel	Closed	1995	24.95	25
1995	Sleepyhead Angel	12/96		24.95	25
1995	Stardust Angel	12/96		24.95	25
1995	Tuck-Me-In Angel	12/96		24.95	25

Sooo Big - M. Tretter
1993	Jimmy	Closed	1994	59.95	60
1994	Kimmy	Closed	1995	59.95	60

Special Edition Tour 1993 - Y. Bello
1993	Miguel	Closed	1993	69.95	70
1993	Rosa	Closed	1993	69.95	70

Stepping Out - Akers/Girardi
1991	Millie	Closed	1992	99.00	125

Tender Moments - L. Tierney
1995	Tender Love	12/96		49.95	50
1995	Tender Heart	12/96		49.95	50
1995	Tender Care	12/96		49.95	50

Together Forever - S. Krey
1994	Kirsten	Closed	1995	59.95	60
1994	Courtney	Closed	1995	59.95	60
1994	Kim	Closed	1995	59.95	60

Treasured Togetherness - M. Tretter
1994	Tender Touch	Closed	1995	99.95	100
1994	Touch of Love	Closed	1995	99.95	100

Tumbling Tots - K. Barry-Hippensteel
1993	Roly Poly Polly	Closed	1994	69.95	70
1994	Handstand Harry	Closed	1995	69.95	70

Two Much To Handle - K. Barry-Hippensteel
1993	Julie (Flowers For Mommy)	Closed	1994	59.95	60
1993	Kevin (Clean Hands)	Closed	1995	59.95	145

Under Her Wings - P. Bomar
1995	Guardian Angel	12/98		79.95	80

Victorian Dreamers - K. Barry-Hippensteel
1995	Rock-A-Bye/Good Night	12/96		49.95	50
1995	Victorian Storytime	12/96		49.95	50

Victorian Lace - C. Layton
1993	Alicia	Closed	1994	79.95	125
1994	Colleen	Closed	1995	79.95	80
1994	Olivia	Closed	1995	79.95	80

Victorian Nursery Heirloom - C. McClure
1994	Victorian Lullaby	Closed	1995	129.95	130
1995	Victorian Highchair	12/96		129.95	130
1995	Victorian Playtime	12/96		139.95	140
1995	Victorian Bunny Buggy	12/96		139.95	140

Visions Of Our Lady - B. Deval
1996	Our Lady of Grace	12/99		99.95	100

What Little Girls Are Made Of - D. Effner
1994	Peaches and Cream	Closed	1995	69.95	70
1995	Lavender & Lace	12/98		69.95	70
1995	Sunshine & Lollipops	12/98		69.95	70

Where Do Babies Come From - T. Tomescu
1996	Special Delivery	12/99		79.95	80

Winter Wonderland - K. Barry-Hippensteel
1994	Annie	Closed	1995	59.95	60
1994	Bobby	Closed	1995	59.95	60

Winterfest - S. Sherwood
1991	Brian	Closed	1992	89.00	125
1992	Michelle	Closed	1993	89.95	125
1993	Bradley	Closed	1993	89.95	90

The Wonderful Wizard of Oz - M. Tretter
1994	Dorothy	Closed	1995	79.95	80
1994	Scarecrow	Closed	1995	79.95	80
1994	Tin Man	Closed	1995	79.95	80
1994	The Cowardly Lion	12/96		79.95	80

Year Book Memories - Akers/Girardi
1991	Peggy Sue	Closed	1992	87.00	95
1993	Going Steady (Patty Jo)	Closed	1994	89.95	90
1993	Prom Queen (Betty Jean)	Closed	1993	92.00	92

Yesterday's Dreams - M. Oldenburg
1990	Andy	Closed	1993	68.00	68
1991	Janey	Closed	1993	69.00	69

Yolanda's Heaven Scent Babies - Y. Bello
1993	Meagan Rose	Closed	1994	49.95	80
1993	Daisy Anne	Closed	1994	49.95	50
1993	Morning Glory	Closed	1995	49.95	50
1993	Sweet Carnation	Closed	1995	54.95	55
1993	Lily	Closed	1995	54.95	55
1993	Cherry Blossom	Closed	1995	54.95	55

Yolanda's Lullaby Babies - Y. Bello
1991	Christy (Rock-a-Bye)	Closed	1993	69.00	75
1992	Joey (Twinkle, Twinkle)	Closed	1994	69.00	75
1993	Amy (Brahms Lullaby)	Closed	1994	75.00	75
1993	Eddie (Teddy Bear Lullaby)	Closed	1994	75.00	75
1993	Jacob (Silent Night)	Closed	1994	75.00	75
1994	Bonnie (You Are My Sunshine)	Closed	1994	80.00	80

Yolanda's Picture - Perfect Babies - Y. Bello
1985	Jason	Closed	1988	48.00	600
1986	Heather	Closed	1988	48.00	230-260
1987	Jennifer	Closed	1989	58.00	225-275
1987	Matthew	Closed	1990	58.00	195
1987	Sarah	Closed	1990	58.00	95-125
1988	Amanda	Closed	1990	63.00	125
1989	Jessica	Closed	1993	63.00	75-85
1990	Michael	Closed	1992	63.00	125
1990	Lisa	Closed	1992	63.00	95-110
1991	Emily	Closed	1992	63.00	125
1991	Danielle	Closed	1993	69.00	125

Yolanda's Playtime Babies - Y. Bello
1993	Todd	Closed	1994	59.95	60
1993	Lindsey	Closed	1994	59.95	65
1993	Shawna	Closed	1994	59.95	60

Yolanda's Precious Playmates - Y. Bello
1992	David	Closed	1994	69.95	125
1993	Paul	Closed	1994	69.95	125
1994	Johnny	Closed	1994	69.95	70

Young Love - J.W. Smith
1993	First Kiss	Closed	1993	118.00	118
1993	Buttercups	Closed	1994	Set	Set

Attic Babies

Attic Babies' Collector Club - M. Maschino-Walker
1992	Burtie Buzbee, SNL		Retrd.	1992	40.00	40
1993	Izzie B. Ruebottom, SNL	277	1993	35.00	35
1994	Sunflower Flossie, SNL		Retrd.	1994	42.00	42
1995	Tricia Kay Yum-Yum, SNL		Retrd.	1995	40.00	40
1996	Baby Savannah, SNL		12/96	39.95	40

Baggie Collection - M. Maschino-Walker
1991	Americana Baggie Bear	Retrd.	1994	19.95	22
1991	Americana Baggie Girl	Retrd.	1994	19.95	22
1991	Americana Baggie Rabbit	Retrd.	1994	19.95	22
1991	Americana Baggie Santa	Retrd.	1994	19.95	22
1991	Christmas Baggie Girl	Retrd.	1994	19.95	22
1991	Christmas Baggie Rabbit	Retrd.	1994	19.95	22
1991	Christmas Baggie Santa	Retrd.	1994	19.95	22
1991	Country Baggie Bear	Retrd.	1994	19.95	22
1991	Country Baggie Girl	Retrd.	1994	19.95	22
1991	Country Baggie Rabbit	Retrd.	1994	19.95	22

Baggie Collection - M. Maschino-Walker-Walker
1991	Christmas Baggie Bear	Retrd.	1994	19.95	22

Mother's Day Angels - M. Maschino-Walker
1994	Nattie Fae Tucker, SNL	757	1994	64.95	65

Retired Dolls - M. Maschino-Walker
1994	Abner Abernathy		Retrd.	1995	55.95	75
1994	Addie Abernathy		Retrd.	1995	61.95	75
1992	Americana Raggedy Santa (1st ed.), SNL		Retrd.	1992	85.95	150
1992	Americana Raggedy Santa (2nd ed.), SNL		Retrd.	1992	89.95	90
1989	Artilma Hunnicut		Retrd.	1995	43.95	70-110
1992	Artilma Hunnicut		Retrd.	1995	73.95	74
1990	Beary Harriete Bear		Retrd.	1995	87.95	88
1990	Beary Harry Bear		Retrd.	1995	87.95	88
1987	Bessie Jo		Retrd.	1989	31.95	98
1987	Beth Sue		Retrd.	1991	27.95	75
1989	Bouncing Baby Roy		Retrd.	1995	49.95	65
1988	Bunnifer		Retrd.	1990	39.95	82
1988	Buttons		Retrd.	1991	27.95	28
1992	Candy Applebee		Retrd.	1994	15.95	18
1992	Christopher Columbus SNL		Retrd.	1992	79.95	200-250
1989	Cloddy Clyde		Retrd.	1995	65.95	70
1989	Cotton Pickin' Ninny		Retrd.	1992	47.95	100
1987	Country Clyde		Retrd.	1988	27.95	28
1992	Daddy's Lil Punkin Patty, SNL		Retrd.	1993	79.95	175
1992	Darcie Duckworth		Retrd.	1995	59.95	60
1987	Dirty Harry		Retrd.	1991	27.95	55-100
1994	Dollie Boots (1st ed.)	100	1994	79.95	300-395
1995	Dollie Boots (2nd ed.)	2,000	1995	84.95	85
1990	Duckie Dinkle		Retrd.	1991	95.95	96
1992	Durwin Duckworth		Retrd.	1995	59.95	60
1988	Fester Chester		Retrd.	1994	39.95	50
1989	Flakey Jakey		Retrd.	1991	59.95	76
1990	Frannie Farkle		Retrd.	1991	129.95	130
1990	Frizzy Lizzy		Retrd.	1992	95.95	250
1995	Fuzzy Sweezy (1st ed.)	2,000	1995	77.95	78
1990	Gabbie Abbie		Retrd.	1995	109.95	110
1988	Hannah Lou		Retrd.	1992	39.95	50
1990	Happy Huck		Retrd.	1992	47.95	102
1993	Happy Pappy Claus SNL	805	1994	73.95	85

DOLLS

YEAR ISSUE		EDITION LIMIT	YEAR RETD.	ISSUE PRICE	*QUOTE U.S.$
1987	Harold	Retrd.	1990	27.95	80
1995	Hazel Lynora Grimsley	2,000	1995	68.95	69
1989	Heavenly Heather	Retrd.	1992	59.95	100
1988	Heffy Cheffy	Retrd.	1994	75.95	125
1990	Homer Hare	Retrd.	1995	147.95	225
1990	Hunnie Bunnie	Retrd.	1995	147.95	148
1989	Itsy Bitsy Mitzy	Retrd.	1995	49.95	50
1993	Itty Bitty Santa	Retrd.	1993	5.95	6
1990	Ivan Ivie	Retrd.	1991	129.95	230
1987	Jacob	Retrd.	1988	27.95	100
1993	Jammy Mammy Claus SNL	653	1994	67.95	85
1987	Jenny Lou	Retrd.	1992	35.95	36
1989	Jingle Jangle Jo	Retrd.	1995	69.95	85
1989	Jolly Jim	Retrd.	1992	31.95	32
1990	Jumpin Pumkin Jill	Retrd.	1994	55.95	56
1988	Katy	Retrd.	1995	59.95	60
1990	Lampsie Divie Ivie	Retrd.	1991	129.95	285
1995	Lani Frumpet (1st ed.)	2,000	1995	56.95	57
1988	Lazy Daisy	Retrd.	1992	39.95	60
1988	Lazy Liza Jane	Retrd.	1991	47.95	48
1995	Lily Lumpbucket	2,000	1995	61.95	62
1988	Little Dove	Retrd.	1988	39.95	40
1994	Lollie Ann	Retrd.	1994	39.95	40
1987	Maggie Mae	Retrd.	1991	25.95	28
1991	Maizie Mae	Retrd.	1994	51.95	52
1991	Mandi Mae	Retrd.	1994	51.95	52
1991	Memsie Mae	Retrd.	1994	51.95	52
1993	Merry Beary Raggady Santy	1,000	1995	113.95	114
1994	Merry Ole Farley Fagan Dooberry, SNL	Retrd.	1994	131.95	132
1987	Messy Tessy	Retrd.	1995	43.95	44
1993	Millie Wilset	2,000	1994	39.95	40
1987	Miss Pitty Pat	Retrd.	1988	27.95	100
1988	Molly Bea	Retrd.	1990	39.95	45-80
1995	Monty Thumpet	2,000	1995	56.95	57
1988	Moosey Matilda	Retrd.	1990	39.95	150-300
1989	Mr. Gardner	Retrd.	1995	109.95	110
1993	Mr. Kno Mo Sno, SNL	1,800	1994	51.95	68
1991	Mr. Raggedy Claus, SNL	Retrd.	1992	69.95	85
1989	Mrs. Gardner	Retrd.	1995	109.95	110
1991	Mrs. Raggedy Claus, SNL	Retrd.	1992	69.95	85
1989	Ms. Waddles	Retrd.	1990	47.95	48
1987	Muslin Bunny	Retrd.	1993	7.95	8
1987	Muslin Teddy	Retrd.	1993	7.95	8
1988	Nathan	Retrd.	1995	59.95	60
1988	Naughty Nellie	Retrd.	1990	31.95	85
1990	Nerdie Nelda	Retrd.	1995	69.95	70
1994	Old Raggady Noah	2,500	1995	139.95	140
1993	Old St. Knickerbocker, SNL	Retrd.	1993	79.95	80
1992	Old St. Nick, SNL	Retrd.	1993	95.95	130
1989	Old Tyme Santy	Retrd.	1989	79.95	80
1995	Pea Pod Sweezy (1st ed.)	2,000	1995	74.95	75
1990	Phylbert Farkle	Retrd.	1991	129.95	225
1991	Pippy Pat	Retrd.	1994	47.95	52
1988	Prissy Missy	Retrd.	1991	31.95	32
1987	Rachel	Retrd.	1988	29.95	85
XX	Raggady Cornell G. Hockenberry Workbench	Retrd.	1996	38.00	38
XX	Raggady Cornell G. Hockenberry, SNL			66.00	66
1987	Raggady Kitty	Retrd.	1988	29.95	30
1995	Raggady Old Wooly Tackitt	2,000	1995	46.95	47
1990	Raggady Ole Chris Cringle (1st ed.)	Retrd.	1990	189.95	262
1990	Raggady Ole Chris Cringle (2nd ed.)	Retrd.	1991	189.95	190
1994	Raggady P. Shagnasty	Retrd.	1995	139.95	140
1988	Raggady Sam (1st ed.)	Retrd.	1991	55.95	115
1991	Raggady Sam (2nd ed.)	500	1995	399.95	500
1987	Raggady Santy (1st ed.)	Retrd.	1988	75.95	200
1990	Raggady Santy (2nd ed.)	Retrd.	1991	89.95	90
1987	Raggady Teddy	Retrd.	1988	9.95	10
1989	Rammy Sammy	Retrd.	1990	43.95	44
1987	Rose Ann	Retrd.	1991	39.95	40
1988	Rotten Wilber	Retrd.	1990	35.95	140
1988	Rufus	Retrd.	1992	35.95	70-80
1987	Sally Francis	Retrd.	1993	35.95	62
1987	Sara	Retrd.	1992	39.95	86
1992	Scary Larry Scarecrow, SNL	Retrd.	1994	79.95	80
1988	Silly Willie	Retrd.	1990	39.95	76
1989	Skitty Kitty	Retrd.	1991	43.95	140
1990	Sollie Ollie Otis	Retrd.	1991	129.95	130
1995	Spirit of Christmas Santy	Retrd.	1995	87.95	88
1988	Spring Santy	Retrd.	1989	47.95	48
1988	Sweet William	Retrd.	1989	35.95	152
1992	Teeny Weenie Christmas Angel	Retrd.	1994	9.95	15
1992	Teeny Weenie Country Angel	Retrd.	1994	9.95	15
1987	Toddy Sue	Retrd.	1990	27.95	87
1995	Tootie Twinkles (1st ed.)	5,000	1995	59.95	60
1990	Verlie Mae	Retrd.	1995	49.95	50
1988	Wacky Jackie	Retrd.	1990	39.95	40
1995	Willa Thumpet	2,000	1995	73.95	74
1991	Winkie Binkie	Retrd.	1993	53.95	54
1992	Witchy Wanda, SNL	Retrd.	1994	79.95	80
1989	Wood Doll, black-large	Retrd.	1991	36.00	36
1989	Wood Doll, white-large	Retrd.	1991	36.00	36
1989	Wood Doll-medium	Retrd.	1991	31.95	32
1989	Wood Doll-small	Retrd.	1991	23.95	24
1990	Yankee Doodle Debbie	Retrd.	1993	95.95	150
1990	Zitty Zelda, SNL	Retrd.	1993	89.95	176

Tour Babies - M. Maschino-Walker

YEAR ISSUE		EDITION LIMIT	YEAR RETD.	ISSUE PRICE	*QUOTE U.S.$
1992	Tour Baby-old man 1992	Retrd.	1992	19.95	20
1992	Tour Baby-old woman 1992	Retrd.	1992	19.95	20
1992	Tour Baby-young boy 1992	Retrd.	1992	19.95	20
1992	Tour Baby-young girl 1992	Retrd.	1992	19.95	20
1993	Tour Baby 1993	Retrd.	1993	19.95	22
1994	Tour Baby 1994	Retrd.	1994	24.95	25
1995	Tour Baby 1995	Retrd.	1995	26.95	27
1996	Tour Baby 1996	12/96		12.95	13

Valentine Collection - M. Maschino-Walker

YEAR ISSUE		EDITION LIMIT	YEAR RETD.	ISSUE PRICE	*QUOTE U.S.$
1993	Valentine Bear-Girl	Retrd.	1993	39.95	40
1993	Valentine Bear-Boy	Retrd.	1993	39.95	40
1994	Herwin Heaps-O Hugs	613	1994	39.95	50
1994	Lottie Lots-A Hugs	825	1994	39.95	50
1995	Ruthie Claire	Retrd.	1995	39.95	45

The Collectables Inc.

Collector's Club Doll - P. Parkins

YEAR ISSUE		EDITION LIMIT	YEAR RETD.	ISSUE PRICE	*QUOTE U.S.$
1991	Mandy	Closed	1991	360.00	360
1992	Kallie	Closed	1992	410.00	410
1993	Mommy and Me	Closed	1993	810.00	810
1994	Krystal	Closed	1994	380.00	380
1995	Taylor	Closed	1995	380.00	380

Cherished Memories - P. Parkins, unless otherwise noted

YEAR ISSUE		EDITION LIMIT	YEAR RETD.	ISSUE PRICE	*QUOTE U.S.$
1986	Amy and Andrew	S/O	1986	220.00	325
1988	Brittany	Closed	1988	240.00	300
1990	Cassandra	Closed	1990	500.00	550
1989	Generations	Closed	1989	480.00	500
1988	Heather	Closed	1988	280.00	300-350
1988	Jennifer	Closed	1988	380.00	500-600
1988	Leigh Ann And Leland	Closed	1988	250.00	250-300
1988	Tea Time - D. Effner	S/O	1986	380.00	450
1990	Twinkles	Closed	1991	170.00	275

The Collectibles Inc. Dolls - P. Parkins, unless otherwise noted

YEAR ISSUE		EDITION LIMIT	YEAR RETD.	ISSUE PRICE	*QUOTE U.S.$
1991	Adrianna	Closed	1992	1350.00	1350
1994	Afternoon Delight	500	1995	410.00	410
1995	Alexus	150		770.00	770
1993	Amber	500	1994	330.00	330
1994	Amber Hispanic	500	1994	340.00	340
1992	Angel on My Shoulder (Lillianne w/CeCe)	500	1993	530.00	530
1990	Bassinet Baby	2,000	1990	130.00	375-425
1991	Bethany	Closed	1992	450.00	450
1995	Brianna	150	1995	590.00	590
1995	Christine	350		390.00	390
1990	Danielle	1,000	1990	400.00	475
1994	Earth Angel	500		195.00	195
1993	Haley	500	1994	330.00	330
1990	In Your Easter Bonnet	1,000	1990	350.00	350
1992	Karlie	500	1992	380.00	380
1991	Kelsie	500	1991	320.00	320
1991	Lauren	S/O	1991	490.00	490
1993	Little Dumpling (Black)	500	1994	190.00	190
1993	Little Dumpling (White)	500	1994	190.00	190
1990	Lizbeth Ann - D. Effner	1,000	1990	420.00	420
1994	Madison	250		350.00	350
1994	Madison Sailor	250	1995	370.00	370
1993	Maggie	500	1994	330.00	330
1992	Marissa	300	1992	350.00	350
1992	Marty	250	1992	190.00	190
1992	Matia	250	1992	190.00	190
1989	Michelle	250	1990	270.00	400-450
1992	Missy	Open		59.00	59
1992	Molly	450	1993	350.00	350
1994	Morgan	250	1995	390.00	390
1994	Morgan in Red	250	1995	390.00	390
1995	A Mother's Love	450		770.00	770
1995	My Little Angel Boy	250		450.00	450
1995	My Little Angel Girl	250		450.00	450
1991	Natasha	Closed	1992	510.00	510
1992	Shelley	300	1992	450.00	450
1987	Storytime By Sarah Jane	S/O	1990	330.00	475-525
1994	Sugar Plum Fairy	500		250.00	250
1987	Tasha	S/O	1987	290.00	1400
1986	Tatiana	S/O	1986	270.00	1000
1989	Welcome Home - D. Effner	1,000	1990	330.00	475-675
1991	Yvette	300	1992	580.00	580

Fairy - P. Parkins

YEAR ISSUE		EDITION LIMIT	YEAR RETD.	ISSUE PRICE	*QUOTE U.S.$
1988	Tabatha	1,500	1989	370.00	400-450

Mother's Little Treasures - D. Effner

YEAR ISSUE		EDITION LIMIT	YEAR RETD.	ISSUE PRICE	*QUOTE U.S.$
1985	1st Edition	S/O	1985	380.00	1000
1990	2nd Edition	S/O	1990	440.00	475-595

Yesterday's Child - D. Effner, unless otherwise noted

YEAR ISSUE		EDITION LIMIT	YEAR RETD.	ISSUE PRICE	*QUOTE U.S.$
1986	Ashley - P. Parkins	Closed	1987	220.00	275
1983	Chad And Charity	Closed	1984	190.00	190
1982	Cleo	Closed	1983	180.00	250
1982	Columbine	Closed	1983	180.00	250
1982	Jason And Jessica	Closed	1983	150.00	300
1984	Kevin And Karissa	Closed	1985	190.00	250-300
1983	Noel	Closed	1984	190.00	240
1984	Rebecca	Closed	1985	250.00	250-300
1986	Todd And Tiffany	Closed	1987	220.00	250

Department 56

Heritage Village Doll Collection - Department 56

YEAR ISSUE		EDITION LIMIT	YEAR RETD.	ISSUE PRICE	*QUOTE U.S.$
1987	Christmas Carol Dolls 1000-6 set/4 (Tiny Tim, Bob Crachet, Mrs. Crachet, Scrooge)	250	1988	1500.00	1500
1987	Christmas Carol Dolls 5907-2 set/4 (Tiny Tim, Bob Crachet, Mrs. Crachet, Scrooge)	Closed	1993	250.00	265-300
1988	Christmas Carol Dolls 1001-4 set/4 (Tiny Tim, Bob Crachet, Mrs. Crachet, Scrooge)	350	1989	1600.00	1600
1988	Mr. & Mrs. Fezziwig 5594-8 set/2	Open		172.00	172

Snowbabies Dolls - Department 56

YEAR ISSUE		EDITION LIMIT	YEAR RETD.	ISSUE PRICE	*QUOTE U.S.$
1988	Allison & Duncan-Set /2, 7730-5	Closed	1989	200.00	650-750

Dolls by Jerri

Dolls by Jerri - J. McCloud

YEAR ISSUE		EDITION LIMIT	YEAR RETD.	ISSUE PRICE	*QUOTE U.S.$
1986	Alfalfa	1,000		350.00	350
1986	Allison	1,000		350.00	450
1986	Amber	1,000		350.00	850
1986	Annabelle	300		600.00	585
1986	Ashley	1,000		350.00	500
1986	Audrey	300		550.00	550
1982	Baby David	538		290.00	2000
XX	Boy	1,000		350.00	425
1985	Bride	1,000		350.00	400
1986	Bridgette	300		500.00	500
1985	Candy	1,000		340.00	2000
1986	Cane	1,000		350.00	1200
1986	Charlotte	1,000		330.00	450
1984	Clara	1,000		320.00	1200-1500
1986	Clown-David 3 Yrs. Old	1,000		340.00	450
1986	Danielle	1,000		330.00	500
1986	David-2 Years Old	1,000		330.00	550
1986	David-Magician	1,000		350.00	450
XX	Denise	1,000		380.00	550
1986	Elizabeth	1,000		340.00	350
1984	Emily	1,000		330.00	2500
1986	The Fool	1,000		350.00	350
XX	Gina	1,000		350.00	475
XX	Goldilocks	1,000		370.00	600-650
1989	Goose Girl, Guild	Closed		300.00	700
1986	Helenjean	1,000		350.00	500-650
1988	Holly	1,000		370.00	825
1986	Jacqueline	300		500.00	500
XX	Jamie	800		380.00	450
1986	Joy	1,000		350.00	350
XX	Laura	1,000		350.00	500
1989	Laura Lee	1,000		370.00	575
XX	Little Bo Peep	1,000		340.00	450
XX	Little Miss Muffet	1,000		340.00	450
1986	Lucianna	300		500.00	500
1986	Mary Beth	1,000		350.00	350
XX	Megan	750		420.00	550
XX	Meredith	750		430.00	600
1985	Miss Nanny	1,000		160.00	275
1986	Nobody	1,000		350.00	550-650
1986	Princess and the Unicorn	1,000		370.00	400
1986	Samantha	1,000		350.00	550
1985	Scotty	1,000		340.00	1800
1986	Somebody	1,000		350.00	550-750
1985	Tammy	1,000		350.00	900
1985	Uncle Joe	1,000		160.00	250-300
XX	Uncle Remus	500		290.00	450
1986	Yvonne	300		500.00	500

Elke's Originals, Ltd.

Elke Hutchens - E. Hutchens

YEAR ISSUE		EDITION LIMIT	YEAR RETD.	ISSUE PRICE	*QUOTE U.S.$
1991	Alicia	250		595.00	700-995
1989	Annabelle	250		575.00	1300-1600
1989	Aubra	250		575.00	850-995
1990	Aurora	250		595.00	850-950
1991	Bellinda	400		595.00	800-895
1992	Bethany	400		595.00	700-895
1991	Braelyn	400		595.00	1300-1700
1991	Brianna	400		595.00	895
1992	Cecilia	435		635.00	750-895
1992	Charles	435		635.00	450-800
1992	Cherie	435		635.00	700
1992	Clarissa	435		635.00	800-895
1993	Daphne	435		675.00	500-800
1993	Deidre	435		675.00	500-800
1993	Desirée	435		675.00	550-800
1990	Kricket	500		575.00	400
1992	Laurakaye	435		550.00	550
1990	Little Liebchen	250		475.00	1000
1990	Victoria	400		645.00	645

Enesco Corporation

Precious Moments Dolls - S. Butcher

YEAR ISSUE		EDITION LIMIT	YEAR RETD.	ISSUE PRICE	*QUOTE U.S.$
1981	Mikey, 18"- E-6214B	Suspd.		150.00	225
1981	Debbie, 18"- E-6214G	Suspd.		150.00	200-225
1982	Cubby, 18"- E-7267B	5,000		200.00	350-400
1982	Tammy, 18"- E-7267G	5,000		300.00	400-500
1983	Katie Lynne, 16"- E-0539	Suspd.		165.00	175
1984	Mother Sew Dear, 18"- E-2850	Retrd.	1985	350.00	350

YEAR ISSUE	EDITION LIMIT	YEAR RETD.	ISSUE PRICE	*QUOTE U.S.$
1984 Kristy, 12"- E-2851	Suspd.		150.00	175
1984 Timmy, 12"- E-5397	Suspd.		125.00	160
1985 Aaron, 12"- 12424	Suspd.		135.00	150
1985 Bethany, 12"- 12432	Suspd.		135.00	150
1985 P.D., 7"- 12475	Suspd.		50.00	75
1985 Trish, 7"-12483	Suspd.		50.00	75
1986 Bong Bong, 13"-100455	12,000		150.00	265
1986 Candy, 13"-100463	12,000		150.00	275
1986 Connie, 12"-102253	7,500		160.00	240
1987 Angie, The Angel of Mercy-12491	12,500		160.00	275
1990 The Voice of Spring-408786	2-Yr.		150.00	150
1990 Summer's Joy-408794	2-Yr.		150.00	150
1990 Autumn's Praise-408808	2-Yr.		150.00	150
1990 Winter's Song-408816	2-Yr.		150.00	170
1991 You Have Touched So Many Hearts- 427527	2-Yr.		90.00	90
1991 May You Have An Old Fashioned Christmas-417785	2-Yr.		150.00	175
1991 The Eyes Of The Lord Are Upon You (Boy Action Musical)-429570	Suspd.		65.00	65
1991 The Eyes Of The Lord Are Upon You (Girl Action Musical)-429589	Suspd.		65.00	65

Precious Moments-Jack-In-The-Boxes - S. Butcher

1991 You Have Touched So Many Hearts-422282	2-Yr.		175.00	175
1991 May You Have An Old Fashioned Christmas-417777	2-Yr.		200.00	200

Precious Moments-Jack-In-The-Boxes-4 Seasons - S. Butcher

1990 Voice of Spring-408735	2-Yr.		200.00	200
1990 Summer's Joy-408743	2-Yr.		200.00	200
1990 Autumn's Praise-408751	2-Yr.		200.00	200
1990 Winter's Song-408778	2-Yr.		200.00	200

Ganz

Cowtown - C. Thammavongsa

1994 Buffalo Bull Cody	Open		20.00	20
1994 Old MooDonald	Open		20.00	20
1994 Santa Cows	Open		25.00	25

Little Cheesers/Cheeserville Picnic Collection - G.D.A. Group

1992 Sweet Cicely Musical Doll In Basket	Closed	1996	85.00	85

Georgetown Collection, Inc.

Age of Romance - J. Reavey

1994 Catherine	100-day		150.00	150

American Diary Dolls - L. Mason

1991 Bridget Quinn	100-day		129.25	130
1991 Christina Merovina	100-day		129.25	130
1990 Jennie Cooper	100-day		129.25	130-155
1994 Lian Ying	100-day		130.00	130
1991 Many Stars	100-day		129.25	130
1992 Rachel Williams	100-day		129.25	130
1993 Sarah Turner	100-day		130.00	130
1992 Tulu	100-day		129.25	130

Baby Kisses - T. DeHetre

1992 Michelle	100-day		118.60	119

Blessed Are The Children - J. Reavey

1994 Faith	100-day		83.00	83

Boys Will Be Boys - J. Reavey

1996 Just Like Dad	100-day		96.00	96
1994 Mr. Mischief	100-day		96.00	96

Children of the Great Spirit - C. Theroux

1993 Buffalo Child	100-day		140.00	140
1994 Golden Flower	100-day		130.00	130
1994 Little Fawn	100-day		114.00	114
1993 Winter Baby	100-day		160.00	160

Class Portraits - J. Kissling

1995 Anna	100-day		140.00	140

Country Quilt Babies - B. Prusseit

1996 Hannah	100-day		104.00	104

Dreams Come True - M. Sirko

1995 Amanda	100-day		120.00	120

Faerie Princess - B. Deval

1989 Faerie Princess	Closed	N/A	248.00	248

Fanciful Dreamers - A. Timmerman

1995 Sweetdreams & Moonbeams	100-day		130.00	130

Faraway Friends - S. Skille

1994 Dara	100-day		140.00	140
1993 Kristin	100-day		140.00	140
1994 Mariama	100-day		140.00	140

YEAR ISSUE	EDITION LIMIT	YEAR RETD.	ISSUE PRICE	*QUOTE U.S.$
Favorite Friends - K. Murawska				
1995 Christina	100-day		130.00	130
1996 Samantha	100-day		130.00	130
Georgetown Collection - Various				
1995 Buffalo Boy - C. Theroux	100-day		130.00	130
1993 Quick Fox - L. Mason	100-day		138.95	139
1994 Silver Moon - L. Mason	100-day		140.00	140
Gifts From Heaven - B. Prusseit				
1994 Good as Gold	100-day		88.00	88
1995 Sweet Pea	100-day		88.00	88
Hearts in Song - J. Galperin				
1994 Angelique	100-day		150.00	150
1992 Grace	100-day		149.60	150
1993 Michael	100-day		150.00	150
Heavenly Messages - M. Sirko				
1996 David	100-day		104.00	104
1995 Gabrielle	100-day		104.00	104
Kindergarten Kids - V. Walker				
1992 Nikki	100-day		129.60	130
Let's Play - T. DeHetre				
1992 Eentsy Weentsy Willie	100-day		118.60	119
1992 Peek-A-Boo Beckie	100-day		118.60	119
Linda's Little Ladies - L. Mason				
1993 Shannon's Holiday	100-day		169.95	170
Little Artists of Africa - C. Massey				
1996 Oluwa Fumike	100-day		130.00	130
Little Bit of Heaven - A. Timmerman				
1994 Arielle	100-day		130.00	130
1995 Cupid	100-day		135.00	135
1995 Noelle	100-day		130.00	130
Little Bloomers - J. Reavey				
1995 Darling Daisy	100-day		104.00	104
Little Dreamers - A. DiMartino				
1994 Beautiful Buttercup	100-day		130.00	130
1995 Julie	100-day		130.00	130
1996 Nicole	100-day		130.00	130
Little Loves - B. Deval				
1988 Emma	Closed	N/A	139.20	140
1989 Katie	Closed	N/A	139.20	140
1990 Laura	Closed	N/A	139.20	140
1989 Megan	Closed	N/A	138.00	160
Little Performers - M. Sirko				
1996 Tickled Pink	100-day		100.00	100
Maud Humphrey's Little Victorians - M. Humphrey				
1996 Papa's Little Sailor	100-day		130.00	130
Messengers of the Great Spirit - Various				
1994 Noatak - L. Mason	100-day		150.00	150
1994 Prayer for the Buffalo - C. Theroux	100-day		120.00	120
Miss Ashley - P. Thompson				
1989 Miss Ashley	Closed	N/A	228.00	228
Naturally Curious Kids - A. Hollis				
1996 Jennifer	100-day		100.00	100
Nursery Babies - T. DeHetre				
1990 Baby Bunting	Closed	N/A	118.20	150
1991 Diddle, Diddle	Closed	N/A	118.20	119
1991 Little Girl	100-day		118.20	119
1990 Patty Cake	Closed	N/A	118.20	119
1991 Rock-A-Bye Baby	100-day		118.20	119
1991 This Little Piggy	100-day		118.20	119
Nutcracker Sweethearts - S. Skille				
1995 Sugar Plum	100-day		130.00	130
Pictures of Innocence - J. Reavey				
1994 Clarissa	100-day		137.50	138
Portraits of Enchantment - A. Timmerman				
1996 Sleeping Beauty	100-day		150.00	150
Portraits of Perfection - A. Timmerman				
1993 Apple Dumpling	100-day		149.60	150
1994 Blackberry Blossom	100-day		149.60	150
1993 Peaches & Cream	100-day		149.60	150
1993 Sweet Strawberry	100-day		149.60	150
Prayers From The Heart - S. Skille				
1995 Hope	100-day		115.00	115
Russian Fairy Tales Dolls - B. Deval				
1993 Vasilisa	100-day		190.00	190

YEAR ISSUE	EDITION LIMIT	YEAR RETD.	ISSUE PRICE	*QUOTE U.S.$
Small Wonders - B. Deval				
1991 Abbey	100-day		97.60	98
1990 Corey	100-day		97.60	98
1992 Sarah	100-day		97.60	98
Songs of Innocence - J. Reavey				
1995 Kelsey	100-day		104.00	104
1996 Meagan	100-day		104.00	104
Sugar & Spice - L. Mason				
1992 Little Sunshine	100-day		141.10	142
1991 Little Sweetheart	100-day		118.25	119
1991 Red Hot Pepper	100-day		118.25	119
Sweethearts of Summer - P. Phillips				
1994 Caroline	100-day		140.00	140
1995 Jessica	100-day		140.00	140
1995 Madeleine & Harry	100-day		140.00	140
Sweets For the Sweet - V. Ohms				
1996 Elise	100-day		130.00	130
Tansie - P. Coffer				
1988 Tansie	Closed	N/A	81.00	81
Victorian Fantasies - L. Mason				
1995 Amber Afternoon	100-day		150.00	150
1995 Lavender Dreams	100-day		150.00	150
1996 Reflections of Rose	100-day		150.00	150
Victorian Innocence - L. Mason				
1994 Annabelle	100-day		130.00	130
Victorian Splendor - J. Reavey				
1994 Emily	100-day		130.00	130
What a Beautiful World - R. Hockh				
1996 Marisa	100-day		130.00	130
Yesterday's Dreams - P. Phillips				
1994 Mary Elizabeth	100-day		130.00	130
1996 Sophie	100-day		130.00	130

Goebel of North America

Bob Timberlake Dolls - B. Ball

1996 Abby Liz-911350	2,000		195.00	195
1996 Ann-911352	2,000		195.00	195
1996 Carter-911351	2,000		195.00	195
1996 Kate-911353	2,000		195.00	195

Cindy Guyer Romance Dolls - B. Ball

1996 Cordelia-911824	1,000		225.00	225
1996 Cynthia-911830	1,000		225.00	225
1996 Mackenzie-911825	1,000		225.00	225

Dolly Dingle - B. Ball

1995 Melvis Bumps-911617	1,000		99.00	99

Goebel Dolls - B. Ball

1995 Brother Murphy-911100	2,000		125.00	125

Hummel Dolls - B. Ball

1996 Little Scholar, 14" 911211	N/A		200.00	200
1997 School Girl, 14" 911212	N/A		200.00	200

United States Historical Society - B. Ball

1995 Mary-911155	1,500		195.00	195

Victoria Ashlea® Birthstone Dolls - K. Kennedy

1995 January-Garnet-912471	2,500		29.50	30
1995 February-Amethyst-912472	2,500		29.50	30
1995 March-Aquamarine-912473	2,500		29.50	30
1995 April-Diamond-912474	2,500		29.50	30
1995 May-Emerald-912475	2,500		29.50	30
1995 June -Lt. Amethyst-912476	2,500		29.50	30
1995 July-Ruby-912477	2,500		29.50	30
1995 August-Peridot-912478	2,500		29.50	30
1995 September-Sapphire-912479	2,500		29.50	30
1995 October-Rosestone-912480	2,500		29.50	30
1995 November-Topaz-912481	2,500		29.50	30
1995 December-Zircon-912482	2,500		29.50	30

Victoria Ashlea® Originals - B. Ball, unless otherwise noted

1985 Adele-901172	Closed	1989	145.00	275
1989 Alexa-912214	Closed	1991	195.00	195
1989 Alexandria-912273	Closed	1991	275.00	275
1987 Alice-901212	Closed	1991	95.00	135
1990 Alice-912296 - K. Kennedy	Closed	1992	65.00	65
1992 Alicia-912388	500	1994	135.00	135
1992 Allison-912358	Closed	1993	160.00	165
1987 Amanda Pouty-901209	Closed	1991	150.00	215
1988 Amanda-912246	Closed	1991	180.00	180
1993 Amanda-912409	2,000	1996	40.00	40
1984 Amelia-933006	Closed	1988	100.00	100
1990 Amie-912313 - K. Kennedy	Closed	1993	150.00	150
1990 Amy-901262	Closed	1993	110.00	110
1990 Angela-912324 - K. Kennedy	Closed	1994	130.00	135
1988 Angelica-912204	Closed	1991	150.00	150
1992 Angelica-912339	1,000	1995	145.00	145

DOLLS

YEAR ISSUE	EDITION LIMIT	YEAR RETD.	ISSUE PRICE	*QUOTE U.S.$
1990 Annabelle-912278	Closed	1992	200.00	200
1988 Anne-912213	Closed	1991	130.00	150
1990 Annette-912333 - K. Kennedy	Closed	1993	85.00	85
1988 April-901239	Closed	1992	225.00	225
1989 Ashlea-901250	Closed	1992	550.00	550
1988 Ashley-901235	Closed	1991	110.00	110
1992 Ashley-911004	Closed	1994	99.00	105
1986 Ashley-912147	Closed	1989	125.00	125
1986 Baby Brook Beige Dress-912103	Closed	1989	60.00	60
1986 Baby Courtney-912124	Closed	1990	120.00	120
1988 Baby Daryl-912200	Closed	1991	85.00	85
1987 Baby Doll-912184	Closed	1990	75.00	75
1988 Baby Jennifer-912210	Closed	1992	75.00	75
1988 Baby Katie-912222	Closed	1993	70.00	70
1986 Baby Lauren Pink-912086	Closed	1991	120.00	120
1987 Baby Lindsay-912190	Closed	1990	80.00	80
1984 Barbara-901108	Closed	1987	57.00	110
1990 Baryshnicat-912298 - K. Kennedy	Closed	1991	25.00	25
1988 Bernice-901245	Closed	1991	90.00	90
1993 Beth-912430 - K. Kennedy	2,000	1996	45.00	45
1992 Betsy-912390	500	1994	150.00	150
1990 Bettina-912310	Closed	1993	100.00	105
1988 Betty Doll-912220	Closed	1993	90.00	90
1987 Bonnie Pouty-901207	Closed	1990	100.00	100
1988 Brandon-901234	Closed	1992	90.00	90
1990 Brandy-912304 - K. Kennedy	Closed	1992	150.00	150
1987 Bride Allison-901218	Closed	1993	180.00	180
1988 Brittany-912207	Closed	1990	130.00	145
1992 Brittany-912365 - K. Kennedy	Closed	1993	140.00	145
1987 Caitlin-901228	Closed	1991	260.00	260
1988 Campbell Kid-Boy-758701	Closed	1988	13.80	14
1988 Campbell Kid-Girl-758700	Closed	1988	13.80	14
1989 Candace-912288 - K. Kennedy	Closed	1992	70.00	70
1992 Carol-912387 - K. Kennedy	1,000	1996	140.00	140
1987 Caroline-912191	Closed	1990	80.00	80
1990 Carolyn-901261 - K. Kennedy	Closed	1993	200.00	200
1992 Cassandra-912355 - K. Kennedy	1,000	1996	165.00	165
1988 Cat Maude-901247	Closed	1993	85.00	85
1986 Cat/Kitty Cheerful Gr Dr-901179	Closed	1990	60.00	60
1987 Catanova-901227	Closed	1991	75.00	75
1988 Catherine-901242	Closed	1992	240.00	240
XX Charity-912244	Closed	1990	70.00	70
1982 Charleen-912094	Closed	1986	65.00	65
1985 Chauncey-912085	Closed	1988	75.00	110
1988 Christina-901229	Closed	1991	350.00	400
1987 Christine-912168	Closed	1989	75.00	75
1992 Cindy-912384	1,000	1994	185.00	190
1985 Claire-901158	Closed	1988	115.00	160
1984 Claude-901032	Closed	1987	110.00	225
1984 Claudette-901033	Closed	1987	110.00	225
1989 Claudia-901257 - K. Kennedy	Closed	1993	225.00	225
1987 Clementine-901226	Closed	1991	75.00	75
1986 Clown Calypso-912104	Closed	1990	70.00	70
1985 Clown Casey-912078	Closed	1988	40.00	40
1986 Clown Cat Cadwalader-912132	Closed	1988	55.00	55
1987 Clown Champagne-912180	Closed	1989	95.00	95
1986 Clown Christabel-912095	Closed	1988	100.00	150
1985 Clown Christie-912084	Closed	1988	60.00	90
1986 Clown Clarabella-912096	Closed	1989	80.00	80
1986 Clown Clarissa-912123	Closed	1990	75.00	110
1988 Clown Cotton Candy-912199	Closed	1990	67.00	67
1986 Clown Cyd-912093	Closed	1988	70.00	70
1985 Clown Jody-912079	Closed	1988	100.00	150
1982 Clown Jolly-912181	Closed	1991	70.00	70
1986 Clown Kitten-Cleo-912133	Closed	1989	50.00	50
1986 Clown Lollipop-912127	Closed	1989	125.00	225
1984 Clown-901136	Closed	1988	90.00	120
1988 Crystal-912226	Closed	1992	75.00	75
1983 Deborah-901107	Closed	1987	220.00	400
1990 Debra-912319 - K. Kennedy	Closed	1992	120.00	120
1992 Denise-912362 - K. Kennedy	1,000	1994	145.00	175-225
1989 Diana Bride-912277	Closed	1992	180.00	180
1984 Diana-901119	Closed	1987	55.00	135
1988 Diana-912218	Closed	1992	270.00	270
1987 Dominique-901219	Closed	1991	170.00	225
1987 Doreen-912198	Closed	1990	75.00	75
1985 Dorothy-901157	Closed	1988	130.00	275
1992 Dottie-912393 - K. Kennedy	1,000	1996	160.00	160
1988 Elizabeth-901214	Closed	1991	90.00	90
1988 Ellen-901246	Closed	1991	100.00	100
1990 Emily-912303	Closed	1992	150.00	150
1988 Erin-901241	Closed	1991	170.00	170
1990 Fluffer-912293	Closed	1994	135.00	150-225
1985 Garnet-901183	Closed	1988	160.00	295
1990 Gigi-912306 - K. Kennedy	Closed	1994	150.00	150
1986 Gina-901176	Closed	1989	300.00	300
1989 Ginny-912287 - K. Kennedy	Closed	1993	140.00	140
1986 Girl Frog Freda-912105	Closed	1989	20.00	20
1988 Goldilocks-912234 - K. Kennedy	Closed	1992	65.00	65
1986 Googley German Astrid-912109	Closed	1989	60.00	60
1988 Heather-912247	Closed	1990	135.00	150
1990 Heather-912322	Closed	1992	150.00	150
1990 Heidi-901266	2,000	1993	150.00	150
1989 Helene-912249 - K. Kennedy	Closed	1991	160.00	160
1990 Helga-912337	Closed	1994	325.00	325
1984 Henri-901035	Closed	1986	100.00	200
1984 Henrietta-901036	Closed	1986	100.00	200
1992 Hilary-912353	Closed	1993	130.00	135
1992 Holly Belle-912380	500	1994	125.00	125
1982 Holly-901233	Closed	1985	160.00	200
1989 Holly-901254	Closed	1992	180.00	180
1989 Hope Baby w/ Pillow-912292	Closed	1992	110.00	110
1992 Iris-912389 - K. Kennedy	500	1995	165.00	165
1987 Jacqueline-912192	Closed	1990	80.00	80
1990 Jacqueline-912329 - K. Kennedy	Closed	1993	136.00	150-225
1984 Jamie-912061	Closed	1987	65.00	100
1984 Jeannie-901062	Closed	1987	200.00	550
1988 Jennifer-901248	Closed	1991	150.00	150
1988 Jennifer-912221	Closed	1990	80.00	80
1992 Jennifer-912374 - K. Kennedy	Closed	1993	150.00	150
1988 Jesse-912231	Closed	1994	110.00	115
1987 Jessica-912195	Closed	1990	120.00	135
1993 Jessica-912410	2,000	1994	40.00	40
1990 Jillian-912323	Closed	1993	150.00	150
1989 Jimmy Baby w/ Pillow-912291 - K. Kennedy	Closed	1992	165.00	165
1989 Jingles-912271	Closed	1991	60.00	60
1990 Joanne-912307 - K. Kennedy	Closed	1992	165.00	165
1987 Joy-912155	Closed	1989	50.00	50
1989 Joy-912289 - K. Kennedy	Closed	1992	110.00	110
1987 Julia-912174	Closed	1989	80.00	80
1990 Julia-912334 - K. Kennedy	Closed	1993	85.00	85
1993 Julie-912435 - K. Kennedy	2,000	1995	45.00	45
1990 Justine-901256	Closed	1992	200.00	200
1988 Karen-912205	Closed	1991	200.00	250
1993 Katie-912412	2,000	1994	40.00	40
1993 Kaylee-912433 - K. Kennedy	2,000	1994	45.00	45
1992 Kelli-912361	1,000	1995	160.00	165
1990 Kelly-912331	Closed	1991	95.00	95
1990 Kimberly-912341	1,000	1996	140.00	145
1987 Kittle Cat-912167	Closed	1989	55.00	55
1987 Kitty Cuddles-901201	Closed	1990	65.00	65
1992 Kris-912345 - K. Kennedy	Closed	1992	160.00	160
1989 Kristin-912285 - K. Kennedy	Closed	1994	90.00	95
1984 Laura-901106	Closed	1987	300.00	575
1988 Laura-912225	Closed	1991	135.00	135
1988 Lauren-912212	Closed	1991	110.00	110
1992 Lauren-912363 - K. Kennedy	1,000	1996	190.00	195
1993 Lauren-912413	2,000	1996	40.00	40
1993 Leslie-912432 - K. Kennedy	2,000	1994	45.00	45
1989 Licorice-912290	Closed	1991	75.00	75
1987 Lillian-901199	Closed	1990	85.00	100
1989 Lindsey-901263	Closed	1991	100.00	100
1989 Lisa-912275	Closed	1991	160.00	160
1989 Loni-912276	Closed	1993	125.00	150-185
1985 Lynn-912144	Closed	1988	90.00	135
1992 Margaret-912354 - K. Kennedy	1,000	1994	150.00	150
1989 Margot-912269	Closed	1991	110.00	110
1989 Maria-912265	Closed	1990	90.00	90
1982 Marie-901231	Closed	1985	95.00	95
1989 Marissa-901252 - K. Kennedy	Closed	1993	225.00	225
1988 Maritta Spanish-912224	Closed	1990	140.00	140
1992 Marjorie-912357	Closed	1993	135.00	135
1990 Marshmallow-912294 - K. Kennedy	Closed	1992	75.00	75
1985 Mary-912126	Closed	1988	60.00	90
1990 Matthew-901251	Closed	1993	100.00	100
1989 Megan-901260	Closed	1993	120.00	120
1987 Megan-912148	Closed	1989	70.00	70
1989 Melanie-912284 - K. Kennedy	Closed	1992	135.00	135
1990 Melinda-912309 - K. Kennedy	Closed	1991	70.00	70
1988 Melissa-901230	Closed	1991	110.00	110
1988 Melissa-912208	Closed	1992	125.00	125
1989 Merry-912249	Closed	1990	200.00	200
1987 Michelle-901222	Closed	1991	90.00	90
1985 Michelle-912066	Closed	1989	100.00	225
1992 Michelle-912381 - K. Kennedy	Closed	1992	175.00	175
1985 Millie-912135	Closed	1988	70.00	125
1989 Missy-912283	Closed	1993	110.00	115
1988 Molly-912211 - K. Kennedy	Closed	1992	75.00	75
1990 Monica-912336 - K. Kennedy	Closed	1993	100.00	105
1990 Monique-912335 - K. Kennedy	Closed	1993	85.00	85
1988 Morgan-912239 - K. Kennedy	Closed	1992	75.00	75
1990 Mrs. Katz-912301	Closed	1993	140.00	145
1993 Nadine-912431 - K. Kennedy	2,000	1995	45.00	45
1989 Nancy-912266	Closed	1991	110.00	110
1987 Nicole-901225	Closed	1991	575.00	575
1993 Nicole-912411	2,000	1996	40.00	40
1987 Noel-912170	Closed	1989	125.00	125
1992 Noelle-912360 - K. Kennedy	1,000	1994	165.00	170
1990 Pamela-912302	Closed	1991	95.00	95
1986 Patty Artic Flower Print-901185	Closed	1990	140.00	140
1990 Paula-912316	Closed	1992	100.00	100
1988 Paulette-901244	Closed	1991	90.00	90
1990 Penny-912325 - K. Kennedy	Closed	1993	130.00	150-225
1986 Pepper Rust Dr/Appr-901184	Closed	1990	125.00	200
1985 Phyllis-912067	Closed	1989	60.00	60
1989 Pinky Clown-912268 - K. Kennedy	Closed	1993	70.00	75
1988 Polly-912206	Closed	1990	100.00	125
1990 Priscilla-912300	Closed	1993	185.00	190
1988 Rebecca-901258	Closed	1992	250.00	250
1988 Renae-912245	Closed	1990	120.00	120
1990 Robin-912321	Closed	1993	160.00	165
1985 Rosalind-912087	Closed	1988	145.00	225
1985 Roxanne-901174	Closed	1988	155.00	275
1984 Sabina-901155	Closed	1988	75.00	N/A
1990 Samantha-912314	Closed	1993	185.00	190
1988 Sandy-901240 - K. Kennedy	Closed	1993	115.00	115
1989 Sara-912279	Closed	1991	175.00	175
1988 Sarah w/Pillow-912219	Closed	1992	105.00	105
1987 Sarah-901203	Closed	1990	350.00	350
1993 Sarah-912408	2,000	1996	40.00	40
1993 Shannon-912434 - K. Kennedy	2,000	1996	45.00	45
1990 Sheena-912338	Closed	1992	115.00	115
1984 Sheila-912060	Closed	1988	75.00	135
1990 Sheri-912305 - K. Kennedy	Closed	1992	115.00	115
1992 Sherise-912383 - K. Kennedy	Closed	1992	145.00	145
1989 Sigrid-912282	Closed	1992	145.00	145
1988 Snow White-912235 - K. Kennedy	Closed	1992	65.00	65
1987 Sophia-912173	Closed	1989	40.00	40
1988 Stephanie-912238	Closed	1992	200.00	200
1990 Stephanie-912312	Closed	1993	150.00	150
1984 Stephanie-933012	Closed	1988	115.00	115
1988 Susan-901243	Closed	1991	100.00	100
1990 Susie-912328	Closed	1993	115.00	120
1987 Suzanne-901200	Closed	1990	85.00	100
1989 Suzanne-912286	Closed	1992	120.00	120
1989 Suzy-912295	Closed	1991	110.00	110
1992 Tamika-912382	500	1994	185.00	185
1989 Tammy-912264	Closed	1990	110.00	110
1987 Tasha-901221	Closed	1990	115.00	130
1990 Tasha-912299 - K. Kennedy	Closed	1992	25.00	25
1989 Terry-912281	Closed	1994	125.00	130
1987 Tiffany Pouty-901211	Closed	1991	120.00	160
1990 Tiffany-912326 - K. Kennedy	Closed	1992	180.00	180
1984 Tobie-912023	Closed	1987	30.00	30
1992 Toni-912367 - K. Kennedy	Closed	1993	120.00	120
1990 Tracie-912315	Closed	1993	125.00	125
1992 Trudie-912391	500	1996	135.00	135
1982 Trudy-901232	Closed	1985	100.00	100
1992 Tulip-912385 - K. Kennedy	500	1994	145.00	145
1989 Valerie-901255	Closed	1994	175.00	175
1989 Vanessa-912272	Closed	1991	110.00	110
1984 Victoria-901068	Closed	1987	200.00	1500
1992 Wendy-912330 - K. Kennedy	1,000	1995	125.00	130
1988 Whitney Blk-912232	Closed	1994	62.50	65

Victoria Ashlea® Originals-Birthday Babies - K. Kennedy

YEAR ISSUE	EDITION LIMIT	YEAR RETD.	ISSUE PRICE	*QUOTE U.S.$
1996 January-913017	2,500		30.00	30
1996 February-913018	2,500		30.00	30
1996 March-913019	2,500		30.00	30
1996 April-913020	2,500		30.00	30
1996 May-913021	2,500		30.00	30
1996 June-913022	2,500		30.00	30
1996 July-913023	2,500		30.00	30
1996 August-913024	2,500		30.00	30
1996 September-913025	2,500		30.00	30
1996 October-913026	2,500		30.00	30
1996 November-913027	2,500		30.00	30
1996 December-913028	2,500		30.00	30

Victoria Ashlea® Originals-Collectible Cats - K. Kennedy

YEAR ISSUE	EDITION LIMIT	YEAR RETD.	ISSUE PRICE	*QUOTE U.S.$
1996 Charmer-913005	2,000		39.50	40
1996 Copper-913006	2,000		39.50	40
1996 Cuddles-913007	2,000		39.50	40
1996 Fluffy-913008	2,000		39.50	40
1996 Lollipop-913009	2,000		39.50	40
1996 Mittens-913010	2,000		39.50	40
1996 Patches-913011	2,000		39.50	40
1996 Pebbles-913012	2,000		39.50	40
1996 Pepper-913013	2,000		39.50	40
1996 Ruffles-913014	2,000		39.50	40
1996 Tumbles-913015	2,000		39.50	40
1996 Whiskers-913016	2,000		39.50	40

Victoria Ashlea® Originals-Holiday Babies - K. Kennedy

YEAR ISSUE	EDITION LIMIT	YEAR RETD.	ISSUE PRICE	*QUOTE U.S.$
1996 Boo!-913001	1,000		30.00	30
1996 Happy Easter-913002	1,000		30.00	30
1996 Happy Holidays-913003	1,000		30.00	30
1996 I Love You-913004	1,000		30.00	30

Victoria Ashlea® Originals-Tiny Tot Clowns - K. Kennedy

YEAR ISSUE	EDITION LIMIT	YEAR RETD.	ISSUE PRICE	*QUOTE U.S.$
1994 Danielle-912461	2,000		45.00	45
1994 Lindsey-912463	2,000	1996	45.00	45
1994 Lisa-912458	2,000	1996	45.00	45
1994 Marie-912462	2,000	1996	45.00	45
1994 Megan-912460	2,000	1996	45.00	45
1994 Stacy-912459	2,000	1996	45.00	45

Victoria Ashlea® Originals-Tiny Tot School Girls - K. Kennedy

YEAR ISSUE	EDITION LIMIT	YEAR RETD.	ISSUE PRICE	*QUOTE U.S.$
1994 Andrea- 912456	2,000	1996	47.50	48
1994 Christine- 912450	2,000	1996	47.50	48
1994 Monique- 912455	2,000	1996	47.50	48
1994 Patricia- 912453	2,000	1996	47.50	48
1994 Shawna- 912449	2,000	1996	47.50	48
1994 Susan- 912457	2,000	1996	47.50	48

Goebel/M.I. Hummel

M.I. Hummel Collectible Dolls - M.I. Hummel

YEAR ISSUE	EDITION LIMIT	YEAR RETD.	ISSUE PRICE	*QUOTE U.S.$
1964 Chimney Sweep 1908	Closed	N/A	55.00	120-150
1964 For Father 1917	Closed	N/A	55.00	100-150
1964 Goose Girl 1914	Closed	N/A	55.00	100-150
1964 Gretel 1901	Closed	N/A	55.00	150
1964 Hansel 1902	Closed	N/A	55.00	150
1964 Little Knitter 1905	Closed	N/A	55.00	100-150
1964 Lost Stocking 1926	Closed	N/A	55.00	150
1964 Merry Wanderer 1906	Closed	N/A	55.00	125-150
1964 Merry Wanderer 1925	Closed	N/A	55.00	125-150
1964 On Secret Path 1928	Closed	N/A	55.00	100-150
1964 Rosa-Blue Baby 1904/B	Closed	N/A	45.00	100
1964 Rosa-Pink Baby 1904/P	Closed	N/A	45.00	100

YEAR ISSUE		EDITION LIMIT	YEAR RETRD.	ISSUE PRICE	*QUOTE U.S.$
1964	School Boy 1910	Closed	N/A	55.00	125-150
1964	School Girl 1909	Closed	N/A	55.00	125-150
1964	Visiting and Invalid 1927	Closed	N/A	55.00	125-150

M. I. Hummel Porcelain Dolls - M. I. Hummel

1984	Birthday Serenade/Boy	Closed	N/A	225.00	275-300
1984	Birthday Serenade/Girl	Closed	N/A	225.00	275-300
1985	Carnival	Closed	N/A	225.00	275-300
1985	Easter Greetings	Closed	N/A	225.00	275-300
1985	Lost Sheep	Closed	N/A	225.00	275-300
1984	On Holiday	Closed	N/A	225.00	275-300
1984	Postman	Closed	N/A	225.00	275-300
1985	Signs of Spring	Closed	N/A	225.00	275-300

Good-Krüger

Limited Edition - J. Good-Krüger

1990	Alice	Retrd.	1991	250.00	250
1992	Anne with an E	Retrd.	1992	240.00	400
1990	Annie-Rose	Retrd.	1990	219.00	425
1994	Christmas Carols	1,000	1995	240.00	240
1990	Christmas Cookie	Retrd.	1993	199.00	225
1995	Circus Trainer	500	1995	250.00	250
1990	Cozy	Retrd.	1990	179.00	275-375
1990	Daydream	Retrd.	1990	199.00	350
1994	Heidi	1,000	1994	250.00	250
1992	Jeepers Creepers (Porcelain)	Retrd.	1992	725.00	800
1991	Johnny-Lynn	Retrd.	1991	240.00	500
1995	Letter to Santa	1,000	1995	250.00	250
1995	Little Princess	1,500	1995	250.00	250
1991	Moppett	Retrd.	1991	179.00	275
1994	Mother's Love	1,000	1994	275.00	275
1994	Stuffed Animal Zoo	1,000	1994	189.00	189
1990	Sue-Lynn	Retrd.	1990	240.00	300
1991	Teachers Pet	Retrd.	1991	199.00	250
1995	Tiny Newborns	500	1995	225.00	225
1991	Victorian Christmas	Retrd.	1992	219.00	275

Gorham

Beverly Port Designer Collection - B. Port

1988	The Amazing Calliope Merriweather 17"	Closed	1990	275.00	1200-1400
1988	Baery Mab 9-1/2"	Closed	1990	110.00	300
1987	Christopher Paul Bearkin 10"	Closed	1990	95.00	450
1988	Hollybeary Kringle 15"	Closed	1990	350.00	500
1987	Kristobear Kringle 17"	Closed	1990	200.00	500
1988	Miss Emily 18"	Closed	1990	350.00	1500
1987	Molly Melinda Bearkin 10"	Closed	1990	95.00	300
1987	Silver Bell 17"	Closed	1990	175.00	350
1988	T.R. 28-1/2"	Closed	1990	400.00	625
1987	Tedward Jonathan Bearkin 10"	Closed	1990	95.00	350
1987	Tedwina Kimelina Bearkin 10"	Closed	1990	95.00	300
1988	Theodore B. Bear 14"	Closed	1990	175.00	550

Bonnets & Bows - B. Gerardi

1988	Belinda	Closed	1990	195.00	450
1988	Annemarie	Closed	1990	195.00	450
1988	Allessandra	Closed	1990	195.00	350
1988	Lisette	Closed	1990	285.00	495
1988	Bettina	Closed	1994	285.00	495
1988	Ellie	Closed	1994	285.00	495
1988	Alicia	Closed	1994	385.00	700
1988	Bethany	Closed	1994	385.00	1350
1988	Jesse	Closed	1994	525.00	675
1988	Francie	Closed	1994	625.00	800

Celebrations Of Childhood - L. Di Leo

1992	Happy Birthday Amy	Closed	1994	160.00	225

Children Of Christmas - S. Stone Aiken

1989	Clara, 16"	Closed	1994	325.00	650
1990	Natalie, 16"	1,500	1994	350.00	500
1991	Emily	1,500	1994	375.00	400
1992	Virginia	1,500	1994	375.00	400

Dollie And Me - J. Pilallis

1991	Dollie's First Steps	Closed	1994	160.00	225

Gifts of the Garden - S. Stone Aiken

1991	Alisa	Closed	1994	125.00	250
1991	Deborah	Closed	1994	125.00	250
1991	Holly (Christmas)	Closed	1994	150.00	250
1991	Irene	Closed	1994	125.00	250
1991	Joelle (Christmas)	Closed	1994	150.00	250
1991	Lauren	Closed	1994	125.00	250
1991	Maria	Closed	1994	125.00	250
1991	Priscilla	Closed	1994	125.00	250
1991	Valerie	Closed	1994	125.00	250

Gorham Baby Doll Collection - Aiken/Matthews

1987	Christening Day	Closed	1990	245.00	350
1987	Leslie	Closed	1990	245.00	350
1987	Matthew	Closed	1990	245.00	350

Gorham Dolls - S. Stone Aiken, unless otherwise noted

1985	Alexander, 19"	Closed	1990	275.00	400
1981	Alexandria, 18"	Closed	1990	250.00	500
1986	Alissa	Closed	1990	245.00	300
1985	Amelia, 19"	Closed	1990	275.00	325

YEAR ISSUE		EDITION LIMIT	YEAR RETRD.	ISSUE PRICE	*QUOTE U.S.$
1982	Baby in Apricot Dress, 16"	Closed	1990	175.00	375
1982	Baby in Blue Dress, 12"	Closed	1990	150.00	300
1982	Baby in White Dress, 18" - Gorham	Closed	1990	250.00	350
1982	Benjamin, 18"	Closed	1990	200.00	600
1981	Cecile, 16"	Closed	1990	200.00	800
1981	Christina, 16"	Closed	1990	200.00	425
1981	Christopher, 19"	Closed	1990	250.00	500
1982	Corrine, 21"	Closed	1990	250.00	500
1981	Danielle, 14"	Closed	1990	150.00	300
1981	Elena, 14"	Closed	1990	150.00	650
1982	Ellice, 18"	Closed	1990	200.00	400
1986	Emily, 14"	Closed	1990	175.00	395
1986	Fleur, 19"	Closed	1990	300.00	450
1985	Gabrielle, 19"	Closed	1990	225.00	350
1983	Jennifer, 19" Bridal Doll	Closed	1990	325.00	750
1982	Jeremy, 23"	Closed	1990	300.00	700
1986	Jessica	Closed	1990	195.00	275
1981	Jillian, 16"	Closed	1990	200.00	400
1986	Julia, 16"	Closed	1990	225.00	350
1987	Juliet	Closed	1990	325.00	400
1982	Kristin, 23"	Closed	1990	300.00	575
1986	Lauren, 14"	Closed	1990	175.00	350
1985	Linda, 19"	Closed	1990	275.00	600
1982	M. Anton, 12" - Unknown	Closed	1990	125.00	175
1982	Melanie, 23"	Closed	1990	300.00	600
1981	Melinda, 14"	Closed	1990	150.00	300
1986	Meredith	Closed	1990	295.00	350
1982	Mlle. Jeanette, 12"	Closed	1990	125.00	175
1982	Mlle. Lucille, 12"	Closed	1990	125.00	375
1982	Mlle. Marsella, 12" - Unknown	Closed	1990	125.00	275
1982	Mlle. Monique, 12"	Closed	1990	125.00	275
1982	Mlle. Yvonne, 12" - Unknown	Closed	1990	125.00	375
1985	Nanette, 12"	Closed	1990	325.00	325
1985	Odette, 19"	Closed	1990	250.00	450
1981	Rosemond, 18"	Closed	1990	250.00	750
1981	Stephanie, 18"	Closed	1990	250.00	2000

Gorham Holly Hobbie Childhood Memories - Holly Hobbie

1985	Mother's Helper	Closed	1990	45.00	175
1985	Best Friends	Closed	1994	45.00	175
1985	First Day of School	Closed	1994	45.00	175
1985	Christmas Wishes	Closed	1994	45.00	175

Gorham Holly Hobbie For All Seasons - Holly Hobbie

1984	Summer Holly 12"	Closed	1994	42.50	195
1984	Fall Holly 12"	Closed	1994	42.50	195
1984	Winter Holly 12"	Closed	1994	42.50	195
1984	Spring Holly 12"	Closed	1994	42.50	195
1984	Set of 4	Closed	1994	170.00	750

Holly Hobbie - Holly Hobbie

1983	Blue Girl, 14"	Closed	1994	80.00	245
1983	Blue Girl, 18"	Closed	1994	115.00	295
1983	Christmas Morning, 14"	Closed	1994	80.00	245
1983	Heather, 14"	Closed	1994	80.00	275
1983	Little Amy, 14"	Closed	1994	80.00	245
1983	Robbie, 14"	Closed	1994	80.00	275
1983	Sunday Best, 18"	Closed	1994	115.00	295
1983	Sweet Valentine, 16"	Closed	1994	100.00	295
1983	Yesterday's Memories, 18"	Closed	1994	125.00	375

Joyful Years - B. Gerardi

1989	Katrina	Closed	1994	295.00	375
1989	William	Closed	1994	295.00	375

Kezi Doll For All Seasons - Kezi

1985	Ariel 16"	Closed	1994	135.00	500
1985	Aubrey 16"	Closed	1994	135.00	500
1985	Amber 16"	Closed	1994	135.00	500
1985	Adrienne 16"	Closed	1994	135.00	500
1985	Set of 4	Closed	1994	540.00	1900

Kezi Golden Gifts - Kezi

1984	Charity 16"	Closed	1990	85.00	175
1984	Faith 18"	Closed	1990	95.00	195
1984	Felicity 18"	Closed	1990	95.00	195
1984	Grace 16"	Closed	1990	85.00	175
1984	Hope 16"	Closed	1990	85.00	175
1984	Merrie 16"	Closed	1990	85.00	175
1984	Patience 18"	Closed	1990	95.00	195
1984	Prudence 18"	Closed	1990	95.00	195

Les Belles Bebes Collection - S. Stone Aiken

1993	Camille	1,500	1994	375.00	395
1991	Cherie	Closed	1994	375.00	475
1991	Desiree	1,500	1994	375.00	395

Limited Edition Dolls - S. Stone Aiken

1982	Allison, 19"	Closed	1990	300.00	4500
1983	Ashley, 19"	Closed	1990	350.00	1000
1984	Nicole, 19"	Closed	1990	350.00	875
1984	Holly (Christmas), 19"	Closed	1990	300.00	850
1985	Lydia, 19"	Closed	1990	550.00	1800
1985	Joy (Christmas), 19"	Closed	1990	350.00	695
1986	Noel (Christmas), 19"	Closed	1990	400.00	750
1987	Jacqueline, 19"	Closed	1990	500.00	700
1987	Merrie (Christmas), 19"	Closed	1990	500.00	750
1988	Andrew, 19"	Closed	1990	475.00	750
1988	Christa (Christmas), 19"	Closed	1990	550.00	1500
1990	Amey (10th Anniversary Edition)	Closed	1994	650.00	1100

YEAR ISSUE		EDITION LIMIT	YEAR RETRD.	ISSUE PRICE	* QUOTE U.S.$

Limited Edition Sister Set - S. Stone Aiken

1988	Kathleen	Closed	1994	550.00	750
1988	Katelin	Set	1994	Set	Set

Little Women - S. Stone Aiken

1983	Amy, 16"	Closed	1994	225.00	500
1983	Beth, 16"	Closed	1994	225.00	500
1983	Jo, 19"	Closed	1994	275.00	575
1983	Meg, 19"	Closed	1994	275.00	650

Precious as Pearls - S. Stone Aiken

1986	Colette	Closed	1994	400.00	1500
1987	Charlotte	Closed	1994	425.00	750
1988	Chloe	Closed	1994	525.00	850
1989	Cassandra	Closed	1994	525.00	1250
XX	Set	Closed	1994	1875.00	4000

Southern Belles - S. Stone Aiken

1985	Amanda, 19"	Closed	1990	300.00	1400
1986	Veronica, 19"	Closed	1990	325.00	750
1987	Rachel, 19"	Closed	1990	375.00	800
1988	Cassie, 19"	Closed	1990	500.00	875

Special Moments - E. Worrell

1991	Baby's First Christmas	Closed	1994	135.00	235
1992	Baby's First Steps	Closed	1994	135.00	135

Sporting Kids - R. Schrubbe

1993	Up At Bat	Closed	1994	49.50	80

Times To Treasure - L. Di Leo

1991	Bedtime	Closed	1994	195.00	250
1993	Playtime	Closed	1994	195.00	250
1990	Storytime	Closed	1994	195.00	250

Valentine Ladies - P. Valentine

1987	Anabella	Closed	1994	145.00	395
1987	Elizabeth	Closed	1994	145.00	450
1988	Felicia	Closed	1994	225.00	325
1987	Jane	Closed	1994	145.00	350
1988	Judith Anne	Closed	1994	195.00	325
1989	Julianna	Closed	1994	225.00	275
1987	Lee Ann	Closed	1994	145.00	325
1988	Maria Theresa	Closed	1994	225.00	350
1987	Marianna	Closed	1994	160.00	400
1987	Patrice	Closed	1994	145.00	325
1988	Priscilla	Closed	1994	195.00	325
1987	Rebecca	Closed	1994	145.00	325
1987	Rosanne	Closed	1994	145.00	325
1989	Rose	Closed	1994	225.00	275
1987	Sylvia	Closed	1994	160.00	350

Victorian Cameo Collection - B. Gerardi

1990	Victoria	1,500	1994	375.00	425
1991	Alexandra	Closed	1994	375.00	425

Victorian Children - S. Stone Aiken

1992	Sara's Tea Time	1,000	1994	495.00	750
1993	Catching Butterflies	1,000	1994	495.00	495

The Victorian Collection - E. Woodhouse

1992	Victoria's Jubilee	Yr.Iss.	1994	295.00	350

H & G Studios

Brenda Burke Dolls - B. Burke

1989	Adelaine	25	1989	1795.00	3600
1989	Alexandra	125	1990	995.00	2000
1989	Alicia	125	1990	895.00	1800
1989	Amanda	25	1989	1995.00	6000
1989	Angelica	50	1989	1495.00	3000
1989	Arabella	500	1990	695.00	1400
1989	Beatrice	85	1991	2395.00	2395
1990	Belinda	12	1990	3695.00	3695
1990	Bethany	45	1990	2995.00	2995
1989	Brittany	75	1990	2695.00	2695
1991	Charlotte	20	1991	2395.00	2395
1991	Clarissa	15	1992	3595.00	3595
1992	Dorothea	500		395.00	395
1993	Giovanna	1	1993	7800.00	7800
1993	Melissa	1	1993	7750.00	7750
1991	Sleigh Ride	20	1991	3695.00	3695
1991	Tender Love	25	1991	3295.00	3295

Hallmark

Special Edition Hallmark Barbie Dolls

1994	Victorian Elegance Barbie	Yr.Iss.	1994	40.00	110-150
1995	Holiday Memories Barbie	Yr.Iss.	1995	45.00	45

Hamilton Collection

Abbie Williams Doll Collection - A. Williams

1992	Molly	Closed	N/A	155.00	200

American Country Doll Collection - N/A

1995	Carson	Open		95.00	95
1995	Bonnie	Open		195.00	195
1996	Patsy	Open		95.00	95

DOLLS

YEAR ISSUE		EDITION LIMIT	YEAR RETD.	ISSUE PRICE	*QUOTE U.S.$
1996	Delaney	Open		95.00	95
1996	Arizona	Open		95.00	95
1996	Kendra	Open		195.00	195

Annual Connoisseur Doll - N/A

1992	Lara	7,450		295.00	295

The Antique Doll Collection - Unknown

1989	Nicole	Closed	N/A	195.00	300
1990	Colette	Closed	1996	195.00	195
1991	Lisette	Closed	1996	195.00	225
1991	Katrina	Closed	1996	195.00	195

Baby Portrait Dolls - B. Parker

1991	Melissa	Closed	1993	135.00	175-200
1992	Jenna	Closed	N/A	135.00	200-250
1992	Bethany	Closed	1996	135.00	135
1993	Mindy	Closed	1996	135.00	135

Belles of the Countryside - C. Heath Orange

1992	Erin	Open		135.00	135
1992	Rose	Open		135.00	135
1993	Lorna	Open		135.00	135
1994	Gwyn	Open		135.00	135

The Bessie Pease Gutmann Doll Collection - B.P. Gutmann

1989	Love is Blind	Closed	N/A	135.00	220
1989	He Won't Bite	Closed	N/A	135.00	135
1991	Virginia	Closed	1996	135.00	135
1991	First Dancing Lesson	Closed	1996	195.00	195
1991	Good Morning	Closed	1996	195.00	195
1991	Love At First Sight	Closed	1996	195.00	195

Best Buddies - C.M. Rolfe

1994	Jodie	Open		69.00	69
1994	Brandy	Open		69.00	69
1995	Joey	Open		69.00	69
1996	Stacey	Open		69.00	69

Boehm Christening - Boehm Studio

1994	Elena's First Portrait	Open		155.00	155

Boehm Dolls - N/A

1994	Elena	Open		155.00	155

Bridal Elegance - Boehm

1994	Camille	Closed	1996	195.00	195

Bride Dolls - Unknown

1991	Portrait of Innocence	Closed	1996	195.00	195
1992	Portrait of Loveliness	Closed	1996	195.00	195

Brooker Tickler - Harris/Brooker

1995	Nellie	Open		95.00	95
1996	Callie	Open		95.00	95

Brooks Wooden Dolls - P. Ryan Brooks

1993	Waiting For Santa	15,000	1994	135.00	200-250
1993	Are You the Easter Bunny?	15,000		135.00	135
1994	Be My Valentine	Open		135.00	135
1995	Shh! I Only Wanna Peek	Open		135.00	135

Byi Praying Dolls - C. Byi

1996	Mark & Mary	Open		89.95	90

Catherine Mather Dolls - C. Mather

1993	Justine	15,000		155.00	155

Central Park Skaters - Unknown

1991	Central Park Skaters	Closed	1996	245.00	245

A Child's Menagerie - B. Van Boxel

1993	Becky	Closed	1996	69.00	69
1993	Carrie	Open		69.00	69
1994	Mandy	Open		69.00	69
1994	Terry	Open		69.00	69

Children To Cherish - N/A

1991	A Gift of Innocence	Yr.Iss.		135.00	135
1991	A Gift of Beauty	Closed	1996	135.00	135

Ciambra - M. Ciambra

1995	Chloe	Open		155.00	155
1996	Lydia	Open		155.00	155

Cindy Marschner Rolfe Dolls - C. M. Rolfe

1993	Shannon	Open		95.00	95
1993	Julie	Open		95.00	95
1993	Kayla	Open		95.00	95
1994	Janey	Open		95.00	95

Cindy Marschner Rolfe Twins - C. M. Rolfe

1995	Shelby & Sydney	Open		190.00	190

Connie Walser Derek Baby Dolls - C.W. Derek

1990	Jessica	Closed	1993	155.00	300-500
1991	Sara	Closed	N/A	155.00	180
1991	Andrew	Closed	1996	155.00	155
1991	Amanda	Closed	1996	155.00	155
1992	Samantha	Closed	1996	155.00	155

Connie Walser Derek Baby Dolls II - C. W. Derek

1992	Stephanie	Closed	1996	95.00	95
1992	Beth	Closed	1996	95.00	95

Connie Walser Derek Baby Dolls III - C. W. Derek

1994	Chelsea	Open		79.00	79
1995	Tina	Open		79.00	79
1995	Tabitha	Open		79.00	79
1995	Ginger	Open		79.00	79

Connie Walser Derek Dolls - C. W. Derek

1992	Baby Jessica	Closed	1996	75.00	75
1993	Baby Sara	Closed	1996	75.00	75

Connie Walser Derek Toddlers - C. W. Derek

1994	Jessie	Closed	1996	79.00	79
1994	Casey	Open		79.00	79
1995	Angie	Open		79.00	79
1995	Tori	Open		79.00	79

Daddy's Little Girls - M. Snyder

1992	Lindsay	Closed	1996	95.00	95
1993	Cassie	Closed	1996	95.00	95
1993	Dana	Open		95.00	95
1994	Tara	Open		95.00	95

Dey Recital Dolls - P. Dey

1996	Mallory	9,500		195.00	195

Dolls by Autumn Berwick - A. Berwick

1993	Laura	Open		135.00	135

Dolls By Kay McKee - K. McKee

1992	Shy Violet	Closed	1993	135.00	200-250
1992	Robin	Open		135.00	135
1993	Katie Did It!	Open		135.00	135
1993	Ryan	Open		135.00	135

Dolls of America's Colonial Heritage - A. Elekfy

1986	Katrina	Closed	1996	55.00	55
1986	Nicole	Closed	1996	55.00	55
1987	Maria	Closed	1996	55.00	55
1987	Priscilla	Closed	1996	55.00	55
1987	Colleen	Closed	1996	55.00	55
1988	Gretchen	Closed	1996	55.00	55

Elaine Campbell Dolls - E. Campbell

1994	Emma	Closed	1996	95.00	95
1995	Abby	Open		95.00	95
1995	Jana	Open		95.00	95
1995	Molly	Open		95.00	95

Eternal Friends Doll Collection - N/A

1996	Love One Another	Open		135.00	135
1997	Friendship Hits The Spot	Open		135.00	135

First Recital - N/A

1993	Hillary	Open		135.00	135
1994	Olivia	Open		135.00	135

Grobben Ethnic Babies - J. Grobben

1994	Jasmine	Open		135.00	135
1995	Taiya	Open		135.00	135

Grothedde Dolls - N. Grothedde

1994	Cindy	Open		69.00	69
1995	Holly	Open		69.00	69

Hargrave Dolls - M. Hargrave

1994	Angela	Open		79.00	79
1995	April	Open		79.00	79

Heath Babies - C. Heath Orange

1995	Hayley	Open		95.00	95
1996	Ellie	Open		95.00	95

Heavenly Clowns Doll Collection - K. McKee

1996	Blue Moon	Open		95.00	95

Helen Carr Dolls - H. Carr

1994	Claudia	Open		135.00	135
1995	Jillian	Open		135.00	135
1996	Abigail	Open		135.00	135
1996	Rosalee	Open		135.00	135

Helen Kish II Dolls - H. Kish

1992	Vanessa	Open		135.00	135
1994	Jordan	Open		95.00	95

Holiday Carollers - U. Lepp

1992	Joy	Closed	1996	155.00	155
1993	Noel	Closed	1996	155.00	155

Honkytonk Gals Doll Collection - C. Johnston

1996	Kendall	Open		95.00	95
1997	Logan	Open		95.00	95

Huckleberry Hill Kids - B. Parker

1994	Gabrielle	Open		95.00	95
1994	Alexandra	Open		95.00	95

1995	Jeremiah	Open		95.00	95
1996	Sarah	Open		95.00	95

I Love Lucy (Porcelain) - Unknown

1990	Lucy	Closed	N/A	95.00	240-300
1991	Ricky	Closed	N/A	95.00	350
1992	Queen of the Gypsies	Closed	N/A	95.00	245
1992	Vitameatavegamin	Closed	N/A	95.00	200-300

I Love Lucy (Vinyl) - Unknown

1988	Ethel	Closed	N/A	40.00	100
1988	Fred	Closed	N/A	40.00	100
1990	Lucy	Closed	N/A	40.00	100
1991	Ricky	Closed	N/A	40.00	150
1992	Queen of the Gypsies	Open		40.00	40
1992	Vitameatavegamin	Open		40.00	40

I'm So Proud Doll Collection - L. Cobabe

1992	Christina	Closed	1996	95.00	95
1993	Jill	Closed	1996	95.00	95
1994	Tammy	Closed	1996	95.00	95
1994	Shelly	Closed	1996	95.00	95

Inga Manders - I. Manders

1995	Miss Priss	Open		79.00	79
1995	Miss Hollywood	Open		79.00	79
1995	Miss Glamour	Open		79.00	79
1996	Miss Sweetheart	Open		79.00	79

International Children - C. Woodie

1991	Miko	Closed	N/A	49.50	80
1991	Anastasia	Closed	1996	49.50	50
1991	Angelina	Closed	1996	49.50	50
1992	Lian	Closed	1996	49.50	50
1992	Monique	Closed	1996	49.50	50
1992	Lisa	Closed	1996	49.50	50

Jane Zidjunas Party Dolls - J. Zidjunas

1991	Kelly	Open		135.00	135
1992	Katie	Open		135.00	135
1993	Meredith	Open		135.00	135

Jane Zidjunas Sleeping Dolls - J. Zidjunas

1995	Annie	Open		79.00	79
1995	Jamie	Open		79.00	79

Jane Zidjunas Toddler Dolls - J. Zidjunas

1991	Jennifer	Closed	1996	135.00	135
1991	Megan	Open		135.00	160
1992	Kimberly	Open		135.00	135
1992	Amy	Closed	1996	135.00	135

Jane Zidjunas Victorian - J. Zidjunas

1996	Constance	9,500		195.00	195

Jeanne Wilson Dolls - J. Wilson

1994	Priscilla	Open		155.00	155

Johnston Cowgirls - C. Johnston

1994	Savannah	Open		79.00	79
1994	Skyler	Open		79.00	79
1995	Cheyene	Open		79.00	79
1995	Austin	Open		79.00	79

Join The Parade - N/A

1992	Betsy	Closed	1996	49.50	50
1994	Peggy	Open		55.00	55
1994	Sandy	Open		55.00	55
1995	Brian	Open		49.50	50

Joke Grobben Dolls - J. Grobben

1992	Heather	Open		69.00	69
1993	Kathleen	Open		69.00	69
1993	Brianna	Open		69.00	69
1994	Bridget	Open		69.00	69

Joke Grobben Tall Dolls - J. Grobben

1995	Jade	Open		135.00	135
1996	Raven	Open		135.00	135

Just Like Mom - H. Kish

1991	Ashley	Closed	1993	135.00	250-300
1992	Elizabeth	Open		135.00	135
1992	Hannah	Open		135.00	135
1993	Margaret	Open		135.00	135

Kay McKee Downsized Dolls - K. McKee

1995	Kyle	Open		79.00	79
1996	Cody	Open		79.00	79

Kay McKee Klowns - K. McKee

1993	The Dreamer	15,000		155.00	155
1994	The Entertainer	15,000		155.00	155

Kuck Fairy - S. Kuck

1994	Tooth Fairy	Closed	1996	135.00	135

Laura Cobabe Dolls - L. Cobabe

1992	Amber	Closed	1996	195.00	195
1992	Brooke	Closed	1996	195.00	195

YEAR ISSUE	EDITION LIMIT	YEAR RETD.	ISSUE PRICE	*QUOTE U.S.$
Laura Cobabe Dolls II - L. Cobabe				
1993 Kristen	Open		75.00	75
Laura Cobabe Ethnic - L. Cobabe				
1995 Nica	Open		95.00	95
1996 Kenu	Open		95.00	95
Laura Cobabe Indians - L. Cobabe				
1994 Snowbird	Open		135.00	135
1995 Little Eagle	Open		135.00	135
1995 Desert Bloom	Open		135.00	135
1996 Call of the Coyote	Open		135.00	135
Laura Cobabe Tall Dolls - L. Cobabe				
1994 Cassandra	Open		195.00	195
1994 Taylor	Open		195.00	195
Laura Cobabe's Costume Kids - L. Cobabe				
1994 Lil' Punkin	Closed 1996		79.00	79
1994 Little Ladybug	Open		79.00	79
1995 Miss Dinomite	Open		79.00	79
1995 Miss Flutterby	Open		79.00	79
Little Gardners - J. Galperin				
1996 Daisy	Open		95.00	95
Little Rascals™ - S./J. Hoffman				
1992 Spanky	Open		75.00	75
1993 Alfalfa	Open		75.00	75
1994 Darla	Open		75.00	75
1994 Buckwheat	Open		75.00	75
1994 Stymie	Open		75.00	75
1995 Pete The Pup	Open		75.00	75
Littlest Members of the Wedding - J. Esteban				
1993 Matthew & Melanie	Open		195.00	195
Lucy Dolls - Unknown				
1996 Lucy	Open		95.00	95
Maud Humphrey Bogart Dolls - Unknown				
1992 Playing Bridesmaid	Closed N/A		195.00	225
Maud Humphrey Bogart Doll Collection - M.H. Bogart				
1989 Playing Bride	Closed N/A		135.00	225
1990 First Party	Closed N/A		135.00	150
1990 The First Lesson	Closed N/A		135.00	149
1991 Seamstress	Closed N/A		135.00	149
1991 Little Captive	Closed 1996		135.00	135
1992 Kitty's Bath	Closed 1996		135.00	135
Mavis Snyder Dolls - M. Snyder				
1994 Tara	Open		95.00	95
Parker Carousel - B. Parker				
1996 Annelise's Musical Ride	4,500		295.00	295
Parker Fairy Tale - B. Parker				
1995 Claire	Open		155.00	155
1996 Marissa	Open		155.00	155
Parker Levi Toddlers - B. Parker				
1992 Courtney	Open		135.00	135
1992 Melody	Open		135.00	135
Parkins Baby - P. Parkins				
1995 Baby Alyssa	Open		225.00	225
Parkins Connisseur - S. Kuck				
1993 Faith	Open		135.00	135
Parkins Portraits - P. Parkins				
1993 Lauren	Open		79.00	79
1993 Kelsey	Open		79.00	79
1994 Morgan	Open		79.00	79
1994 Cassidy	Closed 1996		79.00	79
Parkins Toddler Angels - P. Parkins				
1995 Celeste	Open		135.00	135
1996 Charity	Open		135.00	135
1996 Charisse	Open		135.00	135
1996 Chantelle	Open		135.00	135
Parkins Treasures - P. Parkins				
1992 Tiffany	Closed 1994		55.00	95-120
1992 Dorothy	Closed N/A		55.00	55
1993 Charlotte	Open		55.00	55
1993 Cynthia	Open		55.00	55
Phyllis Parkins Dolls - P. Parkins				
1992 Swan Princess	9,850		195.00	220-250
Phyllis Parkins II Dolls - P. Parkins				
1995 Dakota	Open		135.00	135
1996 Kerrie	Open		135.00	135
1996 Ginny	Open		135.00	135
1996 Dixie	Open		135.00	135
Phyllis Parkins Musical Dolls - P. Parkins				
1995 Nite, Nite Pony	Open		95.00	95

YEAR ISSUE	EDITION LIMIT	YEAR RETD.	ISSUE PRICE	*QUOTE U.S.$
1996 Twice As Nice	Open		95.00	95
1996 Sleep Tight, Sweetheart	Open		95.00	95
1996 Cradled in Love	Open		95.00	95
Picnic In The Park - J. Esteban				
1991 Rebecca	Closed 1995		155.00	155
1992 Emily	Closed 1995		155.00	155
1992 Victoria	Closed 1995		155.00	155
1993 Benjamin	Closed 1995		155.00	155
Pitter Patter Doll Collection - C. W. Derek				
1996 Bobbie Jo	Open		79.00	79
1997 Mary Anne	Open		79.00	79
Precious Moments - S. Butcher				
1994 Tell Me the Story of Jesus	Open		79.00	79
1995 God Loveth a Cheerful Giver	Open		79.00	79
1995 Mother Sew Dear	Open		79.00	79
1996 You Are the Type I Love	Open		79.00	79
Precious Moments Christening - S. Butcher				
1996 Anna	Open		95.00	95
1996 Elise	Open		95.00	95
Proud Indian Nation - N/A				
1992 Navajo Little One	Closed 1993		95.00	200
1993 Dressed Up For The Pow Wow	Closed 1996		95.00	95
1993 Autumn Treat	Open		95.00	95
1994 Out with Mama's Flock	Open		95.00	95
Rachel Cold Toddlers - R. Cold				
1995 Jenny	Open		95.00	95
1996 Trudy	Open		95.00	95
The Royal Beauty Dolls - Unknown				
1991 Chen Mai	Open		195.00	195
Russian Czarra Dolls - Unknown				
1991 Alexandra	Closed N/A		295.00	350
Sandra Kuck Dolls - S. Kuck				
1993 A Kiss Goodnight	Open		79.00	79
1994 Teaching Teddy	Open		79.00	79
1995 Reading With Teddy	Open		79.00	79
1996 Picnic With Teddy	Open		79.00	79
Santa's Little Helpers - C.W. Derek				
1992 Nicholas	Closed 1996		155.00	155
1993 Hope	Closed 1996		155.00	155
Schmidt Babies - J. Schmidt				
1995 Baby	Open		79.00	79
1996 Snookums	Open		79.00	79
Schmidt Dolls - J. Schmidt				
1994 Kaitlyn	Open		79.00	79
1995 Kara	Open		79.00	79
1995 Kathy	Open		79.00	79
1996 Karla	Open		79.00	79
Schrubbe Santa Dolls - R. Schrubbe				
1994 Jolly Old St. Nick	Open		135.00	135
Sentiments From the Garden - M. Severino				
1996 Fairy of Innocence	Open		59.00	59
1997 Fairy of Loveliness	Open		59.00	59
Shelton II Doll - V. Shelton				
1996 Josie	Open		79.00	79
Shelton Indians - V. Shelton				
1995 Little Cloud	Open		95.00	95
1996 Little Basketweaver	Open		95.00	95
1996 Little Warrior	Open		95.00	95
1996 Little Skywatcher	Open		95.00	95
Simon Indians - S. Simon				
1994 Meadowlark	Open		95.00	95
1995 Tashee	Open		95.00	95
1996 Star Dreamer	Open		95.00	95
1996 Sewanka	Open		95.00	95
Songs of the Seasons Hakata Doll Collection - T. Murakami				
1985 Winter Song Maiden	9,800		75.00	75
1985 Spring Song Maiden	9,800		75.00	75
1985 Summer Song Maiden	9,800		75.00	75
1985 Autumn Song Maiden	9,800		75.00	75
Star Trek Doll Collection - E. Daub				
1988 Mr. Spock	Closed N/A		75.00	150
1988 Captain Kirk	Closed N/A		75.00	120
1989 Dr. Mc Coy	Closed N/A		75.00	120
1989 Scotty	Closed N/A		75.00	120
1990 Sulu	Closed N/A		75.00	120
1990 Chekov	Closed N/A		75.00	120
1991 Uhura	Closed N/A		75.00	120
Storybook Dolls - L. Di Leo				
1991 Alice in Wonderland	Closed 1996		75.00	75

YEAR ISSUE	EDITION LIMIT	YEAR RETD.	ISSUE PRICE	*QUOTE U.S.$
Summertime Beauties - C. Marschner				
1995 Sally	Open		95.00	95
1996 Lacey	Open		95.00	95
Through The Eyes of Virginia Turner - V. Turner				
1992 Michelle	Closed 1993		95.00	130-180
1992 Danielle	Open		95.00	95
1993 Wendy	Closed 1995		95.00	95
1994 Dawn	Closed 1996		95.00	95
Toddler Days Doll Collection - D. Schurig				
1992 Erica	Open		95.00	95
1993 Darlene	Open		95.00	95
1994 Karen	Open		95.00	95
1995 Penny	Open		95.00	95
Treasured Toddlers - V. Turner				
1992 Whitney	Closed 1996		95.00	95
1993 Natalie	Closed 1996		95.00	95
Vickie Walker 1st's - V. Walker				
1995 Leah	Open		79.00	79
1995 Leslie	Open		79.00	79
1995 Lily	Open		79.00	79
1995 Leanna	Open		79.00	79
Victorian Treasures - C.W. Derek				
1992 Katherine	Closed 1996		155.00	155
1993 Madeline	Closed 1996		155.00	155
Virginia Turner Dolls - V. Turner				
1995 Amelia	Open		95.00	95
1995 Mckenzie	Open		95.00	95
1996 Grace	Open		95.00	95
1996 Alexis	Open		95.00	95
Virginia Turner Little Sisters - V. Turner				
1996 Allie	Open		95.00	95
Wooden Dolls - N/A				
1991 Gretchen	9,850	1995	225.00	280
1991 Heidi	9,850	1995	225.00	200-250
Wright Indian Dolls - D. Wright				
1994 Sacajawea	Open		135.00	135
1994 Minnehaha	Open		135.00	135
1995 Pine Leaf	Open		135.00	135
1995 Lozen	Open		135.00	135
Year Round Fun - D. Schurig				
1992 Allison	Open		95.00	95
1993 Christy	Open		95.00	95
1993 Paula	Open		95.00	95
1994 Kaylie	Open		95.00	95
Zolan Dolls - D. Zolan				
1991 A Christmas Prayer	Closed 1993		95.00	250-280
1992 Winter Angel	Closed 1996		95.00	95
1992 Rainy Day Pals	Closed 1996		95.00	95
1992 Quiet Time	Closed 1996		95.00	95
1993 For You	Closed 1996		95.00	95
1993 The Thinker	Closed 1996		95.00	95
Zolan Double Dolls - D. Zolan				
1993 First Kiss	Closed 1995		155.00	155
1994 New Shoes	Open		155.00	155

Jan McLean Originals

YEAR ISSUE	EDITION LIMIT	YEAR RETD.	ISSUE PRICE	*QUOTE U.S.$
Flowers of the Heart Collection - J. McLean				
1991 Marigold	100	N/A	2400.00	2900-3200
1990 Pansy	100		2200.00	2800-2900
1990 Pansy (bobbed blonde)	Retrd.	N/A	2200.00	2800-3000
1990 Pansy A/P	Retrd.	N/A	4300	4800
1990 Poppy	100		2200.00	2700
1991 Primrose	100		2500.00	2500-2600
Jan McLean Originals - J. McLean				
1991 Lucrezia	15		6000.00	6000
1990 Phoebe I	25	N/A	2700.00	3300-3600

Kurt S. Adler, Inc.

YEAR ISSUE	EDITION LIMIT	YEAR RETD.	ISSUE PRICE	*QUOTE U.S.$
Royal Heritage Collection - J. Mostrom				
1993 Anastasia J5746	3,000	1996	125.00	125
1993 Good King Wenceslas W2928	2,000	1996	130.00	130
1993 Medieval King of Christmas W2981	2,000	1994	390.00	390
1994 Nicholas on Skates J5750	3,000		120.00	120
1994 Sasha on Skates J5749	3,000	1996	130.00	130
Small Wonders - J. Mostrom				
1995 America-Hollie Blue W3162	Open		30.00	30
1995 America-Texas Tyler W3162	Open		30.00	30
1995 Ireland-Cathleen W3082	Open		28.00	28
1995 Ireland-Michael W3082	Open		28.00	28
1995 Kwanza-Mufaro W3161	Open		28.00	28
1995 Kwanza-Shani W3161	Open		28.00	28

When I Grow Up - J. Mostrom

YEAR ISSUE	EDITION LIMIT	YEAR RETD.	ISSUE PRICE	*QUOTE U.S.$
1995 Dr. Brown W3079	Open		27.00	27
1995 Freddy the Fireman W3163	Open		28.00	28
1995 Melissa the Teacher W3081	Open	1996	28.00	28
1995 Nurse Nancy W3079	Open		27.00	27
1995 Scott the Golfer W3080	Open	1996	28.00	28

Ladie and Friends

Lizzie High Society™ Members-Only Dolls - B.K. Wisber

YEAR ISSUE	EDITION LIMIT	YEAR RETD.	ISSUE PRICE	*QUOTE U.S.$
1993 Audrey High-1301	Closed	1992	59.00	300
1993 Becky High-1330	Closed	1994	96.00	275
1994 Chloe Valentine-1351	Closed	1995	79.00	79
1996 Dottie Bowman-1371	Closed	1996	78.00	78

The Christmas Concert - B.K. Wisber

YEAR ISSUE	EDITION LIMIT	YEAR RETD.	ISSUE PRICE	*QUOTE U.S.$
1990 Claire Valentine-1262	Open		56.00	60
1993 James Valentine-1310	Open		60.00	63
1992 Judith High-1292	Open		70.00	74
1993 Stephanie Bowman-1309	Open		74.00	77

The Christmas Pageant™ - B.K. Wisber

YEAR ISSUE	EDITION LIMIT	YEAR RETD.	ISSUE PRICE	*QUOTE U.S.$
1985 "Earth" Angel-1122	Closed	1989	30.00	80-100
1985 "Noel" Angel (1st Ed.)-1126	Closed	1989	30.00	100
1989 "Noel" Angel (2nd Ed.)-1126	Open		48.00	52
1985 "On" Angel-1121	Closed	1989	30.00	100
1985 "Peace" Angel (1st Ed.)-1120	Closed	1989	30.00	100
1989 "Peace" Angel (2nd Ed.)-1120	Open		48.00	52
1985 Christmas Wooly Lamb-1133	Closed	1991	11.00	35
1985 Joseph and Donkey-1119	Open		30.00	39
1985 Mary and Baby Jesus-1118	Open		30.00	39
1996 Meredith High-1383	Open		79.50	80
1996 Phillip Valentine-1384	Open		79.50	80
1986 Shepherd-1193	Open		32.00	39
1985 Wiseman #1-1123	Closed	1996	30.00	39
1985 Wiseman #2-1124	Closed	1996	30.00	39
1985 Wiseman #3-1125	Closed	1996	30.00	39
1985 Wooden Creche-1132	Open		28.00	33

The Family and Friends of Lizzie High® - B.K. Wisber

YEAR ISSUE	EDITION LIMIT	YEAR RETD.	ISSUE PRICE	*QUOTE U.S.$
1987 Abigail Bowman-1199	Closed	1994	40.00	90
1996 Adam Valentine-1380	Open		69.50	70
1987 Addie High-1202	Closed	1996	37.00	43
1990 Albert Valentine-1260	Closed	1995	42.00	45
1986 Alice Valentine (1st Ed.)-1148	Closed	1987	32.00	100
1995 Alice Valentine (2nd Ed.)-1148	Open		56.00	58
1988 Allison Bowman-1229	Closed	1996	56.00	62
1985 Amanda High (1st Ed.)-1111	Closed	1988	30.00	100
1990 Amanda High (2nd Ed.)-1111	Closed	1995	54.00	58
1989 Amelia High-1248	Open		45.00	50
1987 Amy Bowman-1201	Closed	1994	37.00	82
1986 Andrew Brown-1157	Closed	1988	45.00	125
1991 Annabelle Bowman-1267	Open		68.00	72
1986 Annie Bowman (1st Ed.)-1150	Closed	1989	32.00	100
1993 Annie Bowman (2nd Ed.)-1150	Open		68.00	71
1993 Ashley Bowman-1304	Open		48.00	50
1992 Barbara Helen-1274	Closed	1996	58.00	62
1985 Benjamin Bowman (Santa)-1134	Closed	1996	34.00	42
1985 Benjamin Bowman-1129	Closed	1987	30.00	100
1988 Bess High-1241	Closed	1996	45.00	50
1988 Betsy Valentine-1245	Closed	1996	42.00	46
1996 Beverly Ann Bowman-1379	Open		69.50	70
1994 Bonnie Valentine-1323	Open		35.00	37
1987 Bridget Bowman (1st Ed.)-1222	Closed	1994	40.00	95
1996 Bridget Bowman (2nd Ed.)-1222	Open		76.00	76
1992 Carol Anne Bowman-1282	Closed	1994	70.00	142
1986 Carrie High (1st Ed.)-1190	Closed	1989	45.00	100
1989 Carrie High (2nd Ed.)-1190	Open		46.00	50
1986 Cassie Yocum (1st Ed.)-1179	Closed	1988	36.00	150
1993 Cassie Yocum (2nd Ed.)-1179	Open		80.00	83
1987 Cat on Chair-1217	Closed	1991	16.00	35
1996 Cecelia Brown (alone)-1366A	Open		27.50	28
1996 Cecelia Brown (w/Mother)-1366	Open		101.00	101
1987 Charles Bowman (1st Ed.)-1221	Closed	1990	34.00	100
1992 Charles Bowman (2nd Ed.)-1221	Closed	1995	46.00	48
1996 Charlotte High-1370	Open		73.50	74
1985 Christian Bowman-1110	Closed	1987	30.00	100
1994 Christine Bowman-1332	Open		62.00	65
1993 Christmas Tree w/Cats-1293A	Open		42.00	44
1986 Christopher High-1182	Closed	1992	34.00	72
1985 Cora High-1115	Closed	1987	30.00	110
1991 Cynthia High-1127A	Closed	1995	60.00	62
1996 Daniel Brown (alone)-1367A	Open		27.50	28
1996 Daniel Brown (w/Mother)-1367	Open		101.00	101
1988 Daphne High-1235	Closed	1994	38.00	40
1996 Darlene Bowman-1368	Open		77.50	78
1986 David Yocum-1195	Closed	1995	33.00	37
1986 Delia Valentine-1153	Closed	1988	32.00	100
1991 The Department Store Santa-1270	Closed	1996	76.00	80
1986 Dora Valentine (1st Ed.)-1152	Closed	1989	30.00	100
1992 Dora Valentine (2nd Ed.)-1152	Open		48.00	51
1986 Edward Bowman (1st Ed.)-1158	Closed	1988	45.00	125
1994 Edward Bowman (2nd Ed.)-1158	Open		76.00	79
1992 Edwin Bowman-1281	Closed	1994	70.00	71
1995 Edwina High-1343	Open		56.00	58
1985 Elizabeth Sweetland (1st Ed.)-1109	Closed	1987	30.00	100
1991 Elizabeth Sweetland (2nd Ed.)-1109	Open		56.00	60
1994 Elsie Bowman-1325	Open		64.00	67
1986 Emily Bowman (1st Ed.)-1185	Closed	1990	34.00	100
1990 Emily Bowman (2nd Ed.)-1185	Closed	1996	48.00	51
1985 Emma High (1st Ed.)-1103	Closed	1988	30.00	100
1996 Emma High (2nd Ed.)-1103	Open		69.50	70
1989 Emmy Lou Valentine-1251	Open		45.00	49
1985 Esther Dunn (1st Ed.)-1127	Closed	1987	45.00	N/A
1991 Esther Dunn (2nd Ed.)-1127	Closed	1995	60.00	62
1988 Eunice High-1240	Closed	1994	56.00	58
1985 Flossie High (1st Ed.)-1128	Closed	1988	45.00	100-125
1989 Flossie High (2nd Ed.)-1128	Open		54.00	59
1987 The Flower Girl-1204	Closed	1995	17.00	24
1996 Francine Bowman-1381	Open		60.00	60
1993 Francis Bowman-1305	Open		48.00	50
1994 Gilbert High-1335	Open		65.00	68
1996 Glenda Brown-1382	Open		60.00	60
1986 Grace Valentine (1st Ed.)-1146	Closed	1989	32.00	100
1991 Grace Valentine (2nd Ed.)-1146	Open		48.00	51
1987 Gretchen High-1216	Closed	1994	40.00	44
1994 Gwendolyn High-1342	Open		56.00	59
1985 Hannah Brown-1131	Closed	1988	45.00	125
1988 Hattie Bowman-1239	Closed	1996	40.00	46
1985 Ida Valentine-1116	Closed	1988	30.00	80
1987 Imogene Bowman-1206	Closed	1994	37.00	80
1988 Jacob High-1230	Closed	1994	44.00	46
1994 Jamie Bowman-1324	Open		35.00	37
1988 Janie Valentine-1231	Closed	1996	37.00	43
1989 Jason High (alone)-1254A	Closed	1996	20.00	25
1989 Jason High (with Mother)-1254	Closed	1996	58.00	63
1986 Jenny Valentine-1181	Closed	1989	34.00	110
1986 Jeremy Bowman-1192	Closed	1991	36.00	80
1989 Jessica High (alone)-1253A	Closed	1996	20.00	25
1989 Jessica High (with Mother)-1253	Closed	1996	58.00	63
1995 Jillian Bowman ((2nd Ed.))-1180	Open		90.00	92
1986 Jillian High (1st Ed.)-1180	Closed	1990	34.00	110
1992 Joanie Valentine-1295	Open		48.00	51
1989 Johann Bowman-1250	Open		40.00	44
1986 Johanna Bowman-1198	Closed	1988	37.00	100
1992 Joseph Valentine-1283	Closed	1995	62.00	64
1994 Josie Valentine-1322	Open		76.00	79
1986 Juliet Valentine (1st Ed.)-1147	Closed	1988	32.00	100
1990 Juliet Valentine (2nd Ed.)-1147	Closed	1996	48.00	52
1993 Justine Valentine-1302	Open		84.00	87
1986 Karl Valentine (1st Ed.)-1161	Closed	1988	30.00	100
1994 Karl Valentine (2nd Ed.)-1161	Open		54.00	57
1987 Katie and Barney-1219	Closed	1996	38.00	43
1986 Katie Bowman-1178	Closed	1994	36.00	82
1985 Katrina Valentine-1135	Closed	1989	30.00	100
1988 Kinch Bowman-1237	Closed	1996	47.00	51
1987 Laura Valentine-1223	Closed	1994	36.00	80
1995 Leona High-1355	Open		68.00	70
1986 Little Ghosts-1197	Closed	1996	15.00	20
1987 Little Witch-1225	Closed	1996	17.00	24
1985 Lizzie High® (1st Ed.)-1100	Closed	1995	30.00	45
1996 Lizzie High® (2nd Ed.)-1100	Open		92.00	92
1985 Louella Valentine-1112	Closed	1991	30.00	100
1989 Lucy Bowman-1255	Open		45.00	49
1985 Luther Bowman (1st Ed.)-1108	Closed	1987	30.00	100
1993 Luther Bowman (2nd Ed.)-1108	Open		60.00	63
1995 Lydia Bowman-1347	Open		54.00	55
1986 Madeleine Valentine (1st Ed.)-1187	Closed	1989	34.00	90
1989 Madeleine Valentine (2nd Ed.)-1187	Open		37.00	41
1986 Maggie High-1160	Closed	1988	30.00	100
1987 Margaret Bowman-1213	Closed	1996	35.00	43
1986 Marie Valentine (1st Ed.)-1184	Closed	1990	47.00	125
1992 Marie Valentine (2nd Ed.)-1184	Closed	1996	68.00	72
1986 Marisa Valentine (alone)-1194A	Closed	1996	33.00	40
1986 Marisa Valentine (w/ Brother Petey)-1194	Closed	1996	45.00	51
1994 Marisa Valentine-1333	Open		58.00	61
1986 Marland Valentine-1183	Closed	1990	33.00	100
1990 Marlene Valentine-1259	Closed	1995	48.00	51
1986 Martha High-1151	Closed	1989	32.00	75-100
1985 Martin Bowman (1st Ed.)-1117	Closed	1992	30.00	43-85
1996 Martin Bowman (2nd Ed.)-1117	Open		64.00	64
1988 Mary Ellen Valentine-1236	Closed	1996	40.00	45
1985 Mary Valentine-1105	Closed	1988	30.00	85-100
1986 Matthew Yocum-1186	Closed	1988	33.00	100
1995 Mattie Dunn-1344	Open		56.00	58
1988 Megan Valentine-1227	Closed	1994	44.00	94
1987 Melanie Bowman (1st Ed.)-1220	Closed	1990	36.00	125
1992 Melanie Bowman (2nd Ed.)-1220	Closed	1995	46.00	48
1991 Michael Bowman-1268	Open		52.00	55
1994 Minnie Valentine-1336	Open		64.00	67
1989 Miriam High-1256	Open		46.00	50
1986 Molly Yocum (1st Ed.)-1189	Closed	1989	34.00	80-100
1989 Molly Yocum (2nd Ed.)-1189	Open		39.00	43
1993 Mommy-1312	Open		48.00	50
1989 Mrs. Claus-1258	Open		42.00	46
1990 Nancy Bowman-1261	Open		48.00	52
1987 Naomi Valentine-1200	Closed	1993	40.00	88
1992 Natalie Valentine-1284	Closed	1995	62.00	64
1995 Nathan Bowman-1354	Open		70.00	72
1985 Nettie Brown (1st Ed.)-1102	Closed	1987	30.00	100
1988 Nettie Brown (2nd Ed.)-1102	Closed	1995	36.00	39
1985 Nettie Brown (Christmas) (1st Ed.)-1114	Closed	1987	30.00	100
1996 Nettie Brown (Christmas) (2nd Ed.)-1114	Open		66.00	66
1996 Nicholas Valentine (alone)-1365A	Open		27.50	28
1996 Nicholas Valentine (w/Mother)-1365	Open		101.00	101
1987 Olivia High-1205	Closed	1993	37.00	43
1987 Patsy Bowman-1214	Closed	1995	50.00	53
1988 Pauline Bowman-1228	Closed	1996	44.00	50
1993 Pearl Bowman-1303	Open		56.00	59
1989 Peggy Bowman-1252	Closed	1995	58.00	70
1987 Penelope High-1208	Closed	1991	40.00	100
1993 Penny Valentine-1308	Open		60.00	63
1985 Peter Valentine (1st Ed.)-1113	Closed	1991	30.00	75
1995 Peter Valentine (2nd Ed.)-1113	Open		55.00	57
1988 Phoebe High-1246	Closed	1994	48.00	90
1995 Priscilla High-1226	Closed	1995	56.00	62
1986 Rachel Bowman (1st Ed.)-1188	Closed	1989	34.00	100
1989 Rachel Bowman (2nd Ed.)-1188	Open		34.00	39
1986 Ramona Brown-1215	Closed	1989	40.00	50
1985 Rebecca Bowman (1st Ed.)-1104	Closed	1988	30.00	100
1989 Rebecca Bowman (2nd Ed.)-1104	Open		56.00	62
1987 Rebecca's Mother-1207	Closed	1995	37.00	54
1995 Regina Bowman-1353	Open		70.00	72
1985 Robert Bowman-1348	Open		64.00	66
1985 Russell Dunn-1107	Closed	1987	30.00	100
1988 Ruth Anne Bowman-1232	Closed	1994	44.00	92
1988 Sabina Valentine (1st Ed.)-1101	Closed	1988	30.00	100
1988 Sabina Valentine (2nd Ed.)-1101	Closed	1996	40.00	44
1986 Sadie Valentine-1163	Closed	1988	45.00	50
1986 Sally Bowman (1st Ed.)-1155	Closed	1991	32.00	110
1996 Sally Bowman (2nd Ed.)-1155	Open		75.50	76
1988 Samantha Bowman-1238	Closed	1996	47.00	51
1987 Santa (with Tub)-1257	Open		58.00	64
1987 Santa Claus (sitting)-1224	Closed	1991	50.00	61
1985 Santa Claus-1311	Open		48.00	50
1991 Santa's Helper-1271	Closed	1996	52.00	55
1986 Sara Valentine-1154	Closed	1994	32.00	38-76
1986 Shirley Bowman-1334	Open		63.00	66
1986 Sophie Valentine (1st Ed.)-1164	Closed	1991	45.00	125
1996 Sophie Valentine (alone)-1164A	Open		27.50	28
1996 Sophie Valentine (w/Mother) (2nd Ed.)-1164	Open		101.00	101
1995 St. Nicholas-1356	Open		98.00	100
1986 Susanna Bowman-1149	Closed	1988	45.00	125
1986 Thomas Bowman-1159	Closed	1988	30.00	100
1986 Tillie Brown-1156	Closed	1988	32.00	100
1992 Timothy Bowman-1294	Open		56.00	60
1991 Trudy Valentine-1269	Open		64.00	68
1996 Tucker Bowman-1369	Open		77.50	78
1989 Vanessa Bowman-1247	Closed	1996	45.00	50
1989 Victoria Bowman-1249	Open		40.00	44
1987 The Wedding (Bride)-1203	Closed	1995	37.00	54
1987 The Wedding (Groom)-1203A	Closed	1995	34.00	37
1985 Wendel Bowman (1st Ed.)-1106	Closed	1987	30.00	100
1992 Wendel Bowman (2nd Ed.)-1106	Closed	1996	60.00	64
1992 Wendy Bowman-1293	Open		78.00	82
1985 William Valentine-1191	Closed	1992	36.00	72
1986 Willie Bowman-1162	Closed	1992	30.00	60

The Grummels of Log Hollow™ - B.K. Wisber

YEAR ISSUE	EDITION LIMIT	YEAR RETD.	ISSUE PRICE	*QUOTE U.S.$
1986 Aunt Gertie Grummel™-1171	Closed	1988	34.00	70-110
1986 Aunt Hilda Grummel™-1174	Closed	1988	34.00	70-110
1986 Aunt Polly Grummel™-1169	Closed	1988	34.00	70-110
1986 Cousin Lottie Grummel™-1170	Closed	1988	36.00	70-110
1986 Cousin Miranda Grummel™-1165	Closed	1988	47.00	70-110
1986 Grandma Grummel™-1173	Closed	1988	45.00	70-110
1986 Grandpa Grummel™-1176	Closed	1988	36.00	180
1986 The Little Ones-Grummels™ (boy/girl)-1196	Closed	1988	15.00	40
1986 Ma Grummel™-1167	Closed	1988	36.00	70-110
1986 Pa Grummel™-1172	Closed	1988	34.00	70-110
1986 Sister Nora Grummel™-1177	Closed	1988	34.00	70-100
1986 Teddy Bear Bed-1168	Closed	1988	15.00	70-110
1986 Uncle Hollis Grummel™-1166	Closed	1988	34.00	70-110
1986 Washline-1175	Closed	1988	15.00	70-100

The Little Ones at Christmas-Nativity™ - B.K. Wisber

YEAR ISSUE	EDITION LIMIT	YEAR RETD.	ISSUE PRICE	*QUOTE U.S.$
1995 Donkey-1362	Open		17.00	18
1995 Little Angel-1359	Open		36.00	37
1995 Little Joseph-1358	Open		31.00	32
1995 Little Mary w/Baby in Manger-1357	Open		33.00	34
1995 Little Ones' Creche-1361	Open		24.00	25
1995 Little Shepherd w/Lamb-1360	Open		45.00	46

The Little Ones at Christmas™ - B.K. Wisber

YEAR ISSUE	EDITION LIMIT	YEAR RETD.	ISSUE PRICE	*QUOTE U.S.$
1990 Girl (black) w/Basket of Greens-1263	Closed	1996	22.00	27
1990 Girl (white) w/Cookie-1264	Open		22.00	27
1990 Girl (white) w/Gift-1266	Open		22.00	27
1990 Girl (white) w/Tree Garland-1265	Open		22.00	27
1991 Boy (black) w/Santa Photo-1273A	Closed	1996	24.00	29
1991 Boy (white) w/Santa Photo-1273	Closed	1996	24.00	29
1991 Girl (black) w/Santa Photo-1272A	Closed	1996	24.00	29
1991 Girl (white) w/Santa Photo-1272	Closed	1996	24.00	29
1993 Boy Peeking (Alone)-1314	Open		22.00	24
1993 Boy Peeking w/Tree-1313	Open		60.00	63
1993 Girl w/Baking Table-1317	Open		38.00	40
1993 Girl w/Note for Santa-1318	Open		36.00	38
1993 Girl Peeking (Alone)-1316	Open		22.00	24
1993 Girl Peeking w/Tree-1315	Open		60.00	63
1994 Girl w/Greens on Table-1337	Open		46.00	48
1996 Boy Tangled in Lights-1390	Open		31.00	31
1996 Girl Tangled in Lights-1389	Open		35.00	35
1996 Boy with Ornament-1388	Open		26.00	26
1996 Girl with Ornament-1387	Open		30.00	30
1995 Little Santa-1364	Open		50.00	51

YEAR ISSUE		EDITION LIMIT	YEAR RETD.	ISSUE PRICE	*QUOTE U.S. $

The Little Ones™ - B.K. Wisber

1985	Boy (black) (1st Ed.)-1130	Closed	1989	15.00	45-65
1985	Boy (white) (1st Ed.)-1130	Closed	1989	15.00	45-65
1985	Girl (black) (1st Ed.)-1130	Closed	1989	15.00	45-65
1985	Girl (white) (1st Ed.)-1130	Closed	1989	15.00	45-65
1989	Boy (black) (2nd Ed.)-1130I	Closed	1994	20.00	23
1989	Boy (white) (2nd Ed.)-1130H	Closed	1994	20.00	23
1989	Girl (black)-country color (2nd Ed.)-1130G	Closed	1994	20.00	23
1989	Girl (black)-pastels (2nd Ed.)-1130E	Closed	1994	20.00	23
1989	Girl (white)-country color (2nd Ed.)-1130F	Closed	1994	20.00	23
1989	Girl (white)-pastels (2nd Ed.)-1130H	Closed	1994	20.00	23
1992	Boy w/Sled-1289	Open		30.00	33
1992	Clown-1290	Open		32.00	35
1992	Girl Reading-1286	Open		36.00	39
1992	Girl w/Apples-1277	Open		26.00	29
1992	Girl w/Beach Bucket-1275	Open		26.00	29
1992	Girl w/Birthday Gift-1279	Open		26.00	29
1992	Girl w/Christmas Lights-1287	Open		34.00	37
1992	Girl w/Easter Eggs-1276	Open		26.00	29
1992	Girl w/Kitten and Milk-1280	Open		32.00	35
1992	Girl w/Kitten and Yarn-1278	Open		34.00	37
1992	Girl w/Snowman-1288	Open		36.00	39
1992	Girl w/Valentine-1291	Open		30.00	33
1993	4th of July Boy-1307	Open		28.00	30
1993	Ballerina-1321	Open		40.00	42
1993	Boy w/Easter Flowers-1306	Open		30.00	32
1993	Bunny-1297	Open		36.00	38
1993	Girl Picnicking w/ Teddy Bear-1320	Open		34.00	36
1993	Girl w/Easter Flowers-1296	Open		34.00	36
1993	Girl w/Mop-1300	Open		36.00	38
1993	Girl w/Spinning Wheel-1299	Open		36.00	38
1993	Girl w/Violin-1319	Open		28.00	30
1993	4th of July Girl-1298	Open		30.00	32
1994	Boy Dyeing Eggs-1327	Open		30.00	32
1994	Boy w/Pumpkin-1341	Open		29.00	31
1994	Girl Dyeing Eggs-1326	Open		30.00	32
1994	Girl w/Laundry Basket-1338	Open		38.00	40
1994	Girl w/Puppy in Tub-1339	Open		43.00	45
1994	Girl w/Pumpkin Wagon-1340	Open		42.00	44
1994	Nurse-1328	Open		40.00	42
1994	Teacher-1329	Open		38.00	40
1995	Basketweaver-1363	Open		48.00	49
1996	Girl w/Sunflower-1373	Open		37.00	37
1996	Bride-1374	Open		41.50	42
1996	Groom-1375	Open		23.50	24
1996	White Girl Rollerskating-1376	Open		40.00	40
1996	Black Girl Rollerskating-1377	Open		40.00	40
1996	Girl Hopscotching-1385	Open		45.00	45
1996	Pumpkin Girl-1386	Open		34.00	34

The Pawtuckets of Sweet Briar Lane™ - B.K. Wisber

1994	Aunt Lillian Pawtucket™ (2nd Ed.)-1141			58.00	61
1986	Aunt Lillian Pawtucket™ (1st Ed.)-1141	Closed	1989	32.00	110
1987	Aunt Mabel Pawtucket™ -212	Closed	1989	45.00	130
1986	Aunt Minnie Pawtucket™ (1st Ed.)-1136	Closed	1989	45.00	110
1994	Aunt Minnie Pawtucket™ (2nd Ed.)-1136	Open		72.00	75
1986	Brother Noah Pawtucket™ -1140	Closed	1989	32.00	110
1987	Bunny Bed-1218	Closed	1989	16.00	110
1987	Cousin Alberta Pawtucket™ -1210	Closed	1989	36.00	110
1986	Cousin Clara Pawtucket™ (1st Ed.)-1144	Closed	1989	32.00	110
1987	Cousin Isabel Pawtucket™ -1209	Closed	1989	36.00	110
1988	Cousin Jed Pawtucket™ -1234	Closed	1990	34.00	110
1988	Cousin Winnie Pawtucket™ -1233	Closed	1990	49.00	110
1994	Flossie Pawtucket™ -1136A	Open		33.00	35
1986	Grammy Pawtucket™ (1st Ed.)-1137	Closed	1989	32.00	110
1995	Grammy Pawtucket™ (2nd Ed.)-1137	Open		68.00	71
1995	The Little Ones Bunnies (1995) -female w/laundry baske-1211A	Open		33.00	34
1986	The Little One Bunnies-boy (1st Ed.)-1145	Closed	1989	15.00	20
1994	The Little One Bunnies-boy (2nd Ed.)-1145A	Open		33.00	35
1986	The Little One Bunnies-girl (1st Ed.)-1145	Closed	1989	15.00	50
1994	The Little One Bunnies-girl (2nd Ed.)-1145	Open		33.00	35
1986	Mama Pawtucket™ (1st Ed.)-1142	Closed	1989	34.00	110
1994	Mama Pawtucket™ (2nd Ed.)-1142	Open		86.00	89
1986	Pappy Pawtucket™ (1st Ed.)-1143	Closed	1989	32.00	110
1995	Pappy Pawtucket™ (2nd Ed.)-1143	Open		56.00	58
1994	Pawtucket™ Bunny Hutch-1141A	Open		38.00	40
1995	Pawtucket™ Wash Line-1211B	Open		20.00	21
1987	Sister Clemmie Pawtucket™ (1st Ed.)-1211	Closed	1989	34.00	110
1995	Sister Clemmie Pawtucket™ (2nd Ed.)-1211	Open		60.00	62
1987	Sister Flora Pawtucket™ (1st Ed.)-1139	Closed	1989	32.00	110
1996	Sister Flora Pawtucket™ (2nd Ed.)-1139	Open		63.50	64
1986	Uncle Harley Pawtucket™ (1st Ed.)-1138	Closed	1989	32.00	110
1994	Uncle Harley Pawtucket™ (2nd Ed.)-1138	Open		74.00	77

Special Editions - B.K. Wisber

1992	Kathryn Bowman™-1992 (Limited Edition)-1285	3,000	1992	140.00	500
1994	Prudence Valentine™-1994 (Limited Edition)-1331	4,000	1994	180.00	180
1995	Little Lizzie High®-Anniversary Special Event Edition	Yr.Iss.	1995	40.00	40
1995	Lizzie High®-10th Anniversary Signature Edition-1100A	Yr.Iss.	1995	90.00	90
1996	Little Rebecca Bowman™-1996 Special Event Edition-1372	Yr.Iss.		37.00	37
1996	Lizzie & The Pawtuckets™-1378	3,000	1996	180.00	180

The Thanksgiving Play - B.K. Wisber

1988	Indian Squaw-1244	Closed	1995	36.00	39
1988	Pilgrim Boy-1242	Closed	1995	40.00	45
1988	Pilgrim Girl-1243	Closed	1995	48.00	51

Lawtons

Guild Dolls - W. Lawton

1989	Baa Baa Black Sheep	1,003	1989	395.00	650
1990	Lavender Blue	781	1990	395.00	400
1991	To Market, To Market	683	1991	495.00	495
1992	Little Boy Blue	510	1992	395.00	395
1993	Lawton Logo Doll	575	1993	350.00	500
1994	Wee Handful	540	1994	250.00	250
1995	Uniquely Yours	500	1995	395.00	395
1996	Teddy And Me	Yr.Iss.		450.00	450

Cherished Customs - W. Lawton

1990	The Blessing/Mexico	500	1990	395.00	1000
1992	Carnival/Brazil	750	1992	425.00	425
1992	Cradleboard/Navajo	750	1993	425.00	425
1991	Frolic/Amish	500	1991	395.00	395
1990	Girl's Day/Japan	500	1990	395.00	395
1990	High Tea/Great Britain	500	1990	395.00	450-550
1994	Kwanzaa/Africa	500	1994	425.00	425
1990	Midsommar/Sweden	500	1990	395.00	395
1993	Nalauqataq-Eskimo	500	1993	395.00	395
1991	Ndeko/Zaire	500	1991	395.00	550
1992	Pascha/Ukraine	750	1992	495.00	495
1995	Piping the Haggis	350	1995	495.00	495
1993	Topeng Klana-Java	250	1993	495.00	495

Childhood Classics® - W. Lawton

1983	Alice In Wonderland	100	1983	225.00	2000
1986	Anne Of Green Gables	250	1986	325.00	1600-2400
1991	The Bobbsey Twins: Flossie	350	1991	364.50	500
1991	The Bobbsey Twins: Freddie	350	1991	364.50	500
1985	Hans Brinker	250	1985	325.00	1800
1984	Heidi	250	1984	325.00	650
1991	Hiawatha	500	1991	395.00	500
1989	Honey Bunch	250	1989	350.00	550
1987	Just David	250	1987	325.00	700
1986	Laura Ingalls	250	1986	325.00	500
1991	Little Black Sambo	500	1991	395.00	650
1988	Little Eva	250	1988	350.00	500-1000
1989	Little Princess	250	1989	395.00	600
1990	Mary Frances	350	1990	350.00	350
1987	Mary Lennox	250	1987	325.00	500
1987	Polly Pepper	250	1987	325.00	450
1986	Pollyanna	250	1986	325.00	1600
1990	Poor Little Match Girl	350	1990	350.00	500
1988	Rebecca	250	1988	350.00	450
1988	Topsy	250	1988	350.00	750

The Children's Hour - W. Lawton

1991	Edith With Golden Hair	500	1991	395.00	475
1991	Grave Alice	500	1991	395.00	475
1991	Laughing Allegra	500	1991	395.00	475

Christmas Dolls - W. Lawton

1988	Christmas Joy	500	1988	325.00	750-1200
1989	Noel	500	1989	325.00	375
1990	Christmas Angel	500	1990	325.00	325
1991	Yuletide Carole	500	1991	395.00	395
1996	The Bird's Christmas Carol	500		450.00	450

Newcomer Collection - W. Lawton

| 1987 | Ellin Elizabeth, Eyes Closed | 49 | 1987 | 335.00 | 750-1000 |
| 1987 | Ellin Elizabeth, Eyes Open | 19 | 1987 | 335.00 | 900-1200 |

Playthings Past - W. Lawton

1989	Edward And Dobbin	500	1989	395.00	495-600
1989	Elizabeth And Baby	500	1989	395.00	495-650
1989	Victoria And Teddy	500	1989	395.00	395

Special Edition - W. Lawton

1993	Flora McFlimsey	250	1993	895.00	1000
1988	Marcella And Raggedy Ann	2,500	1989	395.00	700-750
1994	Mary Chilton	350	1994	395.00	395
1995	Through The Looking Glass	180	1995	N/A	N/A

Special Occasion - W. Lawton

1990	First Birthday	500	1990	295.00	350
1989	First Day Of School	500	1989	325.00	525
1988	Nanthy	500	1988	325.00	525

Sugar 'n' Spice - W. Lawton

| 1987 | Ginger | 454 | 1987 | 275.00 | 395-550 |

1986	Jason	27	1986	250.00	800-1700
1986	Jessica	30	1986	250.00	800-1700
1986	Kersten	103	1986	250.00	550-800
1986	Kimberly	87	1986	250.00	550-800
1987	Marie	208	1987	275.00	450

Timeless Ballads® - W. Lawton

1987	Annabel Lee	250	1987	550.00	600-695
1987	Highland Mary	250	1987	550.00	600-875
1988	She Walks In Beauty	250	1988	550.00	600-800
1987	Young Charlotte	250	1987	550.00	850-900

Wee Bits - W. Lawton

1989	Wee Bit O'Bliss	250	1989	295.00	350
1988	Wee Bit O'Heaven	250	1988	295.00	350
1988	Wee Bit O'Sunshine	250	1988	295.00	350
1988	Wee Bit O'Woe	250	1988	295.00	350
1989	Wee Bit O'Wonder	250	1989	295.00	350

Lenox Collections

Bolshoi Nutcracker Dolls - Unknown

| 1991 | Clara | Closed | 1993 | 195.00 | 195 |

Children of the World - Unknown

1991	Amma-The African Girl	Closed	1993	119.00	119
1992	Gretchen, German Doll	Closed	1993	119.00	119
1989	Hannah, The Little Dutch Maiden	Closed	1993	119.00	119
1990	Heather, Little Highlander	Closed	1993	119.00	119
1991	Sakura-The Japanese Girl	Closed	1993	119.00	119

Children With Toys Dolls - Unknown

| 1991 | Tea For Teddy | Closed | 1993 | 136.00 | 136 |

China Dolls - Cloth Bodies - J. Grammer

1985	Amy, 14"	Closed	1990	250.00	N/A
1985	Annabelle, 14"	Closed	1990	250.00	N/A
1985	Elizabeth, 14"	Closed	1990	250.00	N/A
1985	Jennifer, 14"	Closed	1990	250.00	N/A
1985	Miranda, 14"	Closed	1990	250.00	N/A
1985	Sarah, 14"	Closed	1990	250.00	N/A

Country Decor Dolls - Unknown

| 1991 | Molly | Closed | 1994 | 150.00 | 150 |

Ellis Island Dolls - P. Thompson

1992	Angelina	Closed	1994	150.00	150
1992	Anna	Closed	1994	152.00	152
1992	Catherine	Closed	1994	152.00	152
1991	Megan	Closed	1994	150.00	150
1991	Stefan	Closed	1994	150.00	150

First Collector Doll - Unknown

| 1992 | Lauren | Closed | 1993 | 152.00 | 152 |

Inspirational Doll - Unknown

| 1992 | Blessed Are The Peacemakers | Closed | 1993 | 119.00 | 119 |

International Baby Doll - Unknown

| 1992 | Natalia, Russian Baby | Closed | 1993 | 119.00 | 119 |

Lenox China Dolls - J. Grammer

1984	Abigail, 20"	Closed	1990	425.00	N/A
1984	Amanda, 16"	Closed	1990	385.00	N/A
1984	Jessica, 20"	Closed	1990	450.00	N/A
1984	Maggie, 16"	Closed	1990	375.00	N/A
1984	Maryanne, 20"	Closed	1990	425.00	N/A
1984	Melissa, 16"	Closed	1990	450.00	N/A
1984	Rebecca, 16"	Closed	1990	375.00	N/A
1984	Samantha, 16"	Closed	1990	500.00	N/A

Lenox Victorian Dolls - Unknown

1990	Christmas Doll, Elizabeth	Closed	1993	195.00	195
1992	Lady at Gala	Closed	1993	295.00	295
1989	The Victorian Bride	Closed	1993	295.00	295
1991	Victorian Christening Doll	Closed	1993	295.00	295

Little Women - Unknown

| 1992 | Amy, The Inspiring Artist | Closed | 1993 | 152.00 | 152 |

Musical Baby Dolls - Unknown

| 1991 | Patrick's Lullabye | Closed | 1993 | 95.00 | 95 |

Nutcracker Dolls - Unknown

| 1993 | Nutcracker | Closed | 1993 | 195.00 | 195 |
| 1992 | Sugarplum | Closed | 1993 | 195.00 | 195 |

Prima Ballerina Collection - Unknown

| 1992 | Odette, Queen of the Swans | Closed | 1992 | 195.00 | 195 |

Sibling Dolls - A. Lester

| 1991 | Skating Lesson | Closed | 1993 | 195.00 | 195 |

Mattel

35th Anniversary Dolls by Mattel - Mattel

1994	Blonde	Retrd.	1994	39.99	40-50
1994	Brunette	Retrd.	1994	39.99	60-80
1994	Gift Pack	Retrd.	1994	79.97	125-140

YEAR ISSUE		EDITION LIMIT	YEAR RETD.	ISSUE PRICE	*QUOTE U.S.$

Annual Holiday (white) Barbie Dolls - Mattel

1988	Holiday Barbie		Retrd. 1990	24.95	675-900
1989	Holiday Barbie		Retrd. 1991	N/A	200-300
1990	Holiday Barbie		Retrd. 1991	N/A	150-225
1991	Holiday Barbie		Retrd. 1993	N/A	125-225
1992	Holiday Barbie		Retrd. 1992	N/A	125-150
1993	Holiday Barbie		Retrd. 1993	N/A	100-175
1994	Holiday Barbie		Retrd. 1994	44.95	125-195
1995	Holiday Barbie		Retrd. 1995	44.95	75-125

Bob Mackie Barbie Dolls - B. Mackie

1992	Empress Bride Barbie 4247		Retrd. 1992	232.00	800-1000
1990	Gold Barbie 5405		Retrd. 1990	120.00	550-800
1993	Masquerade		Retrd. 1993	175.00	800-1000
1992	Neptune Fantasy Barbie 4248		Retrd. 1993	160.00	600-800
1991	Platinum Barbie 2703		Retrd. 1991	153.00	225-250
1994	Queen of Hearts		Retrd. 1994	175.00	600-900
1991	Starlight Splendor Barbie 2704		Retrd. 1991	135.00	750-950

Classique Collection - Various

1992	Benefit Ball - C. Spencer		Retrd. 1994	59.95	175-200
1993	City Style - J. Goldblatt		Retrd. 1994	59.95	125
1993	Opening Night - J. Goldblatt		Retrd. 1994	59.95	100-125

Golden Jubilee - C. Spencer

| 1994 | Golden Jubilee | | Retrd. 1994 | 299.00 | 600-950 |

Great Eras - Mattel

| 1993 | Flapper | | Retrd. 1995 | 54.00 | 125-200 |
| 1993 | Gibson Girl | | Retrd. 1995 | 54.00 | 100-110 |

Nostalgic Porcelain Barbie Dolls - Mattel

1990	Solo in the Spotlight 7613		Retrd. 1990	198.00	200-250
1990	Sophisticated Lady 5313		Retrd. 1990	198.00	200-295
1989	Wedding Day Barbie 2641		Retrd. 1989	198.00	500-600

The Winter Princess Collection - Mattel

1994	Evergreen Princess		Retrd. 1994	59.95	120-175
1994	Evergreen Princess (Red Head)		Retrd. 1994	59.95	300-500
1995	Peppermint Princess		Retrd. 1995	59.95	75
1993	Winter Princess		Retrd. 1993	59.95	400-600

Middleton Doll Company

Christmas Angel Collection - L. Middleton

1987	Christmas Angel 1987	4,174	1987	130.00	400-500
1988	Christmas Angel 1988	8,969	1988	130.00	200-250
1989	Christmas Angel 1989	7,500	1991	150.00	190
1990	Christmas Angel 1990	5,000	1991	150.00	190
1991	Christmas Angel 1991	5,000	1992	180.00	200
1992	Christmas Angel 1992	5,000	1995	190.00	190
1993	Christmas Angel 1993-Girl	3,144	1995	190.00	190
1993	Christmas Angel 1993 (set)	1,000	1993	390.00	500
1994	Christmas Angel 1994	5,000		190.00	190
1995	Christmas Angel 1995 (wh. or bl.)	3,000		190.00	190

First Moments Series - L. Middleton

1984	First Moments (Sleeping)	40,861	1990	69.00	200
1992	First Moments Awake in Blue	1,230	1994	170.00	170
1992	First Moments Awake in Pink	856	1994	170.00	170
1986	First Moments Blue Eyes	14,494	1990	120.00	150
1987	First Moments Boy	6,075	1989	130.00	160
1986	First Moments Brown Eyes	5,324	1989	120.00	150
1987	First Moments Christening (Asleep)	9,377	1992	160.00	250
1987	First Moments Christening (Awake)	16,384	1992	160.00	180
1993	First Moments Heirloom	1,372	1995	190.00	190
1991	First Moments Sweetness	6,323	1995	180.00	180
1994	Sweetness-Newborn		Retrd. 1995	190.00	190

Porcelain Collector Series - L. Middleton

1992	Beloved & Bé Bé	362	1994	590.00	590
1993	Cherish - Lilac & Lace	141	1994	500.00	500
1992	Sencerity II - Country Fair	253	1994	500.00	500

Porcelain Limited Edition Series - L. Middleton

1990	Baby Grace	500	1990	500.00	500
1994	Blossom	86	1995	500.00	500
1994	Bride	200	1994	1390.00	1390
1988	Cherish -1st Edition	750	1988	350.00	500
1989	Devan	543	1991	500.00	500
1995	Elise - 1860's Fashion	200		1790.00	1790
1991	Johanna	381	1992	500.00	500
1991	Molly Rose	500	1991	500.00	500
1989	My Lee	655	1991	500.00	500
1988	Sincerity -1st Edition -Nettie/Simplicity	750	1988	330.00	350-600
1995	Tenderness - Baby Clown	250		590.00	590
1994	Tenderness-Petite Pierrot	250	1994	500.00	500

Vinyl Collectors Series - L. Middleton

1987	Amanda - 1st Edition	3,778	1989	140.00	160
1985	Angel Face	20,200	1989	90.00	150
1994	Angel Kisses Boy	Open		98.00	98
1994	Angel Kisses Girl	Open		98.00	98
1992	Beth	1,414	1994	160.00	160
1986	Bubba Chubbs	5,550	1988	100.00	150-200
1988	Bubba Chubbs Railroader	7,925	1994	140.00	170
1988	Cherish	14,790	1992	160.00	250
1994	Country Boy	Open		118.00	118

1994	Country Boy (Dark Flesh)	Open		118.00	118
1994	Country Girl	Open		118.00	118
1994	Country Girl (Dark Flesh)	Open		118.00	118
1986	Dear One - 1st Edition	4,935	1988	90.00	250
1989	Devan	8,336	1991	170.00	170
1993	Echo	Open		180.00	180
1995	Hershey's Kisses - Gold	Open		99.50	100
1994	Hershey's Kisses - Silver	Open		99.50	100
1986	Little Angel - 3rd Edition	15,158	1992	90.00	110
1992	Little Angel Boy	Open		130.00	130
1992	Little Angel Girl	Open		130.00	130
1987	Missy	11,855	1991	100.00	120
1989	My Lee	3,794	1991	170.00	170
1992	Polly Esther	2,137	1994	160.00	160
1995	Polly Esther - Hershey's Country Girl	Open		130.00	130
1988	Sincerity - Limited 1st Ed. - Nettie/Simplicity	3,711	1989	160.00	200-250
1989	Sincerity-Schoolgirl	6,622	1992	180.00	200
1994	Town Boy	Open		118.00	118
1994	Town Boy (Dark Flesh)	Open		118.00	118
1994	Town Girl	Open		118.00	118
1994	Town Girl (Dark Flesh)	Open		118.00	118

Original Appalachian Artworks

Collectors Club Editions - X. Roberts

1987	Baby Otis	Closed	1987	250.00	500
1989	Anna Ruby	Closed	1989	250.00	400-650
1990	Lee Ann	Closed	1990	250.00	400-500
1991	Richard Russell	Closed	1991	250.00	400-650
1992	Baby Dodd	Closed	1992	250.00	300-500
1993	Patti w/ Cabbage Bud Boutonnier	Closed	1993	280.00	280
1994	Mother Cabbage	Closed	1995	150.00	150
1995	Rosie	Closed	1996	275.00	275
1996	Gabriella	Closed	1996	265.00	265

Cabbage Patch Kids - X. Roberts

1982	Amy	Closed	1982	125.00	500-700
1983	Andre/Madeira	Closed	1982	250.00	1200
1982	Billie	Closed	1982	125.00	450-600
1982	Bobbie	Closed	1982	125.00	450-600
1984	Daddy's Darlins' Kitten	Closed	1984	300.00	400-500
1984	Daddy's Darlins' Princess	Closed	1984	300.00	500-750
1984	Daddy's Darlins' Pun'kin	Closed	1983	300.00	400-500
1984	Daddy's Darlins' Tootsie	Closed	1984	300.00	400-500
1984	Daddy's Darlins', set of 4	Closed	1984	1600.00	1000-2000
1982	Dorothy	Closed	1982	125.00	700
1982	Gilda	Closed	1982	125.00	700-2500
1994	Little People 27" (Boy)	Closed	1994	325.00	750
1993	Little People 27" (Girl)	Closed	1993	325.00	850
1982	Marilyn	Closed	1982	125.00	700-800
1994	Mountain Laurel 'Kids™	Closed	1994	210.00	210
1994	Mountain Laurel Baby Sidney & Baby Lanier	100	1994	390.00	390
1994	Mountain Laurel Easter	200	1994	210.00	210
1994	Mountain Laurel Mysterious Barry	Closed	1994	225.00	375
1994	Mountain Laurel Norma Jean	Closed	1994	225.00	425
1994	Mountain Laurel-St. Patrick Boys	100	1994	210.00	210
1994	Mountain Laurel-St. Patrick Girls	200	1994	210.00	210
1995	Mt. Yonah	Closed	1995	210.00	210
1995	Mt. Yonah Easter	Closed	1995	215.00	215
1995	Mt. Yonah Valentine	Closed	1995	200.00	200
1995	OlympiKids™	Open		275.00	275
1982	Otis	Closed	1982	125.00	700
1982	Rebecca	Closed	1982	125.00	700
1982	Sybil	Closed	1982	125.00	450-700
1984	Tiger's Eye-Mother's Day	Closed	1984	150.00	300-375
1988	Tiger's Eye-Valentine's Day	Closed	1984	150.00	300-375
1982	Tyler	Closed	1982	125.00	2000-3000
1993	Unicoi Edition	1,500	1993	210.00	210

Cabbage Patch Kids Circus Parade - X. Roberts

1987	Big Top Clown-Baby Cakes	2,000	1987	180.00	450-550
1989	Happy Hobo-Bashful Billy	1,000	1989	180.00	350
1991	Mitzi	1,000	1991	220.00	200-400

Cabbage Patch Kids International - X. Roberts

1983	American Indian/Pair	Closed	1983	300.00	1200
1984	Bavarian/Pair	Closed	1984	300.00	450-800
1983	Hispanic/Pair	Closed	1983	300.00	400
1983	Irish/Pair	Closed	1985	320.00	320
1983	Oriental/Pair	Closed	1983	300.00	1000

Christmas Collection - X. Roberts

1979	X Christmas/Pair	Closed	1979	300.00	5500
1980	Christmas-Nicholas/Noel	Closed	1980	400.00	1200
1982	Christmas-Baby Rudy/Christy Nicole	Closed	1982	400.00	1600
1983	Christmas-Holly/Berry	Closed	1983	400.00	800
1984	Christmas-Carole/Chris	Closed	1984	400.00	600
1985	Christmas-Baby Sandy/Claude	Closed	1985	400.00	400
1986	Christmas-Hilliary/Nigel	Closed	1986	400.00	425
1987	Christmas-Katrina/Misha	Closed	1987	500.00	500
1988	Christmas-Kelly/Kane	Closed	1988	500.00	500-600
1989	Christmas-Joy	Closed	1989	250.00	600
1990	Christmas-Krystina	Closed	1990	250.00	250
1991	Christmas-Nick	Closed	1991	275.00	275
1992	Christmas-Christy Claus	Closed	1992	285.00	285
1993	Christmas-Rudolph	Closed	1993	275.00	275

1994	Christmas-Natalie	Closed	1994	275.00	275
1995	Christmas-Treena	Closed	1995	275.00	275
1996	Sammy The Snowman	Yr.Iss.		275.00	275

Convention Baby - X. Roberts

1989	Ashley	Closed	1989	150.00	600-800
1990	Bradley	Closed	1990	175.00	500-600
1991	Caroline	Closed	1991	200.00	500
1992	Duke	Closed	1992	225.00	375-400
1993	Ellen	Closed	1993	225.00	300-400
1994	Justin	Closed	1994	238.50	300-400
1995	Fifi	Closed	1995	250.00	450-700
1996	Gina	200	1996	275.00	275

Happily Ever After - X. Roberts

| 1993 | Bride | Closed | 1993 | 230.00 | 275 |
| 1993 | Groom | Closed | 1993 | 230.00 | 275 |

Little People - X. Roberts

1978	"A" Blue	Closed	1978	125.00	7000-8500
1978	"B" Red	Closed	1978	100.00	4500-6000
1978	"C" Burgundy	Closed	1978	100.00	1500-1800
1979	"D" Purple	Closed	1979	100.00	1000-1500
1979	"E" Bronze	Closed	1979	125.00	750-850
1982	"PE" New 'Ears Preemie	Closed	1982	140.00	300-450
1981	"PR II" Preemie	Closed	1981	130.00	350-450
1980	"SP" Preemie	Closed	1980	100.00	600-800
1982	"U" Unsigned	Closed	1982	125.00	300-450
1980	"U" Unsigned	Closed	1981	125.00	300-450
1980	Celebrity	Closed	1982	200.00	550
1980	Grand Edition	Closed	1986	1000.00	1000
1978	Helen Blue	Closed	1978	150.00	8000-11000
1981	New 'Ears	Closed	1981	125.00	250
1981	Standing Edition	Closed	1986	300.00	350-375

Reco International

Childhood Doll Collection - S. Kuck

1994	A Kiss Goodnight		Retrd. 1995	79.00	79
1995	Reading With Teddy		Retrd. 1995	79.00	79
1994	Teaching Teddy His Prayers	Open		79.00	79
1996	Teddy's Picnic	Open		79.00	79

Children's Circus Doll Collection - J. McClelland

1991	Johnny The Strongman		Yr.Iss.	83.00	83
1991	Katie The Tightrope Walker		Yr.Iss.	78.00	78
1992	Maggie The Animal Trainer		Yr.Iss.	83.00	83
1991	Tommy The Clown		Yr.Iss.	78.00	78

Precious Memories of Motherhood - S. Kuck

1993	Bedtime		Retrd. 1994	149.00	149
1992	Expectant Moments		Retrd. 1993	149.00	149
1990	Loving Steps		Retrd. 1992	125.00	150-195
1991	Lullaby		Retrd. 1995	125.00	125

Roman, Inc.

Abbie Williams Collection - E. Williams

| 1991 | Molly | 5,000 | | 155.00 | 155 |

A Christmas Dream - E. Williams

| 1990 | Carole | 5,000 | | 125.00 | 125 |
| 1990 | Chelsea | 5,000 | | 125.00 | 125 |

Classic Brides of the Century - E. Williams

1991	Flora-The 1900's Bride		Yr.Iss. 1991	145.00	145
1992	Jennifer-The 1980's Bride		Yr.Iss. 1992	149.00	149
1993	Kathleen-The 1930's Bride		Yr.Iss. 1993	149.00	149

Ellen Williams Doll - E. Williams

| 1989 | Noelle | 5,000 | | 125.00 | 125 |
| 1989 | Rebecca 999 | 7,500 | | 195.00 | 195 |

Sarah's Attic, Inc.

Heirlooms from the Attic - Sarah's Attic

1991	Adora 1823	500	1991	90.00	200
1991	All Cloth Muffin Bl. Doll 1820	Closed	1991	90.00	200
1991	All Cloth Puffin Bl. Doll 1821	Closed	1991	90.00	200
1991	Enos 1822	500	1991	90.00	200
1993	Granny Quilting Lady Doll 3576	Closed	1993	130.00	150
1992	Harpster w/Banjo 3591	Closed	1993	250.00	250
1990	Hickory-Americana 1771	Closed	1993	140.00	170
1990	Hickory-Beachtime 1769	2,000	1993	140.00	150-175
1991	Hickory-Christmas 1810	2,000	1993	140.00	150-175
1990	Hickory-Playtime 1768	2,000	1993	140.00	175
1990	Hickory-School Days 1766	2,000	1993	140.00	175
1991	Hickory-Springtime 1814	2,000	1993	150.00	195
1990	Hickory-Sunday's Best 1770	2,000	1993	150.00	195
1990	Hickory-Sweet Dreams 1767	2,000	1993	140.00	175
1986	Holly Bl. Angel 0410		Retrd. 1986	34.00	200
1992	Kiah Guardian Angel 3570	2,000	1993	170.00	200
1993	Lilla Quilting Lady Doll 3581	Closed	1993	130.00	150
1986	Maggie Cloth Doll 0012	Closed	1989	70.00	120
1986	Matt Cloth Doll 0011	Closed		70.00	120
1993	Millie Quilting Lady Doll 3586	Closed	1993	130.00	130
1992	Peace on Earth Santa 3564	200	1992	175.00	350
1986	Priscilla Doll 0030	Closed	1989	140.00	300
1990	Sassafras-Americana 1685	2,000	1993	150.00	175

YEAR ISSUE		EDITION LIMIT	YEAR RETD.	ISSUE PRICE	*QUOTE U.S.$
1990	Sassafras-Beachtime 1683	2,000	1993	140.00	175
1991	Sassafras-Christmas 1809	2,000	1993	150.00	150-175
1990	Sassafras-Playtime 1682	2,000	1993	140.00	175
1989	Sassafras-School Days 1680	2,000	1993	140.00	175
1991	Sassafras-Springtime 1813	2,000	1993	150.00	195
1990	Sassafras-Sunday's Best 1684	2,000	1993	150.00	175
1990	Sassafras-Sweet Dreams 1681	2,000	1993	140.00	195
1988	Smiley Clown Doll 3050	Closed	1988	126.00	126
1986	Twinkie Doll 0039A	Closed	1986	32.00	32
1986	Whimpy Doll 0039E	Closed	1986	32.00	32
1992	Whoopie 3597	Closed	1992	200.00	200
1992	Wooster 3602	Closed	1992	160.00	160

Seymour Mann, Inc.

Connoisseur Doll Collection - E. Mann

YEAR ISSUE		EDITION LIMIT	YEAR RETD.	ISSUE PRICE	QUOTE U.S.$
1991	Abby 16" Pink Dress-C3145	Closed	1993	100.00	100
1995	Abby C-3229	2,500		30.00	30
1994	Abby YK-4533	3,500		135.00	135
1994	Abigail-EP-3	Closed	1993	100.00	100
1991	Abigal-WB-72WM	Closed	1993	75.00	75
1994	Adak PS-412	2,500		150.00	150
1993	Adrienne C-3162	Closed	1994	135.00	135
1995	Aggie PS-435	2,500		80.00	80
1991	Alexis 24" Beige Lace-EP32	Closed	1993	220.00	220
1994	Alice GU-32	2,500		150.00	150
1994	Alice IND-508	2,500	1995	115.00	115
1992	Alice-JNC-4013	Closed	1993	90.00	90
1994	Alicia C-3235	2,500		65.00	65
1991	Alicia-YK-4215	Closed	1993	90.00	90
1995	Allison CD-18183	2,500		35.00	35
1995	Allison TR-92	2,500		125.00	125
1994	Ally FH-556	2,500	1995	115.00	115
1994	Alyssa C-3201	2,500	1995	110.00	110
1994	Alyssa PP-1	2,500		275.00	275
1991	Amanda Toast-OM-182	Closed	1993	260.00	260
1995	Amanda TR-96	2,500		135.00	135
1989	Amber-DOM-281A	Closed	1993	85.00	85
1991	Amelia-TR-47	Closed	1993	105.00	105
1991	Amy C-3147	Closed	1993	135.00	135
1995	Amy GU-300A	2,500	1995	30.00	30
1995	Amy OC-43M	2,500		115.00	115
1992	Amy OM-06	2,500	1993	150.00	150
1990	Anabelle C-3080	Closed	1992	85.00	85
1990	Angel DOM-335	Closed	1992	105.00	105
1995	Angel FH-291DP	2,500		70.00	70
1994	Angel LL-956	2,500	1996	90.00	90
1994	Angel SP-460	2,500		140.00	140
1990	Angela C-3084	Closed	1992	105.00	105
1990	Angela C-3084M	Closed	1992	115.00	115
1995	Angela Doll 556	2,500		35.00	35
1995	Angela FH-511	2,500		85.00	85
1995	Angela OM-87	2,500		150.00	150
1995	Angelica FH-291B	2,500		70.00	70
1994	Angelica FH-291E	2,500		85.00	85
1995	Angelica FH-511B	2,500		85.00	85
1995	Angelina FH-291S	2,500		70.00	70
1994	Angelina FH-291S	2,500		85.00	85
1995	Angeline FH-291WG	2,500		75.00	75
1994	Angeline FH-291WG	2,500		85.00	85
1995	Angelina OM-84	2,500		100.00	100
1995	Angelique	2,500		150.00	150
1995	Angelita FH-291G	2,500		70.00	70
1995	Angelita FH-291G	2,500		85.00	85
1994	Angelo OC-57	2,500		135.00	135
1990	Anita FH-277G	Closed	1992	65.00	65
1991	Ann TR-52	Closed	1993	135.00	135
1995	Anna Doll 550	2,500		60.00	60
1995	Annette FH-635	2,500		110.00	110
1991	Annette-TR-59	Closed	1993	130.00	130
1991	Annie YK-4214	Closed	1993	145.00	145
1991	Antoinette FH-452	Closed	1993	100.00	100
1993	Antonia OM-227	2,500	1993	350.00	350
1994	Antonia OM-42	2,500	1996	150.00	150
1995	April CD-2212B	2,500		50.00	50
1991	Arabella-C-3163	Closed	1993	135.00	135
1991	Ariel 34" Blue/White-EP-33	Closed	1993	175.00	175
1995	Ariel OM-81	2,500		185.00	185
1994	Arlene LL-940	2,500	1994	90.00	90
1993	Arlene SP-421	Closed	1993	100.00	100
1988	Ashley C-278	Closed	1990	80.00	80
1993	Ashley C-278	Closed	1993	80.00	80
1990	Ashley FH-325	Closed	1993	75.00	75
1995	Ashley OC-76	2,500		40.00	40
1995	Ashley PS-433	2,500		110.00	110
1994	Atanak PS-414	2,500	1994	150.00	150
1994	Audrey FH-455	2,500	1993	125.00	125
1990	Audrey YK-4089	Closed	1992	125.00	125
1987	Audrina YK-200	Closed	1986	85.00	140
1991	Aurora Gold 22"-OM-181	2,500	1993	260.00	260
1991	Azure AM-15	2,500	1993	175.00	175
1994	Baby Belle C-3193	2,500	1994	150.00	150
1991	Baby Beth-DOLL-406P	2,500	1993	27.50	28
1995	Baby Betsy Doll 336	2,500		75.00	75
1990	Baby Betty YK-4087	Closed	1991	125.00	125
1991	Baby Bonnie SP-341	Closed	1993	55.00	55
1990	Baby Bonnie SP-341	Closed	1991	55.00	55
1990	Baby Bonnie w/Walker Music-DOLL-409	2,500	1993	40.00	40
1991	Baby Brent EP-15	Closed	1993	85.00	85
1990	Baby Brent EP-15	Closed	1991	85.00	85
1991	Baby Carrie DOLL-402P	2,500	1993	27.50	28
1990	Baby Ecru WB-17	Closed	1991	65.00	65
1991	Baby Ecru WB-17	Closed	1991	65.00	65
1991	Baby Ellie Ecru Musical DOLL-402E	2,500	1993	27.50	28
1991	Baby Gloria Black Baby PS-289	Closed	1993	75.00	75
1991	Baby John PS-498	Closed	1993	85.00	85
1989	Baby John PS-49B	Closed	1991	85.00	85
1990	Baby Kate WB-19	Closed	1991	85.00	85
1991	Baby Linda-DOLL-406E	2,500	1993	27.50	28
1990	Baby Nelly-PS-163	Closed	1991	95.00	95
1994	Baby Scarlet C-3194	2,500	1994	115.00	115
1991	Baby Sue-DOLL-402B	2,500	1993	27.50	28
1990	Baby Sue-DOLL-402B	Closed	1992	27.50	28
1990	Baby Sunshine-C-3055	Closed	1992	90.00	90
1995	Barbara PS-439	2,500		65.00	65
1995	Beige Angel FH-291E	2,500		70.00	70
1991	Belinda-C-3164	Closed	1993	150.00	150
1991	Bernetta-EP-40	Closed	1993	115.00	115
1995	Beth OC-74	2,500		40.00	40
1992	Beth-OM-05	2,500	1993	135.00	135
1990	Beth-YK-4099A/B	Closed	1992	125.00	125
1995	Betsy C-3224	2,500		45.00	45
1995	Betsy OM-89B	2,500		125.00	125
1995	Betsy RDK-230	2,500		35.00	35
1991	Betsy-AM-6	Closed	1993	105.00	105
1992	Bette-OM-01	2,500	1993	115.00	115
1990	Bettina-TR-4	Closed	1991	125.00	125
1991	Bettina-YK-4144	Closed	1993	105.00	105
1995	Betty LL-996	2,500		115.00	115
1989	Betty-PS27G	Closed	1993	65.00	125
1990	Beverly-DOLL-335	Closed	1992	110.00	110
1995	Bianca CD-1450C	2,500		35.00	35
1990	Billie-YK-4056V	Closed	1992	65.00	65
1993	Blaine C-3167	Closed	1993	100.00	100
1991	Blaine-TR-61	Closed	1993	115.00	115
1994	Blair YK-4532	3,500	1994	150.00	150
1991	Blythe-CH-15V	Closed	1993	135.00	135
1991	Bo-Peep w/Lamb-C-3128	Closed	1993	105.00	105
1994	Bobbi NM-30	2,500	1994	135.00	135
1994	Brandy YK-4537	3,500	1995	165.00	165
1995	Brenda Doll 551	2,500		60.00	60
1989	Brett-PS27B	Closed	1993	65.00	125
1995	Brianna GU-300B	2,500		30.00	30
1991	Bridget-SP-379	2,500	1993	105.00	105
1995	Brie C-3230	2,500		30.00	30
1995	Brie CD-16310C	2,500		30.00	30
1995	Brie OM-89W	2,500		125.00	125
1995	Britt OC-77	2,500		40.00	40
1995	Brittany Doll 558	2,500		35.00	35
1989	Brittany-TK-4	Closed	1993	150.00	150
1988	Brittany-TK-5	Closed	1990	120.00	120
1994	Bronwyn IND-517	2,500	1994	140.00	140
1991	Brooke-FH-461	2,500	1993	115.00	115
1995	Bryna Doll 555	2,500		35.00	35
1991	Bryna-AM-100B	2,500	1993	70.00	70
1995	Bunny TR-97	2,500		85.00	85
1994	Cactus Flower Indian LL-944	2,500	1994	105.00	105
1990	Caillin-DOLL-11PH	Closed	1992	60.00	60
1995	Caitlin LL-997	2,500		115.00	115
1990	Caitlin-YK-4051V	Closed	1992	90.00	90
1994	Callie TR-76	2,500	1994	140.00	140
1994	Calypso LL-942	2,500	1994	150.00	150
1991	Camellia-FH-457	2,500	1993	100.00	100
1986	Camelot Fairy-C-84	Closed	1988	75.00	225
1993	Camille OM-230	2,500	1994	250.00	250
1995	Candice TR-94	2,500	1995	135.00	135
1990	Carole-YK-4085W	Closed	1992	125.00	125
1991	Caroline-LL-838	2,500	1993	110.00	110
1991	Caroline-LL-905	2,500	1993	110.00	110
1995	Carlotta OM-80	2,500		175.00	175
1995	Carrie C-3231	2,500		30.00	30
1994	Casey C-3197	2,500		140.00	140
1995	Catherine RDK-231	2,500		30.00	30
1994	Cathy GU-41	2,500	1994	140.00	140
1995	Cecily Doll 552	2,500		60.00	60
1995	Celene FH-618	2,500		120.00	120
1995	Celestine LL-982	2,500		100.00	100
1990	Charlene-YK-4112	Closed	1992	90.00	90
1992	Charlotte-FH-484	2,500	1993	115.00	115
1995	Chelsea Doll 560	2,500		35.00	35
1992	Chelsea-IND-397	Closed	1993	85.00	85
1995	Cherry FH-616	2,500	1994	100.00	100
1991	Cheryl-TR-49	Closed	1993	120.00	120
1991	Chin Chin-YK-4211	Closed	1993	85.00	85
1990	Chin Fa-C-3061	Closed	1992	95.00	95
1990	Chinook-WB-24	Closed	1992	85.00	85
1994	Chris FH-561	2,500	1993	85.00	85
1994	Chrissie FH-562	2,500	1993	85.00	85
1990	Chrissie-WB-2	Closed	1992	75.00	75
1991	Christina-PS-261	Closed	1993	115.00	115
1985	Christmas Cheer-125	Closed	1988	40.00	100
1995	Christmas Kitten IND-530	2,500		100.00	100
1991	Cindy Lou-FH-464	2,500	1993	85.00	85
1994	Cindy OC-58	2,500		140.00	140
1993	Cinnamon JNC-4014	Closed	1993	90.00	90
1988	Cissie-DOM263	Closed	1990	65.00	135
1991	Cissy-EP-56	Closed	1993	95.00	95
1995	Clancy GU-54	2,500	1995	80.00	80
1994	Clara IND-518	2,500	1994	140.00	140
1994	Clara IND-524	2,500	1994	150.00	150
1993	Clare FH-497	2,500	1993	100.00	100
1991	Clare-DOLL-465	Open	1993	100.00	100
1994	Claudette TR-81	2,500	1995	150.00	150
1991	Claudine-C-3146	Closed	1993	95.00	95
1993	Clothilde FH-469	2,500	1993	125.00	125
1995	Cody FH-629	2,500	1995	120.00	120
1991	Colette-WB-7	Closed	1993	65.00	65
1991	Colleen-YK-4163	Closed	1993	120.00	120
1991	Cookie-GU-6	2,500	1993	110.00	110
1994	Copper YK-4546C	3,500		150.00	150
1994	Cora FH-565	2,500		140.00	140
1992	Cordelia-OM-009	2,500	1993	250.00	250
1992	Cordelia-OM-09	2,500	1993	250.00	250
1994	Cory FH-564	2,500	1994	115.00	115
1991	Courtney-LL-859	2,500	1993	150.00	150
1991	Creole-AM-17	2,500	1993	160.00	160
1989	Crying Courtney-PS-75	Closed	1993	115.00	115
1988	Crying Courtney-PS75	Closed	1990	115.00	115
1991	Crystal-YK-4237	3,500	1993	125.00	125
1995	Cynthia GU-300C	2,500		30.00	30
1988	Cynthia-DOM-211	3,500	1990	85.00	85
1987	Cynthia-DOM-211	Closed	1986	85.00	85
1990	Daisy-EP-6	Closed	1992	90.00	90
1994	Dallas PS-403	2,500	1994	150.00	150
1995	Danielle MER-808	2,500		65.00	65
1995	Danielle PS-432	2,500		100.00	100
1991	Danielle-AM-5	Closed	1993	125.00	125
1990	Daphne Ecru-C-3025	Closed	1992	85.00	85
1989	Daphne Ecru/Mint Green-C3025	Closed	1990	85.00	85
1995	Darcy FH-636	2,500	1996	80.00	80
1995	Darcy LL-986	2,500		110.00	110
1991	Darcy-EP-47	Closed	1993	110.00	110
1991	Darcy-FH-451	2,500	1993	105.00	105
1991	Daria-C-3122	Closed	1993	110.00	110
1995	Darla LL-988	2,500	1996	100.00	100
1991	Darlene-DOLL-444	2,500	1993	75.00	75
1994	Daryl LL-947	2,500	1994	150.00	150
1991	Dawn-C-3135	Closed	1993	130.00	130
1987	Dawn-C185	Closed	1986	75.00	175
1992	Debbie-JNC-4006	Open	1993	90.00	90
1994	Dee LL-948	2,500	1994	110.00	110
1992	Deidre-FH-473	2,500	1993	115.00	115
1992	Deidre-YK-4083	Closed	1993	95.00	95
1994	Delilah C-3195	2,500	1994	150.00	150
1995	Denise LL-994	2,500	1996	105.00	105
1991	Denise-LL-852	2,500	1993	105.00	105
1991	Dephine SP-308	Closed	1993	135.00	135
1991	Desiree-LL-898	2,500	1993	120.00	120
1995	Diana RDK-221A	2,500		35.00	35
1995	Diane PS-444	2,500		110.00	110
1990	Diane-FH-275	Closed	1992	90.00	90
1990	Dianna-TK-31	Closed	1992	175.00	175
1995	Dinah OC-79	2,500		40.00	40
1988	Doll Oliver-FH392	Closed	1990	100.00	100
1990	Domino-C-3050	Closed	1992	145.00	200
1992	Dona-FH-494	2,500	1993	100.00	100
1993	Donna DOLL-447	2,500	1993	85.00	85
1995	Donna GU-300D	2,500		30.00	30
1990	Dorothy-TR-10	Closed	1992	135.00	150
1990	Dorri-DOLL-16PH	Closed	1992	85.00	85
1991	Duanane-SP-366	Closed	1993	85.00	85
1995	Dulcie FH-622	2,500		110.00	110
1991	Dulcie-YK-4131V	Closed	1993	100.00	100
1991	Dwayne-C-3123	Closed	1993	120.00	120
1991	Edie -YK-4177	Closed	1993	115.00	115
1990	Eileen-FH-367	Closed	1992	100.00	100
1995	Elaine CD-02210	2,500		50.00	50
1995	Eleanor C16669	2,500		35.00	35
1991	Elisabeth and Lisa-C-3095	2,500	1993	195.00	195
1989	Elisabeth-OM-32	Closed	1990	120.00	120
1991	Elise -PS-259	Closed	1993	105.00	105
1995	Elizabeth Doll 553	2,500		35.00	35
1991	Elizabeth-AM-32	2,500	1993	105.00	105
1989	Elizabeth-C-246P	Closed	1990	150.00	200
1993	Ellen YK-4223	3,500	1994	150.00	150
1995	Ellie FH-621	2,500		125.00	125
1989	Emily-PS-48	Closed	1993	110.00	110
1988	Emily-YK-243V	Closed	1990	70.00	70
1995	Emma Doll 559	2,500		35.00	35
1995	Emma GU-300E	2,500		30.00	30
1991	Emmaline Beige/Lilac-OM-197	Closed	1993	300.00	300
1991	Emmaline-OM-191	2,500	1993	300.00	300
1991	Emmy-C-3099	Closed	1993	125.00	125
1995	Erin RDK-223	2,500		30.00	30
1991	Erin-DOLL-4PH	Closed	1993	60.00	60
1992	Eugenie-OM-225	2,500	1993	300.00	300
1991	Evalina-C-3124	Closed	1993	135.00	135
1994	Faith IND-522	2,500	1994	135.00	135
1994	Faith OC-60	2,500	1994	115.00	115
1995	Fawn C-3228	2,500		55.00	55
1995	Felicia GU-300F	2,500		30.00	30
1990	Felicia-TR-9	Closed	1992	115.00	115
1991	Fifi-AM-100F	Closed	1993	70.00	70
1995	Fleur C16415	2,500		30.00	30
1991	Fleurette-PS-286	2,500	1993	75.00	75
1994	Flora FH-583	2,500	1994	115.00	115
1991	Flora-TR-46	Closed	1993	125.00	125
1994	Florette IND-519	2,500	1994	140.00	140
1988	Frances-C-233	Closed	1990	80.00	125
1989	Frances-C233	Closed	1990	80.00	125

YEAR ISSUE		EDITION LIMIT	YEAR RETD.	ISSUE PRICE	*QUOTE U.S.$
1991	Francesca-AM-14	2,500	1993	175.00	175
1990	Francesca-C-3021	Closed	1992	175.00	175
1994	Gardiner PS-405	2,500		150.00	150
1993	Gena OM-229	Closed	1994	250.00	250
1994	Georgia IND-510	2,500	1995	220.00	220
1995	Georgia IND-528	2,500		125.00	125
1994	Georgia SP-456	2,500		115.00	115
1991	Georgia-YK-4131	Closed	1993	100.00	100
1991	Georgia-YK-4143	Closed	1993	150.00	150
1990	Gerri Beige-YK4094	Closed	1992	95.00	140
1991	Gigi-C-3107	Closed	1993	135.00	135
1991	Ginger-LL-907	Closed	1993	115.00	115
1995	Ginnie FH-619	2,500		110.00	110
1990	Ginny-YK-4119	Closed	1995	100.00	100
1988	Giselle on Goose-FH176	Closed	1990	105.00	225
1992	Giselle-OM-02	Closed	1993	90.00	90
1991	Gloria-AM-100G	2,500	1993	70.00	70
1991	Gloria-YK-4166	Closed	1993	105.00	105
1995	Gold Angel FH-511G	2,500		85.00	85
1995	Green Angel FH-511C	2,500		85.00	85
1995	Gretchen FH-620	2,500	1995	120.00	120
1991	Gretchen-DOLL-446	Open	1993	45.00	45
1991	Gretel-DOLL-434	Closed	1993	60.00	60
1995	Guardian Angel TR-98	2,500		85.00	85
1995	Guardian Angel OM-91	2,500		150.00	150
1991	Hansel and Gretel-DOLL-448V	Closed	1993	60.00	60
1989	Happy Birthday-C3012	Closed	1990	80.00	125
1993	Happy FH-479	2,500	1994	105.00	105
1995	Happy RDK-238	2,500		25.00	25
1994	Hatty/Matty IND-514	2,500		165.00	165
1995	Heather LL-991	2,500		115.00	115
1995	Heather PS-436	2,500		115.00	115
1994	Heather YK-4531	3,500		165.00	165
1993	Hedy FH-449	Closed	1994	95.00	95
1989	Heidi-260	Closed	1990	50.00	95
1991	Helene-AM-29	2,500	1993	150.00	150
1995	Holly CD-16526	2,500		30.00	30
1991	Holly-CH-6	Closed	1993	100.00	100
1991	Honey Bunny-WB-9	Closed	1993	70.00	70
1994	Honey LL-945	2,500		150.00	150
1991	Honey-FH-401	Closed	1993	100.00	100
1991	Hope-FH-434	2,500	1993	90.00	90
1990	Hope-YK-4118	Closed	1992	90.00	90
1995	Hyacinth C-3227	2,500		130.00	130
1994	Hyacinth YK-4166	2,500	1995	90.00	90
1990	Hyacinth-DOLL-15PH	Closed	1992	85.00	85
1990	Indian Doll-FH-295	Closed	1992	60.00	60
1994	Indian IND-520	2,500		115.00	115
1991	Indira-AM-4	2,500	1993	125.00	125
1995	Irene GU-56	2,500		85.00	85
1995	Irina RDK-237	2,500		35.00	35
1993	Iris FH-483	2,500	1994	95.00	95
1991	Iris-TR-58	Closed	1993	120.00	120
1995	Ivana RDK-233	2,500		35.00	35
1994	Ivy C-3203	2,500		85.00	85
1991	Ivy-PS-307	Closed	1993	75.00	75
1994	Jacqueline C-3202	2,500		150.00	150
1995	Jamaica LL-989	2,500		75.00	75
1993	Jan Dress-Up OM-12	2,500	1994	135.00	135
1994	Jan FH-584R	2,500		115.00	115
1992	Jan-OM-012	9,200	1993	135.00	135
1991	Jane-PS-243L	Closed	1993	115.00	115
1992	Janet-FH-496	2,500	1993	120.00	120
1990	Janette-DOLL-385	Closed	1992	85.00	85
1991	Janice-OM-194	2,500	1993	300.00	300
1994	Janis FH-584B	2,500		115.00	115
1989	Jaqueline-DOLL-254M	Closed	1990	85.00	85
1995	Jennifer PS-446	2,500		145.00	145
1995	Jenny CD-16673B	2,500		35.00	35
1994	Jenny OC-36M	2,500		115.00	115
1995	Jerri PS-434	2,500		100.00	100
1995	Jessica RDK-225	2,500		30.00	30
1988	Jessica-DOM-267	Closed	1990	90.00	90
1991	Jessica-FH-423	2,500	1993	95.00	95
1992	Jet-FH-478	2,500	1993	115.00	115
1995	Jewel TR-100	2,500		110.00	110
1994	Jillian C-3196	2,500		150.00	150
1993	Jillian SP-428	Closed	1994	165.00	165
1990	Jillian-DOLL-41PH	Closed	1992	90.00	90
1994	Jo YK-4539	3,500	1995	150.00	150
1988	Joanne Cry Baby-PS-50	Closed	1990	100.00	100
1989	Joanne Cry Baby-PS-50	2,500	1991	100.00	100
1990	Joanne-TR-12	Closed	1992	175.00	175
1992	Jodie-FH-495	2,500	1993	115.00	115
1995	Joella CD-16779	2,500		35.00	35
1988	Jolie-C231	Closed	1990	65.00	150
1994	Jordan SP-455	2,500		150.00	150
1995	Joy CD-1450A	2,500		35.00	35
1995	Joy TR-99	2,500		85.00	135
1991	Joy-EP-23V	Closed	1993	130.00	130
1991	Joyce-AM-100J	2,500	1993	35.00	35
1995	Julia C-3234	2,500		100.00	100
1995	Julia RDK-222	2,500		35.00	35
1991	Julia-C-3102	Closed	1993	135.00	135
1988	Julie-C245A	Closed	1990	65.00	160
1990	Julie-WB-35	Closed	1992	70.00	70
1988	Juliette Bride Musical-C246LTM	Closed	1990	150.00	200
1993	Juliette OM-8	2,500	1994	175.00	175
1992	Juliette-OM-08	2,500	1993	175.00	175
1991	Juliette-OM-192	2,500	1993	300.00	300
1995	June CD-2212	2,500		50.00	50
1991	Karen-EP-24	Closed	1993	115.00	115
1990	Karen-PS-198	Closed	1992	150.00	150
1991	Karmela-EP-57	2,500	1993	120.00	120
1995	Karyn RDK-224	2,500		35.00	35
1994	Kate OC-55	2,500		150.00	150
1990	Kate-C-3060	Closed	1992	95.00	95
1990	Kathy w/Bear-TE1	Closed	1992	70.00	70
1994	Katie IND-511	2,500		110.00	110
1989	Kayoko-PS-24	Closed	1991	75.00	175
1994	Kelly YK-4536	3,500		150.00	150
1991	Kelly-AM-8	Closed	1993	125.00	125
1995	Kelsey Doll 561	2,500		35.00	35
1993	Kendra FH-481	2,500	1994	115.00	115
1991	Kerry-FH-396	Closed	1993	100.00	100
1994	Kevin MS-25	2,500		150.00	150
1994	Kevin YK-4543	3,500		140.00	140
1990	Kiku-EP-4	Closed	1992	100.00	100
1991	Kim-AM-100K	2,500	1993	70.00	70
1995	Kimmie CD-15816	2,500		30.00	30
1991	Kinesha-SP-402	2,500	1993	110.00	110
1988	Kirsten-PS-40G	Closed	1990	70.00	70
1989	Kirsten-PS-40G	Closed	1991	70.00	70
1993	Kit SP-426	Closed	1994	55.00	55
1994	Kit YK-4547	3,500		115.00	115
1994	Kitten IND-512	2,500	1996	110.00	110
1995	Kitty IND-527	2,500	1996	40.00	40
1991	Kristi-FH-402	Closed	1993	100.00	100
1991	Kyla-YK-4137	Closed	1993	95.00	95
1994	Lady Caroline LL-938	2,500		120.00	120
1994	Lady Caroline LL-939	2,500		120.00	120
1994	Laughing Waters PS-410	2,500		150.00	150
1990	Laura-DOLL-25PH	Closed	1992	55.00	55
1992	Laura-OM-010	2,500	1993	250.00	250
1991	Laura-WB-110P	Closed	1993	85.00	85
1994	Lauren SP-458	2,500		125.00	125
1990	Lauren-SP-300	Closed	1993	85.00	85
1992	Laurie-JNC-4004	Open	1993	90.00	90
1990	Lavender Blue-YK-4024	Closed	1993	95.00	135
1991	Leigh-DOLL-457	2,500	1993	95.00	95
1991	Leila-AM-2	Closed	1993	125.00	125
1995	Lenore FH-617	2,500		120.00	120
1995	Lenore RDK-229	2,500		50.00	50
1991	Lenore-LL-911	2,500	1993	105.00	105
1991	Lenore-YK-4218	3,500	1995	135.00	135
1995	Leslie LL-983	2,500		105.00	105
1995	Leslie MER-809	2,500		65.00	65
1991	Libby-EP-18	Closed	1993	85.00	85
1990	Lien Wha-YK-4092	Closed	1992	100.00	100
1995	Lila GU-55	2,500		55.00	55
1991	Lila-AM-10	2,500	1993	125.00	125
1991	Lila-FH-404	2,500	1993	100.00	100
1995	Lili CD-16888	2,500		30.00	30
1995	Lily FH-630	2,500		120.00	120
1995	Lily in pink stripe IND-533	2,500	1995	85.00	85
1993	Linda SP-435	Closed	1994	95.00	95
1987	Linda-C190	Closed	1986	60.00	120
1995	Lindsay PS-442	2,500		175.00	175
1994	Lindsay SP-462	2,500		150.00	150
1991	Lindsey-C-3127	Closed	1993	135.00	135
1991	Linetta-C-3166	Closed	1993	135.00	135
1990	Ling-Ling-DOLL	Closed	1992	50.00	50
1989	Ling-Ling-PS-87G	Closed	1991	90.00	90
1988	Lionel-FH206B	Closed	1990	50.00	120
1990	Lisa Beige Accordion Pleat-YK4093	Closed	1992	125.00	125
1991	Lisa-AM-100L	2,500	1993	70.00	70
1990	Lisa-FH-379	Closed	1992	100.00	100
1995	Lisette LL-993	2,500		105.00	105
1995	Little Bobby RDK-235	2,500		25.00	25
1991	Little Boy Blue-C-3159	Closed	1993	100.00	100
1995	Little Lisa OM-86	2,500		125.00	125
1995	Little Lori RDK-228	2,500		20.00	20
1995	Little Lou RDK-227	2,500		20.00	20
1995	Little Mary RDK-234	2,500		25.00	25
1995	Little Patty PS-429	2,500		50.00	50
1994	Little Red Riding Hood FH-557	2,500		140.00	140
1989	Liz -YK-269	Closed	1991	70.00	100
1991	Liz-C-3150	2,500	1993	100.00	100
1990	Liza-C-3053	Closed	1992	100.00	100
1991	Liza-YK-4226	3,500	1993	35.00	35
1991	Lola-SP-363	2,500	1993	90.00	90
1990	Lola-SP-79	Closed	1992	105.00	105
1991	Loni-FH-448	2,500	1993	100.00	100
1994	Loretta SP-457	2,500		140.00	140
1990	Loretta-FH-321	Closed	1992	90.00	90
1991	Lori-EP-52	2,500	1993	95.00	95
1990	Lori-WB-72BM	Closed	1992	75.00	75
1991	Louise-LL-908	2,500	1993	105.00	105
1995	Lucie MER-607	2,500		65.00	65
1989	Lucinda -DOM-293	Closed	1990	90.00	90
1994	Lucinda PS-406	2,500		150.00	150
1988	Lucinda-DOM-293	Closed	1990	90.00	90
1991	Lucinda-C-853	Closed	1993	80.00	80
1992	Lydia-OM-226	2,500	1993	250.00	250
1993	Lynn FH-498	2,500	1994	120.00	120
1995	Lynn LL-995	2,500		105.00	105
1990	Madame De Pompadour-C-3088	Closed	1992	250.00	250
1991	Madeleine-C-3106	Closed	1993	95.00	95
1995	Mae PS-431	2,500		70.00	70
1995	Maggie IND-532	2,500		80.00	80
1992	Maggie-FH-505	Closed	1993	125.00	125
1990	Maggie-PS-151P	Closed	1992	90.00	90
1990	Maggie-WB-51	Closed	1992	105.00	105
1994	Magnolia FH-558	2,500		150.00	150
1989	Mai-Ling-PS-79	2,500	1991	100.00	100
1994	Maiden PS-409	2,500	1995	150.00	150
1994	Marcey YK-4548	3,500		115.00	115
1989	Marcey-YK-4005	3,500	1995	90.00	90
1991	Marcy-TR-55	Closed	1993	135.00	135
1987	Marcy-YK122	Closed	1986	55.00	100
1994	Margaret C-3204	2,500		150.00	150
1989	Margaret-245	Closed	1991	100.00	100
1994	Maria GU-35	2,500		115.00	115
1990	Maria-YK-4116	Closed	1992	85.00	85
1993	Mariah LL-909	2,500		135.00	135
1991	Mariel 18" Ivory-C-3119	Closed	1993	125.00	125
1995	Marielle PS-443	2,500		175.00	175
1995	Marta PS-437	2,500		125.00	125
1995	Martina RDK-232	2,500		35.00	35
1995	Mary Ann FH-633	2,500		110.00	110
1994	Mary Ann TR-79	2,500		125.00	125
1994	Mary Elizabeth OC-51	2,500	1996	50.00	50
1994	Mary Jo FH-552	2,500		150.00	150
1994	Mary Lou FH-565	2,500		135.00	135
1994	Mary OC-56	2,500		135.00	135
1991	Maude-AM-100M	2,500	1993	70.00	70
1989	Maureen-PS-84	Closed	1990	90.00	90
1995	Maxine C-3225	2,500		125.00	125
1995	Mc Kenzie LL-987	2,500		100.00	100
1995	Megan C-3192	2,500		150.00	150
1995	Megan RDK-220	2,500		30.00	30
1989	Meimei-PS22	Closed	1990	75.00	225
1990	Melanie-YK-4115	Closed	1992	80.00	80
1991	Melissa-AM-9	Closed	1993	120.00	120
1991	Melissa-CH-3	Closed	1993	110.00	110
1990	Melissa-DOLL-390	Closed	1992	75.00	75
1989	Melissa-LL-794	Closed	1993	95.00	95
1991	Melissa-LL-901	Closed	1993	135.00	135
1992	Melissa-OM-03	2,500	1993	135.00	135
1995	Meredith MER-806	2,500	1996	65.00	65
1991	Meredith-FH-391-P	Closed	1993	95.00	95
1995	Merri MER-810	2,500		65.00	65
1990	Merry Widow 20"-C-3040M	Closed	1992	140.00	140
1990	Merry Widow-C-3040	Closed	1992	145.00	145
1991	Meryl-FH-463	2,500	1993	95.00	95
1991	Michael w/School Books -FH-439B	2,500	1993	95.00	95
1988	Michelle & Marcel-YK176	Closed	1990	70.00	150
1991	Michelle Lilac/Green-EP36	Closed	1993	95.00	95
1991	Michelle w/School Books-FH-439G	Closed	1993	95.00	95
1995	Mindi PS-441	2,500	1995	125.00	125
1995	Mindy LL-990	2,500		75.00	75
1995	Miranda C16456B	2,500		30.00	30
1995	Miranda TR-91	2,500		135.00	135
1991	Miranda-DOLL-9PH	Closed	1993	75.00	75
1984	Miss Debutante Debi	Closed	1987	75.00	180
1994	Miss Elizabeth SP-459	2,500		150.00	150
1989	Miss Kim-PS-25	Closed	1990	75.00	175
1994	Missy FH-567	2,500	1996	140.00	140
1991	Missy-DOLL-464	Closed	1993	70.00	70
1991	Missy-PS-258	Closed	1993	90.00	90
1991	Mon Yun w/Parasol-TR33	2,500	1993	115.00	115
1995	Monica TR-95	2,500		135.00	135
1994	Morning Dew Indian PS-404	2,500		150.00	150
1994	Musical Doll OC-45M	2,500		140.00	140
1991	Nancy -WB-73	2,500	1993	65.00	65
1991	Nancy 21" Pink w/Rabbit-EP-31	Closed	1993	165.00	165
1995	Nancy FH-615	2,500		100.00	100
1992	Nancy-JNC-4001	Open	1993	90.00	90
1990	Nanook-WB-23	Closed	1992	75.00	75
1995	Natasha TR-90	2,500		125.00	125
1990	Natasha-PS-102	Closed	1992	100.00	100
1991	Nellie-EP-1B	Closed	1993	75.00	75
1991	Nicole-AM-12	Closed	1993	135.00	135
1994	Nikki PS-401	2,500	1995	150.00	150
1994	Nikki SP-461	2,500		150.00	150
1993	Nina YK-4232	3,500	1995	135.00	135
1987	Nirmala-YK-210	Closed	1995	50.00	50
1994	Noel MS-27	2,500		150.00	150
1994	Noelle C-3199	2,500		195.00	195
1994	Noelle MS-28	2,500		150.00	150
1991	Noelle-PS-239V	Closed	1993	95.00	95
1994	Norma C-3226	2,500		135.00	135
1990	Odessa-FH-362	Closed	1992	65.00	65
1994	Odetta IND-521	2,500	1995	140.00	140
1994	Oona TR-57	Closed	1993	135.00	135
1994	Oriana IND-515	2,500		140.00	140
1995	Our First Skates RDK-226/BG	2,500		50.00	50
1994	Paige GU-33	2,500		150.00	150
1995	Paige IND-529	2,500		80.00	80
1994	Pamela LL-949	2,500		115.00	115
1994	Pan Pan GU-52	2,500		60.00	60
1994	Panama OM-43	2,500		195.00	195
1989	Patricia/Patrick-215GBB	Closed	1993	105.00	135
1991	Patti-DOLL-440	2,500	1993	65.00	65
1995	Patty C-3220	2,500		60.00	60
1994	Patty GU-34	2,500		115.00	115
1991	Patty-YK-4221	3,500	1993	125.00	125
1989	Paula-PS-56	Closed	1990	75.00	75
1995	Paulette PS-430	2,500		80.00	80
1989	Pauline Bonaparte-OM68	Closed	1990	120.00	120
1995	Pauline PS-440	2,500		65.00	65
1988	Pauline-YK-230	Closed	1990	90.00	90
1994	Payson YK-4541	3,500		135.00	135

YEAR ISSUE	EDITION LIMIT	YEAR RETD.	ISSUE PRICE	*QUOTE U.S.$
1994 Payton PS-407	2,500	1995	150.00	150
1995 Peaches IND-531	2,500		80.00	80
1994 Pearl IND-523	2,500	1996	275.00	275
1994 Pegeen C-3205	2,500	1996	150.00	150
1994 Peggy TR-75	2,500		185.00	185
1991 Pepper-PS-277	Closed	1993	130.00	130
1994 Petula C-3191	2,500		140.00	140
1991 Pia-PS-246L	Closed	1993	115.00	115
1990 Ping-Ling-DOLL-363RV	Closed	1992	50.00	50
1990 Polly-DOLL-22PH	Closed	1992	90.00	90
1990 Princess Fair Skies-FH-268B	Closed	1992	75.00	75
1994 Princess Foxfire PS-411	2,500		150.00	150
1990 Princess Moonrise YK-4542	3,500		140.00	140
1990 Princess Red Feather-PS-189	Closed	1992	90.00	90
1994 Princess Snow Flower PS-402	2,500	1995	150.00	150
1991 Princess Summer Winds-FH-427	2,500	1993	120.00	120
1994 Priscilla YK-4538	3,500		135.00	135
1990 Priscilla-WB-50	Closed	1992	105.00	105
1991 Prissy White/Blue-C-3140	Closed	1993	100.00	100
1995 Rainie LL-984	2,500	1996	125.00	125
1989 Ramona-PS-31B	Closed	1992	80.00	80
1991 Rapunzel-C-3157	2,500	1993	150.00	150
1987 Rapunzel-C158	Closed	1986	95.00	165
1987 Rebecca C-3177	2,500		135.00	135
1993 Rebecca C-3177	2,500		135.00	135
1989 Rebecca-PS-34V	Closed	1992	45.00	45
1991 Red Wing-AM-30	2,500	1993	165.00	165
1994 Regina OM-41	2,500		150.00	150
1994 Rita FH-553	2,500	1996	115.00	115
1994 Robby NM-29	2,500		135.00	135
1995 Robin C-3236	2,500		60.00	60
1991 Robin-AM-22	Closed	1993	120.00	120
1991 Rosalind-C-3090	Closed	1992	150.00	150
1989 Rosie-290M	Closed	1992	55.00	85
1989 Rusty CD-1450B	2,500		35.00	35
1988 Sabrina -C-208	Closed	1992	65.00	95
1987 Sabrina-C208	Closed	1986	65.00	95
1987 Sabrina-C3050	Closed		105.00	105
1987 Sailorette-DOM217	Closed	1986	70.00	150
1992 Sally-FH-492	2,500	1993	105.00	105
1992 Sally-WB-20	Closed	1993	95.00	95
1991 Samantha-GU-3	Closed	1992	100.00	100
1991 San San GU-53	2,500		60.00	60
1991 Sandra-DOLL-6-PHE	2,500	1994	65.00	65
1992 Sapphires-OM-223	2,500	1993	250.00	250
1992 Sara Ann-FH-474	2,500	1993	115.00	115
1995 Sarah C-3214	2,500		110.00	110
1994 Saretta SP-423	2,500		100.00	100
1994 Saretta SP-423	2,500	1993	100.00	100
1995 Sasha GU-57	2,500		75.00	75
1991 Scarlett-FH-399	2,500	1992	100.00	100
1991 Scarlett-FH-436	2,500		135.00	135
1992 Scarlett-FH-471	2,500		120.00	120
1993 Shaka TR-45	2,500	1993	100.00	100
1991 Shaka TR-45	2,500		100.00	100
1991 Shaka-SP-401	2,500		110.00	110
1991 Sharon 21" Blue-EP-34	Closed	1992	120.00	120
1995 Sharon C-3237	2,500		95.00	95
1991 Shau Chen-GU-2	2,500		85.00	85
1991 Shelley-CH-1	2,500		110.00	110
1995 Shimmering Caroline LL-992	2,500		115.00	115
1991 Shirley-WB-37	Closed	1992	65.00	65
1988 Sister Agnes 14"-C250	Closed	1990	75.00	75
1988 Sister Ignatius Notre Dame-FH184	Closed	1990	75.00	75
1989 Sister Mary-C-249	Closed	1992	75.00	125
1990 Sister Mary-WB-15	Closed	1992	70.00	70
1991 Sister Suzie IND-509	2,500	1995	95.00	95
1988 Sister Teresa-FH187	Closed	1990	80.00	80
1995 Sleeping Beauty OM-88	2,500		115.00	115
1992 Sonja-FH-486	2,500	1994	125.00	125
1995 Sophia PS-445	2,500		125.00	125
1991 Sophie-OM-1	Closed	1992	65.00	65
1991 Sophie-TR-53	2,500	1992	135.00	135
1995 Southern Belle Bride FH-637	2,500		160.00	160
1994 Southern Belle FH-570	2,500		140.00	140
1994 Sparkle OM-40	2,500	1996	150.00	150
1995 Stacy FH-634	2,500		110.00	110
1994 Stacy OC-75	2,500		40.00	40
1991 Stacy-DOLL-6PH	Closed	1992	65.00	65
1991 Stacy-TR-5	Closed		105.00	105
1991 Stephanie Pink & White-OM-196	Closed	1992	300.00	300
1991 Stephanie-AM-11	Closed	1992	105.00	105
1991 Stephanie-FH-467	Closed		95.00	95
1994 Stephie OC-41M	2,500		115.00	115
1990 Sue Chuen-C-3061G	Closed	1992	95.00	95
1991 Sue Kwei TR-73	2,500		110.00	110
1992 Sue-JNC-4003	Closed	1994	90.00	90
1994 Sugar Plum Fairy OM-39	2,500	1996	150.00	150
1990 Summer-AM-33	Closed	1992	200.00	200
1990 Sunny-FH-331	Closed	1992	70.00	70
1990 Sunny-PS-59V	Closed	1992	71.00	71
1990 Susan-DOLL-364MC	Closed	1992	75.00	75
1995 Suzanna Doll 554	2,500		35.00	35
1994 Suzanna LL-943	2,500		105.00	105
1994 Suzie GU-38	2,500		135.00	135
1995 Suzie OC-80	2,500		50.00	50
1994 Suzie SP-422	2,500	1993	164.00	164
1994 Suzie SP-422	2,500		164.00	164
1989 Suzie-PS-32	Closed	1992	80.00	80
1991 Sweet Pea LL-981	2,500	1996	90.00	90
1991 Sybil 20" Beige-C-3131	Closed	1992	135.00	135

YEAR ISSUE	EDITION LIMIT	YEAR RETD.	ISSUE PRICE	*QUOTE U.S.$
1991 Sybil Pink-DOLL-12PHMC	2,500	1992	75.00	75
1995 Sylvie CD-16634B	2,500		35.00	35
1995 Tabitha C-3233	2,500		50.00	50
1994 Taffy TR-80	2,500		150.00	150
1994 Tallulah OM-44	2,500		275.00	275
1991 Tamara-OM-187	Closed	1992	135.00	135
1992 Tania-DOLL-376P	Closed	1992	65.00	65
1989 Tatiana Pink Ballerina-OM-60	Closed	1991	120.00	175
1994 Teresa C-3198	2,500	1995	110.00	110
1995 Terri OM-78	2,500		150.00	150
1989 Terri-PS-104	Closed	1991	85.00	85
1991 Terri-TR-62	Closed	1992	75.00	75
1991 Tessa-AM-19	Closed	1992	135.00	135
1994 Tiffany OC-44M	2,500	1996	140.00	140
1992 Tiffany-OM-014	2,500	1994	150.00	150
1995 Tina OM-79	2,500		150.00	150
1991 Tina-AM-16	Closed	1992	130.00	130
1990 Tina-DOLL-371	Closed	1992	85.00	85
1990 Tina-WB-32	Closed	1992	65.00	65
1994 Tippy LL-946	2,500	1995	110.00	110
1991 Tobey C-3232	2,500		50.00	50
1994 Todd YK-4540	3,500		45.00	45
1990 Tommy-C-3064	Closed	1992	75.00	75
1994 Topaz TR-74	2,500	1995	195.00	195
1988 Tracy-C-3006	Closed	1990	95.00	150
1992 Trina-OM-011	2,500	1994	165.00	165
1994 Trixie TR-77	2,500		110.00	110
1991 Vanessa-AM-34	Closed	1992	90.00	90
1991 Vicki-C-3101	Closed	1992	200.00	200
1991 Violet-EP-41	Closed	1992	135.00	135
1991 Violet-OM-186	2,500	1992	270.00	270
1992 Violette-FH-503	2,500	1994	120.00	120
1991 Virginia TR-78	2,500		195.00	195
1991 Virginia-SP-359	Closed	1992	120.00	120
1992 Vivian-C-201P	Closed	1990	80.00	80
1988 Vivian-C201P	Closed	1990	80.00	80
1991 Wah-Ching Watching Oriental Toddler YK-4175	Closed	1992	110.00	110
1995 Wei Lin GU-44	2,500		70.00	70
1994 Wendy MS-26	2,500		150.00	150
1985 Wendy-C120	Closed	1987	45.00	150
1989 Wendy-PS-51	Closed	1991	105.00	105
1990 Wendy-TE-3	Closed	1992	75.00	75
1990 Wilma-PS-174	Closed	1992	75.00	75
1995 Windy in Rose Print FH-626	2,500	1995	200.00	200
1995 Winnie LL-985	2,500		75.00	75
1995 Winter Wonderland RDK-301	2,500		35.00	35
1995 Woodland Sprite OM-90	2,500		100.00	100
1995 Yelena RDK-236	2,500		35.00	35
1990 Yen Yen-YK-4091	Closed	1992	95.00	95
1992 Yvette-OM-015	2,500	1994	150.00	150

Signature Doll Series - Various

YEAR ISSUE	EDITION LIMIT	YEAR RETD.	ISSUE PRICE	*QUOTE U.S.$
1992 Abigail-MS-11 - M. Severino	5,000	1994	125.00	125
1995 Adak PPA-21 - P. Phillips	5,000		110.00	110
1992 Adora-MS-14 - M. Severino	5,000	1994	185.00	185
1995 Alain PPA-19 - P. Phillips	2,500		100.00	100
1992 Alexandria-PAC-19 - P. Aprile	5,000	1995	300.00	300
1991 Alice-MS-7 - M. Severino	5,000		120.00	120
1995 Amanda KSFA-1 - K. Fitzpatrick	5,000		175.00	175
1991 Amber-MS-1 - M. Severino	Closed	1994	95.00	95
1992 Amelia PAC-28 - P. Aprile	5,000		130.00	130
1995 Amy Rose HKHF-200 - H.K. Hyland	5,000		125.00	125
1992 Baby Cakes -PK-CRUMBS - P. Kolesar	5,000		17.50	18
1992 Baby Cakes Crumbs/Black -PK-CRUMBS/B - P. Kolesar	5,000		17.50	18
1991 Becky-MS-2 - M. Severino	5,000	1994	95.00	95
1991 Bianca-PK-101 - P. Kolesar	Closed	1994	120.00	120
1993 Bonnett Baby MS-17W - M. Severino	5,000	1996	175.00	175
1991 Brad HKH-15 - H.K. Hyland	5,000		85.00	85
1992 Bride & Flower Girl-PAC-6 - P. Aprile	5,000		600.00	600
1991 Bridgette-PK-104 - P. Kolesar	Closed	1994	120.00	120
1995 Brie PPA-26 - P. Aprile	5,000		180.00	180
1995 Cara DALI-1 - E. Dali	5,000		400.00	400
1995 Casey PPA-23 - P. Phillips	5,000		85.00	85
1992 Cassandra-PAC-8 - P. Aprile	Closed	N/A	450.00	450
1992 Cassie Flower Girl-PAC-9 - P. Aprile	Closed	N/A	175.00	175
1991 Celine-PAC-11 - P. Aprile	5,000		165.00	165
1991 Clair-Ann-PK-252 - P. Kolesar	5,000		100.00	100
1992 Clarissa-PAC-3 - P. Aprile	5,000	1996	165.00	165
1992 Cody-MS-19 - M. Severino	Closed	1993	120.00	120
1992 Creole Black-HP-202 - H. Payne	5,000	1993	250.00	250
1992 Cynthia-PAC-10 - P. Aprile	5,000	1993	165.00	165
1991 Daddy's Little Darling-MS-8 - M. Severino	5,000		165.00	165
1992 Darla-HP-204 - H. Payne	5,000		250.00	250
1991 Dozy Elf w/ Featherbed -MAB-100 - M.A. Byerly	Closed	1991	110.00	110
1991 Duby Elf w/ Featherbed -MAB-103 - M.A. Byerly	Closed	1991	110.00	110
1991 Dudley Elf w/ Featherbed -MAB-101 - M.A. Byerly	Closed	1991	110.00	110
1991 Duffy Elf w/ Featherbed -MAB-102 - M.A. Byerly	Closed	1991	110.00	110
1992 Dulcie-HP-200 - H. Payne	5,000	1993	250.00	250
1992 Dustin-HP-201 - H. Payne	5,000	1993	250.00	250
1995 Eleanore GMNA-100 - G. McNeil	5,000		225.00	225
1992 Enoc-PK-100 - P. Kolesar	5,000		100.00	100
1992 Eugenie Bride-PAC-1 - P. Aprile	5,000	1996	165.00	165
1992 Evening Star-PAC-5 - P. Aprile	Closed	1993	500.00	500

YEAR ISSUE	EDITION LIMIT	YEAR RETD.	ISSUE PRICE	*QUOTE U.S.$
1995 Ginny LR-2 - L. Randolph	5,000		360.00	360
1993 Grace HKH-2 - H. Kahl-Hyland	5,000		250.00	250
1995 Happy JFC-100 - K. Fitzpatrick	5,000		120.00	120
1993 Helene HKH-1 - H. Kahl-Hyland	5,000	1996	250.00	250
1995 Holly GMN-202 - G. McNeil	5,000		150.00	150
1995 Iman PPA-24 - P. Aprile	5,000	1996	110.00	110
1992 Kate-MS-15 - M. Severino	Closed	1993	190.00	190
1995 Latisha PPA-25 - P. Phillips	5,000		110.00	110
1995 Laurel HKH-17R - H.K. Hyland	5,000		110.00	110
1995 Lauren HKH-202 - H.K. Hyland	5,000		150.00	150
1995 Lena PPA-20 - P. Phillips	5,000		120.00	120
1995 Lenore LRC-100 - L. Randolph	5,000		140.00	140
1992 Little Match Girl-HP-205 - H. Payne	Closed	1994	150.00	150
1992 Little Turtle Indian-PK-110 - P. Kolesar	Closed	1993	150.00	150
1995 Lucy HKH-14 - H.K. Hyland	5,000		105.00	105
1992 Megan-MS-12 - M. Severino	5,000	1995	125.00	125
1992 Melanie-PAC-14 - P. Aprile	Closed	1993	300.00	300
1995 Meredith LR-3 - L. Randolph	5,000		375.00	375
1991 Mikey-MS-3 - M. Severino	5,000	1994	95.00	95
1991 Mommy's Rays of Sunshine MS-9 - M. Severino	5,000		165.00	165
1992 Nadia-PAC-18 - P. Aprile	Closed	1993	175.00	175
1995 Natasha HKH-17P - H.K. Hyland	5,000		110.00	110
1995 Nikki HKHF-20 - H.K. Hyland	5,000		125.00	125
1992 Olivia-PAC-12 - P. Aprile	Closed	1993	300.00	300
1995 Patricia DALI-3 - E. Dali	5,000		280.00	280
1991 Paulette-PAC-2 - P. Aprile	5,000		250.00	250
1991 Paulette-PAC-4 - P. Aprile	5,000		250.00	250
1992 Pavlova-PAC-17 - P. Aprile	5,000	1994	145.00	145
1992 Polly-HP-206 - H. Payne	5,000		120.00	120
1991 Precious Baby-SB-100 - S. Bilotto	5,000		250.00	250
1991 Precious Pary Time-SB-102 - S. Bilotto	5,000		250.00	250
1991 Precious Spring Time-SB-104 - S. Bilotto	Closed	N/A	250.00	250
1992 Raven Eskimo-PK-106 - P. Kolesar	Closed	1993	130.00	130
1992 Rebecca Beige Bonnet-MS-17B - M. Severino	5,000	1995	175.00	175
1993 Reilly HKH-3 - H. Kahl-Hyland	5,000		260.00	260
1992 Ruby-MS-18 - M. Severino	5,000		135.00	135
1992 Sally-MS-25 - M. Severino	5,000	1994	110.00	110
1995 Shao Ling PPA-22 - P. Phillips	5,000		110.00	110
1991 Shun Lee-PK-102 - P. Kolesar	Closed	N/A	120.00	120
1994 Sis JAG-110 - J. Grammer	5,000	1994	110.00	110
1992 Spanky-HP-25 - H. Payne	5,000		250.00	250
1991 Sparkle-PK-250 - P. Kolesar	5,000		250.00	250
1995 Stacy DALI-2 - E. Dali	5,000		360.00	360
1992 Stacy-MS-24 - M. Severino	Closed	1993	110.00	110
1991 Stephie-MS-6 - M. Severino	Closed		125.00	125
1991 Su Lin-MS-5 - M. Severino	5,000	1994	105.00	105
1991 Susan Marie-PK-103 - P. Kolesar	Closed	1991	120.00	120
1995 Suzie HKH-16 - H.K. Hyland	5,000		100.00	100
1991 Sweet Pea-PK-251 - P. Kolesar	Closed		100.00	100
1995 Tammy LR-4 - L. Randolph	5,000		325.00	325
1994 Tex JAG-114 - J. Grammer	5,000		110.00	110
1995 Tiffany LR-1 - L. Randolph	5,000	1996	370.00	370
1994 Tracy JAG-111 - J. Grammer	5,000	1994	150.00	150
1994 Trevor JAG-112 - J. Grammer	5,000	1996	115.00	115
1992 Vanessa-PAC-15 - P. Aprile	Closed	1993	300.00	300
1992 Victoria w/Blanket-MS-10 - M. Severino	Closed		110.00	110
1992 Violetta PAC-16 - P. Aprile	5,000		165.00	165
1991 Yawning Kate-MS-4 - M. Severino	Closed	1994	105.00	105

Susan Wakeen Doll Co. Inc.

The Littlest Ballet Company - S. Wakeen

YEAR ISSUE	EDITION LIMIT	YEAR RETD.	ISSUE PRICE	*QUOTE U.S.$
1985 Cynthia	375		198.00	350
1987 Elizabeth	250		425.00	1000
1985 Jeanne	375		198.00	800
1985 Jennifer	250		750.00	750
1987 Marie Ann	50		1000.00	1000
1985 Patty	375		198.00	400-500

Timeless Creations

Barefoot Children - A. Himstedt

YEAR ISSUE	EDITION LIMIT	YEAR RETD.	ISSUE PRICE	*QUOTE U.S.$
1987 Bastian	Closed	1989	329.00	700-800
1987 Beckus	Closed	1989	329.00	1200-1500
1987 Ellen	Closed	1989	329.00	800-900
1987 Fatou	Closed	1989	329.00	900-1100
1987 Fatou (Cornroll)	Closed	1989	329.00	1200-1500
1987 Kathe	Closed	1989	329.00	800
1987 Lisa	Closed	1989	329.00	800
1987 Paula	Closed	1989	329.00	700-800

Blessed Are The Children - A. Himstedt

YEAR ISSUE	EDITION LIMIT	YEAR RETD.	ISSUE PRICE	*QUOTE U.S.$
1988 Friederike	Closed	1990	499.00	1800-2200
1988 Kasimir	Closed	1990	499.00	1500-2000
1988 Makimura	Closed	1990	499.00	900-1400
1988 Malin	Closed	1990	499.00	1400-1600
1988 Michiko	Closed	1990	499.00	1200-1500

Faces of Friendship - A. Himstedt

YEAR ISSUE	EDITION LIMIT	YEAR RETD.	ISSUE PRICE	*QUOTE U.S.$
1991 Liliane (Netherlands)	2-Yr.	1993	598.00	600-700
1991 Neblina (Switzerland)	2-Yr.	1993	598.00	650
1991 Shireem (Bali)	2-Yr.	1993	598.00	598

Fiene And The Barefoot Babies - A. Himstedt

YEAR ISSUE	EDITION LIMIT	YEAR RETD.	ISSUE PRICE	*QUOTE U.S.$
1990 Annchen-German Baby Girl	2-Yr.	1992	498.00	700

YEAR ISSUE	EDITION LIMIT	YEAR RETD.	ISSUE PRICE	*QUOTE U.S.$
1990 Fiene-Belgian Girl	2-Yr.	1992	598.00	800-900
1990 Mo-American Baby Boy	2-Yr.	1992	498.00	550-600
1990 Taki-Japanese Baby Girl	2-Yr.	1992	498.00	800-1100

Heartland Series - A. Himstedt
1988 Timi	Closed		329.00	400-500
1988 Toni	Closed		329.00	400-500

Images of Childhood - A. Himstedt
1993 Kima (Greenland)	2-Yr.	1995	599.00	600-650
1993 Lona (California)	2-Yr.	1995	599.00	600-650
1993 Tara (Germany)	2-Yr.	1995	599.00	600-650

Reflection of Youth - A. Himstedt
1989 Adrienne (France)	Closed	1991	558.00	800-900
1989 Ayoka (Africa)	Closed	1991	558.00	950-1100
1989 Janka (Hungry)	Closed	1991	558.00	800-900
1989 Kai (German)	Closed	1991	558.00	700-900

Summer Dreams - A. Himstedt
1992 Enzo	2-Yr.	1994	599.00	600-650
1992 Jule	2-Yr.	1994	599.00	650-700
1992 Pemba	2-Yr.	1994	599.00	599
1992 Sanga	2-Yr.	1994	599.00	599

FIGURINES/COTTAGES

Ace Product Management Group, Inc.

Harley-Davidson Archive Pewter Figurines - Ace
1994 Catch Of The Day 99450-93Z	1,500	1996	150.00	150
1996 On Patrol 99169-96Z	1,500		150.00	150

Harley-Davidson Christmas Figurines - Ace
1989 Perfect Tree 99420-90Z	3,000	1989	99.95	100
1990 Mainstreet U.S.A. 99421-91Z	3,000	1990	129.95	130
1991 Joy Of Giving 99423-92Z	3,000	1991	134.95	135
1992 Home For The Holidays 99422-93Z	3,000	1992	145.00	145
1993 Rural Delivery 99423-94Z	3,000	1993	155.00	155
1994 29 Days 'Til Christmas 99089-95Z	3,000	1994	170.00	170
1995 Skating Party 99417-96Z	3,000	1995	185.00	185
1996 Surprise Visit 99934-97Z	3,000		185.00	185

Harley-Davidson Mini-Plate Figurines - Ace
1992 Letters To Santa 99415-93Z	Yr.Iss	1992	25.00	25
1993 Santa's Predicament 99420-94Z	Yr.Iss.	1993	18.00	18
1994 Not A Creature Was Stirring 99447-95Z	Yr.Iss	1994	20.00	20
1995 Planning The Route 99476-96Z	Yr.Iss.	1995	22.00	22
1996 Reviewing the Plan 99946-97Z	Yr.Iss.		22.00	22

Harley-Davidson Sculptures - M. Patrick
1993 90th Anniversary -The Reunion 99215-93Z	2,500	1993	495.00	495
1993 90th Anniversary-Bronze The Reunion 99216-93ZB	90	1993	3495.00	3495
1993 Milwaukee Ride 99497-94Z	1,500	1995	350.00	350
1994 Old Soldier 99403-95Z	1,500	1995	350.00	350
1995 Just Hitched 99079-96Z	1,500	1995	350.00	350
1996 Daytona Bound 99164-96Z	1,500		350.00	350

Harley-Davidson Young Rider Figurines - Ace
1992 The Jacket 99370-93Z	3,000	1994	25.00	25
1993 Free Wheelin' 99371-93Z	3,000	1995	25.00	25
1993 The Enthusiast 99372-94Z	3,000	1995	25.00	25
1994 Engine Lesson 99376-95Z	3,000		28.00	28
1995 Harley Rides-5 Cents 99377-95Z	3,000		28.00	28
1995 Treehouse Christening 99296-96Z	3,000		32.00	32

Holiday Memories Holiday Music Boxes - Ace
1994 Under The Mistletoe 99459-95Z	7,500	1994	85.00	85
1995 Late Arrival 99496-96Z	7,500	1995	90.00	90

All God's Children

Collectors' Club - M. Root
1989 Molly -1524	Retrd.	1990	38.00	300-600
1990 Joey -1539	Retrd.	1991	32.00	300-475
1991 Mandy -1540	Retrd.	1992	36.00	250-300
1992 Olivia -1562	Retrd.	1993	36.00	175-250
1993 Garrett -1567	Retrd.	1994	36.00	125-200
1993 Peek-a-Boo	Retrd.	1994	Gift	50-85
1994 Alexandria -1575	Retrd.	1995	36.00	95-120
1994 Lindy	Retrd.	1995	Gift	50-75
1995 Zamika -1581	Retrd.	1996	36.00	50-70
1995 Zizi	Retrd.	1996	Gift	30
1996 Donnie -1585	5/97		36.00	36
1996 Dinky	5/97		Gift	N/A

All God's Children - M. Root
1985 Abe -1357	Retrd.	1988	25.00	1475
1989 Adam - 1526	Open		36.00	37
1987 Amy - 1405W	Retrd.	1996	22.00	50-65
1987 Angel - 1401W	Retrd.	1995	20.00	40-70
1986 Annie Mae 6" -1311	Retrd.	1989	19.00	110-175
1986 Annie Mae 8 1/2" -1310	Retrd.	1989	27.00	150-260
1987 Aunt Sarah - blue -1440	Retrd.	1989	45.00	200-300
1987 Aunt Sarah - red-1440	Retrd.	1989	45.00	300-400
1992 Barney - 1557	Retrd.	1995	32.00	75-95
1988 Bean (Clear Water)-1521	Retrd.	1992	36.00	250-325
1992 Bean (Painted Water)-1521	Retrd.	1993	36.00	125-150
1987 Becky - 1402W	Retrd.	1995	22.00	40-70
1987 Becky with Patch - 1402W	Retrd.	N/A	19.00	225-245
1987 Ben - 1504	Retrd.	1988	22.00	350-425
1991 Bessie & Corkie - 1547	Open		70.00	70
1992 Beth - 1558	Retrd.	1995	32.00	75-90
1988 Betsy (Clear Water)- 1513	Retrd.	1992	36.00	250-325
1992 Betsy (Painted Water)- 1513	Retrd.	1993	36.00	125-150
1989 Beverly (sm.)- 1525	Retrd.	1990	50.00	400-635
1991 Billy (lg. stars raised)- 1545	Retrd.	1993	36.00	110-155
1991 Billy (stars imprinted)- 1545	Retrd.	1993	36.00	120-160
1987 Blossom - blue - 1500	Retrd.	1989	60.00	345-425
1987 Blossom - red - 1500	Retrd.	1989	60.00	800
1989 Bo - 1530	Retrd.	1994	22.00	55-90
1987 Bonnie & Buttons - 150	Retrd.	1992	24.00	120-165
1985 Booker T - 1320	Retrd.	1988	19.00	1300-1450
1989 Boone - 1510	Retrd.	1989	16.00	100-180
1989 Bootsie - 1529	Retrd.	1994	22.00	55-70
1992 Caitlin - 1554	Retrd.	1994	36.00	80-124
1985 Callie 2 1/4" - 1362	Retrd.	1988	12.00	275-300
1985 Callie 4 1/2" - 1361	Retrd.	1988	19.00	500
1987 Calvin - 777	Retrd.	1988	200.00	1700-2100
1987 Cassie - 1503	Retrd.	1989	22.00	150-195
1994 Chantel 1573	Open		39.00	39
1987 Charity - 1408	Retrd.	1994	28.00	65-120
1996 Charles - 1588	Open		36.00	36
1994 Cheri 1574	Open		38.00	38
1989 David - 1528	Open		28.00	30
1996 Debi - 1584	Open		N/A	N/A
1991 Dori (green dress) - 1544	Retrd.	N/A	30.00	350-410
1991 Dori (peach dress) - 1544	Open		28.00	30
1987 Eli - 1403W	Open		26.00	28
1992 Emma - 1322	Retrd.	1988	27.00	1750-1950
1992 Faith - 1555	Retrd.	1993	32.00	60-115
1995 Gina - 1579	Open		38.00	38
1987 Ginnie - 1508	Retrd.	1988	22.00	375-445
1986 Grandma - 1323	Retrd.	1987	30.00	3300-3700
1988 Hannah - 1515	Open		36.00	37
1988 Hope - 1519	Open		36.00	37
1987 Jacob - 1407W	Retrd.	1996	26.00	35-70
1989 Jeremy - 1523	800	1993	195.00	750-895
1989 Jerome - 1532	Open		30.00	32
1989 Jessica - 1522	800	1993	195.00	700-890
1989 Jessica and Jeremy -1522-1523	Retrd.	1993	390.00	1800-1875
1987 Jessie (no base) -1501W	Retrd.	1989	19.00	350-450
1989 Jessie - 1501	Open		30.00	32
1988 John -1514	Retrd.	1990	30.00	150-225
1989 Joseph - 1537	Open		30.00	30
1991 Joy - 1548	Open		30.00	30
1994 Justin - 1576	Open		37.00	37
1989 Kacie - 1533	Open		38.00	38
1988 Kezia - 1518	Open		36.00	37
1986 Lil' Emmie 3 1/2"-1345	Retrd.	1989	14.00	125-175
1986 Lil' Emmie 4 1/2" -1344	Retrd.	1989	18.00	155-200
1986 Lisa-1512	Retrd.	1991	36.00	125-250
1989 Mary - 1536	Open		30.00	30
1988 Maya - 1520	Retrd.	1988	36.00	100-145
1988 Meg (beige dress) -1505	Retrd.	1988	21.00	1000-1225
1988 Meg (blue dress, long hair) -1505	Retrd.	1988	21.00	450
1988 Meg (blue dress, short hair) -1505	Retrd.	1988	21.00	875
1992 Melissa - 1556	Retrd.	1995	32.00	60-95
1992 Merci - 1559	Open		36.00	37
1986 Michael & Kim - 1517	Open		36.00	38
1988 Moe & Pokey - 1552	Retrd.	1993	16.00	70-98
1987 Moses - 1506	Retrd.	1992	30.00	129-169
1993 Nathaniel-11569	Open		36.00	36
1991 Nellie - 1546	Retrd.	1993	36.00	120-160
1994 Niambi- 1577	Open		34.00	34
1987 Paddy Paw & Lucy - 1553	Suspd.		24.00	75-90
1987 Paddy Paw & Luke - 1551	Suspd.		24.00	75-90
1988 Peanut -1509	Retrd.	1990	16.00	125-180
1989 Preshus -1538	Open		24.00	24
1987 Primas Jones (w/base) -1377	Retrd.	1988	40.00	725-845
1987 Primas Jones -1377	Retrd.	1988	40.00	725-845
1986 Prissy (Bear) - 1558	Open		18.00	25
1986 Prissy (Moon Pie) - 1557	Open		20.00	32
1986 Prissy with Basket -1346	Retrd.	1989	16.00	150-175
1986 Prissy w/Yarn Hair (6 strands)-1343	Retrd.	1989	19.00	250-300
1986 Prissy w/Yarn Hair (9 strands) -1343	Retrd.	1989	19.00	450-525
1987 Pud - 1550	Retrd.	1988	11.00	1250-1350
1987 Rachel -1404W	Open		20.00	28
1992 Rakiya - 1561	Open		36.00	36
1988 Sally -1507	Retrd.	1989	19.00	165-200
1991 Samantha -1542	Retrd.	1994	38.00	85-130
1991 Samuel - 1541	Retrd.	1994	32.00	100-125
1989 Sasha - 1531	Open		30.00	32
1986 Selina Jane (6 strands) -1338	Retrd.	1989	21.95	255-300
1986 Selina Jane (9 strands) -1338	Retrd.	1989	21.95	525-625
1995 Shani - 1583	Open		33.00	33
1996 Shani - 1583	Open		38.00	38
1986 St. Nicholas-B -1316	Retrd.	1990	30.00	125-165
1986 St. Nicholas-W -1315	Retrd.	1990	30.00	135-150
1992 Stephen (Nativity Shepherd) - 1563	Open		36.00	36
1988 Sunshine -1535	Open		38.00	38
1993 Sylvia -1564	Open		36.00	37
1988 Tansi & Tedi (green socks, collar, cuffs)-1516	Retrd.	N/A	30.00	250-325
1988 Tansy & Tedi - 1516	Open		N/A	37
1989 Tara -1527	Open		36.00	37
1989 Tess - 1534	Open		30.00	32
1990 Thaliyah- 778	Retrd.	1990	200.00	1675-1875
1991 Thomas - 1549	Open		30.00	32
1996 Tia - 1587	Open		22.50	23
1987 Tiffany - 1511	Open		32.00	33
1994 Tish 1572	Open		38.00	38
1986 Toby 3 1/2"- 1332	Retrd.	1989	13.00	135-175
1986 Toby 4 1/2"- 1331	Retrd.	1989	16.00	195
1985 Tom- 1353	Retrd.	1988	16.00	350-450
1986 Uncle Bud 6"- 1304	Retrd.	1990	19.00	125-200
1986 Uncle Bud 8 1/2"- 1303	Retrd.	1991	27.00	250-375
1992 Valerie - 1560	Open		36.00	37
1995 William - 1580	Open		38.00	38
1987 Willie - 1406W	Retrd.	1996	22.00	28
1987 Willie - 1406W (no base)	Retrd.	1987	22.00	456
1993 Zack - 1566	Open		34.00	34

All God's Children Ragbabies - M. Root
1995 Honey - 4005	Open		33.00	33
1995 Issie - 4004	Open		33.00	33
1995 Ivy - 4008	Open		33.00	33
1995 Josie - 4003	Open		33.00	33
1995 Mitzi - 4000	Open		33.00	33
1995 Muffin - 4001	Open		33.00	33
1995 Puddin - 4006	Open		33.00	33
1995 Punkin - 4007	Open		33.00	33
1995 Sweetie - 4002	Open		33.00	33

Angelic Messengers - M. Root
1994 Cieara 2500	Open		38.00	38
1996 Demetrious - 2503	Open		38.00	38
1994 Mariah 2501	Open		38.00	38
1994 Mariah 2501 (scratched in letters)	Retrd.	N/A	38.00	85
1995 Sabrina - 2502	Open		38.00	38

Christmas - M. Root
1987 1987 Father Christmas-W -1750	Retrd.	N/A	145.00	625-735
1987 1987 Father Christmas-B -1751	Retrd.	N/A	145.00	625-735
1988 1988 Father Christmas-W -1757	Retrd.	N/A	195.00	500-630
1988 1988 Father Christmas-B -1758	Retrd.	N/A	195.00	500-630
1988 Santa Claus-W -1767	Retrd.	N/A	185.00	500-650
1988 Santa Claus-B -1768	Retrd.	N/A	185.00	500-650
1989 1989 Father Christmas-W -1769	Retrd.	N/A	195.00	500-700
1989 1989 Father Christmas-B -1770	Retrd.	N/A	195.00	500-700
1990 1990-91 Father Christmas-W -1771	Retrd.	N/A	195.00	550-675
1990 1990-91 Father Christmas-B -1772	Retrd.	N/A	195.00	550-675
1991 1991-92 Father Christmas-W -1773	Retrd.	N/A	195.00	350-475
1991 1991-92 Father Christmas-B -1774	Retrd.	N/A	195.00	400-475
1992 Father Christmas Bust-W -1775	Retrd.	N/A	145.00	300-370
1992 Father Christmas Bust-B -1776	Retrd.	N/A	145.00	300-350

Event Piece - M. Root
1994 Uriel 2000	Yr.Iss.	1994	45.00	120-155
1995 Jane - 2001 (ten year Anniversary)	Yr.Iss.	1995	45.00	100-125
1996 Patti - 2002-Spring (rose colored dress/girl, green colored doll)	Yr.Iss.		45.00	45
1996 Patti - 2002-Fall (dark blue dress/girl, peach colored dress/doll)	Yr.Iss.		45.00	45

Historical Series - M. Root
1994 Augustus Walley (Buffalo Soldier) - 1908	Retrd.	1995	95.00	175-225
1994 Bessie Smith- 1909	Open		70.00	70
1992 Dr. Daniel Williams - 1903	Retrd.	1995	70.00	135-165
1992 Frances Harper - 1905	Open		70.00	70
1991 Frederick Douglass - 1902	Open		70.00	70
1992 George Washington Carver - 1907	Open		70.00	70
1989 Harriet Tubman - 1900	Retrd.	1994	65.00	150-225
1992 Ida B. Wells - 1906	Retrd.	1996	70.00	70
1992 Mary Bethune (misspelled) - 1904	Retrd.	1992	70.00	250-275
1992 Mary Bethune - 1904	Open		70.00	70
1995 Mary Mahoney - 1911	Open		65.00	65
1995 Richard Allen - 1910	Open		70.00	70
1990 Sojourner Truth - 1901	Open		65.00	65

International Series - M. Root
1987 Juan - 1807	Retrd.	1993	26.00	125-155
1987 Kameko - 1802	Open.		26.00	28
1987 Karl - 1808	Retrd.	1996	26.00	28
1987 Katrina - 1803	Retrd.	1993	26.00	120-160
1987 Kelli - 1805	Open		30.00	30
1987 Little Chief - 1804	Open		32.00	32
1993 Minnie - 1568	Open		36.00	36
1987 Pike - 1806	Open		30.00	32
1987 Tat - 1801	Retrd.	1996	30.00	35-70

Little Missionary Series - M. Root
1994 Nakia 3500	Retrd.	1995	40.00	110
1994 Nakia 3500 (Mat.)	Retrd.	1995	40.00	100

Sugar And Spice - M. Root
1987 Blessed are the Peacemakers (Eli) -1403	Retrd.	1988	22.00	530
1987 Friend Show Love (Becky) -1402	Retrd.	1988	22.00	530
1987 Friendship Warms the Heart (Jacob) -1407	Retrd.	1988	22.00	530
1987 God is Love (Angel) -1401	Retrd.	1988	22.00	530
1987 Jesus Loves Me (Amy) -1405	Retrd.	1989	22.00	530
1987 Old Friends are Best (Rachel) -1404	Retrd.	1988	22.00	530
1987 Sharing w/Friends (Willie) -1406	Retrd.	1988	22.00	530

Through His Eyes - M. Root
1993 Simon & Andrew - 1565	Open		45.00	45
1995 Jewel & Judy - 1582	Open		45.00	45

FIGURINES/COTTAGES

YEAR ISSUE	EDITION LIMIT	YEAR RETD.	ISSUE PRICE	*QUOTE U.S.$
Amaranth Productions				
Angels - L. West				
1995 Andre-Victorian 4261	250		590.00	590
1995 Anna- Victorian 4262	250		590.00	590
1996 Katherine-Caroler 4267	250		590.00	590
1996 Nathanael, Caroler 4266	250		590.00	590
Bears - L. West				
1991 Ashley Bearsley 5005	300	1991	500.00	500
1990 Duchess Tinchin 4900	100	1990	750.00	750
1991 Mr. Santa B. Claws 5000	300	1991	500.00	500
1991 Mrs. Santa B. Claws 5001	300	1991	500.00	500
1989 Princess Simsong and Pl 3100	150	1989	750.00	750
1989 Sara Bearsley 5006	300	1991	500.00	500
1994 Su-Lin and Son 9001	Retrd.	1994	300.00	300
1989 Wee Woo Wong 2500	Retrd.	1988	750.00	750
Christmas Elves - L. West				
1988 Bayberry 2304	300	1988	250.00	500
1989 Bayberry 3503	300	1989	278.00	500
1994 Brandy 8103	150	1994	230.00	230
1991 D'Light 4505	350	1992	500.00	500
1993 Dominick 4531	350	1994	420.00	420
1994 Forrest 8101	150	1994	210.00	210
1995 Giuseppe-Christmas Elf 4515	150		900.00	900
1995 Goldwin 4525	150	1995	950.00	950
1990 Half Note 4603	500	1992	278.00	475
1988 Holly 1988 2302	300	1988	230.00	230
1989 Holly 3501	300	1989	250.00	250
1994 Jolly Holiday 4540	200		950.00	950
1994 Krister 4541	250		510.00	510
1994 Nate 8102	150	1994	220.00	220
1992 Oliver 2452	200	1993	470.00	470
1992 Patches 4605	500	1993	278.00	500
1992 Pepe Mint 4510	350	1992	850.00	850
1993 Raffael 4530	350	1994	390.00	390
1990 Rocky 4602	500	1992	278.00	278
1991 Rump-Papa-Pum 4604	500	1992	278.00	278
1990 Russell The Wrapper 4500	350	1992	480.00	480
1990 Skeeter 4601	500	1992	278.00	278
1993 T'Winkle 4520	200	1994	950.00	1200-1400
1992 Timothy 2453	200	1994	590.00	590
1988 Wassail 2303	300	1988	250.00	250
1989 Wassail 3502	300	1989	250.00	375
1993 Wolfie 4532	350	1995	390.00	390
Christmas Scenes - L. West				
1993 Checking It Twice 2350	150	1995	3590.00	3590
1992 Christmas Memories Set 2450	200	1994	2390.00	2390
1991 Merry Little Christmas 2400	200	1993	1990.00	1990
1989 Tree Top Angel 3600	Retrd.	1989	500.00	500
1989 Up On The Roof Top 2305	100	1991	1300.00	1300
Faeries - L. West				
1994 Asteroid 4221	300	1995	284.00	284
1992 Baubles 4211	500	1993	284.00	430
1990 Berry 4201	500	1991	278.00	470
1990 Blueberry 4101	500	1990	270.00	270
1995 Borealis 4224	300	1995	310.00	310
1994 Cadence 4222	300	1995	284.00	284
1992 Cardinal 4213	500	1993	284.00	284
1996 Dreamweaver 4230	110		330.00	330
1990 Dusty 4103	500	1991	270.00	270
1991 Eggburt 4112	500	1993	278.00	430
1990 Emerald 4102	500	1992	270.00	270
1993 Evergreen 4219	300	1995	284.00	284
1992 Fiddler 4210	500	1993	284.00	430
1995 Figaro 4225	300	1995	310.00	310
1996 Gardino 4232	250		330.00	330
1992 Golden Frost 4214	500	1993	284.00	284
1996 Gumdrop 4233	250		330.00	330
1993 Jack 4218	300	1994	284.00	430
1990 Jingles 4202	500	1992	278.00	278
1996 Jubilee 4231	250		330.00	330
1992 Ludwig 4216	500	1993	284.00	284
1994 Mendicino 7020	200	1995	510.00	510
1991 Mistletoe 4205	500	1993	284.00	430
1991 Raddish 4111	500	1992	278.00	430
1995 Sean-Custom Faerie/Neiman Marcus 101	38	1995	310.00	310
1995 Serenade 4223	300	1995	310.00	310
1990 Snowflake 4203	500	1991	278.00	278
1992 Spring Mist 4215	500	1993	284.00	284
1992 Tealberry 4217	500	1994	284.00	284
1994 Timber 4220	300	1995	284.00	284
1991 Tweetle Berry 4204	500	1992	284.00	284
1995 Winsor-Custom Faerie/Neiman Marcus 100	38	1995	310.00	310
1992 Woodie 4212	500	1993	284.00	284
Father Christmas - L. West				
1994 Anniversary Father Christmas 4330	300	1995	750.00	750
1992 Christmas Glory 4310	350	1993	750.00	750
1989 Christmas Majesty 2300	250	1988	750.00	750
1993 Christmas Majesty Special Ed. 4270	100	1993	1590.00	2500
1994 Christmas Peace 4275	100	1994	1450.00	2950
1993 Father Christmas with Staff 4250	200	1994	1300.00	2100
1991 Father Nikolai 4305	500	1993	750.00	750
1989 Grand Father Christmas 3520	300	1991	750.00	750
1996 Old World Santa 4340	250		750.00	750

YEAR ISSUE	EDITION LIMIT	YEAR RETD.	ISSUE PRICE	*QUOTE U.S.$
1993 Special Delivery 4320	350	1993	750.00	750
1994 Victorian Saint Nicholas 4255	150	1995	1300.00	1800-2600
1995 Victorian Winter Father Christmas 4260	250		1450.00	1450
1990 Winter Majesty 4300	350	1992	750.00	950
1996 Yuletide Saint Nick 4265	250		1450.00	1450
Forest Fantasies - L. West				
1994 Captain Surewood 7025	200	1995	950.00	950
1992 Father Earth 7000	350	1993	830.00	830
1995 Frederick-Music School 7006	100	1995	490.00	490
1993 Hermes 7010	200	1993	790.00	790
1992 Leopole 7002	350	1993	470.00	470
1995 Professer Wind Chime 7005	100	1995	1190.00	1190
1991 Sullivan 4110	350	1992	480.00	480
1990 Telltale and Teabu 7001	350	1992	670.00	1200-1500
1990 Wee Willie 4000	350	1991	480.00	600
1993 Whiskers and Wink 7015	200	1993	590.00	800
Home Bred Folks - L. Gill				
1995 Aunt Ruthie with Quilt 1000	250	1995	430.00	430
1996 Belle, HomeBred Angel 1007	250		350.00	350
1995 Dottie Ellen with Bread 1006	250	1995	430.00	430
1995 Hazel Jane with Birds 1001	250	1995	430.00	430
1995 Jake and His Dog 1003	250	1995	430.00	430
1995 Margaret with Vegetables 1004	250	1995	430.00	430
1995 Marie And Her Dog 1002	250	1995	430.00	430
1995 Miss Henrieta with Eggs 1005	250	1995	430.00	430
Lynniputs - L. West				
1994 Chestnut-Lynniputs 7032	350	1995	450.00	450
1995 Fern-Lynniputs 7035	350	1995	450.00	450
1995 Frostie-Lynniputs 7034	350		450.00	450
1994 Nester-Lynniputs 7030	350	1995	450.00	450
1994 Noel-Lynniputs 7033	350	1995	450.00	450
1994 Pops-Lynniputs 7031	350	1995	450.00	450
Old Time Santa Series - L. West				
1992 Old Time Santa-1st in Series 3540	300	1993	530.00	700
1993 Still Fits-2nd in Series 3545	300	1993	700.00	900
1994 Old Time Santa and Tree-3rd in Series 3546	250	1995	650.00	925
Santa Elves Series - L. West				
1995 Franz, Santa's Helper 3555	300	1995	330.00	330
1996 Herbie, Holiday Helper 3602	250		350.00	350
Santas - L. West				
1992 Classic Santa With Chair 2451	200	1993	1450.00	1850
1988 Kris Kringle Special Edition 1115	50	1988	2000.00	2000
1990 Large Santa 4400	250	1993	700.00	700
1991 Last Minute Details w/ Beard 6005BRD	950	1992	550.00	700
1991 Last Minute Details-M.B. 6005	950	1992	430.00	430
1995 Lynn West's Santa Claus 3550	250		550.00	550
1991 Saint Nick 6000	950	1992	370.00	370
1989 Santa At The North Pole 3535	300	1991	450.00	450
1988 Spencer 2301	150	1991	850.00	850
1994 Standing Santa w/Toypack 9002	Retrd.	1994	450.00	450
1996 Woodland Santa & Herbie 3600	250		1650.00	1650
1996 Woodland Santa on wooden base 3601	250		690.00	690
Toys With Affection - D. Thibault				
1995 Father Folk Art 2004	250	1995	260.00	260
1995 Good Tidings Santa 2003	250	1995	380.00	380
1995 Jolly Jack 2002	250	1995	290.00	290
1995 The Melon Man 2001	250	1995	290.00	290
1995 Santa And His Sled 2005	250	1995	380.00	380
1995 True Blue Santa 2000	250	1995	250.00	250
Amazze				
Century Lights - S.N. Meyers				
1994 Admiralty Head, WA	3,995		66.00	66
1995 Assateague, VA	4,975		62.00	62
1994 Barnegat, NJ	10,000		58.00	58
1995 Block Island, RI	4,896		86.00	86
1994 Boston Harbor, MA	3,475		58.00	58
1994 Buffalo, NY	3,475		54.00	54
1994 Burrows Island, WA	2,995		66.00	66
1994 Cape Blanco, OR	2,995	1996	58.00	58
1994 Cape Hatteras, NC	10,000		58.00	58
1994 Cape Henry, VA	3,996		62.00	62
1996 Cape Lookout, NC	3,996		62.00	62
1995 Cape May, NJ	4,975		58.00	58
1994 Charlotte-Genesee, NY	3,475		40.00	40
1995 Chicago Harbor, IL	4,250		66.00	66
1994 Coquille River, OR	2,995		66.00	66
1994 Diamond Head, HI	10,000		54.00	54
1996 East Brother Island, CA	3,996		69.00	69
1995 East Quoddy Head, Canada	2,475		58.00	58
1994 Fort Gratiot, MI	3,475		58.00	58
1994 Great Point, MA	2,475		58.00	58
1994 Hilton Head, SC	10,000		54.00	54
1996 Hog Island, RI	3,996		62.00	62
1994 Holland, MI	4,975		66.00	66
1995 Jupiter Inlet, FL	7,500		58.00	58
1995 Lorain Light, OH	3,195		66.00	66
1994 Marblehead, OH	7,500		54.00	54
1994 Montauk Point, NY	3,475		54.00	54
1995 Nauset Beach, MA	4,995		56.00	56

YEAR ISSUE	EDITION LIMIT	YEAR RETD.	ISSUE PRICE	*QUOTE U.S.$
1994 Ned Point, MA	2,475	1996	40.00	40
1994 North Head, WA	2,995		58.00	58
1995 Ocracoke Island Light, NC	3,975		54.00	54
1994 Old Point Loma, CA	4,550		66.00	66
1994 Plymouth, MA	3,475		58.00	58
1994 Ponce De Leon, FL	3,475		54.00	54
1995 Port Isabel, TX	3,975		58.00	58
1995 Rose Island, RI	4,111		68.00	68
1996 Round Island, MI	3,996		69.00	69
1994 Sand Point, MI	3,475		66.00	66
1995 Sandy Hook, NJ	4,975		58.00	58
1995 Split Rock, MN	4,449		66.00	66
1995 St. Augustine, FL	10,000		62.00	62
1995 St. George Reef, CA	4,500		62.00	62
1995 St. Simmons, GA	3,975		56.00	56
1994 Tybee Island, GA	3,475		58.00	58
1994 Umpqua, OR	2,995		58.00	58
1995 West Quoddy Head, ME	4,995		66.00	66
1995 Yaquina Head, OR	4,500		60.00	60
Centuryville - S.N. Meyers				
1995 Bed & Breakfast	1,975	1996	56.00	56
1994 Cathedral	2,950	1995	70.00	70
1994 Centuryville B&O	3,250	1996	56.00	56
1994 Cranes Eye Point	3,750	1996	60.00	60
1995 Fire Station	1,975	1996	60.00	60
1994 Foggy Point	4,998	1996	50.00	50
1994 Gothic Church	3,436	1996	60.00	60
1995 Lawrence Keith	1,975	1996	64.00	64
1994 Mr. John Johnson	2,960	1996	50.00	50
1994 Mr. Lyle E. Wilson	2,960	1996	50.00	50
1995 Ms. Hilda Grant	2,960	1996	60.00	60
1994 Ms. Marv William	1,975	1996	60.00	60
1994 Ms. Mary Thompson	2,342	1996	50.00	50
1994 Richard & Jan Smith	2,960	1996	50.00	50
1994 Schoolhouse	3,250	1995	56.00	56
1995 Ship Island Miss	1,975	1995	48.00	48
1995 Sweet Shoppe	1,975	1996	56.00	56
1994 Village Church	3,250	1996	60.00	60
The Chocolate Town, U.S.A.! ™Collection - Innes/Meyers				
1996 Chocolate Town™ Cinema	9,988		84.00	84
1996 Chocolate Town™ Post Office	9,988		69.00	69
1996 Hershey's™ 5 and 10 Cent Store	9,988		68.00	68
1996 Hershey's™ Chocolate Shoppe	9,988		76.00	76
1996 Hershey's™ Gallery	9,988		98.00	98
1996 Mr. Goodbar™ Cafe	9,988		66.00	66
Evergreen Village - S.N. Meyers				
1994 Candymakers	2,475	1996	36.00	36
1994 Carpenters	2,475	1996	36.00	36
1994 Cobblers	2,475	1996	36.00	36
1994 Cottage Point	2,675	1995	36.00	36
1994 Evergreen Church	2,475	1995	50.00	50
1994 Train Conductors	2,475	1996	36.00	36
American Artists				
Fred Stone Figurines - F. Stone				
1986 Arab Mare & Foal	2,500		150.00	225
1985 The Black Stallion, bronze	1,500		150.00	175
1985 The Black Stallion, porcelain	2,500		125.00	260
1987 Rearing Black Stallion (Bronze)	1,250		175.00	195
1987 Rearing Black Stallion (Porcelain)	3,500		150.00	175
1986 Tranquility	2,500		175.00	275
Anheuser-Busch, Inc.				
Anheuser-Busch Collectible Figurines - Various				
1994 Buddies N4575 - M. Urdahl	7,500		65.00	65
1995 Horseplay F1 - P. Radtke	7,500		65.00	65
1995 "Bud-weis-er Frogs" F4 - A. Busch, Inc.	Open		30.00	30
ANRI				
Club ANRI - Various				
1983 Welcome, 4" - J. Ferrandiz	Yr.Iss.	1984	110.00	395
1984 My Friend, 4" - J. Ferrandiz	Yr.Iss.	1985	110.00	400
1984 Apple of My Eye, 4 1/2" - S. Kay	Yr.Iss.	1985	135.00	385
1985 Harvest Time, 4" - J. Ferrandiz	Yr.Iss.	1986	125.00	175-385
1985 Dad's Helper, 4 1/2" - S. Kay	Yr.Iss.	1986	135.00	150-375
1986 Harvest's Helper, 4" - J. Ferrandiz	Yr.Iss.	1987	135.00	175-335
1986 Romantic Notions, 4" - S. Kay	Yr.Iss.	1987	135.00	175-310
1986 Celebration March, 5" - J. Ferrandiz	Yr.Iss.	1987	165.00	225-295
1987 Will You Be Mine, 4" - J. Ferrandiz	Yr.Iss.	1988	175.00	175-310
1987 Make A Wish, 4" - S. Kay	Yr.Iss.	1988	165.00	215-325
1987 A Young Man's Fancy, 4" - S. Kay	Yr.Iss.	1988	135.00	165-265
1988 Forever Yours, 4" - J. Ferrandiz	Yr.Iss.	1989	170.00	250
1988 I've Got a Secret, 4" - S. Kay	Yr.Iss.	1989	170.00	205
1988 Maestro Mickey, 4 1/2" - Disney Studio	Yr.Iss.	1989	170.00	175
1989 Diva Minnie, 4 1/2" - Disney Studio	Yr.Iss.	1990	190.00	190
1989 I'll Never Tell, 4" - S. Kay	Yr.Iss.	1990	190.00	190
1989 Twenty Years of Love, 4" - J. Ferrandiz	Yr.Iss.	1990	190.00	190
1990 You Are My Sunshine, 4" - J. Ferrandiz	Yr.Iss.	1991	220.00	220
1990 A Little Bashful, 4" - S. Kay	Yr.Iss.	1991	220.00	220

YEAR ISSUE	EDITION LIMIT	YEAR RETD.	ISSUE PRICE	*QUOTE U.S.$
1990 Dapper Donald, 4" - Disney Studio	Yr.Iss.	1991	199.00	199
1991 With All My Heart, 4" - J. Ferrandiz	Yr.Iss.	1992	250.00	250
1991 Kiss Me, 4" - S. Kay	Yr.Iss.	1992	250.00	250
1991 Daisy Duck, 4 1/2" - Disney Studio	Yr.Iss.	1992	250.00	250

ANRI Club - Various

YEAR ISSUE	EDITION LIMIT	YEAR RETD.	ISSUE PRICE	*QUOTE U.S.$
1992 You Are My All, 4" - J. Ferrandiz	Yr.Iss.	1993	260.00	260
1992 My Present For You, 4" - S. Kay	Yr.Iss.	1993	270.00	270
1992 Gift of Love - S. Kay	Yr.Iss.	1993	Gift	N/A
1993 Truly Yours, 4" - J. Ferrandiz	Yr.Iss.	1994	290.00	290
1993 Sweet Thoughts, 4" - S. Kay	Yr.Iss.	1994	300.00	300
1993 Just For You - S. Kay	Yr.Iss.	1994	Gift	N/A
1994 Sweet 'N Shy, 4" - J. Ferrandiz	Yr.Iss.	1994	250.00	250
1994 Snuggle Up, 4" - S. Kay	Yr.Iss.	1994	300.00	300
1994 Dapper 'N Dear, 4" - J. Ferrandiz	Yr.Iss.	1994	250.00	250

ANRI Collectors' Society- Various

YEAR ISSUE	EDITION LIMIT	YEAR RETD.	ISSUE PRICE	*QUOTE U.S.$
1995 On My Own, 4" - S. Kay	Yr.Iss.	1996	175.00	175
1995 Sealed With A Kiss - J. Ferrandiz	Yr.Iss.		275.00	275
1995 ANRI Artists' Tree House - ANRI	Yr.Iss.		695.00	695
1996 On Cloud Nine - J. Ferrandiz	Yr.Iss.		275.00	275
1996 Sweet Tooth - S. Kay	Yr.Iss.		199.50	200

Bernardi Reflections - U. Bernardi

YEAR ISSUE	EDITION LIMIT	YEAR RETD.	ISSUE PRICE	*QUOTE U.S.$
1996 Learning the Skills, 4"	500		275.00	275
1996 Learning the Skills, 6"	250		550.00	550
1994 Master Carver, 4"	500		350.00	350
1994 Master Carver, 6"	250	1995	600.00	600
1995 Planning the Tour, 4"	500		450.00	450
1995 Planning the Tour, 6"	250		300.00	300

Disney Studios Mickey Mouse Thru The Ages - Disney Studios

YEAR ISSUE	EDITION LIMIT	YEAR RETD.	ISSUE PRICE	*QUOTE U.S.$
1991 The Mad Dog, 4"	1,000	1991	500.00	375-500
1990 Steam Boat Willie, 4"	1,000	1990	295.00	450-550

Disney Woodcarving - Disney Studio

YEAR ISSUE	EDITION LIMIT	YEAR RETD.	ISSUE PRICE	*QUOTE U.S.$
1991 Bell Boy Donald, 4" 656029	Closed	1991	250.00	250
1991 Bell Boy Donald, 6" 656110	500	1991	400.00	400
1990 Chef Goofy, 2 1/2" 656222	Closed	1991	125.00	150-175
1990 Chef Goofy, 5" 656227	Closed	1991	265.00	265
1989 Daisy, 4" 656021	Closed	1991	190.00	225
1990 Donald & Daisy, 6" 656108	500	1991	700.00	700
1988 Donald Duck, 1 3/4" 656209	Closed	1990	80.00	125
1988 Donald Duck, 2" 656204	Closed	1990	85.00	100-135
1987 Donald Duck, 4" 656004	Closed	1989	150.00	200-265
1988 Donald Duck, 4" 656014	Closed	1990	180.00	200-295
1988 Donald Duck, 6" 656102	500	1988	350.00	500
1989 Donald, 4" 656020	Closed	1991	190.00	200-250
1988 Goofy, 1 3/4" 656210	Closed	1990	80.00	100-150
1988 Goofy, 2" 656205	Closed	1990	85.00	100-150
1987 Goofy, 4" 656005	Closed	1989	150.00	200-250
1988 Goofy, 4" 656015	Closed	1990	180.00	200-250
1989 Goofy, 4" 656022	Closed	1991	190.00	200-250
1988 Goofy, 6" 656103	500	1988	380.00	575
1989 Mickey & Minnie Set, 6" 656106	500	1991	700.00	750-950
1989 Mickey & Minnie, 20" matched set	50	1991	7000.00	7000
1987 Mickey & Minnie, 6" 656101	500	1987	625.00	1000
1988 Mickey Mouse, 1 3/4" 656206	Closed	1990	80.00	200-250
1988 Mickey Mouse, 2" 656201	Closed	1990	85.00	100-150
1990 Mickey Mouse, 2" 656220	Closed	1991	100.00	200-400
1987 Mickey Mouse, 4" 656001	Closed	1989	150.00	200-300
1988 Mickey Mouse, 4" 656011	Closed	1990	180.00	200-300
1990 Mickey Mouse, 4" 656025	Closed	1991	199.00	250-295
1991 Mickey Skating, 2" 656224	Closed	1991	120.00	250-295
1991 Mickey Skating, 4" 656030	Closed	1991	190.00	250
1988 Mickey Sorcerer's Apprentice, 2" 656211	Closed	1991	80.00	200
1988 Mickey Sorcerer's Apprentice, 4" 656016	Closed	1991	180.00	199
1988 Mickey Sorcerer's Apprentice, 6" 656105	500	1991	350.00	650
1989 Mickey, 10" 656800	250	1991	700.00	850-1000
1989 Mickey, 20" 656850	50	1991	3500.00	3500
1989 Mickey, 4" 656018	Closed	1991	190.00	250-350
1988 Mini Donald, 1 3/4" 656204	Closed	1991	85.00	150
1989 Mini Donald, 2" 656215	Closed	1991	85.00	150
1988 Mini Goofy, 1 3/4" 656205	Closed	1991	85.00	175
1989 Mini Goofy, 2" 656217	Closed	1991	85.00	175
1988 Mini Mickey, 1 3/4" 656201	Closed	1991	85.00	185
1989 Mini Mickey, 2" 656213	Closed	1991	85.00	185
1988 Mini Minnie, 1 3/4" 656202	Closed	1991	85.00	185
1989 Mini Minnie, 2" 656214	Closed	1991	85.00	185
1989 Mini Pluto, 2" 656218	Closed	1991	85.00	100-125
1988 Minnie Daisy, 2" 656216	Closed	1991	85.00	100-125
1990 Minnie Mouse, 2" 656202	Closed	1990	85.00	100-125
1990 Minnie Mouse, 2" 656221	Closed	1991	100.00	100-125
1987 Minnie Mouse, 4" 656002	Closed	1989	150.00	250
1990 Minnie Mouse, 4" 656026	Closed	1991	199.00	200
1988 Minnie Pinocchio, 1 3/4" 656203	Closed	1991	85.00	200-300
1991 Minnie Skating, 2" 656225	Closed	1991	120.00	125
1991 Minnie Skating, 4" 656031	Closed	1991	250.00	350
1989 Minnie, 10" 656801	250	1991	700.00	900-1100
1989 Minnie, 20" 656851	50	1991	3500.00	3500
1989 Minnie, 4" 656019	Closed	1991	190.00	300
1988 Pinocchio, 4" 656208	Closed	1991	80.00	200-300
1989 Pinocchio, 10" 656802	250	1991	700.00	1000
1988 Pinocchio, 2" 656203	Closed	1990	85.00	85
1989 Pinocchio, 2" 656219	Closed	1991	85.00	100
1989 Pinocchio, 20" 656851	50	1991	3500.00	3500
1987 Pinocchio, 4" 656003 (apple)	Closed	1989	150.00	400
1988 Pinocchio, 4" 656013	Closed	1990	180.00	199
1989 Pinocchio, 4" 656024	Closed	1991	190.00	199
1989 Pinocchio, 6" 656107	500	1991	350.00	350
1988 Pluto, 1 3/4" 656207	Closed	1990	80.00	125-145
1988 Pluto, 4" 656012	Closed	1990	180.00	250-275
1989 Pluto, 4" 656023	Closed	1991	190.00	250-275
1988 Pluto, 6" 656104	500	1991	350.00	450-500
1990 Sorcerer's Apprentice w/ crystal, 2" 656223	Closed	1991	125.00	450-700
1990 Sorcerer's Apprentice w/ crystal, 4" 656028	Closed	1991	265.00	350
1990 Sorcerer's Apprentice w/ crystal, 6" 656109	1,000	1991	475.00	600-800
1990 Sorcerer's Apprentice w/ crystal, 8" 656803	350	1991	790.00	800-900
1990 Sorcerer's Apprentice w/ crystal,16" 656853	100	1991	3500.00	3500

Ferrandiz Boy and Girl - J. Ferrandiz

YEAR ISSUE	EDITION LIMIT	YEAR RETD.	ISSUE PRICE	*QUOTE U.S.$
1983 Admiration, 6"	2,250	1983	220.00	295
1990 Alpine Friend, 3"	1,500	1990	225.00	365
1990 Alpine Friend, 6"	1,500	1990	450.00	610
1990 Alpine Music, 3"	1,500	1990	225.00	225
1990 Alpine Music, 6"	1,500	1990	450.00	580
1989 Baker Boy, 3"	1,500	1989	170.00	170
1989 Baker Boy, 6"	1,500	1989	340.00	340
1978 Basket of Joy, 6"	1,500	1978	140.00	350-450
1983 Bewildered, 6"	2,250	1983	196.00	295
1991 Catalonian Boy, 3"	1,500	1993	227.50	228
1991 Catalonian Boy, 6"	1,500	1993	500.00	500
1991 Catalonian Girl, 3"	1,500	1993	227.50	228
1991 Catalonian Girl, 6"	1,500	1993	500.00	500
1976 Cowboy, 6"	1,500	1976	75.00	500-600
1987 Dear Sweetheart, 3"	2,250	1989	130.00	130
1987 Dear Sweetheart, 6"	2,250	1989	250.00	250
1988 Extra, Extra!, 3"	1,500	1988	145.00	145
1988 Extra, Extra!, 6"	1,500	1988	320.00	320
1979 First Blossom, 6"	2,250	1979	135.00	345-375
1987 For My Sweetheart, 3"	2,250	1989	130.00	130
1987 For My Sweetheart, 6"	2,250	1989	250.00	250
1984 Friendly Faces, 3"	2,250	1984	93.00	110
1984 Friendly Faces, 6"	2,250	1984	210.00	225-295
1980 Friends, 6"	2,250	1980	200.00	300-350
1986 Golden Sheaves, 3"	2,250	1986	125.00	125
1986 Golden Sheaves, 6"	2,250	1986	245.00	245
1982 Guiding Light, 6"	2,250	1982	225.00	275-350
1979 Happy Strummer, 6"	2,250	1979	160.00	395
1976 Harvest Girl, 6"	1,500	1976	75.00	400-800
1977 Leading the Way, 6"	1,500	1977	100.00	300-375
1992 May I, Too?, 3"	1,000	1993	230.00	230
1992 May I, Too?, 6"	1,000	1993	440.00	440
1980 Melody for Two, 6"	2,250	1980	200.00	350
1981 Merry Melody, 6"	2,250	1981	210.00	300-350
1989 Pastry Girl, 3"	1,500	1989	170.00	170
1989 Pastry Girl, 6"	1,500	1989	340.00	340
1978 Peace Pipe, 6"	1,500	1978	140.00	325-450
1985 Peaceful Friends, 3"	2,250	1985	120.00	120
1985 Peaceful Friends, 6"	2,250	1985	250.00	295
1986 Season's Bounty, 3"	2,250	1986	125.00	125
1986 Season's Bounty, 6"	2,250	1986	245.00	245
1988 Sunny Skies, 3"	1,500	1988	145.00	145
1988 Sunny Skies, 6"	1,500	1988	320.00	320
1985 Tender Love, 3"	2,250	1985	100.00	125
1985 Tender Love, 6"	2,250	1985	225.00	250
1981 Tiny Sounds, 6"	2,250	1981	210.00	300-350
1982 To Market, 6"	1,500	1982	220.00	295
1977 Tracker, 6"	1,500	1977	100.00	400
1984 Wanderer's Return, 3"	2,250	1984	93.00	135
1984 Wanderer's Return, 6"	2,250	1984	196.00	250
1992 Waste Not, Want Not, 3"	1,000	1993	190.00	200
1992 Waste Not, Want Not, 6"	1,000	1993	430.00	430

Ferrandiz Circus - J. Ferrandiz

YEAR ISSUE	EDITION LIMIT	YEAR RETD.	ISSUE PRICE	*QUOTE U.S.$
1986 Balancing Ballerina, 2 1/2"	Closed	1988	100.00	100
1986 Balancing Ballerina, 5"	3,000	1988	150.00	150
1986 Ballerina on Horse, 2 1/2"	Closed	1988	125.00	125
1986 Ballerina on Horse, 5"	3,000	1988	200.00	200
1986 Cat on Stool, 2 1/2"	Closed	1988	50.00	50
1986 Cat on Stool, 5"	3,000	1988	110.00	110
1986 Clown on Elephant, 2 1/2"	Closed	1988	125.00	125
1986 Clown on Elephant, 5"	3,000	1988	200.00	200
1986 Clown on Unicycle, 2 1/2"	Closed	1988	80.00	80
1986 Clown on Unicycle, 5"	3,000	1988	175.00	175
1987 Clown w/Bunny, 2 1/2"	Closed	1988	80.00	80
1987 Clown w/Bunny, 5"	3,000	1988	175.00	175
1986 Clown w/Sax, 2 1/2"	Closed	1988	80.00	80
1986 Clown w/Sax, 5"	3,000	1988	175.00	175
1987 Clown w/Umbrella, 2 1/2"	Closed	1988	80.00	80
1987 Clown w/Umbrella, 5"	3,000	1988	175.00	175
1986 Lion Tamer, 2 1/2"	Closed	1988	80.00	80
1986 Lion Tamer, 5"	3,000	1988	175.00	175
1986 Ring Master, 2 1/2"	Closed	1988	80.00	80
1986 Ring Master, 5"	3,000	1988	175.00	175

Ferrandiz Message Collection - J. Ferrandiz

YEAR ISSUE	EDITION LIMIT	YEAR RETD.	ISSUE PRICE	*QUOTE U.S.$
1990 Christmas Carillon, 4 1/2"	2,500	1992	299.00	299
1990 Count Your Blessings, 4 1/2"	5,000	1992	300.00	300
1990 God's Creation, 4 1/2"	5,000	1992	300.00	300
1989 God's Miracle, 4 1/2"	5,000	1991	300.00	300
1989 God's Precious Gift, 4 1/2"	5,000	1991	300.00	300
1989 He Guides Us, 4 1/2"	5,000	1991	300.00	300
1989 He is the Light, 4 1/2"	5,000	1991	300.00	300
1989 He is the Light, 9"	5,000	1991	600.00	600
1989 Heaven Sent, 4 1/2"	5,000	1991	300.00	300
1989 Light From Within, 4 1/2"	5,000	1991	300.00	300
1989 Love Knows No Bounds, 4 1/2"	5,000	1991	300.00	300
1989 Love So Powerful, 4 1/2"	5,000	1991	300.00	300

Ferrandiz Mini Nativity Set - J. Ferrandiz

YEAR ISSUE	EDITION LIMIT	YEAR RETD.	ISSUE PRICE	*QUOTE U.S.$
1985 Baby Camel, 1 1/2"	Closed	1993	45.00	53
1985 Camel Guide, 1 1/2"	Closed	1993	45.00	53
1985 Camel, 1 1/2"	Closed	1993	45.00	53
1988 Devotion, 1 1/2"	Closed	1993	53.00	53
1985 Harmony, 1 1/2"	Closed	1993	45.00	53
1984 Infant, 1 1/2"	Closed	1993	Set	Set
1988 Jolly Gift, 1 1/2"	Closed	1992	53.00	53
1984 Joseph, 1 1/2"	Closed	1993	Set	Set
1984 Leading the Way, 1 1/2"	Closed	1993	Set	Set
1988 Long Journey, 1 1/2"	Closed	1993	53.00	53
1984 Mary, 1 1/2"	Closed	1993	300.00	540
1986 Mini Angel, 1 1/2"	Closed	1993	45.00	53
1986 Mini Balthasar, 1 1/2"	Closed	1993	45.00	53
1986 Mini Caspar, 1 1/2"	Closed	1993	45.00	53
1986 Mini Free Ride, plus Mini Lamb, 1 1/2"	Closed	1993	45.00	53
1986 Mini Melchoir, 1 1/2"	Closed	1993	45.00	53
1986 Mini Star Struck, 1 1/2"	Closed	1993	45.00	53
1986 Mini The Hiker, 1 1/2"	Closed	1993	45.00	53
1986 Mini The Stray, 1 1/2"	Closed	1993	45.00	53
1986 Mini Weary Traveller, 1 1/2"	Closed	1993	45.00	53
1984 Ox Donkey, 1 1/2"	Closed	1993	Set	Set
1985 Rest, 1 1/2"	Closed	1993	45.00	53
1985 Reverence, 1 1/2"	Closed	1993	45.00	53
1984 Sheep Kneeling, 1 1/2"	Closed	1993	Set	Set
1984 Sheep Standing, 1 1/2"	Closed	1993	Set	Set
1985 Small Talk, 1 1/2"	Closed	1993	45.00	53
1988 Sweet Dreams, 1 1/2"	Closed	1993	53.00	53
1988 Sweet Inspiration, 1 1/2"	Closed	1992	53.00	53
1985 Thanksgiving, 1 1/2"	Closed	1993	45.00	53

Ferrandiz Shepherds of the Year - J. Ferrandiz

YEAR ISSUE	EDITION LIMIT	YEAR RETD.	ISSUE PRICE	*QUOTE U.S.$
1982 Companions, 6"	2,250	1982	220.00	275-300
1984 Devotion, 3"	2,250	1984	82.50	125
1984 Devotion, 6"	2,250	1984	180.00	200-250
1979 Drummer Boy, 3"	Yr.Iss.	1979	80.00	250
1979 Drummer Boy, 6"	Yr.Iss.	1979	220.00	400-425
1980 Freedom Bound, 3"	Yr.Iss.	1980	90.00	225
1980 Freedom Bound, 6"	Yr.Iss.	1980	225.00	400
1977 Friendship, 3"	Yr.Iss.	1977	53.50	330
1977 Friendship, 6"	Yr.Iss.	1977	110.00	500-675
1983 Good Samaritan, 6"	2,250	1983	200.00	300-320
1981 Jolly Piper, 6"	2,250	1981	225.00	375
1978 Spreading the Word, 3"	Yr.Iss.	1978	115.00	250-275
1978 Spreading the Word, 6"	Yr.Iss.	1978	270.50	500

Ferrandiz Woodcarvings - J. Ferrandiz

YEAR ISSUE	EDITION LIMIT	YEAR RETD.	ISSUE PRICE	*QUOTE U.S.$
1988 Abracadabra, 3"	1,500	1991	145.00	165
1988 Abracadabra, 6"	1,500	1991	315.00	345
1976 Adoration, 12"	Closed	1987	350.00	350
1981 Adoration, 20"	250	1987	3200.00	3200
1976 Adoration, 3"	Closed	1987	45.00	45
1976 Adoration, 6"	Closed	1987	100.00	100
1987 Among Friends, 3"	3,000	1990	125.00	151
1987 Among Friends, 6"	3,000	1990	245.00	291
1969 Angel Sugar Heart, 6"	Closed	1973	25.00	2500
1974 Artist, 3"	Closed	1981	30.00	195
1970 Artist, 6"	Closed	1981	25.00	350
1982 Bagpipe, 3"	Closed	1983	80.00	95
1982 Bagpipe, 6"	Closed	1983	175.00	190
1978 Basket of Joy, 6"	Closed	1983	65.00	120
1984 Bird's Eye View, 3"	Closed	1989	88.00	129
1984 Bird's Eye View, 6"	Closed	1989	216.00	700
1987 Black Forest Boy, 3"	3,000	1990	125.00	151
1987 Black Forest Boy, 6"	3,000	1990	250.00	301
1987 Black Forest Girl, 3"	3,000	1990	125.00	151
1987 Black Forest Girl, 6"	3,000	1990	250.00	300-350
1977 The Blessing, 3"	Closed	1982	45.00	150
1977 The Blessing, 6"	Closed	1982	250.00	250
1988 Bon Appetit, 3"	3,000	1990	175.00	195
1988 Bon Appetit, 6"	500	1991	395.00	440
1974 The Bouquet, 3"	Closed	1981	35.00	175
1974 The Bouquet, 6"	Closed	1981	75.00	325
1982 Bundle of Joy, 3"	Closed	1990	100.00	300
1982 Bundle of Joy, 6"	Closed	1990	225.00	323
1985 Butterfly Boy, 3"	Closed	1990	95.00	140
1985 Butterfly Boy, 6"	Closed	1990	220.00	322
1976 Catch a Falling Star, 3"	Closed	1983	35.00	150
1976 Catch a Falling Star, 6"	Closed	1983	75.00	250
1986 Celebration March, 11"	750	1987	495.00	495
1986 Celebration March, 20"	200	1987	2700.00	2700
1982 The Champion, 3"	Closed	1985	98.00	110
1982 The Champion, 6"	Closed	1985	225.00	250
1975 Cherub, 2"	Open		32.00	90
1975 Cherub, 4"	Open		32.00	275
1993 Christmas Time, 5"	750		360.00	420
1982 Circus Serenade, 3"	Closed	1988	100.00	160
1982 Circus Serenade, 6"	Closed	1988	220.00	220
1982 Clarinet, 3"	Closed	1983	80.00	100
1982 Clarinet, 6"	Closed	1983	175.00	200
1982 Companions, 3"	Closed	1984	95.00	115
1975 Courting, 3"	Closed	1982	70.00	235
1975 Courting, 6"	Closed	1982	150.00	450
1984 Cowboy, 10"	Closed	1989	370.00	500
1983 Cowboy, 20"	250	1989	2100.00	2100

YEAR ISSUE	EDITION LIMIT	YEAR RETD.	ISSUE PRICE	*QUOTE U.S.$
1976 Cowboy, 3"	Closed	1989	35.00	140-160
1994 Donkey Driver, 3"	Open		160.00	160
1994 Donkey Driver, 6"	Open		360.00	360
1994 Donkey, 3"	Open		200.00	200
1994 Donkey, 6"	Open		450.00	450
1980 Drummer Boy, 3"	Closed	1988	130.00	200
1980 Drummer Boy, 6"	Closed	1988	300.00	400
1970 Duet, 3"	Closed	1991	36.00	165
1970 Duet, 6"	Closed	1991	Unkn.	355
1986 Edelweiss, 10"	Open		500.00	1000
1986 Edelweiss, 20"	250		3300.00	5420
1983 Edelweiss, 3"	Open		95.00	205
1983 Edelweiss, 6"	Open		220.00	500
1982 Encore, 3"	Closed	1984	100.00	115
1982 Encore, 6"	Closed	1984	225.00	235
1979 First Blossom, 3"	Closed	1985	70.00	110
1974 Flight Into Egypt, 3"	Closed	1986	35.00	125
1974 Flight Into Egypt, 6"	Closed	1986	70.00	500
1976 Flower Girl, 3"	Closed	1988	40.00	40
1976 Flower Girl, 6"	Closed	1988	90.00	310
1982 Flute, 3"	Closed	1983	80.00	95
1982 Flute, 6"	Closed	1983	175.00	190
1976 Gardener, 3"	Closed	1984	32.00	195
1976 Gardener, 6"	Closed	1982	65.00	275-350
1975 The Gift, 3"	Closed	1982	40.00	195
1975 The Gift, 6"	Closed	1982	70.00	295
1973 Girl in the Egg, 3"	Closed	1988	30.00	127
1973 Girl in the Egg, 6"	Closed	1988	60.00	272
1973 Girl with Dove, 3"	Closed	1984	30.00	110
1973 Girl with Dove, 6"	Closed	1984	50.00	175-200
1976 Girl with Rooster, 3"	Closed	1982	32.50	175
1976 Girl with Rooster, 6"	Closed	1982	60.00	275
1986 God's Little Helper, 2"	3,500	1991	170.00	255
1986 God's Little Helper, 4"	2,000	1991	425.00	550
1975 Going Home, 3"	Closed	1988	40.00	175
1975 Going Home, 6"	Closed	1988	70.00	325
1986 Golden Blossom, 10"	Open		500.00	1000
1986 Golden Blossom, 20"	250		3300.00	5420
1983 Golden Blossom, 3"	Open		95.00	205
1986 Golden Blossom, 40"	50	1994	8300.00	12950
1983 Golden Blossom, 6"	Open		220.00	500
1982 The Good Life, 3"	Closed	1984	100.00	200
1982 The Good Life, 6"	Closed	1984	225.00	295
1969 The Good Sheperd, 3"	Closed	1988	12.50	121
1971 The Good Shepherd, 10"	Closed	1988	90.00	90
1969 The Good Shepherd, 6"	Closed	1988	25.00	237
1974 Greetings, 3"	Closed	1976	30.00	300
1974 Greetings, 6"	Closed	1976	55.00	475
1982 Guiding Light, 3"	Closed	1984	100.00	115-150
1982 Guitar, 3"	Closed	1983	80.00	95
1982 Guitar, 6"	Closed	1983	175.00	190
1979 Happy Strummer, 3"	Closed	1986	75.00	110
1973 Happy Wanderer, 10"	Closed	1985	120.00	500
1974 Happy Wanderer, 3"	Closed	1986	40.00	105
1974 Happy Wanderer, 6"	Closed	1986	70.00	200
1982 Harmonica, 3"	Closed	1983	80.00	95
1982 Harmonica, 3"	Closed	1983	80.00	95
1982 Harmonica, 6"	Closed	1983	175.00	190
1978 Harvest Girl, 3"	Closed	1986	75.00	110-140
1979 He's My Brother, 3"	Closed	1984	70.00	130
1979 He's My Brother, 6"	Closed	1984	155.00	240
1987 Heavenly Concert, 2"	3,000	1991	200.00	200
1987 Heavenly Concert, 4"	2,000	1991	450.00	550
1969 Heavenly Gardener, 6"	Closed	1973	25.00	2000
1969 Heavenly Quintet, 6"	Closed	1973	25.00	2000
1969 The Helper, 3"	Closed	1987	12.50	13
1969 The Helper, 5"	Closed	1987	25.00	25
1974 Helping Hands, 3"	Closed	1976	30.00	350
1974 Helping Hands, 6"	Closed	1976	55.00	700
1984 High Hopes, 3"	Closed	1986	81.00	81-100
1984 High Hopes, 6"	Closed	1986	170.00	255
1979 High Riding, 3"	Closed	1984	145.00	200
1979 High Riding, 6"	Closed	1984	340.00	475
1974 The Hiker, 3"	Closed	1993	36.00	36
1974 The Hiker, 6"	Closed	1993	80.00	80
1982 Hitchhiker, 3"	Closed	1986	98.00	85-110
1982 Hitchhiker, 6"	Closed	1986	125.00	230
1993 Holiday Greetings, 3"	1,000	1993	200.00	200
1993 Holiday Greetings, 6"	1,000	1993	450.00	450
1975 Holy Family, 3"	Closed	1988	75.00	250
1975 Holy Family, 6"	Closed	1988	200.00	670
1996 Homeward Bound, 3"	Open		155.00	155
1996 Homeward Bound, 6"	Open		410.00	410
1977 Hurdy Gurdy, 3"	Closed	1988	53.00	150
1977 Hurdy Gurdy, 6"	Closed	1988	112.00	390
1975 Inspector, 3"	Closed	1981	40.00	250
1975 Inspector, 6"	Closed	1981	80.00	395
1988 Jolly Gift, 3"	Closed	1991	129.00	129
1988 Jolly Gift, 6"	Closed	1991	296.00	296
1981 Jolly Piper, 3"	Closed	1984	100.00	120
1977 Journey, 3"	Closed	1983	67.50	175
1977 Journey, 6"	Closed	1983	120.00	400
1977 Leading the Way, 3"	Closed	1984	62.50	120
1976 The Letter, 3"	Closed	1988	40.00	40
1976 The Letter, 6"	Closed	1988	90.00	600
1982 Lighting the Way, 3"	Closed	1984	105.00	150
1982 Lighting the Way, 6"	Closed	1984	225.00	295
1974 Little Mother, 3"	Closed	1981	136.00	290
1974 Little Mother, 6"	Closed	1981	85.00	285
1989 Little Sheep Found, 3"	Open		120.00	180
1989 Little Sheep Found, 6"	Open		275.00	335
1993 Lots of Gifts, 3"	1,000	1993	200.00	200
1993 Lots of Gifts, 6"	1,000	1993	450.00	450
1975 Love Gift, 3"	Closed	1982	40.00	175
1975 Love Gift, 6"	Closed	1982	70.00	295
1969 Love Letter, 3"	Closed	1982	12.50	150
1969 Love Letter, 6"	Closed	1982	25.00	250
1983 Love Message, 3"	Closed	1990	105.00	151
1983 Love Message, 6"	Closed	1990	240.00	366
1969 Love's Messenger, 6"	Closed	1973	25.00	2000
1992 Madonna With Child, 3"	1,000	1994	190.00	190
1992 Madonna With Child, 6"	1,000	1994	370.00	370
1981 Merry Melody, 3"	Closed	1984	90.00	115
1989 Mexican Boy, 3"	1,500	1993	170.00	175
1989 Mexican Boy, 6"	1,500	1993	340.00	350
1989 Mexican Girl, 3"	1,500	1993	170.00	175
1989 Mexican Girl, 6"	1,500	1993	340.00	350
1975 Mother and Child, 3"	Closed	1983	45.00	150
1975 Mother and Child, 6"	Closed	1983	90.00	295
1981 Musical Basket, 3"	Closed	1984	90.00	115
1981 Musical Basket, 6"	Closed	1984	200.00	225
1986 A Musical Ride, 4"	Closed	1990	165.00	237
1986 A Musical Ride, 8"	Closed	1990	395.00	559
1973 Nature Girl, 3"	Closed	1988	30.00	30
1973 Nature Girl, 6"	Closed	1988	60.00	272
1987 Nature's Wonder, 3"	3,000	1990	125.00	151
1987 Nature's Wonder, 6"	3,000	1990	245.00	291
1974 New Friends, 3"	Closed	1976	30.00	275
1974 New Friends, 6"	Closed	1976	55.00	550
1977 Night Night, 3"	Closed	1983	45.00	120
1977 Night Night, 6"	Closed	1983	67.50	250-315
1992 Pascal Lamb, 3"	1,000	1993	210.00	210
1992 Pascal Lamb, 6"	1,000	1993	460.00	460
1988 Peace Maker, 3"	1,500	1991	180.00	200
1988 Peace Maker, 6"	1,500	1991	360.00	395
1983 Peace Pipe, 10"	Closed	1986	460.00	495
1984 Peace Pipe, 20"	250	1986	2200.00	3500
1979 Peace Pipe, 3"	Closed	1986	85.00	120
1988 Picnic for Two, 3"	500	1991	190.00	210
1988 Picnic for Two, 6"	500	1991	425.00	465
1982 Play It Again, 3"	Closed	1984	100.00	120
1982 Play It Again, 6"	Closed	1984	250.00	255
1977 Poor Boy, 3"	Closed	1986	50.00	110
1977 Poor Boy, 6"	Closed	1986	125.00	215
1977 Proud Mother, 3"	Closed	1988	52.50	150
1977 Proud Mother, 6"	Closed	1988	130.00	350
1971 The Quintet, 10"	Closed	1990	100.00	750
1971 The Quintet, 20"	Closed	1990	Unkn.	4750
1969 The Quintet, 3"	Closed	1990	12.50	175
1969 The Quintet, 6"	Closed	1990	25.00	395
1970 Reverance, 3"	Closed	1991	30.00	30
1970 Reverance, 6"	Closed	1991	56.00	56
1977 Riding Thru the Rain, 10"	Open		400.00	1190
1985 Riding Thru the Rain, 20"	100	1988	3950.00	3950
1977 Riding Thru the Rain, 5"	Open		145.00	470
1976 Rock A Bye, 3"	Closed	1987	60.00	60
1976 Rock A Bye, 6"	Closed	1987	125.00	125
1974 Romeo, 3"	Closed	1981	50.00	250
1974 Romeo, 6"	Closed	1981	85.00	395
1993 Santa and Teddy, 5"	750		360.00	380
1994 Santa Resting on Bag, 5"	750		400.00	400
1987 Serenity, 3"	3,000	1989	125.00	151
1987 Serenity, 6"	3,000	1989	245.00	291
1976 Sharing, 3"	Closed	1983	32.50	130
1976 Sharing, 6"	Closed	1983	32.50	225-275
1984 Shipmates, 3"	Closed	1989	81.00	119
1984 Shipmates, 6"	Closed	1989	170.00	248
1978 Spreading the Word, 3"	Closed	1989	115.00	194
1978 Spreading the Word, 6"	Closed	1989	270.00	495
1980 Spring Arrivals, 10"	Open		435.00	770
1980 Spring Arrivals, 20"	250		2000.00	3360
1973 Spring Arrivals, 3"	Open		30.00	160
1973 Spring Arrivals, 6"	Open		50.00	350
1978 Spring Dance, 12"	Closed	1984	950.00	1750
1978 Spring Dance, 24"	Closed	1984	4750.00	6200
1974 Spring Outing, 3"	Closed	1976	30.00	625
1974 Spring Outing, 6"	Closed	1976	55.00	900
1982 Star Bright, 3"	Closed	1984	110.00	125
1982 Star Bright, 6"	Closed	1984	250.00	295
1982 Star Struck, 10"	Closed	1987	490.00	490
1982 Star Struck, 20"	250	1987	2400.00	2400
1974 Star Struck, 3"	Closed	1987	97.50	98
1974 Star Struck, 6"	Closed	1987	210.00	210
1981 Stepping Out, 3"	Closed	1984	95.00	110-145
1981 Stepping Out, 6"	Closed	1984	220.00	275
1979 Stitch in Time, 3"	Closed	1984	75.00	125
1979 Stitch in Time, 6"	Closed	1984	150.00	235
1975 Stolen Kiss, 3"	Closed	1987	80.00	80
1975 Stolen Kiss, 6"	Closed	1987	150.00	150
1969 Sugar Heart, 3"	Closed	1973	12.50	450
1969 Sugar Heart, 6"	Closed	1973	25.00	525
1975 Summertime, 3"	Closed	1989	35.00	35
1975 Summertime, 6"	Closed	1989	70.00	258
1982 Surprise, 3"	Closed	1988	100.00	150
1982 Surprise, 6"	Closed	1988	225.00	325
1973 Sweeper, 3"	Closed	1981	35.00	130
1973 Sweeper, 6"	Closed	1981	75.00	425
1981 Sweet Arrival Blue, 3"	Closed	1985	105.00	110
1981 Sweet Arrival Blue, 6"	Closed	1985	225.00	255
1981 Sweet Arrival Pink, 3"	Closed	1985	105.00	110
1981 Sweet Arrival Pink, 6"	Closed	1985	225.00	225
1981 Sweet Dreams, 3"	Closed	1990	100.00	140
1982 Sweet Dreams, 6"	Closed	1990	225.00	330
1989 Sweet Inspiration, 3"	Closed	1991	129.00	129
1989 Sweet Inspiration, 6"	Closed	1991	296.00	296
1982 Sweet Melody, 3"	Closed	1985	80.00	90
1982 Sweet Melody, 6"	Closed	1985	198.00	210
1989 Swiss Boy, 3"	Closed	1993	180.00	180
1986 Swiss Boy, 3"	Closed	1993	122.00	162
1986 Swiss Boy, 6"	Closed	1993	380.00	380
1986 Swiss Boy, 6"	Closed	1993	245.00	324
1989 Swiss Girl, 3"	Closed	1993	200.00	200
1986 Swiss Girl, 3"	Closed	1993	122.00	122
1986 Swiss Girl, 6"	Closed	1993	245.00	304
1986 Swiss Girl, 6"	Closed	1993	470.00	470
1971 Talking to Animals, 20"	Closed	1989	Unkn.	3000
1971 Talking to the Animals, 10"	Closed	1989	90.00	600
1969 Talking to the Animals, 3"	Closed	1989	12.50	125
1969 Talking to the Animals, 6"	Closed	1989	45.00	250
1995 Tender Care, 3" 55710/52	Open		125.00	135
1995 Tender Care, 6" 55700/52	Open		275.00	295
1974 Tender Moments, 3"	Closed	1976	30.00	375
1974 Tender Moments, 6"	Closed	1976	55.00	575
1981 Tiny Sounds, 3"	Closed	1984	90.00	105
1982 To Market, 3"	Closed	1984	95.00	115
1977 Tracker, 3"	Closed	1984	70.00	120-200
1982 Treasure Chest w/6 mini figurines	10,000	1984	300.00	300
1980 Trumpeter, 10"	Closed	1986	500.00	500
1980 Trumpeter, 20"	250	1986	2350.00	3050
1973 Trumpeter, 3"	Closed	1986	69.00	115
1973 Trumpeter, 6"	Closed	1986	120.00	240
1980 Umpapa, 4"	Closed	1984	125.00	140
1982 Violin, 3"	Closed	1983	80.00	95
1982 Violin, 6"	Closed	1983	175.00	195
1976 Wanderlust, 3"	Closed	1983	32.50	125
1975 Wanderlust, 6"	Closed	1983	70.00	450
1972 The Weary Traveler, 3"	Closed	1989	24.00	24
1972 The Weary Traveler, 6"	Closed	1989	48.00	48
1988 Winter Memories, 3"	1,500	1991	180.00	195
1988 Winter Memories, 6"	1,500	1991	398.00	440

Limited Edition Couples - J. Ferrandiz

YEAR ISSUE	EDITION LIMIT	YEAR RETD.	ISSUE PRICE	*QUOTE U.S.$
1985 First Kiss, 8"	750	1985	590.00	950
1987 Heart to Heart, 8"	750	1985	590.00	850
1988 A Loving Hand, 8"	750	1991	795.00	850
1986 My Heart Is Yours, 8"	750	1991	590.00	850
1985 Springtime Stroll, 8"	750	1990	590.00	950
1986 A Tender Touch, 8"	750	1990	590.00	850

Sarah Kay Christmas Firsts - S. Kay

YEAR ISSUE	EDITION LIMIT	YEAR RETD.	ISSUE PRICE	*QUOTE U.S.$
1994 Sarah Kay's First Christmas, 4"	500		350.00	350
1994 Sarah Kay's First Christmas, 6"	250	1995	600.00	600
1995 First Christmas Stocking, 4" 57553	500		250.00	250
1995 First Christmas Stocking, 6" 57554	250		395.00	395
1996 All I Want For Christmas, 4" 57555	500		325.00	325
1996 All I Want For Christmas, 6" 57556	250		550.00	550

Sarah Kay Figurines - S. Kay

YEAR ISSUE	EDITION LIMIT	YEAR RETD.	ISSUE PRICE	*QUOTE U.S.$
1985 Afternoon Tea, 11"	750	1993	650.00	770
1985 Afternoon Tea, 20"	100	1993	3100.00	3500
1985 Afternoon Tea, 4"	4,000	1990	95.00	185
1985 Afternoon Tea, 6"	4,000	1990	195.00	325-365
1987 All Aboard, 1 1/2"	7,500	1990	50.00	90
1987 All Aboard, 4"	4,000	1990	130.00	185
1987 All Aboard, 6"	2,000	1990	265.00	355
1987 All Mine, 1 1/2"	7,500	1988	49.50	95
1987 All Mine, 4"	4,000	1988	130.00	225
1987 All Mine, 6"	4,000	1988	245.00	465
1986 Always By My Side, 1 1/2"	7,500	1988	45.00	95
1986 Always By My Side, 4"	4,000	1988	95.00	195
1986 Always By My Side, 6"	4,000	1988	195.00	375
1990 Batter Up, 1 1/2"	3,750	1991	90.00	95
1990 Batter Up, 4"	2,000		220.00	265
1990 Batter Up, 6"	2,000		440.00	515
1983 Bedtime, 1 1/2"	7,500	1984	45.00	110
1983 Bedtime, 4"	Closed	1987	95.00	230
1983 Bedtime, 6"	4,000	1987	195.00	435
1994 Bubbles & Bows, 4"	1,000		300.00	300
1994 Bubbles & Bows, 6"	1,000		600.00	600
1986 Bunny Hug, 1 1/2"	7,500	1989	45.00	85
1986 Bunny Hug, 4"	4,000	1989	95.00	172
1986 Bunny Hug, 6"	2,000	1989	210.00	395
1989 Cherish, 1 1/2"	Closed	1991	80.00	95
1989 Cherish, 4"	2,000	1994	199.00	290
1989 Cherish, 6"	2,000	1994	398.00	560
1993 Christmas Basket, 4"	1,000		310.00	290
1993 Christmas Basket, 6"	1,000		600.00	580
1994 Christmas Wonder, 4"	1,000		370.00	370
1994 Christmas Wonder, 6"	1,000		700.00	700
1994 Clowning Around, 4"	1,000		300.00	300
1994 Clowning Around, 6"	1,000		550.00	550
1987 Cuddles, 1 1/2"	7,500	1988	49.50	95
1987 Cuddles, 4"	4,000	1988	130.00	225
1987 Cuddles, 6"	4,000	1988	245.00	465
1984 Daydreaming, 1 1/2"	7,500	1984	45.00	125
1984 Daydreaming, 4"	4,000	1988	95.00	235
1984 Daydreaming, 6"	4,000	1988	195.00	445
1991 Dress Up, 1 1/2"	3,750	1991	110.00	110
1991 Dress Up, 4"	2,000	1993	270.00	270
1991 Dress Up, 6"	2,000	1993	550.00	570
1983 Feeding the Chickens, 1 1/2"	7,500	1984	45.00	110
1983 Feeding the Chickens, 4"	Closed	1987	95.00	250
1983 Feeding the Chickens, 6"	4,000	1987	195.00	450
1991 Figure Eight, 1 1/2"	3,750	1991	110.00	110
1991 Figure Eight, 4"	2,000		270.00	365

*Quotes have been rounded up to nearest dollar

YEAR ISSUE		EDITION LIMIT	YEAR RETD.	ISSUE PRICE	*QUOTE U.S.$
1991	Figure Eight, 6"	2,000		550.00	660
1984	Finding Our Way, 1 1/2"	7,500	1984	45.00	135
1984	Finding Our Way, 4"	4,000	1988	95.00	245
1984	Finding Our Way, 6"	2,000	1984	210.00	495
1986	Finishing Touch, 1 1/2"	7,500	1989	45.00	85
1986	Finishing Touch, 4"	4,000	1989	95.00	172
1986	Finishing Touch, 6"	4,000	1989	195.00	312
1989	First School Day, 1 1/2"	Closed	1991	85.00	95
1989	First School Day, 4"	2,000	1993	290.00	350
1989	First School Day, 6"	2,000	1993	550.00	650
1989	Fisherboy, 1 1/2"	Closed	1991	85.00	95
1989	Fisherboy, 4"	2,000	1994	220.00	250
1989	Fisherboy, 6"	1,000	1994	440.00	475
1984	Flowers for You, 1 1/2"	7,500	1984	45.00	125
1984	Flowers for You, 4"	4,000	1988	95.00	250
1984	Flowers for You, 6"	4,000	1988	195.00	450
1991	Fore!!, 1 1/2"	3,750	1991	110.00	115
1991	Fore!!, 4"	2,000		270.00	325
1991	Fore!!, 6"	2,000		550.00	580
1992	Free Skating, 4"	1,000		310.00	325
1992	Free Skating, 6"	1,000		590.00	620
1983	From the Garden, 1 1/2"	7,500	1984	45.00	110
1983	From the Garden, 4"	Closed	1987	95.00	235
1983	From the Garden, 6"	4,000	1987	195.00	450
1989	Garden Party, 1 1/2"	Closed	1991	85.00	95
1989	Garden Party, 4"	2,000	1993	220.00	240
1989	Garden Party, 6"	2,000	1993	440.00	475
1985	Giddyap!, 4"	4,000	1990	95.00	250
1985	Giddyap!, 6"	4,000	1990	195.00	325
1988	Ginger Snap, 1 1/2"	Closed	1990	70.00	90
1988	Ginger Snap, 4"	2,000	1990	150.00	185
1988	Ginger Snap, 6"	1,000	1990	300.00	355
1986	Good As New, 1 1/2"	7,500	1991	45.00	90
1986	Good As New, 4"	4,000	1994	95.00	290
1986	Good As New, 6"	4,000	1994	195.00	500
1996	Head of the Class, 4"	500		295.00	295
1996	Head of the Class, 6"	250		495.00	495
1983	Helping Mother, 1 1/2"	7,500	1983	45.00	110
1983	Helping Mother, 4"	Closed	1983	95.00	300
1983	Helping Mother, 6"	2,000	1983	210.00	495
1988	Hidden Treasures, 1 1/2"	Closed	1990	70.00	90
1988	Hidden Treasures, 4"	2,000	1990	150.00	185
1988	Hidden Treasures, 6"	1,000	1990	300.00	355
1990	Holiday Cheer, 1 1/2"	3,750	1991	90.00	95
1990	Holiday Cheer, 4"	2,000		225.00	320
1990	Holiday Cheer, 6"	1,000		450.00	610
1989	House Call, 1 1/2"	Closed	1991	85.00	95
1989	House Call, 4"	2,000	1991	190.00	195
1989	House Call, 6"	2,000	1991	390.00	390
1995	I Know, I Know, 4" 57701	500		250.00	275
1995	I Know, I Know, 6" 57702	250		395.00	450
1993	Innocence, 4"	1,000		345.00	315
1993	Innocence, 6"	1,000		630.00	630
1994	Jolly Pair, 4"	1,000		350.00	350
1994	Jolly Pair, 6"	1,000		650.00	650
1993	Joy to the World, 4"	1,000		310.00	290
1993	Joy to the World, 6"	1,000		600.00	580
1987	Let's Play, 1 1/2"	7,500	1990	49.50	90
1987	Let's Play, 4"	4,000	1990	130.00	185
1987	Let's Play, 6"	2,000	1990	265.00	355
1994	Little Chimney Sweep, 4"	1,000		300.00	310
1994	Little Chimney Sweep, 6"	1,000		600.00	600
1987	Little Nanny, 1 1/2"	7,500	1990	49.50	90
1987	Little Nanny, 4"	4,000		150.00	200
1987	Little Nanny, 6"	4,000	1990	295.00	400
1987	A Loving Spoonful, 1 1/2"	7,500	1991	49.50	90
1987	A Loving Spoonful, 4"	4,000	1994	150.00	290
1987	A Loving Spoonful, 6"	4,000	1994	295.00	550
1992	Merry Christmas, 1 1/2"	3,750	1994	110.00	115
1992	Merry Christmas, 4"	1,000	1994	350.00	350
1992	Merry Christmas, 6"	1,000	1994	580.00	580
1995	Mom's Joy, 5" 57902	250	1995	297.00	297
1983	Morning Chores, 1 1/2"	7,500	1983	45.00	110
1983	Morning Chores, 4"	Closed	1983	95.00	300
1983	Morning Chores, 6"	2,000	1983	210.00	550
1993	Mr. Santa, 4"	750		375.00	390
1993	Mr. Santa, 6"	750		695.00	730
1993	Mrs. Santa, 4"	750		375.00	390
1993	Mrs. Santa, 6"	750		695.00	730
1993	My Favorite Doll, 4"	1,000		315.00	315
1993	My Favorite Doll, 6"	1,000		600.00	600
1988	My Little Brother, 1 1/2"	Closed	1991	70.00	90
1988	My Little Brother, 4"	2,000	1991	195.00	225
1988	My Little Brother, 6"	2,000	1991	375.00	450
1988	New Home, 1 1/2"	Closed	1991	70.00	90
1988	New Home, 4"	2,000	1991	185.00	240
1988	New Home, 6"	2,000	1991	365.00	500
1985	Nightie Night, 4"	4,000	1990	95.00	185
1985	Nightie Night, 6"	4,000	1990	195.00	325
1984	Off to School, 1 1/2"	7,500	1984	45.00	125
1984	Off to School, 11"	750		590.00	880
1984	Off to School, 20"	100		2900.00	4200
1984	Off to School, 4"	4,000		95.00	240
1984	Off to School, 6"	4,000		195.00	450
1986	Our Puppy, 1 1/2"	7,500	1990	45.00	90
1986	Our Puppy, 4"	4,000	1990	95.00	185
1986	Our Puppy, 6"	2,000	1990	210.00	355
1988	Penny for Your Thoughts, 1 1/2"	Closed	1991	70.00	90
1988	Penny for Your Thoughts, 4"	2,000		185.00	275
1988	Penny for Your Thoughts, 6"	2,000		365.00	570
1983	Playtime, 1 1/2"	7,500	1984	45.00	110
1983	Playtime, 4"	Closed	1987	95.00	250
1983	Playtime, 6"	4,000	1987	195.00	495
1988	Purrfect Day, 4"	2,000	1991	184.00	215
1988	Purrfect Day, 1 1/2"	Closed	1991	70.00	90
1988	Purrfect Day, 6"	2,000	1991	265.00	455
1992	Raindrops, 1 1/2"	3,750	1994	110.00	110
1992	Raindrops, 4"	1,000	1994	350.00	350
1992	Raindrops, 6"	1,000	1994	640.00	640
1988	School Marm, 6"	2,000	1988	398.00	398
1991	Season's Joy, 1 1/2"	3,750	1991	110.00	115
1991	Season's Joy, 4"	2,000		270.00	350
1991	Season's Joy, 6"	1,000		550.00	690
1990	Seasons Greetings, 1 1/2"	3,750	1991	90.00	95
1990	Seasons Greetings, 4"	2,000		225.00	285
1990	Seasons Greetings, 6"	1,000		450.00	610
1990	Shootin' Hoops, 4"	2,000	1993	220.00	250
1990	Shootin' Hoops, 6"	2,000	1993	440.00	450
1990	Shootin' Hoops, 1 1/2"	3,750	1991	90.00	95
1985	A Special Day, 4"	4,000	1990	95.00	195
1985	A Special Day, 6"	4,000	1990	195.00	325
1984	Special Delivery, 1 1/2"	7,500	1984	45.00	125
1984	Special Delivery, 4"	4,000	1989	95.00	187
1984	Special Delivery, 6"	4,000	1989	195.00	312-350
1990	Spring Fever, 1 1/2"	3,750	1991	90.00	95
1990	Spring Fever, 4"	2,000		225.00	325
1990	Spring Fever, 6"	2,000		450.00	610
1983	Sweeping, 1 1/2"	7,500	1984	45.00	110
1983	Sweeping, 4"	Closed	1987	95.00	230
1983	Sweeping, 6"	4,000	1987	195.00	435
1986	Sweet Treat, 1 1/2"	7,500	1989	45.00	85
1986	Sweet Treat, 4"	4,000	1989	95.00	172
1986	Sweet Treat, 6"	4,000	1989	195.00	312
1996	Sweets for My Sweet, 6"	250		399.00	399
1984	Tag Along, 4"	4,000	1988	95.00	225
1984	Tag Along, 6"	4,000	1988	195.00	290
1984	Tag Along, 1 1/2"	7,500	1984	45.00	130
1989	Take Me Along, 1 1/2"	Closed	1991	85.00	95
1992	Take Me Along, 11"	400		950.00	950
1992	Take Me Along, 20"	100		4550.00	4550
1989	Take Me Along, 4"	2,000		220.00	285
1989	Take Me Along, 6"	1,000		440.00	565
1993	Ten Roses For You, 4"	1,000		290.00	290
1993	Ten Roses For You, 6"	1,000		525.00	525
1990	Tender Loving Care, 1 1/2"	3,750	1991	90.00	95
1990	Tender Loving Care, 4"	2,000	1993	220.00	240
1990	Tender Loving Care, 6"	2,000	1993	440.00	475
1985	Tis the Season, 4"	4,000	1993	95.00	250
1985	Tis the Season, 6"	2,000	1985	210.00	425
1986	To Love and To Cherish, 1 1/2"	7,500	1989	45.00	85
1986	To Love and To Cherish, 11"	1,000	1989	Unkn.	667
1986	To Love and To Cherish, 20"	200	1989	Unkn.	3600
1986	To Love and To Cherish, 4"	4,000	1989	95.00	172
1986	To Love And To Cherish, 6"	4,000	1989	195.00	312
1991	Touch Down, 1 1/2"	3,750	1994	110.00	110
1991	Touch Down, 4"	2,000	1994	270.00	310
1991	Touch Down, 6"	2,000	1994	550.00	550
1992	Tulips For Mother, 4"	1,000		310.00	325
1992	Tulips For Mother, 6"	1,000		590.00	620
1983	Waiting for Mother, 1 1/2"	7,500	1984	45.00	110
1983	Waiting for Mother, 11"	750	1987	495.00	795
1983	Waiting for Mother, 4"	Closed	1987	95.00	230
1983	Waiting for Mother, 6"	4,000	1987	195.00	445
1984	Wake Up Kiss, 1 1/2"	7,500	1984	45.00	550
1984	Wake Up Kiss, 4"	4,000	1993	95.00	195
1983	Wake Up Kiss, 6"	2,000		210.00	550
1984	Watchful Eye, 4"	4,000	1988	95.00	235
1984	Watchful Eye, 6"	4,000	1988	195.00	445
1984	Watchful Eye, 1 1/2"	7,500	1984	45.00	125
1992	Winter Cheer, 4"	2,000	1993	300.00	300
1992	Winter Cheer, 6"	1,000	1993	580.00	580
1991	Winter Surprise, 1 1/2"	3,750	1994	110.00	110
1991	Winter Surprise, 4"	2,000	1994	270.00	290
1991	Winter Surprise, 6"	1,000	1994	550.00	570
1986	With This Ring, 1 1/2"	7,500	1989	45.00	85
1986	With This Ring, 11"	1,000	1989	Unkn.	668
1986	With This Ring, 20"	200	1989	Unkn.	3600
1986	With This Ring, 4"	4,000	1989	95.00	172
1986	With This Ring, 6"	4,000	1989	195.00	312
1989	Yearly Check-Up, 1 1/2"	Closed	1991	85.00	95
1989	Yearly Check-Up, 4"	2,000	1991	190.00	195
1989	Yearly Check-Up, 6"	2,000	1991	390.00	390
1985	Yuletide Cheer, 4"	4,000	1993	95.00	250
1985	Yuletide Cheer, 6"	Closed	1985	210.00	435

Sarah Kay Koalas - S. Kay

1986	Green Thumb, 3"	3,500	1986	81.00	81
1985	Green Thumb, 5"	2,000	1986	165.00	165
1986	Honey Bunch, 3"	3,500	1986	75.00	75
1985	Honey Bunch, 5"	2,000	1986	165.00	165
1985	A Little Bird Told Me, 3"	3,500	1986	75.00	75
1985	A Little Bird Told Me, 5"	2,000	1986	165.00	165
1985	Party Time, 3"	3,500	1986	75.00	75
1985	Party Time, 5"	2,000	1986	165.00	165
1986	Scout About, 3"	3,500	1986	81.00	81
1986	Scout About, 5"	2,000	1986	178.00	178
1986	A Stitch with Love, 3"	3,500	1986	81.00	81
1986	A Stitch with Love, 5"	2,000	1986	178.00	178

Sarah Kay Mini Santas - S. Kay

1992	Father Christmas, 1 1/2"	2,500	1993	110.00	110
1992	A Friend to All, 1 1/2"	2,500	1993	110.00	110
1991	Jolly Santa, 1 1/2"	2,500	1993	110.00	110
1991	Jolly St. Nick, 1 1/2"	2,500	1993	110.00	110
1991	Kris Kringle, 1 1/2"	2,500	1993	110.00	110
1991	Sarah Kay Santa, 1 1/2"	2,500	1993	110.00	110

Sarah Kay Santas - S. Kay

1995	Checking It Twice, 4" 57709	500		250.00	270
1995	Checking It Twice, 6" 57710	250		395.00	450
1992	Father Christmas, 4"	750	1994	350.00	350
1992	Father Christmas, 6"	750	1994	590.00	590
1991	A Friend To All, 4"	750	1994	300.00	300
1991	A Friend To All, 6"	750	1994	590.00	590
1989	Jolly Santa, 12"	150	1990	1300.00	1300
1988	Jolly Santa, 4"	750	1989	235.00	300-350
1988	Jolly Santa, 6"	750	1989	480.00	600
1988	Jolly St. Nick, 4"	750	1989	199.00	300-550
1988	Jolly St. Nick, 6"	750	1989	398.00	850
1990	Kris Kringle Santa, 4"	750	1990	275.00	350
1990	Kris Kringle Santa, 6"	750	1990	550.00	550
1989	Santa, 4"	750	1990	235.00	350
1989	Santa, 6"	750	1990	480.00	480
1996	Workshop Santa, 4"	500		295.00	295
1996	Workshop Santa, 6"	250		495.00	495

Arcadian Pewter, Inc.

Arcade Toys - N. Lindblade

1996	A-Express Truck	10,000		45.95	46
1995	Aeroplane Monocoupe	10,000		45.95	46
1995	Bus-Safety Coach	10,000		45.95	46
1995	Coffee Mill	10,000		49.95	50
1996	Cottage Bank	10,000		29.95	30
1995	Coupe A-Rumble Seat	10,000		49.95	50
1995	Coupe Model T	10,000		45.95	46
1995	Express Flyer Wagon	10,000		45.95	46
1995	Fire Engine Auto	10,000		55.95	56
1995	Firewagon (Horsedrawn)	10,000		69.95	70
1995	Mail Box (Special Edition)	2,500		39.95	40
1996	Motorcycle Cop	10,000		45.95	46
1996	No. 1501 Sedan	10,000		29.95	30
1996	No. 1810 Fire Engine	10,000		45.95	46
1996	Prancing Horse Bank	10,000		39.95	40
1996	Rocking Chair	10,000		29.95	30
1996	Row Crop Truck	10,000		45.95	46
1995	Sedan A Tudor	10,000		45.95	46
1995	Sedan T-Fordor	10,000		45.95	46
1995	State Bank	10,000		49.95	50
1995	Steamboat	10,000		49.95	50
1995	Tractor	10,000		45.95	46
1995	Truck A-Stakes Sides	10,000		45.95	46
1995	Truck T-Stake Sides	10,000		55.95	56
1996	Two-Man Racer	10,000		45.95	46
1996	Wheelbarrow with Toys	10,000		45.95	46

Red Oak II - N. Lindblade

1995	Leapin' Lizard	10,000		89.95	90
1995	Privy	10,000		29.95	30

Armani

G. Armani Society Members Only Figurine - G. Armani

1990	Awakening 591C	Closed	1990	137.50	1000-1250
1991	Ruffles 745E	Closed	1991	139.00	315-400
1992	Ascent 866C	Closed	1992	195.00	250-425
1993	Venus 881C	Closed	1993	225.00	400-500
1993	Lady Rose (Bonus) 197C	Closed	1993	125.00	200-250
1993	Julie (Bonus) 293P	Closed	1993	90.00	135-200
1993	Juliette (Bonus) 294P	Closed	1994	90.00	225-265
1994	Flora 212C	Closed	1994	225.00	300-350
1994	Aquarius (Bonus) 248C	Closed	1994	125.00	125-155
1994	Harlequin (Bonus) 490C	Closed	1994	300.00	350-450
1995	Melody 656C	Closed	1995	250.00	325
1995	Scarlett (Bonus) 698C	Closed	1995	200.00	200-250
1995	Lady w/Doves mini 546C	Closed	1995	Gift	N/A
1995	Arianna (Bonus) 400C	Yr.Iss.		125.00	125
1996	Allegra 345C	Yr.Iss.		250.00	250
1996	Lady Jane (Figurine of the Year) 390C	Yr.Iss.		200.00	200

G. Armani Society Members Only Event - G. Armani

1990	My Fine Feathered Friends (Bonus)122S	Closed	1991	175.00	350
1991	Peace & Harmony (Bonus) 824C	7,500	1992	300.00	325-360
1992	Springtime 961C	Closed	1992	250.00	395-500
1992	Boy w/Dog (Bonus) 407S	Closed	1992	200.00	200
1993	Loving Arms 880E	Closed	1993	250.00	350-400
1994	Daisy 202E	Closed	1994	250.00	325-450
1995	Iris 628E	Closed	1995	250.00	300
1996	Rose 678C	Yr.Iss.		250.00	250

Can-Can Dancers - G. Armani

1989	Two Can-Can Dancers 516C	Closed	1994	820.00	975

Capodimonte - G. Armani

1995	Easy Ride 334C	Open		350.00	350
1995	Easy Ride 334F	Open		220.00	220
1995	Flowers For Sale 333C	Open		500.00	500
1995	Flowers For Sale 333F	Open		300.00	300
1995	Gentle Swing 335C	Open		550.00	550
1995	Gentle Swing 335F	Open		350.00	350
1995	Spring Water 381C	Open		300.00	300
1995	Spring Water 381F	Open		170.00	170
1995	Sweet Apple 369C	Open		600.00	600

Collectors' Information Bureau

*Quotes have been rounded up to nearest dollar

YEAR ISSUE		EDITION LIMIT	YEAR RETD.	ISSUE PRICE	*QUOTE U.S.$
1995	Sweet Apple 369F	Open		420.00	420
1995	Wild Flower 367C	Open		560.00	560
1995	Wild Flower 367F	Open		400.00	400
1995	Young Hearts 679C	1,500		900.00	900

Clown Series - G. Armani

1991	Bust of Clown 725E	5,000		500.00	550
1995	Charlie 644C	Open		175.00	175
1994	The Happy Fiddler 478C	Open		360.00	360
1995	Jerry 643C	Open		200.00	200
1994	Sound the Trumpet 476C	Open		300.00	300

Country Series - G. Armani

1994	Back From the Fields 473F	Open		360.00	360
1993	Boy With Accordion 177C	Open		170.00	170
1993	Boy With Accordion 177F	Open		75.00	75
1993	Boy With Flute 890C	Open		175.00	175
1993	Boy With Flute 890F	Open		90.00	90
1994	Country Girl with Grapes 215C	Open		230.00	230
1994	Country Girl with Grapes 215F	Open		120.00	120
1994	Fresh Fruits 471F	Open		250.00	250
1993	Girl Tending Flowers 466C	Open		210.00	210
1993	Girl With Chicks 889C	Open		155.00	155
1993	Girl With Chicks 889F	Open		75.00	75
1993	Girl With Sheep 178C	Open		150.00	150
1993	Girl With Sheep 178F	Open		65.00	65
1993	Girl w/Wheelbarrow /Flowers 468C	Open		240.00	240
1994	Laundry Girl 214C	Open		230.00	230
1994	Laundry Girl 214F	Open		120.00	120

Etruscan - G. Armani

1993	Lady with Bag 2149E	Retrd. 1996		350.00	365

Florence/Disney - G. Armani

1993	Snow White 209C	Open		425.00	425
1993	Dopey 200C	Open		150.00	150
1994	Sneezy 914C	Open		150.00	150
1994	Sleepy 915C	Open		150.00	150
1994	Bashful 916C	Open		150.00	150
1994	Grumpy 917C	Open		150.00	150
1995	Doc 326C	Open		150.00	150
1995	Happy 327C	Open		150.00	150

Florentine Garden - G. Armani

1995	Wisteria 626C	Open		350.00	350
1995	Wisteria 626F	Open		275.00	275

Four Seasons - G. Armani

1990	Lady on Seashore (Summer) 540C	Open		440.00	440
1990	Lady With Bicycle (Spring) 539C	Open		550.00	550
1992	Lady With Fruit (Summer) 182B	Open		135.00	135
1992	Lady With Fruit (Summer) 182C	Open		275.00	275
1992	Lady With Grapes (Fall) 183C	Open		275.00	275
1992	Lady With Grapes (Fall)182B	Open		135.00	135
1990	Lady w/Ice Skates (Winter) 542C	Open		400.00	400
1992	Lady With Roses (Spring)181B	Open		135.00	135
1992	Lady With Roses (Spring)181C	Open		275.00	275
1990	Lady With Umbrella (Fall) 541C	Open		475.00	475
1992	Lady w/Vegetables (Winter)183B	Open		135.00	135
1992	Lady w/Vegetables (Winter)183C	Open		275.00	275

Galleria Collection: Distinguished Dealers - G. Armani

1996	Eros 406T	1,500		750.00	750
1994	The Falconer 224S	3,000		1000.00	1000
1994	Leda & The Swan 1012T	1,500		500.00	650
1993	The Sea Wave 1006T	1,500	1994	500.00	500
1993	Spring Herald 1009T	1,500	1994	500.00	500
1993	Spring Water 1007T	1,500	1994	500.00	500
1993	Zephyr 1010T	1,500	1994	500.00	500

Garden Series - G. Armani

1994	Lady At Well 222C	Open		275.00	275
1994	Lady At Well 222F	Open		150.00	150
1991	Lady with Cornucopie 870C	10,000	1996	600.00	600
1991	Lady with Harp 874C	10,000	1996	500.00	500
1991	Lady with Peacock 871C	10,000	1996	585.00	585
1991	Lady with Violin 872C	10,000	1996	560.00	560

Golden Age - G. Armani

1995	Christine 348C	Open		300.00	300
1995	Christine 348F	Open		200.00	200
1995	Claire 654C	Open		250.00	250
1995	Claire 654F	Open		100.00	100
1995	Dear Friends 532F	Open		100.00	100
1995	Eloise 350C	Open		285.00	285
1995	Eloise 350F	Open		170.00	170
1995	Florence 535C	Open		250.00	250
1995	Florence 535F	Open		155.00	155
1996	Fragrance 340C	3,000		500.00	500
1996	Fragrance 340F	Open		300.00	300
1995	Gloria 655C	Open		250.00	250
1995	Gloria 655F	Open		100.00	100
1995	Love and Peace 538C	Open		125.00	125
1996	Promenade 339C	3,000		600.00	600
1996	Promenade 339F	Open		400.00	400
1995	Serena 349C	Open		300.00	300
1995	Serena 349F	Open		200.00	200
1996	Soiree 338C	3,000		600.00	600
1996	Soiree 338F	Open		350.00	350
1996	Spring Morning 337C	3,000		600.00	600
1996	Spring Morning 337F	Open		370.00	370

YEAR ISSUE		EDITION LIMIT	YEAR RETD.	ISSUE PRICE	*QUOTE U.S.$
1995	Stormy Weather 533C	Open		260.00	260
1995	Stormy Weather 533F	Open		135.00	135
1995	Sunday Drive 531C	Open		275.00	275
1995	Sunday Drive 531F	Open		140.00	140
1995	Sunshine Dream 529C	Open		165.00	165
1995	Sunshine Dream 529F	Open		90.00	90
1995	Sweet Dreams 536C	Open		225.00	225
1995	Sweet Dreams 536F	Open		135.00	135
1995	Vanessa 347C	Open		350.00	350
1995	Vanessa 347F	Open		220.00	220

Gulliver's World - G. Armani

1994	The Barrel 659T	1,000		225.00	225
1994	Cowboy 657T	1,000	1995	125.00	125
1994	Getting Clean 661T	1,000		130.00	130
1994	Ray of Moon 658T	1,000		100.00	100
1994	Serenade 660T	1,000		200.00	200

Gypsy Series - G. Armani

1994	Esmeralda-Gypsy Girl 198C	Open		400.00	400
1994	Esmeralda-Gypsy Girl 198F	Open		215.00	215

Impressions - G. Armani

1990	Bittersweet 528P	Retrd. 1993		275.00	350-375
1990	Masquerade 527P	Retrd. 1993		300.00	325

Little Treasures - G. Armani

1994	Bathtime 357T	Open		50.00	50
1994	Clean Sweep 373T	Open		50.00	50
1994	Girl at the Telephone 364T	Open		50.00	50
1994	Girl with Ice Cream 365T	Open		50.00	50
1994	Little Fisher Boy 362T	Open		37.00	37
1994	Playing the Piano 376T	Open		50.00	50
1994	Sweet Dreams 360T	Open		35.00	35
1994	A Woman's Work 363T	Open		50.00	50

Masterworks - G. Armani

1996	Aurora 680C	1,500		3500.00	3500

Moonlight Masquerade - G. Armani

1990	Harlequin Lady 740C	7,500	1994	450.00	465
1990	Lady Clown with Cane 742C	7,500	1994	390.00	415
1990	Lady Clown with Doll 743C	7,500	1994	410.00	410
1990	Lady Pierrot 741C	7,500	1994	390.00	490
1990	Queen of Hearts 744C	7,500	1994	450.00	595

Motherhood - G. Armani

1994	Black Maternity 502C	5,000		500.00	500
1994	Black Maternity 502F	Open		335.00	335
1993	Garden Maternity 188C	Open		210.00	210
1993	Garden Maternity 188F	Open		115.00	115
1994	Kneeling Maternity 216C	Open		275.00	275
1994	Kneeling Maternity 216F	Open		135.00	135
1993	Maternity Embracing 190C	Open		250.00	250
1993	Maternity Embracing 190F	Open		160.00	160
1994	Mother & Child 470F	Open		150.00	150
1992	Mother with Child (Mother's Day) 185B	Open		235.00	235
1992	Mother with Child (Mother's Day) 185C	Open		400.00	400
1994	Mother's Hand 479F	Open		215.00	215
1993	Mother/Child 792C	Open		385.00	385
1993	Mother/Child 792C	Open		250.00	250
1995	Perfect Love 652C	3,000		1200.00	1200
1995	Perfect Love 652F	Open		800.00	800

My Fair Ladies™ - G. Armani

1995	At Ease 634C	5,000		650.00	650
1995	At Ease 634F	Open		400.00	400
1995	Awaiting 631C	Open		170.00	170
1995	Awaiting 631F	Open		90.00	90
1993	Elegance 195C	5,000	1996	525.00	525
1993	Elegance 195F	Open		300.00	300
1993	Fascination 192C	5,000	1996	500.00	500
1993	Fascination 192F	Open		250.00	250
1987	Flamenco Dancer 389C	5,000		400.00	450
1996	Georgia 414C	5,000		550.00	550
1996	Grace 383C	5,000		475.00	475
1996	In Love 382C	5,000		450.00	450
1995	Isadora 633C	3,000		920.00	920
1995	Isadora 633F	Open		500.00	500
1987	Lady with Book 384C	5,000		300.00	450
1987	Lady with Compact 386C	Retrd. 1993		300.00	750-950
1987	Lady with Fan 387C	5,000		400.00	450
1987	Lady with Fan 387E	Retrd. 1995		400.00	420
1987	Lady with Great Dane 429C	5,000	1996	365.00	475
1987	Lady with Muff 388C	5,000		250.00	450
1989	Lady with Parrot 616C	5,000	1996	400.00	600-1000
1987	Lady with Peacock 385C	Retrd. 1992		380.00	2000-3200
1994	Lady with Umbrella 196C	5,000		335.00	335
1994	Lady with Umbrella 196F	Open		200.00	200
1996	Lara 433C	5,000		450.00	450
1993	Mahogany 194C	5,000	1995	500.00	650-950
1993	Mahogany 194F	Open		360.00	360
1993	Morning Rose 193C	5,000		450.00	450
1993	Morning Rose 193F	Open		225.00	225
1987	Mother & Child 405C	5,000		410.00	550
1995	Promenade 630C	Open		185.00	185
1995	Promenade 630F	Open		90.00	90
1995	Starry Night 632C	Open		185.00	185
1995	Starry Night 632F	Open		90.00	90

Pearls Of The Orient - G. Armani

YEAR ISSUE		EDITION LIMIT	YEAR RETD.	ISSUE PRICE	QUOTE U.S.$
1989	Chu Chu San 612C	10,000	1994	500.00	550
1989	Lotus Blossom 613C	10,000	1994	450.00	475
1989	Madame Butterfly 610C	10,000	1994	450.00	500
1989	Turnadot 611C	10,000	1994	475.00	500

Premiere Ballerina - G. Armani

1988	Ballerina 508C	10,000	1994	430.00	530
1988	Ballerina Group in Flight 518C	7,500	1994	810.00	1000-1200
1988	Ballerina in Flight 503C	10,000	1994	420.00	500
1988	Ballerina with Drape 504C	10,000	1994	450.00	575
1991	Dancer w/Peacock 727C	7,500	1993	460.00	510
1990	Fly Dancer 585F	7,500	1993	190.00	210
1988	Kneeling Ballerina 517C	10,000	1994	325.00	385
1988	Two Ballerinas 515C	7,500	1994	620.00	775

Professionals - G. Armani

1995	Nurse 693C	Open		250.00	250
1995	Nurse 693F	Open		175.00	175
1995	Teacher 694C	Open		310.00	310
1995	Teacher 694F	Open		175.00	175

Religious - G. Armani

1995	The Assumption 697C	5,000		675.00	675
1994	Baby Jesus 1020C	1,000		175.00	175
1987	Choir Boys 900	5,000	1996	350.00	620
1990	Crucifix Plaque 711C	15,000	1996	265.00	265
1987	Crucifix 1158C	10,000	1990	155.00	750-900
1993	Crucifix 786C	7,500		250.00	250
1991	Crucifix 790C	15,000		180.00	180
1996	The Crucifixion 780C	5,000		500.00	500
1994	Donkey 1027C	1,000		185.00	185
1996	The Holy Family 788C	5,000		1000.00	1000
1994	Joseph 1021C	1,000		500.00	500
1994	La Pieta 802C	5,000		950.00	950
1994	La Pieta 802F	Open		550.00	550
1992	Madonna with Child 787B	Open		260.00	260
1992	Madonna with Child 787C	Open		425.00	425
1992	Madonna with Child 787F	Open		265.00	265
1994	Magi King Gold 1023C	1,000		600.00	600
1994	Magi King Incense 1024C	1,000		600.00	600
1994	Magi King Myrrh 1025C	1,000		450.00	450
1994	Mary 1022C	1,000		365.00	365
1995	Moses 606C	2,500		365.00	365
1994	Moses 812C	Open		220.00	220
1994	Moses 812F	Open		115.00	115
1994	Ox 1026C	1,000		300.00	300
1994	Renaissance Crucifix 1017T	5,000		250.00	250

Renaissance - G. Armani

1992	Abundance 870C	5,000		600.00	600
1992	Abundance 870F	Retrd. 1994		420.00	420
1994	Ambrosia 482C	5,000		435.00	435
1994	Angelica 484C	5,000		575.00	575
1992	Aurora-Girl With Doves 884B	Open		220.00	220
1992	Aurora-Girl With Doves 884C	7,500		370.00	370
1991	Bust of Eve 590T	1,000	1991	250.00	550-950
1992	Dawn 874C	5,000		500.00	500
1996	Ebony 372C	5,000		550.00	550
1993	Freedom-Man And Horse 906C	3,000		850.00	850
1992	Liberty-Girl On Horse 903B	Open		450.00	450
1992	Liberty-Girl On Horse 903C	5,000	1996	750.00	750
1992	Lilac & Roses-Girl w/Flowers 882B	Open		220.00	220
1992	Lilac & Roses-Girl w/Flowers 882C	7,500		410.00	410
1992	Twilight 872C	5,000		560.00	560
1992	Vanity 871C	5,000		585.00	585
1993	Wind Song-Girl With Sail 904C	5,000		520.00	520

Romantic - G. Armani

1994	The Embrace 480C	3,000	1996	1450.00	1450
1993	Girl w/Dog At Fence 886C	Open		350.00	350
1993	Girl w/Dog At Fence 886F	Open		175.00	175
1993	Girl With Ducks 887C	Open		320.00	320
1993	Girl With Ducks 887F	Open		160.00	160
1992	Lady with Doves 858E	1,000	1993	250.00	450
1993	Lovers 191C	3,000	1996	450.00	450
1993	Lovers 879C	3,000		570.00	570
1993	Lovers 879F	Open		325.00	325
1993	Lovers On A Swing 942C	Open		410.00	410
1993	Lovers On A Swing 942F	Open		265.00	265
1993	Lovers With Roses 888C	Open		300.00	300
1993	Lovers With Roses 888F	Open		155.00	155
1993	Lovers With Wheelbarrow 891C	Open		370.00	370
1993	Lovers With Wheelbarrow 891F	Open		190.00	190

Romantic Motherhood - G. Armani

1993	Maternity On Swing 941C	Open		360.00	360
1993	Maternity On Swing 941F	Open		220.00	220

Siena Collection - G. Armani

1993	Back From The Fields 1002T	1,000	1995	400.00	450
1994	Country Boy 1014T	2,500		135.00	135
1993	Encountering 1003T	1,000	1995	350.00	370
1993	Fresh Fruit 1001T	2,500	1995	155.00	350
1993	Happy Fiddler 1005T	1,000		225.00	225
1993	Mother's Hand 1008T	2,500		250.00	300-400
1996	Pearl 1019T	1,000		550.00	550
1993	Soft Kiss 1000T	2,500	1995	155.00	250
1993	Sound The Trumpet! 1004T	1,000	1995	225.00	250

---

*Quotes have been rounded up to nearest dollar

Special Issues - G. Armani

Year Issue	Description	Edition Limit	Year Retd.	Issue Price	*Quote U.S.$
1991	Discovery of America Plaque 867C	2,500	1994	400.00	400
1993	Mother's Day Plaque 899C	Closed	1993	100.00	100
1994	Mother's Day Plaque-The Swing 254C	Closed	1994	120.00	120
1995	Mother's Day Plaque -Love/Peace 538C	Closed	1995	125.00	125
1996	Mother's Day Plaque/Mother's Rosebud 341C	Yr.Iss.		150.00	150

Special Times - G. Armani

Year Issue	Description	Edition Limit	Year Retd.	Issue Price	*Quote U.S.$
1982	Card Players (Cheaters) 3280	Open		400.00	1200
1991	Couple in Car 862C	5,000		1000.00	1000
1991	Doctor in Car 848C	2,000	1995	800.00	800
1994	The Encounter 472F	Open		315.00	315
1994	The Fairy Tale 219C	Open		335.00	335
1994	The Fairy Tale 219F	Open		175.00	175
1982	Girl with Chicks 5122E	Suspd.		95.00	165
1982	Girl with Sheep Dog 5117E	Retrd.	1992	100.00	210
1994	Grandpa's Nap 251C	Open		225.00	225
1994	Lady Doctor 249C	Open		200.00	200
1994	Lady Doctor 249F	Open		105.00	105
1994	Lady Graduate-Lawyer 253C	Open		225.00	225
1994	Lady Graduate-Lawyer 253F	Open		120.00	120
1991	Lady with Car 861C	3,000	1995	900.00	900
1994	Old Acquaintance 252C	Open		275.00	275
1982	Shy Kiss 5138E	Retrd.	1992	125.00	285
1982	Sledding 5111E	Retrd.	1992	115.00	250
1982	Soccer Boy 5109	Retrd.	1995	75.00	180
1994	Story Time 250C	Open		275.00	275

Special Walt Disney Production - G. Armani

Year Issue	Description	Edition Limit	Year Retd.	Issue Price	*Quote U.S.$
1992	Cinderella 783C	Retrd.	1992	500.00	3400-4500
1993	Snow White 199C	Retrd.	1993	750.00	1000-1500
1994	Ariel (Little Mermaid) 505C	1,500	1994	750.00	1050-1300
1995	Beauty and the Beast 543C	2,000	1995	975.00	1050-1250
1996	Jasmine & Rajah 410C	1,200		800.00	800

Sports - G. Armani

Year Issue	Description	Edition Limit	Year Retd.	Issue Price	*Quote U.S.$
1992	Lady Equestrian 910C	Open		315.00	315
1992	Lady Equestrian 910F	Open		155.00	155
1992	Lady Golfer 911C	Open		325.00	325
1992	Lady Golfer 911F	Open		170.00	170
1992	Lady Skater 913C	Open		300.00	300
1992	Lady Skater 913F	Open		170.00	170
1992	Lady Tennis 912C	Retrd.	1996	275.00	275
1992	Lady Tennis 912F	Open		175.00	175

Terra Cotta - G. Armani

Year Issue	Description	Edition Limit	Year Retd.	Issue Price	*Quote U.S.$
1994	Ambrosia 1013T	Open		275.00	275
1994	Angelica 1016T	Open		450.00	450
1994	Country Boy w/Mushrooms 1014T	2,500		135.00	135
1994	The Embrace 1011T	Open		930.00	930
1994	La Pieta 1015T	Open		550.00	550

Vanity - G. Armani

Year Issue	Description	Edition Limit	Year Retd.	Issue Price	*Quote U.S.$
1992	Beauty at the Mirror 850P	Retrd.	1994	300.00	325
1992	Beauty w/Perfume 853P	Retrd.	1994	370.00	380

Via Veneto - G. Armani

Year Issue	Description	Edition Limit	Year Retd.	Issue Price	*Quote U.S.$
1995	Alessandra 648C	5,000		370.00	370
1995	Marina 649C	5,000		475.00	475
1995	Nicole 651C	5,000		515.00	515
1995	Valentina 647C	5,000		420.00	420

Wedding - G. Armani

Year Issue	Description	Edition Limit	Year Retd.	Issue Price	*Quote U.S.$
1994	Black Bride 500C	Open		170.00	170
1994	Black Bride 500F	Open		115.00	115
1994	Black Wedding Waltz 501C	3,000		750.00	750
1994	Black Wedding Waltz 501F	Open		450.00	450
1988	Bride & Groom Wedding 475P	Open		270.00	285
1994	Bride With Column & Vase 488C	Open		260.00	260
1994	Bride With Column & Vase 488F	Open		200.00	200
1992	Bride With Doves 885C	Open		280.00	280
1992	Bride With Doves 885F	Open		220.00	220
1994	Bride With Flower Vase 489C	Open		135.00	135
1994	Bride With Flower Vase 489F	Open		90.00	90
1993	Carriage Wedding 902C	2,500		1000.00	1000
1993	Carriage Wedding 902F	Open		500.00	500
1993	Garden Wedding 189C	Open		225.00	225
1993	Garden Wedding 189F	Open		120.00	120
1989	Just Married 827C	5,000		950.00	1000
1996	Tenderness 418C	5,000		950.00	950
1996	Tomorrow's Dream 336C	5,000		700.00	700
1987	Wedding Couple 407C	Open		525.00	550
1982	Wedding Couple 5132	Open		110.00	190
1991	Wedding Couple At Threshold 813C	7,500		400.00	400
1993	Wedding Couple At Wall 201C	Open		225.00	225
1993	Wedding Couple At Wall 201F	Open		115.00	115
1993	Wedding Couple Forever 791F	Open		250.00	250
1991	Wedding Couple Kissing 815C	7,500		500.00	500
1991	Wedding Couple w/Bicycle 814C	7,500		600.00	600
1993	Wedding Flowers To Mary 187C	Open		225.00	225
1993	Wedding Flowers To Mary 187F	Open		115.00	115
1994	Wedding Waltz 493C	3,000		750.00	750
1994	Wedding Waltz 493F	Open		450.00	450

Wildlife - G. Armani

Year Issue	Description	Edition Limit	Year Retd.	Issue Price	*Quote U.S.$
1988	Bird Of Paradise 454S	5,000		475.00	500
1990	Bird of Paradise 718S	5,000	1996	550.00	575
1996	Companions (2 Collies) 302S	3,000		900.00	900
1993	Doves With Vase 204S	3,000	1996	375.00	375
1983	Eagle Bird of Prey 3213	Open		210.00	425
1995	Elegance in Nature (Herons) 226S	3,000		1000.00	1000
1996	Feed Us! (Mother/Baby Owls) 305S	1,500		950.00	950
1991	Flamingo 713S	5,000		420.00	420
1991	Flying Duck 839S	5,000		470.00	470
1993	Galloping Horse 905S	7,500		465.00	465
1991	Great Argus Pheasant 717S	3,000	1996	600.00	600
1993	Horse Head 205S	Open		140.00	140
1996	The Hunt 290S	3,000		850.00	850
1991	Large Owl 842S	5,000		520.00	520
1996	Lone Wolf 284S	3,000		600.00	600
1996	Mid Night (Wolf) 285S	3,000		550.00	550
1995	Midnight 284S	3,000		600.00	600
1996	Night Vigil (Owl) 306S	3,000		1050.00	1050
1996	Nocturne 976S	1,500		1000.00	1000
1993	Parrot with Vase 736S	3,000	1996	460.00	460
1988	Peacock 455S	5,000		600.00	675
1988	Peacock 458S	5,000		630.00	700
1993	Peacock with Vase 735S	3,000		375.00	375
1996	Proud Watch (Lion) 278S	1,500		700.00	700
1993	Rearing Horse 909S	7,500		515.00	515
1983	Royal Eagle with Babies 3553	Open		215.00	400
1994	Running Free (Greyhounds) 972S	3,000		870.00	870
1993	Show Horse 907S	7,500		550.00	550
1993	Silent Watch (Mtn. Lion) 291S	Open		700.00	700
1982	Snow Bird 5548	Open		100.00	180
1993	Soaring Eagle 970S	5,000	1996	620.00	700
1991	Swan 714S	5,000		550.00	550
1990	Three Doves 996S	5,000		670.00	750
1996	Vantage Point (Eagle) 270S	3,000		600.00	600
1996	Wild Hearts (Horses) 282S	3,000		2000.00	2000
1996	Wisdom (Owl) 281S	3,000		1250.00	1250
1995	Wisdom 281S	3,000		1250.00	1250

Yesteryears - G. Armani

Year Issue	Description	Edition Limit	Year Retd.	Issue Price	*Quote U.S.$
1993	Country Doctor In Car 848C	2,000	1995	800.00	800
1994	Summertime-Lady on Swing 485C	5,000		650.00	650
1994	Summertime-Lady on Swing 485F	Open		450.00	450

Zodiac Collection - G. Armani

Year Issue	Description	Edition Limit	Year Retd.	Issue Price	*Quote U.S.$
1996	Aquarius 426C	5,000		600.00	600
1996	Gemini 427C	5,000		600.00	600
1996	Virgo 425C	5,000		600.00	600

Armstrong's

Armstrong's/Ron Lee - R. Skelton

Year Issue	Description	Edition Limit	Year Retd.	Issue Price	*Quote U.S.$
1984	Captain Freddie	7,500		85.00	350-450
1984	Freddie the Torchbearer	7,500		110.00	375-450

Happy Art - W. Lantz

Year Issue	Description	Edition Limit	Year Retd.	Issue Price	*Quote U.S.$
1982	Woody's Triple Self-Portrait	5,000		95.00	325

Pro Autographed Ceramic Baseball Card Plaque - Unknown

Year Issue	Description	Edition Limit	Year Retd.	Issue Price	*Quote U.S.$
1985	Brett, Garvey, Jackson, Rose, Seaver, auto, 3-1/4X5	1,000		150.00	250

The Red Skelton Collection - R. Skelton

Year Issue	Description	Edition Limit	Year Retd.	Issue Price	*Quote U.S.$
1981	Clem Kadiddlehopper	7,500		75.00	150
1981	Freddie in the Bathtub	7,500		80.00	100
1981	Freddie on the Green	7,500		80.00	150
1981	Freddie the Freeloader	7,500		70.00	150
1981	Jr., The Mean Widdle Kid	7,500		75.00	150
1981	San Fernando Red	7,500		75.00	150
1981	Sheriff Deadeye	7,500		75.00	150

The Red Skelton Porcelain Plaque - R. Skelton

Year Issue	Description	Edition Limit	Year Retd.	Issue Price	*Quote U.S.$
1991	All American	1,500		495.00	1500
1994	Another Day	1,994		675.00	725-800
1992	Independance Day?	1,500		525.00	600-800
1993	Red & Freddie Both Turned 80	1,993		595.00	1200-1500

Artaffects

Members Only Limited Edition Redemption Offerings - G. Perillo

Year Issue	Description	Edition Limit	Year Retd.	Issue Price	*Quote U.S.$
1983	Apache Brave (Bust)	Closed		50.00	150
1986	Painted Pony	Closed		125.00	175
1991	Chief Crazy Horse	Closed		195.00	250

Limited Edition Free Gifts to Members - G. Perillo

Year Issue	Description	Edition Limit	Year Retd.	Issue Price	*Quote U.S.$
1986	Dolls	Closed		Gift	35
1991	Sunbeam	Closed		Gift	35
1992	Little Shadow	Closed		Gift	35

The Chieftains - G. Perillo

Year Issue	Description	Edition Limit	Year Retd.	Issue Price	*Quote U.S.$
1983	Crazy Horse	5,000		65.00	200
1983	Geronimo	5,000		65.00	135
1983	Joseph	5,000		65.00	250
1983	Red Cloud	5,000		65.00	275
1983	Sitting Bull	5,000		65.00	200

Pride of America's Indians - G. Perillo

Year Issue	Description	Edition Limit	Year Retd.	Issue Price	*Quote U.S.$
1988	Brave and Free	10-day		50.00	150
1989	Dark Eyed Friends	10-day		45.00	75
1989	Kindred Spirits	10-day		45.00	50
1989	Loyal Alliance	10-day		45.00	75
1989	Noble Companions	10-day		45.00	50
1989	Peaceful Comrades	10-day		45.00	50
1989	Small & Wise	10-day		45.00	50
1989	Winter Scouts	10-day		45.00	50

Special Issue - G. Perillo

Year Issue	Description	Edition Limit	Year Retd.	Issue Price	*Quote U.S.$
1984	Apache Boy Bust	Closed	N/A	40.00	75
1984	Apache Girl Bust	Closed	N/A	40.00	75
1985	Lovers	Closed	N/A	70.00	125
1984	Papoose	325		500.00	500
1982	The Peaceable Kingdom	950		750.00	750

The Storybook Collection - G. Perillo

Year Issue	Description	Edition Limit	Year Retd.	Issue Price	*Quote U.S.$
1981	Cinderella	10,000		65.00	95
1982	Goldilocks & 3 Bears	10,000		80.00	110
1982	Hansel and Gretel	10,000		80.00	110
1980	Little Red Ridinghood	10,000		65.00	95

The Tribal Ponies - G. Perillo

Year Issue	Description	Edition Limit	Year Retd.	Issue Price	*Quote U.S.$
1984	Arapaho	1,500		65.00	175-200
1984	Comanche	1,500		65.00	175-200
1984	Crow	1,500		65.00	175-200

The War Pony - G. Perillo

Year Issue	Description	Edition Limit	Year Retd.	Issue Price	*Quote U.S.$
1983	Apache War Pony	495		150.00	175-200
1983	Nez Perce War Pony	495		150.00	175-200
1983	Sioux War Pony	495		150.00	175-200

Artists of the World

DeGrazia Annual Christmas Collection - T. DeGrazia

Year Issue	Description	Edition Limit	Year Retd.	Issue Price	*Quote U.S.$
1992	Feliz Navidad	1,992		195.00	225
1993	Fiesta Angels	1,993	1995	295.00	300-400
1994	Littlest Angel	1,994		165.00	165
1995	Bethlehem Bound	1,995		195.00	195
1996	Christmas Serenade	1,996		145.00	145

DeGrazia Figurine - T. DeGrazia

Year Issue	Description	Edition Limit	Year Retd.	Issue Price	*Quote U.S.$
1990	Alone	S/O	N/A	395.00	475-595
1988	Beautiful Burden	Closed	1990	175.00	250-300
1990	Biggest Drum	Closed	1992	110.00	130
1986	The Blue Boy	Suspd.		70.00	130
1990	Crucifixion	S/O	1995	295.00	350
1990	Desert Harvest	S/O	N/A	135.00	150
1986	Festival Lights	Suspd.		75.00	110
1984	Flower Boy	Closed	1992	65.00	250-300
1988	Flower Boy Plaque	Closed	1990	80.00	110
1984	Flower Girl	Suspd.		65.00	250
1984	Flower Girl Plaque	Closed	1985	45.00	85
1985	Little Madonna	Closed	1993	80.00	250-300
1988	Los Ninos	S/O	N/A	595.00	1200-1500
1989	Los Ninos (Artist's Edition)	S/O	N/A	695.00	2000-3500
1987	Love Me	Closed	1992	95.00	200-350
1988	Merrily, Merrily, Merrily	Closed	1991	95.00	230
1989	My First Arrow	Closed	1992	95.00	250-300
1984	My First Horse	Closed	1990	65.00	250-300
1990	Navajo Boy	Closed	1992	110.00	150-300
1992	Navajo Madonna	Closed	1993	135.00	200
1991	Navajo Mother	3,500	1995	295.00	325
1985	Pima Drummer Boy	Closed	1991	65.00	200-300
1984	Sunflower Boy	Closed	1985	65.00	300
1990	Sunflower Girl	Closed	1993	95.00	200
1987	Wee Three	Closed	1990	180.00	200-300
1984	White Dove	Closed	1992	45.00	150
1984	Wondering	Closed	1987	85.00	280

DeGrazia Nativity Collection - T. DeGrazia

Year Issue	Description	Edition Limit	Year Retd.	Issue Price	*Quote U.S.$
1988	Christmas Prayer Angel (red)	Closed	1991	70.00	295
1990	El Burrito	Closed	N/A	60.00	90-125
1990	Little Prayer Angel (white)	Closed	1992	85.00	300
1989	Two Little Lambs	Closed	1992	70.00	220-300

DeGrazia Pendants - R. Olszewski

Year Issue	Description	Edition Limit	Year Retd.	Issue Price	*Quote U.S.$
1987	Festival of Lights 562-P	Suspd.		90.00	275
1985	Flower Girl Pendant 561-P	Suspd.		125.00	200

DeGrazia Village Collection - T. DeGrazia

Year Issue	Description	Edition Limit	Year Retd.	Issue Price	*Quote U.S.$
1992	The Listener	Closed	1992	48.00	75
1992	Little Feather	Closed	1992	53.00	53
1992	Medicine Man	Closed	1995	75.00	75
1992	Standing Tall	Closed	1996	65.00	65
1992	Telling Tales	Closed	1995	48.00	75
1992	Tiny Treasure	Closed	1995	53.00	53
1993	Water Wagon	Closed	1995	295.00	295

DeGrazia: Goebel Miniatures - R. Olszewski

Year Issue	Description	Edition Limit	Year Retd.	Issue Price	*Quote U.S.$
1988	Adobe Display 948D	Suspd.		45.00	60-90
1990	Adobe Hacienda (lg.) Display 958-D	Suspd.		85.00	95-150
1989	Beautiful Burden 554-P	Suspd.		110.00	110-150
1990	Chapel Display 971-D	Suspd.		95.00	125
1986	Festival of Lights 507-P	Suspd.		85.00	145-200
1985	Flower Boy 502-P	Suspd.		85.00	145-200
1985	Flower Girl 501-P	Suspd.		85.00	145-200
1986	Little Madonna 552-P	Suspd.		93.00	225
1989	Merry Little Indian 508-P (new style)	Suspd.		110.00	150-175
1987	Merry Little Indian 508-P (old style)	Closed		95.00	250-300
1991	My Beautiful Rocking Horse 555-P	Suspd.		110.00	175-200
1985	My First Horse 503-P	Suspd.		85.00	150-165
1986	Pima Drummer Boy 506-P	Suspd.		85.00	250-300
1985	Sunflower Boy 551- P	Suspd.		93.00	165

YEAR ISSUE	EDITION LIMIT	YEAR RETD.	ISSUE PRICE	*QUOTE U.S.$
1985 White Dove 504-P	Suspd.		80.00	125
1985 Wondering 505-P	Suspd.		93.00	150-175

Autom

Lisi Martin Resin - L. Martin

1995 Barefoot Buddies	Open		38.00	38
1995 Celebrate The Season	Open		29.00	29
1995 Come Let Us Adore Him	Open		36.00	36
1995 Dress Rehearsal	Open		32.00	32
1995 First Love	Open		38.00	38
1995 Garden Secrets	Open		38.00	38
1995 Gifts Galore	Open		38.00	38
1995 Greetings	Open		34.00	34
1995 Just Friends	Open		38.00	38
1995 Mother's Little Helper	Open		36.00	36
1995 My First Kitten	Open		29.00	29
1995 Nap Time	Open		36.00	36
1996 Newborn Baby	1996		49.00	49
1995 Pampered Puppies	Open		38.00	38
1995 Peaceful Glow	Open		34.00	34
1995 Playful Pals	Open		36.00	36
1995 Sing A Song Of Joy	Open		29.00	29
1995 Snowy Sleigh Ride	Open		34.00	34
1995 Springtime Friends	Open		14.50	15
1995 Study Break	Open		36.00	36
1995 Wrapped In Love	Open		36.00	36

Lisi Martin Wood - L. Martin

1990 Come Let Us Adore Him	5,000		240.00	240
1990 Garden Secrets	5,000		195.00	195
1990 Littlest Santa	5,000		195.00	195
1990 Mother's Little Helper	5,000		195.00	195
1990 My First Kitten	5,000		220.00	220
1990 Peaceful Glow	5,000		195.00	195
1990 Sleepyhead	5,000		220.00	220
1990 Snowy Sleigh Ride	5,000		220.00	220
1990 Springtime Friends	5,000		195.00	195
1990 Springtime Shower	5,000		195.00	195
1990 Study Break	5,000		220.00	220
1990 Wrapped In Love	5,000		220.00	220

Lisi Water Globes - L. Martin

1995 Birdland Cafe	Open		39.00	39
1995 Littlest Santa	Open		39.00	39
1995 My First Kitten	Open		39.00	39
1995 Pampered Puppies	Open		39.00	39
1995 Playful Pals	Open		39.00	39
1995 Snowy Sleigh Ride	Open		39.00	39

Matteo Nativity Resin - Matteo Comploi

1995 Baby Jesus	Open		14.95	15
1995 Black Wise Man	Open		29.95	30
1995 Camel	Open		39.95	40
1995 Camel Driver	Open		29.95	30
1995 Gloria Angel	Open		29.95	30
1995 Gray Donkey	Open		29.95	30
1995 Joseph	Open		29.95	30
1995 Kneeling Shepherd	Open		29.95	30
1995 Kneeling Wise Man	Open		29.95	30
1995 Mary	Open		29.95	30
1995 Ox	Open		14.95	15
1995 Ram	Open		14.95	15
1995 Shepherd w/ Bagpipes	Open		29.95	30
1995 Shepherd w/ Ducks	Open		29.95	30
1995 Shepherd w/Hat	Open		29.95	30
1995 Shepherdess w/ Basket	Open		29.95	30
1995 Shepherdess w/Boy	Open		29.95	30
1995 Standing Sheep	Open		14.95	15
1995 Wise Man	Open		29.95	30

Band Creations, Inc.

"America's County Barns" - Band Creations

1996 Double Crib Barn	Open		29.95	30
1996 Dutch Barn	Open		29.95	30
1996 English Barn	Open		29.95	30
1996 Gambrel Roof Barn	Open		29.95	30
1996 Log Barn	Open		29.95	30
1996 Pennsylvania Dutch Barn	Open		29.95	30
1996 Polygonal Barn	Open		29.95	30
1996 Round Barn	Open		29.95	30

"America's Covered Bridges" - Band Creations

1995 Billie Creek, Parke County, IN	Open		29.95	30
1995 Bridge at the Green, Bennington County, VT	Open		29.95	30
1995 Bunker Hill, Catawba County, NC	Open		29.95	30
1995 Burfordville, Cape Giradeai County, MO	Open		39.95	40
1995 Cedar Creek, Ozaukee County, WI	Open		29.95	30
1995 Chiselville, Bennington County, VT	Open		29.95	30
1995 Elder's Mill, Oconee County, GA	Open		29.95	30
1995 Elizabethton, Carter County, TN	Open		29.95	30
1995 Fallasburg, Kent County, MI	Open		29.95	30
1995 Gilliland, Etowah County, AL	Open		29.95	30
1995 Humpback, Allegheny County, VA	Open		29.95	30
1995 Knox, Chester County, PA	Open		29.95	30
1995 Narrows, Parke County, IN	Open		29.95	30
1995 Old Blenheim, Schoharie County, NY	Open		39.95	40

1995 Philippi, Barbour County, WV	Open		39.95	40
1995 Roberts, Preble County, OH	Open		29.95	30
1995 Robyville, Penobscot County, ME	Open		29.95	30
1995 Roseman, Madison County, IA	Open		29.95	30
1995 Shimenak, Linn County, OR	Open		29.95	30
1995 Thompson Mill, Shelly County, IL	Open		29.95	30
1995 Wawona, Mariposa County, CA	Open		29.95	30
1995 Zumbrota, Goodhue County, MN	Open		29.95	30

Best Friends Angel Pins - Richards/Penfield

1996 Angel on Your Shoulder	Open		5.00	5
1996 Aunt	Open		5.00	5
1996 Childcare Angel	Open		5.00	5
1995 Daughter	Open		5.00	5
1996 Daughter-in-law	Open		5.00	5
1995 Friend	Open		5.00	5
1995 Grandmother	Open		5.00	5
1996 Mom-to-Be	Open		5.00	5
1995 Mother	Open		5.00	5
1995 Nurse	Open		5.00	5
1996 Secret Pal	Open		5.00	5
1995 Sister	Open		5.00	5
1996 Sweetheart	Open		5.00	5
1995 Teacher	Open		5.00	5
1995 Teammate	Open		5.00	5
1996 Volunteer	Open		5.00	5

Best Friends-Angel Wishes - Richards/Penfield

1994 Anniversary	Open		12.00	12
1994 Best Wishes	Open		12.00	12
1994 Bride and Groom	Open		12.00	12
1994 Congratulations	Open		12.00	12
1994 Create A Wish	Open		12.00	12
1994 Get Well	Open		12.00	12
1994 Good Luck	Open		12.00	12
1994 Happy Birthday	Open		12.00	12
1994 Inspirational	Open		12.00	12
1994 New Baby	Open		12.00	12

Best Friends-Angels Of The Month - Richards/Penfield

1993 January	Open		10.00	10
1993 February	Open		10.00	10
1993 March	Open		10.00	10
1993 April	Open		10.00	10
1993 May	Open		10.00	10
1993 June	Open		10.00	10
1993 July	Open		10.00	10
1993 August	Open		10.00	10
1993 September	Open		10.00	10
1993 October	Open		10.00	10
1993 November	Open		10.00	10
1993 December	Open		10.00	10

Best Friends-Celebrate Around the World Santas - Richards/Penfield

1996 England	Open		12.00	12
1996 Germany	Open		12.00	12
1996 Mexico	Open		12.00	12
1996 Norway	Open		12.00	12
1996 Russia	Open		12.00	12
1996 United States (African American)	Open		12.00	12
1996 United States (white)	Open		12.00	12

Best Friends-Celebrate Around the World Trees - Richards/Penfield

1996 Around the World Tree	Open		18.00	18
1996 British Tree	Open		19.50	20
1996 Germany Tree	Open		19.50	20
1996 Scandinavian Tree	Open		19.50	20
1996 United States Tree	Open		19.50	20

Best Friends-Christmas Pageant - Richards/Penfield

1996 Angel-peace/joy	Open		6.00	6
1996 Bench	Open		4.00	4
1996 Boy with Star	Open		6.00	6
1996 Donkey	Open		4.00	4
1996 Girl with Tree	Open		6.00	6
1996 Joseph	Open		6.00	6
1996 Mary and Baby Jesus	Open		6.00	6
1996 Sheep	Open		4.00	4
1996 Sign	Open		4.00	4
1996 Stage	Open		14.00	14
1996 Christmas Pageant 10 pc set	Open		60.00	60

Best Friends-Earth Angels - Richards/Penfield

1996 Angel Potsitter Bird Nest	Open		10.00	10
1996 Angel Potsitter Front	Open		8.00	8
1996 Angel Potsitter Left	Open		9.00	9
1996 Angel with Aster	Open		10.00	10
1996 Angel with Calendula	Open		10.00	10
1996 Angel with Carnation	Open		10.00	10
1996 Angel with Chrysanthemum	Open		10.00	10
1996 Angel with Gladiolous	Open		10.00	10
1996 Angel with Jonquil	Open		10.00	10
1996 Angel with Larkspur	Open		10.00	10
1996 Angel with Lily of the Valley	Open		10.00	10
1996 Angel with Narcissus	Open		10.00	10
1996 Angel with Rose	Open		10.00	10
1996 Angel with Sweet Pea	Open		10.00	10
1996 Angel with Violet	Open		10.00	10

Best Friends-First Friends Begin At Childhood - Richards/Penfield

1993 Castles In The Sand (4 pc set)	Retrd.	1996	16.00	16
1993 Checking It Twice (2 pc set)	Retrd.	1996	15.00	15
1993 Dad's Best Pal	Retrd.	1996	15.00	15
1993 Feathered Friends	Retrd.	1996	13.00	13
1993 Fishing Friends	Retrd.	1996	18.00	18
1993 Grandma's Favorite	Retrd.	1996	15.00	15
1993 My "Beary" Best Friend	Retrd.	1996	12.00	12
1993 My Best Friend (2 pc set)	Retrd.	1996	24.00	24
1993 Oh So Pretty	Retrd.	1996	14.00	14
1993 Purr-Fit Friends	Retrd.	1996	12.00	12
1993 Quiet Time	Retrd.	1996	15.00	15
1993 Rainbow Of Friends	Retrd.	1996	24.00	24
1993 Santa's First Visit	Retrd.	1996	15.00	15
1993 Santa's Surprise	Retrd.	1996	14.00	14
1993 Sharing Is Caring	Retrd.	1996	12.00	12
1993 A Wagon Full Of Fun (2 pc set)	Retrd.	1996	15.00	15

Best Friends-Happy Hearts - Richards/Penfield

1996 Angels in the Snow	Open		35.00	35
1996 Best Friends	Open		35.00	35
1996 A Guiding Star	Open		35.00	35
1996 Just Married	Open		35.00	35
1996 Making New Friends	Open		35.00	35
1996 Thanksgiving Friends	Open		35.00	35

Best Friends-Heavenly Helpers - Richards/Penfield

1996 Childcare	Open		12.00	12
1996 Emergency Medical Team	Open		12.00	12
1996 Fireman	Open		12.00	12
1996 Nurse	Open		12.00	12
1996 Policeman	Open		12.00	12
1996 Teacher	Open		12.00	12
1996 Volunteer	Open		12.00	12

Best Friends-Noah's Ark - Richards/Penfield

1995 Animals (set of 10)	Open		20.00	20
1995 Noah's Ark & Raft	Open		42.00	42
1996 Noah's Ark Pin	Open		4.95	5

Best Friends-O Joyful Night Nativity - Richards/Penfield

1994 3 Kings (set/3)	Open		18.00	18
1994 Angel on Stable (wall)	Open		16.00	16
1996 Camel	Open		6.00	6
1994 Camel and Donkey (set/2)	Retrd.	1996	8.00	8
1995 Camel Standing	Open		6.00	6
1996 Cow	Open		4.00	4
1996 Donkey	Open		4.00	4
1994 Holy Family (Joseph, Mary & Jesus)	Open		16.00	16
1994 Shepherd Boy	Retrd.	1996	8.00	8
1995 Shepherd with Sheep (set/7)	Open		8.00	8

Best Friends-Rainbow of Friends - Richards/Penfield

1996 Rainbow of Friends	Open		24.00	24
1996 Rainbow of Friends, music Box	Open		17.50	18

Best Friends-RiverSong - Richards/Penfield

1994 3 Assorted Carolers	Open		22.00	22
1995 Brick House	Open		19.95	20
1993 Carolers Set (3 carolers, 1 lamp post, 1 dog)	Open		30.00	30
1995 Church	Open		19.95	20
1995 Double Angels	Open		8.00	8
1995 Gingerbread House	Open		19.95	20
1995 Skaters Sitting (set/2)	Open		12.00	12
1995 Skaters Standing (set/2)	Open		12.00	12
1995 Snowball Fight (set/3)	Open		15.00	15
1995 Snowmen (set/3)	Open		12.95	13
1995 Stucco House	Open		19.95	20
1995 Wood House	Open		19.95	20

Best Friends-Winter Wonderland - Richards/Penfield

1994 3 Assorted White Trees	Open		18.00	18
1994 Accessories; rabbits, teddies, presents (set/3)	Open		4.00	4
1994 Mr. Santa	Open		9.00	9
1994 Mrs. Santa	Open		9.00	9
1994 Reindeer (1 standing, 1 sitting) (set/2)	Open		10.00	10

Country Time Clocks - Band Creations

1996 Cow	Open		23.95	24
1996 Hen	Open		23.95	24
1996 Home Sweet Home	Open		29.50	30
1996 Pig	Open		23.95	24
1996 Water Can	Open		23.95	24

Bing & Grondahl

Centennial Anniversary Commemoratives - F.A. Hallin

1995 Centennial Vase: Behind the Frozen Window	1,250	1995	295.00	295

Boyds Collection Ltd.

The Bearstone Collection ™ - G.M. Lowenthal

1994 Agatha & Shelly-'Scardy Cat' 2246	Open		16.25	17-60

YEAR ISSUE		EDITION LIMIT	YEAR RETRD.	ISSUE PRICE	*QUOTE U.S.$
1995	Amelia's Enterprise 'Carrot Juice' 2258	Open		16.25	17-55
1995	Angelica...'the Guardian' 2266	Open		17.95	18-45
1995	Angelica...the Guardian Angel Water Globe 2702	Open		37.50	38-50
1993	Arthur...with Red Scarf 2003-03	Retrd.	1994	10.50	50-110
1994	Bailey & Emily...'Forever Friends' 2018	12/96		34.10	34-100
1994	Bailey & Wixie 'To Have and To Hold' 2017	Open		15.75	16-150
1994	Bailey at the Beach 2020-09	Retrd.	1995	15.75	90-125
1993	Bailey Bear with Suitcase (old version) 2000	Retrd.	1993	14.20	285-375
1993	Bailey Bear with Suitcase (revised version) 2000	Open		14.20	15-90
1994	Bailey's Birthday 2014	Open		15.95	16-100
1995	Bailey...'The Baker with Sweetie Pie' 2254	Open		12.50	13-55
1995	Bailey...'The Baker with Sweetie Pie' 2254CL	3,600	1995	15.00	150-225
1995	Bailey...'the Cheerleader' 2268	Open		15.95	16-50
1995	Bailey...'The Honeybear' 2260	Open		15.75	16-70
1996	Bailey...Heart's Desire 2272	Open		15.00	15-65
1993	Bailey...in the Orchard 2006	12/96		14.20	15-150
1995	Baldwin...as the Child 2403	Open		14.95	15
1994	Bessie the Santa Cow 2239	12/96		15.75	16-60
1993	Byron & Chedda w/Catmint 2010	Retrd.	1994	14.20	45-100
1994	Celeste...'The Angel Rabbit' 2230	Open		16.25	17-150
1994	Charlotte & Bebe...'The Gardeners' 2229	Retrd.	1995	15.75	45-85
1993	Christian by the Sea 2012	Open		14.20	15-75
1994	Clara...'The Nurse' 2231	Open		16.25	17-225
1994	Clarence Angel Bear (rust) 2029-11	Retrd.	1995	12.60	50-80
1995	Cookie Catberg...'Knittin' Kitten' 2250	Open		18.75	19-40
1994	Cookie the Santa Cat 2237	Retrd.	1995	15.25	35-50
1995	Daphne and Eloise...'Women's Work' 2251	Open		18.00	18-45
1993	Daphne Hare & Maisey Ewe 2011	Retrd.	1995	14.20	75-90
1994	Daphne...The Reader Hare 2226	Open		14.20	15-90
1994	Edmond & Bailey...'Gathering Holly' 2240	Open		24.25	25-120
1994	Elgin the Elf Bear 2236	Open		14.20	15-70
1994	Elliot & Snowbeary 2242	Open		15.25	16-50
1994	Elliot & The Tree 2241	Open		16.25	17-150
1995	Elliot & the Tree Water Globe 2704	Open		35.00	35-50
1996	Elliot...the Hero 2280	Open		16.75	17-38
1996	Emma & Bailey...Afternoon Tea 2277	Open		18.00	18-40
1995	Emma...'the Witchy Bear' 2269	Open		16.75	17-50
1996	Ewell/Walton Manitoba Moosemen BC2228	12,000		24.99	25
1993	Father Chrisbear and Son 2008	Retrd.	1993	15.00	200-300
1994	Grenville & Beatrice...'Best Friends' 2016	Open		26.25	27-175
1996	Grenville & Beatrice...True Love 2274	Open		36.00	36-80
1995	Grenville & Knute...Football Buddies 2255	Open		19.95	20-60
1993	Grenville & Neville...'The Sign' (prototype) 2099	Retrd.	1993	15.75	60-110
1993	Grenville & Neville...'The Sign' 2099	Open		15.75	16-60
1994	Grenville the Santabear 2030	Retrd.	1996	14.20	250-400
1996	Grenville the Santabear Musical Waterball 2700	12/96		35.75	36-50
1996	Grenville with Matthew & Bailey...Sunday Afternoon 2281	Open		34.50	35-60
1994	Grenville...'The Graduate' 2233	12/96		16.25	17-70
1995	Grenville...'The Storyteller' 2265	Retrd.	1995	50.00	50-125
1993	Grenville...with Green Scarf 2003-04	Retrd.	1994	10.50	200-350
1993	Grenville...with Red Scarf 2003-08	Retrd.	1995	10.50	50-110
1994	Homer on the Plate 2225	Open		15.75	16-75
1994	Homer on the Plate BC2210	Open		24.99	25-85
1995	Hop-a-Long...'The Deputy' 2247	Open		14.00	14-75
1994	Juliette Angel Bear (ivory) 2029-10	Retrd.	1995	12.60	60-100
1994	Justina & M. Harrison...'Sweetie Pie' 2015	Open		26.25	27-75
1996	Justina...The Message "Bearer" 2273	Open		16.00	16-40
1994	Knute & The Gridiron 2225	Open		16.25	17-75
1994	Kringle & Bailey with List 2235	Open		14.20	15-55
1996	Kringle And Company 2283	Open		17.45	18-38
1995	Lefty...'On the Mound' 2253	Open		15.00	15-80
1995	Lefty...'On the Mound' BC2056	Open		24.99	25-90
1994	Lucy Big Pig, Little Pig BC2250	Retrd.	1996	24.99	50-100
1996	M. Harrison's Birthday 2275	Open		17.00	17-50
1994	Manheim the 'Eco-Moose' 2243	Open		15.25	16-75
1994	Maynard the Santa Moose 2238	Open		15.25	16-60
1995	Miss Bruin & Bailey 'The Lesson' 2259	Open		18.45	19-85
1996	Momma Mcbear...Anticipation 2282	Open		14.95	15
1993	Moriarty-'The Bear in the Cat Suit' 2005	Retrd.	1995	13.75	50-100
1996	Ms. Griz...Monday Morning 2276	Open		34.00	34-80
1995	Neville...the Bear 2401	Open		14.95	15
1993	Neville...The 'Bedtime Bear' 2002	12/96		14.20	15-95
1996	Noah & Co...Art Builders 2278	12/96		61.00	61-100
1996	Noah & Company (waterglobe) 2706	6,000		50.95	51
1995	Otis...'Taxtime' 2262	Open		18.75	19-55

YEAR ISSUE		EDITION LIMIT	YEAR RETRD.	ISSUE PRICE	*QUOTE U.S.$
1995	Otis...'The Fisherman' 2249-06	Open		15.75	16-55
1994	Sebastian's Prayer 2227	12/96		16.25	17-90
1994	Sherlock & Watson-In Disguise 2019	Retrd.	1996	15.75	16-95
1995	Simone & Bailey...'Helping Hands' 2267	Open		25.95	26-55
1996	Simone and Bailey...Helping Hands 2705	Open		34.80	35
1993	Simone De Beavoire and Her Mom 2001	12/96		14.20	15-210
1996	Sir Edmund... Persistence 2279	Open		20.75	21
1995	The Stage...the School Pagent 2425	Open		34.95	35
1994	Ted & Teddy 2223	Open		15.75	16-90
1995	Theresa...as Mary 2402	Open		14.95	15
1995	Union Jack...'Love Letters' 2263	Open		18.95	19-50
1993	Victoria...'The Lady' 2004	Open		18.40	19-150
1994	Wilson at the Beach 2020-06	Open		15.75	16-90
1994	Wilson the "Perfesser" 2222	Open		16.25	17-75
1993	Wilson with Love Sonnets 2007	Open		12.60	13-375
1995	Wilson...'the Wonderful Wizard of Wuz' 2261	Open		15.95	16-60
1994	Xmas Bear Elf with List BC2051	1,865	1994	24.99	365-420

The Dollstone Collection ™ - G.M. Lowenthal

YEAR ISSUE		EDITION LIMIT	YEAR RETRD.	ISSUE PRICE	*QUOTE U.S.$
1996	Betsey and Edmund with Union Jack BC35031	Open		24.99	25-65
1995	Betsey & Edmund 3503PE	Retrd.	1995	19.50	60-105
1995	Katherine, Amanda & Edmund 3505PE	Retrd.	1995	19.50	60-105
1995	Meagan 3504PE	Retrd.	1995	19.50	100-200
1995	Victoria with Samantha 3502PE	Retrd.	1995	19.50	50-125
1995	Set of 4 PE	Retrd.	1995	78.00	300-600
1996	Anne...the Masterpiece 3599	Open		24.25	25
1996	Ashley with Chrissie...Dress Up 3506	Open		20.50	21
1996	Betsey with Edmond...The Patriots 3503	Open		20.00	20-50
1996	Candice w/Matthew...Gathering Apples 3514	Open		18.95	19
1996	Courtney with Phoebe...over the River and Thru the Woods 3512	Open		24.25	25
1996	Emily with Kathleen & Otis...The Future 3508	Open		30.00	30-65
1996	Jean with Elliot & Debbie...The Bakers 3510	Open		19.50	20
1996	Jennifer with Priscilla...The Doll in the Attic 3500	Open		20.50	21-60
1996	Katherine with Amanda & Edmond...Kind Hearts 3505	Open		20.00	20-60
1996	Megan with Elliot & Annie...Christmas Carol 3504	Open		19.50	20
1996	Megan with Elliot...Christmas Carol (waterglobe) 2720	Open		39.45	40
1996	Michelle with Daisy...Reading is Fun 3511	Open		17.95	18
1996	Patricia with Molly...Attic Treasures 3501	Open		14.00	14-65
1996	Rebecca with Elliot...Birthday 3509	Open		20.50	21-55
1996	Sara & Heather with Elliot & Amelia...Tea for Four 3507	12/96		46.00	46-100
1996	Victoria w/Samantha...Victorian 3500	Open		20.00	20-75

The Folkstone Collection ™ - G.M. Lowenthal

YEAR ISSUE		EDITION LIMIT	YEAR RETRD.	ISSUE PRICE	*QUOTE U.S.$
1995	Abigail...Peaceable Kingdom 2829	Open		18.95	19-40
1996	Alvin T. Mac Barker...Dogface 2872	Open		19.00	19-40
1994	Angel of Freedom 2820	12/96		16.75	17-70
1994	Angel of Love 2821	12/96		16.75	17-70
1994	Angel of Peace 2822	Open		16.75	17-70
1996	Athena...The Wedding Angel 28202	Open		19.00	19-35
1995	Beatrice-Birthday Angel 2825	Open		20.00	20-30
1995	Beatrice...the Giftgiver 2836	Open		17.95	18-30
1996	Bernie... I Got Wat I wanted St. Bernard Santa 2873	Open		17.75	18
1996	Betty Cocker 2870	Open		19.00	19-55
1996	Boowinkle Vonhindenmoose...2831	Open		17.95	18-35
1996	Buster Goes A' Courtin' 2844	Open		19.00	19-40
1994	Chilly & Son with Dove 2811	Open		17.75	18-50
1996	Cosmos...The Gardening Angel 28201	Open		19.00	19-38
1996	Egon...the Skier 2837	Open		17.75	18
1994	Elmer-Cow on Haystacks 2851	Open		19.00	19-35
1996	Elmo "Tex" Beefcake...On the Range 2853	Open		19.00	19-35
1995	Ernest Hemmingmoose...the Hunter 2835	Open		17.95	18-40
1995	Esmeralda...the Wonderful Witch 2860	Open		17.95	18-40
1996	Fixit...Santa's Faerie 3600	Open		17.45	18
1996	Flora & Amelia...The Gardeners 2843	Open		19.00	19-35
1996	Flora, Amelia & Eloise...The Tea Party 2846	Open		19.00	19-40
1994	Florence-Kitchen Angel 2824	12/96		20.00	20-32
1996	G.M.'s Choice, Etheral...Angel of Light 28203-06	7,200		18.25	19-100
1995	Icabod Mooselman...the Pilgrim 2833	Open		17.95	18-40
1994	Ida & Bessie-The Gardeners 2852	Open		19.00	19-35
1996	Illumina...Angel of Light 28203	Open		18.45	19-35
1996	Jean Claude & Jacque...the Skiers (waterglobe) 2710	Open		37.50	38-45
1995	Jean Claude & Jacques...the Skiers 2815	Open		16.95	17-40
1994	Jill-Language of Love 2842	Open		19.00	19-50
1994	Jingle Moose 2830	12/96		17.75	18-65
1994	Jingles & Son with Wreath 2812	12/96		17.75	18-60

YEAR ISSUE		EDITION LIMIT	YEAR RETRD.	ISSUE PRICE	*QUOTE U.S.$
1994	Lizzie Shopping Angel 2827	Open		20.00	20-30
1996	Loretta Moostein..."Yer Cheatin' Heart" 2854	Open		19.00	19-40
1994	Minerva-Baseball Angel 2826	Open		20.00	20-28
1994	Myrtle-Believe 2840	Open		20.00	20-28
1995	Na-Nick of the North 2804	Open		17.95	18-40
1996	Nanick & Siegfried the Plan 2807	10,000		32.50	33-90
1996	Nanny...the Snowmom 2817	Open		17.95	18
1994	Nicholai with Tree 2800	Open		17.75	18-65
1994	Nicholas with Book 2802	12/96		17.75	18-35
1995	Nick on Ice (1st ed. GCC) 3001	3,600	1995	49.95	75
1994	Nick on Ice 3001	Open		32.95	33
1996	Nicknoak...Santa with Ark 2806	Open		17.95	18
1994	Nikki with Candle 2801	Open		17.75	18-45
1996	No-No Nick...Bad Boy Santa 2805	Open		17.95	18
1995	Northbound Wille 2814	Open		16.95	17-40
1994	Oceana-Ocean Angel 2823	Open		16.75	17-60
1994	Peter-The Whopper 2841	Open		19.00	19-40
1995	Prudence Mooselmaid...the Pilgrim 2834	Open		17.95	18-40
1996	Robin...the Snowbird Lover 2816	Open		17.95	18
1994	Rufus-Hoedown 2850	Open		19.00	19-28
1994	Santa's Challenge (1st ed. GCC) 3002	3,600	1995	49.95	75
1994	Santa's Challenge 3002	Open		32.95	33
1994	Santa's Flight Plan (1st ed. GCC) 3000	3,600	1995	49.95	75
1995	Santa's Flight Plan (waterglobe) 2703	12/96		37.00	37
1994	Santa's Flight Plan 3000	Open		32.95	33
1996	Seraphina with Jacob & Rachael...the Choir Angels 2828	Open		19.95	20-35
1996	Serenity...the Mother's Angel 28204	Open		18.25	19
1995	Siegfried and Egon...the Sign 2899	Open		18.95	19-45
1995	Sliknick the Chimney Sweep 2803	Open		17.95	18-55
1996	Sparky McPlug 2871	Open		19.00	19-40
1996	Too Loose Lapin...The Arteest 2845	Open		19.00	19-40
1994	Windy with Book 2810	12/96		17.75	18-75

Brandywine Collectibles

Accessories - M. Whiting

YEAR ISSUE		EDITION LIMIT	YEAR RETRD.	ISSUE PRICE	*QUOTE U.S.$
1992	Apple Tree/Tire Swing	Open		10.00	10
1991	Baggage Cart	Open		10.50	11
1990	Bandstand	Closed	1992	10.50	11
1994	Elm Tree with Benches	Open		16.00	16
1988	Flag	Open		10.00	10
1990	Flower Cart	Open		13.00	13
1990	Gate & Arbor	Closed	1992	9.00	9
1990	Gooseneck Lamp	Open		7.50	8
1989	Horse & Carriage	Open		13.00	13
1994	Lamp with Barber Pole	Open		10.50	11
1988	Lampost, Wall & Fence	Open		11.00	11
1989	Mailbox, Tree & Fence	Open		10.00	10
1989	Pumpkin Wagon	Open		11.50	12
1991	Street Sign	Open		8.00	8
1987	Summer Tree with Fence	Open		7.00	7
1991	Town Clock	Open		7.50	8
1992	Tree with Birdhouse	Open		10.00	10
1989	Victorian Gas Light	Open		6.50	7
1990	Wishing Well	Open		10.00	10

Barnsville Collection - M. Whiting

YEAR ISSUE		EDITION LIMIT	YEAR RETRD.	ISSUE PRICE	*QUOTE U.S.$
1991	B & O Station	Open		28.00	28
1992	Barnesville Church	Open		44.00	44
1991	Bradfield House	Closed	1996	32.00	32
1990	Candace Bruce House	Closed	1996	30.00	30
1990	Gay 90's Mansion	Closed	1996	32.00	32
1992	Plumtree Bed & Breakfast	Open		44.00	44
1990	Thompson House	Closed	1996	32.00	32
1990	Treat-Smith House	Closed	1996	32.00	32
1991	Whiteley House	Closed	1996	32.00	32

Country Lane - M. Whiting

YEAR ISSUE		EDITION LIMIT	YEAR RETRD.	ISSUE PRICE	*QUOTE U.S.$
1995	Berry Farm	Open		30.00	30
1995	Country School	Open		30.00	30
1995	Dairy Farm	Open		30.00	30
1995	Farm House	Open		30.00	30
1995	The General Store	Open		30.00	30

Country Lane II - M. Whiting

YEAR ISSUE		EDITION LIMIT	YEAR RETRD.	ISSUE PRICE	*QUOTE U.S.$
1995	Antiques & Crafts	Open		30.00	30
1995	Basketmaker	Open		30.00	30
1995	Country Church	Open		30.00	30
1995	Fishing Lodge	Open		30.00	30
1995	Herb Farm	Open		30.00	30
1995	Olde Mill	Open		30.00	30
1995	Spinners & Weavers	Open		30.00	30

Country Lane III - M. Whiting

YEAR ISSUE		EDITION LIMIT	YEAR RETRD.	ISSUE PRICE	*QUOTE U.S.$
1996	Airport	Open		30.00	30
1996	Country Club	Open		30.00	30
1996	Country Fair	Open		30.00	30
1996	Firehouse	Open		30.00	30
1996	Old Orchard	Open		30.00	30
1996	Post Office	Open		30.00	30

Country Lane IV - M. Whiting

YEAR ISSUE		EDITION LIMIT	YEAR RETRD.	ISSUE PRICE	*QUOTE U.S.$
1996	Candles & Country	Open		30.00	30
1996	Country Inn	Open		30.00	30
1996	Farmer's Market	Open		30.00	30
1996	Lighthouse	Open		30.00	30

YEAR ISSUE		EDITION LIMIT	YEAR RETD.	ISSUE PRICE	*QUOTE U.S.$
1996	Train Station	Open		30.00	30
1996	Valley Stables	Open		30.00	30

Custom Collection - M. Whiting

1988	Burgess Museum	Open		15.50	16
1992	Cumberland County Courthouse	Open		15.00	15
1990	Doylestown Public School	Open		32.00	32
1991	Jamestown Tower	Closed	1991	9.00	9
1990	Jared Coffin House	Open		32.00	32
1989	Lorain Lighthouse	Closed	1992	11.00	11
1992	Loudon County Courthouse	Open		15.00	15
1988	Princetown Monument	Closed	1989	9.70	10
1991	Smithfield VA. Courthouse	Closed	1992	12.00	12
1989	Yankee Candle Co.	Open		13.50	14

Hilton Village - M. Whiting

1987	Dutch House	Closed	1991	8.50	9
1987	English House	Closed	1991	8.50	9
1987	Georgian House	Closed	1991	8.50	9
1987	Gwen's House	Closed	1991	8.50	9
1987	Hilton Firehouse	Closed	1991	8.50	9

Hometown I - M. Whiting

1990	Barber Shop	Closed	1992	14.00	14
1990	General Store	Closed	1992	14.00	14
1990	School	Closed	1992	14.00	14
1990	Toy Store	Closed	1992	14.00	14

Hometown II - M. Whiting

1991	Church	Closed	1993	14.00	14
1991	Dentist	Closed	1993	14.00	14
1991	Ice Cream Shop	Closed	1993	14.00	14
1991	Stitch-N-Sew	Closed	1993	14.00	14

Hometown III - M. Whiting

1991	Basket Shop	Closed	1993	15.50	16
1991	Dairy	Closed	1993	15.50	16
1991	Firehouse	Closed	1993	15.50	16
1991	Library	Closed	1993	15.50	16

Hometown IV - M. Whiting

1992	Bakery	Closed	1994	21.00	21
1992	Country Inn	Closed	1994	21.50	22
1992	Courthouse	Closed	1994	21.50	22
1992	Gas Station	Closed	1994	21.00	21

Hometown V - M. Whiting

1992	Antiques Shop	Closed	1995	22.00	22
1992	Gift Shop	Closed	1995	22.00	22
1992	Pharmacy	Closed	1995	22.00	22
1992	Sporting Goods	Closed	1995	22.00	22
1992	Tea Room	Closed	1995	22.00	22

Hometown VI - M. Whiting

1993	Church	Closed	1995	24.00	24
1993	Diner	Closed	1995	24.00	24
1993	General Store	Closed	1995	24.00	24
1993	School	Closed	1995	24.00	24
1993	Train Station	Closed	1995	24.00	24

Hometown VII - M. Whiting

1993	Candy Shop	Closed	1996	24.00	24
1993	Dress Shop	Closed	1996	24.00	24
1993	Flower Shop	Closed	1996	24.00	24
1993	Pet Shop	Closed	1996	24.00	24
1993	Post Office	Closed	1996	24.00	24
1993	Quilt Shop	Closed	1996	24.00	24

Hometown VIII - M. Whiting

1994	Barber Shop	Closed	1996	28.00	28
1994	Country Store	Closed	1996	28.00	28
1994	Fire Company	Closed	1996	28.00	28
1994	Professional Building	Closed	1996	28.00	28
1994	Sewing Shop	Closed	1996	26.00	26

Hometown IX - M. Whiting

1994	Bed & Breakfast	Open		29.00	29
1994	Cafe/Deli	Open		29.00	29
1994	Hometown Bank	Open		29.00	29
1994	Hometown Gazette	Open		29.00	29
1994	Teddys & Toys	Open		29.00	29

Hometown X - M. Whiting

1995	Brick Church	Open		29.00	29
1995	The Doll Shoppe	Open		29.00	29
1995	General Hospital	Open		29.00	29
1995	The Gift Box	Open		29.00	29
1995	Police Station	Open		29.00	29

Hometown XI - M. Whiting

1995	Antiques	Open		29.00	29
1995	Church II	Open		29.00	29
1995	Grocer	Open		29.00	29
1995	Pharmacy II	Open		29.00	29
1995	School II	Open		29.00	29

Hometown XII - M. Whiting

1996	Bridal & Dress Shoppe	Open		29.00	29
1996	Five & Dime	Open		29.00	29
1996	Hometown Theater	Open		29.00	29
1996	Post Office	Open		29.00	29

YEAR ISSUE		EDITION LIMIT	YEAR RETD.	ISSUE PRICE	*QUOTE U.S.$
1996	Travel Agency	Open		29.00	29

Hometown XIII - M. Whiting

1996	Baby Shoppe	Open		29.00	29
1996	Beauty Shoppe	Open		29.00	29
1996	Gem Shoppe	Open		29.00	29
1996	House of Flowers	Open		29.00	29
1996	Robins & Roses	Open		29.00	29

North Pole Collection - M. Whiting, unless otherwise noted

1992	3 Winter Trees - D. Whiting	Open		10.50	11
1993	Candy Cane Factory	Open		24.00	24
1991	Claus House	Open		24.00	24
1993	Elf Club	Open		24.00	24
1992	Elves Workshop	Closed	1996	24.00	24
1991	Gingerbread House	Open		24.00	24
1995	New Reindeer Barn	Open		24.00	24
1996	North Pole Chapel	Open		25.50	26
1994	Post Office	Open		25.00	25
1991	Reindeer Barn	Closed	1996	24.00	24
1992	Snowflake Lodge	Open		24.00	24
1992	Snowman with St. Sign	Open		11.50	12
1995	Stocking Shop	Open		24.00	24
1992	Sugarplum Bakery	Open		24.00	24
1993	Teddybear Factory	Open		24.00	24
1993	Town Christmas Tree	Open		20.00	20
1994	Town Hall	Open		25.00	25
1996	Trim-a-Tree Shop	Open		25.50	26

Old Salem Collection - M. Whiting

1987	Boys School	Open		18.50	19
1987	First House	Open		12.80	13
1987	Home Moravian Church	Open		18.50	19
1987	Miksch Tobacco Shop	Closed	1993	12.00	12
1987	Salem Tavern	Open		20.50	21
1987	Schultz Shoemaker	Open		10.50	11
1987	Vogler House	Open		20.50	21
1987	Winkler Bakery	Open		20.50	21

Patriots Collection - M. Whiting

1992	Betsy Ross House	Open		17.50	18
1992	Washingtons Headquarters	Open		24.00	24

Seymour Collection - M. Whiting

1991	Anderson House	Open		20.00	20
1991	Blish Home	Open		20.00	20
1992	Majestic Theater	Open		22.00	22
1991	Seymour Church	Open		19.00	19
1991	Seymour Library	Open		20.00	20

Treasured Times - M. Whiting

1994	Birthday House	750		32.00	32
1994	Halloween House	750		32.00	32
1994	Mother's Day House	750		32.00	32
1994	New Baby Boy House	750		32.00	32
1994	New Baby Girl House	750		32.00	32
1994	Valentine House	750		32.00	32

Victorian Collection - M. Whiting

1989	Broadway House	Closed	1994	22.00	22
1989	Elm House	Closed	1994	25.00	25
1989	Fairplay Church	Closed	1994	19.50	20
1989	Hearts Ease Cottage	Closed	1994	15.30	16
1989	Old Star Hook & Ladder	Closed	1994	23.00	23
1989	Peachtree House	Closed	1994	22.50	23
1989	Seabreeze Cottage	Closed	1994	15.30	16
1989	Serenity Cottage	Closed	1994	15.30	16
1989	Skippack School	Closed	1994	22.50	23

Williamsburg Collection - M. Whiting

1993	Campbell's Tavern	Open		28.00	28
1988	Colonial Capitol	Open		43.50	44
1988	Court House of 1770	Open		26.50	27
1988	Governor's Palace	Open		37.50	38
1993	Kings Arms Tavern	Open		25.00	25
1988	The Magazine	Open		23.50	24
1988	Wythe House	Open		25.00	25

Yorktown Collection - M. Whiting

1987	Custom House	Open		17.50	18
1993	Digges House	Open		22.00	22
1987	Grace Church	Open		19.00	19
1987	Medical Shop	Open		13.00	13
1987	Moore House	Open		22.00	22
1987	Nelson House	Open		22.00	22
1987	Pate House	Open		19.00	19
1987	Swan Tavern	Open		22.00	22

Byers' Choice Ltd.

Accessories - J. Byers

1995	Cat in Hat	Open		10.00	10
1996	Dog with Hat	Open		18.50	19
1995	Dog with Sausages	Closed	1995	18.00	20

Carolers - J. Byers

1988	Children with Skates	Open		40.00	49
1988	Singing Cats	Open		13.50	16
1986	Singing Dogs	Open		13.00	16
1996	Teenagers (Traditional)	Open		46.00	46
1996	Teenagers (Victorian)	Open		49.00	49

YEAR ISSUE		EDITION LIMIT	YEAR RETD.	ISSUE PRICE	* QUOTE U.S.$
1976	Traditional Adult (1976-80)	Closed	1980	N/A	475
1981	Traditional Adult (1981-current)	Open		45.00	45-300
XX	Traditional Adult (undated)	Closed	N/A	N/A	400-700
1978	Traditional Colonial Lady (w/ hands)	Closed	1978	N/A	1500
1986	Traditional Grandparents	Open		35.00	45
1982	Victorian Adult (1st ed.)	Closed	1982	32.00	400
1982	Victorian Adult (2nd ed./dressed alike)	Closed	1983	46.00	300-400
1983	Victorian Adult (assorted) (2nd ed.)	Open		35.00	48
1982	Victorian Child (1st ed. w/floppy hats)	Closed	1982	32.00	300-375
1983	Victorian Child (2nd ed./sailor suit)	Closed	1983	33.00	300-400
1983	Victorian Child (assorted)	Open		33.00	48
1988	Victorian Grand Parent	Open		40.00	48

Children of The World - J. Byers

1993	Bavarian Boy	Closed	1993	50.00	175-250
1992	Dutch Boy	Closed	1992	50.00	225-325
1992	Dutch Girl	Closed	1992	50.00	225-325
1994	Irish Girl	Closed	1994	50.00	150-250
1996	Saint Lucia	Open		52.00	52

Cries Of London - J. Byers

1991	Apple Lady (red stockings)	Closed	1991	80.00	850-1100
1991	Apple Lady (red/wh stockings)	Closed	1991	80.00	975-1200
1992	Baker	Closed	1992	62.00	125-200
1993	Chestnut Roaster	Closed	1993	64.00	150-350
1996	Children Buying Gingerbread	Open		46.00	46
1995	Dollmaker	Closed	1995	64.00	64-100
1994	Flower Vendor	Closed	1994	64.00	115-200
1996	Gingerbread Vendor	Open		75.00	75
1995	Girl Holding Doll	Closed	1995	48.00	55-100

Dickens Series - J. Byers

1990	Bob Cratchit & Tiny Tim (1st ed.)	Closed	1990	84.00	125
1991	Bob Cratchit & Tiny Tim (2nd ed.)	Open		86.00	275
1991	Happy Scrooge (1st ed.)	Closed	1991	50.00	175-300
1992	Happy Scrooge (2nd ed.)	Closed	1992	50.00	100-225
1986	Marley's Ghost (1st ed.)	Closed	1986	40.00	300-450
1987	Marley's Ghost (2nd ed.)	Closed	1992	42.00	150-300
1985	Mr. Fezziwig (1st ed.)	Closed	1985	43.00	450-750
1986	Mr. Fezziwig (2nd ed.)	Closed	1990	43.00	450-750
1984	Mrs. Cratchit (1st ed.)	Closed	1984	38.00	900-1200
1985	Mrs. Cratchit (2nd ed.)	Open		39.00	49
1985	Mrs. Fezziwig (1st ed.)	Closed	1985	43.00	600-750
1986	Mrs. Fezziwig (2nd ed.)	Closed	1990	43.00	300-500
1983	Scrooge (1st ed.)	Closed	1983	36.00	1000-1400
1984	Scrooge (2nd ed.)	Open		38.00	49
1989	Spirit of Christmas Future (1st ed.)	Closed	1989	46.00	275-375
1990	Spirit of Christmas Future (2nd ed.)	Closed	1991	48.00	225-350
1987	Spirit of Christmas Past (1st ed.)	Closed	1987	42.00	325-375
1988	Spirit of Christmas Past (2nd ed.)	Closed	1991	46.00	275-375
1987	Spirit of Christmas Present (1st ed.)	Closed	1988	44.00	300-375
1989	Spirit of Christmas Present (2nd ed.)	Closed	1991	48.00	200-350

Display Figures - J. Byers

1986	Display Adults	Closed	1987	170.00	500
1983	Display Carolers	Closed	1983	200.00	500
1985	Display Children (Boy & Girl)	Closed	1987	140.00	1100-1400
1982	Display Drummer Boy-1st	Closed	1983	96.00	800-1200
1985	Display Drummer Boy-2nd	Closed	1986	160.00	400-600
1981	Display Lady	Closed	1981	N/A	2000
1981	Display Man	Closed	1981	N/A	2000
1985	Display Old World Santa	Closed	1985	260.00	500
1982	Display Santa	Closed	1983	96.00	600
1990	Display Santa-bayberry	Closed	1990	250.00	450-500
1990	Display Santa-red	Closed	1990	250.00	425-500
1984	Display Working Santa	Closed	1985	260.00	500
1987	Mechanical Boy with Drum	Closed	1987	N/A	600-800
1987	Mechanical Girl with Bell	Closed	1987	N/A	600-800

Musicians - J. Byers

1991	Boy with Mandolin	Closed	1991	48.00	175-275
1985	Horn Player	Closed	1985	38.00	550-750
1985	Horn Player, chubby face	Closed	1985	37.00	500-900
1991	Musician with Accordian	Closed	1991	48.00	200-275
1989	Musician with Clarinet	Closed	1989	44.00	450-650
1992	Musician with French Horn	Closed	1992	52.00	100-250
1990	Musician with Mandolin	Closed	1990	46.00	175-300
1986	Victorian Girl with Violin	Closed	1986	39.00	275-300
1983	Violin Player Man (1st ed.)	Closed	1983	38.00	1500
1984	Violin Player Man (2nd ed.)	Closed	1984	38.00	1500

Nativity - J. Byers

1989	Angel Gabriel	Closed	1991	37.00	150-200
1987	Angel-Great Star (Blonde)	Closed	1991	40.00	250
1987	Angel-Great Star (Brunette)	Closed	1991	40.00	250
1987	Angel-Great Star (Red Head)	Closed	1991	40.00	200-250
1987	Black Angel	Closed	1987	36.00	225-310
1990	Holy Family with stable	Closed	1991	119.00	250-350
1989	King Balthasar	Closed	1991	40.00	95
1989	King Gaspar	Closed	1991	40.00	95
1989	King Melchior	Closed	1991	40.00	95
1987	Shepherds	Closed	1991	37.00	95

The Nutcracker - J. Byers

1996	Drosselmeier w/Music Box (1st ed.)	Open		83.00	83
1994	Fritz (1st ed.)	Closed	1994	56.00	100-200
1995	Fritz (2nd ed.)	Open		57.00	57
1995	Louise Playing Piano (1st ed.)	Closed	1995	82.00	125
1996	Louise Playing Piano (2nd ed.)	Open		83.00	83

*Quotes have been rounded up to nearest dollar

Byers' Choice Ltd.

YEAR ISSUE	EDITION LIMIT	YEAR RETRD.	ISSUE PRICE	*QUOTE U.S.$
1993 Marie (1st ed.)	Closed	1993	52.00	115-200
1994 Marie (2nd ed.)	Open		53.00	54

Salvation Army Band - J. Byers

YEAR ISSUE	EDITION LIMIT	YEAR RETRD.	ISSUE PRICE	*QUOTE U.S.$
1995 Girl with War Cry	Open		55.00	55
1996 Man with Bass Drum	Open		60.00	60
1993 Man with Cornet	Open		54.00	56
1992 Woman with Kettle	Open		64.00	67
1992 Woman with Kettle (1st ed.)	Closed	1992	64.00	175
1993 Woman with Tambourine	Closed	1995	58.00	75-110

Santas - J. Byers

YEAR ISSUE	EDITION LIMIT	YEAR RETRD.	ISSUE PRICE	*QUOTE U.S.$
1991 Father Christmas	Closed	1992	48.00	120-190
1988 Knecht Ruprecht (Black Peter)	Closed	1989	38.00	145-175
1996 Knickerbocker Santa	Open		58.00	58
1984 Mrs. Claus	Closed	1991	38.00	250-350
1992 Mrs. Claus (2nd ed.)	Closed	1993	50.00	135-150
1986 Mrs. Claus on Rocker	Closed	1986	73.00	400
1995 Mrs. Claus' Needlework	Open		70.00	100-200
1994 Old Befana	Open		53.00	54
1978 Old World Santa	Closed	1986	33.00	375-440
1989 Russian Santa	Closed	1989	85.00	400-450
1988 Saint Nicholas	Closed	1992	44.00	140-200
1982 Santa in a Sleigh (1st ed.)	Closed	1983	46.00	800
1984 Santa in Sleigh (2nd ed.)	Closed	1985	70.00	750
1993 Skating Santa	Closed	1993	60.00	100-125
1987 Velvet Mrs. Claus	Open		44.00	53
1978 Velvet Santa	Closed	1993	Unkn.	300
1994 Velvet Santa w/Stocking (2nd ed.)	Open		47.00	51
1986 Victorian Santa	Closed	1989	39.00	250-300
1990 Weihnachtsmann (German Santa)	Closed	1990	56.00	120-190
1992 Working Santa	Open		52.00	55
1983 Working Santa (1st yr. issue)	Closed	1991	38.00	175-275
1992 Working Santa (1st yr. issue)	Closed	1992	50.00	150-250

Skaters - J. Byers

YEAR ISSUE	EDITION LIMIT	YEAR RETRD.	ISSUE PRICE	*QUOTE U.S.$
1991 Adult Skaters	Closed	1994	50.00	100-125
1991 Adult Skaters (1991 ed.)	Closed	1991	50.00	115-130
1993 Boy Skater on Log	Closed	1993	55.00	100-125
1992 Children Skaters	Open		50.00	52
1992 Children Skaters (1992 ed.)	Closed	1992	50.00	150
1993 Grandparent Skaters	Closed	1993	50.00	65-125
1993 Grandparent Skaters (1993 ed.)	Closed	1993	50.00	145
1995 Man Holding Skates	Open		52.00	52
1995 Woman Holding Skates	Open		52.00	52

Special Characters - J. Byers

YEAR ISSUE	EDITION LIMIT	YEAR RETRD.	ISSUE PRICE	*QUOTE U.S.$
1996 Actress	Open		52.00	52
1979 Adult Male "Icabod"	Closed	1979	32.00	2400-2600
1988 Angel Tree Top	100	1988	Unkn.	275-375
1994 Baby in Basket	Closed	1994	7.50	30
1989 Black Boy w/skates	Closed	N/A	N/A	400-450
1989 Black Drummer Boy	Closed	N/A	N/A	500
1989 Black Girl w/skates	Closed	N/A	N/A	400-450
1983 Boy on Rocking Horse	300	1983	85.00	2400-2600
1987 Boy on Sled	Closed	1987	50.00	300-375
1991 Boy with Apple	Closed	1991	41.00	150-275
1994 Boy with Goose	Closed	1995	49.50	50-100
1996 Boy with Lamb	Open		52.00	52
1995 Boy with Skis	Open		49.50	50
1991 Boy with Tree	Closed	1994	49.00	125
1995 Butcher	Closed	1995	54.00	110-125
1987 Caroler with Lamp	Closed	1987	40.00	175-200
1984 Chimney Sweep-Adult	Closed	1994	36.00	1200-1500
1991 Chimney Sweep-Child	Closed	1994	50.00	75-125
1982 Choir Children, boy and girl set	Closed	1986	32.00	600-700
1993 Choir Director, lady/music stand	Closed	1995	56.00	58
1982 Conductor	Closed	1992	32.00	125
1994 Constable	Open		53.00	54
1995 Couple in Sleigh	Closed	1995	110.00	175-200
1982 Drummer Boy	Closed	1992	34.00	150
1982 Easter Boy	Closed	1983	32.00	450-550
1982 Easter Girl	Closed	1983	32.00	450-550
1996 Girl Holding Holly Basket	Open		52.00	52
1991 Girl with Apple	Closed	1991	41.00	150-250
1991 Girl with Apple/coin purse	Closed	1991	41.00	350-500
1989 Girl with Hoop	Closed	1990	44.00	155-185
1995 Girl with Skis	Open		49.50	50
1982 Icabod	Closed	1982	32.00	1150
1993 Lamplighter	Open		48.00	50
1993 Lamplighter (1st yr. issue)	Closed	1993	48.00	100-220
1982 Leprechauns	Closed	1982	34.00	1200-2000
1988 Mother Holding Baby	Closed	1993	44.00	100-175
1987 Mother's Day	225	1987	125.00	250-350
1988 Mother's Day (Daughter)	Closed	1988	125.00	450-600
1988 Mother's Day (Son)	Closed	1988	125.00	450-600
1989 Mother's Day (with Carriage)	3,000	1989	75.00	450-600
1994 Nanny	Open		66.00	67
1989 Newsboy with Bike	Closed	1992	78.00	175-225
1985 Pajama Children (painted flannel)	Closed	1989	35.00	180-300
1985 Pajama Children (red flannel)	Closed	1989	35.00	200-300
1990 Parson	Closed	1993	44.00	100-150
1996 Pilgrims	Open		53.00	53
1990 Postman	Closed	1993	45.00	115-175
1996 Puppeteer	Open		54.00	54
1994 Sandwich Board Man (red board)	Closed	1994	52.00	100
1994 Sandwich Board Man (wh. board)	Open		52.00	53
1993 School Kids	Closed	1994	48.00	75-125
1992 Schoolteacher	Closed	1994	48.00	75-125
1995 Shopper-Man	Closed	1995	56.00	75
1995 Shopper-Woman	Closed	1995	56.00	75
1996 Shoppers - Grandparents	Open		56.00	56
1981 Thanksgiving Lady (Clay Hands)	Closed	1981	Unkn.	2000
1981 Thanksgiving Man (Clay Hands)	Closed	1981	Unkn.	2000
1994 Treetop Angel	Closed	1996		50-80
1982 Valentine Boy	Closed	1983	32.00	450-550
1982 Valentine Girl	Closed	1983	32.00	450-550
1990 Victorian Girl On Rocking Horse (blonde)	Closed	1991	70.00	150-200
1990 Victorian Girl On Rocking Horse (brunette)	Closed	1991	70.00	150-225
1992 Victorian Mother with Toddler (Fall/Win-green)	Closed	1993	60.00	125-200
1993 Victorian Mother with Toddler (Spr/Sum-blue)	Closed	1993	61.00	125-150
1992 Victorian Mother with Toddler (Spr/Sum-white)	Closed	1993	60.00	120-150

Store Exclusives-Christmas Loft - J. Byers

YEAR ISSUE	EDITION LIMIT	YEAR RETRD.	ISSUE PRICE	*QUOTE U.S.$
1991 Russian Santa	40	1991	100.00	600-850

Store Exclusives-Country Christmas - J. Byers

YEAR ISSUE	EDITION LIMIT	YEAR RETRD.	ISSUE PRICE	*QUOTE U.S.$
1988 Toymaker	600	1988	59.00	850-1000

Store Exclusives-Foster's Exclusives - J. Byers

YEAR ISSUE	EDITION LIMIT	YEAR RETRD.	ISSUE PRICE	*QUOTE U.S.$
1995 American Boy	100	1995	50.00	500

Store Exclusives-Long's Jewelers - J. Byers

YEAR ISSUE	EDITION LIMIT	YEAR RETRD.	ISSUE PRICE	*QUOTE U.S.$
1981 Leprechaun (with bucket)	Closed	N/A	N/A	2000

Store Exclusives-Port-O-Call - J. Byers

YEAR ISSUE	EDITION LIMIT	YEAR RETRD.	ISSUE PRICE	*QUOTE U.S.$
1986 Cherub Angel-blue	Closed	1987	N/A	275-400
1986 Cherub Angel-cream	Closed	1987	N/A	400
1986 Cherub Angel-pink	Closed	1987	N/A	275-400
1987 Cherub Angel-rose	Closed	1987	N/A	275-400

Store Exclusives-Snow Goose - J. Byers

YEAR ISSUE	EDITION LIMIT	YEAR RETRD.	ISSUE PRICE	*QUOTE U.S.$
1988 Man with Goose	600	1988	60.00	300

Store Exclusives-Stacy's Gifts & Collectibles - J. Byers

YEAR ISSUE	EDITION LIMIT	YEAR RETRD.	ISSUE PRICE	*QUOTE U.S.$
1987 Santa in Rocking Chair with Boy	100	1987	130.00	1000
1987 Santa in Rocking Chair with Girl	100	1987	130.00	1000

Store Exclusives-Talbots - J. Byers

YEAR ISSUE	EDITION LIMIT	YEAR RETRD.	ISSUE PRICE	*QUOTE U.S.$
1990 Victorian Family of Four	Closed	N/A	N/A	375-450
1993 Skating Girl/Boy	Retrd.	N/A	N/A	450
1994 Man w/Log Carrier	Closed	N/A	N/A	130-150
1994 Family of Four/Sweaters	Retrd.	N/A	N/A	500-550
1995 Santa in Sleigh	1,625	1995	88.00	150-175

Store Exclusives-Tudor Cottage Exclusives - J. Byers

YEAR ISSUE	EDITION LIMIT	YEAR RETRD.	ISSUE PRICE	*QUOTE U.S.$
1993 Penny Children (boy/girl)	Closed	1993	42.00	500

Store Exclusives-Wayside Country Store Exclusives - J. Byers

YEAR ISSUE	EDITION LIMIT	YEAR RETRD.	ISSUE PRICE	*QUOTE U.S.$
1988 Colonial Lady s/n	600	1988	49.00	500-600
1986 Colonial Lamplighter s/n	600	1986	46.00	750-900
1987 Colonial Watchman s/n	600	1987	49.00	700-800
1995 Sunday School Boy	150	1995	55.00	200
1995 Sunday School Girl	150	1995	55.00	200

Store Exclusives-Wooden Soldier - J. Byers

YEAR ISSUE	EDITION LIMIT	YEAR RETRD.	ISSUE PRICE	*QUOTE U.S.$
XX Victorian Lamp Lighter	Closed	N/A	N/A	100-150

Store Exclusives-Woodstock Inn - J. Byers

YEAR ISSUE	EDITION LIMIT	YEAR RETRD.	ISSUE PRICE	*QUOTE U.S.$
1987 Skier Boy	200	1987	40.00	250-350
1987 Skier Girl	200	1987	40.00	250-350
1991 Sugarin Kids (Woodstock)	Closed	1991	41.00	300
1988 Woodstock Lady	Closed	1988	41.00	350
1988 Woodstock Man	Closed	1988	41.00	350

Toddlers - J. Byers

YEAR ISSUE	EDITION LIMIT	YEAR RETRD.	ISSUE PRICE	*QUOTE U.S.$
1996 Book - "Night Before Christmas"	Open		20.00	20
1996 Doll - "Night Before Christmas"	Open		20.00	20
1993 Gingerbread Boy	Closed	1994	18.50	25
1993 Package	Closed	1993	18.50	35
1992 Shovel	Closed	1993	17.00	35
1994 Skis	Open		19.00	20
1994 Sled (black toddler)	Closed	1994	19.00	19
1992 Sled (white toddler)	Closed	1993	17.00	20
1995 Sled (white toddler-2nd ed.)	Open		19.00	20
1991 Sled with Dog/toddler	Closed	1991	30.00	125-200
1992 Snowball	Closed	1994	17.00	35
1994 Snowflake	Closed	1994	18.00	18
1993 Teddy Bear	Closed	1993	18.50	35
1995 Toddler with Wagon	Open		19.50	20
1994 Tree	Open		18.00	20
1996 Tricycle	Open		20.00	20
1995 Victorian Boy Toddler	Open		19.50	20
1995 Victorian Girl Toddler	Open		19.50	20

Calabar Creations

Angelic Pigasus - P. Apsit

YEAR ISSUE	EDITION LIMIT	YEAR RETRD.	ISSUE PRICE	*QUOTE U.S.$
1996 Acapella & Atto AP75424	Open		25.00	25
1995 Adagio AP75364	Open		18.00	18
1996 Adagio Mini Waterglobe AP76053	Open		8.50	9
1994 Alba AP75353	6/96		12.00	12
1995 Allegria AP75395	Open		24.00	24
1996 Allegria Mini Waterglobe AP76033	Open		8.50	9
1995 Ambrose AP75374	Open		22.00	22
1996 Ambrose Mini Waterglobe AP76043	Open		8.50	9
1995 Andante AP75384	Open		18.00	18
1994 Angelica AP75315	Open		24.00	24
1996 Angelica Mini Waterglobe AP76063	Open		8.50	9
1995 Angelo AP75335	Open		5.00	5
1994 Angelo AP75335	Open		24.00	24
1996 Angelo Mini Waterglobe AP76083	Open		8.50	9
1996 Anna & Allegria Mini Waterglobe AP76094	Open		20.00	20
1994 Anna AP75324	Retrd.	1995	22.00	22
1996 Anna Mini Waterglobe AP76073	Open		8.50	9
1994 Aria AP75343	Retrd.	1996	12.00	12
1996 Arpeggio AP75414	Open		22.00	22
1995 Signature Piece AP75405	Open		24.00	24

Daddy's Girl - P. Apsit

YEAR ISSUE	EDITION LIMIT	YEAR RETRD.	ISSUE PRICE	*QUOTE U.S.$
1994 All Aboard! DA74804	5,000		20.00	20
1994 Discovery DA74816	5,000		28.00	28
1994 Moil DA74834	5,000		20.00	20
1994 Peek-A-Boo DA74843	5,000		20.00	20
1994 Spring Harvest DA74856	5,000		28.00	28
1995 Summer DA74866	5,000		34.00	34
1994 Teddy Talks DA74826	5,000		40.00	40

Days of Innocence - P. Apsit

YEAR ISSUE	EDITION LIMIT	YEAR RETRD.	ISSUE PRICE	*QUOTE U.S.$
1995 Dear God DI74975	5,000		28.00	28
1995 A Letter From Grandma DI74966	5,000		40.00	40
1995 To Grandma's DI74956	5,000		28.00	28

Grandpions - P. Apsit

YEAR ISSUE	EDITION LIMIT	YEAR RETRD.	ISSUE PRICE	*QUOTE U.S.$
1995 Alex the Great OM77144	Open		13.00	13
1995 Alley King OM77313	Open		13.00	13
1995 Blue Baron OM77294	Open		13.00	13
1995 Chained OM77234	Open		13.00	13
1995 Doc OM77184	Open		13.00	13
1996 Dr. Tooth OM 77544	Open		13.00	13
1995 The Finest OM77174	Open		13.00	13
1995 Harleyson OM77164	Open		15.00	15
1996 Hazel (Waitress) OM 77384	Open		13.00	13
1995 Ice Proof OM77133	Open		13.00	13
1995 Lady Hope OM77304	Open		13.00	13
1995 Marathon Man OM77224	Open		13.00	13
1995 Martiny OM77264	Open		13.00	13
1995 Mazuma OM77244	Open		13.00	13
1996 Ms. Brown (Teacher) OM 77374	Open		13.00	13
1996 Ms. Ellie S. Crow (Real Estate Agent) OM 77394	Open		13.00	13
1996 Ms. Will Do (Secretary) OM 77404	Open		13.00	13
1995 Oh Gee! OM77203	Open		13.00	13
1995 Old Red OM77154	Open		13.00	13
1996 Peleman OM77274	Open		13.00	13
1995 Ratchet OM77254	Open		13.00	13
1995 Rocky Road OM77283	Open		13.00	13
1995 See The Birdy OM77193	Open		13.00	13
1995 Struck OM77214	Open		13.00	13
1995 Weed Child OM77323	Open		13.00	13

Junior Murphy's Law - P. Apsit

YEAR ISSUE	EDITION LIMIT	YEAR RETRD.	ISSUE PRICE	*QUOTE U.S.$
1995 Extra Topping JM75216	5,000		40.00	40
1995 Fast Food JM75196	5,000		46.00	46
1995 Lucky Me! JM75176	5,000		40.00	40
1995 Milk Fan JM75205	5,000		44.00	44
1995 Robin Tell JM75226	5,000		40.00	40

Little Farmers - P. Apsit

YEAR ISSUE	EDITION LIMIT	YEAR RETRD.	ISSUE PRICE	*QUOTE U.S.$
1994 Apple Delivery LF73127	5,000		54.00	54
1993 Between Chores LF73105	5,000		40.00	40
1993 Caring Friend LF73066	5,000		57.00	57
1993 Going Home LF73027	5,000		64.00	64
1993 It's Not For You LF73038	5,000		64.00	64
1994 LF Signature Piece LF73147	Open		40.00	40
1993 Little Lumber Joe LF73077	5,000		64.00	64
1994 Lunch Express LF73117	5,000		76.00	76
1993 Oops! LF73058	5,000		64.00	64
1993 Piggy Ride LF73097	5,000		45.00	45
1993 Playful Kittens LF73016	5,000		64.00	64
1993 Surprise! LF73046	5,000		60.00	60
1993 True Love LF73087	5,000		45.00	45
1994 Vita-Veggie Vendor LF73137	5,000		62.00	62

Little Professionals - P. Apsit

YEAR ISSUE	EDITION LIMIT	YEAR RETRD.	ISSUE PRICE	*QUOTE U.S.$
1994 Little Angelo LP75057	5,000		38.00	38
1995 Little Count LP75084	5,000		36.00	36
1995 Little Desi LP75135	5,000		18.00	18
1994 Little Florence LP75065	5,000		44.00	44
1995 Little Gypsy LP75115	5,000		18.00	18
1995 Little Louis LP75106	5,000		18.00	18
1994 Little Miss Market LP75046	5,000		40.00	40
1995 Little Red LP75075	5,000		38.00	38
1995 Little Ringo LP75094	5,000		18.00	18

Pig Hollow - P. Apsit

YEAR ISSUE	EDITION LIMIT	YEAR RETRD.	ISSUE PRICE	*QUOTE U.S.$
1994 The After Picture PH75544	Open		12.00	12
1995 Armchair/buttons PH75752	Open		7.00	7
1994 Barn Fun PH75474	Open		15.00	15
1995 Bathroom Vanity PH75703	Open		6.00	6
1995 Double Bed PH75722	Open		9.00	9
1994 Dresser/2-drawer PH75714	Open		8.00	8
1995 Going South PH75533	Open		11.00	11
1994 Just Cute PH75442	Open		9.00	9
1995 Kitchen Counter PH75684	Open		19.00	19

YEAR ISSUE		EDITION LIMIT	YEAR RETD.	ISSUE PRICE	*QUOTE U.S. $
1995	Large Armchair PH75742	Open		8.00	8
1994	Mary Pig PH75524	Open		11.00	11
1994	Move Please PH75462	Open		11.00	11
1994	Nap Time PH75492	Open		11.00	11
1994	Old McPig PH75513	Open		11.00	11
1995	Par PH75674	Open		15.00	15
1995	Pauline PH75873	Open		9.00	9
1995	Pelota PH75612	Open		8.00	8
1995	Pendleton PH75822	Open		10.00	10
1995	Pepin PH75842	Open		9.00	9
1995	Pieball PH75633	Open		9.00	9
1995	Pig Kahuna PH75602	Open		9.00	9
1995	Pigmobile PH75853	Open		34.00	34
1995	Pilar PH75832	Open		9.00	9
1994	Pillow Talk PH75453	Open		12.00	12
1995	Plopsy PH75642	Open		8.00	8
1995	Pluckster PH75812	Open		9.00	9
1995	Poirot PH75622	Open		8.00	8
1995	Poof PH75592	Open		8.00	8
1995	Pot Belly PH75883	Open		12.00	12
1995	Pristine Pig PH75573	Open		10.00	10
1995	Prof PH75583	Open		9.00	9
1995	Proof PH75862	Open		12.00	12
1995	Prude Jr. PH75652	Open		8.00	8
1995	Prude PH75663	Open		9.00	9
1994	Reddie PH75554	Open		12.00	12
1994	Sidetable/1 book PH75773	Open		8.00	8
1995	Sidetable/2 doors PH75782	Open		6.00	6
1994	Signature Piece PH75565	Open		19.00	19
1995	Sofa PH75762	Open		14.00	14
1995	Stove/Oven PH75693	Open		7.00	7
1994	Sweet Corn PH75503	Open		9.00	9
1995	Time For School PH75484	Open		15.00	15
1995	TV Console PH75793	Open		7.00	7
1995	Twin Bed PH75732	Open		9.00	9

Santaventure - P. Apsit

1994	Almost Done SV73836	5,000		50.00	50
1993	Cart O' Plenty SV73737	5,000		66.00	66
1993	Hooray For Santa SV73757	5,000		59.00	59
1993	In His Dream SV73816	5,000		78.00	78
1994	The Last Mile SV73806	5,000		54.00	54
1993	Nuts For You SV73787	5,000		59.00	59
1993	Pilgrim Santa SV73748	5,000		59.00	59
1993	A Pinch of Advice SV73768	5,000		68.00	68
1994	Reindeer's Strike SV73827	5,000		54.00	54
1993	Santa Tested SV73778	5,000		68.00	68
1993	Santa's Sack Attack SV73796	5,000		60.00	60
1994	Signature Piece SV73577	5,000		60.00	60
1994	Viola! SV73847	5,000		50.00	50

Tee Club - P. Apsit

1993	Certain-Tee TC73898	5,000		100.00	100
1993	Naugh-Tee TC73908	5,000		56.00	56
1993	Old Tee-Mer TC73887	5,000		78.00	78
1993	Prac-Tees TC73858	5,000		66.00	66
1993	Putt-Teeing TC73868	5,000		66.00	66
1993	Teed-Off TC73877	5,000		60.00	60

Yesterday's Friends - P. Apsit

1993	Bayou Boys RW74456	3,500		80.00	80
1993	Bluester RW74446	7,500		44.00	44
1993	Buddies RW74466	7,500		50.00	50
1994	Caddie Chris RW74527	7,500		34.00	34
1994	Cornered RW74707	7,500		54.00	54
1993	Dinner For Two RW74496	7,500		38.00	38
1994	Equipment Manager RW74596	7,500		34.00	34
1994	Excess RW74726	7,500		50.00	50
1993	Freewheeling RW74436	7,500		48.00	48
1994	Funny Frog RW74745	7,500		44.00	44
1995	Goose Loose RW74635	7,500		40.00	40
1995	High Fly RW74795	7,500		28.00	28
1993	Hop-a-Long Pete RW74539	3,500		80.00	80
1994	Interference RW74506	7,500		42.00	42
1993	Jazzy Bubble RW74486	7,500		37.00	37
1993	Me Big Chief RW74548	7,500		56.00	56
1993	Mike's Magic RW74475	7,500		37.00	37
1995	Out! RW74766	7,500		34.00	34
1994	Parade RW74716	7,500		60.00	60
1995	Pop Up! RW74755	7,500		34.00	34
1994	Read All About It RW74616	7,500		70.00	70
1994	Read-A-Thon RW74694	7,500		40.00	40
1994	Scrub-a-Swine RW74606	7,500		48.00	48
1994	Signature Piece RW74737	Open		54.00	54
1994	Strike So Sweet RW74517	7,500		42.00	42
1994	Tuba Notes RW74688	7,500		54.00	54
1993	Tug-a-Leg RW74557	7,500		56.00	56
1993	What A Smile RW74626	7,500		40.00	40

Cardew Design

"English Bettys" - P. Cardew

1995	Cat Got the Cream-Brown Betty	Open		50.00	50
1996	Chess-Black Betty	Open		50.00	50
1996	Gardening-Green Betty	Open		50.00	50
1996	Golf-White Betty	Open		50.00	50
1996	Harvest Pies-Brown Betty	Open		50.00	50
1996	London Touring-Black Betty	Open		50.00	50
1996	Magician-Black Betty	Open		50.00	50
1995	Ploughman's Lunch-Brown Betty	Open		50.00	50
1995	Rise & "Shoe" Shine-Brown Betty	Open		50.00	50

YEAR ISSUE		EDITION LIMIT	YEAR RETD.	ISSUE PRICE	*QUOTE U.S. $
1995	Summer Picnic-Brown Betty	Open		50.00	50
1995	Tea Table-Brown Betty	Open		50.00	50
1996	Teddy Bear's Picnic-Yellow Betty	Open		50.00	50

Bloomingdales Exclusive - P. Cardew

1996	Botanic Garden Christmas Fireplace	Open		49.00	49

Event Piece - P. Cardew

1996	"Travellers Return"	5,000	1996	45.00	45

Limited Edition Full Sized Teapots - P. Cardew

1996	Farmhouse Welsh Dresser	5,000		175.00	175
1995	Kitchen Sink	5,000		175.00	175
1995	Ladies Dressing Table	5,000		175.00	175
1996	Lilliput Lane Market Stall	Yr.Iss.		250.00	250
1996	Moving Day	5,000		175.00	175
1995	Refrigerator	5,000		175.00	175
1995	Teapot Market Stall	5,000	1996	199.00	199
1996	Teapot Martket Stall Mark II	5,000		199.00	199
1995	Teddy Bear's Picnic	5,000		175.00	175
1995	Washing Machine	5,000		175.00	175

Market Stall Series - P. Cardew

1993	Antiques Market Stall	Open		160.00	160
1993	China Market Stall	Open		160.00	160
1993	Hardware Market Stall	Open		160.00	160
1995	Shoe Market Stall	Open		160.00	160

One-Cup Teapot Collection - P. Cardew

1996	Bloomingdales	Open		45.00	45
1995	China Stall	Open		45.00	45
1995	Christmas Presents	Open		45.00	45
1996	Christmas Tree	Open		45.00	45
1996	Egg Cup	Open		45.00	45
1996	Fireplace	Open		45.00	45
1996	Gardening	Open		45.00	45
1996	Golf Bag	Open		45.00	45
1996	Grandfather Clock	Open		45.00	45
1995	Kitchen Sink	Open		45.00	45
1995	Lady's Dressing Table	Open		45.00	45
1995	Moving Day	Open		45.00	45
1996	Outward Bound	Open		45.00	45
1995	Refrigerator	Open		45.00	45
1996	Romance/Heart	Open		45.00	45
1996	Santa Claus	Open		45.00	45
1995	Sewing Machine	Open		45.00	45
1995	Tea Chest	Open		45.00	45
1995	Tea Shop Counter	Open		45.00	45
1995	Teddy Bear's Picnic	Open		45.00	45
1995	Toy Box	Open		45.00	45
1995	Victorian Tea Table	Open		45.00	45
1995	Washing Machine	Open		45.00	45
1995	Washing Mangle	Open		45.00	45
1995	Welsh Dresser	Open		45.00	45

Standard Teapots - P. Cardew

1991	50's Stove	Open		140.00	140
1992	Baking Day	Open		140.00	140
1992	Crime Writer's Desk	Open		140.00	140
1992	Sewing Machine	Open		140.00	140
1991	Toy Box	Open		140.00	140
1992	Victorian Tea Table	Open		140.00	140
1992	Washing Mangle	Open		140.00	140

Tiny Teapots - P. Cardew

1995	50's Stove	Open		12.00	12
1995	Baking Day	Open		12.00	12
1995	Crime Writer's Desk	Open		12.00	12
1995	Kitchen Sink	Open		12.00	12
1995	Refrigerator	Open		12.00	12
1995	Sewing Machine	Open		12.00	12
1995	Tea Shop Counter	Open		12.00	12
1995	Teddy Bear's Picnic	Open		12.00	12
1995	Toy Box	Open		12.00	12
1995	Victorian Wash Stand	Open		12.00	12
1995	Washing Machine	Open		12.00	12
1995	Washing Mangle	Open		12.00	12
1996	Golf Trolley	Open		12.00	12
1996	Petrol Pump	Open		12.00	12
1996	Heart	Open		12.00	12
1996	Radio	Open		12.00	12
1996	Safe	Open		12.00	12
1996	50's TV	Open		12.00	12
1996	Fireplace	Open		12.00	12
1996	Grandfather's Clock	Open		12.00	12
1996	Lady's Dressing Table	Open		12.00	12
1996	Night Stand	Open		12.00	12
1996	Victorian Tea Table	Open		12.00	12
1996	Welsh Dresser	Open		12.00	12

Cast Art Industries

Dreamsicles Club - K. Haynes

1993	A Star is Born-CD001	Retrd.	1993	Gift	100
1994	Daydream Believer-CD100	Retrd.	1994	29.95	60
1994	Join The Fun-CD002	Retrd.	1994	Gift	35
1994	Makin' A List-CD101	Retrd.	1994	47.95	75
1995	Three Cheers-CD003	Retrd.		Gift	50
1995	Town Crier-CD102	Retrd.	1995	24.95	25
1995	Snowbound-CD103	Retrd.	1996	24.95	25

YEAR ISSUE		EDITION LIMIT	YEAR RETD.	ISSUE PRICE	* QUOTE U.S. $
1996	Star Shower-CD004	12/96		Gift	N/A
1996	Heavenly Flowers-CD104	Yr.Iss.		24.95	25

Dreamsicles - K. Haynes

1995	The 1995 International Collectible Exposition Commemorative Figurine	Retrd.	1995	34.95	150-200
1992	Baby Love-DC147	Retrd.	1995	7.00	10
1991	Best Pals-DC103	Retrd.	1994	15.00	50
1994	Birthday Party-DC171	Suspd.		13.50	14
1992	Bluebird On My Shoulder-DC115	Retrd.	1995	19.00	23
1994	Boxful of Stars-DC224	Suspd.		16.00	16
1992	Bundle of Joy-DC142	Retrd.	1995	7.00	10
1992	Bunny Wall Plaque-5018	Suspd.		22.00	22
1992	Bunny Wall Plaque-5019	Suspd.		22.00	22
1993	By the Silvery Moon-DC253	10,000	1994	100.00	350
1992	Caroler - Center Scroll-DC216	Retrd.	1995	19.00	22
1992	Caroler - Left Scroll-DC218	Retrd.	1995	19.00	22
1992	Caroler - Right Scroll-DC217	Retrd.	1995	19.00	22
1994	Carousel-DC174	Suspd.		35.00	35
1991	Cherub and Child-DC100	Retrd.	1995	15.00	35
1994	Cherub Bowl-Stars-DC161	Suspd.		9.50	10
1992	Cherub For All Seasons-DC114	Retrd.	1995	23.00	50
1991	Cherub Wall Plaque-5130	Suspd.		15.00	15
1991	Cherub Wall Plaque-5131	Suspd.		15.00	15
1992	Cherub-DC111	10,000	1992	50.00	75
1992	Cherub-DC112	10,000	1993	50.00	75
1996	A Child Is Born-DC256	10,000		95.00	95
1992	A Child's Prayer-DC145	Retrd.	1995	7.00	7
1994	Cuddle Blanket-DC153	Retrd.	1995	6.50	7
1992	Cupid's Bow-DC202	Suspd.		27.00	27
1992	Dance Ballerina Dance-DC140	Retrd.	1995	37.00	42
1992	Dream A Little Dream-DC144	Retrd.	1995	7.00	10
1994	Eager to Please-DC154	Retrd.	1995	6.50	10
1992	Flying Lesson-DC251	10,000	1993	80.00	370
1991	Forever Friends-DC102	Retrd.	1994	15.00	50
1991	Forever Yours-DC110	Retrd.	1995	44.00	75
1994	Good Shepherd-DC104	Suspd.		15.00	15
1994	Happy Birthday w/hat-DC133	Suspd.		13.50	14
1991	Heavenly Dreamer-DC106	Retrd.	1996	11.50	12
1994	Here's Looking at You-DC172	Retrd.	1995	25.00	27
1994	I Can Read-DC151	Retrd.	1995	6.50	10
1991	King Heart "I Love You" Box-5850	Suspd.		37.50	38
1991	King Oval Cow Box-5860	Suspd.		55.00	55
1993	Lg. Candle Holder Boy-DC138	Suspd.		20.00	22
1993	Lg. Candle Holder Girl-DC139	Suspd.		20.00	22
1992	Life Is Good-DC119	Retrd.	1996	10.00	12
1992	Little Darlin'-DC146	Retrd.	1995	7.00	10
1993	Little Dickens-DC127	Retrd.	1995	24.00	24
1992	Littlest Angel-DC143	Retrd.	1995	7.00	10
1993	Long Fellow-DC126	Retrd.	1995	24.00	24
1993	Me And My Shadow-DC116	Retrd.	1996	19.00	22
1991	Medium Heart Cherub Box-5751	Suspd.		14.00	14
1991	Mischief Maker-DC105	Retrd.	1996	10.00	10
1993	Miss Morningstar-DC141	Retrd.	1995	25.00	25
1991	Musician w/Cymbals-5154	Suspd.		22.00	22
1991	Musician w/Drums-5152	Suspd.		22.00	22
1991	Musician w/Flute-5153	Suspd.		22.00	22
1991	Musician w/Trumpet-5151	Suspd.		22.00	22
1992	My Funny Valentine-DC201	Suspd.		17.00	28
1994	Newborn Cherub-DC168	Suspd.		9.50	10
1995	Nursery Rhyme-DC229	Suspd.		42.00	50
1991	Octagonal Ballerina Box-5700	Suspd.		9.00	9
1994	Open Me First-DC243	Suspd.		13.00	13
1995	Picture Perfect-DC255	10,000	1995	100.00	112
1991	Queen Octagonal Cherub Box -5804	Suspd.		26.00	26
1991	Queen Rectangle Cat Box-5800	Suspd.		28.75	29
1991	Queen Round Bears Box-5801	Suspd.		28.75	29
1994	The Recital-DC254	10,000	1994	135.00	175-250
1994	Side By Side-DC169	Retrd.	1995	31.50	32
1991	Sitting Pretty-DC101	Retrd.	1996	9.50	12
1992	Sleigh Ride-DC122	Suspd.		15.50	16
1993	Small Candle Holder #1-DC136	Suspd.		11.50	12
1993	Small Candle Holder #2-DC137	Suspd.		11.50	12
1991	Small Cherub with Hanging Ribbon-5104	Suspd.		10.00	10
1991	Small Heart "I Love You" Box -5701	Suspd.		9.00	9
1991	Small Rectangle "Dicky Duck" Box -5703	Suspd.		9.00	9
1991	Small Square Dinosaur Box -5702	Suspd.		9.00	9
1994	Snowflake-DC117	Suspd.		10.00	14
1994	Sock Hop-DC222	Suspd.		16.00	16
1991	Speed Racer Box-5750	Suspd.		14.00	14
1994	Sucking My Thumb-DC156	Retrd.	1995	6.50	10
1994	Surprise Gift-DC152	Retrd.	1995	6.50	10
1993	Sweet Dreams-DC125	Retrd.	1995	29.00	29
1994	Sweet Gingerbread-DC223	Suspd.		16.00	16
1993	Teeter Tots-DC252	10,000	1993	100.00	175
1993	Thinking of You-DC129	Open		42.00	42
1991	Train Box-5803	Suspd.		28.75	29
1994	Up All Night-DC155	Suspd.		6.50	10
1991	Wild Flower-DC107	Retrd.	1996	10.00	10
1991	You're Special Box-5802	Suspd.		28.75	29

Dreamsicles Animals - K. Haynes

1991	Armadillo-5176	Suspd.		14.00	14
1992	Beach Baby-DA615	Suspd.		26.00	26
1994	Beary Sweet-DA455	Suspd.		15.00	15
1992	Blowfish-DA608	Suspd.		10.00	10

FIGURINES/COTTAGES

YEAR ISSUE		EDITION LIMIT	YEAR RETD.	ISSUE PRICE	*QUOTE U.S.$
1991	Buddy Bear-DA451	Suspd.		7.50	8
1992	Bunny Bookends-DA122	Suspd.		44.00	44
1991	Bunny Hop-DA105	Retrd.	1995	19.50	20
1991	Carnation-DA379	Retrd.	1996	16.00	16
1992	Cat Nap-DA551	Suspd.		10.00	10
1992	The Cat's Meow-DA552	Suspd.		10.00	10
1993	Country Bear-DA458	Suspd.		14.00	14
1992	Crabby-DA607	Suspd.		8.00	8
1992	Cute As A Button-DA553	Suspd.		10.00	10
1991	Dairy Delight-DA381	Retrd.	1995	28.00	30
1991	Dimples (girl)-DA100	Retrd.	1995	6.00	6
1992	Dino-DA480	Suspd.		14.00	14
1992	Dodo-DA482	Suspd.		9.00	9
1992	Double fish-DA611	Suspd.		8.00	8
1992	Fat Cat-DA555	Suspd.		26.00	26
1992	Free Ride-DA631	Suspd.		13.00	13
1991	Gathering Flowers-DA320	Retrd.	1995	18.00	18
1991	Hambone-DA344	Retrd.	1996	10.00	10
1991	Hamlet-DA342	Retrd.	1996	10.00	10
1992	Helga-DA112	Retrd.	1995	8.00	8
1994	Henrietta-DA383	Retrd.	1996	28.00	28
1991	Hey Diddle Diddle-DA380	Retrd.	1996	16.00	16
1991	Hippity Hop- DA106	Suspd.		31.00	31
1991	Honey Bun (boy)-DA101	Retrd.	1995	6.00	6
1992	Hound Dog-DA568	Suspd.		11.00	11
1991	King Rabbit-DA124	Suspd.		66.00	66
1991	Kitchen Pig-DA345	Suspd.		31.50	32
1991	Lambie Pie-DA328	Suspd.		9.00	9
1992	Largemouth-DA609	Suspd.		8.00	8
1992	Lazy Bones-DA605	Suspd.		14.00	14
1993	Li'l Chick-DA385	Suspd.		7.00	7
1993	Li'l Duck-DA388	Suspd.		7.00	7
1991	Mama Bear-DA452	Suspd.		9.00	9
1992	Man's Best Friend-DA560	Suspd.		11.00	11
1991	Mother Mouse-DA477	Suspd.		10.00	10
1991	Mouse on Skis-DA475	Suspd.		17.00	17
1991	Mr. Bunny- DA107	Suspd.		27.00	27
1991	Mrs. Bunny- DA108	Suspd.		27.00	27
1991	Mutton Chops-DA326	Suspd.		7.50	8
1992	Needlenose-DA610	Suspd.		8.00	8
1992	Octopus' Garden-DA606	Suspd.		10.00	10
1991	P.J. Mouse-DA476	Suspd.		10.00	10
1993	Pal Joey-DA104	Retrd.	1995	13.50	14
1992	Papa Pelican-DA602	Suspd.		22.00	22
1993	Party Bunny-DA116	Suspd.		19.00	19
1992	Pelican Jr.- DA601	Suspd.		9.00	9
1993	Pierre The Bear-DA453	Suspd.		14.00	14
1991	Piglet-DA343	Retrd.	1996	10.00	10
1991	Pigmalion-DA340	Retrd.	1995	6.00	6
1991	Pigtails-DA341	Retrd.	1995	6.00	6
1994	Potpourri Bunnies-DA117	Suspd.		15.50	16
1994	Potpourri Pals-DA118	Suspd.		15.50	16
1992	Pretty Kitty-DA554	Suspd.		15.00	15
1992	Pumpkin Harvest-DA322	Suspd.		19.00	19
1992	Puppy Love-DA562	Suspd.		12.00	12
1992	Red Rover-DA566	Suspd.		17.00	17
1992	Rhino-DA481	Suspd.		14.00	14
1991	Ricky Raccoon-5170	Suspd.		27.00	27
1992	Sarge-DA111	Retrd.	1995	8.00	8
1992	Scooter-DA567	Suspd.		11.00	11
1992	Sir Hareold-DA123	Retrd.	1996	49.00	49
1992	Slow Poke-DA630	Suspd.		13.00	13
1991	Soap Box Bunny-DA221	Retrd.	1995	15.00	15
1991	Socrates the Sheep-5029	Suspd.		18.00	18
1992	Splash-DA616	Suspd.		26.00	26
1992	St. Peter Rabbit-DA243	Suspd.		29.00	29
1991	Sweet Cream-DA382	Retrd.	1996	29.00	29
1992	Teddy Bear-DA456	Suspd.		14.00	14
1991	Tiny Bunny-DA102	Retrd.	1996	7.50	10
1991	Trick or Treat-DA651	Retrd.	1996	11.00	11
1992	Winter's Comin'-DA471	Suspd.		10.00	10
1991	Wooly Bully-DA327	Suspd.		9.00	9

Dreamsicles Calendar Collection - K. Haynes

1994	Winter Wonderland (January) -DC180	Retrd.	1995	24.00	24
1994	Special Delivery (February) -DC181	Retrd.	1995	24.00	27
1994	Ride Like The Wind (March) -DC182	Retrd.	1995	24.00	27
1994	Springtime Frolic (April)-DC183	Retrd.	1995	24.00	27
1994	Love In Bloom (May)-DC184	Retrd.	1995	24.00	27
1994	Among Friends (June)-DC185	Retrd.	1995	24.00	27
1994	Pool Pals (July)-DC186	Retrd.	1995	24.00	27
1994	Nature's Bounty (August)-DC187	Retrd.	1995	24.00	27
1994	School Days (September) -DC188	Retrd.	1995	24.00	27
1994	Autumn Leaves (October) -DC189	Retrd.	1995	24.00	27
1994	Now Give Thanks (November) -DC190	Retrd.	1995	24.00	27
1994	Holiday Magic (December) -DC191	Retrd.	1995	24.00	27

Dreamsicles Christmas - K. Haynes

1992	Baby Love-DX147	Retrd.	1995	7.00	7
1995	Best Buddies-DX159	Suspd.		14.50	15
1992	Bluebird On My Shoulder-DX115	Retrd.	1995	19.00	19
1991	Bright Eyes-DX108	Suspd.	1993	10.00	10
1992	Bundle of Joy-DX142	Retrd.	1995	7.00	7
1992	Caroler - Center Scroll-DX216	Retrd.	1995	19.00	22
1992	Caroler - Left Scroll-DX218	Retrd.	1995	19.00	22
1992	Caroler - Right Scroll-DX217	Retrd.	1995	19.00	22

YEAR ISSUE		EDITION LIMIT	YEAR RETD.	ISSUE PRICE	*QUOTE U.S.$
1991	Cherub and Child-DX100	Retrd.	1995	14.00	30
1992	A Child's Prayer-DX145	Retrd.	1995	7.00	7
1992	Dream A Little Dream-DX144	Retrd.	1995	7.00	7
1993	The Finishing Touches-DX248 (2nd Ed.)	Retrd.	1994	85.00	150
1991	Forever Yours-DX110	Retrd.	1995	44.00	44
1995	Forty Winks-DX233	Suspd.		12.50	13
1995	Free Bird-DX234	Suspd.		12.50	13
1995	Grandma's Or Bust-DX227	Suspd.		15.50	16
1995	Granny's Cookies-DX228	Suspd.		12.50	13
1995	Happy Feet-DX164	Suspd.		10.00	10
1991	Heavenly Dreamer-DX106	Retrd.	1996	11.00	11
1994	Here's Looking at You-DX172	Retrd.	1995	25.00	28
1994	Holiday on Ice-DX249 (3rd Ed.)	Retrd.	1995	85.00	100
1996	Homeward Bound-DX251 (5th Ed.)	Yr.Iss.		80.00	80
1995	Hushaby Baby-DX303	Suspd.		15.50	16
1995	I Love Mommy-DX226	Suspd.		12.50	13
1995	I Love You-DX225	Suspd.		15.50	16
1995	Let's Play Fetch-DX237	Suspd.		15.50	16
1992	Life Is Good-DX119	Retrd.	1995	10.50	12
1992	Little Darlin'-DX146	Retrd.	1995	7.00	10
1993	Little Dickens-DX127	Retrd.	1995	24.00	25
1992	Little Drummer Boy-DX241	Suspd.		32.00	32
1992	Littlest Angel-DX143	Retrd.	1995	7.00	7
1993	Long Fellow-DX126	Retrd.	1995	24.00	25
1993	Love My Kitty-DX130	Suspd.		15.50	16
1993	Love My Puppy-DX131	Suspd.		14.50	15
1993	Love My Teddy-DX132	Suspd.		15.50	16
1992	Make A Wish-DX118	Suspd.		14.50	15
1993	Me And My Shadow-DX116	Retrd.	1996	19.50	20
1991	Mischief Maker-DX105	Suspd.		10.50	11
1993	Miss Morningstar-DX141	Retrd.	1996	25.50	28
1994	Moon Dance-DX210	Suspd.		30.00	30
1995	Moonglow-DX235	Suspd.		13.50	14
1992	My Prayer-DX121	Suspd.		14.00	14
1994	Newborn Cherub-DX168	Suspd.		10.00	10
1995	Nite Nite-DX238	Suspd.		15.50	16
1994	Over The Rainbow-DX209	Suspd.		36.00	36
1995	Poetry In Motion-DX113	Suspd.		82.00	100
1995	Purr-fect Pals-DX239	Suspd.		15.50	16
1995	Rainbow Rider-DX236	Suspd.		14.00	14
1995	Range Rider-DX305	Suspd.		15.50	16
1995	Read Me A Story-DX123	Suspd.		13.50	14
1991	Santa Bunny-DX203	Retrd.	1994	32.00	32
1992	Santa In Dreamsicle Land-DX247 (1st Ed.)	Retrd.	1993	85.00	225-350
1991	Santa's Elf-DX240	Retrd.	1996	19.00	22
1995	Santa's Kingdom-DX250 (4th Ed.)	Retrd.	1995	80.00	90
1994	Share The Fun-DX178	Suspd.		14.00	14
1994	Side By Side-DX169	Retrd.	1995	31.50	32
1991	Sitting Pretty-DX101	Retrd.	1996	10.00	10
1991	Snowman-DX252	Suspd.		10.00	10
1994	Stolen Kiss-DX162	Suspd.		12.50	14
1995	Swan Lake-DX163	Suspd.		13.50	14
1993	Sweet Dreams-DX125	Retrd.	1995	29.00	29
1994	Swing On A Star-DX208	Suspd.		30.00	30
1993	Teacher's Pet-DX124	Suspd.		11.50	12
1993	Thinking of You-DX129	Suspd.		45.00	45
1994	Three Amigos-DX179	Suspd.		14.00	14
1991	Wildflower-DX107	Retrd.	1996	10.50	15
1991	Wishin' On A Star-DX120	Suspd.		10.50	12
1994	You've Got A Friend-DX170	Suspd.		27.00	27

Dreamsicles Day Event- K. Haynes

1995	1995 Dreamsicles Event Figurine-DC075	Retrd.	1995	20.00	35
1996	Glad Tidings-DD100	Yr.Iss.		15.95	16

Dreamsicles Heavenly Classics - K. Haynes & S. Hackett

1995	The Dedication-DC351	10,000		118.00	125

The Cat's Meow

Collector Club Gift - Houses - F. Jones

1989	1989 Betsy Ross House	Retrd.	1989	Gift	200
1990	1990 Amelia Earhart	Retrd.	1990	Gift	100
1991	1991 Limberlost Cabin	Retrd.	1991	Gift	50
1992	1992 Abigail Adams Birthplace	Retrd.	1992	Gift	50
1993	1993 Pearl S. Buck House	Retrd.	1993	Gift	50
1994	1994 Lillian Gish	Retrd.	1994	Gift	30
1995	1995 Eleanor Roosevelt	Retrd.	1995	Gift	N/A
1996	1996 Mother's Day Church	12/96		Gift	N/A

Collector Club - Famous Authors - F. Jones

1989	Harriet Beecher Stowe	Retrd.	1989	8.75	N/A
1989	Orchard House	Retrd.	1989	8.75	N/A
1989	Longfellow House	Retrd.	1989	8.75	N/A
1989	Herman Melville's Arrowhead	Retrd.	1989	8.75	800
1989	Set	Retrd.	1989	35.00	800

Collector Club - Great Inventors - F. Jones

1990	Thomas Edison	Retrd.	1990	9.25	N/A
1990	Ford Motor Co.	Retrd.	1990	9.25	N/A
1990	Seth Thomas Clock Co.	Retrd.	1990	9.25	75
1990	Wright Cycle Co.	Retrd.	1990	9.25	50
1990	Set	Retrd.	1990	37.00	350-500

Collector Club - American Songwriters - F. Jones

1991	Benjamin R. Hanby House	Retrd.	1991	9.25	N/A
1991	Anna Warner House	Retrd.	1991	9.25	N/A

YEAR ISSUE		EDITION LIMIT	YEAR RETD.	ISSUE PRICE	*QUOTE U.S.$
1991	Stephen Foster Home	Retrd.	1991	9.25	22
1991	Oscar Hammerstein House	Retrd.	1991	9.25	22
1991	Set	Retrd.	1991	37.00	200-300

Collector Club - Signers of the Declaration - F. Jones

1992	Josiah Bartlett Home	Retrd.	1992	9.75	N/A
1992	George Clymer Home	Retrd.	1992	9.75	N/A
1992	Stephen Hopkins Home	Retrd.	1992	9.75	N/A
1992	John Witherspoon Home	Retrd.	1992	9.75	N/A
1992	Set	Retrd.	1992	39.00	200

Collector Club -19th Century Master Builders - F. Jones

1993	Henry Hobson Richardson	Retrd.	1993	10.25	N/A
1993	Samuel Sloan	Retrd.	1993	10.25	N/A
1993	Alexander Jackson Davis	Retrd.	1993	10.25	N/A
1993	Andrew Jackson Downing	Retrd.	1993	10.25	N/A
1993	Set	Retrd.	1993	41.00	100

Collector Club - Williamsburg Merchants - F. Jones

1994	East Carlton Wigmaker	Retrd.	1994	11.15	12
1994	J. Geddy Silversmith	Retrd.	1994	11.15	12
1994	Craig Jeweler	Retrd.	1994	11.15	12
1994	M. Hunter Millinery	Retrd.	1994	11.15	12
1994	Set	Retrd.	1994	44.60	75

Collector Club - Mt. Rushmore Presidential Series - F. Jones

1995	George Washington Birthplace	Retrd.	1995	12.00	12
1995	Metamora Courthouse	Retrd.	1995	12.00	12
1995	Theodore Roosevelt Birthplace	Retrd.	1995	12.00	12
1995	Tuckahoe Plantation	Retrd.	1995	12.00	12
1995	Set	Retrd.	1995	48.00	48

Collector Club - American Holiday Series - F. Jones

1996	And to all a Goodnight	12/96		11.00	11
1996	Boo to You	12/96		11.00	11
1996	Easter's On Its Way	12/96		11.00	11
1996	Let Freedom Ring	12/96		11.00	11

Accessories - F. Jones

1990	1909 Franklin Limousine	Retrd.	1995	4.00	7
1990	1913 Peerless Touring Car	Retrd.	1995	4.00	7
1990	1914 Fire Pumper	Retrd.	1995	4.00	7
1983	5" Hedge	Retrd.	1988	3.00	20-35
1983	5" Iron Fence	Retrd.	1988	3.00	33
1987	5" Picket Fence	Retrd.	1992	3.00	15-25
1990	5" Wrought Iron Fence	Retrd.	1995	3.00	7
1983	8" Hedge	Retrd.	1988	3.25	40-50
1983	8" Iron Fence	Retrd.	1988	3.25	30-50
1983	8" Picket Fence	Retrd.	1988	3.25	40
1989	Ada Belle	Retrd.	1994	4.00	11
1990	Amish Buggy	Retrd.	1995	4.00	8
1991	Amish Garden	12/96		4.00	5
1987	Band Stand	Retrd.	1992	6.50	18
1991	Barnyard	12/96		4.00	5
1990	Blue Spruce	Retrd.	1995	4.00	7
1990	Bus Stop	Retrd.	1995	4.00	7
1987	Butch & T.J.	Retrd.	1992	4.00	10-20
1986	Cable Car	Retrd.	1991	4.00	9-18
1986	Carolers	Retrd.	1991	4.00	15
1987	Charlie & Co.	Retrd.	1992	4.00	10
1985	Cherry Tree	Retrd.	1990	4.00	50
1991	Chessie Hopper Car	12/96		4.00	5
1986	Chickens	Retrd.	1991	3.25	15
1990	Christmas Tree Lot	Retrd.	1995	4.00	7
1989	Clothesline	Retrd.	1994	4.00	9
1988	Colonial Bread Wagon	Retrd.	1993	4.00	12
1991	Concert in the Park	12/96		4.00	18
1986	Cows	Retrd.	1991	4.00	15
1986	Dairy Wagon	Retrd.	1991	4.00	15
1986	Ducks	Retrd.	1991	3.25	13
1990	Eugene	Retrd.	1995	4.00	7
1985	Fall Tree	Retrd.	1990	4.00	25
1987	FJ Express	Retrd.	1992	4.00	15
1986	FJ Real Estate Sign	Retrd.	1991	3.00	15-24
1988	Flower Pots	Retrd.	1993	4.00	11
1988	Gas Light	Retrd.	1993	4.00	10
1990	Gerstenslager Buggy	Retrd.	1995	4.00	7
1989	Harry's Hotdogs	Retrd.	1994	4.00	10
1986	Horse & Carriage	Retrd.	1991	4.00	13
1987	Horse & Sleigh	Retrd.	1992	4.00	13
1986	Ice Wagon	Retrd.	1991	4.00	13
1983	Iron Gate	Retrd.	1988	4.00	40-50
1991	Jack The Postman	12/96		3.25	5
1986	Liberty St. Sign	Retrd.	1991	3.25	13
1983	Lilac Bushes	Retrd.	1988	3.00	200-400
1990	Little Red Caboose	Retrd.	1995	4.00	9
1988	Mail Wagon	Retrd.	1993	4.00	10
1988	Main St. Sign	Retrd.	1993	3.25	10
1991	Marble Game	12/96		4.00	5
1986	Market St. Sign	Retrd.	1991	3.25	5
1991	Martin House	12/96		3.25	5
1987	Nanny	Retrd.	1992	4.00	10
1991	On Vacation	12/96		4.00	5
1989	Passenger Train Car	Retrd.	1994	4.00	9
1985	Pine Tree	Retrd.	1990	4.00	30
1988	Pony Express Rider	Retrd.	1993	4.00	11
1991	Popcorn Wagon	12/96		4.00	5
1985	Poplar Tree	Retrd.	1990	4.00	25-35
1989	Pumpkin Wagon	Retrd.	1994	3.25	9
1989	Quaker Oats Train Car	Retrd.	1994	4.00	9
1987	Railroad Sign	Retrd.	1992	3.00	13

*Quotes have been rounded up to nearest dollar

YEAR ISSUE		EDITION LIMIT	YEAR RETRD.	ISSUE PRICE	*QUOTE U.S.$
1990	Red Maple Tree	Retrd.	1995	4.00	8
1989	Rose Trellis	Retrd.	1994	3.25	9
1989	Rudy & Aldine	Retrd.	1994	4.00	9
1990	Santa & Reindeer	Retrd.	1995	4.00	7
1991	Scarey Harry (Scarecrow)	12/96		4.00	5
1991	School Bus	12/96		4.00	5
1991	Ski Party	12/96		4.00	5
1988	Skipjack	Retrd.	1993	6.50	15
1996	Smucker Train Car	Retrd.	1996	5.00	15
1989	Snowmen	Retrd.	1994	4.00	9
1988	Street Clock	Retrd.	1993	4.00	10
1985	Summer Tree	Retrd.	1990	4.00	35
1989	Tad & Toni	Retrd.	1994	4.00	9
1988	Telephone Booth	Retrd.	1993	4.00	10
1986	Touring Car	Retrd.	1991	4.00	10
1990	Tulip Tree	Retrd.	1995	4.00	10
1988	U.S. Flag	Retrd.	1993	4.00	7
1991	USMC War Memorial	12/96		6.50	7
1990	Veterinary Wagon	Retrd.	1995	4.00	7
1990	Victorian Outhouse	Retrd.	1995	4.00	7
1991	Village Entrance Sign	12/96		6.50	7
1990	Watkins Wagon	Retrd.	1995	4.00	7
1986	Wells, Fargo Wagon	Retrd.	1991	4.00	15
1987	Windmill	Retrd.	1992	3.25	10
1986	Wishing Well	Retrd.	1991	3.25	23
1987	Wooden Gate (two-sided)	Retrd.	1992	3.00	15
1985	Xmas Pine Tree	Retrd.	1990	4.00	25-35
1985	Xmas Pine Tree w/Red Bows	Retrd.	1990	3.00	150-200
1990	Xmas Spruce	Retrd.	1995	4.00	7

American Barns - F. Jones

1992	Bank Barn	5-Yr.		8.50	10
1992	Crib Barn	5-Yr.		8.50	10
1992	Ohio Barn	5-Yr.		8.50	10
1992	Vermont Barn	5-Yr.		8.50	10

Bed & Breakfast Series - F. Jones

1995	Glen Iris	5-Yr.		10.00	10
1995	Kinter House Inn	5-Yr.		10.00	10
1995	Southmoreland	5-Yr.		10.00	10
1995	Victorian Mansion	5-Yr.		10.00	10

Black Heritage Series - F. Jones

1994	Dexter Avenue Baptist Church	5-Yr.		8.00	8
1994	Frederick Douglass Home	5-Yr.		8.00	8
1994	George Washington Carver Museum	5-Yr.		8.00	8
1994	Martin Luther King Birthplace	Retrd.	1994	8.00	50

California Mission Series - F. Jones

1995	Mission Dolores	5-Yr.		10.00	10
1995	Mission San Buenaventura	5-Yr.		10.00	10
1995	Mission San Juan Bautista	5-Yr.		10.00	10
1995	Mission San Luis Rey	5-Yr.		10.00	10

Chippewa Amusement Park - F. Jones

1993	Ballroom	5-Yr.		9.00	10
1993	Bath House	5-Yr.		9.00	10
1993	Midway	5-Yr.		9.00	10
1993	Pavilion	5-Yr.		9.00	10

Christmas '83-Williamsburg - F. Jones

1983	Christmas Church	Retrd.	1983	6.00	N/A
1983	Federal House	Retrd.	1983	6.00	N/A
1983	Garrison House	Retrd.	1983	6.00	N/A
1983	Georgian House	Retrd.	1983	6.00	450
1983	Set	Retrd.	1983	24.00	N/A

Christmas '84-Nantucket - F. Jones

1984	Christmas Shop	Retrd.	1984	6.50	N/A
1984	Powell House	Retrd.	1984	6.50	350
1984	Shaw House	Retrd.	1984	6.50	350
1984	Wintrop House	Retrd.	1984	6.50	250
1984	Set	Retrd.	1984	26.00	1600

Christmas '85-Ohio Western Reserve - F. Jones

1985	Bellevue House	Retrd.	1985	7.00	175
1985	Gates Mills Church	Retrd.	1985	7.00	200
1985	Olmstead House	Retrd.	1985	7.00	175
1985	Western Reserve Academy	Retrd.	1985	7.00	175
1985	Set	Retrd.	1985	27.00	600-975

Christmas '86-Savannah - F. Jones

1986	J.J. Dale Row House	Retrd.	1986	7.25	150
1986	Lafayette Square House	Retrd.	1986	7.25	140-150
1986	Liberty Inn	Retrd.	1986	7.25	200
1986	Simon Mirault Cottage	Retrd.	1986	7.25	200
1986	Set	Retrd.	1986	29.00	850-925

Christmas '87-Maine - F. Jones

1987	Cappy's Chowder House	Retrd.	1987	7.75	250
1987	Captain's House	Retrd.	1987	7.75	250
1987	Damariscotta Church	Retrd.	1987	7.75	250
1987	Portland Head Lighthouse	Retrd.	1987	7.75	250
1987	Set	Retrd.	1987	31.00	800-1050

Christmas '88-Philadelphia - F. Jones

1988	Elfreth's Alley	Retrd.	1988	7.75	150-200
1988	Graff House	Retrd.	1988	7.75	150-200
1988	The Head House	Retrd.	1988	7.75	150-200
1988	Hill-Physick-Keith House	Retrd.	1988	7.75	150-200

YEAR ISSUE		EDITION LIMIT	YEAR RETRD.	ISSUE PRICE	*QUOTE U.S.$
1988	Set	Retrd.	1988	31.00	400-650

Christmas '89-In New England - F. Jones

1989	Hunter House	Retrd.	1989	8.00	50-80
1989	The Old South Meeting House	Retrd.	1989	8.00	80-125
1989	Sheldon's Tavern	Retrd.	1989	8.00	125
1989	The Vermont Country Store	Retrd.	1989	8.00	80-125
1989	Set	Retrd.	1989	32.00	250-450

Christmas '90-Colonial Virginia - F. Jones

1990	Dulany House	Retrd.	1990	8.00	50-100
1990	Rising Sun Tavern	Retrd.	1990	8.00	70-100
1990	Shirley Plantation	Retrd.	1990	8.00	50-75
1990	St. John's Church	Retrd.	1990	8.00	100
1990	St. John's Church (blue)	Retrd.	1990	8.00	150-200
1990	Set	Retrd.	1990	32.00	300-400

Christmas '91-Rocky Mountain - F. Jones

1991	First Presbyterian Church	Retrd.	1991	8.20	25-50
1991	Tabor House	Retrd.	1991	8.20	55-75
1991	Western Hotel	Retrd.	1991	8.20	25-55
1991	Wheller-Stallard House	Retrd.	1991	8.20	25-55
1991	Set	Retrd.	1991	32.80	125-200

Christmas '92-Hometown - F. Jones

1992	August Imgard House	Retrd.	1992	8.50	35-50
1992	Howey House	Retrd.	1992	8.50	30-50
1992	Overholt House	Retrd.	1992	8.50	30-50
1992	Wayne Co. Courthouse	Retrd.	1992	8.50	30-50
1992	Set	Retrd.	1992	34.00	100-120

Christmas '93-St. Charles - F. Jones

1993	Lewis & Clark Center	Retrd.	1993	9.00	15-20
1993	Newbill-McElhiney House	Retrd.	1993	9.00	15-20
1993	St. Peter's Catholic Church	Retrd.	1993	9.00	15-20
1993	Stone Row	Retrd.	1993	9.00	15-20
1993	Set	Retrd.	1993	36.00	70-90

Christmas '94-New Orleans Series - F. Jones

1994	Beauregard-Keyes House	Retrd.	1994	10.00	14-20
1994	Gallier House	Retrd.	1994	10.00	14-20
1994	Hermann-Grima House	Retrd.	1994	10.00	14-20
1994	St. Patrick's Church	Retrd.	1994	10.00	14-20
1994	Set	Retrd.	1994	40.00	50

Christmas '95-New York Series - F. Jones

1995	Clement C. Moore House	Retrd.	1995	10.00	10-15
1995	Fraunces Taver	Retrd.	1995	10.00	10-15
1995	Fulton Market	Retrd.	1995	10.00	10-15
1995	St. Marks-In-the-Bowery	Retrd.	1995	10.00	10-15
1995	Set	Retrd.	1995	40.00	55

Christmas '96-Atlanta Series - F. Jones

1996	Callanwolde	12/96		11.00	11
1996	First Baptist Church	12/96		11.00	11
1996	Fox Theatre	12/96		11.00	11
1996	Margaret Mitchell House	12/96		11.00	11

Circus Series - F. Jones

1996	Ferris Wheel	12/96		10.00	10
1995	Sideshow	Retrd.	1995	10.00	17

Covered Bridge Series - F. Jones

1995	Creamery Bridge	Retrd.	1995	10.00	17
1996	Kennedy Bridge	12/96		10.00	10

Daughters of the Painted Lady Series - F. Jones

1995	Barber Cottage	5-Yr.		10.00	10
1995	The Fan House	5-Yr.		10.00	10
1995	Hall Cottage	5-Yr.		10.00	10
1995	The Painted Lady	5-Yr.		10.00	10

Duke of Gloucester Series - F. Jones

1994	Cole Shop	5-Yr.		10.00	10
1994	Nicolson Store	5-Yr.		10.00	10
1994	Pasteur & Galt Apothecary	5-Yr.		10.00	10
1994	Prentis Shop	5-Yr.		10.00	10

Elm Street Series - F. Jones

1994	Blumenthal's	5-Yr.		10.00	10
1994	Clyde's Shoe Repair	5-Yr.		10.00	10
1994	First Congregational Church	5-Yr.		10.00	10
1994	Jim's Hunting & Fishing	5-Yr.		10.00	10

Fairy Tale Series - F. Jones

1996	Gingerbread House	5-Yr.		10.00	10
1996	Grandmother's House	5-Yr.		10.00	10
1996	Seven Dwarf's House	5-Yr.		10.00	10
1996	Three Bear's House	5-Yr.		10.00	10

Fall - F. Jones

1986	Golden Lamb Buttery	Retrd.	1991	8.00	35-50
1986	Grimm's Farmhouse	Retrd.	1991	8.00	45
1986	Mail Pouch Barn	Retrd.	1991	8.00	55-75
1986	Vollant Mills	Retrd.	1991	8.00	35-65
1986	Set	Retrd.	1991	32.00	135-180

Firehouse Series - F. Jones

1994	David Crockett No. 1	5-Yr.		10.00	10
1994	Denver No. 1	5-Yr.		10.00	10
1994	Toledo No. 18	5-Yr.		10.00	10

YEAR ISSUE		EDITION LIMIT	YEAR RETRD.	ISSUE PRICE	* QUOTE U.S.$
1994	Vigilant 1891	5-Yr.		10.00	10

Galveston Series - F. Jones

1996	Ashton Villa	5-Yr.		10.00	10
1996	Lemuel Burr House	5-Yr.		10.00	10
1996	Sacred Heart Church	5-Yr.		10.00	10
1996	Trueheart - Adriance Building	5-Yr.		10.00	10

General Store Series - F. Jones

1993	Calef's Country Store	5-Yr.		10.00	10
1993	Davoll's General Store	5-Yr.		10.00	10
1993	Peltier's Market	5-Yr.		10.00	10
1993	S. Woodstock Country Store	5-Yr.		10.00	10

Great Americans Series - F. Jones

1996	Daniel Boone Home	12/96		10.00	10

Green Gables Series - F. Jones

1996	Green Gables House	12/96		10.00	10

Greenwich Village Series - F. Jones

1996	Hudson Gormet	5-Yr.		10.00	10
1996	Mc Nulty's Tea & Coffee	5-Yr.		10.00	10
1996	Three Lives Books	5-Yr.		10.00	10
1996	Vesuvio Bakery	5-Yr.		10.00	10

Hagerstown - F. Jones

1988	J Hager House	Retrd.	1993	8.00	17-25
1988	Miller House	Retrd.	1993	8.00	17-25
1988	Woman's Club	Retrd.	1993	8.00	17-25
1988	The Yule Cupboard	Retrd.	1993	8.00	17-25
1988	Set	Retrd.	1993	32.00	60-75

Historic Nauvoo Series - F. Jones

1995	Cultural Hall	5-Yr.		10.00	10
1995	J. Browning Gunsmith	5-Yr.		10.00	10
1995	Printing Office	5-Yr.		10.00	10
1995	Stoddard Home & Tinsmith	5-Yr.		10.00	10

Liberty St. - F. Jones

1988	County Courthouse	Retrd.	1993	8.00	17-31
1988	Graf Printing Co.	Retrd.	1993	8.00	17-31
1988	Wilton Railway Depot	Retrd.	1993	8.00	17-31
1988	Z. Jones Basketmaker	Retrd.	1993	8.00	20-40

Lighthouse - F. Jones

1990	Admiralty Head	Retrd.	1995	8.00	15
1990	Cape Hatteras Lighthouse	Retrd.	1995	8.00	15
1990	Sandy Hook Lighthouse	Retrd.	1995	8.00	15
1990	Split Rock Lighthouse	Retrd.	1995	8.00	15

Limited Edition Promotional Items - F. Jones

1993	Convention Museum	Retrd.	1993	12.95	13
1993	FJ Factory	Open		12.95	13
1994	FJ Factory/5 Yr. Banner	Retrd.	1994	10.00	18
1993	FJ Factory/Gold Cat Edition	Retrd.	1993	12.95	490
1994	FJ Factory/Home Banner	Retrd.	1994	10.00	10
1990	Frycrest Farm Homestead	Retrd.	1991	8.00	125
1992	Glen Pine	Retrd.	1993	8.00	27
1993	Nativity Cat on the Fence	Retrd.	1993	19.95	30

Main St. - F. Jones

1987	Franklin Library	Retrd.	1992	8.00	35
1987	Garden Theatre	Retrd.	1992	8.00	45
1987	Historical Museum	Retrd.	1992	8.00	25
1987	Telegraph/Post Office	Retrd.	1992	8.00	25
1987	Set	Retrd.	1992	32.00	100

Mark Twain's Hannibal Series - F. Jones

1995	Becky Thatcher House	Retrd.	1995	10.00	17
1996	Hickory Stick	12/96		10.00	10

Market St. - F. Jones

1989	Schumacher Mills	Retrd.	1993	8.00	17-25
1989	Seville Hardware Store	Retrd.	1993	8.00	17-25
1989	West India Goods Store	Retrd.	1993	8.00	17-25
1989	Yankee Candle Company	Retrd.	1993	8.00	17-35

Martha's Vineyard Series - F. Jones

1995	John Coffin House	Retrd.	1995	10.00	10-15
1996	West Chop Lighthouse	12/96		10.00	10

Miscellaneous - F. Jones

1985	Pencil Holder	Retrd.	1988	3.95	210
1985	Recipe Holder	Retrd.	1988	3.95	250
1986	School Desk-blue	Retrd.	1988	12.00	N/A
1986	School Desk-red	Retrd.	1988	12.00	175

Nantucket - F. Jones

1987	Jared Coffin House	Retrd.	1992	8.00	25
1987	Maria Mitchell House	Retrd.	1992	8.00	25
1987	Nantucket Atheneum	Retrd.	1992	8.00	25
1987	Unitarian Church	Retrd.	1992	8.00	25
1987	Set	Retrd.	1992	32.00	100

Nautical - F. Jones

1987	H & E Ships Chandlery	Retrd.	1992	8.00	25
1987	Lorain Lighthouse	Retrd.	1992	8.00	25
1987	Monhegan Boat Landing	Retrd.	1992	8.00	25
1987	Yacht Club	Retrd.	1992	8.00	25
1987	Set	Retrd.	1992	32.00	100

*Quotes have been rounded up to nearest dollar

FIGURINES/COTTAGES

YEAR ISSUE		EDITION LIMIT	YEAR RETD.	ISSUE PRICE	*QUOTE U.S.$
Neighborhood Event Series - F. Jones					
1995	Peter Seitz Tavern & Stagecoach	Retrd.	1995	12.95	18
1995	Birely Place	Retrd.	1995	12.95	18
1996	Sea-Chimes	12/96		12.95	13
1996	Bailey-Gombert House	12/96		12.95	13
Nursery Rhyme Series - F. Jones					
1994	Crooked House	5-Yr.		10.00	10
1994	House That Jack Built	5-Yr.		10.00	10
1994	Old Woman in the Shoe	5-Yr.		10.00	10
1994	Peter, Peter Pumpkin Eater	5-Yr.		10.00	10
Ohio Amish - F. Jones					
1991	Ada Mae's Quilt Barn	5-Yr.		8.00	10
1991	Brown School	5-Yr.		8.00	10
1991	Eli's Harness Shop	5-Yr.		8.00	10
1991	Jonas Troyer Home	5-Yr.		8.00	10
Painted Ladies - F. Jones					
1988	Andrews Hotel	Retrd.	1993	8.00	16-25
1988	Lady Amanda	Retrd.	1993	8.00	16-25
1988	Lady Elizabeth	Retrd.	1993	8.00	16-25
1988	Lady Iris	Retrd.	1993	8.00	16-25
1988	Set	Retrd.	1993	32.00	60
Postage Stamp Lighthouse Series - F. Jones					
1996	The Great Lakes Postage Stamp Lighthouse, set/5	6,000	1996	75.00	75
Roscoe Village - F. Jones					
1986	Canal Company	Retrd.	1991	8.00	45-65
1986	Jackson Twp. Hall	Retrd.	1991	8.00	45-65
1986	Old Warehouse Rest.	Retrd.	1991	8.00	45-65
1986	Roscoe General Store	Retrd.	1991	8.00	45-65
1986	Set	Retrd.	1991	32.00	150
Series I - F. Jones					
1983	Antique Shop	Retrd.	1988	8.00	100-125
1983	Apothecary	Retrd.	1988	8.00	100-125
1983	Barbershop	Retrd.	1988	8.00	80-125
1983	Book Store	Retrd.	1988	8.00	50-125
1983	Cherry Tree Inn	Retrd.	1988	8.00	N/A
1983	Federal House	Retrd.	1988	8.00	60-125
1983	Florist Shop	Retrd.	1988	8.00	60-125
1983	Garrison House	Retrd.	1988	8.00	125
1983	Red Whale Inn	Retrd.	1988	8.00	N/A
1983	School	Retrd.	1988	8.00	85-100
1983	Sweetshop	Retrd.	1988	8.00	125
1983	Toy Shoppe	Retrd.	1988	8.00	125
1983	Victorian House	Retrd.	1988	8.00	50-125
1983	Wayside Inn	Retrd.	1988	8.00	N/A
1983	Set of 12 w/1 Inn	Retrd.	1988	96.00	850-1450
1983	Set of 14 w/ 3 Inns	Retrd.	1988	112.00	2000-3000
Series II - F. Jones					
1984	Attorney/Bank	Retrd.	1989	8.00	95-150
1984	Brocke House	Retrd.	1989	8.00	40-95
1984	Church	Retrd.	1989	8.00	40-95
1984	Eaton House	Retrd.	1989	8.00	150-175
1984	Grandinere House	Retrd.	1989	8.00	95-150
1984	Millinery/Quilt	Retrd.	1989	8.00	150-200
1984	Music Shop	Retrd.	1989	8.00	100-125
1984	S&T Clothiers	Retrd.	1989	8.00	150-175
1984	Tobacconist/Shoemaker	Retrd.	1989	8.00	95-150
1984	Town Hall	Retrd.	1989	8.00	150
1984	Set	Retrd.	1989	96.00	500-850
Series III - F. Jones					
1985	Allen-Coe House	Retrd.	1990	8.00	60
1985	Connecticut Ave. FireHouse	Retrd.	1990	8.00	40-75
1985	Dry Goods Store	Retrd.	1990	8.00	50-75
1985	Edinburgh Times	Retrd.	1990	8.00	40-75
1985	Fine Jewelers	Retrd.	1990	8.00	40-50
1985	Hobart-Harley House	Retrd.	1990	8.00	50-75
1985	Kalorama Guest Home	Retrd.	1990	8.00	30-40
1985	Main St. Carriage Shop	Retrd.	1990	8.00	50-75
1985	Opera House	Retrd.	1990	8.00	50-75
1985	Ristorante	Retrd.	1990	8.00	50-75
1985	Set	Retrd.	1990	80.00	350-400
Series IV - F. Jones					
1986	Bennington-Hull House	Retrd.	1991	8.00	30-40
1986	Chagrin Falls Popcorn Shop	Retrd.	1991	8.00	30-40
1986	Chepachet Union Church	Retrd.	1991	8.00	30-40
1986	John Belville House	Retrd.	1991	8.00	30-40
1986	Jones Bros. Tea Co.	Retrd.	1991	8.00	30-40
1986	The Little House Giftables	Retrd.	1991	8.00	30-40
1986	O'Malley's Livery Stable	Retrd.	1991	8.00	30-40
1986	Vandenberg House	Retrd.	1991	8.00	30-40
1986	Village Clock Shop	Retrd.	1991	8.00	30-40
1986	Westbrook House	Retrd.	1991	8.00	30-40
1986	Set	Retrd.	1991	80.00	320
Series V - F. Jones					
1987	Amish Oak/Dixie Shoe	Retrd.	1992	8.00	20-30
1987	Architect/Tailor	Retrd.	1992	8.00	20-30
1987	Congruity Tavern	Retrd.	1992	8.00	20-30
1987	Creole House	Retrd.	1992	8.00	20-30
1987	Dentist/Physician	Retrd.	1992	8.00	20-30
1987	M. Washington House	Retrd.	1992	8.00	20-30
1987	Markethouse	Retrd.	1992	8.00	20-30

YEAR ISSUE		EDITION LIMIT	YEAR RETD.	ISSUE PRICE	*QUOTE U.S.$
1987	Murray Hotel	Retrd.	1992	8.00	20-30
1987	Police Department	Retrd.	1992	8.00	20-30
1987	Southport Bank	Retrd.	1992	8.00	20-30
1987	Set	Retrd.	1992	80.00	200-250
Series VI - F. Jones					
1988	Burton Lancaster House	Retrd.	1993	8.00	20
1988	City Hospital	Retrd.	1993	8.00	20
1988	First Baptist Church	Retrd.	1993	8.00	20
1988	Fish/Meat Market	Retrd.	1993	8.00	20
1988	Lincoln School	Retrd.	1993	8.00	20
1988	New Masters Gallery	Retrd.	1993	8.00	20
1988	Ohliger House	Retrd.	1993	8.00	20
1988	Pruyn House	Retrd.	1993	8.00	20
1988	Stiffenbody Funeral Home	Retrd.	1993	8.00	20
1988	Williams & Sons	Retrd.	1993	8.00	20
1988	Set	Retrd.	1993	80.00	150-175
Series VII - F. Jones					
1989	Black Cat Antiques	Retrd.	1994	8.00	15
1989	Hairdressing Parlor	Retrd.	1994	8.00	15
1989	Handcrafted Toys	Retrd.	1994	8.00	15
1989	Justice of the Peace	Retrd.	1994	8.00	15
1989	Octagonal School	Retrd.	1994	8.00	15
1989	Old Franklin Book Shop	Retrd.	1994	8.00	15
1989	Thorpe House Bed & Breakfast	Retrd.	1994	8.00	15
1989	Village Tinsmith	Retrd.	1994	8.00	15
1989	Williams Apothecary	Retrd.	1994	8.00	15
1989	Winkler Bakery	Retrd.	1994	8.00	15
1989	Set	Retrd.	1994	80.00	100
Series VIII - F. Jones					
1990	FJ Realty Company	Retrd.	1995	8.00	15
1990	Globe Corner Bookstore	Retrd.	1995	8.00	15
1990	Haberdashers	Retrd.	1995	8.00	15
1990	Medina Fire Department	Retrd.	1995	8.00	15
1990	Nell's Stems & Stitches	Retrd.	1995	8.00	15
1990	Noah's Ark Veterinary	Retrd.	1995	8.00	15
1990	Piccadilli Pipe & Tobacco	Retrd.	1995	8.00	15
1990	Puritan House	Retrd.	1995	8.00	15
1990	Victoria's Parlour	Retrd.	1995	8.00	15
1990	Walldorff Furniture	Retrd.	1995	8.00	15
1990	Set	Retrd.	1995	80.00	100
Series IX - F. Jones					
1991	All Saints Chapel	12/96		8.00	10
1991	American Red Cross	12/96		8.00	10
1991	Central City Opera House	12/96		8.00	10
1991	City Hall	12/96		8.00	10
1991	CPA/Law Office	12/96		8.00	10
1991	Gov. Snyder Mansion	12/96		8.00	10
1991	Jeweler/Optometrist	12/96		8.00	10
1991	Osbahr's Upholstery	12/96		8.00	10
1991	Spanky's Hardware Co.	12/96		8.00	10
1991	The Treble Clef	12/96		8.00	10
Series X - F. Jones					
1992	City News	5-Yr.		8.50	10
1992	Fudge Kitchen	5-Yr.		8.50	10
1992	Grand Haven	5-Yr.		8.50	10
1992	Henyan's Athletic Shop	5-Yr.		8.50	10
1992	Leppert's 5 &10	5-Yr.		8.50	10
1992	Madeline's Dress Shop	5-Yr.		8.50	10
1992	Owl And The Pussycat	5-Yr.		8.50	10
1992	Pickles Pub	5-Yr.		8.50	10
1992	Pure Gas Station	5-Yr.		8.50	10
1993	Shrimplin & Jones Produce	5-Yr.		9.00	10
1992	United Church of Acworth	5-Yr.		8.50	10
Series XI - F. Jones					
1993	Barbershop/Gallery	5-Yr.		9.00	10
1993	Haddonfield Bank	5-Yr.		9.00	10
1993	Immanuel Church	5-Yr.		9.00	10
1993	Johann Singer Boots & Shoes	5-Yr.		9.00	10
1993	Pet Shop/Gift Shop	5-Yr.		9.00	10
1993	Police-Troop C	5-Yr.		9.00	10
1993	Stone's Restaurant	5-Yr.		9.00	10
1993	U.S. Armed Forces	5-Yr.		9.00	10
1993	U.S. Post Office	5-Yr.		9.00	10
Series XII - F. Jones					
1994	Arnold-Lynch Funeral Home	5-Yr.		10.00	10
1994	Bedford County Courthouse	5-Yr.		10.00	10
1994	Boyd's Drug Strore	5-Yr.		10.00	10
1994	Christmas Tree Hill Gifts	5-Yr.		10.00	10
1994	Foorman-Morrison House	5-Yr.		10.00	10
1994	Haddon Hts. Train Depot	5-Yr.		10.00	10
1994	Historical Society	5-Yr.		10.00	10
1994	Masonic Temple	5-Yr.		10.00	10
1994	Ritz Theater	5-Yr.		10.00	10
1994	Spread Eagle Tavern	5-Yr.		10.00	10
Series XIII - F. Jones					
1995	Alvanas & Coe Barbers	5-Yr.		10.00	10
1995	Cedar School	5-Yr.		10.00	10
1995	Hospital	5-Yr.		10.00	10
1995	Needleworker	5-Yr.		10.00	10
1995	Public Library	5-Yr.		10.00	10
1995	Schneider's Bakery	5-Yr.		10.00	10
1995	Susquehanna Antiques	5-Yr.		10.00	10
1995	YMCA	5-Yr.		10.00	10

YEAR ISSUE		EDITION LIMIT	YEAR RETD.	ISSUE PRICE	*QUOTE U.S.$
Series XIV - F. Jones					
1996	3 Guys Pizzeria	5-Yr.		10.00	10
1996	Dr. Goodbody III	5-Yr.		10.00	10
1996	Mc Auley School	5-Yr.		10.00	10
1996	Rosie's Fish & Chips	5-Yr.		10.00	10
1996	Stabler Apothecary	5-Yr.		10.00	10
1996	Wayside Inn Grist Mill	5-Yr.		10.00	10
1996	Willa Cather Home	5-Yr.		10.00	10
1996	Winter Clove Inn	5-Yr.		10.00	10
Shaker Village Series - F. Jones					
1995	Great Stone Dwelling	5-Yr.		10.00	10
1995	Meetinghouse	5-Yr.		10.00	10
1995	Round Barn	5-Yr.		10.00	10
1995	Trustees Office	5-Yr.		10.00	10
Southern Belles Series - F. Jones					
1996	Auburn	12/96		10.00	10
Special Item - F. Jones					
1996	Discus Thrower	12/96		10.00	10
1996	Smithsonian Castle/Stamp Edition	12/96		15.00	15
1995	Smokey Bear	Retrd.	1995	8.95	14
1994	Smokey Bear w/ 50th stamp	Retrd.	1994	8.95	14
Tradesman - F. Jones					
1988	Buckeye Candy & Tobacco	Retrd.	1993	8.00	20
1988	C.O. Wheel Company	Retrd.	1993	8.00	20
1988	Hermannhof Winery	Retrd.	1993	8.00	20
1988	Jenney Grist Mill	Retrd.	1993	8.00	20
1988	Set	Retrd.	1993	32.00	60
Washington - F. Jones					
1991	National Archives	12/96		8.00	10
1991	U.S. Capitol	12/96		8.00	10
1991	U.S. Supreme Court	12/96		8.00	10
1991	White House	12/96		8.00	10
Waterfront Series - F. Jones					
1994	Arnold Transit Company	5-Yr.		10.00	10
1994	Lowell's Boat Shop	5-Yr.		10.00	10
1994	Sand Island Lighthouse	5-Yr.		10.00	10
1994	Seaside Market	5-Yr.		10.00	10
West Coast Lighthouse Series - F. Jones					
1994	East Brother Lighthouse	5-Yr.		10.00	10
1994	Heceta Head Light	5-Yr.		10.00	10
1994	Mukilteo Light	5-Yr.		10.00	10
1994	Point Pinos Light	5-Yr.		10.00	10
Wild West - F. Jones					
1989	Drink 'em up Saloon	Retrd.	1993	8.00	15
1989	F.C. Zimmermann's Gun Shop	Retrd.	1993	8.00	15
1989	Marshal's Office	Retrd.	1993	8.00	15
1989	Wells, Fargo & Co.	Retrd.	1993	8.00	15
1989	Wells, Fargo & Co.	Retrd.	1993	32.00	60
Williamsburg Series - F. Jones					
1993	Bruton Parish	5-Yr.		10.00	10
1993	Governor's Palace	5-Yr.		10.00	10
1993	Grissell Hay Lodging House	5-Yr.		10.00	10
1993	Raleigh Tavern	5-Yr.		10.00	10
Wine Country Series - F. Jones					
1996	Charles Krug Winery	12/96		10.00	10

Cavanagh Group Intl.

Coca-Cola Brand Heritage Collection - Various

YEAR ISSUE		EDITION LIMIT	YEAR RETD.	ISSUE PRICE	*QUOTE U.S.$
1995	Always - CGI	Open		30.00	30
1995	Always-Musical - CGI	Open		50.00	50
1995	Boy at Well - N. Rockwell	5,000		60.00	60
1995	Boy Fishing - N. Rockwell	5,000		60.00	60
1996	Busy Man's Pause - Sundblom	Open		80.00	80
1994	Calendar Girl 1916-Music Box - CGI	500		60.00	60
1996	Coca-Cola Stand - CGI	Open		45.00	45
1996	Cool Break - CGI	Open		40.00	40
1994	Dear Santa, Please Pause Here - Sundblom	2,500	1995	80.00	85
1994	Dear Santa, Please Pause Here-Musical - Sundblom	2,500	1995	100.00	100
1996	Decorating The Tree - CGI	Open		45.00	45
1994	Eight Polar Bears on Wood - CGI	5,000		100.00	100
1994	Eight Polar Bears on Wood -Musical - CGI	10,000		150.00	150
1995	Elaine - CGI	2,500		100.00	100
1994	Extra Bright Refreshment -Snowglobe - Sundblom	2,500		50.00	50
1996	For Me - Sundblom	Open		40.00	40
1995	Girl on Swing - CGI	2,500		100.00	100
1996	Gone Fishing - CGI	Open		60.00	60
1994	Good Boys and Girl - Sundblom	2,500	1995	80.00	80
1994	Good Boys and Girls-Musical - Sundblom	2,500	1995	100.00	100
1994	Good Boys and Girls-Snowglobe - Sundblom	2,000	1995	45.00	45
1994	Hilda Clark 1901-Music Box - CGI	500		60.00	60
1994	Hilda Clark 1903-Music Box - CGI	500		60.00	60
1996	Hollywood-Snowglobe - CGI	Open		50.00	50
1995	The Homecoming - S. Stearman	2,500	1995	125.00	125

Collectors' Information Bureau

*Quotes have been rounded up to nearest dollar

Column headers (all tables): YEAR ISSUE | EDITION LIMIT | YEAR RETD. | ISSUE PRICE | *QUOTE U.S.$

YEAR ISSUE	Item	EDITION LIMIT	YEAR RETD.	ISSUE PRICE	*QUOTE U.S.$
1995	Hospitality - Sundblom	5,000		35.00	35
1995	Playing with Dad - CGI	Open		40.00	40
1996	A Refreshing Break - N. Rockwell	Open		60.00	60
1996	Refreshing Treat - CGI	Open		45.00	45
1994	Santa at His Desk - Sundblom	5,000		80.00	80
1994	Santa at His Desk-Musical - Sundblom	5,000		100.00	100
1994	Santa at His Desk-Snowglobe - Sundblom	Open		45.00	45
1994	Santa at the Fireplace - Sundblom	5,000		80.00	80
1994	Santa at the Fireplace-Musical - Sundblom	5,000		100.00	100
1994	Santa at the Lamppost-Snowglobe - Sundblom	Open		50.00	50
1996	Santa with Polar Bear-Snowglobe - CGI	Open		50.00	50
1996	Say Uncle-Snowglobe - CGI	Open		50.00	50
1994	Single Polar Bear on Ice-Snowglobe - CGI	Open		40.00	40
1996	Sshh!-Musical - Sundblom	Open		55.00	55
1995	They Remember Me-Musical - Sundblom	5,000		50.00	50
1994	Two Polar Bears on Ice - CGI	Open		25.00	25
1994	Two Polar Bears on Ice-Musical -CGI	Open		45.00	45

Coca-Cola Brand Heritage Collection Polar Bear Cubs - CGI

YEAR	Item	LIMIT	RETD.	PRICE	QUOTE
1996	Balancing Act	Open		16.00	16
1996	The Bear Cub Club	Open		20.00	20
1996	Bearing Gifts of Love & Friendship	10,000		30.00	30
1996	The Big Catch	Open		16.00	16
1996	A Christmas Wish	Open		10.00	10
1996	Friends Are Forever	Open		16.00	16
1996	Giving Is Better Than Receiving	Open		12.00	12
1996	A Helping Hand	Open		20.00	20
1996	I'm Not Sleepy...Really	Open		10.00	10
1996	It's My Turn to Hide	Open		12.00	12
1996	Look What I Can Do	Open		12.00	12
1996	Ride 'em Cowboy	Open		20.00	20
1996	Skating Rink Romance	Open		16.00	16
1996	Snowday Adventure	Open		12.00	12
1996	Sweet Dreams	Open		12.00	12
1996	To Grandmother's House We Go	Open		12.00	12
1996	Who Says Girls Can't Throw	Open		16.00	16

Coca-Cola Brand Musical - Various

1993	Dear Santa, Please Pause Here - Sundblom	Open		50.00	50
1994	Santa's Soda Shop - CGI	Open		50.00	50

Coca-Cola Brand North Pole Bottling Works - CGI

1995	All in a Day's Work	Open		25.00	25
1996	Art Department	Open		50.00	50
1996	An Artist's Touch	Open		25.00	25
1996	Big Ambitions	Open		25.00	25
1995	Checking His List	Open		30.00	30
1996	Delivery for Mrs. Claus	Open		25.00	25
1996	Elf in Training	Open		25.00	25
1995	An Elf's Favorite Chore	Open		30.00	30
1995	Filling Operations	Open		45.00	45
1995	Front Office	Open		50.00	50
1995	The Kitchen Corner	Open		55.00	55
1995	Maintenance Mischief	Open		25.00	25
1995	Making the Secret Syrup	Open		30.00	30
1996	Oops!	Open		25.00	25
1996	Order Department	Open		55.00	55
1996	Precious Cargo	Open		25.00	25
1996	Quality Control	Open		25.00	25
1996	Shipping Department	Open		55.00	55
1996	Special Delivery	Open		25.00	25
1996	A Stroke of Genius	Open		25.00	25
1995	Top Secret	Open		30.00	30

Coca-Cola Brand Santa Animations - Sundblom

1991	Ssshh! (1st Ed.)	Closed	1992	99.99	275-365
1992	Santa's Pause for Refreshment (2nd Ed.)	Closed	1993	99.99	175-265
1993	Trimming the Tree (3rd Ed.)	Closed	1994	99.99	150-235
1995	Santa at the Lamppost (4th Ed.)	Open		110.00	110

Coca-Cola Brand Town Square Collection - CGI

1992	Candler's Drugs	Closed	1993	40.00	50-70
1996	Carlson's General Store	Open		40.00	40
1996	Chandler's Ski Resort	Open		40.00	40
1993	City Hall	Closed	1994	40.00	70-90
1996	Clara's Christmas Shop	Open		40.00	40
1995	Coca-Cola Bottling Works	Closed	1995	40.00	40
1996	Cooper's Tree Farm	Open		20.00	20
1992	Dee's Boarding House	Closed	1993	40.00	350-550
1996	Diamond Service Station	Open		40.00	40
1992	Dick's Luncheonette	Closed	1993	40.00	50-70
1994	Flying "A" Service Station	Open		40.00	40
1992	Gilbert's Grocery	Closed	1993	40.00	60-90
1995	Grist Mill	Closed	1995	40.00	40
1992	Howard Oil	Closed	1993	40.00	125-165
1993	Jacob's Pharmacy	5,000	1993	25.00	350-550
1995	Jenny's Sweet Shoppe	Closed	1995	40.00	40
1994	Lighthouse Point Snack Bar	Open		40.00	40
1994	McMahon's General Store	Closed	1995	40.00	40
1993	Mooney's Antique Barn	Closed	1994	40.00	60-90
1995	Plaza Drugs	Closed	1995	20.00	40

(Town Square Collection continued)

1993	Route 93 Covered Bridge	Closed	1995	20.00	29
1996	Scooter's Drive In	Open		40.00	40
1994	Station #14 Firehouse	Open		40.00	40
1994	Strand Theatre	Open		40.00	40
1993	T. Taylor's Emporium	Closed	1994	40.00	50-60
1993	The Tick Tock Diner	Closed	1995	40.00	60
1996	Town Barber Shop	Open		40.00	40
1994	Town Gazebo	Closed	1995	20.00	29
1992	Train Depot	Closed	1993	40.00	250-300
1996	Walton's 5 & 10	Open		40.00	40

Coca-Cola Brand Town Square Collection Accessories - CGI

1992	Ad Car "Coca-Cola"	Closed	1993	9.00	25
1992	After Skating	Closed	1993	8.00	13
1995	Boys with Snowballs	Closed	1995	11.00	11
1992	Bringing It Home	Closed	1993	8.00	17
1994	Checker Players	Closed	1995	15.00	15
1994	Crowley Cab Co.	Closed	1995	11.00	15
1992	Delivery Man	Closed	1993	8.00	15
1992	Delivery Truck "Coca-Cola"	Closed	1993	15.00	28
1993	Extra! Extra!	Closed	1994	7.00	13
1992	Gil the Grocer	Closed	1993	8.00	13
1993	Gone Fishing	Closed	1994	11.00	15
1994	Homeward Bound	Closed	1995	8.00	8
1992	Horse-Drawn Wagon	Closed	1993	12.00	30-50
1995	Lunch Wagon	Closed	1995	15.00	15
1993	Officer Pat	Closed	1995	7.00	10
1993	Old Number Seven	Closed	1995	15.00	15
1994	Sledders	Closed	1995	11.00	11
1994	Sleigh Ride	Closed	1995	15.00	15
1993	Soda Jerk	Closed	1995	7.00	12
1993	Street Vendor	Closed	1994	11.00	17
1992	Thirsty the Snowman	Closed	1993	9.00	20

Cody

The Animal Spirits Collection - B. Austin

1996	Spirit of the Antelope	2,500		150.00	150
1996	Spirit of the Bear	2,500		130.00	130
1996	Spirit of the Buffalo	2,500		130.00	130
1996	Spirit of the Eagle	2,500		130.00	130
1996	Spirit of the Wolf	2,500		130.00	130

The Animal Tracks Collection - K. Cantrell

1995	Cougar	3,500		125.00	125
1995	Eagle	3,500		125.00	125
1995	Grizzly Bear	3,500		125.00	125
1995	Wolf	3,500		125.00	125

The Canine Collection - K. Cantrell

1996	Cocker Spaniel	2,500		140.00	140
1996	Dalmation	2,500		140.00	140
1996	German Shepherd	2,500		140.00	140
1996	Golden Retriever	2,500		140.00	140
1996	Labrador Retriever (black)	2,500		140.00	140
1996	Labrador Retriever (yellow)	2,500		140.00	140
1996	Rottweiler	2,500		140.00	140

The Equinus Collection - K. Cantrell

1995	Arabian	2,500		150.00	150
1996	Arabian Mare and Foal	2,500		190.00	190
1996	Clydesdale	2,500		190.00	190
1995	Quarterhorse	2,500		150.00	150
1995	Thoroughbred	2,500		150.00	150

Native American Spirits - W. Whitten

1994	Buffalo Dreamer	1,250		250.00	250
1995	Calling the Buffalo	1,250		250.00	250
1994	Cheyenne War Shield	1,250		250.00	250
1995	Flying Shield	1,250		250.00	250
1994	Peace Pipe	1,250		250.00	250
1994	War Bonnet	1,250		250.00	250
1995	Wolf Headdress	1,250		290.00	290

The Noble Americans Collection - C. Pardell

1995	Crazy Horse	2,500		150.00	150
1995	Pocahontas	2,500		150.00	150
1995	Red Cloud	2,500		150.00	150
1995	Sacajewca	2,500		150.00	150
1995	Sitting Bull	2,500		190.00	190

The North American Collection - K. Cantrell

1995	Artful Dodger	2,500		160.00	160
1995	Buffalo Spirit	2,500		160.00	160
1995	Eagles Realm	2,500		160.00	160
1995	Elusive	2,500		160.00	160
1995	Northern Express	2,500		160.00	160
1995	Spirit of the Wolf	2,500		160.00	160
1995	Wild Music	2,500		160.00	160
1995	Wind Blown	2,500		160.00	160

The Western Hats Collection - D. Lemon

1996	The Plainsman-1860's	2,500		150.00	150
1996	The Plainsman-1870's	2,500		150.00	150
1996	The Montana Peak-1880's	2,500		150.00	150
1996	The Bowler-1890's	2,500		150.00	150
1996	The Sombrero-1900's	2,500		150.00	150
1996	The Tom Mix-1920's	2,500		150.00	150
1996	The Buckaroo-1980's	2,500		150.00	150
1996	The Stetson-1990's	2,500		150.00	150

Crystal World

Animal Friends Collection - R. Nakai, unless otherwise noted

1983	Alligator	Closed	N/A	46.00	46
1996	Baby Bird Bath	Open		45.00	45
1990	Baby Dinosaur - T. Suzuki	Closed	N/A	50.00	50
1990	Barney Dog - T. Suzuki	Closed	N/A	32.00	32
1984	Beaver	Closed	N/A	30.00	30
1990	Betsy Bunny - T. Suzuki	Closed	N/A	32.00	32
1984	Butterfly	Closed	N/A	36.00	36
1994	Cheese Mouse	Open		53.00	53
1990	Clara Cow - T. Suzuki	Closed	N/A	32.00	32
1984	Dachshund	Closed	N/A	28.00	28
1984	Dog	Closed	N/A	28.00	28
1984	Donkey	Closed	N/A	40.00	40
1987	Duckling - T. Suzuki	Closed	N/A	60.00	60
1983	Elephant	Closed	N/A	40.00	40
1995	Fido the Dog - T. Suzuki	Open		27.00	27
1995	Frisky Fido - T. Suzuki	Closed	1996	27.00	27
1990	Georgie Giraffe - T. Suzuki	Closed	N/A	32.00	32
1990	Henry Hippo - T. Suzuki	Closed	N/A	32.00	32
1990	Jumbo Elephant - T. Suzuki	Open		32.00	32
1984	Koala Bear	Closed	N/A	50.00	50
1987	Large Circus Puppy	Closed	N/A	50.00	50
1985	Large Elephant	Closed	N/A	54.00	54
1984	Large Hippo	Closed	N/A	50.00	50
1984	Large Kangaroo	Closed	N/A	50.00	50
1985	Large Lion	Closed	N/A	60.00	60
1983	Large Mouse	Closed	N/A	36.00	36
1987	Large Panda	Closed	1995	45.00	45
1983	Large Pig	Closed	N/A	50.00	50
1987	Large Playful Pup	Closed	N/A	85.00	85
1987	Large Poodle	Closed	N/A	64.00	64
1983	Large Rabbit	Closed	N/A	50.00	50
1987	Large Rabbit with Carrot	Closed	N/A	55.00	55
1984	Large Racoon	Closed	N/A	44.00	44
1987	Large Snowbunny	Closed	N/A	45.00	45
1983	Large Turtle	Closed	N/A	56.00	56
1995	Ling Ling - T. Suzuki	Open		53.00	53
1983	Medium Mouse	Closed	N/A	28.00	28
1983	Medium Pig	Closed	N/A	32.00	32
1983	Medium Turtle	Closed	N/A	38.00	38
1990	Mikey Monkey - T. Suzuki	Closed	N/A	32.00	32
1986	Mini Butterfly - N. Mulargia	Closed	N/A	15.00	15
1986	Mini Dachshund - N. Mulargia	Closed	N/A	15.00	15
1986	Mini Frog Mushroom - N. Mulargia	Closed	N/A	15.00	15
1986	Mini Koala - N. Mulargia	Closed	N/A	15.00	15
1986	Mini Mouse - N. Mulargia	Closed	N/A	15.00	15
1986	Mini Rabbit - N. Mulargia	Closed	N/A	15.00	15
1989	Mini Rainbow Dog	Closed	N/A	25.00	25
1989	Mini Rainbow Owl	Closed	N/A	25.00	25
1989	Mini Rainbow Penguin	Closed	N/A	25.00	25
1989	Mini Rainbow Squirrel	Closed	N/A	25.00	25
1986	Mini Swan - N. Mulargia	Open		15.00	28
1984	Mini Turtle	Closed	N/A	18.00	18
1987	Mother Koala and Cub	Closed	N/A	55.00	55
1983	Mouse Standing	Closed	N/A	34.00	34
1994	Mozart - T. Suzuki	Open		48.00	48
1996	Noah and Friends - N. Mulargia	Open		150.00	150
1994	Owls - N. Mulargia	Open		53.00	53
1984	Peacock	Closed	N/A	50.00	50
1984	Penguin	Closed	N/A	34.00	34
1987	Penguin On Cube	Closed	1996	30.00	30
1995	Percy Piglet - T. Suzuki	Open		19.00	19
1993	Pig - N. Mulargia	Closed	1995	50.00	50
1994	Playful Pup - T. Suzuki	Open		53.00	53
1993	Playful Seal - T. Suzuki	Open		42.00	42
1984	Poodle	Closed	N/A	30.00	30
1984	Porcupine	Closed	N/A	42.00	42
1987	Posing Penguin	Closed	N/A	85.00	85
1990	Puppy Love - T. Suzuki	Closed	N/A	45.00	45
1993	Puppy-Gram - T. Suzuki	Open		58.00	58
1985	Racoon	Closed	N/A	50.00	50
1987	Rhinoceros	Closed	N/A	55.00	55
1994	Seal	Closed	1996	46.00	46
1987	Small Circus Puppy	Closed	N/A	28.00	28
1984	Small Hippo	Closed	N/A	30.00	30
1984	Small Kangaroo	Closed	N/A	34.00	34
1984	Small Koala	Closed	N/A	28.00	28
1985	Small Lion	Closed	N/A	36.00	36
1983	Small Mouse	Closed	N/A	20.00	20
1987	Small Panda	Closed	N/A	30.00	30
1983	Small Pig	Closed	N/A	22.00	22
1987	Small Playful Pup	Closed	1995	32.00	32
1987	Small Poodle	Closed	1994	35.00	35
1983	Small Rabbit	Closed	N/A	28.00	28
1987	Small Rabbit with Carrot	Closed	N/A	32.00	32
1987	Small Racoon	Closed	N/A	30.00	30
1984	Small Racoon	Closed	N/A	30.00	30
1987	Small Snowbunny	Closed	N/A	25.00	25
1983	Small Turtle	Closed	N/A	28.00	28
1987	Small Walrus - T. Suzuki	Closed	N/A	60.00	60
1991	Spike	Closed	N/A	50.00	50
1991	Spot	Closed	N/A	50.00	50
1985	Squirrel	Closed	1994	30.00	30
1994	Sweetie - T. Suzuki	Open		28.00	28
1995	Tea Time	Open		50.00	50
1992	Trumpeting Elephant - T. Suzuki	Closed	1996	50.00	50

YEAR ISSUE		EDITION LIMIT	YEAR RETD.	ISSUE PRICE	*QUOTE U.S.$
1993	Turtle	Closed	1996	65.00	65
1986	Unicorn	Closed	1994	110.00	110
1987	Walrus	Closed	N/A	70.00	70
1996	Wanna Play? - T. Suzuki	Open		65.00	65
1995	Wilbur in Love - N. Mulargia	Open		90.00	90
1994	Wilbur the Pig - T. Suzuki	Open		48.00	48

Bird Collection - R. Nakai, unless otherwise noted

YEAR ISSUE		EDITION LIMIT	YEAR RETD.	ISSUE PRICE	*QUOTE U.S.$
1986	Bird Bath - N. Mulargia	Closed	1989	54.00	75
1984	Bird Family	Closed	1990	22.00	35
1984	Love Bird	Closed	1988	44.00	65
1986	Love Birds	Closed	1992	54.00	75
1990	Ollie Owl - T. Suzuki	Closed	1993	32.00	40
1983	Owl Standing	Closed	1987	40.00	70
1983	Owl-Large	Closed	1987	44.00	75
1983	Owl-Small	Closed	1987	22.00	36
1991	Parrot Couple	Closed	1992	90.00	100
1985	Parrot-Extra Large	Closed	1988	300.00	450
1987	Parrot-Large	Closed	1993	130.00	170
1987	Parrot-Small	Closed	1989	30.00	45
1985	Parrot-Small	Closed	1989	100.00	110
1990	Tree Top Owls - T. Suzuki	Closed	1993	96.00	96
1990	Wise Owl - T. Suzuki	Closed	1993	55.00	65
1990	Wise Owl-Small - T. Suzuki	Closed	1993	40.00	65

By The Beautiful Sea Collection - R. Nakai, unless otherwise noted

YEAR ISSUE		EDITION LIMIT	YEAR RETD.	ISSUE PRICE	*QUOTE U.S.$
1992	Baby Seal - T. Suzuki	Open		21.00	21
1991	Beaver	Closed	1996	47.00	47
1996	Crabbie le Crab	Open		38.00	38
1992	Cute Crab - T. Suzuki	Open		27.00	32
1988	Dancing Dolphin	Closed	N/A	130.00	130
1993	Extra Large Oyster with Pearl	Closed	1996	75.00	75
1984	Fish	Closed	N/A	36.00	36
1996	Freddy Frog	Open		30.00	30
1996	Frieda Frog	Open		37.00	37
1993	Harbor Lighthouse - N. Mulargia	Open		75.00	79
1988	Hatching Sea Turtle - T. Suzuki	Open		45.00	47
1983	Large Crab	Closed	N/A	20.00	20
1988	Large Island Paradise	Closed	N/A	90.00	90
1988	Large Lighthouse	Closed	1994	150.00	150
1983	Large Oyster	Closed	1994	30.00	30
1983	Mini Oyster	Closed	N/A	12.00	12
1994	Oscar Otter - T. Suzuki	Open		53.00	53
1987	Palm Tree	Closed	N/A	160.00	160
1996	Pelican	Open		65.00	65
1996	Penguin On Cube	Open		48.00	48
1991	Penguin On Cube	Closed	1996	40.00	40
1996	Playful Dolphin	Open		125.00	125
1992	Playful Dolphins - T. Suzuki	Closed	1996	60.00	60
1993	Playful Seal - T. Suzuki	Open		45.00	45
1993	Sailboat	Open		100.00	115
1994	Seal	Closed	1996	47.00	47
1992	Seaside Pelican - T. Suzuki	Closed	1995	55.00	55
1983	Small Crab	Closed	N/A	28.00	28
1988	Small Dolphin	Closed	N/A	55.00	55
1988	Small Island Paradise	Closed	N/A	50.00	50
1988	Small Lighthouse	Open		80.00	80
1983	Small Oyster	Closed	1994	18.00	18
1996	Small Playful Dolphin	Open		75.00	75
1992	Tropical Fish	Closed	1995	95.00	95
1992	Tuxedo Penguin	Closed	1995	75.00	75
1992	The Whales - T. Suzuki	Closed	1994	60.00	60

By The Lake Collection - R. Nakai, unless otherwise noted

YEAR ISSUE		EDITION LIMIT	YEAR RETD.	ISSUE PRICE	*QUOTE U.S.$
1985	Butterfly Caterpillar	Closed	N/A	40.00	40
1985	Butterfly on Daisy	Closed	N/A	30.00	30
1984	Duck	Closed	N/A	30.00	30
1990	Duck Family	Closed	N/A	70.00	70
1984	Frog & Mushroom	Closed	N/A	46.00	46
1987	King Swan	Closed	N/A	110.00	110
1983	Large Frog	Closed	N/A	30.00	30
1996	Large Love Swans - N. Mulargia	Open		252.00	252
1987	Large Swan	Closed	1996	70.00	70
1985	Large Swan	Closed	N/A	70.00	70
1983	Large Swan	Closed	N/A	44.00	44
1986	Love Swan - N. Mulargia	Closed	N/A	70.00	70
1995	Love Swans - N. Mulargia	Open		83.00	83
1987	Medium Swan	Open		45.00	63
1985	Medium Swan	Closed	N/A	54.00	54
1983	Mini Frog	Closed	N/A	14.00	14
1985	Mini Swan	Open		28.00	29
1983	Small Frog	Closed	N/A	26.00	26
1985	Small Swan	Closed	N/A	44.00	44
1983	Small Swan	Closed	N/A	28.00	28
1987	Small Swan	Open		32.00	47
1990	Swan Family - T. Suzuki	Closed	N/A	70.00	70

Castles and Legends - R. Nakai, unless otherwise noted

YEAR ISSUE		EDITION LIMIT	YEAR RETD.	ISSUE PRICE	*QUOTE U.S.$
1991	Castle In The Sky	Closed	1994	150.00	150
1994	Castle Rainbow Rainbow Mtn. Bs.	Open		1575.00	1575
1994	Castle Royale/Clear Mountain Bs	Open		1300.00	1300
1989	Dragon Baby	Closed	1994	80.00	80
1996	Emerald Castle	Open		105.00	105
1990	I Love You Unicorn - N. Mulargia	Closed	N/A	58.00	58
1987	Ice Castle	Closed	N/A	150.00	150
1988	Imperial Castle	Open		320.00	345
1988	Imperial Ice Castle	Open		320.00	320
1993	Large Fantasy Castle	Open		230.00	245
1995	Large Fantasy Coach - N. Mulargia	Open		368.00	368
1989	Magic Fairy	Closed	N/A	40.00	40

YEAR ISSUE		EDITION LIMIT	YEAR RETD.	ISSUE PRICE	*QUOTE U.S.$
1991	Majestic Castle - A. Kato	Open		390.00	390
1993	Medium Fantasy Castle	Open		130.00	142
1995	Medium Fantasy Coach - N. Mulargia	Open		158.00	158
1992	Mini Fantasy Castle - N. Mulargia	Open		40.00	40
1995	Mini Mouse Coach - N. Mulargia	Open		52.00	52
1989	Mini Rainbow Castle	Open		60.00	62
1988	Mystic Castle	Open		90.00	90
1988	Mystic Ice Castle	Closed	N/A	90.00	90
1990	Pegasus - N. Mulargia	Closed	N/A	50.00	50
1987	Rainbow Castle	Open		150.00	184
1990	Rainbow Unicorn - N. Mulargia	Open		50.00	58
1992	Small Fantasy Castle	Open		85.00	95
1995	Small Fantasy Coach - N. Mulargia	Open		100.00	100
1995	Small Mouse Coach - N. Mulargia	Open		95.00	95
1989	Star Fairy	Closed	N/A	65.00	65
1989	Starlight Castle	Closed	1994	155.00	155
1995	Treasure Chest	Open		63.00	63
1989	Unicorn & Friend	Closed	N/A	100.00	100
1990	Unicorn - N. Mulargia	Closed	1994	38.00	38

Clown Collection - R. Nakai, unless otherwise noted

YEAR ISSUE		EDITION LIMIT	YEAR RETD.	ISSUE PRICE	*QUOTE U.S.$
1985	Acrobatic Clown	Closed	N/A	50.00	50
1992	Baby Clown - N. Mulargia	Closed	N/A	30.00	30
1985	Baseball Clown	Closed	N/A	54.00	54
1996	Bo-Bo The Clown - N. Mulargia	Open		53.00	53
1984	Clown	Closed	N/A	42.00	42
1985	Clown On Unicycle	Closed	N/A	54.00	54
1992	Flower Clown - N. Mulargia	Closed	N/A	70.00	70
1985	Golf Clown	Closed	N/A	54.00	54
1985	Juggler	Closed	N/A	54.00	54
1985	Large Clown	Closed	N/A	42.00	42
1985	Large Jack In The Box	Closed	N/A	64.00	64
1985	Small Clown	Closed	N/A	30.00	30
1985	Small Jack In The Box	Closed	N/A	24.00	24
1985	Tennis Clown	Closed	N/A	54.00	54

Decorative Item Collection (Paperweights) - Various

YEAR ISSUE		EDITION LIMIT	YEAR RETD.	ISSUE PRICE	*QUOTE U.S.$
1993	100 mm Diamond - R. Nakai	Open		525.00	525
1996	40 mm Diamond - R. Nakai	Open		48.00	48
1993	50 mm Diamond - R. Nakai	Open		70.00	70
1993	75 mm Diamond - R. Nakai	Open		285.00	285
1990	Baseball - I. Nakamura	Closed	N/A	170.00	170
1995	Boston "Cityscape" Paperweight - R. Nakai	Open		105.00	105
1989	Chicago - I. Nakamura	Open		150.00	150
1996	Crystal Egg & Stand - R. Nakai	Open		83.00	83
1991	Dallas Skyline - I. Nakamura	Open		180.00	180
1988	Empire State - G. Veith	Closed	N/A	120.00	120
1996	Fabulous Fifties Jukebox - N. Mulargia	Open		79.00	79
1990	Fishing - I. Nakamura	Closed	N/A	170.00	170
1990	Golfing - I. Nakamura	Closed	N/A	170.00	170
1992	Heart Clock - R. Nakai	Closed	N/A	100.00	100
1993	Manatee - R. Nakai	Open		125.00	130
1992	Manhattan Reflections - R. Nakai	Open		95.00	95
1995	Med. Boston Skyline Paperweight - R. Nakai	Open		80.00	80
1995	Med. Chicago Skyline Clock Paperweight - R. Nakai	Closed	1996	158.00	158
1994	Med. NY Skyline Paperweight - G. Veith	Open		80.00	80
1995	Med. Philadelphia Skyline Paperweight - R. Nakai	Open		80.00	80
1994	Med. San Francisco Skyline Pwght. - G. Veith	Open		80.00	80
1994	Med. Wash. DC Skyline Paperweight - G. Veith	Open		80.00	80
1988	N.Y. Skyline - G. Veith	Open		100.00	100
1988	Nativity - R. Nakai	Closed	1994	100.00	100
1992	Niagara Falls Pwght. - R. Nakai	Open		85.00	85
1994	NY "Cityscape" Pwght. - G. Veith	Open		105.00	105
1994	NY Dome Paperweight - G. Veith	Closed	1995	75.00	75
1994	NY Skyline Clock Paperweight - R. Nakai	Closed	1996	158.00	158
1995	Philadelphia "Cityscape" Paperweight - R. Nakai	Open		105.00	105
1991	Polar Bear - R. Nakai	Open		98.00	98
1994	S.F. Skyline Clock Paperweight - R. Nakai	Closed	1996	158.00	158
1994	San Francisco "Cityscape" Pwght. - G. Veith	Open		105.00	105
1989	San Francisco - I. Nakamura	Open		150.00	150
1994	San Francisco Dome Paperweight - G. Veith	Closed	1995	75.00	75
1995	San Francisco Skyline Clock Paperweight - R. Nakai	Closed	1996	158.00	158
1992	Small NY - G. Veith	Open		45.00	45
1993	Small San Francisco Skyline	Open		45.00	45
1990	Tennis - I. Nakamura	Closed	N/A	170.00	170
1994	Wash. DC "Cityscape" Paperweight - R. Nakai	Open		105.00	105
1994	Wash. DC Skyline Clock Paperweight - R. Nakai	Closed	1996	158.00	158
1989	Washington - I. Nakamura	Open		150.00	150
1994	Washington DC Dome Paperweight - G. Veith	Closed	1995	75.00	75
1994	Washington Vietnam Memorial Pwt. - R. Nakai	Closed	1996	105.00	105

Fruit Collection - R. Nakai

YEAR ISSUE		EDITION LIMIT	YEAR RETD.	ISSUE PRICE	*QUOTE U.S.$
1985	Large Apple	Open		44.00	68
1991	Large Pineapple	Open		42.00	42
1985	Medium Apple	Open		30.00	39
1993	Medium Apple with Red Heart	Open		37.00	39
1991	Medium Pineapple	Closed	N/A	27.00	27

YEAR ISSUE		EDITION LIMIT	YEAR RETD.	ISSUE PRICE	*QUOTE U.S.$
1987	Mini Apple	Open		15.00	16
1985	Pear	Closed	N/A	30.00	30
1996	Pineapple	Open		53.00	53
1985	Small Apple	Open		15.00	15
1993	Small Apple with Red Heart	Open		21.00	22
1991	Small Pineapple	Closed	N/A	16.00	16
1985	Strawberries	Closed	N/A	28.00	28

The Gambler Collection - R. Nakai, unless otherwise noted

YEAR ISSUE		EDITION LIMIT	YEAR RETD.	ISSUE PRICE	*QUOTE U.S.$
1993	Large Rolling Dice	Open		60.00	60
1993	Large Slot Machine - T. Suzuki	Open		83.00	83
1991	Lucky 7	Closed	N/A	50.00	50
1994	Lucky Roll	Open		95.00	95
1993	Medium Rolling Dice	Open		48.00	48
1992	Mini Rolling Dice	Open		32.00	32
1991	Mini Slot Machine	Open		30.00	30
1996	One Arm Bandit	Open		70.00	70
1991	Rolling Dice - T. Suzuki	Closed	N/A	110.00	110
1991	Small Dice	Open		27.00	27
1993	Small Rolling Dice	Closed	1996	40.00	40
1991	Small Slot Machine - T. Suzuki	Open		58.00	58
1994	Super Slot	Open		295.00	295

Holiday Treasure Collection - R. Nakai, unless otherwise noted

YEAR ISSUE		EDITION LIMIT	YEAR RETD.	ISSUE PRICE	*QUOTE U.S.$
1984	Angel	Closed	N/A	28.00	28
1994	Cathedral w/Rainbow Base	Open		104.00	104
1994	Country Church	Open		53.00	53
1994	Country Church w/Rainbow Base	Open		63.00	63
1994	Extra Large Christmas Tree	Open		315.00	315
1996	Frosty	Open		41.00	41
1995	Happy Birthday Cake	Open		63.00	63
1991	Holy Angel Blowing A Trumpet - T. Suzuki	Open		38.00	38
1991	Holy Angel Holding A Candle - T. Suzuki	Open		38.00	38
1991	Holy Angel Playing A Harp - T. Suzuki	Open		38.00	38
1995	Large Angel	Open		53.00	53
1985	Large Angel	Closed	N/A	30.00	30
1985	Large Christmas Tree	Open		126.00	126
1987	Large Rainbow Christmas Tree	Closed	1995	40.00	40
1985	Mini Angel	Closed	1996	16.00	16
1985	Mini Christmas Tree	Closed	N/A	10.00	10
1986	Nativity - N. Mulargia	Open		150.00	179
1985	Small Christmas Tree	Open		50.00	68
1991	Small Nativity - T. Suzuki	Open		85.00	90
1987	Small Rainbow Christmas Tree	Closed	1993	25.00	25
1984	Snowman	Closed	N/A	38.00	38
1990	Trumpeting Angel	Closed	N/A	60.00	60

Kitty Land Collection - T. Suzuki, unless otherwise noted

YEAR ISSUE		EDITION LIMIT	YEAR RETD.	ISSUE PRICE	*QUOTE U.S.$
1991	Calamity Kitty	Open		60.00	60
1984	Cat - R. Nakai	Closed	N/A	36.00	36
1990	Cat N Mouse	Closed	1996	45.00	45
1992	Country Cat	Open		60.00	62
1990	The Curious Cat	Open		62.00	62
1991	Hello Birdie	Open		65.00	68
1992	Kitten in Basket - C. Kido	Open		35.00	40
1993	Kitty Kare	Closed	1995	70.00	70
1991	Kitty with Butterfly	Closed	N/A	60.00	60
1991	Kitty with Heart	Open		27.00	29
1987	Large Cat with Ball - R. Nakai	Closed	N/A	70.00	70
1991	Large Curious Cat	Open		90.00	90
1993	Large Playful Kitty	Closed	1996	50.00	50
1990	Moonlight Cat - R. Nakai	Closed	1993	100.00	100
1995	Moonlight Kitties	Open		83.00	83
1991	Peekaboo Kitties	Open		65.00	65
1993	Pinky	Closed	1996	50.00	50
1992	Playful Kitty	Open		32.00	32
1989	Rainbow Mini Cat - R. Nakai	Closed	N/A	25.00	25
1991	Rockabye Kitty - R. Nakai	Open		80.00	83
1992	See Saw Pals - A. Kato	Open		40.00	41
1987	Small Cat with Ball - R. Nakai	Closed	1993	32.00	32
1991	Strolling Kitties	Closed	1993	65.00	65

Limited Edition Collection Series - Various

YEAR ISSUE		EDITION LIMIT	YEAR RETD.	ISSUE PRICE	*QUOTE U.S.$
1986	Airplane -T. Suzuki	Closed	1992	400.00	500
1995	Classic Motorcycle -T. Suzuki	950		420.00	420
1993	Country Gristmill -T. Suzuki	1,250		320.00	340
1986	Crucifix - N. Mulargia	Closed	1992	300.00	400
1991	Cruise Ship -T. Suzuki	1000		2000.00	2100
1989	Dream Castle - R. Nakai	500		9000.00	10000
1986	The Eiffel Tower -T. Suzuki	2000		1000.00	1300
1991	Ellis Island - R. Nakai	Closed	1992	450.00	500
1996	The Empire State Bldg. - R. Nakai	475		1315.00	1315
1993	Enchanted Castle - R. Nakai	750		800.00	895
1985	Extra Large Empire State Bldg. - R. Nakai	Closed	1992	1000.00	1300
1989	Grand Castle - R. Nakai	Closed	1996	2500.00	2500
1995	Independence Hall - R. Nakai	750		370.00	370
1987	Lg. Empire State Bldg. - R. Nakai	2000		650.00	700
1987	Large US Capitol Bldg. -T. Suzuki	Closed	1992	1000.00	1100
1987	Manhattanscape - G. Veith	Closed	1992	1000.00	1100
1996	Merry-Go-Round - N. Mulargia	750		280.00	280
1993	Riverboat - N. Mulargia	350		570.00	600
1992	Santa Maria - N. Mulargia	Closed	1993	1000.00	1050
1988	Small Eiffel Tower -T. Suzuki	2000		500.00	600
1989	Space Shuttle Launch -T. Suzuki	Closed	1992	900.00	1000

YEAR ISSUE	EDITION LIMIT	YEAR RETD.	ISSUE PRICE	*QUOTE U.S.$
1987 Taj Mahal - T. Suzuki	2000		2000.00	2100
1990 Tower Bridge - T. Suzuki	Closed	1992	600.00	650
1993 Victorian House - N. Mulargia	Closed	1996	190.00	190
1992 The White House - R. Nakai	200	1993	3000.00	3000

New York Collection - R. Nakai, unless otherwise noted

1995 Chrysler Building	Open		275.00	275
1993 Holiday Empire State Bldg. - N. Mulargia	Open		205.00	205
1992 Large Contemp. Empire State Bldg. - A. Kato	Closed	1996	475.00	475
1989 Liberty Island - N. Mulargia	Open		75.00	75
1990 Manhattan Island	Open		240.00	240
1992 Med. Contemp. Empire State Bldg.	Open		170.00	170
1987 Medium Empire State Bldg.	Open		250.00	250
1987 Medium Statue of Liberty	Open		120.00	120
1991 Mini Empire State Bldg.	Open		60.00	60
1992 Mini Empire State Bldg. w/Windows	Open		74.00	74
1992 Mini Statue Of Liberty	Open		50.00	50
1992 Sm. Contemp. Empire State Bldg.	Closed	1996	95.00	95
1992 Sm. Contemp. Empire State Bldg, MV	Open		95.00	95
1987 Small Empire State Bldg.	Open		120.00	120
1993 Sm. Manhattan Island - N. Mulargia	Open		105.00	105
1993 Small Rainbow Contemp. Empire	Open		95.00	95
1987 Sm. Statue of Liberty - N. Mulargia	Open		50.00	50
1992 Small Twin Towers	Open		130.00	130
1985 The Statue of Liberty	Open		250.00	250
1991 World Trade Center Bldg.	Open		170.00	170

Nostalgia Collection - Various

1996 Pinocchio - T. Suzuki	Open		150.00	150
1996 Sm. Merry-Go-Round - N. Mulargia	Open		150.00	150

Religious Moment Collection - N. Mulargia, unless otherwise noted

1987 Church - T. Suzuki	Closed	N/A	40.00	40
1987 Cross On Mountain	Closed	N/A	30.00	30
1992 Cross with Rose	Closed	N/A	30.00	30
1987 Crucifix	Closed	N/A	50.00	50
1987 Crucifix On Mountain	Closed	N/A	40.00	40
1987 Face Of Christ - R. Nakai	Closed	N/A	35.00	35
1987 Large Cross On Mountain	Closed	N/A	85.00	85
1992 Peace On Earth - I. Nakamura	Closed	1995	95.00	95
1987 Small Cross	Closed	1993	40.00	40
1987 Star Of David - R. Nakai	Closed	1993	40.00	40

Spring Parade Collection - Various

1990 African Violet - I. Nakamura	Open		32.00	32
1996 American Beauty Rose - N. Mulargia	Open		53.00	53
1992 Barrel Cactus - I. Nakamura	Closed	1995	45.00	45
1991 Blossom Bunny - T. Suzuki	Open		42.00	42
1991 Bunnies On Ice - T. Suzuki	Closed	1996	58.00	58
1991 Bunny Buddy with Carrot - T. Suzuki	Open		32.00	32
1992 Candleholder - N. Mulargia	Closed	1995	125.00	125
1991 Cheep Cheep - T. Suzuki	Open		35.00	35
1990 Crocus - R. Nakai	Closed	N/A	45.00	45
1992 Cute Bunny - T. Suzuki	Closed	1995	38.00	38
1995 Desert Cactus - N. Mulargia	Open		48.00	48
1994 The Enchanted Rose - R. Nakai	Open		126.00	126
1985 Flower Basket - R. Nakai	Closed	1995	36.00	36
1992 Flowering Cactus - I. Nakamura	Closed	1996	58.00	58
1992 Half Dozen Flower Arrangement - N. Mulargia	Closed	1996	20.00	20
1992 Happy Heart - N. Mulargia	Closed	1996	25.00	25
1992 Hummingbird - T. Suzuki	Open		58.00	58
1990 Hyacinth - I. Nakamura	Open		50.00	50
1989 Large Windmill - R. Nakai	Closed	1991	160.00	160
1992 Long Stem Rose - N. Mulargia	Open		35.00	35
1994 Long Stem Rose in Vase - R. Nakai	Open		82.00	82
1992 Loving Hearts - N. Mulargia	Open		35.00	35
1995 Medium Wedding Couple - N. Mulargia	Open		63.00	63
1992 Mini Hummingbird - T. Suzuki	Open		29.00	29
1992 Mini Wedding Couple - N. Mulargia	Open		30.00	30
1995 Pink Rose - R. Nakai	Open		53.00	53
1995 Pink Rose in Vase - R. Nakai	Open		41.00	41
1991 Rainbow Mini Butterfly - R. Nakai	Open		27.00	27
1994 Rainbow Rose - N. Mulargia	Open		82.00	82
1987 Red Rose - R. Nakai	Open		35.00	35
1992 Rose Bouquet - I. Nakamura	Closed	N/A	100.00	100
1987 Small Flower Basket - R. Nakai	Closed	N/A	40.00	40
1996 Small Rose Bouquet - N. Mulargia	Open		45.00	45
1989 Small Windmill - R. Nakai	Closed	1993	90.00	90
1993 Songbirds - I. Nakamura	Open		90.00	90
1995 Spring Butterfly - R. Nakai	Open		62.00	62
1989 Spring Chick - R. Nakai	Open		50.00	53
1992 Spring Flowers - T. Suzuki	Open		40.00	40
1996 Water Lily, Medium, AB - R. Nakai	Open		210.00	210
1992 Waterfront Village - N. Mulargia	Open		190.00	190
1989 Wedding Couple - N. Mulargia	Open		75.00	75
1985 Wedding Couple - R. Nakai	Closed	N/A	38.00	38
1987 White Rose - R. Nakai	Closed	N/A	35.00	35

Teddyland Collection - Various

1995 Baby Bear's Christmas - T. Suzuki	Open		48.00	48
1990 Baron Von Teddy - T. Suzuki	Closed	1993	60.00	60
1987 Beach Teddies - N. Mulargia	Open		60.00	60
1992 Billard Buddies - T. Suzuki	Open		70.00	70
1993 Black Jack Teddies - N. Mulargia	Open		97.00	97
1990 Choo Choo Teddy - T. Suzuki	Closed	1993	100.00	100
1991 Christmas Wreath Teddy - T. Suzuki	Closed	1993	70.00	70
1995 CompuBear - N. Mulargia	Open		63.00	63
1996 Cuddly Bear - R. Nakai	Open		48.00	48
1993 Flower Teddy - T. Suzuki	Open		50.00	50
1995 Fly A Kite Teddy - T. Suzuki	Open		41.00	41
1995 Get Well Teddy - R. Nakai	Closed	1996	48.00	48
1989 Golfing Teddies - R. Nakai	Open		100.00	100
1991 Gumball Teddy - T. Suzuki	Closed	1996	63.00	63
1989 Happy Birthday Teddy - R. Nakai	Open		50.00	50
1991 Heart Bear - T. Suzuki	Open		27.00	27
1991 High Chair Teddy - T. Suzuki	Closed	1993	75.00	75
1988 I Love You Teddy - N. Mulargia	Open		50.00	50
1994 I Love You Teddy Couple - N. Mulargia	Open		95.00	95
1995 I Love You Teddy w/lg. Heart - R. Nakai	Open		48.00	48
1992 Ice Cream Teddies - N. Mulargia	Open		55.00	55
1988 Large Bouquet Teddy - N. Mulargia	Closed	N/A	50.00	50
1988 Large Surfing Teddy - R. Nakai	Closed	N/A	80.00	80
1983 Large Teddy Bear - R. Nakai	Open		68.00	68
1987 Loving Teddies - N. Mulargia	Open		75.00	75
1991 Luck Of The Irish - R. Nakai	Closed	1993	60.00	60
1983 Medium Teddy Bear - R. Nakai	Open		44.00	44
1991 Merry Christmas Teddy - T. Suzuki	Open		55.00	55
1986 Mini Teddy - N. Mulargia	Closed	1993	15.00	15
1985 Mother and Cub - R. Nakai	Closed	N/A	64.00	64
1990 Mountaineer Teddy - N. Mulargia	Closed	1993	80.00	80
1991 My Favorite Picture - T. Suzuki	Open		45.00	45
1992 Patriotic Teddy - N. Mulargia	Open		30.00	30
1991 Play It Again Ted - T. Suzuki	Open		65.00	65
1991 Playground Teddy - R. Kido	Closed	N/A	90.00	90
1989 Rainbow Mini Bear - R. Nakai	Closed	N/A	25.00	25
1990 Rainbow Teddies - N. Mulargia	Closed	1993	95.00	95
1990 Rocking Horse Teddy - N. Mulargia	Closed	N/A	80.00	80
1987 Sailing Teddies - N. Mulargia	Open		100.00	100
1991 Santa Bear Christmas - T. Suzuki	Open		70.00	70
1991 Santa Bear Sleighride - T. Suzuki	Open		70.00	70
1991 School Bears - H. Serino	Closed	1993	75.00	75
1991 Scuba Bear - T. Suzuki	Closed	1993	65.00	65
1989 Shipwreck Teddies - N. Mulargia	Closed	1993	100.00	100
1992 Singing Baby Bear - T. Suzuki	Open		55.00	55
1987 Skateboard Teddy - R. Nakai	Closed	1993	30.00	30
1987 Skiing Teddy - R. Nakai	Open		50.00	50
1992 Sm. Beach Teddies - N. Mulargia	Open		55.00	55
1988 Sm. Bouquet Teddy - N. Mulargia	Open		35.00	35
1990 Sm. Loving Teddies - N. Mulargia	Open		60.00	60
1983 Small Teddy Bear - R. Nakai	Closed	N/A	28.00	28
1989 Speedboat Teddies - R. Nakai	Open		90.00	90
1990 Storytime Teddies - T. Suzuki	Open		70.00	70
1987 Surfing Teddy - R. Nakai	Closed	1993	45.00	45
1991 Swinging Teddy - N. Mulargia	Open		100.00	100
1988 Teddies At Eight - N. Mulargia	Open		100.00	100
1988 Teddies With Heart - R. Nakai	Open		45.00	45
1989 Teddy Balloon - R. Nakai	Closed	1993	70.00	70
1994 Teddy Bear - R. Nakai	Open		63.00	63
1987 Teddy Bear Christmas - R. Nakai	Open		100.00	100
1994 Teddy Bear with Rainbow Base - R. Nakai	Open		75.00	75
1988 Teddy Family - N. Mulargia	Closed	1993	50.00	50
1995 Teddy's Self Portrait - T. Suzuki	Open		53.00	53
1987 Teeter Totter Teddies - N. Mulargia	Closed	1993	65.00	65
1988 Touring Teddies - N. Mulargia	Open		90.00	90
1990 Tricycle Teddy - T. Suzuki	Closed	1993	40.00	40
1991 Trim A Tree Teddy - R. Nakai	Closed	1996	50.00	50
1989 Vanity Teddy - R. Nakai	Closed	1993	100.00	100
1989 Windsurf Teddy - R. Nakai	Closed	1993	85.00	85
1988 Winter Teddy - N. Mulargia	Closed	N/A	90.00	90

The Voyage Collection - Various

1995 Amish Buggy - R. Nakai	Open		160.00	160
1995 Amish Buggy w/Wood Base - R. Nakai	Open		190.00	190
1994 Bermuda Rig Sailboat - R. Nakai	Open		105.00	105
1984 Classic Car - T. Suzuki	Closed	N/A	160.00	160
1993 Express Train - N. Mulargia	Closed	1993	95.00	95
1992 Fire Engine - T. Suzuki	Open		100.00	100
1991 Large Cable Car - T. Suzuki	Open		130.00	130
1993 Large San Francisco Cable Car - R. Nakai	Open		59.00	59
1990 Large Train Set - T. Suzuki	Closed	N/A	480.00	480
1984 Limousine - R. Nakai	Closed	N/A	46.00	46
1994 Mainsail Sailboat - R. Nakai	Open		230.00	230
1992 Mini Bi-Plane - T. Suzuki	Open		65.00	65
1992 Mini Cable Car - T. Suzuki	Closed	1996	40.00	40
1995 Mini Cruise Ship - N. Mulargia	Open		105.00	105
1990 Orbiting Space Shuttle - T. Suzuki	Open		300.00	300
1984 Pickup Track - R. Nakai	Closed	N/A	38.00	38
1991 The Rainbow Express - N. Mulargia	Closed	1993	125.00	125
1992 Sailing Ship - N. Mulargia	Open		38.00	38
1991 Schooner - N. Mulargia	Closed	1995	95.00	95
1990 Small Airplane - T. Suzuki	Closed	1993	200.00	200
1991 Small Cable Car - T. Suzuki	Open		70.00	70
1996 Sm. Classic Motorcycle - T. Suzuki	Open		210.00	210
1994 Small Cruise Ship - T. Suzuki	Open		575.00	575
1991 Sm. Orbiting Space Shuttle - T. Suzuki	Open		90.00	90
1994 Small Riverboat - N. Mulargia	Open		210.00	210
1993 Small San Francisco Cable Car - R. Nakai	Open		40.00	40
1990 Small Space Shuttle Launch - T. Suzuki	Closed	1996	265.00	265
1990 Small Train Set - T. Suzuki	Open		100.00	100
1994 Spinnaker Sailboat - R. Nakai	Open		265.00	265
1984 Sports Car - T. Suzuki	Closed	N/A	140.00	140
1990 Square Rigger - R. Nakai	Open		250.00	250
1995 Tall Ship - R. Nakai	Open		395.00	395
1984 Touring Car - T. Suzuki	Closed	N/A	140.00	140
1984 Tractor Trailer - R. Nakai	Closed	N/A	40.00	40

Wonders of the World Collection - R. Nakai, unless otherwise noted

1991 Chicago Water Tower w/Base - T. Suzuki	Open		300.00	300
1991 Chicago Water Tower w/o Base - T. Suzuki	Closed	1996	280.00	280
1986 Large Space Needle	Closed	1996	160.00	160
1990 Le Petit Eiffel - T. Suzuki	Open		240.00	240
1995 The Liberty Bell	Open		160.00	160
1995 Medium Taj Mahal	Open		790.00	790
1993 Sears Tower	Open		150.00	150
1993 Sm. Capitol Building - N. Mulargia	Open		100.00	100
1986 Sm. Space Needle - N. Mulargia	Closed	N/A	50.00	50
1995 Small Taj Mahal	Open		215.00	215
1994 Small White House w/Oct. Mirror - N. Mulargia	Open		185.00	185
1986 Taj Mahal	Open		1050.00	1050
1987 U.S. Capitol Building	Open		250.00	250

Dave Grossman Creations

6" Gone With The Wind Series - Unknown

1994 Ashley GWW-102	Open		40.00	40
1994 Rhett GW-104	Open		40.00	40
1994 Scarlett GWW-101	Open		40.00	40

Gone With The Wind Series - Unknown

1993 Belle Waiting GWW-10	Open		70.00	70
1994 Gerald O'Hara GWW-15	Open		70.00	70
1988 Mammy GWW-6	Retrd.		70.00	70
1991 Prissy GWW-8	Open		50.00	50
1993 Rhett & Bonnie GWW-11	Open		80.00	80
1993 Rhett in White Suit GWW-12	Open		70.00	70
1994 Scarlett in Bar B Que Dress GWW-14	Open		70.00	70
1992 Scarlett in Green Dress GWW-9	Open		70.00	70
1987 Tara GWW-5	Retrd.	N/A	70.00	70

Norman Rockwell America Collection - Rockwell-Inspired

1993 After The Prom NRP-916	7,500		75.00	75
1989 Bottom of the Sixth NRC-607	Retrd.	N/A	140.00	140
1989 Doctor and Doll NRP-600	Retrd.	N/A	90.00	60
1989 First Day Home NRC-606	Retrd.	N/A	80.00	60
1989 First Haircut NRC-604	Retrd.	N/A	75.00	75
1989 First Visit NRC-605	Retrd.	N/A	110.00	110
1993 Gone Fishing NRP-915	7,500		65.00	65
1989 Locomotive NRC-603	Retrd.	N/A	110.00	110
1993 Missed NRP-914	7,500		110.00	110
1989 Runaway NRC-610	Retrd.	N/A	140.00	140
1989 Weigh-In NRC-611	Retrd.	N/A	120.00	120

Norman Rockwell America Collection-Lg. Ltd. Edition - Rockwell-Inspired

1989 Bottom of the Sixth NRP-307	Retrd.	N/A	190.00	190
1989 Doctor and Doll NRP-300	Retrd.	N/A	150.00	150
1989 Runaway NRP-310	Retrd.	N/A	190.00	190
1989 Weigh-In NRP-311	Retrd.	N/A	190.00	175

Norman Rockwell America Collection-Miniatures - Rockwell-Inspired

1989 First Day Home MRC-906	Retrd.	N/A	45.00	45
1989 First Haircut MRC-904	Retrd.	N/A	45.00	45

Saturday Evening Post - Rockwell-Inspired

1992 After the Prom NRP-916	Open		75.00	75
1994 Almost Grown Up NRC-609	Open		75.00	75
1993 Baby's First Step NRC-604	Open		100.00	100
1993 Bed Time NRP-606	Open		100.00	100
1993 Bedside Manner NRP-904	Open		65.00	65
1990 Big Moment NRP-906	Retrd.	N/A	100.00	135
1990 Bottom of the Sixth NRP-908	Open		165.00	165
1993 Bride & Groom NRC-605	Open		100.00	100
1991 Catching The Big One NRP-909	Open		75.00	75
1992 Choosin Up NRP-912	Retrd.	N/A	110.00	140-150
1990 Daydreamer NRP-902	Open		55.00	55
1990 Doctor and Doll NRP-907	Open		110.00	150
1992 For A Good Boy NRC-608	Open		100.00	100
1992 Gone Fishing NRP-915	Open		65.00	65
1991 Gramps NRP-910	Open		85.00	85
1992 Little Mother NRC-607	Open		75.00	75
1992 Locomotive NRC-603	Open		110.00	110
1992 Missed NRP-914	Open		110.00	110
1990 No Swimming NRP-901	Retrd.	N/A	50.00	50
1991 The Pharmacist NRP-911	Open		70.00	70
1990 Prom Dress NRP-903	Retrd.	N/A	60.00	60

YEAR ISSUE	EDITION LIMIT	YEAR RETD.	ISSUE PRICE	*QUOTE U.S.$
1990 Runaway NRP-905	Open		130.00	130
1994 A Visit with Rockwell (100th Anniversary)-NRP-100	1,994		100.00	100

Saturday Evening Post-Miniatures - Rockwell-Inspired

YEAR ISSUE	EDITION LIMIT	YEAR RETD.	ISSUE PRICE	*QUOTE U.S.$
1991 A Boy Meets His Dog BMR-01	Retrd.	N/A	35.00	35
1991 Downhill Daring BMR-02	Retrd.	N/A	40.00	40
1991 Flowers in Tender Bloom BMR-03	Retrd.	N/A	32.00	32
1991 Fondly Do We Remember BMR-04	Retrd.	N/A	30.00	30
1991 In His Spirit BMR-05	Retrd.	N/A	30.00	30
1991 Pride of Parenthood BMR-06	Retrd.	N/A	35.00	35
1991 Sweet Serenade BMR-07	Retrd.	N/A	32.00	32
1991 Sweet Song So Young BMR-08	Retrd.	N/A	30.00	32

Dave Grossman Designs

Lladró-Norman Rockwell Collection Series - Rockwell-Inspired

YEAR ISSUE	EDITION LIMIT	YEAR RETD.	ISSUE PRICE	*QUOTE U.S.$
1982 Court Jester RL-405G	5,000	N/A	600.00	1300
1982 Daydreamer RL-404G	5,000	N/A	450.00	1300-1500
1982 Lladró Love Letter RL-400G	5,000	N/A	650.00	1000-1200
1982 Practice Makes Perfect RL-402G	5,000	N/A	725.00	800-1000
1982 Springtime RL-406G	5,000	N/A	450.00	1200-1500
1982 Summer Stock RL-401G	5,000	N/A	750.00	800-900
1982 Young Love RL-403G	5,000	N/A	450.00	1350-1750

See also Lladró-Norman Rockwell Collection

Norman Rockwell Collection - Rockwell-Inspired

YEAR ISSUE	EDITION LIMIT	YEAR RETD.	ISSUE PRICE	*QUOTE U.S.$
1982 American Mother NRG-42	Retrd.	N/A	100.00	125
1978 At the Doctor NR-29	Retrd.	N/A	108.00	150-275
1979 Back From Camp NR-33	Retrd.	N/A	96.00	120
1973 Back To School NR-02	Retrd.	N/A	20.00	40-45
1975 Barbershop Quartet NR-23	Retrd.	N/A	100.00	1400
1974 Baseball NR-16	Retrd.	N/A	45.00	160
1975 Big Moment NR-21	Retrd.	N/A	60.00	125
1973 Caroller NR-03	Retrd.	N/A	22.50	75
1975 Circus NR-22	Retrd.	N/A	55.00	145
1983 Country Critic NR-43	Retrd.	N/A	75.00	125
1982 Croquet NR-41	Retrd.	N/A	100.00	135
1973 Daydreamer NR-04	Retrd.	N/A	22.50	60
1975 Discovery NR-20	Retrd.	N/A	55.00	175
1973 Doctor & Doll NR-12	Retrd.	N/A	65.00	150-285
1979 Dreams of Long Ago NR-31	Retrd.	N/A	100.00	125
1976 Drum For Tommy NRC-24	Retrd.	N/A	40.00	95
1980 Exasperated Nanny NR-35	Retrd.	N/A	96.00	100
1978 First Day of School NR-27	Retrd.	N/A	100.00	150
1974 Friends In Need NR-13	Retrd.	N/A	45.00	100
1983 Graduate NR-44	Retrd.	N/A	30.00	75
1979 Grandpa's Ballerina NR-32	Retrd.	N/A	100.00	110
1980 Hankerchief NR-36	Retrd.	N/A	110.00	100-110
1973 Lazybones NR-08	Retrd.	N/A	30.00	250
1973 Leapfrog NR-09	Retrd.	N/A	50.00	600-700
1973 Love Letter NR-06	Retrd.	N/A	25.00	60
1973 Lovers NR-07	Retrd.	N/A	45.00	70
1978 Magic Potion NR-28	Retrd.	N/A	84.00	235
1973 Marble Players NR-11	Retrd.	N/A	60.00	400-450
1973 No Swimming NR-05	Retrd.	N/A	25.00	65-145
1977 Pals NR-25	Retrd.	N/A	60.00	120
1986 Red Cross NR-47	Retrd.	N/A	67.00	100
1973 Redhead NR-01	Retrd.	N/A	20.00	210
1980 Santa's Good Boys NR-37	Retrd.	N/A	90.00	100
1973 Schoolmaster NR-10	Retrd.	N/A	55.00	225
1984 Scotty's Home Plate NR-46	Retrd.	N/A	30.00	60
1983 Scotty's Surprise NRS-20	Retrd.	N/A	25.00	50-60
1974 See America First NR-17	Retrd.	N/A	50.00	125
1981 Spirit of Education NR-38	Retrd.	N/A	96.00	125
1974 Springtime '33 NR-14	Retrd.	N/A	30.00	65
1977 Springtime '35 NR-19	Retrd.	N/A	50.00	65
1974 Summertime '33 NR-15	Retrd.	N/A	45.00	65
1974 Take Your Medicine NR-18	Retrd.	N/A	50.00	100
1979 Teacher's Pet NRA-30	Retrd.	N/A	35.00	100
1980 The Toss NR-34	Retrd.	N/A	110.00	150-225
1982 A Visit With Rockwell NR-40	Retrd.	N/A	120.00	100-120
1988 Wedding March NR-49	Retrd.	N/A	110.00	150
1978 Young Doctor NRD-26	Retrd.	N/A	100.00	120
1987 Young Love NR-48	Retrd.	N/A	70.00	120

Norman Rockwell Collection-American Rockwell Series - Rockwell-Inspired

YEAR ISSUE	EDITION LIMIT	YEAR RETD.	ISSUE PRICE	*QUOTE U.S.$
1981 Breaking Home Ties NRV-300	Retrd.	N/A	2000.00	2300
1982 Lincoln NRV-301	Retrd.	N/A	300.00	375
1982 Thanksgiving NRV-302	Retrd.	N/A	2500.00	2650

Norman Rockwell Collection-Boy Scout Series - Rockwell-Inspired

YEAR ISSUE	EDITION LIMIT	YEAR RETD.	ISSUE PRICE	*QUOTE U.S.$
1981 Can't Wait BSA-01	Retrd.	N/A	30.00	50
1981 Good Friends BSA-04	Retrd.	N/A	58.00	65
1981 Good Turn BSA-05	Retrd.	N/A	65.00	100
1982 Guiding Hand BSA-07	Retrd.	N/A	58.00	60
1981 Physically Strong BSA-03	Retrd.	N/A	56.00	150
1981 Scout Is Helpful BSA-02	Retrd.	N/A	38.00	45
1981 Scout Memories BSA-06	Retrd.	N/A	65.00	70
1983 Tomorrow's Leader BSA-08	Retrd.	N/A	45.00	55

Norman Rockwell Collection-Country Gentlemen Series - Rockwell-Inspired

YEAR ISSUE	EDITION LIMIT	YEAR RETD.	ISSUE PRICE	*QUOTE U.S.$
1982 Bringing Home the Tree CG-02	Retrd.	N/A	60.00	75
1982 The Catch CG-04	Retrd.	N/A	50.00	60
1982 On the Ice CG-05	Retrd.	N/A	50.00	60
1982 Pals CG-03	Retrd.	N/A	36.00	45
1982 Thin Ice CG-06	Retrd.	N/A	50.00	60
1982 Turkey Dinner CG-01	Retrd.	N/A	85.00	90

Norman Rockwell Collection-Huck Finn Series - Rockwell-Inspired

YEAR ISSUE	EDITION LIMIT	YEAR RETD.	ISSUE PRICE	*QUOTE U.S.$
1980 Listening HF-02	Retrd.	N/A	110.00	120
1980 No Kings HF-03	Retrd.	N/A	110.00	110
1979 The Secret HF-01	Retrd.	N/A	110.00	130
1980 Snake Escapes HF-04	Retrd.	N/A	110.00	120

Norman Rockwell Collection-Large Limited Editions - Rockwell-Inspired

YEAR ISSUE	EDITION LIMIT	YEAR RETD.	ISSUE PRICE	*QUOTE U.S.$
1975 Baseball NR-102	Retrd.	N/A	125.00	450
1982 Circus NR-106	Retrd.	N/A	500.00	500
1974 Doctor and Doll NR-100	Retrd.	N/A	300.00	1400
1981 Dreams of Long Ago NR-105	Retrd.	N/A	500.00	750
1979 Leapfrog NR-104	Retrd.	N/A	440.00	750
1984 Marble Players NR-107	Retrd.	N/A	500.00	750
1975 No Swimming NR-101	Retrd.	N/A	150.00	550-600
1974 See America First NR-103	Retrd.	N/A	100.00	500-550

Norman Rockwell Collection-Miniatures - Rockwell-Inspired

YEAR ISSUE	EDITION LIMIT	YEAR RETD.	ISSUE PRICE	*QUOTE U.S.$
1984 At the Doctor's NR-229	Retrd.	N/A	35.00	35
1979 Back To School NR-202	Retrd.	N/A	18.00	25
1982 Barbershop Quartet NR-223	Retrd.	N/A	40.00	50
1980 Baseball NR-216	Retrd.	N/A	40.00	50
1982 Big Moment NR-221	Retrd.	N/A	36.00	40
1979 Caroller NR-203	Retrd.	N/A	20.00	25
1982 Circus NR-222	Retrd.	N/A	35.00	40
1979 Daydreamer NR-204	Retrd.	N/A	20.00	30
1982 Discovery NR-220	Retrd.	N/A	35.00	45
1979 Doctor and Doll NR-212	Retrd.	N/A	40.00	40
1984 Dreams of Long Ago NR-231	Retrd.	N/A	35.00	40
1982 Drum For Tommy NRC-224	Retrd.	N/A	25.00	30
1984 First Day of School NR-227	Retrd.	N/A	35.00	35
1980 Friends In Need NR-213	Retrd.	N/A	35.00	40
1979 Lazybones NR-208	Retrd.	N/A	22.00	50
1979 Leapfrog NR-209	Retrd.	N/A	32.00	32
1979 Love Letter NR-206	Retrd.	N/A	26.00	50
1979 Lovers NR-207	Retrd.	N/A	28.00	30
1984 Magic Potion NR-228	Retrd.	N/A	40.00	40
1979 Marble Players NR-211	Retrd.	N/A	36.00	38
1979 No Swimming NR-205	Retrd.	N/A	22.00	30
1984 Pals NR-225	Retrd.	N/A	25.00	25
1979 Redhead NR-201	Retrd.	N/A	18.00	50
1983 Santa On the Train NR-245	Retrd.	N/A	35.00	55
1979 Schoolmaster NR-210	Retrd.	N/A	34.00	45
1980 See America First NR-217	Retrd.	N/A	28.00	50
1980 Springtime '33 NR-214	Retrd.	N/A	24.00	80
1982 Springtime '35 NR-219	Retrd.	N/A	24.00	30
1980 Summertime '33 NR-215	Retrd.	N/A	22.00	25
1980 Take Your Medicine NR-218	Retrd.	N/A	36.00	40
1984 Young Doctor NRD-226	Retrd.	N/A	30.00	50

Norman Rockwell Collection-Pewter Figurines - Rockwell-Inspired

YEAR ISSUE	EDITION LIMIT	YEAR RETD.	ISSUE PRICE	*QUOTE U.S.$
1980 Back to School FP-02	Retrd.	N/A	25.00	25
1980 Barbershop Quartet FP-23	Retrd.	N/A	25.00	25
1980 Big Moment FP-21	Retrd.	N/A	25.00	25
1980 Caroller FP-03	Retrd.	N/A	25.00	25
1980 Circus FP-22	Retrd.	N/A	25.00	25
1980 Doctor and Doll FP-12	Retrd.	N/A	25.00	25
1980 Figurine Display Rack FDR-01	Retrd.	N/A	60.00	60
1980 Grandpa's Ballerina FP-32	Retrd.	N/A	25.00	25
1980 Lovers FP-07	Retrd.	N/A	25.00	25
1980 Magic Potion FP-28	Retrd.	N/A	25.00	25
1980 No Swimming FP-05	Retrd.	N/A	25.00	25
1980 See America First FP-17	Retrd.	N/A	25.00	25
1980 Take Your Medicine FP-18	Retrd.	N/A	25.00	25

Norman Rockwell Collection-Rockwell Club Series - Rockwell-Inspired

YEAR ISSUE	EDITION LIMIT	YEAR RETD.	ISSUE PRICE	*QUOTE U.S.$
1982 Diary RCC-02	Retrd.	N/A	35.00	75
1984 Gone Fishing RCC-04	Retrd.	N/A	30.00	55
1983 Runaway Pants RCC-03	Retrd.	N/A	65.00	75
1981 Young Artist RCC-01	Retrd.	N/A	96.00	105

Norman Rockwell Collection-Select Collection, Ltd. - Rockwell-Inspired

YEAR ISSUE	EDITION LIMIT	YEAR RETD.	ISSUE PRICE	*QUOTE U.S.$
1982 Boy & Mother w/Puppies SC-1001	Retrd.	N/A	27.50	28
1982 Father With Child SC-1005	Retrd.	N/A	22.00	22
1982 Football Player SC-1004	Retrd.	N/A	22.00	22
1982 Girl Bathing Dog SC-1006	Retrd.	N/A	26.50	27
1982 Girl With Dolls In Crib SC-1002	Retrd.	N/A	26.50	27
1982 Helping Hand SC-1007	Retrd.	N/A	32.00	32
1982 Lemonade Stand SC-1008	Retrd.	N/A	32.00	32
1982 Save Me SC-1010	Retrd.	N/A	35.00	35
1982 Shaving Lesson SC-1009	Retrd.	N/A	30.00	30
1982 Young Couple SC-1003	Retrd.	N/A	27.50	28

Norman Rockwell Collection-Tom Sawyer Miniatures - Rockwell-Inspired

YEAR ISSUE	EDITION LIMIT	YEAR RETD.	ISSUE PRICE	*QUOTE U.S.$
1983 First Smoke TSM-02	Retrd.	N/A	40.00	45
1983 Lost In Cave TSM-05	Retrd.	N/A	40.00	50
1983 Take Your Medicine TSM-04	Retrd.	N/A	40.00	45
1983 Whitewashing the Fence TSM-01	Retrd.	N/A	40.00	50

Norman Rockwell Collection-Tom Sawyer Series - Rockwell-Inspired

YEAR ISSUE	EDITION LIMIT	YEAR RETD.	ISSUE PRICE	*QUOTE U.S.$
1976 First Smoke TS-02	Retrd.	N/A	60.00	235
1978 Lost In Cave TS-04	Retrd.	N/A	70.00	175
1977 Take Your Medicine TS-03	Retrd.	N/A	63.00	235
1975 Whitewashing the Fence TS-01	Retrd.	N/A	60.00	235

Dear Artistic Sculpture, Inc.

Art Gallery Collection - A. Belcari

YEAR ISSUE	EDITION LIMIT	YEAR RETD.	ISSUE PRICE	*QUOTE U.S.$
1995 Autumn	3,000		500.00	500
1995 Black Mother Swing	2,000		750.00	750
1995 Canada Geese	1,000		1700.00	1700
1994 Carriage	2,000		1350.00	1350
1995 Couple on Horse	2,000		1100.00	1100
1993 Eagle Trunk	1,200		1050.00	1050
1993 Eagle Trunk, white	800		500.00	500
1995 Eagle, lg.	2,000		1250.00	1250
1995 Eagle, lg., white	2,000		750.00	750
1992 Eagle, white	1,000		475.00	475
1995 Elk	1,000		700.00	700
1996 Flamingo	3,000		800.00	800
1996 Giraff w/Young	1,000		800.00	800
1994 Group of Doves	2,000		850.00	850
1996 Hawk	1,000		1075.00	1075
1996 Heron	3,000		750.00	750
1995 Horse Head	2,000		650.00	650
1995 Horse Head, bronze	2,000		650.00	650
1994 Lady on Horse	1,000		850.00	850
1994 Lady on Horse	1,000		750.00	750
1996 Macaw	1,000		1650.00	1650
1996 Owls on Books	3,000		1050.00	1050
1995 Peacock	1,000		700.00	700
1996 Peacock, lg.	2,000		1150.00	1150
1996 Pegasus, lg.	3,000		675.00	675
1996 Pegasus, lg., white	3,000		575.00	575
1996 Pelican	1,000		775.00	775
1995 Snow Geese	1,000		1450.00	1450
1995 Spring	3,000		550.00	550
1995 Summer	3,000		500.00	500
1993 Two Eagles	1,200		1050.00	1050
1993 Two Eagles, white	800		450.00	450
1995 Two Gulls	1,000		1100.00	1100
1996 Two Ibis	3,000		1275.00	1275
1995 Two Swans	1,000		1250.00	1250
1995 Winter	3,000		500.00	500

Department 56

All Through The House - Department 56

YEAR ISSUE	EDITION LIMIT	YEAR RETD.	ISSUE PRICE	*QUOTE U.S.$
1992 Aunt Martha With Turkey 9317-3	Closed	1995	27.50	28
1992 Dinner Table 9313-0	Closed	1995	65.00	65
1992 Mr. & Mrs. Bell at Dinner 9314-9, set/2	Closed	1995	40.00	40
1992 Nicholas, Natallie, & Spot The Dog 9315-7, set/3	Closed	1995	45.00	45
1992 Sideboard 9316-5	Closed	1995	45.00	45

Alpine Village Series - Department 56

YEAR ISSUE	EDITION LIMIT	YEAR RETD.	ISSUE PRICE	*QUOTE U.S.$
1987 Alpine Church 6541-2	Closed	1991	32.00	155-195
1992 Alpine Shops 5618-9, set/2 (Metternniche Wurst, Kukuck Uhren)	Open		75.00	75
1986 Alpine Village 6540-4, set/5 (Bessor Bierkeller, Gasthof Eisl, Apotheke, E. Staubr Backer, Milch-Kase)	Open		150.00	195
1990 Bahnhof 5615-4	Closed	1993	42.00	65-95
1994 Bakery & Chocolate Shop 5614-6	Open		37.50	38
1988 Grist Mill 5953-6	Open		42.00	45
1987 Josef Engel Farmhouse 5952-8	Closed	1989	33.00	860-1100
1995 Kamm Haus 5617-1	Open		42.00	42
1993 Sport Laden, 5612-0	Open		50.00	50
1991 St. Nikolaus Kirche 5617-0	Open		37.50	38

Christmas In the City Series - Department 56

YEAR ISSUE	EDITION LIMIT	YEAR RETD.	ISSUE PRICE	*QUOTE U.S.$
1989 5607 Park Avenue Townhouse 5977-3	Closed	1992	48.00	65-100
1989 5609 Park Avenue Townhouse 5978-1	Closed	1992	48.00	65-100
1991 All Saints Corner Church 5542-5	Open		96.00	110
1991 Arts Academy 5543-3	Closed	1993	45.00	50-85
1995 Brighton School 5887-6	Open		52.00	52
1994 Brokerage House, 5881-5	Open		48.00	48
1995 Brownstones on the Square 5887-7, set/2 (Beekman House, Pickford Place)	Open		90.00	90
1987 The Cathedral 5962-5	Closed	1990	60.00	300-385
1992 Cathedral Church of St. Mark 5549-2	3,024	1993	120.00	1700-2300
1988 Chocolate Shoppe 5968-4	Closed	1991	40.00	100-145
1987 Christmas In The City 6512-9, set/3	Closed	1990	112.00	435-550
1987 • Bakery 6512-9	Closed	1990	37.50	95-130
1987 • Tower Restaurant 6512-9	Closed	1990	37.50	200-285
1987 • Toy Shop and Pet Store 6512-9	Closed	1990	37.50	220-275
1988 City Hall (small) 5969-2	Closed	1991	65.00	175-240
1988 City Hall (standard) 5969-2	Closed	1991	65.00	155-225
1991 The Doctor's Office 5544-1	Closed	1994	60.00	75-125
1989 Dorothy's Dress Shop 5974-9	12,500	1991	70.00	300-385
1994 First Metropolitan Bank 5882-3	Open		60.00	60
1988 Hank's Market 5970-6	Closed	1992	40.00	65-100
1994 Heritage Museum of Art 5883-1	Open		96.00	96

*Quotes have been rounded up to nearest dollar

FIGURINES/COTTAGES

YEAR ISSUE	EDITION LIMIT	YEAR RETD.	ISSUE PRICE	*QUOTE U.S.$
1991 Hollydale's Department Store 5534-4	Open		75.00	85
1995 Holy Name Church 5887-5	Open		96.00	96
1995 Ivy Terrace Apartments 5887-4	Open		60.00	60
1991 Little Italy Ristorante 5538-7	Closed	1995	50.00	55-95
1987 Palace Theatre 5963-3	Closed	1989	45.00	800-1150
1990 Red Brick Fire Station 5536-0	Closed	1995	55.00	60-100
1989 Ritz Hotel 5973-0	Closed	1994	55.00	60-110
1987 Sutton Place Brownstones 5961-7	Closed	1989	80.00	825-950
1992 Uptown Shoppes 5531-0, set/3 (Haberdashery, City Clockworks, Music Emporium)	Open		150.00	150
1988 Variety Store 5972-2	Closed	1990	45.00	150-190
1996 Washington Street Post Office 58880	Open		52.00	52
1993 West Village Shops 5880-7, set/2 (Potters' Tea Seller, Spring St. Coffee House)	Open		90.00	90
1990 Wong's In Chinatown 5537-9	Closed	1994	55.00	60-95

Dickens' Village Series - Department 56

YEAR ISSUE	EDITION LIMIT	YEAR RETD.	ISSUE PRICE	*QUOTE U.S.$
1991 Ashbury Inn 5555-7	Closed	1995	55.00	50-85
1987 Barley Bree 5900-5, set/2 (Farmhouse, Barn)	Closed	1989	60.00	350-395
1990 Bishops Oast House 5567-0	Closed	1992	45.00	60-100
1995 Blenham Street Bank, 5833-0	Open		60.00	60
1986 Blythe Pond Mill House 6508-0	Closed	1990	37.00	245-300
1986 By The Pond Mill House 6508-0	Closed	1990	37.00	125-200
1994 Boarding & Lodging School, 5810-6	Open		48.00	48
1993 Boarding and Lodging School, 5809-2 (Christmas Carol Commemorative Piece)	Yr.Iss.	1993	48.00	125-195
1987 Brick Abbey 6549-8	Closed	1989	33.00	345-425
1996 Butter Tub Barn 58338	Open		48.00	48
1996 Butter Tub Farmhouse 58337	Open		40.00	40
1988 C. Fletcher Public House 5904-8	12,500	1989	35.00	525-595
1986 Chadbury Station and Train 6528-5	Closed	1989	65.00	345-395
1987 Chesterton Manor House 6568-4	7,500	1988	45.00	1500-1800
1986 Christmas Carol Cottages 6500-5, set/3	Closed	1995	75.00	100-145
1986 • The Cottage of Bob Cratchit & Tiny Tim 6500-5	Closed	1995	25.00	45-65
1986 • Fezziwig's Warehouse 6500-5	Closed	1995	25.00	25-55
1986 • Scrooge and Marley Counting House 6500-5	Closed	1995	25.00	33-55
1996 The Christmas Carol Cottages (revisited) 58339	Open		60.00	60
1988 Cobblestone Shops 5924-2, set/3	Closed	1990	95.00	250-440
1988 • Booter and Cobbler 5924-2	Closed	1990	32.00	100-135
1988 • T. Wells Fruit & Spice Shop 5924-2	Closed	1990	32.00	80-130
1988 • The Wool Shop 5924-2	Closed	1990	32.00	160-200
1989 Cobles Police Station 5583-2	Closed	1991	37.50	130-170
1988 Counting House & Silas Thimbleton Barrister 5902-1	Closed	1990	32.00	70-120
1992 Crown & Cricket Inn (Charles Dickens' Signature Series), 5750-9	Yr.Iss.	1992	100.00	150-200
1989 David Copperfield 5550-6, set/3	Closed	1992	125.00	170-240
1989 • Betsy Trotwood's Cottage 5550-6	Closed	1992	42.50	45-75
1989 • Peggotty's Seaside Cottage 5550-6 (green boat)	Closed	1992	42.50	45-75
1989 • Mr. Wickfield Solicitor 5550-6	Closed	1992	42.50	85-100
1989 David Copperfield 5550-6, set/3 with tan boat	Closed	1992	125.00	250-275
1989 Peggotty's Seaside Cottage 5550-6 (tan boat)	Closed	1992	42.50	120-175
1994 Dedlock Arms, 5752-5 (Charles Dickens' Signature Series)	Yr.Iss.	1994	100.00	110-180
1985 Dickens' Cottages 6518-8 set3	Closed	1988	75.00	800-1050
1985 • Stone Cottage 6518-8	Closed	1988	25.00	375-450
1985 • Thatched Cottage 6518-8	Closed	1988	25.00	175-200
1985 • Tudor Cottage 6518-8	Closed	1988	25.00	355-450
1986 Dickens' Lane Shops 6507-2, set/3	Closed	1989	80.00	400-600
1986 • Cottage Toy Shop 6507-2	Closed	1989	27.00	200-225
1986 • Thomas Kersey Coffee House 6507-2	Closed	1989	27.00	155-225
1986 • Tuttle's Pub 6507-2	Closed	1989	27.00	200-245
1984 Dickens' Village Church (cream) 6516-1	Closed	1989	35.00	300-420
1985 Dickens' Village Church(dark) 6516-1	Closed	1989	35.00	160-250
1985 Dickens' Village Church(green) 6516-1	Closed	1989	35.00	375-475
1985 Dickens' Village Church(tan) 6516-1	Closed	1989	35.00	165-225
1985 Dickens' Village Mill 6519-6	2,500	1986	35.00	3800-4800
1995 Dudden Cross Church 5834-3	Open		45.00	45
1995 Dursley Manor, 5832-9	Open		50.00	50
1991 Fagin's Hide-A-Way 5552-2	Closed	1995	68.00	75-90
1989 The Flat of Ebenezer Scrooge 5587-5	Open		37.50	38
1994 Giggelswick Mutton & Ham, 5822-0	Open		48.00	48
1996 The Grapes Inn, 5753-4 (Charles Dickens' Signature Series)	Yr.Iss.		120.00	120
1993 Great Denton Mill, 5812-2	Open		50.00	50
1989 Green Gate Cottage 5586-7	22,500	1990	65.00	250-300
1994 Hather Harness 5823-8	Open		48.00	48
1992 Hembleton Pewterer, 5800-9	Closed	1995	72.00	75-100
1988 Ivy Glen Church 5927-7	Closed	1991	35.00	75-95
1995 J.D. Nichols Toy Shop, 5832-8	Open		48.00	48
1987 Kenilworth Castle 5916-1	Closed	1988	70.00	625-700
1992 King's Road Post Office, 5801-7	Open		45.00	45
1993 Kingford's Brewhouse, 5811-4	Open		45.00	45
1990 Kings Road 5568-9, set/2 (Tutbury Printer, C.H. Watt Physician)	Open		72.00	80
1989 Knottinghill Church 5582-4	Closed	1995	50.00	60-100

YEAR ISSUE	EDITION LIMIT	YEAR RETD.	ISSUE PRICE	*QUOTE U.S.$
1995 The Maltings 5833-5	Open		50.00	50
1988 Merchant Shops 5926-9, set/5	Closed	1993	150.00	200-290
1988 • Geo. Weeton Watchmaker 5926-9	Closed	1993	30.00	45-70
1988 • The Mermaid Fish Shoppe 5926-9	Closed	1993	30.00	65-75
1988 • Poulterer 5926-9	Closed	1993	30.00	50-80
1988 • Walpole Tailors 5926-9	Closed	1993	30.00	40-75
1988 • White Horse Bakery 5926-9	Closed	1993	30.00	45-65
1991 Nephew Fred's Flat 5557-3	Closed	1994	35.00	65-75
1988 Nicholas Nickleby 5925-0, set/2	Closed	1991	72.00	170-200
1988 • Nicholas Nickleby Cottage 5925-0	Closed	1991	36.00	65-95
1988 • Wackford Squeers Boarding School 5925-0	Closed	1991	36.00	70-100
1988 Nickolas Nickleby Cottage 5925-0-misspelled	Closed	1991	36.00	80-105
1988 Nickolas Nickleby set/2, 5925-0-misspelled	Closed	1991	36.00	200-225
1986 Norman Church 6502-1	3,500	1987	40.00	3000-3800
1987 The Old Curiosity Shop 5905-6	Open		32.00	42
1992 Old Michaelchurch, 5562-0	Open		42.00	48
1991 Oliver Twist 5553-0, set/2	Closed	1993	75.00	80-150
1991 • Brownlow House 5553-0	Closed	1993	38.00	55-80
1991 • Maylie Cottage 5553-0	Closed	1993	38.00	40-80
1984 The Original Shops of Dickens' Village, 6515-3, set of 7	Closed	1988	175.00	1200-1400
1984 • Abel Beesley Butcher 6515-3	Closed	1988	25.00	115-150
1984 • Bean And Son Smithy Shop 6515-3	Closed	1988	25.00	175-195
1984 • Candle Shop 6515-3	Closed	1988	25.00	165-195
1984 • Crowntree Inn 6515-3	Closed	1988	25.00	290-350
1984 • Golden Swan Baker 6515-3	Closed	1988	25.00	155-175
1984 • Green Grocer 6515-3	Closed	1988	25.00	185-215
1984 • Jones & Co. Brush & Basket Shop 6515-3	Closed	1988	25.00	280-345
1993 The Pied Bull Inn (Charles Dickens' Signature Series), 5751-7	Closed	1993	100.00	130-200
1994 Portobello Road Thatched Cottages 5824-6, set/3 (Mr. & Mrs. Pickle, Cobb Cottage, Browning Cottage)	Open		120.00	120
1993 Pump Lane Shoppes 5808-4, set/3 (Bumpstead Nye Cloaks & Canes, Lomas Ltd. Molasses, W.M. Wheat Cakes & Puddings)	Open		112.00	112
1996 Ramsford Palace 58336, set/17 (Ramsford Palace, Palace Guards, set/2 Accessory, Palace Gate Accessory, Palace Fountain Accessory, Wall Hedge, set/8 Accessory, Corner Wall Topiaries, set/4 Accessory)	27,500		175.00	175
1989 Ruth Marion Scotch Woolens 5585-9	17,500	1990	65.00	375-450
1995 Sir John Falstaff Inn 5753-3 (Charles Dickens' Signature Series)	Closed	1995	100.00	120-165
1995 Start A Tradition Set 5832-7, set/13 (The Town Square Shops-Faversham Lamps & Oil, Morston Steak and Kidney Pie, The Town Square Carolers Accessory, set/3, 6 Sisal Trees, Bag of Real Plastic Snow, Cobblestone Road)	Open		85.00	85
1989 Theatre Royal 5584-0	Closed	1992	45.00	65-95
1989 Victoria Station 5574-3	Open		100.00	112
1994 Whittlesbourne Church, 5821-1	Open		85.00	85
1995 Wrenbury Shops 5833-1, set/3 (Wrenbury Baker, The Chop Shop, T. Puddlewick Spectacle Shop)	Open		100.00	100

Disney Parks Village Series - Department 56

YEAR ISSUE	EDITION LIMIT	YEAR RETD.	ISSUE PRICE	*QUOTE U.S.$
1994 Fire Station No. 105 5352-0 Disneyland, CA	Closed	1996	45.00	45
1994 Mickey's Christmas Shop 5350-3, set/2 Disney World, FL	Closed	1996	144.00	144
1994 Olde World Antiques 5351-1, set/2 Disney World, FL	Closed	1996	90.00	90
1995 Silversmith 5352-1 Disney World, FL	Closed	1996	50.00	50-75
1995 Tinker Bell's Treasures 5352-2 Disney World, FL	Closed	1996	60.00	60-90

Disney Parks Village Series Accessories - Department 56

YEAR ISSUE	EDITION LIMIT	YEAR RETD.	ISSUE PRICE	*QUOTE U.S.$
1995 The Balloon Seller 5353-9, set/2	Closed	1996	25.00	25-35
1994 Disney Parks Family, set/3 5354-6	Closed	1996	32.50	33
1994 Mickey and Minnie 5353-8, set/2	Closed	1996	22.50	23-30
1994 Olde World Antiques Gate 5355-4	Closed	1996	15.00	15

Easter Collectibles - Department 56

YEAR ISSUE	EDITION LIMIT	YEAR RETD.	ISSUE PRICE	*QUOTE U.S.$
1995 Bisque Chick, Large 2464-3	Closed	1996	8.50	10
1995 Bisque Chick, Small, 2465-1	Closed	1996	6.50	8
1993 Bisque Duckling, set	Closed	1993	15.00	26-36
1993 Bisque Duckling, Large 3.5" 7282-6	Closed	1993	8.50	18
1993 Bisque Duckling, Small 2.75" 7281-8	Closed	1993	6.50	15
1994 Bisque Fledgling in Nest, Large 2.75" 2400-7	Closed	1994	6.00	11-16
1994 Bisque Fledgling in Nest, Small 2.5" 2401-5	Closed	1994	5.00	10
1991 Bisque Lamb, set	Closed	1991	12.50	66-85
1991 Bisque Lamb, Large 4" 7392-0	Closed	1991	7.50	26-42
1991 Bisque Lamb, Small 2.5" 7393-8	Closed	1991	5.00	24-42
1992 Bisque Rabbit, set	Closed	1992	14.00	40-70
1992 Bisque Rabbit, Large 5" 7498-5	Closed	1992	8.00	22-28
1992 Bisque Rabbit, Small 4" 7499-3	Closed	1992	6.00	14-25
1996 Bisque Rabbit, Large 2765-0	Open		8.50	9
1996 Bisque Rabbit, Small 2764-2	Open		7.50	8

Event Piece - Heritage Village Collection Accessory - Department 56

YEAR ISSUE	EDITION LIMIT	YEAR RETD.	ISSUE PRICE	* QUOTE U.S.$
1992 Gate House 5530-1	Closed	1992	22.50	45-100
1996 Christmas Bells 98711	Open		35.00	35

Little Town of Bethlehem Series - Department 56

YEAR ISSUE	EDITION LIMIT	YEAR RETD.	ISSUE PRICE	* QUOTE U.S.$
1987 Little Town of Bethlehem 5975-7, set/12	Open		150.00	150

Merry Makers - Department 56

YEAR ISSUE	EDITION LIMIT	YEAR RETD.	ISSUE PRICE	* QUOTE U.S.$
1991 Charles The Cellist 9355-6	Closed	1995	19.00	19
1991 Clarence The Concertinist 9353-0	Closed	1995	19.00	19
1991 Frederick The Flutist 9352-1	Closed	1995	19.00	19
1991 Horatio The Hornblower 9351-3	Closed	1995	19.00	19
1991 Martin The Mandolinist 9350-5	Closed	1995	19.00	19
1991 Sidney The Singer 9354-8	Closed	1995	19.00	19

New England Village Series - Department 56

YEAR ISSUE	EDITION LIMIT	YEAR RETD.	ISSUE PRICE	* QUOTE U.S.$
1993 A. Bieler Farm 5648-0, set/2 (Pennsylvania Dutch Farmhouse, Pennsylvania Dutch Barn)	Open		92.00	95
1988 Ada's Bed and Boarding House (lemon yellow) 5940-4	Closed	1991	36.00	250-320
1988 Ada's Bed and Boarding House (pale yellow) 5940-4	Closed	1991	36.00	120-175
1996 Apple Valley School 56172	Open		35.00	35
1994 Arlington Falls Church, 5651-0	Open		40.00	42
1989 Berkshire House (medium blue) 5942-0	Closed	1991	40.00	145-165
1989 Berkshire House (teal) 5942-0	Closed	1991	40.00	100-125
1993 Blue Star Ice Co., 5647-2	Open		45.00	48
1992 Bluebird Seed and Bulb, 5642-1	Open		48.00	48
1995 Brewster Bay Cottage 5657-0, set/2 (Jeremiah Brewster House, Thomas T. Julian House)	Open		90.00	90
1994 Cape Keag Cannery 5652-9	Open		48.00	48
1990 Captain's Cottage 5947-1	Open		40.00	44
1988 Cherry Lane Shops 5939-0, set/3	Closed	1990	80.00	250-325
1988 • Anne Shaw Toys 5939-0	Closed	1990	27.00	145-185
1988 • Ben's Barbershop 5939-0	Closed	1990	27.00	100-115
1988 • Otis Hayes Butcher Shop 5939-0	Closed	1990	27.00	75-95
1987 Craggy Cove Lighthouse 5930-7	Closed	1994	35.00	50-100
1995 Chowder House 5657-1	Open		40.00	40
1986 Jacob Adams Farmhouse and Barn 6538-2	Closed	1989	65.00	450-600
1989 Jannes Mullet Amish Barn 5944-7	Closed	1992	48.00	80-110
1989 Jannes Mullet Amish Farm House 5943-9	Closed	1992	32.00	95-130
1991 McGrebe-Cutters & Sleighs 5640-5	Closed	1995	45.00	48-55
1986 New England Village 6530-7, set/7	Closed	1989	170.00	1000-1300
1986 • Apothecary Shop 6530-7	Closed	1989	25.00	95
1986 • Brick Town Hall 6530-7	Closed	1989	25.00	170-270
1986 • General Store 6530-7	Closed	1989	25.00	310-375
1986 • Livery Stable & Boot Shop 6530-7	Closed	1989	25.00	115-155
1986 • Nathaniel Bingham Fabrics 6530-7	Closed	1989	25.00	145-160
1986 • Red Schoolhouse 6530-7	Closed	1989	25.00	250-285
1986 • Steeple Church (Original) 6530-7	Closed	1989	25.00	160-180
1988 Old North Church 5932-3	Open		40.00	45
1995 Pierce Boat Works 5657-3	Open		55.00	55
1994 Pigeonhead Lighthouse 5653-7	Open		50.00	50
1990 Shingle Creek House 5946-3	Closed	1994	37.50	45-95
1990 Sleepy Hollow 5954-4, set/3	Closed	1993	96.00	100-185
1990 • Ichabod Crane's Cottage 5954-4	Closed	1993	32.00	35-80
1990 • Sleepy Hollow School 5954-4	Closed	1993	32.00	75-100
1990 • Van Tassel Manor 5954-4	Closed	1993	32.00	40-85
1990 Sleepy Hollow Church 5955-2	Closed	1993	36.00	45-85
1987 Smythe Woolen Mill 5643-9	7,500	1988	42.00	1000-1100
1986 Steeple Church (Second Version) 6539-0	Closed	1990	30.00	85-115
1992 Stoney Brook Town Hall 5644-8	Closed	1995	42.00	42-60
1987 Timber Knoll Log Cabin 6544-7	Closed	1990	28.00	150-175
1987 Weston Train Station 5931-5	Closed	1989	42.00	245-300
1995 Woodbridge Post Office 5657-2	Open		40.00	40
1992 Yankee Jud Bell Casting 5643-0	Closed	1995	44.00	42-60

North Pole Series - Department 56

YEAR ISSUE	EDITION LIMIT	YEAR RETD.	ISSUE PRICE	* QUOTE U.S.$
1994 Beard Barber Shop 5634-0	Open		27.50	28
1992 Elfie's Sleds & Skates 5625-1	Open		48.00	48
1995 Elfin Forge & Assembly Shop 5638-6	Open		65.00	65
1994 Elfin Snow Cone Works 5633-2	Open		40.00	40
1995 Elves' Trade School 5638-7	Open		50.00	50
1993 Express Depot 5627-8	Open		48.00	48
1991 Neenee's Dolls & Toys 5620-0	Closed	1995	37.50	50-85
1990 North Pole 5601-4, set/2 (Reindeer Barn, Elf Bunkhouse)	Open		70.00	80
1993 North Pole Chapel 5626-0	Open		45.00	45
1994 North Pole Dolls & Santa's Bear Works 5635-9, set/3 (North Pole Dolls, Santa's Bear Works, Entrance)	Open		96.00	96
1992 North Pole Post Office 5623-5	Open		45.00	50
1991 North Pole Shops 5621-9, set/2	Closed	1995	75.00	95-110
1991 • Orly's Bell & Harness Supply	Closed	1995	37.50	50-75
1991 • Rimpy's Bakery	Closed	1995	37.50	55-85
1992 Obbie's Books & Letrinka's Candy 5624-3	Open		70.00	70
1996 Popcorn & Cranberry House 56388	Open		45.00	45
1996 Santa's Bell Repair 56389	Open		45.00	45
1993 Santa's Lookout Tower 5629-4	Open		45.00	48

FIGURINES/COTTAGES

YEAR ISSUE	EDITION LIMIT	YEAR RETD.	ISSUE PRICE	*QUOTE U.S.$
1995 Santa's Rooming House 5638-6	Open		50.00	50
1993 Santa's Woodworks 5628-6	Open		42.00	45
1990 Santa's Workshop 5600-6	Closed	1993	72.00	400-485
1996 Start a Tradition Set 56390, set/12 (Candy Cane & Peppermint Shop, Gift Wrap & Ribbons, Candy Cane Elves, set/2 Accessory)	Open		85.00	85
1991 Tassy's Mittens & Hassel's Woolies 5622-7	Closed	1995	50.00	60-100
1995 Tin Soldier Shop 5638-3	Open		42.00	42
1995 Weather & Time Observatory 5638-5	Open		50.00	50

The Original Snow Village Collection - Department 56

YEAR ISSUE	EDITION LIMIT	YEAR RETD.	ISSUE PRICE	*QUOTE U.S.$
1986 2101 Maple 5043-1	Closed	1986	32.00	310-400
1990 56 Flavors Ice Cream Parlor 5151-9	Closed	1992	42.00	75-120
1979 Adobe House 5066-6	Closed	1980	18.00	2000-2300
1992 Airport 5439-9	Open		60.00	60
1992 Al's TV Shop 5423-2	Closed	1995	40.00	40-60
1986 All Saints Church 5070-9	Open		38.00	45
1986 Apothecary 5076-8	Closed	1990	34.00	75-125
1981 Bakery 5077-6	Closed	1983	30.00	185-250
1986 Bakery 5077-6	Closed	1991	35.00	75-100
1982 Bank 5024-5	Closed	1983	34.00	550-650
1981 Barn 5074-1	Closed	1984	32.00	360-400
1984 Bayport 5015-6	Closed	1986	30.00	210-250
1986 Beacon Hill House 5065-2	Closed	1988	31.00	150-180
1995 Beacon Hill Victorian 5485-7	Open		60.00	60
1979 Brownstone 5056-7	Closed	1981	36.00	535-635
1996 Boulder Springs House 54873	Open		60.00	60
1995 Bowling Alley 5485-8	Open		42.00	42
1978 Cape Cod 5013-8	Closed	1980	20.00	365-380
1994 Carmel Cottage 5466-6	Open		48.00	48
1982 Carriage House 5021-0	Closed	1984	28.00	305-375
1986 Carriage House 5071-7	Closed	1988	29.00	100-125
1987 Cathedral Church 5019-9	Closed	1990	50.00	95-125
1980 Cathedral Church 5067-4	Closed	1981	36.00	2200-3000
1982 Centennial House 5020-2	Closed	1984	32.00	305-375
1983 Chateau 5084-9	Closed	1984	35.00	385-500
1995 Christmas Cove Lighthouse 5483-6	Open		60.00	60
1991 The Christmas Shop 5097-0	Open		37.50	38
1985 Church of the Open Door 5048-2	Closed	1988	34.00	95-150
1988 Cobblestone Antique Shop 5123-3	Closed	1992	36.00	55-80
1994 Coca-Cola® Brand Bottling Plant 5469-0	Open		65.00	65
1995 Coca-Cola® Brand Corner Drugstore 5484-4	Open		55.00	55
1989 Colonial Church 5119-5	Closed	1992	60.00	60-110
1980 Colonial Farm House 5070-9	Closed	1982	30.00	255-325
1984 Congregational Church 5034-2	Closed	1985	28.00	575-650
1988 Corner Cafe 5124-1	Closed	1991	37.00	75-100
1981 Corner Store 5076-8	Closed	1983	30.00	200-270
1976 Country Church 5004-7	Closed	1979	18.00	340-375
1979 Countryside Church 5051-8 Meadowland Series	Closed	1980	25.00	700-760
1979 Countryside Church 5058-3	Closed	1984	27.50	220-350
1989 Courthouse 5144-6	Closed	1993	65.00	145-170
1992 Craftsman Cottage (American Architecture Series), 5437-2	Closed	1995	55.00	55-75
1987 Cumberland House 5024-5	Closed	1995	42.00	45-75
1993 Dairy Barn 5446-1	Open		55.00	55
1984 Delta House 5012-1	Closed	1986	32.00	220-325
1985 Depot and Train w/2 Train Cars 5051-2	Closed	1988	65.00	90-125
1993 Dinah's Drive-In 5447-0	Open		45.00	45
1989 Doctor's House 5143-8	Closed	1992	56.00	90-120
1991 Double Bungalow 5407-0	Closed	1994	45.00	45-75
1985 Duplex 5050-4	Closed	1987	35.00	115-145
1995 Dutch Colonial 5485-6 (American Architecture Series)	Open		45.00	45
1981 English Church 5078-4	Closed	1982	30.00	365-400
1981 English Cottage 5073-3	Closed	1982	25.00	245-290
1983 English Tudor 5033-4	Closed	1985	30.00	215-275
1987 Farm House 5089-0	Closed	1992	40.00	50-85
1994 Federal House (American Architecture Series) 5465-8	Open		50.00	50
1991 Finklea's Finery: Costume Shop 5405-4	Closed	1993	45.00	50-85
1983 Fire Station 5032-6	Closed	1984	32.00	525-650
1987 Fire Station No. 2 5091-1	Closed	1989	40.00	155-185
1994 Fisherman's Nook Cabins 5461-5, set/2, (Fisherman's Nook Bass Cabin, Fisherman's Nook Trout Cabin)	Open		50.00	50
1994 Fisherman's Nook Resort 5460-7	Open		75.00	75
1982 Flower Shop 5082-2	Closed	1983	25.00	485
1976 Gabled Cottage 5002-1	Closed	1979	20.00	330-375
1982 Gabled House 5081-4	Closed	1983	30.00	350-425
1984 Galena House 5009-1	Closed	1985	32.00	330-400
1978 General Store (tan) 5012-0	Closed	1980	25.00	675
1978 General Store (white) 5012-0	Closed	1980	25.00	440-500
1979 Giant Trees 5065-8	Closed	1982	20.00	300-400
1983 Gingerbread HouseBank (Non-lighted) 5025-3	Closed	1984	24.00	330-400
1994 Glenhaven House 5468-2	Open		45.00	45
1992 Good Shepherd Chapel & Church School 5424-0, set/2	Open		72.00	72
1983 Gothic Church 5028-8	Closed	1986	36.00	220-300
1991 Gothic Farmhouse (American Architecture Series), 5404-6	Open		48.00	48
1983 Governor's Mansion 5003-2	Closed	1985	32.00	300
1992 Grandma's Cottage 5420-8	Open		42.00	45
1983 Grocery 5001-6	Closed	1985	35.00	345-400
1992 Hartford House 5426-7	Closed	1995	55.00	60-70
1984 Haversham House 5008-3	Closed	1987	37.00	220-320
1986 Highland Park House 5063-6	Closed	1988	35.00	125
1995 Holly Brothers Garage 5485-4	Open		48.00	48
1988 Home Sweet Home/House & Windmill 5126-8	Closed	1991	60.00	100-130
1978 Homestead 5011-2	Closed	1984	30.00	240-275
1991 Honeymooner Motel 5401-1	Closed	1993	42.00	65-95
1993 Hunting Lodge 5445-3	Open		50.00	50
1976 The Inn 5003-9	Closed	1979	20.00	420
1989 J. Young's Granary 5149-7	Closed	1992	45.00	75-95
1991 Jack's Corner Barber Shop 5406-2	Closed	1994	42.00	55-80
1987 Jefferson School 5082-2	Closed	1991	36.00	125-180
1989 Jingle Belle Houseboat 5114-4	Closed	1991	42.00	95-120
1988 Kenwood House 5054-7	Closed	1990	50.00	125-150
1979 Knob Hill (gold) 5055-9	Closed	1981	30.00	330-400
1979 Knob Hill 5055-9	Closed	1981	30.00	175-300
1981 Large Single Tree 5080-6	Closed	1989	17.00	35-55
1987 Lighthouse 5030-0	Closed	1988	36.00	500-700
1986 Lincoln Park Duplex 5060-1	Closed	1988	33.00	125
1979 Log Cabin 5057-5	Closed	1981	22.00	440-500
1984 Main Street House 5005-9	Closed	1986	27.00	235-275
1990 Mainstreet Hardware Store 5153-5	Closed	1993	42.00	60-85
1977 Mansion 5008-8	Closed	1979	30.00	440-550
1988 Maple Ridge Inn 5121-7	Closed	1990	55.00	60-125
1994 Marvel's Beauty Salon 5470-4	Open		37.50	38
1986 Mickey's Diner 5078-4	Closed	1987	22.00	600-690
1979 Mission Church 5062-5	Closed	1980	30.00	1000-1200
1979 Mobile Home 5063-3	Closed	1980	18.00	2100-2300
1990 Morningside House 5152-7	Closed	1992	45.00	50-65
1993 Mount Olivet Church, 5442-9	Open		65.00	65
1976 Mountain Lodge 5001-3	Closed	1979	20.00	375
1978 Nantucket 5014-6	Closed	1986	25.00	250-280
1993 Nantucket Renovation 5441-0	Closed	1993	55.00	70-100
1984 New School House 5037-7	Closed	1986	35.00	225-325
1982 New Stone Church 5083-0	Closed	1984	32.00	375
1996 Nick's Tree Farm 54871, set/10 (Nick's Tree Farm, Nick The Tree Farmer Accessory)	Open		40.00	40
1989 North Creek Cottage 5120-9	Closed	1992	45.00	60-80
1991 Oak Grove Tudor 5400-3	Closed	1994	42.00	44-60
1994 The Original Snow Village Starter Set 5462-3 (Shady Oak Church, Sunday School Serenade Accessory, 3 assorted Sisal Trees, 1.5 oz. bag of real plastic snow)	Open		50.00	50
1986 Pacific Heights House 5066-0	Closed	1988	33.00	90-125
1988 Palos Verdes 5141-1	Closed	1990	37.50	65-90
1989 Paramount Theater 5142-0	Closed	1993	42.00	90-130
1984 Parish Church 5039-3	Closed	1986	32.00	220-300
1983 Parsonage 5029-6	Closed	1985	35.00	225-350
1995 Peppermint Porch Day Care 5485-2	Open		45.00	45
1989 Pinewood Log Cabin 5150-0	Closed	1995	37.50	38-65
1982 Pioneer Church 5022-9	Closed	1984	30.00	275-350
1995 Pisa Pizza 5485-1	Open		35.00	35
1985 Plantation House 5047-4	Closed	1987	37.00	88-115
1992 Post Office 5422-4	Closed	1995	35.00	40-55
1990 Prairie House (American Architecture Series), 5156-0	Closed	1993	42.00	45-70
1992 Print Shop & Village News 5425-9	Closed	1994	37.50	45-65
1990 Queen Anne Victorian (American Architecture Series), 5157-8	Open		48.00	50
1986 Ramsey Hill House 5067-9	Closed	1989	36.00	85-125
1987 Red Barn 5081-4	Closed	1992	38.00	75-95
1988 Redeemer Church 5127-6	Closed	1992	42.00	50-80
1996 Reindeer Bus Depot 54874	Open		42.00	42
1985 Ridgewood 5052-0	Closed	1987	35.00	125-170
1984 River Road House 5010-5	Closed	1987	36.00	170-250
1995 Ryman Auditorium 5485-5	Open		75.00	75
1986 Saint James Church 5068-7	Closed	1988	37.00	140-180
1979 School House 5060-9	Closed	1982	30.00	320-375
1988 Service Station 5128-4	Closed	1991	37.50	230-295
1988 Single Car Garage 5125-0	Closed	1990	22.00	40-80
1994 Skate & Ski Shop 5467-4	Open		50.00	50
1982 Skating Pond 5017-2	Closed	1984	25.00	300-400
1978 Skating Rink, Duck Pond (set) 5015-3	Closed	1979	16.00	1200-1500
1976 Small Chalet 5006-2	Closed	1979	15.00	380-475
1978 Small Double Trees w/ blue birds 5016-1	Closed	1989	13.50	170
1978 Small Double Trees w/ red birds 5016-1	Closed	1989	13.50	35-70
1996 Smokey Mountain Retreat 54872	Open		65.00	65
1995 Snow Carnival Ice Palace 5485-0	Open		95.00	95
1987 Snow Village Factory 5013-0	Closed	1989	45.00	120-145
1987 Snow Village Resort Lodge 5092-0	Closed	1989	55.00	120-150
1993 Snowy Hills Hospital 5448-8	Open		48.00	48
1986 Sonoma House 5062-8	Closed	1988	33.00	120-150
1991 Southern Colonial (American Architecture Series), 5403-8	Closed	1994	48.00	60-85
1990 Spanish Mission Church 5155-1	Closed	1992	42.00	60-95
1987 Springfield House 5027-0	Closed	1990	40.00	50-80
1985 Spruce Place 5049-0	Closed	1987	33.00	225-285
1987 St. Anthony Hotel & Post Office 5006-7	Closed	1989	40.00	105-135
1992 St. Luke's Church 5421-6	Closed	1994	45.00	50-65
1995 Starbucks Coffee 5485-9	Open		48.00	48
1976 Steepled Church 5005-4	Closed	1979	25.00	550
1977 Stone Church (10") 5009-6	Closed	1979	35.00	520-600
1979 Stone Church (8") 5059-1	Closed	1980	32.00	1050
1980 Stone Mill House 5068-2	Closed	1982	30.00	465-525
1988 Stonehurst House 5140-3	Closed	1994	37.50	45-70
1984 Stratford House 5007-5	Closed	1986	28.00	175
1982 Street Car 5019-9	Closed	1984	16.00	400-450
1985 Stucco Bungalow 5045-8	Closed	1986	30.00	365-400
1984 Summit House 5036-9	Closed	1985	28.00	345
1982 Swiss Chalet 5023-7	Closed	1984	28.00	440-475
1979 Thatched Cottage 5050-0 Meadowland Series	Closed	1980	30.00	600-675
1980 Town Church 5071-7	Closed	1982	33.00	375-450
1983 Town Hall 5000-8	Closed	1984	32.00	330-375
1986 Toy Shop 5073-3	Closed	1990	36.00	85-100
1980 Train Station w/ 3 Train Cars 5085-6	Closed	1985	100.00	300-375
1984 Trinity Church 5035-0	Closed	1986	32.00	200-275
1979 Tudor House 5061-7	Closed	1981	25.00	250-400
1983 Turn of the Century 5004-0	Closed	1986	36.00	210-275
1986 Twin Peaks 5042-3	Closed	1986	32.00	385-425
1979 Victorian 5054-2	Closed	1982	30.00	320-400
1983 Victorian Cottage 5002-4	Closed	1985	35.00	330-400
1977 Victorian House 5007-0	Closed	1979	30.00	465
1983 Village Church 5026-1	Closed	1984	30.00	425
1991 Village Greenhouse 5402-0	Closed	1995	35.00	36-55
1988 Village Market 5044-0	Closed	1991	39.00	65-80
1995 Village Police Station 5485-3	Open		48.00	48
1993 Village Public Library, 5443-7	Open		55.00	55
1990 Village Realty 5154-3	Closed	1993	42.00	55-70
1992 Village Station 5438-0	Open		65.00	65
1992 Village Station and Train 5122-5	Closed	1992	65.00	85-125
1992 Village Vet and Pet Shop 5427-5	Closed	1995	32.00	44-55
1989 Village Warming House 5145-4	Closed	1992	42.00	55-85
1986 Waverly Place 5041-5	Closed	1986	35.00	290-325
1994 Wedding Chapel 5464-0	Open		55.00	55
1985 Williamsburg House 5046-6	Closed	1988	37.00	138
1993 Woodbury House 5444-5	Open		45.00	45
1983 Wooden Church 5031-8	Closed	1984	30.00	300-400
1981 Wooden Clapboard 5072-5	Closed	1984	32.00	175-250

The Original Snow Village Collection Accessories Retired - Department 56

YEAR ISSUE	EDITION LIMIT	YEAR RETD.	ISSUE PRICE	*QUOTE U.S.$
1987 3 Nuns With Songbooks 5102-0	Closed	1988	6.00	120-130
1988 Apple Girl/Newspaper Boy 5129-2, set/2	Closed	1990	11.00	20-28
1979 Aspen Trees 5052-6, Meadowland Series	Closed	1980	16.00	450-500
1989 Bringing Home The Tree 5169-1	Closed	1992	15.00	17-30
1989 Calling All Cars 5174-8, set/2	Closed	1991	15.00	30-45
1979 Carolers 5064-1	Closed	1986	12.00	120-145
1987 Caroling Family 5105-5, set/3	Closed	1990	20.00	25-35
1980 Ceramic Car 5069-0	Closed	1986	5.00	55
1981 Ceramic Sleigh 5079-2	Closed	1986	5.00	55
1993 Check It Out Bookmobile 5451-8, set/3	Closed	1995	25.00	27
1987 Children In Band 5104-7	Closed	1989	15.00	23-35
1989 Choir Kids 5147-0	Closed	1992	15.00	20-28
1991 Christmas Cadillac 5413-5	Closed	1994	9.00	15
1987 Christmas Children 5107-1, set/4	Closed	1990	20.00	30
1991 Cold Weather Sports 5410-0, set/4	Closed	1994	27.50	33
1991 Come Join The Parade 5411-9	Closed	1992	13.00	23
1991 Country Harvest 5415-1	Closed	1993	13.00	20-28
1988 Doghouse/Cat In Garbage Can 5131-4, set/2	Closed	1992	15.00	22-29
1990 Down the Chimney He Goes, 5158-6	Closed	1993	6.50	10
1992 Early Morning Delivery 5431-3, set/3	Closed	1995	27.50	28
1985 Family Mom/Kids, Goose/Girl 5057-1	Closed	1988	11.00	25-42
1987 For Sale Sign 5108-0	Closed	1989	3.50	12
1990 Fresh Frozen Fish 5163-2, set/2	Closed	1993	20.00	35
1986 Girl/Snowman, Boy 5095-4	Closed	1987	11.00	55-65
1988 Hayride 5117-9	Closed	1990	30.00	55-70
1990 Here We Come A Caroling 5161-6, set/3	Closed	1992	18.00	25
1987 Home Delivery 5162-4, set/2	Closed	1992	16.00	22-35
1986 Kids Around The Tree (large) 5094-6	Closed	1990	15.00	45-70
1986 Kids Around The Tree (small) 5094-6	Closed	1990	15.00	35-57
1990 Kids Decorating the Village Sign 5134-9	Closed	1993	13.00	25
1989 Kids Tree House 5168-3	Closed	1991	25.00	50-65
1988 Man On Ladder Hanging Garland 5116-0	Closed	1992	7.50	12-18
1984 Monks-A-Caroling (brown) 5040-7	Closed	1988	6.00	32-45
1983 Monks-A-Caroling (butterscotch) 6459-9	Closed	1984	6.00	67
1992 Nanny and the Preschoolers 5430-5, set/2	Closed	1994	27.50	22-35
1987 Park Bench (green) 5109-8	Closed	1993	3.00	9
1987 Praying Monks 5103-9	Closed	1988	6.00	38-48
1992 Round & Round We Go! 5433-0, set/2	Closed	1995	18.00	24
1985 Santa/Mailbox 5059-8	Closed	1988	11.00	35-50
1994 Santa Comes To Town, 1995 5477-1	Closed	1995	30.00	35-55
1988 School Bus, Snow Plow 5137-3, set/2	Closed	1991	16.00	50
1988 School Children 5118-7, set/3	Closed	1990	15.00	14-25
1984 Scottie With Tree 5038-5	Closed	1985	3.00	150-240
1979 Sheep, 9 White, 3 Black 5053-4 Meadowland Series	Closed	1980	12.00	400
1986 Shopping Girls w/Packages (large) 5096-2	Closed	1988	11.00	30-42
1986 Shopping Girls w/Packages (small) 5096-2	Closed	1988	11.00	40-55
1985 Singing Nuns 5053-9	Closed	1987	6.00	135-150
1988 Sisal Tree Lot 8183-3	Closed	1991	45.00	80-130
1989 Skate Faster Mom 5170-5	Closed	1991	13.00	15-28
1990 Sleighride 5160-8	Closed	1992	30.00	40-60
1990 Sno-Jet Snowmobile, 5159-0	Closed	1993	15.00	21-29
1987 Snow Kids 5113-6, set/4	Closed	1990	20.00	40-55
1985 Snow Kids Sled, Skis 5056-3	Closed	1987	11.00	40-60

FIGURINES/COTTAGES

YEAR ISSUE		EDITION LIMIT	YEAR RETD.	ISSUE PRICE	*QUOTE U.S.$
1991	Snowball Fort 5414-3, set/3	Closed	1993	28.00	25-40
1982	Snowman With Broom 5018-0	Closed	1990	3.00	12
1989	Statue of Mark Twain 5173-0	Closed	1993	15.00	30-45
1990	SV Special Delivery 5197-7, set/2	Closed	1992	16.00	20-35
1989	Through the Woods 5172-1, set/2	Closed	1991	18.00	20-35
1990	A Tree For Me 5164-0, set/2	Closed	1995	8.00	8
1989	US Mailbox 5179-9	Closed	1990	3.50	11-20
1989	US Special Delivery 5148-9, set/2	Closed	1990	16.00	30-50
1989	Village Birds 5180-2, set/6	Closed	1993	3.50	9
1989	Village Gazebo 5146-2	Closed	1995	30.00	30-45
1991	Village Greetings 5418-6, set/3	Closed	1994	5.00	9
1991	Village Marching Band 5412-7, set/3	Closed	1992	30.00	48
1988	Water Tower 5133-0	Closed	1991	20.00	60-75
1989	Water Tower-John Deere 568-0	Closed	1991	20.00	660-725
1992	We're Going to a Christmas Pageant 5435-6	Closed	1994	15.00	18
1991	Winter Fountain 5409-7	Closed	1993	25.00	35-55
1992	Winter Playground 5436-4	Closed	1995	20.00	22
1988	Woodsman and Boy 5136-2, set/2	Closed	1991	13.00	24-34
1988	Woody Station Wagon 5136-5	Closed	1990	6.50	28
1991	Wreaths For Sale 5408-9,set/4	Closed	1994	27.50	30-40

Retired Heritage Village Collection Accessories - Department 56

YEAR ISSUE		EDITION LIMIT	YEAR RETD.	ISSUE PRICE	*QUOTE U.S.$
1991	All Around the Town 5545-0, set/2	Closed	1993	18.00	25-35
1987	Alpine Village Sign 6571-4	Closed	1993	6.00	18-28
1986	Alpine Villagers 6542-0, set/3	Closed	1992	13.00	35
1990	Amish Buggy 5949-8	Closed	1992	22.00	40-65
1990	Amish Family 5948-0, set/3	Closed	1992	20.00	30-40
1990	Amish Family, w/Moustache 5948-0, set/3	Closed	1992	20.00	40-50
1991	Baker Elves 5603-0, set/3	Closed	1995	27.50	28-40
1992	The Bird Seller 5803-3, set/3	Closed	1995	25.00	22-32
1987	Blacksmith 5934-0, set/3	Closed	1990	20.00	70-85
1990	Busy Sidewalks 5535-2, set/4	Closed	1992	28.00	40-55
1992	Buying Bakers Bread 5619-7, set/2	Closed	1995	20.00	25
1990	Carolers on the Doorstep 5570-0, set/4	Closed	1993	25.00	30-45
1984	Carolers, w/ Lamppost (bl) 6526-9, set/4	Closed	1990	10.00	28-45
1984	Carolers, w/ Lamppost (wh) 6526-9, set/4	Closed	1990	10.00	85-130
1988	Childe Pond and Skaters 5903-0, set/4	Closed	1991	30.00	70-90
1986	Christmas Carol Figures 6501-3, set/3	Closed	1990	12.50	50-90
1987	Christmas in the City Sign, 5960-9	Closed	1993	6.00	15
1992	Churchyard Gate and Fence 5563-8, set/3	Closed	1992	15.00	55
1988	City Bus & Milk Truck 5983-8, set/2	Closed	1991	15.00	20-35
1988	City Newsstand 5971-4, set/4	Closed	1991	25.00	40-55
1987	City People 5965-0, set/5	Closed	1990	27.50	50-90
1987	City Workers 5967-6, set/4	Closed	1988	15.00	35-45
1991	Come into the Inn, 5560-3	Closed	1994	22.00	28-40
1989	Constables 5579-4, set/3	Closed	1991	17.50	65
1986	Covered Wooden Bridge 6531-5	Closed	1990	10.00	35-50
1989	David Copperfield Characters 5551-4, set/5	Closed	1992	32.50	30-50
1987	Dickens' Village Sign 6569-2	Closed	1993	6.00	10-20
1992	Don't Drop The Presents! 5532-8, set/2	Closed	1995	25.00	25-35
1987	Dover Coach 6590-0	Closed	1990	18.00	55-85
1987	Dover Coach w/o Mustache 6590-0	Closed	1990	18.00	85-95
1989	Farm Animals 5945-5, set/4	Closed	1991	15.00	30-50
1987	Farm People And Animals 5901-3, set/5	Closed	1989	24.00	75-90
1988	Fezziwig and Friends 5928-5, set/3	Closed	1990	12.50	45-65
1991	The Fire Brigade 5546-8, set/2	Closed	1995	20.00	20-35
1991	Fire Truck, "City Fire Dept." 5547-6, set/2	Closed	1995	18.00	20-30
1992	Harvest Seed Cart 5645-6, set/3	Closed	1995	27.50	30-40
1989	Heritage Village Sign 9953-8	Closed	1990	10.00	25
1992	Letters for Santa 5604-9, set/3	Closed	1994	30.00	40-55
1986	Lighted Tree With Children & Ladder 6510-2	Closed	1989	35.00	275-325
1987	Maple Sugaring Shed 6589-7, set/3	Closed	1989	19.00	225
1991	Market Day 5641-3,set/3	Closed	1993	35.00	30-45
1987	New England Village Sign 6570-6	Closed	1993	6.00	12
1986	New England Winter set 6532-3, set/5	Closed	1990	18.00	38-48
1988	Nicholas Nickleby Characters 5929-3, set/4	Closed	1991	20.00	30-50
1992	The Old Puppeteer 5802-5, set/3	Closed	1995	32.00	40-55
1991	Oliver Twist Characters 5554-9, set/3	Closed	1993	35.00	40-55
1988	One Horse Open Sleigh 5982-0	Closed	1991	20.00	30-40
1989	Organ Grinder 5957-9, set/3	Closed	1991	21.00	30-45
1987	Ox Sled (blue pants) 5951-0	Closed	1989	20.00	120-170
1987	Ox Sled (tan pants) 5951-0	Closed	1989	20.00	245-275
1989	Popcorn Vendor 5958-7, set/3	Closed	1992	22.00	25-40
1986	Porcelain Trees 6537-4,set/2	Closed	1991	14.00	35
1994	Postern, 9871-0, (Dickens' Village Ten Year Accessory Anniversary Piece)	Closed	1994	17.50	20-30
1991	Poultry Market 5559-0, set/3	Closed	1995	32.00	30-40
1988	Red Covered Bridge 5987-0	Closed	1990	17.00	20-40
1989	River Street Ice House Cart 5959-5	Closed	1991	20.00	35-50
1989	Royal Coach 5578-6	Closed	1992	55.00	65-90
1988	Salvation Army Band 5985-4, set/6	Closed	1991	24.00	75-90
1990	Santa's Little Helpers 5610-3, set/3	Closed	1993	28.00	45-55

YEAR ISSUE		EDITION LIMIT	YEAR RETD.	ISSUE PRICE	*QUOTE U.S.$
1987	Shopkeepers 5966-8, set/4	Closed	1988	15.00	30-50
1987	Silo And Hay Shed 5950-1	Closed	1989	18.00	145-175
1987	Skating Pond 6545-5	Closed	1990	24.00	70-95
1990	Sleepy Hollow Characters 5956-0, set/3	Closed	1992	27.50	41
1986	Sleighride 6511-0	Closed	1990	19.50	45-60
1988	Snow Children 5938-2	Closed	1994	17.00	28
1987	Stone Bridge 6546-3	Closed	1990	12.00	60-90
1990	Tis the Season 5539-5	Closed	1994	12.95	25
1992	Town Tinker 5646-4, set/2	Closed	1995	24.00	25
1991	Toymaker Series 5602-2, set/3	Closed	1995	27.50	28-45
1990	Trimming the North Pole 5608-1	Closed	1993	10.00	25
1989	U.S. Mail Box and Fire Hydrant 5517-4	Closed	1990	5.00	18
1989	Village Blvd. 5516-6, set/14	Closed	1993	25.00	45-55
1987	Village Express Train (electric, black) 5997-8	Closed	1988	89.95	270-350
1993	Village Express Van (black) 9951-1	Closed	1993	25.00	100-135
1993	Village Express Van (gold) 9977-5 (promotional)	Closed	1993	N/A	750-1000
1994	Village Express Van-Bachman's 729-3	Closed	1994	22.50	75-100
1994	Village Express Van-Bronner's 737-4	Closed	1994	22.50	40-75
1995	Village Express Van-Canadian 2163-7	Closed	1995	N/A	70
1994	Village Express Van-Christmas Dove 730-7	Closed	1994	25.00	50-65
1994	Village Express Van-European Imports 739-0	Closed	1994	22.50	50-70
1994	Village Express Van-Fortunoff's 735-8	Closed	1994	22.50	122
1994	Village Express Van-Limited Edition 733-1	Closed	1994	25.00	110
1994	Village Express Van-Lock, Stock & Barrel 731-5	Closed	1994	22.50	120-135
1994	Village Express Van-North Pole City 736-6	Closed	1994	25.00	50-65
1995	Village Express Van-Park West 0755-2	Closed	1995	N/A	50-70
1994	Village Express Van-Robert's Christmas Wonderland 734-0	Closed	1994	22.50	50-55
1994	Village Express Van-Stat's 741-2	Closed	1994	22.50	55
1994	Village Express Van-The Incredible Christmas (Pigeon Forge) 732-3	Closed	1994	24.98	45-65
1994	Village Express Van-The Lemon Tree 721-8	Closed	1994	30.00	52
1994	Village Express Van-William Glen, 738-2	Closed	1994	22.50	50-60
1994	Village Express Van-Windsor Shoppe, 740-4	Closed	1994	25.00	53
1988	Village Harvest People 5941-2, set/4	Closed	1991	27.50	40-50
1989	Village Sign w/Snowman 5572-7	Closed	1994	10.00	15
1992	Village Street Peddlers 5804-1, set/2	Closed	1994	16.00	20-30
1985	Village Train Brighton 6527-7, set/3	Closed	1986	12.00	400-500
1988	Village Train Trestle 5981-1	Closed	1991	17.00	50-75
1987	Village Well and Holy Cross 6547-1, set/2	Closed	1989	13.00	140-150
1989	Violet Vendor/Carolers/Chestnut Vendor 5580-8, set/3	Closed	1989	23.00	30-45
1992	Welcome Home 5533-6, set/3	Closed	1995	27.50	35
1988	Woodcutter And Son 5986-2, set/2	Closed	1990	10.00	40-49
1993	Woodsmen Elves 5630-8, set/3	Closed	1995	25.00	35-55

Snowbabies - Department 56

YEAR ISSUE		EDITION LIMIT	YEAR RETD.	ISSUE PRICE	*QUOTE U.S.$
1989	All Fall Down 7984-7, set/4	Closed	1992	36.00	55-85
1990	All Tired Out, waterglobe 7937-5	Closed	1992	55.00	60-100
1988	Are All These Mine? 7977-4	Open		10.00	13
1995	Are You On My List? 6875-6	Open		25.00	25
1995	Are You On My List?, waterglobe 6879-7	Open		32.50	33
1986	Best Friends 7958-8	Closed	1989	12.00	115-170
1994	Bringing Starry Pines 6862-4	Open		35.00	35
1992	Can I Help, Too? 6806-3	18,500	1992	48.00	70-110
1993	Can I Open it Now? 6838-1 (Event Piece)	Closed	1993	15.00	35-50
1986	Catch a Falling Star, waterglobe 7967-7	Closed	1987	18.00	660
1996	Climb Every Mountain 68816	22,500		75.00	75
1986	Climbing on Snowball, Bisque Votive w/Candle 7965-0	Closed	1989	15.00	95-118
1987	Climbing On Tree 7971-5, set/2	Closed	1989	25.00	810-880
1993	Crossing Starry Skies 6834-9	Open		35.00	35
1991	Dancing to a Tune 6808-0, set/3	Closed	1995	30.00	45
1987	Don't Fall Off 7968-5	Closed	1990	12.50	85-125
1987	Down The Hill We Go 7960-0	Open		20.00	23
1989	Finding Fallen Stars 7985-5	6,000	1994	32.50	140-200
1991	Fishing For Dreams 6809-8	Closed	1994	28.00	33-45
1992	Fishing For Dreams, waterglobe 6832-2	Closed	1994	32.50	45-57
1986	Forest Accessory "Frosty Forest" 7963-4, set/3	Open		15.00	20
1988	Frosty Frolic 7981-2	4,800	1989	35.00	725-990
1989	Frosty Fun 7983-9	Closed	1991	27.50	45-70
1995	Frosty Pines 76687, set/3	Open		12.50	13
1986	Give Me A Push 7955-3	Closed	1990	12.00	60-75
1986	Hanging Pair 7966-9	Closed	1989	15.00	145-175
1992	Help Me, I'm Stuck 6817-9	Closed	1994	32.50	40-60
1989	Helpful Friends 7982-0	Closed	1993	30.00	38-55
1986	Hold On Tight 7956-1	Open		14.00	14
1995	I Can't Find Him 68800	Open		37.50	38
1995	I Found The Biggest Star of All! 6874-8	Open		16.00	16

YEAR ISSUE		EDITION LIMIT	YEAR RETD.	ISSUE PRICE	* QUOTE U.S.$
1993	I Found Your Mittens 6836-5, set/2	Open		30.00	30
1991	I Made This Just For You 6802-0	Open		15.00	15
1992	I Need A Hug 6813-6	Open		20.00	20
1995	I See You! 6878-0, set/2	Open		27.50	28
1995	I'll Hug You Goodnight, waterglobe 68798	Open		32.50	33
1995	I'll Play A Christmas Tune 68801	Open		16.00	16
1991	I'll Put Up The Tree 6800-4	Closed	1995	24.00	25-33
1993	I'll Teach You A Trick 6835-7	Open		24.00	24
1993	I'm Making an Ice Sculpture 6842-0	Open		30.00	30
1986	I'm Making Snowballs 7962-6	Closed	1992	12.00	30
1994	I'm Right Behind You! 6852-7	Open		60.00	60
1996	I'm So Sleepy 68810	Open		16.00	16
1989	Icy Igloo 7987-1	Open		37.50	38
1991	Is That For Me 6803-9, set/2	Closed	1993	32.50	35-55
1996	Jack Frost...A Sleighride Through the Stars 68811, set/3	Open		110.00	110
1994	Jack Frost...A Touch of Winter's Magic 6854-3	Open		90.00	95
1992	Join the Parade 6824-1	Closed	1994	37.50	45-55
1992	Just One Little Candle 6823-3	Open		15.00	15
1989	Let It Snow, waterglobe 7992-8	Closed	1993	25.00	45
1993	Let's All Chime In! 6845-4, set/2	Closed	1995	37.50	47
1994	Let's Go Skating 6860-8	Open		16.50	17
1992	Let's Go Skiing 6815-2	Closed	1994	15.00	20
1994	Lift Me Higher, I Can't Reach 6863-2	Open		75.00	75
1992	Look What I Can Do! 6819-5	Open		16.50	17
1993	Look What I Found 6833-0	Open		45.00	45
1994	Look What I Found, waterglobe 6872-1	Open		32.50	33
1994	Mickey's New Friend 714-5 (Disney Exclusive)	Retrd.	1995	60.00	450-650
1995	Mush 68805	Open		48.00	48
1993	Now I Lay Me Down to Sleep 6839-0	Open		13.50	14
1996	Once Upon A Time... 68815	Open		25.00	25
1992	Over the Milky Way 6828-4	Closed	1995	32.00	38
1995	Parade of Penguins 68804, set/6	Open		15.00	15
1991	Peek-A-Boo, waterglobe 7938-3	Closed	1993	50.00	75
1989	Penguin Parade 7986-3	Closed	1992	25.00	30-70
1994	Pennies from Heaven 6864-0	Open		17.50	18
1994	Planting Starry Pines, waterglobe 6870-5	Open		32.50	33
1991	Play Me a Tune, waterglobe 7936-7	Closed	1993	50.00	60-75
1995	Play Me a Tune, music box 68809	Open		37.50	38
1990	Playing Games Is Fun 7947-2	Closed	1993	30.00	35-50
1988	Polar Express 7978-2	Closed	1992	22.00	65-90
1990	Read Me a Story 7945-6	Open		25.00	25
1992	Read Me a Story, waterglobe 6831-4	Open		32.50	33
1995	Ring The Bells...It's Christmas! 6876-4	Open		40.00	40
1992	Shall I Play For You? 6820-9	Open		16.50	17
1995	Skate With Me, waterglobe 68799	Open		32.50	33
1995	Snowbabies Animated Skating Pond 7668-6, set/14	Open		60.00	60
1993	Snowbabies Picture Frame, Baby's First Smile 6846-2	Open		30.00	30
1987	Snowbabies Riding Sleds, waterglobe 7975-8	Closed	1988	40.00	700
1986	Snowbaby Holding Picture Frame 7970-7, set/2	Closed	1987	15.00	540-650
1986	Snowbaby Nite-Lite 7959-6	Closed	1989	15.00	300-350
1991	Snowbaby Polar Sign 6804-7	Open		20.00	20
1986	Snowbaby Standing, waterglobe 7964-2	Closed	1987	7.50	385-445
1987	Snowbaby with Wings, waterglobe 7973-1	Closed	1988	20.00	460-550
1993	So Much Work To Do 6837-3	Open		18.00	18
1993	Somewhere in Dreamland 6840-3	Open		85.00	85
1990	A Special Delivery 7948-0	Closed	1994	15.00	23-50
1995	Star Gazing 7800 (Starter Set)	Open		40.00	40
1995	A Star in the Box 68803	Open		18.00	18
1992	Starry Pines 6829-2, set/2	Open		17.50	18
1992	Stars-In-A-Row, Tic-Tac-Toe 6822-5	Closed	1995	32.50	35
1994	Stringing Fallen Stars 6861-6	Open		25.00	25
1994	There's Another One! 6853-5	Open		24.00	24
1991	This Is Where We Live 6805-5	Closed	1994	60.00	60-75
1992	This Will Cheer You Up 6816-0	Closed	1994	30.00	35-60
1988	Tiny Trio 7979-0, set/3	Closed	1990	20.00	165-180
1993	Tumbling In the Snow 7957-0, set/5	Closed	1994	35.00	70-90
1990	Twinkle Little Stars 7942-1, set/2	Closed	1994	37.50	40-65
1992	Wait For Me 6812-8	Closed	1994	48.00	48-65
1991	Waiting For Christmas 6807-1	Closed	1994	27.50	30-45
1993	We Make a Great Pair 6843-8	Open		30.00	30
1990	We Will Make it Shine 7946-4	Closed	1992	45.00	48-85
1994	We'll Plant the Starry Pines 6865-9, set/2	Open		37.50	38
1995	We're Building An Icy Igloo 68802	Open		70.00	70
1995	What Shall We Do Today? 6877-2	Open		32.50	33
1987	When You Wish Upon a Star, music box 7972-3	Closed	1993	30.00	35-50
1996	Which Way's Up? 68812	Open		30.00	30
1993	Whistle While You Work, music box 6849-7	Closed	1995	32.50	35
1993	Where Did He Go? 6841-1	Open		35.00	35
1994	Where Did You Come From? 6856-0	Open		40.00	40
1990	Who Are You? 7949-9	12,500	1991	32.50	110-143
1991	Why Don't You Talk To Me 6801-2	Open		24.00	24
1993	Will it Snow Today? 6844-6	Closed	1995	45.00	45-60

*Quotes have been rounded up to nearest dollar

FIGURINES/COTTAGES

YEAR ISSUE		EDITION LIMIT	YEAR RETD.	ISSUE PRICE	*QUOTE U.S.$
1992	Winken, Blinken, and Nod 6814-4	Open		60.00	65
1987	Winter Surprise 7974-0	Closed	1992	15.00	40-50
1990	Wishing on a Star 7943-0	Closed	1994	22.00	30-45
1996	With Hugs & Kisses 68813, set/2	Open		32.50	33
1996	You are My Lucky Star 68814, set/2	Open		35.00	35
1992	You Can't Find Me! 6818-7	Open		45.00	45
1992	You Didn't Forget Me 6821-7	Open		32.50	33

Snowbabies Pewter Miniatures - Department 56

YEAR ISSUE		EDITION LIMIT	YEAR RETD.	ISSUE PRICE	*QUOTE U.S.$
1989	All Fall Down 7617-1, set/4	Closed	1993	25.00	35-55
1989	Are All These Mine? 7605-8	Closed	1992	7.00	15-25
1989	Best Friends 7604-0	Closed	1994	10.00	13-25
1993	Can I Open it Now?, mini music box 7648-1	Closed	1994	20.00	30-40
1991	Dancing to a Tune 7630-9, set/3	Closed	1993	18.00	21-33
1989	Don't Fall Off!, 7603-1	Closed	1994	7.00	10-20
1989	Finding Fallen Stars 7618-0, set/2	Closed	1992	12.50	28-45
1989	Frosty Frolic 7613-9, set/4	Closed	1993	24.00	25-50
1993	Frosty Fun, mini music box 7650-3	Closed	1994	20.00	30-50
1989	Give Me a Push! 7601-5	Closed	1994	7.00	15
1989	Helpful Friends 7608-2, set/4	Closed	1992	13.50	25-35
1991	I Made This Just for You! 7628-7	Closed	1994	7.00	15
1989	Icy Igloo, w/tree 7610-4, set/2	Closed	1992	7.50	22-35
1991	Is That For Me? 7631-7, set/2	Closed	1993	12.50	16-25
1992	Join the Parade, 7645-7, set/4	Closed	1995	22.50	25
1989	Penguin Parade 7616-3, set/4	Closed	1993	12.50	30
1993	Penguin Parade, mini music box 7645-5	Closed	1994	20.00	32-42
1993	Play Me a Tune, mini music box 7651-1	Closed	1994	20.00	35-50
1990	Playing Games is Fun! 7623-6, set/2	Closed	1993	13.50	24-35
1989	Polar Express 7609-0, set2	Closed	1993	13.50	25-45
1993	Reading a Story, mini music box 7649-0	Closed	1994	20.00	42
1990	A Special Delivery 7624-4	Closed	1993	7.00	13-24
1992	This Will Cheer You Up 7639-2	Closed	1995	13.75	21
1989	Tiny Trio 7615-5, set3	Closed	1993	18.00	25-45
1989	Tumbling in the Snow! 7614-7, set/5	Closed	1992	30.00	45-75
1990	Twinkle Little Stars 7621-0, set/2	Closed	1993	15.00	30
1992	Wait For Me!, 7641-4, set/4	Closed	1995	22.50	26
1991	Waiting for Christmas, 7629-5	Closed	1993	13.00	15-30
1989	Winter Surprise!, 7607-4	Closed	1994	13.50	14-30
1991	Wishing on a Star, 7626-0	Closed	1995	10.00	20-30
1992	You Didn't Forget Me!, 7643-0, set/3	Closed	1995	17.50	21

Village CCP Miniatures - Department 56

YEAR ISSUE		EDITION LIMIT	YEAR RETD.	ISSUE PRICE	*QUOTE U.S.$
1987	Christmas Carol Cottages 6561-7, set/3	Closed	1989	30.00	85-125
1987	• The Cottage of Bob Cratchit & Tiny Tim 6561-7	Closed	1989	10.00	35-42
1987	• Fezziwig's Warehouse 6561-7	Closed	1989	10.00	30
1987	• Scrooge/ Marley Countinghouse 6561-7	Closed	1989	10.00	30-40
1987	Dickens' Chadbury Station & Train 6592-7	Closed	1989	27.50	55-80
1987	Dickens' Cottages 6559-5, set/3	Closed	1989	30.00	275-350
1987	• Stone Cottage 6559-5	Closed	1989	10.00	155
1987	• Thatched Cottage 6559-5	Closed	1989	10.00	110-125
1987	• Tudor Cottage 6559-5	Closed	1989	10.00	150-200
1988	Dickens' Kenilworth Castle 6565-0	Closed	1989	30.00	150-165
1987	Dickens' Lane Shops 6591-9, set/3	Closed	1989	30.00	140
1987	• Cottage Toy Shop 6591-9	Closed	1989	10.00	40
1987	• Thomas Kersey Coffee House 6591-9	Closed	1989	10.00	40-50
1987	• Tuttle's Pub 6591-9	Closed	1989	10.00	55
1987	Dickens' Village Assorted 6560-9, set/3	Closed	1989	48.00	140
1987	• Blythe Pond Mill House 6560-9	Closed	1989	16.00	30-50
1987	• Dickens Village Church 6560-9	Closed	1989	16.00	55-70
1987	• Norman Church 6560-9	Closed	1989	16.00	100-125
1987	Dickens' Village Assorted 6562-5, set/4	Closed	1989	60.00	300
1987	• Barley Bree Farmhouse 6562-5	Closed	1989	15.00	55-70
1987	• Brick Abbey 6562-5	Closed	1989	15.00	90-120
1987	• Chesterton Manor House 6562-5	Closed	1989	15.00	120-130
1987	• The Old Curiosity Shop 6562-5	Closed	1989	15.00	70
1987	Dickens' Village Original 6558-7, set/7	Closed	1989	72.00	300
1987	• Abel Beesley Butcher 6558-7	Closed	1989	12.00	30-40
1987	• Bean and Son Smithy Shop 6558-7	Closed	1989	12.00	45
1987	• Candle Shop 6558-7	Closed	1989	12.00	26-36
1987	• Crowntree Inn 6558-7	Closed	1989	12.00	35
1987	• Golden Swan Baker 6558-7	Closed	1989	12.00	22-36
1987	• Green Grocer 6558-7	Closed	1989	12.00	45
1987	• Jones & Co Brush & Basket Shop 6558-7	Closed	1989	12.00	75
1987	Little Town of Bethlehem 5976-8, set/12	Closed	1989	85.00	180
1988	New England Village Assorted 5937-4, set/6	Closed	1989	85.00	400-500
1988	• Craggy Cove Lighthouse 5937-4	Closed	1989	14.50	85-100
1988	• Jacob Adams Barn 5937-4	Closed	1989	14.50	60-85
1988	• Jacob Adams Farmhouse 5937-4	Closed	1989	14.50	45-60
1988	• Maple Sugaring Shed 5937-4	Closed	1989	14.50	40-50
1988	• Smythe Wollen Mill 5937-4	Closed	1989	14.50	80-100
1988	• Timber Knoll Log Cabin 5937-4	Closed	1989	14.50	30-45
1988	New England Village Original 5935-8, set/7	Closed	1989	72.00	600-800
1988	• Apothecary Shop 5935-8	Closed	1989	10.50	45
1988	• Brick Town Hall 5935-8	Closed	1989	10.50	55-65

YEAR ISSUE		EDITION LIMIT	YEAR RETD.	ISSUE PRICE	*QUOTE U.S.$
1988	• General Store 5935-8	Closed	1989	10.50	66-80
1988	• Livery Stable & Boot Shop 5935-8	Closed	1989	10.50	65-80
1988	• Nathaniel Bingham Fabrics 5935-8	Closed	1989	10.50	70
1988	• Red Schoolhouse 5935-8	Closed	1989	10.50	85
1988	• Village Steeple Church 5935-8	Closed	1989	10.50	175-225
1986	Victorian Miniatures, set/2 6564-1	Closed	1987	45.00	275
1986	• Church 6564-1	Closed	1987	22.50	150
1986	• Estate 6564-1	Closed	1987	22.50	175
1986	Victorian Miniatures 6563-3, set/5	Closed	1987	65.00	275
1986	Williamsburg Snowhouse Series, set/6	Closed	1987	60.00	575-650
1986	• Williamsburg Church, White 6566-8	Closed	1987	10.00	125
1986	• Williamsburg House Brown Brick 6566-8	Closed	1987	10.00	60-100
1986	• Williamsburg House, Blue 6566-8	Closed	1987	10.00	60-100
1986	• Williamsburg House, Brown Clapboard	Closed	1987	10.00	60-100
1986	• Williamsburg House, Red 6566-8	Closed	1987	10.00	60-110
1986	• Williamsburg House, White 6566-8	Closed	1987	10.00	85-125

Winter Silhouette - Department 56

YEAR ISSUE		EDITION LIMIT	YEAR RETD.	ISSUE PRICE	*QUOTE U.S.$
1990	Angel Candle Holder w/Candle 6767-9	Closed	1992	32.50	33
1992	Bedtime Stories Waterglobe 7838-7	Closed	1995	30.00	30
1989	Bringing Home The Tree 7790-9, set/4	Closed	1993	75.00	75
1989	Camel w/glass Votive 6766-0	Closed	1993	25.00	50
1987	Carolers 7774-7, set/4	Closed	1993	120.00	130-160
1991	Chimney Sweep 7799-2	Closed	1993	37.50	55
1989	Father Christmas 7788-7	Closed	1993	50.00	50
1991	Grandfather Clock 7797-6	Closed	1995	27.50	28
1989	Joy To The World 5595-6	Closed	1990	42.00	42
1988	Silver Bells Music Box 8271-6	Closed	1990	75.00	140
1991	Skating Couple 7772-0	Closed	1995	35.00	44
1987	Snow Doves 8215-5, set/2	Closed	1992	60.00	60
1992	Snowy White Deer 7837-9, set/2	Closed	1995	55.00	55
1989	Three Kings Candle Holder 6765-2, set/3	Closed	1990	85.00	85
1991	Town Crier 7800-0	Closed	1994	37.50	50

Disneyana

Disneyana Conventions - Various

YEAR ISSUE		EDITION LIMIT	YEAR RETD.	ISSUE PRICE	*QUOTE U.S.$
1992	1947 Mickey Mouse Plush J20967 - Gund	1,000	1992	50.00	350
1992	Big Thunder Mountain A26648 - R. Lee	250	1992	1650.00	2200-2800
1992	Carousel Horse 022482 - PJ's	250	1992	125.00	275-300
1992	Cinderella 022076 - Armani	500	1992	500.00	3000-4500
1992	Cinderella Castle 022077 - John Hine Studio	500	1992	250.00	1100-1200
1992	Cruella DeVil Doll-porcelain 22554 - J. Wols	25	1992	600.00	3000-3500
1992	Disneyana Logo Charger - B. White	25	1992	600.00	2800
1992	Nifty-Nineties Mickey & Minnie 022503 - House of Laurenz	250	1992	650.00	700-850
1992	Pinocchio - R. Wright	250	1992	750.00	1000-2000
1992	Steamboat Willie-Resin - M. Delle	500	1992	125.00	1200-1325
1992	Tinker Bell 022075 - Lladró	1,500	1992	350.00	2100-2600
1992	Two Merry Wanderers 022074 - Goebel	1,500	1992	250.00	950-1250
1992	Walt's Convertible (Cel) - Disney Art Ed.	500	1992	950.00	2300
1993	1947 Minnie Mouse Plush - Gund	1,000	1993	50.00	100
1993	Alice in Wonderland - Malvern	10	1993	8000.00	N/A
1993	Annette Doll - Alexander Doll	1,000	1993	400.00	450
1993	The Band Concert "Maestro Mickey" - Disney Art Ed.	275	1993	2950.00	N/A
1993	The Band Concert-Bronze - B. Toma	25	1993	650.00	2750-3000
1993	Bandleader-Resin - M. Delle	1,500	1993	125.00	225
1993	Family Dinner Figurine - C. Boyer	1,000	1993	600.00	800-1250
1993	Jumper from King Arthur Carousel - PJ's	250	1993	125.00	200-250
1993	Mickey & Pluto Charger - White/Rhodes	25	1993	850.00	3000
1993	Mickey Mouse, the Bandleader - Arribas Brothers	25	1993	700.00	2300-2500
1993	Mickey's Dreams - R. Lee	250	1993	400.00	650-800
1993	Peter Pan - Lladró	2,000	1993	400.00	800-1250
1993	Sleeping Beauty Castle - John Hine Studio	500	1993	250.00	350-600
1993	Snow White - Armani	2,000	1993	750.00	1000-1500
1993	Two Little Drummers - Goebel	1,500	1993	325.00	450-650
1993	Walt's Train Celebration - Disney Art Ed.	950	1993	950.00	1800
1994	Ariel - Armani	1,500	1994	750.00	1050-1300
1994	Cinderella/Godmother - Lladró	2,500	1994	875.00	600-780
1994	Cinderella's Slipper - Waterford	1,200	1994	250.00	300-500
1994	Euro Disney Castle - John Hine Studio	750	1994	250.00	300-500
1994	Jessica & Roger Charger - White/Rhodes	25	1994	2000.00	3000-4000
1994	Mickey Triple Self Portrait - Goebel Miniatures	500	1994	295.00	800-1100
1994	Minnie Ice Cream - Goebel	1,500	1994	395.00	470-650
1994	MM/MN w/House Kinetic - F. Prescott	10	1994	4000.00	N/A
1994	MM/MN/Goofy Limo (Stepin' Out) - Ron Lee	500	1994	500.00	375-500

YEAR ISSUE		EDITION LIMIT	YEAR RETD.	ISSUE PRICE	*QUOTE U.S.$
1994	Scrooge in Money Bin/Bronze - Carl Barks	100	1994	1800.00	3300
1994	Sleeping Beauty - Malvern	10	1994	5500.00	N/A
1994	Sorcerer Mickey-Bronze - B. Toma	100	1994	1000.00	1800-2000
1994	Sorcerer Mickey-Crystal - Arribas Brothers	50	1994	1700.00	2000-2300
1994	Sorcerer Mickey-Resin - M. Delle	2,000	1994	125.00	160-250
1995	Ah, Venice - M. Pierson	100	1995	2600.00	2600
1995	Ariel's Dolphin Ride - Wyland	250	1995	2500.00	2500
1995	Barbershop Quartet - Goebel Miniatures	750	1995	300.00	345-600
1995	Beauty and the Beast - Armani	2,000	1995	975.00	1050-1250
1995	Brave Little Tailor - White/Rhodes	15	1995	2000.00	2850
1995	Celebration-Resin - M. Delle	1,500	1995	125.00	200
1995	Donald Duck Mini-Charger - White/Rhodes	1,000	1995	75.00	125-175
1995	Ear Force One - R. Lee	500	1995	600.00	600
1995	Engine No. One - R. Lee	500	1995	650.00	965
1995	Fire Station 105 - Lilliput Lane	501	1995	195.00	385-550
1995	For Father - Goebel	1,500	1995	450.00	550
1995	Grandpa's Boys - Goebel	1,500	1995	340.00	340
1995	Mad Minnie Charger - White/Rhodes	10	1995	2000.00	4000
1995	Memories - B. Toma	200	1995	1200.00	1300-1650
1995	Neat & Pretty Mickey-Crystal - Arribas	50	1995	1700.00	2900-3200
1995	Neat & Pretty Mickey-Resin - M. Delle	2,000	1995	135.00	155
1995	Plane Crazy - Arribas	50	1995	1750.00	2000
1995	The Prince's Kiss - P Gordon	25	1995	250.00	600
1995	"Proud Pocahontas" Lithogragh - D. Struzan	500	1995	195.00	250
1995	Sheriff of Bullet Valley - Barks/Vought	200	1995	1800.00	2100-2500
1995	Showtime - B. Toma	200	1995	1400.00	2000
1995	Simba - Bolae	200	1995	1500.00	1500
1995	Sleeping Beauty Castle Mirror - Gordon	250	1995	1200.00	1200
1995	Sleeping Beauty Dance - Lladró	1,000	1995	1280.00	1400-1600
1995	Sleeping Beauty's Tiara - Waterford	1,500	1995	250.00	250-395
1995	Snow White's Apple - Waterford	1,500	1995	225.00	220-395
1995	"Snow White & Friends" Brooch/Pendant	25	1995	1500.00	1500
1995	Thru the Mirror - Barks/Vought	200	1995	2600.00	2800-3400
1995	"Uncle Scrooge" Tile - Barks/Vought	50	1995	900.00	2000
1996	Brave Little Tailor - Arribas Brothers	50		1700.00	1700
1996	Brave Little Tailor (resin) - M. Delle	1,500	1996	125.00	125
1996	Brave Little Tailor Inlaid Leather Box - P. Gordon	25	1996	300.00	300
1996	Breakfast of Tycoons-Scrooge (litho) - C. Barks	295	1996	295.00	295
1996	Cinderella's Castle (bronze) - B. Toma	100	1996	1400.00	1400
1996	Flying Dumbo (bronze) - Wolf's Head	N/A	1996	2000.00	2000
1996	Hall of Presidents - Lilliput Lane	500		225.00	225
1996	Heigh Ho - R. Lee	350		500.00	500
1996	Jasmine & Rajah - Armani	1,200		800.00	800
1996	Mickey - Armani	N/A	1996	N/A	N/A
1996	Minnie for Mother - Goebel	1,200	1996	470.00	470
1996	Proud Pongo - Walt Disney Classics	1,200	1996	175.00	175
1996	Puppy Love - Goebel Miniatures	750		325.00	325
1996	Self Control-Donald Duck (bronze) - C. Barks	150	1996	1800.00	1800
1996	Soccer - Waterford	1,200		275.00	275
1996	Uncle Scrooge Charger Plate - B. White	25	1996	2500.00	2500

Duncan Royale

Collector Club - Duncan Royale

YEAR ISSUE		EDITION LIMIT	YEAR RETD.	ISSUE PRICE	*QUOTE U.S.$
1991	Today's Nast	Retrd.	1991	80.00	150
1994	Winter Santa	Retrd.	1994	125.00	150
1995	Santa's Gift	Retrd.	1995	100.00	150
1996	Santa Choir	Yr.Iss.		90.00	90

1990 & 1991 Special Event Piece - Duncan Royale

YEAR ISSUE		EDITION LIMIT	YEAR RETD.	ISSUE PRICE	*QUOTE U.S.$
XX	Nast & Music	Retrd.	1993	79.95	75-125

Duncan Royale Figurines - Duncan Royale

YEAR ISSUE		EDITION LIMIT	YEAR RETD.	ISSUE PRICE	*QUOTE U.S.$
1996	Guardian Angel	2,500		140.00	140
1996	Peace & Harmony	2,500		140.00	140

Ebony Collection - Duncan Royale

YEAR ISSUE		EDITION LIMIT	YEAR RETD.	ISSUE PRICE	*QUOTE U.S.$
1990	Banjo Man	5,000		80.00	80
1993	Ebony Angel	5,000		170.00	170
1991	Female Gospel Singer	5,000		90.00	90
1990	The Fiddler	5,000		90.00	90
1990	Harmonica Man	5,000		80.00	80
1991	Jug Man	5,000		90.00	90
1992	Jug Tooter	5,000		90.00	90
1992	A Little Magic	5,000		80.00	80
1991	Male Gospel Singer	5,000		90.00	90
1996	O' Happy Day (Youth Gospel)	5,000		70.00	71
1996	Pigskin (Youth Football)	5,000		70.00	71
1991	Preacher	5,000		90.00	90
1991	Spoons	5,000	1996	90.00	90

Ebony Collection- History of African Kings & Queens - Duncan Royale

YEAR ISSUE		EDITION LIMIT	YEAR RETD.	ISSUE PRICE	*QUOTE U.S.$
1996	Gbadebo	Yr.Iss.		N/A	N/A

YEAR ISSUE		EDITION LIMIT	YEAR RETD.	ISSUE PRICE	*QUOTE U.S.$
1996	Nandi	5,000	N/A	N/A	
1996	Shaka	5,000	N/A	N/A	
1996	Sunni Ali Bear	5,000	N/A	N/A	
1996	Tenkamenin	5,000	N/A	N/A	

Ebony Collection-Buckwheat - Duncan Royale

1992	O'Tay	5,000		70.00	90
1992	Painter	5,000		80.00	90
1992	Petee & Friend	5,000		90.00	90
1992	Smile For The Camera	5,000	1996	80.00	90

Ebony Collection-Friends & Family - Duncan Royale

1994	Agnes	5,000		100.00	120
1994	Daddy	5,000		120.00	125
1994	Lunchtime	5,000		100.00	100
1994	Millie	5,000		100.00	100
1994	Mommie & Me	5,000		125.00	125

Ebony Collection-Jazzman - Duncan Royale

1992	Bass	5,000		90.00	110
1992	Bongo	5,000		90.00	100
1992	Piano	5,000		130.00	140
1992	Sax	5,000		90.00	100
1992	Trumpet	5,000		90.00	100

Ebony Collection-Jubilee Dancers - Duncan Royale

1993	Bliss	5,000		200.00	200
1993	Fallana	5,000		100.00	100
1993	Keshia	5,000		100.00	100
1993	Lamar	5,000		100.00	100
1993	Lottie	5,000		125.00	125
1993	Wilfred	5,000		100.00	100

Ebony Collection-Special Releases - Duncan Royale

1991	Signature Piece	Open		50.00	50

History of Classic Entertainers - P. Apsit

1987	American		Retrd. 1995	160.00	350
1987	Auguste		Retrd. 1995	220.00	350
1987	Greco-Roman		Retrd. 1995	180.00	350
1987	Grotesque		Retrd. 1995	230.00	350
1987	Harlequin		Retrd. 1995	250.00	350
1987	Jester		Retrd. 1995	410.00	700-800
1987	Pantalone		Retrd. 1995	270.00	300
1987	Pierrot		Retrd. 1995	180.00	225
1987	Pulcinella		Retrd. 1995	220.00	350
1987	Russian		Retrd. 1995	190.00	350
1987	Slapstick		Retrd. 1995	250.00	300
1987	Uncle Sam		Retrd. 1995	160.00	350

History of Classic Entertainers II - P. Apsit

1988	Bob Hope		Retrd. 1995	250.00	250-295
1988	Feste		Retrd. 1995	250.00	250
1988	Goliard		Retrd. 1995	200.00	300
1988	Mime		Retrd. 1995	200.00	300
1988	Mountebank		Retrd. 1995	270.00	300
1988	Pedrolino		Retrd. 1995	200.00	300
1988	Tartaglia		Retrd. 1995	200.00	250
1988	Thomassi		Retrd. 1995	200.00	300
1988	Touchstone		Retrd. 1995	200.00	300
1988	Tramp		Retrd. 1995	200.00	300
1988	White Face		Retrd. 1995	250.00	300
1988	Zanni		Retrd. 1995	200.00	300

History of Classic Entertainers-Special Releases - P. Apsit

1990	Bob Hope-18"		Retrd. 1995	1500.00	1700
1990	Bob Hope-6" porcelain		Retrd. 1995	130.00	130
1990	Mime-18"		Retrd. 1995	1500.00	1500
1988	Signature Piece		Retrd. 1995	50.00	50

History of Santa Claus I - P. Apsit

1983	Black Peter		Retrd. 1991	145.00	300
1983	Civil War	10,000	1988	145.00	350-400
1983	Dedt Moroz		Retrd. 1989	145.00	550-650
1983	Kris Kringle		Retrd. 1988	165.00	1100-1250
1983	Medieval		Retrd. 1988	220.00	1200-1800
1983	Nast		Retrd. 1987	90.00	1800-2200
1983	Pioneer		Retrd. 1989	145.00	275-325
1983	Russian		Retrd. 1989	145.00	550-600
1983	Soda Pop		Retrd. 1988	145.00	1250-1600
1983	St. Nicholas		Retrd. 1989	175.00	1100-1400
1983	Victorian		Retrd. 1990	120.00	300-400
1983	Wassail		Retrd. 1991	90.00	150-300

History of Santa Claus II - P. Apsit

1986	Alsace Angel	10,000		250.00	300
1986	Babouska	10,000		170.00	200
1986	Bavarian	10,000		250.00	300
1986	Befana	10,000		200.00	250
1986	Frau Holda	10,000		160.00	180
1986	Lord of Misrule	10,000		160.00	200
1986	The Magi	10,000		350.00	400
1986	Mongolian/Asian	10,000		240.00	300
1986	Odin	10,000	1996	200.00	250
1986	The Pixie	10,000		140.00	175
1986	Sir Christmas	10,000		150.00	175
1986	St. Lucia	10,000		180.00	225

History of Santa Claus III - Duncan Royale

1990	Druid	10,000	1996	250.00	250
1991	Grandfather Frost & Snow Maiden	10,000		400.00	400

YEAR ISSUE		EDITION LIMIT	YEAR RETD.	ISSUE PRICE	*QUOTE U.S.$
1991	Hoteisho	10,000		200.00	200
1991	Judah Maccabee	10,000		300.00	300
1990	Julenisse	10,000		200.00	200
1991	King Wenceslas	10,000		300.00	300
1991	Knickerbocker	10,000		300.00	300
1991	Samichlaus	10,000		350.00	350
1991	Saturnalia King	10,000	1996	200.00	200
1990	St. Basil	10,000		300.00	300
1990	Star Man	10,000		300.00	300
1990	Ukko	10,000	1996	250.00	250

History of Santa Claus I (6") - P. Apsit

1988	Black Peter-6" porcelain	6,000/yr.		40.00	80
1988	Civil War-6" porcelain	6,000/yr.		40.00	80
1988	Dedt Moroz -6" porcelain	6,000/yr.		40.00	80
1988	Kris Kringle-6" porcelain	6,000/yr.		40.00	80
1988	Medieval-6" porcelain	6,000/yr.		40.00	80
1988	Nast-6" porcelain	6,000/yr.		40.00	80
1988	Pioneer-6" porcelain	6,000/yr.		40.00	80
1988	Russian-6" porcelain	6,000/yr.		40.00	80
1988	Soda Pop-6" porcelain	6,000/yr.		40.00	80
1988	St. Nicholas-6" porcelain	6,000/yr.		40.00	80
1988	Victorian-6" porcelain	6,000/yr.		40.00	80
1988	Wassail-6" porcelain	6,000/yr.		40.00	80

History of Santa Claus II (6") - P. Apsit

1988	Alsace Angel-6" porcelain	6,000/yr		80.00	90
1988	Babouska-6" porcelain	6,000/yr		70.00	80
1988	Bavarian-6" porcelain	6,000/yr		90.00	100
1988	Befana-6" porcelain	6,000/yr		70.00	80
1988	Frau Holda-6" porcelain	6,000/yr		60.00	80
1988	Lord of Misrule-6" porcelain	6,000/yr		60.00	80
1988	Magi-6" porcelain	6,000/yr		130.00	150
1988	Mongolian/Asian-6" porcelain	6,000/yr		80.00	90
1988	Odin-6" porcelain	6,000/yr		80.00	90
1988	Pixie-6" porcelain	6,000/yr		50.00	80
1988	Sir Christmas-6" porcelain	6,000/yr		60.00	80
1988	St. Lucia-6" porcelain	6,000/yr		70.00	80

History of Santa Claus (18") - P. Apsit

1989	Kris Kringle-18"	1,000	1995	1500.00	1500
1989	Medieval-18"	1,000	1995	1500.00	1500
1989	Nast-18"	1,000	1995	1500.00	1500
1989	Russian-18"	1,000	1995	1500.00	1500
1989	Soda Pop-18"	1,000	1995	1500.00	1500
1989	St. Nicholas-18"	1,000	1995	1500.00	1500

History of Santa Claus I -Wood - P. Apsit

1987	Black Peter-8" wood	500	1993	450.00	450
1987	Civil War-8" wood	500	1993	450.00	450
1987	Dedt Moroz-8" wood	500	1993	450.00	450
1987	Kris Kringle-8" wood	500	1993	450.00	450
1987	Medieval-8" wood	500	1993	450.00	1200
1987	Nast-8" wood	500	1993	450.00	1500
1987	Pioneer-8" wood	500	1993	450.00	450
1987	Russian-8" wood	500	1993	450.00	450
1987	Soda Pop-8" wood	500	1993	450.00	850
1987	St. Nicholas-8" wood	500	1993	450.00	700
1987	Victorian-8" wood	500	1993	450.00	450
1987	Wassail-8" wood	500	1993	450.00	450

History Of Santa Claus -Special Releases - Duncan Royale

1992	Nast & Sleigh	5,000		500.00	650
1991	Signature Piece	Open		50.00	50

Painted Pewter Miniatures-Santa 1st Series - Duncan Royale

1986	Black Peter	500		30.00	30
1986	Civil War	500		30.00	30
1986	Dedt Moroz	500		30.00	30
1986	Kris Kringle	500		30.00	30
1986	Medieval	500		30.00	30
1986	Nast	500		30.00	30
1986	Pioneer	500		30.00	30
1986	Russian	500		30.00	30
1986	Soda Pop	500		30.00	30
1986	St. Nicholas	500		30.00	30
1986	Victorian	500		30.00	30
1986	Wassail	500		30.00	30
1986	Set of 12	500		360.00	360-495

Painted Pewter Miniatures-Santa 2nd Series - Duncan Royale

1988	Alsace Angel	500		30.00	30
1988	Babouska	500		30.00	30
1988	Bavarian	500		30.00	30
1988	Befana	500		30.00	30
1988	Frau Holda	500		30.00	30
1988	Lord of Misrule	500		30.00	30
1988	Magi	500		30.00	30
1988	Mongolian	500		30.00	30
1988	Odin	500		30.00	30
1988	Pixie	500		30.00	30
1988	Sir Christmas	500		30.00	30
1988	St. Lucia	500		30.00	30
1988	Set of 12	500		360.00	360-495

Woodland Fairies - Duncan Royale

1988	Almond Blossom		Retrd. 1993	70.00	70
1988	Apple		Retrd. 1994	70.00	70
1988	Calla Lily		Retrd. 1994	70.00	70
1988	Cherry	10,000	1995	70.00	70

YEAR ISSUE		EDITION LIMIT	YEAR RETD.	ISSUE PRICE	* QUOTE U.S.$
1988	Chestnut	10,000	1995	70.00	70
1988	Christmas Tree		Retrd. 1993	70.00	70
1988	Elm	10,000	1995	70.00	70
1988	Guilder Rose		Retrd. 1994	70.00	70
1988	Lime Tree		Retrd. 1993	70.00	70
1988	Mulberry	10,000	1995	70.00	70
1988	Pear Blossom		Retrd. 1993	70.00	70
1988	Pine Tree	10,000	1995	70.00	70
1988	Poplar	10,000	1995	70.00	70
1988	Sycamore		Retrd. 1993	70.00	70

Enchantica

Enchantica Collectors Club - Various

1991	Snappa on Mushroom-2101 - A. Bill		Retrd. 1991	Gift	10-150
1991	Rattajack with Snail-2102 - A. Bill		Retrd. 1991	60.00	85
1992	Jonquil-2103 - A. Hull		Retrd. 1992	Gift	75
1992	Ice Demon-2104 - K. Fallon		Retrd. 1992	85.00	150
1992	Sea Dragon-2106 - A. Bill		Retrd. 1993	99.00	275
1993	White Dragon-2107 - A. Bill		Retrd. 1993	Gift	200
1993	Jonquil's Flight-2108 - A. Bill		Retrd. 1993	140.00	300-375
1994	Verratus-2111 - A. Bill		Retrd. 1994	Gift	60
1994	Mimmer-Spring Fairy-2112 - A. Bill		Retrd. 1994	100.00	165
1994	Gorgoyle Cameo piece-2113 - K. Fallon		Retrd. 1994	Gift	10
1995	Destroyer-2116 - A. Hull		Retrd. 1995	100.00	100
1995	Cloudbreaker-2115 - J. Oliver		Retrd. 1995	Gift	N/A
1996	Sheylag's Trophy-2119		Yr.Iss.	125.00	125
1996	Jacarand-2118 - A. Hull		Yr.Iss.	Gift	N/A

Retired Enchantica Collection - Various

1994	Anaxorg-Six Leg Dragon-2094 - A. Hull		Retrd. 1995	87.00	87
1990	Arangast - Summer Dragon-2026 - K. Fallon	7,500	1992	165.00	350
1991	Bledderag, Goblin Twin-2048 - K. Fallon	15,000	1993	115.00	175
1988	Blick Scoops Crystals-2015 - A. Bill		Retrd. 1991	47.00	70
1992	Breen - Carrier Dragon-2053 - K. Fallon	15,000	1993	156.00	175
1992	Cave Dragon-2065 - A. Bill	7,500	1994	200.00	225
1990	Cellandia-Summer Fairy-2029 - K. Fallon		Retrd. 1992	115.00	170
1996	Changeling-2121 - A. Bill		Retrd. 1996	120.00	120
1989	Chuckwalla-2021 - A. Bill		Retrd. 1994	43.00	60
1994	Coracob-Cobra Dragon-2093 - A. Hull		Retrd. 1995	87.00	87
1994	Daggerback-2114 - K. Fallon		Retrd. 1995	95.00	95
1992	Desert Dragon-2064 - A. Bill	7,500	1994	175.00	200
1994	Escape (5th Anniversary)-2110 - A. Bill		Retrd. 1994	250.00	320
1988	Fantazar- Spring Wizard-2016 - A. Bill	7,500	1991	132.50	400
1991	Flight to Danger-2044 - K. Fallon	450	1991	3000.00	6500
1990	Fossfex - Autumn Fairy-2030 - K. Fallon		Retrd. 1992	115.00	200
1991	Furza - Carrier Dragon-2050 - K. Fallon	15,000	1993	137.50	200
1996	Glostomorg-2122 - A. Bill		Retrd. 1996	250.00	250
1988	Gorgoyle - Spring Dragon-2017 - A. Bill	7,500	1994	132.50	500
1991	Grawlfang '91 Winter Dragon -2046 - A. Bill	15,000	1994	295.00	375
1989	Grawlfang - Winter Dragon-2019 - A. Bill	7,500	1991	132.50	600
1988	Hepna Pushes Truck-2014 - A. Bill		Retrd. 1994	47.00	75
1988	Hest Checks Crystals-2013 - A. Bill		Retrd. 1994	47.00	75
1989	Hobba, Hellbenders Twin Son-2023 - A. Bill		Retrd. 1992	69.00	150
1993	Ice Dragon-2109 - A. Bill		Retrd. 1994	95.00	100
1992	Jonquil and Snappa-2055 - A. Bill		Retrd. 1995	40.00	60
1988	Jonquil- Dragons Footprint-2004 - A. Bill		Retrd. 1991	55.00	90
1992	Manu Manu-Peeper-2105 - A. Bill		Retrd. 1993	40.00	60
1994	Mezereon "Grand Corrupter"-2091 - A. Bill	7,500		187.00	187
1994	Necranon-Raptor Dragon-2095 - A. Bill		Retrd. 1995	105.00	105
1991	Ogrod-Ice Troll-2032 - A. Bill		Retrd. 1994	235.00	325
1991	Okra, Goblin Princess-2031 - K. Fallon		Retrd. 1994	105.00	115
1989	Old Yargle-2020 - A. Bill		Retrd. 1994	55.00	75
1992	Olm & Sylphen, Mer-King & Queen-2059 - A. Bill	9,500	1994	350.00	450
1990	Orolan-Summer Wizard-2025 - A. Bill	7,500	1992	165.00	300
1991	Quillion-Autumn Witch-2045 - A. Bill	15,000	1994	205.00	220
1993	Rattajack "All Alone"-2089 - A. Bill		Retrd. 1995	52.00	52
1993	Rattajack "Gone Fishing"-2090 - A. Bill		Retrd. 1995	77.00	77
1993	Rattajack "Soft Landing"-2088 - A. Bill		Retrd. 1995	53.00	53
1992	Rattajack & Snappa-2056 - A. Bill		Retrd. 1995	73.00	73
1988	Rattajack - Circles-2003 - A. Bill		Retrd. 1993	40.00	60
1988	Rattajack - My Ball-2001 - A. Bill		Retrd. 1993	40.00	70
1988	Rattajack - Please-2000 - A. Bill		Retrd. 1993	40.00	65
1988	Rattajack - Terragon Dreams -2002 - A. Bill		Retrd. 1993	40.00	60
1991	Rattajack-Up & Under-2038 - A. Bill		Retrd. 1994	65.00	70
1995	Saberath-2117 - K. Fallon		Retrd. 1995	100.00	100
1991	Samphire-Carrier Dragon-2049 - A. Bill	15,000	1994	137.50	175
1988	Snappa Climbs High-2008 - A. Bill		Retrd. 1993	25.00	65
1988	Snappa Finds a Collar-2009 - A. Bill		Retrd. 1992	25.00	60
1993	Snappa "Flapping"-2082 - A. Bill		Retrd. 1995	32.50	33
1993	Snappa "If The Cap Fits"-2084 - A. Bill		Retrd. 1995	35.00	35

FIGURINES/COTTAGES

YEAR ISSUE		EDITION LIMIT	YEAR RETD.	ISSUE PRICE	*QUOTE U.S.$
1993	Snappa "Nature Watch"-2086 - A. Bill	Retrd.	1995	28.00	28
1993	Snappa "Rollaball"-2081 - A. Bill	Retrd.	1995	35.00	35
1993	Snappa "w/Enchantica Rose"-2083 - A. Bill	Retrd.	1995	27.00	27
1993	Snappa "What Ball"-2085 - A. Bill	Retrd.	1995	33.00	33
1991	Snappa Caught Napping-2039 - A. Hull	Retrd.	1994	39.50	60
1988	Snappa Dozes Off-2011 - A. Bill	Retrd.	1993	25.00	60
1988	Snappa Hatches Out-2006 - A. Bill	Retrd.	1991	25.00	60
1991	Snappa Nods Off-2043 - A. Hull	Retrd.	1994	30.00	40
1988	Snappa Plays Ball-2010 - A. Bill	Retrd.	1993	25.00	60
1991	Snappa Posing-2042 - A. Hull	Retrd.	1994	30.00	40
1991	Snappa Tumbles-2047 - A. Hull	Retrd.	1994	30.00	40
1988	Snappa's First Feast-2007 - A. Bill	Retrd.	1993	25.00	60
1991	Snappa-Snowdrift-2041 - A. Hull	Retrd.	1994	30.00	40
1991	Snarlgard - Autumn Dragon -2034 - K. Fallon	7,500	1992	337.00	400
1993	Snow Dragon-2066 - A. Bill	7,500	1995	150.00	150
1992	Sorren & Gart-2054 - K. Fallon	9,500	1994	220.00	350
1992	Spring Wizard and Yim-2060 - A. Bill	9,500	1993	410.00	450
1990	The Swamp Demon-2028 - K. Fallon	Retrd.	1992	69.00	95
1988	Tarbet with Sack-2012 - A. Bill	Retrd.	1991	47.00	60
1992	Thrace-Gladiator-2061 - K. Fallon	9,500	1993	280.00	350
1992	The Throne Citadel-2063 - J. Woodward	950	1994	2000.00	2000
1990	Tuatara-Evil Witch-2027 - A. Bill	9,500	1994	174.00	185
1989	Vrorst - The Ice Sorcerer-2018 - A. Bill	7,500	1991	155.00	650
1991	Vrorst-Ice Sorcerer on Throne -2040 - A. Bill	15,000	1995	500.00	500
1994	Vyzauga-Twin Headed Dragon -2092 - A. Bill	Retrd.	1995	87.00	87
1991	Waxifrade - Autumn Wizard -2033 - K. Fallon	7,500	1992	265.00	400
1994	Zorganoid-Crab Dragon-2096 - K. Fallon	Retrd.	1995	99.00	99

Enesco Corporation

Cherished Teddies Club - P. Hillman

YEAR ISSUE		EDITION LIMIT	YEAR RETD.	ISSUE PRICE	*QUOTE U.S.$
1995	Cub E. Bear CT001	Yr.Iss.		Gift	35-50
1995	Mayor Wilson T.Beary CT951	Yr.Iss.		20.00	50
1995	Hilary Hugabear CT952	Yr.Iss.		17.50	35-65
1996	R. Harrison Hartford-New Membear CT002	Yr.Iss.		Gift	N/A
1996	R. Harrison Hartford-Charter Membear CT102	Yr.Iss.		Gift	N/A
1996	Emily E. Claire CT962	Yr.Iss.		17.50	18
1996	Kurtis D. Claw CT961	Yr.Iss.		17.50	18

Cherished Teddies - P. Hillman

YEAR ISSUE		EDITION LIMIT	YEAR RETD.	ISSUE PRICE	*QUOTE U.S.$
1993	Abigail "Inside We're All The Same"-900362	Suspd.		16.00	25-50
1993	Alice "Cozy Warm Wishes Coming Your Way" (9")-903620	Suspd.		100.00	100-150
1993	Alice "Cozy Warm Wishes Coming Your Way" Dated 1993-912875	Yr.Iss.		17.50	75-135
1995	Allison & Alexandria "Two Friends Mean Twice The Love"-127981	Open		25.00	25
1995	Amanda "Here's Some Cheer to Last The Year"-141186	Yr.Iss.		17.50	35-50
1993	Amy "Hearts Quilted With Love"-910732	Open		13.50	15
1996	Andy "You Have A Special Place In My Heart"-176265	Open		18.50	19
1992	Angie "I Brought The Star"-951137	Open		15.00	15
1992	Anna "Hooray For You"-950459	Open		22.50	23
1997	Annie, Brittany, Colby, Danny, Ernie "Strike Up The Band And Give Five Cherished Years A Hand" (5th Anniversary)-205354	Yr.Iss.		75.00	75
1994	Baby Boy Jointed (Musical) -699324	Open		60.00	60
1994	Baby Girl Jointed (Musical) -699322	Open		60.00	60
1993	Baby in Cradle (Musical)-914320	Open		60.00	60
1995	Bea "Bee My Friend"-141348	Open		15.00	18
1994	Bear as Bunny Jointed (Musical) -625302	Retrd.	1996	60.00	100-150
1995	Bear Cupid Girl 2AT-103640	Suspd.		15.00	30
1994	Bear Holding Harp (Musical)-916323	Open		40.00	40
1996	Bear In Bunny Outfit Resin Egg Dated 1996-156507	Yr.Iss.		8.50	20
1992	Bear on Rocking Reindeer (Musical)-950815	Suspd.		60.00	65-80
1993	Bear Playing w/Train (Musical) -912964	Open		40.00	40
1994	Bear w/ Goose (Musical) -627445	Open		45.00	45
1994	Bear w/Horse (Musical)-628565	Retrd.	1996	150.00	150
1994	Bear w/Rocking Reindeer (Musical)-629618	Open		165.00	165
1994	Bear w/Toy Chest (Musical) -627453	Open		60.00	60
1995	Beary Scary Halloween House -152382	Open		20.00	20
1994	Becky "Springtime Happiness" -916331	Suspd.		20.00	35-65
1992	Benji "Life Is Sweet, Enjoy" -950548	Retrd.	1995	13.50	35-65
1994	Bessie "Some Bunny Loves You" -916404	Suspd.		15.00	100-140
1995	The Best Is Yet To Come -127949	Open		12.50	14

YEAR ISSUE		EDITION LIMIT	YEAR RETD.	ISSUE PRICE	*QUOTE U.S.$
1995	The Best Is Yet To Come -127957	Open		12.50	14
1992	Beth "Bear Hugs"-950637	Retrd.	1995	17.50	35-75
1992	Beth "Happy Holidays, Deer Friend"-950807	Suspd.		22.50	35-50
1994	Betty "Bubblin' Over With Love" -626066	Open		18.50	20
1994	Billy "Everyone Needs A Cuddle", Betsey "First Step To Love" Bobbie "A Little Friendship To Share"-624896	Open		12.50	13
1992	Blossom & Beth "Friends Are Never Far Apart" w/butterfly-950564	Retrd.	1992	50.00	150
1992	Blossom & Beth "Friends Are Never Far Apart"-950564	Open		50.00	50
1995	Boy Bear Cupid-103551	Suspd.		17.50	31-50
1995	Boy Bear Flying Cupid-103608	Suspd.		13.00	25
1993	Boy Praying (Musical)-914304	Open		37.50	38
1994	Boy/Girl in Laundry Basket (Musical)-624926	Open		60.00	60
1994	Boy/Girl in Sled (Musical) -651435	Open		100.00	100
1994	Breanna "Pumpkin Patch Pals"-617180	Open		15.00	15
1994	Bride/Groom (Musical)-699349	Open		50.00	50
1993	Buckey & Brenda "How I Love Being Friends With You"-912816	Retrd.	1995	15.00	75
1995	Bunny "Just In Time For Spring"-103802	Open		13.50	14
1996	Butch "Can I Be Your Football Hero?"-156388	Open		15.00	15
1992	Camille "I'd Be Lost Without You"-950424	Open		20.00	20
1993	Carolyn "Wishing You All Good Things"-912921	Suspd.		22.50	25-50
1995	Carrie "The Future 'Beareth' All Things"-141321	Open		18.50	19
1995	Celeste "An Angel To Watch Over You"-141267	Open		20.00	20
1993	Charity "I Found A Friend In Ewe"-910678	Suspd.		20.00	75-150
1992	Charlie "The Spirit of Friendship Warms The Heart"-950742	Suspd		22.50	35-60
1993	Chelsea "Good Friends Are A Blessing"-910694	Retrd.	1995	15.00	200-300
1996	Cheryl & Carl "Wishing You A Cozy Christmas"-141216	Open		25.00	25
1995	Christian "My Prayer Is For You"-103837	Open		18.50	19
1995	Christine "My Prayer Is For You"-103845	Open		18.50	19
1992	Christopher "Old Friends Are The Best Friends" 950483	Open		20.00	50
1993	Connie "You're A Sweet Treat"-912794	Suspd.		15.00	15
1992	Couple in Basket/Umbrella (Musical)-950645	Open		60.00	60
1994	Courtney "Springtime Is A Blessing From Above"-916390	Suspd.		15.00	65-100
1992	Creche & Quilt-951218	Open		50.00	50
1995	Cupid Baby on Pillow 2 Asst -103659	Suspd.		13.50	14
1995	Cupid Boy Sitting 2 Asst-869074	Suspd.		13.50	14
1995	Cupid Boy/Girl Double 2 Asst -869082	Suspd.		18.50	19
1995	Cupid Boy/Girl Double-103594	Suspd.		25.00	30-50
1993	Daisy "Friendship Blossoms With Love"-910651	Retrd.	1996	15.00	500-780
1996	Daniel "You're My Little Pumpkin"-176214	Open		22.50	23
1996	Debbie "Let's Hear It For Friendship!"-156361	Open		15.00	15
1995	Donald "Friends Are Egg-ceptional Blessings"-103799	Open		20.00	20
1992	Douglas "Let's Be Friends"-950661	Retrd.	1995	20.00	40-85
1995	Earl "Warm Hearted Friends"-131873	Open		17.50	18
1994	Elizabeth & Ashley "My Beary Best Friend"-916277	Retrd.	1996	25.00	50-100
1994	Eric "Bear Tidings Of Joy"-622796	Open		22.50	25
1996	Erica "Friends Are Always Pulling For You"-176028	Open		22.50	23
1994	Faith "There's No Bunny Like You"-916412	Suspd.		20.00	55-100
1993	Freda & Tina "Our Friendship Is A Perfect Blend"- 911747	Open		35.00	35
1993	Friends Like You Are Precious And Few-904309	Open		30.00	30
1993	Friendship Pulls Us Through & Ewe Make Being Friends Special-912867	Open		13.50	14
1995	Gail "Catching the First Blooms of Friendship"-103772	Open		20.00	20
1993	Gary "True Friendships Are Scarce"-912786	Suspd.		18.50	25
1995	Girl Bear Cupid-103586	Suspd.		15.00	40-50
1995	Girl Bear Flying Cupid-103616	Suspd.		13.00	25
1995	Girl Bear on Ottoman Musical-128058	Open		55.00	55
1993	Girl Praying (Musical)-914312	Open		37.50	38
1993	Gretel "We Make Magic, Me And You"-912778	Open		18.50	20
1993	Hans "Friends In Toyland"-912956	Retrd.	1995	20.00	55-110
1993	Heidi & David "Special Friends"-910708	Suspd.		25.00	45-55
1993	Henrietta "A Basketful of Wings"-910686	Suspd.		22.50	75-125
1994	Henry "Celebrating Spring With You"-916420	Suspd.		20.00	55-100
1995	Hope "Our Love Is Ever-Blooming"-103764	Open		20.00	20

YEAR ISSUE		EDITION LIMIT	YEAR RETD.	ISSUE PRICE	*QUOTE U.S.$
1994	Ingrid "Bundled Up With Warm Wishes" Dated 1994-617237	Yr.Iss.		20.00	35-50
1992	Jacob "Wishing For Love"-950734	Suspd.		22.50	40-75
1996	Jamie & Ashley "I'm All Wrapped Up In Your Love"-141224	Open		25.00	25
1992	Jasmine " You Have Touched My Heart"-950475	Suspd.		22.50	30-55
1994	Jedediah "Giving Thanks For Friends"-617091	Open		17.50	18
1995	Jennifer "Gathering The Blooms of Friendship"-103810	Open		22.50	23
1992	Jeremy "Friends Like You Are Precious And Few"-950521	Retrd.	1995	15.00	25-60
1996	Jessica "A Mother's Heart Is Full of Love" GCC Early Introduction-155438A	Yr.Iss.		25.00	100-150
1997	Jessica "A Mother's Heart Is Full of Love"-155438	Open		25.00	25
1993	Jointed Bear Christmas (Musical)-903337	Suspd.		60.00	60
1992	Joshua "Love Repairs All"-950556	Open		20.00	20
1994	Kathleen "Luck Found Me A Friend In You"-916447	Open		12.50	13
1992	Katie "A Friend Always Knows When You Need A Hug"-950440	Open		20.00	20
1994	Kelly "You're My One And Only" -916307	Suspd.		15.00	60-100
1995	Kevin "Good Luck To You"-103896	Retrd.	1996	12.50	35
1995	Kiss The Hurt And Make It Well-127965	Open		15.00	15
1996	Kittie "You Make Wishes Come True" 1996 Adoption Center Event-131865	Yr.Iss.		17.50	18
1995	Kristen "Hugs of Love And Friendship"-141194	Open		20.00	20
1996	Laura "Friendship Makes It All Better"-156396	Open		15.00	15
1996	Linda "ABC And 1-2-3, You're A Friend To Me!"-156426	Open		15.00	15
1995	Lisa "My Best Is Always You"-103780	Open		20.00	20
1995	Madeline "A Cup Full of Friendship"-135593	Open		20.00	20
1992	Mandy "I Love You Just The Way You Are"-950572	Retrd.	1995	15.00	35-65
1995	Margaret "A Cup Full of Love"-103667	Open		20.00	20
1992	Maria, Baby & Josh "A Baby Is God's Gift of Love" "Everyone Needs a Daddy"- 950688	Open		35.00	35
1993	Marie "Friendship Is A Special Treat"-910767	Open		20.00	20
1995	Marilyn "A Cup Full of Cheer"-135682	Open		20.00	20
1993	Mary "A Special Friend Warms The Season"-912840	Open		25.00	25
1995	Maureen "Lucky Friend"-135690	Retrd.	1996	12.50	35
1995	Melissa "Every Bunny Needs A Friend"-103829	Open		20.00	20
1993	Michael & Michelle "Friendship Is A Cozy Feeling"-910775	Suspd.		30.00	40-75
1994	Miles "I'm Thankful For A Friend Like You"-912751	Open		17.00	18
1995	Millie, Christy, Dorothy "A. Love Me Tender, B. Take Me To Your Heart, C. Love Me True"-128023	Retrd.	1996	37.50	100-160
1993	Mindy "Friendship Keeps Me On My Toes"-156418	Open		15.00	15
1993	Molly "Friendship Softens A Bumpy Ride"-910759	Retrd.	1996	30.00	35-75
1994	Nancy "Your Friendship Makes My Heart Sing"-916315	Retrd.	1996	15.00	75-125
1992	Nathaniel & Nellie "It's Twice As Nice With You"-950513	Retrd.	1996	30.00	60-75
1993	Nativity (Musical)-912859	Suspd.		60.00	100
1994	Nativity Cow "That's What Friends Are For"-651095	Open		22.50	23
1996	Nativity Prayer Plaque-176362	Open		13.50	14
1994	Nils "Near And Dear For Christmas"-617245	Suspd.		22.50	30-40
1996	Olga "Feel The Peace...Hold The Joy...Share The Love"-182966	Yr.Iss.		50.00	50
1996	Park Bench w/Bears 1996 National Event Piece-CRT240	Yr.Iss.		12.50	20
1995	Pat "Falling For You"-141313	Open		22.50	23
1994	Patience "Happiness Is Homemade"-617105	Open		17.50	18
1993	Patrice "Thank You For The Sky So Blue"-911429	Open		18.50	20
1993	Patrick "Thank You For A Friend That's True"-911410	Open		18.50	20
1995	Peter "You're Some Bunny Special-104973	Open		17.50	18
1994	Phoebe "A Little Friendship Is A Big Blessing"-617113	Retrd.	1995	13.50	30-50
1993	Priscilla "Love Surrounds Our Friendship"-910724	Open		15.00	15
1995	Priscilla & Greta "Our Hearts Belong to You"-128031	19,950		50.00	95-125
1993	Prudence "A Friend To Be Thankful For"-912808	Open		17.00	18
1996	Pumpkins/Corn Stalk/Scarecrow Mini 3 Asst-176206	Open		15.00	15
1992	Richard "My Gift Is Loving", Edward "My Gift Is Caring", Wilbur"My Gift Is Sharing"-950718	Open		55.00	55
1993	Robbie & Rachel "Love Bears All Things"-911402	Open		27.50	30
1996	Robert "Love Keeps Me Afloat"-156272	Open		13.50	14

Year Issue	Description	Edition Limit	Year Retd.	Issue Price	*Quote U.S.$
1994	Ronnie "I'll Play My Drum For You"-912905	Open		13.50	14
1997	Ryan "I'm Green With Envy For You"-203041	Open		20.00	20
1992	Sammy "Little Lambs Are In My Care"-950726	Open		17.50	18
1992	Sara "Lov Ya" Jacki Hugs & Kisses", Karen "Best Buddy"-950432	Open		10.00	10
1995	Sculpted Irish Plaque-110981	Open		13.50	14
1994	Sean "Luck Found Me A Friend In You"-916439	Open		12.50	13
1995	Seth & Sarabeth "We're Beary Good Pals"-128015	Open		25.00	25
1996	Sign/Bunny/Basket of Strawberries Mini 3 Asst.-900931	Open		3.50	4
1992	Signage Plaque-951005	Open		15.00	15
1994	Sonja "Holiday Cuddles"-622818	Open		20.00	20
1994	Stacie "You Lift My Spirit"-617148	Open		18.50	20
1992	Steven "A Season Filled With Sweetness"-951129	Retrd.	1995	20.00	35-75
1996	Stormi "Hark The Herald Angels Sing"-176001	Yr.Iss.		20.00	20
1996	Tabitha "You're The Cat's Meow"-176257	Open		15.00	15
1996	Tasha "In Grandmother's Attic" 1996 Adoption Center Exclusive-156353	19,960		50.00	95-125
1994	Taylor "Sail The Seas With Me"-617156	Suspd.		15.00	22-50
1994	Thanksgiving Quilt -617075	Open		12.00	12
1992	Theadore, Samantha & Tyler "Friends Come In All Sizes"-950505	Open		20.00	20
1993	Theadore, Samantha & Tyler "Friendship Weathers All Storms (9")-912883	Suspd.		160.00	160
1993	Theadore, Samantha & Tyler "Friendship Weathers All Storms" (musical)-904546	Suspd.		170.00	170-190
1992	Theadore, Samantha & Tyler "Friendship Weathers All Storms"-950769	Open		20.00	20
1992	Theadore, Samantha & Tyler (9") "Friends Come In All Sizes"-951196	Open		130.00	130
1993	Thomas "Chuggin' Along", Jonathon "Sail With Me", Harrison "We're Going Places"-911739	Open		15.00	18
1993	Timothy "A Friend Is Forever"-910740	Retrd.	1996	15.00	20-50
1995	Town Tattler Sign-1995 National Event Piece-CRT109	Yr.Iss.		6.00	20
1993	Tracie & Nicole "Side By Side With Friends"-911372	Open		35.00	35
1996	Trunk Full of Bear Hugs-103977	Open		22.50	23
1995	Tucker & Travis "We're in This Together"-127973	Open		25.00	25
1996	Two Boys By Lamp Post Musical-141698	Open		50.00	50
1994	Victoria "From My Heart To Yours"-916293	Suspd.		16.50	80-120
1996	Violet "Blessings Bloom When You Are Near"-156280	Open		15.00	15
1994	Willie "Bears Of A Feather Stay Together" -617164	Open		15.00	15
1994	Winona "Fair Feather Friends"-617172	Open		15.00	15
1994	Wyatt "I'm Called Little Running Bear"-629707	Open		15.00	15
1994	Wylie "I'm Called Little Friend"-617121	Open		15.00	15
1992	Zachary "Yesterday's Memories Are Today's Treasures"-950491	Open		30.00	30
1995	UK Bears, set/4 163481A (Bertie, Gordon, Duncan, Sherlock)	Open		70.00	115-175
1994	Oliver & Olivia "Will You Be Mine?"-916641	Suspd.		25.00	45-70

Cherished Teddies Special Limited Edition - P. Hillman

Year Issue	Description	Edition Limit	Year Retd.	Issue Price	*Quote U.S.$
1993	Holding On To Someone Special-Collector Appreciation Fig.-916285	Yr.Iss.		20.00	250-350
1994	Priscilla Ann "There's No One Like Hue" Collectible Exposition Exclusive available only at Secaucus and South Bend in 1994 and at Long Beach in 1995	Yr.Iss.		24.00	175-300
1993	Teddy & Roosevelt "The Book of Teddies 1903-1993"-624918	Yr.Iss.		20.00	155-200

Cherished Teddies A Christmas Carol - P. Hillman

Year Issue	Description	Edition Limit	Year Retd.	Issue Price	*Quote U.S.$
1994	Bear Cratchit "And A Very Merry Christmas To You Mr. Scrooge"-617326	Open		17.50	18
1994	Counting House-622788	Open		75.00	75
1994	Cratchit's House-651362	Open		75.00	75
1994	Ebearneezer Scrooge "Bah Humbug!"-617296	Open		17.50	18
1994	Gloria "Ghost of Christmas Past," Garland "Ghost Of Christmas Present", Gabriel "Ghost of Christmas Yet To Come"-614807	Open		55.00	55
1994	Jacob Bearly "You Will Be Haunted By Three Spirits"-614785	Open		17.50	18
1994	Mrs. Cratchit "A Beary Christmas And Happy New Year!"-617318	Open		18.50	19
1994	Tiny Ted-Bear "God Bless Us Every One"-614777	Open		10.00	10

Cherished Teddies Across The Seas - P. Hillman

Year Issue	Description	Edition Limit	Year Retd.	Issue Price	*Quote U.S.$
1996	Bob "Our Friendship Is From Sea To Shining Sea"-202444	Open		15.00	15
1996	Carlos "I Found An Amigo In You"-202339	Open		15.00	15
1996	Claudette "Our Friendship Is Bon Appetit!"-197254	Open		15.00	15
1996	Fernando "You Make Everday A Fiesta"-202355	Open		15.00	15
1996	Johann "I'd Climb The Highest Alp For You"-202436	Open		15.00	15
1996	Katrinka "Tulips Blossom With Friendship"-202401	Open		15.00	15
1996	Kerstin "You're The Swedish of Them All"-197289	Open		15.00	15
1996	Lian "Our Friendship Spans Many Miles"-202347	Open		15.00	15
1996	Lorna "Our Love Is In The Highlands"-202452	Open		15.00	15
1996	Machiko "Love Fans A Beautiful Friendship"-202312	Open		15.00	15
1996	Nadia "From Russia, With Love"-202320	Open		15.00	15
1996	Preston "Riding Across The Great White North"-216739	Open		15.00	15
1996	Rajul "You're The Jewel Of My Heart"-202398	Open		15.00	15
1996	Winston "Friendship Is Elementary My Dear"-202878	Open		15.00	15

Cherished Teddies Blossoms of Friendship - P. Hillman

Year Issue	Description	Edition Limit	Year Retd.	Issue Price	*Quote U.S.$
1997	Dahlia "You're The Best Pick of the Bunch"-202932	Open		15.00	15
1997	Iris "You're The Iris of My Eye"-202908	Open		15.00	15
1997	Rose "Everything's Coming Up Roses"-202886	Open		15.00	15
1997	Susan "Love Stems From Our Friendship"-202894	Open		15.00	15

Cherished Teddies By The Sea, By The Sea - P. Hillman

Year Issue	Description	Edition Limit	Year Retd.	Issue Price	*Quote U.S.$
1997	Gregg "Everything Pails in Comparison To Friends"-203505	Open		20.00	20
1997	Jerry "Ready To Make a Splash"-203475	Open		17.50	18
1997	Jim and Joey "Underneath It All We're Forever Friends"-203513	Open		25.00	25
1997	Judy "I'm Your Bathing Beauty"-203491	Open		35.00	35
1997	Sandy "There's Room In My Sand Castle For You"-203467	Open		20.00	20

Cherished Teddies Circus Tent - P. Hillman

Year Issue	Description	Edition Limit	Year Retd.	Issue Price	*Quote U.S.$
1996	"Seal of Friendship"-137596	Open		10.00	10
1996	Bruno "Step Right Up And Smile"-103713	Open		17.50	18
1996	Claudia "You Take Center Ring With Me"-103721	Open		17.50	18
1996	Clown on Ball Musical-111430	Open		40.00	40
1997	Dudley "Just Clowning Around"-103748	Open		17.50	18
1997	Lion-"You're My Mane Attraction"-203548	Open		12.50	13
1997	Logan "Love Is A Bear Necessity"-103756	Yr.Iss.		17.50	18
1997	Shelby "Friendship Keeps You Popping"-203572	Open		17.50	18
1997	Tonya "Friends Are Bear Essentials"-103942	Open		20.00	20
1996	Wally "You're The Tops With Me"-103934	Open		17.50	18

Cherished Teddies Down Strawberry Lane - P. Hillman

Year Issue	Description	Edition Limit	Year Retd.	Issue Price	*Quote U.S.$
1997	Diane "I Picked The Beary Best For You"-202991	Yr.Iss.		25.00	25
1996	Ella "Love Grows in My Heart"-156329	Open		15.00	15
1996	Jenna "You're Berry Special To Me"-156337	Open		15.00	15
1996	Matthew "A Dash of Love Sweetens Any Day!"-156299	Open		15.00	15
1996	Tara "You're My Berry Best Friend!"-156310	Open		15.00	15
1996	Thelma "Cozy Tea For Two" -156302	Open		22.50	23

Cherished Teddies Family - P. Hillman

Year Issue	Description	Edition Limit	Year Retd.	Issue Price	*Quote U.S.$
1994	Father "A Father Is The Bearer Of Strength"-624888	Open		13.50	14
1994	Mother "A Mother's Love Bears All Things"-624861	Open		20.00	20
1994	Older Daughter "Child Of Love" -624845	Open		10.00	10
1994	Older Son "Child Of Pride" -624829	Open		10.00	10
1994	Young Daughter "Child Of Kindness"-624853	Open		9.00	9
1994	Young Son "Child of Hope" -624837	Open		9.00	9

Cherished Teddies Holiday Dangling - P. Hillman

Year Issue	Description	Edition Limit	Year Retd.	Issue Price	*Quote U.S.$
1996	Holden "Catchin' The Holiday Spirit"-176095	Open		15.00	15
1996	Jeffrey "Striking Up Another Year" Dated 1996-176044	Yr.Iss.		17.50	18
1996	Jolene "Dropping You A Holiday Greeting"-176133	Open		20.00	20
1996	Joy "You Always Bring Joy" -176087	Open		15.00	15
1996	Noel "An Old Fashioned Noel To You"-176109	Open		15.00	15
1996	Nolan "A String Of Good Tidings" -176141	Open		20.00	20

Cherished Teddies Love Letters From Teddie Mini - P. Hillman

Year Issue	Description	Edition Limit	Year Retd.	Issue Price	*Quote U.S.$
1997	Bear w/ "I Love Bears" Blocks -902950	Open		7.50	8
1997	Bear w/ "I Love Hugs" Blocks -902969	Open		7.50	8
1997	Bear w/ "I Love You" Blocks -156515	Open		7.50	8
1997	Bear w/Heart Dangling Blocks -203084	Open		13.50	14
1997	Bears w/ "Love" Double-203076	Open		13.50	14

Cherished Teddies Monthly - P. Hillman

Year Issue	Description	Edition Limit	Year Retd.	Issue Price	*Quote U.S.$
1993	Jack January Monthly-914754 (Also available through Hamilton Collection)	Open		15.00	15
1993	Phoebe February Monthly -914762 (Also available through Hamilton Collection)	Open		15.00	15
1993	Mark March Monthly-914770 (Also available through Hamilton Collection)	Open		15.00	15
1993	Alan April Monthly-914789 (Also available through Hamilton Collection)	Open		15.00	15
1993	May May Monthly-914797 (Also available through Hamilton Collection)	Open		15.00	15
1993	June June Monthly-914800 (Also available through Hamilton Collection)	Open		15.00	15
1993	Julie July Monthly-914819 (Also available through Hamilton Collection)	Open		15.00	15
1993	Arthur August Monthly-914827 (Also available through Hamilton Collection)	Open		15.00	15
1993	Seth September Monthly -914835 (Also available through Hamilton Collection)	Open		15.00	15
1993	Oscar October Monthly-914843 (Also available through Hamilton Collection)	Open		15.00	15
1993	Nicole November Monthly -914851 (Also available through Hamilton Collection)	Open		15.00	15
1993	Denise December Monthly -914878 (Also available through Hamilton Collection)	Open		15.00	15

Cherished Teddies Nursery Rhyme - P. Hillman

Year Issue	Description	Edition Limit	Year Retd.	Issue Price	*Quote U.S.$
1994	Jack & Jill "Our Friendship Will Never Tumble"-624772	Open		30.00	30
1994	Little Bo Peep "Looking For A Friend Like You"-624802	Open		22.50	23
1994	Little Jack Horner "I'm Plum Happy You're My Friend"-624780	Open		20.00	20
1994	Little Miss Muffet "I'm Never Afraid With You At My Side"-624799	Open		20.00	20
1994	Mary, Mary Quite Contrary "Friendship Blooms With Loving Care"-626074	Open		22.50	23
1994	Tom, Tom The Piper's Son "Wherever You Go I'll Follow"-624810	Open		20.00	20

Cherished Teddies Santa Express - P. Hillman

Year Issue	Description	Edition Limit	Year Retd.	Issue Price	*Quote U.S.$
1996	Car of Toys "Riding Along With Friends and Smiles"-219096	Open		17.50	18
1996	Casey "Friendship Is The Perfect End To The Holidays"-219525	Open		22.50	23
1996	Colin "He Knows If You've Been Bad or Good"-219088	Open		17.50	18
1996	Lionel "All Aboard the Santa Express"-219061	Open		22.50	23
1996	Tony "A First Class Delivery For You"-219487	Open		17.50	18

Cherished Teddies Santa's Workshop - P. Hillman

Year Issue	Description	Edition Limit	Year Retd.	Issue Price	*Quote U.S.$
1995	Ginger "Painting Your Holidays With Love"-141127	Open		22.50	23
1995	Holly "A Cup of Homemade Love"-141119	Open		18.50	19
1996	Klaus "Bearer of Good Tidings"-176036	Yr.Iss.		20.00	20
1995	Meri "Handsewn Holidays"-141135	Open		20.00	20
1995	Nickolas "You're At The Top Of My List"-141100	Yr.Iss.	1996	20.00	25-50
1996	Ornaments/Mailsack/North Pole Sign Mini 3 Asst.-176079	Open		15.00	15
1995	Santa's Workshop Nightlight-141925	Open		75.00	75
1995	Yule "Building a Sturdy Friendship"-141143	Open		22.50	23

Cherished Teddies Sweetheart Ball - P. Hillman

Year Issue	Description	Edition Limit	Year Retd.	Issue Price	*Quote U.S.$
1996	Craig & Cheri "Sweethearts Forever"-156485	Open		25.00	25
1996	Darla "My Heart Wishes For You"-156469	Open		20.00	20
1996	Darrel "Love Unveils A Happy Heart"-156450	Open		17.50	18
1996	Jilly "Won't You Be My Sweetheart?"-156477	Open		17.50	18
1996	Marian "You're The Hero Of My Heart"-156442	Open		20.00	20
1996	Robin "You Steal My Heart Away"-156434	Open		17.50	18

YEAR ISSUE	EDITION LIMIT	YEAR RETRD	ISSUE PRICE	*QUOTE U.S.$
1997 Romeo & Juliet "There's No Rose Sweeter Than You" Wherefore Art Thou Romeo?"-203114			60.00	60

Cherished Teddies T Is For Teddy - P. Hillman

YEAR ISSUE	EDITION LIMIT	YEAR RETRD	ISSUE PRICE	*QUOTE U.S.$
1995 Bear w/"A" Block-158488A	Open		5.00	5
1995 Bear w/"B" Block-158488B	Open		5.00	5
1995 Bear w/"C" Block-158488C	Open		5.00	5
1995 Bear w/"D" Block-158488D	Open		5.00	5
1995 Bear w/"E" Block-158488E	Open		5.00	5
1995 Bear w/"F" Block-158488F	Open		5.00	5
1995 Bear w/"G" Block-158488G	Open		5.00	5
1995 Bear w/"H" Block-158488H	Open		5.00	5
1995 Bear w/"I" Block-158488I	Open		5.00	5
1995 Bear w/"J" Block-158488J	Open		5.00	5
1995 Bear w/"K" Block-158488K	Open		5.00	5
1995 Bear w/"L" Block-158488L	Open		5.00	5
1995 Bear w/"M" Block-158488M	Open		5.00	5
1995 Bear w/"N" Block-158488N	Open		5.00	5
1995 Bear w/"O" Block-158488O	Open		5.00	5
1995 Bear w/"P" Block-158488P	Open		5.00	5
1995 Bear w/"Q" Block-158488Q	Open		5.00	5
1995 Bear w/"R" Block-158488R	Open		5.00	5
1995 Bear w/"S" Block-158488S	Open		5.00	5
1995 Bear w/"T" Block-158488T	Open		5.00	5
1995 Bear w/"U" Block-158488U	Open		5.00	5
1995 Bear w/"V" Block-158488V	Open		5.00	5
1995 Bear w/"W" Block-158488W	Open		5.00	5
1995 Bear w/"X" Block-158488X	Open		5.00	5
1995 Bear w/"Y" Block-158488Y	Open		5.00	5
1995 Bear w/"Z" Block-158488Z	Open		5.00	5

Cherished Teddies Through The Years - P. Hillman

YEAR ISSUE	EDITION LIMIT	YEAR RETRD	ISSUE PRICE	*QUOTE U.S.$
1993 "Beary Special One" Age 1 -911348	Open		13.50	14
1995 "Chalking Up Six Wishes" Age 6 -911283	Open		16.50	17
1993 "Color Me Five" Age 5-911291	Open		15.00	15
1993 "Cradled With Love" Baby -911356	Open		16.50	17
1993 "Three Cheers For You" Age 3 -911313	Open		15.00	15
1993 "Two Sweet Two Bear" Age 2 -911348	Open		13.50	14
1993 "Unfolding Happy Wishes Four You" Age 4-911305	Open		15.00	15

Cherished Teddies We Bear Thanks - P. Hillman

YEAR ISSUE	EDITION LIMIT	YEAR RETRD	ISSUE PRICE	*QUOTE U.S.$
1996 Barbara "Giving Thanks For Our Family"-141305	Open		12.50	13
1996 Dina "Bear In Mind, You're Special"-141275	Open		15.00	15
1996 John "Bear In Mind, You're Special"-141283	Open		15.00	15
1996 Rick "Suited Up For The Holidays"-141291	Open		12.50	13
1996 Table With Food / Dog-141542	Open		30.00	30

Maud Humphrey Bogart - Collectors' Club Members Only - M. Humphrey

YEAR ISSUE	EDITION LIMIT	YEAR RETRD	ISSUE PRICE	*QUOTE U.S.$
1991 Friends For Life MH911	Closed	N/A	60.00	100
1992 Nature's Little Helper MH921	Closed	N/A	65.00	60-65
1993 Sitting Pretty MH931	Yr.Iss.		60.00	60

Maud Humphrey Bogart - Symbol Of Membership Figurines - M. Humphrey

YEAR ISSUE	EDITION LIMIT	YEAR RETRD	ISSUE PRICE	*QUOTE U.S.$
1991 A Flower For You H5596	Closed	N/A	Unkn.	30
1992 Sunday Best M0002	Closed	N/A	Unkn.	30-53
1993 Playful Companions M0003	Yr.Iss.		Unkn.	Unkn.

Maud Humphrey Bogart - M. Humphrey

YEAR ISSUE	EDITION LIMIT	YEAR RETRD	ISSUE PRICE	*QUOTE U.S.$
1988 Tea And Gossip H1301	Retrd.	N/A	65.00	70-95
1988 Cleaning House H1303	Retrd.	N/A	60.00	55
1988 Susanna H 1305	Retrd.	N/A	60.00	75-100
1988 Little Chickadees H1306	Retrd.	N/A	65.00	60
1988 The Magic Kitten H1308	Retrd.	N/A	66.00	60
1988 Seamstress H1309	Retrd.	N/A	66.00	84
1988 A Pleasure To Meet You H1310	Retrd.	N/A	65.00	80-125
1988 My First Dance H1311	Retrd.	N/A	60.00	85-100
1988 Sarah H1312	Retrd.	N/A	60.00	245-295
1988 Sealed With A Kiss H1316	Retrd.	N/A	45.00	60
1988 Special Friends H1317	Retrd.	N/A	66.00	76
1988 School Days H1318	Retrd.	N/A	42.50	45-55
1988 Gift Of Love H1319	Retrd.	N/A	65.00	40
1988 My 1st Birthday H1320	Retrd.	N/A	47.00	47
1989 Winter Fun H1354	Retrd.	N/A	46.00	53
1992 Stars and Stripes Forever 910201	Retrd.	N/A	75.00	80
1993 Playing Mama 5th Anniv. Figurine 915963	Retrd.	N/A	80.00	110
1993 Playing Mama Event Figurine 915963R	Retrd.	N/A	80.00	90-110

Maud Humphrey Bogart Victorian Village - M. Humphrey

YEAR ISSUE	EDITION LIMIT	YEAR RETRD	ISSUE PRICE	*QUOTE U.S.$
1994 Christmas Scene-655457	Open		50.00	50

Memories of Yesterday - Society Figurines - M. Attwell

YEAR ISSUE	EDITION LIMIT	YEAR RETRD	ISSUE PRICE	*QUOTE U.S.$
1991 Welcome To Your New Home-MY911	Yr.Iss.		30.00	45
1991 I Love My Friends-MY921	Yr.Iss.		32.50	35
1993 Now I'm The Fairest Of Them All-MY931	Yr.Iss.		35.00	35
1993 A Little Love Song for You -MY941	Yr.Iss.		35.00	35
1994 Wot's All This Talk About Love-MY942	Yr.Iss.		27.50	28
1995 Sharing the Common Thread of Love- MY951	Yr.Iss.		100.00	100
1995 A Song For You From One That's True-MY952	Yr.Iss.		37.50	38
1996 You've Got My Vote-MY961	Yr.Iss.		40.00	40
1996 Peace, Heavenly Peace-MY962	Yr.Iss.		30.00	30

Memories of Yesterday - Exclusive Membership Figurine - M. Attwell

YEAR ISSUE	EDITION LIMIT	YEAR RETRD	ISSUE PRICE	*QUOTE U.S.$
1991 We Belong Together-S0001	Yr.Iss.		Gift	35
1992 Waiting For The Sunshine-S0002	Yr.Iss.		Gift	35
1993 I'm The Girl For You-S0003	Yr.Iss.		Gift	40
1994 Blowing a Kiss to a Dear I Miss -S0004	Yr.Iss.		Gift	N/A
1995 Time to Celebrate-S0005	Yr.Iss.		Gift	N/A
1996 Forget-Me-Not!-S0006	Yr.Iss.		Gift	N/A

Memories of Yesterday - Exclusive Charter Membership Figurine - M. Attwell

YEAR ISSUE	EDITION LIMIT	YEAR RETRD	ISSUE PRICE	*QUOTE U.S.$
1992 Waiting For The Sunshine-S0102	Yr.Iss.		Gift	N/A
1993 I'm The Girl For You-S0103	Yr.Iss.		Gift	N/A
1994 Blowing a Kiss to a Dear I Miss -S0104	Yr.Iss.		Gift	N/A
1995 Time to Celebrate-S0105	Yr.Iss.		Gift	N/A
1996 Forget-Me-Not!-S0106	Yr.Iss.		Gift	N/A

Memories of Yesterday - M. Attwell

YEAR ISSUE	EDITION LIMIT	YEAR RETRD	ISSUE PRICE	*QUOTE U.S.$
1995 A Friend Like You Is Hard To Find-101176	Open		45.00	45
1995 A Helping Hand For You-101192	Open		40.00	40
1995 Won't You Skate With Me? -134864	5,000		35.00	35
1995 Dear Old Dear, Wish You Were Here-134872	5,000		37.50	38
1995 You're My Sunshine On A Rainy Day-137626	Open		37.50	38
1995 Boo-Boo's Band Set/5-137758	Open		25.00	25
1996 We're In Trouble Now!-162299	7,500		37.50	38
1996 A Basket Full of Love-162582	Open		50.00	50
1996 Just Longing To See You -162620	7,500		27.50	28
1996 We Are All His Children-162639	Open		30.00	30
1996 Just Like Daddy-162698	7,500		27.50	28
1996 How Good of God To Make Us All-164135	5,000		50.00	50
1990 Collection Sign-513156	Closed	1993	7.00	7
1989 Blow Wind, Blow-520012	Open		40.00	40
1990 Hold It! You're Just Swell -520020	Suspd.		50.00	50
1990 Kiss The Place And Make It Well-520039	Suspd.		50.00	50
1989 Let's Be Nice Like We Was Before-520047	Suspd.		50.00	50
1991 Who Ever Told Mother To Order Twins?-520063	Open		33.50	34
1989 I'se Spoken For-520071	Retrd.	1991	30.00	30-50
1993 You Do Make Me Happy-520098	Open		27.50	28
1990 Where's Muvver?-520101	Retrd.	1994	30.00	30
1990 Here Comes The Bride And Groom God Bless 'Em!-520136 (musical)	Suspd.		80.00	80
1989 Daddy, I Can Never Fill Your Shoes-520187	Open		30.00	30
1989 This One's For You, Dear-520195	Suspd.		50.00	50
1989 Should I . . . ?-520209	Suspd.		50.00	50
1990 Luck At Last! He Loves Me-520217	Retrd.	1992	35.00	36-58
1989 Here Comes The Bride-God Bless Her! -9"-520527	Retrd.	1990	95.00	95-100
1989 We's Happy! How's Yourself?-520616	Retrd.	1991	70.00	85-150
1989 Here Comes The Bride & Groom (musical) God Bless 'Em-520896	Open		50.00	50
1989 The Long and Short of It-522384	Retrd.	1994	32.50	33
1989 As Good As His Mother Ever Made-522392	Open		32.50	32-40
1989 Must Feed Them Over Christmas-522406	Retrd.	1996	38.50	39
1989 Knitting You A Warm & Cozy Winter-522414	Suspd.		37.50	38
1989 Joy To You At Christmas-522449	Retrd.	1996	45.00	45
1991 For Fido And Me-522457	Open		70.00	70
1991 Wishful Thinking-522597	Open		45.00	45
1991 Why Don't You Sing Along?-522600	Retrd.	1995	55.00	55
1995 You Brighten My Day With A Smile-522627	Open		30.00	30
1991 Tying The Knot-522678	Open		60.00	60
1991 Wherever I Am, I'm Dreaming of You-522686	Suspd.		40.00	40
1993 Will You Be Mine?-522694	Open		30.00	30
1991 Sitting Pretty-522708	Retrd.	1993	40.00	40
1993 Here's A Little Song From Me To You Musical-522716	Open		70.00	70
1992 A Whole Bunch of Love For You-522732	Retrd.	1996	40.00	40
1992 I'se Such A Good Little Girl Sometimes-522759	Suspd.		30.00	30
1992 Things Are Rather Upside Down-522775	Suspd.		30.00	30
1991 Pull Yourselves Together Girls, Waists Are In-522783	Open		30.00	30
1993 Bringing Good Luck To You-522791	Retrd.	1996	30.00	30
1995 I Comfort Fido And Fido Comforts Me-522813	5,000		50.00	50
1992 A Kiss From Fido-523119	Suspd.		35.00	35
1994 Bless 'Em!-523127	Open		35.00	35
1994 Bless 'Em!-523232	Open		35.00	35
1990 I'm Not As Backwards As I Looks-523240	Open		32.50	33
1990 I Pray The Lord My Soul To Keep-523259	Open		25.00	25
1990 He Hasn't Forgotten Me-523267	Suspd.		30.00	30
1990 Time For Bed 9"-523275	Retrd.	1991	95.00	125
1991 Just Thinking 'bout You-523461 (musical)	Suspd.		70.00	70
1992 Now Be A Good Dog Fido -524581	Open		45.00	45
1991 Them Dishes Nearly Done -524611	Suspd.		50.00	50
1995 Join Me For A Little Song -524654	5,000		37.50	38
1990 Let Me Be Your Guardian Angel -524670	Open		32.50	33
1990 A Lapful Of Luck-524689	Open		15.00	15
1990 Not A Creature Was Stirrin' -524697	Suspd.		45.00	45
1990 I'se Been Painting-524700	Suspd.		37.50	38
1992 The Future-God Bless "Em! -524719	Open		37.50	38
1990 A Dash of Something With Something For the Pot-524727	Open		55.00	55
1991 Opening Presents Is Much Fun! -524735	Suspd.		37.50	38
1992 You'll Always Be My Hero -524743	Open		50.00	50
1990 Got To Get Home For The Holidays-524751(musical)	Retrd.	1994	100.00	100
1990 Hush-A-Bye Baby-524778	Open		80.00	80
1990 The Greatest Treasure The World Can Hold-524808	Open		50.00	50
1994 With A Heart That's True, I'll Wait For You-524816	Retrd.	1996	50.00	50
1990 Hoping To See You Soon -524824	Suspd.		30.00	30
1991 I Must Be Somebody's Darling -524832	Retrd.	1993	30.00	30
1991 We All Loves A Cuddle-524832	Retrd.	1992	30.00	35
1991 He Loves Me -9"-525022	Retrd.	1992	100.00	100
1993 Now I Lay Me Down To Sleep-525413 (musical)	Suspd.		65.00	65
1992 Making Something Special For You-525472	Suspd.		45.00	45
1991 I'm As Comfy As Can Be-525480	Suspd.		50.00	50
1992 I'm Hopin' You're Missing Me Too-525499	Suspd.		55.00	55
1993 The Jolly Ole Sun Will Shine Again-525502	Retrd.	1994	55.00	55
1991 Friendship Has No Boundaries (Special Understamp)-525545	Yr.Iss.	1991	30.00	30-50
1992 Home's A Grand Place To Get Back To Musical-525553	Retrd.	1995	100.00	100
1991 Give It Your Best Shot-525561	Open		35.00	35
1992 I Pray The Lord My Soul To Keep (musical)-525596	Suspd.		65.00	65
1991 Could You Love Me For Myself Alone?-525618	Retrd.	1994	30.00	30
1996 Whenever I Get A Moment-I Think of You-525626	7,500		37.50	38
1992 Good Night and God Bless You In Every Way!-525634	Suspd.		50.00	50
1992 Five Years Of Memories -525669 (Five Year Anniversary Figurine)	Yr.Iss.	1992	50.00	65
1992 Five Years Of Memories Celebrating Our Five Years 1992-525669A	500		N/A	N/A
1996 Loving You One Stitch At A Time-525677	5,000		50.00	50
1993 May Your Flowers Be Even Better Than The Pictures On The Packets-525685	Open		37.50	38
1995 Let's Sail Away Together-525707	Open		32.50	33
1993 You Won't Catch Me Being A Golf Widow-525715	Open		30.00	30
1995 Good Friends Are Great Gifts-525723	Open		50.00	50
1994 Taking After Mother-525731	Open		40.00	40
1994 Too Shy For Words-525758	Retrd.	1996	50.00	50
1991 Good Morning, Little Boo-Boo-525766	Retrd.	1996	40.00	40
1992 Hurry Up For the Last Train to Christmas-525863	Suspd.		40.00	40
1992 I'se So Happy You Called-526401	Retrd.	1993	100.00	100
1994 Pleasant Dreams and Sweet Repose-(musical)-526592	Open		80.00	80
1996 Put Your Best Foot Forward-526983	5,000		50.00	50
1994 Bobbed-526991	Retrd.	1995	32.50	33
1996 Can I Keep Her, Mommy? -527025	Open		13.50	14
1992 Time For Bed-527076	Open		30.00	30
1991 S'no Use Lookin' Back Now! -527203	Yr.Iss.	1991	75.00	75
1992 Collection Sign-527300	Open		30.00	30
1993 Having A Wash And Brush Up -527424	Open		35.00	35
1994 Having a Good Ole Laugh -527432	Open		50.00	50
1993 A Bit Tied Up Just Now-But Cheerio-527467	Open		45.00	45
1992 Send All Life's Little Worries Skipping-527505	Open		30.00	30
1994 Don't Wait For Wishes to Come True-Go Get Them!-527645	Open		37.50	38
1993 Hullo! Did You Come By Underground?-527653	Yr.Iss.	1993	40.00	40
1993 Hullo! Did You Come By Underground? Commemorative Issue: 1913-1993 -527653A	500		N/A	N/A
1993 Look Out-Something Good Is Coming Your Way!-528781	Suspd.		37.50	38

YEAR ISSUE		EDITION LIMIT	YEAR RETD.	ISSUE PRICE	*QUOTE U.S.$
1992	Merry Christmas, Little Boo-Boo-528803	Open		37.50	38
1994	Do Be Friends With Me-529117	Open		40.00	40
1994	Good Morning From One Cheery Soul To Another-529141	Open		30.00	30
1994	May Your Birthday Be Bright And Happy-529575	Open		35.00	35
1996	God Bless Our Future-529583	5,000		45.00	45
1993	Strikes Me, I'm Your Match -529656	Open		27.50	28
1993	Wot's All This Talk About Love? -529737	Retrd.	1994	100.00	100
1994	Thank God For Fido-529753	2-Yr.		100.00	100
1994	Making the Right Connection -529907	Yr.Iss.	1994	30.00	30
1994	Still Going Strong-530344	Open		27.50	28
1993	Do You Know The Way To Fairyland?-530379	Retrd.	1996	50.00	50
1996	We'd Do Anything For You, Dear-530905	5,000		50.00	50
1994	Comforting Thoughts-531367	Open		32.50	33
1995	Love To You Always-602752	Open		30.00	30
1995	Wherever You Go, I'll Keep In Touch-602760	Retrd.	1996	30.00	30
1995	Love Begins With Friendship -602914	Open		50.00	50
1994	The Nativity Pageant-602949	Open		90.00	90
1995	May You Have A Big Smile For A Long While-602965	Open		30.00	30
1995	Love To You Today-602973	Open		30.00	30
1996	You Warm My Heart-603007	7,500		35.00	35

Memories of Yesterday A Loving Wish For You - M. Attwell

1995	Happiness Is Our Wedding Wish -135178	Open		25.00	25
1995	A Blessed Day For You-135186	Open		25.00	25
1995	Wishing You A Bright Future-135194	Open		25.00	25
1995	An Anniversary Is Love-135208	Open		25.00	25
1995	A Birthday Wish For You-135216	Open		25.00	25
1995	Bless You, Little One-135224	Open		25.00	25
1996	You Are My Shining Star-164585	Open		25.00	25
1996	You Brighten My Days-164615	Open		25.00	25

Memories of Yesterday Charter 1988 - M. Attwell

1988	Mommy, I Teared It-114480	Open		25.00	40-143
1988	Now I Lay Me Down To Sleep -114499	Open		20.00	25-65
1988	We's Happy! How's Yourself? -114502	Retrd.	1996	40.00	45-60
1988	Hang On To Your Luck!-114510	Suspd.		25.00	27-70
1988	How Do You Spell S-O-R-R-Y? -114529	Retrd.	1990	25.00	50-95
1988	What Will I Grow Up To Be? -114537	Suspd.		40.00	45
1988	Can I Keep Her Mommy? -114545	Retrd.	1995	25.00	27-70
1988	Hush!-114553	Retrd.	1990	45.00	75-125
1988	It Hurts When Fido Hurts-114561	Retrd.	1992	30.00	32-75
1988	Anyway, Fido Loves Me-114588	Suspd.		30.00	32-75
1988	If You Can't Be Good, Be Careful-114596	Retrd.	1993	50.00	55-90
1988	Welcome Santa-114960	Suspd.		45.00	50-100
1988	Special Delivery-114979	Retrd.	1991	30.00	32-70
1988	How 'bout A Little Kiss?-114987	Retrd.	1995	25.00	27-85
1988	Waiting For Santa-114995	Open		40.00	40-50
1988	Dear Santa. . .-115002	Suspd.		50.00	50
1988	I Hope Santa Is Home . . . -115010	Open		30.00	33-45
1988	It's The Thought That Counts -115029	Suspd.		25.00	29-75
1988	Is It Really Santa?-115347	Retrd.	1996	50.00	55-60
1988	He Knows If You've Been Bad Or Good-115355	Suspd.		40.00	45-75
1988	Now He Can Be Your Friend, Too!-115363	Suspd.		45.00	50-70
1988	We Wish You A Merry Christmas-115371 (musical)	Suspd.		70.00	70
1988	Good Morning Mr. Snowman -115401	Retrd.	1992	75.00	80-170
1988	Mommy, I Teared It, 9"-115924	Retrd.	1990	85.00	140-195

Memories of Yesterday Event Item Only - M. Attwell

1994	I'll Always Be Your Truly Friend -525693	Yr.Iss.		30.00	30
1995	Wrapped In Love And Happiness 602930	Yr.Iss.		35.00	35
1996	A Sweet Treat For You-115126	Yr.Iss.		30.00	30

Memories of Yesterday Exclusive Heritage Dealer Figurine - M. Attwell

1991	A Friendly Chat and a Cup of Tea-525510	Yr.Iss.	1991	50.00	100
1993	I'm Always Looking Out For You -527440	Yr.Iss.		55.00	55
1994	Loving Each Other Is The Nicest Thing We've Got- 522430	Yr.Iss.		60.00	60
1995	A Little Help From Fairyland 529133	1,995	1995	55.00	55
1995	Friendship Is Meant To Be Shared-602922	Yr.Iss.		50.00	50
1995	Bedtime Tales-set-153400	2,000	1996	60.00	60
1996	Tucking My Dears All Safe Away -130095	Yr.Iss.		50.00	50
1996	I Do Like My Holiday Crews -522805	1,996		100.00	100
1996	Peter Pan Collector's Set 174564	1,000		150.00	150

YEAR ISSUE		EDITION LIMIT	YEAR RETD.	ISSUE PRICE	*QUOTE U.S.$

Memories of Yesterday Friendship - M. Attwell

1996	I'll Miss You-179183	Open		25.00	25
1996	I Love You This Much!-179191	Open		25.00	25
1996	Thinking of You-179213	Open		25.00	25
1996	You And Me-179205	Open		25.00	25

Memories of Yesterday Holiday Snapshots - M. Attwell

1995	I'll Help You Mommy 144673	Open		25.00	25
1995	Isn't She Pretty? 144681	Open		25.00	25
1995	I Didn't Mean To Do It 144703	Open		25.00	25
1995	Can I Open Just One? 144711	Open		25.00	25

Memories of Yesterday Memories Of A Special Day - M. Attwell

1994	Monday's Child...-531421	Open		35.00	35
1994	Tuesday's Child...-531448	Open		35.00	35
1994	Wednesday's Child...-531405	Open		35.00	35
1994	Thursday's Child...-531413	Open		35.00	35
1994	Friday's Child...-531391	Open		35.00	35
1994	Saturday's Child...-531383	Open		35.00	35
1994	Sunday's Child...-531480	Open		35.00	35
1994	Collector's Commemorative Edition Set of 7, Hand-numbered-528056	1,994	1994	250.00	250

Memories of Yesterday Nativity - M. Attwell

1994	Nativity Set of 4 602949	Open		90.00	90
1995	Innkeeper 602892	Open		27.50	28
1996	Shepherd-602906	Open		27.50	28

Memories of Yesterday Once Upon A Fairy Tale™... - M. Attwell

1992	Mother Goose-526428	18,000		50.00	50
1993	Mary, Mary Quite Contrary -526436	18,000		45.00	45
1993	Little Miss Muffett-526444	18,000		50.00	50
1992	Simple Simon-526452	18,000		35.00	35
1992	Mary Had A Little Lamb-526479	18,000		45.00	45
1994	Tweedle Dum & Tweedle Dee -526462	10,000		50.00	50

Memories of Yesterday Peter Pan - M. Attwell

1996	John-165441	Open		25.00	25
1996	Michael-165425	Open		30.00	30
1996	Peter Pan-164666	Open		25.00	25
1996	Wendy-164674	Open		25.00	25

Memories of Yesterday Special Edition - M. Attwell

1989	As Good As His Mother Ever Made-523925	9,600	1989	32.50	114-150
1988	Mommy, I Teared It-523488	10,000	1988	25.00	175-325
1990	A Lapful of Luck -525014	5,000	1990	30.00	114-180
1990	Set of Three	N/A		87.50	735

Memories of Yesterday When I Grow Up - M. Attwell

1995	When I Grow Up, I Want To Be A Doctor-102997	Open		25.00	25
1995	When I Grow Up, I Want To Be A Mother-103195	Open		25.00	25
1995	When I Grow Up, I Want To Be A Ballerina-103209	Open		25.00	25
1995	When I Grow Up, I Want To Be A Teacher-103357	Open		25.00	25
1995	When I Grow Up, I Want To Be A Fireman-103462	Open		25.00	25
1995	When I Grow Up, I Want To Be A Nurse-103535	Open		25.00	25
1996	When I Grow Up, I Want To Be A Businessman-164623	Open		25.00	25
1996	When I Grow Up, I Want To Be A Businesswoman-164631	Open		25.00	25

Miss Martha's Collection - M. Holcombe

1993	Erin-Don't Worry Santa Won't Forget Us-307246	Retrd.	1994	55.00	110
1993	Amber-Mr. Snowman! (waterglobe)-310476	Closed	1994	50.00	100
1993	Kekisha-Heavenly Peace Musical-310484	Closed	1994	60.00	120
1993	Whitney-Let's Have Another Party-321559	Closed	1994	45.00	60-90
1993	Megan-My Birthday Cake!-321567	Closed	1994	60.00	100-120
1993	Doug-I'm Not Showin' Off-321575	Closed	1994	40.00	80
1993	Francie-Such A Precious Gift!-321583	Closed	1994	50.00	100
1993	Alicia-A Blessing From God-321591	Closed	1994	40.00	80
1993	Anita-It's For You, Mama!-321605	Closed	1994	45.00	75-90
1994	Jeffrey-Bein' A Fireman Sure Is Hot & Thirsty Work-350206	Closed	1994	40.00	80
1993	Jess-I Can Fly-350516	Retrd.	1994	45.00	80
1993	Ruth-Littlest Angel Figurine-350524	Closed	1994	40.00	80
1993	Stephen-I'll Be The Best Shepherd In The World!-350540	Closed	1994	40.00	80
1993	Jonathon-Maybe I Can Be Like Santa-350550	Closed	1994	45.00	90
1994	Charlotte-You Can Be Whatever You Dream-353191	Closed	1994	40.00	60-80
1992	Lillie-Christmas Dinner!-369373	Retrd.	1993	55.00	110
1992	Eddie-What A Nice Surprise!-369381	Retrd.	1994	50.00	100
1992	Kekisha-Heavenly Peace-421456	Closed	1994	40.00	80
1992	Angela-I Have Wings-421464	Closed	1994	45.00	90

YEAR ISSUE		EDITION LIMIT	YEAR RETD.	ISSUE PRICE	* QUOTE U.S.$
1992	Amber-Mr. Snowman-421472	Closed		60.00	120
1992	Mar/Jsh/Christopher-Hush Baby! It's Your B-day! Musical-431362	Closed	1994	80.00	160
1992	Carrie-God Bless America-440035	Closed	1994	45.00	90
1993	Hallie-Sing Praises To The Lord -443166	Retrd.	1993	60.00	90-120
1991	Jana-Plant With Love-443174	Closed	1994	40.00	80
1991	Hallie-Sing Praises To The Lord -443182	Closed	1994	37.50	75
1992	Belle-Maize-Not Now, Muffin -443204	Retrd.	1993	50.00	100
1991	Sammy/Leisha-Sister's First Day Of School-443190	Retrd.	1993	55.00	80-110
1991	Nate-Hope You Hear My Prayer, Lord-443212	Closed	1994	17.50	55
1991	Sadie-They Can't Find Us Here -443220	Retrd.	1993	45.00	90
1992	Patsy-Clean Clothes For Dolly -443239	Retrd.	1993	50.00	100
1991	Dawn-Pretty Please, Mama -443247	Closed	1994	40.00	70-80
1991	Tonya-Hush, Puppy Dear -443255	Closed	1994	50.00	80-100
1991	Jenny/Jeremiah-Birthday Biscuits, With Love...-443263	Retrd.	1993	60.00	95-120
1991	Suzi-Mama, Watch Me!-443271	Retrd.	1993	35.00	50-70
1992	Mattie-Sweet Child-443298	Retrd.	1993	30.00	50-60
1992	Sara Lou-Here, Lammie-443301	Retrd.	1993	50.00	80-100
1992	Angel Tree Topper-446521	Closed	1994	80.00	160
1992	Mar/Jsh/Christopher-Hush, Baby! It's Your B-day Figurine-448354	Closed	1994	55.00	110

Precious Moments Collectors Club Welcome Gift - S. Butcher

1982	But Love Goes On Forever -Plaque-E-0202	Yr.Iss.		Unkn.	75-90
1983	Let Us Call the Club to Order -E-0303	Yr.Iss.		Unkn.	45-65
1984	Join in on the Blessings-E-0404	Yr.Iss.		Unkn.	35-55
1985	Seek and Ye Shall Find-E-0005	Yr.Iss.		Unkn.	35-50
1986	Birds of a Feather Collect Together-E-0006	Yr.Iss.		Unkn.	30-45
1987	Sharing Is Universal-E-0007	Yr.Iss.		Unkn.	30-40
1988	A Growing Love-E-0008	Yr.Iss.		Unkn.	30-40
1989	Always Room For One More -C-0009	Yr.Iss.		Unkn.	30-55
1990	My Happiness-C-0010	Yr.Iss.		Unkn.	45
1991	Sharing the Good News Together-C-0011	Yr.Iss.		Unkn.	25-50
1992	The Club That's Out Of This World-C-0012	Yr.Iss.		Unkn.	30-45
1993	Loving, Caring, and Sharing Along the Way-C-0013	Yr.Iss.		Unkn.	35
1994	You Are the End of My Rainbow-C-0014	Yr.Iss.		Unkn.	25-30
1995	You're The Sweetest Cookie In The Batch-C-0015	Yr.Iss.		Unkn.	28
1996	You're As Pretty As A Picture-C-0016	Yr.Iss.		Unkn.	Unkn.

Precious Moments Inscribed Charter Member Renewal Gift - S. Butcher

1981	But Love Goes on Forever -E-0001	Yr.Iss.		Unkn.	115-170
1982	But Love Goes on Forever -Plaque-E-0102	Yr.Iss.		Unkn.	60-125
1983	Let Us Call the Club to Order -E-0103	Yr.Iss.		25.00	50-65
1984	Join in on the Blessings-E-0104	Yr.Iss.		25.00	35-60
1985	Seek and Ye Shall Find-E-0105	Yr.Iss.		25.00	35-50
1986	Birds of a Feather Collect Together-E-0106	Yr.Iss.		25.00	30-50
1987	Sharing Is Universal-E-0107	Yr.Iss.		25.00	30-50
1988	A Growing Love-E-0108	Yr.Iss.		25.00	30-50
1989	Always Room For One More -C-0109	Yr.Iss.		35.00	30-50
1990	My Happiness-C-0110	Yr.Iss.		Unkn.	35
1991	Sharing The Good News Together-C-0111	Yr.Iss.		Unkn.	30-45
1992	The Club That's Out Of This World-C-0112	Yr.Iss.		Unkn.	35-45
1993	Loving, Caring, and Sharing Along the Way-C-0113	Yr.Iss.		Unkn.	20-35
1994	You Are the End of My Rainbow-C-0114	Yr.Iss.		Unkn.	28
1995	You're The Sweetest Cookie In The Batch-C-0115	Yr.Iss.		Unkn.	30

Precious Moments Special Edition Members' Only - S. Butcher

1981	Hello, Lord, It's Me Again -PM-811	Yr.Iss.		25.00	300-425
1982	Smile, God Loves You-PM-821	Yr.Iss.		25.00	200-275
1983	Put on a Happy Face-PM-822	Yr.Iss.		25.00	175-200
1983	Dawn's Early Light-PM-831	Yr.Iss.		27.50	75-90
1984	God's Ray of Mercy-PM-841	Yr.Iss.		25.00	55-75
1984	Trust in the Lord to the Finish -PM-842	Yr.Iss.		25.00	55-85
1985	The Lord is My Shepherd -PM-851	Yr.Iss.		25.00	70-95
1985	I Love to Tell the Story-PM-852	Yr.Iss.		27.50	60-80
1986	Grandma's Prayer-PM-861	Yr.Iss.		25.00	70-100
1986	I'm Following Jesus-PM-862	Yr.Iss.		25.00	50-90
1987	Feed My Sheep-PM-871	Yr.Iss.		25.00	45-65
1987	In His Time-PM-872	Yr.Iss.		25.00	40-65
1987	Loving You Dear Valentine-PM-873	Yr.Iss.		25.00	35-50

YEAR ISSUE	EDITION LIMIT	YEAR RETRD.	ISSUE PRICE	*QUOTE U.S.$
1987 Loving You Dear Valentine -PM-874	Yr.Iss.		25.00	35-50
1988 God Bless You for Touching My Life-PM-881	Yr.Iss.		27.50	40-55
1988 You Just Can't Chuck A Good Friendship-PM-882	Yr.Iss.		27.50	35-50
1989 You Will Always Be My Choice - PM-891	Yr.Iss.		27.50	35-55
1989 Mow Power To Ya-PM-892	Yr.Iss.		27.50	40-65
1990 Ten Years And Still Going Strong-PM-901	Yr.Iss.		30.00	30-55
1990 You Are A Blessing To Me -PM-902	Yr.Iss.		30.00	40-60
1991 One Step At A Time-PM-911	Yr.Iss.		33.00	45
1991 Lord, Keep Me In TeePee Top Shape-PM-912	Yr.Iss.		33.00	40-50
1992 Only Love Can Make A Home -PM-921	Yr.Iss.		30.00	40-75
1992 Sowing The Seeds of Love -PM-922	Yr.Iss.		30.00	45
1993 His Little Treasure-PM-931	Yr.Iss.		30.00	40
1993 Loving PM-932	Yr.Iss.		30.00	50-70
1994 Caring PM-941	Yr.Iss.		35.00	50
1994 Sharing PM-942	Yr.Iss.		35.00	45-55
1995 You're One In A Million To Me PM-951	Yr.Iss.		35.00	35
1995 Take Time To Pray PM-952	Yr.Iss.		35.00	35
1996 Teach Us To Love One Another PM-961	Yr.Iss.		40.00	40
1996 Our Club is Soda-licious PM-962	Yr.Iss.		35.00	35

Precious Moments Club 5th Anniversary Commemorative Edition - S. Butcher

YEAR ISSUE	EDITION LIMIT	YEAR RETRD.	ISSUE PRICE	*QUOTE U.S.$
1985 God Bless Our Years Together -12440	Yr.Iss.		175.00	225-300

Precious Moments Club 10th Anniversary Commemorative Edition - S. Butcher

YEAR ISSUE	EDITION LIMIT	YEAR RETRD.	ISSUE PRICE	*QUOTE U.S.$
1988 The Good Lord has Blessed Us Tenfold-114022	Yr.Iss.		90.00	120-175

Precious Moments Club 15th Anniversary Commemorative Edition - S. Butcher

YEAR ISSUE	EDITION LIMIT	YEAR RETRD.	ISSUE PRICE	*QUOTE U.S.$
1993 15 Happy Years Together: What A Tweet-530786	Yr.Iss.		100.00	100
1993 A Perfect Display of 15 Happy Years-127817	Yr.Iss.		100.00	100

Precious Moments - S. Butcher

YEAR ISSUE	EDITION LIMIT	YEAR RETRD.	ISSUE PRICE	*QUOTE U.S.$
1983 Sharing Our Season Together -E-0501	Suspd.		50.00	115-155
1983 Jesus is the Light that Shines -E-0502	Suspd.		23.00	40-65
1983 Blessings from My House to Yours-E-0503	Suspd.		27.00	85-105
1983 Christmastime Is for Sharing-E-0504	Retrd.	1990	37.00	55-85
1983 Surrounded with Joy-E-0506	Retrd.	1989	21.00	55-75
1983 God Sent His Son-E-0507	Suspd.		32.50	65-90
1983 Prepare Ye the Way of the Lord-E-0508	Suspd.		75.00	100-130
1983 Bringing God's Blessing to You-E-0509	Suspd.		35.00	70-100
1983 Tubby's First Christmas-E-0511	Suspd.		12.00	30-45
1983 It's a Perfect Boy-E-0512	Suspd.		18.50	45-65
1983 Onward Christian Soldiers-E-0523	Open		24.00	35-59
1983 You Can't Run Away from God-E-0525	Retrd.	1989	28.50	75-100
1983 He Upholdeth Those Who Fall-E-0526	Suspd.		35.00	70-90
1987 His Eye Is On The Sparrow-E-0530	Retrd.	1987	28.50	85-125
1979 Jesus Loves Me-E-1372B	Open		7.00	28-125
1979 Jesus Loves Me-E-1372G	Open		7.00	28-130
1979 Smile, God Loves You-E-1373B	Retrd.	1984	7.00	60-135
1979 Jesus is the Light-E-1373G	Retrd.	1988	7.00	60-125
1979 Praise the Lord Anyhow-E-1374B	Retrd.	1982	8.00	85-125
1979 Make a Joyful Noise-E-1374G	Open		8.00	28-125
1979 Love Lifted Me-E-1375A	Retrd.	1993	11.00	75-120
1979 Prayer Changes Things-E-1375B	Suspd.		11.00	135-215
1979 Love One Another-E-1376	Open		10.00	40-120
1979 He Leadeth Me-E-1377A	Suspd.		9.00	85-130
1979 He Careth For You-E-1377B	Suspd.		9.00	85-115
1979 God Loveth a Cheerful Giver-E-1378	Retrd.	1981	11.00	700-800
1979 Love is Kind-E-1379A	Suspd.		8.00	80-125
1979 God Understands-E-1379B	Suspd.		8.00	85-135
1979 O, How I Love Jesus-E-1380B	Retrd.	1984	8.00	90-150
1979 His Burden Is Light-E-1380G	Retrd.	1984	8.00	85-150
1979 Jesus is the Answer-E-1381	Suspd.		11.50	130-150
1979 We Have Seen His Star-E-2010	Suspd.		8.00	75-250
1979 Come Let Us Adore Him-E-2011	Retrd.	1981	10.00	180-250
1979 Jesus is Born-E-2012	Suspd.		12.00	75-105
1979 Unto Us a Child is Born-E-2013	Suspd.		12.00	70-120
1982 May Your Christmas Be Cozy -E-2345	Suspd.		23.00	70-130
1982 May Your Christmas Be Warm -E-2348	Suspd.		30.00	100-140
1982 Tell Me the Story of Jesus -E-2349	Suspd.		30.00	100-135
1982 Dropping in for Christmas-E-2350	Suspd.		18.00	65-110
1987 Holy Smokes!-E-2351	Retrd.	1987	27.00	100-145
1982 O Come All Ye Faithful-E-2353	Retrd.	1986	27.50	70-100
1982 I'll Play My Drum for Him-E-2356	Suspd.		30.00	60-95
1982 I'll Play My Drum for Him-E-2360	Open		16.00	30-40
1982 Christmas Joy from Head to Toe-E-2361	Suspd.		25.00	55-80
1982 Camel Figurine-E-2363	Open		20.00	33-50
1982 Goat Figurine-E-2364	Open		10.00	35-65
1982 The First Noel-E-2365	Suspd.		16.00	40-75
1982 The First Noel-E-2366	Suspd.		16.00	45-65
1982 Bundles of Joy-E-2374	Retrd.	1993	27.50	50-75
1982 Dropping Over for Christmas -E-2375	Retrd.	1991	30.00	50-100
1982 Our First Christmas Together -E-2377	Suspd.		35.00	75-150
1982 3 Mini Nativity Houses & Palm Tree-E-2387	Open		45.00	75-110
1982 Come Let Us Adore Him-E-2395 (11pc. set)	Open		80.00	130-175
1980 Come Let Us Adore Him-E2800 (9 pc. set)	Open		70.00	125-175
1980 Jesus is Born-E-2801	Suspd.		37.00	150-250
1980 Christmas is a Time to Share-E-2802	Suspd.		20.00	60-90
1980 Crown Him Lord of All-E-2803	Suspd.		20.00	65-85
1980 Peace on Earth-E-2804	Suspd.		20.00	120-135
1980 Wishing You a Season Filled w/ Joy-E-2805	Retrd.	1985	20.00	80-110
1984 You Have Touched So Many Hearts-E-2821	Open		25.00	38-52
1984 This is Your Day to Shine -E-2822	Retrd.	1988	37.50	90-100
1984 To God Be the Glory-E-2823	Suspd.		40.00	75-120
1984 To a Very Special Mom-E-2824	Open		27.50	38-57
1984 To a Very Special Sister-E-2825	Open		37.50	55-65
1984 May Your Birthday Be a Blessing-E-2826	Suspd.		37.50	75-130
1984 I Get a Kick Out of You-E-2827	Suspd.		50.00	145-210
1984 Precious Memories-E-2828	Open		45.00	45-70
1984 I'm Sending You a White Christmas-E-2829	Open		37.50	55-60
1984 God Bless the Bride-E-2832	Open		35.00	50-60
1986 Sharing Our Joy Together-E-2834	Suspd.		30.00	40-60
1987 Baby Figurines (set of 6)-E-2852	Closed	N/A	15.00	115-200
1987 Boy Standing-E-2852A	Suspd.		13.50	25
1987 Girl Standing-E-2852B	Suspd.		13.50	25
1987 Boy Sitting Up-E-2852C	Suspd.		13.50	25
1987 Girl Sitting Clapping-E-2852D	Suspd.		13.50	25
1987 Boy Crawling-E-2852E	Suspd.		13.50	25
1987 Girl Laying Down-E-2852F	Suspd.		13.50	25
1980 Blessed Are the Pure in Heart-E-3104	Suspd.		9.00	30-40
1980 He Watches Over Us All-E-3105	Suspd.		11.00	60-85
1980 Mother Sew Dear-E-3106	Open		13.00	28-80
1980 Blessed are the Peacemakers-E-3107	Retrd.	1985	13.00	75-130
1980 The Hand that Rocks the Future-E-3108	Suspd.		13.00	70-95
1980 The Purr-fect Grandma-E-3109	Open		13.00	28-75
1980 Loving is Sharing-E-3110B	Retrd.	1993	13.00	60-100
1980 Loving is Sharing-E-3110G	Open		13.00	30-100
1980 Be Not Weary In Well Doing-E-3111	Retrd.	1985	14.00	80-125
1980 God's Speed-E-3112	Retrd.	1983	14.00	50-90
1980 Thou Art Mine-E-3113	Open		16.00	40-65
1980 The Lord Bless You and Keep You-E-3114	Suspd.		16.00	45-65
1980 But Love Goes on Forever-E-3115	Open		16.50	38-77
1980 Thee I Love-E-3116	Retrd.	1983	16.50	50-120
1980 Walking By Faith-E-3117	Open		35.00	70-125
1980 Eggs Over Easy-E-3118	Retrd.	1983	12.00	60-115
1980 It's What's Inside that Counts -E-3119	Suspd.		13.00	90-120
1980 To Thee With Love-E-3120	Suspd.		13.00	70-140
1981 The Lord Bless You and Keep You-E-4720	Suspd.		14.00	45-75
1981 The Lord Bless You and Keep You-E-4721	Open		14.00	33-80
1981 Love Cannot Break a True Friendship E-4722	Suspd.		22.50	100-170
1981 Peace Amid the Storm-E-4723	Suspd.		22.50	75-120
1981 Rejoicing with You-E-4724	Open		25.00	45-99
1981 Peace on Earth-E-4725	Suspd.		25.00	70-110
1981 Bear Ye One Another's Burdens-E-5200	Suspd.		20.00	70-105
1981 Love Lifted Me-E-5201	Suspd.		25.00	75-125
1981 Thank You for Coming to My Ade-E-5202	Suspd.		22.50	130-200
1981 Let Not the Sun Go Down Upon Your Wrath-E-5203	Suspd.		22.50	115-165
1981 To A Special Dad-E-5212	Open		20.00	35-79
1981 God is Love-E-5213	Suspd.		17.00	55-104
1981 Prayer Changes Things-E-5214	Suspd.		35.00	100-165
1984 May Your Christmas Be Blessed-E-5376	Suspd.		37.50	55-85
1984 Love is Kind-E-5377	Retrd.	1987	27.50	70-95
1984 Joy to the World-E-5378	Suspd.		18.00	40-50
1984 Isn't He Precious?-E-5379	Open		20.00	30-48
1984 A Monarch is Born-E-5380	Suspd.		33.00	60-75
1984 His Name is Jesus-E-5381	Suspd.		45.00	95-120
1984 For God So Loved the World-E-5382	Suspd.		70.00	115-130
1984 Wishing You a Merry Christmas-E-5383	Yr.Iss.		17.00	45
1984 I'll Play My Drum for Him-E-5384	Open		10.00	16-30
1984 Oh Worship the Lord (B)-E-5385	Suspd.		10.00	25-55
1984 Oh Worship the Lord (G)-E-5386	Suspd.		10.00	55-70
1981 Come Let Us Adore Him-E-5619	Suspd.		10.00	30-45
1981 Donkey Figurine-E-5621	Open		6.00	15-30
1981 They Followed the Star-E-5624	Open		130.00	200-270
1981 Wee Three Kings-E-5635	Open		40.00	75-125
1981 Rejoice O Earth-E-5636	Open		15.00	30-70
1981 The Heavenly Light-E-5637	Open		15.00	30-60
1981 Cow with Bell Figurine-E-5638	Open		16.00	30-50
1981 Isn't He Wonderful (B)-E-5639	Suspd.		12.00	50-75
1981 Isn't He Wonderful (G)-E-5640	Suspd.		12.00	45-75
1981 They Followed the Star-E-5641	Suspd.		75.00	175-230
1981 Nativity Wall (2 pc. set)-E-5644	Open		60.00	120-145
1984 God Sends the Gift of His Love-E-6613	Suspd.		22.50	70-150
1982 God is Love, Dear Valentine-E-7153	Suspd.		16.00	22-40
1982 God is Love, Dear Valentine-E-7154	Suspd.		16.00	22-40
1982 Thanking Him for You-E-7155	Suspd.		16.00	60
1982 I Believe in Miracles-E-7156	Suspd.		17.00	95-120
1987 I Believe in Miracles-E-7156R	Retrd.	1992	22.50	65-100
1982 There is Joy in Serving Jesus-E-7157	Retrd.	1986	17.00	45-85
1982 Love Beareth All Things-E-7158	Open		25.00	38-70
1982 Lord Give Me Patience-E-7159	Suspd.		25.00	40-85
1982 The Perfect Grandpa-E-7160	Suspd.		25.00	45-85
1982 His Sheep Am I-E-7161	Suspd.		25.00	55-85
1982 Love is Sharing-E-7162	Suspd.		25.00	135-175
1982 God is Watching Over You -E-7163	Suspd.		27.50	75-115
1982 Bless This House-E-7164	Suspd.		45.00	180-225
1982 Let the Whole World Know -E-7165	Suspd.		45.00	75-110
1997 And A Child Shall Lead Them-E-8287R	Open		50.00	50
1983 If God Be for Us, Who Can Be Against Us-E-9285	Suspd.		27.50	55-70
1983 Love is Patient-E-9251	Suspd.		35.00	60-100
1983 Forgiving is Forgetting-E-9252	Suspd.		37.50	60-100
1983 The End is in Sight-E-9253	Suspd.		25.00	40-85
1983 Praise the Lord Anyhow-E-9254	Retrd.	1994	35.00	75-90
1983 Bless You Two-E-9255	Open		21.00	40-50
1983 We are God's Workmanship -E-9258	Open		19.00	33-50
1983 We're In It Together-E-9259	Suspd.		24.00	60-90
1983 God's Promises are Sure-E-9260	Suspd.		30.00	55-90
1983 Seek Ye the Lord-E-9261	Suspd.		21.00	40-50
1983 Seek Ye the Lord-E-9262	Suspd.		21.00	50
1983 How Can Two Walk Together Except They Agree-E-9263	Suspd.		35.00	125-160
1963 Press On-E-9265	Open		40.00	55-100
1973 Animal Collection, Teddy Bear-E-9267A	Suspd.		6.50	21-30
1983 Animal Collection, Dog W/ Slippers-E-9267B	Suspd.		6.50	18-25
1983 Animal Collection, Bunny W/ Carrot-E-9267C	Suspd.		6.50	18-31
1983 Animal Collection, Kitty With Bow-E-9267D	Suspd.		6.50	18-22
1983 Animal Collection, Lamb With Bird-E-9267E	Suspd.		6.50	19-25
1983 Animal Collection, Pig W/ Patches-E-9267F	Suspd.		6.50	18-25
1983 Nobody's Perfect-E-9268	Retrd.	1990	21.00	55-90
1987 Let Love Reign-E-9273	Retrd.	1987	27.50	65-85
1983 Taste and See that the Lord is Good-E-9274	Retrd.	1986	22.50	40-75
1983 Jesus Loves Me-E-9278	Open		9.00	17-34
1983 Jesus Loves Me-E-9279	Open		9.00	17-32
1983 To Some Bunny Special -E-9282A	Suspd.		8.00	18-35
1983 You're Worth Your Weight In Gold-E-9282B	Suspd.		8.00	15-30
1983 Especially For Ewe-E-9282C	Suspd.		8.00	15-35
1983 Peace on Earth-E-9287	Suspd.		37.50	100-160
1983 Sending You a Rainbow-E-9288	Suspd.		22.50	70-95
1983 Trust in the Lord-E-9289	Suspd.		21.00	55-75
1985 Love Covers All-12009	Open		27.50	50-65
1985 Part of Me Wants to be Good -12149	Suspd.		19.00	40-80
1987 This Is The Day Which The Lord Has Made-12157	Suspd.		20.00	35-65
1985 Get into the Habit of Prayer-12203	Suspd.		19.00	35-45
1985 Miniature Clown-12238A	Suspd.		13.50	22-32
1985 Miniature Clown-12238B	Suspd.		13.50	19-32
1985 Miniature Clown-12238C	Suspd.		13.50	19-32
1985 Miniature Clown-12238D	Suspd.		13.50	19-32
1985 It is Better to Give than to Receive-12297	Suspd.		19.00	125-225
1985 Love Never Fails-12300	Open		25.00	35-57
1985 God Bless Our Home-12319	Open		40.00	55-65
1986 You Can Fly-12335	Open		25.00	55-80
1985 Jesus is Coming Soon-12343	Suspd.		22.50	35-70
1985 Halo, and Merry Christmas -12351	Open		40.00	175
1985 May Your Christmas Be Delightful-15482	Suspd.		25.00	35-52
1985 Honk if You Love Jesus-15490	Open		13.00	20-35
1985 Baby's First Christmas-15539	Yr.Iss.		13.00	25-40
1985 Baby's First Christmas-15547	Yr.Iss.		13.00	35-45
1985 God Sent His Love-15881	Yr.Iss.		17.00	25-60
1986 To My Favorite Paw-100021	Suspd.		22.50	45-65
1987 To My Deer Friend-100048	Open		33.00	50-92
1986 Sending My Love-100056	Suspd.		22.50	40-65
1986 O Worship the Lord-100064	Open		24.00	38-49
1986 To My Forever Friend-100072	Open		33.00	44-80
1987 He's The Healer Of Broken Hearts-100080	Open		33.00	55-90
1987 Make Me A Blessing-100102	Retrd.	1990	35.00	75-110
1986 Lord I'm Coming Home-100110	Open		22.50	33-55
1986 Lord, Keep Me On My Toes -100129	Retrd.	1988	22.50	75-100

YEAR ISSUE	EDITION LIMIT	YEAR RETRD.	ISSUE PRICE	*QUOTE U.S.$
1986 The Joy of the Lord is My Strength-100137	Open		35.00	50-89
1986 God Bless the Day We Found You-100145	Suspd.		37.50	85-125
1995 God Bless the Day We Found You(Girl)-100145R	Open		60.00	60
1986 God Bless the Day We Found You-100153	Suspd.		37.50	45-85
1995 God Bless the Day We Found You(Boy)-100153R	Open		60.00	60
1986 Serving the Lord-100161	Suspd.		19.00	45-65
1986 I'm a Possibility-100188	Retrd.	1993	21.00	35-75
1987 The Spirit Is Willing But The Flesh Is Weak-100196	Retrd.	1991	19.00	45-75
1987 The Lord Giveth & the Lord Taketh Away-100226	Retrd.	1995	33.50	50-70
1986 Friends Never Drift Apart-100250	Open		35.00	55-75
1986 Help, Lord, I'm In a Spot-100269	Retrd.	1989	18.50	55-65
1986 He Cleansed My Soul-100277	Open		24.00	38-60
1986 Serving the Lord-100293	Suspd.		19.00	35-55
1987 Scent From Above-100528	Retrd.	1991	19.00	50-75
1986 Brotherly Love-100544	Suspd.		37.00	65-90
1987 No Tears Past The Gate-101826	Open		40.00	70-85
1987 Smile Along The Way-101842	Retrd.	1991	30.00	135-165
1987 Lord, Help Us Keep Our Act Together-101850	Retrd.	1992	35.00	110-140
1986 O Worship the Lord-102229	Open		24.00	38-42
1986 Shepherd of Love-102261	Open		10.00	16-24
1986 Three Mini Animals-102296	Suspd.		13.50	19-30
1986 Wishing You a Cozy Christmas-102342	Yr.Iss.		17.00	30-45
1986 Love Rescued Me-102393	Open		21.00	38-40
1986 Angel of Mercy-102482	Open		19.00	19-40
1986 Sharing our Christmas Together-102490	Suspd.		35.00	55-75
1987 We Are All Precious In His Sight-102903	Yr.Iss.		30.00	70-110
1986 God Bless America-102938	Yr.Iss.		30.00	65-75
1986 It's the Birthday of a King-102962	Suspd.		18.50	35-50
1987 I Would Be Sunk Without You-102970	Open		15.00	20-30
1987 My Love Will Never Let You Go-103497	Open		25.00	38-45
1986 I Believe in the Old Rugged Cross-103632	Open		25.00	35-47
1986 Come Let Us Adore Him-104000 (9 pc. set w/cassette)	Open		95.00	130
1987 With this Ring I...-104019	Open		40.00	60-70
1987 Love Is The Glue That Mends-104027	Suspd.		33.50	40-70
1987 Cheers To The Leader-104035	Open		22.50	30-39
1987 Happy Days Are Here Again-104396	Suspd.		25.00	60-70
1987 A Tub Full of Love-104817	Open		22.50	30-42
1987 Sitting Pretty-104825	Suspd.		22.50	30-50
1987 Have I Got News For You-105635	Suspd.		22.50	30-55
1988 Something's Missing When You're Not Around-105643	Suspd.		32.50	45-75
1987 To Tell The Tooth You're Special-105813	Suspd.		38.50	85-150
1988 Hallelujah Country-105821	Open		35.00	45-65
1988 We're Pulling For You-106151	Suspd.		40.00	55-75
1987 God Bless You Graduate-106194	Open		20.00	33-35
1987 Congratulations Princess-106208	Open		20.00	33-35
1987 Lord Help Me Make the Grade-106216	Suspd.		25.00	35-55
1988 Heaven Bless Your Togetherness-106755	Open		65.00	80-87
1988 Precious Memories-106763	Open		37.50	50-55
1988 Puppy Love Is From Above-106798	Retrd.	1995	45.00	55-65
1988 Happy Birthday Poppy-106836	Suspd.		27.50	35-50
1988 Sew In Love-106844	Open		45.00	55-80
1987 They Followed The Star-108243	Open		75.00	120
1987 The Greatest Gift Is A Friend-109231	Open		30.00	38-55
1988 Believe the Impossible-109487	Suspd.		35.00	45-100
1988 Happiness Divine-109584	Retrd.	1992	25.00	40-75
1987 Wishing You A Happy Christmas-109754	Suspd.		35.00	50-70
1987 We Gather Together to Ask The Lord's Blessing-109762	Retrd.	1995	130.00	150-200
1988 Meowie Christmas-109800	Open		30.00	40-50
1987 Oh What Fun It Is To Ride-109819	Open		85.00	110-135
1988 Wishing You A Happy Easter-109886	Open		23.00	35
1988 Wishing You A Basket Full Of Blessings-109924	Open		23.00	30
1988 Sending You My Love-109967	Open		35.00	45-60
1988 Mommy, I Love You-109975	Open		22.50	30-34
1987 Love Is The Best Gift of All -110930	Yr.Iss.		22.50	35-45
1988 Faith Takes The Plunge-111155	Open		27.50	40-50
1988 Tis the Season-111163	Suspd.		27.50	40-50
1987 O Come Let Us Adore Him (4 pc. 9" Nativity)-111333	Suspd.		200.00	225-275
1988 Mommy, I Love You-112143	Open		22.50	30-36
1988 A Tub Full of Love-112313	Open		22.50	30-36
1988 This Too Shall Pass-114014	Open		23.00	28-37
1988 Some Bunny's Sleeping-115274	Open		15.00	20-30
1988 Our First Christmas Together-115290	Suspd.		50.00	60-80
1988 Time to Wish You a Merry Christmas-115339	Yr.Iss.		24.00	35-50
1995 Love Blooms Eternal-127019 (1st in dated cross series)	Yr.Iss.		35.00	35
1995 Dreams Really Do Come True -128309	Open		37.50	38
1995 Another Year More Grey Hares -128686	Open		17.50	18
1995 Happy Hula Days-128694	Open		30.00	30
1995 I Give You My Love Forever True-129100	Open		70.00	70
1995 He Hath Made Everything Beautiful in His Time-129151	Open		50.00	50
1997 Love Letters in The Sand -129488	Open		35.00	35
1995 He Covers the Earth With His Beauty-142654	Yr.Iss.		30.00	30
1995 Come Let Us Adore Him-142735 (large nativity)	Open		50.00	50
1995 Come Let Us Adore Him-142743 (small nativity)	Open		35.00	35
1995 Making A Trail to Bethlehem-142751	Open		30.00	30
1995 I'll Give Him My Heart-150088	Open		40.00	40
1995 Soot Yourself To A Merry Christmas-150096	Open		35.00	35
1995 Making Spirits Bright-150118	Open		37.50	38
1996 Standing In The Presence Of The Lord-163732 (2nd in dated cross series)	Yr.Iss.		37.50	38
1996 Take It To The Lord In Prayer-163767	Open		30.00	30
1996 The Sun Is Always Shining Somewhere-163775	Open		37.50	38
1996 Sewing Seeds of Kindness-163856 (1st in Growing In God's Garden Of Love Series)	Open		37.50	38
1996 Some Plant, Some Water, But God Giveth The Increase-176958 (2nd in Growing In God's Garden Of Love Series)	Open		37.50	38
1996 It May Be Greener, But It's Just As Hard to Cut-163899	Open		37.50	38
1996 Peace On Earth...Anyway -183342	Yr.Iss.		32.50	33
1996 Angels On Earth-Boy Making Snow Angel-183776	Open		40.00	40
1996 Snowbunny Loves You Like I Do-183792	Open		18.50	19
1996 Sing In Excelsis Deo Tree Topper-183830	Open		125.00	125
1996 Color Your World With Thanksgiving-183857	Open		50.00	50
1996 Shepard/Standing White Lamb/Sitting Black Lamb 3pc. Nativity set -183954	Open		40.00	40
1996 Making a Trail to Bethlehem-Mini Nativity-184004	Open		18.50	19
1996 All Sing His Praises-Large Nativity-184012	Open		32.50	33
1997 A Bouquet From God's Garden Of Love-184268 (3rd in God's Garden of Love series)	Open		37.50	38
1997 You're A Life Saver To Me-204854	Open		35.00	35
1996 Three Kings-Mini Nativity set-213624	Open		55.00	55
1997 Lead Me To Calvary-260916 (3rd in dated cross series)	Yr.Iss.		37.50	38
1997 Friends From The Very Beginning-261068	Open		50.00	50
1997 You Have Touched So Many Hearts-261084	Open		37.50	38
1997 Lettuce Pray-261122	Open		17.50	18
1997 Have You Any Room For Jesus-261130	Open		35.00	35
1997 Say I Do-261149	Open		35.00	35
1997 We All Have Our Bad Hair Days-261157	Open		35.00	35
1997 TBA-261564	Open		40.00	40
1988 Rejoice O Earth-520268	Open		13.00	17-27
1988 Jesus the Savior Is Born-520357	Suspd.		25.00	30-40
1992 The Lord Turned My Life Around-520535	Suspd.		35.00	40
1991 In The Spotlight Of His Grace-520543	Suspd.		35.00	50
1990 Lord, Turn My Life Around-520551	Suspd.		35.00	40-50
1992 You Deserve An Ovation-520578	Open		35.00	35
1989 My Heart Is Exposed With Love-520624	Open		45.00	55-60
1989 A Friend Is Someone Who Cares-520632	Retrd.	1995	30.00	55-70
1989 I'm So Glad You Fluttered Into My Life-520640	Retrd.	1991	40.00	250-400
1995 Wishing You A Happy Bear Hug-520659	Suspd.		27.50	30
1989 Eggspecially For You-520667	Open		45.00	50-60
1989 Your Love Is So Uplifting-520675	Open		60.00	65-79
1989 Sending You Showers Of Blessings-520683	Retrd.	1992	32.50	45
1989 Just A Line To Wish You A Happy Day-520721	Suspd.		65.00	80
1989 Friendship Hits The Spot-520748	Open		55.00	60-68
1989 Jesus Is The Only Way-520756	Suspd.		40.00	60-75
1989 Puppy Love-520764	Open		12.50	45-70
1989 Many Moons In Same Canoe, Blessum You-520772	Retrd.	1990	50.00	220-250
1989 Wishing You Roads Of Happiness-520780	Open		60.00	75
1989 Someday My Love-520799	Retrd.	1992	40.00	55-90
1989 My Days Are Blue Without You-520802	Suspd.		65.00	80-125
1989 We Need A Good Friend Through The Ruff Times-520810	Suspd.		35.00	40-60
1989 You Are My Number One -520829	Open		25.00	33-42
1989 The Lord Is Your Light To Happiness-520837	Open		50.00	65
1989 Wishing You A Perfect Choice -520845	Open		55.00	60-67
1989 I Belong To The Lord-520853	Suspd.		25.00	30-45
1990 Heaven Bless You-520934	Open		35.00	30-150
1993 There Is No Greater Treasure Than To Have A Friend Like You -521000	Open		30.00	30
1989 Hello World-521175	Open		15.00	17
1990 That's What Friends Are For -521183	Open		45.00	45-49
1997 Lord, Spare Me-521191	Open		50.00	50
1990 Hope You're Up And On The Trail Again-521205	Suspd.		35.00	35-55
1993 The Fruit of the Spirit is Love-521213	Yr.Iss.		30.00	33
1996 Enter His Court With Thanksgiving-521221	Open		35.00	35
1991 Take Heed When You Stand-521272	Suspd.		55.00	55-70
1990 Happy Trip-521280	Suspd.		35.00	35-60
1991 Hug One Another-521299	Retrd.	1995	45.00	50
1990 Yield Not To Temptation-521310	Suspd.		27.50	30-45
1990 Faith Is A Victory-521396	Retrd.	1993	25.00	120-175
1990 I'll Never Stop Loving You-521418	Open		37.50	38-53
1991 To A Very Special Mom & Dad-521434	Suspd.		35.00	35-45
1990 Lord, Help Me Stick To My Job-521450	Open		30.00	30-48
1989 Tell It To Jesus-521477	Open		35.00	38-60
1991 There's A Light At The End Of The Tunnel-521485	Suspd.		55.00	65
1991 A Special Delivery-521493	Open		30.00	30
1991 Thumb-body Loves You-521698	Suspd.		55.00	60
1996 My Love Blooms For You -521779	Open		50.00	50
1990 Sweep All Your Worries Away -521779	Open		40.00	40-110
1990 Good Friends Are Forever -521817	Open		50.00	55-62
1990 Love Is From Above-521841	Suspd.		45.00	45-59
1989 The Greatest of These Is Love -521866	Suspd.		27.50	35-60
1990 Easter's On Its Way-521892	Open		60.00	65-75
1994 Hoppy Easter Friend-521906	Open		40.00	40-43
1991 Perfect Harmony-521914	Open		55.00	55
1993 Safe In The Arms Of Jesus -521922	Open		30.00	30
1989 Wishing You A Cozy Season -521949	Suspd.		42.50	45-62
1990 High Hopes-521957	Suspd.		30.00	30-45
1991 To A Special Mum-521965	Open		30.00	30-33
1996 Marching To The Beat of Freedom's Drum-521981	Open		35.00	35
1993 To The Apple Of God's Eye-522015	Yr.Iss.		32.50	35
1979 May Your Life Be Blessed With Touchdowns-522023	Open		45.00	50-55
1989 Thank You Lord For Everything -522031	Suspd.		55.00	60-90
1994 Now I Lay Me Down To Sleep -522058	Open		30.00	33
1991 May Your World Be Trimmed With Joy-522082	Open		55.00	55-65
1990 There Shall Be Showers Of Blessings-522090	Open		60.00	70
1992 It's No Yolk When I Say I Love You-522104	Suspd.		60.00	65
1989 Don't Let the Holidays Get You Down-522112	Retrd.	1993	42.50	55-110
1989 Wishing You A Very Successful Season-522120	Open		60.00	65-70
1989 Bon Voyage!-522201	Suspd.		75.00	85-110
1989 He Is The Star Of The Morning -522252	Suspd.		55.00	60-75
1989 To Be With You Is Uplifting -522260	Retrd.	1994	20.00	20-30
1991 A Reflection Of His Love-522279	Open		50.00	50
1990 Thinking Of You Is What I Really Like To Do-522287	Suspd.		30.00	30-42
1989 Merry Christmas Deer-522317	Open		50.00	55-80
1996 Sweeter As The Years Go By-522333	Open		60.00	60
1995 Just A Line To Say You're Special-522864	Open		50.00	50
1997 On My Way To A Perfect Day -522872	Open		45.00	30-45
1989 Isn't He Precious-522988	Suspd.		15.00	20-45
1990 Some Bunny's Sleeping-522996	Suspd.		12.00	12-28
1989 Jesus Is The Sweetest Name I Know-523097	Suspd.		22.50	25-36
1991 Joy On Arrival-523178	Open		50.00	50-60
1990 The Good Lord Always Delivers-523453	Open		27.50	28-35
1990 This Day Has Been Made In Heaven-523496	Open		30.00	33-45
1990 God Is Love Dear Valentine -523518	Open		27.50	28-45
1991 I Will Cherish The Old Rugged Cross-523534	Yr.Iss.		27.50	30
1992 You Are The Type I Love-523542	Open		40.00	40
1993 The Lord Will Provide-523593	Yr.Iss.		40.00	40-55
1991 Good News Is So Uplifting-523615	Open		60.00	65
1992 I'm So Glad That God Has Blessed Me With A Friend Like You -523623	Retrd.	1995	50.00	65-75
1994 I Will Always Be Thinking Of You-523631	Open		45.00	45
1990 Time Heals-523739	Open		37.50	38

*Quotes have been rounded up to nearest dollar

YEAR ISSUE		EDITION LIMIT	YEAR RETRD.	ISSUE PRICE	*QUOTE U.S.$
1990	Blessings From Above-523747	Retrd.	1994	45.00	50-80
1994	Just Poppin' In To Say Halo-523755	Open		45.00	45
1991	I Can't Spell Success Without You-523763	Suspd.		40.00	45-60
1990	Once Upon A Holy Night-523836	Yr.Iss.		25.00	30-45
1996	Love Never Leaves A Mother's Arms-523941	Open		40.00	40
1992	My Warmest Thoughts Are You-524085	Open		55.00	60
1991	Good Friends Are For Always-524123	Open		27.50	33
1994	Lord Teach Us to Pray-524158	Yr.Iss.		35.00	35-40
1991	May Your Christmas Be Merry-524166	Yr.Iss.		27.50	35
1995	Walk In The Sonshine-524212	Open		35.00	35
1991	He Loves Me-524263	Yr.Iss.		35.00	35-50
1992	Friendship Grows When You Plant A Seed-524271	Retrd.	1994	40.00	80-115
1993	May Your Every Wish Come True-524298	Open		50.00	50-60
1991	May Your Birthday Be A Blessing-524301	Open		30.00	33-48
1992	What The World Needs Now -524352	Open		50.00	50
1997	Something Precious From Above-524360	Open		50.00	50
1991	May You Have Good Things Come Your Way-524425	Open		30.00	38
1993	Sealed With A Kiss-524441	Open		50.00	55
1993	A Special Chime For Jesus -524468	Yr.Iss.		32.50	33
1994	God Cared Enough To Send His Best-524476	Open		50.00	50
1990	Happy Birthday Dear Jesus -524875	Suspd.		13.50	14-27
1992	It's So Uplifting To Have A Friend Like You-524905	Open		40.00	45
1990	We're Going To Miss You -524913	Open		50.00	50-65
1991	Angels We Have Heard On High -524921	Open		60.00	60
1992	Tubby's First Christmas-525278	Open		10.00	10
1991	It's A Perfect Boy-525286	Open		16.50	17
1993	May Your Future Be Blessed -525316	Open		35.00	38
1992	Ring Those Christmas Bells-525898	Open		95.00	100
1992	Going Home-525979	Open		60.00	60-70
1996	A Prince Of A Guy-526038	Open		35.00	35
1996	Pretty As A Princess-526053	Open		35.00	35
1992	I Would Be Lost Without You-526142	Open		27.50	28
1994	Friends 'Til The Very End -526150	Open		40.00	40
1992	You Are My Happiness-526185	Yr.Iss.		37.50	45-80
1994	You Suit Me to a Tee-526193	Open		35.00	35
1994	Sharing Sweet Moments Together-526487	Open		45.00	45
1991	How Could I Ever Forget You -526924	Open		15.00	17
1996	The Lord Is With You-526835	Open		27.50	28
1991	We Have Come From Afar-526959	Suspd.		17.50	20
1993	Bless-Um You-527335	Open		35.00	35
1992	You Are My Favorite Star-527378	Open		55.00	55
1992	Bring The Little Ones To Jesus-527556	Open		90.00	90-110
1992	God Bless The U.S.A.-527564	Yr.Iss.		32.50	35-45
1993	Tied Up For The Holidays-527580	Yr.Iss.		40.00	40
1993	Bringing You A Merry Christmas-527599	Retrd.	1995	45.00	45-80
1992	Wishing You A Ho Ho Ho -527629	Open		40.00	40
1992	But The Greatest of These Is Love-527688	Yr.Iss.		27.50	35
1992	Wishing You A Comfy Christmas-527750	Open		30.00	30
1993	I Only Have Arms For You -527769	Open		15.00	16
1992	This Land Is Our Land-527777	Yr.Iss.		35.00	35-45
1994	Nativity Cart-528072	Open		16.00	16
1994	Have I Got News For You-528137	Open		16.00	17
1994	To a Very Special Sister-528633	Open		60.00	60
1993	America You're Beautiful-528862	Yr.Iss.		35.00	35
1996	My True Love Gave To Me -529273	Open		40.00	40
1993	Ring Out The Good News -529966	Yr.Iss.		27.50	30
1993	Wishing You the Sweetest Christmas-530166	Yr.Iss.		27.50	40
1994	You're As Pretty As A Christmas Tree-530425	Yr.Iss.		27.50	28
1994	Serenity Prayer Girl-530697	Open		35.00	35
1994	Serenity Prayer Boy-530700	Open		35.00	35
1995	We Have Come From Afar -530913	Open		12.00	12
1995	I Only Have Ice For You-530956	Open		27.50	28
1997	Sometimes You're Next To Impossible-530964	Open		50.00	50
1997	Potty Time-531022	Open		25.00	25
1996	I Haven't Seen Much of You Lately-531057	Open		13.50	14
1995	What The World Needs Is Love -531065	Open		45.00	45
1994	Money Isn't The Only Green Thing Worth Saving-531073	Open		50.00	50
1996	What A Difference You've Made In My Life-531138	Open		50.00	50
1995	Vaya Con Dios (To Go With God)-531146	Open		32.50	33-55
1995	Bless Your Sole-531162	Open		25.00	25
1997	Who's Gonna Fill You're Shoes-531634	Open		37.50	38
1996	You Deserve a Halo—Thank You-531693	Open		55.00	55
1994	The Lord is Counting on You -531707	Open		32.50	33
1994	Dropping In For The Holidays-531952	Open		40.00	40
1995	Hallelujah For The Cross-532002	Open		35.00	35
1995	Sending You Oceans Of Love -532010	Open		35.00	35
1995	I Can't Bear To Let You Go -532037	Open		50.00	50
1995	Lord Help Me To Stay On Course-532096	Open		35.00	35
1994	The Lord Bless You and Keep You-532118	Open		40.00	45
1994	The Lord Bless You and Keep You-532126	Open		30.00	33
1994	The Lord Bless You and Keep You-532134	Open		30.00	33
1994	Luke 2:10-11-532916	Open		35.00	35
1994	Nothing Can Dampen The Spirit of Caring-603864	Open		35.00	35
1995	A Poppy For You-604208	Open		35.00	35

Precious Moments Anniversary Figurines - S. Butcher

YEAR ISSUE		EDITION LIMIT	YEAR RETRD.	ISSUE PRICE	*QUOTE U.S.$
1984	God Blessed Our Years Together With So Much Love And Happiness-E-2853	Open		35.00	50-60
1984	God Blessed Our Year Together With So Much Love And Happiness (1st)-E-2854	Open		35.00	50-60
1984	God Blessed Our Years Together With So Much Love And Happiness (5th)-E-2855	Suspd.		35.00	50-55
1984	God Blessed Our Years Together With So Much Love And Happiness (10th)-E-2856	Suspd.		35.00	50-55
1984	God Blessed Our Years Together With So Much Love And Happiness (25th)-E-2857	Open		35.00	50-65
1984	God Blessed Our Years Together With So Much Love And Happiness (40th)-E-2859	Open		35.00	50-65
1984	God Blessed Our Years Together With So Much Love And Happiness (50th)-E-2860	Open		35.00	50-65
1994	I Still Do-530999	Open		30.00	30
1994	I Still Do-531006	Open		30.00	30

Precious Moments Baby's First - S. Butcher

YEAR ISSUE		EDITION LIMIT	YEAR RETRD.	ISSUE PRICE	*QUOTE U.S.$
1984	Baby's First Step-E-2840	Suspd.		35.00	70-100
1984	Baby's First Picture-E-2841	Retrd.	1986	45.00	120-200
1985	Baby's First Haircut-12211	Suspd.		32.50	100-175
1986	Baby's First Trip-16012	Suspd.		32.50	150-275
1989	Baby's First Pet-520705	Suspd.		45.00	50-85
1990	Baby's First Meal-524077	Open		35.00	35-45
1990	Baby's First Word-527238	Open		24.00	24-28
1993	Baby's First Birthday-524069	Open		25.00	25

Precious Moments Birthday Club Figurines - S. Butcher

YEAR ISSUE		EDITION LIMIT	YEAR RETRD.	ISSUE PRICE	*QUOTE U.S.$
1986	Fishing For Friends-BC-861	Yr.Iss.		10.00	140-160
1987	Hi Sugar-BC-871	Yr.Iss.		11.00	90-110
1988	Somebunny Cares-BC-881	Yr.Iss.		13.50	50-75
1989	Can't Bee Hive Myself Without You-BC-891	Yr.Iss.		13.50	40-65
1990	Collecting Makes Good Scents -BC-901	Yr.Iss.		15.00	35-55
1990	I'm Nuts Over My Collection-BC-902	Yr.Iss.		15.00	40
1991	Love Pacifies-BC-911	Yr.Iss.		15.00	30-40
1991	True Blue Friends-BC-912	Yr.Iss.		15.00	29-40
1992	Every Man's House Is His Castle-BC-921	Yr.Iss.		16.50	35-45
1993	I Got You Under My Skin -BC-922	Yr.Iss.		16.00	35
1994	Put a Little Punch In Your Birthday-BC-931	Yr.Iss.		15.00	25
1994	Owl Always Be Your Friend -BC-932	Yr.Iss.		16.00	25
1994	God Bless Our Home-BC-941	Yr.Iss.		16.00	20-35
1995	Yer A Pel-I-Can Count On-BC-942	Yr.Iss.		16.00	20
1996	There's A Spot In My Heart For You-BC-951	Yr.Iss.		15.00	15

Precious Moments Birthday Club Inscribed Charter Membership Renewal Gift - S. Butcher

YEAR ISSUE		EDITION LIMIT	YEAR RETRD.	ISSUE PRICE	*QUOTE U.S.$
1987	A Smile's the Cymbal of Joy -B-0102	Yr.Iss.		Unkn.	55-80

Precious Moments Birthday Club Inscribed Charter Membership Renewal Gift - S. Butcher

YEAR ISSUE		EDITION LIMIT	YEAR RETRD.	ISSUE PRICE	*QUOTE U.S.$
1988	The Sweetest Club Around -B-0103	Yr.Iss.		Unkn.	50-70
1989	Have A Beary Special Birthday -B-0104	Yr.Iss.		Unkn.	30-60
1990	Our Club Is A Tough Act To Follow-B-0105	Yr.Iss.		Unkn.	30-50
1991	Jest To Let You Know You're Tops-B-0106	Yr.Iss.		Unkn.	45-60
1992	All Aboard For Birthday Club Fun-B-0107	Yr.Iss.		Unkn.	30-50
1994	Happiness Is Belonging-B-0108	Yr.Iss.		Unkn.	20-35
1994	Can't Get Enough of Our Club -B-0109	Yr.Iss.		Unkn.	25

YEAR ISSUE		EDITION LIMIT	YEAR RETRD.	ISSUE PRICE	*QUOTE U.S.$
1995	Hoppy Birthday-B-0110	Yr.Iss.		Unkn.	Unkn.
1996	Scootin' By Just To Say Hi! -B-0111	Yr.Iss.		Unkn.	Unkn.

Precious Moments Birthday Club Welcome Gift - S. Butcher

YEAR ISSUE		EDITION LIMIT	YEAR RETRD.	ISSUE PRICE	*QUOTE U.S.$
1986	Our Club Can't Be Beat-B-0001	Yr.Iss.		Unkn.	70-85
1987	A Smile's The Cymbal of Joy -B-0002	Yr.Iss.		Unkn.	55-70
1988	The Sweetest Club Around -B-0003	Yr.Iss.		Unkn.	45
1989	Have A Beary Special Birthday -B-0004	Yr.Iss.		Unkn.	30-40
1990	Our Club Is A Tough Act To Follow-B-0005	Yr.Iss.		Unkn.	25-35
1991	Jest To Let You Know You're Tops-B-0006	Yr.Iss.		Unkn.	40-55
1992	All Aboard For Birthday Club Fun-B-0007	Yr.Iss.		Unkn.	30-40
1994	Happiness Is Belonging-B-0008	Yr.Iss.		Unkn.	20-30
1994	Can't Get Enough of Our Club-B-0009	Yr.Iss.		Unkn.	25
1995	Hoppy Birthday-B-0010	Yr.Iss.		Unkn.	Unkn.
1996	Scootin' By Just To Say Hi! -B-0011	Yr.Iss.		Unkn.	Unkn.

Precious Moments Birthday Series - S. Butcher

YEAR ISSUE		EDITION LIMIT	YEAR RETRD.	ISSUE PRICE	*QUOTE U.S.$
1988	Friends To The End-104418	Suspd.		15.00	20-30
1987	Showers Of Blessings-105945	Retrd.	1993	16.00	30-50
1988	Brighten Someone's Day-105953	Suspd.		12.50	20-30
1990	To My Favorite Fan-521043	Suspd.		16.00	25-40
1989	Hello World!-521175	Open		13.50	15-30
1993	Hope You're Over The Hump-521671	Suspd.		16.00	16
1990	Not A Creature Was Stirring -524484	Suspd.		17.00	20-30
1991	Can't Be Without You-524492	Open		16.00	17-29
1991	How Can I Ever Forget You -526924	Open		15.00	15
1992	Let's Be Friends-527270	Open		15.00	15-20
1992	Happy Birdie-527343	Suspd.		8.00	17
1993	Happy Birthday Jesus-530492	Open		20.00	20
1994	Oinky Birthday-524506	Open		13.50	14
1995	Wishing You A Happy Bear Hug-520659	Suspd.		27.50	28
1996	I Haven't Seen Much of You Lately 531057	Open		13.50	14
1997	From The First Time I Spotted You I Knew We'd Be Friends-260940	Open		18.50	19

Precious Moments Birthday Train Figurines - S. Butcher

YEAR ISSUE		EDITION LIMIT	YEAR RETRD.	ISSUE PRICE	*QUOTE U.S.$
1988	Isn't Eight Just Great-109460	Open		18.50	23
1988	Wishing You Grr-eatness -109479	Open		18.50	23-38
1986	May Your Birthday Be Warm -15938	Open		10.00	16-35
1986	Happy Birthday Little Lamb -15946	Open		10.00	15-39
1986	Heaven Bless Your Special Day -15954	Open		11.00	18-23
1986	God Bless You On Your Birthday-15962	Open		11.00	18-37
1986	May Your Birthday Be Gigantic -15970	Open		12.50	20-38
1986	This Day Is Something To Roar About-15989	Open		13.50	23-40
1986	Keep Looking Up-15997	Open		13.50	23-35
1986	Bless The Days Of Our Youth -16004	Open		15.00	23-38
1992	May Your Birthday Be Mammoth-521825	Open		25.00	25-40
1992	Being Nine Is Just Divine-521833	Open		25.00	25-40

Precious Moments Bless Those Who Serve Their Country - S. Butcher

YEAR ISSUE		EDITION LIMIT	YEAR RETRD.	ISSUE PRICE	*QUOTE U.S.$
1991	Bless Those Who Serve Their Country (Navy) 526568	Suspd.		32.50	80-135
1991	Bless Those Who Serve Their Country (Army) 526576	Suspd.		32.50	40-60
1991	Bless Those Who Serve Their Country (Air Force) 526584	Suspd.		32.50	40-60
1991	Bless Those Who Serve Their Country (Girl Soldier) 527289	Suspd.		32.50	45
1991	Bless Those Who Serve Their Country (Soldier) 527297	Suspd.		32.50	40-65
1991	Bless Those Who Serve Their Country (Marine) 527521	Suspd.		32.50	50-60
1995	You Will Always Be Our Hero 136271	Yr.Iss.		40.00	40

Precious Moments Bridal Party - S. Butcher

YEAR ISSUE		EDITION LIMIT	YEAR RETRD.	ISSUE PRICE	*QUOTE U.S.$
1984	Bridesmaid-E-2831	Open		13.50	22-30
1985	Ringbearer-E-2833	Open		11.00	17-30
1985	Flower Girl-E-2835	Open		11.00	17-25
1984	Groomsman-E-2836	Open		13.50	22-30
1986	Groom-E-2837	Open		13.50	20-40
1987	This is the Day That the Lord Hath Made-E-2838	Open		185.00	185
1985	Junior Bridesmaid-E-2845	Open		12.50	20-30
1987	Bride-E-2846	Open		18.00	25-30
1987	God Bless Our Family (Parents of the Groom)-100498	Open		35.00	50-55
1987	God Bless Our Family (Parents of the Bride)-100501	Open		35.00	50-60
1987	Wedding Arch-102369	Suspd.		22.50	40-45

Precious Moments Calendar Girl - S. Butcher

YEAR ISSUE		EDITION LIMIT	YEAR RETRD.	ISSUE PRICE	*QUOTE U.S.$
1988	January-109983	Open		37.50	40-67

Collectors' Information Bureau *Quotes have been rounded up to nearest dollar

YEAR ISSUE		EDITION LIMIT	YEAR RETD.	ISSUE PRICE	*QUOTE U.S. $
1988	February-109991	Open		27.50	38-67
1988	March-110019	Open		27.50	38-50
1988	April-110027	Open		30.00	38-100
1988	May-110035	Open		25.00	30-225
1988	June-110043	Open		40.00	50-112
1988	July-110051	Open		35.00	45-58
1988	August-110078	Open		40.00	45-58
1988	September-110086	Open		27.50	38-50
1988	October-110094	Open		35.00	45-59
1988	November-110108	Open		32.50	38-50
1988	December-110116	Open		27.50	35-75

Precious Moments Clown - S. Butcher

XX	I Get a Bang Out of You-12262	Open		30.00	45-55
1986	Lord Keep Me On the Ball-12270	Open		30.00	45-65
1986	Waddle I Do Without You-12459	Retrd.	1989	30.00	80-100
1986	The Lord Will Carry You Through-12467	Retrd.	1988	30.00	75-115

Precious Moments Commemorative 500th Columbus Anniversary - S. Butcher

1992	This Land Is Our Land-527386	Yr.Iss.		350.00	350-425

Precious Moments Commemorative Easter Seal - S. Butcher

1988	Jesus Loves Me-9" Fig.-104531	1,000		N/A	1800-2000
1987	He Walks With Me-107999	Yr.Iss.		25.00	35-75
1988	Blessed Are They That Overcome-115479	Yr.Iss.		27.50	30-60
1989	Make A Joyful Noise-9" Fig.-520322	1,500		N/A	900-950
1989	His Love Will Shine On You-522376	Yr.Iss.		30.00	50-65
1990	You Have Touched So Many Hearts-9" fig.-523283	2,000		N/A	600-775
1991	We Are God's Workmanship-9" fig.-523879	2,000		N/A	650-725
1990	Always In His Care-524522	Yr.Iss.		30.00	40-55
1992	You Are Such A Purr-fect Friend 9" fig.-526010	2,000		N/A	600-700
1991	Sharing A Gift Of Love-527114	Yr.Iss.		30.00	40-65
1992	A Universal Love-527173	Yr.Iss.		32.50	40-60
1993	Gather Your Dreams-9" fig.-529680	2,000		N/A	600
1993	You're My Number One Friend-530026	Yr.Iss.		30.00	40
1994	It's No Secret What God Can Do-531111	Yr.Iss.		30.00	35
1994	You Are The Rose of His Creation-9" fig.-531243	2,000		N/A	N/A
1995	Take Time To Smell the Flowers-524387	Yr.Iss.		30.00	30
1995	He's Got The Whole World In His Hands-9" fig.-526886	Yr.Iss.		N/A	N/A
1996	He Loves Me 9" fig.-152277	2,000		N/A	N/A
1996	You Can Always Count on Me-526827	Yr.Iss.		30.00	30

Precious Moments Events Figurines - S. Butcher

1988	You Are My Main Event-115231	Yr.Iss.		30.00	40-70
1989	Sharing Begins In The Heart-520861	Yr.Iss.		25.00	50-75
1990	I'm A Precious Moments Fan-523526	Yr.Iss.		25.00	40-50
1990	Good Friends Are Forever-525049	Yr.Iss.		25.00	N/A
1991	You Can Always Bring A Friend-527122	Yr.Iss.		27.50	35-50
1992	An Event Worth Wading For-527319	Yr.Iss.		32.50	35-45
1993	An Event For All Seasons-530158	Yr.Iss.		30.00	30-45
1994	Memories Are Made of This-529982	Yr.Iss.		30.00	30-40
1995	Follow Your Heart-528080	Yr.Iss.		30.00	30
1996	Hallelujah Hoedown-163864	Yr.Iss.		32.50	33

Precious Moments Family Christmas Scene - S. Butcher

1985	May You Have the Sweetest Christmas-15776	Suspd.		17.00	25-45
1985	The Story of God's Love-15784	Suspd.		22.50	35-60
1985	Tell Me a Story-15792	Suspd.		10.00	20-30
1985	God Gave His Best-15806	Suspd.		13.00	30-45
1985	Silent Night-15814	Suspd.		37.50	75-120
1986	Sharing Our Christmas Together-102490	Suspd.		40.00	55-75
1989	Have A Beary Merry Christmas-522856	Suspd.		15.00	20-40
1990	Christmas Fireplace-524883	Suspd.		37.50	40-70

Precious Moments Four Seasons - S. Butcher

1985	The Voice of Spring-12068	Yr.Iss.		30.00	225-295
1985	Summer's Joy-12076	Yr.Iss.		30.00	100
1986	Autumn's Praise-12084	Yr.Iss.		30.00	85
1986	Winter's Song-12092	Yr.Iss.		30.00	100-115
1986	Set			120.00	550

Precious Moments Growing In Grace - S. Butcher

1995	Infant Angel With Newspaper -136204	Open		22.50	23
1995	Age 1 Baby With Cake-136190	Open		25.00	25
1995	Age 2 Girl With Blocks-136212	Open		25.00	25
1995	Age 3 Girl With Flowers-136220	Open		25.00	25
1995	Age 4 Girl With Doll-136239	Open		27.50	28
1995	Age 5 Girl With Lunch Box-136247	Open		27.50	28
1995	Age 6 Girl On Bicycle-136255	Open		30.00	30
1996	Age 7 Girl Dressed As Nurse -163740	Open		32.50	33

YEAR ISSUE		EDITION LIMIT	YEAR RETD.	ISSUE PRICE	*QUOTE U.S. $
1996	Age 8 Girl Shooting Marbles -163759	Open		32.50	33
1995	Age 16 Sweet Sixteen Girl Holding Sixteen Roses-136263	Open		45.00	45
1996	Age 9 Girl With Charm Bracelet-183865	Open		30.00	30
1996	Age 10 Girl Bowling-183873	Open		37.50	38
1997	Age 11 Girl With Ice Cream Cone-260924	Open		37.50	38
1997	Age 12 Girl/Puppy Holding Clock-260932	Open		37.50	38

Precious Moments Musical Figurines - S. Butcher

1983	Sharing Our Season Together-E-0519	Retrd.	1986	70.00	120-145
1983	Wee Three Kings-E-0520	Suspd.		60.00	110-125
1983	Let Heaven And Nature Sing-E-2346	Suspd.		55.00	115-130
1982	O Come All Ye Faithful-E-2352	Suspd.		50.00	140-200
1982	I'll Play My Drum For Him-E-2355	Suspd.		45.00	175-225
1979	Christmas Is A Time To Share-E-2806	Retrd.	1984	35.00	140-170
1979	Crown Him Lord Of All-E-2807	Suspd.		35.00	93-110
1979	Unto Us A Child Is Born-E-2808	Suspd.		35.00	95-125
1980	Jesus Is Born-E-2809	Suspd.		35.00	105-125
1980	Come Let Us Adore Him-E-2810	Suspd.		45.00	100-120
1980	Peace On Earth-E-4726	Suspd.		45.00	122-132
1980	The Hand That Rocks The Future-E-5204	Open		30.00	55-85
1980	My Guardian Angel-E-5205	Suspd.		22.50	70-100
1981	My Guardian Angel-E-5206	Suspd.		22.50	65-95
1984	Wishing You A Merry Christmas-E-5394	Suspd.		55.00	80-120
1980	Silent Knight-E-5642	Suspd.		45.00	250-300
1981	Rejoice O Earth-E-5645	Retrd.	1988	35.00	60-120
1981	The Lord Bless You And Keep You-E-7180	Open		55.00	80-100
1981	Mother Sew Dear-E-7182	Open		35.00	55-95
1981	The Purr-fect Grandma-E-7184	Suspd.		35.00	60-80
1981	Love Is Sharing-E-7185	Retrd.	1985	40.00	120-170
1981	Let the Whole World Know-E-7186	Suspd.		60.00	125-190
1985	Lord Keep My Life In Tune (G) (2/set)-12165	Suspd.		50.00	80-125
1984	We Saw A Star-12408	Suspd.		50.00	70-115
1987	Lord Keep My Life In Tune (B) (2/set)-12580	Suspd.		50.00	200-300
1985	God Sent You Just In Time-15504	Retrd.	1989	60.00	85-120
1993	Silent Night-15814	Open		55.00	55-89
1985	Heaven Bless You-100285	Suspd.		45.00	60-75
1986	Our 1st Christmas Together-101702	Retrd.	1992	50.00	70-110
1993	Let's Keep In Touch-102520	Open		85.00	85-115
1993	Peace On Earth-109746	Suspd.		120.00	130
1987	I'm Sending You A White Christmas-112402	Retrd.	1993	55.00	75-110
1987	You Have Touched So Many Hearts-112577	Suspd.		50.00	50-60
1991	Lord Keep My Life In Balance-520691	Suspd.		60.00	65-75
1993	The Light Of The World Is Jesus-521507	Open		65.00	65-87
1992	Do Not Open Till Christmas-522244	Suspd.		75.00	85-110
1992	This Day Has Been Made In Heaven-523682	Open		60.00	60
1993	Wishing You Were Here-526916	Open		100.00	100

Precious Moments Rejoice in the Lord - S. Butcher

1987	Lord Keep My Life In Tune -12165	Suspd.		37.50	80-110
1985	There's a Song in My Heart -12173	Suspd.		11.00	25-45
1985	Happiness is the Lord-12378	Suspd.		15.00	25-40
1985	Lord Give Me a Song-12386	Suspd.		15.00	23-40
1985	He is My Song-12394	Suspd.		17.50	30-40

Precious Moments Sammy's Circus - S. Butcher

1994	Markie-528099	Suspd.		18.50	19
1994	Dusty-529176	Suspd.		22.50	23
1994	Katie-529184	Suspd.		17.00	17
1994	Tippy-529192	Suspd.		12.00	12
1994	Collin-529214	Suspd.		20.00	20
1994	Sammy-529222	Yr.Iss.		20.00	45
1994	Circus Tent-528196 (Nite-Lite)	Suspd.		90.00	90
1994	Jordan-529168	Suspd.		20.00	20
1996	Jennifer-163708	Suspd.		20.00	20

Precious Moments Spring Catalog - S. Butcher

1993	Happiness Is At Our Fingertips -529931	Yr.Iss.	1993	35.00	45-80
1994	So Glad I Picked You As A Friend-524379	Yr.Iss.	1994	40.00	40
1995	Sending My Love Your Way -528609	Yr.Iss.		40.00	40
1996	Have I Toad You Lately That I Love You-521329	Yr.Iss.		30.00	30

Precious Moments Sugartown - S. Butcher

1992	Chapel-529621	Retrd.	1994	85.00	85-125
1992	Christmas Tree-528684	Retrd.	1994	15.00	15-25
1992	Grandfather-529516	Retrd.	1994	15.00	20
1992	Nativity-529508	Retrd.	1994	20.00	25
1992	Philip-529494	Retrd.	1994	17.00	35
1992	Aunt Ruth & Aunt Dorothy-529486	Retrd.	1994	20.00	20
1992	Sam Butcher-529567 (1st sign)	Yr.Iss.		22.50	125-225

YEAR ISSUE		EDITION LIMIT	YEAR RETD.	ISSUE PRICE	*QUOTE U.S. $
1993	7 pc. Sam's House Collector's Set-531774	Open		189.00	189
1993	Sam's House Night-Light-529605	Open		80.00	85
1993	Fence-529796	Open		10.00	10
1993	Sammy-528668	Open		17.00	17
1993	Katy Lynne-529524	Open		20.00	20
1993	Sam Butcher-529842 (2nd sign)	Yr.Iss.		22.50	55
1993	Dusty-529435	Open		17.00	17
1993	Sam's Car-529443	Open		22.50	23
1993	Sugar Town Chapel-530484	Yr.Iss.		17.50	18
1994	Dr. Sam Sugar-530850	Open		17.00	17
1994	Doctor's Office Night Light -529869	Open		80.00	85
1994	Sam's House-530468	Yr.Iss.		17.50	18
1994	Jan-529826	Open		17.00	17
1994	Sugar & Her Dog House-533165	Open		20.00	20
1994	Stork With Baby Sam-529788	Yr.Iss.		22.50	25-50
1994	Free Christmas Puppies-528064	Open		18.50	19
1994	7 pc. Doctor's Office Collectors Set-529781	Yr.Iss.		189.00	190-225
1994	Leon & Evelyn Mae-529818	Open		20.00	20
1994	Village Town Hall Clock-532908	Open		80.00	85
1995	Sam the Conductor-150169	Yr.Iss.		20.00	20
1995	Train Station Night Light -150150	Open		50.00	50
1995	Railroad Crossing Sign -150177	Open		12.00	12
1995	Tammy and Debbie -531812	Open		22.50	23
1995	Donny -531871	Open		22.50	23
1995	Luggage Cart With Kitten And Tag -150185	Open		13.00	13
1995	6 pc. Train Station Collector Set-150193	Yr.Iss.		190.00	190
1996	Sugar Town Skating Sign-184020	Yr.Iss.		15.00	15
1996	Skating Pond-184047	Open		40.00	40
1996	Mazie-184055	Open		18.50	19
1996	Cocoa-184063	Open		7.50	8
1996	Leroy-184071	Open		18.50	19
1996	Hank and Sharon-184098	Open		25.00	25
1996	Lighted Warming Hut-192341	Open		60.00	60

Precious Moments Sugartown Enhancements - S. Butcher

1994	Lamp Post-529559	Open		8.00	8
1994	Mailbox-531847	Open		5.00	5
1994	Single Tree-533173	Open		10.00	10
1994	Cobble Stone Bridge-533203	Open		17.00	17
1994	Straight Sidewalk-533157	Open		10.00	10
1994	Double Tree-533181	Open		10.00	10
1994	Curved Sidewalk-533149	Open		10.00	10
1995	Street Sign-532185	Open		5.00	5
1995	Dog And Kitten On Park Bench -529540	Open		13.00	13
1995	Bus Stop-150207	Open		8.50	9
1995	Bird Bath-150223	Open		8.50	9
1995	Fire Hydrant-150215	Open		5.00	5
1995	Sugartown Enhancement Pack, set/5-152269	Open		45.00	45
1996	Flag Pole w/Kitten-184136	Open		15.00	15
1996	Tree Night Light-184039	Open		45.00	45
1996	Wooden Barrel Hot Cocoa Stand-184144	Open		15.00	15
1996	Bonfire with Bunnies-184152	Open		10.00	10

Precious Moments To Have And To Hold - S. Butcher

1996	Love Vows To Always Bloom-1st Anniversary Couple With Flowers-129097	Open		70.00	70
1996	A Year Of Blessings-1st Anniversary Couple With Cake-163783	Open		70.00	70
1996	Each Hour Is Precious With You-5th Anniversary Couple With Clock-163791	Open		70.00	70
1996	Ten Years Heart To Heart-10th Anniversary Couple With Pillow-163805	Open		70.00	70
1996	A Silver Anniversary To Share-25th Anniversary Couple With Silver Platter-163813	Open		70.00	70
1996	Forty Years Of Precious Moments-40th Anniversary Couple With Photo Album-163281	Open		70.00	70
1996	Fifty Years As Precious As Gold-50th Anniversary Couple With Gift Box-163848	Open		70.00	70

Precious Moments Two By Two - S. Butcher

1993	Noah, Noah's Wife, & Noah's Ark (lighted)-530042	Open		125.00	125-195
1993	Sheep (mini double fig.) -530077	Open		10.00	10
1993	Pigs (mini double fig.) -530085	Open		12.00	12
1993	Giraffes (mini double fig.) -530115	Open		16.00	16
1993	Bunnies (mini double fig.) -530123	Open		9.00	9
1993	Elephants (mini double fig.) -530131	Open		18.00	18
1993	Eight Piece Collector's Set -530948	Open		190.00	190
1994	Llamas-531375	Open		15.00	15
1995	Congratulations You Earned Your Stripes-127809	Open		15.00	15
1996	I'd Goat Anywhere With You -163694	Open		10.00	10

FIGURINES/COTTAGES

Precious Moments You Are Always There For Me - S. Butcher

YEAR ISSUE		EDITION LIMIT	YEAR RETD.	ISSUE PRICE	*QUOTE U.S.$
1996	Mother Kissing Daughter's Owie -163600	Open		50.00	50
1996	Father Helping Son Bat-163627	Open		50.00	50
1996	Sister Consoling Sister-163635	Open		50.00	50
1997	Mother Kissing Son's Owie -163619	Open		50.00	50
1997	Father Bandaging Daughter's Doll-163597	Open		50.00	50

Ertl Collectibles

American Country Barn Series - L. Davis

YEAR ISSUE		EDITION LIMIT	YEAR RETD.	ISSUE PRICE	*QUOTE U.S.$
1996	Gambrel Roofed Bank Barn F910	Yr.Iss.		50.00	50
1996	Western Log Barn F904	Yr.Iss.		50.00	50
1996	Victorian Barn F909	Yr.Iss.		50.00	50
1997	Round Barn H093	Yr.Iss.		50.00	50

Ertl Elves - Ertl

YEAR ISSUE		EDITION LIMIT	YEAR RETD.	ISSUE PRICE	*QUOTE U.S.$
1996	Santa's Workshop H113	5,000		70.00	70

Farm Country Christmas - L. Davis

YEAR ISSUE		EDITION LIMIT	YEAR RETD.	ISSUE PRICE	*QUOTE U.S.$
1996	Barn H045	Open		90.00	90
1996	Cat & Bird House H053	Open		25.00	25
1996	Dinner Bell H091	Open		25.00	25
1996	Farm House H046	Open		85.00	85
1996	Mailbox H056	Open		25.00	25
1996	Silo H052	Open		65.00	65
1996	Smokehouse H054	Open		70.00	70

Fenton Art Glass Company

Collectors Club - Fenton

YEAR ISSUE		EDITION LIMIT	YEAR RETD.	ISSUE PRICE	*QUOTE U.S.$
1978	Cranberry Opalescent Baskets w/variety of spot moulds	Yr.Iss.	1978	20.00	75-125
1979	Vasa Murrhina Vases (Variety of colors)	Yr.Iss.	1979	25.00	60-110
1980	Velva Rose Bubble Optic "Melon" Vases	Yr.Iss.	1980	30.00	60-110
1981	Amethyst w/White Hanging Hearts Vases	Yr.Iss.	1981	37.50	130-175
1982	Overlay Baskets in pastel shades (Swirl Optic)	Yr.Iss.	1982	40.00	75-110
1983	Cranberry Opalescent 1 pc. Fairy Lights	Yr.Iss.	1983	40.00	150-295
1984	Blue Burmese w/peloton Treatment Vases	Yr.Iss.	1984	25.00	75-150
1985	Overlay Vases in Dusty Rose w/Mica Flecks	Yr.Iss.	1985	25.00	95
1986	Ruby Iridized Art Glass Vase	Yr.Iss.	1986	30.00	100-195
1987	Dusty Rose Overlay/Peach Blow Interior w/dark blue Crest Vase	Yr.Iss.	1987	38.00	75-95
1988	Teal Green and Milk marble Basket	Yr.Iss.	1988	30.00	75-110
1989	Mulberry Opalescent Basket w/Coin Dot Optic	Yr.Iss.	1989	37.50	100-225
1990	Sea Mist Green Opalescent Fern Optic Basket	Yr.Iss.	1990	40.00	50-75
1991	Rosalene Leaf Basket and Peacock & Dahlia Basket	Yr.Iss.	1991	65.00	95
1992	Blue Bubble Optic Vases	Yr.Iss.	1992	35.00	50-75
1993	Cranberry Opalescent "Jonquil" Basket	Yr.Iss.	1993	35.00	70-110
1994	Cranberry Opalescent Jacqueline Pitcher	Yr.Iss.	1994	55.00	85-135
1994	Rosalene Tulip Vase-1994 Convention Pc.	Yr.Iss.	1994	45.00	110
1995	Fairy Light-Blue Burmese-1995 Convention Pc.	Yr.Iss.	1995	45.00	125

Glass Messenger Subscribers Only - M. Reynolds

YEAR ISSUE		EDITION LIMIT	YEAR RETD.	ISSUE PRICE	*QUOTE U.S.$
1996	Basket, Roselle on Cranberry	Yr.Iss.		89.00	89

1983 Connoisseur Collection - Fenton

YEAR ISSUE		EDITION LIMIT	YEAR RETD.	ISSUE PRICE	*QUOTE U.S.$
1983	Basket, 9" Vasa Murrhina	1,000	1983	75.00	125
1983	Craftsman Stein, White Satin Carnival	1,500	1983	35.00	50
1983	Cruet/Stopper Vasa Murrhina	1,000	1983	75.00	195
1983	Epergne Set, 5 pc. Burmese	500	1983	200.00	550-795
1983	Vase, 4 1/2" Sculptured Rose Quartz	2,000	1983	32.50	75-95
1983	Vase, 7" Sculptured Rose Quartz	1,500	1983	50.00	120
1983	Vase, 9" Sculptured Rose Quartz	850	1983	75.00	175-220

1984 Connoisseur Collection - Fenton, unless otherwise noted

YEAR ISSUE		EDITION LIMIT	YEAR RETD.	ISSUE PRICE	*QUOTE U.S.$
1984	Basket, 10" Plated Amberina Velvet	1,250	1984	85.00	195
1984	Candy Box w/cover, 3 pc. Blue Burmese	1,250	1984	75.00	200-250
1984	Cane, 18" Plated Amberina Velvet	Yr.Iss.	1984	35.00	195
1984	Top Hat, 8" Plated Amberina Velvet	1,500	1984	65.00	175-195
1984	Vase, 9" Rose Velvet Hndpt. Floral - L. Everson	750	1984	75.00	150-175
1984	Vase, 9" Rose Velvet-Mother/Child	750	1984	125.00	175-225
1984	Vase, Swan, 8" Gold Azure	1,500	1984	65.00	175-225

1985 Connoisseur Collection - Fenton, unless otherwise noted

YEAR ISSUE		EDITION LIMIT	YEAR RETD.	ISSUE PRICE	*QUOTE U.S.$
1985	Basket, 8 1/2" Buremese, Hndpt. - L. Everson	1,250	1985	95.00	175-200
1985	Epergne Set, 4 pc. Diamond Lace Green Opal.	1,000	1985	95.00	150-195
1985	Lamp, 22" Burmese-Butterfly, Hndpt. - L. Everson	350	1985	300.00	595-695

YEAR ISSUE		EDITION LIMIT	YEAR RETD.	ISSUE PRICE	*QUOTE U.S.$
1985	Punch Set, 14 pc. Green Opalescent	500	1985	250.00	295
1985	Vase, 12" Gabrielle Scul. French Opal.	800	1985	150.00	195
1985	Vase, 7 1/2" Burmese-Shell - D. Barbour	950	1985	135.00	250
1985	Vase, 7 1/2" Chrysanthemums/ Circlet, Hndpt. - L. Everson	1,000	1985	125.00	150

1986 Connoisseur Collection - Fenton, unless otherwise noted

YEAR ISSUE		EDITION LIMIT	YEAR RETD.	ISSUE PRICE	*QUOTE U.S.$
1986	Basket, Top hat Wild Rose/Teal Overlay	1,500	1986	49.00	110
1986	Boudoir Lamp, Cranberry Pearl	750	1986	145.00	250-295
1986	Cruet/Stopper, Cranberry Pearl	1,000	1986	75.00	250-295
1986	Handled Urn, 13" Cranberry Satin	1,000	1986	185.00	300
1986	Handled Vase, 7" French Royale	1,000	1986	100.00	175
1986	Lamp, 20" Burmese Shells Hndpt. - D. Barbour	500	1986	350.00	600-695
1986	Vanity Set, 4 pc. Blue Ridge	1,000	1986	125.00	250-295
1986	Vase 10 1/2" Danielle Sandcarved - R. Delaney	1,000	1986	95.00	195
1986	Vase, 10 1/2" Misty Morn, Hndpt. - L. Everson	1,000	1986	95.00	195

1987 Connoisseur Collection - Various

YEAR ISSUE		EDITION LIMIT	YEAR RETD.	ISSUE PRICE	*QUOTE U.S.$
1987	Pitcher, 8" Enameled Azure Hndpt.- L. Everson	950	1987	85.00	125
1987	Vase, 7 1/4" Blossom/Bows on Cranberry Hndpt.- D. Barbour	950	1987	95.00	175

1988 Connoisseur Collection - Fenton, unless otherwise noted

YEAR ISSUE		EDITION LIMIT	YEAR RETD.	ISSUE PRICE	*QUOTE U.S.$
1988	Basket, Irid. Teal Cased Vasa Murrhina	2,500	1988	65.00	125-150
1988	Candy, Wave Crest	2,000	1988	95.00	150-195
1988	Pitcher, Cased Cranberry/Opal Teal Ring Hndpt. - L. Everson	3,500	1988	60.00	125-150
1988	Vase, 6" Cased Cranberry/Opal Teal/Irid.	3,500	1988	50.00	100-125

1989 Connoisseur Collection - Fenton, unless otherwise noted

YEAR ISSUE		EDITION LIMIT	YEAR RETD.	ISSUE PRICE	*QUOTE U.S.$
1989	Basket, 7" Cranberry w/Crystal Ring Hndpt.- L. Everson	2,500	1989	85.00	100-150
1989	Candy Box, w/cover, Cranberry, Hndpt. - L. Everson	2,500	1989	85.00	150-195
1989	Epergne Set 5 pc., Rosalene	2,000	1989	250.00	400-495
1989	Lamp, 21" Rosalene Satin Hndpt. - L. Everson	1,000	1989	250.00	300-395
1989	Pitcher, Diamond Optic, Rosalene	2,500	1989	55.00	100
1989	Vase, Basketweave, Rosalene	2,500	1989	45.00	85
1989	Vase, Pinch, 8" Vasa Murrhina	2,000	1989	65.00	100

1990-85th Anniversary Collection - Various

YEAR ISSUE		EDITION LIMIT	YEAR RETD.	ISSUE PRICE	*QUOTE U.S.$
1990	Basket, 5 1/2" Trees on Burmese, Hndpt.- Piper/F. Burton	Closed	1990	57.50	110
1990	Basket, 7" Raspberry on Burmese, Hndpt. - L. Everson	Closed	1990	75.00	150-195
1990	Cruet/Stopper Petite Floral on Burmese, Hndpt. - L. Everson	Closed	1990	85.00	150-195
1990	Epergne Set, 2 pc. Pt. Floral on Burmese, Hndpt. - L. Everson	Closed	1990	125.00	200-295
1990	Lamp, 20" Rose Burmese, Hndpt. - Piper/D. Barbour	Closed	1990	250.00	350-450
1990	Lamp, 21" Raspberry on Burmese, Hndpt. - L. Everson	Closed	1990	295.00	450
1990	Vase, 6 1/2" Rose Burmese, Hndpt. - Piper/D. Barbour	Closed	1990	45.00	90
1990	Vase, 9" Trees on Burmese, Hndpt. - Piper/F. Burton	Closed	1990	75.00	150-200
1990	Vase, Fan 6" Rose Burmese, Hndpt. - Piper/D. Barbour	Closed	1990	49.50	95
1990	Water Set, 7 pc. Raspberry on Burmese, Hndpt. - L. Everson	Closed	1990	275.00	500-695

1991 Connoisseur Collection - Various

YEAR ISSUE		EDITION LIMIT	YEAR RETD.	ISSUE PRICE	*QUOTE U.S.$
1991	Basket, Floral on Rosalene, Hndpt. - M. Reynolds	1,500	1991	64.00	100
1991	Candy Box, 3 pc. Favrene - Fenton	1,000	1991	90.00	200
1991	Fish, Paperweight, Rosalene - Fenton	2,000	1991	30.00	60
1991	Lamp, 20" Roses on Burmese, Hndpt. - Piper/F. Burton	500	1991	275.00	450
1991	Vase, 7 1/2" Raspberry on Burmese, Hndpt. - L. Everson	1,500	1991	65.00	100
1991	Vase, Floral on Favrene, Hndpt. - M. Reynolds	850	1991	125.00	350
1991	Vase, Fruit on Favrene, Hndpt. - F. Burton	850	1991	125.00	300-350

1992 Connoisseur Collection - Various

YEAR ISSUE		EDITION LIMIT	YEAR RETD.	ISSUE PRICE	*QUOTE U.S.$
1992	Covered Box, Poppy/Daisy, Hndpt. - F. Burton	1,250	1992	95.00	200
1992	Pitcher, 4 1/2" Berries on Burmese, Hndpt. - M. Reynolds	1,500	1992	65.00	120
1992	Pitcher, 9" Empire on Cranberry, Hndpt. - M. Reynolds	950	1992	110.00	150
1992	Vase, 6 1/2" Raspberry on Burmese, Hndpt. - L. Everson	1,500	1992	45.00	95
1992	Vase, 8" Seascape, Hndpt. - F. Burton	750	1992	150.00	175
1992	Vase, Twining Floral Rosalene Satin, Hndpt. - M. Reynolds	950	1992	110.00	175

1993 Connoisseur Collection - Various

YEAR ISSUE		EDITION LIMIT	YEAR RETD.	ISSUE PRICE	*QUOTE U.S.$
1993	Amphora w/Stand, Favrene, Hndpt. - M. Reynolds	850	1993	285.00	350

YEAR ISSUE		EDITION LIMIT	YEAR RETD.	ISSUE PRICE	*QUOTE U.S.$
1993	Bowl, Ruby Stretch w/Gold Scrolls, Hndpt. - M. Reynolds	1,250	1993	95.00	125
1993	Lamp, Spring Woods Reverse Hndpt. - F. Burton	500	1993	595.00	595
1993	Owl Figurine, 6" Favrene - Fenton	1,500	1993	95.00	125
1993	Perfume/Stopper, Rose Trellis Rosalene, Hndpt. - F. Burton	1,250	1993	95.00	125
1993	Vase, 9" Gold Leaves Sandcarved on Plum Irid., - M. Reynolds	950	1993	175.00	225
1993	Vase, Victorian Roses Persian Blue Opal., Hndpt. - M. Reynolds	950	1993	125.00	180

1993 Family Signature Collection - Various

YEAR ISSUE		EDITION LIMIT	YEAR RETD.	ISSUE PRICE	*QUOTE U.S.$
1993	Basket, 8 1/2" Lilacs - Bill Fenton	Closed	1993	65.00	90
1993	Vase, 9" Alpine Thistle/Ruby Carnival - Frank M. Fenton	Closed	1993	105.00	175
1993	Vase, 9" Cottage Scene - Shelley Fenton	Closed	1993	90.00	150
1993	Vase, 10" Vintage on Plum - Don Fenton	Closed	1993	80.00	110
1993	Vase, 11" Cranberry Dec. - George Fenton	Closed	1993	110.00	140

1994 Connoisseur Collection - Various

YEAR ISSUE		EDITION LIMIT	YEAR RETD.	ISSUE PRICE	*QUOTE U.S.$
1994	Bowl, 14" Cranberry Cameo Sandcarved - Reynolds/Delaney	500	1994	390.00	390
1994	Clock, 4 1/2" Favrene, Hndpt. - F. Burton	850	1994	150.00	175
1994	Lamp, Hummingbird Reverse, Hndpt. - F. Burton	300	1994	590.00	750
1994	Pitcher, 10" Lattice on Burmese, Hndpt. - F. Burton	750	1994	165.00	225
1994	Vase, 7" Favrene, Hndpt. - M. Reynolds	850	1994	185.00	200
1994	Vase, 8" Plum Opalescent, Hndpt. - M. Reynolds	750	1994	165.00	175
1994	Vase, 11" Gold Amberina, Hndpt. - M. Reynolds	750	1994	175.00	225

1994 Family Signature Collection - Various

YEAR ISSUE		EDITION LIMIT	YEAR RETD.	ISSUE PRICE	*QUOTE U.S.$
1994	Basket, 7 1/2" Lilacs - Shelley Fenton	Closed	1994	65.00	95
1994	Basket, 8" Stiegel Green - Bill Fenton	Closed	1994	60.00	95
1994	Basket, 8 1/2" Ruby Carnival - Tom Fenton	Closed	1994	60.00	95
1994	Basket, 11" Autumn Gold Opal - Frank Fenton	Closed	1994	70.00	90
1994	Candy w/cover, 9 1/2" Autumn Leaves - Don Fenton	Closed	1994	60.00	75
1994	Pitcher, 6 1/2" Cranberry - Frank M. Fenton	Closed	1994	85.00	125
1994	Vase, 9 1/2" Pansies on Cranberry - Bill Fenton	Closed	1994	95.00	125
1994	Vase, 10" Fuchsia - George Fenton	Closed	1994	95.00	125

1995 Connoisseur Collection - M. Reynolds, unless otherwise noted

YEAR ISSUE		EDITION LIMIT	YEAR RETD.	ISSUE PRICE	*QUOTE U.S.$
1995	Amphora w/stand, 10 1/4" Royal Purple, Hndpt.	890	1995	195.00	300
1995	Ginger Jar, 3 Pc. 8 1/2" Favrene, Hndpt.	790	1995	275.00	400
1995	Lamp, 21" Butterfly/Floral Reverse, Hndpt. - F. Burton	300	1995	595.00	700-800
1995	Pitcher, 9 1/2" Victorian Art Glass, Hndpt.	490	1995	250.00	250
1995	Vase, 7" Aurora Wild Rose, Hndpt.	890	1995	125.00	175

1995 Family Signature Collection - Various

YEAR ISSUE		EDITION LIMIT	YEAR RETD.	ISSUE PRICE	*QUOTE U.S.$
1995	Basket, 8 1/2" Trellis - Lynn Fenton	Closed	1995	85.00	85
1995	Basket, 9 1/2" Coralene Floral - Frank M./Bill Fenton	Closed	1995	75.00	75
1995	Candy w/cover, 9" Red Carnival - Mike Fenton	Closed	1995	65.00	65
1995	Pitcher, 9 1/2" Thistle - Don Fenton	Closed	1995	125.00	125
1995	Vase, 7" Gold Pansies on Cranberry - George Fenton	Closed	1995	75.00	75
1995	Vase, 9" Summer Garden on Spruce - Don Fenton	Closed	1995	85.00	85
1995	Vase, 9 1/2" Golden Flax on Cobalt - Shelley Fenton	Closed	1995	95.00	95

1996 Connoisseur Collection - Various

YEAR ISSUE		EDITION LIMIT	YEAR RETD.	ISSUE PRICE	*QUOTE U.S.$
1996	Covered Box, 7" Mandarin Red, Hndpt. - K. Plauche	1,250	1996	150.00	150
1996	Lamp, 33" Reverse Painted Poppies, Hndpt. - F. Burton	400	1996	750.00	750
1996	Pitcher, 8" Dragonfly on Burmese, Hndpt. - F. Burton	1,450	1996	165.00	165
1996	Vase, 11" Berries on Wildrose, Hndpt. - M. Reynolds	1,250	1996	195.00	195
1996	Vase, 11" Queen's Bird on Burmese, Hndpt. - M. Reynolds	1,350	1996	250.00	250
1996	Vase, 7 1/2" Favrene Cut-Back Sandcarved - M. Reynolds	1,250	1996	195.00	195
1996	Vase, 8" Trout on Burmese, Hndpt. - R. Spindler	1,450	1996	135.00	135

1996 Family Signature Collection - Various

YEAR ISSUE		EDITION LIMIT	YEAR RETD.	ISSUE PRICE	*QUOTE U.S.$
1996	Basket, 7 1/2" Starflower on Cran. Pearl - M. Fenton	Closed	1996	75.00	75
1996	Basket, 8" Mountain Berry - Don Fenton	Closed	1996	85.00	85
1996	Candy Box w/cover Pansies - Shelley Fenton	Closed	1996	65.00	65
1996	Pitcher, 6 1/2" Asters - Lynn Fenton	Closed	1996	70.00	70

YEAR ISSUE	EDITION LIMIT	YEAR RETD.	ISSUE PRICE	*QUOTE U.S.$
1996 Vase, 10" Magnolia & Berry on Spruce - Tom Fenton	Closed	1996	85.00	85
1996 Vase, 11" Meadow Beauty - Nancy Fenton	Closed	1996	95.00	95
1996 Vase, 8 1/2" Blush Rose on Opaline - George Fenton	Closed	1996	75.00	75

American Classic Series - M. Dickinson

YEAR ISSUE	EDITION LIMIT	YEAR RETD.	ISSUE PRICE	*QUOTE U.S.$
1986 Jupiter Train on Opal Satin, Lamp, 23"	1,000	1986	295.00	350
1986 Studebaker-Garford Car on Opal Satin, Lamp, 16"	1,000	1986	235.00	300

Christmas - Various

YEAR ISSUE	EDITION LIMIT	YEAR RETD.	ISSUE PRICE	*QUOTE U.S.$
1978 Christmas Morn, Lamp, 16" - M. Dickinson	Yr.Iss.	1978	125.00	250
1978 Christmas Morn, Fairy Light - M. Dickinson	Yr.Iss.	1978	25.00	75
1979 Nature's Christmas, Lamp, 16" - K. Cunningham	Yr.Iss.	1979	150.00	250
1979 Nature's Christmas, Fairy Light - K. Cunningham	Yr.Iss.	1979	30.00	95
1980 Going Home, Lamp, 16" - D. Johnson	Yr.Iss.	1980	165.00	250
1980 Going Home, Fairy Light - D. Johnson	Yr.Iss.	1980	32.50	65
1981 All Is Calm, Lamp, 16" - D. Johnson	Yr.Iss.	1981	175.00	295
1981 All Is Calm, Lamp, 20" - D. Johnson	Yr.Iss.	1981	225.00	295
1981 All Is Calm, Fairy Light - D. Johnson	Yr.Iss.	1981	35.00	65
1982 Country Christmas, Lamp, 16" - R. Spindler	Yr.Iss.	1982	175.00	295
1982 Country Christmas, Lamp, 21" - R. Spindler	Yr.Iss.	1982	225.00	350
1982 Country Christmas, Fairy Light - R. Spindler	Yr.Iss.	1982	35.00	65
1983 Anticipation, Fairy Light - D. Johnson	7,500	1983	35.00	65
1984 Expectation, Lamp, 10 1/2" - D. Johnson	7,500	1984	75.00	275
1984 Expectation, Fairy Light - D. Johnson	7,500	1984	37.50	65
1985 Heart's Desire, Fairy Light - D. Johnson	7,500	1986	37.50	65
1987 Sharing The Spirit, Fairy Light - L. Everson	Yr.Iss.	1987	37.50	65
1987 Cardinal in the Churchyard, Lamp, 18 1/2" - D. Johnson	500	1987	250.00	295
1987 Cardinal in the Churchyard, Fairy Light - D. Johnson	4,500	1987	29.50	95
1988 A Chickadee Ballet, Lamp, 21" - D. Johnson	500	1988	274.00	295
1988 A Chickadee Ballet, Fairy Light - D. Johnson	4,500	1988	29.50	95
1989 Downy Pecker, Lamp, 16" - Chiseled Song - D. Johnson	500	1989	250.00	295
1989 Downy Pecker, Fairy Light - Chiseled Song - D. Johnson	4,500	1989	29.50	95
1990 A Blue Bird in Snowfall, Lamp, 21" - D. Johnson	500	1990	250.00	295
1990 A Blue Bird in Snowfall, Fairy Light - D. Johnson	4,500	1990	29.50	95
1990 Sleigh Ride, Lamp, 16"- F. Burton	1,000	1990	250.00	295
1990 Sleigh Ride, Fairy Light - F. Burton	3,500	1990	39.00	75
1991 Christmas Eve, Lamp, 16" - F. Burton	1,000	1991	250.00	295
1991 Christmas Eve, Fairy Light - F. Burton	3,500	1991	39.00	95
1992 Family Tradition, Lamp, 20" - F. Burton	1,000	1992	250.00	295
1992 Family Tradition, Fairy Light - F. Burton	3,500	1992	39.00	75
1993 Family Holiday, Lamp, 16" - F. Burton	1,000	1993	265.00	295
1993 Family Holiday, Fairy Light - F. Burton	3,500	1993	39.00	75
1994 Silent Night, Lamp, 16" - F. Burton	500	1994	275.00	325
1994 Silent Night, Fairy Light - F. Burton	1,500	1994	45.00	45
1994 Silent Night, Egg on Stand - F. Burton	1,500	1994	45.00	45
1995 Our Home Is Blessed, Lamp, 21" - F. Burton	500	1995	275.00	275
1995 Our Home Is Blessed, Egg - F. Burton	1,500	1995	45.00	45
1995 Our Home Is Blessed, Fairy Light - F. Burton	1,500	1995	45.00	45
1996 Star of Wonder, Lamp, 16" - F. Burton	750	1996	175.00	175
1996 Star of Wonder, Egg - F. Burton	1,750		45.00	45
1996 Star of Wonder, Fairy Light - F. Burton	1,750		48.00	48

Christmas Limited Edition - M. Reynolds, unless otherwise noted

YEAR ISSUE	EDITION LIMIT	YEAR RETD.	ISSUE PRICE	*QUOTE U.S.$
1992 Egg, 3 1/2" Manager Scene on Ruby	2,500	1992	30.00	30
1992 Egg, 3 1/2" Poinsettia on Crystal Irid.	2,500	1992	30.00	30
1993 Egg, 3 1/2" Angel on Green	2,500	1993	35.00	35
1993 Egg, 3 1/2" Woods on White	2,500	1993	35.00	35
1994 Egg, 3 1/2" Magnolia on Gold	1,500	1994	35.00	35
1994 Egg, 3 1/2" Partridge on Ruby	1,500	1994	35.00	35
1995 Egg, 3 1/2" Bow & Holly on Ivory	900	1995	35.00	35
1995 Egg, 3 1/2" Chickadee on Gold	900	1995	35.00	35
1995 Egg, 3 1/2" Iced Poinsettia on Ruby	900	1995	39.50	40
1995 Angel, Radiant-Musical Base	900	1995	85.00	85
1995 Pitcher, Golden Holiday Pine Cones	900	1995	79.00	79
1996 Egg, 3 1/2" Holly Berries on Gold	1,500		37.50	38
1996 Egg, 3 1/2" Golden Partridge on Spruce	1,500		35.00	35
1996 Egg, 3 1/2" Moonlit Meadow on Ruby - R. Spindler	1,500		39.50	40
1996 Fairy Light, Nativity Scene on Ivory - R. Spindler	1,500		37.50	38
1996 Fairy Light, Golden Winged Angel	2,000		39.50	40
1996 Egg, 3 1/2" Golden Winged Angel	1,500		37.50	38
1996 Radiant Golden Winged Angel, 7 1/2"	1,000		59.50	60

Collectible Eggs - M. Reynolds, unless otherwise noted

YEAR ISSUE	EDITION LIMIT	YEAR RETD.	ISSUE PRICE	*QUOTE U.S.$
1991 Egg, Gold Design/Salem Blue Irid.	1,500	1991	29.50	30
1991 Egg, Partridge/Seamist Green Irid.	1,500	1991	29.50	30
1991 Egg, Poinsettias/Special Milk Glass	1,500	1991	29.50	30
1991 Egg, Shell/Favrene	1,500	1991	35.00	45
1991 Egg, Skater/Ruby	1,500	1991	29.50	30
1991 Egg, Snow Scene/Sp. Milk	1,500	1991	29.50	30
1991 Egg, White Scene/Black	1,500	1991	29.50	30
1992 Egg, Butterflies/Black	2,500	1992	30.00	30
1992 Egg, Croquet/Clear Carnival	2,500	1992	30.00	30
1992 Egg, Floral & Bronze/Special Milk Glass	2,500	1992	30.00	30
1992 Egg, Iris/Seamist Green	2,500	1992	30.00	30
1992 Egg, Pink Floral/Dusty Rose	2,500	1992	30.00	30
1992 Egg, Unicorn/Twilight Blue	2,500	1992	30.00	30
1993 Egg, Cottage/White Opal	2,500	1993	30.00	30
1993 Egg, Fuchsia Floral/White	2,500	1993	30.00	30
1993 Egg, Paisley/Dusty Rose	2,500	1993	30.00	30
1993 Egg, Sandcarved/Black	1,500	1993	35.00	35
1993 Egg, Scrolling Floral/Green - K. Plauche	2,500	1993	30.00	30
1993 Egg, Sea Gulls/Ocean Blue	2,500	1993	30.00	30
1993 Egg, w/gold on Plum - K. Plauche	2,500	1993	35.00	35
1993 Egg, w/gold on Ruby	2,500	1993	30.00	30
1994 Egg, Cascading Floral/Pink - S. Jackson	2,500	1994	32.50	33
1994 Egg, Metallic Floral/Plum - K. Plauche	2,500	1994	32.50	33
1994 Egg, Enameled Flowers/Blue - F. Burton	2,500	1994	37.50	38
1994 Egg, Scrolls/Gold	2,500	1994	32.50	33
1994 Egg, Spring Landscape/Opal - S. Jackson	2,500	1994	32.50	33
1994 Egg, Tulips/Sea Mist - S. Jackson	2,500	1994	32.50	33
1994 Egg, Violets/Milk Pearl - S. Jackson	2,500	1994	32.50	33
1995 Egg, Floral/Blue	2,500	1995	32.50	33
1995 Egg, Floral/Gold	2,500	1995	32.50	33
1995 Egg, Floral/Green	2,500	1995	32.50	33
1995 Egg, Floral/White	2,500	1995	32.50	33
1995 Egg, Hummingbird/Dusty Rose	2,500	1995	35.00	35
1995 Egg, Scene/White	2,500	1995	32.50	33
1995 Egg, Scrolls/Black	2,500	1995	32.50	33
1996 Egg, Honeysuckle - R. Spindler	2,500	1996	37.50	38
1996 Egg, Hummingbird	2,500	1996	37.50	38
1996 Egg, Butterflies - R. Spindler	2,500	1996	37.50	38
1996 Egg, Morning Glories - R. Spindler	2,500	1996	37.50	38
1996 Egg, Lake Scene	2,500	1996	37.50	38
1996 Egg, Jeweled	2,500	1996	37.50	38
1996 Egg, Fish - R. Spindler	2,500	1996	37.50	38

Designer Series - Various

YEAR ISSUE	EDITION LIMIT	YEAR RETD.	ISSUE PRICE	*QUOTE U.S.$
1983 Lighthouse Point, Lamp, 23 1/2", - M. Dickinson	150	1983	350.00	450
1983 Lighthouse Point, Lamp, 25 1/2", - M. Dickinson	150	1983	350.00	575
1983 Down Home, Lamp, 21" - G. Finn	300	1983	300.00	450
1984 Smoke 'N Cinders, Lamp, 16" - M. Dickinson	250	1984	195.00	325
1984 Smoke 'N Cinders, Lamp, 23" - M. Dickinson	250	1984	350.00	400
1984 Majestic Flight, Lamp, 16" - B. Cumberledge	250	1984	195.00	295
1984 Majestic Flight, Lamp, 23 1/2" - B. Cumberledge	250	1984	350.00	450
1985 In Season, Lamp, 16" - M. Dickinson	250	1985	225.00	325
1985 In Season, Lamp, 23" - M. Dickinson	250	1985	295.00	395
1985 Nature's Grace, Lamp, 16" - B. Cumberland	250	1985	225.00	325
1985 Nature's Grace, Lamp, 23" - B. Cumberland	295	1985	295.00	400

Easter Series - M. Reynolds

YEAR ISSUE	EDITION LIMIT	YEAR RETD.	ISSUE PRICE	*QUOTE U.S.$
1995 Fairy Light	Closed	1995	49.00	49

Fenton Miniatures - Fenton

YEAR ISSUE	EDITION LIMIT	YEAR RETD.	ISSUE PRICE	*QUOTE U.S.$
1996 Epergne, 4 1/2" Opaline	Closed	1996	35.00	35
1996 Punch Bowl Set, 5" x 3 3/4" high	Closed	1996	59.00	59

Mary Gregory - M. Reynolds

YEAR ISSUE	EDITION LIMIT	YEAR RETD.	ISSUE PRICE	*QUOTE U.S.$
1994 Basket, 7 1/2" Oval	Closed	1994	59.00	59
1995 Basket, 7 1/2" Oval	Closed	1995	65.00	65
1995 Egg on stand, 4" - Butterfly Delight	Closed	1995	37.50	38
1996 Hat Basket on Cranberry, 6 1/2"	2,000	1996	95.00	95
1996 Vase on Cranberry, 9"	1,500	1996	135.00	135

Mouthblown Eggs - M. Reynolds, unless otherwise noted

YEAR ISSUE	EDITION LIMIT	YEAR RETD.	ISSUE PRICE	*QUOTE U.S.$
1991 Egg, 3 1/2" Mother of Pearl	Closed	1991	49.00	49
1991 Egg, 4 1/2" Mother of Pearl	Closed	1991	59.00	59
1992 Egg, 5" Petal Pink Iridized - F. Burton	Closed	1992	65.00	65
1992 Egg, 5" Seamist Green Iridized - F. Burton	Closed	1992	65.00	65
1993 Egg, 5" Ocean Blue	Closed	1993	69.00	69
1993 Egg, 5" Plum	Closed	1993	69.00	125
1994 Egg, 5" Blue - F. Burton	Closed	1994	75.00	75
1994 Egg, 5" Rose	Closed	1994	75.00	125
1995 Egg, 5" Gold	Closed	1995	75.00	75
1995 Egg, 5" Spruce	Closed	1995	75.00	75
1996 Egg, 5" Cranberry	Closed	1996	95.00	125
1996 Egg, 5" French Opalescent	Closed	1996	75.00	125

Valentine's Day Series - Fenton, unless otherwise noted

YEAR ISSUE	EDITION LIMIT	YEAR RETD.	ISSUE PRICE	*QUOTE U.S.$
1992 Basket, 6" Cranberry Opal/Heart Optic	Closed	1992	50.00	85
1992 Vase, 4" Cranberry Opal/Heart Optic	Closed	1992	35.00	60
1992 Perfume, w/oval stopper Cranberry Opal/Heart Optic	Closed	1992	60.00	125
1993 Basket, 7" Caprice Cranberry Opal/Heart Optic	Closed	1993	59.00	85
1993 Trinket Box, 5" Cranberry Opal/Heart Optic	Closed	1993	79.00	95
1993 Vase, 5 1/2" Melon Cranberry Opal/Heart Optic	Closed	1993	45.00	70
1993 Southern Girl, 8", Hndpt. Opal Satin - M. Reynolds	Closed	1993	49.00	90
1993 Southern Girl, 8", Rose Pearl Irid.	Closed	1993	45.00	95
1994 Basket, 7" Cranberry Opal/Heart Optic	Closed	1994	65.00	95
1994 Vase, 5 1/2" Ribbed Cranberry Opal/Heart Optic	Closed	1994	47.50	60
1994 Perfume, w/ stopper, 5" Cranberry Opal/Heart Optic	Closed	1994	75.00	125
1995 Basket, 8" Melon Cranberry Opal/Heart Optic	Closed	1995	69.00	95
1995 Pitcher, 5 1/2" Melon Cranberry Opal/Heart Optic	Closed	1995	69.00	95
1995 Perfume, w/ heart stopper, Kristen's Floral Hndpt. - M. Reynolds	2,500	1995	49.00	75
1995 Doll, 7", Kristen's Floral Hndpt. Ivory Satin - M. Reynolds	2,500	1995	49.00	70
1996 Basket, 8" Melon Cranberry Opalescent	Closed	1996	75.00	75
1996 Perfume, 5" Melon Cranberry Opalescent	Closed	1996	95.00	95
1996 Fairy Light, 3 pc. Cranberry Opalescent	Closed	1996	135.00	135
1996 Vanity Set, 4 pc. Tea Rose - M. Reynolds	1,500		250.00	250
1996 Doll, w/Musical Base Tea Rose - M. Reynolds	2,500		55.00	55

FFSC, Inc.

Charming Tails Autumn Harvest Figurines - D. Griff

YEAR ISSUE	EDITION LIMIT	YEAR RETD.	ISSUE PRICE	*QUOTE U.S.$
1993 Acorn Built For Two	Open		10.00	10
1996 Bag of Tricks...Or Treats	Open		15.50	16
1996 Blinkey's Acorn Costume	Open		11.50	12
1995 Candy Apples	Open		16.00	16
1995 Candy Corn Vampire	Closed	1996	18.00	18
1993 Caps Off to You	Open		10.00	10
1996 Chauncey's Pear Costume	Open		12.00	12
1993 Cornfield Feast	Closed	1994	15.00	65
1993 Fall Frolicking	Closed	1996	13.00	13
1994 Frosting Pumpkins	Closed	1996	16.00	16
1995 Garden Naptime	Open		18.00	18
1995 Giving Thanks	Open		16.00	16
1993 Gourd Slide	Open		16.00	16
1994 Harvest Fruit	Closed	1995	16.00	30-40
1995 Horn of Plenty	Open		20.00	20
1996 Indian Impostor	Open		14.00	14
1994 Jumpin' Jack O' Lanterns	Open		16.00	16
1995 Let's Get Crackin'	Open		20.00	20
1996 Look! No Hands	Open		15.50	16
1996 Maxine's Pumpkin Costume	Open		12.00	12
1996 Oops, I Missed	Open		12.00	12
1994 Open Pumpkin	Closed	1994	15.00	25-45
1994 Painting Leaves	Closed	1996	16.00	16
1994 Pear Candleholder	Closed	1995	14.00	30
1996 Pickin' Time	Open		16.00	16
1995 Pilgrim's Progress	Open		13.50	14
1995 Pumpkin Pie	Closed	1996	16.00	16
1994 Pumpkin Slide	Closed	1994	16.00	25-40
1994 Pumpkin Votive	Closed	1995	13.50	30-45
1995 Reginald's Hideaway	Open		14.00	14
1994 Stump Candleholders	Closed	1996	20.00	75
1996 You're Not Scary	Open		14.00	14
1996 You're Nutty	Open		12.00	12

Charming Tails Easter Basket Figurines - D. Griff

YEAR ISSUE	EDITION LIMIT	YEAR RETD.	ISSUE PRICE	*QUOTE U.S.$
1995 After the Hunt	Open		18.00	18
1993 Animals in Eggs	Closed	1996	11.00	11
1995 Binkey's Bouncing Bundle	7,500	1995	18.00	18
1994 Bunny Imposter	Open		12.00	12
1995 Bunny Love	Open		18.00	18
1993 Duckling in Egg with Mouse	Closed	1996	15.00	100
1994 Easter Parade	Closed	1996	10.00	10
1995 Gathering Treats	Open		12.00	12
1994 Jelly Bean Feast	Open		14.00	14
1995 Look Out Below	Open		20.00	20
1996 No Thanks, I'm Stuffed	Open		15.00	15
1993 Peek-a-boo	Closed	1996	12.00	12
1994 Wanna Play?	2,500	1994	15.00	75-150

FIGURINES/COTTAGES

YEAR ISSUE		EDITION LIMIT	YEAR RETD.	ISSUE PRICE	*QUOTE U.S.$
1995	Want a Bite	Open		18.00	18
1996	What's Hatchin'	Open		16.00	16

Charming Tails Event Piece - D. Griff

1996	Take Me Home	Closed	1996	20.00	20

Charming Tails Everyday Figurines - D. Griff

1996	Ach-Choo, Get Well Soon	Open		12.00	12
1994	After Lunch Snooze	Open		15.00	15
1996	The Berry Best	Open		16.00	16
1994	Binkey Growing Carrots	Closed	1995	15.00	50
1993	Binkey in a Lily	Closed	1996	16.00	16
1994	Binkey in the Berry Patch	Closed	1996	12.00	12
1995	Binkey's First Cake	Open		16.00	16
1994	Binkey's New Pal	Open		14.00	14
1996	Bunny Buddies	Open		20.00	20
1994	Butterfly Smelling Zinnia	Closed	1995	15.00	65
1994	Can I Keep Him?	2,500	1994	13.00	135-225
1995	Catchin' Butterflies	Open		16.00	16
1996	Cattail Catapult	Open		16.00	16
1996	Charming Tails Display Sign	Open		20.00	20
1996	The Chase is On	Open		16.00	16
1994	Chauncey Growing Tomatoes	Closed	1995	15.00	45
1995	Feeding Time	Closed	1996	16.00	16
1996	Flower Friends	Open		16.00	15
1995	Gardening Break	Open		16.00	16
1994	Get Well Soon	Open		15.00	15
1994	Good Luck	Open		15.00	15
1996	Hangin' Around	Open		18.00	18
1994	Happy Birthday	Open		15.00	15
1995	Hello, Sweet Pea	Open		12.00	12
1993	Hide and Seek	Closed	1994	13.50	65-95
1994	Hope You're Feeling Better	Open		15.00	15
1996	Hoppity Hop	Open		16.00	16
1994	How Do You Measure Love	Open		15.00	15
1996	I Have a Question for You	Open		16.00	16
1994	I Love You	Open		15.00	15
1996	I See Things Clearly Now	Open		14.00	14
1995	I'm Berry Happy	Open		15.00	15
1995	I'm Full	Open		15.00	15
1994	I'm So Sorry	Open		15.00	15
1996	It's Not the Same Without You	Open		15.00	15
1996	Just "Plane" Friends	Open		18.00	18
1993	King of the Mushroom	Closed	1996	16.00	16
1996	Love Doesn't Come With Instructions	15,000		18.00	18
1993	Love Mice	Closed	1994	15.00	50-95
1994	Mackenzie Growing Beans	Closed	1995	15.00	35
1994	Maxine's Butterfly Ride	Open		16.50	17
1994	Mender of Broken Hearts	Closed	1996	15.00	15
1996	Mid-day Snooze	Open		18.00	18
1993	Mouse on a Bee	Closed	1994	16.50	95-200
1993	Mouse on a Dragonfly	Closed	1994	16.50	100-200
1993	Mouse on a Grasshopper	Closed	1994	15.00	100
1994	New Arrival	Open		15.00	15
1995	One for Me...	Open		16.00	16
1995	One for You...	Open		16.00	16
1995	Picking Peppers	Open		12.00	12
1993	Rabbit/Daffodil Candleholder	Closed	1995	13.50	85
1994	Reach for the Stars	Open		15.00	15
1994	Slumber Party	Closed	1996	16.00	16
1993	Spring Flowers	Closed	1996	16.00	16
1994	Springtime Showers	Closed	1996	10.00	10
1995	Surrounded By Friends	Open		16.00	16
1996	Taggin' Along	Open		14.00	14
1996	Take Time To Reflect	Open		16.00	16
1994	Thanks for Being There	Closed	1996	15.00	15
1995	This Is Hot!	Open		15.00	15
1996	Training Wings	Open		16.00	16
1995	Tuggin' Twosome	10,000		18.00	18
1993	Two Peas in a Pod	Closed	1996	14.00	14
1996	The Waterslide	Open		20.00	20
1994	We'll Weather the Storm Together	Open		15.00	15
1995	Why, Hello There!	Open		14.00	14
1995	You Are Not Alone	Closed	1996	20.00	20
1996	You Couldn't Be Sweeter	Open		16.00	16
1996	You Love me-You Love Me Not	Open		16.00	16

Charming Tails Musicals and Waterglobes - D. Griff

1994	Jawbreakers Musical	Closed	1995	40.00	75
1994	Letter to Santa Waterglobe	Closed	1994	45.00	75
1995	Me Next! Musical	Closed	1995	45.00	45
1994	Mini Surprise Waterglobe	Closed	1994	22.00	22
1994	My Hero! Waterglobe	Closed	1995	45.00	45
1995	Pumpkin Playtime Musical	Closed	1995	35.00	35
1993	Rocking Mice Musical	Closed	1994	65.00	115
1994	Sailing Away Waterglobe	Closed	1995	50.00	50
1994	Sharing the Warmth Waterglobe	Closed	1995	40.00	40
1993	Skating Mice Musical	Closed	1994	25.00	25
1994	Sweet Dreams Waterglobe	Closed	1995	40.00	40
1994	Together at Christmas, Mini Waterglobe	Closed	1995	30.00	30
1994	Trimming the Tree Waterglobe	Closed	1994	45.00	45
1994	Underwater Explorer Waterglobe	Closed	1995	45.00	45
1994	Up, Up and Away Musical	Closed	1995	70.00	70

Charming Tails Squashville Figurines - D. Griff

1996	Airmail	Open		16.00	16
1996	All I Can Give You is Me	Closed	1996	15.00	15
1996	All Snug in Their Beds Waterglobe	Closed	1996	30.00	30
1996	Angel of Light	Open		12.00	12

YEAR ISSUE		EDITION LIMIT	YEAR RETD.	ISSUE PRICE	*QUOTE U.S.$
1996	Baby's First Christmas Waterglobe	Closed	1996	28.00	28
1996	Binkey in a Bed of Flowers	Closed	1996	15.00	15
1995	Binkey Snow Shoeing	Open		14.00	14
1995	Binkey's 1995 Ice Sculpture	Yr.Iss.	1995	20.00	20
1996	Building a Snowbunny	Open		16.00	16
1995	Charming Choo-Choo & Cabbose	Open		35.00	35
1996	Chauncey's Noisemakers	Open		12.00	12
1995	Christmas Pageant Stage	Open		30.00	30
1996	Christmas Stroll	Open		16.00	16
1996	The Drum Major	Open		12.00	12
1996	Extra! Extra!	Open		14.00	14
1996	Farmer Mackenzie	Open		16.00	16
1996	The Float Driver	Open		12.00	12
1995	Flying Leaf Saucer	Open		16.00	16
1996	Follow in my Footsteps	Open		12.00	12
1996	Holiday Trumpeteer	Open		12.00	12
1995	Holy Family Players	Open		20.00	20
1994	Hot Doggin'	Closed	1995	20.00	40
1996	Jingle Bells	Open		15.00	15
1994	Lady Bug Express	Closed	1994	18.00	115-125
1996	Lil' Drummer Mouse	Open		12.00	12
1996	Little Drummer Boy	Open		12.00	12
1994	Mackenzie and Maxine Caroling	Closed	1995	18.00	30-65
1994	Mackenzie Building a Snowmouse	7,500	1994	18.00	50-125
1996	Mackenzie Claus on Parade	Open		22.00	22
1995	Mail Mouse	Open		12.00	12
1994	Manger Animals	Open		20.00	20
1994	Maxine Makin Snow Angels	Open		20.00	20
1996	My New Toy	Open		14.00	14
1996	Oops! Did I Do That?	Open		14.00	14
1996	Parade Banner	Open		16.00	16
1995	Pear Taxi	Open		16.00	16
1996	Peeking at Presents	Open		13.00	13
1996	Reginald's Newstand	Open		20.00	20
1995	Sleigh Ride	7,500	1995	16.00	50-125
1996	Snack for the Reindeer	Open		13.00	13
1995	Snow Plow	Open		16.00	16
1996	The Snowball Fight	Open		18.00	18
1995	Stewart's Choo Choo Ride	Open		17.50	18
1995	Teamwork Helps	Open		16.00	16
1995	Testing the Lights	Open		14.00	14
1995	Three Wise Mice	Open		20.00	20
1996	Town Crier	Open		14.00	14
1996	Waiting For Christmas	14,000		16.00	16
1997	You Melted My Heart	Open		20.00	20

Charming Tails Squashville Lighted Village - D. Griff

1994	Acorn Street Lamp	Open		5.00	5
1995	Butternut Squash Dairy	7,500	1996	45.00	45
1995	Candy Apple Candy Store	9,000		45.00	45
1996	Cantaloupe Cathedral	Open		45.00	45
1995	Carrot Post Office	Closed	1996	45.00	45
1994	Chestnut Chapel	Closed	1996	45.00	45
1995	Great Oak Town Hall	Open		45.00	45
1995	Leaf Fence	Open		6.00	6
1995	Mail Box, Bench	Open		11.00	11
1994	Mushroom Depot	Open		45.00	45
1994	Old Cob Mill	7,500		45.00	45
1994	Pumpkin Inn	Open		45.00	45
1995	Street Light/Sign	Open		11.00	11
1994	Village Sign	Open		30.00	30

Fitz And Floyd, Inc. : See Silvestri, Inc.

Flambro Imports

Emmett Kelly Jr. Members Only Figurine - Undisclosed

1990	Merry-Go-Round	Closed	1990	125.00	400-500
1991	10 Years Of Collecting	Closed	1991	100.00	200
1992	All Aboard	Closed	1992	75.00	200
1993	Ringmaster	Closed	1993	125.00	125
1994	Birthday Mail	Closed	1994	100.00	175-225
1995	Salute To Our Vets	Closed	1995	75.00	75
1996	I Love You	Closed	1996	95.00	95

EKJ Professionals - Undisclosed

1987	Accountant	Retrd.	1994	50.00	125
1991	Barber	Retrd.	1995	50.00	75-100
1988	Bowler	Retrd.	1994	50.00	100
1996	Bowler	Open		55.00	55
1991	Carpenter	Open		50.00	50
1991	The Chef	Retrd.	1994	50.00	100
1995	Coach	Open		55.00	55
1990	Computer Whiz	Open		50.00	50
1987	Dentist	Retrd.	1995	50.00	75-100
1996	Dentist	Open		55.00	55
1987	Doctor	Retrd.	1995	50.00	100
1995	Doctor	Open		55.00	55
1991	Engineer	Retrd.	1995	50.00	100
1987	Executive	Open		50.00	50
1996	Farmer	Open		55.00	55
1988	Fireman	Open		55.00	55
1988	Fireman	Retrd.	1994	50.00	75-100
1990	Fisherman	Open		50.00	50
1988	Golfer	Open		55.00	55
1988	Golfer	Open		50.00	50
1990	Hunter	Open		50.00	50
1990	Lawyer	Open		55.00	55
1987	Lawyer	Retrd.	1995	50.00	75-100

YEAR ISSUE		EDITION LIMIT	YEAR RETD.	ISSUE PRICE	*QUOTE U.S.$
1996	Mailman	Open		55.00	55
1988	Mailman	Retrd.	1995	50.00	100
1993	On Maneuvers	Open		50.00	50
1991	Painter	Open		50.00	50
1991	Pharmacist	Open		50.00	50
1990	Photographer	Open		50.00	50
1993	Pilot	Open		50.00	50
1991	Plumber	Retrd.	1994	50.00	100
1995	Policeman	Open		55.00	55
1988	Policeman	Retrd.	1994	50.00	75-100
1990	The Putt	Open		50.00	50
1993	Realtor	Open		50.00	50
1988	Skier	Retrd.	1995	50.00	100
1996	Skier	Open		55.00	55
1987	Stockbrocker	Open		50.00	50
1987	Teacher	Retrd.	1995	50.00	100
1993	Veterinarian	Open		50.00	50

Emmett Kelly Jr. - Undisclosed, unless otherwise noted

1995	20th Anniversary of All Star Circus	5,000	1995	240.00	240
1995	35 Years of Clowning	5,000	1995	240.00	240
1989	65th Birthday Commemorative	1,989	1989	300.00	1200-1600
1993	After The Parade	7,500		190.00	190
1988	Amen	12,000	1991	120.00	350
1996	American Circus Extravaganza	5,000		240.00	240
1991	Artist At Work	7,500		285.00	285
1992	Autumn - D. Rust	Retrd.	1996	60.00	100
1983	The Balancing Act	10,000	1985	75.00	700-800
1983	Balloons For Sale	10,000	1985	75.00	600-700
1990	Balloons for Sale II	7,500		250.00	250
1986	Bedtime	12,000	1991	198.00	175-250
1984	Big Business	9,500	1987	110.00	800-900
1990	Convention-Bound	7,500		225.00	230
1986	Cotton Candy	12,000	1987	98.00	375
1996	Daredevil Thrill Motor Show	5,000		240.00	240
1988	Dining Out	12,000	1991	120.00	200-300
1984	Eating Cabbage	12,000	1986	75.00	475
1985	Emmett's Fan	12,000	1986	80.00	475
1986	The Entertainers	12,000	1991	120.00	150-200
1986	Fair Game	2,500	1987	450.00	1650
1991	Finishing Touch	7,500		230.00	230
1991	Follow The Leader	7,500		200.00	200
1994	Forest Friends	7,500		190.00	190
1983	Hole In The Sole	10,000	1986	75.00	600
1989	Hurdy-Gurdy Man	9,500	1991	150.00	200-350
1985	In The Spotlight	12,000	1988	103.00	400
1993	Kittens For Sale	7,500		190.00	190
1994	Let Him Eat Cake	3,500	1995	300.00	550
1994	The Lion Tamer	7,500		190.00	190
1981	Looking Out To See	12,000	1982	75.00	2400-2700
1986	Making New Friends	9,500	1989	140.00	350
1989	Making Up	7,500	1995	200.00	250-450
1985	Man's Best Friend	9,500	1989	98.00	550-650
1990	Misfortune?	3,500	1989	350.00	500-600
1987	My Favorite Things	9,500	1988	109.00	600-700
1989	No Loitering	7,500	1994	200.00	400
1985	No Strings Attached	9,500	1991	98.00	200-350
1992	No Use Crying	7,500		200.00	200
1987	On The Road Again	9,500	1991	109.00	450
1988	Over a Barrel	9,500	1991	130.00	250-450
1992	Peanut Butter?	7,500		200.00	200
1984	Piano Player	9,500	1988	160.00	500-600
1992	Ready-Set-Go	7,500		200.00	200
1987	Saturday Night	7,500	1988	153.00	500-600
1983	Spirit of Christmas I	3,500	1984	125.00	2600
1984	Spirit of Christmas II	3,500	1985	270.00	500-600
1985	Spirit of Christmas III	3,500	1989	220.00	525
1986	Spirit of Christmas IV	3,500	1989	150.00	400-550
1987	Spirit of Christmas V	2,400	1989	170.00	400-550
1988	Spirit of Christmas VI	2,400	1989	194.00	400-600
1990	Spirit of Christmas VII	3,500	1990	275.00	425
1991	Spirit of Christmas VIII	3,500	1992	250.00	350
1993	Spirit of Christmas IX	3,500		200.00	200
1993	Spirit of Christmas X	3,500		200.00	200
1994	Spirit of Christmas XI	3,500	1995	200.00	225-250
1995	Spirit of Christmas XII	3,500		200.00	200
1996	Spirit of Christmas XIII	3,500		200.00	200
1992	Spring - D. Rust	Retrd.	1996	60.00	60
1992	Summer - D. Rust	Retrd.	1996	60.00	60
1981	Sweeping Up	12,000	1982	75.00	1500-1700
1982	The Thinker	15,000	1986	60.00	1100
1987	Toothache	12,000	1995	98.00	125-250
1990	Watch the Birdie	9,500		200.00	225
1982	Wet Paint	15,000	1983	80.00	800
1988	Wheeler Dealer	7,500	1990	160.00	250-300
1982	Why Me?	15,000	1984	60.00	475-600
1983	Wishful Thinking	10,000	1985	65.00	500-700
1993	World Traveler	7,500		190.00	190

Emmett Kelly Jr. A Day At The Fair - Undisclosed

1990	75¢ Please	Retrd.	1994	65.00	85-125
1991	Coin Toss	Retrd.	1994	65.00	85-125
1990	Look At You	Retrd.	1994	65.00	85-125
1991	Popcorn!	Retrd.	1994	65.00	85-125
1990	Ride The Wild Mouse	Retrd.	1994	65.00	85-125
1990	Step Right Up	Retrd.	1994	65.00	85-125
1992	Stilt Man	Retrd.	1994	65.00	85-125
1990	The Stilt Man	Retrd.	1994	65.00	85-125
1990	Thanks Emmett	Retrd.	1994	65.00	85-125
1990	Three For A Dime	Retrd.	1994	65.00	85-125

Collectors' Information Bureau

*Quotes have been rounded up to nearest dollar

YEAR ISSUE	EDITION LIMIT	YEAR RETRD.	ISSUE PRICE	*QUOTE U.S.$
1991 The Trouble With Hot Dogs		Retrd. 1994	65.00	85-125
1990 You Can Do It, Emmett		Retrd. 1994	65.00	85-125
1990 You Go First, Emmett		Retrd. 1994	65.00	85-125

Emmett Kelly Jr. Appearance Figurine - Undisclosed

YEAR ISSUE	EDITION LIMIT	YEAR RETRD.	ISSUE PRICE	*QUOTE U.S.$
1992 Now Appearing	Open		100.00	100
1993 The Vigilante	Open		75.00	75
1996 Going My Way	Open		90.00	90

Emmett Kelly Jr. Event Figurine - Undisclosed

1996 EKJ For President	12/96		60.00	60

Emmett Kelly Jr. Images of Emmett - Undisclosed

YEAR ISSUE	EDITION LIMIT	YEAR RETRD.	ISSUE PRICE	*QUOTE U.S.$
1994 Baby's First Christmas	Open		80.00	80
1994 Best of Friends	Open		55.00	55
1994 Healing Heart	Open		90.00	90
1994 Holding The Future		Retrd. 1996	65.00	65
1994 Learning Together	Open		85.00	85
1994 Tightrope	Open		70.00	70
1994 Why Me, Again?	Open		60.00	60

Emmett Kelly Jr. Miniatures - Undisclosed

YEAR ISSUE	EDITION LIMIT	YEAR RETRD.	ISSUE PRICE	*QUOTE U.S.$
1994 65th Birthday		Retrd. 1994	70.00	75-95
1996 Amen	Open		35.00	35
1986 Balancing Act		Retrd. 1992	25.00	125
1986 Balloons for Sale		Retrd. 1993	25.00	105
1995 Bedtime	Open		35.00	35
1988 Big Business		Retrd. 1995	35.00	90-100
1989 Cotton Candy		Retrd. 1991	30.00	75
1995 Dining Out	Open		35.00	35
1987 Eating Cabbage		Retrd. 1990	30.00	50-75
1987 Emmett's Fan		Retrd. 1994	30.00	100
1995 The Entertainers	Open		45.00	45
1994 Fair Game	Open		75.00	75
1986 Hole in the Sole		Retrd. 1989	25.00	100
1995 Hurdy Gurdy Man	Open		40.00	40
1991 In The Spotlight		Retrd. 1996	35.00	85
1986 Looking Out To See		Retrd. 1987	25.00	150-175
1992 Making New Friends		Retrd. 1996	40.00	40
1996 Making Up	Open		55.00	55
1989 Man's Best Friend?		Retrd. 1994	35.00	85
1996 Misfortune	Open		60.00	60
1990 My Favorite Things		Retrd. 1995	45.00	90
1995 No Loitering	Open		50.00	50
1991 No Strings Attached		Retrd. 1996	35.00	35
1992 On the Road Again	Numbrd.		35.00	35
1994 Over a Barrel	Open		30.00	30
1992 Piano Player	Numbrd.		50.00	50
1990 Saturday Night		Retrd. 1995	50.00	65-100
1988 Spirit of Christmas I		Retrd. 1990	40.00	150
1992 Spirit of Christmas II		Retrd. 1995	50.00	75
1990 Spirit Of Christmas III		Retrd. 1993	50.00	75-125
1993 Spirit of Christmas IV	Numbrd.		40.00	40
1994 Spirit of Christmas V	Open		50.00	50
1996 Spirit of Christmas VI	Open		55.00	55
1986 Sweeping Up		Retrd. 1987	25.00	175-200
1986 The Thinker		Retrd. 1991	25.00	75
1996 The Toothache	Open		35.00	35
1986 Wet Paint		Retrd. 1993	25.00	125
1996 Wheeler Dealer	Open		65.00	65
1986 Why Me?		Retrd. 1989	25.00	110
1986 Wishful Thinking		Retrd. 1988	25.00	90

Emmett Kelly Jr. Real Rags Collection - Undisclosed

YEAR ISSUE	EDITION LIMIT	YEAR RETRD.	ISSUE PRICE	*QUOTE U.S.$
1993 Big Business II		Retrd. 1996	140.00	140
1993 Checking His List	Closed	N/A	100.00	200
1994 Eating Cabbage 2	3,000		100.00	100
1994 A Good Likeness	3,000		120.00	120
1993 Looking Out To See II	Open		100.00	100
1994 On in Two	3,000		100.00	100
1994 Rudolph Has A Red Nose, Too	3,000	1996	135.00	135
1993 Sweeping Up II	Open		100.00	100
1993 Thinker II	Open		120.00	120

Little Emmetts - M. Wu

YEAR ISSUE	EDITION LIMIT	YEAR RETRD.	ISSUE PRICE	*QUOTE U.S.$
1996 Balancing Act	Open		25.00	25
1996 Balloons for Sale	Open		25.00	25
1994 Birthday Haul	Open		30.00	30
1995 Dance Lessons	Open		50.00	50
1994 Little Artist Picture Frame	Open		22.00	22
1994 Little Emmett Fishing	Open		35.00	35
1995 Little Emmett Noel, Noel	Open		40.00	40
1994 Little Emmett Shadow Show	Open		40.00	40
1995 Little Emmett Someday	Open		50.00	50
1994 Little Emmett w/Blackboard	Open		30.00	30
1994 Little Emmett, Counting Lession (Musical)	Open		30.00	30
1994 Little Emmett, Country Road (Musical)	Open		35.00	35
1994 Little Emmett, Raindrops (Musical)	Open		35.00	35
1994 Little Emmett, You've Got a Friend (Musical)	Open		33.00	33
1996 Long Distance	Open		50.00	50
1995 Looking Back Musical Waterglobe	Open		75.00	75
1995 Looking Forward Musical Waterglobe	Open		75.00	75
1996 Looking Out To See	Open		25.00	25
1994 Playful Bookends	Open		40.00	40
1996 Sweeping Up	Open		25.00	25
1996 Thinker	Open		25.00	25
1996 Wet Paint	Open		40.00	40

YEAR ISSUE	EDITION LIMIT	YEAR RETRD.	ISSUE PRICE	*QUOTE U.S.$
1994 EKJ, Age 1	Open		9.00	9
1994 EKJ, Age2	Open		9.50	10
1994 EKJ, Age 3	Open		12.00	12
1994 EKJ, Age 4	Open		12.00	12
1994 EKJ, Age 5	Open		15.00	15
1994 EKJ, Age 6	Open		15.00	15
1994 EKJ, Age 7	Open		17.00	17
1994 EKJ, Age 8	Open		21.00	21
1994 EKJ, Age 9	Open		22.00	22
1994 EKJ, Age 10	Open		25.00	25
1996 January-New Years	Open		35.00	35
1996 February-Valentine's Day	Open		35.00	35
1996 March-St. Patrick's Day	Open		35.00	35
1996 April-April Showers	Open		35.00	35
1996 May-May Flowers	Open		35.00	35
1996 June-School Is Out	Open		35.00	35
1996 July-Independence Day	Open		35.00	35
1996 August-Summer Picnic	Open		35.00	35
1996 September-School Is In	Open		35.00	35
1996 October-Pumpkins for Fall & Halloween	Open		35.00	35
1996 November-Thanksgiving	Open		35.00	35
1996 December-Snow Sledding w/Friends	Open		35.00	35

Pleasantville 1893 - J. Berg Victor

YEAR ISSUE	EDITION LIMIT	YEAR RETRD.	ISSUE PRICE	*QUOTE U.S.$
1990 1st Church Of Pleasantville		Retrd. 1994	35.00	35
1992 Apothecary/Ice Cream Shop	Open		36.00	36
1992 Ashbey House	Open		40.00	40
1993 Balcomb's Barn	Open		40.00	40
1993 Balcomb's Farm (out buildings)	Open		40.00	40
1993 Balcomb's Farmhouse	Open		40.00	40
1990 The Band Stand		Retrd. 1992	12.00	15
1992 Bank/Real Estate Office		Retrd. 1995	36.00	36
1993 Blacksmith Shop	Open		40.00	40
1991 Court House	Open		36.00	36
1992 Covered Bridge		Retrd. 1995	36.00	36
1990 Department Store		Retrd. 1993	25.00	29
1991 Fire House	Open		40.00	40
1994 Gazebo/Bandstand	Open		25.00	25
1990 The Gerber House		Retrd. 1993	30.00	30
1992 Library	Open		32.00	32
1993 Livery Stable and Residence	Open		40.00	40
1990 Mason's Hotel and Saloon	Open		35.00	35
1991 Methodist Church	Open		40.00	40
1992 Miss Fountains Boarding House	Open		48.00	48
1990 Pleasantville Library	Open		32.00	32
1992 Post Office		Retrd. 1995	40.00	40
1992 Railroad Station	Open		40.00	40
1990 Reverend Littlefield's House	Open		34.00	34
1994 Sacred Heart Catholic Church	Open		40.00	40
1994 Sacred Heart Rectory	Open		40.00	40
1991 School House	Open		36.00	36
1990 Sweet Shoppe & Bakery	Open		40.00	40
1990 Toy Store		Retrd. 1992	30.00	45
1992 Tubbs, Jr. House	Open		40.00	40

Pleasantville 1893 Members Only - J. Berg Victor

1992 Pleasantville Gazette Building	Open		30.00	30

Pocket Dragon Collector Club - R. Musgrave

YEAR ISSUE	EDITION LIMIT	YEAR RETRD.	ISSUE PRICE	*QUOTE U.S.$
1991 Collecting Butterflies		Retrd. 1992	Gift	135
1992 The Key to My Heart		Retrd. 1993	Gift	110
1993 Want A Bite?		Retrd. 1994	Gift	55-65
1993 Bitsy		Retrd. 1994	Gift	N/A
1994 Friendship Pin	Open		Gift	85
1994 Blue Ribbon Dragon		Retrd. 1995	Gift	80
1995 Making Time For You		Retrd. 1996	Gift	N/A
1996 Good News	5/97		Gift	N/A

Pocket Dragon Members Only Pieces - R. Musgrave

YEAR ISSUE	EDITION LIMIT	YEAR RETRD.	ISSUE PRICE	*QUOTE U.S.$
1991 A Spot of Tea Won't You Join Us (set)		Retrd. 1992	75.00	350
1991 Wizard's House Print		Retrd. 1993	39.95	85-100
1992 Book Nook		Retrd. 1993	140.00	200
1993 Pen Pals		Retrd. 1994	90.00	110-135
1994 The Best Seat in the House		Retrd. 1995	75.00	105-175
1995 Party Time		Retrd. 1996	75.00	75
1996 Looking For The Right Words	5/97		80.00	80

Pocket Dragon Appearance Figurines - R. Musgrave

YEAR ISSUE	EDITION LIMIT	YEAR RETRD.	ISSUE PRICE	*QUOTE U.S.$
1993 A Big Hug		Retrd. 1994	35.00	50-65
1994 Packed and Ready		Retrd. 1995	47.00	60-95
1995 Attention to Detail		Retrd. 1996	24.00	24
1996 On The Road Again	Open		30.00	30

Pocket Dragon Christmas Editions - R. Musgrave

YEAR ISSUE	EDITION LIMIT	YEAR RETRD.	ISSUE PRICE	*QUOTE U.S.$
1992 A Pocket-Sized Tree		Retrd. 1992	18.95	80-90
1993 Christmas Angel		Retrd. 1993	45.00	65
1991 I've Been Very Good		Retrd. 1991	37.50	95-125
1989 Putting Me on the Tree		Retrd. 1994	52.50	75
1994 Dear Santa		Retrd. 1995	50.00	65-95
1995 Chasing Snowflakes		Retrd. 1995	35.00	45-55
1996 Christmas Skates		Retrd. 1996	36.00	36

Pocket Dragons - R. Musgrave

YEAR ISSUE	EDITION LIMIT	YEAR RETRD.	ISSUE PRICE	*QUOTE U.S.$
1990 The Apprentice		Retrd. 1994	22.50	50
1989 Attack		Retrd. 1992	45.00	105
1989 Baby Brother		Retrd. 1992	19.50	55
1993 Bath Time		Retrd. 1995	90.00	95-105
1993 The Book End		Retrd. 1996	90.00	90
1994 A Book My Size	Open		30.00	30

YEAR ISSUE	EDITION LIMIT	YEAR RETRD.	ISSUE PRICE	*QUOTE U.S.$
1992 Bubbles		Retrd. 1996	55.00	55
1995 But I am Too Little!	Open		14.50	15
1994 Butterfly Kissess	Open		29.50	30
1994 Candy Cane	Open		55.00	55
1995 Classical Dragon	Open		80.00	80
1994 Coffee Please	Open		24.00	24
1996 D-Pressing	Open		28.00	28
1994 Dance Partner	Open		23.00	23
1992 A Different Drummer		Retrd. 1994	32.50	50-85
1989 Do I Have To?		Retrd. 1994	45.00	45
1991 Dragons in the Attic		Retrd. 1995	120.00	120-135
1989 Drowsy Dragon		Retrd. 1996	27.50	28
1995 Elementary My Dear	Open		35.00	35
1989 Flowers For You		Retrd. 1992	42.50	75-100
1991 Friends	Open		55.00	55
1993 Fuzzy Ears	Open		16.50	17
1989 The Gallant Defender		Retrd. 1992	36.50	105
1989 Gargoyle Hoping For Raspberry Teacakes		Retrd. 1990	139.50	485-550
1994 Gargoyles Just Wanna Have Fun	Open		30.00	30
1989 A Good Egg		Retrd. 1991	36.50	175
1996 He Ain't Heavy...He's My Puffin	Open		34.00	34
1995 Hedgehog's Joke	Open		27.00	27
1996 Hopalong Gargoyle	Open		42.00	42
1993 I Ate the Whole Thing		Retrd. 1996	32.50	33
1991 I Didn't Mean To	Open		32.50	33
1991 I'm A Kitty		Retrd. 1993	37.50	60-75
1996 I'm So Pretty	Open		22.50	23
1994 In Trouble Again	Open		35.00	35
1995 It's a Present	Open		21.00	21
1994 It's Dark Out There	Open		45.00	45
1994 It's Magic	Open		31.00	31
1991 A Joyful Noise		Retrd. 1996	16.50	17
1992 The Juggler	Open		32.50	33
1993 Let's Make Cookies		Retrd. 1996	90.00	90
1992 The Library Cat		Retrd. 1994	38.50	65-100
1993 Little Bit (lapel pin)		Retrd. 1994	16.50	17
1993 Little Jewel (brooch)		Retrd. 1994	19.50	30
1994 A Little Security	Open		20.00	20
1989 Look at Me		Retrd. 1994	42.50	175
1992 Mitten Toes		Retrd. 1996	16.50	17
1994 My Big Cookie	Open		35.00	35
1992 Nap Time	Open		15.00	15
1989 New Bunny Shoes		Retrd. 1992	28.50	50-85
1989 No Ugly Monsters Allowed		Retrd. 1992	47.50	80
1993 Oh Goody!	Open		16.50	17
1996 Oh Happy Day	Open		22.00	22
1990 One-Size-Fits-All		Retrd. 1993	16.50	35
1992 Oops!		Retrd. 1996	16.50	17
1989 Opera Gargoyle		Retrd. 1991	85.00	225
1992 Percy		Retrd. 1994	70.00	105-135
1991 Pick Me Up		Retrd. 1995	16.50	17
1996 Pillow Fight	3,500		157.00	157
1989 Pink 'n' Pretty		Retrd. 1994	23.90	35-65
1994 Playing Dress Up	Open		30.00	30
1991 Playing Footsie		Retrd. 1994	16.50	25-35
1989 Pocket Dragon Countersign		Retrd. 1993	50.00	200
1989 The Pocket Minstrel		Retrd. 1991	36.50	125
1996 Pocket Piper	Open		37.00	37
1992 Pocket Posey		Retrd. 1996	16.50	17-25
1993 Pocket Rider (brooch)		Retrd. 1995	19.50	20-30
1991 Practice Makes Perfect		Retrd. 1993	32.50	50
1991 Putt Putt		Retrd. 1993	37.50	55-100
1996 Quartet	Open		80.00	80
1994 Raiding the Cookie Jar	3,500	1995	200.00	225-275
1993 Reading the Good Parts	Open		70.00	70
1996 Red Ribbon	Open		16.50	17
1991 Scales of Injustice	Open		45.00	45
1989 Scribbles		Retrd. 1994	32.50	45-60
1989 Sea Dragon		Retrd. 1991	45.00	175
1995 Sees All, Knows All	Open		35.00	35
1989 Sir Nigel Smythebe-Smoke		Retrd. 1993	120.00	200-225
1991 Sleepy Head		Retrd. 1995	37.50	50
1994 Snuggles	Open		35.00	35
1989 Stalking the Cookie Jar	Open		27.50	28
1989 Storytime at Wizard's House		Retrd. 1993	375.00	495
1996 Sweetie Pie	Open		28.00	28
1990 Tag-A-Long		Retrd. 1993	15.00	40
1989 Teddy Magic		Retrd. 1991	85.00	135-155
1995 Telling Secrets	Open		48.00	48
1991 Thimble Foot		Retrd. 1994	38.50	45-75
1991 Tickle		Retrd. 1996	27.50	28
1996 Tiny Bit Tired	Open		16.00	16
1989 Toady Goldtrayler		Retrd. 1993	55.00	85-105
1993 Treasure	Open		90.00	90
1995 Tumbly	Open		21.00	21
1991 Twinkle Toes		Retrd. 1995	16.50	20
1992 Under the Bed	2,500	1995	450.00	475-500
1989 Walkies		Retrd. 1992	65.00	175
1996 Watcha Doin	Open		22.50	23
1995 Watson	Open		22.50	23
1993 We're Very Brave		Retrd. 1996	37.50	38
1989 What Cookie?	Open		38.50	39
1989 Wizardry for Fun and Profit		Retrd. 1992	375.00	500-600
1993 You Can't Make Me	Open		15.00	15
1989 Your Paint is Stirred		Retrd. 1991	42.50	125
1992 Zoom Zoom	Open		37.50	38

Wizards & Dragons - H. Henriksen

YEAR ISSUE	EDITION LIMIT	YEAR RETRD.	ISSUE PRICE	*QUOTE U.S.$
1995 Alkmyne	2,500		135.00	135
1996 Apothes	1,500		195.00	195
1996 Archimedes	1,500		195.00	195

*Quotes have been rounded up to nearest dollar

YEAR ISSUE		EDITION LIMIT	YEAR RETD.	ISSUE PRICE	*QUOTE U.S.$
1995	Atnanticus	Retrd.	1996	150.00	150
1995	Confrontation	1,500		295.00	295
1996	Conversation	1,500		175.00	175
1996	Laidley Worm	1,500		150.00	150
1995	Pelryn	2,500		175.00	175
1995	Rammis	2,500		150.00	150
1996	Storm Bringer	1,500		150.00	150
1996	Tholief	1,500		250.00	250
1994	The Travellers	1,500		295.00	295

Forma Vitrum

Annual Christmas - B. Job

1995	Confectioner's Cottage 41101	2,500	1995	100.00	110
1996	Lollipop Shoppe 41102	2,500	1996	110.00	110

Coastal Classics - B. Job

1995	Bayside Beacon Lighthouse 21013	Open		65.00	65
1996	Cape Hope Lighthouse 21014	Open		100.00	100
1993	Carolina Lighthouse 21003	Open		65.00	65
1996	Cozy Cottage 21500	Open		70.00	70
1994	Lookout Point Lighthouse 21012	Open		60.00	60
1993	Maine Lighthouse 21002	Open		50.00	50
1993	Michigan Lighthouse 21001	Open		50.00	50
1994	Patriot's Point 29010	Open		70.00	70
1994	Sailor's Knoll Lighthouse 21011	Open		65.00	65

Coastal Heritage - B. Job

1996	Barnegat (NJ) 25006	2,996		85.00	85
1996	Cape Hatteras (NC) 25102	3,867		120.00	120
1995	Cape Neddick (ME) 25002	1,995	1995	140.00	155
1996	Fire Island (NY) 25005	2,996		150.00	150
1996	Holland Harbor (MI) 25203	1,996		125.00	125
1995	Marble Head (OH) 25201	1,995	1995	75.00	90
1996	New London (CT) 25004	2,996		145.00	145
1995	North Head (WA) 25302	1,995	1995	100.00	100
1995	Old Point Loma (CA) 25301	1,995	1995	100.00	100
1996	Peggy's Cove (NS) 25501	2,500		75.00	75
1995	Pigeon Point (CA) 25303	2,996		125.00	125
1995	Portland Head (ME) 25003	1,995	1995	140.00	160
1995	Sandy Hook (NJ) 25001	3,759	1995	140.00	155
1996	Split Rock (MN) 25202	2,996		130.00	130
1996	St. Augustine (FL) 25103	2,996		130.00	130
1995	St. Simon's (GA) 25101	1,995	1995	120.00	120

Special Production - B. Job

1993	The Bavarian Church 11503	Retrd.	1994	90.00	125
1994	Gingerbread House 19111	1,020	1994	100.00	175-300
1995	Miller's Mill (Musical) 11304	Open		115.00	115
1993	Pillars of Faith 11504	Retrd.	1994	90.00	135-175

Vitreville™ - B. Job

1993	Breadman's Bakery 11301	Retrd.	1996	70.00	72
1995	Brookview Bed & Breakfast 11303	1,250	1995	295.00	425-500
1993	Candlemaker's Delight 11801	Retrd.	1996	60.00	65
1993	Candymaker's Cottage 11102	Retrd.	1996	65.00	70
1994	Community Chapel 19510	Open		95.00	95
1993	Country Church 11502	12,500	1995	100.00	115
1993	Doctor's Domain 11201	Open		70.00	74
1996	Edgewater Inn 11305	1,500	1996	310.00	310
1995	Fire Station 11403	Open		100.00	100
1996	First Bank & Trust 11405	Open		110.00	110
1996	Kramer Building 11404	Open		100.00	100
1994	Maplewood Elementary School 11401	Open		100.00	100
1995	Mayor's Manor 11205	Open		85.00	85
1993	Painter's Place 11202	Open		70.00	74
1993	Pastor's Place 11101	Open		65.00	70
1993	Roofer's Roost 11203	Retrd.	1994	70.00	75
1993	Tailor's Townhouse 11204	Retrd.	1995	70.00	75
1994	Thompson's Drug 11302	5,000	1995	140.00	160-190
1993	Tiny Town Church 11501	Open		95.00	100
1994	Trinity Church 11511	7,000		130.00	130
1994	Vitreville Post Office 11402	Open		90.00	90

Woodland Village™ - B. Job

1993	Badger House 31003	Retrd.	1996	80.00	85
1993	Chipmunk House 31005	Retrd.	1996	80.00	85
1993	Owl House 31004	Retrd.	1996	80.00	85
1993	Rabbit House 31001	Retrd.	1996	90.00	94
1993	Racoon House 31002	Retrd.	1996	80.00	85

Franklin Mint

Joys of Childhood - N. Rockwell

1976	Coasting Along	3,700		120.00	175
1976	Dressing Up	3,700		120.00	175
1976	The Fishing Hole	3,700		120.00	175
1976	Hopscotch	3,700		120.00	175
1976	The Marble Champ	3,700		120.00	175
1976	The Nurse	3,700		120.00	175
1976	Ride 'Em Cowboy	3,700		120.00	175
1976	The Stilt Walker	3,700		120.00	175
1976	Time Out	3,700		120.00	175
1976	Trick or Treat	3,700		120.00	175

Ganz

Back to Basics Collection - C. Thammavongsa

1996	Back to Basics Cabin	Open		25.00	25

YEAR ISSUE		EDITION LIMIT	YEAR RETD.	ISSUE PRICE	*QUOTE U.S.$
1996	Campfire	Open		23.00	23
1996	Camping Out	Open		17.00	17
1996	Canoe Trip	Open		20.00	20
1996	Cub Scout	Open		8.50	9
1996	Family Picnic	Open		25.00	25
1996	Fishing Buddies	Open		23.00	23
1996	Honey Bear	Open		19.00	19
1996	Nature Walk	Open		15.00	15
1996	Sweet Tooth	Open		15.00	15
1996	Under the Stars	Open		12.00	12
1996	Wild Berries	Open		12.00	12

Blazing Spirits Collection - Ganz

1995	Freedom's Foal	Open		75.00	75
1995	Racing The Wind	Open		55.00	55
1995	Wild Stallion	Open		55.00	55

Carnival Classico Collection - Ganz

1995	Columbina	Open		52.00	52
1995	Harlequin	Open		52.00	52
1995	Jester	Open		52.00	52
1995	Pierrot	Open		52.00	52
1995	Spaventa	Open		52.00	52
1995	Tartaglia	Open		52.00	52

Cock-A-Doodle Corners Collection - C.Thammavongsa

1995	Cock-a-Doodle Corners Sign	Open		16.00	16
1995	Coffee Clutch	Open		24.00	24
1995	Country Courting	Open		20.00	20
1995	Follow the Leader	Open		24.00	24
1995	Fresh-Baked	Open		16.50	17
1995	Great Eggspectations	Open		15.00	15
1995	Hen Packed	Open		17.00	17
1995	Home Remedy	Open		21.00	21
1995	Master Craftsman	Open		18.00	18
1995	New Arrival	Closed	1996	10.00	10
1995	Organically Grown	Open		22.00	22
1995	Poultry Patrol	Open		16.50	17

Cottage Collectibles Collection - Ganz

1995	Bath Time	Open		17.00	17
1995	Best Friends	Open		16.00	16
1995	Circus Parade	Open		23.00	23
1995	First Love	Open		20.00	20
1995	Goin' Fishin'	Open		16.00	16
1995	Grandma's Treasures	Open		25.00	25
1995	A Job Well Done...	Open		25.00	25
1995	My Favorite Things	Open		16.00	16
1995	Naptime	Open		23.00	23
1995	Play Time	Open		23.00	23
1995	School Days	Open		16.00	16
1995	Tea Time	Open		23.00	23

Cowtown Collection - C.Thammavongsa

1994	Amoolia Steerheart	Open		25.00	25
1995	Bedtime Dairy Tales	Open		19.00	19
1993	Buffalo Bull Cody	Open		15.00	15
1996	Bull Cassidy & The Sundance Calf	Open		20.00	20
1993	Bull Masterson	Open		15.00	15
1993	Bull Rogers	Open		17.00	17
1993	Bull Ruth	Retrd.	1994	13.00	13
1995	Buster Cowtown	Open		15.00	15
1993	Buttermilk & Buttercup	Open		16.00	16
1995	A Calf's Best Friend	Open		12.00	12
1993	Cowlamity Jane	Open		15.00	15
1994	Cowsey Jones & The Cannonbull Express	Open		26.50	27
1993	Daisy Moo	Open		11.00	11
1995	Dracowla	Open		15.00	15
1995	Francowstein	Open		12.50	13
1994	Geronimoo	Open		17.00	17
1993	Gloria Bovine & Rudolph Bullentino	Open		20.00	20
1995	Grandma Mooses	Open		15.00	15
1994	Heiferella	Open		16.50	17
1995	Hicowatha & Moonehaha	Open		18.50	19
1995	Holy Mootrimoony	Open		20.00	20
1995	Jack-Cow-Lantern	Open		11.00	11
1993	Jethro Bovine	Retrd.	1994	15.00	15
1994	King Cowmooamooa	Open		16.50	17
1993	Lil' Orphan Angus	Open		11.00	11
1996	Lone-Wrangler	Open		15.00	15
1994	Ma & Pa Cattle	Open		23.50	24
1993	Moo West	Open		15.00	15
1995	Moother's Li'l Rascow	Open		20.00	20
1993	Old MooDonald	Open		13.50	14
1994	Pocowhantis	Open		15.00	15
1995	Scarecow	Open		11.50	12
1994	Set of Three Cacti	Open		17.00	17
1995	Steershot Annie	Open		16.50	17
1995	Supercow	Open		15.00	15
1994	Tchaicowsky	Open		19.00	19
1994	Tender Loving Cow	Open		12.50	13
1994	Texas Lonesteer	10,000		50.00	50
1995	Will Bull Hickock	Open		17.00	17
1995	Yellowsteer National Park	Open		20.00	20

Cowtown/Christmas Collection - C. Thammavongsa, unless otherwise noted

1994	Billy the Calf	Open		14.00	14
1996	Calf Ton Pickup - Chiemlowski	Open		10.00	10
1994	Christmas Cactus	Open		13.50	14

YEAR ISSUE		EDITION LIMIT	YEAR RETD.	ISSUE PRICE	*QUOTE U.S.$
1995	Ellie-Moo's Angel	Open		11.00	11
1995	Here Comes Santa Cow	Open		17.50	18
1995	John Steere	Closed	1996	11.00	11
1995	Milk & Cookies	Open		14.50	15
1995	Moo Claus	Open		17.00	17
1995	Polar Bull	Open		17.50	18
1994	Saint Nicowlas	Open		16.00	16
1994	Santa Cows	Open		18.00	18
1994	Santa's Little Heifer	Open		12.50	13
1996	Snowbull and Friends - Chiemlowski	Open		18.00	18
1995	Twinkle Twinkle Little Steer	Open		12.00	12

Cowtown/Fall, Halloween Collection - C. Thammavongsa, unless otherwise noted

1995	Dracowla	Open		15.00	15
1996	Footbull Jersey - Chiemlowski	Open		10.00	10
1995	Francowstein	Open		12.50	13
1995	Jack-Cow-Lantern	Open		11.00	11
1996	The Mooflowers - Chiemlowski	Open		20.00	20
1995	Scarecow	Open		11.50	12

Cowtown/Valentine Collection - C.Thammavongsa

1994	I Love Moo	Open		15.00	15
1994	Robin Hoof & Maid Mooian	Open		23.00	23
1994	Romecow & Mooliet	Open		22.00	22
1994	Wanted: A Sweetheart	Open		16.00	16

Ferggie Polliwog & Friends Collection - Ganz/B. Lemaire

1995	Band-Aids	Open		15.00	15
1996	Beach Buddies	Open		14.00	14
1996	Frog Prince	Open		15.00	15
1996	Froggie Tales	Open		19.00	19
1996	Hi-Ho Fishy!	Open		19.00	19
1996	The Jitterbug Band	Open		21.00	21
1996	Lawnmower Man	Open		15.00	15
1996	Leap Frog	Open		15.00	15
1995	Lilypad League	Open		17.00	17
1996	Moonlight Serenade	Open		20.00	20
1996	No Fishing! Sign	Open		16.00	16
1996	No Place Like Home	Open		17.00	17

Grandma's Attic Collection - C.Thammavongsa

1995	Balderdash	Open		25.00	25
1995	Bumblebeary	Open		10.00	10
1995	Coco & Jiffy	Open		11.00	11
1995	Crumples & Creampuff	Open		13.50	14
1995	Dilly-Dally	Open		13.50	14
1995	Dumblekin	Open		19.00	19
1995	Jelly-Belly	Open		12.00	12
1995	Molly-Coddle	Open		16.00	16
1995	Prince Fuddle-Duddle & Princess Dazzle	Open		17.00	17
1995	Sprinkles	Open		15.00	15
1995	Tootoo	Open		10.00	10

Grandma's Attic/Easter, Springtime Collection - C.Thammavongsa

1995	Hucklebeary	Open		14.50	15
1995	Lambie-Pie	Open		14.50	15
1995	Slugger	Open		13.00	13

Grandma's Attic/Valentine Collection - C.Thammavongsa

1995	Abracadabra	Closed	1996	14.00	14
1995	Cuddles	Closed	1996	12.00	12
1995	Skippy and Marmalade	Closed	1996	23.00	23
1995	Tickles and Giggles	Closed	1996	20.00	20

The Lacewing Fairies Collection - Ganz/B. Lemaire

1995	Lacewing Fairies Sign	Open		10.00	10
1995	Liana & Her Spellbounde Prince	Open		37.00	37
1995	Liana - Spirit of the Woodes	Open		30.00	30
1995	Liana - The Butterflye Maiden	Open		26.50	27
1995	Salina - Enchantress of the Sea	Open		35.00	35
1995	Salina - Midsummer Night's Dreame	Open		36.00	36
1995	Salina - the Faerie Queene	Open		37.00	37

Little Cheesers/Collectors' Club Pieces - C.Thammavongsa

1993	Charter Member	Closed	1994	27.00	27
1994	Fireweed Fox	Closed	1995	15.00	15
1995	Welcome to the Club	Closed	1996	27.00	27
1995	The Invention	Closed	1996	15.00	15

Little Cheesers/Cheeserville Fall - C.Thammavongsa

1995	Bewitched	Open		8.50	9
1995	Candy Bandit	Open		8.50	9
1995	Cornucopia	Open		10.00	10
1995	Peace Offering	Open		8.50	9
1995	Pilgrims	Open		15.50	16
1995	Pumpkin Patch	Open		8.00	8

Little Cheesers/Cheeserville Picnic Collection - G.D.A. Group, unless otherwise noted

1991	Auntie Marigold Eating Cookie	Open		13.00	13
1991	Baby Cicely	Retrd.	1995	8.00	8
1991	Baby Truffle	Open		8.00	8
1991	Blossom & Hickory In Love	Open		19.00	19

YEAR ISSUE	EDITION LIMIT	YEAR RETD.	ISSUE PRICE	*QUOTE U.S. $
1995 Cheeserville Tales - C.Thammavongsa	Open		7.50	8
1993 Chuckles The Clown - C.Thammavongsa	Open		16.00	16
1993 Clownin' Around - C.Thammavongsa	Open		10.50	11
1991 Cousin Woody With Bread & Fruit	Open		14.00	14
1991 Fellow With Picnic Hamper	Retrd. 1991		13.00	13
1991 Fellow With Plate Of Cookies	Retrd. 1991		13.00	13
1994 Fiddle-Dee-Dee - C.Thammavongsa	Open		13.00	13
1993 For Someone Special - C.Thammavongsa	Open		13.50	14
1991 Grandmama Thistledown Holding Bread	Open		14.00	14
1991 Grandpapa Thistledown Carrying Basket	Open		13.00	13
1991 Harley Harvestmouse Waving	Open		13.00	13
1991 Harriet Harvestmouse	Retrd. 1993		13.00	13
1995 Hush-A-Bye Baby - C.Thammavongsa	Open		14.00	14
1991 Jenny Butterfield Kneeling	Open		13.00	13
1991 Jeremy Butterfield	Open		13.00	13
1995 Joyful Beginnings - C.Thammavongsa	Open		15.00	15
1991 Lady With Grapes	Retrd. 1991		14.00	14
1993 Little Cheesers Display Plaque - C.Thammavongsa	Open		25.00	25
1991 Little Truffle Eating Grapes	Open		8.00	8
1991 Little Truffle Smelling Flowers	Retrd. 1995		16.50	17
1991 Mama Fixing Sweet Cicely's Hair	Retrd. 1993		16.50	17
1991 Mama With Rolling Pin	Open		13.00	13
1991 Mama Woodsworth With Crate	Retrd. 1992		14.00	14
1991 Marigold Thistledown Picking Up Jar	Open		14.00	14
1991 Medley Meadowmouse w/Bouquet	Open		13.00	13
1994 Melody Maker	Retrd. 1995		17.00	17
1994 Ooom-Pah-Pah - C.Thammavongsa	Open		13.00	13
1991 Papa Woodsworth	Open		13.00	13
1991 Picnic Buddies	Open		19.00	19
1995 Picnic with Papa - C.Thammavongsa	Open		14.00	14
1995 Playtime - C.Thammavongsa	Open		14.00	14
1995 Read Me A Story - C.Thammavongsa	Open		15.00	15
1993 The Storyteller - C.Thammavongsa	10,000		25.00	25
1994 Strummin' Away - C.Thammavongsa	Open		13.00	13
1993 Sunday Drive - C.Thammavongsa	Open		40.00	40
1993 Sweet Dreams - C.Thammavongsa	Open		27.50	28
1994 Swingin' Sax - C.Thammavongsa	Open		13.00	13
1991 Violet With Peaches	Open		13.00	13
1994 Washboard Blues - C.Thammavongsa	Open		13.00	13
1994 What a Hoot! - C.Thammavongsa	Open		13.00	13
1993 Willy's Toe-Tappin' Tunes	Open		15.00	15
1993 Words Of Wisdom - C.Thammavongsa	Open		14.00	14

Little Cheesers/Cheeserville Picnic Collection Accessories - G.D.A. Group

YEAR ISSUE	EDITION LIMIT	YEAR RETD.	ISSUE PRICE	*QUOTE U.S. $
1994 Mayflower Meadow Base	Open		50.00	50

Little Cheesers/Cheeserville Picnic Mini-Food Accessories - G.D.A. Group

YEAR ISSUE	EDITION LIMIT	YEAR RETD.	ISSUE PRICE	*QUOTE U.S. $
1991 Basket Of Apples	Open		2.25	3
1991 Basket Of Peaches	Open		2.00	2
1991 Blueberry Cake	Retrd. 1994		2.50	3
1991 Bread Basket	Open		2.50	3
1991 Candy	Open		2.00	2
1991 Cherry Mousse	Open		2.00	2
1991 Cherry Pie	Retrd. 1991		2.00	2
1991 Chocolate Cake	Open		2.50	3
1991 Chocolate Cheesecake	Open		2.00	2
1991 Doughnut Basket	Open		2.50	3
1991 Egg Tart	Open		1.00	1
1991 Food Basket With Blue Cloth	Retrd. 1994		6.50	7
1991 Food Basket With Green Cloth	Open		7.50	8
1991 Food Basket With Pink Cloth	Retrd. 1994		6.00	6
1991 Food Basket With Purple Cloth	Open		6.00	6
1991 Food Trolley	Retrd. 1991		12.00	12
1991 Hazelnut Roll	Retrd. 1991		2.00	2
1991 Honey Jar	Retrd. 1991		2.00	2
1991 Hot Dog	Open		2.25	3
1991 Ice Cream Cup	Open		2.00	2
1991 Lemon Cake	Retrd. 1991		2.00	2
1991 Napkin In Can	Retrd. 1991		2.00	2
1991 Set Of Four Bottles	Retrd. 1991		10.00	10
1991 Strawberry Cake	Open		2.00	2
1991 Sundae	Open		2.00	2
1991 Wine Glass	Retrd. 1995		1.25	2

Little Cheesers/Cheeserville Picnic Musicals - G.D.A. Group

YEAR ISSUE	EDITION LIMIT	YEAR RETD.	ISSUE PRICE	*QUOTE U.S. $
1994 The Bandstand Base	Open		48.50	49
1991 Blossom & Hickory Musical Jewelry Box	Closed 1992		65.00	65
1991 Mama & Sweet Cicely Waterglobe	Closed 1992		55.00	55
1991 Medley Meadowmouse Waterglobe	Retrd. 1995		47.00	47

YEAR ISSUE	EDITION LIMIT	YEAR RETD.	ISSUE PRICE	*QUOTE U.S. $
1993 Musical "Secret Treasures" Trinket Box	Open		36.00	36
1991 Musical Basket Trinket Box	Open		30.00	30
1991 Musical Floral Trinket Box	Open		32.00	32
1991 Musical Medley Meadowmouse Cookie Jar	Retrd. 1992		75.00	75
1991 Musical Picnic Base	Open		60.00	60
1991 Musical Sunflower Base	Closed 1993		65.00	65
1991 Musical Violet Woodsworth Cookie Jar	Retrd. 1992		75.00	75
1992 Sweet Cicely Musical Doll Basket	Closed 1996		85.00	85
1993 Wishing Well Musical	Open		50.00	50

Little Cheesers/Christmas Collection - C. Thammavongsa, unless otherwise noted

YEAR ISSUE	EDITION LIMIT	YEAR RETD.	ISSUE PRICE	*QUOTE U.S. $
1991 Abner Appleton Ringing Bell - G.D.A. Group	Retrd. 1993		14.00	14
1993 All I Want For Christmas	Open		18.00	18
1994 Angel	Open		8.00	8
1991 Auntie Blossom With Ornaments - G.D.A. Group	Open		14.00	14
1994 Baby Jesus	Retrd. 1996		6.50	7
1991 Cheeser Snowman - G.D.A. Group	Retrd. 1994		7.50	8
1993 Christmas Greetings	Open		16.50	17
1991 Cousin Woody Playing Flute - G.D.A. Group	Retrd. 1996		14.00	14
1994 First Wiseman	Retrd. 1996		11.00	11
1991 Frowzy Roquefort III Skating - G.D.A. Group	Retrd. 1993		14.00	14
1991 Grandmama & Little Truffle - G.D.A. Group	Retrd. 1993		19.00	19
1991 Grandpapa & Sweet Cicely - G.D.A. Group	Retrd. 1996		19.00	19
1991 Grandpapa Blowing Horn - G.D.A. Group	Retrd. 1994		14.00	14
1991 Great Aunt Rose With Tray - G.D.A. Group	Open		14.00	14
1991 Harley & Harriet Dancing - G.D.A. Group	Retrd. 1993		19.00	19
1991 Hickory Playing Cello - G.D.A. Group	Retrd. 1994		14.00	14
1991 Jenny On Sleigh - G.D.A. Group	Open		16.00	16
1991 Jeremy With Teddy Bear - G.D.A. Group	Open		12.00	12
1994 Joseph	Retrd. 1996		10.00	10
1995 Joy to the World	Open		8.00	8
1991 Little Truffle With Stocking - G.D.A. Group	Open		8.00	8
1991 Mama Pouring Tea - G.D.A. Group	Retrd. 1994		14.00	14
1991 Marigold & Oscar Stealing A Christmas Kiss - G.D.A. Group	Retrd. 1994		19.00	19
1994 Mary	Retrd. 1996		10.00	10
1991 Medley Playing Drum - G.D.A. Group	Open		8.00	8
1991 Myrtle Meadowmouse With Book - G.D.A. Group	Retrd. 1994		14.00	14
1991 Santa Cheeser - G.D.A. Group	Open		13.00	13
1994 Santa's Sleigh	10,000		22.00	22
1994 Second Wiseman	Retrd. 1996		11.00	11
1994 Shepherd	Retrd. 1996		8.50	9
1993 Sleigh Ride	Retrd. 1995		11.00	11
1995 Tending The Flocks	Open		9.00	9
1994 Third Wiseman	Retrd. 1996		10.50	11
1991 Violet With Snowball - G.D.A. Group	Retrd. 1994		8.00	8

Little Cheesers/Christmas Collection Accessories - C. Thammavongsa, unless otherwise noted

YEAR ISSUE	EDITION LIMIT	YEAR RETD.	ISSUE PRICE	*QUOTE U.S. $
1993 Candleholder-Santa Cheeser	Open		19.00	19
1993 Candy Cane	Open		2.00	2
1994 Christmas Collection Base	Open		50.00	50
1993 Christmas Gift	Open		3.00	3
1993 Christmas Stocking	Open		3.00	3
1991 Christmas Tree - G.D.A. Group	Open		9.00	9
1994 Creche Base	Retrd. 1996		28.50	29
1993 Gingerbread House	Open		3.00	3
1993 Ice Pond Base	Open		5.50	6
1991 Lamp Post - G.D.A. Group	Open		8.50	9
1995 Little Cheeser Tree Topper	Open		34.00	34
1991 Outdoor Scene Base - G.D.A. Group	Retrd. 1993		35.00	35
1991 Parlor Scene Base - G.D.A. Group	Open		37.50	38
1993 Toy Soldier	Open		3.00	3
1993 Toy Train	Open		3.00	3

Little Cheesers/Christmas Collection Musicals - Various

YEAR ISSUE	EDITION LIMIT	YEAR RETD.	ISSUE PRICE	*QUOTE U.S. $
1992 Jenny Butterfield Christmas Waterglobe - GDA /Thammavongsa	Closed 1992		55.00	55
1992 Little Truffle Christmas Waterglobe - G.D.A. Group	Retrd. 1995		45.00	45
1992 Musical Santa Cheeser Roly-Poly - G.D.A. Group	Suspd.		55.00	55
1993 Rotating Round Wood Base "I'll be Home for X'mas" - C.Thammavongsa	Open		30.00	30
1993 Round Wood Base "We Wish You a Merry X'mas" - C.Thammavongsa	Open		25.00	25

Little Cheesers/Circus Party Collection - C.Thammavongsa

YEAR ISSUE	EDITION LIMIT	YEAR RETD.	ISSUE PRICE	*QUOTE U.S. $
1995 Balancing Act	Open		8.00	8
1995 Beep-Beep	Open		13.50	14
1995 Cheeserville Choo-Choo	Open		21.00	21
1995 Easy As Cake	Open		15.00	15
1995 Look Ma-No Hands	Open		18.00	18

YEAR ISSUE	EDITION LIMIT	YEAR RETD.	ISSUE PRICE	*QUOTE U.S.$
1995 Woops!	Open		10.50	11

Little Cheesers/Little Hoppers Collection - C.Thammavongsa

YEAR ISSUE	EDITION LIMIT	YEAR RETD.	ISSUE PRICE	*QUOTE U.S.$
1994 Bubble Bath	Open		7.50	8
1994 Let's Play Ball	Open		7.00	7
1994 Somebunny Loves You	Open		7.50	8
1994 Sweet Nothings	Open		15.00	15
1994 Tender Loving Care	Open		10.00	10
1994 Tricycle Built for Two	Open		16.00	16

Little Cheesers/Springtime In Cheeserville Accessories - C.Thammavongsa

YEAR ISSUE	EDITION LIMIT	YEAR RETD.	ISSUE PRICE	*QUOTE U.S.$
1992 April Showers Bring May Flowers	Open		7.50	8
1992 Decorated With Love	Open		7.50	8
1992 For Somebunny Special	Open		7.50	8

Little Cheesers/Springtime In Cheeserville Musicals - GDA/Thammavongsa

YEAR ISSUE	EDITION LIMIT	YEAR RETD.	ISSUE PRICE	*QUOTE U.S.$
1992 Tulips & Ribbons Musical Trinket Box	Closed 1994		28.00	28

Little Cheesers/Springtime In Cheeserville Collection - C.Thammavongsa

YEAR ISSUE	EDITION LIMIT	YEAR RETD.	ISSUE PRICE	*QUOTE U.S.$
1992 A Basket Full Of Joy	Open		16.00	16
1994 Birthday Party	Retrd. 1995		22.00	22
1993 Blossom Has A Little lamb	Open		16.50	17
1993 First Kiss	Open		24.00	24
1993 For My Sweatheart	Open		22.00	22
1993 Friends Forever	Open		22.00	22
1995 Fuzzy Friends	Open		9.00	9
1993 Gently Down The Stream	10,000		27.00	27
1994 Get Well	Open		22.00	22
1993 Gift From Heaven	Retrd. 1996		10.00	10
1994 Hip Hip Hooray	Open		22.00	22
1992 Hippity-Hop. It's Eastertime!	Open		16.00	16
1993 Hugs & Kisses	Open		11.00	11
1993 I Love You	Open		22.00	22
1995 Little Miracles	Open		8.00	8
1993 Playing Cupid	Open		10.00	10
1992 Springtime Delights	Open		12.00	12
1994 Sugar & Spice	Open		24.00	24
1993 Sunday Stroll	Open		22.00	22
1992 A Wheelbarrow Of Sunshine	Open		17.00	17

Little Cheesers/Valentine Collection - C.Thammavongsa

YEAR ISSUE	EDITION LIMIT	YEAR RETD.	ISSUE PRICE	*QUOTE U.S.$
1993 Ballerina Sweetheart	Retrd. 1996		10.00	10
1995 Be My Angel	Open		10.50	11
1993 First Kiss	Open		24.00	24
1993 For My Sweetheart	Open		22.00	22
1993 Friends Forever	Open		22.00	22
1993 Gently Down the Stream	10,000		27.00	27
1993 Hugs & Kisses	Open		11.00	11
1993 I Love You	Open		22.00	22
1995 My L'il Sweetheart	Open		9.00	9
1993 Playing Cupid	Open		10.00	10
1993 Sugar & Spice	Open		24.00	24
1993 Sunday Stroll	Open		22.00	22

Little Cheesers/Wedding Collection - GDA/Thammavongsa, unless otherwise noted

YEAR ISSUE	EDITION LIMIT	YEAR RETD.	ISSUE PRICE	*QUOTE U.S.$
1993 The Big Day - C. Thammavongsa	Open		20.00	20
1992 Blossom Thistledown (bride)	Open		16.00	16
1992 Cousin Woody & Little Truffle	Open		20.00	20
1992 Frowzy Roquefort III With Gramophone	Open		20.00	20
1992 Grandmama & Grandpapa Thistledown	Retrd. 1994		20.00	20
1992 Great Aunt Rose Beside Table	Open		20.00	20
1992 Harley & Harriet Harvestmouse	Open		20.00	20
1992 Hickory Harvestmouse (groom)	Open		16.00	16
1992 Jenny Butterfield/Sweet Cicely (bridesmaids)	Retrd. 1995		20.00	20
1992 Little Truffle (ringbearer)	Open		10.00	10
1992 Mama & Papa Woodsworth Dancing	Open		20.00	20
1992 Marigold Thistledown & Oscar Bobbins	Open		20.00	20
1992 Myrtle Meadowmouse w/Medley	Closed 1992		20.00	20
1992 Pastor Smallwood	Open		16.00	16
1992 Wedding Procession	Open		40.00	40

Little Cheesers/Wedding Collection Accessories - C. Thammavongsa

YEAR ISSUE	EDITION LIMIT	YEAR RETD.	ISSUE PRICE	*QUOTE U.S.$
1993 Banquet Table	Open		14.00	14
1993 Gazebo Base	Open		42.00	42

Little Cheesers/Wedding Collection Mini-Food Accessories - G.D.A. Group, unless otherwise noted

YEAR ISSUE	EDITION LIMIT	YEAR RETD.	ISSUE PRICE	*QUOTE U.S.$
1992 Bible Trinket Box - GDA/Thammavongsa	Open		16.50	17
1992 Big Chocolate Cake	Retrd. 1994		4.50	5
1992 Bride Candleholder - GDA/Thammavongsa	Open		20.00	20
1992 Cake Trinket Box - GDA/Thammavongsa	Open		14.00	14
1992 Candles	Open		3.00	3
1992 Cherry Jello	Open		3.00	3
1992 Chocolate Pastry	Retrd. 1992		2.00	2
1992 Chocolate Pudding	Open		2.50	3
1992 Flour Bag	Retrd. 1992		2.00	2

FIGURINES/COTTAGES

YEAR ISSUE		EDITION LIMIT	YEAR RETD.	ISSUE PRICE	*QUOTE U.S.$
1992	Flower Vase	Retrd.	1994	3.00	3
1992	Fruit Salad	Open		3.00	3
1993	Gooseberry Champagne - C. Thammavongsa	Open		3.00	3
1992	Grass Base - GDA/Thammavongsa	Suspd.		3.50	4
1992	Groom Candleholder - GDA/Thammavongsa	Open		20.00	20
1992	Honey Pot	Open		2.00	2
1992	Ring Cake	Open		3.00	3
1992	Salt Can	Retrd.	1992	2.00	2
1992	Souffle	Retrd.	1992	2.50	3
1992	Soup Pot	Open		3.00	3
1992	Tea Pot Set	Retrd.	1994	3.00	3
1992	Teddy Mouse	Retrd.	1994	2.00	2
1993	Wedding Cake - C. Thammavongsa	Open		4.50	5

Little Cheesers/Wedding Collection Musicals - Various

1993	Blossom & Hickory Musical - C. Thammavongsa	Retrd.	1994	50.00	50
1992	Musical Blossom & Hickory Wedding Waterglobe - GDA/Thammavongsa	Open		55.00	55
1992	Musical Wedding Base - GDA/Thammavongsa	Open		32.00	32
1992	Musical Wooden Base For Wedding Processional - G.D.A. Group	Open		25.00	25
1993	White Musical Wood Base For Gazebo Base "Evergreen" - C. Thammavongsa	Open		25.00	25

Magic of Saint Nicholas Collection - Ganz

1996	Holly Jolly Holidays	Open		60.00	60
1996	Magical Melodies	Open		60.00	60
1996	Twinkling Lights	Open		60.00	60

Perfect Little Place Collection - C. Thammavongsa

1995	All Star Angel	Open		14.00	14
1995	Angel Face	Open		15.00	15
1995	Angel's Food	Open		15.00	15
1996	Bless This Marriage	Open		20.00	20
1995	Divine Intervention	Open		15.00	15
1995	Heaven & Nature	Open		14.00	14
1996	Heaven Makes All Things New	Open		18.00	18
1995	Heavenly Grace	Open		14.00	14
1995	Match Made in Heaven	Open		18.00	18
1995	Paradise	Open		13.00	13
1995	Perfect Little Place	Open		16.00	16
1995	Pray the Lord My Soul to Keep	Open		13.00	13
1995	Ride Like The Wind	Open		15.00	15
1996	Showered With Love	Open		16.00	16
1995	Sweet Sleep, Angel Mild	Open		13.50	14

Perfect Little Place/Christmas Collection - C. Thammavongsa

1996	Angels in the Snow	Open		15.00	15
1995	Bearer of Blessings	Open		17.00	17
1996	Celestial Wonders	Open		17.00	17
1995	A Child is Born	Open		21.00	21
1996	Songs of Praise	Open		17.00	17

Perfect Little Place/Valentine Collection - C. Thammavongsa

1995	Be My Angel	Open		16.00	16
1995	Sweet Innocence	Open		16.00	16
1995	Whispers of Love	Open		21.00	21

Pigsville Accessories - C. Thammavongsa

1995	Bale of Straw	Open		10.00	10
1994	Barn	Open		35.00	35
1995	Outhouse	Open		10.00	10
1994	Silo	Open		15.00	15

Pigsville Collection - C. Thammavongsa, unless otherwise noted

1993	Bakin' at the Beach	Open		11.00	11
1994	Bedtime	Open		9.50	10
1994	Birthday Surprise	Open		9.50	10
1993	Ice Cream Anyone? - G.D.A. Group	Retrd.	1994	9.00	9
1995	Juke Box	Open		12.00	12
1993	Me & My Ice Cream - G.D.A. Group	Retrd.	1994	17.00	17
1996	Melon Patch	Open		11.00	11
1993	Mother Love - G.D.A. Group	Open		13.00	13
1995	Mr. Fix It	Open		14.00	14
1993	Nap Time - G.D.A. Group	Retrd.	1995	11.00	11
1994	Ole Fishing Hole	Open		16.00	16
1995	Open Roads	Open		14.00	14
1993	P.O.P Display Sign	Open		8.00	8
1995	Paradise	Open		10.00	10
1993	Pig at the Beach - G.D.A. Group	Open		9.00	9
1996	Pig Pen Blues	Open		11.00	11
1996	Pig Tails	Open		10.00	10
1995	Piggy Back	Open		10.50	11
1994	Play Ball	Open		11.50	12
1994	Pretty Piglet	Open		8.00	8
1993	Prima Ballerina	Retrd.	1994	11.00	11
1994	Sandcastle	Open		12.00	12
1995	Scrub-A-Dub-Dub	Open		13.50	14
1995	Seeds of Love	Open		14.50	15
1994	Snacktime	Open		11.50	12

YEAR ISSUE		EDITION LIMIT	YEAR RETD.	ISSUE PRICE	*QUOTE U.S.$
1993	Soap Suds - G.D.A. Group	Open		12.00	12
1994	Special Treat	Open		11.50	12
1993	Squeaky Clean - G.D.A. Group	Retrd.	1995	11.00	11
1994	Storytime	Open		13.00	13
1993	Tipsy - G.D.A. Group	Open		9.00	9
1995	Touchdown	Open		11.00	11
1993	True Love	Open		12.00	12
1993	Wedded Bliss	Open		16.00	16
1993	Wee Little Piggy	Open		8.00	8
1996	Yard Work	Open		13.00	13

Pigsville/Christmas Collection - C. Thammavongsa, unless otherwise noted

1996	Christmas Rush - Chiemlowski	Open		14.00	14
1994	Christmas Trimmings	10,000		24.00	24
1995	Dear Santa	Open		10.00	10
1996	Holiday Hog - Chiemlowski	Open		16.00	16
1994	Joy to the World	Open		10.00	10
1994	Let It Snow	Open		12.00	12
1994	Mistletoe Magic	Open		14.00	14
1995	Mrs. Claus	Open		11.00	11
1995	Oh Christmas Tree	Open		10.50	11
1994	Santa Pig	Open		11.00	11
1995	Tucked into Bed	Open		12.00	12
1994	Yuletide Carols	Open		19.00	19

Pigsville/Fall, Halloween Collection - C. Thammavongsa, unless otherwise noted

1995	Apple Bobbing	Open		10.00	10
1995	Giving Thanks	Open		10.00	10
1996	Hell's Angel - Chiemlowski	Open		10.00	10
1996	Hobo Clown - Chiemlowski	Open		10.00	10
1995	Pumpkin Pig	Open		11.00	11
1995	Scarecrow	Open		11.00	11

Pigsville/Valentine Collection - C. Thammavongsa

1995	Barn Dance	Open		14.50	15
1994	Champagne & Roses	Open		14.00	14
1995	The Hayloft	Open		11.00	11
1994	I Love You	Open		9.50	10
1994	I'm All Yours	Open		11.50	12
1995	Lover's Lane	Open		17.00	17
1994	Lovestruck	Open		10.00	10
1995	Popping The Question	Open		10.00	10
1995	Secret Admirer	Open		11.00	11
1995	Serenade	Open		10.50	11
1994	Sweetheart Pig	Open		8.00	8
1994	Together Forever	Open		15.00	15

Portraits of a People Collection - Ganz/B. Galvin

1996	"Crazy Horse" Chief of Oglala Sioux	Open		35.00	35
1996	"Ouanah Parker" Comanche Chief	Open		24.00	24
1996	"Ouray" Ute Chief Round Plaque	Open		15.00	15
1996	"Pontiac" Ottawa Chief Square Plaque	Open		15.00	15
1996	"Sitting Bull"	Open		33.00	33
1996	"Tecumseh" Shawnee Chief	Open		25.00	25
1996	"White Arrow" Cherokee SW	Open		24.00	24
1996	"Winema" (Toby Riddle)	Open		25.00	25
1996	Cheyenne Buffalo-Horn Bonnet	Open		21.00	21

The Precious Steeples Collection - Ganz/L. Sunarth

1995	Display Sign	Open		15.00	15
1995	Florence Cathedral	Open		40.00	40
1995	Notre Dame Cathedral	Open		40.00	40
1995	St. Patrick's Cathedral	Open		40.00	40
1995	St. Paul's Cathedral	Open		40.00	40
1995	St. Peter's Basilica	Open		40.00	40
1995	Westminster Abbey	Open		40.00	40

Trains Gone By Collection - Ganz

1996	C.P. Huntington Train	3,000		70.00	70
1996	C.P. Huntington Train with sound	2,000		85.00	85
1995	Display Sign	Open		24.00	24
1995	The General Train	4,000		70.00	70
1995	The General Train with sound	1,000		85.00	85
1995	New York Central Train	3,000		70.00	70
1995	New York Central Train w/sound	2,000		85.00	85
1995	Pennsylvania Train	4,000		70.00	70
1995	Pennsylvania Train with sound	1,000		85.00	85
1995	Santa Fe Train with sound	1,000		85.00	85
1995	Santa Fe Train	4,000		70.00	70

Watching Over You Collection - C. Thammavongsa

1995	Angelic Teachings	Open		42.00	42
1996	It Is Written...	Open		40.00	40
1995	New Borne Babe	Open		40.00	40
1995	Sweet Dreams Little One	Open		38.00	38

Watching Over You Collection Musicals - C. Thammavongsa

1996	Sweet Music Fills the Air	Open		60.00	60

Woodland Santas Collection - C. Thammavongsa

1995	Forest Friends	Open		45.00	45
1995	Lake of the Woods	Open		45.00	45
1995	Santa's Sanctuary	Open		41.00	41

Zoological Zodiac Collection - Ganz/B. Lemaire

1996	Aries	Open		25.00	25
1996	Taurus	Open		25.00	25

YEAR ISSUE		EDITION LIMIT	YEAR RETD.	ISSUE PRICE	*QUOTE U.S.$
1996	Gemini	Open		25.00	25
1996	Cancer	Open		25.00	25
1996	Leo	Open		25.00	25
1996	Virgo	Open		25.00	25
1996	Libra	Open		25.00	25
1996	Scorpio	Open		25.00	25
1996	Sagittarius	Open		25.00	25
1996	Capricorn	Open		25.00	25
1996	Aquarius	Open		25.00	25
1996	Pisces	Open		25.00	25

Gartlan USA

Members Only Figurine - Various

1990	Wayne Gretzky-Home Uniform - L. Heyda	Closed	1991	75.00	225
1991	Joe Montana-Road Uniform - F. Barnum	Closed	1992	75.00	150-250
1991	Kareem Abdul-Jabbar - L. Heyda	Closed	1993	75.00	175-250
1992	Mike Schmidt - J. Slockbower	Closed	1993	79.00	150-200
1993	Hank Aaron - J. Slockbower	Closed	1994	79.00	100-125
1994	Shaquille O'Neal - L. Cella	Closed	1995	39.95	75-100

Kareem Abdul-Jabbar Sky-Hook Collection - L. Heyda

1989	Kareem Abdul-Jabbar "The Captain", signed	1,989	1990	175.00	300-550
1989	Kareem Abdul-Jabbar, A/P	100	1990	200.00	550-700
1989	Kareem Abdul-Jabbar, Commemorative	33	1990	275.00	4700-5300

Leave It To Beaver - Noble Studio

1995	Jerry Mathers, (5")	5,000		49.95	50
1995	Jerry Mathers, (7 1/2"), signed	1,963		195.00	195
1996	Jerry Mathers, A/P (7 1/2"), signed	234		250.00	250

Magic Johnson Gold Rim Collection - R. Sun

1988	Magic Johnson "Magic in Motion"	1,737	1989	125.00	500-1000
1988	Magic Johnson A/P "Magic in Motion", signed	250	1989	175.00	2500
1988	Magic Johnson Commemorative	32	1989	275.00	7500

Mike Schmidt "500th" Home Run Edition - R. Sun

1987	Mike Schmidt "500th" Home Run, A/P signed	20	1988	275.00	1400-1700
1987	Mike Schmidt "500th" Home Run, signed	1,987	1988	150.00	750-850

Plaques - Various

1986	George Brett-"Royalty in Motion", signed - J. Martin	2,000	1987	75.00	275
1987	Mike Schmidt-"Only Perfect", A/P - Paluso	20	1988	200.00	550
1987	Mike Schmidt-"Only Perfect", signed - Paluso	500	1988	150.00	225-400
1985	Pete Rose-"Desire to Win", signed - T. Sizemore	4,192	1986	75.00	325
1986	Reggie Jackson A/P-The Roundtripper, signed - J. Martin	44	1987	175.00	400-475
1986	Reggie Jackson-"The Roundtripper" signed - J. Martin	500	1987	150.00	350-400
1987	Roger Staubach, signed - C. Soileau	1,979	1988	85.00	250-325

Ringo Starr - J. Hoffman

1996	Ringo Starr with drums, (6")	5,000		150.00	150
1996	Ringo Starr, (4")	10,000		49.95	50
1996	Ringo Starr, (8 1/2") A/P signed	250		600.00	600
1996	Ringo Starr, (8 1/2") signed	1,000		350.00	350

Signed Figurines - Various

1991	Al Barlick - V. Bova	1,989	1995	195.00	195
1993	Bob Cousy - L. Heyda	950	1995	150.00	150
1991	Bobby Hull - The Golden Jet - L. Heyda	1,983	1995	250.00	250-300
1992	Bobby Hull, A/P - L. Heyda	300	1994	350.00	400-600
1991	Brett Hull - The Golden Brett - L. Heyda	1,986	1995	250.00	250-300
1992	Brett Hull, A/P - L. Heyda	300	1994	350.00	400-600
1989	Carl Yastrzemski-"Yaz", A/P - L. Heyda	250	1990	150.00	500-800
1989	Carl Yastrzemski-"Yaz" - L. Heyda	1,989	1990	150.00	400
1992	Carlton Fisk - J. Slockbower	1,972	1995	225.00	225
1990	Darryl Strawberry - L. Heyda	2,500	1995	100.00	100
1994	Eddie Matthews - R. Sun	1,978	1995	195.00	200-300
1994	Frank Thomas - D. Carroll	500	1995	225.00	350
1990	George Brett - F. Barnum	2,250	1995	225.00	225
1992	Gordie Howe - L. Heyda	2,358	1994	225.00	250-350
1990	Gordie Howe, signed A/P - L. Heyda	250	1994	395.00	395
1992	Hank Aaron - F. Barnum	1,982	1994	225.00	225
1992	Hank Aaron Commemorative w/displ. case - F. Barnum	755	1994	275.00	400
1991	Hull Matched Figurines - L. Heyda	950	1995	500.00	500-700
1989	Joe DiMaggio - L. Heyda	2,214	1990	275.00	1500
1990	Joe DiMaggio- Pinstripe Yankee Clipper - L. Heyda	325	1990	695.00	2600
1990	Joe DiMaggio- Pinstripe Yankee Clipper, A/P - L. Heyda	12	1990	1500.00	4000-8000
1991	Joe Montana - F. Barnum	2,250	1991	325.00	675
1991	Joe Montana, A/P - F. Barnum	250	1991	500.00	700-1100
1989	John Wooden-Coaching Classics - L. Heyda	1,975	1990	175.00	175
1989	John Wooden-Coaching Classics, A/P - L. Heyda	250	1995	350.00	350
1989	Johnny Bench - L. Heyda	1,989	1990	150.00	225
1989	Johnny Bench, A/P - L. Heyda	250	1990	150.00	500-725

*Quotes have been rounded up to nearest dollar

YEAR ISSUE	EDITION LIMIT	YEAR RETD.	ISSUE PRICE	*QUOTE U.S.$
1994 Ken Griffey Jr., - J. Slockbower	1,989	1995	225.00	275
1993 Kristi Yamaguchi - K. Ling Sun	950	1995	195.00	195
1990 Luis Aparicio - J. Slockbower	1,984	1995	225.00	225
1991 Monte Irvin - V. Bova	1,973	1995	195.00	195
1991 Negro League, Set/3	950	1995	500.00	500
1985 Pete Rose-"For the Record", signed - H. Reed	4,192	1987	125.00	1100-1500
1992 Ralph Kiner - J. Slockbower	1,975	1995	225.00	225
1991 Rod Carew - Hitting Splendor - J. Slockbower	1,991	1995	225.00	225
1994 Sam Snead - L. Cella	950	1995	225.00	225
1994 Shaquille O'Neal - R. Sun	500	1995	225.00	300-500
1992 Stan Musial - J. Slockbower	1,969	1995	325.00	325
1992 Stan Musial, A/P - J. Slockbower	300	1995	425.00	425
1989 Steve Carlton - L. Heyda	3,290	1992	175.00	225-325
1989 Steve Carlton, A/P - L. Heyda	300	1992	350.00	400-500
1989 Ted Williams - L. Heyda	2,654	1990	295.00	400-800
1989 Ted Williams, A/P - L. Heyda	250	1990	650.00	700-1000
1992 Tom Seaver - J. Slockbower	1,992	1995	225.00	225
1994 Troy Aikman - V. Davila	500	1995	225.00	300
1991 Warren Spahn - J. Slockbower	1,973	1995	225.00	275
1989 Wayne Gretzky - L. Heyda	1,851	1989	225.00	600-1000
1989 Wayne Gretzky, A/P - L. Heyda	300	1989	695.00	1800-2300
1990 Whitey Ford - S. Barnum	2,360	1995	225.00	225
1990 Whitey Ford, A/P - S. Barnum	250	1995	350.00	350
1989 Yogi Berra - F. Barnum	2,150	1994	225.00	225
1989 Yogi Berra, A/P - F. Barnum	250	1994	350.00	350

Genesis

Aquatics Collection - K. Cantrell

YEAR ISSUE	EDITION LIMIT	YEAR RETD.	ISSUE PRICE	*QUOTE U.S.$
1994 Ancient Mariner (Sea Turtles)	950		950.00	990
1994 Bringing Up Baby (Humpback Whales)	950		950.00	990
1994 Old Men of the Sea (Sea Otters)	950		990.00	990
1994 Sea Wolves (Killer Whales)	950		950.00	990
1994 Splish Splash (Dolphins)	950		950.00	990

Arctic Collection - K. Cantrell

1995 Arctic Hares	2,500	1995	98.00	98
1995 Arctic Owl	2,500	1995	98.00	98
1995 Arctic Wolves	2,500	1995	98.00	98
1995 Harp Seal	2,500	1995	98.00	98
1995 Polar Bear	2,500	1995	98.00	98

Bear Cubs Collection - K. Cantrell

1996 Black Bear	500		250.00	250
1996 Grizzly Bear	500		250.00	250
1996 Polar Bear	500		250.00	250

Birds of Prey - K. Cantrell

1994 Bald Eagle	1,250		350.00	350
1994 Great Horned Owl	1,250		350.00	350

The Lighthouse Collection - L. Steorts

1995 Boston Light	2,500		170.00	170
1995 Cape Hatteras	2,500		170.00	170
1996 North Head	2,500		170.00	170
1996 Old Point Loma	2,500		170.00	170

Neptune's Children - K. Cantrell

1995 Neptune's Children	1,250		290.00	290
1995 Tranquil Waters	1,250		290.00	290

Ocean Realm - K. Cantrell

1994 Dolphins	1,250	1996	240.00	250
1994 Humpback Whales	1,250		240.00	250
1994 Manta Ray	1,250		240.00	250
1994 Marlins	1,250		240.00	250
1994 Otters	1,250		240.00	250

River Dwellers - K. Cantrell

1994 Construction Crew	950		990.00	990
1994 Ice Follies	950		890.00	950
1994 Salmon Supper	950		990.00	990

Sea Scapes Collection - K. Cantrell

1996 Exuberant	500		750.00	750
1996 Fluid Motion	500		750.00	750

Special Commission - K. Cantrell

1994 Fragile Planet	950		350.00	350
1995 Heavenly Waters	950		690.00	690
1996 Wave Dance	950		990.00	990

Geo. Zoltan Lefton Company

Colonial Village - Lefton

1993 Antiques & Curiosities 00723	Open		50.00	50
1995 Applegate-CVRA Exclusive 01327	Closed	1995	50.00	95
1990 The Ardmore House 07338	Closed	1995	45.00	110
1993 Baldwin's Fine Jewelry 00722	Open		50.00	50
1991 Belle-Union Saloon 07482	Closed	1994	45.00	85-125
1989 Bijou Theatre 06897	Closed	1990	40.00	250-300
1994 Black Sheep Tavern 01003	Open		50.00	50
1993 Blacksmith 00720	Open		47.00	47
1992 Brenner's Apothecary 07961	Open		45.00	45
1996 The Brookfield 11996	5,500		75.00	75
1994 Brown's Book Shop 01001	Open		50.00	50
1993 Burnside 00717	Open		50.00	50
1989 Capper's Millinery 06904	Suspd.		40.00	130
1988 City Hall 06340	Suspd.		40.00	200-300
1989 Cobb's Bootery 06903	Suspd.		40.00	140
1990 Coffee & Tea Shoppe 07342	Open		45.00	47
1996 Collectors Set 10740	Open		100.00	100
1994 Cole's Barn 06750	Closed	1994	40.00	150
1995 Colonial Savings and Loan 01321	Open		50.00	50
1995 Colonial Village News 01002	Open		50.00	50
1990 Country Post Office 07341	Closed	1994	45.00	65-150
1992 County Courthouse 00233	Open		45.00	50
1991 Daisy's Flower Shop 07478	Open		45.00	47
1993 Dentist's Office 00724	Open		50.00	50
1993 Doctor's Office 00721	Open		45.00	50
1992 Elegant Lady Dress Shop 00232	Open		45.00	50
1988 Engine Co. No. 5 Firehouse 06342	Open		40.00	50
1996 Fairbanks House 10397	Open		50.00	50
1988 Faith Church 06333	Closed	1991	40.00	125-250
1990 Fellowship Church 07334	Open		45.00	47
1990 The First Church 07333	Open		45.00	47
1988 First Post Office 06343	Open		40.00	50
1996 Franklin College 10393	Open		50.00	50
1988 Friendship Chapel 06334	Closed	1994	40.00	125-150
1993 Green's Grocery 00725	Open		50.00	50
1988 Greystone House 06339	Closed	1995	40.00	110
1989 Gull's Nest Lighthouse 06747	Open		40.00	47
1990 Hampshire House 07336	Open		45.00	50
1990 Hillside Church 11991	Closed	1991	60.00	350-500
1995 Historical Society Museum 01328	Open		50.00	50
1988 House of Blue Gables 06337	Closed	1995	40.00	70-110
1988 Johnson's Antiques 06346	Closed	1993	40.00	125-200
1993 Joseph House 00718	Open		50.00	50
1993 Kirby House-CVRA Exclusive 00716	Closed	1994	50.00	100-115
1992 Lakehurst House 11992	Closed	1992	55.00	300
1996 Lattimore House-CVRA Exclusive 10391	Open		50.00	50
1992 Main St. Church 00230	Open		45.00	50
1989 The Major's Manor 06902	Open		40.00	47
1989 Maple St. Church 06748	Closed	1993	40.00	500-700
1993 Mark Hall 00719	Open		40.00	50
1989 Miller Bros. Silversmiths 06905	Suspd.		40.00	155
1994 Mt. Zion Church 11994	Closed	1994	70.00	115-200
1990 Mulberry Station 07344	Open		50.00	65
1995 Mundt Manor 01008	Open		50.00	50
1988 New Hope Church (Musical) 06470	Closed	N/A	40.00	125-200
1990 The Nob Hill 07337	Closed	1995	45.00	85-110
1992 Northpoint School 07960	Open		45.00	50
1994 Notfel Cabin 01320	Open		50.00	50
1995 O'Doul's Ice House 01324	Open		50.00	50
1988 Old Time Station 06335	Open		40.00	50
1986 Original Set of 6	Unkn.		210.00	N/A
1986 · Charity Chapel 05895	Closed	1989	35.00	400-650
1986 · King's Cottage 05890	Open		35.00	50
1986 · McCauley House 05892	Closed	1988	35.00	275
1986 · Nelson House 05891	Closed	1989	35.00	250-450
1986 · Old Stone Church 05825	Open		35.00	47
1986 · The Welcome Home 05824	Open		35.00	47
1986 Original Set of 6	Unkn.		210.00	N/A
1986 · Church of the Golden Rule 05820	Open		35.00	50
1986 · General Store 05823	Closed	1988	35.00	450-500
1986 · Lil Red School House 05821	Open		35.00	50
1986 · Penny House 05893	Closed	1988	35.00	275-500
1986 · Ritter House 05894	Closed	1989	35.00	400-650
1986 · Train Station 05822	Closed	1989	35.00	150-200
1995 Patriot Bridge 01325	Open		50.00	50
1990 Pierpont-Smithe's Curios 07343	Closed	1993	45.00	110-175
1995 Queensgate 01329	Open		50.00	50
1989 Quincy's Clock Shop 06899	Open		40.00	47
1995 Rainy Days Barn 01323	Open		50.00	50
1994 Real Estate Office -CVRA Exclusive 01006	Open		50.00	50
1988 The Ritz Hotel 06341	Suspd.		40.00	105-250
1994 Rosamond 00988	Open		50.00	50
1990 Ryman Auditorium-Special Edition 08010	Open		50.00	55
1992 San Sebastian Mission 00231	Closed	1995	45.00	100-125
1991 Sanderson's Mill 07927	Open		45.00	47
1990 Ship's Chandler's Shop 07339	Suspd.		45.00	50
1994 Smith and Jones Drug Store 01007	Open		50.00	50
1991 Smith's Smithy 07476	Closed	1991	45.00	400-500
1994 Springfield 00989	Open		50.00	50
1993 St. James Cathedral 11993	Closed	1993	75.00	200-275
1996 St. Paul's Church 10735	Open		50.00	50
1993 St. Peter's Church w/Speaker 00715	Open		60.00	60
1988 The State Bank 06345	Open		40.00	50
1992 Stearn's Stable 00228	Open		45.00	50
1988 The Stone House 06338	Open		40.00	47
1991 Sweet Shop 07481	Open		45.00	47
1989 Sweetheart's Bridge 06751	Open		50.00	50
1996 Town Hall-Events Only 10390	Yr.Iss.		50.00	50
1991 The Toy Maker's Shop 07477	Open		45.00	47
1993 Trader Tom's Gen'l Store 06336	Open		45.00	47
1996 Trading Post 10732	Open		50.00	50
1996 Treviso House 10392	Open		50.00	50
1990 The Victoria House 07335	Closed	1993	45.00	85-100
1989 Victorian Apothecary 06900	Closed	1991	40.00	175
1991 Victorian 07925	Open		45.00	45
1989 The Village Bakery 06898	Open		40.00	47
1989 Village Barber Shop 06901	Open		40.00	47
1986 Village Express 05826	Closed	N/A	27.00	100-145
1992 Village Green Gazebo 00227	Open		22.00	22
1990 Village Hardware 07340	Open		45.00	50
1994 Village Hospital 01004	Open		50.00	50
1992 The Village Inn 07962	Open		45.00	50
1989 Village Library 06752	Open		40.00	47
1988 Village Police Station 06344	Open		40.00	50
1989 Village School 06749	Closed	1991	40.00	300-400
1991 Watt's Candle Shop 07479	Closed	1994	45.00	150
1994 White's Butcher Shop 01005	Open		50.00	50
1991 Wig Shop 07480	Suspd.		45.00	86-110
1992 Windmill 00229	Open		45.00	47
1995 Wycoff Manor 11995	5,500		75.00	130-150
1995 Zachary Peters Cabinet Maker 01322	Open		50.00	50

Colonial Village Special Event - Lefton

1995 Bayside Inn 01326	Yr.Iss.		50.00	120

Great American Carousel Collection - T. Fraley

1995 Am Spirit/Heartland 8620	4,500		115.00	115
1995 Am Spirit/Heartland 8624	4,500		125.00	125
1995 Am Spirit/Liberty-Lincoln 8621	4,500		115.00	115
1995 Am Spirit/Liberty/Lincoln 8625	4,500		125.00	125
1995 Am Spirit/Sage 8623	4,500		115.00	115
1995 Am Spirit/Sage 8627	4,500		125.00	125
1995 Am Spirit/Southern Bell 8622	4,500		115.00	115
1995 Am Spirit/Southern Bell 8626	4,500		125.00	125

Historic American Lighthouse Collection - Lefton

1995 1716 Boston Lighthouse 08607	7,500	1995	50.00	50
1994 Admirality Head, WA 01126	Open		40.00	40
1992 Assateague, VA 00137	Open		40.00	40
1995 Barneget, NJ 01333	Open		40.00	40
1993 Big Sable Point, MI 00885	Open		40.00	40
1994 Block Island, RI 10105	Open		50.00	50
1994 Bodie Island, NC 01118	Open		40.00	40
1993 Boston Harbor, MA 00881	Open		40.00	40
1996 Buffalo, NY 10076	Open		40.00	40
1994 Cana Island, WI 01117	Open		40.00	40
1993 Cape Cod, MA 00882	Open		40.00	40
1994 Cape Florida, FL 01125	Open		40.00	40
1992 Cape Hatteras, NC 00133	Open		40.00	40
1992 Cape Henry, VA 00135	Open		40.00	40
1992 Cape Lookout, NC 00134	Open		40.00	40
1994 Cape May, NJ 01013	Closed	1995	40.00	85
1994 Cape May, NJ 01013R	Open		40.00	40
1996 Cape Neddick, ME 10106	Open		47.00	47
1994 Chicago Harbor, IL 01010	Open		40.00	40
1996 Destruction Island, WA 10108	Open		40.00	40
1995 Fire Island, NY 01334	Open		40.00	40
1994 Ft. Gratiot, MI 01123	Open		40.00	40
1993 Gray's Harbor, WA 00880	Open		40.00	40
1994 Heceta Head, OR 01122	Open		40.00	40
1996 Holland Harbor, MI 10104	Open		45.00	45
1995 Jupiter Inlet, FL 01336	Open		40.00	40
1996 Key West, FL 10075	Open		40.00	40
1996 Los Angeles Harbor, CA 10109	Open		45.00	45
1993 Marblehead, OH 00879	Open		40.00	40
1993 Montauk, NY 00884	Open		40.00	40
1994 New London Ledge, CT 01119	Open		40.00	40
1994 Ocracoke, NC 01124	Open		40.00	40
1996 Old Cape Henry, VA 08619	7,500	1996	47.00	75
1994 Old Point Loma, CA 01011	Open		40.00	40
1995 Pigeon Point, CA 01289	Open		40.00	40
1995 Point Betsie, MI 01335	Open		47.00	47
1995 Point Cabrillo, CA 01330	Open		47.00	47
1993 Point Wilson, WA 00883	Open		40.00	40
1995 Ponce De Leon, FL 01332	Open		40.00	40
1994 Portland Head, ME 01121	Open		40.00	40
1996 Pt. Isabel, TX 10074	Open		40.00	40
1992 Sandy Hook, NJ 00132	Open		40.00	40
1994 Split Rock, MN 01009	Open		40.00	40
1994 St. Augustine, FL 01015	Open		40.00	40
1994 St. Simons, GA 01012	Open		40.00	40
1996 Thomas Point, MO 10107	Open		45.00	45
1995 Toledo Harbor, OH 01331	Open		47.00	47
1994 Tybee Island, GA 01014	Open		40.00	40
1992 West Quoddy Head, ME 00136	Open		40.00	40
1993 White Shoal, MI 00878	Open		40.00	40
1994 Yerba Buena, CA 01120	Open		40.00	40

Glynda Turley Prints

Turley - G. Turley

1995 Circle of Friends	4,800		67.00	67
1995 The Courtyard II	4,800		99.00	99
1995 Flowers For Mommy	4,800		85.00	85
1994 Old Mill Stream	4,800		64.00	64
1995 Past Times	4,800		78.00	78
1995 Playing Hookie Again	4,800		83.00	83
1995 Secret Garden II	4,800		95.00	95

Goebel of North America

Charlot Byj Blondes - C. Byj

1968 Bless Us All	Closed	1987	6.00	6
1968 A Child's Prayer	Closed	1987	6.00	6
1968 Evening Prayer	Closed	1986	8.00	8
1969 Her Shining Hour	Closed	1988	14.00	14
1969 Little Prayers Are Best	Closed	1987	12.00	12
1972 Love Bugs	Closed	1986	38.00	38
XX Love Bugs (music box)	Closed	1986	80.00	80

YEAR ISSUE		EDITION LIMIT	YEAR RETD.	ISSUE PRICE	*QUOTE U.S.$
1968	Madonna of the Doves	Closed	1993	25.00	25
1968	Mother Embracing Child	Closed	N/A	12.00	12
1968	Rock-A-Bye-Baby	Closed	N/A	7.50	8
XX	Rock-A-Bye-Baby (music box)	Closed	1985	50.00	50
1968	Sitting Pretty	Closed	1983	9.00	9
1968	Sleepy Head	Closed	1986	9.00	9
1968	Tender Shepherd	Closed	1974	8.00	8
1968	The Way To Pray	Closed	1988	8.50	9

Charlot Byj Redheads - C. Byj

YEAR ISSUE		EDITION LIMIT	YEAR RETD.	ISSUE PRICE	*QUOTE U.S.$
1982	1-2 Ski-Doo	Closed	1986	75.00	75
1985	All Gone	Closed	1988	42.00	42
1987	Almost There	Closed	1988	45.00	48
1987	Always Fit	Closed	1988	45.00	45
1968	Atta Boy	Closed	1984	6.50	7
1972	Baby Sitter	Closed	1983	28.00	28
1972	Bachelor Degree	Closed	1983	18.00	18
1975	Barbeque	Closed	1983	55.00	55
1985	Bedtime Boy	Closed	1987	26.00	26
1985	Bedtime Girl	Closed	1987	26.00	26
1975	Bird Watcher	Closed	1983	48.00	48
1971	Bongo Beat	Closed	1980	18.50	19
1975	Camera Shy	Closed	1983	48.00	48
1984	Captive Audience	Closed	1988	55.00	55
1968	Cheer Up	Closed	1988	8.00	8
1987	Come Along	Closed	1988	47.50	48
1970	Copper Topper	Closed	1986	10.00	10
1968	Daisies Won't Tell	Closed	1986	6.00	6
1983	A Damper on the Camper	Closed	1986	75.00	75
1983	Dear Sirs	Closed	1988	40.00	40
1968	Dropping In	Closed	1986	6.00	6
1968	E-e-eek	Closed	1986	8.00	8
1985	Farm Friends	Closed	1988	46.00	46
1987	Figurine Collector	Closed	1988	64.00	64
1972	First Degree	Closed	1986	18.00	18
1968	Forbidden Fruit	Closed	1978	7.00	7
1975	Fore	Closed	1983	48.00	48
1983	Four Letter Word For Ouch	Closed	1988	40.00	40
1983	A Funny Face From Outer Space	Closed	1987	65.00	65
1968	Gangway	Closed	1986	8.50	9
1968	Good News	Closed	1988	6.00	6
1988	Greetings	Closed	1988	55.00	55
1968	Guess Who	Closed	1979	8.50	9
1983	Heads or Tails	Closed	1986	60.00	60
1968	The Kibitzer	Closed	1983	7.50	8
1975	Lazy Day	Closed	1986	55.00	55
1969	Let It Rain	Closed	1988	26.00	26
1968	Little Miss Coy	Closed	1986	6.00	6
1968	Little Prayers Are Best	Closed	1969	13.00	13
1969	Little Shopper	Closed	1978	13.00	13
1968	Lucky Day	Closed	1986	5.50	6
1984	Not Yet a Vet	Closed	1988	65.00	65
1983	Nothing Beats a Pizza	Closed	1988	55.00	55
1971	The Nurse	Closed	1988	13.00	13
1968	O'Hair For President	Closed	1983	6.00	6
1968	Off Key	Closed	1986	7.50	8
1984	Once Upon a Time	Closed	1988	55.00	55
1984	One Puff's Enough (Yech)	Closed	1988	55.00	55
1968	Oops	Closed	1988	8.00	8
1987	Please Wait	Closed	1988	47.50	48
1968	Plenty of Nothing	Closed	1986	5.50	6
1987	The Practice	Closed	1988	64.00	64
1968	Putting on the Dog	Closed	1986	9.00	9
1968	The Roving Eye	Closed	1986	6.00	6
1972	Say A-a-a-aah	Closed	1986	19.00	19
1982	Sea Breeze	Closed	1986	65.00	65
1988	Shall We Dance?	Closed	1988	72.50	73
1985	Sharing Secrets	Closed	1988	44.00	44
1968	Shear Nonsense	Closed	1986	10.00	10
1970	Skater's Waltz	Closed	1986	15.00	15
XX	Skater's Waltz	Closed	1986	70.00	70
1983	Something Tells Me	Closed	1987	40.00	40
1988	A Special Friend (Black Angel)	Closed	1988	55.00	55
1968	Spellbound	Closed	1986	12.00	12
1968	Spring Time	Closed	1983	7.50	8
1968	The Stolen Kiss	Closed	1978	13.00	13
1968	Strike	Closed	1986	6.00	6
1968	Super Service	Closed	1979	9.00	9
1985	Sweet Snack	Closed	1988	40.00	40
1971	Swinger	Closed	1983	15.00	15
1969	Trim Lass	Closed	1978	14.00	14
1971	Trouble Shooter (This Won't Hurt)	Closed	1986	13.00	13
1975	Wash Day	Closed	1986	55.00	55
1984	Yeah Team	Closed	1987	65.00	65
1968	A Young Man's Fancy	Closed	1988	10.00	10

Co-Boy - G. Skrobek

YEAR ISSUE		EDITION LIMIT	YEAR RETD.	ISSUE PRICE	*QUOTE U.S.$
1981	Al the Trumpet Player	Closed	N/A	45.00	50-75
1987	Bank-Pete the Pirate	Closed	N/A	80.00	125-150
1987	Bank-Utz the Money Bank	Closed	N/A	80.00	100-125
1981	Ben the Blacksmith	Closed	N/A	45.00	50-75
XX	Bert the Soccer Player	Closed	N/A	Unkn.	50-75
1971	Bit the Bachelor	Closed	N/A	16.00	50-75
1972	Bob the Bookworm	Closed	N/A	20.00	50-75
1984	Brad the Clockmaker	Closed	N/A	75.00	125-150
1972	Brum the Lawyer	Closed	N/A	20.00	50-75
XX	Candy the Baker's Delight	Closed	N/A	Unkn.	50-75
1980	Carl the Chef	Closed	N/A	49.00	50-75
1984	Chris the Shoemaker	Closed	N/A	45.00	50-75
1987	Chuck on His Pig	Closed	N/A	75.00	75
1984	Chuck the Chimney Sweep	Closed	N/A	45.00	50-75

YEAR ISSUE		EDITION LIMIT	YEAR RETD.	ISSUE PRICE	*QUOTE U.S.$
1987	Clock-Conny the Watchman	Closed	N/A	125.00	125-150
1987	Clock-Sepp and the Beer Keg	Closed	N/A	125.00	125-150
1972	Co-Boy Plaque	Closed	N/A	20.00	50-125
XX	Conny the Night Watchman	Closed	N/A	Unkn.	125-150
1980	Doc the Doctor	Closed	N/A	49.00	50-100
XX	Ed the Wine Cellar Steward	Closed	N/A	Unkn.	50-75
1984	Felix the Baker	Closed	N/A	45.00	50-75
1971	Fips the Foxy Fisherman	Closed	N/A	16.00	50-75
1971	Fritz the Happy Boozer	Closed	N/A	16.00	50-75
1981	George the Gourmand	Closed	N/A	45.00	50-75
1980	Gerd the Diver	Closed	N/A	49.00	125-175
1978	Gil the Goalie	Closed	N/A	34.00	50-85
1981	Greg the Gourmet	Closed	N/A	45.00	50-95
1981	Greta the Happy Housewife	Closed	N/A	45.00	50-75
1980	Herb the Horseman	Closed	N/A	49.00	50-100
1984	Herman the Butcher	Closed	N/A	45.00	50-75
1984	Homer the Driver	Closed	N/A	45.00	50-75
XX	Jack the Village Pharmacist	Closed	N/A	Unkn.	50-75
XX	Jim the Bowler	Closed	N/A	Unkn.	50-75
XX	John the Hawkeye Hunter	Closed	N/A	Unkn.	50-75
1972	Kuni the Painter	Closed	N/A	20.00	50-75
XX	Mark-Safety First	Closed	N/A	Unkn.	120
1984	Marthe the Nurse	Closed	N/A	45.00	50-75
XX	Max the Boxing Champ	Closed	N/A	Unkn.	135
1971	Mike the Jam Maker	Closed	N/A	16.00	50-75
1980	Monty the Mountain Climber	Closed	N/A	49.00	50-75
1981	Nick the Nightclub Singer	Closed	N/A	45.00	50-75
1981	Niels the Strummer	Closed	N/A	45.00	50-75
1978	Pat the Pitcher	Closed	N/A	34.00	50-75
1984	Paul the Dentist	Closed	N/A	45.00	50-75
1981	Peter the Accordionist	Closed	N/A	45.00	50-75
XX	Petrl the Village Angler	Closed	N/A	Unkn.	50-75
1971	Plum the Pastry Chef	Closed	N/A	16.00	50-75
1972	Porz the Mushroom Muncher	Closed	N/A	20.00	50-75
1984	Rick the Fireman	Closed	N/A	45.00	50-75
1971	Robby the Vegetarian	Closed	N/A	16.00	85
1984	Rudy the World Traveler	Closed	N/A	45.00	50-75
1971	Sam the Gourmet	Closed	N/A	16.00	50-75
1972	Sepp the Beer Buddy	Closed	N/A	20.00	50-75
1984	Sid the Vintner	Closed	N/A	45.00	50-75
1980	Ted the Tennis Player	Closed	N/A	49.00	95
1971	Tom the Honey Lover	Closed	N/A	16.00	70
1978	Tommy Touchdown	Closed	N/A	34.00	50-75
XX	Toni the Skier	Closed	N/A	Unkn.	50-75
1972	Utz the Banker	Closed	N/A	20.00	50-75
1981	Walter the Debutant	Closed	N/A	45.00	50-75
1971	Wim the Court Supplier	Closed	N/A	16.00	50-75

Co-Boys-Culinary - Welling/Skrobek

YEAR ISSUE		EDITION LIMIT	YEAR RETD.	ISSUE PRICE	*QUOTE U.S.$
1994	Mike the Jam Maker 301050	Open		30.00	30
1994	Plum the Sweets Maker 301052	Open		30.00	30
1994	Robby the Vegetarian 301054	Open		30.00	30
1994	Sepp the Drunkard 301051	Open		30.00	30
1994	Tom the Sweet Tooth 301053	Open		30.00	30

Co-Boys-Professionals - Welling/Skrobek

YEAR ISSUE		EDITION LIMIT	YEAR RETD.	ISSUE PRICE	*QUOTE U.S.$
1994	Brum the Lawyer 301060	Open		30.00	30
1994	Conny the Nightwatchman 301062	Open		30.00	30
1994	Doc the Doctor 301064	Open		30.00	30
1994	John the Hunter 301063	Open		30.00	30
1994	Utz the Banker 301061	Open		30.00	30

Co-Boys-Sports - Welling/Skrobek

YEAR ISSUE		EDITION LIMIT	YEAR RETD.	ISSUE PRICE	*QUOTE U.S.$
1994	Bert the Soccer Player 301059	Open		30.00	30
1994	Jim the Bowler 301057	Open		30.00	30
1994	Petri the Fisherman 301055	Open		30.00	30
1994	Ted the Tennis Player 301058	Open		30.00	30
1994	Toni the Skier 301056	Open		30.00	30

Goebel Figurines - N. Rockwell

YEAR ISSUE		EDITION LIMIT	YEAR RETD.	ISSUE PRICE	*QUOTE U.S.$
1963	Advertising Plaque 218	Closed	N/A	Unkn.	750-1000
1963	Boyhood Dreams (Adventurers between Adventures) 202	Closed	N/A	12.00	350-400
1963	Buttercup Test (Beguiling Buttercup) 214	Closed	N/A	10.00	350-400
1963	First Love (A Scholarly Pace) 215	Closed	N/A	30.00	350-400
1963	His First Smoke 208	Closed	N/A	9.00	350-400
1963	Home Cure 211	Closed	N/A	16.00	350-400
1963	Little Veterinarian (Mysterious Malady) 201	Closed	N/A	15.00	350-400
1963	Mother's Helper (Pride of Parenthood) 203	Closed	N/A	15.00	350-400
1963	My New Pal (A Boy Meets His Dog) 204	Closed	N/A	12.00	350-400
1963	Patient Anglers (Fisherman's Paradise) 217	Closed	N/A	18.00	350-400
1963	She Loves Me (Day Dreamer) 213	Closed	N/A	8.00	350-400
1963	Timely Assistance (Love Aid) 212	Closed	N/A	16.00	350-400

Miniatures-Americana Series - R. Olszewski

YEAR ISSUE		EDITION LIMIT	YEAR RETD.	ISSUE PRICE	*QUOTE U.S.$
1982	American Bald Eagle 661-B	Closed	1989	45.00	275-300
1986	Americana Display 951-D	Open	1995	80.00	105
1989	Blacksmith 667-P	Closed	1989	55.00	125-150
1986	Carrousel Ride 665-B	Closed	1995	45.00	100-150
1985	Central Park Sunday 664-B	Closed	1995	45.00	75
1986	Eyes on the Horizon 663-B	Closed	1995	45.00	80
1981	The Plainsman 660-B	Closed	1989	45.00	200-250
1983	She Sounds the Deep 662-B	Closed	1995	45.00	75
1987	To The Bandstand 666-B	Closed	1995	45.00	75

Miniatures-Bob Timberlake Signature Series - B. Timberlake

YEAR ISSUE		EDITION LIMIT	YEAR RETD.	ISSUE PRICE	*QUOTE U.S.$
1996	Autumn Afternoons Vignette	500		490.00	490

Miniatures-Children's Series - R. Olszewski

YEAR ISSUE		EDITION LIMIT	YEAR RETD.	ISSUE PRICE	*QUOTE U.S.$
1983	Backyard Frolic 633-P	Closed	1989	65.00	100
1980	Blumenkinder-Courting 630-P	Closed	1989	55.00	200-300
1990	Building Blocks Castle (large) 968-D	Closed	1995	75.00	100
1987	Carrousel Days (plain base) 637-P	Closed	1989	85.00	750-815
1987	Carrousel Days 637-P	Closed	1989	85.00	220-250
1988	Children's Display (small)	Closed	1995	45.00	60
1989	Clowning Around 636-P (new style)	Closed	1995	85.00	100-145
1986	Clowning Around 636-P (old style)	Closed	N/A	85.00	165-200
1984	Grandpa 634-P	Closed	1995	75.00	100
1988	Little Ballerina 638-P	Closed	1995	85.00	125
1982	Out and About 632-P	Closed	1989	85.00	285-300
1985	Snow Holiday 635-P	Closed	1995	75.00	125
1981	Summer Days 631-P	Closed	1989	65.00	300

Miniatures-Classic Clocks - Larsen

YEAR ISSUE		EDITION LIMIT	YEAR RETD.	ISSUE PRICE	*QUOTE U.S.$
1995	Alexis	2,500		200.00	200
1995	Blinking Admiral	2,500		200.00	200
1995	Play	2,500		250.00	250

Miniatures-Disney-Cinderella - Disney

YEAR ISSUE		EDITION LIMIT	YEAR RETD.	ISSUE PRICE	*QUOTE U.S.$
1991	Anastasia 172-P	Suspd.		85.00	150-175
1991	Cinderella 176-P	Suspd.		85.00	150-195
1991	Cinderella's Coach Display 978-D	Suspd.		95.00	150-180
1991	Cinderella's Dream Castle 976-D	Suspd.		95.00	175-200
1991	Drizella 174-P	Suspd.		85.00	150-175
1991	Fairy Godmother 180-P	Suspd.		85.00	150-175
1991	Footman 181-P	Suspd.		85.00	150-175
1991	Gus 177-P	Suspd.		80.00	145-150
1991	Jaq 173-P	Suspd.		80.00	145
1991	Lucifer 175-P	Suspd.		80.00	165
1991	Prince Charming 179-P	Suspd.		85.00	200
1991	Stepmother 178-P	Suspd.		85.00	150-175

Miniatures-Disney-Peter Pan - Disney

YEAR ISSUE		EDITION LIMIT	YEAR RETD.	ISSUE PRICE	*QUOTE U.S.$
1994	Captain Hook 188-P	Suspd.		160.00	200-225
1992	John 186-P	Suspd.		90.00	180
1994	Lost Boy-Fox 191-P	Suspd.		130.00	195-225
1994	Lost Boy-Rabbit 192-P	Suspd.		130.00	195-225
1992	Michael 187-P	Suspd.		90.00	150-165
1992	Nana 189-P	Suspd.		95.00	155-165
1994	Neverland Display 997-D	Suspd.		150.00	175-215
1992	Peter Pan 184-P	Suspd.		90.00	150-215
1992	Peter Pan's London 986-D	Suspd.		125.00	175-215
1994	Smee 190-P	Suspd.		140.00	160-195
1992	Wendy 185-P	Suspd.		90.00	150-195

Miniatures-Disney-Pinocchio - Disney

YEAR ISSUE		EDITION LIMIT	YEAR RETD.	ISSUE PRICE	*QUOTE U.S.$
1991	Blue Fairy 693-P	Suspd.		95.00	150-175
1991	Geppetto's Toy Shop Display 965-D	Suspd.		95.00	200
1990	Geppetto/Figaro 682-P	Suspd.		90.00	180
1990	Gideon 683-P	Suspd.		75.00	165
1990	J. Worthington Foulfellow 684-P	Suspd.		95.00	160-195
1990	Jiminy Cricket 685-P	Suspd.		75.00	160-185
1991	Little Street Lamp Display 964-D	Suspd.		65.00	135-180
1992	Monstro The Whale 985-D	Suspd.		120.00	270
1990	Pinocchio 686-P	Suspd.		75.00	195-205
1991	Stromboli 694-P	Suspd.		95.00	165-185
1991	Stromboli's Street Wagon 979-D	Suspd.		105.00	195-210

Miniatures-Disney-Snow White - Disney

YEAR ISSUE		EDITION LIMIT	YEAR RETD.	ISSUE PRICE	*QUOTE U.S.$
1987	Bashful 165-P	Suspd.		60.00	150-165
1991	Castle Courtyard Display 981-D	Suspd.		105.00	155
1987	Cozy Cottage Display 941-D	Suspd.		35.00	325-365
1987	Doc 162-P	Suspd.		60.00	150-165
1987	Dopey 167-P	Suspd.		60.00	150-215
1987	Grumpy 166-P	Suspd.		60.00	150-165
1987	Happy 164-P	Suspd.		60.00	150-165
1988	House In The Woods Display 944-D	Suspd.		60.00	175-195
1992	Path In The Woods 996-D	Suspd.		140.00	225-250
1987	Sleepy 163-P	Suspd.		60.00	150-160
1987	Sneezy 161-P	Suspd.		60.00	150-165
1987	Snow White 168-P	Suspd.		60.00	175-225
1990	Snow White's Prince 170-P	Suspd.		80.00	175-225
1992	Snow White's Queen 182-P	Suspd.		100.00	160-180
1992	Snow White's Witch 183-P	Suspd.		100.00	195
1990	The Wishing Well Display 969-D	Suspd.		65.00	195

Miniatures-Disneyana Convention -P. Larsen

YEAR ISSUE		EDITION LIMIT	YEAR RETD.	ISSUE PRICE	*QUOTE U.S.$
1994	Mickey Self Portrait	500	1994	295.00	800-1100
1995	Barbershop Quartet	750	1995	325.00	345-600
1996	Puppy Love	750	1996	325.00	325

Miniatures-Historical Series - R. Olszewski

YEAR ISSUE		EDITION LIMIT	YEAR RETD.	ISSUE PRICE	*QUOTE U.S.$
1985	Capodimonte 600-P (new style)	Suspd.		90.00	150-200
1980	Capodimonte 600-P (old style)	Closed	1987	90.00	400-600
1983	The Cherry Pickers 602-P	Suspd.		85.00	225-250
1990	English Country Garden 970-D	Open		85.00	110
1989	Farmer w/Doves 607-P	Open		85.00	115
1990	Floral Bouquet Pompadour 604-P	Open		85.00	120
1990	Gentleman Fox Hunt 616-P	Suspd.		145.00	170-200
1988	Historical Display 943-D	Open		45.00	65
1981	Masquerade-St. Petersburg 601-P	Closed	1989	65.00	245-260

FIGURINES/COTTAGES

YEAR ISSUE	EDITION LIMIT	YEAR RETD.	ISSUE PRICE	*QUOTE U.S.$
1987 Meissen Parrot 605-P	Open		85.00	115
1988 Minton Rooster 606-P	7,500		85.00	115
1984 Moor With Spanish Horse 603-P	Open		85.00	115
1992 Poultry Seller 608-G	1,500		200.00	245

Miniatures-Jack & The Beanstalk - R. Olszewski

YEAR ISSUE	EDITION LIMIT	YEAR RETD.	ISSUE PRICE	*QUOTE U.S.$
1994 Beanseller 742-P	5,000		200.00	210
1994 Jack & The Beanstalk Display 999-D	5,000		225.00	260
1994 Jack and the Cow 743-P	5,000		180.00	195
1994 Jack's Mom 741-P	5,000		145.00	180

Miniatures-Mickey Mouse - Disney

YEAR ISSUE	EDITION LIMIT	YEAR RETD.	ISSUE PRICE	*QUOTE U.S.$
1990 Fantasia Living Brooms 972-D	Suspd.		85.00	275-325
1990 The Sorcerer's Apprentice 171-P	Suspd.		80.00	225-295
1990 Set	Suspd.		165.00	350-500

Miniatures-Nativity Collection - R. Olszewski

YEAR ISSUE	EDITION LIMIT	YEAR RETD.	ISSUE PRICE	*QUOTE U.S.$
1992 3 Kings Display 987-D	Open		85.00	105
1992 Balthazar 405-P	Open		135.00	200
1994 Camel & Tender 819292	Open		380.00	395
1992 Caspar 406-P	Open		135.00	200
1994 Final Nativity Display 991-D	Open		260.00	275
1994 Guardian Angel 407-P	Open		200.00	225
1991 Holy Family Display 982-D	Open		85.00	95
1991 Joseph 401-P	Open		95.00	130
1991 Joyful Cherubs 403-P	Open		130.00	185
1992 Melchoir 404-P	Open		135.00	200
1991 Mother/Child 440-P	Open		120.00	155
1994 Sheep & Shepherd 819290	Open		230.00	240
1991 The Stable Donkey 402-P	Open		95.00	130

Miniatures-Nature's Moments - Yenawine

YEAR ISSUE	EDITION LIMIT	YEAR RETD.	ISSUE PRICE	*QUOTE U.S.$
1995 Bathing Beauties	Open		95.00	95
1995 Fish Paradise	Open		110.00	110
1995 Gathering Goodies	Open		95.00	95
1995 Hide and Seek	Open		110.00	110
1995 Penguins Plunge	Open		95.00	95
1995 Polar Playground	Open		110.00	110
1995 Preparing for Flight	Open		80.00	80
1995 Robyn Refresher	Open		95.00	95
1995 Summer Surprise	Open		95.00	95
1995 Touch and Go	Open		95.00	95

Miniatures-Night Before Christmas (1st Edition) - R. Olszewski

YEAR ISSUE	EDITION LIMIT	YEAR RETD.	ISSUE PRICE	*QUOTE U.S.$
1990 Eight Tiny Reindeer 691-P	5,000		110.00	135
1990 Mama & Papa 692-P	5,000		110.00	140
1990 St. Nicholas 690-P	5,000		95.00	125
1990 Sugar Plum Boy 687-P	5,000		70.00	100
1990 Sugar Plum Girl 689-P	5,000		70.00	100
1991 Up To The Housetop 966-D	5,000		95.00	115
1990 Yule Tree 688-P	5,000		90.00	110

Miniatures-Oriental Series - R. Olszewski

YEAR ISSUE	EDITION LIMIT	YEAR RETD.	ISSUE PRICE	*QUOTE U.S.$
1986 The Blind Men and the Elephant 643-P	Suspd.		70.00	175-195
1990 Chinese Temple Lion 646-P	Open		90.00	115-175
1987 Chinese Water Dragon 644-P	Suspd.		70.00	150-195
1990 Empress' Garden Display 967-D	Open		95.00	135
1982 The Geisha 641-P	Suspd.		65.00	175-250
1984 Kuan Yin 640-W (new style)	Suspd.		45.00	125-225
1980 Kuan Yin 640-W (old style)	Closed	1992	40.00	225-250
1987 Oriental Display (small) 945-D	Open		45.00	70
1985 Tang Horse 642-P	Open		65.00	100
1989 Tiger Hunt 645-P	Open		85.00	105

Miniatures-Pendants - R. Olszewski

YEAR ISSUE	EDITION LIMIT	YEAR RETD.	ISSUE PRICE	*QUOTE U.S.$
1986 Camper Bialosky 151-P	Closed	1988	95.00	255-275
1991 Chrysanthemum Pendant 222-P	Open		135.00	155
1991 Daffodil Pendant 221-P	Open		135.00	155
1990 Hummingbird 697-P	Open		125.00	155
1988 Mickey Mouse 169-P	5,000	1989	92.00	285-310
1991 Poinsettia Pendant 223-P	Open		135.00	155
1991 Rose Pendant 220-P	Open		135.00	155

Miniatures-Portrait of America/Saturday Evening Post - N. Rockwell

YEAR ISSUE	EDITION LIMIT	YEAR RETD.	ISSUE PRICE	*QUOTE U.S.$
1989 Bottom Drawer 366-P	7,500	1995	85.00	95
1988 Bottom of the Sixth 365-P	Suspd.		85.00	125-195
1988 Check-Up 363-P	Suspd.		85.00	95-125
1988 The Doctor and the Doll 361-P	Suspd.		85.00	125-200
1991 Home Coming Vignette -Soldier/Mother 990-D	2,000	1995	190.00	225-300
1988 Marbles Champion (Pewter) 362-P	Closed	1995	85.00	95-125
1988 No Swimming (Pewter) 360-P	Closed	1995	85.00	95-125
1988 Rockwell Display (Pewter) 952-D	Closed	1995	80.00	95-140
1988 Triple Self-Portrait (Pewter) 364-P	Suspd.		85.00	150-225

Miniatures-Precious Moments Series I - Goebel

YEAR ISSUE	EDITION LIMIT	YEAR RETD.	ISSUE PRICE	*QUOTE U.S.$
1995 Fields of Friendship-Diorama (display)	Open		135.00	135
1995 God Loveth a Cheerful Giver	Open		70.00	70
1995 His Burden is Light	Open		70.00	70
1995 I'm Sending You a White Christmas	5,000		100.00	100
1995 Love Is Kind	Open		70.00	70
1995 Love One Another	Open		70.00	70
1995 Make a Joyful Noise	Open		70.00	70
1995 Praise the Lord Anyhow	Open		70.00	70
1995 Prayer Changes Things	Open		70.00	70

Miniatures-Precious Moments Series II - Goebel

YEAR ISSUE	EDITION LIMIT	YEAR RETD.	ISSUE PRICE	*QUOTE U.S.$
1996 Heart & Home-Diorama (display)	Open		150.00	150
1996 Jesus is the Answer	Open		70.00	70
1996 Jesus is the Light	Open		70.00	70
1996 Jesus Loves Me (boy)	Open		70.00	70
1996 Jesus Loves Me (girl)	Open		70.00	70
1996 Merry Christmas Deer	5,000		100.00	100
1996 O, How I Love Jesus	Open		70.00	70
1996 Smile, God Loves You	Open		70.00	70
1996 Unto Us A Child is born	Open		70.00	70

Miniatures-Special Release-Alice in Wonderland - R. Olszewski

YEAR ISSUE	EDITION LIMIT	YEAR RETD.	ISSUE PRICE	*QUOTE U.S.$
1982 Alice In the Garden 670-P	Closed	1982	60.00	600-650
1984 The Cheshire Cat 672-P	Closed	1984	75.00	375-550
1983 Down the Rabbit Hole 671-P	Closed	1983	75.00	450

Miniatures-Special Release-Wizard of Oz - R. Olszewski

YEAR ISSUE	EDITION LIMIT	YEAR RETD.	ISSUE PRICE	*QUOTE U.S.$
1986 The Cowardly Lion 675-P	Closed	1987	85.00	295-325
1992 Dorothy/Glinda 695-P	Closed	1995	135.00	145-165
1992 Good-Bye to Oz Display 980-D	Open		110.00	130-180
1988 The Munchkins 677-P	Closed	1995	85.00	105-140
1987 Oz Display 942-D	Closed	1994	45.00	550-650
1984 Scarecrow 673-P	Closed	1985	75.00	395-495
1985 Tinman 674-P	Closed	1986	80.00	275-325
1987 The Wicked Witch 676-P	Closed	1995	85.00	115-175

Miniatures-Special Releases - R. Olszewski

YEAR ISSUE	EDITION LIMIT	YEAR RETD.	ISSUE PRICE	*QUOTE U.S.$
1994 Dresden Timepiece 450-P	750		1250.00	1300
1991 Portrait Of The Artist (convention) 658-P	Closed	1991	195.00	450-600
1991 Portrait Of The Artist (promotion) 658-P	Open		195.00	210-250
1992 Summer Days Collector Plaque 659-P	Open		130.00	130-175

Miniatures-The American Frontier Collection - Various

YEAR ISSUE	EDITION LIMIT	YEAR RETD.	ISSUE PRICE	*QUOTE U.S.$
1987 American Frontier Museum Display 947-D - R. Olszewski	Suspd.		80.00	115
1987 The Bronco Buster 350-B - Remington	Suspd.		80.00	130-160
1987 Eight Count 310-B - Pounder	Suspd.		75.00	95
1987 The End of the Trail 340-B - Frazier	Suspd.		80.00	95-150
1987 The First Ride 330-B - Rogers	Suspd.		85.00	105
1987 Grizzly's Last Stand 320-B - Jonas	Suspd.		65.00	85
1987 Indian Scout and Buffalo 300-B - Bonheur	Suspd.		95.00	95-140

Miniatures-Three Little Pigs - R. Olszewski

YEAR ISSUE	EDITION LIMIT	YEAR RETD.	ISSUE PRICE	*QUOTE U.S.$
1991 The Hungry Wolf 681-P	7,500		80.00	110
1991 Little Bricks Pig 680-P	7,500		75.00	110
1989 Little Sticks Pig 678-P	7,500		75.00	110
1990 Little Straw Pig 679-P	7,500		75.00	110
1991 Three Little Pigs House 956-D	7,500		50.00	130

Miniatures-Wildlife Series - R. Olszewski

YEAR ISSUE	EDITION LIMIT	YEAR RETD.	ISSUE PRICE	*QUOTE U.S.$
1985 American Goldfinch 625-P	Open		65.00	100
1986 Autumn Blue Jay 626-P	Suspd.		65.00	175-200
1992 Autumn Blue Jay 626-P (Archive release)	Open		125.00	140
1987 Chipping Sparrow 620-P	Suspd.		55.00	350-415
1990 Country Display (small) 940-D	Open		45.00	70
1990 Country Landscape (large) 957-D	Open		85.00	115
1989 Hooded Oriole 629-P	Open		80.00	105
1990 Hummingbird 696-P	Closed	N/A	85.00	175-200
1987 Mallard Duck 627-P	Open		75.00	110
1981 Owl-Daylight Encounter 621-P	Closed	N/A	65.00	275-350
1983 Red-Winged Blackbird 623-P	Closed	N/A	65.00	175-200
1988 Spring Robin 628-P	Closed	N/A	75.00	155-185
1982 Western Bluebird 622-P	Closed	N/A	65.00	165-180
1984 Winter Cardinal 624-P	Closed	N/A	65.00	200-275

Miniatures-Winter Lights - Norrgard

YEAR ISSUE	EDITION LIMIT	YEAR RETD.	ISSUE PRICE	*QUOTE U.S.$
1995 Once Upon a Winter Day	Open		275.00	275

Miniatures-Women's Series - R. Olszewski

YEAR ISSUE	EDITION LIMIT	YEAR RETD.	ISSUE PRICE	*QUOTE U.S.$
1980 Dresden Dancer 610-P	Closed	1989	55.00	525
1985 The Hunt With Hounds (new style) 611-P	Closed	N/A	75.00	225-275
1981 The Hunt With Hounds (old style) 611-P	Closed	1984	75.00	385
1986 I Do 615-P	Closed	N/A	85.00	200-300
1983 On The Avenue 613-P	Closed	1995	65.00	145-195
1982 Precious Years 612-P	Closed	N/A	65.00	200-275
1984 Roses 614-P	Closed	1995	65.00	130-150
1989 Women's Display (small) 950-D	Closed	1995	40.00	95-115

Goebel/M.I. Hummel

M.I. Hummel Collectors Club Exclusives - M. I. Hummel, unless otherwise noted

YEAR ISSUE	EDITION LIMIT	YEAR RETD.	ISSUE PRICE	*QUOTE U.S.$
1977 Valentine Gift 387	Closed	N/A	45.00	575-800
1978 Smiling Through Plaque 690	Closed	N/A	50.00	175-225
1979 Bust of Sister-M.I.Hummel HU-3 - G. Skrobek	Closed	N/A	75.00	250-350
1980 Valentine Joy 399	Closed	N/A	95.00	300-365
1981 Daisies Don't Tell 380	Closed	N/A	80.00	275-350
1982 It's Cold 421	Closed	N/A	80.00	160-275
1983 What Now? 422	Closed	N/A	90.00	280-325
1983 Valentine Gift Mini Pendant 248-P - R. Olszewski	Closed	N/A	85.00	275-350
1984 Coffee Break 409	Closed	N/A	90.00	245-300
1985 Smiling Through 408/0	Closed	N/A	125.00	275-350
1986 Birthday Candle 440	Closed	N/A	95.00	245-350
1986 What Now? Mini Pendant 249-P - R. Olszewski	Closed	N/A	125.00	200-300
1987 Morning Concert 447	Closed	N/A	98.00	200-275
1987 Little Cocopah Indian Girl - T. DeGrazia	Closed	N/A	140.00	200-300
1988 The Surprise 431	Closed	N/A	125.00	200-325
1989 Mickey and Minnie - H. Fischer	Closed	N/A	275.00	350-450
1989 Hello World 429	Closed	N/A	130.00	200-300
1990 I Wonder 486	Closed	N/A	140.00	195-250
1991 Gift From A Friend 485	Closed	N/A	160.00	180-250
1991 Miniature Morning Concert w/ Display 269-P - R. Olszewski	Closed	N/A	175.00	175-250
1992 My Wish Is Small 463/0	Closed	N/A	170.00	175-250
1992 Cheeky Fellow 554	Closed	N/A	120.00	130
1993 I Didn't Do It 626	Closed	1995	175.00	175-220
1993 Sweet As Can Be 541	Closed	1995	125.00	125
1994 Little Visitor 563/0	Closed	1996	180.00	180
1994 Little Troubadour 558	Closed	1996	130.00	130
1994 At Grandpa's 621	10,000		1300.00	1300
1994 Miniature Honey Lover Pendant 247-P	Closed	1996	165.00	165
1995 Country Suitor 760	5/97		195.00	195
1995 Strum Along 557	5/97		135.00	135
1996 A Story From Grandma 620	10,000		1300.00	1300
1996 Valentine Gift Plaque 717	12/96		250.00	250
1996 Celebrate with Song 790	5/98		295.00	295
1996 One, Two, Three 555	5/98		145.00	145

Special Edition Anniversary Figurines For 5/10/15/20 Year Membership - M.I. Hummel

YEAR ISSUE	EDITION LIMIT	YEAR RETD.	ISSUE PRICE	*QUOTE U.S.$
1990 Flower Girl 548 (5 year)	Open		105.00	135
1990 The Little Pair 449 (10 year)	Open		170.00	200
1991 Honey Lover 312 (15 year)	Open		190.00	220
1996 Behave 339 (20 year)	Open		350.00	350

M.I. Hummel Bavarian Village Collection - M.I. Hummel

YEAR ISSUE	EDITION LIMIT	YEAR RETD.	ISSUE PRICE	*QUOTE U.S.$
1996 All Aboard (house)	Open		60.00	60
1995 Angel's Duet (house)	Open		50.00	50
1995 The Bench & Tree Set (accessory)	Open		25.00	30
1995 Christmas Mail (house)	Open		50.00	60
1996 Company's Coming (house)	Open		50.00	60
1996 Little Shoemaker Shop (house)	Open		60.00	60
1996 Off for the Holidays (house)	Open		60.00	60
1995 The Sled and Pine Tree Set (accessory)	Open		25.00	30
1995 The Village Bakery (house)	Open		50.00	60
1995 The Village Bridge (accessory)	Open		25.00	30
1995 Winter's Comfort (house)	Open		50.00	60
1995 The Wishing Well (accessory)	Open		25.00	30

M.I. Hummel Collectibles Century Collection - M.I. Hummel

YEAR ISSUE	EDITION LIMIT	YEAR RETD.	ISSUE PRICE	*QUOTE U.S.$
1986 Chapel Time 442	Closed	N/A	500.00	1500-2800
1987 Pleasant Journey 406	Closed	N/A	500.00	2000-2700
1988 Call to Worship 441	Closed	N/A	600.00	995-1150
1989 Harmony in Four Parts 471	Closed	N/A	850.00	1350-2000
1990 Let's Tell the World 487	Closed	N/A	875.00	1150-1500
1991 We Wish You The Best 600	Closed	N/A	1300.00	1450-1800
1992 On Our Way 472	Closed	N/A	950.00	1100-1200
1993 Welcome Spring 635	Closed	N/A	1085.00	1250-1450
1994 Rock-A-Bye 574	Closed	N/A	1150.00	1200-1350
1995 Strike Up the Band 668	Closed	1995	1200.00	1200
1996 Love's Bounty 751	Yr.Iss.		1200.00	1200

M.I. Hummel Collectibles Christmas Angels - M.I. Hummel

YEAR ISSUE	EDITION LIMIT	YEAR RETD.	ISSUE PRICE	*QUOTE U.S.$
1993 Angel in Cloud 585	Open		25.00	33
1993 Angel with Lute 580	Open		25.00	33
1993 Angel with Trumpet 586	Open		25.00	33
1993 Celestial Musician 578	Open		25.00	33
1993 Festival Harmony with Flute 577	Open		25.00	33
1993 Festival Harmony w/Mandolin 576	Open		25.00	33
1993 Gentle Song 582	Open		25.00	33
1993 Heavenly Angel 575	Open		25.00	33
1993 Prayer of Thanks 581	Open		25.00	33
1993 Song of Praise 579	Open		25.00	33

M.I. Hummel Collectibles Figurines - M.I. Hummel

YEAR ISSUE	EDITION LIMIT	YEAR RETD.	ISSUE PRICE	*QUOTE U.S.$
1988 The Accompanist 453	Open		Unkn.	110
XX Adoration 23/I	Open		Unkn.	380
XX Adoration 23/III	Open		Unkn.	590
XX Adventure Bound 347	Open		Unkn.	3960
XX Angel Duet 261	Open		Unkn.	240
XX Angel Serenade 214/D/I	Open		Unkn.	100
XX Angel Serenade with Lamb 83	Open		Unkn.	240
XX Angel with Accordion 238/B	Open		Unkn.	55
XX Angel with Lute 238/A	Open		Unkn.	55
XX Angel With Trumpet 238/C	Open		Unkn.	55
XX Angelic Song 144	Open		Unkn.	160
1995 The Angler 566	Open		Unkn.	350
1989 An Apple A Day 403	Open		Unkn.	300
XX Apple Tree Boy 142/3/0	Open		Unkn.	155
XX Apple Tree Boy 142/I	Open		Unkn.	300
XX Apple Tree Boy 142/V	Open		Unkn.	1320
XX Apple Tree Girl 141/3/0	Open		Unkn.	155
XX Apple Tree Girl 141/I	Open		Unkn.	300
XX Apple Tree Girl 141/V	Open		Unkn.	1320
1991 Art Critic 318	Open		Unkn.	315
XX Artist, The 304	Open		Unkn.	270
XX Auf Wiedersehen 153/0	Open		Unkn.	270
XX Auf Wiedersehen 153/I	Open		Unkn.	325
XX Autumn Harvest 355	Open		Unkn.	220

YEAR ISSUE		EDITION LIMIT	YEAR RETD.	ISSUE PRICE	*QUOTE U.S.$
XX	Baker 128	Open		Unkn.	215
XX	Baking Day 330	Open		Unkn.	300
XX	Band Leader 129	Open		Unkn.	220
XX	Band Leader 129/4/0	Open		Unkn.	110
XX	Barnyard Hero 195/2/0	Open		Unkn.	180
XX	Barnyard Hero 195/I	Open		Unkn.	330
XX	Bashful 377	Open		Unkn.	215
1990	Bath Time 412	Open		Unkn.	410
XX	Be Patient 197/2/0	Open		Unkn.	215
XX	Be Patient 197/I	Open		Unkn.	325
XX	Begging His Share 9	Open		Unkn.	275
XX	Big Housecleaning 363	Open		Unkn.	315
XX	Bird Duet 169	Open		Unkn.	155
XX	Bird Watcher 300	Open		Unkn.	240
1989	Birthday Cake 338	Open		Unkn.	155
1994	Birthday Present 341/3/0	Open		140.00	155
XX	Birthday Serenade 218/0	Open		Unkn.	325
XX	Birthday Serenade 218/2/0	Open		Unkn.	190
XX	Blessed Event 333	Open		Unkn.	350
1996	Blossom Time 608	Open		155.00	155
XX	Bookworm 3/I	Open		Unkn.	325
XX	Bookworm 8	Open		Unkn.	240
XX	Boots 143/0	Open		Unkn.	220
XX	Boots 143/I	Open		Unkn.	360
XX	Botanist, The 351	Open		Unkn.	220
XX	Boy with Accordion 390	Open		Unkn.	95
XX	Boy with Horse 239/C	Open		Unkn.	60
XX	Boy with Toothache 217	Open		Unkn.	230
XX	Brother 95	Open		Unkn.	220
1988	A Budding Maestro 477	Open		Unkn.	110
XX	Builder, The 305	Open		Unkn.	270
XX	Busy Student 367	Open		Unkn.	175
XX	Call to Glory 739/I	Open		250.00	275
1996	Carefree 490	Open		120.00	120
XX	Carnival 328	Open		Unkn.	240
XX	Celestial Musician 188/0	Open		Unkn.	240
1993	Celestial Musician 188/4/0	Open		Unkn.	100
XX	Celestial Musician 188/I	Open		255.00	280
XX	Chick Girl 57/0	Open		Unkn.	180
XX	Chick Girl 57/2/0	Open		Unkn.	160
XX	Chick Girl 57/I	Open		Unkn.	300
XX	Chicken-Licken 385	Open		Unkn.	310
XX	Chicken-Licken 385/4/0	Open		Unkn.	110
XX	Chimney Sweep 12/2/0	Open		Unkn.	130
XX	Chimney Sweep 12/I	Open		Unkn.	240
1989	Christmas Angel 301	Open		Unkn.	275
XX	Christmas Song 343	Open		Unkn.	240
1996	Christmas Song 343/4/0	Open		115.00	115
XX	Cinderella 337	Open		Unkn.	315
XX	Close Harmony 336	Open		Unkn.	315
1995	Come Back Soon 545	Open		Unkn.	150
XX	Confidentially 314	Open		Unkn.	315
XX	Congratulations 17	Open		Unkn.	220
XX	Coquettes 179	Open		Unkn.	315
1990	Crossroads (Commemorative) 331	20,000		360.00	550-900
XX	Crossroads (Original) 331	Open		Unkn.	440
XX	Culprits 56/A	Open		Unkn.	320
1989	Daddy's Girls 371	Open		Unkn.	250
1996	Delicious 435/3/0	Open		155.00	155
XX	Doctor 127	Open		Unkn.	170
XX	Doll Bath 319	Open		Unkn.	315
XX	Doll Mother 67	Open		Unkn.	230
XX	Easter Greetings 378	Open		Unkn.	220
XX	Easter Time 384	Open		Unkn.	275
1992	Evening Prayer 495	Open		Unkn.	115
XX	Eventide 99	Open		Unkn.	360
XX	A Fair Measure 345	Open		Unkn.	315
XX	Farm Boy 66	Open		Unkn.	250
1996	Fascination 649/0 (Special Event)	25,000		190.00	190
XX	Favorite Pet 361	Open		Unkn.	315
XX	Feathered Friends 344	Open		Unkn.	300
XX	Feeding Time 199/0	Open		Unkn.	215
XX	Feeding Time 199/I	Open		Unkn.	300
1994	Festival Harmony w/Mandolin 172/4/0	Open		95.00	105
XX	Festival Harmony, with Flute 173/0	Open		Unkn.	340
XX	Festival Harmony, with Mandolin 172/0	Open		Unkn.	340
XX	Flower Vendor 381	Open		Unkn.	270
XX	Follow the Leader 369	Open		Unkn.	1320
XX	For Father 87	Open		Unkn.	230
XX	For Mother 257	Open		Unkn.	220
XX	For Mother 257/2/0	Open		Unkn.	130
XX	Forest Shrine 183	Open		Unkn.	585
1993	A Free Flight 569	Open		Unkn.	215
1996	Free Spirit 564	Open		120.00	120
1991	Friend Or Foe 434	Open		Unkn.	240
XX	Friends 136/I	Open		Unkn.	220
XX	Friends 136/V	Open		Unkn.	1320
1993	Friends Together 662/0 (Commemorative)	Open		260.00	300
1993	Friends Together 662/I (Limited)	25,000		475.00	550
1996	From The Heart 761	Open		120.00	120
XX	Gay Adventure 356	Open		Unkn.	210
1995	Gentle Fellowship (Limited) 628	25,000		550.00	550
XX	A Gentle Glow 439	Open		Unkn.	220
XX	Girl with Doll 239/B	Open		Unkn.	60
XX	Girl with Nosegay 239/A	Open		Unkn.	60
XX	Girl with Sheet Music 389	Open		Unkn.	95
XX	Girl with Trumpet 391	Open		Unkn.	95
XX	Going Home 383	Open		Unkn.	340
XX	Going to Grandma's 52/0	Open		Unkn.	290
XX	Good Friends 182	Open		Unkn.	215
XX	Good Hunting 307	Open		Unkn.	270
XX	Good Night 214/C/I	Open		Unkn.	100
XX	Good Shepherd 42	Open		Unkn.	275
XX	Goose Girl 47/0	Open		Unkn.	250
XX	Goose Girl 47/3/0	Open		Unkn.	180
XX	Grandma's Girl 561	Open		Unkn.	160
XX	Grandpa's Boy 562	Open		Unkn.	160
1991	The Guardian 455	Open		Unkn.	180
XX	Guiding Angel 357	Open		Unkn.	95
XX	Happiness 86	Open		Unkn.	145
XX	Happy Birthday 176/0	Open		Unkn.	230
XX	Happy Birthday 176/I	Open		Unkn.	325
XX	Happy Days 150/0	Open		Unkn.	330
XX	Happy Days 150/2/0	Open		Unkn.	190
XX	Happy Days 150/I	Open		Unkn.	500
XX	Happy Pastime 69	Open		Unkn.	175
XX	Happy Traveller 109/0	Open		Unkn.	155
XX	Hear Ye! Hear Ye! 15/0	Open		Unkn.	220
XX	Hear Ye! Hear Ye! 15/2/0	Open		Unkn.	160
XX	Hear Ye! Hear Ye! 15/I	Open		Unkn.	275
1996	Heart and Soul 559	Open		120.00	120
XX	Heavenly Angel 21/0	Open		Unkn.	130
XX	Heavenly Angel 21/0/1/2	Open		Unkn.	240
XX	Heavenly Angel 21/I	Open		Unkn.	275
XX	Heavenly Lullaby 262	Open		Unkn.	200
XX	Heavenly Protection 88/I	Open		Unkn.	470
1995	Hello (Perpetual Calendar) 788A	Open		295.00	295
XX	Hello 124/0	Open		Unkn.	240
XX	Home from Market 198/2/0	Open		Unkn.	160
XX	Home from Market 198/I	Open		Unkn.	230
XX	Homeward Bound 334	Open		Unkn.	360
1990	Horse Trainer 423	Open		Unkn.	240
1989	Hosanna 480	Open		Unkn.	110
1989	I'll Protect Him 483	Open		Unkn.	95
1994	I'm Carefree 633	Open		365.00	410
1989	I'm Here 478	Open		Unkn.	110
1989	In D Major 430	Open		Unkn.	220
XX	In The Meadow 459	Open		Unkn.	220
XX	In Tune 414	Open		Unkn.	310
XX	Is It Raining? 420	Open		Unkn.	280
XX	Joyful 53	Open		Unkn.	130
XX	Joyous News 27/III	Open		Unkn.	240
1995	Just Dozing 451	Open		Unkn.	240
XX	Just Fishing 373	Open		Unkn.	250
XX	Just Resting 112/3/0	Open		Unkn.	160
XX	Just Resting 112/I	Open		Unkn.	310
XX	Kindergartner 467	Open		Unkn.	220
XX	Kiss Me 311	Open		Unkn.	315
XX	Knit One, Purl One 432	Open		Unkn.	125
XX	Knitting Lesson 256	Open		Unkn.	550
1991	Land in Sight 530	30,000		1600.00	1600
XX	Latest News 184	Open		Unkn.	320
XX	Let's Sing 110/0	Open		Unkn.	135
XX	Let's Sing 110/I	Open		Unkn.	180
1993	Little Architect 410/I	Open		Unkn.	330
XX	Little Bookkeeper 306	Open		Unkn.	315
XX	Little Cellist 89/I	Open		Unkn.	230
XX	Little Drummer 240	Open		Unkn.	160
XX	Little Fiddler 2/0	Open		Unkn.	240
XX	Little Fiddler 2/4/0	Open		Unkn.	110
XX	Little Fiddler 4	Open		Unkn.	220
XX	Little Gabriel 32	Open		Unkn.	155
XX	Little Gardener 74	Open		Unkn.	130
XX	Little Goat Herder 200/0	Open		Unkn.	215
XX	Little Goat Herder 200/I	Open		Unkn.	260
XX	Little Guardian 145	Open		Unkn.	160
XX	Little Helper 73	Open		Unkn.	130
XX	Little Hiker 16/2/0	Open		Unkn.	130
XX	Little Hiker 16/I	Open		Unkn.	240
XX	Little Nurse 376	Open		Unkn.	270
XX	Little Pharmacist 322/E	Open		Unkn.	265
XX	Little Scholar 80	Open		Unkn.	230
XX	Little Shopper 96	Open		Unkn.	150
1988	Little Sweeper 171/0	Open		Unkn.	150
XX	Little Sweeper 171/4/0	Open		Unkn.	110
XX	Little Tailor 308	Open		Unkn.	270
XX	Little Thrifty 118	Open		Unkn.	160
XX	Little Tooter 214/H	Open		Unkn.	135
XX	Little Tooter 214/H	Open		Unkn.	110
XX	Lost Stocking 374	Open		Unkn.	155
1995	Lucky Boy (Special Event) 335	25,000		190.00	190
XX	Mail is Here 226	Open		Unkn.	585
1989	Make A Wish 475	Open		Unkn.	220
1996	Making New Friends 2002	Open		595.00	595
XX	March Winds 43	Open		Unkn.	170
XX	Max and Moritz 123	Open		Unkn.	240
XX	Meditation 13/0	Open		Unkn.	240
XX	Meditation 13/2/0	Open		Unkn.	155
XX	Merry Wanderer 11/0	Open		Unkn.	215
XX	Merry Wanderer 11/2/0	Open		Unkn.	150
XX	Merry Wanderer 7/0	Open		Unkn.	300
XX	Mischief Maker 342	Open		Unkn.	300
1994	Morning Stroll 375/3/0	Open		170.00	195
XX	Mother's Darling 175	Open		Unkn.	230
XX	Mother's Helper 133	Open		Unkn.	215
XX	Mountaineer 315	Open		Unkn.	230
1991	A Nap 534	Open		Unkn.	130
1996	Nimble Fingers w/wooden bench 758	Open		225.00	225
1996	No Thank You 535	Open		120.00	120
XX	Not For You 317	Open		Unkn.	265
XX	On Holiday 350	Open		Unkn.	190
XX	On Secret Path 386	Open		Unkn.	270
1989	One For You, One For Me 482	Open		Unkn.	110
1993	One Plus One 556	Open		Unkn.	145
XX	Ooh My Tooth 533	Open		Unkn.	120
XX	Out of Danger 56/B	Open		Unkn.	320
1993	Parade Of Lights 616	Open		Unkn.	275
XX	The Photographer 178	Open		Unkn.	315
1995	Pixie 768	Open		Unkn.	115
XX	Playmates 58/0	Open		Unkn.	180
XX	Playmates 58/2/0	Open		Unkn.	160
XX	Playmates 58/I	Open		Unkn.	300
1994	The Poet 397/I	Open		220.00	250
XX	Postman 119	Open		Unkn.	220
1989	Postman 119/2/0	Open		Unkn.	150
XX	Prayer Before Battle 20	Open		Unkn.	180
1996	Pretty Please 489	Open		120.00	120
1992	The Professor 320	Open		Unkn.	220
1995	Puppy Love Display Plaque 767	Open		Unkn.	265
XX	Retreat to Safety 201/2/0	Open		Unkn.	175
XX	Retreat to Safety 201/I	Open		Unkn.	330
XX	Ride into Christmas 396/2/0	Open		Unkn.	260
XX	Ride into Christmas 396/I	Open		Unkn.	470
XX	Ring Around the Rosie 348	Open		Unkn.	2860
XX	The Run-A-Way 327	Open		Unkn.	275
1992	Scamp 553	Open		Unkn.	120
XX	School Boy 82/0	Open		Unkn.	215
XX	School Boy 82/2/0	Open		Unkn.	155
XX	School Boy 82/II	Open		Unkn.	500
XX	School Boys 170/I	Open		Unkn.	1320
XX	School Girl 81/0	Open		Unkn.	215
XX	School Girl 81/2/0	Open		Unkn.	155
XX	School Girls 177/I	Open		Unkn.	1320
XX	Sensitive Hunter 6/0	Open		Unkn.	215
XX	Sensitive Hunter 6/2/0	Open		Unkn.	160
XX	Sensitive Hunter 6/I	Open		Unkn.	275
XX	Serenade 85/0	Open		Unkn.	145
XX	Serenade 85/4/0	Open		Unkn.	110
XX	Serenade 85/II	Open		Unkn.	500
XX	She Loves Me, She Loves Me Not 174	Open		Unkn.	210
1996	Shepherd Boy 395/0	Open		295.00	295
XX	Shepherd's Boy 64	Open		Unkn.	250
XX	Shining Light 358	Open		Unkn.	95
XX	Sing Along 433	Open		Unkn.	300
XX	Sing With Me 405	Open		Unkn.	340
XX	Singing Lesson 63	Open		Unkn.	135
1995	Sister (Perpetual Calendar) 788B	Open		295.00	295
XX	Sister 98/0	Open		Unkn.	220
XX	Sister 98/2/0	Open		Unkn.	150
XX	Skier 59	Open		Unkn.	220
1990	Sleep Tight 424	Open		Unkn.	240
XX	Smart Little Sister 346	Open		Unkn.	275
XX	Soldier Boy 332	Open		Unkn.	230
XX	Soloist 135	Open		Unkn.	145
XX	Soloist 135/4/0	Open		Unkn.	110
1988	Song of Praise 454	Open		Unkn.	110
1988	Sound the Trumpet 457	Open		Unkn.	110
1988	Sounds of the Mandolin 438	Open		Unkn.	130
XX	Spring Dance 353/0	Open		Unkn.	340
XX	St. George 55	Open		Unkn.	350
XX	Star Gazer 132	Open		Unkn.	225
XX	Stitch in Time 255/4/0	Open		Unkn.	105
XX	Stitch in Time 255/I	Open		Unkn.	315
XX	Stormy Weather 71/2/0	Open		Unkn.	330
XX	Stormy Weather 71/I	Open		Unkn.	495
1992	Storybook Time 458	Open		Unkn.	420
XX	Street Singer 131	Open		Unkn.	210
XX	Surprise 94/3/0	Open		Unkn.	165
XX	Surprise 94/I	Open		Unkn.	315
XX	Sweet Greetings 352	Open		Unkn.	220
XX	Sweet Music 186	Open		Unkn.	220
XX	Telling Her Secret 196/0	Open		Unkn.	325
XX	Thoughtful 415	Open		Unkn.	240
XX	Timid Little Sister 394	Open		Unkn.	470
1995	To Keep You Warm w/ Wooden Chair 759	Open		Unkn.	215
XX	To Market 49/0	Open		Unkn.	315
XX	To Market 49/3/0	Open		Unkn.	175
XX	Trumpet Boy 97	Open		Unkn.	145
1989	Tuba Player 437	Open		Unkn.	290
XX	Tuneful Angel 359	Open		Unkn.	95
1996	A Tuneful Trio	20,000		450.00	450
XX	Umbrella Boy 152/A/0	Open		Unkn.	630
XX	Umbrella Boy 152/A/II	Open		Unkn.	1600
XX	Umbrella Girl 152/B/0	Open		Unkn.	630
XX	Umbrella Girl 152/B/II	Open		Unkn.	1600
XX	Village Boy 51/0	Open		Unkn.	275
XX	Village Boy 51/2/0	Open		Unkn.	155
XX	Village Boy 51/3/0	Open		Unkn.	130
XX	Visiting an Invalid 382	Open		Unkn.	220
XX	Volunteers 50/0	Open		Unkn.	325
XX	Volunteers 50/2/0	Open		Unkn.	240
XX	Waiter 154/0	Open		Unkn.	230
XX	Waiter 154/I	Open		Unkn.	315
1989	Wash Day 321/4/0	Open		Unkn.	110
XX	Wash Day 321/I	Open		Unkn.	315
XX	Watchful Angel 194	Open		Unkn.	340

YEAR ISSUE		EDITION LIMIT	YEAR RETD.	ISSUE PRICE	*QUOTE U.S. $
XX	Wayside Devotion 28/II	Open	Unkn.		450
XX	Wayside Devotion 28/III	Open	Unkn.		600
XX	Wayside Harmony 111/3/0	Open	Unkn.		160
XX	Wayside Harmony 111/I	Open	Unkn.		300
1993	We Come In Peace (Commemorative) 754	Open		385.00	385
XX	We Congratulate 214/E/I	Open	Unkn.		175
XX	We Congratulate 220	Open	Unkn.		165
XX	Weary Wanderer 204	Open	Unkn.		275
1990	What's New? 418	Open	Unkn.		300
XX	Which Hand? 258	Open	Unkn.		215
1992	Whistler's Duet 413	Open	Unkn.		310
XX	Whitsuntide 163	Open	Unkn.		330
1988	A Winter Song 476	Open	Unkn.		120
XX	With Loving Greetings 309	Open	Unkn.		210
XX	Worship 84/0	Open	Unkn.		175

M.I. Hummel Collectibles Figurines Retired - M.I. Hummel

1947	Accordion Boy 185	Closed	1994	Unkn.	200-700
1939	Duet 130	Open	1995	Unkn.	280-850
1937	Farewell 65 TMK1-5	Closed	1993	Unkn.	250-700
1937	Globe Trotter 79 TMK1-7	Closed	1991	Unkn.	200-500
1937	Lost Sheep 68/0 TMK1-7	Closed	1992	Unkn.	235-300
1955	Lost Sheep 68/2/0 TMK2-7	Closed	1992	7.50	125-300
1935	Puppy Love I TMK1-6	Closed	1988	125.00	350-700
1948	Signs Of Spring 203/2/0 TMK2-6	Closed	1990	120.00	250-900
1948	Signs Of Spring 203/I TMK2-6	Closed	1990	155.00	295-750
1935	Strolling Along 5 TMK1-6	Closed	1989	115.00	265-750

M.I. Hummel Collectibles Madonna Figurines - M.I. Hummel

XX	Flower Madonna, color 10/I/II	Open		Unkn.	470
1996	Flower Madonna, white 10 (Commemorative)	12/96		225.00	225
XX	Madonna with Halo, color 45/I/6	Open		Unkn.	135

M.I. Hummel Collectibles Nativity Components - M. I. Hummel, unless otherwise noted

XX	Ox 214/K/I	Open		Unkn.	75
XX	12-Pc. Set Figs. only, Color, 214/A/M/I, B/I, A/K/I, F/I G/I J/I K/I, L/I, M/I, N/I, O/I, 36/6/I	Open		Unkn.	1680
XX	Angel Serenade 214/D/I	Open		Unkn.	100
XX	Camel Kneeling - Goebel	Open		Unkn.	275
XX	Camel Lying - Goebel	Open		Unkn.	275
XX	Camel Standing - Goebel	Open		Unkn.	275
XX	Donkey 214/J/0	Open		Unkn.	55
XX	Donkey 214/J/I	Open		Unkn.	75
XX	Flying Angel/color 366/I	Open		Unkn.	135
XX	Good Night 214/C/I	Open		Unkn.	100
XX	Holy Family, 3 Pcs., Color 214/A/M/0, B/0, A/K/0	Open		Unkn.	330
XX	Holy Family, 3 Pcs., Color 214/A/M/I, B/I, A/K/I	Open		Unkn.	440
XX	Infant Jesus 214/A/K/0	Open		Unkn.	45
XX	Infant Jesus 214/A/K/I	Open		Unkn.	70
XX	King, Kneeling 214/M/I	Open		Unkn.	195
XX	King, Kneeling 214M/0	Open		Unkn.	155
XX	King, Kneeling w/ Box 214/N/0	Open		Unkn.	150
XX	King, Kneeling w/Box 214/N/I	Open		Unkn.	175
XX	King, Moorish 214/L/0	Open		Unkn.	165
XX	King, Moorish 214/L/I	Open		Unkn.	200
XX	Lamb 214/O/0	Open		Unkn.	22
XX	Lamb 214/O/I	Open		Unkn.	22
XX	Little Tooter 214/H/0	Open		Unkn.	110
XX	Little Tooter 214/H/I	Open		Unkn.	135
XX	Madonna 214/A/M/0	Open		Unkn.	145
XX	Madonna 214/A/M/I	Open		Unkn.	195
XX	Ox 214/K/0	Open		Unkn.	55
XX	Shepherd Boy 214/G/I	Open		Unkn.	145
XX	Shepherd Kneeling 214/G/0	Open		Unkn.	130
XX	Shepherd Standing 214/F/0	Open		Unkn.	165
XX	Shepherd with Sheep-1 pc. 214/F/I	Open		Unkn.	195
XX	Small Camel Kneeling - Goebel	Open		Unkn.	220
XX	Small Camel Lying - Goebel	Open		Unkn.	220
XX	Small Camel Standing - Goebel	Open		Unkn.	220
XX	St. Joseph 214/B/0	Open		Unkn.	145
XX	St. Joseph color 214/B/I	Open		Unkn.	195
XX	Stable only fits12 or 16-pc. HUM214/II Set	Open		Unkn.	110
XX	Stable only, fits 16-piece HUM260 Set	Open		Unkn.	440
XX	Stable only, fits 3-pc. HUM214 Set	Open		Unkn.	50
XX	We Congratulate 214/E/I	Open		Unkn.	175

M.I. Hummel Disneyana Figurines - M.I. Hummel

1995	For Father	1,500	1995	450.00	550
1995	Grandpa's Boys	1,500	1995	340.00	340
1994	Minnie Be Patient	1,500	1994	395.00	470-650
1996	Minnie For Mother	1,200	1996	470.00	470
1993	Two Little Drummers	1,500	1993	325.00	450-650
1992	Two Merry Wanderers 022074	1,500	1992	250.00	950-1250

M.I. Hummel First Edition Miniatures - M.I. Hummel

1991	Accordion Boy -37225	Suspd.		105.00	105-135
1989	Apple Tree Boy -37219	Suspd.		115.00	130-200
1990	Baker -37222	Suspd.		100.00	105-130
1992	Bavarian Church (Display) -37370	Closed	N/A	60.00	60-70
1988	Bavarian Cottage (Display) -37355	Closed	N/A	60.00	75-90
1990	Bavarian Marketsquare Bridge(Display) -37358	Closed	N/A	110.00	110-125
1990	Bavarian Village (Display) -37356	Closed	N/A	100.00	105

YEAR ISSUE		EDITION LIMIT	YEAR RETD.	ISSUE PRICE	*QUOTE U.S.$
1991	Busy Student -37226	Suspd.		105.00	105-130
1990	Cinderella -37223	Suspd.		115.00	125
1991	Countryside School (Display) -37365	Closed	N/A	100.00	100
1989	Doll Bath -37214	Suspd.		95.00	110
1995	Festival Harmony 173/4/0	Open		100.00	100
1992	Goose Girl -37238	Suspd.		130.00	180-225
1989	Little Fiddler -37211	Suspd.		90.00	115
1989	Little Sweeper -37212	Suspd.		90.00	115
1990	Marketsquare Flower Stand (Display) -37360	Closed	N/A	35.00	50-80
1990	Marketsquare Hotel (Display) -37359	Closed	N/A	70.00	90-125
1989	Merry Wanderer -37213	Suspd.		95.00	115
1991	Merry Wanderer Dealer Plaque -37229	Closed	N/A	130.00	135
1989	Postman -37217	Suspd.		95.00	120
1991	Roadside Shrine (Display)-37366	Closed	N/A	60.00	60
1992	School Boy -37236	Suspd.		120.00	120-150
1991	Serenade -37228	Suspd.		105.00	105-120
1992	Snow-Covered Mountain (Display)-37371	Closed	N/A	100.00	100
1989	Stormy Weather -37215	Suspd.		115.00	130-150
1992	Trees (Display) -37369	Closed	N/A	40.00	40-50
1989	Visiting an Invalid -37218	Suspd.		105.00	115-130
1990	Waiter -37221	Suspd.		100.00	115-135
1992	Wayside Harmony -37237	Suspd.		140.00	165-180
1991	We Congratulate -37227	Suspd.		130.00	130

M.I. Hummel Hummel Scapes - M.I. Hummel

1996	Heavenly Harmonies	Open		100.00	100
1996	Home Sweet Home	Open		130.00	130
1996	Little Music Makers	Open		130.00	130

M.I. Hummel Pen Pals - M.I. Hummel

1995	For Mother 257/5/0	Open		55.00	55
1995	March Winds 43/5/0	Open		55.00	55
1995	One For You, One For Me 482/5/0	Open		55.00	55
1995	Sister 98/5/0	Open		55.00	55
1995	Soloist 135/5/0	Open		55.00	55
1995	Village Boy 151/5/0	Open		55.00	55

M.I. Hummel Tree Toppers - M.I. Hummel

1994	Heavenly Angel 755	Open		450.00	495

M.I. Hummel Vingettes w/Solitary Domes - M.I. Hummel

1992	Bakery Day w/Baker & Waiter 37726	3,000		225.00	225
1992	The Flower Market w/Cinderella 37729	3,000		135.00	135
1993	The Mail Is Here Clock Tower 826504	Open		495.00	575
1995	Ring Around the Rosie Musical 826101	10,000		675.00	675
1992	Winterfest w/Ride Into Christmas 37728	5,000		195.00	195

M.I. Hummel's Temporarily Out of Production (including trademarks) - M.I. Hummel

XX	16-Pc. Set Figs. only, Color, 214/A/M/I, B/I, A/K/I, C/I, D/I, E/I, F/I, G/I, H/I, J/I, K/I, L/I, M/I, N/I, O/I, 366/I	Suspd.		Unkn.	1990
XX	17-Pc. Set Large Color 16 Figs.& Wooden Stable 260 A-R	Suspd.		Unkn.	4540
XX	Angel Serenade 260/E	Suspd.		Unkn.	345-445
XX	Apple Tree Boy 142/X	Suspd.		Unkn.	17000
XX	Apple Tree Girl 141/X	Suspd.		Unkn.	17000
XX	Blessed Child 78/I/83	Suspd.		Unkn.	35
XX	Blessed Child 78/I/83	Suspd.		Unkn.	50
XX	Blessed Child 78/III/83	Suspd.		Unkn.	60
XX	Bookworm 3/II	Suspd.		Unkn.	675-1350
XX	Bookworm 3/III	Suspd.		Unkn.	1195-2100
XX	Celestial Musician 188/I	Suspd.		Unkn.	255-475
XX	Christ Child 18	Suspd.		Unkn.	130-325
XX	Donkey 260/L	Suspd.		Unkn.	135
XX	Festival Harmony, w/Flute 173/II	Suspd.		Unkn.	400-1000
XX	Festival Harmony, w/Mandolin 172/II	Suspd.		Unkn.	400-1000
XX	Flower Madonna, color 10/III/II	Suspd.		Unkn.	600-750
XX	Flower Madonna, white 10/I/W	Suspd.		Unkn.	165-420
XX	Flower Madonna, white 10/III/W	Suspd.		Unkn.	470-750
XX	Going to Grandma's 52/I	Suspd.		Unkn.	350-900
XX	Good Night 260/D	Suspd.		Unkn.	145
XX	Goose Girl 47/II	Suspd.		Unkn.	410
XX	Happy Traveler 109/II	Suspd.		Unkn.	350-975
XX	Hear Ye! Hear Ye! 15/II	Suspd.		Unkn.	375-1500
XX	Heavenly Angel 21/II	Suspd.		Unkn.	415-1025
XX	Heavenly Protection 88/II	Suspd.		Unkn.	600-900
XX	Hello 124/I	Suspd.		Unkn.	175-385
XX	Holy Child 70	Suspd.		Unkn.	160-400
XX	Hummel Display Plaque 187	Suspd.		Unkn.	125-150
XX	Infant Jesus 260/C	Suspd.		Unkn.	120
1985	Jubilee 416 TMK6	Suspd.		200.00	275-380
XX	King, Kneeling 260/P	Suspd.		Unkn.	480
XX	King, Moorish 260/N	Suspd.		Unkn.	430-500
XX	King, Standing 260/O	Suspd.		Unkn.	300-500
XX	Little Band 392	Suspd.		Unkn.	250-350
XX	Little Cellist 89/II	Suspd.		Unkn.	400-650
XX	Little Fiddler 2/I	Suspd.		Unkn.	400-650
XX	Little Fiddler 2/II	Suspd.		Unkn.	1100-3000
XX	Little Fiddler 2/III	Suspd.		Unkn.	1200-3500
XX	Little Tooter 260/K	Suspd.		Unkn.	170-195
XX	Lullaby 24/III	Suspd.		Unkn.	450-1800

YEAR ISSUE		EDITION LIMIT	YEAR RETD.	ISSUE PRICE	* QUOTE U.S.$
XX	Madonna 260/A	Suspd.		Unkn.	590
XX	Madonna Holding Child, color 151/II	Suspd.		Unkn.	115
XX	Madonna Holding Child, white 151/W	Suspd.		Unkn.	320
XX	Madonna Praying, color 46/III/6	Suspd.		Unkn.	140-400
XX	Madonna Praying, white 46/0/W	Suspd.		Unkn.	40-195
XX	Madonna Praying, white 46/I/W	Suspd.		Unkn.	70-175
XX	Madonna w/o Halo, color 46/I/6	Suspd.		Unkn.	115-300
XX	Madonna w/o Halo, white 45/I/W	Suspd.		Unkn.	70-175
XX	Madonna w/o Halo, white 46/I/W	Suspd.		Unkn.	70-175
XX	Meditation 13/V	Suspd.		Unkn.	1200-5000
XX	Meditation, color 13/II	Suspd.		Unkn.	400-4500
XX	Merry Wanderer 7/II	Suspd.		Unkn.	850-2200
XX	Merry Wanderer 7/III	Suspd.		Unkn.	925-1300
XX	Merry Wanderer 7/X	Suspd.		Unkn.	12000-20000
XX	Merry Wanderer Stepbase 7/I	Suspd.		Unkn.	360-960
1995	Ooh My Tooth (Special Event) 533	Suspd.		Unkn.	120
XX	Ox 260/M	Suspd.		Unkn.	135
XX	School Boys 170/III	Suspd.		Unkn.	1600-2000
XX	School Girls 177/III	Suspd.		Unkn.	1500-2200
XX	Sensitive Hunter 6/II	Suspd.		Unkn.	400-1000
XX	Sheep (Lying) 260/R	Suspd.		Unkn.	100
XX	Sheep (Standing) w/ Lamb 260/H	Suspd.		Unkn.	110
XX	Shepherd Boy, Kneeling 260/J	Suspd.		Unkn.	300
XX	Shepherd, Standing 260/G	Suspd.		Unkn.	525
XX	Spring Cheer 72	Suspd.		Unkn.	165-500
XX	Spring Dance 353/I	Suspd.		Unkn.	500-750
XX	St. Joseph 260/B	Suspd.		Unkn.	520
1984	Supreme Protection 364 TMK6	Suspd.		150.00	350
XX	Telling Her Secret 196/I	Suspd.		Unkn.	430-800
XX	To Market 49/I	Suspd.		Unkn.	300-850
XX	Village Boy 51/I	Suspd.		Unkn.	250-650
XX	Volunteers 50/I	Suspd.		Unkn.	430-1400
XX	We Congratulate 260/F	Suspd.		Unkn.	400
XX	Worship 84/V	Suspd.		Unkn.	800-2800

Gorham

(Four Seasons) A Boy And His Dog - N. Rockwell

1972	A Boy Meets His Dog	2,500	1980	200.00	1300-1575
1972	Adventurers Between Adventures	2,500	1980	Set	Set
1972	The Mysterious Malady	2,500	1980	Set	Set
1972	Pride of Parenthood	2,500	1980	Set	Set

(Four Seasons) A Helping Hand - N. Rockwell

1980	Year End Court	2,500	1980	650.00	650-700
1980	Closed For Business	2,500	1980	Set	Set
1980	Swatter's Right	2,500	1980	Set	Set
1980	Coal Seasons Coming	2,500	1980	Set	Set

(Four Seasons) Dad's Boy - N. Rockwell

1981	Ski Skills	2,500	1990	750.00	750-800
1981	In His Spirit	2,500	1990	Set	Set
1981	Trout Dinner	2,500	1990	Set	Set
1981	Careful Aim	2,500	1990	Set	Set

(Four Seasons) Four Ages of Love - N. Rockwell

1974	Gaily Sharing Vintage Times	2,500	1980	300.00	600-1250
1974	Sweet Song So Young	2,500	1980	Set	Set
1974	Flowers In Tender Bloom	2,500	1980	Set	Set
1974	Fondly Do We Remember	2,500	1980	Set	Set

(Four Seasons) Going On Sixteen - N. Rockwell

1978	Chilling Chore	2,500	1980	400.00	650-675
1978	Sweet Serenade	2,500	1980	Set	Set
1978	Shear Agony	2,500	1980	Set	Set
1978	Pilgrimage	2,500	1980	Set	Set

(Four Seasons) Grand Pals - N. Rockwell

1977	Snow Sculpturing	2,500	1980	350.00	1000-1200
1977	Soaring Spirits	2,500	1980	Set	Set
1977	Fish Finders	2,500	1980	Set	Set
1977	Ghostly Gourds	2,500	1980	Set	Set

(Four Seasons) Grandpa and Me - N. Rockwell

1975	Gay Blades	2,500	1980	300.00	800-1000
1975	Day Dreamers	2,500	1980	Set	Set
1975	Goin' Fishing	2,500	1980	Set	Set
1975	Pensive Pals	2,500	1980	Set	Set

(Four Seasons) Life With Father - N. Rockwell

1983	Big Decision	2,500	1990	250.00	250
1983	Blasting Out	2,500	1990	Set	Set
1983	Cheering The Champs	2,500	1990	Set	Set
1983	A Tough One	2,500	1990	Set	Set

(Four Seasons) Me and My Pal - N. Rockwell

1976	A Licking Good Bath	2,500	1980	300.00	1200
1976	Young Man's Fancy	2,500	1980	Set	Set
1976	Fisherman's Paradise	2,500	1980	Set	Set
1976	Disastrous Daring	2,500	1980	Set	Set

(Four Seasons) Old Buddies - N. Rockwell

1984	Shared Success	2,500	1990	250.00	250
1984	Hasty Retreat	2,500	1990	Set	Set
1984	Final Speech	2,500	1990	Set	Set
1984	Endless Debate	2,500	1990	Set	Set

FIGURINES/COTTAGES

YEAR ISSUE		EDITION LIMIT	YEAR RETD.	ISSUE PRICE	*QUOTE U.S.$
(Four Seasons) Old Timers - N. Rockwell					
1982	Canine Solo	2,500	1990	250.00	250
1982	Sweet Surprise	2,500	1990	Set	Set
1982	Lazy Days	2,500	1990	Set	Set
1982	Fancy Footwork	2,500	1990	Set	Set
(Four Seasons) Tender Years - N. Rockwell					
1979	New Year Look	2,500	1979	500.00	1200
1979	Spring Tonic	2,500	1979	Set	Set
1979	Cool Aid	2,500	1979	Set	Set
1979	Chilly Reception	2,500	1979	Set	Set
(Four Seasons) Traveling Salesman - N. Rockwell					
1985	Horse Trader	2,500	1985	275.00	250-275
1985	Expert Salesman	2,500	1985	Set	Set
1985	Traveling Salesman	2,500	1985	Set	Set
1985	Country Pedlar	2,500	1985	Set	Set
(Four Seasons) Young Love - N. Rockwell					
1973	Downhill Daring	2,500	1973	250.00	1100
1973	Beguiling Buttercup	2,500	1973	Set	Set
1973	Flying High	2,500	1973	Set	Set
1973	A Scholarly Pace	2,500	1973	Set	Set
Miniature Christmas Figurines - Various					
1979	Tiny Tim - N. Rockwell	Yr.Iss.	1979	15.00	20
1980	Santa Plans His Trip - N. Rockwell	Yr.Iss.	1980	15.00	15
1981	Yuletide Reckoning - N. Rockwell	Yr.Iss.	1981	20.00	20
1982	Checking Good Deeds - N. Rockwell	Yr.Iss.	1982	20.00	20
1983	Santa's Friend - N. Rockwell	Yr.Iss.	1983	20.00	20
1984	Downhill Daring - N. Rockwell	Yr.Iss.	1984	20.00	20
1985	Christmas Santa - T. Nast	Yr.Iss.	1985	20.00	20
1986	Christmas Santa - T. Nast	Yr.Iss.	1986	25.00	25
1987	Annual Thomas Nast Santa - T. Nast	Yr.Iss.	1987	25.00	25
Miniatures - N. Rockwell					
1982	The Annual Visit	Closed	1990	50.00	75
1981	At the Vets	Closed	1990	27.50	40
1987	Babysitter	15,000	1990	75.00	75
1981	Beguiling Buttercup	Closed	1990	45.00	45
1985	Best Friends	Closed	1990	27.50	28
1987	Between The Acts	15,000	1990	60.00	60
1981	Boy Meets His Dog	Closed	1990	37.50	38
1984	Careful Aims	Closed	1990	55.00	55
1987	Cinderella	15,000	1990	70.00	75
1981	Downhill Daring	Closed	1990	45.00	75
1985	Engineer	Closed	1990	55.00	55
1981	Flowers in Tender Bloom	Closed	1990	60.00	60
1986	Football Season	Closed	1990	60.00	60
1981	Gay Blades	Closed	1990	45.00	75
1984	Ghostly Gourds	Closed	1990	60.00	60
1984	Goin Fishing	Closed	1990	60.00	60
1986	The Graduate	Closed	1990	30.00	40
1984	In His Spirit	Closed	1990	60.00	80
1984	Independence	Closed	1990	60.00	80
1986	Lemonade Stand	Closed	1990	50.00	60
1986	Little Angel	Closed	1990	60.00	60
1985	Little Red Truck	Closed	1990	25.00	25
1982	Marriage License	Closed	1990	60.00	75
1987	The Milkmaid	15,000	1990	80.00	85
1986	Morning Walk	Closed	1990	60.00	60
1985	Muscle Bound	Closed	1990	30.00	30
1985	New Arrival	Closed	1990	32.50	35
1984	The Oculist	Closed	1990	60.00	60
1986	The Old Sign Painter	Closed	1990	70.00	80
1984	Pride of Parenthood	Closed	1990	50.00	50
1987	The Prom Dress	15,000	1990	75.00	75
1982	The Runaway	Closed	1990	50.00	50
1984	Shear Agony	Closed	1990	60.00	60
1986	Shoulder Ride	Closed	1990	50.00	65
1981	Snow Sculpture	Closed	1990	45.00	70
1985	Spring Checkup	Closed	1990	60.00	60
1987	Springtime	15,000	1990	65.00	75
1987	Starstruck	15,000	1990	75.00	80
1981	Sweet Serenade	Closed	1990	45.00	45
1981	Sweet Song So Young	Closed	1990	55.00	55
1985	To Love & Cherish	Closed	1990	32.50	35
1982	Triple Self Portrait	Closed	1990	60.00	90-175
1983	Trout Dinner	15,000	1990	60.00	60
1982	Vintage Times	Closed	1990	50.00	50
1986	Welcome Mat	Closed	1990	70.00	75
1984	Years End Court	Closed	1990	60.00	60
1981	Young Man's Fancy	Closed	1990	55.00	55
Parasol Lady - Unknown					
1991	On the Boardwalk	Closed	1993	95.00	95
1994	Sunday Promenade	Closed	1993	95.00	95
1994	At The Fair	Closed	1993	95.00	95
Rockwell - N. Rockwell					
1983	Antique Dealer RW48	7,500	1990	130.00	200
1982	April Fool's (At The Curiosity Shop) RW39	Closed	1990	55.00	100-110
1974	At The Vets RW4	Closed	1990	25.00	125
1974	Batter Up RW6	Closed	1990	40.00	150-200
1975	Boy And His Dog RW9	Closed	1990	38.00	150
1974	Captain RW8	Closed	1990	45.00	95
1984	Card Tricks	7,500	1990	110.00	180
1981	Christmas Dancers RW37	7,500	1990	130.00	195
1988	Confrontation	15,000	1990	75.00	75

YEAR ISSUE		EDITION LIMIT	YEAR RETD.	ISSUE PRICE	*QUOTE U.S.$
1988	Cramming	15,000	1990	80.00	80
1981	Day in the Life Boy II RW34	Closed	1990	75.00	85
1982	A Day in the Life Boy III RW40	Closed	1990	85.00	95
1982	A Day in the Life Girl III RW41	Closed	1990	85.00	150
1988	The Diary	15,000	1990	80.00	80
1988	Dolores & Eddie NRM59	15,000	1990	75.00	80
1986	Drum For Tommy RW53	Annual	1986	90.00	N/A
1983	Facts of Life RW45	7,500	1990	110.00	180
1974	Fishing RW5	Closed	1990	50.00	125
1988	Gary Cooper in Hollywood	15,000	1990	90.00	90
1976	God Rest Ye Merry Gentlemen RW13	Closed	1990	50.00	1000-1500
1988	Home for the Holidays	7,500	1990	100.00	100
1976	Independence RW15	Closed	1990	40.00	150
1980	Jolly Coachman RW33	7,500	1990	75.00	175
1982	Marriage License (10 3/4") RW38	5,000	1990	110.00	400-600
1976	Marriage License (6 1/4") RW16	Closed	1990	50.00	275
1982	Merrie Christmas RW43	7,500	1990	75.00	150
1974	Missing Tooth RW2	Closed	1990	30.00	150
1975	No Swimming RW18	Closed	1990	35.00	175
1976	The Oculist RW17	Closed	1990	50.00	175
1975	Old Mill Pond RW11	Closed	1990	45.00	145
1985	The Old Sign Painter	7,500	1990	130.00	210
1985	Puppet Maker	7,500	1990	130.00	130-200
1987	Santa Planning His Annual Visit	7,500	1990	95.00	95
1984	Santa's Friend	7,500	1990	75.00	160
1982	Saying Grace (5 1/2") RW12	Closed	1990	110.00	500-600
1976	Saying Grace (8") RW42	5,000	1990	75.00	275
1982	Serenade	7,500	1990	95.00	165
1974	Skating RW7	Closed	1990	37.50	140
1976	Tackled (Ad Stand)	Closed	1990	35.00	150
1976	Tackled (Rockwell Name Signed) RW8662	Closed	1990	45.00	100
1974	Tiny Tim RW3	Closed	1990	30.00	125
1980	Triple Self Portrait (10 1/2") RW32	5,000	1990	300.00	600
1974	Weighing In RW1	Closed	1990	40.00	150
1981	Wet Sport RW36	Closed	1990	85.00	100

Great American Taylor Collectibles

Great American Collectors' Club - L. Smith, unless otherwise noted

YEAR ISSUE		EDITION LIMIT	YEAR RETD.	ISSUE PRICE	*QUOTE U.S.$
1993	William Claus-USA 700s	Retrd.	1994	35.00	75
1994	Winston-England 716	Retrd.	1995	35.00	60
1995	Timothy Claus-Ireland 717	12/96		35.00	35
1995	Kris Jingle 817 - J. Clement	12/96		70.00	80
1996	Palmer-USA 723	12/97		50.00	50
1996	Big Catch 830 - J. Clement	12/97		60.00	60

Jim Clement Collection - J. Clement

YEAR ISSUE		EDITION LIMIT	YEAR RETD.	ISSUE PRICE	*QUOTE U.S.$
1994	Americana Patriotic Santa 807	Retrd.	1994	20.00	20
1994	Bearded Shorty Santa 812	Retrd.	1994	13.50	16
1994	Mrs. Clement's Santa 808	Retrd.	1994	17.00	17
1994	Santa High Hat 815	Retrd.	1994	30.00	35
1994	Santa w/Tree 804	Retrd.	1994	15.00	18
1994	Day After Christmas 809	Retrd.	1995	16.50	17
1994	Down the Chimney Santa 814	Retrd.	1995	28.00	30
1994	Golfer Santa 806	Retrd.	1995	28.00	33
1994	Mr. Egg Santa 802	Retrd.	1995	19.50	22
1994	Sm. Hobby Horse Santa 803	Retrd.	1995	28.00	33
1994	Big Santa w/Toys 813	12/96		70.00	70
1994	Night After Christmas 810	12/96		16.50	17
1994	Noah Santa 805	12/96		28.00	30
1994	Santa w/Rover 811	12/96		20.00	20
1994	Tennis Santa 816	12/96		28.00	29
1995	Doe a Deer 818	12/97		29.00	30
1995	Ho! Ho! Ho! 819	12/97		11.50	12
1995	Mountain Dream 821	12/97		27.00	30
1995	Silent Night 820	12/97		29.00	32
1995	Visions of Sugar Plums 822	12/97		23.00	25
1996	Heading South 828	12/98		32.00	32
1996	Hogan 827	12/98		29.00	29
1996	Night Cats 825	12/98		30.00	30
1996	Radar 826	12/98		13.00	13
1996	Ted 829	12/98		29.00	29

Lamp Collection - J. Clement

YEAR ISSUE		EDITION LIMIT	YEAR RETD.	ISSUE PRICE	*QUOTE U.S.$
1995	Clementine Cat 55LNKS	12/97		70.00	79
1995	Kris Jingle 817LRS	12/96		99.00	99
1995	Toy Soldier 57LSS	12/97		80.00	89
1995	Uncle Sam 56LRS	12/97		80.00	89

Old World Santas - L. Smith

YEAR ISSUE		EDITION LIMIT	YEAR RETD.	ISSUE PRICE	*QUOTE U.S.$
1988	Jangle Claus-Ireland 335s	Retrd.	1990	20.00	145-160
1988	Hans Von Claus-Germany 337s	Retrd.	1990	20.00	145-160
1988	Ching Chang Claus-China 338s	Retrd.	1990	20.00	145-160
1988	Kris Kringle Claus-Switzerland 339s	Retrd.	1990	20.00	145-160
1988	Jingle Claus-England 336s	Retrd.	1990	20.00	145-160
1989	Rudy Claus-Austria 410s	Retrd.	1991	20.00	130
1989	Noel Claus-Belgium 412s	Retrd.	1991	20.00	130
1989	Pierre Claus-France 414s	Retrd.	1991	20.00	130
1989	Nicholai Claus-Russia 413s	Retrd.	1991	20.00	130
1989	Yule Claus-Germany 411s	Retrd.	1991	20.00	130
1990	Matts Claus-Sweden 430s	Retrd.	1992	20.00	85-105
1990	Vander Claus-Holland 433s	Retrd.	1992	20.00	85-105
1990	Sven Claus-Norway 432s	Retrd.	1992	20.00	85-105
1990	Cedric Claus-England 434s	Retrd.	1992	20.00	85-105
1990	Mario Claus-Italy 431s	Retrd.	1992	20.00	85-105
1991	Mitch Claus-England 437s	Retrd.	1993	25.00	65-80
1991	Samuel Claus-USA 436s	Retrd.	1993	25.00	65-80
1991	Duncan Claus-Scotland 439s	Retrd.	1993	25.00	65-80

YEAR ISSUE		EDITION LIMIT	YEAR RETD.	ISSUE PRICE	*QUOTE U.S.$
1991	Benjamin Claus-Israel 438s	Retrd.	1993	25.00	65-80
1991	Boris Claus-Russia 435s	Retrd.	1993	25.00	65-80
1992	Mickey Claus-Ireland 701s	Retrd.	1994	25.00	55
1992	Jacques Claus-France 702s	Retrd.	1994	25.00	55
1992	Terry Claus-Denmark 703s	Retrd.	1994	25.00	55
1992	José Claus-Spain 704s	Retrd.	1994	25.00	55
1992	Stu Claus-Poland 705s	Retrd.	1994	25.00	55
1993	Otto Claus-Germany 707s	Retrd.	1995	27.50	45
1993	Franz Claus-Switzerland 706s	Retrd.	1995	27.50	45
1993	Bjorn Claus-Sweden 709s	Retrd.	1995	27.50	45
1993	Ryan Claus-Canada 710s	Retrd.	1995	27.50	45
1993	Vito Claus-Italy 708s	Retrd.	1995	27.50	45
1994	Angus Claus-Scotland 713s	12/96		29.00	30
1994	Ivan Claus-Russia 712s	12/96		29.00	30
1994	Desmond Claus-England 715s	12/96		29.00	30
1994	Gord Claus-Canada 714s	12/96		29.00	30
1995	Tomba Claus-South Africa 718s	12/97		29.00	30
1995	Butch Claus-United States 719s	12/97		29.00	30
1995	Lars Claus-Norway 720s	12/97		29.00	30
1995	Stach Claus-Poland 721s	12/97		29.00	30
1995	Raymond Claus-Galapagos Islands 722s	12/97		29.00	30
1996	Gunther-Germany 724s	12/98		30.00	30
1996	Sean-Ireland 725s	12/98		30.00	30
1996	René-France 728s	12/98		30.00	30
1996	Manuel-Mexico 726s	12/98		30.00	30
1996	Zorba-Greece 727s	12/98		30.00	30

Stars & Stripes Collection - J. Clement

YEAR ISSUE		EDITION LIMIT	YEAR RETD.	ISSUE PRICE	*QUOTE U.S.$
1996	American Glory 555	12/98		36.00	36
1996	Flying Sam 553	12/98		29.00	29
1996	Great American Chicken 552	12/98		39.00	39
1996	Small Sam 554	12/98		29.00	29
1996	Tall Sam 551	12/98		39.00	39

Greenwich Workshop

Bronze - Various

YEAR ISSUE		EDITION LIMIT	YEAR RETD.	ISSUE PRICE	*QUOTE U.S.$
1994	Bird Hunters (Bronze) - J. Christensen	50	N/A	4500.00	4500
1990	The Candleman, AP (Bronze) - J. Christensen	100	N/A	737.00	4500
1991	Comanche Rider - K. McCarthy	100	N/A	812.50	813
1989	The Fish Walker (Bronze) - J. Christensen	100	N/A	711.00	4500
1991	Pony Express - K. McCarthy	10	N/A	934.00	934
1994	Thunder of Hooves - K. McCarthy	10	N/A	875.00	875

The Greenwich Workshop Collection - J. Christensen, unless otherwise noted

YEAR ISSUE		EDITION LIMIT	YEAR RETD.	ISSUE PRICE	*QUOTE U.S.$
1996	And They...Crooked House	Open		295.00	295
1996	Another Fish Act	2,500		350.00	350
1997	Bassoonist	2,500		395.00	395
1996	Bed Time Buddies - W. Bullas	Open		75.00	75
1996	Candleman	2,500		295.00	295
1996	Christmas Angel - W. Bullas	Open		75.00	75
1996	Christmas Elf - W. Bullas	Open		75.00	75
1997	Consultant - W. Bullas	Open		95.00	95
1996	The Dare Devil - W. Bullas	Open		75.00	75
1996	Ductor - W. Bullas	Open		75.00	75
1996	Fool and His Bunny - W. Bullas	Open		75.00	75
1997	Forest Fish Rider	1,500		175.00	175
1996	He Bought a Crooked Cat	Open		90.00	90
1996	Head of the Class - W. Bullas	Open		75.00	75
1996	Jack Be Nimble	Open		295.00	295
1996	Jailbirds - W. Bullas	Open		75.00	75
1996	Lawrence Pretended	2,500		350.00	350
1996	Levi Levitates a Stone Fish	2,500		295.00	295
1996	Man Who Minds the Moon	2,500		295.00	295
1996	Mother Goose	Open		275.00	275
1995	Olde World Santa	950	1995	295.00	495
1996	Oldest Angel	2,500		295.00	295
1996	Responsible Woman	2,500		595.00	595
1997	Scholar	3,500		495.00	495
1996	There Was a Crooked Man...	Open		225.00	225
1996	Three Blind Mice: Fluffy	Open		75.00	75
1996	Three Blind Mice: Sniffer	Open		75.00	75
1996	Three Blind Mice: Weevil	Open		75.00	75
1997	Tommy Tucker	Open		295.00	295
1996	Trick or Treat - W. Bullas	Open		75.00	75
1996	The Trick Rider - W. Bullas	Open		75.00	75
1996	Tweedle Dee	1,250		295.00	295
1996	Tweedle Dum	1,250		295.00	295
1996	Zippo...the Fire Eater - W. Bullas	Open		75.00	75

Hallmark Galleries

Kiddie Car Classics - E. Weirick

YEAR ISSUE		EDITION LIMIT	YEAR RETD.	ISSUE PRICE	*QUOTE U.S.$
1996	1935 Steelcraft by Murray® (Luxury Edition) QHG9029	24,500	1996	65.00	65
1994	1936 Steelcraft Lincoln Zephyr by Murray® QHG9015	19,500	1996	50.00	50-80
1995	1937 Steelcraft Auburn Luxury Ed. QHG9021	24,500	1996	65.00	65
1995	1937 Steelcraft Chrysler Airflow by Murray® QHG9024	24,500	1996	65.00	65
1992	1940 Murray Airplane QHG9003	14,500	1996	50.00	195-250
1992	1941 Steelcraft Spitfire Airplane QHG9009	19,500	1996	50.00	80
1995	1948 Murray Pontiac QHG9026	Open		50.00	50
1995	1950 Murray Torpedo QHG9020	Retrd.	1996	50.00	95
1992	1953 Murray Dump Truck QHG9012	14,500	1993	48.00	90-150

YEAR ISSUE		EDITION LIMIT	YEAR RETRD.	ISSUE PRICE	*QUOTE U.S.$
1992	1955 Murray Champion QHG9008	14,500	1993	45.00	195-240
1992	1955 Murray Dump Truck QHG9011	19,500	1996	48.00	65-80
1993	1955 Murray Fire Chief QHG9006	19,500	1996	45.00	45
1992	1955 Murray Fire Truck QHG9001	14,500	1993	50.00	195-240
1992	1955 Murray Fire Truck QHG9010	19,500	1996	50.00	100-125
1993	1955 Murray Ranch Wagon QHG9007	24,500	1996	48.00	65-100
1992	1955 Murray Red Champion QHG9002	19,500	1996	45.00	95
1995	1955 Murray Royal Deluxe QHG9025	29,500		55.00	55
1992	1955 Murray Tractor and Trailer QHG9004	14,500	1993	55.00	195-225
1994	1956 Garton Dragnet Police Car QHG9016	24,500		50.00	50
1994	1956 Garton Kidillac (Sp. Ed.) QHX9094	Retrd.	1994	50.00	50
1994	1956 GARTON Mark V QHG9022	24,500		45.00	45
1994	1958 Murray Atomic Missile QHG9018	24,500		55.00	55
1995	1959 GARTON Deluxe Kidillac QHG9017	Retrd.	1996	55.00	55
1995	1961 GARTON Casey Jones Locomotive QHG9019	Retrd.	1996	55.00	55
1994	1961 Murray Circus Car QHG9014	24,500		48.00	48
1994	1961 Murray Speedway Pace Car 4500QHG9013	24,500		45.00	45
1995	1962 Murray Super Deluxe Fire Truck QHG9095	Open		55.00	55
1995	1964 GARTON Tin Lizzie QHG9023	Open		50.00	50
1993	1968 Murray Boat Jolly Roger QHG9005	19,500	1996	50.00	95

Tender Touches - E. Seale

1990	Baby Bear in Backpack QEC9863	Retrd.	1991	16.00	60
1988	Baby Raccoon QHG7031	Retrd.	1992	20.00	40
1991	Baby's 1st Riding Rocking Bear QEC9349	Retrd.	1991	16.00	16
1989	Bear Decorating Tree QHG7050	Retrd.	1995	18.00	40
1992	Bear Family Christmas QHG7002	9,500	1995	45.00	50-70
1990	Bear Graduate QHG7043	Retrd.	1995	15.00	15
1988	Bear w/ Umbrella QHG7029	Retrd.	1994	16.00	35
1990	Bear's Easter Parade QHG7040	Retrd.	1995	23.00	23
1990	Bears Playing Baseball QHG7039	Retrd.	1994	20.00	20
1990	Bears w/ Gift QEC9461	Retrd.	1991	18.00	50-65
1992	Beaver Growth Chart QHG7007	19,500	1995	20.00	20
1992	Beaver w/ Double Bass QHG7058	Retrd.	1995	18.00	18
1990	Beavers w/Tree QHG7052	Retrd.	1994	23.00	23
1989	Birthday Mouse QHG7010	Retrd.	1993	16.00	45
1992	Breakfast in Bed QHG7059	Retrd.	1995	18.00	18
1989	Bride & Groom QHG7009	Retrd.	1994	20.00	40
1992	Building a Pumpkin Man QHG7061	Retrd.	1995	18.00	18
1990	Bunnies Eating Ice Cream QHG7038	Retrd.	1995	20.00	20
1990	Bunnies w/ Slide QHG7016	Retrd.	1994	20.00	20
1990	Bunny Cheerleader QHG7018	Retrd.	1994	16.00	45
1992	Bunny Clarinet QHG7063	Retrd.	1994	16.00	16
1990	Bunny Hiding Valentine QHG7035	Retrd.	1995	16.00	16
1990	Bunny in Boat QHG7021	Retrd.	1994	18.00	40
1989	Bunny in Flowers QHG7012	Retrd.	1992	16.00	30
1991	Bunny in High Chair QHG7054	Retrd.	1995	16.00	16
1990	Bunny Pulling Wagon QHG7008	Retrd.	1994	23.00	23
1990	Bunny w/ Ice Cream QHG7020	Retrd.	1993	15.00	25
1992	Bunny w/ Kite QHG7006	19,500	1995	19.00	19
1991	Bunny w/ Large Eggs QHG7056	Retrd.	1995	16.00	50
1990	Bunny w/ Stocking QEC9416	Retrd.	1990	15.00	25
1992	Chatting Mice QHG7003	19,500	1995	23.00	40-60
1989	Chipmunk Praying QEC9431	Retrd.	1991	18.00	75
1989	Chipmunk w/Roses QHG7023	Retrd.	1992	16.00	35
1992	Chipmunk w/Album QHG7057	Retrd.	1995	23.00	35
1991	Christmas Bunny Skiing QHG7046	Retrd.	1995	18.00	18
1990	Dad and Son Bears QHG7015	Retrd.	1992	23.00	33
1992	Delightful Fright QHG7067	19,500	1995	23.00	75
1993	Downhill Dash QHG7080	Retrd.	1995	23.00	23
1993	Easter Egg Hunt QEC9866	Retrd.	1991	18.00	28
1993	Easter Stroll QHG7084	Retrd.	1995	21.00	21
1993	Ensemble Chipmunk Kettledrum QHG7087	Retrd.	1994	18.00	18
1991	Father Bear Barbequing QHG7041	Retrd.	1995	23.00	23
1994	Fireman QHG7090	Retrd.	1995	23.00	23
1992	First Christmas Mice @ Piano QEC9357	Retrd.	1991	23.00	23
1992	Fitting Gift QHG7065	Retrd.	1995	23.00	23
1991	Foxes in Rowboat QHG7053	Retrd.	1995	23.00	23
1992	From Your Valentine QHG7071	Retrd.	1995	20.00	20
1993	Garden Capers QHG7078	Retrd.	1995	20.00	20
1994	Golfing QHG7091	Retrd.	1995	23.00	23
1994	Halloween QHG7093	Retrd.	1995	23.00	23
1989	Halloween Trio QEC9714	Retrd.	1990	18.00	130-150
1993	Handling a Big Thirst QHG7076	Retrd.	1995	21.00	21
1994	Happy Campers QHG7092	Retrd.	1995	25.00	25
1994	Jesus, Mary, Joseph QHG7094	Retrd.	1995	23.00	23
1993	Love at First Sight QHG7085	Retrd.	1995	23.00	23

YEAR ISSUE		EDITION LIMIT	YEAR RETRD.	ISSUE PRICE	*QUOTE U.S.$
1991	Love-American Gothic-Farmer Raccoons QHG7047	Retrd.	1995	20.00	20
1993	Making A Splash QHG7088	Retrd.	1995	20.00	20
1988	Mice at Tea Party QHG7028	Retrd.	1993	23.00	23
1991	Mice Couple Slow Waltzing QEC9437	Retrd.	1991	20.00	20
1990	Mice in Red Car QEC9886	Retrd.	1991	20.00	85
1988	Mice in Rocking Chair QHG7030	Retrd.	1994	18.00	18
1990	Mice w/Mistletoe QEC9423	Retrd.	1990	20.00	30
1990	Mice w/Quilt QHG7017	Retrd.	1994	20.00	45
1992	Mom's Easter Bonnet QHG7072	Retrd.	1995	18.00	18
1991	Mother Raccoon Reading Bible Stories QHG7042	Retrd.	1994	20.00	20
1989	Mouse at Desk QEC9434	Retrd.	1990	18.00	50
1991	Mouse Couple Sharing Soda QHG7055	Retrd.	1995	23.00	23
1990	Mouse in Pumpkin QEC9473	Retrd.	1991	18.00	100-135
1992	Mouse Matinee QHG7073	Retrd.	1995	22.00	22
1990	Mouse Nurse QHG7037	Retrd.	1995	15.00	15
1988	Mouse w/Heart QHG7024	Retrd.	1993	18.00	18
1989	Mouse w/Violin QHG7049	Retrd.	1992	16.00	30-50
1993	Mr. Repair Bear QHG7075	Retrd.	1995	18.00	18
1992	New World, Ahoy! QHG7068	Retrd.	1995	25.00	45
1992	Newsboy Bear QHG7060	Retrd.	1995	16.00	16
1993	The Old Swimming Hole QHG7086	9,500	1995	45.00	55-95
1990	Pilgrim Bear Praying QEC9466	Retrd.	1991	18.00	35-65
1989	Pilgrim Mouse QEC9721	Retrd.	1990	16.00	95
1993	Playground Go-Round QHG7089	Retrd.	1995	23.00	23
1989	Rabbit Painting Egg QHG7022	Retrd.	1994	18.00	30
1988	Rabbit w/Ribbon QHG7027	Retrd.	1994	15.00	15
1988	Rabbits at Juice Stand QHG7033	Retrd.	1994	23.00	23
1989	Rabbits Ice Skating QEC9391	Retrd.	1991	18.00	28
1988	Rabbits w/Cake QHG7025	Retrd.	1992	20.00	40
1992	Raccoon in Bath QHG7069	Retrd.	1993	18.00	45
1990	Raccoon Mail Carrier QHG7013	Retrd.	1995	16.00	16
1988	Raccoon w/Cake QEC9724	Retrd.	1991	18.00	48
1990	Raccoon Watering Roses QHG7036	Retrd.	1994	20.00	20
1991	Raccoon Witch QHG7045	Retrd.	1994	16.00	35
1988	Raccoons Fishing QHG7034	Retrd.	1994	18.00	18
1992	Raccoons on Bridge QHG7004	19,500	1995	25.00	25
1988	Raccoons Playing Ball QEC9771	Retrd.	1991	18.00	40
1990	Raccoons w/Flag QHG7044	Retrd.	1994	23.00	45
1990	Raccoons w/Wagon QHG7014	Retrd.	1993	23.00	30
1990	Romeo & Juliet Mice QEC9903	Retrd.	1991	25.00	35
1990	Santa in Chimney QHG7051	Retrd.	1994	18.00	18
1989	Santa Mouse in Chair QEC9394	Retrd.	1990	20.00	150
1993	Sculpting Santa QHG7083	Retrd.	1995	20.00	20
1992	Soapbox Racer QHG7005	19,500	1995	23.00	23
1988	Squirrels w/Bandage QHG7032	Retrd.	1993	18.00	18
1992	Stealing a Kiss QHG7066	19,500	1995	23.00	23
1992	Sweet Sharing QHG7062	Retrd.	1995	20.00	20
1992	Swingtime Love QHG7070	Retrd.	1993	21.00	21
1990	Teacher & Student Chipmunks QHG7019	Retrd.	1992	20.00	30
1988	Teacher w/Student QHG7026	Retrd.	1995	18.00	18
1993	Teeter For Two QHG7077	Retrd.	1995	23.00	23
1992	Tender Touches Tree House QHG7001	9,500	1995	55.00	55
1992	Thanksgiving Family Around Table QHG7048	Retrd.	1995	25.00	25
1990	Tucking Baby in Bed QHG7011	Retrd.	1993	18.00	18
1992	Waiting for Santa QHG7064	Retrd.	1995	20.00	20
1993	Woodland Americana-Liberty Mouse QHG7081	Retrd.	1995	21.00	21
1993	Woodland Americana-Patriot George QHG7082	Retrd.	1995	25.00	25
1993	Woodland Americana-Stitching the Stars and Stripes QHG7079	Retrd.	1995	21.00	21
1992	Younger Than Springtime QHG7074	19,500	1995	35.00	50

Hamilton Collection

American Garden Flowers - D. Fryer

1987	Azalea	15,000		75.00	75
1988	Calla Lilly	15,000		75.00	75
1987	Camelia	9,800		55.00	75
1988	Day Lily	15,000		75.00	75
1987	Gardenia	15,000		75.00	75
1989	Pansy	15,000		75.00	75
1988	Petunia	15,000		75.00	75
1987	Rose	15,000		75.00	75

American Wildlife Bronze Collection - H./N. Deaton

1980	Beaver	7,500		60.00	65
1979	Bobcat	7,500		60.00	75
1979	Cougar	7,500		60.00	125
1980	Polar Bear	7,500		60.00	65
1980	Sea Otter	7,500		60.00	65
1979	White-Tailed Deer	7,500		60.00	105

Arrowhead Spirits - N/A

1996	Path of the Wolf	28-day		29.95	30
1996	Piercing The Night	28-day		29.95	30
1996	Soul of the Hunter	28-day		29.95	30

A Celebration of Roses - N/A

1989	Brandy	Open		55.00	55
1989	Color Magic	Open		55.00	55
1989	Honor	Open		55.00	55
1989	Miss All-American Beauty	Open		55.00	55

YEAR ISSUE		EDITION LIMIT	YEAR RETRD.	ISSUE PRICE	*QUOTE U.S.$
1991	Ole'	Open		55.00	55
1990	Oregold	Open		55.00	55
1991	Paradise	Open		55.00	55
1989	Tiffany	Open		55.00	55

Coral Reef Beauties - Everhart

1996	Coral Paradise	Open		39.95	40
1996	Ocean's Bounty	Open		39.95	40
1996	Sentinel of the Sea	Open		39.95	40

Dreamsicles Heavenly Village - N/A

1996	Flight School	Open		49.95	50
1996	Star Factory	Open		49.95	50

First on Race Day Figurine Collection - N/A

1996	Bill Elliott	Open		45.00	45
1996	Jeff Gordon	Open		45.00	45

Freshwater Challenge - M. Wald

1992	Prized Catch	Open		75.00	75
1991	Rainbow Lure	Open		75.00	75
1991	The Strike	Open		75.00	75
1991	Sun Catcher	Open		75.00	75

Gifts of the Ancient Spirits - S. Kehrli

1996	Talisman of Courage	Open		79.00	79
1996	Talisman of the Buffalo	Open		79.00	79
1996	Talisman of Strength	Open		79.00	79

Gone With The Wind-Porcelain Trading Cards - N/A

1995	Fire and Passion	28-day		14.95	15
1995	Scarlett and Her Suitors	28-day		14.95	15
1996	Portrait of Scarlett	28-day		14.95	15
1996	Portrait of Rhett	28-day		14.95	15
1996	The Proposal	28-day		14.95	15
1996	Scarlett and Mammy	28-day		14.95	15
1996	Rhett at Twelve Oaks	28-day		14.95	15
1996	The Bold Entrance	28-day		14.95	15
1996	Sunset Embrace	28-day		14.95	15
1996	The Jail Scene	28-day		14.95	15
1996	The Exodus	28-day		14.95	15
1996	Anger Turns to Passion	28-day		14.95	15
1996	The Reunion	28-day		14.95	15

Heroes of Baseball-Porcelain Baseball Cards - N/A

1990	Brooks Robinson	Open		19.50	20
1991	Casey Stengel	Open		19.50	20
1990	Duke Snider	Open		19.50	20
1991	Ernie Banks	Open		19.50	20
1991	Gil Hodges	Open		19.50	20
1991	Jackie Robinson	Open		19.50	20
1991	Mickey Mantle	Open		19.50	20
1991	Roberto Clemente	Open		19.50	20
1991	Satchel Page	Open		19.50	20
1991	Whitey Ford	Open		19.50	20
1990	Willie Mays	Open		19.50	20
1991	Yogi Berra	Open		19.50	20

International Santa - N/A

1995	Alpine Santa	Open		55.00	55
1993	Belsnickel	Open		55.00	55
1995	Dedushka Moroz	Open		55.00	55
1992	Father Christmas	Open		55.00	55
1992	Grandfather Frost	Open		55.00	55
1993	Jolly Old St. Nick	Open		55.00	55
1993	Kris Kringle	Open		55.00	55
1994	Pére Noël	Open		55.00	55
1992	Santa Claus	Open		55.00	55
1994	Yuletide Santa	Open		55.00	55

Jeweled Carousel - M. Griffin

1995	Sapphire Jumper	Open		55.00	55
1996	Ruby Prancer	Open		55.00	55
1996	Emerald Stander	Open		55.00	55
1996	Amethyst Jumper	Open		55.00	55

Kitten Mischief - S. Kehrli

1996	Picnic Pirates	Open		19.95	20
1996	Toy Smugglers	Open		19.95	20
1996	Wet Paint!	Open		19.95	20

Little Friends of the Arctic - N/A

1995	The Young Prince	Open		35.00	35
1995	Princely Fishing	Open		35.00	35
1996	Playful Prince	Open		35.00	35
1996	Snoozing Prince	Open		35.00	35
1996	Princely Disguise	Open		35.00	35
1996	Slippery Prince	Open		35.00	35
1996	Prince Charming	Open		35.00	35
1996	Prince of the Mountain	Open		35.00	35

Little Messengers - P. Parkins

1996	Love Is Patient	Open		29.95	30

Little Night Owls - D.T. Lyttleton

1990	Barn Owl	Open		45.00	45
1991	Barred Owl	Open		45.00	45
1991	Great Grey Owl	Open		45.00	45
1991	Great Horned Owl	Open		45.00	45
1991	Short-Eared Owl	Open		45.00	45
1990	Snowy Owl	Open		45.00	45

*Quotes have been rounded up to nearest dollar

FIGURINES/COTTAGES

YEAR ISSUE		EDITION LIMIT	YEAR RETD.	ISSUE PRICE	*QUOTE U.S.$
1990	Tawny Owl	Open		45.00	45
1991	White-Faced Owl	Open		45.00	45

Masters of the Evening Wilderness - N/A

YEAR ISSUE		EDITION LIMIT	YEAR RETD.	ISSUE PRICE	*QUOTE U.S.$
1994	The Great Snowy Owl	Open		37.50	38
1995	Autumn Barn Owls	Open		37.50	38
1995	Great Grey Owl	Open		37.50	38
1995	Great Horned Owl	Open		37.50	38
1996	Barred Owl	Open		37.50	38
1996	Screech Owl	Open		37.50	38
1996	Burrowing Owl	Open		37.50	38
1996	Eagle Owl	Open		37.50	38

Mickey Mantle Collector's Edition-Porcelain Baseball Cards - N/A

YEAR ISSUE		EDITION LIMIT	YEAR RETD.	ISSUE PRICE	*QUOTE U.S.$
1995	1952 Card #311/1969 Card #500	Open		39.90	40
1996	1956 Card #135/1965 Card #350	Open		39.90	40
1996	1953 Card #82/1964 Card #50	Open		39.90	40
1996	1957 Card #95/1959 Card #10	Open		39.90	40
1996	1958 Card #150/1962 Card #318	Open		39.90	40
1996	1959 Card #564/1961 Card #300	Open		39.90	40

Mickey Mantle Figurine Collection - N/A

YEAR ISSUE		EDITION LIMIT	YEAR RETD.	ISSUE PRICE	*QUOTE U.S.$
1995	Mickey Swings Home	Open		45.00	45
1996	The Switch Hitter Connects	Open		45.00	45
1996	The Ultimate Switch Hitter	Open		45.00	45
1996	On Deck	Open		45.00	45
1996	Bunting From the Left	Open		45.00	45

Mickey Mantle Sculpture - N/A

YEAR ISSUE		EDITION LIMIT	YEAR RETD.	ISSUE PRICE	*QUOTE U.S.$
1996	Tribute to a Yankee Legend	Open		195.00	195

Mystic Spirits - S. Douglas

YEAR ISSUE		EDITION LIMIT	YEAR RETD.	ISSUE PRICE	*QUOTE U.S.$
1995	Spirit of the Wolf	Open		55.00	55
1995	Spirit of the Buffalo	Open		55.00	55
1995	Spirit of the Golden Eagle	Open		55.00	55
1996	Spirit of the Bear	Open		55.00	55
1996	Spirit of the Mountain Lion	Open		55.00	55
1996	Hawk Dancer	Open		55.00	55
1996	Wolf Scout	Open		55.00	55
1996	Spirit of the Deer	Open		55.00	55

Nature's Beautiful Bonds - R. Roberts

YEAR ISSUE		EDITION LIMIT	YEAR RETD.	ISSUE PRICE	*QUOTE U.S.$
1996	A Mother's Vigil	Open		29.95	30
1996	A Moment's Peace	Open		29.95	30
1996	A Warm Embrace	Open		29.95	30
1996	Safe By Mother's Side	Open		29.95	30
1996	Curious Cub	Open		29.95	30
1996	Under Mother's Watchful Eye	Open		29.95	30
1996	Time To Rest	Open		29.95	30
1996	Sheltered From Harm	Open		29.95	30

Nature's Majestic Cats - D. Geentz

YEAR ISSUE		EDITION LIMIT	YEAR RETD.	ISSUE PRICE	*QUOTE U.S.$
1995	Tigress and Cubs	Open		55.00	55
1995	Himalayan Snow Leopard	Open		55.00	55
1996	Cougar and Cubs	Open		55.00	55
1996	Pride of the Lioness	Open		55.00	55

Nesting Instincts - R. Willis

YEAR ISSUE		EDITION LIMIT	YEAR RETD.	ISSUE PRICE	*QUOTE U.S.$
1995	By Mother's Side	Open		19.50	20
1995	Learning to Fly	Open		19.50	20
1995	Like Mother, Like Son	Open		19.50	20
1995	A Mother's Pride	Open		19.50	20
1995	Peaceful Perch	Open		19.50	20
1995	Safe and Sound	Open		19.50	20
1995	Under Mother's Wings	Open		19.50	20
1995	A Watchful Eye	Open		19.50	20

Noble American Indian Women - N/A

YEAR ISSUE		EDITION LIMIT	YEAR RETD.	ISSUE PRICE	*QUOTE U.S.$
1994	Falling Star	Open		55.00	55
1995	Lily of the Mohawks	Open		55.00	55
1995	Lozen	Open		55.00	55
1994	Minnehaha	Open		55.00	55
1994	Pine Leaf	Open		55.00	55
1995	Pocahontas	Open		55.00	55
1993	Sacajawea	Open		55.00	55
1993	White Rose	Open		55.00	55

The Noble Swan - G. Granget

YEAR ISSUE		EDITION LIMIT	YEAR RETD.	ISSUE PRICE	*QUOTE U.S.$
1985	The Noble Swan	5,000		295.00	295

Noble Warriors - N/A

YEAR ISSUE		EDITION LIMIT	YEAR RETD.	ISSUE PRICE	*QUOTE U.S.$
1993	Deliverance	Open		135.00	135
1994	Spirit of the Plains	Open		135.00	135
1995	Top Gun	Open		135.00	135
1995	Windrider	Open		135.00	135

The Nolan Ryan Collectors Edition-Porcelain Baseball Cards - N/A

YEAR ISSUE		EDITION LIMIT	YEAR RETD.	ISSUE PRICE	*QUOTE U.S.$
1993	Angels 1972-C #595	Open		19.50	20
1993	Astros 1985-C #7	Open		19.50	20
1993	Mets 1968-C #177	Open		19.50	20
1993	Mets 1969-C #533	Open		19.50	20
1993	Rangers 1990-C #1	Open		19.50	20
1993	Rangers 1992-C #1	Open		19.50	20

North Pole Bears - T. Newsom

YEAR ISSUE		EDITION LIMIT	YEAR RETD.	ISSUE PRICE	*QUOTE U.S.$
1996	All I Want For Christmas	Open		29.95	30
1996	Beary Best Snowman	Open		29.95	30
1996	Beary Started	Open		29.95	30
1996	Papa's Cozy Chair	Open		29.95	30

Ocean Odyssey - W. Youngstrom

YEAR ISSUE		EDITION LIMIT	YEAR RETD.	ISSUE PRICE	*QUOTE U.S.$
1995	Breaching the Waters	Open		55.00	55
1995	Return to Paradise	Open		55.00	55
1995	Riding the Waves	Open		55.00	55
1996	Baja Bliss	Open		55.00	55
1996	Arctic Blue	Open		55.00	55
1996	Splashdown	Open		55.00	55
1996	Free Spirit	Open		55.00	55
1996	Beluga Belles	Open		55.00	55

Playful Penguins - N/A

YEAR ISSUE		EDITION LIMIT	YEAR RETD.	ISSUE PRICE	*QUOTE U.S.$
1996	Look Out Below!	Open		37.50	38

Princess of the Plains - N/A

YEAR ISSUE		EDITION LIMIT	YEAR RETD.	ISSUE PRICE	*QUOTE U.S.$
1995	Mountain Princess	Open		55.00	55
1995	Nature's Guardian	Open		55.00	55
1995	Noble Beauty	Open		55.00	55
1994	Noble Guardian	Open		55.00	55
1995	Proud Dreamer	Open		55.00	55
1994	Snow Princess	Open		55.00	55
1994	Wild Flower	Open		55.00	55
1995	Winter's Rose	Open		55.00	55

Protect Nature's Innocents - R. Manning

YEAR ISSUE		EDITION LIMIT	YEAR RETD.	ISSUE PRICE	*QUOTE U.S.$
1995	African Elephant	Open		14.95	15
1995	Giant Panda	Open		14.95	15
1995	Snow Leopard	Open		14.95	15
1995	Rhinoceros	Open		14.95	15
1996	Orangutan	Open		14.95	15
1996	Key Deer	Open		14.95	15
1996	Bengal Tiger	Open		14.95	15
1996	Pygmy Hippo	Open		14.95	15
1996	Gray Wolf	Open		14.95	15
1996	Fur Seal	Open		14.95	15
1996	Gray Kangaroo	Open		14.95	15
1996	Sea Otter	Open		14.95	15

Puppy Playtime Sculpture Collection - J. Lamb

YEAR ISSUE		EDITION LIMIT	YEAR RETD.	ISSUE PRICE	*QUOTE U.S.$
1991	Cabin Fever	Open		29.50	30
1991	Catch of the Day	Open		29.50	30
1990	Double Take	Open		29.50	30
1991	Fun and Games	Open		29.50	30
1991	Getting Acquainted	Open		29.50	30
1991	Hanging Out	Open		29.50	30
1991	A New Leash on Life	Open		29.50	30
1991	Weekend Gardner	Open		29.50	30

Puss in Boots - P. Cooper

YEAR ISSUE		EDITION LIMIT	YEAR RETD.	ISSUE PRICE	*QUOTE U.S.$
1993	All Dressed Up	Open		35.00	35
1992	Caught Napping	Open		35.00	35
1994	Daydreamer	Open		35.00	35
1993	Hide'n Go Seek	Open		35.00	35
1992	Sitting Pretty	Open		35.00	35
1992	Sweet Dreams	Open		35.00	35
1994	Tee Time	Open		35.00	35
1993	Tennis Anyone?	Open		35.00	35

Ringling Bros. Circus Animals - P. Cozzolino

YEAR ISSUE		EDITION LIMIT	YEAR RETD.	ISSUE PRICE	*QUOTE U.S.$
1983	Acrobatic Seal	9,800		49.50	50
1983	Baby Elephant	9,800		49.50	55
1983	Miniature Show Horse	9,800		49.50	68
1983	Mr. Chimpanzee	9,800		49.50	50
1984	Parade Camel	9,800		49.50	50
1984	Performing Poodles	9,800		49.50	50
1984	Roaring Lion	9,800		49.50	50
1983	Skating Bear	9,800		49.50	50

Santa Clothtique - Possible Dreams

YEAR ISSUE		EDITION LIMIT	YEAR RETD.	ISSUE PRICE	*QUOTE U.S.$
1992	Checking His List	Open		95.00	95
1993	Last Minute Details	Open		95.00	95
1993	Twas the Nap Before Christmas	Open		95.00	95
1994	Upon the Rooftop	Open		95.00	95
1994	O Tannenbaum!	Open		95.00	95
1995	Baking Christmas Cheer	Open		95.00	95
1995	Santa to the Rescue	Open		95.00	95
1996	Toyshop Tally	Open		95.00	95

Shield of the Mighty Warrior - S. Kehrli

YEAR ISSUE		EDITION LIMIT	YEAR RETD.	ISSUE PRICE	*QUOTE U.S.$
1995	Spirit of the Grey Wolf	Open		45.00	45
1996	Spirit of the Bear	Open		45.00	45
1996	Protection of the Cougar	Open		45.00	45
1996	Protection of the Buffalo	Open		45.00	45
1996	Protection of the Bobcat	Open		45.00	45

Snuggle Babies - Jacqueline B.

YEAR ISSUE		EDITION LIMIT	YEAR RETD.	ISSUE PRICE	*QUOTE U.S.$
1988	Baby Bears	Open		35.00	35
1988	Baby Bunnies	Open		35.00	35
1989	Baby Chipmunks	Open		35.00	35
1989	Baby Fawns	Open		35.00	35
1988	Baby Foxes	Open		35.00	35
1989	Baby Raccoons	Open		35.00	35
1988	Baby Skunks	Open		35.00	35
1989	Baby Squirrels	Open		35.00	35

Spirit of the Eagle - T. Sullivan

YEAR ISSUE		EDITION LIMIT	YEAR RETD.	ISSUE PRICE	*QUOTE U.S.$
1994	Spirit of Independence	Open		55.00	55
1995	Blazing Majestic Skies	Open		55.00	55
1995	Noble and Free	Open		55.00	55
1995	Proud Symbol of Freedom	Open		55.00	55
1996	Legacy of Freedom	Open		55.00	55
1996	Protector of Liberty	Open		55.00	55

STAR TREK® : Captain James T. Kirk Autographed Wall Plaque - N/A

YEAR ISSUE		EDITION LIMIT	YEAR RETD.	ISSUE PRICE	*QUOTE U.S.$
1995	Captain James T. Kirk	5,000		195.00	195

STAR TREK® : Captain Jean-Luc Picard Autographed Wall Plaque - N/A

YEAR ISSUE		EDITION LIMIT	YEAR RETD.	ISSUE PRICE	*QUOTE U.S.$
1994	Captain Jean-Luc Picard	5,000		195.00	175-200

STAR TREK® : First Officer Spock® Autographed Wall Plaque - N/A

YEAR ISSUE		EDITION LIMIT	YEAR RETD.	ISSUE PRICE	*QUOTE U.S.$
1994	First Officer Spock®	2,500		195.00	195

STAR TREK® : The Spock® Commemorative Wall Plaque - N/A

YEAR ISSUE		EDITION LIMIT	YEAR RETD.	ISSUE PRICE	*QUOTE U.S.$
1993	Spock®/STAR TREK VI The Undiscovered Country	2,500		195.00	195

STAR TREK®: The Next Generation-Porcelain Cards - S. Hillios

YEAR ISSUE		EDITION LIMIT	YEAR RETD.	ISSUE PRICE	*QUOTE U.S.$
1996	Deanna Troi & Data	28-day		39.90	40
1997	Inner Light & All Good Things	28-day		39.90	40
1996	Jean-Luc Picard & Q	28-day		39.90	40
1996	Ship In a Bottle & Best of Both Worlds	28-day		39.90	40
1996	USS Enterprise NCC-1701-D & William T. Riker	28-day		39.90	40
1997	Worf & Klingon Bird-of-Prey	28-day		39.90	40

STAR TREK®: The Voyagers-Porcelain Cards - K. Birdsong

YEAR ISSUE		EDITION LIMIT	YEAR RETD.	ISSUE PRICE	*QUOTE U.S.$
1996	Klingon Bird-of-Prey & Cardassian Galor Warship	28-day		39.90	40
1996	Triple Nacelled USS Enterprise & USS Excelsior	28-day		39.90	40
1996	USS Enterprise NCC-1701 & Klingon Battlecruiser	28-day		39.90	40
1996	USS Enterprise NCC-1701-A & Ferengi Marauder	28-day		39.90	40
1996	USS Enterprise NCC-1701-D & Romulan Warbird	28-day		39.90	40
1996	USS Voyager NCC-74656 & USS Defiant NX-74205	28-day		39.90	40

Star Wars: A New Hope-Porcelain Cards - N/A

YEAR ISSUE		EDITION LIMIT	YEAR RETD.	ISSUE PRICE	*QUOTE U.S.$
1996	Leia in Detention & Luke Skywalker	28-day		39.90	40
1996	Millennium Falcon Cockpit & Capture of Leia's Ship	28-day		39.90	40
1996	Obi-wan Kenobi & C-3PO and R2-D2	28-day		39.90	40

Tropical Treasures - M. Wald

YEAR ISSUE		EDITION LIMIT	YEAR RETD.	ISSUE PRICE	*QUOTE U.S.$
1990	Beaked Coral Butterfly Fish	Open		37.50	38
1990	Blue Girdled Angel Fish	Open		37.50	38
1989	Flag-tail Surgeonfish	Open		37.50	38
1989	Pennant Butterfly Fish	Open		37.50	38
1989	Sail-finned Surgeonfish	Open		37.50	38
1989	Sea Horse	Open		37.50	38
1990	Spotted Angel Fish	Open		37.50	38
1990	Zebra Turkey Fish	Open		37.50	38

Unbridled Spirits - C. DeHaan

YEAR ISSUE		EDITION LIMIT	YEAR RETD.	ISSUE PRICE	*QUOTE U.S.$
1994	Wild Fury	Open		135.00	135

Visions of Christmas - M. Griffin

YEAR ISSUE		EDITION LIMIT	YEAR RETD.	ISSUE PRICE	*QUOTE U.S.$
1995	Gifts From St. Nick	Open		135.00	135
1994	Mrs. Claus' Kitchen	Open		135.00	135
1993	Santa's Delivery	Open		135.00	135
1993	Toys in Progress	Open		135.00	135

Warrior's Quest - S. Kehrli

YEAR ISSUE		EDITION LIMIT	YEAR RETD.	ISSUE PRICE	*QUOTE U.S.$
1996	Cry of the Eagle	Open		95.00	95
1996	Strength of the Wolf	Open		95.00	95

The Way of the Warrior - J. Pyre

YEAR ISSUE		EDITION LIMIT	YEAR RETD.	ISSUE PRICE	*QUOTE U.S.$
1995	One With the Eagle	Open		45.00	45
1996	Star Shooter	Open		45.00	45
1996	Bear Warrior	Open		45.00	45
1996	Beckoning Back the Buffalo	Open		45.00	45

Wild and Free - C. De Haan

YEAR ISSUE		EDITION LIMIT	YEAR RETD.	ISSUE PRICE	*QUOTE U.S.$
1996	Wild and Free	Open		195.00	195

Wild Ducks of North America - C. Burgess

YEAR ISSUE		EDITION LIMIT	YEAR RETD.	ISSUE PRICE	*QUOTE U.S.$
1988	American Widgeon	15,000		95.00	95
1988	Bufflehead	15,000		95.00	95
1987	Common Mallard	15,000		95.00	95
1987	Green Winged Teal	15,000		95.00	95
1987	Hooded Merganser	15,000		95.00	95
1988	Northern Pintail	15,000		95.00	95
1988	Ruddy Duck Drake	15,000		95.00	95
1987	Wood Duck	15,000		95.00	95

Wolves of the Wilderness - D. Geenty

YEAR ISSUE		EDITION LIMIT	YEAR RETD.	ISSUE PRICE	*QUOTE U.S.$
1995	A Wolf's Pride	Open		55.00	55
1995	Mother's Watch	Open		55.00	55
1996	Time For Play	Open		55.00	55
1996	Morning Romp	Open		55.00	55
1996	First Adventure	Open		55.00	55
1996	Tumbling Twosome	Open		55.00	55

Harbour Lights

Harbour Lights Collector's Society - Harbour Lights

YEAR ISSUE		EDITION LIMIT	YEAR RETD.	ISSUE PRICE	*QUOTE U.S. $
1995	Point Fermin CA 501 (Charter Member Piece)	Retrd.	1996	80.00	150-200
1996	Stonington Harbour CT 502	4/97		70.00	70
1996	Spyglass Collection CT 503	4/97		Gift	30

Chesapeake Series - Harbour Lights

1996	Concord MD 186	9,500		66.00	66
1996	Sandy Point MD 167	9,500		70.00	70
1996	Sharp's Island MD 185	9,500		70.00	70
1996	Thomas Point MD 181	9,500	1996	99.00	99

Event Piece - Harbour Lights

1996	Sunken Rock NY 602	Yr.Iss.		25.00	25

Great Lakes Region - Harbour Lights

1992	Buffalo NY 122	5,500	1996	60.00	125-175
1992	Cana Island WI 119	5,500	1995	60.00	120-150
1996	Charlotte-Genesee NY 165	9,500		77.00	77
1991	Fort Niagara NY 113	5,500	1995	60.00	125-150
1992	Grosse Point IL 120	5,500		60.00	62
1994	Holland (Big Red) MI 142	5,500	1995	60.00	125-175
1992	Marblehead OH 121	5,500	1995	60.00	110-150
1992	Michigan City IN 123	5,500	1996	60.00	62
1992	Old Mackinac Point MI 118	5,500	1995	65.00	125-170
1995	Round Island MI 153	9,500		85.00	85
1991	Sand Island WI 112	5,500	1996	60.00	65-100
1995	Selkirk NY 157	9,500		75.00	75
1992	Split Rock MI 124 (misspelled)	Closed	1992	60.00	1800-2200
1992	Split Rock MN 124	Retrd.	1995	60.00	120-150
1992	Tawas Pt. MI 152	5,500		75.00	75
1995	Wind Point WI 154	9,500		78.00	78

Great Lighthouses of the World - Harbour Lights

1995	Boston Harbor MA 402	Open		50.00	50
1994	Cape Hatteras NC 401	Open		50.00	50
1995	Portland Head ME 404	Open		50.00	50
1996	Sandy Hook NJ 418	Open		50.00	50
1995	Southeast Block Island RI 403	Open		50.00	50

Gulf Coast Region - Harbour Lights

1995	Biloxi MS 149	5,500		60.00	60
1995	Bolivar TX 146	5,500		70.00	70
1995	New Canal LA 148	5,500	1996	65.00	65
1995	Pensacola FL 150	9,000		80.00	80
1995	Port Isabel TX 147	5,500		65.00	65

International Series - Harbour Lights

1996	Peggy's Cove Canada 169	9,500		68.00	68

Lady Lightkeepers - Harbour Lights

1996	Chatham MA 172	9,500		70.00	70
1996	Ida Lewis RI 174	9,500		70.00	70
1996	Matinicus ME 173	9,500		77.00	77
1996	Point Piños CA 170	9,500		70.00	70
1996	Saugerties NY 171	9,500		75.00	75
1996	Toledo OH 179	9,500		85.00	85

Northeast Region - Harbour Lights

1994	Barnegat NJ 139	5,500	1995	60.00	150-185
1991	Boston Harbor MA 117	5,500	1995	60.00	125-150
1995	Brant Point MA 162	9,500		66.00	66
1996	Cape May NJ 168	9,500		75.00	75
1994	Cape Neddick (Nubble) ME 141	5,500	1995	66.00	125-200
1991	Castle Hill RI 116	5,500	1996	60.00	60
1996	Fire Island NY 176	9,500		70.00	70
1991	Gt. Captain's Island CT 114	5,500	1994	60.00	70-120
1995	Highland MA 161	9,500		75.00	75
1992	Minot's Ledge MA 131	5,500		60.00	60
1992	Montauk NY 143	5,500	1995	85.00	195-225
1992	Nauset MA 126	5,500	1995	66.00	125-175
1992	New London Ledge CT 129	5,500	1995	66.00	120-150
1992	Pemaquid ME 164	9,500		90.00	90
1992	Portland Breakwater ME 130	5,500	1996	60.00	75-125
1992	Portland Head ME 125	5,500	1994	66.00	375-480
1991	Sandy Hook NJ 104	Retrd.	1994	60.00	140-200
1996	Scituate MA 166	9,500		77.00	77
1992	Southeast Block Island RI 128	5,500	1994	71.00	150-200
1991	West Quoddy Head ME 103	5,500	1995	60.00	110-170
1992	Whaleback NH 127	5,500	1996	60.00	115

Southeast Region - Harbour Lights

1994	Assateague VA 145-mold one	988	1994	69.00	300-425
1994	Assateague VA 145-mold two	4,512	1995	69.00	105-140
1996	Bald Head NC 155	9,500		75.00	75
1996	Bodie NC 159	9,500		77.00	77
1996	Cape Canaveral FL 163	9,500	1996	80.00	100-120
1991	Cape Hatteras NC 102 (w/ house)	Retrd.	1991	60.00	4000-4400
1992	Cape Hatteras NC 102R	Retrd.	1993	60.00	500-675
1992	Cape Lookout NC 175			64.00	64
1995	Currituck NC 158	9,500		80.00	80
1993	Hilton Head SC 136	5,500	1994	60.00	250-300
1995	Jupiter FL 151	9,500		77.00	77
1993	Key West FL 134	5,500	1995	60.00	150
1993	Ocracoke FL 135	5,500	1995	60.00	120-145
1993	Ponce de Leon FL 132	5,500	1994	60.00	175-210
1993	St. Augustine FL 138	5,500	1994	71.00	175-250
1993	St. Simons GA 137	5,500		66.00	150-175
1993	Tybee GA 133	5,500	1995	60.00	125-165

Special Editions - Harbour Lights

1995	Christmas 1995 - Big Bay Point MI 700	5,000	1995	75.00	150-250
1996	Christmas 1996 - Colchester VT 701			75.00	125-150
1995	Legacy Light (red) 600	Retrd.	1996	65.00	150-225
1995	Legacy Light 601	Open		65.00	65

Stamp Series - Harbour Lights

1995	Marblehead OH	Open		50.00	50
1995	Spectacle Reef MI	9,500		60.00	60
1995	Split Rock MN	Open		60.00	60
1995	St. Joseph MI	9,500		60.00	60
1995	Thirty Mile Point NY	9,500		62.00	62
1995	Five Piece Matched Numbered Set 400	5,800		275.00	275-350

Western Region - Harbour Lights

1991	Admirality Head WA 101(misspelled)	Closed	1994	60.00	125-175
1996	Admiralty Head WA 101	Retrd.	1994	60.00	130-200
1996	Alcatraz CA 177	9,500	1996	77.00	110-175
1991	Burrows Island OR 108 (misspelled)	Closed	1991	60.00	900-1200
1991	Burrows Island WA 108	Retrd.	1994	60.00	130-200
1991	Cape Blanco OR 109	5,500		60.00	60
1996	Cape Meares OR 160	9,500		68.00	68
1991	Coquille River OR 111	1,138	1993	60.00	2100-2300
1994	Diamond Head HI 140	5,500	1995	60.00	120-150
1994	Heceta Head OR 144	5,500	1996	65.00	75-100
1996	Mukilteo WA 178	9,500		55.00	55
1991	North Head WA 106	5,500		60.00	60
1991	Old Point Loma CA 105	5,500	1995	60.00	120
1995	Pt. Arena CA 156	9,500	1996	80.00	125-175
1991	St. George's Reef CA 115	5,500		60.00	60
1991	Umpqua River OR 107	5,500	1996	60.00	110
1991	Yaquina Head WA 110	5,500		60.00	62

Harmony Kingdom

Royal Watch Society - Various

1996	Big Blue - P. Calvestert	Open		75.00	75
1996	The Big Day - P. Calvestert	Open		Gift	N/A
1996	Purrfect Fit - D. Lawrence	Open		Gift	N/A

Angelique - D. Lawrence

1996	Fleur-de-lis	Open		35.00	35
1996	Gentil Homme	Open		35.00	35
1996	Ingenue	Open		35.00	35
1996	Joie De Vivre	Open		35.00	35

Garden Party - P. Calvesbert

1996	Baroness Trotter	Open		17.50	18
1996	Courtiers At Rest	Open		17.50	18
1996	Garden Prince	Open		17.50	18
1996	Ladies In Waiting	Open		17.50	18
1996	Royal Flotilla	Open		17.50	18
1996	Yeoman Of The Guard	Open		17.50	18

Harmony Circus - D. Lawrence

1996	The Audience	Open		150.00	150
1996	Ball Brothers	Open		35.00	35
1996	Beppo And Barney The Clowns	Open		35.00	35
1996	Circus Ring	Open		100.00	100
1996	Clever Constantine	Open		35.00	35
1996	Great Escapo	Open		35.00	35
1996	Harmony Circus Arch	Open		80.00	80
1996	Henry The Human Cannonball	Open		35.00	35
1996	Il Bendi	Open		35.00	35
1996	Lionel Loveless	Open		35.00	35
1996	Mr. Sediments	Open		35.00	35
1996	Olde Time Carousel	Open		35.00	35
1996	Pavareata The Little Big Girl	Open		35.00	35
1996	The Ringmaster	Open		35.00	35
1996	Road Dogs	Open		35.00	35
1996	Suave St. John	Open		35.00	35
1996	Top Hat	Open		35.00	35
1996	Vlad The Impaler	Open		35.00	35
1996	Winston The Lion Tamer	Open		35.00	35

Hi-Jinx - P. Calvesbert

1994	Antarctic Antics	Open		100.00	100
1994	Hold That Line	Open		100.00	100
1994	Mad Dogs and Englishmen	Open		100.00	100
1995	Open Mike	Open		100.00	100

Holiday Edition - D. Lawrence, unless otherwise noted

1995	Chatelaine	Retrd.	1995	35.00	55
1996	Bon Enfant	12/96		35.00	35
1996	Nick Of Time - P. Calvesbert	12/96		35.00	35

Large Treasure Jestr - P. Calvesbert

1991	Awaiting A Kiss	Open		55.00	55
1990	Drake's Fancy	Open		55.00	55
1995	Holding Court	Open		55.00	55
1991	Horn A' Plenty	Open		55.00	55
1991	Journey Home	Open		55.00	55
1990	Keeping Current	Open		55.00	55
1992	On A Roll	Open		55.00	55
1994	One Step Ahead	Open		55.00	55
1991	Pen Pals	Open		55.00	55

1990	Pondering	Open		55.00	55
1993	Pride And Joy	Open		55.00	55
1990	Quiet Waters	Open		55.00	55
1993	Standing Guard	Open		55.00	55
1993	Step Aside	Open		55.00	55
1991	Straight From The Hip	Open		55.00	55
1991	Sunnyside Up	Open		55.00	55
1991	Tea For Two	Open		55.00	55

Limited Editions - P. Calvesbert

1995	Noah's Lark	5,000		400.00	400
1995	Unbearables	2,500		400.00	400

Paradoxicals - P. Calvesbert

1995	Paradise Found	Open		35.00	35
1995	Paradise Lost	Open		35.00	35

Rather Large Series - P. Calvesbert

1996	Rather Large Friends	Open		65.00	65
1996	Rather Large Hop	Open		65.00	65
1996	Rather Large Huddle	Open		65.00	65
1996	Rather Large Safari	Open		65.00	65

Small Treasure Jestr - P. Calvesbert

1994	All Angles Covered	Open		35.00	35
1993	All Ears	Open		35.00	35
1993	All Tied Up	Open		35.00	35
1993	At Arm's Length	Retrd.	1996	35.00	42
1995	At The Hop	Open		35.00	35
1993	Baby on Board	Open		35.00	35
1993	Back Scratch	Retrd.	1995	35.00	35
1995	Beak To Beak	Open		35.00	35
1996	Brean Sands	Open		35.00	35
1996	Changing of the Guard	Open		35.00	35
1996	Close Shave	Open		35.00	35
1995	Damnable Plot	Open		35.00	35
1993	Day Dreamer	Retrd.	1996	35.00	35
1995	Den Mothers	Open		35.00	35
1994	Dog Days	Open		35.00	35
1995	Ed's Safari	Open		35.00	35
1994	Family Tree	Open		35.00	35
1992	Forty Winks	Open		35.00	35
1995	Fur Ball	Open		35.00	35
1994	Group Therapy	Open		35.00	35
1993	Hammin' It Up	Open		35.00	35
1996	Hog Heaven	Open		35.00	35
1995	Horse Play	Retrd.	1996	35.00	42
1994	Inside Joke	Open		35.00	35
1993	It's A Fine Day	Retrd.	1996	35.00	42
1995	Jersey Belles	Open		35.00	35
1993	Jonah's Hideaway	Retrd.	1996	35.00	35
1994	Let's Do Lunch	Retrd.	1995	35.00	35
1996	Liberty and Justice	Open		45.00	45
1995	Life's a Picnic	Open		35.00	35
1994	Love Seat	Open		35.00	35
1995	Major's Mousers	Open		45.00	45
1995	Mud Bath	Open		35.00	35
1994	Neighborhood Watch	Open		35.00	35
1993	Of The Same Stripe	Open		35.00	35
1991	Panda	100		35.00	35
1996	Pink Paradise	Open		35.00	35
1994	Play School	Open		35.00	35
1992	Princely Thoughts	Retrd.	1996	35.00	42
1995	Puddle Huddle	Open		35.00	35
1994	Purrfect Friends	Open		35.00	35
1991	Ram	100	1995	35.00	35
1993	Reminiscence	Open		35.00	35
1996	Rumble Seat	Open		45.00	45
1993	School's Out	Open		35.00	35
1991	Shark	100	1995	35.00	35
1993	Shell Game	Open		35.00	35
1993	Side Steppin'	Open		35.00	35
1994	Sunday Swim	Open		35.00	35
1993	Swamp Song	Open		35.00	35
1995	Sweet Serenade	Open		35.00	35
1994	Teacher's Pet	Open		35.00	35
1996	Tin Cat	Open		35.00	35
1994	Tongue And Cheek	Open		35.00	35
1994	Too much Of A Good Thing	Open		35.00	35
1993	Top Banana	Open		35.00	35
1996	Trumpeter's Ball	Open		45.00	45
1993	Trunk Show	Open		35.00	35
1995	Unbridled & Groomed	Open		35.00	35
1994	Unexpected Arrival	Open		35.00	35
1994	Untouchable	Retrd.	1995	35.00	55
1993	Who'd A Thought	Retrd.	1995	35.00	55
1995	Wise Guys	Open		35.00	35

Special Edition - P. Calvesbert

1995	Primordial Soup	Open		150.00	150

Hawthorne Village

Anne of Green Gables - Hawthorne

1996	Green Gables	Open		49.95	50

Baseball Stadiums - Hawthorne

1998	Wrigley Field-D. Kessinger	Open		49.95	50
1995	Wrigley Field-Ernie Banks	Open		99.95	100
1996	Wrigley Field-Ernie signature/cert.	Open		49.95	50

FIGURINES/COTTAGES

YEAR ISSUE		EDITION LIMIT	YEAR RETD.	ISSUE PRICE	*QUOTE U.S.$
1997	Wrigley Field-R. Huntley	Open		49.95	50
1999	Wrigley Field-R. Rushell	Open		49.95	50
1996	Wrigley Field-R. Santo	Open		49.95	50

Beacons of Freedom - Unknown
1995	Portland Head Lighthouse	Closed	1996	39.90	40
1996	Sandy Hook Lighthouse	Open		39.90	40
1995	West Quoddy Head Lighthouse	Open		39.90	40

Bedford Falls-Christmas in Bedford Falls (Illuminated) - Hawthorne
1995	Baily Bros. Building & Loan	Open		39.90	40
1995	The Old Granville Place	Open		39.90	40

Bedford Falls-It's a Wonderful Life Accessories - Hawthorne
1996	George & Mary	Open		21.90	22
1996	Uncle Billy & Clarence	Open		21.90	22

Chestnut Hill Station - K.&H. LeVan
1994	Bicycle Shop	Closed	1995	29.90	30
1994	Chestnut Hill Depot	Closed	1994	29.90	30
1993	Parkside Cafe	Closed	1995	29.90	30
1993	Wishing Well Cottage	Closed	1994	29.90	30

Colonial Accessories - K.&H. LeVan
1996	Colonial Pageant	Open		21.90	22

Colonial Christmas - K.&H. LeVan
1996	The Bruton Parish Church	Open		39.90	40
1995	Margaret Hunter's Shop	Open		39.90	40
1995	Market Square Tavern	Open		39.90	40

Concord: The Hometown of American Literature - K.&H. LeVan
1993	Alcott's Orchard House	Closed	1995	39.90	40
1992	Emerson's Old Manse	Closed	1995	39.90	40
1992	Hawthorne's Wayside Retreat	Closed	1995	39.90	40

Corinne Layton's Victoriana - C. Layton
1995	May Cottage	Open		29.95	30
1996	Rose Manor	Open		29.95	30

Currier & Ives Stocking Holders - C&I Inspired
1995	Holder for American Winter	Open		9.90	10
1995	Holder for Early Winter	Open		9.90	10
1995	Holder for Old Grist Mill	Open		9.90	10
1995	Holder for Winter Moonlight	Open		9.90	10
1995	Holder w/American Winter	Open		39.90	40
1995	Holder w/Early Winter	Open		39.90	40
1995	Holder w/Old Grist Mill	Open		39.90	40
1995	Holder w/Winter Moonlight	Open		39.90	40

Currier & Ives Summer - C&I Inspired
1995	American Homestead Summer	Open		29.90	30
1995	Home on the Mississippi	Open		29.90	30

Currier & Ives: The Art of America - C&I Inspired
1994	American Homestead Winter	Open		29.90	30
1995	A Cold Morning	Open		29.90	30
1995	Early Winter	Open		29.90	30
1995	Feeding the Chickens	Open		29.90	30
1995	The Old Grist Mill	Open		29.90	30
1994	The Snow Storm	Open		29.90	30
1995	Winter Evenings	Open		29.90	30
1995	Winter Moonlight	Open		29.90	30

England of My Dreams - R. Dowding
1994	Mayfair Hill	Closed	1994	59.90	60

The Fairytale Forest - S. Smith
1994	Goldilocks and the Three Bears/Figurines	Closed	1996	24.90	25
1994	Goldilocks and the Three Bears/Sculpture	Closed	1996	24.90	25
1994	Little Red Riding Hood/Sculp. & Figurine	Closed	1996	49.80	50

Gone With the Wind (Illuminated) - Hawthorne
1994	Atlanta Church	Closed	1996	39.90	40
1995	Butler's Mansion	Open		39.90	40
1994	Kennedy Store	Open		39.90	40
1994	Red Horse Saloon	Open		39.90	40
1993	Tara	Closed	1996	39.90	40
1994	Twelve Oaks	Open		39.90	40

Gone With the Wind Accessories - Hawthorne
1995	The Barbeque	Open		24.90	25
1995	The Butlers	Open		24.90	25
1995	Escape	Open		24.90	25
1995	Helping the Wounded	Open		24.90	25
1995	The O'Haras	Open		24.90	25
1995	Rebel Charge	Open		24.90	25
1995	Rhett & Scarlett	Open		24.90	25
1995	The Riding Lesson	Open		24.90	25
1995	Scarlett & Ashley	Open		24.90	25

Gone With the Wind Collection - K.&H. LeVan
1993	Against Her Will	Closed	1996	42.90	43
1994	Alone	Closed	1996	45.90	46
1995	Ashley's Safe	Closed	1996	45.90	46
1995	Dignity & Respect	Closed	1995	45.90	46

1994	Hope for a New Tomorrow	Closed	1994	42.90	43
1994	I Have Done Enough	Closed	1996	45.90	46
1994	Kennedy House	Open		45.90	46
1994	Merriweather House	Open		45.90	46
1993	A Message for Captain Butler	Closed	1996	42.90	43
1995	Revenge on Shantytown	Open		45.90	46
1993	Rhett Returns	Closed	1996	39.90	40
1994	Surrender at Last	Open		47.90	50
1994	Swept Away	Closed	1996	45.90	46
1994	Take Me to Tara	Closed	1995	45.90	46
1992	Tara . . .Scarlett's Pride	Closed	1995	39.90	40
1992	Twelve Oaks: The Romance Begins	Closed	1995	39.90	40

Gone With the Wind Miniatures - Hawthorne
1996	Ashley's Safe/Train Station	Open		29.95	30
1996	Message for Capt. Butler/Hope	Open		29.95	30
1996	Revenge/Dignity & Respect	Open		29.95	30
1996	Rhett's Return/Against Her Will	Open		29.95	30
1995	Scarlett's Pride/Romance	Open		29.95	30
1996	Springhouse/Carriage House	Open		29.95	30
1996	Swept Away/Alone	Open		29.95	30
1996	Take Me to Tara/Done Enough	Open		29.95	30
1996	Tara Mill/Stable	Open		29.95	30

Gone With the Wind-Special Edition - Hawthorne
1994	Burning of Atlanta	10,000		79.95	80

Helen Steiner Rice Accessories - S. Smith
1995	Boy w/Lantern, Singing, Lg. Tree	Open		19.90	20
1995	Girl Snowangel, sign, tree	Open		19.90	20
1995	Lamps	Open		19.90	20

Helen Steiner Rice: Windows of Gold - S. Smith
1994	Inspiration Point Lighthouse	Open		34.90	35
1994	Peace of Faith	Open		39.90	40
1994	Winter's Warmth	Open		39.90	40

Hershey, PA: An American Dream Comes True - Hawthorne
1995	Birthplace of Milton Hershey	Closed	1996	29.90	30
1995	Derry Church School	Open		29.90	30

Hometown America - Rockwell Inspired
1993	Evergreen Cottage	Open		34.95	35
1994	Evergreen General Store	Open		39.95	40
1994	Evergreen Valley Church	Open		37.95	38
1993	Evergreen Valley School	Closed	1995	34.95	35
1995	Happy Holidays	Open		39.95	40
1993	The Village Bakery	Closed	1994	37.95	38
1994	Waiting For Santa	Closed	1995	39.95	40
1994	Woodcutter's Rest	Open		37.95	38

Hummel's Bavarian Village Accessories - Unknown
1995	Large Tree/Sled	Open		24.90	25
1995	Small Tree/Bench	Open		24.90	25
1995	Village Bridge	Open		24.90	25
1995	Wishing Well	Open		24.90	25

Hummel's Bavarian Village Christmas - M.I. Hummel Inspired
1994	All Aboard	Open		49.90	50
1996	Angel's Duet	Open		49.90	50
1994	The Bakery	Open		49.90	50
1995	Christmas Mail	Open		49.90	50
1995	Company's Coming	Open		49.90	50
1996	Little Shoemaker	Open		49.90	50
1996	Off For The Holidays	Open		49.90	50
1995	Winter's Comfort	Open		49.90	50

Inside Gone With the Wind Collection - K.&H. LeVan
1996	Ashley I Love You	Open		39.90	40
1994	Pride and Passion	Open		39.90	40

Kinkade's Candlelight Cottages (Illuminated) - Kinkade-Inspired
1993	Chandler's Cottage	Closed	1994	29.90	30
1992	Olde Porterfield Tea Room	Closed	1994	29.90	30

Kinkade's Candlelight Cottages - Kinkade-Inspired
1994	Candlelit Cottage	Open		29.90	30
1995	Cedar Nook Cottage	Open		29.90	30
1993	Chandler's Cottage	Open		24.90	25
1993	Merritt's Cottage	Open		27.90	28
1992	Olde Porterfield Tea Room	Open		24.90	25
1994	Seaside Cottage	Open		27.90	28
1993	Swanbrooke Cottage	Open		24.90	25
1994	Sweetheart Cottage	Open		27.90	28

Kinkade's Christmas Memories - Kinkade-Inspired
1995	Home Before Christmas	Open		34.90	35
1995	Home to Grandma's	Open		34.90	35
1995	Homespun Holiday	Open		34.90	35
1995	Old Porterfield Gift & Shoppe	Open		34.90	35
1995	Silent Night	Open		34.90	35
1996	Stonehearth Hutch	Open		34.90	35
1995	Warmth of Home	Open		34.90	35

Kinkade's Enchanted Cottages - Kinkade-Inspired
1996	Cottage By the Sea	Open		29.90	30
1995	Heather's Hutch	Open		29.90	30
1995	Julianne's Cottage	Open		29.90	30

1995	McKenna's Cottage	Open		29.90	30
1995	Miller's Cottage	Open		29.90	30
1996	Sweetheart's Cottage	Open		29.90	30

Kinkade's Home for the Holidays - Kinkade-Inspired
1996	Christmas Eve	Open		29.95	30
1996	Moonlit Church	Open		29.95	30
1996	Victorian Christmas	Open		29.95	30
1996	Victorian Homestead	Open		29.95	30

Kinkade's Lamplight Lane - Kinkade-Inspired
1995	Kinkade's Cottage	Open		49.90	50
1996	Stonebrooke Cottage	Open		49.90	50

Kinkade's Lamplight Village (Illuminated) - Kinkade-Inspired
1996	Filkin's Cottage	Open		29.95	30
1996	Grantham's Cottage	Open		29.95	30
1996	Kinkade's Cottage	Open		29.95	30
1996	Lamplight Inn	Open		29.95	30
1996	Stonebrooke Cottage	Open		29.95	30
1996	Windermere Cottage	Open		29.95	30

Kinkade's St. Nicholas Square (Illuminated) - Kinkade-Inspired
1994	Evergreen Apothecary	Closed	1995	39.90	40
1994	The Firehouse	Closed	1995	39.90	40
1994	Holly House Inn	Closed	1995	39.90	40
1994	Kringle Brothers	Closed	1995	39.90	40
1994	Mrs. C. Bakery	Closed	1995	39.90	40
1994	Noel Chapel (free sign in box)	Closed	1995	39.90	40
1994	S.C. Toy Maker	Closed	1996	39.90	40
1993	Town Hall	Closed	1996	39.90	40

Lost Victorians of Old San Francisco - Hawthorne
1992	Empress of Russian Hill	Closed	1993	34.90	35
1991	Grande Dame of Nob Hill	Closed	1994	34.90	35
1993	Princess of Pacific Heights	Closed	1993	34.90	35

Marty Bell-Martha's Vineyard - M. Bell
1996	Summerland	Open		39.95	40

Mc-Memories - Hawthorne
1995	McDonald's Restaurant	Open		39.95	40

Nativity - Hawthorne
1995	Camels, Beasts & Mary's Donkey	Open		24.90	25
1995	Nativity	Open		39.90	40
1995	Palm Trees	Open		24.90	25
1995	Stable Keeper & Standing Carmel	Open		24.90	25

North Pole Accessories - Hawthorne
1994	Cookies for Kiddies	Open		23.90	24
1994	Getting Ready for Xmas (Santa/Tree)	Open		23.90	24
1994	Letters for Santa Set (Mailman/Deer)	Open		23.90	24
1994	Santa's Helpers Set	Closed	1996	23.90	24
1994	Sweet Delights Set (Elf/Candy Cane)	Open		23.90	24

On the Water - K.&H. LeVan
1995	Artists Delight	Open		34.90	35
1994	Sunrise Cove	Open		34.90	35

P.O. #1, North Pole Collection - G. Hoover
1995	Santa's Candy Shop	Open		39.90	40
1995	Santa's Gift Wrap Central	Closed	1996	39.90	40
1994	Santa's Post Office	Open		39.90	40
1994	Santa's Toy Shoppe with Sign	Open		39.90	40

Peaceable Kingdom - K.&H. LeVan
1993	Squire Boone's Homestead	Closed	1996	34.90	35
1994	White Horse Inn	Closed	1996	34.90	35

Peppercricket Grove - C. Wysocki
1996	Budzen's Roadside Food Stand	Open		49.90	50
1996	Evening Sled Ride	Open		49.90	50
1995	Peppercricket Farm	Open		44.90	45
1995	Peppercricket Farm, signed	Open		99.90	100
1996	Pumpkin Hollow	Open		49.90	50
1995	Virginia's Nest	Open		49.90	50

Rockwell Minis - Rockwell-Inspired
1996	Church on the Green/The Bank	Open		29.95	30
1996	Country Store/Rockwell Studio	Open		29.95	30
1996	Firehouse/Old Corner House	Open		29.95	30
1996	Grey Stone Church/Plain School	Open		29.95	30
1996	The Parsonage/The Mission House	Open		29.95	30
1996	The Red Lion Inn/Citizen's Hall	Open		29.95	30
1995	Rockwell Residence/Antique Shop	Open		29.95	30
1996	The Town Offices/The Bell Tower	Open		29.95	30
1996	The Train Station/The Library	Open		29.95	30

Rockwell Print Town - Rockwell-Inspired
1996	The Diner	Open		49.95	50

Rockwell's Four Freedoms (Illuminated) - Rockwell-Inspired
1994	Freedom of Worship: Arlington Church	Open		39.90	40

Collectors' Information Bureau

*Quotes have been rounded up to nearest dollar

YEAR ISSUE		EDITION LIMIT	YEAR RETD.	ISSUE PRICE	*QUOTE U.S.$
1994	Freedom from Fear: The Rockwell Homestead	Open		39.90	40
1995	Freedom of Speech: Town Hall	Open		39.90	40
1995	Freedom from Want: The Farmhouse	Open		39.90	40
1996	Freedom is Knowledge: The Library	Open		39.90	40

Rockwell's Heart of Stockbridge (Illuminated) - Rockwell-Inspired

1995	Bell Tower	Open		39.90	40
1995	Church on the Green	Open		39.90	40
1995	Firehouse	Open		39.90	40
1995	Rockwell's Home	Open		39.90	40
1995	Rockwell's Studio	Open		39.90	40

Rockwell's Home for the Holidays - Rockwell-Inspired

1992	Bringing Home the Christmas Tree	Closed	1994	34.90	35
1992	Carolers In The Church Yard	Closed	1996	37.90	38
1992	Christmas Eve at the Studio	Closed	1994	34.90	35
1994	A Golden Memory	Closed	1995	41.90	42
1994	Late for the Dance	Closed	1996	41.90	42
1993	Letters to Santa	Closed	1995	39.90	40
1993	Over the River	Closed	1995	37.90	38
1995	Ready & Waiting	Closed	1995	41.90	42
1993	A Room at the Inn	Closed	1994	39.90	40
1993	School's Out	Closed	1994	39.90	40
1993	Three-Day Pass	Closed	1996	37.90	38
1994	A White Christmas	Closed	1995	41.90	42

Rockwell's Hometown Collection - Rockwell-Inspired

1991	The Bell Tower	Closed	1995	36.95	37
1992	Berkshire Playhouse	Closed	1993	42.95	43
1991	The Church on the Green	Closed	1995	39.95	40
1992	Citizen's Hall	Closed	1994	42.95	43
1991	The Fire House	Closed	1995	36.95	37
1991	Grey Stone Church	Closed	1995	34.95	35
1992	The Mission House	Closed	1995	42.95	43
1992	The Old Corner House	Closed	1995	42.95	43
1994	Old Rectory	Closed	1994	42.95	43
1993	Parsonage Cottage	Closed	1995	42.95	43
1993	Plain School	Closed	1995	42.95	43
1990	Rockwell's Residence	Closed	1995	34.95	35
1992	Towne Hall	Closed	1993	39.95	40
1993	Train Station	Closed	1995	42.95	43

Rockwell's Main Street (Illuminated) - Rockwell-Inspired

1993	The Antique Shop	Open		29.90	30
1993	The Bank	Open		29.90	30
1993	The Country Store	Open		29.90	30
1993	The Library	Open		29.90	30
1993	The Red Lion Inn	Open		29.90	30
1993	Rockwell's Studio	Open		29.90	30
1993	The Town Offices	Open		29.90	30

Rockwell's Main Street - Rockwell-Inspired

1992	Bringing Home the Tree	Closed	1994	34.90	35
1992	Carolers in the Churchyard	Closed	1994	37.90	38
1992	Christmas Eve at the Studio	Closed	1993	34.90	35
1995	A Golden Memory	Closed	1995	41.90	42
1994	Late for the Dance	Open		41.90	42
1992	Letters to Santa	Open		39.90	40
1993	Over the River	Closed	1995	37.90	38
1995	Ready & Waiting	Open		41.90	42
1993	A Room at the Inn	Open		39.90	40
1993	School's Out	Closed	1994	37.90	38
1993	Three-Day Pass	Open		37.90	38
1994	A White Christmas	Closed	1995	41.90	42

Rockwell's Main Street Accessories - Rockwell-Inspired

1995	Autumn Trees	Open		29.90	30
1995	Backyard Barbeque	Open		21.90	22
1994	Bringing Home the Tree Set	Open		21.90	22
1995	Christmas Shopping Set	Open		29.90	30
1994	Country Farmstand	Open		21.90	22
1994	Decorating the Tree Set	Open		21.90	22
1995	Early Morning Delivery	Open		21.90	22
1996	Festive Holiday Street Lamps	Open		23.90	24
1995	Fire Drill	Open		23.90	24
1996	Footbridge, Bench, & Wishing Well	Open		21.90	22
1994	Greetings & Games Set	Open		21.90	22
1995	Holiday Mail	Open		21.90	22
1995	Last Day of School Before Christmas	Open		21.90	22
1995	Laundry Day	Open		21.90	22
1994	Norman Rockwell & Trio of Carollers	Open		21.90	22
1994	Old Fashioned Street Lights Set	Open		21.90	22
1995	Out for a Stroll	Open		21.90	22
1995	Picking Out a Pumpkin	Open		39.90	40
1995	Refreshments	Open		21.90	22
1994	Roaring Roadsters Set	Open		21.90	22
1995	Shopkeeper & Travelers Set	Open		21.90	22
1996	Sidewalk Racer	Open		23.90	24
1995	Sidewalk Sellers	Open		21.90	22
1994	The Skating Pond	Open		23.90	24
1994	Slipping & Sliding Set	Open		21.90	22
1994	Snow Covered Evergreens Set	Open		21.90	22
1994	Snowman & Tree Set	Open		21.90	22
1995	Summer Trees	Open		21.90	22

YEAR ISSUE		EDITION LIMIT	YEAR RETD.	ISSUE PRICE	*QUOTE U.S.$
1996	The Swimming Hole	Open		29.90	30
1996	The Village Clock	Open		29.90	30
1994	Village Vehicles Set	Open		21.90	22
1994	Vintage V-8s Set	Open		21.90	22

Rockwell's Neighborhood Collection - Rockwell-Inspired

1994	Fido's New Home	Closed	1995	29.90	30
1993	The Lemonade Stand	Open		29.90	30
1994	Sidewalk Speedster	Open		29.90	30

Small Town Christmas - C. Wysocki

1995	Ye Very Olde Fruitcake Shoppe	Open		39.90	40

Springtime on Main Street - Rockwell-Inspired

1993	Rockwell's Studio	Open		29.95	30

Stonefield Valley - K.&H. LeVan

1992	Church in the Glen	Closed	1994	37.90	38
1993	Ferryman's Cottage	Closed	1994	39.90	40
1993	Hillside Country Store	Closed	1994	39.90	40
1992	Meadowbrook School	Closed	1994	34.90	35
1993	Parson's Cottage	Closed	1994	37.90	38
1992	Springbridge Cottage	Closed	1994	34.90	35
1993	Valley View Farm	Closed	1994	39.90	40
1992	Weaver's Cottage	Closed	1994	37.90	38

Strolling Through Colonial America - K.&H. LeVan

1992	Captain Lee's Grammar School	Closed	1995	39.90	40
1992	Court House on the Green	Closed	1995	37.90	38
1992	Eastbrook Church	Closed	1995	37.90	38
1993	Everett's Joiner Shop	Closed	1993	39.90	40
1992	Higgins' Grist Mill	Closed	1995	37.90	38
1991	Jefferson's Ordinarie	Closed	1995	34.90	35
1992	Millrace Store	Closed	1995	34.90	35
1992	The Village Smithy	Closed	1993	39.90	40

Tara: The Only Thing Worth Fighting For Plantation - K.&H. LeVan

1994	Carriage House	Closed	1996	29.90	30
1993	A Dream Remembered	Closed	1996	29.90	30
1994	Kitchen & Gateway	Closed	1995	29.90	30
1994	The Mill	Closed	1996	29.90	30
1994	Spring House & Hideaway	Closed	1995	29.90	30
1995	The Stable	Closed	1996	29.90	30

Thatcher's Crossing - R. Dowding

1993	Chapel Crossing	Closed	1995	29.90	30
1993	Midsummer's Cottage	Closed	1995	29.90	30
1993	Rose Arbour Cottage	Closed	1994	29.90	30
1994	Woodcutter's Cottage	Closed	1995	29.90	30

Victorian Grove Collection - K.&H. LeVan

1993	Cherry Blossom	Closed	1994	34.90	35
1992	Lilac Cottage	Closed	1995	34.90	35
1992	Rose Haven	Closed	1994	34.90	35

Welcome to Mayberry - Unknown

1994	The Courthouse	Open		39.90	40
1994	Floyd's Barber Shop	Open		39.90	40
1994	Mayberry Methodist Church	Open		39.90	40
1994	Post Office	Open		39.90	40
1994	The Taylor Home	Open		39.90	40
1994	Wally's Filling Station	Open		39.90	40

Welcome to Mayberry Accessories - Unknown

1995	Andy & Barney	Open		21.90	22
1995	Aunt Bee & Opie	Open		21.90	22
1996	Barney's Sidecar	Open		23.90	24
1996	Fishin' with Pa	Open		29.90	30
1996	Have a Great Day	Open		21.90	22
1995	Patrol Car & Gas Pumps	Open		21.90	22

Wizard of Oz - Unknown

1995	The Journey Begins (Diorama)	Open		149.50	150

John Hine N.A. Ltd.

Alpine Christmas™ - G. Davison

1995	The Commons	Open		55.00	55
1995	Endcaps and Transformers	Open		39.00	39
1995	Hans Gasthof	Open		75.00	75
1995	Her Stuben's Sausagehaus	Open		80.00	80
1995	Herr Bergermeister's Retreat	Open		75.00	75
1995	The Manor	Open		80.00	80
1995	St. Peter's Church	Open		99.00	99
1995	The Village Hall	Open		99.00	99

Alpine Christmas™ Accessories - A. Stadden

1995	Carolers	Open		25.00	25
1995	Carolers with Lantern	Open		25.00	25
1995	Horse & Carriage, blue	Open		30.00	30
1995	Horse & Carriage, green	Open		30.00	30
1995	Minister and Nativity	Open		15.00	15
1995	Skating Couple and Children	Open		20.00	20
1995	Skating Couple and Sledders	Open		20.00	20
1995	Skier and Christmas Tree	Open		15.00	15

David Winter Collectors Guild Exclusives - D. Winter

1987	The Village Scene	Closed	1987	Gift	225-400

YEAR ISSUE		EDITION LIMIT	YEAR RETD.	ISSUE PRICE	* QUOTE U.S.$
1987	Robin Hood's Hideaway	Closed	1987	54.00	250-450
1987	Queen Elizabeth Slept Here	Closed	1987	183.00	200-400
1988	Black Bess Inn	Closed	1988	60.00	150-200
1988	The Pavillion	Closed	1988	52.00	100
1988	Street Scene	Closed	1988	Gift	100
1989	Home Guard	Closed	1989	105.00	105
1989	Coal Shed	Closed	1989	112.00	100-150
1990	The Plucked Ducks	Closed	1990	Gift	45-85
1990	The Cobblers Cottage	Closed	1990	40.00	60-90
1990	The Pottery	Closed	1990	40.00	65
1990	Cartwright's Cottage	Closed	1990	45.00	65-100
1991	Pershore Mill	Closed	1991	Gift	50-75
1991	Tomfool's Cottage	Closed	1991	100.00	75-110
1991	Will-O' The Wisp	Closed	1991	120.00	115-140
1992	Irish Water Mill	Closed	1992	Gift	50-125
1992	Patrick's Water Mill	Closed	1992	Gift	150-225
1992	Candlemaker's	Closed	1992	65.00	75
1992	Beekeeper's	Closed	1992	65.00	65-100
1993	On The River Bank	Closed	1993	Gift	55
1993	Thameside	Closed	1993	79.00	80
1993	Swan Upping Cottage	Closed	1993	69.00	75
1993	Horatio Pernickety's Amorous Intent	9,900	1993	375.00	275-375
1994	15 Lawnside Road	Closed	1994	Gift	55
1994	While Away Cottage	Closed	1994	70.00	70
1994	Ashe Cottage	Closed	1994	62.00	70
1995	Buttercup Cottage	Closed	1995	60.00	60
1995	The Flowershop	Closed	1995	150.00	150
1995	Gardener's Cottage	Closed	1995	Gift	50
1996	Punch Stables	Yr.Iss.		150.00	150
1996	Plough Farmstead	Yr.Iss.		125.00	125

David Winter Special Event Pieces - D. Winter

1992	Birthstone Wishing Well	Closed	1992	40.00	60
1993	Birthday Cottage	Closed	1994	55.00	60
1994	Wishing Falls Cottage	Closed	1995	65.00	65
1995	Whisper Cottage	Closed	1995	65.00	65
1996	Primrose Cottage	Yr.Iss.		65.00	65

David Winter Tour Special Event Piece - D. Winter

1993	Arches Thrice	Closed	1993	150.00	100-175

David Winter Appearance Piece - D. Winter

1994	Winter Arch	Closed	1995	N/A	N/A
1995	Grumbleweed's Potting Shed	Closed	1995	99.00	100-125

David Winter At The Centre of the Village Collection - D. Winter

1983	The Bakehouse	Open		31.40	60
1984	The Chapel	Closed	1992	48.80	70
1985	The Cooper Cottage	Closed	1993	57.90	60-80
1983	The Green Dragon Inn	Open		31.40	60
1982	Ivy Cottage	Closed	1992	22.00	45-65
1980	Little Market	Closed	1993	28.90	50
1980	Market Street	Open		48.80	90
1984	Parsonage	Open		390.00	560
1980	Rose Cottage	Open		28.90	55
1984	Spinner's Cottage	Closed	1991	28.90	40-60
1982	The Village Shop	Open		22.00	35
1980	The Wine Merchant	Closed	1993	28.90	40

David Winter British Traditions - D. Winter

1990	Blossom Cottage	Closed	1995	59.00	40-70
1990	The Boat House	Closed	1995	37.50	60
1990	Bull & Bush	Closed	1995	37.50	52
1990	Burns' Reading Room	Closed	1995	31.00	50
1990	Grouse Moor Lodge	Closed	1995	48.00	50-70
1990	Guy Fawkes	Closed	1995	31.00	50
1990	Harvest Barn	Closed	1995	31.00	50
1990	Knight's Castle	Closed	1995	59.00	85
1991	The Printers and The Bookbinders	Closed	1994	120.00	150
1990	Pudding Cottage	Closed	1995	78.00	60
1990	St. Anne's Well	Closed	1995	48.00	60-75
1990	Staffordshire Vicarage	Closed	1995	48.00	55-70
1990	Stonecutters Cottage	Closed	1995	48.00	70

David Winter Cameos - D. Winter

1992	Barley Malt Kilns	Open		12.50	15
1992	Brooklet Bridge	Open		12.50	15
1992	Diorama-Bright	Open		50.00	50
1992	Diorama-Light	Closed	1992	30.00	50
1992	Greenwood Wagon	Open		12.50	15
1992	Lych Gate	Open		12.50	15
1992	Market Day	Open		12.50	15
1992	One Man Jail	Open		12.50	15
1992	Penny Wishing Well	Open		12.50	15
1992	The Potting Shed	Open		12.50	15
1992	Poultry Ark	Open		12.50	15
1992	The Privy	Open		12.50	15
1992	Saddle Steps	Open		12.50	15
1992	Welsh Pig Pen	Open		12.50	15

David Winter Castle Collection - D. Winter

1995	Bishopsgate	Open		175.00	175
1995	Bishopsgate Premier	3,500		225.00	225
1994	Castle Wall	Open		65.00	65
1996	Christmas Castle	2,950		160.00	160
1996	Guinevere's Castle	4,300		299.00	299
1996	Guinevere's Castle Premier	2,200		350.00	350

David Winter Celebration Cottages - D. Winter

Year	Issue	Edition Limit	Year Retd.	Issue Price	*Quote U.S.$
1994	Celebration Chapel	Open		75.00	75
1994	Celebration Chapel Premier	3,500		150.00	150
1995	Mother's Cottage	Open		65.00	65
1995	Mother's Cottage Premier	3,500		89.50	90
1994	Spring Hollow	Open		65.00	65
1994	Spring Hollow Premier	3,500		125.00	125
1995	Stork Cottage Boy	Open		65.00	65
1995	Stork Cottage Girl	Open		65.00	65
1994	Sweetheart Haven	Open		60.00	60
1994	Sweetheart Haven Premier	3,500		115.00	115

David Winter Dicken's Christmas - D. Winter

Year	Issue	Edition Limit	Year Retd.	Issue Price	*Quote U.S.$
1987	Ebenezer Scrooge's Counting House	Closed	1988	96.90	150-200
1988	Christmas in Scotland & Hogmanay	Closed	1988	100.00	135-185
1989	A Christmas Carol	Closed	1989	135.00	150-225
1990	Mr. Fezziwig's Emporium	Closed	1990	135.00	100-155
1991	Fred's Home: "A Merry Christmas, Uncle Ebenezer saids Scrooge's Nephew Fred, and a Happy New Year.	Closed	1991	145.00	100-120
1992	Scrooge's School	Closed	1992	160.00	125-175
1993	Old Joe's Beetling Shop A Veritable Den of Iniquity!	Closed	1993	175.00	175-190
1994	Scrooge's Family Home	Closed	1994	175.00	215
1994	Scrooge's Family Home Premier	Closed	1994	230.00	250
1994	Scrooge's Family Home, Plaque	3,500	1994	125.00	180
1995	Miss Belle's Cottage	Closed	1995	185.00	195
1995	Miss Belle's Cottage Premier	2,200	1995	235.00	235
1995	Miss Belle's Christmas Plaque	4,000	1995	120.00	125
1996	Tiny Tim	Yr.Iss.		150.00	150
1996	Tiny Tim Premier	2,200		180.00	180
1996	Tiny Tim Christmas Plaque	4,000		110.00	110

David Winter English Village - D. Winter

Year	Issue	Edition Limit	Year Retd.	Issue Price	*Quote U.S.$
1994	Cat & Pipe	Open		53.00	53
1994	Chandlery	Open		53.00	53
1994	Church & Vestry	Open		57.00	57
1994	Constabulary	Open		60.00	60
1994	Crystal Cottage	Open		53.00	53
1994	Engine House	Open		55.00	55
1994	Glebe Cottage	Open		53.00	53
1994	Guardian Castle	8,490	1994	275.00	495
1994	Guardian Castle Premier	1,500	1994	350.00	510-600
1993	The Hall	Open		55.00	55
1993	One Acre Cottage	Open		55.00	55
1994	The Post Office	Open		53.00	53
1994	The Quack's Cottage	Open		57.00	57
1993	The Rectory	Open		55.00	55
1994	The Seminary	Open		57.00	57
1993	The Smithy	Open		50.00	50
1993	The Tannery	Open		50.00	50

David Winter Garden Cottages of England - D. Winter

Year	Issue	Edition Limit	Year Retd.	Issue Price	*Quote U.S.$
1995	Spencer Hall Gardens	4,300		395.00	395
1995	Spencer Hall Gardens, Premier	2,200		495.00	495
1995	Willow Gardens	4,300	1995	225.00	225
1995	Willow Gardens, Premier	2,200	1995	299.00	299

David Winter Heart of England Series - D. Winter

Year	Issue	Edition Limit	Year Retd.	Issue Price	*Quote U.S.$
1985	The Apothecary Shop	Closed	1995	24.10	50
1985	Blackfriars Grange	Closed	1994	24.10	50
1985	Craftsmen's Cottage	Closed	1995	24.10	40
1985	The Hogs Head Tavern	Closed	1995	24.10	50
1985	Meadowbank Cottages	Closed	1995	24.10	40
1985	The Schoolhouse	Closed	1995	24.10	50
1985	Shirehall	Closed	1995	24.10	50
1985	St. George's Church	Closed	1995	24.10	45
1985	The Vicarage	Closed	1995	24.10	45
1985	The Windmill	Closed	1995	37.50	50
1985	Yeoman's Farmhouse	Closed	1995	24.10	40

David Winter In The Country Collection - D. Winter

Year	Issue	Edition Limit	Year Retd.	Issue Price	*Quote U.S.$
1983	The Bothy	Open		31.40	60
1982	Brookside Hamlet	Closed	1991	74.80	60-70
1982	Drover's Cottage	Open		22.00	35
1983	Fisherman's Wharf	Open		31.40	60
1994	Guardian Gate	Open		150.00	150
1994	Guardian Gate Premier	3,500		199.00	199
1987	John Benbow's Farmhouse	Closed	1993	78.00	85-95
1996	Lover's Tryst	Open		125.00	125
1983	Pilgrim's Rest	Closed	1993	48.80	60
1984	Snow Cottage	Closed	1992	24.80	85-125
1986	There was a Crooked House	Open		96.90	155
1996	There was a Narrow House	Open		115.00	115
1984	Tollkeeper's Cottage	Closed	1992	87.00	95-125

David Winter Irish Collection - D. Winter

Year	Issue	Edition Limit	Year Retd.	Issue Price	*Quote U.S.$
1992	Fogartys	Closed	1994	75.00	85
1992	Irish Round Tower	Open		65.00	70
1992	Murphys	Open		100.00	110
1992	O'Donovan's Castle	Open		145.00	170
1991	Only A Span Apart	Closed	1993	80.00	80
1991	Secret Shebeen	Closed	1993	70.00	70

David Winter Landowners - D. Winter

Year	Issue	Edition Limit	Year Retd.	Issue Price	*Quote U.S.$
1984	Castle Gate	Closed	1992	155.00	220-250
1982	The Dower House	Closed	1993	22.00	45
1988	The Grange	Closed	1989	120.00	800-1050
1985	Squire Hall	Closed	1990	92.30	100

Year	Issue	Edition Limit	Year Retd.	Issue Price	*Quote U.S.$
1981	Tudor Manor House	Closed	1992	48.80	75-125

David Winter Main Collection - D. Winter

Year	Issue	Edition Limit	Year Retd.	Issue Price	*Quote U.S.$
1983	The Alms Houses	Closed	1987	59.90	225-425
1992	Audrey's Tea Room	Closed	1992	90.00	150-250
1992	Audrey's Tea Shop	Closed	1992	90.00	225-325
1982	Blacksmith's Cottage	Closed	1986	22.00	250
1991	Castle in the Air	Closed	1996	675.00	710
1981	Castle Keep	Closed	1982	30.00	900-1200
1981	Chichester Cross	Closed	1981	50.00	3200-3700
1980	The Coaching Inn	Closed	1983	165.00	3600
1981	Cornish Cottage	Closed	1986	30.00	825
1983	Cornish Tin Mine	Closed	1989	22.00	65
1983	Cotton Mill	Closed	1989	41.30	465-600
1981	Double Oast	Closed	1982	60.00	3300
1980	Dove Cottage	Closed	1983	60.00	1690
1982	Fairytale Castle	Closed	1989	115.00	300-450
1986	Falstaff's Manor	10,000	1990	242.00	225-325
1980	The Forge	Closed	1983	60.00	1200-1700
1996	Golf Clubhouse	Open		160.00	160
1996	Haunted House	4,900		325.00	325
1983	The Haybarn	Closed	1987	22.00	200
1985	Hermit's Humble Home	Closed	1988	87.00	200-300
1984	House of the Master Mason	Closed	1988	74.80	175-300
1988	House on Top	Closed	1988	92.30	195-325
1991	Inglenook Cottage	Open		60.00	75
1988	Jim'll Fixit	Closed	1988	350.00	2300-2600
1994	Kingmaker's Castle	Closed	1994	225.00	250-295
1980	Little Forge	Closed	1983	40.00	1200-1500
1980	Little Mill	Closed	1980	40.00	1200
1980	Little Mill-remodeled	Closed	1983	Unkn.	1600
1992	Mad Baron Fourthrite's Folly	Closed	1992	275.00	200
1980	Mill House	Closed	1980	50.00	2500
1980	Mill House-remodeled	Closed	1983	50.00	1800
1982	Miner's Cottage	Closed	1987	22.00	175-225
1991	Moonlight Haven	Open		120.00	155
1982	Moorland Cottage	Closed	1987	22.00	150-225
1995	Newtown Millhouse	4,500		195.00	195
1981	The Old Curiosity Shop	Closed	1983	40.00	1200
1980	Quayside	Closed	1985	60.00	1100-1500
1994	Quindene Manor	3,000	1994	695.00	700
1994	Quindene Manor Premier	1,500	1994	850.00	900
1982	Sabrina's Cottage	Closed	1984	30.00	2000-2350
1981	St. Paul's Cathedral	Closed	1982	40.00	1300-1900
1985	Suffolk House	Closed	1989	48.80	65
1980	Three Duck Inn	Closed	1983	60.00	1450
1981	Tythe Barn	Closed	1986	39.30	1450
1981	The Village	Open		362.00	580
1991	The Weaver's Lodgings	Open		65.00	75
1995	Welcome Home Cottage	Closed	1995	99.00	125-150
1995	Welcome Home Cottage Military	Closed	1995	99.00	99
1982	William Shakespeare's Birthplace (large)	Closed	1984	60.00	1300
1983	Woodcutter's Cottage	Closed	1988	87.00	250-400

David Winter Midlands Collection - D. Winter

Year	Issue	Edition Limit	Year Retd.	Issue Price	*Quote U.S.$
1988	Bottle Kilns	Closed	1991	78.00	78
1988	Coal Miner's Row	Open		90.00	120
1988	Derbyshire Cotton Mill	Closed	1994	65.00	90-125
1988	The Gunsmiths	Open		78.00	100
1988	Lacemaker's Cottage	Open		120.00	155
1988	Lock-keepers Cottage	Open		65.00	85

David Winter Porridge Pot Alley - D. Winter

Year	Issue	Edition Limit	Year Retd.	Issue Price	*Quote U.S.$
1995	Cob's Bakery	Open		125.00	125
1995	Cob's Bakery Premier	3,500		165.00	165
1995	Porridge Pot Arch	Open		50.00	50
1995	Sweet Dreams	Open		79.00	79
1995	Sweet Dreams Premier	3,500		99.00	99
1995	Tartan Teahouse	Open		99.00	99
1995	Tartan Teahouse Premier	3,500		129.00	129

David Winter Regions Collection - D. Winter

Year	Issue	Edition Limit	Year Retd.	Issue Price	*Quote U.S.$
1981	Cotswold Cottage	Open		22.00	35
1982	Cotswold Village	Closed	1990	59.90	65-75
1983	Hertford Court	Closed	1992	87.00	125-140
1985	Kent Cottage	Open		48.80	110
1981	Single Oast	Closed	1993	22.00	30-52
1981	Stratford House	Open		47.80	130
1981	Sussex Cottage	Open		22.00	50
1981	Triple Oast (old version)	Closed	1994	59.90	100-140

David Winter Scenes - Cameo Guild, unless otherwise noted

Year	Issue	Edition Limit	Year Retd.	Issue Price	*Quote U.S.$
1992	At Rose cottage Vignette - D. Winter	5,000		39.00	39
1992	Daughter - D. Winter	5,000		30.00	30
1992	Father	5,000		45.00	45
1992	Mother	5,000		50.00	50
1992	Son	5,000		30.00	30
1992	At The Bake House Vignette - D. Winter	5,000		35.00	35
1992	Girl Selling Eggs	5,000		30.00	30
1992	Hot Cross Bun Seller	5,000		60.00	60
1992	Lady Customer	5,000		45.00	45
1992	Small Boy And Dog	5,000		45.00	45
1992	Woman At Pump	5,000		45.00	45
1992	At The Bothy Vignette Base - D. Winter	5,000		39.00	39
1992	Farm Hand And Spade	5,000		40.00	40
1992	Farmer And Plough	5,000		60.00	60
1992	Farmer's Wife	5,000		45.00	45
1992	Goose Girl	5,000		45.00	45

Year	Issue	Edition Limit	Year Retd.	Issue Price	*Quote U.S.$
1993	Christmas Snow Vignette - D. Winter	5,000		50.00	50
1993	Bob Cratchit And Tiny Tim	5,000		50.00	50
1993	Ebenezer Scrooge	5,000		45.00	45
1993	Fred	5,000		35.00	35
1993	Miss Belle	5,000		35.00	35
1993	Mrs. Fezziwig	5,000		35.00	35
1993	Tom The Street Shoveler	5,000		60.00	60

David Winter Scottish Collection - D. Winter

Year	Issue	Edition Limit	Year Retd.	Issue Price	*Quote U.S.$
1986	Crofter's Cottage	Closed	1989	51.00	55-75
1989	Gatekeeper's Cottage	Open		65.00	85
1990	Gillie's Cottage	Open		65.00	85
1989	The House on the Loch	Closed	1994	65.00	80-90
1989	MacBeth's Castle	Open		200.00	260
1982	Old Distillery	Closed	1993	312.00	500
1992	Scottish Crofter's	Open		42.00	65

David Winter Seaside Boardwalk - D. Winter

Year	Issue	Edition Limit	Year Retd.	Issue Price	*Quote U.S.$
1995	The Barnacle Theatre	4,500		175.00	175
1995	Dock Accessory	Open		Gift	N/A
1995	The Fisherman's Shanty	Open		110.00	110
1995	Harbour Master's Watch-House	Open		125.00	125
1995	Jolly Roger Tavern	Open		199.00	199
1995	Lodgings and Sea Bathing	Open		165.00	165
1995	Trinity Lighthouse	Open		135.00	135
1995	Waterfront Market	Open		125.00	125

David Winter Sherwood Forest Collection - D. Winter

Year	Issue	Edition Limit	Year Retd.	Issue Price	*Quote U.S.$
1995	Friar Tuck's Sanctum	Open		45.00	45
1995	King Richard's Bower	Open		45.00	45
1995	Little John's Riverloft	Open		45.00	45
1995	Loxley Castle	Open		150.00	150
1995	Maid Marian's Retreat	Open		49.50	50
1995	Much's Mill	Open		45.00	45
1995	Sherwood Forest Diorama	Open		100.00	100
1995	Will Scarlett's Den	Open		49.50	50

David Winter Shires Collection - D. Winter

Year	Issue	Edition Limit	Year Retd.	Issue Price	*Quote U.S.$
1993	Berkshire Milking Byre	Closed	1995	38.00	38
1993	Buckinghamshire Bull Pen	Closed	1994	38.00	38
1993	Cheshire Kennels	Closed	1995	36.00	36
1993	Derbyshire Dovecote	Closed	1995	36.00	36
1993	Gloucestershire Greenhouse	Open		40.00	40
1993	Hampshire Hutches	Closed	1995	34.00	34
1993	Lancashire Donkey Shed	Closed	1995	38.00	38
1993	Oxfordshire Goat Yard	Open	1994	32.00	32
1993	Shropshire Pig Shelter	Closed	1995	32.00	32
1993	Staffordshire Stable	Closed	1995	36.00	36
1993	Wiltshire Waterwheel	Open		34.00	34
1993	Yorkshire Sheep Fold	Closed	1995	38.00	38

David Winter Tiny Series - D. Winter

Year	Issue	Edition Limit	Year Retd.	Issue Price	*Quote U.S.$
1980	Anne Hathaway's Cottage	Closed	1982	Unkn.	750
1980	Cotswold Farmhouse	Closed	1982	Unkn.	450-700
1980	Crown Inn	Closed	1982	Unkn.	600-700
1980	St. Nicholas' Church	Closed	1982	Unkn.	600-900
1980	Sulgrave Manor	Closed	1982	Unkn.	450-700
1980	William Shakespeare's Birthplace	Closed	1982	Unkn.	750

David Winter Welsh Collection - D. Winter

Year	Issue	Edition Limit	Year Retd.	Issue Price	*Quote U.S.$
1993	A Bit of Nonsense	Open		50.00	50
1993	Pen-y-Craig	Open		88.00	90
1993	Tyddyn Siriol	Closed	1995	88.00	95
1993	Y' Ddraig Goch	Closed	1994	88.00	88

David Winter West Country Collection - D. Winter

Year	Issue	Edition Limit	Year Retd.	Issue Price	*Quote U.S.$
1988	Cornish Engine House	Open		120.00	155
1988	Cornish Harbour	Open		120.00	155
1986	Devon Combe	Closed	1994	73.00	110
1987	Devon Creamery	Open		62.90	110
1986	Orchard Cottage	Closed	1991	91.30	125
1987	Smuggler's Creek	Open		390.00	520
1987	Tamar Cottage	Open		45.30	75
1996	Wreckers Cottages	4,300		225.00	225
1996	Wreckers Cottages Premier	2,200		275.00	275

David Winter Winterville Collection - D. Winter

Year	Issue	Edition Limit	Year Retd.	Issue Price	*Quote U.S.$
1996	At Home with Comfort & Joy	5,750		110.00	110
1996	At Home with Comfort & Joy Premier	1,750		145.00	145
1994	The Christmastime Clockhouse	Open		165.00	165
1994	The Christmastime Clockhouse Premier	3,500	1994	215.00	215
1995	St. Stephen's	5,750		150.00	150
1995	St. Stephen's Premier	1,750	1995	195.00	195
1994	Toymaker	Open		135.00	135
1994	Toymaker Premier	3,500	1994	175.00	175
1995	Winterville Square	Open		75.00	75
1995	Ye Merry Gentlemen's Lodgings	5,750		125.00	125
1995	Ye Merry Gentlemen's Lodgings Premier	1,750	1995	170.00	170

Disneyana Convention - John Hine Studio

Year	Issue	Edition Limit	Year Retd.	Issue Price	*Quote U.S.$
1992	Cinderella Castle	500	1992	250.00	1100-1200
1993	Sleeping Beauty Castle	500	1993	250.00	350-600
1994	Euro Disney Castle	500	1994	250.00	300-350

Father Christmas - J. King

Year	Issue	Edition Limit	Year Retd.	Issue Price	*Quote U.S.$
1988	Falling	Closed	N/A	70.00	70
1988	Feet	Closed	N/A	70.00	70

YEAR ISSUE		EDITION LIMIT	YEAR RETD.	ISSUE PRICE	*QUOTE U.S.$
1988	Standing	Closed	N/A	70.00	70

Father Time Clocks - J. Herbert

YEAR ISSUE		EDITION LIMIT	YEAR RETD.	ISSUE PRICE	*QUOTE U.S.$
1995	Captain's Keep	5,000		199.00	199
1991	Castle	Open		110.00	110
1995	Cupid's Clock	Open		55.00	55
1991	Farmhouse	Open		99.00	99
1996	Father Christmas	Open		75.00	75
1994	Hokus Pokus	Open		79.90	80
1991	Little Thatched	Open		78.00	78
1991	The Manor	Open		90.00	90
1994	Marshland Castle	Open		99.00	99
1996	Nursery Clock	Open		110.00	110
1994	Riverside Haven	Open		99.00	99
1996	Santa Clock	Open		60.00	60
1995	Schoolhouse Clock	Open		55.00	55
1994	Small Farmhouse Clock	Open		79.90	80
1996	Snowman Clock	Open		60.00	60
1995	A Time To Remember	Open		70.00	70
1991	Treehouse	Open		99.00	99
1995	Tudor Falls	Open		55.00	55
1995	Tudor Hall	Open		55.00	55
1994	Tudor Ruin	Open		94.00	94
1991	Watermill	Open		99.00	99
1991	Windmill	Open		120.00	120

Great British Pubs - M. Cooper

YEAR ISSUE		EDITION LIMIT	YEAR RETD.	ISSUE PRICE	*QUOTE U.S.$
1989	The Bell	Closed	N/A	79.50	100-350
1989	Black Swan	Closed	1990	79.50	100-200
1989	Blue Bell	Closed	N/A	57.50	58
1989	Coach & Horses	Closed	N/A	79.50	80
1989	The Crown Inn	Closed	N/A	79.50	80
1989	Dickens Inn	Closed	N/A	100.00	100
1989	The Feathers	Closed	N/A	200.00	200
1989	The George	Closed	N/A	57.50	58
1989	George Somerset	Closed	N/A	100.00	100
1989	Hawkeshead	Closed	N/A	Unkn.	900
1989	Jamaica Inn	Closed	N/A	39.50	40
1989	King's Arms	Closed	N/A	28.00	28
1989	The Lion	Closed	N/A	57.50	58
1989	Montague Arms	Closed	N/A	57.50	58
1989	Old Bridge House	Closed	N/A	37.50	38
1989	Old Bull Inn	Closed	N/A	87.50	88
1989	The Plough	Closed	N/A	28.00	95
1989	Sherlock Holmes	Closed	N/A	100.00	200
1989	Smith's Arms	Closed	N/A	28.00	28
1989	White Horse	Closed	N/A	39.50	40
1989	White Tower	Closed	N/A	35.00	35
1989	Ye Grapes	Closed	N/A	87.50	88
1989	Ye Olde Spotted Horse	Closed	N/A	79.50	80

Great British Pubs -Yard of Pubs - M. Cooper

YEAR ISSUE		EDITION LIMIT	YEAR RETD.	ISSUE PRICE	*QUOTE U.S.$
1989	Black Friars	Closed	N/A	25.00	25
1989	Dirty Duck	Closed	N/A	25.00	25
1989	The Eagle	Closed	N/A	35.00	35
1989	Falkland Arms	Closed	N/A	25.00	25
1989	The Falstaff	Closed	N/A	35.00	35
1989	George & Pilgrims	Closed	N/A	25.00	25
1989	The Green Man	Closed	N/A	Unkn.	75
1989	Grenadier	Closed	N/A	25.00	25
1989	Lygon Arms	Closed	N/A	35.00	35
1989	Suffolk Bull	Closed	N/A	35.00	35
1989	The Swan	Closed	N/A	35.00	35
1989	Wheatsheaf	Closed	N/A	35.00	35

Heartstrings - S. Kuck

YEAR ISSUE		EDITION LIMIT	YEAR RETD.	ISSUE PRICE	*QUOTE U.S.$
1992	Day Dreaming	Closed	N/A	92.50	93
1992	Hush, It's Sleepytime	Closed	N/A	97.50	98
1992	Taking Tea	Closed	N/A	92.50	93
1992	Watch Me Waltz	Closed	N/A	97.50	98

London By Gaslight - B. Russell

YEAR ISSUE		EDITION LIMIT	YEAR RETD.	ISSUE PRICE	*QUOTE U.S.$
1995	Banker's House	Open		75.00	75
1995	Birdcage Walk	Open		75.00	75
1995	Chelsea House	Open		65.00	65
1995	Cockney Corner Shop	Open		59.00	59
1995	The Iron Duke	Open		69.00	69
1995	Knightsbridge Mansion	Open		80.00	80
1995	L.B.G. Transformer	Open		19.50	20
1995	St. Bartholomew's Church Gate	Open		69.00	69
1995	Streatham House	Open		59.00	59
1995	Thameside Walk	Open		65.00	65

London By Gaslight Accessories - A. Stadden

YEAR ISSUE		EDITION LIMIT	YEAR RETD.	ISSUE PRICE	*QUOTE U.S.$
1995	Barrowman & Woman	Open		25.00	25
1995	Children Playing	Open		15.00	15
1995	Couple/Postbox	Open		15.00	15
1995	Empty Hansom Cab	Open		30.00	30
1995	Fire Engine	Open		35.00	35
1995	Flower Seller/Lamplighter	Open		15.00	15
1995	Goods Wagon	Open		25.00	25
1995	Hansom Cab with Passengers	Open		30.00	30
1995	Lawyers/Man with Trolleycart	Open		20.00	20
1995	Organ Grinder	Open		25.00	25
1995	Policeman/Holmes & Daphne	Open		20.00	20
1995	Trees	Open		25.00	25
1995	Two Couples	Open		15.00	15

Mushrooms - C. Lawrence

YEAR ISSUE		EDITION LIMIT	YEAR RETD.	ISSUE PRICE	*QUOTE U.S.$
1989	The Cobblers	Closed	N/A	265.00	265
1989	The Constables	Closed	N/A	200.00	200

YEAR ISSUE		EDITION LIMIT	YEAR RETD.	ISSUE PRICE	*QUOTE U.S.$
1989	The Elders Mushroom	Closed	N/A	175.00	175
1989	The Gift Shop	Closed	N/A	350.00	420
1989	The Ministry	Closed	N/A	185.00	185
1989	The Mush Hospital for Malingerers	Closed	N/A	250.00	250
1989	The Princess Palace	Closed	N/A	600.00	730
1989	Royal Bank of Mushland	Closed	N/A	235.00	235

Once Upon A Story - M. Danko

YEAR ISSUE		EDITION LIMIT	YEAR RETD.	ISSUE PRICE	*QUOTE U.S.$
1995	Annabelle-Pioneer Girl	Open		75.00	75
1995	Bethany-The Royal Visit	Open		80.00	80
1995	Catherine-Circus Memories	2,750		99.00	99
1995	Faith-The Little Angel	Open		75.00	75
1995	Nicholas-A Perfect Christmas	Open		80.00	80
1995	Sarah-The Wedding Day	Open		80.00	80

Santa's Big Day - J. King

YEAR ISSUE		EDITION LIMIT	YEAR RETD.	ISSUE PRICE	*QUOTE U.S.$
1992	Booting Up	Closed	N/A	40.00	40
1992	Feet First	Closed	N/A	55.00	55
1992	Heave Ho!	Closed	N/A	70.00	70
1992	Home Rudolph	Closed	N/A	50.00	50
1992	Ready Boys?	Closed	N/A	80.00	80
1992	Reindeer Breakfast	Closed	N/A	50.00	50
1992	Rest-a-while	Closed	N/A	60.00	60
1992	Santa's Night Ride	Closed	N/A	55.00	55
1992	Tight Fit!	Closed	N/A	55.00	55
1992	Wakey, Wakey!	Closed	N/A	55.00	55
1992	Whoops!	Closed	N/A	60.00	60
1992	Zzzzz...	Closed	N/A	85.00	85

The Shoemaker's Dream - J. Herbert

YEAR ISSUE		EDITION LIMIT	YEAR RETD.	ISSUE PRICE	*QUOTE U.S.$
1991	Baby Booty (blue)	Open		45.00	45
1991	Baby Booty (pink)	Open		45.00	45
1991	Castle Boot	Open		55.00	55
1991	The Chapel	Open		55.00	55
1992	Christmas Boot	Open		55.00	55
1994	Christmas Presence	Open		55.00	55
1991	The Clocktower Boot	Open		60.00	60
1992	Clown Boot	Open		45.00	45
1991	The Crooked Boot	Open		35.00	35
1995	Dovecote Shoehouse	Open		65.00	65
1996	Garden Boot	Open		65.00	65
1991	The Gate Lodge	Open		65.00	65
1991	The Golf Shoe	Open		35.00	40
1991	The Jester Boot	Closed	1994	29.00	29
1995	Kitty Boot	Open		65.00	65
1991	River Shoe Cottage	Closed	1994	55.00	55
1991	Rosie's Cottage	Closed	1994	40.00	40
1993	Shiver me Timbers	Open		45.00	55
1991	Shoemaker's Palace	Open		50.00	50
1992	The Sports Shoe	Open		35.00	40
1994	Sweetheart's Shoe	Open		55.00	55
1991	Tavern Boot	Open		55.00	55
1992	Upside Down Boot	Open		45.00	45
1991	Watermill Boot	Closed	1994	60.00	60
1993	Wedding Bells	Open		45.00	50
1991	Windmill Boot	Open		65.00	65
1992	Wishing Well Shoe	Open		32.00	32
1993	The Woodcutter's Shoe	Open		40.00	40

Wideman - M. Wideman

YEAR ISSUE		EDITION LIMIT	YEAR RETD.	ISSUE PRICE	*QUOTE U.S.$
1992	Moe's Clubhouse	Closed	1993	40.00	250

Wideman-American Collection - M. Wideman

YEAR ISSUE		EDITION LIMIT	YEAR RETD.	ISSUE PRICE	*QUOTE U.S.$
1989	Band Stand	Closed	1993	90.00	72-90
1989	Barber Shop	Closed	1993	40.00	30
1989	The Blockhouse	Closed	1993	25.00	16-55
1989	Cajun Cottage	Closed	1993	50.00	40
1989	California Winery	Closed	1993	180.00	215-225
1989	Cherry Hill School	Closed	1993	45.00	46-96
1991	Church in the Dale	Closed	1993	130.00	90
1989	Colonial Wellhouse	Closed	1993	15.00	14-30
1991	Desert Storm Tent	Closed	1991	75.00	75-120
1989	Dog House	Closed	1993	10.00	14
1991	Fire Station	Closed	1993	160.00	125-275
1989	Forty-Niner Cabin	Closed	1993	50.00	40-60
1989	Garconniere	Closed	1993	25.00	12-20
1989	The Gingerbread House	Closed	1993	60.00	50-60
1992	Grain Elevator	Closed	1993	110.00	110-150
1989	Hacienda	Closed	1993	51.00	40-80
1989	Haunted House	Closed	1993	100.00	100-175
1989	Hawaiian Grass Hut	Closed	1992	45.00	45
1991	Joe's Service Station	Closed	1993	90.00	108
1989	King William Tavern	Closed	1993	99.00	80-150
1991	The Kissing Bridge	Closed	1992	50.00	40-50
1989	The Log Cabin	Closed	1993	45.00	40-60
1989	The Maple Sugar Shack	Closed	1993	50.00	40-50
1991	Milk House	Closed	1993	20.00	24
1989	The Mission	Closed	1993	99.00	80-100
1991	Mo At Work	Closed	1991	35.00	35-75
1989	Moe's Diner	Closed	1993	100.00	300-700
1989	The New England Church	Closed	1993	79.00	72-80
1989	New England Lighthouse	Closed	1993	99.00	80-120
1992	News Stand	Closed	1993	30.00	30-72
1989	Octagonal House	Closed	1993	40.00	25-40
1989	The Old Mill	Closed	1993	100.00	80-125
1989	The Opera House	Closed	1992	89.00	72-90
1989	The Out House	Closed	1993	15.00	15-30
1989	Oxbow Saloon	Closed	1993	90.00	65-90
1989	The Pacific Lighthouse	Closed	1992	89.00	80-175
1991	Paul Revere's House	Closed	1992	90.00	72-95
1989	Plantation House	Closed	1993	119.00	90-195

YEAR ISSUE		EDITION LIMIT	YEAR RETD.	ISSUE PRICE	* QUOTE U.S.$
1989	Prairie Forge	Closed	1993	65.00	85-135
1989	Railhead Inn	Closed	1993	250.00	195-250
1989	The River Bell	Closed	1993	99.00	95-120
1989	Seaside Cottage	Closed	1992	225.00	190
1989	Sierra Mine	Closed	1992	120.00	90-120
1989	Sod House	Closed	1992	40.00	25-40
1989	Star Cottage	Closed	1993	30.00	24
1989	Sweetheart Cottage	Closed	1993	45.00	35-45
1992	Telephone Booth	Closed	1993	15.00	25
1989	Tobacconist	Closed	1993	45.00	40
1992	Topper's Drive-In	Closed	1993	120.00	125-145
1989	Town Hall	Closed	1993	129.00	125-150
1989	Tree House	Closed	1993	45.00	40-80
1992	Village Mercantile	Closed	1993	60.00	60-175
1989	Wisteria	Closed	1993	15.00	20

Wideman-First Nation Collection - M. Wideman

YEAR ISSUE		EDITION LIMIT	YEAR RETD.	ISSUE PRICE	*QUOTE U.S.$
1993	Elm Bark Longhouse	Closed	1993	56.00	56
1993	The First Nation Collection, set /8	Closed	1993	500.00	990-1200
1993	Igloo	Closed	1993	60.00	100
1993	Mandan Earth Lodge	Closed	1993	56.00	225-350
1993	Plains Teepee	Closed	1993	68.00	200-300
1993	Stilt House	Closed	1993	60.00	60
1993	Sweat Lodge	Closed	1993	34.00	60-75
1993	West Coast Longhouse	Closed	1993	100.00	100
1993	Wigwam	Closed	1993	65.00	200-275

Woodly Wise - T. Slack

YEAR ISSUE		EDITION LIMIT	YEAR RETD.	ISSUE PRICE	*QUOTE U.S.$
1995	Arbor Stone	Open		55.00	55
1995	Brambly Perch	Open		49.00	49
1995	Chimney Pot Lodge	Open		79.00	79
1995	Crooked Climb	Open		55.00	55
1995	Roundabout	Open		29.00	29
1995	Snow Chapel	2,950		99.00	99
1995	Timberskeep	Open		79.00	79
1995	Water's End	Open		55.00	55
1995	Wendy House	2,950		99.00	99

June McKenna Collectibles, Inc.

Black Folk Art - J. McKenna

YEAR ISSUE		EDITION LIMIT	YEAR RETD.	ISSUE PRICE	*QUOTE U.S.$
1987	Aunt Bertha - 3D	Closed	1991	36.00	75-100
1983	Black Boy With Watermelon, available in 3 colors	Closed	1988	12.00	75-125
1986	Black Butler	Closed	1989	13.00	75
1983	Black Girl With Watermelon, available in 3 colors	Closed	1988	12.00	75-125
1984	Black Man With Pig, available in 3 colors	Closed	1988	13.00	100-150
1984	Black Woman With Broom, available in 3 colors	Closed	1988	13.00	100-125
1989	Delia	Closed	1991	16.00	65
1989	Jake	Closed	1991	16.00	65
1985	Kids in a Tub - 3D	Closed	1991	30.00	110
1985	Kissing Cousins - sill sitter	Closed	1990	36.00	100-150
1990	Let's Play Ball -3D	Closed	1993	45.00	75-100
1987	Lil' Willie -3D	Closed	1991	36.00	75-100
1984	Mammie Cloth Doll	Closed	1988	90.00	450-500
1985	Mammie With Kids - 3D	Closed	1990	90.00	150-200
1985	Mammie With Spoon	Closed	1989	13.00	250
1988	Netty	Closed	1991	16.00	65
1984	Remus Cloth Doll	Closed	1988	90.00	375-500
1988	Renty	Closed	1991	16.00	65
1990	Sunday's Best -3D	Closed	1993	45.00	75-100
1987	Sweet Prissy -3D	Closed	1991	36.00	75-100
1990	Tasha	Closed	1991	17.00	65
1985	Toaster Cover	Closed	1988	50.00	350
1990	Tyree	Closed	1991	17.00	65
1987	Uncle Jacob- 3D	Closed	1991	36.00	75-100
1985	Watermelon Patch Kids	Closed	1990	24.00	100-150

Carolers - J. McKenna

YEAR ISSUE		EDITION LIMIT	YEAR RETD.	ISSUE PRICE	*QUOTE U.S.$
1985	Boy Caroler	Closed	1989	36.00	75-100
1992	Carolers, Grandparents	Closed	1994	70.00	85
1991	Carolers, Man With Girl	Closed	1994	50.00	65
1991	Carolers, Woman With Boy	Closed	1994	50.00	65
1985	Girl Caroler	Closed	1989	36.00	75-100
1985	Man Caroler	Closed	1989	36.00	75-100
1985	Woman Caroler	Closed	1989	36.00	75-100

June McKenna Figurines - J. McKenna

YEAR ISSUE		EDITION LIMIT	YEAR RETD.	ISSUE PRICE	*QUOTE U.S.$
1989	16th Century Santa - 3D, blue	Closed	1989	60.00	200-250
1989	16th Century Santa - 3D, green	Closed	1989	60.00	250-350
1989	17th Century Santa - 3D, red	Closed	1991	70.00	200-250
1993	Angel Name Plaque	Open		70.00	100
1983	Boy Rag Doll	Closed	1983	12.00	300-450
1985	Bride w/o base -3D	Closed	1987	25.00	150-225
1985	Bride -3D	Closed	1987	25.00	200
1993	Children Ice Skaters	Closed	1994	60.00	75
1992	Choir of Angels	Closed	1993	60.00	75
1992	Christmas Santa	Closed	1993	60.00	100-125
1987	Country Rag Boy (sitting)	Closed	1990	40.00	155
1987	Country Rag Girl (sitting)	Closed	1990	40.00	155
1985	Father Times - 3D	Closed	1991	40.00	150-175
1983	Girl Rag Doll	Closed	1983	12.00	300-450
1993	A Good Night's Sleep	Closed	1994	70.00	100-125
1985	Groom w/o base -3D	Closed	1985	25.00	175-235
1985	Groom -3D	Closed	1987	25.00	150-200
1989	Jolly Ole Santa - 3D	Closed	1991	44.00	150-175
1986	Little St. Nick -3D	Closed	1990	50.00	175-200
1986	Male Angel	Closed	1986	44.00	1300-1700
1988	Mr. Santa - 3D	Closed	1991	44.00	100

YEAR ISSUE		EDITION LIMIT	YEAR RETD.	ISSUE PRICE	*QUOTE U.S.$
1993	Mr. Snowman	Closed	1994	40.00	65
1988	Mrs. Santa - 3D	Closed	1989	50.00	200-250
1987	Name Plaque	Closed	1992	50.00	120-150
1990	Noel - 3D	Closed	1992	50.00	125
1987	Patriotic Santa	Closed	1989	60.00	300-350
1993	Santa Name Plaque	Closed	1995	70.00	100
1993	The Snow Family	Closed	1994	40.00	65
1985	Soldier	Closed	1988	60.00	175-200
1992	Taking A Break	Closed	1995	60.00	85-100
1984	Tree Topper	Closed	1987	70.00	350-400

Limited Edition - J. McKenna

1988	Bringing Home Christmas	4,000	1990	170.00	300-400
1987	Christmas Eve	4,000	1989	170.00	375-400
1992	Christmas Gathering	4,000	1996	220.00	300
1991	Coming to Town	4,000	1994	220.00	300
1983	Father Christmas	4,000	1986	90.00	2500-3000
1987	Kris Kringle	4,000	1990	350.00	650-750
1990	Night Before Christmas	1,500	1993	750.00	750-800
1984	Old Saint Nick	4,000	1986	100.00	600-900
1988	Remembrance of Christmas Past	4,000	1992	400.00	400
1991	Santa's Hot Air Balloon	1,500	1993	800.00	800
1989	Santa's Wardrobe	1,500	1992	750.00	850-1000
1989	Seasons Greetings	4,000	1992	200.00	325-350
1986	Victorian	4,000	1988	150.00	450-650
1990	Wilderness	4,000	1994	200.00	275-300
1985	Woodland	4,000	1987	140.00	500-750

Limited Edition 7" - J. McKenna

1991	Christmas Bishop	7,500	1993	110.00	150-200
1993	Christmas Cheer 1st ed.	7,500	1993	120.00	350-400
1993	Christmas Cheer 2nd. ed.	7,500	1995	120.00	150-200
1990	Christmas Delight	7,500	1992	100.00	125-200
1995	Christmas Lullaby, red	7,500	1996	120.00	125-350
1988	Christmas Memories	7,500	1991	90.00	250
1992	Christmas Wizard	7,500	1994	110.00	150-200
1990	Ethnic Santa	7,500	1992	100.00	150-200
1988	Joyful Christmas	7,500	1991	90.00	175-225
1989	Old Fashioned Santa	7,500	1992	100.00	150-200
1989	Santa's Bag of Surprises	7,500	1991	100.00	225-250

Limited Edition Flatback - J. McKenna

1991	Bag of Stars	10,000	1993	34.00	45-65
1993	Bells of Christmas	10,000	1995	40.00	45-65
1989	Blue Christmas	10,000	1991	32.00	100
1992	Deck The Halls	10,000	1994	34.00	45-65
1991	Farewell Santa	10,000	1993	34.00	55-65
1992	Good Tidings	10,000	1994	34.00	45-65
1990	Medieval Santa	10,000	1992	34.00	65
1988	Mystical Santa	10,000	1991	30.00	100
1990	Old Time Santa	10,000	1992	34.00	65
1993	Santa's Love	10,000	1995	40.00	55-65
1988	Toys of Joy	10,000	1991	30.00	70-100
1989	Victorian	10,000	1991	32.00	120

Personal Appearance Figurines - J. McKenna

1989	Father Christmas	Closed	1993	30.00	100-200
1990	Old Saint Nick	Closed	1994	30.00	100-150
1991	Woodland	Closed	1995	35.00	75-125
1992	Victorian	Closed	1996	35.00	50-100
1993	Christmas Eve	4-Yr.		35.00	35
1994	Bringing Home Christmas	4-Yr.		35.00	35
1995	Seasons Greetings	4-Yr.		35.00	35
1996	Wilderness	4-Yr.		35.00	35

Registered Edition - J. McKenna

1991	Checking His List	Closed	1994	230.00	300-350
1986	Colonial	Closed	1990	150.00	300-400
1992	Forty Winks	Closed	1994	250.00	300
1988	Jolly Ole St. Nick	Closed	1990	170.00	300-400
1993	Tomorrow's Christmas	Closed	1995	250.00	275
1990	Toy Maker	Closed	1993	200.00	400
1989	Traditional	Closed	1991	180.00	300-400
1987	White Christmas	Closed	1990	170.00	900-1100

Special Limited Edition - J. McKenna

1995	All Aboard-Toy Car	Closed	1996	250.00	275
1993	Baking Cookies	2,000	1995	450.00	450
1991	Bedtime Stories	2,000	1994	500.00	500
1990	Christmas Dreams	4,000	1992	280.00	400-500
1990	Christmas Dreams (Hassock)	63	1990	280.00	1600-2000
1989	Last Gentle Nudge	4,000	1991	280.00	350-450
1989	Santa & His Magic Sleigh	4,000	1992	280.00	350-450
1992	Santa's Arrival	2,000	1994	300.00	350-450
1990	Santa's Reindeer	1,500	1993	400.00	400-450
1990	Up On The Rooftop	4,000	1992	280.00	400-450
1994	Welcome to the World	2,000	1995	400.00	450

Victorian Limited Edition - J. McKenna

1990	Edward - 3D	1,000	1991	180.00	450
1990	Elizabeth - 3D	1,000	1991	180.00	450
1990	Joseph - 3D	Closed	1991	50.00	50-250
1990	Victoria - 3D	Closed	1991	50.00	50-250

Kurt S. Adler, Inc.

Angel Darlings - N. Bailey

1996	Almost Fits H4765/1	Open		15.00	15
1996	Bottoms Up H4765/6	Open		15.00	15
1996	Buddies H4765/3	Open		15.00	15
1996	Cuddles H4765/5	Open		15.00	15

1996	Dream Builders H4765/4	Open		15.00	15
1996	Peek-A-Boo H4765/2	Open		15.00	15

Christmas Legends - P.F. Bolinger

1994	Aldwyn of the Greenwood J8196	Open		145.00	145
1994	Berwyn the Grand J8198	Open		175.00	175
1995	Bountiful J8234	Open		164.00	164
1994	Caradoc the Kind J8199	Open		70.00	70
1994	Florian of the Berry Bush J8199	Open		70.00	70
1994	Gustave the Gutsy J8199	Open		70.00	70
1995	Luminatus J8241	Open		136.00	136
1994	Silvanus the Cheerful J8197	Open		165.00	165

The Fabriché™ Bear & Friends Series - KSA Design Team

1992	Laughing All The Way W1567	Retrd.	1994	83.00	83
1992	Not A Creature Was Stirring W1534	Retrd.	1996	67.00	67
1993	Teddy Bear Parade W1601	Retrd.	1996	73.00	73

Fabriché™ Angel Series - K.S. Adler

1992	Heavenly Messenger W1584	Retrd.	1994	41.00	41

Fabriché™ Camelot Figure Series - P. Mauk

1994	King Arthur J3372	7,500		110.00	110
1993	Merlin the Magician J7966	7,500	1996	120.00	120
1993	Young Arthur J7967	7,500	1996	120.00	120

Fabriché™ Holiday Figurines - KSA Design Team, unless otherwise noted

1995	All Aboard For Christmas W1679	Retrd.	1996	56.00	56
1994	All Star Santa W1652	Open		56.00	56
1993	All That Jazz W1620	Retrd.	1994	67.00	67
1992	An Apron Full of Love W1582 - M. Rothenberg	Retrd.	1996	75.00	75
1995	Armchair Quarterback W1693	Open		90.00	90
1994	Basket of Goodies W1650	Retrd.	1996	60.00	60
1992	Bringing in the Yule Log W1589 - M. Rothenberg	5,000	1996	200.00	200
1993	Bringing the Gifts W1605	Retrd.	1996	60.00	60
1992	Bundles of Joy W1578	Retrd.	1994	78.00	78
1995	Captain Claus W1680	Open		56.00	56
1994	Checking His List W1643	Retrd.	1996	60.00	60
1993	Checking It Twice W1604	Open		56.00	56
1992	Christmas is in the Air W1590	Retrd.	1995	110.00	125
1995	Diet Starts Tomorrow W1691	Open		60.00	60
1995	Father Christmas W1687	Open		56.00	56
1994	Firefighting Friends W1654	Open		72.00	72
1993	Forever Green W1607	Retrd.	1994	56.00	56
1994	Friendship W1642	Retrd.	1996	65.00	65
1995	Gift From Heaven W1694	Retrd.	1996	60.00	60
1992	He Did It Again J7944 - T. Rubel	Retrd.	1996	160.00	160
1993	Here Kitty W1618 - M. Rothenberg	Retrd.	1994	90.00	125
1994	Ho, Ho, Ho Santa W1632	Retrd.	1996	56.00	56
1993	Holiday Express W1636	Open		100.00	100
1992	Homeward Bound W1568	Open		61.00	65
1993	Hugs and Kisses W1531	Retrd.	1994	67.00	67
1992	I'm Late, I'm Late J7947 - T. Rubel	Retrd.	1995	100.00	100
1992	It's Time To Go J7943 - T. Rubel	Retrd.	1994	150.00	150
1995	Kris Kringle W1685	Open		55.00	55
1994	Mail Must Go Through W1667 - KSA/WRG	Open		110.00	110
1992	Merry Kissmas W1548 - M. Rothenberg	Retrd.	1993	140.00	140
1995	Merry Memories W1735	Open		56.00	56
1994	Merry St. Nick W1641 - Giordano	Open		100.00	100
1995	Mrs. Santa Caroller W1690 - M. Rothenberg	Open		70.00	70
1995	Night Before Christmas W1692 - Wood River Gallery	Open		60.00	60
1994	Officer Claus W1677	Open		56.00	56
1993	Par For The Claus W1603	Open		60.00	60
1994	Peace Santa W1631	Open		60.00	60
1995	Pere Noel W1686	Open		55.00	55
1993	Playtime For Santa W1619	Retrd.	1994	67.00	67
1994	Santa Calls W1678 - W. Joyce	Retrd.	1996	55.00	55
1995	Santa Caroller W1689 - M. Rothenberg	Open		70.00	70
1991	Santa Fiddler W1549 - M. Rothenberg	Retrd.	1992	100.00	100
1992	Santa Steals A Kiss & A Cookie W1581 - M. Rothenberg	Retrd.	1994	150.00	175
1992	Santa's Cat Nap W1504 - M. Rothenberg	Retrd.	1992	98.00	110
1994	Santa's Fishtales W1640	Open		60.00	60
1992	Santa's Ice Capades W1588 - M. Rothenberg	Retrd.	1995	110.00	110
1994	Schussing Claus W1651	Retrd.	1996	78.00	78
1992	St. Nicholas The Bishop W1532	Open		78.00	78
1994	Star Gazing Santa W1656 - M. Rothenberg	Open		120.00	120
1993	Stocking Stuffer W1622	Retrd.	1994	56.00	56
1995	Strike Up The Band W1681	Retrd.	1996	55.00	55
1994	Tee Time W1734	Open		60.00	60
1993	Top Brass W1630	Retrd.	1995	67.00	67
1993	With All The Trimmings W1616	Open		76.00	76
1995	Woodland Santa W1731 - R. Volpi	Retrd.	1996	67.00	67

Fabriché™ Santa at Home Series - M. Rothenberg

1995	Baby Burping Santa W1732	Retrd.	1996	80.00	80
1994	The Christmas Waltz 1635	Open		135.00	135
1995	Family Portrait W1727	Retrd.	1996	140.00	140
1993	Grandpa Santa's Piggyback Ride W1621	7,500		84.00	84
1994	Santa's Horsey Ride W1728	Open		80.00	80
1994	Santa's New Friend W1655	Open		110.00	110

Fabriché™ Santa's Helpers Series - M. Rothenberg

1993	Little Olde Clockmaker W1629	5,000	1996	134.00	134
1992	A Stitch in Time W1591	5,000		135.00	135

Fabriché™ Smithsonian Museum Series - KSA/Smithsonian

1992	Holiday Drive W1556	Retrd.	1995	155.00	155
1993	Holiday Flight W1617	Retrd.	1995	144.00	144
1992	Peace on Earth Angel Treetop W1583	Retrd.	1995	52.00	52
1992	Peace on Earth Flying Angel W1585	Retrd.	1995	49.00	49
1991	Santa On A Bicycle W1527	Retrd.	1994	150.00	150
1995	Toys For Good Boys and Girls W1696	Open		75.00	75

Fabriché™ Thomas Nast Figurines - KSA Design Team

1992	Caught in the Act W1577	Retrd.	1993	133.00	133
1992	Christmas Sing-A-Long W1576	12,000		110.00	110
1993	Dear Santa W1602	Retrd.	1993	110.00	110
1991	Hello! Little One W1552	12,000	1994	90.00	90

Gallery of Angels - KSA Design Team

1994	Guardian Angel M1099	2,000	1996	150.00	150
1994	Unspoken Word M1100	2,000		150.00	150

Halloween - P.F. Bolinger

1996	Dr. Punkinstein HW535	Open		50.00	50
1996	Eat at Drac's HW493	Open		22.00	22
1996	Pumpkin Grumpkin HW494	Open		18.00	18
1996	Pumpkin Plumpkin HW494	Open		18.00	18
1996	Pumpkins Are Us HW534	Open		17.00	17

Helping Hand Santas - P. Bolinger

1996	Harmonious J6509	Open		115.00	115
1996	Noah J6487	Open		56.00	56
1996	Uncle Sam J6488	Open		56.00	56

Ho Ho Ho Gang - P.F. Bolinger

1996	Box of Chocolate J6510	Open		33.00	33
1994	Christmas Goose J8201	Open		22.00	22
1996	Christmas Shopping Santa J6497	Open		22.00	22
1996	Claus-A-Lounger J6478	Open		33.00	33
1995	Cookie Claus J8286	Open		39.00	39
1995	Do Not Disturb J8233	Open		34.00	34
1996	Fire Department North Pole J6508	Open		50.00	50
1994	Fireman Santa J6476	Open		28.00	28
1994	Holy Mackerel J8201	Open		22.00	22
1994	Joy of Cooking J6496	Open		28.00	28
1996	Love Santa J6493	Open		18.00	18
1995	No Hair Day J8287	Open		50.00	50
1996	Noel Roly Poly J6489	Open		20.00	20
1995	North Pole (large) J8237	Open		56.00	56
1995	North Pole (small) J8238	Open		45.00	45
1996	North Pole Pro-Am J6479	Open		28.00	28
1996	On Strike For More Cookies J6506	Open		33.00	33
1996	Police Department North Pole J6507	Open		50.00	50
1996	Policeman Santa J6475	Open		28.00	28
1994	Santa Cob J8203	Retrd.	1995	28.00	28
1996	Save The Reindeer J6498	Open		28.00	28
1996	Some Assembly Required J6477	Open		53.00	53
1996	Surprise J8201	Open		22.00	22
1994	Will He Make It? J8203	Retrd.	1995	28.00	28
1995	Will Work For Cookies J8235	Open		40.00	40
1995	Wishful Thinking J8239	Open		32.00	32

Holly Bearies - H. Adler

1996	Angel Bear J7342	Open		14.00	14
1996	Mother's Day Bear J7318	Open		15.00	15
1996	Teddy Tower J7221	Open		23.00	23

Holly Bearies Calendar Bears - H. Adler

1996	Clairmont, Dempsey & Pete J7215/Jul	Open		16.00	16
1996	Clara & Carnation The Kitty J7215/Oct	Open		16.00	16
1996	Fergus & Fritzi's Frosty Frolic J7215/Jan	Open		16.00	16
1996	Grandma Gladys J7215/Dec	Open		16.00	16
1996	Nicole & Nicholas Sun Bearthing J7215/Aug	Open		16.00	16
1996	Petunia & Nathan Plant Posies J7215/May	Open		16.00	16
1996	Philo's Pot O Gold J7215/Mar	Open		16.00	16
1996	Pinky & Victoria Are Sweeties J7215/Feb	Open		16.00	16
1996	Skeeter & Sigourney Start School J7215/Sep	Open		16.00	16
1996	Sunshine Catching Raindrops J7215/Apr	Open		16.00	16
1996	Thorndike & Filbert Catch Fish J7215/Jun	Open		16.00	16
1996	Thorndike All Dressed Up J7215/Nov	Open		16.00	16

Jim Henson's Muppet Nutcrackers - KSA/JHP

1993	Kermit The Frog H1223	Retrd.	1995	90.00	90

Mickey Unlimited - KSA/Disney

1994	Donald Duck Drummer W1671	Open		45.00	45
1993	Donald Duck H1235	Open		90.00	90
1992	Goofy H1216	Open		78.00	78
1994	Mickey Bandleader W1669	Open		45.00	45

YEAR ISSUE		EDITION LIMIT	YEAR RETD.	ISSUE PRICE	*QUOTE U.S.$
1992	Mickey Mouse Soldier H1194	Open		72.00	72
1992	Mickey Mouse Sorcerer H1221	Open		100.00	100
1993	Mickey Mouse w/Gift Boxes W1608	Open		78.00	78
1994	Mickey Santa Nutcracker H1237	Open		90.00	90
1994	Minnie With Cymbals Nutcrackers H1236	Open		90.00	90
1994	Minnie With Cymbals W1670	Open		45.00	45
1993	Pinnochio H1222	Open		110.00	110

Old World Santa Series - J. Mostrom

1992	Chelsea Garden Santa W2721	Retrd.	1994	33.50	34
1993	Good King Wenceslas W2928	3,000		134.00	134
1992	Large Black Forest Santa W2717	Retrd.	1994	110.00	110
1992	Large Father Christmas W2719	Retrd.	1994	106.00	106
1993	Medieval King of Christmas W2881	3,000	1994	390.00	390
1992	Mrs. Claus W2714	5,000	1996	37.00	37
1992	Patriotic Santa W2720	3,000	1994	128.00	128
1992	Pere Noel W2723	Retrd.	1994	33.50	34
1992	Small Black Forest Santa W2712	Retrd.	1994	40.00	40
1992	Small Father Christmas W2712	Retrd.	1994	33.50	34
1992	Small Father Frost W2716	Retrd.	1994	43.00	43
1992	Small Grandfather Frost W2718	Retrd.	1994	106.00	106
1992	St. Nicholas W2713	Retrd.	1994	30.00	30
1992	Workshop Santa W2715	5,000		43.00	43

Sesame Street Series - KSA/JHP

1993	Big Bird Fabrich, Figurine J7928	Retrd.	1996	60.00	60
1993	Big Bird Nutcracker H1199	Retrd.	1994	60.00	60

Snow People - P.F. Bolinger

1996	Coola Hula J6430	Open		20.00	20
1996	Snowpoke J6431	Open		28.00	28
1996	Snowy J6429	Open		28.00	28

Steinbach Camelot Smoking Figure Series - KSA/Steinbach

1993	King Arthur ES832	7,500	1996	175.00	175
1992	Merlin The Magician ES830	7,500		150.00	150

Steinbach Nutcracker Collectors' Club - KSA/Steinbach

1995	King Wenceslaus	12/96		225.00	225
1995	The Town Crier	12/96		Gift	N/A

Steinbach Nutcracker American Presidents Series - KSA/Steinbach

1992	Abraham Lincoln ES622	12,000	1995	195.00	200-400
1993	Ben Franklin ES635	12,000	1996	225.00	225
1992	George Washington ES623	12,000	1994	195.00	500
1993	Teddy Roosevelt ES644	10,000		225.00	225
1996	Thomas Jefferson ES866	7,500		260.00	260

Steinbach Nutcracker Biblical - KSA/Steinbach

1996	Noah ES893	10,000		260.00	260

Steinbach Nutcracker Camelot Series - KSA/Steinbach

1992	King Arthur ES621	Retrd.	1993	195.00	500-1500
1991	Merlin The Magician ES610	Retrd.	1991	185.00	2500-4200
1995	Queen Guenevere ES869	10,000		245.00	245
1994	Sir Galahad ES862	12,000		225.00	225
1993	Sir Lancelot ES638	12,000		225.00	225
1994	Sir Lancelot Smoker ES833	7,500		150.00	150

Steinbach Nutcracker Christmas Legends Series - KSA/Steinbach

1995	1930s Santa Claus ES891	7,500		245.00	245
1993	Father Christmas ES645	7,500		225.00	225
1994	St. Nicholas, The Bishop ES865	7,500	1995	225.00	225

Steinbach Nutcracker Collection - KSA/Steinbach

1991	Columbus ES697	Retrd.	1992	194.00	225
1992	Happy Santa ES601	Open		190.00	220
1984	Oil Sheik	Retrd.	1985	100.00	500

Steinbach Nutcracker Famous Chieftans Series - KSA/Steinbach

1995	Black Hawk ES889	7,500		245.00	245
1993	Chief Sitting Bull ES637	8,500	1995	225.00	300-600
1994	Chief Sitting Bull Smoker ES834	7,500		150.00	150
1994	Red Cloud ES864	8,500		225.00	225

Steinbach Nutcracker Mini Series - KSA/Steinbach

1996	Merlin ES335	15,000		50.00	50
1996	Robin Hood ES338	10,000	1996	50.00	50

Steinbach Nutcracker Tales of Sherwood Forest - KSA/Steinbach

1995	Friar Tuck ES890	7,500		245.00	245
1992	Robin Hood ES863	7,500	1996	225.00	225
1996	Sherif of Nottingham ES892	7,500		260.00	260

Steinbach Nutcracker Three Muskateers - KSA/Steinbach

1996	Aramis ES722	7,500		130.00	130

Visions Of Santa Series - KSA Design Team

1992	Santa Coming Out Of Fireplace J1023	Retrd.	1993	29.00	29
1992	Santa Holding Child J826		1993	24.50	25
1992	Santa Spilling Bag Of Toys J1022	7,500	1994	25.50	26
1992	Santa w/Little Girls On Lap J1024	7,500	1996	24.50	25

1992	Santa w/Sack Holding Toy J827	7,500	1994	24.50	25
1992	Workshop Santa J825	7,500	1994	27.00	27

Zuber Nutcracker Series - KSA/Zuber

1992	The Annapolis Midshipman EK7	5,000	1994	125.00	125
1992	The Bavarian EK16	5,000	1994	130.00	130
1992	Bronco Billy The Cowboy EK1	5,000	1994	125.00	125
1992	The Chimney Sweep EK6	5,000	1993	125.00	125
1992	The Country Singer EK19	5,000	1994	125.00	125
1992	The Fisherman EK17	5,000	1996	125.00	125
1994	The Gardner EK26	2,500	1996	150.00	150
1992	Gepetto, The Toymaker EK9	5,000	1994	125.00	125
1992	The Gold Prospector EK18	5,000	1994	125.00	125
1992	The Golfer EK5	5,000	1994	125.00	125
1993	Herr Drosselmeir Nutcracker EK21	5,000	1996	150.00	300-450
1993	The Ice Cream Vendor EK24	5,000	1996	150.00	150
1992	The Indian EK15	5,000		135.00	135
1994	Jazz Player EK25	2,500		145.00	145
1994	Kurt the Traveling Salesman EK28	2,500	1994	155.00	155
1994	Mouse King EK31	2,500		150.00	150
1993	Napoleon Bonaparte EK23	5,000		150.00	150
1992	The Nor' Easter Sea Captain EK3	5,000		125.00	125
1992	Paul Bunyan The Lumberjack EK2	5,000	1993	125.00	125
1994	Peter Pan EK28	2,500		145.00	145
1992	The Pilgrim EK14	5,000		125.00	125
1993	The Pizzamaker EK22	5,000		150.00	150
1994	Scuba Diver EK27	2,500		150.00	150
1994	Soccer Player EK30	2,500		145.00	145
1992	TheTyrolean EK4	5,000	1994	125.00	125
1992	The West Point Cadet With Canon EK8	5,000	1994	130.00	130

Ladie and Friends

Lizzie High® Figurines - B.& P. Wisber

1996	Amanda High-111	2-Yr.		28.00	28
1996	Cassie Yocum-179	2-Yr.		29.50	29
1996	Edward Bowman-158	2-Yr.		28.00	28
1996	Grace Valentine-146	2-Yr.		25.00	25
1996	Katie Bowman-178	2-Yr.		28.00	28
1996	Lizzie High Sign-090	2-Yr.		37.00	37
1996	Lizzie High-100	2-Yr.		26.50	27
1996	Marisa Valentine-333	2-Yr.		25.00	25
1996	Megan Valentine-227	2-Yr.		35.00	35
1996	Minnie Valentine-336	2-Yr.		29.50	30
1996	Nancy Bowman-261	2-Yr.		24.00	24
1996	Natalie Valentine-284	2-Yr.		28.00	28
1996	Rebeca Bowman-104	2-Yr.		37.00	37

Lalique Society of America

Lalique Society Annual Series - Various

1989	Degas Box 10585 - R. Lalique	Yr.Iss.		295.00	725
1990	Hestia Medallion 61051 - M.C. Lalique	Yr.Iss.		295.00	700
1991	Lily of Valley (perfume bottle) 61053 - R. Lalique	Yr.Iss.		275.00	450
1992	La Patineuse (paperweight) 61054 - M.C. Lalique	Yr.Iss.		325.00	375
1993	Enchantment (figurine) 61055 - M.C. Lalique	Yr.Iss.		395.00	395
1994	Eclipse (perfume bottle) - M.C. Lalique	Yr.Iss.		395.00	395

Lance Corporation

Chilmark MetalART™ The Great Chiefs - J. Slockbower

1992	Chief Joseph	750	1992	975.00	15-1900
1993	Crazy Horse	750		975.00	975
1992	Geronimo	750	1992	975.00	1300-1850
1993	Sitting Bull	750		1075.00	1075

Chilmark MetalART™ Mickey & Co. On the Road - Staff

1994	Beach Bound	350	1994	350.00	800-1300
1992	Cruising	350	1992	275.00	2000-3500
1993	Sunday Drive	350	1993	325.00	1200-1800
1993	Matched Numbrd. set/3	350	1993	950.00	8000-9000
1993	Mixed & Matched Numbrd. set/3	350	1993	950.00	5000-8000

Chilmark MetalART™ The Seekers - A. McGrory

1993	Bear Vision	500		1375.00	1375
1992	Buffalo Vision	500	1993	1075.00	1075
1993	Eagle Vision	500		1250.00	1250

Chilmark MetalART™ To The Great Spirit - T. Sullivan

1993	Gray Elk	950		775.00	775
1992	Shooting Star	950	1994	775.00	775
1994	Thunder Cloud	950		775.00	775
1993	Two Eagles	950		775.00	775

Chilmark Pewter Adversaries - F. Barnum

1991	Robert E. Lee	950	1992	350.00	1250-1400
1992	Stonewall Jackson	950	1992	375.00	500
1992	Ulysses S. Grant	950	1992	350.00	600-1000
1993	Wm. Tecumseh Sherman	950	1993	375.00	375-675
1993	Set of 4		1993	1450.00	3200-4000

Chilmark Pewter American West - D. Polland, unless otherwise noted

1981	Ambushed	294	1991	2370.00	2700

1987	Appeal to the Great Spirit - F. Barnum	Retrd.	1995	275.00	275
1985	Bear Meet - S. York	Retrd.	1992	500.00	600-800
1983	Bison's Fury - M. Boyett	Retrd.	1995	495.00	495
1982	Blood Brothers - M. Boyett	717	1993	250.00	610-995
1979	Border Rustlers	500	1989	1295.00	1500
1983	Bounty Hunter	264	1987	250.00	300-600
1976	Buffalo Hunt	2,250	1980	300.00	1625
1982	Buffalo Prayer	2,500	1989	95.00	225-400
1990	Buffalo Spirit	2,500	1993	110.00	185
1979	Cavalry Officer - D. LaRocca	500	1985	125.00	400-650
1974	Cheyenne	2,800	1980	200.00	3000
1976	Cold Saddles, Mean Horses	2,800	1986	200.00	800
1974	Counting Coup	2,800	1980	225.00	1600-2000
1979	Cowboy - D. LaRocca	950	1984	125.00	500-750
1974	Crow Scout	3,000	1983	250.00	1000-1700
1978	Dangerous Encounter - B. Rodden	746	1977	475.00	600-950
1985	The Doctor - M. Boyett	Retrd.	1994	750.00	750
1990	Eagle Dancer (deNatura)	614	1993	300.00	300
1981	Enemy Tracks	2,500	1988	225.00	720
1984	Flat Out for Red River Station - M. Boyett	2,500	1991	3000.00	4500-7200
1979	Getting Acquainted	950	1988	215.00	800-1100
1985	Horse of A Different Color - S. York	Retrd.	1992	500.00	600-800
1979	Indian Warrior - D. LaRocca	1,186	1988	95.00	400
1982	Jemez Eagle Dancer	2,500	1989	95.00	250-450
1991	Kiowa Princess (deNatura)	444	1993	300.00	300
1982	Last Arrow	2,500	1989	95.00	300-400
1983	Line Rider	2,500	1988	195.00	975
1979	Mandan Hunter	5,000	1985	65.00	780-900
1988	Marauders	Retrd.	1989	850.00	850
1975	Maverick Calf	2,500	1981	250.00	1300-1700
1976	Monday Morning Wash	2,500	1986	200.00	1000
1979	Mountain Man - D. LaRocca	764	1988	95.00	500-650
1983	The Mustanger - D. Polland	Retrd.	1995	425.00	425
1983	Now or Never	693	1991	265.00	800
1975	The Outlaws	2,500	1989	450.00	900-1180
1976	Painting the Town	2,250	1983	300.00	1500-1700
1990	Pequot Wars	950	1990	395.00	800
1981	Plight of the Huntsman - M. Boyett	950	1987	495.00	850
1985	Postal Exchange - S. York	Retrd.	1992	300.00	400-600
1990	Red River Wars	950	1990	425.00	700-850
1976	Rescue	2,500	1980	275.00	1150
1979	Running Battle - B. Rodden	761	1987	400.00	750-900
1990	Running Wolf (deNatura)	720	1993	350.00	350
1982	Sioux War Chief	2,500	1989	95.00	240-480
1991	The Storyteller - D. Polland	Retrd.	1995	150.00	150
1990	Tecumseh's Rebellion	950	1990	350.00	700
1983	Too Many Aces	1,717	1993	400.00	600-850
1981	U.S. Marshal	1,500	1986	95.00	450
1981	War Party	1,066	1991	550.00	975-1150
1981	When War Chiefs Meet	2,500	1988	300.00	800
1983	The Wild Bunch	285	1987	200.00	225-400
1982	Yakima Salmon Fisherman	2,500	1987	200.00	700
1991	Yellow Boy (deNatura)	460	1993	350.00	350

Chilmark Pewter American West Christmas Special - D. Polland

1991	Merry Christmas Neighbor	1,240	1991	395.00	600
1992	Merry Christmas My Love	819	1992	350.00	350-450
1993	Almost Home	520	1994	375.00	375
1994	Cowboy Christmas	427	1994	250.00	250

Chilmark Pewter American West Event Specials - D. Polland, unless otherwise noted

1991	Uneasy Truce	737	1991	125.00	175-195
1992	Irons In The Fire	612	1992	125.00	125
1994	Bacon 'N' Beans Again?	458	1994	150.00	150
1994	Buffalo Skull - J. Slockbower	Yr. Iss.	1994	125.00	125
1995	Renegade Apache	Closed	1995	150.00	150

Chilmark Pewter American West Redemption Specials - D. Polland, unless otherwise noted

1983	The Chief	2,459	1984	275.00	1400-1900
1984	Unit Colors	1,394	1985	250.00	1200-1700
1985	Oh Great Spirit	3,180	1986	300.00	1000-1300
1986	Eagle Catcher - M. Boyett	1,840	1987	300.00	850-1200
1987	Surprise Encounter - F. Barnum	1,534	1988	250.00	600-800
1988	I Will Fight No More Forever (Chief Joseph)	3,404	1989	300.00	850
1989	Geronimo	1,866	1990	375.00	650-750
1990	Cochise	1,778	1991	400.00	500-600
1991	Crazy Horse	2,067	1992	295.00	600-700
1992	Strong Hearts to the Front	1,252	1993	425.00	600
1993	Sacred Ground Reclaimed	861	1994	495.00	550-650
1994	Horse Breaking	504	1995	395.00	395
1995	The Rainmaker - M. Boyett	Yr.Iss.		350.00	350

Chilmark Pewter Americana - L. Davis

1993	Skedaddlin'	350	1995	2000.00	2000

Chilmark Pewter Cavalry Generals - F. Barnum

1993	George Armstrong Custer	950		375.00	375
1992	J.E.B. Stuart	950	1992	375.00	500
1993	Nathan Bedford Forrest	950		375.00	400-650
1994	Philip Sheridan	950		375.00	375

Chilmark Pewter Civil War - F. Barnum

1993	Abraham Lincoln Bust (Bronze)	50	1993	2000.00	2250

FIGURINES/COTTAGES

YEAR ISSUE	EDITION LIMIT	YEAR RETD.	ISSUE PRICE	*QUOTE U.S.$
1988 A Father's Farewell	2,500	1994	150.00	275
1988 Johnny Shiloh	2,500	1994	100.00	220-285
1992 Kennesaw Mountain	350	1992	650.00	1500
1992 Parson's Battery	500	1993	495.00	575-700
1987 Pickett's Charge	Retrd.	1994	350.00	450
1987 The Rescue	Retrd.	1995	275.00	350-400
1987 Saving The Colors	Retrd.	1992	350.00	485-650

Chilmark Pewter Civil War Christmas Specials - F. Barnum

YEAR ISSUE	EDITION LIMIT	YEAR RETD.	ISSUE PRICE	*QUOTE U.S.$
1992 Merry Christmas Yank	810	1992	350.00	500-600
1993 Silent Night	591	1993	350.00	475-600
1994 Christmas Truce	Retrd.	1994	295.00	325-600
1995 Peace on Earth	Retrd.	1995	350.00	350

Chilmark Pewter Civil War Event Specials - F. Barnum

YEAR ISSUE	EDITION LIMIT	YEAR RETD.	ISSUE PRICE	*QUOTE U.S.$
1991 Boots and Saddles	437	1991	95.00	200-450
1992 140th NY Zouave	389	1992	95.00	150-300
1993 Johnny Reb	889	1993	95.00	150-190
1994 Billy Yank	Retrd.	1994	95.00	125
1995 Seaman, CSS Alabama	Retrd.	1995	95.00	95
1996 The Forager	Yr.Iss.		110.00	110

Chilmark Pewter Civil War Redemption Specials - F. Barnum

YEAR ISSUE	EDITION LIMIT	YEAR RETD.	ISSUE PRICE	*QUOTE U.S.$
1989 Lee To The Rear	1,088	1990	300.00	700-800
1990 Lee And Jackson	1,040	1991	375.00	550-1000
1991 Stonewall Jackson	1,169	1992	295.00	450
1992 Zouaves 1st Manassas	640	1993	375.00	500-600
1993 Letter to Sarah	Retrd.	1994	395.00	425-625
1994 Angel of Fredericksburg	Retrd.	1995	275.00	275
1995 Rebel Yell	Yr.Iss.		475.00	475

Chilmark Pewter Confederates - F. Barnum

YEAR ISSUE	EDITION LIMIT	YEAR RETD.	ISSUE PRICE	*QUOTE U.S.$
1995 The Cavalier (Bronze)	75		1500.00	1500
1995 The Cavalier (Pewter)	750		625.00	625
1993 The Gentleman Soldier (Bronze)	75		1500.00	1500
1993 The Gentleman Soldier (Pewter)	750	1995	625.00	625
1994 Old Jack (Bronze)	75		1500.00	1500
1994 Old Jack (Pewter)	750		625.00	625

Chilmark Pewter Eagles - Various

YEAR ISSUE	EDITION LIMIT	YEAR RETD.	ISSUE PRICE	*QUOTE U.S.$
1991 Cry of Freedom - S. Knight	Suspd.	1993	395.00	395
1981 Freedom Eagle - G. deLodzia	2,500	1983	195.00	750-900
1989 High and Mighty - A. McGrory	Suspd.	1993	185.00	200
1987 Winged Victory - J. Mullican	Suspd.	1993	275.00	315
1982 Wings of Liberty - M. Boyett	950	1986	625.00	1200

Chilmark Pewter Horses - Various

YEAR ISSUE	EDITION LIMIT	YEAR RETD.	ISSUE PRICE	*QUOTE U.S.$
1980 Affirmed - M. Jovine	145	1987	850.00	1275
1980 Born Free - B. Rodden	950	1988	250.00	675
1977 The Challenge - B. Rodden	1,600	1977	175.00	250-300
1981 Clydesdale Wheel Horse - C. Keim	2,808	1989	120.00	430
1978 Paddock Walk - A. Petitto	1,277	1991	85.00	215
1977 Rise and Shine - B. Rodden	1,500	1977	135.00	200
1976 Running Free - B. Rodden	2,500	1977	75.00	300
1976 Stallion - B. Rodden	2,500	1977	75.00	260
1982 Tender Persuasion - J. Mootry	155	1987	950.00	1250
1985 Wild Stallion - D. Polland	179	1988	145.00	350

Chilmark Pewter Kindred Spirits Collection - A. McGrory

YEAR ISSUE	EDITION LIMIT	YEAR RETD.	ISSUE PRICE	*QUOTE U.S.$
1994 Brother Wolf	500	1995	500.00	500
1995 Buffalo Hide	500		750.00	750
1996 Secret Hunter	500		500.00	500

Chilmark Pewter Legacy of Courage - M. Boyett

YEAR ISSUE	EDITION LIMIT	YEAR RETD.	ISSUE PRICE	*QUOTE U.S.$
1983 Along the Cherokee Trace	624	1991	295.00	720
1981 Apache Signals	765	1987	175.00	550-575
1982 Arapaho Sentinel	678	1991	195.00	500
1981 Blackfoot Snow Hunter	984	1988	175.00	650
1981 Buffalo Stalker	1,034	1991	175.00	560
1983 Circling the Enemy	Retrd.	1992	295.00	395
1981 Comanche	1,553	1991	175.00	530-670
1982 Dance of the Eagles	Retrd.	1992	150.00	215
1983 Forest Watcher	658	1991	215.00	540
1981 Iroquois Warfare	1,477	1991	125.00	600
1982 Kiowa Scout	292	1991	195.00	525
1982 Listening For Hooves	883	1991	150.00	400
1982 Mandan Buffalo Dancer	1,494	1991	195.00	450-600
1983 Moment of Truth	1,145	1991	295.00	550-620
1982 Plains Talk-Pawnee	421	1987	195.00	625
1983 Rite of the Whitetail	Retrd.	1992	295.00	400
1982 Shoshone Eagle Catcher	2,500	1985	225.00	1600-2000
1982 The Tracker Nez Perce	686	1988	150.00	575
1981 Unconquered Seminole	1,021	1991	175.00	540
1981 Victor Cheyenne	1,299	1991	175.00	500
1983 A Warrior's Tribute	Retrd.	1992	335.00	635
1983 Winter Hunt	756	1991	295.00	400

Chilmark Pewter Masters of the American West - Various

YEAR ISSUE	EDITION LIMIT	YEAR RETD.	ISSUE PRICE	*QUOTE U.S.$
1985 Bronco Buster (Large) - C. Rousell	766	1989	400.00	400
1986 Buffalo Hunt - A. McGrory	172	1991	550.00	800
1984 Cheyenne (Remington) - C. Rousell	285	1988	400.00	600
1987 Coming Through the Rye - A. McGrory	Retrd.	1995	750.00	750
1986 End of the Trail (lg.) - A. McGrory	Retrd.	1995	450.00	450
1988 End of the Trail (Mini) - A. McGrory	2,500	1992	225.00	325

Chilmark Pewter Mickey & Co. - Staff

YEAR ISSUE	EDITION LIMIT	YEAR RETD.	ISSUE PRICE	*QUOTE U.S.$
1989 "Gold Edition" Hollywood Mickey	Retrd.	1994	200.00	400-750
1995 California or Bust! (Pewter)	250	1995	1250.00	1750
1989 Hollywood Mickey	Suspd.	1991	165.00	200-300
1994 Lights, Camera, Action (Bronze)	50		3250.00	3250
1994 Lights, Camera, Action (Pewter)	500		1500.00	1500
1994 Mickey on Parade (Bronze)	50	1994	950.00	1450-1600
1994 Mickey on Parade (MetalART))	350	1994	500.00	600-900
1994 Mickey on Parade (Pewter)	750	1996	375.00	400
1991 Mickey's Carousel Ride	2,500		150.00	160
1992 Minnie's Carousel Ride	2,500		150.00	160
1994 Mouse in a Million (Bronze)	50	1994	1250.00	1500-2000
1994 Mouse in a Million (MetalART)	250	1994	650.00	800-1000
1994 Mouse in a Million (Pewter)	500	1994	500.00	600-900
1994 Puttin' on the Ritz (Bronze)	50	1994	2000.00	2200
1994 Puttin' on the Ritz (MetalART))	250		1000.00	1000
1994 Puttin' on the Ritz (Pewter)	350		750.00	750

Chilmark Pewter Mickey & Co. Annual Christmas Special - Staff

YEAR ISSUE	EDITION LIMIT	YEAR RETD.	ISSUE PRICE	*QUOTE U.S.$
1993 Hanging the Stockings	Annual	1993	295.00	350
1994 Trimming the Tree	Annual	1994	350.00	400-450
1995 Holiday Harmony?	Annual	1995	395.00	395

Chilmark Pewter Mickey & Co. Annual Santa - Staff

YEAR ISSUE	EDITION LIMIT	YEAR RETD.	ISSUE PRICE	*QUOTE U.S.$
1993 Checking it Twice	Annual	1993	195.00	300-400
1994 Just For You	Annual	1994	265.00	300-400
1995 Surprise, Santa!	Annual	1995	225.00	245

Chilmark Pewter Mickey & Co. Annual Special - Staff

YEAR ISSUE	EDITION LIMIT	YEAR RETD.	ISSUE PRICE	*QUOTE U.S.$
1994 Bicycle Built For Two	Retrd.	1995	195.00	225-400
1995 Riding the Rails	Retrd.	1996	295.00	295

Chilmark Pewter Mickey & Co. Comic Capers - Staff

YEAR ISSUE	EDITION LIMIT	YEAR RETD.	ISSUE PRICE	*QUOTE U.S.$
1995 Crack the Whip (Bronze)	50		2000.00	2000
1995 Crack the Whip (Pewter)	500		750.00	750
1994 Foursome Follies (Bronze)	50	1994	2000.00	2000
1994 Foursome Follies (Pewter)	500	1994	750.00	700-1000
1994 Matched Numbrd set	500	1994	N/A	3100-3500
1994 Un-Matched Numbrd set	500	1994	N/A	2700-2900

Chilmark Pewter Mickey & Co. Generations of Mickey - Staff

YEAR ISSUE	EDITION LIMIT	YEAR RETD.	ISSUE PRICE	*QUOTE U.S.$
1987 Antique Mickey	2,500	1990	95.00	700-1200
1990 The Band Concert	2,500		185.00	195
1990 The Band Concert (Painted)	500	1993	215.00	400-600
1990 Disneyland Mickey	2,500		150.00	160
1989 Mickey's Gala Premiere	2,500		150.00	160
1991 The Mouse-1935	1,200		185.00	195
1991 Plane Crazy-1928	2,500		175.00	185
1989 Sorcerer's Apprentice	2,500	1993	150.00	300-600
1989 Steamboat Willie	2,500	1993	165.00	300-600

Chilmark Pewter Mickey & Co. Mickey and Friends - Staff

YEAR ISSUE	EDITION LIMIT	YEAR RETD.	ISSUE PRICE	*QUOTE U.S.$
1994 Donald (Bronze)	75	1994	325.00	400
1994 Donald (Pewter)	1,500		150.00	150
1994 Goofy (Bronze)	75	1994	375.00	450
1994 Goofy (Pewter)	1,500		175.00	175
1994 Mickey (Bronze)	75	1994	325.00	400
1994 Mickey (Pewter)	1,500		150.00	150
1994 Minnie (Bronze)	75	1994	325.00	400
1994 Minnie (Pewter)	1,500		150.00	150
1994 Pluto (Bronze)	75	1994	325.00	400
1994 Pluto (Pewter)	1,500		150.00	150

Chilmark Pewter Mickey & Co. Sweethearts - Staff

YEAR ISSUE	EDITION LIMIT	YEAR RETD.	ISSUE PRICE	*QUOTE U.S.$
1994 Jitterbugging	500	1994	450.00	600-900
1995 Mice on Ice	500	1995	425.00	500-700
1994 Rowboat Serenade	500	1994	495.00	500-700

Chilmark Pewter Mickey & Co. The Sorcerer's Apprentice - Staff

YEAR ISSUE	EDITION LIMIT	YEAR RETD.	ISSUE PRICE	*QUOTE U.S.$
1990 The Whirlpool	Retrd.	1995	225.00	275
1990 The Dream	Retrd.	1995	225.00	240
1990 The Incantation	Retrd.	1995	150.00	175
1990 The Repentant Apprentice	Retrd.	1995	195.00	300-500
1990 The Sorcerer's Apprentice	Retrd.	1995	225.00	240
1990 Matched Numbrd set	Retrd.	1995	225.00	1800-2200

Chilmark Pewter Mickey & Co. Two Wheeling - Staff

YEAR ISSUE	EDITION LIMIT	YEAR RETD.	ISSUE PRICE	*QUOTE U.S.$
1994 Get Your Motor Runnin' (Bronze)	50	1994	1200.00	1300-1600
1994 Get Your Motor Runnin' (MetalART)	950	1994	475.00	600-1000
1994 Head Out on the Highway (Bronze)	50	1996	1200.00	1200-1300
1994 Head Out on the Highway (MetalART)	950		475.00	475
1995 Looking For Adventure (Bronze)	50		1200.00	1200
1995 Looking For Adventure (MetalART)	950		475.00	475

Chilmark Pewter OffCanvas™ - A. T. McGrory

YEAR ISSUE	EDITION LIMIT	YEAR RETD.	ISSUE PRICE	*QUOTE U.S.$
1991 Blanket Signal	350	1993	750.00	850
1990 Smoke Signal	950	1990	345.00	550-700
1990 Vigil	950	1990	345.00	500-700
1990 Warrior	950	1990	300.00	350-600

Chilmark Pewter Sculptures - Various

YEAR ISSUE	EDITION LIMIT	YEAR RETD.	ISSUE PRICE	*QUOTE U.S.$
1981 Budweiser Wagon - Keim/Hazen	890	1989	2000.00	3000
1986 Camelot Chess Set - P. Jackson	Retrd.	1991	2250.00	2250
1979 Carousel - R. Sylvan	950	1983	115.00	115
1980 Charge of the 7th Cavalry - B. Rodden	394	1988	600.00	950
1983 Dragon Slayer - D. LaRocca	290	1988	385.00	500
1985 Moby Dick - J. Royce	Retrd.	1995	350.00	350
1979 Moses - B. Rodden	2,500	1989	140.00	235
1979 Pegasus - R. Sylvan	527	1981	95.00	175
1979 Unicorn - R. Sylvan	2,500	1982	115.00	550

Chilmark Pewter Turning Points - F. Barnum

YEAR ISSUE	EDITION LIMIT	YEAR RETD.	ISSUE PRICE	*QUOTE U.S.$
1994 Clashing Sabers	500	1995	600.00	600
1993 The High Tide	500	1993	600.00	900
1996 Last Resort	500		600.00	600
1995 The Swinging Gate	500		600.00	600

Chilmark Pewter Wildlife - Various

YEAR ISSUE	EDITION LIMIT	YEAR RETD.	ISSUE PRICE	*QUOTE U.S.$
1978 Buffalo - B. Rodden	950	1986	170.00	375-400
1980 Duel of the Bighorns - M. Boyett	137	1987	650.00	1200
1979 Elephant - D. Polland	750	1987	315.00	450-550
1979 Giraffe - D. Polland	414	1981	145.00	145
1979 Kudu - D. Polland	204	1981	160.00	160
1980 Lead Can't Catch Him - M. Boyett	397	1987	645.00	845
1980 Prairie Sovereign - M. Boyett	247	1981	550.00	800
1979 Rhino - D. Polland	142	1981	135.00	135-550
1980 Ruby-Throated Hummingbird - V. Hayton	500	1983	275.00	350
1980 Voice of Experience - M. Boyett	174	1987	645.00	850

Chilmark Pewter/MetalART™ The Medicine Men - D. Polland

YEAR ISSUE	EDITION LIMIT	YEAR RETD.	ISSUE PRICE	*QUOTE U.S.$
1992 False Face (MetalART)	1,000		550.00	550
1992 False Face (pewter)	500	1992	375.00	375

Chilmark Pewter/MetalART™ The Warriors - D. Polland

YEAR ISSUE	EDITION LIMIT	YEAR RETD.	ISSUE PRICE	*QUOTE U.S.$
1995 Keeper of the Eastern Door (pewter)	500		375.00	375
1995 Keeper of the Eastern Door (MetalART)	1,000		500.00	500
1993 Son of the Morning Star (MetalART)	1,000		495.00	495
1993 Son of the Morning Star (pewter)	500	1993	375.00	460
1995 Soul of the Forest (pewter)	500		375.00	375
1995 Soul of the Forest (MetalART)	1,000		500.00	500
1992 Spirit of the Wolf (MetalART)	1,000	1996	500.00	500
1992 Spirit of the Wolf (pewter)	500	1993	350.00	850

Chilmark Polland Collectors Society Annual Redemption Special - Various

YEAR ISSUE	EDITION LIMIT	YEAR RETD.	ISSUE PRICE	*QUOTE U.S.$
1995 Thunder Pipe	Closed	1996	395.00	395
1996 Two For the Price of One	Yr.Iss.		260.00	260

Chilmark Polland Collectors Society Membership Sculptures - D. Polland

YEAR ISSUE	EDITION LIMIT	YEAR RETD.	ISSUE PRICE	*QUOTE U.S.$
1995 Mystic Medicine Man	Closed	1996	Gift	N/A
1996 Training Session	Yr.Iss.		Gift	N/A

See also Polland Studios Collector Society

Hudson Pewter Figures - P.W. Baston, unless otherwise noted

YEAR ISSUE	EDITION LIMIT	YEAR RETD.	ISSUE PRICE	*QUOTE U.S.$
1972 Benjamin Franklin	Closed	1974	15.00	75-100
1969 Betsy Ross	Closed	1971	30.00	100-125
1969 Colonial Blacksmith	Closed	1971	30.00	100-125
1975 Declaration Wall Plaque	100	1975	Unkn.	300-500
1975 The Favored Scholar - P.W. Baston	6	1975	Unkn.	600-1000
1972 George Washington	Closed	1974	15.00	75-100
1969 George Washington (Cannon)	Closed	1971	35.00	75-100
1972 James Madison	Closed	1974	15.00	50-75
1969 John Adams	Closed	1971	15.00	75-100
1969 John Hancock	Closed	1971	15.00	100-125
1975 Lee's Ninth General Order	Closed	1975	Unkn.	300-400
1975 Lincoln's Gettysburg Address	Closed	1975	Unkn.	300-400
1975 Neighboring Pews	6	1975	Unkn.	600-1000
1975 Spirit of '76 - P.W. Baston	12	1975	Unkn.	750-1500
1972 Thomas Jefferson - P.W. Baston	Closed	1974	15.00	75-100
1975 Washington's Letter of Acceptance - P.W. Baston	Closed	1975	Unkn.	300-400
1975 Weighing the Baby - P.W. Baston	6	1975	Unkn.	600-1000

Hudson Pewter Mickey & Co. - Staff

YEAR ISSUE	EDITION LIMIT	YEAR RETD.	ISSUE PRICE	*QUOTE U.S.$
1989 Fantasia	Retrd.	1995	19.00	19
1988 Happy Birthday Mickey	Yr.Iss.	1989	60.00	150
1988 Soncerer's Apprentice	Retrd.	1995	25.00	25
1986 Soncerer's Apprentice (lg.)	Retrd.	1995	25.00	25
1988 Soncerer's Apprentice/Music Train	Retrd.	1995	28.00	28
1990 Soncerer's Apprentice/No. 9 Birthday Train	Retrd.	1995	25.00	25
1990 Soncerer's Apprentice/No. 9 Birthday Train-painted	Retrd.	1995	27.00	27

Hudson Pewter Mickey & Co. -Registered - Staff

YEAR ISSUE	EDITION LIMIT	YEAR RETD.	ISSUE PRICE	*QUOTE U.S.$
1994 Be My Valentine	Closed	1994	65.00	75-125
1994 Christmas Waltz	Closed	1994	65.00	100-200

Hudson Pewter World of Mickey - Staff

YEAR ISSUE	EDITION LIMIT	YEAR RETD.	ISSUE PRICE	*QUOTE U.S.$
1991 Mouse Waltz	Retrd.	1994	41.00	41
1988 Sweethearts	Retrd.	1993	45.00	45

Pere Noel Collection - C. Smith

YEAR ISSUE	EDITION LIMIT	YEAR RETD.	ISSUE PRICE	*QUOTE U.S.$
1994 Checking His List	3,500		70.00	75
1994 Christ Kindle	3,500		85.00	95
1994 Father Christmas	Closed	1994	150.00	150
1994 Grandfather Frost	3,500		65.00	75
1995 Kriss Kringle	3,500		75.00	75
1994 Pere Noel	3,500		65.00	75
1994 Santa Claus	3,500		75.00	75
1995 Santa McClaus	750		110.00	110
1994 Sinter Klaas	3,500		70.00	75

YEAR ISSUE		EDITION LIMIT	YEAR RETRD.	ISSUE PRICE	*QUOTE U.S.$
1995	St. Nikkolo	3,500		65.00	65
1995	Stars & Stripes Santa	3,500		85.00	85

Sebastian Miniatures Collectors Society - P.W. Baston, unless otherwise noted

1980	S.M.C. Society Plaque ('80 Charter)	11,914	1980	Gift	20-35
1981	S.M.C. Society Plaque	4,957	1981	Gift	20-30
1982	S.M.C. Society Plaque	1,530	1982	Gift	20-30
1983	S.M.C. Society Plaque	1,167	1983	Gift	20-30
1984	S.M.C. Society Plaque	505	1984	Gift	50-75
1984	Self Portrait	Retrd.	1994	Gift	45
1995	Grace - P.W. Baston, Jr.	Annual	1995	Gift	N/A

Sebastian Miniatures Holiday Memories-Member Only - P.W. Baston, Jr.

1990	Thanksgiving Helper	Yr.iss.	1991	39.50	40
1990	Leprechaun	Yr.iss.	1991	27.50	35-40
1991	Trick or Treat	Yr.iss.	1992	25.50	50-75
1993	Father Time	Yr.iss.	1994	27.50	28
1993	New Year Baby	Yr.iss.	1994	27.50	28
1994	Look What the Easter Bunny Left Me	Yr.iss.	1995	27.50	28
1995	On Parade	Yr.iss.		N/A	N/A

Sebastian Miniatures Member Only - P.W. Baston, Jr.

1989	The Collectors	Yr.iss.	1990	39.50	40
1992	Christopher Columbus	Yr.iss.	1993	28.50	29

Sebastian Miniature Figurines - P.W. Baston, Jr.

1991	America Salutes Desert Storm -bronze	Retrd.	1994	26.50	100
1991	America Salutes Desert Storm -painted	350	1991	49.50	200-250
1990	America's Hometown	4,750		34.00	34
1994	Boston Light	3,500		45.00	45
1994	Egg Rock Light	3,500		55.00	55
1992	Firefighter	500	1992	28.00	50
1991	Happy Hood Holidays	2,000	1991	32.50	95-105
1983	Harry Hood	1,000	1983	Unkn.	200-250
1992	I Know I Left It Here Somewhere	1,000		28.50	29
1985	It's Hoods (Wagon)	3,250	1985	N/A	75-100
1994	A Job Well Done	1,000		27.50	28
1993	The Lamplighter	1,000		28.00	28
1994	Nubble Light	3,500		45.00	45
1993	Pumpkin Island Light	3,500		55.00	55
1993	Soap Box Derby	500		45.00	45
1986	Statue of Liberty (AT & T)	1,000	1986	N/A	200-225
1987	White House (Gold, Oval Base)	250	1987	17.00	35-50

Sebastian Miniatures America Remembers - P.W. Baston

1979	Family Sing	7,358	1979	29.50	125-150
1980	Family Picnic	16,527	1980	29.50	60-100
1981	Family Reads Aloud	21,027	1981	34.50	50-75
1982	Family Fishing	8,734	1982	34.50	50-100
1983	Family Feast	4,147	1983	37.50	125-150

Sebastian Miniatures Children At Play - P.W. Baston

1979	Building Days Boy	10,000	1980	19.50	30-50
1979	Building Days Girl	10,000	1980	19.50	30-50
1981	Sailing Days Boy	10,000	1981	19.50	30-50
1981	Sailing Days Girl	10,000	1981	19.50	30-50
1982	School Days Boy	10,000	1982	19.50	40-60
1982	School Days Girl	10,000	1982	19.50	40-60
1978	Sidewalk Days Boy	10,000	1980	19.50	40-60
1978	Sidewalk Days Girl	10,000	1980	19.50	40-60
1980	Snow Days Boy	10,000	1980	19.50	40-60
1980	Snow Days Girl	10,000	1980	19.50	40-60

Sebastian Miniatures Christmas - P.W. Baston, Jr.

1993	Caroling With Santa	1,000		29.00	29
1993	Harmonizing With Santa	1,000		27.00	27
1994	Victorian Christmas Skaters	1,000		32.50	33
1995	Midnight Snacks	1,000		28.50	29

Sebastian Miniatures Exchange Figurines - P.W. Baston, Jr., unless otherwise noted

1984	First Things First	1,267	1985	30.00	45
1987	It's About Time	576	1988	25.00	40
1986	News Wagon	1,422	1987	35.00	45
1983	Newspaper Boy - P.W. Baston	1,708	1984	28.50	60-95
1985	Newstand	1,454	1986	30.00	45

Sebastian Miniatures Firefighter Collection - P.W. Baston, Jr.

1993	Firefighter No. 1	950	1995	48.00	48
1994	Firefighter No. 2	950		48.00	48
1994	Firefighter No. 3	950		48.00	48
1995	Firefighter No. 4	950		48.00	48

Sebastian Miniatures Jimmy Fund - P.W. Baston, Jr., unless otherwise noted

1993	Boy With Ducks	500	1993	27.50	28
1984	Catcher - P.W. Baston	1,872	1988	24.50	35-75
1987	Football Player	1,270	1988	26.50	27
1995	Girl in Riding Outfit	500		28.00	28
1994	Girl on Bench	500	1994	28.00	28
1985	Hockey Player	1,836	1986	24.50	35-50
1995	Santa	500	1988	32.50	33
1983	Schoolboy - P.W. Baston	3,567	1984	24.50	25-35
1986	Soccer Player	1,166	1987	25.00	25

Sebastian Miniatures Private Label - P.W. Baston Jr.

1993	Adams Academy w/ Steeple	75	N/A	100.00	200-225
1993	Adams Academy w/o Steeple	750	N/A	30.00	30

Sebastian Miniatures Shakespearean-Member Only - P.W. Baston, unless otherwise noted

1984	Anne Boleyn	3,897	1984	17.50	35
1984	Henry VIII	4,578	1984	19.50	35
1985	Falstaff	3,357	1985	19.50	35
1985	Mistress Ford	2,836	1985	17.50	35
1986	Juliet	2,620	1986	17.50	35
1986	Romeo	2,853	1986	19.50	35
1987	Countess Olivia	1,893	1987	19.50	35
1987	Malvolio	2,093	1987	21.50	35
1988	Audrey	1,548	1988	22.50	35
1988	Shakespeare - P.W. Baston, Jr.	Retrd.	1989	23.50	35
1988	Touchstone	1,770	1988	22.50	35
1989	Cleopatra	Retrd.	1989	27.00	35
1989	Mark Antony	Retrd.	1989	27.00	35

Sebastian Miniatures Washington Irving-Member Only - P.W. Baston

1980	Rip Van Winkle	12,005	1983	19.50	35
1981	Ichabod Crane	9,069	1983	19.50	35
1981	Dame Van Winkle	11,217	1983	19.50	35
1982	Brom Bones (Headless Horseman)	6,610	1983	22.50	35
1982	Katrina Van Tassel	7,367	1983	19.50	35
1983	Diedrich Knickerbocker	5,528	1983	22.50	35

Legends

Annual Collectors Edition - C. Pardell

1990	The Night Before	500	1991	990.00	2000-2500
1991	Medicine Gift of Manhood	500	1992	990.00	2000
1992	Spirit of the Wolf	500	1992	950.00	2000
1993	Tomorrow's Warrior	500	1993	590.00	1000-1600
1994	Guiding Hand	500	1994	990.00	875-1100
1995	Gift of the Sacred Calf	500	1995	650.00	650-900
1996	Spirit and Image	500		750.00	750

Collectors Only - Various

1993	Give Us Peace - C. Pardell	1,250	1993	270.00	370-500
1994	First Born - C. Pardell	1,250	1994	350.00	370-500
1994	River Bandits - K. Cantrell	1,250	1995	350.00	350
1995	Sonata - K. Cantrell	1,250	1996	250.00	290
1995	Daydreams of Manhood - C. Pardell	2,500	1995	390.00	390
1996	Innocence Remembered - C. Pardell	12/96		490.00	490

American Heritage - D. Edwards

1987	Grizz Country (Bronze)	Retrd.	1990	350.00	350
1987	Grizz Country (Pewter)	Retrd.	1990	370.00	370
1987	Winter Provisions (Bronze)	Retrd.	1990	340.00	340
1987	Winter Provisions (Pewter)	Retrd.	1990	370.00	370
1987	Wrangler's Dare (Bronze)	Retrd.	1990	630.00	630
1987	Wrangler's Dare (Pewter)	Retrd.	1990	660.00	660

American Indian Dance Premier Edition - C. Pardell

1996	Dancing Ground	750		2500.00	2500
1993	Drum Song	750	1995	2800.00	3000-3200
1994	Footprints of the Butterfly	750		1800.00	1990
1994	Image of the Eagle	750		1900.00	2100
1995	Spirit of the Mountain	750		1750.00	1850

American West Premier Edition - C. Pardell

1992	American Horse	950	1995	1300.00	1300
1992	Defending the People	950		1350.00	1450
1991	First Coup	950	1993	1150.00	1500
1993	Four Bears' Challenge	950	1996	990.00	1050
1994	Season of Victory	950		1500.00	1580
1991	Unexpected Rescuer	950	1991	990.00	1500-1700

Animal Dreamer - M. Boyett

1995	Breaking of the War Horse	950		590.00	590
1995	Buffalo Runner	950		550.00	570
1995	He Hunts with the Eagle Medicine	950		490.00	500
1995	In the Path of the Wolf Spirit	950		490.00	500
1995	Receiving The Cougar Spirit	950		590.00	590

Classic Equestrian Collection - C. Pardell

1988	Lippizzaner (Bronze)	Retrd.	N/A	200.00	200

The Classics Premier Edition - C. Pardell

1995	Indomitable	750		1590.00	1590

Clear Visions - Various

1993	Salmon Falls - W. Whitten	950	1995	950.00	980
1994	Saving Their Skins - C. Pardell	950		1590.00	1630

Counting Coup Collection - C. Pardell

1996	Telling The Tale	500		850.00	850

Culture Covenant Premier Edition - C. Pardell

1995	Each, to the Other	500		1300.00	1350
1995	Our Kind, with All Others	500		1300.00	1350
1994	Our Past, to Our Future	500	1996	1350.00	1450

The Endangered Wildlife Collection - K. Cantrell

1993	Big Pine Survivor	950		390.00	390
1990	Forest Spirit	950	1991	290.00	1500
1991	Mountain Majesty	950		350.00	390
1991	Old Tusker	950		390.00	390
1992	Plains Monarch	950		350.00	390
1994	Prairie Phantom	950		370.00	390
1990	Savannah Prince	950		290.00	350
1993	Silvertip	950		370.00	390
1992	Songs of Autumn	950	1995	390.00	390
1992	Spirit Song	950	1992	350.00	500-1000
1994	Twilight	950		290.00	310
1992	Unchallenged	950		350.00	390

Endangered Wildlife Eagle Series - K. Cantrell

1989	Aquila Libre	2,500	1995	280.00	350-450
1993	Defiance	2,500		350.00	350
1989	Food Fight	2,500		650.00	750
1989	Outpost	2,500	1995	280.00	350-400
1989	Sentinel	2,500	1993	280.00	350-500
1993	Spiral Flight	2,500		290.00	300
1992	Sunday Brunch	2,500		550.00	650
1989	Unbounded	2,500	1994	280.00	350-450

Gallery Editions - Various

1994	Center Fire - W. Whitten	350		2500.00	2600
1994	Mountain Family - D. Lemon	150		7900.00	8300
1996	On Wings of Eagles - D. Lemon	250		3700.00	3700
1993	Over the Rainbow - K. Cantrell	600	1995	2900.00	3000-3300
1993	Over the Rainbow AP - K. Cantrell	Retrd.	1996	4000.00	5000
1992	Resolute - C. Pardell	250	1992	7950.00	12000-15000
1993	Visionary - C. Pardell	350		7500.00	8300
1993	The Wanderer - K. Cantrell	350		3500.00	3700
1996	Wind on Still Water - C. Pardell	350	1996	2500.00	3000-3500

The Great Outdoorsman - C. Pardell

1988	Both Are Hooked (Bronze)	Retrd.	N/A	320.00	320
1988	Both Are Hooked (Pewter)	Retrd.	N/A	320.00	320

Happy Trails Collection - W. Whitten

1994	Cowboy Soul	750		450.00	450

Hidden Images Collection - D. Lemon

1994	In Search of Bear Rock	350	1995	1300.00	1300
1995	Sensed, But Unseen	350	1995	990.00	990
1995	Spirit	350		990.00	990

Indian Arts Collection - C. Pardell

1990	Chief's Blanket	1,500	1992	350.00	575-700
1990	Indian Maiden	1,500		240.00	240
1990	Indian Potter	1,500		260.00	260
1990	Kachina Carver	1,500	1993	270.00	400-550
1990	Story Teller	1,500	1993	290.00	450-550

The Jazz Musicians Collection - P. Wegner

1996	Face The Music	500		1200.00	1200
1996	Improv	500		1500.00	1500
1996	Play It Again	500		750.00	750
1996	'Round Midnight	500		590.00	590

Kachina Dancers Collection - C. Pardell

1991	Ahote	2,500		370.00	390
1991	Angakchina	2,500		370.00	390
1994	Deer Kachina	2,500		390.00	390
1994	Eototo	2,500		390.00	390
1991	Hilili	2,500		390.00	390
1993	Koshari	2,500		390.00	390
1991	Koyemsi	2,500		370.00	390
1992	Kwahu	2,500		390.00	390
1993	Mongwa	2,500		390.00	390
1994	Palhik Mana	2,500		390.00	390
1992	Tawa	2,500		390.00	390
1994	Wiharu	2,500		390.00	390

The Legacies Of The West Premier Edition - C. Pardell

1991	Defiant Comanche	950	1991	1300.00	1300-1800
1993	Eminent Crow	950	1994	1500.00	1500
1994	Enduring	950	1996	1250.00	1350
1992	Esteemed Warrior	950	1992	1750.00	2500-2800
1990	Mystic Vision	950	1990	990.00	2800-3800
1991	No More, Forever	950	1990	1500.00	1700
1992	Rebellious	950		1500.00	1600
1990	Victorious	950	1990	1275.00	3500-3900

The Legendary West Collection - C. Pardell

1992	Beating Bad Odds	2,500		390.00	410
1989	Bustin' A Herd Quitter	2,500		590.00	660
1993	Cliff Hanger	2,500		990.00	1050
1992	Crazy Horse	2,500	1992	390.00	800-1100
1989	Eagle Dancer	2,500		370.00	410
1993	Hunter's Brothers	2,500		590.00	660
1989	Johnson's Last Fight	2,500	1991	590.00	1200-1300
1990	Keeper of Eagles	2,500		370.00	410
1987	Pony Express (Bronze)	2,500	N/A	320.00	320-450
1989	Pony Express (Mixed Media)	2,500		320.00	410
1987	Pony Express (Pewter)	2,500	N/A	320.00	320-450
1989	Sacajawea	2,500	1995	380.00	495
1990	Shhh	2,500		390.00	410
1990	Stand of the Sash Wearer	2,500	1996	390.00	410
1989	Tables Turned	2,500		680.00	750

YEAR ISSUE		EDITION LIMIT	YEAR RETRD.	ISSUE PRICE	*QUOTE U.S.$
1990	Unbridled	2,500	1996	290.00	290
1991	Warning	2,500		390.00	410
1989	White Feather's Vision	2,500	1991	390.00	1000-1300

The Legendary West Premier Edition - C. Pardell

1990	Crow Warrior	750	1990	1225.00	2000-3000
1992	The Final Charge	750	1992	1250.00	1500-2000
1989	Pursued	750	1989	750.00	2000-4000
1988	Red Cloud's Coup	750	1988	480.00	5000-6700
1989	Songs of Glory	750	1989	850.00	3500-4300
1991	Triumphant	750	1991	1150.00	1700-2200

Mystical Quest Collection - D. Medina

1993	Hunter's Quest	950		990.00	1050
1994	Peace Quest	950	1996	1150.00	1200
1992	Vision Quest	950	1995	990.00	990

The North & South Collection - W. Whitten

1993	Brother Against Brother	950	1995	550.00	550
1993	The Noble Heart	950	1995	450.00	450
1994	Stonewall	950	1995	450.00	450
1992	Victory at Hand	950	1995	390.00	390

North American Wildlife - D. Edwards

1988	Defenders of Freedom (Bronze)	Retrd.	N/A	340.00	340
1988	Defenders of Freedom (Pewter)	Retrd.	N/A	370.00	370
1988	Double Trouble (Bronze)	Retrd.	N/A	300.00	300
1988	Double Trouble (Pewter)	Retrd.	N/A	320.00	320
1988	Downhill Run (Bronze)	Retrd.	N/A	330.00	330
1988	Downhill Run (Pewter)	Retrd.	N/A	340.00	340
1988	Grizzly Solitude (Bronze)	Retrd.	N/A	310.00	310
1988	Grizzly Solitude (Pewter)	Retrd.	N/A	330.00	330
1988	Last Glance (Bronze)	Retrd.	N/A	300.00	300
1988	Last Glance (Pewter)	Retrd.	N/A	320.00	320
1988	The Proud American (Bronze)	Retrd.	N/A	330.00	330
1988	The Proud American (Pewter)	Retrd.	N/A	340.00	340
1988	Ridge Runners (Bronze)	Retrd.	N/A	300.00	300
1988	Ridge Runners (Pewter)	Retrd.	N/A	310.00	310
1988	Sudden Alert (Bronze)	Retrd.	N/A	300.00	300
1988	Sudden Alert (Pewter)	Retrd.	N/A	320.00	320

Oceanic World - D. Medina

1989	Freedom's Beauty (Bronze)	Retrd.	N/A	330.00	330
1989	Freedom's Beauty (Pewter)	Retrd.	N/A	130.00	130
1989	Together (Bronze)	Retrd.	N/A	140.00	140
1989	Together (Pewter)	Retrd.	N/A	130.00	130

Relics of the Americas - W. Whitten

1993	Dream Medicine	950		1150.00	1290
1994	Flared Glory	950	1996	1350.00	1350
1995	Walks With Wolves	950		1250.00	1300

Special Commissions - Various

1988	Alpha Pair (Bronze) - C. Pardell	Retrd.	N/A	330.00	330
1988	Alpha Pair (Mixed Media) - C. Pardell	S/O	N/A	390.00	500-1000
1988	Alpha Pair (Pewter) - C. Pardell	Retrd.	N/A	330.00	330
1991	American Allegiance - D. Edwards	1,250	1996	570.00	625
1995	Father-The Power Within - D. Medina	350		1500.00	1590
1990	Lakota Love Song - C. Pardell	Retrd.	1990	380.00	1950
1987	Mama's Joy (Bronze) - D. Edwards	Retrd.	N/A	200.00	200
1987	Mama's Joy (Pewter) - D. Edwards	Retrd.	N/A	250.00	250
1996	Proud Heritage - K. Cantrell	2,500		290.00	290
1995	Rapture - W. Whitten	350		1750.00	1850
1995	Scent in the Air - K. Cantrell	750		990.00	1050
1991	Symbols of Freedom - K. Cantrell	2,500		490.00	550
1987	Wild Freedom (Bronze) - D. Edwards	Retrd.	N/A	320.00	320
1987	Wild Freedom (Pewter) - D. Edwards	Retrd.	N/A	330.00	330
1992	Yellowstone Bound - K. Cantrell	600	1994	2500.00	3600-3900

Spirit Helpers Collection - C. Pardell

1996	Sees An Eagle	950		490.00	490

Warriors of the Plains - B. Austin

1996	Battle Cry of The Warrior	500		490.00	490
1996	Unconquered Spirit	500		490.00	490

Warriors of the Sacred Circle - W. Whitten

1993	Coup Feather	950	1995	450.00	450
1992	Dog Soldier	950	1995	450.00	450
1992	Peace Offering	950	1995	550.00	550
1994	Traditional Weapons	950	1995	550.00	550
1993	Yellow Boy	950	1995	450.00	450

Way of the Cat Collection - K. Cantrell

1996	Cat's Cradle	500		790.00	790
1995	Encounter	500	1995	750.00	1000-1200

Way of the Eagle Collection - K. Cantrell

1996	Aerial Display	950		750.00	750

Way of the Warrior Collection - C. Pardell

1991	Clan Leader	1,600	1994	170.00	225
1991	Elder Chief	1,600	1994	170.00	225
1991	Medicine Dancer	1,600	1994	170.00	225
1991	Rite of Manhood	1,600	1994	170.00	225
1991	Seeker of Visions	1,600	1994	170.00	225

YEAR ISSUE		EDITION LIMIT	YEAR RETRD.	ISSUE PRICE	*QUOTE U.S.$
1991	Tribal Defender	1,600	1994	170.00	225

Way of the Wolf Collection - K. Cantrell

1993	Courtship	500	1993	590.00	1500-2000
1995	Gossip Column	500		1250.00	1250
1994	Missed by a Hare	500	1994	700.00	850-1300
1994	Renewal	500	1994	700.00	950-1700
1995	Stink Bomb	500	1995	750.00	950-1300

Western Memories Premier Edition - D. Lemon

1996	Coulter's Escape	500		1250.00	1250
1995	Ole Mossy Horns	500		1450.00	1530
1994	Vacant Thunder	500		1900.00	1990
1995	Winds of Memory	500		1750.00	1850

Wild Realm Collection - C. Pardell

1988	Fly Fisher (Bronze)	Retrd.	N/A	330.00	330
1988	Fly Fisher (Pewter)	Retrd.	N/A	330.00	330

Wild Realm Premier Edition - C. Pardell

1989	High Spirit	1,600	1996	870.00	990
1991	Speed Incarnate	1,600	N/A	790.00	790

Lenox Collections

American Fashion - Unknown

1986	Belle of the Ball	Open		95.00	95
1987	Centennial Bride	Open		95.00	95
1984	First Waltz	Open		95.00	95
1987	Gala at the Whitehouse	Open		95.00	95
1985	Governor's Garden Party	Open		95.00	95
1986	Grand Tour	Open		95.00	95
1992	Royal Reception	Open		95.00	95
1983	Springtime Promenade	Open		95.00	95
1984	Tea at the Ritz	Open		95.00	95

Baby Bears - Unknown

1991	Polar Bear	Open		45.00	45

Baby Bird Pairs - Unknown

1992	Chickadee	Closed	1994	64.00	64
1992	Orioles	Closed	1994	64.00	64
1991	Robins	Closed	1994	64.00	64

Breed Puppies - Unknown

1995	Dachshund	Open		75.00	75

Carousel Animals - Unknown

1992	Camelot Horse	Open		152.00	152
1990	Carousel Charger	Open		136.00	152
1989	Carousel Circus Horse	Open		136.00	152
1990	Carousel Elephant	Open		136.00	152
1987	Carousel Horse	Open		136.00	152
1990	Carousel Lion	Open		136.00	152
1991	Carousel Polar Bear	Open		152.00	152
1989	Carousel Reindeer	Open		136.00	152
1988	Carousel Unicorn	Open		136.00	152
1992	Christmas Horse 1992	Yr.Iss.	1992	156.00	156
1993	Christmas Horse 1993	Yr.Iss.	1993	156.00	156
1994	Christmas Horse 1994	Yr.Iss.	1994	156.00	156
1994	Midnight Charger	9,500		156.00	156
1993	Nautical Horse	Open		156.00	156
1991	Pride of America	Closed	1991	152.00	152
1993	Rose Prancer	9,500		156.00	156
1993	Statement Horse #1 Victorian Romance	2,500		395.00	395
1994	Statement Horse #2 Ribbons & Roses	2,500		395.00	395
1992	Statement Piece	Open		395.00	395
1992	Tropical Horse	Open		156.00	156
1992	Victorian Romance Horse	Open		156.00	156
1991	Western Horse	Open		152.00	152

Carousels - Unknown

1995	Carousel Courtship (Spec. Ed.)	5,500		195.00	195
1995	Jeweled Prancer Carousel	Open		154.00	154

Classical Goddesses - Unknown

1992	Aphrodite	Closed	1994	95.00	95
1992	Aphrodite, Painted	Closed	1994	136.00	136

Crystal Animal Pairs - Unknown

1994	Lord & Lady, Wolves	Open		76.00	76
1994	Preen & Serene, Cats	Open		76.00	76
1993	Prim & Proper, Cats	Open		76.00	76
1993	Silk & Satin, Rabbits	Open		76.00	76

Crystal Eagles - Unknown

1994	Soaring Majesty	Open		195.00	195
1995	Wings of the Sun	Open		195.00	195

Doves & Roses - Unknown

1992	Doves of Honor	Open		119.00	119
1993	Doves of Love	Open		119.00	119
1991	Doves of Peace	Open		95.00	95
1991	Love's Promise	Open		95.00	95

Endangered Baby Animals - Unknown

1991	Baby Florida Panther	Open		57.00	57
1991	Baby Grey Wolf	Open		57.00	57
1994	Baby Orangatan	Open		58.00	58

YEAR ISSUE		EDITION LIMIT	YEAR RETRD.	ISSUE PRICE	*QUOTE U.S.$
1992	Baby Rhinocerous	Open		57.00	57
1994	Bridled Nail-Tailed Wallaby Joey	Open		58.00	58
1994	Burmese Deer	Open		58.50	59
1991	Elephant	Open		57.00	57
1993	Indian Elephant Calf	Open		57.00	57
1990	Panda	Open		39.00	39
1994	Pigmy Hippo	Open		58.00	58
1994	Sumatra Tiger Cub	Open		58.00	58

Exotic Birds - Unknown

1993	"Plum Headed" Parakeet	Open		49.50	50
1991	Cockatoo	Open		45.00	45

Floral Sculptures - Unknown

1987	Iris	Open		119.00	136
1988	Magnolia	Open		119.00	136
1988	Peace Rose	Open		119.00	136
1986	Rubrum Lily	Open		119.00	136

Garden Birds - Unknown

1987	American Goldfinch	Open		39.00	45
1990	Baltimore Oriole	Open		45.00	45
1993	Barn Swallow	Open		45.00	45
1986	Blue Jay	Open		39.00	45
1991	Broadbilled Hummingbird	Open		45.00	45
1987	Cardinal	Open		39.00	45
1988	Cedar Waxwing	Open		39.00	45
1985	Chickadee	Open		39.00	45
1990	Chipping Sparrow	Open		45.00	45
1993	Chipping Sparrow	Open		45.00	45
1994	Christmas Dove	Yr.Iss.		45.00	45
1991	Dark Eyed Junco	Open		45.00	45
1989	Downy Woodpecker	Open		39.00	45
1986	Eastern Bluebird	Open		39.00	45
1994	Female BlueJay	Open		45.00	45
1993	Female Cardinal	Open		45.00	45
1994	Female Chickadee	Open		45.00	45
1993	Female Kinglet	Open		45.00	45
1991	Golden Crowned Kinglet	Open		45.00	45
1988	Hummingbird	Open		39.00	45
1993	Indigo Bunting	Open		45.00	45
1992	Magnificent Hummingbird	Open		45.00	45
1990	Marsh Wren	Open		45.00	45
1993	Mockingbird	Open		45.00	45
1993	Mountain Bluebird	Open		45.00	45
1991	Purple Finch	Open		45.00	45
1994	Purple Martin	Open		45.00	45
1993	Red Winged Blackbird	Open		45.00	45
1987	Red-Breasted Nuthatch	Open		39.00	45
1989	Robin	Open		39.00	45
1991	Rose Grosbeak	Open		45.00	45
1989	Saw Whet Owl	Open		45.00	45
1992	Scarlet Tanger	Open		45.00	45
1993	Statement Piece	Open		45.00	45
1986	Tufted Titmouse	Open		39.00	45
1987	Turtle Dove	Open		39.00	45
1994	Vermillion Flycatcher	Open		45.00	45
1992	Western Meadowlark	Open		45.00	45
1994	Western Tanager	Open		45.00	45
1990	Wood Duck	Open		45.00	45
1993	Yellow Warbler	Open		45.00	45

Garden Flowers - Unknown

1991	Calla Lily	Open		45.00	45
1991	Camelia	Open		45.00	45
1990	Carnation	Open		45.00	45
1988	Cattleya Orchid	Open		39.00	45
1995	Crocus	Open		39.00	39
1990	Daffodil	Open		45.00	45
1990	Day Lily	Open		45.00	45
1995	Gardenia	Open		39.00	39
1995	Gladiolus	Open		39.00	39
1989	Iris	Open		45.00	45
1995	Keepsake Rose (Statement)	Open		95.00	95
1991	Magnolia	Open		45.00	45
1991	Morning Glory	Open		45.00	45
1988	Parrot Tulip	Open		39.00	39
1991	Poinsettia	Open		39.00	39
1993	Red Rose	Open		45.00	45
1988	Tea Rose	Open		39.00	45

Gentle Majesty - Unknown

1990	Bear Hug Polar Bear	Open		76.00	76
1991	Keeping Warm (Foxes)	Open		76.00	76
1990	Penguins	Open		76.00	76

Hunters of the Sky - Unknown

1993	Challenge of the Eagles, Double Eagles	Open		275.00	275
1994	Challenge of the Red Tailed Hawks	Open		295.00	295
1994	Golden Conquerors	Open		295.00	295
1994	Masters of the Wind, Peregian Falcons	Open		295.00	295

International Brides - Unknown

1992	Japanese Bride, Kiyoshi	Closed	1993	136.00	136
1990	Russian Bride	Closed	1993	136.00	136

International Horse Sculptures - Unknown

1990	Appaloosa	Open		136.00	136
1988	Arabian Knight	Open		136.00	136
1990	Lippizan	Open		136.00	136

YEAR ISSUE		EDITION LIMIT	YEAR RETRD.	ISSUE PRICE	*QUOTE U.S.$
1989	Thoroughbred	Open		136.00	136

International Songbirds - Unknown

YEAR ISSUE		EDITION LIMIT	YEAR RETRD.	ISSUE PRICE	*QUOTE U.S.$
1992	American Goldfinch	Open		152.00	152
1992	European Goldfinch	Open		152.00	152

Jessie Willcox Smith - J.W.Smith

1991	Feeding Kitty	Closed	1993	60.00	60
1991	Rosebuds	Closed	1993	60.00	60

Kings of the Sky - Unknown

1991	Defender of Freedom, American Bald Eagle	Closed		234.00	234
1991	Eagle of Glory, Golden Eagle	Open		234.00	234
1994	Eagle of Splendor, American Bald Eagle	Open		252.00	252
1993	Foundation of Freedom	Open		252.00	252
1989	Lord of Skies, American Bald Eagle	Open		195.00	195
1992	Wings of Majesty, American Bald Eagle	Open		252.00	252
1993	Wings of Power, Golden Eagle	Open		252.00	252
1994	Wings of Pride, Golden Eagle	Open		252.00	252

Legendary Princesses - Unknown

1988	Cinderella	Open		136.00	136
1990	Cleopatra	Open		136.00	136
1994	Fairy Godmother	9,500		156.00	156
1992	Firebird	Open		156.00	156
1994	Frog Princess	Open		156.00	156
1990	Guinevere	Open		136.00	136
1990	Juliet	Open		136.00	136
1993	Little Mermaid, Princess of the Sea	Open		156.00	156
1994	Maid Marion	Open		156.00	156
1991	Peacock Maiden	Open		136.00	136
1991	Pocahontas	9,500	1992	156.00	165
1993	Princes Beauty	Open		156.00	156
1993	Princess and the Pea	Open		156.00	156
1985	Rapunzel	Open		119.00	136
1992	Sheherazade	Open		156.00	156
1986	Sleeping Beauty	Open		119.00	136
1987	Snow Queen	Open		119.00	136
1989	Snow White	Open		136.00	136
1989	Swan Princess	Open		136.00	136

Lenox Baby Book - Unknown

1991	Baby's First Christmas	Closed	1994	57.00	57
1992	Baby's First Portrait	Closed	1994	57.00	57
1990	Baby's First Shoes	Closed	1994	57.00	57
1991	Baby's First Steps	Closed	1994	57.00	57

Lenox Breed Puppies - Unknown

1990	Beagle	Open		76.00	76
1991	Cocker Spaniel	Open		76.00	76
1994	German Shepherd	Open		75.00	75
1995	Labrador Retriever	Open		76.00	76
1992	Poodle	Open		76.00	76

Lenox Sea Animals - Unknown

1994	Adventure of Fur Seals	Open		136.00	136
1991	Dance of the Dolphins	Open		119.00	119
1993	Flight of the Dolphins	Open		119.00	119
1993	Journey of the Whales	Open		136.00	136
1993	Otter Escapade	Open		136.00	136
1994	Penguins at Play	Open		136.00	136
1992	Song of the Whales	Open		136.00	136
1994	Voyage of the Sea Turtles	Open		136.00	136

Life of Christ - Unknown

1992	A Child's Comfort	Open		95.00	95
1992	A Child's Prayer	Open		95.00	95
1993	Children's Adoration	Open		95.00	95
1990	The Children's Blessing	Open		95.00	95
1992	Childrens's Devotion (Painted)	Open		195.00	195
1990	The Good Shepherd	Open		95.00	95
1993	Jesus, The Carpenter	Open		95.00	95
1991	Jesus, The Teacher	9,500		95.00	95
1990	Madonna And Child	Open		95.00	95
1992	Mary & Christ Child (Painted)	Open		195.00	195
1991	The Savior	Open		95.00	95

Miniature Santas Around the World-8" - Unknown

1993	Americana Santa	Open		19.50	20
1993	Bavarian Santa	Open		19.50	20
1994	Befona	Open		19.50	20
1994	Christkindle	Open		19.50	20
1993	Father Christmas	Open		19.50	20
1993	Grandfather Frost	Open		19.50	20
1993	Kris Kringle	Open		19.50	20
1994	Patriotic Santa	Open		19.50	20
1993	Pere Noel	Open		19.50	20
1994	Sanct Herr Nikolaus	Open		19.50	20
1994	Santa Lucia	Open		19.50	20
1994	Sinterklaus	Open		19.50	20
1994	St. Mikulase	Open		19.50	20
1994	St. Nick	Open		19.50	20
1993	Victorian Santa	Open		19.50	20

Mother & Child - Unknown

1991	Afternoon Stroll	7,500		136.00	136
1990	Bedtime Prayers	Open		119.00	119
1986	Cherished Moment	Open		119.00	119
1989	Christening	Open		119.00	119
1991	Evening Lullaby	7,500		136.00	136
1992	Morning Playtime	Open		136.00	136
1988	The Present	Open		119.00	119
1987	Storytime	Open		119.00	119
1986	Sunday in the Park	Open		119.00	119

Nativity - Unknown

1989	Angels of Adoration	Open		136.00	152
1988	Animals of the Nativity	Open		119.00	152
1990	Children of Bethlehem	Open		136.00	152
1986	Holy Family	Open		119.00	136
1988	Shepherds	Open		119.00	152
1991	Standing Camel & Driver	9,500		152.00	152
1987	Three Kings	Open		119.00	152
1991	Townspeople of Bethlehem	Open		136.00	152

Nature's Beautiful Butterflies - Unknown

1991	Adonis	Open		45.00	45
1993	American Painted Lady	Open		45.00	45
1993	Black Swallowtail	Open		45.00	45
1989	Blue Temora	Open		39.00	45
1993	Great Orange Wingtip	Open		45.00	45
1991	Malachite	Open		45.00	45
1990	Monarch	Open		39.00	45
1990	Purple Emperor	Open		45.00	45
1994	Rainforest Dazzler	Open		45.00	45
1990	Yellow Swallowtail	Open		39.00	45

North American Bird Pairs - Unknown

1991	Blue Jay Pairs	Open		119.00	119
1992	Cardinal	Open		119.00	119
1991	Chickadees	Open		119.00	119
1990	Hummingbirds	Open		119.00	119

North American Wildlife - Unknown

1991	White Tailed Deer	Closed	1993	195.00	195

Owls of America - Unknown

1989	Barn Owl	Open		136.00	136
1991	Great Horned Owl	9,500		136.00	136
1990	Screech Owl	Open		136.00	136
1988	Snowy Owl	Open		136.00	136

Parent & Child Bird Pairs - Unknown

1992	Blue Jay Pairs	Open		119.00	119

Porcelain Duck Collection - Unknown

1992	Blue Winged Teal Duck	Open		45.00	45
1991	Mallard Duck	Open		45.00	45
1993	Pintail Duck	Open		45.00	45
1991	Wood Duck	Open		45.00	45

Religious Sculptures - Unknown

1994	Footsteps in the Sand	Open		152.00	152
1993	Last Supper	Open		152.00	152
1992	Moses	Open		95.00	95
1994	Pieta	Open		152.00	152
1995	Praying Hands	Open		95.00	95

Renaissance Nativity - Unknown

1991	Angels	Open		195.00	195
1995	Angels of Harmony	Open		195.00	195
1991	Animals of the Nativity	Open		195.00	195
1993	Camel & Driver	9,500		195.00	195
1994	Children of Bethlehem	9,500		195.00	195
1991	Holy Family	Open		195.00	195
1991	Shepherds of Bethlehem	Open		195.00	195
1991	Three Kings	Open		195.00	195

Santa Claus Collection - Unknown

1991	Americana Santa	Open		136.00	156
1994	Bavarian Santa	Open		136.00	156
1990	Father Christmas	Open		136.00	156
1992	Grandfather Frost	Open		136.00	156
1991	Kris Kringle	Open		136.00	156
1992	Pere Noel	Open		136.00	156
1993	St. Nick	Open		136.00	156
1994	Victorian Santa	Open		136.00	156

Street Crier Collection - Unknown

1991	Belgian Lace Maker	Closed	1993	136.00	136
1990	French Flower Maiden	Closed	1993	136.00	136

Unicorns - Unknown

1995	Celestial Unicorn (Statement #2)	4,500		295.00	295
1993	Eternal Enchantment (Statement #1)	Open		245.00	245
1994	Golden Grace	Open		149.00	149
1995	Love's Celebration (Anniversary/Spec. Ed.)	9,500		136.00	136
1994	Love's Magic	Open		119.00	119
1994	Love's Messenger (Valentine)	Open		119.00	119
1993	Love's Paradise	Open		119.00	119
1993	Love's Pride	Open		119.00	119
1995	Mid-Summer's Night Unicorn (Spec. Ed.)	9,500		149.00	149
1994	Platinum Purity	Open		149.00	149
1994	Royal Court Unicorn	Open		136.00	136
1994	Unicorn of Summer	Open		119.00	119
1992	Yuletide Blessing (Christmas)	Yr.Iss.	1992	119.00	119
1993	Yuletide Magic (Christmas)	Yr.Iss.	1993	119.00	119
1994	Yuletide Splendor (Christmas)	Yr.Iss.	1994	119.00	119

Wildlife of the Seven Continents - Unknown

1988	African Lion	Open		136.00	136
1987	Antarctic Seals	Open		136.00	136
1985	Asian Elephant	Open		120.00	120
1985	Australian Koala	Open		120.00	120
1987	European Red Deer	Open		136.00	136
1984	North American Bighorn Sheep	Open		120.00	120
1986	South American Puma	Open		120.00	120

Woodland Animals - Unknown

1991	Autumn Adventure (Chipmunk)	Open		39.00	39
1993	Autumn Splendor (Fawn)	Open		45.00	45
1992	Daybreak Discovery (Rabbit)	Open		39.00	39
1994	Early Morning Surprise (Fox)	Open		45.00	45
1995	Forest Friends (Statement)	Open		97.00	97
1994	Nature's Reward (Mouse)	Open		45.00	45
1994	Playful Pursuit (Black Bear)	Open		45.00	45
1993	Scent of Spring (Skunk)	Open		45.00	45
1995	Spring Shadow (Ground Hog)	Open		45.00	45
1995	Springtime Skamper (Red Squirrel)	Open		39.00	39
1994	Summer Delight (Chipmunk)	Open		45.00	45
1990	Twilight Mischief (Raccoon)	Open		39.00	39
1994	Woodland Worker (Beaver)	Open		45.00	45

Lilliput Lane Ltd.

Collectors Club Specials - Various

1986	Packhorse Bridge - D. Tate	Retrd.	1987	Gift	700
1986	Packhorse Bridge (dealer) - D. Tate	Retrd.	1987	Gift	450-750
1986	Crendon Manor - D. Tate	Retrd.	1989	285.00	850
1986	Gulliver - Unknown	Retrd.	1986	65.00	325
1987	Little Lost Dog - D. Tate	Retrd.	1988	Gift	225-450
1987	Yew Tree Farm - D. Tate	Retrd.	1988	160.00	230
1988	Wishing Well - D. Tate	Retrd.	1989	Gift	105
1989	Dovecot - D. Tate	Retrd.	1990	Gift	95
1989	Wenlock Rise - D. Tate	Retrd.	1989	175.00	150
1990	Cosy Corner - D. Tate	Retrd.	1991	Gift	75-125
1990	Lavender Cottage - D. Tate	Retrd.	1991	50.00	50-90
1990	Bridle Way - D. Tate	Retrd.	1991	100.00	150-225
1991	Puddlebrook - D. Tate	Retrd.	1992	Gift	60-100
1991	Gardeners Cottage - D. Tate	Retrd.	1992	120.00	175-250
1991	Wren Cottage - D. Tate	Retrd.	1993	13.95	70-110
1992	Pussy Willow - D. Tate	Retrd.	1993	Gift	50-95
1992	Forget-Me-Not - D. Tate	Retrd.	1993	130.00	175-250
1993	The Spinney - Lilliput Lane	Retrd.	1994	Gift	100-125
1993	Heaven Lea Cottage - Lilliput Lane	Retrd.	1994	150.00	250
1993	Curlew Cottage - Lilliput Lane	Retrd.	1995	18.95	50-65
1994	Petticoat Cottage - Lilliput Lane	Retrd.	1995	Gift	70
1994	Woodman's Retreat - Lilliput Lane	Retrd.	1995	135.00	150-200
1995	Thimble Cottage - Lilliput Lane	Retrd.	1996	Gift	N/A
1995	Porlock Down - Lilliput Lane	Retrd.	1996	135.00	135
1996	Wash Day - Lilliput Lane	4/97		Gift	N/A
1996	Meadowsweet Cottage - Lilliput Lane	4/97		110.00	110
1996	Nursery Cottage - Lilliput Lane	4/97		Gift	N/A
1996	Winnows - Lilliput Lane	4/97		22.50	23

Anniversary Special - Lilliput Lane

1992	Honeysuckle Cottage	Yr.Iss.	1992	195.00	300-450
1993	Cotman Cottage	Yr.Iss.	1993	220.00	250-350
1994	Watermeadows	Yr.Iss.	1994	189.00	200-250
1995	Gertrude's Garden	Yr.Iss.	1995	192.00	200
1996	Cruck End	Yr.Iss.		130.00	130

South Bend Dinner Collection - Various

1989	Commemorative Medallion - D. Tate	Retrd.	1989	N/A	130-200
1990	Rowan Lodge - D. Tate	Retrd.	1990	N/A	200-400
1991	Gamekeepers Cottage - D. Tate	Retrd.	1991	N/A	250-400
1992	Ashberry Cottage - D. Tate	Retrd.	1992	N/A	200-400
1993	Magnifying Glass - Lilliput Lane	Retrd.	1993	N/A	N/A

Special Event Collection - Lilliput Lane

1990	Rowan Lodge	Retrd.	1990	50.00	120
1991	Gamekeepers Cottage	Retrd.	1991	75.00	200
1992	Ploughman's Cottage	Retrd.	1992	75.00	75
1993	Aberford Gate	Retrd.	1993	95.00	160
1994	Leagrave Cottage	Retrd.	1994	75.00	75
1995	Vanbrugh Lodge	Retrd.	1995	60.00	60
1996	Amberly Rose	Yr.Iss.		45.00	45

American Collection - D. Tate

1984	Adobe Church	Retrd.	1985	22.50	700-1100
1984	Adobe Village	Retrd.	1985	60.00	900-1500
1984	Cape Cod	Retrd.	1985	22.50	570-910
1984	Country Church	Retrd.	1985	22.50	500-800
1984	Covered Bridge	Retrd.	1985	22.50	1000-2000
1984	Forge Barn	Retrd.	1985	22.50	550-660
1984	General Store	Retrd.	1985	22.50	600-800
1984	Grist Mill	Retrd.	1985	22.50	500-785
1984	Light House	Retrd.	1985	22.50	650-800
1984	Log Cabin	Retrd.	1985	22.50	625-1100
1984	Midwest Barn	Retrd.	1985	22.50	275
1984	San Francisco House	Retrd.	1985	22.50	850
1984	Wallace Station	Retrd.	1985	22.50	400

Blaise Hamlet Classics - Lilliput Lane

1993	Circular Cottage	Retrd.	1995	95.00	125-175
1993	Dial Cottage	Retrd.	1995	95.00	125-175

Year Issue	Item	Edition Limit	Year Retd.	Issue Price	*Quote U.S.$
1993	Diamond Cottage	Retrd.	1995	95.00	95
1993	Double Cottage	Retrd.	1995	95.00	95
1993	Jasmine Cottage	Retrd.	1995	95.00	125-175
1993	Oak Cottage	Retrd.	1995	95.00	105
1993	Rose Cottage	Retrd.	1995	95.00	150
1993	Sweet Briar Cottage	Retrd.	1995	95.00	125-175
1993	Vine Cottage	Retrd.	1995	95.00	135

Blaise Hamlet Collection - D. Tate

Year Issue	Item	Edition Limit	Year Retd.	Issue Price	*Quote U.S.$
1989	Circular Cottage	Retrd.	1993	110.00	150-200
1990	Dial Cottage	Retrd.	1995	110.00	150-175
1989	Diamond Cottage	Retrd.	1993	110.00	125-175
1991	Double Cottage	Retrd.	1995	200.00	150-200
1991	Jasmine Cottage	Retrd.	1996	140.00	110-150
1989	Oak Cottage	Retrd.	1993	110.00	150-200
1991	Rose Cottage	Open		140.00	110-140
1990	Sweetbriar Cottage	Retrd.	1995	110.00	150-175
1990	Vine Cottage	Retrd.	1995	110.00	135-150

Christmas Church - Lilliput Lane

Year Issue	Item	Edition Limit	Year Retd.	Issue Price	*Quote U.S.$
1996	St. Stephen's Church	Yr.Iss.		100.00	100

Christmas Collection - Various

Year Issue	Item	Edition Limit	Year Retd.	Issue Price	*Quote U.S.$
1992	Chestnut Cottage	Retrd.	1996	46.50	35-50
1992	Cranberry Cottage	Retrd.	1996	46.50	35-50
1988	Deer Park Hall - D. Tate	Retrd.	1993	120.00	200-300
1993	The Gingerbread Shop	3/97		50.00	35-50
1992	Hollytree House	Retrd.	1996	46.50	35-50
1991	The Old Vicarage at Christmas - D. Tate	Retrd.	1992	180.00	180-300
1993	Partridge Cottage	3/97		50.00	35-50
1994	Ring O' Bells	Open		50.00	35-50
1993	St. Joseph's Church	Open		70.00	50-70
1994	St. Joseph's School	Open		50.00	35-50
1989	St. Nicholas Church - D. Tate	Retrd.	1990	130.00	155-275
1994	The Vicarage	Open		50.00	35-50
1990	Yuletide Inn - D. Tate	Retrd.	1991	145.00	120-150

Christmas Lodge Collection - Lilliput Lane

Year Issue	Item	Edition Limit	Year Retd.	Issue Price	*Quote U.S.$
1993	Eamont Lodge	Retrd.	1993	180.00	200-300
1992	Highland Lodge	Retrd.	1992	180.00	200-300
1995	Kerry Lodge	Retrd.	1995	160.00	120-160
1994	Snowdon Lodge	Retrd.	1994	175.00	175

Countryside Scene Plaques - D. Simpson

Year Issue	Item	Edition Limit	Year Retd.	Issue Price	*Quote U.S.$
1989	Bottle Kiln	Retrd.	1991	49.50	50
1989	Cornish Tin Mine	Retrd.	1991	49.50	50
1989	Country Inn	Retrd.	1991	49.50	50
1989	Cumbrian Farmhouse	Retrd.	1991	49.50	50
1989	Lighthouse	Retrd.	1991	49.50	50
1989	Norfolk Windmill	Retrd.	1991	49.50	50
1989	Oasthouse	Retrd.	1991	49.50	50
1989	Old Smithy	Retrd.	1991	49.50	50
1989	Parish Church	Retrd.	1991	49.50	50
1989	Post Office	Retrd.	1991	49.50	50
1989	Village School	Retrd.	1991	49.50	50
1989	Watermill	Retrd.	1991	49.50	50

Disneyana Convention - R. Day

Year Issue	Item	Edition Limit	Year Retd.	Issue Price	*Quote U.S.$
1995	Fire Station 105	501	1995	195.00	385-595
1996	The Hall of Presidents	500	1996	225.00	225

Dutch Collection - D. Tate

Year Issue	Item	Edition Limit	Year Retd.	Issue Price	*Quote U.S.$
1991	Aan de Amstel	Open		79.00	60-85
1991	Begijnhof	Open		55.00	35-60
1991	Bloemenmarkt	Open		79.00	60-85
1991	De Branderij	Open		72.50	55-80
1991	De Diamantair	Open		79.00	60-85
1991	De Pepermolen	Open		55.00	35-60
1991	De Wolhandelaar	Open		72.50	55-80
1991	De Zijdewever	Open		79.00	60-85
1991	Rembrant van Rijn	Open		120.00	85-130
1991	Rozengracht	Open		72.50	50-80

English Cottages - D. Tate, unless otherwise noted

Year Issue	Item	Edition Limit	Year Retd.	Issue Price	*Quote U.S.$
1982	Acorn Cottage-Mold 1	Retrd.	1983	30.00	250-350
1983	Acorn Cottage-Mold 2	Retrd.	1987	30.00	60
1996	The Anchor - Lilliput Lane	Open		85.00	85
1982	Anne Hathaway's-Mold 1	Retrd.	1983	40.00	2500
1983	Anne Hathaway's-Mold 2	Retrd.	1984	40.00	400-600
1984	Anne Hathaway's-Mold 3	Retrd.	1988	40.00	375
1989	Anne Hathaway's-Mold 4	3/97		130.00	130
1991	Anne of Cleves	Retrd.	1996	360.00	250-395
1994	Applejack Cottage - Lilliput Lane	Open		45.00	35-45
1982	April Cottage-Mold 1	Retrd.	1984	Unkn.	350-500
1982	April Cottage-Mold 2	Retrd.	1989	Unkn.	100
1991	Armada House	3/97		175.00	130-185
1989	Ash Nook	Retrd.	1995	47.50	60
1986	Bay View	Retrd.	1988	39.50	90-125
1987	Beacon Heights	Retrd.	1992	125.00	150
1989	Beehive Cottage	Retrd.	1995	72.50	95
1996	Birchwood Cottage - Lilliput Lane	Open		55.00	55
1993	Birdlip Bottom - Lilliput Lane	Open		80.00	50-80
1996	Blue Boar - Lilliput Lane	Open		85.00	85
1996	Bluebell Farm - Lilliput Lane	Open		250.00	250
1992	Bow Cottage	Retrd.	1995	128.00	135
1996	Boxwood Cottage - Lilliput Lane	Open		30.00	30
1990	Bramble Cottage	Retrd.	1995	55.00	100
1988	Bredon House	Retrd.	1990	145.00	150-275
1989	The Briary	Retrd.	1995	47.50	60
1982	Bridge House-Mold 1	Retrd.	N/A	15.95	450
1982	Bridge House-Mold 2	Retrd.	1990	15.95	175
1991	Bridge House-Mold 3	Open		25.00	20-30
1988	Brockbank	Retrd.	1993	58.00	90
1985	Bronte Parsonage	Retrd.	1987	72.00	80
1982	Burnside	Retrd.	1985	30.00	550
1990	Buttercup Cottage	Retrd.	1992	40.00	65
1989	Butterwick	Retrd.	1996	52.50	60-70
1995	Button Down - Lilliput Lane	Open		37.50	30-38
1996	Calendar Cottage - Lilliput Lane	Open		55.00	55
1994	Camomile Lawn - Lilliput Lane	3/97		125.00	90-125
1982	Castle Street	Retrd.	1986	130.00	240-350
1993	Cat's Coombe Cottage - Lilliput Lane	Retrd.	1995	95.00	95
1996	Chalk Down - Lilliput Lane	Open		35.00	35
1991	Chatsworth View	Retrd.	1996	250.00	170-275
1995	Cherry Blossom Cottage - Lilliput Lane	Open		128.00	95-128
1990	Cherry Cottage	Retrd.	1995	33.50	45
1989	Chiltern Mill	Retrd.	1995	87.50	110
1989	Chine Cot-Mold 1	Retrd.	1989	36.00	N/A
1989	Chine Cot-Mold 2	Retrd.	1996	35.00	35-50
1995	Chipping Campden - Lilliput Lane	3,000		525.00	525
1992	The Chocolate House - Lilliput Lane	Open		130.00	90-140
1985	Clare Cottage	Retrd.	1993	30.00	30
1993	Cley-next-the-sea - Lilliput Lane	2,500		725.00	725
1987	Clover Cottage	Retrd.	1994	27.50	58
1982	Coach House	Retrd.	1985	100.00	1100-1895
1986	Cobblers Cottage - D. Hall	Retrd.	1994	42.00	65
1990	Convent in The Woods	Retrd.	1996	175.00	175-220
1983	Coopers	Retrd.	1986	15.00	440-825
1996	Cradle Cottage - Lilliput Lane	Open		100.00	100
1994	Creel Cottage - Lilliput Lane	3/97		40.00	35-40
1996	Crispin Cottage - Lilliput Lane	Open		50.00	50
1988	Crown Inn	Retrd.	1992	120.00	120-215
1996	The Cuddy - Lilliput Lane	Open		30.00	30
1991	Daisy Cottage	Open		37.50	30-40
1982	Dale Farm-Mold 1	Retrd.	1986	30.00	1300
1982	Dale Farm-Mold 2	Retrd.	1986	30.00	875
1986	Dale Head	Retrd.	1988	75.00	85-200
1982	Dale House	Retrd.	1986	25.00	840
1996	The Dalesman - Lilliput Lane	Open		95.00	95
1992	Derwent-le-Dale - Lilliput Lane	Open		75.00	55-80
1983	Dove Cottage-Mold 1	Retrd.	1984	35.00	725-1800
1984	Dove Cottage-Mold 2	Retrd.	1988	35.00	55-85
1991	Dovetails	Retrd.	1996	90.00	100
1982	Drapers-Mold 1	Retrd.	1983	15.95	5000
1982	Drapers-Mold 2	Retrd.	1983	15.95	4025
1995	Duckdown Cottage - Lilliput Lane	3/97		95.00	70-95
1994	Elm Cottage - Lilliput Lane	3/97		65.00	50-65
1985	Farriers	Retrd.	1990	40.00	55-85
1991	Farthing Lodge	Retrd.	1996	37.50	40
1996	Fiddlers Folly - Lilliput Lane	Open		35.00	35
1992	Finchingfields - Lilliput Lane	Retrd.	1995	82.50	95
1985	Fisherman's Cottage	Retrd.	1989	30.00	60
1989	Fiveways	Retrd.	1995	42.50	55
1991	The Flower Sellers	Retrd.	1996	110.00	110
1996	Flowerpots - Lilliput Lane	Open		55.00	55
1987	Four Seasons - M. Adkinson	Retrd.	1991	70.00	125
1993	Foxglove Fields - Lilliput Lane	3/97		130.00	85-130
1996	Fry Days - Lilliput Lane	Open		70.00	70
1996	Fuchsia Cottage - Lilliput Lane	Open		30.00	30
1987	The Gables - Lilliput Lane	Retrd.	1992	145.00	145
1996	Gossip Gate - Lilliput Lane	Open		170.00	170
1992	Granny Smiths	Retrd.	1996	60.00	45-65
1992	Grantchester Meadows - Lilliput Lane	Retrd.	1995	275.00	195-275
1989	Greensted Church	Retrd.	1995	72.50	95
1994	Gulliver's Gate - Lilliput Lane	Open		45.00	35-45
1996	Harriet's Cottage - Lilliput Lane	Open		85.00	85
1989	Helmere Cottage	Retrd.	1995	65.00	80-125
1992	High Ghyll Farm - Lilliput Lane	Open		360.00	250-395
1982	Holly Cottage	Retrd.	1988	42.50	85
1987	Holme Dyke	Retrd.	1990	50.00	65
1996	Honey Pot Cottage - Lilliput Lane	Open		60.00	60
1982	Honeysuckle Cottage	Retrd.	1987	45.00	200
1991	Hopcroft Cottage	Retrd.	1995	120.00	130
1987	Inglewood	Retrd.	1994	27.50	40
1987	Izaak Waltons Cottage	Retrd.	1989	75.00	80-125
1991	John Barleycorn Cottage	Retrd.	1995	130.00	140
1993	Junk and Disorderly - Lilliput Lane	Open		150.00	110-150
1987	Keepers Lodge	Retrd.	1988	75.00	75-120
1985	Kentish Oast	Retrd.	1990	55.00	75-125
1990	The King's Arms	Retrd.	1995	450.00	550
1991	Lace Lane	3/97		90.00	70-95
1995	Ladybird Cottage - Lilliput Lane	Open		40.00	35-40
1982	Lakeside House-Mold 1	Retrd.	1983	40.00	1500
1982	Lakeside House-Mold 2	Retrd.	1986	40.00	810-940
1991	Lapworth Lock	Retrd.	1993	82.50	85-100
1995	Larkrise - Lilliput Lane	Open		50.00	45-50
1995	Lazy Days - Lilliput Lane	Open		60.00	60
1994	Lenora's Secret - Lilliput Lane	2,500	1995	350.00	400-450
1995	Little Hay - Lilliput Lane	Open		55.00	50-55
1996	Little Lupins - Lilliput Lane	Open		40.00	40
1995	Little Smithy - Lilliput Lane	Open		65.00	60-65
1987	Loxdale Cottage - Lilliput Lane	Open		35.00	35
1987	Magpie Cottage	Retrd.	1990	70.00	100-115
1993	Marigold Meadow - Lilliput Lane	Open		120.00	80-120
1991	Micklegate Antiques	Open		90.00	80-95
1995	Milestone Cottage - Lilliput Lane	Open		40.00	35-40
1983	Millers	Retrd.	1986	15.00	120-150
1983	Miners-Mold 1	Retrd.	1985	15.00	590
1983	Miners-Mold 2	Retrd.	1985	15.00	400-500
1991	Moonlight Cove	Retrd.	1989	82.50	60-85
1985	Moreton Manor	Retrd.	1989	55.00	65-100
1990	Mrs. Pinkerton's Post Office	Open		72.50	70-85
1992	The Nutshell - Lilliput Lane	Open		75.00	80
1982	Oak Lodge-Mold 1	Retrd.	N/A	40.00	1000
1982	Oak Lodge-Mold 2	Retrd.	1987	40.00	65-100
1985	Oakwood Smithy	Open		450.00	300-475
1985	Old Curiosity Shop	Retrd.	1989	62.50	100-125
1982	Old Mine	Retrd.	1983	15.95	6500
1993	Old Mother Hubbard's - Lilliput Lane	Open		185.00	120-185
1982	The Old Post Office	Retrd.	1986	35.00	500
1984	Old School House	Retrd.	1985	25.00	1000-1400
1991	Old Shop at Bignor	Retrd.	1995	215.00	220
1991	Olde York Toll	Retrd.	1991	82.50	125
1994	Orchard Farm Cottage - Lilliput Lane	Open		145.00	110-145
1985	Ostlers Keep	Retrd.	1991	55.00	75
1990	Otter Reach	Retrd.	1996	33.50	30-45
1991	Paradise Lodge	Retrd.	1996	130.00	95-160
1988	Pargetters Retreat	Retrd.	1990	75.00	115
1991	Pear Tree House	Retrd.	1995	82.50	75
1990	Penny's Post - Lilliput Lane	Open		55.00	50-55
1990	Periwinkle Cottage	Retrd.	1996	165.00	165-220
1995	Pipit Toll - Lilliput Lane	Open		64.00	50-64
1990	Pixie House	Retrd.	1995	55.00	60
1996	Potter's Beck - Lilliput Lane	Open		35.00	35
1991	The Priest's House	Retrd.	1995	180.00	195-225
1992	Primrose Hill	Retrd.	1996	46.50	50
1992	Puffin Row	3/97		128.00	95-135
1993	Purbeck Stores - Lilliput Lane	Open		55.00	35-55
1996	Railway Cottage - Lilliput Lane	Open		60.00	60
1983	Red Lion Inn	Retrd.	1987	125.00	360
1988	Reflections of Jade - Lilliput Lane	3,950		350.00	350
1988	Rising Sun	Retrd.	1992	58.00	84-105
1987	Riverview	Retrd.	1994	27.50	35-55
1996	Robin's Gate	Open		33.50	50
1996	Rosemary Cottage - Lilliput Lane	Open		70.00	70
1988	Royal Oak	Retrd.	1991	145.00	150-300
1992	Runswick House	Open		62.50	55-80
1992	Rustic Root House	3/97		110.00	80-120
1995	The Rustlings - Lilliput Lane	Open		128.00	95-128
1987	Rydal View	Retrd.	1989	220.00	200
1987	Saddlers Inn - M. Adkinson	Retrd.	1989	50.00	75-125
1994	Saffron House - Lilliput Lane	Open		220.00	170-220
1985	Sawrey Gill	Retrd.	1992	30.00	125-200
1991	Saxham St. Edmunds	Retrd.		1550.00	1850
1986	Saxon Cottage	Retrd.	1989	245.00	200-400
1986	Scroll on the Wall	Retrd.	1987	55.00	150-175
1987	Secret Garden - M. Adkinson	Retrd.	1994	145.00	175-225
1987	Ship Inn - Lilliput Lane	Retrd.	1992	210.00	228-325
1988	Smallest Inn	Retrd.	1991	42.50	75-125
1996	Sore Paws - Lilliput Lane	Open		70.00	70
1996	The Spindles - Lilliput Lane	Open		85.00	85
1986	Spring Bank	Retrd.	1991	42.00	50-70
1994	Spring Gate Cottage - Lilliput Lane	3/97		130.00	95-130
1996	St. John the Baptist - Lilliput Lane	Open		75.00	75
1989	St. Lawrence Church	Open		110.00	85-140
1991	St. Marks	Retrd.	1991	75.00	150-225
1985	St. Mary's Church	Retrd.	1988	40.00	75-125
1991	St. Peter's Cove	Retrd.	1991	1375.00	1500-2000
1993	Stocklebeck Mill - Lilliput Lane	Open		325.00	195-325
1982	Stone Cottage-Mold 1	Retrd.	1983	40.00	1500
1982	Stone Cottage-Mold 2	Retrd.	1986	40.00	185
1982	Stone Cottage-Mold 3	Retrd.	1986	40.00	200
1987	Stoneybeck	Retrd.	1992	45.00	60-75
1993	Stradling Priory - Lilliput Lane	3/97		130.00	85-130
1996	Strawberry Cottage	Open		36.00	35-45
1987	Street Scene No. 1 - Unknown	Retrd.	1987	45.00	120
1987	Street Scene No. 2 - Unknown	Retrd.	1987	45.00	120
1987	Street Scene No. 3 - Unknown	Retrd.	1987	45.00	120
1987	Street Scene No. 4 - Unknown	Retrd.	1987	45.00	120
1987	Street Scene No. 5 - Unknown	Retrd.	1987	40.00	120
1987	Street Scene No. 6 - Unknown	Retrd.	1987	40.00	120
1987	Street Scene No. 7 - Unknown	Retrd.	1987	40.00	120
1987	Street Scene No. 8 - Unknown	Retrd.	1987	40.00	120
1987	Street Scene No. 9 - Unknown	Retrd.	1987	45.00	120
1987	Street Scene No. 99 - Unknown	Retrd.	1987	45.00	120
1987	Street Scene Set - Unknown	Retrd.	1987	425.00	800-1000
1990	Sulgrave Manor	Retrd.	1992	120.00	125-195
1987	Summer Haze	Retrd.	1993	90.00	110
1994	Sunnyside - Lilliput Lane	3/97		40.00	35-40
1982	Sussex Mill	Retrd.	1985	25.00	325-450
1988	Swan Inn	Retrd.	1992	120.00	175-225
1994	Sweet Pea Cottage - Lilliput Lane	3/97		40.00	35-40
1988	Swift Hollow	Open		75.00	90
1987	Tanglewood Lodge	Retrd.	1992	97.00	150-200
1987	Tanners Cottage	Retrd.	1992	27.50	45
1994	Teacaddy Cottage - Lilliput Lane	Open		79.00	60-79
1983	Thatcher's Rest	Retrd.	1988	185.00	250
1986	Three Feathers	Retrd.	1989	115.00	200-250
1987	Tillers Green	Open		60.00	65
1984	Tintagel	Retrd.	1988	39.50	110-170
1994	Tired Timbers - Lilliput Lane	Open		80.00	60-80
1996	Titmouse Cottage	Retrd.	1995	92.50	120
1993	Titwillow Cottage - Lilliput Lane	3/97		70.00	45-70
1983	Toll House	Retrd.	1985	15.00	75-165
1995	Tranquillity	2,500	1995	425.00	425
1983	Troutbeck Farm	Retrd.	1987	125.00	300
1983	Tuck Shop	Retrd.	1985	35.00	650-900
1986	Tudor Court - Lilliput Lane	Retrd.	1992	260.00	275-350
1994	Two Hoots - Lilliput Lane	3/97		75.00	55-75

YEAR ISSUE		EDITION LIMIT	YEAR RETD.	ISSUE PRICE	*QUOTE U.S. $
1989	Victoria Cottage	Retrd.	1993	52.50	80
1991	Village School	Retrd.	1996	120.00	85-130
1983	Warwick Hall-Mold 1	Retrd.	1983	185.00	3000-4000
1983	Warwick Hall-Mold 2	Retrd.	1985	185.00	1300-1800
1985	Watermill	Retrd.	1993	40.00	50-75
1994	Waterside Mill - Lilliput Lane	Open		65.00	50-65
1987	Wealden House	Retrd.	1990	125.00	140
1992	Wedding Bells - Lilliput Lane	Open		75.00	50-80
1991	Wellington Lodge	Retrd.	1995	55.00	60
1992	Wheyside Cottage - Lilliput Lane	Open		46.50	35-50
1989	Wight Cottage	Retrd.	1994	52.50	65
1982	William Shakespeare-Mold 1	Retrd.	1983	55.00	1500-3000
1983	William Shakespeare-Mold 2	Retrd.	1986	55.00	240
1986	William Shakespeare-Mold 3	Retrd.	1989	55.00	215
1989	William Shakespeare-Mold 4	Retrd.	1992	130.00	150
1996	Windy Ridge - Lilliput Lane	Open		50.00	50
1991	Witham Delph	Retrd.	1994	110.00	120
1987	Woodcutters	Retrd.	1987	15.00	140-300

English Tea Room Collection - Lilliput Lane

1995	Bargate Cottage Tea Room	Open		160.00	120-160
1995	Bo-Peep Tea Rooms	Open		120.00	85-120
1995	Grandma Batty's Tea Room	Open		120.00	90-120
1995	Kendal Tea House	Open		120.00	85-120
1995	New Forest Teas	Open		160.00	120-160
1996	Swalesdale Teas	Open		85.00	85

Founders Collection - Lilliput Lane

1996	The Almonry	Yr.Iss.		275.00	275

Framed English Plaques - D. Tate

1990	Ashdown Hall	Retrd.	1991	59.50	70
1990	Battleview	Retrd.	1991	59.50	70
1990	Cat Slide Cottage	Retrd.	1991	59.50	70
1990	Coombe Cot	Retrd.	1991	59.50	70
1990	Fell View	Retrd.	1991	59.50	70
1990	Flint Fields	Retrd.	1991	59.50	70
1990	Huntingdon House	Retrd.	1991	59.50	70
1990	Jubilee Lodge	Retrd.	1991	59.50	70
1990	Stowside	Retrd.	1991	59.50	70
1990	Trevan Cove	Retrd.	1991	59.50	70

Framed Irish Plaques - D. Tate

1990	Ballyteag House	Retrd.	1991	59.50	70
1990	Crockuna Croft	Retrd.	1991	59.50	70
1990	Pearses Cottages	Retrd.	1991	59.50	70
1990	Shannons Bank	Retrd.	1991	59.50	70

Framed Scottish Plaques - D. Tate

1990	Barra Black House	Retrd.	1991	59.50	70
1990	Fife Ness	Retrd.	1991	59.50	70
1990	Kyle Point	Retrd.	1991	59.50	70
1990	Preston Oat Mill	Retrd.	1991	59.50	70

French Collection - D. Tate

1991	L' Auberge d'Armorique	Open		220.00	170-250
1991	La Bergerie du Perigord	Open		230.00	170-250
1991	La Cabane du Gardian	Open		55.00	45-60
1991	La Chaumiere du Verger	Open		120.00	95-130
1991	La Maselle de Nadaillac	Open		130.00	95-140
1991	La Porte Schoenenberg	Open		75.00	60-85
1991	Le Manoir de Champfleuri	Open		265.00	215-295
1991	Le Mas du Vigneron	Open		120.00	85-130
1991	Le Petite Montmartre	Open		130.00	95-140
1991	Locmaria	Open		65.00	50-90

German Collection - D. Tate

1992	Alte Schmiede	Open		175.00	120-185
1987	Das Gebirgskirchlein	Open		120.00	120-140
1988	Das Rathaus	Open		140.00	140-160
1992	Der Bücherwurm	Open		140.00	100-160
1988	Der Familienschrein	Retrd.	1991	52.50	100
1988	Die Kleine Backerei	Retrd.	1994	68.00	80
1987	Haus Im Rheinland	Open		220.00	215-250
1987	Jaghutte	Open		82.50	83-95
1987	Meersburger Weinstube	Open		82.50	70-95
1987	Moselhaus	Open		140.00	140-160
1987	Nurnberger Burgerhaus	Open		140.00	140-160
1992	Rosengartenhaus	Open		120.00	90-130
1987	Schwarzwaldhaus	Open		140.00	120-160
1992	Strandvogthaus	Open		120.00	90-130

Historic Castles of England - Lilliput Lane

1994	Bodiam Castle	Open		129.00	95-129
1994	Castell Coch	Open		149.00	120-149
1995	Penkill Castles	Open		130.00	115-130
1994	Stokesay Castle	Open		99.00	85-99

Irish Cottages - D. Tate

1989	Ballykerne Croft	Retrd.	1996	75.00	70-75
1987	Donegal Cottage	Retrd.	1992	29.00	60
1989	Hegarty's Home	Retrd.	1992	68.00	75
1989	Kennedy Homestead	Retrd.	1996	33.50	30-45
1989	Kilmore Quay	Retrd.	1992	68.00	100
1989	Limerick House	Retrd.	1992	110.00	160-170
1989	Magilligan's	Retrd.	1996	33.50	30-45
1989	O'Lacey's Store	Retrd.	1996	68.00	60-85
1989	Pat Cohan's Bar	Retrd.	1996	110.00	85-140
1989	St. Columba's School	Retrd.	1992	72.50	120
1989	St. Kevin's Church	Retrd.	1996	47.50	40-60
1989	St. Kevin's Church	Retrd.	1996	55.00	55-70

YEAR ISSUE		EDITION LIMIT	YEAR RETD.	ISSUE PRICE	*QUOTE U.S. $
1989	St. Patrick's Church	Retrd.	1993	185.00	185
1989	Thoor Ballylee	Retrd.	1992	105.00	160-170

Lakeland Bridge Plaques - D. Simpson

1989	Aira Force	Retrd.	1991	35.00	35
1989	Ashness Bridge	Retrd.	1991	35.00	35
1989	Birks Bridge	Retrd.	1991	35.00	35
1989	Bridge House	Retrd.	1991	35.00	105-120
1989	Hartsop Packhorse	Retrd.	1991	35.00	35
1989	Stockley Bridge	Retrd.	1991	35.00	35

Lakeland Christmas - Lilliput Lane

1995	Langdale Cottage	Open		48.00	35-48
1995	Patterdale Cottage	Open		48.00	35-48
1995	Rydal Cottage	Open		44.75	35-45
1996	All Saints Watermillock	Open		50.00	50
1996	Borrowdale School	Open		35.00	35
1996	Millbeck Cottage	Open		35.00	35

London Plaques - D. Simpson

1989	Big Ben	Retrd.	1991	39.50	40
1989	Buckingham Palace	Retrd.	1991	39.50	40
1989	Piccadilly Circus	Retrd.	1991	39.50	40
1989	Tower Bridge	Retrd.	1991	39.50	40
1989	Tower of London	Retrd.	1991	39.50	40
1989	Trafalgar Square	Retrd.	1991	39.50	40

Ray Day/American Landmark Series - R. Day

1992	16.9 Cents Per Gallon	Open		150.00	95-150
1995	Afternoon Tea	1,995		495.00	495
1994	Birdsong	Open		120.00	85-120
1990	Country Church	Retrd.	1992	82.50	170
1989	Countryside Barn	Retrd.	1992	75.00	150-200
1990	Covered Memories	Retrd.	1993	110.00	200-300
1989	Falls Mill	Retrd.	1992	130.00	225-325
1991	Fire House 1	Open		87.50	85-140
1994	Fresh Bread	Open		150.00	95-150
1992	Gold Miners' Claim	3/97		110.00	95-120
1992	Gold Miners' Claim (no snow)	Retrd.	N/A	95.00	750
1990	Great Point Light	Open		39.50	45-55
1994	Harvest Mill	3,500		395.00	395
1994	Holy Night	Open		225.00	170-225
1992	Home Sweet Home	Open		120.00	95-130
1990	Hometown Depot	Retrd.	1993	68.00	100-125
1990	Mail Pouch Barn	Retrd.	1993	75.00	100-200
1990	Pepsi Cola Barn	Retrd.	1993	87.00	175-225
1990	Pioneer Barn	Retrd.	1991	30.00	75
1991	Rambling Rose	Retrd.	1995	60.00	100
1990	Riverside Chapel	Retrd.	1993	82.50	135-155
1990	Roadside Coolers	Retrd.	1994	75.00	110-145
1991	School Days	3/97		60.00	60-80
1993	See Rock City	Open		60.00	35-60
1993	Shave and A Haircut	3/97		160.00	95-160
1990	Sign Of The Times	Retrd.	1996	27.50	35
1993	Simply Amish	Open		160.00	110-160
1992	Small Town Library	Retrd.	1995	130.00	140
1994	Spring Victorian	Open		250.00	170-250
1991	Victoriana	Retrd.	1992	295.00	350-650
1992	Winnie's Place	Retrd.	1993	395.00	550-850

Ray Day/Christmas in America - R. Day

1996	Home For the Holidays	2,596		495.00	495

Ray Day/Coca Cola Country - R. Day

1996	A Cherry Coke...Just the Prescription	Open		95.00	95
1996	Country Fresh Pickins	Open		150.00	150
1996	Fill'er Up & Check the Oil	Open		125.00	125
1996	Hazards of the Road	Open		50.00	50
1996	Hook, Line & Sinker	Open		95.00	95
1997	Let the Good Times Roll	Open		N/A	N/A
1997	The Lunch Line	Open		N/A	N/A
1997	Mmmm...Just Like Home	Open		N/A	N/A
1997	Saturday Night Jive	Open		N/A	N/A
1996	We've Got it or They Don't Make it	Open		95.00	95
1997	Wet Your Whistle	Open		N/A	N/A

Ray Day/The Allegiance Collection - R. Day

1997	Home of the Brave	Open		N/A	N/A
1997	I Pledge Allegiance	Open		N/A	N/A
1997	In Remembrance	Open		N/A	N/A
1997	One Nation Under God	Open		N/A	N/A

Scottish Collection - D. Tate, unless otherwise noted

1985	7 St. Andrews Square - A. Yarrington	Retrd.	1986	15.95	85-120
1995	Amisfield Tower - Lilliput Lane	Open		55.00	50-55
1989	Blair Atholl	Retrd.	1992	275.00	375
1985	Burns Cottage	Retrd.	1988	35.00	70-95
1989	Carrick House	Open		47.50	35-60
1990	Cawdor Castle	3,000	1992	295.00	300-455
1989	Claypotts Castle	3/97		72.50	70-95
1989	Craigievar Castle	Retrd.	1991	185.00	300-525
1984	The Croft (renovated)	Retrd.	1991	36.00	65-100
1982	The Croft (without sheep)	Retrd.	1984	29.00	800-1250
1989	Culloden Cottage	Open		36.00	35-45
1992	Culross House	3/97		90.00	70-95
1992	Duart Castle	3,000		450.00	495
1987	East Neuk	Retrd.	1991	29.00	60-75
1993	Edzell Summer House - Lilliput Lane	3/97		110.00	70-110
1990	Eilean Donan	Open		145.00	145-185

YEAR ISSUE		EDITION LIMIT	YEAR RETD.	* QUOTE U.S. $	
1992	Eriskay Croft	Open		50.00	40-55
1990	Fishermans Bothy	Open		36.00	35-45
1990	Glenlochie Lodge	Retrd.	1993	110.00	120
1990	Hebridean Hame	Retrd.	1992	55.00	65-120
1989	Inverlochie Hame	Open		47.50	40-60
1989	John Knox House	Retrd.	1992	68.00	150-200
1989	Kenmore Cottage	Retrd.	1993	87.00	110
1990	Kinlochness	Retrd.	1993	79.00	85-125
1990	Kirkbrae Cottage	Retrd.	1993	55.00	70-95
1994	Ladybank Lodge - Lilliput Lane	Open		80.00	60-80
1992	Mair Haven	Open		46.50	35-50
1985	Preston Mill-Mold 1	Retrd.	1986	45.00	175-200
1986	Preston Mill-Mold 2	Retrd.	1992	62.50	78
1989	Stockwell Tenement	Retrd.	1996	62.50	63-80

Specials - Various

1985	Bermuda Cottage (3 Colors) - D. Tate	Retrd.	1991	29.00	40-50
1985	Bermuda Cottage (3 Colors)-set - D. Tate	Retrd.	1991	87.00	175-345
1983	Bridge House Dealer Sign - D. Tate	Retrd.	1984	N/A	375
1988	Chantry Chapel - D. Tate	Retrd.	1991	N/A	200-250
1983	Cliburn School - D. Tate	Retrd.	1984	Gift	6000-7000
1987	Clockmaker's Cottage - D. Tate	Retrd.	1990	40.00	200-235
1996	Cornflower Cottage	Retrd.	1996	N/A	N/A
1993	Counting House Corner (mounted) - Lilliput Lane	Retrd.	1993	N/A	N/A
1993	Counting House Corner - Lilliput Lane	3,093	1993	N/A	N/A
1987	Guildhall - D. Tate	Retrd.	1989	N/A	145
1996	Honeysuckle Plaque (with doves) - Lilliput Lane	Retrd.	1996	N/A	90
1996	Honeysuckle Plaque (without doves) - Lilliput Lane	12/96		N/A	N/A
1989	Mayflower House - D. Tate	Retrd.	1990	79.50	120-175
1991	Rose Cottage Skirsgill-Mold 1 - Lilliput Lane	200	1991	N/A	700
1991	Rose Cottage Skirsgill-Mold 2 - Lilliput Lane	Retrd.	1991	N/A	250-300
1994	Rose Cottage Skirsgill-Mold 3 - Lilliput Lane	Open		N/A	N/A
1991	Settler's Surprise - Lilliput Lane	Open		135.00	135
1986	Seven Dwarf's Cottage - D. Tate	Retrd.	1986	146.80	700-1100
1994	Wycombe Toll House - Lilliput Lane	Retrd.	1994	33.00	240-330

Studley Royal Collection - Lilliput Lane

1994	Banqueting House	5,000		65.00	65
1995	Fountains Abbey	3,500		395.00	395
1994	Octagon Tower	5,000		85.00	85
1994	St. Mary's Church	5,000		115.00	115
1994	Temple of Piety	5,000		95.00	95

Unframed Plaques - D. Tate

1989	Large Lower Brockhampton	Retrd.	1991	120.00	120
1989	Large Somerset Springtime	Retrd.	1991	130.00	130
1989	Medium Cobble Combe Cottage	Retrd.	1991	68.00	68
1989	Medium Wishing Well	Retrd.	1991	75.00	75
1989	Small Stoney Wall Lea	Retrd.	1991	47.50	48
1989	Small Woodside Farm	Retrd.	1991	47.50	48

Village Shop Collection - Various

1995	The Baker's Shop	Open		120.00	85-120
1995	The Chine Shop	Open		120.00	85-120
1992	The Greengrocers - D. Tate	Open		120.00	80-130
1993	Jones The Butcher	Open		120.00	80-120
1992	Penny Sweets	Open		130.00	80-130
1993	Toy Shop	Open		120.00	80-120

Welsh Collection - Various

1986	Brecon Bach - D. Tate	Retrd.	1993	42.00	55
1991	Bro Dawel - D. Tate	Open		37.50	30-40
1985	Hermitage - D. Tate	Retrd.	1986	30.00	175-300
1987	Hermitage Renovated - D. Tate	Retrd.	1990	42.50	100
1992	St. Govan's Chapel	Open		75.00	50-80
1991	Tudor Merchant - D. Tate	3/97		90.00	70-95
1991	Ugly House - D. Tate	Open		55.00	50-60

A Year In An English Garden - Lilliput Lane

1994	Autumn Hues	Open		120.00	85-120
1995	Spring Glory	Open		120.00	85-120
1995	Summer Impressions	Open		120.00	85-120
1994	Winter's Wonder	Open		120.00	85-120

Lladró

Lladró Collectors Society - Lladró

1985	Little Pals S7600	Closed	1985	95.00	2350-2800
1985	LCS Plaque w/blue writing S7601	Closed	N/A	35.00	75-125
1986	Little Traveler S7602	Closed	1986	95.00	1100-1600
1987	Spring Bouquets S7603	Closed	1987	125.00	625-900
1988	School Days S7604	Closed	1988	125.00	425-700
1988	Flower Song S7607	Closed	1988	175.00	525-625
1989	My Buddy S7609	Closed	1989	145.00	250-450
1990	Can I Play? S7610	Closed	1990	150.00	300-500
1991	Summer Stroll S7611	Closed	1992	195.00	300-400
1991	Picture Perfect S7612	Closed	1991	350.00	400-500
1992	All Aboard S7619	Closed	1992	165.00	250-350
1993	Best Friend S7620	Closed	1993	195.00	225-300
1994	Basket of Love S7622	Closed	1994	225.00	300-450
1995	10 Year Society Anniversary - Ten and Growing S7635	Closed	1995	395.00	425
1995	Afternoon Promenade S7636	Closed	1995	240.00	300

YEAR ISSUE		EDITION LIMIT	YEAR RETD.	ISSUE PRICE	*QUOTE U.S.$
1995	Now and Forever (10 year membership piece) S7642	N/A		395.00	395
1996	Innocence In Bloom S7644	Yr.Iss.		250.00	250
1996	Where Love Begins w/base 7649	4,000		895.00	895

Lladró Event Figurines - Lladró

YEAR ISSUE		EDITION LIMIT	YEAR RETD.	ISSUE PRICE	*QUOTE U.S.$
1991	Garden Classic L7617G	Closed	1991	295.00	400-700
1992	Garden Song L7618G	Closed	1992	295.00	300-500
1993	Pick of the Litter L7621G	Closed	1993	250.00	400-500
1994	Little Riders L7623	Closed	1994	250.00	300-350
1995	For A Perfect Performance L7641	Closed	1995	310.00	400-500
1995	Snow White Wishing Well L7558 (1995 Event)	Closed	1995	1500.00	1850
1996	Destination Big Top L6245	Closed	1996	225.00	225

Capricho - Lladró

YEAR ISSUE		EDITION LIMIT	YEAR RETD.	ISSUE PRICE	*QUOTE U.S.$
1988	Bust w/ Black Veil & base C1538	Open		650.00	975
1988	Small Bust w/ Veil & base C1539	Open		225.00	455
1987	Orchid Arrangement C1541	Closed	1987	500.00	1700-2100
1987	Iris Arrangement C1542	Closed	1990	800.00	1000-1500
1987	Fan C1546	Closed	1987	650.00	900-1600
1987	Fan C1546.3	Closed	1987	650.00	900-1600
1987	Iris with Vase C1551	Closed	1991	110.00	375
1987	Flowers Chest C1572	Open		550.00	900
1987	Flat Basket with Flowers C1575	Closed	1991	450.00	850
1989	White Rosary C1647	Closed	1991	290.00	360
1989	Romantic Lady / Black Veil w/base C1666	Closed	1993	420.00	520
1969	Frosted Angel w/Guitar C4507	Closed	1985	55.00	350
XX	White Bust w/ Veil & base C5927	Open		550.00	865
XX	Special Museum Flower Basket C7606	Closed	1991	N/A	450-750

Crystal Sculptures - Lladró

YEAR ISSUE		EDITION LIMIT	YEAR RETD.	ISSUE PRICE	*QUOTE U.S.$
1983	Frosted Bear, Head Up L04502	Closed	1983	200.00	350
1983	Frosted Bear, Head Down L04503	Closed	1983	205.00	350
1983	Frosted Bear, Head Up L04504	Closed	1983	210.00	350
1983	Frosted Bear, Head Straight L04506	Closed	1983	200.00	350
1983	Frosted Angel w/Guitar L04507	Closed	1983	166.00	375
1983	Frosted Angel w/Cymbal L04508	Closed	1983	165.00	375
1983	Frosted Angel w/Violin L04509	Closed	1983	165.00	375
1983	Frosted Geisha, Praying L04510	Closed	1983	135.00	375
1983	Frosted Geishaw/Fan L04511	Closed	1983	135.00	375
1983	Frosted Geishaw/Flowers L04512	Closed	1983	135.00	375
1983	Clear Bear, Head Straight L04513	Closed	1983	220.00	400
1983	Clear Bear, Head Up L04514	Closed	1983	230.00	400

Limited Edition - Lladró

YEAR ISSUE		EDITION LIMIT	YEAR RETD.	ISSUE PRICE	*QUOTE U.S.$
1971	Hamlet LL1144	750	1973	125.00	2800-4500
1971	Othello and Desdemona LL1145	750	1973	275.00	2500-3000
1971	Antique Auto LL1146	750	1975	1000.00	6000-10000
1971	Floral LL1184	200	1978	400.00	2200
1971	Floral LL1185	200	1974	475.00	1800
1971	Floral LL1186	200	1976	575.00	2200
1972	Eagles LL1189	750	1978	450.00	3200
1972	Sea Birds with Nest LL1194	500	1975	300.00	2750
1972	Turkey Group LL1196	350	1982	325.00	1800
1972	Peace LL1202	150	1973	550.00	7500
1972	Eagle Owl LL1223	750	1983	225.00	1050
1972	Hansom Carriage LL1225	750	1975	1450.00	8000-12000
1973	Buck Hunters LL1238	800	1976	400.00	3000
1973	Turtle Doves LL1240	850	1976	250.00	2300-2500
1973	The Forest LL1243	500	1976	625.00	3300
1974	Soccer Players LL1266	500	1983	1000.00	7500
1974	Man From LaMancha LL1269	1,500	1977	700.00	3800
1974	Queen Elizabeth II LL1275	250	1985	3650.00	5000
1974	Judge LL1281	1,200	1985	325.00	1250
1974	Partridge LL1290G	800	1974	700.00	1200-2000
1974	The Hunt LL1308	750	1984	4750.00	6900
1974	Ducks at Pond LL1317	1,200	1984	4250.00	5700
1976	Impossible Dream LL1318	1,000	1983	1200.00	4400
1976	Comforting Baby LL1329	750	1978	350.00	1050
1976	Mountain Country Lady LL1330	750	1983	900.00	1700
1976	My Baby LL1331	1,000	1981	275.00	900
1978	Flight of Gazelles LL1352	1,500	1984	1225.00	3100
1978	Car in Trouble LL1375	1,500	1987	3000.00	5250-6500
1978	Fearful Flight LL1377	750		7000.00	14500
1978	Henry VIII LL 1384	1,200	1990	650.00	1000-1250
1981	Venus and Cupid LL1392	750	1993	1100.00	1600-2100
1982	First Date w/base LL1393	1,500		3800.00	5900
1982	Columbus LL1432G	1,200	1988	535.00	1300-1700
1983	Venetian Serenade LL1433	750	1989	2600.00	3900
1985	Festival in Valencia w/base LL1457	3,000	1994	1400.00	2350
1985	Camelot LL1458	3,000	1994	950.00	1500
1985	Napoleon Planning Battle w/base LL1459	1,500	1995	825.00	1450
1985	Youthful Beauty w/base LL1461	5,000		750.00	1200
1985	Flock of Birds w/base LL1462	1,500		1060.00	1750
1985	Classic Spring LL1465	1,500	1995	620.00	975
1985	Classic Fall LL1466	1,500	1995	620.00	975
1985	Valencian Couple on Horse LL1472	3,000		885.00	1550
1985	Coach XVIII Century w/base LL1485	500		14000.00	26000
1986	The New World w/base LL1486	4,000		700.00	1350
1986	Fantasia w/base LL1487	5,000		1500.00	2700
1986	Floral Offering w/base LL1490	3,000		2500.00	4450
1986	Oriental Music w/base LL1491	5,000		1350.00	2445
1986	Three Sisters w/base LL1492	3,000		1850.00	3250
1986	At the Stroke of Twelve w/base LL1493	1,500	N/A	4250.00	6300-7500
1986	Hawaiian Festival w/base LL1496	4,000		1850.00	3200

YEAR ISSUE		EDITION LIMIT	YEAR RETD.	ISSUE PRICE	*QUOTE U.S.$
1987	A Sunday Drive w/base LL1510	1,000		3400.00	4000
1987	Listen to Don Quixote w/base LL1520	750		1800.00	2900
1987	A Happy Encounter LL1523	1,500		2900.00	4900
1988	Japanese Vase LL1536	750	1989	2600.00	3450-3750
1988	Garden Party w/base LL1578	500		5500.00	7250
1988	Blessed Lady w/base LL1579	1,000	1991	1150.00	3000
1988	Return to La Mancha w/base LL1580	500		6400.00	8350
1989	Southern Tea LL1597	1,000	1995	1775.00	2300
1989	Kitakami Cruise w/base LL1605	500	1994	5800.00	7500
1989	Mounted Warriors w/base LL1608	500		2850.00	3450
1989	Circus Parade w/base LL1609	1,000		5200.00	6550
1989	"Jesus the Rock" w/base LL1615	1,000		1175.00	1550
1989	Hopeful Group LL1723	1,000	1993	1825.00	1995
1991	Valencian Cruise LL1731	1,000		2700.00	2950
1991	Venice Vows LL1732	1,500		3755.00	4100
1991	Liberty Eagle LL1738	1,500		1000.00	1100
1991	Heavenly Swing LL1739	1,000		1900.00	2050
1991	Columbus, Two Routes LL1740	1,000	1995	1500.00	1650
1991	Columbus Reflecting LL1741	1,000	1994	1850.00	1995
1991	Onward! LL1742	1,000	1993	2500.00	2750-2950
1991	The Prophet LL1743	300		800.00	875
1991	My Only Friend LL1744	200	1993	1400.00	1700-2000
1991	Dawn LL1745	N/A	1993	1200.00	2500
1991	Champion LL1746	300		1800.00	1950
1991	Romantic Lady / Black Veil LL1747	300	1994	800.00	875
1991	Comforting News LL1748	300		1200.00	1325
1991	Baggy Pants LL1749	300	1994	1450.00	1650
1991	Circus Show LL1750	300	1994	1400.00	1525
1991	Maggie LL1751	300	1994	900.00	990
1991	Apple Seller LL1752	300	1994	900.00	1000-1150
1991	The Student LL1753	300		1300.00	1425
1991	Tree Climbers LL1754	300	1994	1500.00	1650
1991	The Princess And The Unicorn LL1755	1,500	1994	1750.00	1950
1992	Outing In Seville LL1756	500		23000.00	24500
1992	Hawaiian Ceremony LL1757	1,000		9800.00	10250
1992	Circus Time LL1758	2,500		9200.00	9650
1992	Tea In The Garden LL1759	2,000		9500.00	9750
1993	Paella Valenciano w/base LL1762	500		10000.00	10000
1993	Trusting Friends w/base LL1763	350		1200.00	1200
1993	He's My Brother w/base LL1764	350		1500.00	1500
1993	The Course of Adventure LL1765	250		1625.00	1625
1993	Ties That Bind LL1766	250		1700.00	1700
1993	Motherly Love LL1767	250		1330.00	1330
1993	Travellers' Respite w/base LL1768	250		1825.00	1825
1993	Fruitful Harvest LL1769	350		1300.00	1300
1993	Gypsy Dancers LL1770	250		2250.00	2400
1993	Country Doctor w/base LL1771	250		1475.00	1475
1993	Back To Back LL1772	350		1450.00	1450
1993	Mischevous Musician LL1773	350		975.00	1045
1993	A Treasured Moment w/base LL1774	350		950.00	950
1993	Oriental Garden w/base LL1775	750		22500.00	22500
1994	Conquered by Love w/base LL1776	2,500		2850.00	2890
1994	Farewell Of The Samurai w/base LL1777	2,500		3950.00	3950
1994	Pegasus w/base LL1778	1,500		1950.00	1950
1994	High Speed w/base LL1779	1,500		3830.00	3830
1994	Indian Princess w/base LL1780	3,000		1630.00	1630
1994	Allegory of Time LL1781	1,500		1290.00	1290
1994	Circus Fanfare w/base LL1783	1,500		14240.00	14240
1994	Flower Wagon w/base LL1784	3,000		3290.00	3290
1994	Cinderella's Arrival w/base LL1785	1,500		25950.00	25950
1994	Floral Figure w/base LL1788	300		2198.00	2198
1994	Natural Beauty LL1795	500		650.00	650
1994	Floral Enchantment w/base LL1796	300		2990.00	2990
1995	Enchanted Outing w/base LL1797	3,000		3950.00	3950
1995	Far Away Thoughts LL1798	1,500		3600.00	3600
1995	Immaculate Virgin w/base LL1799	2,000		2250.00	2250
1995	To the Rim w/base LL1800	1,500		2475.00	2475
1995	Vision of Peace w/base LL1803	1,500		1895.00	1895
1995	Portrait of a Family w/base LL1805	2,500		1750.00	1750
1995	A Family of Love w/base LL1806	2,500		1750.00	1750
1995	A Dream of Peace w/base LL1807	2,000		1160.00	1160
1996	Noah w/base LL1809	1,200		1720.00	1720
1996	Easter Fantasy w/base LL1810	1,000		3500.00	3500
1996	Moses & The Ten Commandments w/base LL1811	1,200		1860.00	1860
1996	La Menina w/base LL1812	1,000		3850.00	3850
1970	Girl with Guitar LL2016	750	1982	325.00	1800
1970	Madonna with Child LL2018	300	1974	450.00	1750
1971	Oriental Man LL2021	500	1983	500.00	1850
1971	Three Girls LL2028	500	1976	950.00	3500
1971	Eve at Tree LL2029	600	1974	450.00	3000
1971	Oriental Horse LL2030	350	1983	1100.00	3500-5000
1971	Lyric Muse LL2031	400	1982	750.00	2100
1973	Madonna and Child LL2043	300	1974	400.00	1500
1973	Peasant Woman LL2049	750	1977	200.00	1300
1973	Passionate Dance LL2051	500	1976	375.00	4500
1977	St. Theresa LL2061	1,200	1987	387.50	1400-1600
1977	Concerto LL2063	1,200	1988	500.00	1235
1977	Flying Partridges LL2064	1,200	1987	1750.00	4300
1987	Christopher Columbus w/base LL2176	1,000	1994	1000.00	1350
1990	Invincible w/base LL2188	300		1100.00	1250
1993	Flight of Fancy w/base LL2243	300		1400.00	1400
1993	The Awakening w/base LL2244	300		1000.00	1250
1993	Inspired Voyage w/base LL2245	1,000		4800.00	4800
1993	Days of Yore w/base LL2248	1,000		1950.00	2050
1993	Holiday Glow w/base LL2249	1,500		750.00	750
1993	Autumn Glow w/base LL2250	1,500		750.00	750

YEAR ISSUE		EDITION LIMIT	YEAR RETD.	ISSUE PRICE	*QUOTE U.S.$
1993	Humble Grace w/base LL2255	2,000		2150.00	2150
1983	Dawn w/base LL3000	300		325.00	550
1983	Monks w/base LL3001	300	1993	1675.00	2550
1983	Waiting w/base LL3002	125	1991	1550.00	1900
1983	Indolence LL3003	150		1465.00	2100
1983	Venus in the Bath LL3005	N/A	1991	1175.00	1450
1987	Classic Beauty w/base LL3012	100		1300.00	1750
1987	Youthful Innocence w/base LL3013	500		1300.00	1750
1987	The Nymph w/base LL3014	250		1000.00	1450
1987	Dignity w/base LL3015	150		1400.00	1900
1988	Passion w/base LL3016	750		865.00	1200
1988	Muse w/base LL3017	300	1993	650.00	875
1988	Cellist w/base LL3018	300	1993	650.00	875
1988	True Affection w/base LL3019	300		750.00	1025
1989	Demureness w/base LL3020	300	1994	400.00	700
1990	Daydreaming w/base LL3022	500		550.00	775
1990	After The Bath w/base LL3023	300	1991	350.00	1250
1990	Discoveries w/Base LL3024	100		1500.00	1750
1991	Resting Nude LL3025	200	1992	650.00	1000-1500
1991	Unadorned Beauty LL3026	200		1700.00	1850
1994	Ebony w/base LL3027	300		1295.00	1295
1994	Modesty w/base LL3028	300		1295.00	1295
1994	Danae LL3029	300		2880.00	2880
1995	Nude Kneeling LL3030	300		975.00	975
1982	Elk LL3501	500	1987	950.00	1200
1978	Nude with Dove LL3503	1,500	1981	250.00	700-1100
1981	The Rescue LL3504	1,500	1987	2900.00	5000
1978	St. Michael w/base LL3515	1,500		2200.00	4690
1980	Turtle Dove Nest w/base LL3519	1,200	1994	3600.00	6050
1980	Turtle Dove Group w/base LL3520	750		6800.00	11900
1981	Philippine Folklore LL3522	1,500	1995	1450.00	2400
1981	Nest of Eagles w/base LL3523	300	1994	6900.00	11500
1982	Drum Beats/Watusi Queen w/base LL3524	1,500	1994	1875.00	3050
1982	Togetherness LL3527	75	1987	375.00	900
1982	Wrestling LL3528	50	1987	950.00	1125
1983	Companionship w/base LL3529	65		1000.00	1790
1983	Anxiety w/base LL3530	125	1993	1075.00	1875
1983	Victory LL3531	90	1988	1500.00	1800
1983	Plentitude LL3532	50	1988	1000.00	1375
1983	The Observer w/base LL3533	115	1993	900.00	1650
1983	In the Distance LL3534	75	1988	525.00	1275
1983	Slave LL3535	50	1988	950.00	1150
1983	Relaxation LL3536	100	1988	525.00	1000
1983	Dreaming w/base LL3537	250	1994	475.00	1475
1983	Youth LL3538	250	1988	525.00	1000
1983	Dantiness LL3539	100	1988	1000.00	1400
1983	Pose LL3540	100	1988	1250.00	1450
1983	Tranquility LL3541	75	1988	1000.00	1400
1983	Yoga LL3542	125	1991	650.00	900
1983	Demure LL3543	100	1988	1250.00	1700
1983	Reflections w/base LL3544	75		650.00	1050
1983	Adoration LL3545	150	1990	1050.00	1600
1983	African Woman LL3546	50		1300.00	2000
1983	Reclining Nude LL3547	75	1988	650.00	875
1983	Serenity w/base LL3548	300	1993	925.00	1550
1983	Reposing LL3549	80	1988	425.00	575
1983	Boxer w/base LL3550	300	1993	850.00	1450
1983	Bather LL3551	300	1988	475.00	1300
1982	Blue God LL3552	1,500	1994	900.00	1575
1982	Fire Bird LL3553	1,500	1994	800.00	1350
1982	Desert People w/base LL3555	750		1680.00	3100
1982	Road to Mandalay LL3556	750	1989	1390.00	2500
1982	Jesus in Tiberias w/base LL3557	1,200		2600.00	4910
1992	The Reader LL3560	200		2650.00	2815
1993	Trail Boss LL3561M	1,500		2450.00	2595
1993	Indian Brave LL3562M	1,500		2250.00	2250
1994	Saint James The Apostle w/base LL3563	1,000		950.00	950
1994	Gentle Moment w/base LL3564	1,000		1795.00	1835
1994	At Peace w/base LL3565	1,000		1650.00	170
1994	Indian Chief w/base LL3566	3,000		1095.00	1095
1994	Trapper w/base LL3567	3,000		950.00	950
1994	American Cowboy w/base LL3568	3,000		950.00	950
1994	A Moment's Pause w/base LL3569	3,500		1495.00	1635
1994	Ethereal Music w/base LL3570	1,000		2450.00	2500
1994	At The Helm w/base LL3571	3,500		1495.00	1495
1995	Proud Warrior w/base LL3572	3,000		995.00	995
1995	Golgotha w/base LL3773	1,000		1650.00	1650
1996	Playing the Blues w/base LL3576	1,000		2160.00	2160
1985	Napoleon Bonaparte LL5338	5,000	1994	275.00	650
1985	Beethoven w/base LL5339	3,000	1993	760.00	1300
1985	Thoroughbred Horse w/base LL5340	1,000	1993	625.00	1000
1985	I Have Found Thee, Dulcinea LL5341	750	1990	1460.00	2800
1985	Pack of Hunting Dogs w/base LL5342	3,000	1994	925.00	2000
1985	Love Boat w/base LL5343	3,000		825.00	1350
1986	Fox Hunt w/base LL5362	1,000		5200.00	8750
1986	Rey De Copas w/base LL5366	2,000	1993	325.00	600
1986	Rey De Oros w/base LL5367	2,000	1993	325.00	600
1986	Rey De Espadas w/base LL5368	2,000	1993	325.00	600
1986	Rey De Bastos w/base LL5369	2,000	1993	325.00	600
1986	Pastoral Scene w/base LL5386	750	1995	1100.00	2290
1987	Inspiration LL5413	500	1993	1200.00	2100
1987	Carnival Time w/base LL5423	1,000	1993	2400.00	3900
1989	"Pious" LL5541	N/A	1991	1075.00	1550
1989	Freedom LL5602	1,500	1989	875.00	950
1990	A Ride In The Park LL5718	N/A	1994	3200.00	3500
1991	Youth LL5800	500	1993	650.00	725
1991	Charm LL5801	500	1994	650.00	725
1991	New World Medallion LL5808	5,000	1994	200.00	225

YEAR ISSUE	EDITION LIMIT	YEAR RETD.	ISSUE PRICE	*QUOTE U.S.$
1992 The Voyage of Columbus LL5847	7,500	1994	1450.00	1450-1650
1992 Sorrowful Mother LL5849	1,500		1750.00	1850
1992 Justice Eagle LL5863	1,500		1700.00	1840
1992 Maternal Joy LL5864	1,500		1600.00	1700
1992 Motoring In Style LL5884	1,500		3700.00	3850
1992 The Way Of The Cross LL5890	2,000		975.00	1050
1992 Presenting Credentials LL5911	1,500		19500.00	20500
1992 Young Mozart LL5915	2,500	1994	500.00	1250-1450
1993 Jester's Serenade w/base LL5932	3,000		1995.00	1995
1993 The Blessing w/base LL5942	2,000		1345.00	1345
1993 Our Lady of Rocio w/base LL5951	2,000		3500.00	3500
1993 Where to Sir w/base LL5952	1,500		5250.00	5250
1993 Discovery Mug LL5967	1,992	1994	90.00	90
1993 Graceful Moment w/base LL6033	3,000		1475.00	1475
1993 The Hand of Justice w/base LL6033	1,000		1250.00	1250
1995 Abraham Lincoln w/base LL7554	2,500		2190.00	2190
1996 Statue of Liberty w/base LL7563	2,000		1620.00	1620

Limited Edition Disneyana - Lladró

YEAR ISSUE	EDITION LIMIT	YEAR RETD.	ISSUE PRICE	*QUOTE U.S.$
1992 Tinkerbell LL7518	1,500	1992	350.00	2100-2600
1993 Peter Pan LL7529	3,000	1993	400.00	800-1250
1994 Cinderella and Fairy Godmother LL7553G	2,500	1994	875.00	600-780
1995 Sleeping Beauty Dance LL7560	1,000	1995	1280.00	1400-1600

Lladró - Lladró

YEAR ISSUE	EDITION LIMIT	YEAR RETD.	ISSUE PRICE	*QUOTE U.S.$
1963 Hunting Dog 308.13	Closed	N/A	N/A	2000
1966 Poodle 325.13	Closed	N/A	N/A	2300
1970 Girl with Pigtails L357.13G	Closed	N/A	N/A	1100
1969 Shepherdess with Goats L1001G	Closed	1987	80.00	675
1969 Shepherdess with Goats L1001M	Closed	1987	80.00	450
1969 Girl's Head L1003G	Closed	1985	150.00	675
1969 Girl's Head L1003M	Closed	1985	150.00	675-800
1969 Pan with Cymbals L1006	Closed	1975	45.00	450-550
1969 Pan with Pipes L1007	Closed	1975	45.00	475-600
1969 Girl With Lamb L1010G	Closed	1993	26.00	200-275
1969 Girl With Pig L1011G	Open		13.00	90
1969 Centaur Girl L1012M	Closed	1989	45.00	400
1969 Centaur Boy L1013M	Closed	1989	45.00	350-450
1969 Two Women w/Water Jugs L1014G	Closed	1985	85.00	650
1969 Dove L1015 G	Closed	1994	21.00	150
1969 Dove L1016 G	Closed	1995	36.00	190
1969 Idyl L1017G	Closed	1991	115.00	700
1969 Idyl L1017M	Closed	1991	115.00	550-615
1969 King Gaspar L1018M	Open		345.00	1895
1969 King Melchior L1019M	Open		345.00	1850
1969 King Baltasar L1020M	Open		345.00	1850
1969 Horse Group L1021G	Closed	1975	950.00	1600
1969 Horse Group/All White L1022M	Open		465.00	2100
1969 Flute Player L1025G	Closed	1978	73.00	750
1969 Clown with Concertina L1027G	Closed	1993	95.00	700
1969 Girl w/Heart L1028G	Closed	1970	37.50	650
1969 Boy w/Bowler L1029G	Closed	1970	37.50	550
1969 Don Quixote w/Stand L1030G	Open		225.00	1450
1969 Sancho Panza L1031G	Closed	1989	65.00	575
1969 Old Folks L1033G	Closed	1985	140.00	1400-1600
1969 Old Folks L1033M	Closed	1985	140.00	1400
1969 Shepherdess with Dog L1034	Closed	1991	30.00	225-275
1969 Girl with Geese L1035G	Closed	1995	37.50	180
1969 Girl With Geese L1035M	Closed	1992	37.50	165
1969 Horseman L1037G	Closed	1970	170.00	2500
1969 Girl with Turkeys L1038G	Closed	1978	95.00	400-550
1969 Violinist and Girl L1039G	Closed	1991	120.00	900-1100
1969 Violinist and Girl L1039M	Closed	1991	120.00	825-1000
1969 Hunters L1048	Closed	1986	115.00	1200-1400
1969 Del Monte (Boy) L1050	Closed	1978	65.00	N/A
1969 Girl with Duck L1052G	Open		30.00	205
1969 Girl with Duck L1052M	Closed	1992	30.00	190
1969 Bird L1053G	Closed	1985	13.00	100
1969 Bird L1054G	Closed	1985	14.00	125
1969 Duck L1056G	Closed	1978	19.00	275
1969 Girl with Pheasant L1055G	Closed	1978	105.00	N/A
1969 Panchito L1059	Closed	1980	28.00	N/A
1969 Bull w/Head Up L1063	Closed	1975	90.00	1100
1969 Deer L1064	Closed	1986	27.50	325
1969 Fox and Cub L1065G	Closed	1985	17.50	400-475
1969 Basset L1066G	Closed	1981	23.50	600
1969 Old dog L1067G	Closed	1978	40.00	600
1969 Great Dane L1068G	Closed	1989	55.00	500
1969 Afghan (sitting) L1069G	Closed	1985	36.00	625
1969 Beagle Puppy L1070G	Closed	1991	16.50	225-350
1969 Beagle Puppy L1071G	Closed	1992	16.50	225-350
1969 Beagle Puppy L1071M	Closed	1992	16.50	200-250
1969 Beagle Puppy L1072G	Closed	1991	16.50	225-300
1969 Dutch Girl L1077G	Closed	1981	57.50	250-450
1969 Herald L1078G	Closed	1970	110.00	1100
1969 Girl With Brush L1081G	Closed	1985	14.50	200-300
1969 Girl Manicuring L1082G	Closed	1985	14.50	200-300
1969 Girl With Doll L1083G	Closed	1985	14.50	200-300
1969 Girl with Mother's Shoe L1084G	Closed	1985	14.50	200-300
1969 Little Green-Grocer L1087G	Closed	1981	40.00	375
1969 Girl Seated with Flowers L1088G	Closed	1989	45.00	700
1971 Lawyer (Face) L1089G	Closed	1973	35.00	950
1971 Girl and Gazelle L1091G	Closed	1975	225.00	1200
1971 Satyr with Snail L1092G	Closed	1975	30.00	425
1969 Beggar L1094G	Closed	1985	65.00	400-650
1971 Girl With Hens L1103G	Closed	1981	50.00	375
1971 La Tarantela L1123G	Closed	1975	550.00	2250
1971 Pelusa (Clown) L1125G	Closed	1978	70.00	875-1150
1971 Clown with Violin L1126G	Closed	1978	71.00	1850
1971 Puppy Love L1127G	Open		50.00	310

YEAR ISSUE	EDITION LIMIT	YEAR RETD.	ISSUE PRICE	*QUOTE U.S.$
1971 Dog in the Basket L1128G	Closed	1985	17.50	450
1971 Faun L1131G	Closed	1972	155.00	1200
1971 Horse L1133G	Closed	1972	115.00	900
1971 Bull L1134G	Closed	1972	130.00	1500
1971 Dog and Snail L1139G	Closed	1981	40.00	450
1971 Girl with Bonnet L1147G	Closed	1985	20.00	275
1971 Girl Shampooing L1148G	Closed	1985	20.00	200-300
1971 Dog's Head L1149G	Closed	1981	27.50	450
1971 Elephants (3) L1150G	Open		100.00	795
1971 Elephants (2) L1151G	Open		45.00	400
1971 Dog Playing Guitar L1152G	Closed	1978	32.50	375-550
1971 Dog Playing Guitar L1153G	Closed	1978	32.50	400-550
1971 Dog Playing Bass Fiddle L1154G	Closed	1978	36.50	400-550
1971 Dog w/Microphone L1155G	Closed	1978	35.00	400-550
1971 Dog Playing Bongos L1156	Closed	1978	32.50	400-550
1971 Seated Torero L1162G	Closed	1973	35.00	700
1971 Kissing Doves L1169G	Open		32.00	145
1971 Kissing Doves L1169M	Closed	N/A	32.00	150
1971 Kissing Doves L1170G	Closed	1988	25.00	250
1971 Girl With Flowers L1172G	Closed	1993	27.00	350
1971 Girl With Domino L1175G	Closed	1981	34.00	350
1971 Girl With Dice L1176G	Closed	1981	25.00	350
1971 Girl With Ball L1177G	Closed	1981	27.50	350-450
1971 Girl With Accordian L1178G	Closed	1981	34.00	350-450
1971 Clown on Domino L1179G	Closed	1981	34.00	375
1971 Little Girl w/Turkeys L1180G	Closed	1981	55.00	450
1971 Platero and Marcelino L1181G	Closed	1985	50.00	350-450
1972 Little Girl with Cat L1187G	Closed	1989	37.00	250-375
1972 Boy Meets Girl L1188G	Closed	1989	310.00	400
1972 Eskimo L1195G	Open		30.00	135
1972 Horse Resting L1203G	Closed	1981	40.00	400-550
1972 Attentive Bear, brown L1204G	Closed	1989	16.00	125
1972 Good Bear, brown L1205G	Closed	1989	16.00	120
1972 Bear Seated, brown L1206G	Closed	1989	16.00	100-125
1972 Attentive Polar Bear, white L1207G	Open		16.00	75
1972 Bear, white L1208G	Open		16.00	75
1972 Bear, white L1209G	Open		16.00	75
1972 Round Fish L1210G	Closed	1981	35.00	450
1972 Girl With Doll L1211G	Closed	1993	72.00	440
1972 Woman Carrying Water L1212G	Closed	1983	100.00	475
1972 Little Jug Magno L1222.3G	Closed	1979	35.00	300
1972 Young Harlequin L1229G	Open		70.00	520
1972 Young Harlequin L1229M	Closed	1991	70.00	550
1972 Friendship L1230G	Closed	1991	68.00	475
1972 Friendship L1230M	Closed	1991	68.00	325
1972 Angel with Lute L1231G	Closed	1988	60.00	425
1972 Angel with Clarinet L1232G	Closed	1988	60.00	400
1972 Angel with Flute L1233G	Closed	1988	60.00	400-450
1972 Little Jesus of Prag L1234G	Closed	1978	70.00	725
1973 Christmas Carols L1239G	Closed	1981	125.00	750
1973 Fluttering Nightingale L1244G	Closed	1981	44.00	375
1973 Girl with Wheelbarrow L1245G	Closed	1981	75.00	500-650
1972 Caress and Rest L1246G	Closed	1990	50.00	300
1974 Happy Harlequin L1247M	Closed	1983	220.00	1100
1974 Honey Lickers L1248G	Closed	1990	100.00	500
1974 The Race L1249G	Closed	1983	450.00	1800-2250
1974 Lovers from Verona L 1250G	Closed	1990	330.00	1300-1600
1974 Pony Ride L1251G	Closed	1979	220.00	1200
1974 Shepherd L1252G	Closed	1981	100.00	N/A
1974 Sad Chimney Sweep L1253G	Closed	1983	180.00	1200
1974 Hamlet and Yorick L1254G	Closed	1983	325.00	1100-1200
1974 Seesaw L1255G	Closed	1993	110.00	575
1974 Mother with Pups L1257G	Closed	1981	50.00	800
1974 Playing Poodles L1258G	Closed	1981	47.50	800
1974 Poodle L1259G	Closed	1985	27.50	400
1974 Flying Duck L1263G	Open		20.00	90
1974 Flying Duck L1264G	Open		20.00	90
1974 Flying Duck L1265G	Open		20.00	90
1974 Girl with Ducks L1267G	Closed	1993	55.00	300
1974 Reminiscing L1270G	Closed	1988	975.00	1375
1974 Thoughts L1272G	Open		87.50	3490
1974 Lovers in the Park L1274G	Closed	1993	450.00	1365
1974 Christmas Seller L1276G	Closed	1981	120.00	675
1974 Feeding Time L1277G	Closed	1993	120.00	350
1974 Feeding Time L1277M	Closed	N/A	120.00	415
1974 Devotion L1278G	Closed	1990	140.00	475
1974 The Wind L1279M	Open		250.00	250
1974 Playtime L1280G	Closed	1983	110.00	550-700
1974 Afghan Standing L1282G	Closed	1985	45.00	450
1974 Little Gardener L1283G	Open		250.00	785
1974 "My Flowers" L1284G	Open		200.00	550
1974 "My Goodness" L1285G	Closed	1995	190.00	415
1974 Flower Harvest L1286G	Open		200.00	495
1974 Picking Flowers L1287G	Open		170.00	440
1974 Aggressive Duck L1288G	Closed	1995	170.00	475
1974 Good Puppy L1289G	Closed	1985	16.60	225
1974 Victorian Girl on Swing L1297G	Closed	1990	520.00	1650
1974 Birds Resting L1298G	Closed	1985	235.00	975
1974 Birds in Nest L1299G	Closed	1985	120.00	750
1974 Valencian Lady with Flowers L1304G	Open		200.00	625
1974 "On the Farm" L1306G	Closed	1990	130.00	240
1974 Ducklings L1307G	Open		47.50	150
1974 Girl with Cats L1309G	Open		120.00	310
1974 Girl w/Puppies in Basket L1311G	Open		120.00	345
1974 Scotland L1313G	Closed	1990	201.00	650
1974 Girl From Scotland L1315G	Closed	1979	450.00	2800
1976 Collie L1316G	Closed	1981	45.00	400
1976 IBIS L1319G	Open		1550.00	2625
1977 Angel with Tamborine L1320G	Closed	1985	125.00	350-450
1977 Angel with Lyre L1321G	Closed	1985	125.00	475

YEAR ISSUE	EDITION LIMIT	YEAR RETD.	ISSUE PRICE	*QUOTE U.S.$
1977 Angel with Song L1322G	Closed	1985	125.00	475
1977 Angel with Accordian L1323G	Closed	1985	125.00	400
1977 Angel with Mandolin L1324G	Closed	1985	125.00	400
1976 The Helmsman L1325M	Closed	1988	600.00	900-1200
1976 Playing Cards L1327 M, numbered series	Open		3800.00	6600
1977 Dove Group L1335G	Closed	1990	950.00	1600
1977 Blooming Roses L1339G	Closed	1988	325.00	550
1977 Male Jockey L1341G	Closed	1979	120.00	450
1977 Wrath of Don Quixote L1343G	Closed	1990	520.00	990
1977 Derby L1344G	Closed	1985	1125.00	2500
1978 Sacristan L1345G	Closed	1979	385.00	2300
1978 Under the Willow L1346G	Closed	1990	1600.00	2150
1978 Mermaid on Wave L1347G	Closed	1983	425.00	1800
1978 Pearl Mermaid L1348G	Closed	1983	225.00	1850
1978 Mermaids Playing L1349G	Closed	1983	425.00	3250
1978 In the Gondola L1350G, numbered series	Open		1850.00	3250
1978 Lady with Girl L1353G	Closed	1985	175.00	700
1978 Growing Roses L1354G	Closed	1988	485.00	635
1978 Phyllis L1356G	Closed	1993	75.00	225
1978 Shelley L1357G	Closed	1993	75.00	225
1978 Beth L1358G	Closed	1993	75.00	225
1978 Heather L1359G	Closed	1993	75.00	225
1978 Laura L1360G	Closed	1993	75.00	225
1978 Julia L1361G	Closed	1993	75.00	185
1978 Swinging L1366G	Closed	1988	825.00	1375
1978 Playful Dogs L1367	Closed	1982	160.00	700
1978 Spring Birds L1368G	Closed	1990	1600.00	2500
1978 Anniversary Waltz L1372G	Open		260.00	570
1978 Chestnut Seller L1373G	Closed	1981	800.00	750-900
1978 Waiting in the Park L1374G	Closed	1993	235.00	450
1978 Watering Flowers L1376G	Closed	1990	400.00	1150
1978 Suzy and Her Doll L1378G	Closed	1985	215.00	625
1978 Debbie and Her Doll L1379G	Closed	1985	215.00	600
1978 Cathy and Her Doll L1380G	Closed	1985	215.00	650
1978 Medieval Girl L1381G	Closed	1985	11.80	400-600
1978 Medieval Boy L1382G	Closed	1985	235.00	650-700
1978 A Rickshaw Ride L1383G	Open		1500.00	2150
1978 The Brave Knight L1385G	Closed	1988	350.00	750
1981 St. Joseph L1386G	Open		250.00	385
1981 Mary L1387G	Open		240.00	385
1981 Baby Jesus L1388G	Open		85.00	140
1981 Donkey L1389G	Open		95.00	190
1981 Cow L1390G	Open		95.00	190
1982 Holy Mary L1394G, numbered series	Open		1000.00	1475
1982 Full of Mischief L1395G	Open		420.00	825
1982 Appreciation L1396G	Open		420.00	825
1982 Second Thoughts L1397G	Open		420.00	820
1982 Reverie L1398G	Open		490.00	970
1982 Dutch Woman w/Tulips L1399G	Closed	1988	750.00	750
1982 Valencian Boy L1400G	Closed	1988	298.00	600
1982 Sleeping Nymph L1401G	Closed	1988	210.00	500-600
1982 Daydreaming Nymph L1402G	Closed	1988	210.00	550
1982 Pondering Nymph L1403G	Closed	1988	210.00	550
1982 Matrimony L1404G	Open		320.00	585
1982 Illusion L1413G	Open		115.00	260
1982 Fantasy L1414G	Open		115.00	260
1982 Mirage L1415G	Open		115.00	260
1982 From My Garden L1416G	Open		140.00	295
1982 Nature's Bounty L1417G	Closed	1995	160.00	340
1982 Flower Harmony L1418G	Closed	1995	130.00	270
1982 A Barrow of Blossoms L1419G	Open		390.00	675
1982 Born Free w/base L1420G	Open		1520.00	3140
1982 Mariko w/base L1421G	Closed	1995	860.00	1575
1982 Miss Valencia L1422G	Open		175.00	395
1982 King Melchior L1423G	Open		225.00	440
1982 King Gaspar L1424G	Open		265.00	475
1982 King Balthasar L1425G	Open		315.00	585
1982 Male Tennis Player L1426M	Closed	1988	200.00	350
1982 Female Tennis Player L1427M	Closed	1988	200.00	350
1982 Afternoon Tea L1428G	Open		115.00	275
1982 Afternoon Tea L1428M	Open		115.00	275
1982 Winter Wonderland w/base L1429G	Open		1025.00	2125
1982 High Society L1430G	Closed	1993	305.00	750
1982 The Debutante L1431G	Open		115.00	275
1982 The Debutante L1431M	Open		115.00	275
1983 Vows L1434G	Closed	1991	600.00	900
1983 Blue Moon L1435G	Closed	1988	98.00	350
1983 Moon Glow L1436G	Closed	1988	98.00	400
1983 Moon Light L1437G	Closed	1988	98.00	400-550
1983 Full Moon L1438G	Closed	1988	115.00	675
1983 "How Do You Do!" L1439G	Open		185.00	295
1983 Pleasantries L1440G	Closed	1991	960.00	1900
1983 A Litter of Love L1441G	Open		385.00	645
1983 Kitty Confrontation L1442G	Open		155.00	285
1983 Bearly Love L1443G	Open		55.00	120
1983 Purr-Fect L1444G	Open		350.00	615
1983 Springtime in Japan L1445G	Open		965.00	1800
1983 "Here Comes the Bride" L1446G	Open		518.00	995
1983 Michiko L1447G	Open		235.00	460
1983 Yuki L1448G	Open		285.00	550
1983 Mayumi L1449G	Open		235.00	495
1983 Kiyoko L1450G	Open		235.00	495
1983 Teruko L1451G	Open		235.00	495
1983 On the Town L1452G	Closed	1993	220.00	475
1983 Golfing Couple L1453G	Open		248.00	530
1983 Flowers of the Season L1454G	Open		1460.00	2550
1983 Reflections of Hamlet L1455G	Closed	1988	1000.00	1600
1983 Cranes w/base L1456G	Open		1000.00	1950
1985 A Boy and His Pony L1460G	Closed	1988	285.00	800

*Quotes have been rounded up to nearest dollar

YEAR ISSUE		EDITION LIMIT	YEAR RETD.	ISSUE PRICE	*QUOTE U.S.$
1985	Carefree Angel w/Flute L1463G	Closed	1988	220.00	650
1985	Carefree Angel w/Lyre L1464G	Closed	1988	220.00	650
1985	Girl on Carousel Horse L1469G	Open		470.00	935
1985	Boy on Carousel Horse L1470G	Open		470.00	935
1985	Wishing On A Star L1475G	Closed	1988	130.00	375-500
1985	Star Light Star Bright L1476G	Closed	1988	130.00	400
1985	Star Gazing L1477G	Closed	1988	130.00	400
1985	Hawaiian Dancer/Aloha! L1478G	Open		230.00	440
1985	In a Tropical Garden L1479G	Closed	1995	230.00	440
1985	Aroma of the Islands L1480G	Open		260.00	480
1985	Sunning L1481G	Closed	1988	145.00	575
1985	Eve L1482	Closed	1988	145.00	700
1985	Free As a Butterfly L1483G	Closed	1988	145.00	550
1986	Lady of the East w/base L1488G	Closed	1993	625.00	1100
1986	Valencian Children L1489G	Open		700.00	1225
1986	My Wedding Day L1494G	Open		800.00	1495
1986	A Lady of Taste L1495G	Open		575.00	1025
1986	Don Quixote & The Windmill L1497G	Open		1100.00	2050
1986	Tahitian Dancing Girls L1498G	Closed	1995	750.00	1500
1986	Blessed Family L1499G	Open		200.00	395
1986	Ragamuffin L1500G	Closed	1991	125.00	350
1986	Ragamuffin L1500M	Closed	1991	125.00	300
1986	Rag Doll L1501G	Closed	1991	125.00	250-300
1986	Rag Doll L1501M	Closed	1991	125.00	300
1986	Forgotten L1502G	Closed	1991	125.00	300
1986	Forgotten L1502M	Closed	1991	125.00	300
1986	Neglected L1503G	Closed	1991	125.00	375-450
1986	Neglected L1503M	Closed	1991	125.00	300
1986	The Reception L1504G	Closed	1990	625.00	1050
1986	Nature Boy L1505G	Closed	1991	100.00	275
1986	Nature Boy L1505M	Closed	1991	100.00	N/A
1986	A New Friend L1506G	Closed	1991	110.00	275-325
1986	A New Friend L1506M	Closed	1991	110.00	260
1986	Boy & His Bunny L1507G	Closed	1991	90.00	275
1986	Boy & His Bunny L1507M	Closed	1991	90.00	N/A
1986	In the Meadow L1508G	Closed	1991	100.00	300
1986	In the Meadow L1508M	Closed	1991	100.00	285
1986	Spring Flowers L1509G	Closed	1991	100.00	300
1986	Spring Flowers L1509M	Closed	1991	100.00	285
1987	Cafe De Paris L1511G	Closed	1995	1900.00	2950
1987	Hawaiian Beauty L1512G	Closed	1990	575.00	1000
1987	A Flower for My Lady L1513G	Closed	1990	1150.00	1750
1987	Gaspar 's Page L1514G	Closed	1990	275.00	300-500
1987	Melchior's Page L1515G	Closed	1990	290.00	650
1987	Balthasar's Page L1516G	Closed	1990	275.00	900-950
1987	Circus Train L1517G	Closed	1994	2900.00	4350
1987	Valencian Garden L1518G	Closed	1991	1100.00	1795
1987	Stroll in the Park L1519G	Open		1600.00	2600
1987	The Landau Carriage L1521G	Open		2500.00	3850
1987	I am Don Quixote! L1522G	Open		2600.00	3950
1987	Valencian Bouquet L1524G	Closed	1991	250.00	400
1987	Valencian Dreams L1525G	Closed	1991	240.00	300-400
1987	Valencian Flowers L1526G	Closed	1991	375.00	550
1987	Tenderness L1527G	Open		260.00	430
1987	I Love You Truly L1528G	Open		375.00	595
1987	Momi L1529G	Closed	1990	275.00	500
1987	Leilani L1530G	Closed	1990	275.00	550
1987	Malia L1531G	Closed	1990	275.00	500
1987	Lehua L1532G	Closed	1990	275.00	600
1987	Not So Fast! L1533G	Open		175.00	265
1988	Little Sister L1534G	Open		180.00	240
1988	Sweet Dreams L1535G	Open		150.00	220
1988	Stepping Out L1537G	Open		230.00	325
1988	Pink Ballet Slippers L1540	Closed	1991	275.00	450-475
1988	White Ballet Slippers L1540.3	Closed	1991	275.00	395
1987	Light Blue Spoon L1548G	Closed	1991	70.00	150
1987	Dark Blue Spoon L1548.1	Closed	1991	70.00	150
1987	White Spoon L1548.3	Closed	1991	70.00	150
1987	Wild Stallions w/base L1566G	Closed	1993	1100.00	1465
1987	Running Free w/base L1567G	Open		1500.00	1600
1987	Grand Dame L1568G	Open		290.00	425
1989	Fluttering Crane L1598G	Open		115.00	145
1989	Nesting Crane L1599G	Open		95.00	115
1989	Landing Crane L1600G	Open		115.00	145
1989	Rock Nymph L1601G	Closed	1995	665.00	795
1989	Spring Nymph L1602G	Closed	1995	665.00	825
1989	Latest Addition L1606G	Open		385.00	480
1989	Flight Into Egypt w/base L1610G	Open		885.00	1150
1989	Courting Cranes L1611G	Open		565.00	695
1989	Preening Crane L1612G	Open		385.00	485
1989	Bowing Crane L1613G	Open		385.00	485
1989	Dancing Crane L1614G	Open		385.00	485
1989	Snow Queen Mask No.11 L1645G	Closed	1991	390.00	250
1989	Medieval Cross No.4 L1652G	Closed	1991	250.00	250
1989	Lavender Lady L1667M	Closed	1991	385.00	550
1989	Lacy Butterfly #1 L1673M	Closed	1991	95.00	150
1989	Beautiful Butterfly #2 L1674M	Closed	1991	100.00	160
1989	Black Butterfly #3 L1675M	Closed	1991	120.00	185
1989	Pink & White Butterfly #4 L1676M	Closed	1991	100.00	175
1989	Black & White Butterfly #5 L1677M	Closed	1991	100.00	175
1989	Large Pink Butterfly #6 L1678M	Closed	1991	100.00	175
1989	Pink & Blue Butterfly #7 L1679M	Closed	1991	80.00	140
1989	Small Pink Butterfly #8 L1680M	Closed	1991	72.50	125
1989	Blue Butterfly #9 L1681M	Closed	1991	185.00	275
1989	Pretty Butterfly #10 L1682M	Closed	1991	185.00	275
1989	Spotted Butterfly #11 L1683M	Closed	1991	175.00	260
1989	Leopard Butterfly #12 L1684M	Closed	1991	165.00	250
1989	Great Butterfly #13 L1685M	Closed	1991	150.00	225
1989	Queen Butterfly #14 L1686M	Closed	1991	125.00	200
1988	Cellist L1700M	Closed	1993	1200.00	1750
1988	Saxophone Player L1701M	Closed	1993	835.00	1840
1988	Boy at the Fair (Decorated) L1708M	Closed	1993	650.00	650
1988	Exodus L1709M	Closed	1993	875.00	875
1988	School Boy L1710M	Closed	1993	750.00	750
1988	School Girl L1711M	Closed	1993	950.00	950
1988	Nanny L1714M	Closed	1993	575.00	700
1988	On Our Way Home (decorated) L1715M	Closed	1993	2000.00	2000
1988	Harlequin with Puppy L1716M	Closed	1993	825.00	1000
1988	Harlequin with Dove L1717M	Closed	1993	900.00	1000
1988	Dress Rehearsal L1718M	Closed	1993	1150.00	1150
1989	Back From the Fair L1719M	Closed	1993	1825.00	1825
1990	Sprite w/base L1720G, numbered series	Open		1200.00	1400
1990	Leprechaun w/base L1721G, numbered series	Open		1200.00	1395
1989	Group Discussion L1722M	Closed	1993	1500.00	1500
1989	Hopeful Group L1723M	Closed	1993	1825.00	1825
1989	Belle Epoque L1724M	Closed	1993	700.00	700
1989	Young Lady w/Parasol L1725M	Closed	1993	950.00	950
1989	Young Lady with Fan L1726M	Closed	1993	750.00	750
1989	Pose L1727M	Closed	1993	725.00	725
1991	Nativity L1730M	Open		725.00	725
1970	Cat L2001G	Closed	1975	27.50	375
1970	Gothic King L2002G	Closed	1975	25.00	450
1970	Gothic Queen L2003G	Closed	1975	25.00	450
1970	Shepherdess with Lamb L2005M	Closed	1981	100.00	710
1970	Water Carrier Girl Lamp L2006M	Closed	1975	30.00	600
1971	Girl with Dog L2013M	Closed	1975	300.00	2200
1971	Little Eagle Owl L2020M	Closed	1985	15.00	425
1971	Boy/Girl Eskimo L2038.3M	Closed	N/A	100.00	275-455
1974	Setter's Head L2045M	Closed	1981	42.50	550
1974	Magistrates L2052M	Closed	1981	135.00	950
1974	Oriental L2056M	Open		35.00	105
1974	Oriental L2057M	Open		30.00	100
1974	Thailandia L2058M	Open		650.00	1885
1974	Muskateer L2059M	Closed	1981	900.00	2000-3000
1977	Monk L2060M	Open		60.00	145
1977	Day Dream L2062M	Closed	1985	400.00	1300
1977	Chinese Farmer w/Staff L2065M	Closed	1985	340.00	
1977	Dogs-Bust L2067M	Closed	1979	280.00	800
1977	Thai Dancers L2069M	Open		300.00	745
1977	A New Hairdo L2070M	Closed	1991	1060.00	1430
1977	Graceful Duo L2073M	Closed	1994	775.00	1650
1977	Nuns L2075M	Open		90.00	250
1978	Lonely L2076M	Open		72.50	185
1978	Rain in Spain L2077M	Closed	1990	190.00	475-550
1978	Woman L2080M	Closed	1985	625.00	625
1978	Woman L2081M	Closed	1985	550.00	1400
1978	Carmen L2083M	Closed	1981	275.00	625
1978	Don Quixote Dreaming L2084M	Closed	1985	550.00	2050
1978	The Little Kiss L2086M	Closed	1985	180.00	475
1978	Girl in Rocking Chair L2089	Closed	1981	235.00	600
1978	Saint Francis L2090	Closed	1981	565.00	N/A
1978	Holy Virgin L2092M	Closed	1981	200.00	N/A
1978	Girl Waiting L2093M	Closed	1995	90.00	185
1978	Tenderness L2094M	Open		100.00	205
1978	Duck Pulling Pigtail L2095M	Open		110.00	275
1978	Nosy Puppy L2096M	Closed	1993	190.00	400
1978	Laundress L2109M	Closed	1983	325.00	325-650
1980	Marujita with Two Ducks L2113M	Closed	1993	240.00	295
1980	Kissing Father L2114M	Closed	1981	575.00	575
1980	Mother's Kiss L2115M	Closed	1981	575.00	700
1980	The Whaler L2121M	Closed	1988	820.00	1050
1981	Lost in Thought L2125M	Closed	1990	210.00	300
1983	Indian Chief L2127M	Closed	1988	525.00	750
1983	Venus L2128M	Closed	N/A	650.00	1150
1983	Waiting for Santa L2129M	Closed	1985	325.00	600
1983	Egyptian Cat L2130M	Closed	1985	75.00	500
1983	Mother & Son L2131M, numbered series	Open		850.00	1550
1983	Spring Sheperdess L2132M	Closed	1985	450.00	N/A
1983	Autumn Sheperdess L2133M	Closed	1985	285.00	N/A
1984	Nautical Watch L2134M	Closed	1988	450.00	800
1984	Mystical Joseph L2135M	Closed	1988	428.00	700
1984	The King L2136M	Closed	1988	570.00	710
1984	Fairy Ballerina L2137M	Closed	1988	500.00	1250
1984	Friar Juniper L2138M	Closed	1993	160.00	400
1984	Aztec Indian L2139M	Closed	1988	553.00	600
1984	Pepita with Sombrero L2140M	Open		97.50	200
1984	Pedro with Jug L2141M	Open		100.00	205
1984	Sea Harvest L2142M	Closed	1990	535.00	700
1984	Aztec Dancer L2143M	Closed	1988	463.00	650
1984	Leticia L2144M	Closed	1995	100.00	225
1984	Gabriela L2145M	Closed	1995	100.00	250
1984	Desiree L2146M	Closed	1995	100.00	225
1984	Alida L2147M	Closed	1995	100.00	250
1984	Head of Congolese Woman L2148M	Closed	1988	55.00	500-700
1985	Young Madonna L2149M	Closed	1988	400.00	675
1985	A Tribute to Peace w/base L2150M	Open		470.00	930
1985	A Bird on Hand L2151M	Open		118.00	210
1985	Chinese Girl L2152M	Closed	1990	90.00	200-250
1985	Chinese Boy L2153	Closed	1990	90.00	200-250
1985	Hawaiian Flower Vendor L2154M	Open		245.00	460
1985	Arctic inter L2156M	Open		75.00	145
1985	Eskimo Girl w/Cold Feet L2157M	Open		140.00	285
1985	Pensive Eskimo Girl L2158M	Open		100.00	210
1985	Pensive Eskimo Boy L2159M	Open		100.00	210
1985	Flower Vendor L2160M	Closed	1995	110.00	215
1985	Fruit Vendor L2161M	Open		120.00	230
1985	Fish Vendor L2162M	Closed	1994	110.00	205
1987	Mountain Shepherd L2163M	Open		120.00	210
1987	My Lost Lamb L2164M	Open		100.00	175
1987	Chiquita L2165M	Closed	1993	100.00	170
1987	Paco L2166M	Closed	1993	100.00	170
1987	Fernando L2167M	Closed	1993	100.00	200
1987	Julio L2168M	Closed	1993	100.00	225
1987	Repose L2169M	Open		120.00	195
1987	Spanish Dancer L2170M	Open		190.00	345
1987	Ahoy Tere L2173M	Open		190.00	325
1987	Andean Flute Player L2174M	Closed	1990	250.00	350
1988	Harvest Helpers L2178M	Open		190.00	265
1988	Sharing the Harvest L2179M	Open		190.00	265
1988	Dreams of Peace w/base L2180M	Open		880.00	1125
1988	Bathing Nymph w/base L2181M	Open		560.00	795
1988	Daydreamer w/base L2182M	Open		560.00	795
1989	Wakeup Kitty L2183M	Closed	1993	225.00	325
1989	Angel and Friend L2184M	Closed	1994	150.00	185
1989	Devoted Reader L2185M	Closed	1994	125.00	160
1989	The Greatest Love L2186M	Open		235.00	320
1989	Jealous Friend L2187M	Closed	1995	275.00	365
1990	Mother's Pride L2189M	Open		300.00	375
1990	To The Well L2190M	Open		250.00	295
1990	Forest Born L2191M	Closed	1991	230.00	450
1990	King Of The Forest L2192M	Closed	1992	290.00	310
1990	Heavenly Strings L2194M	Closed	1993	170.00	235
1990	Heavenly Sounds L2195M	Closed	1993	170.00	215
1990	Heavenly Solo L2196M	Closed	1993	170.00	235
1990	Heavenly Song L2197M	Closed	1993	175.00	185
1990	A King is Born w/base L2198M	Open		750.00	895
1990	Devoted Friends w/base L2199M	Closed	1995	700.00	895
1990	A Big Hug! L2200M	Open		250.00	310
1990	Our Daily Bread L2201M	Closed	1994	150.00	300
1990	A Helping Hand L2202M	Closed	1994	150.00	250
1990	Afternoon Chores L2203M	Closed	1994	150.00	250
1990	Farmyard Grace L2204M	Open		180.00	300
1990	Prayerful Stitch L2205M	Closed	1994	160.00	250
1990	Sisterly Love L2206M	Open		300.00	375
1990	What A Day! L2207M	Open		550.00	640
1991	Let's Rest L2208M	Open		550.00	665
1991	Long Dy L2209M	Open		295.00	340
1991	Lazy Day L2210M	Open		240.00	260
1991	Patrol Leader L2212M	Closed	1993	390.00	420
1991	Nature's Friend L2213M	Closed	1993	390.00	420
1991	Seaside Angel L2214M	Open		150.00	165
1991	Friends in Flight L2215M	Open		165.00	180
1991	Laundry Day L2216M	Open		350.00	400
1991	Gentle Play L2217M	Closed	1993	380.00	415
1991	Costumed Couple L2218M	Closed	1993	680.00	750
1992	Underfoot L2219M	Open		360.00	410
1992	Free Spirit L2220M	Closed	1994	235.00	245
1992	Spring Beauty L2221M	Closed	1994	285.00	295
1992	Tender Moment L2222M	Open		400.00	450
1992	New Lamb L2223M	Open		365.00	385
1992	Cherish L2224M	Open		1750.00	1850
1992	FriendlySparrow L2225M	Open		295.00	325
1992	Boy's Best Friend L2226M	Open		390.00	410
1992	Artic Allies L2227M	Open		585.00	615
1992	Snowy Sunday L2228M	Open		550.00	625
1992	Seasonal Gifts L2229M	Open		450.00	475
1992	Mary's Child L2230M	Closed	1994	525.00	550
1992	Afternoon Verse L2231M	Open		580.00	595
1992	Poor Little Bear L2232M	Open		250.00	265
1992	Guess What I Have L2233M	Open		340.00	375
1992	Playful Push L2234M	Open		850.00	875
1993	Adoring Mother L2235M	Open		405.00	440
1993	Frosty Outing L2236M	Open		375.00	410
1993	The Old Fishing Hole L2237M	Open		625.00	640
1993	Learning Together L2238M	Open		500.00	500
1993	Valencian Courtship L2239M	Open		880.00	895
1993	Winged Love L2240M	Closed	1995	285.00	310
1993	Winged Harmony L2241M	Closed	1995	285.00	310
1993	Away to School L2242M	Open		465.00	465
1993	Lion Tamer L2246M	Closed	1995	375.00	375
1993	Just Us L2247M	Closed	1995	650.00	650
1993	Noella L2251M	Open		405.00	420
1993	Waiting For Father L2252M	Open		660.00	660
1993	Noisy Friend L2253M	Open		280.00	280
1993	Step Aside L2254M	Open		280.00	280
1994	Solitude L2256M	Open		398.00	435
1994	Constant Companions L2257M	Open		575.00	625
1994	Family Love L2258M	Open		450.00	485
1994	Little Fisherman L2259M	Open		298.00	330
1994	Artic Friends L2260M	Open		345.00	380
1995	Jesus and Joseph L2294M	Open		550.00	550
1995	Peaceful Rest L2295M	Open		390.00	390
1995	Life's Small Wonders L2296M	Open		370.00	370
1995	Elephants L2297M	Open		875.00	875
1995	Hindu Children L2298M	Open		450.00	450
1995	Poetic Moment L2299M	Open		465.00	465
1995	Emperor L2300M	Open		765.00	765
1995	Empress L2301M	Open		795.00	795
1995	Twilight Years L2302M	Open		385.00	385
1995	Not So Fast L2303M	Open		350.00	350
1995	Love in Bloom L2304M	Open		420.00	420
1995	Fragrant Bouquet L2305M	Open		330.00	330
1995	Hurray Now L2306M	Open		310.00	310
1995	Happy Birthday L2307M	Open		150.00	150
1995	Let's Make Up L2308M	Open		420.00	420
1995	Windblown Spirit L2309M	Open		320.00	320
1995	Chit-Chat L2310M	Open		270.00	270
1995	Good Night L2311M	Open		280.00	280
1995	Goose Trying to Eat L2312M	Open		325.00	325
1995	Who's the Fairest L2313M	Open		230.00	230

YEAR ISSUE		EDITION LIMIT	YEAR RETD.	ISSUE PRICE	*QUOTE U.S. $
1995	Breezy Afternoon L2314M	Open		220.00	220
1995	On the Green L2315M	Open		575.00	575
1995	Closing Scene L2316M	Open		560.00	560
1995	Talk to Me L2317M	Open		175.00	175
1995	Taking Time L2318M	Open		175.00	175
1995	A Lesson Shared L2319M	Open		215.00	215
1995	Cat Nap L2320M	Open		265.00	265
1995	All Tuckered Out L2321M	Open		275.00	275
1995	Naptime L2322M	Open		275.00	275
1995	Water Girl L2323M	Open		245.00	245
1995	A Basket of Fun L2324M	Open		320.00	320
1995	Spring Splendor L2325M	Open		440.00	440
1995	Physician L2326M	Open		350.00	350
1995	Sad Sax L2327M	Open		225.00	225
1995	Circus Sam L2328M	Open		225.00	225
1995	Daily Chores L2329M	Open		345.00	345
1996	The Shepherdess L2330	Open		410.00	410
1996	Little Peasant Girl (pink) L2331	Open		155.00	155
1996	Little Peasant Girl (blue) L2332	Open		155.00	155
1996	Little Peasant Girl (white) L2333	Open		155.00	155
1996	Asian Melody L2334	Open		690.00	690
1996	Young Fisherman L2335	Open		225.00	225
1996	Young Water Girl L2336	Open		315.00	315
1996	Virgin of Montserrat w/base L2337	Open		1000.00	1000
1996	Sultan's Dream L2338	Open		700.00	700
1996	The Sultan L2339	Open		480.00	480
1996	Oriental Fantasy w/bow L2340	Open		1350.00	1350
1996	Oriental Fantasy w/brooch L2341	Open		1350.00	1350
1996	Returning From the Well w/base L2342	Open		1800.00	1800
1996	Care and Tenderness w/base L2343	Open		860.00	860
1996	Oration L2344	Open		295.00	295
1996	Bedtime Story L2345	Open		360.00	360
1996	Feeding the Ducks L2346	Open		305.00	305
1996	Meditation (blue) L2347	Open		145.00	145
1996	Prayerful Moment (blue) L2348	Open		145.00	145
1996	Sleigh Ride w/base L2349	Open		1520.00	1520
1996	Pensive Clown w/base L2350	Open		680.00	680
1996	Fishing With Gramps w/base L2351	Open		1025.00	1025
1996	Under My Spell L2352	Open		225.00	225
1996	Shot on Goal w/base L2353	Open		935.00	935
1978	Native L3502M	Open		700.00	2450
1978	Letters to Dulcinea L3509M, numbered series	Open		875.00	2175
1978	Horse Heads L3511M	Closed	1990	260.00	700
1978	Girl With Pails L3512M	Open		140.00	285
1978	A Wintry Day L3513M	Closed	1988	525.00	800-1000
1978	Pensive w/ base L3514M	Open		500.00	1050
1978	Jesus Christ L3516M	Closed	1988	1050.00	1450
1978	Nude with Rose w/ base L3517M	Open		225.00	780
1980	Lady Macbeth L3518M	Closed	1981	385.00	700-1200
1980	Mother's Love L3521M	Closed	1990	1000.00	1100
1981	Weary w/ base L3525M	Open		360.00	685
1982	Contemplation w/ base L3526M	Open		265.00	590
1982	Stormy Sea w/base L3554M	Open		675.00	1445
1984	Innocence w/base/green L3558M	Closed	1991	960.00	1650
1984	Innocence w/base/red L3558.3M	Closed	1987	960.00	1200
1985	Peace Offering w/base L3559M	Open		397.00	665
1969	Marketing Day L4502G	Closed	1985	40.00	400
1969	Girl with Lamb L4505G	Open		20.00	125
1969	Boy with Kid L4506M	Closed	1985	22.50	400
1969	Boy with Lambs L4509G	Closed	1981	37.50	275
1969	Girl w/Parasol and Geese L4510G	Closed	1993	40.00	350
1969	Nude L4511M	Closed	1985	45.00	700
1969	Nude L4512G	Closed	1985	44.00	400
1969	Man on Horse L4515G	Closed	1985	180.00	1000
1969	Female Equestrian L4516G	Open		170.00	745
1969	Boy Student L4517G	Closed	1978	57.50	475
1969	Flamenco Dancers L4519G	Closed	1993	150.00	1200
1970	Boy With Dog L4522M	Closed	N/A	25.00	155
1969	Girl With Slippers L4523G	Closed	1993	17.00	100
1969	Girl With Slippers L4523M	Closed	1993	17.00	100
1969	Donkey in Love L4524G	Closed	1985	15.00	350
1969	Donkey in Love L4524M	Closed	1985	15.00	350
1969	Violinist L4527G	Closed	1985	75.00	500
1969	Ballet Lamp L4528G	Closed	1985	120.00	850
1969	Joseph L4533G	Open		60.00	110
1969	Joseph L4533M	Open		60.00	110
1969	Mary L4534G	Open		60.00	85
1969	Mary L4534M	Open		60.00	85
1971	Baby Jesus L4535.3G	Open		60.00	70
1969	Baby Jesus L4535.3M	Open		60.00	70
1969	Angel, Chinese L4536G	Open		45.00	90
1969	Angel, Chinese L4536M	Open		45.00	90
1969	Angel, Black L4537G	Open		13.00	90
1969	Angel, Black L4537M	Open		13.00	90
1969	Angel, Praying L4538G	Open		13.00	90
1969	Angel, Praying L4538M	Open		13.00	90
1969	Angel, Thinking L4539G	Open		13.00	90
1969	Angel, Thinking L4539M	Open		13.00	90
1969	Angel with Horn L4540G	Open		13.00	90
1969	Angel with Horn L4540M	Open		13.00	90
1969	Angel Reclining L4541G	Open		13.00	90
1969	Angel Reclining L4541M	Open		13.00	90
1969	Group of Angels L4542G	Open		31.00	195
1969	Group of Angels L4542M	Open		31.00	195
1969	Troubador L4548G	Closed	1978	67.50	750
1969	Geese Group L4549G	Open		28.50	230
1969	Geese Group L4549M	Closed	1992	28.50	230
1969	Flying Dove L4550G	Open		47.50	265
1969	Flying Dove L4550M	Closed	1992	47.50	165

YEAR ISSUE		EDITION LIMIT	YEAR RETD.	ISSUE PRICE	*QUOTE U.S.$
1969	Ducks, Set/3 asst. L4551-3G	Open		18.00	140
1969	Shepherd L4554	Closed	1972	69.00	N/A
1969	Sad Harlequin L4558G	Closed	1993	110.00	600
1969	Waiting Backstage L4559G	Closed	1990	110.00	500
1970	Llama Group 4561G	Closed	1974	55.00	1600
1969	Couple with Parasol L4563G	Closed	1985	180.00	900
1969	Girl with Geese L4568G	Closed	1985	45.00	350
1969	Girl With Turkey L4569G	Closed	1981	28.50	375
1969	Shepherd Resting L4571G	Closed	1981	60.00	475
1969	Girl with Piglets L4572G	Closed	1985	70.00	400
1969	Girl with Piglets L4572M	Closed	1985	70.00	400
1969	Mother & Child L4575G	Open		50.00	265
1969	New Shepherdess L4576G	Closed	1985	37.50	315
1969	New Shepherd L4577G	Closed	1983	35.00	550
1969	Mardi Gras L4580G	Closed	1975	57.50	2000-2500
1969	Mardi Gras L4580M	Closed	1975	57.50	1800
1969	Girl with Sheep L4584G	Closed	1993	27.00	170
1969	Holy Family L4585G	Closed	1994	18.00	135
1969	Holy Family L4585M	Closed	1994	18.00	135
1969	Madonna L4586G	Closed	1979	32.50	350
1969	White Cockeral L4588G	Closed	1979	17.50	300
1969	Girl with Pitcher L4590G	Closed	1981	47.50	400
1969	Shepherdess w/Basket L4591G	Closed	1993	20.00	275
1969	Lady with Greyhound L4594G	Closed	1981	60.00	800
1969	Fairy L4595G	Closed	1994	27.50	150
1969	Two Horses L4597	Closed	1990	240.00	925-1000
1969	Doctor L4602.3G	Open		33.00	198
1969	Nurse-L4603.3G	Open		35.00	200
1969	Clown with Girl L4605	Closed	1985	160.00	1000
1969	Accordian Player L4606	Closed	1978	60.00	650
1969	Cupid L4607G	Closed	1980	15.00	150
1969	Cook in Trouble L4608	Closed	1985	27.50	650-775
1969	Nuns L4611G	Open		37.50	155
1969	Nuns L4611M	Open		37.50	155
1969	Girl Singer L4612G	Closed	1979	14.00	450
1969	Boy With Cymbals L4613G	Closed	1979	14.00	400
1969	Boy with Guitar L4614G	Closed	1979	19.50	400
1969	Boy with Double Bass L4615G	Closed	1979	22.50	400
1969	Boy With Drum L4616G	Closed	1979	16.50	350
1969	Group of Musicians L4617G	Closed	1979	33.00	500
1969	Clown L4618G	Open		70.00	415
1969	Sea Captain L4621G	Closed	1993	45.00	325
1969	Sea Captain L4621M	Closed	N/A	42.50	300
1969	Old Man with Violin L4622G	Closed	1982	45.00	700
1969	Velazquez Bookend L4626G	Closed	1975	90.00	950
1969	Columbus Bookend L4627G	Closed	1975	90.00	950
1969	Angel with Child L4635G	Open		15.00	110
1969	Honey Peddler L4638G	Closed	1978	60.00	575
1969	Cow With Pig L4640	Closed	1981	42.50	500
1969	Pekinese L4641G	Closed	1985	20.00	450
1969	Dog L4642	Closed	1985	22.50	425
1969	Skye Terrier L4643G	Closed	1985	15.00	450
1969	Andalucians Group L4647G	Closed	1990	412.00	1400
1969	Valencian Couple on Horseback L4648	Closed	1990	900.00	1000
1969	Madonna Head L4649G	Open		25.00	155
1969	Madonna Head L4649M	Open		25.00	155
1969	Girl with Calla Lillies L4650G	Open		18.00	145
1969	Cellist L4651G	Closed	1985	70.00	750
1969	Happy Travelers L4652	Closed	1978	115.00	650
1969	Orchestra Conductor L4653G	Closed	1979	95.00	850
1969	The Grandfather L4654G	Closed	1979	75.00	950-1100
1969	Horses L4655G	Open		110.00	760
1969	Shepherdess L4660G	Closed	1993	21.00	300
1969	Countryman L4664M	Open		50.00	500
1969	Girl with Basket L4665G	Closed	1979	50.00	450
1969	Girl with Basket L4665M	Closed	1979	50.00	550
1969	Birds L4667G	Closed	1985	25.00	200
1969	Maja Head L4668G	Closed	1985	50.00	650
1969	Baby Jesus L4670BG	Open		18.00	55
1969	Mary L4671G	Open		33.00	75
1969	St. Joseph L4672G	Open		33.00	90
1969	King Melchior L4673G	Open		35.00	95
1969	King Gaspar L4674G	Open		35.00	95
1969	King Balthasar L4675G	Open		35.00	95
1969	Shepherd with Lamb L4676G	Open		14.00	110
1969	Girl with Rooster L4677G	Open		14.00	90
1969	Shepherdess w/Basket L4678G	Open		13.00	90
1969	Donkey L4679G	Open		36.50	100
1969	Cow L4680G	Open		36.50	90
1970	Girl with Milkpail L4682G	Closed	1991	28.00	325
1970	Hebrew Student L4684G	Closed	1985	33.00	500-650
1970	Hebrew Student L4684M	Closed	1985	33.00	600
1970	Gothic Queen L4689	Closed	1978	20.00	700
1970	Troubadour in Love L4699	Closed	1975	60.00	1000
1970	Dressmaker L4700G	Closed	1993	45.00	500
1970	Mother & Child L4701G	Open		45.00	295
1970	Girl Jewelry Dish L4713G	Closed	1978	30.00	550
1970	Girl Jewelry Dish L4713M	Closed	1978	30.00	550
1970	Lady Empire L4719G	Closed	1979	150.00	1000
1970	Girl With Tulips L4720G	Closed	1978	65.00	500
1970	Hamlet L4729G	Open		85.00	800
1970	Bird Watcher L4730	Closed	1985	35.00	400-500
1970	German Shepherd w/Pup L4731	Closed	1975	40.00	800
1971	Small Dog L4749	Closed	1985	5.50	90
1971	Romeo and Juliet L4750G	Open		150.00	1250
1971	Doncel With Roses L4757G	Closed	1979	35.00	500
1971	Lady with Dog L4761G	Closed	1993	60.00	400-500
1971	Dentist L4762	Closed	1978	36.00	550
1971	Dentist (Reduced) L4762.3G	Closed	1985	30.00	475
1971	Obstetrician L4763G	Closed	1973	47.50	450
1971	Obstetrician L4763.3G	Open		40.00	255

YEAR ISSUE		EDITION LIMIT	YEAR RETD.	ISSUE PRICE	* QUOTE U.S.$
1971	Don Quixote Vase L4770G	Closed	1975	25.00	750
1971	Don Quixote Vase L4770M	Closed	1975	25.00	750
1971	Rabbit L4772G	Open		17.50	135
1971	Rabbit L4773G	Open		17.50	130
1971	Dormouse L4774	Closed	1983	30.00	375
1972	Girl Tennis Player L4798	Closed	1981	50.00	450
1971	Children, Praying L4779G	Open		36.00	195
1971	Children, Praying L4779M	Closed	1992	36.00	153
1971	Boy with Goat L4780	Closed	1978	80.00	600
1972	Japanese Woman L4799	Closed	1975	45.00	500
1972	Gypsy with Brother L4800G	Closed	1979	36.00	400
1972	The Teacher L4801G	Open		45.00	500
1972	Fisherman L4802G	Closed	1979	70.00	700
1972	Woman with Umbrella L4805G	Closed	1981	100.00	800
1972	Girl with Dog L4806G	Closed	1981	80.00	500
1972	Geisha L4807G	Closed	1993	190.00	475
1972	Wedding L4808G	Open		50.00	190
1972	Wedding L4808M	Open		50.00	190
1972	Going Fishing L4809G	Open		33.00	160
1972	Young Sailor L4810G	Open		33.00	175
1972	Boy with Pails L4811	Closed	1988	30.00	400
1972	Getting Her Goat L4812G	Closed	1988	55.00	450
1972	Girl with Geese L4815G	Closed	1991	72.00	400
1972	Girl with Geese L4815M	Closed	1991	72.00	295
1972	Little Shepherd w/Goat L4817M	Closed	1981	50.00	475
1972	Burro L4821G	Closed	1979	24.00	450
1974	Peruvian Girl with Baby L4822	Closed	1981	65.00	775
1974	Legionary L4823	Closed	1978	55.00	400-500
1972	Male Golfer L4824G	Open		66.00	295
1972	Veterinarian L4825	Closed	1985	48.00	500
1972	Girl Feeding Rabbit L4826G	Closed	1993	40.00	300
1972	Caressing Calf L4827G	Closed	1981	35.00	475
1972	Cinderella L4828G	Open		47.00	245
1975	Swan L4829G	Closed	1983	16.00	400
1972	You and Me L4830G	Closed	1979	112.50	1000
1972	Romance L4831G	Open		175.00	1500
1972	Chess Set Pieces L4833.3G	Closed	1985	410	2500
1972	Shepherdess L4835G	Closed	1991	42.00	225-325
1973	Clean Up Time L4838G	Closed	1993	36.00	250-300
1973	Clean Up Time L4838M	Closed	1992	36.00	250
1973	Oriental Flower Arranger/Girl L4840G	Open		90.00	415
1973	Oriental Flower Arranger/Girl L4840M	Open		90.00	515
1974	Girl from Valencia L4841G	Open		35.00	225
1973	Viola Lesson L4842G	Closed	1981	66.00	450
1973	Donkey Ride L4843	Closed	1981	86.00	650
1973	Pharmacist L4844G	Closed	1985	70.00	1650
1973	Classic Dance L4847G	Closed	1985	60.00	800
1973	Feeding The Ducks L4849G	Closed	1995	60.00	270
1973	Feeding The Ducks L4849M	Closed	1985	60.00	250
1973	Aesthetic Pose L4850G	Closed	1985	110.00	650
1973	Lady Golfer L4851M	Closed	1992	70.00	450
1973	Gardner in Trouble L4852	Closed	1981	65.00	500
1974	Cobbler L4853G	Closed	1985	100.00	600
1973	Don Quixote L4854C	Open		40.00	205
1973	Ballerina L4855G	Open		45.00	330
1983	Ballerina, white L4855.3	Closed	1987	110.00	250
1974	Waltz Time L4856G	Open		65.00	450
1974	Dog L4857G	Closed	1979	40.00	550
1974	Pleasant Encounter L4858M	Closed	1981	60.00	450
1974	Peddler L4859G	Closed	1985	180.00	750
1974	Dutch Girl L4860G	Closed	1985	45.00	250
1974	Horse L4861	Closed	1978	55.00	425
1974	Horse L4862	Closed	1978	55.00	425
1974	Horse L4863	Closed	1978	55.00	400
1974	Embroiderer L4865G	Closed	1994	115.00	700
1974	Girl with Swan and Dog L4866G	Closed	1993	26.00	205
1974	Seesaw L4867G	Open		55.00	350
1974	Girl with Candle L4868G	Open		13.00	90
1974	Girl with Candle L4868M	Closed	1992	13.00	80
1974	Boy Kissing L4869G	Open		13.00	90
1974	Boy Kissing L4869M	Closed	1992	13.00	150-175
1974	Boy Yawning L4870G	Open		13.00	90
1974	Boy Yawning L4870M	Closed	1992	13.00	175
1974	Girl with Guitar L4871G	Open		13.00	80
1974	Girl with Guitar L4871M	Closed	1992	13.00	80
1974	Girl Stretching L4872G	Open		13.00	90
1974	Girl Stretching L4872M	Open		13.00	80
1974	Girl Kissing L4873G	Open		13.00	90
1974	Girl Kissing L4873M	Closed	1992	13.00	80
1974	Boy & Girl L4874G	Open		25.00	150
1974	Boy & Girl L4874M	Closed	1992	25.00	135
1974	Girl with Jugs L4875G	Closed	1985	40.00	300
1974	Boy Thinking L4876G	Closed	1993	20.00	170
1974	Boy Thinking L4876M	Closed	1992	20.00	120
1974	Boy with Flute L4877G	Closed	1981	60.00	450
1974	Lady with Parasol L4879G	Open		48.00	325
1974	Carnival Couple L4882G	Closed	1985	60.00	300
1974	Carnival Couple L4882M	Closed	1991	60.00	375
1974	Lady w/ Young Harlequin L4883G	Closed	1975	100.00	2350
1974	Seraph's Head No.1 L4884	Closed	1985	10.00	100
1974	Seraph's Head No.2 L4885	Closed	1985	10.00	100
1974	Seraph's Head No.3 L4886	Closed	1985	10.00	100
1974	The Kiss L4888C	Closed	1983	150.00	700
1974	Spanish Policeman L4889G	Open		55.00	310
1974	Watching the Pigs L4892G	Closed	1978	160.00	1000
1976	"My Dog" L4893G	Open		85.00	230
1974	Tennis Player Boy L4894	Closed	1980	75.00	350
1974	Ducks L4895G	Open		45.00	95
1974	Ducks L4895M	Closed	1992	45.00	85

FIGURINES/COTTAGES

YEAR ISSUE		EDITION LIMIT	YEAR RETD.	ISSUE PRICE	*QUOTE U.S.$
1974	Boy with Snails L4896G	Closed	1979	50.00	400
1974	Boy From Madrid L4898G	Open		55.00	150
1974	Boy From Madrid L4898M	Closed	1992	55.00	130
1974	Boy with Smoking Jacket L4900	Closed	1983	45.00	200
1974	Barrister L4908G	Closed	1985	100.00	585
1974	Girl With Dove L4909G	Closed	1982	70.00	450
1974	Girl With Lantern L4910G	Closed	1990	85.00	300
1974	Young Lady in Trouble L4912G	Closed	1985	110.00	450
1975	Lady with Shawl L4914G	Open		220.00	730
1975	Girl with Pigeons L4915	Closed	1990	110.00	400
1976	Chinese Noblewoman L4916G	Closed	1978	300.00	2000
1974	A Girl at the Pond L4918G	Closed	1985	85.00	350
1976	Gypsy Woman L4919G	Closed	1981	165.00	1100
1974	Country Lass with Dog L4920G	Closed	1995	185.00	495
1974	Country Lass with Dog L4920M	Closed	1992	185.00	495
1974	Chinese Nobleman L4921G	Closed	1978	325.00	2000
1974	Windblown Girl L4922G	Open		150.00	375
1974	Lanquid Clown L4924G	Closed	1983	200.00	1500
1974	Milk For the Lamb L4926G	Closed	1980	185.00	1300
1974	Medieval Lady L4928G	Closed	1980	275.00	925
1974	Sisters L4930	Closed	1981	250.00	625
1974	Children with Fruits L4931G	Closed	1981	210.00	500
1974	Dainty Lady L4934G	Closed	1985	60.00	475
1974	"Closing Scene" L4935G	Open		180.00	520
1983	"Closing Scene"/white L4935.3M	Closed	1987	213.00	265
1974	Spring Breeze L4936G	Open		145.00	410
1976	Golden Wedding L4937M	Retrd.	1981	285.00	600
1976	Baby's Outing L4938G	Open		250.00	725
1977	Missy L4951M	Closed	1985	300.00	600-850
1977	Meditation L4952M	Closed	1979	200.00	N/A
1977	Tavern Drinkers L4956G	Closed	1985	1125.00	3500
1977	Attentive Dogs L4957G	Closed	1981	350.00	1600
1977	Cherub, Puzzled L4959G	Open		40.00	110
1977	Cherub, Smiling L4960G	Open		40.00	110
1977	Cherub, Dreaming L4961G	Open		40.00	110
1977	Cherub, Wondering L4962G	Open		40.00	110
1977	Cherub, Wondering L4962M	Closed	1992	40.00	100
1977	Infantile Candour L4963G	Closed	1979	285.00	1300-1500
1977	Little Red Riding Hood L4965G	Closed	1983	210.00	575
1977	Tennis Player Puppet L4966G	Closed	1985	60.00	250
1977	Soccer Player L4967G	Closed	1985	65.00	425
1977	Oympic Puppet L4968	Closed	1983	65.00	800
1977	Cowboy & Sheriff Puppet L4969G	Closed	1985	85.00	650
1977	Skier Puppet L4970G	Closed	1983	85.00	500-900
1977	Hunter Puppet L4971G	Closed	1985	95.00	750
1977	Girl w/ Calla Lilies sitting L4972G	Open		65.00	180
1977	Choir Lesson L4973G	Closed	1981	350.00	1850
1977	Dutch Children L4974G	Closed	1981	375.00	1150
1977	Augustina of Aragon L4976G	Closed	1979	475.00	1500-1800
1977	Harlequin Serenade L4977	Closed	1979	185.00	675
1977	Milkmaid w/Wheelbarrow L4979G	Closed	1981	220.00	950
1977	Ironing Time L4981G	Closed	1985	80.00	350
1978	Naughty Dog L4982G	Closed	1995	130.00	275
1978	Gossip L4984G	Closed	1985	260.00	1000
1978	Mimi L4985G	Closed	1980	110.00	625
1978	Attentive Lady L4986G	Closed	1981	635.00	2200
1978	Oriental Spring L4988G	Open		125.00	325
1978	Sayonara L4989G	Open		125.00	300
1978	Chrysanthemum L4990G	Open		125.00	310
1978	Butterfly L4991G	Open		125.00	295
1978	Dancers Resting L4992G	Closed	1983	350.00	850
1978	Gypsy Venders L4993G	Closed	1985	165.00	475
1978	Ready to Go L4996G	Closed	1981	425.00	1500-1700
1978	Don Quixote & Sancho L4998G	Closed	1983	875.00	2900
1978	Reading L5000G	Open		150.00	275
1978	Elk Family L5001G	Closed	1981	550.00	700
1978	Sunny Day L5003G	Closed	1993	193.00	360
1978	Eloise L5005G	Closed	1978	175.00	550
1978	Naughty L5006G	Open		55.00	150
1978	Bashful L5007G	Open		55.00	150
1978	Static-Girl w/Straw Hat L5008G	Open		55.00	150
1978	Curious-Girl w/Straw Hat L5009G	Open		55.00	150
1978	Coiffure-Girl w/Straw Hat L5010G	Open		55.00	150
1978	Trying on a Straw Hat L5011G	Open		55.00	150
1978	Daughters L5013G	Closed	1991	425.00	900
1978	Genteel L5014G	Closed	1981	725.00	2300
1978	Painful Monkey L5018	Closed	1981	135.00	750
1978	Painful Giraffe L5019	Closed	1981	115.00	750
1978	Painful Elephant L5020	Closed	1981	85.00	850
1978	Painful Bear L5021	Closed	1981	75.00	800
1978	Painful Giraffe L5022G	Closed	1981	95.00	800
1978	Painful Kangaroo L5023G	Closed	1981	150.00	850
1978	Woman With Scarf L5024G	Closed	1985	141.00	450
1980	A Clean Sweep L5025G	Closed	1985	100.00	450
1980	Planning the Day L5026G	Closed	1985	90.00	275
1979	Flower Curtsy L5027G	Open		230.00	470
1980	Flowers in Pot L5028G	Closed	1985	325.00	575
1980	Boy with Tricycle & Flowers L5029G	Closed	1985	675.00	1200-1350
1980	Wildflower L5030G	Closed	1994	360.00	695
1979	Little Friskies L5032G	Open		108.00	220
1980	Avoiding the Goose L5033G	Closed	1993	160.00	350
1980	Goose Trying To Eat L5034G	Open		135.00	310
1980	Act II w/base L5035G	Open		700.00	1425
1979	Jockey with Lass L5036G	Open		950.00	2240
1980	Sleighride w/base L5037G	Open		585.00	1140
1979	Girl Bowing L5038G	Closed	1981	185.00	750
1980	Candid L5039G	Closed	1981	145.00	475
1979	Girl Walking L5040G	Closed	1981	150.00	420-450
1980	Girl Kneeling and Tulips L5041G	Closed	1981	160.00	850
1980	Ladies Talking L5042G	Closed	1983	385.00	575-1000

YEAR ISSUE		EDITION LIMIT	YEAR RETD.	ISSUE PRICE	*QUOTE U.S.$
1980	Hind and Baby Deer L5043G	Closed	1981	650.00	3600
1980	Girl with Toy Wagon L5044G	Open		115.00	245
1980	Belinda with Doll L5045G	Closed	1995	115.00	215
1980	Organ Grinder L5046G	Closed	1981	328.00	1600
1980	Teacher Woman L5048G	Closed	1981	115.00	550-675
1980	Dancer L5050G	Open		85.00	205
1980	Samson and Delilah L5051G	Closed	1981	350.00	1600
1980	Clown and Girl/ At the Circus L5052G	Closed	1985	525.00	1250
1980	Festival Time L5053G	Closed	1985	250.00	375
1980	Little Senorita L5054G	Closed	1985	235.00	600
1980	Ship-Boy with Baskets L5055G	Closed	1985	140.00	450
1980	Boy Clown with Clock L5056G	Closed	1985	290.00	850
1980	Boy Clown w/Violin and Top Hat L5057G	Closed	1985	270.00	850
1980	Boy Clown with Concertina L5058G	Closed	1985	290.00	500-600
1980	Boy Clown with Saxophone L5059G	Closed	1985	320.00	600
1980	Girl Clown with Trumpet L5060G	Closed	1985	290.00	550
1980	Girl Bending/March Wind L5061G	Closed	1983	370.00	600
1980	Kristina L5062G	Closed	1985	225.00	400
1980	Dutch Girl With Braids L5063G	Closed	1985	265.00	425-450
1980	Dutch Girl, Hands Akimbo L5064G	Closed	1990	255.00	425
1980	Ingrid L5065G	Closed	1990	370.00	800
1980	Ilsa L5066G	Closed	1990	275.00	600
1981	Snow White with Apple L5067G	Closed	1983	450.00	1500
1980	Fairy Godmother L5068G	Closed	1983	625.00	950-1150
1980	Choir Boys L5070G	Closed	1983	240.00	850
1980	Nostalgia L5071G	Closed	1993	185.00	350
1980	Courtship L5072	Closed	1990	327.00	750
1980	Country Flowers L5073	Closed	1985	315.00	1500
1980	My Hungry Brood L5074G	Open		295.00	415
1980	Little Harlequin "A" L5075G	Closed	1985	217.50	410
1980	Little Harlequin "B" L5076G	Closed	1985	185.00	375
1980	Little Harlequin "C" L5077G	Closed	1985	185.00	500
1980	Teasing the Dog L5078G	Closed	1985	300.00	600
1980	Woman Painting Vase L5079G	Closed	1985	300.00	600-750
1980	Boy Pottery Seller L5080G	Closed	1985	320.00	650-700
1980	Girl Pottery Seller L5081G	Closed	1985	300.00	725
1980	Flower Vendor L5082G	Closed	1985	750.00	3000
1980	A Good Book L5084G	Closed	1985	175.00	350-525
1980	Mother Amabilis L5086G	Closed	1983	275.00	600
1980	Roses for My Mom L5088G	Closed	1988	645.00	1150
1980	Scare-Dy Cat/Playful Cat L5091G	Open		65.00	95
1980	After the Dance L5092G	Closed	1983	165.00	475
1980	A Dancing Partner L5093G	Closed	1983	165.00	500
1980	Ballet First Step L5094G	Closed	1983	165.00	400
1980	Ballet Bowing L5095G	Closed	1983	165.00	300
1989	Her Ladyship, L5097G	Closed	1991	5900.00	6700
1980	Successful Hunt L5098	Closed	1993	5200.00	5200
1982	Playful Tot L5099G	Closed	1985	58.00	265
1982	Cry Baby L5100G	Closed	1985	58.00	275
1982	Learning to Crawl L5101G	Closed	1985	58.00	275-300
1982	Teething L5102G	Closed	1985	58.00	300
1982	Time for a Nap L5103G	Closed	1985	58.00	275
1982	Natalia L5106G	Closed	1985	85.00	350
1982	Little Ballet Girl L5108G	Closed	1985	85.00	400
1982	Little Ballet Girl L5109G	Closed	1985	85.00	400
1982	Dog Sniffing L5110G	Closed	1985	50.00	450-700
1982	Timid Dog L5111G	Closed	1985	44.00	500-600
1982	Play with Me L5112G	Open		40.00	80
1982	Feed Me L5113G	Open		40.00	80
1982	Pet Me L5114G	Open		40.00	80
1982	Little Boy Bullfighter L5115G	Closed	1985	123.00	400
1982	A Victory L5116G	Closed	1985	123.00	400-500
1982	Proud Matador L5117G	Closed	1985	123.00	500
1982	Girl in Green Dress L5118G	Closed	1985	170.00	600
1982	Girl in Bluish Dress L5119G	Closed	1985	170.00	650
1982	Girl in Pink Dress L5120G	Closed	1985	170.00	650
1982	August Moon L5122G	Closed	1993	185.00	350
1982	My Precious Bundle L5123G	Open		150.00	235
1982	Dutch Couple w/Tulips L5124G	Closed	1985	310.00	950
1982	Amparo L5125G	Closed	1985	130.00	330-350
1982	Sewing A Trousseau L5126G	Closed	1990	185.00	400-600
1982	Marcelina L5127G	Closed	1985	255.00	255
1982	Lost Love L5128G	Closed	1988	400.00	700
1982	Jester w/base L5129G	Open		220.00	445
1982	Pensive Clown w/base L5130G	Open		250.00	445
1982	Cervantes L5132G	Closed	1985	925.00	1175
1982	Trophy with Base L5133G	Closed	1983	250.00	650
1982	Girl Soccer Player L5134G	Closed	1983	140.00	575
1982	Billy Football Player L5135G	Closed	1983	140.00	575
1982	Billy Skier L5136G	Closed	1983	140.00	750
1982	Billy Baseball Player L5137G	Closed	1983	140.00	750
1982	Billy Golfer L5138G	Closed	1983	140.00	1000
1982	A New Doll House L5139G	Closed	1983	185.00	750
1982	Feed Her Son L5140G	Closed	1991	170.00	300
1982	Balloons for Sale L5141G	Open		145.00	250
1982	Comforting Daughter L5142G	Closed	1991	195.00	375
1982	Scooting L5143G	Closed	1985	575.00	850-1000
1982	Amy L5145G	Closed	1985	110.00	1600
1982	"E" is for Ellen L5146G	Closed	1985	110.00	1200
1982	Ivez L5147G	Closed	1985	100.00	600
1982	Olivia L5148G	Closed	1985	100.00	400
1982	Ursula L5149G	Closed	1985	100.00	400
1982	Girl's Head L5150G	Closed	1983	435.00	1300
1982	Girl's Head L5151G	Closed	1983	380.00	1400
1982	Girl's Head L5152G	Closed	1983	535.00	2000
1982	Girl's Head L5153G	Closed	1983	475.00	1350
1982	First Prize L5154G	Closed	1985	90.00	N/A

YEAR ISSUE		EDITION LIMIT	YEAR RETD.	ISSUE PRICE	*QUOTE U.S.$
1982	Monks at Prayer L5155M	Open		130.00	275
1982	Susan and the Doves L5156G	Closed	1991	203.00	325-360
1982	Bongo Beat L5157G	Open		135.00	230
1982	A Step In Time L5158G	Open		90.00	195
1982	Harmony L5159G	Open		270.00	495
1982	Rhumba L5160G	Open		113.00	185
1982	Cycling To A Picnic L5161G	Closed	1985	2000.00	2800
1982	Mouse Girl/Mindy L5162G	Closed	1985	125.00	550
1982	Bunny Girl/Bunny L5163G	Closed	1985	125.00	450
1982	Cat Girl/Kitty L5164G	Closed	1985	125.00	450
1982	Sancho with Bottle L5165	Closed	1990	100.00	400
1982	Sea Fever L5166M	Closed	1993	130.00	235
1982	Sea Fever L5166G	Closed	1993	130.00	325
1982	Jesus L5167G	Open		130.00	265
1982	King Solomon L5168G	Open		205.00	900
1982	Abraham L5169G	Closed	1985	155.00	725-750
1982	Moses L5170G	Open		175.00	395
1982	Madonna with Flowers L5171G	Open		173.00	310
1982	Fish A'Plenty L5172G	Closed	1994	190.00	385
1982	Pondering L5173G	Closed	1993	300.00	700
1982	Roaring 20's L5174G	Closed	1993	173.00	425
1982	Flapper L5175G	Closed	1995	185.00	425
1982	Rhapsody in Blue L5176G	Closed	1985	325.00	1850
1982	Dante L5177G	Open		263.00	750
1982	Stubborn Mule L5178G	Closed	1993	250.00	500
1983	Three Pink Roses w/base L5179M	Closed	1990	70.00	110
1983	Dahlia L5180M	Closed	1990	65.00	140
1983	Japanese Camelia w/base L5181M	Closed	1990	60.00	90
1983	White Peony L5182M	Closed	1990	85.00	125
1983	Two Yellow Roses L5183M	Closed	1990	57.50	100
1983	White Carnation L5184M	Closed	1990	65.00	100
1983	Lactiflora Peony L5185M	Closed	1990	65.00	100
1983	Begonia L5186M	Closed	1990	67.50	100
1983	Rhododendrom L5187M	Closed	1990	67.50	190
1983	Miniature Begonia L5188M	Closed	1990	80.00	120
1983	Chrysanthemum L5189M	Closed	1990	100.00	150
1983	California Poppy L5190M	Closed	1990	97.50	180
1985	Predicting the Future L5191G	Closed	1985	135.00	400
1984	Lolita L5192G	Open		80.00	165
1984	Juanita L5193G	Open		80.00	165
1984	Roving Photographer L5194G	Closed	1985	145.00	1400
1983	Say "Cheese!" L5195G	Closed	1990	170.00	600
1983	"Maestro, Music Please!" L5196G	Closed	1988	135.00	500
1983	Female Physician L5197	Open		120.00	260
1984	Boy Graduate L5198G	Open		160.00	290
1984	Girl Graduate L5199G	Open		160.00	285
1984	Male Soccer Player L5200G	Closed	1988	155.00	475
1984	Special Male Soccer Player L5200.3G	Closed	1988	150.00	500
1983	Josefa Feeding Duck L5201G	Closed	1991	125.00	250-300
1983	Aracely with Ducks L5202G	Closed	1991	125.00	250-300
1984	Little Jester L5203G	Closed	1993	75.00	300-325
1984	Little Jester L5203M	Closed	1992	75.00	200-250
1983	Sharpening the Cutlery L5204	Closed	1988	210.00	1250
1983	Lamplighter L5205G	Open		170.00	395
1983	Yachtsman L5206G	Closed	1994	110.00	210
1983	A Tall Yarn L5207G	Open		260.00	545
1983	Professor L5208G	Open		205.00	550-750
1983	School Marm L5209G	Closed	1990	205.00	900
1984	Jolie L5210G	Open		105.00	220
1984	Angela L5211G	Open		105.00	220
1984	Evita L5212G	Open		105.00	195
1984	Lawyer L5213G	Open		250.00	570
1984	Architect L5214G	Closed	1990	140.00	450
1984	Fishing with Gramps w/base L5215G	Open		410.00	850
1984	On the Lake L5216G	Closed	1988	660.00	1000
1984	Spring L5217G	Open		90.00	185
1984	Spring L5217M	Open		90.00	185
1984	Autumn L5218G	Open		90.00	185
1984	Autumn L5218M	Open		90.00	185
1984	Summer L5219G	Open		90.00	185
1984	Summer L5219M	Open		90.00	185
1984	Winter L5220G	Open		90.00	185
1984	Winter L5220M	Open		90.00	185
1984	Sweet Scent L5221G	Open		80.00	145
1984	Sweet Scent L5221M	Open		80.00	145
1984	Pretty Pickings L5222G	Open		80.00	145
1984	Pretty Pickings L5222M	Open		80.00	145
1984	Spring is Here L5223G	Open		80.00	145
1984	Spring is Here L5223M	Open		80.00	145
1984	The Quest L5224G	Open		125.00	295
1984	Male Candleholder L5226	Closed	1985	660.00	1200
1984	Playful Piglets L5228G	Open		80.00	150
1984	Storytime L5229G	Closed	1990	245.00	950
1984	Graceful Swan L5230G	Open		35.00	90
1984	Swan with Wings Spread L5231G	Open		50.00	125
1984	Playful Kittens L5232G	Open		130.00	280
1984	Charlie the Tramp L5233G	Closed	1991	150.00	750-950
1984	Artistic Endeavor L5234G	Closed	1988	225.00	500-650
1984	Ballet Trio L5235G	Open		785.00	1650
1984	Cat and Mouse L5236G	Open		55.00	95
1984	Cat and Mouse L5236M	Closed	1992	55.00	95
1984	School Chums L5237G	Open		225.00	485
1984	Eskimo Boy with Pet L5238G	Open		55.00	115
1984	Eskimo Boy with Pet L5238M	Closed	1992	55.00	95
1984	Wine Taster L5239G	Open		190.00	395
1984	Lady from Majorca L5240G	Closed	1990	120.00	385
1984	Best Wishes L5244G	Closed	1986	185.00	325

Collectors' Information Bureau

*Quotes have been rounded up to nearest dollar

YEAR ISSUE	EDITION LIMIT	YEAR RETD.	ISSUE PRICE	*QUOTE U.S.$
1984 A Thought for Today L5245	Closed	1986	180.00	250
1984 St. Christopher L5246	Closed	1988	265.00	650
1984 Penguin L5247G	Closed	1988	70.00	200
1984 Penguin L5248G	Closed	1988	70.00	200
1984 Penguin L5249G	Closed	1988	70.00	175
1984 Exam Day L5250G	Closed	1994	115.00	210
1984 Torch Bearer L5251G	Closed	1988	100.00	400-500
1984 Dancing the Polka L5252G	Closed	1988	205.00	495
1984 Cadet L5253G	Closed	1984	150.00	550-650
1984 Making Paella L5254G	Closed	1993	215.00	500
1984 Spanish Soldier L5255G	Closed	1988	185.00	475-575
1984 Folk Dancing L5256G	Closed	1990	205.00	475-575
1984 Vase L5257.30	Closed	1988	55.00	200
1984 Vase L5258.30	Closed	1988	55.00	175
1984 Vase L5261.30	Closed	1988	70.00	125
1984 Vase L5262.30	Closed	1988	70.00	125
1984 Centerpiece-Decorated L5265M	Closed	1990	50.00	175
1985 Bust of Lady from Elche L5269M	Closed	1988	432.00	750
1985 Racing Motor Cyclist L5270G	Closed	1988	360.00	800
1985 Gazelle L5271G	Closed	1988	205.00	425-550
1985 Biking in the Country L5272G	Closed	1990	295.00	850
1985 Civil Guard at Attention L5273G	Closed	1988	170.00	500
1985 Wedding Day L5274G	Open		240.00	435
1985 Weary Ballerina L5275G	Closed	1995	175.00	310
1985 Weary Ballerina L5275M	Closed	1988	175.00	310
1985 Sailor Serenades His Girl L5276G	Closed	1988	315.00	950
1985 Pierrot with Puppy L5277G	Open		95.00	160
1985 Pierrot with Puppy and Ball L5278G	Open		95.00	160
1985 Pierrot with Concertina L5279G	Open		95.00	160
1985 Hiker L5280G	Closed	1988	195.00	425
1985 Nativity Scene "Haute Relief" L5281M	Closed	1988	210.00	450
1985 Over the Threshold L5282G	Open		150.00	290
1985 Socialite of the Twenties L5283G	Open		175.00	340
1985 Glorious Spring L5284G	Open		355.00	710
1985 Summer on the Farm L5285G	Open		235.00	455
1985 Fall Clean-up L5286G	Open		295.00	565
1985 Winter Frost L5287G	Open		270.00	520
1985 Mallard Duck L5288G	Closed	1994	310.00	520
1985 Little Leaguer Exercising L5289	Closed	1990	150.00	450
1985 Little Leaguer, Catcher L5290	Closed	1990	150.00	450
1985 Little Leaguer on Bench L5291	Closed	1990	150.00	450
1985 Love in Bloom L5292G	Open		225.00	425
1985 Mother and Child and Lamb L5299G	Closed	1988	180.00	750
1985 Medieval Courtship L5300G	Closed	1990	735.00	800
1985 Waiting to Tee Off L5301G	Open		145.00	295
1985 Antelope Drinking L5302	Closed	1988	215.00	650
1985 Playing w/Ducks at the Pond L5303G	Closed	1990	425.00	875
1985 Children at Play L5304	Closed	1990	220.00	550
1985 A Visit with Granny L5305G	Closed	1993	275.00	625
1985 Young Street Musicians L5306G	Closed	1988	300.00	1500
1985 Mini Kitten L5307G	Closed	1993	35.00	100
1985 Mini Cat L5308G	Closed	1993	35.00	75
1985 Mini Cocker Spaniel Pup L5309G	Closed	1993	35.00	125-450
1985 Mini Cocker Spaniel L5310G	Closed	1993	35.00	85-150
1985 Mini Puppies L5311G	Closed	1990	65.00	175
1985 Mini Bison Resting L5312G	Closed	1990	50.00	150
1985 Mini Bison Attacking L5313G	Closed	1990	57.50	225
1985 Mini Deer L5314G	Closed	1990	40.00	175
1985 Mini Dromedary L5315G	Closed	1990	45.00	150
1985 Mini Giraffe L5316G	Closed	1990	50.00	225
1985 Mini Lamb L5317G	Closed	1990	30.00	175
1985 Mini Seal Family L5318G	Closed	1990	77.50	215
1985 Wistful Centaur Girl L5319G	Closed	1990	157.00	450
1985 Demure Centaur Girl L5320	Closed	1990	157.00	425
1985 Parisian Lady L5321G	Closed	1990	193.00	325
1985 Viennese Lady L5322G	Closed	1994	160.00	295
1985 Milanese Lady L5323G	Closed	1994	180.00	400
1985 English Lady L5324G	Open		225.00	475
1985 Ice Cream Vendor L5325G	Closed	1995	380.00	650
1985 The Tailor L5326G	Closed	1988	335.00	900-1300
1985 Nippon Lady L5327G	Open		325.00	575
1985 Lady Equestrian L5328G	Closed	1988	160.00	450
1985 Gentleman Equestrian L5329G	Closed	1988	160.00	525
1985 Concert Violinist L5330G	Closed	1988	220.00	400
1985 Gymnast with Ring L5331	Closed	1988	95.00	295
1985 Gymnast Balancing Ball L5332	Closed	1988	95.00	375
1985 Gymnast Exercising w/Ball L5333G	Closed	1988	95.00	250
1985 Aerobics Push-Up L5334G	Closed	1988	110.00	295
1985 Aerobics Floor Exercises L5335G	Closed	1988	110.00	300
1985 "La Giaconda" L5337G	Closed	1988	110.00	400
1986 A Stitch in Time L5344G	Open		425.00	795
1986 A New Hat L5345G	Closed	1990	200.00	375
1986 Nature Girl L5346G	Closed	1988	450.00	1000
1986 Bedtime L5347G	Open		300.00	545
1986 On The Scent L5348G	Closed	1990	47.50	300
1986 Relaxing L5349G	Closed	1990	47.50	150
1986 On Guard L5350G	Closed	1990	50.00	200
1986 Woe is Me L5351G	Closed	1990	45.00	200
1986 Hindu Children L5352G	Open		250.00	445
1986 Eskimo Riders L5353G	Open		150.00	250
1986 Eskimo Riders L5353M	Open		150.00	250
1986 A Ride in the Country L5354G	Closed	1993	225.00	415
1986 Consideration L5355M	Closed	1988	100.00	225
1986 Wolf Hound L5356G	Closed	1990	45.00	225
1986 Oration L5357G	Open		170.00	295
1986 Little Sculptor L5358G	Closed	1990	160.00	325-400
1986 El Greco L5359G	Closed	1990	300.00	550
1986 Sewing Circle L5360G	Closed	1990	600.00	1250-1400
1986 Try This One L5361G	Open		225.00	385
1986 Still Life L5363G	Open		180.00	395
1986 Litter of Fun L5364G	Open		275.00	465
1986 Sunday in the Park L5365G	Open		375.00	625
1986 Can Can L5370G	Closed	1990	700.00	1200-1400
1986 Family Roots L5371G	Open		575.00	935
1986 Lolita L5372G	Closed	1993	120.00	250
1986 Carmencita L5373G	Closed	1993	120.00	250
1986 Pepita L5374G	Closed	1993	120.00	350
1986 Teresita L5375G	Closed	1993	120.00	350
1986 This One's Mine L5376G	Closed	1995	300.00	520
1986 A Touch of Class L5377G	Open		475.00	795
1986 Time for Reflection L5378G	Open		425.00	745
1986 Children's Games L5379G	Closed	1991	325.00	700
1986 Sweet Harvest L5380G	Closed	1990	450.00	850
1986 Serenade L5381	Closed	1990	450.00	625
1986 Lovers Serenade L5382G	Closed	1990	350.00	850
1986 Petite Maiden L5383	Closed	1990	110.00	350
1986 Petite Pair L5384	Open		225.00	400
1986 Scarecrow & the Lady L5385G	Open		350.00	680
1986 St. Vincent L5387	Closed	1990	190.00	350
1986 Sidewalk Serenade L5388G	Closed	1988	750.00	1100-1300
1986 Deep in Thought L5389G	Closed	1990	170.00	450
1986 Spanish Dancer L5390G	Closed	1990	170.00	450
1986 A Time to Rest L5391G	Closed	1990	170.00	275-375
1986 Balancing Act L5392G	Closed	1990	35.00	200
1986 Curiosity L5393G	Closed	1990	25.00	150
1986 Poor Puppy L5394G	Closed	1990	25.00	150-175
1986 Valencian Boy L5395G	Closed	1991	200.00	400
1986 The Puppet Painter L5396G	Open		500.00	850
1986 The Poet L5397G	Closed	1988	425.00	900
1986 At the Ball L5398G	Closed	1991	375.00	750
1987 Time To Rest L5399G	Closed	1993	175.00	295
1987 Time To Rest L5399M	Closed	1991	175.00	350
1987 The Wanderer L5400G	Open		150.00	245
1987 My Best Friend L5401G	Closed	1994	150.00	240
1987 Desert Tour L5402G	Closed	1990	950.00	1050
1987 The Drummer Boy L5403G	Open		225.00	400
1987 Cadet Captain L5404G	Closed	1990	175.00	360
1987 The Flag Bearer L5405G	Closed	1990	200.00	450
1987 The Bugler L5406G	Open		175.00	375
1987 At Attention L5407G	Open		175.00	325
1987 Sunday Stroll L5408G	Closed	1990	250.00	600
1987 Courting Time L5409	Closed	1990	425.00	550
1987 Pilar L5410G	Closed	1990	200.00	400
1987 Teresa L5411G	Closed	1990	225.00	430
1987 Isabel L5412G	Closed	1990	225.00	450
1987 Mexican Dancers L5415G	Open		800.00	1195
1987 In the Garden L5416G	Open		200.00	325
1987 Artist's Model L5417	Closed	1990	425.00	475
1987 Short Eared Owl L5418G	Closed	1990	200.00	360
1987 Great Gray Owl L5419G	Closed	1990	190.00	195
1987 Horned Owl L5420G	Closed	1990	150.00	225
1987 Barn Owl L5421G	Closed	1990	120.00	175
1987 Hawk Owl L5422G	Closed	1990	120.00	195-225
1987 Intermezzo L5424	Closed	1990	325.00	550
1987 Studying in the Park L5425G	Closed	1991	675.00	950
1987 Studying in the Park L5425M	Closed	1990	675.00	400-600
1987 One, Two, Three L5426G	Closed	1995	240.00	390
1987 Saint Nicholas L5427G	Closed	1991	425.00	750
1987 Feeding the Pigeons L5428	Closed	1990	490.00	700
1987 Happy Birthday L5429G	Open		100.00	155
1987 Music Time L5430G	Closed	1990	500.00	700
1987 Midwife L5431G	Closed	1990	175.00	650
1987 Midwife L5431M	Closed	1990	175.00	525
1987 Monkey L5432G	Closed	1990	60.00	200
1987 Kangaroo L5433G	Closed	1990	65.00	175-300
1987 Miniature Polar Bear L5434G	Open		65.00	110
1987 Cougar L5435G	Closed	1990	65.00	275
1987 Lion L5436G	Closed	1990	50.00	200-300
1987 Rhino L5437G	Closed	1990	50.00	175
1987 Elephant L5438G	Closed	1990	50.00	250
1987 The Bride L5439G	Closed	1995	250.00	425
1987 Poetry of Love L5442G	Open		500.00	865
1987 Sleepy Trio L5443G	Open		190.00	305
1987 Will You Marry Me? L5447G	Closed	1994	750.00	1250
1987 Naptime L5448G	Open		135.00	250
1987 Naptime L5448M	Open		135.00	250
1987 Goodnight L5449	Open		225.00	375
1987 I Hope She Does L5450G	Open		190.00	345
1988 Study Buddies L5451G	Open		225.00	295
1988 Masquerade Ball L5452G	Closed	1993	220.00	375
1988 Masquerade Ball L5452M	Closed	1992	220.00	265
1988 For You L5453G	Open		450.00	640
1988 For Me? L5454G	Open		290.00	395
1988 Bashful Bather L5455G	Open		150.00	190
1988 Bashful Bather L5455M	Closed	1992	150.00	180
1988 New Playmates L5456G	Open		160.00	230
1988 New Playmates L5456M	Closed	1992	160.00	190
1988 Bedtime Story L5457G	Open		275.00	355
1988 Bedtime Story L5457M	Closed	1992	275.00	330
1988 A Barrow of Fun L5460G	Open		370.00	525
1988 A Barrow of Fun L5460M	Open		370.00	450
1988 Koala Love L5461G	Closed	1993	115.00	200-300
1988 Practice Makes Perfect L5462G	Open		375.00	545
1988 Look At Me! L5465G	Open		375.00	495
1988 Look At Me! L5465M	Closed	1992	375.00	435
1988 "Chit-Chat" L5466G	Open		150.00	198
1988 "Chit-Chat" L5466M	Closed	1992	150.00	180
1988 May Flowers L5467G	Open		160.00	215
1988 May Flowers L5467M	Closed	1992	160.00	190
1988 "Who's The Fairest?" L5468G	Open		150.00	200
1988 "Who's The Fairest?" L5468M	Closed	1992	150.00	180
1988 Lambkins L5469G	Closed	1993	150.00	210
1988 Lambkins L5469M	Closed	1989	150.00	195
1988 Tea Time L5470G	Open		280.00	385
1988 Sad Sax L5471G	Open		175.00	205
1988 Circus Sam L5472G	Open		175.00	205
1988 How You've Grown! L5474G	Open		180.00	250
1988 How You've Grown! L5474M	Closed	1992	180.00	215
1988 A Lesson Shared L5475G	Open		150.00	190
1988 A Lesson Shared L5475M	Closed	1992	150.00	170
1988 St. Joseph L5476G	Open		210.00	270
1988 Mary L5477G	Open		130.00	165
1988 Baby Jesus L5478G	Open		55.00	75
1988 King Melchior L5479G	Open		210.00	265
1988 King Gaspar L5480G	Open		210.00	265
1988 King Balthasar L5481G	Open		210.00	265
1988 Ox L5482G	Open		125.00	175
1988 Donkey L5483G	Open		125.00	175
1988 Lost Lamb L5484G	Open		100.00	140
1988 Shepherd Boy L5485G	Open		140.00	190
1988 Debutantes L5486G	Open		490.00	695
1988 Debutantes L5486M	Closed	1992	490.00	635
1988 Ingenue L5487G	Open		110.00	145
1988 Ingenue L5487M	Closed	1992	110.00	130
1988 Sandcastles L5488G	Closed	1993	160.00	220
1988 Sandcastles L5488M	Closed	1992	160.00	200
1988 Justice L5489G	Closed	1993	675.00	950
1988 Flor Maria L5490G	Open		500.00	635
1988 Heavenly Strings L5491G	Closed	1993	140.00	160
1988 Heavenly Cellist L5492G	Closed	1993	240.00	240
1988 Angel with Lute L5493G	Closed	1993	140.00	160
1988 Angel with Clarinet L5494G	Closed	1993	140.00	160
1988 Angelic Choir L5495G	Closed	1993	300.00	550
1988 Recital L5496G	Open		190.00	285
1988 Dress Rehearsal L5497G	Open		290.00	420
1988 Opening Night L5498G	Open		190.00	285
1988 Pretty Ballerina L5499G	Open		190.00	285
1988 Prayerful Moment (blue) L5500G	Open		90.00	110
1988 Time to Sew (blue) L5501G	Open		90.00	110
1988 Time to Sew (white) L5501.3	Closed	1991	90.00	200
1988 Meditation (blue) L5502G	Open		90.00	110
1988 Hurry Now L5503G	Open		180.00	250
1988 Hurry Now L5503M	Closed	1992	180.00	240
1988 Silver Vase No. 20 L5531.4	Closed	1991	135.00	275
1989 Flowers for Sale L5537G	Open		1200.00	1550
1989 Puppy Dog Tails L5539G	Open		1200.00	1595
1989 An Evening Out L5540G	Closed	1991	350.00	450
1989 Melancholy w/base L5542G	Open		375.00	455
1989 "Hello, Flowers" L5543G	Closed	1993	385.00	545
1989 Reaching the Goal L5546G	Open		215.00	275
1989 Only the Beginning L5547G	Open		215.00	275
1989 Pretty Posies L5548G	Closed	1994	425.00	530
1989 My New Pet L5549G	Open		150.00	185
1989 Serene Moment (blue) L5550G	Closed	1993	115.00	225
1989 Serene Moment (white) L5550.3G	Closed	1991	115.00	225
1989 Serene Moment (white) L5550.3M	Closed	1991	115.00	135
1989 Call to Prayer (blue) L5551G	Closed	1993	100.00	225
1989 Call to Prayer (white) L5551.3G	Closed	1991	100.00	225
1989 Call to Prayer (white) L5551.3M	Closed	1991	100.00	120
1989 Morning Chores (blue) L5552G	Closed	1993	115.00	225
1989 Morning Chores (white) L5552G	Closed	1991	115.00	225
1989 Wild Goose Chase L5553G	Open		175.00	230
1989 Pretty and Prim L5554G	Open		215.00	270
1989 "Let's Make Up" L5555G	Open		215.00	265
1989 Wide Tulip Vase L5560G	Closed	1990	110.00	300
1989 Green Clover Vase L5561G	Closed	1991	130.00	225
1989 Sad Parting L5583G	Open		375.00	525
1989 Daddy's Girl/Father's Day L5584G	Open		315.00	395
1989 Fine Melody w/base L5585G	Closed	1993	225.00	325
1989 Sad Note w/base L5586G	Closed	1993	185.00	375
1989 Wedding Cake L5587G	Open		595.00	750
1989 Blustery Day L5588G	Closed	1993	185.00	230
1989 Pretty Pose L5589G	Closed	1993	185.00	230
1989 Spring Breeze L5590G	Closed	1993	185.00	230
1989 Garden Treasures L5591G	Closed	1993	185.00	230
1989 Male Siamese Dancer L5592G	Closed	1993	345.00	400
1989 Siamese Dancer L5593G	Closed	1993	345.00	420
1989 Playful Romp L5594G	Open		215.00	270
1989 Joy in a Basket L5595G	Open		215.00	270
1989 A Gift of Love L5596G	Open		400.00	495
1989 Summer Soiree L5597G	Open		150.00	180
1989 Bridesmaid L5598G	Open		150.00	180
1989 Coquette L5599G	Open		150.00	180
1989 The Blues w/base L5600G	Closed	1993	265.00	395
1989 "Ole" L5601G	Open		365.00	460
1989 Close To My Heart L5603G	Open		125.00	165
1989 Spring Token L5604G	Open		175.00	230
1989 Floral Treasures L5605G	Open		195.00	250
1989 Quiet Evening L5606G	Closed	1993	125.00	165
1989 Calling A Friend L5607G	Open		125.00	180
1989 Baby Doll L5608G	Open		150.00	180
1989 Playful Friends L5609G	Closed	1995	135.00	170
1989 Star Struck w/base L5610G	Open		335.00	420
1989 Sad Clown w/base L5611G	Open		335.00	420
1989 Reflecting w/base L5612G	Closed	1994	335.00	420
1989 Startled L5614G	Open		425.00	425
1989 Bathing Beauty L5615G	Closed	1991	265.00	350-475
1989 Candleholder L5625G	Closed	1990	105.00	125
1989 Candleholder L5626	Closed	1990	90.00	125

*Quotes have been rounded up to nearest dollar

FIGURINES/COTTAGES

YEAR ISSUE		EDITION LIMIT	YEAR RETD.	ISSUE PRICE	*QUOTE U.S.$
1989	Lladró Vase L5631G	Closed	1990	150.00	300-350
1990	Water Dreamer Vase L5633G	Closed	1990	150.00	350-400
1990	Cat Nap L5640G	Open		125.00	145
1990	The King's Guard w/base L5642G	Closed	1993	950.00	1100
1990	Cathy L5643G	Open		200.00	235
1990	Susan L5644G	Open		190.00	215
1990	Elizabeth L5645G	Open		190.00	215
1990	Cindy L5646G	Open		190.00	215
1990	Sara L5647G	Open		200.00	230
1990	Courtney L5648G	Open		200.00	230
1990	Nothing To Do L5649G	Open		190.00	220
1990	Anticipation L5650G	Closed	1993	300.00	375
1990	Musical Muse L5651G	Open		375.00	440
1989	Marbella Clock L5652	Closed	1994	125.00	235
1989	Avila Clock L5653	Closed	1995	135.00	135
1990	Venetian Carnival L5658G	Closed	1993	500.00	575
1990	Barnyard Scene L5659G	Open		200.00	450
1990	Sunning In Ipanema L5660G	Closed	1993	370.00	440-525
1990	Traveling Artist L5661G	Closed	1994	250.00	290
1990	May Dance L5662G	Open		170.00	210
1990	Spring Dance L5663G	Open		170.00	300
1990	Giddy Up L5664G	Closed	1994	190.00	230
1990	Hang On! L5665G	Closed	1995	225.00	285
1990	Trino At The Beach L5666G	Closed	1995	390.00	500
1990	Valencian Harvest L5668G	Closed	1993	175.00	350-400
1990	Valencian FLowers L5669G	Closed	1993	370.00	375
1990	Valencian Beauty L5670G	Closed	1993	175.00	325
1990	Little Dutch Gardener L5671G	Closed	1993	400.00	475
1990	Hi There! L5672G	Open		450.00	520
1990	A Quiet Moment L5673G	Open		450.00	520
1990	A Faun And A Friend L5674G	Open		450.00	520
1990	Tee Time L5675G	Closed	1993	280.00	315
1990	Wandering Minstrel L5676G	Closed	1993	270.00	310
1990	Twilight Years L5677G	Open		370.00	420
1990	I Feel Pretty L5678G	Open		190.00	230
1990	In No Hurry L5679G	Closed	1994	550.00	640
1990	Traveling In Style L5680G	Closed	1994	425.00	495
1990	On The Road L5681G	Closed	1991	320.00	450-550
1990	Breezy Afternoon L5682G	Open		180.00	195
1990	Breezy Afternoon L5682M	Open		180.00	195
1990	Beautiful Burro L5683G	Closed	1993	280.00	365
1990	Barnyard Reflections L5684G	Closed	1993	460.00	525
1990	Promenade L5685G	Closed	1993	275.00	325
1990	On The Avenue L5686G	Closed	1993	275.00	325
1990	Afternoon Stroll L5687G	Closed	1994	275.00	350
1990	Dog's Best Friend L5688G	Open		250.00	295
1990	Can I Help? L5689G	Open		250.00	325
1990	Marshland Mates w/base L5691G	Open		950.00	1200
1990	Street Harmonies w/base L5692G	Closed	1993	3200.00	3750
1990	Circus Serenade L5694G	Closed	1994	300.00	375
1990	Concertina L5695G	Closed	1994	300.00	360
1990	Mandolin Serenade L5696G	Closed	1994	300.00	360
1990	Over The Clouds L5697G	Open		275.00	310
1990	Don't Look Down L5698G	Open		330.00	395
1990	Sitting Pretty L5699G	Open		300.00	340
1990	Southern Charm L5700G	Open		675.00	1025
1990	Just A Little Kiss L5701G	Open		320.00	375
1990	Back To School L5702G	Closed	1993	350.00	300-445
1990	Behave! L5703G	Closed	1994	230.00	265
1990	Swan Song L5704G	Closed	1995	350.00	410
1990	The Swan And The Princess L5705G	Closed	1994	350.00	425-450
1990	We Can't Play L5706G	Open		200.00	235
1990	After School L5707G	Closed	1993	280.00	315
1990	My First Class L5708G	Closed	1993	280.00	315
1990	Between Classes L5709G	Closed	1993	280.00	315
1990	Fantasy Friend L5710G	Closed	1993	420.00	495
1990	A Christmas Wish L5711G	Open		350.00	410
1990	Sleepy Kitten L5712G	Open		110.00	130
1990	The Snow Man L5713G	Open		300.00	350
1990	First Ballet L5714G	Open		370.00	420
1990	Mommy, it's Cold! L5715G	Closed	1994	360.00	435-450
1990	Land of The Giants L5716G	Closed	1994	275.00	400
1990	Rock A Bye Baby L5717G	Open		300.00	365
1990	Sharing Secrets L5720G	Open		290.00	335
1990	Once Upon A Time L5721G	Open		550.00	650
1990	Follow Me L5722G	Open		140.00	160
1990	Heavenly Chimes L5723G	Open		100.00	120
1990	Angelic Voice L5724G	Open		125.00	145
1990	Making A Wish L5725G	Open		125.00	145
1990	Sweep Away The Clouds L5726G	Open		125.00	145
1990	Angel Care L5727G	Open		190.00	210
1990	Heavenly Dreamer L5728G	Open		100.00	120
1991	Carousel Charm L5731G	Closed	1994	1700.00	1850
1991	Carousel Canter L5732G	Closed	1994	1700.00	1850
1991	Horticulturist L5733G	Closed	1993	450.00	495
1991	Pilgrim Couple L5734G	Closed	1993	490.00	525
1991	Big Sister L5735G	Open		650.00	685
1991	Puppet Show L5736G	Open		280.00	295
1991	Little Prince L5737G	Closed	1993	295.00	315
1991	Best Foot Forward L5738G	Closed	1994	280.00	305
1991	Lap Full of Love L5739G	Closed	1995	275.00	295
1991	Alice In Wonderland L5740G	Open		440.00	485
1991	Dancing Class L5741G	Open		340.00	365
1991	Bridal Portrait L5742G	Closed	1995	480.00	560
1991	Don't Forget Me L5743G	Open		150.00	160
1991	Bull & Donkey L5744G	Open		250.00	275
1991	Baby Jesus L5745G	Open		170.00	185
1991	St. Joseph L5746G	Open		350.00	375
1991	Mary L5747G	Open		275.00	295
1991	Shepherd Girl L5748G	Open		150.00	165
1991	Shepherd Boy L5749G	Open		225.00	245
1991	Little Lamb L5750G	Open		40.00	42
1991	Walk With Father L5751G	Closed	1994	375.00	440
1991	Little Virgin L5752G	Closed	1994	295.00	325
1991	Hold Her Still L5753G	Closed	1993	650.00	700
1991	Singapore Dancers L5754G	Closed	1993	950.00	1195
1991	Claudette L5755G	Closed	1993	265.00	350
1991	Ashley L5756G	Closed	1993	265.00	300
1991	Beautiful Tresses L5757G	Closed	1993	725.00	875
1991	Sunday Best L5758G	Open		725.00	785
1991	Presto! L5759G	Closed	1993	275.00	325
1991	Interrupted Nap L5760G	Closed	1995	325.00	350
1991	Out For A Romp L5761G	Closed	1994	375.00	410
1991	Checking The Time L5762G	Closed	1995	560.00	595
1991	Musical Partners L5763G	Closed	1995	625.00	675
1991	Seeds Of Laughter L5764G	Closed	1995	525.00	575
1991	Hats Off To Fun L5765G	Closed	1995	475.00	510
1991	Charming Duet L5766G	Open		575.00	625
1991	First Sampler L5767G	Closed	1995	625.00	680
1991	Academy Days L5768G	Closed	1993	280.00	310
1991	Faithful Steed L5769G	Closed	1994	370.00	395
1991	Out For A Spin L5770G	Closed	1994	390.00	420
1991	The Magic Of Laughter L5771G	Open		950.00	1050
1991	Little Dreamers L5772G	Open		230.00	240
1991	Little Dreamers L5772M	Open		230.00	240
1991	Graceful Offering L5773G	Closed	1995	850.00	895
1991	Nature's Gifts L5774G	Closed	1994	900.00	975
1991	Gift Of Beauty L5775G	Closed	1995	850.00	1100
1991	Lover's Paradise L5779G	Open		2250.00	2450
1991	Walking The Fields L5780G	Closed	1993	725.00	795
1991	Not Too Close L5781G	Closed	1994	365.00	450
1991	My Chores L5782G	Open		325.00	355
1991	Special Delivery L5783G	Closed	1994	525.00	550
1991	A Cradle Of Kittens L5784G	Open		360.00	385
1991	Ocean Beauty L5785G	Open		625.00	665
1991	Story Hour L5786G	Open		550.00	625
1991	Sophisticate L5787G	Open		185.00	195
1991	Talk Of The Town L5788G	Open		185.00	195
1991	The Flirt L5789G	Open		185.00	195
1991	Carefree L5790G	Open		300.00	325
1991	Fairy Godmother L5791G	Closed	1994	375.00	450
1991	Reverent Moment L5792G	Open		295.00	320
1991	Precocious Ballerina L5793G	Closed	1995	575.00	625
1991	Precious Cargo L5794G	Closed	1994	460.00	495
1991	Floral Getaway L5795G	Closed	1993	625.00	745
1991	Holy Night L5796G	Closed	1994	330.00	340
1991	Come Out And Play L5797G	Closed	1994	275.00	300
1991	Milkmaid L5798G	Closed	1993	450.00	495
1991	Shall We Dance? L5799G	Closed	1993	600.00	750
1991	Elegant Promenade L5802G	Open		775.00	825
1991	Playing Tag L5804G	Closed	1993	170.00	190
1991	Tumbling L5805G	Closed	1993	130.00	140
1991	Tumbling L5805M	Closed	1992	130.00	140
1991	Tickling L5806G	Closed	1993	130.00	145
1991	Tickling L5806M	Closed	1992	130.00	145
1991	My Puppies L5807G	Closed	1993	325.00	360
1991	Musically Inclined L5810G	Closed	1993	235.00	250
1991	Littlest Clown L5811G	Open		225.00	240
1991	Tired Friend L5812G	Open		225.00	245
1991	Having A Ball L5813G	Open		225.00	240
1991	Curtain Call L5814G	Closed	1994	490.00	520
1991	Curtain Call L5814M	Closed	1994	490.00	520
1991	In Full Relave L5815G	Closed	1994	490.00	520
1991	In Full Relave L5815M	Closed	1994	490.00	520
1991	Prima Ballerina L5816G	Closed	1994	490.00	520
1991	Prima Ballerina L5816M	Closed	1994	490.00	520
1991	Backstage Preparation L5817G	Closed	1994	490.00	520
1991	Backstage Preparation L5817M	Closed	1994	490.00	520
1991	On Her Toes L5818G	Closed	1994	490.00	520
1991	On Her Toes L5818M	Closed	1994	490.00	520
1991	Allegory Of Liberty L5819G	Open		1950.00	2100
1991	Dance Of Love L5820G	Closed	1993	575.00	625
1991	Minstrel's Love L5821G	Closed	1993	525.00	575
1991	Little Unicorn L5826G	Open		275.00	295
1991	Little Unicorn L5826M	Open		275.00	295
1991	I've Got It L5827G	Closed	1995	170.00	180
1991	Next At Bat L5828G	Open		170.00	180
1991	Heavenly Harpist L5830	Yr.Iss.	1991	135.00	165
1991	Jazz Horn L5832G	Open		295.00	310
1991	Jazz Sax L5833G	Open		295.00	315
1991	Jazz Bass L5834G	Open		395.00	425
1991	I Do L5835G	Open		165.00	190
1991	Sharing Sweets L5836G	Open		220.00	245
1991	Sing With Me L5837G	Open		240.00	250
1991	On The Move L5838G	Open		340.00	395
1992	A Quiet Afternoon L5843G	Closed	1995	1050.00	1125
1992	Flirtatious Jester L5844G	Open		890.00	925
1992	Dressing The Baby L5845G	Open		295.00	295
1992	All Tuckered Out L5846G	Open		220.00	255
1992	All Tuckered Out L5846M	Open		220.00	255
1992	The Loving Family L5848G	Closed	1994	950.00	985
1992	Inspiring Muse L5850G	Closed	1994	1200.00	1250
1992	Feathered Fantasy L5851G	Open		1200.00	1250
1992	Easter Bonnets L5852G	Closed	1993	265.00	400
1992	Floral Admiration L5853G	Open		690.00	825
1992	Floral Fantasy L5854G	Closed	1995	690.00	710
1992	Afternoon Jaunt L5855G	Closed	1993	420.00	440
1992	Circus Concert L5856G	Open		570.00	595
1992	Grand Entrance L5857G	Closed	1993	265.00	275
1992	Waiting to Dance L5858G	Closed	1993	295.00	335
1992	At The Ball L5859G	Open		295.00	330
1992	Fairy Garland L5860G	Closed	1993	630.00	750
1992	Fairy Flowers L5861G	Closed	1995	630.00	655
1992	Fragrant Bouquet L5862G	Open		350.00	360
1992	Dressing For The Ballet L5865G	Closed	1995	395.00	415
1992	Final Touches L5866G	Closed	1995	395.00	415
1992	Serene Valenciana L5867G	Closed	1994	365.00	385
1992	Loving Valenciana L5868G	Closed	1995	365.00	385
1992	Fallas Queen L5869G	Closed	1995	420.00	440
1992	Olympic Torch w/Fantasy Logo L5870G	Closed	1994	165.00	145
1992	Olympic Champion w/Fantasy Logo L5871G	Closed	1994	165.00	145
1992	Olympic Pride w/Fantasy Logo L5872G	Closed	1994	165.00	495
1992	Modern Mother L5873G	Open		325.00	335
1992	Off We Go L5874G	Closed	1994	365.00	385
1992	Angelic Cymbalist L5876	Yr.Iss.	1992	140.00	165
1992	Guest of Honor L5877G	Open		195.00	200
1992	Sister's Pride L5878G	Open		595.00	615
1992	Shot On Goal L5879G	Open		1100.00	1150
1992	Playful Unicorn L5880G	Open		295.00	320
1992	Playful Unicorn L5880M	Open		295.00	320
1992	Mischievous Mouse L5881G	Open		285.00	295
1992	Restful Mouse L5882G	Open		285.00	295
1992	Loving Mouse L5883G	Open		285.00	295
1992	From This Day Forward L5885G	Open		265.00	285
1992	Hippity Hop L5886G	Closed	1995	95.00	95
1992	Washing Up L5887G	Closed	1995	95.00	95
1992	That Tickles! L5888G	Closed	1995	95.00	105
1992	Snack Time L5889G	Closed	1995	95.00	105
1992	The Aviator L5891G	Open		375.00	415
1992	Circus Magic L5892G	Open		470.00	495
1992	Friendship In Bloom L5893G	Closed	1995	650.00	685
1992	Precious Petals L5894G	Open		395.00	415
1992	Bouquet of Blossoms L5895G	Open		295.00	295
1992	The Loaves & Fishes L5896G	Open		695.00	760
1992	Trimming The Tree L5897G	Open		900.00	925
1992	Spring Splendor L5898G	Open		440.00	450
1992	Just One More L5899G	Open		450.00	495
1992	Sleep Tight L5900G	Open		450.00	495
1992	Surprise L5901G	Open		325.00	335
1992	Easter Bunnies L5902G	Open		240.00	250
1992	Down The Aisle L5903G	Open		295.00	295
1992	Sleeping Bunny L5904G	Open		75.00	75
1992	Attentive Bunny L5905G	Open		75.00	75
1992	Preening Bunny L5906G	Open		75.00	80
1992	Sitting Bunny L5907G	Open		75.00	80
1992	Just A Little More L5908G	Open		370.00	380
1992	All Dressed Up L5909G	Open		440.00	450
1992	Making A Wish L5910G	Open		790.00	825
1992	Swans Take Flight L5912G	Open		2850.00	2950
1992	Rose Ballet L5919G	Open		210.00	215
1992	Swan Ballet L5920G	Open		210.00	215
1992	Take Your Medicine L5921G	Open		360.00	370
1990	Floral Clock L5924	Closed	1995	N/A	165
1990	Garland Quartz Clock L5926	Closed	1995	195.00	195
1992	Jazz Clarinet L5928G	Open		295.00	295
1992	Jazz Drums L5929G	Open		595.00	610
1992	Jazz Duo L5930G	Open		795.00	885
1993	The Ten Commandments w/Base L5933G	Open		930.00	930
1993	The Holy Teacher L5934G	Open		375.00	375
1993	Nutcracker Suite L5935G	Open		620.00	620
1993	Little Skipper L5936G	Open		320.00	320
1993	Riding The Waves L5941G	Open		405.00	405
1993	World of Fantasy L5943G	Closed	1995	295.00	295
1993	The Great Adventure L5944G	Closed	1994	325.00	325
1993	A Mother's Way L5946G	Open		1350.00	1350
1993	General Practitioner L5947G	Open		360.00	360
1993	Physician L5948G	Open		360.00	360
1993	Angel Candleholder w/Lyre L5949G	Open		295.00	315
1993	Angel Candleholder w/Tambourine L5950G	Open		295.00	315
1993	Sounds of Summer L5953G	Open		125.00	142
1993	Sounds of Winter L5954G	Open		125.00	142
1993	Sounds of Fall L5955G	Open		125.00	142
1993	Sounds of Spring L5956G	Open		125.00	142
1993	The Glass Slipper L5957G	Open		475.00	475
1993	Country Ride w/base L5958G	Open		2850.00	2875
1993	It's Your Turn L5959G	Open		365.00	365
1993	On Patrol L5960G	Open		395.00	445
1993	The Great Teacher w/base L5961G	Open		850.00	850
1993	Angelic Melody L5963	Yr.Iss.	1993	145.00	170
1993	The Great Voyage L5964G	Closed	1994	50.00	50
1993	The Clipper Ship w/base L5965M	Open		240.00	250
1993	Flowers Forever w/base L5966G	Open		4150.00	4150
1993	Honeymoon Ride w/base L5968G	Closed	1995	2750.00	2750
1993	A Special Toy L5971G	Open		815.00	815
1993	Before the Dance w/base L5972G	Open		3550.00	3550
1993	Before the Dance w/base L5972M	Open		3550.00	3550
1993	Family Outing w/base L5974G	Open		4275.00	4275
1993	Up and Away w/base L5975G	Open		2850.00	2850
1993	The Fireman L5976G	Open		395.00	445
1993	Revelation w/base (white) L5977G	Closed	1995	310.00	310
1993	Revelation w/base (black) L5978M	Closed	1995	310.00	310
1993	Revelation w/base (sand) L5979M	Closed	1995	310.00	310
1993	The Past w/base (white) L5980G	Closed	1995	310.00	310
1993	The Past w/base (black) L5981M	Closed	1995	310.00	310
1993	The Past w/base (sand) L5982M	Closed	1995	310.00	310

YEAR ISSUE		EDITION LIMIT	YEAR RETD.	ISSUE PRICE	*QUOTE U.S.$
1993	Beauty w/base (white) L5983G	Closed	1995	310.00	310
1993	Beauty w/base (black) L5984M	Closed	1995	310.00	310
1993	Beauty w/base (sand) L5985M	Closed	1995	310.00	310
1993	Sunday Sermon L5986G	Open		425.00	425
1993	Talk to Me L5987G	Open		145.00	165
1993	Taking Time L5988G	Open		145.00	165
1993	A Mother's Touch L5989G	Open		470.00	470
1993	Thoughtful Caress L5990G	Open		225.00	225
1993	Love Story L5991G	Open		2800.00	2800
1993	Unicorn and Friend L5993G	Open		355.00	355
1993	Unicorn and Friend L5993M	Open		355.00	355
1993	Meet My Friend L5994G	Open		695.00	695
1993	Soft Meow L5995G	Open		480.00	515
1993	Bless the Child L5996G	Closed	1994	465.00	465
1993	One More Try L5997G	Open		715.00	715
1993	My Dad L6001G	Closed	1995	550.00	575
1993	Down You Go L6002G	Open		815.00	815
1993	Ready To Learn L6003G	Open		650.00	650
1993	Bar Mitzvah Day L6004G	Open		395.00	430
1993	Christening Day w/base L6005G	Closed	1995	1425.00	1425
1993	Oriental Colonade w/base L6006G	Closed	1995	1875.00	1875
1993	The Goddess & Unicorn w/base L6007G	Open		1675.00	1675
1993	Joyful Event L6008G	Open		825.00	825
1993	Monday's Child (Boy) L6011G	Open		245.00	270
1993	Monday's Child (Girl) L6012G	Open		260.00	290
1993	Tuesday's Child (Boy) L6013G	Open		225.00	250
1993	Tuesday's Child (Girl) L6014G	Open		245.00	270
1993	Wednesday's Child (Boy) L6015G	Open		245.00	270
1993	Wednesday's Child (Girl) L6016G	Open		245.00	270
1993	Thursday's Child (Boy) L6017G	Open		225.00	250
1993	Thursday's Child (Girl) L6018G	Open		245.00	270
1993	Friday's Child (Boy) L6019G	Open		225.00	250
1993	Friday's Child (Girl) L6020G	Open		225.00	250
1993	Saturday's Child (Boy) L6021G	Open		245.00	270
1993	Saturday's Child (Girl) L6022G	Open		245.00	270
1993	Angelic Melody-L5963G	Yr.Iss.	1993	145.00	145-175
1993	Sunday's Child (Boy) L6023G	Open		225.00	250
1993	Sunday's Child (Girl) L6024G	Open		225.00	250
1993	Barnyard See Saw L6025G	Open		500.00	500
1993	My Turn L6026G	Open		515.00	515
1993	Hanukah Lights L6027G	Open		345.00	395
1993	Mazel Tov! L6028G	Open		380.00	395
1993	Hebrew Scholar L6029G	Open		225.00	245
1993	On The Go L6031G	Closed	1995	475.00	485
1993	On The Green L6032G	Open		645.00	645
1993	Monkey Business L6034G	Closed	1994	745.00	745
1993	Young Princess L6036G	Open		240.00	240
1994	Saint James L6084G	Open		310.00	310
1994	Angelic Harmony L6085G	Open		495.00	550
1994	Allow Me L6086G	Open		1625.00	1625
1994	Loving Care L6087G	Open		250.00	270
1994	Communion Prayer (Boy) L6088G	Open		194.00	200
1994	Communion Prayer (Girl) L6089G	Open		198.00	210
1994	Baseball Player L6090G	Open		295.00	310
1994	Basketball Player L6091G	Open		295.00	310
1994	The Prince L6092G	Open		325.00	325
1994	Songbird L6093G	Open		395.00	395
1994	The Sportsman L6096G	Open		495.00	540
1994	Sleeping Bunny w/Flowers L6097G	Open		110.00	110
1994	Attentive Bunny w/Flowers L6098G	Open		140.00	140
1994	Preening Bunny w/Flowers L6099G	Open		140.00	140
1994	Sitting Bunny With Flowers L6100G	Open		110.00	110
1994	Follow Us L6101G	Open		198.00	215
1994	Mother's Little Helper L6102G	Open		275.00	285
1994	Beautiful Ballerina L6103G	Open		250.00	270
1994	Finishing Touches L6104	Open		240.00	250
1994	Spring Joy L6106G	Open		795.00	795
1994	Football Player L6107	Open		295.00	310
1994	Hockey Player L6108G	Open		295.00	310
1994	Meal Time L6109G	Open		495.00	515
1994	Medieval Maiden L6110G	Open		150.00	165
1994	Medieval Soldier L6111G	Open		225.00	245
1994	Medieval Lord L6112G	Open		285.00	300
1994	Medieval Lady L6113G	Open		225.00	225
1994	Medieval Princess L6114G	Open		245.00	245
1994	Medieval Prince L6115G	Open		295.00	315
1994	Medieval Majesty L6116G	Open		315.00	325
1994	Constance L6117G	Open		195.00	205
1994	Musketeer Portos L6118G	Open		220.00	230
1994	Musketeer Aramis L6119G	Open		275.00	295
1994	Musketeer Dartagnan L6120G	Open		245.00	270
1994	Musketeer Athos L6121G	Open		245.00	270
1994	A Great Adventure L6122	Open		198.00	215
1994	Out For a Stroll L6123G	Open		198.00	215
1994	Travelers Rest L6124G	Open		275.00	295
1994	Angelic Violinist L6126G	Yr.Iss.	1994	150.00	185
1994	Sweet Dreamers L6127G	Open		280.00	290
1994	Christmas Melodies L6128G	Open		375.00	385
1994	Little Friends L6129G	Open		225.00	235
1996	Spring Enchantment L6130G	Open		245.00	245
1994	Angel of Peace L6131G	Open		345.00	370
1994	Angel with Garland L6133G	Open		345.00	370
1994	Birthday Party L6134G	Open		395.00	425
1994	Football Star L6135	Open		295.00	295
1994	Basketball Star L6136G	Open		295.00	295
1994	Baseball Star L6137G	Open		295.00	295
1994	Globe Paperweight L6138M	Open		95.00	95
1994	Springtime Friends L6140G	Open		485.00	485
1994	Kitty Cart L6141G	Open		750.00	795
1994	Indian Pose L6142G	Open		475.00	475
1994	Indian Dancer L6143G	Open		475.00	475
1995	Caribbean Kiss L6144G	Open		340.00	340
1994	Heavenly Prayer L6145	Open		675.00	695
1994	Spring Angel L6146G	Open		250.00	265
1994	Fall Angel L6147G	Open		250.00	265
1994	Summer Angel L6148G	Open		220.00	220
1994	Winter Angel L6149G	Open		250.00	265
1994	Playing The Flute L6150G	Open		175.00	190
1994	Bearing Flowers L6151G	Open		175.00	190
1994	Flower Gazer L6152G	Open		175.00	190
1994	American Love L6153G	Open		225.00	225
1994	African Love L6154G	Open		225.00	225
1994	European Love L6155G	Open		225.00	225
1994	Asian Love L6156G	Open		225.00	225
1994	Polynesian Love L6157G	Open		225.00	225
1995	Fiesta Dancer L6163G	Open		285.00	285
1994	Wedding Bells L6164G	Open		175.00	185
1995	Pretty Cargo L6165G	Open		500.00	500
1995	Dear Santa L6166G	Open		250.00	250
1995	Delicate Bundle L6167G	Open		275.00	275
1994	The Apollo Landing L6168G	Closed	1995	450.00	450
1995	Seesaw Friends L6169G	Open		795.00	795
1995	Under My Spell L6170G	Open		195.00	195
1995	Magical Moment L6171G	Open		180.00	180
1995	Coming of Age L6172G	Open		345.00	345
1995	A Moment's Rest L6173G	Open		130.00	130
1995	Graceful Pose L6174G	Open		195.00	195
1995	Graceful Pose L6174M	Open		195.00	195
1995	White Swan L6175G	Open		90.00	90
1995	Communion Bell L6176G	Open		85.00	85
1995	Asian Scholar L6177G	Open		315.00	315
1995	Little Matador L6178G	Open		245.00	245
1995	Peaceful Moment L6179G	Open		385.00	385
1995	Sharia L6180G	Open		235.00	235
1995	Velisa L6181G	Open		180.00	180
1996	Wanda L6182	Open		205.00	205
1995	Preparing For The Sabbath L6183G	Open		385.00	385
1995	For a Better World L6186G	Open		575.00	575
1995	European Boy L6187G	Open		185.00	185
1995	Asian Boy L6188G	Open		225.00	225
1995	African Boy L6189G	Open		195.00	195
1995	Polynesian Boy L6190G	Open		250.00	250
1995	All American L6191G	Open		225.00	225
1995	American Indian Boy L6192G	Open		225.00	225
1995	Summer Serenade L6193G	Open		375.00	375
1995	Summer Serenade L6193M	Open		375.00	375
1996	Christmas Wishes L6194	Open		245.00	245
1995	Carnival Companions L6195G	Open		650.00	650
1995	Seaside Companions L6196G	Open		230.00	230
1995	Seaside Serenade L6197G	Open		275.00	275
1995	Soccer Practice L6198G	Open		195.00	195
1995	In The Procession L6199G	Open		250.00	250
1995	In The Procession L6199M	Open		250.00	250
1995	Bridal Bell L6200G	Open		125.00	125
1995	Cuddly Kitten L6201G	Open		270.00	270
1995	Daddy's Little Sweetheart L6202G	Open		595.00	595
1995	Grace and Beauty L6204G	Open		325.00	325
1995	Grace and Beauty L6204M	Open		325.00	325
1995	Graceful Dance L6205G	Open		340.00	340
1995	Reading the Torah L6208G	Open		535.00	535
1995	The Rabbi L6209G	Open		250.00	250
1995	Gentle Surprise L6210G	Open		125.00	125
1995	New Friend L6211G	Open		120.00	120
1995	Little Wonder L6212G	Open		115.00	115
1995	Lady Of Nice L6213G	Open		198.00	198
1995	Lady Of Nice L6213M	Open		198.00	198
1995	Leo L6214G	Open		198.00	198
1995	Virgo L6215G	Open		198.00	198
1995	Aquarius L6216G	Open		198.00	198
1995	Sagittarius L6217G	Open		198.00	198
1995	Taurus L6218G	Open		198.00	198
1995	Gemini L6219G	Open		198.00	198
1995	Libra L6220G	Open		198.00	198
1995	Aries L6221G	Open		198.00	198
1995	Capricorn L6222G	Open		198.00	198
1995	Pisces L6223G	Open		198.00	198
1995	Cancer L6224G	Open		198.00	198
1995	Scorpio L6225G	Open		198.00	198
1995	Snuggle Up L6226G	Open		170.00	170
1995	Trick or Treat L6227G	Open		250.00	250
1995	Special Gift L6228G	Open		265.00	265
1995	Contented Companion L6229G	Open		195.00	195
1995	Oriental Dance L6230G	Open		198.00	198
1995	Oriental Lantern L6231G	Open		198.00	198
1995	Oriental Beauty L6232G	Open		198.00	198
1995	Chef's Apprentice L6233G	Open		260.00	260
1995	Chef's Apprentice L6233M	Open		260.00	260
1995	The Great Chef L6234G	Open		195.00	195
1995	The Great Chef L6234M	Open		195.00	195
1995	Dinner is Served L6235G	Open		185.00	185
1995	Dinner is Served L6235M	Open		185.00	185
1995	Lady of Monaco L6236G	Open		250.00	250
1995	Lady of Monaco L6236M	Open		250.00	250
1995	The Young Jester-Mandolin L6237G	Open		235.00	235
1995	The Young Jester-Mandolin L6237M	Open		235.00	235
1995	The Young Jester-Trumpet L6238G	Open		235.00	235
1995	The Young Jester-Trumpet L6238M	Open		235.00	235
1995	The Young Jester-Singer L6239G	Open		235.00	235
1995	The Young Jester-Singer L6239M	Open		235.00	235
1995	Graceful Ballet L6240G	Open		795.00	795
1995	Graceful Ballet L6240M	Open		795.00	795
1995	Allegory of Spring L6241G	Open		735.00	735
1995	Allegory of Spring L6241M	Open		735.00	735
1996	Winged Companions L6242G	Open		270.00	270
1996	Winged Companions L6242M	Open		270.00	270
1996	Sweet Symphony L6243	Open		450.00	450
1996	Pumpkin Ride L6244	Open		695.00	695
1996	Sunday's Best L6246	Open		370.00	370
1995	Challenge L6247M	Yr.Iss.		350.00	350
1995	Regatta L6248G	Yr.Iss.		695.00	695
1995	Delphica L6249	Open		1200.00	1200
1996	Springtime Harvest L6250	Open		760.00	760
1996	Nature's Beauty w/base L6252	Open		770.00	770
1996	Making Rounds L6256	Open		295.00	295
1996	Pierrot in Preparation L6257	Open		195.00	195
1996	Pierrot in Love L6258	Open		195.00	195
1996	Pierrot Rehearsing L6259	Open		195.00	195
1996	Our Lady "Caridid Del Cobre" w/base L6268	Open		1355.00	1355
1996	Diana Goddess of the Hunt w/base L6269	Open		1550.00	1550
1996	Commencement L6270	Open		200.00	200
1996	Cap and Gown L6271	Open		200.00	200
1996	Going Forth L6272	Open		200.00	200
1996	Pharmacist L6273	Open		290.00	290
1996	Daisy L6274	Open		150.00	150
1996	Rose L6275	Open		150.00	150
1996	Iris L6276	Open		150.00	150
1996	Young Mandolin Player L6278	Open		330.00	330
1996	Flowers of Paris L6279	Open		525.00	525
1996	Paris in Bloom L6280	Open		525.00	525
1996	Coqueta L6281G	Open		435.00	435
1996	Coqueta L6281M	Open		435.00	435
1996	Medic L6282G	Open		225.00	225
1996	Medic L6282M	Open		225.00	225
1996	Temis L6283G	Open		435.00	435
1996	Temis L6283M	Open		435.00	435
1996	Quione L6284G	Open		435.00	435
1996	Quione L6284M	Open		435.00	435
1996	Dreams of Aladdin w/base L6285	Open		1440.00	1440
1996	Tennis Champion w/base L6286G	Open		350.00	350
1996	Tennis Champion w/base L6286M	Open		350.00	350
1996	Restless Dove L6287G	Open		105.00	105
1996	Restless Dove L6287M	Open		105.00	105
1996	Taking Flight L6288G	Open		150.00	150
1996	Taking Flight L6288M	Open		150.00	150
1996	Peaceful Dove L6289G	Open		105.00	105
1996	Peaceful Dove L6289M	Open		105.00	105
1996	Proud Dove L6290G	Open		105.00	105
1996	Proud Dove L6290M	Open		105.00	105
1996	Love Nest L6291G	Open		260.00	260
1996	Love Nest L6291M	Open		260.00	260
1996	Sweethearts L6296	Open		900.00	900
1996	Little Bear L6299	Open		285.00	285
1996	Rubber Ducky L6300	Open		285.00	285
1996	Care and Tenderness w/base L6301			850.00	850
1996	Thena L6302G	Open		485.00	485
1996	Thena L6302M	Open		485.00	485
1996	Tuba Player L6303	Open		315.00	315
1996	Bass Drummer L6304	Open		400.00	400
1996	Trumpet Player L6305	Open		270.00	270
1996	Majorette L6306	Open		310.00	310
1996	Young Nurse L6307	Open		185.00	185
1996	Natural Wonder L6308	Open		220.00	220
1996	Nature's Treasures L6309	Open		220.00	220
1996	Nature's Song L6310	Open		230.00	230
1996	Cupid L6311	Open		200.00	200
1996	The Harpist L6312	Open		820.00	820
1996	Lost in Dreams L6313	Open		420.00	420
1996	Little Sailor Boy L6314	Open		225.00	225
1996	Dreaming of You L6315	Open		1280.00	1280
1996	Carnevale L6316	Open		840.00	840
1996	Making House Calls L6317	Open		260.00	260
1996	Little Distraction L6318	Open		350.00	350
1996	Beautiful Rhapsody L6319	Open		450.00	450
1996	Architect L6320	Open		330.00	330
1996	Serenading Colombina L6322	Open		415.00	415
1996	Stage Presence L6323	Open		355.00	355
1996	Princess of Peace L6324	Open		830.00	830
1996	Curtains Up L6325	Open		255.00	255
1996	Virgin of Carmen w/base L6326	Open		1270.00	1270
1996	Medieval Romance w/base L6327	Open		2250.00	2250
1996	Venice Festival w/base L6328	Open		5350.00	5350
1996	Blushing Bride L6329G	Open		370.00	370
1996	Blushing Bride L6329M	Open		370.00	370
1996	Refreshing Pause L6330	Open		170.00	170
1996	Bridal Bell L6331	Open		155.00	155
1996	Concerto L6332	Open		490.00	490
1996	Medieval Chess Set L6333	Open		2120.00	2120
1996	Country Sounds L6339	Open		750.00	750
1996	Sweet Country L6340	Open		750.00	750
1985	Lladró Plaque L7116	Open		17.50	18
1985	Lladró Plaque L7118	Closed	N/A	17.00	18
1992	Special Torch L7513G	Open		165.00	165
1992	Special Champion L7514G	Open		165.00	165
1992	Special Pride L7515G	Open		165.00	165

*Quotes have been rounded up to nearest dollar

YEAR ISSUE		EDITION LIMIT	YEAR RETD.	ISSUE PRICE	*QUOTE U.S.$
1993	Courage L7522G	Open		195.00	200
1994	Dr. Martin Luther King, Jr. L7528G	Open		345.00	345
1994	Spike L7543G	Open		95.00	105
1994	Brutus L7544G	Open		125.00	140
1994	Rocky L7545G	Open		110.00	120
1994	Stretch L7546G	Open		125.00	140
1994	Rex L7547G	Open		125.00	140
1994	Snow White L7555G (Disney -back stamp Theme Park issue)	Closed	N/A	295.00	650-800
1995	16th Century Globe Paperweight	Open		105.00	105
1989	Starting Forward/Lolo L7605G	Closed	1989	125.00	350
1996	By My Side L7645	Open		250.00	250
1996	Chess Board L8036	Open		145.00	145

Lladró Limited Edition Egg Series - Lladró

1993	1993 Limited Edition Egg L6083M	Closed	1993	145.00	240
1994	1994 Limited Edition Egg L7532M	Closed	1994	150.00	175
1995	1995 Limited Edition Egg L7548M	Closed	1995	150.00	155-175
1996	1996 Limited Edition Egg L7550	Yr.Iss.		155.00	155

Norman Rockwell Collection - Rockwell-Inspired

1982	Lladró Love Letter RL-400G	5,000	N/A	650.00	1000-1200
1982	Summer Stock RL-401G	5,000	N/A	750.00	800-900
1982	Practice Makes Perfect RL-402G	5,000	N/A	725.00	800-1000
1982	Young Love RL-403G	5,000	N/A	450.00	1350-1750
1982	Daydreamer RL-404G	5,000	N/A	450.00	1300-1500
1982	Court Jester RL-405G	5,000	N/A	600.00	1300
1982	Springtime RL-406G	5,000	N/A	450.00	1200-1500

See also Dave Grossman Designs-Lladró Norman Rockwell Collection

Lowell Davis Farm Club

Lowell Davis Farm Club - L. Davis

1986	The Bride 221001 / 20993	Yr.Iss.	1987	45.00	400-450
1987	The Party's Over 221002 / 20994	Yr.Iss.	1988	50.00	175-190
1988	Chow Time 221003 / 20995	Yr.Iss.	1989	55.00	100-150
1989	Can't Wait 221004 / 20996	Yr.Iss.	1990	75.00	125
1990	Pit Stop 221005 / 20997	Yr.Iss.	1991	75.00	100-150
1991	Arrival Of Stanley 221006 / 20998	Yr.Iss.	1992	100.00	100
1991	Don't Pick The Flowers 221007/ 21007	Yr.Iss.	1992	100.00	145
1992	Hog Wild	Yr.Iss.	1993	100.00	100
1992	Check's in the Mail	Yr.Iss.	1993	100.00	110
1993	The Survivor 25371	Yr.Iss.	1994	70.00	70
1993	Summer Days	Yr.Iss.	1994	100.00	100
1994	Dutch Treat	Yr.Iss.	1995	100.00	100
1995	Free Kittens	Yr.Iss.	1996	40.00	40
1996	Sunnyside Up	9/97		70.00	70

Lowell Davis Farm Club Renewal Figurine - L. Davis

1986	Thirsty? 892050 / 92050	Yr.Iss.	1987	Gift	20-75
1987	Cackle Berries 892051 / 92051	Yr.Iss.	1989	Gift	85-120
1988	Ice Cream Churn 892052 / 92052	Yr.Iss.	1990	Gift	50-70
1990	Not A Sharing Soul 892053 / 92053	Yr.Iss.	1991	Gift	50-70
1991	New Arrival 892054 / 92054	Yr.Iss.	1992	Gift	65
1992	Garden Toad 92055	Yr.Iss.	1993	Gift	45-65
1993	Luke 12:6 25372	Yr.Iss.	1994	Gift	65
1994	Feathering Her Nest	Yr.Iss.	1995	Gift	30-50
1995	After the Rain	Yr.Iss.	1996	Gift	25-60
1996	A Gift For You	6/97		Gift	N/A

Davis Cat Tales Figurines - L. Davis

1982	Company's Coming 25205	Closed	1986	60.00	270
1982	Flew the Coop 25207	Closed	1986	60.00	365
1982	On the Move 25206	Closed	1986	70.00	600-650
1982	Right Church, Wrong Pew 25204	Closed	1986	70.00	350

Davis Country Christmas Figurines - L. Davis

1983	Hooker at Mailbox with Presents 23550	Closed	1984	80.00	750
1984	Country Christmas 23551	Closed	1985	80.00	450
1985	Christmas at Fox Fire Farm 23552	Closed	1986	80.00	275
1986	Christmas at Red Oak 23553	Closed	1987	80.00	200-225
1987	Blossom's Gift 23554	Closed	1988	150.00	300-475
1988	Cutting the Family Christmas Tree 23555	Closed	1989	80.00	350
1989	Peter and the Wren 23556	Closed	1990	165.00	450
1990	Wintering Deer 23557	Closed	1991	165.00	200-300
1991	Christmas At Red Oak II 23558	Closed	1992	250.00	250
1992	Born on a Starry Night 23559	2,500	1993	225.00	225
1993	Waiting For Mr. Lowell 23606	2,500	1994	250.00	250
1994	Visions of Sugar Plums	2,500	1995	250.00	250
1995	Bah Humbug	2,500		200.00	200

Davis Country Pride - L. Davis

1981	Bustin' with Pride 25202	Closed	1985	100.00	250-300
1981	Duke's Mixture 25203	Closed	1985	100.00	300
1981	Plum Tuckered Out 25201	Closed	1985	100.00	950
1981	Surprise in the Cellar 25200	Closed	1985	100.00	400-900

Davis Farm Set - L. Davis

1985	Barn 25352	Closed	1987	47.50	425-450
1985	Chicken House 25358	Closed	1987	19.00	50
1985	Corn Crib and Sheep Pen 25354	Closed	1987	25.00	65
1985	Garden and Wood Shed 25359	Closed	1987	25.00	65
1985	Goat Yard and Studio 25353	Closed	1987	32.50	85
1985	Hen House 25356	Closed	1987	32.50	80
1985	Hog House 25355	Closed	1987	27.50	85
1985	Main House 25351	Closed	1987	42.50	100

YEAR ISSUE		EDITION LIMIT	YEAR RETD.	ISSUE PRICE	*QUOTE U.S.$
1985	Privy 25348	Closed	1987	12.50	35
1985	Remus' Cabin 25350	Closed	1987	42.50	95
1985	Smoke House 25357	Closed	1987	12.50	65
1985	Windmill 25349	Closed	1987	25.00	45

Davis Friends of Mine - L. Davis

1992	Cat and Jenny Wren 23633	5,000	1993	170.00	175-200
1992	Cat and Jenny Wren Mini Figurine 23634	Open	1993	35.00	40
1989	Sun Worshippers 23620	5,000	1993	120.00	133
1989	Sun Worshippers Mini Figurine 23621	5,000	1993	32.50	40
1990	Sunday Afternoon Treat 23625	5,000	1993	120.00	175-200
1990	Sunday Afternoon Treat Mini Figurine 23626	Closed	1993	32.50	43
1991	Warm Milk 23629	Closed	1993	120.00	200
1991	Warm Milk Mini Figurine 23630	5,000	1993	32.50	43

Davis Little Critters - L. Davis

1992	Charivari 25707	950	1993	250.00	250
1991	Christopher Critter 25514	1,192	1993	150.00	150
1992	Double Yolker 25516	Yr.Iss.	1993	70.00	70
1989	Gittin' a Nibble 25294	Closed	1993	50.00	60
1991	Great American Chicken Race 25500	2,500	1993	225.00	250
1991	Hittin' The Sack 25510	Closed	1993	70.00	70
1990	Home Squeezins 25504	Closed	1993	90.00	90
1991	Itiskit, Itasket 25511	Closed	1993	45.00	45
1990	Milk Mouse 25503	2,500	1993	175.00	230
1992	Miss Private Time 25517	Yr.Iss.	1993	35.00	35
1990	Outing With Grandpa 25502	2,500	1993	200.00	250
1990	Private Time 25506	Closed	1993	18.00	40
1990	Punkin' Pig 25505	2,500	1993	250.00	300
1991	Punkin' Wine 25501	Closed	1993	100.00	120
1991	Toad Strangler 25509	Closed	1993	57.00	57
1991	When Coffee Never Tasted So Good (Music box) 809225	1,250	1993	800.00	800
1991	When Coffee Never Tasted So Good 25507	1,250	1993	800.00	800
1992	A Wolf in Sheep's Clothing 25518	Yr.Iss.	1993	110.00	110

Davis Pen Pals - L. Davis

1993	The Old Home Place 25802	1,200	1995	200.00	200

Davis Promotional Figurine - L. Davis

1991	Leavin' The Rat Race 225512	Yr.Iss.	1991	80.00	150
1992	Hen Scratch Prom 225968	Yr.Iss.	1992	90.00	95
1993	Leapin' Lizard 225969	Yr.Iss.	1993	80.00	80
1994	Don't Forget Me 227130	Yr.Iss.	1994	70.00	70
1995	Nasty Stuff 95103	Yr.Iss.	1995	40.00	40

Davis RFD America - L. Davis

1984	Anybody Home 25239	Closed	1987	35.00	100
1994	Attic Antics	Closed	1995	100.00	150
1982	Baby Blossom 25227	Closed	1984	40.00	325
1982	Baby Bobs 25222	Closed	1984	47.50	250
1985	Barn Cats 25257	Closed	1990	39.50	90
1993	Be My Valentine 27561	Open		35.00	40
1986	Bit Off More Than He Could Chew 25279	Closed	1987	15.00	60
1979	Blossom 25032	Closed	1983	180.00	1800
1993	Blossom 96846 (15th Anniversary)	Closed	1993	80.00	80
1982	Blossom and Calf 25326	Closed	1986	250.00	850
1995	Blossom's Best	750	1995	300.00	400
1987	Bottoms Up 25270	Closed	1992	80.00	105
1989	Boy's Night Out 25339	1,500	1992	190.00	250
1982	Brand New Day 25226	Closed	1984	23.50	150-175
1979	Broken Dreams 25035	Closed	1983	165.00	1000-1300
1993	Broken Dreams 96847 (15th Anniversary)	Closed	1993	80.00	80
1988	Brothers 25286	Closed	1990	55.00	75
1984	Catnapping Too? 25247	Closed	1991	70.00	150
1987	Chicken Thief 25338	Closed	1988	200.00	300-375
1983	City Slicker 25329	Closed	1990	150.00	270
1991	Cock Of The Walk 25347	2,500	1993	300.00	325
1986	Comfy? 25273	Open		40.00	80
1994	Companion pc. And Down the Hatch	6 mo.	1994	135.00	145
1994	Companion pc. Open The Lid	6 mo.	1994	135.00	145
1989	Coon Capers 25291	Open		67.50	90
1990	Corn Crib Mouse 25295	Closed	1993	35.00	45
1983	Counting the Days 25233	Closed	1992	40.00	60
1981	Country Boy 25213	Closed	1984	37.50	300-375
1985	Country Cousins 25266	Closed	1995	42.50	90
1982	Country Crook 25280	Closed	1984	37.50	330
1985	Country Crooner 25256	Closed	1995	25.00	50
1984	Country Kitty 25246	Closed	1987	52.00	115-125
1979	Country Road 25030	Closed	1983	100.00	900
1993	Country Road 96842 (15th Anniversary)	Closed	1993	65.00	65
1984	Courtin' 25220	Closed	1987	45.00	125
1980	Creek Bank Bandit 25038	Closed	1985	37.50	400
1995	Cussin' Up a Storm	Closed	1995	45.00	45
1993	Don't Open Till Christmas 27562	Open		35.00	35
1992	Don't Play With Fire 25319	Open		120.00	120
1985	Don't Play with Your Food 25258	Closed	1992	28.50	100
1981	Double Trouble 25211	Closed	1984	35.00	475
1981	Dry as a Bone 25216	Closed	1984	45.00	300-325
1993	Dry Hole 25374	Closed	1995	30.00	35
1987	Easy Pickins 25269	Closed	1990	45.00	85
1993	End of the Trail 81000A	100	1993	100.00	600
1983	Fair Weather Friend 25236	Closed	1987	25.00	85

YEAR ISSUE		EDITION LIMIT	YEAR RETD.	ISSUE PRICE	*QUOTE U.S.$
1983	False Alarm 25237	Closed	1985	65.00	150-185
1989	Family Outing 25289	Closed	1995	45.00	60
1994	Favorite Sport 25381	Closed	1995	230.00	230
1985	Feelin' His Oats 25275	1,500	1990	150.00	300-345
1990	Finder's Keepers 25299	Open		39.50	45
1991	First Offense 25304	Closed	1993	70.00	70
1994	First Outing	Open		65.00	65
1988	Fleas 25272	Open		20.00	30
1980	Forbidden Fruit 25022	Closed	1985	25.00	150
1990	Foreplay 25300	Closed	1993	59.50	80
1979	Fowl Play 25033	Closed	1983	100.00	275-325
1993	Fowl Play 96845 (15th Anniversary)	Closed	1993	60.00	60
1992	Free Lunch 25321	Open		85.00	85
1993	The Freeloaders 95042	1,250	1995	230.00	230
1985	Furs Gonna Fly 25335	1,500	1989	145.00	175-300
1994	Get Well 96902	Open		35.00	40
1987	Glutton for Punishment 25268	Closed	1991	95.00	160
1988	Goldie and Her Peeps 25283	Closed	1991	25.00	37
1984	Gonna Pay for His Sins 25243	Closed	1989	27.50	50
1980	Good, Clean Fun 25020	Closed	1985	40.00	150
1984	Gossips 25248	Closed	1987	110.00	250
1992	The Grass is Always Greener 25367	Closed	1995	195.00	195
1991	Gun Shy 25305	Closed	1993	70.00	70
1990	Hanky Panky 25298	Closed	1993	65.00	80
1994	Happy Anniversary 95089	Open		35.00	40
1993	Happy Birthday My Sweet 27560	Open		35.00	40
1988	Happy Hour 25287	Open		57.50	80
1983	Happy Hunting Ground 25330	Closed	1990	160.00	235
1984	Headed Home 25240	Closed	1991	25.00	50
1992	Headed South 25327	Closed	1993	45.00	45
1991	Heading For The Persimmon Grove 25306	Closed	1993	80.00	80
1994	Helpin Himself	Closed	1995	65.00	65
1983	Hi Girls, The Name's Big Jack 25328	Closed	1987	200.00	390
1981	Hightailing It 25214	Closed	1984	50.00	400-450
1983	His Eyes Are Bigger Than His Stomach 25332	Closed	1989	235.00	350
1984	His Master's Dog 25244	Closed	1988	45.00	150
1994	Hittin The Trail	1,250	1995	250.00	250
1985	Hog Heaven 25336	1,500	1988	165.00	300-400
1992	The Honeymoon's Over 25370	1,950	1994	300.00	300
1995	Hook, Line & Sinker 25382	Open		35.00	35
1984	Huh? 25242	Closed	1989	40.00	150
1993	I'm Thankful For You 27563	Open		35.00	40
1982	Idle Hours 25230	Closed	1985	37.50	300-450
1993	If You Can't Beat Em Join Em 25379	1,750	1995	250.00	250
1979	Ignorance is Bliss 25031	Closed	1983	165.00	1250-1300
1993	Ignorance is Bliss 96843 (15th Anniversary)	Closed	1993	75.00	75
1988	In a Pickle 25284	Closed	1995	40.00	50
1989	Itching Post 25037	Closed	1995	30.00	75-115
1980	King of The Mountain 25380	750	1995	500.00	500
1991	Kissin' Cousins 25307	Closed	1993	80.00	80
1990	The Last Straw 25301	Closed	1993	125.00	180
1989	Left Overs 25290	Open		90.00	95
1983	Licking Good 25234	Closed	1995	35.00	200-250
1991	Little Black Lamb (Baba) 25297	Closed	1993	30.00	38
1990	Long Days, Cold Nights 25344	2,500	1993	175.00	190
1991	Long, Hot Summer 25343	1,950	1995	250.00	250
1985	Love at First Sight 25267	Closed	1992	70.00	115
1992	Lowell Davis Profile 25366	Open		75.00	75
1984	Mad As A Wet Hen 25334	Closed	1986	185.00	600-800
1987	Mail Order Bride 25263	Closed	1991	150.00	200-325
1983	Makin' Tracks 25238	Closed	1989	70.00	125-185
1984	Making a Bee Line 25274	Open		75.00	125
1994	Mama Can Willie Stay For Supper	1,250	1995	200.00	220
1983	Mama's Prize Leghorn 25235	Closed	1988	55.00	135
1982	Mama? 25277	Closed	1991	15.00	45
1989	Meeting of Sheldon 25293	Closed	1992	120.00	125
1980	Milking Time 25023	Closed	1985	20.00	240
1991	Missouri Spring 25278	Closed	1992	115.00	175
1982	Moon Raider 25325	Closed	1986	190.00	325
1995	The Morning After 10000	Closed	1995	60.00	120
1993	Mother Hen 25292	Open		37.50	50
1993	Mother's Day 95088	Open		35.00	40
1982	Moving Day 25225	Closed	1984	43.50	325
1992	My Favorite Chores 25362	1,500	1994	750.00	750
1980	New Day 25025	Closed	1984	20.00	165
1993	New Friend 25288	Closed	1994	45.00	60
1993	No Hunting 25375	1,000	1995	95.00	95
1988	No Private Time 25316	Closed	1992	200.00	300-350
1994	Not a Happy Camper	Open		75.00	75
1994	Oh Mother What is it?	1,000	1995	250.00	250
1992	OH Sheeeit . . . 25363	Closed	1995	120.00	135
1993	Oh Where is He Now 95041	1,250	1995	250.00	250
1984	One for the Road 25241	Closed	1988	37.50	60-70
1987	The Orphans 25271	Closed	1990	50.00	80
1985	Out-of-Step 25259	Closed	1989	45.00	90
1985	Ozark Belle 25264	Closed	1990	35.00	70
1994	Ozark's Vittles 25318	Open		60.00	60
1984	Pasture Pals 25245	Closed	1990	52.00	130
1993	Peep Show 25376	Open		35.00	35
1982	Perfect Ten 25282	Closed	1990	95.00	180
1990	Piggin' Out 25345	Closed	1993	190.00	250
1994	Pollywogs 25617	750	1994	750.00	850-1000
1993	Prairie Chorus 25333	Closed	1986	135.00	1200-1400
1996	Proud Papa 96002	Yr.Iss.		250.00	250
1985	Punkin' Seeds 25219	Closed	1984	225.00	1500-1700
1994	Qu'est - Ceque C'est?	Closed	1995	200.00	200

Collectors' Information Bureau

*Quotes have been rounded up to nearest dollar

YEAR ISSUE		EDITION LIMIT	YEAR RETD.	ISSUE PRICE	*QUOTE U.S. $
1985	Renoir 25261	Closed	1991	45.00	85
1981	Rooted Out 25217	Closed	1989	45.00	85-115
1992	Safe Haven 25320	Closed	1994	95.00	95
1988	Sawin' Logs 25260	Closed	1993	85.00	105
1981	Scallawags 25221	Closed	1987	65.00	150-200
1992	School Yard Dogs 25369	Closed	1994	100.00	100
1996	See Ya There 96002	Yr.Iss.		330.00	330
1990	Seein' Red (Gus w/shoes) 25296	Closed	1993	35.00	47
1992	She Lay Low 25364	Closed	1995	120.00	120
1993	Sheep Sheerin Time 25388	1,200	1995	500.00	500
1982	A Shoe to Fill 25229	Closed	1986	37.50	150-175
1979	Slim Pickins 25034	Closed	1983	165.00	600-800
1993	Slim Pickins 96846 (15th Anniversary)	Closed	1993	75.00	75
1992	Snake Doctor 25365	Closed	1995	70.00	70
1991	Sooieee 25360	1,500	1994	350.00	350
1981	Split Decision 25210	Closed	1984	45.00	200-300
1995	Sticks and Stones	Open		30.00	30
1983	Stirring Up Trouble 25331	Closed	1988	160.00	260
1980	Strawberry Patch 25021	Closed	1989	25.00	95
1982	Stray Dog 25223	Closed	1988	35.00	75
1981	Studio Mouse 25215	Closed	1984	60.00	360
1980	Sunday Afternoon 25024	Closed	1985	22.50	225-250
1993	Sweet Tooth 25373	Closed	1995	60.00	60
1982	Thinking Big 25231	Closed	1988	35.00	90
1985	Too Good to Waste on Kids 25262	Closed	1989	70.00	130
1982	Treed 25327	Closed	1988	155.00	320
1989	A Tribute to Hooker 25340	Closed	1992	180.00	200-250
1993	Trick or Treat 27565	Open		35.00	50
1990	Tricks Of The Trade 25346	Closed	1994	300.00	300-375
1987	Two in the Bush 25337	Closed	1988	150.00	320
1994	Two Timer	Closed	1995	95.00	95
1982	Two's Company 25224	Closed	1986	43.50	200-225
1981	Under the Weather 25212	Closed	1991	25.00	85
1995	Uninvited Caller	Closed	1995	35.00	35
1981	Up To No Good 25218	Closed	1984	200.00	850-950
1982	Waiting for His Master 25281	Closed	1986	50.00	300
1994	Warmin' Their Buns	1,250		270.00	270
1991	Washed Ashore 25308	Closed	1993	70.00	70
1982	When Mama Gets Mad 25228	Closed	1986	37.50	300-375
1987	When the Cat's Away 25276	Closed	1990	40.00	60
1988	When Three Foot's a Mile 25315	Closed	1991	230.00	300
1980	Wilbur 25029	Closed	1985	100.00	585
1985	Will You Still Respect Me in the Morning 25265	Closed	1993	35.00	75
1988	Wintering Lamb 25317	Closed	1991	200.00	250-275
1988	Wishful Thinking 25285	Closed	1990	55.00	70
1983	Woman's Work 25232	Closed	1989	35.00	80
1989	Woodscolt 25342	Closed	1992	300.00	375-425
1993	You're a Basket Full of Fun 27564	Open		35.00	35

Davis Route 66 - L. Davis

1992	Fresh Squeezed? (w/ wooden base) 25609	350	1995	600.00	700
1992	Fresh Squeezed? 25608	2,500	1995	450.00	550
1992	Going To Grandma's 25619	Closed	1995	80.00	80
1993	Home For Christmas 25621	Closed	1995	80.00	80
1991	Just Check The Air 25600	350	1995	700.00	750
1991	Just Check The Air 25603	2,500	1995	550.00	550
1993	Kickin' Himself 25622	Closed	1995	80.00	80
1991	Little Bit Of Shade 25602	Closed	1995	100.00	100
1991	Nel's Diner 25601	350	1995	700.00	700
1991	Nel's Diner 25604	2,500	1995	550.00	550
1992	Quiet Day at Maple Grove 25618	Closed	1995	130.00	130
1992	Relief 25605	Closed	1995	80.00	80
1993	Summer Days 25607	Yr.Iss.	1995	100.00	100
1992	Welcome Mat (w/ wooden base) 25606	1,500	1995	400.00	400
1992	What Are Pals For? 25620	Closed	1995	100.00	100

Davis Special Edition Figurines - L. Davis

1983	The Critics 23600	Closed	1986	400.00	1500-1700
1989	From A Friend To A Friend 23602	1,200	1992	750.00	1700
1985	Home from Market 23601	Closed	1988	400.00	1500
1992	Last Laff 23604	1,200	1994	900.00	900
1990	What Rat Race? 23603	1,200	1994	800.00	1025

Davis Uncle Remus - L. Davis

1981	Brer Bear 25251	Closed	1984	80.00	900-1200
1981	Brer Coyote 25255	Closed	1984	80.00	500
1981	Brer Fox 25250	Closed	1984	70.00	900-950
1981	Brer Rabbit 25252	Closed	1984	85.00	2000
1981	Brer Weasel 25254	Closed	1984	80.00	700
1981	Brer Wolf 25253	Closed	1984	85.00	500

Maruri USA

African Safari Animals - W. Gaither

1983	African Elephant	Closed	N/A	3500.00	3500
1983	Black Maned Lion	Closed	N/A	1450.00	1450
1983	Cape Buffalo	Closed	N/A	2200.00	2200
1983	Grant's Zebras, pair	500	1995	1200.00	1200
1981	Nyala	300	1995	1450.00	1450
1983	Sable	Closed	N/A	1200.00	1200
1983	Southern Greater Kudu	Closed	N/A	1800.00	1800
1983	Southern Impala			1200.00	1200
1983	Southern Leopard	Closed	1994	1450.00	1450
1983	Southern White Rhino	150		3200.00	3200

American Eagle Gallery - Maruri Studios

1985	E-8501	Closed	1989	45.00	75
1985	E-8502	Open		55.00	65

YEAR ISSUE		EDITION LIMIT	YEAR RETD.	ISSUE PRICE	*QUOTE U.S.$
1985	E-8503	Open		60.00	65
1985	E-8504	Open		65.00	75
1985	E-8505	Closed	1989	65.00	150
1985	E-8506	Open		75.00	90
1985	E-8507	Open		75.00	90
1985	E-8508	Closed	1989	75.00	85
1985	E-8509	Closed	1989	85.00	125
1985	E-8510	Open		85.00	85
1985	E-8511	Closed	1989	85.00	125
1985	E-8512	Open		295.00	325
1987	E-8721	Open		40.00	50
1987	E-8722	Open		45.00	55
1987	E-8723	Closed	1989	55.00	60
1987	E-8724	Open		175.00	195
1989	E-8931	Open		55.00	60
1989	E-8932	Open		75.00	80
1989	E-8933	Open		95.00	95
1989	E-8934	Open		135.00	140
1989	E-8935	Open		175.00	185
1989	E-8936	Open		185.00	195
1991	E-9141 Eagle Landing	Open		60.00	60
1991	E-9142 Eagle w/ Totem Pole	Open		75.00	75
1991	E-9143 Pair in Flight	Open		95.00	95
1991	E-9144 Eagle w/Salmon	Open		110.00	110
1991	E-9145 Eagle w/Snow	Open		135.00	135
1991	E-9146 Eagle w/Babies	Open		145.00	145
1995	E-9551 Eagle	Open		60.00	60
1995	E-9552 Eagle	Open		65.00	65
1995	E-9553 Eagle	Open		75.00	75
1995	E-9554 Eagle	Open		80.00	80
1995	E-9555 Eagle	Open		90.00	90
1995	E-9556 Eagle	Open		110.00	110

Americana - W. Gaither

1981	Grizzley Bear and Indian	Closed	N/A	650.00	650
1982	Sioux Brave and Bison	Closed	N/A	985.00	985

Baby Animals - W. Gaither

1981	African Lion Cubs	1,500	1995	195.00	195
1981	Black Bear Cubs	Closed	N/A	195.00	195
1981	Wolf Cubs	Closed	N/A	195.00	195

Birds of Prey - W. Gaither

1981	Screech Owl	300		960.00	960
1981	American Bald Eagle I	Closed	N/A	165.00	1750
1982	American Bald Eagle II	Closed	N/A	245.00	2750
1983	American Bald Eagle III	Closed	N/A	445.00	1750
1984	American Bald Eagle IV	Closed	N/A	360.00	1750
1986	American Bald Eagle V	Closed	N/A	325.00	1250

Eyes Of The Night - Maruri Studios

1988	Double Barn Owl O-8807	Closed	1993	125.00	130
1988	Double Snowy Owl O-8809	Closed	1993	245.00	250
1988	Single Great Horned Owl O-8803	Closed	1993	60.00	65
1988	Single Great Horned Owl O-8808	Closed	1993	145.00	150
1988	Single Screech Owl O-8801	Closed	1993	50.00	55
1988	Single Screech Owl O-8806	Closed	1993	90.00	95
1988	Single Snowy Owl O-8802	Closed	1993	50.00	55
1988	Single Snowy Owl O-8805	Closed	1993	80.00	85
1988	Single Tawny Owl O-8804	Closed	1993	60.00	65

Gentle Giants - Maruri Studios

1992	Baby Elephant Sitting GG-9252	Open		65.00	65
1992	Baby Elephant Standing GG-9251	Open		50.00	50
1992	Elephant Pair GG-9255	Open		220.00	220
1992	Elephant Pair Playing GG-9253	Open		80.00	80
1992	Mother & Baby Elephant GG-9254	Open		160.00	160

Graceful Reflections - Maruri Studios

1991	Mute Swan w/Baby SW-9152	Closed	1993	95.00	95
1991	Pair-Mute Swan SW-9153	Closed	1993	145.00	145
1991	Pair-Mute Swan SW-9154	Closed	1993	195.00	195
1991	Single Mute Swan SW-9151	Closed	1993	85.00	85

Horses Of The World - Maruri Studios

1993	Arabian HW-9356	Closed	1995	175.00	175
1993	Camargue HW-9354	Closed	1995	150.00	150
1993	Clydesdale HW-9351	Closed	1995	145.00	145
1993	Paint Horse HW-9355	Closed	1995	160.00	160
1993	Quarter Horse HW-9353	Closed	1995	145.00	145
1993	Thoroughbred HW-9352	Closed	1995	145.00	145

Hummingbirds - Maruri Studios

1995	Allen's & Babies w/Rose H-9523	Open		120.00	120
1995	Allen's w/Easter Lily H-9522	Open		95.00	95
1989	Allen's w/Hibiscus H-8906	Open		195.00	195
1989	Anna's w/Lily H-8905	Open		160.00	160
1995	Anna's w/Trumpet Creeper H-9524	Open		130.00	130
1995	Broad-Billed w/Amaryllis H-9526	Open		150.00	150
1989	Calliope w/Azalea H-8904	Open		120.00	120
1989	Ruby-Throated w/Azalea H-8911	Open		75.00	75
1989	Ruby-Throated w/Orchid H-8914	Open		150.00	150
1989	Rufous w/Trumpet Creeper H-8901	Open		70.00	75
1989	Violet-crowned w/Gentian H-8903	Open		90.00	90
1989	Violet-Crowned w/Gentian H-8913	Open		75.00	75
1995	Violet-Crowned w/Iris H-9521	Open		95.00	95
1989	White-eared w/Morning Glory H-8902	Open		85.00	85

YEAR ISSUE		EDITION LIMIT	YEAR RETD.	ISSUE PRICE	* QUOTE U.S.$
1989	White-Eared w/Morning Glory H-8912	Open		75.00	75
1995	White-Eared w/Tulip H-9525	Open		145.00	145

Legendary Flowers of the Orient - Ito

1985	Cherry Blossom	15,000		45.00	55
1985	Chinese Peony	15,000		45.00	55
1985	Chrysanthemum	15,000		45.00	55
1985	Iris	15,000		45.00	55
1985	Lily	15,000		45.00	55
1985	Lotus	15,000		45.00	45
1985	Orchid	15,000		45.00	55
1985	Wisteria	15,000		45.00	55

Majestic Owls of the Night - D. Littleton

1988	Barred Owl	15,000		55.00	55
1987	Burrowing Owl	15,000		55.00	55
1988	Elf Owl	15,000		55.00	55

National Parks - Maruri Studios

1993	Baby Bear NP-9301	12/96		60.00	60
1993	Bear Family NP-9304	12/96		160.00	160
1993	Buffalo NP-9306	12/96		170.00	170
1993	Cougar Cubs NP-9302	12/96		70.00	70
1993	Deer Family NP-9303	12/96		120.00	120
1993	Eagle NP-9307	12/96		180.00	180
1993	Falcon NP-9308	12/96		195.00	195
1993	Howling Wolves NP-9305	12/96		165.00	165

North American Game Animals - W. Gaither

1984	White Tail Deer	950		285.00	285

North American Game Birds - W. Gaither

1983	Bobtail Quail, female	Closed	N/A	375.00	375
1983	Bobtail Quail, male	Closed	N/A	375.00	375
1981	Canadian Geese, pair	Closed	N/A	2000.00	2000
1981	Eastern Wild Turkey	Closed	N/A	300.00	300
1982	Ruffed Grouse	Closed	N/A	1745.00	1745
1983	Wild Turkey Hen with Chicks	Closed	N/A	300.00	300

North American Songbirds - W. Gaither

1982	Bluebird	Closed	N/A	95.00	95
1983	Cardinal, female	Closed	N/A	95.00	95
1982	Cardinal, male	Closed	N/A	95.00	95
1982	Carolina Wren	Closed	N/A	95.00	95
1982	Chickadee	Closed	N/A	95.00	95
1982	Mockingbird	Closed	N/A	95.00	95
1983	Robin	Closed	N/A	95.00	95

North American Waterfowl I - W. Gaither

1981	Blue Winged Teal	200		980.00	980
1981	Canvasback Ducks	Closed	1994	780.00	780
1981	Flying Wood Ducks	Closed		880.00	880
1981	Mallard Drake	Closed	N/A	2380.00	2380
1981	Wood Duck, decoy	950		480.00	480

North American Waterfowl II - W. Gaither

1982	Bufflehead Ducks Pair	1,500		225.00	225
1982	Goldeneye Ducks Pair	Closed	N/A	225.00	225
1983	Loon	Closed	1989	245.00	245
1981	Mallard Ducks Pair	1,500		225.00	225
1982	Pintail Ducks Pair	Closed	1994	225.00	225
1982	Widgeon, female	Closed	N/A	225.00	225
1982	Widgeon, male	Closed	N/A	225.00	225

Polar Expedition - Maruri Studios

1992	Arctic Fox Cubs Playing-P-9223	Open		65.00	65
1990	Baby Arctic Fox-P-9002	Open		50.00	55
1990	Baby Emperor Penguin-P-9001	Open		45.00	50
1992	Baby Harp Seal-P-9221	Open		55.00	55
1990	Baby Harp Seals-P-9005	Open		65.00	70
1990	Emperor Penguins-P-9222	Open		60.00	60
1990	Mother & Baby Emperor Penguins-P-9006	Open		80.00	85
1990	Mother & Baby Harp Seals-P-9007	Open		90.00	95
1990	Mother & Baby Polar Bears-P-9008	Open		125.00	130
1990	Polar Bear Cub Sliding-P-9003	Open		50.00	55
1990	Polar Bear Cubs Playing-P-9004	Open		60.00	65
1992	Polar Bear Family-P-9224	Open		90.00	90
1990	Polar Expedition Sign-PES-001	Open		18.00	18

Precious Panda - Maruri Studios

1992	Lazy Lunch PP-9202	Open		60.00	60
1992	Mother's Cuddle-PP-9204	Open		120.00	120
1992	Snack Time PP-9201	Open		60.00	60
1992	Tug of War PP-9203	Open		70.00	70

Santa's World Travels - Maruri Studios

1996	Cat Nap SWT-9603	7,500		85.00	85
1996	Crossing the Tundra SWT-9605	7,500		145.00	145
1996	Desert Trip SWT-9604	7,500		95.00	95
1996	Santa's Safari SWT-9600	5,000		225.00	225
1996	Trusted Friend SWT-9602	7,500		85.00	85
1996	Wild Ride SWT-9601	7,500		75.00	75

Shore Birds - W. Gaither

1984	Pelican	Closed	N/A	260.00	260
1984	Sand Piper	Closed	N/A	285.00	285

FIGURINES/COTTAGES

YEAR ISSUE		EDITION LIMIT	YEAR RETD.	ISSUE PRICE	*QUOTE U.S.$
Signature Collection - W. Gaither					
1985	American Bald Eagle	Closed	N/A	60.00	60
1985	Canada Goose	Closed	N/A	60.00	60
1985	Hawk	Closed	N/A	60.00	60
1985	Pintail Duck	Closed	N/A	60.00	60
1985	Snow Goose	Closed	N/A	60.00	60
1985	Swallow	Closed	N/A	60.00	60
Songbirds Of Beauty - Maruri Studios					
1991	Bluebird w/ Apple Blossom SB-9105	Closed	1994	85.00	85
1991	Cardinal w/ Cherry Blossom SB-9103	Closed	1994	85.00	85
1991	Chickadee w/ Roses SB-9101	Closed	1994	85.00	85
1991	Dbl. Bluebird w/ Peach Blossom SB-9107	Closed	1994	145.00	145
1991	Dbl. Cardinal w/ Dogwood SB-9108	Closed	1994	145.00	145
1991	Goldfinch w/ Hawthorne SB-9102	Closed	1994	85.00	85
1991	Robin & Baby w/ Azalea SB-9106	Closed	1994	115.00	115
1991	Robin w/ Lilies SB-9104	Closed	1994	85.00	85
Special Commissions - W. Gaither					
1982	Cheetah	Closed	N/A	995.00	995
1983	Orange Bengal Tiger	240		340.00	340
1981	White Bengal Tiger	240		340.00	340
Studio Collection - Maruri Studios					
1990	Majestic Eagles-MS-100	Closed	1994	350.00	800
1991	Delicate Motion-MS-200	3,500		325.00	325
1992	Imperial Panda-MS-300	3,500		350.00	350
1993	Wild Wings-MS-400	3,500		395.00	450
1994	Waltz of the Dolphins-MS-500	3,500		300.00	300
1995	"Independent Spirit" MS-600	3,500		395.00	395
Stump Animals - W. Gaither					
1984	Bobcat	Closed	N/A	175.00	175
1984	Chipmunk	Closed	N/A	175.00	175
1984	Gray Squirrel	1,200	1995	175.00	175
1983	Owl	Closed	N/A	175.00	175
1983	Raccoon	Closed	1989	175.00	175
1982	Red Fox	Closed	N/A	175.00	175
Tribal Spirits - Maruri Studios					
1996	Bear Hunter TS-9653	5,000		140.00	140
1996	Buffalo Hunter TS-9651	5,000		130.00	130
1996	Eagle Messenger TS-9652	5,000		140.00	140
1996	Wolf Guide TS-9654	5,000		150.00	150
Upland Birds - W. Gaither					
1981	Mourning Doves	Closed	N/A	780.00	780
Wings of Love Doves - Maruri Studios					
1987	D-8701 Single Dove w/ Forget-Me-Not	Closed	1994	45.00	55
1987	D-8702 Single Dove w/ Primrose	Open		55.00	65
1987	D-8703 Single Dove w/Buttercup	Closed	1994	65.00	70
1987	D-8704 Double Dove w/Daisy	Open		75.00	85
1987	D-8705 Single Dove w/Blue Flax	Closed	1994	95.00	95
1987	D-8706 Double Dove w/Cherry Blossom	Open		175.00	195
1990	D-9021 Double Dove w/Gentian	Open		50.00	55
1990	D-9022 Double Dove w/Azalea	Open		75.00	75
1990	D-9023 Double Dove w/Apple Blossom	Open		115.00	120
1990	D-9024 Double Dove w/Morning Glory	Open		150.00	160
Wonders of the Sea - Maruri Studios					
1994	Dolphin WS-9401	Open		70.00	70
1994	Great White Shark WS-9406	Open		90.00	90
1994	Green Sea Turtle WS-9405	Open		85.00	85
1994	Humpback Mother & Baby WS-9409	Open		150.00	150
1994	Manatee & Baby WS-9403	Open		75.00	75
1994	Manta Ray WS-9404	Open		80.00	80
1994	Orca Mother & Baby WS-9410	Open		150.00	150
1994	Sea Otter & Baby WS-9402	Open		75.00	75
1994	Three Dolphins WS-9408	Open		135.00	135
1994	Two Dolphins WS-9407	Open		120.00	120

Michael's Limited

YEAR ISSUE		EDITION LIMIT	YEAR RETD.	ISSUE PRICE	*QUOTE U.S.$
Collectors' Corner - B. Baker					
1993	City Cottage (Membership House)-rose/grn.1682	Retrd.	1993	35.00	110
1993	Brian's First House (Redemption House)-red1496	Retrd.	1993	71.00	150-175
1994	Gothic Cottage (Membership Sculpture) 1571	Retrd.	1994	35.00	75-95
1994	Duke of Gloucester Street (Redemption House) 1459	Retrd.	1995	108.00	150-165
1995	Marie's Cottage-grey (Membership Sculpture) 1942	Retrd.	1996	35.00	35
1995	Welcome Home-brick (Redemption House) 1599	Retrd.	1996	65.00	65
1996	Queen Ann Cottage-rose/blue (Membership Sculpture) 1676	3/97		39.00	39
1996	Oak Street-brick/brown (Redemption House) 1685	9/97		65.00	65
Signing Piece - B. Baker					
1995	Joe's Newstand 1348	Yr.Iss.	1995	27.00	27
1996	Yellow Rose Cottage 1444	12/96		62.00	62

YEAR ISSUE		EDITION LIMIT	YEAR RETD.	ISSUE PRICE	*QUOTE U.S.$
Brian Baker's Déjà Vu Collection - B. Baker					
1988	Adam Colonial Cottage -blue/white 1515	Retrd.	1992	53.00	53
1993	Admiralty Head Lighthouse -white 1532	Retrd.	1995	62.00	62
1992	Alpine Ski Lodge-brown/white 1012	Retrd.	1993	62.00	92
1988	Andulusian Village-white 1060	Retrd.	1993	53.00	63
1992	Angel of the Sea-blue/white 1587	Open		67.00	67
1996	Angel of the Sea-blue/white 1592	Open		69.00	69
1992	Angel of the Sea-mauve/white 1586	Open		67.00	67
1996	Angel of the Sea-mauve/white 1591	Open		69.00	69
1989	Antebellum Mansion-blue/rose 1505	Retrd.	1993	53.00	73
1988	Antebellum Mansion-blue/white 1519	Retrd.	1988	49.00	49
1989	Antebellum Mansion-peach 1506	Retrd.	1991	49.00	56
1988	Antebellum Mansion-peach 1517	Retrd.	1988	49.00	49
1988	Antebellum Mansion -white/green 1518	Retrd.	1988	49.00	49
1994	Barber Shop 1164	12/96		53.00	53
1987	Bavarian Church-white 1021	Retrd.	1988	38.00	38
1987	Bavarian Church-yellow 1020	Retrd.	1988	38.00	38
1987	The Bernese Guesthouse -golden br. 1010	Retrd.	1990	49.00	49
1989	Blumen Shop-white/brown 1023	Retrd.	1993	53.00	73
1996	Brick & Brackets-brick 1933	Open		65.00	65
1994	Cabbagetown 1704	Open		65.00	65
1996	Cape Cottage-grey/white 1442	Open		63.00	63
1992	Casa Chiquita-natural 1400	Retrd.	1993	53.00	60
1994	Castle in the Clouds 1090	Retrd.	1995	75.00	85
1993	Charleston Single House-blue/white 1583	Open		60.00	60
1993	Charleston Single House-peach/white 1584	Open		60.00	60
1996	Chateau in the Woods 1683	12/96		79.00	79
1994	Christmas at Church 1223	12/96		63.00	63
1990	Christmas House-blue 1225	Retrd.	1992	51.00	51
1990	Classic Victorian-blue/white 1555	Retrd.	1994	60.00	80
1990	Classic Victorian-peach 1557	Retrd.	1994	60.00	80
1990	Classic Victorian-rose/blue 1556	Retrd.	1994	60.00	80
1991	Colonial Color-brown 1508	Retrd.	1993	62.00	82
1991	Colonial Cottage-white/bue 1509	Retrd.	1994	59.00	80
1987	Colonial House-blue 1510	Retrd.	1988	49.00	70
1987	Colonial House-wine 1511	Retrd.	1987	40.00	60
1987	Colonial Store-brick 1512	Retrd.	1993	53.00	73
1993	Corner Grocery-brick 1141	Open		67.00	67
1987	The Cottage House-blue 1531	Retrd.	1988	42.00	67
1987	The Cottage House-white 1530	Retrd.	1993	47.00	67
1989	Country Barn-blue 1528	Retrd.	1991	49.00	70
1989	Country Barn-red 1527	Retrd.	1993	53.00	73
1994	Country Bridge 1513	Open		69.00	69
1996	Country Christmas-red 1219	Open		68.00	68
1988	Country Church-white/blue 1522	Retrd.	1994	49.00	50-70
1992	Country Station-blue/rust 1156	Open		64.00	64
1994	Country Store 1122	12/96		61.00	61
1994	Craftsman Cottage-cream 1478	Open		56.00	56
1994	Craftsman Cottage-grey 1477	Retrd.	1995	56.00	56
1989	Deja Vu Sign-ivory/brown 1600	Retrd.	1991	21.00	24-29
1992	Deja Vu Sign-ivory/brown 1999	Open		21.00	21
1993	Dinard Mansion-beige/brick 1005	Retrd.	1996	67.00	67
1996	Dixie Landing-white 1740	Open		68.00	68
1994	Ellis Island 1250	Retrd.	1996	62.00	62
1993	Enchanted Cottage-natural 1205	Retrd.	1995	63.00	68
1988	Fairy Tale Cottage-white/brown 1200	Retrd.	1992	46.00	46
1987	The Farm House-beige/blue 1525	Retrd.	1991	49.00	49
1987	The Farm House-spiced tan 1526	Retrd.	1991	49.00	49
1992	Firehouse-brick 1140	Open		60.00	60
1992	Flower Store-tan/green 1145	Open		67.00	67
1988	French Colonial Cottage-beige 1516	Retrd.	1990	42.00	65
1988	Georgian Colonial House-white/blue 1514	Retrd.	1992	53.00	53
1990	Gothic Victorian-blue/mauve 1534	Retrd.	1991	47.00	52-54
1988	Gothic Victorian-peach 1536	Retrd.	1991	51.00	60
1988	Gothic Victorian-sea green 1537	Retrd.	1990	47.00	47
1993	Grandpa's Barn-brown 1498	Open		63.00	63
1988	Hampshire House-brick 1040	Retrd.	1990	49.00	60
1989	Hampshire House-brick 1041	Retrd.	1990	49.00	56
1996	Harbor Sentry-white 1590	Open		59.00	59
1989	Henry VIII Pub-white/brown 1043	Retrd.	1993	56.00	76
1993	Homestead Christmas-red 1224	Retrd.	1995	57.00	57
1987	Hotel Couronne (original) wh./br. 1000	Retrd.	1988	49.00	49
1989	Hotel Couronne-white/brown 1003	Retrd.	1992	55.00	55
1987	Italianate Victorian-brown 1543	Retrd.	1990	52.00	52
1987	Italianate Victorian-lavendar 1550	Retrd.	1988	45.00	45
1987	Italianate Victorian-mauve/blue 1545	Retrd.	1991	49.00	49
1989	Italianate Victorian-peach/teal 1552	Retrd.	1991	51.00	62
1989	Italianate Victorian-rose/blue 1551	Retrd.	1991	51.00	55-58
1987	Italianate Victorian-rust/blue 1544	Retrd.	1988	49.00	49
1987	Japanese House-white/brown 1100	Retrd.	1988	47.00	47
1996	Japanese Tea House -brown/white 1101	Open		59.00	59
1987	The Lighthouse-white 1535	Retrd.	1990	51.00	60
1991	Log Cabin-brown 1501	Retrd.	1994	55.00	75
1992	Looks Like Nantucket-grey 1451	Open		59.00	59
1995	Main Street Cafe-blue 1142	Open		61.00	61
1993	Mansard Lady-blue/rose 1606	Open		64.00	64
1993	Mansard Lady-tan/green 1607	Open		64.00	64
1995	Maple Lane-blue/white 1904	Open		72.00	72
1995	Maple Lane-desert/white 1905	Open		72.00	72
1991	Mayor's Mansion-blue/peach 1585	Retrd.	1994	57.00	77

YEAR ISSUE		EDITION LIMIT	YEAR RETD.	ISSUE PRICE	*QUOTE U.S.$
1996	Mediterranean Ave-cream/tile 1741	Open		65.00	65
1995	Mesa Manor 1733	Open		75.00	75
1994	Mission Dolores (no umbrella) 1435	Retrd.	N/A	47.00	75
1994	Mission Dolores 1435	Open		47.00	47
1993	Monday's Wash-cream/blue 1450	12/96		62.00	62
1993	Monday's Wash-white/blue 1449	12/96		62.00	62
1995	Mountain Homestead-brown 1401	Open		78.00	78
1994	Mukilteo Lighthouse 1569	Open		55.00	55
1989	Norwegian House-brown 1051	Retrd.	1990	51.00	58
1990	Old Country Cottage-blue 1502	Retrd.	1992	51.00	58
1990	Old Country Cottage-peach 1504	Retrd.	1991	47.00	65
1990	Old Country Cottage-red 1503	Retrd.	1992	51.00	65
1996	Old Glory-brick 1567	Open		59.00	59
1994	The Old School House 1439	Open		61.00	61
1987	Old West General Store-white/grey 1520	Retrd.	1991	50.00	68
1987	Old West General Store-yellow/white 1521	Retrd.	1988	50.00	50
1993	Old West Hotel-cream 1120	Open		62.00	62
1995	Old West Sheriff-red 1125	Open		56.00	56
1995	Old White Church-white 1424	Open		65.00	65
1988	One Room School House-red 1524	Retrd.	1993	53.00	73
1994	Orleans Cottage-white/blue 1447	Retrd.	1996	63.00	63
1994	Orleans Cottage-white/red 1448	Retrd.	1996	63.00	63
1990	Palm Villa-desert/green 1421	Retrd.	1995	54.00	61
1990	Palm Villa-white/blue 1420	Retrd.	1995	54.00	61
1994	Paris by the Bay 1004	Retrd.	1996	55.00	55
1989	Parisian Apartment-beige/blue 1002	Retrd.	1993	53.00	73
1987	Parisian Apartment-golden brown 1001	Retrd.	1993	53.00	73
1995	Peggy's Cove Light-white 1533	Open		56.00	56
1996	Pennridge-white/stone 1429	Open		70.00	70
1994	Police Station 1147	Open		55.00	55
1993	Post Office-light green 1146	Open		60.00	60
1987	Queen Ann Victorian-peach/green 1540	Retrd.	1993	53.00	73
1987	Queen Ann Victorian-rose 1541	Retrd.	1993	53.00	73
1987	Queen Ann Victorian-rust/green 1542	Retrd.	1988	49.00	49
1995	Quiet Afternoon-cream/blue 1623	Open		71.00	71
1995	Quiet Afternoon-rose/blue 1622	Open		71.00	71
1995	River Belle Steamer-white 1092	Open		70.00	70
1994	Riverside Mill 1507	Open		65.00	65
1988	Roeder Gate, Rothenburg -brown 1022	Retrd.	1990	49.00	49
1996	Ruby's Watch-blue/white 1630	Open		56.00	56
1996	Ruby's Watch-cream/white 1631	Open		56.00	56
1994	San Francisco Stick-brick/teal 1625	Retrd.	1996	61.00	61
1994	San Francisco Stick-cream/blue 1624	Retrd.	1996	61.00	61
1995	Scenic Route 100-red/green 1426	Open		71.00	71
1995	Scenic Route 100-red/yellow 1425	Open		71.00	71
1996	Seaside Cottage-blue/white 1691	Open		64.00	64
1996	Seaside Cottage-rose/white 1690	Open		64.00	64
1988	Second Empire House-sea grn./desert 1539	Retrd.	1991	50.00	50
1988	Second Empire House -white/blue 1538	Retrd.	1993	54.00	74
1993	Smuggler's Cove-grey/brown 1529	Open		72.00	72
1987	Snow Cabin-brown/white 1500	Retrd.	1993	51.00	70
1995	Southern Exposure-cream/rose 1582	Open		62.00	62
1995	Southern Exposure-tan/green 1581	Open		62.00	62
1995	Southern Mansion-brick 1744	Retrd.	1995	79.00	79
1995	St. Nicholas Church-white/blue 1409	Open		56.00	56
1993	Steiner Street-peach/green 1674	Open		63.00	63
1993	Steiner Street-rose/blue 1675	Open		63.00	63
1993	The Stone House-stone/blue 1453	Open		63.00	63
1988	Stone Victorians-browns 1554	Retrd.	1993	56.00	76
1993	Sunday Afternoon-brick 1523	Retrd.	1995	62.00	62
1989	Swedish House-Swed.red 1050	Retrd.	1990	51.00	58
1991	Teddy's Place-teal/rose 1570	Open		61.00	61
1994	Towered Lady-blue/rose 1688	Open		65.00	65
1994	Towered Lady-rose 1689	Open		65.00	65
1992	Tropical Fantasy-blue/coral 1410	Open		67.00	67
1992	Tropical Fantasy-rose/blue 1411	Open		67.00	67
1992	Tropical Fantasy-yellow/teal 1412	Open		67.00	67
1996	Tropical Paradise-white/brown 1115	Open		65.00	65
1995	Tudor Christmas-red brick 1221	Open		67.00	67
1995	Tudor Home-tan brick 1222	Open		67.00	67
1987	Turreted Victorian-beige/blue 1546	Retrd.	1992	55.00	55
1987	Turreted Victorian-peach 1547	Retrd.	1993	55.00	55
1987	Ultimate Victorian-lt. blue/rose 1549	Retrd.	1993	60.00	80
1987	Ultimate Victorian-maroon/slate 1548	Retrd.	1993	60.00	80
1989	Ultimate Victorian-peach/green 1553	Retrd.	1993	60.00	65
1992	Victorian Bay View-cream/teal 1564	Open		63.00	63
1992	Victorian Bay View-rose/blue 1563	Open		63.00	63
1992	Victorian Charm-cream 1588	12/96		61.00	61
1992	Victorian Charm-mauve 1589	12/96		61.00	61
1990	Victorian Country Estate -desert/br. 1560	Retrd.	1994	62.00	82
1990	Victorian Country Estate -peach/blue 1562	Retrd.	1994	62.00	82
1990	Victorian Country Estate -rose/blue 1561	Retrd.	1994	62.00	82
1991	Victorian Farmhouse -goldenbrown 1565	Retrd.	1994	59.00	90
1995	Victorian Living-clay/white 1927	Open		70.00	70
1995	Victorian Living-teal/tan 1926	Open		70.00	70
1992	Victorian Tower House-blue/maroon 1558	Open		63.00	63
1992	Victorian Tower House -peach/blue 1559	Open		63.00	63

YEAR ISSUE	EDITION LIMIT	YEAR RETRD.	ISSUE PRICE	*QUOTE U.S.$
1996 Village Pharmacy-brick 1157	Open		65.00	65
1996 Willow Road-brick 1713	Open		68.00	68
1991 Wind and Roses-brick 1470	Open		63.00	63
1989 Windmill on the Dike -beige/green 1034	Retrd. 1994		60.00	90
1992 Rose Cottage-grey 1443	Open		59.00	59

Brian Baker's Déjà Vu Collection Accessories - B. Baker

YEAR ISSUE	EDITION LIMIT	YEAR RETRD.	ISSUE PRICE	*QUOTE U.S.$
1995 Apple Tree 1317	Open		36.00	36
1996 Autumn Birch 1323	Open		26.00	26
1996 Autumn Flame 1328	Open		29.00	29
1996 Banana Tree 1318	Open		36.00	36
1996 Blue Spruce 1352	Open		24.00	24
1995 Cactus Garden 1334	Open		27.50	28
1995 Coconut Palms 1319	Open		25.00	25
1995 Date Palm 1320	Open		24.00	24
1995 Doghouse 1306	Open		23.00	23
1996 Farm Truck 1357	Open		47.00	47
1996 Forest Fir 1358	Open		24.00	24
1996 Forest Giant 1333	Open		36.00	36
1996 Garden Trellis 1308	Open		24.00	24
1996 Hemlock 1344	Open		24.00	24
1995 House For Sale 1307	Open		24.00	24
1996 Huckleberry's Cat 1343	Open		20.00	20
1995 In The Park 1340	Open		30.00	30
1996 Japanese Bridge 1330	Open		34.00	34
1996 Japanese Pine 1331	Open		36.00	36
1996 Large Blue Spruce 1361	Open		24.00	24
1995 Long Picket Fence 1309	Open		23.00	23
1995 Members Only 1312	Open		46.00	46
1995 Outhouse 1305	Open		26.00	26
1995 Rope Swing 1311	Open		36.00	36
1995 Route 1 1313	Open		28.00	28
1996 Summer Birch 1322	Open		26.00	26
1996 Summer Shade 1327	Open		29.00	29
1996 Tom's Fence 1342	Open		20.00	20
1995 Weeping Willow 1326	Open		39.00	39
1995 Windy Day 1321	Open		35.00	35
1996 Winter Green 1360	Open		24.00	24
1996 Winter Mantel 1351	Open		24.00	24

Limited Editions From Brian Baker - B. Baker

YEAR ISSUE	EDITION LIMIT	YEAR RETRD.	ISSUE PRICE	*QUOTE U.S.$
1993 American Classic-rose 1566	Retrd. 1993		99.00	550-595
1987 Amsterdam Canal-brown, S/N 1030	Retrd. 1993		79.00	200
1994 Hill Top Mansion 1598	1,200 1995		97.00	97
1993 James River Plantation-brick 1454	Retrd. 1994		108.00	300-500
1996 London 1045	1,000		119.00	119
1994 Painted Ladies 1190	1,200		125.00	125
1995 Philadelphia-brick 1441	1,500		110.00	110
1994 White Point 1596	700 1996		100.00	150

Midwest of Cannon Falls

Belenes Puig Nativity Collection - J.P. Llobera

YEAR ISSUE	EDITION LIMIT	YEAR RETRD.	ISSUE PRICE	*QUOTE U.S.$
1989 Angel 02087-6	Open		50.00	55
1989 Baby Jesus 02085-2	Open		62.00	62
1989 Donkey 02082-1	Open		26.00	26
1989 Joseph 02086-9	Open		62.00	62
1989 Mother Mary 02084-5	Open		62.00	62
1985 Nativity, set/6: Holy Family, Angel, Animals 6 3/4" 00205-6	Open		250.00	250
1989 Ox 02083-8	Open		26.00	26
1990 Resting Camel 04025-6	Open		115.00	115
1986 Sheep, set/3 00475-3	Open		28.00	28
1987 Shepherd & Angel Scene, set/7 06084-1	Open		305.00	305
1989 Shepherd Carrying Lamb 02092-0	Open		56.00	56
1989 Shepherd with Staff 02091-3	Open		56.00	56
1985 Shepherd, set/2 00458-6	Open		110.00	110
1988 Standing Camel 08792-3	Open		115.00	115
1989 Wise Man with Frankincense 02088-3	Open		66.00	66
1989 Wise Man with Frankincense on Camel 02077-7	Open		155.00	156
1989 Wise Man with Gold 02089-0	Open		66.00	66
1989 Wise Man with Gold on Camel 02075-3	Open		155.00	156
1989 Wise Man with Myrrh 02090-6	Open		66.00	66
1989 Wise Man with Myrrh on Camel 02076-0	Open		155.00	156
1985 Wise Men, set/3 00459-3	Open		185.00	185

Cottontail Lane Figurines and Accessories - Midwest

YEAR ISSUE	EDITION LIMIT	YEAR RETRD.	ISSUE PRICE	*QUOTE U.S.$
1993 Arbor w/ Fence Set 02188-0	Open		14.00	15
1993 Birdbath, Bench & Mailbox, 02184-2	Retrd. 1993		4.00	4
1994 Birdhouse, Sundial & Fountain, 3 asst. 00371-8	Open		4.50	5
1993 Bridge & Gazebo, 2 asst. 02182-9	Retrd. 1996		11.50	12
1997 Bunnies on an Afternoon Stroll 18656-5	Open		5.00	5
1996 Bunnies Sitting in Gazebo 15801-2	Open		10.00	10
1996 Bunny Band Quartet, set/4 15799-2	Open		16.00	16
1995 Bunny Chef, 2 asst. 12433-8	Open		4.50	5
1997 Bunny Child Collecting Eggs, 2 asst. 02880-3	Retrd. 1993		4.20	14
1996 Bunny Children Working in Garden, 2 asst. 15796-1	Open		3.50	4
1997 Bunny Clown, 2 asst. 18659-6	Open		4.00	4
1995 Bunny Couple at Cafe Table 12444-4	Open		7.00	7

YEAR ISSUE	EDITION LIMIT	YEAR RETRD.	ISSUE PRICE	*QUOTE U.S.$
1993 Bunny Couple on Bicycle 02978-7	Retrd. 1993		5.30	6
1997 Bunny Flower Girl & Ring Bearer, 2 asst. 18651-0	Open		3.50	4
1995 Bunny Kids at Carrot Juice Stand 12437-6	Open		5.30	6
1997 Bunny Kissing Booth 18660-2	Open		9.00	9
1994 Bunny Marching Band, 6 asst. 00355-8	Open		4.20	5
1995 Bunny Minister, Soloist, 2 asst. 12434-8	Open		5.00	5
1996 Bunny Picnicking, set/4 15798-5	Open		15.00	15
1995 Bunny Playing Piano 12439-0	Open		5.30	6
1995 Bunny Playing, 2 asst. 12442-0	Open		6.50	7
1995 Bunny Popcorn, Balloon Vendor, 2 asst. 12443-7	Open		6.70	7
1994 Bunny Preparing for Easter, 3 asst. 02971-8	Retrd. 1996		4.20	5
1994 Bunny Shopping Couple, 2 asst. 10362-3	Open		4.20	5
1997 Bunny Throwing Pie 18657-2	Open		3.00	3
1997 Bunny Vendor 18658-9	Open		4.00	4
1997 Carrot Fence 19625-0	Open		10.00	10
1994 Cobblestone Road 10072-1	Retrd. 1996		9.00	9
1994 Cone-Shaped Tree Set 10369-2	Retrd. 1996		7.50	8
1997 Cotton Candy Vendor Bunny 18661-9	Open		5.00	5
1994 Cottontail Lane Sign 10063-9	Open		5.00	5
1994 Easter Bunny Figure, 2 asst. 00356-5	Open		4.20	5
1994 Egg Stand & Flower Cart, 2 asst. 10354-8	Open		6.00	6
1995 Electric Street Lamppost, set/4 12461-1	Open		25.00	25
1996 Garden Shopkeeper, set/2 15800-5	Open		10.00	10
1996 Garden Table with Potted Plants and Flowers 15802-9	Open		9.00	9
1996 Garden with Waterfall and Pond 15797-8	Open		15.00	15
1997 Just Married Getaway Car 18650-3	Open		10.00	10
1993 Lamppost, Birdhouse & Mailbox, 3 asst. 02187-3	Retrd. 1993		4.50	5
1995 Mayor Bunny and Bunny with Flag Pole, 2 asst. 12441-3	Open		5.50	6
1995 Outdoor Bunny, 3 asst. 12435-2	Open		5.00	5
1994 Policeman, Conductor Bunny, 2 asst. 00367-1	Open		4.20	5
1995 Professional Bunny, 3 asst. 12438-3	Open		5.00	5
1995 Street Sign, 3 asst. 12433-8	Open		4.50	5
1993 Strolling Bunny, 2 asst. 02976-3	Retrd. 1993		4.20	5
1995 Strolling Bunny, 2 asst. 12440-6	Open		5.50	6
1994 Sweeper & Flower Peddler Bunny Couple, 2 asst. 00359-6	Open		4.20	5
1997 Ticket Vendor 18654-1	Open		10.00	10
1994 Topiary Trees, 3 asst. 00346-6	Retrd. 1994		2.50	3
1994 Train Station Couple, 2 asst. 00357-2	Open		4.20	5
1994 Tree & Shrub, 2 asst. 00382-4	Open		5.00	5
1996 Tree with Painted Flowers, set/3 15924-8	Open		20.00	20
1993 Trees, 3 asst. 02194-1	Retrd. 1994		6.20	7
1997 Wedding Bunny Couple 18652-7	Open		5.00	5
1994 Wedding Bunny Couple, 2 asst. 00347-3	Open		4.20	5

Cottontail Lane Houses - Midwest

YEAR ISSUE	EDITION LIMIT	YEAR RETRD.	ISSUE PRICE	*QUOTE U.S.$
1997 Arcade Booth (lighted) 18655-8	Open		33.00	33
1993 Bakery (lighted) 01396-0	Open		43.00	45
1996 Bandshell (lighted) 15753-4	Open		50.00	50
1994 Bed & Breakfast House (lighted) 00337-4	Open		43.00	45
1995 Boutique and Beauty Shop (lighted) 12301-0	Open		45.00	45
1996 Bungalow (lighted) 15752-7	Open		45.00	45
1997 Bunny Chapel (lighted) 18653-4	Open		40.00	40
1995 Cafe (lighted) 12303-4	Open		45.00	45
1997 Carousel (lighted & musical) 18649-7	5,000		47.00	47
1995 Cathedral (lighted) 12302-7	Open		47.00	47
1994 Chapel (lighted) 00331-2	3,000 1993		43.00	200
1993 Church (lighted) 01385-4	3,000 1993		42.00	140
1992 Confectionary Shop (lighted) 06335-5	Retrd. 1994		43.00	85
1993 Cottontail Inn (lighted) 01394-6	Open		43.00	45
1996 Fire Station w/Figures, set/6 (lighted) 15830-2	5,000		90.00	90
1992 Flower Shop (lighted) 06333-9	Retrd. 1994		43.00	85
1994 General Store (lighted) 00340-4	Open		43.00	45
1993 Painting Studio (lighted) 01395-3	Retrd. 1994		43.00	45
1993 Rose Cottage (lighted) 01386-1	Retrd. 1994		43.00	45
1995 Rosebud Manor (lighted) 12304-1	3,500 1994		43.00	80
1993 Schoolhouse (lighted) 01378-6	Open		43.00	45
1992 Springtime Cottage (lighted) 06329-8	Retrd. 1994		43.00	85
1996 Town Garden Shoppe (lighted) 15751-0	Open		45.00	45
1995 Town Hall (lighted) 12300-3	Open		45.00	45
1994 Train Station (lighted) 00330-5	Open		43.00	45
1997 Tunnel of Love w/Swan (lighted)18648-0	Open		40.00	40
1992 Victorian House (lighted) 06332-1	Open		43.00	45

Creepy Hollow Figurines and Accessories - Midwest

YEAR ISSUE	EDITION LIMIT	YEAR RETRD.	ISSUE PRICE	*QUOTE U.S.$
1994 Black Picket Fence 10685-3	Retrd. 1996		13.50	14
1996 Bone Fence 16961-2	Open		9.50	10

YEAR ISSUE	EDITION LIMIT	YEAR RETRD.	ISSUE PRICE	*QUOTE U.S.$
1992 Bride of Frankenstein 06663-8	Retrd. 1993		5.00	20
1995 Cemetery Gate 13366-8	Open		16.00	16
1996 Covered Bridge 16664-2	Open		22.00	22
1994 Creepy Hollow Sign 10647-1	Open		5.50	6
1993 Dracula (standing) 06707-9	Retrd. 1994		7.30	13
1996 Dragon 16936-0	Open		8.50	9
1995 Flying Witch, Ghost, 2 asst. 13362-0	Retrd. 1996		11.00	11
1993 Frankenstein 06704-8	Retrd. 1994		6.00	11
1994 Ghost, 3 asst. 10652-5	Open		6.00	6
1996 Ghostly King 16659-8	Open		8.00	8
1994 Ghoul Usher 13515-0	Open		6.50	7
1995 Ghoulish Organist Playing Organ 13363-7	Open		13.00	13
1995 Grave Digger, 2 asst. 13360-6	Open		10.00	10
1996 Gypsy 16656-7	Open		8.00	8
1996 Gypsy Witch 16655-0	Open		8.00	8
1992 Halloween Sign, 2 asst. 06709-3	Retrd. 1995		6.00	7
1993 Haunted Tree, 2 asst. 05892-3	Open		7.00	7
1996 Headless Horseman 16658-1	Open		11.00	11
1995 Hearse with Monsters 13364-4	Open		15.00	15
1993 Hinged Dracula's Coffin 08545-5	Open		11.00	11
1995 Hinged Tomb 13516-7	Retrd. 1995		15.00	15
1995 Hunchback 13359-0	Open		9.00	9
1996 Inn Keeper 16660-4	Open		7.00	—7
1994 Mad Scientist 10646-4	Open		6.00	7
1993 Mummy 06705-5	Retrd. 1994		6.00	13
1994 Outhouse 10648-8	Open		7.00	7
1994 Phantom of the Opera 10645-7	Open		6.00	7
1993 Pumpkin Head Ghost 06661-4	Retrd. 1993		5.50	15
1993 Pumpkin Patch Sign, 2 asst. 05898-5	Retrd. 1995		6.50	7
1995 Pumpkin Street Lamp, set/4 13365-1	Retrd. 1996		25.00	25
1993 Resin Skeleton 06651-5	Retrd. 1994		5.50	15
1995 Road of Bones 13371-2	Open		9.00	9
1996 School Teacher 16657-4	Open		8.00	8
1996 Skeleton Butler 16661-1	Open		7.00	7
1994 Street Sign, 2 asst. 10644-0	Retrd. 1996		5.70	6
1993 Street Sign, 3 asst. 13357-6	Open		5.50	6
1995 Theatre Goer, set/2 13358-3	Open		9.00	15
1995 Ticket Seller 13361-3	Open		10.00	10
1994 Tombstone Sign, 3 asst. 10642-6	Open		3.50	4
1993 Trick or Treater, 3 asst. 08591-2	Retrd. 1995		5.50	5
1994 Werewolf 10643-4	Open		6.00	7
1992 Witch 06706-2	Retrd. 1996		6.00	13

Creepy Hollow Houses - Midwest

YEAR ISSUE	EDITION LIMIT	YEAR RETRD.	ISSUE PRICE	*QUOTE U.S.$
1995 Bewitching Belfry (lighted) 13355-2	Open		50.00	50
1993 Blood Bank (lighted) 08548-6	Retrd. 1996		40.00	43
1996 Castle (lighted) 16959-9	5,000		50.00	50
1994 Cauldron Cafe (lighted) 10649-5	Open		40.00	43
1992 Dr. Frankenstein's House (lighted) 01621-3	Retrd. 1995		40.00	65
1992 Dracula's Castle (lighted) 01627-5	Retrd. 1995		40.00	65
1995 Funeral Parlor (lighted) 13356-9	Open		50.00	50
1996 Gypsy Wagon (lighted) 16663-5	Open		45.00	45
1993 Haunted Hotel (lighted) 08549-3	Retrd. 1996		40.00	43
1996 Jack-O' Lant-Inn (lighted) 16665-9	Open		45.00	45
1994 Medical Ghoul School (lighted) 10651-8	Open		40.00	43
1992 Mummy's Mortuary (lighted) 01641-1	Retrd. 1995		40.00	43
1994 Phantom's Opera (lighted) 10650-1	Open		40.00	43
1996 School House (lighted) 16662-8	Open		45.00	45
1993 Shoppe of Horrors (lighted) 08550-9	Retrd. 1995		40.00	43
1995 Skeleton Cinema (lighted) 13354-5	5,000 1996		50.00	85
1992 Witches Cove (lighted) 01665-7	Retrd. 1995		40.00	43

Leo R. Smith III Collection - L. R. Smith

YEAR ISSUE	EDITION LIMIT	YEAR RETRD.	ISSUE PRICE	*QUOTE U.S.$
1996 Angel of the Morning 18232-1	1,000		48.00	50
1995 Angel w/Lion and Lamb 13990-5	1,500 1995		125.00	175
1995 Circle of Nature Wreath 16120-3	500		200.00	200
1991 Cossack Santa 01092-1	1,700 1993		103.00	185
1993 Dancing Santa 09042-8	5,000 1996		170.00	170
1992 Dreams of Night Buffalo 07999-7	1,062		250.00	270
1991 Fisherman Santa 03311-1	4,000 1995		270.00	350-475
1993 Folk Angel 05444-4	2,095 1995		145.00	150
1995 Gardening Angel 16118-0	2,500		130.00	130
1994 Gift Giver Santa 12056-9	1,500 1996		180.00	180
1993 Gnome Santa on Deer 05206-8	1,463		270.00	270
1992 Great Plains Santa 08049-8	5,000 1994		270.00	400-500
1995 Hare Leaping Over the Garden 16121-0	750		100.00	100
1996 Jolly Boatman Santa 17794-5	1,500		180.00	180
1992 Leo Smith Name Plaque 07881-5	5,000		12.00	12
1995 Maize Maiden Angel 13992-9	2,500		45.00	45
1991 Milkmaker 03541-2	5,000 1994		170.00	184
1992 Ms. Liberty 07866-2	5,000 1994		190.00	250-300
1994 Old-World Santa 12053-8	1,500 1996		75.00	200-250
1993 Orchard Santa 13989-9	1,500		125.00	125
1995 Otter Wall Hanging 16122-7	750		150.00	150
1995 Owl Lady 13988-2	1,000 1995		100.00	105
1991 Pilgrim Man 03313-5	5,000 1994		84.00	200
1991 Pilgrim Riding Turkey 03312-8	5,000 1995		230.00	350-500
1991 Pilgrim Woman 03315-9	5,000 1995		84.00	200
1996 Prairie Moon Market 17793-8	750		300.00	300
1993 Santa Fisherman 08979-8	1,748		250.00	300
1996 Santa in Red Convertible 17790-7	2,000		100.00	100
1995 Santa in Sleigh 13987-5	1,500		125.00	125
1992 Santa of Peace 07328-5	5,000 1994		250.00	350-400
1994 Santa Skier 12054-5	1,500 1995		190.00	200
1996 Snowflake in Nature Santa 17791-4	1,500		125.00	125

FIGURINES/COTTAGES

YEAR ISSUE		EDITION LIMIT	YEAR RETRD.	ISSUE PRICE	*QUOTE U.S.$
1994	Star of the Roundup Cowboy 11966-1	1,500		100.00	100
1991	Stars and Stripes Santa 01743-2	5,000	1994	190.00	350-400
1995	Sunbringer Santa 13991-2	1,500	1996	125.00	125
1996	SW Bach Santa 17792-1	1,500		125.00	125
1991	Tis a Witching Time 03544-3	609	1991	140.00	1500
1991	Toymaker 03540-5	5,000	1994	120.00	200
1993	Voyageur 09043-5	788		170.00	170
1994	Weatherwise Angel 12055-2	1,500		150.00	150
1995	Wee Willie Santa 13993-6	2,500	1995	50.00	50
1992	Woodland Brave 07867-9	1,500	1993	87.00	350-450
1991	Woodsman Santa 03310-4	5,000	1995	230.00	300-350

Ore Mountain "A Christmas Carol" Nutcrackers - Midwest

1993	Bob Cratchit, 09421-1	5,000	1995	120.00	130
1994	Ghost of Christmas Future, 10449-1	1,500	1995	116.00	125
1994	Ghost of Christmas Past, 10447-7	1,500	1995	116.00	125
1993	Ghost of Christmas Present 12041-5	1,500	1996	116.00	200
1994	Marley's Ghost, 10448-4	1,500	1995	116.00	125
1993	Scrooge, 05522-9	2,500	1995	104.00	125

Ore Mountain "Nutcracker Fantasy" Nutcrackers - Midwest

1995	Clara, 12801-5	5,000		125.00	137
1991	Clara, 8" 01254-3	Retrd.	1995	77.00	100
1994	Herr Drosselmeyer, 10456-9	5,000		110.00	137
1988	Herr Drosselmeyer, 14 1/2" 07506-7	Retrd.	1996	75.00	115
1993	The Mouse King, 05350-8	5,000		100.00	125
1988	The Mouse King, 10" 07509-8	Open		60.00	85
1994	Nutcracker Prince, 11001-0	5,000		104.00	125
1988	The Prince, 12 3/4" 07507-4	Open		75.00	105
1988	The Toy Soldier, 11" 07508-1	Retrd.	1996	70.00	95
1995	Toy Soldier, 12804-6	5,000		125.00	125

Ore Mountain Easter Nutcrackers - Midwest

1992	Bunny Painter, 06480-1	Retrd.	1993	77.00	80
1991	Bunny with Egg, 00145-5	Retrd.	1993	77.00	80
1984	March Hare, 00312-1	Retrd.	1993	77.00	80

Ore Mountain Nutcracker Collection - Midwest

1995	American Country Santa, 13195-4	Open		165.00	170
1996	Angel with Candle 17010-6	Open		220.00	240
1994	Annie Oakley, 10464-4	Retrd.	1995	128.00	130
1996	Attorney 17012-0	Open		120.00	130
1995	August the Strong, 13185-5	Open		190.00	190
1995	Barbeque Dad, 13193-0	Retrd.	1996	176.00	176
1994	Baseball Player, 10459-0	Open		111.00	120
1995	Basketball Player, 12784-1	Open		135.00	135
1995	Beefeater, 12797-1	Open		175.00	177
1994	Black Santa, 10460-6	Retrd.	1995	74.00	74
1993	Cat Witch, 09426-6	Retrd.	1995	93.00	93
1994	Cavalier, 12952-4	Open		80.00	100
1994	Cavalier, 12953-1	Open		65.00	80
1994	Cavalier, 12958-6	Open		57.00	70
1996	Chimney Sweep 17043-4	Open		120.00	120
1995	Chimney Sweep, 00326-8	Open		70.00	76
1992	Christopher Columbus, 00152-3	Retrd.	1992	80.00	80
1991	Clown, 03561-0	Retrd.	1994	115.00	118
1994	Confederate Soldier, 12837-4	Open		93.00	110
1996	Count Dracula 17050-2	Open		150.00	150
1989	Country Santa, 09326-9	Retrd.	1995	95.00	150
1996	Cow Farmer 17054-0	Open		120.00	145
1992	Cowboy, 00298-8	Open		97.00	150
1995	Downhill Santa Skier, 13197-8	Open		145.00	150
1996	Drummer 17044-1	Open		120.00	120
1996	East Coast Santa 17047-2	Open		200.00	220
1990	Elf, 04154-3	Retrd.	1993	70.00	73
1996	Emergency Medical Technician 17013-7	Open		140.00	140
1994	Engineer, 10454-5	Retrd.	1995	108.00	108
1992	Farmer, 01109-6	Retrd.	1994	65.00	77
1996	Female Farmer 17011-3	1,000		145.00	180
1993	Fireman with Dog, 06592-1	Open		134.00	145
1989	Fisherman, 09327-6	Retrd.	1995	90.00	100
1996	Frankenstein 17009-0	Open		170.00	190
1994	Gardening Lady, 10450-7	Open		104.00	112
1993	Gepetto Santa, 09417-4	Retrd.	1995	115.00	115
1989	Golfer, 09325-2	Retrd.	1994	85.00	90
1996	Guard 17046-5	Open		120.00	120
1995	Handyman, 12806-0	Open		136.00	137
1996	Harlequin Santa 17174-5	Open		150.00	160
1995	Hockey Player, 12783-4	Open		155.00	155
1995	Hunter Nutcraker 12785-8	Open		136.00	136
1992	Indian, 00195-0	Retrd.	1994	96.00	100
1995	Jack Frost, 12803-9	Open		150.00	150
1995	Jolly St. Nick with Toys, 13709-3	Open		135.00	135
1995	King Richard the Lionhearted, 12798-8	Retrd.	1996	165.00	165
1996	King with Sceptor 17045-8	Open		120.00	120
1995	Law Scholar, 12789-6	Retrd.	1996	127.00	127
1996	Male Farmer 17015-1	1,000		145.00	145
1990	Merlin the Magician, 04207-6	Retrd.	1995	67.00	75
1994	Miner, 10493-4	Open		110.00	120
1994	Nature Lover, 10446-0	Retrd.	1995	112.00	112
1988	Nordic Santa, 08872-2	Open		84.00	110
1996	Northwoods Santa 17048-9	Open		200.00	220
1991	Nutcracker-Maker, 03601-3	Retrd.	1993	62.00	65
1995	Peddler, 12805-3	Retrd.	1996	140.00	140
1995	Pierre Le Chef, 12802-2	Retrd.	1996	147.00	147
1992	Pilgrim, 00188-2	Retrd.	1994	96.00	100
1994	Pinecone Santa, 10461-3	Retrd.	1995	92.00	92
1984	Pinocchio, 00160-8	Retrd.	1996	60.00	68

YEAR ISSUE		EDITION LIMIT	YEAR RETRD.	ISSUE PRICE	*QUOTE U.S.$
1995	Pizza Baker, 13194-7	Open		170.00	170
1996	Prince 17038-0	Open		120.00	120
1994	Prince Charming, 10457-6	Retrd.	1994	125.00	130
1994	Pumpkin Head Scarecrow, 10451-1	Retrd.	1996	127.00	140
1994	Regal Prince, 10452-1	Open		140.00	152
1992	Ringmaster, 00196-7	Retrd.	1993	135.00	137
1995	Riverboat Gambler, 12787-2	Open		137.00	140
1995	Royal Lion, 13985-1	Open		130.00	140
1995	Santa at Workbench, 13335-4	Retrd.	1996	130.00	130
1994	Santa in Nightshirt, 10462-0	Retrd.	1995	108.00	120
1996	Santa One-Man Band Musical 17051-9	Open		170.00	175
1988	Santa w/Tree & Toys, 07666-8	Retrd.	1993	76.00	87
1993	Santa with Animals, 09424-2	Retrd.	1994	117.00	117
1994	Santa with Basket, 10472-9	Open		80.00	100
1992	Santa with Skis, 01305-2	Retrd.	1994	100.00	110
1990	Sea Captain, 04157-4	Retrd.	1994	86.00	95
1994	Snow King, 10470-5	Open		108.00	120
1994	Soccer Player, 10494-1	Retrd.	1994	97.00	107
1994	Sorcerer, 10471-2	Retrd.	1995	100.00	100
1996	Sports Fan 17173-8	Open		120.00	125
1994	Sultan King, 10455-2	Retrd.	1996	130.00	145
1995	Teacher, 13196-1	Open		165.00	165
1994	Toy Vendor, 11987-7	Open		124.00	145
1990	Uncle Sam, 04206-9	Retrd.	1993	50.00	62
1994	Union Soldier, 12836-7	Retrd.	1996	93.00	105
1996	Victorian Santa 17172-1	Open		180.00	185
1992	Victorian Santa, 00187-5	Retrd.	1994	130.00	140
1996	Western 17049-6	Open		250.00	250
1993	White Santa, 09533-1	Retrd.	1995	100.00	100
1990	Windsor Club, 04160-4	Retrd.	1994	85.00	87
1990	Witch, 04159-8	Retrd.	1995	75.00	76
1990	Woodland Santa, 04191-8	Retrd.	1995	105.00	150

Wendt and Kuhn Collection - Wendt/Kuhn

1989	Angel at Piano 09403-7	Open		31.00	37
1983	Angel Brass Musicians, set/6 00470-8	Open		92.00	110
1983	Angel Conductor on Stand 00469-2	Open		21.00	28
1990	Angel Duet in Celestial Stars 04158-1	Retrd.	1994	60.00	63
1983	Angel Percussion Musicians set/6 00443-2	Open		110.00	145
1979	Angel Playing Violin 00403-6	Retrd.	1994	34.00	35
1980	Angel Pulling Wagon 00553-8	Retrd.	1995	43.00	50
1983	Angel String & Woodwind Musicians, set/6 00465-4	Open		108.00	140
1983	Angel String Musicians, set/6 00455-5	Retrd.	1995	105.00	120
1979	Angel Trio, set/3 00471-5	Open		140.00	185
1981	Angel w/Tree & Basket 01190-8	Retrd.	1993	24.00	25
1976	Angel with Sled 02940-4	Retrd.	1994	36.50	38
1981	Angels at Cradle, set/4 01193-5	Open		73.00	92
1996	Angels Bearing Gifts 17039-7	Open		120.00	130
1984	Angels Bearing Toys, set/6 00451-7	Retrd.	1995	97.00	110
1979	Bavarian Moving Van 02854-4	Open		134.00	174
1991	Birdhouse 01209-3	Retrd.	1994	22.50	23
1996	Blueberry Children 17040-3	Open		110.00	120
1991	Boy on Rocking Horse, 2 asst. 01202-4	Retrd.	1994	35.00	36
1994	Busy Elf, 3 asst. 12856-5	Open		22.00	25
1987	Child on Skis, 2 asst. 06083-4	Retrd.	1994	28.00	29
1987	Child on Sled 06085-8	Retrd.	1994	25.50	27
1994	Child with Flowers Set 12947-0	Retrd.	1996	45.00	50
1988	Children Carrying Lanterns Procession, set/6 01213-0	Open		117.00	157
1991	Display Base for Wendt & Kuhn Figures, 12 1/2 x 2" 01214-7	Open		32.00	45
1991	Flower Children, set/6 01213-0	Open		130.00	157
1979	Girl w/Cradle, set/2 01203-1	Retrd.	1994	37.50	40
1979	Girl w/Porridge Bowl 01198-0	Open		29.00	34
1979	Girl w/Scissors 01197-3	Open		25.00	32
1983	Girl w/Wagon 01196-6	Retrd.	1994	27.00	29
1991	Girl with Doll 01200-0	Open		31.50	37
1980	Little People Napkin Rings 6 asst. 03504-7	Open		21.00	28
1988	Lucia Parade Figures, set/3 07667-5	Retrd.	1995	75.00	80
1978	Madonna w/Child 01207-9	Open		120.00	153
1979	Magarita Angels, set/6 02938-1	Open		94.00	125
1983	Margarita Birthday Angels, set/3 00480-7	Retrd.	1995	44.00	53
1979	Pied Piper and Children, set/7 02843-8	Retrd.	1994	120.00	130
1981	Santa w/Angel in Sleigh 01192-8	Retrd.	1995	52.00	60
1976	Santa with Angel 00473-9	Open		50.00	55
1994	Santa with Tree 12942-5	Open		29.00	34
1994	Sun, Moon, Star Set 12943-2	Open		69.00	128
1992	Wendt and Kuhn Display Sign w/ Sitting Angel 07535-7	Retrd.	1996	20.00	23
1991	White Angel with Violin 01205-5	Retrd.	1993	25.50	27

Wendt and Kuhn Collection Music Boxes - Wendt/Kuhn

1978	Angel at Pipe Organ 01929-0	Open		176.00	230
1996	Angel Musicians 17036-6	Open		260.00	270
1992	Angel Under Stars Crank 12974-6	300		150.00	190
1991	Angels & Santa Around Tree 01211-6	Open		300.00	370
1996	Children Around Tree 17037-3	Open		330.00	350
1976	Girl Rocking Cradle 09215-6	Retrd.	1994	180.00	190
1978	Rotating Angels 'Round Cradle 01911-5	Open		270.00	336

Wendt and Kuhn Figurines Candleholders - Wendt/Kuhn

1976	Angel Pair 00472-1	Open		70.00	94

YEAR ISSUE		EDITION LIMIT	YEAR RETRD.	ISSUE PRICE	*QUOTE U.S.$
1991	Angel with Friend 01191-1	Retrd.	1994	33.30	34
1994	Angel with Wagon 12860-2	Open		35.00	44
1980	Large Angel Pair 01201-7	Retrd.	1994	270.00	277
1996	Orchestra Stand 17042-7	Open		130.00	145
1986	Pair of Angels 01204-8	Retrd.	1994	30.00	32
1991	Santa 06082-7	Retrd.	1994	53.00	54
1991	Small Angel Pair 01195-9	Retrd.	1994	60.00	63
1991	White Angel 01206-2	Retrd.	1994	28.00	29

Museum Collections, Inc.

American Family I - N. Rockwell

1979	Baby's First Step	22,500		90.00	175-200
1980	Birthday Party	22,500		110.00	150
1981	Bride and Groom	22,500		110.00	125
1980	First Haircut	22,500		90.00	150
1980	First Prom	22,500		90.00	135
1980	Happy Birthday, Dear Mother	22,500		90.00	135
1980	Little Mother	22,500		110.00	125
1981	Mother's Little Helpers	22,500		110.00	135
1980	The Student	22,500		110.00	175
1980	Sweet Sixteen	22,500		90.00	125
1980	Washing Our Dog	22,500		110.00	125
1980	Wrapping Christmas Presents	22,500		90.00	125

Christmas - N. Rockwell

1980	Checking His List	Yr.Iss.		65.00	110
1983	High Hopes	Yr.Iss.		95.00	175
1981	Ringing in Good Cheer	Yr.Iss.		95.00	100
1984	Space Age Santa	Yr.Iss.		65.00	100
1982	Waiting for Santa	Yr.Iss.		95.00	110

Classic - N. Rockwell

1984	All Wrapped Up	Closed		65.00	90-95
1980	Bedtime	Closed		65.00	90-95
1984	The Big Race	Closed		65.00	90-95
1983	Bored of Education	Closed		65.00	90-95
1983	Braving the Storm	Closed		65.00	90-95
1980	The Cobbler	Closed		65.00	125
1982	The Country Doctor	Closed		65.00	90-95
1981	A Dollhouse for Sis	Closed		65.00	90-95
1982	Dreams in the Antique Shop	Closed		65.00	90-95
1983	A Final Touch	Closed		65.00	90-95.
1980	For A Good Boy	Closed		65.00	125
1984	Goin' Fishin'	Closed		65.00	90-95
1983	High Stepping	Closed		65.00	90-95
1982	The Kite Maker	Closed		65.00	100
1980	Lighthouse Keeper's Daughter	Closed		65.00	125
1982	Memories	Closed		65.00	125
1981	The Music Lesson	Closed		65.00	125
1981	Music Master	Closed		65.00	90-95
1981	Off to School	Closed		65.00	90-95
1981	Puppy Love	Closed		65.00	90-95
1984	Saturday's Hero	Closed		65.00	90-95
1983	A Special Treat	Closed		65.00	90-95
1982	Spring Fever	Closed		65.00	90-95
1980	The Toymaker	Closed		65.00	125
1981	While The Audience Waits	Closed		65.00	85
1983	Winter Fun	Closed		65.00	90-95
1982	Words of Wisdom	Closed		65.00	90-95

Commemorative - N. Rockwell

1985	Another Masterpiece by Norman Rockwell	5,000		125.00	200-250
1981	Norman Rockwell Display	5,000		125.00	200-250
1983	Norman Rockwell, America's Artist	5,000		125.00	200-250
1984	Outward Bound	5,000		125.00	200-250
1986	The Painter and the Pups	5,000		125.00	250
1982	Spirit of America	5,000		125.00	200-250

Old World Christmas

Candleholders - E.M. Merck

1989	Angel 9015	Retrd.	1994	7.50	8
1989	Hummingbird 9013	Retrd.	1994	7.50	8
1989	Nutcracker 9016	Retrd.	1994	7.50	8
1989	Rocking Horse 9011	Retrd.	1994	7.50	8
1989	Santa 9012	Retrd.	1992	7.55	10
1989	Teddy Bear 9014	Retrd.	1994	7.50	8

Collectibles - O.W.C., unless otherwise noted

1992	Candle Arch with Church 862	Retrd.	1993	28.50	50
1991	Carved Deer at Feeder, set/3 86104	Retrd.	1996	35.00	35
1990	Carved Deer w/Tree 8653	Retrd.	1996	12.00	12
1991	Carved Goats, set/3 86123 - Helbig	Retrd.	1996	55.00	55
1992	Church w/Choir Candle 8699	Retrd.	1996	40.00	40
1986	Hansel & Gretel Bank 86898	Retrd.	1996	35.00	35
1992	Large Seiffener Candle Arch 8616	Retrd.	1994	450.00	495
1991	Nativity, 12 pc. 8657	Retrd.	1994	145.00	145
1990	Shaved Wood Tree 86020 - K.W.O	Retrd.	1996	12.00	12
1992	Weather House 86109	Retrd.	1994	31.50	37

Halloween - E.M. Merck

1988	Black Cat on Wire 9208	Retrd.	1992	8.35	13
1989	Black Cat/Witch with Cart (A) 9251	Retrd.	1994	10.00	12
1989	Cast Iron Scarecrow 9218	Retrd.	1994	32.50	39
1987	Ghost Light 9205	Open		37.00	75
1989	Ghost Votive 9211	Retrd.	1994	8.50	12
1988	Haunted House Waterglobe 9206	Retrd.	1989	22.50	32
1987	Haunted House with Lights 9203	Retrd.	1994	99.50	125-145

YEAR ISSUE	EDITION LIMIT	YEAR RETD.	ISSUE PRICE	*QUOTE U.S.$
1988 Large Pumpkin Bowl 9273	Retrd.	1994	18.50	20
1987 Lighted Ghost Dish 9204	Retrd.	1994	45.00	50
1988 Pumpkin Head on Wire 9207	Retrd.	1992	7.35	12
1987 Pumpkin Light with Ghosts 9201	Retrd.	1994	39.50	45
1987 Pumpkin Light with Scarecrow 9202	Retrd.	1991	37.00	45
1988 Pumpkin Taper Holder 9272	Retrd.	1992	5.65	9
1988 Pumpkin Votive 9271	Retrd.	1991	8.90	12
1989 Witch on Moon Night Light 9212	Retrd.	1992	37.50	45
1988 Witch Taper Holder 9282	Retrd.	1993	11.00	19
1988 Witch Votive Holder 9281	Retrd.	1994	29.50	350

Night Lights - E.M. Merck

1986 ABC Block 529713	Retrd.	1994	37.00	50
1986 Angel 529703	Retrd.	1992	18.00	97
1990 Father Christmas 529721	Retrd.	1992	45.00	110
1993 Father Christmas w/Toys 529727	Retrd.	1995	65.00	65
1985 Santa 529701	Retrd.	1987	37.00	525
1988 Santa Hugging Tree 529717	Retrd.	1990	42.00	275
1986 Santa in Chimney 529707	Retrd.	1988	37.00	325
1989 Santa on Locomotive 529719	Retrd.	1991	42.00	195
1992 Santa with Nutcracker 529725	Retrd.	1994	45.00	250
1991 Santa with Stocking 529723	Retrd.	1993	45.00	195
1987 Santa with Tree 529715	Retrd.	1989	39.50	255
1986 Snowman 529709	Retrd.	1988	37.00	125
1986 Teddy Bear 529711	Retrd.	1991	37.00	135

Nutcrackers - E.M. Merck, unless otherwise noted

1987 Austrian Musketeer 72048 - K.W.O.	Retrd.	1995	57.50	58
1993 Bohemian Beekeeper 7264	Retrd.	1995	110.00	110
1993 Brandenburger Guard 7250	Retrd.	1995	110.00	125
1987 British Guard 72041 - K.W.O.	Retrd.	1995	60.00	60
1992 Carved Hunter 72213 - O.W.C.	Retrd.	1992	150.00	195
1993 Exceptional Guard 7231 - K.W.O.	50	1995	995.00	995
1992 Exceptional King 7230	50	1994	950.00	1100
1994 Exceptional Santa 7232 - Merten	Retrd.	1995	995.00	995
1993 Falkensteiner Wizard 7261	Retrd.	1995	110.00	110
1991 Inlaid Natural King 7214 - O.W.C.	Retrd.	1992	150.00	195
1991 Inlaid Natural Muskateer 7225 - O.W.C.	Retrd.	1992	150.00	225
1992 Lg. Bavarian Duke 72242 - K.W.O.	Retrd.	1995	130.00	130
1992 Large British Guard 72141 - K.W.O.	Retrd.	1994	90.00	95
1992 Large Carved Santa 7223 - K.W.O.	Retrd.	1994	175.00	180
1992 Large Dutch Guard 72140 - K.W.O.	Retrd.	1994	90.00	96
1991 Large Hunter 7228 - K.W.O.	Retrd.	1994	97.50	105
1993 Large King 72033 - K.W.O.	Retrd.	1994	79.95	85
1992 Lg. Prussian King 72244 - K.W.O.	Retrd.	1994	130.00	135
1992 Large Prussian Sargeant 72145 - K.W.O.	Retrd.	1995	90.00	90
1992 Large Saxon Duke 72241 - K.W.O.	Retrd.	1995	130.00	130
1992 Large Snow Prince 7277	Retrd.	1992	100.00	115
1989 Prussian Corporal 72047 - K.W.O.	Retrd.	1990	42.50	43
1987 Prussian Sergeant 72045 - K.W.O.	Retrd.	1995	60.00	60
1993 Rostocker Pirate 7252	Retrd.	1995	110.00	110
1993 Saalfelder Shepherd 7263	Retrd.	1995	110.00	110
1993 Seiffener Santa 7257	Retrd.	1995	110.00	115
1992 Skier 7294	Retrd.	1992	82.50	83
1993 Teddy Bear 7296	Retrd.	1994	135.00	150
1993 Tegernsee Golfer 7259	Retrd.	1995	135.00	135

Paper Maché - E.M. Merck

1988 52 cm. Father Christmas 9652	Retrd.	1990	175.00	195
1988 Assorted Father Christmas 9615	Retrd.	1989	44.00	50
1989 Assorted Santas 9691	Retrd.	1991	35.00	43
1988 Blue Father Christmas 9602	Retrd.	1988	19.50	27
1988 Father Christmas (A) 9600	Retrd.	1988	19.50	27
1989 Father Christmas 9612	Retrd.	1988	38.50	45
1988 Father Christmas with Gifts 9610	Retrd.	1988	32.50	40
1989 Father Christmas with Pack 9638	Retrd.	1989	40.00	47
1988 Red Father Christmas 9601	Retrd.	1988	19.50	25
1989 Santa in Sleigh 9672	Retrd.	1989	39.50	45
1988 Small Traditional Belznickel 9662	Retrd.	1994	35.00	40
1988 Traditional Belznickel 9661	Retrd.	1994	40.00	50
1988 White Father Christmas 9603	Retrd.	1988	19.50	30
1988 White Father Christmas 9616	Retrd.	1989	50.00	55

Porcelain Christmas - E.M. Merck

1987 Angels, Set/3 9421	Retrd.	1988	15.50	21
1988 Bear on Skates Music Box 9492	Retrd.	1988	44.00	50
1988 Bunny on Skies Music Box 9491	Retrd.	1988	44.00	50
1987 Cast Iron Santa 9419	Retrd.	1993	35.00	47
1987 Cast Iron Santa on Horse 9418	Retrd.	1993	37.50	48
1987 Four Castles of Germany 9450	Retrd.	1988	31.00	52
1995 Mr. C's Roadster 9708			9.95	14
1988 Penguin with Gifts Music Box 9493	Retrd.	1988	44.00	65
1987 Roly-Poly Santa 9440	Retrd.	1987	27.00	35
1987 Santa Head Night Light 9412	Retrd.	1989	19.00	30
1987 Santa Head Stocking Holder 9414	Retrd.	1987	18.00	25
1987 Santa Head Votive 9411	Retrd.	1988	10.00	20
1987 Santa in Chimney Music Box 9413	Retrd.	1987	44.00	47
1988 Santa in Swing 9473	Retrd.	1988	6.25	12
1988 Santa on Polar Bear 9471	Retrd.	1988	6.25	12
1988 Santa on Teeter-Totter 9475	Retrd.	1988	6.25	12
1988 Santa Visiting Igloo 9476	Retrd.	1988	6.25	15
1988 Santa Visiting Lighthouse 9472	Retrd.	1988	6.25	12
1988 Santa with Angel 9474	Retrd.	1988	6.25	15
1995 Swinging into the Season 9705	Retrd.	1994	10.50	13

Pyramids - O.W.C., unless otherwise noted

1992 3-Tier Forest 882	Retrd.	1995	225.00	225
1992 3-Tier Nativity 883	Retrd.	1995	250.00	250
1991 3-Tier Painted Nativity 8818	Retrd.	1993	225.00	260
1992 5ft Hand-Carved 884007	Retrd.	1992	1295.00	1325
1992 6ft Hand-Carved 884006	Retrd.	1992	4000.00	4500-5000
1991 Camel Caravan 8812	Retrd.	1995	92.50	93
1986 Deer w/Tree, Wall Pyramid 88137	Retrd.	1993	65.00	65
1992 Detailed Nativity 8851	Retrd.	1993	175.00	195
1992 Mini-Pyramid, Angels 8811	Retrd.	1994	22.50	23
1992 Mini-Pyramid, Santa 8820	Retrd.	1994	32.50	40
1992 Miniature Choir 885	Retrd.	1995	35.00	35
1992 Miniature Forest 884	Retrd.	1994	35.00	40
1992 Miniature Music Band 886	Retrd.	1993	30.00	30
1991 Musical 4-Tier 8815	Retrd.	1991	775.00	825
1992 Natural with Deer 8821	Retrd.	1995	65.00	65
1992 Santa with Angels 887	Retrd.	1993	175.00	195
1991 Santa with Train 8817	Retrd.	1991	62.50	95
1992 Small Choir 8879	Retrd.	1993	68.50	75
1992 Small Nativity 8822	Retrd.	1993	110.00	110
1992 Small Nativity 889	Retrd.	1993	82.00	90
1991 White 3-Tier 8816	Retrd.	1992	225.00	250
1992 White with Angels 8824	Retrd.	1993	55.00	75

Smoking Men - O.W.C., unless otherwise noted

1992 Alpenhorn Player 7058	Retrd.	1995	70.00	70
1988 Antique Style Coachman 70053 - K.W.O.	Retrd.	1988	28.00	35
1988 Antique Style Cook 70052 - K.W.O.	Retrd.	1989	27.50	33
1986 Artist 7020 - E.M. Merck	Retrd.	1993	55.00	60
1991 Baker 7044	Retrd.	1992	49.50	55
1992 Basket Peddler 7040	Retrd.	1993	130.00	140
1991 Bavarian Hunter 7032	Retrd.	1994	79.50	85
1991 Beer Drinker 7033	Retrd.	1994	67.50	72
1991 Bird Seller 7014	Retrd.	1992	50.00	55
1991 Butcher 7043	Retrd.	1993	49.50	55
1986 Carved Hunter 70100	Retrd.	1991	90.00	97
1992 Carved Hunter 7054	Retrd.	1993	200.00	215
1992 Carved King 7072	Retrd.	1995	68.50	69
1992 Carved Shepherd 7053	Retrd.	1993	150.00	160
1992 Carved Woodsman 7015	Retrd.	1994	67.50	75
1991 Champion Archer 7041	Retrd.	1995	67.50	68
1989 Chimney Sweep 7017 - E.M. Merck	Retrd.	1993	55.00	55
1992 Clock Salesman 7039	Retrd.	1992	275.00	350
1990 Coachman 70062 - K.W.O.	Retrd.	1996	50.00	50
1991 Coachman 7057	Retrd.	1992	60.00	72
1991 Cook 7025	Retrd.	1993	55.00	60
1992 Farmer 7026	Retrd.	1993	55.00	60
1992 Farmer with Crate 7023	Retrd.	1994	150.00	155
1992 Father Christmas 70113-1	Retrd.	1989	45.00	60
1986 Father Christmas 702	Retrd.	1994	60.00	63
1991 Father Christmas 7051	Retrd.	1995	80.00	80
1993 Father Christmas 7063	Retrd.	1993	45.00	50
1986 Father Christmas with Toys 7010	Retrd.	1994	60.00	68
1991 Fisherman 7029	Retrd.	1993	55.00	58
1991 Frosty Snowman 703	Retrd.	1993	22.50	31
1991 Gardener 7045	Retrd.	1992	49.50	56
1991 Gardner 7016 - E.M. Merck	Retrd.	1993	55.00	59
1992 Grandma 702622	Retrd.	1993	42.50	48
1985 Grandpa 702615	Retrd.	1993	42.50	46
1986 Hunter 701	Retrd.	1993	30.00	36
1991 Hunter 7018 - E.M. Merck	Retrd.	1993	55.00	60
1992 Hunter with Crate 7021	Retrd.	1994	150.00	155
1991 Ice Skater 7038 - E.M. Merck	Retrd.	1992	60.00	63
1992 Innkeeper 70268	Retrd.	1993	54.00	60
1991 Innkeeper 7037	Retrd.	1995	60.00	60
1992 King 70229 - E.M. Merck	Retrd.	1993	95.00	104
1986 Large Old World Santa 70203	Retrd.	1988	77.50	83
1992 Minstrel 7061	Retrd.	1994	85.00	85
1991 Mountain Climber 7036	Retrd.	1995	67.50	68
1991 Natural Father Christmas 7012	Retrd.	1994	60.00	69
1991 Natural Santa 706	Retrd.	1994	40.00	48
1991 Nightwatchman 7027	Retrd.	1993	55.00	59
1985 Nightwatchman 7034	Retrd.	1993	32.50	41
1986 Old World Santa 70204	Retrd.	1988	42.50	47
1991 Postman 7028	Retrd.	1993	55.00	59
1991 Prussian Soldier 7056	Retrd.	1993	60.00	63
1989 Santa 7086	Retrd.	1993	55.00	61
1991 Santa Claus 705	Retrd.	1993	45.00	51
1992 Santa in Crate 707	Retrd.	1994	165.00	195
1986 Santa Smoker/Candleholder 704	Retrd.	1994	55.00	58
1992 Skier 702616	Retrd.	1992	54.00	62
1992 Skier 7059	Retrd.	1993	59.50	60
1986 Small Old World Santa 70202	Retrd.	1988	37.50	44
1992 Small Santa 7011	Retrd.	1995	37.50	38
1985 Snowman 702621	Retrd.	1993	30.00	38
1991 Snowman on Skis 7092	Retrd.	1993	30.00	39
1988 Snowman with Bird 708	Retrd.	1993	26.00	35
1992 St. Peter 70228	Retrd.	1993	95.00	105
1991 Toy Peddler 7030	Retrd.	1993	55.00	59
1991 Toy Peddler 7055	Retrd.	1992	60.00	66
1992 Toy Peddler 7060	Retrd.	1994	110.00	120
1992 Tyrolian 702613	Retrd.	1993	45.00	50
1992 Witch 70543 - E.M. Merck	Retrd.	1993	49.50	56
1991 Wood Worker 7031	Retrd.	1994	79.50	85
1987 Woodcarver 70043 - K.W.O.	Retrd.	1990	40.00	47
1991 Woodsman 7013	Retrd.	1993	60.00	64
1991 Woodsman 7019 - E.M. Merck	Retrd.	1993	55.00	60

Olszewski Studios

Olszewski Studios - R. Olszewski

1994 The Grand Entrance SM1	1,500	1994	225.00	325
1994 The Grand Entrance A/P SM1	120	1994	450.00	575
1994 Tinker's Treasure Chest SM2	Closed	1994	235.00	450-495
1994 Tinker's Treasure Chest A/P SM2	120	1994	470.00	470
1994 To Be (included w/Treasure Chest) SM3	Closed	1994	Set	Set
1994 To Be (included w/Treasure Chest) A/P SM3	120	1994	Set	Set
1994 The Little Tinker SM4	750	1995	235.00	295
1994 The Little Tinker A/P SM4	100	1995	470.00	470
1995 Special Treat SM5	800	1995	220.00	225
1995 Special Treat A/P SM5	100	1995	440.00	440
1995 Mocking Bird with Peach Blossoms SM6	800	1995	230.00	230
1995 Mocking Bird with Peach Blossoms A/P SM6	100	1995	460.00	460
1995 Lady With An Urn (brown, green, pink, blue dress) SM7	250	1995	235.00	235
1995 Lady With An Urn (brown, green, pink, blue dress) A/P SM7	124	1995	470.00	470
1995 Castle of Gleaming White Porcelain SM8	750	1995	285.00	285
1995 Castle of Gleaming White Porcelain A/P SM8	100	1995	570.00	570
1996 Spring Dance SM9	750	1996	210.00	210
1996 Spring Dance A/P SM9	100	1996	420.00	420
1996 Oriental Lovers SM11	750	1996	240.00	240
1996 Oriental Lovers A/P SM11	100	1996	480.00	480
1996 Dashing Through the Snow SM12	500	1996	480.00	480
1996 Dashing Through the Snow A/P SM12	100	1996	960.00	960
1996 The Viceroy SM13	750	1996	235.00	235
1996 The Viceroy A/P SM13	100	1996	470.00	470
1996 Little Red Riding Hood SM14	750	1996	225.00	225
1996 Little Red Riding Hood A/P SM14	100	1996	450.00	450
1996 The Departure (Sterling) SM1S	375	1996	325.00	325
1996 The Departure (Sterling) A/P SM1S	27	1996	650.00	650

Pacific Rim Import Corp.

Bristol Township - P. Sebern unless otherwise noted

1990 Bedford Manor	Open		30.00	30
1990 Black Swan Millinery	Open		30.00	30
1991 Bridgestone Church	Retrd.	1993	30.00	30
1990 Bristol Books	Open		35.00	35
1995 Bristol Channel Lighthouse	Open		30.00	30
1996 Bristol Somerset Cathedral - Pacific Rim Team	Open		N/A	N/A
1990 Bristol Township Sign	Open		10.00	10
1993 Chesterfield House	Open		30.00	30
1990 Coventry House	Retrd.	1995	30.00	30
1991 Elmstone House	Retrd.	1993	30.00	45
1991 Flower Shop	Open		30.00	30
1993 Foxdown Manor	Open		30.00	30
1990 Geo. Straith Grocer - R. S. Benson	Open		25.00	25
1991 Hardwicke House	Retrd.	1993	30.00	45
1990 High Gate Mill	Open		40.00	40
1990 Iron Horse Livery	Retrd.	1993	30.00	30
1991 Kilby Cottage	Retrd.	1993	30.00	45
1995 Kings Gate School - Pacific Rim Team	Open		30.00	30
1990 Maps & Charts	Open		25.00	25
1991 Pegglesworth Inn	Retrd.	1995	40.00	40
1990 Queen's Road Church	Open		40.00	40
1994 Shotwick Inn/Surgery	Open		35.00	35
1990 Silversmith	Open		30.00	30
1996 Somerset Cathedral - Pacific Rim Team	Open		50.00	50
1990 Southwick Church	Open		30.00	30
1994 Surrey Road Church	Open		40.00	40
1990 Trinity Church	Retrd.	1993	30.00	30
1990 Violin Shop	Open		30.00	30
1990 Wexford Manor	Open		25.00	25

Bristol Waterfront - P. Sebern unless otherwise noted

1992 Admiralty Shipping - P. Sebern	Open		30.00	30
1992 Avon Fish Co.	Open		30.00	30
1995 Bristol Channel Lighthouse - Pacific Rim Team	Open		30.00	30
1993 Bristol Point Lighthouse	Open		45.00	45
1994 Bristol Tattler	Open		40.00	40
1992 Chandler	Open		30.00	30
1992 Customs House	Open		40.00	40
1992 Hawke Exports	Open		40.00	40
1993 Lower Quay Chapel	Open		40.00	40
1994 Portshead Lighthouse	Open		30.00	30
1992 Quarter Deck Inn	Open		40.00	40
1992 Regent Warehouse	Open		40.00	40
1993 Rusty Knight Inn	Open		35.00	35

Bunny Toes - Pacific Rim Team, unless otherwise noted

1995 Annie With Strawberries - P. Sebern	Open		15.00	15
1996 Betsy-Celebrate	1,440		15.00	15
1995 Bunny Gazebo	Open		50.00	50
1995 Bunny Toes Sign - P. Sebern	Open		20.00	20
1995 Garden Trellis	Open		30.00	30
1995 Hannah Strolls With Carriage	Open		15.00	15
1995 Hannah With Maximillian	Open		13.00	13
1996 Justin-Stars & Stripes	1,440		15.00	15
1994 Mazie at Play	Open		13.00	13
1994 Phoebe Goes Ballooning	Open		7.00	7
1995 Rustic Garden Accessory Group (6 pcs) - P. Sebern	Open		40.00	40

YEAR ISSUE		EDITION LIMIT	YEAR RETD.	ISSUE PRICE	*QUOTE U.S.$
1994	Sophie Pops Out	Open		7.00	7
1995	Spring Garden Accessory Group (6 pcs) - P. Sebern	Open		40.00	40
1994	Sweethearts (lighted)	Open		50.00	50
1994	Tillie Making a Wreath	Open		13.00	13
1995	Tillie With Her Bike	Open		15.00	15
1995	Timothy With Eggs	Open		13.00	13
1994	Timothy With Flower Cart	Open		17.00	17
1994	Timothy With Tulips	Open		13.00	13
1995	Tommy's Joy Ride - P. Sebern	Open		15.00	15
1994	Wendell at the Mail Box	Open		17.00	17
1995	Wendell Play The Cello	Open		13.00	13
1994	Wendell With Eggs in Hat	Open		13.00	13
1995	Wendell With Flowers	Open		13.00	13
1994	Willis & Skeeter	Open		17.00	17
1995	Willis & Skeeter Gardening	Open		15.00	15
1995	Winifred Paints Eggs	Open		15.00	15
1994	Winifred With Blooms	Open		13.00	13

Bunny Toes Birthday Bunnies - P. Sebern

YEAR ISSUE		EDITION LIMIT	YEAR RETD.	ISSUE PRICE	*QUOTE U.S.$
1995	Anabell Gliding Along	Open		20.00	20
1995	Beth Back to School	Open		20.00	20
1995	Callie Bundle Up	Open		20.00	20
1995	Carly Striking a Pose	Open		20.00	20
1995	Charlotte Best of the Bunch	Open		20.00	20
1995	Chester Sharing With Friends	Open		20.00	20
1995	Christopher & Cory The Best Shot	Open		20.00	20
1995	Dinah Irresistible	Open		20.00	20
1995	Douglas Frosty Friends	Open		20.00	20
1995	Goldie Taking Turns	Open		20.00	20
1995	Harvey Giddy-Up and Go	Open		20.00	20
1995	Jeremy Clear Sailing	Open		20.00	20
1995	Joey Autumn Chores	Open		20.00	20
1995	Maggie Joy of Giving	Open		20.00	20
1995	Molly Sweet Wishes	Open		20.00	20
1995	Nicholas Between Tides	Open		20.00	20
1995	Penelope Wishful Thinking	Open		20.00	20
1995	Phoebe First Outing	Open		20.00	20
1995	Pieter Higher Education	Open		20.00	20
1995	Russel & Robby Sharing the Harvest	Open		20.00	20
1995	Violet Thank You Notes	Open		20.00	20
1995	Wilbur Lazy Daze	Open		20.00	20
1995	Wiley Winter Games	Open		20.00	20
1995	Zachary Waitin' on the Wind	Open		20.00	20

When Grandma Was a Girl - Pacific Rim Team

YEAR ISSUE		EDITION LIMIT	YEAR RETD.	ISSUE PRICE	*QUOTE U.S.$
1996	Amanda with 5 Kittens	Open		20.00	20
1996	Ballerina Rebecca	Open		17.00	17
1996	Billy & Josie Bathe Pigs	Open		25.00	25
1996	Eliza & Mama	Open		25.00	25
1996	Ella, Cats & Fishbowl	Open		25.00	25
1996	Jen, Bess & Ann Skip Rope	Open		35.00	35
1996	Jonathan at Bat	Open		15.00	15
1996	Joshua & Grandpa	Open		15.00	15
1996	Mary, Claire & Wagon	Open		35.00	35
1996	Naomi & Hannah	Open		25.00	25
1996	Rose, Luke & Luster	Open		30.00	30
1996	Ruth & Abigail (Musical)	Open		35.00	35
1996	Verna & Thomas at Play	Open		25.00	25

Pemberton & Oakes

Zolan's Children - D. Zolan

YEAR ISSUE		EDITION LIMIT	YEAR RETD.	ISSUE PRICE	*QUOTE U.S.$
1982	Erik and the Dandelion	17,000		48.00	90
1983	Sabina in the Grass	6,800		48.00	115
1985	Tender Moment	10,000		29.00	80
1984	Winter Angel	8,000		28.00	150

PenDelfin

PenDelfin Family Circle Collectors' Club - J. Heap

YEAR ISSUE		EDITION LIMIT	YEAR RETD.	ISSUE PRICE	*QUOTE U.S.$
1993	Herald	Closed	1993	Gift	50
1993	Bosun	Closed	1993	50.00	100
1994	Buttons	Closed	1994	Gift	30
1994	Puffer	Closed	1995	85.00	85
1995	Bellman	Closed	1995	Gift	N/A
1995	Georgie and the Dragon	Closed	1995	125.00	125
1996	Newsie	Yr.Iss.		Gift	N/A
1996	Delia	Yr.Iss.		125.00	125

40th Anniversary Piece - PenDelfin

YEAR ISSUE		EDITION LIMIT	YEAR RETD.	ISSUE PRICE	*QUOTE U.S.$
1994	Aunt Ruby	10,000		275.00	275

Event Piece - J. Heap

YEAR ISSUE		EDITION LIMIT	YEAR RETD.	ISSUE PRICE	*QUOTE U.S.$
1994	Walmsley	Retrd.	1995	75.00	75
1995	Runaway	Retrd.	1995	90.00	90
1996	Event Piece	Yr.Iss.		85.00	85

Nursery Rhymes - Various

YEAR ISSUE		EDITION LIMIT	YEAR RETD.	ISSUE PRICE	*QUOTE U.S.$
1956	Little Bo Peep - J. Heap	Retrd.	1959	2.00	N/A
1956	Little Jack Horner - J. Heap	Retrd.	1959	2.00	N/A
1956	Mary Mary Quite Contrary - J. Heap	Retrd.	1959	2.00	N/A
1956	Miss Muffet - J. Heap	Retrd.	1959	2.00	N/A
1956	Tom Tom the Piper's Son - J. Heap	Retrd.	1959	2.00	N/A
1956	Wee Willie Winkie - J. Heap	Retrd.	1959	2.00	N/A

Retired Figurines - Various

YEAR ISSUE		EDITION LIMIT	YEAR RETD.	ISSUE PRICE	*QUOTE U.S.$
1985	Apple Barrel - J. Heap	Retrd.	1992	N/A	15-25
1963	Aunt Agatha - J. Heap	Retrd.	1965	N/A	1500-2000

YEAR ISSUE		EDITION LIMIT	YEAR RETD.	ISSUE PRICE	*QUOTE U.S.$
1955	Balloon Woman - J. Heap	Retrd.	1956	1.00	N/A
1964	Bandstand - J. Heap	Retrd.	N/A	70.00	85
1967	The Bath Tub - J. Heap	Retrd.	1975	4.50	70-100
1955	Bell Man - J. Heap	Retrd.	1956	1.00	N/A
1984	Blossom - D. Roberts	Retrd.	1989	35.00	60-75
1955	Bobbin Woman - J. Heap	Retrd.	1956	N/A	N/A
1964	Bongo - D. Roberts	Retrd.	1987	31.00	75-150
1966	Cakestand - J. Heap	Retrd.	1972	2.00	250-500
1953	Cauldron Witch - J. Heap	Retrd.	1959	3.50	N/A
1959	Cha Cha - J. Heap	Retrd.	1961	N/A	1000-1200
1990	Charlotte - D. Roberts	Retrd.	1992	25.00	75-90
1989	Chirpy - D. Roberts	Retrd.	1992	31.50	60-100
1985	Christmas Set - D. Roberts	2,000	1989	N/A	450-550
1962	Cornish Prayer (Corny) - J. Heap	Retrd.	1965	N/A	500-900
1980	Crocker - D. Roberts	Retrd.	1989	20.00	60-75
1963	Cyril Squirrel - J. Heap	Retrd.	1965	N/A	750-1300
1955	Daisy Duck - J. Heap	Retrd.	1958	N/A	N/A
1956	Desmond Duck - J. Heap	Retrd.	1958	2.50	N/A
1964	Dodger - J. Heap	Retrd.	1996	24.00	28
1955	Elf - J. Heap	Retrd.	1956	1.00	N/A
1954	Fairy Jardiniere - N/A	Retrd.	1958	N/A	N/A
1953	The Fairy Shop - J. Heap	Retrd.	1958	N/A	N/A
1961	Father Mouse (grey) - J. Heap	Retrd.	1966	N/A	500-750
1955	Flying Witch - J. Heap	Retrd.	1956	1.00	N/A
1993	Forty Winks - D. Roberts	Retrd.	1996	57.00	57
1969	The Gallery Series: Wakey, Pieface, Poppet, Robert, Dodger - J. Heap	Retrd.	1971	N/A	200-400
1961	Grand Stand (mold 1) - J. Heap	Retrd.	1969	35.00	400-775
1992	Grand Stand (mold 2)- J. Heap	Retrd.	1996	150.00	150
1960	Gussie - J. Heap	Retrd.	1968	N/A	400
1989	Honey - D. Roberts	Retrd.	1993	40.00	60
1988	Humphrey Go-Kart - J. Heap	Retrd.	1994	70.00	100
1986	Jim-Lad - D. Roberts	Retrd.	1992	22.50	45-75
1985	Jingle - D. Roberts	Retrd.	1992	11.25	25-45
1986	Little Mo - D. Roberts	Retrd.	1994	35.00	43
1961	Lollipop (grey) (Mouse) - J. Heap	Retrd.	1966	N/A	500-700
1960	Lucy Pocket - J. Heap	Retrd.	1967	4.20	300-400
1956	Manx Kitten - J. Heap	Retrd.	1958	2.00	N/A
1961	Margot - J. Heap	Retrd.	1961	2.00	350-550
1967	Maud - J. Heap	Retrd.	1970	N/A	300-550
1961	Megan - J. Heap	Retrd.	1967	3.00	400-500
1956	Midge (Replaced by Picnic Midge) - J. Heap	Retrd.	1965	2.00	300-600
1966	Milk Jug Stand - J. Heap	Retrd.	1972	2.00	250-500
1960	Model Stand - J. Heap	Retrd.	1964	4.00	400-750
1961	Mother Mouse (grey) - J. Heap	Retrd.	1966	N/A	450-800
1965	Mouse House (bronze) - J. Heap	Retrd.	1969	N/A	300-400
1965	Mouse House (stoneware) - J. Heap	Retrd.	N/A	N/A	500-700
1965	Muncher - D. Roberts	Retrd.	1983	26.00	60-100
1981	Nipper - D. Roberts	Retrd.	1989	20.50	75
1955	Old Adam - J. Heap	Retrd.	1956	4.00	N/A
1955	Old Father (remodeled)- J. Heap	Retrd.	1970	50.	700-1000
1957	Old Mother - J. Heap	Retrd.	1978	6.25	550-800
1984	Oliver - D. Roberts	Retrd.	1996	25.00	30
1955	Original Father - J. Heap	Retrd.	1960	50.00	1000-1500
1956	Original Robert - J. Heap	Retrd.	1967	2.50	200-400
1953	Pendle Witch (stoneware) - J. Heap	Retrd.	1957	4.00	800-1200
1967	Phumf - J. Heap	Retrd.	1985	24.00	75
1955	Phynnoddderee (Commissioned -Exclusive) - J. Heap	Retrd.	N/A	1.00	N/A
1966	Picnic Basket - J. Heap	Retrd.	1968	2.00	350-600
1965	Picnic Stand - J. Heap	Retrd.	1985	62.50	150-175
1967	Picnic Table - J. Heap	Retrd.	1972	N/A	250-600
1966	Pieface - D. Roberts	Retrd.	1987	31.00	60-75
1965	Pixie Bods - J. Heap	Retrd.	1967	N/A	N/A
1953	Pixie House - J. Heap	Retrd.	1958	N/A	N/A
1962	Pooch - D. Roberts	Retrd.	1987	24.50	60-75
1958	Rabbit Book Ends - J. Heap	Retrd.	1965	10.00	1500-2000
1954	Rhinegold Lamp - J. Heap	Retrd.	1956	21.00	N/A
1967	Robert w/lollipop - D. Roberts	Retrd.	1979	12.00	100-250
1959	Rocky - J. Heap	Retrd.	N/A	32.00	37
1957	Romeo & Juliet - J. Heap	Retrd.	1959	11.00	N/A
1960	Shiner w/black eye - J. Heap	Retrd.	1967	2.50	300-500
1981	Shrimp Stand - D. Roberts	Retrd.	1994	70.00	80
1985	Solo - D. Roberts	Retrd.	1993	40.00	50-75
1960	Squeezy - J. Heap	Retrd.	1970	2.50	300-550
1957	Tammy - D. Roberts	Retrd.	1987	24.50	75
1987	Tennyson - D. Roberts	Retrd.	1994	35.00	42
1956	Timber Stand - J. Heap	Retrd.	1982	35.00	150-200
1953	Tipsy Witch - J. Heap	Retrd.	1959	3.50	N/A
1955	Toper - J. Heap	Retrd.	1956	1.00	N/A
1971	Totty - J. Heap	Retrd.	1981	21.00	150-250
1959	Uncle Soames - J. Heap	Retrd.	1985	105.00	300-400
1991	Wordsworth - D. Roberts	Retrd.	1993	60.00	75

Polland Studios

Collector Society - D. Polland

YEAR ISSUE		EDITION LIMIT	YEAR RETD.	ISSUE PRICE	*QUOTE U.S.$
1987	I Come In Peace	Closed	1987	35.00	400-600
1987	Silent Trail	Closed	1987	300.00	1300
1987	I Come In Peace, Silent Trail-Matched Numbered Set	Closed	1987	335.00	15-1895
1988	The Hunter	Closed	1988	35.00	545
1988	Disputed Trail	Closed	1988	300.00	700-1045
1988	The Hunter, Disputed Trail-Matched Numbered Set	Closed	1988	335.00	11-1450
1989	Crazy Horse	Closed	1989	35.00	300-470
1989	Apache Birdman	Closed	1989	300.00	700-970
1989	Crazy Horse, Apache Birdman-Matched Numbered Set	Closed	1989	335.00	13-1700

YEAR ISSUE		EDITION LIMIT	YEAR RETD.	ISSUE PRICE	*QUOTE U.S.$
1990	Chief Pontiac	Closed	1990	35.00	420
1990	Buffalo Pony	Closed	1990	300.00	600-800
1990	Chief Pontiac, Buffalo Pony-Matched Numbered Set	Closed	1990	335.00	900-1350
1991	War Drummer	Closed	1991	35.00	330
1991	The Signal	Closed	1991	350.00	730
1991	War Drummer, The Signal-Matched Numbered Set	Closed	1991	385.00	900-1150
1992	Cabinet Sign	Closed	1992	35.00	125
1992	Warrior's Farewell	Closed	1992	350.00	400
1992	Cabinet Sign, Warrior's Farewell-Matched Numbered Set	Closed	1992	385.00	465
1993	Mountain Man	Closed	1993	35.00	125
1993	Blue Bonnets & Yellow Ribbon	Closed	1993	350.00	350-400
1993	Mountain Man, Blue Bonnets & Yellow Ribbon-Matched Numbered Set	Closed	1993	385.00	385
1994	The Wedding Robe	Closed	1995	45.00	45
1994	The Courtship Race	Closed	1995	375.00	375
1994	The Wedding Robe, The Courtside Race-Matched Numbered Set	Closed	1995	385.00	420

See also Lance Corporation Chilmark Polland Collector Society

Possible Dreams

Santa Claus Network® Collectors Club - Staff

YEAR ISSUE		EDITION LIMIT	YEAR RETD.	ISSUE PRICE	*QUOTE U.S.$
1992	The Gift Giver-805001	Closed	1993	Gift	40
1993	Santa's Special Friend-805050	Closed	1993	59.00	59
1993	Special Delivery-805002	Closed	1994	Gift	N/A
1994	On a Winter's Eve-805051	Closed	1994	65.00	65
1994	Jolly St. Nick-805003	Closed	1994	Gift	N/A
1995	Marionette Santa-805052	Closed	1995	50.00	50
1996	Checking His List-805004	Yr.Iss.		32.00	32

The Citizens of Londonshire® - Unknown

YEAR ISSUE		EDITION LIMIT	YEAR RETD.	ISSUE PRICE	*QUOTE U.S.$
1990	Admiral Waldo-713407	Open		65.00	68
1992	Albert-713426	Closed	1994	65.00	68
1991	Bernie-713414	Open		68.00	71
1992	Beth-713417	Open		35.00	37
1992	Christopher-713418	Open		35.00	37
1992	Countess of Hamlett-713419	Open		65.00	68
1992	David-713423	Open		37.50	39
1992	Debbie-713422	Open		37.50	39
1990	Dianne-713413	Open		33.00	35
1990	Dr. Isaac-713409	Closed	1995	65.00	68
1989	Earl of Hamlett-713400	Closed	1994	65.00	68
1992	Jean Claude-713421	Open		35.00	37
1992	Lady Ashley-713405	Open		65.00	68
1989	Lord Nicholas-713402	Open		72.00	76
1989	Lord Winston of Riverside-713403	Closed	1994	65.00	68
1994	Maggie-713428	Open		57.00	57
1990	Margaret of Foxcroft-713408	Open		65.00	68
1992	Nicole-713420	Open		35.00	37
1990	Nigel As Santa-713427	Open		53.50	56
1990	Officer Kevin-713406	Closed	1994	65.00	68
1992	Phillip-713412	Open		33.00	35
1992	Rebecca-713424	Open		35.00	37
1992	Richard-713425	Open		35.00	37
1990	Rodney-713404	Open		65.00	68
1991	Sir Red-713415	Closed	1994	72.00	76
1989	Sir Robert-713401	Open		65.00	68
1992	Tiffany Sorbet-713416	Open		65.00	68
1990	Walter-713410	Closed	1994	33.00	35
1990	Wendy-713411	Closed	1994	33.00	35

Clothtique® American Artist Collection™ - Various

YEAR ISSUE		EDITION LIMIT	YEAR RETD.	ISSUE PRICE	*QUOTE U.S.$
1996	The 12 Days of Christmas -15052 - M. Monterio	Open		48.00	48
1991	Alpine Christmas-15003 - J. Brett	Closed	1994	129.00	135
1992	An Angel's Kiss-15008 - J. Griffith	Closed	1995	85.00	125
1993	A Beacon of Light-15022 - J. Vaillancourt	Closed	1996	60.00	63
1993	A Brighter Day-15024 - J. St. Denis	Open		67.50	70
1994	Captain Claus-15030 - M. Monterio	Open		77.00	77
1995	Christmas Caller-15035 - J. Vaillancourt	Open		57.50	58
1992	Christmas Company-15011 - T. Browning	Closed	1995	77.00	125
1996	Christmas Light-15055 - D. Wenzel	Open		53.50	54
1996	Christmas Stories-15054 - T. Browning	Open		63.50	64
1994	Christmas Surprise-15033 - M. Alvin	Open		88.00	88
1995	Country Sounds-15042 - M. Monterio	Open		74.00	74
1996	Dressed For the Holidays-15050 - J. Vaillancourt	Open		27.00	27
1993	Easy Putt-15018 - T. Browning	Closed	1996	110.00	115
1991	Father Christmas-15007 - J. Vaillancourt	Closed	1995	59.50	63
1993	Father Earth-15017 - M. Monterio	Open		77.00	80
1995	Fresh From The Oven-15051 - M. Alvin	Open		49.00	49
1991	A Friendly Visit-15005 - T. Browning	Closed	1994	99.50	105
1994	The Gentle Craftsman-15031 - J. Griffith	Open		81.00	81
1994	Gifts from the Garden-15032 - J. Griffith	Closed	1996	77.00	77
1995	Giving Thanks-15045 - M. Alvin	Open		45.50	46
1995	A Good Round-15041 - T. Browning	Open		73.00	73
1992	Heralding the Way-15014 - J. Griffith	Closed	1995	72.00	75

YEAR ISSUE	EDITION LIMIT	YEAR RETD.	ISSUE PRICE	*QUOTE U.S.$
1993 Ice Capers-15025 - T. Browning	Open		99.50	105
1993 Just Scooting Along-15023 - J. Vaillancourt	Open		79.50	83
1992 Lighting the Way-15012 - L. Bywaters	Closed	1996	85.00	89
1991 The Magic of Christmas-15001 - L. Bywaters	Closed	1994	132.00	139
1992 Music Makers-15010 - T. Browning	Closed	1995	135.00	155
1993 Nature's Love-15016 - M. Alvin	Closed	1996	75.00	79
1995 A New Suit For Santa-15053 - T. Browning	Open		90.00	90
1996 Not a Creature Was Stirring -15046 - J. Cleveland	Open		44.00	44
1992 Out of the Forest-15013 - J. Vaillancourt	Closed	1995	60.00	68
1995 Patchwork Santa-15039 - J. Cleveland	Open		67.50	68
1992 Peace on Earth-15009 - M. Alvin	Closed	1995	87.50	92
1991 A Peaceful Eve-15002 - L. Bywaters	Closed	1994	99.50	105
1995 Ready For Christmas-15049 - T. Browning	Open		95.00	95
1995 Refuge From The Storm 15047 - M. Monterio	Open		49.00	49
1995 Riding High-15040 - L. Nillson	Open		115.00	115
1994 Santa and Feathered Friend -15026 - D. Wenzel	Open		84.00	84
1995 Santa and the Ark-15038 - J. Griffith	Open		71.50	72
1992 Santa in Rocking Chair-713090 - M. Monteiro	Closed	1995	85.00	100
1991 Santa's Cuisine-15006 - T. Browning	Closed	1994	138.00	148
1995 Southwest Santa-15043 - V. Wiseman	Open		65.00	65
1994 Spirit of Christmas Past-15036 - J. Vaillancourt	Open		79.00	79
1994 Spirit of Santa-15028 - T. Browning	Open		68.00	68
1995 The Storyteller-15029 - T. Browning	Open		76.00	76
1993 Strumming the Lute-15015 - M. Alvin	Open		79.00	83
1995 Sunflower Santa-15044 - J. Griffith	Open		75.00	75
1994 Tea Time-15034 - M. Alvin	Open		90.00	90
1994 Teddy Love-15037 - J. Griffith	Open		89.00	89
1994 A Touch of Magic-15027 - T. Browning	Open		95.00	95
1991 Traditions-15004 - T. Blackshear	Closed	1994	50.00	75
1993 The Tree Planter-15020 - J. Griffith	Open		79.50	84
1995 Visions of Sugar Plums-15048 - J. Griffith	Open		50.00	50
1993 The Workshop-15019 - T. Browning	Closed	1995	140.00	150

Clothtique® Limited Edition Santas - Unknown

1988 Father Christmas-3001	10,000	1993	240.00	240
1988 Kris Kringle-3002	10,000	1992	240.00	240
1988 Patriotic Santa-3000	10,000	1994	240.00	240
1989 Traditional Santa 40's-3003	10,000	1994	240.00	252

Clothtique® Pepsi® Santa Collection - Various

1994 Holiday Host-3605 - Unknown	Open		62.00	62
1995 Jolly Traveler-3606 - B. Prata	Open		90.00	90
1990 Pepsi Cola Santa 1940's-3601 - Unknown	Open		68.00	74
1992 Pepsi Santa Sitting-3603 - Unknown	Closed	1994	84.00	95
1991 Rockwell Pepsi Santa 1952 -3602 - N. Rockwell	Closed	1994	75.00	82

Clothtique® Santas Collection - Staff, unless otherwise noted

1992 1940's Traditional Santa-713049	Closed	1994	44.00	65
1992 African American Santa-713056	Closed	1995	65.00	68
1993 African-American Santa w/ Doll -713102	Open		40.00	42
1996 Autograph For A Fan-713143	Open		39.00	39
1989 Baby's First Christmas-713042	Closed	1992	42.00	46
1995 Baby's First Noel-713120	Open		62.00	62
1988 Carpenter Santa-713033	Closed	1992	38.00	44
1994 Christmas Cheer-713109	Open		58.00	58
1994 A Christmas Guest-713112	Open		79.00	79
1994 Christmas is for Children-713115	Open		62.00	62
1986 Christmas Man-713027	Closed	1989	34.50	44
1987 Colonial Santa-713032	Closed	1990	38.00	40
1995 Down Hill Santa-713123	Open		66.50	67
1992 Engineer Santa-713057	Closed	1995	130.00	137
1993 European Santa-713095	Open		53.00	55
1989 Exhausted Santa-713043	Closed	1992	60.00	65
1991 Father Christmas-713087	Closed	1993	43.00	47
1995 Finishing Touch-713121	Open		54.70	55
1993 Fireman & Child-713106	Open		55.00	58
1992 Fireman Santa-713053	Closed	1995	60.00	68
1996 For Someone Special-713142	Open		39.00	39
1995 Frisky Friend-713130	Open		45.50	46
1988 Frontier Santa-713034	Closed	1991	40.00	42
1995 Ginger Bread Baker-713135	Open		35.00	35
1993 Good Tidings-713107	Open		51.00	51
1990 Harlem Santa-713046	Closed	1994	46.00	55
1995 Heaven Sent-713138	Open		50.00	50
1993 His Favorite Color-713098	Open		48.00	50
1995 Ho: Ho-Hole in One-713131	Open		43.00	43
1994 Holiday Friend-713110	Open		104.00	104
1995 Home Spun Holidays-713128	Open		49.50	50
1995 Hook Line and Santa-713129	Open		49.70	50
1995 Jumping Jack Santa-713139	Open		45.50	46
1991 Kris Kringle-713088	Closed	1993	43.00	46
1993 A Long Trip-713105	Open		95.00	100
1993 May Your Wishes Come True-713096	Open		59.00	62

YEAR ISSUE	EDITION LIMIT	YEAR RETD.	ISSUE PRICE	*QUOTE U.S.$
1993 The Modern Shopper-713103	Open		40.00	42
1994 A Most Welcome Visitor-713113	Open		63.00	63
1991 Mrs. Claus in Coat -713078	Closed	1995	47.00	71
1989 Mrs. Claus w/doll-713041	Closed	1992	42.00	43
1994 Mrs. Claus-713118	Open		58.00	58
1992 Nicholas-713052	Closed	1994	57.50	60
1994 Our Hero-713116	Open		62.00	62
1989 Pelze Nichol-713039	Closed	1993	40.00	47
1995 Pet Project-713134 - L. Craven	Open		37.00	37
1994 Playmates-713111	Closed	1996	104.00	104
1994 Puppy Love-713117	Open		62.00	62
1988 Russian St. Nicholas-713036	Open		40.00	43
1990 Santa "Please Stop Here"-713045	Closed	1992	63.00	72
1991 Santa Decorating Christmas Tree-713079	Closed	1992	60.00	60
1991 Santa in Bed-713076	Closed	1994	76.00	85
1992 Santa on Motorbike-713054	Closed	1994	115.00	130
1992 Santa on Reindeer-713058	Closed	1995	75.00	83
1992 Santa on Sled-713050	Closed	1994	75.00	79
1992 Santa on Sleigh-713091	Open		79.00	83
1991 Santa Shelf Sitter-713089	Closed	1995	55.50	60
1990 Santa w/Blue Robe-713048	Closed	1992	46.00	50
1989 Santa w/Embroidered Coat -713040	Closed	1991	43.00	43
1993 Santa w/Groceries-713099	Closed	1996	47.50	50
1986 Santa w/Pack-713026	Closed	1989	34.50	35
1996 Shamrock Santa-713140	Open		41.50	42
1991 Siberian Santa-713077	Closed	1993	49.00	52
1990 Skiing Santa -713047	Closed	1993	62.00	65
1995 Sounds of Christmas-713127	Open		57.50	58
1995 A Special Treat-713122	Open		50.50	51
1988 St. Nicholas-713035	Closed	1991	40.00	42
1995 The Stockings Were Hung -713126	Open		N/A	N/A
1995 Three Alarm Santa-713137	Open		42.50	43
1987 Traditional Deluxe Santa-713030	Closed	1994	38.00	38
1986 Traditional Santa-713028	Closed	1989	34.50	125
1989 Traditional-713038	Closed	1992	42.00	43
1991 The True Spirit of Christmas -713075	Closed	1994	97.00	97
1987 Ukko-713031	Closed	1994	38.00	38
1995 Victorian Evergreen-713125	Open		49.00	49
1995 Victorian Puppeteer-713124	Open		51.50	52
1993 Victorian Santa-713097	Closed	1996	55.50	58
1988 Weihnachtsman-713037	Closed	1991	40.00	43
1994 A Welcome Visit-713114	Open		62.00	62
1990 Workbench Santa-713044	Closed	1993	72.00	76
1994 Yuletide Journey-713108	Open		58.00	58

Clothtique® Saturday Evening Post J. C. Leyendecker - J. Leyendecker

1991 Hugging Santa-3599	Closed	1994	129.00	150
1996 Hugging Santa-3650 (smaller re-issue)	Open		52.50	53
1992 Santa on Ladder-3598	Closed	1994	135.00	150
1996 Santa on Ladder-3651 (smaller re-issue)	Open		59.00	59
1991 Traditional Santa-3600	Closed	1992	100.00	125
1996 Traditional Santa-3652 (smaller re-issue)	Open		66.00	66

Clothtique® Saturday Evening Post Norman Rockwell - N. Rockwell

1992 Balancing the Budget-3064	Open		120.00	126
1989 Christmas "Dear Santa"-3050	Closed	1992	160.00	180
1996 Christmas "Dear Santa" (smaller re-issue)-3050	Open		70.50	71
1989 Christmas "Santa with Globe"-3051	Closed	1992	154.00	175
1996 Santa With Globe-3101 (smaller re-issue)	Open		73.00	73
1991 Doctor and Doll-3055	Closed	1994	196.00	206
1991 The Gift-3057	Closed	1996	160.00	168
1990 Gone Fishing-3054	Closed	1995	250.00	263
1991 Gramps at the Reins-3058	Open		290.00	305
1990 Hobo-3052	Open		159.00	167
1990 Love Letters-3053	Open		172.00	180
1991 Man with Geese-3059	Open		120.00	126
1992 Marriage License-3062	Open		195.00	205
1996 Not a Creature was Stirring (smaller re-issue)	Open		44.00	44
1991 Santa Plotting His Course-3060	Open		160.00	168
1992 Santa's Helpers-3063	Closed	1994	170.00	179
1991 Springtime-3056	Closed	1996	130.00	137
1992 Triple Self Portrait-3061	Closed	1995	230.00	250

Clothtique® Signature Series® - Stanley/Chang

1995 Department Store Santa, USA/Circa 1940s-721001	Open		108.00	108
1995 Father Christmas, England/Circa 1890s-721002	Open		90.00	90
1996 St. Nicholas, Myra/Circa 1300s-721004	Open		99.00	99
1996 Kriss Kringle, USA/Circa 1840s-721005	Open		99.00	99

Crinkle Angels - Staff

1996 Crinkle Angel w/Candle-659405	Open		19.80	20
1996 Crinkle Angel w/Dove-659403	Open		19.80	20
1996 Crinkle Angel w/Harp-659402	Open		19.80	20
1996 Crinkle Angel w/Lamb-659401	Open		19.80	20
1996 Crinkle Angel w/Lantern-659400	Open		19.80	20
1996 Crinkle Angel w/Mandolin -659404	Open		19.80	20

Crinkle Claus - Staff

YEAR ISSUE	EDITION LIMIT	YEAR RETD.	ISSUE PRICE	*QUOTE U.S.$
1995 American Santa-657224	Open		15.50	16
1995 Arctic Santa-659107	Open		15.70	16
1995 Austrian Santa-659103	Open		15.80	16
1995 Bell Shape Santa-659008	Open		23.50	24
1996 Bishop of Maya Plaque-659306	Open		19.90	20
1996 Bishop of Maya-659111	Open		19.90	20
1996 Black Forest Gift Giver Plaque-659302	Open		19.90	20
1996 Black Forest Gift Giver-659114	Open		19.90	20
1996 Buckets of Fruit for Good Girls & Boys-659903	5,000		45.00	45
1995 Candle Stick Santa-659121	Open		15.80	16
1996 Carrying The Torch	Open		19.80	20
1996 Catch of The Day-659504	Open		19.90	20
1996 Celtic Santa Plaque-659305	Open		19.90	20
1996 Celtic Santa-659110	Open		19.90	20
1996 Choo-Choo For The Children-659904	5,000		25.00	25
1995 Christmas Tree Santa-659117	Open		19.90	20
1995 Crescent Moon Santa-659119	Open		19.00	19
1996 Crinkle Claus w/Dome-German Santa-659601	Open		45.00	45
1996 Crinkle Claus w/Dome-Santa/Chimney-659600	Open		45.00	45
1996 Crinkle Claus w/Dome-St. Nicholas-659602	Open		45.00	45
1996 A Crown of Antlers	Open		19.70	20
1996 Dashing Through The Snow-659902	5,000		45.00	45
1996 Display Figurine-965003	Open		11.00	11
1995 English Santa-659100	Open		15.80	16
1996 Feeding His Forest Friends-659905	5,000		27.50	28
1995 Forest Santa-657225	Open		15.50	16
1995 French Santa-659108	Open		15.70	16
1995 German Santa-659105	Open		15.80	16
1996 Hard Boiled Santa-659115	Open		13.70	14
1995 High Hat Santa-657134	Open		13.40	14
1995 Hour Glass Santa-659118	Open		15.00	15
1996 Iceland Visitor Plaque-659303	Open		19.90	20
1996 Iceland Visitor-659112	Open		19.90	20
1995 Italian Santa-659116	Open		15.70	16
1995 Jolly St. Nick-659012	Open		15.00	15
1996 Learned Gentleman	Open		19.80	20
1996 Lighting The Way	Open		19.80	20
1996 Low & Behold	Open		13.90	14
1996 Merry Old England Plaque -659301	Open		19.90	20
1996 Merry Old England-659113	Open		19.90	20
1996 The Music Man	Open		19.80	20
1995 Netherlands Santa-659102	Open		15.70	16
1996 Northland Santa Plaque-659304	Open		19.90	20
1996 Northland Santa-659109	Open		19.90	20
1995 Pine Cone Santa-657226	Open		15.50	16
1996 Rag/Doll Delivery-659906	5,000		34.50	35
1995 Roly Poly Santa 3.5"-657138	Open		12.50	13
1995 Roly Poly Santa 4"-659009	Open		23.00	23
1996 Running Down The List-659901	5,000		33.00	33
1995 Russian Santa 3.5"-659101	Open		15.70	16
1995 Russian Santa 4"-657228	Open		15.50	16
1995 Santa on Bag-657508	Retired	1996	15.00	15
1995 Santa on Roof-659006	Open		28.50	29
1995 Santa Sitting Pretty-659116	Open		13.90	14
1995 Santa w/Book-659010	Open		13.80	14
1995 Santa w/Candy Cane 4.5" -657139	Open		13.00	13
1996 Santa w/Candy Cane 5"-657142	Open		27.00	27
1996 Santa w/Candy Cane 6.5" -657135	Open		17.50	18
1995 Santa w/Cane & Bag-657230	Retired	1996	12.00	12
1995 Santa w/Gifts-657143	Retired	1996	27.00	27
1995 Santa w/Lantern & Bag-657229	Retired	1996	15.50	16
1995 Santa w/Lantern 5"-657136	Open		12.50	13
1995 Santa w/Lantern 5"-657144	Retrd.	1996	27.00	27
1995 Santa w/Noah's Ark-657227	Open		15.50	16
1995 Santa w/Patchwork Bag-657232	Open		19.00	19
1995 Santa w/Stars-657140	Open		14.00	14
1995 Santa w/Teddy Bear-657231	Open		16.00	16
1995 Santa w/Tree-659011	Open		14.20	15
1995 Santa w/Wreath-657141	Retired	1996	16.30	17
1995 Santa's Candy Surprise	Open		27.00	27
1995 Scandinavian Santa-659104	Open		15.80	16
1995 Slimline Santa-657137	Retired	1996	12.00	12
1995 Tall Santa	Open		17.50	18
1995 Tick Tock Santa-659120	Open		15.00	15
1995 Tip Top Santa-659007	Open		23.50	24
1996 To The Rescue	Open		19.90	20
1996 Well Rounded Santa	Open		13.70	14

Crinkle Cousins - Staff

1995 Crinkle Cousin w/Clock-659002	Open		15.50	16
1995 Crinkle Cousin w/Clown-659004	Open		15.50	16
1995 Crinkle Cousin w/Dolls-659003	Open		15.50	16
1995 Crinkle Cousin w/Lantern -659001	Open		15.50	16
1995 Crinkle Cousin w/Teddy-659005	Open		15.50	16

Crinkle Crackers - Staff

1995 Admiral Crinkle Cracker-659212	Open		18.50	19
1995 Captain Crinkle Cracker-659213	Open		13.00	13
1995 Corporal Crinkle Cracker-659214	Open		14.60	15
1995 French Crinkle Cracker-659203	Open		22.00	22
1995 French Lieutenant Crinkle Cracker-659205	Open		13.50	14

Year Issue		Edition Limit	Year Retd.	Issue Price	*Quote U.S.$
1995	General Crinkle Cracker-659213	Open		15.50	16
1995	Lieutenant Crinkle Cracker -659209	Open		26.50	27
1995	Major Crinkle Cracker-659215	Open		14.50	15
1995	Private Crinkle Cracker-659210	Open		15.00	15
1995	Roly Poly French Crinkle Cracker-659204	Open		13.90	14
1995	Roly Poly Russian Crinkle Cracker-659207	Open		13.50	14
1995	Roly Poly Sergeant Crinkle Cracker-659216	Open		13.50	14
1995	Roly Poly U.S. Crinkle Cracker-659201	Open		13.90	14
1995	Russian Crinkle Cracker 4" -659208	Open		13.50	14
1995	Russian Crinkle Cracker 7.75" -659206	Open		29.50	30
1995	U.S. Crinkle Cracker 3.75" -659202	Open		13.50	14
1995	U.S.Crinkle Cracker 7.5"-659200	Open		29.00	29

Crinkle Professionals - Staff

Year Issue		Edition Limit	Year Retd.	Issue Price	*Quote U.S.$
1996	Baseball Player-659507	Open		19.50	20
1996	Doctor-659500	Open		19.50	20
1996	Fireman-659503	Open		19.50	20
1996	Fisherman-659504	Open		19.50	20
1996	Football Player-659506	Open		19.50	20
1996	Golfer-659505	Open		19.50	20
1996	Hockey Player-659508	Open		19.50	20
1996	Policeman-659502	Open		19.50	20
1996	Postman-659501	Open		19.50	20
1996	Soccer Player-659509	Open		19.50	20

Crinkle Village - Staff

Year Issue		Edition Limit	Year Retd.	Issue Price	*Quote U.S.$
1996	Crinkle Castle (lighted)-659652	Open		70.00	70
1996	Crinkle Church (lighted) 659651	Open		70.00	70
1996	Crinkle Cottage (lighted) 659653	Open		70.00	70
1996	Crinkle Workshop (lighted) -659650	Open		70.00	70
1996	Santa Castle-659019	Open		15.00	15
1996	Santa Christmas House-659017	Open		15.00	15
1996	Santa Church-659020	Open		15.00	15
1996	Santa Farm House-659018	Open		15.00	15
1996	Santa Palace-659016	Open		15.00	15
1996	Santa Windmill-659021	Open		15.00	15

Floristine Angels® - B. Sargent

Year Issue		Edition Limit	Year Retd.	Issue Price	*Quote U.S.$
1996	Angel of Happiness-668002	Open		100.00	100
1996	An Angel's Prayer-668003	Open		98.00	98
1996	Celestial Garden-668001	Open		98.00	98
1996	Heavenly Harmony-668006	Open		100.00	100
1996	Lessons From Above-668005	Open		100.00	100
1996	My Guardian Angel-668004	Open		112.00	112

The Thickets at Sweetbriar® - B. Ross

Year Issue		Edition Limit	Year Retd.	Issue Price	*Quote U.S.$
1995	Angel Dear-350123	Open		32.00	32
1996	Autumn Peppergrass-350135	Open		31.00	31
1993	The Bride-Emily Feathers -350112	Open		30.00	30
1995	Buttercup-350121	Open		32.00	32
1995	Cecily Pickwick-350125	Open		32.00	32
1995	Clem Jingles-350130	Open		37.00	37
1993	Clovis Buttons-350101	Open		24.15	25
1996	Dainty Whiskers-350136	Open		30.00	30
1996	Goody Pringle-350134	Open		31.00	31
1993	The Groom-Oliver Doone -350111	Closed	1996	30.00	30
1993	Jewel Blossom-350106	Open		36.75	37
1995	Katy Hollyberry-350124	Open		35.00	35
1995	Kris Krinkle-350414	Open		12.50	13
1994	Lady Slipper-350116	Open		20.00	20
1993	Lily Blossom-350105	Closed	1996	36.75	37
1993	Maude Tweedy-350100	Closed	1994	26.25	27
1996	Merry Heart-350131	Open		30.00	30
1994	Morning Dew-350113	Open		30.00	30
1993	Morning Glory-350104	Open		30.45	31
1993	Mr. Claws-350109	Closed	1996	34.00	34
1993	Mrs. Claws-350110	Open		34.00	34
1993	Orchid Beasley-350103	Closed	1996	26.25	27
1995	Parsley Divine-350129	Open		37.00	37
1996	Patience Finney-350133	Open		31.00	31
1993	Peablossom Thorndike-350102	Closed	1994	26.25	27
1995	Penny Pringle-350128	Open		32.00	32
1995	Pittypat-350122	Open		32.00	32
1994	Precious Petals-350115	Open		34.00	34
1993	Raindrop-350108	Open		47.25	48
1995	Riley Pickens-350127	Open		32.00	32
1993	Rose Blossom-350107	Open		36.75	37
1994	Sunshine-350118	Open		33.00	33
1994	Sweetie Flowers-350114	Open		33.00	33
1995	Tillie Lilly-350120	Open		32.00	32
1995	Timmy Evergreen-350126	Open		29.00	29
1996	Velvet Winterberry-350132	Open		30.00	30
1995	Violet Wiggles-350119	Open		32.00	32

Precious Art/Panton

Krystonia Collector's Club - Panton

Year Issue		Edition Limit	Year Retd.	Issue Price	*Quote U.S.$
1989	Pultzr	Retrd.	1990	55.00	500-585
1989	Key	Retrd.	1990	Gift	100-130
1991	Dragons Play	Retrd.	1992	65.00	150-200
1991	Kephrens Chest	Retrd.	1992	Gift	
1992	Vaaston	Retrd.	1993	65.00	120-220
1992	Lantern	Retrd.	1993	Gift	45-75

Year Issue		Edition Limit	Year Retd.	Issue Price	*Quote U.S.$
1993	Sneaking A Peak	Retrd.	1994	Gift	85
1993	Spreading His Wings	Retrd.	1994	60.00	125-145
1994	All Tuckered Out	Retrd.	1995	65.00	65
1994	Filler-Up	Retrd.	1995	Gift	N/A
1995	Twingnuk	Retrd.	1996	55.00	55
1995	Kappah Krystal	Retrd.	1996	Gift	N/A
1996	Quinzet	Yr.Iss		38.00	38
1996	Holy Dragons	Yr.Iss		65.00	65
1996	Frobbit	Yr.Iss		Gift	N/A

Fair Maidens - Panton

Year Issue		Edition Limit	Year Retd.	Issue Price	*Quote U.S.$
1994	Faithful Companion	1,000	1994	325.00	380
1995	Safe Passage	1,000	1996	350.00	350

World of Krystonia - Panton

Year Issue		Edition Limit	Year Retd.	Issue Price	*Quote U.S.$
1992	Azael -3811	Retrd.	1995	85.00	85
1989	Babul -1402	Retrd.	1995	25.00	25
1994	Boll - 3912	Retrd.	1994	52.00	85-125
1989	Caught At Last! -1107	Retrd.	1992	150.00	225
1991	Charcoal Cookie -3451	Retrd.	1996	38.00	38
1991	Culpy -3441	Retrd.	1996	38.00	38
1992	Dubious Alliance -1109	Retrd.	1995	195.00	195
1995	Enough Is Enough -1114	1,500	1996	250.00	250
1991	Flayla w/Sumbly -1105	Retrd.	1995	104.00	104
1980	Gateway to Kystonia - 3301	Retrd.	1994	35.00	75-95
1989	Gorph In Bucket -2801	Retrd.	1996	20.00	20
1989	Gorphylia - 2802	Retrd.	1996	18.00	18
1987	Grackene -1051	Retrd.	1995	50.00	50
1989	Graffyn on Grunch (waterglobe) -9006	Retrd.	1992	42.00	180
1987	Groc -1041	Retrd.	1995	50.00	50
1987	Grumblypeg Grunch -1081	Retrd.	1992	52.00	110
1989	Kephren -2702	Retrd.	1994	56.00	65
1989	Krystonia Sign - 701	Retrd.	1993	N/A	75
1989	Large Bags -703	Retrd.	1996	12.00	12
1987	Large Graffyn on Grumblypeg Grunch -1011	Retrd.	1992	52.00	115
1991	Large Grunch's Toothache -1082	Retrd.	1994	76.00	80
1987	Large Haapf -1901	Retrd.	1991	38.00	100
1987	Large Krak N'Borg -3001	Retrd.	1990	240.00	250-500
1987	Large Moplos -1021	Retrd.	1991	90.00	150-225
1987	Large Myzer -1201	Retrd.	1991	50.00	90
1987	Large N' Chakk -2101	Retrd.	1995	140.00	140
1987	Large N'Borg -1092	Retrd.	1991	98.00	140
1988	Large N'Grall - 2201	Retrd.	1990	108.00	250
1987	Large Rueggan -1701	Retrd.	1989	55.00	100-200
1987	Large Stoope -1103	15,000	1996	98.00	98
1987	Large Turfen -1601	Retrd.	1991	50.00	85-100
1987	Large Wodema -1301	Retrd.	1990	50.00	115
1991	Maj-Dron Migration - 1108	Retrd.	1994	145.00	155
1988	Medium N'Grall -2202	Retrd.	1994	70.00	80
1987	Medium Rueggan -1702	Retrd.	1993	48.00	70
1987	Medium Stoope -1101	Retrd.	1996	52.00	100-200
1987	Medium Wodema -1302	Retrd.	1993	44.00	85
1992	Mini N' Grall - 611	Retrd.	1995	27.00	27
1992	N' Leila-3801	Retrd.	1994	60.00	65
1991	N'Borg-Mini -609	Retrd.	1994	29.00	29
1990	N'Chakk-Mini -607	Retrd.	1994	29.00	29
1989	N'Tormet -2601	15,000	1996	60.00	60
1990	Owhey (waterglobe) -9004	Retrd.	1995	42.00	100
1987	Owhey -1071	Retrd.	1990	32.00	110-150
1990	Shadra -3401	Retrd.	1994	30.00	65
1989	Small Bags -704	Retrd.	1996	4.00	4
1987	Small Graffyn/Grunch -1012	Retrd.	1992	45.00	120-150
1987	Small Groc -1042B	Retrd.	1987	24.00	4600
1987	Small Krak N' Borg -3003	Retrd.	1993	60.00	140
1987	Small N' Borg -1091	Retrd.	1992	50.00	200
1987	Small N' Tormet - 2602	Retrd.	1993	44.00	65
1988	Small Rueggau -1703	Retrd.	1992	42.00	42
1989	Small Scrolls -702	Retrd.	1996	4.00	4
1987	Small Shepf -1152	Retrd.	1990	40.00	120
1987	Small Stoope -1102	Retrd.	1996	46.00	46
1988	Small Tulan Captain -2502	Retrd.	1991	44.00	105
1987	Spyke -1061	Retrd.	1993	50.00	95
1989	Stoope (waterglobe) - 9003	Retrd.	1992	40.00	156
1988	Tarnhold-Med. - 3202	Retrd.	1992	120.00	175
1987	Tarnhold-Small - 3203	Retrd.	1995	60.00	60
1988	Tokkel -2401	Retrd.	1991	42.00	42
1989	Tulan - 2501	15,000	1996	60.00	60

Pulaski Furniture, Inc.

Curios Henry Limited Edition Figurine Series - L. Eisen

Year Issue		Edition Limit	Year Retd.	Issue Price	*Quote U.S.$
1996	Jack Russell Terrier	Yr.Iss.		19.95	20

R.R. Creations, Inc.

Collectors' Club - D. Ross

Year Issue		Edition Limit	Year Retd.	Issue Price	*Quote U.S.$
1994	Cape Cod 9400	Retrd.	1994	9.95	10
1995	Grist Mill 9500	Retrd.	1995	11.95	12
1996	Covered Bridge 9600	Retrd.	1996	13.95	14

Accessories - D. Ross

Year Issue		Edition Limit	Year Retd.	Issue Price	*Quote U.S.$
1989	4" Brick Fence 8913	Retrd.	1991	3.75	4
1987	4" Corral Fence 8726	Retrd.	1992	3.60	4
1989	4" Fence 8917	Open		3.25	5
1991	4" Fence w/ Tree 9124	Open		7.20	8
1989	8" Brick Fence 8912	Retrd.	1991	3.75	4
1990	Cactus 9014	Open		2.80	3
1993	Honey Pine Shelf 9333	Open		9.95	12
1990	Large Flag Pole 9017	Open		2.95	4
1989	Large Lamp Post 8911	Open		2.75	5
1990	Main Street Sign 9018	Open		2.75	4
1990	Natural Windmill 9019	Retrd.	1992	3.60	4
1991	Oak Tree 9123	Open		3.50	5
1992	Pine Tree 9250	Open		3.50	5
1989	Pine Tree w/Bow other side 8915	Retrd.	1991	3.75	4
1989	Shade Tree 8914	Retrd.	1991	3.75	4
1992	Sisters Sled 9252	Open		5.95	7
1992	Small Flag Pole 9251	Retrd.	1994	2.95	3
1992	Small Lamp Post 9254	Retrd.	1994	2.95	3
1990	Sunflower 9016	Open		2.80	4
1992	Trolley 9255	Retrd.	1994	5.95	6
1987	Welcome Mat 8717	Retrd.	1994	1.80	2
1993	Welcome R.R. Sign 9332	Retrd.	1994	4.50	5
1990	Wheat 9015	Open		2.80	4
1987	Windmill 8725	Open		3.60	4

Amish Accessories - D. Ross

Year Issue		Edition Limit	Year Retd.	Issue Price	*Quote U.S.$
1990	Amish Buggy 9013	Open		4.40	7
1991	Amish Family 9120	Open		4.40	7
1993	Amish Garden 9330	Open		5.95	7
1991	Amish Outhouse 9104	Open		4.25	5
1994	Buggies in a Row 9432	Open		6.50	7
1992	Clothesline 9253	Open		2.95	7
1994	Cows 9434	Open		6.50	7
1994	Milk Cans 9433	Open		6.50	7
1994	No Sunday Sales 9431	Open		3.60	4
1991	Slow Moving Vehicle 9121	Open		2.95	4

Amish Collection Series I - D. Ross

Year Issue		Edition Limit	Year Retd.	Issue Price	*Quote U.S.$
1991	Amish Barn 9102	Retrd.	1994	8.95	11
1991	Amish House 9101	Retrd.	1994	8.95	11
1991	Amish School 9103	Retrd.	1994	8.95	11
1992	Barn Raising 9220	Retrd.	1994	8.95	11
1992	Quilt Shop 9204	Retrd.	1994	8.95	11

Amish Collection Series II - D. Ross

Year Issue		Edition Limit	Year Retd.	Issue Price	*Quote U.S.$
1993	Blacksmith 9329	Retrd.	1995	8.95	11
1993	Harness & Buggy 9331	Retrd.	1995	8.95	11
1993	Troyer Bakery 9328	Retrd.	1995	8.95	11

Amish Collection Series III - D. Ross

Year Issue		Edition Limit	Year Retd.	Issue Price	*Quote U.S.$
1994	Barn 9429	2,500		11.00	11
1994	House 9428	2,500		11.00	11

Amish Collection Series IV - D. Ross

Year Issue		Edition Limit	Year Retd.	Issue Price	*Quote U.S.$
1996	Miller Barn Raising 9605	2,500		14.50	15
1996	Miller House 9604	2,500		13.50	14
1996	Miller School House 9603	2,500		13.50	14

Author Collection Series I - D. Ross

Year Issue		Edition Limit	Year Retd.	Issue Price	*Quote U.S.$
1994	Edgar Allan Poe 9403	2,500		11.00	11
1994	Harriet Beecher Stowe 9404	2,500		11.00	11
1994	Mark Twain 9401	2,500		11.00	11

Christmas Accessories - D. Ross

Year Issue		Edition Limit	Year Retd.	Issue Price	*Quote U.S.$
1996	Christmas Tree 9427	Open		6.50	7
1996	Frosty & Wife 9426	Open		6.50	7
1996	St. Nicholas 9425	Open		6.50	7

Christmas Memories Series I - D. Ross

Year Issue		Edition Limit	Year Retd.	Issue Price	*Quote U.S.$
1992	Christmas Chapel 9216	Retrd.	1994	8.95	11
1992	Christmas F Douglass 9218	Retrd.	1994	8.95	11
1992	Daniel Boone 9219	Retrd.	1994	8.95	11

Christmas Memories Series II - D. Ross

Year Issue		Edition Limit	Year Retd.	Issue Price	*Quote U.S.$
1993	Boscobel 9320	Retrd.	1995	8.95	11
1993	Christmas Church 9318	Retrd.	1995	8.95	11
1993	Dell House 9321	Retrd.	1995	8.95	11

Christmas Memories Series III - D. Ross

Year Issue		Edition Limit	Year Retd.	Issue Price	*Quote U.S.$
1995	Apothecary 9513	2,500		11.00	12
1995	Butcher 9515	2,500		11.00	12
1995	Cobbler 9514	2,500		11.00	12

Colonial Collection Series I - D. Ross

Year Issue		Edition Limit	Year Retd.	Issue Price	*Quote U.S.$
1989	Boot & Shoemaker 8910	Retrd.	1993	8.95	9
1989	Colonial Inn 8903	Retrd.	1993	8.95	9
1989	Easton House 8918	Retrd.	1993	8.95	9
1989	Silversmith 8909	Retrd.	1993	8.95	9
1989	Tavern 8908	Retrd.	1993	8.95	9

Colonial Collection Series II - D. Ross

Year Issue		Edition Limit	Year Retd.	Issue Price	*Quote U.S.$
1989	C.L. Edwards 8901	Retrd.	1994	8.95	11
1989	Dry Goods 8904	Retrd.	1994	8.95	11
1989	G. Dressmaker 8920	Retrd.	1994	8.95	11
1989	Kiistner 8902	Retrd.	1994	8.95	11
1989	Town Hall 8906	Retrd.	1994	8.95	11

Courthouse Collection - D. Ross

Year Issue		Edition Limit	Year Retd.	Issue Price	*Quote U.S.$
1989	Chase Country 8924	Retrd.	1993	8.95	9
1990	Franklin County 9011	Retrd.	1993	8.95	9
1990	Mount Holly 9010	Retrd.	1993	8.95	9

Grandpa's Farm Collection Series I (No Open Window/ Printed Both Sides) - D. Ross

Year Issue		Edition Limit	Year Retd.	Issue Price	*Quote U.S.$
1987	Barn 8721	Retrd.	1992	8.95	9
1987	Chicken Coop 8722	Retrd.	1992	6.50	7
1987	Farm House 8720	Retrd.	1992	8.95	9
1987	Outhouse 8724	Retrd.	1992	4.25	5
1987	Wash House 8723	Retrd.	1992	6.00	6

YEAR ISSUE	EDITION LIMIT	YEAR RETD.	ISSUE PRICE	*QUOTE U.S.$
Grandpa's Farm Collection Series II - D. Ross				
1993 Chicken Coop 9326	Retrd.	1995	6.50	11
1993 Hofacre House 9323	Retrd.	1995	8.95	11
1993 New Barn 9324	Retrd.	1995	8.95	11
1992 Outhouse 9327	Retrd.	1995	4.25	5
1993 Wash House 9325	Retrd.	1995	6.50	11
Historical Collection Series I - D. Ross				
1992 Canfield 9205	Retrd.	1994	8.95	11
1992 Hexagon 9208	Retrd.	1994	8.95	11
1992 Lincoln 9217	Retrd.	1994	8.95	11
1992 Smith-Bly 9201	Retrd.	1994	8.95	11
1992 Susan B. Anthony 9222	Retrd.	1994	8.95	11
Historical Collection Series II - D. Ross				
1993 Betsy Ross 9305	Retrd.	1995	8.95	11
1993 Kennedy Home 9308	Retrd.	1995	8.95	11
1993 Stone House 9319	Retrd.	1995	8.95	11
In The Country Series I - D. Ross				
1989 Church 8905	Retrd.	1993	8.95	9
1990 Grist Mill 9001	Retrd.	1993	8.95	9
1989 School 8907	Retrd.	1993	8.95	9
In The Country Series II - D. Ross				
1993 Country Church 9322	Retrd.	1995	8.95	11
1993 Country Livin' Shop 9307	Retrd.	1995	8.95	11
1993 Tollhouse 9301	Retrd.	1995	8.95	11
Inn Collection Series I - D. Ross				
1994 Black Horse Inn 9411	2,500		11.00	11
1994 Herlong Mansion 9412	2,500		11.00	11
1994 Nathaniel Porter Inn 9410	2,500		11.00	11
Landmark Collection Series I - D. Ross				
1994 Locust Grove 9405	2,500		11.00	11
1994 Longfellow 9408	2,500		11.00	11
1994 Melrose 9409	2,500		11.00	11
Lighthouse Collection Series I - D. Ross				
1994 Mystic Seaport 9406	2,500		11.00	11
1994 Old Point Betsie 9402	2,500		11.00	11
1994 Quoddy Head 9407	2,500		11.00	11
Lighthouse Collection Series II - D. Ross				
1996 Block Island S.E. 9506	2,500		13.50	14
1996 Boca Grande 9505	2,500		13.50	14
1996 Drum Point 9504	2,500		13.50	14
Main Street Collection Series I - D. Ross				
1989 Barron Theatre 8922	Retrd.	1993	8.95	9
1989 Gas Station 8923	Retrd.	1993	8.95	9
1989 Kingman Firehouse 8919	Retrd.	1993	8.95	9
1990 Library 9007	Retrd.	1993	8.95	9
1989 Myerstown Depot 8921	Retrd.	1993	8.95	9
1990 Santa Fe Depot 9006	Retrd.	1993	8.95	9
1991 Telephone Company 9107	Retrd.	1993	8.95	9
Main Street Collection Series II - D. Ross				
1992 Bakery 9212	Retrd.	1994	8.95	11
1992 Bank 9211	Retrd.	1994	8.95	11
1992 Beauty Shop 9209	Retrd.	1994	8.95	11
1991 Chautaqua Hills Jelly 9105	Retrd.	1994	8.95	11
1989 Harrold's Hardware 8925	Retrd.	1994	8.95	11
1992 Oakbrook Fire Co. 9207	Retrd.	1994	8.95	11
On the Square I (No Open Window/Printed Both Sides) - D. Ross				
1987 Antique Shop 8708	Retrd.	1992	8.95	9
1987 Bakery 8710	Retrd.	1992	8.95	9
1987 Book Store 8709	Retrd.	1992	8.95	9
1987 Candle Shop 8712	Retrd.	1992	8.95	9
1987 Craft Shop 8711	Retrd.	1992	8.95	9
1988 Flower Shop 8807	Retrd.	1992	8.95	9
1988 Ice Cream Parlor 8806	Retrd.	1992	8.95	9
On the Square II - D. Ross				
1993 Antique Shop 9314	Retrd.	1995	8.95	11
1993 Book Store 9309	Retrd.	1995	8.95	11
1993 Candle Shop 9312	Retrd.	1995	8.95	11
1993 Craft Shop 9313	Retrd.	1995	8.95	11
1993 Flower Shop 9311	Retrd.	1995	9.95	11
1993 Ice Cream Shop 9310	Retrd.	1995	9.95	11
Pre-Open Window Series - D. Ross				
1990 Adobe House 9005	Retrd.	1992	8.50	9
1991 Faulkner House 9108	Retrd.	1992	8.50	9
1990 Fox Theater 9009	Retrd.	1992	8.50	9
1988 Hardesty House 8808	Retrd.	1992	8.95	9
1991 John Hayes House 9109	Retrd.	1992	11.95	12
1991 Memphis Mansion 9110	Retrd.	1992	8.50	9
1990 Mission 9004	Retrd.	1992	8.50	9
1990 Stone Barn 9003	Retrd.	1992	8.50	9
1990 Stone House 9002	Retrd.	1991	8.50	9
1990 Strater Hotel 9008	Retrd.	1992	8.50	9
Victorian Collection Series I - D. Ross				
1992 Chapline 9206	Retrd.	1994	8.95	11
1992 Queen Anne 9203	Retrd.	1994	8.95	11
1991 Victorian Michigan 9106	Retrd.	1994	8.95	11

YEAR ISSUE	EDITION LIMIT	YEAR RETD.	ISSUE PRICE	*QUOTE U.S.$
Wild West Accessories - D. Ross				
1996 Gunfighter 9511	Open		6.50	7
Wild West Collection I - D. Ross				
1996 Great Western Hotel 9508	2,500		13.50	14
1996 J. Collar Dry Goods 9509	2,500		13.50	14
1996 J.P. Allen Drugstore 9507	2,500		13.50	14
1996 Outlaws 9510	2,500		12.00	12
Williamsburg Collection Series I - D. Ross				
1992 Davidson Shop 9213	Retrd.	1994	8.95	11
1992 Orrell House 9214	Retrd.	1994	8.95	11
1992 Tarpley's Shop 9215	Retrd.	1994	8.95	11
Williamsburg Collection Series II - D. Ross				
1993 Capitol 9303	Retrd.	1995	8.95	11
1993 Court House 9302	Retrd.	1995	8.95	11
1993 Governors Palace 9304	Retrd.	1995	8.95	11

Reco International

YEAR ISSUE	EDITION LIMIT	YEAR RETD.	ISSUE PRICE	*QUOTE U.S.$
Clown Figurines by John McClelland - J. McClelland				
1988 Mr. Cool	9,500		35.00	35
1987 Mr. Cure-All	9,500		35.00	35
1988 Mr. Heart-Throb	9,500		35.00	35
1987 Mr. Lovable	9,500		35.00	35
1988 Mr. Magic	9,500		35.00	35
1987 Mr. One-Note	9,500		35.00	35
1987 Mr. Tip	9,500		35.00	35
Faces of Love - J. McClelland				
1988 Cuddles	Open		29.50	33
1988 Sunshine	Open		29.50	33
Granget Crystal Sculpture - G. Granget				
1973 Long Earred Owl, Asio Otus	Retrd.	1974	2250.00	2250
XX Ruffed Grouse	Retrd.	1976	1000.00	1000
Laughables - J. Bergsma				
1995 Annie, Geoge & Harry	Open		17.50	18
1996 Ashley	Open		13.50	14
1995 Cody & Spot	Open		15.00	15
1995 Daffodil & Prince	Open		13.50	14
1995 Daisy & Jeremiah	Open		15.00	15
1996 Felix & Freddie	Open		15.00	15
1995 Joey & Jumper	Open		15.00	15
1996 Jordan & Jessie	Open		15.00	15
1996 Leo & Lindsey	Open		17.50	18
1996 Mattie & Quackers	Open		15.00	15
1995 Merlin & Gemini	Open		15.00	15
1995 Millie & Mittens	Open		15.00	15
1996 Nicholas & Chelsea	Yr.iss.		15.00	15
1995 Patches and Pokey	Open		15.00	15
1995 Patty & Petunia	Open		16.50	17
1996 Peter & Polly	Open		17.50	18
1996 Sammy & Mikey	Open		15.00	15
1995 Sunny	Open		13.50	14
1995 Whiskers & Willie	Open		13.50	14
Porcelains in Miniature by John McClelland - J. McClelland				
XX Alice	10,000		34.50	35
XX Autumn Dreams	Open		29.50	30
XX The Baker	Open		29.50	30
XX Batter Up	Retrd.	1993	29.50	30
XX Center Ice	Open		29.50	30
XX Cheerleader	Open		29.50	30
XX Chimney Sweep	10,000		34.50	35
XX The Clown	Open		29.50	30
XX Club Pro	Open		29.50	30
XX Country Lass	Open		29.50	30
XX Cowboy	Open		29.50	30
XX Cowgirl	Open		29.50	30
XX Doc	Open		29.50	30
XX Dressing Up	10,000		34.50	35
XX The Farmer	Open		29.50	30
XX Farmer's Wife	Open		29.50	30
XX The Fireman	Open		29.50	30
XX First Outing	Open		29.50	30
XX First Solo	Open		29.50	30
XX Highland Fling	7,500		34.50	35
XX John	10,000		34.50	35
XX Lawyer	Open		29.50	30
XX Love 40	Open		29.50	30
XX The Nurse	Open		29.50	30
XX The Painter	Open		29.50	30
XX The Policeman	Open		29.50	30
XX Quiet Moments	Open		29.50	30
XX Smooth Smailing	Open		29.50	30
XX Special Delivery	Open		29.50	30
XX Sudsie Suzie	Open		29.50	30
XX Tuck-Me-In	Open		29.50	30
XX Winter Fun	Open		29.50	30
The Reco Angel Collection - J. McClelland				
1986 Adoration	Open		24.00	24
1986 Devotion	Open		15.00	15
1986 Faith	Retrd.	1995	24.00	24
1986 Gloria	Open		12.00	12
1986 Harmony	Retrd.	1994	12.00	12

YEAR ISSUE	EDITION LIMIT	YEAR RETD.	ISSUE PRICE	* QUOTE U.S.$
1986 Hope	Open		24.00	24
1986 Innocence	Open		12.00	12
1986 Joy	Retrd.	1994	15.00	15
1986 Love	Open		12.00	12
1988 Minstral	Retrd.	1995	12.00	12
1986 Peace	Open		24.00	24
1986 Praise	Open		20.00	20
1988 Reverence	Retrd.	1995	12.00	12
1986 Serenity	Open		24.00	24
The Reco Clown Collection - J. McClelland				
1985 Arabesque	Open		12.00	13
1985 Bow Jangles	Open		12.00	13
1985 Curly	Open		12.00	13
1987 Disco Dan	Open		12.00	13
1987 Domino	Open		12.00	13
1987 Happy George	Open		12.00	13
1985 Hobo	Open		12.00	13
1987 The Joker	Open		12.00	13
1987 Jolly Joe	Open		12.00	13
1987 Love	Open		12.00	13
1987 Mr. Big	Open		12.00	13
1985 The Professor	Open		12.00	13
1985 Ruffles	Open		12.00	13
1985 Sad Eyes	Open		12.00	13
1985 Scamp	Open		12.00	13
1987 Smiley	Open		12.00	13
1985 Sparkles	Open		12.00	13
1985 Top Hat	Open		12.00	13
1987 Tramp	Open		12.00	13
1987 Twinkle	Open		12.00	13
1985 Whoopie	Open		12.00	13
1985 Winkie	Retrd.	1994	12.00	13
1987 Wistful	Open		12.00	13
1987 Zany Jack	Open		12.00	13
Reco Creche Collection - J. McClelland				
1988 Cow	Open		15.00	15
1988 Donkey	Open		16.50	17
1987 Holy Family (3 Pieces)	Open		49.00	49
1988 King/Frankincense	Open		22.50	23
1988 King/Gold	Open		22.50	23
1988 King/Myrrh	Open		22.50	23
1987 Lamb	Open		9.50	10
1987 Shepherd-Kneeling	Open		22.50	23
1987 Shepherd-Standing	Open		22.50	23

Rhodes Studio

YEAR ISSUE	EDITION LIMIT	YEAR RETD.	ISSUE PRICE	QUOTE U.S.$
Rockwell's Age of Wonder - Rockwell-Inspired				
1992 The Birthday Party	Closed	N/A	39.95	40
1991 Hush-A-Bye	Closed	N/A	34.95	35
1991 School Days	Closed	N/A	36.95	37
1991 Splish Splash	Closed	N/A	34.95	35
1991 Stand by Me	Closed	N/A	36.95	37
1991 Summertime	Closed	N/A	39.95	40
Rockwell's Beautiful Dreamers - Rockwell-Inspired				
1991 Dear Diary	Closed	N/A	37.95	38
1992 Debutante's Dance	Closed	N/A	42.95	43
1991 Secret Sonnets	Closed	N/A	39.95	40
1991 Sitting Pretty	Closed	N/A	37.95	38
1991 Springtime Serenade	Closed	N/A	39.95	40
1992 Walk in the Park	Closed	N/A	42.95	43
Rockwell's Gems of Wisdom - Rockwell-Inspired				
1991 Love Cures All	Closed	N/A	39.95	40
1991 Practice Makes Perfect	Closed	N/A	39.95	40
1991 A Stitch In Time	Closed	N/A	42.95	43
Rockwell's Heirloom Santa Collection - Rockwell -Inspired				
1991 Christmas Dream	150-day		49.95	50
1992 Making His List	Closed	N/A	49.95	50
1990 Santa's Workshop	150-day		49.95	50
Rockwell's Hometown - Various				
1991 Bell Tower - Rockwell-Inspired	Closed	N/A	36.95	37
1992 The Berkshire Playhouse - Rockwell-Inspired	Closed	N/A	42.95	43
1991 Church On The Green - Rockwell-Inspired	Closed	N/A	39.95	40
1992 Citizen's Hall - Rockwell-Inspired	Closed	N/A	42.95	43
1991 Firehouse - Rockwell-Inspired	Closed	N/A	36.95	37
1991 Greystone Church - Rhodes	Closed	N/A	34.95	35
1992 Mission House - Rockwell -Inspired	Closed	N/A	42.95	43
1992 Old Corner House - Rockwell -Inspired	Closed	1994	42.95	43
1991 Rockwell's Residence - Rhodes	Closed	N/A	34.95	35
1992 Town Hall - Rockwell-Inspired	Closed	N/A	39.95	40
Rockwell's Main Street - Rockwell-Inspired				
1990 The Antique Shop	150-day		28.00	150
1991 The Bank	150-day		36.00	36
1990 The Country Store	150-day		32.00	36
1991 The Library	150-day		36.00	36
1991 Red Lion Inn	150-day		39.00	39
1990 Rockwell's Studio	150-day		28.00	85
1990 The Town Offices	150-day		32.00	36

Rick Cain Studios

Collectors Guild - R. Cain

YEAR ISSUE		EDITION LIMIT	YEAR RETRD.	ISSUE PRICE	*QUOTE U.S.$
1992	High Point	S/O	1992	82.00	95-125
1992	Visor	Retrd.	1992	Gift	100
1993	Strider	S/O	1993	82.00	105
1993	Star Shadow	Retrd.	1993	Gift	75
1994	Midnight Son	1,225	1994	297.00	500
1994	Arctic Moon II	Retrd.	1994	Gift	75
1995	Family Tree	Retrd.	1995	260.00	260-350
1995	Bonsai	Retrd.	1995	Gift	45-75

Master Series - R. Cain

YEAR ISSUE		EDITION LIMIT	YEAR RETRD.	ISSUE PRICE	*QUOTE U.S.$
1986	Aerial Hunter 1114	5,000	1990	70.40	100
1991	Aerial Victor 1707	2,000	1995	115.00	150-175
1993	Arctic Moon 1917	2,000	1993	231.00	625-900
1993	Arctic Son 1927	2,000	1993	275.00	550-800
1988	The Balance 1302	5,000	1992	374.00	515-550
1992	Bathing Hole 1901	2,000	1994	102.00	153-165
1988	Blackberry Summer 1201	300	1994	165.00	190
1985	Catchmaster 1104	5,000	1990	184.80	325-500
1990	Dark Feather 1501	2,000	1994	86.00	155
1989	Domain 1205	5,000	1992	187.00	255-300
1986	Dragon Sprout 1112	5,000	1990	92.50	300
1987	Dragonflies Dance 1123	5,000	1992	55.00	85
1986	Elder 1113	2,500	1993	550.00	750-900
1988	Fair Atlantis 1130	5,000	1993	319.00	375
1990	Falcon Lore 1406	5,000	1992	86.00	155-200
1985	Featherview 1103	5,000	1993	151.80	330
1988	Guardian 1301	5,000	1995	325.00	370
1989	Hatchling 1205	1,250	1994	85.00	100
1991	Highland Voyager 1805	2,000	1995	120.00	150
1987	Innerview 1203	1,500	1994	84.00	95
1988	Lady Reflecting 1129	5,000	1995	93.00	105
1992	Leading Wolf 1904	2,000	1992	143.00	450
1987	Liquid Universe 1117	5,000	1995	540.00	615
1990	Majestic Cradle 1505	900	1995	440.00	500
1994	Moon Walk 1930	2,000	1994	198.00	300
1985	Nightmaster 1105	5,000	1990	184.80	350
1988	Old Man of the Forest 1126	5,000	1992	132.00	200
1988	Orbit 1127	5,000	1992	108.00	150-250
1992	The Pack 1902	2,000	1992	105.50	400
1988	Paradise Found 1124	575	1994	308.00	425
1990	Pathfinder 1403	2,000	1991	101.00	155-200
1992	Power of One 1909	2,000	1995	77.00	95
1992	Prairie Thunder 1903	2,000	1994	110.00	165
1986	Sandmaster 1115	5,000	1993	93.00	105
1990	Scarlett Wing 1404	365	1994	101.00	185
1985	Sea View 1107	5,000	1993	70.40	115
1990	Searchers 1502	2,000	1994	174.00	350
1987	Sentinel Crest 1119	5,000	1994	121.00	140-170
1992	Seven Bears 1908	2,000	1993	231.00	385
1991	Spirit Dog 1702	2,000	1992	198.00	450-625
1992	Spirit Eagle 1908	2,000	1993	121.00	185
1993	Spirit Totem 1922	2,000	1993	286.00	435-475
1993	Steppin' Wolf 1925	2,000	1993	210.00	315
1987	Teller 1120	5,000	1992	308.00	425
1985	Tidemaster 1108	2,500	1994	242.00	275
1986	Tropical Flame 1111	5,000	1992	209.00	290-350
1989	Universes 1204	5,000	1995	115.00	130
1994	Waiting Wolf 1929	2,000	1994	198.00	210-300
1986	Wind Horse 1108	5,000	1992	70.00	100-150
1987	Winged Fortress 1118	5,000	1994	363.00	400
1993	Wolf Trail 1919	2,000	1993	121.00	210
1990	Wood Flight 1401	2,000	1992	105.50	150
1993	Wood Song 1912	2,000	1993	143.00	220-350
1987	Yore Castle 1121	5,000	1992	165.00	225-250

Vision Quest - R. Cain

YEAR ISSUE		EDITION LIMIT	YEAR RETRD.	ISSUE PRICE	*QUOTE U.S.$
1992	Alphascape 1900	2,000	1993	210.00	400

River Shore

Rockwell Single Issues - N. Rockwell

YEAR ISSUE		EDITION LIMIT	YEAR RETRD.	ISSUE PRICE	*QUOTE U.S.$
1982	Grandpa's Guardian	9,500	N/A	125.00	195
1981	Looking Out To Sea	9,500	N/A	85.00	200

Roman, Inc.

American Santas Through the Decades - Galleria Lucchese Studios

YEAR ISSUE		EDITION LIMIT	YEAR RETRD.	ISSUE PRICE	*QUOTE U.S.$
1994	1800 Cloth-like Santa 7"	Closed	1995	49.50	50
1994	1800 Pencil Santa 8"	Closed	1995	29.50	30
1994	1810 Cloth-like Santa 7"	Closed	1995	49.50	50
1994	1810 Pencil Santa 8"	Closed	1995	29.50	30

Catnippers - I. Spencer

YEAR ISSUE		EDITION LIMIT	YEAR RETRD.	ISSUE PRICE	*QUOTE U.S.$
1985	A Baffling Yarn	15,000		45.00	45
1985	Can't We Be Friends	15,000		45.00	45
1985	A Christmas Mourning	15,000		45.00	50
1985	Flora and Felina	15,000		45.00	50
1985	Flying Tiger-Retired	15,000		45.00	45
1985	The Paw that Refreshes	15,000		45.00	45
1985	Sandy Claws	15,000		45.00	45
1985	A Tail of Two Kitties	15,000		45.00	45

Ceramica Excelsis - Unknown

YEAR ISSUE		EDITION LIMIT	YEAR RETRD.	ISSUE PRICE	*QUOTE U.S.$
1978	Assumption Madonna	5,000		56.00	56
1978	Christ Entering Jerusalem	5,000		96.00	96

YEAR ISSUE		EDITION LIMIT	YEAR RETRD.	ISSUE PRICE	*QUOTE U.S.$
1978	Christ in the Garden of Gethsemane	5,000		40.00	60
1977	Christ Knocking at the Door	5,000		60.00	60
1980	Daniel in the Lion's Den	5,000		80.00	80
1980	David	5,000		77.00	77
1978	Flight into Egypt	5,000		59.00	90
1983	Good Shepherd	5,000		49.00	49
1978	Guardian Angel with Boy	5,000		69.00	69
1978	Guardian Angel with Girl	5,000		69.00	69
1983	Holy Family	5,000		72.00	72
1978	Holy Family at Work	5,000		96.00	96
1978	Infant of Prague	5,000		37.50	60
1981	Innocence	5,000		95.00	95
1979	Jesus Speaks in Parables	5,000		90.00	90
1983	Jesus with Children	5,000		74.00	74
1981	Journey to Bethlehem	5,000		89.00	89
1983	Kneeling Santa	5,000		95.00	95
1977	Madonna and Child with Angels	5,000		60.00	60
1977	Madonna with Child	5,000		65.00	65
1979	Moses	5,000		77.00	77
1979	Noah	5,000		77.00	77
1981	Sermon on the Mount	5,000		56.00	56
1983	St. Anne	5,000		49.00	49
1983	St. Francis	5,000		59.50	60
1977	St. Francis	5,000		60.00	60
1981	Way of the Cross	5,000		59.00	59
1980	Way to Emmaus	5,000		155.00	155
1977	What Happened to Your Hand?	5,000		60.00	60

A Child's World 1st Edition - F. Hook

YEAR ISSUE		EDITION LIMIT	YEAR RETRD.	ISSUE PRICE	*QUOTE U.S.$
1980	Beach Buddies, signed	15,000		29.00	600
1980	Beach Buddies, unsigned	15,000		29.00	450
1980	Helping Hands	Closed	N/A	45.00	85
1980	Kiss Me Good Night	15,000		29.00	40
1980	My Big Brother	Closed	N/A	39.00	200
1980	Nighttime Thoughts	Closed	N/A	25.00	65
1980	Sounds of the Sea	15,000	N/A	45.00	150

A Child's World 2nd Edition - F. Hook

YEAR ISSUE		EDITION LIMIT	YEAR RETRD.	ISSUE PRICE	*QUOTE U.S.$
1981	All Dressed Up	15,000		36.00	70
1981	Cat Nap	15,000	N/A	42.00	125
1981	I'll Be Good	15,000	N/A	36.00	80
1981	Making Friends	15,000		42.00	46
1981	The Sea and Me	15,000	N/A	39.00	80
1981	Sunday School	15,000		39.00	70

A Child's World 3rd Edition - F. Hook

YEAR ISSUE		EDITION LIMIT	YEAR RETRD.	ISSUE PRICE	*QUOTE U.S.$
1981	Bear Hug	15,000		42.00	45
1981	Pathway to Dreams	15,000		47.00	50
1981	Road to Adventure	15,000		47.00	50
1981	Sisters	15,000	N/A	64.00	75
1981	Spring Breeze	15,000	N/A	37.50	50
1981	Youth	15,000		37.50	40

A Child's World 4th Edition - F. Hook

YEAR ISSUE		EDITION LIMIT	YEAR RETRD.	ISSUE PRICE	*QUOTE U.S.$
1982	All Bundled Up	15,000		37.50	40
1982	Bedtime	15,000		35.00	38
1982	Birdie	15,000		37.50	40
1982	Flower Girl	15,000		42.00	45
1982	My Dolly!	15,000		39.00	40
1982	Ring Bearer	15,000		39.00	40

A Child's World 5th Edition - F. Hook

YEAR ISSUE		EDITION LIMIT	YEAR RETRD.	ISSUE PRICE	*QUOTE U.S.$
1983	Brothers	15,000		64.00	70
1983	Finish Line	15,000		39.00	42
1983	Handful of Happiness	15,000		36.00	40
1983	He Loves Me...	15,000		49.00	55
1983	Puppy's Pal	15,000		39.00	42
1983	Ring Around the Rosie	15,000		99.00	105

A Child's World 6th Edition - F. Hook

YEAR ISSUE		EDITION LIMIT	YEAR RETRD.	ISSUE PRICE	*QUOTE U.S.$
1984	Can I Help?	15,000		37.50	40
1984	Future Artist	15,000		42.00	45
1984	Good Doggie	15,000		47.00	50
1984	Let's Play Catch	15,000		33.00	35
1984	Nature's Wonders	15,000		29.00	31
1984	Sand Castles	15,000		37.50	40

A Child's World 7th Edition - F. Hook

YEAR ISSUE		EDITION LIMIT	YEAR RETRD.	ISSUE PRICE	*QUOTE U.S.$
1985	Art Class	15,000		99.00	105
1985	Don't Tell Anyone	15,000		49.00	50
1985	Look at Me!	15,000		42.00	45
1985	Mother's Helper	15,000		45.00	50
1985	Please Hear Me	15,000		29.00	30
1985	Yummm!	15,000		36.00	39

A Child's World 8th Edition - F. Hook

YEAR ISSUE		EDITION LIMIT	YEAR RETRD.	ISSUE PRICE	*QUOTE U.S.$
1985	Chance of Showers	15,000		33.00	35
1985	Dress Rehearsal	15,000		33.00	35
1985	Engine	15,000		36.00	40
1985	Just Stopped By	15,000		36.00	40
1985	Private Ocean	15,000		29.00	31
1985	Puzzling	15,000		36.00	40

A Child's World 9th Edition - F. Hook

YEAR ISSUE		EDITION LIMIT	YEAR RETRD.	ISSUE PRICE	*QUOTE U.S.$
1987	Hopscotch	15,000		67.50	70
1987	Li'l Brother	15,000		60.00	65

Classic Brides of the Century - E. Williams

YEAR ISSUE		EDITION LIMIT	YEAR RETRD.	ISSUE PRICE	*QUOTE U.S.$
1989	1900-Flora	5,000		175.00	175
1989	1910-Elizabeth Grace	5,000		175.00	175

YEAR ISSUE		EDITION LIMIT	YEAR RETRD.	ISSUE PRICE	*QUOTE U.S.$
1989	1920-Mary Claire	5,000		175.00	175
1989	1930-Kathleen	5,000		175.00	175
1989	1940-Margaret	5,000		175.00	175
1989	1950-Barbara Ann	5,000		175.00	175
1989	1960-Dianne	5,000		175.00	175
1989	1970-Heather	5,000		175.00	175
1989	1980-Jennifer	5,000		175.00	175
1992	1990-Stephanie Helen	5,000		175.00	175

Divine Servant - M. Greiner Jr.

YEAR ISSUE		EDITION LIMIT	YEAR RETRD.	ISSUE PRICE	*QUOTE U.S.$
1993	Divine Servant, pewter sculpture	Open		200.00	200
1993	Divine Servant, porcelain sculpture	Open		59.50	60
1993	Divine Servant, resin sculpture	Open		250.00	250

Fontanini Collectors' Club Member's Only - E. Simonetti

YEAR ISSUE		EDITION LIMIT	YEAR RETRD.	ISSUE PRICE	*QUOTE U.S.$
1991	The Pilgrimage	Yr.Iss.	1991	24.95	25
1992	She Rescued Me	Yr.Iss.	1992	23.50	24
1993	Christmas Symphony	Yr.Iss.	1993	13.50	14
1994	Sweet Harmony	Yr.Iss.	1994	13.50	14
1995	Faith: The Fifth Angel	Yr.Iss.	1995	22.50	23

Fontanini Member's Only Nativity Preview - E. Simonetti

YEAR ISSUE		EDITION LIMIT	YEAR RETRD.	ISSUE PRICE	*QUOTE U.S.$
1996	Mara	Yr.Iss.		12.50	13

Fontanini Collector Club Renewal Gift - E. Simonetti

YEAR ISSUE		EDITION LIMIT	YEAR RETRD.	ISSUE PRICE	*QUOTE U.S.$
1993	He Comforts Me	Yr.Iss.	1993	12.50	13
1994	I'm Heaven Bound	Yr.Iss.	1994	12.50	13
1995	Gift of Joy	Yr.Iss.	1995	12.50	13

Fontanini Collector Club Symbol of Membership - E. Simonetti

YEAR ISSUE		EDITION LIMIT	YEAR RETRD.	ISSUE PRICE	*QUOTE U.S.$
1996	Rosannah - Angel of The Roses	Yr.Iss.		Gift	N/A

Fontanini Collector Club Special Event Piece - E. Simonetti

YEAR ISSUE		EDITION LIMIT	YEAR RETRD.	ISSUE PRICE	*QUOTE U.S.$
1990	Gideon	Closed	1995	15.00	15
1995	Dominica	7/96		15.00	15

Fontanini Tour Exclusive - E. Simonetti

YEAR ISSUE		EDITION LIMIT	YEAR RETRD.	ISSUE PRICE	*QUOTE U.S.$
1995	Luke	Yr.Iss.		15.00	15

Fontanini Collector Club First Year Welcome Gift - E. Simonetti

YEAR ISSUE		EDITION LIMIT	YEAR RETRD.	ISSUE PRICE	*QUOTE U.S.$
1990	I Found Him	Closed	1995	Gift	N/A

Fontanini Heirloom Nativity Limited Edition Figurines - E. Simonetti

YEAR ISSUE		EDITION LIMIT	YEAR RETRD.	ISSUE PRICE	*QUOTE U.S.$
1994	14 pc. Golden Edition Heirloom Nativity Set	2,500		375.00	375
1994	Abigail & Peter	25,000	1994	29.50	30
1992	Ariel	Retrd.	1992	29.50	30
1995	Gabriela	25,000	1995	18.00	18
1993	Jeshua & Adin	Retrd.	1993	29.50	30
1996	Raphael	Yr.Iss.		18.00	18

Fontanini Retired 5" Collection - E. Simonetti

YEAR ISSUE		EDITION LIMIT	YEAR RETRD.	ISSUE PRICE	*QUOTE U.S.$
1985	Aaron		Retrd. 1994	12.50	13
1979	Baby Jesus		Retrd. 1992	5.50	12
1979	Balthazar		Retrd. 1993	5.50	12
1979	Gabriel		Retrd. 1993	5.50	12
1979	Gaspar		Retrd. 1993	5.50	12
1979	Joseph		Retrd. 1992	5.50	12
1979	Josiah		Retrd. 1994	5.50	13
1986	Kneeling Angel		Retrd. 1994	5.50	13
1985	Levi		Retrd. 1994	5.50	13
1979	Mary		Retrd. 1992	5.50	12
1979	Melchior		Retrd. 1993	5.50	12
1986	Micah		Retrd. 1995	5.50	13
1985	Miriam		Retrd. 1994	5.50	12
1986	Mordecai		Retrd. 1995	5.50	13
1986	Standing Angel		Retrd. 1994	5.50	13

Fontanini Retired 7.5" Collection - E. Simonetti

YEAR ISSUE		EDITION LIMIT	YEAR RETRD.	ISSUE PRICE	*QUOTE U.S.$
1979	Baby Jesus		Retrd. 1994	13.00	25
1979	Gabriel		Retrd. 1994	13.00	25
1979	Joseph		Retrd. 1994	13.00	25
1982	Kneeling Angel		Retrd. 1995	13.00	25
1979	Mary		Retrd. 1994	13.00	25
1982	Standing Angel		Retrd. 1995	13.00	25

Fontanini, The Collectible Creche - E. Simonetti

YEAR ISSUE		EDITION LIMIT	YEAR RETRD.	ISSUE PRICE	*QUOTE U.S.$
1973	10cm., (15 piece Set)	Closed	1992	63.60	89
1973	12cm., (15 piece Set)	Closed	1992	76.50	102
1979	16cm., (15 piece Set)	Closed	1992	178.50	285
1982	17cm., (15 piece Set)	Closed	1992	189.00	305
1973	19cm., (15 piece Set)	Closed	1992	175.50	280
1980	30cm., (15 piece Set)	Closed	1992	670.00	759

Frances Hook's Four Seasons - F. Hook

YEAR ISSUE		EDITION LIMIT	YEAR RETRD.	ISSUE PRICE	*QUOTE U.S.$
1984	Winter	12,500		95.00	100
1985	Spring	12,500		95.00	100
1985	Summer	12,500		95.00	100
1985	Fall	12,500		95.00	100

Heartbeats - I. Spencer

YEAR ISSUE		EDITION LIMIT	YEAR RETRD.	ISSUE PRICE	*QUOTE U.S.$
1986	Miracle	5,000		145.00	145
1987	Storytime	5,000		145.00	145

Hook - F. Hook

YEAR ISSUE		EDITION LIMIT	YEAR RETRD.	ISSUE PRICE	*QUOTE U.S.$
1986	Carpenter Bust		Retrd. 1986	95.00	95
1986	Carpenter Bust-Heirloom Edition		Retrd. 1986	95.00	95
1987	Little Children, Come to Me	15,000		45.00	45

YEAR ISSUE		EDITION LIMIT	YEAR RETD.	ISSUE PRICE	*QUOTE U.S.$
1987	Madonna and Child	15,000		39.50	40
1982	Sailor Mates	2,000		290.00	315
1982	Sun Shy	2,000		290.00	315

Jam Session - E. Rohn
1985	Banjo Player	7,500		145.00	145
1985	Bass Player	7,500		145.00	145
1985	Clarinet Player	7,500		145.00	145
1985	Coronet Player	7,500		145.00	145
1985	Drummer	7,500		145.00	145
1985	Trombone Player	7,500		145.00	145

The Masterpiece Collection - Various
1979	Adoration - F. Lippe	5,000		73.00	73
1981	The Holy Family - G. delle Notti	5,000		98.00	98
1982	Madonna of the Streets - R. Ferruzzi	5,000		65.00	65
1980	Madonna with Grapes - P. Mignard	5,000		85.00	85

The Museum Collection by Angela Tripi - A. Tripi
1995	The Batter	1,000		95.00	95
1993	Be a Clown	1,000		95.00	95
1994	Blackfoot Woman with Baby	1,000		95.00	95
1991	The Caddie	1,000		135.00	135
1992	Checking It Twice	2,500		95.00	95
1991	Christopher Columbus	1,000		250.00	250
1994	Crow Warrior	1,000		195.00	195
1991	The Fiddler	1,000		175.00	176
1992	Flying Ace	1,000		95.00	95
1993	For My Next Trick	1,000		95.00	95
1992	Fore!	1,000		175.00	175
1992	The Fur Trapper	1,000		175.00	175
1991	A Gentleman's Game	1,000	1994	175.00	175
1992	The Gift Giver	2,500		95.00	95
1994	Iroquois Warrior	1,000		95.00	95
1995	Jesus in Gethsemane	1,000		95.00	95
1993	Jesus, The Good Shepherd	1,000		95.00	95
1992	Justice for All	1,000		95.00	95
1992	Ladies' Day	1,000		175.00	175
1992	Ladies' Tee	1,000		250.00	250
1990	The Mentor	1,000		290.00	291
1994	Native American Chief	1,000		95.00	95
1994	Native American Woman -Cherokee Maiden	1,000		95.00	95
1992	Nativity Set-8 pc.	2,500		425.00	425
1995	Nurse	1,000		95.00	95
1993	One Man Band Clown	1,000		95.00	95
1992	Our Family Doctor	1,000		95.00	95
1995	The Pitcher	1,000		95.00	95
1993	Preacher of Peace	1,000		175.00	175
1992	Prince of the Plains	1,000		175.00	175
1993	Public Protector	1,000		95.00	95
1994	Rhapsody	1,000		95.00	95
1993	Right on Schedule	1,000		95.00	95
1993	Road Show	1,000		95.00	95
1995	The Runner	1,000		95.00	95
1994	Serenade	1,000		95.00	95
1994	Sonata	1,000		95.00	95
1991	St. Francis of Assisi	1,000		175.00	175
1992	The Tannenbaum Santa	2,500		95.00	95
1992	The Tap In	1,000		175.00	175
1995	Teacher	1,000		95.00	95
1991	Tee Time at St. Andrew's	1,000	1993	175.00	175
1992	This Way, Santa	2,500		95.00	95
1992	To Serve and Protect	1,000		95.00	95
1993	Tripi Crucifix-Large	Open		59.00	59
1993	Tripi Crucifix-Medium	Open		35.00	35
1993	Tripi Crucifix-Small	Open		27.50	28

The Richard Judson Zolan Collection - R.J. Zolan
1992	Summer at the Seashore	1,200		125.00	125
1994	Terrace Dancing	1,200		175.00	175

Seraphim Classics™ - Seraphim Studios
1996	Celine - The Morning Star	Open		55.00	55
1994	Cymbeline - Peacemaker	Open		49.50	55
1994	Evangeline - Angel of Mercy	Open		49.50	55
1995	Felcia - Adoring Maiden	Open		49.50	55
1994	Francesca - Loving Guardian	Open		65.00	65
1996	Gabriel - Celestial Messenger	Open		59.50	60
1994	Iris - Rainbow's End	Open		49.50	55
1994	Isabel - Gentle Spirit	Open		49.50	55
1995	Laurice - Wisdom's Child	Open		49.50	55
1996	Lydia - Winged Poet	Open		49.50	55
1996	Mariah - Heavenly Joy	Open		59.50	60
1994	Ophelia - Heart Seeker	Retrd.	1996	49.50	55
1995	Priscilla - Benevolent Guide	Open		49.50	55
1996	Rosalie - Nature's Delight	Open		55.00	55
1995	Sepaphina - Heaven's Helper	Retrd.	1996	49.50	55
1996	Serena - Angel of Peace	Open		65.00	65

Seraphim Classics™ Glitterdome™ - Seraphim Studios
1995	Francesca - Loving Guardian	Open		50.00	50

Seraphim Classics™ Limited Edition Figurines - Seraphim Studios
1995	Alyssa - Nature's Angel	Closed	1995	145.00	145
1996	Vanessa - Heavenly Maiden	Yr.Iss.		150.00	150

Seraphim Classics™ Musical - Seraphim Studios
1994	Francesca - Loving Guardian	Open		75.00	75
1996	Iris - Rainbow's End	Open		65.00	65

Spencer - I. Spencer
YEAR ISSUE		EDITION LIMIT	YEAR RETD.	ISSUE PRICE	*QUOTE U.S.$
1985	Flower Princess	5,000		195.00	195
1985	Moon Goddess	5,000		195.00	195

Ron Lee's World of Clowns

The Ron Lee Collector's Club Gifts - R. Lee
1987	Hooping It Up CCG1	Closed	1987	Gift	95
1988	Pudge CCG2	Closed	1988	Gift	65
1989	Pals CCG3	Closed	1989	Gift	65
1990	Potsie CCG4	Closed	1990	Gift	65
1991	Hi! Ya! CCG5	Closed	1991	Gift	65
1992	Bashful Beau CCG6	Closed	1992	Gift	65
1993	Lit'l Mate CCG7	Closed	1993	Gift	65
1994	Chip Off the Old Block CCG8	Closed	1994	Gift	65
1995	Rock-A-Billy CCG9	Closed	1995	Gift	65

The Ron Lee Collector's Club Renewal Sculptures - R. Lee
1987	Doggin' Along CC1	Yr.Iss.	1987	75.00	115
1988	Midsummer's Dream CC2	Yr.Iss.	1988	97.00	140
1989	Peek-A-Boo Charlie CC3	Yr.Iss.	1989	65.00	125
1990	Get The Message CC4	Yr.Iss.	1990	65.00	125
1991	I'm So Pretty CC5	Yr.Iss.	1991	65.00	125
1992	It's For You CC6	Yr.Iss.	1992	65.00	125
1993	My Son Keven CC7	Yr.Iss.	1993	70.00	125

Around the World With Hobo Joe - R. Lee
1994	Hobo Joe in Caribbean L412	750	1995	110.00	110
1994	Hobo Joe in Egypt L415	750	1995	110.00	110
1994	Hobo Joe in England L411	750	1995	110.00	110
1994	Hobo Joe in France L407	750	1995	110.00	110
1994	Hobo Joe in Italy L406	750	1995	110.00	110
1994	Hobo Joe in Japan L408	750	1995	110.00	110
1994	Hobo Joe in Norway L413	750	1995	110.00	110
1994	Hobo Joe in Spain L414	750	1995	110.00	110
1994	Hobo Joe in Tahiti L410	750	1995	110.00	110
1994	Hobo Joe in the U.S.A L409	750	1995	110.00	110-125

The Betty Boop Collection - R. Lee
1992	Bamboo Isle BB715	1,500		240.00	240
1992	Boop Oop A Doop BB705	1,500		97.00	97
1992	Harvest Moon BB700	1,500		93.00	93
1992	Max's Cafe BB720	1,500		99.00	99
1992	Spicy Dish BB710	1,500		215.00	215

Center Ring - R. Lee
1994	According To L-431SE	750	1995	125.00	125
1994	Aristocrat L-424SE	750	1995	125.00	125
1994	Barella L-423SE	750	1995	125.00	125-140
1994	Belt-a-Loon L-427SE	750	1995	125.00	125
1994	Boo-Boo L-430SE	750	1995	125.00	125
1994	Bubbles L-422SE	750	1995	125.00	125
1994	Carpetbagger L-421SE	750	1995	125.00	125
1994	Daisy L-417SE	750	1995	125.00	125
1994	Forget-Me-Not L-428SE	750	1995	125.00	125
1994	Glamour Boy L-433SE	750	1995	125.00	125
1994	Hoop-De-Doo L-434SE	750	1995	125.00	125
1994	Hot Dog L-418SE	750	1995	125.00	125
1994	Kandy L-419SE	750	1995	125.00	125
1994	Maid in the USA L-432SE	750	1995	125.00	125-140
1994	Mal-Lett L-426SE	750	1995	125.00	125
1994	Poodles L-420SE	750	1995	125.00	125
1994	Puddles L-416SE	750	1995	125.00	125
1994	Rabbit's Foot L-429SE	750	1995	125.00	125
1994	Ruffles L-435SE	750	1995	125.00	125
1994	Snacks L-425SE	750	1995	125.00	125

The Classics - R. Lee
1991	Huckleberry Hound HB815	2,750	1995	90.00	90
1991	Quick Draw McGraw HB805	2,750	1995	90.00	90
1991	Scooby Doo & Shaggy HB810	2,750	1995	114.00	114
1991	Yogi Bear & Boo Boo HB800	2,750	1995	95.00	95

The Commemorative Collection - R. Lee
1995	April 12th L455	2,500		180.00	180
1995	Between Shows L456	2,500		250.00	250
1995	Filet of Sole L460	2,500		180.00	200
1995	The Highwayman L457	2,500		165.00	165
1995	Just Plain Tired L459	2,500		195.00	225
1995	Practice Swing...Not!! L458	2,500		180.00	205

The E.T. Collection - R. Lee
1992	E.T. ET100	1,500	1995	94.00	94
1993	Flight ET115	1,500	1995	325.00	325
1993	Friends ET110	1,500	1995	125.00	125
1992	It's Mee...E.T. ET105	1,500	1995	94.00	94

The Flintstones - R. Lee
1991	Bedrock Serenade HB130	2,750		250.00	250
1991	Bogey Buddies HB150	2,750		143.00	143
1991	Buffalo Brothers HB170	2,750		134.00	134
1991	The Flintstones HB100	2,750		410.00	410
1991	Joyride-A-Saurus HB140	2,750		107.00	107
1991	Saturday Blues HB120	2,750		105.00	105
1991	Vac-A-Saurus HB160	2,750		105.00	110
1991	Yabba-Dabba-Doo HB110	2,750		230.00	230

History of Golf - R. Lee
1994	20th Century GTA700	10,000		150.00	150
1994	Age of Chivalry GTA400	10,000		150.00	150

YEAR ISSUE		EDITION LIMIT	YEAR RETD.	ISSUE PRICE	* QUOTE U.S.$
1994	Caesar GTA300	10,000		150.00	150
1994	Dawn of Man GTA100	10,000		150.00	150
1994	New Frontiers GTA800	10,000		150.00	150
1994	Old West GTA600	10,000		150.00	150
1994	The Pharaoh GTA200	10,000		150.00	150
1994	Plymouth GTA500	10,000		150.00	150

Holiday Special - R. Lee
1995	Santa's Other Sleigh L461	750		195.00	195

The Jetsons - R. Lee
1991	4 O'Clock Tea HB550	2,750	1995	203.00	203
1991	Astro: Cosmic Canine HB520	2,750	1995	275.00	275
1991	The Cosmic Couple HB510	2,750	1995	105.00	105
1991	I Rove Roo HB530	2,750	1995	105.00	105
1991	The Jetsons HB500	2,750	1995	500.00	500
1991	Scare-D-Dog HB540	2,750	1995	160.00	160

Lance Burton - R. Lee
1996	Levitation LB100	950		425.00	425

Musical Clowns in Harmony - R. Lee
1994	Aristocrat L-424	750	1995	175.00	175
1994	Barella L-423	750	1995	175.00	175
1994	Bubbles L-422	750	1995	175.00	175
1994	Carpet Bagger L-421	750	1995	175.00	175
1994	Daisy L-417	750	1995	175.00	175
1994	Hot Dog L-418	750	1995	175.00	175
1994	Kandy L-419	750	1995	175.00	175
1994	Poodles L-420	750	1995	175.00	175
1994	Puddles L-416	750	1995	175.00	175
1994	Snacks L-425	750	1995	175.00	175

The Original Ron Lee Collection-1976 - R. Lee
1976	Alligator Bowling 504	Closed	N/A	15.00	35-78
1976	Bear Fishing 511	Closed	N/A	15.00	35-78
1976	Clown and Dog Act 101	Closed	N/A	48.00	78-140
1976	Clown and Elephant Act 107	Closed	N/A	56.00	85-140
1976	Clown Tightrope Walker 104	Closed	N/A	50.00	82-155
1976	Dog Fishing 512	Closed	N/A	15.00	35-78
1976	Frog Surfing 502	Closed	N/A	15.00	35-78
1976	Hippo on Scooter 505	Closed	N/A	15.00	35-78
1976	Hobo Joe Hitchiking 116	Closed	N/A	55.00	65
1976	Hobo Joe with Balloons 120	Closed	N/A	63.00	90
1976	Hobo Joe with Pal 115	Closed	N/A	63.00	85-170
1976	Hobo Joe with Umbrella 117	Closed	N/A	58.00	65-160
1976	Kangaroos Boxing 508	Closed	N/A	15.00	35-78
1976	Owl With Guitar 500	Closed	N/A	15.00	35-78
1976	Penguin on Snowskis 503	Closed	N/A	15.00	35-78
1976	Pig Playing Violin 510	Closed	N/A	15.00	35-78
1976	Pinky Lying Down 112	Closed	N/A	25.00	145-225
1976	Pinky Sitting 119	Closed	N/A	25.00	145
1976	Pinky Standing 118	Closed	N/A	25.00	145-225
1976	Pinky Upside Down 111	Closed	N/A	25.00	125
1976	Rabbit Playing Tennis 507	Closed	N/A	15.00	35-78
1976	Turtle On Skateboard 501	Closed	N/A	15.00	35-78

The Original Ron Lee Collection-1977 - R. Lee
1977	Bear On Rock 523	Closed	N/A	18.00	30-80
1977	Koala Bear In Tree 514	Closed	N/A	15.00	35-78
1977	Koala Bear On Log 516	Closed	N/A	15.00	35-78
1977	Koala Bear With Baby 515	Closed	N/A	15.00	35-78
1977	Monkey With Banana 521	Closed	N/A	18.00	30-80
1977	Mouse and Cheese 520	Closed	N/A	18.00	30-80
1977	Mr. Penguin 518	Closed	N/A	18.00	39-85
1977	Owl Graduate 519	Closed	N/A	22.00	44-90
1977	Pelican and Python 522	Closed	N/A	18.00	30-80

The Original Ron Lee Collection-1978 - R. Lee
1978	Bobbi on Unicyle 204	Closed	N/A	45.00	65-98
1978	Bow Tie 222	Closed	N/A	67.50	93-215
1978	Butterfly and Flower 529	Closed	N/A	22.00	40-85
1978	Clancy, the Cop 210	Closed	N/A	55.00	72-130
1978	Clara-Bow 205	Closed	N/A	52.00	70-120
1978	Coco-Hands on Hips 218	Closed	N/A	70.00	85-250
1978	Corky, the Drummer Boy 202	Closed	N/A	53.00	85-130
1978	Cuddles 208	Closed	N/A	37.00	55-110
1978	Dolphins 525	Closed	N/A	22.00	40-85
1978	Driver the Golfer 211	Closed	N/A	55.00	200-225
1978	Elephant on Ball 214	Closed	N/A	26.00	42-80
1978	Elephant on Stand 213	Closed	N/A	26.00	42-80
1978	Elephant Sitting 215	Closed	N/A	26.00	42-80
1978	Fancy Pants 224	Closed	N/A	55.00	90-120
1978	Fireman with Hose 216	Closed	N/A	62.00	85-170
1978	Hey Rube 220	Closed	N/A	35.00	53-92
1978	Hummingbird 528	Closed	N/A	22.00	40-85
1978	Jeri In a Barrel 219	Closed	N/A	75.00	175
1978	Jocko with Lollipop 221	Closed	N/A	67.50	93-215
1978	Oscar On Stilts 223	Closed	N/A	55.00	90-120
1978	Pierrot Painting 207	Closed	N/A	50.00	80-170
1978	Polly, the Peacock & Crackers 201	Closed	N/A	63.00	100-170
1978	Poppy with Puppet 209	Closed	N/A	60.00	75-140
1978	Prince Frog 526	Closed	N/A	22.00	40-85
1978	Sad Sack 212	Closed	N/A	48.00	62-210
1978	Sailfish 524	Closed	N/A	18.00	40-95
1978	Sea Otter on Back 531	Closed	N/A	22.00	40-85
1978	Sea Otter on Rock 532	Closed	N/A	22.00	40-85
1978	Seagull 527	Closed	N/A	22.00	40-85
1978	Skippy Swinging 239	Closed	N/A	52.00	65-85
1978	Sparky Skating 206	Closed	N/A	55.00	72-260
1978	Tinker Bowling 203	Closed	N/A	37.00	55-110

YEAR ISSUE		EDITION LIMIT	YEAR RETD.	ISSUE PRICE	*QUOTE U.S.$
1978	Tobi-Hands Outstretched 217	Closed	N/A	70.00	98-260
1978	Turtle on Rock 530	Closed	N/A	22.00	40-85

The Original Ron Lee Collection-1979 - R. Lee

1979	Buttons Bicycling 229	Closed	N/A	75.00	110-150
1979	Carousel Horse 232	Closed	N/A	119.00	130-195
1979	Darby Tipping Hat 238	Closed	N/A	35.00	60-140
1979	Darby with Flower 235	Closed	N/A	35.00	60-140
1979	Darby with Umbrella 236	Closed	N/A	35.00	60-140
1979	Darby With Violin 237	Closed	N/A	35.00	60-140
1979	Doctor Sawbones 228	Closed	N/A	75.00	110-150
1979	Fearless Fred in Cannon 234	Closed	N/A	80.00	105-300
1979	Harry and the Hare 233	Closed	N/A	69.00	102-180
1979	Kelly at the Piano 241	Closed	N/A	185.00	285-510
1979	Kelly in Kar 230	Closed	N/A	164.00	210-380
1979	Kelly's Kar 231	Closed	N/A	75.00	90-280
1979	Lilli 227	Closed	N/A	75.00	105-145
1979	Timmy Tooting 225	Closed	N/A	35.00	52-85
1979	Tubby Tuba 226	Closed	N/A	35.00	50

The Original Ron Lee Collection-1980 - R. Lee

1980	Alexander's One Man Band 261	Closed	N/A	N/A	N/A
1980	Banjo Willie 258	Closed	N/A	68.00	85-195
1980	Carousel Horse 248	Closed	N/A	88.00	115-285
1980	Carousel Horse 249	Closed	N/A	88.00	115-285
1980	Chuckles Juggling 244	Closed	N/A	98.00	105-150
1980	Cubby Holding Balloon 240	Closed	N/A	96.00	65-70
1980	Dennis Playing Tennis 252	Closed	N/A	74.00	95-185
1980	Doctor Jawbones 260	Closed	N/A	85.00	110-305
1980	Donkey What 243	Closed	N/A	60.00	92-250
1980	Emile 257	Closed	N/A	43.00	82-190
1980	Happy Waving 255	Closed	N/A	43.00	82-190
1980	Hobo Joe in Tub 259	Closed	N/A	96.00	240
1980	Horse Drawn Chariot 263	Closed	N/A	N/A	N/A
1980	Jaque Downhill Racer 253	Closed	N/A	74.00	90-210
1980	Jingles Telling Time 242	Closed	N/A	75.00	90-190
1980	Jo-Jo at Make-up Mirror 250	Closed	N/A	86.00	125-185
1980	The Menagerie 262	Closed	N/A	N/A	N/A
1980	Monkey 251	Closed	N/A	60.00	85-210
1980	P. T. Dinghy 245	Closed	N/A	65.00	80-190
1980	Peanuts Playing Concertina 247	Closed	N/A	65.00	150-285
1980	Roni Riding Horse 246	Closed	N/A	115.00	180-290
1980	Ruford 254	Closed	N/A	43.00	80-190
1980	Zach 256	Closed	N/A	43.00	82-190

The Original Ron Lee Collection-1981 - R. Lee

1981	Al at the Bass 284	Closed	N/A	48.00	52-112
1981	Barbella 273	Closed	N/A	N/A	N/A
1981	Bojangles 276	Closed	N/A	N/A	N/A
1981	Bosom Buddies 299	Closed	N/A	135.00	90-280
1981	Bozo On Unicycle 279	Closed	N/A	28.00	99-185
1981	Bozo Playing Cymbols 277	Closed	N/A	28.00	99-185
1981	Bozo Riding Car 278	Closed	N/A	28.00	99-185
1981	Carney and Seal Act 300	Closed	N/A	63.00	75-290
1981	Carousel Horse 280	Closed	N/A	88.00	125-290
1981	Carousel Horse 281	Closed	N/A	88.00	115-290
1981	Cashew On One Knee 275	Closed	N/A	N/A	N/A
1981	Elephant Reading 271	Closed	N/A	N/A	N/A
1981	Executive Hitchiking 267	Closed	N/A	23.00	45-110
1981	Executive Reading 264	Closed	N/A	23.00	45-110
1981	Executive Resting 266	Closed	N/A	23.00	45-110
1981	Executive with Umbrella 265	Closed	N/A	23.00	45-110
1981	Harpo 296	Closed	N/A	120.00	190-350
1981	Hobo Joe Praying 298	Closed	N/A	57.00	65-85
1981	Kevin at the Drums 283	Closed	N/A	50.00	92-150
1981	Larry and His Hotdogs 274	Closed	N/A	76.00	90-200
1981	Louie Hitching A Ride 269	Closed	N/A	47.00	58-135
1981	Louie on Park Bench 268	Closed	N/A	56.00	85-160
1981	Louie On Railroad Car 270	Closed	N/A	77.00	95-180
1981	Mickey With Umbrella 291	Closed	N/A	50.00	75-140
1981	Mickey Tightrope Walker 292	Closed	N/A	50.00	75-140
1981	Mickey Upside Down 293	Closed	N/A	50.00	75-140
1981	My Son Darren 295	Closed	N/A	57.00	72-140
1981	Nicky Sitting on Ball 289	Closed	N/A	39.00	48-92
1981	Nicky Standing on Ball 290	Closed	N/A	39.00	48-92
1981	Perry Sitting With Balloon 287	Closed	N/A	37.00	50-95
1981	Perry Standing With Balloon 288	Closed	N/A	37.00	50-95
1981	Pickles and Pooch 297	Closed	N/A	90.00	200-240
1981	Pistol Pete 272	Closed	N/A	76.00	85-180
1981	Rocketman 294	Closed	N/A	77.00	92-150
1981	Ron at the Piano 285	Closed	N/A	46.00	55-110
1981	Ron Lee Trio 282	Closed	N/A	144.00	280-435
1981	Timothy In Big Shoes 286	Closed	N/A	37.00	50-95

The Original Ron Lee Collection-1982 - R. Lee

1982	Ali on His Magic Carpet 335	Closed	N/A	105.00	150-210
1982	Barnum Feeding Bacon 315	Closed	N/A	120.00	160-270
1982	Beaver Playing Accordian 807	Closed	N/A	23.00	35-92
1982	Benny Pulling Car 310	Closed	N/A	190.00	235-360
1982	Burrito Bandito 334	Closed	N/A	150.00	190-260
1982	Buster in Barrel 308	Closed	N/A	85.00	90-120
1982	Camel 818	Closed	N/A	57.00	75-150
1982	Captain Cranberry 320	Closed	N/A	115.00	145-180
1982	Captain Mis-Adventure 703	Closed	N/A	250.00	300-550
1982	Carney and Dog Act 301	Closed	N/A	63.00	75-149
1982	Charlie Chaplain 701	Closed	N/A	230.00	285-650
1982	Charlie in the Rain 321	Closed	N/A	80.00	90-160
1982	Chico Playing Guitar 336	Closed	N/A	70.00	95-180
1982	Clancy, the Cop and Dog 333	Closed	N/A	115.00	140-250
1982	Clarence - The Lawyer 331	Closed	N/A	100.00	140-230
1982	Denny Eating Ice Cream 305	Closed	N/A	39.00	50-170

YEAR ISSUE		EDITION LIMIT	YEAR RETD.	ISSUE PRICE	*QUOTE U.S.$
1982	Denny Holding Gift Box 306	Closed	N/A	39.00	50-170
1982	Denny Juggling Ball 307	Closed	N/A	39.00	50-170
1982	Dog Playing Guitar 805	Closed	N/A	23.00	35-92
1982	Dr. Painless and Patient 311	Closed	N/A	195.00	240-385
1982	Fireman Watering House 303	Closed	N/A	99.00	99-180
1982	Fish With Shoe 803	Closed	N/A	23.00	35-92
1982	Fox In An Airplane 806	Closed	N/A	23.00	35-92
1982	Georgie Going Anywhere 302	Closed	N/A	95.00	375
1982	Giraffe 816	Closed	N/A	57.00	75-150
1982	Herbie Balancing Hat 327	Closed	N/A	26.00	40-110
1982	Herbie Dancing 325	Closed	N/A	26.00	40-110
1982	Herbie Hands Outstretched 326	Closed	N/A	26.00	40-110
1982	Herbie Legs in Air 329	Closed	N/A	26.00	40-110
1982	Herbie Lying Down 328	Closed	N/A	26.00	40-110
1982	Herbie Touching Ground 330	Closed	N/A	26.00	40-110
1982	Hobo Joe on Cycle 322	Closed	N/A	125.00	170-280
1982	Horse 819	Closed	N/A	57.00	75-150
1982	Kukla and Friend 316	Closed	N/A	100.00	140-210
1982	Laurel & Hardy 700	Closed	N/A	225.00	290-500
1982	Limousine Service 705	Closed	N/A	330.00	375-750
1982	Lion 817	Closed	N/A	57.00	75-150
1982	Marion With Marrionette 317	Closed	N/A	105.00	135-225
1982	Murphy On Unicycle 337	Closed	N/A	115.00	160-288
1982	Nappy Snoozing 346	Closed	N/A	110.00	125-210
1982	Norman Painting Dumbo 314	Closed	N/A	126.00	150-210
1982	Ostrich 813	Closed	N/A	57.00	75-150
1982	Parrot Rollerskating 809	Closed	N/A	23.00	35-92
1982	Pig Brick Layer 800	Closed	N/A	23.00	35-92
1982	Pinball Pal 332	Closed	N/A	150.00	195-287
1982	Quincy Lying Down 304	Closed	N/A	80.00	92-210
1982	Rabbit With Egg 801	Closed	N/A	23.00	35-92
1982	Reindeer 812	Closed	N/A	57.00	75-150
1982	Robin Resting 338	Closed	N/A	110.00	125-210
1982	Ron Lee Carousel	Closed	N/A	1000.00	12500
1982	Rooster 815	Closed	N/A	57.00	75-150
1982	Rooster With Barbell 808	Closed	N/A	23.00	35-92
1982	Sammy Riding Elephant 309	Closed	N/A	90.00	125-250
1982	Seal Blowing His Horns 804	Closed	N/A	23.00	35-92
1982	Self Portrait 702	Closed	N/A	355.00	2500
1982	Slim Charging Bull 313	Closed	N/A	195.00	265-410
1982	Smokey, the Bear 802	Closed	N/A	23.00	35-92
1982	Steppin' Out 704	Closed	N/A	325.00	390-700
1982	Three Man Valentinos 319	Closed	N/A	55.00	70-120
1982	Tiger 814	Closed	N/A	57.00	75-150
1982	Too Loose-L'Artiste 312	Closed	N/A	150.00	180-290
1982	Tou Tou 323	Closed	N/A	70.00	90-190
1982	Toy Soldier 324	Closed	N/A	95.00	250
1982	Turtle With Gun 811	Closed	N/A	57.00	75-150
1982	Two Man Valentinos 318	Closed	N/A	45.00	60-130
1982	Walrus With Umbrella 810	Closed	N/A	23.00	35-92

The Original Ron Lee Collection-1983 - R. Lee

1983	The Bandwagon 707	Closed	N/A	900.00	2000
1983	Beethoven's Fourth Paws 358	Closed	N/A	59.00	110-165
1983	Black Carousel Horse 1001	Closed	N/A	450.00	450-600
1983	Bumbles Selling Balloons 353	Closed	N/A	80.00	170-240
1983	Buster and His Balloons 363	Closed	N/A	47.00	90-125
1983	Captain Freddy 375	Closed	N/A	85.00	425-475
1983	Casey Cruising 351	Closed	N/A	57.00	95-170
1983	Catch the Brass Ring 708	Closed	N/A	510.00	900-1350
1983	Cecil and Sausage 354	Closed	N/A	90.00	200-270
1983	Chef's Cuisine 361	Closed	N/A	57.00	100-110
1983	Chestnut Carousel Horse 1002	Closed	N/A	450.00	700-1100
1983	Cimba the Elephant 706	Closed	N/A	225.00	300-550
1983	Clyde Juggling 339	Closed	N/A	39.00	100-115
1983	Clyde Upside Down 340	Closed	N/A	39.00	100-115
1983	Coco and His Compact 369	Closed	N/A	55.00	145-175
1983	Cotton Candy 377	Closed	N/A	150.00	200-400
1983	Daring Dudley 367	Closed	N/A	65.00	100-200
1983	Door to Door Dabney 373	Closed	N/A	100.00	200-285
1983	Engineer Billie 356	Closed	N/A	190.00	275-550
1983	Flipper Diving 345	Closed	N/A	115.00	200-350
1983	Gazebo 1004	Closed	N/A	750.00	13-1750
1983	Gilbert Tee'd Off 376	Closed	N/A	60.00	225
1983	Hobi in His Hammock 344	Closed	N/A	85.00	175
1983	I Love You From My Heart 360	Closed	N/A	35.00	125
1983	The Jogger 372	Closed	N/A	75.00	120-220
1983	Josephine 370	Closed	N/A	55.00	145-175
1983	Knickers Balancing Feather 366	Closed	N/A	47.00	120-135
1983	The Last Scoop 379	Closed	N/A	175.00	300-475
1983	The Last Scoop 900	Closed	N/A	325.00	300-725
1983	Little Horse - Head Down 342	Closed	N/A	29.00	72
1983	Little Horse - Head Up 341	Closed	N/A	29.00	72
1983	Little Saturday Night 348	Closed	N/A	53.00	200
1983	Lou Proposing 365	Closed	N/A	57.00	120-170
1983	Matinee Jitters 378	Closed	N/A	175.00	200-450
1983	Matinee Jitters 901	Closed	N/A	325.00	355
1983	My Daughter Deborah 357	Closed	N/A	63.00	125-185
1983	No Camping or Fishing 902	Closed	N/A	325.00	350-600
1983	On The Road Again 355	Closed	N/A	220.00	300-650
1983	Riches to Rags 374	Closed	N/A	55.00	200-265
1983	Ride 'em Roni 347	Closed	N/A	125.00	200-375
1983	Rufus and His Refuse 343	Closed	N/A	65.00	160
1983	Say It With Flowers 359	Closed	N/A	35.00	95-110
1983	Singin' In The Rain 362	Closed	N/A	105.00	350
1983	Tatters and Balloons 352	Closed	N/A	65.00	135
1983	Teeter Tottie Scottie 350	Closed	N/A	55.00	105-165
1983	Tottie Scottie 349	Closed	N/A	39.00	75-115
1983	Up, Up and Away 364	Closed	N/A	50.00	250
1983	White Carousel Horse 1003	Closed	N/A	450.00	700-1100
1983	Wilt the Stilt 368	Closed	N/A	49.00	100-155

The Original Ron Lee Collection-1984 - R. Lee

YEAR ISSUE		EDITION LIMIT	YEAR RETD.	ISSUE PRICE	*QUOTE U.S.$
1984	Baggy Pants 387	Closed	N/A	98.00	250-300
1984	Black Circus Horse 711A	Closed	N/A	305.00	350-520
1984	A Bozo Lunch 390	Closed	N/A	148.00	250-400
1984	Bozo's Seal of Approval 389	Closed	N/A	138.00	200-350
1984	Chestnut Circus Horse 710A	Closed	N/A	305.00	350-520
1984	Give a Dog a Bone 383	Closed	N/A	95.00	95-182
1984	Just For You 386	Closed	N/A	110.00	150-250
1984	Look at the Birdy 388	Closed	N/A	138.00	200-300
1984	Mortimer Fishing 382	Closed	N/A	N/A	N/A
1984	My Fellow Americans 391	Closed	N/A	138.00	250-425
1984	No Camping or Fishing 380	Closed	N/A	175.00	275-450
1984	No Loitering 392	Closed	N/A	113.00	150-250
1984	The Peppermints 384	Closed	N/A	150.00	180-250
1984	Rudy Holding Balloons 713	Closed	N/A	230.00	300-550
1984	Saturday Night 714	Closed	N/A	250.00	600-825
1984	T.K. and OH!! 385	Closed	N/A	85.00	200-325
1984	Tisket and Tasket 393	Closed	N/A	93.00	150-250
1984	Wheeler Sheila 381	Closed	N/A	75.00	175-225
1984	White Circus Horse 709	Closed	N/A	305.00	350-520

The Original Ron Lee Collection-1985 - R. Lee

1985	Bull-Can-Rear-You 422	Closed	N/A	120.00	206
1985	Cannonball 466	Closed	N/A	43.00	83
1985	Catch of the Day 441	Closed	N/A	170.00	305
1985	Clowns of the Caribbean PS101	Closed	N/A	1250.00	2-2800
1985	Dr. Sigmund Fraud 457	Closed	N/A	98.00	190
1985	Dr. Timothy DeCay 459	Closed	N/A	98.00	185
1985	Duster Buster 461	Closed	N/A	43.00	90
1985	The Finishing Touch 409	Closed	N/A	178.00	305
1985	Fred Figures 903	Closed	N/A	175.00	595
1985	From Riches to Rags 374	Closed	N/A	108.00	250
1985	Get the Picture 456	Closed	N/A	70.00	140
1985	Gilbert TeeOd OFF 376	Closed	N/A	63.00	55-63
1985	Giraffe Getting a Bath 428	Closed	N/A	160.00	350-450
1985	Ham Track 451	Closed	N/A	240.00	430
1985	Hi Ho Blinky 462	Closed	N/A	53.00	105
1985	One Wheel Winky 464	Closed	N/A	43.00	83
1985	Pee Wee With Balloons 435	Closed	N/A	50.00	100
1985	Pee Wee With Umbrella 434	Closed	N/A	50.00	100
1985	Policy Paul 904	Closed	N/A	175.00	190
1985	Rosebuds 433	Closed	N/A	155.00	315
1985	Twas the Night Before 408	Closed	N/A	235.00	405
1985	Whiskers Bathing 749	Closed	N/A	305.00	500-800
1985	Whiskers Hitchhiking 745	Closed	N/A	240.00	800
1985	Whiskers Holding Balloons 746	Closed	N/A	265.00	500-800
1985	Whiskers Holding Umbrella 747	Closed	N/A	265.00	500-800
1985	Whiskers On The Bench 750	Closed	N/A	230.00	695-895
1985	Whiskers Sweeping 744	Closed	N/A	240.00	700-850
1985	Yo Yo Stravinsky-Attoney at Law 458	Closed	N/A	98.00	200

The Original Ron Lee Collection-1986 - R. Lee

1986	Bathing Buddies 450	Closed	N/A	145.00	375
1986	Bums Day at the Beach L105	Closed	N/A	97.00	N/A
1986	Captain Cranberry 469	Closed	N/A	140.00	175-335
1986	Christmas Morning Magic L107	Closed	N/A	99.00	N/A
1986	Getting Even 485	Closed	N/A	85.00	125-225
1986	Hari and Hare 454	Closed	N/A	57.00	85-135
1986	High Above the Big Top L112	Closed	N/A	162.00	350
1986	The Last Stop L106	Closed	N/A	99.00	N/A
1986	Most Requested Toy L108	Closed	N/A	264.00	N/A
1986	Puppy Love's Portrait L113	Closed	N/A	168.00	325
1986	Ride 'Em Peanuts 463	Closed	N/A	55.00	70-135
1986	Wet Paint 436	Closed	N/A	80.00	150

The Original Ron Lee Collection-1987 - R. Lee

1987	First & Main L110	Closed	N/A	368.00	850
1987	Happines Is L116	Closed	N/A	155.00	185
1987	Heartbroken Harry L101	Closed	N/A	63.00	125-225
1987	Lovable Luke L102	Closed	N/A	70.00	150
1987	Puppy Love L103	Closed	N/A	71.00	150
1987	Show of Shows L115	Closed	N/A	175.00	N/A
1987	Sugarland Express L109	Closed	N/A	342.00	650-895
1987	Would You Like To Ride? L104	Closed	N/A	246.00	350

The Original Ron Lee Collection-1988 - R. Lee

1988	Anchors-A-Way L120	Closed	N/A	195.00	250
1988	Boulder Bay L124	Closed	N/A	700.00	N/A
1988	Bozorina L118	Closed	N/A	95.00	120
1988	Cactus Pete L125	Closed	N/A	495.00	N/A
1988	Dinner for Two L119	Closed	N/A	140.00	N/A
1988	The Fifth Wheel L117	Closed	N/A	250.00	375
1988	Fore! L122	Closed	N/A	135.00	175
1988	New Ron Lee Carousel	Closed	N/A	7000.00	9500
1988	Pumpkuns Galore L121	Closed	N/A	135.00	160-245
1988	To The Rescue L127	Closed	N/A	130.00	160-550
1988	Together Again L126	Closed	N/A	130.00	210
1988	Tunnel of Love L123	Closed	N/A	490.00	600-800
1988	When You're Hot, You're Hot! L128	Closed	N/A	221.00	295

The Original Ron Lee Collection-1989 - R. Lee

1989	The Accountant L173	Closed	N/A	68.00	150-200
1989	The Baseball Player L189	Closed	N/A	72.00	150-200
1989	The Basketball Player L187	Closed	N/A	68.00	150-200
1989	Be Happy L198	Closed	N/A	160.00	195
1989	Be It Ever So Humble L111	Closed	N/A	900.00	950-1250
1989	The Beautician L183	Closed	N/A	68.00	150-200
1989	Beauty Is In The Eye Of L140	Closed	N/A	190.00	400-475
1989	Birdbrain L206	Closed	N/A	110.00	250

Collectors' Information Bureau   *Quotes have been rounded up to nearest dollar

YEAR ISSUE		EDITION LIMIT	YEAR RETD.	ISSUE PRICE	*QUOTE U.S.$
1989	The Bowler L191	Closed	N/A	68.00	150-200
1989	Butt-R-Fly L151	Closed	N/A	47.00	75
1989	Butterflies Are Free L204	Closed	N/A	225.00	250
1989	Candy Apple L155	Closed	N/A	47.00	75
1989	Candy Man L217	Closed	N/A	350.00	595
1989	Catch A Falling Star L148	Closed	N/A	57.00	75
1989	The Chef L178	Closed	N/A	65.00	150-200
1989	The Chiropractor L180	Closed	N/A	68.00	150-200
1989	Circus Little L143	Closed	N/A	990.00	1250
1989	Craps L212	Closed	N/A	530.00	N/A
1989	Dang It L200	Closed	N/A	47.00	N/A
1989	The Dentist L175	Closed	N/A	65.00	150-200
1989	The Doctor L170	Closed	N/A	65.00	150-200
1989	Eye Love You L136	Closed	N/A	68.00	150
1989	The Fireman L169	Closed	N/A	68.00	175
1989	The Fisherman L194	Closed	N/A	72.00	400
1989	The Football Player L186	Closed	N/A	65.00	150-200
1989	Get Well L131	Closed	N/A	79.00	N/A
1989	The Golfer L188	Closed	N/A	72.00	150-200
1989	The Greatest Little Shoe On Earth L210	Closed	N/A	165.00	200-300
1989	Happy Chanakah L162	Closed	N/A	106.00	N/A
1989	Hot Diggity Dog L201	Closed	N/A	47.00	50
1989	The Housewife L181	Closed	N/A	75.00	150-200
1989	Hughie Mungus L144	Closed	N/A	250.00	300-825
1989	I Ain't Got No Money L195	Closed	N/A	325.00	895
1989	I Just Called! L153	Closed	N/A	47.00	75
1989	I Pledge Allegiance L134	Closed	N/A	131.00	150-250
1989	I Should've When I Could've L196	Closed	N/A	325.00	895
1989	I-D-D-D-Do! L215	Closed	N/A	180.00	N/A
1989	If I Were A Rich Man L133	Closed	N/A	315.00	695
1989	If That's Your Drive How's Your Putts L164	Closed	N/A	260.00	N/A
1989	In Over My Head L135	Closed	N/A	95.00	250
1989	Jingles Hitchhiking L209	Closed	N/A	90.00	200
1989	Jingles Holding Balloon L208	Closed	N/A	90.00	200
1989	Jingles With Umbrella L207	Closed	N/A	90.00	175
1989	Just Carried Away L138	Closed	N/A	135.00	230
1989	Just Go! L156	Closed	N/A	47.00	75
1989	The Lawyer 171	Closed	N/A	68.00	150-200
1989	Maestro L132	Closed	N/A	173.00	200
1989	Marcelle L150	Closed	N/A	47.00	N/A
1989	The Mechanic L184	Closed	N/A	68.00	150-200
1989	Memories L197	Closed	N/A	325.00	N/A
1989	Merry Xmas L159	Closed	N/A	94.00	N/A
1989	My Affections L157	Closed	N/A	47.00	75
1989	My First Tree L161	Closed	N/A	92.00	125
1989	My Heart Beats For You L137	Closed	N/A	74.00	150
1989	My Last Chip L213	Closed	N/A	550.00	N/A
1989	My Money's OnThe Bull L142	Closed	N/A	187.00	480
1989	The New Self Portrait L218	Closed	N/A	800.00	2000-3000
1989	No Fishing L130	Closed	N/A	247.00	795
1989	Not A Ghost Of A Chance L145	Closed	N/A	195.00	500
1989	The Nurse L168	Closed	N/A	65.00	95
1989	O' Solo Mia L139	Closed	N/A	85.00	90-150
1989	The Optometrist L174	Closed	N/A	65.00	150-200
1989	Over 21 L214	Closed	N/A	550.00	N/A
1989	The Pharmacist L166	Closed	N/A	65.00	N/A
1989	The Photographer L172	Closed	N/A	68.00	150-200
1989	The Plumber L176	Closed	N/A	65.00	150-200
1989	The Policeman L165	Closed	N/A	68.00	150
1989	Rain Bugs Me L203	Closed	N/A	225.00	N/A
1989	The Real Estate Lady L185	Closed	N/A	70.00	250
1989	The Real Estate Man L177	Closed	N/A	65.00	150-200
1989	Rest Stop L149	Closed	N/A	47.00	75
1989	The Salesman L167	Closed	N/A	68.00	N/A
1989	Santa's Dilemma L160	Closed	N/A	97.00	250
1989	The Secretary L179	Closed	N/A	65.00	95
1989	The Serenade L202	Closed	N/A	47.00	N/A
1989	Sh-h-h-h! L146	Closed	N/A	210.00	450
1989	She Loves Me Not L205	Closed	N/A	225.00	250
1989	The Skier L193	Closed	N/A	75.00	150-200
1989	Slots Of Luck L211	Closed	N/A	90.00	300-375
1989	Snowdrifter L163	Closed	N/A	230.00	695
1989	Stormy Weathers L152	Closed	N/A	47.00	N/A
1989	Sunflower L154	Closed	N/A	47.00	75
1989	The Surfer L192	Closed	N/A	72.00	150-200
1989	Tee for Two L141	Closed	N/A	125.00	150
1989	The Tennis Player L190	Closed	N/A	72.00	150-200
1989	Today's Catch L147	Closed	N/A	230.00	350
1989	Two a.m. Blues L199	Closed	N/A	125.00	180-250
1989	The Veterinarian L182	Closed	N/A	72.00	150-200
1989	Wintertime Pals L158	Closed	N/A	90.00	N/A
1989	Wishful Thinking L114	Closed	N/A	230.00	2000-3000
1989	You Must Be Kidding L216	Closed	N/A	N/A	800

The Original Ron Lee Collection-1990 - R. Lee

1990	All Show No Go L238	1,500		285.00	795
1990	The Big Wheel L236	Closed	N/A	240.00	245
1990	Carousel Horse L219	Closed	N/A	150.00	N/A
1990	Carousel Horse L220	Closed	N/A	150.00	N/A
1990	Carousel Horse L221	Closed	N/A	150.00	N/A
1990	Carousel Horse L222	Closed	N/A	150.00	210
1990	Fill'er Up L248	Closed	N/A	280.00	300
1990	Flapper Riding Carousel L223	Closed	N/A	190.00	N/A
1990	Heart of My Heart L246	5,500	1995	55.00	55
1990	Heartbroken Hobo L233	Closed	N/A	116.00	195
1990	Henry 8-3/4 L260	Closed	N/A	37.00	50
1990	Horsin' Around L262	Closed	N/A	37.00	37-50
1990	I Love You L242	5,500	1995	55.00	55
1990	I.Q. Two L253	2,750	1995	33.00	50
1990	Jo-Jo Riding Carousel L226	Closed	N/A	190.00	N/A

YEAR ISSUE		EDITION LIMIT	YEAR RETD.	ISSUE PRICE	*QUOTE U.S.$
1990	Kiss! Kiss! L251	Closed	N/A	37.00	37
1990	L-O-V-E L245	5,500	1995	55.00	55
1990	Loving You L244	5,500	1996	55.00	55
1990	Me Too!! L231	Closed	1995	70.00	70-80
1990	My Heart's on for You L240	5,500	1995	55.00	55
1990	Na! Na! L252	Closed	N/A	33.00	50
1990	New Pinky Lying Down L228	8,500		42.00	42
1990	New Pinky Sitting L230	8,500		42.00	42
1990	New Pinky Standing L229	8,500		42.00	42
1990	New Pinky Upside Down L227	8,500		42.00	42
1990	Paddle L259	2,750	1995	33.00	50
1990	Par Three L232	2,750	1995	144.00	144
1990	Peaches Riding Carousel L224	Closed	N/A	190.00	N/A
1990	Pitch L261	2,750	1995	35.00	50
1990	Push and Pull L249	Closed	N/A	260.00	280
1990	Q.T. Pie L257	2,750	1995	37.00	50
1990	Rascal Riding Carousel L225	Closed	N/A	190.00	N/A
1990	Same To "U" L255	2,750	1995	37.00	50
1990	Scooter L234	Closed	1995	240.00	275
1990	Skiing My Way L239	2,500	1995	400.00	895
1990	Snowdrifter II L250	Closed	N/A	340.00	795-895
1990	Squirt L258	2,750	1995	37.00	50
1990	Stuck on Me L243	5,500	1995	55.00	55
1990	Swinging on a Star L241	5,500	1995	55.00	55
1990	Tandem Mania L235	Closed	N/A	360.00	360
1990	Uni-Cycle L237	Closed	N/A	240.00	245
1990	Watch Your Step L247	2,500	1996	78.00	78
1990	Yo Mama L256	2,750	1995	35.00	50
1990	Your Heaviness L254	2,750	1995	37.00	50

The Original Ron Lee Collection-1991 - R. Lee

1991	Ain't No Havana L315	500	1995	230.00	400
1991	Anywhere? L269	Closed	N/A	125.00	200
1991	Banjo Willie L293	1,750	1996	90.00	90
1991	Business is Business L266	Closed	1995	110.00	190
1991	Clarence Clarinet L289	1,750		42.00	50
1991	Cruising L265	Closed	N/A	170.00	170-175
1991	Droopy Drummer L290	1,750	1995	42.00	50
1991	Eight Ball-Corner Pocket L311	1,750		224.00	250
1991	Fall L282	1,500		120.00	140
1991	Geronimo L304	1,750		127.00	180
1991	Gilbert's Dilemma L270	Closed	N/A	90.00	125
1991	Give Me Liberty L313	Closed	N/A	155.00	200-250
1991	Happy Birthday Puppy Love L278	Closed	N/A	73.00	85
1991	Harley Horn L291	1,750	1995	42.00	50
1991	Hobi Daydreaming L299	1,750	1996	112.00	112
1991	Hook, Line and Sinker L303	1,750		100.00	100
1991	Hot Dawg! L316	500	1995	255.00	255
1991	I'm Singin' In The Rain L268	Closed	N/A	135.00	165
1991	IRS or Bust L285	1,500	1995	122.00	122
1991	Lit'l Snowdrifter L298	1,750	1996	70.00	150
1991	Makin Tracks L283	1,500	1995	142.00	142
1991	Marcelle I L271	2,250	1995	50.00	50
1991	Marcelle II L272	2,250	1995	50.00	100
1991	Marcelle III L273	2,250	1995	50.00	50
1991	Marcelle IV L274	2,250	1995	50.00	50
1991	New Darby Tipping Hat L310	1,250		57.00	57
1991	New Darby with Flower L307	1,250		57.00	57
1991	New Darby with Umbrella L308	1,250		57.00	57
1991	New Darby with Violin L309	1,250		57.00	57
1991	New Harpo L305	1,250		130.00	130
1991	New Toy Soldier L306	1,250	1995	115.00	115
1991	Our Nation's Pride L312	Closed	N/A	150.00	150
1991	Puppy Love Scootin' L275	Closed	N/A	73.00	85
1991	Puppy Love's Free Ride L276	Closed	N/A	73.00	100
1991	Puppy Love's Treat L277	Closed	N/A	73.00	100
1991	Refugee L267	1,750	1995	88.00	88
1991	Sand Trap L301	1,750		100.00	100
1991	Soap Suds Serenade L284	1,750	1996	85.00	85
1991	Spring L280	1,500		95.00	95
1991	Strike!!! L302	1,750		76.00	76
1991	Summer L281	1,500	N/A	95.00	125
1991	Surf's Up L300	1,750		80.00	80
1991	TA DA L294	Closed	N/A	220.00	200-295
1991	Tender-Lee L264	1,750	1995	96.00	96
1991	This Won't Hurt L296	1,750	1995	110.00	110
1991	Tootie Tuba L286	1,750	1995	42.00	50
1991	Trash Can Sam L295	1,750	1995	118.00	118
1991	Truly Trumpet L287	1,750	1995	42.00	50
1991	Trusty Trombone L288	1,750	1995	42.00	50
1991	Two For Fore L297	1,750	1996	120.00	120
1991	United We Stand L314	Closed	N/A	150.00	150
1991	The Visit L263	1,750	1995	100.00	100
1991	Winter L279	1,500		115.00	115

The Original Ron Lee Collection-1992 - R. Lee

1992	Baloony L350	2,500		26.00	27
1992	Beats Nothin' L357	1,500		145.00	145
1992	Beau Regards L342	2,500		26.00	27
1992	Big Wheel Kop RLC1005	1,750	1995	65.00	99
1992	Birdy The Hard Way L352	1,750		85.00	85
1992	Bo-Bo Balancing RLC1003	1,750	1995	75.00	75
1992	Break Point L335	2,500		26.00	27
1992	Brokenhearted Huey RLC1006	1,750	1995	65.00	65
1992	Buster Too PC100	1,500	1995	65.00	65
1992	Cannonball RLC1009	1,750	1995	95.00	125
1992	Clar-A-Bow L336	2,500		26.00	27
1992	Cyclin' Around L322	2,500		26.00	27
1992	Dreams L332	2,500		26.00	27
1992	Dudley's Dog Act RLC1010	1,750	1995	75.00	75
1992	Dunkin' L328	2,500		26.00	27

YEAR ISSUE		EDITION LIMIT	YEAR RETD.	ISSUE PRICE	* QUOTE U.S.$
1992	Fish in Pail L358	1,500	1996	130.00	235
1992	Flyin' High L340	2,500		26.00	27
1992	Forget Me Not L341	2,500		26.00	27
1992	Gassing Up RLC1004	1,750	1995	70.00	70
1992	Go Man Go L344	2,500		26.00	27
1992	Handy Standy L321	2,500		26.00	27
1992	Heel's Up L329	2,500		26.00	27
1992	Hi-Five L339	2,500		26.00	27
1992	Hippolong Cassidy L320	Closed	N/A	166.00	140
1992	Howdy! L325	2,500		26.00	27
1992	Jo-Jo Juggling RLC1002	1,750	1995	70.00	70
1992	Juggles L347	2,500		26.00	27
1992	Little Pard L349	2,500		26.00	27
1992	Lolly L326	2,500		26.00	27
1992	Love Ya' Baby L355	1,250		190.00	190
1992	Miles PC105	1,500	1995	65.00	65
1992	My Pal L334	2,500		26.00	27
1992	My Portrait L354	Closed	N/A	315.00	595
1992	Myak Kyak L337	2,500		26.00	27
1992	On My Way L348	2,500		26.00	27
1992	Penny Saver L333	2,500		26.00	27
1992	Popcorn & Cotton Candy RLC1001	1,750	1995	70.00	70
1992	Scrub-A- Dub-Dub L319	Closed	N/A	185.00	195
1992	Seven's Up L356	1,250		165.00	165
1992	Shake Jake L324	2,500		26.00	27
1992	Ship Ahoy L345	2,500		26.00	27
1992	Shufflin' L343	2,500		26.00	27
1992	Snowdrifter Blowin' In Wind L317	1,750	1996	77.50	78
1992	Snowdrifter's Special Delivery L318	1,750	1996	136.00	136
1992	Steamer L338	2,500		26.00	27
1992	Stop Cop L331	2,500		26.00	27
1992	Strike Out L323	2,500		26.00	27
1992	Struttin' L346	2,500		26.00	27
1992	Sure-Footed Freddie RLC1007	1,750	1995	80.00	80
1992	To-Tee L327	2,500		26.00	27
1992	Topper PC110	1,500	1995	65.00	65
1992	Twirp Chirp L330	2,500		26.00	27
1992	Vincent Van Clown L353	Closed	N/A	160.00	160
1992	Walking A Fine Line RMB7000	1,750	1995	65.00	65
1992	Webb-ster PC115	1,500	1995	65.00	65
1992	Wrong Hole Clown L351	1,750		125.00	125

The Original Ron Lee Collection-1993 - R. Lee

1993	Andy Jackson L364	950	1995	87.00	115
1993	Anywhere Warm L398	950	1995	90.00	90
1993	Bellboy L390	950	1995	80.00	80
1993	Blinky Lying Down L384	1,200		45.00	45
1993	Blinky Sitting L383	1,200		45.00	45
1993	Blinky Standing L382	1,200		45.00	45
1993	Blinky Upside Down L385	1,200		45.00	45
1993	Bo-Bo L365	950	1995	95.00	95
1993	Britches L377	750		205.00	205
1993	Bumper Fun L403	750		330.00	330
1993	Buster L368	950	1995	87.00	115
1993	Charkles L381	750	1995	220.00	220
1993	Chattanooga Choo-Choo L374	750		420.00	420
1993	Dave Bomber L360	950	1995	90.00	90
1993	Happy Trails L369	950	1995	90.00	90
1993	Honk Honk L370	950	1995	90.00	90
1993	Hot Buns L376	750		175.00	175
1993	Lollipop L363	950	1995	87.00	120
1993	Merry Go Clown L405	750		375.00	375
1993	Moto Kris L380	750		255.00	255
1993	North Pole L396	950	1995	75.00	75
1993	Piggy Backin' L379	750		205.00	205
1993	Pretzels L372	750		195.00	195
1993	Sailin' L366	950	1995	95.00	95
1993	Scrubs L361	950	1995	87.00	115
1993	Sho-Sho L373	750		115.00	115
1993	Shriner Cop L404	750		175.00	175
1993	Skittles L367	950	1995	95.00	95
1993	Snoozin' L399	950		90.00	90
1993	Soft Shoe L400	750		275.00	275
1993	Sole-Full L375	750		250.00	250
1993	Special Occasion L402	750		280.00	280
1993	Taxi L378	750		470.00	470
1993	Tinker And Toy L359	950	1995	95.00	95
1993	Wagone Hes L371	750		210.00	210
1993	Wanderer L401	750		255.00	255
1993	Yo-Yo L362	950	1995	87.00	115

The Original Ron Lee Collection-1995 - R. Lee

1995	Bar Mitzvah L463	950		270.00	270
1995	Bat Mitzvah L462	950		270.00	270
1995	Batter Up L465	500		270.00	270
1995	Cimba's Last Stand L466	950		165.00	165
1995	Fillet of Sole L460	750		180.00	180
1995	Fore! Anyone! L464	500		275.00	275
1995	Santa's Other Sleigh L461	750		195.00	195

The Original Ron Lee Collection-1996 - R. Lee

1996	The Bass Drum L478	950		47.00	47
1996	The Clarinet L476	950		47.00	47
1996	The Cymbols L477	950		47.00	47
1996	Frankie L480	950		95.00	95
1996	The Grand Bandwagon L470	750		1100.00	1100
1996	Johnnie L481	950		95.00	95
1996	Pastime Pals L469	950		135.00	135
1996	Portrait Pals L468	950		135.00	135
1996	Sleepytime Pals L467	950		115.00	115
1996	The Snare Drum L472	950		47.00	47

FIGURINES/COTTAGES

YEAR ISSUE	EDITION LIMIT	YEAR RETD.	ISSUE PRICE	*QUOTE U.S.$
1996 The Sousaphone L471	950		47.00	47
1996 Strike It Rich L479	950		110.00	110
1996 The Trombone L475	950		47.00	47
1996 The Trumpet L474	950		47.00	47
1996 The Tuba L473	950		47.00	47
The Popeye Collection - R. Lee				
1992 Liberty P001	1,750	1995	184.00	184
1992 Men!!! P002	1,750	1995	230.00	230
1992 Oh Popeye P005	1,750	1995	230.00	230
1992 Par Excellence P006	1,750	1995	220.00	220
1992 Strong to The Finish P003	1,750	1995	95.00	95
1992 That's My Boy P004	1,750	1995	145.00	145
Premier Dealer Collection - R. Lee				
1992 Dream On PD002	Closed	N/A	125.00	145
1992 Framed Again PD001	Closed	N/A	110.00	125
1993 Jake-A-Juggling Balls PD008	500		85.00	90
1993 Jake-A-Juggling Clubs PD007	500		85.00	90
1993 Jake-A-Juggling Cylinder PD006	500		85.00	90
1994 Joe's Feline Friend PD009	500		105.00	105
1994 Just Big Enough PD010	500		115.00	115
1992 Moonlighting PD004	Closed	N/A	125.00	125
1992 Nest to Nothing PD003	Closed	N/A	110.00	125
1994 Off The Toe PD011	500		120.00	120
1993 Pockets PD005	500		175.00	175
1994 Storm Warning PD012	500		115.00	115
1994 Trading Places PD013	500		190.00	190
Rocky & Bullwinkle And Friends Collection - R. Lee				
1992 Dudley Do-Right RB610	1,750	1995	175.00	175
1992 KA-BOOM! RB620	1,750	1995	175.00	175
1992 My Hero RB615	1,750	1995	275.00	330
1992 Rocky & Bullwinkle RB600	1,750	1995	120.00	140
1992 The Swami RB605	1,750	1995	175.00	175
The Ron Lee Disney Collection Exclusives - R. Lee				
1993 Aladdin MM560	500	1996	550.00	550
1996 Alice In Wonderland MM840	750		295.00	295
1995 Autopia MM770	750		220.00	220
1992 Bambi MM330	2,750		195.00	195
1990 The Bandleader MM100	Closed	N/A	75.00	75
1992 Beauty & The Beast (shadow box) DIS100	500		1650.00	1650
1994 Beauty & The Beast MM610	800	1996	170.00	170
1992 Captain Hook MM320	2,750		175.00	175
1995 The Carousel MM730	750		125.00	125
1992 Christmas '92 MM420	1,500		145.00	145
1993 Cinderella's Slipper MM510	1,750	1995	115.00	150-165
1993 Darkwing Duck MM470	1,750		105.00	105
1991 Decorating Donald MM210	2,750		60.00	60
1992 The Dinosaurs MM370	2,750		195.00	195
1991 Dopey MM120	2,750	1995	80.00	135
1996 Dumbo & The Ringmaster MM860	750		195.00	195
1990 Dumbo MM600	2,750		110.00	110
1995 Fantasyland MM780	750		285.00	285
1992 Finishing Touch MM440	1,500		85.00	85
1993 Flying With Dumbo MM530	1,000		330.00	330
1995 Frontierland MM740	750		160.00	160
1992 Genie MM450	2,750		110.00	110
1991 Goofy MM110	2,750		115.00	115
1991 Goofy's Gift MM230	2,750		70.00	70
1994 Grumpy Playing Organ MM590	800	1995	150.00	200
1995 Home Improvements MM820	750		170.00	170
1996 Hunchback of Notre Dame MM910	950		185.00	185
1991 Jiminy's List MM250	2,750		60.00	60
1991 Lady and the Tramp MM280	1,500	1995	295.00	295
1993 Letters to Santa MM550	1,500		170.00	170
1991 Lion Around MM270	2,750		140.00	140
1994 The Lion King MM640	1,750	1996	170.00	250
1992 Lit'l Sorcerer MM340	2,750		57.00	57
1992 Little Mermaid MM310	2,750		230.00	230
1992 Lumiere & Cogsworth MM350	2,750		145.00	145
1995 Main Street MM710	750		120.00	120
1995 The Matterhorn MM750	750		240.00	240
1991 Mickey & Minnie at the Piano MM180	2,750		195.00	195
1996 Mickey & The Caddie MM890	1,250		195.00	195
1991 Mickey's Adventure MM150	2,750		195.00	195
1990 Mickey's Christmas MM400	2,750		95.00	95
1991 Mickey's Delivery MM220	2,750		70.00	70
1994 Mickey, Brave Little Tailor MM570	1,750	1995	72.00	100
1991 Minnie Mouse MM170	2,750		80.00	80
1994 Minnie, Brave Little Tailor MM580	1,750	1995	72.00	72
1992 Mrs. Potts & Chip MM360	2,750		125.00	125
1991 Mt. Mickey MM900	2,750		175.00	175
1994 New Tinkerbell MM680	300	1995	99.00	99
1994 Official Conscience MM620	300	1995	65.00	65
1995 The People Mover MM760	750		190.00	190
1990 Pinocchio MM500	2,750	1995	85.00	85
1991 Pluto's Treat MM240	2,750		60.00	60
1994 Pongo & Pups MM670	800	1995	124.00	124
1995 Pooh & The Cookie Jar MM830	750		190.00	190
1996 Pooh & The Honey Pot MM870	1,250		120.00	120
1996 Pooh In The Honey Tree MM850	750		300.00	300
1996 Pooh, Eeyore & Piglet MM880	1,250		150.00	150
1995 Reflections MM810	750	1996	99.00	99
1993 Santa's Workshop MM540	1,500		170.00	170
1994 Snow White & Doc MM630	800		135.00	135
1990 Snow White & Grumpy MM800	2,750		140.00	140
1993 Snow White & The Seven Dwarfs (shadow box) DIS200	250		1800.00	1800
1990 The Sorcerer MM200	Closed	N/A	85.00	120
1992 Sorcerer's Apprentice MM290	2,750		125.00	125
1990 Steamboat Willie MM300	2,750	1995	95.00	95
1992 Stocking Stuffer MM410	1,500	1996	63.00	63
1991 The Tea Cup Ride (Disneyland Exclusive) MM260	1,250	1996	225.00	225
1994 Tigger on Rabbit MM660	800	1995	110.00	110
1993 Tinker Bell MM490	1,750	1995	85.00	85
1995 The Topiary MM720	750		145.00	145
1996 Toy Story MM930	950		197.00	197
1991 Tugboat Mickey MM160	2,750		180.00	180
1996 TV Buddies MM920	1,250		199.00	199
1991 Two Gun Mickey MM140	2,750		115.00	115
1990 Uncle Scrooge MM700	2,750		110.00	110
1993 Winnie The Pooh MM480	1,750	1996	125.00	150-200
1992 Winnie The Pooh & Tigger MM390	2,750	1995	105.00	105
1992 Wish Upon A Star MM430	1,500		80.00	80
1991 The Witch MM130	2,750		115.00	115
1992 Workin' Out MM380	2,750		95.00	95
The Ron Lee Disneyana Collection Exclusives - R. Lee				
1992 Big Thunder Mountain MM460	250	1995	1650.00	2200-2800
1993 Mickey's Dream MM520	250	1993	400.00	650-800
1994 MM/MN/Goofy Limo MM650	500	1994	500.00	375-500
1995 Ear Force One MM790	500	1995	600.00	600
1995 Engine Number One MM690	500	1995	650.00	965
1996 Heigh-ho MM940	500		500.00	500
The Ron Lee Emmett Kelly, Sr. Collection - R. Lee				
1991 Emmett Kelly, Sr. Sign E208	Closed	N/A	110.00	110
1991 God Bless America EK206	Closed	N/A	130.00	250
1991 Help Yourself EK202	Closed	N/A	145.00	350
1991 Love at First Sight EK204	Closed	N/A	197.00	197
1991 My Protege EK207	Closed	N/A	160.00	165
1991 Spike's Uninvited Guest EK203	Closed	N/A	165.00	295
1991 That-A-Way EK201	Closed	N/A	125.00	135
1991 Time for a Change EK205	Closed	N/A	190.00	305
The Ron Lee Gallery Collection - R. Lee				
1996 The Juggler KL100	500		350.00	350
1996 Toad Bo Joe KL300	500		195.00	195
The Ron Lee Looney Tunes Collection - R. Lee				
1991 1940 Bugs Bunny LT165	Closed	N/A	85.00	100
1991 Bugs Bunny LT150	Closed	N/A	123.00	135
1991 Daffy Duck LT140	Closed	N/A	80.00	80-85
1991 Elmer Fudd LT125	Closed	N/A	87.00	87-90
1991 Foghorn Leghorn & Henry Hawk LT160	Closed	N/A	115.00	115
1991 Marvin the Martian LT170	Closed	N/A	75.00	75
1991 Michigan J. Frog LT110	Closed	N/A	115.00	115
1991 Mt. Yosemite LT180	850		160.00	160-300
1991 Pepe LePew & Penelope LT145	Closed	N/A	115.00	115
1991 Porky Pig LT115	Closed	N/A	97.00	100
1991 Sylvester & Tweety LT135	Closed	N/A	110.00	110-115
1991 Tasmanian Devil LT120	Closed	N/A	105.00	105
1991 Tweety LT155	Closed	N/A	110.00	110-115
1991 Western Daffy Duck LT105	Closed	N/A	87.00	90
1991 Wile E. Coyote & Roadrunner LT175	Closed	N/A	165.00	175
1991 Yosemite Sam LT130	Closed	N/A	110.00	110
The Ron Lee Looney Tunes Collection - R. Lee				
1992 Beep Beep LT220	1,500		115.00	115
1992 Ditty Up LT200	2,750		110.00	110
1992 For Better or Worse LT190	1,500		285.00	285
1992 Leopold & Giovanni LT205	1,500		225.00	225
1992 No Pain No Gain LT210	950		270.00	270
1992 Rackin' Frackin' Varmint LT225	950		260.00	260
1992 Speedy Gonzales LT185	2,750		73.00	73
1992 Van Duck LT230	950		335.00	335
1992 The Virtuosos LT235	950		350.00	350
1992 What The ...? LT195	1,500		240.00	240
1992 What's up Doc? LT215	950		270.00	270
The Ron Lee Looney Tunes Collection - R. Lee				
1992 Bugs Bunny w/ Horse LT245	1,500		105.00	105
1992 Cowboy Bugs LT290	1,500		70.00	70
1992 Daffy Duck w/ Horse LT275	1,500		105.00	105
1992 Elmer Fudd w/ Horse LT270	1,500		105.00	105
1992 Pepe Le Pew w/ Horse LT285	1,500		105.00	105
1992 Porky Pig w/ Horse LT260	1,500		105.00	105
1992 Sylvester w/ Horse LT250	1,500		105.00	105
1992 Tasmanian Devil w/ Horse LT255	1,500		105.00	105
1992 Wile E. Coyote w/ Horse LT280	1,500		105.00	105
1992 Yosemite Sam w/ Horse LT265	1,500		105.00	105
The Ron Lee Looney Tunes Collection - R. Lee				
1993 Bugs LT330	1,200		79.00	79
1993 A Christmas Carrot LT320	1,200		175.00	175
1993 The Essence of Love LT310	1,200		145.00	145
1993 Martian's Best Friend LT305	1,200		140.00	140
1993 Me Deliver LT295	1,200		110.00	110
1993 Puttin' on the Glitz LT325	1,200		79.00	79
1993 The Rookie LT315	1,200		75.00	75
1993 Yo-Ho-Ho- LT300	1,200		105.00	105
The Ron Lee Looney Tunes Collection - R. Lee				
1994 Bugs LT330	1,200		79.00	79
1994 A Carrot a Day LT350	1,200		85.00	85
1994 Guilty LT345	1,200		80.00	80
1994 Ma Cherie LT340	1,200		185.00	185
1994 No H20 LT355	1,200		160.00	160
1994 Puttin' on the Glitz LT325	1,200		79.00	79
1994 Smashing LT335	1,200		80.00	80
1994 Taz On Ice LT360	1,200		115.00	115
The Ron Lee Looney Tunes Collection - R. Lee				
1994 Bugs Pharoah LT370	500	1996	130.00	130
1994 Cleopatra's Barge LT400	500	1996	550.00	550
1994 Cruising Down the Nile LT385	500	1996	295.00	295
1994 King Bugs and Friends LT395	500	1996	480.00	480
1994 Ramases & Son LT380	500	1996	230.00	230
1994 Tweety Pharoah LT365	500	1996	110.00	110
1994 Warrior Taz LT375	500	1996	140.00	140
1994 Yosemite's Chariot LT390	500	1996	310.00	310
The Ron Lee Looney Tunes Collection - R. Lee				
1995 The Baron LT475	750		235.00	235
1995 Daffy Scuba Diving LT470	750		170.00	170
1995 Drive..Drive!! Putt..Putt!! LT450	750		120.00	120
1995 The Great Chase LT485	750		385.00	385
1995 Highway My Way LT460	750		280.00	280
1995 The Hustler LT465	750		397.00	397
1995 Ice Dancing LT440	750		180.00	180
1995 King Pin LT445	750		165.00	165
1995 Slam Dunk LT455	750		190.00	190
1995 Speedy Tweety LT480	750		225.00	225
The Ron Lee Looney Tunes Sports Collection - R. Lee				
1996 The Baron LT475	750		235.00	235
1996 The Chase LT485	750		385.00	385
1996 Daffy Scuba Diving LT470	750		170.00	170
1996 The Hustler LT465	750		397.00	397
1996 Ice Dancing LT440	750		180.00	180
1996 King Pin LT445	750		165.00	165
1996 Slam Dunk LT455	750		190.00	190
1996 Speedy Tweety LT480	750		225.00	225
The Ron Lee Looney Tunes Western Collection - R. Lee				
1995 Acme Junction LT435	500		290.00	290
1995 Bwanding Iron LT420	500		210.00	210
1995 Heap Big Chief LT415	500		230.00	230
1995 Lit'l Trooper LT405	500		157.00	157
1995 Roadrunner Express LT425	500		240.00	240
1995 Saturday Serenade LT430	500		255.00	255
1995 Whoa!! LT410	500		215.00	215
The Ron Lee Warner Bros. Collection - R. Lee				
1995 Animaniacs WBA100	750		170.00	170
1996 Bugs At The Door WB007	500		98.00	98
1993 Courtly Gent WB003	1,000		102.00	102
1992 Dickens' Christmas WB400	850		198.00	198
1993 Duck Dodgers WB005	1,000		300.00	300
1993 Gridiron Glory WB002	1,000		102.00	102
1993 Hair-Raising Hare WB006	1,000		300.00	300
1993 Hare Under Par WB001	1,000		102.00	102
1993 Home Plate Heroes WB004	1,000		102.00	102
1991 The Maltese Falcon WB100	Closed	N/A	175.00	175
1996 Marvin and The Maggott WB008	750		140.00	140
1995 Pinky And The Brain WB105	750		170.00	170
1991 Robin Hood Bugs WB200	1,000		190.00	190
1996 Speedy Playing Soccer WB009	750		135.00	135
1996 Spokeshphibian WB500	750		205.00	205
1992 Yankee Doodle Bugs WB300	850		195.00	195
Shriner Clowns - R. Lee				
1994 Bubbles L437	1,750		120.00	120
1994 Helping Hand L436	1,750		145.00	145
Sports & Professionals - R. Lee				
1994 The Baseball Player L448	2,500		77.00	77
1994 The Basketball Player L450	2,500		74.00	74
1994 The Chef L441	2,500		74.00	74
1994 The Dentist L446	2,500		70.00	70
1994 The Doctor L439	2,500		70.00	70
1994 The Fireman L444	2,500		90.00	90
1994 The Fisherman L452	2,500		77.00	77
1994 The Football Player L449	2,500		74.00	74
1994 The Golfer L447	2,500		77.00	77
1994 The Hockey Player L454	2,500		80.00	80
1994 The Lawyer L445	2,500		70.00	70
1994 The Nurse L443	2,500		74.00	74
1994 The Pilot L440	2,500		74.00	74
1994 The Policeman L442	2,500		77.00	77
1994 The Skier L453	2,500		77.00	77
1994 The Teacher L438	2,500		70.00	70
1994 The Tennis Player L451	2,500		74.00	74
Superman I - R. Lee				
1993 Help Is On The Way SP100	750	1995	280.00	280
1993 Meteor Moment SP115	750	1995	314.00	314
1993 Metropolis SP110	750	1995	320.00	320
1993 Proudly We Wave SP105	750	1995	185.00	185
Superman II - R. Lee				
1994 Good and Evil SP135	750	1995	190.00	190
1994 More Powerful SP130	750	1995	420.00	420
1994 Quick Change SP120	750	1995	125.00	125
1994 To The Rescue SP125	750	1995	195.00	195

Year Issue	Description	Edition Limit	Year Retrd.	Issue Price	Quote U.S.$
	The Wizard of Oz Collection - R. Lee				
1992	The Cowardly Lion WZ425	750	1996	620.00	620
1992	Kansas WZ400	750	1996	550.00	550
1992	The Munchkins WZ405	750	1996	620.00	620
1992	The Ruby Slippers WZ410	750	1996	620.00	620
1992	The Scarecrow WZ415	750	1996	510.00	510
1992	The Tin Man WZ420	750	1996	530.00	530
	Wizard of Oz II - R. Lee				
1994	The Cowardly Lion WZ445	500		130.00	130
1994	Dorothy WZ430	500		150.00	150
1994	Glinda WZ455	500		225.00	225
1994	The Scarecrow WZ435	500		130.00	130
1994	The Tinman WZ440	500		110.00	110
1994	The Wicked Witch WZ450	500		125.00	125
	The Woody Woodpecker And Friends Collection - R. Lee				
1992	1940 Woody Woodpecker WL020	1,750	1996	73.00	75
1992	Andy and Miranda Panda WL025	1,750	1996	140.00	140
1992	Birdy for Woody WL005	1,750	1996	117.00	125
1992	Pals WL030	1,750	1996	179.00	179
1992	Peck of My Heart WL010	1,750	1996	370.00	495
1992	Woody Woodpecker WL015	1,750	1996	73.00	73

Royal Doulton

Royal Doulton International Collectors' Club - Various

Year Issue	Description	Edition Limit	Year Retrd.	Issue Price	Quote U.S.$
1980	John Doulton Jug (8 O'Clock) D6656 - E. Griffiths	Yr.Iss.	1981	70.00	125
1981	Sleepy Darling Figure HN2953 - P. Parsons	Yr.Iss.	1982	100.00	195
1982	Dog of Fo-Flambe - N/A	Yr.Iss.	1983	50.00	175
1982	Prized Possessions Figure HN2942 - R. Tabbenor	Yr.Iss.	1983	125.00	450
1983	Loving Cup - N/A	Yr.Iss.	1984	75.00	150
1983	Springtime HN3033 - A. Hughes	Yr.Iss.	1984	125.00	325
1984	Sir Henry Doulton Jug D6703 - E. Griffiths	Yr.Iss.	1985	50.00	125
1984	Pride & Joy Figure HN2945 - R. Tabbenor	Yr.Iss.	1985	125.00	295
1985	Top of the Hill HN2126 - P. Gee	Yr.Iss.	1986	35.00	100
1985	Wintertime Figure HN3060 - A. Hughes	Yr.Iss.	1986	125.00	225
1986	Albert Sagger Toby Jug - W. Harper	Yr.Iss.	1987	35.00	85
1986	Auctioneer Figure HN2988 - R. Tabbenor	Yr.Iss.	1987	150.00	300-350
1987	Collector Bunnykins DB54 - D. Lyttleton	Yr.Iss.	1988	40.00	450-650
1987	Summertime Figurine HN3137 - P. Parsons	Yr.Iss.	1988	140.00	150
1988	Top of the Hill Miniature Figurine HN2126 - P. Gee	Yr.Iss.	1989	95.00	125
1988	Beefeater Tiny Jug - R. Tabbenor	Yr.Iss.	1989	25.00	125
1988	Old Salt Tea Pot - N/A	Yr.Iss.	1989	135.00	300
1989	Geisha Flambe Figure HN3229	Yr.Iss.	1990	195.00	195
1989	Flower Sellers Children Plate - N/A	Yr.Iss.	1990	65.00	70-100
1990	Autumntime Figure HN3231 - P. Parsons	Yr.Iss.	1991	190.00	195
1990	Jester Mini Figure HN3335 - C.J. Noke	Yr.Iss.	1991	115.00	125
1990	Old King Cole Tiny Jug - H. Fenton	Yr.Iss.	1991	35.00	125
1991	Bunny's Bedtime Figure HN3370 - N. Pedley	9,500	1992	195.00	225
1991	Charles Dickens Jug D6901 - W. Harper	Yr.Iss.	1992	100.00	125
1991	L'Ambiteuse Figure (Tissot Lady) HN3359 - V. Annand	5,000	1992	295.00	385
1991	Christopher Columbus Jug D6911 - S. Taylor	Yr.Iss.	1992	95.00	125
1992	Discovery Figure HN3428 - A. Munslow	Yr.Iss.	1993	160.00	100
1992	King Edward Jug D6923 - W. Harper	Yr.Iss.	1993	250.00	260
1992	Master Potter Bunnykins DB131 - W. Platt	Yr.Iss.	1993	50.00	85
1992	Eliza Farren Prestige Figure HN3442 - N/A	Yr.Iss.	1993	335.00	250-325
1993	Barbara Figure - N/A	Yr.Iss.	1994	285.00	350-450
1993	Lord Mountbatten L/S Jug - S. Taylor	5,000	1994	225.00	225
1993	Punch & Judy Double Sided Jug - S. Taylor	2,500	1994	400.00	465
1993	Flambe Dragon HN3552 - N/A	Retrd.	1994	260.00	260
1994	Diane HN3604 - N/A	Retrd.	1995	250.00	250
1995	Le Bal HN3702 - N/A	Retrd.	1996	350.00	350
1995	George Tinworth Jug, sm. D7000 - W. Harper	Retrd.	1996	99.00	99
1995	Partners in Collecting Bunnykins DB151	Retrd.	1996	45.00	45
1996	Special Delivery Plate - N/A	Retrd.	1996	45.00	45
1996	Welcome - N/A	Retrd.	1996	80.00	80
1996	Pamela HN3756 - T. Potts	Yr.Iss.		275.00	275
1996	Mr. Pickwick Jug, sm. D7025 - M. Alcock	Yr.Iss.		138.00	138

Age of Innocence - N. Pedley

Year Issue	Description	Edition Limit	Year Retrd.	Issue Price	Quote U.S.$
1991	Feeding Time HN3373	9,500	1994	245.00	390
1992	First Outing HN3377	9,500	1994	275.00	390
1991	Making Friends HN3372	9,500	1994	270.00	390
1991	Puppy Love HN3371	9,500	1994	270.00	390

Beatrix Potter Figures - Various

Year Issue	Description	Edition Limit	Year Retrd.	Issue Price	Quote U.S.$
1967	Amiable Guinea Pig P2061 - A. Hallam	Retrd.	1983	29.95	395

Year Issue	Description	Edition Limit	Year Retrd.	Issue Price	Quote U.S.$
1992	And This Pig Had None P3319 - M. Alcock	Open		29.95	33
1963	Anna Maria P1851 - A. Hallam	Retrd.	1983	29.95	395
1971	Appley Dapply P2333 - A. Hallam	Open		29.95	33
1970	Aunt Pettitoes P2276 - A. Hallam	Retrd.	1993	29.95	75-110
1989	Babbity Bumble P2971 - W. Platt	Retrd.	1993	29.95	85
1992	Benjamin Ate a Lettuce Leaf P3317 - M. Alcock	Open		29.95	33
1948	Benjamin Bunny P1105 - A. Gredington	Open		29.95	33
1983	Benjamin Bunny Sat on a Bank P2803 - D. Lyttleton	Open		29.95	33
1975	Benjamin Bunny with Peter Rabbit P2509 - A. Musiankowski	Retrd.	1995	39.95	75
1995	Benjamin Bunny-large size P3403 - M. Alcock	Open		65.00	73
1991	Benjamin Wakes Up P3234 - A. Hughes-Lubeck	Open		29.95	33
1965	Cecily Parsley P1941 - A. Gredington	Retrd.	1993	29.95	85-110
1979	Chippy Hackee P2627 - D. Lyttleton	Retrd.	1993	29.95	50
1991	Christmas Stocking P3257 - M. Alcock	Retrd.	1994	65.00	65
1985	Cottontail at Lunchtime P2878 - D. Lyttleton	Retrd.	1996	29.95	33
1970	Cousin Ribby P2284 - A. Hallam	Retrd.	1993	29.95	45-65
1982	Diggory Diggory Delvet P2713 - D. Lyttleton	Open		29.95	33
1955	Dutchess P1355 - G. Orwell	Retrd.	1967	29.95	200
1995	F.W. Gent-large size P3450 - M. Alcock	Open		65.00	73
1977	Fierce Bad Rabbit P2586 - D. Lyttleton	Open		29.95	33
1954	Flopsy Mopsy and Cottontail P1274 - A. Gredington	Open		29.95	33
1990	Foxy Reading Country News P3219 - A. Hughes-Lubeck	Open		49.95	55
1954	Foxy Whiskered Gentleman P1277 - A. Gredington	Open		29.95	33
1990	Gentleman Mouse Made a Bow P3200 - T. Chawner	Retrd.	1996	29.95	33
1976	Ginger P2559 - D. Lyttleton	Retrd.	1982	29.95	495
1986	Goody and Timmy Tiptoes P2957 - D. Lyttleton	Retrd.	1996	49.95	75
1961	Goody Tiptoes P1675 - A. Gredington	Open		29.95	33
1951	Hunca Munca P1198 - A. Gredington	Open		29.95	33
1992	Hunca Munca Spills the Beads P3288 - M. Alcock	Retrd.	1996	29.95	33
1977	Hunca Munca Sweeping P2584 - D. Lyttleton	Open		29.95	33
1990	Jemema Puddleduck-Foxy Whiskered Gentleman P3193 - T. Chawner	Open		55.00	55
1983	Jemima Puddleduck Made a Feather Nest-P2823 - D. Lyttleton	Open		29.95	33
1948	Jemima Puddleduck P1092 - A. Gredington	Open		29.95	33
1993	Jemima Puddleduck-Large size P3373 - M. Alcock	Open		49.95	73
1988	Jeremy Fisher Digging P3090 - T. Chawner	Retrd.	1994	50.00	200
1950	Jeremy Fisher P1157 - A. Gredington	Open		29.95	33
1995	Jeremy Fisher-large size P3372 - M. Alcock	Open		65.00	73
1990	John Joiner P2965 - G. Tongue	Open		29.95	33
1954	Johnny Townmouse P1276 - A. Gredington	Retrd.	1993	29.95	45-55
1988	Johnny Townmouse with Bag P3094 - T. Chawner	Retrd.	1994	50.00	200
1990	Lady Mouse Made a Curtsy P3220 - A. Hughes-Lubeck	Open		29.95	33
1950	Lady Mouse P1183 - A. Gredington	Open		29.95	33
1977	Little Black Rabbit P2585 - D. Lyttleton	Open		29.95	33
1987	Little Pig Robinson Spying P3031 - T. Chawner	Retrd.	1993	29.95	150-175
1991	Miss Dormouse P3251 - M. Alcock	Retrd.	1995	29.95	65
1978	Miss Moppet P1275 - A. Gredington	Open		32.50	33
1990	Mittens & Moppet P3197 - T. Chawner	Retrd.	1994	50.00	75
1989	Mother Ladybird P2966 - W. Platt	Retrd.	1993	29.95	33
1973	Mr. Alderman Ptolemy P2424 - G. Tongue	Open		29.95	33
1965	Mr. Benjamin Bunny P1940 - A. Gredington	Open		29.95	33
1979	Mr. Drake Puddleduck P2628 - D. Lyttleton	Open		29.95	33
1974	Mr. Jackson P2453 - A. Hallam	Open		29.95	33
1995	Mr. McGregor P3506 - M. Alcock	Open		42.50	43
1988	Mr. Tod P3091 - T. Chawner	Retrd.	1993	29.95	95
1965	Mrs. Flopsy Bunny P1942 - A. Gredington	Open		29.95	33
1992	Mrs. Rabbit Cooking P3278 - M. Alcock	Open		29.95	33
1951	Mrs. Rabbit P1200 - A. Gredington	Open		29.95	33
1976	Mrs. Rabbit with Bunnies P2543 - D. Lyttleton	Open		29.95	33
1995	Mrs. Rabbit-large size P3398 - M. Alcock	Open		65.00	73
1951	Mrs. Ribby P1199 - A. Gredington	Open		29.95	33
1948	Mrs. Tittlemouse P1103 - A. Gredington	Retrd.	1993	29.95	95
1992	No More Twist P3325 - M. Alcock	Open		29.95	33
1986	Old Mr. Bouncer P2956	Retrd.	1995	29.95	65
1963	Old Mr. Brown P1796 - A. Hallam	Open		29.95	33
1983	Old Mr. Pricklepin P2767 - D. Lyttleton	Retrd.	1982	29.95	85

Year Issue	Description	Edition Limit	Year Retrd.	Issue Price	Quote U.S.$
1959	Old Woman Who Lived in a Shoe P1545 - C. Melbourne	Open		29.95	33
1983	Old Woman Who Lived in a Shoe, Knitting P2804 - D. Lyttleton	Open		29.95	33
1991	Peter & The Red Handkerchief P3242 - M. Alcock	Open		39.95	43
1995	Peter in Bed P3473 - M. Alcock	Open		39.95	43
1989	Peter Rabbit in the Gooseberry Net P3157 - D. Lyttleton	Retrd.	1995	39.95	50
1948	Peter Rabbit P1098 - A. Gredington	Open		29.95	33
1993	Peter Rabbit-large size P3356 - M. Alcock	Open		65.00	73
1996	Peter with Daffodils P3597 - A. Hughes-Lubeck	Open		42.50	43
1996	Peter with Postbag P3591 - A. Hughes-Lubeck	Open		42.50	43
1996	Peter with Red Pocket Handkerchief, lg. P3592 - A. Hughes-Lubeck	Open		75.00	75
1971	Pickles P2334 - A. Hallam	Retrd.	1982	29.95	375
1948	Pig Robinson P1104 - A. Gredington	Open		29.95	33
1972	Pig Wig P2381 - A. Hallam	Retrd.	1982	29.95	395
1955	Pigling Bland P1365 - G. Orwell	Open		29.95	33
1991	Pigling Eats Porridge P3252 - M. Alcock	Retrd.	1994	50.00	50
1976	Poorly Peter Rabbit P2560 - D. Lyttleton	Open		29.95	33
1981	Rebeccah Puddleduck P2647 - D. Lyttleton	Open		29.95	33
1992	Ribby and the Patty Pan P3280 - M. Alcock	Open		29.95	33
1974	Sally Henry Penney P2452 - A. Hallam	Retrd.	1993	29.95	95
1948	Samuel Whiskers P1106 - A. Gredington	Retrd.	1995	29.95	50
1975	Simpkin P2508 - A. Maslankowski	Retrd.	1983	29.95	650
1973	Sir Isaac Newton P2425 - G. Tongue	Retrd.	1984	29.95	350
1948	Squirrel Nutkin P1102 - A. Gredington	Open		29.95	33
1961	Tabitha Twitchit P1676 - A. Gredington	Retrd.	1995	29.95	30
1976	Tabitha Twitchitt with Miss Moppett P2544 - D. Lyttleton	Retrd.	1993	29.95	125
1949	Tailor of Gloucester P1108 - A. Gredington	Open		29.95	33
1995	Tailor of Gloucester-large size P3449 - M. Alcock	Open		65.00	73
1948	Tiggy Winkle P1107 - A. Gredington	Open		29.95	33
1985	Tiggy Winkle Takes Tea P2877 - D. Lyttleton	Open		29.95	33
1948	Timmy Tiptoes P1101 - A. Gredington	Open		29.95	33
1949	Timmy Willie P1109 - A. Gredington	Retrd.	1993	29.95	45-195
1986	Timmy Willie Sleeping P2996 - G. Tongue	Retrd.	1996	29.95	33
1948	Tom Kitten P1100 - A. Gredington	Open		29.95	33
1995	Tom Kitten-lg. size P3405 - M. Alcock	Open		65.00	73
1987	Tom Kitten and Butterfly P3030 - T. Chawner	Retrd.	1994	50.00	175
1987	Tom Thumb P2989 - W. Platt	Open		29.95	33
1955	Tommy Brock P1348 - G. Orwell	Open		29.95	33

British Sporting Heritage - V. Annand

Year Issue	Description	Edition Limit	Year Retrd.	Issue Price	Quote U.S.$
1994	Ascot HN3471	5,000		475.00	475
1993	Henley HN3367	5,000		475.00	475
1995	Wimbledon HN3366	5,000		475.00	475

Bunnykins - Various

Year Issue	Description	Edition Limit	Year Retrd.	Issue Price	Quote U.S.$
1995	Bathtime DB148 - M. Alcock	Open		40.00	40
1987	Be Prepared DB56 - D. Lyttleton	Retrd.	1995	40.00	75
1987	Bed Time DB55 - D. Lyttleton	Open		40.00	40
1995	Boy Skater DB152 - M. Alcock	Open		40.00	40
1991	Bride DB101 - A. Hughes	Open		40.00	40
1987	Brownie DB61 - W. Platt	Retrd.	1993	39.00	75
1994	Christmas Surprise DB146 - W. Platt	Open		50.00	50
1990	Cook DB85- W. Platt	Retrd.	1994	35.00	65
1995	Easter Greetings DB149 - M. Alcock	Open		50.00	50
1996	Father Bunnykin DB154 - M. Alcock	Retrd.	1996	50.00	50
1988	Father, Mother, Victoria DB68 - M. Alcock	Retrd.	1995	40.00	40
1989	Fireman DB75 - M. Alcock	Open		40.00	40
1990	Fisherman DB84- W. Platt	Retrd.	1993	39.00	75
1996	Gardener DB156 - W. Platt	Open		40.00	40
1995	Girl Skater DB153 - M. Alcock	Open		40.00	40
1995	Goodnight DB157 - S. Ridge	Open		40.00	40
1991	Groom DB102 - M. Alcock	Open		40.00	40
1993	Halloween Bunnykin DB132 - M. Alcock	Open		50.00	50
1983	Happy Birthday DB21 - G. Tongue	Open		40.00	40
1988	Harry DB73 - M. Alcock	Retrd.	1993	34.00	75
1972	Helping Mother DB2 - A. Hallam	Retrd.	1993	34.00	65
1986	Home Run DB43 - D. Lyttleton	Retrd.	1993	39.00	125
1990	Ice Cream DB82 - W. Platt	Retrd.	1993	39.00	75
1996	Mother's Day DB155 - S. Ridge	Open		50.00	50
1982	Mr. Bunnykin Easter Parade (pink ribbons) DB18 - G. Tongue	Retrd.	N/A	39.00	550
1982	Mr. Bunnykin Easter Parade DB18 - G. Tongue	Retrd.	1993	39.00	65
1982	Mrs. Bunnykin Easter Parade (pink ribbons) DB19 - G. Tongue	Retrd.	N/A	40.00	650
1982	Mrs. Bunnykin Easter Parade DB19 - G. Tongue	Retrd.	1995	40.00	65
1995	New Baby DB158 - G. Tongue	Open		40.00	40
1989	Nurse DB74 - M. Alcock	Open		35.00	40

YEAR ISSUE		EDITION LIMIT	YEAR RETD.	ISSUE PRICE	*QUOTE U.S.$
1989	Paper Boy DB77 - M. Alcock	Retrd.	1993	39.00	65
1972	Playtime DB8 - A Hallam	Retrd.	1993	34.00	75
1988	Policeman DB69 - M. Alcock	Open		40.00	40
1988	Polly DB71 - M. Alcock	Retrd.	1993	34.00	40-65
1995	Rainy Day DB147 - M. Alcock	Open		40.00	40
1981	Santa Bunnykins DB17 - D. Lyttleton	Retrd.	1995	40.00	40
1987	School Days DB57 - D. Lyttleton	Retrd.	1994	40.00	55
1982	School Master DB60 - W. Platt	Retrd.	1995	40.00	55
1974	Sleepytime DB15 - A. Musiankowski	Retrd.	1993	39.00	65
1972	Sleigh Ride DB4 - A Hallam	Open		40.00	40
1972	Story Time DB9 - A Hallam	Open		35.00	40
1988	Susan DB70 - M. Alcock	Retrd.	1993	34.00	40-60
1992	Sweetheart Bunnykin DB130 - W. Platt	Open		40.00	40
1988	Tom DB72 - M. Alcock	Retrd.	1993	34.00	65
1986	Uncle Sam DB50 - D. Lyttleton	Open		40.00	40
1988	William DB69 - M. Alcock	Retrd.	1993	34.00	40-65

Character Jugs: See Stein Section-Royal Doulton

Character Sculptures - Various

1996	Bill Sikes HN3785 - A. Dobson	Open		306.25	307
1996	Bowls Player HN3780 - J. Jones	Open		137.50	138
1993	Captain Hook - R. Tabbenor	Open		250.00	269
1995	Cyrano de Bergerac HN3751 - D. Biggs	Open		268.75	269
1994	D'Artagnan - R. Tabbenor	Open		260.00	269
1993	Dick Turpin - R. Tabbenor	Open		250.00	269
1995	Fagin HN3752 - A. Dobson	Open		268.75	269
1995	Gulliver - D. Biggs	Open		285.00	307
1993	Long John Silver - A. Maslankowski	Open		250.00	269
1996	Oliver Twist and Artful Dodger HN3786 - A. Dobson	Open		275.00	275
1994	Pied Piper - A. Maslankowski	Open		260.00	269
1993	Robin Hood - A. Maslankowski	Open		250.00	269
1995	Sherlock Holmes HN3639 - R. Tabbenor	Open		268.75	269
1996	Sir Francis Drake HN3770 - D. Biggs	Open		275.00	275
1995	Wizard HN3722 - A. Maslankowski	Open		306.25	307

Diamond Anniversary Tinies - Various

1994	John Barleycorn - C. Noke	2,500	1994	350.00	450
1994	Simon The Cellarer - Noke/Fenton	2,500	1994	set	Set
1994	Dick Turpin - W. Harper	2,500	1994	set	Set
1994	Granny - W. Harper	2,500	1994	set	Set
1994	Jester - C. Noke	2,500	1994	set	Set
1994	Parson Brown - W. Harper	2,500	1994	set	Set

Femmes Fatales - P. Davies

1979	Cleopatra HN2868	750		750.00	1350
1984	Eve HN2466	750		1250.00	1250
1981	Helen of Troy HN2387	750	1993	1250.00	1350
1985	Lucrezia Borgia HN2342	750	1993	1250.00	1400
1982	Queen of Sheba HN2328	750		1250.00	1300-1400
1983	Tz'u-Hsi HN2391	750		1250.00	1250

Figure of the Year - Various

1991	Amy HN3316 - P. Gee	Closed	1991	195.00	400-500
1992	Mary HN3375 - P. Gee	Closed	1992	225.00	375-475
1993	Patricia HN3365 - V. Annand	Closed	1993	250.00	350-475
1994	Jennifer HN3447 - P. Gee	Closed	1994	250.00	290
1995	Deborah HN3644 - N. Pedley	Closed	1995	225.00	225
1996	Belle HN3703 - V. Annand	Yr.Iss.		231.25	232

The Four Seasons - V. Annand

1993	Springtime HN3477	Open		325.00	350
1994	Summertime HN3478	Open		325.00	350
1993	Autumntime HN3621	Open		325.00	350
1993	Wintertime HN3622	Open		325.00	350

Gainsborough Ladies - P. Gee

1991	Countess of Sefton HN3010	5,000	1994	650.00	650
1991	Hon Frances Duncombe HN3009	5,000	1994	650.00	650-700
1991	Lady Sheffield HN3008	5,000	1994	650.00	650-700
1990	Mary, Countess Howe HN3007	5,000	1994	650.00	650

Great Lovers - R. Jefferson

1995	Antony and Cleopatra HN3114	150		5250.00	5250
1996	Lancelot and Guinevere HN3112	150		5250.00	5250
1994	Robin Hood and Maid Marian HN3111	150		5250.00	5250
1993	Romeo and Juliet HN3113	150		5250.00	5250

Images - Various

1991	Bride & Groom HN3281 - R. Tabbenor	Open		85.00	94
1991	Bridesmaid HN3280 - R. Tabbenor	Open		85.00	94
1993	Brother & Sister HN3460 - A. Hughes	Retrd.	N/A	52.50	107
1991	Brothers HN3191 - E. Griffiths	Open		90.00	107
1981	Family HN2720 - E. Griffiths	Open		187.50	200
1988	First Love HN2747 - D. Tootle	Open		170.00	200
1991	First Steps HN3282	Open		142.00	200
1993	Gift of Freedom HN3443 - N/A	Open		90.00	107
1989	Happy Anniversary HN3254 - D. Tootle	Open		187.50	200
1981	Lovers HN2762 - D. Tootle	Open		187.50	200

YEAR ISSUE		EDITION LIMIT	YEAR RETD.	ISSUE PRICE	*QUOTE U.S.$
1980	Mother & Daughter HN2841 - E. Griffiths	Open		187.50	200
1993	Our First Christmas HN3452 - N/A	Open		185.00	200
1989	Over the Threshold HN3274 - R. Tabbenor	Open		187.50	200
1983	Sisters HN3018 - P. Parson	Open		90.00	107
1987	Wedding Day HN2748 - D. Tootle	Open		187.50	200

Limited Edition Figurines - Various

1992	Christopher Columbus HN3392 - A. Maslankowski	1,492	N/A	1950.00	1950
1993	Duke of Wellington HN3432 - A. Maslankowski	1,500		1750.00	1750
1996	Eastern Grace Flambe HN3683 - P. Parsons	2,500		493.75	494
1994	Field Marshal Montgomery HN3405 - N/A	1,944	N/A	1100.00	1100
1993	General Robert E. Lee HN3404 - R. Tabbenor	5,000	1995	1175.00	1175
1993	Lt. General Ulysses S. Grant HN3403 - R. Tabbenor	5,000	1995	1175.00	1175
1992	Napoleon at Waterloo HN3429 - A. Maslankowski	1,500		1900.00	1900
1992	Samurai Warrior HN3402 - R. Tabbenor	950		500.00	500
1993	Vice Admiral Lord Nelson HN3489 - A. Maslankowski	950		1750.00	1750
1993	Winston S. Churchill HN3433 - A. Maslankowski	5,000		595.00	595

Myths & Maidens - R. Jefferson

1986	Diana The Huntress HN2829	300	N/A	2950.00	3000
1985	Europa & Bull HN2828	300	N/A	2950.00	3000
1984	Juno & Peacock HN2827	300	N/A	2950.00	3000
1982	Lady & Unicorn HN2825	300	N/A	2500.00	2500
1983	Leda & Swan HN2826	300	N/A	2950.00	3000

Prestige Figures - Various

1996	Charge of the Light Brigade HN3718 - A. Maslankowski	Open		17500.00	17500
1982	Columbine HN2738 - D. Tootle	Open		1250.00	1350
1982	Harlequin HN2737 - D. Tootle	Open		1250.00	1350
1964	Indian Brave HN2376 - M. Davis	500	1993	2500.00	5500
1952	Jack Point HN2080 - C.J. Noke	Open		2900.00	3400
1950	King Charles HN2084 - C.J. Noke	Open		2500.00	2500
1964	Matador & Bull HN2324 - M. Davis	Open		21500.00	25200
1952	The Moor HN2082 - C.J. Noke	Open		2500.00	3000
1964	The Palio HN2428 - M. Davis	500	1993	2500.00	6500
1952	Princess Badoura HN2081 - H. Stanton	Open		28000.00	33000
1978	St George and Dragon HN2856 - W.K. Harper	Open		13600.00	14500

Queens of Realm - P. Parsons

1989	Mary, Queen of Scots HN3142	S/O	N/A	550.00	850
1988	Queen Anne HN3141	S/O	N/A	525.00	700
1986	Queen Elizabeth I HN3099	S/O	N/A	495.00	700-900
1987	Queen Victoria HN3125	S/O	N/A	495.00	1100-1300
1987	Set of 4			2065.00	3000

Reynolds Collection - P. Gee

1992	Countess Harrington HN3317	5,000		550.00	595
1993	Countess Spencer HN3320	5,000		595.00	595
1991	Lady Worsley HN3318	5,000		550.00	595
1992	Mrs. Hugh Bonfoy HN3319	5,000		550.00	595

Royal Doulton Figurines - Various

1933	Beethoven - R. Garbe	25	N/A	N/A	6500
1987	Life Boatman HN2764 - W. Harper	Closed	N/A	N/A	225
1975	The Milkmaid HN2057A - L. Harradine	Closed	N/A	N/A	225
1924	Tony Weller HN684 - C. Noke	Closed	N/A	N/A	1800

Royalty - Various

1986	Duchess Of York HN3086 - E. Griffiths	1,500		495.00	650
1981	Duke Of Edinburgh HN2386 - P. Davis	750		395.00	450
1982	Lady Diana Spencer HN2885 - E. Griffiths	1,500		395.00	600
1981	Prince Of Wales HN2883 - E. Griffiths	1,500		395.00	450
1981	Prince Of Wales HN2884 - E. Griffiths	1,500		750.00	1000
1982	Princess Of Wales HN2887 - E. Griffiths	1,500		750.00	1500
1973	Queen Elizabeth II HN2502 - P. Davis	750		N/A	1800
1982	Queen Elizabeth II HN2878 - E. Griffiths	2,500		N/A	450
1992	Queen Elizabeth II, 2nd Version HN3440 - P. Gee	3,500		460.00	460
1989	Queen Elizabeth, the Queen Mother as the Duchess of York HN3230 - P. Parsons	9,500		N/A	450
1990	Queen Elizabeth, the Queen Mother HN3189 - E. Griffiths	2,500		N/A	450
1980	Queen Mother HN2882 - P. Davis	1,500		650.00	1250

Salvino Inc.

Collector Club Figurines - Salvino

1993	6" Mario Lemieux-Painted Away Uniform (Unsigned)	Closed	N/A	70.00	90
1993	Joe Montana-"KC" Away Uniform (Hand Signed)	Closed	N/A	275.00	275

YEAR ISSUE		EDITION LIMIT	YEAR RETD.	ISSUE PRICE	*QUOTE U.S.$

Boston Celtic Greats - Salvino

1991	Larry Bird	S/O	N/A	285.00	395
1993	Larry Bird (Special Edition)	S/O	N/A	375.00	400-450

Boxing Greats - Salvino

1990	Muhammed Ali	S/O	N/A	250.00	250
1990	Muhammed Ali (Special Edition)	S/O	N/A	375.00	350-700

Brooklyn Dodger - Salvino

1989	Don Drysdale	S/O	N/A	185.00	200-300
1989	Don Drysdale AP	300	N/A	200.00	400
1993	Duke Snider	1,000		275.00	275
1990	Roy Campanella	2,000	N/A	395.00	350-500
1990	Roy Campanella (Special Edition)			550.00	500
1989	Sandy Koufax	S/O	N/A	195.00	225-300
1989	Sandy Koufax AP	500	N/A	200.00	400

Collegiate Series - Salvino

1992	Joe Montana	S/O	N/A	275.00	325
1992	OJ Simpson	1,000		275.00	350

Dealer Special Series - Salvino

1992	Joe Namath	S/O	N/A	700.00	700
1992	Mickey Mantle #6	S/O	N/A	700.00	1350
1992	Mickey Mantle #7	S/O	N/A	700.00	1400
1993	Willie Mays	S/O	N/A	700.00	700

Heroes of the Diamond - Salvino

1993	Brooks Robinson	1,000		275.00	275
1992	Mickey Mantle Batting	S/O	N/A	395.00	595-700
1992	Mickey Mantle Batting-Right Hand (Away)	S/O	N/A	545.00	695-995
1992	Mickey Mantle Batting-Right Hand (Home)	S/O	N/A	545.00	895-995
1992	Mickey Mantle Fielding	S/O	N/A	395.00	595-700
1991	Rickey Henderson (Away)	600		275.00	275
1991	Rickey Henderson (Home)	S/O	N/A	275.00	275
1991	Rickey Henderson (Special Edition)	550		375.00	375
1992	Willie Mays New York	750		395.00	395
1992	Willie Mays San Francisco	750		395.00	395

Hockey Greats - Salvino

1991	Mario Lemieux	S/O	N/A	275.00	300-600
1992	Mario Lemieux (Special Editon)	S/O	N/A	285.00	400
1994	Wayne Gretzky	S/O	N/A	395.00	395

NFL Superstar - Salvino

1990	Jim Brown	S/O	N/A	275.00	275-325
1990	Jim Brown (Special Edition)	S/O	N/A	525.00	450-550
1990	Joe Montana	S/O	N/A	275.00	275-325
1990	Joe Montana (Special Edition)	S/O	N/A	395.00	395
1993	Joe Montana 49'er	1,000		275.00	275
1993	Joe Montana Chiefs	450		275.00	400
1990	Joe Namath	2,500		275.00	275
1990	Joe Namath (Special Edition)	500		375.00	375-475
1990	OJ Simpson	1,000		250.00	300-400

Racing Legends - Salvino

1991	AJ Foyt	S/O	N/A	250.00	250
1991	Darrell Waltrip	S/O	N/A	250.00	250
1991	Richard Petty	S/O	N/A	250.00	250
1991	Richard Petty (Special Edition)	S/O	N/A	279.00	350-400
1993	Richard Petty Farewell Tour	2,500		275.00	275

Sarah's Attic, Inc.

Collector's Club Promotion - Sarah's Attic

1991	Diamond 3497	Closed	1992	36.00	100
1991	Ruby 3498	Closed	1992	42.00	150
1992	Christmas Love Santa 3522	Closed	1992	45.00	65
1992	Forever Frolicking Friends 3523	Closed	1992	Gift	75
1992	Love One Another 3561	Closed	1992	60.00	60
1992	Sharing Dreams 3562	Closed	1993	75.00	100
1992	Life Time Friends 3563	Closed	1993	75.00	125
1992	Love Starts With Children 3607	Closed	1993	Gift	75
1993	First Forever Friend Celebration 3903	Closed	1993	50.00	50
1993	Pledge of Allegiance 3749	Closed	1993	45.00	90
1993	Love Starts With Children II 3837	Closed	1994	Gift	65
1993	Gem Wh. Girl w/Basket 3842	Closed	1994	33.00	150
1993	Rocky Bk. Boy w/Marbles 3843	Closed	1994	25.00	65
1994	America Boy 4191	Closed	1994	25.00	25
1994	America Girl 4192	Closed	1994	25.00	25
1994	Forever Friends 4286	Closed	1994	45.00	45
1994	Saturday Night Round Up 4232	Closed	1995	Gift	25
1994	Billy Bob 4233	Closed	1995	38.00	38
1994	Jimmy Dean 4234	Closed	1995	38.00	38
1994	Sally/Jack 4235	Closed	1995	55.00	55
1994	Ellie/T.J. 4236	Closed	1995	55.00	55
1995	Flags in Heaven 4386	Closed	1995	45.00	45
1995	Friends Forever 4444	12/96		60.00	60
1995	Playtime Pals 4446	2/97		65.00	70
1995	Horsin' around 4445	2/97		65.00	65
1996	Abigail 4543	12/96		36.00	36
1996	Aretha 4542	12/96		36.00	36

Angels In The Attic - Sarah's Attic

1989	Abbee-Angel-2336	Closed	1991	10.00	20
1990	Adora Girl Angel Standing 3276	4,000	1990	35.00	125-150
1991	Angel Adora With Bunny 3390	Closed	1993	50.00	65

YEAR ISSUE	EDITION LIMIT	YEAR RETD.	ISSUE PRICE	*QUOTE U.S.$
1991 Angel Enos With Frog 3391	10,000	1993	50.00	65
1996 Angels on Assignment 4544	12/96		65.00	65
1989 Ashbee-Angel 2337	Closed	1991	10.00	25
1991 Bert Angel 3416	1,000	1992	60.00	120
1990 Billi-Angel 3295	Closed	1991	18.00	22
1993 Blessed is He 3952	1,994	1994	48.00	120
1994 Blessed is He II 4189	2,500		66.00	75
1995 Blessed is He III 4387	4,000		60.00	60
1990 Cindi-Angel 3296	Closed	1991	18.00	22
1989 Clyde-Angel 2329	Closed	1991	17.00	20
1992 Contentment 3500	500	1992	100.00	200
1992 Enos & Adora-Small 3671	5,000	1993	35.00	60-125
1990 Enos Boy Angel Sitting 3275	4,000	1990	33.00	100
1993 Faith-Bk. Angel 3953	1,994		40.00	40
1989 Floppy-Angel 2330	Closed	1990	10.00	20
1990 Flossy-Angel 3301	Closed	1991	15.00	24
1989 Gramps Angel 2357	Closed	1990	17.00	40
1989 Grams Angel 2356	Closed	1990	17.00	40
1992 Heavenly Caring 3661	2,500	1993	70.00	90
1992 Heavenly Giving 3663	Closed	1993	70.00	90
1992 Heavenly Loving 3664	2,500	1993	70.00	90
1993 Heavenly Peace 3833	2,500	1994	47.00	50
1992 Heavenly Sharing 3662	2,500	1993	70.00	90
1993 Heavenly Uniting 3794	2,500	1994	45.00	45
1992 Hope Angel 3659	Closed	1994	40.00	45
1996 Karissa Wh. Angel 4480	1,200	1996	34.00	34
1996 Karita Bk. Angel 4479	1,200	1996	34.00	34
1990 Lena-Angel 3297	Closed	1991	36.00	40
1990 Louise-Angel 3300	Closed	1991	17.00	24
1992 Love 3501	500	1992	80.00	200
1995 Prayer of Love 4437	500	1995	85.00	170
1992 Priscilla-Angel 3511	5,000	1993	46.00	60
1989 Saint Willie Bill 2360	Closed	1991	30.00	40
1989 St. Anne 2323	Closed	1991	29.00	32
1989 St. Gabbe 2322	Closed	1991	30.00	33
1990 Trapper-Angel 3299	Closed	1991	17.00	40
1989 Wendall-Angel 2324	Closed	1991	10.00	45
1989 Wilbur-Angel 2327	Closed	1991	10.00	25

Beary Adorables Collection - Sarah's Attic

YEAR ISSUE	EDITION LIMIT	YEAR RETD.	ISSUE PRICE	*QUOTE U.S.$
1987 Abbee Bear 2005	Closed	1989	6.00	12
1987 Alex Bear 2003	Closed	1989	6.00	12
1987 Amelia Bear 2004	Closed	1989	8.00	12
1988 Americana Bear 3047	Closed	1990	50.00	75
1989 Angel Bear 3105	Closed	1990	24.00	25
1988 Arti Boy Bear 6319	Closed	1990	7.00	15
1987 Ashbee Bear 2006	Closed	1989	6.00	12
1990 Belinda 50's Girl Bear 3253	4,000	1991	25.00	35
1989 Betsy Bear w/Flag 3097	Closed	1990	22.00	40
1989 Colonial Bear w/Hat 3098	Closed	1990	22.00	40
1989 Daisy Bear 3101	Closed	1990	48.00	55
1991 Dudley Bear 3355	2,500	1992	32.00	60
1988 Ghost Bear 3028	Closed	1989	9.00	25
1989 Griswald Bear 3102	Closed	1990	48.00	55
1988 Honey Ma Bear 6316	Closed	1990	16.00	20
1988 Marti Girl Bear 6318	Closed	1990	12.00	20
1989 Mikey Bear 3104	Closed	1990	26.00	30
1989 Missy Bear 3103	Closed	1990	26.00	30
1988 Rufus Pa Bear 6317	Closed	1990	15.00	20
1989 Sammy Boy Bear 3111	Closed	1990	12.00	15
1989 Sid Papa Bear 3092	Closed	1990	18.00	25
1989 Sophie Mama Bear 3093	Closed	1990	18.00	25
1989 Spice Bear Crawling 3109	Closed	1990	12.00	15

Black Heritage Collection - Sarah's Attic

YEAR ISSUE	EDITION LIMIT	YEAR RETD.	ISSUE PRICE	*QUOTE U.S.$
1991 Bl. Baby Tansy 3388	Closed	1992	40.00	50
1992 Booker T. Washington 3648	3,000	1993	80.00	100
1992 Boys Night Out 3660	2,000	1994	350.00	450-695
1990 Brotherly Love 3336	5,000	1991	80.00	175
1992 Buffalo Soldier 3524	5,000	1993	80.00	125
1991 Caleb w/ Football 3485	6,000	1993	40.00	55
1990 Caleb-Lying Down 3232	Closed	1994	23.00	35
1992 Calvin Prayer Time 3510	5,000	1993	46.00	55
1991 Corporal Pervis 3366	8,000	1993	60.00	125
1992 Esther w/Butter Churn 3536	Closed	1994	70.00	70
1987 Gramps 5104	Closed	1988	16.00	100
1987 Grams 5105	Closed	1988	16.00	100
1992 Granny Wynne & Olivia 3535	5,000	1994	85.00	95
1990 Harpster w/Banjo 3257	4,000	1990	60.00	250
1991 Harpster w/Harmonica II 3384	8,000	1993	60.00	125
1992 Harriet Tubman 3687	3,000	1993	60.00	125
1991 Hattie Quilting 3483	6,000	1993	60.00	125
1990 Hattie-Knitting 3233	4,000	1990	40.00	75-100
1992 Ida B. Wells & Frederick Douglass 3642	3,000	1993	160.00	250
1990 Libby w/Overalls 3259	4,000	1990	36.00	175
1991 Libby w/Puppy 3386	10,000	1993	50.00	100
1991 Lucas w/Dog 3387	10,000	1993	50.00	100
1990 Lucas w/Overalls 3260	4,000	1990	36.00	175
1993 Miles Boy Angel 3752	2,500	1995	27.00	40
1993 Moriah Girl Angel 3759	2,500	1994	27.00	45
1992 Muffy-Prayer Time 3509	5,000	1993	46.00	55
1992 Music Masters 3533	1,000	1992	300.00	350
1992 Music Masters II 3621	1,000	1992	250.00	300
1993 Nat Love Cowboy (Isom Dart) 3792	2,500	1993	45.00	300-350
1991 Nighttime Pearl 3362	Closed	1993	50.00	65
1991 Nighttime Percy 3363	Closed	1993	50.00	65
1996 Noah's Ark 4529	500		130.00	130
1993 Otis Redding 3793	Closed	1994	70.00	300
1989 Pappy Jake 3100	Closed	1990	40.00	100
1990 Pearl-Blk. Girl Dancing 3291	5,000	1992	45.00	100
1990 Percy-Blk. Boy Dancing 3292	5,000	1993	45.00	100

YEAR ISSUE	EDITION LIMIT	YEAR RETD.	ISSUE PRICE	*QUOTE U.S.$
1992 Porter 3525	5,000	1993	80.00	125
1990 Portia Reading Book 3256	Closed	1991	30.00	45-65
1990 Praise the Lord I (Preacher I) 3277	4,000	1991	55.00	150
1991 Praise the Lord II w/Kids 3376	5,000	1994	100.00	100
1993 Praise the Lord III 3753	2,500	1994	44.00	55
1989 Quilting Ladies 3099	Closed	1991	90.00	250-300
1992 Sojourner Truth 3629	3,000	1993	80.00	125
1991 Uncle Reuben 3389	8,000	1993	70.00	95
1993 Vanessa Gospel Singer (Upside down book) 3756	12/96		40.00	100
1990 Whoophe & Wooster 3255	4,000	1990	50.00	295
1991 Whoopie & Wooster II 3385	8,000	1993	70.00	95

Classroom Memories - Sarah's Attic

YEAR ISSUE	EDITION LIMIT	YEAR RETD.	ISSUE PRICE	*QUOTE U.S.$
1988 Miss Pritchet 6505	Closed	1993	28.00	35

Cotton Tale Collection - Sarah's Attic

YEAR ISSUE	EDITION LIMIT	YEAR RETD.	ISSUE PRICE	*QUOTE U.S.$
1988 Americana Bunny 3048	Closed	1990	58.00	190
1988 Billi Rabbit 6283	Closed	1990	27.00	35
1987 Bonnie 5727	Closed	1989	30.00	125
1988 Cindi Rabbit 6282	Closed	1990	27.00	35
1987 Clyde 5728	Closed	1989	30.00	125
1989 Cookie Rabbit 3078	Closed	1990	29.00	125
1989 Crumb Rabbit 3077	Closed	1990	29.00	35-43
1989 Nana Rabbit 3080	Closed	1990	50.00	60-75
1990 Ollie Rabbit w/Vest 3239	Closed	1991	75.00	150
1989 Papa Rabbit 3079	Closed	1990	50.00	60-75
1989 Sleepy Rabbit 3088	Closed	1990	16.00	25
1991 Tabitha Victorian Rabbit 3371	Closed	1993	30.00	45
1991 Tessy Victorian Rabbit 3370	Closed	1993	20.00	35
1989 Thelma Rabbit 3084	Closed	1990	33.00	40
1989 Thomas Rabbit 3085	Closed	1990	33.00	40
1991 Toby Victorian Rabbit 3369	Closed	1993	40.00	55
1988 Wendall Mini Rabbit 6268	Closed	1990	8.00	12
1987 Wendall Rabbit 5285	Closed	1989	14.00	25
1988 Wendy Mini Rabbit 6270	Closed	1990	8.00	12
1987 Wendy Rabbit 5286	Closed	1989	15.00	25
1988 Wilbur Mini Rabbit 6269	Closed	1990	8.00	12
1987 Wilbur Rabbit 5287	Closed	1989	13.00	25
1990 Zeb Pa Rabbit w/Carrots 3217	500	1991	18.00	32
1990 Zeb Sailor Dad 3319	Closed	1992	28.00	32
1990 Zeke Boy Rabbit w/Carrots 3219	500	1991	17.00	32
1990 Zelda Ma Rabbit w/Carrots 3218	500	1991	18.00	32
1987 Zoe Girl Rabbit w/Carrots 3220	500	1991	17.00	32

Daisy Collection - Sarah's Attic

YEAR ISSUE	EDITION LIMIT	YEAR RETD.	ISSUE PRICE	*QUOTE U.S.$
1990 Bomber-Tom 3309	Closed	1993	52.00	57
1990 Jack Boy Ball & Glove 3249	Closed	1993	40.00	44
1993 Jack Boy w/Broken Arm 3970	2,000	1994	30.00	60
1990 Jewel-Julie 3310	Closed	1993	62.00	68
1989 Sally Booba 2344	Closed	1993	40.00	60
1990 Sparky-Mark 3307	Closed	1993	55.00	60
1990 Spike-Tim 3308	Closed	1993	46.00	51
1990 Stretch-Mike 3311	Closed	1993	52.00	57

Dreams of Tomorrow - Sarah's Attic

YEAR ISSUE	EDITION LIMIT	YEAR RETD.	ISSUE PRICE	*QUOTE U.S.$
1991 Benjamin w/Drums 3487	10,000	1993	46.00	55
1992 Bubba-Doctor 3506	6,000	1993	60.00	66
1992 Bubba-Policeman 3685	3,000	1993	46.00	51
1992 Bud-Fireman 3668	6,000	1993	50.00	55
1991 Charity Sewing Flags 3486	10,000	1993	46.00	55
1992 Pansy-Ballerina 3682	3,000	1993	46.00	55
1992 Pansy-Nurse 3505	6,000	1993	46.00	51
1993 Rachel-Photographer 3871	2,000	1995	27.00	32
1992 Shelby-Executive 3666	6,000	1993	46.00	50
1993 Tillie-Photographer 3870	12/96		27.00	32
1993 Twinkie-Pilot 3869	12/96		27.00	35
1992 Willie-Fireman 3667	6,000	1993	46.00	50

Matt & Maggie - Sarah's Attic

YEAR ISSUE	EDITION LIMIT	YEAR RETD.	ISSUE PRICE	*QUOTE U.S.$
1988 Large Matt 3029	4,000	1989	48.00	58
1986 Maggie 2029	4,000	1989	14.00	28
1989 Maggie Bench Sitter 3083	Closed	1990	32.00	42
1987 Maggie on Heart 5145	Closed	1989	9.00	15
1987 Matt & Maggie w/ Bear 5730	100	1987	100.00	150
1986 Matt 2030	Closed	1989	14.00	28
1989 Matt Bench Sitter 3082	Closed	1990	32.00	42
1987 Matt on Heart 5144	Closed	1989	9.00	15
1989 Mini Maggie 2314	Closed	1990	6.00	12
1989 Mini Matt 2313	Closed	1990	6.00	12
1988 Small Sitting Maggie 5284	Closed	1989	11.50	35
1988 Small Sitting Matt 5283	Closed	1989	11.50	35
1987 Standing Maggie 2014	Closed	1989	11.00	15
1987 Standing Matt 2013	Closed	1989	11.00	15

Santas Of The Month-Series A - Sarah's Attic

YEAR ISSUE	EDITION LIMIT	YEAR RETD.	ISSUE PRICE	*QUOTE U.S.$
1988 January Wh. Santa	Closed	1990	50.00	135-150
1988 January Bk. Santa	Closed	1990	50.00	200-300
1988 February Wh. Santa	Closed	1990	50.00	135-150
1988 February Bk. Santa	Closed	1990	50.00	200-300
1988 March Wh. Santa	Closed	1990	50.00	135-150
1988 March Bk. Santa	Closed	1990	50.00	200-300
1988 April Wh. Santa	Closed	1990	50.00	135-150
1988 April Bk. Santa	Closed	1990	50.00	200-300
1988 May Wh. Santa	Closed	1990	50.00	135-150
1988 May Bk. Santa	Closed	1990	50.00	200-300
1988 June Wh. Santa	Closed	1990	50.00	135-150
1988 June Bk. Santa	Closed	1990	50.00	200-300
1988 July Wh. Santa	Closed	1990	50.00	175
1988 July Bk. Santa	Closed	1990	50.00	200-300
1988 August Wh. Santa	Closed	1990	50.00	135-150

YEAR ISSUE	EDITION LIMIT	YEAR RETD.	ISSUE PRICE	*QUOTE U.S.$
1988 August Bk. Santa	Closed	1990	50.00	200-300
1988 September Wh. Santa	Closed	1990	50.00	135-150
1988 September Bk. Santa	Closed	1990	50.00	200-300
1988 October Wh. Santa	Closed	1990	50.00	135-150
1988 October Bk. Santa	Closed	1990	50.00	200-300
1988 November Wh. Santa	Closed	1990	50.00	135-150
1988 November Bk. Santa	Closed	1990	50.00	200-300
1988 December Wh. Santa	Closed	1990	50.00	135-150
1988 December Bk. Santa	Closed	1990	50.00	225-375
1988 Mini January Wh. Santa	Closed	1990	14.00	33-35
1988 Mini January Bk. Santa	Closed	1990	14.00	35
1988 Mini February Wh. Santa	Closed	1990	14.00	33-35
1988 Mini February Bk. Santa	Closed	1990	14.00	35
1988 Mini March Wh. Santa	Closed	1990	14.00	33-35
1988 Mini March Bk. Santa	Closed	1990	14.00	35
1988 Mini April Wh. Santa	Closed	1990	14.00	33-35
1988 Mini April Bk. Santa	Closed	1990	14.00	35
1988 Mini May Wh. Santa	Closed	1990	14.00	33-35
1988 Mini May Bk. Santa	Closed	1990	14.00	35
1988 Mini June Wh. Santa	Closed	1990	14.00	33-35
1988 Mini June Bk. Santa	Closed	1990	14.00	35
1988 Mini July Wh. Santa	Closed	1990	14.00	40
1988 Mini July Bk. Santa	Closed	1990	14.00	50
1988 Mini August Wh. Santa	Closed	1990	14.00	33-35
1988 Mini August Bk. Santa	Closed	1990	14.00	35
1988 Mini September Wh. Santa	Closed	1990	14.00	33-35
1988 Mini September Bk. Santa	Closed	1990	14.00	35
1988 Mini October Wh. Santa	Closed	1990	14.00	33-35
1988 Mini October Bk. Santa	Closed	1990	14.00	35
1988 Mini November Wh. Santa	Closed	1990	14.00	33-35
1988 Mini November Bk. Santa	Closed	1990	14.00	35
1988 Mini December Wh. Santa	Closed	1990	14.00	33-35
1988 Mini December Bk. Santa	Closed	1990	14.00	35

Santas Of The Month-Series B - Sarah's Attic

YEAR ISSUE	EDITION LIMIT	YEAR RETD.	ISSUE PRICE	*QUOTE U.S.$
1990 Jan. Santa Winter Fun 7135	Closed	1991	80.00	100
1990 Feb. Santa Cupids Help 7136	Closed	1991	120.00	120
1990 Mar. Santa Irish Delight 7137	Closed	1991	120.00	150
1990 Apr. Santa Spring/Joy 7138	Closed	1991	150.00	150
1990 May Santa Par For Course 7139	Closed	1991	100.00	125
1990 June Santa Graduation 7140	Closed	1991	70.00	70
1990 July Santa God Bless 7141	Closed	1991	100.00	125
1990 Aug. Santa Summers Tranquility 7142	Closed	1991	110.00	130
1990 Sep. Santa Touchdown 7143	Closed	1991	90.00	90
1990 Oct. Santa Seasons Plenty 7144	Closed	1991	120.00	120
1990 Nov. Santa Give Thanks 7145	Closed	1991	90.00	90
1990 Dec. Santa Peace 7146	Closed	1991	120.00	125
1990 Jan.Mrs. Winter Fun 7147	Closed	1991	80.00	100
1990 Feb. Mrs. Cupid's Helper 7148	Closed	1991	110.00	110
1990 March Mrs. Irish Delight7149	Closed	1991	80.00	100
1990 April Mrs. Spring Joy 7150	Closed	1991	110.00	110
1990 May Mrs. Par for the Course 7151	Closed	1991	80.00	100
1990 June Mrs. Graduate 7152	Closed	1991	70.00	100
1990 July Mrs. God Bless America 7153	Closed	1991	100.00	125
1990 Aug. Mrs. Summer Tranquility 7154	Closed	1991	90.00	112
1990 Sept. Mrs. Touchdown 7155	Closed	1991	90.00	100
1990 Oct. Mrs. Seasons of Plenty 7156	Closed	1991	90.00	112
1990 Nov. Mrs. Give Thanks 7157	Closed	1991	90.00	112
1990 Dec. Mrs. Peace 7158	Closed	1991	110.00	137

Sarah's Gang Collection - Sarah's Attic

YEAR ISSUE	EDITION LIMIT	YEAR RETD.	ISSUE PRICE	*QUOTE U.S.$
1989 Baby Rachel 2306	Closed	1994	20.00	30
1990 Baby Rachel-Beachtime 3248	Closed	1992	35.00	50
1988 Cupcake 4027	Closed	1994	20.00	25
1989 Cupcake Clown 3144	Closed	1989	21.00	35
1987 Cupcake on Heart 5140	Closed	1989	9.00	20
1993 Cupcake w/Snowman 3822	2,500	1994	35.00	40
1989 Cupcake-Americana 2304	Closed	1993	21.00	30
1990 Cupcake-Beachtime 3244	Closed	1992	35.00	53
1986 Cupcake-Original 2034	Closed	1988	14.00	20-75
1989 Cupcake-Small School 2309	Closed	1990	11.00	20
1990 Katie & Whimpy-Beachtime 3243	Closed	1992	60.00	60-75
1987 Katie On Heart 5141	Closed	1989	9.00	20
1987 Katie Sitting 2002	Closed	1987	14.00	20
1989 Katie-Americana 2302	Closed	1993	21.00	25
1991 Katie-Bride 3431	Closed	1994	47.00	52
1986 Katie-Original 2032	Closed	1988	14.00	20
1989 Katie-Small Sailor 2307	Closed	1990	14.00	20
1990 Katie-Witch 3312	Closed	1992	40.00	50
1991 Percy-Minister 3440	Closed	1994	50.00	55
1991 Pug-Ringbearer 3439	Closed	1994	40.00	44
1990 Rachel-Flower Girl 3432	Closed	1994	40.00	43
1990 Rachel-Pumpkin 3318	Closed	1992	40.00	50
1991 Rachel-Thanksgiving 3474	10,000	1993	32.00	35
1988 Tillie 4032	Closed	1994	20.00	25
1991 Tillie Masquerade 3412	Closed	1993	45.00	50
1987 Tillie On Heart 5150	Closed	1989	9.00	20
1989 Tillie-Americana 2301	Closed	1993	21.00	25
1990 Tillie-Beachtime 3247	Closed	1992	35.00	53
1990 Tillie-Clown 3316	Closed	1992	40.00	50
1986 Tillie-Original 2027	Closed	1988	14.00	20
1989 Tillie-Small Country 2312	Closed	1992	18.00	26
1989 Twinkie Clown 3145	Closed	1989	19.00	35
1987 Twinkie On Heart 5143	Closed	1989	9.00	20
1989 Twinkie-Americana 2305	Closed	1993	21.00	25
1990 Twinkie-Beachtime 3245	Closed	1992	35.00	53
1990 Twinkie-Devil 3315	Closed	1992	40.00	50
1986 Twinkie-Original 2033	Closed	1988	14.00	20
1990 Twinkie-Small School 2310	Closed	1990	11.00	20
1991 Tyler-Ring Bearer 3433	Closed	1994	40.00	44

YEAR ISSUE	EDITION LIMIT	YEAR RETD.	ISSUE PRICE	*QUOTE U.S.$
1988 Whimpy 4030	Closed	1994	20.00	25
1987 Whimpy on Heart 5142	Closed	1989	9.00	20
1987 Whimpy Sitting 2001	Closed	1987	14.00	20
1989 Whimpy-Americana 2303	Closed	1993	21.00	25
1991 Whimpy-Groom 3430	Closed	1994	47.00	52
1986 Whimpy-Original 2031	Closed	1988	14.00	20
1989 Whimpy-Small Sailor 2308	Closed	1990	14.00	20
1991 Whimpy-Thanksgiving 3469	10,000	1993	32.00	35
1988 Willie 4031	Closed	1994	20.00	25
1987 Willie On Heart 5151	Closed	1989	9.00	20
1989 Willie-Americana 2300	Closed	1993	21.00	30
1990 Willie-Beachtime 3246	Closed	1992	35.00	53
1990 Willie-Clown 3317	Closed	1992	40.00	50
1986 Willie-Original 2028	Closed	1988	14.00	20-75
1989 Willie-Small Country 2311	Closed	1992	18.00	26

Sarah's Neighborhood Friends - Sarah's Attic

YEAR ISSUE	EDITION LIMIT	YEAR RETD.	ISSUE PRICE	*QUOTE U.S.$
1991 Babes-Nativity Jesus 3427	Closed	1994	20.00	22
1990 Bubba w/Lantern 3268	Closed	1992	40.00	45
1991 Bubba w/Lemonade Stand 3382	Closed	1992	54.00	108
1991 Bud Nativity (Joseph) 3420	Closed	1994	34.00	36
1990 Bud w/Book 3270	Closed	1992	40.00	45
1995 Chilly-Snowman 4418	1,000		44.00	44
1991 Dolly Nativity (Jesus) 3418	Closed	1994	20.00	22
1993 Emily & Gideon-Small 3670	Closed	1993	40.00	75
1989 Jennifer & Max 2319	4,000	1990	57.00	85
1991 Pansy-Nativity Angel 3425	Closed	1994	30.00	32
1988 Trudy-w/Teacup 3042	Closed	1990	34.00	50
1990 Tyler Victorian Boy 3327	Closed	1992	40.00	65

Snowflake Collection - Sarah's Attic

YEAR ISSUE	EDITION LIMIT	YEAR RETD.	ISSUE PRICE	*QUOTE U.S.$
1989 Boo Mini Snowman 3200	Closed	1993	6.00	12
1992 Christmas Love-Small 3674	5,000	1992	30.00	33
1989 Flurry 2342	Closed	1993	12.00	20
1990 Old Glory Snowman 3225	4,000	1992	24.00	26
1989 Winter Frolic 3209	Closed	1992	60.00	70

Spirit of America - Sarah's Attic

YEAR ISSUE	EDITION LIMIT	YEAR RETD.	ISSUE PRICE	*QUOTE U.S.$
1988 Betsy Ross 3024	Closed	1992	34.00	40
1991 Bright Sky Mother Indian 3345	Closed	1992	70.00	90-140
1991 Iron Hawk Father Indian 3344	Closed	1992	70.00	90-140
1991 Little Dove Girl Indian 3346	Closed	1992	40.00	60-85
1988 Pilgrim Boy 4009	Closed	1990	12.00	20
1988 Pilgrim Girl 4010	Closed	1990	12.00	24
1994 Shine-Boy Indian 3980	1,000	1994	25.00	50
1994 Siyah-Girl Indian 3979	1,000	1994	25.00	50
1991 Spotted Eagle Boy Indian 3347	Closed	1992	30.00	45-85

Spirit of Christmas Collection - Sarah's Attic

YEAR ISSUE	EDITION LIMIT	YEAR RETD.	ISSUE PRICE	*QUOTE U.S.$
1994 Jeb-Christmas 94 4155	Closed	1994	28.00	30
1994 LOL-Christmas 4151	Closed	1994	30.00	35
1987 Long Journey 2051	Closed	1989	19.00	35
1987 Mini Santa w/Cane 5123	Closed	1990	8.00	20
1989 Papa Santa Sitting 3180	Closed	1990	30.00	40
1989 Papa Santa Stocking 3182	Closed	1990	50.00	60
1988 Santa in Chimney 4020	4,000	1990	110.00	150
1991 Santa Tex 3392	500	1990	30.00	75
1987 Santa's Workshop 3006	Closed	1990	50.00	100
1991 Sharing Love Santa 3491	3,000	1993	120.00	140
1989 Silent Night 2343	6,000	1991	33.00	50
1989 Woodland Santa 2345	7,500	1992	100.00	150

Tender Moments - Sarah's Attic

YEAR ISSUE	EDITION LIMIT	YEAR RETD.	ISSUE PRICE	*QUOTE U.S.$
1992 Bk. Baby Boy Birth 3516	Closed	1993	50.00	55
1992 Bk. Baby Girl 1-2 3517	Closed	1993	50.00	55
1993 Bk. Girl 3-4/Tricycle 3744	Open		40.00	60
1992 Generations of Love	Closed	1994	293.00	425
1993 Joy of Motherhood Bk. Pregnant Woman 3791	1,000	1994	55.00	70
1993 Little Blessing Bk. Couple 3839	2,500	1994	75.00	90
1993 Love of Life-Bk. Couple 3788	1,000	1994	70.00	75-100
1993 True Love-Wh. Couple 3789	1,000	1994	70.00	80
1992 Wh. Baby Boy 1 3527	Closed	1993	60.00	66
1992 Wh. Baby Girl 1 3528	Closed	1993	60.00	66
1992 Wh. Boy 2-3 3624	Closed	1993	60.00	65
1992 Wh. Girl 2-3 3623	Closed	1993	60.00	66

United Hearts Collection - Sarah's Attic

YEAR ISSUE	EDITION LIMIT	YEAR RETD.	ISSUE PRICE	*QUOTE U.S.$
1992 Adora Angel-May 3632	Closed	1993	50.00	75
1991 Adora Christmas-December 3479	Closed	1992	36.00	60
1991 Barney the Great-October 3466	Closed	1992	40.00	48
1991 Bibi & Biff Clowns-October 3467	Closed	1992	35.00	42
1991 Bibi-Miss Liberty Bear-July 3457	Closed	1992	30.00	36
1991 Bubba Beach-August 3461	Closed	1992	34.00	41
1992 Carrotman-January 3619	Closed	1993	30.00	40
1991 Chilly Snowman-January 3443	Closed	1992	33.00	40
1992 Cookie-July 3638	Closed	1993	34.00	34
1991 Crumb on Stool-September 3463	Closed	1992	32.00	39
1992 Cupcake-November 3649	Closed	1992	35.00	40
1991 Cupcake-Thanksgiving 3470	Closed	1993	36.00	36
1991 Emily-Springtime May 3452	Closed	1992	53.00	60
1992 Ethan Angel-August 3641	Closed	1993	46.00	60
1991 Gideon-Springtime May 3453	Closed	1992	40.00	43
1991 Hewett w/Leprechaun-March 3448	Closed	1992	56.00	67
1991 Noah w/Pot of Gold-March 3447	Closed	1992	36.00	43
1991 Pansy Beach-August 3459	Closed	1992	34.00	41
1991 Papa Barney & Biff-July 3458	Closed	1992	64.00	76
1991 Sally Booba Graduation-June 3454	Closed	1992	45.00	50
1991 Shelby w/Shamrock-March 3446	Closed	1992	36.00	43
1991 Tillie-January 3441	Closed	1992	32.00	40
1991 Willie-January 3442	Closed	1992	32.00	40

Schmid: See Lowell Davis Farm Club

Sebastian Studios

Large Ceramastone Figures - P.W. Baston

YEAR ISSUE	EDITION LIMIT	YEAR RETD.	ISSUE PRICE	*QUOTE U.S.$
1963 Abraham Lincoln Toby Jug	Closed	N/A	Unkn.	600-1000
1963 Anne Boleyn	Closed	N/A	Unkn.	600-1000
1940 Basket	Closed	N/A	Unkn.	300-400
1973 Blacksmith	Closed	N/A	Unkn.	300-400
1940 Breton Man	Closed	N/A	Unkn.	1000-1500
1940 Breton Woman	Closed	N/A	Unkn.	1000-1500
1973 Cabinetmaker	Closed	N/A	Unkn.	300-400
1940 Candle Holder	Closed	N/A	Unkn.	300-400
1940 Caroler	Closed	N/A	Unkn.	300-400
1973 Clockmaker	Closed	N/A	Unkn.	300-400
1964 Colonial Boy	Closed	N/A	Unkn.	600-1000
1964 Colonial Girl	Closed	N/A	Unkn.	600-1000
1964 Colonial Man	Closed	N/A	Unkn.	600-1000
1964 Colonial Woman	Closed	N/A	Unkn.	600-1000
1963 David Copperfield	Closed	N/A	Unkn.	600-1000
1965 The Dentist	Closed	N/A	Unkn.	600-1000
1963 Dora	Closed	N/A	Unkn.	600-1000
1963 George Washington Toby Jug	Closed	N/A	Unkn.	600-1000
1966 Guitarist	Closed	N/A	Unkn.	600-1000
1963 Henry VIII	Closed	N/A	Unkn.	600-1000
1940 Horn of Plenty	Closed	N/A	Unkn.	300-400
1964 IBM Father	Closed	N/A	Unkn.	600-1000
1964 IBM Mother	Closed	N/A	Unkn.	600-1000
1964 IBM Photographer	Closed	N/A	Unkn.	600-1000
1964 IBM Son	Closed	N/A	Unkn.	600-1000
1964 IBM Woman	Closed	N/A	Unkn.	600-1000
1967 Infant of Prague	Closed	N/A	Unkn.	600-1000
1956 Jell-O Cow Milk Pitcher	Closed	N/A	Unkn.	175-225
1940 Jesus	Closed	N/A	Unkn.	300-400
1963 John F. Kennedy Toby Jug	Closed	N/A	Unkn.	600-1000
1940 Lamb	Closed	N/A	Unkn.	300-400
1947 Large Victorian Couple	Closed	N/A	Unkn.	600-1000
1940 Mary	Closed	N/A	Unkn.	600-1000
1963 Mending Time	Closed	N/A	Unkn.	600-1000
1975 Minuteman	Closed	N/A	Unkn.	600-1000
1978 Mt. Rushmore	Closed	N/A	Unkn.	400-500
1965 N.E. Home For Little Wanderers	Closed	N/A	Unkn.	600-1000
1939 Paul Revere Plaque	Closed	N/A	Unkn.	400-500
1973 Potter	Closed	N/A	Unkn.	300-400
XX Santa Fe...All The Way	Closed	N/A	Unkn.	600-1000
XX St. Francis (Plaque)	Closed	N/A	Unkn.	600-1000
1965 Stanley Music Box	Closed	N/A	Unkn.	300-500
1958 Swift Instrument Girl	Closed	N/A	Unkn.	500-750
1963 Tom Sawyer	Closed	N/A	Unkn.	600-1000
1959 Wasp Plaque	Closed	N/A	Unkn.	500-750
1948 Woody at Three	Closed	N/A	Unkn.	600-1000

Sebastian Miniatures - P.W. Baston

YEAR ISSUE	EDITION LIMIT	YEAR RETD.	ISSUE PRICE	*QUOTE U.S.$
1956 77th Bengal Lancer (Jell-O)	Closed	N/A	Unkn.	600-1000
1942 Accordion	Closed	N/A	Unkn.	325-375
1952 Aerial Tramway	Closed	N/A	Unkn.	300-600
1959 Alcoa Wrap PS	Closed	N/A	Unkn.	350-400
1959 Alexander Smith Weaver	Closed	N/A	Unkn.	350-425
1956 Alike, But Oh So Different	Closed	N/A	Unkn.	300-350
1957 Along the Albany Road PS	Closed	N/A	Unkn.	600-1000
1940 Ann Styvyesant	Closed	N/A	Unkn.	75-100
1940 Annie Oakley	Closed	N/A	Unkn.	75-100
1956 Arthritic Hands (J & J)	Closed	N/A	Unkn.	600-1000
XX Babe Ruth	Closed	N/A	Unkn.	600-1000
1952 Baby (Jell-O)	Closed	N/A	Unkn.	525-600
1939 Benjamin Franklin	Closed	N/A	Unkn.	75-100
1962 Big Brother Bob Emery	Closed	N/A	Unkn.	600-1000
1953 Blessed Julie Billart	Closed	N/A	Unkn.	400-500
1962 Blue Belle Highlander	Closed	N/A	Unkn.	200-250
1954 Bluebird Girl	Closed	N/A	Unkn.	400-450
XX Bob Hope	Closed	N/A	Unkn.	600-1000
1957 Borden's Centennial (Elsie the Cow)	Closed	N/A	Unkn.	600-1000
1971 Boston Gas Tank	Closed	N/A	Unkn.	300-500
1953 Boy Jesus in the Temple	Closed	N/A	Unkn.	350-400
1949 Boy Scout Plaque	Closed	N/A	Unkn.	300-350
1940 Buffalo Bill	Closed	N/A	Unkn.	75-100
1961 Bunky Knudsen	Closed	N/A	Unkn.	600-1000
1954 Campfire Girl	Closed	N/A	Unkn.	400-450
1955 Captain Doliber	Closed	N/A	Unkn.	300-350
1968 Captain John Parker	Closed	N/A	Unkn.	300-350
1951 Carl Moore (WEEI)	Closed	N/A	Unkn.	200-300
1951 Caroline Cabot (WEEI)	Closed	N/A	Unkn.	200-350
1940 Catherine LaFitte	Closed	N/A	Unkn.	75-100
1958 CBS Miss Columbia PS	Closed	N/A	Unkn.	600-1000
1951 Charles Ashley (WEEI)	Closed	N/A	Unkn.	200-350
1951 Chief Pontiac	Closed	N/A	Unkn.	400-700
1951 Chiquita Banana	Closed	N/A	Unkn.	350-400
1951 Christopher Columbus	Closed	N/A	Unkn.	250-300
1958 Cliquot Club Eskimo PS	Closed	N/A	Unkn.	10-2300
1957 Colonial Fund Doorway PS	Closed	N/A	Unkn.	600-1000
1958 Commodore Stephen Decatur	Closed	N/A	Unkn.	125-175
1958 Connecticut Bank & Trust	Closed	N/A	Unkn.	225-275
1939 Coronado	Closed	N/A	Unkn.	75-100
1939 Coronado's Senora	Closed	N/A	Unkn.	75-100
XX Coronation Crown	Closed	N/A	Unkn.	600-1000
1942 Cymbals	Closed	N/A	Unkn.	325-375
1954 Dachshund (Audiovox)	Closed	N/A	Unkn.	300-350
1947 Dahl's Fisherman	Closed	N/A	Unkn.	150-175
1940 Dan'l Boone	Closed	N/A	Unkn.	75-100
1953 Darned Well He Can	Closed	N/A	Unkn.	300-350
1955 Davy Crockett	Closed	N/A	Unkn.	225-275

YEAR ISSUE	EDITION LIMIT	YEAR RETD.	ISSUE PRICE	*QUOTE U.S.$
1939 Deborah Franklin	Closed	N/A	Unkn.	75-100
1948 Democratic Victory	Closed	N/A	Unkn.	350-500
1963 Dia-Mel Fat Man	Closed	N/A	Unkn.	375-400
1947 Dilemma	Closed	N/A	Unkn.	275-300
1967 Doc Berry of Berwick (yellow shirt)	Closed	N/A	Unkn.	300-350
1941 Doves	Closed	N/A	Unkn.	600-1000
1947 Down East	Closed	N/A	Unkn.	125-150
1942 Drum	Closed	N/A	Unkn.	325-375
1941 Ducklings	Closed	N/A	Unkn.	600-1000
1949 Dutchman's Pipe	Closed	N/A	Unkn.	175-225
1951 E. B. Rideout (WEEI)	Closed	N/A	Unkn.	200-350
XX Eagle Plaque	Closed	N/A	Unkn.	1000-1500
1956 Eastern Paper Plaque	Closed	N/A	Unkn.	350-400
1940 Elizabeth Monroe	Closed	N/A	Unkn.	150-175
1956 Elsie the Cow Billboard	Closed	N/A	Unkn.	600-1000
1949 Emmett Kelly	Closed	N/A	Unkn.	200-300
1949 Eustace Tilly	Closed	N/A	Unkn.	750-1500
1939 Evangeline	Closed	N/A	Unkn.	100-125
1952 The Fat Man (Jell-O)	Closed	N/A	Unkn.	525-600
1952 The Favored Scholar	Closed	N/A	Unkn.	200-300
1959 Fiorello LaGuardia	Closed	N/A	Unkn.	125-175
1947 First Cookbook Author	Closed	N/A	Unkn.	125-150
1952 The First House, Plimoth Plantation	Closed	N/A	Unkn.	150-195
1947 Fisher Pair PS	Closed	N/A	Unkn.	400-1000
1959 Fleischman's Margarine PS	Closed	N/A	Unkn.	225-325
1939 Gabriel	Closed	N/A	Unkn.	100-125
1966 Gardener Man	Closed	N/A	Unkn.	250-300
1966 Gardener Women	Closed	N/A	Unkn.	250-300
1966 Gardeners (Thermometer)	Closed	N/A	Unkn.	300-400
1949 Gathering Tulips	Closed	N/A	Unkn.	225-250
1972 George & Hatchet	Closed	N/A	Unkn.	400-450
1939 George Washington	Closed	N/A	Unkn.	35-75
1949 Giant Royal Bengal Tiger	Closed	N/A	Unkn.	1000-1500
1959 Giovanni Verrazzano	Closed	N/A	Unkn.	125-175
1955 Giraffe (Jell-O)	Closed	N/A	Unkn.	350-375
1956 Girl on Diving Board	Closed	N/A	Unkn.	400-450
1951 Great Stone Face	Closed	N/A	Unkn.	600-1000
1956 The Green Giant	Closed	N/A	Unkn.	400-500
1959 H.P. Hood Co. Cigar Store Indian	Closed	N/A	Unkn.	600-1000
1958 Hannah Duston PS	Closed	N/A	Unkn.	250-325
1940 Hannah Penn	Closed	N/A	Unkn.	100-150
1959 Harvard Trust Co. Town Crier	Closed	N/A	Unkn.	350-400
1958 Harvard Trust Colonial Man	Closed	N/A	Unkn.	275-325
1948 A Harvey Girl	Closed	N/A	Unkn.	250-300
1959 Henry Hudson	Closed	N/A	Unkn.	125-175
1965 Henry Wadsworth Longfellow	Closed	N/A	Unkn.	275-325
1953 Holgrave the Daguerrotypist	Closed	N/A	Unkn.	200-250
1954 Horizon Girl	Closed	N/A	Unkn.	400-450
1942 Horn	Closed	N/A	Unkn.	325-375
1955 Horse Head PS	Closed	N/A	Unkn.	350-375
1947 Howard Johnson Pieman	Closed	N/A	Unkn.	300-450
1957 IBM 305 Ramac	Closed	N/A	Unkn.	400-450
1939 Indian Maiden	Closed	N/A	Unkn.	100-125
1939 Indian Warrior	Closed	N/A	Unkn.	100-125
1960 The Infantryman	Closed	N/A	Unkn.	600-1000
1951 The Iron Master's House	Closed	N/A	Unkn.	350-500
1958 Jackie Gleason	Closed	N/A	Unkn.	600-1000
1963 Jackie Kennedy Toby Jug	Closed	N/A	Unkn.	600-1000
1940 James Monroe	Closed	N/A	Unkn.	150-175
1957 Jamestown Church	Closed	N/A	Unkn.	400-450
1957 Jamestown Ships	Closed	N/A	Unkn.	350-475
1940 Jean LaFitte	Closed	N/A	Unkn.	75-100
1951 Jesse Buffman (WEEI)	Closed	N/A	Unkn.	200-350
1939 John Alden	Closed	N/A	Unkn.	35-50
1963 John F. Kennedy Toby Jug	Closed	N/A	Unkn.	600-1000
1940 John Harvard	Closed	N/A	Unkn.	125-150
1940 John Smith	Closed	N/A	Unkn.	75-100
1958 Jordan Marsh Observer	Closed	N/A	Unkn.	175-275
1948 Jordan Marsh Observer	Closed	N/A	Unkn.	150-175
1951 Jordan Marsh Observer Rides the A.W. Horse	Closed	N/A	Unkn.	300-325
1951 Judge Pyncheon	Closed	N/A	Unkn.	175-225
1954 Kernel-Fresh Ashtray	Closed	N/A	Unkn.	400-450
XX The King	Closed	N/A	Unkn.	600-1000
1941 Kitten (Sitting)	Closed	N/A	Unkn.	600-1000
1941 Kitten (Sleeping)	Closed	N/A	Unkn.	600-1000
1953 Lion (Jell-O)	Closed	N/A	Unkn.	350-375
1966 Little George	Closed	N/A	Unkn.	350-450
1952 Lost in the Kitchen (Jell-O)	Closed	N/A	Unkn.	350-375
1942 Majorette	Closed	N/A	Unkn.	325-375
1952 Marblehead High School Plaque	Closed	N/A	Unkn.	200-300
1939 Margaret Houston	Closed	N/A	Unkn.	75-100
1960 Marine Memorial	Closed	N/A	Unkn.	300-400
1949 The Mark Twain Home in Hannibal, MO	Closed	N/A	Unkn.	600-1000
1972 Martha & the Cherry Pie	Closed	N/A	Unkn.	350-400
1939 Martha Washington	Closed	N/A	Unkn.	35-75
1948 Mary Lyon	Closed	N/A	Unkn.	250-300
1960 Masonic Bible	Closed	N/A	Unkn.	300-400
1966 Massachusetts SPCA	Closed	N/A	Unkn.	250-350
1957 Mayflower PS	Closed	N/A	Unkn.	300-325
1949 Menotomy Indian	Closed	N/A	Unkn.	175-250
1961 Merchant's Warren Sea Capt.	Closed	N/A	Unkn.	200-250
1960 Metropolitan Life Tower PS	Closed	N/A	Unkn.	350-400
1956 Michigan Millers PS	Closed	N/A	Unkn.	200-275
1951 Mit Seal	Closed	N/A	Unkn.	350-375
1954 Moose (Jell-O)	Closed	N/A	Unkn.	350-375
1951 Mother Parker (WEEI)	Closed	N/A	Unkn.	200-350
1947 Mr. Beacon Hill	Closed	N/A	Unkn.	50-75
1950 Mr. Obocell	Closed	N/A	Unkn.	75-125
1948 Mr. Rittenhouse Square	Closed	N/A	Unkn.	150-175

YEAR ISSUE	EDITION LIMIT	YEAR RETD.	ISSUE PRICE	*QUOTE U.S.$
1948 Mr. Sheraton	Closed	N/A	Unkn.	400-500
1947 Mrs. Beacon Hill	Closed	N/A	Unkn.	50-75
1940 Mrs. Dan'l Boone	Closed	N/A	Unkn.	75-100
1940 Mrs. Harvard	Closed	N/A	Unkn.	125-150
1956 Mrs. Obocell	Closed	N/A	Unkn.	400-450
1948 Mrs. Rittenhouse Square	Closed	N/A	Unkn.	150-175
1959 Mrs. S.O.S.	Closed	N/A	Unkn.	300-350
1958 Mt. Vernon	Closed	N/A	Unkn.	400-500
1957 Nabisco Buffalo Bee	Closed	N/A	Unkn.	600-1000
1957 Nabisco Spoonmen	Closed	N/A	Unkn.	600-1000
1948 Nathaniel Hawthorne	Closed	N/A	Unkn.	175-200
1950 National Diaper Service	Closed	N/A	Unkn.	250-300
1963 Naumkeag Indian	Closed	N/A	Unkn.	225-275
1952 Neighboring Pews	Closed	N/A	Unkn.	200-300
1956 NYU Grad School of Bus. Admin. Bldg.	Closed	N/A	Unkn.	300-350
1951 The Observer & Dame New England.	Closed	N/A	Unkn.	325-375
1952 Old Powder House	Closed	N/A	Unkn.	250-300
1953 Old Put Enjoys a Licking	Closed	N/A	Unkn.	300-350
1955 Old Woman in the Shoe (Jell-O)	Closed	N/A	Unkn.	500-600
1957 Olde James Fort	Closed	N/A	Unkn.	250-300
XX Ortho Gynecic	Closed	N/A	Unkn.	600-1000
1967 Ortho-Novum	Closed	N/A	Unkn.	600-1000
1952 Our Lady of Good Voyage	Closed	N/A	Unkn.	200-250
1954 Our Lady of Laleche	Closed	N/A	Unkn.	300-350
1965 Panti-Legs Girl PS	Closed	N/A	Unkn.	250-300
1949 Patrick Henry	Closed	N/A	Unkn.	100-125
1949 Paul Bunyan	Closed	N/A	Unkn.	150-250
1966 Paul Revere Plaque (W.T. Grant)	Closed	N/A	Unkn.	300-350
1941 Peacock	Closed	N/A	Unkn.	600-1000
1956 Permacel Tower of Tape Ashtray	Closed	N/A	Unkn.	600-1000
1960 Peter Stvyvesant	Closed	N/A	Unkn.	125-175
1940 Peter Stvyvesant	Closed	N/A	Unkn.	75-100
1941 Pheasant	Closed	N/A	Unkn.	600-1000
1950 Phoebe, House of 7 Gables	Closed	N/A	Unkn.	150-175
1940 Pocohontas	Closed	N/A	Unkn.	75-150
1961 Pope John 23rd	Closed	N/A	Unkn.	400-450
1965 Pope Paul VI	Closed	N/A	Unkn.	400-500
1956 Praying Hands	Closed	N/A	Unkn.	250-300
1947 Prince Philip	Closed	N/A	Unkn.	200-300
1947 Princess Elizabeth	Closed	N/A	Unkn.	200-300
1939 Priscilla	Closed	N/A	Unkn.	35-50
1951 Priscilla Fortesue (WEEI)	Closed	N/A	Unkn.	200-350
1946 Puritan Spinner	Closed	N/A	Unkn.	500-1000
1953 R.H. Stearns Chestnut Hill Mall	Closed	N/A	Unkn.	225-275
1954 Rabbit (Jell-O)	Closed	N/A	Unkn.	350-375
1956 Rarical Blacksmith	Closed	N/A	Unkn.	300-500
1948 Republican Victory	Closed	N/A	Unkn.	600-1000
1954 Resolute Ins. Co. Clipper PS	Closed	N/A	Unkn.	300-325
1956 Robin Hood & Friar Tuck	Closed	N/A	Unkn.	400-500
1956 Robin Hood & Little John	Closed	N/A	Unkn.	400-500
1958 Romeo & Juliet	Closed	N/A	Unkn.	400-500
1941 Rooster	Closed	N/A	Unkn.	600-1000
1958 Salem Savings Bank	Closed	N/A	Unkn.	250-300
1939 Sam Houston	Closed	N/A	Unkn.	75-100
1955 Santa (Jell-O)	Closed	N/A	Unkn.	500-600
1949 Sarah Henry	Closed	N/A	Unkn.	100-125
1946 Satchel-Eye Dyer	Closed	N/A	Unkn.	125-150
1953 The Schoolboy of 1850	Closed	N/A	Unkn.	350-400
1952 Scottish Girl (Jell-O)	Closed	N/A	Unkn.	350-375
1954 Scuba Diver	Closed	N/A	Unkn.	400-450
1962 Seaman's Bank for Savings	Closed	N/A	Unkn.	300-350
1951 Seb. Dealer Plaque (Marblehead)	Closed	N/A	Unkn.	300-350
1955 Second Bank-State St. Trust PS	Closed	N/A	Unkn.	300-325
1941 Secrets	Closed	N/A	Unkn.	600-1000
1938 Shaker Lady	Closed	N/A	Unkn.	50-100
1938 Shaker Man	Closed	N/A	Unkn.	50-100
1959 Siesta Coffee PS	Closed	N/A	Unkn.	600-1000
1951 Sir Frances Drake	Closed	N/A	Unkn.	250-300
1948 Sitzmark	Closed	N/A	Unkn.	175-200
1948 Slalom	Closed	N/A	Unkn.	175-200
1960 Son of the Desert	Closed	N/A	Unkn.	200-275
1957 Speedy Alka Seltzer	Closed	N/A	Unkn.	600-1000
1952 St. Joan d'Arc	Closed	N/A	Unkn.	300-350
1961 St. Jude Thaddeus	Closed	N/A	Unkn.	400-500
1954 St. Pius X	Closed	N/A	Unkn.	400-475
1952 St. Sebastian	Closed	N/A	Unkn.	300-350
1953 St. Teresa of Lisieux	Closed	N/A	Unkn.	225-275
1965 State Street Bank Globe	Closed	N/A	Unkn.	250-300
1954 Stimalose (Men)	Closed	N/A	Unkn.	600-1000
1954 Stimalose (Woman)	Closed	N/A	Unkn.	175-200
1952 Stork (Jell-O)	Closed	N/A	Unkn.	425-525
1960 Supp-Hose Lady	Closed	N/A	Unkn.	300-500
1941 Swan	Closed	N/A	Unkn.	600-1000
1954 Swan Boat Brooch-Enpty Seats	Closed	N/A	Unkn.	600-1000
1954 Swan Boat Brooch-Full Seats	Closed	N/A	Unkn.	600-1000
1948 Swedish Boy	Closed	N/A	Unkn.	250-500
1948 Swedish Girl	Closed	N/A	Unkn.	250-500
XX Sylvania Electric-Bulb Display	Closed	N/A	Unkn.	600-1000
1952 Tabasco Sauce	Closed	N/A	Unkn.	400-500
1956 Texcel Tape Boy	Closed	N/A	Unkn.	350-425
1949 The Thinker	Closed	N/A	Unkn.	175-250
1956 Three Little Kittens (Jell-O)	Closed	N/A	Unkn.	375-400
1947 Tollhouse Town Crier	Closed	N/A	Unkn.	125-175
1961 Tony Piet	Closed	N/A	Unkn.	600-1000
1966 Town Lyne Indian	Closed	N/A	Unkn.	600-1000
1971 Town Meeting Plaque	Closed	N/A	Unkn.	350-400
1942 Tuba	Closed	N/A	Unkn.	325-375
1949 Uncle Mistletoe	Closed	N/A	Unkn.	250-300
1970 Uncle Sam in Orbit	Closed	N/A	Unkn.	350-400

YEAR ISSUE	EDITION LIMIT	YEAR RETD.	ISSUE PRICE	*QUOTE U.S.$
1968 Watermill Candy Plaque	Closed	N/A	Unkn.	600-1000
1952 Weighing the Baby	Closed	N/A	Unkn.	200-300
1954 Whale (Jell-O)	Closed	N/A	Unkn.	350-375
1954 William Penn	Closed	N/A	Unkn.	175-225
1940 William Penn	Closed	N/A	Unkn.	100-150
1939 Williamsburg Governor	Closed	N/A	Unkn.	75-100
1939 Williamsburg Lady	Closed	N/A	Unkn.	75-100
1962 Yankee Clipper Sulfide	Closed	N/A	Unkn.	600-1000

Seymour Mann, Inc.

Bunny Musical Figurines - Kenji

YEAR ISSUE	EDITION LIMIT	YEAR RETD.	ISSUE PRICE	*QUOTE U.S.$
1991 Bunny In Teacup MH-781	Open		25.00	25
1991 Bunny In Teapot MH-780	Open		25.00	25

Cat Musical Figurines - Kenji

YEAR ISSUE	EDITION LIMIT	YEAR RETD.	ISSUE PRICE	*QUOTE U.S.$
1990 Bride/Groom Cat MH-738	Closed	1995	37.50	38
1991 Brown Cat in Bag	Closed	1995	30.00	30
1987 Brown Cat in Bag MH-617B/6	Closed	1995	30.00	30
1991 Brown Cat in Hat	Closed	1995	35.00	35
1988 Brown Cat in Hat MH-634B/6	Closed	1995	35.00	35
1991 Brown Cat in Teacup	Closed	1995	30.00	30
1987 Brown Cat in Teacup MH-600VGB16	Closed	1995	30.00	30
1987 Cat in Garbage Can MH-490	Closed	1995	35.00	35
1987 Cat in Rose Teacup MH-600VG	Closed	1995	30.00	30
1990 Cat Asleep MH-735	Closed	1995	17.50	18
1990 Cat Calico in Easy Chair MH-743VG	Closed	1995	27.50	28
1991 Cat in Bag	Closed	1995	30.00	30
1991 Cat in Bag	Closed	1995	30.00	30
1987 Cat in Bag MH-614	Closed	1995	30.00	30
1987 Cat in Bag MH-617	Closed	1995	30.00	30
1989 Cat in Basinet MH-714	Closed	1995	35.00	35
1989 Cat in Basket MH-713B	Closed	1995	35.00	35
1991 Cat in Basket MH-768	Closed	1995	35.00	35
1991 Cat in Bootie	Closed	1995	35.00	35
1990 Cat in Bootie MH-728	Closed	1995	35.00	35
1990 Cat in Dress MH-751VG	Closed	1995	37.50	38
1989 Cat in Flower MH-709	Closed	1995	35.00	35
1991 Cat in Garbage Can	Closed	1995	35.00	35
1989 Cat in Gift Box Musical MH-732	Closed	1995	40.00	40
1991 Cat in Hat	Closed	1995	35.00	35
1991 Cat in Hat Box	Closed	1995	35.00	35
1988 Cat in Hat Box MH-634	Closed	1995	35.00	35
1988 Cat in Hat MH-634B	Closed	1995	35.00	35
1991 Cat in Rose Teacup	Closed	1995	30.00	30
1989 Cat in Shoe MH-718	Closed	1995	30.00	30
1991 Cat in Teacup	Closed	1995	30.00	30
1987 Cat in Teacup MH-600VGG	Closed	1995	30.00	30
1991 Cat in Teapot Brown	Closed	1995	30.00	30
1987 Cat in Teapot Brown MH-600VGB	Closed	1995	30.00	30
1989 Cat in Water Can Musical MH-712	Closed	1995	35.00	35
1991 Cat Momma MH-758	Closed	1995	35.00	35
1989 Cat on Basket MH-713	Closed	1995	35.00	35
1990 Cat on Gift Box Music MH-740	Closed	1995	40.00	40
1990 Cat on Pillow MH-731	Closed	1995	17.50	18
1991 Cat on Tipped Garbage Can	Closed	1995	35.00	35
1987 Cat on Tipped Garbage Can MH-498	Closed	1995	35.00	35
1990 Cat Sailor in Rocking Boat MH-734	Closed	1995	45.00	45
1990 Cat w/Bow on Pink Pillow MH-741P	Closed	1995	33.50	34
1989 Cat w/Coffee Cup Musical MH-706	Closed	1995	35.00	35
1990 Cat w/Parrot Musical MH-730	Closed	1995	37.50	38
1989 Cat w/Swing Musical MH-710	Closed	1995	35.00	35
1991 Cat Watching Butterfly MH-784	Closed	1995	17.50	18
1991 Cat Watching Canary MH-783	Closed	1995	25.00	25
1991 Cat With Bow on Pink Pillow MH-741P	Closed	1995	33.50	34
1991 Cats Ball Shape	Closed	1995	25.00	25
1985 Cats Ball Shape MH-303A/G	Closed	1995	25.00	25
1990 Cats Graduation MH-745	Closed	1995	27.50	28
1989 Cats in Basket XMAS-664	Closed	1995	7.50	8
1991 Cats w/Ribbon	Closed	1995	30.00	30
1986 Cats w/Ribbon MH-481A/C	Closed	1995	30.00	30
1991 Family Cat MH-770	Closed	1995	35.00	35
1991 Grey Cat in Bootie	Closed	1995	35.00	35
1990 Grey Cat in Bootie MH-728G/6	Closed	1995	35.00	35
1991 Kitten Picking Tulips MH-756	Closed	1995	40.00	40
1990 Kitten Trio in Carriage MH-742	Closed	1995	37.50	38
1991 Kittens w/Balls of Yarn	Closed	1995	35.00	35
1987 Kittens w/Balls of Yarn MH-612	Closed	1995	30.00	30
1991 Musical Bear	Closed	1995	27.50	28
1987 Musical Bear MH-602	Closed	1995	27.50	28
1991 Revolving Cat with Butterfly MH-759	Closed	1995	40.00	40
1991 Teapot Cat	Closed	1995	30.00	30
1987 Teapot Cat MH-631	Closed	1995	30.00	30
1987 Valentine Cat in Bag Musical MH-600	Closed	1995	33.50	34
1987 Valentine Cat in Teacup MH-600VLT	Closed	1995	33.50	34

Christmas Collection - Various

YEAR ISSUE	EDITION LIMIT	YEAR RETD.	ISSUE PRICE	*QUOTE U.S.$
1991 2 Tone Stone Church MER-360B - J. White	Closed	1993	35.00	35
1986 Antique Santa Musical XMAS-364 - J. White	Closed	1987	20.00	20
1990 Antique Shop Lite Up House MER-376 - J. White	Closed	1993	27.50	28
1991 Apothecary Lite Up CJ-128 - Jaimy	Closed	1993	33.50	34
1990 Bakery Lite Up House MER-373 - J. White	Closed	1993	27.50	28
1991 Beige Church Lite Up House MER-360A - Jaimy	Closed	1993	35.00	35
1990 Bethlehem Lite Up Set 3 CP-59893 - J. White	Closed	1993	120.00	120
1991 Boy and Girl on Bell CJ-132 - Jaimy	Closed	1993	13.50	14
1991 Boy on Horse CJ-457 - Jaimy	Closed	1993	6.00	6
1990 Brick Church Lite Up House MER-360C - J. White	Closed	1993	35.00	35
1991 Carolers Under Lamppost CJ-114A - Jaimy	Closed	1993	7.50	8
1989 Cat in Teacup Musical XMAS-600 - J. White	Closed	1992	30.00	30
1990 Cathedral Lite Up House MER-362 - J. White	Closed	1993	37.50	38
1991 Church Lite Up MER-410 - J. White	Closed	1993	17.50	18
1990 Church Lite Up House MER-310 - J. White	Closed	1993	27.50	28
1991 Church w/Blue Roof Lite Up House MER-360E - J. White	Closed	1993	35.00	35
1991 Covered Bridge CJ-101 - Jaimy	Closed	1993	27.50	28
1990 Deep Gold Church Lite Up House MER-360D - J. White	Closed	1993	35.00	35
1990 Double Store Lite Up House MER-311 - J. White	Closed	1993	27.50	28
1991 Elf w/Doll House CB-14 - E. Mann	Closed	1993	30.00	30
1991 Elf w/Hammer CB-11 - E. Mann	Closed	1993	30.00	30
1991 Elf w/Reindeer CJ-422 - Jaimy	Closed	1993	9.00	9
1991 Elf w/Rocking Horse CB-10 - E. Mann	Closed	1993	30.00	30
1991 Elf w/Teddy Bear CB-12 - E. Mann	Closed	1993	30.00	30
1991 Emily's Toys CJ-127 - Jaimy	Closed	1993	35.00	35
1991 Father and Mother w/Daughter CJ-133 - Jaimy	Closed	1993	13.50	14
1991 Father Christmas CJ-233	Closed	1993	33.50	34
1991 Father Christmas w/Holly CJ-239 - Jaimy	Closed	1993	35.00	35
1991 Fire Station CJ-129 - Jaimy	Closed	1993	50.00	50
1990 Fire Station Lite Up House XMS-1550C - E.Mann	Closed	1993	25.00	25
1991 Four Men Talking CJ-138 - Jaimy	Closed	1993	27.50	28
1991 Gift Shop Lite Up CJ-125 - Jaimy	Closed	1993	33.50	34
1991 Girls w/Instruments CJ-131 - Jaimy	Closed	1993	13.50	14
1990 Grist Mill Lite Up House MER-372 - J. White	Closed	1993	27.50	28
1991 Horse and Coach CJ-207 - Jaimy	Closed	1993	25.00	25
1990 Inn Lite Up House MER-316 - J. White	Closed	1993	27.50	28
1986 Jumbo Santa/Toys XMAS-38 - J. White	Closed	1987	45.00	45
1991 Kids Building Igloo CJ-137 - Jaimy	Closed	1993	13.50	14
1991 Lady w/Dogs CJ-208 - Jaimy	Closed	1993	13.50	14
1990 Leatherworks Lite Up House MER-371 - J. White	Closed	1993	27.50	28
1990 Library Lite Up House MER-317 - J. White	Closed	1993	27.50	28
1990 Light House Lite Up House MER-370 - J. White	Closed	1993	27.50	28
1991 Man w/Wheelbarrow CJ-134 - Jaimy	Closed	1993	13.50	14
1990 Mansion Lite Up House MER-319 - J. White	Closed	1993	27.50	28
1990 Mr/Mrs Santa Musical CJ-281 - Jaimy	Closed	1993	37.50	38
1990 New England Church Lite Up House MER-375 - J. White	Closed	1993	27.50	28
1990 New England General Store Lite Up House MER-377 - J. White	Closed	1993	27.50	28
1991 Newsboy Under Lamppost CJ-144B - Jaimy	Closed	1993	15.00	15
1991 Old Curiosity Lite Up CJ-201 - Jaimy	Closed	1993	37.50	38
1991 Playhouse Lite Up CJ-122 - Jaimy	Closed	1993	50.00	50
1991 Public Library Lite Up CJ-121 - Jaimy	Closed	1993	45.00	45
1990 Railroad Station Lite Up House MER-374 - J. White	Closed	1993	27.50	28
1991 Reindeer Barn Lite Up House CJ-421 - Jaimy	Closed	1993	55.00	55
1991 Restaurant Lite Up House MER-354 - J. White	Closed	1993	27.50	28
1990 Roly Poly Santa 3 Asst. CJ-253/4/7 - Jaimy	Closed	1993	17.50	18
1991 Santa Cat Roly Poly CJ-252 - Jaimy	Closed	1993	17.50	18
1991 Santa Fixing Sled CJ-237 - Jaimy	Closed	1993	35.00	35
1991 Santa In Barrel Waterball CJ-243 - Jaimy	Closed	1993	33.50	34
1989 Santa in Sled w/Reindeer CJ-3 - Jaimy	Closed	1993	25.00	25
1991 Santa In Toy Shop CJ-441 - Jaimy	Closed	1993	33.50	34
1989 Santa Musicals CJ-1/4 - Jaimy	Closed	1993	27.50	28
1990 Santa on Chimney Musical CJ-212 - Jaimy	Closed	1993	33.50	34
1989 Santa on Horse CJ-33A - Jaimy	Closed	1993	33.50	34
1990 Santa on See Saw TR-14 - E. Mann	Closed	1993	30.00	30
1991 Santa On Train CJ-458 - Jaimy	Closed	1993	6.00	6
1991 Santa On White Horse CJ-338 - E. Mann	Closed	1993	33.50	34
1991 Santa Packing Bag CJ-210 - Jaimy	Closed	1993	33.50	34
1990 Santa Packing Bag CJ-210 - Jaimy	Closed	1993	33.50	34
1991 Santa Packing Bag CJ-236 - Jaimy	Closed	1993	35.00	35
1991 Santa Sleeping Musical CJ-214 - Jaimy	Closed	1993	30.00	30
1991 Santa w/Bag and List CJ-431 - Jaimy	Closed	1993	33.50	34
1991 Santa w/Deer Musical CJ-21R - Jaimy	Closed	1993	33.50	34
1991 Santa w/Girl Waterball CJ-241 - Jaimy	Closed	1993	33.50	34

*Quotes have been rounded up to nearest dollar

FIGURINES/COTTAGES

YEAR ISSUE		EDITION LIMIT	YEAR RETD.	ISSUE PRICE	*QUOTE U.S.$
1991	Santa w/Lantern Musical CJ-211 - Jaimy	Closed	1993	33.50	34
1990	Santa w/List CJ-23 - Jaimy	Closed	1993	27.50	28
1989	Santa w/List CJ-23 - Jaimy	Closed	1992	27.50	28
1991	Santa w/List CJ-23R - Jaimy	Closed	1993	27.50	28
1990	School Lite Up House MER-320 - J. White	Closed	1993	27.50	28
1991	The Skaters CJ-205 - Jaimy	Closed	1993	25.00	25
1991	Snowball Fight CJ-124B - Jaimy	Closed	1993	25.00	25
1991	Soup Seller Waterball CJ-209 - Jaimy	Closed	1993	25.00	25
1991	Stone Cottage Lite Up CJ-100 - Jaimy	Closed	1993	37.50	38
1991	Stone House Lite Up CJ-102 - Jaimy	Closed	1993	45.00	45
1991	The Story Teller CJ-204 - Jaimy	Closed	1993	20.00	20
1991	Teddy Bear On Wheels CB-42 - E. Mann	Closed	1993	25.00	25
1991	Three Ladies w/Food CJ-136 - Jaimy	Closed	1993	13.50	14
1990	Town Hall Lite Up House MER-315 - J. White	Closed	1993	27.50	28
1991	The Toy Seller CJ-206 - Jaimy	Closed	1993	13.50	14
1991	Toy Store Lite Up House MER-355 - J. White	Closed	1993	27.50	28
1991	Trader Santa Musical CJ-442 - Jaimy	Closed	1993	30.00	30
1991	Train Set MER-378 - J. White	Closed	1993	25.00	25
1985	Trumpeting Angel w/Jesus XMAS-527 - J. White	Closed	1987	40.00	40
1991	Two Old Men Talking CJ-107 - Jaimy	Closed	1993	13.50	14
1991	Village Mill Lite Up CJ-104 - Jaimy	Closed	1993	30.00	30
1991	Village People CJ-116A - Jaimy	Closed	1993	60.00	60
1985	Virgin w/Christ Musical XMAS-528 - J. White	Closed	1987	33.50	34
1991	Woman w/Cow CJ-135 - Jaimy	Closed	1993	15.00	15
1991	Ye Olde Town Tavern CJ-130 - Jaimy	Closed	1993	45.00	45

Christmas In America - Various

1990	Cart With People - E. Mann	Closed	1992	25.00	35
1988	Doctor's Office Lite Up - E. Mann	Closed	1990	27.50	28
1991	New England Church Lite Up House MER-375 - J. White	Closed	1992	27.50	28
1991	New England General Store Lite Up House MER-377 - J. White	Closed	1992	27.50	28
1989	Santa in Sleigh - E. Mann	Closed	1990	25.00	45
1988	Set/3, Capitol, White House, Mt. Vernon - E. Mann	Closed	1990	75.00	150

Christmas Village - L. Sciola

1991	Away, Away	Closed	1993	30.00	30
1991	Counsil House	Closed	1993	60.00	60
1991	Curiosity Shop	Closed	1993	45.00	45
1991	Emily's Toys	Closed	1993	45.00	45
1991	The Fire Station	Closed	1993	60.00	60
1991	On Thin Ice	Closed	1993	30.00	30
1991	The Playhouse	Closed	1993	60.00	60
1991	Public Library	Closed	1993	50.00	50
1991	Scrooge/Marley's Counting House	Closed	1993	45.00	45
1991	Story Teller	Closed	1993	20.00	20
1991	Ye Old Gift Shoppe	Closed	1993	50.00	50

Dickens Collection - Various

1990	Black Swan Inn Lite Up XMS-7000E - J. White	Closed	1993	30.00	30
1990	Cratchit Family MER-121 - J. White	Closed	1993	37.50	38
1991	Cratchit's Lite Up House CJ-200 - Jaimy	Closed	1993	37.50	38
1991	Cratchit/Tiny Tim Musical CJ-117 - Jaimy	Closed	1993	33.50	34
1990	Cratchit/Tiny Tim Musical MER-105 - J. White	Closed	1993	33.50	34
1989	Cratchits Lite Up XMS-7000A - J. White	Closed	1991	30.00	30
1989	Fezziwigs Lite Up XMS-7000C - J. White	Closed	1991	30.00	30
1989	Gift Shoppe Lite Up XMS-7000D - J. White	Closed	1991	30.00	30
1990	Hen Poultry Lite Up XMS-7000H - J. White	Closed	1993	30.00	30
1991	Scrooge Musical CJ-118 - Jaimy	Closed	1993	30.00	30
1991	Scrooge/Marley Counting House CJ-202 - Jaimy	Closed	1993	37.50	38
1989	Scrooge/Marley Lite Up XMS-7000B - J. White	Closed	1991	30.00	30
1990	Tea and Spice Lite Up XMS-7000F - J. White	Closed	1993	30.00	30
1990	Waite Fish Store Lite Up XMS-7000G - J. White	Closed	1993	30.00	30

Gingerbread Christmas Collection - J. Sauerbrey

1991	Gingerbread Angel CJ-411	Closed	1993	7.50	8
1991	Gingerbread Church Lite Up House CJ-403	Closed	1993	65.00	65
1991	Gingerbread House CJ-416	Closed	1993	7.50	8
1991	Gingerbread House Lite Up CJ-404	Closed	1993	65.00	65
1991	Gingerbread Man CJ-415	Closed	1993	7.50	8
1991	Gingerbread Mansion Lite Up CJ-405	Closed	1993	70.00	70
1991	Gingerbread Mouse/Boot CJ-409	Closed	1993	7.50	8
1991	Gingerbread Mrs. Claus CJ-414	Closed	1993	7.50	8
1991	Gingerbread Reindeer CJ-410	Closed	1993	7.50	8
1991	Gingerbread Rocking Horse Music CJ-460	Closed	1993	33.50	34
1991	Gingerbread Santa CJ-408	Closed	1993	7.50	8
1991	Gingerbread Sleigh CJ-406	Closed	1993	7.50	8

1991	Gingerbread Snowman CJ-412	Closed	1993	7.50	8
1991	Gingerbread Swan Musical CJ-462	Closed	1993	33.50	34
1991	Gingerbread Sweet Shop Lite Up House	Closed	1993	60.00	60
1991	Gingerbread Teddy Bear Music CJ-461	Closed	1993	33.50	34
1991	Gingerbread Toy Shop Lite Up House CJ-402	Closed	1993	60.00	60
1991	Gingerbread Tree CJ-407	Closed	1993	7.50	8
1991	Gingerbread Village Lite Up House CJ-400	Closed	1993	60.00	60

Victorian Christmas Collection - Various

1991	Antique Shop Lite Up House MER-353 - J. White	Closed	1993	27.50	28
1991	Beige Church Lite Up House MER-351 - J. White	Closed	1993	35.00	35
1991	Book Store Lite Up House MER-351 - J. White	Closed	1993	27.50	28
1991	Town Lite Up House MER-350 - J. White	Closed	1993	37.50	38
1991	Country Store Lite Up House MER-356 - J. White	Closed	1993	27.50	28
1993	Couple Against Wind CJ-420 - Jaimy	Closed	1994	15.00	15
1991	Inn Lite Up House MER-352 - J. White	Closed	1993	27.50	28
1991	Little Match Girl CJ-419 - Jaimy	Closed	1993	9.00	9
1990	Toy/Doll House Lite Up MER-314 - J. White	Closed	1993	27.50	28
1990	Two Boys w/Snowman CJ-106 - Jaimy	Closed	1993	12.00	12
1990	Victorian House Lite Up House MER-312 - J. White	Closed	1993	27.50	28
1990	Yarn Shop Lite Up House MER-313 - J. White	Closed	1993	27.50	28

Wizard Of Oz - 40th Anniversary - E. Mann

1979	Dorothy, Scarecrow, Lion, Tinman	Closed	1981	7.50	45
1979	Dorothy, Scarecrow, Lion, Tinman, Musical	Closed	1981	12.50	75

Shelia's Collectibles

Shelia's Collectors' Society - S. Thompson

1993	Anne Peacock House SOC01	Retrd.	1994	16.00	100-120
1993	Susan B. Anthony CGA93	Retrd.	1994	Gift	75-125
1993	Anne Peacock House Print	Retrd.	1994	Gift	N/A
1994	Seaview Cottage SOC02	Retrd.	1995	17.00	70
1994	Helen Keller's Birthplace-Ivy Green CGA94	Retrd.	1995	Gift	55
1994	Collector's Society T-Shirt	Retrd.	1995	Gift	N/A
1995	Pink Lady SOC03	Retrd.	1996	20.00	25
1995	Red Cross CGA95	Retrd.	1996	Gift	25
1995	Collector's Society T-Shirt & Collector's Society Pin	Retrd.	1996	Gift	N/A
1996	Tinker Toy House SOC04	6/97		20.00	N/A
1996	Tatman House CGA96	4/97		Gift	N/A
1996	Tinker Toy House Ornament	4/97		Gift	N/A

Accessories - S. Thompson

1994	Amish Quilt Line COL12	Retrd.	1994	18.00	30-48
1993	Apple Tree COL09	Retrd.	1996	12.00	20
1996	Autumn Tree ACC09	Open		14.00	14
1996	Barber Gazebo ACC05	Open		13.00	13
1993	Dogwood Tree COL08	Retrd.	1996	12.00	16
1992	Fence 5" COL04	Retrd.	1993	9.00	30
1992	Fence 7" COL05	Retrd.	1993	10.00	30
1995	Flower Garden ACC02	Open		13.00	30-50
1994	Formal Garden COL13	Retrd.	1994	18.00	45
1992	Gazebo w/Victorian Lady COL02	Retrd.	1995	11.00	20-35
1996	Grazing Cows ACC04	Open		12.00	12
1992	Lake With Swan COL06	Retrd.	1995	11.00	25-35
1992	Oak Bower COL03	Retrd.	1993	11.00	25-50
1996	Palm Tree ACC07	Open		14.00	14
1995	Real Estate Sign ACC03	Open		12.00	12
1996	Sailboat ACC06	Open		12.00	12
1996	Spring Tree ACC10	Open		14.00	14
1996	Summertime Picket Fence ACC08	Open		12.00	12
1994	Sunrise At 80 Meeting COL10	Retrd.	1994	18.00	25-35
1992	Tree With Bush COL07	Retrd.	1996	10.00	15-30
1994	Victorian Arbor COL11	Retrd.	1994	18.00	30
1995	Wisteria Arbor ACC01	Open		12.00	12
1992	Wrought Iron Gate With Magnolias COL01	Retrd.	1993	11.00	30-50

American Barns - S. Thompson

1995	Casey Barn BAR04	Open		18.00	18
1995	Mail Pouch Barn BAR03	Open		18.00	18
1996	Mr. Peanut Barn BAR05	Open		19.00	19
1996	Mr. Peanut Barn, AP BAR05	97	1996	24.00	24
1995	Pennsylvania Dutch Barn AP BAR02	Retrd.	1995	20.00	40
1995	Pennsylvania Dutch Barn BAR02	Retrd.		18.00	30
1994	Rock City Barn AP BAR01	Retrd.	1994	20.00	30-40
1994	Rock City Barn BAR01	Open		18.00	18

Amish Village - S. Thompson

1994	Amish Barn (renovated) AMS04II	Open		17.00	17
1993	Amish Barn AMS04	Open		17.00	17
1993	Amish Barn, AP AMS04	Retrd.	1993	20.00	40
1994	Amish Buggy (renovated) AMS05II	Open		12.00	12
1993	Amish Buggy AMS05	Open		12.00	12
1993	Amish Buggy, AP AMS05	Retrd.	1993	16.00	33

1994	Amish Home (renovated) AMS01II	Open		17.00	17
1993	Amish Home AMS01	Open		17.00	17
1993	Amish Home, AP AMS01	Retrd.	1993	20.00	25-35
1994	Amish School (renovated) AMS02II	Open		15.00	15
1993	Amish School AMS02	Open		15.00	15
1993	Amish School, AP AMS02	Retrd.	1993	20.00	25-35
1994	Covered Bridge (renovated) AMS03II	Open		16.00	16
1993	Covered Bridge AMS03	Open		16.00	16
1993	Covered Bridge, AP AMS03	Retrd.	1993	20.00	25-35
1995	Roadside Stand AMS06	Open		17.00	17
1995	Roadside Stand, AP AMS06	Retrd.	1995	24.00	30-40

Arkansas Ladies - S. Thompson

1996	Handford Terry House ARK02	Open		19.00	19
1996	Pillow-Thompson House ARK04	Open		19.00	19
1996	Rosalie House ARK01	Open		19.00	19
1996	Wings ARK03	Open		19.00	19

Art Deco - S. Thompson

1996	Berkeley Shore DEC03	Open		19.00	19
1996	Berkeley Shore, AP DEC03	95	1996	24.00	24
1996	The Carlyle DEC02	Open		19.00	19
1996	The Carlyle, AP DEC02	97	1996	24.00	24
1996	Hotel Webster DEC01	Open		19.00	19
1996	Hotel Webster, AP DEC01	99	1996	24.00	24
1996	Marlin DEC04	Open		19.00	19
1996	Marlin, AP DEC04	89	1996	24.00	24

Atlanta - S. Thompson

1995	Fox Theatre ATL06	Open		19.00	19
1995	Hammond's House ATL05	Open		18.00	18
1996	Margaret Mitchell House ATL07	Open		19.00	19
1996	Margaret Mitchell House, AP ATL07	89	1996	24.00	24
1995	Swan House ATL03	Open		18.00	18
1995	Tullie Smith House ATL01	Open		17.00	17
1995	Victorian Playhouse ATL02	Open		17.00	17
1995	Wren's Nest ATL04	Open		19.00	19

Charleston - S. Thompson

1994	#2 Meeting Street (renovated) CHS06II	Open		16.00	16
1991	#2 Meeting Street CHS06	Open		15.00	15
1990	90 Church St. CHS17	Retrd.	1993	12.00	25-50
1994	Ashe House (renovated) CHS51II	Open		16.00	16
1993	Ashe House CHS51	Open		16.00	16
1991	Beth Elohim Temple CHS20	Retrd.	1993	15.00	22-35
1994	The Citadel (renovated) CHS22II	Open		16.00	16
1993	The Citadel CHS22	Open		16.00	16
1993	City Hall (No banner) CHS21	Retrd.	1993	15.00	80-100
1993	City Hall (without Spuleto colors) CHS21	Retrd.	1993	15.00	200
1993	City Hall CHS21	Retrd.	1993	15.00	80-150
1991	City Market (closed gates) CHS07	Retrd.	1991	15.00	25-60
1991	City Market (open gates) CHS07	Open		15.00	15
1994	City Market (renovated) CHS07II	Open		15.00	15
1994	College of Charleston (renovated) CHS40II	Retrd.	1996	16.00	30
1993	College of Charleston CHS40	Retrd.	1996	16.00	30
1993	College of Charleston, AP CHS40	Retrd.	1996	20.00	40
1992	Dock Street Theater (chimney) CHS08	Retrd.	1993	15.00	30
1991	Dock Street Theater (no chimney) CHS08	Retrd.	1992	15.00	65
1994	Edmonston-Alston (renovated) CHS04II	Retrd.	1996	16.00	50
1991	Edmonston-Alston CHS04	Retrd.	1995	15.00	50
1990	Exchange Building CHS15	Retrd.	1994	15.00	30-50
1990	Heyward-Washington House CHS02	Retrd.	1993	15.00	25-50
1994	John Rutledge House Inn (renovated) CHS50II	Open		16.00	16
1993	John Rutledge House Inn CHS50	Open		16.00	16
1991	Magnolia Plantation House (beige curtains) CHS03	Retrd.	1996	16.00	25
1994	Magnolia Plantation House (renovated) CHS03II	Open		16.00	21
1991	Magnolia Plantation House (white curtains) CHS03	Retrd.	1996	16.00	16
1990	Manigault House CHS01	Retrd.	1993	15.00	25-40
1990	Middleton Plantation CHS19	Retrd.	1991	9.00	200
1990	Pink House CHS18	Retrd.	1993	12.00	15-25
1990	Powder Magazine CHS16	Retrd.	1991	9.00	125-200
1994	Single Side Porch (renovated) CHS30II	Open		16.00	16
1993	Single Side Porch CHS30	Open		16.00	16
1993	Single Side Porch, AP CHS30	Retrd.	1993	20.00	36
1990	St. Michael's Church CHS14	Retrd.	1994	15.00	35
1994	St. Philip's Church (renovated) CHS05II	Retrd.	1996	15.00	20
1991	St. Philip's Church CHS05	Retrd.	1996	15.00	25
1991	St. Phillip's Church (misspelling Phillips) CHS05	Retrd.	1996	15.00	40

Charleston Battery - S. Thompson

1996	22 South Battery CHB01	Open		19.00	19
1996	22 South Battery, AP CHB01	109	1996	24.00	40
1996	24 South Battery CHB02	Open		19.00	19
1996	24 South Battery, AP CHB02	99	1996	24.00	40
1996	26 South Battery CHB03	Open		19.00	19
1996	26 South Battery, AP CHB03	74	1996	24.00	40
1996	28 South Battery CHB04	Open		19.00	19
1996	28 South Battery, AP CHB04	74	1996	24.00	40

YEAR ISSUE		EDITION LIMIT	YEAR RETRD.	ISSUE PRICE	*QUOTE U.S.$

Charleston Gold Seal - S. Thompson

1988	90 Church St. CHS17	Retrd.	1990	9.00	50
1988	CHS31 Rainbow Row-rust	Retrd.	1990	9.00	N/A
1988	CHS32 Rainbow Row-tan	Retrd.	1990	9.00	N/A
1988	CHS33 Rainbow Row-cream	Retrd.	1990	9.00	N/A
1988	CHS34 Rainbow Row-green	Retrd.	1990	9.00	N/A
1988	CHS35 Rainbow Row-lavender	Retrd.	1990	9.00	N/A
1988	CHS36 Rainbow Row-pink	Retrd.	1990	9.00	N/A
1988	CHS37 Rainbow Row-blue	Retrd.	1990	9.00	N/A
1988	CHS38 Rainbow Row-lt. yellow	Retrd.	1990	9.00	N/A
1988	CHS39 Rainbow Row-lt. pink	Retrd.	1990	9.00	N/A
1988	Exchange Building CHS15	Retrd.	1990	9.00	N/A
1988	Middleton Plantation CHS19	Retrd.	1990	9.00	150
1988	Pink House CHS18	Retrd.	1990	9.00	36
1988	Powder Magazine CHS16	Retrd.	1990	9.00	250
1988	St. Michael's Church CHS14	Retrd.	1990	9.00	N/A

Charleston II - S. Thompson

1995	Boone Hall Plantation CHS56	Open		18.00	18
1995	Boone Hall Plantation, AP CHS56	Retrd.	1995	24.00	40
1994	Drayton House CHS52	Open		18.00	18
1994	Drayton House, AP CHS52	Retrd.	1994	24.00	40-75
1996	Huguenot Church CHS58	Open		19.00	19
1996	Huguenot Church, AP CHS58	95	1996	24.00	40
1996	Magnolia Garden CHS57	Open		19.00	19
1995	O'Donnell's Folly CHS55	Open		18.00	18
1995	O'Donnell's Folly, AP CHS55	Retrd.	1995	24.00	45
1996	Sotile CHS59	Open		19.00	19
1996	Sotile, AP CHS59	98	1996	24.00	40

Charleston Rainbow Row - S. Thompson

1990	CHS31 Rainbow Row-rust	Retrd.	1993	9.00	40
1990	CHS32 Rainbow Row-cream	Retrd.	1993	9.00	20-35
1990	CHS33 Rainbow Row-tan	Retrd.	1993	9.00	25
1990	CHS34 Rainbow Row-green	Retrd.	1993	9.00	23
1990	CHS35 Rainbow Row-lavender	Retrd.	1993	9.00	33
1990	CHS36 Rainbow Row-pink	Retrd.	1993	9.00	23-35
1990	CHS37 Rainbow Row-blue	Retrd.	1993	9.00	25-40
1990	CHS38 Rainbow Row-lt. yellow	Retrd.	1993	9.00	25-40
1990	CHS39 Rainbow Row-lt. pink	Retrd.	1993	9.00	25
1993	CHS41 Rainbow Row-aurora	Open		13.00	13
1994	CHS41II Rainbow Row-aurora (renovated)	Open		13.00	13
1993	CHS42 Rainbow Row-off-white	Open		13.00	13
1994	CHS42II Rainbow Row-off-white (renovated)	Open		13.00	13
1993	CHS43 Rainbow Row-cream	Open		13.00	13
1994	CHS43II Rainbow Row-cream (renovated)	Open		13.00	13
1993	CHS44 Rainbow Row-green	Open		13.00	13
1994	CHS44II Rainbow Row-green (renovated)	Open		13.00	13
1993	CHS45 Rainbow Row-lavender	Open		13.00	13
1994	CHS45II Rainbow Row-lavender (renovated)	Open		13.00	13
1993	CHS46 Rainbow Row-pink	Open		13.00	13
1994	CHS46II Rainbow Row-pink (renovated)	Open		13.00	13
1993	CHS47 Rainbow Row-blue	Open		13.00	13
1994	CHS47II Rainbow Row-blue (renovated)	Open		13.00	13
1993	CHS48 Rainbow Row-yellow	Open		13.00	13
1994	CHS48 Rainbow Row-yellow (renovated)	Open		13.00	13
1993	CHS49 Rainbow Row-gray	Open		13.00	13
1994	CHS49II Rainbow Row-gray (renovated)	Open		13.00	13
1993	Rainbow Row Sign	Retrd.	N/A	12.50	20

Dicken's Village - S. Thompson

1991	Butcher Shop XMS03	Retrd.	1993	15.00	30
1991	Evergreen Tree XMS08	Retrd.	1993	11.00	20-40
1991	Gazebo & Carolers XMS06	Retrd.	1993	12.00	17-40
1991	Scrooge & Marley's Shop XMS01	Retrd.	1993	15.00	25-40
1991	Scrooge's Home XMS05	Retrd.	1993	15.00	20-40
1991	Toy Shoppe XMS04	Retrd.	1993	15.00	25-35
1991	Victorian Apartment Building XMS02	Retrd.	1993	15.00	30-40
1992	Victorian Church XMS09	Retrd.	1993	15.00	25-50
1991	Victorian Skaters XMS07	Retrd.	1993	12.00	25
1992	Set	Retrd.	1993	125.00	185-200

Galveston - S. Thompson

1995	Beissner House GLV04	Open		18.00	18
1995	Dancing Pavillion GLV03	Open		18.00	18
1995	Frenkel House GLV01	Open		18.00	18
1995	Reymershoffer House GLV02	Open		18.00	18

George Barber - S. Thompson

1996	Newton House GFB03	Open		19.00	19
1996	Phillippi House GFB02	Open		19.00	19
1996	Pine Crest GFB04	Open		19.00	19
1996	Renaissance GFB01	Open		19.00	19

Ghost House Series - S. Thompson

1996	31 Legare St. GHO06	Open		19.00	19
1995	Gaffos House GHO04	Open		19.00	19
1994	Inside-Outside House GHO01	Retrd.	1996	18.00	25
1994	Inside-Outside House, AP GHO01	Retrd.	1994	20.00	30-40
1996	Kings Tavern GHO05	Open		19.00	19
1996	Kings Tavern, AP GHO05	102	1996	24.00	24
1994	Pirates' House GHO02	Retrd.	1996	18.00	20-40

| 1994 | Pirates' House, AP GHO02 | Retrd. | 1994 | 20.00 | 25-40 |
| 1995 | Red Castle GHO03 | Open | | 19.00 | 19 |

Gone with the Wind - S. Thompson

1995	Aunt Pittypat's GWW03	12/96		24.00	24
1995	Aunt Pittypat's, AP GWW03	Retrd.	1995	30.00	40
1995	General Store GWW04	12/96		24.00	24
1995	General Store, AP GWW04	Retrd.	1995	30.00	40
1995	Loew's Grand GWW05	Retrd.	1995	24.00	35
1995	Loew's Grand, AP GWW05	Retrd.	1995	30.00	25-75
1996	Silhouette GWW06	12/96		16.00	16
1995	Tara GWW01	12/96		24.00	24
1995	Tara, AP GWW01	Retrd.	1995	30.00	25-75
1995	Twelve Oaks GWW02	12/96		24.00	24
1995	Twelve Oaks, AP GWW02	Retrd.	1995	30.00	40
1995	Set of 5, AP	Retrd.	1995	150.00	250

Inventor Series - S. Thompson

1993	Ford Motor Company (green) INV01	Retrd.	1993	17.00	45-65
1993	Ford Motor Company (grey) INV01	Retrd.	1994	17.00	40-60
1993	Ford Motor Company, AP INV01	Retrd.	1993	20.00	40
1993	Menlo Park Laboratory (cream) INV02	Retrd.	1993	16.00	30-50
1993	Menlo Park Laboratory (grey) INV02	Retrd.	1994	16.00	25
1993	Menlo Park Laboratory, AP INV02	Retrd.	1993	20.00	30-40
1993	Noah Webster House INV03	Retrd.	1994	15.00	30
1993	Noah Webster House, AP INV03	Retrd.	1993	20.00	35-45
1993	Wright Cycle Shop INV04	Retrd.	1994	17.00	30
1993	Wright Cycle Shop, AP INV04	Retrd.	1993	20.00	35-45

Jazzy New Orleans Series - S. Thompson

1994	Beauregard-Keyes House JNO04	Retrd.	1996	18.00	30
1994	Beauregard-Keyes House, AP JNO04	Retrd.	1994	20.00	45
1994	Gallier House JNO02	Open		18.00	18
1994	Gallier House, AP JNO02	Retrd.	1994	20.00	50
1994	La Branche Building JNO01	Open		18.00	18
1994	La Branche Building, AP JNO01	Retrd.	1994	20.00	50
1994	LePretre House JNO03	Open		18.00	18
1994	LePretre House, AP JNO03	Retrd.	1994	20.00	50

Key West - S. Thompson

1995	Artist House KEY06	Open		19.00	19
1995	Artist House, AP KEY06	Retrd.	1995	24.00	40
1995	Eyebrow House KEY01	Open		18.00	18
1995	Eyebrow House, AP KEY01	Retrd.	1995	24.00	40
1995	Hemingway House KEY07	Open		19.00	19
1995	Hemingway House, AP KEY07	Retrd.	1995	24.00	40
1995	Illingsworth Gingerbread House KEY05	Open		19.00	19
1995	Illingsworth Gingerbread House, AP KEY05	Retrd.	1995	24.00	40
1995	Shotgun House KEY03	Open		17.00	17
1995	Shotgun House, AP KEY03	Retrd.	1995	24.00	40
1995	Shotgun Sister KEY04	Open		17.00	17
1995	Shotgun Sister, AP KEY04	Retrd.	1995	24.00	40
1995	Southernmost House KEY02	Open		19.00	19
1995	Southernmost House, AP KEY02	Retrd.	1995	24.00	40
1996	Southernmost Point KEY08	Open		12.00	12

Ladies By The Sea - S. Thompson

1996	Abbey II LBS01	Open		19.00	19
1996	Abbey II, AP LBS01	93	1996	24.00	40
1996	Centennial Cottage LBS02	Open		19.00	19
1996	Centennial Cottage, AP LBS02	94	1996	24.00	24
1996	Hall Cottage LBS04	Open		19.00	19
1996	Hall Cottage, AP LBS04	108	1996	24.00	24
1996	Heart Blossom LBS03	Open		19.00	19
1996	Heart Blossom, AP LBS03	107	1996	24.00	24

Lighthouse Series - S. Thompson

1991	Anastasia Lighthouse (burgundy) FL103	Retrd.	1991	15.00	20
1991	Anastasia Lighthouse (red) FL103	Retrd.	1994	15.00	30
1993	Assateague Island Light LTS07	Open		17.00	17
1994	Assateague Island Light, AP LTS07	Retrd.	1994	20.00	40
1995	Cape Hatteras Light LTS09	Open		17.00	17
1995	Cape Hatteras Light, AP LTS09	Retrd.	1995	24.00	40
1991	Cape Hatteras Lighthouse NC103	Retrd.	1994	15.00	35
1994	Charleston Light (renovated) LTS01	Retrd.	1995	15.00	30
1993	Charleston Light LTS01	Retrd.	1995	15.00	25
1993	New London Ledge Light LTS08	Retrd.	1996	17.00	20
1994	New London Ledge Light, AP LTS08	Retrd.	1994	20.00	40-75
1993	Round Island Light LTS06	Open		17.00	17
1994	Round Island Light, AP LTS06	Retrd.	1994	20.00	40
1990	Stage Harbor Lighthouse NEW06	Retrd.	1993	15.00	70-115
1993	Thomas Point Light LTS05	Open		17.00	17
1994	Thomas Point Light, AP LTS05	Retrd.	1994	20.00	45
1990	Tybee Lighthouse SAV07	Retrd.	1994	15.00	25-35

Limited Edition American Gothic - S. Thompson

1993	Gothic Revival Cottage ACL01	Retrd.	1993	20.00	25-45
1993	Mele House ACL04	Retrd.	1993	20.00	43
1993	Perkins House ACL02	Retrd.	1993	20.00	45
1993	Rose Arbor ACL05	Retrd.	1993	14.00	25-45
1993	Roseland Cottage ACL03	Retrd.	1993	20.00	30
1993	Set of 5	Retrd.	1993	94.00	140

Limited Edition Barber Houses - S. Thompson

| 1995 | Banta House | 4,000 | 1995 | 24.00 | 24 |

1995	Greenman House	4,000	1995	24.00	24
1995	Riley-Cutler House	4,000	1995	24.00	24
1995	Weller House	4,000	1995	24.00	24

Limited Edition Mail-Order Victorians (Barber Houses) - S. Thompson

1994	Brehaut House ACL09	3,300	1994	24.00	30-40
1994	Goeller House ACL08	3,300	1994	24.00	31-45
1994	Henderson House ACL07	3,300	1994	24.00	30-50
1994	Titman House ACL06	3,300	1994	24.00	33-40
1994	Set of 4	3,300	1994	96.00	100-145

Limited Pieces - S. Thompson

1991	Bridgetown Library NJ102	Retrd.	N/A	16.00	25
1993	Comly-Rich House XXX01	Retrd.	N/A	12.00	25-75
1991	Delphos City Hall OH101	Retrd.	N/A	15.00	125
1991	Historic Burlington County Clubhouse NJ101	Retrd.	N/A	16.00	N/A
1991	Mark Twain Boyhood Home MO101	Retrd.	N/A	15.00	N/A
1990	Newton County Court House GA101	Retrd.	N/A	16.00	200

Mackinac - S. Thompson

1996	Amberg Cottage MAK01	Open		19.00	19
1996	Amberg Cottage, AP MAK01	102	1996	24.00	40
1996	Anne Cottage MAK02	Open		19.00	19
1996	Anne Cottage, AP MAK02	95	1996	24.00	40
1996	Grand Hotel (3 pc. set) MAK05	Open		57.00	57
1996	Rearick Cottage MAK03	Open		19.00	19
1996	Rearick Cottage, AP MAK03	103	1996	24.00	40
1996	Windermere Hotel MAK04	Open		19.00	19
1996	Windermere Hotel, AP MAK04	105	1996	24.00	40

Martha's Vineyard - S. Thompson

1994	Alice's Wonderland (renovated) MAR08II	Open		16.00	16
1993	Alice's Wonderland MAR08	Open		16.00	16
1993	Alice's Wonderland, AP MAR08	Retrd.	1993	20.00	30
1995	Blue Cottage MAR13	Open		17.00	17
1995	Blue Cottage, AP MAR13	Retrd.	1995	24.00	30-40
1994	Campground Cottage (renovated) MAR07II	Retrd.	1995	16.00	16
1993	Campground Cottage MAR07	Retrd.	1995	16.00	30-50
1993	Campground Cottage, AP MAR07	Retrd.	1993	20.00	30
1994	Gingerbread Cottage-grey (renovated) MAR09II	Retrd.	1996	16.00	18
1993	Gingerbread Cottage-grey AP MAR09	Retrd.	1993	20.00	30
1993	Gingerbread Cottage-grey MAR09	Retrd.	1996	16.00	30
1995	Trails End MAR11	Open		17.00	17
1995	Trails End, AP MAR11	Retrd.	1995	24.00	30-40
1995	White Cottage MAR12	Open		17.00	17
1995	White Cottage, AP MAR12	Retrd.	1995	24.00	30-40
1994	Wood Valentine (renovated) MAR10II	Open		16.00	16
1993	Wood Valentine MAR10	Open		16.00	16
1993	Wood Valentine, AP MAR10	Retrd.	1993	20.00	30-40

New England - S. Thompson

1991	Faneuil Hall NEW09	Retrd.	1993	15.00	25-75
1990	Longfellow's House NEW01	Retrd.	1993	15.00	25-50
1990	Malden Mass. Victorian Inn NEW05	Retrd.	1992	10.00	60-100
1990	Martha's Vineyard Cottage-blue/mauve MAR06	Retrd.	1993	15.00	30-75
1990	Martha's Vineyard Cottage-blue/orange MAR05	Retrd.	1993	15.00	50
1990	Motif #1 Boathouse NEW02	Retrd.	1993	15.00	20-70
1990	Old North Church NEW04	Retrd.	1993	15.00	25-85
1990	Paul Revere's Home NEW03	Retrd.	1993	15.00	30-70
1991	President Bush's Home NEW07	Retrd.	1993	15.00	40-95
1991	Wedding Cake House NEW08	Retrd.	1993	15.00	30-60

North Carolina - S. Thompson

1990	Josephus Hall House NC101	Retrd.	1993	15.00	25-45
1990	Presbyterian Bell Tower NC102	Retrd.	1993	15.00	50
1991	The Tryon Palace NC104	Retrd.	1993	15.00	25-75

Old-Fashioned Christmas - S. Thompson

1994	Conway Scenic Railroad Station OFC04	Open		18.00	18
1994	Conway Scenic Railroad Station, AP OFC04	Retrd.	1994	20.00	35-45
1994	Dwight House OFC02	Retrd.	1996	18.00	25
1994	Dwight House, AP OFC02	Retrd.	1994	20.00	50-85
1994	General Merchandise OFC03	Open		18.00	18
1994	General Merchandise, AP OFC03	Retrd.	1994	20.00	40-50
1994	Old First Church OFC01	Open		18.00	18
1994	Old First Church, AP OFC01	Retrd.	1994	20.00	40-50
1994	Set of 4 1994 AP	Retrd.	1994	80.00	199
1995	Christmas Inn OFC05	Open		18.00	18
1995	Town Square Tree OFC06	Open		18.00	18

Painted Ladies I - S. Thompson

1990	The Abbey LAD08	Retrd.	1992	10.00	115-150
1990	Atlanta Queen Anne LAD07	Retrd.	1992	10.00	150-200
1990	Cincinnati Gothic LAD05	Retrd.	1992	10.00	75-125
1990	Colorado Queen Anne LAD04	Retrd.	1992	10.00	75-125
1990	Mira Vista LAD06	Retrd.	1992	10.00	385-450
1990	San Francisco Italianate-yellow LAD03	Retrd.	1991	10.00	125-150
1990	San Francisco Stick House-blue LAD02	Retrd.	1991	10.00	60-80

YEAR ISSUE		EDITION LIMIT	YEAR RETD.	ISSUE PRICE	*QUOTE U.S.$
1990	San Francisco Stick House-yellow LAD01	Retrd.	1991	10.00	85-125
1990	Painted Ladies I Sign	Retrd.	N/A	12.50	20

Painted Ladies II - S. Thompson

1994	Cape May Gothic (renovated) LAD13II	Retrd.	1995	16.00	35
1992	Cape May Gothic LAD13	Retrd.	1995	15.00	25-35
1994	Cape May Victorian Pink House (renovated) LAD16II	Retrd.	1996	16.00	20
1992	Cape May Victorian Pink House LAD16	Retrd.	1996	15.00	22
1994	The Gingerbread Mansion (renovated) LAD09II	Retrd.	1994	16.00	25-35
1992	The Gingerbread Mansion LAD09	Retrd.	1993	15.00	20-30
1994	Morningstar Inn (renovated) LAD15II	Retrd.	1994	16.00	25-35
1992	Morningstar Inn LAD15	Retrd.	1994	15.00	25-35
1994	Pitkin House (renovated) LAD10II	Retrd.	1996	16.00	20
1992	Pitkin House LAD10	Retrd.	1996	15.00	20
1994	Queen Anne Townhouse (renovated) LAD12II	Retrd.	1994	16.00	35
1992	Queen Anne Townhouse LAD12	Retrd.	1994	15.00	25-35
1994	The Victorian Blue Rose (renovated) LAD14II	Retrd.	1996	16.00	20
1992	The Victorian Blue Rose LAD14	Retrd.	1996	15.00	21
1994	The Young-Larson House (renovated) LAD11II	Retrd.	1996	16.00	20
1992	The Young-Larson House LAD11	Retrd.	1996	15.00	20

Painted Ladies III - S. Thompson

1994	Cape May Green Stockton Row (renovated) LAD20II	Retrd.	1995	16.00	25
1993	Cape May Green Stockton Row LAD20	Retrd.	1995	16.00	25
1994	Cape May Linda Lee (renovated) LAD17II	Retrd.	1996	16.00	25
1993	Cape May Linda Lee LAD17	Retrd.	1996	16.00	20
1994	Cape May Pink Stockton Row (renovated) LAD19II	Open		16.00	16
1993	Cape May Pink Stockton Row LAD19	Open		16.00	16
1994	Cape May Tan Stockton Row (renovated) LAD18II	Open		16.00	16
1993	Cape May Tan Stockton Row LAD18	Open		16.00	16
1996	Cream Stockton LAD22	Open		19.00	19
1996	Cream Stockton, AP LAD22	101	1996	24.00	24
1995	Steiner Cottage LAD21	Open		17.00	17
1995	Steiner Cottage, AP LAD21	Retrd.	1995	24.00	40

Panaramic Lights - S. Thompson

1996	Jeffrys Hook Light PLH02	Open		19.00	19
1996	Jeffrys Hook Light, AP PLH02	97	1996	24.00	40
1996	New Canal Light PLH03	Open		19.00	19
1996	New Canal Light, AP PLH03	104	1996	24.00	40
1996	Quoddy Head Light PLH04	Open		19.00	19
1996	Quoddy Head Light, AP PLH04	102	1996	24.00	40
1996	Split Rock Light PLH01	Open		19.00	19
1996	Split Rock Light, AP PLH01	105	1996	24.00	40

Philadelphia - S. Thompson

1990	"Besty" Ross House (misspelling) PHI03	Retrd.	1990	15.00	20-45
1990	Betsy Ross House PHI03	Retrd.	1993	15.00	45
1990	Carpenter's Hall PHI01	Retrd.	1993	15.00	35
1990	Elphreth's Alley PHI05	Retrd.	1993	15.00	30-65
1990	Graff House PHI07	Retrd.	1993	15.00	35-60
1990	Independence Hall PHI04	Retrd.	1993	15.00	35-50
1990	Market St. Post Office PHI02	Retrd.	1993	15.00	35
1990	Old City Hall PHI06	Retrd.	1993	15.00	25-35
1990	Old Tavern PHI08	Retrd.	1993	15.00	33

Plantations - S. Thompson

1996	Dickey House PLA05	Open		19.00	19
1995	Farley PLA04	Retrd.	1996	18.00	18
1995	Farley, AP PLA04	Retrd.	1995	24.00	40-65
1995	Longwood PLA02	Open		19.00	19
1995	Longwood, AP PLA02	Retrd.	1995	24.00	30-40
1995	Merry Sherwood PLA03	Open		18.00	18
1995	Merry Sherwood, AP PLA03	Retrd.	1995	24.00	30-40
1995	San Francisco PLA01	Open		19.00	19
1995	San Francisco, AP PLA01	Retrd.	1995	24.00	40-50

San Francisco - S. Thompson

1995	Brandywine SF101	Open		18.00	18
1995	Brandywine, AP SF101	Retrd.	1995	24.00	30-40
1995	Eclectic Blue SF103	Open		19.00	19
1995	Eclectic Blue, AP SF103	Retrd.	1995	24.00	40-50
1995	Edwardian Green SF104	Open		18.00	18
1995	Edwardian Green, AP SF104	Retrd.	1995	24.00	30-40
1995	Queen Rose SF102	Open		19.00	19
1995	Queen Rose, AP SF102	Retrd.	1995	24.00	30-40

Savannah - S. Thompson

1990	Andrew Low Mansion SAV02	Retrd.	1994	15.00	25-35
1996	Asendorf SAV13	Open		19.00	19
1996	Asendorf, AP SAV13	100	1996	24.00	24
1994	Cathedral of St. John (renovated) SAV09II	Retrd.	1995	16.00	30-40
1992	Cathedral of St. John SAV09	Retrd.	1995	16.00	40-95
1994	Chestnut House SAV11	Open		18.00	18
1994	Chestnut House, AP SAV11	Retrd.	1994	24.00	75
1990	Davenport House SAV03	Retrd.	1994	15.00	25-35
1990	Herb House SAV05	Retrd.	1993	15.00	16-30

YEAR ISSUE		EDITION LIMIT	YEAR RETD.	ISSUE PRICE	*QUOTE U.S.$
1994	Juliette Low House (renovated) SAV04II	Open		15.00	15
1990	Juliette Low House (w/logo) SAV04	Open		15.00	15
1990	Juliette Low House (w/o logo) SAV04	Retrd.	1990	15.00	100
1995	Mercer House SAV12	Open		18.00	18
1995	Mercer House, AP SAV12	Retrd.	1995	24.00	40-75
1990	Mikve Israel Temple SAV06	Retrd.	1994	15.00	35-85
1994	Olde Pink House (renovated) SAV01II	Retrd.	1996	15.00	25
1990	Olde Pink House SAV01	Retrd.	1996	15.00	35-45
1994	Owens Thomas House (renovated) SAV10II	Retrd.	1996	16.00	25-35
1993	Owens Thomas House AP SAV10	Retrd.	1993	20.00	75
1993	Owens Thomas House SAV10	Retrd.	1996	16.00	30-45
1990	Savannah Gingerbread House I SAV08	Retrd.	1996	15.00	265-300
1990	Savannah Gingerbread House II SAV08	Retrd.	1992	15.00	375

Shadow Play Silhouettes - S. Thompson

1996	Girl w/Hoop & Boy w/Dog SPO03	Open		12.00	12
1996	Horse and Carriage SPO01	Open		15.00	15
1996	Victorian Couple & Bicycle SPO02	Open		15.00	15

Show Pieces - S. Thompson

| 1995 | Baldwin House SHW01 | Retrd. | 1995 | 20.00 | 20 |
| 1996 | The Winnie Watson House SHW02 | Retrd. | 1996 | 20.00 | 25 |

Signing Only Pieces - S. Thompson

1994	Star Barn SOP01	Retrd.	1994	24.00	35-60
1995	Shelia's Real Estate Office SOP02	Retrd.	1995	20.00	45
1996	Thompson's Mercantile SOP03	12/96		24.00	24

South Carolina - S. Thompson

1991	All Saints' Church SC105	Retrd.	1993	15.00	30-45
1990	The Governor's Mansion (misspelling) SC102	Retrd.	1990	15.00	15
1994	The Governor's Mansion (renovated) SC102II	Retrd.	1995	15.00	35
1990	The Governor's Mansion SC102	Retrd.	1995	15.00	15
1994	The Hermitage (renovated) SC101II	Retrd.	1995	15.00	22
1990	The Hermitage SC101	Retrd.	1995	15.00	25-35
1994	The Lace House (renovated) SC103II	Retrd.	1995	15.00	15
1990	The Lace House SC103	Retrd.	1995	15.00	40-50
1994	The State Capitol (renovated) SC104II	Retrd.	1994	15.00	50-70
1991	The State Capitol SC104	Retrd.	1994	15.00	30

South Carolina Ladies - S. Thompson

1996	Cinnamon Hill SCL04	Open		19.00	19
1996	Cinnamon Hill, AP SCL04	93	1996	24.00	40
1996	Davis-Johnsey House SCL02	Open		19.00	19
1996	Davis-Johnsey House, AP SCL02	104	1996	24.00	40
1996	Inman House SCL01	Open		19.00	19
1996	Inman House, AP SCL01	107	1996	24.00	40
1996	Montgomery House SCL03	Open		19.00	19
1996	Montgomery House, AP SCL03	105	1996	24.00	40

St. Augustine - S. Thompson

1991	Anastasia Lighthousekeeper's House FL104	Retrd.	1993	15.00	35-45
1991	Mission Nombre deDios FL105	Retrd.	1993	15.00	30-50
1991	Old City Gates FL102	Retrd.	1993	15.00	30
1991	The "Oldest House" FL101	Retrd.	1993	15.00	30-50

Texas - S. Thompson

1990	The Alamo TEX01	Retrd.	1993	15.00	150-200
1990	Mission Concepcion TEX04	Retrd.	1993	15.00	50-75
1990	Mission San Francisco TEX03	Retrd.	1993	15.00	35-75
1990	Mission San Jose' TEX02	Retrd.	1993	15.00	40-75
1990	Texas Sign	Retrd.	N/A	12.50	20

Victorian Springtime - S. Thompson

1993	Heffron House VST03	Retrd.	1996	17.00	23
1993	Heffron House, AP VST03	Retrd.	1996	20.00	30-40
1993	Jacobsen House VST04	Retrd.	1996	17.00	23
1993	Jacobsen House, AP VST04	Retrd.	1996	20.00	30-40
1993	Ralston House VST01	Retrd.	1996	17.00	25-75
1993	Ralston House, AP VST01	Retrd.	1993	20.00	40
1993	Sessions House VST02	Retrd.	1996	17.00	25-75
1993	Sessions House, AP VST02	Retrd.	1993	20.00	40
1993	Set of 4, AP	Retrd.	1993	100.00	180

Victorian Springtime II - S. Thompson

1995	Dragon House VST07	Open		18.00	18
1995	Dragon House, AP VST07	Retrd.	1995	24.00	40
1995	E.B. Hall House VST08	Open		19.00	19
1995	E.B. Hall House, AP VST08	Retrd.	1995	24.00	40
1995	Gibney Home VST09	Open		18.00	18
1995	Gibney Home, AP VST09	Retrd.	1995	24.00	40
1995	Ray Home VST05	Open		18.00	18
1995	Ray Home, AP VST05	Retrd.	1995	24.00	40
1995	Victoria VST06	Open		18.00	18
1995	Victoria, AP VST06	Retrd.	1995	24.00	40

Victorian Springtime III - S. Thompson

| 1996 | Clark House VST14 | Open | | 19.00 | 19 |

YEAR ISSUE		EDITION LIMIT	YEAR RETD.	ISSUE PRICE	*QUOTE U.S.$
1996	Clark House, AP VST14	96	1996	24.00	40
1996	Goodwill House VST13	Open		19.00	19
1996	Goodwill House, AP VST13	88	1996	24.00	40
1996	Queen-Anne Mansion VST12	Open		19.00	19
1996	Queen-Anne Mansion, AP VST12	103	1996	24.00	40
1996	Sheppard House VST11	Open		19.00	19
1996	Sheppard House, AP VST11	98	1996	24.00	40
1996	Urfer House VST10	Open		19.00	19
1996	Urfer House, AP VST10	71	1996	24.00	40

Washington D.C. - S. Thompson

1992	Cherry Trees DC005	Retrd.	1993	12.00	40-70
1992	Library of Congress DC002	Retrd.	1993	16.00	47
1991	National Archives DC001	Retrd.	1993	16.00	35
1991	Washington Monument DC004	Retrd.	1993	16.00	30-50
1992	White House DC003	Retrd.	1993	16.00	105-175
1992	Set of 5	Retrd.	1993	76.00	250-375

West Coast Lighthouse Series - S. Thompson

1995	East Brother Light WCL01	Open		19.00	19
1995	East Brother Light, AP WCL01	Retrd.	1995	24.00	40
1995	Mukilteo Light WCL02	Open		18.00	18
1995	Mukilteo Light, AP WCL02	Retrd.	1995	24.00	40
1995	Point Fermin Light WCL04	Open		18.00	18
1995	Point Fermin Light, AP WCL04	Retrd.	1995	24.00	40
1995	Yaquina Bay Light WCL03	Open		18.00	18
1995	Yaquina Bay Light, AP WCL03	Retrd.	1995	24.00	40

Williamsburg - S. Thompson

1990	Apothecary WIL09	Retrd.	1994	12.00	25
1994	Bruton Parish Church (renovated) WIL13II	Open		15.00	15
1992	Bruton Parish Church WIL13	Open		15.00	15
1995	Capitol WIL15	Open		18.00	18
1995	Capitol, AP WIL15	Retrd.	1995	24.00	30-40
1994	Courthouse (renovated) WIL11II	Retrd.	1995	15.00	25
1990	Courthouse WIL11	Retrd.	1995	15.00	25
1990	The Golden Ball Jeweler WIL07	Retrd.	1994	12.00	30
1994	Governor's Palace (renovated) WIL04II	Open		15.00	15
1990	Governor's Palace WIL04	Open		15.00	15
1994	Homesite (renovated) WIL12II	Retrd.	1996	15.00	22
1990	Homesite WIL12	Retrd.	1996	15.00	22
1994	King's Arm Tavern (renovated) WIL10II	Retrd.	1995	15.00	25-35
1990	King's Arm Tavern WIL10	Retrd.	1995	15.00	25
1990	Milliner WIL06	Retrd.	1994	12.00	25
1990	Nicolson Shop WIL08	Retrd.	1994	12.00	25
1990	The Printing Offices WIL05	Retrd.	1993	12.00	25
1995	Raleigh Tavern WIL14	Open		18.00	18
1995	Raleigh Tavern, AP WIL14	Retrd.	1995	24.00	30-40

Shube's Manufacturing, Inc.

Busts - P. Sedlow

1995	General Grant	750		380.00	380
1995	General Lee	750		380.00	380
1995	Kennedy	750		380.00	380
1995	Lincoln	750		380.00	380

Fantasy - Various

1992	Behold - P. Sedlow	2,500		280.00	280
1987	Castle - N/A	Retrd.	1992	N/A	N/A
1992	Crystal Fortress - Sedlow/Wimberly	2,500		480.00	480
1987	Dragon - N/A	Retrd.	1992	N/A	N/A
1991	Dragon Lord - P. Sedlow	4,500		330.00	330
1991	Guardian of the Crystal - D. Wimberly	2,500		870.00	870
1990	Immortal Power - R. Gonzales	3,500		280.00	280
1991	Keeper of the Fire Lamp - P. Sedlow	4,500		330.00	330
1992	Pinnacle - P. Sedlow	Retrd.	1995	280.00	280
1991	Winged Splendor - P. Sedlow	4,500		420.00	420
1989	Wizard - N/A	Retrd.	1992	N/A	N/A
1991	Wizards Spell - P. Sedlow	4,500		330.00	330

Frontier - P. Sedlow

| 1991 | High Desert Ambush | Retrd. | 1995 | 550.00 | 550 |
| 1991 | Summit Confrontation | Retrd. | 1995 | 480.00 | 480 |

Great Chiefs and Leaders - P. Sedlow

1992	Chief Joseph	2,500		240.00	240
1992	CrazyHorse	2,500		240.00	240
1992	Geronimo	2,500		240.00	240
1992	Quanna Parker	2,500		240.00	240
1992	Red Cloud	2,500		240.00	240
1992	Sitting Bull	2,500		240.00	240

Limited Edition Figurine - N/A

| 1990 | Entrancing Carousel | 4,500 | | 240.00 | 240 |

Native American - Various

1993	Battleground - P. Sedlow	900		380.00	380
1991	Blood Bros - P. Sedlow	4,500		330.00	330
1994	End of the Trail (classic pewter) - P. Sedlow	500		800.00	800
1994	End of the Trail - P. Sedlow	250		650.00	650
1994	Heritage (classic pewter) - P. Sedlow	300		380.00	380
1994	Heritage - P. Sedlow	700		480.00	480
1991	Moon Bear (diamond cut) - P. Sedlow	3,500		750.00	750

YEAR ISSUE		EDITION LIMIT	YEAR RETD.	ISSUE PRICE	*QUOTE U.S.$
1991	Moon Bear - P. Sedlow	3,500		680.00	680
1990	Noble Flight - R. Gonzales	Retrd.	1995	240.00	240
1994	Offering (classic pewter) - P. Sedlow	250		650.00	650
1994	Offering (diamond cut) - P. Sedlow	250		870.00	870
1994	Offering - P. Sedlow	1,200		800.00	800
1994	Old Enemies (classic pewter) - M. Phelps	250		550.00	550
1994	Old Enemies (diamond cut) - M. Phelps	250		330.00	330
1994	Old Enemies - M. Phelps	1,200		700.00	700
1994	Pueblo Dancer (classic pewter) - M. Phelps	350		280.00	280
1994	Pueblo Dancer - M. Phelps	750		380.00	380
1990	Saga on the Plains - P. Sedlow	4,500		430.00	430
1995	Scout - P. Sedlow	750		170.00	170
1994	Sitting Bull (classic pewter) - P. Sedlow	300		1500.00	1500
1992	Sitting Bull (classic pewter) - P. Sedlow	400		170.00	170
1994	Sitting Bull - P. Sedlow	500		2000.00	2000
1993	Smoke Signal - P. Sedlow	900		380.00	380
1994	Traditional Dancer (classic pewter) - M. Phelps	350		280.00	280
1994	Traditional Dancer - M. Phelps	750		380.00	380
1993	Victorious - P. Sedlow	900		380.00	380
1990	Whitewater Rush - P. Sedlow	4,500		430.00	430

Wildlife - Various

YEAR ISSUE		EDITION LIMIT	YEAR RETD.	ISSUE PRICE	*QUOTE U.S.$
1990	American Eagle - D. Wimberly	S/O	1995	430.00	430
1990	Bugling Monarch (diamond cut) - D. Wimberly	4,500		280.00	280
1990	Bugling Monarch - D. Wimberly	4,500		240.00	240
1993	Catch of the Day (classic pewter) - P. Sedlow	450		240.00	240
1993	Catch of the Day (diamond cut) - P. Sedlow	2,500		330.00	330
1993	Catch of the Day - P. Sedlow	2,500		280.00	280
1991	Dancers of the Land (diamond cut) - D. Wimberly	4,500		480.00	480
1991	Dancers of the Land - D. Wimberly	4,500		430.00	430
1990	Duel - P. Sedlow	Retrd.	1995	280.00	280
1990	Family Frolic - H. Freidland	Retrd.	1992	N/A	N/A
1993	Freedom's Cry (classic pewter) - P. Sedlow	450		280.00	280
1993	Freedom's Cry (diamond cut) - P. Sedlow	1,800		380.00	380
1993	Freedom's Cry - P. Sedlow	1,800		330.00	330
1994	Lobo - P. Sedlow	750		240.00	240
1990	Master of the Night - P. Sedlow	Retrd.	1995	330.00	330
1991	Morning Solitude - D. Wimberly	Retrd.	1995	330.00	330
1993	Night Song (diamond cut) - P. Sedlow	1,800		430.00	430
1993	Night Song - P. Sedlow	1,800		380.00	380
1993	Soaring Spirit (classic pewter) - D. Wimberly	450		330.00	330
1993	Soaring Spirit (diamond cut) - D. Wimberly	1,800		430.00	430
1993	Soaring Spirit - D. Wimberly	1,800		380.00	380
1990	Unbridled Majesty - P. Sedlow	Retrd.	1992	N/A	N/A
1993	Warhorse (diamond cut) - P. Sedlow	1,800		430.00	430
1993	Warhorse - P. Sedlow	1,800		380.00	380

Silvestri, Inc.

Holiday Hamlet® -Accessories - V. Balcou

YEAR ISSUE		EDITION LIMIT	YEAR RETD.	ISSUE PRICE	*QUOTE U.S.$
1993	Blizzard Express Train	Open		95.00	95
1993	Carols in the Snow	Open		30.00	30
1993	Christmas Tree, large	Open		45.00	45
1993	Christmas Tree, small	Open		30.00	30
1994	Hand Car	Open		35.00	35
1993	Silent Night Singers	Closed	1994	30.00	35
1993	Village Sign	Open		40.00	40
1993	Village Square Clock	Open		50.00	50

Holiday Hamlet® -Figurines - V. Balcou

YEAR ISSUE		EDITION LIMIT	YEAR RETD.	ISSUE PRICE	*QUOTE U.S.$
1993	Baby Squirrel	Closed	1995	15.00	30
1993	Bell Choir Bunny	Open		15.00	15
1993	Bell Choir Fox	Open		10.00	10
1994	Blessed Mother/Joseph Players	Open		25.00	25
1993	Christmas Carolers	Open		20.00	20
1993	Christmas Carolers, waterglobe	Open		45.00	45
1993	Christmas Treats	Open		15.00	15
1993	The Conductor	Open		10.00	10
1993	Delivering Gifts	Open		20.00	20
1993	Dollmaker	Open		15.00	15
1993	Dollmaker's Apprentice	Closed	1994	15.00	30
1993	Dr. B. Well	Open		15.00	15
1993	Dr. Quack & Patient	Open		15.00	15
1993	Gathering Apples	Open		15.00	15
1993	Gathering Pine Boughs	Open		10.00	10
1994	Holiday Hamlet, waterglobe	Open		75.00	75
1994	Little Angels	Open		30.00	30
1993	Mr. Grizzly	Open		20.00	20
1994	Mr. Winterberry, Pie Vendor	2,500	1995	25.00	50
1993	Mrs. Grizzly	Open		20.00	20
1993	Nanny Rabbit & Bunnies	Open		20.00	20
1993	Old Royal Elf	Open		20.00	20
1993	The Parson	Open		10.00	10
1993	Pastry Vendor	Open		10.00	10
1994	Poor Shepherds	Open		15.00	15
1994	The Porter	Closed	1995	25.00	25
1994	Proud Mother/Father	Open		20.00	20

YEAR ISSUE		EDITION LIMIT	YEAR RETD.	ISSUE PRICE	*QUOTE U.S.$
1993	Santa Claus	Open		25.00	25
1993	Skaters	Open		20.00	20
1993	Squirrel Family	Closed	1994	15.00	30
1994	Three Wisemen	Open		20.00	20
1993	Tying the Christmas Garland	Closed	1994	20.00	20
1993	Waving Elf	Open		10.00	10
1993	Welcome Banner	Open		20.00	20
1993	Welcoming Elf	Closed	1995	10.00	10

Holiday Hamlet®-Lighted Houses - V. Balcou

YEAR ISSUE		EDITION LIMIT	YEAR RETD.	ISSUE PRICE	*QUOTE U.S.$
1994	Christmas Pageant Stage	Open		75.00	75
1993	Doctor's Office	Open		75.00	75
1993	Dollmaker's Cottage	Open		125.00	125
1993	Holiday Hamlet Chapel	Open		75.00	75
1993	Holiday Manor	Closed	1994	75.00	125
1994	Mr. Winterberry's Pie Shop	2,500	1995	100.00	200-350
1993	Railroad Station	Closed	1994	125.00	300-475
1994	Snowman Supply Hut	Open		65.00	65
1993	Stocking Stuffer's Workshop	Open		45.00	45
1993	Tavern in the Woods	Closed	1995	125.00	200-350
1993	Toymaker's Workshop	Open		45.00	45
1994	Whistlestop Junction Train Stop	Open		65.00	65
1994	World's Best Snowman	Open		55.00	55

Sports Impressions/Enesco

Collectors' Club Members Only - Various

YEAR ISSUE		EDITION LIMIT	YEAR RETD.	ISSUE PRICE	*QUOTE U.S.$
1990	The Mick-Mickey Mantle 5000-1	Yr.Iss.	N/A	75.00	200
1991	Rickey Henderson-Born to Run 5001-11	Yr.Iss.	N/A	49.95	50
1991	Nolan Ryan-300 Wins 5002-01	Yr.Iss.	N/A	125.00	125
1991	Willie, Mickey & Duke plate 5003-04	Yr.Iss.	N/A	39.95	40
1992	Babe Ruth 5006-11	Yr.Iss.	N/A	40.00	40
1992	Walter Payton 5015-01	Yr.Iss.	N/A	50.00	50
1993	The 1927 Yankees plate - R.Tanenbaum	Yr.Iss.	N/A	60.00	75

Collectors' Club Symbol of Membership - Sports Impressions

YEAR ISSUE		EDITION LIMIT	YEAR RETD.	ISSUE PRICE	*QUOTE U.S.$
1991	Mick/7 plate 5001-02	Yr.Iss.	N/A	Gift	70
1992	USA Basketball team plate 5008-30	Yr.Iss.	N/A	Gift	N/A
1993	Nolan Ryan porcelain card	Yr.Iss.	N/A	Gift	25

Baseball Superstar Figurines - Sports Impressions

YEAR ISSUE		EDITION LIMIT	YEAR RETD.	ISSUE PRICE	*QUOTE U.S.$
1988	Al Kaline	2,500	N/A	90.00	125
1988	Andre Dawson	2,500	N/A	90.00	125-200
1988	Bob Feller	2,500	N/A	90.00	125-200
1992	Cubs Ryne Sandberg Home 1118-23	975	1993	150.00	195
1987	Don Mattingly	Closed	N/A	90.00	250
1987	Don Mattingly (Franklin glove variation)	Closed	N/A	90.00	750
1989	Duke Snider	2,500	N/A	90.00	125
1994	Giants Barry Bonds (signed) 1160-46	975	1995	150.00	150
1992	Johnny Bench (hand signed) 1126-23	975	1994	150.00	150
1988	Jose Canseco	Closed	N/A	90.00	125-200
1987	Keith Hernandez	2,500	N/A	90.00	125-200
1989	Kirk Gibson	Closed	N/A	90.00	125-200
1987	Mickey Mantle	Closed	N/A	90.00	175-295
1996	Mickey Mantle "The Greatest Switch Hitter" (hand signed) 1228-46 - T. Treadway	975	1995	395.00	500
1990	Nolan Ryan	Closed	N/A	50.00	50
1992	Nolan Ryan Figurine/plate/stand 1134-31	500	1994	260.00	260
1990	Nolan Ryan Kings of K	Closed	N/A	125.00	125
1990	Nolan Ryan Mini	Closed	N/A	50.00	50
1990	Nolan Ryan Supersize	Closed	N/A	250.00	250
1993	Oakland A's Reggie Jackson (signed) 1048-46	975	1994	150.00	150
1993	Rangers Nolan Ryan (signed) 1127-46	975	1994	175.00	175
1994	Rangers Nolan Ryan (signed) Farewell 1161-49	975	1994	150.00	250
1990	Ted Williams	Closed	N/A	90.00	475-625
1987	Wade Boggs	Closed	N/A	90.00	150-225
1989	Will Clark	Closed	N/A	90.00	125-250
1993	Yankees Mickey Mantle (signed) 1038-46	975	1993	195.00	350

Basketball Superstar Figurines - Sports Impressions

YEAR ISSUE		EDITION LIMIT	YEAR RETD.	ISSUE PRICE	*QUOTE U.S.$
1993	Julius Erving 76ers (hand signed) 4102-46	975	1994	150.00	150
1993	Julius Erving 76ers (hand signed) 4102-61	76	1994	295.00	295

Football Superstar Figurines - Sports Impressions

YEAR ISSUE		EDITION LIMIT	YEAR RETD.	ISSUE PRICE	*QUOTE U.S.$
1993	Gale Sayers Bears (hand signed) 3029-23	975	1994	150.00	150
1992	John Unitas Colts (hand signed) 3016-23	975	1994	150.00	150
1993	Kenny Stabler Raiders (hand signed) 3026-23	975	1994	150.00	150
1993	Walter Payton Bears (hand signed) 3028-23	975	1994	150.00	150

NASCAR - Sports Impressions

YEAR ISSUE		EDITION LIMIT	YEAR RETD.	ISSUE PRICE	*QUOTE U.S.$
1995	Bill Elliott (hand signed) 8100-46	975		150.00	150
1994	Jeff Gordon (hand signed) 8101-46	975	1995	150.00	150

Plaques - Various

YEAR ISSUE		EDITION LIMIT	YEAR RETD.	ISSUE PRICE	*QUOTE U.S.$
1995	Life of a Legend Mickey Mantle 1228-71 - T. Fogarty	Open		40.00	40
1995	Profiles in Courage Mickey Mantle 1231-62 - M. Petronella	Open		40.00	40

Swarovski America Limited

Collectors Society Editions - Various

YEAR ISSUE		EDITION LIMIT	YEAR RETD.	ISSUE PRICE	*QUOTE U.S.$
1987	Togetherness-The Lovebirds - Schreck/Stocker	Yr.Iss.	1987	150.00	3500-4500
1988	Sharing-The Woodpeckers - A. Stocker	Yr.Iss.	1988	165.00	1400-2100
1988	Mini Cactus	Yr.Iss.	1988	Gift	225-300
1989	Amour-The Turtledoves - A. Stocker	Yr.Iss.	1989	195.00	900-1200
1989	SCS Key Chain	Yr.Iss.	1989	Gift	80-135
1990	Lead Me-The Dolphins - M. Stamey	Yr.Iss.	1990	225.00	1100-1500
1990	Mini Chaton	Yr.Iss.	1990	Gift	65-80
1991	Save Me-The Seals - M. Stamey	Yr.Iss.	1991	225.00	450-600
1991	Dolphin Brooch	Yr.Iss.	1991	75.00	100-150
1991	SCS Pin	Yr.Iss.	1991	Gift	50-75
1992	Care For Me - The Whales - M. Stamey	Yr.Iss.	1992	265.00	450-700
1992	SCS Pen	Yr.Iss.	1992	Gift	35-75
1992	5th Anniversary Edition-The Birthday Cake - G. Stamey	Yr.Iss.	1992	85.00	135-225
1993	Inspiration Africa-The Elephant - M. Zendron	Yr.Iss.	1993	325.00	1150-1500
1993	Elephant Brooch	Yr.Iss.	1993	85.00	100-150
1993	Leather Luggage Tag	Yr.Iss.	1993	Gift	25-55
1994	Inspiration Africa-The Kudu - M. Stamey	Yr.Iss.	1994	295.00	450-650
1994	Leather Double Picture Frame	Yr.Iss.	1994	Gift	20-40
1995	Inspiration Africa-The Lion - A. Stocker	Yr.Iss.	1995	325.00	400-650
1995	Centenary Swan Brooch	Yr.Iss.	1995	125.00	150-225
1995	Miniature Crystal Swan	Yr.Iss.	1995	Gift	60-120
1996	Fabulous Creatures-The Unicorn - M. Zendron	Yr.Iss.		325.00	325

Swarovski Silver Crystal Worldwide Limited Editions - A. Stocker

YEAR ISSUE		EDITION LIMIT	YEAR RETD.	ISSUE PRICE	*QUOTE U.S.$
1995	Eagle	10,000	1995	1750.00	7000-8900

African Wildlife - Various

YEAR ISSUE		EDITION LIMIT	YEAR RETD.	ISSUE PRICE	*QUOTE U.S.$
1995	Baby Elephant - M. Zendron	Open		155.00	155
1994	Cheetah - M. Stamey	Open		275.00	275
1989	Elephant-Small - A. Stocker	Open		50.00	65

Among Flowers And Foliage - C. Schneiderbauer, unless otherwise noted

YEAR ISSUE		EDITION LIMIT	YEAR RETD.	ISSUE PRICE	*QUOTE U.S.$
1992	Bumblebee	Open		85.00	85
1994	Butterfly on Leaf	Open		75.00	85
1995	Dragonfly	Open		85.00	85
1992	Hummingbird	Open		195.00	210
1996	Snail on Vine-Leaf - E. Mair	Open		65.00	65

Barnyard Friends - Various

YEAR ISSUE		EDITION LIMIT	YEAR RETD.	ISSUE PRICE	*QUOTE U.S.$
1993	Mother Goose - A. Stocker	Open		75.00	75
1993	Tom Gosling - A. Stocker	Open		37.50	38
1993	Dick Gosling - A. Stocker	Open		37.50	38
1993	Harry Gosling - A. Stocker	Open		37.50	38
1984	Medium Pig - M. Schreck	Open		35.00	55
1988	Mini Chicks (Set/3) - G. Stamey	Open		35.00	45
1987	Mini Hen - G. Stamey	Open		35.00	45
1982	Mini Pig - M. Schreck	Open		16.00	30
1987	Mini Rooster - G. Stamey	Open		35.00	55

Beauties of the Lake - Various

YEAR ISSUE		EDITION LIMIT	YEAR RETD.	ISSUE PRICE	*QUOTE U.S.$
1983	Drake-Mini - M. Schreck	Open		20.00	45
1994	Frog - G. Stamey	Open		49.50	50
1996	Goldfish-Mini - M. Stamey	Open		45.00	45
1989	Mallard-Giant - M. Stamey	Open		2000.00	4500
1986	Standing Duck-Mini - A. Stocker	Open		22.00	38
1977	Swan-Large - M. Schreck	Open		55.00	95
1995	Swan-Maxi - A. Hirzinger	Open		4500.00	4500
1977	Swan-Medium - M. Schreck	Open		44.00	85
1989	Swan-Small - M. Schreck	Open		35.00	55
1986	Swimming Duck-Mini - A. Stocker	Open		16.00	38

Centenary Edition - A. Hirzinger

YEAR ISSUE		EDITION LIMIT	YEAR RETD.	ISSUE PRICE	*QUOTE U.S.$
1995	Centenary Swan	Yr.Iss.	1995	150.00	250-300

Commemorative Single Issues - Team

YEAR ISSUE		EDITION LIMIT	YEAR RETD.	ISSUE PRICE	*QUOTE U.S.$
1990	Elephant, 7640NR100 (Introduced by Swarovski America as a commemorative item during Design Celebration/January '90 in Walt Disney World)	Closed	N/A	125.00	1000-1500
1993	Elephant, 7640NR100001 (Introduced by Swarovski America as a commemorative item during Design Celebration/January '93 in Walt Disney World)	Closed	1993	150.00	250-400

Crystal Melodies - M. Zendron, unless otherwise noted

YEAR ISSUE		EDITION LIMIT	YEAR RETD.	ISSUE PRICE	*QUOTE U.S.$
1993	Grand Piano	Open		250.00	260
1992	Harp	Open		175.00	210
1992	Lute	Open		125.00	140
1996	Violin - G. Stamey	Open		140.00	140

YEAR ISSUE		EDITION LIMIT	YEAR RETD.	ISSUE PRICE	*QUOTE U.S.$
Decorative Items For The Desk (Paperweights) - M. Schreck					
1990	Chaton-Giant 7433NR180000	Open		4500.00	4500
1987	Chaton-Large 7433NR80	Open		190.00	260
1987	Chaton-Small 7433NR50	Open		50.00	65
1987	Pyramid-Small Crystal Cal. 7450NR40095	Open		100.00	125
1987	Pyramid-Small Vitrail Med. 7450NR40087	Open		100.00	125
Endangered Species - Various					
1993	Baby Panda - A. Stocker	Open		24.50	25
1993	Mother Panda - A. Stocker	Open		120.00	125
1991	Kiwi - M. Stamey	12/96		37.50	45
1987	Koala - A. Stocker	Open		50.00	65
1989	Mini Koala - A. Stocker	Open		35.00	45
1992	Mother Beaver - A. Stocker	12/96		110.00	125
1992	Sitting Baby Beaver - A. Stocker	Open		47.50	50
1993	Mother Kangaroo with Baby - G. Stamey	Open		95.00	95
1981	Turtle-Giant - M. Schreck	Open		2500.00	4500
1977	Turtle-Large - M. Schreck	Open		48.00	75
1977	Turtle-Small - M. Schreck	12/96		35.00	50
Exquisite Accents - Various					
1995	Angel - A. Stocker	Open		210.00	210
1980	Birdbath - M. Schreck	Open		150.00	210
1987	Birds' Nest - Team	12/96		90.00	125
1987	Dinner Bell-Medium - M. Schreck	Open		80.00	95
1987	Dinner Bell-Small - M. Schreck	Open		60.00	65
1995	The Orchid-pink - M. Stamey	Open		140.00	140
1995	The Orchid-yellow - M. Stamey	Open		140.00	140
1992	The Rose - M. Stamey	Open		150.00	155
1996	Sleigh - M. Zendron	Open		295.00	295
Feathered Friends - Various					
1995	Baby Lovebirds - A. Stocker	Open		155.00	155
1995	Dove - E. Mair	Open		55.00	55
1993	Pelican - A. Hirzinger	Open		37.50	38
Game of Kings - M. Schreck					
1984	Chess Set	Open		950.00	1375
Horses on Parade - M. Zendron					
1993	White Stallion	Open		250.00	260
In A Summer Meadow - Various					
1994	Field Mice (Set/3) - A. Stocker	Open		42.50	45
1991	Field Mouse - A. Stocker	Open		47.50	50
1985	Hedgehog-Large - M. Schreck	12/96		120.00	140
1985	Hedgehog-Medium - M. Schreck	Open		70.00	85
1987	Hedgehog-Small - M. Schreck	Open		50.00	55
1995	Ladybug - E. Mair	Open		29.50	30
1988	Mini Sitting Rabbit - A. Stocker	Open		35.00	45
1988	Mother Rabbit - A. Stocker	Open		60.00	75
1992	Sparrow - C. Schneiderbauer	Open		29.50	30
1982	Butterfly - Team	Open		44.00	85
1986	Mini Butterfly - Team	Open		16.00	45
Kingdom Of Ice And Snow - Various					
1986	Large Polar Bear - A. Stocker	Open		140.00	210
1996	Madame Penguin - A. Stocker	Open		85.00	85
1986	Mini Baby Seal - A. Stocker	Open		30.00	45
1984	Mini Penguin - M. Schreck	Open		16.00	38
1995	Sir Penguin - A. Stocker	Open		85.00	85
Our Candleholders - Various					
1987	Star-Large 7600NR143 - Team	12/96		250.00	375
1989	Star-Medium 7600NR143001 - Team	Open		200.00	260
1985	Water Lily-Large 7600NR125 - M. Schreck	Open		200.00	375
1983	Water Lily-Medium 7600NR123 - M. Schreck	Open		150.00	260
1985	Water Lily-Small 7600NR124 - M. Schreck	Open		100.00	175
Our Woodland Friends - Various					
1981	Bear-Large - M. Schreck	Open		75.00	95
1985	Bear-Mini - M. Schreck	Open		16.00	55
1987	Fox - A. Stocker	Open		50.00	75
1988	Mini Running Fox - A. Stocker	12/96		35.00	45
1988	Mini Sitting Fox - A. Stocker	Open		35.00	45
1989	Mushrooms - A. Stocker	Open		35.00	45
1996	Night Owl - A. Hirzinger	Open		85.00	85
1983	Owl-Giant - M. Schreck	Open		1200.00	2000
1979	Owl-Large - M. Schreck	Open		90.00	125
1979	Owl-Mini - M. Schreck	Open		16.00	30
1995	Owlet - A. Hirzinger	Open		45.00	45
1994	Roe Deer Fawn - E. Mair	Open		75.00	75
1985	Squirrel - M. Schreck	Open		35.00	45
Pets' Corner - Various					
1993	Beagle Playing - A. Stocker	Open		49.50	50
1990	Beagle Puppy - A. Stocker	Open		40.00	50
1992	Poodle - A. Stocker	Open		125.00	140
1990	Scotch Terrier - A. Stocker	12/96		60.00	75
1991	Sitting Cat - M. Stamey	Open		75.00	85
1993	Sitting Poodle - A. Stocker	Open		85.00	85
1996	St. Bernard - E. Mair	Open		95.00	95
1995	Tomcat - A. Hirzinger	Open		45.00	45

YEAR ISSUE		EDITION LIMIT	YEAR RETD.	ISSUE PRICE	*QUOTE U.S.$
South Sea - Various					
1987	Blowfish-Mini - Team	Open		22.00	30
1986	Blowfish-Small - Team	Open		35.00	55
1991	Butterfly Fish - M. Stamey	Open		150.00	175
1995	Dolphin - M. Stamey	Open		210.00	210
1988	Open Shell w/Pearl - M. Stamey	Open		120.00	175
1993	Sea Horse - M. Stamey	Open		85.00	85
1995	Shell - M. Stamey	Open		45.00	45
1995	Starfish - M. Stamey	Open		29.50	30
1995	Conch - M. Stamey	Open		29.50	30
1995	Maritime Trio (Shell, Starfish, Conch) - M. Stamey	Open		104.00	104
1993	Three South Sea Fish - M. Stamey	Open		135.00	140
Sparkling Fruit - Various					
1991	Apple - M. Stamey	12/96		175.00	185
1995	Grapes - Team	Open		375.00	375
1991	Pear - M. Stamey	Open		175.00	185
1981	Pineapple-Giant /Gold - M. Schreck	Open		1750.00	3250
1981	Pineapple-Large /Gold - M. Schreck	Open		150.00	260
1986	Pineapple-Small /Gold - M. Schreck	Open		55.00	85
When We Were Young - Various					
1988	Locomotive - G. Stamey	Open		150.00	155
1990	Petrol Wagon - G. Stamey	Open		75.00	95
1988	Tender - G. Stamey	Open		55.00	55
1993	Tipping Wagon - G. Stamey	Open		95.00	95
1988	Wagon - A. Stamey	Open		85.00	95
1990	Airplane - A. Stocker	Open		135.00	155
1996	Baby Carriage - G. Stamey	Open		140.00	140
1993	Kris Bear - M. Zendron	Open		75.00	75
1995	Kris Bear on Skates - M. Zendron	Open		75.00	75
1994	Replica Cat - Team	Open		37.50	38
1994	Replica Hedgehog - Team	Open		37.50	38
1994	Replica Mouse - Team	Open		37.50	38
1994	Starter Set - Team	Open		112.50	113
1994	Sailboat - G. Stamey	Open		195.00	210
1991	Santa Maria - G. Stamey	Open		375.00	375
1994	Rocking Horse - G. Stamey	Open		125.00	125
1995	Train-Mini - G. Stamey	Open		125.00	125
Retired Candleholders - Various					
XX	Candleholder 7600NR101		Retrd. 1982	23.00	150-300
XX	Candleholder 7600NR102		Retrd. 1987	35.00	100-150
XX	Candleholder 7600NR103		Retrd. 1988	40.00	100-175
XX	Candleholder 7600NR104		Retrd. 1988	95.00	200-300
XX	Candleholder 7600NR106		Retrd. 1986	85.00	300-400
XX	Candleholder 7600NR107		Retrd. 1986	100.00	350-400
XX	Candleholder 7600NR109		Retrd. 1986	37.00	125
XX	Candleholder 7600NR110		Retrd. 1987	40.00	125-200
XX	Candleholder 7600NR111		Retrd. 1986	100.00	185-300
XX	Candleholder 7600NR112		Retrd. 1986	75.00	200-300
XX	Candleholder 7600NR114		Retrd. 1986	37.00	150-300
XX	Candleholder 7600NR115		Retrd. 1987	185.00	450-600
XX	Candleholder 7600NR116		Retrd. 1986	350.00	1000-1400
XX	Candleholder 7600NR119		Retrd. 1989	N/A	275-475
XX	Candleholder 7600NR122		Retrd. 1987	85.00	200-250
XX	Candleholder 7600NR127		Retrd. 1987	65.00	200-250
XX	Candleholder 7600NR128		Retrd. 1987	100.00	250-300
XX	Candleholder 7600NR129		Retrd. 1987	120.00	275-350
XX	Candleholder 7600NR130		Retrd. 1986	275.00	1100-1700
XX	Candleholder 7600NR131 (Set/6)		Retrd. N/A	43.00	500-800
XX	Candleholder 7600NR138		Retrd. 1987	160.00	450-600
XX	Candleholder 7600NR139		Retrd. 1987	140.00	300-600
XX	Candleholder 7600NR140		Retrd. 1987	120.00	400-600
XX	Candleholder-Baroque 7600NR121		Retrd. 1987	150.00	250-450
XX	Candleholder-European Style 7600NR103		Retrd. 1991	N/A	450-500
XX	Candleholder-European Style 7600NR108		Retrd. 1990	N/A	300-650
XX	Candleholder-European Style 7600NR141		Retrd. 1991	N/A	500-700
XX	Candleholder-European Style 7600NR142		Retrd. 1990	N/A	250-450
XX	Candleholder-Global-Kg. Sz. 7600NR135		Retrd. 1989	50.00	175-250
XX	Candleholder-Global-Lg. 7600NR134		Retrd. 1991	40.00	80-100
XX	Candleholder-Global-Med. (2) 7600NR133		Retrd. 1991	40.00	70-120
XX	Candleholder-Global-Sm. (4) 7600NR132		Retrd. 1990	60.00	150-250
1990	Candleholder-Neo-Classic-Lg. 7600NR144090 - A. Stocker		Retrd. 1993	220.00	225-275
1990	Candleholder-Neo-Classic-Med. 7600NR144080 - A. Stocker		Retrd. 1993	190.00	195-225
1990	Candleholder-Neo-Classic-Sm. 7600NR144070 - A. Stocker		Retrd. 1993	170.00	175-200
XX	Candleholder-Pineapple 7600NR136G		Retrd. 1987	150.00	250-400
XX	Candleholder-Pineapple 7600NR136R		Retrd. 1987	150.00	275-450
XX	Candleholder-w/Flowers-Lg. 7600NR137		Retrd. 1991	150.00	225-300
XX	Candleholder-w/Flowers-Sm. 7600NR120		Retrd. 1987	60.00	350
XX	Candleholder-w/Leaves-Sm. 7600NR126		Retrd. 1987	100.00	250-350
Retired - Various					
1992	Angel 6475NR000009		Retrd. 1994	65.00	75-115

YEAR ISSUE		EDITION LIMIT	YEAR RETD.	ISSUE PRICE	*QUOTE U.S.$
XX	Apple Photo Stand-Kg. Sz. (Gold) 7504NR060G		Retrd. 1989	120.00	350-450
XX	Apple Photo Stand-Kg. Sz. (Rhodium) 7504NR060R - M. Schreck		Retrd. 1989	120.00	400-500
XX	Apple Photo Stand-Lg. 7504NR050R		Retrd. 1987	80.00	250-450
XX	Apple Photo Stand-Lg. (Gold) 7504NR050G		Retrd. 1991	80.00	180-300
XX	Apple Photo Stand-Sm. (Gold) 7504NR030G		Retrd. 1991	40.00	180-250
XX	Apple Photo Stand-Sm. 7504NR030R		Retrd. 1987	40.00	190-275
XX	Ashtray 7461NR100		Retrd. 1991	45.00	250-300
XX	Ashtray 7501NR061		Retrd. 1991	45.50	700-1300
XX	Bear-Giant Size 7637NR112 - M. Schreck		Retrd. 1988	125.00	1575-1800
XX	Bear-Kg Sz 7637NR92 - M. Schreck		Retrd. 1987	95.00	1400-1600
1984	Bear-Mini 7670NR32 - M. Schreck		Retrd. 1989	16.00	125-200
1982	Bear-Sm 7637NR054000 - M. Schreck		Retrd. 1995	44.00	50-90
1992	Beaver-Baby Lying 7616NR000003 - A. Stocker		Retrd. 1995	47.50	45-55
1985	Bee (Gold) 7553NR100		Retrd. 1989	200.00	1100-1500
1985	Bee (Rhodium) 7553NR200		Retrd. 1987	200.00	1600-2200
XX	Beetle Bottle Opener (Gold) 7505NR76		Retrd. 1984	80.00	1100-1800
XX	Beetle Bottle Opener (Rhodium) 7505NR76		Retrd. 1984	80.00	1000-1650
1984	Blowfish-Lg. 7644NR41		Retrd. 1992	40.00	90-170
1985	Butterfly (Gold) 7551NR100		Retrd. 1989	200.00	1000-1200
1985	Butterfly (Rhodium) 7551NR200		Retrd. 1989	200.00	1400-2100
XX	Butterfly-Mini 7671NR30		Retrd. 1989	16.00	125-150
XX	Cardholders-Lg. , Set/4 -7403NR30095		Retrd. 1990	45.00	250-400
XX	Cardholders-Sm., Set/4-7403NR20095		Retrd. 1990	25.00	150-200
1977	Cat-Lg 7634NR70 - M. Schreck		Retrd. 1992	44.00	90-125
19XX	Cat-Medium 7634NR52		Retrd. 1987	38.00	300-400
1982	Cat-Mini 7659NR31 - M. Schreck		Retrd. 1992	16.00	45-80
1981	Chess Set/Wooden Board 7550NR432032		Retrd. 1987	950.00	1200-2000
XX	Chicken-Mini 7651NR20		Retrd. 1989	16.00	50-100
XX	Cigarette Box 7503NR050		Retrd. 1982	136.00	1800-2500
XX	Cigarette Holder 7463NR062		Retrd. 1991	85.00	175-225
1991	City Gates 7474NR000023 - G. Stamey		Retrd. 1995	95.00	100-125
1991	City Tower 7474NR000022 - G. Stamey		Retrd. 1995	37.50	50-70
1984	Dachshund-Lg. 7641NR75 - M. Schreck		Retrd. 1992	48.00	100-125
XX	Dachshund-Mini 7672NR42 - A. Stocker		Retrd. 1989	20.00	80-150
1987	Dachshund-Mini 7672NR042000 - A. Stocker		Retrd. 1995	20.00	50-80
1981	Dinner Bell-Lg. 7467NR071000 - M. Schreck		Retrd. 1987	80.00	125-150
XX	Dog (standing) 7635NR70		Retrd. 1991	44.00	90-150
XX	Duck-Lg 7653NR75		Retrd. 1987	44.00	250-350
XX	Duck-Medium 7653NR55		Retrd. 1988	38.00	125
XX	Duck-Mini 7653NR45		Retrd. 1989	16.00	70-100
XX	Elephant 7640NR55		Retrd. 1990	90.00	225-275
1988	Elephant-Lg. 7640NR060000 - A. Stocker		Retrd. 1995	70.00	110-150
1984	Falcon Head-Lg. 7645NR100		Retrd. 1992	600.00	1000-1500
1986	Falcon Head-Sm. 7645NR45 - M. Schreck		Retrd. 1992	60.00	120-200
1984	Frog (black eyes) 7642NR48		Retrd. 1992	30.00	100-200
1984	Frog (clear eyes) 7642NR48		Retrd. 1992	30.00	550-800
1985	Grapes-Large 7550NR30015		Retrd. 1989	250.00	900-1300
1985	Grapes-Med. 7550NR20029		Retrd. 1995	300.00	375-500
1985	Grapes-Sm. 7550NR20015		Retrd. 1995	200.00	250-300
XX	Hedgehog-Kg. Sz. 7630NR60 - M. Schreck		Retrd. 1987	98.00	350-550
XX	Hedgehog-Lg. 7630NR50 - M. Schreck		Retrd. 1987	65.00	150-275
XX	Hedgehog-Med. 7630NR40 - M. Schreck		Retrd. 1987	44.00	90-175
XX	Hedgehog-Sm. 7630NR30 - M. Schreck		Retrd. 1987	38.00	335-400
1988	Hippopotamus 7626NR65 - A. Stocker		Retrd. 1993	70.00	110-150
1989	Hippopotamus-Sm. 7626NR055000 - A. Stocker		Retrd. 1995	70.00	80
1991	Holy Family w/Arch 7475NR001		Retrd. 1994	250.00	250-300
1985	Hummingbird (Gold) 7552NR100		Retrd. 1989	200.00	1200-1450
1985	Hummingbird (Rhodium) 7552NR200		Retrd. 1987	200.00	1700-2200
1990	Kingfisher 7621NR000001 - M. Stamey		Retrd. 1993	75.00	125-150
1991	Kitten 7634NR028000 - M. Stamey		Retrd. 1995	47.50	50
XX	Lighter 7462NR062		Retrd. 1991	160.00	180-275
XX	Lighter 7500NR050		Retrd. 1982	160.00	2000
1986	Mallard 7647NR80 - M. Schreck		Retrd. 1995	80.00	150-200
XX	Mouse-Kg. Sz. 7631NR60 - M. Schreck		Retrd. 1987	95.00	550-650
XX	Mouse-Lg. 7631NR50 - M. Schreck		Retrd. 1987	69.00	225-300
1976	Mouse-Med. 7631NR040000 - M. Schreck		Retrd. 1995	48.00	85
XX	Mouse-Mini 7655NR23		Retrd. 1989	16.00	75-90
XX	Mouse-Sm. 7631NR30 - M. Schreck		Retrd. 1992	35.00	75-100
1989	Old Timer Automobile 7473NR000001 - G. Stamey		Retrd. 1995	130.00	175-190
1989	Owl 7621NR000003 - M. Stamey		Retrd. 1993	70.00	125-175
1979	Owl-Sm. 7636NR046000 - M. Schreck		Retrd. 1995	59.00	90

Collectors' Information Bureau

*Quotes have been rounded up to nearest dollar

YEAR ISSUE		EDITION LIMIT	YEAR RETD.	ISSUE PRICE	*QUOTE U.S.$
1989	Parrot 7621NR000004 - M. Stamey	Retrd.	1993	70.00	125-150
1987	Partridge 7625NR50 - A. Stocker	Retrd.	1991	85.00	140-180
1984	Penguin-Lg. 7643NR085000 - M. Schreck	Retrd.	1995	44.00	95-140
XX	Picture Frame/Oval 7505NR75G	Retrd.	1990	90.00	250-350
XX	Picture Frame/Square 7506NR60G	Retrd.	1990	100.00	250-300
XX	Pig-Lg. 7638NR65 - M. Schreck	Retrd.	1987	50.00	250-350
1985	Pineapple/Rhodium-Giant 7507NR26002 - M. Schreck	Retrd.	1987	1750.00	2700-3700
1982	Pineapple/Rhodium-Lg. 7507NR105002 - M. Schreck	Retrd.	1987	150.00	350-450
1987	Pineapple/Rhodium-Sm. 7507NR060002 - M. Schreck	Retrd.	1987	55.00	150
XX	Pprwgt-Atomic-Crystal Cal 7454NR60095	Retrd.	1985	80.00	1200-1750
XX	Pprwgt-Atomic-Vitrl Med. 7454NR60087	Retrd.	1985	80.00	1200-1700
XX	Pprwgt-Barrel-Crystal Cal 7453NR60095	Retrd.	1989	80.00	200-400
XX	Pprwgt-Barrel-Vitrl Med. 7453NR60087	Retrd.	1989	80.00	250
XX	Pprwgt-Carousel-Crystal Cal 7451NR60095	Retrd.	1985	80.00	1000-1200
XX	Pprwgt-Carousel-Vitrl Med. 7451NR60087	Retrd.	1985	80.00	1200-1500
1982	Pprwgt-Cone Crystal Cal 7452NR60095 - M. Schreck	Retrd.	1993	80.00	200-400
1982	Pprwgt-Cone Vitrl Med. 7452NR60087 - M. Schreck	Retrd.	1993	80.00	220-250
1981	Pprwgt-Egg 7458NR63069 - M. Schreck	Retrd.	1993	60.00	125-200
XX	Pprwgt-Geometric 7432NR57002N	Retrd.	1991	75.00	175-225
XX	Pprwgt-Octron-Crystal Cal 7456NR41	Retrd.	1992	75.00	150-180
XX	Pprwgt-Octron-Vitrl Med. 7456NR41087	Retrd.	1992	75.00	130-250
XX	Pprwgt-One Ton 7495NR65	Retrd.	1991	75.00	140-170
XX	Pprwgt-Rd.-Berm Blue 7404NR30MM	Retrd.	N/A	15.00	150-250
XX	Pprwgt-Rd.-Berm Blue 7404NR40MM	Retrd.	N/A	20.00	175-300
XX	Pprwgt-Rd.-Berm Blue 7404NR50MM	Retrd.	N/A	40.00	200-350
XX	Pprwgt-Rd.-Crystal Cal 7404NR30095/30MM	Retrd.	1989	15.00	60-75
XX	Pprwgt-Rd.-Crystal Cal 7404NR40095/40MM	Retrd.	1989	20.00	80-125
XX	Pprwgt-Rd.-Crystal Cal 7404NR50095/50MM	Retrd.	1989	40.00	150-200
XX	Pprwgt-Rd.-Crystal Cal 7404NR60095/60MM	Retrd.	1989	50.00	200-250
XX	Pprwgt-Green 7404NR30	Retrd.	N/A	15.00	100-250
XX	Pprwgt-Green 7404NR40	Retrd.	N/A	20.00	150-240
XX	Pprwgt-Green 7404NR50	Retrd.	N/A	40.00	255
XX	Pprwgt-Rd.-Sahara 7404NR30	Retrd.	1983	15.00	200-300
XX	Pprwgt-Rd.-Sahara 7404NR40	Retrd.	1982	20.00	250
XX	Pprwgt-Rd.-Sahara 7404NR50	Retrd.	1983	40.00	300-400
XX	Pprwgt-Rd.-Vitrl Med. 7404NR30087/30MM	Retrd.	1989	15.00	60-70
XX	Pprwgt-Rd.-Vitrl Med. 7404NR40087/40MM	Retrd.	1989	20.00	95-125
XX	Pprwgt-Rd.-Vitrl Med. 7404NR50087/50MM	Retrd.	1989	40.00	100-200
XX	Pprwgt-Rd.-Vitrl Med. 7404NR60087/60MM	Retrd.	1989	50.00	125-225
1987	Pyramid-Lg.-Crystal Cal 7450NR50095 - M. Schreck	Retrd.	1994	90.00	195
1987	Pyramid-Lg.-Vitrl Med. 7450NR50087 - M. Schreck	Retrd.	1994	90.00	200-275
XX	Rabbit-Lg. 7652NR45	Retrd.	1988	38.00	200-300
XX	Rabbit-Mini 7652NR20	Retrd.	1989	16.00	95
1988	Rabbit-Mini Lying 7678NR030000 - A. Stocker	Retrd.	1995	35.00	45
1988	Rhinoceros 7622NR70 - A. Stocker	Retrd.	1993	70.00	120-150
1990	Rhinoceros-Sm. 7622NR060000 - A. Stocker	Retrd.	1995	70.00	80-90
XX	Salt and Pepper Shakers 7508NR068034	Retrd.	1989	80.00	285
XX	Schnapps Glasses, Set/6-7468NR039000	Retrd.	1991	150.00	250-350
1985	Seal-Large 7646NR085000 - M. Schreck	Retrd.	1995	44.00	110-150
1992	Shepherd 7475NR000007	Retrd.	1994	65.00	90-100
1990	Silver Crystal City-Cathedral 7474NR000021 - G. Stamey	Retrd.	1995	95.00	110-130
1990	Silver Crystal City-Houses I & II (Set/2) 7474NR100000 - G. Stamey	Retrd.	1995	75.00	75-125
1990	Silver Crystal City-Houses III & IV (Set/2) 7474NR200000 - G. Stamey	Retrd.	1995	75.00	75-125
1990	Silver Crystal City-Poplars (Set/3) 7474NR020003 - G. Stamey	Retrd.	1995	40.00	60-75
1986	Snail 7648NR030000 - M. Stamey	Retrd.	1995	35.00	60
1991	South Sea Shell 7624NR72000 - M. Stamey	Retrd.	1995	110.00	120-140
X	Sparrow-Lg. 7650NR32	Retrd.	1988	38.00	120
1979	Sparrow-Mini 7650NR20 - M. Schreck	Retrd.	1992	16.00	80
X	Swan-Mini 7658NR27	Retrd.	1989	16.00	115-130
X	Table Magnifyer (no chain) 7510NR01G	Retrd.	1984	70.00	1000-1400
X	Table Magnifyer (no chain) 7510NR01R	Retrd.	1984	80.00	1000-1400
X	Table Magnifyer (with chain) 7510NR01R	Retrd.	1984	80.00	1200-1500
389	Toucan 7621NR000002 - M. Stamey	Retrd.	1993	70.00	125-140
993	Town Hall 7474NR000027 - G. Stamey	Retrd.	1995	135.00	125-200

YEAR ISSUE		EDITION LIMIT	YEAR RETD.	ISSUE PRICE	*QUOTE U.S.$
XX	Treasure Box (Heart/Butterfly)7465NR52/100	Retrd.	1991	80.00	185-250
XX	Treasure Box (Heart/Flower)7465NR52/100	Retrd.	1989	80.00	185-250
XX	Treasure Box (Heart/Flower)7465NR52	Retrd.	1989	80.00	225-300
XX	Treasure Box (Oval/Butterfly)7466NR063100	Retrd.	1991	80.00	225-270
XX	Treasure Box (Oval/Flower) 7466NR063000	Retrd.	1989	80.00	225-280
XX	Treasure Box (Round/Butterfly) 7464NR50/100	Retrd.	1991	80.00	225-250
XX	Treasure Box (Round/Flower) 7464NR50	Retrd.	1988	58.00	225-300
XX	Turtle-King Sz. 7632NR75 - M. Schreck	Retrd.	1991	50.00	125-175
XX	Vase 7511NR70	Retrd.	1994	120.00	150-200
1989	Walrus 7620NR100000 - M. Stamey	Retrd.	1992	70.00	150-170
1988	Whale 7628NR80 - M. Stamey	Retrd.	1994	175.00	175-225
1992	Wise Men (Set/3) 7475NR200000				

The Tudor Mint Inc.

Arthurian Legend - M. Locker, unless otherwise noted

YEAR ISSUE		EDITION LIMIT	YEAR RETD.	ISSUE PRICE	*QUOTE U.S.$
1990	3200 Merlin	Open		18.60	34
1990	3201 Into Merlin's Care Mold 1	Closed	N/A	25.40	250-340
1990	3201 Into Merlin's Care Mold 2	Closed	1993	25.40	85
1990	3202 Excaliber - M.L./R.G.	Open		18.60	34
1990	3203 Camelot	Open		25.40	42
1990	3204 King Arthur - M.L./R.G.	Open		18.60	34
1990	3205 Queen Guinevere	Open		18.60	34
1990	3206 Sir Percival & the Grail	Closed	1993	18.60	250-340
1990	3207 Morgan Le Fey	Open		25.40	42
1990	3208 Sir Lancelot	Open		25.40	42
1992	3209 Vigil of Sir Galahad - A. Slocombe	Open		31.45	42
1992	3210 Sir Mordred - R. Gibbons	Open		23.70	34
1992	3211 Return of Excalibur	Open		23.70	34
1993	3212 Sir Gawain - A. Slocombe	Open		25.40	34
1993	3213 King Arthur/Sir Bedevere	12/96		33.90	42

Dark Secrets - Various

YEAR ISSUE		EDITION LIMIT	YEAR RETD.	ISSUE PRICE	*QUOTE U.S.$
1994	6201 Dark Secrets - A. Slocombe	Open		84.90	112
1994	6202 Guardian of the Skulls - R. Gibbons	Open		30.18	40
1994	6203 The Skull Gateway - M. Locker	Open		33.90	44
1994	6204 The Tortured Skull - M. Locker	Open		33.90	44
1994	6205 The Serpent of the Skulls - S. Darnley	Open		33.90	44
1994	6206 The Altar of the Skulls - M. Locker	Open		25.40	36
1994	6207 The Skull Master - R. Gibbons	Open		33.90	44
1994	6208 The Vampire of the Skulls - A. Slocombe	Open		25.40	36
1994	6209 The Chamber of the Skulls - A. Slocombe	Open		101.90	142
1994	6210 The Guardian of the Demons - M. Locker	Open		30.18	40
1994	6211 The Ice Demon - S. Darnley	Open		25.40	36
1994	6212 The Demon of the Pit - S. Darnley	Open		25.40	36
1994	6213 The Demon of the Night - M. Locker	Open		25.40	36
1994	6214 The Demon of the Catacombs - R. Gibbons	Open		25.40	36
1994	6215 The Demon Slayer - M. Locker	Open		25.40	36
1994	6216 The Demon Jailer - S. Darnley	Open		25.40	36
1994	6217 The Chamber of the Demons - A. Slocombe	Open		101.90	142
1994	6218 The Guardian of Skeletons - R. Gibbons	Open		30.51	42
1994	6219 The Vigil of the Skeleton - R. Gibbons	Open		25.40	36
1994	6220 The Forgotten Skeleton - R. Gibbons	Open		30.51	42
1994	6221 The Prisoners of the Sword - A. Slocombe	Open		30.51	42
1994	6222 The Executioner - M. Locker	Open		30.51	42
1994	6223 The Finder of the Treasure - A. Slocombe	Open		25.40	36
1994	6224 The Skeleton Warrior - S. Darnley	Open		30.51	42
1994	6225 The Chamber of Skeletons - A. Slocombe	Open		101.90	142
1996	6226 The Sabre-Toothed Skull - S.R./A.S.	Open		48.00	48
1996	6227 The Dragon Skull - S.R./R.G.	Open		48.00	48
1996	6228 The Scorpion Skull - J.W./M.L.	Open		48.00	48
1996	6229 The Flying Skull - J.W./A.S.	Open		48.00	48

Dinosaur Collection - Various

YEAR ISSUE		EDITION LIMIT	YEAR RETD.	ISSUE PRICE	*QUOTE U.S.$
1993	6001 Pteranodon - M. Locker	Closed	1994	25.40	50-70
1993	6002 Triceratops - A. Slocombe	Closed	1994	25.40	50-70
1993	6003 Stegosaurus - A. Slocombe	Closed	1994	25.40	50-70
1993	6004 Brontosaurus - M. Locker	Closed	1994	25.40	50-70
1993	6005 Tyrannosaurus Rex - A. Slocombe	Closed	1994	25.40	50-70
1993	6006 Spinosaurus - R. Gibbons	Closed	1994	25.40	50-70

Hobbit Collection - A. Slocombe, unless otherwise noted

YEAR ISSUE		EDITION LIMIT	YEAR RETD.	ISSUE PRICE	*QUOTE U.S.$
1991	5001 Bilbo Baggins - R. Gibbons	Open		23.70	38
1991	5002 Gandalf	Open		42.41	64

YEAR ISSUE		EDITION LIMIT	YEAR RETD.	ISSUE PRICE	*QUOTE U.S.$
1991	5003 Thorn Oakenshield - R. Gibbons	Closed	1992	23.70	50-80
1991	5004 The Great Goblin - R. Gibbons	Closed	1993	23.70	55
1991	5005 Gollum	Open		29.75	46
1991	5006 Beorn	Closed	1992	42.41	85
1991	5007 The Elven King	Closed	1993	29.75	90-160
1991	5008 Smaug the Dragon	Closed	1993	93.41	175-220
1991	5009 Bard - M. Locker	Closed	1992	23.70	100
1991	5010 'Good Morn.' at Bag End - R. Gibbons	Closed	1993	67.90	150
1991	5011 Moon Letters	Closed	1992	93.41	150-200
1991	5012 Finding the 'Precious' - R. Gibbons	Closed	1992	67.90	155
1991	5013 The Capture of Bilbo	Closed	1992	67.90	150-200
1991	5014 'Riddles in the Dark'	Closed	1992	56.01	150
1991	5015 Escape From the Wargs - R. Gibbons	Closed	1992	67.90	150-200
1991	5016 Barrels Out of Bond - M. Locker	Closed	1993	67.90	150-200
1991	5017 The 'Courage of the Bilbo'	Closed	1993	56.01	150
1991	5018 Prisoner of Elven King	Closed	1992	67.90	150
1991	5019 The Enchanted Door - M. Locker	Closed	1992	93.41	200-250
1991	5020 The Wrath of Beorn - M. Locker	Closed	1992	67.90	150-185
1991	5021 Journey's End - R. Gibbons	Closed	1993	67.90	150
1991	5022 The Troll's Clearing - R. Gibbons	Closed	1992	251.51	750-1000
1991	5023 Burglar Steals Smaug's - R. Gibbons	Closed	1993	254.91	750-1000
1991	5024 Farewell, King Under Mt. - M. Locker	Closed	1992	254.91	750-1000

Lord of the Rings - Various

YEAR ISSUE		EDITION LIMIT	YEAR RETD.	ISSUE PRICE	*QUOTE U.S.$
1992	5025 Frodo Baggins - R. Gibbons	Open		25.40	38
1992	5026 Bilbo's Tale - M. Locker	12/96		25.40	38
1992	5027 Gimli the Dwarf - M. Locker	12/96		25.40	38
1992	5028 Sam Gamgee - R. Gibbons	12/96		25.40	38
1992	5029 Aragorn (Strider) - A. Slocombe	Open		25.40	38
1992	5030 An Orc - R. Gibbons	Closed	1994	30.51	60
1992	5031 Legolas the Elf - A. Slocombe	Open		30.51	46
1992	5032 The Mirror of Galadriel - R. Gibbons	Open		30.51	46
1992	5033 Saruman - A. Slocombe	Closed	1994	43.78	80
1992	5034 The Balrog - R. Gibbons	Open		67.90	100
1992	5035 Gandalf & Shadowfax - M. Locker	Open		67.90	100
1992	5036 A Black Rider - A. Slocombe	Open		67.90	100
1992	5037 Pippin - A. Slocombe	Closed	1994	25.40	48
1992	5038 Merry - A. Slocombe	Closed	1994	25.40	48
1992	5039 Boromir - R. Gibbons	Closed	1994	25.40	48
1992	5040 Treebeard (Fangorn) - R. Gibbons	Closed	1994	43.78	65

Myth & Magic Club - Various

YEAR ISSUE		EDITION LIMIT	YEAR RETD.	ISSUE PRICE	*QUOTE U.S.$
1990	9001 The Quest For the Truth - R.G./M.L.	Closed	1991	84.90	675-1100
1991	9002 The Game of Strax	Closed	1991	25.40	600-900
1991	9003 The Well of Aspirations - A. Slocombe	Closed	1992	84.90	750-890
1992	9004 Playmates - R. Gibbons	Closed	1992	28.80	100-175
1992	9005 Friends - A. Slocombe	Closed	1993	32.20	100-175
1992	9006 The Enchanted Pool - R. Gibbons	Closed	1993	84.90	150-225
1993	9007 The Mystical Encounter - A. Slocombe	Closed	1994	33.58	60-85
1994	9008 Keeper of the Dragons - R. Gibbons	Closed	1994	84.90	125
1994	9009 The Crystal Shield - M. Locker	Closed	1995	44.00	63
1994	9010 Battle for the Crystal - A. Slocombe	Closed	1995	108.00	130
1995	9011 Starstruck - S. Darnley	Closed	1996	44.00	44
1996	9012 Cauldron of Fire - A. Slocombe	Closed	1996	108.00	108
1996	9013 When Is It Our Turn? - H.C./S.D.	6/97		44.00	44
1996	9014 The Peacemakers - S.R./A.S.	6/97		N/A	N/A
1990	CC01 The Protector - R. Gibbons	Closed	1991	Gift	500-750
1991	CC02 The Jovial Wizard - M. Locker	Closed	1992	Gift	275-450
1992	CC03 Dragon of Destiny - R. Gibbons	Closed	1993	Gift	175-200
1993	CC04 Dragon of Methtintdour - A. Slocombe	Closed	1994	Gift	80-100
1994	CC05 The Dreamy Dragon - M. Locker	Closed	1995	Gift	50
1995	CC06 The Regal Dragon - A. Slocombe	Closed	1996	Gift	N/A
1996	CC07 Contemplation - S.R./M.L.	6/97		Gift	N/A

Myth & Magic One Year Only Piece - R. Gibbons, unless otherwise noted

YEAR ISSUE		EDITION LIMIT	YEAR RETD.	ISSUE PRICE	*QUOTE U.S.$
1993	OY93 The Flying Dragon - A. Slocombe	Closed	1993	67.90	375
1994	OY94 Dragon of Underworld - R. Gibbons	Closed	1994	70.55	375
1995	OY95 Guardian of the Crystal - A. Slocombe	Closed	1995	84.90	110-160
1996	OY96 The Enchanted Dragon - J. Watson	Yr.Iss.		114.00	114

Myth & Magic Promotion - Various

YEAR ISSUE		EDITION LIMIT	YEAR RETD.	ISSUE PRICE	*QUOTE U.S.$
1993	3601 Dactrius - R.G./M.L./A.S.	Closed	1993	67.90	495
1994	3603 Vexius - A. Slocombe	Closed	1994	70.55	122
1995	3606 Viamphe - M. Locker	Closed	1995	73.42	110

YEAR ISSUE		EDITION LIMIT	YEAR RETD.	ISSUE PRICE	*QUOTE U.S.$
1995	3607 Quargon - A. Slocombe	Closed	1995	26.32	50
1996	3609 Aurora - H.C./A.S.	12/96		108.00	108
1996	3610 Lepidorus - J.W./R.G.	12/96		48.00	48

Myth & Magic Colleggtibles - R. Gibbons

1996	1049 The Protector	Open		38.00	38
1996	1050 The Supreme Dragon	Open		38.00	38
1996	1051 The Family of Dragons	Open		38.00	38
1996	1052 The Dragon of Justice	Open		38.00	38
1996	1053 The Paternal Dragon	Open		38.00	38
1996	1054 The Sleepy Lizards	Open		38.00	38
1996	1055 The Castle of Unicorns	Open		38.00	38
1996	1056 The Fairy Rider	Open		38.00	38
1996	1057 The Leaping Pegasus	Open		38.00	38
1996	1058 The Fairy Glade	Open		38.00	38
1996	1059 The Damsel & Unicorn	Open		38.00	38
1996	1060 The Wizard's Cauldron	Open		38.00	38

Myth & Magic Extravaganza Study - Various

1992	3600 Sauria - A. Slocombe	Closed	1992	33.90	700
1993	3602 Deinos - R. Gibbons	Closed	1993	33.90	600
1994	3604 Lithia - M. Locker	Closed	1994	31.92	32
1995	3608 Imperia - S. Darnley	Closed	1995	41.25	42

Myth & Magic Large - Various

1990	3300 The Dragon Master - R. Gibbons	7,500		297.50	404
1990	3301 The Magical Encounter - R. Gibbons	Open		30.50	42
1990	3302 The Keeper of the Magic - R. Gibbons	Closed	1995	59.40	110-130
1990	3303 Summoning the Elements - R. Gibbons	Closed	1993	59.40	325-475
1990	3304 Sorceror's Apprentice - R. Gibbons	Closed	1991	59.40	465
1990	3305 The Nest of Dragons - M. Locker	Closed	1993	59.40	175-225
1990	3306 Meeting of the Unicorns - M. Locker	Open		59.40	86
1990	3307 Sentinels at the Portal - R. Gibbons	Closed	1991	59.40	465
1990	3308 The VII Seekers of Knowledge - M. Locker	7,500		297.50	404
1990	3309 Le Morte D'Arthur - A. Slocombe	Open		84.90	122
1990	3310 The Magical Vision - A. Slocombe	Closed	1995	84.90	125-185
1990	3311 The Dance of the Dolphins - R. Gibbons	1,537	1993	297.50	500
1991	3312 Altar of Enlightenment - M. Locker	Open		84.90	122
1991	3313 Power of the Crystal - A. Slocombe	3,500		595.00	595
1992	3314 The Awakening - J. Pickering	Closed	1995	64.50	125-190
1992	3315 The Crystal Dragon - A. Slocombe	Open		101.90	122
1992	3318 The Gathering of the Unicorns - A.S./R.G.	5,000		314.50	110-185
1993	3319 The Invocation - M. Locker	Closed	1995	84.90	150-190
1993	3320 The Fighting Dragons - A. Slocombe	12/96		67.90	86
1993	3321 The Playful Dolphins - M. Locker	Open		56.95	68
1993	3322 The Dragon of Darkness - A. Slocombe	Open		67.90	90
1994	3323 The Destroyer of the Crystal - S. Darnley	Open		84.90	114
1994	3324 A Tranquil Moment - M. Locker	Open		84.90	114
1994	3325 Great Earth Dragon - R. Gibbons	Open		101.90	136
1995	3326 The Great Sun Dragon - A. Slocombe	Open		136.00	136
1995	3327 The Great Moon Dragon - R. Gibbons	Open		136.00	136
1995	3328 The Great Sea Dragon - M. Locker	Open		136.00	136
1996	3329 The Destroyer of Evil - H.C./R.G.	Open		136.00	136
1996	3330 The Portal of Life - H.C./S.D.	Open		136.00	136
1996	3331 The Warlord - S.R./A.S.	2,500		210.00	210

Myth & Magic Miniatures - R. Gibbons, unless otherwise noted

1989	3500 The Incantation	Closed	1991	8.42	125-165
1989	3501 The Book of Spells - R.G./M.L.	Closed	1995	8.42	25
1989	3502 The Enchanted Castle	Closed	1993	8.42	28
1989	3503 The Cauldron of Light - M.L./R.G	Open		8.42	12
1989	3504 The Winged Serpent	Closed	1995	8.42	25
1989	3505 The White Witch - R.G./M.L.	Closed	1991	8.42	83
1989	3506 The Master Wizard	Closed	1995	8.42	25
1989	3507 The Guardian Dragon	Open		8.42	12
1989	3508 The Unicorn	Open		8.42	12
1989	3509 Pegasus	Open		8.42	12
1989	3510 The Castle of Dreams	Closed	1993	8.42	25
1989	3511 The Light of Knowledge - R.G./M.L.	Closed	1991	8.42	25-80
1990	3512 The Siren	Closed	1991	8.42	200-275
1990	3513 The Crystal Queen	Closed	1991	8.76	28-50
1990	3514 The Astronomer - R.G./M.L.	Closed	1991	8.76	50-100
1990	3515 The Alchemist - R.G./M.L.	Closed	1991	8.76	50-100
1990	3516 The Minotaur	Closed	1991	8.76	150-175
1990	3517 The Grim Reaper - R.G./M.L.	Closed	1995	8.76	25
1990	3518 The Castle of Souls	Closed	1993	8.76	41
1990	3519 The Dragon Gateway	Closed	1995	8.76	25
1990	3520 The Dragon Rider - R.G./M.L.	Closed	1991	8.76	175-220

YEAR ISSUE		EDITION LIMIT	YEAR RETD.	ISSUE PRICE	*QUOTE U.S.$
1990	3521 The Dragon's Kiss	Closed	1992	8.76	65
1990	3522 The Witch & Familiar	Closed	1991	8.76	28
1990	3523 The Oriental Dragon - R.G./M.L.	Closed	1993	8.76	30
1990	3524 The Reborn Dragon	Open		8.76	12
1990	3525 The Fire Dragon - R.G./M.L.	Closed	1994	8.76	28
1990	3526 The Giant Sorceror - R.G./M.L.	Closed	1991	8.76	125-160
1990	3527 The Wizard of Light	Closed	1994	8.76	28
1990	3528 Keeper of the Treasure	Closed	1992	8.76	82
1990	3529 The Old Hag	Closed	1991	8.76	250-375
1991	3530 Mother Nature	Closed	1994	9.44	25
1991	3531 The Earth Wizard - R.G./M.L.	Closed	1992	9.44	74
1991	3532 The Fire Wizard	Closed	1994	9.44	28
1991	3533 The Water Wizard	Closed	1992	9.44	20
1991	3534 The Air Wizard	Closed	1992	9.44	70
1991	3535 The Dragon of the Lake	Closed	1994	9.44	35
1991	3536 The Dragon's Spell - R.G./M.L.	Closed	1991	9.44	20-30
1991	3537 Merlin - M. Locker	Open		9.44	12
1991	3538 Excalibur - M.L./R.G.	Closed	1993	9.44	25
1991	3539 Camelot - M. Locker	Open		9.44	12
1991	3540 King Arthur - M.L./R.G.	Open		9.44	12
1991	3541 Queen Guinevere - M. Locker	Closed	1993	9.44	30
1992	3542 Dragon of the Forest	Closed	1995	10.11	25
1992	3543 Dragon of the Moon	Closed	1995	10.11	25
1992	3544 Wizard of Winter	Closed	1995	10.11	25
1992	3545 Dragon of Wisdom	Closed	1995	10.11	25
1992	3546 Dragon of the Sun - M. Locker	Closed	1995	10.11	25
1992	3547 Dragon of the Clouds - M. Locker	Closed	1995	10.11	25
1993	3548 Moon Wizard - A. Slocombe	Open		10.62	12
1993	3549 Unicorn of Light - A. Slocombe	Open		10.62	12
1993	3550 Return of Excalibur - M. Locker	Closed	1994	10.62	28
1993	3551 Magical Encounter	Open		10.62	12
1993	3552 Ice Dragon - A. Slocombe	Closed	1995	10.62	25
1993	3553 Sleepy Dragon - M. Locker	Open		10.62	12
1994	3554 Keeper of the Skulls	Open		10.80	12
1994	3555 The Dark Dragon - A. Slocombe	Open		10.80	12
1994	3556 Protector of the Young - M.L./R.G.	Open		10.80	12
1994	3557 Dragon of Light - R.G./A.S.	Open		10.80	12
1994	3558 Unicorns of Freedom	Open		10.80	12
1994	3559 Defender of the Crystal	Open		10.80	12
1995	3560 The Loving Dragons - N/A	Open		12.00	12
1995	3561 The Wizard of the Lake - N/A	Open		12.00	12
1995	3562 The Hatch Wings - N/A	Open		12.00	12
1995	3563 Dragon of the Treasure - N/A	Open		12.00	12
1995	3564 The Armoured Dragon - N/A	Open		12.00	12
1995	3565 The Sword Master - N/A	Open		12.00	12
1996	3566 The Dragon of the Ice Crystals - S. Riley	Open		14.00	14
1996	3567 The Mischievous Dragon - S. Riley	Open		14.00	14
1996	3568 The Summoner of Light - S. Riley	Open		14.00	14
1996	3569 The Proud Pegasus - S. Riley	Open		14.00	14
1996	3570 The Crystal Unicorn - S. Riley	Open		14.00	14
1996	3571 The Majestic Dragon - S. Riley	Open		14.00	14
1996	3572 The Celtic Dragon - H. Coventry	Open		14.00	14
1996	3573 The Dragon Warrior - H. Coventry	Open		14.00	14
1996	3574 The Dragon Thief - J. Watson	Open		14.00	14
1996	3575 The Crystal Serpent - S. Riley	Open		14.00	14
1996	3576 The Dragon's Nest - J. Watson	Open		14.00	14
1996	3577 The Guardian of Light - J. Watson	Open		14.00	14

Myth & Magic Standard - R. Gibbons, unless otherwise noted

1989	3001 The Incantation	Open		16.90	34
1989	3002 The Siren	Closed	1995	16.90	45-70
1989	3003 The Evil of Greed	Closed	1989	16.90	300-425
1989	3004 The Book of Spells - M. Locker	Open		16.90	34
1989	3005 The Enchanted Castle	Closed	1991	16.90	90
1989	3006 The Cauldron of Light - M.L./R.G.	Open		16.90	34
1989	3007 The Winged Serpent	Closed	1991	16.90	100
1989	3008 The White Witch - M. Locker	Closed	1991	16.90	85-100
1989	3009 The Master Wizard	Closed	1993	16.90	85
1989	3010 The Infernal Demon	Closed	1989	16.90	375
1989	3011 The Warrior Knight Mold 1	Closed	N/A	16.90	400-600
1989	3011 The Warrior Knight Mold 2	Closed	1990	16.90	375
1989	3012 The Deadly Combat	Closed	1989	16.90	375
1989	3013 The Old Hag Mold 1	Closed	N/A	16.90	400-900
1989	3013 The Old Hag Mold 2	Closed	1990	16.90	200-250
1989	3014 The Crystal Queen	Closed	1993	16.90	95
1989	3015 The Astronomer - M. Locker	Closed	1990	16.90	275
1989	3016 The Pipes of Pan	Closed	1990	16.90	225-350
1989	3017 Mischievous Goblin	Closed	1990	16.90	175-250
1989	3018 The Gorgon Medusa - R.G./M.L.	Closed	1990	16.90	200
1989	3019 The Alchemist - M. Locker	Closed	1990	16.90	200-600
1989	3020 The Merman - M. Locker	Closed	1990	16.90	200
1989	3021 The Guardian Dragon	Closed	1995	16.90	60-70
1989	3022 The Minotaur	Closed	1990	16.90	200-375
1989	3023 The Grim Reaper	Open		16.90	34

YEAR ISSUE		EDITION LIMIT	YEAR RETD.	ISSUE PRICE	*QUOTE U.S.$
1989	3024 The Unicorn	Open		16.90	34
1989	3027 The Castle of Souls	Closed	1995	22.00	65-75
1989	3028 The Dragon Gateway	Closed	1995	22.00	65-75
1989	3029 The Dragon Rider - M. Locker	Closed	1995	16.90	55-85
1989	3030 The Dragon's Kiss Mold 1 - M. Locker	Closed	N/A	16.90	100
1989	3030 The Dragon's Kiss Mold 2 - M. Locker	Closed	1993	16.90	82
1989	3031 The Witch and Familiar	Closed	1990	16.90	250-325
1989	3032 The Oriental Dragon Mold 1 - M. Locker	Closed	N/A	16.90	600
1989	3032 The Oriental Dragon Mold 2 - M. Locker	Closed	N/A	16.90	480
1989	3032 The Oriental Dragon Mold 3 - M. Locker	Closed	1993	16.90	295
1989	3033 The Reborn Dragon	Open		16.90	34
1989	3034 The Fire Dragon - M. Locker	Closed	1993	16.90	90
1989	3035 The Giant Sorceror	Closed	1993	16.90	90
1989	3036 The Wizard of Light	Closed	1995	16.90	70-85
1989	3037 The Light of Knowledge - M. Locker	Closed	1991	16.90	175-220
1989	3038 Pegasus	Open		16.90	34
1990	3039 The Earth Wizard	Closed	1991	18.60	100
1990	3040 The Fire Wizard	Closed	1994	18.60	90
1990	3041 The Water Wizard	Closed	1991	18.60	100
1990	3042 The Air Wizard	Closed	1991	18.60	100
1990	3043 Mother Nature	Open		18.60	34
1990	3044 The Dragon of the Lake	Closed	1993	26.10	125-250
1990	3045 The Dragon's Spell	Closed	1992	18.60	100
1990	3046 The Keeper of the Treasure	Closed	1995	18.60	60-85
1990	3047 George & the Dragon	Closed	1990	18.60	550-775
1990	3048 Dragon of the Sea	Closed	1993	18.60	88
1990	3049 Dragon of the Forest	Closed	1994	18.65	88
1990	3050 Dragon of Wisdom	Open		18.60	34
1990	3051 Spirits of the Forest	Closed	1995	18.60	65-85
1990	3052 Virgin and Unicorn	Closed	1993	26.10	88
1991	3053 The Wizard of Autumn	Open		22.00	34
1991	3054 The Wizard of Winter	Open		22.00	34
1991	3055 The Wizard of Spring - A. Slocombe	Closed	1995	22.00	60-85
1991	3056 The Wizard of Summer	Open		22.00	34
1991	3057 The Dragon of the Moon	Open		22.00	34
1991	3058 The Sun Dragon - M. Locker	Open		22.00	34
1991	3059 Dragon of the Clouds - M. Locker	Open		22.00	34
1991	3060 The Spirited Pegasus	Closed	1994	22.00	88
1991	3061 The Castle of Spires - A. Slocombe	Closed	1993	29.75	100
1991	3062 The Castle in the Clouds - A. Slocombe	Closed	1992	22.00	88
1991	3063 The Moon Wizard - A. Slocombe	Open		22.00	34
1991	3064 Dragon of the Stars - M. Locker	Closed	1995	29.75	65-85
1991	3065 The Sorceress of Light - M. Locker	Closed	1994	22.00	70
1991	3066 The Jewelled Dragon - A. Slocombe	Closed	1995	29.75	65-85
1991	3067 Old Father Time - M. Locker	Closed	1993	29.75	100-110
1991	3068 Runelore	12/96		29.75	42
1992	3069 The Fairy Queen - A. Slocombe	Closed	1993	23.70	88
1992	3070 The Dragon Queen - A. Slocombe	12/96		32.20	42
1992	3071 The Ice Dragon - A. Slocombe	Open		23.70	34
1992	3072 The Sleepy Dragon - M. Locker	Open		23.70	34
1992	3073 Unicorn of Light - A. Slocombe	Open		23.70	34
1992	3074 Starspell - M. Locker	Open		23.70	34
1992	3075 The Visionary	Open		32.20	42
1992	3076 The Crystal Spell - M. Locker	Closed	1995	23.70	60-75
1992	3077 Unicorn Rider - A. Slocombe	Open		23.70	34
1992	3078 The Loremaker - A. Slocombe	Open		23.70	34
1992	3079 Dragon's Enchantress - A. Slocombe	Closed	1994	32.20	88
1992	3080 The Leaf Spirit	Closed	1994	23.70	70
1992	3081 The Wizard of the Future	Open		23.70	34
1992	3082 The Swamp Dragon - A. Slocombe	12/96		23.70	34
1992	3083 The Dragon of the Skulls - A. Slocombe	12/96		23.70	34
1992	3084 The Dark Dragon - A. Slocombe	Open		23.70	34
1992	3085 The Dragon of Light - R.G./A.S.	Open		23.70	34
1993	3092 The Fountain of Light - A. Slocombe	Closed	1995	25.00	60-75
1993	3093 The Dawn of the Dragon - R. Gibbons	12/96		25.00	34
1993	3094 The Dragon of Prehistory - A. Slocombe	Closed	1995	25.00	60-75
1993	3095 Defender of the Crystal - A. Slocombe	Open		25.00	34
1993	3096 Rising of the Phoenix - M. Locker	Closed	1995	25.00	58
1993	3097 The Protector of Young - M. Locker	Open		25.00	34
1993	3098 The Unicorns of Freedom - A. Slocombe	Open		25.00	34
1993	3099 The Keeper of the Skulls	Open		33.60	42
1993	3100 The Wizard of the Serpents - M. Locker	12/96		25.00	34
1993	3101 The Loving Dragons - M. Locker	Open		25.00	34
1993	3102 The Sword Master - A. Slocombe	Open		25.00	34

YEAR ISSUE	EDITION LIMIT	YEAR RETRD.	ISSUE PRICE	*QUOTE U.S.$
1993 3103 Dragon of Mystery - M. Locker	12/96		25.00	34
1994 3104 The Wizard of the Skies - M. Locker	Open		25.40	36
1994 3105 The Dragon of the Treasure - A. Slocombe	Open		25.40	36
1994 3106 The Wizard of the Lake	Open		25.40	36
1994 3107 Banishing the Dragon - S. Darnley	Open		25.40	36
1994 3108 The Dragon's Castle	Open		25.40	44
1994 3109 The Mystical Traveller - M. Locker	Open		25.40	36
1994 3110 The Armoured Dragon - S. Darnley	Open		25.40	36
1994 3111 The Hatchlings - S. Darnley	Open		25.40	36
1994 3112 Dragon of Ice Crystals - A. Slocombe	Open		30.50	42
1994 3113 Mischievous Dragon - S. Darnley	Open		25.40	36
1994 3114 The Crystal Unicorn - S. Darnley	Open		30.50	42
1994 3115 Summoner of Light - M. Locker	Open		30.50	42
1994 3116 The Majestic Dragon - A. Slocombe	Open		30.50	42
1994 3117 The Proud Pegasus	Open		25.40	36
1995 3118 The Dragon Warrior - S. Darnley	Open		40.00	42
1995 3119 The Crystal Serpent - M. Locker	Open		54.00	54
1995 3120 The Dragon of the Deep - M. Locker	Open		34.00	34
1995 3121 The Celtic Dragon - A. Slocombe	Open		42.00	42
1995 3122 The Unicorn of Justice - A. Slocombe	Open		34.00	34
1995 3123 The Dragon King - M. Locker	Open		64.00	64
1995 3124 The Castle of Light	Open		34.00	34
1995 3125 The Dragon's Nest - A. Slocombe	Open		42.00	42
1995 3126 The Mischievous Dragonets	Open		42.00	42
1995 3127 The Guardian of Light	Open		54.00	54
1995 3128 The Dragon Thief	Open		42.00	42
1995 3129 The Earth Dragon - A. Slocombe	Open		54.00	54
1995 3130 The Studious Dragon - A. Slocombe	Open		42.00	42
1995 3131 Finding the Dragonets - M. Locker	Open		34.00	34
1995 3132 Learning to Fly	Open		34.00	34
1995 3133 The Wizard's Best Friend	Open		34.00	34
1995 3134 Reflections - M. Locker	Open		42.00	42
1995 3135 The Lord of the Wizards - A. Slocombe	Open		42.00	42
1995 3136 The Solar Dragon - S. Darnley	Open		54.00	54
1995 3137 The Lunar Dragon	Open		54.00	54
1995 3138 Wizard Mountain	Open		28.00	28
1995 3139 The Crystal Chalice	Open		32.00	32
1995 3140 The Wizard's Scroll - A. Slocombe	Open		28.00	28
1995 3141 The Magic Glade - S. Darnley	Open		32.00	32
1995 3142 The Magic Staff - M. Locker	Open		28.00	28
1995 3143 The Wrong Spell - M. Locker	Open		32.00	32
1996 3144 The Sea Dragon - S. Riley	Open		35.00	35
1996 3145 The First Born - J. Watson	Open		35.00	35
1996 3146 Way Out Dragon - H. Coventry	Open		35.00	35
1996 3147 Dragons At Play - H. Coventry	Open		46.00	46
1996 3148 The Nursery - H. Coventry	Open		35.00	35
1996 3149 Snoozing Wizard - H. Coventry	Open		35.00	35
1996 3150 The Fairy Princess - H. Coventry	Open		46.00	46
1996 3151 Follow Me Kids! - H. Coventry	Open		35.00	35
1996 3152 Don't Push Me! - S. Riley	Open		35.00	35
1996 3153 The Artist - S.R./S.D.	Open		46.00	46
1996 3154 The Magical World - S.R./A.S.	Open		38.00	38
1996 3155 The Biker - S.R./M.L.	Open		38.00	38
1996 3156 Behave! - S.R./R.G.	Open		38.00	38
1996 3157 The Looking Glass - H.C./S.D.	Open		46.00	46
1996 3158 Bestowing the Magic Power - J.W./A.S.	Open		46.00	46
1996 3159 A Bicycle Made For Two - J.W./R.G.	Open		38.00	38
1996 3160 'Out of Tune' - H.C./M.L.	Open		38.00	38
1996 3161 The Holder of the Skull - J.W./A.S.	Open		46.00	46

United Design Corp.

Angels Collection - D. Newburn, unless otherwise noted

YEAR ISSUE	EDITION LIMIT	YEAR RETRD.	ISSUE PRICE	*QUOTE U.S.$
1993 Angel of Flight AA-032 - K. Memoli	10,000		100.00	100
1993 Angel w/ Birds AA-034	10,000	1995	75.00	75
1994 Angel w/ Book AA-058	10,000		84.00	84
1994 Angel w/ Christ Child AA-061 - K. Memoli	10,000		84.00	84
1993 Angel w/ Lilies AA-033	10,000	1996	80.00	80
1993 Angel w/ Lilies, Crimson AA-040	10,000		80.00	80
1992 Angel, Lamb & Critters AA-021 - S. Bradford	10,000		90.00	95
1996 Angel, Lion & Fawn AA-093 - K. Memoli	20,000		280.00	280
1992 Angel, Lion & Lamb AA-020 - K. Memoli	10,000	1994	135.00	300

YEAR ISSUE	EDITION LIMIT	YEAR RETRD.	ISSUE PRICE	*QUOTE U.S.$
1994 Angel, Roses and Bluebirds AA-054	10,000		65.00	65
1996 Angels, Roses & Doves AA-112	10,000		75.00	75
1993 Autumn Angel AA-035	10,000	1996	70.00	70
1993 Autumn Angel, Emerald AA-041	10,000	1996	70.00	70
1995 Celestial Guardian Angel AA-069 - S. Bradford	10,000		120.00	120
1991 Christmas Angel AA-003 - S. Bradford	10,000	1994	125.00	125
1991 Classical Angel AA-005 - S. Bradford	10,000		79.00	79
1994 Dreaming of Angels AA-060 - K. Memoli	10,000		120.00	120
1996 Dreaming of Angels, pastel AA-111 - K. Memoli	10,000		120.00	120
1994 Earth Angel AA-059 - S. Bradford	10,000		84.00	84
1991 The Gift AA-009 - S. Bradford	2,500	1991	135.00	645
1992 The Gift '92 AA-018 - S. Bradford	3,500	1992	140.00	295
1993 The Gift '93 AA-037 - S. Bradford	3,500	1993	120.00	225
1994 The Gift '94 AA-057	5,000	1994	140.00	195
1995 The Gift '95 AA-067	5,000	1995	140.00	140
1996 The Gift '96 AA-094	5,000		140.00	140
1995 Guardian Angel, Lion & Lamb AA-083 - S. Bradford	10,000		165.00	165
1995 Guardian Angel, Lion & Lamb, lt. AA-068 - S. Bradford	10,000		165.00	165
1994 Harvest Angel AA-063 - S. Bradford	10,000		84.00	84
1991 Heavenly Shepherdess AA-008 - S. Bradford	10,000		99.00	99
1992 Joy To The World AA-016	10,000	1996	90.00	95
1995 A Little Closer to Heaven AA-081 - K. Memoli	10,000		230.00	230
1995 A Little Closer to Heaven, lt. AA-085 - K. Memoli	10,000		230.00	230
1993 Madonna AA-031 - K. Memoli	10,000		100.00	100
1991 Messenger of Peace AA-006 - S. Bradford	10,000		75.00	79
1992 Peaceful Encounter AA-017	10,000		100.00	100
1995 Starlight Starbright AA-066	10,000		70.00	70
1991 Trumpeter Angel AA-004 - S. Bradford	10,000		99.00	99
1992 Winter Angel AA-019	10,000		75.00	75
1991 Winter Rose Angel AA-007 - S. Bradford	10,000	1994	65.00	65

Backyard Birds™ - Various

YEAR ISSUE	EDITION LIMIT	YEAR RETRD.	ISSUE PRICE	*QUOTE U.S.$
1994 Allen's on Pink Flowers BB-044 - P.J. Jonas	Open		22.00	22
1994 Allen's on Purple Morning Glory BB-051 - P.J. Jonas	Open		22.00	22
1989 Baltimore Oriole BB-024 - S. Bradford	Retrd.	1996	19.50	22
1989 Blue Jay BB-026 - S. Bradford	Open		19.50	22
1989 Blue Jay, Baby BB-027	Retrd.	1996	15.00	15
1990 Bluebird (Upright) BB-031 - S. Bradford	Open		20.00	20
1988 Bluebird BB-009 - S. Bradford	Open		15.00	21
1988 Bluebird Hanging BB-017 - S. Bradford	Retrd.	1990	11.00	17
1988 Bluebird, Small BB-001 - S. Bradford	Open		10.00	11
1994 Broadbill on Blue Morning Glory BB-053 - P.J. Jonas	Open		22.00	22
1994 Broadbill on Trumpet Vine BB-043 - P.J. Jonas	Open		22.00	22
1994 Broadbill on Yellow Fuscia BB-055 - P.J. Jonas	Open		22.00	22
1994 Broadbill Pair on Yellow Flowers BB-048 - P.J. Jonas	Open		30.00	30
1988 Cardinal Hanging BB-018 - S. Bradford	Retrd.	1990	11.00	11
1988 Cardinal, Female BB-011 - S. Bradford	Open		15.00	17
1988 Cardinal, Male BB-013 - S. Bradford	Open		15.00	18
1988 Cardinal, Small BB-002 - S. Bradford	Open		10.00	11
1990 Cedar Waxwing Babies BB-033 - S. Bradford	Retrd.	1996	22.00	22
1990 Cedar Waxwing BB-032 - S. Bradford	Retrd.	1996	20.00	20
1988 Chickadee BB-010 - S. Bradford	Open		15.00	18
1988 Chickadee Hanging BB-019 - S. Bradford	Retrd.	1990	11.00	11
1988 Chickadee, Small BB-003 - S. Bradford	Open		10.00	11
1990 Evening Grosbeak BB-034 - S. Bradford	Retrd.	1996	22.00	22
1989 Goldfinch BB-028 - S. Bradford	Open		16.50	20
1989 Hoot Owl BB-025 - S. Bradford	Open		15.00	20
1988 Humingbird BB-012 - S. Bradford	Open		15.00	18
1988 Hummingbird Female, Small BB-005 - S. Bradford	Retrd.	1991	10.00	10
1988 Hummingbird Flying, Small BB-004 - S. Bradford	Open		10.00	11
1988 Hummingbird Sm., Hanging BB-022 - S. Bradford	Retrd.	1990	11.00	11
1988 Hummingbird, Lg., Hanging BB-023 - S. Bradford	Retrd.	1990	15.00	15
1990 Indigo Bunting BB-036 - S. Bradford	Retrd.	1996	20.00	20
1990 Indigo Bunting, Female BB-039 - S. Bradford	Retrd.	1996	20.00	20
1994 Magnificent Pair on Trumpet Vlne BB-046 - P.J. Jonas	Open		30.00	30
1990 Nuthatch, White-throated BB-037 - S. Bradford	Retrd.	1996	20.00	20
1990 Painted Bunting BB-040 - S. Bradford	Retrd.	1996	20.00	20
1990 Painted Bunting, Female BB-041 - S. Bradford	Retrd.	1996	20.00	20

YEAR ISSUE	EDITION LIMIT	YEAR RETRD.	ISSUE PRICE	*QUOTE U.S.$
1990 Purple Finch BB-038 - S. Bradford	Retrd.	1996	20.00	20
1988 Red-winged Blackbird BB-014 - S. Bradford	Retrd.	1991	15.00	17
1988 Robin Babies BB-008 - S. Bradford	Open		15.00	19
1988 Robin Baby, Small BB-006 - S. Bradford	Open		10.00	11
1988 Robin BB-015 - S. Bradford	Open		15.00	21
1988 Robin Hanging BB-020 - S. Bradford	Retrd.	1990	11.00	11
1990 Rose Breasted Grosbeak BB-042 - S. Bradford	Retrd.	1996	20.00	20
1994 Rubythroat on Pink Fuscia BB-054 - P.J. Jonas	Open		22.00	22
1994 Rubythroat on Red Morning Glory BB-052 - P.J. Jonas	Open		22.00	22
1994 Rubythroat on Thistle BB-049 - P.J. Jonas	Open		16.50	17
1994 Rubythroat on Yellow Flowers BB-045 - P.J. Jonas	Open		22.00	22
1994 Rubythroat Pair on Pink Flowers BB-047 - P.J. Jonas	Open		30.00	30
1989 Saw-Whet Owl BB-029 - S. Bradford	Open		15.00	18
1988 Sparrow BB-016 - S. Bradford	Open		15.00	17
1988 Sparrow Hanging BB-021 - S. Bradford	Retrd.	1990	11.00	11
1988 Sparrow, Small BB-007 - S. Bradford	Retrd.	1996	10.00	11
1989 Woodpecker BB-030 - S. Bradford	Open		16.50	20

Easter Bunny Family™ - D. Kennicutt

YEAR ISSUE	EDITION LIMIT	YEAR RETRD.	ISSUE PRICE	*QUOTE U.S.$
1994 All Hidden SEC-045	Retrd.	1996	24.50	25
1989 Auntie Bunny SEC-008	Retrd.	1992	20.00	23
1992 Auntie Bunny w/Cake SEC-033R	Retrd.	1994	20.00	22
1991 Baby in Buggy, Boy SEC-027R	Retrd.	1994	20.00	22
1991 Baby in Buggy, Girl SEC-029R	Retrd.	1994	20.00	22
1994 Babysitter SEC-049	Open		24.50	25
1994 Bath Time SEC-044	Open		24.50	25
1995 Bed Time SEC-057	Open		24.00	24
1992 Boy Bunny w/Large Egg SEC-034R	Retrd.	1994	20.00	22
1991 Bubba In Wheelbarrow SEC-021	Retrd.	1993	20.00	20
1990 Bubba w/Wagon SEC-016	Retrd.	1993	16.50	18
1988 Bunnies, Basket Of SEC-001	Retrd.	1991	13.00	18
1991 Bunny Boy w/Basket SEC-025	Retrd.	1993	20.00	20
1988 Bunny Boy w/Duck SEC-002	Retrd.	1991	13.00	18
1988 Bunny Girl w/Hen SEC-004	Retrd.	1991	13.00	18
1989 Bunny w/Prize Egg SEC-010	Retrd.	1993	19.50	22
1988 Bunny, Easter SEC-003	Retrd.	1991	15.00	18
1993 Christening Day SEC-040	Retrd.	1995	20.00	22
1989 Ducky w/Bonnet, Blue SEC-015	Retrd.	1992	10.00	12
1989 Ducky w/Bonnet, Pink SEC-014	Retrd.	1992	10.00	12
1996 Easter Bunny In Evening Clothes-SEC-064	Open		20.00	20
1992 Easter Bunny w/Back Pack SEC-030	Open		20.00	22
1990 Easter Bunny w/Crystal SEC-017	Retrd.	1995	23.00	25
1993 Easter Bunny, Chocolate Egg SEC-041	Retrd.	1996	23.00	25
1995 Easter Cookies SEC-052	Open		24.00	24
1989 Easter Egg Hunt SEC-012	Retrd.	1995	16.50	22
1996 Easter Pageant - SEC-059	Open		17.00	17
1996 Easter Parade - SEC-063	Open		25.00	25
1993 Egg Roll SEC-036	Open		23.00	25
1991 Fancy Find SEC-028	Retrd.	1995	20.00	22
1996 First Kiss - SEC-061	Open		20.00	20
1995 First Outing SEC-054	Open		19.00	19
1994 First Steps SEC-048	Open		24.50	25
1994 Gift Carrot SEC-046	Open		20.00	22
1993 Girl Bunny w/Basket SEC-039	Open		20.00	22
1992 Girl Bunny w/Large Egg SEC-035R	Retrd.	1994	20.00	22
1993 Grandma & Quilt SEC-037	Open		23.00	25
1992 Grandma w/ Bible SEC-031	Retrd.	1996	20.00	22
1996 Grandma's Dress Makers Form-1996-SEC-066	Yr.Iss.		25.00	25
1992 Grandpa w/Carrots SEC-032R	Retrd.	1994	20.00	22
1996 Grandpa w/Sunflowers SEC-065	Open		20.00	20
1990 Hen w/Chick SEC-018	Retrd.	1992	23.00	23
1994 Large Prize Egg SEC-047	Open		22.00	22
1989 Little Sis w/Lolly SEC-009	Retrd.	1992	14.50	18
1993 Lop Ear Dying Eggs SEC-042	Open		23.00	25
1996 Lop Girl w/Gift Box - SEC-060	Open		20.00	20
1991 Lop-Ear w/Crystal SEC-022	Open		23.00	25
1993 Mom Storytime SEC-043	Open		23.00	25
1996 Mom w/Chocolate Egg SEC-062	Open		25.00	25
1990 Momma Making Basket SEC-019	Retrd.	1992	23.00	25
1990 Mother Goose SEC-020	Retrd.	1992	16.50	20
1991 Nest of Bunny Eggs SEC-023	Open		17.50	22
1995 Printing Lessons SEC-053	Open		19.00	19
1995 Quality Inspection SEC-055	Open		19.00	19
1988 Rabbit, Grandma SEC-005	Retrd.	1991	15.00	20
1988 Rabbit, Grandpa SEC-006	Retrd.	1991	15.00	20
1988 Rabbit, Momma w/Bonnet SEC-007	Retrd.	1991	15.00	20
1989 Rock-A-Bye Bunny SEC-013	Retrd.	1995	20.00	25
1993 Rocking Horse SEC-038	Retrd.	1996	20.00	25
1989 Sis & Bubba Sharing SEC-011	Retrd.	1996	22.50	25
1995 Spring Flying SEC-058	Open		19.00	19
1995 Team Work SEC-051	Open		24.00	24
1995 Two in a Basket SEC-056	Open		24.00	24
1991 Victorian Auntie Bunny SEC-026	Retrd.	1993	20.00	25
1991 Victorian Momma SEC-024	Retrd.	1993	20.00	25
1994 Wheelbarrow SEC-050	Open		24.50	25

Easter Bunny Family™ Babies - D. Kennicutt

YEAR ISSUE	EDITION LIMIT	YEAR RETRD.	ISSUE PRICE	*QUOTE U.S.$
1995 Baby in Basket SEC-815	Open		8.00	8

YEAR ISSUE	EDITION LIMIT	YEAR RETD.	ISSUE PRICE	*QUOTE U.S.$
1994 Baby on Blanket, Naptime SEC-807	Open		6.50	7
1996 Baby w/Diaper & Bottle, Blue - SEC-825	Open		8.00	8
1996 Baby w/Diaper & Bottle, Pink - SEC-817	Open		8.00	8
1996 Baby w/Diaper & Bottle, Yellow - SEC-824	Open		8.00	8
1995 Basket of Carrots SEC-812	Open		8.00	8
1994 Boy Baby w/Blocks SEC-805	Open		6.50	7
1994 Boy w/Baseball Bat SEC-801	Open		6.50	7
1996 Boy w/Baseball Mitt - SEC-822	Open		8.00	8
1994 Boy w/Basket and Egg SEC-802	Open		6.50	7
1996 Boy w/Big Teddy - SEC-819	Open		8.00	8
1995 Boy w/Butterfly SEC-814	Open		8.00	8
1994 Boy w/Stick Horse SEC-803	Open		6.50	7
1996 Boy w/Train Engine - SEC-816	Open		8.00	8
1996 Dress Up Girl - SEC-821	Open		8.00	8
1996 Egg Delivery - SEC-823	Open		8.00	8
1995 Gift Egg SEC-808	Open		8.00	8
1996 Girl w/Apron Full - SEC-820	Open		8.00	8
1994 Girl w/Big Egg SEC-806	Open		6.50	7
1994 Girl w/Blanket SEC-800	Open		6.50	7
1996 Girl w/Book - SEC-818	Open		8.00	8
1994 Girl w/Toy Rabbit SEC-804	Open		6.50	7
1995 Hostess SEC-810	Open		8.00	8
1995 Lop Ear & Flower Pot SEC-809	Open		8.00	8
1995 Spring Flowers SEC-813	Open		8.00	8
1995 Tea Party SEC-811	Open		8.00	8

Legend of Santa Claus™ - L. Miller, unless otherwise noted

YEAR ISSUE	EDITION LIMIT	YEAR RETD.	ISSUE PRICE	*QUOTE U.S.$
1992 Arctic Santa CF-035 - S. Bradford	7,500		90.00	100-140
1988 Assembly Required CF-017	7,500	1994	79.00	120
1991 Blessed Flight CF-032 - K. Memoli	7,500	1994	159.00	260
1996 Blessing Santa CF-066 - K. Memoli	10,000		160.00	160
1987 Checking His List CF-009	15,000	1994	75.00	120
1989 Christmas Harmony CF-020 - S. Bradford	7,500	1992	85.00	130
1992 The Christmas Tree CF-038	7,500	1995	90.00	90
1993 Dear Santa CF-046 - K. Memoli	7,500	1996	170.00	170
1995 Dear Santa, Vict. CF-063	10,000		170.00	170
1987 Dreaming Of Santa CF-008 - S. Bradford	15,000	1988	65.00	325
1992 Earth Home Santa CF-040 - S. Bradford	7,500		135.00	140
1986 Elf Pair CF-005	10,000	1992	60.00	130
1988 Father Christmas CF-018	7,500	1993	75.00	115
1991 For Santa CF-029	7,500		99.00	135
1990 Forest Friends CF-025	7,500	1993	90.00	110
1995 Getting Santa Ready CF-056	10,000		170.00	170
1996 High Country Santa CF-064	15,000		190.00	190
1989 Hitching Up CF-021	7,500	1993	90.00	110
1995 Into the Wind CF-061	10,000		140.00	140
1995 Into the Wind, Vict. CF-062	10,000		140.00	140
1993 Jolly St. Nick CF-045 - K. Memoli	7,500		130.00	130
1993 Jolly St. Nick, Victorian CF-050 - K. Memoli	7,500		120.00	120
1986 Kris Kringle CF-002	10,000	1991	60.00	160
1992 Letters to Santa CF-036	7,500	1995	125.00	130
1988 Load 'Em Up CF-016	7,500	1990	79.00	350
1987 Loading Santa's Sleigh CF-010	15,000	1993	100.00	110
1992 Loads of Happiness CF-041 - K. Memoli	7,500	1996	100.00	110
1994 Long Stocking Dilemma, Victorian CF-055 - K. Memoli	7,500		170.00	170
1994 Longstocking Dilemma CF-052 - K. Memoli	7,500		170.00	170
1987 Mrs. Santa CF-006 - S. Bradford	15,000	1991	60.00	225
1993 The Night Before Christmas CF-043	7,500	1996	100.00	100
1993 Northwoods Santa CF-047 - S. Bradford	7,500	1996	100.00	100
1987 On Santa's Knee CF007 - S. Bradford	15,000	1994	65.00	120
1996 Pause For a Tale CF-065	10,000		190.00	190
1996 Pause For a Tale, Victorian CF-069 - K. Memoli	10,000		190.00	190
1990 Puppy Love CF-024	7,500	1996	100.00	220
1989 A Purrr-Fect Christmas CF-019 - S. Bradford	7,500	1994	95.00	135
1991 Reindeer Walk CF-031 - K. Memoli	7,500		150.00	165
1995 The Ride CF-057	10,000		130.00	130
1986 Rooftop Santa CF-004 - S. Bradford	10,000	1991	65.00	170
1990 Safe Arrival CF-027 - Memoli/Jonas	7,500	1996	150.00	175
1996 Santa & Blitzen CF-067 - K. Memoli	10,000		140.00	140
1996 Santa & Blitzen, Victorian CF-070 - K. Memoli	10,000		140.00	140
1992 Santa and Comet CF-037	7,500	1995	110.00	110
1992 Santa and Mrs. Claus CF-039 - K. Memoli	7,500		150.00	150
1992 Santa and Mrs. Claus, Victorian CF-042 - K. Memoli	7,500		135.00	140
1986 Santa At Rest CF-001	10,000	1988	70.00	600
1991 Santa At Work CF-030	7,500	1995	99.00	110
1987 Santa On Horseback CF-011 - S. Bradford	15,000	1990	75.00	295
1994 Santa Riding Dove CF-053	7,500		120.00	120
1986 Santa w/Pups CF-003 - S. Bradford	10,000	1988	65.00	570
1993 Santa's Friends CF-044	7,500	1996	100.00	100
1995 Santa, Dusk & Dawn CF-060	10,000		150.00	150
1988 St. Nicholas CF-015	7,500	1992	75.00	125
1994 Star Santa w/ Polar Bear CF-054 - S. Bradford	7,500		130.00	130
1995 Starlight Express CF-059	10,000		170.00	170
1994 The Story of Christmas CF-051 - K. Memoli	10,000		180.00	180
1996 The Story of Christmas, Victorian CF-068 - K. Memoli	10,000		180.00	180
1993 Victorian Lion & Lamb Santa CF-048 - S. Bradford	7,500		100.00	100
1990 Victorian Santa CF-028 - S. Bradford	7,500	1992	125.00	325
1991 Victorian Santa w/ Teddy CF-033 - S. Bradford	7,500		150.00	160
1990 Waiting For Santa CF-026 - S. Bradford	7,500	1995	100.00	225

Legend Of The Little People™ - L. Miller

YEAR ISSUE	EDITION LIMIT	YEAR RETD.	ISSUE PRICE	*QUOTE U.S.$
1989 Adventure Bound LL-002	Retrd.	1993	35.00	50
1989 Caddy's Helper LL-007	Retrd.	1993	35.00	50
1991 The Easter Bunny's Cart LL-020	Retrd.	1994	45.00	50
1991 Fire it Up LL-023	Retrd.	1994	50.00	55
1990 Fishin' Hole LL-012	Retrd.	1994	35.00	50
1989 A Friendly Toast LL-003	Retrd.	1993	35.00	50
1990 Gathering Acorns LL-014	Retrd.	1994	100.00	100
1991 Got It LL-021	Retrd.	1994	45.00	50
1990 Hedgehog In Harness LL-010	Retrd.	1994	45.00	50
1990 Husking Acorns LL-008	Retrd.	1994	60.00	65
1991 It's About Time LL-022	Retrd.	1994	55.00	60
1990 A Little Jig LL-018	Retrd.	1994	45.00	50
1990 A Look Through The Spyglass LL-015	Retrd.	1994	40.00	50
1989 Magical Discovery LL-005	Retrd.	1993	45.00	50
1990 Ministral Magic LL-017	Retrd.	1993	45.00	50
1990 A Proclamation LL-013	Retrd.	1994	45.00	55
1989 Spring Water Scrub LL-006	Retrd.	1993	35.00	50
1990 Traveling Fast LL-009	Retrd.	1994	35.00	50
1989 Treasure Hunt LL-004	Retrd.	1993	45.00	50
1991 Viking LL-019	Retrd.	1994	45.00	50
1989 Woodland Cache LL-001	Retrd.	1993	35.00	50
1990 Woodland Scout LL-011	Retrd.	1994	40.00	50
1990 Writing The Legend LL-016	Retrd.	1994	35.00	65

Lil' Doll™ - Various

YEAR ISSUE	EDITION LIMIT	YEAR RETD.	ISSUE PRICE	*QUOTE U.S.$
1992 Clara & The Nutcracker LD-017 - D. Newburn	Retrd.	1994	35.00	35
1991 The Nutcracker LD-006 - P.J. Jonas	Retrd.	1994	35.00	35

Music Makers™ - Various

YEAR ISSUE	EDITION LIMIT	YEAR RETD.	ISSUE PRICE	*QUOTE U.S.$
1991 A Christmas Gift MM-015 - D. Kennicutt	Retrd.	1993	59.00	59
1991 Crystal Angel MM-017 - D. Kennicutt	Retrd.	1993	59.00	59
1991 Dashing Through The Snow MM-013 - D. Kennicutt	Retrd.	1993	59.00	59
1989 Evening Carolers MM-005 - D. Kennicutt	Retrd.	1993	69.00	69
1989 Herald Angel MM-011 - S. Bradford	Retrd.	1993	79.00	79
1991 Nutcracker MM-024 - P.J. Jonas	Retrd.	1994	69.00	69
1991 Peace Descending MM-025 - P.J. Jonas	Retrd.	1993	69.00	69
1991 Renaissance Angel MM-028 - P.J. Jonas	Retrd.	1994	69.00	69
1989 Santa's Sleigh MM-004 - L. Miller	Retrd.	1993	69.00	69
1991 Teddy Bear Band #2 MM-023 - D. Kennicutt	Retrd.	1994	90.00	90
1989 Teddy Bear Band MM-012 - S. Bradford	Retrd.	1993	99.00	100
1989 Teddy Drummers MM-009 - D. Kennicutt	Retrd.	1993	69.00	69
1991 Teddy Soldiers MM-018 - D. Kennicutt	Retrd.	1993	69.00	84
1991 Victorian Santa MM-026 - L. Miller	Retrd.	1993	69.00	69

Party Animals™ - L. Miller, unless otherwise noted

YEAR ISSUE	EDITION LIMIT	YEAR RETD.	ISSUE PRICE	*QUOTE U.S.$
1992 Democratic Donkey ('92) - K. Memoli	Retrd.	1994	20.00	20
1984 Democratic Donkey ('84) - D. Kennicutt	Retrd.	1986	14.50	16
1986 Democratic Donkey ('86)	Retrd.	1988	14.50	15
1988 Democratic Donkey ('88)	Retrd.	1990	14.50	16
1990 Democratic Donkey ('90) - D. Kennicutt	Retrd.	1992	16.00	16
1984 GOP Elephant ('84)	Retrd.	1986	14.50	16
1986 GOP Elephant ('86)	Retrd.	1988	14.50	15
1988 GOP Elephant ('88)	Retrd.	1990	14.50	16
1990 GOP Elephant ('90) - D. Kennicutt	Retrd.	1992	16.00	16
1992 GOP Elephant ('92) - K. Memoli	Retrd.	1994	20.00	20

PenniBears™ - P.J. Jonas

YEAR ISSUE	EDITION LIMIT	YEAR RETD.	ISSUE PRICE	*QUOTE U.S.$
1992 After Every Meal PB-058	Retrd.	1994	22.00	22
1992 Apple For Teacher PB-069	Retrd.	1994	24.00	24
1992 Attic Fun PB-019	Retrd.	1992	20.00	40
1989 Baby Hugs PB-007	Retrd.	1992	20.00	35
1991 Baking Goodies PB-043	Retrd.	1993	26.00	30
1989 Bathtime Buddies PB-023	Retrd.	1992	20.00	25
1992 Batter Up PB-066	Retrd.	1994	22.00	22
1991 Bear Footin' it PB-037	Retrd.	1993	24.00	24
1992 Bear-Capade PB-073	Retrd.	1994	22.00	22
1991 Beasly Awake PB-033	Retrd.	1993	22.00	25
1989 Beautiful Bride PB-004	Retrd.	1992	20.00	35
1993 Big Chief Little Bear PB-088	12/96		28.00	28
1989 Birthday Bear PB-013	Retrd.	1992	20.00	40
1991 Boo Hoo Bear PB-050	Retrd.	1994	22.00	22
1990 Boooo Bear PB-025	Retrd.	1993	20.00	22
1991 Bountiful Harvest PB-045	Retrd.	1994	24.00	24
1989 Bouquet Boy PB-003	Retrd.	1992	20.00	45
1989 Bouquet Girl PB-001	Retrd.	1992	20.00	45
1991 Bump-bear-Crop PB-035	Retrd.	1993	26.00	30
1991 Bunny Buddies PB-042	Retrd.	1993	22.00	25
1989 Butterfly Bear PB-005	Retrd.	1992	20.00	45-50
1990 Buttons & Bows PB-012	Retrd.	1992	20.00	45
1992 Christmas Cookies PB-075	Retrd.	1994	22.00	22
1991 Christmas Reinbear PB-046	Retrd.	1994	28.00	28
1992 Cinderella PB-056	Retrd.	1994	22.00	22
1992 Clowning Around PB-065	Retrd.	1994	22.00	22
1989 Cookie Bandit PB-006	Retrd.	1992	20.00	30
1990 Count Bearacula PB-027	Retrd.	1993	22.00	24
1991 Country Lullabye PB-036	Retrd.	1993	24.00	25
1990 Country Quilter PB-030	Retrd.	1993	22.00	30
1990 Country Spring PB-013	Retrd.	1992	20.00	45
1991 Curtain Call PB-049	Retrd.	1994	24.00	24
1992 Decorating The Wreath PB-076	Retrd.	1994	22.00	22
1989 Doctor Bear PB-008	Retrd.	1992	20.00	30
1992 Downhill Thrills PB-070	Retrd.	1994	24.00	24
1990 Dress Up Fun PB-028	Retrd.	1993	22.00	30
1992 Dust Bunny Roundup PB-062	Retrd.	1994	22.00	22
1992 First Prom PB-064	Retrd.	1994	22.00	22
1990 Garden Path PB-014	Retrd.	1992	20.00	45-50
1993 Getting 'Round On My Own PB-085	12/96		26.00	26
1990 Giddiap Teddy PB-011	Retrd.	1992	20.00	35
1991 Goodnight Little Prince PB-041	Retrd.	1993	26.00	30
1991 Goodnight Sweet Princess PB-040	Retrd.	1993	26.00	30
1993 Gotta Try Again PB-082	12/96		24.00	24
1989 Handsome Groom PB-015	Retrd.	1992	20.00	40
1993 Happy Birthday PB-084	12/96		26.00	26
1993 A Happy Camper PB-077	12/96		28.00	28
1991 Happy Hobo PB-051	Retrd.	1994	26.00	26
1989 Honey Bear PB-002	Retrd.	1992	20.00	45
1992 I Made It Boy PB-061	Retrd.	1994	22.00	22
1992 I Made It Girl PB-060	Retrd.	1994	22.00	22
1989 Lazy Days PB-009	Retrd.	1992	20.00	25
1992 Lil' Devil PB-071	Retrd.	1994	24.00	24
1991 Lil' Mer-teddy PB-034	Retrd.	1994	24.00	24
1992 Lil' Sis Makes Up PB-074	Retrd.	1994	22.00	22
1993 Little Bear Peep PB-083	12/96		24.00	24
1993 Making It Better PB-087	12/96		24.00	24
1993 May Joy Be Yours PB-080	12/96		24.00	24
1993 My Forever Love PB-078	12/96		28.00	28
1989 Nap Time PB-016	Retrd.	1992	20.00	22
1989 Nurse Bear PB-017	Retrd.	1992	20.00	35
1992 On Your Toes PB-068	Retrd.	1994	24.00	24
1989 Petite Mademoiselle PB-010	Retrd.	1992	20.00	40
1991 Pilgrim Provider PB-047	Retrd.	1994	32.00	32
1991 Pot O' Gold PB-059	Retrd.	1994	22.00	22
1992 Puddle Jumper PB-057	Retrd.	1994	24.00	24
1989 Puppy Bath PB-020	Retrd.	1992	20.00	25
1989 Puppy Love PB-021	Retrd.	1992	20.00	25
1993 Rest Stop PB-079	12/96		24.00	24
1992 Sandbox Fun PB-063	Retrd.	1994	22.00	22
1990 Santa Bear-ing Gifts PB-031	Retrd.	1993	24.00	30
1993 Santa's Helper PB-081	12/96		28.00	28
1990 Scarecrow Teddy PB-029	Retrd.	1993	24.00	25
1992 Smokey's Nephew PB-055	Retrd.	1994	22.00	22
1990 Sneaky Snowball PB-026	Retrd.	1993	20.00	25
1989 Southern Belle PB-024	Retrd.	1992	20.00	35
1992 Spanish Rose PB-053	Retrd.	1994	24.00	24
1990 Stocking Surprise PB-032	Retrd.	1993	22.00	26
1993 Summer Belle PB-086	12/96		24.00	24
1991 Summer Sailing PB-039	Retrd.	1993	26.00	30
1991 Sweet Lil 'Sis PB-048	Retrd.	1994	22.00	22
1991 Sweetheart Bears PB-044	Retrd.	1994	28.00	30
1992 Tally Ho! PB-054	Retrd.	1994	22.00	22
1992 Touchdown PB-072	Retrd.	1994	22.00	22
1989 Tubby Teddy PB-022	Retrd.	1992	20.00	22
1991 A Wild Ride PB-052	Retrd.	1994	26.00	26
1992 Will You Be Mine? PB-067	Retrd.	1994	22.00	22
1991 Windy Day PB-038	Retrd.	1993	24.00	24

PenniBears™ Collector's Club Members Only Editions - P.J. Jonas

YEAR ISSUE	EDITION LIMIT	YEAR RETD.	ISSUE PRICE	*QUOTE U.S.$
1990 1990 First Collection PB-C90	Retrd.	1990	26.00	125
1991 1991 Collecting Makes Cents PB-C91	Retrd.	1991	26.00	150
1992 1992 Today's Pleasures, Tomorrow's Treasures PB-C92	Retrd.	1992	26.00	100
1993 1993 Chalkin Up Another Year PB-C93	Retrd.	1993	26.00	35
1994 1994 Artist's Touch-Collector's Treasure PB-C94	Retrd.	1994	26.00	26

Storytime Rhymes & Tales - H. Henriksen

YEAR ISSUE	EDITION LIMIT	YEAR RETD.	ISSUE PRICE	*QUOTE U.S.$
1991 Humpty Dumpty SL-008	Retrd.	1993	64.00	64
1991 Little Jack Horner SL-007	Retrd.	1993	50.00	50
1991 Little Miss Muffet SL-006	Retrd.	1993	64.00	64
1991 Mistress Mary SL-002	Retrd.	1993	64.00	64
1991 Mother Goose SL-001	Retrd.	1993	64.00	64
1991 Owl & Pussy Cat SL-004	Retrd.	1993	100.00	100
1991 Simple Simon SL-003	Retrd.	1993	90.00	90
1991 Three Little Pigs SL-005	Retrd.	1993	100.00	100

Teddy Angels™ - P.J. Jonas

YEAR ISSUE	EDITION LIMIT	YEAR RETD.	ISSUE PRICE	*QUOTE U.S.$
1995 Bruin & Bluebirds "Nurture nature." BA-013	Open		19.00	19
1995 Bruin Making Valentines "Holidays start within the heart." BA-012	Open		15.00	15

United Design Corp.

YEAR ISSUE		EDITION LIMIT	YEAR RETD.	ISSUE PRICE	*QUOTE U.S.$
1995	Bruin With Harp Seal "Make your corner of the world a little warmer." BA-021	Open		15.00	15
1995	Bunny's Picnic "Make a feast of friendship." BA-007	Open		19.00	19
1995	Casey & Honey Reading "Friends are the best recipe for relaxation." BA-023	Open		15.00	15
1995	Casey Tucking Honey In "There is magic in the simplest things we do." BA-008	Open		19.00	19
1995	Cowboy Murray "Have a Doo Da Day." BA-002	Open		19.00	19
1995	Honey "Love gives our hearts wings." BA-014	Open		13.00	13
1995	Ivy & Blankie "Nothing is as comfortable as an old friend." BA-003	Open		13.00	13
1995	Ivy In Garden "Celebrate the little things." BA-009	Open		15.00	15
1995	Ivy With Locket "You're always close at heart." BA-028	Open		13.00	13
1995	Murray & Little Bit "Imagination can take you anywhere." BA-004	Open		19.00	19
1995	Murray Mending Bruin "Everybody needs a helping hand." BA-005	Open		15.00	15
1995	Murray With Angel "I believe in you, too." BA-022	Open		22.00	22
1995	Nicholas With Stars "Dreams are never too far away to catch." BA-024	Open		15.00	15
1995	Old Bear "Always remember your way home." BA-011	Open		19.00	19
1995	Old Bear & Little Bit Gardening "The well-watered garden produces a great harvest." BA-026	Open		15.00	15
1995	Old Bear & Little Bit Reading "Love to learn and learn to love." BA-006	Open		15.00	15
1995	Rufus Helps Bird "We could all use a little lift." BA-027	Open		15.00	15
1995	Sweetie "Come tell me all about it." - BA-001	Open		15.00	15
1995	Sweetie With Kitty Cats "Always close-knit." BA-025	Open		15.00	15
1995	Tilli & Murray "Friendship is a bridge between hearts." BA-010	Open		15.00	15

Teddy Angels™ Christmas - P.J. Jonas

YEAR ISSUE		EDITION LIMIT	YEAR RETD.	ISSUE PRICE	*QUOTE U.S.$
1995	Casey "You're a bright & shining star." BA-019	Open		13.00	13
1995	Ivy "Enchantment glows in winter snows." BA-020	Open		13.00	13
1995	Sweetie & Santa Bear "Tis the season of surprises." BA-016	Open		22.00	22
1995	Tilli & Doves "A wreath is a circle of love." BA-015	Open		19.00	19

WACO Products Corp.

Melody In Motion/Collector's Society - S. Nakane, unless otherwise noted

YEAR ISSUE		EDITION LIMIT	YEAR RETD.	ISSUE PRICE	*QUOTE U.S.$
1992	Amazing Willie the One-Man Band 07152	Retrd.	1994	130.00	250-300
1992	Willie The Conductor	Retrd.	1994	Gift	35
1993	Charmed Bunnies	Retrd.	1993	Gift	45
1993	Willie The Collector 07170	Retrd.	1995	200.00	200
1994	Springtime	Retrd.	1994	Gift	45
1995	Best Friends	Retrd.	1995	Gift	45
1996	Willie The Entertainer 07199	Yr. Iss.		200.00	200
1996	'86 Santa Replica - K. Maeda	Yr. Iss.		Gift	N/A

Melody In Motion - S. Nakane, unless otherwise noted

YEAR ISSUE		EDITION LIMIT	YEAR RETD.	ISSUE PRICE	*QUOTE U.S.$
1985	Willie The Trumpeter 07000	Open		90.00	175
1985	Willie The Hobo (Memories) 07001	2,500	1985	90.00	175
1985	Willie The Hobo (Show Me...) 07001	Retrd.	1996	90.00	175
1985	Willie The Whistler (Show Me...) 07002	2,500	1985	90.00	175
1985	Willie The Whistler (Memories) 07002	Open		90.00	175
1985	Salty 'N' Pepper 07010	Retrd.	1992	90.00	400
1986	The Cellist 07011	Retrd.	1995	100.00	180
1986	Santa Claus 1986 07012	20,000	1986	100.00	2500
1986	The Guitarist 07013	Retrd.	1994	100.00	200
1986	The Fiddler 07014	Retrd.	1995	100.00	160
1987	Lamppost Willie 07051	Open		85.00	150
1987	The Organ Grinder 07053	Retrd.	1994	100.00	200
1987	Violin Clown 07055	Retrd.	1992	85.00	200
1987	Clarinet Clown 07056	Retrd.	1991	85.00	300
1987	Saxophone Clown 07057	Retrd.	1991	85.00	250
1987	Accordion Clown 07058	Retrd.	1991	85.00	250
1987	Santa Claus 1987 07060	16,000	1987	110.00	700-2000
1987	Balloon Clown 07061	Open		85.00	150
1987	The Carousel (1st Edition) 07065	Retrd.	1993	190.00	260
1987	Madame Violin 07075	Retrd.	1991	130.00	130
1987	Madame Mandolin 07076	Retrd.	1994	130.00	130
1987	Madame Cello 07077	Retrd.	1991	130.00	130
1987	Madame Flute 07078	Retrd.	1992	130.00	130
1987	Madame Harpsichord 07080	Retrd.	1991	130.00	130
1987	Madame Lyre 07081	Retrd.	1994	130.00	130
1987	Madame Harp 07079	Open		130.00	130
1988	Spotlight Clown Cornet 07082	Retrd.	1992	120	125-200
1988	Spotlight Clown Banjo 07083	Retrd.	1992	120.00	200
1988	Spotlight Clown Trombone 07084	Retrd.	1992	120.00	200
1988	Spotlight Clown Bingo 07085	Retrd.	1992	130.00	160
1988	Spotlight Clown Tuba 07086	Retrd.	1992	120.00	200
1988	Spotlight Clown Bass 07087	Retrd.	1994	130.00	160
1988	Peanut Vendor 07088	Retrd.	1994	140.00	200

YEAR ISSUE		EDITION LIMIT	YEAR RETD.	ISSUE PRICE	*QUOTE U.S.$
1988	Ice Cream Vendor 07089	Retrd.	1994	140.00	200
1988	Santa Claus 1988 07090	12,000	1988	130.00	1000
1989	Clockpost Willie 07091			150.00	220
1989	Santa Claus 1989 (Willie) 07092	12,000	1989	130.00	N/A
1989	Lull'aby Willie 07093	Retrd.	1992	170.00	170
1989	The Grand Carousel 07094	Retrd.	1995	3000.00	3000
1989	Grandfather's Clock 07096	Retrd.	1994	200.00	295
1990	Santa Claus 1990 07097	12,000	1990	150.00	200-225
1990	Shoemaker 07130	3,700	1993	110.00	200
1990	Blacksmith 07131	3,700	1993	110.00	200
1990	Woodchopper 07132	3,700	1993	110.00	200
1990	Accordion Boy 07133	4,100	1992	120.00	200
1990	Hunter 07134	Retrd.	1994	110.00	150
1990	Robin Hood 07135 - C. Johnson	2,000	1991	180.00	350
1990	Little John 07136 - C. Johnson	2,000	1992	180.00	300
1990	Clockpost Willie II (European) 07140	Retrd.	1990	N/A	N/A
1990	Clockpost Clown 07141	Open		220.00	220
1990	Lull' A Bye Willie II (European) 07142	Retrd.	1990	N/A	N/A
1991	The Carousel (2nd Edition) 07065	Retrd.	1995	240.00	350
1991	Victoria Park Carousel 07143	Open		300.00	360
1991	Hunter Timepiece 07144	Retrd.	1994	250.00	320
1991	Santa Claus 1991 07146	7,000	1991	150.00	150
1992	Wall Street Willie 07147	Open		180.00	240
1991	Willie The Fisherman 07148	Open		150.00	200
1992	King of Clowns Carousel 07149	Open		740.00	850
1992	Golden Mountain Clock 07150	Open		250.00	280
1992	Santa Claus 1992 07151	11,000	1992	160.00	180
1992	Dockside Willie 07153	Open		160.00	190
1993	Wild West Willie 07154	Open		175.00	200
1993	Alarm Clock Post 07155	Open		N/A	N/A
1993	Lamplight Willie 07156	Retrd.	1996	220.00	220
1993	Madame Cello Player, glaze 07157	200	1993	170.00	170
1993	Madame Flute, glaze 07158	200	1993	170.00	170
1993	Madame Harpsichord, glaze 07159	200	1993	170.00	170
1993	Madame Harp, glaze	150	1993	190.00	190
1993	Santa Claus 1993 Coke 07161	6,000	1993	180.00	225
1993	Wall Street (Japanese) 07162	Retrd.	1993	N/A	N/A
1993	Santa Claus 1993 (European) 07163	1,000	1993	N/A	N/A
1993	Willie The Golfer - Alarm 07164	Retrd.	1995	240.00	240
1993	The Artist 07165	Open		240.00	240
1993	Heartbreak Willie 07166	Open		180.00	190
1993	South of the Border 07167	Retrd.	1996	180.00	180
1993	When I Grow Up 07171	Open		200.00	200
1994	Low Press Job-Alarm 07168	Retrd.	1996	240.00	240
1994	Day's End-Alarm 07169	Open		240.00	240
1994	Santa '94 Coca-Cola 07174	9,000	1994	190.00	225
1994	Smooth Sailing 07175	Open		200.00	200
1994	Santa Claus 1994 (European) 07176	700	1994	N/A	N/A
1994	The Longest Drive 07177	Open		150.00	150
1994	Happy Birthday Willie 07178	Open		170.00	170
1994	Chattanooga Choo Choo 07179	Open		180.00	190
1994	Jackpot Willie 07180	Open		180.00	190
1994	Caroler Boy 07189	10,000		172.00	180
1994	Caroler Girl 07190	10,000		172.00	180
1994	Willie the Yodeler 07192	Open		158.00	160
1994	Willie the Golfer- Clock 07264	Open		240.00	240
1994	Day's End-Clock 07269	Open		240.00	240
1995	Campfire Cowboy 07172	Retrd.	1995	180.00	180
1995	Blue Danube Carousel 07173	Open		280.00	300
1995	Willie the Conductor (10th Anniversary) 07181	10,000		220.00	220
1995	Coca-Cola Norman Rockwell 07194	Open		194.00	200
1995	Santa Claus '95 07195	6,000	1995	190.00	190
1995	Gaslight Willie 07197	Open		190.00	190
1995	Coca Cola Polar Bear 07198	6,000		180.00	180
1995	Low Pressure Job-Clock 07268	Open		240.00	240
1995	Willie The Fireman 07271	1,500		200.00	200
1996	The Candy Factory-I Love Lucy 07203 - Willingham/Maeda	Open		250.00	250
1996	Willie On The Road 07204 - K. Maeda	Open		180.00	180
1996	Marionette Clown 07205 - K. Maeda	Open		200.00	200
1996	Willie the Racer 07206 - K. Maeda	Open		180.00	180
1996	Willie the Organ Grinder 07207	3,000		200.00	200
1996	Santa Claus '96 07208 - K. Maeda	7,000		220.00	220
1996	Willie the Champion 07209 - K. Maeda	Open		180.00	180
1996	Willie the Photographer 07211 - K. Maeda	Open		220.00	220

Walnut Ridge Collectibles

Autumn Figurines - K. Bejma

YEAR ISSUE		EDITION LIMIT	YEAR RETD.	ISSUE PRICE	*QUOTE U.S.$
1996	Black Cat-410	Open		24.00	24
1996	Ghost with Pumpkin-417	Open		30.00	30
1996	Jack-O-Lantern Man-416	Open		40.00	40
1996	Jack-O-Lantern-414	Open		28.00	28
1991	Oak Leaf, set/2-420	Open		28.00	28
1996	Owl-411	Open		22.00	22
1996	Pilgrim Set-400	Open		80.00	80
1996	Pumpkin Kids, set/2-415	Open		56.00	56
1991	Pumpkin, set/3-404	Open		22.00	22
1996	Pumpkin-large-412	Open		48.00	48
1996	Pumpkin-small-413	Open		28.00	28
1996	Turkey-large-419	Open		44.00	44
1996	Turkey-medium-418	Open		36.00	36
1991	Turkey-small-401	Open		20.00	20
1996	Witch-large-407	Open		68.00	68

YEAR ISSUE		EDITION LIMIT	YEAR RETD.	ISSUE PRICE	*QUOTE U.S.$
1996	Witch-medium-408	Open		48.00	48
1996	Witch-small-409	Open		44.00	44

Cat Figurines - K. Bejma

YEAR ISSUE		EDITION LIMIT	YEAR RETD.	ISSUE PRICE	*QUOTE U.S.$
1993	Basket of Kittens-309	Open		70.00	70
1991	Calico Cat-306	Open		40.00	40
1991	Goodrich Cat-300	Open		50.00	50
1994	Tabby Cat-310	Open		50.00	50
1991	Tiny Cat-304	Open		24.00	24

Christmas Figurines - K. Bejma

YEAR ISSUE		EDITION LIMIT	YEAR RETD.	ISSUE PRICE	*QUOTE U.S.$
1996	Alpine Tree-1001	Open		24.00	24
1988	Belsnickle-102	Open		32.00	32
1988	Belsnickle-104	12/96		48.00	48
1988	Belsnickle-105	12/96		32.00	32
1989	Belsnickle-124	12/96		30.00	30
1991	Belsnickle-140	12/96		40.00	40
1994	Belsnickle-176	12/96		28.00	28
1988	Belsnickle-mini-116	Open		22.00	22
1994	Belsnickle/Tree-174	Open		32.00	32
1994	Children on Sled-172	Open		48.00	48
1995	Crying Snowman-189	Open		44.00	44
1994	Father Christmas-175	Open		28.00	28
1992	Father Christmas-large-161	Open		270.00	270
1988	Father Christmas-Apples-122	12/96		48.00	48
1988	Father Christmas/Bag-114	12/96		34.00	34
1993	Father Christmas/Bag-163	12/96		38.00	38
1994	Father Christmas/Bag-166	12/96		30.00	30
1994	Father Christmas/Bag-178	12/96		42.00	42
1988	Father Christmas/Basket-100R	12/96		120.00	120
1988	Father Christmas/Basket-100W	12/96		120.00	120
1994	Father Christmas/Girl/Doll-165	12/96		52.00	52
1993	Father Christmas/Holly-164	12/96		52.00	52
1990	Father Christmas/Toys/Switch-136	12/96		120.00	120
1991	Gnome/Rabbit-148	12/96		32.00	32
1990	Jolly St. Nick-135	12/96		52.00	52
1994	Primitive Snowman-173	Open		32.00	32
1990	Rocking Santa-129	12/96		36.00	36
1992	Santa/Horse-small-158	Open		24.00	24
1991	Santa/Walking Stick-152	12/96		56.00	56
1996	Snow Children-1002	Open		56.00	56
1994	Snowflake Belsnickle-177	Open		36.00	36
1994	Snowman & Boy-181	Open		34.00	34
1996	Snowman in Forest-1003	Open		70.00	70
1993	Snowman with Scarf-162	Open		28.00	28
1995	Snowman with Twig Arms-188	Open		32.00	32
1990	Snowman-127	12/96		32.00	32
1994	Snowman-large-182	Open		44.00	44
1990	Snowman-medium-131	Open		28.00	28
1991	Snowman-small-139	12/96		22.00	22
1996	Snowman/Snowflake Scarf-1004	Open		44.00	44
1992	Snowman/Twigs-156	Open		30.00	30
1995	Tall Tree-190	Open		28.00	28
1992	Tree Set-160	Open		44.00	44
1996	Tree-197	Open		26.00	26
1996	Tree-198	Open		22.00	22
1996	Tree-199	Open		18.00	18
1994	Walking Santa-180	12/96		90.00	90

Gossamer Wings - K. Bejma

YEAR ISSUE		EDITION LIMIT	YEAR RETD.	ISSUE PRICE	*QUOTE U.S.$
1994	Addie-167	Open		40.00	40
1995	Alexandra-183	Open		54.00	54
1996	Deborah-192	Open		50.00	50
1994	Elizabeth-170	Open		52.00	52
1996	Gabriella-194	Open		64.00	64
1994	Hannah-169	Open		50.00	50
1995	Julia-184	Open		38.00	38
1996	Kathleen-193	Open		56.00	56
1995	Lucia-187	Open		62.00	62
1995	Lydia-185	Open		58.00	58
1994	Meghan-168	Open		46.00	46
1996	Olivia-196	Open		56.00	56
1995	Tatiana-186	Open		58.00	58
1996	Thomas-195	Open		64.00	64
1996	Victoria-191	Open		54.00	54

Herr Belsnickle Collection - K. Bejma

YEAR ISSUE		EDITION LIMIT	YEAR RETD.	ISSUE PRICE	*QUOTE U.S.$
1993	Herr Dieter-807	Open		90.00	90
1993	Herr Franz-805	Open		90.00	90
1993	Herr Fritz-803	Open		100.00	100
1993	Herr Gottfried-806	Open		90.00	90
1994	Herr Gregor-818	Open		90.00	90
1993	Herr Gunther-809	Open		70.00	70
1993	Herr Heinrich-810	Open		60.00	60
1993	Herr Hermann-813	Open		48.00	48
1995	Herr Johann-820	Open		230.00	230
1993	Herr Karl-801	Open		150.00	150
1993	Herr Klaus-800	Open		180.00	180
1993	Herr Ludwig-811	Open		60.00	60
1993	Herr Nicholas-802	Open		130.00	130
1993	Herr Oskar-816	Open		44.00	44
1993	Herr Peter-815	Open		44.00	44
1993	Herr Reiner-812	Open		60.00	60
1994	Herr Rudolph-819	Open		230.00	230
1995	Herr Rutger-822	Open		150.00	150
1995	Herr Sebastian-821	Open		70.00	70
1994	Herr Viktor-817	Open		64.00	64
1993	Herr Wilhelm-804	Open		100.00	100
1993	Herr Willi-814	Open		44.00	44
1993	Herr Wolfgang-808	Open		70.00	70

*Quotes have been rounded up to nearest dollar

FIGURINES/COTTAGES

Limited Edition Collector's Series - K. Bejma

YEAR ISSUE		EDITION LIMIT	YEAR RETD.	ISSUE PRICE	*QUOTE U.S.$
1996	Christkindl-635	2,000		68.00	68
1996	Christmas Aglow-629	1,000		48.00	48
1996	Dash Away All-628	1,500		108.00	108
1995	Downhill Racer-618	2,500		48.00	48
1994	Egg Cottage-603	1,500		80.00	80
1994	Egyptian Egg/Rabbits-600	1,500		48.00	48
1995	Happy Christmas-622	2,000		50.00	50
1995	Hareratio-613	1,500		42.00	42
1994	Hemlocks And Holly-610	750		260.00	260
1996	Hitching a Ride-625	750		44.00	44
1996	Holiday Rider-631	1,000		68.00	68
1995	Holiday Sledding-620	2,500		52.00	52
1994	Holy Night-612	750		250.00	250
1995	Jacqueline-614	1,500		48.00	48
1995	Jeffrey-615	1,500		48.00	48
1994	Keeping Secrets-605	3,500		52.00	52
1994	Kimbra-609	10,000		24.00	24
1996	Life is but a Dream-627	1,000		42.00	42
1994	Lite The Way-604	3,500		52.00	52
1995	Magnolias in Bloom-616	1,500		90.00	90
1996	A Midnight Clear-634	1,250		52.00	52
1994	Miles To Go-607	10,000		52.00	52
1995	O' Tannenbaum-621	1,500		56.00	56
1995	Père Noel-619	1,500		90.00	90
1994	Rabbits At Home Egg-602	1,500		80.00	80
1996	Robin Tracks-624	1,000		48.00	48
1995	Santa Express-617	2,000		56.00	56
1996	Sharing The Spirit-630	1,000		90.00	90
1994	Shhh...-606	5,000		44.00	44
1994	Silent Night-611	750		120.00	120
1995	St. Nick's Visit-623	750		380.00	380
1996	The Stocking Was Hung-633	1,500		68.00	68
1994	Strolling Rabbits Egg-601	1,500		80.00	80
1996	Sweet Messenger-632	1,500		52.00	52
1994	Up On The Rooftop-608	5,000		56.00	56
1996	Violets for Mary-626	500		64.00	64

Nativity Collection - K. Bejma

YEAR ISSUE		EDITION LIMIT	YEAR RETD.	ISSUE PRICE	*QUOTE U.S.$
1995	Elephant	Open		120.00	120
1995	Group I Stable, Joseph, Mary, Baby Jesus, Angel	Open		324.00	324
1995	Group II Wise Men, set/3	Open		190.00	190
1995	Group III Shepards and Wanderer, set/4	Open		190.00	190
1995	Group IV Farm Animals, Sheep/2, Goat, Donkey, Cow	Open		130.00	130
1995	Laying Camel	Open		120.00	120
1995	Standing Camel	Open		120.00	120

Spring Figurines - K. Bejma

YEAR ISSUE		EDITION LIMIT	YEAR RETD.	ISSUE PRICE	*QUOTE U.S.$
1991	Bavarian Rabbit Set-226	Open		90.00	90
1996	Bunny in Shamrocks-268	Open		52.00	52
1996	Bunny with Carrots on Base-272	Open		48.00	48
1995	Bunny with Colored Eggs-263	Open		28.00	28
1990	Bunny/Acorns/Carrots-202	Open		32.00	32
1991	Bunny/Basket-227	12/96		26.00	26
1993	Bunny/Cabbage-233	Open		24.00	24
1994	Chick with Egg-257	Open		48.00	48
1994	Chicks, set/3 -260	Open		64.00	64
1995	Country Rabbit-large-265	Open		70.00	70
1996	Egg Wagon-275	Open		44.00	44
1996	Farmer Rabbit w/Carrots-270	Open		56.00	56
1992	Folksy/Rabbit-231	Open		48.00	48
1994	Hatching Chick-259	Open		20.00	20
1993	Hatching Rabbit-234	Open		34.00	34
1995	Hiking Bunny w/Egg Basket-262	Open		28.00	28
1994	Lady Vendor Rabbit-256	Open		42.00	42
1994	Laying Sheep-245	Open		44.00	44
1995	Meadow Rabbit-266	Open		90.00	90
1991	Mother Rabbit/Basket-215	12/96		48.00	48
1990	Mother Rabbit/Six Babies-200	Open		120.00	120
1990	Mother/Bowl of Eggs-207	12/96		30.00	30
1993	Mr. Rabbit/Two Children-244	12/96		44.00	44
1994	Professor Rabbit/Chicks-236	Open		30.00	30
1990	Rabbit Holding Basket-220	12/96		50.00	50
1994	Rabbit Holding Carrot-253	Open		52.00	52
1994	Rabbit in Flower Garden-246	Open		64.00	64
1996	Rabbit on Scooter-271	Open		44.00	44
1991	Rabbit Riding Rooster-209	Open		36.00	36
1996	Rabbit w/Ferns and Lillies-269	Open		120.00	120
1994	Rabbit with Basket-255	Open		52.00	52
1994	Rabbit with Vest-254	Open		38.00	38
1991	Rabbit/Basket Eggs-224	Open		46.00	46
1991	Rabbit/Basket/Bow-225	Open		46.00	46
1994	Rabbit/Hat/Stick-239	Open		28.00	28
1990	Rabbit/Holding Basket-203	Open		30.00	30
1990	Rabbit/Umbrella-208	12/96		30.00	30
1994	Rabbits on See-Saw-252	Open		44.00	44
1990	Running Rabbit-205	Open		32.00	32
1996	Shamrock Cart-226	Open		36.00	36
1990	Sitting Bunny-204	12/96		24.00	24
1995	Sitting Bunny-261	Open		24.00	24
1990	Sitting Bunny-large-216	Open		68.00	68
1994	Sitting Rabbit-251	Open		36.00	36
1993	Sitting Rabbit-large-235	Open		44.00	44
1994	Squirrel on Pinecone-249	Open		40.00	40
1996	Squirrel-large-276	Open		48.00	48
1996	Squirrel-medium-277	Open		44.00	44
1994	Standing Chick-258	Open		24.00	24
1994	Standing Rabbit-237	12/96		44.00	44
1990	Standing Sheep-211	12/96		36.00	36

YEAR ISSUE		EDITION LIMIT	YEAR RETD.	ISSUE PRICE	*QUOTE U.S.$
1996	Tan Rabbit w/Basket on Back-267	Open		90.00	90
1990	Two Rabbits/Basket-219	Open		52.00	52
1996	Wheelbarrow Egg-274	Open		48.00	48
1994	Wheelbarrow Rabbit-250	Open		44.00	44
1995	Woodland Rabbit-264	Open		48.00	48

Walt Disney

Walt Disney Collectors Society - Disney Studios

YEAR ISSUE		EDITION LIMIT	YEAR RETD.	ISSUE PRICE	*QUOTE U.S.$
1993	Jiminy Cricket Kit	Closed	1993	Gift	200-275
1993	Jiminy Cricket 4" /wheel	Closed	1993	Gift	175-250
1993	Jiminy Cricket/clef	Closed	1993	Gift	150-225
1993	Brave Little Tailor 7 1/4"	Closed	1994	160.00	240-325
1994	Cheshire Cat 4 3/4" / clef	Closed	1994	Gift	85-125
1994	Cheshire Cat 4 3/4" / flower			Gift	75-125
1994	Pecos Bill 9 1/2"	Closed	1994	650.00	500-750
1994	Admiral Duck 6 1/4"	Closed	1994	165.00	250-175
1995	Dumbo			Gift	75-100
1995	Cruella De Vil 10 1/4"	Closed	1995	250.00	275-350
1995	Dumbo Ornament	Closed	1995	20.00	40-75
1995	Slue Foot Sue 41075	Closed	1995	695.00	550-695
1996	Winnie the Pooh 41091	12/96		Gift	N/A
1996	Princess Minnie 41095	12/96		165.00	165
1996	Winnie the Pooh Ornament 41096	12/96		25.00	25
1996	Casey at the Bat 41107	Yr.Iss.		395.00	395

Classics Collection-Special Event - Disney Studios

YEAR ISSUE		EDITION LIMIT	YEAR RETD.	ISSUE PRICE	*QUOTE U.S.$
1993	Flight of Fancy 3" 41051	Closed	1994	35.00	40-50
1994	Mr. Smee 5" 41062	Closed	1995	90.00	80-125
1994	Mr. Smee 5" 41062 (teal stamp)	Closed	1995	90.00	90-125
1995	Lucky 41080	Closed	1995	40.00	50-75
1995	Wicked Witch 41084	Closed	1995	130.00	150-165
1996	Tinkerbell Ornament	Closed	1996	50.00	90
1996	Fairy Godmother 41108	12/96		125.00	125

Classics Collection-3 Caballeros - Disney Studios

YEAR ISSUE		EDITION LIMIT	YEAR RETD.	ISSUE PRICE	*QUOTE U.S.$
1995	Amigo Donald 7" 41076	Retrd.	1996	180.00	180
1995	Amigo Jose 7" 41077	Retrd.	1996	180.00	180
1995	Amigo Panchito 7" 41078	Retrd.	1996	180.00	180

Classics Collection-Bambi - Disney Studios

YEAR ISSUE		EDITION LIMIT	YEAR RETD.	ISSUE PRICE	*QUOTE U.S.$
1992	Bambi 6" 41033	Open		195.00	195
1992	Bambi 6" 41033/ wheel	Closed	1992	195.00	200-250
1992	Bambi & Flower 6" 41010	10,000	1993	298.00	450-595
1992	Field Mouse-not touching 5 3/5" 41012	7,500	1993	195.00	1450-1750
1992	Field Mouse-touching 5 3/5" 41012	7,500	1993	195.00	1000-1450
1992	Flower 3" 41034	Open		78.00	78
1992	Flower 3" 41034/ wheel	Closed	1992	78.00	110-150
1992	Friend Owl 8 3/5" 41011	Open		195.00	195
1992	Friend Owl 8 3/5" 41011/ wheel	Closed	1992	195.00	125-225
1992	Thumper 3" 41013	Open		55.00	55
1992	Thumper 3" 41013/ wheel	Closed	1992	55.00	60-75
1992	Thumper's Sisters 3 3/5" 41014	Open		69.00	69
1992	Thumper's Sisters 3 3/5" 41014/ wheel	Closed	1992	69.00	75-90
1992	Bambi-Opening Title 41015	Open		29.00	29
1992	Bambi-Opening Title 41015 /wheel	Closed	1992	29.00	30-45

Classics Collection-Cinderella - Disney Studios

YEAR ISSUE		EDITION LIMIT	YEAR RETD.	ISSUE PRICE	*QUOTE U.S.$
1993	A Dress For Cinderelly 41030/ wheel & clef	5,000	1993	800.00	1750-2300
1992	Birds With Sash 6 2/5" 41005	Closed	1994	149.00	150-195
1992	Chalk Mouse 3 2/5" 41006	Closed	1994	65.00	70-100
1992	Cinderella 6" 41000/ clef	Closed	1993	195.00	295-425
1992	Cinderella 6" 41000/ wheel	Closed	1992	195.00	325-425
1995	Cinderella & The Prince 41079	Open		275.00	295
1992	Cinderella, Lucifer, Bruno, Set/3	Closed	1993	333.00	500-620
1992	Gus 3 2/5" 41007	Closed	1994	65.00	80-120
1992	Bruno 4 2/5" 41002/ wheel & clef	Closed	1994	69.00	95-150
1992	Jaq 4 1/5" 41008	Closed	1994	65.00	85-115
1992	Lucifer 2 3/5" 41001/ wheel & clef	Closed	1994	69.00	95-145
1992	Needle Mouse 5 4/5" 41004	Closed	1994	69.00	80-110
1992	Sewing Book 41003	Closed	1994	69.00	70-110
1992	Sewing Book 41003/ no mark	Closed	1994	69.00	75-100
1992	Cinderella-Opening Title 41009	Open		29.00	29
1992	Cinderella-Opening Title -Technicolor 41009	Closed	1993	29.00	35-50

Classics Collection-Fantasia - Disney Studios

YEAR ISSUE		EDITION LIMIT	YEAR RETD.	ISSUE PRICE	*QUOTE U.S.$
1993	Blue Centaurette-Beauty in Bloom 7 1/2" 41041	Retrd.	1995	195.00	155-200
1992	Broom, 5 4/5" 41017	Retrd.	1995	75.00	100
1992	Broom, w/water spots 5 4/5" 41017/ wheel	Closed	1992	75.00	85-195
1996	Ben Ali Gator 7 1/2" 41118	Open		185.00	185
1994	Hop Low 2 3/4" 41067	Open		35.00	35
1996	Hyacinth Hippo 5 1/2" 41117	Open		195.00	195
1993	Love's Little Helpers 8" 41042	Retrd.	1995	290.00	290
1994	Mushroom Dancer-Medium 4 1/4" 41068	Open		50.00	50
1994	Mushroom Dancer-Medium 4 1/4" 41068/teal stamp	Open		50.00	65-75
1994	Mushroom Dancer-Large 4 3/4" 41058	Open		60.00	60-75
1994	Mushroom Dancer-Large 4 3/4" 41058/ teal stamp	Closed	1994	60.00	60-90
1994	Mushroom Dancer-Small 41067	Open		35.00	155-200
1993	Pink Centaurette-Romantic Reflections 7 1/2" 41040	Retrd.	1995	175.00	225-295
1992	Sorcerer Mickey 5 1/8" 41016	Retrd.	1995	195.00	215-250

YEAR ISSUE		EDITION LIMIT	YEAR RETD.	ISSUE PRICE	*QUOTE U.S.$
1992	Fantasia-Opening Title 41018	Open		29.00	40-50
1992	Fantasia-Opening Title-blank 41018	Closed	1994	29.00	40-50
1992	Fantasia-Opening Title -Technicolor 41018	Closed	1993	29.00	175

Classics Collection-Holiday Series - Disney Studios

YEAR ISSUE		EDITION LIMIT	YEAR RETD.	ISSUE PRICE	*QUOTE U.S.$
1995	Presents For My Pals 41086	Closed	1995	150.00	175
1996	Pluto Helps Decorate 41112	Yr.Iss.		150.00	150

Classics Collection-Lady and The Tramp - Disney Studios

YEAR ISSUE		EDITION LIMIT	YEAR RETD.	ISSUE PRICE	*QUOTE U.S.$
1996	Lady 4 1/2" 41089	Open		120.00	120
1996	Tramp 1/2" 41090	Open		100.00	100
1996	Lady and the Tramp-Opening Title 41099	Open		29.00	29

Classics Collection-Mr. Duck - Disney Studios

YEAR ISSUE		EDITION LIMIT	YEAR RETD.	ISSUE PRICE	*QUOTE U.S.$
1993	Donald & Daisy 6 3/5" 41024/ clef	5,000	1993	298.00	500-650
1993	Donald & Daisy 6 3/5" 41024/ wheel	5,000	1993	298.00	660-900
1993	Mr. Duck Steps Out-Opening Title 41023	Retrd.	1996	29.00	29
1993	Mr. Duck Steps Out-Opening Title 41023/ clef	Closed	1993	29.00	35
1993	Nephew Duck-Dewey 4" 41025	Retrd.	1996	65.00	65
1993	Nephew Duck-Dewey 4" 41025/ wheel	Closed	1993	65.00	70-95
1993	Nephew Duck-Huey 4" 41049	Retrd.	1996	65.00	65
1993	Nephew Duck-Huey 4" 41049/clef	Closed	1993	65.00	65-85
1993	Nephew Duck-Louie 4" 41050	Retrd.	1996	65.00	65
1993	Nephew Duck-Louie 4" 41050/ clef	Closed	1993	65.00	65-80
1994	With Love From Daisy 6 1/4" 41060	Retrd.	1996	180.00	180-200

Classics Collection-Peter Pan - Disney Studios

YEAR ISSUE		EDITION LIMIT	YEAR RETD.	ISSUE PRICE	*QUOTE U.S.$
1993	Captain Hook 8" 41044	Open		275.00	275
1993	Captain Hook 8" 41044/ clef	Closed	1994	275.00	700-800
1993	The Crocodile 6 1/4" 41054	Open		315.00	315
1993	Peter Pan 7 1/2" 41043	Open		165.00	165
1993	Peter Pan 7 1/2" 41043/ clef	Closed	1994	165.00	180-220
1993	Tinkerbell 5" 41045/ clef	12,500	1994	215.00	450-600
1993	Tinkerbell 5" 41045/ flower	12,500	1994	215.00	375-450
1993	Peter Pan-Opening Title 41047	Open		29.00	29
1993	Peter Pan-Opening Title 41047/ clef	Closed	1994	29.00	40-50

Classics Collection-Pinocchio - Disney Studios

YEAR ISSUE		EDITION LIMIT	YEAR RETD.	ISSUE PRICE	*QUOTE U.S.$
1996	Figaro 41111	Open		55.00	55
1996	Geppetto 41114	Open		145.00	145
1996	Jiminy Cricket 41109	Open		85.00	85
1996	Pinocchio 41110	Open		125.00	125
1996	Pinocchio-Opening Title 41116	Open		29.00	29

Classics Collection-Pocahontas - Disney Studios

YEAR ISSUE		EDITION LIMIT	YEAR RETD.	ISSUE PRICE	*QUOTE U.S.$
1996	Pocahontas 6 1/2" (dealer prototype) 41098	Closed	1996	225.00	450-550
1996	Pocahontas 6 1/2" 41098	Closed	1996	225.00	225-250

Classics Collection-Snow White - Disney Studios

YEAR ISSUE		EDITION LIMIT	YEAR RETD.	ISSUE PRICE	*QUOTE U.S.$
1994	Snow White 8 1/4" 41063/ flower	Closed	1994	165.00	180-220
1994	Snow White 8 1/4" 41063	Open		165.00	165
1995	Bashful 5" 91069	Open		85.00	85
1995	Doc 5 1/4" 41071	Open		95.00	95
1995	Dopey 5" 41074	Open		95.00	95
1995	Grumpy 7 3/4" 41065	Open		180.00	180
1995	Happy 5 1/2" 41064	Open		125.00	125
1995	Sleepy 3 1/4" 41066	Open		95.00	95
1995	Sneezy 4 1/2" 41073	Open		90.00	90
1995	Snow White-Opening Title 41083	Open		29.00	29

Classics Collection-Song of the South - Disney Studios

YEAR ISSUE		EDITION LIMIT	YEAR RETD.	ISSUE PRICE	*QUOTE U.S.$
1996	Brer Bear 7 1/2" 41112	Open		175.00	175
1996	Brer Fox 4" 41101	Open		120.00	120
1996	Brer Rabbit 4 3/4" 41103	Open		150.00	150
1996	Song of the South-Opening Title 41104	Open		29.00	29

Classics Collection-Symphony Hour - Disney Studios

YEAR ISSUE		EDITION LIMIT	YEAR RETD.	ISSUE PRICE	*QUOTE U.S.$
1993	Clarabelle 6 4/5" 41027/ wheel	Closed	1993	198.00	225-245
1993	Clarabelle 6 4/5" 41027	Open		198.00	198
1994	Clara Cluck 41061	Open		185.00	185
1993	Goofy 6 4/5" 41026/ clef	Closed	1993	198.00	230-250
1993	Goofy 6 4/5" 41026/ wheel	Closed	1993	198.00	1200-1650
1993	Goofy 6 4/5" 41026	Open		198.00	235
1996	Donald Duck 8 1/4" 41105	Open		225.00	225
1993	Horace 6 4/5" 41028	Open		198.00	198
1993	Horace 6 4/5" 41028/ wheel	Closed	1993	198.00	225
1993	Mickey Conductor 7 3/8" 41029	Open		185.00	185
1996	Sylvester Macaroni 41106	12,500		395.00	395
1993	Mickey Conductor 7 3/8" 41029/ wheel	Closed	1993	185.00	225-250
1993	Symphony Hour-Opening Title 41031	Open		29.00	29
1993	Symphony Hour-Opening Title 41031/ clef	Closed	1993	29.00	35-45

Classics Collection-The Delivery Boy - Disney Studios

YEAR ISSUE		EDITION LIMIT	YEAR RETD.	ISSUE PRICE	*QUOTE U.S.$
1992	Delivery Boy-Opening Title 41019	Open		29.00	29
1992	Delivery Boy-Opening Title 41019/ clef	Closed	1993	29.00	35-45

*Quotes have been rounded up to nearest dollar

YEAR ISSUE	EDITION LIMIT	YEAR RETD.	ISSUE PRICE	*QUOTE U.S. $
1992 Mickey 6" 41020	Open		125.00	135
1992 Mickey 6" 41020/ wheel	Closed	1992	125.00	150-200
1992 Minnie 6" 41021	Open		125.00	135
1992 Minnie 6" 41021/ wheel	Closed	1992	125.00	145-175
1992 Pluto (raised letters) 3 3/5" 41020/ wheel	Closed	1992	125.00	280-350
1992 Pluto 3 3/5" 41022	Open		125.00	125
1992 Pluto 3 3/5" 41022/ wheel	Closed	1992	125.00	150-200

Classics Collection-The Reluctant Dragon - Disney Studios
1996 The Reluctant Dragon 7" 41072	7,500	1996	695.00	800-925

Classics Collection-Three Little Pigs - Disney Studios
1993 Big Bad Wolf 41039 (short straight teeth/ cone base) 1st version	S/O	1994	295.00	1100-1300
1993 Big Bad Wolf 41039 (short straight teeth/ flat base) 2nd version	S/O	1994	295.00	850-990
1993 Big Bad Wolf 41039 (long/short curved teeth) 3rd version	S/O	1994	295.00	700-900
1996 Big Bad Wolf 41094	Open		225.00	225
1993 Fiddler Pig 4 1/2" 41038	Open		75.00	75
1993 Fiddler Pig 4 1/2" 41038/ clef	Closed	1993	75.00	85
1993 Fifer Pig 4 1/2" 41037	Open		75.00	75
1993 Fifer Pig 4 1/2" 41037/ clef	Closed	1993	75.00	85
1993 Practical Pig 4 1/2" 41036	Open		75.00	75
1993 Practical Pig 4 1/2" 41036/ clef	Closed	1993	75.00	85
1993 Three Little Pigs-Opening Title 41046	Open		29.00	30-40
1993 Three Little Pigs-Opening Title 41046/ clef	Closed	1993	29.00	35

Classics Collection-Tribute Series - Disney Studios
1995 Pals Forever 41085	Closed	1995	175.00	200-250

Disney's Enchanted Places - Disney Studios
1996 Beast's Castle 41225	Open		245.00	245
1996 Captain Hook 41209	Open		475.00	475
1996 Cinderella's Coach 41208	Open		265.00	265
1996 Fiddler Pig's Stick House 41204	Open		85.00	85
1996 Fifer Pig's Straw House 41205	Open		85.00	85
1996 Geppetto's Toy Shop 41207	Open		150.00	150
1996 Grandpa's House 41211	Open		125.00	125
1996 Practical Pig's Brick House 41206	Open		115.00	115
1995 Seven Dwarf's Cottage 41200	Open		180.00	180
1995 Seven Dwarf's Jewel Mine 41203	Open		190.00	190
1995 White Rabbit's House 41202	Open		175.00	175
1995 Woodcutter's Cottage 41201	Open		170.00	170

Disney's Enchanted Places Miniatures - Disney Studios
1996 Briar Rose 41214	Open		50.00	50
1996 Captain Hook 41219	Open		50.00	50
1996 Dopey 41215	Open		50.00	50
1996 Fiddler Pig 41224	Open		50.00	50
1996 Fifer Pig 41223	Open		50.00	50
1996 Gus 41218	Open		50.00	50
1996 Peter 41221	Open		50.00	50
1996 Pinocchio 41217	Open		50.00	50
1996 Practical Pig 41216	Open		50.00	50
1996 Snow White 41212	Open		50.00	50
1996 The White Rabbit 41213	Open		50.00	50

Wee Forest Folk

Animals - A. Petersen, unless otherwise noted
1974 Baby Hippo H-2	Closed	1977	7.00	N/A
1978 Beaver Wood Cutter BV-1 - W. Petersen	Closed	1980	8.00	400-500
1974 Miss and Baby Hippo H-3	Closed	1977	15.00	N/A
1973 Miss Ducky D-1	Closed	1977	6.00	N/A
1974 Miss Hippo H-1	Closed	1977	8.00	N/A
1977 Nutsy Squirrel SQ-1 - W. Petersen	Closed	1977	3.00	N/A
1979 Turtle Jogger TS-1	Closed	1980	4.00	N/A

Bears - A. Petersen
1978 Big Lady Bear BR-4	Closed	1980	7.50	N/A
1977 Blueberry Bears BR-1	Closed	1982	8.75	500-700
1977 Boy Blueberry Bear BR-3	Closed	1982	4.50	400-550
1977 Girl Blueberry Bear BR-2	Closed	1982	4.25	400-550
1978 Traveling Bear BR-5	Closed	1980	8.00	500-750

Book / Figurine - W. Petersen
1988 Tom & Eon BK-1	Suspd.	1991	45.00	200-275

Bunnies - A. Petersen, unless otherwise noted
1977 Batter Bunny B-9	Closed	1982	4.50	275-500
1973 Broom Bunny B-6	Closed	1978	9.50	N/A
1972 Double Bunnies B-1	Closed	1980	4.25	N/A
1972 Housekeeping Bunny B-2	Closed	1980	4.50	N/A
1973 Market Bunny B-8	Closed	1977	9.00	N/A
1973 Muff Bunny B-7	Closed	1980	9.00	N/A
1973 The Professor B-4	Closed	1980	4.75	N/A
1980 Professor Rabbit B-11	Closed	1981	14.00	N/A
1973 Sir Rabbit B-3 - W. Petersen	Closed	1980	4.50	N/A
1973 Sunday Bunny B-5	Closed	1980	4.75	N/A
1977 Tennis Bunny BS-1	Closed	1980	3.75	300-400
1985 Tiny Easter Bunny B-12 - D. Petersen	Closed	1992	25.00	85
1978 Wedding Bunnies B-10 - W. Petersen	Closed	1981	12.50	700-1000

YEAR ISSUE	EDITION LIMIT	YEAR RETD.	ISSUE PRICE	*QUOTE U.S.$

Christmas Carol Series - A. Petersen
1988 The Fezziwigs CC-7	Closed	1996	65.00	82

Cinderella Series - A. Petersen
1988 Cinderella's Slipper (with Prince) C-1	Closed	1989	62.00	250-275
1989 Cinderella's Slipper C-1a	Closed	1994	32.00	90-105
1988 Cinderella's Wedding C-5	Closed	1994	62.00	175-200
1989 The Fairy Godmother C-7	Closed	1994	69.00	175
1988 Flower Girl C-6	Closed	1994	22.00	75-95
1988 The Flower Girls C-4	Closed	1994	42.00	95-115
1988 The Mean Stepmother C-3	Closed	1994	32.00	90-140
1988 The Ugly Stepsisters C-2	Closed	1994	62.00	125-150

Fairy Tale Series - A. Petersen
1980 Red Riding Hood & Wolf FT-1	Closed	1982	29.00	1200-1450
1980 Red Riding Hood FT-2	Closed	1982	13.00	400-600

Forest Scene - W. Petersen
1990 Mousie Comes A-Calling FS-3	Closed	1996	128.00	146
1988 Woodland Serenade FS-1	Closed	1995	125.00	250-350

Foxes - A. Petersen
1978 Barrister Fox FX-3	Closed	1979	7.50	600-900
1977 Dandy Fox FX-2	Closed	1979	6.00	450-500
1977 Fancy Fox FX-1	Closed	1979	4.75	350-475

Frogs - A. Petersen, unless otherwise noted
1977 Frog Friends F-3 - W. Petersen	Closed	1981	5.75	400-600
1974 Frog on Rock F-2	Closed	1977	6.00	N/A
1977 Grampa Frog F-5 - W. Petersen	Closed	1981	6.00	700-1100
1974 Prince Charming F-1 - W. Petersen	Closed	1977	7.50	N/A
1978 Singing Frog F-6	Closed	1979	5.50	N/A
1977 Spring Peepers F-4	Closed	1979	3.50	N/A

Limited Edition - A. Petersen, unless otherwise noted
1981 Beauty and the Beast (color variations) BB-1 - W. Petersen	Closed	1981	89.00	8000-20000
1985 Helping Hand LTD-2	Closed	1985	62.00	550-750
1984 Postmouster LTD-1 - W. Petersen	Closed	1984	46.00	450-750
1987 Statue in the Park LTD-3 - W. Petersen	Closed	1987	93.00	700-950
1988 Uncle Sammy LTD-4	Closed	1988	85.00	225-295

Mice - A. Petersen, unless otherwise noted
1988 Aloha! M-158	Closed	1994	32.00	95-125
1982 Arty Mouse M-71	Closed	1991	19.00	100-175
1985 Attic Treasure M-126	Closed	1995	42.00	100-150
1977 Baby Sitter M-19	Closed	1981	5.75	350-450
1982 Baby Sitter M-66	Closed	1983	23.50	100-150
1981 Barrister Mouse M-57	Closed	1982	16.00	500-800
1987 Bat Mouse M-154	Closed	1994	25.00	65-95
1982 Beach Mousey M-76	Closed	1993	19.00	100-125
1981 Blue Devil M-61	Closed	N/A	12.50	125-175
1982 Boy Sweetheart M-81	Closed	1982	13.50	350-500
1975 Bride Mouse M-9	Closed	1978	4.50	450-600
1978 Bridge Club Mouse M-20	Closed	1979	6.00	600-800
1978 Bridge Club Mouse Partner M-21	Closed	1979	6.00	600-800
1984 Campfire Mouse M-109	Closed	1986	26.00	300-450
1981 The Carolers M-63	Closed	1981	29.00	900-2000
1980 Carpenter Mouse M-49	Closed	1981	15.00	600-800
1983 Chief Geronimouse M-107a	Closed	1995	21.00	70-110
1978 Chief Nip-a-Way Mouse M-26	Closed	1981	7.00	600-800
1987 Choir Mouse M-147 - W. Petersen	Closed	1990	23.00	60-90
1979 Chris-Miss M-32	Closed	1981	9.00	250-395
1979 Chris-Mouse M-33	Closed	1982	9.00	250-395
1983 Christmas Morning M-92	Closed	1987	35.00	175-300
1983 Clown Mouse M-98	Closed	1986	22.00	300-400
1986 Come & Get It! M-141	Closed	1988	34.00	125-150
1985 Come Play! M-131	Closed	1991	18.00	65-150
1989 Commencement Day M-161 - W. Petersen	Closed	1992	28.00	36
1980 Commo-Dormouse M-42 - W. Petersen	Closed	1981	14.00	600-900
1978 Cowboy Mouse M-25	Closed	1981	6.00	550-850
1981 Doc Mouse & Patient M-55 - W. Petersen	Closed	1981	14.00	500-750
1987 Don't Cry! M-149	Closed	1990	33.00	125-150
1986 Down the Chimney M-143	Closed	1988	48.00	250-300
1987 Drummer M-153b - W. Petersen	Closed	1989	29.00	50-75
1989 Elf Tales M-163	Closed	1995	48.00	95
1985 Family Portrait M-127	Closed	1987	54.00	225-350
1976 Fan Mouse M-10	Closed	1979	5.75	N/A
1974 Farmer Mouse M-5	Closed	1979	3.75	550-700
1983 First Christmas M-93	Closed	1986	16.00	225-350
1984 First Day of School M-112	Closed	1985	27.00	350-450
1986 First Haircut M-137 - W. Petersen	Closed	1992	58.00	150-250
1993 First Kiss! M-192	Closed	1996	65.00	65
1980 Fishermouse M-41	Closed	1981	16.00	550-700
1981 Flower Girl M-53	Closed	1983	15.00	350-400
1988 Forty Winks M-159 - W. Petersen	Closed	1992	36.00	46
1979 Gardener Mouse M-37	Closed	1981	12.00	600-800
1983 Get Well Soon! M-96	Closed	1983	15.00	500-600
1974 Good Knight Mouse M-4 - W. Petersen	Closed	1977	7.50	N/A
1981 Graduate Mouse M-58	Closed	1988	15.00	85-115
1991 Grammy-Phone M-176	Closed	1996	75.00	88
1992 Greta M-169b	Closed	1993	35.00	75
1992 Hans M-169a	Closed	1993	35.00	75
1990 Hans & Greta M-169	Closed	1992	64.00	150-200
1983 Harvest Mouse M-104 - W. Petersen	Closed	1984	23.00	250-450

YEAR ISSUE	EDITION LIMIT	YEAR RETD.	ISSUE PRICE	* QUOTE U.S.$
1992 High on the Hog M-186	Closed	1995	52.00	115-125
1976 June Belle M-13	Closed	1979	4.25	400
1977 King "Tut" Mouse TM-1	Closed	1979	4.50	450-600
1982 Lamplight Carolers M-86	Closed	1987	35.00	250-350
1982 Little Fire Chief M-77 - W. Petersen	Closed	1984	29.00	375-750
1982 Little Sledders M-85	Closed	1984	24.00	200-350
1982 Littlest Angel M-88	Closed	1986	15.00	95-125
1987 Littlest Witch M-156	Closed	1993	24.00	65-100
1981 Lone Caroler M-64	Closed	1981	15.50	800-1500
1993 Lord & Lady Mousebatten M-195	Closed	1995	85.00	125-150
1995 Lord Mousebatten M-195a	Closed	1996	46.00	46
1976 Mama Mouse with Baby M-18	Closed	1979	6.00	375-450
1987 Market Mouse M-150 - W. Petersen	Closed	1993	49.00	125-150
1972 Market Mouse M-1a	Closed	1978	4.25	120-150
1976 May Belle M-12	Closed	1980	4.25	300-400
1983 Merry Chris-Miss M-90	Closed	1985	17.00	250-350
1983 Merry Chris-Mouse M-91	Closed	1985	16.00	350
1972 Miss Mouse M-1	Closed	1978	4.25	N/A
1972 Miss Mousey M-2	Closed	1978	4.00	N/A
1972 Miss Mousey w/ Bow Hat M-2b	Closed	1979	4.25	N/A
1972 Miss Mousey w/ Straw Hat M-2a	Closed	1980	4.25	250-350
1973 Miss Nursey Mouse M-3	Closed	1980	4.00	400
1980 Miss Polly Mouse M-46	Closed	1984	23.00	375-450
1982 Miss Teach & Pupil M-73	Closed	1984	29.50	350-475
1980 Miss Teach M-45	Closed	1984	18.00	500-700
1982 Moon Mouse M-78	Closed	1984	15.50	350-500
1981 Mother's Helper M-52	Closed	1983	11.00	250-300
1979 Mouse Artiste M-39	Closed	1981	12.50	350-500
1979 Mouse Ballerina M-38	Closed	1981	12.50	700-900
1983 Mouse Call M-97 - W. Petersen	Closed	1983	24.00	600-800
1979 Mouse Duet M-29	Closed	1982	25.00	550-700
1986 Mouse on Campus M-139 - W. Petersen	Closed	1988	25.00	95-125
1979 Mouse Pianist M-30	Closed	1984	17.00	300-550
1985 Mouse Talk M-130	Closed	1993	44.00	100-150
1979 Mouse Violinist M-31	Closed	1984	9.00	250-350
1976 Mouse with Muff M-16	Closed	1977	9.00	N/A
1979 Mousey Baby M-34	Closed	1982	9.50	300-350
1981 Mousey Express M-65	Closed	1993	22.00	100-150
1983 Mousey's Cone M-100	Closed	1994	22.00	75-100
1983 Mousey's Dollhouse M-102	Closed	1985	30.00	325-425
1988 Mousey's Easter Basket M-160	Closed	N/A	32.00	80-150
1982 Mousey's Teddy M-75	Closed	1985	29.00	300-450
1976 Mrs. Mousey M-15	Closed	1978	4.00	N/A
1976 Mrs. Mousey w/ Hat M-15a	Closed	1979	4.25	N/A
1980 Mrs. Tidy M-51	Closed	1981	19.50	325-400
1980 Mrs. Tidy and Helper M-50	Closed	1981	24.00	450-600
1976 Nightie Mouse M-14	Closed	1979	4.75	400-500
1981 Nursery Mousey M-54	Closed	1982	14.00	350-500
1982 Office Mousey M-68	Closed	1984	23.00	375-450
1983 Pack Mouse M-106 - W. Petersen	Closed	1984	19.00	300-400
1985 Pageant Shepherds M-122	Closed	1985	35.00	200-275
1985 Pageant Wiseman M-121	Closed	1985	58.00	200-275
1981 Pearl Knit Mouse M-59	Closed	1985	20.00	200-275
1984 Pen Pal Mousey M-114	Closed	1985	26.00	275-350
1993 Peter Pumpkin Eater M-190	Closed	1995	98.00	110-175
1984 Peter's Pumpkin M-118	Closed	1992	19.00	60-85
1980 Photographer Mouse M-48 - W. Petersen	Closed	1981	23.00	500-800
1978 Picnic Mice M-23 - W. Petersen	Closed	1979	7.25	500-700
1985 Piggy-Back Mousey M-129 - W. Petersen	Closed	1986	28.00	300-400
1978 Pirate Mouse M-27	Closed	1979	6.50	800-1100
1980 Pirate Mouse M-47 - W. Petersen	Closed	1981	16.00	500-700
1990 Polly's Parasol M-170	Closed	1993	39.00	85-150
1982 Poorest Angel M-89	Closed	1986	15.00	95-125
1984 Prudence Pie Maker M-119	Closed	1992	18.50	60-85
1977 Queen "Tut" Mouse TM-2	Closed	1979	4.50	450-600
1979 Raggedy and Mouse M-36	Closed	1981	12.00	350-400
1987 The Red Wagon M-151 - W. Petersen	Closed	1991	54.00	200-250
1979 Rock-a-bye Baby Mouse M-35	Closed	1982	17.00	350-500
1983 Rocking Tot M-103	Closed	1984	19.00	700-100
1983 Rope 'em Mousey M-108	Closed	1984	19.00	300-500
1980 Santa Mouse M-43	Closed	1985	12.00	200-350
1984 Santa's Trainee M-116	Closed	1984	36.50	450-600
1982 Say "Cheese" M-72 - W. Petersen	Closed	1983	15.50	400-600
1981 School Marm Mouse M-56	Closed	1981	19.50	500-750
1987 Scooter Mouse M-152 - W. Petersen	Closed	1996	34.00	43
1978 Secretary Miss Pell M-22	Closed	1981	4.50	375-425
1976 Shawl Mouse M-17	Closed	1977	9.00	N/A
1987 Skeleton Mousey M-157	Closed	1993	27.00	50-100
1982 Snowmouse & Friend M-84	Closed	1985	23.50	375-450
1990 Stars & Stripes M-168	Closed	1996	34.00	40
1985 Sunday Drivers M-132 - W. Petersen	Closed	1994	58.00	250-300
1986 Sweet Dreams M-136	Closed	1992	58.00	125-225
1982 Sweethearts M-79	Closed	1985	26.00	400-500
1982 Tea for Two M-74	Closed	1984	26.00	350-450
1976 Tea Mouse M-11	Closed	1979	5.75	300-400
1985 Tidy Mouse M-113	Closed	1985	38.00	500-700
1978 Town Crier Mouse M-28	Closed	1979	10.50	900
1984 Traveling Mouse M-110	Closed	1987	28.00	250-350
1987 Trumpeter M-153a - W. Petersen	Closed	1989	29.00	85-95
1987 Tuba Player M-153c - W. Petersen	Closed	1989	29.00	85-95
1992 Tuckered Out! M-136a	Closed	1993	46.00	150-250
1975 Two Mice with Candle M-7	Closed	1979	4.50	450-600
1975 Two Tiny Mice M-8	Closed	1979	4.50	450-600
1986 Waltzing Matilda M-135 - W. Petersen	Closed	1993	48.00	95-125

FIGURINES/COTTAGES/GRAPHICS

YEAR ISSUE	EDITION LIMIT	YEAR RETD.	ISSUE PRICE	*QUOTE U.S.$
1983 Wash Day M-105	Closed	1984	23.00	300-350
1978 Wedding Mice M-24 - W. Petersen	Closed	1981	7.50	500-600
1982 Wedding Mice M-67 - W. Petersen	Closed	1993	29.50	100-125
1980 Witch Mouse M-44	Closed	1983	12.00	175-275
1984 Witchy Boo! M-120	Closed	1995	21.00	40-75
1974 Wood Sprite M-6a	Closed	1978	4.00	500
1974 Wood Sprite M-6b	Closed	1978	4.00	500
1974 Wood Sprite M-6c	Closed	1978	4.00	500

Minutemice - A. Petersen, unless otherwise noted

YEAR ISSUE	EDITION LIMIT	YEAR RETD.	ISSUE PRICE	*QUOTE U.S.$
1974 Concordian On Drum w/Glasses MM-4	Closed	1977	9.00	N/A
1974 Concordian Wood Base w/Hat MM-4b	Closed	1977	8.00	N/A
1974 Concordian Wood Base w/Tan Coat MM-4a	Closed	1977	7.50	N/A
1974 Little Fifer on Drum MM-5b	Closed	1977	8.00	N/A
1974 Little Fifer on Drum with Fife MM-5	Closed	1977	8.00	N/A
1974 Little Fifer on Wood Base MM-5a	Closed	1977	8.00	N/A
1974 Mouse Carrying Large Drum MM-3	Closed	1977	8.00	N/A
1974 Mouse on Drum w/Black Hat MM-2	Closed	1977	9.00	N/A
1974 Mouse on Drum with Fife MM-1	Closed	1977	9.00	N/A
1974 Mouse on Drum w/Fife Wood Base MM-1a	Closed	1977	9.00	N/A

Moles - A. Petersen

YEAR ISSUE	EDITION LIMIT	YEAR RETD.	ISSUE PRICE	*QUOTE U.S.$
1978 Mole Scout MO-1	Closed	1980	4.25	300-400

Mouse Sports - A. Petersen, unless otherwise noted

YEAR ISSUE	EDITION LIMIT	YEAR RETD.	ISSUE PRICE	*QUOTE U.S.$
1975 Bobsled Three MS-1	Closed	1977	12.00	N/A
1985 Fishin' Chip MS-14 - W. Petersen	Closed	1992	46.00	250-275
1981 Golfer Mouse MS-10	Closed	1984	15.50	350-450
1977 Golfer Mouse MS-7	Closed	1980	5.25	400-500
1984 Land Ho! MS-12	Closed	1987	36.50	250-350
1976 Mouse Skier MS-3	Closed	1979	4.25	400-500
1975 Skater Mouse MS-2	Closed	1980	4.50	300-400
1980 Skater Mouse MS-8	Closed	1983	16.50	250-550
1977 Skating Star Mouse MS-6	Closed	1979	3.75	250-350
1980 Skier Mouse (Early Colors) MS-9	Closed	1983	13.00	225-400
1984 Tennis Anyone? MS-13	Closed	1988	18.00	125-150
1976 Tennis Star MS-4	Closed	1978	3.75	250-300
1976 Tennis Star MS-5	Closed	1981	3.75	250-300

Owls - A. Petersen, unless otherwise noted

YEAR ISSUE	EDITION LIMIT	YEAR RETD.	ISSUE PRICE	*QUOTE U.S.$
1975 Colonial Owls O-4	Closed	1977	11.50	N/A
1979 Grad Owl O-5 - W. Petersen	Closed	1979	4.25	400-600
1980 Graduate Owl (On Books) O-6 - W. Petersen	Closed	1980	12.00	550
1974 Mr. and Mrs. Owl O-1	Closed	1981	6.00	500-600
1974 Mr. Owl O-3	Closed	1981	3.25	300-400
1974 Mrs. Owl O-2	Closed	1981	3.00	300-400

Piggies - A. Petersen

YEAR ISSUE	EDITION LIMIT	YEAR RETD.	ISSUE PRICE	*QUOTE U.S.$
1978 Boy Piglet/ Picnic Piggy P-6	Closed	1981	4.00	250-300
1978 Girl Piglet/Picnic Piggy P-5	Closed	1981	4.00	250-300
1981 Holly Hog P-11	Closed	1981	25.00	600-800
1978 Jolly Tar Piggy P-3	Closed	1979	4.50	300-350
1978 Miss Piggy School Marm P-1	Closed	1979	4.50	300-600
1980 Nurse Piggy P-10	Closed	1981	15.50	300-400
1978 Picnic Piggies P-4	Closed	1981	7.75	400-600
1980 Pig O' My Heart P-9	Closed	1981	12.00	300-400
1978 Piggy Baker P-2	Closed	1981	4.50	300-350
1980 Piggy Ballerina P-7	Closed	1981	15.50	300-500
1978 Piggy Jogger PS-1	Closed	1981	4.50	400-600
1980 Piggy Policeman P-8	Closed	1981	17.50	300-500

Raccoons - A. Petersen

YEAR ISSUE	EDITION LIMIT	YEAR RETD.	ISSUE PRICE	*QUOTE U.S.$
1978 Bird Watcher Raccoon RC-3	Closed	1981	6.50	600-800
1977 Hiker Raccoon RC-2	Closed	1980	4.50	500-700
1977 Mother Raccoon RC-1	Closed	1980	4.50	400-600
1978 Raccoon Skater RCS-1	Closed	1980	4.75	400-700
1978 Raccoon Skier RCS-2	Closed	1980	6.00	400-600

Rats - A. Petersen, unless otherwise noted

YEAR ISSUE	EDITION LIMIT	YEAR RETD.	ISSUE PRICE	*QUOTE U.S.$
1975 Doc Rat R-2 - W. Petersen	Closed	1980	5.25	500-700
1975 Seedy Rat R-1	Closed	1977	5.25	N/A

Robin Hood Series - A. Petersen

YEAR ISSUE	EDITION LIMIT	YEAR RETD.	ISSUE PRICE	*QUOTE U.S.$
1990 Friar Tuck RH-3	Closed	1994	32.00	75-100
1990 Maid Marion RH-2	Closed	1994	32.00	75-100
1990 Robin Hood RH-1	Closed	1994	37.00	75-100

Single Issues - A. Petersen, unless otherwise noted

YEAR ISSUE	EDITION LIMIT	YEAR RETD.	ISSUE PRICE	*QUOTE U.S.$
1980 Cave Mice - W. Petersen	Closed	N/A	N/A	550-800
1972 Party Mouse in Plain Dress	Closed	N/A	N/A	N/A
1972 Party Mouse in Polka-Dot Dress	Closed	N/A	N/A	N/A
1972 Party Mouse in Sailor Suit	Closed	N/A	N/A	N/A
1972 Party Mouse with Bow Tie	Closed	N/A	N/A	N/A
1980 Screech Owl - W. Petersen	Closed	1982	N/A	N/A

Tiny Teddies - D. Petersen

YEAR ISSUE	EDITION LIMIT	YEAR RETD.	ISSUE PRICE	*QUOTE U.S.$
1984 Boo Bear T-3	Suspd.		20.00	75-125
1987 Christmas Teddy T-10	Suspd.		26.00	100-125
1984 Drummer Bear T-4	Suspd.		22.00	75-125
1988 Hansel & Gretel Bears @ Witch's House T-11	Suspd.		175.00	150-250
1986 Huggy Bear T-8	Suspd.		26.00	75-125
1984 Little Teddy T-1	Closed	1986	20.00	75-125
1989 Momma Bear T-12	Suspd.		27.00	100-150
1985 Ride 'em Teddy! T-6	Suspd.		32.00	95-125
1984 Sailor Teddy T-2	Suspd.		20.00	75-125

YEAR ISSUE	EDITION LIMIT	YEAR RETD.	ISSUE PRICE	*QUOTE U.S.$
1984 Santa Bear T-5	Suspd.		27.00	95-125
1985 Seaside Teddy T-7	Suspd.		28.00	75-125
1983 Tiny Teddy TT-1	Closed	1983	16.00	N/A
1987 Wedding Bears T-9	Suspd.		54.00	150-200

Wind in the Willows - A. Petersen, unless otherwise noted

YEAR ISSUE	EDITION LIMIT	YEAR RETD.	ISSUE PRICE	*QUOTE U.S.$
1982 Badger WW-2	Closed	1983	18.00	300-450
1982 Mole WW-1	Closed	1983	18.00	300-400
1982 Ratty WW-4	Closed	1983	18.00	300-450
1982 Toad WW-3 - W. Petersen	Closed	1983	18.00	300-450

GRAPHICS

American Artists

Fred Stone - F. Stone

YEAR ISSUE	EDITION LIMIT	YEAR RETD.	ISSUE PRICE	*QUOTE U.S.$
1979 Affirmed, Steve Cauthen Up	750	N/A	100.00	600
1988 Alysheba	950	N/A	195.00	650
1992 The American Triple Crown I, 1948-1978	1,500		325.00	325
1993 The American Triple Crown II, 1937-1946	1,500		325.00	325
1993 The American Triple Crown III, 1919-1935	1,500		225.00	225
1983 Andalusian, The	750	N/A	150.00	350
1981 Arabians, The	750	N/A	115.00	525
1989 Battle For The Triple Crown	950	N/A	225.00	650
1980 The Belmont-Bold Forbes	500	N/A	100.00	375
1991 Black Stallion	1,500		225.00	250
1988 Cam-Fella	950	N/A	175.00	350
1981 Contentment	750	N/A	115.00	525
1992 Dance Smartly-Pat Day Up	950	N/A	225.00	325
1995 Dancers, canvas litho	350		375.00	375
1995 Dancers, print	Open		60.00	60
1983 The Duel	750	N/A	150.00	400
1985 Eternal Legacy	950	N/A	175.00	950
1980 Exceller-Bill Shoemaker	500	N/A	90.00	800
1990 Final Tribute- Secretariat	1,150		265.00	1300
1987 The First Day	950	N/A	175.00	225
1991 Forego	1,150		225.00	250
1986 Forever Friends	950	N/A	175.00	725
1985 Fred Stone Paints the Sport of Kings (Book)	750	N/A	265.00	750
1980 Genuine Risk	500	N/A	100.00	700
1991 Go For Wand-A Candle in the Wind	1,150		225.00	225
1986 Great Match Race-Ruffian & Foolish Pleasure	950	N/A	175.00	375
1995 Holy Bull, canvas litho	350		375.00	375
1995 Holy Bull, litho	1,150		225.00	225
1981 John Henry-Bill Shoemaker Up	595	N/A	160.00	1500
1985 John Henry-McCarron Up	750	N/A	175.00	500-750
1995 Julie Krone - Colonial Affair	1,150		225.00	225
1985 Kelso	950	N/A	175.00	750
1980 The Kentucky Derby	750	N/A	100.00	650
1980 Kidnapped Mare-Franfreluche	750	N/A	115.00	575
1987 Lady's Secret	950	N/A	175.00	425
1982 Man O'War "Final Thunder"	750	N/A	175.00	2500-3100
1979 Mare and Foal	500	N/A	90.00	500
1979 The Moment After	500	N/A	90.00	350
1986 Nijinski II	950	N/A	175.00	275
1984 Northern Dancer	950	N/A	175.00	625
1982 Off and Running	750	N/A	125.00	250-350
1990 Old Warriors Shoemaker-John Henry	1,950	N/A	265.00	595
1979 One, Two, Three	500	N/A	100.00	1000
1980 The Pasture Pest	500	N/A	100.00	875
1979 Patience	1,000	N/A	90.00	1200
1989 Phar Lap	950	N/A	195.00	275
1982 The Power Horses	750	N/A	125.00	250
1987 The Rivalry-Alysheba and Bet Twice	950	N/A	195.00	550
1979 The Rivals-Affirmed & Alydar	500	N/A	90.00	500
1983 Ruffian-For Only a Moment	750	N/A	175.00	1100
1983 Secretariat	950	N/A	175.00	995-1200
1989 Shoe Bald Eagle	950	N/A	195.00	675
1981 The Shoe-8,000 Wins	395	N/A	200.00	7000
1980 Spectacular Bid	500	N/A	65.00	350-400
1995 Summer Days, canvas litho	350		375.00	375
1995 Summer Days, litho	1,150		225.00	225
XX Sunday Silence	950	N/A	195.00	425
1981 The Thoroughbreds	750	N/A	115.00	425
1983 Tranquility	750	N/A	150.00	525
1984 Turning For Home	750	N/A	150.00	425
1982 The Water Trough	750	N/A	125.00	575

Anheuser-Busch, Inc.

Anheuser-Busch - H. Droog

YEAR ISSUE	EDITION LIMIT	YEAR RETD.	ISSUE PRICE	*QUOTE U.S.$
1994 Gray Wolf Mirror N4570	2,500		135.00	150

Endangered Species Fine Art Prints - B. Kemper

YEAR ISSUE	EDITION LIMIT	YEAR RETD.	ISSUE PRICE	*QUOTE U.S.$
1996 Bald Eagle Print, framed N9995	2,500		159.00	159
1996 Bald Eagle, unframed N9995U	2,500		79.00	79
1996 Cougar Print, framed N9993	2,500		159.00	159
1996 Cougar Print, unframed N9993U	2,500		79.00	79
1996 Gray Wolf Print, framed N9992	2,500		159.00	159
1996 Gray Wolf Print, unframed N9992U	2,500		79.00	79
1996 Panda Print, framed N9994	2,500		159.00	159
1996 Panda Print, unframed N9994U	2,500		79.00	79

Armani

Wall Art - G. Armani

YEAR ISSUE	EDITION LIMIT	YEAR RETD.	ISSUE PRICE	*QUOT U.S.$
1994 Abiding Love 105A	675		475.00	475
1994 Abiding Love A/P 111A	25	1995	675.00	675
1994 The Embrace 103A	675	1995	475.00	475
1994 The Embrace A/P 109A	25	1995	675.00	675
1994 La Pieta 102A	675		475.00	475
1994 La Pieta A/P 108A	25	1995	675.00	675
1994 Lady w/ Mirror 101A	675		475.00	475
1994 Lady w/ Mirror A/P 107A	25	1995	675.00	675
1994 Lady w/ Peacock 100A	675		475.00	475
1994 Lady w/ Peacock A/P 106A	25	1995	675.00	675
1994 Wind Song 104A	675		475.00	475
1994 Wind Song A/P 110A	25	1995	675.00	675

Circle Fine Art

Rockwell - N. Rockwell

YEAR ISSUE	EDITION LIMIT	YEAR RETD.	ISSUE PRICE	*QUOT U.S.$
XX American Family Folio	200		Unkn.	17500
XX The Artist at Work	130		Unkn.	3500
XX At the Barber	200		Unkn.	4900
XX Autumn	200		Unkn.	3500
XX Autumn/ Japon	25		Unkn.	3600
XX Aviary	200		Unkn.	4200
XX The Barbershop Quartet	200		Unkn.	4200
XX Baseball	200		Unkn.	3600
XX Ben Franklin's Philadelphia	200		Unkn.	3600
XX Ben's Belles	200		Unkn.	3500
XX The Big Day	200		Unkn.	3400
XX The Big Top	148		Unkn.	2800
XX Blacksmith Shop	200		Unkn.	6300
XX Bookseller	200		Unkn.	2700
XX Bookseller/ Japon	25		Unkn.	2750
XX The Bridge	200		Unkn.	3100
XX Cat	200		Unkn.	3400
XX Cat/Collotype	200		Unkn.	4000
XX Cheering	200		Unkn.	3600
XX Children at Window	200		Unkn.	3600
XX Church	200		Unkn.	3400
XX Church/ Collotype	200		Unkn.	4000
XX Circus	200		Unkn.	2650
XX County Agricultural Agent	200		Unkn.	3900
XX The Critic	200		Unkn.	4650
XX Day in the Life of a Boy	200		Unkn.	6200
XX Day in the Life of a Boy/ Japon	25		Unkn.	6500
XX Debut	200		Unkn.	3600
XX Discovery	200		Unkn.	5900
XX Doctor and Boy	200		Unkn.	9400
XX Doctor and Doll-Signed	200		Unkn.	11900
XX Dressing Up/ Ink	60		Unkn.	4400
XX Dressing Up/ Pencil	200		Unkn.	3700
XX The Drunkard	200		Unkn.	3600
XX The Expected and Unexpected	200		Unkn.	3700
XX Family Tree	200		Unkn.	5900
XX Fido's House	200		Unkn.	3600
XX Football Mascot	200		Unkn.	3700
XX Four Seasons Folio	200		Unkn.	13500
XX Four Seasons Folio/Japon	25		Unkn.	14000
XX Freedom from Fear-Signed	200		Unkn.	6400
XX Freedom from Want-Signed	200		Unkn.	6400
XX Freedom of Religion-Signed	200		Unkn.	6400
XX Freedom of Speech-Signed	200		Unkn.	6400
XX Gaiety Dance Team	200		Unkn.	4300
XX Girl at Mirror-Signed	200		Unkn.	8400
XX The Golden Age	200		Unkn.	3500
XX Golden Rule-Signed	200		Unkn.	4400
XX Golf	200		Unkn.	3600
XX Gossips	200		Unkn.	5000
XX Gossips/ Japon	25		Unkn.	5100
XX Grotto	200		Unkn.	3400
XX Grotto/ Collotype	200		Unkn.	4000
XX High Dive	200		Unkn.	3400
XX The Homecoming	200		Unkn.	3700
XX The House	200		Unkn.	3700
XX Huck Finn Folio	200		Unkn.	35000
XX Ichabod Crane	200		Unkn.	6700
XX The Inventor	200		Unkn.	4100
XX Jerry	200		Unkn.	4700
XX Jim Got Down on His Knees	200		Unkn.	4500
XX Lincoln	200		Unkn.	11400
XX Lobsterman	200		Unkn.	5500
XX Lobsterman/Japon	25		Unkn.	5750
XX Marriage License	200		Unkn.	6900
XX Medicine	200		Unkn.	3400
XX Medicine/ Color Litho	200		Unkn.	4000
XX Miss Mary Jane	200		Unkn.	4500
XX Moving Day	200		Unkn.	3900
XX Music Hath Charms	200		Unkn.	4200
XX My Hand Shook	200		Unkn.	4500
XX Out the Window	200		Unkn.	3400
XX Out the Window/ Collotype	200		Unkn.	4000
XX Outward Bound-Signed	200		Unkn.	7900
XX Poor Richard's Almanac	200		Unkn.	24000
XX Prescription	200		Unkn.	4900
XX Prescription/Japon	25		Unkn.	5000
XX The Problem We All Live With	200		Unkn.	4500
XX Puppies	200		Unkn.	3700
XX Raleigh the Dog	200		Unkn.	3900
XX Rocket Ship	200		Unkn.	3650
XX The Royal Crown	200		Unkn.	3500

YEAR ISSUE		EDITION LIMIT	YEAR RETD.	ISSUE PRICE	*QUOTE U.S. $
XX	Runaway	200	Unkn.	3800
XX	Runaway/ Japon	200	Unkn.	5700
XX	Safe and Sound	200	Unkn.	3800
XX	Saturday People	200	Unkn.	3300
XX	Save Me	200	Unkn.	3600
XX	Saying Grace-Signed	200	Unkn.	7400
XX	School Days Folio	200	Unkn.	14000
XX	Schoolhouse	200	Unkn.	4500
XX	Schoolhouse/ Japon	25	Unkn.	4650
XX	See America First	200	Unkn.	5650
XX	See America First/ Japon	25	Unkn.	6100
XX	Settling In	200	Unkn.	3600
XX	Shuffelton's Barbershop	200	Unkn.	7400
XX	Smoking	200	Unkn.	3400
XX	Smoking/ Collotype	200	Unkn.	4000
XX	Spanking	200	Unkn.	3400
XX	Spanking/ Collotype	200	Unkn.	4000
XX	Spelling Bee	200	Unkn.	6500
XX	Spring	200	Unkn.	3500
XX	Spring Flowers	200	Unkn.	5200
XX	Spring/ Japon	25	Unkn.	3600
XX	Study for the Doctor's Office	200	Unkn.	6000
XX	Studying	200	Unkn.	3600
XX	Summer	200	Unkn.	3500
XX	Summer Stock	200	Unkn.	4900
XX	Summer Stock/ Japon	25	Unkn.	5000
XX	Summer/ Japon	25	Unkn.	3600
XX	The Teacher	200	Unkn.	3400
XX	Teacher's Pet	200	Unkn.	3600
XX	The Teacher/ Japon	25	Unkn.	3500
XX	The Texan	200	Unkn.	3700
XX	Then For Three Minutes	200	Unkn.	4500
XX	Then Miss Watson	200	Unkn.	4500
XX	There Warn't No Harm	200	Unkn.	4500
XX	Three Farmers	200	Unkn.	3600
XX	Ticketseller	200	Unkn.	4200
XX	Ticketseller/Japon	25	Unkn.	4400
XX	Tom Sawyer Color Suite	200	Unkn.	30000
XX	Tom Sawyer Folio	200	Unkn.	26500
XX	Top of the World	200	Unkn.	4200
XX	Trumpeter	200	Unkn.	3900
XX	Trumpeter/Japon	25	Unkn.	4100
XX	Two O'Clock Feeding	200	Unkn.	3600
XX	The Village Smithy	200	Unkn.	3500
XX	Welcome	200	Unkn.	3500
XX	Wet Paint	200	Unkn.	3800
XX	When I Lit My Candle	200	Unkn.	4500
XX	White Washing	200	Unkn.	3400
XX	Whitewashing the Fence/Collotype	200	Unkn.	4000
XX	Window Washer	200	Unkn.	4800
XX	Winter	200	Unkn.	3500
XX	Winter/Japon	25	Unkn.	3600
XX	Ye Old Print Shoppe	200	Unkn.	3500
XX	Your Eyes is Lookin'	200	Unkn.	4500

Cross Gallery, Inc.

Bandits & Bounty Hunters - P.A. Cross

| 1996 | Bandits | 865 | | 225.00 | 225 |
| 1994 | Bounty Hunter | 865 | | 225.00 | 225 |

The Gift - P.A. Cross

| 1989 | B' Achua Dlubh-bia Bii Noskiiyahi The Gift, Part II | | S/O 1989 | 225.00 | 650 |
| 1993 | The Gift, Part III | | S/O 1993 | 225.00 | 350-1000 |

Half Breed Series - P.A. Cross

1989	Ach-hua Dlubh: (Body Two), Half Breed		S/O 1989	190.00	1450
1990	Ach-hua Dlubh: (Body Two), Half Breed II		S/O 1990	225.00	800-1100
1991	Ach-hua Dlubh: (Body Two), Half Breed III		S/O 1991	225.00	850
1995	Ach-hua Dlubh: (Body Two), Half Breed IV	865		225.00	225

Limited Edition Original Graphics - P.A. Cross

1991	Bia-A-Hoosh (A Very Special Woman), Stone Lithograph		S/O 1991	500.00	500
1987	Caroline, Stone Lithograph		S/O 1987	300.00	600
1988	Maidenhood Hopi, Stone Lithograph		S/O 1988	950.00	1150
1990	Nighteyes, I, Serigraph		S/O 1990	225.00	425
1989	The Red Capote, Serigraph		S/O 1989	750.00	1150
1989	Rosapina, Etching	74		1200.00	1200
1991	Wooltalkers, Serigraph	275		750.00	750

Limited Edition Prints - P.A. Cross

1991	Ashpahdua Hagay Ashae-Gyoke (My Home & Heart Is Crow)		S/O 1991	225.00	225-350
1983	Ayla-Sah-Xuh-Xah (Pretty Colours, Many Designs)		S/O 1983	150.00	450
1990	Baape Ochia (Night Wind, Turquoise)		S/O 1990	185.00	370
1990	Biaachee-itah Bah-achbeh (Medicine Woman Scout)		S/O 1990	225.00	525
1984	Blue Beaded Hair Ties		S/O 1984	85.00	330
1991	The Blue Shawl		S/O 1991	185.00	275
1987	Caroline		S/O 1987	45.00	145
1989	Chey-ayjeh: Prey		S/O 1989	190.00	325-600
1988	Dance Apache		S/O 1988	190.00	360
1987	Dii-tah-shteh Ee-wihza-ahook (A Coat of much Value)		S/O 1987	90.00	740

YEAR ISSUE		EDITION LIMIT	YEAR RETD.	ISSUE PRICE	*QUOTE U.S. $
1989	The Dreamer		S/O 1989	190.00	600
1987	The Elkskin Robe		S/O 1987	190.00	640
1990	Eshte		S/O 1990	185.00	200
1986	Grand Entry		S/O 1986	85.00	85
1983	Isbaaloo Eetshiileehcheek (Sorting Her Beads)		S/O 1983	150.00	1750
1990	Ishia-Kahda #1 (Quiet One)		S/O 1990	185.00	400
1988	Ma-a-luppis-she-La-dus (She is above everything, nothing can touch her)		S/O 1988	190.00	525
1984	Profile of Caroline		S/O 1984	85.00	185
1986	The Red Capote		S/O 1986	150.00	850
1987	The Red Necklace		S/O 1987	90.00	210
1989	Teesa Waits To Dance		S/O 1989	135.00	180
1984	Thick Lodge Clan Boy: Crow Indian	475		85.00	85
1987	Tina		S/O 1987	45.00	110
1985	The Water Vision		S/O 1985	150.00	325
1984	Whistling Water Clan Girl: Crow Indian		S/O 1984	85.00	85
1993	Winter Girl Bride	1,730		225.00	225
1986	Winter Morning		S/O 1986	185.00	1450
1986	The Winter Shawl		S/O 1986	150.00	1600

Miniature Line - P.A. Cross

1991	BJ		S/O 1995	80.00	80
1993	Braids	447		80.00	80
1993	Daybreak	447		80.00	80
1991	The Floral Shawl		S/O 1995	80.00	80
1991	Kendra		S/O 1995	80.00	80
1993	Ponytails	447		80.00	80
1993	Sundown	447		80.00	80
1991	Watercolour Study #2 For Half Breed		S/O 1995	80.00	80

The Painted Ladies' Suite - P.A. Cross

1992	Acoria (Crow; Seat of Honor)		S/O 1995	185.00	185
1992	Avisola		S/O 1995	185.00	185
1992	Dah-say (Crow; Heart)		S/O 1995	185.00	185
1992	Itza-chu (Apache; The Eagle)		S/O 1995	185.00	185
1992	Kel'hoya (Hopi; Little Sparrow Hawk)		S/O 1995	185.00	185
1992	The Painted Ladies		S/O 1992	225.00	1200
1997	Sus(h)gah-daydus(h) (Crow; Quick)	447		185.00	185
1997	Tze-go-juni (Chiricahua Apache)	447		185.00	185

Star Quilt Series - P.A. Cross

1988	The Quilt Makers		S/O 1988	190.00	1200
1986	Reflections		S/O 1986	185.00	865
1985	Winter Warmth		S/O 1985	150.00	900-1215

Wolf Series - P.A. Cross

1990	Agnjnaug Amaguut;Inupiag (Women With Her Wolves)		S/O 1993	325.00	350-750
1993	Ahmah-ghut, Tuhtu-loo; Eelahn-nuht Kah-auhk (Wolves and Caribou; My Furs and My Friends)	1,050		255.00	255
1996	Bia Ukbah Chedah Noskiiyah (Woman with wolves at the edge of the water)	865		225.00	225
1989	Biagoht Eecuebeh Hehsheesh-Checah: (Red Ridinghood & Her Wolves), Gift I		S/O 1989	225.00	1500-2500
1985	Dii-tah-shteh Bii-wik; Chedah-bah Iiidah (My Very Own Protective Covering; Walks w/the Wolf Woman)		S/O 1985	185.00	3275
1987	The Morning Star Gives Long Otter His Hoop Medicine Power		S/O 1987	190.00	1800-2500

Flambro Imports

Emmett Kelly Jr. Lithographs - B. Leighton-Jones

1995	All Star Circus	2 Yr.		150.00	150
1994	EKJ 70th Birthday Commemorative	1,994		150.00	150
1994	I Love You	2 Yr.		90.00	90
1994	Joyful Noise	2 Yr.		90.00	90
1994	Picture Worth 1,000 Words	2 Yr.		90.00	90

Gartlan USA

Lithograph - Various

1986	George Brett-"The Swing" - J. Martin	2,000		85.00	200
1991	Joe Montana - M. Taylor	500 1994		495.00	600-700
1989	Kareem Abdul Jabbar-The Record Setter - M. Taylor	1,989 1993		85.00	395
1991	Negro League 1st World Series (print) - Unknown	1,924 1993		109.00	125
1987	Roger Staubach - C. Soileau	1,979 1992		85.00	200-300

Glynda Turley Prints

Turley - Canvas - G. Turley

1996	Abundance III	350		190.00	190
1992	Courtyard II	200		140.00	140
1994	Courtyard III	350		140.00	140
1988	Elegance	350		130.00	130
1991	Floral Fancy	150		130.00	130
1992	Flower Garden	350		130.00	130
1990	Garden Room	250		130.00	130
1992	The Garden Wreath II	200		130.00	130
1994	The Garden Wreath III	350		140.00	140
1994	Georgia Sweet	350		140.00	140

YEAR ISSUE		EDITION LIMIT	YEAR RETD.	ISSUE PRICE	* QUOTE U.S. $
1992	Grand Glory I	350		160.00	160
1992	Grand Glory II	350		160.00	160
1995	Grand Glory III	350		160.00	160
1995	Grand Glory IV	350		160.00	160
1992	In Full Bloom	200		160.00	160
1992	In Full Bloom	200 N/A		160.00	160
1994	In Full Bloom II	350		160.00	160
1988	Iris Basket II	350		130.00	130
1990	Iris Basket III	50		130.00	130
1991	Iris Basket IV	25		130.00	130
1989	Iris Parade	350		130.00	130
1988	La Belle IV	25		130.00	130
1995	Mabry In Spring	350		160.00	160
1992	Old Mill Stream	350 N/A		130.00	130
1993	Old Mill Stream II	350 N/A		130.00	130
1994	Old Mill Stream III	350		190.00	190
1988	Once Upon A Time	200		130.00	130
1989	Petals In Pink	100		190.00	190
1989	Pretty Pickings I	350		130.00	130
1989	Pretty Pickings II	300		130.00	130
1989	Pretty Pickings III	100		130.00	130
1993	Primrose Lane II	300		130.00	130
1995	Remember When	350		190.00	190
1991	Secret Garden	350		130.00	130
1994	Secret Garden II	350		130.00	130
1996	Secret Garden III	350		160.00	160
1991	Simply Southern	350		160.00	160
1992	Southern Sunday	200		140.00	140
1995	Southern Sunday II	350		190.00	190
1993	A Southern Tradition II	350		190.00	190
1994	A Southern Tradition III	350		190.00	190
1995	A Southern Tradition V	350		190.00	190
1993	Spring's Promise II	300		130.00	130
1988	Spring's Return	350		130.00	130
1995	Summer in Victoria	350		130.00	130
1994	Summer Stroll	350		160.00	160
1990	Sweet Nothings	350		130.00	130

Turley - Print - G. Turley

1996	Abundance III	7,500		73.00	73
1996	Abundance III A/P	50		109.50	110
1995	Almost An Angel	7,500		56.00	56
1995	Almost An Angel A/P	50		84.00	84
1986	Attic Curiosity	2,000 N/A		15.00	15
1986	Attic Curiosity A/P	50 N/A		25.00	25
1986	Busy Bodies I	2,000 N/A		25.00	25
1986	Busy Bodies I A/P	50 N/A		40.00	40
1986	Busy Bodies II	2,000 N/A		25.00	25
1986	Busy Bodies II A/P	50 N/A		40.00	40
1986	Callie And Company	2,000 N/A		30.00	30
1986	Callie And Company A/P	50 N/A		50.00	50
1987	Callie And Company II	3,000 N/A		30.00	30
1987	Callie And Company II A/P	50 N/A		50.00	50
1988	Calling On Callie	5,000		30.00	30
1988	Calling On Callie A/P	50		45.00	45
1990	Childhood Memories I	3,500		30.00	30
1990	Childhood Memories I A/P	50		45.00	45
1990	Childhood Memories II	3,500		30.00	30
1990	Childhood Memories II A/P	50		45.00	45
1988	Circle of Friends	5,000		25.00	25
1988	Circle Of Friends A/P	50 N/A		40.00	40
1990	The Coming Out Party	3,500		35.00	35
1991	The Courtyard	2,500 N/A		47.00	47
1991	The Courtyard A/P	50 N/A		70.50	71
1992	The Courtyard II	2,500 N/A		50.00	50
1992	The Courtyard II A/P	50		75.00	75
1994	The Courtyard III A/P	50		91.50	92
1990	Dear To My Heart	3,500		35.00	35
1990	Dear To My Heart A/P	50		52.50	53
1988	Elegance	5,000		30.00	30
1988	Elegance A/P	50		45.00	45
1986	A Family Affair	2,500 N/A		25.00	25
1986	A Family Affair A/P	50 N/A		40.00	40
1984	Feeding Time	1,000 N/A		50.00	50
1984	Feeding Time A/P	50 N/A		75.00	75
1984	Feeding Time II	1,000 N/A		25.00	25
1984	Feeding Time II A/P	50 N/A		40.00	40
1987	Fence Row Gathering	3,000 N/A		30.00	30
1987	Fence Row Gathering A/P	50 N/A		50.00	50
1988	Fence Row Gathering II	5,000 N/A		30.00	30
1988	Fence Row Gathering II A/P	50 N/A		50.00	50
1991	Floral Fancy	3,500 N/A		40.00	40
1991	Floral Fancy A/P	50		60.00	60
1992	The Flower Garden	2,500		43.00	43
1992	The Flower Garden A/P	50		64.50	65
1986	Flowers And Lace	3,000 N/A		25.00	25
1986	Flowers And Lace A/P	50 N/A		40.00	40
1988	Flowers For Mommy	5,000 N/A		25.00	25
1988	Flowers For Mommy A/P	50 N/A		40.00	40
1990	Forever Roses	3,500		30.00	30
1990	Forever Roses A/P	50		45.00	45
1987	The Garden Gate	3,000 N/A		30.00	30
1987	The Garden Gate A/P	50 N/A		50.00	50
1990	Garden Room	3,500 N/A		40.00	40
1991	The Garden Wreath	2,500 N/A		47.00	47
1991	The Garden Wreath A/P	50 N/A		60.00	60
1992	The Garden Wreath II	2,500 N/A		50.00	50
1992	The Garden Wreath II A/P	50 N/A		75.00	75
1994	The Garden Wreath III	5,000		61.00	61
1994	The Garden Wreath III A/P	50		91.50	92
1994	Georgia Sweet	2,500		50.00	50

YEAR ISSUE		EDITION LIMIT	YEAR RETD.	ISSUE PRICE	*QUOTE U.S.$
1994	Georgia Sweet A/P	50		75.00	75
1995	Glynda's Garden	7,500		73.00	73
1995	Glynda's Garden A/P	50		109.50	110
1993	Grand Glory I	2,500	N/A	53.00	53
1992	Grand Glory I A/P	50		79.50	80
1993	Grand Glory II	2,500	N/A	53.00	53
1992	Grand Glory II A/P	50		79.50	80
1995	Grand Glory III	7,500		65.00	65
1995	Grand Glory III A/P	50		97.50	98
1995	Grand Glory IV	7,500		65.00	65
1995	Grand Glory IV A/P	50		97.50	98
1984	Heading Home I	1,000	N/A	25.00	25
1984	Heading Home I A/P	50	N/A	40.00	40
1984	Heading Home II	1,000	N/A	25.00	25
1984	Heading Home II A/P	50	N/A	40.00	40
1984	Heading Home III	1,000	N/A	25.00	25
1984	Heading Home III A/P	50	N/A	40.00	40
1987	Heart Wreath	3,000	N/A	25.00	25
1987	Heart Wreath A/P	50	N/A	40.00	40
1988	Heart Wreath II	3,500	N/A	25.00	25
1988	Heart Wreath II A/P	50	N/A	40.00	40
1989	Heart Wreath III	3,500	N/A	25.00	25
1989	Heart Wreath III A/P	50	N/A	40.00	40
1987	Hollyhocks	3,000	N/A	30.00	30
1987	Hollyhocks A/P	50	N/A	50.00	50
1990	Hollyhocks II	3,500	N/A	25.00	25
1990	Hollyhocks II A/P	50	N/A	60.00	60
1995	Hollyhocks III	7,500		69.00	69
1995	Hollyhocks III A/P	50		103.50	104
1992	In Full Bloom	2,500	N/A	53.00	53
1992	In Full Bloom A/P	50	N/A	79.50	80
1994	In Full Bloom II	3,500	N/A	65.00	65
1994	In Full Bloom II A/P	50		97.50	98
1995	In Full Bloom III	7,500		64.00	64
1995	In Full Bloom III A/P	50		96.00	96
1984	In One Ear And Out The Other	950	N/A	50.00	50
1984	In One Ear And Out The Other A/P	50	N/A	75.00	75
1987	Iris Basket	3,000	N/A	30.00	30
1987	Iris Basket A/P	50	N/A	50.00	50
1988	Iris Basket II	3,500	N/A	30.00	30
1988	Iris Basket II A/P	50	N/A	50.00	50
1990	Iris Basket III	3,500	N/A	35.00	35
1990	Iris Basket III A/P	50	N/A	52.50	53
1991	Iris Basket IV	2,500		35.00	35
1991	Iris Basket IV A/P	50		52.50	53
1989	Iris Parade	3,500		35.00	35
1989	Iris Parade A/P	50		52.50	53
1985	La Belle	750	N/A	25.00	25
1985	La Belle A/P	50	N/A	40.00	40
1986	La Belle II	2,000	N/A	25.00	25
1986	La Belle II A/P	50	N/A	40.00	40
1986	La Belle III	3,500	N/A	25.00	25
1986	La Belle III A/P	50	N/A	40.00	40
1988	La Belle IV	5,000	N/A	30.00	30
1988	La Belle IV A/P	50	N/A	50.00	50
1995	Little Red River	7,500		73.00	73
1995	Little Red River A/P	50		109.50	110
1995	Mabry In Spring	7,500		65.00	65
1995	Mabry In Spring A/P	50		97.50	98
1987	Mauve Iris I	3,000	N/A	10.00	10
1987	Mauve Iris I A/P	50	N/A	25.00	25
1987	Mauve Iris II	3,000	N/A	10.00	10
1987	Mauve Iris II A/P	50	N/A	25.00	25
1983	Now I Lay Me	1,000	N/A	50.00	50
1983	Now I Lay Me A/P	50	N/A	75.00	75
1989	Old Favorites	3,500	N/A	35.00	35
1989	Old Favorites A/P	50	N/A	52.50	53
1988	Old Friends	5,000	N/A	30.00	30
1988	Old Friends A/P	50	N/A	50.00	50
1992	Old Mill Stream	2,500	N/A	40.00	40
1992	Old Mill Stream A/P	50		60.00	60
1993	Old Mill Stream II	2,500	N/A	43.00	43
1993	Old Mill Stream II A/P	50		64.50	65
1994	Old Mill Stream III	3,500	N/A	69.00	69
1994	Old Mill Stream III A/P	50		103.50	104
1988	Once Upon A Time	5,000	N/A	30.00	30
1988	Once Upon A Time A/P	50		45.00	45
1988	Past Times	5,000	N/A	30.00	30
1988	Past Times A/P	50	N/A	50.00	50
1988	Peeping Tom	5,000	N/A	35.00	35
1988	Peeping Tom A/P	50	N/A	55.00	55
1989	Petals In Pink	3,500	N/A	30.00	30
1989	Petals In Pink A/P	50	N/A	79.50	80
1987	Playing Hookie	3,000	N/A	30.00	30
1987	Playing Hookie A/P	50	N/A	50.00	50
1988	Playing Hookie Again	5,000	N/A	30.00	30
1988	Playing Hookie Again A/P	50	N/A	50.00	50
1988	The Porch	5,000	N/A	30.00	30
1988	The Porch A/P	50	N/A	50.00	50
1989	Pretty Pickings I	3,500	N/A	30.00	30
1989	Pretty Pickings I A/P	50		45.00	45
1989	Pretty Pickings II	3,500		35.00	35
1989	Pretty Pickings II A/P	50		52.50	53
1989	Pretty Pickings III	3,500		30.00	30
1989	Pretty Pickings III A/P	50		45.00	45
1991	Primrose Lane	3,500	N/A	40.00	40
1991	Primrose Lane A/P	50	N/A	60.00	60
1993	Primrose Lane II	2,500	N/A	43.00	43
1993	Primrose Lane II A/P	50		64.50	65
1995	Remember When	7,500		73.00	73
1995	Remember When A/P	50		109.50	110
1983	Sad Face Clown	950	N/A	50.00	50

YEAR ISSUE		EDITION LIMIT	YEAR RETD.	ISSUE PRICE	*QUOTE U.S.$
1983	Sad Face Clown A/P	50	N/A	75.00	75
1991	Secret Garden	3,500	N/A	40.00	40
1991	Secret Garden A/P	50		60.00	60
1994	Secret Garden II A/P	50		79.50	80
1996	Secret Garden III	7,500		65.00	65
1996	Secret Garden III A/P	50		97.50	98
1991	Simply Southern	3,500	N/A	53.00	53
1991	Simply Southern A/P	50	N/A	79.50	80
1985	Snips N Snails	750	N/A	25.00	25
1985	Snips N Snails A/P	50	N/A	40.00	40
1992	Southern Sunday	2,500	N/A	50.00	50
1992	Southern Sunday A/P	50		75.00	75
1995	Southern Sunday II	7,500		73.00	73
1995	Southern Sunday II A/P	50		109.50	110
1993	A Southern Tradition II	3,500	N/A	60.00	60
1993	A Southern Tradition II A/P	50	N/A	90.00	90
1994	A Southern Tradition IV	5,000	N/A	69.00	69
1994	A Southern Tradition IV A/P	50		103.50	104
1995	A Southern Tradition V	7,500		73.00	73
1995	A Southern Tradition V A/P	50		109.50	110
1988	A Special Time	5,000	N/A	30.00	30
1988	A Special Time A/P	50		45.00	45
1993	Spring's Promise II	2,500		43.00	43
1993	Spring's Promise III A/P	50		64.50	65
1988	Spring's Return	5,000		35.00	35
1988	Spring's Return A/P	50		52.50	53
1983	Stepping Out	1,000	N/A	50.00	50
1983	Stepping Out A/P	50	N/A	75.00	75
1985	Sugar N Spice	750	N/A	25.00	25
1985	Sugar N Spice A/P	50	N/A	40.00	40
1987	A Summer Day	3,000	N/A	30.00	30
1987	A Summer Day A/P	50	N/A	50.00	50
1995	Summer In Victoria	7,500		53.00	53
1995	Summer In Victoria A/P	50		79.50	80
1994	Summer Stroll	3,500	N/A	65.00	65
1994	Summer Stroll A/P	50		97.50	98
1990	Sweet Nothings	3,500		40.00	40
1990	Sweet Nothings A/P	50		60.00	60
1987	Victorian Bouquet	3,500	N/A	25.00	25
1987	Victorian Bouquet A/P	50	N/A	40.00	40
1989	Victorian Bouquet II	3,500		25.00	25
1986	White Iris	2,000	N/A	25.00	25
1986	White Iris A/P	50	N/A	40.00	40
1987	Wild Roses	3,000	N/A	30.00	30
1987	Wild Roses A/P	50	N/A	50.00	50
1990	Wild Roses II	3,500		35.00	35
1990	Wild Roses II A/P	50		52.50	53

Greenwich Workshop

Ballantyne - Ballantyne

YEAR ISSUE		EDITION LIMIT	YEAR RETD.	ISSUE PRICE	*QUOTE U.S.$
1995	John's New Pup	850		150.00	150
1995	Kate and Her Fiddle	850		150.00	150

Bama - J. Bama

YEAR ISSUE		EDITION LIMIT	YEAR RETD.	ISSUE PRICE	*QUOTE U.S.$
1996	After the Council	1,000		195.00	195
1993	Art of James Bama Book with Chester Medicine Crow Fathers Flag Print	2,500	N/A	345.00	345
1981	At a Mountain Man Wedding	1,500	N/A	145.00	145-200
1981	At Burial Gallager and Blind Bill	1,650	N/A	135.00	150
1988	Bittin' Up-Rimrock Ranch	1,250	N/A	195.00	800-995
1992	Blackfeet War Robe	1,000		195.00	195
1995	Blackfoot Ceremonial Headdress	200		850.00	850
1987	Buck Norris-Crossed Sabres Ranch	1,000	N/A	195.00	700
1990	Buffalo Bill	1,250	N/A	210.00	210
1993	The Buffalo Dance	1,000		195.00	195
1991	Ceremonial Lance	1,250		225.00	225
1996	Cheyene Split Horn Headdress	200		850.00	850
1994	Cheyenne Dog Soldier	1,000		225.00	225
1991	Chuck Wagon	1,000		225.00	225
1975	Chuck Wagon in the Snow	1,000	N/A	50.00	1125-1395
1992	Coming' Round the Bend	1,000		195.00	195
1978	Contemporary Sioux Indian	1,000	N/A	75.00	1675
1995	A Cowboy Named Anne	1,000		185.00	185
1992	Crow Cavalry Scout	1,000		195.00	195
1977	A Crow Indian	1,000	N/A	65.00	95-125
1982	Crow Indian Dancer	1,250		150.00	150
1988	Crow Indian From Lodge Grass	1,250		225.00	225
1988	Dan-Mountain Man	1,250	N/A	195.00	195
1983	The Davilla Brothers-Bronc Riders	1,250		145.00	145
1983	Don Walker-Bareback Rider	1,250	N/A	85.00	85
1991	The Drift on Skull Creek Pass	1,500		225.00	225
1979	Heritage	1,500	N/A	75.00	300-395
1978	Indian at Crow Fair	1,500	N/A	75.00	75
1988	Indian Wearing War Medicine Bonnet	1,000	N/A	225.00	225
1980	Ken Blackbird	1,500	N/A	95.00	95
1974	Ken Hunder, Working Cowboy	1,000	N/A	55.00	600
1989	Little Fawn-Cree Indian Girl	1,250	N/A	195.00	195
1979	Little Star	1,500	N/A	80.00	900-995
1993	Magua-"The Last of the Mohicans"	1,000		225.00	225
1993	Making Horse Medicine	1,000		225.00	225
1978	Mountain Man	1,000		400.00	400
1980	Mountain Man 1820-1840 Period	1,500	N/A	115.00	295-375
1979	Mountain Man and His Fox	1,500	N/A	90.00	400
1982	Mountain Man with Rifle	1,250	N/A	135.00	135-150
1978	A Mountain Ute	1,000	N/A	75.00	500-595
1992	Northern Cheyene Wolf Scout	1,000		195.00	195
1981	Old Arapaho Story-Teller	1,500	N/A	135.00	135

YEAR ISSUE		EDITION LIMIT	YEAR RETD.	ISSUE PRICE	*QUOTE U.S.$
1980	Old Saddle in the Snow	1,500	N/A	75.00	595
1980	Old Sod House	1,500	N/A	80.00	300-395
1981	Oldest Living Crow Indian	1,500	N/A	135.00	135
1993	On the North Fork of the Shoshoni	1,000		195.00	195
1990	Paul Newman as Butch Cassidy & Video	2,000		250.00	250
1981	Portrait of a Sioux	1,500	N/A	135.00	135
1979	Pre-Columbian Indian with Atlatl	1,500	N/A	75.00	75
1991	Ready to Rendezvous	1,000		225.00	225
1995	Ready to Ride	1,000		185.00	185
1990	Ridin' the Rims	1,250	N/A	210.00	210
1991	Riding the High Country	1,250		225.00	225
1978	Rookie Bronc Rider	1,000	N/A	75.00	150
1976	Sage Grinder	1,000	N/A	65.00	1050-1495
1980	Sheep Skull in Drift	1,500	N/A	75.00	150
1974	Shoshone Chief	1,000	N/A	65.00	650
1982	Sioux Indian with Eagle Feather	1,250	N/A	150.00	150
1992	Sioux Subchief	1,000		195.00	195
1994	Slim Warren, The Old Cowboy	1,000		125.00	125
1983	Southwest Indian Father & Son	1,250		145.00	145
1977	Timber Jack Joe	1,000	N/A	65.00	650-895
1988	The Volunteer	1,500		225.00	225
1996	The Warrior (Ink-Jet)	200		550.00	550
1987	Winter on Trout Creek	1,000	N/A	150.00	400
1981	Winter Trapping	1,500	N/A	150.00	520-595
1980	Young Plains Indian	1,500	N/A	125.00	1050-1500
1990	Young Sheepherder	1,500		225.00	225

Bean - A. Bean

YEAR ISSUE		EDITION LIMIT	YEAR RETD.	ISSUE PRICE	*QUOTE U.S.$
1993	Conrad Gordon and Bean:The Fantasy	1,000		385.00	595
1987	Helping Hands	850		150.00	150
1995	Houston, We Have a Problem	1,000		500.00	500
1988	How It Felt to Walk on the Moon	850	N/A	150.00	150
1992	In Flight	850		385.00	385
1994	In The Beginning Apollo 25 C/S	1,000	N/A	450.00	600-895

Blackshear - T. Blackshear

YEAR ISSUE		EDITION LIMIT	YEAR RETD.	ISSUE PRICE	*QUOTE U.S.$
1994	Beauty and the Beast	1,000		225.00	225
1996	Dance of the Wind & Storm	850		195.00	195
1996	Golden Breeze	850		225.00	225
1993	Hero Frederick Douglass	746		20.00	20
1993	Hero Harriet Tubman	753		20.00	20
1993	Hero Martin Luther King, Jr.	762		20.00	20
1993	Heroes of Our Heritage Portfolio	5,000		35.00	35
1995	Intimacy	550		850.00	850
1995	Night in Day	850		195.00	195
1995	Swansong	1,000		175.00	175

Blake - B. Blake

YEAR ISSUE		EDITION LIMIT	YEAR RETD.	ISSUE PRICE	*QUOTE U.S.$
1995	The Old Double Diamond	850		175.00	175
1994	West of the Moon	650		195.00	195

Blossom - C. Blossom

YEAR ISSUE		EDITION LIMIT	YEAR RETD.	ISSUE PRICE	*QUOTE U.S.$
1987	After the Last Drift	950		145.00	145
1984	Ah Your Majesty	N/A	N/A	45.00	45
1985	Allerton on the East River	650	N/A	145.00	145
1996	Arthur James Heading Out	850		150.00	150
1988	Black Rock	950		150.00	150
1984	December Moonrise	650	N/A	135.00	135
1984	December Moonrise (remarqued)	25	N/A	175.00	175
1990	Ebb Tide	950		175.00	175
1983	First Out	450	N/A	90.00	90
1983	First Out (remarqued)	25	N/A	190.00	190
1987	Gloucester Mackerel Seiners	950		145.00	145
1989	Harbor Light	950		165.00	165
1988	Heading Home	950	N/A	150.00	250
1985	Off Palmer Land	850		145.00	145
1992	Port of Call	850		175.00	175
1986	Potomac By Moonlight	950	N/A	145.00	145
1987	San Francisco-Eve of the Gold Rush	950		150.00	150
1992	Silhouette	850		175.00	175
1986	Southport @ Twilight	950		145.00	145
1985	Tranquil Dawn	650		95.00	95
1994	Traveling in Company	850		175.00	175
1994	Traveling in Company, Remarque	100		415.00	415
1992	Windward	950		175.00	175
1986	Winter Dawn @ Boston Wharf	850		85.00	85

Bralds - B. Bralds

YEAR ISSUE		EDITION LIMIT	YEAR RETD.	ISSUE PRICE	*QUOTE U.S.$
1995	Bag Ladies	2,500	1995	150.00	335-500
1996	Basket Cases	2,500	1996	150.00	150
1996	Cabinet Meeting	2,000	1996	150.00	150

Bullas - W. Bullas

YEAR ISSUE		EDITION LIMIT	YEAR RETD.	ISSUE PRICE	*QUOTE U.S.$
1995	The Big Game	1,500		95.00	95
1993	Billy the Pig	850		95.00	172
1995	The Chimp Shot	1,000		95.00	95
1994	Clucks Unlimited	850		95.00	95
1995	The Consultant	1,000		95.00	95
1994	Court of Appeals	850	1995	95.00	95
1995	Dog Byte	1,000		95.00	95
1994	Ductor	850		95.00	95
1995	fowl ball...	1,500		95.00	95
1994	Fridays After Five	850		95.00	95
1995	Legal Eagles	1,000		95.00	95
1993	Mr. Harry Buns	850	N/A	95.00	95
1993	Our Ladies of the Front Lawn	850		95.00	95
1993	The Pale Prince	850		110.00	110
1993	Sand Trap Pro	850		95.00	95

YEAR ISSUE		EDITION LIMIT	YEAR RETD.	ISSUE PRICE	*QUOTE U.S. $
1993	Some Set of Buns	850		95.00	95
1995	tennis, anyone?	1,000		95.00	95
1993	Wine-Oceros	850		95.00	95
1993	You Rang, Madam?	850		95.00	114

Christensen - J. Christensen

1989	The Annunciation	850	N/A	175.00	200-225
1995	Balancing Act	3,500	N/A	185.00	185
1996	The Bassonist	2,500		125.00	125
1996	The Believer's Etching Edition	1,000		840.00	840
1990	The Burden of the Responsible Man	850	N/A	145.00	1000-1300
1991	The Candleman	850		160.00	250-700
1993	College of Magical Knowledge	4,500	N/A	185.00	250-300
1993	College of Magical Knowledge, remarque	500	N/A	252.50	325-395
1996	Court of the Faeries	3,500		245.00	245
1991	Diggery Diggery Dare-Etching	75	N/A	210.00	465
1994	Evening Angels	4,000	N/A	195.00	195
1994	Evening Angels w/Art Furnishings Frame	200	N/A	800.00	800
1989	Fantasies of the Sea-poster	Open		35.00	35
1995	Fishing	2,500	N/A	145.00	145
1993	Getting it Right	4,000	N/A	185.00	185
1985	The Gift For Mrs. Claus	3,500	N/A	80.00	475-695
1991	Jack Be Nimble-Etching	75	N/A	210.00	425
1986	Jonah	850	N/A	95.00	325-395
1991	Lawrence and a Bear	850	N/A	145.00	695
1987	Low Tech-Poster	Open		35.00	35
1991	Man in the Moon-Etching	75	N/A	210.00	450-600
1988	The Man Who Minds the Moon	850	N/A	145.00	700
1991	Mother Goose-Etching	75	N/A	210.00	450
1987	Old Man with a Lot on His Mind	850	N/A	85.00	800-1200
1986	Olde World Santa	3,500	N/A	80.00	600-800
1992	The Oldest Angel	850	N/A	125.00	700-1000
1991	Once Upon a Time	1,500	N/A	175.00	1200-1500
1991	Once Upon a Time, remarque	500	N/A	220.00	1400-1650
1996	One Light	1,500		125.00	125
1991	Pelican King	850	N/A	115.00	275-395
1991	Peter Peter Pumpkin Eater-Etching	75	N/A	210.00	450-600
1995	Piscatorial Percussionist	3,000	N/A	125.00	125
1992	The Reponsible Woman	2,500	N/A	175.00	300-400
1990	Rhymes & Reasons w/Booklet	Open		150.00	240
1990	Rhymes & Reasons w/Booklet, remarque	500	N/A	208.00	150
1993	The Royal Music Barque	2,750	N/A	375.00	375
1992	The Royal Processional	1,500	N/A	185.00	185-300
1992	The Royal Processional, remarque	500	N/A	252.50	375-450
1993	The Scholar	3,250	N/A	125.00	125
1995	Serenade For an Orange Cat	3,000	N/A	125.00	125
1987	The Shakespearean Poster	Open		35.00	35
1995	Sisters of the Sea	2,000	N/A	195.00	195
1994	Six Bird Hunters-Full Camouflage 3	4,662	N/A	165.00	165
1994	Sometimes the Spirit Touches w/book	3,600	N/A	195.00	195
1991	Three Blind Mice-Etching	75	N/A	210.00	450
1991	Three Wise Men of Gotham-Etching	75	N/A	210.00	450
1991	Tweedle Dee & Tweedle Dum-Etching	75	N/A	210.00	400
1994	Two Angels Discussing Botticelli	2,950	N/A	145.00	145
1990	Two Sisters	650	N/A	325.00	325
1996	The Voyage of the Basset Collector's Edition Book & The Oldest Professor	2,500		195.00	195
1987	Voyage of the Basset w/Journal	850	N/A	225.00	2500-3500
1993	Waiting for the Tide	2,250	N/A	150.00	150
1988	The Widows Mite	850	N/A	145.00	2800
1986	Your Plaice, or Mine?	850	N/A	125.00	200-395

Combes - S. Combes

1992	African Oasis	650	N/A	375.00	600-895
1981	Alert	1,000		95.00	95
1987	The Angry One	850		95.00	95
1988	Bushwhacker	850	N/A	145.00	145
1983	Chui	275	N/A	250.00	250
1988	Confrontation	850		145.00	145
1988	The Crossing	1,250	N/A	245.00	245
1994	Disdain	850		110.00	110
1980	Facing the Wind	1,500	N/A	75.00	75-125
1993	Fearful Symmetry	850	N/A	110.00	110
1995	Golden Silhouette	950		175.00	175
1990	The Guardian (Silverback)	1,000		185.00	185
1992	The Hypnotist	1,250		145.00	145
1994	Indian Summer	950		175.00	175
1980	Interlude	1,500	N/A	85.00	85
1995	Jungle Phantom	950		175.00	175
1991	Kilimanjaro Morning	850		185.00	185
1981	Leopard Cubs	1,000	N/A	95.00	95
1992	Lookout	1,250		95.00	95
1980	Manyara Afternoon	1,500	N/A	75.00	325
1989	Masai-Longonot, Kenya	850		145.00	145
1992	Midday Sun (Lioness & Cubs)	850		125.00	125
1989	Mountain Gorillas	550	N/A	135.00	135
1991	Mountain Myth	950		175.00	175
1995	Pride	950		175.00	175
1980	Serengeti Monarch	1,500	N/A	85.00	85
1995	Serious Intent	950		175.00	175
1995	Siberian Winter	950		175.00	175
1996	The Siberians	850		175.00	175
1988	Simba	850		125.00	125
1995	Snow Tracker	950		175.00	175
1980	Solitary Hunter	1,500	N/A	75.00	75

YEAR ISSUE		EDITION LIMIT	YEAR RETD.	ISSUE PRICE	*QUOTE U.S. $
1990	Standoff	850	N/A	375.00	600-695
1991	Study in Concentration	850	N/A	185.00	225
1987	Tall Shadows	850	N/A	150.00	375-495
1985	Tension at Dawn	825	N/A	145.00	1000-1150
1985	Tension at Dawn, remarque	25	N/A	275.00	1150-1295
1989	The Watering Hole	850		225.00	225
1986	The Wildebeest Migration	450	N/A	350.00	1350-2000

Crowley - D. Crowley

1981	Afterglow	1,500		110.00	110
1992	Anna Thorne	650		160.00	160
1980	Apache in White	1,500	N/A	85.00	85
1979	Arizona Mountain Man	1,500	N/A	85.00	85
1980	Beauty and the Beast	1,500	N/A	85.00	85
1992	Colors of the Sunset	650		175.00	175
1979	Desert Sunset	1,500	N/A	75.00	75
1978	Dorena	1,000	N/A	75.00	75
1994	The Dreamer	650		150.00	150
1981	Eagle Feathers	1,500	N/A	95.00	95
1988	Ermine and Beads	550	N/A	85.00	85
1989	The Gunfighters	3,000	N/A	35.00	35
1981	The Heirloom	1,000	N/A	125.00	125
1982	Hopi Butterfly	275		350.00	350
1978	Hudson's Bay Blanket	1,000	N/A	75.00	75
1980	The Littlest Apache	275	N/A	325.00	850
1994	Plumes and Ribbons	650		160.00	160
1979	Security Blanket	1,500	N/A	65.00	65
1981	Shannandoah	275	N/A	325.00	325
1978	The Starquilt	1,000	N/A	65.00	500
1986	The Trapper	550		75.00	75

Dawson - J. Dawson

1992	The Attack (Cougars)	850		175.00	175
1993	Berry Contented	850		150.00	150
1993	Berry Contented (Remarque)	100		235.00	235
1994	The Face Off (Right & Left Panel)	850		150.00	150
1993	Looking Back	850		110.00	110
1993	Otter Wise	850		150.00	150
1993	Taking a Break	850	N/A	150.00	150

Doolittle - B. Doolittle

1983	Art of Camouflage, signed	2,000	1983	55.00	325
1980	Bugged Bear	1,000	1980	85.00	4200-4600
1987	Calling the Buffalo	8,500	1987	245.00	800-1000
1983	Christmas Day, Give or Take a Week	4,581	1983	80.00	1150-1400
1988	Doubled Back	15,000	1988	245.00	1150-1450
1992	Eagle Heart	48,000	1992	285.00	285
1982	Eagle's Flight	1,500	1982	185.00	3100-3850
1983	Escape by a Hare	1,500	1983	80.00	600-795
1984	Forest Has Eyes, The	8,544	1984	175.00	4000-4600
1980	Good Omen, The	1,000	1980	85.00	3700-4400
1987	Guardian Spirits	13,238	1987	295.00	800-900
1990	Hide and Seek (Composite & Video)	25,000	1990	1200.00	1500
1984	Let My Spirit Soar	1,500	1984	195.00	4500-5000
1979	Pintos	1,000	1979	65.00	8500-11000
1993	Prayer for the Wild Things	65,000	1993	325.00	225-275
1983	Runs With Thunder	1,500	1983	150.00	1200-1450
1983	Rushing War Eagle	1,500	1983	150.00	1200-1400
1991	Sacred Circle (Print & Video)	40,192	1991	325.00	500
1989	Sacred Ground	69,996	1989	265.00	600-850
1987	Season of the Eagle	36,548	1987	245.00	625-850
1991	The Sentinel	35,000	1991	275.00	500-700
1981	Spirit of the Grizzly	1,500	1981	150.00	3200-4300
1995	Spirit Takes Flight	48,000		225.00	225
1996	Three More for Breakfast	20,000	1996	245.00	245
1986	Two Bears of the Blackfeet	2,650	1986	225.00	850-1100
1985	Two Indian Horses	12,253	1985	225.00	3450-4300
1995	Two More Indian Horses	48,000	1995	225.00	475-595
1981	Unknown Presence	1,500	1981	135.00	3200-3300
1992	Walk Softly (Chapbook)	40,192	1992	225.00	225
1994	When The Wind Had Wings	57,500	1994	325.00	325
1986	Where Silence Speaks, Doolittle The Art of Bev Doolittle	3,500	1986	650.00	2450-2700
1980	Whoo !?	1,000	1980	75.00	1250-2300
1993	Wilderness? Wilderness!	50,000	1993	65.00	65-95
1985	Wolves of the Crow	2,650	1985	225.00	1450-2000
1981	Woodland Encounter	1,500	1981	145.00	9200-11000

Dubowski - E. Dubowski

1996	Aspen Flowers	850		145.00	145
1996	Fresh From the Garden	850		145.00	145

Ferris - K. Ferris

1990	The Circus Outbound	1,000		225.00	225
1991	Farmer's Nightmare	850		185.00	185
1991	Linebacker in the Buff	1,000		225.00	225
1983	Little Willie Coming Home	1,000	N/A	145.00	1750
1994	Real Trouble	1,000		195.00	195
1995	Schweinfurt Again	1,000		195.00	195
1982	Sunrise Encounter	1,000	N/A	145.00	145
1993	A Test of Courage	850		185.00	185
1991	Too Little, Too Late w/Video	1,000		245.00	245

Frederick - R. Frederick

1990	Autumn Leaves	1,250	N/A	175.00	175
1996	Autumn Trail	850		195.00	195
1989	Barely Spring	1,500		165.00	165
1994	Beeline (C)	1,000		195.00	195
1987	Before the Storm (Diptych)	550	N/A	350.00	600-900
1991	Breaking the Ice	2,750	N/A	235.00	235

YEAR ISSUE		EDITION LIMIT	YEAR RETD.	ISSUE PRICE	* QUOTE U.S.$
1989	Colors of Home	1,500	N/A	165.00	275-295
1995	Drifters	850		175.00	175
1985	Early Evening Gathering	475	N/A	325.00	355
1992	An Early Light Breakfast	1,750	N/A	235.00	265-300
1990	Echoes of Sunset	1,750	N/A	235.00	700-800
1987	Evening Shadows (White-Tail Deer)	1,500	N/A	125.00	125
1992	Fast Break	2,250		235.00	235
1992	Fire and Ice (Suite of 2)	1,750		175.00	175
1984	First Moments of Gold	825	N/A	145.00	225
1984	First Moments of Gold, remarque	25	N/A	172.50	265
1984	From Timber's Edge	850	N/A	125.00	140-165
1996	Geyser Basin	850		175.00	175
1989	Gifts of the Land #2	500	N/A	150.00	150
1988	Gifts of the Land w/Wine & Wine Label	500	N/A	150.00	150
1988	Glimmer of Solitude	1,500		145.00	145
1993	Glory Days	1,750		115.00	115
1986	Great Horned Owl	1,250	N/A	115.00	135
1995	High Country Harem	1,000		185.00	185
1985	High Society	950	N/A	115.00	425
1995	Jaywalkers	850		175.00	175
1991	The Long Run	1,750	N/A	235.00	250-395
1991	The Long Run, AP	200	N/A	167.50	495
1985	Los Colores De Chiapas	950	N/A	85.00	85
1994	The Lost World	1,000		175.00	175
1985	Misty Morning Lookout	950	N/A	145.00	145
1984	Misty Morning Sentinel	850	N/A	125.00	145
1989	Monarch of the North	2,000		150.00	150
1990	Morning Surprise	1,750	N/A	165.00	165
1991	Morning Thunder	1,750	N/A	185.00	185-200
1988	The Nesting Call	2,500		150.00	150
1988	The Nesting Call, remarque	1,000	N/A	165.00	165
1993	New Heights	1,950		195.00	195
1987	Northern Light	1,500	N/A	165.00	165
1986	Out on a Limb	1,250	N/A	145.00	300-375
1993	Point of View	1,000		235.00	235
1992	Rain Forest Rendezvous	1,500	N/A	225.00	225
1988	Rim Walk	1,500	N/A	90.00	90
1988	Shadows of Dusk	1,500	N/A	165.00	165
1990	Silent Watch (High Desert Museum)	2,000	N/A	35.00	35
1994	Snow Pack	1,000		175.00	175
1992	Snowstorm	1,750		195.00	195
1990	Snowy Reflections (Snowy Egret)	1,500		150.00	150
1986	Sounds of Twilight	1,500	N/A	135.00	250-295
1991	Summer's Song (Triptych)	2,500		225.00	225
1993	Temple of the Jaguar	1,500		225.00	225
1988	Timber Ghost w/Mini Wine Label	3,000	N/A	150.00	150
1994	Tropic Moon	850		165.00	165
1987	Tundra Watch (Snowy Owl)	1,500	N/A	145.00	145
1994	Way of the Caribou	1,235		235.00	235
1987	Winter's Brilliance (Cardinal)	1,500	N/A	135.00	135
1986	Winter's Call	1,250	N/A	165.00	550
1986	Winter's Call Raptor, AP	100	N/A	165.00	600
1987	Woodland Crossing (Caribou)	1,500	N/A	145.00	145
1988	World of White	2,500	N/A	150.00	150

Gurney - J. Gurney

1992	Birthday Pageant	2,500	N/A	60.00	60
1992	Birthday Pageant, remarque	300	N/A	275.00	295
1995	Cottage Reflections	3,000		195.00	195
1991	Dinosaur Boulevard	2,000	N/A	125.00	125
1991	Dinosaur Boulevard, remarque	250	N/A	196.00	425-525
1990	Dinosaur Parade	1,995	1995	125.00	125
1990	Dinosaur Parade, remarque	150	N/A	130.00	3200
1992	Dream Canyon	N/A	N/A	125.00	125
1992	Dream Canyon, remarque	150	N/A	196.00	475
1993	The Excursion	3,500		175.00	175
1993	Garden of Hope	3,500		175.00	175
1990	Morning in Treetown	1,500	N/A	175.00	275-295
1993	Palace in the Clouds	3,500	N/A	175.00	175
1993	Ring Riders	2,500	N/A	175.00	175
1995	Rumble & Mist	2,500		175.00	175
1990	Seaside Romp	1,000	N/A	175.00	225-350
1992	Skyback Print w/Dinotopia Book	3,500	N/A	295.00	295
1994	Small Wonder	3,299	N/A	75.00	75
1994	Steep Street	3,500		95.00	95
1991	Waterfall City	3,000	N/A	125.00	125
1991	Waterfall City, remarque	250	N/A	186.00	400-650
1995	The World Beneath Collectors' Book w/ print	3,000		195.00	195

Gustafson - S. Gustafson

1995	The Alice in Wonderland Suite	4,000		195.00	195
1994	Frog Prince	3,500	1994	125.00	125
1993	Goldilocks and the Three Bears	3,500	1993	125.00	325-400
1995	Hansel & Gretel	3,000		125.00	125
1993	Humpty Dumpty	3,500	1993	125.00	125
1995	Jack in the Beanstalk	3,500		125.00	125
1993	Little Red Riding Hood	3,500	1993	125.00	125
1996	Old King Cole	2,750		125.00	125
1994	Pat-A-Cake	4,000	1994	125.00	125
1996	Puss in Boots	2,750		145.00	145
1995	Rumpelstiltskin	2,750		125.00	125
1993	Snow White and the Seven Dwarfs	3,500	1993	165.00	225-300
1995	Touched by Magic	4,000		185.00	185

Hartough - L. Hartough

1996	11th Hole, "White Dogwood", Augusta National Golf Club	850		225.00	225

YEAR ISSUE		EDITION LIMIT	YEAR RETD.	ISSUE PRICE	*QUOTE U.S.$
1995	14th Hole, St. Andrews	850	1995	225.00	225
1996	15th Hole, "Firethorn", Augusta National Golf Club	850		325.00	325
1996	18th Hole, Royal Lytham & St. Annes Golf Club	850		225.00	225
1995	7th Hole, Pebble Beach Golf Links	850		225.00	225

Holm - J. Holm

1996	Slipper Thief	850		95.00	95

Johnson - J. Johnson

1994	Moose River	650		175.00	175
1994	Sea Treasures	650		125.00	125
1994	Winter Thaw	650		150.00	150
1993	Wolf Creek	550	N/A	165.00	200

Kennedy - S. Kennedy

1988	After Dinner Music	2,500	N/A	175.00	230
1995	Alaskan Malamute	1,000		125.00	125
1992	Aurora	2,250	N/A	195.00	195
1991	A Breed Apart	2,750	N/A	225.00	225
1992	Cabin Fever	2,250		175.00	175
1995	Cliff Dwellers	850		175.00	175
1988	Distant Relations	950	N/A	200.00	300
1988	Eager to Run	950	N/A	200.00	1400-1790
1990	Fish Tales	5,500	N/A	225.00	225
1991	In Training	3,350	N/A	165.00	295
1991	In Training, remarque	150	N/A	215.50	345
1996	Keeping Watch	850		150.00	150
1995	The Lesson	1,000		125.00	125
1996	Looking For Trouble	850		125.00	125
1993	Midnight Eyes	1,750		125.00	125
1993	Never Alone	2,250		225.00	225
1993	Never Alone, remarque	250	N/A	272.50	273
1990	On the Edge	4,000		225.00	225
1995	On the Heights	850		175.00	175
1994	Quiet Time Companions -Samoyed	1,000		125.00	125
1994	Quiet Time Companions -Siberian Husky	1,000	N/A	125.00	125
1994	Silent Observers	1,250	N/A	165.00	165
1996	Snow Buddies	850		125.00	125
1989	Snowshoes	4,000	N/A	185.00	185
1994	Spruce and Fur	1,500		165.00	165
1995	Standing Watch	850		175.00	175
1993	The Touch	1,500		115.00	115
1989	Up a Creek	2,500	N/A	185.00	185

Kodera - C. Kodera

1986	The A Team (K10)	850		145.00	145
1995	A.M. Sortie	1,000		225.00	225
1996	Canyon Starliner	850		185.00	185
1991	Darkness Visible (Stealth)	2,671	N/A	40.00	40
1987	Fifty Years a Lady	550	N/A	150.00	450-500
1988	The Great Greenwich Balloon Race	1,000		145.00	145
1990	Green Light-Jump!	650	N/A	145.00	200
1992	Halsey's Surprise	850		95.00	95
1994	Last to Fight	1,000		225.00	225
1995	Lonely Flight to Destiny	1,000	1995	347.00	1200
1992	Looking For Nagumo	1,000		225.00	225
1996	The Lost Squadron	850		275.00	275
1992	Memphis Belle/Dauntless Dotty	1,250		245.00	245
1990	A Moment's Peace	1,250		150.00	150
1988	Moonlight Intruders	1,000		125.00	125
1995	Only One Survived	1,000		245.00	245
1989	Springtime Flying in the Rockies	550	N/A	95.00	95
1996	Stratojet Shakedown	1,000		265.00	265
1992	Thirty Seconds Over Tokyo	1,000	N/A	275.00	325
1991	This is No Drill w/Video	1,000		225.00	225
1994	This is No Time to Lose an Engine	850		150.00	150
1994	Tiger's Bite	850		150.00	150
1987	Voyager: The Skies Yield	1,500		225.00	225

Landry - P. Landry

1996	Afternoon Tea	450	1996	495.00	495
1993	The Antique Shop	1,250	N/A	125.00	125
1992	Apple Orchard	1,250		150.00	150
1992	Aunt Martha's Country Farm	1,500	N/A	185.00	300
1995	Autumn Market	1,000		185.00	185
1987	Bluenose Country	550	N/A	115.00	175
1992	Boardwalk Promenade	1,250		175.00	175
1989	A Canadian Christmas	1,250		125.00	125
1989	Cape Cod Welcome Cameo	850	N/A	75.00	275
1990	The Captain's Garden	1,000	N/A	165.00	425
1993	Christmas at Mystic Seaport	2,000		125.00	125
1992	Christmas at the Flower Market	2,500		125.00	125
1994	Christmas Carousel Pony	2,000		125.00	125
1990	Christmas Treasures	2,500		165.00	165
1992	Cottage Garden	1,250	N/A	160.00	160
1995	Cottage Reflections	850		135.00	135
1994	An English Cottage	850		150.00	150
1994	Flower Barn	1,000		175.00	175
1988	Flower Boxes	550	N/A	75.00	250
1991	Flower Market	1,500	N/A	185.00	1000
1990	Flower Wagon	1,500	N/A	165.00	165
1994	Flowers For Mary Hope	1,250		165.00	165
1995	Harbor Garden	1,000		160.00	160
1993	Hometown Parade	1,250		165.00	165
1996	It's a Wonderful Christmas	1,250		165.00	165
1996	Joseph's Corner	450		495.00	495
1996	Joseph's Corner, Artist Touch	100		795.00	795
1995	Lantern Skaters	1,500		135.00	135

YEAR ISSUE		EDITION LIMIT	YEAR RETD.	ISSUE PRICE	*QUOTE U.S.$
1990	Morning Papers	1,250	N/A	135.00	145
1994	Morning Walk	850		135.00	135
1991	Nantucket Colors	1,500		150.00	150
1993	Paper Boy	1,500		150.00	150
1993	A Place in the Park	1,500		185.00	185
1984	Regatta	500	N/A	75.00	150
1984	Regatta, remarque	50	N/A	97.50	145
1990	Seaside Carousel	1,500	N/A	165.00	200
1988	Seaside Cottage	550	N/A	125.00	125
1986	Seaside Mist	450	N/A	85.00	200
1985	The Skaters	500		75.00	75
1985	The Skaters, remarque	50	N/A	97.50	98
1995	Spring Song	2,500		145.00	145
1996	Summer Buddies	950		135.00	135
1991	Summer Concert	1,500		195.00	195
1989	Summer Garden	850	N/A	125.00	400
1995	Summer Mist (Fine Art Original Lithograph)	550		750.00	850
1992	Sunflowers	1,250	N/A	125.00	125
1991	The Toymaker	1,500	N/A	165.00	165
1991	Victorian Memories	1,500	N/A	150.00	150
1996	Winter Memories w/The Captain's Garden Collector's Edition Book	2,000		195.00	195

Lovell - T. Lovell

1988	The Battle of the Crater	1,500	N/A	225.00	225
1988	Berdan's Sharpshooters -Gettysburg	1,500		225.00	225
1986	Blackfeet Wall	450	N/A	325.00	1295
1981	Carson's Boatyard	1,000		150.00	150
1985	Chiricahua Scout	650		90.00	90
1981	The Deceiver	1,000		150.00	150
1990	Dry Goods and Molasses	1,000		225.00	225
1981	Fires Along the Oregon Trail	1,000	N/A	150.00	295
1993	The Handwarmer	1,000		225.00	225
1988	The Hunter	1,000		150.00	150
1982	Invitation to Trade	1,000	N/A	150.00	150
1989	The Lost Rag Doll	1,000		225.00	225
1988	Mr. Bodmer's Music Box	5,000		40.00	40
1975	The Mud Owl's Warning	1,000	N/A	150.00	175
1988	North Country Rider	2,500		95.00	95
1976	Quicksand at Horsehead	1,000		150.00	150
1976	Shotgun Toll	1,000		150.00	150
1983	Sugar In The Coffee	650	N/A	165.00	165
1987	Surrender at Appomattox	1,000	N/A	225.00	1695
1992	Target Practice	2,000		25.00	25
1976	Time of Cold-Maker	1,000		150.00	150
1989	Union Fleet Passing Vicksburg	1,500		225.00	225
1982	Walking Coyote & Buffalo Orphans	650	N/A	165.00	195
1982	The Wheelsoakers	1,000		150.00	150
1984	Winter Holiday	850		95.00	95
1989	Youth's Hour of Glory	1,500		175.00	175

Lyman - S. Lyman

1990	Among The Wild Brambles	1,750	1990	185.00	400
1985	Autumn Grandeur	850	N/A	115.00	700-850
1996	Beach Bonfire	6,500	1996	225.00	225
1985	Bear & Blossoms (C)	850	N/A	75.00	625
1987	Canadian Autumn	1,500	1987	165.00	325
1995	Cathedral Snow	4,000	1996	245.00	245
1989	Color In The Snow (Pheasant)	1,500	N/A	165.00	395
1996	The Crossing	2,500	1996	195.00	195
1991	Dance of Cloud and Cliff	1,500	1991	225.00	475
1991	Dance of Water and Light	3,000	1991	225.00	225
1983	Early Winter In The Mountains	850	N/A	95.00	625-825
1987	An Elegant Couple (Wood Ducks)	1,000	N/A	125.00	325-385
1991	Embers at Dawn	3,500	1991	225.00	1400-1700
1983	End Of The Ridge	850	N/A	95.00	700-950
1990	Evening Light	2,500	1990	225.00	2600-2725
1995	Evening Star w/collector's edition book	9,500	1995	195.00	275
1993	Fire Dance	8,500	1993	235.00	500-550
1984	Free Flight	850	N/A	70.00	150-200
1987	High Creek Crossing	1,000	N/A	165.00	1350-1565
1989	High Light	1,250	1989	165.00	400-450
1986	High Trail At Sunset	1,000	N/A	125.00	975
1988	The Intruder	1,500	N/A	150.00	225-275
1993	Lake of the Shining Rocks	2,250	1993	235.00	485-520
1992	Lantern Light Print w/ Firelight Chapbook	10,000	1993	195.00	195
1989	Last Light of Winter	1,500	1989	175.00	1675
1995	Midnight Fire	8,500	1996	245.00	245
1994	Moon Fire	7,500	1994	245.00	750-920
1987	Moon Shadows	1,500	N/A	135.00	175-200
1994	Moonlit Flight on Christmas Night	2,750	1994	165.00	165-200
1996	Morning Light	8,000	1996	245.00	245
1986	Morning Solitude	850	N/A	115.00	550-800
1990	A Mountain Campfire	1,500	1990	195.00	2700-2895
1994	New Kid on the Rock	2,250	1996	185.00	185
1987	New Territory (Grizzly & Cubs)	1,000	N/A	135.00	425
1984	Noisy Neighbors	675	N/A	95.00	1300
1984	Noisy Neighbors, remarque	25	N/A	127.50	1800
1994	North Country Shores	3,000	1994	225.00	325
1983	The Pass	850	N/A	95.00	1150-1240
1989	Quiet Rain	1,500	N/A	165.00	1000
1988	The Raptor's Watch	1,500	N/A	150.00	900-975
1991	Return Of The Falcon	1,500	N/A	150.00	350
1993	Riparian Riches	2,500	1993	235.00	235
1992	River of Light (Geese)	2,950	N/A	225.00	225
1991	Secret Watch (Lynx)	2,250	N/A	150.00	325
1990	Silent Snows	1,750	N/A	210.00	200

YEAR ISSUE		EDITION LIMIT	YEAR RETD.	ISSUE PRICE	*QUOTE U.S.$
1988	Snow Hunter	1,500	N/A	135.00	725-1000
1986	Snowy Throne (C)	850	N/A	85.00	250-400
1993	The Spirit of Christmas	2,750	1993	165.00	250
1996	Sunset Fire (PC)	N/A	1996	245.00	245
1995	Thunderbolt	7,000	N/A	235.00	500-600
1987	Twilight Snow (C)	950	N/A	85.00	400-600
1988	Uzumati: Great Bear of Yosemite	1,750	N/A	150.00	200-275
1992	Warmed by the View	8,500	1992	235.00	450-500
1992	Wilderness Welcome	8,500	N/A	235.00	800
1992	Wildflower Suite (Hummingbird)	2,250	N/A	175.00	275
1992	Woodland Haven	2,500	N/A	195.00	195

Marris - B. Marris

1987	Above the Glacier	850	N/A	145.00	145
1986	Best Friends	850	N/A	85.00	235-295
1994	Big Gray's Barn and Bistro	1,000		125.00	125
1989	Bittersweet	1,000	N/A	135.00	135
1990	Bugles and Trumpets!	1,000	N/A	175.00	175
1996	Catch The Wind	850		165.00	165
1992	The Comeback	1,250		175.00	175
1991	Cops & Robbers	1,000	N/A	165.00	165
1988	Courtship	850	N/A	145.00	145
1995	Dairy Queens	1,000		125.00	125
1995	The Dartmoor Ponies	1,000		165.00	165
1987	Desperados	850	N/A	135.00	135
1991	End of the Season	1,000		165.00	165
1985	The Fishing Lesson	1,000		145.00	145
1995	The Gift	1,000		125.00	125
1987	Honey Creek Whitetales	850	N/A	145.00	145
1985	Kenai Dusk	1,000	N/A	145.00	800
1994	Lady Marmalade's Bed & Breakfast	1,000		125.00	125
1996	A Little Pig with a Big Heart	1,000	1996	95.00	95
1990	Mom's Shadow	1,000		165.00	165
1994	Moonshine	1,000		95.00	95
1989	New Beginnings	1,000	N/A	175.00	375
1990	Of Myth and Magic	1,500	N/A	175.00	175
1986	Other Footsteps	950		75.00	75
1989	The Playground Showoff	850	N/A	165.00	165
1992	Security Blanket	1,250		175.00	175
1993	Spring Fever	1,000		165.00	165
1991	The Stillness (Grizzzly & Cubs)	1,000	N/A	165.00	165
1992	Sun Bath	1,000		95.00	95
1992	To Stand and Endure	1,000	N/A	195.00	275-395
1991	Under the Morning Star	1,500		175.00	175
1988	Waiting For the Freeze	1,000	N/A	125.00	125
1995	Where Best Friends Are Welcome	850	1996	95.00	195

McCarthy - F. McCarthy

1996	After the Council	550		850.00	850
1984	After the Dust Storm	1,000	N/A	145.00	295
1982	Alert	1,000		135.00	135
1984	Along the West Fork	1,000	N/A	175.00	225
1995	Ambush at the Ancient Rocks	1,000		225.00	225
1978	Ambush, The	1,000	N/A	125.00	300
1982	Apache Scout	1,000	N/A	165.00	165
1988	Apache Trackers (C)	1,000	N/A	95.00	95
1992	The Art of Frank McCarthy	10,418	N/A	60.00	60
1982	Attack on the Wagon Train	1,400	N/A	150.00	150
1977	The Beaver Men	1,000	N/A	75.00	350
1980	Before the Charge	1,000	N/A	115.00	150
1978	Before the Norther	1,000		90.00	325
1990	Below The Breaking Dawn	1,250	N/A	225.00	225
1994	Beneath the Cliff (Petraglyphs)	1,500		295.00	295
1989	Big Medicine	1,000	N/A	225.00	350
1983	Blackfeet Raiders	1,000	N/A	90.00	300
1992	Breaking the Moonlit Silence	650	N/A	375.00	375
1986	The Buffalo Runners	1,000	N/A	195.00	170
1980	Burning the Way Station	1,000	N/A	125.00	250
1993	By the Ancient Trails They Passed	1,000	N/A	245.00	245
1989	Canyon Lands	1,250	N/A	225.00	225
1982	The Challenge	1,000	N/A	175.00	275-450
1995	Charge of the Buffalo Soldiers	1,000	1995	195.00	285
1985	Charging the Challenger	1,000	N/A	150.00	425
1991	The Chase	1,000		225.00	225
1986	Children of the Raven	1,000	N/A	185.00	550
1987	Chiricahua Raiders	1,000	N/A	165.00	225
1977	Comanche Moon	1,000	N/A	75.00	235
1992	Comanche Raider-Bronze	100		812.50	813
1986	Comanche War Trail	1,000	N/A	165.00	170
1989	The Coming Of The Iron Horse	1,500	N/A	225.00	225
1989	The Coming Of The Iron Horse (Print/Pewter Train Special Pub. Ed.)	100	N/A	1500.00	1600-2150
1981	The Coup	1,000	N/A	125.00	500
1981	Crossing the Divide (The Old West)	1,500	N/A	850.00	450-750
1984	The Decoys	450	N/A	325.00	500
1977	Distant Thunder	1,500	N/A	75.00	500
1989	Down From The Mountains	1,000	N/A	245.00	245
1986	The Drive (C)	1,000	N/A	95.00	95-175
1977	Dust Stained Posse	1,000	N/A	75.00	650
1985	The Fireboat	1,000	N/A	175.00	175
1994	Flashes of Lighting-Thunder of Hooves	550		435.00	435
1987	Following the Herds	1,000	N/A	195.00	265
1980	Forbidden Land	1,000	N/A	125.00	125
1978	The Fording	1,000	N/A	75.00	250
1987	From the Rim	1,000	N/A	225.00	225
1981	Headed North	1,500	N/A	150.00	275
1992	Heading Back	1,000		225.00	225
1995	His Wealth	850		225.00	225
1990	Hoka Hey: Sioux War Cry	1,250	N/A	225.00	225
1987	The Hostile Land	1,000	N/A	225.00	235

Year Issue	Title	Edition Limit	Year Retd.	Issue Price	*Quote U.S.$
1976	The Hostiles	1,000	N/A	75.00	475
1984	Hostiles, signed	1,000	N/A	55.00	55
1974	The Hunt	1,000	N/A	75.00	450
1988	In Pursuit of the White Buffalo	1,500	N/A	225.00	425-525
1992	In the Land of the Ancient Ones	1,250	N/A	245.00	265
1983	In The Land Of The Sparrow Hawk People	1,000	N/A	165.00	175
1987	In The Land Of The Winter Hawk	1,000	N/A	225.00	400-495
1978	In The Pass	1,500	N/A	90.00	265
1985	The Last Crossing	550	N/A	350.00	350
1989	The Last Stand: Little Big Horn	1,500	N/A	225.00	225
1984	Leading the Charge, signed	1,000	N/A	55.00	80
1979	Lone Sentinel	1,000	N/A	55.00	1000
1979	The Loner	1,000	N/A	75.00	225
1974	Long Column	1,000	N/A	75.00	400
1985	The Long Knives	1,000	N/A	175.00	350
1989	Los Diablos	1,250	N/A	225.00	225
1995	Medicine Man	850	1996	165.00	165
1983	Moonlit Trail	1,000	N/A	90.00	295
1992	Navajo Ponies Comanchie Warriors	1,000		225.00	225
1978	Night Crossing	1,000	N/A	75.00	200
1974	The Night They Needed a Good Ribbon Man	1,000	N/A	65.00	300
1977	An Old Time Mountain Man	1,000	N/A	65.00	200
1990	On The Old North Trail (Triptych)	650	N/A	550.00	675
1979	On the Warpath	1,000	N/A	75.00	150-175
1983	Out Of The Mist They Came	1,000	N/A	165.00	235
1990	Out Of The Windswept Ramparts	1,250	N/A	225.00	225
1976	Packing In	1,000	N/A	65.00	400
1991	Pony Express	1,000		225.00	225
1979	The Prayer	1,500	N/A	90.00	450
1991	The Pursuit	650	N/A	550.00	550
1981	Race with the Hostiles	1,000	N/A	135.00	135
1987	Red Bull's War Party	1,000	N/A	165.00	165
1979	Retreat to Higher Ground	2,000	N/A	90.00	240-360
1975	Returning Raiders	1,000	N/A	75.00	300
1980	Roar of the Norther	1,000	N/A	90.00	200
1977	Robe Signal	850	N/A	60.00	375
1988	Saber Charge	2,250	N/A	225.00	225-250
1984	The Savage Taunt	1,000	N/A	225.00	275
1985	Scouting The Long Knives	1,400	N/A	195.00	270
1993	Shadows of Warriors (3 Print Suite)	1,000		225.00	225
1994	Show of Defiance	1,000		195.00	195
1993	Sighting the Intruders	1,000		225.00	225
1995	Single File	1,000	N/A	75.00	850
1976	Sioux Warriors	650	N/A	55.00	250
1975	Smoke Was Their Ally	1,000	N/A	75.00	225
1980	Snow Moon	1,000	N/A	115.00	225
1995	Splitting the Herd	550		465.00	465
1986	Spooked	1,400	N/A	195.00	195
1981	Surrounded	1,000	N/A	150.00	350-395
1975	The Survivor	1,000	N/A	65.00	275
1980	A Time Of Decision	1,150	N/A	125.00	225
1978	To Battle	1,000	N/A	75.00	350-400
1985	The Traders	1,000	N/A	195.00	195
1996	The Trek	850		175.00	175
1980	The Trooper	1,000	N/A	90.00	165
1988	Turning The Leaders	1,500	N/A	225.00	225
1983	Under Attack	5,676	N/A	125.00	375-500
1981	Under Hostile Fire	1,000	N/A	150.00	160
1975	Waiting for the Escort	1,000	N/A	75.00	100
1976	The Warrior	650	N/A	55.00	350
1982	The Warriors	1,000	N/A	150.00	150
1984	Watching the Wagons	1,400	N/A	175.00	750
1995	The Way of the Ancient Migrations	1,250		245.00	245
1987	When Omens Turn Bad	1,000	N/A	165.00	425-500
1992	When the Land Was Theirs	1,000		225.00	225
1992	Where Ancient Ones Had Hunted	1,000	N/A	245.00	245
1992	Where Others Had Passed	1,000	N/A	245.00	245
1995	Where Tracks Will Be Lost	550	N/A	350.00	350
1982	Whirling He Raced to Meet the Challenge	1,000	N/A	175.00	400-525
1991	The Wild Ones	1,000	N/A	225.00	225
1990	Winter Trail	1,500	N/A	235.00	235
1993	With Pistols Drawn	1,000		195.00	195

Mitchell - D. Mitchell

Year Issue	Title	Edition Limit	Year Retd.	Issue Price	*Quote U.S.$
1994	Bonding Years	550		175.00	175
1993	Country Church	550		175.00	175
1995	Innocence	1,000		150.00	150
1995	Let Us Pray	850		175.00	175
1993	Psalms 4:1	550	N/A	195.00	195
1992	Rowena	550	N/A	195.00	300

Mo Da-Feng - M. Da-Feng

Year Issue	Title	Edition Limit	Year Retd.	Issue Price	*Quote U.S.$
1990	Family Boat	888		235.00	235
1993	First Journey	650		150.00	150
1989	Fishing Hut	888		235.00	235
1994	Ocean Mist	850		150.00	150

Parker, Ed. - E. Parker

Year Issue	Title	Edition Limit	Year Retd.	Issue Price	*Quote U.S.$
1996	Acadia Tea and Tennis Society	850		135.00	135
1995	The Glorious 4th	850		150.00	150
1996	St. Duffer's Golf Club	850		135.00	135
1995	A Visit From St. Nicholas	850		125.00	125

Parker, Ron. - R. Parker

Year Issue	Title	Edition Limit	Year Retd.	Issue Price	*Quote U.S.$
1995	The Breakfast Club	850		125.00	125
1995	Coastal Morning	850		195.00	195
1995	Evening Solitude	850		195.00	195
1994	Forest Flight	850		195.00	195

Year Issue	Title	Edition Limit	Year Retd.	Issue Price	*Quote U.S.$
1994	Grizzlies at the Falls	850		225.00	225
1994	Morning Flight	4,000		20.00	20
1996	Summer Memories	850		125.00	125
1996	Summer Reading	850		125.00	125
1995	Tea For Two	850		125.00	125

Phillips - W. Phillips

Year Issue	Title	Edition Limit	Year Retd.	Issue Price	*Quote U.S.$
1982	Advantage Eagle	1,000	N/A	135.00	300-400
1992	Alone No More	850		195.00	195
1988	America on the Move	1,500	N/A	185.00	185
1994	Among the Columns of Thor	1,000		295.00	295
1993	And Now the Trap	850		175.00	175
1986	Changing of the Guard	500		100.00	100
1993	Chasing the Daylight	850		185.00	185
1994	Christmas Leave When Dreams Come True	1,500	N/A	185.00	185
1996	Clipper at the Gate	850		185.00	185
1986	Confrontation at Beachy Head	1,000		150.00	150
1991	Dauntless Against a Rising Sun	850	N/A	195.00	195
1995	Dawn The World Forever Changed	1,000	1996	347.50	348
1995	The Dream Fulfilled	1,750		195.00	195
1991	Fifty Miles Out	1,000		175.00	175
1983	The Giant Begins to Stir	1,250	N/A	185.00	1600-1850
1990	Going in Hot w/Book	1,500		250.00	250
1985	Heading For Trouble	1,000	N/A	125.00	250
1984	Hellfire Corner	1,225	N/A	185.00	600
1984	Hellfire Corner, remarque	25	N/A	225.80	800
1990	Hunter Becomes the Hunted w/video	1,500		265.00	265
1992	I Could Never Be So Lucky Again	850	N/A	295.00	750-1150
1993	If Only in My Dreams	1,000	N/A	175.00	750
1984	Into the Teeth of the Tiger	975	N/A	135.00	925
1984	Into the Teeth of the Tiger, remarque	25	N/A	167.50	2000
1994	Into the Throne Room of God w/book "The Glory of Flight"	750	N/A	195.00	600
1991	Intruder Outbound	1,000		225.00	225
1991	Last Chance	1,000	N/A	165.00	350
1985	Lest We Forget	1,250	N/A	195.00	250
1994	Lethal Encounter	1,000		225.00	225
1996	The Lightkeepers Gift	1,000		175.00	175
1988	The Long Green Line	3,500		185.00	185
1992	The Long Ride Home (P-51D)	850	N/A	195.00	195
1991	Low Pass For the Home Folks, BP	1,000	N/A	175.00	175
1996	The Moonwatchers	1,750		185.00	185
1986	Next Time Get 'Em All	1,500	N/A	225.00	275
1989	No Empty Bunks Tonight	1,500	N/A	165.00	165
1989	No Flying Today	1,500		185.00	185
1989	Over the Top	1,000		165.00	165
1985	The Phantoms and the Wizard	850	N/A	145.00	800
1992	Ploesti: Into the Fire and Fury	850		195.00	195
1987	Range Wars	1,000		160.00	160
1996	Return of the Red Gremlin	1,000		350.00	350
1987	Shore Birds at Point Lobos	1,250	N/A	175.00	175
1989	Sierra Hotel	1,250	N/A	175.00	175
1995	Summer of '45	1,750		195.00	195
1987	Sunward We Climb	1,000		175.00	175
1983	Those Clouds Won't Help You Now	625	N/A	135.00	500
1983	Those Clouds Won't Help You Now, remarque	25	N/A	275.00	675
1987	Those Last Critical Moments	1,250	N/A	185.00	300
1993	Threading the Eye of the Needle	1,000		195.00	195
1996	Thunder and Lightning	850		185.00	185
1986	Thunder in the Canyon	1,000	N/A	165.00	600
1990	A Time of Eagles	1,250	1996	245.00	245
1989	Time to Head Home	1,500		165.00	165
1986	Top Cover for the Straggler	1,000	N/A	145.00	325
1983	Two Down, One to Go	3,000	N/A	15.00	15
1982	Welcome Home Yank	1,000	N/A	135.00	800
1993	When Prayers are Answered	850		245.00	245
1991	When You See Zeros, Fight Em'	1,500		245.00	245

Poskas - P. Poskas

Year Issue	Title	Edition Limit	Year Retd.	Issue Price	*Quote U.S.$
1996	Yellow Moon Rising	850		175.00	175

Reynolds - J. Reynolds

Year Issue	Title	Edition Limit	Year Retd.	Issue Price	*Quote U.S.$
1994	Arizona Cowboys	850	N/A	195.00	245
1994	Cold Country, Hot Coffee	1,000		185.00	185
1994	The Henry	850	N/A	195.00	195
1995	Mystic of the Plains	1,000		195.00	195
1994	Quiet Place	1,000	N/A	185.00	185
1994	Spring Showers	1,000		225.00	225
1996	A Strange Sign	550		750.00	750
1996	The Summit	950		195.00	195

Simpkins - J. Simpkins

Year Issue	Title	Edition Limit	Year Retd.	Issue Price	*Quote U.S.$
1994	All My Love	850		125.00	125
1993	Angels	850		225.00	225
1994	Gold Falls	1,750		195.00	195
1995	Mrs. Tenderhart	1,000		175.00	175
1995	Pavane in Gold	2,500		175.00	175
1996	Pavane von Khint	1,000		195.00	195
1994	Reverence For Life w/ border & card	750	N/A	175.00	335
1994	Reverence For Life w/frame	100	N/A	600.00	600
1995	Where Love Resides (Premiere Ed.)	1,000		450.00	450
1995	Where Love Resides (Studio Ed.)	1,000		225.00	225

Smith - T. Smith

Year Issue	Title	Edition Limit	Year Retd.	Issue Price	*Quote U.S.$
1992	The Challenger	1,300		185.00	185
1995	The Refuge	1,000		245.00	245

Terpning - H. Terpning

Year Issue	Title	Edition Limit	Year Retd.	Issue Price	*Quote U.S.$
1992	Against the Coldmaker	1,000	1992	195.00	195
1993	The Apache Fire Makers	1,000	1993	235.00	235
1993	Army Regulations	1,000		235.00	235
1987	Blackfeet Among the Aspen	1,000	1987	225.00	250-300
1985	Blackfeet Spectators	475	1985	350.00	925-1250
1988	Blood Man	1,250	1988	95.00	300-350
1982	CA Set Pony Soldiers/Warriors	1,000	1982	200.00	750
1985	The Cache	1,000		175.00	175
1992	Capture of the Horse Bundle	1,250		235.00	235
1982	Chief Joseph Rides to Surrender	1,000	1982	150.00	2600-3000
1996	Color of Sun	1,000		175.00	175
1986	Comanche Spoilers	1,000		195.00	195
1990	Cree Finery	1,000		225.00	225
1996	Crossing Below the Falls	1,000	1996	245.00	245
1983	Crossing Medicine Lodge Creek	1,000	1983	150.00	400
1994	Crow Camp, 1864	1,000	1994	235.00	235
1984	Crow Pipe Holder	1,000		150.00	150
1991	Digging in at Sappa Creek MW	650	1991	375.00	300-500
1994	The Feast	1,850	1994	245.00	285
1992	Four Sacred Drummers	1,000	1992	225.00	225
1988	Hope Springs Eternal-Ghost Dance	2,250		225.00	400
1994	Isdzan-Apache Woman	1,000	1994	175.00	195
1991	The Last Buffalo	1,000		225.00	225
1991	Leader of Men	1,250	1991	235.00	300-500
1984	The Long Shot, signed	1,000	1984	55.00	75
1984	Medicine Man of the Cheyene	450	1984	350.00	2550-3400
1993	Medicine Pipe	1,000	1993	150.00	185
1985	One Man's Castle	1,000		150.00	150
1995	Opening the Sacred Bundle	550	1995	850.00	1700-2500
1983	Paints	1,000	1983	140.00	200-295
1992	Passing Into Womanhood	650	1992	375.00	500
1987	The Ploy	1,000	1987	195.00	600-695
1992	Prairie Knights	1,000	1992	225.00	225
1996	Prairie Shade	1,000		225.00	225
1987	Preparing for the Sun Dance	1,000	1987	175.00	300-375
1988	Pride of the Cheyene	1,250		195.00	195
1993	Profile of Wisdom	1,000		175.00	175
1989	Scout's Report	1,250		225.00	225
1985	The Scouts of General Crook	1,000	1985	175.00	250-275
1988	Search For the Pass	1,000	1988	225.00	250
1982	Search For the Renegades	1,000	1982	150.00	195
1989	Shepherd of the Plains Cameo	1,250		125.00	125
1982	Shield of Her Husband	1,000	1982	150.00	600-900
1983	Shoshonis	1,250	1983	85.00	200-225
1985	The Signal	1,250	1985	90.00	400-600
1981	Sioux Flag Carrier	1,000	1981	125.00	165
1981	Small Comfort	1,000	1981	135.00	400-450
1993	Soldier Hat	1,000		235.00	235
1981	The Spectators	1,000	1981	135.00	295-325
1994	Spirit of the Rainmaker	1,500		235.00	235
1983	Staff Carrier	1,250	1983	90.00	550-850
1986	Status Symbols	1,000	1986	185.00	1250-1600
1981	Stones that Speak	1,000	1981	150.00	950-1200
1989	The Storyteller w/Video & Book	1,500	1989	950.00	1150
1992	The Strength of Eagles	1,250		235.00	235
1988	Sunday Best	1,250		195.00	195
1995	Talking Robe	1,250		235.00	235
1990	Telling of the Legends	1,250	1990	225.00	800-1200
1986	Thunderpipe and the Holy Man	550	1986	350.00	500-800
1995	Trading Post at Chadron Creek	1,000		225.00	225
1991	Transferring the Medicine Shield	850	1991	375.00	1300-1800
1996	The Trophy	1,000		925.00	925
1981	The Victors	1,000	1981	150.00	650-825
1985	The Warning	1,650	1985	175.00	550-750
1986	Watching the Column	1,250	1986	90.00	400
1990	When Careless Spelled Disaster	1,000	1990	225.00	375-450
1987	Winter Coat	1,250	1987	95.00	195
1996	With Mother Earth	1,250		245.00	245
1984	Woman of the Sioux	1,000	1984	165.00	925-1200

Townsend - B. Townsend

Year Issue	Title	Edition Limit	Year Retd.	Issue Price	*Quote U.S.$
1994	Autumn Hillside	1,000		175.00	175
1993	Dusk	1,250		195.00	195
1995	Gathering of the Herd	1,000		195.00	195
1993	Hailstorm Creek	1,250		195.00	195
1994	Mountain Light	1,000		195.00	195
1992	Open Ridge	1,500	N/A	225.00	225
1993	Out of the Shadows	1,500		195.00	195
1996	Out of the Valley	850		185.00	185
1992	Riverbend	1,000	N/A	185.00	300

Weiss - J. Weiss

Year Issue	Title	Edition Limit	Year Retd.	Issue Price	*Quote U.S.$
1995	All Is Well	1,250		165.00	165
1984	Basset Hound Puppies	1,000	N/A	65.00	325-350
1988	Black Labrador Head Study Cameo	1,000		90.00	90
1984	Cocker Spaniel Puppies	1,000	N/A	75.00	200-295
1992	Cuddle Time	850		95.00	95
1993	A Feeling of Warmth	1,000	N/A	165.00	475
1994	Forever Friends	1,000	1994	95.00	255
1983	Golden Retriever Puppies	1,000	N/A	65.00	800
1988	Goldens at the Shore	850	N/A	145.00	525-725
1995	I Didn't Do It	1,250		125.00	125
1982	Lab Puppies	1,000	N/A	65.00	195-250
1996	New Friends	1,000	1996	125.00	125
1992	No Swimming Lessons Today	1,000		140.00	140
1984	Old English Sheepdog Puppies	1,000	N/A	65.00	325
1993	Old Friends	1,000	1993	95.00	800-950
1986	One Morning in October	850	N/A	125.00	525-650

Greenwich Workshop (continued)

YEAR ISSUE		EDITION LIMIT	YEAR RETD.	ISSUE PRICE	*QUOTE U.S.$
1985	Persian Kitten	1,000	N/A	65.00	80-95
1982	Rebel & Soda	1,000	N/A	45.00	135
1991	Wake Up Call	850		165.00	165
1988	Yellow Labrador Head Study Cameo	1,000		90.00	90

Williams - B.D. Williams

YEAR ISSUE		EDITION LIMIT	YEAR RETD.	ISSUE PRICE	*QUOTE U.S.$
1993	Avant Garde S&N	500	N/A	60.00	60
1993	Avant Garde unsigned	2,603	N/A	30.00	30

Wootton - F. Wootton

YEAR ISSUE		EDITION LIMIT	YEAR RETD.	ISSUE PRICE	*QUOTE U.S.$
1990	Adlertag, 15 August 1940 & Video	1,500	N/A	245.00	245
1993	April Morning:France, 1918	850		245.00	245
1983	The Battle of Britain	850	N/A	150.00	300
1988	Encounter with the Red Baron	850	N/A	165.00	200
1985	Huntsmen and Hounds	650		115.00	115
1982	Knights of the Sky	850	N/A	165.00	375
1993	Last Combat of the Red Baron	850		185.00	185
1992	The Last of the First F. Wooten	850		235.00	235
1994	Peenemunde	850		245.00	245
1986	The Spitfire Legend	850	N/A	195.00	195

Wysocki - C. Wysocki

YEAR ISSUE		EDITION LIMIT	YEAR RETD.	ISSUE PRICE	*QUOTE U.S.$
1987	'Twas the Twilight Before Christmas	7,500	N/A	95.00	150
1988	The Americana Bowl	3,500		295.00	295
1983	Amish Neighbors	1,000	N/A	150.00	1150-1650
1989	Another Year At Sea	2,500	N/A	175.00	450-750
1983	Applebutter Makers	1,000	N/A	135.00	600
1987	Bach's Magnificat in D Minor	2,250	N/A	150.00	650-825
1991	Beauty And The Beast	2,000	N/A	125.00	125
1990	Belly Warmers	2,500		150.00	195-200
1984	Bird House Cameo	1,000	N/A	85.00	300
1985	Birds of a Feather	1,250	N/A	145.00	400
1989	Bostonians And Beans (PC)	6,711	N/A	225.00	650
1979	Butternut Farms	1,000	N/A	75.00	1000
1980	Caleb's Buggy Barn	1,000	N/A	80.00	435
1984	Cape Cod Cold Fish Party	1,000	N/A	150.00	150
1986	Carnival Capers	620		200.00	200
1981	Carver Coggins	1,000	N/A	145.00	900
1989	Christmas Greeting	11,000	N/A	125.00	100
1982	Christmas Print, 1982	2,000	N/A	80.00	500
1984	Chumbuddies, signed	1,000		55.00	55
1985	Clammers at Hodge's Horn	1,000	N/A	150.00	1250
1983	Commemorative Print, 1983	2,000	N/A	55.00	55
1983	Commemorative Print, 1984	2,000		55.00	55
1984	Commemorative Print, 1985	2,000		55.00	55
1985	Commemorative Print, 1986	2,000		55.00	55
1984	Cotton Country	1,000	N/A	150.00	300-350
1983	Country Race	1,000	N/A	150.00	235-395
1986	Daddy's Coming Home	1,250	N/A	150.00	1100-1200
1987	Dahalia Dinalhaven Makes a Dory Deal	2,250	N/A	150.00	300-475
1986	Dancing Pheasant Farms	1,750	N/A	165.00	475
1980	Derby Square	1,000	N/A	90.00	1100
1986	Devilbelly Bay	1,000	N/A	145.00	250
1986	Devilstone Harbor/An American Celebration (Print & Book)	3,500	N/A	195.00	400
1989	Dreamers	3,000	N/A	175.00	425
1992	Ethel the Gourmet	10,179	N/A	150.00	400-530
1979	Fairhaven by the Sea	1,000	N/A	75.00	600
1988	Feathered Critics	2,500		150.00	150
1979	Fox Run	1,000	N/A	75.00	1250-1500
1984	The Foxy Fox Outfoxes the Fox Hunters	1,500	N/A	150.00	425
1992	Frederick the Literate	6,500	N/A	150.00	2000-2300
1989	Fun Lovin' Silly Folks	3,000	N/A	185.00	285-300
1984	The Gang's All Here	Open		65.00	65
1984	The Gang's All Here, remarque	250		90.00	90
1992	Gay Head Light	2,500		165.00	165
1986	Hickory Haven Canal	1,500	N/A	165.00	900-1100
1988	Home Is My Sailor	2,500	N/A	150.00	150
1985	I Love America	2,000	N/A	20.00	20
1990	Jingle Bell Teddy and Friends	5,000		125.00	125
1980	Jolly Hill Farms	1,000	N/A	75.00	600
1986	Lady Liberty's Independence Day Enterprising Immigrants	1,500	N/A	140.00	250
1992	Love Letter From Laramie	1,500		150.00	150
1989	The Memory Maker	2,500		165.00	135
1985	Merrymakers Serenade	1,250	N/A	135.00	135
1986	Mr. Swallobark	2,000	N/A	145.00	1200
1982	The Nantucket	1,000	N/A	145.00	275
1981	Olde America	1,500	N/A	125.00	500
1981	Page's Bake Shoppe	1,000	N/A	115.00	385
1983	Plum Island Sound, signed	1,000		55.00	55
1983	Plum Island Sound, unsigned	Open		40.00	40
1981	Prairie Wind Flowers	1,000	N/A	125.00	1375-1495
1992	Proud Little Angler	2,750	N/A	150.00	200
1994	Remington w/Book-Heartland	15,000		195.00	195
1990	Robin Hood	2,000		165.00	165
1991	Rockland Breakwater Light	2,500	N/A	165.00	295
1985	Salty Witch Bay	475	N/A	350.00	2400
1991	Sea Captain's Wife Abiding	1,500	N/A	150.00	150
1979	Shall We?	1,000	N/A	75.00	850-1000
1982	Sleepy Town West	1,500	N/A	150.00	550
1984	Storin' Up	450		325.00	725
1982	Sunset Hills, Texas Wildcatters	1,000	N/A	125.00	150
1984	Sweetheart Chessmate	1,000	N/A	95.00	1200
1983	Tea by the Sea	1,000	N/A	145.00	1000-1300
1993	The Three Sisters of Nauset, 1880	2,500	N/A	165.00	165
1984	A Warm Christmas Love	3,951	N/A	80.00	325
1990	Wednesday Night Checkers	2,500		175.00	175
1991	West Quoddy Head Light, Maine	2,500		165.00	165
1990	Where The Bouys Are	2,750	N/A	175.00	175
1991	Whistle Stop Christmas	5,000		125.00	125
1980	Yankee Wink Hollow	1,000	N/A	95.00	1150
1987	Yearning For My Captain	2,000	N/A	150.00	235-295
1987	You've Been So Long at Sea, Horatio	2,500	N/A	150.00	230

Hadley House

Capser - M. Capser

YEAR ISSUE		EDITION LIMIT	YEAR RETD.	ISSUE PRICE	*QUOTE U.S.$
1993	Briar and Brambles	999		100.00	100
1992	Comes the Dawn	600		100.00	100
1994	Dashing Through the Snow	999		100.00	100
1994	Down the Lane	Open		30.00	30
1995	Enchanted Waters	999		100.00	100
1995	Grapevine Estates	999		100.00	100
1994	The Lifting Fog	Open		30.00	30
1995	Mariner's Point	999		100.00	100
1994	Nappin'	999		100.00	100
1994	A Night's Quiet	999		100.00	100
1995	On Gentle Wings	999		100.00	100
1993	Pickets & Vines	999	1994	100.00	100
1992	Reflections	600	1993	100.00	100
1993	Rock Creek Spring	999		80.00	80
1994	September Blush	999		100.00	100
1992	Silence Unbroken	600		100.00	100
1993	Skyline Serenade	600	1994	100.00	100
1995	Spring Creek Fever	999		100.00	100
1993	A Summer's Glow	999		60.00	60
1994	A Time For Us	999		125.00	125
1994	To Search Again	Open		30.00	30
1992	The Watch	600	1993	100.00	150
1994	The Way Home	Open		30.00	30
1993	Whispering Wings	1,500	1994	100.00	100

Franca - O. Franca

YEAR ISSUE		EDITION LIMIT	YEAR RETD.	ISSUE PRICE	*QUOTE U.S.$
1988	The Apache	950	1990	70.00	175
1990	Blue Navajo	1,500	1991	125.00	210
1990	Blue Tranquility	999	1990	100.00	450
1988	Cacique	950	1990	70.00	175
1990	Cecy	1,500	1992	125.00	225
1990	Destiny	999	1990	100.00	100
1991	Early Morning	3,600		125.00	225
1993	Evening In Taos	4,000		80.00	80
1988	Feathered Hair Ties	600	1990	80.00	1595
1990	Feathered Hair Ties II	999	1990	100.00	200
1991	The Lovers	2,400	1991	125.00	900
1991	The Model	1,500	1991	125.00	495
1992	Navajo Daydream	3,600	1993	175.00	425
1989	Navajo Fantasy	999	1989	80.00	150
1992	Navajo Meditating	4,000		80.00	125
1992	Navajo Reflection	4,000	1992	80.00	225
1990	Navajo Summer	999	1988	100.00	240
1991	Olympia	1,500	1991	125.00	250
1989	Pink Navajo	999	1989	80.00	250
1988	The Red Shawl	600	1990	80.00	300
1991	Red Wolf	1,500	1991	125.00	125
1990	Santa Fe	1,500	1991	125.00	300
1988	Sitting Bull	950	1990	70.00	200
1988	Slow Bull	950	1990	70.00	200
1990	Turqoise Necklace	999	1990	100.00	275
1990	Wind Song	999	1990	100.00	195
1992	Wind Song II	4,000	1992	80.00	175-225
1989	Winter	999	1989	80.00	175
1989	Young Warrior	999	1989	80.00	595

Hanks - S. Hanks

YEAR ISSUE		EDITION LIMIT	YEAR RETD.	ISSUE PRICE	*QUOTE U.S.$
1994	All Gone Awry	2,000		150.00	150
1994	All In a Row	2,000	1994	150.00	150
1995	A Captive Audience	1,500		150.00	150
1995	Cat's Lair	1,500		150.00	150
1993	Catching The Sun	999	1993	150.00	495
1992	Conferring With the Sea	999	1993	125.00	495
1990	Contemplation	999		100.00	150
1995	Country Comfort	999		100.00	100
1995	Drip Castles	4,000		30.00	30
1991	Duet	999	1993	150.00	545
1990	Emotional Appeal	999		150.00	225
1993	Gathering Thoughts	1,500	1995	150.00	345
1992	An Innocent View	999	1992	150.00	495
1994	The Journey Is The Goal	1,500	1995	150.00	150
1995	Kali	Open		25.00	25
1993	Little Black Crow	1,500		150.00	150
1994	Michaela and Friends/Book	2,500		200.00	200
1993	The New Arrival	1,500		150.00	200
1995	Pacific Sanctuary	1,500		150.00	150
1993	Peeking Out	Open		40.00	40
1993	Places I Remember	1,500		150.00	150
1990	Quiet Rapport	999		150.00	300
1993	A Sense of Belonging	1,500		150.00	150
1995	Small Miracle	1,500		125.00	125
1992	Sometimes It's the Little Things	999		125.00	225
1994	Southwestern Bedroom	999		150.00	180-225
1992	Stepping Stones	999	1993	150.00	295
1991	Sunday Afternoon	Open		40.00	40
1992	Things Worth Keeping	999	1991	125.00	1495
1993	The Thinkers	1,500		150.00	150
1994	Water Lilies In Bloom	750		295.00	295
1993	When Her Blue Eyes Close	999		100.00	100
1994	Where The Light Shines Brightest	1,500		150.00	150
1991	A World For Our Children	999	1992	125.00	1595

Hulings - C. Hulings

YEAR ISSUE		EDITION LIMIT	YEAR RETD.	ISSUE PRICE	*QUOTE U.S.$
1990	Ancient French Farmhouse	999		150.00	225
1989	Chechaquene-Morocco Market Square	999	1993	150.00	250
1992	Cuernavaca Flower Market	580		225.00	225
1988	Ile de la Cite-Paris	580	1990	150.00	225
1990	The Lonely Man	999	1993	150.00	150
1988	Onteniente	580	1989	150.00	425
1991	Place des Ternes	580	1991	195.00	700
1989	Portuguese Vegetable Woman	999	1993	85.00	85
1994	The Red Raincoat	580		225.00	225
1990	Spanish Shawl	999	1994	125.00	125
1993	Spring Flowers	580		225.00	225
1992	Sunday Afternoon	580		195.00	275
1988	Three Cats on a Grapevine	580	1989	65.00	225
1993	Washday In Provence	580		225.00	225

Redlin - T. Redlin

YEAR ISSUE		EDITION LIMIT	YEAR RETD.	ISSUE PRICE	*QUOTE U.S.$
1981	1981 MN Duck Stamp Print	7,800	1981	125.00	150
1982	1982 MN Trout Stamp Print	960	1982	125.00	600
1983	1983 ND Duck Stamp Print	3,438	1983	135.00	150
1984	1984 Quail Conservation	1,500	1984	135.00	135
1985	1985 MN Duck Stamp	4,385	1985	135.00	135
1985	Afternoon Glow	960	1985	150.00	1495
1979	Ageing Shoreline	960	1979	40.00	395
1981	All Clear	960	1981	150.00	395
1994	America, America	29,500		250.00	250
1994	And Crown Thy Good w/ Brotherhood	29,500		250.00	250
1977	Apple River Mallards	Retrd.	1977	10.00	100
1981	April Snow	960	1981	100.00	595
1989	Aroma of Fall	6,800	1989	200.00	1600
1987	Autumn Afternoon	4,800	1987	100.00	795
1993	Autumn Evening	29,500		250.00	250
1980	Autumn Run	960	1980	60.00	375
1983	Autumn Shoreline	Retrd.	1983	50.00	325
1978	Back from the Fields	720	1978	40.00	345
1985	Back to the Sanctuary	960	1986	150.00	475
1978	Backwater Mallards	720	1978	40.00	945
1983	Backwoods Cabin	960	1983	150.00	965
1990	Best Friends (AP)	570	1993	1000.00	1895
1982	The Birch Line	960	1982	100.00	1295
1984	Bluebill Point (AP)	240	1984	300.00	785
1988	Boulder Ridge	4,800		150.00	150
1980	Breaking Away	960	1980	60.00	430
1985	Breaking Cover	960	1985	150.00	500
1981	Broken Covey	960	1981	100.00	525
1985	Brousing	960	1985	150.00	895
1994	Campfire Tales	29,500		250.00	250
1988	Catching the Scent	2,400		200.00	200
1986	Changing Seasons-Autumn	960	1986	150.00	425
1987	Changing Seasons-Spring	960	1987	200.00	475
1984	Changing Seasons-Summer	960	1984	150.00	1400
1986	Changing Seasons-Winter	960	1986	200.00	600
1985	Clear View	1,500	1985	300.00	1195
1980	Clearing the Rail	960	1980	60.00	650-850
1984	Closed for the Season	960	1984	150.00	495
1979	Colorful Trio	960	1979	40.00	800
1991	Comforts of Home	22,900	N/A	175.00	800
1986	Coming Home	2,400	1986	100.00	1800
1992	The Conservationists	29,500		175.00	175
1988	Country Neighbors	4,800	1988	150.00	600
1980	Country Road	960	1980	60.00	650-745
1987	Deer Crossing	2,400	1987	200.00	1195
1985	Delayed Departure	1,500	1985	150.00	500-1000
1980	Drifting	960	1980	60.00	400
1987	Evening Chores (print & book)	2,400	1988	400.00	775-1000
1985	Evening Company	960	1985	150.00	500
1983	Evening Glow	960	1983	150.00	2250
1987	Evening Harvest	960	1987	200.00	1350
1982	Evening Retreat (AP)	300	1982	400.00	3000
1990	Evening Solitude	9,500	1990	200.00	800
1983	Evening Surprise	960	1983	150.00	1000
1990	Evening With Friends	19,500	1991	225.00	1500
1990	Family Traditions	Retrd.	1993	80.00	100
1979	Fighting a Headwind	960	1979	30.00	350
1991	Flying Free	14,500		200.00	200
1993	For Amber Waves of Grain	29,500		250.00	250
1993	For Purple Mountains Majesty	29,500		250.00	250
1995	From Sea to Shining Sea	29,500		250.00	250
1994	God Shed His Grace on Thee	29,500		250.00	250
1987	Golden Retreat (AP)	500	1986	800.00	2000
1995	Harvest Moon Ball	9,500	1995	275.00	395
1986	Hazy Afternoon	2,560	1986	200.00	850
1990	Heading Home	Retrd.	1993	80.00	200
1983	Hidden Point	960	1983	150.00	600
1981	High Country	960	1981	100.00	600
1981	Hightailing	960	1981	75.00	350
1980	The Homestead	960	1980	60.00	640
1988	Homeward Bound	Retrd.	1993	70.00	150
1989	Homeward Bound	Retrd.	1994	80.00	250
1988	House Call	6,800	1990	175.00	1000
1991	Hunter's Haven (A/P)	1,000	N/A	175.00	1000
1989	Indian Summer	4,800	1989	200.00	600-725
1980	Intruders	960	1980	60.00	320
1982	The Landing	Retrd.	1982	30.00	80
1981	The Landmark	960	1981	100.00	400
1984	Leaving the Sanctuary	960	1984	150.00	475
1994	Lifetime Companions	29,500		250.00	250
1988	Lights of Home	9,500	1988	125.00	850
1979	The Loner	960	1979	40.00	300
1990	Master of the Valley	6,800		200.00	200

YEAR ISSUE		EDITION LIMIT	YEAR RETD.	ISSUE PRICE	*QUOTE U.S.$
1988	The Master's Domain	2,400	1988	225.00	800
1988	Moonlight Retreat (A/P)	530	N/A	1000.00	1600
1979	Morning Chores	960	1979	40.00	1350
1984	Morning Glow	960	1984	150.00	1400
1981	Morning Retreat (AP)	240	N/A	400.00	3000
1989	Morning Rounds	6,800	1992	150.00	595
1991	Morning Solitude	12,107	1991	250.00	600
1984	Night Harvest	960	1984	150.00	1795
1985	Night Light	1,500	1985	300.00	1195
1986	Night Mapling	960	1986	125.00	550
1995	A Night on the Town	29,500		150.00	150
1980	Night Watch	2,400	1980	60.00	1000
1984	Nightlight (AP)	360	1984	600.00	2200
1982	October Evening	960	1982	100.00	1000
1989	Office Hours	6,800	1991	175.00	1000
1992	Oh Beautiful for Spacious Skies	29,500		250.00	250
1978	Old Loggers Trail	720	1978	40.00	950-1200
1983	On the Alert	960	1983	125.00	400
1977	Over the Blowdown	Retrd.	1977	20.00	595
1978	Over the Rushes	720	1978	40.00	450
1981	Passing Through	960	1981	100.00	225
1983	Peaceful Evening	960	1983	100.00	350
1991	Pleasures of Winter	24,500	1992	150.00	245
1986	Prairie Monuments	960	1986	200.00	795
1988	Prairie Morning	4,800	1988	150.00	500
1984	Prairie Skyline	960	1984	150.00	600
1983	Prairie Springs	960	1983	150.00	595
1987	Prepared for the Season	Retrd.	1994	70.00	100
1990	Pure Contentment	9,500	1989	150.00	600
1978	Quiet Afternoon	720	1978	40.00	695
1988	Quiet of the Evening	4,800	1988	150.00	700
1982	Reflections	960	1982	100.00	600
1985	Riverside Pond	960	1985	150.00	525
1984	Rural Route	960	1984	150.00	395
1983	Rushing Rapids	960	1983	125.00	750
1980	Rusty Refuge I	960	1980	60.00	295
1981	Rusty Refuge II	960	1980	100.00	495
1984	Rusty Refuge III	960	1984	150.00	595
1985	Rusty Refuge IV	960	1985	150.00	695
1980	Secluded Pond	960	1980	60.00	295
1982	Seed Hunters	960	1982	100.00	575
1985	Sharing Season I	Retrd.	1993	60.00	150
1986	Sharing Season II	Retrd.	1993	60.00	150
1981	Sharing the Bounty	960	1981	100.00	1500
1994	Sharing the Evening	29,500		175.00	175
1987	Sharing the Solitude	2,400	1987	125.00	900
1986	Silent Flight	960	1986	150.00	335
1980	Silent Sunset	960	1980	60.00	780
1984	Silent Wings Suite (set of 4)	960	1984	200.00	750
1981	Soft Shadows	960	1984	100.00	325
1989	Special Memories (AP)	570		1000.00	1000
1982	Spring Mapling	960	1982	100.00	975
1981	Spring Run-Off	1,700	1981	125.00	695
1980	Spring Thaw	960	1980	60.00	460
1980	Squall Line	960	1980	60.00	300
1978	Startled	720	1978	30.00	995
1986	Stormy Weather	1,500	1986	200.00	550
1992	Summertime	24,900		225.00	225
1984	Sundown	960	1984	300.00	575
1986	Sunlit Trail	960	1986	150.00	350
1984	Sunny Afternoon	960	1984	150.00	700
1987	That Special Time	2,400	1987	125.00	700-1000
1987	Together for the Season	Open		70.00	100
1995	Total Comfort	9,500	1995	275.00	275
1986	Twilight Glow	960	1986	200.00	700
1988	Wednesday Afternoon	6,800	1989	175.00	900
1990	Welcome to Paradise	14,500	1990	150.00	700
1985	Whistle Stop	960	1985	150.00	785
1979	Whitecaps	960	1979	40.00	445
1982	Whitewater	960	1982	100.00	400
1982	Winter Haven	500	1982	85.00	800
1977	Winter Snows	Retrd.	1977	20.00	595
1984	Winter Windbreak	960	1984	150.00	750
1992	Winter Wonderland	29,500	1993	150.00	275

Hamilton Collection

Mickey Mantle - R. Tanenbaum

1996	An All American Legend-The Mick	Open		95.00	95

Hawthorne Village

Rockwell's Main Street - Rockwell-Inspired

1993	Rockwell's Main Street	Open		69.95	70

Imperial Graphics, Ltd.

Chang - L. Chang

1988	Egrets with Lotus S/N	1,950		10.00	10
1988	Flamingos with Catail S/N	1,950		10.00	10

Irvine - G. Irvine

1995	Pansies	Open		8.00	8
1995	Violets	Open		8.00	8

Lee - H.C. Lee

1988	Blue Bird of Paradise S/N	950		35.00	35
1988	Cat & Callas S/N	1,950		30.00	30
1990	Double Red Hibiscus S/N	1,950		16.00	16
1988	Hummingbird I S/N	1,950		16.00	16

YEAR ISSUE		EDITION LIMIT	YEAR RETD.	ISSUE PRICE	*QUOTE U.S.$
1988	Hummingbird II S/N	1,950		16.00	16
1990	Maroon & Mauve Peonies S/N	950		60.00	60
1990	Maroon & Peach Peonies S/N	950		60.00	60
1990	Maroon Peony S/N	2,950		20.00	20
1990	Peacock w/Tulip & Peony S/N	1,950		105.00	105
1990	Peonies & Butterflies S/N	2,950		40.00	40
1990	Pink Peony S/N	2,950		20.00	20
1990	Single Red Hibiscus S/N	1,950		16.00	16
1988	White Bird of Paradise S/N	950		35.00	35
1988	White Peacocks w/Peonies S/N	950		65.00	65

Liu - Celestial Symphony Series - L. Liu

1995	Flute Interlude S/N	5,500		40.00	40
1995	French Horn Melody S/N	5,500		40.00	40
1995	Piano Sonata S/N	5,500		40.00	40
1995	Violin Concerto S/N	5,500		40.00	40

Liu - Celestial Symphony Series Unframed Canvas Transfers - L. Liu

1995	Flute Interlude S/N	300		145.00	145
1995	French Horn Melody S/N	300		145.00	145
1995	Piano Sonata S/N	300		145.00	145
1995	Violin Concerto S/N	300		145.00	145

Liu - L. Liu

1989	Abundance of Lilies (poster)	Closed	1993	30.00	30
XX	Afternoon Nap S/N	1,000		45.00	45
XX	Aiming High S/N	950	N/A	65.00	65
1994	Allen's Hummingbird w/Columbine S/N	3,300	1994	30.00	50
1987	Amaryllis S/N	1,950	N/A	16.00	60
1996	Angel with Harp S/N	5,500		40.00	40
1996	Angel with Trumpet S/N	5,500		40.00	40
1993	Anna's Hummingbird w/Fuchsia S/N	3,300	1993	30.00	30
XX	At Peace S/N	950	N/A	45.00	45
1989	Autumn Melody S/N	1,950	1993	45.00	45
1990	Azalea Path S/N	2,500		85.00	85
1990	Azalea w/Dogwood S/N	2,500		55.00	55
1988	Baby Bluebirds S/N	1,950	N/A	16.00	30
1990	Baby Bluebirds w/Plum Tree S/N	2,500	N/A	18.00	18
1988	Baby Chickadees S/N	1,950	N/A	16.00	30
1990	Baby Chickadees w/Pine Tree S/N	2,500	N/A	18.00	18
XX	Basket of Begonias S/N	2,500	N/A	40.00	40
1993	Basket of Calla Lilies S/N	3,300	1994	50.00	50
1991	Basket of Grapes & Raspberries S/N	2,500	N/A	25.00	30
1993	Basket of Hydrangi S/N	3,300	1995	50.00	60
1989	Basket of Irises & Lilacs S/N	1,950	N/A	45.00	45
1993	Basket of Magnolias S/N	3,300	1993	50.00	50
1993	Basket of Orchids S/N	3,300		50.00	50
1992	Basket of Pansies & Lilacs S/N	2,950	N/A	50.00	50
XX	Basket of Pansies S/N	2,500	N/A	40.00	40
1991	Basket of Peonies S/N	2,500	N/A	40.00	40
1992	Basket of Roses & Hydrangeas S/N	2,950	N/A	50.00	50
1991	Basket of Roses S/N	2,500	N/A	40.00	40
1991	Basket of Strawberries & Grapes A/P	50		35.00	35
1991	Basket of Strawberries & Grapes S/N	2,500	N/A	25.00	25
1991	Basket of Sweet Peas S/N	2,500		25.00	25
1989	Basket of Tulips & Lilacs S/N	1,950	N/A	45.00	45
1991	Basket of Wild Roses S/N	2,500	N/A	25.00	25
1991	Baskets of Primroses A/P	50		35.00	35
1991	Baskets of Primroses S/N	2,500	N/A	25.00	25
1986	Bearded Irises S/N	1,950	N/A	45.00	45
XX	Begonia w/Ribbon S/N	2,500	N/A	16.00	16
1994	Berries & Cherries S/N	3,500		30.00	30
XX	Blue & Peach Irises S/N	1,950	N/A	35.00	65
XX	Blue Peacock S/N	950	N/A	65.00	65
1990	Bluebirds & Dandelion S/N	2,500	N/A	40.00	40
1990	Bluebirds & Dandelion A/P	50	N/A	55.00	70
XX	Bluebirds S/N	950	N/A	35.00	35
1986	Bluebirds w/Plum Blossoms S/N	1,950	N/A	35.00	35
1988	Bluebirds w/Rhododendrons S/N	1,950		40.00	40
1990	Bouquet of Peonies S/N	2,500		50.00	50
1990	Bouquet of Poppies S/N	2,500	N/A	50.00	50
1992	Bouquet of Roses A/P	50		25.00	25
1992	Bouquet of Roses S/N	2,950	1994	20.00	20
1992	Breath of Spring S/N	2,950		135.00	135
1993	Broad-Billed HB w/Petunias S/N	3,300		30.00	30
1995	Burgundy Irises w/Foxgloves S/N	5,500		60.00	60
XX	Butterfly & Morning Glories S/N	950	N/A	35.00	35
XX	Butterfly & Poppies S/N	950	N/A	35.00	35
1995	Butterfly Garden I S/N	5,500		50.00	50
1995	Butterfly Garden II S/N	5,500		50.00	50
1994	Butterfly Kisses S/N	3,500		50.00	50
1990	Butterfly w/Clematis A/P	50		55.00	55
1990	Butterfly w/Clematis S/N	2,500	1994	40.00	40
1990	Butterfly w/Wild Rose S/N	2,500	1993	40.00	50
1987	Calla Lily S/N	1,950		35.00	35
1994	Calliope Hummingbird w/Trumpet Vine S/N	3,300		30.00	30
1990	Cardinal & Queen Anne's Lace S/N	2,500	1994	40.00	40-90
XX	Cardinal S/N	950	N/A	35.00	35
XX	Cat & Hummer S/N	1,000		45.00	45
1989	Cherries & Summer Bouquet S/N	2,500	N/A	45.00	45
1993	Cherub Orchestra S/N	3,300	1994	80.00	90
1991	Cherubim w/Ivy S/N	2,500	1993	20.00	20
XX	Chickadees S/N	950	N/A	35.00	50
1988	Chickadees w/Cherry Blossoms S/N	1,950		40.00	40
1992	Conservatory A/P	50		110.00	110
1992	Conservatory S/N	2,950	1994	80.00	100
1987	Daylily S/N	1,950	N/A	35.00	35

YEAR ISSUE		EDITION LIMIT	YEAR RETD.	ISSUE PRICE	* QUOTE U.S.$
1989	Daylily w/Hummingbird S/N	2,500	N/A	18.00	18
1987	Dogwood S/N	1,950	N/A	30.00	30
1986	The Dreamer S/N	950		65.00	65
1991	Dried-Floral Bouquet S/N	2,500		25.00	25
1991	The Drying Room S/N	2,500		75.00	75
1992	Early Spring S/N	2,950	1993	85.00	85
1988	Eastern Black Swallowtail w/ Milkweed S/N	1,950		45.00	45
1991	Egret's w/Queen Anne's Lace S/N	2,500	1995	60.00	60
1992	Entryway S/N	2,950		40.00	40
1993	Fairy Ballet S/N	3,300		80.00	80
1986	Fall S/N	950		35.00	35
1994	Fancy Fiddle S/N	5,500	1994	80.00	80
1988	Feathered Harmony S/N	1,950	N/A	60.00	60
1991	Field of Irises A/P	50		115.00	115
1991	Field of Irises S/N	2,500	1994	85.00	85
1989	First Landing S/N	1,950	N/A	16.00	25
1991	Floral Arch S/N	2,500		25.00	25
1988	Floral Symphony S/N	1,950	N/A	95.00	95
XX	Flying Free S/N	950	N/A	45.00	45
1990	Forest Azalea S/N	2,500	N/A	55.00	55
1992	Forest Stream S/N	2,950	1995	85.00	85
1992	Fountain S/N	2,950		40.00	40
1986	Free Flight I -Rust Butterfly S/N	950		60.00	60
1986	Free Flight II -Pink Butterfly S/N	950		60.00	60
1989	Fritillaries w/ Violet S/N	2,500		18.00	18
1989	Fruit & Spring Basket S/N	1,500	N/A	45.00	45
1988	Garden Blossoms I S/N	1,950	N/A	35.00	35
1988	Garden Blossoms II S/N	1,950	N/A	35.00	35
1991	Garden Peonies S/N	2,500		60.00	60
1991	Garden Poppies S/N	2,500		60.00	60
1986	Garden Poppies S/N	2,000		45.00	45
1992	Garden Seat S/N	2,950		40.00	40
1991	The Gathering S/N	2,500	N/A	75.00	75
1996	Guardian Angel S/N	5,500		125.00	125
1988	Harmonious Flight S/N	1,950		50.00	50
1994	Heavenly Tulips S/N	3,300	1994	80.00	80
1987	Herons & Irises S/N	1,950		65.00	65
1987	Hibiscus & Hummer S/N	1,950	1995	45.00	45
1988	Hummingbird & Hollyhock S/N	1,950	N/A	40.00	40
XX	Hummingbird & Columbine S/N	950	N/A	35.00	35
1989	Hummingbird & Floral I A/P	50	1994	60.00	60
1989	Hummingbird & Floral I S/N	2,500	1994	35.00	35
1989	Hummingbird & Floral II S/N	2,500	1994	35.00	35
XX	Hummingbird & Hibiscus S/N	950	N/A	45.00	45
XX	Hummingbird & Trumpet Vine S/N	950	N/A	35.00	35
1988	Hummingbirds & Iris S/N	1,950	N/A	40.00	40
1988	Hydrangea Bouquet S/N	2,500		30.00	30
1989	Innocents S/N	1,950		16.00	16
1993	Iris Garden II S/N	3,300	1994	105.00	105
XX	Iris Garden S/N	1,950	N/A	45.00	45
1989	Iris Profusion (poster)	Closed	1995	30.00	30
1987	Iris S/N	1,950	N/A	16.00	16
XX	Iris S/N	950	N/A	45.00	45
1991	Irises in Bloom S/N	2,500	N/A	85.00	85
1992	Ivy & Fragrant Flowers S/N	3,300	1993	60.00	60
1992	Ivy & Honeysuckle S/N	3,300	1993	50.00	75
1992	Ivy & Sweetpea A/P	50		65.00	65
1992	Ivy & Sweetpea S/N	3,300	1994	50.00	75
1988	Kingfisher & Iris S/N	1,950		45.00	45
XX	Kingfisher & Lotus S/N	950	N/A	45.00	45
1986	Kingfisher S/N	950		35.00	35
1995	Lilac Breezes S/N	5,500		80.00	80
1986	Lily Pond S/N	950		35.00	35
1987	Lily S/N	1,950	N/A	16.00	16
1994	Love Notes S/N	5,500	1994	80.00	80
1995	Magnolia Path S/N	5,500		135.00	135
1987	Magnolia S/N	1,950	N/A	30.00	30
1995	Magnolias & Day Lilies S/N	5,500		80.00	80
1995	Magnolias & Hydrangeas S/N	5,500		80.00	80
1986	Mauve Veiltail S/N	950		35.00	35
1994	Mermaid Callas S/N	5,500		60.00	60
1996	Messengers of Love S/N	5,500		60.00	60
XX	Misty Valley S/N	1,950		45.00	45
1990	Mixed Irises I S/N	2,500	N/A	50.00	50
1990	Mixed Irises II S/N	2,500	N/A	50.00	50
1988	Moonlight Splendor S/N	1,950	N/A	60.00	60
1990	Morning Glories & Hummer S/N	1,950	N/A	45.00	45
1989	The Morning Room S/N	2,500	N/A	95.00	95
1987	Motherlove S/N	1,950	N/A	45.00	45
1987	Motif Orientale S/N	1,950	N/A	95.00	95
1994	Mystic Bouquet S/N	3,300		80.00	80
1995	Nun's Retreat S/N	5,500		145.00	145
1986	Nuthatch w/Dogwood S/N	1,950	N/A	35.00	35
1992	Old Stone House S/N	2,950		50.00	50
1986	Opera Lady S/N	950	N/A	95.00	95
1989	Orange Tip & Blossoms S/N	2,500		18.00	18
XX	Orchid S/N	950	N/A	45.00	45
1989	Oriental Screen S/N	2,500	N/A	95.00	95
1996	Oriental Splendor S/N	5,500		145.00	145
1988	Painted Lady w/Thistle S/N	1,950		45.00	45
1988	Pair of Finches S/N	1,950	N/A	35.00	35
1992	Palladian Windows S/N	2,950	1993	80.00	80
1990	Pansies & Ivy S/N	2,500		18.00	18
1992	Pansies & Lilies of the Valley S/N	2,950	1993	20.00	20
1992	Pansies & Sweet Peas S/N	2,950	1994	20.00	20
1991	Pansies in a Basket S/N	2,500	N/A	25.00	25
1993	Pansies w/Blue Stardrift A/P	50		35.00	35
1993	Pansies w/Blue Stardrift S/N	2,950	1995	25.00	25
1993	Pansies w/Daisies S/N	2,950		25.00	25
XX	Pansies w/Ribbon S/N	2,500	N/A	16.00	16
1991	Pansies w/Sweet Pea S/N	2,500	N/A	16.00	16

YEAR ISSUE		EDITION LIMIT	YEAR RETD.	ISSUE PRICE	*QUOTE U.S.$
1991	Pansies w/Violets S/N	2,500	N/A	16.00	16
1987	Parenthood S/N	1,950	N/A	45.00	45
1992	Patio S/N	2,950		40.00	40
1993	Peach & Purple Irises S/N	3,300	1994	50.00	50
1993	Peach & Yellow Roses S/N	3,300		50.00	50
1986	Peach Veiltail S/N	950		35.00	35
1994	Peaches & Fruits S/N	3,500		30.00	30
1991	Peacock Duet-Serigraph S/N	325		550.00	550
1987	Peacock Fantasy S/N	950		65.00	65
1991	Peacock Solo-Serigraph S/N	325		550.00	550
1988	Peonies & Azaleas S/N	1,950	N/A	35.00	35
1988	Peonies & Forsythia S/N	1,950	N/A	35.00	35
1988	Peonies & Waterfall S/N	1,950	N/A	65.00	65
1993	Peonies S/N	3,300	1995	30.00	40
1990	Petunias & Ivy S/N	2,500		18.00	18
1989	Phlox w/Hummingbird S/N	2,500		18.00	18
1990	Potted Beauties S/N	2,500		105.00	105
1996	Protectors of Peace S/N	5,500		60.00	60
1995	Purple Irises w/Foxgloves S/N	5,500		60.00	60
1991	Putti w/Column S/N	2,500		20.00	20
1990	Quiet Moment S/N	2,500	N/A	105.00	175
1989	Romantic Abundance S/N	1,950	N/A	95.00	95
1989	Romantic Garden (poster)	Open		35.00	35
1994	Romantic Reflection S/N	5,950		145.00	185
1993	Rose Bouquet w/Tassel S/N	3,300	1995	25.00	25
1994	Rose Fairies S/N	5,500		80.00	80
1989	Roses & Lilacs S/N	2,500		30.00	30
1992	Roses & Violets A/P	50		25.00	25
1992	Roses & Violets S/N	2,950	1993	20.00	20
1993	Roses in Bloom S/N	3,300	1995	105.00	105
1990	Royal Garden S/N	1,950		95.00	95
1990	Royal Retreat S/N	1,950	N/A	95.00	95
1995	Ruby Throated Hummingbird w/Hibiscus S/N	5,800		40.00	40
1993	Rufous Hummingbird w/Foxgloves S/N	3,300	1993	30.00	30
1988	Snapdragon S/N	1,950	N/A	16.00	16
1987	Solitude S/N	1,950	N/A	60.00	60
1993	Southern Magnolia S/N	3,300	1993	30.00	30
XX	Spring Blossoms I S/N	1,950		45.00	45
XX	Spring Blossoms II S/N	1,950		45.00	45
1989	Spring Bouquet (poster)	Closed	1995	30.00	30
1989	Spring Bouquet (poster-signed)	Closed	1995	45.00	45
1996	Spring Bulbs S/N	5,500		50.00	50
1994	Spring Conservatory S/N	3,300		105.00	105
XX	Spring Duet S/N	1,950	N/A	60.00	60
1986	Spring Fairy S/N	950		35.00	35
1990	Spring Floral S/N	2,500	N/A	105.00	105
XX	Spring Forest S/N	2,500	N/A	75.00	75
1995	Spring Garden S/N	5,500		125.00	125
1986	Spring S/N	950		35.00	35
XX	Spring Song S/N	1,950		60.00	60
1986	Spring Tulips S/N	1,950	N/A	45.00	45
1989	Spring Tulips S/N	2,500	N/A	45.00	45
XX	Stream w/Blossoms S/N	1,950		45.00	45
1992	Study for a Breath of Spring S/N	2,950		105.00	105
1996	Summer Bouquet S/N	5,500		50.00	50
XX	Summer Garden S/N	2,500	N/A	75.00	75
1986	Summer Glads S/N	1,950	N/A	45.00	45
1988	Summer Lace w/Blue Chicory S/N	1,950	1991	45.00	45
1987	Summer Lace w/Chicadees S/N	950	N/A	65.00	65
1988	Summer Lace w/Chickadees II A/P	50	1991	85.00	85
1988	Summer Lace w/Chickadees II S/N	1,950	1991	65.00	65
1988	Summer Lace w/Daisies A/P	50	1991	60.00	60
1988	Summer Lace w/Daisies S/N	1,950	1991	45.00	45
1987	Summer Lace w/Dragon Fly S/N	950	N/A	45.00	45
1987	Summer Lace w/Lady Bug S/N	950	N/A	45.00	45
1989	Summer Rose S/N	2,500	N/A	45.00	45
1986	Summer S/N	950		35.00	35
1987	Swans & Callas S/N	1,950	1994	65.00	65
1991	Swans w/Daylilies S/N	2,500	1993	60.00	60
1989	Swans w/Dogwood S/N	1,950	N/A	65.00	65
1995	Sweet Bounty S/N	5,500		80.00	80
1994	Sweet Delight S/N	3,500		50.00	50
1988	Sweet Pea Floral S/N	1,950	N/A	16.00	16
XX	Sweet Pea w/Ribbon S/N	2,500	N/A	16.00	16
1986	Three Little Deer S/N	950		35.00	35
1987	Togetherness S/N	1,950	N/A	60.00	60
1988	Trio of Sparrows S/N	1,950	N/A	35.00	35
1993	Tulip Bouquet w/Tassel A/P	50		35.00	35
1993	Tulip Bouquet w/Tassel S/N	3,300	1995	25.00	30
1987	Tulips S/N	1,950	N/A	16.00	16
1993	Two Burgundy Irises S/N	3,300	1994	50.00	50
XX	Two Peach Irises S/N	1,950	N/A	35.00	65
1990	Two White Irises S/N	2,500	N/A	40.00	40
1992	Victorian Pavilion S/N	2,950		50.00	50
1992	Vintage Bouquet S/N	2,950	1994	135.00	135
1993	Violet Crowned HB w/Morning Glories S/N	3,300		30.00	30
XX	Violets w/Ribbon A/P	50		22.00	22
XX	Violets w/Ribbon S/N	2,500	N/A	16.00	20
XX	Waterfall I S/N	950	N/A	60.00	60
XX	Waterfall II S/N	950	N/A	60.00	60
XX	Waterfall w/Blossoms S/N	1,950	N/A	65.00	65
1989	Waterfall w/Dogwood S/N	1,950		45.00	45
1989	Waterfall w/White & Pink Dogwood S/N	1,950		45.00	45
1990	White & Blue Irises S/N	2,500	N/A	40.00	40
1993	White & Burgundy Roses A/P	50		65.00	65
1993	White & Burgundy Roses S/N	3,300	1995	50.00	50
1995	White Eared Hummingbird w/Hydrangea S/N	5,800		40.00	40
XX	White Peacock S/N	950	N/A	65.00	65

YEAR ISSUE		EDITION LIMIT	YEAR RETD.	ISSUE PRICE	*QUOTE U.S.$
1991	Wild Flowers w/ Single Butterfly S/N	2,500		50.00	50
1991	Wild Flowers w/ Two Butterflies S/N	2,500		50.00	50
1986	Winter S/N	950		35.00	35
1993	Woodland Path S/N	3,300	1994	135.00	135
1993	Woodland Steps S/N	3,300	1995	85.00	85
1993	Woodland View A/P	50		115.00	115
1993	Woodland View S/N	3,300	1995	85.00	85
XX	Woodpecker S/N	950	N/A	35.00	35
1995	Wreath of Lilies S/N	5,500		55.00	55
1995	Wreath of Pansies S/N	5,500		55.00	55
1994	Wreath of Peonies S/N	3,500		55.00	55
1995	Wreath of Roses S/N	3,500	1995	55.00	80

Liu - The Music Room - L. Liu

YEAR ISSUE		EDITION LIMIT	YEAR RETD.	ISSUE PRICE	*QUOTE U.S.$
1991	The Music Room I S/N	2,500	1992	135.00	750-975
1992	The Music Room II-Nutcracker S/N	4,500	1993	200.00	300-495
1994	The Music Room III-Composer's Retreat S/N	5,500	1994	145.00	300-425
1995	The Music Room IV-Swan Melody S/N	6,500		150.00	150

Liu - Unframed Canvas Transfers - L. Liu

YEAR ISSUE		EDITION LIMIT	YEAR RETD.	ISSUE PRICE	*QUOTE U.S.$
1996	Angel with Harp S/N	300		145.00	145
1996	Angel with Trumpet S/N	300		145.00	145
1993	Basket of Calla Lilies S/N	300	1995	195.00	195
1993	Basket of Magnolias S/N	300	1995	195.00	195
1993	Cherub Orchestra S/N	300	1995	295.00	400-550
1992	Conservatory S/N	300	1995	295.00	295
1993	Fairy Ballet S/N	300	1995	295.00	295
1994	Fancy Fiddle S/N	300		295.00	295
1996	Guardian Angel S/N	300		395.00	395
1993	Iris Garden II S/N	300	1995	395.00	395-475
1995	Lilac Breezes A/P	25		355.00	355
1995	Lilac Breezes S/N	300		295.00	295
1994	Love Notes S/N	300		295.00	295
1995	Magnolia Path A/P	25		455.00	455
1995	Magnolia Path S/N	300		395.00	395
1994	Mermaid Callas S/N	300		295.00	295
1995	Nature's Retreat S/N	300		395.00	395
1992	Old Stone House S/N	300		195.00	195
1996	Oriental Splendor S/N	300		395.00	395
1992	Palladian Windows S/N	300	1993	295.00	295-395
1994	Romantic Reflection S/N	500		395.00	395
1994	Rose Fairies S/N	300		295.00	295
1993	Roses in Bloom S/N	300	1995	395.00	395
1996	Spring Bulbs S/N	300		195.00	195
1994	Spring Conservatory S/N	300	1995	395.00	395
1995	Spring Garden A/P	25		435.00	435
1995	Spring Garden S/N	300		395.00	395
1996	Summer Bouquet S/N	300		195.00	195
1995	Sweet Bounty A/P	25		355.00	355
1995	Sweet Bounty S/N	300		295.00	295
1992	Victorian Pavillion S/N	300		195.00	195
1992	Vintage Bouquet S/N	300	1995	395.00	395
1993	Woodland Path S/N	300		495.00	495

Liu - Unframed Canvas Transfers The Music Room - L. Liu

YEAR ISSUE		EDITION LIMIT	YEAR RETD.	ISSUE PRICE	*QUOTE U.S.$
1991	The Music Room S/N	300	1992	395.00	700-900
1992	The Music Room II-Nutcracker S/N	300	1993	395.00	600
1994	The Music Room III-Composer's Retreat S/N	300	1994	395.00	500
1995	Music Room IV - Swan Melody S/N	300		425.00	425
1995	Music Room IV A/P	25		485.00	485

McDonald - M. McDonald

YEAR ISSUE		EDITION LIMIT	YEAR RETD.	ISSUE PRICE	*QUOTE U.S.$
1988	Amaryllis Dancer S/N	1,000		55.00	55
1988	Lily Queen S/N	1,000		55.00	55

John Hine N.A. Ltd.

Rambles - A. Wyatt

YEAR ISSUE		EDITION LIMIT	YEAR RETD.	ISSUE PRICE	*QUOTE U.S.$
1989	Blue Tit	Closed	N/A	33.00	33
1989	Bluebell Cottage	Closed	N/A	50.00	50
1989	Castle Street	Closed	N/A	42.00	42
1989	Frog	Closed	N/A	33.00	33
1989	Garden Gate	Closed	N/A	59.90	60
1989	Hedgerow	Closed	N/A	59.90	60
1989	Kingfisher	Closed	N/A	33.00	33
1989	Lobster Pot	Closed	N/A	50.00	50
1989	Otter's Holt	Closed	N/A	50.00	50
1989	Puffin Rock	Closed	N/A	50.00	50
1989	Riverbank	Closed	N/A	59.90	60
1989	Shirelarm	Closed	N/A	42.00	42
1989	St. Mary's Church	Closed	N/A	42.00	42
1989	Summer Harvest	Closed	N/A	59.90	60
1989	The Swan	Closed	N/A	42.00	42
1989	Two for Joy	Closed	N/A	59.90	60
1989	Waters Edge	Closed	N/A	59.90	60
1989	Wren	Closed	N/A	33.00	33

Lightpost Publishing

Kinkade Member's Only Collectors' Society - T. Kinkade

YEAR ISSUE		EDITION LIMIT	YEAR RETD.	ISSUE PRICE	*QUOTE U.S.$
1992	Skater's Pond	Closed	N/A	295.00	400-525
1992	Morning Lane	Closed	N/A	Gift	125
1994	Collector's Cottage I	Closed	1995	315.00	335-425
1994	Painter of Light Book	Closed	1995	Gift	50-80
1995	Lochavan Cottage	Closed	1995	295.00	295-400

YEAR ISSUE		EDITION LIMIT	YEAR RETD.	ISSUE PRICE	*QUOTE U.S.$
1995	Gardens Beyond Autumn Gate-pencil sketch	Closed	1995	Gift	100
1996	Julianne's Cottage-Keepsake Box	12/96		Gift	70

Kinkade-Archival Paper/Canvas -Combined Edition -Framed - T. Kinkade

YEAR ISSUE		EDITION LIMIT	YEAR RETD.	ISSUE PRICE	*QUOTE U.S.$
1989	Blue Cottage (Paper)		Retrd. 1993	125.00	200-400
1989	Blue Cottage (Canvas)		Retrd. 1993	495.00	900-1400
1990	Moonlit Village (Paper)	Closed	N/A	225.00	700-1200
1990	Moonlit Village (Canvas)	Closed	N/A	595.00	2500-3400
1986	New York, 1932 (Paper)	Closed	N/A	225.00	700-1500
1986	New York, 1932 (Canvas)	Closed	N/A	595.00	2200-3500
1989	Skating in the Park (Paper) S/N	750	1994	225.00	1200-1500
1989	Skating in the Park (Canvas) S/N	750	1994	595.00	1250-2000

Kinkade-Canvas Editions-Framed - T. Kinkade

YEAR ISSUE		EDITION LIMIT	YEAR RETD.	ISSUE PRICE	*QUOTE U.S.$
1991	Afternoon Light, Dogwood A/P	98	1991	595.00	2100-2500
1991	Afternoon Light, Dogwood S/N	980	N/A	495.00	1600-2200
1992	Amber Afternoon A/P	595	1992	715.00	1000-1700
1992	Amber Afternoon S/N	980	N/A	615.00	1000-1500
1994	Autumn at Ashley's Cottage A/P	395		590.00	600-800
1994	Autumn at Ashley's Cottage S/N	3,950		440.00	465
1991	The Autumn Gate A/P	200	N/A	695.00	3300-3900
1991	The Autumn Gate R/P		Retrd. 1992	695.00	3300-4300
1991	The Autumn Gate S/N	980	N/A	595.00	2800-3800
1995	Autumn Lane A/P	295		800.00	800
1995	Autumn Lane G/P	1,240		750.00	800
1995	Autumn Lane S/N	2,950		650.00	650
1994	Beacon of Hope A/P	275	1994	765.00	900-1400
1994	Beacon of Hope S/N	2,750	1994	615.00	750-1000
1996	Beginning of a Perfect Day A/P	295		1025.00	1025
1996	Beginning of a Perfect Day G/P	740		1240.00	1240
1996	Beginning of a Perfect Day S/N	2,950		1090.00	1090
1993	Beside Still Waters A/P	400	N/A	745.00	1300-1800
1993	Beside Still Waters G/P	490	N/A	745.00	1300-1800
1993	Beside Still Waters S/N	980	N/A	595.00	1200-1600
1995	Beside Still Waters S/N		Retrd. N/A	2325.00	2500
1993	Beyond Autumn Gate A/P	600	1993	915.00	3100-3800
1993	Beyond Autumn Gate G/P	500	N/A	915.00	3600-4000
1993	Beyond Autumn Gate S/N	1,750	N/A	815.00	2600-3400
1995	Beyond Autumn Gate S/P		Retrd. N/A	N/A	3850-5000
1993	The Blessings of Autumn A/P	300	1994	715.00	910-1200
1993	The Blessings of Autumn G/P	250	1994	715.00	915-1400
1993	The Blessings of Autumn S/N	1,250	1994	615.00	700-1200
1994	The Blessings of Spring A/P	275	1994	665.00	825
1994	The Blessings of Spring G/P	685	1994	665.00	825
1994	The Blessings of Spring S/N	2,750	1994	515.00	550-700
1995	Blessings of Summer A/P	495		1015.00	1070
1995	Blessings of Summer G/P	1,240		965.00	965
1995	Blessings of Summer S/N	4,950		865.00	920
1995	Blossom Bridge A/P	295		730.00	730
1995	Blossom Bridge G/P	740		685.00	685
1995	Blossom Bridge S/N	2,950		580.00	580
1992	Blossom Hill Church A/P	200	1994	695.00	815-1300
1992	Blossom Hill Church R/P		Retrd. 1993	695.00	1000-1600
1992	Blossom Hill Church S/N	980	1994	595.00	700-1200
1991	Boston A/P	50	N/A	595.00	1400-2300
1991	Boston S/N	550	N/A	495.00	1100-2200
1992	Broadwater Bridge A/P	200	N/A	595.00	2100-2400
1992	Broadwater Bridge G/P	200	N/A	645.00	2100-2500
1992	Broadwater Bridge S/N	980	N/A	495.00	1400-2000
1995	Brookside Hideaway A/P	395	1995	695.00	695-945
1995	Brookside Hideaway G/P	990	1995	695.00	795-945
1995	Brookside Hideaway S/N	3,950	1996	545.00	580-700
1991	Carmel, Delores Street and the Tuck Box Tea Room A/P	200	1994	745.00	3100-3400
1991	Carmel, Delores Street and the Tuck Box Tea Room R/P		Retrd. 1992	745.00	3200-3400
1991	Carmel, Delores Street and the Tuck Box Tea Room S/N	980	1992	645.00	1600-3000
1989	Carmel, Ocean Avenue A/P	Closed	N/A	795.00	5300-5800
1989	Carmel, Ocean Avenue S/N	Closed	N/A	645.00	3800-5000
1991	Cedar Nook Cottage R/P	200	1991	295.00	700-800
1991	Cedar Nook Cottage S/N	1,960	1991	195.00	350-450
1990	Chandler's Cottage S/N	550	N/A	495.00	1900-2800
1992	Christmas At the Ahwahnee A/P	200		615.00	730
1992	Christmas At the Ahwahnee S/N	980		495.00	580
1990	Christmas Cottage 1990 A/P	550	1990	295.00	1800-2200
1990	Christmas Cottage 1990 S/N	550	N/A	295.00	1000-2000
1991	Christmas Eve A/P	200	1991	495.00	1000-1400
1991	Christmas Eve R/P		Retrd. 1991	495.00	1700-1900
1991	Christmas Eve S/N	980	N/A	395.00	700-1300
1994	Christmas Memories A/P	345	N/A	695.00	695-900
1994	Christmas Memories G/P	860		695.00	800-1000
1994	Christmas Memories S/N	3,450	1995	545.00	600-750
1994	Christmas Tree Cottage A/P	395		590.00	615
1994	Christmas Tree Cottage G/P	990		590.00	615
1994	Christmas Tree Cottage S/N	3,950		440.00	465
1992	Cottage-By-The-Sea A/P	200	1992	695.00	1700-2000
1992	Cottage-By-The-Sea G/P	200	N/A	745.00	1800-2300
1992	Cottage-By-The-Sea S/N	980	N/A	595.00	1000-2000
1992	Country Memories A/P	200	1992	495.00	800-1050
1992	Country Memories G/P	200		545.00	695
1992	Country Memories S/N	980	1994	395.00	695-900
1994	Creekside Trail A/P	198	1994	840.00	840-890
1994	Creekside Trail G/P	500		840.00	840
1994	Creekside Trail S/N	1,984		690.00	690
1994	Days of Peace A/P	198	1994	840.00	840
1994	Days of Peace G/P	500		840.00	840
1994	Days of Peace S/N	1,984		690.00	690
1995	Deer Creek Cottage A/P	295		615.00	615
1995	Deer Creek Cottage G/P	740		565.00	565

YEAR ISSUE	EDITION LIMIT	YEAR RETD.	ISSUE PRICE	*QUOTE U.S.$
1995 Deer Creek Cottage S/N	2,950		465.00	465
1994 Dusk in the Valley A/P	198		840.00	840
1994 Dusk in the Valley G/P	500		840.00	840
1994 Dusk in the Valley S/N	1,984		690.00	690
1994 Emerald Isle Cottage A/P	275	1994	665.00	765
1994 Emerald Isle Cottage G/P	685		665.00	665
1994 Emerald Isle Cottage S/N	2,750		515.00	580
1993 End of a Perfect Day I A/P	400	N/A	615.00	1500-2300
1993 End of a Perfect Day I G/P	300	N/A	665.00	1600-2300
1993 End of a Perfect Day I S/N	1,250	N/A	515.00	1400-2100
1995 End of a Perfect Day I S/P	91	1996	2325	2400-3000
1994 End of a Perfect Day II A/P	275	1994	765.00	1200-2300
1994 End of a Perfect Day II G/P	685	1994	765.00	1400-2300
1994 End of a Perfect Day II S/N	2,750	1995	815.00	1100-2200
1995 End of a Perfect Day III A/P	495	1995	1145.00	1145-1650
1995 End of a Perfect Day III G/P	1,240		1145.00	1245
1995 End of a Perfect Day III S/N	4,950		995.00	1055
1989 Entrance to the Manor House A/P	Closed	N/A	595.00	1900
1989 Entrance to the Manor House S/N	550	N/A	495.00	1700
1989 Evening at Merritt's Cottage A/P	Closed	N/A	595.00	2495-3200
1989 Evening at Merritt's Cottage S/N	550	N/A	495.00	2295-3000
1992 Evening at Swanbrooke Cottage Thomashire A/P	Closed	N/A	595.00	1995-2895
1992 Evening at Swanbrooke Cottage Thomashire G/P	Closed	N/A	645.00	1995-3000
1992 Evening at Swanbrooke Cottage Thomashire S/N	980	N/A	495.00	1895-2500
1992 Evening Carolers A/P	200		415.00	505
1992 Evening Carolers G/P	200		415.00	505
1992 Evening Carolers S/N	1,960		295.00	355
1995 Evening in the Forest A/P	495		695.00	730
1995 Evening in the Forest G/P	1,250		645.00	680
1995 Evening in the Forest S/N	4,950		545.00	580
1993 Fisherman's Wharf San Francisco A/P	275	1993	1065.00	1165-1500
1993 Fisherman's Wharf San Francisco G/P	550	N/A	1065.00	1200-1500
1993 Fisherman's Wharf San Francisco S/N	2,750	N/A	965.00	1000-1300
1991 Flags Over The Capitol A/P	200	N/A	695.00	715-850
1991 Flags Over The Capitol R/P	Retrd.	N/A	695.00	1000-1300
1991 Flags Over The Capitol S/N	980		595.00	690
1993 The Garden of Promise A/P	300	N/A	715.00	1200-1900
1993 The Garden of Promise G/P	400	N/A	715.00	1900-2100
1993 The Garden of Promise S/N	1,250	1994	615.00	1000-1700
1995 The Garden of Promise S/P	Retrd.	N/A	2800	3000-4000
1992 The Garden Party A/P	200		595.00	650
1992 The Garden Party G/P	200		595.00	615
1992 The Garden Party S/N	980		495.00	580
1994 Gardens Beyond Autumn Gate S/N	Closed	1996	1025.00	900-1300
1993 Glory of Evening A/P	400	1993	365.00	515-600
1993 Glory of Evening G/P	490		365.00	415
1993 Glory of Evening S/N	1,980	1994	315.00	415-500
1993 Glory of Morning A/P	400	1993	365.00	515-600
1993 Glory of Morning G/P	490	1993	365.00	515-650
1993 Glory of Morning S/N	1,980	1994	315.00	415-500
1993 Glory of Winter A/P	300		715.00	715-765
1993 Glory of Winter G/P	250		715.00	840
1993 Glory of Winter S/N	1,250		615.00	690
1995 Golden Gate Bridge, San Francisco A/P	395		1240.00	1240
1995 Golden Gate Bridge, San Francisco G/P	990		1190.00	1190
1995 Golden Gate Bridge, San Francisco S/N	3,950	1996	1090.00	1095-1400
1994 Guardian Castle A/P	475		1015.00	1070
1994 Guardian Castle G/P	1,190		1015.00	1070
1994 Guardian Castle S/N	4,750		865.00	920
1993 Heather's Hutch A/P	400	1993	515.00	515-800
1993 Heather's Hutch G/P	300	N/A	515.00	665-750
1993 Heather's Hutch S/N	1,250	N/A	415.00	665-800
1994 Hidden Arbor A/P	375		665.00	730
1994 Hidden Arbor G/P	685		665.00	730
1994 Hidden Arbor S/N	3,750		515.00	580
1990 Hidden Cottage I A/P	100	N/A	595.00	1100-2200
1990 Hidden Cottage I S/N	550	N/A	495.00	1100-2100
1993 Hidden Cottage II A/P	400	1993	615.00	750-900
1993 Hidden Cottage II G/P	400	1995	665.00	750-1000
1993 Hidden Cottage II S/N	1,480	1994	515.00	700-900
1994 Hidden Gazebo A/P	240	1994	665.00	765-1100
1994 Hidden Gazebo G/P	600	1994	665.00	765-1100
1994 Hidden Gazebo S/N	2,400	1994	515.00	575-900
1996 Hollyhock House A/P	395		730.00	730
1996 Hollyhock House G/P	990		730.00	730
1996 Hollyhock House S/N	3,850		580.00	580
1991 Home For The Evening A/P	200	1994	295.00	600-895
1991 Home For The Evening S/N	980	N/A	195.00	500-695
1991 Home For The Holidays A/P	200	1991	695.00	2200-2800
1991 Home For The Holidays R/P	N/A	1991	695.00	3000
1991 Home For The Holidays S/N	980	N/A	595.00	1500-2500
1992 Home is Where the Heart Is A/P	200	N/A	695.00	1800-2200
1992 Home is Where the Heart Is G/P	200	N/A	695.00	2000-2300
1992 Home is Where the Heart Is S/N	980	N/A	595.00	1500-2000
1993 Homestead House A/P	300		715.00	715
1993 Homestead House G/P	250		715.00	840
1993 Homestead House S/N	1,250	1996	615.00	690-895
1995 Hometown Chapel A/P	495		1045.00	1100
1995 Hometown Chapel G/P	1,240		995.00	1050
1995 Hometown Chapel S/N	4,950		895.00	950
1995 Hometown Memories I A/P	495	1995	1015.00	1050-1250
1995 Hometown Memories I G/P	1,240		1015.00	1020
1995 Hometown Memories I S/N	4,950	1996	865.00	900-1100

YEAR ISSUE	EDITION LIMIT	YEAR RETD.	ISSUE PRICE	*QUOTE U.S.$
1992 Julianne's Cottage A/P	200	N/A	495.00	1400-2000
1992 Julianne's Cottage G/P	200	N/A	545.00	1400-2000
1992 Julianne's Cottage S/N	980	N/A	395.00	1375-1800
1996 Lamplight Bridge A/P	295		730.00	730
1996 Lamplight Bridge G/P	740		730.00	730
1996 Lamplight Bridge S/N	2,950		580.00	580
1993 Lamplight Brooke A/P	400	1994	715.00	1300-2200
1993 Lamplight Brooke G/P	330	1994	715.00	1700-2300
1993 Lamplight Brooke S/N	1,650	1994	615.00	1100-2100
1994 Lamplight Inn A/P	275	1994	765.00	865-1000
1994 Lamplight Inn G/P	685	1994	765.00	850-1000
1994 Lamplight Inn S/N	2,750	1994	615.00	615-845
1993 Lamplight Lane A/P	200	N/A	695.00	2800-3600
1993 Lamplight Lane G/P	200	1994	695.00	3200-3800
1993 Lamplight Lane S/N	980	N/A	615.00	2800-3500
1995 Lamplight Lane S/P	Retrd.	N/A	N/A	2600-3500
1995 Lamplight Village A/P	495	1995	800.00	900-1145
1995 Lamplight Village G/P	1,240		800.00	900
1995 Lamplight Village S/N	4,950	1995	650.00	750-1000
1995 A Light in the Storm A/P	395	1995	800.00	800-925
1995 A Light in the Storm G/P	1,240		750.00	750
1995 A Light in the Storm S/N	3,950		650.00	650
1995 The Lights of Home S/N	2,500		195.00	195
1996 Lilac Gazebo A/P	295		615.00	615
1996 Lilac Gazebo G/P	740		615.00	615
1996 Lilac Gazebo S/N	2,950		465.00	465
1991 The Lit Path A/P	200	1991	395.00	395-595
1991 The Lit Path R/P	Retrd.	1991	395.00	495-700
1991 The Lit Path S/N	1,960	1994	195.00	300-500
1995 Main Street Celebration A/P	125	1995	800.00	650-850
1995 Main Street Celebration S/N	1,250		650.00	650
1995 Main Street Courthouse A/P	125	1995	800.00	850
1995 Main Street Courthouse S/N	1,250		650.00	690
1995 Main Street Matinee A/P	125	1995	800.00	850
1995 Main Street Matinee S/N	1,250		650.00	690
1995 Main Street Trolley A/P	125	1995	800.00	850
1995 Main Street Trolley S/N	1,250		650.00	690
1991 McKenna's Cottage A/P	100		595.00	730
1991 McKenna's Cottage R/P	200	N/A	615.00	700-1000
1991 McKenna's Cottage S/N	980	1995	495.00	500-700
1996 Meadowood Cottage S/N	4,950		310.00	310
1992 Miller's Cottage, Thomashire A/P	200	N/A	595.00	1000-1350
1992 Miller's Cottage, Thomashire G/P	200	N/A	595.00	1000-1450
1992 Miller's Cottage, Thomashire S/N	980	1994	495.00	900-1300
1994 Moonlight Lane I A/P	240	1995	665.00	665-720
1994 Moonlight Lane I G/P	600		665.00	665
1994 Moonlight Lane I S/N	2,400		515.00	580
1992 Moonlit Sleigh Ride A/P	200	1995	395.00	500-695
1992 Moonlit Sleigh Ride S/N	1,960	1995	295.00	315-500
1995 Morning Dogwood A/P	495		645.00	675
1995 Morning Dogwood G/P	1,240		645.00	645
1995 Morning Dogwood S/N	4,950		495.00	525
1995 Morning Glory Cottage A/P	495		695.00	730
1995 Morning Glory Cottage G/P	1,240		645.00	680
1995 Morning Glory Cottage S/N	4,950		545.00	580
1990 Morning Light A/P	N/A	N/A	695.00	1500-2400
1992 Olde Porterfield Gift Shoppe A/P	200	1995	595.00	615-900
1992 Olde Porterfield Gift Shoppe G/P	200		595.00	615
1992 Olde Porterfield Gift Shoppe S/N	980	1994	495.00	495-700
1991 Olde Porterfield Tea Room A/P	200	N/A	595.00	1100-1700
1991 Olde Porterfield Tea Room R/P	Retrd.	1991	595.00	1400-2000
1991 Olde Porterfield Tea Room S/N	980	N/A	495.00	900-1500
1991 Open Gate, Sussex A/P	100	1994	295.00	365-600
1991 Open Gate, Sussex R/P	Retrd.	1992	295.00	500-700
1991 Open Gate, Sussex S/N	980	N/A	195.00	315-400
1993 Paris, City of Lights A/P	600	1994	765.00	1400-1900
1993 Paris, City of Lights G/P	600	N/A	815.00	1900-2100
1993 Paris, City of Lights S/N	1,980	N/A	615.00	1200-1800
1994 Paris, Eiffel Tower A/P	275	1994	945.00	945-1395
1994 Paris, Eiffel Tower G/P	685	1995	945.00	1400
1994 Paris, Eiffel Tower S/N	2,750	1994	795.00	800-1200
1995 Petals of Hope A/P	395		730.00	730
1995 Petals of Hope G/P	990		680.00	680
1995 Petals of Hope S/N	3,950		580.00	580
1994 The Power & The Majesty A/P	275		765.00	840
1994 The Power & The Majesty G/P	685		765.00	840
1994 The Power & The Majesty S/N	2,750		615.00	690
1991 Pye Corner Cottage A/P	200		295.00	395
1991 Pye Corner Cottage R/P	Retrd.	N/A	295.00	395
1991 Pye Corner Cottage S/N	1,960	1996	195.00	275-350
1990 Rose Arbor A/P	98	N/A	595.00	1900
1990 Rose Arbor S/N	935	N/A	495.00	700-1500
1996 Rose Gate A/P	295		615.00	615
1996 Rose Gate G/P	740		615.00	615
1996 Rose Gate S/N	2,950		465.00	465
1994 San Francisco Market Street A/P	750	1994	945.00	945-1050
1994 San Francisco Market Street G/P	1,875		945.00	945-1045
1994 San Francisco Market Street S/N	7,500		795.00	800
1992 San Francisco, Nob Hill (California St.) A/P	Closed	N/A	715.00	3900-5300
1992 San Francisco, Nob Hill (California St.) P/P	Closed	N/A	815.00	5500-5800
1992 San Francisco, Nob Hill (California St.) S/N	980	N/A	645.00	3400-5000
1989 San Francisco, Union Square A/P	Closed	N/A	795.00	4400-5500
1989 San Francisco, Union Square S/N	Closed	N/A	595.00	5000-5300
1992 Silent Night A/P	200	N/A	495.00	850-1200
1992 Silent Night G/P	200	N/A	495.00	900-1300
1992 Silent Night S/N	980	N/A	395.00	800-1000
1995 Simpler Times I A/P	345		840.00	840
1995 Simpler Times I G/P	870		790.00	790
1995 Simpler Times I S/N	3,450		690.00	690

YEAR ISSUE	EDITION LIMIT	YEAR RETD.	ISSUE PRICE	*QUOTE U.S.$
1990 Spring At Stonegate A/P	50	N/A	395.00	515-800
1990 Spring At Stonegate S/N	550	1995	295.00	415-600
1996 Spring Gate A/P	395		1240.00	1240
1996 Spring Gate G/P	990		1240.00	1240
1996 Spring Gate S/N	3,950		1090.00	1090
1994 Spring in the Alps A/P	198		725.00	730
1994 Spring in the Alps G/P	500		725.00	730
1994 Spring in the Alps S/N	1,984		575.00	580
1993 St. Nicholas Circle A/P	420	1995	715.00	715-1000
1993 St. Nicholas Circle G/P	350	1995	715.00	915-1100
1993 St. Nicholas Circle S/N	1,750	1994	615.00	695-900
1995 Stepping Stone Cottage A/P	295		840.00	840
1995 Stepping Stone Cottage G/P	740		840.00	840
1995 Stepping Stone Cottage S/N	2,950		690.00	690
1993 Stonehearth Hutch A/P	300	N/A	515.00	700-900
1993 Stonehearth Hutch G/P	300	1994	515.00	700-950
1993 Stonehearth Hutch S/N	1,650	N/A	415.00	550-700
1993 Studio in the Garden A/P	400		515.00	615
1993 Studio in the Garden G/P	600		515.00	600
1993 Studio in the Garden S/N	1,480		415.00	465
1992 Sunday at Apple Hill A/P	200	1993	595.00	1200-1400
1992 Sunday at Apple Hill G/P	200	N/A	595.00	1200-1500
1992 Sunday at Apple Hill S/N	980	1993	495.00	1050-1200
1993 Sunday Outing A/P	200	N/A	595.00	1100-1600
1993 Sunday Outing G/P	200	N/A	595.00	1100-1600
1993 Sunday Outing S/N	980	N/A	495.00	995-1300
1996 Sunset on Riverbend Farm A/P	495		840.00	840
1996 Sunset on Riverbend Farm G/P	1,240		840.00	840
1996 Sunset on Riverbend Farm S/N	4,950		690.00	690
1992 Sweetheart Cottage I A/P	200	1992	595.00	1295-1400
1992 Sweetheart Cottage I G/P	200		595.00	1150-1500
1992 Sweetheart Cottage I S/N	980	N/A	495.00	900-1200
1993 Sweetheart Cottage II A/P	400	1993	695.00	1500-1700
1993 Sweetheart Cottage II G/P	490	N/A	745.00	1450-1750
1993 Sweetheart Cottage II S/N	980	N/A	615.00	1400-1600
1994 Sweetheart Cottage III A/P	165	1994	765.00	865-1045
1994 Sweetheart Cottage III G/P	410	1994	765.00	865-1045
1994 Sweetheart Cottage III S/N	1,650	1994	615.00	615-895
1996 Venice A/P	495		1240.00	1240
1996 Venice G/P	1,240		1240.00	1240
1996 Venice S/N	4,950		1090.00	1090
1992 Victorian Christmas I A/P	200	1992	695.00	2000-2600
1992 Victorian Christmas I G/P	200	1992	695.00	2600-3000
1992 Victorian Christmas I S/N	980	1992	595.00	1800-2500
1993 Victorian Christmas II A/P	400	1994	715.00	1500-2000
1993 Victorian Christmas II G/P	300	1994	715.00	1500-2100
1993 Victorian Christmas II S/N	980	1994	615.00	1200-1800
1994 Victorian Christmas III A/P	395	1994	800.00	800
1994 Victorian Christmas III G/P	990		800.00	800
1994 Victorian Christmas III S/N	3,950	1995	650.00	650
1995 Victorian Christmas IV S/N	2,330	1995	650.00	650
1991 Victorian Evening	980	1993	495.00	900-1500
1992 Victorian Garden A/P	200	1993	895.00	2100-2600
1992 Victorian Garden G/P	200	1993	895.00	2200-2700
1992 Victorian Garden S/N	980	1993	795.00	2000-2500
1993 Village Inn A/P	400	1996	615.00	615-815
1993 Village Inn G/P	400		615.00	730
1993 Village Inn S/N	1,200	1994	515.00	600-700
1994 The Warmth of Home A/P	345		590.00	615
1994 The Warmth of Home G/P	860		590.00	615
1994 The Warmth of Home S/N	3,450		440.00	465
1992 Weathervane Hutch A/P	200	1995	395.00	395-645
1992 Weathervane Hutch G/P	200		395.00	415
1992 Weathervane Hutch S/N	1,960	1995	295.00	400-515
1996 Winsor Manor A/P	395		1070.00	1070
1996 Winsor Manor G/P	990		1120.00	1120
1996 Winsor Manor S/N	3,950		920.00	920
1993 Winter's End A/P	400		715.00	840
1993 Winter's End G/P	490		715.00	840
1993 Winter's End S/N	1,450		615.00	690
1991 Woodman's Thatch A/P	200	1995	295.00	475-600
1991 Woodman's Thatch R/P	200	N/A	295.00	600-800
1991 Woodman's Thatch S/N	1,960	1994	195.00	300-450
1992 Yosemite A/P	200		695.00	840
1992 Yosemite G/P	200		695.00	840
1992 Yosemite S/N	980		595.00	690

Kinkade-Premium Paper-Unframed - T. Kinkade

YEAR ISSUE	EDITION LIMIT	YEAR RETD.	ISSUE PRICE	*QUOTE U.S.$
1991 Afternoon Light, Dogwood A/P	98	N/A	295.00	400-900
1991 Afternoon Light, Dogwood S/N	980	N/A	185.00	350-700
1992 Amber Afternoon S/N	980		225.00	265
1994 Autumn at Ashley's Cottage A/P	245		335.00	395
1994 Autumn at Ashley's Cottage S/N	2,450		185.00	195
1991 The Autumn Gate S/N	980	1994	225.00	500-1000
1995 Autumn Lane A/P	285		400.00	400
1995 Autumn Lane S/N	2,850		250.00	250
1994 Beacon of Hope S/N	2,750		235.00	265
1996 Beginning of a Perfect Day A/P	285		475.00	475
1996 Beginning of a Perfect Day S/N	2,850		325.00	325
1993 Beside Still Waters S/N	1,280	1994	185.00	400-800
1993 Beyond Autumn Gate S/N	1,750	1994	285.00	400-800
1985 Birth of a City S/N	Closed	N/A	150.00	300-900
1993 The Blessings of Autumn S/N	1,250		235.00	265
1994 The Blessings of Spring A/P	275		345.00	370
1994 The Blessings of Spring S/N	2,750		195.00	220
1995 Blessings of Summer A/P	485		450.00	450
1995 Blessings of Summer S/N	4,850		300.00	300
1995 Blossom Bridge S/N	2,850		205.00	205
1992 Blossom Hill Church S/N	980		225.00	265
1991 Boston S/N	550	1994	175.00	350-750
1992 Broadwater Bridge S/N	980	1994	225.00	350-700

YEAR ISSUE		EDITION LIMIT	YEAR RETD.	ISSUE PRICE	*QUOTE U.S.$
1995	Brookside Hideaway A/P	385		355.00	355
1995	Brookside Hideaway S/N	3,850		205.00	220
1991	Carmel, Delores Street and the Tuck Box Tea Room S/N	980	1994	275.00	500-1000
1989	Carmel, Ocean Avenue S/N	Closed	N/A	225.00	1100-2100
1990	Chandler's Cottage S/N	550	N/A	125.00	850-1200
1992	Christmas At the Ahwahnee S/N	980		175.00	220
1990	Christmas Cottage 1990 S/N	550	N/A	95.00	350-700
1991	Christmas Eve S/N	980		125.00	185
1994	Christmas Tree Cottage A/P	295		335.00	395
1994	Christmas Tree Cottage S/N	2,950		185.00	195
1992	Cottage-By-The-Sea S/N	980	N/A	250.00	300-800
1992	Country Memories S/N	980		185.00	195
1994	Creekside Trail A/P	198		425.00	425
1994	Creekside Trail S/N	1,984		275.00	275
1984	Dawson S/N	Closed	N/A	150.00	350-950
1994	Days of Peace A/P	198		425.00	425
1994	Days of Peace S/N	1,984		275.00	275
1995	Deer Creek Cottage A/P	285		335.00	335
1995	Deer Creek Cottage S/N	2,850		185.00	185
1994	Dusk in the Valley A/P	198		425.00	425
1994	Dusk in the Valley S/N	1,984		275.00	275
1994	Emerald Isle Cottage A/P	275		345.00	355
1994	Emerald Isle Cottage S/N	2,750		195.00	220
1993	End of a Perfect Day I S/N	1,250	1994	195.00	400-900
1994	End of a Perfect Day II A/P	275		385.00	435
1994	End of a Perfect Day II S/N	2,750		235.00	265
1995	End of a Perfect Day III A/P	485		475.00	475
1995	End of a Perfect Day III S/N	4,850		325.00	345
1989	Entrance to the Manor House	550	N/A	125.00	600-1000
1989	Evening at Merritt's Cottage	550	N/A	125.00	800-1200
1992	Evening at Swanbrooke Cottage, S/N	980	1994	250.00	600-1000
1995	Evening in the Forest A/P	485		355.00	355
1995	Evening in the Forest S/N	4,850		205.00	205
1985	Evening Service S/N	Closed	N/A	90.00	400-1000
1991	Flags Over The Capitol S/N	1,991		195.00	265
1993	The Garden of Promise S/N	1,250	1994	235.00	450-900
1992	The Garden Party S/N	980		175.00	220
1994	Gardens Beyond Autumn Gate S/N	Closed	1996	325.00	325-500
1993	Glory of Winter S/N	1,250		235.00	265
1995	Golden Gate Bridge, San Francisco A/P	385		475.00	475
1995	Golden Gate Bridge, San Francisco S/N	3,850		325.00	325
1994	Guardian Castle A/P	275		450.00	450
1994	Guardian Castle G/P	685		450.00	450
1994	Guardian Castle S/N	2,750		300.00	320
1993	Heather's Hutch S/N	1,250		175.00	195
1994	Hidden Arbor S/N	2,750	N/A	195.00	195-295
1993	Hidden Cottage II S/N	1,480		195.00	195
1990	Hidden Cottage S/N	550	N/A	125.00	1000
1994	Hidden Gazebo A/P	275		345.00	355
1994	Hidden Gazebo, S/N	2,400		195.00	195
1996	Hollyhock House A/P	385		355.00	355
1996	Hollyhock House S/N	3,850		205.00	205
1991	Home For The Evening S/N	980	N/A	100.00	300-375
1991	Home For The Holidays S/N	980	1994	225.00	450-900
1992	Home is Where the Heart Is S/N	980	1994	225.00	500-900
1993	Homestead House S/N	1,250		235.00	265
1995	Hometown Memories I A/P	485		450.00	470
1995	Hometown Memories I S/N	4,850		300.00	320
1992	Julianne's Cottage S/N	980	N/A	185.00	400-800
1996	Lamplight Bridge A/P	285		355.00	355
1996	Lamplight Bridge S/N	2,850		205.00	205
1993	Lamplight Brook S/N	1,650	1995	235.00	300-700
1994	Lamplight Inn A/P	275	1995	385.00	415
1994	Lamplight Inn S/N	2,750		235.00	265
1993	Lamplight Lane S/N	980	N/A	225.00	500-1000
1995	Lamplight Village A/P	485		400.00	415
1995	Lamplight Village S/N	4,850		250.00	265
1995	A Light in the Storm A/P	385		415.00	415
1995	A Light in the Storm S/N	3,850		265.00	265
1995	The Lights of Home A/P	250		225.00	225
1996	Lilac Gazebo A/P	285		335.00	335
1996	Lilac Gazebo S/N	2,850		185.00	185
1995	Main Street Celebration A/P	195		400.00	400
1995	Main Street Celebration S/N	1,950		250.00	250
1995	Main Street Courthouse A/P	195		400.00	400
1995	Main Street Courthouse S/N	1,950		250.00	250
1995	Main Street Matinee A/P	195		400.00	400
1995	Main Street Matinee S/N	1,950		250.00	250
1995	Main Street Trolley A/P	195		400.00	400
1995	Main Street Trolley S/N	1,950		250.00	250
1991	McKenna's Cottage S/N	980		150.00	220
1996	Meadowood Cottage S/N	950		95.00	95
1992	Miller's Cottage S/N	980	1995	175.00	200-350
1994	Moonlight Lane I A/P	240		345.00	345
1994	Moonlight Lane I S/N	2,400		195.00	195
1985	Moonlight on the Riverfront S/N	750	N/A	150.00	300-1000
1995	Morning Dogwood A/P	485		345.00	345
1995	Morning Dogwood S/N	4,850		195.00	205
1995	Morning Glory Cottage A/P	485		355.00	355
1995	Morning Glory Cottage S/N	4,850		205.00	205
1986	New York, 6th Avenue S/N	Closed	N/A	150.00	1350-2000
1992	Olde Porterfield Gift Shoppe S/N	980		175.00	195
1991	Olde Porterfield Tea Room S/N	980		150.00	205
1991	Open Gate, Sussex S/N	980		100.00	115
1993	Paris, City of Lights S/N	1,980		285.00	295
1994	Paris, Eiffel Tower A/P	275		445.00	445
1994	Paris, Eiffel Tower S/N	2,750		295.00	310
1995	Petals of Hope A/P	385		355.00	355
1995	Petals of Hope S/N	3,850		205.00	205

YEAR ISSUE		EDITION LIMIT	YEAR RETD.	ISSUE PRICE	*QUOTE U.S.$
1984	Placerville, 1916 S/N	Closed	N/A	90.00	1100-2000
1994	The Power & The Majesty A/P	275		385.00	385
1994	The Power & The Majesty S/N	2,750		235.00	265
1988	Room with a View S/N	Closed	N/A	150.00	400-1000
1990	Rose Arbor S/N	935	1994	125.00	350-800
1996	Rose Gate A/P	285		335.00	335
1996	Rose Gate S/N	2,850		185.00	185
1994	San Francisco Market Street A/P	750		525.00	550
1994	San Francisco Market Street S/N	7,500		375.00	400
1986	San Francisco, 1909 S/N	Closed	N/A	150.00	1450
1993	San Francisco, Fisherman's Wharf S/N	2,750		305.00	305
1992	San Francisco, Nob Hill (California St.) S/N	980	N/A	275.00	900-2000
1989	San Francisco, Union Square S/N	Closed	N/A	225.00	1300-2100
1992	Silent Night S/N	980	1994	175.00	375
1995	Simpler Time I A/P	335		400.00	400
1995	Simpler Time I S/N	3,350		250.00	250
1990	Spring At Stonegate S/N	550		95.00	95
1996	Spring Gate A/P	385		475.00	475
1996	Spring Gate S/N	3,850		325.00	325
1994	Spring in the Alps A/P	198		375.00	375
1994	Spring in the Alps S/N	1,984		225.00	225
1993	St. Nicholas Circle S/N	1,750	1995	235.00	265
1995	Stepping Stone Cottage A/P	285		400.00	400
1995	Stepping Stone Cottage S/N	2,850		250.00	250
1993	Stonehearth Hutch S/N	1,650	1995	175.00	195
1993	Studio in the Garden S/N	980	1995	175.00	175
1992	Sunday At Apple Hill, S/N	980	1994	175.00	350-400
1993	Sunday Outing S/N	980	1995	175.00	250-300
1996	Sunset on Riverbend Farm A/P	485		400.00	400
1996	Sunset on Riverbend Farm S/N	4,850		250	250
1992	Sweetheart Cottage I S/N	980	1995	150.00	200-400
1993	Sweetheart Cottage II S/N	980	1994	150.00	350-450
1993	Sweetheart Cottage III A/P	165	1995	385.00	400
1993	Sweetheart Cottage III S/N	1,650		235.00	265
1996	Venice A/P	485		475.00	475
1996	Venice S/N	4,850		325.00	325
1992	Victorian Christmas I S/N	980	N/A	235.00	400-700
1993	Victorian Christmas II S/N	1,650		235.00	250
1994	Victorian Christmas III S/N	2,950	1995	250.00	250
1995	Victorian Christmas IV S/N	750	1995	250.00	250
1991	Victorian Evening, S/N	Retrd.	1993	150.00	250-450
1992	Victorian Garden, S/N	980	1994	275.00	500-1000
1993	Village Inn S/N	1,200		195.00	220
1994	The Warmth of Home A/P	245		335.00	345
1994	The Warmth of Home S/N	2,450		185.00	195
1996	Winsor Manor A/P	385		450.00	450
1996	Winsor Manor S/N	3,850		300.00	300
1993	Winter's End S/N	875		235.00	265
1992	Yosemite S/N	980		225.00	265

Lightpost Publishing/ Recollections

American Heroes Collection-Framed - Recollections

YEAR ISSUE		EDITION LIMIT	YEAR RETD.	ISSUE PRICE	*QUOTE U.S.$
1992	Abraham Lincoln	7,500		150.00	150
1993	Babe Ruth	2,250	1996	95.00	95
1993	Ben Franklin	1,000		95.00	95
1994	Dwight D. Eisenhower	Open		30.00	30
1994	Eternal Love (Civil War)	1,861		195.00	195
1994	Franklin D. Roosevelt	Open		30.00	30
1992	George Washington	7,500		150.00	150
1994	George Washington	Open		30.00	30
1992	John F. Kennedy	7,500		150.00	150
1994	John F. Kennedy	Open		30.00	30
1992	Mark Twain	7,500		150.00	150
1994	A Nation Divided	1,000		150.00	150
1993	A Nation United	1,000		150.00	150

Cinema Classics Collection - Recollections

YEAR ISSUE		EDITION LIMIT	YEAR RETD.	ISSUE PRICE	*QUOTE U.S.$
1993	As God As My Witness Classic Clip	Closed	1995	40.00	40
1994	Attempted Deception Classic Clip	Open		30.00	30
1994	A Chance Meeting Classic Clip	Open		30.00	30
1993	A Dream Remembered Classic Clip	Closed	1995	40.00	40
1993	The Emerald City Classic Clip	Closed	1995	40.00	40
1993	Follow the Yellow Brick Road Classic Clip	Closed	1995	40.00	40
1993	Frankly My Dear Classic Clip	Closed	1995	40.00	40
1994	The Gift Classic Clip	Open		30.00	30
1993	Gone With the Wind-Movie Ticket Classic Clip	2,000		40.00	40
1994	If I Only Had a Brain Classic Clip	Open		30.00	30
1994	If I Only Had a Heart Classic Clip	Open		30.00	30
1994	If I Only Had the Nerve Classic Clip	Open		30.00	30
1993	The Kiss Classic Clip	Closed	1995	40.00	40
1993	Not A Marrying Man	12,500		150.00	150
1993	Over The Rainbow	7,500		150.00	150
1994	The Proposal Classic Clip	Open		30.00	30
1993	The Ruby Slippers Classic Clip	Closed	1995	40.00	40
1993	Scarlett & Her Beaux	12,500		150.00	150
1994	There's No Place Like Home Classic Clip	Open		30.00	30
1993	We're Off to See the Wizard Classic Clip	Closed	1995	40.00	40
1993	You Do Waltz Divinely	12,500		195.00	195
1993	You Need Kissing	12,500		195.00	195

The Elvis Collection - Recollections

YEAR ISSUE		EDITION LIMIT	YEAR RETD.	ISSUE PRICE	*QUOTE U.S.$
1994	Celebrity Soldier/Regular G.I.	Open		30.00	30
1994	Dreams Remembered/Dreams Realized	Open		30.00	30
1994	Elvis the King	2,750		195.00	195
1994	Elvis the Pelvis	2,750		195.00	195

YEAR ISSUE		EDITION LIMIT	YEAR RETD.	ISSUE PRICE	*QUOTE U.S.$
1994	The King/The Servant	Open		30.00	30
1994	Lavish Spender/Generous Giver	Open		30.00	30
1994	Professional Artist/Practical Joker	Open		30.00	30
1994	Public Image/Private Man	Open		30.00	30
1994	Sex Symbol/Boy Next Door	Open		30.00	30
1994	To Elvis with Love	2,750		195.00	195
1994	Vulgar Showman/Serious Musician	Open		30.00	30

Gone With the Wind - Recollections

1995	Final Parting Classic Clip	Open		30.00	30
1995	A Parting Kiss Classic Clip	Open		30.00	30
1995	The Red Dress Classic Clip	Open		30.00	30
1995	Sweet Revenge Classic Clip	Open		30.00	30

The Wizard of Oz - Recollections

1995	Glinda the Good Witch	Open		30.00	30
1995	Toto	Open		30.00	30
1995	The Wicked Witch	Open		30.00	30
1995	The Wizard	Open		30.00	30

Marty Bell

Members Only Collectors Club - M. Bell

1991	Little Thatch Twilight	Closed	1992	288.00	350
1991	Charter Rose, The	Closed	1992	Gift	N/A
1992	Candle At Eventide	Closed	1993	Gift	N/A
1992	Blossom Lane	Closed	1993	288.00	350
1993	Laverstoke Lodge	Closed	1994	328.00	328
1993	Chideock Gate	Closed	1994	Gift	N/A
1994	Hummingbird Hill	Closed	1995	320.00	450-495
1994	The Hummingbird	Closed	1995	Gift	N/A
1995	The Bluebird Victorian	Closed	1996	320.00	340
1995	The Bluebird	Closed	1996	Gift	N/A
1996	Goldfinch Garden	Yr.Iss.		220.00	220
1996	The Goldfinch	Yr.Iss.		Gift	N/A

America the Beautiful - M. Bell

1993	Jones Victorian	750	1994	400.00	1300
1995	The Tuck Box Tea Room, Carmel	500	1995	456.00	1295
1993	Turlock Spring	114	1995	700.00	750

Christmas - M. Bell

1989	Fireside Christmas	500	1989	136.00	750
1990	Ready For Christmas	700	1990	148.00	495
1991	Christmas in Rochester	900	1991	148.00	275-350
1992	McCoy's Toy Shoppe	900	1992	148.00	350
1993	Christmas Treasures	900	1993	200.00	200
1995	Tuck Box Christmas	750	1995	250.00	250

England - M. Bell

1987	Alderton Village	500	1988	235.00	650
1992	Antiques of Rye	1,100	1996	220.00	234
1990	Arbor Cottage	900	1993	130.00	150-250
1993	Arundel Row	282	1995	130.00	138
1991	Bay Tree Cottage, Rye	1,100	1992	230.00	230-520
1981	Bibury Cottage	500	1988	280.00	800-1000
1981	Big Daddy's Shoe	700	1989	64.00	150-300
1988	The Bishop's Roses	900	1989	220.00	695
1989	Blush of Spring	1,200	1990	96.00	120-160
1988	Bodiam Twilight	900	1991	520.00	900-1100
1988	Brendon Hills Lane	860	1995	304.00	318
1992	Briarwood	217	1993	220.00	220
1993	Broadway Cottage	122	1995	330.00	350
1987	Broughton Village	900	1988	128.00	400-500
1984	Brown Eyes	312	1993	296.00	296
1990	Bryants Puddle Thatch	900	1990	130.00	150-295
1986	Burford Village Store	500	1988	106.00	595
1981	Castle Combe Cottage	500	1988	230.00	895
1993	The Castle Tearoom	900	1993	88.00	98
1987	The Chaplains Garden	500	1987	235.00	1000-2000
1991	Childswickham Morning	305	1993	396.00	396
1987	Chippenham Farm	500	1988	120.00	300-900
1988	Clove Cottage	900	1988	128.00	500
1988	Clover Lane Cottage	1,800	1988	272.00	500
1991	Cobblestone Cottage	652	1995	374.00	404
1993	Coln St. Aldwyn's	1,000	1995	730.00	800-1000
1986	Cotswold Parish Church	500	1988	98.00	1500-2000
1988	Cotswold Twilight	900	1988	128.00	200-495
1991	Cozy Cottage	900	1991	130.00	130
1982	Crossroads Cottage	S/O	1987	38.00	200
1992	Devon Cottage	472	1995	374.00	404
1991	Devon Roses	1,200	1991	96.00	195-500
1991	Dorset Roses	1,200	1991	96.00	195
1987	Dove Cottage Garden	900	1990	260.00	304-495
1987	Driftstone Manor	500	1988	440.00	1500-1800
1987	Ducksbridge Cottage	500	1988	400.00	400
1987	Eashing Cottage	900	1988	120.00	200-400
1992	East Sussex Roses (Archival)	1,200	1993	96.00	96
1985	Fiddleford Cottage	500	1986	78.00	1950
1988	Friday Street Lane	1,800	1992	280.00	600
1989	The Game Keeper's Cottage	900	1989	560.00	1800-2000
1992	Garlands Flower Shop	900	1994	220.00	220
1988	Ginger Cottage	1,800	1988	320.00	550-800
1989	Glory Cottage	911	1993	96.00	96
1989	Goater's Cottage	900	1991	368.00	400-560
1990	Gomshall Flower Shop	900	1990	396.00	2900-3300
1987	Halfway Cottage	900	1988	260.00	300-500
1992	Hollybush	1,200	1994	560.00	795
1991	Horsham Farmhouse	593	1995	180.00	200
1986	Housewives Choice	500	1987	98.00	750-1000
1988	Icomb Village Garden	900	1988	620.00	1300-1500

Marty Bell (continued)

YEAR ISSUE	EDITION LIMIT	YEAR RETD.	ISSUE PRICE	*QUOTE U.S.$
1988 Jasmine Thatch	900	1991	272.00	495
1989 Larkspur Cottage	900	1989	220.00	495
1985 Little Boxford	500	1987	78.00	300-900
1991 Little Timbers	900	1992	130.00	130
1987 Little Tulip Thatch	500	1988	120.00	400-700
1990 Little Well Thatch	950	1990	130.00	150-250
1990 Longparish Cottage	900	1991	368.00	650
1990 Longstock Lane	900	1990	130.00	295
1986 Lorna Doone Cottage	500	1987	380.00	7000-8000
1990 Lower Brockhampton Manor	900	1990	640.00	1800
1988 Lullabye Cottage	900	1988	220.00	300-400
1987 May Cottage	900	1988	120.00	200-699
1988 Meadow School	816	1993	220.00	350
1985 Meadowlark Cottage	500	1987	78.00	450-699
1987 Millpond, Stockbridge, The	500	1987	120.00	1100
1987 Morning Glory Cottage	500	1988	120.00	450-599
1988 Morning's Glow	1,800	1989	280.00	320-650
1988 Murrle Cottage	1,800	1988	220.00	450-650
1983 Nestlewood	500	1987	300.00	2500
1989 Northcote Lane	1,160	1993	88.00	88
1989 Old Beams Cottage	900	1990	368.00	650
1988 Old Bridge, Grasmere	453	1993	640.00	640
1990 Old Hertfordshire Thatch	900	1990	396.00	2000
1993 Old Mother Hubbard's Cottage	2-Yr.	1995	230.00	250
1989 Overbrook	827	1993	220.00	350
1992 Pangbourne on Thames	900	1994	304.00	675
1984 Penshurst Tea Rooms (Archival)	1,000	1988	335.00	950
1984 Penshurst Tea Rooms (Canvas)	500	1987	335.00	1500-3600
1989 Pride of Spring	1,200	1990	96.00	200-400
1988 Rodway Cottage	900	1989	694.00	700-1500
1989 Rose Bedroom, The	515	1993	388.00	388
1990 Sanctuary	900	1992	220.00	450
1982 Sandhills Cottage	S/O	1987	38.00	38
1988 Sandy Lane Thatch	375	1993	380.00	500
1982 School Lane Cottage	S/O	1987	38.00	38
1993 Selborne Cottage	750	1995	300.00	318
1988 Shere Village Antiques	900	1988	272.00	304-699
1981 Spring in the Santa Ynez	500	1984	400.00	1100
1991 Springtime at Scotney	1,200	1992	730.00	950-1200
1989 St. Martin's Ashurst	243	1993	344.00	344
1990 Summer's Garden	900	1990	78.00	400-800
1985 Summers Glow	500	1987	98.00	600-1000
1987 Sunrise Thatch	900	1988	120.00	200-300
1985 Surrey Garden House	500	1986	98.00	850-1499
1985 Sweet Pine Cottage	500	1987	78.00	350-1499
1988 Sweet Twilight	900	1988	220.00	350-600
1990 Sweetheart Thatch	900	1993	220.00	375
1991 Tea Time	900	1991	130.00	300
1994 Tea With Miss Teddy	350	1995	128.00	128
1982 Thatchcolm Cottage	S/O	1987	38.00	38
1989 The Thimble Pub	641	1993	344.00	344
1993 Tithe Barn Cottage	308	1995	368.00	398
1991 Upper Chute	900	1991	496.00	1200
1987 The Vicar's Gate	500	1988	110.00	700-900
1987 Wakehurst Place	900	1988	480.00	1750
1987 Well Cottage, Sandy Lane	500	1988	440.00	650-1500
1991 Wepham Cottage	1,200	1991	396.00	1200
1984 West Kington Dell	500	1988	215.00	650
1992 West Sussex Roses (Archival)	1,200	1993	96.00	96
1990 Weston Manor	900	1995	694.00	742
1987 White Lilac Thatch	900	1988	260.00	400-700
1992 Wild Rose Cottage	155	1993	248.00	248
1985 Windsong Cottage	500	1987	156.00	350-799
1991 Windward Cottage, Rye	1,100	1991	228.00	895
1986 York Garden Shop	500	1988	98.00	250-999

Mill Pond Press

Bateman - R. Bateman

YEAR ISSUE	EDITION LIMIT	YEAR RETD.	ISSUE PRICE	*QUOTE U.S.$
1982 Above the River-Trumpeter Swans	950	1984	200.00	750-850
1984 Across the Sky-Snow Geese	950	1985	220.00	675-825
1980 African Amber-Lioness Pair	950	1980	175.00	425-475
1979 African Glow-Snowy Owl	950	1979	125.00	500
1990 Air, The Forest and The Watch	42,558	N/A	325.00	325
1984 Along the Ridge-Grizzly Bears	950	1984	200.00	825-1000
1984 American Goldfinch-Winter Dress	950	1984	75.00	125
1979 Among the Leaves-Cottontail Rabbit	950	1980	75.00	1000
1980 Antarctic Elements	950	1980	125.00	170
1991 Arctic Cliff-White Wolves	13,000	1991	325.00	345
1982 Arctic Evening-White Wolf	950	1982	185.00	1025
1980 Arctic Family-Polar Bears	950	1980	150.00	1200-1300
1992 Arctic Landscape-Polar Bear	5,000	N/A	345.00	345
1992 Arctic Landscape-Polar Bear-Premier Ed.	450		800.00	800
1982 Arctic Portrait-White Gyrfalcon	950	1982	175.00	325
1985 Arctic Tern Pair	950	1985	175.00	175
1981 Artist and His Dog	950	1983	150.00	450
1980 Asleep on Hemlock-Screech Owl	950	1980	125.00	585
1991 At the Cliff-Bobcat	12,500	1991	325.00	325
1992 At the Feeder-Cardinal	950	1992	125.00	150
1987 At the Nest-Secretary Birds	950	1987	290.00	290
1982 At the Roadside-Red-Tailed Hawk	950	1984	185.00	850
1980 Autumn Overture-Moose	950	1980	245.00	2000
1980 Awesome Land-American Elk	950	1980	245.00	2350
1989 Backlight-Mute Swan	950	1989	275.00	450
1982 Bald Eagle Portrait	950	1983	185.00	280
1982 Baobab Tree and Impala	950	1986	245.00	300
1980 Barn Owl in the Churchyard	950	1981	125.00	700
1989 Barn Swallow and Horse Collar	950	N/A	225.00	225
1984 Barn Swallows in August	950	N/A	245.00	350
1992 Beach Grass and Tree Frog	1,250		345.00	350

YEAR ISSUE	EDITION LIMIT	YEAR RETD.	ISSUE PRICE	*QUOTE U.S.$
1985 Beaver Pond Reflections	950	1985	185.00	250
1984 Big Country, Pronghorn Antelope	950	1985	185.00	185
1986 Black Eagle	950	1986	200.00	200
1993 Black Jaguar-Premier Edition	450	N/A	850.00	1000
1986 Black-Tailed Deer in the Olympics	950	1986	245.00	245
1986 Blacksmith Plover	950	1986	185.00	185
1991 Bluebird and Blossoms	4,500		235.00	235
1991 Bluebird and Blossoms-Prestige Ed.	450		625.00	625
1980 Bluffing Bull-African Elephant	950	1981	135.00	1100
1981 Bright Day-Atlantic Puffins	950	1985	175.00	875
1989 Broad-Tailed Hummingbird Pair	950	1989	225.00	225
1980 Brown Pelican and Pilings	950	1980	165.00	1500
1979 Bull Moose	950	1979	125.00	650
1978 By the Tracks-Killdeer	950	1980	75.00	1025-1150
1983 Call of the Wild-Bald Eagle	950	1983	200.00	200
1985 Canada Geese Family(stone lithograph)	260	1985	350.00	1200
1985 Canada Geese Over the Escarpment	950	1985	135.00	225
1986 Canada Geese With Young	950	1986	195.00	215
1981 Canada Geese-Nesting	950	1981	295.00	2000
1993 Cardinal and Sumac	2,510	N/A	235.00	235
1988 Cardinal and Wild Apples	12,183	1988	235.00	235
1989 Catching The Light-Barn Owl	2,000	1990	295.00	295
1988 Cattails, Fireweed and Yellowthroat	950	1988	235.00	235
1989 Centennial Farm	950	1989	295.00	295
1988 The Challenge-Bull Moose	10,671		325.00	325
1980 Chapel Doors	950	1985	135.00	375
1986 Charging Rhino	950	1986	325.00	650-900
1982 Cheetah Profile	950	1985	245.00	350
1978 Cheetah With Cubs	950	1980	95.00	450
1988 Cherrywood with Juncos	950	1988	245.00	245
1990 Chinstrap Penguin	810	1991	150.00	150
1992 Clan of the Raven	950	1992	235.00	425-540
1981 Clear Night-Wolves	950	1981	245.00	4600-5200
1988 Colonial Garden	950	1988	245.00	245
1987 Continuing Generations-Spotted Owls	950	1987	525.00	600
1991 Cottage Lane-Red Fox	950	1991	285.00	250
1984 Cougar Portrait	950	1984	95.00	250
1979 Country Lane-Pheasants	950	1981	85.00	600
1981 Courting Pair-Whistling Swans	950	1981	245.00	300
1981 Courtship Display-Wild Turkey	950	1981	175.00	225
1980 Coyote in Winter Sage	950	1980	245.00	2000-3100
1992 Cries of Courtship-Red Crowned Cranes	950	1992	350.00	500-600
1980 Curious Glance-Red Fox	950	1980	135.00	600-975
1986 Dark Gyrfalcon	950	1986	225.00	300
1993 Day Lilies and Dragonflies	1,250		345.00	345
1982 Dipper By the Waterfall	950	1985	165.00	600
1989 Dispute Over Prey	950		325.00	325
1989 Distant Danger-Raccoon	1,600	1989	225.00	225
1984 Down for a Drink-Morning Dove	950	1985	135.00	250
1978 Downy Woodpecker on Goldenrod Gall	950	1979	50.00	900-1200
1988 Dozing Lynx	950	1988	335.00	1250-1495
1986 Driftwood Perch-Striped Swallows	950		195.00	195
1983 Early Snowfall-Ruffed Grouse	950	1985	195.00	225
1983 Early Spring-Bluebird	950	1984	185.00	600-875
1981 Edge of the Ice-Ermine	950	1981	175.00	250-400
1982 Edge of the Woods-Whitetail Deer, w/Book	950	1983	745.00	1300
1991 Elephant Cow and Calf	950	1991	300.00	375
1986 Elephant Herd and Sandgrouse	950	1986	235.00	320
1991 Encounter in the Bush-African Lions	950	1991	295.00	295
1987 End of Season-Grizzly	950	1987	325.00	575-600
1991 Endangered Spaces-Grizzly	4,008	1991	325.00	325
1985 Entering the Water-Common Gulls	950	1986	195.00	200
1986 European Robin and Hydrangeas	950		130.00	275
1989 Evening Call-Common Loon	950	1989	235.00	450-540
1980 Evening Grosbeak	950	1980	125.00	700
1983 Evening Idyll-Mute Swans	950	1984	245.00	650
1981 Evening Light-White Gyrfalcon	950	1981	245.00	775-975
1979 Evening Snowfall-American Elk	950	1980	150.00	1200
1987 Everglades	950	1987	360.00	360
1980 Fallen Willow-Snowy Owl	950	1980	200.00	500-700
1987 Farm Lane and Blue Jays	950	1987	225.00	400
1986 Fence Post and Burdock	950	1987	130.00	130
1991 Fluid Power-Orca	290		2500.00	2500
1980 Flying High-Golden Eagle	950	1980	150.00	1000
1982 Fox at the Granary	950	1985	165.00	275
1982 Frosty Morning-Blue Jay	950	1982	185.00	800-900
1982 Gallinule Family	950		135.00	135
1981 Galloping Herd-Giraffes	950	1981	175.00	1200
1985 Gambel's Quail Pair	950	1985	95.00	300
1982 Gentoo Penguins and Whale Bones	950	1986	205.00	550-600
1983 Ghost of the North-Great Gray Owl	950	1983	200.00	1700
1982 Golden Crowned Kinglet and Rhododendron	950	1982	150.00	1900
1979 Golden Eagle	950	1981	150.00	235
1985 Golden Eagle Portrait	950	1987	115.00	175
1989 Goldfinch In the Meadow	1,600	1990	150.00	150
1983 Goshawk and Ruffed Grouse	950	1984	185.00	500
1988 Grassy Bank-Great Blue Heron	950	1988	285.00	285
1981 Gray Squirrel	950	1981	180.00	650
1979 Great Blue Heron	950	1980	125.00	800-1200
1987 Great Blue Heron in Flight	950	1987	295.00	400
1988 Great Crested Grebe	950	1987	135.00	135
1987 Great Egret Preening	950	1987	315.00	600-725
1983 Great Horned Owl in the White Pine	950	1983	225.00	450
1987 Greater Kudu Bull	950	1987	145.00	145

YEAR ISSUE	EDITION LIMIT	YEAR RETD.	ISSUE PRICE	*QUOTE U.S.$
1993 Grizzly and Cubs	2,250		335.00	400
1991 Gulls on Pilings	1,950		265.00	265
1988 Hardwood Forest-White-Tailed Buck	630	1988	300.00	1500-1600
1988 Harlequin Duck-Bull Kelp-Executive Ed.	623	1988	550.00	550
1988 Harlequin Duck-Bull Kelp-Gold Plated	950	1988	300.00	300
1980 Heron on the Rocks	950	1980	75.00	300
1981 High Camp at Dusk	950	1985	245.00	450
1979 High Country-Stone Sheep	950	1982	125.00	600
1987 High Kingdom-Snow Leopard	950	1987	325.00	500
1990 Homage to Ahmed	290		3300.00	3300
1984 Hooded Mergansers in Winter	950	1984	210.00	400
1984 House Finch and Yucca	950	1984	95.00	170
1986 House Sparrow	950	1986	125.00	225
1987 House Sparrows and Bittersweet	950	1987	220.00	350-400
1986 Hummingbird Pair Diptych	950	1986	330.00	650
1987 Hurricane Lake-Wood Ducks	950		135.00	200
1981 In for the Evening	950	1981	150.00	1750-1850
1994 In His Prime-Mallard	950	N/A	195.00	250-350
1984 In the Brier Patch-Cottontail	950	1985	165.00	350
1986 In the Grass-Lioness	950	1986	245.00	245
1985 In the Highlands-Golden Eagle	950	1985	235.00	350
1985 In the Mountains-Osprey	950	1987	95.00	150
1992 Intrusion-Mountain Gorilla	2,250		325.00	325
1990 Ireland House	950	1990	265.00	265
1985 Irish Cottage and Wagtail	950	1990	175.00	200
1992 Junco in Winter	1,250	1992	185.00	185
1990 Keeper of the Land	290		3300.00	3300
1993 Kestrel and Grasshopper	1,250		335.00	335
1979 King of the Realm	950	1979	125.00	600
1987 King Penguins	950	1987	130.00	150
1981 Kingfisher and Aspen	950	1981	225.00	950
1980 Kingfisher in Winter	950	1981	175.00	1000
1980 Kittiwake Greeting	950	1980	75.00	335-380
1981 Last Look-Bighorn Sheep	950	1986	195.00	225
1987 Late Winter-Black Squirrel	950	1987	165.00	165
1981 Laughing Gull and Horseshoe Crab	950	1981	125.00	125
1982 Leopard Ambush	950	1986	245.00	450
1988 Leopard and Thomson Gazelle Kill	950	1988	275.00	275
1985 Leopard at Seronera	950	1985	175.00	250
1980 Leopard in a Sausage Tree	950	1980	150.00	2300-2600
1984 Lily Pads and Loon	950	1984	200.00	1250-1400
1987 Lion and Wildebeest	950	1987	265.00	265
1980 Lion at Tsavo	950	1983	150.00	295
1978 Lion Cubs	950	1981	125.00	295
1987 Lioness at Serengeti	950	1987	325.00	325
1985 Lions in the Grass	950	1985	265.00	800
1981 Little Blue Heron	950	1981	95.00	200
1982 Lively Pair-Chickadees	950	1982	160.00	330-400
1983 Loon Study	950	1983	200.00	850
1990 Lunging Heron	1,250	1990	225.00	225
1978 Majesty on the Wing-Bald Eagle	950	1979	150.00	2200-2500
1988 Mallard Family at Sunset	950	1988	235.00	235
1986 Mallard Family-Misty Marsh	950	1986	130.00	130
1986 Mallard Pair-Early Winter	41,740	1986	135.00	200
1985 Mallard Pair-Early Winter 24K Gold	950	1986	1650.00	2000
1986 Mallard Pair-Early Winter Gold Plated	7,691	1986	250.00	375
1989 Mangrove Morning-Roseate Spoonbills	2,000	1989	325.00	325
1991 Mangrove Shadow-Common Egret	1,250		285.00	285
1993 Marbled Murrelet	55	1993	1200.00	1200
1986 Marginal Meadow	950	1986	220.00	220
1979 Master of the Herd-African Buffalo	950	1980	150.00	1950
1984 May Maple-Scarlet Tanager	950	1984	175.00	600
1982 Meadow's Edge-Mallard	950	1982	175.00	600
1982 Merganser Family in Hiding	950	1982	200.00	575
1994 Meru Dusk-Lesser Kudu	950		135.00	135
1989 Midnight-Black Wolf	25,352	1989	325.00	1350-1600
1980 Mischief on the Prowl-Raccoon	950	1980	85.00	200
1980 Misty Coast-Gulls	950	1980	135.00	400
1984 Misty Lake-Osprey	950	1985	95.00	200
1981 Misty Morning-Loons	950	1981	150.00	1400
1986 Moose at Water's Edge	950	1986	130.00	260
1990 Morning Cove-Common Loon	950	1990	165.00	165
1985 Morning Dew-Roe Deer	950	1985	175.00	175
1983 Morning on the Flats-Bison	950	1983	200.00	300
1984 Morning on the River-Trumpeter Swans	950	1984	185.00	350
1990 Mossy Branches-Spotted Owl	4,500	1990	300.00	385-425
1990 Mowed Meadow	950	1990	190.00	190
1986 Mule Deer in Aspen	950	1986	175.00	175
1983 Mule Deer in Winter	950	1983	200.00	250
1988 Muskoka Lake-Common Loons	2,500	1988	265.00	300
1989 Near Glenburnie	950		265.00	265
1983 New Season-American Robin	950	1983	200.00	375
1986 Northern Reflections-Loon Family	8,631	1986	255.00	1300
1985 Old Whaling Base and Fur Seals	950	1985	195.00	200
1987 Old Willow and Mallards	950	1987	325.00	325
1980 On the Alert-Chipmunk	950	1980	60.00	350
1993 On the Brink-River Otters	1,250		345.00	345
1985 On the Garden Wall	950	1985	115.00	300
1985 Orca Procession	950	1985	245.00	2250
1981 Osprey Family	950	1981	245.00	245
1983 Osprey in the Rain	950	1983	110.00	500
1987 Otter Study	950	1987	235.00	425-475
1981 Pair of Skimmers	950	1981	150.00	150
1988 Panda's At Play (stone lithograph)	160	1988	400.00	1200
1994 Path of the Panther	1,950		295.00	295
1984 Peregrine and Ruddy Turnstones	950	1985	200.00	425-500
1985 Peregrine Falcon and White-Throated Swifts	950	1985	245.00	550

GRAPHICS

YEAR ISSUE		EDITION LIMIT	YEAR RETD.	ISSUE PRICE	*QUOTE U.S.$
1987	Peregrine Falcon on the Cliff-Stone Litho	525	1988	350.00	350
1983	Pheasant in Cornfield	950	1983	200.00	300-395
1988	Pheasants at Dusk	950	1988	325.00	485-550
1982	Pileated Woodpecker on Beech Tree	950	1982	175.00	900
1990	Pintails in Spring	9,651	1989	135.00	300
1982	Pioneer Memories-Magpie Pair	950	1982	175.00	175
1987	Plowed Field-Snowy Owl	950	1987	145.00	325
1990	Polar Bear	290	1990	3300.00	3300
1982	Polar Bear Profile	950	1982	210.00	1700-1900
1982	Polar Bears at Bafin Island	950	1982	245.00	875
1990	Power Play-Rhinoceros	950	1990	320.00	350
1980	Prairie Evening-Short-Eared Owl	950	1983	150.00	325
1994	Predator Portfolio-Black Bear	950		475.00	475
1992	Predator Portfolio/Cougar	950		465.00	465
1993	Predator Portfolio/Grizzly	950		475.00	475
1993	Predator Portfolio/Polar Bear	950		485.00	485
1993	Predator Portfolio/Wolf	950	N/A	475.00	475
1988	Preening Pair-Canada Geese	950	1988	235.00	235
1987	Pride of Autumn-Canada Goose	15,294	1987	135.00	245
1986	Proud Swimmer-Snow Goose	950	1986	185.00	185
1989	Pumpkin Time	950		195.00	
1982	Queen Anne's Lace and American Goldfinch	950	1982	150.00	700-800
1984	Ready for Flight-Peregrine Falcon	950	1984	185.00	450
1982	Ready for the Hunt-Snowy Owl	950	1982	245.00	550
1993	Reclining Snow Leopard	1,250		335.00	335
1988	Red Crossbills	950	1988	125.00	125
1984	Red Fox on the Prowl	950	1984	245.00	550-650
1982	Red Squirrel	950	1982	175.00	325
1986	Red Wolf	950	1986	250.00	275
1981	Red-Tailed Hawk by the Cliff	950	1981	245.00	500-600
1981	Red-Winged Blackbird and Rail Fence	950	1981	195.00	225
1984	Reeds	950	1984	185.00	425
1986	A Resting Place-Cape Buffalo	950	1986	265.00	265
1986	Resting Place-Cape Buffalo	950		265.00	265
1987	Rhino at Ngoro Ngoro	950	1988	325.00	325
1993	River Otter-North American Wilderness	350		325.00	500
1993	River Otters	290		1500.00	1500
1986	Robins at the Nest	950	1986	185.00	195
1987	Rocky Point-October	950	1987	195.00	225
1980	Rocky Wilderness-Cougar	950	1980	175.00	975-1100
1990	Rolling Waves-Lesser Scaup	3,330		125.00	125
1993	Rose-breasted Grosbeak	290		450.00	450
1981	Rough-Legged Hawk in the Elm	950	1991	175.00	175
1981	Royal Family-Mute Swans	950	1981	245.00	750
1983	Ruby Throat and Columbine	950	1983	150.00	2200
1987	Ruddy Turnstones	950	1987	175.00	175
1994	Salt Spring Sheep	1,250		235.00	235
1981	Sarah E. with Gulls	950	1981	245.00	2200
1993	Saw Whet Owl and Wild Grapes	950		185.00	185
1991	The Scolding-Chickadees & Screech Owl	12,500		235.00	235
1991	Sea Otter Study	950	1991	150.00	225
1993	Shadow of the Rain Forest	9,000	1993	345.00	435-500
1981	Sheer Drop-Mountain Goats	950	1981	245.00	1700-2400
1988	Shelter	950	1988	325.00	800-1275
1992	Siberian Tiger	4,500		325.00	325
1984	Smallwood	950	1985	200.00	500
1990	Snow Leopard	290	1990	2500.00	1550-2400
1985	Snowy Hemlock-Barred Owl	950	1985	245.00	245
1994	Snowy Nap-Tiger	950	1994	185.00	475-600
1994	Snowy Owl	150	N/A	265.00	600-750
1987	Snowy Owl and Milkweed	950	1987	235.00	600
1983	Snowy Owl on Driftwood	950	1983	245.00	650
1984	Spirits of the Forest	950	1984	170.00	2250
1986	Split Rails-Snow Buntings	950	1986	220.00	220
1980	Spring Cardinal	950	1980	125.00	400-500
1982	Spring Marsh-Pintail Pair	950	1982	200.00	300
1980	Spring Thaw-Killdeer	950	1980	85.00	150
1982	Still Morning-Herring Gulls	950	1982	200.00	200
1987	Stone Sheep Ram	950	1987	175.00	175
1985	Stream Bank June	950	1986	160.00	175
1984	Stretching-Canada Goose	950	1984	225.00	2300
1985	Strutting-Ring-Necked Pheasant	950	1985	225.00	450
1985	Sudden Blizzard-Red-Tailed Hawk	950	1985	245.00	475
1990	Summer Morning Pasture	950	1990	175.00	175
1984	Summer Morning-Loon	950	1984	185.00	1000
1986	Summertime-Polar Bears	950	1986	225.00	250
1979	Surf and Sanderlings	950	1980	65.00	1200-1800
1981	Swift Fox	950	1981	175.00	300
1986	Swift Fox Study	950	1986	115.00	150
1987	Sylvan Stream-Mute Swans	950	1987	125.00	175
1984	Tadpole Time	950	1985	135.00	400-500
1988	Tawny Owl In Beech	950		325.00	325
1992	Tembo (African Elephant)	1,550		350.00	350
1984	Tiger at Dawn	950	1984	225.00	1800
1983	Tiger Portrait	950	1983	130.00	425
1988	Tree Swallow over Pond	950	1988	290.00	290
1991	Trumpeter Swan Family	290		2500.00	2500
1985	Trumpeter Swans and Aspen	950	1985	245.00	450
1979	Up in the Pine-Great Horned Owl	950	1981	150.00	650-750
1980	Vantage Point	950	1980	245.00	800-975
1993	Vigilance	9,500		330.00	330
1989	Vulture And Wildebeest	550		295.00	295
1981	Watchful Repose-Black Bear	950	1981	245.00	475
1985	Weathered Branch-Bald Eagle	950	1985	115.00	300
1991	Whistling Swan-Lake Erie	1,950		325.00	375
1979	White Encounter-Polar Bear	950	1980	245.00	3750
1990	White on White-Snowshoe Hare	950	1990	195.00	400

YEAR ISSUE		EDITION LIMIT	YEAR RETD.	ISSUE PRICE	*QUOTE U.S.$
1982	White World-Dall Sheep	950	1982	200.00	600
1985	White-Breasted Nuthatch on a Beech Tree	950	1985	175.00	300
1980	White-Footed Mouse in Wintergreen	950	1980	60.00	650
1982	White-Footed Mouse on Aspen	950	1983	90.00	180
1992	White-Tailed Deer Through the Birches	10,000		335.00	335
1984	White-Throated Sparrow and Pussy Willow	950	1984	150.00	575
1991	Wide Horizon-Tundra Swans	2,862		325.00	350
1991	Wide Horizon-Tundra Swans Companion	2,862		325.00	325
1986	Wildbeest	950		185.00	185
1982	Willet on the Shore	950	N/A	125.00	185
1979	Wily and Wary-Red Fox	950	1979	265.00	1025
1984	Window into Ontario	950	1984	265.00	1300
1983	Winter Barn	950	1984	170.00	400
1979	Winter Cardinal	950	1979	75.00	1000-2000
1992	Winter Coat	1,250		245.00	245
1985	Winter Companion	950	1985	175.00	600-850
1980	Winter Elm-American Kestrel	950	1980	135.00	800
1986	Winter in the Mountains-Raven	950	1987	200.00	200
1981	Winter Mist-Great Horned Owl	950	1981	245.00	550
1980	Winter Song-Chickadees	950	1980	95.00	550
1984	Winter Sunset-Moose	950	1984	245.00	1600
1992	Winter Trackers	4,500	1992	335.00	335
1981	Winter Wren	950	1981	135.00	400
1983	Winter-Lady Cardinal	950	1983	200.00	1100
1979	Winter-Snowshoe Hare	950	1980	95.00	1050
1987	Wise One, The	950	1987	325.00	450-595
1979	Wolf Pack in Moonlight	950	1979	95.00	2150
1994	Wolf Pair in the Snow	290		795.00	795
1994	Wolverine Porfolio	950		275.00	275
1983	Wolves on the Trail	950	1983	225.00	400-475
1985	Wood Bison Portrait	950	1985	165.00	200
1983	Woodland Drummer-Ruffed Grouse	950	1984	185.00	200
1981	Wrangler's Campsite-Gray Jay	950	1981	195.00	700
1979	Yellow-Rumped Warbler	950	1980	50.00	425-490
1978	Young Barn Swallow	950	1979	75.00	575
1983	Young Elf Owl-Old Saguaro	950	1983	95.00	325
1991	Young Giraffe	290		850.00	850
1989	Young Kittiwake	950		195.00	195
1988	Young Sandhill-Cranes	950	1988	325.00	325
1989	Young Snowy Owl	950	1990	195.00	195

Brenders - C. Brenders

YEAR ISSUE		EDITION LIMIT	YEAR RETD.	ISSUE PRICE	*QUOTE U.S.$
1986	The Acrobat's Meal-Red Squirrel	950	1989	65.00	465-600
1988	Apple Harvest	950	1989	115.00	350-580
1989	The Apple Lover	1,500	1990	125.00	250-275
1987	Autumn Lady	950	1989	150.00	800
1991	The Balance of Nature	1,950		225.00	225
1993	Black Sphinx	950		235.00	235
1986	Black-Capped Chickadees	950	1989	40.00	200-400
1990	Blond Beauty	1,950	1990	185.00	185
1986	Bluebirds	950	1989	40.00	225
1988	California Quail	950	1989	95.00	350-450
1991	Calm Before the Challenge -Moose	1,950	1991	225.00	225
1988	Close to Mom	950	1988	150.00	1200
1993	Collectors Group (Butterfly Collections)	290		375.00	375
1986	Colorful Playground-Cottontails	950	1989	75.00	550
1989	The Companions	18,036	1989	200.00	500-800
1994	Dall Sheep Portrait	950		115.00	115
1992	Den Mother-Pencil Sketch	2,500	1992	135.00	135
1992	Den Mother-Wolf Family	25,000	1992	250.00	250-400
1986	Disturbed Daydreams	950	1989	95.00	425
1987	Double Trouble-Raccoons	950	1988	120.00	600-750
1993	European Group (Butterfly Collections)	290		375.00	375
1993	Exotic Group (Butterfly Collections)	290		375.00	375
1989	Forager's Reward-Red Squirrel	1,250	1989	135.00	135
1988	Forest Sentinel-Bobcat	950	1988	135.00	550
1990	Full House-Fox Family	20,106	1990	235.00	235
1990	Ghostly Quiet-Spanish Lynx	1,950	1990	200.00	200
1986	Golden Season-Gray Squirrel	950	1987	85.00	600-700
1986	Harvest Time-Chipmunk	950	1989	65.00	270-400
1988	Hidden In the Pines-Immature Great Hor	950	1988	175.00	1000-1125
1988	High Adventure-Black Bear Cubs	950	1989	105.00	400
1988	A Hunter's Dream	950	1989	165.00	1100
1993	In Northern Hunting Grounds	1,750		375.00	375
1992	Island Shores-Snowy Egret	2,500		250.00	250
1987	Ivory-Billed Woodpecker	950	1989	95.00	600
1988	Long Distance Hunters	950	1988	175.00	1350-1900
1989	Lord of the Marshes	1,250	1989	135.00	135
1986	Meadowlark	950	1989	40.00	320-400
1989	Merlins at the Nest	1,250	1989	165.00	200-375
1985	Mighty Intruder	950	1989	95.00	250
1987	Migration Fever-Barn Swallows	950	1989	150.00	275
1990	The Monarch is Alive	4,071	1990	265.00	275-375
1993	Mother of Pearls	5,000		275.00	275
1990	Mountain Baby-Bighorn Sheep	1,950		165.00	165
1987	Mysterious Visitor-Barn Owl	950	1989	150.00	325
1993	Narrow Escape-Chipmunk	1,750		150.00	150
1991	The Nesting Season-House Sparrow	1,950	1991	195.00	200
1989	Northern Cousins-Black Squirrels	950	1989	150.00	150-225
1984	On the Alert-Red Fox	950	1986	95.00	350
1990	On the Old Farm Door	1,500	1990	225.00	250
1991	One to One-Gray Wolf	10,000	1991	245.00	400-500
1992	Pathfinder-Red Fox	5,000	1992	245.00	245

YEAR ISSUE		EDITION LIMIT	YEAR RETD.	ISSUE PRICE	*QUOTE U.S.$
1984	Playful Pair-Chipmunks	950	1987	60.00	500
1994	Power and Grace	2,500	1994	265.00	500-795
1989	The Predator's Walk	1,250	1989	150.00	150
1992	Red Fox Study	1,250	1992	125.00	125
1994	Riverbank Kestrel	2,500		225.00	225
1988	Roaming the Plains-Pronghorns	950	1989	150.00	150
1986	Robins	950	1989	40.00	125
1993	Rocky Camp-Cougar Family	5,000		275.00	275
1993	Rocky Camp-Cubs	950		225.00	225
1992	Rocky Kingdom-Bighorn Sheep	1,750		255.00	255
1991	Shadows in the Grass-Young Cougars	1,950	1991	235.00	235
1990	Shoreline Quartet-White Ibis	1,950		265.00	265
1984	Silent Hunter-Great Horned Owl	950	1987	95.00	450
1984	Silent Passage	950	1988	150.00	400
1990	Small Talk	1,500	1990	125.00	125
1992	Snow Leopard Portrait	1,750	1993	150.00	150
1990	Spring Fawn	1,500	1990	125.00	300
1990	Squirrel's Dish	1,950		110.00	110
1989	Steller's Jay	1,250	1989	135.00	175
1991	Study for One to One	1,950		120.00	200
1993	Summer Roses-Winter Wren	1,500	1993	250.00	500
1989	The Survivors-Canada Geese	1,500	1989	225.00	475-700
1994	Take Five-Canadian Lynx	1,500		245.00	245
1988	Talk on the Old Fence	950	1988	165.00	600-800
1990	A Threatened Symbol	1,950	1990	145.00	145-195
1989	Tundra Summit-Arctic Wolves	6,061	1994	265.00	335
1984	Waterside Encounter	950	1987	95.00	1000
1987	White Elegance-Trumpeter Swans	950	1989	115.00	500
1993	White Wolves-North American Wilderness Portfolio	350		325.00	475
1988	Witness of a Past-Bison	950	1990	110.00	110
1992	Wolf Scout #1	2,500	1992	105.00	105
1992	Wolf Scout #2	2,500	1992	105.00	105
1991	Wolf Study	950	1991	125.00	125
1987	Yellow-Bellied Marmot	950	1989	95.00	375-750
1989	A Young Generation	1,250	1989	165.00	275-400

Calle - P. Calle

YEAR ISSUE		EDITION LIMIT	YEAR RETD.	ISSUE PRICE	*QUOTE U.S.$
1981	Almost Home	950	1981	150.00	150
1991	Almost There	950	1991	165.00	165
1989	And A Good Book For Company	950	1990	135.00	435
1993	And A Grizzly Claw Necklace	750		150.00	150
1981	And Still Miles to Go	950	1981	245.00	400
1981	Andrew At The Falls	950	1981	150.00	150
1989	The Beaver Men	950		125.00	125
1984	A Brace for the Spit	950	1985	110.00	275
1980	Caring for the Herd	950	1981	110.00	110
1985	The Carrying Place	950	1990	195.00	195
1984	Chance Encounter	950	1986	225.00	325
1981	Chief High Pipe (Color)	950	1981	265.00	265
1980	Chief High Pipe (Pencil)	950	1980	75.00	175
1980	Chief Joseph-Man of Peace	950	1980	135.00	165
1990	Children of Walpi	350		160.00	160
1990	The Doll Maker	950		95.00	95
1982	Emerging from the Woods	950	1987	110.00	110
1981	End of a Long Day	950	1981	150.00	225
1984	Fate of the Late Migrant	950	1985	110.00	375
1983	Free Spirits	950	1985	195.00	475
1983	Free Trapper Study	550	1985	75.00	125-300
1981	Fresh Tracks	950	1985	150.00	150
1981	Friend of Foe	950		125.00	125
1981	Friends	950	1987	150.00	150
1985	The Frontier Blacksmith	950		245.00	245
1989	The Fur Trapper	550		75.00	175
1982	Generations in the Valley	950	1987	245.00	245
1985	The Grandmother	950	1987	400.00	400
1989	The Great Moment	950		350.00	350
1992	Hunter of Geese	950		125.00	125
1993	I Call Him Friend	950		235.00	235
1983	In Search of Beaver	950	1983	225.00	600
1991	In the Beginning . . . Friends	1,250	1993	250.00	275
1987	In the Land of the Giants	950	1988	245.00	900
1990	Interrupted Journey	1,750	1991	265.00	265
1990	Interrupted Journey-Prestige Ed.	290	1991	465.00	465
1987	Into the Great Alone	950	1988	245.00	700-850
1981	Just Over the Ridge	950	1982	245.00	245
1980	Landmark Tree	950	1980	125.00	225
1991	Man of the Fur Trade	550		110.00	110
1984	Mountain Man	550	1988	95.00	225
1993	Mountain Man-North American Wilderness Portfolio	350		325.00	N/A
1989	The Mountain Men	300	1989	400.00	400
1989	Navajo Madonna	650		95.00	95
1988	A New Day	950		150.00	150
1981	One With The Land	950	1981	245.00	250
1992	Out of the Silence	2,500		265.00	265
1992	Out of the Silence-Prestige	290		465.00	465
1981	Pause at the Lower Falls	950	1981	110.00	250
1980	Prayer to the Great Mystery	950	1980	245.00	245
1982	Return to Camp	950	1982	245.00	500
1991	The Silenced Honkers	1,250		250.00	250
1980	Sioux Chief	950	1980	85.00	140
1986	Snow Hunter	950	1988	150.00	225
1980	Something for the Pot	950		175.00	1100
1990	Son of Sitting Bull	950		95.00	675
1985	Storyteller of the Mountains	950	1985	225.00	675
1983	Strays From the Flyway	950	1983	195.00	225
1981	Teton Friends	950		125.00	125
1991	They Call Me Matthew	950		125.00	125
1992	Through the Tall Grass	950		175.00	175
1988	Trapper at Rest	550		95.00	95

YEAR	ISSUE	EDITION LIMIT	YEAR RETD.	ISSUE PRICE	*QUOTE U.S. $
1982	Two from the Flock	950	1982	245.00	500
1980	View from the Heights	950	1980	245.00	245
1988	Voyageurs and Waterfowl...Constant	950	1988	265.00	700-900
1980	When Snow Came Early	950	1980	85.00	250-340
1984	When Trails Cross	950	1984	245.00	750
1991	When Trails Grow Cold	2,500		265.00	265
1991	When Trails Grow Cold-Prestige Ed.	290	1991	465.00	465
1994	When Trappers Meet	750		165.00	165
1989	Where Eagles Fly	1,250	1990	265.00	350
1989	A Winter Feast	1,250	1989	265.00	375
1989	A Winter Feast-Prestige Ed.	290	1989	465.00	465
1981	Winter Hunter (Color)	950	1981	245.00	800
1980	Winter Hunter (Pencil)	950	1980	65.00	450
1983	A Winter Surprise	950	1984	195.00	500

Cross - T. Cross

1994	April	750		55.00	55
1994	August	750		55.00	55
1993	Ever Green	750		135.00	135
1993	Flame Catcher	750	1993	185.00	185
1993	Flicker, Flash and Twirl	525		165.00	165
1994	July	750		55.00	55
1994	June	750		55.00	55
1994	March	750		55.00	55
1994	May	750		55.00	55
1992	Shell Caster	750	1993	150.00	150
1993	Sheperds of Magic	750		135.00	135
1993	Spellbound	750		85.00	85
1994	Spring Forth	750		145.00	145
1992	Star Weaver	750	1993	150.00	150
1994	Summer Musings	750		145.00	145
1993	The Summons...And Then They Are One	750	1993	195.00	195
1994	When Water Takes to Air	750		135.00	135
1993	Wind Sifter	750	1993	150.00	150

Daly - J. Daly

1990	The Big Moment	1,500		125.00	125
1991	Cat's Cradle-Prestige Edition	950		450.00	450
1994	Catch of My Dreams	4,500		45.00	45
1994	Childhood Friends	950		110.00	110
1990	Confrontation	1,500	1992	85.00	85
1990	Contentment	1,500	1990	95.00	300-500
1992	Dominoes	1,500		155.00	155
1992	Favorite Gift	2,500	1992	175.00	175
1987	Favorite Reader	950	1990	85.00	250
1986	Flying High	950	1988	50.00	450-525
1992	The Flying Horse	950		325.00	325
1993	Good Company	1,500		155.00	155
1992	Her Secret Place	1,500	1992	135.00	200
1991	Home Team: Zero	1,500		150.00	150
1991	Homemade	1,500		125.00	125
1990	Honor and Allegiance	1,500	1993	110.00	110
1990	The Ice Man	1,500	1992	125.00	250-300
1992	The Immigrant Spirit	5,000		125.00	125
1992	The Immigrant Spirit-Prestige Ed.	950		125.00	125
1989	In the Doghouse	950	1990	75.00	300-425
1990	It's That Time Again	1,500		120.00	120
1992	Left Out	1,500		110.00	110
1989	Let's Play Ball	1,500	1991	75.00	200
1990	Make Believe	1,500	1990	75.00	275-400
1994	Mud Mates	950		150.00	150
1994	My Best Friends	950		85.00	85
1991	A New Beginning	5,000		125.00	125
1993	The New Citizen	5,000		125.00	125
1993	The New Citizen-Prestige Edition	950		125.00	125
1987	Odd Man Out	950	1988	85.00	85
1988	On Thin Ice	950	1993	95.00	295
1991	Pillars of a Nation-Charter Ed.	20,000		175.00	175
1992	Playmates	1,500	1992	155.00	350-395
1990	Radio Daze	1,500		150.00	150
1983	Saturday Night	950	1985	85.00	1125
1990	The Scholar	1,500	N/A	110.00	110
1993	Secret Admirer	1,500		150.00	150
1994	Slugger	950		75.00	75
1982	Spring Fever	950	1988	85.00	600
1993	Sunday Afternoon	1,500		150.00	150
1988	Territorial Rights	950	1990	85.00	350
1989	The Thief	1,500	1990	95.00	350-480
1989	The Thorn	1,500		125.00	350
1988	Tie Breaker	950	1990	95.00	220
1991	Time-Out	1,500	1993	125.00	125
1993	To All a Good Night	1,500		160.00	160
1992	Walking the Rails	1,500		175.00	175
1993	When I Grow Up	1,500		175.00	175
1994	Wind-Up, The	950		75.00	75
1988	Wiped Out	1,250	1990	125.00	375-500

Morrissey - D. Morrissey

1994	The Amazing Time Elevator	950		195.00	195
1993	Charting the Skies	1,250	1993	195.00	195
1993	Charting the Skies-Caprice Ed.	550	1993	375.00	375
1993	Draft of a Dream	175	1993	250.00	250
1994	The Dreamer's Trunk	1,500		195.00	195
1993	Drifting Closer	1,250		175.00	175
1993	The Mystic Mariner	750	1993	150.00	150
1993	The Redd Rocket	1,250		175.00	375
1994	The Redd Rocket-Pre-Flight	950	1993	110.00	110
1992	The Sandman's Ship of Dreams	750	1993	150.00	150
1994	Sighting off the Stern	950		135.00	135
1993	Sleeper Flight	1,250	1993	195.00	195

YEAR	ISSUE	EDITION LIMIT	YEAR RETD.	ISSUE PRICE	*QUOTE U.S.$
1993	The Telescope of Time	5,000		195.00	195

Olsen - G. Olsen

1993	Airship Adventures	750		150.00	150
1993	Angels of Christmas	750	1993	135.00	135
1993	Dress Rehearseal	750	1993	165.00	800
1993	The Fraternity Tree	750		195.00	195
1994	Little Girls Will Mothers Be	750	N/A	135.00	135
1994	Mother's Love	750	1994	165.00	165
1994	Summerhouse	750		165.00	165

Seerey-Lester - J. Seerey-Lester

1994	Abandoned	950		175.00	175
1986	Above the Treeline-Cougar	950	1986	130.00	130
1986	After the Fire-Grizzly	950	1990	95.00	95
1986	Along the Ice Floe-Polar Bears	950		200.00	200
1987	Alpenglow-Artic Wolf	950	1987	200.00	200
1987	Amboseli Child-African Elephant	950		160.00	160
1984	Among the Cattails-Canada Geese	950	1985	130.00	375
1984	Artic Procession-Willow Ptarmigan	950	1988	220.00	500
1990	Artic Wolf Pups	290		500.00	500
1987	Autumn Mist-Barred Owl	950	1987	160.00	160
1987	Autumn Thunder-Muskoxen	950		150.00	150
1985	Awakening Meadow-Cottontail	950		50.00	50
1992	Banyan Ambush- Black Panther	950	1992	235.00	235
1984	Basking-Brown Pelicans	950	1988	115.00	125
1988	Bathing-Blue Jay	950		95.00	95
1987	Bathing-Mute Swan	950	1992	175.00	275
1989	Before The Freeze-Beaver	950		165.00	165
1990	Bittersweet Winter-Cardinal	1,250	1990	150.00	150-175
1992	Black Jade	1,950	1992	275.00	500
1992	Black Magic-Panther	750	1992	195.00	225
1993	Black Wolf-North American Wilderness	350		325.00	N/A
1984	Breaking Cover-Black Bear	950	N/A	130.00	150
1987	Canyon Creek-Cougar	950	1987	195.00	435
1992	The Chase-Snow Leopard	950		200.00	200
1994	Child of the Outback	950		175.00	175
1985	Children of the Forest-Red Fox Kits	950	1985	110.00	325
1985	Children of the Tundra-Artic Wolf Pup	950	1985	110.00	325-395
1988	Cliff Hanger-Bobcat	950		200.00	200
1984	Close Encounter-Bobcat	950	1989	130.00	130
1988	Coastal Clique-Harbor Seals	950		160.00	160
1986	Conflict at Dawn-Heron and Osprey	950	1989	130.00	325
1983	Cool Retreat-Lynx	950	1988	85.00	125
1986	Cottonwood Gold-Baltimore Oriole	950		85.00	85
1985	Cougar Head Study	950		60.00	60
1989	Cougar Run	950	1989	185.00	225
1994	The Courtship	950		175.00	175
1993	Dark Encounter	3,500	N/A	200.00	200
1990	Dawn Majesty	1,250	1991	185.00	225-275
1987	Dawn on the Marsh-Coyote	950		200.00	200
1985	Daybreak-Moose	950		135.00	135
1991	Denali Family-Grizzly Bear	950	1991	195.00	235
1986	Early Arrivals-Snow Buntings	950		75.00	75
1983	Early Windfall-Gray Squirrels	950		85.00	85
1988	Edge of the Forest-Timber Wolves	950	1988	500.00	500-700
1989	Evening Duet-Snowy Egrets	1,250		185.00	185
1991	Evening Encounter-Grizzly & Wolf	1,250		185.00	185
1988	Evening Meadow-American Goldfinch	950		150.00	150
1991	Face to Face	1,250		200.00	200
1985	Fallen Birch-Chipmunk	950	1985	60.00	375
1985	First Light-Gray Jays	950	1985	130.00	175
1983	First Snow-Grizzly Bears	950	1984	95.00	325
1987	First Tracks-Cougar	950		150.00	150
1989	Fluke Sighting-Humback Whales	950	1989	185.00	185
1993	Freedom I	350		500.00	500
1993	Frozen Moonlight	2,500	1993	225.00	200
1995	Gathering-Gray Wolves, The	950	1987	165.00	250
1989	Gorilla	290	1989	400.00	450
1993	Grizzly Impact	950	N/A	225.00	300-385
1990	Grizzly Litho	290	1990	400.00	400-600
1989	Heavy Going-Grizzly	950	1989	175.00	240
1986	Hidden Admirer-Moose	950	1986	165.00	275
1988	Hiding Place-Saw-Whet Owl	950		95.00	95
1989	High and Mighty-Gorilla	950	1989	185.00	185
1986	High Country Champion-Grizzly	950	1986	175.00	375
1984	High Ground-Wolves	950	1984	130.00	225
1987	High Refuge-Red Squirrel	950		120.00	120
1984	Icy Outcrop-White Gyrfalcon	950	1986	115.00	200
1987	In Deep-Black Bear Cub	950	N/A	135.00	250
1990	In Their Presence	1,250		200.00	200
1985	Island Sanctuary-Mallards	950	1987	95.00	150
1986	Kenyan Family-Cheetahs	950		130.00	130
1986	Lakeside Family-Canada Geese	950		75.00	75
1988	Last Sanctuary-Florida Panther	950	1993	175.00	350
1983	Lone Fisherman-Great Blue Heron	950	1985	85.00	375
1993	Loonlight	1,500		225.00	225
1986	Low Tide-Bald Eagles	950		130.00	130
1987	Lying in Wait-Arctic Fox	950		175.00	175
1984	Lying Low-Cougar	950	1986	85.00	550
1991	Monsoon-White Tiger	950	1994	195.00	195
1991	Moonlight Chase-Cougar	1,250		195.00	195-220
1988	Moonlight Fishermen-Raccoons	950	1990	175.00	175
1988	Moose Hair	950	N/A	165.00	225
1988	Morning Display-Common Loons	3,395	1988	135.00	135
1986	Morning Forage-Ground Squirrel	950	1988	75.00	75
1993	Morning Glory-Bald Eagle	1,250	N/A	225.00	225
1984	Morning Mist-Snowy Owl	950	1988	95.00	180
1990	Mountain Cradle	1,250		200.00	200

YEAR	ISSUE	EDITION LIMIT	YEAR RETD.	ISSUE PRICE	* QUOTE U.S.$
1988	Night Moves-African Elephants	950		150.00	150
1990	Night Run-Artic Wolves	1,250	1990	200.00	200
1993	Night Specter	1,250		195.00	195
1986	Northwoods Family-Moose	950		75.00	75
1987	Out of the Blizzard-Timber Wolves	950	1987	215.00	450
1992	Out of the Darkness	290		200.00	200
1987	Out of the Mist-Grizzly	950	1990	200.00	375
1991	Out on a Limb-Young Barred Owl	950		185.00	185
1991	Panda Trilogy	950		375.00	375
1993	Phantoms of the Tundra	950		235.00	235
1984	Plains Hunter-Prairie Falcon	950		95.00	95
1990	The Plunge-Northern Sea Lions	1,250		200.00	200
1986	Racing the Storm-Artic Wolves	950	1986	200.00	300
1987	Rain Watch-Belted Kingfisher	950		125.00	125
1993	The Rains-Tiger	950		225.00	225
1992	Ranthambhore Rush	950		225.00	225
1983	The Refuge-Raccoon	950	1983	85.00	275
1992	Regal Majesty	290		200.00	200
1985	Return to Winter-Pintails	950	1990	135.00	135-200
1983	River Watch-Peregrine Falcon	950		85.00	85
1988	Savana Siesta-African Lions	950		165.00	165
1990	Seasonal Greeting-Cardinal	1,250		150.00	150
1993	Seeking Attention	950		200.00	200
1991	Sisters-Artic Wolves	1,250		185.00	185
1989	Sneak Peak	950		185.00	185
1986	Snowy Excursion-Red Squirrel	950		75.00	75
1988	Snowy Watch-Great Gray Owl	950		175.00	175
1989	Softly, Softly-White Tiger	950	1989	220.00	400-500
1991	Something Stirred (Bengal Tiger)	950		195.00	195
1988	Spanish Mist-Young Barred-Owl	950		175.00	175
1984	Spirit of the North-White Wolf	950	1986	130.00	185
1990	Spout	290		500.00	500
1989	Spring Flurry-Adelie Penguins	950		185.00	185
1986	Spring Mist-Chickadees	950	1986	105.00	150
1990	Suitors-Wood Ducks	3,313	1989	135.00	135
1990	Summer Rain-Common Loons	4,500	1990	200.00	200
1990	Summer Rain-Common Loons (Prestige)	450		425.00	425
1987	Sundown Alert-Bobcat	950	N/A	150.00	195
1985	Sundown Reflections-Wood Ducks	950		85.00	85
1990	Their First Season	1,250	1990	200.00	200
1986	Togetherness	1,250		125.00	185
1986	Treading Thin Ice-Chipmunk	950		75.00	75
1988	Tundra Family-Arctic Wolves	950		200.00	200
1985	Under the Pines-Bobcat	950	1986	95.00	275
1989	Water Sport-Bobcat	950	1989	185.00	185
1990	Whitetail Spring	1,250	1990	185.00	185
1988	Winter Grazing-Bison	950		185.00	185
1986	Winter Hiding-Cottontail	950		75.00	75
1983	Winter Lookout-Cougar	950	1985	85.00	600-700
1986	Winter Perch-Cardinal	950	1986	85.00	150
1985	Winter Rendezvous-Coyotes	950	1985	140.00	140
1988	Winter Spirit-Gray Wolf	950		200.00	200
1987	Winter Vigil-Great Horned Owl	950	1990	175.00	175
1993	Wolong Whiteout	950		225.00	225
1986	The Young Explorer-Red Fox Kit	950	N/A	75.00	95

Smith - D. Smith

1993	African Ebony-Black Leopard	1,250		195.00	195
1992	Armada	950		195.00	195
1993	Catching the Scent-Polar Bear	950		175.00	175
1994	Curious Presence-Whitetail Deer	950		195.00	195
1991	Dawn's Early Light-Bald Eagles	950		185.00	185
1993	Echo Bay-Loon Family	1,150		185.00	250
1992	Eyes of the North	2,500		225.00	225
1993	Guardians of the Den	1,500	N/A	195.00	195-240
1991	Icy Reflections-Pintails	500		250.00	250
1992	Night Moves-Cougar	950		185.00	185
1994	Parting Reflections	950		185.00	185
1993	Shrouded Forest-Bald Eagle	950	N/A	150.00	750-975
1991	Twilight's Calling-Common Loons	950	1991	175.00	250
1993	What's Bruin	1,750		185.00	185

New Masters Publishing

Bannister - P. Bannister

1982	Amaryllis	500	N/A	285.00	1900
1988	Apples and Oranges	485	N/A	265.00	600
1982	April	300	N/A	200.00	1100
1984	April Light	950	N/A	150.00	600
1987	Autumn Fields	950	N/A	150.00	150
1978	Bandstand	250	N/A	75.00	450
1992	Bed of Roses	663	N/A	265.00	265
1995	Bridesmaids	950	N/A	265.00	265
1991	Celebration	662	N/A	350.00	700
1989	Chapter One	485	N/A	265.00	1300
1991	Crossroads	485	N/A	295.00	590
1993	Crowning Glory	485	N/A	265.00	265
1992	Crystal Bowl	485	N/A	265.00	265
1989	Daydreams	485	N/A	265.00	530
1993	Deja Vu	663	N/A	265.00	265
1983	The Duchess	500	N/A	250.00	1800
1980	Dust of Autumn	200	N/A	200.00	1225
1981	Easter	300	N/A	260.00	950
1982	Emily	500	N/A	285.00	800
1980	Faded Glory	200	N/A	200.00	1225
1984	The Fan Window	950	N/A	195.00	450
1987	First Prize	950	N/A	115.00	175
1988	Floribunda	485	N/A	265.00	550
1994	Fountain	485	N/A	265.00	265
1994	From Russia With Love	950	N/A	165.00	165

New Masters Publishing

YEAR ISSUE		EDITION LIMIT	YEAR RETRD.	ISSUE PRICE	*QUOTE U.S.$
1980	Gift of Happiness	200	N/A	200.00	2000
1980	Girl on the Beach	200	N/A	200.00	1200
1990	Good Friends	485	N/A	265.00	750
1988	Guinevere	485	N/A	265.00	1000
1993	Into The Woods	485	N/A	265.00	265
1982	Ivy	500	N/A	285.00	700
1982	Jasmine	500	N/A	285.00	650
1981	Juliet	300	N/A	260.00	5000
1990	Lavender Hill	485	N/A	265.00	625
1992	Love Letters	485	N/A	265.00	265
1988	Love Seat	485	N/A	230.00	500
1989	Low Tide	485	N/A	265.00	550
1995	Magnolias	950	N/A	265.00	265
1982	Mail Order Brides	500	N/A	325.00	2300
1984	Make Believe	950	N/A	150.00	600
1989	March Winds	485	N/A	265.00	530
1983	Mementos	950	N/A	150.00	1400
1982	Memories	500	N/A	235.00	500
1992	Morning Mist	485	N/A	265.00	265
1981	My Special Place	300	N/A	260.00	1850
1982	Nuance	500	N/A	235.00	470
1994	Once Upon A Time	950	N/A	265.00	265
1983	Ophelia	950	N/A	150.00	675
1989	Peace	485	N/A	265.00	1100
1981	Porcelain Rose	300	N/A	260.00	2000
1982	The Present	500	N/A	260.00	800
1986	Pride & Joy	950	N/A	150.00	300
1991	Pudding & Pies	485	N/A	265.00	265
1987	Quiet Corner	950	N/A	115.00	300
1989	The Quilt	485	N/A	265.00	900
1993	Rambling Rose	485	N/A	265.00	265
1981	Rehearsal	300	N/A	260.00	1850
1990	Rendezvous	485	N/A	265.00	650
1984	Scarlet Ribbons	950	N/A	150.00	325
1980	Sea Haven	300	N/A	260.00	1100
1990	Seascapes	485	N/A	265.00	550
1987	September Harvest	950	N/A	150.00	300
1980	The Silver Bell	200	N/A	200.00	2000
1990	Sisters	485	N/A	265.00	950
1990	Songbird	485	N/A	265.00	550
1991	String of Pearls	485	N/A	265.00	850
1988	Summer Choices	300	N/A	250.00	800
1991	Teatime	485	N/A	295.00	600
1980	Titania	350	N/A	260.00	900
1991	Wildflowers	485	N/A	295.00	590
1983	Window Seat	950	N/A	150.00	600

Past Impressions

Limited Edition Canvas Transfers - A. Maley

YEAR ISSUE		EDITION LIMIT	YEAR RETRD.	ISSUE PRICE	*QUOTE U.S.$
1990	Cafe Royale	100	N/A	665.00	665
1992	Circle of Love	250	N/A	445.00	925
1992	An Elegant Affair	250	N/A	595.00	1000-2000
1992	Evening Performance	100	N/A	295.00	800-1200
1990	Festive Occasion	100	N/A	595.00	200-300
1990	Gracious Era	100	N/A	645.00	1700-2000
1995	The Letter	250	N/A	465.00	600-995
1987	Love Letter	75	N/A	445.00	1000-1100
1994	New Years Eve	250	N/A	445.00	650-1000
1994	Parisian Beauties	250	N/A	645.00	750
1993	Rags and Riches	250	N/A	445.00	550-750
1994	The Recital	250	N/A	595.00	1550-2500
1990	Romantic Engagement	100	N/A	445.00	995
1993	Sleigh Bells	250	N/A	595.00	600-800
1991	Summer Carousel	250	N/A	345.00	1250
1994	Summer Elegance	250	N/A	595.00	950
1995	Summer Romance	250	N/A	465.00	750-900
1993	Visiting The Nursery	250	N/A	445.00	1400
1992	A Walk in the Park	250	N/A	595.00	1000-1895
1989	Winter Impressions	100	N/A	595.00	1150-2200

Limited Edition Paper Prints - A. Maley

YEAR ISSUE		EDITION LIMIT	YEAR RETRD.	ISSUE PRICE	*QUOTE U.S.$
1989	Alexandra	750	1994	125.00	125
1989	Beth	750	1994	125.00	125
1988	The Boardwalk	500	N/A	250.00	325
1989	Catherine	750	1994	125.00	200
1987	Day Dreams	500	N/A	200.00	300
1989	English Rose	750	N/A	250.00	400
1990	Festive Occasion	750	N/A	250.00	900
1984	Glorious Summer	350	N/A	150.00	650
1989	In Harmony	750	1995	250.00	250
1988	Joys of Childhood	500	N/A	250.00	250
1987	Love Letter	450	N/A	200.00	425-500
1988	Opening Night	500	N/A	250.00	2000
1985	Passing Elegance	350	N/A	150.00	900
1987	The Promise	450	N/A	200.00	400
1984	Secluded Summer	350	N/A	150.00	970
1985	Secret Thoughts	350	N/A	150.00	850
1990	Summer Pastime	750	N/A	250.00	300
1986	Tell Me	450	N/A	150.00	800
1988	Tranquil Moment	500	N/A	250.00	300
1989	Victoria	750	1994	125.00	125
1988	Victorian Trio	500	N/A	250.00	380
1986	Winter Romance	450	N/A	150.00	1000

Pemberton & Oakes

Membership-Miniature Lithographs - D. Zolan

YEAR ISSUE		EDITION LIMIT	YEAR RETRD.	ISSUE PRICE	*QUOTE U.S.$
1992	Brotherly Love	Retrd.	N/A	18.00	68
1993	New Shoes	Retrd.	N/A	18.00	42
1993	Country Walk	Retrd.	N/A	22.00	40

YEAR ISSUE		EDITION LIMIT	YEAR RETRD.	ISSUE PRICE	*QUOTE U.S.$
1994	Enchanted Forest	Retrd.	N/A	22.00	40

Zolan's Children-Lithographs - D. Zolan

YEAR ISSUE		EDITION LIMIT	YEAR RETRD.	ISSUE PRICE	*QUOTE U.S.$
1989	Almost Home	Retrd.	N/A	98.00	255
1991	Autumn Leaves	Retrd.	N/A	98.00	120
1993	The Big Catch	Retrd.	N/A	98.00	130
1989	Brotherly Love	Retrd.	N/A	98.00	295
1982	By Myself	Retrd.	N/A	98.00	230
1989	Christmas Prayer	Retrd.	N/A	98.00	175-225
1990	Colors of Spring	Retrd.	N/A	98.00	175-240
1990	Crystal's Creek	Retrd.	N/A	98.00	175
1989	Daddy's Home	Retrd.	N/A	98.00	310
1988	Day Dreamer	Retrd.	N/A	35.00	130
1992	Enchanted Forest	Retrd.	N/A	98.00	110-135
1982	Erik and the Dandelion	Retrd.	N/A	98.00	400
1990	First Kiss	Retrd.	N/A	98.00	240
1991	Flowers for Mother	Retrd.	N/A	98.00	160
1993	Grandma's Garden	Retrd.	N/A	98.00	135
1989	Grandma's Mirror	Retrd.	N/A	98.00	140-195
1990	Laurie and the Creche	Retrd.	N/A	98.00	115-165
1989	Mother's Angels	Retrd.	N/A	98.00	175-240
1992	New Shoes	Retrd.	N/A	98.00	150
1989	Rodeo Girl	Retrd.	N/A	98.00	160
1984	Sabina in the Grass	Retrd.	N/A	98.00	625
1988	Small Wonder	Retrd.	N/A	98.00	250
1989	Snowy Adventure	Retrd.	N/A	98.00	205
1991	Summer Suds	Retrd.	N/A	98.00	140-175
1989	Summer's Child	Retrd.	N/A	98.00	225
1986	Tender Moment	Retrd.	N/A	98.00	275
1988	Tiny Treasures	Retrd.	N/A	150.00	215
1987	Touching the Sky	Retrd.	N/A	98.00	175-225
1988	Waiting to Play	Retrd.	N/A	35.00	135
1988	Winter Angel	Retrd.	N/A	98.00	230

Reco International

Fine Art Canvas Reproduction - J. McClelland

YEAR ISSUE		EDITION LIMIT	YEAR RETRD.	ISSUE PRICE	*QUOTE U.S.$
1990	Beach Play	350		80.00	80
1991	Flower Swing	350		100.00	100
1991	Summer Conversation	350		80.00	80

Limited Edition Print - S. Kuck

YEAR ISSUE		EDITION LIMIT	YEAR RETRD.	ISSUE PRICE	*QUOTE U.S.$
1986	Ashley	500		85.00	150
1985	Heather	Retrd.	1987	75.00	150
1984	Jessica	Retrd.	1986	60.00	400

McClelland - J. McClelland

YEAR ISSUE		EDITION LIMIT	YEAR RETRD.	ISSUE PRICE	*QUOTE U.S.$
XX	I Love Tammy	500		75.00	100
XX	Just for You	300		155.00	155
XX	Olivia	300		175.00	175
XX	Reverie	300		110.00	110
XX	Sweet Dreams	300		145.00	145

Roman, Inc.

Abble Williams - A. Williams

YEAR ISSUE		EDITION LIMIT	YEAR RETRD.	ISSUE PRICE	*QUOTE U.S.$
1988	Mary, Mother of the Carpenter	Closed	N/A	100.00	100

The Discovery of America Miniature Art Print - I. Spencer

YEAR ISSUE		EDITION LIMIT	YEAR RETRD.	ISSUE PRICE	*QUOTE U.S.$
1991	The Discovery of America	Open		2.00	2

Divine Servant - M. Greiner Jr.

YEAR ISSUE		EDITION LIMIT	YEAR RETRD.	ISSUE PRICE	*QUOTE U.S.$
1993	Divine Servant, print of drawing	Open		35.00	35
1994	Divine Servant, print of painting	Closed	1994	150.00	150
1994	Divine Servant, print of painting	Closed	1994	75.00	75
1994	Divine Servant, print of painting w/remarque	Closed	1994	75.00	75
1994	Divine Servant, print of painting w/remarque	Closed	1994	150.00	150

Fishers of Men - M. Greiner, Jr.

YEAR ISSUE		EDITION LIMIT	YEAR RETRD.	ISSUE PRICE	*QUOTE U.S.$
1994	Fishers of Men 8x10	Open		10.00	10
1994	Fishers of Men 11x14	Open		20.00	20
1994	Fishers of Men 16x20	Open		35.00	35

Hook - F. Hook

YEAR ISSUE		EDITION LIMIT	YEAR RETRD.	ISSUE PRICE	*QUOTE U.S.$
1982	Bouquet	1,200		70.00	350
1981	The Carpenter	Closed	1981	100.00	1000
1981	The Carpenter (remarque)	Closed	1981	100.00	3000
1982	Frolicking	1,200		60.00	350
1982	Gathering	1,200		60.00	350-450
1982	Little Children, Come to Me	1,950		50.00	500
1982	Little Children, Come to Me, remarque	50		100.00	500
1982	Posing	1,200		70.00	350
1982	Poulets	1,200		60.00	350
1982	Surprise	1,200		50.00	350

Portraits of Love - F. Hook

YEAR ISSUE		EDITION LIMIT	YEAR RETRD.	ISSUE PRICE	*QUOTE U.S.$
1988	Expectation	2,500		25.00	25
1988	In Mother's Arms	2,500		25.00	25
1988	My Kitty	2,500		25.00	25
1988	Remember When...	2,500		25.00	25
1988	Sharing	2,500		25.00	25
1988	Sunkissed Afternoon	2,500		25.00	25

V.F. Fine Arts

Kuck - S. Kuck

YEAR ISSUE		EDITION LIMIT	YEAR RETRD.	ISSUE PRICE	*QUOTE U.S.$
1994	'95 Angel Collection, S/N	750	1995	198.00	198

YEAR ISSUE		EDITION LIMIT	YEAR RETRD.	ISSUE PRICE	*QUOTE U.S.$
1995	'96 Angel Collection, S/N	750		198.00	198
1993	Best Friend, proof	250	N/A	175.00	225
1993	Best Friends, Canvas Transfer	250	N/A	500.00	600
1993	Best Friends, S/N	2,500	N/A	145.00	150
1994	Best of Days, S/N	750	1994	160.00	175
1989	Bundle of Joy, S/N	1,000	1989	125.00	250
1993	Buttons & Bows, proof	95	N/A	125.00	150
1993	Buttons & Bows, S/N	950	N/A	95.00	125
1990	Chopsticks, proof	150	1991	120.00	150
1990	Chopsticks, remarque	25	1991	160.00	200
1990	Chopsticks, S/N	1,500	1990	80.00	95
1995	Christmas Magic, S/N	950		80.00	80
1987	The Daisy, proof	90	1988	40.00	175
1987	The Daisy, S/N	900	1988	30.00	125
1989	Day Dreaming, proof	90	1989	225.00	250
1989	Day Dreaming, remarque	50	1989	300.00	395
1989	Day Dreaming, S/N	900	1989	150.00	200
1994	Dear Santa, S/N	950	1994	95.00	125
1992	Duet, Canvas Framed	500	1994	255.00	325
1992	Duet, proof	95	N/A	175.00	200
1992	Duet, S/N	950	N/A	125.00	135
1988	First Recital, proof	25	1988	250.00	750
1988	First Recital, remarque	25	1988	400.00	1000
1988	First Recital, S/N	150	1988	200.00	500
1990	First Snow, proof	50	1990	150.00	250
1990	First Snow, remarque	25	1990	200.00	350
1990	First Snow, S/N	500	1990	95.00	150
1987	The Flower Girl, proof	90	1987	50.00	125
1987	The Flower Girl, S/N	900	1987	40.00	95
1994	Garden Memories, Canvas Transfer	250	N/A	500.00	500
1994	Garden Memories, S/N	2,500	N/A	145.00	175
1991	God's Gift, proof	150	N/A	150.00	175
1991	God's Gift, S/N	1,500	1993	125.00	125
1993	Good Morning, Canvas	250	1993	500.00	500
1993	Good Morning, proof	50	N/A	175.00	200
1993	Good Morning, S/N	2,500	N/A	145.00	165
1996	Hidden Garden, Canvas Transfer	395		379.00	379
1996	Hidden Garden, S/N	950	1996	95.00	95
1995	Homecoming, proof	95	1995	172.50	173
1995	Homecoming, S/N	1,150	1995	125.00	125
1989	Innocence, proof	90	1989	225.00	275
1989	Innocence, remarque	50	1989	300.00	395
1989	Innocence, S/N	900	1989	150.00	220
1992	Joyous Day, Canvas Transfer	250	N/A	250.00	295
1992	Joyous Day, proof	120	N/A	175.00	200
1992	Joyous Day, S/N	1,200	1993	125.00	150
1988	The Kitten, proof	50	1988	150.00	1000
1988	The Kitten, remarque	25	1988	250.00	1200
1988	The Kitten, S/N	350	1988	120.00	1000
1990	Le Beau, proof	150	1990	120.00	225
1990	Le Beau, remarque	25	1990	160.00	275
1990	Le Beau, S/N	1,500	1990	80.00	175
1987	Le Papillion, proof	35	1990	110.00	175
1987	Le Papillion, remarque	7	1990	150.00	250
1987	Le Papillion, S/N	350	1990	90.00	150
1990	Lilly Pond, color remarque	125	1990	500.00	500
1990	Lilly Pond, proof	75	1990	200.00	200
1990	Lilly Pond, S/N	750	1990	150.00	150
1988	Little Ballerina, proof	25	1988	150.00	350
1988	Little Ballerina, remarque	25	1988	225.00	450
1988	Little Ballerina, S/N	150	1988	110.00	275
1987	The Loveseat, proof	90	1987	40.00	150
1987	The Loveseat, S/N	900	1987	30.00	100
1991	Memories, S/N	5,000	1991	195.00	250
1987	Mother's Love, proof	12	1987	225.00	1200
1987	Mother's Love, S/N	150	1987	195.00	750
1988	My Dearest, proof	50	1988	200.00	900
1988	My Dearest, remarque	25	1988	325.00	1200
1988	My Dearest, S/N	350	1988	160.00	700
1995	Night Before Christmas, S/N	1,150		95.00	95
1995	Playful Kitten	950	1995	95.00	95
1989	Puppy, proof	50	1989	180.00	500
1989	Puppy, remarque	50	1989	240.00	750
1989	Puppy, S/N	500	1989	120.00	400
1987	A Quiet Time, proof	90	1987	50.00	100
1987	A Quiet Time, S/N	900	1987	40.00	75
1987	The Reading Lesson, proof	90	1987	70.00	200
1987	The Reading Lesson, S/N	900	1987	60.00	150
1995	Rhapsody & Lace	1,150		95.00	100
1989	Rose Garden, proof	50	1989	150.00	400
1989	Rose Garden, remarque	50	1989	200.00	500
1989	Rose Garden, S/N	500	1989	95.00	390
1986	Silhouette, proof	25	1987	90.00	250
1986	Silhouette, S/N	250	1987	80.00	200
1989	Sisters, proof	90	1989	150.00	550
1989	Sisters, remarque	50	1989	200.00	650
1989	Sisters, S/N	900	1988	95.00	300
1989	Sonatina, proof	90	1989	225.00	700
1989	Sonatina, remarque	50	1989	300.00	850
1989	Sonatina, S/N	900	1989	150.00	400
1986	Summer Reflections, proof	90	1987	70.00	300
1986	Summer Reflections, S/N	900	1987	60.00	250
1986	Tender Moments, proof	50	1986	80.00	300
1986	Tender Moments, S/N	500	1986	70.00	200
1993	Thinking of You, Canvas Transfer	250	1993	500.00	500
1993	Thinking of You, S/N	2,500	N/A	145.00	175
1988	Wild Flowers, proof	50	1988	175.00	300
1988	Wild Flowers, remarque	25	1988	250.00	400
1988	Wild Flowers, S/N	350	1988	160.00	250
1992	Yesterday, Canvas Framed	550	N/A	195.00	200
1992	Yesterday, proof	95	N/A	150.00	150
1992	Yesterday, S/N	950	N/A	95.00	95

Collectors' Information Bureau

*Quotes have been rounded up to nearest dollar

ORNAMENTS

Ace Product Management Group, Inc.

Harley-Davidson Child's Ornaments - Ace

YEAR ISSUE		EDITION LIMIT	YEAR RETD.	ISSUE PRICE	*QUOTE U.S.$
1991	For The Young At Heart 99433-92Z	Yr.Iss.	1991	14.95	15
1992	The Gift 99466-93Z	Yr.Iss.	1992	15.00	15
1993	First Harley 99429-94Z	Yr.Iss.	1993	15.00	15
1994	Daddy's Boots 99442-95Z	Yr.Iss.	1994	15.00	15
1995	Little Stocking Stuffer 99448-96Z	Yr.Iss.	1995	15.00	15
1996	1996 Commemorative 99940-97Z	Yr.Iss.		15.00	15

Harley-Davidson Christmas Ornaments - Ace

1981	Ornament 99407-82V	Yr.Iss.	1981	5.95	5
1983	Ornament 99407-84V	Yr.Iss.	1983	6.50	7
1984	Ornament 99408-85Z	Yr.Iss.	1984	6.95	7
1985	Ornament 99406-86Z	Yr.Iss.	1985	6.95	7
1986	Ornament 99407-87Z	Yr.Iss.	1986	6.95	7
1987	Ornament 99406-88Z	Yr.Iss.	1987	6.95	7
1988	Ornament 99408-89Z	Yr.Iss.	1988	6.95	7
1989	Ornament 99435-90Z	Yr.Iss.	1989	6.95	7
1990	Ornament 99435-91Z	Yr.Iss.	1990	6.95	7
1991	Skating Party 99436-92Z	Yr.Iss.	1991	6.95	7
1992	Surprise Visit 99437-93Z	Yr.Iss.	1992	7.00	7
1993	Xmas Vacation 99427-94Z	Yr.Iss.	1993	8.00	8

Harley-Davidson Holiday Memories - Ace

1994	Under The Mistletoe 99091-95Z	Yr.Iss.	1994	8.00	8
1995	Late Arrival 99495-96Z	Yr.Iss.	1995	8.00	8
1996	After The Pageant 99948-97Z	Yr.Iss.		8.00	8

Harley-Davidson Mini-Plate Ornaments - Ace

1989	1989 99440-90Z	Yr.Iss.	1989	10.00	10
1990	Santa's Predicament 99442-91Z	Yr.Iss.	1990	9.95	10
1991	Not A Creature 99443-92Z	Yr.Iss.	1991	10.00	10
1992	Finding The Way 99441-93Z	Yr.Iss.	1992	10.00	10
1993	Pulling Together 99416-94Z	Yr.Iss.	1993	10.00	10
1994	Sorry Guys 99445-95Z	Yr.Iss.	1994	10.00	10
1995	Ratchet The Elf 99480-96Z	Yr.Iss.	1995	10.00	10
1996	Reviewing the Plan 99947-97Z	Yr.Iss.		10.00	10

Harley-Davidson Pewter Ornaments - Ace

1988	Santa's Secret 99409-89Z	Yr.Iss.	1988	6.95	7
1989	Santa's Workshop 99438-90Z	Yr.Iss.	1989	6.95	7
1990	Stocking Stuffer 99438-91Z	Yr.Iss.	1990	8.95	9
1991	Finishing Touches 99439-92Z	Yr.Iss.	1991	10.95	11
1992	Batteries Not Included 99426-93Z	Yr.Iss.	1992	12.00	12
1993	Joy Ride 99428-94Z	Yr.Iss.	1993	12.00	12
1993	90th Anniversary-"The Reunion" 99430-94Z	7,500	1993	35.00	35
1994	Cleared For Takeoff 99463-95Z	Yr.Iss.	1994	14.00	14
1995	Night Flight 99455-96Z	Yr.Iss.	1995	15.00	15
1996	V-Twin 99940-97Z	Yr.Iss.		15.00	15

All God's Children

Angel Dumpling - M. Root

1993	Eric-1570		Retrd. 1994	22.50	40-60
1994	Erica-1578		Retrd. 1995	22.50	35-45

Christmas Ornaments - M. Root

1987	Cameo Ornaments (set/12)- D1912		Retrd. 1988	144.00	1500-2000
1987	Doll Ornaments (set /24) - D1924		Retrd. 1988	336.00	2000-3000
1993	Santa with Scooty-1571		Retrd. 1994	22.50	40-60

Amaranth Productions

Christmas Ornaments - L. West

1994	Mr. Santa 8010	500	1995	110.00	110
1994	St. Nick (burgundy) 8020	500	1995	120.00	120
1994	Angel 8030	500	1995	120.00	120
1994	Jester 8040	500	1995	120.00	350
1995	Mrs. Claus 8015	500	1995	110.00	110
1995	Harlequin 8045	500	1995	110.00	110
1995	St. Nick (white) 8025	500	1995	120.00	120

Anheuser-Busch, Inc.

A & Eagle Collector Ornament Series - A.-Busch, Inc.

1991	Budweiser Girl-Circa 1890's N3178	Retrd. N/A	15.00	15
1992	1893 Columbian Exposition N3649	Retrd. N/A	15.00	15
1993	Greatest Triumph N4089	Retrd. N/A	15.00	15

Christmas Ornaments - Various

1992	Clydesdales Mini Plate Ornaments N3650 - S. Sampson	Retrd. N/A	23.00	23
1993	Budweiser Six-Pack Mini Plate Ornaments N4220 - M. Urdahl	Retrd. 1994	10.00	10

Annalee Mobilitee Dolls, Inc.

Christmas Ornaments - A. Thorndike

1985	Clown Head	5,701	N/A	6.95	175
1986	3" Clown	3,369	1986	11.95	200
1987	3" Elf	1,950	1989	12.95	325
1992	3" Skier	8,332	N/A	14.45	175

ANRI

Disney Four Star Collection - Disney Studios

1989	Maestro Mickey	Yr.Iss.	1989	25.00	75-95
1990	Minnie Mouse	Yr.Iss.	1990	25.00	50

Ferrandiz Message Collection - J. Ferrandiz

1989	Let the Heavens Ring	1,000	1992	215.00	215
1990	Hear The Angels Sing	1,000	1992	225.00	225

Ferrandiz Woodcarvings - J. Ferrandiz

1988	Heavenly Drummer	1,000	1992	175.00	225
1989	Heavenly Strings	1,000	1992	190.00	190

Sarah Kay's First Christmas - S. Kay

1994	Sarah Kay's First Christmas	500		140.00	195
1995	First Xmas Stocking 57502	500		99.00	195
1996	All I Want for Xmas 57503	500		195.00	195

Armani

Christmas - G. Armani

1991	Christmas Ornament 799A	Retrd. 1991	11.50	45
1992	Christmas Ornament 788F	Retrd. 1992	23.50	24
1993	Christmas Ornament 892P	Retrd. 1993	25.00	25
1994	Christmas Ornament 801P	Retrd. 1994	25.00	30
1995	Christmas Ornament-Gifts & Snow 640P	Retrd. 1995	30.00	30
1996	Christmas Ornament-A Sweet Christmas 355P	Yr.Iss.	30.00	30

Artists of the World

De Grazia Annual Ornaments - T. De Grazia

1986	Pima Indian Drummer Boy	Yr.Iss.	1986	28.00	350
1987	White Dove	Yr.Iss.	1987	30.00	95-140
1988	Flower Girl	Yr.Iss.	1988	33.00	85-100
1989	Flower Boy	Yr.Iss.	1989	35.00	85-100
1990	Pink Papoose	Yr.Iss.	1990	35.00	80-120
1990	Merry Little Indian	10,000	1990	88.00	95-110
1991	Christmas Prayer (Red)	Yr.Iss.	1991	50.00	75-95
1992	Bearing Gift	Yr.Iss.	1992	55.00	65-85
1993	Lighting the Way	Yr.Iss.	1993	58.00	75-95
1994	Warm Wishes	Yr.Iss.	1994	65.00	65-75
1995	Little Prayer (White)	Yr.Iss.	1995	49.50	65-75
1995	Heavenly Flowers	Yr.Iss.	1995	65.00	65
1995	My Beautiful Rocking Horse	Yr.Iss.	1995	125.00	125
1996	Oh Holy Night	Yr.Iss		67.50	70

Attic Babies

Christmas Decorations- M. Maschino-Walker

1993	Raggedy Santa Wreath		Retrd. 1994	101.95	102
1992	Stocking		Retrd. 1994	55.95	56

Wooden Ornaments - M. Maschino-Walker

1993	Angel		Retrd. 1994	21.95	22
1993	Snowman		Retrd. 1994	17.95	18
1993	Stocking		Retrd. 1994	25.95	26

Band Creations, Inc.

Best Friends - Angels - Richards/Penfield

1994	4 Assorted Angel Ornaments	Open	5.00	5
1995	Double Angels	Open	8.00	8
1996	4 Assorted African American Angel Ornaments	Open	5.00	5

Best Friends-A Star is Born - Richards/Penfield

1995	Baseball Boy	Open	6.00	6
1996	Baseball Boy (African American)	Open	10.00	10
1995	Baseball Girl	Open	6.00	6
1996	Baseball Girl (African American)	Open	10.00	10
1995	Basketball Boy	Open	6.00	6
1996	Basketball Boy (African American)	Open	10.00	10
1995	Basketball Girl	Open	6.00	6
1996	Basketball Girl (African American)	Open	10.00	10
1996	Biker Boy	Open	6.00	6
1996	Biker Girl	Open	6.00	6
1995	Cheerleader Girl	Open	6.00	6
1996	Cheerleader Girl (African American)	Open	10.00	10
1996	Fisher Boy	Open	6.00	6
1996	Fisher Girl	Open	6.00	6
1995	Football Boy	Open	6.00	6
1996	Football Boy (African American)	Open	10.00	10
1995	Golfer Boy	Open	6.00	6
1995	Golfer Girl	Open	6.00	6
1995	Hockey Boy	Open	6.00	6
1996	Skier Boy	Open	6.00	6
1996	Skier Girl	Open	6.00	6
1996	Soccer Boy	Open	6.00	6
1995	Soccer Girl	Open	6.00	6
1996	Swimmer Boy	Open	6.00	6
1995	Swimmer Girl	Open	6.00	6
1996	Tennis Boy	Open	6.00	6
1996	Tennis Girl	Open	6.00	6

Best Friends-Monthly Messengers - Richards/Penfield

1996	January	Open	10.00	10
1996	February	Open	10.00	10
1996	March	Open	10.00	10
1996	April	Open	10.00	10
1996	May	Open	10.00	10
1996	June	Open	10.00	10
1996	July	Open	10.00	10
1996	August	Open	10.00	10
1996	September	Open	10.00	10
1996	October	Open	10.00	10
1996	November	Open	10.00	10
1996	December	Open	10.00	10

Kringle Toppers - Band Creations

1996	America, Santa Claus	Open	10.00	10
1996	Austria, Christkind	Open	10.00	10
1996	England, Father Christmas	Open	10.00	10
1996	France, Pere Noel	Open	10.00	10
1996	Germany, Pelsnickel	Open	10.00	10
1996	Netherlands, St. Nickolas	Open	10.00	10
1996	Russia, Father Frost	Open	10.00	10
1996	Scandinavia, Julnisse	Open	10.00	10

Snowman/Sport Toppers - Band Creations

1996	Beach/Boating	Open	6.00	6
1996	Fishing	Open	6.00	6
1996	Golf	Open	6.00	6
1996	Skiing	Open	6.00	6
1996	Snowman	Open	6.00	6
1996	Tennis	Open	6.00	6

Bing & Grondahl

Christmas - Various

1985	Christmas Eve at the Farmhouse - E. Jensen	Closed	1985	19.50	20
1986	Silent Night, Holy Night - E. Jensen	Closed	1986	19.50	30
1987	The Snowman's Christmas Eve - E. Jensen	Closed	1987	22.50	23
1988	In the King's Garden - E. Jensen	Closed	1988	25.00	25
1989	Christmas Anchorage - E. Jensen	Closed	1989	27.00	27
1990	Changing of the Guards - E. Jensen	Closed	1990	32.50	35
1991	Copenhagen Stock Exchange - E. Jensen	Closed	1991	34.50	35
1992	Christmas at the Rectory - J. Steensen	Closed	1992	36.50	37
1993	Father Christmas in Copenhagen - J. Nielsen	Closed	1993	36.50	37
1994	A Day at the Deer Park - J. Nielsen	Closed	1994	36.50	37
1995	The Towers of Copenhagen - J. Nielsen	Closed	1995	37.50	38
1996	Winter at the Old Mill - J. Nielsen	12/96		37.50	38
1997	Country Christmas - J. Nielsen	Yr.Iss.		37.50	38

Christmas In America - J. Woodson

1986	Christmas Eve in Williamsburg	Closed	1986	12.50	50-100
1987	Christmas Eve at the White House	Closed	1987	15.00	25-60
1988	Christmas Eve at Rockefeller Center	Closed	1988	18.50	19
1989	Christmas in New England	Closed	1989	20.00	20
1990	Christmas Eve at the Capitol	Closed	1990	20.00	35
1991	Independence Hall	Closed	1991	23.50	24
1992	Christmas in San Francisco	Closed	1992	25.00	35
1993	Coming Home For Christmas	Closed	1993	25.00	30
1994	Christmas Eve in Alaska	Closed	1994	25.00	45
1995	Christmas Eve in Mississippi	Closed	1995	25.00	25

Santa Around the World - H. Hansen

1995	Santa in Greenland	Yr.Iss.	1995	25.00	25
1996	Santa in Orient	12/96		25.00	25
1997	Santa in Russia	Yr.Iss.		25.00	25

Santa Claus - Unknown

1989	Santa's Workshop	Yr.Iss.	1989	20.00	60
1990	Santa's Sleigh	Yr.Iss.	1990	20.00	60
1991	The Journey	Yr.Iss.	1991	24.00	45
1992	Santa's Arrival	Yr.Iss.	1992	25.00	36
1993	Santa's Gifts	Yr.Iss.	1993	25.00	36
1994	Christmas Stories	Yr.Iss.	1994	25.00	25

Boyds Collection Ltd.

The Bearstone Collection™ - G. M. Lowenthal

1994	'Charity'-Angel Bear with Star 2502	12/96	9.45	10
1994	'Faith'-Angel Bear w/Trumpet 2500	12/96	9.45	10
1994	'Hope'-Angel Bear w/Wreath 2501	12/96	9.45	10
1995	'Edmund'...Believe 2505	Open	9.45	10
1995	'Elliot with Tree 2507	Open	9.45	10
1995	'Manheim' the Moose with Wreath 2506	Open	9.45	10

The Folkstone Collection™ - G.M. Lowenthal

1995	Father Christmas 2553	Open	9.45	10
1995	Jean Claude & Jacque...the Skiers 2561	Open	9.45	10
1995	Jingles the Snowman with Wreath 2562	Open	9.45	10
1995	Nicholai with Tree 2550	Open	9.45	10
1995	Nicholas the Giftgiver 2551	Open	9.45	10
1995	Olaf...Let it Snow 2560	Open	9.45	10
1995	Sliknick in the Chimney 2552	Open	9.45	10

Brandywine Collectibles

Custom Collection - M. Whiting

YEAR ISSUE	EDITION LIMIT	YEAR RETD.	ISSUE PRICE	*QUOTE U.S.$
1989 Lorain Lighthouse	Closed	1992	9.00	9
1994 Smithfield Clerk's Office	Closed	1995	9.00	9
1991 Smithfield VA. Courthouse	Closed	1992	9.00	9

Williamsburg Ornaments - M. Whiting

YEAR ISSUE	EDITION LIMIT	YEAR RETD.	ISSUE PRICE	*QUOTE U.S.$
1988 Apothocary	Closed	1991	9.00	9
1988 Bootmaker	Closed	1991	9.00	9
1989 Cole Shop	Closed	1991	9.00	9
1988 Finnie Quarter	Closed	1991	9.00	9
1989 Gunsmith	Closed	1991	9.00	9
1994 Gunsmith	360	1994	9.50	10
1989 Music Teacher	Closed	1991	9.00	9
1988 Nicolson Shop	Closed	1991	9.00	9
1988 Tarpley's Store	Closed	1991	9.00	9
1988 Wigmaker	Closed	1991	9.00	9
1989 Windmill	Closed	1991	9.00	9

Calabar Creations

Angelic Pigasus - P. Apsit

YEAR ISSUE	EDITION LIMIT	YEAR RETD.	ISSUE PRICE	*QUOTE U.S.$
1995 Adagio AP75361	Open		5.00	5
1995 Alba AP75351	Open		5.00	5
1995 Ambrose AP75372	Open		5.00	5
1995 Andante AP75381	Open		5.00	5
1995 Angelica AP75312	Open		5.00	5
1995 Anna AP75321	Open		5.00	5
1995 Aria AP75341	Open		5.00	5

Carlton Cards

1988 Summit Heirloom Collection - Carlton

YEAR ISSUE	EDITION LIMIT	YEAR RETD.	ISSUE PRICE	*QUOTE U.S.$
1988 1st Christmas Together 053-047-6	Closed	1988	4.50	5
1988 Animals 053-049-2	Closed	1988	4.50	5
1988 Baby's First Christmas 053-026-3	Closed	1988	5.00	5
1988 Bundles of Joy 053-041-7	Closed	1989	11.00	11
1988 Carousel Magic 053-023-9	Closed	1988	8.00	48-58
1988 Christmas Charmer 053-038-7	Closed	1988	7.50	8
1988 Christmas Confection 053-044-1	Closed	1988	7.00	7
1988 Christmas Dreams 053-012-3	Closed	1988	12.00	12
1988 Christmas Magic 053-022-0	Closed	1988	8.00	8
1988 Christmas Wishes 053-060-3	Closed	1988	4.50	5
1988 Country Cheer 053-919-8	Closed	1988	7.50	38-45
1988 Cozy Kitten 053-053-0	Closed	1988	10.00	10
1988 Cuddly Christmas (A Good Roommate) 053-055-7	Closed	1988	6.50	60
1988 Favorite Things 053-039-5	Closed	1991	10.00	10
1988 Fluffy 053-017-4	Closed	1988	4.50	5
1988 Forever Friends 053-016-6	Closed	1988	9.50	10
1988 Friends Forever 053-032-8	Closed	1988	5.50	6
1988 Giddyap Teddy! 053-019-0	Closed	1988	9.50	10
1988 Grandma Twinkle 053-030-1	Closed	1988	N/A	N/A
1988 Happy Holly Days 053-054-9	Closed	1988	8.00	8
1988 Havin' Fun 053-037-9	Closed	1988	6.50	125-200
1988 Home, Sweet Home 053-015-8	Closed	1988	N/A	N/A
1988 Just Us 053-029-8	Closed	1988	9.50	10
1988 Kiss-Moose 053-025-5			5.50	6
1988 Little One 053-027-1	Closed	1989	9.50	10
1988 Manger 053-051-4	Closed	1988	5.00	10-15
1988 Merry Christmas Grandson 053-046-8	Closed	1988	7.50	8
1988 Merry Heartwarming 053-048-4	Closed	1988	N/A	N/A
1988 O Holy Night 053-057-3	Closed	1989	9.50	10
1988 Old-Time Santa 053-040-9	Closed	1988	8.50	75
1988 Perky Penguin 053-058-1	Closed	1988	6.50	28
1988 Ring in Christmas 053-020-4	Closed	1988	6.00	6
1988 Roses 053-049-2	Closed	1988	4.50	5
1988 Song of Christmas 053-034-4	Closed	1988	4.50	5
1988 Special Delivery (dated) 053-018-2	Closed	1989	11.00	35
1988 Star of Wonder 053-024-7	Closed	1988	N/A	N/A
1988 The Sweetest Angel 053-043-3	Closed	1988	6.00	6
1988 Teacher's Treat 053-021-2	Closed	1988	5.50	6
1988 Winter Friend 053-056-5	Closed	1989	4.00	24
1988 Wonderland Waltz 053-013-1	Closed	1988	12.00	12
1988 Wood Decoy 053-036-0	Closed	1988	N/A	N/A

1989 Summit/Carlton Heirloom Collection - Carlton

YEAR ISSUE	EDITION LIMIT	YEAR RETD.	ISSUE PRICE	*QUOTE U.S.$
1989 Arctic Antics 058-131-3	Closed	1989	5.50	6
1989 Best Friends 058-109-7	Closed	1989	9.50	10
1989 Bundles of Joy 058-104-5	Closed	1989	11.00	11
1989 Christmas Charmer 058-094-5	Closed	1989	6.50	7
1989 Christmas Confection 058-105-4	Closed	1989	6.50	7
1989 Christmas Dreams 058-096-1	Closed	1989	12.00	12
1989 Christmas Fantasy 058-119-4	Closed	1989	5.00	5
1989 Country Christmas 058-127-5	Closed	1989	5.00	5
1989 A Daughter Is A Joy 058-128-3	Closed	1989	5.00	5
1989 Forever Friends 058-041-7	Closed	1989	9.50	10
1989 Gentle Hearts 058-118-6	Closed	1989	6.50	7
1989 Giddyap Teddy! 058-093-7	Closed	1989	9.50	10
1989 A Gift From Heaven 058-111-9	Closed	1989	8.50	9
1989 Golden Snowflake 058-137-2	Closed	1989	5.00	5
1989 Havin' Fun 058-092-9	Closed	1989	6.50	7
1989 Hello Moon! 058-103-8	Closed	1989	7.50	8
1989 Here Comes Santa! 058-099-6	Closed	1990	7.50	8
1989 Home, Tweet, Home 058-112-7	Closed	1989	9.50	10
1989 Honey Love 058-117-8	Closed	1989	6.50	7
1989 In the Workshop 058-100-3	Closed	1990	11.00	11
1989 Jolly Holiday Bell 058-136-4	Closed	1989	6.50	7
1989 Joy To The World 058-138-0	Closed	1989	7.50	8
1989 Just Us 058-091-0	Closed	1989	9.50	10
1989 Kiss-Moose 058-107-0	Closed	1989	5.50	6
1989 Little Frostee 058-115-1	Closed	1989	8.50	9
1989 Little One 058-098-8	Closed	1989	9.50	10
1989 A Little Shepherd 058-130-5	Closed	1989	5.00	5
1989 Merrie Old Christmas 058-135-6	Closed	1989	5.50	6
1989 Merry Old Santa Claus 053-035-2	Closed	1992	12.00	45
1989 Pa-Rum-Pa-Pum-Pum 058-113-5	Closed	1989	9.50	10
1989 Perky Penguin 058-121-6	Closed	1989	6.50	7
1989 Ring In The Holidays 058-134-9	Closed	1989	7.50	8
1989 School Days 058-125-9	Closed	1989	7.50	8
1989 A Season of Fun 058-108-9	Closed	1989	7.50	8
1989 Season Of Love 058-126-7	Closed	1989	5.00	5
1989 A Sister Is A Friend 058-129-1	Closed	1989	5.00	5
1989 Special Delivery 058-090-2	Closed	1989	11.00	11
1989 To A Special Mom 058-132-1	Closed	1989	7.50	8
1989 Wonderland Waltz 058-095-3	Closed	1992	12.00	12

1990 Summit/Carlton Collector's Series - Carlton

YEAR ISSUE	EDITION LIMIT	YEAR RETD.	ISSUE PRICE	*QUOTE U.S.$
1990 Christmas Express 102-355-1	Closed	1990	12.00	12
1990 Christmas Go-Round 102-346-2	Closed	1990	13.00	13
1990 Christmas Hello 102-352-7	Closed	1990	13.00	13
1990 A Little Bit Of Christmas 102-340-3	Closed	1990	10.50	11
1990 Santa's Roommate 102-361-6	Closed	1990	7.50	8

1990 Summit/Carlton Heirloom Collection - Carlton

YEAR ISSUE	EDITION LIMIT	YEAR RETD.	ISSUE PRICE	*QUOTE U.S.$
1990 Beary Christmas 102-375-6	Closed	1990	7.50	8
1990 Best Friends 102-376-4	Closed	1990	9.50	10
1990 Bunny Love 102-359-4	Closed	1991	9.50	11
1990 Checkin' It Twice 102-323-4	Closed	1991	12.00	12
1990 Christmas Angel 102-331-4	Closed	1990	7.50	8
1990 Christmas At Heart 102-322-5	Closed	1990	12.00	12
1990 Christmas Blessings 102-353-5	Closed	1991	8.00	8
1990 Christmas Caring 102-338-1	Closed	1990	8.00	8
1990 Christmas Confection 102-337-3	Closed	1990	7.00	7
1990 Christmas Dreams 102-363-2	Closed	1990	12.00	12
1990 Christmas Flight 102-329-2	Closed	1990	6.00	6
1990 Christmas Is Special 102-313-6	Closed	1990	6.50	7
1990 Christmas Means Togetherness 102-369-1	Closed	1990	8.50	9
1990 Christmas Memories 102-347-0	Closed	1990	5.25	6
1990 A Christmas Shared 102-354-3	Closed	1991	10.50	11
1990 Christmas Surprise 102-312-8	Closed	1990	7.50	8
1990 Christmas Whirl 102-378-9	Closed	1990	11.00	11
1990 Cool Yule 102-310-1	Closed	1990	9.50	10
1990 Country Friend 102-326-8	Closed	1990	7.00	7
1990 Cozy Kitten 102-341-1	Closed	1990	10.50	11
1990 Crystal Thoughts 102-335-7	Closed	1990	6.50	7
1990 Favorite Things 102-344-6	Closed	1991	11.00	11
1990 Friendship Is A Gift 102-377-2	Closed	1990	5.50	6
1990 Gentle Hearts 102-330-6	Closed	1990	7.00	7
1990 Giddyap Teddy! 102-364-0	Closed	1990	9.50	10
1990 Giddyap Teddy! 102-365-9	Closed	1990	9.50	10
1990 A Gift From Heaven 102-368-3	Closed	1990	7.50	8
1990 Gifts 'N' Good Wishes 102-345-4	Closed	1990	10.50	11
1990 A Grandmother Is Special 102-382-9	Closed	1990	5.50	6
1990 Grandparents Are Always 102-383-7	Closed	1990	5.25	6
1990 Heavenly Flight 102-358-6	Closed	1990	7.50	8
1990 Hi-Ho Holidays 102-321-7	Closed	1990	9.50	10
1990 A Holiday Hi 102-360-8	Closed	1990	10.00	10
1990 Holiday Magic 102-328-4	Closed	1990	6.50	7
1990 Holiday Purr-fection 102-323-3	Closed	1990	6.50	7
1990 Home For The Holidays 102-357-8	Closed	1990	10.50	11
1990 Home, Tweet, Home 102-374-8	Closed	1990	9.50	10
1990 In The Workshop 102-343-8	Closed	1990	13.00	13
1990 Just Us 102-371-3	Closed	1990	9.50	10
1990 Little Frostee 102-379-9	Closed	1990	8.00	8
1990 Little One 102-367-5	Closed	1990	10.50	11
1990 Love is A Gift 102-320-9	Closed	1990	7.50	8
1990 Merry Little Christmas 102-380-2	Closed	1990	11.00	11
1990 Merry Magic 102-324-1	Closed	1990	6.00	6
1990 A Mother Is Love 102-381-0	Closed	1990	7.50	8
1990 Not A Creature Was Stirring 102-348-9	Closed	1992	13.00	13
1990 The Nutcracker 102-327-6	Closed	1990	9.00	9
1990 Pa-Rum-Pa-Pum-Pum 102-366-7	Closed	1990	9.50	10
1990 Pandabelle 102-386-1	Closed	1990	7.50	8
1990 Peace, Hope, Love 102-333-0	Closed	1990	5.25	6
1990 Perky Penguin 102-332-2	Closed	1990	6.50	7
1990 Remembering Christmas 102-384-5	Closed	1990	9.00	9
1990 Rocking Horse Fun 102-316-0	Closed	1990	10.50	11
1990 Sing A Song Of Christmas 102-336-5	Closed	1990	6.00	6
1990 Sound Of Christmas 102-317-9	Closed	1990	7.00	7
1990 Special Christmas Moments 102-385-3	Closed	1990	8.50	9
1990 A Special Gift Photo Holder 102-314-4	Closed	1990	7.50	8
1990 The Stockings Were Hung 102-349-7	Closed	1990	8.00	8
1990 Thoughts Of Christmas 102-334-9	Closed	1990	5.25	6
1990 Together Forever 102-372-1	Closed	1990	11.00	11
1990 Up On The Roof Top 102-309-8	Closed	1990	11.00	11
1990 Up, Up, Away 102-350-0	Closed	1990	10.00	10
1990 Visions Of Sugar Plums 102-351-9			9.50	10
1990 Winter Filigree 102-315-2	Closed	1990	6.50	7
1990 Wonderland Waltz 102-370-5	Closed	1990	13.00	13
1990 Wrapped Up In Christmas 102-318-7	Closed	1990	10.00	10
1990 Ziggy 102-319-5	Closed	1990	5.25	6

1991 Carlton Collector's Series - Carlton

YEAR ISSUE	EDITION LIMIT	YEAR RETD.	ISSUE PRICE	*QUOTE U.S.$
1991 Christmas Express 114-826-5	Closed	1991	14.00	14
1991 Christmas Express 114-857-3	Closed	1991	14.00	14
1991 Christmas Go-Round 114-830-3	Closed	1991	14.00	25
1991 A Little Bit Of Christmas 114-831-1	Closed	1991	11.00	11
1991 Santa's Roommate 114-828-1	Closed	1991	8.00	8

1991 Carlton Heirloom Collection - Carlton

YEAR ISSUE	EDITION LIMIT	YEAR RETD.	ISSUE PRICE	*QUOTE U.S.$
1991 And Away We Go 114-879-6	Closed	1992	9.00	9
1991 Bunny Love 114-836-2	Closed	1992	10.00	10
1991 Catch The Christmas Spirit 114-856-7	Closed	1992	8.50	9
1991 Checkin' It Twice 114-844-3	Closed	1991	12.00	12
1991 Christmas Blessing 114-842-7	Closed	1991	8.50	9
1991 Christmas By The Heartful 114-857-5	Closed	1991	9.00	9
1991 Christmas Caring 114-852-4	Closed	1991	8.00	8
1991 Christmas Charmer 114-804-4	Closed	1991	11.00	11
1991 Christmas Couple 114-861-3	Closed	1991	13.00	13
1991 Christmas Cuddles 114-817-6	Closed	1991	10.50	11
1991 Christmas Cutie 114-811-7	Closed	1991	10.00	10
1991 Christmas Darlings 114-806-0	Closed	1991	12.00	12
1991 Christmas Dreams 114-807-9	Closed	1991	13.00	13
1991 Christmas Fantasy 114-872-9	Closed	1991	11.00	11
1991 Christmas Greetings	Closed	1991		
1991 Christmas Is In The Air 114-878-8	Closed	1992	11.00	11
1991 A Christmas Shared 114-841-9	Closed	1991	10.50	11
1991 Christmas Sweetie 114-855-9	Closed	1991	9.50	10
1991 A Christmas To Remember 114-822-2	Closed	1991	9.00	9
1991 Christmas Wishes 114-869-9	Closed	1992	14.00	14
1991 Christmastime For Two 114-816-8	Closed	1991	14.00	14
1991 Elfkin 114-870-2	Closed	1992	9.50	10
1991 Favorite Things 114-837-0	Closed	1991	12.00	12
1991 Friends At Heart 114-825-7	Closed	1991	8.00	8
1991 Frosty Friend 114-835-4	Closed	1991	8.50	9
1991 Gentle Hearts 114-866-4	Closed	1991	11.00	11
1991 A Gift From Heaven 114-805-2	Closed	1991	8.00	8
1991 God Bless Us All! 114-858-3	Closed	1992	10.00	10
1991 Happiness Is All Around! 114-876-1	Closed	1991	9.00	9
1991 Happy Christmas To All 114-840-0	Closed	1991	8.50	9
1991 Happy Holidays 114-818-4	Closed	1991	8.00	8
1991 Heavenly Flight 114-853-2	Closed	1991	8.00	8
1991 Here Comes Santa! 114-845-1	Closed	1991	9.00	9
1991 Holiday Beauty 114-860-5	Closed	1991	9.00	9
1991 Holiday Fun 114-867-2	Closed	1991	9.50	10
1991 Holiday Hobby Horse 114-812-5	Closed	1991	10.50	11
1991 Holiday Memories 114-808-7	Closed	1991	9.50	10
1991 Holiday Treat 114-881-8	Closed	1992	10.00	10
1991 Hollie Hobbie Christmas At Heart 114-838-9	Closed	1991	12.00	12
1991 Home For Christmas 114-884-2	Closed	1991	10.50	11
1991 Home For The Holidays 114-839-9	Closed	1991	10.50	11
1991 In The Workshop 114-847-8	Closed	1991	13.00	13
1991 A Jolly Old Elf 114-859-1	Closed	1991	10.00	10
1991 Just Us 114-813-3	Closed	1991	11.00	11
1991 Little Christmas Wishes 114-810-9	Closed	1991	11.00	11
1991 Little Drummer Bear 114-864-8	Closed	1991	9.50	10
1991 Little Starflight 114-868-0	Closed	1991	11.00	11
1991 A Little Taste Of Christmas 114-862-1	Closed	1991	13.00	13
1991 Love Is All Around 114-823-0	Closed	1991	11.00	11
1991 A Mother Is Love 114-819-2	Closed	1991	11.00	11
1991 North Pole Parade 114-874-5	Closed	1991	14.00	14
1991 Not A Creature Was Stirring 114-850-8	Closed	1991	14.00	14
1991 Purr-fect Holidays 114-871-0	Closed	1991	11.00	11
1991 Reindeer Games 114-865-6	Closed	1991	10.00	10
1991 Ring In the Holidays 114-821-4	Closed	1991	10.00	10
1991 Rocking Horse Fun 114-848-6	Closed	1991	11.00	11
1991 Sing A Song Of Christmas 114-873-7	Closed	1991	12.00	12
1991 Small Surprises 114-809-5	Closed	1991	10.50	11
1991 Snowflake Friends 114-824-9	Closed	1991	11.00	11
1991 A Special Gift 114-820-6	Closed	1991	9.00	9
1991 A Special Photo Holder 114-834-6	Closed	1991	9.00	9
1991 Stocking Full Of Love 114-854-0	Closed	1991	9.00	9
1991 There Is A Santa! 114-833-8	Closed	1991	14.00	14
1991 Together Forever 114-814-1	Closed	1991	12.00	12
1991 Up On The Roof Top 114-843-5	Closed	1991	11.00	11
1991 Visions Of Sugar Plums 114-849-4	Closed	1992	9.50	10
1991 The Wonder Of Christmas 114-875-3	Closed	1992	9.00	9

1992 Carlton Collector's Series - Carlton

YEAR ISSUE	EDITION LIMIT	YEAR RETD.	ISSUE PRICE	*QUOTE U.S.$
1992 Christmas Express Caboose (2nd) 120539-0	Closed	1993	15.00	15
1992 Christmas Express Coal Tender (3rd) 120478-5	Closed	1992	15.00	15
1992 Christmas Express Engine (1st) 120477-7	Closed	1992	15.00	15
1992 Christmas Go-Round (3rd) 120479-3	Closed	1992	14.00	14
1992 Christmas Sweets (1st) 120486-6	Closed	1992	11.00	20
1992 Ice Pals (1st) 120483-1	Closed	1992	10.00	10
1992 A Little Bit Of Christmas (3rd) 120481-5	Closed	1992	13.00	13

YEAR ISSUE	EDITION LIMIT	YEAR RETD.	ISSUE PRICE	*QUOTE U.S.$
1992 North Pole Parade (1st) 120482-3	Closed	1992	14.00	14
1992 Rodrick & Sam's Winter Fun (1st) 120485-8	Closed	1992	13.00	13

1992 Carlton Heirloom Collection - Carlton

YEAR ISSUE	EDITION LIMIT	YEAR RETD.	ISSUE PRICE	*QUOTE U.S.$
1992 Alpine Adventure 120469-6	Closed	1992	11.00	11
1992 Bundles of Joy 120509-9	Closed	1992	14.00	14
1992 Bunny Love 120519-6	Closed	1992	11.00	11
1992 Catch The Christmas Spirit 120522-6	Closed	1992	8.50	9
1992 Cherished Memories 120457-2	Closed	1992	11.00	11
1992 A Child's Christmas 120532-3	Closed	1992	11.00	11
1992 A Child's Christmas 120533-1	Closed	1992	11.00	11
1992 Christmas Blessing 120513-7	Closed	1992	9.50	10
1992 Christmas Charmer 120441-6	Closed	1992	11.00	11
1992 Christmas Couple 120511-0	Closed	1992	14.00	14
1992 Christmas Cuddles 120461-0	Closed	1992	11.00	11
1992 Christmas Fantasy 120524-2	Closed	1992	11.00	11
1992 The Christmas Star 120527-7	Closed	1992	9.50	10
1992 Christmas Swingtime 120505-6	Closed	1992	10.00	10
1992 A Christmas to Remember 120538-2	Closed	1992	12.00	12
1992 Christmas Twirl 120455-6	Closed	1992	14.00	14
1992 Christmas Warmth 120452-1	Closed	1992	9.00	9
1992 Christmas Whirl 120448-3	Closed	1992	12.00	12
1992 Christmas Wishes 120516-1	Closed	1992	14.00	14
1992 Circle of Love 120439-4	Closed	1992	11.00	11
1992 Cuddly Christmas 120445-9	Closed	1992	10.00	10
1992 Curious Cutie 11.00				11
1992 Elfkin 120497-1	Closed	1992	10.00	10
1992 Family Ties 120459-9	Closed	1992	10.00	10
1992 Frosted Fantasy 120502-1	Closed	1992	9.00	9
1992 Frosty Fun 120440-8	Closed	1992	12.00	12
1992 Giddyap, Teddy!	Closed	1992	11.00	11
1992 A Gift From The Heart 120530-7	Closed	1993	9.50	10
1992 Ginger 120476-9	Closed	1992	9.50	10
1992 Happiness Is All Around 120518-8	Closed	1992	9.00	9
1992 Heart Full of Christmas 120446-7	Closed	1992	10.00	10
1992 Heart Full of Love 120463-7	Closed	1992	13.00	13
1992 Heart to Heart 120454-8	Closed	1992	11.00	11
1992 Heartfelt Christmas 120471-8	Closed	1992	10.00	10
1992 Heartwarming Holidays 120528-5	Closed	1992	9.00	9
1992 Heaven Sent 120535-8	Closed	1992	9.50	10
1992 High-Flying Holiday 11.00				11
1992 Holiday Harmony 120490-4	Closed	1992	13.00	13
1992 Holiday Heirloom 120450-5	Closed	1992	11.00	11
1992 Holiday Helpers 120491-2	Closed	1992	13.00	13
1992 A Holiday Hi 120525-0	Closed	1992	11.00	11
1992 Holiday Treat 120523-4	Closed	1992	11.00	11
1992 Home, Tweet Home 120468-8	Closed	1992	10.00	10
1992 Honey Bunny Christmas 120494-7	Closed	1992	12.00	12
1992 Jolly Holidays 120456-4	Closed	1992	12.00	12
1992 Joy 120474-2	Closed	1992	9.50	10
1992 Just Us 120460-2	Closed	1992	11.00	11
1992 Kitty Caper 120493-9	Closed	1992	11.00	11
1992 Little Starlight 120537-4	Closed	1992	12.00	12
1992 Made With Love 15.00				15
1992 Magic of Christmas 120451-3	Closed	1992	12.00	12
1992 Merry Christmas to All 120506-4	Closed	1992	8.50	9
1992 Merry Marionettes 120487-4	Closed	1992	15.00	15
1992 Noelle 120475-0	Closed	1992	9.50	
1992 North Pole Putter 120473-4	Closed	1992	11.00	11
1992 Not A Creature Was Stirring 120514-5	Closed	1992	14.00	14
1992 Picture Perfect 120529-3	Closed	1992	8.50	9
1992 Polar Pals 120512-9	Closed	1992	11.00	11
1992 Pom Pom The Clown 120531-5	Closed	1992	9.50	10
1992 Precious Heart 120444-0	Closed	1992	10.00	10
1992 Purr-fect Holidays 120507-2	Closed	1992	11.00	11
1992 Ringing In Christmas 120536-6	Closed	1992	12.00	12
1992 Rock-A-Bye Baby 120442-4	Closed	1992	13.00	13
1992 Rocking Horse Fun 120504-8	Closed	1992	11.00	11
1992 Santa's Helpers 120495-5	Closed	1992	15.00	15
1992 Santa's Roommate (3rd) 120480-7	Closed	1992	9.00	9
1992 Santa's Surprises 120449-1	Closed	1992	11.00	11
1992 School Days 120472-6	Closed	1992	10.00	10
1992 The Season of Love 120464-5	Closed	1992	9.00	9
1992 A Silver Celebration 120466-1	Closed	1992	10.00	10
1992 Special Surprise 120489-0	Closed	1992	12.00	12
1992 Spirit of St. Nick 120458-0	Closed	1992	9.00	9
1992 Stocking Full of Love 120508-0	Closed	1992	9.00	9
1992 Times to Treasure 120465-3	Closed	1992	9.00	9
1992 Tiny Toy Shop 15.00				15
1992 Together Forever 120462-9	Closed	1992	12.00	12
1992 Visions of Sugar Plums 10.00				10
1992 Warmhearted Holidays 120526-9	Closed	1992	9.50	10
1992 Winter Funtime 120501-3	Closed	1992	11.00	11
1992 The Wonder of Christmas 120510-2	Closed	1992	10.00	10

1993 Carlton Collector's Series - Carlton

YEAR ISSUE	EDITION LIMIT	YEAR RETD.	ISSUE PRICE	*QUOTE U.S.$
1993 Book of Carols (1st) 126005-7	Closed	1993	13.50	14
1993 Christmas Express Caboose (2nd) 126037-5	Closed	1993	15.00	15
1993 Christmas Express Coal Tender Car (3rd) 126038-3	Closed	1993	15.00	15
1993 Christmas Express Engine (1st) 126036-7	Closed	1993	15.00	15
1993 Christmas Express Reindeer Coach (4th) 126010-3	Closed	1993	15.00	15
1993 Christmas Sweets (2nd) 126035-9	Closed	1993	12.00	12

YEAR ISSUE	EDITION LIMIT	YEAR RETD.	ISSUE PRICE	*QUOTE U.S.$
1993 Christmas-Go-Round (4th) 126013-8	Closed	1993	14.00	14
1993 Ice Pals (2nd) 126006-5	Closed	1993	10.50	11
1993 A Little Bit of Christmas 126007-3	Closed	1993	13.00	13
1993 North Pole Parade (2nd) 126011-1	Closed	1993	14.00	14
1993 Rodrick & Sam's Winter Fun (2nd) 126008-1	Closed	1993	13.00	13
1993 Santa's Roommate (4th) 126039-1	Closed	1993	9.00	9
1993 Santa's Wheels 125986-5	Closed	1993	10.00	10
1993 Sewing Circle Sweetie 126102-9	Closed	1993	12.50	13
1993 Special Surprise 126084-7	Closed	1993	13.00	13
1993 Tiny Toymaker (1st) 126034-0	Closed	1993	12.50	13

1993 Carlton Heirloom Collection - Carlton

YEAR ISSUE	EDITION LIMIT	YEAR RETD.	ISSUE PRICE	*QUOTE U.S.$
1993 10 Yrs. Together Christmas Bell 126002-0	Closed	1993	11.00	11
1993 25 Yrs. Together Christmas Bell 126003-0	Closed	1993	11.00	11
1993 5 Yrs. Together Christmas Bell 126001-4	Closed	1993	11.00	11
1993 Airmail Delivery 126069-3	Closed	1993	12.50	13
1993 All Decked Out 126015-4	Closed	1993	12.50	13
1993 And Away We Go 126073-1	Closed	1993	12.00	12
1993 Baby Kermit's Sleighride 125968-7	Closed	1993	10.50	11
1993 Baby Magic 125981-4	Closed	1993	11.00	11
1993 Baby Miss Piggy's Christmas Star 125966-0	Closed	1993	10.50	11
1993 Beary Merry Balloon 125971-7	Closed	1993	10.00	10
1993 A Beary Snowy Day 126053-7	Closed	1993	18.00	18
1993 Bundles of Joy 126086-3	Closed	1993	14.50	15
1993 Chef's Delight 126096-0	Closed	1993	11.50	12
1993 Christmas Cuddles 125995-4	Closed	1993	11.00	11
1993 Christmas Fantasy 126094-4	Closed	1993	12.00	12
1993 Christmas Parade 126018-9	Closed	1993	13.00	13
1993 The Christmas Star 126098-7	Closed	1993	9.50	10
1993 Christmas Surprise 125972-5	Closed	1993	10.00	10
1993 Christmas Waltz 126063-4	Closed	1993	16.00	16
1993 Christmas Wishes 126076-6	Closed	1993	14.00	14
1993 Circle of Love 125963-6	Closed	1993	11.00	11
1993 Cozy Moments 125993-8	Closed	1993	11.00	11
1993 Curious Cutie 126070-7	Closed	1993	12.00	12
1993 December 24th Deadline 126059-6	Closed	1993	13.50	14
1993 Do Not Disturb Til Christmas 126044-8	Closed	1993	11.50	12
1993 Festive Lace 125998-5	Closed	1993	8.50	9
1993 Frosty and Friend 125999-7	Closed	1993	10.50	11
1993 A Gift From The Heart 126090-1	Closed	1993	9.50	10
1993 Ginger 126029-4	Closed	1993	10.00	10
1993 Gingerbread Treat 126042-1	Closed	1993	10.50	11
1993 Good Catch! 126040-5	Closed	1993	10.00	10
1993 Happy Home 125991-1	Closed	1993	10.50	11
1993 Heavenly Love 125982-2	Closed	1993	9.50	10
1993 Holiday Harmony 126083-9	Closed	1993	14.00	14
1993 Holiday Helpers 126078-2	Closed	1993	14.00	14
1993 A Holiday Hi 126087-1	Closed	1993	12.00	12
1993 Holiday Treat 126089-8	Closed	1993	12.00	12
1993 Holly Hippo 126101-0	Closed	1993	11.50	12
1993 Home For Christmas 125990-3	Closed	1993	10.00	10
1993 Homemade Happiness 126064-2	Closed	1993	12.50	13
1993 Honeybunny Christmas 126085-5	Closed	1993	12.50	13
1993 Hooked A Good One 126004-9	Closed	1993	11.50	12
1993 It's A Small World 126052-9	Closed	1993	16.00	16
1993 Joy 126028-6	Closed	1993	10.00	10
1993 Just A Few Lines 126048-0	Closed	1993	11.00	11
1993 Just Us 125977-0	Closed	1993	12.00	12
1993 Kermit's Christmas 126032-4	Closed	1993	11.00	11
1993 Kitty Caper 126081-2	Closed	1993	11.00	11
1993 Letter To Santa 126045-6	Closed	1993	12.00	12
1993 Li'l Artist 126056-1	Closed	1993	11.50	12
1993 Li'l Chimney Sweep 126100-2	Closed	1993	11.00	11
1993 Li'l Feathered Friend 126020-0	Closed	1993	8.00	8
1993 Love Birds 125996-2	Closed	1993	13.00	13
1993 Loving Wishes 125987-3	Closed	1993	11.00	11
1993 Made With Love 127072-3	Closed	1993	15.00	15
1993 Magic of the Season 126097-9			11.50	12
1993 Making Music 126058-8	Closed	1993	11.50	12
1993 Memories to Keep 125985-7	Closed	1993	10.00	10
1993 Merry Marionettes 126095-2	Closed	1993	15.00	15
1993 Miss Piggy's Waltz 126031-6	Closed	1993	12.00	12
1993 A Muppet Christmas 126033-2	Closed	1993	6.50	7
1993 Next Stop, North Pole 125984-9	Closed	1993	11.00	11
1993 Noelle 126030-8	Closed	1993	10.00	10
1993 North Pole Putter 126082-8	Closed	1993	12.00	12
1993 On Top of The Whirl 126067-7	Closed	1993	14.50	15
1993 One Last Touch! 126051-0	Closed	1993	14.00	14
1993 Peppermint Panda 126079-0	Closed	1993	9.50	10
1993 Peppermint Waltz 126047-2	Closed	1993	11.50	12
1993 The Perfect Package 126065-0	Closed	1993	14.00	14
1993 Polar Pals 126093-6	Closed	1993	12.50	13
1993 Pom Pom 126105-3	Closed	1993	10.00	10
1993 Pop-Up Fun! 125964-4	Closed	1993	11.00	11
1993 Precious Heart 125970-9	Closed	1993	10.00	10
1993 Pretty Bubbler 126050-2	Closed	1993	13.00	13
1993 Purr-fect Holidays 126016-2	Closed	1993	12.00	12
1993 Rocking Horse Fun 126017-0	Closed	1993	12.00	12
1993 Santa's Boy 125969-5	Closed	1993	13.00	13
1993 Santa's Helpers 126080-4	Closed	1993	15.00	15
1993 Stocking Full of Love 126082-0	Closed	1993	9.00	9
1993 Sweet Season 125973-3	Closed	1993	10.00	10
1993 Swinging On A Star 126041-3	Closed	1993	10.00	10

YEAR ISSUE	EDITION LIMIT	YEAR RETD.	ISSUE PRICE	*QUOTE U.S.$
1993 Teacher's Pet 126000-6	Closed	1993	7.50	8
1993 Tiny Toyshop 126071-5	Closed	1993	15.00	15
1993 A Token of Love 125983-0	Closed	1993	12.00	12
1993 Trimming The Tree 125988-1	Closed	1993	9.00	9
1993 Two Together 125994-6	Closed	1993	13.50	14
1993 Up on the House Top 126061-8	Closed	1993	17.00	17
1993 Visions of Sugarplums 126075-8	Closed	1994	10.00	10
1993 Waiting For Santa 126066-9	Closed	1994	15.00	15
1993 Wake Me When It's Christmas 126049-9	Closed	1993	13.00	13
1993 Warm 'N Toasty 126054-5	Closed	1993	16.00	16
1993 Warmhearted Holidays 126099-5	Closed	1993	9.50	10
1993 Wee Whatnots 126062-6	Closed	1993	17.50	18
1993 Winter Funtime 126077-4	Closed	1993	11.00	11
1993 Winterland Fun 126055-3	Closed	1993	17.00	17
1993 Wishes On The Way 126068-5	Closed	1993	8.50	9

1994 Carlton Collector's Series - Carlton

YEAR ISSUE	EDITION LIMIT	YEAR RETD.	ISSUE PRICE	*QUOTE U.S.$
1994 Big Fun (1st) ORN001L	Closed	1994	13.50	14
1994 Book of Carols (2nd) ORN004L	Closed	1994	13.50	14
1994 Christmas Express Caboose (2nd) ORN010L	Closed	1994	15.00	15
1994 Christmas Express Coach (4th) ORN011L	Closed	1994	15.00	15
1994 Christmas Express Engine (1st) ORN009L	Closed	1994	15.00	15
1994 Christmas Express Tanker (5th) ORN012L	Closed	1994	15.00	15
1994 Christmas Go-Round (5th) ORN013L	Closed	1994	15.00	15
1994 Christmas Sweets (3rd) ORN006L	Closed	1994	14.50	15
1994 Ice Pals (3rd) ORN007L	Closed	1994	12.50	13
1994 A Little Bit Of Christmas (5th) ORN014L	Closed	1994	13.50	14
1994 Rodrick & Sam's Winter Fun (3rd) ORN008L	Closed	1994	12.50	13
1994 Santa's Roommate (5th) ORN015L	Closed	1994	10.50	11
1994 Santa's Toy Shop (1st) ORN003L	Closed	1994	17.00	17
1994 Snug In Their Beds (1st) ORN002L	Closed	1994	16.00	16
1994 Tiny Toymaker (2nd) ORN005L	Closed	1994	12.50	13

1994 Carlton Heirloom Collection - Carlton

YEAR ISSUE	EDITION LIMIT	YEAR RETD.	ISSUE PRICE	*QUOTE U.S.$
1994 All Decked Out ORN118L	Closed	1994	12.50	13
1994 Artistic Wishes ORN092L	Closed	1994	14.50	15
1994 Baby's First Christmas ORN022L	Closed	1994	11.50	12
1994 Baby's First Christmas ORN023L	Closed	1994	14.50	15
1994 Baby's First Christmas ORN024L	Closed	1994	13.50	14
1994 Baby's First Christmas ORN025L	Closed	1994	13.50	14
1994 Baby's Second Christmas ORN027L	Closed	1994	10.50	11
1994 A Basketful Of Goodies ORN077L	Closed	1994	10.50	11
1994 Bears On Parade ORN081L	Closed	1995	18.00	18
1994 Beary Merry Wishes ORN075L	Closed	1994	9.50	10
1994 Brother ORN040L	Closed	1994	15.00	15
1994 Bunny Delight ORN112L	Closed	1994	15.00	15
1994 Candy-Gram ORN103L	Closed	1994	8.50	9
1994 Caregiver ORN046L	Closed	1994	11.50	12
1994 Catch The Christmas Spirit ORN116L	Closed	1994	8.50	9
1994 Changin' For Christmas ORN109L	Closed	1994	13.50	14
1994 Chester's Heartfelt Holiday ORN063L	Closed	1994	10.50	11
1995 A Child's Christmas ORN135L	Closed	1994	11.50	12
1994 Child's Fourth Christmas ORN029L	Closed	1994	10.50	11
1994 Child's Third Christmas ORN028L	Closed	1994	10.50	11
1994 Christmas Bell ORN127L	Closed	1994	13.50	14
1994 Christmas By The Heartful ORN021L	Closed	1994	12.50	13
1994 Christmas Catch ORN069L	Closed	1994	11.50	12
1994 Christmas Countdown ORN089L	Closed	1995	14.50	15
1994 Christmas In The Country ORN129L	Closed	1994	8.50	9
1994 Christmas Spin ORN054L	Closed	1994	17.00	17
1994 The Christmas Star ORN076L	Closed	1994	9.50	10
1994 Circle Of Love ORN026L	Closed	1994	11.50	12
1994 Clowning Around ORN090L	Closed	1994	13.50	14
1994 Co-Worker ORN045L	Closed	1994	10.50	11
1994 Dad ORN035L	Closed	1994	12.50	13
1994 Dashing Through The Snow ORN057L	Closed	1994	16.00	16
1994 Daughter N/A				13
1994 December 24th Deadline ORN085L	Closed	1994	13.50	14
1994 Downhill Delight ORN070L	Closed	1994	13.50	14
1994 Finishing Touches ORN073L	Closed	1994	12.50	13
1994 First Christmas Together ORN016L	Closed	1994	11.50	12
1994 First Christmas Together ORN017L	Closed	1994	18.00	18
1994 First Christmas Together ORN018L	Closed	1994	13.50	14
1994 Folk Angel ORN132l	Closed	1994	7.50	8
1994 Folk Santa ORN071L	Closed	1994	13.50	14
1994 Friend ORN047L	Closed	1994	9.50	10
1994 Friends Around The World ORN132L	Closed	1994	7.50	8
1994 Gift Exchange ORN078L	Closed	1994	11.50	12
1994 Godchild ORN033L	Closed	1994	10.50	11
1994 Grand-Daughter's First Christmas ORN030L	Closed	1994	11.50	12
1994 Grand-Mother ORN041L	Closed	1994	11.50	12
1994 Grandparents ORN042L	Closed	1994	9.50	10

ORNAMENTS

YEAR ISSUE	EDITION LIMIT	YEAR RETD.	ISSUE PRICE	*QUOTE U.S.$
1994 Grandson's First Christmas ORN031L	Closed	1994	11.50	15
1994 High Flying Fun ORN106L	Closed	1994	12.50	13
1994 High Lights ORN107L	Closed	1994	12.50	13
1994 Holiday Gardner ORN088L	Closed	1994	12.50	13
1994 Holiday Sentiment ORN128L	Closed	1994	11.50	12
1994 Holiday Swing Time ORN108L	Closed	1994	13.50	14
1994 Holiday Time ORN052L	Closed	1995	16.00	16
1994 Homemade Happiness ORN083L	Closed	1995	12.50	13
1994 Hook, Line and Singers ORN067L	Closed	1995	13.50	14
1994 Hoppy Holidays ORN111L	Closed	1994	13.50	14
1994 It's A Small World ORN100L	Closed	1994	16.00	16
1994 Jogging Santa ORN068L	Closed	1994	11.50	12
1994 Juggling Jester ORN050L	Closed	1994	13.50	14
1994 Jumbo Wishes ORN117L	Closed	1994	12.50	13
1994 L'il Artist ORN080L	Closed	1994	11.50	12
1994 Lion & Lamb ORN133L	Closed	1994	13.50	14
1994 Madonna Child ORN131L	Closed	1994	12.50	13
1994 Magic Of The Season ORN124L	Closed	1994	12.50	13
1994 Many Happy Returns ORN061L	Closed	1994	13.50	14
1994 Merry Old Santa ORN074L	Closed	1994	14.50	15
1994 Moo-ey Christmas ORN102L	Closed	1994	8.50	9
1994 Mother ORN034L	Closed	1994	11.50	15
1994 Mouse With Gifts ORN086L	Closed	1994	11.50	12
1994 Music Box Dancers ORN053L	Closed	1994	18.00	18
1994 Nature's Friends ORN125L	Closed	1994	9.50	10
1994 New Home ORN043L	Closed	1994	12.50	13
1994 Noah's Ark ORN134L	Closed	1994	13.50	15
1994 North Pole Pals ORN122L	Closed	1994	14.50	15
1994 O. Opus Tree ORN058L	Closed	1994	12.50	15
1994 Off For A Spin ORN091L	Closed	1994	14.50	15
1994 On Top Of The Whirl ORN097L	Closed	1994	14.50	15
1994 One Last Touch ORN096L	Closed	1994	14.50	15
1994 Our Christmas Together ORN019L	Closed	1994	14.50	15
1994 Our House To Your House ORN044L	Closed	1994	10.50	11
1994 Paddling Pals ORN064L	Closed	1994	11.50	12
1994 Parents ORN036L	Closed	1994	14.50	15
1994 Parents To-Be ORN032L	Closed	1994	11.50	12
1994 Peppermint Waltz ORN119L	Closed	1994	11.50	12
1994 The Perfect Package ORN098L	Closed	1994	14.50	15
1994 Picture Perfect ORN126L	Closed	1994	7.50	8
1994 Playin A Holiday Tune ORN110L	Closed	1995	13.50	14
1994 The Polar Bear Club ORN079L	Closed	1995	13.50	14
1994 Pretty Bubbler ORN084L	Closed	1994	13.50	14
1994 Puffin ORN104L	Closed	1994	11.50	12
1994 Purr-fect Holidays ORN115L	Closed	1994	12.50	13
1994 Rocking Horse Fun ORN123L	Closed	1994	12.50	13
1994 Santa's Hotline ORN114L	Closed	1995	13.50	14
1994 Santa-In-The-Box ORN072L	Closed	1994	15.00	15
1994 Servin' Up Christmas Cheer ORN066L	Closed	1994	10.50	11
1994 Sew Much Love ORN087L	Closed	1994	12.50	13
1994 Sister ORN039L	Closed	1994	10.50	11
1994 SNOWDOME! Winterland Fun ORN113L			17.00	17
1994 Soccer Star ORN065L	Closed	1995	9.50	10
1994 Son ORN038L	Closed	1995	11.50	12
1994 St. Bernard ORN105L	Closed	1994	8.50	9
1994 Sugar Cone Castle ORN120L	Closed	1994	15.00	15
1994 Surprise! ORN049L	Closed	1994	12.50	13
1994 Sweet Season ORN082L	Closed	1994	10.50	11
1994 Sweetheart ORN020L	Closed	1994	10.50	11
1994 Swinging On A Star ORN094L	Closed	1994	10.50	11
1994 Teacher ORN048L	Closed	1994	7.50	8
1994 Tenderheart Bear ORN062L	Closed	1994	10.50	11
1994 Twinkle, Twinkle Christmas Stars ORN121L	Closed	1995	13.50	14
1994 Twirling Fun ORN051L	Closed	1994	18.00	18
1994 Up On The Housetop ORN055L	Closed	1994	17.00	17
1994 Visions Of Sugarplums ORN095L	Closed	1994	10.50	11
1994 Waiting For Santa ORN099L	Closed	1994	15.00	15
1994 Warm 'N Toasty ORN056L	Closed	1994	16.00	16
1994 Wee Whatnots ORN101L	Closed	1994	17.00	17
1994 Yuletide News ORN093L	Closed	1994	15.00	15
1994 Ziggy ORN059L	Closed	1994	12.50	13
1994 Ziggy ORN060L	Closed	1994	12.50	13

1995 Carlton Collector's Series - Carlton

YEAR ISSUE	EDITION LIMIT	YEAR RETD.	ISSUE PRICE	*QUOTE U.S.$
1995 Book of Carols (3rd) ORN004M	Closed	1995	13.75	14
1995 Christmas Express Handcar (6th) ORN010M	Closed	1995	15.75	18
1995 Christmas Go Round (6th) ORN013M	Closed	1995	15.75	16
1995 Christmas Sweets (4th) ORN006M	Closed	1995	14.75	15
1995 Christmas Town Lane (1st) ORN011M	Closed	1995	14.75	20
1995 Holiday Garden (1st) ORN125M	Closed	1995	14.75	15
1995 Holiday Town (2nd) ORN003M	Closed	1995	17.75	18
1995 Ice Pals (4th) ORN007M	Closed	1995	12.75	13
1995 A Little Bit of Christmas (6th) ORN014M	Closed	1995	13.75	14
1995 Pinecone Cottage (2nd) ORN002M	Closed	1995	16.75	17
1995 Rodrick and Sam's Winter Fun (4th) ORN008M	Closed	1995	12.75	13
1995 Roommate Bear (6th) ORN009M	Closed	1995	12.75	13
1995 Santa's Music Makers (2nd) ORN001M	Closed	1995	13.75	14
1995 Tiny Toymaker (3rd) ORN005M	Closed	1995	12.75	13
1995 Year By Year (1st) ORN126M	Closed	1995	12.75	13

1995 Carlton Heirloom Collection - Carlton

YEAR ISSUE	EDITION LIMIT	YEAR RETD.	ISSUE PRICE	*QUOTE U.S.$
1995 25th Wedding Anniversary ORN056M	Closed	1995	13.75	14
1995 Airmail Delivery ORN100M	Closed	1995	17.75	18
1995 All Around The Workshop ORN074M	Closed	1995	34.00	34
1995 Artistic Wishes ORN092M	Closed	1995	11.75	12
1995 Away In A Manger ORN093M	Closed	1995	11.75	12
1995 Baby Boy's First Christmas ORN025M	Closed	1995	13.75	14
1995 Baby Boy's First Christmas ORN131M	Closed	1995	10.75	11
1995 Baby Girl's First Christmas ORN024M	Closed	1995	14.75	15
1995 Baby Girl's First Christmas ORN130M	Closed	1995	10.75	11
1995 Baby Photoholder ORN026M	Closed	1995	9.75	10
1995 Baby's First Christmas ORN022M	Closed	1995	11.75	12
1995 Baby's First Christmas ORN023M	Closed	1995	14.75	15
1995 Baby's Second Christmas ORN027M	Closed	1995	10.75	11
1995 Bears on Parade ORN081M	Closed	1995	17.75	18
1995 Beary Merry Treasures ORN054M	Closed	1995	13.75	15
1995 Brother ORN040M	Closed	1995	16.75	17
1995 Bunny Delight ORN112M	Closed	1995	13.75	14
1995 Care Bears Bedtime Bear ORN107M	Closed	1995	11.75	12
1995 Caregiver ORN046M	Closed	1995	8.75	9
1995 Changin' for Christmas ORN109M	Closed	1995	18.75	19
1995 Child's Fourth Christmas ORN029M	Closed	1995	10.75	11
1995 Child's Third Christmas ORN028M	Closed	1995	11.75	12
1995 A Christmas Celebration ORN084M	Closed	1995	16.75	17
1995 Christmas Countdown ORN089M			14.75	15
1995 Christmas is Coming ORN076M	Closed	1995	32.00	32
1995 Christmas Poinsettia ORN079M	Closed	1995	10.75	11
1995 Christmas Spin ORN090M	Closed	1995	14.75	15
1995 The Christmas Star ORN118M	Closed	1995	8.75	9
1995 Clowning Around ORN090M	Closed	1995	13.75	14
1995 Dad ORN035M	Closed	1995	14.75	15
1995 Dancin' Prancin' Bear ORN116M	Closed	1995	14.75	15
1995 Danglin' Darlin's ORN129M	Closed	1995	8.75	9
1995 Daughter ORN037M	Closed	1995	13.75	14
1995 Do Not Disturb 'Til Christmas ORN049M	Closed	1995	8.75	9
1995 Elvis-Blue Christmas (1st) ORN073M	Closed	1995	25.00	50
1995 A Feeling of Christmas ORN075M	Closed	1995	34.00	34
1995 First Christmas Together ORN012M	Closed	1995	13.75	14
1995 First Christmas Together ORN016M	Closed	1995	11.75	12
1995 First Christmas Together ORN017M	Closed	1995	13.75	14
1995 First Christmas Together ORN018M	Closed	1995	14.75	15
1995 Friend ORN047M	Closed	1995	10.75	11
1995 Get Your Pop-Corn Here! ORN083M			21.00	21
1995 Gift Exchange ORN078M	Closed	1995	11.75	12
1995 Godchild ORN033M	Closed	1995	10.75	11
1995 Godchild ORN071M	Closed	1995	12.75	13
1995 Godmother ORN015M	Closed	1995	11.75	12
1995 Grandaughter's First Christmas ORN030M	Closed	1995	11.75	12
1995 Grandmother ORN041M	Closed	1995	10.75	11
1995 Grandparents ORN042M	Closed	1995	13.75	14
1995 Grandson's First Christmas ORN031M	Closed	1995	11.75	12
1995 Greetings To You ORN070M	Closed	1995	28.00	28
1995 The Heart of Christmas ORN102M	Closed	1995	12.75	13
1995 Hershey's Express ORN098M	Closed	1995	17.75	18
1995 High-Flyin' Santa ORN077M	Closed	1995	28.00	28
1995 Holiday Gardner ORN088M	Closed	1995	13.75	14
1995 Holiday Harmony ORN128M	Closed	1995	14.75	15
1995 Holiday Time ORN052M	Closed	1995	14.75	15
1995 Hook, Line and Singers ORN067M	Closed	1995	12.75	13
1995 Hoppy Holidays ORN111M	Closed	1995	13.75	14
1995 Juggling Jester ORN050M	Closed	1995	12.75	13
1995 Jukebox Jingles ORN080M	Closed	1995	23.00	23
1995 Li'l Feathered Friend ORN117M	Closed	1995	16.75	17
1995 Love at Christmas ORN021M	Closed	1995	10.75	11
1995 Magic of the Season ORN124M	Closed	1995	14.75	15
1995 Merry Matinee ORN082M	Closed	1995	21.00	21
1995 Merry Meister ORN087M	Closed	1995	18.75	19
1995 Mother ORN034M	Closed	1995	14.75	15
1995 Music Box Dancers ORN053M	Closed	1995	18.75	19
1995 New Home ORN043M	Closed	1995	12.75	13
1995 New Home ORN057M	Closed	1995	12.75	13
1995 North Pole Pals ORN122M	Closed	1995	13.75	14
1995 Off For A Spin ORN091M	Closed	1995	13.75	14
1995 Oh, Sew Merry! ORN064M	Closed	1995	13.75	14
1995 Opus Flashin' Through the Snow! ORN104M	Closed	1995	12.75	13
1995 Our Christmas Together ORN019M	Closed	1995	11.75	12
1995 Our Family Photoholder ORN135M	Closed	1995	9.75	10
1995 Our House To Your House ORN044M	Closed	1995	13.75	14
1995 Parents ORN036M	Closed	1995	15.75	16
1995 Parents To Be ORN032M	Closed	1995	11.75	12
1995 Pet Photoholder ORN055M	Closed	1995	9.75	10
1995 Pillsbury Poppin' Fresh Christmas ORN097M	Closed	1995	13.75	14
1995 Playin' A Holiday Tune ORN110M	Closed	1995	13.75	14
1995 Purr-Fect Holidays ORN115M	Closed	1995	13.75	14
1995 Rocking Horse Fun ORN123M	Closed	1995	9.75	10
1995 Rocky and Bullwinkle Merry Fishmas ORN096M	Closed	1995	15.75	16
1995 Santa's Hotline ORN114M	Closed	1995	13.75	14
1995 Santa's On His Way! ORN127M	Closed	1995	9.75	10
1995 Santa-In-The-Box ORN072M	Closed	1995	15.75	16
1995 Sister ORN039M	Closed	1995	11.75	12
1995 Sister To Sister ORN133M	Closed	1995	13.75	14
1995 A Sleighful Of Joys ORN128M	Closed	1995	15.75	16
1995 Snow Bunnies ORN103M	Closed	1995	12.75	13
1995 Snow Sculpturing ORN105M	Closed	1995	12.75	13
1995 Son ORN038M	Closed	1995	11.75	12
1995 St. Bernard ORN119M	Closed	1995	10.75	11
1995 Stocking Full Of Fun ORN099M	Closed	1995	12.75	13
1995 Sugar Cone Castle ORN120M	Closed	1995	17.75	18
1995 Sweetheart ORN020M	Closed	1995	12.75	13
1995 Swinging Into Christmas ORN085M	Closed	1995	14.75	15
1995 Teacher ORN048M	Closed	1995	8.75	9
1995 To Grandma Photoholder ORN134M	Closed	1995	9.75	10
1995 Twinkle, Twinkle Christmas Star ORN121M	Closed	1995	13.75	14
1995 Twirling Fun ORN051M	Closed	1995	14.75	15
1995 Visit With Santa Photoholder ORN132M	Closed	1995	9.75	10
1995 Volkswagon On Our Merry Way! ORN094M	Closed	1995	21.00	21
1995 Wake Me When It's Christmas ORN106M	Closed	1995	11.75	12
1995 Westward Ho Holidays ORN108M	Closed	1995	17.75	18
1995 The Wisemen's Journey ORN101M	Closed	1995	12.75	13
1995 Workplace Wishes ORN045M	Closed	1995	12.75	13
1995 Ziggy's Merry Tree-Some ORN095M	Closed	1995	13.75	14

1996 Carlton Collector's Series - Carlton

YEAR ISSUE	EDITION LIMIT	YEAR RETD.	ISSUE PRICE	*QUOTE U.S.$
1996 Book of Carols (4th) CXOR-004T	Open		13.95	14
1996 Candy Cane Cabin (1st) CXOR-108T	Open		13.95	14
1996 Christmas Go Round (7th) CXOR-011T	Open		15.95	16
1996 Christmas Sweets (5th) CXOR-005T	Open		14.95	15
1996 Christmas Tidings (2nd) CXOR-100T	Open		13.95	14
1996 Country Cow (1st) CXOR-105T	Open		11.95	12
1996 Gingerbread Farm (3rd) CXOR-110T	Open		13.95	14
1996 Holiday Fun (3rd) CXOR-101T	Open		13.95	14
1996 Holiday Garden (2nd) CXOR-010T	Open		14.95	15
1996 Holiday Recollections (1st) CXOR-099T	Open		13.95	14
1996 Holiday Town (3rd) CXOR-003T	Open		18.95	19
1996 Ice Pals (5th) CXOR-006T	Open		12.95	13
1996 Jolly Old St. Nick (1st) CXOR-015T	Open		15.95	16
1996 Joy (1st) CXOR-102T	Open		11.95	12
1996 Joy Is In The Air (1st) CXOR-007T	Open		16.95	17
1996 Love (3rd) CXOR-104T	Open		11.95	12
1996 Merry (2nd) CXOR-103T	Open		11.95	12
1996 Merry Mischief (1st) CXOR-012T	Open		14.95	15
1996 O Holy Night (1st) CXOR-014T	Open		17.95	18
1996 Perky Pig (3rd) CXOR-107T	Open		11.95	12
1996 Pinecone Cottage (3rd) CXOR-002T	Open		17.95	18
1996 Prancing Pony (3rd)	Open		11.95	12
1996 Santa's Music Makers (3rd) CXOR-001T	Open		13.95	14
1996 Song of Hope (2nd) CXOR-097T	Open		12.95	13
1996 Song of Joy (3rd) CXOR-098T	Open		12.95	13
1996 Song of Peace (1st) CXOR-096T	Open		12.95	13
1996 Sugarplum Chapel (2nd) CXOR-109T	Open		13.95	14
1996 Wonderland Express (1st) CXOR-008T	Open		15.95	16
1996 Year By Year (2nd) CXOR-013T	Open		12.95	13

1996 Carlton Heirloom Collection - Carlton

YEAR ISSUE	EDITION LIMIT	YEAR RETD.	ISSUE PRICE	*QUOTE U.S.$
1996 25th Wedding Anniversary CXOR-027T	Open		14.95	15
1996 All Around The Workshop CXOR-074T	Open		34.00	34
1996 Another Magical Season CXOR-087T	Open		15.95	16
1996 Baby Boy's First Christmas CXOR-032T	Open		13.95	14
1996 Baby Girl's First Christmas CXOR-030T	Open		13.95	14
1996 Baby Photo Holder CXOR-059T	Open		9.95	10
1996 Baby's First Christmas CXOR-028T	Open		14.95	15
1996 Baby's First Christmas CXOR-133T	Open		15.95	16
1996 Baby's Second Christmas CXOR-036T	Open		11.95	12
1996 Bainbridge Bear CXOR-031T	Open		11.95	12
1996 Bainbridge Bear CXOR-033T	Open		11.95	12
1996 A Brief Message CXOR-086T	Open		12.95	13
1996 Brother CXOR-049T	Open		12.95	13
1996 Campbell's, A Hearty Christmas CXOR-079T	Open		17.95	18
1996 Caregiver CXOR-053T	Open		10.95	11
1996 A Child's Christmas CXOR-124T	Open		13.95	14
1996 Child's Fourth Christmas CXOR-038T	Open		11.95	12

YEAR ISSUE		EDITION LIMIT	YEAR RETD.	ISSUE PRICE	*QUOTE U.S.$
1996	Child's Third Christmas CXOR-037T	Open		11.95	12
1996	Christmas All Around CXOR-072T	Open		32.00	32
1996	A Christmas Celebration CXOR-080T	Open		16.95	17
1996	Christmas Countdown CXOR-024T	Open		14.95	15
1996	Christmas Kickoff CXOR-113T	Open		11.95	12
1996	Christmas Town Inn CXOR-009T	Open		14.95	15
1996	Clubhouse Christmas CXOR-129T	Open		13.95	14
1996	Counting The Days 'Til Christmas CXOR-118T	Open		10.95	11
1996	Cozy Little Christmas CXOR-079T	Open		15.95	16
1996	Cyclin' Santa CXOR-114T	Open		14.95	15
1996	Dad CXOR-043T	Open		13.95	14
1996	Dancing 'Til Daylight CXOT-073T	Open		32.00	32
1996	Daughter CXOR-045T	Open		13.95	14
1996	Do Not Disturb 'Til Christmas CXOR-121T	Open		11.95	12
1996	Elvis CXOR-093T	Open		30.00	30
1996	Finishing Touches CXOR-071T	Open		28.00	28
1996	First Christmas Together CXOR-019T	Open		11.95	12
1996	First Christmas Together CXOR-020T	Open		18.95	19
1996	First Christmas Together CXOR-021T	Open		14.95	15
1996	First Christmas Together CXOR-022T	Open		12.95	13
1996	Friend CXOR-054T	Open		9.95	10
1996	Friend CXOR-055T	Open		10.95	11
1996	Friends Around The World CXOR-062T	Open		11.95	12
1996	Get Your Pup-Corn Here! CXOR-078T	Open		21.00	21
1996	Goal For It! CXOR-116T	Open		12.95	13
1996	Godchild CXOR-039T	Open		10.95	11
1996	Godchild CXOR-040T	Open		13.95	14
1996	Godmother CXOR-052T	Open		14.95	15
1996	Grandaughter's First Christmas CXOR-034T	Open		10.95	11
1996	Grandmother CXOR-050T	Open		14.95	15
1996	Grandparents CXOR-051T	Open		14.95	15
1996	Grandson's First Christmas CXOR-035T	Open		10.95	11
1996	Greetings To You CXOR-127T	Open		28.00	28
1996	Happy Holidaze! CXOR-085T	Open		15.95	16
1996	Happy, Happy! Joy, Joy! CXOR-111TT	Open		15.95	16
1996	Hershey's Hugs 'N Kisses CXOR-084T	Open		15.95	16
1996	High Lights CXOR-120T	Open		13.95	14
1996	High Powered Holidays! CXOR-095T	Open		16.95	17
1996	Holiday Debut CXOR-115T	Open		9.95	10
1996	A Holiday Hello CXOR-075T	Open		15.95	16
1996	Holiday Hoopla CXOR-119T	Open		13.95	14
1996	Holiday Sentiment CXOR-029T	Open		11.95	12
1996	Holiday Surprise! CXOR-08lT	Open		14.95	15
1996	Holiday Waltz CXOR-070T	Open		34.00	34
1996	Homerun Holiday CXOR-112T	Open		12.95	13
1996	It's Showtime! CXOR-077T	Open		21.00	21
1996	Jukebox Jingles CXOR-067T	Open		23.95	24
1996	Little Cup of Dreams CXOR-135T	Open		14.95	15
1996	Little Treasures-Boy CXOR-132T	Open		11.95	12
1996	Little Treasures-Girl CXOR-131T	Open		11.95	12
1996	Magic Of The Season CXOR-123T	Open		12.95	13
1996	Marilyn CXOR-094T	Open		17.95	18
1996	Merry Birthday CXOR-128T	Open		12.95	13
1996	Mother CXOR-042T	Open		13.95	14
1996	New Home CXOR-016T	Open		12.95	13
1996	New Home CXOR-017T	Open		13.95	14
1996	Noah's Ark CXOR-125T	Open		13.95	14
1996	Nonstop Wishes CXOR-069T	Open		28.00	28
1996	North Pole or Bust CXOR-082T	Open		16.95	17
1996	Our Christmas Together CXOR-025T	Open		12.95	13
1996	Our Christmas Together CXOR-026T	Open		13.95	14
1996	Our Family Photo Holder CXOR-061T	Open		9.95	10
1996	Our House to Your House CXOR-018T	Open		13.95	14
1996	Paddington Bear, Gliding Into Christmas CXOR-089T	Open		14.95	15
1996	Parents CXOR-044T	Open		14.95	15
1996	Parents To Be CXOR-041T	Open		12.95	13
1996	Pet Photo Holder CXOR-063T	Open		9.95	10
1996	Puppy Pals CXOR-083T	Open		14.95	15
1996	Purr-Fect Holidays CXOR-122T	Open		12.95	13
1996	Rocking Horse Fun CXOR-126T	Open		13.95	14
1996	Santa's Little Friends CXOR-068T	Open		15.95	16
1996	Santa's Network CXOR-058T	Open		13.95	14
1996	Season of Giving CXOR-134T	Open		14.95	15
1996	Sister CXOR-047T	Open		13.95	14
1996	Sister To Sister CXOR-048T	Open		14.95	15
1996	Son CXOR-046T	Open		14.95	15
1996	Sweetheart CXOR-023T	Open		14.95	15
1996	Sweetheart CXOR-130T	Open		16.95	17
1996	Teacher CXOR-056T	Open		9.95	10
1996	Teacher CXOR-057T	Open		11.95	12

YEAR ISSUE		EDITION LIMIT	YEAR RETD.	ISSUE PRICE	*QUOTE U.S.$
1996	Ten-Pin Christmas CXOR-111T	Open		10.95	11
1996	Tender Loving Care CXOR-064T	Open		11.95	12
1996	Tenderheart Bear CXOR-088T	Open		11.95	12
1996	That's The Spirit! CXOR-117T	Open		11.95	12
1996	To Grandma Photo Holder CXOR-060T	Open		9.95	10
1996	To The Rescue CXOR-065T	Open		12.95	13
1996	Up On The Housetop CXOR-066T	Open		17.95	18
1996	You're A Winner CXOR-076T	Open		16.95	17

Cast Art Industries

Dreamsicles Ornaments - K. Haynes

1992	Bear-DX274	Suspd.		6.00	6
1992	Bunny-DX270	Suspd.		6.00	6
1992	Cherub On Cloud-DX263	Suspd.		6.00	6
1992	Cherub With Moon-DX260	Suspd.		6.00	6
1992	Cherub With Star-DX262	Suspd.		6.00	6
1992	Lamb-DX275	Suspd.		6.00	6
1992	Piggy-DX271	Suspd.		6.00	6
1992	Praying Cherub-DX261	Suspd.		6.00	6
1992	Raccoon-DX272	Suspd.		6.00	6
1992	Squirrel-DX273	Suspd.		6.00	6

The Cat's Meow

1986 Christmas Ornaments - F. Jones

1986	Bancroft House	Retrd. 1986		4.00	40
1986	Chapel	Retrd. 1986		4.00	N/A
1986	Grayling House	Retrd. 1986		4.00	40
1986	Morton House	Retrd. 1986		4.00	N/A
1986	Rutledge House	Retrd. 1986		4.00	75
1986	School	Retrd. 1986		4.00	N/A

1988 Christmas Ornaments - F. Jones

1988	Blacksmith Shop	Retrd. 1988		5.00	60
1988	District #17 School	Retrd. 1988		5.00	60
1988	Globe Corner Bookstore	Retrd. 1988		5.00	60
1988	Kennedy Birthplace	Retrd. 1988		5.00	26-75
1988	Set/4	Retrd. 1988		20.00	175-200

1995 Christmas Ornaments - F. Jones

1995	Carnegie Library	Retrd. 1995		8.75	13
1995	Holly Hill Farmhouse	Retrd. 1995		8.75	13
1995	North Central School	Retrd. 1995		8.75	13
1995	St. James General Store	Retrd. 1995		8.75	13
1995	Unitarian Church	Retrd. 1995		8.75	13
1995	Yaquina Bay Light	Retrd. 1995		8.75	13

1996 Christmas Ornaments - F. Jones

1996	Christ Church	12/96		9.00	9
1996	Deerfield Post Office	12/96		9.00	9
1996	Gimbel & Sons Country Store	12/96		9.00	9
1996	Hook Windmill	12/96		9.00	9
1996	Maple Manor	12/96		9.00	9
1996	Parsonage	12/96		9.00	9

Cavanagh Group Intl.

Coca-Cola Christmas Collectors Society Members' Only - Sundblom, unless otherwise noted

1993	Ho Ho Ho	Closed 1993		Gift	25-35
1994	Fishing Bear - CGI	Closed 1994		Gift	28
1995	Hospitality	Closed 1995		Gift	25
1996	Sprite	12/96		Gift	N/A
1997	Carousel Capers	12/97		Gift	N/A

Coca-Cola Brand Heritage Collection - Sundblom

1995	Christmas Is Love (polyresin)	Open		10.00	10
1996	Hospitality in Your Refrigerator (porcelain & brass)	10,000		25.00	25
1996	It Will Refresh You, Too (porcelain & brass)	10,000		25.00	25
1996	Please Pause Here (porcelain & brass)	10,000		25.00	25
1995	Santa at the Mantle (polyresin)	Open		10.00	10
1995	Ssshhh! (polyresin)	Open		10.00	10

Coca-Cola Brand Heritage Collection Polar Bear - CGI

1996	Baby's First Christmas (porcelain)	Open		12.00	12
1996	Our First Christmas (porcelain)	Open		12.00	12
1996	Stocking Stuffers (porcelain)	Open		12.00	12

Coca-Cola Brand Historical Building - CGI

1991	1930's Service Station	Closed 1994		10.00	20
1991	Early Coca-Cola Bottling Company	Closed 1994		10.00	20
1991	Jacob's Pharmacy	Closed 1994		10.00	20
1991	The Pemberton House	Closed 1994		10.00	20

Coca-Cola Brand North Pole Bottling Works - CGI

1995	Barrel of Bears	Open		9.00	9
1993	Blast Off	Closed 1995		9.00	13
1993	Delivery for Santa	Open		9.00	9
1993	Fill 'er Up	Closed 1994		9.00	15-25
1995	Fountain Glass Follies	Open		9.00	9
1993	Ice Sculpting	Closed 1995		9.00	13
1993	Long Winter's Nap	Closed 1995		9.00	13
1993	North Pole Express	Closed 1994		9.00	15-25
1995	North Pole Flying School	Open		9.00	9

YEAR ISSUE		EDITION LIMIT	YEAR RETD.	ISSUE PRICE	*QUOTE U.S.$
1994	Power Drive	Open		9.00	9
1996	Refreshing Surprise	Open		9.00	9
1996	Rush Delivery	Open		9.00	9
1994	Santa's Refreshment	Closed 1995		9.00	13
1994	Seltzer Surprise	Closed 1995		9.00	13
1993	Thirsting for Adventure	Closed 1994		9.00	15
1996	To: Mrs. Claus	Open		9.00	9
1994	Tops Off Refreshment	Closed 1995		9.00	9
1993	Tops On Refreshment	Closed 1995		9.00	13

Coca-Cola Brand Polar Bear - CGI

1996	The Christmas Star	Open		9.00	9
1994	Downhill Sledder	Open		9.00	9
1996	Hollywood	Open		9.00	9
1994	North Pole Delivery	Closed 1995		9.00	13
1995	Polar Bear in Bottle Opener	Open		9.00	9
1994	Skating Coca-Cola Polar Bear	Closed 1995		9.00	13
1995	Snowboardin' Bear	Open		9.00	9
1994	Vending Machine Mischief	Open		9.00	9

Coca-Cola Brand Trim A Tree Collection - Sundblom

1990	Away with a Tired and Thirsty Face	Closed 1993		10.00	25
1994	Busy Man's Pause	Open		10.00	10
1991	Christmas Is Love	Closed 1992		10.00	25
1993	Decorating the Tree	Closed 1994		10.00	20
1993	Extra Bright Refreshment	Closed 1994		10.00	15-20
1994	For Sparkling Holidays	Closed 1995		10.00	10
1992	Happy Holidays	Closed 1992		10.00	25
1990	Hospitality	Closed 1993		10.00	15
1995	It Will Refresh You Too	Open		10.00	10
1990	Merry Christmas and a Happy New Year	Closed 1991		10.00	40
1996	The Pause That Refreshes	Open		10.00	10
1995	Please Pause Here	Open		10.00	10
1990	Santa on Stool	Closed 1993		10.00	20
1990	Season's Greetings	Closed 1991		10.00	15
1992	Sshhh!	Closed 1993		10.00	20-35
1996	They Remembered Me	Open		10.00	10
1994	Things Go Better with Coke	Open		10.00	10
1991	A Time to Share	Closed 1993		10.00	25
1993	Travel Refreshed	Closed 1995		10.00	13

Christopher Radko

Christopher Radko Family of Collectors - C. Radko

1993	Angels We Have Heard on High SP1	Retrd. 1993		50.00	450-575
1994	Starbuck Santa SP3	Retrd. 1994		75.00	185-350
1995	Dash Away All SP7	Retrd. 1995		34.00	75
1995	Purrfect Present SP8	Retrd. 1995		Gift	50
1996	Christmas Magic SP13	Yr.Iss.		50.00	50
1996	Frosty Weather SP14	Yr.Iss.		Gift	N/A

10 Year Anniversary - C. Radko

1995	On Top of the World SP6	Yr.Iss. 1995		32.00	50-125

1987 Holiday Collection - C. Radko

1987	Memphis 18	Retrd. N/A		15.00	125

1988 Holiday Collection - C. Radko

1988	Alpine Flowers 8822	Retrd. N/A		16.00	100
1988	Baby Balloon 8832	Retrd. N/A		7.95	125
1988	Birdhouse 8873	Retrd. 1987		10.00	130
1988	Buds in Bloom (pink) 8824	Retrd. N/A		16.00	125
1988	Celestial 884	Retrd. N/A		15.00	75
1988	Christmas Fanfare 8850	Retrd. 1988		15.00	125
1988	Circle of Santas 8811	Retrd. N/A		16.95	120
1988	Cornucopia/Pear Branch 8839	Retrd. N/A		15.00	360
1988	Crown Jewels 8874	Retrd. 1993		15.00	175
1988	Double Royal Star 8856	Retrd. 1991		23.00	160
1988	Exclamation Flask 8871	Retrd. N/A		7.50	90
1988	Faberge Oval 883	Retrd. N/A		15.00	30
1988	Gilded Leaves 8813	Retrd. N/A		16.00	125
1988	Grecian Column 8842	Retrd. 1990		9.95	95
1988	Hot Air Balloon 885	Retrd. N/A		15.00	150-200
1988	Lilac Sparkle 1814	Retrd. N/A		15.00	125
1988	Mushroom in Winter 8862	Retrd. 1993		12.00	85
1988	Ripples on Oval 8844	Retrd. 1987		6.00	85
1988	Royal Diadem 8860	Retrd. 1987		25.00	135
1988	Royal Porcelain 8812	Retrd. 1991		16.00	100-175
1988	Russian St. Nick 8823	Retrd. N/A		15.00	150
1988	Satin Scepter 8847	Retrd. 1987		8.95	110
1988	Simply Cartiere 8817	Retrd. N/A		16.95	125
1988	Stained Glass 8816	Retrd. 1990		16.00	50
1988	Striped Balloon 8877	Retrd. N/A		16.95	50
1988	Tiger 886	Retrd. N/A		15.00	500
1988	Tree on Ball 8864	Retrd. N/A		9.00	95
1988	Twin Finial 8857	Retrd. N/A		23.50	135
1988	Zebra 886	Retrd. N/A		15.00	150-175

1989 Holiday Collection - C. Radko

1989	Alpine Flowers 9-43	Retrd. N/A		17.00	30
1989	Baroque Angel 9-11	Retrd. 1989		17.00	125-150
1989	Charlie Chaplin (blue hat) 9-55	Retrd. 1990		8.50	75
1989	Double Top 9-71	Retrd. N/A		7.00	90
1989	Elf on Ball (matte) 9-62	Retrd. 1990		9.50	60
1989	Fisher Frog 9-65	Retrd. 1991		7.00	40
1989	Grecian Urn 9-69	Retrd. 1989		17.00	35
1989	The Holly 9-49	Retrd. 1989		17.00	90
1989	Hurricane Lamp 9-67	Retrd. 1989		7.00	45
1989	The Ivy 9-47	Retrd. N/A		16.50	120

YEAR ISSUE	EDITION LIMIT	YEAR RETD.	ISSUE PRICE	*QUOTE U.S.$
1989 Joey Clown (light pink) 9-58	Retrd.	1992	9.00	65
1989 Kim Ono 9-57	Retrd.	1990	6.50	50-65
1989 King Arthur (Lt. Blue) 9-103	Retrd.	1991	12.00	45
1989 Lilac Sparkle 9-7	Retrd.	1989	17.00	30
1989 Lucky Fish 9-73	Retrd.	1989	6.50	30
1989 Parachute 9-68	Retrd.	1989	6.50	75-95
1989 Royal Rooster 9-18	Retrd.	1993	17.00	95
1989 Royal Star Tree Finial 108	Retrd.	N/A	42.00	95
1989 Seahorse 9-54	Retrd.	1992	10.00	100
1989 Serpent 9-72	Retrd.	N/A	7.00	18
1989 Shy Kitten 9-66	Retrd.	N/A	7.00	45
1989 Shy Rabbit 9-61	Retrd.	N/A	7.00	53
1989 Small Reflector 9-76	Retrd.	N/A	7.50	32
1989 Smiling Sun 9-59	Retrd.	N/A	7.00	45
1989 Tiffany 44	Retrd.	N/A	17.00	650-750
1989 Vineyard 9-51	Retrd.	N/A	17.00	115
1989 Walrus 9-63	Retrd.	1990	8.00	65-120
1989 Zebra 9-10	Retrd.	1991	17.50	100-150

1990 Holiday Collection - C. Radko

YEAR ISSUE	EDITION LIMIT	YEAR RETD.	ISSUE PRICE	*QUOTE U.S.$
1990 Angel on Harp 46	Retrd.	1990	9.00	85
1990 Ballooning Santa 87	Retrd.	1991	20.00	95-145
1990 Bathing Baby 70	Retrd.	N/A	11.00	65
1990 Calla Lilly 38	Retrd.	N/A	7.00	50
1990 Carmen Miranda 18	Retrd.	1991	19.00	125
1990 Christmas Cardinals 16	Retrd.	1992	18.00	125
1990 Conch Shell 65	Retrd.	1991	9.00	100
1990 Crowned Prince 56	Retrd.	1990	14.00	45
1990 Dublin Pipe 40	Retrd.	1990	14.00	50
1990 Eagle Medallion 67	Retrd.	1990	9.00	85
1990 Early Winter 24	Retrd.	1990	10.00	40
1990 Emerald City 92	Retrd.	1990	7.50	95
1990 Fat Lady 35	Retrd.	N/A	7.00	35
1990 Father Christmas 76	Retrd.	1990	7.00	45
1990 Frog Under Balloon 58	Retrd.	1991	14.00	75
1990 Golden Puppy 73	Retrd.	1990	8.00	95
1990 Google Eyes 44	Retrd.	1990	9.00	75
1990 Happy Gnome 77	Retrd.	1991	8.00	40
1990 Holly Ball 4	Retrd.	N/A	19.00	125
1990 Joey Clown (red striped) 55	Retrd.	1990	14.00	90
1990 Kim Ono 79	Retrd.	1990	6.00	55
1990 King Arthur (Red) 72	Retrd.	N/A	16.00	110
1990 Lullaby 47	Retrd.	1990	9.00	65
1990 Maracca 94	Retrd.	1990	9.00	125
1990 Mother Goose (blue bonnet/pink shawl) 52	Retrd.	N/A	10.00	65
1990 Nativity 36	Retrd.	1990	6.00	60
1990 Peacock (on snowball) 74	Retrd.	N/A	18.00	50
1990 Pierre Le Berry	Retrd.	N/A	10.00	75
1990 Polish Folk Dance 13	Retrd.	N/A	19.00	150
1990 Proud Peacock 74	Retrd.	N/A	18.00	50
1990 Roly Poly Santa (Red bottom) 69	Retrd.	N/A	13.00	60
1990 Rose Lamp 96	Retrd.	N/A	14.00	95
1990 Santa on Ball 80	Retrd.	1991	16.00	100
1990 Silent Movie (black hat) 75	Retrd.	1990	8.50	75
1990 Small Nautilus Shell 78	Retrd.	N/A	7.00	22
1990 Smiling Kite 63	Retrd.	1990	14.00	100-125
1990 Snowball Tree 71	Retrd.	1990	17.00	60-115
1990 Snowman on Ball 45	Retrd.	1990	14.00	75
1990 Southwest Indian Ball 19	Retrd.	N/A	19.00	240
1990 Spin Top 90	Retrd.	N/A	11.00	95
1990 Sunburst Fish (green/yellow) 68	Retrd.	N/A	13.00	28
1990 Trumpet Player 85	Retrd.	N/A	18.00	100
1990 Tuxedo Penguin 57	Retrd.	N/A	8.00	750
1990 Walrus 59	Retrd.	1990	8.50	120
1990 Yarn Fight 23	Retrd.	N/A	17.00	125-150

1991 Holiday Collection - C. Radko

YEAR ISSUE	EDITION LIMIT	YEAR RETD.	ISSUE PRICE	*QUOTE U.S.$
1991 All Weather Santa 137	Retrd.	1992	32.00	275
1991 Altar Boy 18	Retrd.	1992	16.00	35
1991 Anchor America 65	Retrd.	1992	21.50	65
1991 Apache 42	Retrd.	N/A	8.50	50
1991 Aspen 76	Retrd.	1992	20.50	125
1991 Aztec 141	Retrd.	1991	21.50	100
1991 Aztec Bird 41	Retrd.	1992	20.00	90
1991 Ballooning Santa 110	Retrd.	1991	23.00	100-200
1991 Barnum Clown 56	Retrd.	1991	15.00	85
1991 Bishop 22	Retrd.	N/A	15.00	40
1991 Blue Rainbow 136	Retrd.	1992	21.50	150
1991 Bowery Kid 50	Retrd.	1991	14.50	70
1991 By the Nile 124	Retrd.	1992	21.50	60-100
1991 Chance Encounter 104	Retrd.	1992	13.50	40
1991 Chief Sitting Bull 107	Retrd.	1992	16.00	75
1991 Chimney Santa 12	Retrd.	N/A	14.50	70
1991 Clown Drum 33	Retrd.	1991	14.00	85
1991 Comet 62	Retrd.	1991	9.00	75
1991 Cosette 16	Retrd.	1991	16.00	60-100
1991 Dapper Shoe 89	Retrd.	1991	10.00	40-60
1991 Dawn & Dust 34	Retrd.	N/A	14.00	24-35
1991 Deco Floral 133	Retrd.	1991	22.00	60
1991 Deco Sparkle 134	Retrd.	1992	21.00	95
1991 Dutch Boy 27	Retrd.	N/A	11.00	55-75
1991 Dutch Girl 28	Retrd.	1991	11.00	55-75
1991 Edwardian Lace 82	Retrd.	1991	21.50	100
1991 Einstein Kite 98	Retrd.	N/A	20.00	130
1991 Elephant on Ball (striped) 115	Retrd.	N/A	23.00	192
1991 Elf Reflector 135	Retrd.	1992	23.00	50
1991 Fanfare 126	Retrd.	1992	21.50	98
1991 Fisher Frog 44	Retrd.	1991	11.00	65-125
1991 Florentine 83	Retrd.	N/A	22.00	40
1991 Flower Child 90	Retrd.	1991	13.00	65
1991 Frog Under Balloon 53	Retrd.	N/A	16.00	45
1991 Fruit in Balloon 40	Retrd.	N/A	22.00	150-200
1991 Fu Manchu 11	Retrd.	N/A	15.00	75
1991 Galaxy 120	Retrd.	1991	21.50	75
1991 Grapefruit Tree 113	Retrd.	N/A	23.00	100-250
1991 Harvest 3	Retrd.	N/A	13.50	25
1991 Hatching Duck 35	Retrd.	1991	14.00	50
1991 Hearts & Flowers Finial 158	Retrd.	1993	53.00	235
1991 Her Majesty 39	Retrd.	1991	21.00	100
1991 Her Purse 88	Retrd.	N/A	10.00	60
1991 Holly Ball 156	Retrd.	N/A	22.00	60
1991 Irish Laddie 10	Retrd.	1991	12.00	60
1991 Jemima's Child 111	Retrd.	1991	16.00	75
1991 Jemima's Child 111	Retrd.	N/A	16.00	75
1991 King Arthur (Blue) 95	Retrd.	1991	18.50	95
1991 Lion's Head 31	Retrd.	N/A	16.00	35
1991 Madeleine's Puppy 25	Retrd.	N/A	11.00	70
1991 Madonna & Child 103	Retrd.	N/A	15.00	85
1991 Melon Slice 99	Retrd.	N/A	18.00	31
1991 Mother Goose 57	Retrd.	N/A	11.00	40
1991 Olympiad 125	Retrd.	1992	22.00	125
1991 Peruvian 74	Retrd.	1991	21.50	100-240
1991 Pierre Le Berry 2	Retrd.	1993	14.00	70
1991 Pink Clown on Ball 32	Retrd.	N/A	14.00	55
1991 Pink Elephants 70	Retrd.	N/A	21.50	100-130
1991 Pipe Smoking Monkey 54	Retrd.	1991	11.00	75
1991 Polish Folk Art 116	Retrd.	N/A	20.50	100
1991 Prince on Ball (pink/blue/green) 51	Retrd.	N/A	15.00	80
1991 Prince Umbrella 21	Retrd.	1991	15.00	80-125
1991 Proud Peacock 37	Retrd.	N/A	23.00	37
1991 Rainbow Bird 92	Retrd.	1991	16.00	45
1991 Raspberry & Lime 96	Retrd.	1991	12.00	50
1991 Red Star 129	Retrd.	1991	21.50	40
1991 Sally Ann 43	Retrd.	1991	8.00	40
1991 Santa Bootie 55	Retrd.	1993	10.00	55
1991 Shirley 15	Retrd.	1991	16.00	95-125
1991 Shy Elf 1	Retrd.	1991	10.00	40-70
1991 Sleepy Time Santa 52	Retrd.	N/A	15.00	125-185
1991 Star Quilt 139	Retrd.	1991	21.50	100
1991 Sunburst Fish 108	Retrd.	N/A	15.00	28
1991 Sunshine 67	Retrd.	N/A	22.00	40
1991 Tabby 46	Retrd.	1991	8.00	30-50
1991 Tiffany 68	Retrd.	1991	22.00	50
1991 Tiger 5	Retrd.	N/A	15.00	35
1991 Trigger 114	Retrd.	1991	15.00	105-125
1991 Trumpet Man 100	Retrd.	1992	21.00	75
1991 Tulip Fairy 63	Retrd.	1992	16.00	65
1991 Vienna 1901 127	Retrd.	1992	21.50	200
1991 Villandry 87	Retrd.	1991	21.00	185
1991 Woodland Santa 38	Retrd.	N/A	14.00	55
1991 Zebra (glittered) 79	Retrd.	1991	22.00	400-500

1992 Holiday Collection - C. Radko

YEAR ISSUE	EDITION LIMIT	YEAR RETD.	ISSUE PRICE	*QUOTE U.S.$
1992 Alpine Flowers 162	Retrd.	1992	28.00	100
1992 Alpine Village 105	Retrd.	N/A	24.00	125
1992 Aspen 120	Retrd.	1992	26.00	50
1992 Barbie's Mom 69	Retrd.	N/A	18.00	70-130
1992 Benjamin's Nutcrackers 185	Retrd.	N/A	58.00	150-185
1992 Butterfly Bouquet 119	Retrd.	1992	26.50	95
1992 By the Nile 139	Retrd.	1992	27.00	75-100
1992 Cabaret (see-through) 159	Retrd.	1993	28.00	60
1992 Candy Trumpet Men (pink/blue) 98	Retrd.	N/A	27.00	75
1992 Candy Trumpet Men (red) w/ white glitter 98	Retrd.	1992	27.00	95
1992 Celestial 129	Retrd.	N/A	26.00	100
1992 Cheerful Sun 50	Retrd.	N/A	18.00	60
1992 Chevron 160	Retrd.	1992	28.00	40
1992 Choir Boy 114	Retrd.	1992	24.00	50
1992 Christmas Cardinals 123	Retrd.	1992	26.00	95
1992 Christmas Rose 143	Retrd.	1992	25.50	75
1992 Circus lady 54	Retrd.	1992	12.00	15
1992 Clown Snake 62	Retrd.	N/A	22.00	75
1992 Country Star Quilt 176	Retrd.	1992	12.00	100
1992 Cowboy Santa 94	Retrd.	N/A	24.00	100
1992 Delft Design 124	Retrd.	1992	26.50	75-175
1992 Diva 73	Retrd.	1992	17.00	65-135
1992 Dolly Madison 115	Retrd.	1992	17.00	65
1992 Downhill Racer 76	Retrd.	1992	34.00	140
1992 Elephant on Parade 141	Retrd.	1992	26.00	85-100
1992 Elephant Reflector 181	Retrd.	N/A	17.00	50
1992 Elf Reflectors 136	Retrd.	1992	28.00	36
1992 Faberge 148	Retrd.	N/A	26.50	55
1992 Faith, Hope & Love 183	Retrd.	1992	12.00	30
1992 Festive Smitty	Retrd.	N/A	N/A	75
1992 Floral Cascade Tier Drop 175	Retrd.	1992	32.00	41-45
1992 Florentine 131	Retrd.	1992	27.00	40
1992 Flutter By's 201 (Set/4)	Retrd.	1992	11.00	40
1992 Folk Art Set 95	Retrd.	1992	10.00	13
1992 Forest Friends 103	Retrd.	1992	14.00	18
1992 French Country 121	Retrd.	1992	26.00	65
1992 Fruit in Balloon 83	Retrd.	1992	28.00	250-325
1992 Gabriel's Trumpets 188	Retrd.	N/A	20.00	25
1992 Harlequin Tier Drop 74	Retrd.	1992	36.00	65
1992 Harold Lloyd Reflector 218	Retrd.	1992	70.00	200-450
1992 Her Slipper 56	Retrd.	1992	17.00	22
1992 Holly Finial 200	Retrd.	N/A	70.00	83
1992 Ice Pear 241	Retrd.	N/A	20.00	30-50
1992 Ice Poppies 127	Retrd.	1992	26.00	60
1992 Jumbo 99	Retrd.	N/A	31.00	45
1992 King of Prussia 149	Retrd.	N/A	27.00	100
1992 Kitty Rattle 166	Retrd.	1993	18.00	85
1992 Little League 53	Retrd.	1992	20.00	50-100
1992 Merry Christmas Maiden 137	Retrd.	1992	26.00	N/A
1992 Mother Goose 37	Retrd.	N/A	15.00	25
1992 Mr. & Mrs. Claus 59	Retrd.	N/A	18.00	200
1992 Mushroom Elf 87	Retrd.	N/A	18.00	58
1992 Neopolitan Angels 152 (Set/3)	Retrd.	1992	27.00	300-400
1992 Norweigian Princess 170	Retrd.	1992	15.00	60
1992 Pierre Winterberry 64	Retrd.	1993	17.00	75
1992 Pink Lace Ball (See Through) 158	Retrd.	1992	28.00	100-200
1992 Polar Bear 184	Retrd.	N/A	16.00	50
1992 Primary Colors 108	Retrd.	1992	30.00	150
1992 Quilted Hearts (Old Salem Museum) 194	Retrd.	N/A	27.50	100
1992 Rainbow Parasol 90	Retrd.	1992	30.00	100
1992 Royal Scepter 77	Retrd.	1992	36.00	95
1992 Russian Imperial 112	Retrd.	1992	25.00	75
1992 Russian Jewel Hearts 146	Retrd.	N/A	27.00	130
1992 Russian Star 130	Retrd.	1992	26.00	32-40
1992 Sail Away 215	Retrd.	N/A	22.00	50
1992 Santa in Winter White 106	Retrd.	N/A	28.00	95
1992 Seahorse (pink) 92	Retrd.	1992	20.00	86
1992 Serpents of Paradise 97	Retrd.	N/A	13.00	30
1992 Siberian Sleighride (pink) 154	Retrd.	N/A	27.00	95
1992 Sitting Bull 93	Retrd.	1992	26.00	75
1992 Sleepytime Santa (pink) 81	Retrd.	N/A	18.00	95
1992 Sloopy Snowman 328	Retrd.	1992	19.90	75
1992 Snowflakes 209	Retrd.	N/A	10.00	40
1992 Sputniks 134	Retrd.	1992	25.50	65-125
1992 St. Nickcicle 107	Retrd.	N/A	26.00	35
1992 Star of Wonder 177	Retrd.	1992	27.00	35
1992 Starbursts 214	Retrd.	N/A	12.00	75
1992 Stardust Joey 110	Retrd.	1992	16.00	75
1992 Starlight Santa (powder blue) 180	Retrd.	N/A	18.00	50
1992 Talking Pipe (black stem) 104	Retrd.	N/A	26.00	110
1992 Thunderbolt 178	Retrd.	1992	60.00	75
1992 Tiffany Bright Harlequin 161	Retrd.	1992	28.00	100
1992 Tiffany Pastel Harlequin 163	Retrd.	1992	28.00	100
1992 To Grandma's House 239	Retrd.	N/A	20.00	55
1992 Topiary 117	Retrd.	N/A	30.00	250-400
1992 Tropical Fish 109	Retrd.	1992	17.00	60
1992 Tulip Fairy 57	Retrd.	1992	18.00	45
1992 Tuxedo Santa 88	Retrd.	1993	22.00	125-170
1992 Two Sided Santa Reflector 102	Retrd.	1992	28.00	125
1992 Umbrella Santa 182	Retrd.	1992	60.00	125-190
1992 Victorian Santa & Angel Balloon 122	Retrd.	1992	68.00	500-600
1992 Vienna 1901 128	Retrd.	1992	27.00	150
1992 Virgin Mary 46	Retrd.	1992	20.00	29
1992 Wacko's Brother, Doofus 55	Retrd.	N/A	20.00	70-150
1992 Water Lilies 133	Retrd.	1992	26.00	95-180
1992 Wedding Bells 217	Retrd.	N/A	40.00	165
1992 Winter Wonderland 156	Retrd.	1992	26.00	110
1992 Woodland Santa 111	Retrd.	N/A	20.00	55-75
1992 Ziegfeld Follies 126	Retrd.	1992	27.00	75-130

1993 Holiday Collection - C. Radko

YEAR ISSUE	EDITION LIMIT	YEAR RETD.	ISSUE PRICE	*QUOTE U.S.$
1993 1939 World's Fair 149	Retrd.	N/A	26.80	100
1993 Accordian Elf 189	Retrd.	N/A	21.00	65
1993 Aladdin's Lamp 237	Retrd.	N/A	20.00	60
1993 Alpine Village 420	Retrd.	1993	23.80	125
1993 Anassazi 172	Retrd.	N/A	26.60	90-180
1993 Angel of Peace 132	Retrd.	1993	17.00	60
1993 Apache 357	Retrd.	1993	13.90	47
1993 Auld Lang Syne 246	Retrd.	1993	15.00	35
1993 Bavarian Santa 335	Retrd.	1993	23.00	45
1993 Bedtime Buddy 239	Retrd.	N/A	29.00	125
1993 Bell House Boy 291	Retrd.	1993	21.00	32
1993 Beyond the Stars 108	Retrd.	1993	18.50	35
1993 Bishop of Myra 327	Retrd.	1993	19.90	50
1993 Blue Top 114	Retrd.	1993	16.00	47
1993 Bowzer 228	Retrd.	N/A	22.80	140
1993 By Jiminy 285	Retrd.	N/A	16.40	85
1993 Calla Lilly 314	Retrd.	N/A	12.90	23
1993 Carnival Rides 303	Retrd.	N/A	18.00	95
1993 Celeste 271	Retrd.	N/A	26.00	100-200
1993 Celestial Peacock Finial 322	Retrd.	N/A	69.00	200-295
1993 Center Ring (Exclusive) 192	Retrd.	1993	30.80	38
1993 Centurian 224	Retrd.	1993	25.50	200
1993 Chimney Sweep Bell 294	Retrd.	1993	26.00	180
1993 Christmas Express 394 (Garland)	Retrd.	N/A	58.00	220
1993 Christmas Stars 342	Retrd.	N/A	14.00	32
1993 Church Bell 295	Retrd.	N/A	24.00	35
1993 Cinderella's Bluebirds 145	Retrd.	1993	25.90	100
1993 Circle of Santas Finial 413	Retrd.	1993	69.00	163
1993 Circus Seal 249	Retrd.	1993	28.00	65-90
1993 Class Clown 332	Retrd.	N/A	21.00	66
1993 Clowning Around 84	Retrd.	N/A	42.50	68
1993 Confucius 363	Retrd.	N/A	19.00	28
1993 Cool Cat 184	Retrd.	N/A	21.00	60
1993 Copenhagen 166	Retrd.	1993	26.80	75-100
1993 Crowned Passion 299	Retrd.	1993	23.00	60
1993 Crystal Rainbow 308	Retrd.	1993	29.90	100-200
1993 Deco Snowfall 147	Retrd.	1993	26.80	33
1993 Deer Drop 304	Retrd.	1993	30.00	175
1993 Downhill Racer 195	Retrd.	1993	30.00	120
1993 Eggman 241	Retrd.	N/A	22.50	40
1993 Emerald Wizard 279	Retrd.	N/A	18.00	65
1993 Emperor's Pet 253	Retrd.	1993	22.00	150-230
1993 Enchanted Gardens 341	Retrd.	1993	5.50	13
1993 English Kitchen 234	Retrd.	N/A	26.00	50
1993 Epiphany 421	Retrd.	N/A	29.00	100
1993 Evening Star Santa 409	Retrd.	1993	59.00	95
1993 Fiesta Ball 316	Retrd.	N/A	26.40	85

YEAR ISSUE		EDITION LIMIT	YEAR RETRD.	ISSUE PRICE	*QUOTE U.S.$
1993	Flora Dora 255	Retrd.	N/A	25.00	75
1993	Forest Friends 250	Retrd.	1993	28.00	35
1993	French Rose 152	Retrd.	1993	26.60	27-33
1993	Fruit in Balloon 115	Retrd.	1993	27.90	115
1993	Geisha Girls 261	Retrd.	1993	11.90	35
1993	Gold Fish 158	Retrd.	1993	25.80	26
1993	Goofy Garden 191 (Set/4)	Retrd.	N/A	15.00	150-200
1993	Grandpa Bear 260	Retrd.	N/A	12.80	13-20
1993	Grecian Urn 231	Retrd.	1993	23.00	50
1993	Gypsy Girl 371	Retrd.	1993	16.00	35
1993	Holiday Spice 422	Retrd.	1993	24.00	24
1993	Honey Bear 352	Retrd.	1993	13.90	55
1993	Ice Star Santa 405	Retrd.	1993	38.00	225-350
1993	Jack Frost (blue) 333	Retrd.	N/A	23.00	30
1993	Jaques Le Berry 356	Retrd.	N/A	16.90	85
1993	Joey B. Clown 135	Retrd.	N/A	26.00	75
1993	Just Like Grandma Lg. 200	Retrd.	N/A	7.20	28
1993	Just Like Grandmas Sm. 200	Retrd.	N/A	7.20	20
1993	Kissing Cousins 245 (Pair)	Retrd.	N/A	30.00	200-250
1993	Kitty Rattle 374	Retrd.	N/A	17.80	90
1993	Letter to Santa 188	Retrd.	N/A	22.00	55
1993	Light in the Windows 229	Retrd.	1994	24.50	30
1993	Little Doggie 180	Retrd.	1993	7.00	30
1993	Little Eskimo 355	Retrd.	N/A	13.90	21
1993	Majestic Reflector 312	Retrd.	1993	70.00	175
1993	Mediterranean Sunshine 156	Retrd.	N/A	26.90	65
1993	Midas Touch 162	Retrd.	N/A	27.80	70
1993	Monkey Man 97	Retrd.	1993	16.00	75-175
1993	Monterey 290	Retrd.	N/A	15.00	40-90
1993	Mr. & Mrs. Claus 121	Retrd.	1993	17.90	80-125
1993	Mushroom Elf 267	Retrd.	N/A	17.90	38
1993	Nellie (Italian ornament) 225	Retrd.	1993	27.50	200
1993	North Woods 317	Retrd.	1993	26.80	45
1993	One Small Leap 222	Retrd.	N/A	26.00	100
1993	Pagoda 258	Retrd.	N/A	8.00	15
1993	Pennsylvania Dutch 146	Retrd.	1993	26.80	33
1993	Piggly Wiggly 101	Retrd.	N/A	11.00	40
1993	Pineapple Quilt 150	Retrd.	N/A	26.80	85
1993	Pinocchio 248	Retrd.	N/A	26.00	65
1993	Pixie Santa 186	Retrd.	N/A	16.00	50
1993	Poinsetta Santa 269	Retrd.	N/A	19.80	76
1993	Polar Bears 112A	Retrd.	1993	15.50	16
1993	Pompadour 344	Retrd.	N/A	8.80	18
1993	Prince Albert 263	Retrd.	N/A	23.00	80
1993	Purse 389	Retrd.	N/A	15.60	16
1993	Quartet 392	Retrd.	N/A	3.60	11
1993	Rainbow Reflector 154	Retrd.	1993	26.60	30-40
1993	Rainbow Shark 277	Retrd.	N/A	18.00	70
1993	Rainy Day Friend 206	Retrd.	N/A	22.00	50-95
1993	Regal Rooster 177	Retrd.	N/A	25.80	75
1993	Rose Pointe Finial 323	Retrd.	N/A	34.00	40
1993	Sail by Starlight 339	Retrd.	1993	11.80	14-19
1993	Santa in Space 127	Retrd.	N/A	39.00	200
1993	Santa Tree 320	Retrd.	N/A	66.00	300
1993	Saraband 140	Retrd.	1993	27.80	125-225
1993	Serenade Pink 157	Retrd.	1993	26.80	55-100
1993	Shy Rabbit 280	Retrd.	N/A	14.00	40-75
1993	Silent Night 120	Retrd.	N/A	18.00	55
1993	The Skating Bettinas 242	Retrd.	N/A	29.00	60-125
1993	Ski Baby 99	Retrd.	N/A	21.00	45
1993	Sloopy Snowman 328	Retrd.	1993	19.90	55
1993	Smitty 378	Retrd.	N/A	17.90	50-120
1993	Snow Dance 247	Retrd.	N/A	29.00	125
1993	Snowday Santa 98	Retrd.	1993	20.00	70
1993	Snowman by Candlelight 155	Retrd.	N/A	26.50	60
1993	Southern Colonial 171	Retrd.	N/A	26.90	135
1993	Spider & the Fly 393	Retrd.	1993	6.40	14
1993	St. Nick's Pipe 330	Retrd.	N/A	4.40	30-75
1993	St. Nickcicle 298	Retrd.	N/A	25.90	35
1993	Star Children 208	Retrd.	1993	18.00	60
1993	Star Fire 175	Retrd.	N/A	26.80	60
1993	Starlight Santa 348	Retrd.	N/A	11.90	19
1993	Stocking Stuffers 236	Retrd.	1993	16.00	23
1993	Sweetheart 202	Retrd.	1993	16.00	40
1993	Talking Pipe 373	Retrd.	N/A	26.00	55-90
1993	Texas Star 338	Retrd.	N/A	7.50	8
1993	Thomas Nast Santa 217	Retrd.	N/A	23.00	50
1993	Tuxedo Santa 117	Retrd.	1993	21.90	100
1993	Tweeter 94	Retrd.	1993	3.20	6
1993	Twinkle Tree 254	Retrd.	N/A	15.50	45
1993	Twister 214	Retrd.	N/A	16.80	65
1993	U-Boat 353	Retrd.	N/A	15.50	50
1993	V.I.P. 230	Retrd.	1993	23.00	150
1993	Waddles 95	Retrd.	N/A	3.80	35
1993	Winterbirds 164	Retrd.	1993	26.80	55

1994 Holiday Collection - C. Radko

1994	Accordion Elf 127	Retrd.	N/A	23.00	65
1994	Andy Gump 48	Retrd.	N/A	18.00	45
1994	Baby Booties (pink) 236	Retrd.	N/A	17.00	35
1994	Bird Brain 254	Retrd.	N/A	33.00	70-95
1994	Bright Heavens Above 136	Retrd.	N/A	56.00	70-95
1994	Chic of Araby 220	Retrd.	N/A	17.00	57
1994	Cool Cat 219	Retrd.	N/A	26.00	45
1994	Corn Husk 336	Retrd.	N/A	13.00	20
1994	Crescent Moons 195	Retrd.	N/A	29.00	75
1994	Einstein's Kite 375	Retrd.	N/A	29.90	45
1994	Elephant Prince 170	Retrd.	N/A	14.50	25
1994	Fleet's In 281	Retrd.	N/A	38.00	75
1994	French Country 192	Retrd.	N/A	29.00	65
1994	Glow Worm 275	Retrd.	N/A	32.00	36

YEAR ISSUE		EDITION LIMIT	YEAR RETRD.	ISSUE PRICE	*QUOTE U.S.$
1994	Golden Crescendo Finial 384	Retrd.	N/A	42.00	125-175
1994	Hieroglyph 194	Retrd.	N/A	29.00	55-120
1994	Honey Belle 156	Retrd.	N/A	74.00	95
1994	House Sitting Santa 240	Retrd.	N/A	26.00	30
1994	Ice Man Cometh 63	Retrd.	N/A	22.00	45
1994	Jockey Pipe 51	Retrd.	N/A	36.00	95-130
1994	Just Like Us 324	Retrd.	N/A	29.50	115-160
1994	Kayo 165	Retrd.	N/A	14.00	25
1994	King of Kings 18	Retrd.	N/A	22.00	45
1994	Kitty Tamer 331	Retrd.	N/A	65.00	350
1994	Leader of the Band 94-915D (wh pants) - signed	Retrd.	1994	25.00	360
1994	Leader of the Band 94-915D (wh pants) - unsigned	Retrd.	1994	25.00	85
1994	Lemon Twist 28	Retrd.	N/A	14.00	25
1994	Letter to Santa 77	Retrd.	N/A	31.00	55
1994	The Los Angeles 155	Retrd.	N/A	26.00	45
1994	Martian Holiday 326	Retrd.	N/A	42.00	60
1994	Masquerade 45	Retrd.	N/A	16.00	25
1994	Medium Nautilus (gold) 103	Retrd.	N/A	16.00	25
1994	Moon Martian 298	Retrd.	N/A	26.00	65
1994	Moon Mullins 230	Retrd.	N/A	18.00	45
1994	Mr. Smedley Drysdale 37	Retrd.	N/A	44.00	180-250
1994	Nighty Night 299	Retrd.	N/A	36.00	65-125
1994	On The Run (Original) 247	Retrd.	N/A	45.00	75-125
1994	Owl Reflector 40	Retrd.	N/A	54.00	75
1994	Papa's Jamboree 427	Retrd.	N/A	29.00	45
1994	Party Hopper 274	Retrd.	N/A	37.00	200
1994	Pickled 317	Retrd.	N/A	26.00	55
1994	Piggly Wiggly 169	Retrd.	N/A	14.00	40
1994	Pinecone Santa 118	Retrd.	N/A	29.50	30
1994	Pixie Santa 218	Retrd.	N/A	20.00	50
1994	President Taft 74	Retrd.	N/A	18.00	50
1994	Prince Philip 909	Retrd.	N/A	N/A	150
1994	Private Eye 163	Retrd.	N/A	18.00	35
1994	Quick Draw 330	Retrd.	N/A	65.00	300
1994	Santa Copter 306	Retrd.	N/A	47.00	54
1994	Santa's Helper 131	Retrd.	N/A	19.90	25
1994	Ships Ahoy 263	Retrd.	N/A	38.00	48
1994	Shivers 262	Retrd.	N/A	25.00	200
1994	Silent Night 129	Retrd.	N/A	27.00	55
1994	Smiley 52	Retrd.	N/A	16.00	35
1994	Soldier Boy 142	Retrd.	N/A	19.00	100-125
1994	Stocking Sam 108	Retrd.	N/A	23.00	35
1994	Swami 128	Retrd.	N/A	18.00	25
1994	Sweet Pear 59	Retrd.	N/A	24.00	60
1994	Terrance 53	Retrd.	N/A	16.00	45
1994	Tiny Nautilus (gold) 100	Retrd.	N/A	12.00	45
1994	Vaudeville Sam 57	Retrd.	N/A	18.00	30
1994	Wedded Bliss 94	Retrd.	N/A	88.00	195
1994	Wednesday 120	Retrd.	N/A	42.00	63
1994	White Nights 197	Retrd.	N/A	26.00	70
1994	Wings and a Snail 301	Retrd.	N/A	32.00	44
1994	Xenon 304	Retrd.	N/A	38.00	125-175

1995 Holiday Collection - C. Radko

1995	Farmer Boy 108	Retrd.	N/A	28.00	50
1995	Flying High 8	Retrd.	N/A	22.00	45
1995	Frog Lady 26	Retrd.	N/A	24.00	45
1995	Gunther 233	Retrd.	N/A	32.00	135
1995	Here Boy 222	Retrd.	N/A	12.00	25
1995	Imperial Helmet 240	Retrd.	N/A	22.00	35
1995	Jumbo Walnut 249	Retrd.	N/A	18.00	35
1995	Little Red 214	Retrd.	N/A	22.00	40
1995	Little Toy Maker 167	Retrd.	N/A	32.00	35
1995	Off to Market 223	Retrd.	N/A	24.00	35
1995	Personal Delivery 116	Retrd.	N/A	36.00	70
1995	Sister Act-set 140	Retrd.	N/A	18.00	65
1995	Sweet Madame 192	Retrd.	N/A	48.00	108
1995	Turtle Bird 121	Retrd.	N/A	22.00	45

Aids Awareness - C. Radko

1993	A Shy Rabbit's Heart 462	Retrd.	1993	15.00	75-95
1994	Frosty Cares SP5	Retrd.	1994	25.00	60
1995	On Wings of Hope SP10	Retrd.	1995	30.00	30
1996	A Winter Bear's Heart SP15	Yr.Iss.		34.00	34

Disney Gallery Ornaments - C. Radko

1996	Best Friends DIS10	10,000		60.00	60
1996	By Jiminy DIS11	7,500		38.00	38
1996	Cruella De Vil DIS13	10,000		55.00	55
1995	Mickey's Tree DIS1	2,500	1995	45.00	300-350
1996	Pinocchio DIS9	5,000	1996	45.00	130-180
1995	Pooh's Favorite Gift DIS2	2,500	1995	45.00	300-350
1996	Tinker Bell DIS12	10,000		55.00	55

Event Only - C. Radko

1993	Littlest Snowman 347S (store & C. Radko event)	Retrd.	1993	15.00	65
1994	Roly Poly 94125E (store & C. Radko event)	Retrd.	1994	22.00	70
1995	Forever Lucy 91075E (store & C. Radko event)	Retrd.	1995	32.00	45
1996	Poinsettia Elegance 287E (store event)	Yr.Iss.		32.00	32
1996	A Job Well Done SP18 (C. Radko event)	Yr.Iss.		30.00	30

Limited Edition Ornaments - C. Radko

1995	And Snowy Makes Eight 169 (set of 8)	15,000	1996	125.00	125
1996	Russian Rhapsody RUS (Set/6)	7,500		150.00	150

Matt Berry Memorial Soccer Fund - C. Radko

YEAR ISSUE		EDITION LIMIT	YEAR RETRD.	ISSUE PRICE	*QUOTE U.S.$
1995	Matthew's Game 158-0	Open		12.00	12

Nativity Series - C. Radko

1995	Three Wise Men WM (Set/3)	15,000	1996	90.00	100-125
1996	Holy Family HF (Set/3)	15,000		70.00	70

Nutcracker Series - C. Radko

1995	Nutcracker Suite I NC1 (Set/3)	15,000	1996	90.00	100-125
1996	Nutcracker Suite II NC2 (Set/3)	15,000		90.00	90

Pediatrics Cancer Research - C. Radko

1994	A Gifted Santa 70	Retrd.	1994	25.00	60-80
1995	Christmas Puppy Love SP11	Retrd.	1995	30.00	50
1996	Bearly Awake SP16	Yr.Iss.		34.00	34

South Bend Special - C. Radko

1995	Polar Express (lilac) 95-076SB	Retrd.	1995	24.95	60-75

Starlight Store Exclusives - C. Radko

1996	Baby Bear (Christmas Dove) 322-0	N/A		30.00	30
1996	Far Away Places (Christmas Village) 321-0	N/A		40.00	40
1996	Frosty Bear (Christmas House) 326-0	N/A		30.00	30
1996	Kitty Christmas (Tuck's) 323-0	N/A		30.00	30
1996	Little St. Mick (Roger's Gardens) DIS7	N/A		45.00	45
1996	On His Way (Geary's) 319-0	N/A		30.00	30
1996	Ruffles (Christmas Attic) 320-0	N/A		30.00	30
1996	Snow Fun (Vinny's) 324-0	N/A		30.00	30
1996	Tweedle Dee (Glass Pheasant) 325-0	N/A		40.00	40
1996	Winter Kitten (Margo's) 327-0	N/A		30.00	30

Sunday Brunch - C. Radko

1996	Hansel & Gretel and Witch HG1	7,500		50.00	50

Twelve Days of Christmas - C. Radko

1993	Partridge in a Pear Tree SP2	5,000	1993	35.00	750-1000
1994	Two Turtle Doves SP4	10,000	1994	28.00	125-195
1995	Three French Hens SP9	10,000	1995	34.00	100-125
1996	Four Calling Birds SP12	10,000		44.00	44

Warner Brothers - C. Radko

1996	Little Angel Tweety WB10	5,000		45.00	45
1995	Santa's Bugs Bunny WB1	Retrd.	1995	45.00	75-135
1996	Superman WB7	7,500		48.00	48
1996	Sylvester Sprite WB9	5,000		45.00	45
1996	Taz & Bugs Stockings WB4	5,000		65.00	65
1995	Taz Angel WB2	Retrd.	1995	40.00	75-135
1995	Tweety's Sprite WB3	Retrd.	1995	45.00	140-185

Dave Grossman Creations

Gone With the Wind Ornaments - Various

1987	Ashley - D. Geenty	Closed	N/A	15.00	45
1994	Gold Plated GWO-00 - Unknown	Open		13.00	13
1994	Limited Edition GWO-94 - Unknown	Yr.Iss.		25.00	25
1989	Mammy - D. Geenty	Closed	N/A	20.00	20
1991	Prissy - Unknown	Closed	N/A	20.00	20
1993	Rhett (White Suit) GWO-93 - Unknown	Closed	N/A	20.00	20
1987	Rhett - D. Geenty	Closed	N/A	15.00	45
1988	Rhett and Scarlett - D. Geenty	Closed	N/A	20.00	40
1992	Scarlett (Green Dress) - Unknown	Closed	N/A	20.00	20
1990	Scarlett (Red Dress) - D. Geenty	Closed	N/A	20.00	20
1987	Scarlett - D. Geenty	Closed	N/A	15.00	45
1994	Scarlett GWO-94 - Unknown	Yr.Iss.		20.00	20
1987	Tara - D. Geenty	Closed	N/A	15.00	45

Rockwell Collection-Annual Rockwell Ball - Rockwell-Inspired

1975	Santa with Feather Quill NRO-01	Retrd.	N/A	3.50	25
1976	Santa at Globe NRO-02	Retrd.	N/A	4.00	25
1977	Grandpa on Rocking Horse NRO-03	Retrd.	N/A	4.00	12
1978	Santa with Map NRO-04	Retrd.	N/A	4.50	12
1979	Santa at Desk with Mail Bag NRO-05	Retrd.	N/A	5.00	12
1980	Santa Asleep with Toys NRO-06	Retrd.	N/A	5.00	10
1981	Santa with Boy on Finger NRO-07	Retrd.	N/A	5.00	10
1982	Santa Face on Winter Scene NRO-08	Retrd.	N/A	5.00	10
1983	Coachman with Whip NRO-9	Retrd.	N/A	5.00	10
1984	Christmas Bounty Man NRO-10	Retrd.	N/A	5.00	10
1985	Old English Trio NRO-11	Retrd.	N/A	5.00	10
1986	Tiny Tim on Shoulder NRO-12	Retrd.	N/A	5.00	10
1987	Skating Lesson NRO-13	Retrd.	N/A	5.00	10
1988	Big Moment NRO-14	Retrd.	N/A	5.50	10
1989	Discovery NRO-15	Retrd.	N/A	6.00	10
1990	Bringing Home The Tree NRO-16	Retrd.	N/A	6.00	10
1991	Downhill Daring NRO-17	Retrd.	N/A	6.00	10
1992	On The Ice NRO-18	Retrd.	N/A	6.00	10
1993	Gramps NRO-19	Retrd.	N/A	6.00	10
1994	Triple Self Portrait -Commemorative NRO-20	Yr.Iss.		6.00	10

Rockwell Collection-Annual Rockwell Figurine Ornaments - Rockwell-Inspired

1978	Caroler NRX-03	Retrd.	N/A	15.00	45

YEAR ISSUE		EDITION LIMIT	YEAR RETRD.	ISSUE PRICE	*QUOTE U.S.$
1979	Drum for Tommy NRX-24	Retrd.	N/A	20.00	30
1980	Santa's Good Boys NRX-37	Retrd.	N/A	20.00	30
1981	Letters to Santa NRX-39	Retrd.	N/A	20.00	30
1982	Cornettist NRX-32	Retrd.	N/A	20.00	30
1983	Fiddler NRX-83	Retrd.	N/A	20.00	30
1984	Christmas Bounty NRX-84	Retrd.	N/A	20.00	30
1985	Jolly Coachman NRX-85	Retrd.	N/A	20.00	30
1986	Grandpa on Rocking Horse NRX-86	Retrd.	N/A	20.00	30
1987	Skating Lesson NRX-87	Retrd.	N/A	20.00	30
1988	Big Moment NRX-88	Retrd.	N/A	20.00	30
1989	Discovery NRX-89	Retrd.	N/A	20.00	30
1990	Bringing Home The Tree NRX-90	Retrd.	N/A	20.00	30
1991	Downhill Daring B NRX-91	Retrd.	N/A	20.00	30
1992	On The Ice	Retrd.	N/A	20.00	30
1993	Granps NRX-93	Retrd.	N/A	24.00	30
1993	Marriage License First Christmas Together NRX-m1	Retrd.	N/A	30.00	30
1994	Merry Christmas NRX-94	Yr.Iss.		24.00	24

Department 56

Bisque Light-Up, Clip-on Ornaments - Department 56

1986	Angelic Lite-up 8260-0	Open		4.00	4
1987	Anniversary Love Birds, (pair) w/brass ribbon 8353-4	Closed	1988	4.00	4
1986	Dessert, 6 asst. 7100-5	Closed	1987	5.00	25-35
1985	Humpty Dumpty 3525-4	Closed	1986	4.50	5
1990	Owl w/clip 8344-5	Closed	1994	5.00	14
1986	Plum Pudding 7101-3	Closed	1987	4.50	30-45
1989	Pond-Frog w/clip 8347-0	Closed	1991	5.00	35
1989	Pond-Snail w/clip 8347-0	Closed	1991	5.00	40-55
1988	Rabbit w/clip 8350-0	Open		4.00	17
1987	Shells, set/4 8349-6	Closed	1991	14.00	50-80
1986	Shooting Star 7106-4	Closed	1987	5.50	22
1985	Snowbirds, (pair) w/clip 8357-7	Open		5.00	5
1985	Snowbirds, set/6 8367-4	Closed	1988	15.00	15
1985	Snowbirds, set/8 8358-5	Closed	1988	20.00	20
1985	Snowmen, 3 asst. 8360-7	Closed	1988	10.50	11
1986	Teddy Bear w/clip 8262-7	Closed	1991	5.00	18
1986	Truffles Sampler, set/4 7102-1	Closed	1987	17.50	35
1986	Winged Snowbird 8261-9	Closed	1988	2.50	3
1989	Woodland-Field Mouse w/clip 8348-8	Closed	1991	5.00	40-55
1989	Woodland-Squirrel w/clip 8348-8	Closed	1991	5.00	42-55

CCP Ornaments-Flat -Department 56

1986	Christmas Carol Houses, set/3 (6504-8)	Closed	1989	13.00	45
1986	• The Cottage of Bob Cratchit & Tiny Tim	Closed	1989	4.35	N/A
1986	• Fezziwig's Warehouse	Closed	1989	4.35	N/A
1986	• Scrooge and Marley Countinghouse	Closed	1989	4.35	N/A
1986	New England Village, set/7 (6536-6)	Closed	1989	25.00	300
1986	• Apothecary Shop	Closed	1989	3.50	25
1986	• Brick Town Hall	Closed	1989	3.50	50
1986	• General Store	Closed	1989	3.50	55
1986	• Livery Stable & Boot Shop	Closed	1989	3.50	25
1986	• Nathaniel Bingham Fabrics	Closed	1989	3.50	25
1986	• Red Schoolhouse	Closed	1989	3.50	40-70
1986	• Steeple Church	Closed	1989	3.50	150-225

Christmas Carol Character Ornaments-Flat -Department 56

1986	Christmas Carol Characters, set/3 (6505-6)	Closed	1987	13.00	45
1986	• Bob Cratchit & Tiny Tim	Closed	1987	4.35	65
1986	• Poulterer	Closed	1987	4.35	30
1986	• Scrooge	Closed	1987	4.35	35-75

Merry Makers - Department 56

1992	Tolland The Toller 9369-6	Closed	1995	11.00	11

Miscellaneous Ornaments - Department 56

1983	Snow Village Wood Ornaments, set/6, 5099-7	Closed	1984	30.00	N/A
1983	• Carriage House	Closed	1984	5.00	50
1983	• Centennial House	Closed	1984	5.00	100
1983	• Countryside Church	Closed	1984	5.00	125
1983	• Gabled House	Closed	1984	5.00	75
1983	• Pioneer Church	Closed	1984	5.00	75-125
1983	• Swiss Chalet	Closed	1984	5.00	75
1984	Dickens 2-sided Tin Ornaments, set/6, 6522-6	Closed	1985	12.00	440
1984	• Abel Beesley Butcher	Closed	1985	2.00	45
1984	• Bean and Son Smithy Shop	Closed	1985	2.00	45
1984	• Crowntree Inn	Closed	1985	2.00	45
1984	• Golden Swan Baker	Closed	1985	2.00	45
1984	• Green Grocer	Closed	1985	2.00	45
1984	• Jones & Co. Brush & Basket Shop	Closed	1985	2.00	45
1986	Cherub on Brass Ribbon, 8248-1	Closed	1988	8.00	72
1986	Teddy Bear on Brass Ribbon 8263-5	Closed	1988	7.00	75
1988	Balsam Bell Brass Dickens' Candlestick 6244-8	Closed	1989	3.00	15
1988	Christmas Carol- Bob & Mrs. Cratchit 5914-5	Closed	1989	18.00	36-45
1988	Christmas Carol- Scrooge's Head 5912-9	Closed	1989	13.00	30-35
1988	Christmas Carol- Tiny Tim's Head 5913-7	Closed	1989	10.00	25-35

YEAR ISSUE		EDITION LIMIT	YEAR RETRD.	ISSUE PRICE	*QUOTE U.S.$
1994	Dickens Village Dedlock Arms 9872-8, (porcelain, gift boxed)	Closed	1994	12.50	15-25
1995	Sir John Falstaff 9870-1 (Charles Dickens' Signature Series)	Closed	1995	15.00	15
1996	The Grapes Inn 98729	Yr.Iss.		15.00	15
1996	Crown & Cricket Inn 98730	Yr.Iss.		15.00	15
1996	The Pied Bull Inn 98731	Yr.Iss.		15.00	15

Snowbabies Mercury Glass Ornaments - Department 56

1996	Snowbaby Drummer The Night Before Christmas 68983	Open		18.00	18
1996	Snowbaby On Package The Night Before Christmas 68981	Open		18.00	18
1996	Snowbaby Soldier The Night Before Christmas 68982	Open		18.00	18
1996	Snowbaby With Wreath The Night Before Christmas 68980	Open		18.00	18

Snowbabies Ornaments - Department 56

1994	Be My Baby 6866-7	Open		15.00	15
1986	Crawling, Lite-Up, Clip-On, 7953-7	Closed	1992	7.00	23-30
1994	First Star Jinglebaby, 6858-6	Open		10.00	11
1994	Gathering Stars in the Sky, 6855-1	Open		12.50	13
1995	Joy 68807, set/3	Open		32.50	33
1994	Juggling Stars in the Sky 6867-5	Open		15.00	15
1994	Just For You Jinglebaby 6869-1	Open		11.00	11
1994	Little Drummer Jinglebaby, 6859-4	Open		10.00	11
1987	Mini, Winged Pair, Lite-Up, Clip-On, 7976-6	Open		9.00	12
1987	Moon Beams, 7951-0	Open		7.50	9
1991	My First Star, 6811-0	Open		7.00	8
1989	Noel, 7988-0	Open		7.50	8
1995	One Little Candle Jinglebaby 68806	Open		11.00	11
1995	Overnight Delivery, 759-5 (Event Piece)	Closed	1995	10.00	25-32
1995	Overnight Delivery, 68808	Open		10.00	10
1990	Penguin, Lite-Up, Clip-On, 7940-5	Closed	1992	5.00	20-32
1990	Polar Bear, Lite-Up, Clip-On, 7941-3	Closed	1992	5.00	12-18
1990	Rock-A-Bye Baby, 7939-1	Closed	1995	7.00	8
1996	Sitting, Lite-Up, Clip-On, 7952-9	Closed	1990	7.00	40
1992	Snowbabies Icicle With Star, 6825-0	Closed	1995	16.00	16
1987	Snowbaby Adrift Lite-Up, Clip-On, 7969-3	Closed	1990	8.50	105-135
1986	Snowbaby on Brass Ribbon, 7961-8	Closed	1989	8.00	155
1993	Sprinkling Stars in the Sky, 6848-9	Open		12.50	13
1989	Star Bright, 7990-1	Open		7.50	8
1992	Starry, Starry Night, 6830-6	Open		12.50	13
1994	Stars in My Stocking Jinglebaby 6868-3	Open		11.00	11
1991	Surprise, 7989-8	Closed	1994	12.00	18-23
1991	Swinging On a Star, 6810-1	Open		9.50	10
1988	Twinkle Little Star, 7980-4	Closed	1990	7.00	70-125
1993	Wee...This is Fun!, 6847-0	Open		13.50	14
1995	Winged, Lite-Up, Clip-On, 7954-5	Closed	1990	7.00	40

Village Light-Up Ornaments - Department 56

1987	Christmas Carol Cottages, set/3 (6513-7)	Closed	1989	17.00	60
1987	• The Cottage of Bob Cratchit & Tiny Tim	Closed	1989	6.00	20
1987	• Fezziwig's Warehouse	Closed	1989	6.00	17-35
1987	• Scrooge & Marley Countinghouse	Closed	1989	6.00	20
1987	Dickens' Village, set/14 (6521-8, 6520-0)	Closed	1989	84.00	400
1987	Dickens' Village, set/6 (6520-0)	Closed	1989	36.00	85-175
1987	• Barley Bree Farmhouse	Closed	1989	6.00	15-38
1987	• Blythe Pond Mill House	Closed	1989	6.00	40
1987	• Brick Abbey	Closed	1989	6.00	85
1987	• Chesterton Manor House	Closed	1989	6.00	33-54
1987	• Kenilworth Castle	Closed	1989	6.00	36-42
1987	• The Old Curiosity Shop	Closed	1989	6.00	50
1987	Dickens' Village, set/8 (6521-8)	Closed	1989	48.00	200
1985	• Abel Beesley Butcher	Closed	1989	6.00	23
1985	• Bean and Son Smithy Shop	Closed	1989	6.00	20-35
1985	• Candle Shop	Closed	1989	6.00	23
1985	• Crowntree Inn	Closed	1989	6.00	35
1985	• Dickens' Village Church	Closed	1989	6.00	48-55
1985	• Golden Swan Baker	Closed	1989	6.00	23
1985	• Green Grocer	Closed	1989	6.00	29
1985	• Jones & Co. Brush & Basket Shop	Closed	1989	6.00	28-36
1987	New England Village, set/13 (6533-1, 6534-0)	Closed	1989	78.00	700-750
1987	New England Village, set/6 (6534-0)	Closed	1989	36.00	200-275
1987	• Craggy Cove Lighthouse	Closed	1989	6.00	150
1987	• Jacob Adams Barn	Closed	1989	6.00	53
1987	• Jacob Adams Farmhouse	Closed	1989	6.00	38-48
1987	• Smythe Woolen Mill	Closed	1989	6.00	80-125
1987	• Timber Knoll Log Cabin	Closed	1989	6.00	115-125
1987	• Weston Train Station	Closed	1989	6.00	45
1986	New England Village, set/7 (6533-1)	Closed	1989	42.00	325
1986	• Apothecary Shop	Closed	1989	6.00	19
1986	• Brick Town Hall	Closed	1989	6.00	35
1986	• General Store	Closed	1989	6.00	35
1986	• Livery Stable & Boot Shop	Closed	1989	6.00	25
1986	• Nathaniel Bingham Fabrics	Closed	1989	6.00	22-36
1986	• Red Schoolhouse	Closed	1989	6.00	65-75
1986	• Steeple Church	Closed	1989	6.00	130

Duncan Royale

History Of Santa Claus - Duncan Royale

1992	Santa I (set of 12)	Open		144.00	144
1992	Santa II (set of 12)	Open		144.00	144

Enesco Corporation

Cherished Teddies - P. Hillman

1993	Angel, 3 Asst.-912980	Suspd.		12.50	20-35
1992	Angel-950777	Suspd.		12.50	30-55
1995	Baby Angel on Cloud-141240	Open		13.50	14
1993	Baby Boy dated 1993-913014	Yr.Iss.		12.50	25-35
1993	Baby Girl dated 1993-913006	Yr.Iss.		12.50	25-35
1992	Bear In Stocking, dated 1992-950653	Yr.Iss.		16.00	25-65
1996	Bear w/Dangling Mittens -177768	Open		12.50	13
1994	Beary Christmas Dated 1994 -617253	Yr.Iss.		15.00	18-30
1992	Beth On Rocking Reindeer -950793	Suspd.		20.00	35-60
1995	Boy Bear Flying Cupid-103608	Suspd.		13.00	25
1995	Boy/Girl with Banner-141259	Suspd.		13.50	14
1994	Bundled Up For The Holidays -617229	Open		15.00	15
1992	Christmas Sister Bears, 3 Asst.-951226	Suspd.		12.50	13-20
1994	Drummer Boy Dated 1994-912891	Yr.Iss.		10.00	20-35
1995	Elf Bear W/Doll-625434	Suspd.		12.50	13
1995	Elf Bear W/Stuffed Reindeer-625442	Suspd.		12.50	13
1995	Elf Bears/Candy Cane-651389	Suspd.		12.50	13
1995	Girl Bear Flying Cupid-103616	Suspd.		13.00	25
1993	Girl w/Muff (Alice) dated 1993-912832	Yr.Iss.		13.50	30-50
1993	Jointed Teddy Bear -914894	Suspd.		12.50	25
1995	Mrs Claus Xmas Holding Tray/Cookies-625426	Suspd.		12.50	25
1996	Santa Bear 2 asst.-176168	Open		12.50	13
1995	Teddies Santa Bear 651370	Open		12.50	13
1995	Teddy with Ice Skates dated 95-141232	Yr.Iss.		12.50	28-38
1996	Toy Soldier (dated)-176052	Yr.Iss.		12.50	13

Memories of Yesterday Society Member's Only - M. Attwell

1992	With Luck And A Friend, I's In Heaven-MY922	Yr.Iss.		16.00	20
1993	I'm Bringing Good Luck-Wherever You Are	Yr.Iss.		16.00	22

Memories of Yesterday - M. Attwell

1988	Baby's First Christmas 1988 -520373	Yr.Iss.	1988	13.50	40-60
1988	Special Delivery! 1988-520381	Yr.Iss.	1988	13.50	35-45
1989	Baby's First Christmas-522465	Retrd.	1996	15.00	15-20
1989	A Surprise for Santa-522473 (1989)	Yr.Iss.	1989	13.50	15-25
1989	Christmas Together-522562	Open		15.00	15-25
1995	Happy Landings (Dated 1995) 522619	Yr.Iss.	1995	16.00	16
1990	Time For Bed-524638	Yr.Iss.		15.00	15-30
1990	New Moon-524646	Suspd.		15.00	15-25
1994	Just Dreaming of You-524786	Open		16.00	16
1990	Moonstruck-524794	Retrd.	1992	15.00	15-25
1991	Just Watchin' Over You-525421	Retrd.	1994	17.50	18
1991	Lucky Me-525448	Retrd.	1993	16.00	20
1993	Wish I Could Fly To You-525790 (dated)	Yr.Iss.	1993	16.00	16
1992	I'll Fly Along To See You Soon-525804 (1992 Dated Bisque)	Yr.Iss.		16.00	16
1991	Star Fishin'-525820	Open		16.00	16
1993	May All Your Finest Dreams Come True-528811	Open		16.00	16
1991	Lucky You-525847	Retrd.	1993	16.00	16
1995	Now I Lay Me Down to Sleep 527009	Open		15.00	15
1995	I Pray the Lord My Soul to Keep 527017	Open		15.00	15
1992	Mommy, I Teared It -527041(Five Year Anniversary Limited Edition)	Yr.Iss.		15.00	20
1991	S'no Use Lookin' Back Now!-527181(dated)	Yr.Iss.	1991	17.50	28
1992	Merry Christmas, Little Boo-Boo-528803	Open		37.50	38
1992	Star Light. Star Bright-528838	Open		16.00	16
1994	Give Yourself a Hug From Me!-529109 ('94 Dated)	Yr.Iss.		17.50	18
1992	Swinging Together -580481(1992 Dated Artplas)	Yr.Iss.	1992	17.50	22
1992	Sailin' With My Friends-587575 (Artplas)	Open		25.00	25
1993	Bringing Good Wishes Your Way-592846 (Artplas)	Open		25.00	25
1994	Bout Time I Came Along to See You-592854 (Artplas)	Open		17.50	18

Memories of Yesterday Event Item Only - Enesco

1993	How 'Bout A Little Kiss?-527068	Closed	1993	16.50	50
1996	Hoping To See You Soon-527033	Yr.Iss.		15.00	15

Memories of Yesterday Friendship - Enesco

1996	I Love You This Much!-185809	Open		13.50	14

Memories of Yesterday Peter Pan - Enesco

1996	Tinkerbell-164682	Open		20.00	20

YEAR ISSUE	EDITION LIMIT	YEAR RETD.	ISSUE PRICE	*QUOTE U.S.$

Miss Martha's Collection - M. Holcombe

YEAR ISSUE		EDITION LIMIT	YEAR RETD.	ISSUE PRICE	*QUOTE U.S.$
1993	Caroline - Always Someone Watching Over Me-350532	Closed	1994	25.00	50
1993	Arianna - Heavenly Sounds H/O-350567	Closed	1994	25.00	50
1992	Baby in Basket-369454	Closed	1994	25.00	50
1992	Baby In Swing-421480	Retrd.	1993	25.00	50
1992	Girl Holding Stocking DTD 1992-421499	Closed	1994	25.00	50
1992	Girl/Bell In Hand-421502	Retrd.	1993	25.00	50

Precious Moments - S. Butcher

YEAR ISSUE		EDITION LIMIT	YEAR RETD.	ISSUE PRICE	*QUOTE U.S.$
1983	Surround Us With Joy-E-0513	Yr.Iss.		9.00	50-60
1983	Mother Sew Dear-E-0514	Open		9.00	17-25
1983	To A Special Dad-E-0515	Suspd.		9.00	30-54
1983	The Purr-fect Grandma-E-0516	Open		9.00	17-40
1983	The Perfect Grandpa-E-0517	Suspd.		9.00	16-30
1983	Blessed Are The Pure In Heart -E-0518	Yr.Iss.		9.00	45
1983	O Come All Ye Faithful-E-0531	Suspd.		10.00	45-60
1983	Let Heaven And Nature Sing -E-0532	Retrd.	1986	9.00	30-40
1983	Tell Me The Story Of Jesus-E-0533	Suspd.		9.00	36-57
1983	To Thee With Love-E-0534	Retrd.	1989	9.00	25-40
1983	Love Is Patient-E-0535	Suspd.		9.00	46-59
1983	Love Is Patient-E-0536	Suspd.		9.00	55-69
1983	Jesus Is The Light That Shines - E-0537	Suspd.		9.00	60-75
1982	Joy To The World-E-2343	Suspd.		9.00	35-65
1982	I'll Play My Drum For Him -E-2359	Yr.Iss.		9.00	95
1982	Baby's First Christmas-E-2362	Suspd.		9.00	25-50
1982	The First Noel-E-2367	Suspd.		9.00	50-70
1982	The First Noel-E-2368	Retrd.	1984	9.00	20-40
1982	Dropping In For Christmas-E-2369	Retrd.	1986	9.00	36-50
1982	Unicorn-E-2371	Retrd.	1988	10.00	50-65
1982	Baby's First Christmas-E-2372	Suspd.		9.00	35-45
1982	Dropping Over For Christmas -E-2376	Retrd.	1985	9.00	29-55
1982	Mouse With Cheese-E-2381	Suspd.		9.00	100-125
1982	Our First Christmas Together -E-2385	Suspd.		10.00	20-50
1982	Camel, Donkey & Cow (3 pc. set)-E2386	Suspd.		25.00	65-100
1984	Wishing You A Merry Christmas-E-5387	Yr.Iss.		10.00	35-55
1984	Joy To The World-E-5388	Retrd.	1987	10.00	20-45
1984	Peace On Earth-E-5389	Suspd.		10.00	20-45
1984	May God Bless You With A Perfect Holiday Season-E-5390	Suspd.		10.00	20-40
1984	Love Is Kind-E-5391	Suspd.		10.00	24-35
1984	Blessed Are The Pure In Heart -E-5392	Yr.Iss.		10.00	20
1981	But Love Goes On Forever-E-5627	Suspd.		6.00	90-130
1981	But Love Goes On Forever -E-5628	Suspd.		6.00	90-140
1981	Let The Heavens Rejoice-E-5629	Yr.Iss.		6.00	200
1981	Unto Us A Child Is Born-E-5630	Suspd.		6.00	40-70
1981	Baby's First Christmas-E-5631	Suspd.		6.00	40-60
1981	Baby's First Christmas-E-5632	Suspd.		6.00	40-65
1981	Come Let Us Adore Him (4pc. set)-E-5633	Suspd.		22.00	115-150
1981	Wee Three Kings (3pc. set) -E-5634	Suspd.		19.00	100-129
1981	We Have Seen His Star-E-6120	Retrd.	1984	6.00	20-45
1985	Have A Heavenly Christmas -12416	Open		12.00	19-30
1995	He Covers The Earth With His Beauty-142689	Yr.Iss.		30.00	30
1995	He Covers The Earth With His Beauty-142662	Yr.Iss.		17.00	17
1995	Our First Christmas Together-142700	Yr.Iss.		18.50	19
1995	Baby's First Christmas-142719	Yr.Iss.		17.50	18
1995	Baby's First Christmas-142727	Yr.Iss.		17.50	18
1985	God Sent His Love-15768	Yr.Iss.		10.00	35
1985	May Your Christmas Be Happy-15822	Suspd.		10.00	30-48
1985	Happiness Is The Lord-15830	Suspd.		10.00	30-37
1985	May Your Christmas Be Delightful-15849	Suspd.		10.00	15-35
1985	Honk If You Love Jesus-15857	Suspd.		10.00	20-35
1985	Baby's First Christmas-15903	Yr.Iss.		10.00	40
1985	Baby's First Christmas-15911	Yr.Iss.		10.00	20-40
1986	Shepherd of Love-102288	Suspd.		10.00	35
1986	Wishing You A Cozy Christmas -102326	Yr.Iss.		10.00	35-45
1986	Our First Christmas Together -102350	Yr.Iss.		10.00	20-35
1986	Trust And Obey-102377	Open		10.00	17-25
1986	Love Rescued Me-102385	Open		10.00	17-23
1986	Angel Of Mercy-102407	Open		10.00	17-30
1986	It's A Perfect Boy-102415	Open		10.00	25
1986	Lord Keep Me On My Toes -102423	Retrd.	1990	10.00	25-50
1986	Serve With A Smile-102431	Suspd.		10.00	18-30
1986	Serve With A Smile-102458	Suspd.		10.00	32
1986	Reindeer-102466	Yr.Iss.		11.00	160-225
1986	Rocking Horse-102474	Open		10.00	25
1986	Baby's First Christmas-102504	Yr.Iss.		10.00	30
1986	Baby's First Christmas-102512	Yr.Iss.		10.00	30
1987	Bear The Good News Of Christmas-104515	Yr.Iss.		12.50	30
1987	Baby's First Christmas-109401	Yr.Iss.		12.00	37
1987	Baby's First Christmas-109428	Yr.Iss.		12.00	30

YEAR ISSUE		EDITION LIMIT	YEAR RETD.	ISSUE PRICE	*QUOTE U.S.$
1987	Love Is The Best Gift Of All -109770	Yr.Iss.		11.00	20
1987	I'm A Possibility-111120	Suspd.		11.00	25
1987	You Have Touched So Many Hearts-112356	Open		11.00	17-30
1987	Waddle I Do Without You -112364	Open		11.00	17-30
1987	I'm Sending You A White Christmas-112372	Open		11.00	20-25
1987	He Cleansed My Soul-112380	Open		12.00	17-25
1987	Our First Christmas Together -112399	Yr.Iss.		11.00	25-35
1988	To My Forever Friend-113956	Open		16.00	19-35
1988	Smile Along The Way-113964	Suspd.		15.00	20-40
1988	God Sent You Just In Time -113972	Suspd.		13.50	25-38
1988	Rejoice O Earth-113980	Retrd.	1991	13.50	30-40
1988	Cheers To The Leader-113999	Suspd.		13.50	32-38
1988	My Love Will Never Let You Go -114006	Suspd.		13.50	15-30
1988	Baby's First Christmas-115282	Yr.Iss.		15.00	20-30
1988	Time To Wish You A Merry Christmas-115320	Yr.Iss.		13.00	45
1996	Owl Be Home For Christmas -128708	Yr.Iss.		18.50	19
1995	He Covers The Earth With His Beauty (ball)-142489	Yr.Iss.		30.00	30
1995	He Covers The Earth With His Beauty-142662	Yr.Iss.		17.00	17
1995	Our First Christmas Together -142700	Yr.Iss.		18.50	19
1995	Baby's First Christmas-142719	Yr.Iss.		17.50	18
1995	Baby's First Christmas-142727	Yr.Iss.		17.50	18
1995	Joy From Head To Mistletoe -150126	Open		18.50	19
1995	You're "A" Number One In My Book, Teacher-150142	Open		18.50	19
1995	Joy To The World-150320	Open		20.00	20
1996	Joy To The World-153338	Open		20.00	20
1996	Peace On Earth...Anyway (Ball)-183350	Yr.Iss.		30.00	30
1996	Peace On Earth...Anyway -183369	Yr.Iss.		18.50	19
1996	God's Precious Gift-183881	Open		20.00	20
1996	Puppy In Ice Skate-183903	Open		18.50	19
1996	Our First Christmas Together -183911	Yr.Iss.		22.50	23
1996	Baby's First Christmas-183938	Yr.Iss.		17.50	18
1996	Baby's First Christmas-183946	Yr.Iss.		17.50	18
1988	Our First Christmas Together -520233	Yr.Iss.		13.00	21
1988	Baby's First Christmas-520241	Yr.Iss.		15.00	25
1988	You Are My Gift Come True -520276	Yr.Iss.		12.50	50-60
1988	Hang On For The Holly Days -520292	Yr.Iss.		13.00	25-35
1992	I'm Nuts About You-520411	Yr.Iss.		15.00	20
1995	Hippo Holidays-520403	Yr.Iss.		17.00	20
1991	Sno-Bunny Falls For You Like I Do-520438	Yr.Iss.		15.00	20-29
1989	Christmas is Ruff Without You -520462	Yr.Iss.		13.00	20-40
1993	Slow Down & Enjoy The Holidays-520489	Yr.Iss.		16.00	18
1990	Wishing You A Purr-fect Holiday -520497	Yr.Iss.		15.00	20-45
1989	May All Your Christmases Be White-521302 (dated)	Suspd.		15.00	20-30
1989	Our First Christmas Together-521558	Yr.Iss.		17.50	30
1990	Glide Through the Holidays -521566	Retrd.	1992	13.50	20-30
1990	Dashing Through the Snow -521574	Suspd.		15.00	20-32
1990	Don't Let the Holidays Get You Down-521590	Retrd.	1994	15.00	20-40
1989	Oh Holy Night-522848	Yr.Iss.		13.50	25-45
1989	Make A Joyful Noise-522910	Suspd.		15.00	17
1990	Love One Another-522929	Open		17.50	19-25
1990	Friends Never Drift Apart-522937	Retrd.	1995	17.50	19-27
1991	Our First Christmas Together -522945	Yr.Iss.		17.50	18-25
1989	I Believe In The Old Rugged Cross-522953	Suspd.		15.00	25-40
1989	Peace On Earth-523062	Yr.Iss.		25.00	60-70
1989	Baby's First Christmas-523194	Yr.Iss.		15.00	25
1989	Baby's First Christmas-523208	Yr.Iss.		15.00	20-30
1991	Happy Trails Is Trusting Jesus-523224	Suspd.		15.00	16-30
1990	May Your Christmas Be A Happy Home-523704	Yr.Iss.		27.50	40
1990	Baby's First Christmas-523798	Yr.Iss.		15.00	25
1990	Baby's First Christmas-523771	Yr.Iss.		15.00	25
1990	Once Upon A Holy Night-523852	Yr.Iss.		15.00	20
1992	Good Friends Are For Always -524004	Open		15.00	17
1991	May Your Christmas Be Merry -524174	Yr.Iss.		15.00	25
1990	Bundles of Joy-525057	Yr.Iss.		15.00	30-40
1990	Our First Christmas Together -525324	Yr.Iss.		17.50	18-25
1992	Lord, Keep Me On My Toes -525332	Open		15.00	17-18
1991	May Your Christmas Be Merry (on Base)-526940	Yr.Iss.		30.00	35
1991	Baby's First Christmas (Boy) -527084	Yr.Iss.		15.00	20
1991	Baby's First Christmas (Girl) -527092	Yr.Iss.		15.00	20
1991	The Good Lord Always Delivers - 527165	Suspd.		15.00	20-30
1993	Share in The Warmth of Christmas-527211	Open		15.00	17

YEAR ISSUE		EDITION LIMIT	YEAR RETD.	ISSUE PRICE	*QUOTE U.S.$
1994	Onward Christmas Soldiers -527327	Open		16.00	16
1992	Baby's First Christmas-527475	Yr.Iss.		15.00	20
1992	Baby's First Christmas-527483	Yr.Iss.		15.00	17
1992	But The Greatest Of These Is Love-527696	Yr.Iss.		15.00	20-30
1992	But The Greatest Of These Is Love-527734 (on Base)	Yr.Iss.		30.00	35
1994	Sending You A White Christmas -528218	Open		16.00	16
1994	Bringing You A Merry Christmas -528226	Open		16.00	16
1993	It's So Uplifting to Have a friend Like You-528846	Open		16.00	17
1992	Our First Christmas-528870	Yr.Iss.		17.50	18-25
1994	Our 1st Christmas Together -529206	Yr.Iss.		18.50	19-25
1993	Wishing You the Sweetest Christmas-530190	Yr.Iss.		30.00	35
1993	Wishing You the Sweetest Christmas-530212	Yr.Iss.		15.00	35
1994	Baby's First Christmas-530255	Yr.Iss.		16.00	16
1994	Baby's First Christmas-530263	Yr.Iss.		16.00	16
1994	You're As Pretty As A Christmas Tree-530387	Yr.Iss.		30.00	30
1994	You're As Pretty As A Christmas Tree-530395	Yr.Iss.		16.00	25-40
1993	Our First Christmas Together -530506	Yr.Iss.		17.50	18
1993	Baby's First Christmas-530859	Yr.Iss.		15.00	15
1993	Baby's First Christmas-530867	Yr.Iss.		15.00	15
1994	You Are Always In My Heart-530972	Yr.Iss.		16.00	16-28

Precious Moments Club 15th Anniversary Commemorative Edition - S. Butcher

YEAR ISSUE		EDITION LIMIT	YEAR RETD.	ISSUE PRICE	*QUOTE U.S.$
1993	15 Years Tweet Music Together -530840	Yr.Iss.		15.00	20-30

Precious Moments DSR Open House Weekend Ornaments - S. Butcher

YEAR ISSUE		EDITION LIMIT	YEAR RETD.	ISSUE PRICE	*QUOTE U.S.$
1992	The Magic Starts With You -529648	Yr.Iss.		16.00	25
1993	An Event For All Seasons -529974	Yr.Iss.		15.00	20
1994	Take A Bow Cuz You're My Christmas Star-520470	Yr.Iss.	1994	16.00	22
1995	Merry Chrismoose-150134	Yr.Iss.		17.00	17
1996	Wishing you a Bearie Merry Christmas-531200	Yr.Iss.	1996	17.50	18

Precious Moments Easter Seal Commemorative Ornaments - S. Butcher

YEAR ISSUE		EDITION LIMIT	YEAR RETD.	ISSUE PRICE	*QUOTE U.S.$
1994	It's No Secret What God Can Do-244570	Yr.Iss.		6.50	7
1995	Take Time To Smell The Flowers-128899	Yr.Iss.		7.50	8
1996	You Can Always Count on Me-152579	Yr.Iss.		6.50	7

Precious Moments Special Edition Members' Only - S. Butcher

YEAR ISSUE		EDITION LIMIT	YEAR RETD.	ISSUE PRICE	*QUOTE U.S.$
1993	Loving, Caring And Sharing Along The Way-PM040 (Club Appreciation)	Yr.Iss.		12.50	15-25
1994	You Are The End of My Rainbow-PM041	Yr.Iss.		15.00	20

Precious Moments Sugartown - S. Butcher

YEAR ISSUE		EDITION LIMIT	YEAR RETD.	ISSUE PRICE	*QUOTE U.S.$
1993	Sugartown Chapel -530484	Yr.Iss.		17.50	18
1994	Sam's House-530468	Yr.Iss.		17.50	18
1995	Dr. Sugar's Office-530441	Yr.Iss.		17.50	18
1996	Train Station-184101	Yr.Iss.		18.50	19

Treasury of Christmas Ornaments Collectors' Club - Enesco, unless otherwise noted

YEAR ISSUE		EDITION LIMIT	YEAR RETD.	ISSUE PRICE	*QUOTE U.S.$
1993	The Treasury Card - T0001 - Gilmore	Yr.Iss.	1993	20.00	20
1993	Together We Can Shoot For The Stars-TR931 - Hahn	Yr.Iss.	1993	17.50	35
1993	Can't Weights For The Holidays -TR932	Yr.Iss.	1993	18.50	35
1994	Seedlings Greetings-TR933 - Hahn	Yr.Iss.	1994	22.50	23
1994	Spry Fry (Club)-TR934	Yr.Iss.	1994	15.00	15
1995	You're the Perfect Fit-T0002 - Hahn	Yr.Iss.	1995	Gift	20.00
1995	You're the Perfect Fit-T0102 (Charter Members) - Hahn	Yr.Iss.	1995	Gift	20.00
1995	Things Go Better With Coke™ - TR951	Yr.Iss.	1995	15.00	15
1995	Buttoning Up Our Holiday Best-TR952 - Gilmore	Yr.Iss.	1995	22.50	23
1995	Holiday High-Light- TR953 - Gilmore	Yr.Iss.	1995	15.00	15
1995	First Class Christmas- TR954 - Gilmore	Yr.Iss.	1995	22.50	23
1996	Yo Ho Holidays-T0003	Yr.Iss.		Gift	20.00
1996	Yo Ho Holidays-T0103 (Charter Members)	Yr.Iss.		Gift	20.00
1996	Coca Colar Choo Choo- TR961	Yr.Iss.		35.00	35
1996	Friends Are Tea-riffic- TR962	Yr.Iss.		25.00	25
1996	On Track With Coke™- TR963	Yr.Iss.		25.00	25
1996	Riding High- TR964 - Hahn	Yr.Iss.		20.00	20

Treasury of Christmas Ornaments - Enesco, unless otherwise noted

YEAR ISSUE		EDITION LIMIT	YEAR RETD.	ISSUE PRICE	*QUOTE U.S.$
1983	Wide Open Throttle-E-0242	3-Yr.	1985	12.00	35

YEAR ISSUE		EDITION LIMIT	YEAR RETD.	ISSUE PRICE	*QUOTE U.S.$
1983	Baby's First Christmas-E-0271	Yr.Iss.	1983	6.00	N/A
1983	Grandchild's First Christmas-E-0272	Yr.Iss.	1983	5.00	N/A
1983	Baby's First Christmas-E-0273	3-Yr.	1985	9.00	N/A
1983	Toy Drum Teddy-E-0274	4-Yr.	1986	9.00	N/A
1983	Watching At The Window-E-0275	3-Yr.	1985	13.00	N/A
1983	To A Special Teacher-E-0276	7-Yr.	1989	5.00	15
1983	Toy Shop-E-0277	7-Yr.	1989	8.00	50
1983	Carousel Horse-E-0278	7-Yr.	1989	9.00	20
1981	Look Out Below-E-6135	2-Yr.	1982	6.00	N/A
1982	Flyin' Santa Christmas Special 1982-E-6136	Yr.Iss.	1982	9.00	75
1981	Flyin' Santa Christmas Special 1981-E-6136	Yr.Iss.	1981	9.00	N/A
1981	Sawin' Elf Helper-E-6138	2-Yr.	1982	6.00	40
1981	Snow Shoe-In Santa-E-6139	2-Yr.	1982	6.00	35
1981	Baby's First Christmas 1981-E-6145	Yr.Iss.	1981	6.00	N/A
1981	Our Hero-E-6146	2-Yr.	1982	4.00	N/A
1981	Whoops-E-6147	2-Yr.	1982	3.50	N/A
1981	Whoops, It's 1981-E-6148	Yr.Iss.	1981	7.50	75
1981	Not A Creature Was Stirring-E-6149	2-Yr.	1982	4.00	25
1984	Joy To The World-E-6209	2-Yr.	1985	9.00	35
1984	Letter To Santa-E-6210	2-Yr.	1985	5.00	30
1984	Lucy & Me Photo Frames-E-6211	3-Yr.	1986	5.00	N/A
1984	Lucy & Me Photo Frames-E-6211	3-Yr.	1986	5.00	N/A
1984	Lucy & Me Photo Frames-E-6211	3-Yr.	1986	5.00	N/A
1984	Lucy & Me Photo Frames-E-6211	3-Yr.	1986	5.00	N/A
1984	Lucy & Me Photo Frames-E-6211	3-Yr.	1986	5.00	N/A
1984	Lucy & Me Photo Frames-E-6211	3-Yr.	1986	5.00	N/A
1984	Baby's First Christmas 1984-E-6212 - Gilmore	Yr.Iss.	1984	10.00	30
1984	Merry Christmas Mother-E-6213	3-Yr.	1986	10.00	30
1984	Baby's First Christmas 1984-E-6215	Yr.Iss.	1984	6.00	N/A
1984	Ferris Wheel Mice-E-6216	2-Yr.	1985	9.00	30
1984	Cuckoo Clock-E-6217	2-Yr.	1985	8.00	40
1984	Muppet Babies Baby's First Christmas-E6222 - J. Henson	Yr.Iss.	1984	10.00	45
1984	Muppet Babies Baby's First Christmas-E6223 -J. Henson	Yr.Iss.	1984	10.00	45
1984	Garfield Hark! The Herald Angel-E-6224 - J. Davis	2-Yr.	1985	7.50	35
1984	Fun In Santa's Sleigh-E-6225 - J. Davis	2-Yr.	1985	12.00	35
1984	Deer! Odie-E-6226 -J. Davis	2-Yr.	1985	6.00	30
1984	Garfield The Snow Cat-E-6227 - J. Davis	2-Yr.	1985	12.00	35
1984	Peek-A-Bear Baby's First Christmas-E-6228	3-Yr.	1986	10.00	N/A
1984	Peek-A-Bear Baby's First Christmas-E-6229	3-Yr.	1986	9.00	N/A
1984	Owl Be Home For Christmas-E-6230	2-Yr.	1985	10.00	23
1984	Santa's Trolley-E-6231	3-Yr.	1986	11.00	50
1984	Holiday Penguin-E-6240	3-Yr.	1986	1.50	15-20
1984	Little Drummer-E-6241	5-Yr.	1988	2.00	N/A
1984	Happy Holidays-E-6248	2-Yr.	1985	2.00	N/A
1984	Christmas Nest-E-6249	2-Yr.	1985	3.00	25
1984	Bunny's Christmas Stocking-E-6251	Yr.Iss.	1984	2.00	15
1984	Santa On Ice-E-6252	3-Yr.	1986	2.50	25
1984	Treasured Memories The New Sled-E-6256	2-Yr.	1985	7.00	N/A
1984	Penguins On Ice-E-6280	2-Yr.	1985	7.50	N/A
1984	Up On The House Top-E-6281	6-Yr.	1989	9.00	N/A
1984	Grandchild's First Christmas 1984-E-6286	Yr.Iss.	1984	5.00	N/A
1984	Grandchild's First Christmas1984-E-6286	Yr.Iss.	1984	5.00	N/A
1984	Godchild's First Christmas-E-6287	3-Yr.	1986	7.00	N/A
1984	Santa In The Box-E-6292	2-Yr.	1985	6.00	N/A
1984	Carousel Horse-E-6913	2-Yr.	1985	1.50	N/A
1983	Arctic Charmer-E-6945	2-Yr.	1984	7.00	N/A
1982	Victorian Sleigh-E-6946	4-Yr.	1985	9.00	15
1983	Wing-A-Ding Angel-E-6948	3-Yr.	1985	7.00	50
1982	A Saviour Is Born This Day-E-6949	8-Yr.	1989	9.00	18
1982	Crescent Santa-E-6950 - Gilmore	4-Yr.	1985	10.00	50
1982	Baby's First Christmas 1982-E-6952	Yr.Iss.	1982	10.00	N/A
1982	Polar Bear Fun Whoops, It's 1982-E-6953	Yr.Iss.	1982	10.00	75
1982	Holiday Skier-E-6954 - J. Davis	5-Yr.	1986	7.00	N/A
1982	Toy Soldier 1982-E-6957	Yr.Iss.	1982	6.50	N/A
1982	Merry Christmas Grandma-E-6975	3-Yr.	1984	5.00	N/A
1982	Carousel Horses-E-6958	3-Yr.	1984	8.00	20-40
1982	Dear Santa-E-6959 - Gilmore	8-Yr.	1989	10.00	25
1982	Penguin Power-E-6977	2-Yr.	1983	6.00	15
1982	Bunny Winter Playground 1982-E-6978	Yr.Iss.	1982	10.00	N/A
1982	Baby's First Christmas 1982-E-6979	Yr.Iss.	1982	10.00	N/A
1983	Carousel Horses-E-6980	4-Yr.	1986	8.00	N/A
1982	Grandchild's First Christmas 1982-E-6983	Yr.Iss.	1982	5.00	73
1982	Merry Christmas Teacher-E-6984	4-Yr.	1985	7.00	N/A
1983	Garfield Cuts The Ice-E-8771 - J. Davis	3-Yr.	1985	6.00	45

YEAR ISSUE		EDITION LIMIT	YEAR RETD.	ISSUE PRICE	*QUOTE U.S.$
1984	A Stocking Full For 1984-E-8773 - J. Davis	Yr.Iss.	1984	6.00	N/A
1983	Stocking Full For 1983-E-8773 - J. Davis	Yr.Iss.	1983	6.00	N/A
1985	Santa Claus Balloon-55794	Yr.Iss.	1985	8.50	20
1985	Carousel Reindeer-55808	4-Yr.	1988	12.00	33
1985	Angel In Flight-55816	4-Yr.	1988	8.00	23
1985	Christmas Penguin-55824	4-Yr.	1988	7.50	43
1985	Merry Christmas Godchild-55832 - Gilmore	5-Yr.	1988	8.00	N/A
1985	Baby's First Christmas-55840	2-Yr.	1986	15.00	N/A
1985	Old Fashioned Rocking Horse-55859	2-Yr.	1986	10.00	15
1985	Child's Second Christmas-55867	5-Yr.	1989	11.00	N/A
1985	Fishing For Stars-55875	5-Yr.	1989	9.00	25
1985	Baby Blocks-55883	2-Yr.	1986	12.00	N/A
1985	Christmas Toy Chest-55891	5-Yr.	1989	10.00	N/A
1985	Grandchild's First Ornament-55921	5-Yr.	1989	7.00	30
1985	Joy Photo Frame-55956	Yr.Iss.	1985	6.00	N/A
1985	We Three Kings-55964	Yr.Iss.	1985	4.50	20
1985	The Night Before Christmas-55972	2-Yr.	1986	5.00	N/A
1985	Baby's First Christmas 1985-55980	Yr.Iss.	1985	6.00	N/A
1985	Baby Rattle Photo Frame-56006	2-Yr.	1986	5.00	N/A
1985	Baby's First Christmas 1985-56014 - Gilmore	Yr.Iss.	1985	10.00	N/A
1985	Christmas Plane Ride-56049 - L. Rigg	6-Yr.	1990	10.00	N/A
1985	Scottie Celebrating Christmas-56065	5-Yr.	1989	7.50	25
1985	North Pole Native-56073	2-Yr.	1986	9.00	N/A
1985	Skating Walrus-56081	2-Yr.	1986	9.00	20
1985	Ski Time-56111 - J. Davis	Yr.Iss.	1985	13.00	N/A
1985	North Pole Express-56138	Yr.Iss.	1985	12.00	N/A
1985	Merry Christmas Mother-56146 - J. Davis	Yr.Iss.	1985	8.50	N/A
1985	Hoppy Christmas-56154 - J. Davis	Yr.Iss.	1985	8.00	N/A
1985	Merry Christmas Teacher-56170 - J. Davis	Yr.Iss.	1985	6.00	N/A
1985	Garfield-In-The-Box-56189 - J. Davis	Yr.Iss.	1985	6.50	25
1985	Merry Christmas Grandma-56197	Yr.Iss.	1985	7.00	N/A
1985	Christmas Lights-56200	2-Yr.	1986	8.00	N/A
1985	Victorian Doll House-56251	Yr.Iss.	1985	13.00	40
1985	Tobaoggan Ride-56286	4-Yr.	1988	6.00	15
1985	Look Out Below-56375	Yr.Iss.	1985	8.50	40
1985	Flying Santa Christmas Special-56383	2-Yr.	1986	10.00	N/A
1985	Sawin Elf Helper-56391	Yr.Iss.	1985	8.00	N/A
1985	Snow Shoe-In Santa-56405	2-Yr.	1986	8.00	50
1985	Our Hero-56413	Yr.Iss.	1985	5.50	N/A
1985	Not A Creature Was Stirring-56421	2-Yr.	1986	4.00	N/A
1985	Merry Christmas Teacher-56448	Yr.Iss.	1985	9.00	N/A
1985	A Stocking Full For 1985-56464 - J. Davis	Yr.Iss.	1985	6.00	25
1985	St. Nicholas Circa 1910-56659	5-Yr.	1989	6.00	15
1985	Christmas Tree Photo Frame-56811	4-Yr.	1988	10.00	N/A
1988	Making A Point-489212 - G.G. Santiago	3-Yr.	1990	10.00	N/A
1988	Mouse Upon A Pipe-489220 - G.G. Santiago	2-Yr.	1989	10.00	12
1988	North Pole Deadline-489387	3-Yr.	1990	13.50	25
1988	Christmas Pin-Up-489409	2-Yr.	1989	11.00	30
1988	Airmail For Teacher-489425	3-Yr.	1990	13.50	N/A
1986	1st Christmas Together 1986-551171	Yr.Iss.	1986	9.00	15-35
1986	Elf Stringing Popcorn-551198	4-Yr.	1989	10.00	20-30
1986	Christmas Scottie-551201	4-Yr.	1989	7.00	15-30
1986	Santa and Child-551236	4-Yr.	1989	13.50	25-50
1986	The Christmas Angel-551244	4-Yr.	1989	22.50	75
1986	Carousel Unicorn-551252 - Gilmore	4-Yr.	1989	12.00	38
1986	Have a Heavenly Holiday-551260	4-Yr.	1989	9.00	N/A
1986	Siamese Kitten-551279	4-Yr.	1989	9.00	36
1986	Old Fashioned Doll House-551287	4-Yr.	1989	15.00	N/A
1986	Holiday Fisherman-551309	3-Yr.	1988	8.00	40
1986	Antique Toy-551317	3-Yr.	1988	9.00	10
1986	Time For Christmas-551325	4-Yr.	1989	13.00	N/A
1986	Christmas Calendar-551333	2-Yr.	1987	7.00	12
1986	Merry Christmas-551341 - Gilmore	3-Yr.	1988	8.00	50
1986	The Santa Claus Shoppe Circa 1905-551562 - J. Grossman	4-Yr.	1989	8.00	15
1986	Baby Bear Sleigh-551651 - Gilmore	3-Yr.	1988	9.00	30
1986	Baby's First Christmas 1986-551678 - Gilmore	Yr.Iss.	1986	10.00	20
1986	First Christmas Together-551708	3-Yr.	1988	6.00	10
1986	Baby's First Christmas-551716	3-Yr.	1988	5.50	10
1986	Baby's First Christmas 1986-551724	Yr.Iss.	1986	6.50	30
1986	Peek-A-Bear Grandchild's First Christmas	Yr.Iss.	1986	6.00	23
1986	Peek-A-Bear Present-552089	4-Yr.	1989	2.50	N/A
1986	Peek-A-Bear Present-552089	4-Yr.	1989	2.50	N/A
1986	Peek-A-Bear Present-552089	4-Yr.	1989	2.50	N/A
1986	Peek-A-Bear Present-552089	4-Yr.	1989	2.50	N/A
1986	Merry Christmas 1986-552186 - L. Rigg	Yr.Iss.	1986	8.00	N/A

YEAR ISSUE		EDITION LIMIT	YEAR RETD.	ISSUE PRICE	*QUOTE U.S.$
1986	Merry Christmas 1986-552534 - L. Rigg	Yr.Iss.	1986	8.00	N/A
1986	Lucy & Me Christmas Tree-552542 - L. Rigg	3-Yr.	1988	7.00	25
1986	Santa's Helpers-552607	3-Yr.	1988	2.50	N/A
1986	My Special Friend-552615	3-Yr.	1988	6.00	10
1986	Christmas Wishes From Panda-552623	3-Yr.	1988	6.00	N/A
1986	Lucy & Me Ski Time-552658 - L. Rigg	2-Yr.	1987	6.50	30
1986	Merry Christmas Teacher-552666	3-Yr.	1988	6.50	N/A
1986	Country Cousins Merry Christmas, Mom	3-Yr.	1988	7.00	23
1986	Country Cousins Merry Christmas, Dad	3-Yr.	1988	7.00	23
1986	Country Cousins Merry Christmas, Mom-552712	4-Yr.	1989	7.00	23
1986	Country Cousins Merry Christmas, Dad-552712	4-Yr.	1989	7.00	23
1986	Grandmother's Little Angel-552747	4-Yr.	1989	8.00	N/A
1987	Puppy's 1st Christmas-552909	2-Yr.	1988	4.00	N/A
1987	Kitty's 1st Christmas-552917	2-Yr.	1988	4.00	25
1987	Merry Christmas Puppy-552925	2-Yr.	1988	3.50	N/A
1987	Merry Christmas Kitty-552933	2-Yr.	1988	3.50	N/A
1986	I Love My Grandparents-553263	Yr.Iss.	1986	6.00	N/A
1986	Merry Christmas Mom & Dad-553271	Yr.Iss.	1986	6.00	N/A
1986	S. Claus Hollycopter-553344	4-Yr.	1989	13.50	35
1986	From Our House To Your House-553360	3-Yr.	1988	15.00	40
1986	Christmas Rattle-553379	3-Yr.	1988	8.00	35
1986	Bah, Humbug!-553387	4-Yr.	1989	9.00	N/A
1986	God Bless Us Everyone-553395	4-Yr.	1989	10.00	15
1987	Carousel Mobile-553409	3-Yr.	1989	15.00	50
1986	Holiday Train-553417	4-Yr.	1989	10.00	N/A
1986	Lighten Up!-553603 - J. Davis	5-Yr.	1990	10.00	N/A
1986	Gift Wrap Odie-553611 - J. Davis	Yr.Iss.	1986	7.00	20
1986	Merry Christmas-553646	4-Yr.	1989	8.00	N/A
1987	M.V.B. (Most Valuable Bear)-554219	2-Yr.	1988	3.00	N/A
1987	M.V.B. (Most Valuable Bear)-554219	2-Yr.	1988	3.00	N/A
1987	M.V.B. (Most Valuable Bear)-554219	2-Yr.	1988	3.00	N/A
1987	M.V.B. (Most Valuable Bear)-554219	2-Yr.	1988	3.00	N/A
1988	1st Christmas Together-554537 - Gilmore	3-Yr.	1990	15.00	N/A
1988	An Eye On Christmas-554545 - Gilmore	3-Yr.	1990	22.50	60
1988	A Mouse Check-554553 - Gilmore	3-Yr.	1990	13.50	45
1988	Merry Christmas Engine-554561	2-Yr.	1989	22.50	35
1989	Sardine Express-554588 - Gilmore	2-Yr.	1990	17.50	30
1988	1st Christmas Together 1988-554596	Yr.Iss.	1988	10.00	N/A
1988	Forever Friends-554626 - Gilmore	2-Yr.	1989	12.00	27
1988	Santa's Survey-554642	2-Yr.	1989	35.00	75-100
1989	Old Town's Church-554871 - Gilmore	2-Yr.	1990	17.50	20
1988	A Chipmunk Holiday-554898	3-Yr.	1990	11.00	25
1988	Christmas Is Coming-554901	3-Yr.	1990	12.00	12
1988	Baby's First Christmas 1988-554928	Yr.Iss.	1988	7.50	N/A
1988	Baby's First Christmas 1988-554936 - Gilmore	Yr.Iss.	1988	10.00	25
1988	The Christmas Train-554944	3-Yr.	1990	15.00	N/A
1988	Li'l Drummer Bear-554952	3-Yr.	1990	12.00	12
1987	Baby's First Christmas-555061	3-Yr.	1989	12.00	N/A
1987	Baby's First Christmas-555088	3-Yr.	1989	7.50	N/A
1987	Baby's First Christmas-555118	3-Yr.	1989	6.00	N/A
1987	Sugar Plum Bearies-555193	2-Yr.	1988	4.50	N/A
1987	Garfield Merry Kissmas-555215 - J. Davis	3-Yr.	1989	8.50	30
1987	Sleigh Away-555401	3-Yr.	1989	12.00	N/A
1987	Merry Christmas 1987-555428 - L. Rigg	Yr.Iss.	1987	8.00	N/A
1987	Merry Christmas 1987-555436 - L. Rigg	Yr.Iss.	1987	8.00	N/A
1987	Lucy & Me Storybook Bear-555444 - L. Rigg	3-Yr.	1989	6.50	N/A
1987	Time For Christmas-555452 - L. Rigg	3-Yr.	1989	12.00	20
1987	Lucy & Me Angel On A Cloud-555487 - L. Rigg	3-Yr.	1989	8.00	35
1987	Teddy's Stocking-555940 - Gilmore	3-Yr.	1989	10.00	N/A
1987	Kitty's Jack-In-The-Box-555959 - Gilmore	3-Yr.	1989	11.00	30
1987	Merry Christmas Teacher-555967	3-Yr.	1989	7.50	N/A
1987	Mouse In A Mitten-555975	3-Yr.	1989	7.50	N/A
1987	Boy On A Rocking Horse-555983	3-Yr.	1989	12.00	18
1987	Peek-A-Bear Letter To Santa-555991	2-Yr.	1988	8.00	30
1987	Garfield Sugar Plum Fairy-556009 - J. Davis	3-Yr.	1989	8.50	15
1987	Garfield The Nutcracker-556017 - J. Davis	4-Yr.	1990	8.50	20
1987	Carousel Lion-556025 - Gilmore	3-Yr.	1989	12.00	25
1987	Home Sweet Home-556033 - Gilmore	3-Yr.	1989	15.00	N/A
1987	Baby's First Christmas-556041	4-Yr.	1990	10.00	20
1990	Deck The Halls-566063	3-Yr.	1992	12.50	N/A
1987	Little Sailor Elf-566068	3-Yr.	1989	10.00	20
1987	Carousel Goose-556076	3-Yr.	1989	17.00	40

YEAR ISSUE	EDITION LIMIT	YEAR RETD.	ISSUE PRICE	*QUOTE U.S.$
1987 Night Caps-556084	2-Yr.	1988	5.50	N/A
1987 Night Caps-556084	2-Yr.	1988	5.50	N/A
1987 Night Caps-556084	2-Yr.	1988	5.50	N/A
1987 Night Caps-556084	2-Yr.	1988	5.50	N/A
1987 Rocking Horse Past Joys -556157	3-Yr.	1989	10.00	20
1987 Partridge In A Pear Tree -556173 - Gilmore	3-Yr.	1989	9.00	35
1987 Skating Santa 1987-556211	Yr.Iss.	1987	13.50	75
1987 Baby's First Christmas 1987 -556238 - Gilmore	Yr.Iss.	1987	10.00	25
1987 Baby's First Christmas 1987 -556254	Yr.Iss.	1987	7.00	25
1987 Teddy's Suspenders-556262	4-Yr.	1990	8.50	22
1987 Baby's First Christmas 1987 -556297	Yr.Iss.	1987	2.00	N/A
1987 Baby's First Christmas 1987 -556297	Yr.Iss.	1987	2.00	N/A
1987 Beary Christmas Family-556300	2-Yr.	1988	2.00	N/A
1987 Beary Christmas Family-556300	2-Yr.	1988	2.00	N/A
1987 Beary Christmas Family-556300	2-Yr.	1988	2.00	N/A
1987 Beary Christmas Family-556300	2-Yr.	1988	2.00	N/A
1987 Beary Christmas Family-556300	2-Yr.	1988	2.00	N/A
1987 Beary Christmas Family-556300	2-Yr.	1988	2.00	N/A
1987 Merry ChristmasTeacher-556319	2-Yr.	1988	2.00	N/A
1987 Merry ChristmasTeacher-556319	2-Yr.	1988	2.00	N/A
1987 Merry ChristmasTeacher-556319	2-Yr.	1988	2.00	N/A
1987 Merry ChristmasTeacher-556319	2-Yr.	1988	2.00	N/A
1987 1st ChristmasTogether 1987 -556335	Yr.Iss.	1987	9.00	18
1987 Country Cousins Katie Goes Ice Skating	3-Yr.	1989	8.00	30
1987 Country Cousins Scooter Snowman-556386	3-Yr.	1989	8.00	30
1987 Santa's List-556394	3-Yr.	1989	7.00	23
1987 Kitty's Bed-556408	3-Yr.	1989	12.00	30
1987 Grandchild's First Christmas -556416	3-Yr.	1989	10.00	N/A
1987 Two Turtledoves-556432 - Gilmore	3-Yr.	1989	9.00	30
1987 Three French Hens-556440 - Gilmore	3-Yr.	1989	9.00	30
1988 Four Calling Birds-556459 - Gilmore	3-Yr.	1990	11.00	30
1987 Teddy Takes A Spin-556467	4-Yr.	1990	13.00	35
1987 Tiny Toy Thimble Mobile-556475	2-Yr.	1988	12.00	35
1987 Bucket O'Love-556491	2-Yr.	1988	2.50	N/A
1987 Bucket O'Love-556491	2-Yr.	1988	2.50	N/A
1987 Puppy Love-556505	2-Yr.	1988	6.00	N/A
1987 Peek-A-Bear My Special Friend -556513	4-Yr.	1990	6.00	30
1987 Our First Christmas Together-556548	3-Yr.	1989	13.00	20
1987 Three Little Bears-556556	3-Yr.	1989	7.50	15
1987 Lucy & Me Mailbox Bear-556564 - L. Rigg	4-Yr.	1990	3.00	N/A
1987 Twinkle Bear-556572 - Gilmore	3-Yr.	1989	8.00	N/A
1987 I'm Dreaming Of A Bright Christmas-556602	2-Yr.	1988	2.50	N/A
1987 I'm Dreaming Of A Bright Christmas-556602	2-Yr.	1988	2.50	N/A
1987 Christmas Train-557196	3-Yr.	1989	10.00	N/A
1988 Dairy Christmas-557501 - M. Cook	2-Yr.	1989	10.00	30
1988 Merry Christmas 1988-557595 - L. Rigg	Yr.Iss.	1988	10.00	N/A
1988 Merry Christmas 1988-557609 - L. Rigg	Yr.Iss.	1988	10.00	N/A
1988 Toy Chest Keepsake-558206 - L. Rigg	3-Yr.	1990	12.50	30
1988 Teddy Bear Greetings-558214 - L. Rigg	3-Yr.	1990	8.00	30
1988 Jester Bear-558222 - L. Rigg	2-Yr.	1989	8.00	N/A
1988 Night-Watch Cat-558362 - J. Cook	3-Yr.	1990	13.00	35
1988 Christmas Thim-bell-558389	Yr.Iss.	1988	4.00	30
1988 Christmas Thim-bell-558389	Yr.Iss.	1988	4.00	N/A
1988 Christmas Thim-bell-558389	Yr.Iss.	1988	4.00	N/A
1988 Christmas Thim-bell-558389	Yr.Iss.	1988	4.00	N/A
1988 Baby's First Christmas 558397 - D. Parker	3-Yr.	1990	16.00	N/A
1988 Christmas Tradition-558400 - Gilmore	2-Yr.	1989	10.00	25
1988 Stocking Story-558419 - G.G. Santiago	3-Yr.	1990	10.00	23
1988 Winter Tale-558427 - G.G. Santiago	2-Yr.	1989	6.00	N/A
1988 Party Mouse-558435 - G.G. Santiago	3-Yr.	1990	12.00	30
1988 Christmas Watch-558443 - G.G. Santiago	2-Yr.	1989	11.00	32
1988 Christmas Vacation-558451 - G.G. Santiago	3-Yr.	1990	8.00	23
1988 Sweet Cherub-558478 - G.G. Santiago	3-Yr.	1990	7.00	8
1988 Time Out-558486 - G.G. Santiago	2-Yr.	1989	11.00	N/A
1988 The Ice Fairy-558516 - G.G. Santiago	3-Yr.	1990	23.00	45-55
1988 Santa Turtle-558559	2-Yr.	1989	10.00	35
1988 The Teddy Bear Ball-558567	3-Yr.	1990	10.00	25
1988 Turtle Greetings-558583	2-Yr.	1989	8.50	25
1988 Happy Howladays-558605	Yr.Iss.	1988	7.00	15
1988 Special Delivery-558699 - J. Davis	2-Yr.	1989	9.00	30
1988 Deer Garfield-558702 - J. Davis	3-Yr.	1990	12.00	20
1988 Garfield Bags O' Fun-558761 - J. Davis	Yr.Iss.	1988	3.30	N/A
1988 Gramophone Keepsake-558818	2-Yr.	1989	13.00	20
1988 North Pole Lineman-558834 - Gilmore	2-Yr.	1989	10.00	50
1988 Five Golden Rings-559121 - Gilmore	3-Yr.	1990	11.00	25
1988 Six Geese A-Laying-559148 - Gilmore	3-Yr.	1990	11.00	25
1988 Pretty Baby-559156 - R. Morehead	3-Yr.	1990	12.50	25
1988 Old Fashioned Angel-559164 - R. Morehead	3-Yr.	1990	12.50	20
1988 Two For Tea-559776 - Gilmore	3-Yr.	1990	20.00	35-40
1988 Merry Christmas Grandpa -560065	3-Yr.	1990	8.00	N/A
1990 Reeling In The Holidays-560405 - M. Cook	2-Yr.	1991	8.00	15
1991 Walkin' With My Baby-561029 - M. Cook	2-Yr.	1992	10.00	N/A
1989 Scrub-A-Dub Chipmunk-561037 - M. Cook	2-Yr.	1991	8.00	20
1989 Christmas Cook-Out-561045 - M. Cook	2-Yr.	1991	9.00	20
1989 Bunkie-561835 - S. Zimnicki	3-Yr.	1991	22.50	30
1989 Sparkles-561843 - S. Zimnicki	3-Yr.	1991	17.50	25-28
1992 Sparky & Buffer-561851 - S. Zimnicki	3-Yr.	1994	25.00	25
1989 Popper-561878 - S. Zimnicki	3-Yr.	1991	12.00	25
1989 Seven Swans A-Swimming -562742 - Gilmore	3-Yr.	1991	12.00	23
1989 Eight Maids A-Milking-562750 - Gilmore	3-Yr.	1991	12.00	23
1989 Nine Dancers Dancing-562769 - Gilmore	3-Yr.	1991	15.00	23
1989 Baby's First Christmas 1989-562807	Yr.Iss.	1989	8.00	20
1989 Baby's First Christmas 1989 -562815 - Gilmore	Yr.Iss.	1989	10.00	N/A
1989 First Christmas Together 1989 -562823	Yr.Iss.	1989	11.00	N/A
1989 Travelin' Trike-562882 - Gilmore	3-Yr.	1991	15.00	15
1989 Victorian Sleigh Ride-562890	3-Yr.	1991	22.50	23
1991 Santa Delivers Love-562904 - Gilmore	2-Yr.	1992	17.50	18
1989 Chestnut Roastin'-562912	2-Yr.	1990	13.00	13
1990 Th-Ink-In' Of You-562920 - Gilmore	2-Yr.	1991	20.00	30
1989 Ye Olde Puppet Show-562939	2-Yr.	1990	17.50	34
1989 Static In The Attic-562947	2-Yr.	1990	13.00	25
1989 Mistle-Toast 1989-562963 - Gilmore	Yr.Iss.	1989	15.00	25
1989 Merry Christmas Pops-562971 - Gilmore	3-Yr.	1991	12.00	12
1990 North Pole Or Bust-562998 - Gilmore	2-Yr.	1991	25.00	25
1989 By The Light Of The Moon -563005 - Gilmore	3-Yr.	1991	12.00	24
1989 Stickin' To It-563013 - Gilmore	2-Yr.	1990	10.00	12
1989 Christmas Cookin'-563048 - Gilmore	3-Yr.	1991	22.50	25
1989 All Set For Santa-563080 -Gilmore	3-Yr.	1991	17.50	25
1990 Santa's Sweets-563196 - Gilmore	2-Yr.	1991	20.00	20
1990 Purr-Fect Pals-563218	2-Yr.	1991	8.00	8
1989 The Pause That Refreshes -563226	3-Yr.	1991	15.00	75
1989 Ho-Ho Holiday Scrooge-563234 - J. Davis	3-Yr.	1991	13.50	30
1989 God Bless Us Everyone-563242 - J. Davis	3-Yr.	1991	13.50	20
1989 Scrooge With The Spirit-563250 - J. Davis	3-Yr.	1991	13.50	30
1989 A Chains Of Pace For Odie -563269 - J. Davis	3-Yr.	1991	12.00	25
1990 Jingle Bell Rock 1990-563390 - G. Armgardt	Yr.Iss.	1990	13.50	30
1989 Joy Ridin'-563463 - J. Davis	2-Yr.	1991	15.00	30
1989 Just What I Wanted-563668 - M. Peters	3-Yr.	1991	13.50	14
1990 Pucker Up!-563676 - M. Peters	3-Yr.	1992	11.00	11
1989 What's The Bright Idea-563684 - M. Peters	3-Yr.	1991	13.50	14
1990 Fleas Navidad-563978 - M. Peters	3-Yr.	1992	13.50	25
1990 Tweet Greetings-564044 - J. Davis	2-Yr.	1991	15.00	20
1990 Trouble On 3 Wheels-564052 - J. Davis	3-Yr.	1992	20.00	25
1989 Mine, All Mine!-564079 - J. Davis	Yr.Iss.	1989	15.00	25
1989 Star of Stars-564389 - J. Jonik	3-Yr.	1991	9.00	15
1990 Hang Onto Your Hat-564397 - J. Jonik	3-Yr.	1992	15.00	15
1990 Fireplace Frolic-564435 - N. Teiber	2-Yr.	1991	25.00	32
1989 Hoe! Hoe! Hoe!-564761	Yr.Iss.	1989	20.00	35
1991 Double Scoop Snowmouse -564796 - M. Cook	3-Yr.	1993	13.50	14
1990 Christmas Is Magic-564826 - M. Cook	2-Yr.	1991	10.00	10
1990 Lighting Up Christmas-564834 - M. Cook	2-Yr.	1991	10.00	10
1989 Feliz Navidad! 1989-564842 - M. Cook	Yr.Iss.	1989	11.00	40
1989 Spreading Christmas Joy -564850 - M. Cook	3-Yr.	1991	10.00	10
1989 Yuletide Tree House-564915 - J. Jonik	3-Yr.	1991	20.00	20
1990 Brewing Warm Wishes-564974	3-Yr.	1991	10.00	10
1990 Yippie-I-Yuletide-564982 - Hahn	3-Yr.	1992	15.00	15
1990 Coffee Break-564990 - Hahn	3-Yr.	1992	15.00	15
1990 You're Sew Special-565008 - Hahn	Yr.Iss.	1990	20.00	35
1989 Full House Mouse-565016 - Hahn	2-Yr.	1990	13.50	75
1989 I Feel Pretty-565024 - Hahn	3-Yr.	1991	20.00	30
1990 Warmest Wishes-565032 - Hahn	3-Yr.	1992	15.00	15
1990 Baby's Christmas Feast-565040 - Hahn	3-Yr.	1992	13.50	14
1990 Bumper Car Santa-565083 - G.G. Santiago	Yr.Iss.	1990	20.00	40
1989 Special Delivery (Proof Ed.) -565091 - G.G. Santiago	Yr.Iss.	1989	12.00	15
1990 Ho! Ho! Yo-Yo! (Proof Ed.) -565105 - G.G. Santiago	Yr.Iss.	1990	12.00	15
1989 Weightin' For Santa-565148 - G.G. Santiago	3-Yr.	1991	7.50	8
1989 Holly Fairy-565199 - C.M. Baker	Yr.Iss.	1989	15.00	45
1990 The Christmas Tree Fairy -565202 - C.M. Baker	Yr.Iss.	1990	15.00	40
1989 Christmas 1989-565210 - L. Rigg	Yr.Iss.	1989	12.00	38
1989 Top Of The Class-565237 - L. Rigg	3-Yr.	1991	11.00	11
1989 Deck The Hogs-565490 - M. Cook	2-Yr.	1991	12.00	14
1989 Pinata Ridin'-565504 - M. Cook	2-Yr.	1990	11.00	N/A
1989 Hangin' In There 1989-565598 - K. Wise	Yr.Iss.	1989	10.00	20
1990 Meow-y Christmas 1990-565601 - K. Wise	Yr.Iss.	1990	10.00	25
1990 Seaman's Greetings-566047	2-Yr.	1991	11.00	24
1990 Hang In Three-566055	3-Yr.	1992	13.50	14
1991 Pedal Pushin' Santa-566071	Yr.Iss.	1991	20.00	30
1990 Merry Christmas Teacher -566098	2-Yr.	1991	11.00	11
1990 Festive Flight-566101	2-Yr.	1991	11.00	11
1993 I'm Dreaming of a White-Out Christmas-566144	2-Yr.	1994	22.50	23
1990 Santa's Suitcase-566160	3-Yr.	1992	25.00	25
1989 The Purr-Fect Fit!-566462	3-Yr.	1991	15.00	35
1990 Tumbles 1990-566519 - S. Zimnicki	Yr.Iss.	1990	16.00	25
1990 Twiddles-566551 - S. Zimnicki	3-Yr.	1992	15.00	30
1991 Snuffy-566578 - S. Zimnicki	3-Yr.	1993	17.50	18
1990 All Aboard-567671 - Gilmore	2-Yr.	1991	17.50	18
1989 Gone With The Wind-567698	Yr.Iss.	1989	13.50	30
1989 Dorothy-567760	Yr.Iss.	1989	12.00	35
1989 The Tin Man-567779	Yr.Iss.	1989	12.00	12
1989 The Cowardly Lion-567787	Yr.Iss.	1989	12.00	12
1989 The Scarecrow-567795	Yr.Iss.	1989	12.00	12
1990 Happy Holiday Readings-568104	2-Yr.	1991	8.00	8
1989 Christmas 1989-568325 - L. Rigg	Yr.Iss.	1989	12.00	N/A
1991 Holiday Ahoy-568368	2-Yr.	1992	12.50	13
1991 Christmas Countdown-568376	3-Yr.	1993	20.00	20
1989 Clara-568406	Yr.Iss.	1989	12.50	20
1990 The Nutcracker-568414	2-Yr.	1991	12.50	30
1991 Clara's Prince-568422	Yr.Iss.	1991	12.50	18
1989 Santa's Little Reindear-568430	2-Yr.	1990	15.00	25
1991 Tuba Totin' Teddy-568449	3-Yr.	1993	15.00	15
1990 A Calling Home At Christmas -568457	2-Yr.	1991	15.00	15
1991 Love Is The Secret Ingredient -568562 - L. Rigg	2-Yr.	1992	15.00	15
1990 A Spoonful of Love-568570 - L. Rigg	2-Yr.	1991	10.00	10
1990 Christmas Swingtime 1990 -568597 - L. Rigg	Yr.Iss.	1990	13.00	N/A
1990 Christmas Swingtime 1990 -568600 - L. Rigg	Yr.Iss.	1990	13.00	N/A
1990 Bearing Holiday Wishes-568619 - L. Rigg	3-Yr.	1992	22.50	23
1992 Moonlight Swing-568627 - L. Rigg	3-Yr.	1994	15.00	15
1990 Smitch-570184 - S. Zimnicki	3-Yr.	1992	22.50	23
1992 Carver-570192 - S. Zimnicki	Yr.Iss.	1992	17.50	18
1991 Twinkle & Sprinkle-570206 - S. Zimnicki	3-Yr.	1993	22.50	23
1990 Blinkie-570214 - S. Zimnicki	3-Yr.	1992	15.00	15
1990 Have A Coke And A Smile™ -571512	3-Yr.	1992	15.00	55
1990 Fleece Navidad-571903 - M. Cook	2-Yr.	1991	13.50	25
1990 Have a Navaho-Ho-Ho 1990 -571970 - M. Cook	Yr.Iss.	1990	15.00	35
1990 Cheers 1990-572411 - T. Wilson	Yr.Iss.	1990	13.50	22
1990 A Night Before Christmas -572438 - T. Wilson	2-Yr.	1991	17.50	18
1990 Merry Kissmas-572446 - T. Wilson	2-Yr.	1991	10.00	30
1992 A Rockin' GARFIELD Christmas -572527 - J. Davis	2-Yr.	1993	17.50	18
1991 Here Comes Santa Paws -572535 - J. Davis	3-Yr.	1993	20.00	20
1990 Frosty Garfield 1990-572551 - J. Davis	Yr.Iss.	1990	13.50	35
1990 Pop Goes The Odie-572578 - J. Davis	2-Yr.	1991	15.00	30
1991 Sweet Beams-572586 - J. Davis	2-Yr.	1992	13.50	14
1990 An Apple A Day-572594 - J. Davis	2-Yr.	1991	12.00	12
1990 Dear Santa-572608 - J. Davis	3-Yr.	1992	17.00	17
1991 Have A Ball This Christmas -572616 - J. Davis	Yr.Iss.	1991	15.00	15
1990 Oh Shoosh!-572624 - J. Davis	3-Yr.	1992	17.00	17
1990 Little Red Riding Cat-572632 - J. Davis	Yr.Iss.	1990	13.50	33
1991 All Decked Out-572659 - J. Davis	2-Yr.	1992	13.50	14
1990 Over The Rooftops-572721 - J. Davis	2-Yr.	1991	17.50	28-35
1990 Garfield NFL Los Angeles Rams -572764 - J. Davis	2-Yr.	1991	12.50	13
1993 Born To Shop-572942	Yr.Iss.	1993	26.50	35
1990 Garfield NFL Cincinnati Bengals -573000 - J. Davis	2-Yr.	1991	12.50	13
1990 Garfield NFL Cleveland Browns -573019 - J. Davis	2-Yr.	1991	12.50	13

*Quotes have been rounded up to nearest dollar

ORNAMENTS

YEAR ISSUE		EDITION LIMIT	YEAR RETD.	ISSUE PRICE	*QUOTE U.S.$
1990	Garfield NFL Houston Oilers -573027 - J. Davis	2-Yr.	1991	12.50	13
1990	Garfield NFL Pittsburg Steelers -573035 - J. Davis	2-Yr.	1991	12.50	13
1990	Garfield NFL Denver Broncos -573043 - J. Davis	2-Yr.	1991	12.50	13
1990	Garfield NFLKansas City Chiefs -573051 - J. Davis	2-Yr.	1991	12.50	13
1990	Garfield NFL Los Angeles Raiders-573078 - J. Davis	2-Yr.	1991	12.50	13
1990	Garfield NFL San Diego Chargers-573086 - J. Davis	2-Yr.	1991	12.50	13
1990	Garfield NFL Seattle Seahawks -573094 - J. Davis	2-Yr.	1991	12.50	13
1990	Garfield NFL Buffalo Bills -573108 - J. Davis	2-Yr.	1991	12.50	13
1990	Garfield NFL Indianapolis Colts -573116 - J. Davis	2-Yr.	1991	12.50	13
1990	Garfield NFL Miami Dolphins -573124 - J. Davis	2-Yr.	1991	12.50	13
1990	Garfield NFL New England Patriots-573132 - J. Davis	2-Yr.	1991	12.50	13
1990	Garfield NFL New York Jets -573140 - J. Davis	2-Yr.	1991	12.50	13
1990	Garfield NFL Atlanta Falcons -573159 - J. Davis	2-Yr.	1991	12.50	13
1990	Garfield NFL New Orleans Saints-573167 - J. Davis	2-Yr.	1991	12.50	13
1990	Garfield NFL San Francisco 49ers-573175 - J. Davis	2-Yr.	1991	12.50	13
1990	Garfield NFL Dallas Cowboys -573183 - J. Davis	2-Yr.	1991	12.50	13
1990	Garfield NFL New York Giants -573191 - J. Davis	2-Yr.	1991	12.50	13
1990	Garfield NFL Philadelphia Eagles-573205 - J. Davis	2-Yr.	1991	12.50	13
1990	Garfield NFL Phoenix Cardinals -573213 - J. Davis	2-Yr.	1991	12.50	13
1990	Garfield NFL Washington Redskins-573221 - J. Davis	2-Yr.	1991	12.50	13
1990	Garfield NFL Chicago Bears -573248 - J. Davis	2-Yr.	1991	12.50	13
1990	Garfield NFL Detroit Lions -573256 - J. Davis	2-Yr.	1991	12.50	13
1990	Garfield NFL Green Bay Packers-573264 - J. Davis	2-Yr.	1991	12.50	13
1990	Garfield NFLMinnesota Vikings -573272 - J. Davis	2-Yr.	1991	12.50	13
1990	Garfield NFL Tampa Bay Buccaneers-573280 - J. Davis	2-Yr.	1991	12.50	13
1991	Tea For Two-573299 - Hahn	3-Yr.	1993	30.00	50
1991	Hot Stuff Santa-573523	Yr.Iss.	1992	25.00	30
1990	Merry Moustronauts-573558 - M. Cook	3-Yr.	1992	20.00	40
1991	Santa Wings It-573612 - J. Jonik	3-Yr.	1993	13.00	13
1990	All Eye Want For Christmas -573647 - Gilmore	3-Yr.	1992	27.50	32
1990	Stuck On You-573655 - Gilmore	2-Yr.	1991	12.50	13
1990	Professor Michael Bear, The One Bear Band-573663 - Gilmore	3-Yr.	1992	22.50	28
1990	A Caroling Wee Go-573671 - Gilmore	3-Yr.	1992	12.00	12
1990	Merry Mailman-573698 - Gilmore	2-Yr.	1991	15.00	30
1990	Deck The Halls-573701 - Gilmore	3-Yr.	1992	22.50	25
1992	Sundae Ride-583707	2-Yr.	1993	20.00	20
1990	You're Wheel Special-573728 - Gilmore	3-Yr.	1992	15.00	15
1991	Come Let Us Adore Him -573736 - Gilmore	2-Yr.	1992	9.00	9
1991	Moon Beam Dreams-573760 - Gilmore	3-Yr.	1993	12.00	12
1991	A Song For Santa-573779 - Gilmore	3-Yr.	1993	25.00	25
1990	Warmest Wishes-573825 - Gilmore	Yr.Iss.	1990	17.50	25
1991	Kurious Kitty-573868 - Gilmore	3-Yr.	1993	17.50	18
1990	Old Mother Mouse-573922 - Gilmore	2-Yr.	1991	17.50	20-32
1990	Railroad Repairs-573930 - Gilmore	2-Yr.	1991	12.50	25
1990	Ten Lords A-Leaping-573949 - Gilmore	3-Yr.	1992	15.00	25
1990	Eleven Drummers Drumming -573957 - Gilmore	3-Yr.	1992	15.00	25
1990	Twelve Pipers Piping-573965 - Gilmore	3-Yr.	1992	15.00	25
1990	Baby's First Christmas 1990 -573973 - Gilmore	Yr.Iss.	1990	10.00	N/A
1990	Baby's First Christmas 1990 -573981 - Gilmore	Yr.Iss.	1990	12.00	N/A
1991	Peter, Peter Pumpkin Eater -574015 - Gilmore	2-Yr.	1992	20.00	30
1992	The Nutcracker-574023	3-Yr.	1994	25.00	25
1990	Little Jack Horner-574058 - Gilmore	2-Yr.	1991	17.50	35
1991	Mary, Mary Quite Contrary -574066 - Gilmore	2-Yr.	1992	22.50	33
1992	Humpty Dumpty-574244 - Gilmore	2-Yr.	1993	25.00	25
1991	Through The Years-574252 - Gilmore	Yr.Iss.	1991	17.50	18
1991	Holiday Wing Ding-574333	3-Yr.	1993	22.50	23
1991	North Pole Here I Come-574597	3-Yr.	1993	10.00	10
1991	Christmas Caboose-574856 - Gilmore	2-Yr.	1992	25.00	30
1990	Bubble Trouble-575038 - Hahn	3-Yr.	1992	20.00	35
1991	Merry Mother-To-Be-575046 - Hahn	2-Yr.	1992	13.50	14
1990	A Holiday 'Scent' Sation-575054 - Hahn	3-Yr.	1992	15.00	30
1990	Catch Of The Day-575070 - Hahn	2-Yr.	1992	25.00	25

YEAR ISSUE		EDITION LIMIT	YEAR RETD.	ISSUE PRICE	*QUOTE U.S.$
1990	Don't Open 'Til Christmas -575089 - Hahn	3-Yr.	1992	17.50	18
1990	I Can't Weight 'Til Christmas -575119 - Hahn	3-Yr.	1992	16.50	30
1991	Deck The Halls-575127 - Hahn	2-Yr.	1992	15.00	25
1992	Music Mice-Trol-575143	2-Yr.	1993	12.00	12
1990	Mouse House-575186	3-Yr.	1992	16.00	16
1991	Dream A Little Dream-575593	2-Yr.	1992	17.50	18
1991	Christmas Two-gether-575615 - L. Rigg	3-Yr.	1993	22.50	23
1992	On Target Two-Gether-575623	Yr.Iss.	1992	17.00	17
1991	Christmas Trimmings-575631	2-Yr.	1992	17.00	17
1991	Gumball Wizard-575658 - Gilmore	2-Yr.	1992	13.00	13
1991	Crystal Ball Christmas-575666 - Gilmore	2-Yr.	1992	22.50	23
1990	Old King Cole-575682 - Gilmore	2-Yr.	1991	20.00	29
1991	Tom, Tom The Piper's Son -575690 - Gilmore	2-Yr.	1992	15.00	33
1992	Rock-A-Bye Baby-575704 - Gilmore	2-Yr.	1993	13.50	14
1992	Queen of Hearts-575712 - Gilmore	2-Yr.	1992	17.50	18
1993	Toy To The World-575763	2-Yr.	1994	25.00	25
1992	Tasty Tidings-575836 - L. Rigg	Yr.Iss.	1992	13.50	14
1991	Tire-d Little Bear-575852 - L. Rigg	Yr.Iss.	1991	12.50	13
1990	Baby Bear Christmas 1990-575860 - L. Rigg	Yr.Iss.	1990	12.00	28
1991	Crank Up The Carols-575887 - L. Rigg	2-Yr.	1992	17.50	18
1990	Beary Christmas 1990-576158 - L. Rigg	Yr.Iss.	1990	12.00	12
1991	Christmas Swingtime 1991 -576166 - L. Rigg	Yr.Iss.	1991	13.00	13
1991	Christmas Swingtime 1991 -576174 - L. Rigg	Yr.Iss.	1991	13.00	13
1991	Christmas Cutie-576182	3-Yr.	1993	13.50	14
1991	Meow Mates-576220	3-Yr.	1993	12.00	12
1991	Frosty The Snowmant-576425	3-Yr.	1993	15.00	15
1991	Ris-ski Business-576719 - T. Wilson	2-Yr.	1992	10.00	10
1991	Pinocchio-577391 - J. Davis	3-Yr.	1993	15.00	15
1990	Yuletide Ride 1990-577502 - Gilmore	Yr.Iss.	1990	13.50	50
1990	Tons of Toys-577510	Yr.Iss.	1990	13.00	30
1990	McHappy Holidays-577529	2-Yr.	1991	17.50	25
1990	Heading For Happy Holidays-577537	3-Yr.	1992	17.50	18
1990	'Twas The Night Before Christmas-577545	3-Yr.	1992	17.50	18
1990	Over One Million Holiday Wishes!-577553	Yr.Iss.	1990	17.50	30
1990	You Malt My Heart-577596	2-Yr.	1991	25.00	25
1991	All I Want For Christmas-577618	2-Yr.	1992	20.00	20
1992	Bearly Sleepy-578029 - Gilmore	Yr.Iss.	1992	17.50	18
1992	Spreading Sweet Joy-580465	Yr.Iss.	1992	13.50	14
1991	Things Go Better With Coke™ -580597	3-Yr.	1993	17.00	25
1991	Christmas To Go-580600 - M. Cook	Yr.Iss.	1991	22.50	23
1991	Have A Mariachi Christmas -580619 - M. Cook	2-Yr.	1992	13.50	14
1993	Bearly Balanced-580724	2-Yr.	1994	15.00	15
1992	Ring My Bell-580740 - J. Davis	Yr.Iss.	1992	13.50	14
1992	4 x 4 Holiday Fun-580783 - J. Davis	2-Yr.	1993	20.00	20
1991	Christmas Is In The Air-581453	Yr.Iss.	1991	15.00	15
1991	Holiday Treats-581542	Yr.Iss.	1991	17.50	18
1991	Christmas Is My Goal-581550	2-Yr.	1992	17.50	18
1991	A Quarter Pounder With Cheer®-581569	3-Yr.	1993	20.00	20
1992	The Holidays Are A Hit-581577	2-Yr.	1993	17.50	18
1991	From The Same Mold-581798 - Gilmore	3-Yr.	1993	17.00	17
1991	The Glow Of Christmas-581801	2-Yr.	1992	20.00	20
1992	Tip Top Tidings-581828	2-Yr.	1993	13.00	13
1992	Christmas Lifts The Spirits -582018	2-Yr.	1993	25.00	25
1993	Joyeux Noel-582026	2-Yr.	1994	24.50	25
1992	A Pound Of Good Cheers -582034	2-Yr.	1993	17.50	18
1993	Holiday Mew-Sic-582107	2-Yr.	1994	20.00	20
1993	Santa's Magic Ride-582115	2-Yr.	1994	24.00	24
1993	Warm And Hearty Wishes -582344	Yr.Iss.	1993	17.50	18
1993	Cool Yule-582352	Yr.Iss.	1993	12.00	12
1993	Have A Holly Jell-O Christmas-582387	Yr.Iss.	1993	45.00	45
1993	Festive Firemen-582565	2-Yr.	1994	17.00	17
1991	All Caught Up In Christmas -583537	2-Yr.	1992	10.00	10
1991	Lights..Camera..Kissmas!-583626 - Gilmore	Yr.Iss.	1991	15.00	35
1991	Sweet Steed-583634 - Gilmore	3-Yr.	1993	15.00	15
1992	Sweet as Cane Be-583642 - Gilmore	3-Yr.	1994	15.00	15
1991	Dreamin' Of A White Christmas -583669 - Gilmore	2-Yr.	1992	15.00	15
1991	Merry Millimeters-583677 - Gilmore	2-Yr.	1992	17.00	17
1991	Here's The Scoop-583693	2-Yr.	1992	13.50	20
1991	Happy Mealr On Wheels-583715	3-Yr.	1993	22.50	23
1991	Christmas Kayak-583723	2-Yr.	1992	13.50	14
1993	Light Up Your Holidays With Coke-583758	Yr.Iss.	1993	27.50	28
1992	The Cold, Crisp Taste Of Coke -583766	3-Yr.	1994	17.00	20
1991	Marilyn Monroe-583774	Yr.Iss.	1991	20.00	20
1992	Sew Christmasy-583820	3-Yr.	1994	25.00	25

YEAR ISSUE		EDITION LIMIT	YEAR RETD.	ISSUE PRICE	*QUOTE U.S.$
1991	A Christmas Carol-583928 - Gilmore	3-Yr.	1993	22.50	23
1991	Checking It Twice-583936	2-Yr.	1992	25.00	25
1992	Catch A Falling Star-583944 - Gilmore	2-Yr.	1993	15.00	15
1992	Swingin' Christmas-584096	2-Yr.	1993	15.00	15
1993	Pool Hall-idays-584851	2-Yr.	1994	19.90	20
1992	Mc Ho, Ho, Ho-585181	3-Yr.	1994	22.50	23
1991	Merry Christmas Go-Round -585203 - J. Davis	3-Yr.	1994	20.00	20
1992	Holiday On Ice-585254 - J. Davis	3-Yr.	1994	17.50	18
1991	Holiday Hideout-585270 - J. Davis	2-Yr.	1992	15.00	15
1992	Fast Track Cat-585289 - J. Davis	3-Yr.	1994	17.50	18
1992	Holiday Cat Napping-585319 - J. Davis	2-Yr.	1993	20.00	20
1993	Bah Humbug-585394 - Davis	Yr.Iss.	1993	15.00	15
1992	The Finishing Touches-585610 - T. Wilson	2-Yr.	1993	17.50	18
1992	Jolly Ol' Gent-585645 - J. Jonik	3-Yr.	1994	13.50	14
1991	Our Most Precious Gift-585726	Yr.Iss.	1991	17.50	18
1991	Christmas Cheer-585769	2-Yr.	1992	13.50	14
1993	Chimer-585777 - Zimnicki	Yr.Iss.	1993	25.00	25
1993	Sweet Whiskered Wishes -585807	Yr.Iss.	1993	17.00	17
1993	Grade "A" Wishes From Garfield -585823 - Davis	2-Yr.	1994	20.00	20
1993	Baby's First Christmas 1993 -585823 - Gilmore	Yr.Iss.	1993	17.50	18
1992	A Child's Christmas-586358	3-Yr.	1994	25.00	25
1992	Festive Fiddlers-586501	2-Yr.	1992	20.00	25
1992	La Luminaria-586579 - M. Cook	2-Yr.	1993	13.50	14
1991	Fired Up For Christmas-586587	2-Yr.	1992	32.50	33
1991	One Foggy Christmas Eve -586625 - Gilmore	3-Yr.	1993	30.00	30
1991	For A Purr-fect Mom-586641 - Gilmore	Yr.Iss.	1991	12.00	12
1991	For A Special Dad-586668 - Gilmore	Yr.Iss.	1991	17.50	18
1991	With Love-586676 - Gilmore	Yr.Iss.	1991	13.00	13
1991	For A Purr-fect Aunt-586692 - Gilmore	Yr.Iss.	1991	12.00	12
1991	For A Dog-Gone Great Uncle -586706 - Gilmore	Yr.Iss.	1991	12.00	12
1991	Peddling Fun-586714 - Gilmore	Yr.Iss.	1991	16.00	16
1991	Special Keepsakes-586722	Yr.Iss.	1991	13.50	14
1992	Cozy Chrismas Carriage -586730 - Gilmore	2-Yr.	1993	22.50	23
1992	Small Fry's First Christmas -586749	2-Yr.	1993	17.00	17
1991	Hats Off To Christmas-586757 - Hahn	Yr.Iss.	1991	22.50	23
1992	Friendships Preserved-586765 - Hahn	Yr.Iss.	1992	22.50	23
1993	Tree For Two-586781 - Gilmore	2-Yr.	1994	17.50	18
1993	A Bright Idea-586803 - Gilmore	2-Yr.	1994	22.50	23
1992	Window Wish List-586854 - Gilmore	2-Yr.	1993	30.00	30
1992	Through The Years-586862 - Gilmore	Yr.Iss.	1992	17.50	18
1993	My Special Christmas-586900	Yr.Iss.	1993	17.50	18
1991	Baby's First Christmas 1991 -586935	Yr.Iss.	1991	12.50	13
1992	Baby's First Christmas 1992 -586943	Yr.Iss.	1992	12.50	13
1992	Firehouse Friends-586951 - Gilmore	Yr.Iss.	1992	22.50	23
1992	Bubble Buddy-586978 - Gilmore	2-Yr	1993	13.50	14
1992	The Warmth Of The Season -586994	2-Yr.	1993	20.00	20
1993	Baby's First Christmas Dinner -587001	Yr.Iss.	1993	12.00	12
1991	Jugglin' The Holidays-587028	2-Yr.	1992	13.00	13
1991	Santa's Steed-587044	Yr.Iss.	1991	15.00	15
1991	A Decade of Treasures-587052 - Gilmore	Yr.Iss.	1991	37.50	75
1992	It's A Go For Christmas-587095 - Gilmore	2-Yr.	1993	15.00	15
1991	Mr. Mailmouse-587109 - Gilmore	2-Yr.	1992	17.00	17
1992	Post-Mouster General-587117 - Gilmore	2-Yr.	1993	20.00	20
1992	To A Deer Baby-587168	Yr.Iss.	1992	18.50	19
1991	Starry Eyed Santa-587176	2-Yr.	1993	15.00	15
1992	Moon Watch-587184	2-Yr.	1993	20.00	20
1992	Guten Cheers-587192	Yr.Iss.	1992	22.50	23
1992	Put On A Happy Face-588237	2-Yr.	1993	15.00	15
1992	Beginning To Look A Lot Like Christmas-588253	2-Yr.	1993	15.00	15
1992	A Christmas Toast-588261	2-Yr.	1993	20.00	20
1992	Merry Mistle-Toad-588288	2-Yr.	1993	15.00	15
1992	Tic-Tac-Mistle-Toe-588296	3-Yr.	1994	23.00	23
1993	A Pause For Claus-588318	2-Yr.	1994	22.50	23
1992	Heaven Sent-588423 - J. Penchoff	Yr.Iss.	1993	12.50	13
1992	Holiday Happenings-588555 - Gilmore	3-Yr.	1994	30.00	30
1992	Seed-son's Greetings-588571 - Gilmore	3-Yr.	1994	27.00	27
1992	Santa's Midnight Snack-588598 - Gilmore	2-Yr.	1993	20.00	20
1992	Trunk Of Treasures-588636	Yr.Iss.	1992	30.00	30
1993	Terrific Toys-588644	2-Yr.	1994	20.00	20
1993	Christmas Dancer-588652	2-Yr.	1993	15.00	15
1993	Not A Creature Was Stirring...-588663 - Gilmore	2-Yr.	1994	27.50	28
1991	Lighting The Way-588776	2-Yr.	1992	20.00	20
1991	Rudolph-588784	2-Yr.	1992	17.50	18
1992	Festive Newsflash-588792	2-Yr.	1993	17.50	17

YEAR ISSUE		EDITION LIMIT	YEAR RETD.	ISSUE PRICE	*QUOTE U.S.$
1992	A-B-C-Son's Greetings-588806	2-Yr.	1993	16.50	17
1992	Hoppy Holidays-588814	Yr.Iss.	1992	13.50	14
1992	Fireside Friends-588830	2-Yr.	1993	20.00	20
1992	Christmas Eve-mergency-588849	2-Yr.	1993	27.00	27
1992	A Sure Sign Of Christmas-588857	2-Yr.	1993	22.50	23
1992	Holidays Give Me A Lift-588865	2-Yr.	1993	30.00	30
1992	Yule Tide Together-588903	2-Yr.	1993	20.00	20
1992	Have A Soup-er Christmas-588911	2-Yr.	1993	17.50	18
1992	Christmas Cure-Alls-588938	2-Yr.	1993	20.00	20
1993	Countin' On A Merry Christmas-588954	2-Yr.	1994	22.50	23
1993	To My Gem-589004	Yr.Iss.	1993	27.50	28
1993	Christmas Mall Call-589012	2-Yr.	1993	20.00	20
1993	Spreading Joy-589047	2-Yr.	1994	27.50	28
1993	Pitter-Patter Post Office-589055	2-Yr.	1994	20.00	20
1993	Happy Haul-idays-589098	2-Yr.	1994	30.00	30
1993	Hot Off The Press-589292	2-Yr.	1994	27.50	28
1993	Designed With You In Mind-589306	2-Yr.	1994	16.00	16
1992	Dial 'S' For Santa-589373	2-Yr.	1993	25.00	25
1993	Seeing Is Believing-589381 - Gilmore	2-Yr.	1994	20.00	20
1992	Joy To The Whirled-589551	2-Yr.	1993	20.00	20
1992	Merry Make-Over-589586 - Hahn	3-Yr.	1994	20.00	20
1992	Campin' Companions-590282 - Hahn	3-Yr.	1994	20.00	20
1992	Fur-Ever Friends-590797 - Gilmore	2-Yr.	1993	13.50	14
1993	Roundin' Up Christmas Together-590800	Yr.Iss.	1993	25.00	25
1992	Tee-rific Holidays-590827	3-Yr.	1993	25.00	25
1992	Spinning Christmas Dreams-590908 - Hahn	3-Yr.	1994	22.50	23
1992	Christmas Trimmin'-590932	3-Yr.	1994	17.00	17
1993	Toasty Tidings-590940	2-Yr.	1994	20.00	20
1993	Focusing On Christmas-590983 - Gilmore	2-Yr.	1994	27.50	28
1993	Dunk The Halls-591009	2-Yr.	1994	18.50	19
1993	Mice Capades-591386 - Hahn	2-Yr.	1994	26.50	27
1993	25 Points For Christmas-591750	Yr.Iss.	1993	25.00	25
1993	Carving Christmas Wishes-592625 - Gilmore	2-Yr.	1994	25.00	25
1993	Celebrating With A Splash-592692	Yr.Iss.	1993	17.00	17
1993	Slimmin' Santa-592722	Yr.Iss.	1993	18.50	24
1993	Plane Ol' Holiday Fun-592773	Yr.Iss.	1993	27.50	28
1992	Wrappin' Up Warm Wishes-593141	Yr.Iss.	1992	17.50	18
1992	Christmas Biz-593168	2-Yr.	1993	22.50	23
1993	Smooth Move, Mom-593176	Yr.Iss.	1993	20.00	20
1993	Tool Time, Yule Time-593192	Yr.Iss.	1993	18.50	19
1993	Speedy-593370 - Zimnicki	2-Yr.	1994	25.00	25
1992	Holiday Take-Out-593508	Yr.Iss.	1992	17.50	18
1992	A Christmas Yarn-593516 - Gilmore	Yr.Iss.	1992	20.00	20
1993	On Your Mark, Set, Is That To Go?-593524	Yr.Iss.	1993	13.50	14
1993	Do Not Open 'Til Christmas-593737 - Hahn	2-Yr.	1994	15.00	15
1993	Greetings In Stereo-593745 - Hahn	Yr.Iss.	1993	19.50	20
1992	Treasure The Earth-593826 - Hahn	2-Yr.	1993	25.00	25
1993	Tangled Up For Christmas-593974	2-Yr.	1994	14.50	15
1992	Toyful' Rudolph-593982	2-Yr.	1993	22.50	23
1992	Take A Chance On The Holidays-594075	3-Yr.	1994	20.00	20
1993	Sweet Season's Eatings-594202	Yr.Iss.	1993	22.50	23
1993	Have A Darn Good Christmas-594229 - Gilmore	2-Yr.	1994	21.00	21
1993	The Sweetest Ride-594253 - Gilmore	2-Yr.	1994	18.50	19
1992	Lights..Camera..Christmas!-594369	3-Yr.	1994	20.00	20
1993	Lights...Camera...Christmas-594369	Yr.Iss.	1993	20.00	20
1992	Spirited Stallion-594407	Yr.Iss.	1992	15.00	15
1993	Have A Cheery Christmas, Sister-594687	Yr.Iss.	1993	13.50	14
1993	Say Cheese-594962 - Gilmore	2-Yr.	1994	13.50	14
1993	Christmas Kicks-594989	Yr.Iss.	1993	17.50	18
1993	Time For Santa-594997 - Gilmore	2-Yr.	1994	17.50	18
1993	Holiday Orders-595004	Yr.Iss.	1993	20.00	20
1993	T'Was The Night Before Christmas-595012	Yr.Iss.	1993	22.50	23
1993	Sugar Chef Shoppe-595055 - Gilmore	2-Yr.	1994	23.50	24
1993	Merry Mc-Choo-Choo-595063	Yr.Iss.	1993	30.00	30
1993	Basketful of Friendship-595098	Yr.Iss.	1993	20.00	20
1993	Rockin' With Santa-595195	Yr.Iss.	1993	13.50	14
1993	Christmas-To-Go-595217	Yr.Iss.	1993	25.50	26
1993	Sleddin' Mr. Snowman-595275	Yr.Iss.	1993	13.00	13
1993	A Kick Out Of Christmas-595373	2-Yr.	1994	10.00	10
1993	Friends Through Thick And Thin-595381	2-Yr.	1994	10.00	10
1993	See-Saw Sweethearts-595403	2-Yr.	1994	10.00	10
1993	Special Delivery For Santa-595411	2-Yr.	1994	10.00	10
1993	Top Marks For Teacher-595438	2-Yr.	1994	10.00	10
1993	Home Tweet Home-595446	2-Yr.	1994	10.00	10
1993	Clownin' Around-595454	2-Yr.	1994	10.00	10
1993	Heart Filled Dreams-595462	2-Yr.	1994	10.00	10
1993	Merry Christmas Baby-595470	2-Yr.	1994	10.00	10
1993	Your A Hit With Me, Brother-595535 - Hahn	Yr.Iss.	1993	10.00	10
1993	For A Sharp Uncle-595543	Yr.Iss.	1993	10.00	10
1993	Paint Your Holidays Bright-595551 - Hahn	2-Yr.	1994	10.00	10
1992	A Watchful Eye-595713	Yr.Iss.	1992	15.00	15
1992	Good Catch-595721	Yr.Iss.	1992	12.50	13
1993	You Got To Treasure The Holidays, Man'-596051	Yr.Iss.	1993	22.50	23
1992	Squirrelin' It Away-595748 - Hahn	Yr.Iss.	1992	12.00	12
1992	Checkin' His List-595756	Yr.Iss.	1992	12.50	13
1992	Christmas Cat Nappin'-595764	Yr.Iss.	1992	12.00	12
1992	Bless Our Home-595772	Yr.Iss.	1992	12.00	12
1992	Salute The Season-595780 - Hahn	Yr.Iss.	1992	12.00	12
1992	Fired Up For Christmas-595799	Yr.Iss.	1992	12.00	12
1992	Speedin' Mr. Snowman-595802 - M. Rhyner	Yr.Iss.	1992	12.00	12
1992	Merry Christmas Mother Earth-595810 - Hahn	Yr.Iss.	1992	11.00	11
1992	Wear The Season With A Smile-595829	Yr.Iss.	1992	10.00	10
1992	Jesus Loves Me-595837 - Hahn	Yr.Iss.	1992	10.00	10
1989	Bottom's Up 1989-830003	Yr.Iss.	1989	11.00	32
1990	Sweetest Greetings 1990-830011 - Gilmore	Yr.Iss.	1990	12.00	27
1990	First Class Christmas-830038 - Gilmore	3-Yr.	1992	12.00	10
1989	Caught In The Act-830046 - Gilmore	3-Yr.	1991	12.50	13
1989	Readin' & Ridin'-830054 - Gilmore	3-Yr.	1991	13.50	34
1991	Beary Merry Mailman-830151 - L. Rigg	3-Yr.	1993	13.50	14
1990	Here's Looking at You!-830259 - Gilmore	2-Yr.	1992	17.50	18
1991	Stamper-830267 - S. Zimnicki	Yr.Iss.	1991	13.50	14
1991	Santa's Key Man-830461	2-Yr.	1992	11.00	11
1991	Tie-dings of Joy-830488 - Gilmore	Yr.Iss.	1991	12.00	12
1990	Have a Cool Yule-830496 - Gilmore	3-Yr.	1992	12.00	27
1990	Slots of Luck-830518 - Hahn	2-Yr.	1991	13.50	45-60
1991	Straight To Santa-830534 - J. Davis	2-Yr.	1992	13.50	14
1991	Letters To Santa-830925 - Gilmore	2-Yr.	1992	15.00	15
1991	Sneaking Santa's Snack-830933 - Gilmore	3-Yr.	1993	13.00	13
1991	Aiming For The Holidays-830941 - Gilmore	2-Yr.	1992	12.00	12
1993	Ode To Joy-830968 - Gilmore	3-Yr.	1994	10.00	10
1991	Fittin' Mittens-830976 - Gilmore	3-Yr.	1993	12.00	12
1992	Merry Kisses-831166	2-Yr.	1993	17.50	18
1992	Christmas Is In The Air-831174	2-Yr.	1993	25.00	25
1992	To The Point-831182	2-Yr.	1993	13.50	14
1992	Poppin' Hoppin' Holidays-831263 - Gilmore	Yr.Iss.	1992	25.00	25
1992	Tankful Tidings-831271	2-Yr.	1993	30.00	30
1991	The Finishing Touch-831530	Yr.Iss.	1991	10.00	10
1992	Ginger-Bred Greetings-831581	Yr.Iss.	1992	12.00	12
1991	A Real Classic-831603 - Gilmore	Yr.Iss.	1991	10.00	10
1991	Christmas Fills The Air-831921 - Gilmore	3-Yr.	1993	12.00	12
1992	A Gold Star For Teacher-831948 - Gilmore	3-Yr.	1994	15.00	15
1992	A Tall Order-832758 - Gilmore	2-Yr.	1993	12.00	12
1992	Candlelight Serenade-832766 - Gilmore	2-Yr.	1993	12.00	12
1992	Holiday Glow Puppet Show-832774 - Gilmore	3-Yr.	1994	15.00	15
1992	Christopher Columouse-832782 - Gilmore	Yr.Iss.	1992	12.00	12
1992	Cartin' Home Holiday Treats-832790	2-Yr.	1993	13.50	14
1992	Making Tracks To Santa-832804	2-Yr.	1993	15.00	15
1992	Special Delivery-832812	2-Yr.	1993	12.00	12
1992	A Mug Full Of Love-832928	Yr.Iss.	1992	13.50	14
1992	Have A Cool Christmas-832944	Yr.Iss.	1992	13.50	14
1992	Knitten' Kittens-832952 - Gilmore	Yr.Iss.	1992	17.50	18
1992	Holiday Honors-833029 - Gilmore	Yr.Iss.	1992	15.00	15
1992	Christmas Nite Cap-834424	3-Yr.	1994	13.50	14
1992	North Pole Peppermint Patrol-840157 - Gilmore	2-Yr.	1993	25.00	25
1992	A Boot-iful Christmas-840165 - Gilmore	2-Yr.	1993	20.00	20
1992	Watching For Santa-840432	2-Yr.	1993	25.00	25
1992	Special Delivery-840440	Yr.Iss.	1992	22.50	23
1991	Deck The Halls-860573 - M. Peters	3-Yr.	1993	12.00	12
1991	Bathing Beauty-860581 - Hahn	3-Yr.	1993	13.50	13
1993	Ariel's Under-the-Sea Tree-596078	Yr.Iss.	1993	20.00	20
1993	Here Comes Santa Claws-596086	Yr.Iss.	1993	22.50	35
1993	You're Tea-Lighting, Mom!-596094	Yr.Iss.	1993	17.50	18
1993	Hearts A Glow-596108	Yr.Iss.	1993	18.50	35
1993	Love's Sweet Dance-596116	Yr.Iss.	1993	25.00	25
1993	Holiday Wishes-596124	Yr.Iss.	1993	15.00	15
1993	Hangin Out For The Holidays-596132	Yr.Iss.	1993	15.00	35
1993	Magic Carpet Ride-596140	Yr.Iss.	1993	20.00	20
1993	Holiday Treasures-596159	Yr.Iss.	1993	18.50	35
1993	Happily Ever After-596167	Yr.Iss.	1993	22.50	23
1993	The Fairest Of Them All-596175	Yr.Iss.	1993	18.50	19
1993	December 25...Dear Diary-596809 - Hahn	2-Yr.	1994	10.00	10
1993	Wheel Merry Wishes-596930 - Hahn	2-Yr.	1994	15.00	15
1993	Good Grounds For Christmas-596957 - Hahn	Yr.Iss.	1993	24.50	25
1993	Ducking The Season's Rush-597597	Yr.Iss.	1993	17.50	18
1993	Here Comes Rudolph-597686	2-Yr.	1994	17.50	18
1993	It's Beginning To Look A Lot Like Christmas-597694	Yr.Iss.	1993	22.50	23
1993	Christmas In The Making-597716	Yr.Iss.	1993	20.00	20
1993	Mickey's Holiday Treasure-597759	Yr.Iss.	1993	12.00	12
1993	Dream Wheels-597856	Yr.Iss.	1993	29.50	50-75
1993	All You Add Is Love-598429	Yr.Iss.	1993	18.50	19
1993	Goofy About Skiing-598631	Yr.Iss.	1993	22.50	23
1989	Tea For Two-693758 - N. Teiber	2-Yr.	1990	12.50	30
1990	Holiday Tea Toast-694770 - N. Teiber	2-Yr.	1991	13.50	14
1991	It's Tea-lightful-694789	2-Yr.	1992	13.50	14
1989	Tea Time-694797 - N. Teiber	2-Yr.	1990	12.50	30
1993	A Toast Ladled With Love-830828 - Hahn	2-Yr.	1994	15.00	15
1993	Christmas Is In The Air-831174	2-Yr.	1994	25.00	35
1993	Delivered to The Nick In Time-831808 - Gilmore	2-Yr.	1994	13.50	14
1993	Sneaking A Peek-831840 - Gilmore	2-Yr.	1994	10.00	10
1993	Jewel Box Ballet-831859 - Hahn	2-Yr.	1994	20.00	20
1993	A Mistle-Tow-831867 - Gilmore	2-Yr.	1994	15.00	15
1993	Grandma's Liddle Griddle-832936 - Gilmore	Yr.Iss.	1993	10.00	10
1993	To A Grade "A" Teacher-833037 - Gilmore	2-Yr.	1994	10.00	10
1993	Have A Cool Christmas-834467 - Gilmore	2-Yr.	1994	10.00	10
1993	For A Star Aunt-834556 - Gilmore	Yr.Iss.	1993	12.00	12
1993	Watching For Santa-840432	2-Yr.	1994	25.00	30
1994	Sending You A Season's Greetings-550140 - Butcher	Yr.Iss.	1994	25.00	25
1994	Goofy Delivery-550639	Yr.Iss.	1994	22.50	23
1994	Happy Howl-idays-550647	Yr.Iss.	1994	22.50	23
1994	Christmas Crusin'-550655	Yr.Iss.	1994	22.50	23
1994	Holiday Honeys-550663	Yr.Iss.	1994	20.00	20
1994	May Your Holiday Be Brightened With Love-550698	Yr.Iss.	1994	15.00	15
1994	May All Your Wishes Come True-550701 - Butcher	Yr.Iss.	1994	20.00	20
1994	Baby's First Christmas-550728 - Butcher	Yr.Iss.	1994	20.00	20
1994	Baby's First Christmas-550736 - Butcher	Yr.Iss.	1994	20.00	20
1994	Our First Christmas Together-550744 - Butcher	Yr.Iss.	1994	25.00	25
1994	Drumming Up A Season Of Joy-550752 - Butcher	Yr.Iss.	1994	18.50	19
1994	Friendships Warm The Holidays-550760 - Butcher	Yr.Iss.	1994	20.00	20
1994	Dropping In For The Holidays-550779 - Butcher	Yr.Iss.	1994	20.00	20
1994	Ringing Up Holiday Wishes-550787 - Butcher	Yr.Iss.	1994	18.50	19
1994	A Child Is Born-550795 - Butcher	Yr.Iss.	1995	25.00	25
1994	Tis The Season To Go Shopping-550817 - Butcher	Yr.Iss.	1994	22.50	23
1994	The Way To A Mouse's Heart-550922	Yr.Iss.	1994	15.00	15
1994	Teed-Off Donald-550930	Yr.Iss.	1994	15.00	15
1994	Holiday Show-Stopper-550949	Yr.Iss.	1995	15.00	15
1994	Answering Christmas Wishes-551023	Yr.Iss.	1994	17.50	18
1994	Pure Christmas Pleasure-551066	Yr.Iss.	1995	20.00	20
1994	Good Tidings, Tidings, Tidings-551333	Yr.Iss.	1995	20.00	20
1994	From Our House To Yours-551384 - Gilmore	Yr.Iss.	1994	25.00	25
1994	Sugar 'N' Spice For Someone Nice-551406 - Gilmore	Yr.Iss.	1994	30.00	30
1994	Picture Perfect Christmas-551465	Yr.Iss.	1994	15.00	15
1994	Toodles-551503 - Zimnicki	Yr.Iss.	1994	25.00	25
1994	A Bough For Belle!-551554	Yr.Iss.	1995	18.50	19
1994	Ariel's Christmas Surprise!-551570	Yr.Iss.	1994	20.00	20
1994	Merry Little Two-Step-551589	Yr.Iss.	1995	12.50	13
1994	Sweets For My Sweetie-551600	Yr.Iss.	1994	15.00	15
1994	Friends Are The Spice of Life-551619 - Hahn	Yr.Iss.	1995	20.00	20
1994	Cool Cruise-551635	19,640	1994	20.00	20
1994	A Christmas Tail-551759	Yr.Iss.	1995	20.00	20
1994	Merry Mischief-551767	Yr.Iss.	1994	15.00	15
1994	L'il Stocking Stuffer-551791	Yr.Iss.	1994	17.50	18
1994	Once Upon A Time-551805	Yr.Iss.	1994	15.00	15
1994	Wishing Upon A Star-551813	Yr.Iss.	1994	18.50	19
1994	A Real Boy For Christmas-551821	Yr.Iss.	1995	15.00	15
1994	Minnie's Holiday Treasure-552216	Yr.Iss.	1994	12.00	12
1994	Sweet Holidays-552259 - Butcher	Yr.Iss.	1994	11.00	11
1994	Special Delivery-561657	Yr.Iss.	1994	20.00	20
1994	Merry Miss Merry-564508 - Hahn	Yr.Iss.	1994	12.00	12
1994	Santa Delivers-564567	Yr.Iss.	1994	12.00	12

*Quotes have been rounded up to nearest dollar

YEAR ISSUE	EDITION LIMIT	YEAR RETD.	ISSUE PRICE	*QUOTE U.S.$
1994 Buttons 'N' Bow Boutique-578363 - Gilmore	Yr.Iss.	1995	22.50	23
1994 A Sign of Peace-581992	Yr.Iss.	1994	18.50	19
1994 Wishing You Well At Christmas -582050	Yr.Iss.	1994	25.00	25
1994 Ahoy Joy!-582085	Yr.Iss.	1994	20.00	20
1994 Santa...Phone Home-582166	Yr.Iss.	1994	25.00	25
1994 Christmas Swishes-582379	Yr.Iss.	1994	17.50	18
1994 The Latest Scoop From Santa -582395 - Gilmore	Yr.Iss.	1994	18.50	19
1994 Chiminy Cheer-582409 - Gilmore	Yr.Iss.	1994	22.50	23
1994 Cozy Candlelight Dinner-582417 - Gilmore	Yr.Iss.	1994	25.00	25
1994 Fine Feathered Festivities -582425 - Gilmore	Yr.Iss.	1994	22.50	23
1994 Joy From Head To Hose -582433 - Gilmore	Yr.Iss.	1994	15.00	15
1994 Yuletide Yummies-584835	Yr.Iss.	1994	20.00	20
1994 Merry Christmas Tool You, Dad -584886	Yr.Iss.	1994	22.50	23
1994 Exercising Good Taste-584967	Yr.Iss.	1994	17.50	18
1994 Holiday Chew-Chew-584983 - Gilmore	Yr.Iss.	1994	22.50	23
1994 Mine, Mine, Mine-585815 - Davis	Yr.Iss.	1994	20.00	20
1994 To The Sweetest Baby-588725 - Gilmore	Yr.Iss.	1994	18.50	19
1994 Rockin' Ranger-588970	Yr.Iss.	1994	25.00	25
1994 Peace On Earthworm-588989	Yr.Iss.	1994	20.00	20
1994 Good Things Crop Up At Christmas-589071	Yr.Iss.	1994	25.00	25
1994 Christmas Crossroads-589128	Yr.Iss.	1994	20.00	20
1994 Have A Ball At Christmas -590673	Yr.Iss.	1994	15.00	15
1994 Have A Totem-ly Terrific Christmas-590819	Yr.Iss.	1994	30.00	30
1994 Cocoa 'N' Kisses For Santa - 591939	Yr.Iss.	1995	22.50	23
1994 On The Road With Coke™ -592528	Yr.Iss.	1995	25.00	25
1994 What's Shakin' For Christmas -592668	Yr.Iss.	1994	18.50	19
1994 "A" For Santa-592676	Yr.Iss.	1994	17.50	18
1994 Christmas Fly-By-592714	Yr.Iss.	1994	15.00	15
1994 Santa...You're The Pops!-593761	Yr.Iss.	1994	22.50	23
1994 Purdy Packages, Pardner! -593834	Yr.Iss.	1994	20.00	20
1994 Handle With Care-593842	Yr.Iss.	1994	20.00	20
1994 To Coin A Phrase, Merry Christmas-593877	Yr.Iss.	1994	20.00	20
1994 Featured Presentation-593885	Yr.Iss.	1994	20.00	20
1994 Christmas Fishes From Santa Paws-593893	Yr.Iss.	1994	18.50	19
1994 Melted My Heart-594237 - Gilmore	Yr.Iss.	1994	15.00	15
1994 Finishing First-594342 - Gilmore	Yr.Iss.	1994	20.00	20
1994 Yule Fuel-594385	Yr.Iss.	1994	20.00	20
1994 Toy Tinker Topper-595047 - Gilmore	Yr.Iss.	1994	20.00	20
1994 Santa Claus Is Comin'-595209	Yr.Iss.	1994	20.00	20
1994 Seasoned With Love-595268	Yr.Iss.	1994	22.50	23
1994 Sweet Dreams-595489	Yr.Iss.	1994	12.50	13
1994 Peace On Earth-595497	Yr.Iss.	1994	12.50	13
1994 Christmas Two-gether-595500	Yr.Iss.	1994	12.50	13
1994 Santa's L'il Helper-595519	Yr.Iss.	1994	12.50	13
1994 Expecting Joy-595527 - Hahn	Yr.Iss.	1994	12.50	13
1994 Sweet Greetings-595578	Yr.Iss.	1994	12.50	13
1994 Ring In The Holidays-595586 - Hahn	Yr.Iss.	1994	12.50	13
1994 Grandmas Are Sew Special -595594	Yr.Iss.	1994	12.50	13
1994 Holiday Catch-595608 - Hahn	Yr.Iss.	1994	12.50	13
1994 Bubblin' with Joy-595616	Yr.Iss.	1994	12.50	13
1994 Good Friends Are Forever -595950 - Gilmore	Yr.Iss.	1994	13.50	14
1994 Christmas Tee-596256	Yr.Iss.	1995	25.00	25
1994 Have a Merry Dairy Christmas -596264	Yr.Iss.	1994	22.50	23
1994 Happy Holi-date-596272 - Hahn	Yr.Iss.	1995	22.50	23
1994 O' Come All Ye Faithful-596280 - Hahn	Yr.Iss.	1994	15.00	15
1994 One Small Step...-596299 - Hahn	19,690	1994	25.00	45
1994 To My Favorite V.I.P.-596698	Yr.Iss.	1994	20.00	20
1994 Building Memories-596876 - Hahn	Yr.Iss.	1994	25.00	25
1994 Open For Business-596906 - Hahn	Yr.Iss.	1994	17.50	18
1994 Twas The Nite Before Christmas -597643 - Gilmore	Yr.Iss.	1994	18.50	19
1994 I Can Bear-ly Wait For A Coke™ -597724	Yr.Iss.	1995	18.50	19
1994 Gallant Greeting- 598313	Yr.Iss.	1994	15.00	20
1994 Merry Menage-598321	Yr.Iss.	1994	20.00	20
1994 Bundle Of Joy-598992	Yr.Iss.	1994	10.00	15
1994 Bundle Of Joy-599018	Yr.Iss.	1994	10.00	10
1994 Have A Dino-mite Christmas -599026 - Hahn	Yr.Iss.	1994	18.50	19
1994 Good Fortune To You-599034	Yr.Iss.	1994	25.00	25
1994 Building a Sew-man-599042	Yr.Iss.	1994	18.50	19
1994 Merry Memo-ries-599050	Yr.Iss.	1994	22.50	23
1994 Ski-son's Greetings-599069	Yr.Iss.	1994	20.00	20
1994 Holiday Freezer Teaser-599085 - Gilmore	Yr.Iss.	1994	25.00	25
1994 Almost Time For Santa-599093 - Gilmore	Yr.Iss.	1994	25.00	25
1994 Santa's Secret Test Drive -599107 - Gilmore	Yr.Iss.	1994	20.00	20
1994 You're A Wheel Cool Brother -599115 - Gilmore	Yr.Iss.	1994	22.50	23

YEAR ISSUE	EDITION LIMIT	YEAR RETD.	ISSUE PRICE	*QUOTE U.S.$
1994 Hand-Tossed Tidings-599166	Yr.Iss.	1994	17.50	18
1994 Tasty Take Off-599174	Yr.Iss.	1994	20.00	20
1994 Formula For Love-599530 - Olsen	Yr.Iss.	1994	10.00	10
1994 Santa's Ginger-bred Doe -599697 - Gilmore	Yr.Iss.	1994	15.00	15
1994 Nutcracker Sweetheart-599700	Yr.Iss.	1994	15.00	15
1994 Merry Reindeer Ride-599719	Yr.Iss.	1994	20.00	20
1994 Santa's Sing-A-Long-599727 - Gilmore	Yr.Iss.	1994	20.00	20
1994 A Holiday Opportunity-599735	Yr.Iss.	1995	20.00	20
1994 Holiday Stars-599743	Yr.Iss.	1995	20.00	20
1994 The Latest Mews From Home-653977	Yr.Iss.	1994	16.00	16
1994 You're A Winner Son!-834564 - Gilmore	Yr.Iss.	1994	18.50	19
1994 Especially For You-834580 - Gilmore	Yr.Iss.	1994	27.50	28
1995 How...Do I Love Thee-104949	Yr.Iss.	1995	22.50	23
1995 Swishing You Sweet Greetings -105201	Yr.Iss.	1995	20.00	20
1995 Planely Delicious-109665	Yr.Iss.		20.00	20
1996 Spice Up The Season-111724	Yr.Iss.		20.00	20
1995 Home For The Howl-i-days -111732	Yr.Iss.	1995	20.00	20
1995 Time For Refreshment-111872	Yr.Iss.	1995	20.00	20
1995 Holiday Bike Hike 111937	Yr.Iss.	1995	20.00	20
1996 Santa's Sacks-111945 - Hahn	Yr.Iss.		15.00	18
1995 Ho, Ho, Hole in One!-111953	Yr.Iss.	1995	20.00	20
1995 No Time To Spare at Christmas -111961	Yr.Iss.	1995	20.00	20
1995 Hustling Up Some Cheer-112038	Yr.Iss.	1995	20.00	20
1995 Scoring Big at Christmas-112046	Yr.Iss.	1995	20.00	20
1995 Serving Up the Best 112054	Yr.Iss.	1995	17.50	18
1995 Sea-sons Greetings, Teacher 112070 - Gilmore	Yr.Iss.	1995	17.50	18
1995 Siesta Santa-112089 - Gilmore	Yr.Iss.	1995	25.00	25
1995 We've Shared Sew Much -112097 - Gilmore	Yr.Iss.	1995	25.00	25
1995 Toys To Treasure-112119	Yr.Iss.	1995	20.00	20
1995 To Santa, Post Haste-112151 - Gilmore	Yr.Iss.	1995	15.00	15
1995 Yule Logon For Christmas Cheer - 122513	Yr.Iss.	1995	20.00	20
1995 Pretty Up For The Holidays-125830	Yr.Iss.	1995	20.00	20
1995 You Bring The Love to Christmas-125849 - Butcher	Yr.Iss.	1995	15.00	15
1995 Happy Birthday Jesus-125857 - Butcher	Yr.Iss.	1995	15.00	15
1995 Let's Snuggle Together For Christmas-125865 - Butcher	Yr.Iss.	1995	15.00	15
1995 I'm In A Spin Over You-125873 - Butcher	Yr.Iss.	1995	15.00	15
1995 Our First Christmas Together -125881 - Butcher	Yr.Iss.	1995	22.50	23
1995 Twinkle, Twinkle Christmas Star -125903 - Butcher	Yr.Iss.	1995	17.50	18
1995 Bringing Holiday Wishes To You -125911 - Butcher	Yr.Iss.	1995	22.50	23
1995 You Pull The Strings To My Heart-125938 - Butcher	Yr.Iss.	1995	20.00	20
1995 Baby's First Christmas-125946 - Butcher	Yr.Iss.	1995	15.00	15
1995 Baby's First Christmas-125954 - Butcher	Yr.Iss.	1995	15.00	15
1995 Friends Are The Greatest Treasure-125962 - Butcher	20,000	1995	25.00	25
1995 4-Alarm Christmas-128767 - Gilmore	Yr.Iss.	1995	17.50	18
1995 Truckin'-128813	Yr.Iss.	1995	25.00	25
1995 T-Bird-128821	19,550	1995	20.00	28
1995 57 HVN-128848	Yr.Iss.	1995	20.00	22
1995 Corvette-128856	Yr.Iss.	1995	20.00	22
1995 Mom's Taxi-128872	Yr.Iss.	1995	25.00	25
1995 Choc Full of Wishes-128945	Yr.Iss.	1995	20.00	20
1995 Have a Coke and a Smile™-128953	Yr.Iss.	1995	22.50	23
1995 Trunk Full of Treasures-128961	20,000	1995	25.00	25
1995 Make Mine a Coke™-128988	Yr.Iss.	1995	25.00	25
1995 Dashing Through the Snow-128996	Yr.Iss.	1995	20.00	20
1995 Happy Yuleglide-129003	Yr.Iss.	1995	17.50	18
1995 Santa's Speedway-129011	Yr.Iss.	1995	20.00	20
1995 You're My Cup of Tea-129038	Yr.Iss.		20.00	20
1995 Crackin' a Smile-129046	Yr.Iss.	1995	17.50	18
1995 Rx:Mas Greetings-129054	Yr.Iss.	1995	17.50	18
1996 Special Bear-Livery-129062	Yr.Iss.		15.00	15
1995 Merry McMeal-129070	Yr.Iss.		17.50	18
1995 Above the Crowd-129089	Yr.Iss.	1995	20.00	20
1995 Mickey at the Helm-132063	Yr.Iss.	1995	17.50	18
1995 Caddy-132705	Yr.Iss.		20.00	22
1996 Catch Of The Holiday-132888 - Hahn	Yr.Iss.		20.00	20
1996 Jackpot Joy!-132896 - Hahn	Yr.Iss.	1995	17.50	18
1995 Get in the Spirit...Recycle-132918 - Hahn	Yr.Iss.		17.50	18
1995 Miss Merry's Secret-132934 - Hahn	Yr.Iss.	1995	20.00	20
1995 ...Good Will Toward Men -132942 - Hahn	19,450	1995	25.00	25
1995 Friendships Bloom Through All Seasons-132950 - Hahn	Yr.Iss.	1995	22.50	23
1995 Merry Monopoly-132969	Yr.Iss.		22.50	23
1995 The Night B 4 Christmas -134848 - Hahn	Yr.Iss.	1995	20.00	20
1995 A Cup Of Cheer-135070 - Gilmore	Yr.Iss.		25.00	25
1995 Bubblin' With Joy-136581	Yr.Iss.	1995	15.00	15
1996 Steppin' With Minnie-136603	Yr.Iss.		13.50	14

YEAR ISSUE	EDITION LIMIT	YEAR RETD.	ISSUE PRICE	*QUOTE U.S.$
1995 Minnie's Merry Christmas -136611	Yr.Iss.	1995	20.00	20
1996 Motorcycle Mickey-136654	Yr.Iss.		25.00	25
1995 Makin' Tracks With Mickey-136662	Yr.Iss.	1995	20.00	20
1995 Mickey's Airmail-136670	Yr.Iss.		20.00	20
1995 Holiday Bound-136689	Yr.Iss.		20.00	20
1995 Goofed-Up!-136697	Yr.Iss.		20.00	20
1995 On The Ball At Christmas -136700	Yr.Iss.		15.00	15
1995 Sweet on You-136719	Yr.Iss.	1995	22.50	23
1995 Nutty About Christmas-137030	Yr.Iss.	1995	22.50	23
1995 Tinkertoy Joy-137049	Yr.Iss.		20.00	20
1995 Starring Roll At Christmas -137057	Yr.Iss.	1995	17.50	18
1995 A Thimble of the Season -137243 - Gilmore	Yr.Iss.		22.50	23
1995 A Little Something Extra...Extra-137251	10,000	1995	25.00	25
1995 The Maze Of Our Lives-139599 - Hahn	Yr.Iss.	1995	17.50	18
1995 A Sip For Good Measure-139610 - Hahn	Yr.Iss.	1995	17.50	18
1995 Christmas Fishes, Dad-139629 - Hahn	Yr.Iss.		17.50	18
1995 Christmas Is In The Bag-139645	Yr.Iss.	1995	17.50	18
1995 Gotta Have a Clue-139653	Yr.Iss.	1995	20.00	20
1995 Fun In Hand-139661	Yr.Iss.	1995	17.50	18
1995 Christmas Cuddle-139688	Yr.Iss.		20.00	20
1995 Dreaming Of the One I Love-139696	Yr.Iss.		25.00	25
1995 Sneaking a Peek-139718	Yr.Iss.		22.50	23
1995 Christmas Eve Mischief-139726	Yr.Iss.	1995	17.50	18
1995 All Tucked In-139734	Yr.Iss.	1995	15.00	15
1995 Merry Christmas To Me-139742	Yr.Iss.	1995	20.00	20
1995 Looking Our Holiday Best-139750	Yr.Iss.		20.00	25
1995 Christmas Vacation-142158	Yr.Iss.		20.00	20
1995 Just Fore Christmas-142174	Yr.Iss.		15.00	15
1995 Christmas Belle-142182	Yr.Iss.		20.00	20
1995 Tail Waggin' Wishes-142190	Yr.Iss.		17.50	18
1995 Holiday Ride-142204	Yr.Iss.		17.50	18
1995 A Carousel For Ariel-142212	Yr.Iss.	1995	17.50	18
1995 On The Move At Christmas -142220 - Hahn	Yr.Iss.	1995	17.50	18
1995 T-Bird-146838	Yr.Iss.	1995	20.00	22
1996 Swinging On A Star-166642	Yr.Iss.		20.00	20
1996 A-Joy Matie, Throw Me A Lifesavers-166677	Yr.Iss.		20.00	20
1996 It's Plane To See...Coke Is It -166723	Yr.Iss.		25.00	25
1996 A Century Of Good Taste -166774	Yr.Iss.		25.00	25
1996 Servin' Up Joy-166847	Yr.Iss.		20.00	20
1996 In-Line To Help Santa-166855	Yr.Iss.		20.00	20
1996 I Love My Daughter-166863	Yr.Iss.		9.00	9
1996 I Love Grandma-166898	Yr.Iss.		9.00	9
1996 I Love Dad-166901	Yr.Iss.		9.00	9
1996 I Love Mom-166928	Yr.Iss.		9.00	9
1996 I Love My Godchild-166936	Yr.Iss.		9.00	9
1996 Baby's 1st Christmas-166944	Yr.Iss.		9.00	9
1996 A Boot Full Of Cheer-166952	Yr.Iss.		20.00	20
1996 Summons For A Merry Christmas-166960	Yr.Iss.		22.50	23
1996 An Appointment With Santa-166979	Yr.Iss.		20.00	20
1996 Play It Again, Nick-166987	Yr.Iss.		17.50	18
1996 Holiday Tinkertoy Tree-166995	Yr.Iss.		17.50	18
1996 A Picture Perfect Pair-167002	Yr.Iss.		25.00	25
1996 Santa's On The Line-167037	Yr.Iss.		25.00	25
1996 Downhill Delivery-167053	Yr.Iss.		25.00	25
1996 On A Roll With Diet Coke -167061	Yr.Iss.		20.00	20
1996 Hold On, Santa!-167088	Yr.Iss.		25.00	25
1996 There's A Friendship Brewing -167096 - Hahn	Yr.Iss.		25.00	25
1996 Tails A' Waggin'-167126	Yr.Iss.		20.00	20
1996 In Store For More-167134	15,000		22.50	23
1996 Jeep Grand Cherokee-167215	Yr.Iss.		22.50	23
1996 Chevy Blazer-167223	Yr.Iss.		22.50	23
1996 Ford Explorer-167231	Yr.Iss.		22.50	23
1996 Dodge Ram Truck-167258	Yr.Iss.		22.50	23
1996 Trees To Please-168378	Yr.Iss.		25.00	25
1996 Plane Crazy-168386	Yr.Iss.		22.50	23
1996 I Love My Son-168432	Yr.Iss.		9.00	9
1996 #1 Coach-168440	Yr.Iss.		9.00	9
1996 Goin' Fishin'-168459	Yr.Iss.		22.50	23
1996 Gifts From Mickey-168467	Yr.Iss.		20.00	20
1996 All Fired Up For Christmas -168475	Yr.Iss.		25.00	25
1996 Minnie's Mall Haul-168491	Yr.Iss.		25.00	25
1996 A Magic Moment-172197	Yr.Iss.		17.50	18
1996 Happy's Holiday-172200	Yr.Iss.		17.50	18
1996 Sitting Pretty-172219	Yr.Iss.		25.00	25
1996 Life's Sweet Choices-172634	Yr.Iss.		25.00	25
1996 Holiday In Bloom-172669	Yr.Iss.		25.00	25
1996 Have A Cracker Jack Christmas -172979	Yr.Iss.		25.00	25
1996 Hair's The Place-173093 - Hahn	Yr.Iss.		25.00	25
1996 Merry Manicure-173339 - Hahn	Yr.Iss.		25.00	25
1996 100 Years...And Still On A Roll -173770	19,960		17.50	18
1996 Tracking Reindeer Pause -173789 - Hahn	Yr.Iss.		25.00	25
1996 Holiday Dreams Of Green -173797 - Hahn	Yr.Iss.		15.00	15
1996 1965 Ford Mustang-173800	Yr.Iss.		22.50	23
1996 Toyland, Joyland-173878	Yr.Iss.		20.00	20

YEAR ISSUE	EDITION LIMIT	YEAR RETD.	ISSUE PRICE	*QUOTE U.S.$
1996 Tobin's Debut Dancer-173886	20,000		20.00	20
1996 Thou Art My Lamp, O Lord	Yr.Iss.		25.00	25
1996 'Tis The Season To Be Nutty-175234	Yr.Iss.		17.50	18
1996 1956 Chevy Corvette-175269	19,560		22.50	23
1996 A World Of Good Taste-175420	18,600		20.00	20
1996 It's Time For Christmas-175455	Yr.Iss.		25.00	25
1996 15 Years Of Hits-175463	10,000		25.00	25
1996 Sew Darn Cute-176761 - Hahn	Yr.Iss.		25.00	25
1996 Decked Out For Christmas -176796 - Hahn	Yr.Iss.		25.00	25
1996 Campaign For Christmas-176818	19,960		17.50	18
1996 Delivering Holiday Cheers -177318	Yr.Iss.		25.00	25
1996 A Splash Of Cool Yule-213713	Yr.Iss.		20.00	20
1995 Sweet Harmony-586773 - Gilmore	Yr.Iss.	1995	17.50	18
1995 Yule Tide Prancer-588660	Yr.Iss.	1995	15.00	15
1995 Baby's Sweet Feast-588733 - Gilmore	Yr.Iss.	1995	17.50	19
1995 A Well, Balanced Meal For Santa-592633	Yr.Iss.	1995	17.50	18
1995 Salute-593133	Yr.Iss.	1995	22.50	23
1995 Filled To The Brim-595039 - Gilmore	Yr.Iss.	1995	25.00	25

Ertl Collectibles

Sparrowsville - L. Davis

YEAR ISSUE	EDITION LIMIT	YEAR RETD.	ISSUE PRICE	*QUOTE U.S.$
1996 Bachelor Pad H109	Open		25.00	25
1996 The Hayloft H108	Open		25.00	25
1996 Hearthside Manor H111	Open		25.00	25
1996 Home Sweet Home H110	Open		25.00	25
1996 Leather Nest H106	Open		25.00	25
1996 Love Nest H107	Open		25.00	25
1996 The Smith's H104	Open		25.00	25
1996 Snowbirds H103	Open		25.00	25
1996 Winter Retreat H105	Open		25.00	25

Fenton Art Glass Company

Christmas Limited Edition - M. Reynolds

YEAR ISSUE	EDITION LIMIT	YEAR RETD.	ISSUE PRICE	*QUOTE U.S.$
1996 Golden Winged Angel, Hndpt. 3 1/2"	2,000		27.50	28

FFSC, Inc.

Charming Tails Deck The Halls - D. Griff

YEAR ISSUE	EDITION LIMIT	YEAR RETD.	ISSUE PRICE	*QUOTE U.S.$
1992 Catching ZZZ's	Closed	1995	12.00	12
1992 The Drifters	Closed	1995	12.00	12
1992 Fresh Fruit	Closed	1995	12.00	12
1992 Mice/Rabbit Ball, set/2	Closed	1995	12.00	25
1993 Hang in There	Closed	1996	10.00	10
1993 Holiday Wreath	Closed	1995	12.00	12
1993 Mackenzie Napping	Closed	1995	12.00	12
1993 Maxine Lights a Candle	Closed	1995	11.00	11
1993 Mouse on Snowflake (lighted)	Closed	1995	11.00	25
1994 Baby's First Christmas	Yr.Iss.	1994	12.00	12
1994 Binkey & Reginald on Ice	Closed	1994	10.00	10
1994 Friends in Flight	Closed	1994	18.00	18
1994 The Grape Escape	Closed	1994	18.00	18
1994 High Flying Mackenzie	Open		20.00	20
1994 Holiday Lights	Closed	1995	10.00	10
1994 Horsin' Around	Open		18.00	18
1994 Mackenzie and Binkey's Snack (cherry & plum)	Closed	1994	12.00	70-100
1994 Mackenzie Blowing Bubble	Closed	1994	12.00	35-50
1994 Mackenzie on Ice	Open		10.00	10
1994 Mackenzie's Bubble Ride	Closed	1996	13.00	13
1994 Mackenzie's Snowball (dated)	Yr.Iss.	1994	10.00	50
1994 Maxine and Mackenzie	Closed	1996	12.00	12
1994 Reginald's Bubble Ride	Closed	1994	12.00	12
1994 Mouse on Yellow Bulb (lighted)	Closed	1995	10.00	20-29
1994 Mouse Star Treetop	Closed	1995	10.00	20-29
1994 Sticky Situations	Closed	1996	16.00	16
1995 1995 Annual	Yr.Iss.	1995	16.00	16
1995 Binkey's Poinsettia	Open		12.00	12
1995 Christmas Cookies	Open		10.00	10
1995 Christmas Flowers	Open		12.00	12
1995 Holiday Balloon Ride	Open		16.00	16
1995 Mackenzie's Whirligig	Open		20.00	20
1995 Peppermint Party	Open		10.00	10
1995 Reginald in Leaves	Open		10.00	10
1995 Stewart at Play	Closed	1995	12.00	12
1995 Stewart's Winter Fun	Closed	1995	10.00	10
1996 1996 Annual-All Wrapped Up	Yr.Iss.		12.00	12
1996 Baby's First Christmas	Yr.Iss.		13.00	13
1996 Our First Christmas (dated)	Yr.Iss.		18.00	18
1996 Christmas Stamps	Open		12.00	12
1996 Fallen Angel	Open		12.00	12
1996 Flights of Fancy	Open		12.00	12
1996 Frequent Flyer	Open		12.00	12
1996 Letter to Santa	Open		12.00	12
1996 Stamp Dispenser	Open		12.00	12
1996 Weeeeee!	Open		12.00	12

Flambro Imports

Emmett Kelly Jr. Christmas Ornaments - Undis.

YEAR ISSUE	EDITION LIMIT	YEAR RETD.	ISSUE PRICE	*QUOTE U.S.$
1989 65th Birthday	Yr.Iss.	1989	24.00	100-150
1990 30 Years Of Clowning	Yr.Iss.	1990	30.00	135
1991 EKJ With Stocking And Toys	Yr.Iss.	1991	30.00	30
1992 Home For Christmas	Yr.Iss.	1992	24.00	70
1993 Christmas Mail	Yr.Iss.	1993	25.00	70
1994 '70 Birthday Commemorative	Yr.Iss.	1994	24.00	55-90
1995 20th Anniversary All Star Circus	Yr.Iss.	1995	25.00	25
1996 Christmas Pageant	Yr.Iss.		29.00	29

Little Emmett Ornaments - M. Wu

YEAR ISSUE	EDITION LIMIT	YEAR RETD.	ISSUE PRICE	*QUOTE U.S.$
1995 Little Emmett Christmas Wrap	Open		11.50	12
1995 Little Emmett Deck the Neck	Open		11.50	12
1996 Little Emmett Singing Carols	Open		13.00	13
1996 Little Emmett Your Present	Open		13.00	13
1996 Little Emmett Baby 1st Christmas	Open		13.00	13
1996 Little Emmett on Rocking Horse	Open		25.00	25

Ganz

Cowtown/The Christmas Collection - C. Thammavongsa

YEAR ISSUE	EDITION LIMIT	YEAR RETD.	ISSUE PRICE	*QUOTE U.S.$
1995 Bells on Cowtail Ring	Open		11.50	12
1994 Bronco Bully	Open		13.00	13
1995 Buckets of Joy	Open		12.00	12
1994 Calf-in-the Box	Open		12.50	13
1994 Christmoos Eve	Open		12.00	12
1995 Dairy Christmas	Open		11.50	12
1994 Downhill Dare Debull	Open		12.00	12
1994 Hallemooah	Open		12.00	12
1995 Holy Cow	Open		12.00	12
1994 Jingle Bull	Open		15.50	16
1994 Li'l Red Gliding Hoof	Open		12.00	12
1994 Little Drummer Calf	Open		12.00	12
1995 Moo, Moo, Moo	Open		11.50	12

Little Cheesers/The Christmas Collection - C. Thammavongsa, unless otherwise noted

YEAR ISSUE	EDITION LIMIT	YEAR RETD.	ISSUE PRICE	*QUOTE U.S.$
1992 Abner Appleton - GDA/Thammavongsa	Open		15.00	15
1994 All I Want For Christmas	Closed	1994	13.50	14
1994 Angel	Open		8.00	8
1995 Annual Angel 1995	Open		10.50	11
1993 Baby's First X'mas Ornament	Retrd.	1995	12.50	13
1994 Candy Cane Caper	Open		9.00	9
1994 Cheeser Snowman	Closed	1994	5.00	5
1994 Chelsea's Stocking Bell	Open		15.50	16
1994 Cousin Woody Playing Flute	Closed	1994	10.00	10
1993 Dashing Through the Snow	Open		11.00	11
1994 Grandpa Blowing Horn	Closed	1994	10.00	10
1994 Hickory Playing Cello	Closed	1994	10.00	10
1992 Jenny Butterfield - GDA/Thammavongsa	Open		17.00	17
1992 Jeremy With Teddy Bear - GDA/Thammavongsa	Open		13.00	13
1995 Light of the World Bell	Open		16.00	16
1993 Little Stocking Stuffer	Open		10.50	11
1992 Little Truffle - GDA/Thammavongsa	Open		9.50	10
1995 Mama Claus' Special Recipe	Open		11.50	12
1993 Medley Meadowmouse X'mas Bell	Closed	1996	17.00	17
1994 Medley Playing Drum	Closed	1994	5.50	6
1992 Myrtle Meadowmouse - GDA/Thammavongsa	Closed	1996	15.00	15
1995 Noel	Closed	1996	10.50	11
1993 Our First Christmas Together	Open		18.50	19
1994 Peace on Earth	Open		8.00	8
1992 Santa Cheeser - GDA/Thammavongsa	Open		14.00	14
1993 Santa's Little Helper	Open		11.00	11
1994 Santa's Workshop	Closed	1994	10.00	10
1993 Skating Into Your Heart	Open		10.00	10
1995 Skiing Santa	Open		10.00	10
1994 Sleigh Ride	Closed	1994	9.00	9
1995 Snow Cheeser II	Open		6.50	7
1994 Swinging in the Season	Open		11.00	11
1996 Swinging on the Moon - Chiemlowski	Open		10.00	10
1994 Violet With Snowball	Closed	1994	5.50	6

Little Cheesers/The Silverwoods - C. Thammavongsa

YEAR ISSUE	EDITION LIMIT	YEAR RETD.	ISSUE PRICE	*QUOTE U.S.$
1995 Angel Above	Open		8.50	9
1994 Christmas Surprise	Open		8.50	9
1994 Comfort and Joy	Open		6.00	6
1994 Deck the Halls	Closed	1996	9.50	10
1994 Giddy Up!	Open		8.50	9
1995 Harps of Gold	Open		8.50	9
1994 Hickory Dickory Dock	Open		9.50	10
1995 Joyful Sounds	Closed	1996	8.50	9
1994 Mrs. Claus	Closed	1996	9.00	9
1995 Over The Hills	Open		8.50	9
1994 Santa Silverwood	Closed	1996	9.00	9
1994 Xmas Express	Open		9.50	10

Perfect Little Place/Christmas Collection - C.Thammavongsa

YEAR ISSUE	EDITION LIMIT	YEAR RETD.	ISSUE PRICE	*QUOTE U.S.$
1995 Angel of Light	Open		12.00	12

Pigsville/The Christmas Collection - C. Thammavongsa

YEAR ISSUE	EDITION LIMIT	YEAR RETD.	ISSUE PRICE	*QUOTE U.S.$
1994 Caroler	Open		10.00	10
1994 Christmas Treats	Open		9.00	9
1994 Drummer Pig	Open		10.00	10
1995 Fa-La-La-La-La	Open		9.50	10
1995 Heaven Sent	Closed	1996	10.50	11
1994 Joy to the World	Open		10.00	10
1994 Lovestruck	Open		10.50	11
1994 Santa Pig	Open		11.00	11
1994 Wheeeeeee! Piggy	Open		9.00	9

The Precious Steeples Collection - Ganz/L. Sunarth

YEAR ISSUE	EDITION LIMIT	YEAR RETD.	ISSUE PRICE	*QUOTE U.S.$
1995 Florence Cathedral	Open		11.00	11
1995 Notre-Dame Cathedral	Open		11.00	11
1995 St. Patrick's Cathedral	Open		11.00	11
1995 St. Paul's Cathedral	Open		11.00	11
1995 St. Peter's Basilica	Open		11.00	11
1995 Westminster Abbey	Open		11.00	11

Trains Gone By/Christmas Collection - Ganz

YEAR ISSUE	EDITION LIMIT	YEAR RETD.	ISSUE PRICE	*QUOTE U.S.$
1996 C.P. Huntington Train	4,896		10.00	10
1996 General Train	4,896		10.00	10
1996 New York Central Train	4,896		10.00	10
1996 Pennsylvania Train	4,896		10.00	10

Goebel of North America

Angel Bell 3" - Goebel

YEAR ISSUE	EDITION LIMIT	YEAR RETD.	ISSUE PRICE	*QUOTE U.S.$
1994 Angel w/Clarinet - Red	Closed	1994	17.50	18
1995 Angel w/Harp - Blue	Closed	1995	17.50	18
1996 Angel w/Mandolin - Champagne	Closed	1996	18.00	18
1997 Angel w/Accordian-Rose	Yr.Iss.		18.00	18

Angel Bells - 3 Asst. Colors - Goebel

YEAR ISSUE	EDITION LIMIT	YEAR RETD.	ISSUE PRICE	*QUOTE U.S.$
1976 Angel Bell w/Clarinet (3 colors)	Closed	1976	8.00	8
1976 Angel Bell w/Clarinet (white bisque)	Closed	1976		6
1977 Angel Bell w/Mandolin (3 colors)	Closed	1977	8.50	9
1977 Angel Bell w/Mandolin (white bisque)	Closed	1977	6.50	7
1978 Angel Bell w/Harp (3 colors)	Closed	1978	9.00	9
1978 Angel Bell w/Harp (white bisque)	Closed	1978	7.00	7
1979 Angel Bell w/Accordion (3 colors)	Closed	1979	9.50	10
1979 Angel Bell w/Accordion (white bisque)	Closed	1979	7.50	8
1980 Angel Bell w/Saxaphone (3 colors)	Closed	1980	10.00	10
1980 Angel Bell w/Saxaphone (white bisque)	Closed	1980	8.00	8
1981 Angel Bell w/Music (3 colors)	Closed	1981	11.00	11
1981 Angel Bell w/Music (white bisque)	Closed	1981	9.00	9
1982 Angel Bell w/French Horn (3 colors)	Closed	1982	11.75	12
1982 Angel Bell w/French Horn (white bisque)	Closed	1982	9.75	10
1983 Angel Bell w/Flute (3 colors)	Closed	1983	12.50	13
1983 Angel Bell w/Flute (white bisque)	Closed	1983	10.50	11
1984 Angel Bell w/Drum (3 colors)	Closed	1984	14.00	14
1984 Angel Bell w/Drum (white bisque)	Closed	1984	12.00	12
1985 Angel Bell w/Trumpet (3 colors)	Closed	1985	14.00	14
1985 Angel Bell w/Trumpet (white bisque)	Closed	1985	12.00	12
1986 Angel Bell w/Bells (3 colors)	Closed	1986	15.00	15
1986 Angel Bell w/Bells (white bisque)	Closed	1986	12.50	13
1987 Angel Bell w/Conductor (3 colors)	Closed	1987	16.50	17
1987 Angel Bell w/Conductor (white bisque)	Closed	1987	13.50	14
1988 Angel Bell w/Candle (3 colors)	Closed	1988	17.50	18
1988 Angel Bell w/Candle (white bisque)	Closed	1988	15.00	15
1989 Angel Bell w/Star (3 colors)	Closed	1989	20.00	20
1989 Angel Bell w/Star (white bisque)	Closed	1989	17.50	18
1990 Angel Bell w/Lantern (3 colors)	Closed	1990	22.50	23
1990 Angel Bell w/Lantern (white bisque)	Closed	1990	20.00	20
1991 Angel Bell w/Teddy (3 colors)	Closed	1991	25.00	25
1991 Angel Bell w/Teddy (white bisque)	Closed	1991	22.50	23
1992 Angel Bell w/Doll (3 colors)	Closed	1992	27.50	28
1992 Angel Bell w/Doll (white bisque)	Closed	1992	25.00	25
1993 Angel Bell w/Rocking Horse (3 colors)	Closed	1993	30.00	30
1993 Angel Bell w/Rocking Horse (white bisque)	Closed	1993	27.50	28
1994 Angel Bell w/Clown (3 colors)	Closed	1994	34.50	35
1994 Angel Bell w/Clown (white bisque)	Closed	1994	29.50	30
1995 Angel Bell w/Train (3 colors)	Closed	1995	37.00	37
1995 Angel Bell w/Train (white bisque)	Closed	1995	30.50	31
1996 Angel Bell w/Puppy (3 colors)	Closed	1996	40.00	40
1996 Angel Bell w/Puppy (white bisque)	Closed	1996	32.00	32
1997 Angel Bell w/Kitten (3 colors)	Open		42.50	43
1997 Angel Bell w/Kitten (white bisque)	Open		32.50	33

Goebel/M.I. Hummel

M.I. Hummel Annual Figurine Ornaments - M.I. Hummel

YEAR ISSUE	EDITION LIMIT	YEAR RETD.	ISSUE PRICE	*QUOTE U.S.$
1988 Flying High 452	Closed	N/A	75.00	95-150
1989 Love From Above 481	Closed	N/A	75.00	75-125
1990 Peace on Earth 484	Closed	N/A	80.00	95-140
1991 Angelic Guide 571	Closed	N/A	75.00	95-140
1992 Light Up The Night 622	Closed	N/A	100.00	100-125
1993 Herald on High 623	Closed	N/A	155.00	155-160

M.I. Hummel Collectibles Christmas Bell Ornaments - M.I. Hummel

YEAR ISSUE	EDITION LIMIT	YEAR RETD.	ISSUE PRICE	*QUOTE U.S.$
1989 Ride Into Christmas 775	Closed	1989	35.00	50-70
1990 Letter to Santa Claus 776	Closed	1990	37.50	40-70
1991 Hear Ye, Hear Ye 777	Closed	1991	40.00	40-70
1992 Harmony in Four Parts 778	Closed	1992	50.00	50-70
1993 Celestial Musician 779	Closed	1993	50.00	50-60
1994 Festival Harmony w/Mandolin 780	Closed	1994	50.00	50-60
1995 Festival Harmony w/Flute 781	Closed	1995	55.00	55
1996 Christmas Song 782	Yr.Iss.		65.00	65

YEAR ISSUE		EDITION LIMIT	YEAR RETD.	ISSUE PRICE	*QUOTE U.S.$
M.I. Hummel Collectibles Miniature Ornaments - M.I. Hummel					
1993	Celestial Musician 646	Open		90.00	110
1994	Festival Harmony w/Mandolin 647	Open		95.00	110
1995	Festival Harmony w/Flute 648	Open		100.00	110
1996	Christmas Song 645	Open		115.00	115

Gorham

Annual Crystal Ornaments - Gorham

1985	Crystal Ornament	Closed	1985	22.00	22
1986	Crystal Ornament	Closed	1986	25.00	25
1987	Crystal Ornament	Closed	1987	25.00	25
1988	Crystal Ornament	Closed	1988	28.00	28
1989	Crystal Ornament	Closed	1989	28.00	28
1990	Crystal Ornament	Closed	1990	30.00	30
1991	Crystal Ornament	Closed	1991	35.00	35
1992	Crystal Ornament	Closed	1992	32.50	33
1993	Crystal Ornament	Closed	1993	32.50	33

Annual Snowflake Ornaments - Gorham

1970	Sterling Snowflake	Closed	1970	10.00	400-600
1971	Sterling Snowflake	Closed	1971	10.00	85-150
1972	Sterling Snowflake	Closed	1972	10.00	110-150
1973	Sterling Snowflake	Closed	1973	11.00	75-130
1974	Sterling Snowflake	Closed	1974	18.00	80-110
1975	Sterling Snowflake	Closed	1975	18.00	35-85
1976	Sterling Snowflake	Closed	1976	20.00	55-110
1977	Sterling Snowflake	Closed	1977	23.00	85
1978	Sterling Snowflake	Closed	1978	23.00	85
1979	Sterling Snowflake	Closed	1979	33.00	85-100
1980	Silverplated Snowflake	Closed	1980	15.00	300-450
1981	Sterling Snowflake	Closed	1981	50.00	300-450
1982	Sterling Snowflake	Closed	1982	38.00	80-130
1983	Sterling Snowflake	Closed	1983	45.00	95-130
1984	Sterling Snowflake	Closed	1984	45.00	85-130
1985	Sterling Snowflake	Closed	1985	45.00	85-130
1986	Sterling Snowflake	Closed	1986	45.00	75-100
1987	Sterling Snowflake	Closed	1987	50.00	75-130
1988	Sterling Snowflake	Closed	1988	50.00	65
1989	Sterling Snowflake	Closed	1989	50.00	65
1990	Sterling Snowflake	Closed	1990	50.00	65
1991	Sterling Snowflake	Closed	1991	55.00	60
1992	Sterling Snowflake	Closed	1992	50.00	75-110
1993	Sterling Snowflake	Closed	1993	50.00	50
1994	Sterling Snowflake	Closed	1994	50.00	50
1995	Sterling Snowflake	Closed	1995	50.00	50

Archive Collectible - Gorham

1988	Victorian Heart	Closed	1988	50.00	50
1989	Victorian Wreath	Closed	1989	50.00	50
1990	Elizabethan Cupid	Closed	1990	60.00	65
1991	Baroque Angels	Closed	1991	55.00	60
1992	Madonna and Child	Closed	1992	50.00	50-60
1993	Angel With Mandolin	Closed	1993	50.00	50-60

Baby's First Christmas Crystal - Gorham

| 1991 | Baby's First Rocking Horse | Closed | 1994 | 35.00 | 35 |

Greenwich Workshop

The Greenwich Workshop Collection - J. Christensen

| 1995 | Angel's Gift | Yr.Iss. | 1995 | 50.00 | 95 |
| 1996 | Angel | Yr.Iss. | | 75.00 | 75 |

Hallmark Keepsake Ornaments

1973 Hallmark Keepsake Collection - Keepsake

1973	Betsey Clark XHD100-2	Yr.Iss.	1973	2.50	60-85
1973	Betsey Clark-(1st Ed.) XHD 100-2	Yr.Iss.	1973	2.50	125
1973	Christmas Is Love XHD106-2	Yr.Iss.	1973	2.50	80
1973	Elves XHD103-5	Yr.Iss.	1973	2.50	75
1973	Manger Scene XHD102-2	Yr.Iss.	1973	2.50	85-125
1973	Santa with Elves XHD101-5	Yr.Iss.	1973	2.50	85

1973 Keepsake Yarn Ornaments - Keepsake

1973	Angel XHD78-5	Yr.Iss.	1973	1.25	23
1973	Blue Girl XHD85-2	Yr.Iss.	1973	1.25	23
1973	Boy Caroler XHD83-2	Yr.Iss.	1973	1.25	30
1973	Choir Boy XHD80-5	Yr.Iss.	1973	1.25	28
1973	Elf XHD79-2	Yr.Iss.	1973	1.25	25
1973	Green Girl XHD84-5	Yr.Iss.	1973	1.25	25
1973	Little Girl XHD82-5	Yr.Iss.	1973	1.25	20
1973	Mr. Santa XHD74-5	Yr.Iss.	1973	1.25	25
1973	Mr. Snowman XHD76-5	Yr.Iss.	1973	1.25	25
1973	Mrs. Santa XHD75-2	Yr.Iss.	1973	1.25	23
1973	Mrs. Snowman XHD77-2	Yr.Iss.	1973	1.25	23
1973	Soldier XHD81-2	Yr.Iss.	1973	1.00	22

1974 Hallmark Keepsake Collection - Keepsake

1974	Angel QX110-1	Yr.Iss.	1974	2.50	75
1974	Betsey Clark-(2nd Ed.) QX 108-1	Yr.Iss.	1974	2.50	47-75
1974	Buttons & Bo (Set/2) QX113-1	Yr.Iss.	1974	3.50	50
1974	Charmers QX109-1	Yr.Iss.	1974	2.50	23-40
1974	Currier & Ives (Set/2) QX112-1	Yr.Iss.	1974	3.50	45
1974	Little Miracles (Set/4) QX115-1	Yr.Iss.	1974	4.50	55
1974	Norman Rockwell QX106-1	Yr.Iss.	1974	2.50	45-85
1974	Norman Rockwell QX111-1	Yr.Iss.	1974	2.50	85
1974	Raggedy Ann and Andy(4/set) QX114-1	Yr.Iss.	1974	4.50	75
1974	Snowgoose QX107-1	Yr.Iss.	1974	2.50	75

YEAR ISSUE		EDITION LIMIT	YEAR RETD.	ISSUE PRICE	*QUOTE U.S.$
1974 Keepsake Yarn Ornaments - Keepsake					
1974	Angel QX103-1	Yr.Iss.	1974	1.50	28
1974	Elf QX101-1	Yr.Iss.	1974	1.50	23
1974	Mrs. Santa QX100-1	Yr.Iss.	1974	1.50	23
1974	Santa QX105-1	Yr.Iss.	1974	1.50	25
1974	Snowman QX104-1	Yr.Iss.	1974	1.50	23
1974	Soldier QX102-1	Yr.Iss.	1974	1.50	23

1975 Handcrafted Ornaments: Adorable - Keepsake

1975	Betsey Clark QX157-1	Yr.Iss.	1975	2.50	225
1975	Drummer Boy QX161-1	Yr.Iss.	1975	2.50	295
1975	Mrs. Santa QX156-1	Yr.Iss.	1975	2.50	275
1975	Raggedy Andy QX160-1	Yr.Iss.	1975	2.50	375
1975	Raggedy Ann QX159-1	Yr.Iss.	1975	2.50	295
1975	Santa QX155-1	Yr.Iss.	1975	2.50	250

1975 Handcrafted Ornaments: Nostalgia - Keepsake

1975	Drummer Boy QX130-1	Yr.Iss.	1975	3.50	115-175
1975	Joy QX132-1	Yr.Iss.	1975	3.50	125-175
1975	Locomotive (dated) QX127-1	Yr.Iss.	1975	3.50	110-175
1975	Peace on Earth (dated) QX131-1	Yr.Iss.	1975	3.50	95-165
1975	Rocking Horse QX128-1	Yr.Iss.	1975	3.50	115
1975	Santa & Sleigh QX129-1	Yr.Iss.	1975	3.50	125

1975 Keepsake Property Ornaments - Keepsake

1975	Betsey Clark (Set/2) QX167-1	Yr.Iss.	1975	3.50	25-45
1975	Betsey Clark (Set/4) QX168-1	Yr.Iss.	1975	4.50	50
1975	Betsey Clark QX163-1	Yr.Iss.	1975	2.50	40
1975	Betsey Clark-(3rd Ed.) QX133-1	Yr.Iss.	1975	3.00	30-75
1975	Buttons & Bo (Set/4) QX139-1	Yr.Iss.	1975	5.00	50
1975	Charmers QX135-1	Yr.Iss.	1975	3.00	30-40
1975	Currier & Ives (Set/2) QX137-1	Yr.Iss.	1975	4.00	40
1975	Currier & Ives (Set/2) QX164-1	Yr.Iss.	1975	2.50	35-40
1975	Little Miracles (Set/4) QX140-1	Yr.Iss.	1975	5.00	40
1975	Marty Links QX136-1	Yr.Iss.	1975	3.00	50
1975	Norman Rockwell QX134-1	Yr.Iss.	1975	3.00	35-45
1975	Norman Rockwell QX166-1	Yr.Iss.	1975	2.50	40-55
1975	Raggedy Ann and Andy(2/set) QX138-1	Yr.Iss.	1975	4.00	65
1975	Raggedy Ann QX165-1	Yr.Iss.	1975	2.50	50-65

1975 Keepsake Yarn Ornaments - Keepsake

1975	Drummer Boy QX123-1	Yr.Iss.	1975	1.75	25
1975	Little Girl QX126-1	Yr.Iss.	1975	1.75	20
1975	Mrs. Santa QX125-1	Yr.Iss.	1975	1.75	22
1975	Raggedy Andy QX122-1	Yr.Iss.	1975	1.75	40
1975	Raggedy Ann QX121-1	Yr.Iss.	1975	1.75	35
1975	Santa QX124-1	Yr.Iss.	1975	1.75	22

1976 Bicentennial Commemoratives - Keepsake

1976	Bicentennial '76 Commemorative QX211-1	Yr.Iss.	1976	2.50	45-60
1976	Bicentennial Charmers QX198-1	Yr.Iss.	1976	3.00	60
1976	Colonial Children (Set/2) 4 QX208-1	Yr.Iss.	1976	4.00	40-65

1976 Decorative Ball Ornaments - Keepsake

| 1976 | Cardinals QX205-1 | Yr.Iss. | 1976 | 2.30 | 50 |
| 1976 | Chickadees QX204-1 | Yr.Iss. | 1976 | 2.30 | 50-65 |

1976 First Commemorative Ornament - Keepsake

| 1976 | Baby's First Christmas QX211-1 | Yr.Iss. | 1976 | 2.50 | 150 |

1976 Handcrafted Ornaments: Nostalgia - Keepsake

1976	Drummer Boy QX130-1	Yr.Iss.	1976	3.50	160-175
1976	Locomotive QX222-1	Yr.Iss.	1976	3.50	165
1976	Peace on Earth QX223-1	Yr.Iss.	1976	3.50	95-175
1976	Rocking Horse QX128-1	Yr.Iss.	1976	3.50	165

1976 Handcrafted Ornaments: Tree Treats - Keepsake

1976	Angel QX176-1	Yr.Iss.	1976	3.00	150-195
1976	Reindeer QX 178-1	Yr.Iss.	1976	3.00	115
1976	Santa QX177-1	Yr.Iss.	1976	3.00	200-225
1976	Shepherd QX175-1	Yr.Iss.	1976	3.00	95

1976 Handcrafted Ornaments: Twirl-Abouts - Keepsake

1976	Angel QX171-1	Yr.Iss.	1976	4.50	132-165
1976	Partridge QX174-1	Yr.Iss.	1976	4.50	195
1976	Santa QX172-1	Yr.Iss.	1976	4.50	103-125
1976	Soldier QX173-1	Yr.Iss.	1976	4.50	95

1976 Handcrafted Ornaments: Yesteryears - Keepsake

1976	Drummer Boy QX184-1	Yr.Iss.	1976	5.00	122-150
1976	Partridge QX183-1	Yr.Iss.	1976	5.00	115
1976	Santa QX182-1	Yr.Iss.	1976	5.00	165
1976	Train QX181-1	Yr.Iss.	1976	5.00	135-160

1976 Property Ornaments - Keepsake

1976	Betsey Clark (Set/3) QX218-1	Yr.Iss.	1976	4.50	50
1976	Betsey Clark QX210-1	Yr.Iss.	1976	2.50	38-42
1976	Betsey Clark-(4th Ed.)QX 195-1	Yr.Iss.	1976	3.00	75-100
1976	Charmers (Set/2) QX215-1	Yr.Iss.	1976	3.50	55
1976	Currier & Ives QX197-1	Yr.Iss.	1976	3.00	55
1976	Currier & Ives QX209-1	Yr.Iss.	1976	2.50	50
1976	Happy the Snowman (Set/2) QX216-1	Yr.Iss.	1976	3.50	55
1976	Marty Links (Set/2) QX207-1	Yr.Iss.	1976	4.00	65
1976	Norman Rockwell QX196-1	Yr.Iss.	1976	3.00	65
1976	Raggedy Ann QX212-1	Yr.Iss.	1976	2.50	65
1976	Rudolph and Santa QX213-1	Yr.Iss.	1976	2.50	75

YEAR ISSUE		EDITION LIMIT	YEAR RETD.	ISSUE PRICE	*QUOTE U.S.$
1976 Yarn Ornaments - Keepsake					
1976	Caroler QX126-1	Yr.Iss.	1976	1.75	28
1976	Drummer Boy QX123-1	Yr.Iss.	1976	1.75	23
1976	Mrs. Santa QX125-1	Yr.Iss.	1976	1.75	22
1976	Raggedy Andy QX122-1	Yr.Iss.	1976	1.75	40
1976	Raggedy Ann QX121-1	Yr.Iss.	1976	1.75	35
1976	Santa QX124-1	Yr.Iss.	1976	1.75	24

1977 Christmas Expressions Collection - Keepsake

1977	Bell QX154-2	Yr.Iss.	1977	3.50	35
1977	Mandolin QX157-5	Yr.Iss.	1977	3.50	65
1977	Ornaments QX155-5	Yr.Iss.	1977	3.50	65
1977	Wreath QX156-2	Yr.Iss.	1977	3.50	65

1977 Cloth Doll Ornaments - Keepsake

| 1977 | Angel QX220-2 | Yr.Iss. | 1977 | 1.75 | 40-50 |
| 1977 | Santa QX221-5 | Yr.Iss. | 1977 | 1.75 | 55-80 |

1977 Colors of Christmas - Keepsake

1977	Bell QX200-2	Yr.Iss.	1977	3.50	35-45
1977	Candle QX203-5	Yr.Iss.	1977	3.50	55
1977	Joy QX201-5	Yr.Iss.	1977	3.50	45
1977	Wreath QX202-2	Yr.Iss.	1977	3.50	35-55

1977 Commemoratives - Keepsake

1977	Baby's First Christmas QX131-5	Yr.Iss.	1977	3.50	55-75
1977	First Christmas Together QX132-2	Yr.Iss.	1977	3.50	65
1977	For Your New Home QX263-5	Yr.Iss.	1977	3.50	120
1977	Granddaughter QX208-2	Yr.Iss.	1977	3.50	150
1977	Grandmother QX260-2	Yr.Iss.	1977	3.50	150
1977	Grandson QX209-5	Yr.Iss.	1977	3.50	150
1977	Love QX262-2	Yr.Iss.	1977	3.50	95
1977	Mother QX261-5	Yr.Iss.	1977	3.50	75

1977 Decorative Ball Ornaments - Keepsake

1977	Christmas Mouse QX134-2	Yr.Iss.	1977	3.50	65
1977	Rabbit QX139-5	Yr.Iss.	1977	2.50	95
1977	Squirrel QX138-2	Yr.Iss.	1977	2.50	95
1977	Stained Glass QX152-2	Yr.Iss.	1977	3.50	40-70

1977 Holiday Highlights - Keepsake

1977	Drummer Boy QX312-2	Yr.Iss.	1977	3.50	45-65
1977	Joy QX310-2	Yr.Iss.	1977	3.50	45
1977	Peace on Earth QX311-5	Yr.Iss.	1977	3.50	65
1977	Star QX313-5	Yr.Iss.	1977	3.50	45

1977 Metal Ornaments - Keepsake

| 1977 | Snowflake Collection (Set/4) QX 210-2 | Yr.Iss. | 1977 | 5.00 | 95 |

1977 Nostalgia Collection - Keepsake

1977	Angel QX182-2	Yr.Iss.	1977	5.00	95-125
1977	Antique Car QX180-2	Yr.Iss.	1977	5.00	65
1977	Nativity QX181-5	Yr.Iss.	1977	5.00	140
1977	Toys QX183-5	Yr.Iss.	1977	5.00	135

1977 Peanuts Collection - Keepsake

1977	Peanuts (Set/2) QX163-5	Yr.Iss.	1977	4.00	75
1977	Peanuts QX135-5	Yr.Iss.	1977	3.50	60
1977	Peanuts QX162-2	Yr.Iss.	1977	2.50	60

1977 Property Ornaments - Keepsake

1977	Betsey Clark -(5th Ed.) QX264-2	Yr.Iss.	1977	3.50	470
1977	Charmers QX153-5	Yr.Iss.	1977	3.50	50
1977	Currier & Ives QX130-2	Yr.Iss.	1977	3.50	55
1977	Disney (Set/2) QX137-5	Yr.Iss.	1977	4.00	75
1977	Disney QX133-5	Yr.Iss.	1977	3.50	45
1977	Grandma Moses QX150-2	Yr.Iss.	1977	3.50	100-175
1977	Norman Rockwell QX151-5	Yr.Iss.	1977	3.50	70

1977 The Beauty of America Collection - Keepsake

1977	Desert QX159-5	Yr.Iss.	1977	2.50	25
1977	Mountains QX158-2	Yr.Iss.	1977	2.50	15
1977	Seashore QX160-2	Yr.Iss.	1977	2.50	50
1977	Wharf QX161-5	Yr.Iss.	1977	2.50	30-50

1977 Twirl-About Collection - Keepsake

1977	Bellringer QX192-2	Yr.Iss.	1977	6.00	45-55
1977	Della Robia Wreath QX193-5	Yr.Iss.	1977	4.50	90-115
1977	Snowman QX190-2	Yr.Iss.	1977	4.50	60-75
1977	Weather House QX191-5	Yr.Iss.	1977	6.00	45

1977 Yesteryears Collection - Keepsake

1977	Angel QX172-2	Yr.Iss.	1977	6.00	85
1977	House QX170-2	Yr.Iss.	1977	6.00	100-125
1977	Jack-in-the-Box QX171-5	Yr.Iss.	1977	6.00	100-125
1977	Reindeer QX173-5	Yr.Iss.	1977	6.00	110-140

1978 Colors of Christmas - Keepsake

1978	Angel QX354-3	Yr.Iss.	1978	3.50	40
1978	Candle QX357-6	Yr.Iss.	1978	3.50	85
1978	Locomotive QX356-3	Yr.Iss.	1978	3.50	48
1978	Merry Christmas QX355-6	Yr.Iss.	1978	3.50	50

1978 Commemoratives - Keepsake

1978	25th Christmas Together QX269-3	Yr.Iss.	1978	3.50	35
1978	Baby's First Christmas QX200-3	Yr.Iss.	1978	3.50	65-85
1978	First Christmas Together QX218-3	Yr.Iss.	1978	3.50	45
1978	For Your New Home QX217-6	Yr.Iss.	1978	3.50	75
1978	Granddaughter QX216-3	Yr.Iss.	1978	3.50	55
1978	Grandmother QX267-6	Yr.Iss.	1978	3.50	50

YEAR ISSUE		EDITION LIMIT	YEAR RETD.	ISSUE PRICE	*QUOTE U.S.$
1978	Grandson QX215-6	Yr.Iss.	1978	3.50	45
1978	Love QX268-3	Yr.Iss.	1978	3.50	55
1978	Mother QX266-3	Yr.Iss.	1978	3.50	25-35

1978 Decorative Ball Ornaments - Keepsake

1978	Drummer Boy QX252-3	Yr.Iss.	1978	3.50	35-45
1978	Hallmark's Antique Card Collection Design QX220-3	Yr.Iss.	1978	3.50	40
1978	Joy QX254-3	Yr.Iss.	1978	3.50	20-40
1978	Merry Christmas (Santa) QX202-3	Yr.Iss.	1978	3.50	45-55
1978	Nativity QX253-6	Yr.Iss.	1978	3.50	150
1978	The Quail QX251-6	Yr.Iss.	1978	3.50	45
1978	Yesterday's Toys QX250-3	Yr.Iss.	1978	3.50	55

1978 Handcrafted Ornaments - Keepsake

1978	Angel QX139-6	Yr.Iss.	1981	4.50	85-95
1978	Angels QX150-3	Yr.Iss.	1978	8.00	345
1978	Animal Home QX149-6	Yr.Iss.	1978	6.00	125-175
1978	Calico Mouse QX137-6	Yr.Iss.	1978	4.50	95
1978	Carrousel Series-(1st Ed.) QX146-3	Yr.Iss.	1978	6.00	400
1978	Dough Angel QX139-6	Yr.Iss.	1981	5.50	65-95
1978	Dove QX190-3	Yr.Iss.	1978	4.50	65-85
1978	Holly and Poinsettia Ball QX147-6	Yr.Iss.	1978	6.00	85
1978	Joy QX138-3	Yr.Iss.	1978	4.50	75-85
1978	Panorama Ball QX145-6	Yr.Iss.	1978	6.00	135
1978	Red Cardinal QX144-3	Yr.Iss.	1978	4.50	152-175
1978	Rocking Horse QX148-3	Yr.Iss.	1978	6.00	85
1978	Schneeberg Bell QX152-3	Yr.Iss.	1978	8.00	190
1978	Skating Raccoon QX142-3	Yr.Iss.	1978	6.00	85-95

1978 Holiday Chimes - Keepsake

1978	Reindeer Chimes QX320-3	Yr.Iss.	1980	4.50	60

1978 Holiday Highlights - Keepsake

1978	Dove QX310-3	Yr.Iss.	1978	3.50	125
1978	Nativity QX309-6	Yr.Iss.	1978	3.50	70-80
1978	Santa QX307-6	Yr.Iss.	1978	3.50	75
1978	Snowflake QX308-3	Yr.Iss.	1978	3.50	65

1978 Little Trimmers - Keepsake

1978	Drummer Boy QX136-3	Yr.Iss.	1978	2.50	75
1978	Praying Angel QX134-3	Yr.Iss.	1978	2.50	90
1978	Santa QX135-6	Yr.Iss.	1978	2.50	60
1978	Set/4 - QX355-6	Yr.Iss.	1978	10.00	400-425
1978	Thimble Series (Mouse)-(1st Ed.) QX133-6	Yr.Iss.	1978	2.50	265-295

1978 Peanuts Collection - Keepsake

1978	Peanuts QX203-6	Yr.Iss.	1978	2.50	50
1978	Peanuts QX204-3	Yr.Iss.	1978	2.50	60
1978	Peanuts QX205-6	Yr.Iss.	1978	3.50	65
1978	Peanuts QX206-3	Yr.Iss.	1978	3.50	50

1978 Property Ornaments - Keepsake

1978	Betsey Clark-(6th Ed.) QX201-6	Yr.Iss.	1978	3.50	60
1978	Disney QX207-6	Yr.Iss.	1978	3.50	60
1978	Joan Walsh Anglund QX221-6	Yr.Iss.	1978	3.50	65
1978	Spencer Sparrow QX219-6	Yr.Iss.	1978	3.50	50

1978 Yarn Collection - Keepsake

1978	Green Boy QX123-1	Yr.Iss.	1979	2.00	25
1978	Green Girl QX126-1	Yr.Iss.	1979	2.00	20
1978	Mr. Claus QX340-3	Yr.Iss.	1979	2.00	23
1978	Mrs. Claus QX125-1	Yr.Iss.	1979	2.00	22

1979 Collectible Series - Keepsake

1979	Bellringer-(1st Ed.) QX147-9	Yr.Iss.	1979	10.00	400
1979	Carousel-(2nd Ed.) QX146-7	Yr.Iss.	1979	6.50	165-185
1979	Here Comes Santa-(1st Ed.) QX155-9	Yr.Iss.	1979	9.00	425-695
1979	Snoopy and Friends QX141-9	Yr.Iss.	1979	8.00	95-120
1979	Thimble-(2nd Ed.) QX131-9	Yr.Iss.	1980	3.00	150-175

1979 Colors of Christmas - Keepsake

1979	Holiday Wreath QX353-9	Yr.Iss.	1979	3.50	35-45
1979	Partridge in a Pear Tree QX351-9	Yr.Iss.	1979	3.50	35-45
1979	Star Over Bethlehem QX352-7	Yr.Iss.	1979	3.50	75
1979	Words of Christmas QX350-7	Yr.Iss.	1979	3.50	85

1979 Commemoratives - Keepsake

1979	Baby's First Christmas QX154-7	Yr.Iss.	1979	8.00	175
1979	Baby's First Christmas QX208-7	Yr.Iss.	1979	3.50	22-30
1979	Friendship QX203-9	Yr.Iss.	1979	3.50	18
1979	Granddaughter QX211-9	Yr.Iss.	1979	3.50	25
1979	Grandmother QX252-7	Yr.Iss.	1979	3.50	10
1979	Grandson QX210-7	Yr.Iss.	1979	3.50	35
1979	Love QX258-7	Yr.Iss.	1979	3.50	17-25
1979	Mother QX251-9	Yr.Iss.	1979	3.50	15-23
1979	New Home QX212-7	Yr.Iss.	1979	3.50	45
1979	Our First Christmas Together QX209-9	Yr.Iss.	1979	3.50	50-75
1979	Our Twenty-Fifth Anniversary QX 250-7	Yr.Iss.	1979	3.50	17-28
1979	Teacher QX213-9	Yr.Iss.	1979	3.50	15

1979 Decorative Ball Ornaments - Keepsake

1979	Behold the Star QX255-9	Yr.Iss.	1979	3.50	40
1979	Black Angel QX207-9	Yr.Iss.	1979	3.50	25
1979	Christmas Chickadees QX204-7	Yr.Iss.	1979	3.50	30
1979	Christmas Collage QX257-9	Yr.Iss.	1979	3.50	25-35
1979	Christmas Traditions QX253-9	Yr.Iss.	1979	3.50	35

1979	The Light of Christmas QX256-7	Yr.Iss.	1979	3.50	18-30
1979	Night Before Christmas QX214-7	Yr.Iss.	1979	3.50	40

1979 Handcrafted Ornaments - Keepsake

1979	Christmas Eve Surprise QX157-9	Yr.Iss.	1979	6.50	65
1979	Christmas Heart QX140-7	Yr.Iss.	1979	6.50	105-115
1979	Christmas is for Children QX135-9	Yr.Iss.	1980	5.00	83-95
1979	A Christmas Treat QX134-7	Yr.Iss.	1980	5.00	85
1979	The Downhill Run QX145-9	Yr.Iss.	1979	6.50	135-175
1979	The Drummer Boy QX143-9	Yr.Iss.	1979	8.00	90-125
1979	Holiday Scrimshaw QX152-9	Yr.Iss.	1979	4.00	225
1979	Outdoor Fun QX150-7	Yr.Iss.	1979	8.00	125-135
1979	Raccoon QX142-3	Yr.Iss.	1979	6.50	65
1979	Ready for Christmas QX133-9	Yr.Iss.	1979	6.50	95-150
1979	Santa's Here QX138-7	Yr.Iss.	1979	5.00	55-75
1979	The Skating Snowman QX139-9	Yr.Iss.	1980	5.00	65-80

1979 Holiday Chimes - Keepsake

1979	Reindeer Chimes QX320-3	Yr.Iss.	1979	4.50	75
1979	Star Chimes QX137-9	Yr.Iss.	1979	4.50	85

1979 Holiday Highlights - Keepsake

1979	Christmas Angel QX300-7	Yr.Iss.	1979	3.50	95
1979	Christmas Cheer QX303-9	Yr.Iss.	1979	3.50	95
1979	Christmas Tree QX302-7	Yr.Iss.	1979	3.50	75
1979	Love QX304-7	Yr.Iss.	1979	3.50	88
1979	Snowflake QX301-9	Yr.Iss.	1979	3.50	40

1979 Little Trimmer Collection - Keepsake

1979	Angel Delight QX130-7	Yr.Iss.	1979	3.00	80-95
1979	A Matchless Christmas QX132-7	Yr.Iss.	1979	4.00	65-85
1979	Santa QX135-6	Yr.Iss.	1979	3.00	55
1979	Thimble Series-Mouse QX133-6	Yr.Iss.	1979	3.00	150-225

1979 Property Ornaments - Keepsake

1979	Betsey Clark-(7th Ed.) QX 201-9	Yr.Iss.	1979	3.50	33-40
1979	Joan Walsh Anglund QX205-9	Yr.Iss.	1979	3.50	35
1979	Mary Hamilton QX203-7	Yr.Iss.	1979	3.50	20
1979	Peanuts (Time to Trim) QX202-7	Yr.Iss.	1979	3.50	40
1979	Spencer Sparrow QX200-7	Yr.Iss.	1979	3.50	30
1979	Winnie-the-Pooh QX206-7	Yr.Iss.	1979	3.50	40

1979 Sewn Trimmers - Keepsake

1979	Angel Music QX343-9	Yr.Iss.	1980	2.00	20
1979	Merry Santa QX342-7	Yr.Iss.	1980	2.00	20
1979	The Rocking Horse QX340-7	Yr.Iss.	1980	2.00	23
1979	Stuffed Full Stocking QX341-9	Yr.Iss.	1980	2.00	18-25

1979 Yarn Collection - Keepsake

1979	Green Boy QX123-1	Yr.Iss.	1979	2.00	20
1979	Green Girl QX126-1	Yr.Iss.	1979	2.00	18
1979	Mr. Claus QX340-1	Yr.Iss.	1979	2.00	20
1979	Mrs. Claus QX125-1	Yr.Iss.	1979	2.00	20

1980 Collectible Series - Keepsake

1980	The Bellringers-(2nd Ed.) QX157-4	Yr.Iss.	1980	15.00	60-85
1980	Carrousel-(3rd Ed.) QX141-4	Yr.Iss.	1980	7.50	140-165
1980	Frosty Friends-(1st Ed.) QX 137-4	Yr.Iss.	1980	6.50	625
1980	Here Comes Santa-(2nd Ed.) QX 143-4	Yr.Iss.	1980	12.00	170
1980	Norman Rockwell-(1st Ed.) QX306-1	Yr.Iss.	1980	6.50	250
1980	Snoopy & Friends-(2nd Ed.) QX154-1	Yr.Iss.	1980	9.00	100-125
1980	Thimble-(3rd Ed.) QX132-1	Yr.Iss.	1980	4.00	175

1980 Colors of Christmas - Keepsake

1980	Joy QX350-1	Yr.Iss.	1980	4.00	20

1980 Commemoratives - Keepsake

1980	25th Christmas Together QX206-1	Yr.Iss.	1980	4.00	15
1980	Baby's First Christmas QX156-1	Yr.Iss.	1980	12.00	50
1980	Baby's First Christmas QX200-1	Yr.Iss.	1980	4.00	23-35
1980	Beauty of Friendship QX303-4	Yr.Iss.	1980	4.00	60
1980	Black Baby's First Christmas QX229-4	Yr.Iss.	1980	4.00	40
1980	Christmas at Home QX210-1	Yr.Iss.	1980	4.00	35
1980	Christmas Love QX207-4	Yr.Iss.	1980	4.00	40
1980	Dad QX214-1	Yr.Iss.	1980	4.00	9-18
1980	Daughter QX212-1	Yr.Iss.	1980	4.00	40
1980	First Christmas Together QX205-4	Yr.Iss.	1980	4.00	25-40
1980	First Christmas Together QX305-4	Yr.Iss.	1980	4.00	30-55
1980	Friendship QX208-1	Yr.Iss.	1980	4.00	10-20
1980	Granddaughter QX202-1	Yr.Iss.	1980	4.00	35
1980	Grandfather QX231-4	Yr.Iss.	1980	4.00	10-20
1980	Grandmother QX204-1	Yr.Iss.	1980	4.00	20
1980	Grandparents QX213-4	Yr.Iss.	1980	4.00	40
1980	Grandson QX201-4	Yr.Iss.	1980	4.00	18-30
1980	Love QX302-1	Yr.Iss.	1980	4.00	65
1980	Mother and Dad QX230-1	Yr.Iss.	1980	4.00	11-20
1980	Mother QX203-4	Yr.Iss.	1980	4.00	11-23
1980	Mother QX304-1	Yr.Iss.	1980	4.00	35
1980	Son QX211-4	Yr.Iss.	1980	4.00	27-35
1980	Teacher QX209-4	Yr.Iss.	1980	4.00	10-20

1980 Decorative Ball Ornaments - Keepsake

1980	Christmas Cardinals QX224-1	Yr.Iss.	1980	4.00	35
1980	Christmas Choir QX228-1	Yr.Iss.	1980	4.00	85
1980	Christmas Time QX226-1	Yr.Iss.	1980	4.00	30
1980	Happy Christmas QX222-1	Yr.Iss.	1980	4.00	30
1980	Jolly Santa QX227-4	Yr.Iss.	1980	4.00	30

1980	Nativity QX225-4	Yr.Iss.	1980	4.00	125
1980	Santa's Workshop QX223-4	Yr.Iss.	1980	4.00	15-30

1980 Frosted Images - Keepsake

1980	Dove QX308-1	Yr.Iss.	1980	4.00	25-35
1980	Drummer Boy QX309-4	Yr.Iss.	1980	4.00	25
1980	Santa QX310-1	Yr.Iss.	1980	4.00	22

1980 Handcrafted Ornaments - Keepsake

1980	The Animals' Christmas QX150-1	Yr.Iss.	1980	8.00	40-65
1980	Caroling Bear QX140-1	Yr.Iss.	1980	7.50	120-150
1980	Christmas is for Children QX135-9	Yr.Iss.	1980	5.50	95
1980	A Christmas Treat QX134-7	Yr.Iss.	1980	5.50	75
1980	A Christmas Vigil QX144-1	Yr.Iss.	1980	9.00	185
1980	Drummer Boy QX147-4	Yr.Iss.	1980	5.50	75-95
1980	Elfin Antics QX142-1	Yr.Iss.	1980	9.00	225
1980	A Heavenly Nap QX139-4	Yr.Iss.	1981	6.50	40
1980	Heavenly Sounds QX152-1	Yr.Iss.	1980	7.50	72-95
1980	Santa 1980 QX146-1	Yr.Iss.	1980	5.50	95
1980	Santa's Flight QX138-1	Yr.Iss.	1980	5.50	105-115
1980	Skating Snowman QX139-9	Yr.Iss.	1980	5.50	80
1980	The Snowflake Swing QX133-4	Yr.Iss.	1980	4.00	45
1980	A Spot of Christmas Cheer QX153-4	Yr.Iss.	1980	8.00	145

1980 Holiday Chimes - Keepsake

1980	Reindeer Chimes QX320-3	Yr.Iss.	1980	5.50	25
1980	Santa Mobile QX136-1	Yr.Iss.	1981	5.50	25-50
1980	Snowflake Chimes QX165-4	Yr.Iss.	1981	5.50	30

1980 Holiday Highlights - Keepsake

1980	Three Wise Men QX300-1	Yr.Iss.	1980	4.00	30
1980	Wreath QX301-4	Yr.Iss.	1980	4.00	85

1980 Little Trimmers - Keepsake

1980	Christmas Owl QX131-4	Yr.Iss.	1982	4.00	40
1980	Christmas Teddy QX135-4	Yr.Iss.	1980	2.50	80-125
1980	Clothespin Soldier QX134-1	Yr.Iss.	1980	3.50	40
1980	Merry Redbird QX160-1	Yr.Iss.	1980	3.50	50-65
1980	Swingin' on a Star QX130-1	Yr.Iss.	1980	4.00	75-85
1980	Thimble Series-A Christmas Salute QX131-9	Yr.Iss.	1980	4.00	175

1980 Old-Fashioned Christmas Collection - Keepsake

1980	In a Nutshell QX469-7	Yr.Iss.	1988	5.50	24-33

1980 Property Ornaments - Keepsake

1980	Betsey Clark QX307-4	Yr.Iss.	1980	6.50	55
1980	Betsey Clark's Christmas QX194-4	Yr.Iss.	1980	7.50	35
1980	Betsey Clark-(8th Ed.) QX 215-4	Yr.Iss.	1980	4.00	24-30
1980	Disney QX218-1	Yr.Iss.	1980	4.00	30
1980	Joan Walsh Anglund QX217-4	Yr.Iss.	1980	4.00	23-25
1980	Marty Links QX221-4	Yr.Iss.	1980	4.00	11-23
1980	Mary Hamilton QX219-4	Yr.Iss.	1980	4.00	20
1980	Muppets QX220-1	Yr.Iss.	1980	4.00	40
1980	Peanuts QX216-1	Yr.Iss.	1980	4.00	30

1980 Sewn Trimmers - Keepsake

1980	Angel Music QX343-9	Yr.Iss.	1980	2.00	20
1980	Merry Santa QX342-7	Yr.Iss.	1980	2.00	20
1980	The Rocking Horse QX340-7	Yr.Iss.	1980	2.00	22
1980	Stuffed Full Stocking QX341-9	Yr.Iss.	1980	2.00	25

1980 Special Editions - Keepsake

1980	Checking it Twice QX158-4	Yr.Iss.	1981	20.00	175-195
1980	Heavenly Minstrel QX156-7	Yr.Iss.	1980	15.00	345

1980 Yarn Ornaments - Keepsake

1980	Angel QX162-1	Yr.Iss.	1981	3.00	10
1980	Santa QX161-4	Yr.Iss.	1981	3.00	9
1980	Snowman QX163-4	Yr.Iss.	1981	3.00	9
1980	Soldier QX164-1	Yr.Iss.	1981	3.00	9

1981 Collectible Series - Keepsake

1981	Bellringer-(3rd Ed.) QX441-5	Yr.Iss.	1981	15.00	70-95
1981	Carrousel-(4th Ed.) QX427-5	Yr.Iss.	1981	9.00	95
1981	Frosty Friends-(2nd Ed.) QX433-5	Yr.Iss.	1981	8.00	365-425
1981	Here Comes Santa-(3rd Ed. QX438-2	Yr.Iss.	1981	13.00	205-295
1981	Norman Rockwell-(2nd Ed.) QX 511-5	Yr.Iss.	1981	8.50	35-50
1981	Rocking Horse-(1st Ed.) QX 422-2	Yr.Iss.	1981	9.00	625
1981	Snoopy and Friends-(3rd Ed.) QX436-2	Yr.Iss.	1981	12.00	95
1981	Thimble-(4th Ed.) QX413-5	Yr.Iss.	1981	4.50	150

1981 Commemoratives - Keepsake

1981	25th Christmas Together QX504-2	Yr.Iss.	1981	5.50	15
1981	25th Christmas Together QX707-5	Yr.Iss.	1981	4.50	15
1981	50th Christmas QX708-2	Yr.Iss.	1981	4.50	38
1981	Baby's First Christmas QX440-2	Yr.Iss.	1981	13.00	15
1981	Baby's First Christmas QX513-5	Yr.Iss.	1981	8.50	11-20
1981	Baby's First Christmas QX516-2	Yr.Iss.	1981	5.50	30
1981	Baby's First Christmas-Black QX602-2	Yr.Iss.	1981	4.50	25
1981	Baby's First Christmas-Boy QX 601-5	Yr.Iss.	1981	4.50	20-30
1981	Baby's First Christmas-Girl QX 600-2	Yr.Iss.	1981	4.50	16-30
1981	Daughter QX607-5	Yr.Iss.	1981	4.50	20-30
1981	Father QX609-5	Yr.Iss.	1981	4.50	10-30

YEAR ISSUE		EDITION LIMIT	YEAR RETD.	ISSUE PRICE	*QUOTE U.S.$
1981	First Christmas Together QX505-5	Yr.Iss.	1981	5.50	15-35
1981	First Christmas Together QX706-2	Yr.Iss.	1981	4.50	25-35
1981	Friendship QX503-5	Yr.Iss.	1981	5.50	17-25
1981	Friendship QX704-2	Yr.Iss.	1981	4.50	17-30
1981	The Gift of Love QX705-5	Yr.Iss.	1981	4.50	14-20
1981	Godchild QX603-5	Yr.Iss.	1981	4.50	10-20
1981	Granddaughter QX605-5	Yr.Iss.	1981	4.50	13-30
1981	Grandfather QX701-5	Yr.Iss.	1981	4.50	20
1981	Grandmother QX702-2	Yr.Iss.	1981	4.50	10-20
1981	Grandparents QX703-5	Yr.Iss.	1981	4.50	11-20
1981	Grandson QX604-2	Yr.Iss.	1981	4.50	13-30
1981	Home QX709-5	Yr.Iss.	1981	4.50	20
1981	Love QX502-2	Yr.Iss.	1981	5.50	40-50
1981	Mother and Dad QX700-2	Yr.Iss.	1981	4.50	11-25
1981	Mother QX608-2	Yr.Iss.	1981	4.50	6-15
1981	Son QX606-2	Yr.Iss.	1981	4.50	14-30
1981	Teacher QX800-2	Yr.Iss.	1981	4.50	7-15

1981 Crown Classics - Keepsake

1981	Angel QX507-5	Yr.Iss.	1981	4.50	11-20
1981	Tree Photoholder QX515-5	Yr.Iss.	1981	5.50	17-30
1981	Unicorn QX516-5	Yr.Iss.	1981	8.50	15-25

1981 Decorative Ball Ornaments - Keepsake

1981	Christmas 1981 QX809-5	Yr.Iss.	1981	4.50	15-25
1981	Christmas in the Forest QX813-5	Yr.Iss.	1981	4.50	145
1981	Christmas Magic QX810-2	Yr.Iss.	1981	4.50	15-25
1981	Let Us Adore Him QX811-5	Yr.Iss.	1981	4.50	30-60
1981	Merry Christmas QX814-2	Yr.Iss.	1981	4.50	10-20
1981	Santa's Coming QX812-2	Yr.Iss.	1981	4.50	12-27
1981	Santa's Surprise QX815-5	Yr.Iss.	1981	4.50	25
1981	Traditional (Black Santa) QX801-5	Yr.Iss.	1981	4.50	45-90

1981 Fabric Ornaments - Keepsake

1981	Calico Kitty QX403-5	Yr.Iss.	1981	3.00	20
1981	Cardinal Cutie QX400-2	Yr.Iss.	1981	3.00	9-20
1981	Gingham Dog QX402-2	Yr.Iss.	1981	3.00	11-20
1981	Peppermint Mouse QX401-5	Yr.Iss.	1981	3.00	35

1981 Frosted Images - Keepsake

1981	Angel QX509-5	Yr.Iss.	1981	4.00	50-65
1981	Mouse QX508-2	Yr.Iss.	1981	4.00	25
1981	Snowman QX510-2	Yr.Iss.	1981	4.00	25

1981 Hand Crafted Ornaments - Keepsake

1981	Candyville Express QX418-2	Yr.Iss.	1981	7.50	83-95
1981	Checking It Twice QX158-4	Yr.Iss.	1981	23.00	195
1981	Christmas Dreams QX437-5	Yr.Iss.	1981	12.00	200-225
1981	Christmas Fantasy QX155-4	Yr.Iss.	1982	13.00	68-85
1981	Dough Angel QX139-6	Yr.Iss.	1981	5.50	80
1981	Drummer Boy QX148-1	Yr.Iss.	1981	2.50	43
1981	The Friendly Fiddler QX434-2	Yr.Iss.	1981	8.00	75
1981	A Heavenly Nap QX139-4	Yr.Iss.	1981	6.50	50
1981	Ice Fairy QX431-5	Yr.Iss.	1981	6.50	85-100
1981	The Ice Sculptor QX432-2	Yr.Iss.	1982	8.00	90-100
1981	Love and Joy QX425-2	Yr.Iss.	1981	9.00	75-95
1981	Mr. & Mrs. Claus QX448-5	Yr.Iss.	1981	12.00	120-135
1981	Sailing Santa QX439-5	Yr.Iss.	1981	13.00	225-290
1981	Space Santa QX430-2	Yr.Iss.	1981	6.50	70-100
1981	St. Nicholas QX446-2	Yr.Iss.	1981	5.50	40-50
1981	Star Swing QX421-5	Yr.Iss.	1981	5.50	60
1981	Topsy-Turvy Tunes QX429-5	Yr.Iss.	1981	7.50	68-80
1981	A Well-Stocked Stocking QX154-7	Yr.Iss.	1981	9.00	85

1981 Holiday Chimes - Keepsake

1981	Santa Mobile QX136-1	Yr.Iss.	1981	5.50	40
1981	Snowflake Chimes QX165-4	Yr.Iss.	1981	5.50	25
1981	Snowman Chimes QX445-5	Yr.Iss.	1981	5.50	25-30

1981 Holiday Highlights - Keepsake

1981	Christmas Star QX501-5	Yr.Iss.	1981	5.50	17-30
1981	Shepherd Scene QX500-2	Yr.Iss.	1981	5.50	16-27

1981 Little Trimmers - Keepsake

1981	Clothespin Drummer Boy QX408-2	Yr.Iss.	1981	4.50	30-45
1981	Jolly Snowman QX407-5	Yr.Iss.	1981	3.50	40-60
1981	Perky Penguin QX409-5	Yr.Iss.	1982	3.50	45-60
1981	Puppy Love QX406-2	Yr.Iss.	1981	3.50	25-40
1981	The Stocking Mouse QX412-2	Yr.Iss.	1981	4.50	85-100

1981 Plush Animals - Keepsake

1981	Christmas Teddy QX404-2	Yr.Iss.	1981	5.50	22
1981	Raccoon Tunes QX405-5	Yr.Iss.	1981	5.50	15-23

1981 Property Ornaments - Keepsake

1981	Betsey Clark Cameo QX512-2	Yr.Iss.	1981	8.50	20-30
1981	Betsey Clark QX423-5	Yr.Iss.	1981	9.00	50-75
1981	Betsey Clark-(9th Ed.)QX 802-2	Yr.Iss.	1981	4.50	23-35
1981	Disney QX805-5	Yr.Iss.	1981	4.50	15-30
1981	The Divine Miss Piggy QX425-5	Yr.Iss.	1982	12.00	80-95
1981	Joan Walsh Anglund QX804-2	Yr.Iss.	1981	4.50	16-30
1981	Kermit the Frog QX424-2	Yr.Iss.	1981	9.00	80-95
1981	Marty Links QX808-2	Yr.Iss.	1981	4.50	27
1981	Mary Hamilton QX806-2	Yr.Iss.	1981	4.50	10-20
1981	Muppets QX807-5	Yr.Iss.	1981	4.50	15-30
1981	Peanuts QX803-5	Yr.Iss.	1981	4.50	20-40

1982 Brass Ornaments - Keepsake

1982	Brass Bell QX460-6	Yr.Iss.	1982	12.00	18-25
1982	Santa and Reindeer QX467-6	Yr.Iss.	1982	9.00	40-50
1982	Santa's Sleigh QX478-6	Yr.Iss.	1982	9.00	15-30

1982 Collectible Series - Keepsake

YEAR ISSUE		EDITION LIMIT	YEAR RETD.	ISSUE PRICE	*QUOTE U.S.$
1982	The Bellringer-(4th Ed.) QX455-6	Yr.Iss.	1982	15.00	80-95
1982	Carrousel Series-(5th Ed.) QX478-3	Yr.Iss.	1982	10.00	90
1982	Clothespin Soldier-(1st Ed.) QX458-3	Yr.Iss.	1982	5.00	115-125
1982	Frosty Friends-(3rd Ed.) QX452-3	Yr.Iss.	1982	8.00	270-300
1982	Here Comes Santa-(4th Ed.) QX464-3	Yr.Iss.	1982	15.00	105-145
1982	Holiday Wildlife-(1st Ed.) QX313-3	Yr.Iss.	1982	7.00	375-450
1982	Rocking Horse-(2nd Ed.) QX 502-3	Yr.Iss.	1982	10.00	425
1982	Snoopy and Friends-(4th Ed.) QX478-3	Yr.Iss.	1982	13.00	85-125
1982	Thimble-(5th Ed.) QX451-3	Yr.Iss.	1982	5.00	60-75
1982	Tin Locomotive-(1st Ed.) QX460-3	Yr.Iss.	1982	13.00	575-600

1982 Colors of Christmas - Keepsake

1982	Nativity QX308-3	Yr.Iss.	1982	4.50	37-50
1982	Santa's Flight QX308-6	Yr.Iss.	1982	4.50	35

1982 Commemoratives - Keepsake

1982	25th Christmas Together QX211-6	Yr.Iss.	1982	4.50	6-20
1982	50th Christmas Together QX212-3	Yr.Iss.	1982	4.50	6-20
1982	Baby's First Christmas (Boy) QX 216-3	Yr.Iss.	1982	4.50	21-30
1982	Baby's First Christmas (Girl) QX 207-3	Yr.Iss.	1982	4.50	20-28
1982	Baby's First Christmas QX302-3	Yr.Iss.	1982	5.50	20-35
1982	Baby's First Christmas QX455-3	Yr.Iss.	1982	13.00	38-50
1982	Baby's First Christmas-Photoholder QX312-6	Yr.Iss.	1982	6.50	22
1982	Christmas Memories QX311-6	Yr.Iss.	1982	6.50	20
1982	Daughter QX204-6	Yr.Iss.	1982	4.50	20-30
1982	Father QX205-6	Yr.Iss.	1982	4.50	8-20
1982	First Christmas Together QX211-3	Yr.Iss.	1982	4.50	35
1982	First Christmas Together QX302-6	Yr.Iss.	1982	5.50	10-30
1982	First Christmas Together QX306-6	Yr.Iss.	1982	8.50	15-40
1982	First Christmas Together-Locket QX456-3	Yr.Iss.	1982	15.00	25-40
1982	Friendship QX208-6	Yr.Iss.	1982	4.50	8-18
1982	Friendship QX304-6	Yr.Iss.	1982	5.50	15-25
1982	Godchild QX222-6	Yr.Iss.	1982	4.50	11-22
1982	Granddaughter QX224-3	Yr.Iss.	1982	4.50	12-28
1982	Grandfather QX207-6	Yr.Iss.	1982	4.50	8-20
1982	Grandmother QX200-3	Yr.Iss.	1982	4.50	7-18
1982	Grandparents QX214-6	Yr.Iss.	1982	4.50	12-18
1982	Grandson QX224-6	Yr.Iss.	1982	4.50	11-30
1982	Love QX209-6	Yr.Iss.	1982	4.50	8-20
1982	Love QX304-3	Yr.Iss.	1982	5.50	20-30
1982	Moments of Love QX209-3	Yr.Iss.	1982	4.50	7-17
1982	Mother and Dad QX222-3	Yr.Iss.	1982	4.50	8-20
1982	Mother QX205-3	Yr.Iss.	1982	4.50	7-17
1982	New Home QX212-6	Yr.Iss.	1982	4.50	8-22
1982	Sister QX208-3	Yr.Iss.	1982	4.50	13-30
1982	Son QX204-3	Yr.Iss.	1982	4.50	11-30
1982	Teacher QX214-3	Yr.Iss.	1982	4.50	6-15
1982	Teacher QX312-3	Yr.Iss.	1982	6.50	10-18
1982	Teacher-Apple QX301-6	Yr.Iss.	1982	5.50	8-14

1982 Decorative Ball Ornaments - Keepsake

1982	Christmas Angel QX220-6	Yr.Iss.	1982	4.50	10-25
1982	Currier & Ives QX201-3	Yr.Iss.	1982	4.50	10-25
1982	Santa QX221-6	Yr.Iss.	1982	4.50	12-20
1982	Season for Caring QX221-3	Yr.Iss.	1982	4.50	23

1982 Designer Keepsakes - Keepsake

1982	Merry Christmas QX225-6	Yr.Iss.	1982	4.50	10-22
1982	Old Fashioned Christmas QX227-6	Yr.Iss.	1982	4.50	40
1982	Old World Angels QX226-3	Yr.Iss.	1982	4.50	23
1982	Patterns of Christmas QX226-6	Yr.Iss.	1982	4.50	15-22
1982	Stained Glass QX228-3	Yr.Iss.	1982	4.50	12-22
1982	Twelve Days of Christmas QX203-6	Yr.Iss.	1982	4.50	30

1982 Handcrafted Ornaments - Keepsake

1982	Baroque Angel QX456-6	Yr.Iss.	1982	15.00	175
1982	Christmas Fantasy QX155-4	Yr.Iss.	1982	13.00	59
1982	Cloisonne Angel QX145-4	Yr.Iss.	1982	12.00	95
1982	Cowboy Snowman QX480-6	Yr.Iss.	1982	8.00	53
1982	Cycling Santa QX435-5	Yr.Iss.	1983	20.00	120-150
1982	Elfin Artist QX457-3	Yr.Iss.	1982	9.00	42-50
1982	Embroidered Tree - QX494-6	Yr.Iss.	1982	6.50	40
1982	Ice Sculptor QX432-2	Yr.Iss.	1982	8.00	75
1982	Jogging Santa QX457-6	Yr.Iss.	1982	8.00	32-50
1982	Jolly Christmas Tree QX465-3	Yr.Iss.	1982	6.50	80
1982	Peeking Elf QX419-5	Yr.Iss.	1982	6.50	24-40
1982	Pinecone Home QX461-3	Yr.Iss.	1982	8.00	160-175
1982	Raccoon Surprises QX479-3	Yr.Iss.	1982	9.00	132-145
1982	Santa Bell QX148-7	Yr.Iss.	1982	15.00	45-60
1982	Santa's Workshop QX450-3	Yr.Iss.	1982	10.00	78-85
1982	The Spirit of Christmas QX452-6	Yr.Iss.	1982	10.00	107-125
1982	Three Kings QX307-3	Yr.Iss.	1982	8.50	17-27
1982	Tin Soldier QX483-6	Yr.Iss.	1982	6.50	30-50

1982 Holiday Chimes - Keepsake

1982	Bell Chimes QX494-3	Yr.Iss.	1982	5.50	30

YEAR ISSUE		EDITION LIMIT	YEAR RETD.	ISSUE PRICE	*QUOTE U.S.$
1982	Tree Chimes QX484-6	Yr.Iss.	1982	5.50	50

1982 Holiday Highlights - Keepsake

1982	Angel QX309-6	Yr.Iss.	1982	5.50	16-35
1982	Christmas Magic QX311-3	Yr.Iss.	1982	5.50	22-30
1982	Christmas Sleigh QX309-3	Yr.Iss.	1982	5.50	55-75

1982 Ice Sculptures - Keepsake

1982	Arctic Penguin QX300-3	Yr.Iss.	1982	4.00	8-20
1982	Snowy Seal QX300-6	Yr.Iss.	1982	4.00	13-20

1982 Little Trimmers - Keepsake

1982	Christmas Kitten QX454-3	Yr.Iss.	1982	4.00	35
1982	Christmas Owl QX131-4	Yr.Iss.	1982	4.50	35
1982	Cookie Mouse QX454-6	Yr.Iss.	1982	4.50	49-60
1982	Dove Love QX462-3	Yr.Iss.	1982	4.50	47-55
1982	Jingling Teddy QX477-6	Yr.Iss.	1982	4.00	23-40
1982	Merry Moose QX415-5	Yr.Iss.	1982	5.50	38-60
1982	Musical Angel QX459-6	Yr.Iss.	1982	5.50	112-125
1982	Perky Penguin QX409-5	Yr.Iss.	1982	4.00	35

1982 Property Ornaments - Keepsake

1982	Betsey Clark QX305-6	Yr.Iss.	1982	8.50	17-25
1982	Betsey Clark-(10th Ed.) QX215-6	Yr.Iss.	1982	4.50	24-34
1982	Disney QX217-3	Yr.Iss.	1982	4.50	20-35
1982	The Divine Miss Piggy QX425-5	Yr.Iss.	1982	12.00	125
1982	Joan Walsh Anglund QX219-3	Yr.Iss.	1982	4.50	8-20
1982	Kermit the Frog QX495-6	Yr.Iss.	1982	11.00	62-95
1982	Mary Hamilton QX217-6	Yr.Iss.	1982	4.50	10-22
1982	Miss Piggy and Kermit QX218-3	Yr.Iss.	1982	4.50	28-40
1982	Muppets Party QX218-6	Yr.Iss.	1982	4.50	31-40
1982	Norman Rockwell QX202-3	Yr.Iss.	1982	4.50	10-28
1982	Norman Rockwell-(3rd Ed.) QX305-3	Yr.Iss.	1982	8.50	28
1982	Peanuts QX200-6	Yr.Iss.	1982	4.50	19-30

1983 Collectible Series - Keepsake

1983	The Bellringer-(5th Ed.)QX 403-9	Yr.Iss.	1983	15.00	95-135
1983	Carrousel-(6th Ed.) QX401-9	Yr.Iss.	1983	11.00	49
1983	Clothespin Soldier-(2nd Ed.) QX402-9	Yr.Iss.	1983	5.00	34-50
1983	Frosty Friends-(4th Ed.) QX400-7	Yr.Iss.	1983	8.00	215-295
1983	Here Comes Santa-(5th Ed.) QX 403-7	Yr.Iss.	1983	13.00	250-295
1983	Holiday Wildlife-(2nd Ed.) QX 309-9	Yr.Iss.	1983	7.00	51-75
1983	Porcelain Bear-(1st Ed.) QX428-9	Yr.Iss.	1983	7.00	50-75
1983	Rocking Horse-(3rd Ed.) QX417-7	Yr.Iss.	1983	10.00	298
1983	Snoopy and Friends-(5th Ed.) QX416-9	Yr.Iss.	1983	13.00	85
1983	Thimble-(6th Ed.) QX401-7	Yr.Iss.	1983	5.00	30
1983	Tin Locomotive-(2nd Ed.) QX404-9	Yr.Iss.	1983	13.00	275-295

1983 Commemoratives - Keepsake

1983	25th Christmas Together QX224-7	Yr.Iss.	1983	4.50	18
1983	Baby's First Christmas QX200-7	Yr.Iss.	1983	4.50	20-30
1983	Baby's First Christmas QX200-9	Yr.Iss.	1983	4.50	20-28
1983	Baby's First Christmas QX301-9	Yr.Iss.	1983	7.50	8-18
1983	Baby's First Christmas QX302-9	Yr.Iss.	1983	7.00	15-35
1983	Baby's First Christmas QX402-7	Yr.Iss.	1983	14.00	30-40
1983	Baby's Second Christmas QX226-7	Yr.Iss.	1983	4.50	25-35
1983	Child's Third Christmas QX226-9	Yr.Iss.	1983	4.50	30
1983	Daughter QX203-7	Yr.Iss.	1983	4.50	30-43
1983	First Christmas Together QX208-9	Yr.Iss.	1983	4.50	30
1983	First Christmas Together QX301-7	Yr.Iss.	1983	7.50	25-35
1983	First Christmas Together QX306-9	Yr.Iss.	1983	6.00	10-25
1983	First Christmas Together QX310-7	Yr.Iss.	1983	6.00	12-25
1983	First Christmas Together-Brass Locket QX 432-9	Yr.Iss.	1983	15.00	30-45
1983	Friendship QX207-7	Yr.Iss.	1983	4.50	20
1983	Friendship QX305-9	Yr.Iss.	1983	6.00	8-20
1983	Godchild QX201-7	Yr.Iss.	1983	4.50	12-18
1983	Grandchild's First Christmas QX 312-9	Yr.Iss.	1983	6.00	10-23
1983	Grandchild's First Christmas QX430-9	Yr.Iss.	1983	14.00	21-38
1983	Granddaughter QX202-7	Yr.Iss.	1983	4.50	30
1983	Grandmother QX205-7	Yr.Iss.	1983	4.50	19
1983	Grandparents QX429-9	Yr.Iss.	1983	6.50	11-22
1983	Grandson QX201-9	Yr.Iss.	1983	4.50	12-30
1983	Love Is a Song QX223-9	Yr.Iss.	1983	4.50	30
1983	Love QX207-9	Yr.Iss.	1983	4.50	43
1983	Love QX305-7	Yr.Iss.	1983	6.00	9-19
1983	Love QX310-9	Yr.Iss.	1983	6.00	40
1983	Love QX422-7	Yr.Iss.	1983	13.00	16-40
1983	Mom and Dad QX429-7	Yr.Iss.	1983	6.50	14-24
1983	Mother QX306-7	Yr.Iss.	1983	6.00	20
1983	New Home QX210-7	Yr.Iss.	1983	4.50	15-30
1983	Sister QX206-9	Yr.Iss.	1983	4.50	23
1983	Son QX202-9	Yr.Iss.	1983	4.50	25-35
1983	Teacher QX224-9	Yr.Iss.	1983	4.50	8-17
1983	Teacher QX304-9	Yr.Iss.	1983	6.00	13
1983	Tenth Christmas Together QX430-7	Yr.Iss.	1983	6.50	30

1983 Crown Classics - Keepsake

1983	Enameled Christmas Wreath QX 311-9	Yr.Iss.	1983	9.00	7-15
1983	Memories to Treasure QX303-7	Yr.Iss.	1983	7.00	25

YEAR ISSUE	EDITION LIMIT	YEAR RETD.	ISSUE PRICE	*QUOTE U.S.$
1983 Mother and Child QX302-7	Yr.Iss.	1983	7.50	20-40

1983 Decorative Ball Ornaments - Keepsake

YEAR ISSUE	EDITION LIMIT	YEAR RETD.	ISSUE PRICE	*QUOTE U.S.$
1983 1983 QX220-9	Yr.Iss.	1983	4.50	17-30
1983 Angels QX219-7	Yr.Iss.	1983	5.00	24
1983 The Annunciation QX216-7	Yr.Iss.	1983	4.50	30
1983 Christmas Joy QX216-9	Yr.Iss.	1983	4.50	15-30
1983 Christmas Wonderland QX221-9	Yr.Iss.	1983	4.50	95
1983 Currier & Ives QX215-9	Yr.Iss.	1983	4.50	8-19
1983 Here Comes Santa QX217-7	Yr.Iss.	1983	4.50	38
1983 An Old Fashioned Christmas QX2217-9	Yr.Iss.	1983	4.50	30
1983 Oriental Butterflies QX218-7	Yr.Iss.	1983	4.50	30
1983 Season's Greeting QX219-9	Yr.Iss.	1983	4.50	10-22
1983 The Wise Men QX220-7	Yr.Iss.	1983	4.50	30-40

1983 Handcrafted Ornaments - Keepsake

YEAR ISSUE	EDITION LIMIT	YEAR RETD.	ISSUE PRICE	*QUOTE U.S.$
1983 Angel Messenger QX408-7	Yr.Iss.	1983	6.50	75-95
1983 Baroque Angels QX422-9	Yr.Iss.	1983	13.00	130
1983 Bell Wreath QX420-9	Yr.Iss.	1983	6.50	35
1983 Brass Santa QX423-9	Yr.Iss.	1983	9.00	23
1983 Caroling Owl QX411-7	Yr.Iss.	1983	4.50	25-40
1983 Christmas Kitten QX454-3	Yr.Iss.	1983	4.00	35
1983 Christmas Koala QX419-9	Yr.Iss.	1983	4.00	20-33
1983 Cycling Santa QX435-5	Yr.Iss.	1983	20.00	195
1983 Embroidered Heart QX421-7	Yr.Iss.	1983	6.50	25
1983 Embroidered Stocking QX479-6	Yr.Iss.	1983	6.50	10-22
1983 Hitchhiking Santa QX424-7	Yr.Iss.	1983	8.00	40
1983 Holiday Puppy QX412-7	Yr.Iss.	1983	3.50	16-30
1983 Jack Frost QX407-9	Yr.Iss.	1983	9.00	60
1983 Jolly Santa QX425-9	Yr.Iss.	1983	3.50	21-35
1983 Madonna and Child QX428-7	Yr.Iss.	1983	12.00	26-45
1983 Mailbox Kitten QX415-7	Yr.Iss.	1983	6.50	40-60
1983 Mountain Climbing Santa QX407-7	Yr.Iss.	1984	6.50	22-40
1983 Mouse in Bell QX419-7	Yr.Iss.	1983	10.00	65
1983 Mouse on Cheese QX413-7	Yr.Iss.	1983	6.50	35-45
1983 Old-Fashioned Santa QX409-9	Yr.Iss.	1983	11.00	54-65
1983 Peppermint Penguin QX408-9	Yr.Iss.	1983	6.50	29-49
1983 Porcelain Doll, Diana QX423-7	Yr.Iss.	1983	9.00	16-32
1983 Rainbow Angel QX416-7	Yr.Iss.	1983	5.50	112-125
1983 Santa's Many Faces QX311-6	Yr.Iss.	1983	4.50	30
1983 Santa's on His Way QX426-9	Yr.Iss.	1983	10.00	35
1983 Santa's Workshop QX450-3	Yr.Iss.	1983	10.00	60
1983 Scrimshaw Reindeer QX424-9	Yr.Iss.	1983	8.00	17-35
1983 Skating Rabbit QX409-7	Yr.Iss.	1983	8.00	55
1983 Ski Lift Santa QX418-7	Yr.Iss.	1983	8.00	50-75
1983 Skiing Fox QX420-7	Yr.Iss.	1983	8.00	30-40
1983 Sneaker Mouse QX400-9	Yr.Iss.	1983	4.50	30-40
1983 Tin Rocking Horse QX414-9	Yr.Iss.	1983	6.50	50
1983 Unicorn QX426-7	Yr.Iss.	1983	10.00	40-65

1983 Holiday Highlights - Keepsake

YEAR ISSUE	EDITION LIMIT	YEAR RETD.	ISSUE PRICE	*QUOTE U.S.$
1983 Christmas Stocking QX303-9	Yr.Iss.	1983	6.00	15-40
1983 Star of Peace QX304-7	Yr.Iss.	1983	6.00	20
1983 Time for Sharing QX307-7	Yr.Iss.	1983	6.00	40

1983 Holiday Sculptures - Keepsake

YEAR ISSUE	EDITION LIMIT	YEAR RETD.	ISSUE PRICE	*QUOTE U.S.$
1983 Heart QX307-9	Yr.Iss.	1983	4.00	50
1983 Santa QX308-7	Yr.Iss.	1983	4.00	17-35

1983 Property Ornaments - Keepsake

YEAR ISSUE	EDITION LIMIT	YEAR RETD.	ISSUE PRICE	*QUOTE U.S.$
1983 Betsey Clark QX404-7	Yr.Iss.	1983	6.50	35
1983 Betsey Clark QX440-1	Yr.Iss.	1983	9.00	35
1983 Betsey Clark-(11th Ed.) QX211-9	Yr.Iss.	1983	4.50	30
1983 Disney QX212-9	Yr.Iss.	1983	4.50	45
1983 Kermit the Frog QX495-6	Yr.Iss.	1983	11.00	35
1983 Mary Hamilton QX213-7	Yr.Iss.	1983	4.50	40
1983 Miss Piggy QX405-7	Yr.Iss.	1983	13.00	225
1983 The Muppets QX214-7	Yr.Iss.	1983	4.50	40-50
1983 Norman Rockwell QX215-7	Yr.Iss.	1983	4.50	50
1983 Norman Rockwell-(4th Ed.) QX 300-7	Yr.Iss.	1983	7.50	35
1983 Peanuts QX212-7	Yr.Iss.	1983	4.50	14-38
1983 Shirt Tales QX214-9	Yr.Iss.	1983	4.50	25

1984 Collectible Series - Keepsake

YEAR ISSUE	EDITION LIMIT	YEAR RETD.	ISSUE PRICE	*QUOTE U.S.$
1984 Art Masterpiece-(1st Ed.) QX349-4	Yr.Iss.	1984	6.50	18
1984 The Bellringer-(6th & Final Ed.) QX438-4	Yr.Iss.	1984	15.00	30-45
1984 Betsey Clark-(12th Ed.) QX249-4	Yr.Iss.	1984	5.00	24-34
1984 Clothespin Soldier-(3rd Ed.) QX447-1	Yr.Iss.	1984	5.00	20-30
1984 Frosty Friends-(5th Ed.) QX437-1	Yr.Iss.	1984	8.00	65-85
1984 Here Comes Santa-(6th Ed.) QX438-4	Yr.Iss.	1984	13.00	65-90
1984 Holiday Wildlife-(3rd Ed.) QX 347-4	Yr.Iss.	1984	7.25	20-30
1984 Norman Rockwell-(5th Ed.) QX341-1	Yr.Iss.	1984	7.50	24-34
1984 Nostalgic Houses and Shops-(1st Ed.) QX 448-1	Yr.Iss.	1984	13.00	180-190
1984 Porcelain Bear-(2nd Ed.) QX454-1	Yr.Iss.	1984	7.00	35-45
1984 Rocking Horse-(4th Ed.) QX435-4	Yr.Iss.	1984	10.00	58-95
1984 Thimble-(7th Ed.) QX430-4	Yr.Iss.	1984	5.00	40-60
1984 Tin Locomotive-(3rd Ed.) QX440-4	Yr.Iss.	1984	14.00	65-90
1984 The Twelve Days of Christmas-(1st Ed.) QX 3484	Yr.Iss.	1984	6.00	285
1984 Wood Childhood Ornaments-(1st Ed.) QX 439-4	Yr.Iss.	1984	6.50	45

1984 Commemoratives - Keepsake

YEAR ISSUE	EDITION LIMIT	YEAR RETD.	ISSUE PRICE	*QUOTE U.S.$
1984 Baby's First Christmas QX300-1	Yr.Iss.	1984	7.00	25-35
1984 Baby's First Christmas QX340-1	Yr.Iss.	1984	6.00	20-40
1984 Baby's First Christmas QX438-1	Yr.Iss.	1984	14.00	40-50
1984 Baby's First Christmas QX904-1	Yr.Iss.	1984	16.00	65
1984 Baby's First Christmas-Boy QX240-4	Yr.Iss.	1984	4.50	20-28
1984 Baby's First Christmas-Girl QX340-1	Yr.Iss.	1984	4.50	20-40
1984 Baby's Second Christmas QX241-1	Yr.Iss.	1984	4.50	25-35
1984 Baby-sitter QX253-1	Yr.Iss.	1984	4.50	6-14
1984 Child's Third Christmas QX261-1	Yr.Iss.	1984	4.50	30
1984 Daughter QX244-4	Yr.Iss.	1984	4.50	30
1984 Father QX257-1	Yr.Iss.	1984	6.00	20
1984 First Christmas Together QX245-1	Yr.Iss.	1984	4.50	20-30
1984 First Christmas Together QX340-4	Yr.Iss.	1984	7.50	25-35
1984 First Christmas Together QX342-1	Yr.Iss.	1984	6.00	20-30
1984 First Christmas Together QX436-4	Yr.Iss.	1984	15.00	35-45
1984 First Christmas Together QX904-4	Yr.Iss.	1984	16.00	45-65
1984 Friendship QX248-1	Yr.Iss.	1984	4.50	15
1984 From Our Home to Yours QX248-4	Yr.Iss.	1984	4.50	50
1984 The Fun of Friendship QX343-1	Yr.Iss.	1984	6.00	10-30
1984 A Gift of Friendship QX260-4	Yr.Iss.	1984	4.50	25
1984 Godchild QX242-1	Yr.Iss.	1984	4.50	20
1984 Grandchild's First Christmas QX257-4	Yr.Iss.	1984	4.50	7-17
1984 Grandchild's First Christmas QX460-1	Yr.Iss.	1984	11.00	30
1984 Granddaughter QX243-1	Yr.Iss.	1984	4.50	30
1984 Grandmother QX244-1	Yr.Iss.	1984	4.50	13-18
1984 Grandparents QX256-1	Yr.Iss.	1984	4.50	18
1984 Grandson QX242-4	Yr.Iss.	1984	4.50	18-30
1984 Gratitude QX344-4	Yr.Iss.	1984	6.00	12
1984 Heartful of Love QX443-4	Yr.Iss.	1984	10.00	45
1984 Love QX255-4	Yr.Iss.	1984	4.50	25
1984 Love...the Spirit of Christmas QX247-4	Yr.Iss.	1984	4.50	15-40
1984 The Miracle of Love QX342-4	Yr.Iss.	1984	6.00	33
1984 Mother and Dad QX258-1	Yr.Iss.	1984	6.50	18
1984 Mother QX343-4	Yr.Iss.	1984	6.00	12-25
1984 New Home QX245-4	Yr.Iss.	1984	4.50	85
1984 Sister QX259-4	Yr.Iss.	1984	6.50	20-32
1984 Son QX243-4	Yr.Iss.	1984	4.50	10-30
1984 Teacher QX249-1	Yr.Iss.	1984	4.50	6-15
1984 Ten Years Together QX258-4	Yr.Iss.	1984	6.50	11-25
1984 Twenty-Five Years Together QX259-1	Yr.Iss.	1984	6.50	20

1984 Holiday Humor - Keepsake

YEAR ISSUE	EDITION LIMIT	YEAR RETD.	ISSUE PRICE	*QUOTE U.S.$
1984 Bell Ringer Squirrel QX443-1	Yr.Iss.	1984	10.00	20-40
1984 Christmas Owl QX444-1	Yr.Iss.	1984	6.00	20-33
1984 A Christmas Prayer QX246-1	Yr.Iss.	1984	4.50	10-23
1984 Flights of Fantasy QX256-4	Yr.Iss.	1984	4.50	20
1984 Fortune Cookie Elf QX452-4	Yr.Iss.	1984	4.50	37
1984 Frisbee Puppy QX444-4	Yr.Iss.	1984	5.00	40-50
1984 Marathon Santa QX456-4	Yr.Iss.	1984	8.00	43
1984 Mountain Climbing Santa QX407-7	Yr.Iss.	1984	6.50	35
1984 Musical Angel QX434-4	Yr.Iss.	1984	5.50	70
1984 Napping Mouse QX435-1	Yr.Iss.	1984	5.50	38-50
1984 Peppermint 1984 QX452-1	Yr.Iss.	1984	4.50	55
1984 Polar Bear Drummer QX430-1	Yr.Iss.	1984	4.50	30
1984 Raccoon's Christmas QX447-7	Yr.Iss.	1984	9.00	34-55
1984 Reindeer Racetrack QX254-4	Yr.Iss.	1984	4.50	10-23
1984 Roller Skating Rabbit QX457-1	Yr.Iss.	1985	5.00	18-35
1984 Santa Mouse QX433-4	Yr.Iss.	1984	4.50	47
1984 Santa Star QX450-4	Yr.Iss.	1984	5.50	33-40
1984 Snowmobile Santa QX431-4	Yr.Iss.	1984	6.50	35-40
1984 Snowshoe Penguin QX453-1	Yr.Iss.	1984	6.50	50-60
1984 Snowy Seal QX450-1	Yr.Iss.	1985	4.00	12-24
1984 Three Kittens in a Mitten QX431-1	Yr.Iss.	1985	8.00	32-50

1984 Keepsake Magic Ornaments - Keepsake

YEAR ISSUE	EDITION LIMIT	YEAR RETD.	ISSUE PRICE	*QUOTE U.S.$
1984 All Are Precious QLX704-1	Yr.Iss.	1985	8.00	13-25
1984 Brass Carrousel QLX707-1	Yr.Iss.	1984	9.00	95
1984 Christmas in the Forest QLX703-4	Yr.Iss.	1984	8.00	15
1984 City Lights QLX701-4	Yr.Iss.	1984	10.00	47-53
1984 Nativity QLX700-1	Yr.Iss.	1984	12.00	18-30
1984 Santa's Arrival QLX702-4	Yr.Iss.	1984	13.00	47-65
1984 Santa's Workshop QLX700-4	Yr.Iss.	1984	13.00	45-62
1984 Stained Glass QLX703-1	Yr.Iss.	1984	8.00	20
1984 Sugarplum Cottage QLX701-1	Yr.Iss.	1986	11.00	40
1984 Village Church QLX702-1	Yr.Iss.	1985	15.00	35-50

1984 Limited Edition - Keepsake

YEAR ISSUE	EDITION LIMIT	YEAR RETD.	ISSUE PRICE	*QUOTE U.S.$
1984 Classical Angel QX459-1	Yr.Iss.	1984	28.00	65-100

1984 Property Ornaments - Keepsake

YEAR ISSUE	EDITION LIMIT	YEAR RETD.	ISSUE PRICE	*QUOTE U.S.$
1984 Betsey Clark Angel QX462-4	Yr.Iss.	1984	9.00	19-35
1984 Currier & Ives QX250-1	Yr.Iss.	1984	4.50	23
1984 Disney QX250-4	Yr.Iss.	1984	4.50	23-43
1984 Katybeth QX463-1	Yr.Iss.	1984	9.00	17-33
1984 Kit QX453-4	Yr.Iss.	1984	5.50	28
1984 Muffin QX442-1	Yr.Iss.	1984	5.50	25-33
1984 The Muppets QX251-1	Yr.Iss.	1984	4.50	20-35
1984 Norman Rockwell QX251-4	Yr.Iss.	1984	4.50	35
1984 Peanuts QX252-1	Yr.Iss.	1984	4.50	20-33
1984 Shirt Tales QX252-4	Yr.Iss.	1984	4.50	17
1984 Snoopy and Woodstock QX439-1	Yr.Iss.	1984	7.50	95

1984 Traditional Ornaments - Keepsake

YEAR ISSUE	EDITION LIMIT	YEAR RETD.	ISSUE PRICE	*QUOTE U.S.$
1984 Alpine Elf QX452-1	Yr.Iss.	1984	6.00	32-40

YEAR ISSUE	EDITION LIMIT	YEAR RETD.	ISSUE PRICE	*QUOTE U.S.$
1984 Amanda QX432-1	Yr.Iss.	1984	9.00	20-30
1984 Chickadee QX451-4	Yr.Iss.	1984	6.00	33-40
1984 Christmas Memories Photoholder QX300-4	Yr.Iss.	1984	6.50	25
1984 Cuckoo Clock QX455-1	Yr.Iss.	1984	10.00	47
1984 Gift of Music QX451-2	Yr.Iss.	1984	15.00	62-95
1984 Holiday Friendship QX445-1	Yr.Iss.	1984	13.00	30
1984 Holiday Jester QX437-4	Yr.Iss.	1984	11.00	20-35
1984 Holiday Starburst QX253-4	Yr.Iss.	1984	5.00	20
1984 Madonna and Child QX344-1	Yr.Iss.	1984	6.00	50
1984 Needlepoint Wreath QX459-4	Yr.Iss.	1984	6.50	13
1984 Nostalgic Sled QX442-4	Yr.Iss.	1984	6.00	12-30
1984 Old Fashioned Rocking Horse QX346-4	Yr.Iss.	1984	7.50	10-20
1984 Peace on Earth QX341-4	Yr.Iss.	1984	4.50	33
1984 Santa QX458-4	Yr.Iss.	1984	7.50	10-20
1984 Santa Sulky Driver QX436-1	Yr.Iss.	1984	9.00	20-35
1984 A Savior is Born QX254-1	Yr.Iss.	1984	4.50	33
1984 Twelve Days of Christmas QX 415-9	Yr.Iss.	1984	15.00	95
1984 Uncle Sam QX449-1	Yr.Iss.	1984	6.00	50
1984 White Christmas QX905-1	Yr.Iss.	1984	16.00	70-95

1985 Collectible Series - Keepsake

YEAR ISSUE	EDITION LIMIT	YEAR RETD.	ISSUE PRICE	*QUOTE U.S.$
1985 Art Masterpiece-(2nd Ed.) QX377-2	Yr.Iss.	1985	6.75	15
1985 Betsey Clark-(13th & final Ed.)) QX263-2	Yr.Iss.	1985	5.00	24-35
1985 Clothespin Soldier-(4th Ed.) QX471-5	Yr.Iss.	1985	5.50	20-30
1985 Frosty Friends-(6th Ed.) QX482-2	Yr.Iss.	1985	8.50	45-65
1985 Here Comes Santa-(7th Ed.) QX496-5	Yr.Iss.	1985	14.00	45-65
1985 Holiday Wildlife-(4th Ed.) QX376-5	Yr.Iss.	1985	7.50	20-30
1985 Miniature Creche-(1st Ed.) QX482-5	Yr.Iss.	1985	8.75	20-40
1985 Norman Rockwell-(6th Ed.) QX374-5	Yr.Iss.	1985	7.50	20-29
1985 Nostalgic Houses and Shops-(2nd Ed.) QX497-5	Yr.Iss.	1985	13.75	90-130
1985 Porcelain Bear-(3rd Ed.) QX479-2	Yr.Iss.	1985	7.50	36-60
1985 Rocking Horse-(5th Ed.) QX493-2	Yr.Iss.	1985	10.75	50-80
1985 Thimble-(8th Ed.) QX472-5	Yr.Iss.	1985	5.50	24-35
1985 Tin Locomotive-(4th Ed.) QX497-2	Yr.Iss.	1985	14.75	50-80
1985 Twelve Days of Christmas-(2nd Ed.) QX371-2	Yr.Iss.	1985	6.50	50-70
1985 Windows of the World-(1st Ed.) QX490-2	Yr.Iss.	1985	9.75	82-97
1985 Wood Childhood Ornaments-(2nd Ed.) QX472-2	Yr.Iss.	1985	7.00	34-50

1985 Commemoratives - Keepsake

YEAR ISSUE	EDITION LIMIT	YEAR RETD.	ISSUE PRICE	*QUOTE U.S.$
1985 Baby Locket QX401-2	Yr.Iss.	1985	16.00	35-38
1985 Baby's First Christmas QX260-2	Yr.Iss.	1985	5.00	20-30
1985 Baby's First Christmas QX370-2	Yr.Iss.	1985	5.75	22
1985 Baby's First Christmas QX478-2	Yr.Iss.	1985	7.00	18
1985 Baby's First Christmas QX499-2	Yr.Iss.	1985	15.00	40-50
1985 Baby's First Christmas QX499-5	Yr.Iss.	1985	16.00	50
1985 Baby's Second Christmas QX478-5	Yr.Iss.	1985	6.00	25-35
1985 Baby-sitter QX264-2	Yr.Iss.	1985	4.75	13
1985 Child's Third Christmas QX475-5	Yr.Iss.	1985	6.00	25
1985 Daughter QX503-2	Yr.Iss.	1985	5.50	15-25
1985 Father QX376-2	Yr.Iss.	1985	6.50	10
1985 First Christmas Together QX261-2	Yr.Iss.	1985	4.75	30
1985 First Christmas Together QX370-5	Yr.Iss.	1985	6.75	15
1985 First Christmas Together QX400-5	Yr.Iss.	1985	16.75	25-35
1985 First Christmas Together QX493-5	Yr.Iss.	1985	13.00	30-40
1985 First Christmas Together QX507-2	Yr.Iss.	1985	8.00	17
1985 Friendship QX378-5	Yr.Iss.	1985	6.75	18
1985 Friendship QX506-2	Yr.Iss.	1985	7.75	15
1985 From Our House to Yours QX520-2	Yr.Iss.	1985	7.75	15
1985 Godchild QX380-2	Yr.Iss.	1985	6.75	15
1985 Good Friends QX265-2	Yr.Iss.	1985	4.75	15-30
1985 Grandchild's First Christmas QX260-5	Yr.Iss.	1985	5.00	15
1985 Grandchild's First Christmas QX495-5	Yr.Iss.	1985	11.00	20
1985 Granddaughter QX263-5	Yr.Iss.	1985	4.75	30
1985 Grandmother QX262-5	Yr.Iss.	1985	4.75	18
1985 Grandparents QX380-5	Yr.Iss.	1985	7.00	10
1985 Grandson QX262-2	Yr.Iss.	1985	4.75	10-25
1985 Heart Full of Love QX378-2	Yr.Iss.	1985	6.75	10-20
1985 Holiday Heart QX498-2	Yr.Iss.	1985	8.00	10-20
1985 Love at Christmas QX371-5	Yr.Iss.	1985	5.75	25-40
1985 Mother and Dad QX509-2	Yr.Iss.	1985	7.75	15
1985 Mother QX372-2	Yr.Iss.	1985	6.75	10-20
1985 New Home QX269-5	Yr.Iss.	1985	4.75	30
1985 Niece QX520-5	Yr.Iss.	1985	5.75	11
1985 Sister QX506-5	Yr.Iss.	1985	7.25	20
1985 Son QX502-5	Yr.Iss.	1985	5.50	38
1985 Special Friends QX372-5	Yr.Iss.	1985	5.75	10
1985 Teacher QX505-2	Yr.Iss.	1985	6.00	20
1985 Twenty-Five Years Together QX500-5	Yr.Iss.	1985	8.00	20
1985 With Appreciation QX375-2	Yr.Iss.	1985	6.75	10

1985 Country Christmas Collection - Keepsake

YEAR ISSUE	EDITION LIMIT	YEAR RETD.	ISSUE PRICE	*QUOTE U.S.$
1985 Country Goose QX518-5	Yr.Iss.	1985	7.75	14
1985 Old-Fashioned Doll QX519-5	Yr.Iss.	1985	15.00	40
1985 Rocking Horse Memories QX518-2	Yr.Iss.	1985	10.00	14
1985 Sheep at Christmas QX517-5	Yr.Iss.	1985	8.25	30

Column headers: YEAR ISSUE | EDITION LIMIT | YEAR RETD. | ISSUE PRICE | *QUOTE U.S.$

1985	Whirligig Santa QX519-2	Yr.Iss.	1985	13.00	25

1985 Heirloom Christmas Collection - Keepsake

1985	Charming Angel QX512-5	Yr.Iss.	1985	9.75	10-25
1985	Keepsake Basket QX514-5	Yr.Iss.	1985	15.00	15
1985	Lacy Heart QX511-2	Yr.Iss.	1985	8.75	15-30
1985	Snowflake QX510-5	Yr.Iss.	1985	6.50	18
1985	Victorian Lady QX513-2	Yr.Iss.	1985	9.50	25

1985 Holiday Humor - Keepsake

1985	Baker Elf QX491-2	Yr.Iss.	1986	5.75	30
1985	Beary Smooth Ride QX480-5	Yr.Iss.	1985	6.50	20
1985	Bottlecap Fun Bunnies QX481-5	Yr.Iss.	1985	7.75	33
1985	Candy Apple Mouse QX470-5	Yr.Iss.	1985	6.50	65-75
1985	Children in the Shoe QX490-5	Yr.Iss.	1985	9.50	45
1985	Dapper Penguin QX477-2	Yr.Iss.	1985	5.00	30
1985	Do Not Disturb Bear QX481-2	Yr.Iss.	1985	7.75	16-33
1985	Doggy in a Stocking QX474-2	Yr.Iss.	1985	5.50	25-40
1985	Engineering Mouse QX473-5	Yr.Iss.	1985	5.50	15-25
1985	Ice-Skating Owl QX476-5	Yr.Iss.	1985	5.00	15-25
1985	Kitty Mischief QX474-5	Yr.Iss.	1985	5.00	15-25
1985	Lamb in Legwarmers QX480-2	Yr.Iss.	1985	7.00	15-25
1985	Merry Mouse QX403-2	Yr.Iss.	1985	4.50	20-30
1985	Mouse Wagon QX476-2	Yr.Iss.	1985	5.75	37-60
1985	Nativity Scene QX264-5	Yr.Iss.	1985	4.75	30
1985	Night Before Christmas QX449-4	Yr.Iss.	1985	13.00	20-40
1985	Roller Skating Rabbit QX457-1	Yr.Iss.	1985	5.00	19
1985	Santa's Ski Trip QX496-2	Yr.Iss.	1985	12.00	41-60
1985	Skateboard Raccoon QX473-2	Yr.Iss.	1986	6.50	25-43
1985	Snow-Pitching Snowman QX470-2	Yr.Iss.	1986	4.50	25
1985	Snowy Seal QX450-1	Yr.Iss.	1985	4.00	16
1985	Soccer Beaver QX477-5	Yr.Iss.	1986	6.50	15-25
1985	Stardust Angel QX475-2	Yr.Iss.	1985	5.75	30
1985	Sun and Fun Santa QX492-2	Yr.Iss.	1985	7.75	40
1985	Swinging Angel Bell QX492-5	Yr.Iss.	1985	11.00	40
1985	Three Kittens in a Mitten QX431-1	Yr.Iss.	1985	8.00	35
1985	Trumpet Panda QX471-2	Yr.Iss.	1985	4.50	15-25

1985 Keepsake Magic Ornaments - Keepsake

1985	All Are Precious QLX704-1	Yr.Iss.	1985	8.00	12-25
1985	Baby's First Christmas QLX700-5	Yr.Iss.	1985	17.00	30-40
1985	Chris Mouse-(1st Ed.) QLX703-2	Yr.Iss.	1985	13.00	88
1985	Christmas Eve Visit QLX710-5	Yr.Iss.	1985	12.00	33
1985	Katybeth QLX710-2	Yr.Iss.	1985	10.75	30-43
1985	Little Red Schoolhouse QLX711-2	Yr.Iss.	1985	15.75	70-95
1985	Love Wreath QLX702-5	Yr.Iss.	1985	8.50	19-30
1985	Mr. and Mrs. Santa QLX705-2	Yr.Iss.	1985	15.00	73-90
1985	Nativity 1200 QLX700-1	Yr.Iss.	1985	12.00	18-30
1985	Santa's Workshop QLX700-4	Yr.Iss.	1985	13.00	58
1985	Season of Beauty QLX712-2	Yr.Iss.	1985	8.00	19-29
1985	Sugarplum Cottage QLX701-1	Yr.Iss.	1985	11.00	45
1985	Swiss Cheese Lane QLX706-5	Yr.Iss.	1985	13.00	34-50
1985	Village Church QLX702-1	Yr.Iss.	1985	15.00	35-50

1985 Limited Edition - Keepsake

| 1985 | Heavenly Trumpeter QX405-2 | Yr.Iss. | 1985 | 28.00 | 75-100 |

1985 Property Ornaments - Keepsake

1985	Betsey Clark QX508-5	Yr.Iss.	1985	8.50	30
1985	A Disney Christmas QX271-2	Yr.Iss.	1985	4.75	30
1985	Fraggle Rock Holiday QX265-5	Yr.Iss.	1985	4.75	23
1985	Hugga Bunch QX271-5	Yr.Iss.	1985	5.00	15-30
1985	Kit the Shepherd QX484-5	Yr.Iss.	1985	5.75	28
1985	Merry Shirt Tales QX267-2	Yr.Iss.	1985	4.75	20
1985	Muffin the Angel QX483-5	Yr.Iss.	1985	5.75	24
1985	Norman Rockwell QX266-2	Yr.Iss.	1985	4.75	30
1985	Peanuts QX266-5	Yr.Iss.	1985	4.75	35
1985	Rainbow Brite and Friends QX 268-2	Yr.Iss.	1985	4.75	10-20
1985	Snoopy and Woodstock QX491-5	Yr.Iss.	1985	7.50	65

1985 Traditional Ornaments - Keepsake

1985	Candle Cameo QX374-2	Yr.Iss.	1985	6.75	15
1985	Christmas Treats QX507-5	Yr.Iss.	1985	5.50	10-18
1985	Nostalgic Sled QX442-4	Yr.Iss.	1985	6.00	20
1985	Old-Fashioned Wreath QX373-5	Yr.Iss.	1985	7.50	25
1985	Peaceful Kingdom QX373-2	Yr.Iss.	1985	5.75	20-30
1985	Porcelain Bird QX479-5	Yr.Iss.	1985	6.50	20-30
1985	Santa Pipe QX494-2	Yr.Iss.	1985	9.50	15-25
1985	Sewn Photoholder QX379-5	Yr.Iss.	1985	7.00	10-25
1985	The Spirit of Santa Claus -(Special Ed.) QX 498-5	Yr.Iss.	1985	23.00	75-95

1986 Christmas Medley Collection - Keepsake

1986	Christmas Guitar QX512-6	Yr.Iss.	1986	7.00	15
1986	Favorite Tin Drum QX514-3	Yr.Iss.	1986	8.50	30
1986	Festive Treble Clef QX513-3	Yr.Iss.	1986	8.75	10-28
1986	Holiday Horn QX514-6	Yr.Iss.	1986	8.00	17-33
1986	Joyful Carolers QX513-6	Yr.Iss.	1986	9.75	30-40

1986 Collectible Series - Keepsake

1986	Art Masterpiece-(3rd & Final Ed.) QX350-6	Yr.Iss.	1986	6.75	23
1986	Betsey Clark: Home for Christmas-(1st Ed.) QX277-6	Yr.Iss.	1986	5.00	20-35
1986	Clothespin Soldier-(5th Ed.) QX406-3	Yr.Iss.	1986	5.50	23
1986	Frosty Friends-(7th Ed.) QX405-3	Yr.Iss.	1986	8.50	62-70
1986	Here Comes Santa-(8th Ed.) QX404-3	Yr.Iss.	1986	14.00	43-65

1986	Holiday Wildlife-(5th Ed.) QX321-6	Yr.Iss.	1986	7.50	20-30
1986	Miniature Creche-(2nd Ed.) QX407-6	Yr.Iss.	1986	9.00	35-45
1986	Mr. and Mrs. Claus-(1st Ed.) QX402-6	Yr.Iss.	1986	13.00	85-100
1986	Norman Rockwell-(7th Ed.) QX321-3	Yr.Iss.	1986	7.75	20-28
1986	Nostalgic Houses and Shops-(3rd Ed.) QX403-3	Yr.Iss.	1986	13.75	200-300
1986	Porcelain Bear-(4th Ed.) QX405-6	Yr.Iss.	1986	7.75	35-45
1986	Reindeer Champs-(1st Ed.) QX422-3	Yr.Iss.	1986	7.50	115-145
1986	Rocking Horse-(6th Ed.) QX401-6	Yr.Iss.	1986	10.75	60-75
1986	Thimble-(9th Ed.) QX406-6	Yr.Iss.	1986	5.75	20-30
1986	Tin Locomotive-(5th Ed.) QX403-6	Yr.Iss.	1986	14.75	50-75
1986	Twelve Days of Christmas-(3rd Ed.) QX378-6	Yr.Iss.	1986	6.50	45-55
1986	Windows of the World-(2nd Ed.) QX408-3	Yr.Iss.	1986	10.00	20-55
1986	Wood Childhood Ornaments-(3rd Ed.) QX407-3	Yr.Iss.	1986	7.50	21-33

1986 Commemoratives - Keepsake

1986	Baby Locket QX412-3	Yr.Iss.	1986	16.00	27-35
1986	Baby's First Christmas Photoholder QX379-2	Yr.Iss.	1986	8.00	25-30
1986	Baby's First Christmas QX271-3	Yr.Iss.	1986	5.50	15-25
1986	Baby's First Christmas QX380-3	Yr.Iss.	1986	6.00	22
1986	Baby's First Christmas QX412-6	Yr.Iss.	1986	9.00	35
1986	Baby's Second Christmas QX413-3	Yr.Iss.	1986	6.50	25
1986	Baby-Sitter QX275-6	Yr.Iss.	1986	4.75	7-12
1986	Child's Third Christmas QX413-6	Yr.Iss.	1986	6.50	25
1986	Daughter QX430-6	Yr.Iss.	1986	5.75	32-50
1986	Father QX431-3	Yr.Iss.	1986	6.50	8-15
1986	Fifty Years Together QX400-6	Yr.Iss.	1986	10.00	20
1986	First Christmas Together QX270-3	Yr.Iss.	1986	4.75	30
1986	First Christmas Together QX379-3	Yr.Iss.	1986	7.00	20
1986	First Christmas Together QX400-3	Yr.Iss.	1986	16.00	28
1986	First Christmas Together QX409-6	Yr.Iss.	1986	12.00	35
1986	Friends Are Fun QX272-3	Yr.Iss.	1986	4.75	40
1986	Friendship Greeting QX427-3	Yr.Iss.	1986	8.00	15
1986	Friendship's Gift QX381-6	Yr.Iss.	1986	6.00	15
1986	From Our Home to Yours QX383-3	Yr.Iss.	1986	6.00	15
1986	Godchild QX271-6	Yr.Iss.	1986	4.75	15
1986	Grandchild's First Christmas QX411-6	Yr.Iss.	1986	10.00	15
1986	Granddaughter QX273-6	Yr.Iss.	1986	4.75	25
1986	Grandmother QX274-3	Yr.Iss.	1986	4.75	8-16
1986	Grandparents QX432-3	Yr.Iss.	1986	7.50	10-23
1986	Grandson QX273-3	Yr.Iss.	1986	4.75	25
1986	Gratitude QX432-6	Yr.Iss.	1986	6.00	10
1986	Husband QX383-6	Yr.Iss.	1986	8.00	14-25
1986	Joy of Friends QX382-3	Yr.Iss.	1986	6.75	18
1986	Loving Memories QX409-3	Yr.Iss.	1986	9.00	35
1986	Mother and Dad QX431-6	Yr.Iss.	1986	7.50	18
1986	Mother QX382-6	Yr.Iss.	1986	7.00	10-20
1986	Nephew QX381-3	Yr.Iss.	1986	6.25	10
1986	New Home QX274-6	Yr.Iss.	1986	4.75	65
1986	Niece QX426-6	Yr.Iss.	1986	6.00	10
1986	Season of the Heart QX270-6	Yr.Iss.	1986	4.75	10-18
1986	Sister QX380-6	Yr.Iss.	1986	6.75	15
1986	Son QX430-3	Yr.Iss.	1986	5.75	25-35
1986	Sweetheart QX409-6	Yr.Iss.	1986	11.00	50-70
1986	Teacher QX275-3	Yr.Iss.	1986	4.75	6-12
1986	Ten Years Together QX401-3	Yr.Iss.	1986	7.50	25
1986	Timeless Love QX379-6	Yr.Iss.	1986	6.00	30
1986	Twenty-Five Years Together QX410-3	Yr.Iss.	1986	8.00	25

1986 Country Treasures Collection - Keepsake

1986	Country Sleigh QX511-3	Yr.Iss.	1986	10.00	25
1986	Little Drummers QX511-6	Yr.Iss.	1986	12.50	18-35
1986	Nutcracker Santa QX512-3	Yr.Iss.	1986	10.00	25-50
1986	Remembering Christmas QX510-6	Yr.Iss.	1986	8.75	30
1986	Welcome, Christmas QX510-3	Yr.Iss.	1986	8.25	20-35

1986 Holiday Humor - Keepsake

1986	Acorn Inn QX424-3	Yr.Iss.	1986	8.50	28
1986	Beary Smooth Ride QX480-5	Yr.Iss.	1986	6.50	20
1986	Chatty Penguin QX417-6	Yr.Iss.	1986	5.75	15-25
1986	Cookies for Santa QX414-6	Yr.Iss.	1986	4.50	17-30
1986	Do Not Disturb Bear QX481-2	Yr.Iss.	1986	7.75	15-25
1986	Happy Christmas to Owl QX418-3	Yr.Iss.	1986	6.00	15-25
1986	Heavenly Dreamer QX417-3	Yr.Iss.	1986	5.75	22-35
1986	Jolly Hiker QX483-2	Yr.Iss.	1987	5.00	20-30
1986	Kitty Mischief QX474-5	Yr.Iss.	1986	5.00	25
1986	Li'l Jingler QX419-3	Yr.Iss.	1987	6.75	22-40
1986	Merry Koala QX415-3	Yr.Iss.	1987	5.00	23
1986	Merry Mouse QX403-2	Yr.Iss.	1986	4.50	22
1986	Mouse in the Moon QX416-6	Yr.Iss.	1987	5.50	20
1986	Open Me First QX422-6	Yr.Iss.	1986	7.25	15-30
1986	Playful Possum QX425-3	Yr.Iss.	1986	11.00	33
1986	Popcorn Mouse QX421-3	Yr.Iss.	1986	6.75	40-55
1986	Puppy's Best Friend QX420-3	Yr.Iss.	1986	6.50	17-30
1986	Rah Rah Rabbit QX421-6	Yr.Iss.	1986	7.00	40
1986	Santa's Hot Tub QX426-3	Yr.Iss.	1986	12.00	58
1986	Skateboard Raccoon QX473-2	Yr.Iss.	1986	6.50	40
1986	Ski Tripper QX420-6	Yr.Iss.	1986	6.75	12-22
1986	Snow Buddies QX423-6	Yr.Iss.	1986	8.00	38
1986	Snow-Pitching Snowman QX470-2	Yr.Iss.	1986	4.50	23

1986	Soccer Beaver QX477-5	Yr.Iss.	1986	6.50	25
1986	Special Delivery QX415-6	Yr.Iss.	1986	5.00	17-30
1986	Tipping the Scales QX418-6	Yr.Iss.	1986	6.75	15-30
1986	Touchdown Santa QX423-3	Yr.Iss.	1986	8.00	42
1986	Treetop Trio QX424-6	Yr.Iss.	1987	11.00	32
1986	Walnut Shell Rider QX419-6	Yr.Iss.	1986	6.00	18-30
1986	Wynken, Blynken and Nod QX424-6	Yr.Iss.	1986	9.75	42

1986 Lighted Ornament Collection - Keepsake

1986	Baby's First Christmas QLX710-3	Yr.Iss.	1986	19.50	45
1986	Chris Mouse-(2nd Ed.) QLX705-6	Yr.Iss.	1986	13.00	75
1986	Christmas Classics-(1st Ed.) QLX704-3	Yr.Iss.	1986	17.50	85
1986	Christmas Sleigh Ride QLX701-2	Yr.Iss.	1986	24.50	120-145
1986	First Christmas Together QLX707-3	Yr.Iss.	1986	14.00	43
1986	General Store QLX705-3	Yr.Iss.	1986	15.75	43-60
1986	Gentle Blessings QLX708-3	Yr.Iss.	1986	15.00	110-175
1986	Keep on Glowin' QLX707-6	Yr.Iss.	1987	10.00	37-50
1986	Merry Christmas Bell QLX709-3	Yr.Iss.	1986	8.50	15-25
1986	Mr. and Mrs. Santa QLX705-2	Yr.Iss.	1986	14.50	65-95
1986	Santa and Sparky-(1st Ed.) QLX703-3	Yr.Iss.	1986	22.00	95
1986	Santa On His Way QLX711-5	Yr.Iss.	1986	15.00	63-75
1986	Santa's Snack QLX706-6	Yr.Iss.	1986	10.00	58
1986	Sharing Friendship QLX706-3	Yr.Iss.	1986	8.50	16
1986	Sugarplum Cottage QLX701-1	Yr.Iss.	1986	11.00	45
1986	Village Express QLX707-2	Yr.Iss.	1987	24.50	87-125

1986 Limited Edition - Keepsake

| 1986 | Magical Unicorn QX429-3 | Yr.Iss. | 1986 | 27.50 | 90 |

1986 Property Ornaments - Keepsake

1986	Heathcliff QX436-3	Yr.Iss.	1986	7.50	20-33
1986	Katybeth QX435-3	Yr.Iss.	1986	7.00	25
1986	Norman Rockwell QX276-3	Yr.Iss.	1986	4.75	25
1986	Paddington Bear QX436-6	Yr.Iss.	1986	6.00	25
1986	Peanuts QX276-6	Yr.Iss.	1986	4.75	30
1986	Shirt Tales Parade QX277-3	Yr.Iss.	1986	4.75	18
1986	Snoopy and Woodstock QX434-6	Yr.Iss.	1986	8.00	50
1986	The Statue of Liberty QX384-3	Yr.Iss.	1986	6.00	10-25

1986 Special Edition - Keepsake

| 1986 | Jolly St. Nick QX429-6 | Yr.Iss. | 1986 | 22.50 | 50-75 |

1986 Traditional Ornaments - Keepsake

1986	Bluebird QX428-3	Yr.Iss.	1986	7.25	40-50
1986	Christmas Beauty QX322-3	Yr.Iss.	1986	6.00	10
1986	Glowing Christmas Tree QX428-6	Yr.Iss.	1986	7.00	15
1986	Heirloom Snowflake QX515-3	Yr.Iss.	1986	6.75	10-22
1986	Holiday Jingle Bell QX404-6	Yr.Iss.	1986	16.00	30-55
1986	The Magi QX272-6	Yr.Iss.	1986	4.75	15
1986	Mary Emmerling:American Country Collection QX275-2	Yr.Iss.	1986	7.95	23
1986	Memories to Cherish QX427-6	Yr.Iss.	1986	7.50	25
1986	Star Brighteners QX322-6	Yr.Iss.	1986	6.00	17

1987 Artists' Favorites - Keepsake

1987	Beary Special QX455-7	Yr.Iss.	1987	4.75	15-30
1987	December Showers QX448-7	Yr.Iss.	1987	5.50	36
1987	Three Men in a Tub QX454-7	Yr.Iss.	1987	8.00	20-30
1987	Wee Chimney Sweep QX451-9	Yr.Iss.	1987	6.25	18-30

1987 Christmas Pizzazz Collection - Keepsake

1987	Christmas Fun Puzzle QX467-9	Yr.Iss.	1987	8.00	15-30
1987	Doc Holiday QX467-7	Yr.Iss.	1987	8.00	43
1987	Happy Holidata QX471-7	Yr.Iss.	1988	6.50	15-30
1987	Holiday Hourglass QX470-7	Yr.Iss.	1987	8.00	25
1987	Jolly Follies QX466-9	Yr.Iss.	1987	8.50	40
1987	Mistletoad QX468-7	Yr.Iss.	1987	7.00	30
1987	St. Louie Nick QX453-9	Yr.Iss.	1988	7.75	16-33

1987 Collectible Series - Keepsake

1987	Betsey Clark:Home for Christmas-(2nd Ed.) QX272-7	Yr.Iss.	1987	5.00	17-25
1987	Clothespin Soldier-(6th & Final Ed.) QX480-7	Yr.Iss.	1987	5.50	20-30
1987	Collector's Plate-(1st Ed.) QX481-7	Yr.Iss.	1987	8.00	65
1987	Frosty Friends-(8th Ed.) QX440-9	Yr.Iss.	1987	8.50	43-60
1987	Here Comes Santa-(9th Ed.) QX484-7	Yr.Iss.	1987	14.00	45-75
1987	Holiday Heirloom-(1st Ed./ limited Ed.)QX485-7	Yr.Iss.	1987	25.00	48
1987	Holiday Wildlife-(6th Ed.) QX371-9	Yr.Iss.	1987	7.50	15-25
1987	Miniature Creche-(3rd Ed.) QX481-9	Yr.Iss.	1987	9.00	30-38
1987	Mr. and Mrs. Claus-(2nd Ed.) QX483-7	Yr.Iss.	1987	13.25	42-65
1987	Norman Rockwell-(8th Ed.) QX370-7	Yr.Iss.	1987	7.75	20-25
1987	Nostalgic Houses and Shops-(4th Ed.) QX483-9	Yr.Iss.	1987	14.00	57-75
1987	Porcelain Bear-(5th Ed.) QX442-7	Yr.Iss.	1987	7.75	25-40
1987	Reindeer Champs-(2nd Ed.) QX480-9	Yr.Iss.	1987	7.50	35-55
1987	Rocking Horse-(7th Ed.) QX482-9	Yr.Iss.	1987	10.75	41-70
1987	Thimble-(10th Ed.) QX441-9	Yr.Iss.	1987	5.75	20-30

YEAR ISSUE	EDITION LIMIT	YEAR RETD.	ISSUE PRICE	*QUOTE U.S.$
1987 Tin Locomotive-(6th Ed.) QX484-9	Yr.Iss.	1987	14.75	45-65
1987 Twelve Days of Christmas -(4th Ed.) QX370-9	Yr.Iss.	1987	6.50	27-35
1987 Windows of the World-(3rd Ed.) QX482-7	Yr.Iss.	1987	10.00	25
1987 Wood Childhood Ornaments-(4th Ed.) QX441-7	Yr.Iss.	1987	7.50	17-27

1987 Commemoratives - Keepsake

YEAR ISSUE	EDITION LIMIT	YEAR RETD.	ISSUE PRICE	*QUOTE U.S.$
1987 Baby Locket QX461-7	Yr.Iss.	1987	15.00	25-35
1987 Baby's First Christmas Photoholder QX4661-9	Yr.Iss.	1987	7.50	30
1987 Baby's First Christmas QX372-9	Yr.Iss.	1987	6.00	20
1987 Baby's First Christmas QX411-3	Yr.Iss.	1987	9.75	30
1987 Baby's First Christmas-Baby Boy QX274-9	Yr.Iss.	1987	4.75	20
1987 Baby's First Christmas-Baby Girl QX274-7	Yr.Iss.	1987	4.75	20
1987 Baby's Second Christmas QX460-7	Yr.Iss.	1987	5.75	32
1987 Babysitter QX279-7	Yr.Iss.	1987	4.75	10-20
1987 Child's Third Christmas QX459-9	Yr.Iss.	1987	5.75	30
1987 Dad QX462-9	Yr.Iss.	1987	6.00	40
1987 Daughter QX463-7	Yr.Iss.	1987	5.75	30-35
1987 Fifty Years Together QX443-7	Yr.Iss.	1987	8.00	25
1987 First Christmas Together QX272-9	Yr.Iss.	1987	4.75	25
1987 First Christmas Together QX371-9	Yr.Iss.	1987	6.50	25
1987 First Christmas Together QX445-9	Yr.Iss.	1987	8.00	20-38
1987 First Christmas Together QX446-7	Yr.Iss.	1987	9.50	38
1987 First Christmas Together QX446-9	Yr.Iss.	1987	15.00	30
1987 From Our Home to Yours QX279-9	Yr.Iss.	1987	4.75	50
1987 Godchild QX276-7	Yr.Iss.	1987	4.75	20
1987 Grandchild's First Christmas QX460-9	Yr.Iss.	1987	9.00	25
1987 Granddaughter QX374-7	Yr.Iss.	1987	6.00	15-25
1987 Grandmother QX277-9	Yr.Iss.	1987	4.75	20
1987 Grandparents QX277-7	Yr.Iss.	1987	4.75	18
1987 Grandson QX276-9	Yr.Iss.	1987	4.75	30
1987 Heart in Blossom QX372-7	Yr.Iss.	1987	6.00	25
1987 Holiday Greetings QX375-7	Yr.Iss.	1987	6.00	13
1987 Husband QX373-9	Yr.Iss.	1987	7.00	12
1987 Love is Everywhere QX278-7	Yr.Iss.	1987	4.75	25
1987 Mother and Dad QX462-7	Yr.Iss.	1987	7.00	20
1987 Mother QX373-7	Yr.Iss.	1987	6.50	25
1987 New Home QX376-7	Yr.Iss.	1987	6.00	30
1987 Niece QX275-9	Yr.Iss.	1987	4.75	13
1987 Sister QX474-7	Yr.Iss.	1987	6.00	15
1987 Son QX463-9	Yr.Iss.	1987	5.75	45
1987 Sweetheart QX447-9	Yr.Iss.	1987	11.00	15-30
1987 Teacher QX466-7	Yr.Iss.	1987	5.75	21
1987 Ten Years Together QX444-7	Yr.Iss.	1987	7.00	25
1987 Time for Friends QX280-7	Yr.Iss.	1987	4.75	22
1987 Twenty-Five Years Together QX443-9	Yr.Iss.	1987	7.50	15-30
1987 Warmth of Friendship QX375-9	Yr.Iss.	1987	6.00	12
1987 Word of Love QX447-7	Yr.Iss.	1987	8.00	10-22

1987 Holiday Humor - Keepsake

YEAR ISSUE	EDITION LIMIT	YEAR RETD.	ISSUE PRICE	*QUOTE U.S.$
1987 Bright Christmas Dreams QX440-7	Yr.Iss.	1987	7.25	75-85
1987 Chocolate Chipmunk QX456-7	Yr.Iss.	1987	6.00	50
1987 Christmas Cuddle QX453-7	Yr.Iss.	1987	5.75	25-35
1987 Dr. Seuss:The Grinch's Christmas QX278-3	Yr.Iss.	1987	4.75	50-60
1987 Fudge Forever QX444-9	Yr.Iss.	1987	5.00	25-40
1987 Happy Santa QX456-9	Yr.Iss.	1987	4.75	30
1987 Hot Dogger QX471-9	Yr.Iss.	1987	6.50	25-30
1987 Icy Treat QX450-9	Yr.Iss.	1987	4.50	20-30
1987 Jack Frosting QX449-9	Yr.Iss.	1987	7.00	30-50
1987 Jammie Pies QX283-9	Yr.Iss.	1987	4.75	18
1987 Jogging Through the Snow QX457-7	Yr.Iss.	1987	7.25	25-40
1987 Jolly Hiker QX483-2	Yr.Iss.	1987	5.00	18
1987 Joy Ride QX440-7	Yr.Iss.	1987	11.50	45-55
1987 Let It Snow QX458-9	Yr.Iss.	1987	6.50	15-25
1987 Li'l Jingler QX419-3	Yr.Iss.	1987	6.75	22-36
1987 Merry Koala QX415-3	Yr.Iss.	1987	5.00	17
1987 Mouse in the Moon QX416-6	Yr.Iss.	1987	5.50	21
1987 Nature's Decorations QX273-9	Yr.Iss.	1987	4.75	35
1987 Night Before Christmas QX451-7	Yr.Iss.	1988	6.50	19-33
1987 Owliday Wish QX455-9	Yr.Iss.	1988	6.50	14-25
1987 Paddington Bear QX472-7	Yr.Iss.	1987	5.50	25-30
1987 Peanuts QX281-9	Yr.Iss.	1987	4.75	34
1987 Pretty Kitten QX448-9	Yr.Iss.	1987	11.00	35
1987 Raccoon Biker QX458-7	Yr.Iss.	1987	7.00	15-30
1987 Reindoggy QX452-7	Yr.Iss.	1988	5.75	20-35
1987 Santa at the Bat QX457-9	Yr.Iss.	1987	7.75	20-30
1987 Seasoned Greetings QX454-9	Yr.Iss.	1987	6.25	15-30
1987 Sleepy Santa QX450-7	Yr.Iss.	1987	6.25	35-40
1987 Snoopy and Woodstock QX472-9	Yr.Iss.	1987	7.25	40-50
1987 Spots 'n Stripes QX452-9	Yr.Iss.	1987	5.50	15-25
1987 Treetop Dreams QX459-7	Yr.Iss.	1988	6.75	15-30
1987 Treetop Trio QX425-6	Yr.Iss.	1987	11.00	25
1987 Walnut Shell Rider QX419-6	Yr.Iss.	1987	6.00	18

1987 Keepsake Collector's Club - Keepsake

YEAR ISSUE	EDITION LIMIT	YEAR RETD.	ISSUE PRICE	*QUOTE U.S.$
1987 Carrousel Reindeer QXC580-7	Yr.Iss.	1987	Unkn.	55-65
1987 Wreath of Memories QXC580-9	Yr.Iss.	1988	Unkn.	55

1987 Keepsake Magic Ornaments - Keepsake

YEAR ISSUE	EDITION LIMIT	YEAR RETD.	ISSUE PRICE	*QUOTE U.S.$
1987 Angelic Messengers QLX711-3	Yr.Iss.	1987	18.75	53-60
1987 Baby's First Christmas QLX704-9	Yr.Iss.	1987	13.50	45
1987 Bright Noel QLX705-9	Yr.Iss.	1987	7.00	18-33
1987 Chris Mouse-(3rd Ed.) QLX705-7	Yr.Iss.	1987	11.00	60
1987 Christmas Classics-(2nd Ed.) QLX702-9	Yr.Iss.	1987	16.00	50-75
1987 Christmas Morning QLX701-3	Yr.Iss.	1988	24.50	33-50
1987 First Christmas Together QLX708-7	Yr.Iss.	1987	11.50	45
1987 Good Cheer Blimp QLX704-6	Yr.Iss.	1987	16.00	52-59
1987 Keeping Cozy QLX704-7	Yr.Iss.	1987	11.75	30-37
1987 Lacy Brass Snowflake QLX709-7	Yr.Iss.	1987	11.50	20
1987 Loving Holiday QLX701-6	Yr.Iss.	1987	22.00	38-55
1987 Memories are Forever Photoholder QLX706-7	Yr.Iss.	1987	8.50	33
1987 Meowy Christmas QLX708-9	Yr.Iss.	1987	10.00	45-63
1987 Santa and Sparky-(2nd Ed.) QLX701-9	Yr.Iss.	1987	19.50	65-75
1987 Season for Friendship QLX706-9	Yr.Iss.	1987	8.50	11-20
1987 Train Station QLX703-9	Yr.Iss.	1987	12.75	50

1987 Lighted Ornament Collection - Keepsake

YEAR ISSUE	EDITION LIMIT	YEAR RETD.	ISSUE PRICE	*QUOTE U.S.$
1987 Keep on Glowin' QLX707-6	Yr.Iss.	1987	10.00	37
1987 Village Express QLX707-2	Yr.Iss.	1987	24.50	87-120

1987 Limited Edition - Keepsake

YEAR ISSUE	EDITION LIMIT	YEAR RETD.	ISSUE PRICE	*QUOTE U.S.$
1987 Christmas is Gentle QX444-9	Yr.Iss.	1987	17.50	45-85
1987 Christmas Time Mime QX442-9	Yr.Iss.	1987	27.50	45-55

1987 Old-Fashioned Christmas Collection - Keepsake

YEAR ISSUE	EDITION LIMIT	YEAR RETD.	ISSUE PRICE	*QUOTE U.S.$
1987 Country Wreath QX470-9	Yr.Iss.	1987	5.75	30
1987 Folk Art Santa QX474-9	Yr.Iss.	1987	5.25	20-33
1987 In a Nutshell QX469-7	Yr.Iss.	1988	5.50	25-34
1987 Little Whittler QX469-9	Yr.Iss.	1987	6.00	25-33
1987 Nostalgic Rocker QX468-9	Yr.Iss.	1987	6.50	26-33

1987 Special Edition - Keepsake

YEAR ISSUE	EDITION LIMIT	YEAR RETD.	ISSUE PRICE	*QUOTE U.S.$
1987 Favorite Santa QX445-7	Yr.Iss.	1987	22.50	35-45

1987 Traditional Ornaments - Keepsake

YEAR ISSUE	EDITION LIMIT	YEAR RETD.	ISSUE PRICE	*QUOTE U.S.$
1987 Christmas Keys QX473-9	Yr.Iss.	1987	5.75	20-33
1987 Currier & Ives: American Farm Scene QX282-9	Yr.Iss.	1987	4.75	30
1987 Goldfinch QX464-9	Yr.Iss.	1987	7.00	55-85
1987 Heavenly Harmony QX465-9	Yr.Iss.	1987	15.00	30
1987 I Remember Santa QX278-9	Yr.Iss.	1987	4.75	33
1987 Joyous Angels QX465-7	Yr.Iss.	1987	7.75	25
1987 Norman Rockwell:Christmas Scenes QX282-7	Yr.Iss.	1987	4.75	30
1987 Promise of Peace QX374-9	Yr.Iss.	1987	6.50	17-25
1987 Special Memories Photoholder QX464-7	Yr.Iss.	1987	6.75	15-27

1988 Artist Favorites - Keepsake

YEAR ISSUE	EDITION LIMIT	YEAR RETD.	ISSUE PRICE	*QUOTE U.S.$
1988 Baby Redbird QX410-1	Yr.Iss.	1988	5.00	20
1988 Cymbals of Christmas QX411-1	Yr.Iss.	1988	5.50	17-30
1988 Little Jack Horner QX408-1	Yr.Iss.	1988	8.00	14-28
1988 Merry-Mint Unicorn QX423-4	Yr.Iss.	1988	8.50	20
1988 Midnight Snack QX410-4	Yr.Iss.	1988	6.00	21
1988 Very Strawbeary QX409-1	Yr.Iss.	1988	4.75	20

1988 Christmas Pizzazz Collection - Keepsake

YEAR ISSUE	EDITION LIMIT	YEAR RETD.	ISSUE PRICE	*QUOTE U.S.$
1988 Happy Holidata QX471-7	Yr.Iss.	1988	6.50	15-30
1988 Mistletoad QX468-7	Yr.Iss.	1988	7.00	20-30
1988 St. Louie Nick QX453-9	Yr.Iss.	1988	7.75	15-22

1988 Collectible Series - Keepsake

YEAR ISSUE	EDITION LIMIT	YEAR RETD.	ISSUE PRICE	*QUOTE U.S.$
1988 Betsey Clark: Home for Christmas-(3rd Ed.) QX271-4	Yr.Iss.	1988	5.00	18-25
1988 Collector's Plate-(2nd Ed.) QX406-4	Yr.Iss.	1988	8.00	50
1988 Five Golden Rings-(5th Ed.) QX371-4	Yr.Iss.	1988	6.50	20
1988 Frosty Friends-(9th Ed.) QX403-1	Yr.Iss.	1988	8.75	45-65
1988 Here Comes Santa-(10th Ed.) QX400-1	Yr.Iss.	1988	14.00	47
1988 Holiday Heirloom-(2nd Ed.) QX406-4	Yr.Iss.	1988	25.00	24
1988 Holiday Wildlife -(7th Ed.)QX371-1	Yr.Iss.	1988	7.75	16-25
1988 Mary's Angels-(1st Ed.) QX407-4	Yr.Iss.	1988	5.00	55
1988 Miniature Creche-(4th Ed.) QX403-4	Yr.Iss.	1988	8.50	21
1988 Mr. and Mrs. Claus -(3rd Ed.)QX401-1	Yr.Iss.	1988	13.00	40-55
1988 Norman Rockwell-(9th Ed.) QX370-4	Yr.Iss.	1988	7.75	17
1988 Nostalgic Houses and Shops-(5th Ed.) QX401-4	Yr.Iss.	1988	14.50	50-60
1988 Porcelain Bear-(6th Ed.) QX404-4	Yr.Iss.	1988	8.00	25-40
1988 Reindeer Champs-(3rd Ed.) QX405-1	Yr.Iss.	1988	7.50	37
1988 Rocking Horse-(8th Ed.) QX402-4	Yr.Iss.	1988	10.75	30-60
1988 Thimble-(11th Ed.) QX405-4	Yr.Iss.	1988	5.75	25
1988 Tin Locomotive-(7th Ed.) QX400-4	Yr.Iss.	1988	14.75	38-60
1988 Windows of the World-(4th Ed.) QX402-1	Yr.Iss.	1988	10.00	22-35
1988 Wood Childhood-(5th Ed.) QX404-1	Yr.Iss.	1988	7.50	23

1988 Commemoratives - Keepsake

YEAR ISSUE	EDITION LIMIT	YEAR RETD.	ISSUE PRICE	*QUOTE U.S.$
1988 Baby's First Christmas (Boy) QX272-1	Yr.Iss.	1988	4.75	17-25
1988 Baby's First Christmas (Girl) QX272-4	Yr.Iss.	1988	4.75	25
1988 Baby's First Christmas QX372-1	Yr.Iss.	1988	6.00	25
1988 Baby's First Christmas QX470-1	Yr.Iss.	1988	9.75	35
1988 Baby's First Christmas QX470-4	Yr.Iss.	1988	7.50	28
1988 Baby's Second Christmas QX471-1	Yr.Iss.	1988	6.00	33
1988 Babysitter QX279-1	Yr.Iss.	1988	4.75	10
1988 Child's Third Christmas QX471-4	Yr.Iss.	1988	6.00	25
1988 Dad QX414-1	Yr.Iss.	1988	7.00	25
1988 Daughter QX415-1	Yr.Iss.	1988	5.75	50
1988 Fifty Years Together QX374-1	Yr.Iss.	1988	6.75	10-20
1988 First Christmas Together QX274-1	Yr.Iss.	1988	4.75	23
1988 First Christmas Together QX373-1	Yr.Iss.	1988	6.75	20-30
1988 First Christmas Together QX489-4	Yr.Iss.	1988	9.00	32
1988 Five Years Together QX274-4	Yr.Iss.	1988	4.75	6-20
1988 From Our Home to Yours QX279-4	Yr.Iss.	1988	4.75	17
1988 Godchild QX278-4	Yr.Iss.	1988	4.75	10-20
1988 Granddaughter QX277-4	Yr.Iss.	1988	4.75	20
1988 Grandmother QX276-4	Yr.Iss.	1988	4.75	20
1988 Grandparents QX277-1	Yr.Iss.	1988	4.75	20
1988 Grandson QX278-1	Yr.Iss.	1988	4.75	15-25
1988 Gratitude QX375-4	Yr.Iss.	1988	6.00	12
1988 Love Fills the Heart QX374-4	Yr.Iss.	1988	6.00	25
1988 Love Grows QX275-4	Yr.Iss.	1988	4.75	31
1988 Mother and Dad QX414-4	Yr.Iss.	1988	8.00	18
1988 Mother QX375-1	Yr.Iss.	1988	6.50	20
1988 New Home QX376-1	Yr.Iss.	1988	6.00	25
1988 Sister QX499-4	Yr.Iss.	1988	8.00	15-32
1988 Son QX415-4	Yr.Iss.	1988	5.75	45
1988 Spirit of Christmas QX276-1	Yr.Iss.	1988	4.75	22
1988 Sweetheart QX490-1	Yr.Iss.	1988	9.75	11-22
1988 Teacher QX417-1	Yr.Iss.	1988	6.25	20
1988 Ten Years Together QX275-1	Yr.Iss.	1988	4.75	10-21
1988 Twenty-Five Years Together QX373-4	Yr.Iss.	1988	6.75	10-20
1988 Year to Remember QX416-4	Yr.Iss.	1988	7.00	25

1988 Hallmark Handcrafted Ornaments - Keepsake

YEAR ISSUE	EDITION LIMIT	YEAR RETD.	ISSUE PRICE	*QUOTE U.S.$
1988 Americana Drum QX488-1	Yr.Iss.	1988	7.75	15-25
1988 Arctic Tenor QX472-1	Yr.Iss.	1988	4.00	10-20
1988 Christmas Cardinal QX494-1	Yr.Iss.	1988	4.75	15
1988 Christmas Cuckoo QX480-1	Yr.Iss.	1988	8.00	30
1988 Christmas Memories QX372-4	Yr.Iss.	1988	6.50	25
1988 Christmas Scenes QX273-1	Yr.Iss.	1988	4.75	18
1988 Cool Juggler QX487-4	Yr.Iss.	1988	6.50	20
1988 Feliz Navidad QX416-1	Yr.Iss.	1988	6.75	20
1988 Filled with Fudge QX419-1	Yr.Iss.	1988	4.75	16-33
1988 Glowing Wreath QX492-1	Yr.Iss.	1988	6.00	15
1988 Go For The Gold QX417-4	Yr.Iss.	1988	8.00	16-30
1988 Goin' Cross-Country QX476-4	Yr.Iss.	1988	8.50	26
1988 Gone Fishing QX479-4	Yr.Iss.	1989	5.00	16
1988 Hoe-Hoe-Hoe! QX422-1	Yr.Iss.	1988	5.00	11-20
1988 Holiday Hero QX423-1	Yr.Iss.	1988	5.00	20
1988 Jingle Bell Clown QX477-4	Yr.Iss.	1988	15.00	20-37
1988 Jolly Walrus QX473-1	Yr.Iss.	1988	4.50	23
1988 Kiss from Santa QX482-1	Yr.Iss.	1989	4.50	23
1988 Kiss the Claus QX486-1	Yr.Iss.	1988	5.00	10-18
1988 Kringle Moon QX495-1	Yr.Iss.	1988	5.00	35
1988 Kringle Portrait QX496-1	Yr.Iss.	1988	7.50	25-40
1988 Kringle Tree QX495-4	Yr.Iss.	1988	6.50	35-40
1988 Love Santa QX486-4	Yr.Iss.	1988	5.00	20
1988 Loving Bear QX493-4	Yr.Iss.	1988	4.75	15
1988 Nick the Kick QX422-4	Yr.Iss.	1988	5.00	23
1988 Noah's Ark QX490-4	Yr.Iss.	1988	8.50	20
1988 Old-Fashioned Church QX498-1	Yr.Iss.	1988	4.00	24
1988 Old-Fashioned School House QX497-1	Yr.Iss.	1988	4.00	23
1988 Oreo QX481-4	Yr.Iss.	1988	4.00	17
1988 Par for Santa QX479-1	Yr.Iss.	1988	5.00	20
1988 Party Line QX476-1	Yr.Iss.	1989	8.75	20-30
1988 Peanuts QX280-1	Yr.Iss.	1988	4.75	35-50
1988 Peek-a-boo Kittens QX487-1	Yr.Iss.	1989	7.50	20
1988 Polar Bowler QX478-4	Yr.Iss.	1988	5.00	10-20
1988 Purrfect Snuggle QX474-4	Yr.Iss.	1988	6.25	25
1988 Sailing! Sailing! QX491-1	Yr.Iss.	1988	8.50	27
1988 Santa Flamingo QX483-4	Yr.Iss.	1988	4.75	16-33
1988 Shiny Sleigh QX492-4	Yr.Iss.	1988	5.75	20
1988 Slipper Spaniel QX472-4	Yr.Iss.	1988	4.50	17
1988 Snoopy and Woodstock QX474-1	Yr.Iss.	1988	6.00	35-46
1988 Soft Landing QX475-1	Yr.Iss.	1988	7.00	15-25
1988 Sparkling Tree QX483-1	Yr.Iss.	1988	6.00	19
1988 Squeaky Clean QX475-4	Yr.Iss.	1988	6.75	15
1988 Starry Angel QX494-4	Yr.Iss.	1988	4.75	20
1988 Sweet Star QX418-4	Yr.Iss.	1988	5.00	20-32
1988 Teeny Taster QX418-1	Yr.Iss.	1989	4.75	27
1988 The Town Crier QX473-4	Yr.Iss.	1988	5.50	15-25
1988 Travels with Santa QX477-1	Yr.Iss.	1988	10.00	26-40
1988 Uncle Sam Nutcracker QX488-4	Yr.Iss.	1988	7.00	20-40
1988 Winter Fun QX478-1	Yr.Iss.	1988	8.50	17-27

1988 Hallmark Keepsake Ornament Collector's Club - Keepsake

YEAR ISSUE	EDITION LIMIT	YEAR RETD.	ISSUE PRICE	*QUOTE U.S.$
1988 Angelic Minstrel QXC408-4	Yr.Iss.	1988	27.50	45-60
1988 Christmas is Sharing QXC407-1	Yr.Iss.	1988	17.50	31-49
1988 Hold on Tight QXC570-4	Yr.Iss.	1988	Unkn.	75
1988 Holiday Heirloom-(2nd Ed.) QXC406-4	Yr.Iss.	1988	25.00	23-37
1988 Our Clubhouse QXC580-4	Yr.Iss.	1988	Unkn.	40-50
1988 Sleighful of Dreams QC580-1	Yr.Iss.	1988	8.00	50-75

1988 Holiday Humor - Keepsake

YEAR ISSUE	EDITION LIMIT	YEAR RETD.	ISSUE PRICE	*QUOTE U.S.$
1988 Night Before Christmas QX451-7	Yr.Iss.	1988	6.50	18-33
1988 Owliday Wish QX455-9	Yr.Iss.	1988	6.50	14-25
1988 Reindoggy QX452-7	Yr.Iss.	1988	5.75	20-25

YEAR ISSUE		EDITION LIMIT	YEAR RETD.	ISSUE PRICE	*QUOTE U.S.$
1988	Treetop Dreams QX459-7	Yr.Iss.	1988	6.75	15-25

1988 Keepsake Magic Ornaments - Keepsake

1988	Baby's First Christmas QLX718-4	Yr.Iss.	1988	24.00	40-60
1988	Bearly Reaching QLX715-1	Yr.Iss.	1988	9.50	40
1988	Chris Mouse-(4th Ed.) QLX715-4	Yr.Iss.	1988	8.75	60
1988	Christmas Classics-(3rd Ed.) QLX716-1	Yr.Iss.	1988	15.00	30
1988	Christmas is Magic QLX717-1	Yr.Iss.	1988	12.00	35-55
1988	Christmas Morning QX701-3	Yr.Iss.	1988	24.50	33-50
1988	Circling the Globe QLX712-4	Yr.Iss.	1988	10.50	45
1988	Country Express QLX721-1	Yr.Iss.	1988	24.50	67-75
1988	Festive Feeder QLX720-4	Yr.Iss.	1988	11.50	45
1988	First Christmas Together QLX702-7	Yr.Iss.	1988	12.00	37
1988	Heavenly Glow QLX711-4	Yr.Iss.	1988	11.75	19-29
1988	Kitty Capers QLX716-4	Yr.Iss.	1988	13.00	45
1988	Kringle's Toy Shop QLX701-7	Yr.Iss.	1988	25.00	35-65
1988	Last-Minute Hug QLX718-1	Yr.Iss.	1988	19.50	47
1988	Moonlit Nap QLX713-4	Yr.Iss.	1988	8.75	21-30
1988	Parade of the Toys QLX719-4	Yr.Iss.	1988	22.00	53
1988	Radiant Tree QLX712-1	Yr.Iss.	1988	11.75	24
1988	Santa and Sparky-(3rd Ed.) QLX719-1	Yr.Iss.	1988	19.50	43
1988	Skater's Waltz QLX720-1	Yr.Iss.	1988	19.50	36-62
1988	Song of Christmas QLX711-1	Yr.Iss.	1988	8.50	15-30
1988	Tree of Friendship QLX710-4	Yr.Iss.	1988	8.50	25

1988 Keepsake Miniature Ornaments - Keepsake

1988	Baby's First Christmas	Yr.Iss.	1988	6.00	12
1988	Brass Angel	Yr.Iss.	1988	1.50	10-20
1988	Brass Star	Yr.Iss.	1988	1.50	20
1988	Brass Tree	Yr.Iss.	1988	1.50	20
1988	Candy Cane Elf	Yr.Iss.	1988	3.00	15-20
1988	Country Wreath	Yr.Iss.	1988	4.00	11
1988	Family Home-(1st Ed.)	Yr.Iss.	1988	8.50	35-40
1988	First Christmas Together	Yr.Iss.	1988	4.00	11
1988	Folk Art Lamb	Yr.Iss.	1988	2.50	14-23
1988	Folk Art Reindeer	Yr.Iss.	1988	2.50	13-20
1988	Friends Share Joy	Yr.Iss.	1988	2.00	15
1988	Gentle Angel	Yr.Iss.	1988	2.00	15
1988	Happy Santa	Yr.Iss.	1988	4.50	19
1988	Holy Family	Yr.Iss.	1988	8.50	13
1988	Jolly St. Nick	Yr.Iss.	1988	8.00	20
1988	Joyous Heart	Yr.Iss.	1988	3.50	12-23
1988	Kittens in Toyland-(1st Ed.)	Yr.Iss.	1988	5.00	20-30
1988	Little Drummer Boy	Yr.Iss.	1988	4.50	20-27
1988	Love is Forever	Yr.Iss.	1988	2.00	15
1988	Mother	Yr.Iss.	1988	3.00	12
1988	Penguin Pal-(1st Ed.)	Yr.Iss.	1988	3.75	20-28
1988	Rocking Horse-(1st Ed.)	Yr.Iss.	1988	4.50	35-45
1988	Skater's Waltz	Yr.Iss.	1988	7.00	15
1988	Sneaker Mouse	Yr.Iss.	1988	4.00	15
1988	Snuggly Skater	Yr.Iss.	1988	4.50	27
1988	Sweet Dreams	Yr.Iss.	1988	7.00	18
1988	Three Little Kitties	Yr.Iss.	1988	6.00	13-19

1988 Old Fashioned Christmas Collection - Keepsake

1988	In A Nutshell QX469-7	Yr.Iss.	1988	5.50	24-33

1988 Special Edition - Keepsake

1988	The Wonderful Santacycle QX411-4	Yr.Iss.	1988	22.50	34-45

1989 Artists' Favorites - Keepsake

1989	Baby Partridge QX452-5	Yr.Iss.	1989	6.75	10-15
1989	Bear-i-Tone QX454-2	Yr.Iss.	1989	4.75	10-20
1989	Carousel Zebra QX451-5	Yr.Iss.	1989	9.25	15-20
1989	Cherry Jubilee QX453-2	Yr.Iss.	1989	5.00	25
1989	Mail Call QX452-2	Yr.Iss.	1989	8.75	12-20
1989	Merry-Go-Round Unicorn QX447-2	Yr.Iss.	1989	10.75	16
1989	Playful Angel QX453-5	Yr.Iss.	1989	6.75	20

1989 Collectible Series - Keepsake

1989	Betsey Clark:Home for Christmas-(4th Ed.) QX230-2	Yr.Iss.	1989	5.00	20-28
1989	Christmas Kitty (1st Ed.) QX544-5	Yr.Iss.	1989	14.75	20-32
1989	Collector's Plate-(3rd Ed.) QX461-2	Yr.Iss.	1989	8.25	30
1989	Crayola Crayon (1st Ed.) QX435-2	Yr.Iss.	1989	8.75	45
1989	Frosty Friends-(10th Ed.) QX457-2	Yr.Iss.	1989	9.25	35-50
1989	The Gift Bringers (1st Ed.) QX279-5	Yr.Iss.	1989	5.00	20
1989	Hark! It's Herald (1st Ed.) QX455-5	Yr.Iss.	1989	6.75	15-25
1989	Here Comes Santa (11th Ed.) QX458-5	Yr.Iss.	1989	14.75	31-50
1989	Mary's Angels-(2nd Ed.) QX454-5	Yr.Iss.	1989	5.75	75-100
1989	Miniature Creche (5th Ed.) QX459-2	Yr.Iss.	1989	9.25	17
1989	Mr. and Mrs. Claus-(4th Ed.) QX457-5	Yr.Iss.	1989	13.25	33-50
1989	Nostalgic Houses and Shops-(6th Ed.) QX458-2	Yr.Iss.	1989	14.25	57
1989	Porcelain Bear (7th Ed.) QX461-5	Yr.Iss.	1989	8.75	20-40
1989	Reindeer Champs-(4th Ed.) QX456-2	Yr.Iss.	1989	7.75	17-27
1989	Rocking Horse (9th Ed.) QX462-2	Yr.Iss.	1989	10.75	40-50
1989	Thimble (12th Ed.) QX455-5	Yr.Iss.	1989	5.75	13-25
1989	Tin Locomotive (8th Ed.) QX460-2	Yr.Iss.	1989	14.75	31-60

YEAR ISSUE		EDITION LIMIT	YEAR RETD.	ISSUE PRICE	*QUOTE U.S.$
1989	Twelve Days of Christmas (6th Ed.) QX381-2	Yr.Iss.	1989	6.75	16
1989	Windows of the World (5th Ed.) QX462-5	Yr.Iss.	1989	10.75	21-33
1989	Winter Surprise (1st Ed.) QX427-2	Yr.Iss.	1989	10.75	25-33
1989	Wood Childhood Ornaments-(6th Ed.) QX459-5	Yr.Iss.	1989	7.75	15-25

1989 Commemoratives - Keepsake

1989	Baby's Fifth Christmas QX543-5	Yr.Iss.	1989	6.75	25
1989	Baby's First Christmas Photoholder QX468-2	Yr.Iss.	1989	6.25	50
1989	Baby's First Christmas QX381-5	Yr.Iss.	1989	6.75	18
1989	Baby's First Christmas QX449-2	Yr.Iss.	1989	7.25	70
1989	Baby's First Christmas-Baby Boy QX272-5	Yr.Iss.	1989	4.75	23
1989	Baby's First Christmas-Baby Girl QX272-2	Yr.Iss.	1989	4.75	23
1989	Baby's Fourth Christmas QX543-2	Yr.Iss.	1989	6.75	25
1989	Baby's Second Christmas QX449-5	Yr.Iss.	1989	6.75	30-40
1989	Baby's Third Christmas QX469-5	Yr.Iss.	1989	6.75	28
1989	Brother QX445-2	Yr.Iss.	1989	6.25	17
1989	Dad QX442-5	Yr.Iss.	1989	7.25	12-20
1989	Daughter QX443-2	Yr.Iss.	1989	6.25	20-30
1989	Festive Year QX384-2	Yr.Iss.	1989	7.75	10-20
1989	Fifty Years Together Photoholder QX486-2	Yr.Iss.	1989	8.75	17
1989	First Christmas Together QX273-2	Yr.Iss.	1989	4.75	15-25
1989	First Christmas Together QX383-2	Yr.Iss.	1989	6.75	23
1989	First Christmas Together QX485-2	Yr.Iss.	1989	9.75	15-25
1989	Five Years Together QX273-5	Yr.Iss.	1989	4.75	14-23
1989	Forty Years Together Photoholder QX545-2	Yr.Iss.	1989	8.75	15
1989	Friendship Time QX413-2	Yr.Iss.	1989	9.75	25-33
1989	From Our Home to Yours QX384-5	Yr.Iss.	1989	6.25	15
1989	Godchild QX311-2	Yr.Iss.	1989	6.25	20
1989	Granddaughter QX278	Yr.Iss.	1989	4.75	23
1989	Granddaughter's First Christmas QX382-2	Yr.Iss.	1989	6.75	10-23
1989	Grandmother QX277-5	Yr.Iss.	1989	4.75	18
1989	Grandparents QX277-2	Yr.Iss.	1989	4.75	15
1989	Grandson QX278-5	Yr.Iss.	1989	4.75	17
1989	Grandson's First Christmas QX382-5	Yr.Iss.	1989	6.75	15
1989	Gratitude QX385-2	Yr.Iss.	1989	6.75	14
1989	Language of Love QX383-5	Yr.Iss.	1989	6.25	22
1989	Mom and Dad QX442-2	Yr.Iss.	1989	9.75	20
1989	Mother QX440-5	Yr.Iss.	1989	9.75	20-30
1989	New Home QX275-5	Yr.Iss.	1989	4.75	20
1989	Sister QX279-2	Yr.Iss.	1989	4.75	17
1989	Son QX444-5	Yr.Iss.	1989	6.25	25
1989	Sweetheart QX486-5	Yr.Iss.	1989	9.75	33
1989	Teacher QX412-5	Yr.Iss.	1989	5.75	14-24
1989	Ten Years Together QX274-2	Yr.Iss.	1989	4.75	30
1989	Twenty-five Years Together Photoholder QX485-5	Yr.Iss.	1989	8.75	17
1989	World of Love QX274-5	Yr.Iss.	1989	4.75	35

1989 Hallmark Handcrafted Ornaments - Keepsake

1989	Peek-a-boo Kittens QX487-1	Yr.Iss.	1989	7.50	21

1989 Hallmark Keepsake Ornament Collector's Club - Keepsake

1989	Christmas is Peaceful QXC451-2	Yr.Iss.	1989	18.50	45
1989	Collect a Dream QXC428-5	Yr.Iss.	1989	9.00	55-65
1989	Holiday Heirloom-(3rd Ed.) QXC460-2	Yr.Iss.	1989	25.00	35
1989	Noelle QXC448-3	Yr.Iss.	1989	19.75	50-60
1989	Sitting Purrty QXC581-2	Yr.Iss.	1989	Unkn.	45
1989	Visit from Santa QXC580-2	Yr.Iss.	1989	Unkn.	45-55

1989 Holiday Traditions - Keepsake

1989	Camera Claus QX546-5	Yr.Iss.	1989	5.75	15
1989	A Charlie Brown Christmas QX276-5	Yr.Iss.	1989	4.75	25
1989	Cranberry Bunny QX426-2	Yr.Iss.	1989	5.75	11-18
1989	Deer Disguise QX426-5	Yr.Iss.	1989	5.75	17-25
1989	Feliz Navidad QX439-2	Yr.Iss.	1989	6.75	20-30
1989	The First Christmas QX547-5	Yr.Iss.	1989	7.75	14-16
1989	Gentle Fawn QX548-5	Yr.Iss.	1989	7.75	13-20
1989	George Washington Bicentennial QX386-2	Yr.Iss.	1989	6.75	9-20
1989	Gone Fishing QX479-4	Yr.Iss.	1989	5.75	17
1989	Gym Dandy QX418-5	Yr.Iss.	1989	5.75	15
1989	Hang in There QX430-5	Yr.Iss.	1989	5.25	15-25
1989	Here's the Pitch QX545-5	Yr.Iss.	1989	5.75	15
1989	Hoppy Holidays QX469-2	Yr.Iss.	1989	7.75	13-24
1989	Joyful Trio QX437-2	Yr.Iss.	1989	9.75	15
1989	A Kiss™ From Santa QX482-1	Yr.Iss.	1989	4.50	20
1989	Kristy Claus QX424-5	Yr.Iss.	1989	5.75	12
1989	Norman Rockwell QX276-2	Yr.Iss.	1989	4.75	25
1989	North Pole Jogger QX546-2	Yr.Iss.	1989	5.75	15
1989	Old-World Gnome QX434-5	Yr.Iss.	1989	7.75	15-30
1989	On the Links QX419-2	Yr.Iss.	1989	5.75	17
1989	Oreo® Chocolate Sandwich Cookies QX481-4	Yr.Iss.	1989	4.00	15
1989	Owliday Greetings QX436-5	Yr.Iss.	1989	4.00	15
1989	Paddington Bear QX429-2	Yr.Iss.	1989	5.75	15-30
1989	Party Line QX476-1	Yr.Iss.	1989	8.75	27
1989	Peek-a-Boo Kitties QX487-1	Yr.Iss.	1989	7.50	16-22
1989	Polar Bowler QX478-4	Yr.Iss.	1989	5.75	17
1989	Sea Santa QX415-5	Yr.Iss.	1989	5.75	15

YEAR ISSUE		EDITION LIMIT	YEAR RETD.	ISSUE PRICE	*QUOTE U.S.$
1989	Snoopy and Woodstock QX433-2	Yr.Iss.	1989	6.75	25-35
1989	Snowplow Santa QX420-5	Yr.Iss.	1989	5.75	12-22
1989	Special Delivery QX432-5	Yr.Iss.	1989	5.25	12-25
1989	Spencer Sparrow, Esq. QX431-2	Yr.Iss.	1990	6.75	14-23
1989	Stocking Kitten QX456-5	Yr.Iss.	1990	6.75	15
1989	Sweet Memories Photoholder QX438-5	Yr.Iss.	1989	6.75	25
1989	Teeny Taster QX418-1	Yr.Iss.	1989	4.75	17

1989 Keepsake Magic Collection - Keepsake

1989	Angel Melody QLX720-2	Yr.Iss.	1989	9.50	25
1989	The Animals Speak QLX723-2	Yr.Iss.	1989	13.50	78-100
1989	Baby's First Christmas QLX727-2	Yr.Iss.	1989	30.00	50
1989	Backstage Bear QLX721-5	Yr.Iss.	1989	13.50	30
1989	Busy Beaver QLX724-5	Yr.Iss.	1989	17.50	35-45
1989	Chris Mouse-(5th Ed.) QLX722-5	Yr.Iss.	1989	9.50	50-60
1989	Christmas Classics-(4th Ed.) QLX724-2	Yr.Iss.	1989	13.50	27-43
1989	First Christmas Together QLX734-2	Yr.Iss.	1989	17.50	35-45
1989	Forest Frolics-(1st Ed.) QLX728-2	Yr.Iss.	1989	24.50	85
1989	Holiday Bell QLX722-2	Yr.Iss.	1989	17.50	29-35
1989	Joyous Carolers QLX729-5	Yr.Iss.	1989	30.00	47-70
1989	Kringle's Toy Shop QLX701-7	Yr.Iss.	1989	24.50	40-60
1989	Loving Spoonful QLX726-2	Yr.Iss.	1989	19.50	35
1989	Metro Express QLX727-5	Yr.Iss.	1989	28.00	75
1989	Moonlit Nap QLX713-4	Yr.Iss.	1989	8.75	24
1989	Rudolph the Red-Nosed Reindeer QLX725-2	Yr.Iss.	1989	19.50	50-70
1989	Spirit of St. Nick QLX728-5	Yr.Iss.	1989	24.50	72
1989	Tiny Tinker QLX717-4	Yr.Iss.	1989	19.50	63
1989	Unicorn Fantasy QLX723-5	Yr.Iss.	1989	9.50	20

1989 Keepsake Miniature Ornaments - Keepsake

1989	Acorn Squirrel QXM568-2	Yr.Iss.	1989	4.50	9
1989	Baby's First Christmas QXM573-2	Yr.Iss.	1989	6.00	10
1989	Brass Partridge QXM572-5	Yr.Iss.	1989	3.00	10
1989	Brass Snowflake QXM570-2	Yr.Iss.	1989	4.50	13
1989	Bunny Hug QXM577-5	Yr.Iss.	1989	3.00	8
1989	Country Wreath QXM573-1	Yr.Iss.	1989	4.50	12
1989	Cozy Skater QXM573-5	Yr.Iss.	1989	4.50	11
1989	First Christmas Together QXM564-2	Yr.Iss.	1989	8.50	10
1989	Folk Art Bunny QXM569-2	Yr.Iss.	1989	4.50	10
1989	Happy Bluebird QXM566-2	Yr.Iss.	1989	4.50	13
1989	Holiday Deer QXM577-2	Yr.Iss.	1989	3.00	11
1989	Holy Family QXM561-1	Yr.Iss.	1989	8.50	15
1989	Kittens in Toyland-(2nd Ed.) QXM561-2	Yr.Iss.	1989	4.50	15
1989	Kitty Cart QXM572-2	Yr.Iss.	1989	3.00	7
1989	The Kringles-(1st Ed.) QXM562-2	Yr.Iss.	1989	6.00	26
1989	Little Soldier QXM567-5	Yr.Iss.	1989	4.50	23
1989	Little Star Bringer QXM562-2	Yr.Iss.	1989	6.00	17
1989	Load of Cheer QXM574-5	Yr.Iss.	1989	6.00	15
1989	Lovebirds QXM563-5	Yr.Iss.	1989	6.00	12
1989	Merry Seal QXM575-5	Yr.Iss.	1989	6.00	10
1989	Mother QXM564-5	Yr.Iss.	1989	6.00	11
1989	Noel R.R.-(1st Ed.) QXM576-2	Yr.Iss.	1989	8.50	35
1989	Old English Village-(2nd Ed.) QXM561-5	Yr.Iss.	1989	8.50	26
1989	Old-World Santa QXM569-5	Yr.Iss.	1989	3.00	6
1989	Penguin Pal-(2nd Ed.) QXM560-2	Yr.Iss.	1989	4.50	16
1989	Pinecone Basket QXM573-4	Yr.Iss.	1989	4.50	7
1989	Puppy Cart QXM571-5	Yr.Iss.	1989	3.00	20
1989	Rejoice QXM578-2	Yr.Iss.	1989	3.00	9
1989	Rocking Horse-(2nd Ed.) QXM560-5	Yr.Iss.	1989	4.50	23-30
1989	Roly-Poly Pig QXM571-2	Yr.Iss.	1989	3.00	15
1989	Roly-Poly Ram QXM570-5	Yr.Iss.	1989	3.00	13
1989	Santa's Magic Ride QXM563-2	Yr.Iss.	1989	8.50	15
1989	Santa's Roadster QXM566-5	Yr.Iss.	1989	6.00	15
1989	Scrimshaw Reindeer QXM568-5	Yr.Iss.	1989	4.50	6
1989	Sharing a Ride QXM576-5	Yr.Iss.	1989	8.50	11
1989	Slow Motion QXM575-2	Yr.Iss.	1989	6.00	12
1989	Special Friend QXM565-2	Yr.Iss.	1989	4.50	12
1989	Starlit Mouse QXM565-5	Yr.Iss.	1989	4.50	12
1989	Stocking Pal QXM567-2	Yr.Iss.	1989	4.50	10
1989	Strollin' Snowman QXM574-2	Yr.Iss.	1989	4.50	12
1989	Three Little Kitties QXM569-4	Yr.Iss.	1989	6.00	19

1989 New Attractions - Keepsake

1989	Balancing Elf QX489-5	Yr.Iss.	1989	6.75	21
1989	Cactus Cowboy QX411-2	Yr.Iss.	1989	6.75	33-44
1989	Claus Construction QX488-5	Yr.Iss.	1990	7.75	25-35
1989	Cool Swing QX487-5	Yr.Iss.	1989	6.25	35
1989	Country Cat QX467-2	Yr.Iss.	1989	6.25	16
1989	Festive Angel QX463-5	Yr.Iss.	1989	6.75	20
1989	Goin' South QX410-5	Yr.Iss.	1989	4.25	22
1989	Graceful Swan QX464-2	Yr.Iss.	1989	6.75	20
1989	Horse Weathervane QX463-2	Yr.Iss.	1989	5.75	15
1989	Let's Play QX488-2	Yr.Iss.	1989	7.25	28
1989	Nostalgic Lamb QX466-5	Yr.Iss.	1989	6.75	11
1989	Nutshell Dreams QX465-5	Yr.Iss.	1989	5.75	14-23
1989	Nutshell Holiday QX465-2	Yr.Iss.	1990	5.75	17-27
1989	Nutshell Workshop QX487-2	Yr.Iss.	1989	5.75	15-23
1989	Peppermint Clown QX450-5	Yr.Iss.	1989	24.75	35
1989	Rodney Reindeer QX407-2	Yr.Iss.	1989	6.75	12
1989	Rooster Weathervane QX467-5	Yr.Iss.	1989	5.75	18-24
1989	Sparkling Snowflake QX547-2	Yr.Iss.	1989	7.75	25
1989	TV Break QX409-2	Yr.Iss.	1989	6.25	17
1989	Wiggly Snowman QX489-2	Yr.Iss.	1989	6.75	25-35

1989 Special Edition - Keepsake

YEAR ISSUE	EDITION LIMIT	YEAR RETD.	ISSUE PRICE	*QUOTE U.S.$
1989 The Ornament Express QX580-5	Yr.Iss.	1989	22.00	40

1990 Artists' Favorites - Keepsake

YEAR ISSUE	EDITION LIMIT	YEAR RETD.	ISSUE PRICE	*QUOTE U.S.$
1990 Angel Kitty QX4746	Yr.Iss.	1990	8.75	25
1990 Donder's Diner QX4823	Yr.Iss.	1990	13.75	22
1990 Gentle Dreamers QX4756	Yr.Iss.	1990	8.75	17-30
1990 Happy Woodcutter QX4763	Yr.Iss.	1990	9.75	17-25
1990 Mouseboat QX4753	Yr.Iss.	1990	7.75	15
1990 Welcome, Santa QX4773	Yr.Iss.	1990	11.75	19-30

1990 Collectible Series - Keepsake

YEAR ISSUE	EDITION LIMIT	YEAR RETD.	ISSUE PRICE	*QUOTE U.S.$
1990 Betsey Clark: Home for Christmas-(5th Ed.) QX2033	Yr.Iss.	1990	5.00	15-25
1990 Christmas Kitty-(2nd Ed.) QX4506	Yr.Iss.	1990	14.75	23
1990 Cinnamon Bear-(8th Ed.) QX4426	Yr.Iss.	1990	8.75	20
1990 Cookies for Santa-(4th Ed.) QX4436	Yr.Iss.	1990	8.75	25
1990 CRAYOLA Crayon-Bright Moving Colors-(2nd Ed.) QX4586	Yr.Iss.	1990	8.75	35-40
1990 Fabulous Decade-(1st Ed.) QX4466	Yr.Iss.	1990	7.75	25-37
1990 Festive Surrey-(12th Ed.) QX4923	Yr.Iss.	1990	14.75	30
1990 Frosty Friends-(11th Ed.) QX4396	Yr.Iss.	1990	9.75	21
1990 The Gift Bringers-St. Lucia-(2nd Ed.) QX2803	Yr.Iss.	1990	5.00	14-23
1990 Greatest Story-(1st Ed.) QX4656	Yr.Iss.	1990	12.75	26-35
1990 Hark! It's Herald-(2nd Ed.) QX4463	Yr.Iss.	1990	6.75	15-20
1990 Heart of Christmas-(1st Ed.) QX4726	Yr.Iss.	1990	13.75	55-65
1990 Holiday Home-(7th Ed.) QX4696	Yr.Iss.	1990	14.75	62
1990 Irish-(6th Ed.) QX4636	Yr.Iss.	1990	10.75	20
1990 Mary's Angels-Rosebud-(3rd Ed.) QX4423	Yr.Iss.	1990	5.75	35
1990 Merry Olde Santa-(1st Ed.) QX4736	Yr.Iss.	1990	14.75	65-70
1990 Popcorn Party-(5th Ed.) QX4393	Yr.Iss.	1990	13.75	60
1990 Reindeer Champs-Comet-(5th Ed.) QX4433	Yr.Iss.	1990	7.75	20-30
1990 Rocking Horse-(10th Ed.) QX4646	Yr.Iss.	1990	10.75	60-95
1990 Seven Swans A-Swimming-(7th Ed.) QX3033	Yr.Iss.	1990	6.75	20-30
1990 Winter Surprise-(2nd Ed.) QX4443	Yr.Iss.	1990	10.75	19-29

1990 Commemoratives - Keepsake

YEAR ISSUE	EDITION LIMIT	YEAR RETD.	ISSUE PRICE	*QUOTE U.S.$
1990 Across The Miles QX3173	Yr.Iss.	1990	6.75	15
1990 Baby's First Christmas QX3036	Yr.Iss.	1990	6.75	10-20
1990 Baby's First Christmas QX4853	Yr.Iss.	1990	9.75	18-28
1990 Baby's First Christmas QX4856	Yr.Iss.	1990	7.75	30-38
1990 Baby's First Christmas-Baby Boy QX2063	Yr.Iss.	1990	4.75	19
1990 Baby's First Christmas-Baby Girl QX2066	Yr.Iss.	1990	4.75	17
1990 Baby's First Christmas-Photo Holder QX4843	Yr.Iss.	1990	7.75	23-30
1990 Baby's Second Christmas QX4683	Yr.Iss.	1990	6.75	33
1990 Brother QX4493	Yr.Iss.	1990	5.75	12
1990 Child Care Giver QX3166	Yr.Iss.	1990	6.75	14
1990 Child's Fifth Christmas QX4876	Yr.Iss.	1990	6.75	15-23
1990 Child's Fourth Christmas QX4873	Yr.Iss.	1990	6.75	15-28
1990 Child's Third Christmas QX4866	Yr.Iss.	1990	6.75	18-28
1990 Copy of Cheer QX4486	Yr.Iss.	1990	7.75	17
1990 Dad QX4533	Yr.Iss.	1990	6.75	13-25
1990 Dad-to-Be QX4913	Yr.Iss.	1990	5.75	18
1990 Daughter QX4496	Yr.Iss.	1990	5.75	17-25
1990 Fifty Years Together QX4906	Yr.Iss.	1990	9.75	18
1990 Five Years Together QX2103	Yr.Iss.	1990	4.75	19
1990 Forty Years Together QX4903	Yr.Iss.	1990	9.75	20
1990 Friendship Kitten QX4142	Yr.Iss.	1990	6.75	17-25
1990 From Our Home to Yours QX2166	Yr.Iss.	1990	4.75	20
1990 Godchild QX3167	Yr.Iss.	1990	6.75	11-20
1990 Granddaughter QX2286	Yr.Iss.	1990	4.75	15
1990 Granddaughter's First Christmas QX3106	Yr.Iss.	1990	6.75	20
1990 Grandmother QX2236	Yr.Iss.	1990	4.75	17
1990 Grandparents QX2253	Yr.Iss.	1990	4.75	15
1990 Grandson QX2293	Yr.Iss.	1990	4.75	15
1990 Grandson's First Christmas QX3063	Yr.Iss.	1990	6.75	17
1990 Jesus Loves Me QX3156	Yr.Iss.	1990	6.75	11
1990 Mom and Dad QX4593	Yr.Iss.	1990	8.75	20
1990 Mom-to-Be QX4916	Yr.Iss.	1990	5.75	25
1990 Mother QX4536	Yr.Iss.	1990	8.75	30
1990 New Home QX4343	Yr.Iss.	1990	6.75	25
1990 Our First Christmas Together QX2136	Yr.Iss.	1990	4.75	20
1990 Our First Christmas Together QX3146	Yr.Iss.	1990	6.75	20
1990 Our First Christmas Together QX4883	Yr.Iss.	1990	9.75	32
1990 Our First Christmas Together-Photo Holder Ornament QX4886	Yr.Iss.	1990	7.75	25
1990 Peaceful Kingdom QX2106	Yr.Iss.	1990	4.75	20
1990 Sister QX2273	Yr.Iss.	1990	4.75	19
1990 Son QX4516	Yr.Iss.	1990	5.75	25
1990 Sweetheart QX4893	Yr.Iss.	1990	11.75	20
1990 Teacher QX4483	Yr.Iss.	1990	7.75	13
1990 Ten Years Together QX2153	Yr.Iss.	1990	4.75	19
1990 Time for Love QX2133	Yr.Iss.	1990	4.75	10-22
1990 Twenty-Five Years Together QX4896	Yr.Iss.	1990	9.75	18

1990 Holiday Traditions - Keepsake

YEAR ISSUE	EDITION LIMIT	YEAR RETD.	ISSUE PRICE	*QUOTE U.S.$
1990 Spencer Sparrow, Esq. QX431-2	Yr.Iss.	1990	6.75	15
1990 Stocking Kitten QX456-5	Yr.Iss.	1990	6.75	11-15

1990 Keepsake Collector's Club - Keepsake

YEAR ISSUE	EDITION LIMIT	YEAR RETD.	ISSUE PRICE	*QUOTE U.S.$
1990 Armful of Joy QXC445-3	Yr.Iss.	1990	8.00	42
1990 Christmas Limited 1975 QXC476-6	38700	1990	19.75	80-120
1990 Club Hollow QXC445-6	Yr.Iss.	1990	Unkn.	36
1990 Crown Prince QXC560-3	Yr.Iss.	1990	Unkn.	39
1990 Dove of Peace QXC447-6	25400	1990	24.75	50-70
1990 Sugar Plum Fairy QXC447-3	25400	1990	27.75	55

1990 Keepsake Magic Ornaments - Keepsake

YEAR ISSUE	EDITION LIMIT	YEAR RETD.	ISSUE PRICE	*QUOTE U.S.$
1990 Baby's First Christmas QLX7246	Yr.Iss.	1990	28.00	55
1990 Beary Short Nap QLX7326	Yr.Iss.	1990	10.00	24-30
1990 Blessings of Love QLX7363	Yr.Iss.	1990	14.00	47
1990 Children's Express QLX7243	Yr.Iss.	1990	28.00	65-75
1990 Chris Mouse Wreath QLX7296	Yr.Iss.	1990	10.00	35-45
1990 Christmas Memories QLX7276	Yr.Iss.	1990	25.00	47
1990 Deer Crossing QLX7213	Yr.Iss.	1990	18.00	40-50
1990 Elf of the Year QLX7356	Yr.Iss.	1990	10.00	16-25
1990 Elfin Whittler QLX7265	Yr.Iss.	1990	20.00	40-55
1990 Forest Frolics QLX7236	Yr.Iss.	1990	25.00	75
1990 Holiday Flash QLX7333	Yr.Iss.	1990	18.00	25-40
1990 Hop 'N Pop Popper QLX7353	Yr.Iss.	1990	20.00	85-95
1990 Letter to Santa QLX7226	Yr.Iss.	1990	14.00	28-35
1990 The Littlest Angel QLX7303	Yr.Iss.	1990	14.00	28-40
1990 Mrs. Santa's Kitchen QLX7263	Yr.Iss.	1990	25.00	50-80
1990 Our First Christmas Together QLX7255	Yr.Iss.	1990	18.00	40-47
1990 Partridges in a Pear QLX7212	Yr.Iss.	1990	14.00	30
1990 Santa's Ho-Ho-Hoedown QLX7256	Yr.Iss.	1990	25.00	90
1990 Song and Dance QLX7253	Yr.Iss.	1990	20.00	60-95
1990 Starlight Angel QLX7306	Yr.Iss.	1990	14.00	27-37
1990 Starship Christmas QLX7336	Yr.Iss.	1990	18.00	35-55

1990 Keepsake Miniature Ornaments - Keepsake

YEAR ISSUE	EDITION LIMIT	YEAR RETD.	ISSUE PRICE	*QUOTE U.S.$
1990 Acorn Wreath QXM5686	Yr.Iss.	1990	6.00	10
1990 Air Santa QXM5656	Yr.Iss.	1990	4.50	10
1990 Baby's First Christmas QXM5703	Yr.Iss.	1990	8.50	16
1990 Basket Buddy QXM5696	Yr.Iss.	1990	6.00	10
1990 Bear Hug QXM5633	Yr.Iss.	1990	6.00	12
1990 Brass Bouquet 600QMX5776	Yr.Iss.	1990	6.00	6
1990 Brass Horn QXM5793	Yr.Iss.	1990	3.00	8
1990 Brass Peace QXM5796	Yr.Iss.	1990	3.00	8
1990 Brass Santa QXM5786	Yr.Iss.	1990	3.00	7
1990 Brass Year QXM5833	Yr.Iss.	1990	3.00	8
1990 Busy Carver QXM5673	Yr.Iss.	1990	4.50	8
1990 Christmas Dove QXM5636	Yr.Iss.	1990	4.50	12
1990 Cloisonne Poinsettia QMX5533	Yr.Iss.	1990	10.75	25-35
1990 Coal Car QXM5756	Yr.Iss.	1990	8.50	23
1990 Country Heart QXM5693	Yr.Iss.	1990	4.50	9
1990 First Christmas Together QXM5536	Yr.Iss.	1990	6.00	12
1990 Going Sledding QXM5683	Yr.Iss.	1990	4.50	12
1990 Grandchild's First Christmas QXM5723	Yr.Iss.	1990	6.00	11
1990 Holiday Cardinal QXM5526	Yr.Iss.	1990	3.00	10
1990 Kittens in Toyland QXM5736	Yr.Iss.	1990	4.50	18
1990 The Kringles QXM5753	Yr.Iss.	1990	6.00	22
1990 Lion and Lamb QXM5676	Yr.Iss.	1990	4.50	8
1990 Loving Hearts QXM5523	Yr.Iss.	1990	3.00	8
1990 Madonna and Child QXM5643	Yr.Iss.	1990	6.00	15
1990 Mother QXM5716	Yr.Iss.	1990	4.50	15
1990 Nativity QXM5706	Yr.Iss.	1990	4.50	15
1990 Nature's Angels QMX5733	Yr.Iss.	1990	4.50	20-27
1990 Panda's Surprise QXM5616	Yr.Iss.	1990	4.50	12
1990 Penguin Pal QXM5746	Yr.Iss.	1990	4.50	10-20
1990 Perfect Fit QXM5516	Yr.Iss.	1990	4.50	8
1990 Puppy Love QXM5666	Yr.Iss.	1990	6.00	10
1990 Rocking Horse QXM5743	Yr.Iss.	1990	4.50	17-25
1990 Ruby Reindeer QXM5816	Yr.Iss.	1990	6.00	10
1990 Santa's Journey QXM5826	Yr.Iss.	1990	8.50	18
1990 Santa's Streetcar QXM5766	Yr.Iss.	1990	8.50	15
1990 School QXM5763	Yr.Iss.	1990	8.50	25
1990 Snow Angel QXM5773	Yr.Iss.	1990	6.00	12
1990 Special Friends QXM5726	Yr.Iss.	1990	6.00	12
1990 Stamp Collector QXM5623	Yr.Iss.	1990	4.50	9
1990 Stringing Along QXM5606	Yr.Iss.	1990	8.50	16
1990 Sweet Slumber QXM5663	Yr.Iss.	1990	4.50	10
1990 Teacher QXM5653	Yr.Iss.	1990	4.50	8
1990 Thimble Bells QXM5543	Yr.Iss.	1990	6.00	20
1990 Type of Joy QXM5646	Yr.Iss.	1990	4.50	9
1990 Warm Memories QXM5713	Yr.Iss.	1990	4.50	10
1990 Wee Nutcracker QXM5843	Yr.Iss.	1990	8.50	14

1990 New Attractions - Keepsake

YEAR ISSUE	EDITION LIMIT	YEAR RETD.	ISSUE PRICE	*QUOTE U.S.$
1990 Baby Unicorn QX5486	Yr.Iss.	1990	9.75	12
1990 Bearback Rider QX5483	Yr.Iss.	1990	9.75	20-32
1990 Beary Good Deal QX4733	Yr.Iss.	1990	6.75	12
1990 Billboard Bunny QX5196	Yr.Iss.	1990	7.75	15
1990 Born to Dance QX5043	Yr.Iss.	1990	7.75	15
1990 Chiming In QX4366	Yr.Iss.	1990	9.75	20
1990 Christmas Croc QX4373	Yr.Iss.	1990	7.75	13
1990 Christmas Partridge QX5246	Yr.Iss.	1990	7.75	13-23
1990 Claus Construction QX4885	Yr.Iss.	1990	7.75	15-20
1990 Country Angel QX5046	Yr.Iss.	1990	6.75	75-115
1990 Coyote Carols QX4993	Yr.Iss.	1990	8.75	20
1990 Cozy Goose QX4966	Yr.Iss.	1990	5.75	14
1990 Feliz Navidad QX5173	Yr.Iss.	1990	6.75	17-25
1990 Garfield QX2303	Yr.Iss.	1990	4.75	20
1990 Gingerbread Elf QX5033	Yr.Iss.	1990	5.75	14-20
1990 Goose Cart QX5236	Yr.Iss.	1990	7.75	14
1990 Hang in There QX4713	Yr.Iss.	1990	6.75	17
1990 Happy Voices QX4645	Yr.Iss.	1990	6.75	14
1990 Holiday Cardinals QX5243	Yr.Iss.	1990	7.75	14-23
1990 Home for the Owldays QX5183	Yr.Iss.	1990	6.75	11
1990 Hot Dogger QX4976	Yr.Iss.	1990	7.75	16
1990 Jolly Dolphin QX4683	Yr.Iss.	1990	6.75	20
1990 Joy is in the Air QX5503	Yr.Iss.	1990	7.75	20
1990 King Klaus QX4106	Yr.Iss.	1990	7.75	13
1990 Kitty's Best Pal QX4716	Yr.Iss.	1990	6.75	15
1990 Little Drummer Boy QX5233	Yr.Iss.	1990	7.75	19
1990 Long Winter's Nap QX4703	Yr.Iss.	1990	6.75	15-20
1990 Lovable Dears QX5476	Yr.Iss.	1990	8.75	15
1990 Meow Mart QX4446	Yr.Iss.	1990	7.75	16
1990 Mooy Christmas QX4933	Yr.Iss.	1990	6.75	25
1990 Norman Rockwell Art QX2296	Yr.Iss.	1990	4.75	20
1990 Nutshell Chat QX5193	Yr.Iss.	1990	6.75	14-25
1990 Nutshell Holiday QX465-2	Yr.Iss.	1990	5.75	17-28
1990 Peanuts QX2233	Yr.Iss.	1990	4.75	25
1990 Pepperoni Mouse QX4973	Yr.Iss.	1990	6.75	15
1990 Perfect Catch QX4693	Yr.Iss.	1990	7.75	13
1990 Polar Jogger QX4666	Yr.Iss.	1990	5.75	9
1990 Polar Pair QX4626	Yr.Iss.	1990	5.75	15
1990 Polar Sport QX5156	Yr.Iss.	1990	7.75	12
1990 Polar TV QX5166	Yr.Iss.	1990	7.75	12
1990 Polar V.I.P. QX4663	Yr.Iss.	1990	5.75	12
1990 Polar Video QX4633	Yr.Iss.	1990	5.75	9
1990 Poolside Walrus QX4986	Yr.Iss.	1990	7.75	15
1990 S. Claus Taxi QX4686	Yr.Iss.	1990	11.75	25
1990 Santa Schnoz QX4983	Yr.Iss.	1990	6.75	30
1990 Snoopy and Woodstock QX4723	Yr.Iss.	1990	6.75	35-40
1990 Spoon Rider QX5496	Yr.Iss.	1990	9.75	15
1990 Stitches of Joy QX5186	Yr.Iss.	1990	7.75	16-30
1990 Stocking Kitten QX456-5	Yr.Iss.	1990	6.75	7
1990 Stocking Pals QX5493	Yr.Iss.	1990	10.75	20
1990 Three Little Piggies QX4996	Yr.Iss.	1990	7.75	15
1990 Two Peas in a Pod QX4926	Yr.Iss.	1990	4.75	25

1990 Special Edition - Keepsake

YEAR ISSUE	EDITION LIMIT	YEAR RETD.	ISSUE PRICE	*QUOTE U.S.$
1990 Dickens Caroler Bell-Mr. Ashbourne QX5056	Yr.Iss.	1990	21.75	45

1991 Artists' Favorites - Keepsake

YEAR ISSUE	EDITION LIMIT	YEAR RETD.	ISSUE PRICE	*QUOTE U.S.$
1991 Fiddlin' Around QX4387	Yr.Iss.	1991	7.75	17
1991 Hooked on Santa QX4109	Yr.Iss.	1991	7.75	21
1991 Noah's Ark QX4867	Yr.Iss.	1991	13.75	45
1991 Polar Circus Wagon QX4399	Yr.Iss.	1991	13.75	15-30
1991 Santa Sailor QX4389	Yr.Iss.	1991	9.75	22
1991 Tramp and Laddie QX4397	Yr.Iss.	1991	7.75	25-30

1991 Club Limited Editions - Keepsake

YEAR ISSUE	EDITION LIMIT	YEAR RETD.	ISSUE PRICE	*QUOTE U.S.$
1991 Galloping Into Christmas QXC4779	28,400	1991	19.75	75-100
1991 Secrets for Santa QXC4797	28,700	1991	23.75	35-48

1991 Collectible Series - Keepsake

YEAR ISSUE	EDITION LIMIT	YEAR RETD.	ISSUE PRICE	*QUOTE U.S.$
1991 1957 Corvette-(1st Ed.) QX4319	Yr.Iss.	1991	12.75	140-195
1991 Betsey Clark: Home for Christmas (6th Ed.) QX2109	Yr.Iss.	1991	5.00	20
1991 Checking His List (6th Ed.) QX4339	Yr.Iss.	1991	13.75	25-40
1991 Christmas Kitty-(3rd Ed.) QX4377	Yr.Iss.	1991	14.75	27
1991 CRAYOLA CRAYON-Bright Vibrant Carols-(3rd Ed.) QX4219	Yr.Iss.	1991	9.75	30
1991 Eight Maids A-Milking-(8th Ed.) QX3089	Yr.Iss.	1991	6.75	20
1991 Fabulous Decade-(2nd Ed.) QX4119	Yr.Iss.	1991	7.75	20-30
1991 Fire Station-(8th Ed.) QX4139	Yr.Iss.	1991	14.75	45
1991 Frosty Friends-(12th Ed.) QX4327	Yr.Iss.	1991	9.75	28-35
1991 The Gift Bringers-Christkind (3rd Ed.) QX2117	Yr.Iss.	1991	5.00	15
1991 Greatest Story-(2nd Ed.) QX4129	Yr.Iss.	1991	12.75	15-24
1991 Hark! It's Herald (3rd Ed.) QX4379	Yr.Iss.	1991	6.75	12-19
1991 Heart of Christmas-(2nd Ed.) QX4357	Yr.Iss.	1991	13.75	27-35
1991 Heavenly Angels-(1st Ed.) QX4367	Yr.Iss.	1991	7.75	20-30
1991 Let It Snow! (5th Ed.) QX4369	Yr.Iss.	1991	8.75	19
1991 Mary's Angels-Iris (4th Ed.) QX4279	Yr.Iss.	1991	6.75	15-25
1991 Merry Olde Santa-(2nd Ed.) QX4359	Yr.Iss.	1991	14.75	57-75
1991 Peace on Earth-Italy (1st Ed.) QX5129	Yr.Iss.	1991	11.75	20-26
1991 Puppy Love-(1st Ed.) QX5379	Yr.Iss.	1991	7.75	45
1991 Reindeer Champ-Cupid (6th Ed.) QX4347	Yr.Iss.	1991	7.75	20
1991 Rocking Horse-(11th Ed.) QX4147	Yr.Iss.	1991	10.75	27
1991 Santa's Antique Car-(13th Ed.) QX4349	Yr.Iss.	1991	14.75	32-40
1991 Winter Surprise-(3rd Ed.) QX4277	Yr.Iss.	1991	10.75	20-35

1991 Commemoratives - Keepsake

YEAR ISSUE	EDITION LIMIT	YEAR RETD.	ISSUE PRICE	*QUOTE U.S.$
1991 Across the Miles QX3157	Yr.Iss.	1991	6.75	13

ORNAMENTS

YEAR ISSUE	EDITION LIMIT	YEAR RETD.	ISSUE PRICE	*QUOTE U.S.$
1991 Baby's First Christmas QX4889	Yr.Iss.	1991	7.75	35
1991 Baby's First Christmas QX5107	Yr.Iss.	1991	17.75	45
1991 Baby's First Christmas-Baby Boy QX2217	Yr.Iss.	1991	4.75	15
1991 Baby's First Christmas-Baby Girl QX2227	Yr.Iss.	1991	4.75	15
1991 Baby's First Christmas-Photo Holder QX4869	Yr.Iss.	1991	7.75	25
1991 Baby's Second Christmas QX4897	Yr.Iss.	1991	6.75	35
1991 The Big Cheese QX5327	Yr.Iss.	1991	6.75	18
1991 Brother QX5479	Yr.Iss.	1991	6.75	18
1991 A Child's Christmas QX4887	Yr.Iss.	1991	9.75	15
1991 Child's Fifth Christmas QX4909	Yr.Iss.	1991	6.75	18
1991 Child's Fourth Christmas QX4907	Yr.Iss.	1991	6.75	18
1991 Child's Third Christmas QX4899	Yr.Iss.	1991	6.75	30
1991 Dad QX5127	Yr.Iss.	1991	7.75	19
1991 Dad-to-Be QX4879	Yr.Iss.	1991	5.75	20
1991 Daughter QX5477	Yr.Iss.	1991	5.75	25
1991 Extra-Special Friends QX2279	Yr.Iss.	1991	4.75	15
1991 Fifty Years Together QX4947	Yr.Iss.	1991	8.75	18
1991 Five Years Together QX4927	Yr.Iss.	1991	7.75	16
1991 Forty Years Together QX4939	Yr.Iss.	1991	7.75	18
1991 Friends Are Fun QX5289	Yr.Iss.	1991	9.75	33
1991 From Our Home to Yours QX2287	Yr.Iss.	1991	4.75	15
1991 Gift of Joy QX5319	Yr.Iss.	1991	8.75	20
1991 Godchild QX5489	Yr.Iss.	1991	6.75	19
1991 Granddaughter QX2299	Yr.Iss.	1991	4.75	20
1991 Granddaughter's First Christmas QX5119	Yr.Iss.	1991	6.75	18
1991 Grandmother QX2307	Yr.Iss.	1991	4.75	15-20
1991 Grandparents QX2309	Yr.Iss.	1991	4.75	15
1991 Grandson QX2297	Yr.Iss.	1991	4.75	14
1991 Grandson's First Christmas QX5117	Yr.Iss.	1991	6.75	14
1991 Jesus Loves Me QX3147	Yr.Iss.	1991	7.75	14
1991 Mom and Dad QX5467	Yr.Iss.	1991	9.75	21
1991 Mom-to-Be QX4877	Yr.Iss.	1991	5.75	22
1991 Mother QX5457	Yr.Iss.	1991	9.75	25-35
1991 New Home QX5449	Yr.Iss.	1991	6.75	20
1991 Our First Christmas Together QX2229	Yr.Iss.	1991	4.75	20
1991 Our First Christmas Together QX3139	Yr.Iss.	1991	6.75	15
1991 Our First Christmas Together QX4919	Yr.Iss.	1991	8.75	30
1991 Our First Christmas Together-Photo Holder QX4917	Yr.Iss.	1991	8.75	25
1991 Sister QX5487	Yr.Iss.	1991	6.75	18
1991 Son QX5469	Yr.Iss.	1991	5.75	20
1991 Sweetheart QX4957	Yr.Iss.	1991	9.75	18
1991 Teacher QX2289	Yr.Iss.	1991	4.75	12
1991 Ten Years Together QX4929	Yr.Iss.	1991	7.75	15
1991 Terrific Teacher QX5309	Yr.Iss.	1991	6.75	16
1991 Twenty -Five Years Together QX4937	Yr.Iss.	1991	8.75	16
1991 Under the Mistletoe QX4949	Yr.Iss.	1991	8.75	19

1991 Keepsake Collector's Club - Keepsake

1991 Beary Artistic QXC7259	Yr.Iss.	1991	10.00	32-40
1991 Hidden Treasure/Li'l Keeper QXC4769	Yr.Iss.	1991	15.00	38

1991 Keepsake Magic Ornaments - Keepsake

1991 Angel of Light QLT7239	Yr.Iss.	1991	30.00	60
1991 Arctic Dome QLX7117	Yr.Iss.	1991	25.00	45-55
1991 Baby's First Christmas QLX7247	Yr.Iss.	1991	30.00	45-65
1991 Bringing Home the Tree-QLX7249	Yr.Iss.	1991	28.00	51-65
1991 Chris Mouse Mail QLX7207	Yr.Iss.	1991	10.00	25-40
1991 Elfin Engineer QLX7209	Yr.Iss.	1991	10.00	25
1991 Father Christmas QLX7147	Yr.Iss.	1991	14.00	29-39
1991 Festive Brass Church QLX7179	Yr.Iss.	1991	14.00	30
1991 Forest Frolics QLX7219	Yr.Iss.	1991	25.00	68
1991 Friendship Tree QLX7169	Yr.Iss.	1991	10.00	24
1991 Holiday Glow QLX7177	Yr.Iss.	1991	14.00	30
1991 It's A Wonderful Life QLX7237	Yr.Iss.	1991	20.00	60-75
1991 Jingle Bears QLX7323	Yr.Iss.	1991	25.00	45-55
1991 Kringles's Bumper Cars-QLX7119	Yr.Iss.	1991	25.00	45-55
1991 Mole Family Home QLX7149	Yr.Iss.	1991	20.00	35-50
1991 Our First Christmas Together QXL7137	Yr.Iss.	1991	25.00	40-50
1991 PEANUTS QLX7229	Yr.Iss.	1991	18.00	75
1991 Salvation Army Band QLX7273	Yr.Iss.	1991	30.00	55-75
1991 Santa Special QLX7167	Yr.Iss.	1992	40.00	75
1991 Santa's Hot Line QLX7159	Yr.Iss.	1991	18.00	32-42
1991 Ski Trip QLX7266	Yr.Iss.	1991	28.00	50-60
1991 Sparkling Angel QLX7157	Yr.Iss.	1991	18.00	27-37
1991 Toyland Tower QLX7129	Yr.Iss.	1991	20.00	37-45

1991 Keepsake Miniature Ornaments - Keepsake

1991 All Aboard QXM5869	Yr.Iss.	1991	4.50	17
1991 Baby's First Christmas QXM5799	Yr.Iss.	1991	6.00	20
1991 Brass Church QXM5979	Yr.Iss.	1991	3.00	9
1991 Brass Soldier QXM5987	Yr.Iss.	1991	3.00	9
1991 Bright Boxers QXM5877	Yr.Iss.	1991	4.50	10-16
1991 Busy Bear QXM5939	Yr.Iss.	1991	4.50	12
1991 Cardinal Cameo QXM5957	Yr.Iss.	1991	6.00	17
1991 Caring Shepherd QXM5949	Yr.Iss.	1991	6.00	17
1991 Cool 'n' Sweet QXM5867	Yr.Iss.	1991	4.50	23
1991 Country Sleigh QXM5999	Yr.Iss.	1991	4.50	6-13
1991 Courier Turtle QXM5857	Yr.Iss.	1991	4.50	14
1991 Fancy Wreath QXM5917	Yr.Iss.	1991	4.50	6-13
1991 Feliz Navidad QXM5887	Yr.Iss.	1991	6.00	15

YEAR ISSUE	EDITION LIMIT	YEAR RETD.	ISSUE PRICE	*QUOTE U.S.$
1991 Fly By QXM5859	Yr.Iss.	1991	4.50	17
1991 Friendly Fawn QXM5947	Yr.Iss.	1991	6.00	17
1991 Grandchild's First Christmas QXM5697	Yr.Iss.	1991	4.50	14
1991 Heavenly Minstrel QXM5687	Yr.Iss.	1991	9.75	25
1991 Holiday Snowflake QXM5997	Yr.Iss.	1991	3.00	12
1991 Inn-(4th Ed.) QXM5627	Yr.Iss.	1991	8.50	20
1991 Key to Love QXM5689	Yr.Iss.	1991	4.50	17
1991 Kittens in Toyland-(4th Ed.) QXM5639	Yr.Iss.	1991	4.50	15
1991 Kitty in a Mitty QXM5879	Yr.Iss.	1991	4.50	13
1991 The Kringles-(3rd Ed.) QXM5647	Yr.Iss.	1991	6.00	20
1991 Li'l Popper QXM5897	Yr.Iss.	1991	4.50	15
1991 Love Is Born QXM5959	Yr.Iss.	1991	6.00	18
1991 Lulu & Family QXM5677	Yr.Iss.	1991	6.00	20
1991 Mom QXM5699	Yr.Iss.	1991	6.00	17
1991 N. Pole Buddy QXM5927	Yr.Iss.	1991	4.50	18
1991 Nature's Angels-(2nd Ed.) QXM5657	Yr.Iss.	1991	4.50	15
1991 Noel QXM5989	Yr.Iss.	1991	3.00	12
1991 Our First Christmas Together QXM5819	Yr.Iss.	1991	6.00	17
1991 Passenger Car-(3rd Ed.) QXM5649	Yr.Iss.	1991	8.50	25
1991 Penquin Pal-(4th Ed.) QXM5629	Yr.Iss.	1991	4.50	17
1991 Ring-A-Ding Elf QXM5669	Yr.Iss.	1991	8.50	18
1991 Rocking Horse-(4th Ed.) QXM5637	Yr.Iss.	1991	4.50	15-25
1991 Seaside Otter QXM5909	Yr.Iss.	1991	4.50	13
1991 Silvery Santa QXM5679	Yr.Iss.	1991	9.75	7-21
1991 Special Friends QXM5797	Yr.Iss.	1991	8.50	18
1991 Thimble Bells-(2nd Ed.) QXM5659	Yr.Iss.	1991	6.00	10-20
1991 Tiny Tea Party (set/6) QXM5827	Yr.Iss.	1991	29.00	142-160
1991 Top Hatter QXM5889	Yr.Iss.	1991	6.00	10-16
1991 Treeland Trio QXM5899	Yr.Iss.	1991	8.50	15
1991 Upbeat Bear QXM5907	Yr.Iss.	1991	6.00	15
1991 Vision of Santa QXM5937	Yr.Iss.	1991	4.50	14
1991 Wee Toymaker QXM5967	Yr.Iss.	1991	8.50	10-15
1991 Woodland Babies QXM5667	Yr.Iss.	1991	6.00	12-22

1991 New Attractions - Keepsake

1991 All-Star QX5329	Yr.Iss.	1991	6.75	17
1991 Basket Bell Players QX5377	Yr.Iss.	1991	7.75	21
1991 Bob Cratchit QX4997	Yr.Iss.	1991	13.75	23
1991 Chilly Chap QX5339	Yr.Iss.	1991	6.75	17
1991 Christmas Welcome QX5299	Yr.Iss.	1991	9.75	21
1991 Christopher Robin QX5579	Yr.Iss.	1991	9.75	37
1991 Cuddly Lamb QX5199	Yr.Iss.	1991	6.75	20
1991 Dinoclaus QX5277	Yr.Iss.	1991	7.75	16
1991 Ebenezer Scrooge QX4989	Yr.Iss.	1991	13.75	30
1991 Evergreen Inn QX5389	Yr.Iss.	1991	8.75	15
1991 Fanfare Bear QX5337	Yr.Iss.	1991	8.75	19
1991 Feliz Navidad QX5279	Yr.Iss.	1991	6.75	15
1991 Folk Art Reindeer QX5359	Yr.Iss.	1991	8.75	14
1991 GARFIELD QX5177	Yr.Iss.	1991	7.75	20
1991 Glee Club Bears QX4969	Yr.Iss.	1991	8.75	18
1991 Holiday Cafe QX5399	Yr.Iss.	1991	8.75	14
1991 Jolly Wolly Santa QX5419	Yr.Iss.	1991	7.75	15-22
1991 Jolly Wolly Snowman QX5427	Yr.Iss.	1991	7.75	21
1991 Jolly Wolly Soldier QX5429	Yr.Iss.	1991	7.75	17
1991 Joyous Memories-Photoholder QX5369	Yr.Iss.	1991	6.75	16
1991 Kanga and Roo QX5617	Yr.Iss.	1991	9.75	18-40
1991 Look Out Below QX4959	Yr.Iss.	1991	8.75	18
1991 Loving Stitches QX4987	Yr.Iss.	1991	8.75	30
1991 Mary Engelbreit QX2237	Yr.Iss.	1991	4.75	28
1991 Merry Carolers QX4799	Yr.Iss.	1991	29.75	95
1991 Mrs. Cratchit QX4999	Yr.Iss.	1991	13.75	30
1991 Night Before Christmas QX5307	Yr.Iss.	1991	9.75	21
1991 Norman Rockwell Art QX2259	Yr.Iss.	1991	5.00	24
1991 Notes of Cheer QX5357	Yr.Iss.	1991	5.75	14
1991 Nutshell Nativity QX5176	Yr.Iss.	1991	6.75	20
1991 Nutty Squirrel QX4833	Yr.Iss.	1991	5.75	14
1991 Old-Fashioned Sled QX4317	Yr.Iss.	1991	8.75	18
1991 On a Roll QX5347	Yr.Iss.	1991	6.75	18
1991 Partridge in a Pear Tree QX5297	Yr.Iss.	1991	9.75	18
1991 PEANUTS QX2257	Yr.Iss.	1991	5.00	15-20
1991 Piglet and Eeyore QX5577	Yr.Iss.	1991	9.75	20-40
1991 Plum Delightful QX4977	Yr.Iss.	1991	8.75	19
1991 Polar Classic QX5287	Yr.Iss.	1991	6.75	18
1991 Rabbit QX5607	Yr.Iss.	1991	9.75	25-32
1991 Santa's Studio QX5397	Yr.Iss.	1991	8.75	15
1991 Ski Lift Bunny QX5447	Yr.Iss.	1991	6.75	17
1991 Snoopy and Woodstock QX5197	Yr.Iss.	1991	6.75	37
1991 Snow Twins QX4979	Yr.Iss.	1991	8.75	20
1991 Snowy Owl QX5269	Yr.Iss.	1991	7.75	18
1991 Sweet Talk QX5367	Yr.Iss.	1991	8.75	17
1991 Tigger QX5609	Yr.Iss.	1991	9.75	95-105
1991 Tiny Tim QX5037	Yr.Iss.	1991	10.75	24-35
1991 Up 'N'Down Journey QX5047	Yr.Iss.	1991	9.75	20
1991 Winnie-the Pooh QX5569	Yr.Iss.	1991	9.75	55
1991 Yule Logger QX4967	Yr.Iss.	1991	8.75	17-27

1991 Special Edition - Keepsake

1991 Dickens Caroler Bell -Mrs. Beaumont QX5039	Yr.Iss.	1991	21.75	40-50
1991 Starship Enterprise QLX7199	Yr.Iss.	1991	20.00	300-500

1992 Artists' Favorites - Keepsake

1992 Elfin Marionette QX5931	Yr.Iss.	1992	11.75	23
1992 Mother Goose QX4984	Yr.Iss.	1992	13.75	27
1992 Polar Post QX4914	Yr.Iss.	1992	8.75	18
1992 Stocked With Joy QX5934	Yr.Iss.	1992	7.75	15

YEAR ISSUE	EDITION LIMIT	YEAR RETD.	ISSUE PRICE	*QUOTE U.S.$
1992 Turtle Dreams QX4991	Yr.Iss.	1992	8.75	20-28
1992 Uncle Art's Ice Cream QX5001	Yr.Iss.	1992	8.75	22-30

1992 Collectible Series - Keepsake

1992 1966 Mustang-(2nd Ed.) QX4284	Yr.Iss.	1992	12.75	45
1992 Betsey's Country Christmas -(1st Ed.) QX2104	Yr.Iss.	1992	5.00	25
1992 CRAYOLA CRAYON-Bright Colors (4th Ed.) QX4264	Yr.Iss.	1992	9.75	32
1992 Fabulous Decade-(3rd Ed.) QX4244	Yr.Iss.	1992	7.75	35
1992 Five-and-Ten-Cent Store (9th Ed.) QX4254	Yr.Iss.	1992	14.75	30
1992 Frosty Friends (13th Ed.) QX4291	Yr.Iss.	1992	9.75	25
1992 The Gift Bringers-Kolyada (4th Ed.) QX2124	Yr.Iss.	1992	5.00	15
1992 Gift Exchange (7th Ed.) QX4294	Yr.Iss.	1992	14.75	33
1992 Greatest Story (3rd Ed.) QX4251	Yr.Iss.	1992	12.75	15-25
1992 Hark! It's Herald (4th Ed.) QX4464	Yr.Iss.	1992	7.75	12-20
1992 Heart of Christmas (3rd Ed.) QX4411	Yr.Iss.	1992	13.75	30
1992 Heavenly Angels (2nd Ed.) QX4454	Yr.Iss.	1992	7.75	30
1992 Kringle Tours (14th Ed.) QX4341	Yr.Iss.	1992	14.75	30
1992 Mary's Angels-Lily (5th Ed.) QX4274	Yr.Iss.	1992	6.75	48
1992 Merry Olde Santa (3rd Ed.) QX4414	Yr.Iss.	1992	14.75	35
1992 Nine Ladies Dancing (9th Ed.) QX3031	Yr.Iss.	1992	6.75	20
1992 Owliver (1st Ed.) QX4544	Yr.Iss.	1992	7.75	17
1992 Peace On Earth-Spain (2nd Ed.) QX5174	Yr.Iss.	1992	11.75	25
1992 Puppy Love (2nd Ed.) QX4484	Yr.Iss.	1992	7.75	25-40
1992 Reindeer Champs-Donder (7th Ed.) QX5284	Yr.Iss.	1992	8.75	30
1992 Rocking Horse (12th Ed.) QX4261	Yr.Iss.	1992	10.75	25-35
1992 Sweet Holiday Harmony (6th Ed.) QX4461	Yr.Iss.	1992	8.75	19-30
1992 Tobin Fraley Carousel (1st Ed.) QX4891	Yr.Iss.	1992	28.00	65
1992 Winter Surprise (4th Ed.) QX4271	Yr.Iss.	1992	11.75	30

1992 Collectors' Club - Keepsake

1992 Chipmunk Parcel Service QXC5194	Yr.Iss.	1992	6.75	21
1992 Rodney Takes Flight QXC5081	Yr.Iss.	1992	9.75	22
1992 Santa's Club List QXC7291	Yr.Iss.	1992	15.00	36

1992 Commemoratives - Keepsake

1992 Across the Miles QX3044	Yr.Iss.	1992	6.75	14
1992 Anniversary Year QX4851	Yr.Iss.	1992	9.75	25
1992 Baby's First Christmas QX4641	Yr.Iss.	1992	7.75	22
1992 Baby's First Christmas QX4644	Yr.Iss.	1992	7.75	25
1992 Baby's First Christmas-Baby Boy QX2191	Yr.Iss.	1992	4.75	15
1992 Baby's First Christmas-Baby Girl QX2204	Yr.Iss.	1992	4.75	13
1992 Baby's First Christmas QX4581	Yr.Iss.	1992	18.75	25-38
1992 Baby's Second Christmas QX4651	Yr.Iss.	1992	6.75	40
1992 Brother QX4684	Yr.Iss.	1992	6.75	14
1992 A Child's Christmas QX4574	Yr.Iss.	1992	9.75	18
1992 Child's Fifth Christmas QX4664	Yr.Iss.	1992	6.75	15
1992 Child's Fourth Christmas QX4661	Yr.Iss.	1992	6.75	20
1992 Child's Third Christmas QX4654	Yr.Iss.	1992	6.75	30
1992 Dad QX4674	Yr.Iss.	1992	7.75	18
1992 Dad-to-Be QX4611	Yr.Iss.	1992	6.75	17
1992 Daughter QX5031	Yr.Iss.	1992	6.75	20
1992 For My Grandma QX5184	Yr.Iss.	1992	7.75	15
1992 For The One I Love QX4884	Yr.Iss.	1992	9.75	20
1992 Friendly Greetings QX5041	Yr.Iss.	1992	7.75	16
1992 Friendship Line QX5034	Yr.Iss.	1992	9.75	27
1992 From Our Home To Yours QX2131	Yr.Iss.	1992	4.75	15
1992 Godchild QX5941	Yr.Iss.	1992	6.75	18
1992 Grandaughter QX5604	Yr.Iss.	1992	6.75	15
1992 Grandaughter's First Christmas QX4634	Yr.Iss.	1992	6.75	14
1992 Grandmother QX2011	Yr.Iss.	1992	4.75	15
1992 Grandparents QX2004	Yr.Iss.	1992	4.75	17
1992 Grandson QX5611	Yr.Iss.	1992	6.75	16
1992 Grandson's First Christmas QX4621	Yr.Iss.	1992	6.75	15
1992 Holiday Memo QX5044	Yr.Iss.	1992	7.75	14
1992 Love To Skate QX4841	Yr.Iss.	1992	8.75	14
1992 Mom and Dad QX4671	Yr.Iss.	1992	9.75	35
1992 Mom QX5164	Yr.Iss.	1992	7.75	18
1992 Mom-to-Be QX4614	Yr.Iss.	1992	6.75	20
1992 New Home QX5191	Yr.Iss.	1992	8.75	25
1992 Our First Christmas Together QX4694	Yr.Iss.	1992	8.75	25
1992 Our First Christmas Together QX3011	Yr.Iss.	1992	6.75	15
1992 Our First Christmas Together QX5061	Yr.Iss.	1992	9.75	25
1992 Secret Pal QX5424	Yr.Iss.	1992	7.75	15
1992 Sister QX4681	Yr.Iss.	1992	6.75	15
1992 Son QX5024	Yr.Iss.	1992	6.75	17-25
1992 Special Cat QX5414	Yr.Iss.	1992	7.75	17
1992 Special Dog QX5421	Yr.Iss.	1992	7.75	30
1992 Teacher QX2264	Yr.Iss.	1992	4.75	17
1992 V. P. of Important Stuff QX5051	Yr.Iss.	1992	6.75	14
1992 World-Class Teacher QX5054	Yr.Iss.	1992	7.75	20

Collectors' Information Bureau
*Quotes have been rounded up to nearest dollar

YEAR ISSUE	EDITION LIMIT	YEAR RETD.	ISSUE PRICE	*QUOTE U.S.$
1992 Easter Ornaments - Keepsake				
1992 Easter Parade (1st Ed.) 675QEO8301	Yr.Iss.	1992	6.75	28
1992 Egg in Sports (1st Ed.) 675QEO9341	Yr.Iss.	1992	6.75	30
1992 Limited Edition Ornaments - Keepsake				
1992 Christmas Treasures QXC5464	15,500	1992	22.00	22
1992 Victorian Skater (w/ base) QXC4067	14,700	1992	25.00	35
1992 Magic Ornaments - Keepsake				
1992 Angel Of Light QLT7239	Yr.Iss.	1992	30.00	30
1992 Baby's First Christmas QLX7281	Yr.Iss.	1992	22.00	90
1992 Chris Mouse Tales (8th Ed.) QLX7074	Yr.Iss.	1992	12.00	27
1992 Christmas Parade QLX7271	Yr.Iss.	1992	30.00	55
1992 Continental Express QLX7264	Yr.Iss.	1992	32.00	58-70
1992 The Dancing Nutcracker QLX7261	Yr.Iss.	1992	30.00	40-60
1992 Enchanted Clock QLX7274	Yr.Iss.	1992	30.00	60
1992 Feathered Friends QLX7091	Yr.Iss.	1992	14.00	29
1992 Forest Frolics-(4th Ed.) QLX7254	Yr.Iss.	1992	28.00	50-65
1992 Good Sledding Ahead QLX7244	Yr.Iss.	1992	28.00	55
1992 Lighting the Way QLX7231	Yr.Iss.	1992	18.00	39-49
1992 Look! It's Santa QLX7094	Yr.Iss.	1992	14.00	30-40
1992 Nut Sweet Nut QLX7081	Yr.Iss.	1992	10.00	22
1992 Our First Christmas Together QLX7221	Yr.Iss.	1992	20.00	40-45
1992 PEANUTS (2nd Ed.) QLX7214	Yr.Iss.	1992	18.00	55
1992 Santa Special QLX7167	Yr.Iss.	1992	40.00	80
1992 Santa Sub QLX7321	Yr.Iss.	1992	18.00	34-40
1992 Santa's Answering Machine QLX7241	Yr.Iss.	1992	22.00	43
1992 Under Construction QLX7324	Yr.Iss.	1992	18.00	37
1992 Watch Owls QLX7084	Yr.Iss.	1992	12.00	26
1992 Yuletide Rider QLX7314	Yr.Iss.	1992	28.00	55
1992 Miniature Ornaments - Keepsake				
1992 A+ Teacher QXM5511	Yr.Iss.	1992	3.75	8
1992 Angelic Harpist QXM5524	Yr.Iss.	1992	4.50	13
1992 Baby's First Christmas QXM5494	Yr.Iss.	1992	4.50	18
1992 The Bearymores (1st Ed.) QXM5544	Yr.Iss.	1992	5.75	15-20
1992 Black-Capped Chickadee QXM5484	Yr.Iss.	1992	3.00	10
1992 Box Car (4th Ed.) Noel R.R. QXM5441	Yr.Iss.	1992	7.00	20
1992 Bright Stringers QXM5841	Yr.Iss.	1992	3.75	5-14
1992 Buck-A-Roo QXM5814	Yr.Iss.	1992	4.50	10
1992 Christmas Bonus QXM5811	Yr.Iss.	1992	3.00	7
1992 Christmas Copter QXM5844	Yr.Iss.	1992	5.75	15
1992 Church (5th Ed.) Old English V. QXM5384	Yr.Iss.	1992	7.00	20-30
1992 Coca-Cola Santa QXM5884	Yr.Iss.	1992	5.75	10-16
1992 Cool Uncle Sam QXM5561	Yr.Iss.	1992	3.00	14
1992 Cozy Kayak QXM5551	Yr.Iss.	1992	3.75	12
1992 Fast Finish QXM5301	Yr.Iss.	1992	3.75	12
1992 Feeding Time QXM5481	Yr.Iss.	1992	5.75	16
1992 Friendly Tin Soldier QXM5874	Yr.Iss.	1992	4.50	13
1992 Friends Are Tops QXM5521	Yr.Iss.	1992	4.50	10
1992 Gerbil Inc. QXM5924	Yr.Iss.	1992	3.75	11
1992 Going Places QXM5871	Yr.Iss.	1992	3.75	10
1992 Grandchild's First Christmas QXM5501	Yr.Iss.	1992	5.75	13
1992 Grandma QXM5514	Yr.Iss.	1992	4.50	10
1992 Harmony Trio-Set/3 QXM5471	Yr.Iss.	1992	11.75	13-21
1992 Hickory, Dickory, Dock QXM5861	Yr.Iss.	1992	3.75	13
1992 Holiday Holly QXM5364	Yr.Iss.	1992	9.75	28
1992 Holiday Splash QXM5834	Yr.Iss.	1992	5.75	12
1992 Hoop It Up QXM5831	Yr.Iss.	1992	4.50	11
1992 Inside Story QXM5881	Yr.Iss.	1992	7.25	17
1992 Kittens in Toyland (5th Ed.) QXM5391	Yr.Iss.	1992	4.50	15
1992 The Kringles-(4th Ed.) QXM5381	Yr.Iss.	1992	6.00	20
1992 Little Town of Bethlehem QXM5864	Yr.Iss.	1992	3.00	18
1992 Minted For Santa QXM5854	Yr.Iss.	1992	3.75	14
1992 Mom QXM5504	Yr.Iss.	1992	4.50	14
1992 Nature's Angels (3rd Ed.) QXM5451	Yr.Iss.	1992	4.50	18
1992 The Night Before Christmas QXM5541	Yr.Iss.	1992	13.75	28-35
1992 Perfect Balance QXM5571	Yr.Iss.	1992	3.00	12
1992 Polar Polka QXM5534	Yr.Iss.	1992	4.50	14
1992 Puppet Show QXM5574	Yr.Iss.	1992	3.00	12
1992 Rocking Horse (5th Ed.) QXM5454	Yr.Iss.	1992	4.50	15
1992 Sew Sew Tiny (set/6) QXM5794	Yr.Iss.	1992	29.00	45-50
1992 Ski For Two QXM5821	Yr.Iss.	1992	4.50	14
1992 Snowshoe Bunny QXM5564	Yr.Iss.	1992	3.75	12
1992 Snug Kitty QXM5554	Yr.Iss.	1992	3.75	13
1992 Spunky Monkey QXM5921	Yr.Iss.	1992	3.00	13
1992 Thimble Bells (3rd Ed.) QXM5461	Yr.Iss.	1992	6.00	18
1992 Visions Of Acorns QXM5851	Yr.Iss.	1992	4.50	15
1992 Wee Three Kings QXM5531	Yr.Iss.	1992	5.75	15
1992 Woodland Babies (2nd Ed.) QXM5444	Yr.Iss.	1992	6.00	14
1992 New Attractions - Keepsake				
1992 Bear Bell Champ QX5071	Yr.Iss.	1992	7.75	16
1992 Caboose QX5321	Yr.Iss.	1992	9.75	20
1992 Cheerful Santa QX5154	Yr.Iss.	1992	9.75	30
1992 Coal Car QX5401	Yr.Iss.	1992	9.75	19

YEAR ISSUE	EDITION LIMIT	YEAR RETD.	ISSUE PRICE	*QUOTE U.S.$
1992 Cool Fliers QX5474	Yr.Iss.	1992	10.75	20
1992 Deck the Hogs QX5204	Yr.Iss.	1992	8.75	12-22
1992 Down-Under Holiday QX5144	Yr.Iss.	1992	7.75	18
1992 Egg Nog Nest QX5121	Yr.Iss.	1992	7.75	14
1992 Eric the Baker QX5244	Yr.Iss.	1992	8.75	18
1992 Feliz Navidad QX5181	Yr.Iss.	1992	6.75	16
1992 Franz the Artist QX5261	Yr.Iss.	1992	8.75	18
1992 Freida the Animals' Friend QX5264	Yr.Iss.	1992	8.75	20
1992 Fun on a Big Scale QX5134	Yr.Iss.	1992	10.75	21
1992 GARFIELD QX5374	Yr.Iss.	1992	7.75	19
1992 Genius at Work QX5371	Yr.Iss.	1992	10.75	20
1992 Golf's a Ball QX5984	Yr.Iss.	1992	6.75	10-26
1992 Gone Wishin' QX5171	Yr.Iss.	1992	8.75	19
1992 Green Thumb Santa QX5101	Yr.Iss.	1992	7.75	15
1992 Hello-Ho-Ho QX5141	Yr.Iss.	1992	9.75	16-23
1992 Holiday Teatime QX5431	Yr.Iss.	1992	14.75	26
1992 Holiday Wishes QX5131	Yr.Iss.	1992	7.75	17
1992 Honest George QX5064	Yr.Iss.	1992	7.75	18
1992 Jesus Loves Me QX3024	Yr.Iss.	1992	7.75	15
1992 Locomotive QX5311	Yr.Iss.	1992	9.75	60
1992 Loving Shepherd QX5151	Yr.Iss.	1992	7.75	15
1992 Ludwig the Musician QX5281	Yr.Iss.	1992	8.75	18
1992 Mary Engelbreit Santa Jolly Wolly QX5224	Yr.Iss.	1992	7.75	8
1992 Max the Tailor QX5251	Yr.Iss.	1992	8.75	20
1992 Memories to Cherish QX5161	Yr.Iss.	1992	10.75	20
1992 Merry "Swiss" Mouse QX5114	Yr.Iss.	1992	7.75	15
1992 Norman Rockwell Art QX2224	Yr.Iss.	1992	5.00	20
1992 North Pole Fire Fighter QX5104	Yr.Iss.	1992	9.75	21
1992 Otto the Carpenter QX5254	Yr.Iss.	1992	8.75	20
1992 Owl QX5614	Yr.Iss.	1992	9.75	15-25
1992 Partridge In a Pear Tree QX5234	Yr.Iss.	1992	8.75	19
1992 PEANUTS® QX2244	Yr.Iss.	1992	5.00	20
1992 Please Pause Here QX5291	Yr.Iss.	1992	14.75	31
1992 Rapid Delivery QX5094	Yr.Iss.	1992	8.75	21
1992 Santa's Hook Shot QX5434	Yr.Iss.	1992	12.75	28
1992 Santa's Roundup QX5084	Yr.Iss.	1992	8.75	20
1992 A Santa-Full! QX5991	Yr.Iss.	1992	9.75	14-30
1992 Silver Star QX5324	Yr.Iss.	1992	28.00	53
1992 Skiing 'Round QX5214	Yr.Iss.	1992	8.75	18
1992 SNOOPY® and WOODSTOCK QX5954	Yr.Iss.	1992	8.75	23
1992 Spirit of Christmas Stress QX5231	Yr.Iss.	1992	8.75	18
1992 Stock Car QX5314	Yr.Iss.	1992	9.75	19
1992 Tasty Christmas QX5994	Yr.Iss.	1992	9.75	19
1992 Toboggan Tail QX5459	Yr.Iss.	1992	7.75	16
1992 Tread Bear QX5091	Yr.Iss.	1992	8.75	23
1992 Special Edition - Keepsake				
1992 Dickens Caroler Bell-Lord Chadwick (3rd Ed.) QX4554	Yr.Iss.	1992	21.75	35
1992 Special Issues - Keepsake				
1992 Elvis QX562-4	Yr.Iss.	1992	14.75	20
1992 Santa Maria QX5074	Yr.Iss.	1992	12.75	20
1992 Shuttlecraft Galileo 2400QLX733-1	Yr.Iss.	1992	24.00	55
1993 Anniversary Edition - Keepsake				
1993 Frosty Friends QX5682	Yr.Iss.	1993	20.00	20-50
1993 Glowing Pewter Wreath QX5302	Yr.Iss.	1993	18.75	38
1993 Shopping With Santa QX5675	Yr.Iss.	1993	24.00	25-50
1993 Tannenbaum's Dept. Store QX5612	Yr.Iss.	1993	26.00	54-60
1993 Artists' Favorites - Keepsake				
1993 Bird Watcher QX5252	Yr.Iss.	1993	9.75	15-20
1993 Howling Good Time QX5255	Yr.Iss.	1993	9.75	18
1993 On Her Toes QX5265	Yr.Iss.	1993	8.75	18
1993 Peek-a-Boo Tree QX5245	Yr.Iss.	1993	10.75	25
1993 Wake-Up Call QX5262	Yr.Iss.	1993	8.75	17
1993 Collectible Series - Keepsake				
1993 1956 Ford Thunderbird (3rd Ed.) QX5275	Yr.Iss.	1993	12.75	35
1993 Betsey's Country Christmas (2nd Ed.) QX2062	Yr.Iss.	1993	5.00	20
1993 Cozy Home (10th Ed.) QX4175	Yr.Iss.	1993	14.75	33-45
1993 CRAYOLA CRAYON-Bright Shining Castle (5th Ed.) QX4422	Yr.Iss.	1993	11.00	30
1993 Fabulous Decade (4th Ed.) QX4475	Yr.Iss.	1993	7.75	17
1993 A Fitting Moment (8th Ed.) QX4202	Yr.Iss.	1993	14.75	30
1993 Frosty Friends (14th Ed.) QX4142	Yr.Iss.	1993	9.75	22-30
1993 The Gift Bringers-The Magi (5th Ed.) QX2065	Yr.Iss.	1993	5.00	16
1993 Happy Haul-idays (15th Ed.) QX4102	Yr.Iss.	1993	14.75	30
1993 Heart Of Christmas-(4th Ed.) QX4482	Yr.Iss.	1993	14.75	28
1993 Heavenly Angels (3rd Ed.) QX4945	Yr.Iss.	1993	7.75	18
1993 Humpty-Dumpty (1st Ed.) QX5282	Yr.Iss.	1993	13.75	35
1993 Mary's Angels-Ivy (6th Ed.) QX4282	Yr.Iss.	1993	6.75	15
1993 Merry Olde Santa (4th Ed.) QX4842	Yr.Iss.	1993	14.75	27
1993 Owliver (2nd Ed.) QX5425	Yr.Iss.	1993	7.75	17
1993 Peace On Earth-Poland (3rd Ed.) QX5242	Yr.Iss.	1993	11.75	22
1993 Peanuts (1st Ed.) QX5315	Yr.Iss.	1993	9.75	35-60
1993 Puppy Love (3rd Ed.) QX5045	Yr.Iss.	1993	7.75	27

YEAR ISSUE	EDITION LIMIT	YEAR RETD.	ISSUE PRICE	*QUOTE U.S.$
1993 Reindeer Champs-Blitzen (8th Ed.) QX4331	Yr.Iss.	1993	8.75	21
1993 Rocking Horse (13th Ed.) QX4162	Yr.Iss.	1993	10.75	30
1993 Ten Lords A-Leaping (10th Ed.) QX3012	Yr.Iss.	1993	6.75	15
1993 Tobin Fraley Carousel (2nd Ed.) QX5502	Yr.Iss.	1993	28.00	40-55
1993 U.S. Christmas Stamps (1st Ed.) QX5292	Yr.Iss.	1993	10.75	32-42
1993 Commemoratives - Keepsake				
1993 Across the Miles QX5912	Yr.Iss.	1993	8.75	18
1993 Anniversary Year QX5972	Yr.Iss.	1993	9.75	18
1993 Apple for Teacher QX5902	Yr.Iss.	1993	7.75	16
1993 Baby's First Christmas QX5512	Yr.Iss.	1993	18.75	40
1993 Baby's First Christmas QX5515	Yr.Iss.	1993	10.75	25
1993 Baby's First Christmas QX5522	Yr.Iss.	1993	7.75	21
1993 Baby's First Christmas QX5525	Yr.Iss.	1993	7.75	30
1993 Baby's First Christmas-Baby Boy QX2105	Yr.Iss.	1993	4.75	13
1993 Baby's First Christmas-Baby Girl QX2092	Yr.Iss.	1993	4.75	15
1993 Baby's Second Christmas QX5992	Yr.Iss.	1993	6.75	25
1993 Brother QX5542	Yr.Iss.	1993	6.75	13
1993 A Child's Christmas QX5882	Yr.Iss.	1993	9.75	20
1993 Child's Fifth Christmas QX5222	Yr.Iss.	1993	6.75	18
1993 Child's Fourth Christmas QX5215	Yr.Iss.	1993	6.75	15-25
1993 Child's Third Christmas QX5995	Yr.Iss.	1993	6.75	20
1993 Coach QX5935	Yr.Iss.	1993	6.75	15
1993 Dad QX5855	Yr.Iss.	1993	7.75	17
1993 Dad-to-Be QX5532	Yr.Iss.	1993	6.75	18
1993 Daughter QX5872	Yr.Iss.	1993	6.75	20
1993 Godchild QX5875	Yr.Iss.	1993	8.75	18
1993 Grandchild's First Christmas QX5552	Yr.Iss.	1993	6.75	15
1993 Granddaughter QX5635	Yr.Iss.	1993	6.75	13
1993 Grandmother QX5665	Yr.Iss.	1993	6.75	13
1993 Grandparents QX2085	Yr.Iss.	1993	4.75	15
1993 Grandson QX5632	Yr.Iss.	1993	6.75	13
1993 Mom and Dad QX5845	Yr.Iss.	1993	9.75	17
1993 Mom QX5852	Yr.Iss.	1993	7.75	17
1993 Mom-to-Be QX5535	Yr.Iss.	1993	6.75	14
1993 Nephew QX5735	Yr.Iss.	1993	6.75	13
1993 New Home QX5905	Yr.Iss.	1993	7.75	37
1993 Niece QX5732	Yr.Iss.	1993	6.75	14
1993 Our Christmas Together QX5942	Yr.Iss.	1993	10.75	22
1993 Our Family QX5892	Yr.Iss.	1993	7.75	17
1993 Our First Christmas Together QX3015	Yr.Iss.	1993	6.75	15
1993 Our First Christmas Together QX5642	Yr.Iss.	1993	9.75	25
1993 Our First Christmas Together QX5952	Yr.Iss.	1993	8.75	25
1993 Our First Christmas Together QX5955	Yr.Iss.	1993	18.75	38
1993 People Friendly QX5932	Yr.Iss.	1993	8.75	16
1993 Sister QX5545	Yr.Iss.	1993	6.75	16-23
1993 Sister to Sister QX5885	Yr.Iss.	1993	9.75	30
1993 Son QX5865	Yr.Iss.	1993	6.75	20
1993 Special Cat QX5235	Yr.Iss.	1993	7.75	14
1993 Special Dog QX5962	Yr.Iss.	1993	7.75	15
1993 Star Teacher QX5645	Yr.Iss.	1993	5.75	13
1993 Strange and Wonderful Love QX5965	Yr.Iss.	1993	8.75	16
1993 To My Grandma QX5555	Yr.Iss.	1993	7.75	16
1993 Top Banana QX5925	Yr.Iss.	1993	7.75	15
1993 Warm and Special Friends QX5895	Yr.Iss.	1993	10.75	25
1993 Easter Ornaments - Keepsake				
1993 Easter Parade (2nd Ed.) QEO8325	Yr.Iss.	1993	6.75	17
1993 Egg in Sports (2nd Ed.) QEO8332	Yr.Iss.	1993	6.75	17
1993 Springtime Bonnets (1st Ed.) QEO8322	Yr.Iss.	1993	7.75	25
1993 Keepsake Collector's Club - Keepsake				
1993 It's In The Mail QXC5272	Yr.Iss.	1993	10.00	10-20
1993 Trimmed With Memories QXC5432	Yr.Iss.	1993	12.00	38
1993 Keepsake Magic Ornaments - Keepsake				
1993 Baby's First Christmas QLX7365	Yr.Iss.	1993	22.00	37
1993 Bells Are Ringing QLX7402	Yr.Iss.	1993	28.00	54-65
1993 Chris Mouse Flight (9th Ed.) QLX7152	Yr.Iss.	1993	12.00	15-25
1993 Dog's Best Friend QLX7172	Yr.Iss.	1993	12.00	23
1993 Dollhouse Dreams QLX7372	Yr.Iss.	1993	22.00	45
1993 Forest Frolics (5th Ed.) QLX7165	Yr.Iss.	1993	25.00	45-53
1993 Home On The Range QLX7395	Yr.Iss.	1993	32.00	63
1993 The Lamplighter QLX7192	Yr.Iss.	1993	18.00	36
1993 Last-Minute Shopping QLX7385	Yr.Iss.	1993	28.00	40-50
1993 North Pole Merrython QLX7392	Yr.Iss.	1993	25.00	46
1993 Our First Christmas Together QLX7355	Yr.Iss.	1993	20.00	40
1993 PEANUTS (3rd Ed.) QLX7155	Yr.Iss.	1993	18.00	38-50
1993 Radio News Flash QLX7362	Yr.Iss.	1993	22.00	40-50
1993 Raiding The Fridge QLX7185	Yr.Iss.	1993	16.00	40
1993 Road Runner and Wile E. Coyote QLX7415	Yr.Iss.	1993	30.00	70
1993 Santa's Snow-Getter QLX7352	Yr.Iss.	1993	18.00	39
1993 Santa's Workshop QLX7375	Yr.Iss.	1993	28.00	55
1993 Song Of The Chimes QLX7405	Yr.Iss.	1993	25.00	50

YEAR ISSUE		EDITION LIMIT	YEAR RETD.	ISSUE PRICE	*QUOTE U.S.$
1993	Winnie The Pooh QLX7422	Yr.Iss.	1993	24.00	38-50

1993 Limited Edition Ornaments - Keepsake

YEAR ISSUE		EDITION LIMIT	YEAR RETD.	ISSUE PRICE	*QUOTE U.S.$
1993	Gentle Tidings QXC5442	17,500	1993	25.00	50
1993	Sharing Christmas QXC5435	16,500	1993	20.00	45

1993 Miniature Ornaments - Keepsake

YEAR ISSUE		EDITION LIMIT	YEAR RETD.	ISSUE PRICE	*QUOTE U.S.$
1993	'Round The Mountain QXM4025	Yr.Iss.	1993	7.25	17
1993	Baby's First Christmas QXM5145	Yr.Iss.	1993	5.75	14
1993	The Bearymores (2nd Ed.) QXM5125	Yr.Iss.	1993	5.75	17
1993	Cheese Please QXM4072	Yr.Iss.	1993	3.75	7
1993	Christmas Castle QXM4085	Yr.Iss.	1993	5.75	12
1993	Cloisonne Snowflake QXM4012	Yr.Iss.	1993	9.75	19
1993	Country Fiddling QXM4062	Yr.Iss.	1993	3.75	9
1993	Crystal Angel QXM4015	Yr.Iss.	1993	9.75	54-60
1993	Ears To Pals QXM4075	Yr.Iss.	1993	3.75	8
1993	Flatbed Car (5th Ed.) QXM5105	Yr.Iss.	1993	7.00	10-20
1993	Grandma QXM5162	Yr.Iss.	1993	4.50	12
1993	I Dream Of Santa QXM4055	Yr.Iss.	1993	3.75	6-12
1993	Into The Woods QXM4045	Yr.Iss.	1993	3.75	7
1993	The Kringles (5th Ed.) QXM5135	Yr.Iss.	1993	5.75	8-15
1993	Learning To Skate QXM4122	Yr.Iss.	1993	3.00	8
1993	Lighting A Path QXM4115	Yr.Iss.	1993	3.00	9
1993	March Of The Teddy Bears (1st Ed.) QX2403	Yr.Iss.	1993	4.50	10-20
1993	Merry Mascot QXM4042	Yr.Iss.	1993	3.75	5-10
1993	Mom QXM5155	Yr.Iss.	1993	4.50	10-15
1993	Monkey Melody QXM4092	Yr.Iss.	1993	5.75	13
1993	Nature's Angels (4th Ed.) QXM5122	Yr.Iss.	1993	4.50	13
1993	The Night Before Christmas (2nd Ed.) QXM5115	Yr.Iss.	1993	4.50	15-20
1993	North Pole Fire Truck QXM4105	Yr.Iss.	1993	4.75	10
1993	On The Road (1st Ed.) QXM4002	Yr.Iss.	1993	5.75	10-18
1993	Pear-Shaped Tones QXM4052	Yr.Iss.	1993	3.75	7
1993	Pull Out A Plum QXM4095	Yr.Iss.	1993	5.75	12
1993	Refreshing Flight QXM4112	Yr.Iss.	1993	5.75	14
1993	Rocking Horse (6th Ed.) QXM5112	Yr.Iss.	1993	4.50	14
1993	Secret Pals QXM5172	Yr.Iss.	1993	3.75	10
1993	Snuggle Birds QXM5182	Yr.Iss.	1993	5.75	13
1993	Special Friends QXM5165	Yr.Iss.	1993	4.50	9
1993	Thimble Bells (4th Ed.) QXM5142	Yr.Iss.	1993	5.75	14
1993	Tiny Green Thumbs, set/6, QXM4032	Yr.Iss.	1993	29.00	38-55
1993	Toy Shop (6th Ed.) QXM5132	Yr.Iss.	1993	7.00	15
1993	Visions Of Sugarplums QXM4022	Yr.Iss.	1993	7.25	15
1993	Woodland Babies (3rd Ed.) QXM5102	Yr.Iss.	1993	5.75	13

1993 New Attractions - Keepsake

YEAR ISSUE		EDITION LIMIT	YEAR RETD.	ISSUE PRICE	*QUOTE U.S.$
1993	Beary Gifted QX5762	Yr.Iss.	1993	7.75	18
1993	Big on Gardening QX5842	Yr.Iss.	1993	9.75	16
1993	Big Roller QX5352	Yr.Iss.	1993	8.75	16
1993	Bowling For ZZZ's QX5565	Yr.Iss.	1993	7.75	18
1993	Bugs Bunny QX5412	Yr.Iss.	1993	8.75	12-24
1993	Caring Nurse QX5785	Yr.Iss.	1993	6.75	12-20
1993	Christmas Break QX5825	Yr.Iss.	1993	7.75	18-25
1993	Clever Cookie QX5662	Yr.Iss.	1993	7.75	16
1993	Curly 'n' Kingly QX5285	Yr.Iss.	1993	10.75	21
1993	Dunkin' Roo QX5575	Yr.Iss.	1993	7.75	15
1993	Eeyore QX5712	Yr.Iss.	1993	9.75	20
1993	Elmer Fudd QX5495	Yr.Iss.	1993	8.75	14-20
1993	Faithful Fire Fighter QX5782	Yr.Iss.	1993	7.75	19
1993	Feliz Navidad QX5365	Yr.Iss.	1993	9.75	18
1993	Fills the Bill QX5572	Yr.Iss.	1993	8.75	10-16
1993	Great Connections QX5402	10.75	1993	10.75	22
1993	He Is Born QX5362	Yr.Iss.	1993	9.75	35
1993	High Top-Purr QX5332	Yr.Iss.	1993	8.75	22
1993	Home For Christmas QX5562	Yr.Iss.	1993	7.75	15
1993	Icicle Bicycle QX5835	Yr.Iss.	1993	9.75	18
1993	Kanga and Roo QX5672	Yr.Iss.	1993	9.75	21
1993	Little Drummer Boy QX5372	Yr.Iss.	1993	9.75	21
1993	Look For Wonder QX5685	Yr.Iss.	1993	12.75	25
1993	Lou Rankin Polar Bear QX5745	Yr.Iss.	1993	9.75	21
1993	Makin' Music QX5325	Yr.Iss.	1993	9.75	18
1993	Making Waves QX5775	Yr.Iss.	1993	9.75	22
1993	Mary Engelbreit QX2075	Yr.Iss.	1993	5.00	15
1993	Maxine QX5385	Yr.Iss.	1993	8.75	10-20
1993	One-Elf Marching Band QX5342	Yr.Iss.	1993	12.75	25
1993	Owl QX5695	Yr.Iss.	1993	9.75	15-22
1993	PEANUTS QX2072	Yr.Iss.	1993	5.00	13-18
1993	Peep Inside QX5322	Yr.Iss.	1993	13.75	25
1993	Perfect Match QX5772	Yr.Iss.	1993	8.75	18
1993	The Pink Panther QX5755	Yr.Iss.	1993	12.75	25
1993	Playful Pals QX5742	Yr.Iss.	1993	14.75	26
1993	Popping Good Times QX5392	Yr.Iss.	1993	14.75	27
1993	Porky Pig QX5652	Yr.Iss.	1993	8.75	10-20
1993	Putt-Putt Penguin QX5795	Yr.Iss.	1993	9.75	18
1993	Quick As A Fox QX5792	Yr.Iss.	1993	8.75	16
1993	Rabbit QX5702	Yr.Iss.	1993	9.75	15-22
1993	Ready For Fun QX5124	Yr.Iss.	1993	7.75	16
1993	Room For One More QX5382	Yr.Iss.	1993	8.75	22-45
1993	Silvery Noel QX5305	Yr.Iss.	1993	12.75	21
1993	Smile! It's Christmas QX5335	Yr.Iss.	1993	9.75	16
1993	Snow Bear Angel QX5355	Yr.Iss.	1993	7.75	16
1993	Snowbird QX5765	Yr.Iss.	1993	7.75	15
1993	Snowy Hideaway QX5312	Yr.Iss.	1993	9.75	15-20
1993	Star Of Wonder QX5982	Yr.Iss.	1993	6.75	32
1993	Superman QX5752	Yr.Iss.	1993	12.75	25-45
1993	The Swat Team QX5395	Yr.Iss.	1993	12.75	27

YEAR ISSUE		EDITION LIMIT	YEAR RETD.	ISSUE PRICE	*QUOTE U.S.$
1993	Sylvester and Tweety QX5405	Yr.Iss.	1993	9.75	25-32
1993	That's Entertainment QX5345	Yr.Iss.	1993	8.75	18
1993	Tigger and Piglet QX5705	Yr.Iss.	1993	9.75	25-42
1993	Tin Airplane QX5622	Yr.Iss.	1993	7.75	20-27
1993	Tin Blimp QX5625	Yr.Iss.	1993	7.75	10-15
1993	Tin Hot Air Balloon QX5615	Yr.Iss.	1993	7.75	15
1993	Water Bed Snooze QX5375	Yr.Iss.	1993	9.75	21
1993	Winnie the Pooh QX5715	Yr.Iss.	1993	9.75	22-28

1993 Showcase Folk Art Americana - Keepsake

YEAR ISSUE		EDITION LIMIT	YEAR RETD.	ISSUE PRICE	*QUOTE U.S.$
1993	Angel in Flight QK1052	Yr.Iss.	1993	15.75	45
1993	Polar Bear Adventure QK1055	Yr.Iss.	1993	15.00	60
1993	Riding in the Woods QK1065	Yr.Iss.	1993	15.75	60
1993	Riding the Wind QK1045	Yr.Iss.	1993	15.75	42
1993	Santa Claus QK1072	Yr.Iss.	1993	16.75	225

1993 Showcase Holiday Enchantment - Keepsake

YEAR ISSUE		EDITION LIMIT	YEAR RETD.	ISSUE PRICE	*QUOTE U.S.$
1993	Angelic Messengers QK1032	Yr.Iss.	1993	13.75	40
1993	Bringing Home the Tree QK1042	Yr.Iss.	1993	13.75	35
1993	Journey to the Forest QK1012	Yr.Iss.	1993	13.75	32
1993	The Magi QK1035	Yr.Iss.	1993	13.75	37
1993	Visions of Sugarplums QK1005	Yr.Iss.	1993	13.75	35

1993 Showcase Old-World Silver - Keepsake

YEAR ISSUE		EDITION LIMIT	YEAR RETD.	ISSUE PRICE	*QUOTE U.S.$
1993	Silver Dove of Peace QK1075	Yr.Iss.	1993	24.75	30
1993	Silver Santa QK1092	Yr.Iss.	1993	24.75	30-55
1993	Silver Sleigh QK1082	Yr.Iss.	1993	24.75	33
1993	Silver Stars and Holly QK1085	Yr.Iss.	1993	24.75	33

1993 Showcase Portraits in Bisque - Keepsake

YEAR ISSUE		EDITION LIMIT	YEAR RETD.	ISSUE PRICE	*QUOTE U.S.$
1993	Christmas Feast QK1152	Yr.Iss.	1993	15.75	34
1993	Joy of Sharing QK1142	Yr.Iss.	1993	15.75	34
1993	Mistletoe Kiss QK1145	Yr.Iss.	1993	15.75	32
1993	Norman Rockwell-Filling the Stockings QK1155	Yr.Iss.	1993	15.75	36
1993	Norman Rockwell-Jolly Postman QK1142	Yr.Iss.	1993	15.75	36

1993 Special Editions - Keepsake

YEAR ISSUE		EDITION LIMIT	YEAR RETD.	ISSUE PRICE	*QUOTE U.S.$
1993	Dickens Caroler Bell-Lady Daphne-(4th Ed.) QX5505	Yr.Iss.	1993	21.75	40-50
1993	Julianne and Teddy QX5295	Yr.Iss.	1993	21.75	40

1993 Special Issues - Keepsake

YEAR ISSUE		EDITION LIMIT	YEAR RETD.	ISSUE PRICE	*QUOTE U.S.$
1993	Holiday Barbie-(1st Ed.) QX572-5	Yr.Iss.	1993	14.75	75-125
1993	Messages of Christmas QLX747-6	Yr.Iss.	1993	35.00	45-55
1993	Star Trek® The Next Generation QLX741-2	Yr.Iss.	1993	24.00	55-70

1994 Artists' Favorites - Keepsake

YEAR ISSUE		EDITION LIMIT	YEAR RETD.	ISSUE PRICE	*QUOTE U.S.$
1994	Cock-a-Doodle Christmas QX5396	Yr.Iss.	1994	8.95	20
1994	Happy Birthday Jesus QX5423	Yr.Iss.	1994	12.95	23
1994	Keep on Mowin' QX5413	Yr.Iss.	1994	8.95	17
1994	Kitty's Catamaran QX5416	Yr.Iss.	1994	10.95	17
1994	Making It Bright QX5403	Yr.Iss.	1994	8.95	15

1994 Collectible Series - Keepsake

YEAR ISSUE		EDITION LIMIT	YEAR RETD.	ISSUE PRICE	*QUOTE U.S.$
1994	1957 Chevy (4th Ed.) QX5422	Yr.Iss.	1994	12.95	30
1994	Baseball Heroes-Babe Ruth (1st Ed.) QX5323	Yr.Iss.	1994	12.95	35-65
1994	Betsey's Country Christmas (3rd Ed.) QX2403	Yr.Iss.	1994	5.00	15
1994	Cat Naps (1st Ed.) QX5313	Yr.Iss.	1994	7.95	25
1994	CRAYOLA CRAYON-Bright Playful Colors (6th Ed.) QX5273	Yr.Iss.	1994	10.95	25
1994	Fabulous Decade (5th Ed.) QX5263	Yr.Iss.	1994	7.95	23
1994	Frosty Friends (15th Ed.) QX5293	Yr.Iss.	1994	9.95	25
1994	Handwarming Present (9th Ed.) QX5283	Yr.Iss.	1994	14.95	28
1994	Heart of Christmas (5th Ed.) QX5266	Yr.Iss.	1994	14.95	28
1994	Hey Diddle Diddle (2nd Ed.) QX5213	Yr.Iss.	1994	13.95	25-40
1994	Makin' Tractor Tracks (16th Ed.) QX5296	Yr.Iss.	1994	14.95	47
1994	Mary's Angels-Jasmine (7th Ed.) QX5276	Yr.Iss.	1994	6.95	20
1994	Merry Olde Santa (5th Ed.) QX5256	Yr.Iss.	1994	14.95	32
1994	Murray Blue Champion (1st Ed.) QX5426	Yr.Iss.	1994	13.95	50-75
1994	Neighborhood Drugstore (11th Ed.) QX5286	Yr.Iss.	1994	14.95	30
1994	Owliver-(3rd Ed.) QX5226	Yr.Iss.	1994	7.95	19
1994	PEANUTS-Lucy (2nd Ed.) QX5203	Yr.Iss.	1994	9.95	20-28
1994	Pipers Piping (11th Ed.) QX3183	Yr.Iss.	1994	6.95	18
1994	Puppy Love (4th Ed.) QX5253	Yr.Iss.	1994	7.95	19
1994	Rocking Horse (14th Ed.) QX5016	Yr.Iss.	1994	10.95	22-35
1994	Tobin Fraley Carousel (3rd Ed.) QX5223	Yr.Iss.	1994	28.00	60
1994	Xmas Stamp (2nd Ed.) QX5206	Yr.Iss.	1994	10.95	23
1994	Yuletide Central (1st Ed.) QX5316	Yr.Iss.	1994	18.95	40-48

1994 Commemoratives - Keepsake

YEAR ISSUE		EDITION LIMIT	YEAR RETD.	ISSUE PRICE	*QUOTE U.S.$
1994	Across the Miles QX5656	Yr.Iss.	1994	8.95	17
1994	Anniversary Year QX5683	Yr.Iss.	1994	10.95	20
1994	Baby's First Christmas Photo QX5636	Yr.Iss.	1994	7.95	19
1994	Baby's First Christmas QX5633	Yr.Iss.	1994	18.95	25-35
1994	Baby's First Christmas QX5713	Yr.Iss.	1994	7.95	22

YEAR ISSUE		EDITION LIMIT	YEAR RETD.	ISSUE PRICE	*QUOTE U.S.$
1994	Baby's First Christmas QX5743	Yr.Iss.	1994	12.95	26
1994	Baby's First Christmas-Baby Boy QX2436	Yr.Iss.	1994	5.00	15
1994	Baby's First Christmas-Baby Girl QX2433	Yr.Iss.	1994	5.00	15
1994	Baby's Second Christmas QX5716	Yr.Iss.	1994	7.95	22
1994	Brother QX5516	Yr.Iss.	1994	6.95	15
1994	Child's Fifth Christmas QX5733	Yr.Iss.	1994	6.95	17
1994	Child's Fourth Christmas QX5726	Yr.Iss.	1994	6.95	18
1994	Child's Third Christmas QX5723	Yr.Iss.	1994	6.95	18
1994	Dad QX5463	Yr.Iss.	1994	7.95	16
1994	Dad-To-Be QX5473	Yr.Iss.	1994	7.95	15
1994	Daughter QX5623	Yr.Iss.	1994	6.95	15
1994	Friendly Push QX5686	Yr.Iss.	1994	8.95	18
1994	Godchild QX4453	Yr.Iss.	1994	8.95	21
1994	Godparents QX2423	Yr.Iss.	1994	5.00	17
1994	Grandchild's First Christmas QX5676	Yr.Iss.	1994	7.95	18
1994	Granddaughter QX5523	Yr.Iss.	1994	6.95	15
1994	Grandma Photo QX5613	Yr.Iss.	1994	6.95	7
1994	Grandmother QX5673	Yr.Iss.	1994	7.95	18
1994	Grandpa QX5616	Yr.Iss.	1994	7.95	15
1994	Grandparents QX2426	Yr.Iss.	1994	5.00	13
1994	Grandson QX5526	Yr.Iss.	1994	6.95	15
1994	Mom and Dad QX5666	Yr.Iss.	1994	9.95	16
1994	Mom QX5466	Yr.Iss.	1994	7.95	20
1994	Mom-To-Be QX5506	Yr.Iss.	1994	7.95	16
1994	Nephew QX5546	Yr.Iss.	1994	7.95	15
1994	New Home QX5663	Yr.Iss.	1994	8.95	20
1994	Niece QX5543	Yr.Iss.	1994	7.95	15
1994	Our Family QX5576	Yr.Iss.	1994	7.95	17
1994	Our First Christmas Together Photo QX5653	Yr.Iss.	1994	8.95	20
1994	Our First Christmas Together QX3186	Yr.Iss.	1994	6.95	35
1994	Our First Christmas Together QX4816	Yr.Iss.	1994	9.95	25
1994	Our First Christmas Together QX5643	Yr.Iss.	1994	9.95	20
1994	Our First Christmas Together QX5706	Yr.Iss.	1994	18.95	35
1994	Secret Santa QX5736	Yr.Iss.	1994	7.95	18
1994	Sister QX5513	Yr.Iss.	1994	6.95	16
1994	Sister to Sister QX5533	Yr.Iss.	1994	9.95	21
1994	Son QX5626	Yr.Iss.	1994	6.95	15
1994	Special Cat QX5606	Yr.Iss.	1994	7.95	16
1994	Special Dog QX5603	Yr.Iss.	1994	7.95	16
1994	Thick 'N' Thin QX5693	Yr.Iss.	1994	10.95	23
1994	Tou Can Love QX5646	Yr.Iss.	1994	8.95	18

1994 Easter Ornaments - Keepsake

YEAR ISSUE		EDITION LIMIT	YEAR RETD.	ISSUE PRICE	*QUOTE U.S.$
1994	Baby's First Easter QEO8153	Yr.Iss.	1994	6.75	18
1994	Carrot Trimmers QEO8226	Yr.Iss.	1994	5.00	5
1994	CRAYOLA CRAYON-Colorful Spring QEO8166	Yr.Iss.	1994	7.75	25
1994	Daughter QEO8156	Yr.Iss.	1994	5.75	20
1994	Divine Duet QEO8183	Yr.Iss.	1994	6.75	15
1994	Easter Art Show QEO8193	Yr.Iss.	1994	7.75	16
1994	Egg Car-(1st Ed.) QEO8093	Yr.Iss.	1994	7.75	26
1994	Golf-(3rd Ed.) QEO8133	Yr.Iss.	1994	6.75	18
1994	Horn-(2nd Ed.) QEO8136	Yr.Iss.	1994	6.75	18
1994	Joyful Lamb QEO8206	Yr.Iss.	1994	5.75	14
1994	PEANUTS QEO8176	Yr.Iss.	1994	7.75	25
1994	Peeping Out QEO8203	Yr.Iss.	1994	6.75	14
1994	Riding a Breeze QEO8213	Yr.Iss.	1994	5.75	14
1994	Son QEO8163	Yr.Iss.	1994	5.75	20
1994	Springtime Bonnets-(2nd Ed.) QEO8096	Yr.Iss.	1994	7.75	23
1994	Sunny Bunny Garden, (Set/3) QEO8146	Yr.Iss.	1994	15.00	32
1994	Sweet as Sugar QEO8086	Yr.Iss.	1994	8.75	19
1994	Sweet Easter Wishes Tender Touches QEO8196				
1994	Treetop Cottage QEO8186	Yr.Iss.	1994	9.75	19
1994	Yummy Recipe QEO8143	Yr.Iss.	1994	7.75	20

1994 Keepsake Collector's Club - Keepsake

YEAR ISSUE		EDITION LIMIT	YEAR RETD.	ISSUE PRICE	*QUOTE U.S.$
1994	First Hello QXC4846	Yr.Iss.	1994	5.00	15
1994	Happy Collecting QXC4803	Yr.Iss.	1994	3.00	25
1994	Holiday Pursuit QXC4823	Yr.Iss.	1994	11.75	23
1994	Mrs. Claus' Cupboard QXC4843	Yr.Iss.	1994	55.00	195-210
1994	On Cloud Nine QXC4853	Yr.Iss.	1994	12.00	28
1994	Sweet Bouquet QXC4806	Yr.Iss.	1994	8.50	23
1994	Tilling Time QXC8256	Yr.Iss.	1994	5.00	20-50

1994 Keepsake Magic Ornaments - Keepsake

YEAR ISSUE		EDITION LIMIT	YEAR RETD.	ISSUE PRICE	*QUOTE U.S.$
1994	Away in a Manger QLX7383	Yr.Iss.	1994	16.00	25-40
1994	Baby's First Christmas QLX7466	Yr.Iss.	1994	20.00	35-43
1994	Candy Cane Lookout QLX7376	Yr.Iss.	1994	18.00	46-65
1994	Chris Mouse Jelly-(10th Ed.) QLX7393	Yr.Iss.	1994	12.00	20
1994	Conversations With Santa QLX7426	Yr.Iss.	1994	28.00	25-50
1994	Country Showtime QLX7416	Yr.Iss.	1994	22.00	45
1994	The Eagle Has Landed QLX7486	Yr.Iss.	1994	24.00	45
1994	Feliz Navidad QLX7433	Yr.Iss.	1994	28.00	53
1994	Forest Frolics-(6th Ed.) QLX7436	Yr.Iss.	1994	28.00	55
1994	Gingerbread Fantasy-(Sp. Ed.) QLX7382	Yr.Iss.	1994	44.00	97
1994	Kringle Trolley QLX7413	Yr.Iss.	1994	20.00	32-38
1994	Maxine QLX7503	Yr.Iss.	1994	20.00	40
1994	PEANUTS-(4th Ed.) QLX7406	Yr.Iss.	1994	20.00	35-45
1994	Peekaboo Pup QLX7423	Yr.Iss.	1994	20.00	40
1994	Rock Candy Miner QLX7403	Yr.Iss.	1994	20.00	25

YEAR ISSUE	EDITION LIMIT	YEAR RETD.	ISSUE PRICE	*QUOTE U.S. $
1994 Santa's Sing-Along QLX7473	Yr.Iss.	1994	24.00	35-50
1994 Tobin Fraley-(1st Ed.) QLX7496	Yr.Iss.	1994	32.00	45-60
1994 Very Merry Minutes QLX7443	Yr.Iss.	1994	24.00	45
1994 White Christmas QLX7463	Yr.Iss.	1994	28.00	40-54
1994 Winnie the Pooh Parade QLX7493	Yr.Iss.	1994	32.00	45

1994 Limited Editions - Keepsake

YEAR ISSUE	EDITION LIMIT	YEAR RETD.	ISSUE PRICE	*QUOTE U.S. $
1994 Jolly Holly Santa QXC4833	N/A	1994	22.00	22
1994 Majestic Deer QXC4836	N/A	1994	25.00	25

1994 Miniature Ornaments - Keepsake

YEAR ISSUE	EDITION LIMIT	YEAR RETD.	ISSUE PRICE	*QUOTE U.S. $
1994 Babs Bunny QXM4116	Yr.Iss.	1994	5.75	12
1994 Baby's First Christmas QXM4003	Yr.Iss.	1994	5.75	12
1994 Baking Tiny Treats, (Set/6) QXM4033	Yr.Iss.	1994	29.00	35-58
1994 Beary Perfect Tree QXM4076	Yr.Iss.	1994	4.75	9
1994 The Bearymores-(3rd Ed.) QXM5133	Yr.Iss.	1994	5.75	13
1994 Buster Bunny QXM5163	Yr.Iss.	1994	5.75	12
1994 Centuries of Santa-(1st Ed.) QXM5153	Yr.Iss.	1994	6.00	15-25
1994 Corny Elf QXM4063	Yr.Iss.	1994	4.50	9
1994 Cute as a Button QXM4103	Yr.Iss.	1994	3.75	14
1994 Dazzling Reindeer-(Pr. Ed.) QXM4026	Yr.Iss.	1994	9.75	19
1994 Dizzy Devil QXM4133	Yr.Iss.	1994	5.75	13
1994 Friends Need Hugs QXM4016	Yr.Iss.	1994	4.50	14
1994 Graceful Carousel QXM4056	Yr.Iss.	1994	7.75	10-18
1994 Hamton QXM4126	Yr.Iss.	1994	5.75	6-12
1994 Hat Shop (7th Ed.) QXM5143	Yr.Iss.	1994	7.00	10-20
1994 Have a Cookie QXM5166	Yr.Iss.	1994	5.75	7-15
1994 Hearts A-Sail QXM4006	Yr.Iss.	1994	5.75	13
1994 Jolly Visitor QXM4053	Yr.Iss.	1994	5.75	15
1994 Jolly Wolly Snowman QXM4093	Yr.Iss.	1994	3.75	11
1994 Journey to Bethlehem QXM4036	Yr.Iss.	1994	5.75	13
1994 Just My Size QXM4086	Yr.Iss.	1994	3.75	10
1994 Love Was Born QXM4043	Yr.Iss.	1994	4.50	13
1994 March of the Teddy Bears-(2nd Ed.) QXM5106	Yr.Iss.	1994	4.50	7-14
1994 Melodic Cherub QXM4066	Yr.Iss.	1994	3.75	9
1994 A Merry Flight QXM4073	Yr.Iss.	1994	5.75	6-12
1994 Mom QXM4013	Yr.Iss.	1994	4.50	10
1994 Nature's Angels-(5th Ed.) QXM5126	Yr.Iss.	1994	4.50	12
1994 Night Before Christmas-(3rd Ed.) QXM5123	Yr.Iss.	1994	4.50	13
1994 Noah's Ark (Sp. Ed.) QXM4106	Yr.Iss.	1994	24.50	48-60
1994 Nutcracker Guild-(1st Ed.) QXM5146	Yr.Iss.	1994	5.75	15
1994 On the Road-(2nd Ed.) QXM5103	Yr.Iss.	1994	5.75	13
1994 Plucky Duck QXM4123	Yr.Iss.	1994	5.75	13
1994 Pour Some More QXM5156	Yr.Iss.	1994	5.75	12
1994 Rocking Horse-(7th Ed.) QXM5116	Yr.Iss.	1994	4.50	11-18
1994 Scooting Along QXM5173	Yr.Iss.	1994	6.75	14
1994 Stock Car-(6th Ed.) QXM5113	Yr.Iss.	1994	7.00	14-20
1994 Sweet Dreams QXM4096	Yr.Iss.	1994	3.00	14
1994 Tea With Teddy QXM4046	Yr.Iss.	1994	7.25	15

1994 New Attractions - Keepsake

YEAR ISSUE	EDITION LIMIT	YEAR RETD.	ISSUE PRICE	*QUOTE U.S. $
1994 All Pumped Up QX5923	Yr.Iss.	1994	8.95	18
1994 Angel Hare QX5896	Yr.Iss.	1994	8.95	19
1994 Batman QX5853	Yr.Iss.	1994	12.95	30
1994 Beatles Gift Set QX5373	Yr.Iss.	1994	48.00	55-100
1994 BEATRIX POTTER The Tale of Peter Rabbit QX2443	Yr.Iss.	1994	5.00	15
1994 Big Shot QX5873	Yr.Iss.	1994	7.95	17
1994 Busy Batter QX5876	Yr.Iss.	1994	7.95	16
1994 Candy Caper QX5776	Yr.Iss.	1994	8.95	18
1994 Caring Doctor QX5823	Yr.Iss.	1994	8.95	18
1994 Champion Teacher QX5836	Yr.Iss.	1994	6.95	16
1994 Cheers to You! QX5796	Yr.Iss.	1994	10.95	22-28
1994 Cheery Cyclists QX5786	Yr.Iss.	1994	12.95	20-30
1994 Child Care Giver QX5906	Yr.Iss.	1994	7.95	16
1994 Coach QX5933	Yr.Iss.	1994	7.95	18
1994 Colors of Joy QX5893	Yr.Iss.	1994	7.95	18
1994 Cowardly Lion QX5446	Yr.Iss.	1994	9.95	35
1994 Daffy Duck QX5415	Yr.Iss.	1994	8.95	15-23
1994 Daisy Days QX5986	Yr.Iss.	1994	9.95	10
1994 Deer Santa Mouse (2) QX5806	Yr.Iss.	1994	14.95	29
1994 Dorothy and Toto QX5433	Yr.Iss.	1994	10.95	55-65
1994 Extra-Special Delivery QX5833	Yr.Iss.	1994	7.95	16
1994 Feelin' Groovy QX5953	Yr.Iss.	1994	7.95	21
1994 A Feline of Christmas QX5816	Yr.Iss.	1994	8.95	25
1994 Feliz Navidad QX5793	Yr.Iss.	1994	8.95	20
1994 Follow the Sun QX5846	Yr.Iss.	1994	8.95	18
1994 Fred and Barney QX5003	Yr.Iss.	1994	14.95	28-40
1994 Friendship Sundae QX4766	Yr.Iss.	1994	10.95	20-25
1994 GARFIELD QX5753	Yr.Iss.	1994	12.95	27
1994 Gentle Nurse QX5973	Yr.Iss.	1994	6.95	18
1994 Harvest Joy QX5993	Yr.Iss.	1994	9.95	10
1994 Hearts in Harmony QX4406	Yr.Iss.	1994	10.95	21
1994 Helpful Shepherd QX5536	Yr.Iss.	1994	8.95	18
1994 Holiday Patrol QX5826	Yr.Iss.	1994	8.95	18
1994 Ice Show QX5946	Yr.Iss.	1994	7.95	17
1994 In the Pink QX5763	Yr.Iss.	1994	9.95	21
1994 It's a Strike QX5856	Yr.Iss.	1994	8.95	18
1994 Jingle Bell Band QX5783	Yr.Iss.	1994	10.95	20-27
1994 Joyous Song QX4473	Yr.Iss.	1994	8.95	17
1994 Jump-along Jackalope QX5756	Yr.Iss.	1994	8.95	18
1994 Kickin' Roo QX5916	Yr.Iss.	1994	7.95	16
1994 Kringle's Kayak QX5886	Yr.Iss.	1994	7.95	18

YEAR ISSUE	EDITION LIMIT	YEAR RETD.	ISSUE PRICE	*QUOTE U.S. $
1994 LEGO'S QX5453	Yr.Iss.	1994	10.95	23-30
1994 Lou Rankin Seal QX5456	Yr.Iss.	1994	9.95	19
1994 Magic Carpet Ride QX5883	Yr.Iss.	1994	7.95	23
1994 Mary Engelbreit QX2416	Yr.Iss.	1994	5.00	15
1994 Merry Fishmas QX5913	Yr.Iss.	1994	8.95	18
1994 Mistletoe Surprise (2)QX5996	Yr.Iss.	1994	12.95	26
1994 Norman Rockwell QX2413	Yr.Iss.	1994	5.00	13-20
1994 Open-and-Shut Holiday QX5696	Yr.Iss.	1994	9.95	21
1994 Out of This World Teacher QX5766	Yr.Iss.	1994	7.95	19
1994 Practice Makes Perfect QX5863	Yr.Iss.	1994	7.95	17
1994 Red Hot Holiday QX5843	Yr.Iss.	1994	7.95	18
1994 Reindeer Pro QX5926	Yr.Iss.	1994	7.95	16
1994 Relaxing Moment QX5356	Yr.Iss.	1994	14.95	15-31
1994 Road Runner and Wile E. Coyote QX5602	Yr.Iss.	1994	12.95	20-28
1994 Scarecrow QX5436	Yr.Iss.	1994	9.95	35-60
1994 A Sharp Flat QX5773	Yr.Iss.	1994	10.95	23
1994 Speedy Gonzales QX5343	Yr.Iss.	1994	8.95	15-23
1994 Stamp of Approval QX5703	Yr.Iss.	1994	7.95	16
1994 Sweet Greeting (2) QX5803	Yr.Iss.	1994	10.95	21
1994 Tasmanian Devil QX5605	Yr.Iss.	1994	8.95	45-60
1994 Thrill a Minute QX5866	Yr.Iss.	1994	8.95	18
1994 Time of Peace QX5813	Yr.Iss.	1994	7.95	15
1994 Tin Man QX5443	Yr.Iss.	1994	9.95	33-52
1994 Tulip Time QX5983	Yr.Iss.	1994	9.95	10
1994 Winnie the Pooh/Tigger QX5746	Yr.Iss.	1994	12.95	25-33
1994 Yosemite Sam QX5346	Yr.Iss.	1994	8.95	19
1994 Yuletide Cheer QX5976	Yr.Iss.	1994	9.95	10

1994 Premiere Event - Keepsake

YEAR ISSUE	EDITION LIMIT	YEAR RETD.	ISSUE PRICE	*QUOTE U.S. $
1994 Eager for Christmas QX5336	Yr.Iss.	1994	15.00	15

1994 Showcase Christmas Lights - Keepsake

YEAR ISSUE	EDITION LIMIT	YEAR RETD.	ISSUE PRICE	*QUOTE U.S. $
1994 Home for the Holidays QK1123	Yr.Iss.	1994	15.75	16
1994 Moonbeams QK1116	Yr.Iss.	1994	15.75	16
1994 Mother and Child QK1126	Yr.Iss.	1994	15.75	16
1994 Peaceful Village QK1106	Yr.Iss.	1994	15.75	16

1994 Showcase Folk Art Americana Collection - Keepsake

YEAR ISSUE	EDITION LIMIT	YEAR RETD.	ISSUE PRICE	*QUOTE U.S. $
1994 Catching 40 Winks QK1183	Yr.Iss.	1994	16.75	32
1994 Going to Town QK1166	Yr.Iss.	1994	15.75	35
1994 Racing Through the Snow QK1173	Yr.Iss.	1994	15.75	50
1994 Rarin' to Go QK1193	Yr.Iss.	1994	15.75	35
1994 Roundup Time QK1176	Yr.Iss.	1994	16.75	35

1994 Showcase Holiday Favorites - Keepsake

YEAR ISSUE	EDITION LIMIT	YEAR RETD.	ISSUE PRICE	*QUOTE U.S. $
1994 Dapper Snowman QK1053	Yr.Iss.	1994	13.75	14
1994 Graceful Fawn QK1033	Yr.Iss.	1994	11.75	12
1994 Jolly Santa QK1046	Yr.Iss.	1994	13.75	14
1994 Joyful Lamb QK1036	Yr.Iss.	1994	11.75	12
1994 Peaceful Dove QK1043	Yr.Iss.	1994	11.75	12

1994 Showcase Old World Silver Collection - Keepsake

YEAR ISSUE	EDITION LIMIT	YEAR RETD.	ISSUE PRICE	*QUOTE U.S. $
1994 Silver Bells QK1026	Yr.Iss.	1994	24.75	40
1994 Silver Bows QK1023	Yr.Iss.	1994	24.75	40
1994 Silver Poinsettias QK1006	Yr.Iss.	1994	24.75	59
1994 Silver Snowflakes QK1016	Yr.Iss.	1994	24.75	40

1994 Special Edition - Keepsake

YEAR ISSUE	EDITION LIMIT	YEAR RETD.	ISSUE PRICE	*QUOTE U.S. $
1994 Lucinda and Teddy QX4813	Yr.Iss.	1994	21.75	30-43

1994 Special Issues - Keepsake

YEAR ISSUE	EDITION LIMIT	YEAR RETD.	ISSUE PRICE	*QUOTE U.S. $
1994 Barney QLX7506	Yr.Iss.	1994	24.00	40
1994 Barney QX5966	Yr.Iss.	1994	9.95	20
1994 Holiday Barbie™-(2nd Ed.) QX5216	Yr.Iss.	1994	14.95	45
1994 Klingon Bird of Prey™ QLX7386	Yr.Iss.	1994	24.00	40
1994 Mufasa/Simba-Lion King QX5406	Yr.Iss.	1994	14.95	20
1994 Nostalgic-Barbie™-(1st Ed.) QX5006	Yr.Iss.	1994	14.95	40
1994 Simba/Nala-Lion King (2) QX5303	Yr.Iss.	1994	12.95	20
1994 Simba/Sarabi/Mufasa the Lion King QLX7513	Yr.Iss.	1994	20.00	41-70
1994 Simba/Sarabi/Mufasa the Lion King QLX7513	Yr.Iss.	1994	32.00	41-70
1994 Timon/Pumbaa-Lion King QX5366	Yr.Iss.	1994	8.95	23-30

1995 Anniversary Edition - Keepsake

YEAR ISSUE	EDITION LIMIT	YEAR RETD.	ISSUE PRICE	*QUOTE U.S. $
1995 Pewter Rocking Horse QX6167	Yr.Iss.		20.00	55

1995 Artists' Favorite - Keepsake

YEAR ISSUE	EDITION LIMIT	YEAR RETD.	ISSUE PRICE	*QUOTE U.S. $
1995 Barrel-Back Rider QX5189	Yr.Iss.		9.95	28
1995 Our Little Blessings QX5209	Yr.Iss.		12.95	26

1995 Collectible Series - Keepsake

YEAR ISSUE	EDITION LIMIT	YEAR RETD.	ISSUE PRICE	*QUOTE U.S. $
1995 1956 Ford Truck (1st Ed.) QX5527	Yr.Iss.		13.95	30
1995 1969 Chevrolet Camaro (5th Ed.) QX5239	Yr.Iss.		12.95	20
1995 Bright 'n' Sunny Tepee (7th Ed.) QX5247	Yr.Iss.		10.95	19
1995 Camellia - Mary's Angels (8th Ed.) QX5149	Yr.Iss.		6.95	15
1995 Cat Naps (2nd Ed.) QX5097	Yr.Iss.		7.95	20
1995 A Celebration of Angels (1st Ed.) QX5077	Yr.Iss.		12.95	18-25
1995 Christmas Eve Kiss (10th Ed.) QX5157	Yr.Iss.		14.95	28
1995 Fabulous Decade (6th Ed.) QX5147	Yr.Iss.		7.95	18

YEAR ISSUE	EDITION LIMIT	YEAR RETD.	ISSUE PRICE	*QUOTE U.S. $
1995 Frosty Friends (16th Ed.) QX5169	Yr.Iss.		10.95	21-32
1995 Jack and Jill (3rd Ed.) QX5099	Yr.Iss.		13.95	24
1995 Lou Gehrig (2nd Ed.) QX5029	Yr.Iss.		12.95	20-25
1995 Merry Olde Santa (6th Ed.) QX5139	Yr.Iss.		14.95	21
1995 Murray® Fire Truck (2nd Ed.) QX5027	Yr.Iss.		13.95	25-35
1995 The PEANUTS® Gang (3rd Ed.) QX5059	Yr.Iss.		9.95	20
1995 Puppy Love (5th Ed.) QX5137	Yr.Iss.		7.95	18
1995 Rocking Horse (15th Ed.) QX5167	Yr.Iss.		10.95	25
1995 Santa's Roadster (17th Ed.) QX5179	Yr.Iss.		14.95	23
1995 St. Nicholas (1st Ed.) QX5087	Yr.Iss.		14.95	29
1995 Tobin Fraley Carousel (4th Ed.) QX5069	Yr.Iss.		28.00	40
1995 Town Church (12th Ed.) QX5159	Yr.Iss.		14.95	23
1995 Twelve Drummers Drumming (12th Ed.) QX3009	Yr.Iss.		6.95	17
1995 U.S. Christmas Stamps (3rd Ed.) QX5067	Yr.Iss.		10.95	23
1995 Yuletide Central (2nd Ed.) QX5079	Yr.Iss.		18.95	23

1995 Commemoratives - Keepsake

YEAR ISSUE	EDITION LIMIT	YEAR RETD.	ISSUE PRICE	*QUOTE U.S. $
1995 Across the Miles QX5847	Yr.Iss.		8.95	9
1995 Air Express QX5977	Yr.Iss.		7.95	8
1995 Anniversary Year QX5819	Yr.Iss.		8.95	9
1995 Baby's First Christmas QX5547	Yr.Iss.		18.95	37
1995 Baby's First Christmas QX5549	Yr.Iss.		7.95	18
1995 Baby's First Christmas QX5557	Yr.Iss.		9.95	10
1995 Baby's First Christmas QX5559	Yr.Iss.		7.95	15
1995 Baby's First Christmas-Baby Boy QX2319	Yr.Iss.		5.00	5
1995 Baby's First Christmas-Baby Girl QX2317	Yr.Iss.		5.00	5
1995 Baby's Second Christmas QX5567	Yr.Iss.		7.95	15
1995 Brother QX5679	Yr.Iss.		6.95	7
1995 Child's Fifth Christmas QX5637	Yr.Iss.		6.95	7
1995 Child's Fourth Christmas QX5629	Yr.Iss.		6.95	7
1995 Child's Third Christmas QX5627	Yr.Iss.		7.95	8
1995 Christmas Fever QX5967	Yr.Iss.		7.95	8
1995 Christmas Patrol QX5959	Yr.Iss.		7.95	8
1995 Dad QX5649	Yr.Iss.		7.95	8
1995 Dad-to-Be QX5667	Yr.Iss.		7.95	8
1995 Daughter QX5677	Yr.Iss.		6.95	7
1995 For My Grandma QX5729	Yr.Iss.		6.95	7
1995 Friendly Boost QX5827	Yr.Iss.		8.95	9
1995 Godchild QX5707	Yr.Iss.		7.95	8
1995 Godparent QX2417	Yr.Iss.		5.00	5
1995 Grandchild's First Christmas QX5777	Yr.Iss.		7.95	8
1995 Granddaughter QX5779	Yr.Iss.		6.95	7
1995 Grandmother QX5767	Yr.Iss.		7.95	8
1995 Grandpa QX5769	Yr.Iss.		8.95	9
1995 Grandparents QX2419	Yr.Iss.		5.00	5
1995 Grandson QX5787	Yr.Iss.		6.95	7
1995 Important Memo QX5947	Yr.Iss.		8.95	9
1995 In a Heartbeat QX5817	Yr.Iss.		8.95	9
1995 Mom and Dad QX5657	Yr.Iss.		9.95	10
1995 Mom QX5647	Yr.Iss.		7.95	8
1995 Mom-to-Be QX5659	Yr.Iss.		7.95	8
1995 New Home QX5839	Yr.Iss.		8.95	9
1995 North Pole 911 QX5957	Yr.Iss.		10.95	11
1995 Number One Teacher QX5949	Yr.Iss.		7.95	8
1995 Our Christmas Together QX5809	Yr.Iss.		9.95	10
1995 Our Family QX5709	Yr.Iss.		7.95	8
1995 Our First Christmas Together QX3177	Yr.Iss.		6.95	7
1995 Our First Christmas Together QX5797	Yr.Iss.		16.95	17
1995 Our First Christmas Together QX5799	Yr.Iss.		8.95	9
1995 Our First Christmas Together QX5807	Yr.Iss.		8.95	9
1995 Packed With Memories QX5639	Yr.Iss.		7.95	8
1995 Sister QX5687	Yr.Iss.		6.95	7
1995 Sister to Sister QX5689	Yr.Iss.		8.95	9
1995 Son QX5669	Yr.Iss.		6.95	7
1995 Special Cat QX5717	Yr.Iss.		7.95	8
1995 Special Dog QX5719	Yr.Iss.		7.95	8
1995 Two for Tea QX5829	Yr.Iss.		9.95	10

1995 Easter Ornaments - Keepsake

YEAR ISSUE	EDITION LIMIT	YEAR RETD.	ISSUE PRICE	*QUOTE U.S. $
1995 3 Flowerpot Friends 1495QEO8229	Yr.Iss.		14.95	25
1995 Baby's First Easter QEO8237	Yr.Iss.		7.95	16
1995 Bugs Bunny (Looney Tunes) QEO8279	Yr.Iss.		8.95	20
1995 Bunny w/Crayons (Crayola) QEO8249	Yr.Iss.		7.95	25
1995 Bunny w/Seed Packets (Tender Touches) QEO8259	Yr.Iss.		8.95	20
1995 Bunny w/Water Bucket QEO8253	Yr.Iss.		6.95	14
1995 Collector's Plate-(2nd Ed.) QEO8217	Yr.Iss.		7.95	15
1995 Daughter QEO8239	Yr.Iss.		5.95	14
1995 Easter Beagle (Peanuts) QEO8257	Yr.Iss.		7.95	20
1995 Easter Egg Cottages-(1st Ed.) QEO8207	Yr.Iss.		8.95	25
1995 Garden Club-(1st Ed.) QEO8209	Yr.Iss.		7.95	20
1995 Ham n Eggs QEO8277	Yr.Iss.		7.95	16

YEAR ISSUE	EDITION LIMIT	YEAR RETD.	ISSUE PRICE	*QUOTE U.S.$
1995 Here Comes Easter-(2nd Ed.) QEO8217	Yr.Iss.		7.95	20-25
1995 Lily (Religious) QEO8267	Yr.Iss.		6.95	12
1995 Miniature Train QEO8269	Yr.Iss.		4.95	13
1995 Son Duck QEO8247	Yr.Iss.		5.95	16
1995 Springtime Barbie-(1st Ed.) QEO8069	Yr.Iss.		12.95	35
1995 Springtime Bonnets-(3rd Ed.) QEO8227	Yr.Iss.		7.95	15-20

1995 Keepsake Collector's Club - Keepsake

YEAR ISSUE	EDITION LIMIT	YEAR RETD.	ISSUE PRICE	*QUOTE U.S.$
1995 1958 Ford Edsel Citation Convertible QXC4167			12.95	54
1995 Brunette Debut-1959 QXC5397	Yr.Iss.		14.95	50
1995 Christmas Eve Bake-Off QXC4049	Yr.Iss.		55.00	110-170
1995 Cinderella's Stepsisters QXC4159	Yr.Iss.		3.75	4
1995 Collecting Memories QXC4117	Yr.Iss.		12.00	17
1995 Cool Santa QXC4457	Yr.Iss.		5.75	6
1995 Cozy Christmas QXC4119	Yr.Iss.		8.50	14
1995 Fishing for Fun QXC5207	Yr.Iss.		10.95	17
1995 A Gift From Rodney QXC4129	Yr.Iss.		5.00	10
1995 Home From the Woods QXC1059	Yr.Iss.		15.95	40
1995 May Flower QXC8246	Yr.Iss.		4.95	25

1995 Keepsake Magic Ornaments - Keepsake

YEAR ISSUE	EDITION LIMIT	YEAR RETD.	ISSUE PRICE	*QUOTE U.S.$
1995 Baby's First Christmas QLX7317	Yr.Iss.		22.00	40
1995 Chris Mouse Tree (11th Ed.) QLX7307	Yr.Iss.		12.50	25
1995 Coming to See Santa QLX7369	Yr.Iss.		32.00	60
1995 Forest Frolics (7th Ed.) QLX7299	Yr.Iss.		28.00	53
1995 Fred and Dino QLX7289	Yr.Iss.		28.00	57
1995 Friends Share Fun QLX7349	Yr.Iss.		16.50	36
1995 Goody Gumballs! QLX7367	Yr.Iss.		12.50	30
1995 Headin' Home QLX7327	Yr.Iss.		22.00	45-50
1995 Holiday Swim QLX7319	Yr.Iss.		18.50	36
1995 Jukebox Party QLX7339	Yr.Iss.		24.50	25
1995 Jumping for Joy QLX7347	Yr.Iss.		28.00	53
1995 My First HOT WHEELS™ QLX7279	Yr.Iss.		28.00	39-45
1995 PEANUTS®- (5th Ed.) QLX7277	Yr.Iss.		24.50	40-50
1995 Santa's Diner QLX7337	Yr.Iss.		24.50	30-35
1995 Space Shuttle QLX7396	Yr.Iss.		24.50	28-35
1995 Superman™ QLX7309	Yr.Iss.		28.00	49
1995 Tobin Fraley Holiday Carousel -(2nd Ed.) QLX7269	Yr.Iss.		32.00	40-65
1995 Victorian Toy Box -Special Ed. QLX7357	Yr.Iss.		42.00	55-66
1995 Wee Little Christmas QLX7329	Yr.Iss.		22.00	40-45
1995 Winnie the Pooh Too Much Hunny QLX7297	Yr.Iss.		24.50	40

1995 Miniature Ornaments - Keepsake

YEAR ISSUE	EDITION LIMIT	YEAR RETD.	ISSUE PRICE	*QUOTE U.S.$
1995 Alice in Wonderland- (1st Ed.) QXM4777			6.75	14
1995 Baby's First Christmas QXM4027	Yr.Iss.		4.75	14
1995 Calamity Coyote QXM4467	Yr.Iss.		6.75	15
1995 Centuries of Santa- (2nd Ed.) QXM4789	Yr.Iss.		5.75	14
1995 Christmas Bells- (1st Ed.) QXM4007	Yr.Iss.		4.75	15
1995 Christmas Wishes QXM4087	Yr.Iss.		3.75	13
1995 Cloisonne Partridge QXM4017	Yr.Iss.		9.75	19
1995 Downhill Double QXM4837	Yr.Iss.		4.75	13
1995 Friendship Duet QXM4019	Yr.Iss.		4.75	15
1995 Furrball QXM4459	Yr.Iss.		5.75	15
1995 Grandpa's Gift QXM4829	Yr.Iss.		5.75	13
1995 Heavenly Praises QXM4037	Yr.Iss.		5.75	13
1995 Joyful Santa QXM4089	Yr.Iss.		4.75	13
1995 Little Beeper QXM4469	Yr.Iss.		5.75	15
1995 March of the Teddy Bears (3rd Ed.) QXM4799	Yr.Iss.		4.75	13
1995 Merry Walruses QXM4057	Yr.Iss.		5.75	14
1995 Milk Tank Car (7th Ed.) QXM4817	Yr.Iss.		6.75	15
1995 Miniature Clothespin Soldier (1st Ed.) QXM4097	Yr.Iss.		3.75	13
1995 A Moustershire Christmas QXM4839	Yr.Iss.		24.50	35-48
1995 Murray® "Champion" (1st Ed.) QXM4079	Yr.Iss.		5.75	15
1995 Nature's Angels (6th Ed.) QXM4809	Yr.Iss.		4.75	14
1995 The Night Before Christmas (4th Ed.) QXM4807	Yr.Iss.		4.75	15
1995 Nutcracker Guild (2nd Ed.) QXM4787	Yr.Iss.		5.75	10-15
1995 On the Road (3rd Ed.) QXM4797	Yr.Iss.		5.75	14
1995 Pebbles and Bamm-Bamm QXM4757	Yr.Iss.		9.75	12
1995 Playful Penguins QXM4059	Yr.Iss.		5.75	10-18
1995 Precious Creations QXM4077	Yr.Iss.		9.75	19
1995 Rocking Horse (8th Ed.) QXM4827	Yr.Iss.		4.75	13
1995 Santa's Little Big Top (1st Ed.) QXM4779	Yr.Iss.		6.75	15
1995 Santa's Visit QXM4047	Yr.Iss.		7.75	17
1995 Starlit Nativity QXM4039	Yr.Iss.		7.75	19
1995 Sugarplum Dreams QXM4099	Yr.Iss.		5.75	11
1995 Tiny Treasures (set of 6) QXM4009	Yr.Iss.		29.00	40-45
1995 Tudor House (8th Ed.) QXM4819	Yr.Iss.		6.75	15
1995 Tunnel of Love QXM4029	Yr.Iss.		4.75	12

1995 New Attractions - Keepsake

YEAR ISSUE	EDITION LIMIT	YEAR RETD.	ISSUE PRICE	*QUOTE U.S.$
1995 Acorn 500 QX5929	Yr.Iss.		10.95	18
1995 Batmobile QX5739	Yr.Iss.		14.95	20-30
1995 Betty and Wilma QX5417	Yr.Iss.		14.95	26

YEAR ISSUE	EDITION LIMIT	YEAR RETD.	ISSUE PRICE	*QUOTE U.S.$
1995 Bingo Bear QX5919	Yr.Iss.		7.95	18
1995 Bobbin' Along QX5879	Yr.Iss.		8.95	35-40
1995 Bugs Bunny QX5019	Yr.Iss.		8.95	12-20
1995 Catch the Spirit QX5899	Yr.Iss.		7.95	19
1995 Christmas Morning QX5997	Yr.Iss.		10.95	18
1995 Colorful World QX5519	Yr.Iss.		10.95	19
1995 Cows of Bali QX5999	Yr.Iss.		8.95	18
1995 Delivering Kisses QX4107	Yr.Iss.		10.95	21
1995 Dream On QX6007	Yr.Iss.		10.95	22
1995 Dudley the Dragon QX6209	Yr.Iss.		10.95	21
1995 Faithful Fan QX5897	Yr.Iss.		8.95	19
1995 Feliz Navidad QX5869	Yr.Iss.		7.95	10-18
1995 Forever Friends Bear QX5258	Yr.Iss.		8.95	15-22
1995 GARFIELD QX5007	Yr.Iss.		10.95	23
1995 Glinda, Witch of the North QX5749	Yr.Iss.		13.95	20
1995 Gopher Fun QX5887	Yr.Iss.		9.95	24
1995 Happy Wrappers QX6037	Yr.Iss.		10.95	22
1995 Heaven's Gift QX6057	Yr.Iss.		20.00	40
1995 Hockey Pup QX5917	Yr.Iss.		9.95	25
1995 In Time With Christmas QX6049	Yr.Iss.		12.95	27
1995 Joy to the World QX5867	Yr.Iss.		8.95	19
1995 LEGO® Fireplace With Santa QX4769	Yr.Iss.		10.95	22
1995 Lou Rankin Bear QX4069	Yr.Iss.		9.95	19
1995 The Magic School Bus™ QX5849	Yr.Iss.		10.95	22
1995 Mary Engelbreit QX2409	Yr.Iss.		5.00	15
1995 Merry RV QX6027	Yr.Iss.		12.95	26
1995 Muletide Greetings QX6009	Yr.Iss.		7.95	16
1995 The Olympic Spirit QX3169	Yr.Iss.		7.95	20
1995 On the Ice QX6047	Yr.Iss.		7.95	21
1995 Perfect Balance QX5927	Yr.Iss.		7.95	16
1995 PEZ® Santa QX5267	Yr.Iss.		7.95	15-25
1995 Polar Coaster QX6117	Yr.Iss.		8.95	23
1995 Popeye® QX5257	Yr.Iss.		10.95	19-34
1995 Refreshing Gift QX4067	Yr.Iss.		14.95	28
1995 Rejoice! QX5987	Yr.Iss.		10.95	22
1995 Roller Whiz QX5937	Yr.Iss.		7.95	18
1995 Santa in Paris QX5877	Yr.Iss.		8.95	29
1995 Santa's Serenade QX6017	Yr.Iss.		8.95	18
1995 Santa's Visitors QX2407	Yr.Iss.		5.00	5
1995 Simba, Pumbaa and Timon QX6159	Yr.Iss.		12.95	12-20
1995 Ski Hound QX5909	Yr.Iss.		8.95	20
1995 Surfin' Santa QX6019	Yr.Iss.		9.95	21
1995 Sylvester and Tweety QX5017	Yr.Iss.		13.95	21
1995 Takin' a Hike QX6029	Yr.Iss.		7.95	18
1995 Tennis, Anyone? QX5907	Yr.Iss.		7.95	18
1995 Thomas the Tank Engine-No. 1 QX5857	Yr.Iss.		9.95	20-25
1995 Three Wishes QX5979	Yr.Iss.		7.95	18
1995 Vera the Mouse QX5537	Yr.Iss.		8.95	17
1995 Waiting Up for Santa QX6106	Yr.Iss.		8.95	18
1995 Water Sports QX6039	Yr.Iss.		14.95	28
1995 Wheel of Fortune® QX6187	Yr.Iss.		12.95	15-22
1995 Winnie the Pooh and Tigger QX5009	Yr.Iss.		12.95	25
1995 The Winning Play QX5889	Yr.Iss.		7.95	19

1995 Premiere Event - Keepsake

YEAR ISSUE	EDITION LIMIT	YEAR RETD.	ISSUE PRICE	*QUOTE U.S.$
1995 Wish List QX5859	Yr.Iss.		15.00	15

1995 Showcase All Is Bright Collection - Keepsake

YEAR ISSUE	EDITION LIMIT	YEAR RETD.	ISSUE PRICE	*QUOTE U.S.$
1995 Angel of Light QK1159	Yr.Iss.		11.95	25
1995 Gentle Lullaby QK1157	Yr.Iss.		11.95	25

1995 Showcase Angel Bells Collection - Keepsake

YEAR ISSUE	EDITION LIMIT	YEAR RETD.	ISSUE PRICE	*QUOTE U.S.$
1995 Carole QK1147	Yr.Iss.		12.95	20
1995 Joy QK1137	Yr.Iss.		12.95	27
1995 Noelle QK1139	Yr.Iss.		12.95	20

1995 Showcase Folk Art Americana Collection - Keepsake

YEAR ISSUE	EDITION LIMIT	YEAR RETD.	ISSUE PRICE	*QUOTE U.S.$
1995 Fetching the Firewood QK1057	Yr.Iss.		15.95	35
1995 Fishing Party QK1039	Yr.Iss.		15.95	35
1995 Guiding Santa QK1037	Yr.Iss.		18.95	45
1995 Learning to Skate QK1047	Yr.Iss.		14.95	37

1995 Showcase Holiday Enchantment Collection - Keepsake

YEAR ISSUE	EDITION LIMIT	YEAR RETD.	ISSUE PRICE	*QUOTE U.S.$
1995 Away in a Manger QK1097	Yr.Iss.		13.95	30
1995 Following the Star QK1099	Yr.Iss.		13.95	30

1995 Showcase Invitation to Tea Collection - Keepsake

YEAR ISSUE	EDITION LIMIT	YEAR RETD.	ISSUE PRICE	*QUOTE U.S.$
1995 Cozy Cottage Teapot QK1127	Yr.Iss.		15.95	30
1995 European Castle Teapot QK1129	Yr.Iss.		15.95	30
1995 Victorian Home Teapot QK1119	Yr.Iss.		15.95	30

1995 Showcase Nature's Sketchbook Collection - Keepsake

YEAR ISSUE	EDITION LIMIT	YEAR RETD.	ISSUE PRICE	*QUOTE U.S.$
1995 Backyard Orchard QK1069	Yr.Iss.		18.95	40
1995 Christmas Cardinal QK1077	Yr.Iss.		18.95	50
1995 Raising a Family QK1067	Yr.Iss.		18.95	40
1995 Violets and Butterflies QK1079	Yr.Iss.		16.95	40

1995 Showcase Symbols of Christmas - Keepsake

YEAR ISSUE	EDITION LIMIT	YEAR RETD.	ISSUE PRICE	*QUOTE U.S.$
1995 Jolly Santa QK1087	Yr.Iss.		15.95	35
1995 Sweet Song QK1089	Yr.Iss.		15.95	32

1995 Showcase Turn-of-the-Century Parade - Keepsake

YEAR ISSUE	EDITION LIMIT	YEAR RETD.	ISSUE PRICE	*QUOTE U.S.$
1995 The Fireman QK1027	Yr.Iss.		16.95	40

1995 Special Edition - Keepsake

YEAR ISSUE	EDITION LIMIT	YEAR RETD.	ISSUE PRICE	*QUOTE U.S.$
1995 Beverly and Teddy QX5259	Yr.Iss.		21.75	43

1995 Special Issues - Keepsake

YEAR ISSUE	EDITION LIMIT	YEAR RETD.	ISSUE PRICE	*QUOTE U.S.$
1995 Captain James T. Kirk QXI5539	Yr.Iss.		13.95	29
1995 Captain Jean-Luc Picard QXI5737	Yr.Iss.		13.95	29
1995 Captain John Smith and Meeko QXI6169	Yr.Iss.		12.95	25
1995 Holiday Barbie™ (3rd Ed.) QXI5057	Yr.Iss.		14.95	25-35
1995 Hoop Stars (1st Ed.) QXI5517	Yr.Iss.		14.95	35
1995 Joe Montana (1st Ed.) QXI5759	Yr.Iss.		14.95	35
1995 Percy, Flit and Meeko QXI6179	Yr.Iss.		9.95	20
1995 Pocahontas and Captain John Smith QXI6197	Yr.Iss.		14.95	23
1995 Pocahontas QXI6177	Yr.Iss.		12.95	17
1995 Romulan Warbird™ QXI7267	Yr.Iss.		24.00	25-35
1995 The Ships of Star Trek® QXI4109	Yr.Iss.		19.95	21-35
1995 Solo in the Spotlight-Barbie™ (2nd Ed.) QXI5049	Yr.Iss.		14.95	25-50

1995 Special Offer - Keepsake

YEAR ISSUE	EDITION LIMIT	YEAR RETD.	ISSUE PRICE	*QUOTE U.S.$
1995 Charlie Brown QRP4207	Yr.Iss.		3.95	23
1995 Linus QRP4217	Yr.Iss.		3.95	8-15
1995 Lucy QRP4209	Yr.Iss.		3.95	8-15
1995 SNOOPY QRP4219	Yr.Iss.		3.95	20
1995 Snow Scene QRP4227	Yr.Iss.		3.95	5-15
1995 5-Pc. Set	Yr.Iss.		19.95	50-75

Hamilton Collection

Christmas Angels - S. Kuck

YEAR ISSUE	EDITION LIMIT	YEAR RETD.	ISSUE PRICE	*QUOTE U.S.$
1994 Angel of Charity	Open		19.50	20
1995 Angel of Joy	Open		19.50	20
1995 Angel of Grace	Open		19.50	20
1995 Angel of Faith	Open		19.50	20
1995 Angel of Patience	Open		19.50	20
1995 Angel of Glory	Open		19.50	20
1996 Angel of Gladness	Open		19.50	20
1996 Angel of Innocence	Open		19.50	20
1996 Angel of Beauty	Open		19.50	20
1996 Angel of Purity	Open		19.50	20
1996 Angel of Charm	Open		19.50	20
1996 Angel of Kindness	Open		19.50	20

Derek Darlings - N/A

YEAR ISSUE	EDITION LIMIT	YEAR RETD.	ISSUE PRICE	*QUOTE U.S.$
1995 Jessica, Sara, Chelsea (set)	Open		29.85	30

Hand & Hammer

Annual Ornaments - De Matteo

YEAR ISSUE	EDITION LIMIT	YEAR RETD.	ISSUE PRICE	*QUOTE U.S.$
1987 Silver Bells 737	2,700	1987	38.00	66
1988 Silver Bells 792	3,150	1988	39.50	60
1989 Silver Bells 843	3,150	1989	39.50	63
1990 Silver Bells 865	3,615	1990	39.00	50
1990 Silver Bells Rev. 964	4,490	1990	39.00	40
1991 Silver Bells 1080	4,100	1991	39.50	40
1992 Silver Bells 1148	4,100	1992	39.50	40
1993 Silver Bells 1311	Retrd.	1993	39.50	40
1994 Silver Bells 1463	Retrd.	1994	39.50	40
1995 Silver Bells 1597	Retrd.	1995	39.50	40
1996 Silver Bells 1795	Yr.Iss.		39.50	40
1997 Silver Bells 1904	Yr.Iss.		39.50	40

Hand & Hammer Ornaments - De Matteo

YEAR ISSUE	EDITION LIMIT	YEAR RETD.	ISSUE PRICE	*QUOTE U.S.$
1996 150 Rose Window 1878	Yr.Iss.		39.50	40
1985 Abigail 613	Suspd.		32.00	50
1991 Alice 1119	Open			39
1991 Alice in Wonderland 1159	Open		140.00	140
1992 America At Peace 1245	2,000		85.00	100
1992 Andrea 1163	Retrd.	1994	36.00	40
1992 Angel 1213	2,000		39.00	50
1993 Angel 1342	Suspd.		38.00	38
1993 Angel 1993 1405	Suspd.		45.00	50
1996 Angel 1996 1885	Yr.Iss		39.50	40
1985 Angel 607	225	1989	36.00	50
1985 Angel 612	217	1989	32.00	75
1988 Angel 797 (sp)	Unkn.		13.00	13
1988 Angel 818	Suspd.		32.00	45
1993 Angel Bell 1312	Retrd.	1994	38.00	40
1992 Angel with Double Horn 1212	2,000		39.00	50
1991 Angel with Horn 1026	Open		32.00	40
1987 Angel with Lyre 750	Retrd.	1991	32.00	44
1994 Angel with Star 1480	Open		38.00	40
1990 Angel with Star 871	Suspd.		38.00	38
1990 Angel with Violin 1024	Suspd.		39.00	60
1990 Angels 1039	Retrd.	1992	36.00	47
1991 Appley Dapply 1091	Open		39.50	40
1986 Archangel 684	Retrd.	1990	29.00	60
1987 Art Deco Angel 765	Retrd.	1992	38.00	56
1985 Art Deco Deer 620	Suspd.		34.00	55
1985 Audubon Bluebird 615	Suspd.		48.00	125
1985 Audubon Swallow 614	Suspd.		48.00	125
1995 Augusta Golf 1653	Open		39.00	39
1988 Bank 812	400	1989	40.00	100
1989 Barnesville Buggy (1989) 950 (sp)	Unkn.		13.00	13
1993 Beantown 1344	Suspd.		38.00	50
1986 Bear Claus 692 (sp)	Unkn.		13.00	13
1990 Beardsley Angel 1040	Retrd.	1991	34.00	70
1984 Beardsley Angel 398	Open		28.00	48
1994 Beatrix Potter Noel 1438	Open		39.50	40
1985 Bicycle 669 (sp)	Unkn.		13.00	30

YEAR ISSUE		EDITION LIMIT	YEAR RETD.	ISSUE PRICE	*QUOTE U.S.$
1984	Bird & Cherub 588 (sp)	Unkn.		13.00	30
1995	Bird Swirl 1502	Open		39.00	39
1990	Blake Angel 961	Suspd.		36.00	40
1992	Bob & Tiny Tim 1242	Open		36.00	40
1996	Boston 1796 1847	Open		39.50	40
1990	The Boston Light 1032	Suspd.		39.50	50
1988	Boston State House 819	Open		34.00	40
1987	Buffalo 777	Suspd.		36.00	48
1988	Buggy 817 (sp)	Unkn.		13.00	13
1989	Bugle Bear 935 (sp)	Unkn.		12.00	12
1996	Bugs Bunny 1797	2,500		39.50	40
1984	Bunny 582 (sp)	Unkn.		13.00	30
1985	Butterfly 646	Suspd.		39.00	56
1988	Cable Car 848	Suspd.		38.00	75
1993	Cable Car to the Stars 1363	Suspd.		39.00	50
1983	Calligraphic Deer 511	Suspd.		25.00	38
1985	Camel 655 (sp)	Unkn.		13.00	30
1994	Canterbury Star 1441	Suspd.		35.00	35
1994	Cardinal & Holly 1445	Open		38.00	40
1990	Cardinals 870	Retrd.	1994	39.00	40
1990	Carousel Horse 866	1,915	1992	38.00	40
1991	Carousel Horse 1025	Retrd.	1993	38.00	40
1993	Carousel Horse (1993) 1321	Retrd.	1993	38.00	40
1989	Carousel Horse 811	2,150	1990	34.00	43
1985	Carousel Pony 618 (sp)	Unkn.		13.00	13
1990	Carriage 960 (sp)	Unkn.		13.00	13
1982	Carved Heart 425	Suspd.		29.00	70
1995	Cat & Fiddle 1658	Open		39.00	39
1987	Cat 754	Suspd.		37.00	37
1990	Cat on Pillow 915 (sp)	Unkn.		13.00	13
1993	Celebrate America 1352	Retrd.	1994	38.00	38
1993	Cheer Mouse 1359	Retrd.	1994	39.00	39
1983	Cherub 528	295	1987	29.00	56
1985	Cherub 642	815	1989	37.00	60
1992	Chocolate Pot 1208	Retrd.	1994	49.50	75
1992	Christmas Seal 931	Unkn.		25.00	25
1986	Christmas Tree 708 (sp)	Unkn.		13.00	13
1988	Christmas Tree 798 (sp)	Unkn.		13.00	13
1990	Church 921	Retrd.	1994	37.00	40
1993	Clara with Nutcracker 1316	Suspd.		38.00	50
1987	Clipper Ship 756	Suspd.		35.00	55
1990	Clown w/Dog 958 (sp)	Unkn.		13.00	13
1990	Cockatoo 969 (sp)	Unkn.		13.00	13
1990	Colonial Capitol 965	Suspd.		39.00	75
1991	Columbus 1140	1,500	1993	39.00	50
1990	Conestoga Wagon 1027	Suspd.		38.00	45
1988	Conn. State House 833	Open		38.00	38
1996	Constitution 1870	Open		39.50	40
1988	Coronado 864	Suspd.		38.00	75
1990	Covered Bridge 920	Retrd.	1994	37.00	40
1995	Cow & Moon 1660	Open		39.00	39
1991	Cow Jumped Over The Moon 1055	Suspd.		38.00	38
1992	Cowardly Lion 1287	Retrd.	1993	36.00	50
1985	Crane 606	Suspd.		38.00	65
1993	Creche 1351	Open		38.00	40
1984	Crescent Angel 559	Suspd.		30.00	60
1983	Cross 1622	Open		39.00	40
1990	Currier & Ives Set -Victorian Village 923	2,000	1994	140.00	160
1995	Degas Dancer 1650	Open		39.00	39
1992	Della Robbia Ornament 1219	Retrd.	1994	39.00	44
1992	Dorothy 1284	Retrd.	1993	36.00	50
1983	Dove 522 (sp)	Unkn.		13.00	13
1987	Dove 747 (sp)	Unkn.		13.00	13
1988	Dove 786	112	1991	36.00	60
1988	Drummer Bear 773 (sp)	Unkn.		13.00	13
1990	Ducklings 1114	Suspd.		38.00	50
1983	Eagle 652	375	1989	30.00	125
1983	Egyptian Cat 521 (sp)	Unkn.		13.00	13
1988	Eiffel Tower 861	225	1989	38.00	100
1990	Elk 1023 (sp)	Unkn.		13.00	13
1990	Ember 1124	120		N/A	350
1994	Emperor 1439	Retrd.	1995	38.00	50
1994	Esplanade 1523	Open		39.00	39
1995	Esplanade 1667	Open		39.00	39
1995	Faberge Egg 1618	Open		39.00	40
1996	Faberge Egg 1725	Yr.Iss.		39.50	40
1992	Fairy-Tale Angel 1222	Open		36.00	36
1985	Family 659	915	1989	32.00	53
1983	Faneuil Hall 1399	Suspd.		39.00	40
1993	Faneuil Hall 1412	Open		39.50	40
1990	Farmhouse 919	Retrd.	1994	37.00	40
1995	Father Christmas 1715	Open		39.00	39
1990	Father Christmas 970	Open		36.00	40
1990	Ferrel's Angel (1990) 1084 (sp)	Unkn.		15.00	15
1991	Fir Tree 1145	Retrd.	1995	39.00	50
1983	Fire Angel 473	315	1985	25.00	53
1990	First Baptist Angel 997	200	1992	35.00	75
1987	First Christmas 771 (sp)	Unkn.		13.00	13
1989	First Christmas 842 (sp)	Unkn.		13.00	13
1988	First Christmas Bear 940	Suspd.		35.00	40
1982	Fleur de Lys Angel 343	320	1985	28.00	75
1990	Flopsy Bunnies 995	Suspd.		39.50	40
1990	Florida State Capitol 1044	2,000		39.50	40
1996	Four Calling Birds 1789	Open		39.50	40
1984	Freer Star 553 (sp)	Unkn.		13.00	30
1985	French Quarter Heart 647	Open		37.00	38
1981	Gabriel 320	Suspd.		25.00	60
1981	Gabriel with Liberty Cap 301	275	1986	25.00	60
1990	George Washington 629	Suspd.		35.00	50
1990	Georgia State Capitol 1042	2,000		39.50	40
1997	Gingerbread Man 1914	Open		39.50	40
1994	Golden Gate Bridge 1429	Suspd.		39.50	50
1990	Goose & Wreath 868	Retrd.	1993	37.00	40
1989	Goose 857	650	1993	37.00	55
1990	Governor's Palace 966	Suspd.		39.00	75
1985	Grasshopper 634	Suspd.		32.00	50
1985	Guardian Angel 616	Suspd.		35.00	48
1993	Gurgling Cod 1397	Open		50.00	50
1991	Gus 1195	200		N/A	150
1986	Hallelujah 686	Suspd.		38.00	56
1985	Halley's Comet 621	432	1990	35.00	75
1995	Hart 1501	Open		38.00	38
1990	Heart Angel 959	Suspd.		39.00	39
1992	Heart of Christmas 1301	500		39.00	60
1994	Heart of Christmas 1440	500		39.00	50
1994	Heart of Christmas 1537	500		39.00	39-50
1995	Heart of Christmas 1682	Yr.Iss.		39.00	39
1996	Heart of Xmas 1866	Yr.Iss.		39.50	40
1996	Heavenly Music 1791	Open		39.00	40
1985	Herald Angel 641	Retrd.	1989	36.00	60
1994	Heralding Angel 1481	Open		39.00	40
1994	Holly 1472	Open		38.00	40
1995	Hummingbird 1631	Open		39.00	40
1985	Hosanna 635	715	1988	32.00	64
1987	Hunting Horn 738	Suspd.		37.00	40
1991	I Love Santa 998	Open		36.00	40
1984	Ibex 584	400	1988	29.00	75
1980	Icicle 009	490	1985	27.00	60
1989	Independence Hall 908	Suspd.		38.00	45
1983	Indian 494	190	1985	29.00	58
1988	Jack in the Box 789	Retrd.	1991	39.50	60
1989	Jack in the Box Bear 936 (sp)	Unkn.		12.00	12
1983	Japanese Snowflake 534	350	1989	29.00	60
1994	Jefferson Hotel 1594	Open		39.00	39
1990	Jemima Puddleduck 1020	Unkn.		30.00	30
1992	Jemima Puddleduck (1992) 1167	Retrd.	1992	39.50	40
1990	Jeremy Fisher 992	Open		39.00	40
1990	Joy 1047	Retrd.	1992	39.00	55
1992	Joy 1164	Open		39.50	40
1990	Joy 867	1,140	1993	36.00	40
1995	Kate Greenaway Joy 1651	Open		39.00	39
1995	Kate Greenaway Noel 1515	Open		39.00	39
1996	Kate Greenaway Noel 1841	Open		39.50	40
1995	Kermit Joy 1596	Open		39.00	40
1996	Kittens & Mittens 1868	Open		39.50	40
1990	Koala San Diego Zoo 1095	Suspd.		36.00	40
1986	Kringle Bear 723 (sp)	Unkn.		13.00	30
1995	L&T Santa 1700	Yr.Iss.		39.00	39
1989	L&T Ugly Duckling 917	Retrd.	1995	38.00	75
1985	Lafarge Angel 658	Suspd.		32.00	45
1986	Lafarge Angel 710	Suspd.		31.00	45
1990	Landing Duck 1021 (sp)	Unkn.		13.00	13
1991	Large Jemima Puddleduck 1083	Open		49.50	50
1991	Large Peter Rabbit 1116	Open		49.50	50
1991	Large Tailor of Gloucester 1117	Open		49.50	50
1990	Liberty Bell 1028	Suspd.		38.00	45
1985	Liberty Bell 611	Suspd.		32.00	50
1993	Lion and Lamb 1322	Open		38.00	40
1989	Locket Bear 844	Unkn.		25.00	25
1990	Locomotive 1100	Suspd.		39.00	50
1996	Lombard Street 1889	Open		39.50	40
1994	Loudoun County C.H. 1611	Open		39.00	39
1994	Lyre 1505	Open		39.00	39
1991	Mad Tea Party 1120	Open		39.00	39
1982	Madonna & Child 388	175	1985	28.00	75
1996	Madonna 1790	Open		39.50	40
1985	Madonna 666	227	1990	35.00	75
1988	Madonna 787	600	1992	35.00	60
1988	Madonna 809	Suspd.		39.00	50
1988	Madonna 815	Suspd.		39.00	75
1988	Magi 788	Suspd.		39.50	50
1994	Mandoline 1506	Open		39.00	39
1984	Manger 601	Retrd.	1988	29.00	48
1994	Marengo 1482	Open		39.00	39
1992	Marley's Ghost 1243	Open		36.00	40
1994	Marmion Angels 1443	Suspd.		50.00	75
1994	Mass State House 1540	Open		39.00	39
1985	Mermaid 622	Retrd.	1995	35.00	75
1990	Merry Christmas Locket 948	Unkn.		25.00	25
1989	MFA Angel with Tree 906	Suspd.		36.00	55
1989	MFA Durer Snowflake 907	Suspd.		36.00	44
1989	MFA LaFarge Angel set 937	Suspd.		98.00	110
1989	MFA Noel 905	Suspd.		36.00	44
1992	MFA Snowflake 1246	Retrd.	1993	39.00	44
1991	MFA Snowflake 1991 1143	Retrd.	1991	36.00	44
1985	Militiaman 608	Suspd.		25.00	38
1990	Mill 922	Retrd.	1994	37.00	40
1987	Minuteman 776	Suspd.		35.00	100
1985	Model A Ford 604 (sp)	Unkn.		13.00	30
1990	Mole & Rat Wind in Will 944	Suspd.		36.00	36
1991	Mommy & Baby Kangaroo 1078	Retrd.	1993	36.00	36
1991	Mommy & Baby Koala Bear 1077	Retrd.	1993	36.00	36
1991	Mommy & Baby Panda Bear 1079	Retrd.	1993	36.00	40
1991	Mommy & Baby Seal 1075	Retrd.	1993	36.00	36
1991	Mommy & Baby Wolves 1076	Retrd.	1993	36.00	36
1990	Montpelier 1113	Suspd.		36.00	75
1984	Moravian Star 595	Suspd.		38.00	100
1986	Mother Goose 719	Open		34.00	40
1993	Mouse King 1398	Suspd.		38.00	50
1990	Mouse with Candy Cane 916 (sp)	Unkn.		13.00	13
1992	Mrs. Cratchit 1244	Open		36.00	40
1992	Mrs. Rabbit 1181	Open		39.50	40
1991	Mrs. Rabbit (1991) 1086	Retrd.	1991	39.50	40
1993	Mrs. Rabbit (1993) 1325	Retrd.	1993	39.50	40
1990	Mrs. Rabbit 991	Open		39.50	40
1984	Mt. Vernon Weathervane 602	Suspd.		32.00	50
1990	N. Carolina State Capitol 1043	2,000		39.50	40
1987	Naptime 732	Retrd.	1991	32.00	48
1996	Nast Santa 1842	Open		39.50	40
1991	Nativity 1118	Open		38.00	40
1986	Nativity 679	Retrd.	1991	36.00	55
1988	Nativity 821	Suspd.		32.00	75
1995	Night Before Christmas 1600	Open		160.00	160
1988	Night Before Xmas Col. 841	10,000		160.00	275
1986	Nightingale 716	Retrd.	1995	35.00	75
1984	Nine Hearts 572	275	1985	34.00	66
1992	Noah's Ark 1166	Open		36.00	40
1996	Noahs Ark 1849	Open		39.50	40
1994	Noel 1477	Open		38.00	40
1987	Noel 731	Suspd.		38.00	40
1991	Nutcracker 1151	Open		49.50	50
1991	Nutcracker 1183	Open		38.00	38
1989	Nutcracker (1989) 872	1,790	1990	38.00	75
1985	Nutcracker 609	510	1989	30.00	55
1986	Nutcracker 681	1,356	1988	37.00	61
1991	Nutrcracker Suite 1184	Suspd.		38.00	100
1990	Old Fashioned Santa 971	Suspd.		36.00	40
1987	Old Ironsides 767	Suspd.		35.00	45
1988	Old King Cole 824	Retrd.	1990	34.00	43
1985	Old North Church 661	Open		35.00	39
1991	Olivers Rocking Horse 1085	Retrd.	1993	37.00	40
1994	Palace of Fine Arts 1522	Open		39.50	40
1992	Parrot 1233	Open		37.00	40
1993	Partridge & Pear 1328	Open		38.00	40
1990	Patriotic Santa 972	Suspd.		36.00	40
1991	Paul Revere 1158	Open		39.00	39
1994	Paul Revere Lantern 1541	Open		39.00	39
1993	Peace 1327	Suspd.		36.00	36
1995	Peace on Earth 1503	Open		39.00	36
1994	Peachtree Swan 1612	Open		39.00	39
1985	Peacock 603	470	1989	34.00	65
1990	Pegasus 1037	Retrd.	1991	35.00	40
1987	Pegasus 745 (sp)	Unkn.		13.00	13
1995	Peter Rabbit & B Bunny 1492	Open		39.50	40
1993	Peter Rabbit 100th 1383	Retrd.	1993	39.50	45
1990	Peter Rabbit (1990) 1018	4,315	1994	39.50	40
1994	Peter Rabbit (1994) 1444	Retrd.	1994	39.50	40
1995	Peter Rabbit (1995) 1598	Yr.Iss.		39.50	40
1996	Peter Rabbit (1996) 1699	Yr.Iss.		39.50	40
1990	Peter Rabbit 993	Open		39.50	40
1990	Peter Rabbit Locket Ornament 1019	Unkn.		30.00	30
1991	Peter Rabbit with Book 1093	Open		39.50	40
1990	Peter's First Christmas 994	Suspd.		39.50	40
1986	Phaeton 683 (sp)	Unkn.		13.00	13
1985	Piazza 653	Suspd.		32.00	55
1991	Pig Robinson 1090	Open		39.00	40
1984	Pineapple 558	Suspd.		30.00	53
1995	Plate & Spoon 1659	Open		39.00	39
1983	Pollock Angel 502	Suspd.		33.00	75
1995	Pooh & Christopher Robin 1668	Open		39.00	39
1996	Pooh 1873	Open		39.50	40
1995	Pooh Hunny Pot 1663	Open		39.00	40
1995	Pooh with Balloon 1664	Open		39.00	40
1996	Pooh, Christopher Robin 1865	Open		39.50	40
1986	Prancer 698	Open		38.00	40
1984	Praying Angel 576	Suspd.		29.00	45
1991	Precious Planet 1142	2,000		120.00	200
1990	Presidential Homes 990	Suspd.		350.00	400
1989	Presidential Seal 858	Suspd.		39.00	150
1992	Princess & The Pea 1247	Retrd.	1995	39.00	50
1993	Public Garden 1370	Suspd.		38.00	50
1995	Public Garden Angel 1701	Open		39.00	39
1993	Puss In Boots 1396	Suspd.		40.00	44
1994	Quatrefoil 1542	Open		50.00	50
1991	Queen of Hearts 1122	Open		39.00	39
1994	R.E. Lee Monument 1446	Open		39.00	39
1988	Rabbit 816 (sp)	Unkn.		13.00	13
1997	Reindeer 1900	Open		39.50	40
1985	Reindeer 656 (sp)	Unkn.		13.00	30
1987	Reindeer 752	Retrd.	1991	38.00	45
1992	Revere Teapot 1207	Retrd.	1994	49.50	75
1987	Ride a Cock Horse 757	Retrd.	1991	34.00	43
1984	Rocking Horse 581 (sp)	Unkn.		13.00	13
1996	Rose Window Collection 1751	Open		160.00	160
1984	Rosette 571	220	1988	32.00	65
1992	Round Teapot 1206	Retrd.	1994	49.50	55
1981	Roundel 109	220	1985	25.00	60
1996	Rowers 1845	Open		39.50	40
1996	Rowhouses 1888	Open		39.50	40
1990	S. Carolina State Capitol 1045	2,000		39.50	40
1986	Salem Lamb 712	Retrd.	1989	32.00	75
1985	Samantha 648	Suspd.		35.00	46
1991	San Francisco Heart 1196	Open		39.00	39
1995	San Francisco House 1685	Open		39.00	39
1990	San Francisco Row House 1071	Suspd.		39.50	50
1990	Santa & Reindeer 929	395	1991	39.00	50
1996	Santa 1884	300		100.00	100
1989	Santa (1989) 856	1,715	1989	35.00	60
1990	Santa (1990) 869	2,250	1990	38.00	42
1991	Santa (1991) 1056	3,750	1992	38.00	40
1987	Santa 741 (sp)	Unkn.		13.00	13
1987	Santa and Sleigh 751	Retrd.	1989	32.00	100
1990	Santa in Balloon 973	Open		36.00	40
1990	Santa in the Moon 941	Suspd.		38.00	40

*Quotes have been rounded up to nearest dollar

YEAR ISSUE		EDITION LIMIT	YEAR RETD.	ISSUE PRICE	*QUOTE U.S.$
1990	Santa on Reindeer 974	Suspd.		36.00	100
1986	Santa Skates 715	Suspd.		36.00	45
1987	Santa Star 739	Retrd.	1991	32.00	48
1990	Santa UpTo Date 975	Suspd.		36.00	40
1988	Santa with Scroll 814	250	1991	34.00	44
1983	Sargent Angel 523	690	1987	29.00	56
1992	Scarecrow 1286	Retrd.	1993	36.00	50
1995	Schwarzschild Carillon 1738	Open		39.00	39
1992	Scrooge 1241	Open		36.00	40
1985	Shepherd 617	1,770	1990	35.00	60
1994	Shepherdstown House 1630	Open		39.00	39
1995	SI Angel 1691	Open		39.00	39
1995	SI Teddy Bear 1687	Open		39.00	39
1988	Skaters 790	Retrd.	1991	39.50	50
1994	Skaters in the Park 1617	Open		39.00	40
1995	Skating in the Park 1705	Open		39.00	39
1988	Sleigh 834	Open		34.00	40
1994	Smithsonian Angel 1534	Retrd.	1994	39.00	39
1987	Snow Queen 746	Retrd.	1995	35.00	75
1995	Snowflake 1574	Open		38.00	38
1990	Snowflake (1990) 1033	1,415	1990	36.00	45
1993	Snowflake (1993) 1394	Retrd.	1993	40.00	44
1994	Snowflake (1994) 1486	Retrd.	1994	39.00	39
1995	Snowflake (1995) 1652	Yr.Iss.		39.00	40
1986	Snowflake 713	Retrd.	1990	36.00	55
1994	Snowman 1572	Retrd.	1995	39.00	50
1987	Snowman 753	825	1991	38.00	56
1992	St. John Angel 1236	10,000		39.00	50
1992	St. John Lion 1235	10,000		39.00	50
1985	St. Nicholas 670 (sp)	Unkn.		13.00	30
1995	Star 1591	Open		40.00	40
1996	Star 1867	Yr.Iss.		39.50	40
1997	Star 1906	Yr.Iss.		39.50	40
1994	Star 1994 1462	Retrd.	1994	39.50	40
1996	Star 1996 1796	Open		39.50	40
1988	Star 806	311	1990	50.00	200
1988	Star 854	275	1991	32.00	75
1988	Star of the East 785	Retrd.	1992	35.00	48
1990	Steadfast Tin Soldier 1050	Retrd.	1995	36.00	75
1987	Stocking 772 (sp)	Unkn.		13.00	13
1988	Stocking 774 (sp)	Unkn.		13.00	13
1988	Stocking 827 (sp)	Unkn.		13.00	13
1989	Stocking Bear 835 (sp)	Unkn.		13.00	13
1989	Stocking Bear 955 (sp)	Unkn.		12.00	12
1989	Stocking with Toys 956 (sp)	Unkn.		12.00	12
1982	Straw Star 448	590	1986	25.00	50
1983	Sunburst 543	Unkn.		13.00	50
1996	Swan Boat 1872	Open		39.50	40
1989	Swan Boat 904	Suspd.		38.00	50
1987	Sweetheart Star 740	Retrd.	1991	39.50	58
1991	Tailor of Gloucester 1087	Open		39.50	40
1985	Teddy 637	Suspd.		37.00	47
1986	Teddy 707	Unkn.		13.00	30
1986	Teddy Bear 685	Retrd.	1991	38.00	58
1990	Teddy Bear Locket 949	Unkn.		25.00	25
1996	Teddy Bear Smithsonian 1863	Open		39.50	40
1990	Teddy Bear with Heart 957 (sp)	Unkn.		13.00	13
1996	Thayer Angel Smithsonian 1877	Yr.Iss.		39.50	40
1995	Three Angels 1683	Open		39.50	40
1995	Three French Hens 1621	Open		39.00	40
1988	Thumbelina 803	Retrd.	1995	35.00	75
1992	Tin Man 1285	Retrd.	1993	36.00	50
1990	Toad Wind in Willows 945	Suspd.		38.00	38
1994	Trumpet 1504	Open		39.00	39
1994	Two Turtle Doves 1478	Open		38.00	40
1992	Unicorn 1165	Retrd.	1994	36.00	36
1985	Unicorn 660	Retrd.	1990	37.00	55
1988	US Capitol 820	Open		38.00	40
1984	USHS 1984 Angel 574	Suspd.		35.00	75
1989	USHS Angel (1989) 901	Suspd.		38.00	75
1990	USHS Angel (1990) 1061	Suspd.		39.00	39
1991	USHS Angel (1991) 1139	Suspd.		38.00	50
1995	USHS Angel (1995) 1703	Yr.Iss.		39.00	39
1986	USHS Angel 703	Suspd.		35.00	75
1985	USHS Bluebird 631	Suspd.		29.00	38
1994	USHS Dove 1521	Open		39.00	39
1987	USHS Gloria Angel 748	Suspd.		39.00	75
1985	USHS Madonna 630	Suspd.		35.00	75
1985	USHS Swallow 632	Suspd.		29.00	38
1989	Victorian Heart 954 (sp)	Unkn.		13.00	13
1986	Victorian Santa 724	250	1988	32.00	45
1993	Violin 1340	Retrd.	1993	38.00	90
1991	The Voyages Of Columbus 1141	1,500	1993	39.00	50
1991	Waiting For Santa 1123	Retrd.	1993	38.00	38
1994	Weld Boathouse 1447	Open		39.00	39
1991	White Rabbit 1121	Open		39.00	39
1990	White Tail Deer 1022 (sp)	Unkn.		13.00	13
1984	Wild Swan 592	Retrd.	1995	35.00	75
1993	Window 1360	Retrd.	1994	38.00	38
1986	Winged Dove 680	Retrd.	1993	35.00	54
1983	Wise Man 549	Retrd.	1988	29.00	56
1984	Wreath 575 (sp)	Unkn.		13.00	30
1986	Wreath 714	Suspd.		36.00	38
1992	Xmas Tree & Heart 1162	Retrd.	1994	36.00	36
1993	Xmas Tree 1395	Suspd.		40.00	44
1993	Zig Zag Tree 1343	Suspd.		39.00	39

Harbour Lights

Christmas Ornaments - Harbour Lights

1996	Big Bay Pt. MI 7040	Open		15.00	15

YEAR ISSUE		EDITION LIMIT	YEAR RETD.	ISSUE PRICE	*QUOTE U.S.$
1996	Burrows Island WA 7043	Open		15.00	15
1996	Holland MI 7041	Open		15.00	15
1996	Sand Island WI 7042	Open		15.00	15
1996	Set of 4 702	Open		60.00	60
1996	30 Mile Pt. NY 7044	Open		15.00	15
1996	Cape Neddick ME 7047	Open		15.00	15
1996	New London Ledge CT 7046	Open		15.00	15
1996	S.E. Block Island RI 7045	Open		15.00	15
1996	Set of 4 703	Open		60.00	60

Hawthorne Village

Gone With the Wind - Hawthorne

1995	Red Horse Saloon/Butler Mansion	Open		29.90	30
1995	Tara/ Atlanta Church	Open		29.90	30
1995	Twelve Oaks/Kennedy Store	Open		29.90	30

Kinkade's Candlelight Cottages - Kinkade-Inspired

1995	Cedar Nooke/ Candlelit	Open		29.90	30
1995	Olde Porterfield Tea Room/ Merritt's	Open		29.90	30
1995	Seaside/Sweetheart	Open		29.90	30
1995	Swanbrooke/Chandler's	Closed	1995	29.90	30

Rockwell's Main Street (Illuminated) - Rockwell-Inspired

1994	Antique Shop & Town Offices	Open		29.90	30
1994	Bank & Library	Open		29.90	30
1994	The Red Lion Inn & Rockwell Residence	Open		29.90	30
1994	Studio & Country Store	Open		29.90	30

John Hine N.A. Ltd.

David Winter Ornaments - Various

1991	Christmas Carol - D. Winter	Closed	1991	15.00	15
1991	Christmas in Scotland & Hogmanay - D. Winter	Closed	1991	15.00	15
1991	Mr. Fezziwig's Emporium - D. Winter	Closed	1991	15.00	15
1991	Ebenezer Scrooge's Counting House - D. Winter	Closed	1991	15.00	15
1992	Fairytale Castle - D. Winter	Closed	1992	15.00	15
1992	Fred's Home - D. Winter	Closed	1992	15.00	15
1992	Suffolk House - D. Winter	Closed	1992	15.00	15
1992	Tudor Manor - D. Winter	Closed	1992	15.00	15
1993	The Grange - J. Hine Studios	Closed	1993	15.00	15
1993	Scrooge's School - J. Hine Studios	Closed	1993	15.00	15
1993	Tomfool's Cottage - J. Hine Studios	Closed	1993	15.00	15
1993	Will-O The Wisp - J. Hine Studios	Closed	1993	15.00	15
1994	Old Joe's Beetling Shop - J. Hine Studios	Closed	1994	17.50	18
1994	Scrooge's Family Home - J. Hine Studios	Closed	1994	17.50	18
1994	What Cottage - J. Hine Studios	Open		17.50	18
1995	Buttercup Cottage - J. Hine Studios	Open		17.50	18
1995	The Flowershop - J. Hine Studios	Open		17.50	18
1995	Looking for Santa - J. Hine Studios	Open		17.50	18
1995	Miss Belle's Cottage - J. Hine Studios	Closed	1995	17.50	18
1995	Robin's Merry Mouse - J. Hine Studios	Open		17.50	18
1995	Season's Greetings - J. Hine Studios	Open		17.50	18

June McKenna Collectibles, Inc.

Flatback Ornaments - J. McKenna

1988	1776 Santa	Closed	1991	17.00	55-65
1986	Amish Boy, blue	Closed	1989	13.00	100
1986	Amish Boy, pink	Closed	1986	13.00	200-300
1986	Amish Girl, blue	Closed	1989	13.00	100
1986	Amish Girl, pink	Closed	1986	13.00	300
1985	Amish Man	Closed	1989	13.00	100
1985	Amish Woman	Closed	1989	13.00	100-125
1993	Angel of Peace, white or pink	Closed	1994	30.00	50
1984	Angel with Horn	Closed	1988	14.00	150
1982	Angel With Toys	Closed	1988	14.00	150-175
1995	Angel, Guiding Light, pink, green & white	Closed	1996	30.00	30
1983	Baby Bear in Vest, 5 colors	Closed	1988	11.00	85
1982	Baby Bear, Teeshirt	Closed	1984	11.00	125-175
1985	Baby Pig	Closed	1988	11.00	100-125
1983	Baby, blue trim	Closed	1988	11.00	110
1983	Baby, pink trim	Closed	1988	11.00	70-80
1991	Boy Angel, white	Closed	1992	20.00	100-125
1982	Candy Cane	Closed	1984	10.00	375
1993	Christmas Treat, blue	Closed	1996	30.00	50-65
1982	Colonial Man, 3 colors	Closed	1984	12.00	175
1982	Colonial Woman, 3 colors	Closed	1984	12.00	100-150
1984	Country Boy, 2 colors	Closed	1988	12.00	65
1984	Country Girl, 2 colors	Closed	1988	12.00	65
1993	Elf Bernie	Closed	1994	30.00	30
1990	Elf Jeffrey	Closed	1992	17.00	40
1991	Elf Joey	Closed	1993	20.00	30
1992	Elf Scotty	Closed	1993	25.00	30
1994	Elf-Ricky	Closed	1995	30.00	30
1994	Elf-Tammy	Closed	1995	30.00	30

YEAR ISSUE		EDITION LIMIT	YEAR RETD.	ISSUE PRICE	*QUOTE U.S.$
1988	Elizabeth, sill sitter	Closed	1989	20.00	75
1983	Father Bear in Suit, 3 colors	Closed	1988	12.00	85-100
1985	Father Pig	Closed	1988	12.00	100
1993	Final Notes	Closed	1994	30.00	55-65
1991	Girl Angel, white	Closed	1993	20.00	100-125
1983	Gloria Angel	Closed	1984	14.00	400-500
1989	Glorious Angel	Closed	1992	17.00	55-75
1983	Grandma, 4 colors	Closed	1988	12.00	80
1983	Grandpa, 4 colors	Closed	1988	12.00	85
1988	Guardian Angel	Closed	1991	16.00	40
1990	Harvest Santa	Closed	1992	17.00	65
1990	Ho Ho Ho	Closed	1992	17.00	65
1982	Kate Greenaway Boy, 3 colors	Closed	1983	12.00	155
1982	Kate Greenaway Girl, 3 colors	Closed	1983	12.00	155
1982	Mama Bear, Blue Cape	Closed	1984	12.00	100-175
1983	Mother Bear in Dress, 3 colors	Closed	1988	12.00	85-100
1985	Mother Pig	Closed	1988	12.00	100-125
1984	Mr. Claus	Closed	1988	14.00	75
1984	Mrs. Claus	Closed	1988	14.00	75
1992	Northpole News	Closed	1993	25.00	55-65
1994	Nutcracker	Closed	1995	30.00	30
1993	Old Lamplighter	Closed	1994	30.00	55-65
1984	Old World Santa, 3 colors	Closed	1989	14.00	75-250
1984	Old World Santa, gold	Closed	1986	14.00	200-275
1982	Papa Bear, Red Cape	Closed	1984	12.00	100-175
1992	Praying Angel	Closed	1993	25.00	30
1985	Primitive Santa	Closed	1989	17.00	145-175
1983	Raggedy Andy, 2 colors	Closed	1983	12.00	250
1983	Raggedy Ann, 2 colors	Closed	1983	12.00	325
1994	Ringing in Christmas	Closed	1995	30.00	45-65
1986	Santa with Bag	Closed	1989	16.00	75
1991	Santa with Banner	Closed	1992	20.00	40-65
1992	Santa with Basket	Closed	1993	25.00	40-65
1986	Santa with Bear	Closed	1991	14.00	65
1986	Santa with Bells, blue	Closed	1989	14.00	75
1986	Santa with Bells, green	Closed	1989	14.00	400-450
1988	Santa with Book, blue & red	Closed	1988	17.00	250-300
1991	Santa with Lights, black or white	Closed	1992	20.00	65
1992	Santa with Sack	Closed	1993	25.00	45-65
1989	Santa with Staff	Closed	1991	17.00	45-65
1982	Santa with Toys	Closed	1988	14.00	75
1988	Santa with Toys	Closed	1991	17.00	100-150
1989	Santa with Tree	Closed	1991	17.00	45-75
1988	Santa with Wreath	Closed	1991	17.00	40-75
1995	Santa's Lil' Helper, brown	Closed	1996	30.00	50-75
1983	St. Nick with Lantern (wooden)	Closed	1988	14.00	75-125
1989	Winking Santa	Closed	1991	17.00	65

Kirk Stieff

Colonial Williamsburg - D. Bacorn

1992	Court House	Open		10.00	10
1989	Doll ornament, silverplate	Closed	N/A	22.00	30
1993	Governors Palace	Open		10.00	10
1988	Lamb, silverplate	Closed	N/A	20.00	25
1992	Prentis Store	Open		10.00	10
1987	Rocking Horse, silverplate	Closed	N/A	20.00	35
1987	Tin Drum, silverplate	Closed	N/A	20.00	28
1983	Tree Top Star, silverplate	Closed	N/A	29.50	35
1984	Unicorn, silverplate	Closed	N/A	22.00	30
1992	Wythe House	Open		10.00	10

Kirk Stieff Ornaments - Various

1994	Angel with Star - J. Ferraioli	Open		8.00	8
1993	Baby's Christmas - D. Bacorn	Open		12.00	12
1993	Bell with Ribbon - D. Bacorn	Open		12.00	12
1992	Cat and Ornament - D. Bacorn	Closed	N/A	10.00	10
1993	Cat with Ribbon - D. Bacorn	Open		12.00	12
1983	Charleston Locomotive - D. Bacorn	Closed	N/A	18.00	20
1993	First Christmas Together - D. Bacorn	Closed	N/A	10.00	10
1993	French Horn - D. Bacorn	Closed	N/A	12.00	12
1992	Guardian Angel - J. Ferraioli	Closed	N/A	13.00	13
1986	Icicle, sterling silver - D. Bacorn	Closed	N/A	35.00	65
1994	Kitten with Tassel - J. Ferraioli	Open		12.00	12
1993	Mouse and Ornament - D. Bacorn	Closed	N/A	10.00	10
1992	Repoussé Angel - J. Ferraioli	Open		13.00	13
1992	Repoussé Wreath - J. Ferraioli	Open		13.00	13
1994	Santa with Tassel - J. Ferraioli	Open		12.00	12
1989	Smithsonian Carousel Horse - Kirk Stieff	Closed	N/A	50.00	50
1989	Smithsonian Carousel Seahorse - Kirk Stieff	Closed	N/A	50.00	50
1994	Teddy Bear - D. Bacorn	Open		8.00	8
1990	Toy Ship - Kirk Stieff	Closed	N/A	23.00	35
1984	Unicorn - D. Bacorn	Closed	N/A	18.00	30
1994	Unicorn - D. Bacorn	Open		8.00	8
1994	Victorian Skaters - D. Bacorn	Open		8.00	8
1994	Williamsburg Wreath - D. Bacorn	Open		15.00	15
1993	Wreath with Ribbon - D. Bacorn	Open		12.00	12

Kurt S. Adler, Inc.

Children's Hour - J. Mostrom

1995	Alice in Wonderland J5751	Retrd.	1996	22.50	23
1995	Bow Peep J5753	Open		27.00	27
1995	Cinderella J5752	Retrd.	1996	28.00	28
1995	Little Boy Blue J5755	Retrd.	1995	18.00	18
1995	Miss Muffet J5753	Open		27.00	27
1995	Mother Goose J5754	Retrd.	1996	27.00	27

YEAR ISSUE	EDITION LIMIT	YEAR RETD.	ISSUE PRICE	*QUOTE U.S.$
1995 Red Riding Hood J5751		Retrd. 1996	22.50	23

Christmas in Chelsea Collection - J. Mostrom

YEAR ISSUE	EDITION LIMIT	YEAR RETD.	ISSUE PRICE	*QUOTE U.S.$
1994 Alice, Marguerite W2973		Retrd. 1996	28.00	28
1992 Allison Sitting in Chair W2812		Retrd. 1994	25.50	26
1992 Allison W2729		Retrd. 1993	21.00	21
1992 Amanda W2709		Retrd. 1993	21.00	21
1992 Amy W2729		Retrd. 1993	21.00	21
1992 Christina W2812		Retrd. 1994	25.50	26
1992 Christopher W2709		Retrd. 1994	21.00	21
1992 Delphinium W2728	Open		20.00	20
1995 Edmond With Violin W3078		Retrd. 1996	32.00	32
1994 Guardian Angel With Baby W2974		Retrd. 1995	31.00	31
1992 Holly Hock W2728	Open		20.00	20
1992 Holly W2709		Retrd. 1993	21.00	21
1995 Jose With Violin W3078		Retrd. 1996	32.00	32
1995 Pauline With Violin W3078		Retrd. 1996	32.00	32
1992 Peony W2728	Open		20.00	20
1992 Rose W2728	Open		20.00	20

Cornhusk Mice Ornament Series - M. Rothenberg

YEAR ISSUE	EDITION LIMIT	YEAR RETD.	ISSUE PRICE	*QUOTE U.S.$
1994 3" Father Christmas W2976	Open		18.00	18
1994 9" Father Christmas W2982	Open		25.00	25
1995 Angel Mice W3088	Open		10.00	10
1995 Baby's First Mouse W3087	Open		10.00	10
1993 Ballerina Cornhusk Mice W2700		Retrd. 1994	13.50	14
1994 Clara, Prince W2948	Open		16.00	16
1994 Cowboy W2951	Open		18.00	18
1994 Drosselmeir Fairy, Mouse King W2949	Open		16.00	16
1994 Little Pocahontas, Indian Brave W2950	Open		18.00	18
1995 Miss Tammie Mouse W3086		Retrd. 1996	17.00	17
1995 Mr. Jamie Mouse W3086		Retrd. 1996	17.00	17
1995 Mrs. Molly Mouse W3086		Retrd. 1996	17.00	17
1993 Nutcracker Suite Fantasy Cornhusk Mice W2885		Retrd. 1994	15.50	16

Fabriché™ Ornament Series - KS. Adler, unless otherwise noted

YEAR ISSUE	EDITION LIMIT	YEAR RETD.	ISSUE PRICE	*QUOTE U.S.$
1994 All Star Santa W1665		Retrd. 1996	27.00	27
1992 An Apron Full of Love W1594 - M. Rothenberg		Retrd. 1996	27.00	27
1995 Captain Claus W1711	Open		25.00	25
1994 Checking His List W1634	Open		23.50	24
1992 Christmas in the Air W1593	Open		35.50	36
1994 Cookies For Santa W1639	Open		28.00	28
1994 Firefighting Friends W1668	Open		28.00	28
1992 Hello Little One! W1561		Retrd. 1996	22.00	22
1994 Holiday Flight W1637 - Smithsonian		Retrd. 1996	40.00	40
1993 Homeward Bound W1596		Retrd. 1996	27.00	27
1992 Hugs And Kisses W1560		Retrd. 1996	22.00	22
1993 Master Toymaker W1595		Retrd. 1996	27.00	27
1992 Merry Chrismouse W1565		Retrd. 1994	10.00	10
1992 Not a Creature Was Stirring W1563		Retrd. 1996	22.00	22
1993 Par For the Claus W1625	Open		27.00	27
1993 Santa With List W1510	Open		20.00	20
1994 Santa's Fishtales W1666	Open		29.00	29
1995 Strike Up The Band W1710		Retrd. 1996	25.00	25

Holly Bearies - H. Adler

YEAR ISSUE	EDITION LIMIT	YEAR RETD.	ISSUE PRICE	*QUOTE U.S.$
1996 Angel Starcatcher (Starlight Foundation) J7222	Open		20.00	20

International Christmas - J. Mostrom

YEAR ISSUE	EDITION LIMIT	YEAR RETD.	ISSUE PRICE	*QUOTE U.S.$
1994 Cathy, Johnny W2945	Open		24.00	24
1994 Eskimo-Atom, Ukpik W2967		Retrd. 1996	28.00	28
1994 Germany-Katerina, Hans W2969	Open		27.00	27
1994 Native American-White Dove, Little Wolf W2970		Retrd. 1994	28.00	28
1994 Poland-Marissa, Hedwig W2965	Open		27.00	27
1994 Scotland-Bonnie, Douglas W2966	Open		27.00	27
1994 Spain-Maria, Miguel W2968	Open		27.00	27

Little Dickens - J. Mostrom

YEAR ISSUE	EDITION LIMIT	YEAR RETD.	ISSUE PRICE	*QUOTE U.S.$
1994 Little Bob Crachit W2961	Open		30.00	30
1994 Little Marley's Ghost W2964	Open		33.50	34
1994 Little Mrs. Crachit W2962	Open		27.00	27
1994 Little Scrooge in Bathrobe W2959	Open		30.00	30
1994 Little Scrooge in Overcoat W2960	Open		30.00	30
1994 Little Tiny Tim W2963	Open		22.50	23

Polonaise™ by Komozja - KSA/Komozja, unless otherwise noted

YEAR ISSUE	EDITION LIMIT	YEAR RETD.	ISSUE PRICE	*QUOTE U.S.$
1995 Alarm Clock GP452	Open		25.00	25
1994 Angel w/Bear GP396		Retrd. 1995	20.20	35-40
1996 Antique Cars boxed set GP522	Open		124.00	124
1994 Beer Glass GP366	Open		18.00	18
1996 Betty Boop GP624 - King Features	Open		32.00	32
1995 Blessed Mother GP413	Open		22.50	23
1995 Caesar GP422	Open		25.00	25
1996 Candleholder GP450	Open		20.00	20
1994 Cardinal on Pine Cone GP420		Retrd. 1995	18.00	18
1995 Cat in Boot GP478 - Rothenberg	Open		28.00	28
1994 Cat w/Ball GP390		Retrd. 1995	23.00	40
1995 Cat w/Bow GP443	Open		22.50	22
1995 Christ Child GP414	Open		20.00	20
1995 Christmas Tree GP461	Open		22.50	23
1996 Cinderella 4 pc boxed set GP512	Open		134.00	134
1996 Cinderella 6 pc boxed set GP511	7,500	1996	190.00	190

YEAR ISSUE	EDITION LIMIT	YEAR RETD.	ISSUE PRICE	*QUOTE U.S.$
1996 Cinderella Coach GP487	Open		33.00	33
1996 Cinderella GP488	Open		28.00	28
1995 Clara GP408	Open		20.00	20
1995 Clown Head 4.5" GP460	Open		25.00	25
1996 Coca Cola 4 pc boxed set GP517	Open		135.00	135
1996 Coca Cola Bear GP630 - Coca Cola	Open		37.00	37
1996 Coca Cola Bottle GP631 - Coca Cola	Open		33.00	33
1996 Coca Cola Bottle Top GP633 - Coca Cola	Open		27.00	27
1996 Coca Cola Disk GP632 - Coca Cola	Open		26.00	26
1996 Coca Cola Vending Machine GP634 - Coca Cola	Open		37.00	37
1996 Cossack GP604	Open		35.00	35
1995 Cowboy Head GP462	Open		30.00	30
1995 Creche GP458 - Stefan	Open		28.00	28
1995 Crocodile GP468	Open		28.00	28
1996 Dice boxed set GP509	Open		60.00	60
1994 Dinosaurs GP397	Open		22.50	23
1994 Dinosaurs-brown GP397		Retrd. 1995	22.50	55
1995 Dove on Ball GP472 - Stefan	Open		30.00	30
1995 Eagle GP453	Open		28.00	28
1994 Egyptian (12 pc boxed set) GP500		Retrd. 1995	200.00	360-420
1996 Egyptian Cat GP351	Open		30.00	30
1996 Egyptian II boxed set GP510	Open		170.00	170
1996 Egyptian Princess GP482	Open		33.00	33
1995 Egyptian set 4 pc. boxed GP500/4	Open		110.00	110
1995 Elephant GP 464	Open		28.00	28
1996 Elves GP611/23	Open		30.00	30
1996 Emerald City GP623	Open		32.00	32
1994 Engine GP353	Open		22.50	23
1996 Fire Engine GP605	Open		30.00	30
1995 Fish 4 pc. boxed GP506	Open		110.00	110
1996 French Hen GP626 - Stefan	Open		33.00	33
1996 Gift Boxes GP614	Open		25.00	25
1994 Glass Acorn GP342		Retrd. 1995	11.00	150
1994 Glass Angel GP309	Open		18.00	18
1994 Glass Apple GP339		Retrd. 1995	11.00	11
1994 Glass Church GP369	Open		18.00	18
1994 Glass Clown 4" GP301		Retrd. 1995	13.50	40
1994 Glass Clown 6" GP303		Retrd. 1995	22.50	40
1994 Glass Clown 6.5" GP302		Retrd. 1995	22.50	35
1994 Glass Doll GP377		Retrd. 1995	13.50	35
1994 Glass Gnome GP347		Retrd. 1995	18.00	18
1994 Glass Knight's Helmet GP304		Retrd. 1995	18.00	18
1994 Glass Owl GP328	Open		20.00	20
1996 Glass Slipper GP490	Open		20.00	20
1996 Glass Turkey GP326	Open		20.00	20
1994 Glass White Dice (original-square) GP363		Retrd. 1994	18.00	85-90
1996 Glinda the Good Witch GP621	Open		32.00	32
1994 Golden Head GP372		Retrd. 1994	18.00	75-125
1994 Golden Rocking Horse GP355		Retrd. 1994	22.50	110
1995 Goose w/Wreath GP475 - Stefan	Open		30.00	30
1996 Gramophone GP446	Open		22.50	23
1995 Herr Drosselmeir GP465 - Rothenberg	Open		30.00	30
1995 Holy Family 3 pc. GP504	Open		84.00	84
1994 Holy Family GP371	Open		28.00	28
1996 Horus GP484	Open		33.00	33
1995 Humpty Dumpty GP477 - Stefan	Open		30.00	30
1995 Icicle Santa GP474 - Stefan		Retrd. 1995	25.00	40-45
1995 Indian GP463	Open		30.00	30
1996 King Balthazar GP607	Open		30.00	30
1996 King Neptune GP496	Open		35.00	35
1996 Light Bulb GP449	Open		20.00	20
1996 Little Mermaid GP492	Open		28.00	28
1995 Locomotive GP447	Open		20.00	20
1994 Madonna w/Child GP370	Open		22.50	23
1996 Medieval boxed set GP519	Open		160.00	160
1996 Medieval Dragon GP642	Open		35.00	35
1996 Medieval Knight GP641	Open		35.00	35
1996 Medieval Lady GP643	Open		35.00	35
1994 Merlin GP373		Retrd. 1995	20.00	30
1995 Mickey Mouse GP392		Retrd. 1995	33.00	90-150
1995 Minnie Mouse GP391		Retrd. 1995	33.00	50-100
1994 Mouse King GP406	Open		20.00	20
1996 Mummy GP483	Open		33.00	33
1996 Nefertiti 96 GP485	Open		33.00	33
1994 Nefertiti GP349		Retrd. 1995	25.00	25
1994 Night & Day GP307	Open		22.50	23
1995 Noah's Ark GP469	Open		28.00	28
1994 Nutcracker GP404	Open		20.00	20
1995 Nutcracker Suite 4 pc. boxed GP507	Open		110.00	110
1994 Old Fashioned Car GP380		Retrd. 1995	13.50	20
1994 Parrot GP333		Retrd. 1995	15.50	35
1995 Partridge in a Pear Tree GP467 - Stefan	Open		33.50	34
1994 Peacock 5" GP324	Open		18.00	18
1994 Peacock on Ball 7.5" GP323	Open		28.00	28
1995 Peter Pan 4 pc. boxed set GP503	Open		124.00	124
1995 Peter Pan GP419	Open		22.50	23
1996 Pharaoh GP481	Open		35.00	35
1994 Pierrot Clown GP405	Open		18.00	18
1996 Polonaise Medieval Horse GP640	Open		35.00	35
1995 Polonaise African-American Santa GP389/1	Open		25.00	25
1995 Polonaise Cardinal GP473 - Stefan	Open		30.00	30
1995 Polonaise House GP455	Open		25.00	25
1995 Polonaise Santa GP389	Open		25.00	25
1996 Prince Charming GP489	Open		28.00	28
1994 Puppy (gold) GP333		Retrd. 1994	15.50	35

YEAR ISSUE	EDITION LIMIT	YEAR RETD.	ISSUE PRICE	*QUOTE U.S.$
1994 Pyramid GP352	Open		22.50	23
1996 Raggedy Ann GP321	Open		28.00	28
1994 Rocking Horse 5" GP356	Open		22.50	23
1994 Roly-Poly Santa GP317	Open		22.50	23
1995 Roman 7 pc. boxed set GP402		Retrd. 1995	164.00	164
1994 Roman Centurian GP427	Open		22.50	23
1995 Roman set 4 pc. boxed GP402/4		Retrd. 1995	110.00	110
1996 Russian 5 pc boxed set GP514	Open		190.00	190
1996 Russian Bishop GP603	Open		35.00	35
1996 Russian Woman GP602	Open		35.00	35
1995 Sailing Ship GP415	Open		30.00	30
1994 Saint Nick GP316	Open		28.00	28
1994 Santa Boot GP375	Open		20.00	20
1994 Santa Car GP367	Open		33.00	33
1994 Santa Head 4" GP315		Retrd. 1995	13.50	14
1994 Santa Head 4.5" GP374	Open		18.00	18
1994 Santa in Airplane GP365	Open		33.00	33
1995 Santa Moon GP454 - Stefan	Open		28.00	28
1995 Santa on Goose on Sled GP479	Open		30.00	30
1995 Santa w/Puppy GP442	Open		25.00	25
1996 Sea Horse GP494	Open		25.00	25
1995 Shark GP417		Retrd. 1996	18.00	18
1994 Snowman w/Parcel GP313	Open		22.50	23
1994 Snowman w/Specs GP312		Retrd. 1995	20.00	30
1994 Soldier GP407		Retrd. 1995	15.50	125
1994 Sparrow GP 329		Retrd. 1995	15.50	20
1994 Sphinx GP350		Retrd. 1995	22.50	30
1994 Sphinx GP480	Open		33.00	33
1994 Spinner Top GP359		Retrd. 1995	9.00	28
1996 St. Basils Cathedral GP600	Open		35.00	35
1996 St. Joseph GP412	Open		22.50	23
1995 Star Santa GP470 - Stefan	Open		25.00	25
1996 Star Snowman GP625 - Stefan	Open		32.00	32
1996 Sting Ray GP495	Open		28.00	28
1994 Swan GP325	Open		20.00	20
1994 Teddy Bear (gold) GP338		Retrd. 1994	15.50	35
1995 Telephone GP448	Open		25.00	25
1996 Three Kings boxed set GP516	Open		144.00	144
1994 Train Coaches GP354	Open		15.50	16
1994 Train Set (boxed) GP501	Open		90.00	90
1995 Treasure Chest GP416	Open		20.00	20
1994 Tropical Fish GP409	Open		22.50	23
1996 Tsar Ivan GP601	Open		35.00	35
1995 Turtle Doves GP471 - Stefan	Open		25.00	25
1996 Tutenkhamen #2 GP476	Open		35.00	35
1994 Tutenkhamen GP348	Open		25.00	25
1996 Wicked Witch GP606	Open		32.00	32
1996 Winter Boy GP615	Open		22.50	23
1996 WinterGirl GP615	Open		22.50	23
1994 Wizard in Balloon GP622	Open		32.00	32
1995 Wizard of Oz 4 pc. boxed GP505	Open		124.00	124
1995 Wizard of Oz 6 pc. boxed GP508	5,000	1995	170.00	200-325
1996 Wizard of Oz Dorothy GP434	Open		25.00	25
1996 Wizard of Oz II boxed set GP518	Open		164.00	164
1995 Wizard of Oz Lion GP433	Open		22.50	23
1995 Wizard of Oz Scarecrow GP435	Open		25.00	25
1995 Wizard of Oz Tinman GP436	Open		25.00	25
1994 Zodiac Sun GP381		Retrd. 1995	28.00	28

Polonaise™ Vatican Library Collection - Vatican Library

YEAR ISSUE	EDITION LIMIT	YEAR RETD.	ISSUE PRICE	*QUOTE U.S.$
1996 Cherub Bust Glass GP651	Open		N/A	N/A
1996 Cherubum boxed set, GP 521	Open		N/A	N/A
1996 Dancing Cherubs on Ball GP652	Open		N/A	N/A
1996 Full Body Cherub GP 650	Open		N/A	N/A
1996 Garden of Mary boxed set, GP 520	Open		N/A	N/A
1996 Lily Glass GP655	Open		N/A	N/A
1996 Madonna & Child GP653	Open		N/A	N/A
1996 Rose Glass GP654	Open		N/A	N/A

Royal Heritage Collection - J. Mostrom

YEAR ISSUE	EDITION LIMIT	YEAR RETD.	ISSUE PRICE	*QUOTE U.S.$
1993 Anastasia W2922		Retrd. 1994	28.00	28
1996 Angelique Angel Baby W3278	Open		25.00	25
1995 Benjamin J5756	Open		24.50	25
1995 Blythe J5756	Open		24.50	25
1996 Brianna Ivory W7663	Open		25.00	25
1996 Brianna Pink W7663	Open		25.00	25
1993 Caroline W2924		Retrd. 1994	25.50	26
1993 Charles W2924		Retrd. 1995	25.50	26
1993 Elizabeth W2924		Retrd. 1995	25.50	26
1996 Etoile Angel Baby W3278	Open		25.00	25
1996 Francis Winter Boy W3279	Open		28.00	28
1996 Gabrielle in Pink Coat W3276	Open		28.00	28
1996 Giselle w/ Bow W3279	Open		28.00	28
1996 Giselle Winter Girl w/Package W3279	Open		28.00	28
1994 Ice Fairy, Winter Fairy W2972	Open		25.50	26
1993 Joella W2979		Retrd. 1993	27.00	27
1993 Kelly W2979		Retrd. 1993	27.00	27
1996 Lady Colette in Sled W3301	Open		32.00	32
1996 Laurielle Lady Skater W3281	Open		36.00	36
1996 Miniotte w/Muff W3279	Open		28.00	28
1996 Monique w/Hat Box W3277	Open		28.00	28
1993 Nicholas W2923		Retrd. 1996	25.50	26
1996 Nicole w/ Balloon W3277	Open		28.00	28
1993 Patina W2923		Retrd. 1996	25.50	26
1996 Rene Victorian Lady W3280	Open		36.00	36
1993 Sasha W2923		Retrd. 1996	25.50	26
1994 Snow Princess W2971		Retrd. 1996	28.00	28

Smithsonian Museum Carousel - KSA/Smithsonian

YEAR ISSUE	EDITION LIMIT	YEAR RETD.	ISSUE PRICE	*QUOTE U.S.$
1987 Antique Bunny S3027/2		Retrd. 1992	14.50	15
1992 Antique Camel S3027/12	Open		15.00	15

YEAR ISSUE		EDITION LIMIT	YEAR RETD.	ISSUE PRICE	*QUOTE U.S.$
1989	Antique Cat S3027/6		Retrd. 1995	14.50	15
1992	Antique Elephant S3027/11		Open	14.50	15
1995	Antique Frog S32027/18		Open	15.50	16
1988	Antique Giraffe S3027/4		Retrd. 1993	14.50	15
1987	Antique Goat S3027/1		Retrd. 1992	14.50	15
1991	Antique Horse S3027/10		Open	15.00	15
1993	Antique Horse S3027/14		Open	15.00	15
1988	Antique Horse S3027/3		Retrd. 1993	14.50	15
1989	Antique Lion S3027/5		Retrd. 1994	14.50	15
1994	Antique Pig S3027/16		Open	15.50	16
1994	Antique Reindeer S3027/15		Open	15.50	16
1991	Antique Rooster S3027/9		Retrd. 1994	14.50	15
1990	Antique Seahorse S3027/8		Open	14.50	15
1993	Antique Tiger S3027/13		Open	15.00	15
1990	Antique Zebra S3027/7		Open	14.50	15
1995	Armored Horse S3027/17		Open	15.50	16

Smithsonian Museum Fabriché™ - KSA/Smithsonian

1992	Holiday Drive W1580		Retrd. 1995	38.00	38
1992	Santa On a Bicycle W1547		Open	31.00	31

Steinbach Ornament Series - KS. Adler

1992	The King's Guards ES300		Open	27.00	27

Lance Corporation

Sebastian Christmas Ornaments - P.W. Baston Jr., unless otherwise noted

1943	Madonna of the Chair - P.W. Baston	25	1943	2.00	150-200
1981	Santa Claus - P.W. Baston	5,000	1981	28.50	30
1982	Madonna of the Chair (Reissue of '43) - P.W. Baston	2,165	1982	15.00	30-45
1985	Home for the Holidays		Closed 1993	10.00	13
1986	Holiday Sleigh Ride		Closed 1993	10.00	13
1987	Santa		Closed 1993	10.00	13
1988	Decorating the Tree		Closed 1993	12.50	13
1989	Final Preparations for Christmas		Closed 1993	13.90	14
1990	Stuffing the Stockings		Closed 1993	14.00	14
1990	Christmas Rose-Red on White (Blossom Shop)		Closed 1990	22.00	25-35
1991	Merry Christmas		Closed 1993	14.50	15
1992	Final Check		Closed 1993	14.50	15
1993	Ethnic Santa		Closed 1993	12.50	25-30
1993	Caroling With Santa		Closed 1993	15.00	15
1994	Victorian Christmas Skaters		Closed 1994	17.00	17
1995	Midnight Snacks		Closed 1995	17.00	17

Lenox China

Yuletide - Lenox

1994	Cat		Open	19.50	20
1995	Candle		Open	19.95	20

Lenox Collections

The Christmas Carousel - Lenox

1989	Cat		Open	19.50	20
1989	Elephant		Open	19.50	20
1989	Goat		Open	19.50	20
1989	Hare		Open	19.50	20
1989	Lion		Open	19.50	20
1989	Palomino		Open	19.50	20
1989	Pinto		Open	19.50	20
1989	Polar Bear		Open	19.50	20
1989	Reindeer		Open	19.50	20
1989	Sea Horse		Open	19.50	20
1989	Swan		Open	19.50	20
1989	Tiger		Open	19.50	20
1989	Unicorn		Open	19.50	20
1989	White Horse		Open	19.50	20
1989	Zebra		Open	19.50	20
1989	Black Horse		Open	19.50	20
1990	Camel		Open	19.50	20
1990	Frog		Open	19.50	20
1990	Giraffe		Open	19.50	20
1990	Medieval Horse		Open	19.50	20
1990	Panda		Open	19.50	20
1990	Pig		Open	19.50	20
1990	Rooster		Open	19.50	20
1990	St. Bernard		Open	19.50	20
1990	Set of 24		Open	468.00	468

Lilliput Lane Ltd.

Christmas Ornaments - Lilliput Lane

1992	Mistletoe Cottage		Retrd. 1992	27.50	40-60
1993	Robin Cottage		Retrd. 1993	35.00	45
1994	Ivy House		Retrd. 1994	35.00	45
1995	Plum Cottage		Retrd. 1995	30.00	40
1996	Fir Tree Cottage		Yr.Iss.	30.00	30

Ray Day/Coca Cola Country - R. Day

1996	Santa's Corner	19,960		35.00	35

Lladró

Angels - Lladró

1994	Joyful Offering L6125G		Yr.Iss. 1994	245.00	265
1995	Angel of the Stars L6132G		Yr.Iss. 1995	195.00	195

1996	Rejoice L6321G		Yr.Iss.	220.00	220

Annual Ornaments - Lladró

1988	Christmas Ball-L1603M		Yr.Iss. 1988	60.00	60-80
1989	Christmas Ball-L5656M		Yr.Iss. 1989	65.00	65
1990	Christmas Ball-L5730M		Yr.Iss. 1990	70.00	70
1991	Christmas Ball-L5829M		Yr.Iss. 1991	52.00	68
1992	Christmas Ball-L5914M		Yr.Iss. 1992	52.00	55
1993	Christmas Ball-L6009M		Yr.Iss. 1993	54.00	55
1994	Christmas Ball-L6105M		Yr.Iss. 1994	55.00	55
1995	Christmas Ball-L6207M		Yr.Iss. 1995	55.00	55
1996	Christmas Ball-L6298M		Yr.Iss.	55.00	55

Cherub Ornaments - Lladró

1995	Surprised Cherub L6253G		Open	120.00	120
1995	Playing Cherub L6254G		Open	120.00	120
1995	Thinking Cherub L6255G		Open	120.00	120

Dove Ornaments - Lladró

1995	Landing Dove L6266G		Open	49.00	49
1995	Flying Dove L6267G		Open	49.00	49

Miniature Ornaments - Lladró

1988	Miniature Angels-L1604G, Set/3		Yr.Iss. 1988	75.00	175-250
1989	Holy Family-L5657G, Set/3		Yr.Iss. 1990	79.50	100
1990	Three Kings-L5729G, Set/3		Yr.Iss. 1991	87.50	110
1991	Holy Shepherds-L5809G		Yr.Iss. 1991	97.50	100-110
1993	Nativity Trio-L6095G		Yr.Iss.	115.00	150

Ornaments - Lladró

1991	Our First-1991-L5840G		Yr.Iss. 1991	50.00	57
1992	Snowman-L5841G		Yr.Iss. 1994	50.00	60
1992	Santa-L5842G		Yr.Iss. 1994	55.00	60
1992	Baby's First-1992-L5922G		Yr.Iss. 1992	55.00	55
1992	Our First-1992-L5923G		Yr.Iss. 1992	50.00	50
1992	Elf Ornament-L5938G		Yr.Iss. 1994	50.00	57-75
1992	Mrs. Claus-L5939G		Yr.Iss. 1994	55.00	57
1992	Christmas Morning-L5940G		Yr.Iss. 1994	97.50	100
1993	Nativity Lamb-L5969G		Yr.Iss. 1994	85.00	85
1993	Baby's First 1993-L6037G		Yr.Iss. 1993	57.00	57
1993	Our First-L6038G		Yr.Iss. 1993	52.00	57
1996	Santa's Journey-L6265		Yr.Iss.	49.00	49

Toy Ornaments - Lladró

1995	Christmas Tree L6261G		Open	75.00	75
1995	Rocking Horse L6262G		Open	69.00	69
1995	Doll L6263G		Open	69.00	69
1995	Train L6264G		Open	69.00	69

Tree Topper Ornaments - Lladró

1990	Angel Tree Topper-L5719G-Blue		Yr.Iss. 1990	115.00	200-225
1991	Angel Tree Topper-L5831G-Pink		Yr.Iss. 1991	115.00	150
1992	Angel Tree Topper -L5875G-Green		Yr.Iss. 1992	120.00	150
1993	Angel Tree Topper -L5962G-Lavender		Yr.Iss. 1993	125.00	150

Margaret Furlong Designs

Annual Ornaments - M. Furlong

1980	3" Trumpeter Angel		Closed 1994	12.00	50-125
1980	4" Trumpeter Angel		Closed 1994	21.00	70-150
1982	3" Star Angel		Closed 1994	12.00	50-125
1982	4" Star Angel		Closed 1994	21.00	70-150
1984	3" Dove Angel		Closed 1995	12.00	50-100
1984	4" Dove Angel		Closed 1995	21.00	70-100
1988	3" Butterfly Angel		Closed 1996	12.00	35-75
1988	4" Butterfly Angel		Closed 1996	21.00	70
1996	4" Sunflower Angel		Yr.Iss.	21.00	21

Flora Angelica - M. Furlong

1995	Faith Angel	10,000	1995	45.00	90
1996	Hope Angel	10,000	1996	45.00	50-90

Gifts from God - M. Furlong

1985	1985 The Charis Angel	3,000	1985	45.00	500-900
1986	1986 The Hallelujah Angel	3,000	1986	45.00	600-1000
1987	1987 The Angel of Light	3,000	1987	45.00	300-700
1988	1988 The Celestial Angel	3,000	1988	45.00	300-700
1989	1989 Coronation Angel	3,000	1989	45.00	300-600

Joyeux Noel - M. Furlong

1990	1990 Celebration Angel	10,000	1994	45.00	175-300
1991	1991 Thanksgiving Angel	10,000	1994	45.00	175-290
1992	1992 Joyeux Noel Angel	10,000	1994	45.00	150-250
1993	1993 Star of Bethlehem Angel	10,000	1994	45.00	175-350
1994	1994 Messiah Angel	10,000	1994	45.00	300-600

Madonna and Child - M. Furlong

1996	Madonna of the Cross	20.000		80.00	80

Musical Series - M. Furlong

1980	1980 The Caroler	3,000	1980	50.00	300-700
1981	1981 The Lyrist	3,000	1981	45.00	250-800
1982	1982 The Lutist	3,000	1982	45.00	200-800
1983	1983 The Concertinist	3,000	1983	45.00	150-750
1984	1984 The Herald Angel	3,000	1984	45.00	250-800

Victoria - M. Furlong

1994	Victoria Heart	10,000	1996	24.95	25
1995	Victoria Lily of the Valley	30,000	1996	25.00	25

Midwest of Cannon Falls

Leo R. Smith III Collection - L.R. Smith

1996	Angel of Heaven and Earth 18396-0	3,500		33.00	33
1996	Angel of Light 18076-1	4,000		33.00	33
1996	Angel of Music 18073-4	3,500		33.00	33
1996	Belsnickle Santa 18074-7	4,000		39.00	39
1994	Flying Woodsman Santa 11921-1	2,500	1994	35.00	200-350
1995	Angel of Love 16123-4	3,500		32.00	33
1995	Angel of Peace 16199-9	3,500		32.00	33
1995	Angel of Your Dreams 16130-2	3,500		32.00	33
1995	Partridge Angel 13994-3	3,500		30.00	30
1995	Santa on Reindeer 13780-2	3,500	1996	35.00	50-95
1996	Angel of Dependability 19218-4		Open	37.00	37
1996	Angel of Adventure 19219-1		Open	37.00	37
1996	Angel of Nurturing 19220-7		Open	37.00	37
1996	Angel of Generosity 19221-4		Open	37.00	37
1996	Angel of Knowledge 19222-1		Open	37.00	37
1996	Angel of Sharing 19223-8		Open	37.00	37
1996	Angel of Guidance 19224-5		Open	37.00	37
1996	Angel of Pride 19225-2		Open	37.00	37
1996	Everyday Angel Ornament Stand 19554-3		Open	25.00	25

Wendt and Kuhn Ornaments - Wendt/Kuhn

1978	Angel Clip-on Ornament 00729-7		Retrd. 1995	20.00	24
1989	Trumpeting Angel Ornament, 2 asst. 09402-0		Retrd. 1995	14.00	17
1991	Angel in Ring Ornament 01208-6		Retrd. 1995	12.00	15
1994	Angel on Moon, Star, 12 asst. 12945-6		Open	20.00	22

Old World Christmas

Collector Club - E.M. Merck, unless otherwise noted

1993	Mr. & Mrs. Claus set 1490		Retrd. 1993	Gift	100-200
1993	Glass Christmas Maidens, Set/4, 1491		Retrd. 1993	35.00	85-100
1993	Dresdener Drummer Nutcracker 7258		Retrd. 1993	110.00	175-250
1994	Santa in Moon 1492		Retrd. 1994	Gift	50-75
1994	Large Santa in Chimney 1493		Retrd. 1994	42.50	65-95
1995	Large Christmas Carousel 1587 - Inge-Glas		Retrd. 1995	79.50	95
1995	The Konigsee Nutcracker 7284		Retrd. 1995	125.00	200-300
1995	Cherub on Reflector 1545 - Inge-Glas		Retrd. 1995	Gift	27-75
1996	The Baroque Angel Above Reflector 1082		Yr.Iss.	39.50	40
1996	The Faxon Santa Claus Nutcracker 7211		Yr.Iss.	135.00	135
1996	The Victorian Christmas Stocking 1554		Yr.Iss.	Gift	N/A

Angel & Female - E.M. Merck, unless otherwise noted

1991	Angel of Peace 1033		Retrd. 1995	9.25	10
1990	Angel on Disc 1028		Retrd. 1993	11.70	16
1992	Angel on Form 1044		Retrd. 1995	9.70	10
1990	Antique Style Doll Head 1026		Retrd. 1996	8.45	9
1987	Baby 1009		Retrd. 1995	5.25	6
1988	Baby in Bunting 1015		Retrd. 1990	7.70	14
1991	Baby Jesus 1036		Retrd. 1995	9.25	10
1991	Baroque Angel 1031		Retrd. 1995	12.95	13
1985	Caroling Girl 101062		Retrd. 1990	6.65	19
1993	Chubby Mushroom Girl 1057		Retrd. 1996	8.00	8
1986	Clip-on Angel with Wings 1004		Retrd. 1995	10.00	11
1985	Doll Head 103209		Retrd. 1989	6.40	11
1993	Frau Schneemann 1059		Retrd. 1995	16.90	17
1992	Garden Girl 1040		Retrd. 1996	8.25	9
1985	Girl in Blue Dress 1042227		Retrd. 1996	7.00	7
1987	Girl in Grapes 1010		Retrd. 1995	8.45	20
1990	Girl in Polka Dot Dress 1030		Retrd. 1996	12.60	13
1987	Girl on Snowball with Teddy 1007		Retrd. 1995	9.25	15
1988	Girl Under Tree 1014		Retrd. 1995	7.80	8
1985	Girl with Flowers 101069		Retrd. 1993	7.50	13
1992	Girl with White Kitty 1045		Retrd. 1996	9.25	10
1985	Gold Girl with Tree 1010306		Retrd. 1995	8.25	12
1992	Guardian Angel 1043		Retrd. 1996	8.25	9
1992	Honey Child 1042		Retrd. 1995	7.45	8
1988	Large Blue Angel 1012		Retrd. 1994	13.40	17
1988	Large Doll Head 1013		Retrd. 1995	11.60	12
1985	Light Blue Angel with Wings 101052		Retrd. 1994	9.25	14
1986	Little Red Riding Hood 1001		Retrd. 1993	9.90	16
1991	Little Tyrolean Girl 1037		Retrd. 1996	7.00	7
1989	Little Witch 1020		Retrd. 1996	8.35	9
1990	Miniature Mrs. Claus 1027		Retrd. 1995	4.95	5
1986	Mrs. Santa Claus 1003		Retrd. 1989	8.90	24
1987	Mushroom Girl 1006		Retrd. 1994	9.25	12
1989	Pilgrim Girl 1019		Retrd. 1995	9.25	10
1986	Pink Angel with Wings 1002		Retrd. 1988	8.90	16
1990	Praying Girl 1025		Retrd. 1993	7.80	12
1985	Red Girl with Tree 1010309		Retrd. 1995	8.25	13
1989	Small Girl Head 1022		Retrd. 1995	7.00	7
1985	Small Girl with Tree 101029		Retrd. 1995	5.85	6
1989	Victorian Angel 1018		Retrd. 1995	8.35	9
1985	Victorian Girl 101035		Retrd. 1989	5.30	16

Animals - E.M. Merck, unless otherwise noted

1993	Bear Above Reflector 1279		Retrd. 1995	33.75	36
1986	Bear in Crib 1203		Retrd. 1994	9.00	12
1993	Brilliant Butterfly 1267		Retrd. 1996	10.70	11

YEAR ISSUE		EDITION LIMIT	YEAR RETRD.	ISSUE PRICE	*QUOTE U.S.$
1993	Buster 1266		Retrd. 1996	8.35	9
1985	Butterfly on Form 1237447		Retrd. 1995	7.80	8
1989	Cat and the Fiddle 1221		Retrd. 1994	7.80	11
1986	Cat in Bag 1204		Retrd. 1995	9.00	9
1985	Cat in Show 121103		Retrd. 1994	7.80	11
1991	Christmas Butterfly 1247		Retrd. 1996	7.00	9
1984	Circus Dog 121021		Retrd. 1994	9.00	12
1989	Fat Fish 1223		Retrd. 1995	5.85	6
1991	Goldfish 1249		Retrd. 1996	7.00	7
1985	Grey Elephant 123420		Retrd. 1995	7.00	7
1993	Grizzly Bear 1265		Retrd. 1996	8.35	9
1988	Jumbo Elephant 1213		Retrd. 1995	9.25	10
1989	King Charles Spaniel 1222		Retrd. 1995	9.90	10
1984	Kitten 121004		Retrd. 1995	7.00	7
1989	Large Fish 1214		Retrd. 1993	6.70	14
1991	Large Puppy with Basket 1241		Retrd. 1993	13.25	22
1985	Large Teddy Bear 121089		Retrd. 1988	13.00	18
1985	Large Three-Sided Head 121088		Retrd. 1994	12.95	23
1985	Matte Gold Bear w/Heart 1234356		Retrd. 1996	7.00	7
1986	Monkey 1205		Retrd. 1994	5.85	11
1993	Monkey with Apple 1258		Retrd. 1996	8.80	9
1987	Mouse 1211		Retrd. 1995	9.90	10
1993	My Darling 1276		Retrd. 1996	6.30	7
1991	Panda Bear 1242		Retrd. 1995	9.25	10
1993	Pastel Butterfly 1268		Retrd. 1995	8.45	9
1990	Pastel Fish 1234		Retrd. 1996	6.65	7
1985	Pink Pig 121042		Retrd. 1994	7.80	8
1990	Pink Poodle 1227		Retrd. 1994	8.80	11
1986	Playing Cat 1202		Retrd. 1994	8.80	11
1992	Proud Pug 1250		Retrd. 1996	9.25	10
1984	Puppy 121010		Retrd. 1994	7.00	9
1989	Rabbit in Tree 1219		Retrd. 1995	8.35	9
1991	Rabbit on Heart 1244		Retrd. 1995	8.00	8
1990	Red Butterfly on Form 1231		Retrd. 1994	8.55	9
1990	Sitting Black Cat 1228		Retrd. 1995	7.00	7
1986	Sitting Dog with Pipe 1206		Retrd. 1995	7.80	11
1991	Sitting Puppy 1246		Retrd. 1994	6.75	9
1985	Small Bunny 121090		Retrd. 1994	5.20	8
1986	Smiling Dog 1207		Retrd. 1994	7.80	10
1985	Snail 121041		Retrd. 1993	6.70	18
1989	Teddy Bear with Bow 1218		Retrd. 1990	6.65	17
1984	Three-Sided: Owl, Dog, Cat 121009		Retrd. 1994	8.55	13
1990	West Highland Terrier 1232		Retrd. 1993	7.45	15
1989	White Kitty 1220		Retrd. 1990	7.45	10
1994	Woodland Squirrel 1291		Retrd. 1996	21.00	21

Bead Garlands - E.M. Merck

YEAR ISSUE		EDITION LIMIT	YEAR RETRD.	ISSUE PRICE	*QUOTE U.S.$
1993	Angel Garland 1306		Retrd. 1993	55.00	85
1993	Celestial Garland 1303		Retrd. 1993	55.00	80
1996	Christmas Candy Garland 1324		Retrd. 1996	110.00	110
1993	Clown & Drum Garland 1301		Retrd. 1993	55.00	65
1993	Frog and Fish Garland 1305		Retrd. 1995	55.00	95
1993	Fruit Garland 1302		Retrd. 1993	55.00	70
1993	Pickle Garland 1304		Retrd. 1993	55.00	110
1996	Poinsettia Garland 1323		Retrd. 1996	100.00	100
1993	Santa Garland 1308		Retrd. 1995	55.00	80-110
1996	Santa/Candy Christmas Garland 1322		Retrd. 1996	110.00	110
1996	Shiny Gold Garland 1325		Retrd. 1996	135.00	135
1993	Teddy Bear & Heart Garland 1307		Retrd. 1993	55.00	100
1994	Woodland Christmas Garland 1311		Retrd. 1996	65.00	65

Birgit's Christmas Collection - B. Mueller-Blech

YEAR ISSUE		EDITION LIMIT	YEAR RETRD.	ISSUE PRICE	*QUOTE U.S.$
1996	Guarding My Children 141	5,000 1996		65.00	65
1996	O' Tannenbaum 131		1996	35.00	35
1996	Old Christmas Barn 133		1996	50.00	50

Butterflies - E.M. Merck

YEAR ISSUE		EDITION LIMIT	YEAR RETRD.	ISSUE PRICE	*QUOTE U.S.$
1987	Butterfly, Blue with Blue 1905		Retrd. 1991	20.95	30
1987	Butterfly, Gold with Gold 1906		Retrd. 1991	20.95	30
1987	Butterfly, Orange with Orange 1904		Retrd. 1991	20.95	30
1987	Butterfly, Red with Cream 1903		Retrd. 1991	20.95	30
1987	Butterfly, White with Blue 1902		Retrd. 1991	20.95	30
1987	Butterfly, White with Red 1901		Retrd. 1991	20.95	30

Celestial Figures - E.M. Merck

YEAR ISSUE		EDITION LIMIT	YEAR RETRD.	ISSUE PRICE	*QUOTE U.S.$
1993	Comet on Form 2209		Retrd. 1996	7.65	8
1993	High Noon 2211		Retrd. 1996	5.65	6
1985	Large Gold Star w/Glitter 2237139		Retrd. 1993	7.00	8
1990	Shining Sun 2204		Retrd. 1995	7.00	7
1986	Shooting Star on Ball 2201		Retrd. 1993	6.65	12
1985	Sun/Moon 221027		Retrd. 1993	7.00	10

Churches & Houses - E.M. Merck

YEAR ISSUE		EDITION LIMIT	YEAR RETRD.	ISSUE PRICE	*QUOTE U.S.$
1985	Bavarian House 201059		Retrd. 1994	8.00	13
1993	Castle Tower 2029		Retrd. 1996	9.45	10
1990	Christmas Chalet 2014		Retrd. 1995	8.00	8
1991	Christmas Shop 2020		Retrd. 1996	9.45	10
1990	Church on Disc 2018		Retrd. 1995	12.50	13
1988	Church/Tree on Form 2008		Retrd. 1995	8.35	9
1986	Farm House 2003		Retrd. 1994	8.45	9
1990	Garden House with Gnome 2011		Retrd. 1993	7.80	14
1986	Gingerbread House (A) 2001		Retrd. 1989	6.55	16
1986	House with Peacock 2004		Retrd. 1987	7.45	16
1991	Large Lighthouse/Mill 2023		Retrd. 1995	11.00	11
1985	Marienkirche Church 206790-2		Retrd. 1993	6.45	11
1985	Mill 201094		Retrd. 1990	9.45	25
1991	Mission with Sea Gull 2024		Retrd. 1996	9.45	10
1985	Rathaus 201051		Retrd. 1989	7.00	14
1985	Square House 201040		Retrd. 1995	7.80	8
1991	Thatched Cottage 2019		Retrd. 1995	7.35	8
1992	Watch Tower 2027		Retrd. 1996	9.25	10
1986	Windmill on Form 2006		Retrd. 1988	7.45	22

Clip-On Birds - E.M. Merck

YEAR ISSUE		EDITION LIMIT	YEAR RETRD.	ISSUE PRICE	*QUOTE U.S.$
1991	Advent Bird 1837		Retrd. 1995	8.00	8
1986	Bird in Nest 1801		Retrd. 1995	10.35	11
1985	Bird of Paradise 181101		Retrd. 1994	7.80	10
1985	Blue Bird 181078		Retrd. 1995	6.65	7
1992	Blue Bird with Topnotch 1845		Retrd. 1996	9.45	10
1992	Brilliant Songbird 1841		Retrd. 1995	7.35	8
1991	Canary 1834		Retrd. 1994	7.35	9
1990	Cardinal 1822		Retrd. 1995	9.90	10
1993	Carnival Canary 1852		Retrd. 1996	9.45	10
1990	Christmas Bird 1824		Retrd. 1995	7.00	7
1992	Christmas Finch 1843		Retrd. 1995	7.65	8
1986	Clip-On Rooster 1802		Retrd. 1989	8.00	31
1991	Cockatiel 1838		Retrd. 1995	9.25	10
1985	Cockatoo 181077		Retrd. 1993	8.55	9
1995	Cranberry Peacock 1870		Retrd. 1996	13.95	14
1985	Fancy Peacock 181073		Retrd. 1993	13.50	16
1985	Fancy Pink Peacock 181096		Retrd. 1993	13.95	14
1985	Fantasy Bird w/Tinsel Tail 181075		Retrd. 1995	8.00	8
1987	Fat Burgundy Bird 1813		Retrd. 1995	7.80	8
1985	Fat Songbird 181074		Retrd. 1995	7.80	8
1991	Festive Bird 1832		Retrd. 1995	7.00	7
1993	Festive Sparrow 1853		Retrd. 1995	6.00	6
1992	Forest Bird 1840		Retrd. 1995	8.00	8
1986	Gold Bird with Tinsel Tail 1803		Retrd. 1994	7.45	8
1985	Gold Peacock, Tinsel Tail 1872016		Retrd. 1995	8.25	9
1987	Goldfinch 1808		Retrd. 1996	8.55	9
1995	Harvest Bird 1868		Retrd. 1996	7.50	8
1984	Large Cockatoo 181025		Retrd. 1994	13.95	16
1985	Large Goldfinch 181085		Retrd. 1994	9.25	11
1992	Large Nightingale 1842		Retrd. 1996	8.00	8
1991	Large Peacock with Crown 1830		Retrd. 1994	13.95	19
1992	Large Woodpecker 1846		Retrd. 1996	11.15	12
1987	Lilac Bird 1811		Retrd. 1996	8.70	9
1985	Magnificent Songbird 181086		Retrd. 1994	13.95	16
1985	Medium Peacock with Tinsel Tail 187215		Retrd. 1995	9.00	9
1990	Miniature Parrot 1828		Retrd. 1995	8.45	9
1990	Miniature Peacock 1825		Retrd. 1995	8.35	12
1985	Nightingale 181083		Retrd. 1996	5.55	6
1985	Nuthatch 181076		Retrd. 1995	7.00	7
1987	Partridge 1814		Retrd. 1995	8.80	11
1985	Pink Bird with Blue Wings 181082		Retrd. 1994	5.55	9
1985	Pink Snowbird 181079		Retrd. 1994	7.25	8
1987	Red Breasted Songbird 1812		Retrd. 1995	9.25	10
1987	Red Snowbird 1810		Retrd. 1993	8.70	13
1987	Robin 1819		Retrd. 1994	8.80	13
1991	Rooster 1831		Retrd. 1996	10.50	11
1987	Shiny Gold Bird 1807		Retrd. 1995	5.55	6
1991	Silly Bird 1833		Retrd. 1994	6.75	12
1987	Small Purple Bird 1809		Retrd. 1994	7.00	7
1990	Small Red-Headed Songbird 1823		Retrd. 1995	7.00	7
1987	Snow Owl 1816		Retrd. 1994	9.90	13
1985	Snowbird 181080		Retrd. 1993	8.00	14
1990	Tropical Parrot 1826		Retrd. 1995	10.35	13
1993	Tropical Songbird 1854		Retrd. 1996	7.55	9
1987	White Cockatoo 1805		Retrd. 1995	7.80	8

Clowns & Male Figures - E.M. Merck, unless otherwise noted

YEAR ISSUE		EDITION LIMIT	YEAR RETRD.	ISSUE PRICE	*QUOTE U.S.$
1984	'Shorty Clown' 241011		Retrd. 1988	5.65	14
1984	'Stop' Keystone Cop 241019		Retrd. 1989	6.65	30
1986	Aviator 2402		Retrd. 1994	7.80	11
1986	Baby 2405		Retrd. 1989	6.75	19
1992	Baker 2449		Retrd. 1996	8.35	9
1992	Bavarian 2450		Retrd. 1996	9.25	10
1990	Black Boy 2439		Retrd. 1996	9.00	12
1993	Boxer 2454		Retrd. 1996	7.20	8
1986	Boy Head w/Stocking Cap 2411		Retrd. 1993	5.30	13
1985	Boy in Yellow Sweater 241032		Retrd. 1988	7.00	15
1995	Charlie Chaplin 2487 - Inge-Glas		Retrd. 1995	25.00	60-65
1986	Clip-on Boy Head 2414		Retrd. 1989	6.45	14
1993	Clown Above Ball 2470		Retrd. 1994	42.00	45
1986	Clown Head in Drum 2412		Retrd. 1996	10.25	11
1986	Clown Head w/Burgundy Hat 2418		Retrd. 1994	7.00	10
1984	Clown in Stocking 241006		Retrd. 1988	6.65	14
1984	Clown Playing Bass Fiddle 241005		Retrd. 1993	7.80	8
1986	Clown with Accordion 2409		Retrd. 1995	10.35	11
1986	Clown with Banjo 2407		Retrd. 1995	7.00	7
1986	Clown with Drum 2408		Retrd. 1995	10.35	11
1985	Dutch Boy 243321		Retrd. 1993	7.55	16
1990	English Bobby 2442		Retrd. 1994	8.80	12
1986	Farm Boy 2414		Retrd. 1989	4.95	17
1985	Fat Boy w/Sweater & Cap 2442265		Retrd. 1994	5.85	14
1987	Gnome in Tree 2431		Retrd. 1996	7.80	8
1987	Gnome Under Mushroom 2417		Retrd. 1993	7.00	7
1988	Harpo 2432		Retrd. 1991	6.20	26
1984	Indian Chief w/Peace Pipe 241008		Retrd. 1993	7.45	8
1984	Indian in Canoe 2401		Retrd. 1994	10.95	14
1994	Jack Horner 2471		Retrd. 1996	6.50	7
1987	Jester 2419		Retrd. 1994	7.45	8
1986	Jolly Accordion Player 2443		Retrd. 1994	8.25	9
1987	Jolly Clown Head 2429		Retrd. 1994	12.95	13
1987	Jolly Snowman 2420		Retrd. 1996	8.00	8
1984	Keystone Cop 241003		Retrd. 1994	9.90	19
1987	King 2421		Retrd. 1995	10.60	11
1989	Leprechaun 2435		Retrd. 1994	7.65	10
1993	Miniature Clown 2464		Retrd. 1995	6.00	6
1993	Monk 2467		Retrd. 1996	7.90	10
1987	Mr. Big Nose 2426		Retrd. 1993	8.00	19
1995	Mr. Sci-Fi 2492 - Inge-Glas		Retrd.	29.50	30
1988	Mushroom Gnome 2430		Retrd. 1989	6.20	13
1994	My Buddy 2474		Retrd. 1996	7.75	8
1992	Pirate 2451		Retrd. 1995	7.45	8
1986	Pixie with Accordion 2406		Retrd. 1989	4.95	16
1987	Punch 2424		Retrd. 1996	8.70	9
1984	Roly-Poly Keystone Cop 241015		Retrd. 1988	9.90	26
1995	Sailor Boy 2488 - Inge-Glas		Retrd. 1996	7.95	8
1986	Sailor Head 2404		Retrd. 1989	7.45	29
1986	School Boy 2415		Retrd. 1989	4.95	13
1984	Scotsman 241017		Retrd. 1988	6.20	20
1990	Scout 2440		Retrd. 1995	9.25	10
1987	Scrooge 2427		Retrd. 1995	8.55	11
1989	Small Clown Head 2436		Retrd. 1993	6.65	11
1993	Small Snowman 2462		Retrd. 1995	6.00	6
1991	Snowman in Chimney 2447		Retrd. 1996	10.50	11
1990	Snowman on Reflector 2445		Retrd. 1993	10.35	15
1985	Waiter in Tuxedo 241047		Retrd. 1994	7.00	24
1993	Winking Leprechaun 2453		Retrd. 1996	6.55	7

Collector's Editions - E.M. Merck, unless otherwise noted

YEAR ISSUE		EDITION LIMIT	YEAR RETRD.	ISSUE PRICE	*QUOTE U.S.$
1994	'94 Santa/Moon on Disc 1512		Retrd. 1994	32.50	40
1992	Angel with Tinsel Wire 1522		Retrd. 1993	55.00	75-100
1993	Angel with Wings 1556		Retrd. 1993	12.50	75-100
1993	Christmas Heart 1593		Retrd. 1993	10.00	40-60
1995	Christmas Tree above Star Reflector 1513	2,400 1995		53.00	60-100
1995	Devil Bell 1599		Retrd. 1995	34.95	N/A
1992	Flying Peacock with Wings 1550		Retrd. 1995	22.50	23
1992	Flying Songbird with Wings 1551		Retrd. 1995	21.75	22
1993	Hansel and Gretal 1511	2,400 1995		45.00	100-125
1993	Heavenly Angel 1563		Retrd. 1995	20.00	20
1990	Night Before Christmas Ball 1501	500 1993		72.50	125-200
1992	Nutcracker Ornament 1510		Retrd. 1995	33.75	150-200
1995	Parachuting Santa 1547		Retrd. 1995	59.50	60
1993	Santa with Hot Air Balloon 1570		Retrd. 1995	38.85	39
1992	Santa with Tinsel Wire 1521		Retrd. 1995	55.00	80-100
1992	Santa's Departure 1503	500 1994		72.50	100
1991	Santa's Visit 1502	500 1994		72.50	100
1992	Snowman with Tinsel Wire 1523		Retrd. 1993	32.50	85
1995	Special Event Santa 1560	5,000 1995		15.00	25
1995	Witch 1582		Retrd. 1995	34.95	700-900

Easter - E.M. Merck

YEAR ISSUE		EDITION LIMIT	YEAR RETRD.	ISSUE PRICE	*QUOTE U.S.$
1988	Gentleman Chick 9311		Retrd. 1993	22.50	23
1988	Gentleman Rabbit 9301		Retrd. 1993	25.00	25
1988	Lady Chick 9312		Retrd. 1993	22.50	23

Easter Light Covers - E.M. Merck

YEAR ISSUE		EDITION LIMIT	YEAR RETRD.	ISSUE PRICE	*QUOTE U.S.$
1988	Assorted Easter Egg 9331-1		Retrd. 1993	3.95	7
1988	Assorted Pastel Egg 9335-1		Retrd. 1994	2.95	3
1988	Bunny 9333-4		Retrd. 1994	4.20	8
1988	Bunny in Basket 9333-6		Retrd. 1994	4.20	8
1988	Chick 9333-3		Retrd. 1994	4.20	8
1988	Chick in Egg 9333-5		Retrd. 1994	4.20	8
1988	Hen in Basket 9333-1		Retrd. 1994	4.20	8
1988	Rabbit in Egg 9333-2		Retrd. 1994	4.20	8

Fruits & Vegetables - E.M. Merck, unless otherwise noted

YEAR ISSUE		EDITION LIMIT	YEAR RETRD.	ISSUE PRICE	*QUOTE U.S.$
1990	Apricot 2831		Retrd. 1995	6.55	7
1990	Cherries on Form 2825		Retrd. 1993	9.00	12
1989	Cucumber 2820		Retrd. 1993	6.65	15
1990	Fruit Basket 2838		Retrd. 1996	7.80	8
1985	Grapes on Form 281038		Retrd. 1987	7.00	14
1994	Grapes with Butterfly 2887		Retrd. 1995	9.50	10
1987	Green Pepper 2812		Retrd. 1995	8.00	8
1985	Large Basket of Grapes 281053		Retrd. 1993	10.35	11
1993	Large Candied Apple 2882		Retrd. 1996	12.95	13
1991	Large Fruit Basket 2849		Retrd. 1995	12.50	13
1984	Large Matte Corn 281033		Retrd. 1993	9.25	10
1985	Large Strawberry 2841432		Retrd. 1993	4.20	10
1990	Large Strawberry w/Flower 2841		Retrd. 1993	10.50	19
1993	Large Sugar Pear 2881		Retrd. 1996	12.95	13
1985	Mr. Apple 281071		Retrd. 1988	6.20	20
1984	Mr. Pear 281023		Retrd. 1989	6.75	7
1987	Onion 2810		Retrd. 1989	8.25	80
1986	Pear with Face 2805		Retrd. 1995	7.00	7
1990	Raspberry 2835		Retrd. 1993	6.20	9
1991	Strawberries/Flower on Form 2851		Retrd. 1994	8.55	10
1990	Strawberry Cluster 2836		Retrd. 1995	5.20	6
1991	Very Large Apple 2848		Retrd. 1993	10.60	15
1991	Very Large Pear 2847		Retrd. 1993	10.60	15

Halloween Light Covers - E.M. Merck

YEAR ISSUE		EDITION LIMIT	YEAR RETRD.	ISSUE PRICE	*QUOTE U.S.$
1989	Dancing Scarecrow 9241-3		Retrd. 1994	7.65	9
1987	Devil 9223-5		Retrd. 1993	3.95	8
1987	Ghost w/Pumpkin 9221-2		Retrd. 1993	3.95	8
1987	Haunted House 9223-1		Retrd. 1994	3.95	8
1987	Jack O'Lantern 9221-1		Retrd. 1994	3.95	7
1989	Man in the Moon 9241-5		Retrd. 1993	7.65	20
1989	Pumpkin Face 9241-6		Retrd. 1994	7.65	9
1987	Pumpkin w/Top Hat 9223-6		Retrd. 1993	3.95	7
1987	Sad Pumpkin 9221-5		Retrd. 1993	3.95	7
1987	Scarecrow 9221-3		Retrd. 1993	3.95	7
1987	Six Halloween Light Covers 9221		Retrd. 1994	25.00	36
1987	Six Halloween Light Covers 9223		Retrd. 1993	25.90	36
1987	Skull 9221-6		Retrd. 1994	3.95	7
1987	Smiling Cat 9223-2		Retrd. 1993	3.95	7

YEAR ISSUE		EDITION LIMIT / YEAR RETD.	ISSUE PRICE	*QUOTE U.S.$
1987	Smiling Ghost 9223-4	Retrd. 1994	3.95	7
1989	Spider 9241-1	Retrd. 1994	7.65	8
1987	Standing Witch 9223-3	Retrd. 1994	3.95	7
1987	Witch Head 9221-4	Retrd. 1993	3.95	7
1989	Witch Head 9241-2	Retrd. 1994	7.65	10
1989	Wizard 9241-4	Retrd. 1993	7.65	23

Hanging Birds - E.M. Merck

YEAR ISSUE		EDITION LIMIT / YEAR RETD.	ISSUE PRICE	*QUOTE U.S.$
1988	Bird House 1611	Retrd. 1995	10.35	11
1992	Birdie 1620	Retrd. 1996	8.80	9
1985	Blue Bird with Wings 161100	Retrd. 1991	7.65	10
1992	Brilliant Hanging Snowbird 1625	Retrd. 1996	9.80	10
1985	Cardinal with Wings 161098	Retrd. 1994	10.95	11
1991	Chick on Form 1619	Retrd. 1993	8.00	12
1984	Cock Robin 161012	Retrd. 1995	7.00	7
1990	Duck 1613	Retrd. 1995	6.20	7
1992	Exotic Bird 1623	Retrd. 1995	10.35	11
1985	Fancy Peacock 161066	Retrd. 1995	9.25	10
1987	Fat Rooster 1610	Retrd. 1995	10.35	11
1993	Hanging Parrot 1631	Retrd. 1996	9.60	10
1993	Hanging Pastel Bird 1630	Retrd. 1996	10.50	11
1992	Large German Songbird 1624	Retrd. 1996	11.25	12
1986	Large Owl with Stein 1604	Retrd. 1989	10.00	45
1991	Large Parrot on Ball 1617	Retrd. 1995	11.00	11
1992	Messenger Bird 1626	Retrd. 1996	6.75	7
1986	Owl on Form 1601	Retrd. 1989	11.00	11
1993	Rooster at Hen House 1629	Retrd. 1995	10.25	12
1986	Rooster on Form 1603	Retrd. 1989	6.65	9
1990	Songbird on Form 1614	Retrd. 1994	8.80	10
1991	Songbird on Heart (A) 1618	Retrd. 1993	8.25	11
1986	Songbirds on Ball 1602	Retrd. 1994	9.25	11
1986	Swan on Form 1605	Retrd. 1995	8.35	9
1988	Swans on Lake 1612	Retrd. 1995	7.80	8
1985	Turkey 161058	Retrd. 1989	8.00	13

Hearts - E.M. Merck

YEAR ISSUE		EDITION LIMIT / YEAR RETD.	ISSUE PRICE	*QUOTE U.S.$
1987	Burgundy Heart with Glitter 3004	Retrd. 1995	6.75	7
1992	Heart with Flowers 3010	Retrd. 1993	9.50	13
1985	Large Matte Red Heart 306925	Retrd. 1995	5.30	6
1985	Pink Heart with Glitter 306767	Retrd. 1995	6.75	7
1986	Small Gold Heart with Star 3001	Retrd. 1993	2.85	9
1988	Valentine 3005	Retrd. 1995	5.75	6

Household Items - E.M. Merck

YEAR ISSUE		EDITION LIMIT / YEAR RETD.	ISSUE PRICE	*QUOTE U.S.$
1986	Black Stocking 3203	Retrd. 1993	9.45	36
1994	Cheers 3222	Retrd. 1996	6.95	7
1994	Christmas Cap 3220	Retrd. 1996	6.50	7
1992	Christmas Shoe 3212	Retrd. 1996	8.25	9
1985	Clip-On Candle 321063	Retrd. 1995	12.95	13
1992	Flapper Purse 3211	Retrd. 1996	9.25	10
1991	Money Bag 3206	Retrd. 1994	7.00	10
1985	Pastel Umbrella (A) 321091	Retrd. 1993	11.00	15
1985	Pocket Watch 326729	Retrd. 1995	5.85	6
1986	Red Stocking 3201	Retrd. 1987	9.00	19
1991	Small Cuckoo Clock 3209	Retrd. 1995	7.00	7
1991	Small Wine Barrel 3210	Retrd. 1993	6.30	10
1985	Very Large Pink Umbrella 321103	Retrd. 1986	29.50	49
1985	Wall Clock 321060	Retrd. 1995	11.00	11
1988	Wine Barrel 3204	Retrd. 1990	7.00	13

Icicles - E.M. Merck

YEAR ISSUE		EDITION LIMIT / YEAR RETD.	ISSUE PRICE	*QUOTE U.S.$
1988	Long Champagne Icicle 3401	Retrd. 1988	7.25	15

Light Covers - E.M. Merck

YEAR ISSUE		EDITION LIMIT / YEAR RETD.	ISSUE PRICE	*QUOTE U.S.$
1984	3 Men in a Tub 529007-1	Retrd. 1986	1.60	12
1986	Angel on Bell 529023-5	Retrd. 1991	3.95	11
1985	Apple 529011-5	Retrd. 1989	3.00	10
1986	Assorted Alphabet Blocks 529043-1	Retrd. 1991	4.50	12
1984	Assorted Animals, set of 6 529003	Retrd. 1987	10.35	48
1986	Assorted Bells, set of 6 529023	Retrd. 1993	22.50	48
1988	Assorted Birds 529057-1	Retrd. 1990	3.95	9
1986	Assorted Easter Eggs 529031-1	Retrd. 1993	3.00	8
1988	Assorted Fast Food 529055-1	Retrd. 1991	3.95	12
1984	Assorted Figurals, set of 6 529005	Retrd. 1987	10.35	54
1989	Assorted Fir Cone 529209-1	Retrd. 1991	2.85	8
1993	Assorted Frosty Bell 5275	Retrd. 1993	5.65	8
1985	Assorted Fruit, set of 6 529011	Retrd. 1989	20.00	48
1986	Assorted Peach Roses 529045-4	Retrd. 1990	3.95	27
1986	Assorted Roses, set of 6 529045	Retrd. 1991	22.50	48
1985	Assorted Santas, set of 6 529015	Retrd. 1992	20.00	54
1989	Assorted Sea Shells 529301-1	Retrd. 1993	3.50	12
1991	Assorted Snowmen 529305-1	Retrd. 1993	5.55	10
1986	Assorted Yellow Roses 529045-2	Retrd. 1990	3.95	12
1985	Automobile 529019-3	Retrd. 1988	2.70	12
1985	Balloon 529019-2	Retrd. 1988	2.70	12
1984	Bear 519003-3	Retrd. 1987	2.50	12
1986	Blue Father Christmas 529047-3	Retrd. 1992	3.95	13
1993	Blue Man in the Moon 5206	Retrd. 1993	5.50	6
1986	Bunny 529033-4	Retrd. 1993	3.60	10
1986	Bunny in Basket 529033-6	Retrd. 1993	3.60	8
1985	Cable Car 529019-5	Retrd. 1988	2.70	12
1984	Carousel 529005-3	Retrd. 1987	2.70	12
1986	Chick 529033-3	Retrd. 1993	3.60	8
1986	Chick in Egg 529033-5	Retrd. 1993	3.60	8
1988	Christmas Carol 529053	Retrd. 1991	25.00	54
1993	Christmas House 5205	Retrd. 1993	5.50	6
1988	Christmas Tree 529051-4	Retrd. 1992	3.95	8
1984	Church on Ball 529005-6	Retrd. 1987	2.50	12
1985	Clara-The Doll 529017-1	Retrd. 1989	2.70	10
1985	Clear Icicles, set of 6 529205	Retrd. 1989	20.00	48
1984	Clown 529001-5	Retrd. 1986	1.60	12
1988	Clown 529051-6	Retrd. 1991	3.95	9
1985	Clown Head 529009-1	Retrd. 1988	1.60	10
1988	Cornucopia 529049-1	Retrd. 1992	3.95	10
1988	Doll 529051-2	Retrd. 1993	3.95	10
1993	Doll Head 5202	Retrd. 1993	5.65	10
1985	Doll Head 529009-4	Retrd. 1988	1.60	9
1988	Drum 529051-1	Retrd. 1992	3.95	9
1988	Ear of Corn 529049-6	Retrd. 1992	3.95	10
1984	Elephant 529003-4	Retrd. 1987	1.60	10
1985	Father Christmas 529009-5	Retrd. 1990	3.00	8
1986	Father Christmas Set 529047	Retrd. 1992	25.00	48
1984	Flower Basket 529005-1	Retrd. 1987	1.60	12
1989	Frog 529303-6	Retrd. 1993	6.45	10
1993	Frosty Acorn 5276	Retrd. 1994	5.65	8
1993	Frosty Cone 5271	Retrd. 1994	5.65	8
1993	Frosty Icicle 5272	Retrd. 1993	5.65	8
1993	Frosty Red Rose 5277	Retrd. 1993	5.65	8
1993	Frosty Snowman 5270	Retrd. 1993	5.65	9
1993	Frosty Tree 5273	Retrd. 1993	5.65	8
1984	Gnome 529001-1	Retrd. 1986	1.60	12
1985	Grapes 529011-3	Retrd. 1989	3.00	8
1986	Green Father Christmas 529047-2	Retrd. 1992	3.95	9
1984	Hedgehog 529003-5	Retrd. 1987	1.60	12
1986	Hen on Bell 529033-1	Retrd. 1993	3.60	8
1984	House 529005-2	Retrd. 1987	1.60	10
1988	Indian 529049-5	Retrd. 1992	3.95	10
1993	Jolly Santa Head 5201	Retrd. 1993	5.50	6
1985	King 529013-3	Retrd. 1988	2.70	10
1989	Kitten 529303-3	Retrd. 1993	6.45	10
1984	Lil' Boy Blue 529007-5	Retrd. 1986	1.60	12
1985	Lil' Rascal Head 529009-6	Retrd. 1988	1.60	12
1985	Locomotive 529019-4	Retrd. 1988	2.70	12
1993	Man in the Moon 5204	Retrd. 1993	5.50	6
1985	Marie-The Girl 529017-3	Retrd. 1989	2.70	12
1985	Mouse King 529017-5	Retrd. 1989	2.70	12
1984	Mrs. Claus 529001-4	Retrd. 1986	1.60	12
1985	Nutcracker 529017-4	Retrd. 1989	2.70	10
1986	Nutcracker on Bell 529023-6	Retrd. 1993	3.95	9
1985	Nutcracker Suite Figures, set/6 529017	Retrd. 1989	19.00	54
1985	Orange 529011-6	Retrd. 1989	3.00	7
1984	Owl 529003-2	Retrd. 1987	1.60	10
1989	Panda 529303-1	Retrd. 1994	6.45	9
1985	Pastel Icicles 529207	Retrd. 1989	N/A	N/A
1984	Peacock 519003-6	Retrd. 1987	2.70	10
1993	Peacock 5203	Retrd. 1993	5.65	11
1985	Pear 529011-1	Retrd. 1989	3.00	9
1988	Pilgrim Boy 529049-3	Retrd. 1992	3.95	12
1988	Pilgrim Girl 529049-4	Retrd. 1992	3.95	12
1985	Pineapple 529011-4	Retrd. 1989	3.00	10
1985	Pink Heart 529201-3	Retrd. 1989	2.85	9
1989	Puppy 529303-2	Retrd. 1994	6.45	10
1986	Purple Father Christmas 529047-6	Retrd. 1992	3.95	12
1984	Queen of Heart 529007-3	Retrd. 1986	2.70	12
1986	Rabbit in Egg 529033-2	Retrd. 1993	3.60	9
1986	Red Father Christmas 529047-1	Retrd. 1992	3.95	12
1986	Red Father Christmas 529047-4	Retrd. 1992	3.95	12
1985	Red Heart 529201-1	Retrd. 1990	2.85	9
1984	Red Riding Hood 529009-2	Retrd. 1988	1.60	10
1986	Rocking Horse on Bell 529023-4	Retrd. 1990	3.95	9
1985	Roly-Poly Santa 529015-6	Retrd. 1989	3.00	12
1984	Santa Head 529005-4	Retrd. 1987	2.70	12
1985	Santa Head 529009-3	Retrd. 1988	3.00	10
1986	Santa on Bell 529023-3	Retrd. 1990	3.95	12
1984	Santa on Heart 529005-5	Retrd. 1987	3.00	10
1993	Santa with Tree 5207	Retrd. 1993	5.50	6
1985	Santa with Tree 529015-3	Retrd. 1992	3.00	10
1985	School Bus 529019-6	Retrd. 1991	2.70	13
1985	Six Red & White Hearts 529201	Retrd. 1989	15.00	16
1992	Six Snowmen 529305	Retrd. 1993	29.00	54
1984	Snowman 519001-2	Retrd. 1986	2.50	10
1988	Soldier with Drum 529013-1	Retrd. 1988	2.70	10
1985	Soldier with Gun 529013-2	Retrd. 1988	2.70	10
1985	Soldiers, set of 6 529013	Retrd. 1988	17.95	54
1989	Squirrel 529303-2	Retrd. 1994	6.45	9
1984	Standing Santa 529001-3	Retrd. 1987	3.00	10
1988	Stocking 529051-3	Retrd. 1992	3.95	10
1985	Strawberry 529011-2	Retrd. 1989	3.00	9
1993	Sugar Apple 5254	Retrd. 1993	5.50	6
1993	Sugar Fruit Basket 5256	Retrd. 1994	5.65	8
1993	Sugar Grapes 5252	Retrd. 1993	5.50	6
1993	Sugar Pear 5255	Retrd. 1993	5.50	6
1993	Sugar Plum 5253	Retrd. 1993	5.50	6
1985	Sugar Plum Fairy 529017-6	Retrd. 1989	2.70	10
1993	Sugar Strawberry 5251	Retrd. 1993	5.65	8
1985	Swan 529303-5	Retrd. 1994	6.45	10
1986	Teddy Bear 529023-2	Retrd. 1990	3.95	10
1988	Teddy Bear 529051-5	Retrd. 1992	3.95	9
1986	Teddy Bear with Ball 529041-5	Retrd. 1994	3.95	6
1986	Teddy Bear w/Candy Cane 529041-1	Retrd. 1992	3.95	8
1986	Teddy Bear w/Nightshirt 529041-4	Retrd. 1994	3.95	9
1986	Teddy Bear w/Red Heart 529041-2	Retrd. 1992	3.95	8
1986	Teddy Bear with Tree 529041-3	Retrd. 1992	3.95	10
1986	Teddy Bear with Vest 529041-6	Retrd. 1992	3.95	6
1986	Teddy Bears, set of 6 529041	Retrd. 1991	25.00	54
1988	Thanksgiving, set of 6 529049	Retrd. 1992	25.00	25
1988	Toy, set of 6 529051	Retrd. 1992	25.00	58
1985	Transportation Set 529019	Retrd. 1988	17.90	58
1986	Tree on Bell 529023-1	Retrd. 1991	3.95	9
1988	Tug Boat 529019-1	Retrd. 1992	2.70	12
1988	Turkey 529049-2	Retrd. 1992	3.95	8
1986	White Father Christmas 529047-5	Retrd. 1992	3.95	12
1985	White Heart 529201-2	Retrd. 1989	2.85	8

Miscellaneous Forms - E.M. Merck, unless otherwise noted

YEAR ISSUE		EDITION LIMIT / YEAR RETD.	ISSUE PRICE	*QUOTE U.S.$
1990	Assorted Christmas Flowers 3626	Retrd. 1994	8.00	9
1990	Assorted Christmas Stars 3620	Retrd. 1995	7.00	7
1993	Assorted Fantasy Form w/Wire 3650	Retrd. 1994	20.00	23
1992	Assorted Northern Stars 3640	Retrd. 1995	6.20	7
1992	Assorted Spirals 3636	Retrd. 1995	8.25	9
1992	Christmas Ball with Roses 3634	Retrd. 1995	9.45	10
1991	Christmas Shamrock 3632	Retrd. 1996	9.25	10
1990	Clip-On Pink Rose 3628	Retrd. 1995	10.50	11
1990	Clip-On Pink Rose 3628	Retrd. 1995	10.50	10
1988	Clip-On Tulip (A) 3605	Retrd. 1995	8.70	9
1990	Edelweiss on Form 3618	Retrd. 1995	8.25	9
1995	Firecracker 3663	Retrd. 1996	6.95	7
1986	Flower Basket 3601	Retrd. 1995	10.25	11
1989	Flower with Butterfly 3609	Retrd. 1995	9.75	13
1992	Garden Flowers 3639	Retrd. 1996	9.00	9
1985	Ice Cream Cone 3637164	Retrd. 1988	14.50	24
1990	Large Conical Shell 3629	Retrd. 1995	8.70	12
1991	Large Ribbed Ball w/Roses 3633	Retrd. 1996	7.00	7
1990	Large Sea Shell 3625	Retrd. 1995	8.35	9
1990	Large Snowflake 3622	Retrd. 1995	13.00	13
1993	Lucky Shamrock 3643	Retrd. 1993	7.80	23
1989	Morning Glories 3608	Retrd. 1995	8.90	9
1989	Mr. Sunflower 3612	Retrd. 1996	7.80	8
1990	Poinsettias 3619	Retrd. 1995	9.90	10
1989	Red Rose on Form 3607	Retrd. 1995	5.85	6
1989	Shamrock on Form 3621	Retrd. 1995	5.55	6
1989	Shiny Red Clip-On Tulip 3617	Retrd. 1990	7.45	8
1988	Skull 3606	Retrd. 1995	7.35	8
1994	Stars and Stripes 3657	Retrd. 1996	9.00	9
1990	Sunburst 3624	Retrd. 1993	8.00	8
1993	Tudor Crown 3654	Retrd. 1996	9.00	9
1994	Victorian Floral Drop 3659	Retrd. 1995	22.00	22

Musical Instruments - E.M. Merck

YEAR ISSUE		EDITION LIMIT / YEAR RETD.	ISSUE PRICE	*QUOTE U.S.$
1989	Bell with Flowers 3805	Retrd. 1995	5.85	6
1986	Cello 3801	Retrd. 1995	6.65	7
1989	Christmas Bells on From 3806	Retrd. 1995	8.35	9
1988	Clip-On Drum 383534	Retrd. 1994	8.00	10
1987	Guitar 3802	Retrd. 1995	6.65	7
1988	Harmonica 3820	Retrd. 1996	8.00	8
1988	Large Bell with Acorns 3804	Retrd. 1994	9.00	12
1993	Large Bell with Holly 3819	Retrd. 1995	50.00	50
1990	Large Christmas Bell 3808	Retrd. 1995	10.35	11
1990	Lyre 3809	Retrd. 1995	8.35	9
1990	Small Fancy Drum 3815	Retrd. 1995	7.80	8
1990	Zither 3810	Retrd. 1996	8.35	9

Porcelain Christmas - E.M. Merck

YEAR ISSUE		EDITION LIMIT / YEAR RETD.	ISSUE PRICE	*QUOTE U.S.$
1989	Angel 9435	Retrd. 1994	6.65	12
1995	Angelic Gifts 9712	Retrd. 1995	11.25	12
1988	Bear on Skates 9495	Retrd. 1988	10.00	19
1988	Bunnies on Skies 9494	Retrd. 1988	10.00	19
1987	Father Christmas (A) 9404	Retrd. 1988	11.00	13
1988	Father Christmas w/Cape 9405	Retrd. 1988	11.00	14
1987	Father Christmas w/Toys 9406	Retrd. 1988	11.00	14
1989	Hummingbird 9433	Retrd. 1994	6.65	9
1987	Lighted Angel Tree Top 9420	Retrd. 1992	29.50	37
1989	Nutcracker 9436	Retrd. 1994	6.65	12
1989	Penguin w/Gifts 9496	Retrd. 1994	10.00	19
1989	Rocking Horse 9431	Retrd. 1994	6.65	11
1987	Roly-Poly Santa 9441	Retrd. 1994	6.75	14
1989	Santa 9432	Retrd. 1994	6.65	7
1987	Santa Head 9410	Retrd. 1988	6.55	12
1989	Teddy Bear 9434	Retrd. 1994	6.65	10
1995	Toys Ahoy 9713	Retrd. 1995	11.25	12
1995	Wish Upon a Star 9711	Retrd. 1995	11.25	12

Reflectors - E.M. Merck, unless otherwise noted

YEAR ISSUE		EDITION LIMIT / YEAR RETD.	ISSUE PRICE	*QUOTE U.S.$
1990	Assorted 6 cm Reflectors 4207	Retrd. 1995	7.00	7
1990	Assorted Reflectors w/Diamonds 4206	Retrd. 1995	9.95	12
1992	Flower in Reflector 4212	Retrd. 1995	9.25	10
1986	Horseshoe Reflector 4203	Retrd. 1989	7.80	15
1987	Large Drop with Indents (A) 4204	Retrd. 1994	12.85	17
1995	Patriotic Reflector 4218 - Inge-Glas	Retrd. 1996	8.95	9
1991	Peacock in Reflector 4208	Retrd. 1995	9.25	10
1991	Pears in Reflector 4209	Retrd. 1996	9.25	10
1986	Pink Reflector 4202	Retrd. 1995	9.50	10
1993	Reflector with Tinsel Wire 4215	Retrd. 1995	20.00	20
1992	Scrap Santa in Reflector 4214	Retrd. 1993	8.80	18
1986	Star Pattern Reflector (A) 4201	Retrd. 1995	9.25	14
1986	Strawberry in Reflector 4205	Retrd. 1996	9.25	10

Santas - E.M. Merck, unless otherwise noted

YEAR ISSUE		EDITION LIMIT / YEAR RETD.	ISSUE PRICE	*QUOTE U.S.$
1991	Alpine Santa 4047	Retrd. 1996	7.00	7
1985	Blue Father Christmas 4010498	Retrd. 1995	8.00	10
1990	Blue Victorian St. Nick 4028	Retrd. 1995	9.95	14
1991	Burgundy Father Christmas 4013	Retrd. 1995	7.80	16
1987	Burgundy Santa Claus 4014	Retrd. 1994	13.95	14
1990	Clip-On Victorian St. Nick 4030	Retrd. 1995	11.00	11
1986	Father Christmas Head 4006	Retrd. 1995	7.80	8

YEAR ISSUE		EDITION LIMIT	YEAR RETD.	ISSUE PRICE	*QUOTE U.S.$
1985	Father Christmas Head 403223	Retrd.	1994	7.80	10
1991	Father Christmas on Form 4046	Retrd.	1996	11.00	11
1985	Father Christmas w/Basket 403224	Retrd.	1994	7.80	10
1985	Father Christmas w/Tree 401039	Retrd.	1995	8.00	8
1990	Festive Santa Head 4039	Retrd.	1995	11.00	11
1985	Gold Father Christmas 401045	Retrd.	1995	7.45	8
1992	Gold Weihnachtsmann 4052	Retrd.	1996	9.80	10
1986	Green Clip-On Santa 4007	Retrd.	1995	7.80	8
1985	Jolly Father Christmas 401043	Retrd.	1995	7.00	7
1993	Large Father Christmas Head 4066	Retrd.	1995	22.50	23
1984	Large Santa In Basket 401001	Retrd.	1995	12.95	13
1985	Large Santa with Tree 401055	Retrd.	1995	12.60	13
1991	Large Weihnachtsmann 4042	Retrd.	1996	10.25	11
1990	Light Blue St. Nicholas 4029	Retrd.	1994	6.45	10
1987	Matte Red Roly-Poly Santa 4012	Retrd.	1995	7.90	8
1991	Old Bavarian Santa 4044	Retrd.	1996	12.50	13
1984	Old Father Christmas 401007	Retrd.	1995	7.00	10
1989	Old-Fashioned Santa (A) 4019	Retrd.	1995	5.75	6
1990	Old-Fashioned St. Nicholas 4040	Retrd.	1996	11.00	11
1986	Pink Clip-On Santa 4011	Retrd.	1994	8.35	10
1985	Pink Father Christmas 4010499	Retrd.	1995	8.00	8
1984	Roly-Poly Santa 401002	Retrd.	1994	7.90	11
1990	Round Jolly Santa Head 4035	Retrd.	1995	11.00	11
1992	Round Santa Head 4054	Retrd.	1996	9.00	9
1987	Santa Above Ball 4018	Retrd.	1995	13.95	14
1985	Santa and Tree on Form 401026	Retrd.	1995	9.25	10
1987	Santa in Airplane 4017	Retrd.	1995	13.95	14
1986	Santa In Chimney 4005	Retrd.	1995	8.70	18
1985	Santa in Chimney 406912	Retrd.	1989	11.00	17
1991	Santa in Mushroom 4048	Retrd.	1996	8.70	9
1985	Santa in Tree 401054	Retrd.	1995	7.45	8
1993	Santa in Walnut 4058	Retrd.	1996	7.00	7
1986	Santa On Carriage 4003	Retrd.	1988	10.00	29
1986	Santa On Cone 4002	Retrd.	1993	7.90	16
1986	Santa with Glued-On Tree 4009	Retrd.	1995	9.00	9
1986	Small Blue Santa 4010	Retrd.	1995	5.40	6
1984	Small Old-Fashioned Santa 401022	Retrd.	1994	6.65	9
1985	Small Santa in Basket 401105	Retrd.	1995	9.25	10
1991	Small Santa on Form 4049	Retrd.	1996	8.00	8
1985	Small Santa with Pack 401065	Retrd.	1995	5.40	6
1990	Small Victorian Santa Head 4027	Retrd.	1996	7.35	8
1990	Snowy Santa 4033	Retrd.	1995	10.95	11
1989	St. Nicholas 4020	Retrd.	1995	10.00	10
1986	St. Nicholas Head 4008	Retrd.	1995	6.65	7
1985	St. Nicholas on Horse 401064	Retrd.	1995	13.95	14
1990	Very Large Belznickel 4037	Retrd.	1996	22.50	23
1987	Very Large Santa Head 4015	Retrd.	1995	13.95	14
1991	Victorian Father Christmas 4045	Retrd.	1996	10.00	10
1989	Victorian Santa 4021	Retrd.	1995	8.45	9
1990	Victorian Scrap Santa 4043	Retrd.	1993	9.70	14
1990	Weihnachtsmann 4034	Retrd.	1996	9.00	9
1990	White Clip-On Santa 4026	Retrd.	1995	7.35	8

Toys - E.M. Merck

1995	Bowling Pin 4413	Retrd.	1995	12.75	13
1985	Doll Buggy with Doll 4437138	Retrd.	1994	7.00	9
1986	Dumb-Dumb 4403	Retrd.	1988	6.45	24
1994	Giddy-Up	Retrd.	1996	12.00	12
1990	Large Doll Buggy with Doll 4409	Retrd.	1995	11.50	12
1986	Large Nutcracker 4401	Retrd.	1995	13.50	14
1985	Matte Dice 443793	Retrd.	1993	5.75	6
1988	Nutcracker Guard 4405	Retrd.	1995	8.50	9
1985	Small Carousel 446836	Retrd.	1995	7.00	7
1986	Small Nutcracker 4402	Retrd.	1996	10.00	10
1986	Soccer Ball 4404	Retrd.	1996	7.00	7

Transportation - E.M. Merck, unless otherwise noted

1988	Cable Car 4602	Retrd.	1989	8.45	26
1985	Cable Car 461067	Retrd.	1988	14.95	25
1990	Large Zeppelin 4605	Retrd.	1993	8.25	9
1985	Locomotive 461069	Retrd.	1993	7.00	18
1985	Old-Fashioned Car 463747	Retrd.	1995	6.25	24
1992	Race Car 4609	Retrd.	1995	7.00	7
1986	Rolls Royce 4601	Retrd.	1989	7.90	24
1985	Zeppelin 467265	Retrd.	1996	7.00	7

Tree Tops - E.M. Merck, unless otherwise noted

1987	Angel in Indent Tree Top 5009	Retrd.	1993	27.00	27
1987	Angel w/Crown 5007	Retrd.	1993	50.00	72
1986	Blue Santa 5002	Retrd.	1995	37.50	38
1985	Fancy Gold Spire w/Bells 506266	Retrd.	1993	32.00	46
1985	Fancy Red Spire w/Bells 506269	Retrd.	1993	32.00	46
1992	Large Spire w/Reflectors 5014	Retrd.	1996	69.50	70
1987	Santa in Indent 5008	Retrd.	1995	25.00	25
1993	Very Large Reflector 5017	Retrd.	1996	65.00	65

Trees & Cones - E.M. Merck, unless otherwise noted

1992	Large Christmas Tree 4815	Retrd.	1996	8.00	8
1988	Large Mauve & Champagne Cone 4802	Retrd.	1993	11.85	17
1985	Medium Gold Cone w/Glitter 486712-5	Retrd.	1995	3.85	4
1990	Multi-Colored Tree 4812	Retrd.	1994	5.55	9
1990	Pine Cone Man 4811	Retrd.	1996	8.25	9
1985	Very Large Red & Gold Cones 483612	Retrd.	1995	7.00	7

Wooden Ornaments - Various

1991	Carved Boy on Skis 7872 - Helbig	Retrd.	1996	18.00	18
1991	Carved Girl on Skis 7873 - Helbig	Retrd.	1996	18.00	18
1991	Father Christmas w/Bell 78198-20 - O.W.C.	Retrd.	1996	8.00	8

YEAR ISSUE		EDITION LIMIT	YEAR RETD.	ISSUE PRICE	*QUOTE U.S.$
1992	Six Robins in Loop 784 - O.W.C.	Retrd.	1996	60.00	60

Pacific Rim Import Corp.
Bristol Waterfront - P. Sebern

1995	Portshead Lighthouse	Open		10.00	10

Possible Dreams
Clothtique® Pepsi® Santa Collection - B. Prata

1995	Yule Pop The Top	Open		7.90	8
1995	Christmas Bells & Bubbles	Open		7.40	8
1995	Holiday Cheer on Top	Open		12.20	13
1995	Get Into The Swing	Open		9.90	10
1995	Unfurl The Fun	Open		7.40	8

Crinkle Claus - Staff

1996	Bishop of Maya-659702	Open		7.80	8
1996	Black Forest Santa-659706	Open		7.80	8
1996	Father Christmas-659703	Open		7.80	8
1996	German Santa-659701	Open		7.80	8
1996	Pere Noel Santa-659705	Open		7.80	8
1996	St. Nicholas-659704	Open		7.80	8

The Thickets at Sweetbriar® - B. Ross

1995	Christmas Whiskers-350400	Closed	1996	11.50	12
1995	Jingle Bells-350407	Closed	1996	12.00	12
1996	Snuggles-350416	Open		11.70	12
1996	Nibbley-Do-350415	Open		10.50	11

Reed & Barton
12 Days of Christmas Sterling and Lead Crystal - Reed & Barton

1988	Partridge in a Pear Tree	Yr.Iss.		25.00	40
1989	Two Turtle Doves	Yr.Iss.		25.00	30-40
1990	Three French Hens	Yr.Iss.		27.50	40
1991	Four Colly birds	Yr.Iss.		27.50	40
1992	Five Golden Rings	Yr.Iss.		27.50	30-40
1993	Six Geese A Laying	Yr.Iss.		27.50	40
1994	Seven Swans A 'Swimming	Yr.Iss.		27.50	30
1995	Eight Maids A Milking	Yr.Iss.		30.00	30
1996	Nine Ladies Dancing	Yr.Iss.		30.00	30

Carousel Horse - Reed & Barton

1988	Silverplate-1988	Closed	1988	13.50	20
1988	Gold-covered-1988	Closed	1988	15.00	15
1989	Silverplate-1989	Closed	1989	13.50	18
1989	Gold-covered-1989	Closed	1989	15.00	15
1990	Silverplate-1990	Closed	1990	13.50	18
1990	Gold-covered-1990	Closed	1990	15.00	15
1991	Silverplate-1991	Closed	1991	13.50	18
1991	Gold-covered-1991	Closed	1991	15.00	15
1992	Silverplate-1992	Closed	1992	13.50	18
1992	Gold-covered-1992	Closed	1992	15.00	15
1993	Silverplate-1993	Closed	1993	13.50	18
1993	Gold-covered-1993	Closed	1993	15.00	15
1994	Silverplate-1994	Closed	1994	13.50	18
1994	Gold-covered-1994	Closed	1994	15.00	15
1995	Silverplate-1995	Closed	1995	13.50	18
1995	Gold-covered-1995	Closed	1995	15.00	15
1996	Silverplate-1996	Yr.Iss.		13.50	14
1996	Gold-covered-1996	Yr.Iss.		15.00	15

Christmas Cross - Reed & Barton

1971	Sterling Silver-1971	Closed	1971	10.00	300-350
1971	24Kt. Gold over Sterling-V1971	Closed	1971	17.50	300
1972	Sterling Silver-1972	Closed	1972	10.00	90-125
1972	24Kt. Gold over Sterling-V1972	Closed	1972	17.50	75-175
1973	Sterling Silver-1973	Closed	1973	10.00	90
1973	24Kt. Gold over Sterling-V1973	Closed	1973	17.50	60-85
1974	Sterling Silver-1974	Closed	1974	12.95	90
1974	24Kt. Gold over Sterling-V1974	Closed	1974	20.00	45-75
1975	Sterling Silver-1975	Closed	1975	12.95	90
1975	24Kt. Gold over Sterling-V1975	Closed	1975	20.00	50-60
1976	Sterling Silver-1976	Closed	1976	13.95	75-90
1976	24Kt. Gold over Sterling-V1976	Closed	1976	19.95	45-50
1977	Sterling Silver-1977	Closed	1977	15.00	75-90
1977	24Kt. Gold over Sterling-V1977	Closed	1977	18.50	45-50
1978	Sterling Silver-1978	Closed	1978	16.00	90
1978	24Kt. Gold over Sterling-V1978	Closed	1978	20.00	45-55
1979	Sterling Silver-1979	Closed	1979	20.00	75-90
1979	24Kt. Gold over Sterling-V1979	Closed	1979	24.00	32-57
1980	Sterling Silver-1980	Closed	1980	35.00	150
1980	24Kt. Gold over Sterling-V1980	Closed	1980	40.00	45-50
1981	Sterling Silver-1981	Closed	1981	35.00	150
1981	24Kt. Gold over Sterling-V1981	Closed	1981	40.00	45
1982	Sterling Silver-1982	Closed	1982	35.00	125-190
1982	24Kt. Gold over Sterling-V1982	Closed	1982	40.00	45
1983	Sterling Silver-1983	Closed	1983	35.00	90
1983	24Kt. Gold over Sterling-V1983	Closed	1983	40.00	40-45
1984	Sterling Silver-1984	Closed	1984	35.00	70-90
1984	24Kt. Gold over Sterling-V1984	Closed	1984	45.00	45
1985	Sterling Silver-1985	Closed	1985	35.00	70-90
1985	24Kt. Gold over Sterling-V1985	Closed	1985	40.00	40
1986	Sterling Silver-1986	Closed	1986	38.50	70-90
1986	24Kt. Gold over Sterling-V1986	Closed	1986	40.00	40
1987	Sterling Silver-1987	Closed	1987	35.00	70-90
1987	24Kt. Gold over Sterling-V1987	Closed	1987	40.00	40
1988	Sterling Silver-1988	Closed	1988	35.00	90-120

YEAR ISSUE		EDITION LIMIT	YEAR RETD.	ISSUE PRICE	*QUOTE U.S.$
1988	24Kt. Gold over Sterling-V1988	Closed	1988	40.00	40
1989	Sterling Silver-1989	Closed	1989	35.00	50-90
1989	24Kt. Gold over Sterling-V1989	Closed	1989	40.00	45
1990	Sterling Silver-1990	Closed	1990	40.00	50-90
1990	24Kt. Gold over Sterling-1990	Closed	1990	45.00	45
1991	Sterling Silver-1991	Closed	1991	40.00	50-90
1991	24Kt. Gold over Sterling-1991	Closed	1991	45.00	45
1992	Sterling Silver-1992	Closed	1992	40.00	50
1992	24Kt. Gold over Sterling-1992	Closed	1992	45.00	45
1993	Sterling Silver-1993	Closed	1993	40.00	50
1993	24Kt. Gold over Sterling-1993	Closed	1993	45.00	45
1994	Sterling Silver-1994	Closed	1994	40.00	50
1994	24Kt. Gold over Sterling-1994	Closed	1994	45.00	45
1995	Sterling Silver-1995	Closed	1995	40.00	40
1995	24Kt. Gold over Sterling-1995	Closed	1995	45.00	45
1996	Sterling Silver-1996	Yr.Iss.		40.00	50
1996	Gold Vermiel-1996	Yr.Iss.		45.00	45

Holly Ball - Reed & Barton

1976	1976 Silver plated	Closed	1976	14.00	50
1977	1977 Silver plated	Closed	1977	15.00	50-65
1978	1978 Silver plated	Closed	1978	15.00	30-65
1979	1979 Silver plated	Closed	1979	15.00	45

Holly Bell - Reed & Barton

1980	1980 Bell	Closed	1980	22.50	25-45
1980	Bell, gold plate, V1980	Closed	1980	25.00	45
1981	1981 Bell	Closed	1981	22.50	50
1981	Bell, gold plate, V1981	Closed	1981	27.50	35
1982	1982 Bell	Closed	1982	22.50	75
1982	Bell, gold plate, V1982	Closed	1982	27.50	50
1983	1983 Bell	Closed	1983	23.50	45-75
1983	Bell, gold plate, V1983	Closed	1983	30.00	75
1984	1984 Bell	Closed	1984	25.00	80
1984	Bell, gold plate, V1984	Closed	1984	28.50	50
1985	1985 Bell	Closed	1985	25.00	75
1985	Bell, gold plate, V1985	Closed	1985	28.50	50
1986	1986 Bell	Closed	1986	25.00	75
1986	Bell, gold plate, V1986	Closed	1986	28.50	50
1987	1987 Bell	Closed	1987	27.50	70
1987	Bell, gold plate, V1987	Closed	1987	30.00	50
1988	1988 Bell	Closed	1988	27.50	65
1988	Bell, gold plate, V1988	Closed	1988	30.00	55
1989	1989 Bell	Closed	1989	27.50	55
1989	Bell, gold plate, V1989	Closed	1989	30.00	30
1990	1990 Bell	Closed	1990	27.50	55
1990	Bell, gold plate, V1990	Closed	1990	30.00	30
1991	1991 Bell	Closed	1991	30.00	30
1991	Bell, gold plate, V1991	Closed	1991	27.50	30
1992	1992 Bell	Closed	1992	30.00	30
1992	Bell, silver plate, 1992	Closed	1992	27.50	45
1993	Bell, gold plate, V1993	Closed	1993	30.00	28
1993	Bell, silver plate, 1993	Closed	1993	30.00	45
1994	Bell, gold plate, 1994	Closed	1994	30.00	30
1994	Bell, silver plate, 1994	Closed	1994	27.50	30
1995	Bell, gold plate, 1995	Closed	1995	30.00	30
1995	Bell, silver plate, 1995	Closed	1995	27.50	30
1996	Bell, gold plate, 1996	Yr.Iss.		35.00	35
1996	Bell, silver plate, 1996	Yr.Iss.		30.00	30

Roman, Inc.
Catnippers - I. Spencer

1989	Bow Brummel	Open		15.00	15
1991	Christmas Knight	Open		15.00	15
1988	Christmas Mourning	Open		15.00	15
1991	Faux Paw	Open		15.00	15
1990	Felix Navidad	Open		15.00	15
1989	Happy Holidaze	Open		15.00	15
1991	Holly Days Are Happy Days	Open		15.00	15
1991	Meowy Christmas	Open		15.00	15
1991	Pawtridge in a Purr Tree	Open		15.00	15
1988	Puss in Berries	Open		15.00	15
1988	Ring A Ding-Ding	Open		15.00	15
1989	Sandy Claws	Open		15.00	15
1991	Snow Biz	Open		15.00	15
1990	Sock It to Me Santa	Open		15.00	15
1990	Stuck on Christmas	Open		15.00	15

The Discovery of America - I. Spencer

1991	Kitstopher Kolumbus	1,992		15.00	15
1991	Queen Kitsabella	1,992		15.00	15

Fontanini Limited Edition Ornaments - E. Simonetti

1995	The Annunciation	20,000		20.00	20
1996	Journey to Bethlehem	20,000		20.00	20

Millenium™ Ornament - A. Lucchesi

1992	Silent Night	20,000	1992	20.00	20
1993	The Annunciation	20,000	1993	20.00	20
1994	Peace On Earth	20,000	1994	20.00	20
1995	Cause of Our Joy	20,000	1995	20.00	20
1996	Prince of Peace	20,000	1996	20.00	20

Museum Collection of Angela Tripi - A. Tripi

1994	1994 Annual Angel Ornament	2,500	1994	49.50	50
1995	1995 Annual Angel Ornament	2,500		49.50	50

Seraphim Classics™ - Seraphim Studios

1995	Isabel - Gentle Spirit	Open		15.00	15
1995	Iris - Rainbow's End	Open		15.00	15

YEAR ISSUE		EDITION LIMIT RETD. YEAR	ISSUE PRICE	*QUOTE U.S.$
1995	Lydia - Winged Poet	Open	15.00	15
1995	Cymbeline - Peacemaker	Open	15.00	15
1995	Ophelia - Heart Seeker	Open	15.00	15
1995	Evangeline - Angel of Mercy	Open	15.00	15
1996	Laurie - Wisdom's Child	Open	15.00	15
1996	Felicia - Adoring Maiden	Open	15.00	15
1996	Priscilla - Benevolent Guide	Open	15.00	15
1996	Seraphina - Heaven's Helper	Open	15.00	15

Seraphim Collection by Faro - Faro

1994	Rarest of Heaven	20,000	25.00	25
1995	Heaven's Herald	20,000	25.00	25
1996	Flora, Flower of Heaven	20,000	25.00	25

Vernon Wilson Signature Series - V. Wilson

1995	We Three Kings	Open	34.00	34

Royal Doulton

Bunnykins - Unknown

1992	Caroling	Yr.Iss.	19.00	19
1991	Santa Bunny	Yr.Iss.	19.00	19

Christmas Ornaments - Unknown

1993	Together for Christmas	Yr.Iss.	20.00	20
1994	Home For Christmas	Yr.Iss.	20.00	20

Seymour Mann, Inc.

Christmas Collection - Various

1985	Angel Wall XMAS-523 - J. White	Closed 1988	12.00	12
1989	Christmas Cat in Teacup XMAS-660 - J. White	Closed 1992	13.50	14
1990	Cupid CPD-5 - J. White	Closed 1993	13.50	14
1990	Cupid CPD-6 - J. White	Closed 1993	13.50	14
1986	Cupid Head XMAS-53 - J. White	Closed 1988	25.00	25
1990	Doll Tree Topper OM-124 - J. White	Closed 1993	85.00	85
1991	Elf w/ Reindeer CJ-422 - Jaimy	Closed 1993	9.00	9
1991	Elves w/ Mail CJ-464 - J. White	Closed 1993	30.00	30
1991	Flat Red Santa CJ-115R - Jaimy	Closed 1993	2.88	3
1991	Flat Santa CJ-115 - Jaimy	Closed 1993	7.50	8
1991	Floral Plaque XMAS-911 - J. White	Closed 1993	10.00	10
1991	Flower Basket XMAS-912 - J. White	Closed 1993	10.00	10
1990	Hat w/ Streamers OM-116 - J. White	Closed 1993	20.00	20
1990	Heartlace OM-119 - J. White	Closed 1993	12.00	12
1990	Lace Ball OM-120 - J. White	Closed 1993	10.00	10
1994	Santa w/ Candle CBU-300 - J. White	Open	40.00	40
1994	Santa w/ Child CBU-305 - J. White	Open	40.00	40
1994	Santa w/ Children CBU-304 - J. White	Open	40.00	40
1994	Santa w/ Lamb CBU-301 - J. White	Open	40.00	40
1994	Santa w/ Lantern CBU-303 - J. White	Open	40.00	40
1994	Santa w/ List CBU-307 - J. White	Open	40.00	40
1994	Santa w/ Sled CBU-306 - J. White	Open	40.00	40
1994	Santa w/ Stick CBU-302 - J. White	Open	40.00	40
1986	Santa XMAS-384 - J. White	Closed 1989	7.50	8
1991	Santas, set of 6 CJ-12 - Jaimy	Closed 1993	60.00	60
1990	Tassel OM-118 - J. White	Closed 1993	7.50	8

Christmas Lite-Up Houses - L. Sciola

1994	Lite-up Church XMR-21	Open	30.00	30
1994	Lite-up Country House XMR-22	Open	30.00	30
1994	Lite-up Library XMR-24	Open	30.00	30
1994	Lite-up Mansion XMR-23	Open	30.00	30
1994	Lite-up Restaurant XMR-20	Open	30.00	30
1994	Set/10 Lite-up Houses XMR-10	Open	95.00	95
1994	Set/10 Lite-up Houses XMR-11	Open	95.00	95

Gingerbread Christmas - J. Sauerbrey

1991	Gingerbread Angel CJ-411	Closed 1992	7.50	8
1991	Gingerbread House CJ-416	Closed 1992	7.50	8
1991	Gingerbread Man CJ-415	Closed 1992	7.50	8
1991	Gingerbread Mouse/Boot CJ-409	Closed 1992	7.50	8
1991	Gingerbread Mrs. Claus CJ-414	Closed 1992	7.50	8
1991	Gingerbread Reindeer CJ-410	Closed 1992	7.50	8
1991	Gingerbread Santa CJ-408	Closed 1992	7.50	8
1991	Gingerbread Sleigh CJ-406	Closed 1992	7.50	8
1991	Gingerbread Snowman CJ-412	Closed 1992	7.50	8
1991	Gingerbread Tree CJ-407	Closed 1992	7.50	8

Victorian Christmas Collection - Jaimy

1991	Couple Against Wind CJ-420	Closed 1993	15.00	15

Shelia's Collectibles

Historical Ornament Collection - S. Thompson

1995	Blue Cottage (1st ed.) OR001	Retrd. 1996	15.00	25
1996	Blue Cottage (2nd ed.) OR001	Open	15.00	15
1995	Cape Hatteras Light (1st ed.) OR007	Retrd. 1996	15.00	25
1996	Cape Hatteras Light (2nd ed.) OR007	Open	15.00	15
1995	Chestnut House (1st ed.) OR002	Retrd. 1996	15.00	25

YEAR ISSUE		EDITION LIMIT RETD. YEAR	ISSUE PRICE	*QUOTE U.S.$
1996	Chestnut House (2nd ed.) OR002	Open	15.00	15
1995	Drayton House (1st ed.) OR003	Retrd. 1996	15.00	25
1996	Drayton House (2nd ed.) OR003	Open	15.00	15
1995	East Brother Lighthouse (1st ed.) OR008	Retrd. 1996	15.00	25
1996	East Brother Lighthouse (2nd ed.) OR008	Open	15.00	15
1995	Eclectic Blue (1st ed.) OR004	Retrd. 1996	15.00	30
1996	Eclectic Blue (2nd ed.) OR004	Open	15.00	15
1995	Goeller House (1st ed.) OR005	Retrd. 1996	15.00	25
1996	Goeller House (2nd ed.) OR005	Open	15.00	15
1995	Point Fermin Light (1st ed.) OR009	Retrd. 1996	15.00	15
1996	Point Fermin Light (2nd ed.) OR009	Open	15.00	15
1995	Stockton Row (1st ed.) OR006	Retrd. 1996	15.00	20
1996	Stockton Row (2nd ed.) OR006	Open	15.00	15
1996	Artist House OR015	Open	19.00	19
1996	Capital OR018	Open	19.00	19
1996	Dragon OR010	Open	19.00	19
1996	E.B. Hall House OR011	Open	19.00	19
1996	Mail Pouch Barn OR016	Open	19.00	19
1996	Market OR013	Open	19.00	19
1996	Pink House OR020	Open	19.00	19
1996	Rutledge OR012	Open	19.00	19
1996	St. Philips Church OR022	Open	19.00	19
1996	Thomas Point Light OR019	Open	19.00	19
1996	Titman House OR021	Open	19.00	19
1996	Victoria OR014	Open	19.00	19
1996	White Cottage OR017	Open	19.00	19
1996	Clark House OR023	Open	19.00	19
1996	Urfer House OR024	Open	19.00	19
1996	Queen Anne OR025	Open	19.00	19
1996	Asendorf House OR026	Open	19.00	19
1996	Abbey II OR027	Open	19.00	19
1996	New Canal Light OR028	Open	19.00	19

Swarovski America Limited

Holiday Ornaments - Swarovski

1981	1981 Snowflake 7563NR35	Yr.Iss.	30.00	250-325
1986	1986 Holiday Ornament 92086	Yr.Iss.	N/A	240
1987	1987 Holiday Etching-Candle	Yr.Iss.	20.00	240-260
1988	1988 Holiday Etching-Wreath	Yr.Iss.	25.00	75-100
1989	1989 Holiday Etching-Dove	Yr.Iss.	35.00	240-275
1990	1990 Holiday Etching-Merry Christmas	Yr.Iss.	25.00	100-175
1991	1991 Holiday Ornament-Star	Yr.Iss.	35.00	75-125
1992	1992 Holiday Ornament-Star	Yr.Iss.	37.50	75-90
1993	1993 Holiday Ornament-Star	Yr.Iss.	37.50	100-135
1994	1994 Holiday Ornament-Star	Yr.Iss.	37.50	65-95
1995	1995 Holiday Ornament-Star	Yr.Iss.	40.00	50-75
1996	1996 Holiday Ornament -Snowflake	Yr.Iss.	45.00	50-90

Towle Silversmiths

Christmas Angel Medallions - Towle

1991	1991 Angel	Closed 1991	45.00	65
1992	1992 Angel	Closed 1992	45.00	65
1993	1993 Angel	Closed 1993	45.00	50
1994	1994 Angel	Closed 1994	50.00	55
1995	1995 Angel	Closed 1995	50.00	50
1996	1996 Angel	Closed 1996	50.00	50

Remembrance Collection - Towle

1990	1990 - Old Master Snowflake	Closed 1990	40.00	55-65
1991	1991 - Old Master Snowflake	Closed 1991	40.00	50-62
1992	1992 - Old Master Snowflake	Closed 1992	40.00	50-62
1993	1993 - Old Master Snowflake	Closed 1993	40.00	50-62
1994	1994 - Old Master Snowflake	Closed 1994	50.00	50
1995	1995 - Old Master Snowflake	Closed 1995	50.00	50
1996	1996 - Old Master Snowflake	Closed 1995	50.00	50

Songs of Christmas Medallions - Towle

1978	Silent Night Medallion	Closed 1978	35.00	65-80
1979	Deck The Halls	Closed 1979	35.00	65-80
1980	Jingle Bells	Closed 1980	53.00	80
1981	Hark the Hearld Angels Sing	Closed 1981	53.00	125-150
1982	O Christmas Tree	Closed 1982	35.00	80
1983	Silver Bells	Closed 1983	40.00	65-80
1984	Let It Snow	Closed 1984	30.00	70-80
1985	Chestnuts Roasting on Open Fire	Closed 1985	35.00	70-80
1986	It Came Upon a Midnight Clear	Closed 1986	35.00	70-80
1987	White Christmas	Closed 1987	35.00	70-80

Sterling Cross - Towle

1994	Sterling Cross	Closed 1994	50.00	50-65
1995	Christmas Cross	Closed 1995	50.00	50
1996	1996 Cross	Closed 1996	50.00	50

Sterling Floral Medallions - Towle

1983	Christmas Rose	Closed 1983	40.00	55
1984	Hawthorn/Glastonbury Thorn	Closed 1984	40.00	50
1985	Poinsettia	Closed 1985	35.00	60-70
1986	Laurel Bay	Closed 1986	35.00	60-80
1987	Mistletoe	Closed 1987	35.00	65-95
1988	Holly	Closed 1988	40.00	60-70
1989	Ivy	Closed 1989	35.00	65
1990	Christmas Cactus	Closed 1990	40.00	50
1991	Chrysanthemum	Closed 1991	40.00	50

YEAR ISSUE		EDITION LIMIT RETD. YEAR	ISSUE PRICE	*QUOTE U.S.$
1992	Star of Bethlehem	Closed 1992	40.00	50

Sterling Nativity Medallions - Towle

1988	The Angel Appeared	Closed 1988	40.00	100-150
1989	The Journey	Closed 1989	40.00	60-75
1990	No Room at the Inn	Closed 1990	40.00	50-75
1991	Tidings of Joy	Closed 1991	40.00	50-75
1992	Star of Bethlehem	Closed 1992	40.00	50-75
1993	Mother and Child	Closed 1993	40.00	60
1994	Three Wisemen	Closed 1994	40.00	60
1995	Newborn King	Closed 1995	40.00	50

Sterling Twelve Days of Christmas Medallions - Towle

1971	Partridge in A Pear Tree	Closed 1971	20.00	550-750
1972	Two Turtle Doves	Closed 1972	20.00	275-375
1973	Three French Hens	Closed 1973	20.00	100-125
1974	Four Calling Birds	Closed 1974	30.00	150-200
1975	Five Golden Rings	Closed 1975	30.00	100-150
1975	Five Golden Rings (vermeil)	Closed 1975	30.00	200-300
1976	Six Geese-a-Laying	Closed 1976	30.00	125-150
1977	Seven Swans-a-Swimming	Closed 1977	35.00	100-125
1977	Seven Swans-a-Swimming (turquoise)	Closed 1977	35.00	200-300
1978	Eight Maids-a-Milking	Closed 1978	37.00	100-125
1979	Nine Ladies Dancing	Closed 1979	37.00	100-125
1980	Ten Lords-a-Leaping	Closed 1980	76.00	100-125
1981	Eleven Pipers Piping	Closed 1981	35.00	100-125
1982	Twelve Drummers Drumming	Closed 1982	35.00	100-125

Twelve Days of Christmas - Towle

1991	Partridge in A Pear Tree In A Wreath	Closed 1991	50.00	70
1992	Two Turtle Doves In A Wreath	Closed 1992	50.00	60
1993	Three French Hens In A Wreath	Closed 1993	50.00	60
1994	Four Calling Birds In A Wreath	Closed 1995	50.00	50
1996	Five Golden Rings In A Wreath	Closed 1996	50.00	50
1996	Six Geese A Laying In A Wreath	Closed 1996	50.00	50

United Design Corp.

Angels Collection-Tree Ornaments™ - P.J. Jonas, unless otherwise noted

1992	Angel and Tambourine IBO-422 - S. Bradford	Open	20.00	20
1992	Angel and Tambourine, ivory IBO-425 - S. Bradford	Open	20.00	20
1993	Angel Baby w/ Bunny IBO-426 - D. Newburn	Retrd. 1996	23.00	24
1996	Angel w/Doves on Cloud IBO-472	Open	25.00	25
1996	Angel w/Doves on Cloud, blue IBO-473	Open	25.00	25
1991	Angel Waif, ivory IBO-411	Open	15.00	20
1993	Angel Waif, plum IBO-437	Retrd. 1996	20.00	20
1995	Autumn's Bounty IBO-460	Open	32.00	32
1995	Autumn's Bounty, light IBO-454	Open	32.00	32
1995	Birds of a Feather IBO-457	Open	27.00	27
1990	Crystal Angel IBO-401	Retrd. 1993	20.00	20
1993	Crystal Angel, emerald IBO-446	Open	20.00	20
1990	Crystal Angel, ivory IBO-405	Open	20.00	20
1991	Fra Angelico Drummer, blue IBO-414 - S. Bradford	Open	20.00	20
1991	Fra Angelico Drummer, ivory IBO-420 - S. Bradford	Open	20.00	20
1991	Girl Cupid w/Rose, ivory IBO-413 - S. Bradford	Open	15.00	20
1995	Heavenly Blossoms IBO-458	Open	27.00	27
1993	Heavenly Harmony IBO-428	Open	25.00	30
1993	Heavenly Harmony, crimson IBO-433	Open	22.00	30
1993	Little Angel IBO-430 - D. Newburn	Open	18.00	20
1993	Little Angel, crimson IBO-445 - D. Newburn	Retrd. 1996	18.00	20
1992	Mary and Dove IBO-424 - S. Bradford	Open	20.00	20
1994	Music and Grace IBO-448	Open	24.00	24
1994	Music and Grace, crimson IBO-449	Open	24.00	24
1994	Musical Flight IBO-450	Open	28.00	28
1994	Musical Flight, crimson IBO-451	Open	28.00	28
1991	Peace Descending, ivory IBO-412	Open	20.00	20
1993	Peace Descending, crimson IBO-436	Open	20.00	20
1993	Renaissance Angel IBO-429	Open	24.00	24
1993	Renaissance Angel, crimson IBO-431	Open	24.00	24
1990	Rose of Sharon IBO-402	Retrd. 1993	20.00	20
1993	Rose of Sharon, crimson IBO-439	Open	20.00	20
1990	Rose of Sharon, ivory IBO-406	Open	20.00	20
1993	Rosetti Angel, crimson IBO-434	Open	20.00	24
1991	Rosetti Angel, ivory IBO-410	Open	20.00	24
1995	Special Wishes IBO-456 - D. Newburn	Open	27.00	27
1995	Spring's Rebirth IBO-452	Open	32.00	32
1996	Spring's Rebirth, green IBO-474	Open	25.00	25
1992	St. Francis and Critters IBO-423 - S. Bradford	Open	20.00	20
1994	Star Flight IBO-447	Open	20.00	20
1990	Star Glory IBO-403	Retrd. 1993	15.00	15
1993	Star Glory, crimson IBO-438	Open	20.00	20
1990	Star Glory, ivory IBO-407	Open	15.00	20
1996	Starflight Sapphire IBO-475	Open	20.00	20
1993	Stars & Lace IBO-427	Open	18.00	20

YEAR ISSUE		EDITION LIMIT	YEAR RETRD.	ISSUE PRICE	*QUOTE U.S.$
1993	Stars & Lace, Emerald IBO-432	Open		18.00	20
1995	Summer's Glory IBO-453	Open		32.00	32
1996	Summer's Glory, green IBO-476	Open		25.00	25
1995	Tender Time IBO-459	Open		27.00	27
1990	Victorian Angel IBO-404	Retrd.	1993	15.00	15
1990	Victorian Angel, ivory IBO-408	Open		15.00	20
1993	Victorian Angel, plum IBO-435	Open		18.00	20
1993	Victorian Cupid, crimson IBO-440	Open		15.00	20
1991	Victorian Cupid, ivory IBO-409	Open		15.00	20
1995	Winter's Light IBO-455	Open		32.00	32
1996	Wooden Angel IBO-461 - M. Ramsey	Open		20.00	20

Teddy Angels™ - P.J. Jonas

1995	Casey "You're a bright & shining star." BA-017	Open		13.00	13
1995	Ivy "Enchantment glows in winter snows." BA-018	Open		13.00	13

Wallace Silversmiths

Annual Pewter Bells - Wallace

1992	Angel	Closed	1992	25.00	30
1993	Santa Holding List	Closed	1993	25.00	25
1994	Large Santa Bell	Closed	1994	25.00	25
1995	Santa Bell	Closed	1995	25.00	25
1996	Santa Bell (North Pole)	Yr.Iss.		25.00	25

Annual Silverplated Sleigh Bells - Wallace

1971	1st Edition Sleigh Bell	Closed	1971	12.95	700-1100
1972	2nd Edition Sleigh Bell	Closed	1972	12.95	500-620
1973	3rd Edition Sleigh Bell	Closed	1973	12.95	450-575
1974	4th Edition Sleigh Bell	Closed	1974	13.95	200-350
1975	5th Edition Sleigh Bell	Closed	1975	13.95	150-275
1976	6th Edition Sleigh Bell	Closed	1976	13.95	200-375
1977	7th Edition Sleigh Bell	Closed	1977	14.95	125-225
1978	8th Edition Sleigh Bell	Closed	1978	14.95	85-120
1979	9th Edition Sleigh Bell	Closed	1979	15.95	120-170
1980	10th Edition Sleigh Bell	Closed	1980	18.95	50-75
1981	11th Edition Sleigh Bell	Closed	1981	18.95	80-100
1982	12th Edition Sleigh Bell	Closed	1982	19.95	100-125
1983	13th Edition Sleigh Bell	Closed	1983	19.95	100-125
1984	14th Edition Sleigh Bell	Closed	1984	21.95	90
1985	15th Edition Sleigh Bell	Closed	1985	21.95	75-100
1986	16th Edition Sleigh Bell	Closed	1986	21.95	40-75
1987	17th Edition Sleigh Bell	Closed	1987	21.99	35-60
1988	18th Edition Sleigh Bell	Closed	1988	21.99	40-60
1989	19th Edition Sleigh Bell	Closed	1989	24.99	50-75
1990	20th Edition Sleigh Bell	Closed	1990	25.00	40-55
1990	Special Edition Sleigh Bell, gold	Closed	1990	35.00	75
1991	21st Edition Sleigh Bell	Closed	1991	25.00	40
1992	22th Edition Sleigh Bell	Closed	1992	25.00	45
1993	23rd Edition Sleigh Bell	Closed	1993	25.00	40
1994	24th Edition Sleigh Bell	Closed	1994	25.00	35
1994	Sleigh Bell, gold	Closed	1994	35.00	45
1995	25th Edition Sleigh Bell	Closed	1995	30.00	30
1995	Sleigh Bell, gold	Closed	1995	35.00	35
1996	26th Edition Sleigh Bell	Yr.Iss.		30.00	30
1996	Sleigh Bell, gold	Yr.Iss.		35.00	35

Candy Canes - Wallace

1981	Peppermint	Closed	1981	8.95	125-250
1982	Wintergreen	Closed	1982	9.95	60-110
1983	Cinnamon	Closed	1983	10.95	50-75
1984	Clove	Closed	1984	10.95	50-60
1985	Dove Motif	Closed	1985	11.95	50-70
1986	Bell Motif	Closed	1986	11.95	80-120
1987	Teddy Bear Motif	Closed	1987	12.95	70-110
1988	Christmas Rose	Closed	1988	13.99	45-75
1989	Christmas Candle	Closed	1989	14.99	45
1990	Reindeer	Closed	1990	16.00	30
1991	Christmas Goose	Closed	1991	16.00	35
1992	Angel	Closed	1992	16.00	30
1993	Snowmen	Closed	1993	16.00	30
1994	Canes	Closed	1994	17.00	20
1995	Santa	Closed	1995	18.00	20
1996	Soldiers	Yr. Iss.		18.00	18

Cathedral Ornaments - Wallace

1988	1988-1st Edition	Closed	1988	24.99	45
1989	1989-2nd Edition	Closed	1989	24.99	30
1990	1990-3rd Edition	Closed	1990	25.00	25

Grande Baroque 12 Day Series - Wallace

1988	Partridge	Closed	1988	39.99	75-100
1989	Two Turtle Doves	Closed	1989	39.99	75-100
1990	Three French Hens	Closed	1990	40.00	75-100
1991	Four Colly Birds	Closed	1991	40.00	100
1992	Five Golden Rings	Closed	1992	40.00	75-100
1993	Six Geese-a-Laying	Closed	1993	40.00	70-100
1994	Seven Swans-a-Swimming	Closed	1994	40.00	60
1995	Eight Maids-a-Milking	Closed	1995	40.00	50
1996	Nine Ladies Dancing	Yr. Iss.		40.00	50

Walnut Ridge Collectibles

Gossamer Wings - K. Bejma

1996	Charity Piece - Glimmer of Hope I	Yr.Iss.		40.00	40

Limited Edition Christmas Ornament - K. Bejma

1996	Snowy, Snowy Night-703	Yr.Iss.		56.00	56

Ornament Collection - K. Bejma

1994	Angel Bunny-21	Open		26.00	26
1995	Angel Donkey-24	Open		26.00	26
1995	Angel Elephant-23	Open		26.00	26
1996	Angel Frog-40	Open		22.00	22
1993	Angel Icicle-9	Open		22.00	22
1994	Angel Kitty-20	Open		26.00	26
1994	Angel Pig-22	Open		26.00	26
1996	Angel w/Star on Wand-35	Open		24.00	24
1994	Angels, Set/3-15	Open		66.00	66
1995	Angels, Set/3-18	Open		66.00	66
1993	Baby Snowman Icicle-12	Open		22.00	22
1996	Baby's First-33	Open		30.00	30
1996	Black and White Bunny-28	Open		26.00	26
1996	Calico Cat-27	Open		26.00	26
1995	Carrot-cicle-17	Open		22.00	22
1996	Cat-cicle w/Stocking-37	Open		22.00	22
1996	Cat-cicle-36	Open		22.00	22
1993	Cherub Icicle-8	Open		22.00	22
1996	Crescent Santa-29	Open		28.00	28
1993	Father Christmas Icicle-13	Open		22.00	22
1994	Father Christmas, Set/3-16	Open		66.00	66
1993	Father Snowman Icicle-10	Open		22.00	22
1996	Golden Father Christmas-38	Open		24.00	24
1996	Kitty Angel-34	Open		24.00	24
1993	Mother Snowman Icicle-11	Open		22.00	22
1994	Nutcracker-30	Open		22.00	22
1995	Nutcracker-31	Open		22.00	22
1996	Nutcracker-32	Open		22.00	22
1995	Reindeer-26	Open		22.00	22
1993	Santa Icicle-14	Open		22.00	22
1995	Snow Family, Set/3-19	Open		66.00	66
1996	Snowman, set/2-39	Open		44.00	44
1995	Tabby/Holly Bunch-25	Open		22.00	22

Walt Disney

Classics Collection-Holiday Series - Disney Studios

1995	Presents For My Pals 41087	Closed	1995	50.00	50-55
1996	Pluto Helps Decorate 41113	Yr.Iss.		50.00	50

Disney's Enchanted Places - Disney Studios

1996	Grandpa's House 41222	Open		35.00	35

PLATES

Ace Product Management Group, Inc.

Good Times Together - B. Otero

1995	Road Trip 99276-95Z	10,000		32.00	32

Harley-Davidson Collector Christmas Plates - Ace

1984	1909 V-Twin 99133-85Z	8,500	1984	19.95	20
1985	Perfect Tree 99134-86Z	8,500	1985	22.50	23
1986	Mainstreet 99136-87Z	8,500	1986	24.95	25
1987	Joy Of Giving 99133-88Z	8,500	1987	24.95	25
1988	Home For The Holidays 99134-89Z	8,500	1988	29.95	30
1989	29 Days Till Xmas 99134-90Z	8,500	1989	34.95	35
1990	Rural Delivery 99134-91Z	8,500	1990	34.95	35
1991	Skating Party 99138-92Z	8,500	1991	34.95	35
1992	A Surprise Visit 99135-93Z	9,500	1992	38.00	38
1993	Christmas Vacation 99287-94Z	9,500	1993	38.00	38

Harley-Davidson Collector Pewter Decade Series Plates - Ace

1992	Birth Of Legend-1900's 99139-92Z	3,000	1992	120.00	120
1993	Growth Of Sport-1910's 99129-94Z	3,000	1993	125.00	125
1994	Roaring Into The 20's-1920's 99136-95Z	3,000		130.00	130
1995	Growing Stronger With Time-1930's 99294-96Z	3,000		132.00	132

Harley-Davidson Collector Pewter Plates - Ace

1988	Winter Gathering 99139-89ZP	3,000	1988	74.95	75
1989	1989 Plate 99139-90ZP	3,000	1989	89.95	90
1990	Spring Races 99136-91ZP	3,000	1990	99.95	100
1990	Summer Tradition 99139-91ZP	3,000	1990	99.95	100

Holiday Memories Christmas Plates - B. Otero

1984	Under The Mistletoe 99090-95Z	15,000	1994	38.00	38
1995	Late Arrival 99415-96Z	15,000	1995	38.00	38
1996	After The Pageant 99933-97Z	15,000		38.00	38

American Artists

The Best of Fred Stone-Mares & Foals Series (6 1/2") - F. Stone

1991	Patience	19,500		25.00	25-30
1992	Water Trough	19,500		25.00	25
1992	Pasture Pest	19,500		25.00	25
1992	Kidnapped Mare	19,500		25.00	25
1993	Contentment	19,500		25.00	25
1993	Arabian Mare & Foal	19,500		25.00	25
1994	Diamond in the Rough	19,500		25.00	25
1995	The First Day	19,500		25.00	25

Famous Fillies Series - F. Stone

1987	Lady's Secret	9,500		65.00	70-90
1988	Ruffian	9,500		65.00	90
1988	Genuine Risk	9,500		65.00	90
1992	Go For The Wand	9,500		65.00	80-90

Fred Stone Classic Series - F. Stone

1986	The Shoe-8,000 Wins	9,500		75.00	80-90
1986	The Eternal Legacy	9,500		75.00	95
1988	Forever Friends	9,500		75.00	85
1989	Alysheba	9,500		75.00	75

Gold Signature Series - F. Stone

1990	Secretariat Final Tribute, signed	4,500		150.00	375
1990	Secretariat Final Tribute, unsigned	7,500		75.00	100
1991	Old Warriors, signed	4,500		150.00	425
1991	Old Warriors, unsigned	7,500		75.00	100

Gold Signature Series II - F. Stone

1991	Northern Dancer, double signature	1,500		175.00	250
1991	Northern Dancer, single signature	3,000		150.00	150
1991	Northern Dancer, unsigned	7,500		75.00	75
1991	Kelso, double signature	1,500		175.00	175
1991	Kelso, single signature	3,000		150.00	150
1991	Kelso, unsigned	7,500		75.00	75

Gold Signature Series III - F. Stone

1992	Dance Smartly-Pat Day, Up, double signature	1,500		175.00	175
1992	Dance Smartly-Pat Day, Up, single signature	3,000		150.00	150
1992	Dance Smartly-Pat Day, Up, unsigned	7,500		75.00	75
1993	American Triple Crown-1937-1946, signed	2,500		195.00	195
1993	American Triple Crown-1937-1946, unsigned	7,500		75.00	75
1993	American Triple Crown-1948-1978, signed	2,500		195.00	195
1993	American Triple Crown-1948-1978, unsigned	7,500		75.00	175
1994	American Triple Crown-1919-1935, signed	2,500		95.00	95
1994	American Triple Crown-1919-1935, unsigned	7,500		75.00	75

Gold Signature Series IV - F. Stone

1995	Julie Krone - Colonial Affair	7,500		75.00	75
1995	Julie Krone - Colonial Affair, signed	2,500		150.00	150

The Horses of Fred Stone - F. Stone

1982	Patience	9,500		55.00	75-125
1982	Arabian Mare and Foal	9,500		55.00	175
1982	Safe and Sound	9,500		55.00	125
1983	Contentment	9,500		55.00	125

Mare and Foal Series - F. Stone

1986	Water Trough	12,500		49.50	90-125
1986	Tranquility	12,500		49.50	65
1986	Pasture Pest	12,500		49.50	100
1987	The Arabians	12,500		49.50	55

Mare and Foal Series II - F. Stone

1989	The First Day	Open		35.00	35
1989	Diamond in the Rough	Retrd.		35.00	35

Racing Legends - F. Stone

1989	Phar Lap	9,500		75.00	75
1989	Sunday Silence	9,500		75.00	75
1990	John Henry-Shoemaker	9,500		75.00	75

Sport of Kings Series - F. Stone

1984	Man O'War	9,500		65.00	125-150
1984	Secretariat	9,500		65.00	295
1985	John Henry	9,500		65.00	75-150
1986	Seattle Slew	9,500		65.00	65

The Stallion Series - F. Stone

1983	Black Stallion	19,500		49.50	150
1983	Andalusian	19,500		49.50	150

Anheuser-Busch, Inc.

1992 Olympic Team Series - A-Busch, Inc.

1991	1992 Olympic Team Winter Plate N3180	Retrd.	1994	35.00	35
1992	1992 Olympic Team Summer Plate N3122	Retrd.	1994	35.00	35

Archives Plate Series - D. Langeneckert

1992	1893 Columbian Exposition N3477	25-day		27.50	28
1992	Ganymede N4004	25-day		27.50	28
1995	Budweiser's Greatest Triumph Plate N5195	25-day		27.50	28
1995	Mirror of Truth Plate N5196	25-day		27.50	28

Civil War Series - D. Langeneckert

1992	General Grant N3478	Retrd.	1994	45.00	45
1993	General Robert E. Lee N3590	Retrd.	1994	45.00	45
1993	President Abraham Lincoln N3591	Retrd.	1994	45.00	45

PLATES

Collector Edition Series - M. Urdahl

YEAR ISSUE	EDITION LIMIT	YEAR RETD.	ISSUE PRICE	*QUOTE U.S.$
1995 "This Bud's For You" N4945	25-day		27.50	28

Holiday Plate Series - Various

YEAR ISSUE	EDITION LIMIT	YEAR RETD.	ISSUE PRICE	*QUOTE U.S.$
1989 Winters Day N2295 - B. Kemper	Retrd.	N/A	30.00	65-95
1990 An American Tradition N2767 - S. Sampson	Retrd.	N/A	30.00	35-45
1991 The Season's Best N3034 - S. Sampson	Retrd.	N/A	30.00	30
1992 A Perfect Christmas N3440 - S. Sampson	Retrd.	N/A	27.50	30-40
1993 Special Delivery N4002 - N. Koerber	Retrd.	N/A	27.50	40-80
1994 Hometown Holiday N4572 - B. Kemper	Retrd.	N/A	27.50	28
1995 Lighting the Way Home N5215 - T. Jester	25-day		27.50	28
1996 Budweiser Clydesdales N5778 - J. Raedeke	25-day		27.50	28

Man's Best Friend Series - M. Urdahl

YEAR ISSUE	EDITION LIMIT	YEAR RETD.	ISSUE PRICE	*QUOTE U.S.$
1990 Buddies N2615	Retrd.	N/A	30.00	50-90
1990 Six Pack N3005	Retrd.	N/A	30.00	35-45
1992 Something's Brewing N3147	Retrd.	1994	30.00	30
1993 Outstanding in Their Field N4003	Retrd.	1995	27.50	28

Anna-Perenna Porcelain

American Silhouettes Family Series - P. Buckley Moss

YEAR ISSUE	EDITION LIMIT	YEAR RETD.	ISSUE PRICE	*QUOTE U.S.$
1982 Family Outing	5,000		75.00	95
1982 John and Mary	5,000		75.00	95
1984 Homemakers Quilting	5,000		75.00	85-195
1983 Leisure Time	5,000		75.00	85

American Silhouettes Valley Series - P. Buckley Moss

1982 Frosty Frolic	5,000		75.00	85-95
1984 Hay Ride	5,000		75.00	85
1983 Sunday Ride	5,000		75.00	85-100
1983 Market Day	5,000		75.00	120

American Silhouettes-Childrens Series - P. Buckley Moss

1981 Fiddlers Two	5,000		75.00	95
1982 Mary With The Lambs	5,000		75.00	125-200
1983 Ring-Around-the-Rosie	5,000		75.00	200
1983 Waiting For Tom	5,000		75.00	175

Annual Christmas Plate - P. Buckley Moss

1984 Noel, Noel	5,000		67.50	325
1985 Helping Hands	5,000		67.50	100-125
1986 Night Before Christmas	5,000		67.50	75-100
1987 Christmas Sleigh	5,000		75.00	95
1988 Christmas Joy	7,500		75.00	75
1989 Christmas Carol	7,500		80.00	95
1990 Christmas Eve	7,500		80.00	80
1991 The Snowman	7,500		80.00	80
1992 Christmas Warmth	7,500		85.00	85
1993 Joy to the World	7,500		85.00	85
1994 Christmas Night	5,000		85.00	85
1995 Christmas at Home	5,000		85.00	85

The Celebration Series - P. Buckley Moss

1986 Wedding Joy	5,000		100.00	200-350
1987 The Christening	5,000		100.00	175
1988 The Anniversary	5,000		100.00	100
1990 Family Reunion	5,000		100.00	125

Uncle Tad's Cats - T. Krumeich

1979 Oliver's Birthday	5,000		75.00	75-125
1980 Peaches & Cream	5,000		75.00	85
1981 Princess Aurora	5,000		80.00	80-90
1981 Walter's Window	5,000		80.00	120

ANRI

ANRI Father's Day - Unknown

YEAR ISSUE	EDITION LIMIT	YEAR RETD.	ISSUE PRICE	*QUOTE U.S.$
1972 Alpine Father & Children	Closed	1972	35.00	100
1973 Alpine Father & Children	Closed	1973	40.00	95
1974 Cliff Gazing	Closed	1974	50.00	100
1975 Sailing	Closed	1975	60.00	90

ANRI Mother's Day - Unknown

1972 Alpine Mother & Children	Closed	1972	35.00	50
1973 Alpine Mother & Children	Closed	1973	40.00	50
1974 Alpine Mother & Children	Closed	1974	50.00	55
1975 Alpine Stroll	Closed	1975	60.00	65
1976 Knitting	Closed	1976	60.00	65

Christmas - J. Malfertheiner, unless otherwise noted

1971 St. Jakob in Groden	6,000	1971	37.50	65
1972 Pipers at Alberobello	6,000	1972	45.00	75
1973 Alpine Horn	6,000	1973	45.00	390
1974 Young Man and Girl	6,000	1974	50.00	95
1975 Christmas in Ireland	6,000	1975	60.00	60
1976 Alpine Christmas	6,000	1976	65.00	190
1977 Legend of Heligenblut	6,000	1977	65.00	91
1978 Klockler Singers	6,000	1978	80.00	80
1979 Moss Gatherers - Unknown	6,000	1979	135.00	177
1980 Wintry Churchgoing - Unknown	6,000	1980	165.00	165
1981 Santa Claus in Tyrol - Unknown	6,000	1981	165.00	200
1982 The Star Singers - Unknown	6,000	1982	165.00	165
1983 Unto Us a Child is Born - Unknown	6,000	1983	165.00	310
1984 Yuletide in the Valley - Unknown	6,000	1984	165.00	170
1985 Good Morning, Good Cheer	6,000	1985	165.00	165
1986 A Groden Christmas	6,000	1986	165.00	200
1987 Down From the Alps	6,000	1987	195.00	250
1988 Christkindl Markt	6,000	1988	220.00	230
1989 Flight Into Egypt	6,000	1989	275.00	275
1990 Holy Night	6,000	1990	300.00	300

Disney Four Star Collection - Disney Studios

1989 Mickey Mini Plate	5,000	1989	40.00	65
1990 Minnie Mini Plate	5,000	1990	40.00	95
1991 Donald Mini Plate	5,000	1991	50.00	55

Ferrandiz Christmas - J. Ferrandiz

1972 Christ In The Manger	4,000	1972	35.00	230
1973 Christmas	4,000	1973	40.00	225
1974 Holy Night	4,000	1974	50.00	100
1975 Flight into Egypt	4,000	1975	60.00	95
1976 Tree of Life	4,000	1976	60.00	85
1977 Girl with Flowers	4,000	1977	65.00	185
1978 Leading the Way	4,000	1978	77.50	180
1979 The Drummer	4,000	1979	120.00	175
1980 Rejoice	4,000	1980	150.00	160
1981 Spreading the Word	4,000	1981	150.00	150
1982 The Shepherd Family	4,000	1982	150.00	150
1983 Peace Attend Thee	4,000	1983	150.00	150

Ferrandiz Mother's Day Series - J. Ferrandiz

1972 Mother Sewing	3,000	1972	35.00	200
1973 Alpine Mother & Child	3,000	1973	40.00	150
1974 Mother Holding Child	3,000	1974	50.00	150
1975 Dove Girl	3,000	1975	60.00	150
1976 Mother Knitting	3,000	1976	60.00	200
1977 Alpine Stroll	3,000	1977	65.00	125
1978 The Beginning	3,000	1978	75.00	150
1979 All Hearts	3,000	1979	120.00	170
1980 Spring Arrivals	3,000	1980	150.00	165
1981 Harmony	3,000	1981	150.00	150
1982 With Love	3,000	1982	150.00	150

Ferrandiz Wooden Birthday Plates - J. Ferrandiz

1972 Boy	Unkn.	1972	15.00	150
1972 Girl	Unkn.	1972	15.00	160
1973 Boy	Unkn.	1973	20.00	200
1973 Girl	Unkn.	1973	20.00	150
1974 Boy	Unkn.	1974	22.00	150
1974 Girl	Unkn.	1974	22.00	160

Ferrandiz Wooden Wedding Plates - J. Ferrandiz

1972 Boy and Girl Embracing	Closed	1972	40.00	150
1973 Wedding Scene	Closed	1973	40.00	150
1974 Wedding	Closed	1974	48.00	150
1975 Wedding	Closed	1975	60.00	150
1976 Wedding	Closed	1976	60.00	90-150

Arcadian Pewter, Inc.

Red Oak II - N. Lindblade

YEAR ISSUE	EDITION LIMIT	YEAR RETD.	ISSUE PRICE	*QUOTE U.S.$
1995 Red Oak II	Open		74.95	75

Armstrong's

Classic Memory Collection - R. Skelton

1995 The Donut Dunker (signed)	1,000		375.00	375

Commemorative Issues - R. Skelton

1983 70 Years Young (10 1/2")	15,000		85.00	100-125
1984 Freddie the Torchbearer (8 1/2")	15,000		62.50	63
1994 Red & His Friend	160		700.00	1200

Freedom Collection of Red Skelton - R. Skelton

1990 The All American, (signed)	1,000		195.00	300
1990 The All American	9,000		62.50	63-85
1991 Independence Day? (signed)	1,000		195.00	200
1991 Independence Day?	9,000		62.50	63
1992 Let Freedom Ring, (signed)	1,000		195.00	200
1992 Let Freedom Ring	9,000		62.50	63
1993 Freddie's Gift of Life, (signed)	1,000		195.00	200
1993 Freddie's Gift of Life	9,000		62.50	63

Happy Art Series - W. Lantz

1981 Woody's Triple Self-Portrait, Signed	1,000		100.00	150
1981 Woody's Triple Self-Portrait	9,000		39.50	40
1983 Gothic Woody, Signed	1,000		100.00	150
1983 Gothic Woody	9,000		39.50	40
1984 Blue Boy Woody, Signed	1,000		100.00	150
1984 Blue Boy Woody	9,000		39.50	40

The Signature Collection - R. Skelton

1986 Anyone for Tennis?	9,000		62.50	65
1986 Anyone for Tennis? (signed)	1,000		125.00	450
1987 Ironing the Waves	9,000		62.50	65
1987 Ironing the Waves (signed)	1,000		125.00	300
1988 The Cliffhanger	9,000		62.50	65
1988 The Cliffhanger (signed)	1,000		150.00	300
1988 Hooked on Freddie	9,000		62.50	65
1988 Hooked on Freddie (signed)	1,000		175.00	250

Sports - Schenken

YEAR ISSUE	EDITION LIMIT	YEAR RETD.	ISSUE PRICE	*QUOTE U.S.$
1985 Pete Rose h/s (10 1/4")	1,000		100.00	275
1985 Pete Rose u/s (10 1/4")	10,000		45.00	75

Armstrong's/Crown Parlan

Freddie The Freeloader - R. Skelton

1979 Freddie in the Bathtub	10,000		60.00	200
1980 Freddie's Shack	10,000		60.00	80
1981 Freddie on the Green	10,000		60.00	70
1982 Love that Freddie	10,000		60.00	70

Freddie's Adventures - R. Skelton

1982 Captain Freddie	15,000		60.00	65
1982 Bronco Freddie	15,000		60.00	65
1983 Sir Freddie	15,000		62.50	63
1984 Gertrude and Heathcliffe	15,000		62.50	100-125

Artaffects

Club Member Limited Edition Redemption Offerings - G. Perillo

1992 The Pencil	Yr. Iss.		35.00	75
1992 Studies in Black and White (Set/4)	Yr. Iss.		75.00	100
1993 Watcher of the Wilderness	Yr. Iss.		60.00	60

America's Indian Heritage - G. Perillo

1987 Cheyenne Nation	10-day		24.50	25-50
1988 Arapaho Nation	10-day		24.50	45
1988 Kiowa Nation	10-day		24.50	45
1988 Sioux Nation	10-day		24.50	30
1988 Chippewa Nation	10-day		24.50	45
1988 Crow Nation	10-day		24.50	45
1988 Nez Perce Nation	10-day		24.50	45
1988 Blackfoot Nation	10-day		24.50	35

Chieftains I - G. Perillo

1979 Chief Sitting Bull	7,500		65.00	325
1979 Chief Joseph	7,500		65.00	80-90
1980 Chief Red Cloud	7,500		65.00	120
1980 Chief Geronimo	7,500		65.00	85
1981 Chief Crazy Horse	7,500		65.00	95-125

Chieftains II - G. Perillo

1983 Chief Pontiac	7,500		70.00	85-95
1983 Chief Victorio	7,500		70.00	85
1984 Chief Tecumseh	7,500		70.00	85
1984 Chief Cochise	7,500		70.00	80
1984 Chief Black Kettle	7,500		70.00	110

Council of Nations - G. Perillo

1992 Strength of the Sioux	14-day		29.50	35
1992 Pride of the Cheyenne	14-day		29.50	35
1992 Dignity of the Nez Perce	14-day		29.50	35
1992 Courage of the Arapaho	14-day		29.50	35
1992 Power of the Blackfoot	14-day		29.50	35
1992 Nobility of the Algonquin	14-day		29.50	35
1992 Wisdom of the Cherokee	14-day		29.50	35
1992 Boldness of the Seneca	14-day		29.50	35

Indian Bridal - G. Perillo

1990 Yellow Bird (6 1/2")	14-day		25.00	25
1990 Autumn Blossom (6 1/2")	14-day		25.00	25
1990 Misty Waters (6 1/2")	14-day		25.00	25
1990 Sunny Skies (6 1/2")	14-day		25.00	25

Indian Nations - G. Perillo

1983 Blackfoot	7,500		140.00	350
1983 Cheyenne	7,500		set	Set
1983 Apache	7,500		set	Set
1983 Sioux	7,500		set	Set

March of Dimes: Our Children - G. Perillo

1989 A Time to Be Born	150-day		29.00	40

Mother's Love - G. Perillo

1988 Feelings	Yr.Iss.		35.00	55
1989 Moonlight	Yr.Iss.		35.00	65
1990 Pride & Joy	Yr.Iss.		39.50	50
1991 Little Shadow	Yr.Iss.		39.50	45

Motherhood Series - G. Perillo

1983 Madre	10,000		50.00	75
1984 Madonna of the Plains	3,500		50.00	75
1985 Abuela	3,500		50.00	75
1986 Nap Time	3,500		50.00	75

Native American Christmas - G. Perillo

1993 The Little Shepherd	Annual		35.00	55
1994 Joy to the World	Annual		45.00	45

Nature's Harmony - G. Perillo

1982 The Peaceable Kingdom	12,500		100.00	125-200
1982 Zebra	12,500		50.00	50
1982 Bengal Tiger	12,500		50.00	50
1983 Black Panther	12,500		50.00	70
1983 Elephant	12,500		50.00	80

North American Wildlife - G. Perillo

Year / Issue	Edition Limit	Year Retd.	Issue Price	*Quote U.S.$
1989 Mustang	14-day		29.50	35-55
1989 White-Tailed Deer	14-day		29.50	35
1989 Mountain Lion	14-day		29.50	35
1990 American Bald Eagle	14-day		29.50	35
1990 Timber Wolf	14-day		29.50	35
1990 Polar Bear	14-day		29.50	35
1990 Buffalo	14-day		29.50	35-55
1990 Bighorn Sheep	14-day		29.50	35

Perillo Christmas - G. Perillo

Year / Issue	Edition Limit	Issue Price	*Quote
1987 Shining Star	Yr.Iss.	29.50	35-75
1988 Silent Light	Yr.Iss.	35.00	65-80
1989 Snow Flake	Yr.Iss.	35.00	65-80
1990 Bundle Up	Yr.Iss.	39.50	65-75
1991 Christmas Journey	Yr.Iss.	39.50	40-50

Portraits of American Brides - R. Sauber

Year / Issue	Edition Limit	Issue Price	*Quote
1986 Caroline	10-day	29.50	40-50
1986 Jacqueline	10-day	29.50	45
1987 Elizabeth	10-day	29.50	45
1987 Emily	10-day	29.50	45
1987 Meredith	10-day	29.50	50
1987 Laura	10-day	29.50	45
1987 Sarah	10-day	29.50	45
1987 Rebecca	10-day	29.50	65

Pride of America's Indians - G. Perillo

Year / Issue	Edition Limit	Issue Price	*Quote
1986 Brave and Free	10-day	24.50	35-50
1986 Dark-Eyed Friends	10-day	24.50	30
1986 Noble Companions	10-day	24.50	30
1987 Kindred Spirits	10-day	24.50	30
1987 Loyal Alliance	10-day	24.50	55
1987 Small and Wise	10-day	24.50	40
1987 Winter Scouts	10-day	24.50	24-40
1987 Peaceful Comrades	10-day	24.50	40

The Princesses - G. Perillo

Year / Issue	Edition Limit	Issue Price	*Quote
1982 Lily of the Mohawks	7,500	50.00	175
1982 Pocahontas	7,500	50.00	100
1982 Minnehaha	7,500	50.00	100
1982 Sacajawea	7,500	50.00	100

Proud Young Spirits - G. Perillo

Year / Issue	Edition Limit	Issue Price	*Quote
1990 Protector of the Plains	14-day	29.50	45
1990 Watchful Eyes	14-day	29.50	55
1990 Freedom's Watch	14-day	29.50	35-45
1990 Woodland Scouts	14-day	29.50	35-45
1990 Fast Friends	14-day	29.50	35-45
1990 Birds of a Feather	14-day	29.50	50
1990 Prairie Pals	14-day	29.50	35-45
1990 Loyal Guardian	14-day	29.50	35

Special Issue - G. Perillo

Year / Issue	Edition Limit	Year Retd.	Issue Price	*Quote
1981 Apache Boy	5,000		95.00	175
1983 Papoose	3,000		100.00	125
1983 Indian Style	17,500		50.00	50
1984 The Lovers	Closed	N/A	50.00	100
1984 Navajo Girl	3,500		95.00	175
1986 Navajo Boy	3,500		95.00	175

The Thoroughbreds - G. Perillo

Year / Issue	Edition Limit	Issue Price	*Quote
1984 Whirlaway	9,500	50.00	250
1984 Secretariat	9,500	50.00	350
1984 Man o' War	9,500	50.00	150
1984 Seabiscuit	9,500	50.00	150

The Young Chieftains - G. Perillo

Year / Issue	Edition Limit	Issue Price	*Quote
1985 Young Sitting Bull	5,000	50.00	75-100
1985 Young Joseph	5,000	50.00	75-100
1986 Young Red Cloud	5,000	50.00	75-100
1986 Young Geronimo	5,000	50.00	75-100
1986 Young Crazy Horse	5,000	50.00	75-100

Artists of the World

Celebration Series - T. DeGrazia

Year / Issue	Edition Limit	Year Retd.	Issue Price	*Quote
1993 The Lord's Candle	5,000		39.50	45-75
1993 Pinata Party	5,000		39.50	45-75
1993 Holiday Lullaby	5,000	1995	39.50	45-75
1993 Caroling	5,000	1995	39.50	45-75

Children (Signed) - T. DeGrazia

Year / Issue	Edition Limit	Issue Price	*Quote
1978 Los Ninos, signed	500	100.00	1500-2200
1978 White Dove, signed	500	100.00	450-700
1978 Flower Girl, signed	500	100.00	450-700
1979 Flower Boy, signed	500	100.00	450-700
1980 Little Cocopah Girl, signed	500	100.00	450-650
1981 Beautiful Burden, signed	500	100.00	450-650
1981 Merry Little Indian, signed	500	100.00	450-650

Children - T. DeGrazia

Year / Issue	Edition Limit	Issue Price	*Quote
1976 Los Ninos	5,000	35.00	1100-1550
1977 White Dove	5,000	40.00	150-300
1978 Flower Girl	9,500	45.00	250-350
1979 Flower Boy	9,500	45.00	250-350
1980 Little Cocopah	9,500	50.00	125-200
1981 Beautiful Burden	9,500	50.00	150-200
1982 Merry Little Indian	9,500	55.00	150-200
1983 Wondering	10,000	60.00	160

Year / Issue	Edition Limit	Issue Price	*Quote
1984 Pink Papoose	10,000	65.00	125
1985 Sunflower Boy	10,000	65.00	125

Children at Play - T. DeGrazia

Year / Issue	Edition Limit	Issue Price	*Quote
1985 My First Horse	15,000	65.00	100-125
1986 Girl With Sewing Machine	15,000	65.00	95-125
1987 Love Me	15,000	65.00	95-125
1988 Merrily, Merrily, Merrily	15,000	65.00	95-125
1989 My First Arrow	15,000	65.00	95-125
1990 Away With My Kite	15,000	65.00	95-125

Children Mini-Plates - T. DeGrazia

Year / Issue	Edition Limit	Issue Price	*Quote
1980 Los Ninos	5,000	15.00	300
1981 White Dove	5,000	15.00	100
1982 Flower Girl	5,000	15.00	100
1982 Flower Boy	5,000	15.00	100
1983 Little Cocopah Indian Girl	5,000	15.00	100
1983 Beautiful Burden	5,000	20.00	100
1984 Merry Little Indian	5,000	20.00	100
1984 Wondering	5,000	20.00	100
1985 Pink Papoose	5,000	20.00	100
1985 Sunflower Boy	5,000	20.00	100

Children of the Sun - T. DeGrazia

Year / Issue	Edition Limit	Issue Price	*Quote
1987 Spring Blossoms	150-day	34.50	60-125
1987 My Little Pink Bird	150-day	34.50	60-125
1987 Bright Flowers of the Desert	150-day	37.90	60-125
1988 Gifts from the Sun	150-day	37.90	60-125
1988 Growing Glory	150-day	37.90	60-125
1988 The Gentle White Dove	150-day	37.90	60-125
1988 Sunflower Maiden	150-day	39.90	60-125
1989 Sun Showers	150-day	39.90	60-125

Floral Fiesta - T. DeGrazia

Year / Issue	Edition Limit	Issue Price	*Quote
1994 Little Flower Vendor	5,000	39.50	40-70
1994 Flowers For Mother	5,000	39.50	40-70
1995 Floral Innocence	5,000	39.50	40-70
1995 Floral Bouquet	5,000	39.50	40-70
1996 Floral Celebration	5,000	39.50	40
1996 Floral Fiesta	5,000	39.50	40

Holiday (Signed) - T. DeGrazia

Year / Issue	Edition Limit	Issue Price	*Quote
1976 Festival of Lights, signed	500	100.00	600-850
1977 Bell of Hope, signed	500	100.00	450-700
1978 Little Madonna, signed	500	100.00	450-750
1979 The Nativity, signed	500	100.00	500-850
1980 Little Pima Drummer, signed	500	100.00	450-550
1981 A Little Prayer, signed	500	100.00	450-500
1982 Blue Boy, signed	96	100.00	450-500

Holiday - T. DeGrazia

Year / Issue	Edition Limit	Issue Price	*Quote
1976 Festival of Lights	9,500	45.00	200-400
1977 Bell of Hope	9,500	45.00	125-300
1978 Little Madonna	9,500	45.00	125-350
1979 The Nativity	9,500	50.00	295
1980 Little Pima Drummer	9,500	50.00	125-200
1981 A Little Prayer	9,500	55.00	125-200
1982 Blue Boy	10,000	60.00	125-200
1983 Heavenly Blessings	10,000	65.00	130
1984 Navajo Madonna	10,000	65.00	135
1985 Saguaro Dance	10,000	65.00	125

Holiday Mini-Plates - T. DeGrazia

Year / Issue	Edition Limit	Issue Price	*Quote
1980 Festival of Lights	5,000	15.00	250
1981 Bell of Hope	5,000	15.00	95
1982 Little Madonna	5,000	15.00	95
1982 The Nativity	5,000	15.00	95
1983 Little Pima Drummer	5,000	15.00	25
1983 Little Prayer	5,000	20.00	25
1984 Blue Boy	5,000	20.00	25
1984 Heavenly Blessings	5,000	20.00	25
1985 Navajo Madonna	5,000	20.00	25
1985 Saguaro Dance	5,000	20.00	25

Special Release - T. DeGrazia

Year / Issue	Edition Limit	Issue Price	*Quote
1996 Wedding Party	5,000	49.50	50

Western - T. DeGrazia

Year / Issue	Edition Limit	Issue Price	*Quote
1986 Morning Ride	5,000	65.00	75-150
1987 Bronco	5,000	65.00	90-150
1988 Apache Scout	5,000	65.00	90-150
1989 Alone	5,000	65.00	90-150

Bareuther

Christmas - H. Mueller, unless otherwise noted

Year / Issue	Edition Limit	Issue Price	*Quote
1967 Stiftskirche	10,000	12.00	85
1968 Kapplkirche	10,000	12.00	25
1969 Christkindlesmarkt	10,000	12.00	18
1970 Chapel in Oberndorf	10,000	12.50	22
1971 Toys for Sale - From Drawing By L. Richter	10,000	12.75	27
1972 Christmas in Munich	10,000	14.50	25
1973 Sleigh Ride	10,000	15.00	35
1974 Black Forest Church	10,000	19.00	19
1975 Snowman	10,000	21.50	30
1976 Chapel in the Hills	10,000	23.50	26
1977 Story Time	10,000	24.50	40
1978 Mittenwald	10,000	27.50	31
1979 Winter Day	10,000	35.00	35
1980 Mittenberg	10,000	37.50	39

Year / Issue	Edition Limit	Issue Price	*Quote
1981 Walk in the Forest	10,000	39.50	40
1982 Bad Wimpfen	10,000	39.50	43
1983 The Night before Christmas	10,000	39.50	40
1984 Zeil on the River Main	10,000	42.50	45
1985 Winter Wonderland	10,000	42.50	57
1986 Christmas in Forchheim	10,000	42.50	70
1987 Decorating the Tree	10,000	42.50	85
1988 St. Coloman Church	10,000	52.50	65
1989 Sleigh Ride	10,000	52.50	80-90
1990 The Old Forge in Rothenburg	10,000	52.50	53
1991 Christmas Joy	10,000	56.50	57
1992 Market Place in Heppenheim	10,000	59.50	60
1993 Winter Fun	10,000	59.50	60
1994 Coming Home For Christmas	10,000	59.50	60

Bing & Grondahl

American Christmas Heritage Collection - C. Magadini

Year / Issue	Edition Limit	Issue Price	*Quote
1996 The Statue of Liberty	12//96	47.50	48
1997 Christmas Eve at The Lincoln Memorial	Yr.Iss.	47.50	48

Centennial Anniversary Commemoratives - Various

Year / Issue	Edition Limit	Year Retd.	Issue Price	*Quote
1995 Centennial Plaquettes: Series of 10-5" plates featuring B&G motifs: 1895, 1905, 1919, 1927, 1932, 1945, 1954, 1967, 1974, 1982	Yr.Iss.	1995	250.00	250
1995 Centennial Plate: Behind the Frozen Window - F.A. Hallin	10,000	1995	39.50	40
1995 Centennial Platter: Towers of Copenhagen - J. Nielsen	7,500	1995	195.00	195

Centennial Collection - Various

Year / Issue	Edition Limit	Year Retd.	Issue Price	*Quote
1991 Crows Enjoying Christmas - D. Jensen	Annual	1991	59.50	60
1992 Copenhagen Christmas - H. Vlugenring	Annual	1992	59.50	60
1993 Christmas Elf - H. Thelander	Annual	1993	59.50	72
1994 Christmas in Church - H. Thelander	Annual	1994	59.50	75
1995 Behind The Frozen Window - A. Hallin	Annual	1995	59.50	60

Children's Day Plate Series - Various

Year / Issue	Edition Limit	Year Retd.	Issue Price	*Quote
1985 The Magical Tea Party - C. Roller	Annual	1985	24.50	27-40
1986 A Joyful Flight - C. Roller	Annual	1986	26.50	30-45
1986 The Little Gardeners - C. Roller	Annual	1987	29.50	30-70
1988 Wash Day - C. Roller	Annual	1988	34.50	40
1989 Bedtime - C. Roller	Annual	1989	37.00	40
1990 My Favorite Dress - S. Vestergaard	Annual	1990	37.00	40
1991 Fun on the Beach - S. Vestergaard	Annual	1991	45.00	60
1992 A Summer Day in the Meadow - S. Vestergaard	Annual	1992	45.00	65
1993 The Carousel - S. Vestergaard	Annual	1993	45.00	55
1994 The Little Fisherman - S. Vestergaard	Annual	1994	45.00	47
1995 My First Book - S. Vestergaard	Annual	1995	45.00	45
1996 The Little Racers - S. Vestergaard	Annual		45.00	45

Christmas - Various

Year / Issue	Edition Limit	Year Retd.	Issue Price	*Quote
1895 Behind The Frozen Window - F.A. Hallin	Annual	1895	.50	5000
1896 New Moon - F.A. Hallin	Annual	1896	.50	2200-2500
1897 Sparrows - F.A. Hallin	Annual	1897	.75	1200-1425
1898 Roses and Star - F. Garde	Annual	1898	.75	800-850
1899 Crows - F. Garde	Annual	1899	.75	900-1800
1900 Church Bells - F. Garde	Annual	1900	.75	875-1300
1901 Three Wise Men - S. Sabra	Annual	1901	1.00	450-540
1902 Gothic Church Interior - D. Jensen	Annual	1902	1.00	425-775
1903 Expectant Children - M. Hyldahl	Annual	1903	1.00	300-450
1904 Fredericksberg Hill - C. Olsen	Annual	1904	1.00	150-225
1905 Christmas Night - D. Jensen	Annual	1905	1.00	150-210
1906 Sleighing to Church - D. Jensen	Annual	1906	1.00	115-130
1907 Little Match Girl - E. Plockross	Annual	1907	1.00	120-150
1908 St. Petri Church - P. Jorgensen	Annual	1908	1.00	75-105
1909 Yule Tree - Aarestrup	Annual	1909	1.50	90-135
1910 The Old Organist - C. Ersgaard	Annual	1910	1.50	85-110
1911 Angels and Shepherds - H. Moltke	Annual	1911	1.50	75-95
1912 Going to Church - E. Hansen	Annual	1912	1.50	80-95
1913 Bringing Home the Tree - T. Larsen	Annual	1913	1.50	80-105
1914 Amalienborg Castle - T. Larsen	Annual	1914	1.50	75-95
1915 Dog Outside Window - D. Jensen	Annual	1915	1.50	125-135
1916 Sparrows at Christmas - P. Jorgensen	Annual	1916	1.50	65-90
1917 Christmas Boat - A. Friis	Annual	1917	1.50	65-80
1918 Fishing Boat - A. Friis	Annual	1918	1.50	75-90
1919 Outside Lighted Window - A. Friis	Annual	1919	2.00	70-90
1920 Hare in the Snow - A. Friis	Annual	1920	2.00	75-85
1921 Pigeons - A. Friis	Annual	1921	2.00	60-75
1922 Star of Bethlehem - A. Friis	Annual	1922	2.00	60-90
1923 The Ermitage - A. Friis	Annual	1923	2.00	93
1924 Lighthouse - A. Friis	Annual	1924	2.50	80-90
1925 Child's Christmas - A. Friis	Annual	1925	2.50	80-95
1926 Churchgoers - A. Friis	Annual	1926	2.50	80-90
1927 Skating Couple - A. Friis	Annual	1927	2.50	90-100
1928 Eskimos - A. Friis	Annual	1928	2.50	65-84
1929 Fox Outside Farm - A. Friis	Annual	1929	2.50	75-90
1930 Town Hall Square - H. Flugenring	Annual	1930	2.50	96-110
1931 Christmas Train - A. Friis	Annual	1931	2.50	96
1932 Life Boat - H. Flugenring	Annual	1932	2.50	75-90

YEAR ISSUE		EDITION LIMIT	YEAR RETD.	ISSUE PRICE	*QUOTE U.S.$
1933	Korsor-Nyborg Ferry - H. Flugenring	Annual	1933	3.00	80-95
1934	Church Bell in Tower - H. Flugenring	Annual	1934	3.00	80-90
1935	Lillebelt Bridge - O. Larson	Annual	1935	3.00	75-140
1936	Royal Guard - O. Larson	Annual	1936	3.00	76
1937	Arrival of Christmas Guests - O. Larson	Annual	1937	3.00	90-110
1938	Lighting the Candles - I. Tjerne	Annual	1938	3.00	125-200
1939	Old Lock-Eye, The Sandman - I. Tjerne	Annual	1939	3.00	140-240
1940	Christmas Letters - O. Larson	Annual	1940	4.00	150-180
1941	Horses Enjoying Meal - O. Larson	Annual	1941	4.00	255-370
1942	Danish Farm - O. Larson	Annual	1942	4.00	170-210
1943	Ribe Cathedral - O. Larson	Annual	1943	5.00	150-210
1944	Sorgenfri Castle - O. Larson	Annual	1944	5.00	90-105
1945	The Old Water Mill - O. Larson	Annual	1945	5.00	140-180
1946	Commemoration Cross - M. Hyldahl	Annual	1946	5.00	105
1947	Dybbol Mill - M. Hyldahl	Annual	1947	5.00	100-135
1948	Watchman - M. Hyldahl	Annual	1948	5.50	95-105
1949	Landsoldaten - M. Hyldahl	Annual	1949	5.50	85-100
1950	Kronborg Castle - M. Hyldahl	Annual	1950	5.50	110-150
1951	Jens Bang - M. Hyldahl	Annual	1951	6.00	120-185
1952	Thorsvaldsen Museum - B. Pramvig	Annual	1952	6.00	100-120
1953	Snowman - B. Pramvig	Annual	1953	7.50	95-150
1954	Royal Boat - K. Bonfils	Annual	1954	7.00	112
1955	Kaulundorg Church - K. Bonfils	Annual	1955	8.00	112-150
1956	Christmas in Copenhagen - K. Bonfils	Annual	1956	8.50	140-275
1957	Christmas Candles - K. Bonfils	Annual	1957	9.00	100-165
1958	Santa Claus - K. Bonfils	Annual	1958	9.50	95-112
1959	Christmas Eve - K. Bonfils	Annual	1959	10.00	100-165
1960	Village Church - K. Bonfils	Annual	1960	10.00	100-210
1961	Winter Harmony - K. Bonfils	Annual	1961	10.50	75-105
1962	Winter Night - K. Bonfils	Annual	1962	11.00	60-120
1963	The Christmas Elf - H. Thelander	Annual	1963	11.00	105-155
1964	The Fir Tree and Hare - H. Thelander	Annual	1964	11.50	40-48
1965	Bringing Home the Tree - H. Thelander	Annual	1965	12.00	48-56
1966	Home for Christmas - H. Thelander	Annual	1966	12.00	45-52
1967	Sharing the Joy - H. Thelander	Annual	1967	13.00	37
1968	Christmas in Church - H. Thelander	Annual	1968	14.00	40
1969	Arrival of Guests - H. Thelander	Annual	1969	14.00	23-38
1970	Pheasants in Snow - H. Thelander	Annual	1970	14.50	15-27
1971	Christmas at Home - H. Thelander	Annual	1971	15.00	15-21
1972	Christmas in Greenland - H. Thelander	Annual	1972	16.50	15-22
1973	Country Christmas - H. Thelander	Annual	1973	19.50	20-36
1974	Christmas in the Village - H. Thelander	Annual	1974	22.00	16-25
1975	Old Water Mill - H. Thelander	Annual	1975	27.50	21
1976	Christmas Welcome - H. Thelander	Annual	1976	27.50	22
1977	Copenhagen Christmas - H. Thelander	Annual	1977	29.50	36
1978	Christmas Tale - H. Thelander	Annual	1978	32.00	45
1979	White Christmas - H. Thelander	Annual	1979	36.50	40
1980	Christmas in Woods - H. Thelander	Annual	1980	42.50	45-55
1981	Christmas Peace - H. Thelander	Annual	1981	49.50	30
1982	Christmas Tree - H. Thelander	Annual	1982	54.50	60
1983	Christmas in Old Town - H. Thelander	Annual	1983	54.50	55
1984	The Christmas Letter - E. Jensen	Annual	1984	54.50	55
1985	Christmas Eve at the Farmhouse - E. Jensen	Annual	1985	54.50	55
1986	Silent Night, Holy Night - E. Jensen	Annual	1986	54.50	55
1987	The Snowman's Christmas Eve - E. Jensen	Annual	1987	59.50	60-75
1988	In the Kings Garden - E. Jensen	Annual	1988	64.50	66
1989	Christmas Anchorage - E. Jensen	Annual	1989	59.50	71
1990	Changing of the Guards - E. Jensen	Annual	1990	64.50	72-90
1991	Copenhagen Stock Exchange - E. Jensen	Annual	1991	69.50	65-70
1992	Christmas At the Rectory - J. Steensen	Annual	1992	69.50	99-113
1993	Father Christmas in Copenhagen - J. Nielsen	Annual	1993	69.50	72-96
1994	A Day At The Deer Park - J. Nielsen	Annual	1994	72.50	75-85
1995	The Towers of Copenhagen - J. Nielsen	Annual	1995	72.50	80-90
1996	Winter at the Old Mill - J. Nielsen	12/96		74.50	75
1997	Country Christmas - J. Nielsen	Annual		74.50	75

Christmas In America - J. Woodson

1986	Christmas Eve in Williamsburg	Annual	1986	29.50	150-165
1987	Christmas Eve at the White House	Annual	1987	34.50	35
1988	Christmas Eve at Rockefeller Center	Annual	1988	34.50	60
1989	Christmas In New England	Annual	1989	37.00	55
1990	Christmas Eve at the Capitol	Annual	1990	39.50	55
1991	Christmas Eve at Independence Hall	Annual	1991	45.00	60
1992	Christmas in San Francisco	Annual	1992	47.50	55-60
1993	Coming Home For Christmas	Annual	1993	47.50	48
1994	Christmas Eve In Alaska	Annual	1994	47.50	55-75
1995	Christmas Eve in Mississippi	Annual	1995	47.50	48

Christmas in America Anniversary Plate - J. Woodson

1991	Christmas Eve in Williamsburg	Annual	1991	69.50	75
1995	The Capitol - J. Woodson	Annual	1995	74.50	75

Jubilee-5 Year Cycle - Various

1915	Frozen Window - F.A. Hallin	Annual	1915	Unkn.	190-225
1920	Church Bells - F. Garde	Annual	1920	Unkn.	60
1925	Dog Outside Window - D. Jensen	Annual	1925	Unkn.	160-300
1930	The Old Organist - C. Ersgaard	Annual	1930	Unkn.	225
1935	Little Match Girl - E. Plockross	Annual	1935	Unkn.	450
1940	Three Wise Men - S. Sabra	Annual	1940	Unkn.	1800
1945	Amalienborg Castle - T. Larsen	Annual	1945	Unkn.	90
1950	Eskimos - A. Friis	Annual	1950	Unkn.	90
1955	Dybbol Mill - M. Hyldahl	Annual	1955	Unkn.	210
1960	Kronborg Castle - M. Hyldahl	Annual	1960	25.00	90
1965	Chruchgoers - A. Friis	Annual	1965	25.00	25
1970	Amalienborg Castle - T. Larsen	Annual	1970	30.00	35
1975	Horses Enjoying Meal - O. Larson	Annual	1975	40.00	60
1980	Yule Tree - Aarestrup	Annual	1980	60.00	60
1985	Lifeboat at Work - H. Flugenring	Annual	1985	65.00	65
1990	The Royal Yacht Dannebrog - J. Bonfils	Annual	1990	95.00	85
1995	Centennial Platter - J. Nielsen	7,500	1995	195.00	195

Mother's Day - Various

1969	Dogs and Puppies - H. Thelander	Annual	1969	9.75	385-500
1970	Bird and Chicks - H. Thelander	Annual	1970	10.00	30-45
1971	Cat and Kitten - H. Thelander	Annual	1971	11.00	11
1972	Mare and Foal - H. Thelander	Annual	1972	12.00	20
1973	Duck and Ducklings - H. Thelander	Annual	1973	13.00	20
1974	Bear and Cubs - H. Thelander	Annual	1974	16.50	20
1975	Doe and Fawns - H. Thelander	Annual	1975	19.50	20
1976	Swan Family - H. Thelander	Annual	1976	22.50	23
1977	Squirrel and Young - H. Thelander	Annual	1977	23.50	27
1978	Heron and Young - H. Thelander	Annual	1978	24.50	25
1979	Fox and Cubs - H. Thelander	Annual	1979	27.50	32
1980	Woodpecker and Young - H. Thelander	Annual	1980	29.50	36
1981	Hare and Young - H. Thelander	Annual	1981	36.50	37
1982	Lioness and Cubs - H. Thelander	Annual	1982	39.50	56
1983	Raccoon and Young - H. Thelander	Annual	1983	39.50	45
1984	Stork and Nestlings - H. Thelander	Annual	1984	39.50	48
1985	Bear and Cubs - H. Thelander	Annual	1985	39.50	45
1986	Elephant with Calf - H. Thelander	Annual	1986	39.50	55
1987	Sheep with Lambs - H. Thelander	Annual	1987	42.50	83-90
1988	Crested Plover and Young - H. Thelander	Annual	1988	47.50	75
1988	Lapwing Mother with Chicks - H. Thelander	Annual	1988	49.50	90
1989	Cow With Calf - H. Thelander	Annual	1989	49.50	55
1990	Hen with Chicks - L. Jensen	Annual	1990	52.50	65-90
1991	The Nanny Goat and her Two Frisky Kids - L. Jensen	Annual	1991	54.50	75-112
1992	Panda With Cubs - L. Jensen	Annual	1992	59.50	75-90
1993	St. Bernard Dog and Puppies - A. Therkelsen	Annual	1993	59.50	95-105
1994	Cat with Kittens - A. Therkelsen	Annual	1994	59.50	80-90
1995	Hedgehog with Young - A. Therkelsen	Annual	1995	59.50	60-75
1996	Koala with Young - A. Therkelsen	12/96		59.50	60
1997	Goose with Gooslings - L. Didier	Annual		59.50	60

Mother's Day Jubilee-5 Year Cycle - Thelander

1979	Dog & Puppies	Yr.Iss.	1979	55.00	55
1984	Swan Family	Yr.Iss.	1984	65.00	65
1989	Mare & Colt	Yr.Iss.	1989	95.00	112
1994	Woodpecker & Young	Yr.Iss.	1994	95.00	95

Olympic - Unknown

1972	Munich, Germany	Closed	1972	20.00	15-25
1976	Montreal, Canada	Closed	1976	29.50	60
1980	Moscow, Russia	Closed	1980	43.00	89
1984	Los Angeles, USA	Closed	1984	45.00	259
1988	Seoul, Korea	Closed	1988	60.00	65
1992	Barcelona, Spain	Closed	1992	74.50	75

Santa Around the World - H. Hansen

1995	Santa in Greenland	Yr.Iss.	1995	74.50	75
1996	Santa in Orient	Yr.Iss.		74.50	75
1997	Santa in Russia	Yr.Iss.		74.50	75

Santa Claus Collection - Unknown

1989	Santa's Workshop	Annual	1989	59.50	60
1990	Santa's Sleigh	Annual	1990	59.50	60
1991	Santa's Journey	Annual	1991	69.50	70
1992	Santa's Arrival	Annual	1992	74.50	75
1993	Santa's Gifts	Annual	1993	74.50	75
1994	Christmas Stories	Annual	1994	74.50	75

Statue of Liberty - Unknown

1985	Statue of Liberty	10,000	1985	60.00	80

The Bradford Exchange/Russia

The Nutcracker - N. Zaitseva

1993	Marie's Magical Gift	95-day		39.87	47
1993	Dance of Sugar Plum Fairy	95-day		39.87	50
1994	Waltz of the Flowers	95-day		39.87	50
1994	Battle With the Mice King	95-day		39.87	50

The Bradford Exchange/United States

Alice in Wonderland - S. Gustafson

1993	The Mad Tea Party	Closed		29.90	90
1993	The Cheshire Cat	Closed		29.90	90
1994	Croquet with the Queen	Closed		29.90	62
1994	Advice from a Caterpillar	Closed		29.90	80

Babe Ruth Centennial - P. Heffernan

1994	The 60th Homer	Closed		34.90	42
1995	Ruth's Pitching Debut	Closed		29.90	35
1995	The Final Home Run	Closed		29.90	35
1995	Barnstorming Days	95-day		34.90	35

Baskets of Love - A. Isakov

1993	Andrew and Abbey	Closed		29.90	39
1993	Cody and Courtney	Closed		29.90	33
1993	Emily and Elliott	Closed		32.90	33
1993	Heather and Hannah	95-day		32.90	33
1993	Justin and Jessica	95-day		32.90	33
1993	Katie and Kelly	95-day		34.90	35
1993	Louie and Libby	95-day		34.90	35
1994	Sammy and Sarah	95-day		34.90	35

Chosen Messengers - G. Running Wolf

1994	The Pathfinders	Closed		29.90	35
1994	The Overseers	Closed		29.90	30
1994	The Providers	Closed		32.90	33
1994	The Surveyors	Closed		32.90	33

A Christmas Carol - L. Garrison

1993	God Bless Us Everyone	Closed		29.90	75
1993	Ghost of Christmas Present	Closed		29.90	40
1994	A Merry Christmas to All	Closed		29.90	55
1994	A Visit From Marley's Ghost	Closed		29.90	30
1994	Remembering Christmas Past	Closed		29.90	60
1994	A Spirit's Warning	Closed		29.90	30
1994	The True Spirit of Christmas	95-day		29.90	30
1994	Merry Christmas, Bob	95-day		29.90	30

Christmas Memories - J. Tanton

1993	A Winter's Tale	Closed		29.90	30
1993	Finishing Touch	Closed		29.90	45
1993	Welcome to Our Home	Closed		29.90	55
1993	A Christmas Celebration	Closed		29.90	55

Classic Melodies from the "Sound of Music" - M. Hampshire

1995	Sing Along with Maria	Closed		29.90	38
1995	A Drop of Golden Sun	Closed		29.90	30
1995	The Von Trapp Family Singers	95-day		29.90	30
1995	Alpine Refuge	95-day		29.90	30

Dog Days - J. Gadamus

1993	Sweet Dreams	Closed		29.90	45
1993	Pier Group	Closed		29.90	45
1993	Wagon Train	Closed		32.90	50
1993	First Flush	Closed		32.90	33
1993	Little Rascals	95-day		32.90	33
1993	Where'd He Go	95-day		32.90	33

Family Circles - R. Rust

1993	Great Gray Owl Family	Closed		29.90	30
1994	Great Horned Owl Family	Closed		29.90	30
1994	Barred Owl Family	Closed		29.90	30
1994	Spotted Owl Family	Closed		29.90	30

Favorite Classic Cars - D. Everhart

1993	1957 Corvette	Closed		54.00	75
1993	1956 Thunderbird	Closed		54.00	125
1994	1957 Bel Air	Closed		54.00	54
1994	1965 Mustang	Closed		54.00	54

Field Pup Follies - C. Jackson

1994	Sleeping on the Job	Closed		29.90	30
1994	Hat Check	Closed		29.90	30
1994	Fowl Play	Closed		29.90	30
1994	Tackling Lunch	Closed		29.90	30

Floral Frolics - G. Kurz

1994	Spring Surprises	Closed		29.90	30
1994	Bee Careful	Closed		29.90	30
1995	Fuzzy Fun	Closed		32.90	33
1995	Sunny Hideout	Closed		32.90	33

Footsteps of the Brave - H. Schaare

1993	Noble Quest	Closed		24.90	25
1993	At Storm's Passage	Closed		24.90	45
1993	With Boundless Vision	Closed		27.90	38
1993	Horizons of Destiny	Closed		27.90	37
1993	Path of His Forefathers	Closed		27.90	45
1993	Soulful Reflection	Closed		29.90	45
1993	The Reverent Trail	Closed		29.90	45
1994	At Journey's End	Closed		34.90	50

Gone With The Wind: A Legend in Stained Glass - M. Phalen

1995	Scarlett Radiance	Closed		39.90	60
1995	Rhett's Bright Promise	95-day		39.90	40
1995	Ashley's Smoldering Fire	95-day		39.90	40

Heirloom Memories - A. Pech

1994	Porcelain Treasure	Closed		29.90	40

YEAR ISSUE		EDITION LIMIT	YEAR RETD.	ISSUE PRICE	*QUOTE U.S.$
1994	Rhythms in Lace	Closed		29.90	65
1994	Pink Lemonade Roses	Closed		29.90	45
1994	Victorian Romance	Closed		29.90	45
1994	Teatime Tulips	Closed		29.90	50
1994	Touch of the Irish	Closed		29.90	30

A Hidden Garden - T. Clausnitzer

1993	Curious Kittens	Closed		29.90	40
1994	Through the Eyes of Blue	95-day		29.90	30
1994	Amber Gaze	95-day		29.90	30
1994	Fascinating Find	95-day		29.90	30

A Hidden World - R. Rust

1993	Two by Night, Two by Light	Closed		29.90	50
1993	Two by Steam, Two in Dream	Closed		29.90	30
1993	Two on Sly, Two Watch Nearby	95-day		32.90	33
1993	Hunter Growls, Spirits Prowl	95-day		32.90	33
1993	In Moonglow One Drinks	95-day		32.90	33
1993	Sings at the Moon, Spirits Sing in Tune	95-day		34.90	35
1994	Two Cubs Play As Spirits Show the Way	95-day		34.90	35
1994	Young Ones Hold on Tight As Spirits Stay in Sight	95-day		34.90	35

Hideaway Lake - R. Rust

1993	Rusty's Retreat	Closed		34.90	35
1993	Fishing For Dreams	Closed		34.90	35
1993	Sunset Cabin	Closed		34.90	48
1993	Echoes of Morning	Closed		34.90	50

Keepsakes of the Heart - C. Layton

1993	Forever Friends	Closed		29.90	35
1993	Afternoon Tea	Closed		29.90	40
1993	Riding Companions	Closed		29.90	40
1994	Sentimental Sweethearts	Closed		29.90	60

Kingdom of the Unicorn - M. Ferraro

1993	The Magic Begins	Closed		29.90	39
1993	In Crystal Waters	Closed		29.90	45
1993	Chasing a Dream	Closed		29.90	52
1993	The Fountain of Youth	Closed		29.90	45

The Life of Christ - R. Barrett

1994	The Passion in the Garden	Closed		29.90	40
1994	Jesus Enters Jerusalem	Closed		29.90	30
1994	Jesus Calms the Waters	Closed		32.90	33
1994	Sermon on the Mount	Closed		32.90	41
1994	The Last Supper	Closed		32.90	33
1994	The Ascension	95-day		34.90	35
1994	The Resurrection	95-day		34.90	35
1994	The Crucifixion	95-day		34.90	35

Little Bandits - C. Jagodits

1993	Handle With Care	Closed		29.90	55
1993	All Tied Up	Closed		29.90	55
1993	Everything's Coming Up Daisies	Closed		32.90	45
1993	Out of Hand	Closed		32.90	43
1993	Pupsicles	Closed		32.90	55
1993	Unexpected Guests	Closed		32.90	33

Me & My Shadow - J. Welty

1994	Easter Parade	Closed		29.90	40
1994	A Golden Moment	Closed		29.90	30
1994	Perfect Timing	Closed		29.90	37
1995	Giddyup	Closed		29.90	40

Mysterious Case of Fowl Play - H. Bond

1994	Inspector Clawseau	Closed		29.90	50
1994	Glamourpuss	Closed		29.90	38
1994	Sophisicat	Closed		29.90	45
1994	Kool Cat	Closed		29.90	45
1994	Sneakers & High-Top	Closed		29.90	60
1995	Tuxedo	Closed		29.90	45

New Horizons - R. Copple

1993	Building For a New Generation	Closed		29.90	30
1993	The Power of Gold	95-day		29.90	30
1994	Wings of Snowy Grandeur	95-day		32.90	33
1994	Master of the Chase	95-day		32.90	33
1995	Coastal Domain	95-day		32.90	33
1995	Majestic Wings	95-day		32.90	33

Nightsong: The Loon - J. Hansel

1994	Moonlight Echoes	Closed		29.90	30
1994	Evening Mist	Closed		29.90	30
1994	Nocturnal Glow	Closed		32.90	33
1994	Tranquil Reflections	Closed		32.90	33
1994	Peaceful Waters	Closed		32.90	33
1994	Silently Nestled	95-day		34.90	35
1994	Night Light	95-day		34.90	35
1995	Peaceful Homestead	95-day		34.90	35
1995	Moonlight Cruise	95-day		36.90	37
1995	Serene Sanctuary	95-day		36.90	37
1995	Silent Passage	95-day		34.90	35
1995	Tranquil Refuge	95-day		36.90	37

Nightwatch: The Wolf - D. Ningewance

1994	Moonlight Serenade	Closed		29.90	30
1994	Midnight Guard	Closed		29.90	30
1994	Snowy Lookout	Closed		29.90	30
1994	Silent Sentries	Closed		29.90	30

YEAR ISSUE		EDITION LIMIT	YEAR RETD.	ISSUE PRICE	*QUOTE U.S.$
1994	Song to the Night	Closed		29.90	30
1994	Winter Passage	Closed		29.90	30

Notorious Disney Villains - Disney Studios

1993	The Evil Queen	Closed		29.90	65
1994	Maleficent	Closed		29.90	65
1994	Ursella	Closed		29.90	50
1994	Cruella De Vil	Closed		29.90	75

Panda Bear Hugs - W. Nelson

1993	Rock-A-Bye	Closed		39.90	50
1993	Loving Advice	Closed		39.90	55
1993	A Playful Interlude	Closed		39.90	40
1993	A Taste of Life	Closed		39.90	40

Peace on Earth - D. Geisness

1993	Winter Lullaby	Closed		29.90	90
1994	Heavenly Slumber	Closed		29.90	45
1994	Sweet Embrace	Closed		32.90	50
1994	Woodland Dreams	Closed		32.90	50
1994	Snowy Silence	Closed		32.90	33
1994	Dreamy Whispers	Closed		32.90	33

Practice Makes Perfect - L. Kaatz

1994	What's a Mother to Do?	Closed		29.90	35
1994	The Ones That Got Away	Closed		29.90	35
1994	Pointed in the Wrong Direction	Closed		32.90	55
1994	Fishing for Compliments	95-day		32.90	33
1994	Dandy Distraction	95-day		32.90	33
1995	On The Right Track	95-day		34.90	35
1995	More Than a Mouthful	95-day		34.90	35
1995	On the Right Track	95-day		34.90	35
1995	Missing the Point	95-day		34.90	35

Sacred Circle - K. Randle

1993	Before the Hunt	Closed		29.90	45
1993	Spiritual Guardian	Closed		29.90	30
1993	Ghost Dance	Closed		32.90	60
1994	Deer Dance	Closed		32.90	33
1994	The Wolf Dance	95-day		32.90	33
1994	The Painted House	95-day		34.90	35
1994	Transformation Dance	95-day		34.90	35
1994	Elk Dance	95-day		34.90	35

Sovereigns of the Wild - D. Grant

1993	The Snow Queen	Closed		29.90	60
1994	Let Us Survive	Closed		29.90	50
1994	Cool Cats	Closed		29.90	55
1994	Siberian Snow Tigers	Closed		29.90	30
1994	African Evening	Closed		29.90	30
1994	Sovereigns of the Wild	95-day		29.90	30

Superstars of Country Music - N. Giorgio

1993	Dolly Parton: I Will Always Love You	Closed		29.90	35
1993	Kenny Rogers: Sweet Music Man	Closed		29.90	30
1994	Barbara Mandrell	Closed		32.90	35
1994	Glen Campbell: Rhinestone Cowboy	95-day		32.90	33

Tale of Peter Rabbit & Benjamin Bunny - R. Akers

1994	A Pocket Full of Onions	Closed		39.00	60
1994	Beside His Cousin	95-day		39.00	39
1995	Round that Corner	95-day		39.00	39
1995	Safely Home	95-day		44.00	44
1995	Mr. McGregor's Garden	95-day		44.00	44
1995	Rosemary Tea and Lavender	95-day		44.00	44
1995	Amongst the Flowerpots	95-day		44.00	44
1995	Upon the Scarecrow	95-day		44.00	44

That's What Friends Are For - A. Isakov

1994	Friends Are Forever	Closed		29.90	40
1994	Friends Are Comfort	Closed		29.90	30
1994	Friends Are Loving	Closed		29.90	30
1995	Friends Are For Fun	95-day		29.90	30

Thomas Kinkade's Illuminated Cottages - T. Kinkade

1994	The Flagstone Path	Closed		34.90	35
1995	The Lighted Gate	Closed		37.90	38
1995	Cherry Blossom Hideaway	Closed		34.90	35

Thundering Waters - F. Miller

1994	Niagara Falls	Closed		34.90	45
1994	Lower Falls, Yellowstone	Closed		34.90	50
1994	Bridal Veil Falls	Closed		34.90	60
1995	Havasu Falls	Closed		29.90	50

Trains of the Great West - K. Randle

1993	Moonlit Journey	Closed		29.90	35
1993	Mountain Hideaway	Closed		29.90	43
1993	Early Morning Arrival	Closed		29.90	50
1994	The Snowy Pass	Closed		29.90	42

Untamed Spirits - P. Weirs

1993	Wild Hearts	Closed		29.90	55
1993	Breakaway	Closed		29.90	45
1994	Forever Free	Closed		29.90	70
1994	Distant Thunder	Closed		29.90	45

Vanishing Paradises - G. Dieckhoner

1994	The Rainforest	Closed		29.90	40

YEAR ISSUE		EDITION LIMIT	YEAR RETD.	ISSUE PRICE	*QUOTE U.S.$
1994	The Panda's World	Closed		29.90	50
1994	Splendors of India	Closed		29.90	60
1994	An African Safari	Closed		29.90	60

A Visit to Brambly Hedge - J. Barklem

1994	Summer Story	Closed		39.90	40
1994	Spring Story	Closed		39.90	40
1994	Autumn Story	Closed		39.90	40
1995	Winter Story	Closed		39.90	40

Welcome to the Neighborhood - B. Mock

1994	Ivy Lane	Closed		29.90	30

When All Hearts Come Home - J. Barnes

1993	Oh Christmas Tree	Closed		29.90	30
1993	Night Before Christmas	95-day		29.90	30
1993	Comfort and Joy	95-day		29.90	30
1993	Grandpa's Farm	95-day		29.90	30
1993	Peace on Earth	95-day		29.90	30
1993	Night Departure	95-day		29.90	30
1993	Supper and Small Talk	95-day		29.90	30
1993	Christmas Wish	95-day		29.90	30

Windows on a World of Song - K. Daniel

1993	The Library: Cardinals	Closed		34.90	55
1993	The Den: Black-Capped Chickadees	95-day		34.90	35
1993	The Bedroom: Bluebirds	95-day		34.90	35
1994	The Kitchen: Goldfinches	95-day		34.90	35

The World of the Eagle - J. Hansel

1993	Sentinel of the Night	Closed		29.90	48
1994	Silent Guard	Closed		29.90	50
1994	Night Flyer	Closed		32.90	45
1995	Midnight Duty	Closed		32.90	55

Cavanagh Group Intl.

Coca-Cola Brand Heritage Collection - Various

1995	Boy Fishing - N. Rockwell	5,000		60.00	65
1995	Good Boys and Girls - Sundblom	2,500	1995	60.00	60
1995	Hilda Clark with Roses - CGI	5,000		60.00	65
1996	Travel Refreshed - Sundblom	Open		60.00	60

Dave Grossman Creations

Emmett Kelly Plates - B. Leighton-Jones

1986	Christmas Carol	Yr.Iss.		20.00	400
1987	Christmas Wreath	Yr.Iss.		20.00	225
1988	Christmas Dinner	Yr.Iss.		20.00	49
1989	Christmas Feast	Yr.Iss.		20.00	39
1990	Just What I Needed	Yr.Iss.		24.00	39
1991	Emmett The Snowman	Yr.Iss.		25.00	45
1992	Christmas Tunes	Yr.Iss.		25.00	35
1993	Downhill-Christmas Plate	Yr.Iss.		30.00	30
1994	Holiday Skater EKP-94	Yr.Iss.		30.00	30

Saturday Evening Post Collection - Rockwell-Inspired

1991	Downhill Daring BRP-91	Yr.Iss.		25.00	25
1991	Missed BRP-101	Yr.Iss.		25.00	25
1992	Choosin Up BRP-102	Yr.Iss.		25.00	25

Dave Grossman Designs

Norman Rockwell Collection - Rockwell-Inspired

1979	Leapfrog NRP-79	Retrd.		50.00	50
1980	Lovers NRP-80	Retrd.		60.00	60
1981	Dreams of Long Ago NRP-81	Retrd.		60.00	60
1982	Doctor and Doll NRP-82	Retrd.		65.00	95
1983	Circus NRP-83	Retrd.		65.00	65
1984	Visit With Rockwell NRP-84	Retrd.		65.00	65
1980	Christmas Trio RXP-80	Retrd.		75.00	75
1981	Santa's Good Boys RXP-81	Retrd.		75.00	75
1982	Faces of Christmas RXP-82	Retrd.		75.00	75
1983	Christmas Chores RXP-83	Retrd.		75.00	75
1984	Tiny Tim RXP-84	Retrd.		75.00	75
1980	Back To School RMP-80	Retrd.		24.00	24
1981	No Swimming RMP-81	Retrd.		25.00	25
1982	Love Letter RMP-82	Retrd.		27.00	30
1983	Doctor and Doll RMP-83	Retrd.		27.00	27
1984	Big Moment RMP-84	Retrd.		27.00	27
1979	Butterboy RP-01	Retrd.		40.00	40
1982	American Mother RGP-42	Retrd.		45.00	45
1983	Dreamboat RGP-83	Retrd.		24.00	30
1978	Young Doctor RDP-26	Retrd.		50.00	65

Norman Rockwell Collection-Boy Scout Plates - Rockwell-Inspired

1981	Can't Wait BSP-01	Retrd.		30.00	45
1982	Guiding Hand BSP-02	Retrd.		30.00	35
1983	Tomorrow's Leader BSP-03	Retrd.		30.00	45

Norman Rockwell Collection-Huck Finn Plates - Rockwell-Inspired

1979	Secret HFP-01	Retrd.		40.00	40
1980	Listening HFP-02	Retrd.		40.00	40
1980	No Kings HFP-03	Retrd.		40.00	40
1981	Snake Escapes HFP-04	Retrd.		40.00	40

YEAR ISSUE		EDITION LIMIT	YEAR RETD.	ISSUE PRICE	*QUOTE U.S.$

Norman Rockwell Collection-Tom Sawyer Plates - Rockwell-Inspired

1975	Whitewashing the Fence TSP-01		Retrd.	26.00	35
1976	First Smoke TSP-02		Retrd.	26.00	35
1977	Take Your Medicine TSP-03		Retrd.	26.00	40
1978	Lost in Cave TSP-04		Retrd.	26.00	40

Delphi

The Beatles Collection - N. Giorgio

1991	The Beatles, Live In Concert	Closed		24.75	50
1991	Hello America	Closed		24.75	60
1991	A Hard Day's Night	Closed		27.75	60
1992	Beatles '65	Closed		27.75	70
1992	Help	Closed		27.75	65
1992	The Beatles at Shea Stadium	150-day		29.75	30
1992	Rubber Soul	150-day		29.75	30
1992	Yesterday and Today	150-day		29.75	30

Cars of the '50's - G. Angelini

1993	'57 Red Corvette	Closed		24.75	45
1993	'57 White T-Bird	Closed		24.75	85
1993	'57 Blue Belair	Closed		27.75	50
1993	'59 Cadillac	Closed		27.75	40
1993	'56 Lincoln Premier	Closed		27.75	45
1994	'59 Red Ford Fairlane	Closed		27.75	45

Commemorating The King - M. Stutzman

1993	The Rock and Roll Legend	Closed		29.75	50
1993	Las Vegas, Live	Closed		29.75	45
1993	Blues and Black Leather	95-day		29.75	50
1993	Private Presley	95-day		29.75	30
1993	Golden Boy	95-day		29.75	30
1993	Screen Idol	95-day		29.75	30
1993	Outstanding Young Man	95-day		29.75	30
1993	The Tiger: Faith, Spirit & Discipline	95-day		29.75	30

Dream Machines - P. Palma

1988	'56 T-Bird	Closed		24.75	25
1988	'57 'Vette	Closed		24.75	25
1989	'58 Biarritz	Closed		27.75	28
1989	'56 Continental	Closed		27.75	28
1989	'57 Bel Air	Closed		27.75	50
1989	'57 Chrysler 300C	Closed		27.75	30

Elvis on the Big Screen - B. Emmett

1992	Elvis in Loving You	Closed		29.75	50
1992	Elvis in G.I. Blues	Closed		29.75	80
1992	Viva Las Vegas	Closed		32.75	120
1993	Elvis in Blue Hawaii	Closed		32.75	40
1993	Elvis in Jailhouse Rock	Closed		32.75	40
1993	Elvis in Spinout	Closed		34.75	40
1993	Elvis in Speedway	150-day		34.75	35
1993	Elvis in Harum Scarum	150-day		34.75	35

Elvis Presley: In Performance - B. Emmett

1990	'68 Comeback Special	Closed		24.75	55
1991	King of Las Vegas	Closed		24.75	65
1991	Aloha From Hawaii	Closed		27.75	55
1991	Back in Tupelo, 1956	Closed		27.75	60
1991	If I Can Dream	Closed		27.75	45
1991	Benefit for the USS Arizona	Closed		29.75	45
1991	Madison Square Garden, 1972	Closed		29.75	60
1991	Tampa, 1955	Closed		29.75	50
1991	Concert in Baton Rouge, 1974	Closed		29.75	45
1992	On Stage in Wichita, 1974	Closed		31.75	47
1992	In the Spotlight: Hawaii, '72	Closed		31.75	45
1992	Tour Finale: Indianapolis 1977	Closed		31.75	40

Elvis Presley: Looking At A Legend - B. Emmett

1988	Elvis at/Gates of Graceland	Closed		24.75	85
1989	Jailhouse Rock	Closed		24.75	80
1989	The Memphis Flash	Closed		27.75	60
1989	Homecoming	Closed		27.75	55
1990	Elvis and Gladys	Closed		27.75	65
1990	A Studio Session	Closed		27.75	45
1990	Elvis in Hollywood	Closed		29.75	60
1990	Elvis on His Harley	Closed		29.75	70
1990	Stage Door Autographs	Closed		29.75	55
1991	Christmas at Graceland	Closed		32.75	70
1991	Entering Sun Studio	Closed		32.75	50
1991	Going for the Black Belt	Closed		32.75	45
1991	His Hand in Mine	Closed		32.75	75
1991	Letters From Fans	Closed		32.75	60
1991	Closing the Deal	Closed		34.75	55
1992	Elvis Returns to the Stage	Closed		34.75	55

In the Footsteps of the King - D. Sivavec

1993	Graceland: Memphis, Tenn.	Closed		29.75	41
1994	Elvis' Birthplace: Tupelo, Miss	95-day		29.75	30
1994	Day Job: Memphis, Tenn.	95-day		32.75	33
1994	Flying Circle G. Ranch: Walls, Miss.	95-day		32.75	33
1994	The Lauderdale Courts	95-day		32.75	33
1995	Patriotic Soldier: Bad Nauheim, W. Ger.	95-day		34.75	35

Indiana Jones - V. Gadino

| 1989 | Indiana Jones | Closed | | 24.75 | 25-35 |
| 1989 | Indiana Jones and His Dad | Closed | | 24.75 | 45 |

1990	Indiana Jones/Dr. Schneider	Closed		27.75	45
1990	A Family Discussion	Closed		27.75	50
1990	Young Indiana Jones	Closed		27.75	50
1991	Indiana Jones/The Holy Grail	Closed		27.75	60

The Magic of Marilyn - C. Notarile

1992	For Our Boys in Korea, 1954	Closed		24.75	35
1992	Opening Night	Closed		24.75	30
1993	Rising Star	Closed		27.75	30
1993	Stopping Traffic	Closed		27.75	35
1992	Strasberg's Student	150-day		27.75	28
1993	Photo Opportunity	150-day		29.75	30
1993	Shining Star	150-day		29.75	30
1993	Curtain Call	150-day		29.75	30

The Marilyn Monroe Collection - C. Notarile

1989	Marilyn Monroe/7 Year Itch	Closed		24.75	80-100
1990	Diamonds/Girls Best Friend	Closed		24.75	95
1991	Marilyn Monroe/River of No Return	Closed		27.75	85
1992	How to Marry a Millionaire	Closed		27.75	55-85
1992	There's No Business/Show Business	Closed		27.75	50-75
1992	Marilyn Monroe in Niagra	Closed		29.75	65-80
1992	My Heart Belongs to Daddy	Closed		29.75	50
1992	Marilyn Monroe as Cherie in Bus Stop	Closed		29.75	60-80
1992	Marilyn Monroe in All About Eve	Closed		29.75	60
1992	Marilyn Monroe in Monkey Business	Closed		31.75	60
1992	Marilyn Monroe in Don't Bother to Knock	Closed		31.75	75
1992	Marilyn Monroe in We're Not Married	Closed		31.75	70

Portraits of the King - D. Zwierz

1991	Love Me Tender	Closed		27.75	40
1991	Are You Lonesome Tonight?	Closed		27.75	45
1991	I'm Yours	Closed		30.75	45
1991	Treat Me Nice	Closed		30.75	45
1992	The Wonder of You	Closed		30.75	32
1992	You're a Heartbreaker	150-day		32.75	33
1992	Just Because	150-day		32.75	33
1992	Follow That Dream	150-day		32.75	33

Department 56

A Christmas Carol - R. Innocenti

1991	The Cratchit's Christmas Pudding 5706-1	18,000	1991	60.00	75-125
1992	Marley's Ghost Appears To Scrooge 5721-5	18,000	1992	60.00	65
1993	The Spirit of Christmas Present 5722-3	18,000	1993	60.00	60
1994	Visions of Christmas Past 5723-1	18,000	1994	60.00	60

Dickens' Village - Department 56

| 1987 | Dickens' Village Porcelain Plates, 5917-0 set/4 | Closed | 1990 | 140.00 | 170-200 |

Duncan Royale

History of Santa Claus I - S. Morton

1985	Medieval	Retrd.	N/A	40.00	75
1985	Kris Kringle	Retrd.	N/A	40.00	75
1985	Pioneer	10,000		40.00	40
1986	Russian	Retrd.	N/A	40.00	65
1986	Soda Pop	Retrd.	N/A	40.00	75
1986	Civil War	10,000		40.00	40
1986	Nast	Retrd.	N/A	40.00	75
1987	St. Nicholas	Retrd.	N/A	40.00	75
1987	Dedt Moroz	10,000		40.00	45
1987	Black Peter	10,000		40.00	60
1987	Victorian	Retrd.	N/A	40.00	45
1987	Wassail	Retrd.	N/A	40.00	45
XX	Collection of 12 Plates	Retrd.	N/A	480.00	480

Edna Hibel Studios

Allegro - E. Hibel

| 1978 | Plate & Book | 7,500 | | 120.00 | 150 |

Arte Ovale - E. Hibel

1980	Takara, gold	300		1000.00	4200
1980	Takara, blanco	700		450.00	1200
1980	Takara, cobalt blue	1,000		595.00	2350
1984	Taro-kun, gold	300		1000.00	2700
1984	Taro-kun, blanco	700		450.00	825
1984	Taro-kun, cobalt blue	1,000		995.00	1050

Christmas Annual - E. Hibel

1985	The Angels' Message	Yr.Iss.		45.00	220
1986	Gift of the Magi	Yr.Iss.		45.00	275
1987	Flight Into Egypt	Yr.Iss.		49.00	250
1988	Adoration of the Shepherds	Yr.Iss.		49.00	175
1989	Peaceful Kingdom	Yr.Iss.		49.00	165
1990	The Nativity	Yr.Iss.		49.00	125

David Series - E. Hibel

1979	Wedding of David & Bathsheba	5,000		250.00	650
1980	David, Bathsheba & Solomon	5,000		275.00	425
1982	David the King	5,000		275.00	295

1982	David the King, cobalt A/P	25		275.00	1200
1984	Bathsheba	5,000		275.00	295
1984	Bathsheba, cobalt A/P	100		275.00	1200

Edna Hibel Holiday - E. Hibel

1991	The First Holiday	Yr.Iss.		49.00	85
1991	The First Holiday, gold	1,000		99.00	150
1992	The Christmas Rose	Yr.Iss.		49.00	70
1992	The Christmas Rose, gold	1,000		99.00	125

Eroica - E. Hibel

| 1990 | Compassion | 10,000 | | 49.50 | 65 |
| 1992 | Darya | 10,000 | | 49.50 | 50 |

Famous Women & Children - E. Hibel

1980	Pharaoh's Daughter & Moses, gold	2,500		350.00	625
1980	Pharaoh's Daughter & Moses, cobalt blue	500		350.00	1350
1982	Cornelia & Her Jewels, gold	2,500		350.00	495
1982	Cornelia & Her Jewels, cobalt blue	500		350.00	350
1982	Anna & The Children of the King of Siam, gold	2,500		350.00	495
1982	Anna & The Children of the King of Siam, colbalt blue	500		350.00	1350
1984	Mozart & The Empress Marie Theresa, gold	2,500		350.00	395
1984	Mozart & The Empress Marie Theresa, cobalt blue	500		350.00	975

Flower Girl Annual - E. Hibel

1985	Lily	15,000		79.00	125-175
1986	Iris	15,000		79.00	225
1987	Rose	15,000		79.00	175
1988	Camellia	15,000		79.00	165
1989	Peony	15,000		79.00	100
1992	Wisteria	15,000		79.00	90

International Mother Love French - E. Hibel

| 1985 | Yvette Avec Ses Enfants | 5,000 | | 125.00 | 225 |
| 1991 | Liberte, Egalite, Fraternite | 5,000 | | 95.00 | 95 |

International Mother Love German - E. Hibel

| 1982 | Gesa Und Kinder | 5,000 | | 195.00 | 195 |
| 1983 | Alexandra Und Kinder | 5,000 | | 195.00 | 195 |

March of Dimes: Our Children Our Future - E. Hibel

| 1990 | A Time To Embrace | 150-day | | 29.00 | 29 |

Mother and Child - E. Hibel

1973	Colette & Child	15,000		40.00	725
1974	Sayuri & Child	15,000		40.00	425
1975	Kristina & Child	15,000		50.00	400
1976	Marilyn & Child	15,000		55.00	400
1977	Lucia & Child	15,000		60.00	350
1981	Kathleen & Child	15,000		85.00	275

Mother's Day - E. Hibel

1992	Molly & Annie	Yr.Iss.		39.00	75
1992	Molly & Annie, gold	2,500		95.00	150
1992	Molly & Annie, platinum	500		275.00	275

Mother's Day Annual - E. Hibel

1984	Abby & Lisa	Yr.Iss.		29.50	300
1985	Erica & Jamie	Yr.Iss.		29.50	200
1986	Emily & Jennifer	Yr.Iss.		29.50	150
1987	Catherine & Heather	Yr.Iss.		34.50	200
1988	Sarah & Tess	Yr.Iss.		34.90	175
1989	Jessica & Kate	Yr.Iss.		34.90	100
1990	Elizabeth, Jorday & Janie	Yr.Iss.		36.90	95
1991	Michele & Anna	Yr.Iss.		36.90	65
1992	Olivia & Hildy	Yr.Iss.		39.90	80

Museum Commemorative - E. Hibel

| 1977 | Flower Girl of Provence | 12,750 | | 175.00 | 425 |
| 1980 | Diana | 3,000 | | 350.00 | 395 |

Nobility Of Children - E. Hibel

1976	La Contessa Isabella	12,750		120.00	425
1977	Le Marquis Maurice Pierre	12,750		120.00	225
1978	Baronesse Johanna-Maryke Van Vollendam Tot Marken	12,750		130.00	175
1979	Chief Red Feather	12,750		140.00	200

Nordic Families - E. Hibel

| 1987 | A Tender Moment | 7,500 | | 79.00 | 95 |

Oriental Gold - E. Hibel

1975	Yasuko	2,000		275.00	3000
1976	Mr. Obata	2,000		275.00	2100
1978	Sakura	2,000		295.00	1800
1979	Michio	2,000		325.00	1500

Scandinavian Mother & Child - E. Hibel

1987	Pearl & Flowers	7,500		55.00	225
1989	Anemone & Violet	7,500		75.00	95
1990	Holly & Talia	7,500		75.00	85

To Life Annual - E. Hibel

1986	Golden's Child	5,000		99.00	200-275
1987	Triumph! Everyone A Winner	19,500		55.00	60
1988	The Whole Earth Bloomed as a Sacred Place	15,000		85.00	85
1989	Lovers of the Summer Palace	5,000		65.00	75

Edna Hibel Studios

YEAR ISSUE	EDITION LIMIT	YEAR RETD.	ISSUE PRICE	*QUOTE U.S.$
1992 People of the Fields	5,000		49.00	49

Tribute To All Children - E. Hibel

1984 Giselle	19,500		55.00	95
1984 Gerard	19,500		55.00	95
1985 Wendy	19,500		55.00	70-100
1986 Todd	19,500		55.00	125

The World I Love - E. Hibel

1981 Leah's Family	17,500		85.00	175-200
1982 Kaylin	17,500		85.00	375
1983 Edna's Music	17,500		85.00	195
1983 O' Hana	17,500		85.00	195

Edwin M. Knowles

Aesop's Fables - M. Hampshire

1988 The Goose That Laid the Golden Egg	Closed		27.90	30
1988 The Hare and the Tortoise	Closed		27.90	30
1988 The Fox and the Grapes	Closed		30.90	35
1989 The Lion And The Mouse	Closed		30.90	37
1989 The Milk Maid And Her Pail	Closed		30.90	32
1989 The Jay And The Peacock	Closed		30.90	32

American Innocents - Marsten/Mandrajji

1986 Abigail in the Rose Garden	Closed		19.50	20
1986 Ann by the Terrace	Closed		19.50	20
1986 Ellen and John in the Parlor	Closed		19.50	20
1986 William on the Rocking Horse	Closed		19.50	35

The American Journey - M. Kunstler

1987 Westward Ho	Closed		29.90	30
1988 Kitchen With a View	Closed		29.90	30
1988 Crossing the River	Closed		29.90	30
1988 Christmas at the New Cabin	Closed		29.90	30

Americana Holidays - D. Spaulding

1978 Fourth of July	Closed		26.00	26
1979 Thanksgiving	Closed		26.00	26
1980 Easter	Closed		26.00	26
1981 Valentine's Day	Closed		26.00	26
1982 Father's Day	Closed		26.00	26
1983 Christmas	Closed		26.00	26
1984 Mother's Day	Closed		26.00	27

Amy Brackenbury's Cat Tales - A. Brackenbury

1987 A Chance Meeting: White American Shorthairs	Closed		21.50	30
1987 Gone Fishing: Maine Coons	Closed		21.50	35
1988 Strawberries and Cream: Cream Persians	Closed		24.90	40
1988 Flower Bed: British Shorthairs	Closed		24.90	25
1988 Kittens and Mittens: Silver Tabbies	Closed		24.90	25
1988 All Wrapped Up: Himalayans	Closed		24.90	45

Animals of the American West - N. Glazier

1993 Youngblood	Closed		29.50	30
1993 Cat Nap	Closed		29.90	30
1993 Desert Bighorn Mormon Ridge	Closed		32.90	33
1993 Crown Prince	Closed		32.90	33

Annie - W. Chambers

1983 Annie and Sandy	Closed		19.00	25
1983 Daddy Warbucks	Closed		19.00	19
1983 Annie and Grace	Closed		19.00	19
1984 Annie and the Orphans	Closed		21.00	25
1985 Tomorrow	Closed		21.00	21
1986 Annie and Miss Hannigan	Closed		21.00	21
1986 Annie, Lily and Rooster	Closed		24.00	30
1986 Grand Finale	Closed		24.00	30

Baby Owls of North America - J. Thornbrugh

1991 Peek-A-Whoo: Screech Owls	Closed		27.90	37
1991 Forty Winks: Saw-Whet Owls	Closed		29.90	40
1991 The Tree House: Northern Pygmy Owls	Closed		30.90	45
1991 Three of a Kind: Great Horned Owls	Closed		30.90	35
1991 Out on a Limb: Great Gray Owls	Closed		30.90	40
1991 Beginning to Explore: Boreal Owls	Closed		32.90	50
1992 Three's Company: Long Eared Owls	Closed		32.90	40
1992 Whoo's There: Barred Owl	Closed		32.90	50

Backyard Harmony - J. Thornbrugh

1991 The Singing Lesson	Closed		27.90	35
1991 Welcoming a New Day	Closed		27.90	70
1991 Announcing Spring	Closed		30.90	55
1992 The Morning Harvest	Closed		30.90	45
1992 Spring Time Pride	Closed		30.90	55
1992 Treetop Serenade	Closed		32.90	60
1992 At The Peep Of Day	Closed		32.90	40
1992 Today's Discoveries	Closed		32.90	45

Bambi - Disney Studios

1992 Bashful Bambi	Closed		34.90	40
1992 Bambi's New Friends	Closed		34.90	60
1992 Hello Little Prince	Closed		37.90	40-50
1992 Bambi's Morning Greetings	Closed		37.90	45-60
1992 Bambi's Skating Lesson	Closed		37.90	115
1993 What's Up Possums?	Closed		37.90	60

Biblical Mothers - E. Licea

1983 Bathsheba and Solomon	Closed		39.50	40
1984 Judgment of Solomon	Closed		39.50	40
1984 Pharaoh's Daughter and Moses	Closed		39.50	40
1985 Mary and Jesus	Closed		39.50	40
1985 Sarah and Isaac	Closed		44.50	45
1986 Rebekah, Jacob and Esau	Closed		44.50	45

Birds of the Seasons - S. Timm

1990 Cardinals In Winter	Closed		24.90	30-55
1990 Bluebirds In Spring	Closed		24.90	35
1991 Nuthatches In Fall	Closed		27.90	35
1991 Baltimore Orioles In Summer	Closed		27.90	40
1991 Blue Jays In Early Fall	Closed		27.90	40-48
1991 Robins In Early Spring	Closed		27.90	33
1991 Cedar Waxwings in Fall	Closed		29.90	50-65
1991 Chickadees in Winter	Closed		29.90	60

Call of the Wilderness - K. Daniel

1991 First Outing	Closed		29.90	40
1991 Howling Lesson	Closed		29.90	100
1991 Silent Watch	Closed		32.90	55
1991 Winter Travelers	Closed		32.90	50
1992 Ahead of the Pack	Closed		32.90	55
1992 Northern Spirits	Closed		34.90	50
1992 Twilight Friends	Closed		34.90	50
1992 A New Future	Closed		34.90	50
1992 Morning Mist	Closed		36.90	37
1992 The Silent One	150-day		36.90	37

Carousel - D. Brown

1987 If I Loved You	Closed		24.90	25
1988 Mr. Snow	Closed		24.90	25
1988 The Carousel Waltz	Closed		24.90	25
1988 You'll Never Walk Alone	Closed		24.90	25

Casablanca - J. Griffin

1990 Here's Looking At You, Kid	Closed		34.90	35
1990 We'll Always Have Paris	Closed		34.90	37
1991 We Loved Each Other Once	Closed		37.90	35
1991 Rick's Cafe Americain	Closed		37.90	40
1991 A Franc For Your Thoughts	Closed		37.90	50
1991 Play it Sam	Closed		37.90	55

Castari Grandparent - J. Castari

1980 Bedtime Story	Closed		18.00	18
1981 The Skating Lesson	Closed		20.00	25
1982 The Cookie Tasting	Closed		20.00	25
1983 The Swinger	Closed		20.00	25
1984 The Skating Queen	Closed		22.00	22
1985 The Patriot's Parade	Closed		22.00	22
1986 The Home Run	Closed		22.00	22
1987 The Sneak Preview	Closed		22.00	22

China's Natural Treasures - T.C. Chiu

1992 The Siberian Tiger	Closed		29.90	40
1992 The Snow Leopard	Closed		29.90	40
1992 The Giant Panda	Closed		32.90	45
1992 The Tibetan Brown Bear	Closed		32.90	40
1992 The Asian Elephant	Closed		32.90	50
1992 The Golden Monkey	Closed		34.90	50

Christmas in the City - A. Leimanis

1992 A Christmas Snowfall	Closed		34.90	35
1992 Yuletide Celebration	Closed		34.90	55
1993 Holiday Cheer	Closed		34.90	60
1993 The Magic of Christmas	Closed		34.90	60

Cinderella - Disney Studios

1988 Bibbidi, Bobbidi, Boo	Closed		29.90	50-70
1988 A Dream Is A Wish Your Heart Makes	Closed		29.90	50
1989 Oh Sing Sweet Nightingale	Closed		32.90	60
1989 A Dress For Cinderelly	Closed		32.90	75-100
1989 So This Is Love	Closed		32.90	50-70
1990 At The Stroke Of Midnight	Closed		32.90	60
1990 If The Shoe Fits	Closed		34.90	65
1990 Happily Ever After	Closed		34.90	35

Classic Fairy Tales - S. Gustafson

1991 Goldilocks and the Three Bears	Closed		29.90	50
1991 Little Red Riding Hood	Closed		29.90	50
1991 The Three Little Pigs	Closed		32.90	50
1991 The Frog Prince	Closed		32.90	60
1992 Jack and the Beanstalk	Closed		32.90	50
1992 Hansel and Gretel	Closed		34.90	60
1992 Puss in Boots	Closed		34.90	40
1992 Tom Thumb	Closed		34.90	40

Classic Mother Goose - S. Gustafson

1992 Little Miss Muffet	Closed		29.90	35
1992 Mary had a Little Lamb	Closed		29.90	45
1992 Mary, Mary, Quite Contrary	Closed		29.90	50
1992 Little Bo Peep	Closed		29.90	50

Cozy Country Corners - H. H. Ingmire

1990 Lazy Morning	Closed		24.90	45
1990 Warm Retreat	Closed		24.90	40
1991 A Sunny Spot	Closed		27.90	40
1991 Attic Afternoon	Closed		27.90	45
1991 Mirror Mischief	Closed		27.90	50
1991 Hide and Seek	Closed		29.90	45
1991 Apple Antics	Closed		29.90	65
1991 Table Trouble	Closed		29.90	60

Ency. Brit. Birds of Your Garden - K. Daniel

1985 Cardinal	Closed		19.50	35
1985 Blue Jay	Closed		19.50	20
1985 Oriole	Closed		22.50	25
1986 Chickadees	Closed		22.50	25
1986 Bluebird	Closed		22.50	30
1986 Robin	Closed		22.50	30
1986 Hummingbird	Closed		24.50	25
1987 Goldfinch	Closed		24.50	30
1987 Downy Woodpecker	Closed		24.50	25
1987 Cedar Waxwing	Closed		24.50	35

Eve Licea Christmas - E. Licea

1987 The Annunciation	Closed		44.90	50
1988 The Nativity	Closed		44.90	50
1989 Adoration Of The Shepherds	Closed		49.90	53
1990 Journey Of The Magi	Closed		49.90	50
1991 Gifts Of The Magi	Closed		49.90	50
1992 Rest on the Flight into Egypt	Closed		49.90	65

Fantasia: (The Sorcerer's Apprentice) Golden Anniversary - Disney Studios

1990 The Apprentice's Dream	Closed		29.90	70
1990 Mischievous Apprentice	Closed		29.90	80
1991 Dreams of Power	Closed		32.90	50
1991 Mickey's Magical Whirlpool	Closed		32.90	45
1991 Wizardry Gone Wild	Closed		32.90	45
1991 Mickey Makes Magic	Closed		34.90	63
1991 The Penitent Apprentice	Closed		34.90	40
1992 An Apprentice Again	Closed		34.90	50

Father's Love - B. Bradley

1984 Open Wide	Closed		19.50	20
1984 Batter Up	Closed		19.50	20
1985 Little Shaver	Closed		19.50	20
1985 Swing Time	Closed		22.50	23

Field Puppies - L. Kaatz

1987 Dog Tired-The Springer Spaniel	Closed		24.90	45-60
1987 Caught in the Act-The Golden Retriever	Closed		24.90	40-60
1988 Missing/Point/Irish Setter	Closed		27.90	30-35
1988 A Perfect Set-Labrador	Closed		27.90	35-50
1988 Fritz's Folly-German Shorthaired Pointer	Closed		27.90	35-42
1988 Shirt Tales: Cocker Spaniel	Closed		27.90	40-51
1989 Fine Feathered Friends-English Setter	Closed		29.90	30-42
1989 Command Performance/ Wiemaraner	Closed		29.90	35-40

Field Trips - L. Kaatz

1990 Gone Fishing	Closed		24.90	25
1991 Ducking Duty	Closed		24.90	25
1991 Boxed In	Closed		27.90	28
1991 Pups 'N Boots	Closed		27.90	28
1991 Puppy Tales	Closed		27.90	28
1991 Pail Pals	Closed		29.90	35
1991 Chesapeake Bay Retrievers	Closed		29.90	32
1991 Hat Trick	Closed		29.90	30

First Impressions - J. Giordano

1991 Taking a Gander	Closed		29.90	40
1991 Two's Company	Closed		29.90	35
1991 Fine Feathered Friends	Closed		32.90	45
1991 What's Up?	Closed		32.90	45
1991 All Ears	Closed		32.90	65
1992 Between Friends	Closed		32.90	35

The Four Ancient Elements - G. Lambert

1984 Earth	Closed		27.50	28
1984 Water	Closed		27.50	28
1985 Air	Closed		29.50	30
1985 Fire	Closed		29.50	40

Frances Hook Legacy - F. Hook

1985 Fascination	Closed		19.50	22
1985 Daydreaming	Closed		19.50	22
1986 Discovery	Closed		22.50	25
1986 Disappointment	Closed		22.50	23
1986 Wonderment	Closed		22.50	25
1987 Expectation	Closed		22.50	23

Free as the Wind - M. Budden

1992 Skyward	Closed		29.90	55
1992 Aloft	Closed		29.90	60
1992 Airborne	Closed		32.90	35
1993 Flight	Closed		32.90	50
1993 Ascent	Closed		32.90	40
1993 Heavenward	Closed		32.90	33

Friends I Remember - J. Down

1983 Fish Story	Closed		17.50	18
1984 Office Hours	Closed		17.50	18
1985 A Coat of Paint	Closed		17.50	18
1985 Here Comes the Bride	Closed		19.50	20

Year Issue		Edition Limit/Retd.	Issue Price	*Quote U.S.$
1985	Fringe Benefits	Closed	19.50	20
1986	High Society	Closed	19.50	20
1986	Flower Arrangement	Closed	21.50	22
1986	Taste Test	Closed	21.50	22

Friends of the Forest - K. Daniel

Year	Issue	Edition Limit/Retd.	Issue Price	*Quote U.S.$
1987	The Rabbit	Closed	24.50	27-35
1987	The Raccoon	Closed	24.50	30
1987	The Squirrel	Closed	27.90	30
1988	The Chipmunk	Closed	27.90	30
1988	The Fox	Closed	27.90	30
1988	The Otter	Closed	27.90	30

Garden Secrets - B. Higgins Bond

Year	Issue	Edition Limit/Retd.	Issue Price	*Quote U.S.$
1993	Nine Lives	Closed	24.90	45
1993	Floral Purr-fume	Closed	24.90	50
1993	Bloomin' Kitties	Closed	24.90	50
1993	Kitty Corner	Closed	24.90	50
1993	Flower Fanciers	Closed	24.90	60
1993	Meadow Mischief	Closed	24.90	25
1993	Pussycat Potpourri	150-day	24.90	25
1993	Frisky Business	150-day	24.90	25

Gone with the Wind - R. Kursar

Year	Issue	Edition Limit/Retd.	Issue Price	*Quote U.S.$
1978	Scarlett	Closed	21.50	150-300
1979	Ashley	Closed	21.50	70-100
1980	Melanie	Closed	21.50	40
1981	Rhett	Closed	23.50	35-50
1982	Mammy Lacing Scarlett	Closed	23.50	50-70
1983	Melanie Gives Birth	Closed	23.50	45-70
1984	Scarlet's Green Dress	Closed	25.50	45-70
1985	Rhett and Bonnie	Closed	25.50	70-95
1985	Scarlett and Rhett: The Finale	Closed	29.50	50-70

Great Cats Of The Americas - L. Cable

Year	Issue	Edition Limit/Retd.	Issue Price	*Quote U.S.$
1989	The Jaguar	Closed	29.90	35-50
1989	The Cougar	Closed	29.90	40-50
1989	The Lynx	Closed	32.90	40-50
1990	The Ocelot	Closed	32.90	40-50
1990	The Bobcat	Closed	32.90	40-50
1990	The Jaguarundi	Closed	32.90	40-50
1990	The Margay	Closed	34.90	40-50
1991	The Pampas Cat	Closed	34.90	40-50

Heirlooms And Lace - C. Layton

Year	Issue	Edition Limit/Retd.	Issue Price	*Quote U.S.$
1989	Anna	Closed	34.90	40
1989	Victoria	Closed	34.90	55
1990	Tess	Closed	37.90	70
1990	Olivia	Closed	37.90	100
1991	Bridget	Closed	37.90	85
1991	Rebecca	Closed	37.90	70

Hibel Christmas - E. Hibel

Year	Issue	Edition Limit/Retd.	Issue Price	*Quote U.S.$
1985	The Angel's Message	Closed	45.00	45
1986	The Gifts of the Magi	Closed	45.00	45
1987	The Flight Into Egypt	Closed	49.00	49
1988	Adoration of the Shepherd	Closed	49.00	50-60
1989	Peaceful Kingdom	Closed	49.00	49
1990	Nativity	Closed	49.00	60

Home Sweet Home - R. McGinnis

Year	Issue	Edition Limit/Retd.	Issue Price	*Quote U.S.$
1989	The Victorian	Closed	39.90	40
1989	The Greek Revival	Closed	39.90	40
1989	The Georgian	Closed	39.90	40
1990	The Mission	Closed	39.90	40

It's a Dog's Life - L. Kaatz

Year	Issue	Edition Limit/Retd.	Issue Price	*Quote U.S.$
1992	We've Been Spotted	Closed	29.90	30
1992	Literary Labs	Closed	29.90	30
1993	Retrieving Our Dignity	Closed	32.90	42
1993	Lodging a Complaint	150-day	32.90	33
1993	Barreling Along	150-day	32.90	33
1993	Play Ball	150-day	34.90	35
1993	Dogs and Suds	150-day	34.90	35
1993	Paws for a Picnic	150-day	34.90	35

J. W. Smith Childhood Holidays - J. W. Smith

Year	Issue	Edition Limit/Retd.	Issue Price	*Quote U.S.$
1986	Easter	Closed	19.50	21
1986	Thanksgiving	Closed	19.50	20
1986	Christmas	Closed	19.50	20
1986	Valentine's Day	Closed	22.50	23
1987	Mother's Day	Closed	22.50	23
1987	Fourth of July	Closed	22.50	23

Jerner's Less Traveled Road - B. Jerner

Year	Issue	Edition Limit/Retd.	Issue Price	*Quote U.S.$
1988	The Weathered Barn	Closed	29.90	30
1988	The Murmuring Stream	Closed	29.90	30
1988	The Covered Bridge	Closed	32.90	38
1989	Winter's Peace	Closed	32.90	33
1989	The Flowering Meadow	Closed	32.90	33
1989	The Hidden Waterfall	Closed	32.90	33

Jewels of the Flowers - T.C. Chiu

Year	Issue	Edition Limit/Retd.	Issue Price	*Quote U.S.$
1991	Sapphire Wings	Closed	29.90	30
1991	Topaz Beauties	Closed	29.90	50
1991	Amethyst Flight	Closed	32.90	35
1991	Ruby Elegance	Closed	32.90	45
1991	Emerald Pair	Closed	32.90	50
1991	Opal Splendor	Closed	34.90	40
1992	Pearl Luster	Closed	34.90	55
1992	Aquamarine Glimmer	Closed	34.90	35

Keepsake Rhymes - S. Gustafson

Year	Issue	Edition Limit/Retd.	Issue Price	*Quote U.S.$
1992	Humpty Dumpty	Closed	29.90	35
1993	Peter Pumpkin Eater	Closed	29.90	80
1993	Pat-a-Cake	Closed	29.90	105
1993	Old King Cole	Closed	29.90	50

The King and I - W. Chambers

Year	Issue	Edition Limit/Retd.	Issue Price	*Quote U.S.$
1984	A Puzzlement	Closed	19.50	20
1985	Shall We Dance?	Closed	19.50	30
1985	Getting to Know You	Closed	19.50	20
1985	We Kiss in a Shadow	Closed	19.50	20

Lady and the Tramp - Disney Studios

Year	Issue	Edition Limit/Retd.	Issue Price	*Quote U.S.$
1992	First Date	Closed	34.90	70
1992	Puppy Love	Closed	34.90	70
1992	Dog Pound Blues	Closed	37.90	50
1993	Merry Christmas To All	Closed	37.90	55
1993	Double Siamese Trouble	Closed	37.90	65
1993	Ruff House	Closed	39.90	45
1993	Telling Tails	Closed	39.90	40
1993	Moonlight Romance	Closed	39.90	40

Lincoln, Man of America - M. Kunstler

Year	Issue	Edition Limit/Retd.	Issue Price	*Quote U.S.$
1986	The Gettysburg Address	Closed	24.50	25-30
1987	The Inauguration	Closed	24.50	25
1987	The Lincoln-Douglas Debates	Closed	27.50	28
1987	Beginnings in New Salem	Closed	27.90	28
1988	The Family Man	Closed	27.90	28
1988	Emancipation Proclamation	Closed	27.90	28

Living with Nature-Jerner's Ducks - B. Jerner

Year	Issue	Edition Limit/Retd.	Issue Price	*Quote U.S.$
1986	The Pintail	Closed	19.50	25-40
1986	The Mallard	Closed	19.50	30-40
1987	The Wood Duck	Closed	22.50	30-40
1987	The Green-Winged Teal	Closed	22.50	35
1987	The Northern Shoveler	Closed	22.90	30
1987	The American Widgeon	Closed	22.90	35
1987	The Gadwall	Closed	24.90	30
1988	The Blue-Winged Teal	Closed	24.90	30

Majestic Birds of North America - D. Smith

Year	Issue	Edition Limit/Retd.	Issue Price	*Quote U.S.$
1988	The Bald Eagle	Closed	29.90	30-40
1988	Peregrine Falcon	Closed	29.90	30
1988	The Great Horned Owl	Closed	32.90	33
1989	The Red-Tailed Hawk	Closed	32.90	33
1989	The White Gyrfalcon	Closed	32.90	33
1989	The American Kestral	Closed	32.90	33
1990	The Osprey	Closed	34.90	35
1990	The Golden Eagle	Closed	34.90	35

Mary Poppins - M. Hampshire

Year	Issue	Edition Limit/Retd.	Issue Price	*Quote U.S.$
1989	Mary Poppins	Closed	29.90	50
1989	A Spoonful of Sugar	Closed	29.90	40
1990	A Jolly Holiday With Mary	Closed	32.90	40
1990	We Love To Laugh	Closed	32.90	45
1991	Chim Chim Cher-ee	Closed	32.90	39
1991	Tuppence a Bag	Closed	32.90	50

Mickey's Christmas Carol - Disney Studios

Year	Issue	Edition Limit/Retd.	Issue Price	*Quote U.S.$
1992	Bah Humbug!	Closed	29.90	35
1992	What's So Merry About Christmas?	Closed	29.90	45
1993	God Bless Us Every One	Closed	32.90	50
1993	A Christmas Surprise	Closed	32.90	33
1993	Yuletide Greetings	Closed	32.90	33
1993	Marley's Warning	Closed	34.90	35
1993	A Cozy Christmas	150-day	34.90	35
1993	A Christmas Feast	150-day	34.90	35

Musical Moments From the Wizard of Oz - K. Milnazik

Year	Issue	Edition Limit/Retd.	Issue Price	*Quote U.S.$
1993	Over the Rainbow	Closed	29.90	55
1993	We're Off to See the Wizard	Closed	29.90	65
1993	Munchkin Land	Closed	29.90	65
1994	If I Only Had a Brain	Closed	29.90	75
1994	Ding Dong The Witch is Dead	Closed	29.90	30
1993	The Lullabye League	95-day	29.90	30
1994	If I Were King of the Forest	95-day	29.90	30
1994	Merry Old Land of Oz	95-day	29.90	30

My Fair Lady - W. Chambers

Year	Issue	Edition Limit/Retd.	Issue Price	*Quote U.S.$
1989	Opening Day at Ascot	Closed	24.90	25
1989	I Could Have Danced All Night	Closed	24.90	25
1989	The Rain in Spain	Closed	27.90	28
1989	Show Me	Closed	27.90	28
1990	Get Me To/Church On Time	Closed	27.90	28
1990	I've Grown Accustomed/Face	Closed	27.90	40

Nature's Child - M. Jobe

Year	Issue	Edition Limit/Retd.	Issue Price	*Quote U.S.$
1990	Sharing	Closed	29.90	31
1990	The Lost Lamb	Closed	29.90	30
1990	Seems Like Yesterday	Closed	32.90	35
1990	Faithful Friends	Closed	32.90	55
1990	Trusted Companion	Closed	32.90	50
1991	Hand in Hand	Closed	32.90	55

Nature's Nursery - J. Thornbrugh

Year	Issue	Edition Limit/Retd.	Issue Price	*Quote U.S.$
1992	Testing the Waters	Closed	29.90	50
1993	Taking the Plunge	Closed	29.90	40
1993	Race Ya Mom	Closed	29.90	46
1993	Time to Wake Up	Closed	29.90	50
1993	Hide and Seek	Closed	29.90	45
1993	Piggyback Ride	Closed	29.90	30

Not So Long Ago - J. W. Smith

Year	Issue	Edition Limit/Retd.	Issue Price	*Quote U.S.$
1988	Story Time	Closed	24.90	25
1988	Wash Day for Dolly	Closed	24.90	30
1988	Suppertime for Kitty	Closed	24.90	30
1988	Mother's Little Helper	Closed	24.90	30

Oklahoma! - M. Kunstler

Year	Issue	Edition Limit/Retd.	Issue Price	*Quote U.S.$
1985	Oh, What a Beautiful Mornin'	Closed	19.50	25
1986	Surrey with the Fringe on Top'	Closed	19.50	25
1986	I Cain't Say No	Closed	19.50	25
1986	Oklahoma!	Closed	19.50	25

The Old Mill Stream - C. Tennant

Year	Issue	Edition Limit/Retd.	Issue Price	*Quote U.S.$
1991	New London Grist Mill	Closed	39.90	40
1991	Wayside Inn Grist Mill	Closed	39.90	45
1991	The Red Mill	Closed	39.90	40
1991	Glade Creek Grist Mill	Closed	39.90	45

Old-Fashioned Favorites - M. Weber

Year	Issue	Edition Limit/Retd.	Issue Price	*Quote U.S.$
1991	Apple Crisp	Closed	29.90	75
1991	Blueberry Muffins	Closed	29.90	65
1991	Peach Cobbler	Closed	29.90	98
1991	Chocolate Chip Oatmeal Cookies	Closed	29.90	190

Once Upon a Time - K. Pritchett

Year	Issue	Edition Limit/Retd.	Issue Price	*Quote U.S.$
1988	Little Red Riding Hood	Closed	24.90	25
1988	Rapunzel	Closed	24.90	25
1988	Three Little Pigs	Closed	27.90	30
1989	The Princess and the Pea	Closed	27.90	30
1989	Goldilocks and the Three Bears	Closed	27.90	30
1989	Beauty and the Beast	Closed	27.90	45

Pinocchio - Disney Studios

Year	Issue	Edition Limit/Retd.	Issue Price	*Quote U.S.$
1989	Gepetto Creates Pinocchio	Closed	29.90	55-65
1990	Pinocchio And The Blue Fairy	Closed	29.90	80
1990	It's an Actor's Life For Me	Closed	32.90	50
1990	I've Got No Strings On Me	Closed	32.90	45
1991	Pleasure Island	Closed	32.90	45
1991	A Real Boy	Closed	32.90	50

Portraits of Motherhood - W. Chambers

Year	Issue	Edition Limit/Retd.	Issue Price	*Quote U.S.$
1987	Mother's Here	Closed	29.50	30
1988	First Touch	Closed	29.50	30

Precious Little Ones - M. T. Fangel

Year	Issue	Edition Limit/Retd.	Issue Price	*Quote U.S.$
1988	Little Red Robins	Closed	29.90	30
1988	Little Fledglings	Closed	29.90	30
1988	Saturday Night Bath	Closed	29.90	33
1988	Peek-A-Boo	Closed	29.90	32

Proud Sentinels of the American West - N. Glazier

Year	Issue	Edition Limit/Retd.	Issue Price	*Quote U.S.$
1993	Youngblood	Closed	29.90	55
1993	Cat Nap	Closed	29.90	70
1993	Desert Bighorn-Mormon Ridge	Closed	32.90	50
1993	Crown Prince	Closed	32.90	60

Purrfect Point of View - J. Giordano

Year	Issue	Edition Limit/Retd.	Issue Price	*Quote U.S.$
1992	Unexpected Visitors	Closed	29.90	30
1992	Wistful Morning	Closed	29.90	50
1992	Afternoon Catnap	Closed	29.90	50
1992	Cozy Company	Closed	29.90	35

Pussyfooting Around - C. Wilson

Year	Issue	Edition Limit/Retd.	Issue Price	*Quote U.S.$
1991	Fish Tales	Closed	24.90	25
1991	Teatime Tabbies	Closed	24.90	25
1991	Yarn Spinners	Closed	24.90	30
1991	Two Maestros	Closed	24.90	32

Romantic Age of Steam - R.B. Pierce

Year	Issue	Edition Limit/Retd.	Issue Price	*Quote U.S.$
1992	The Empire Builder	Closed	29.90	35
1992	The Broadway Limited	Closed	29.90	55
1992	Twentieth Century Limited	Closed	32.90	50
1992	The Chief	Closed	32.90	70
1992	The Crescent Limited	Closed	32.90	65
1993	The Overland Limited	Closed	34.90	50
1993	The Jupiter	Closed	34.90	55
1993	The Daylight	Closed	34.90	50

Santa's Christmas - T. Browning

Year	Issue	Edition Limit/Retd.	Issue Price	*Quote U.S.$
1991	Santa's Love	Closed	29.90	40
1991	Santa's Cheer	Closed	29.90	40
1991	Santa's Promise	Closed	32.90	67
1991	Santa's Gift	Closed	32.90	75
1992	Santa's Surprise	Closed	32.90	55
1992	Santa's Magic	Closed	32.90	55

Season For Song - M. Jobe

Year	Issue	Edition Limit/Retd.	Issue Price	*Quote U.S.$
1991	Winter Concert	Closed	34.90	43
1991	Snowy Symphony	Closed	34.90	45
1991	Frosty Chorus	Closed	34.90	70
1991	Silver Serenade	Closed	34.90	50

Seasons of Splendor - K. Randle

Year	Issue	Edition Limit/Retd.	Issue Price	*Quote U.S.$
1992	Autumn's Grandeur	Closed	29.90	40
1992	School Days	Closed	29.90	40
1992	Woodland Mill Stream	Closed	32.90	65
1992	Harvest Memories	Closed	32.90	55
1992	A Country Weekend	Closed	32.90	60
1993	Indian Summer	Closed	32.90	60

Collectors' Information Bureau *Quotes have been rounded up to nearest dollar

YEAR ISSUE	EDITION LIMIT	YEAR RETD.	ISSUE PRICE	*QUOTE U.S. $

Shadows and Light: Winter's Wildlife - N. Glazier

YEAR ISSUE	EDITION LIMIT	YEAR RETD.	ISSUE PRICE	*QUOTE
1993 Winter's Children	Closed		29.90	50
1993 Cub Scouts	Closed		29.90	50
1993 Little Snowman	Closed		29.90	50
1993 The Snow Cave	Closed		29.90	40

Singin' In The Rain - M. Skolsky

1990 Singin' In The Rain	Closed		32.90	35
1990 Good Morning	Closed		32.90	34
1991 Broadway Melody	Closed		32.90	40
1991 We're Happy Again	Closed		32.90	50

Sleeping Beauty - Disney Studios

1991 Once Upon A Dream	Closed		39.90	50
1991 Awakened by a Kiss	Closed		39.90	75-100
1991 Happy Birthday Briar Rose	Closed		42.90	55
1992 Together At Last	Closed		42.90	50

Small Blessings - C. Layton

1992 Now I Lay Me Down to Sleep	Closed		29.90	35
1992 Bless Us O Lord For These, Thy Gifts	Closed		29.90	35
1992 Jesus Loves Me, This I Know	Closed		32.90	40
1992 This Little Light of Mine	Closed		32.90	55
1992 Blessed Are The Pure In Heart	Closed		32.90	45
1993 Bless Our Home	Closed		32.90	40

Snow White and the Seven Dwarfs - Disney Studios

1991 The Dance of Snow White/Seven Dwarfs	Closed		29.90	50-100
1991 With a Smile and a Song	Closed		29.90	40
1991 A Special Treat	Closed		32.90	40
1992 A Kiss for Dopey	Closed		32.90	50
1992 The Poison Apple	Closed		32.90	50-70
1992 Fireside Love Story	Closed		34.90	55
1992 Stubborn Grumpy	Closed		34.90	50
1992 A Wish Come True	Closed		34.90	45
1993 Time to Tidy Up	Closed		34.50	50-60
1993 May I Have This Dance?	Closed		36.90	45
1993 A Surprise in the Clearing	Closed		36.50	50
1993 Happy Ending	Closed		36.90	55

Songs of the American Spirit - H. Bond

1991 The Star Spangled Banner	Closed		29.90	30
1991 Battle Hymn of the Republic	Closed		29.90	45
1991 America the Beautiful	Closed		29.90	35
1991 My Country 'Tis of Thee	Closed		29.90	65

Sound of Music - T. Crnkovich

1986 Sound of Music	Closed		19.50	20
1986 Do-Re-Mi	Closed		19.50	20
1986 My Favorite Things	Closed		22.50	23
1986 Laendler Waltz	Closed		22.50	25
1987 Edelweiss	Closed		22.50	23
1987 I Have Confidence	Closed		22.50	23
1987 Maria	Closed		24.90	25
1987 Climb Ev'ry Mountain	Closed		24.90	30

South Pacific - E. Gignilliat

1987 Some Enchanted Evening	Closed		24.50	25
1987 Happy Talk	Closed		24.50	25
1987 Dites Moi	Closed		24.90	25
1988 Honey Bun	Closed		24.90	25

Stately Owls - J. Beaudoin

1989 The Snowy Owl	Closed		29.90	50
1989 The Great Horned Owl	Closed		29.90	45
1990 The Barn Owl	Closed		32.90	35
1990 The Screech Owl	Closed		32.90	35
1990 The Short-Eared Owl	Closed		32.90	33
1990 The Barred Owl	Closed		32.90	35
1990 The Great Grey Owl	Closed		32.90	35
1991 The Saw-Whet Owl	Closed		34.90	35

Sundblom Santas - H. Sundblom

1989 Santa By The Fire	Closed		27.90	30
1990 Christmas Vigil	Closed		27.90	35
1991 To All A Good Night	Closed		32.90	65
1992 Santa's on His Way	Closed		32.90	65

A Swan is Born - L. Roberts

1987 Hopes and Dreams	Closed		24.50	25
1987 At the Barre	Closed		24.50	25
1987 In Position	Closed		24.50	30
1988 Just For Size	Closed		24.50	45

Sweetness and Grace - J. Welty

1992 God Bless Teddy	Closed		34.90	40
1992 Sunshine and Smiles	Closed		34.90	55
1992 Favorite Buddy	Closed		34.90	45
1992 Sweet Dreams	Closed		34.90	60

Thomas Kinkade's Garden Cottages of England - T. Kinkade

1991 Chandler's Cottage	Closed		27.90	60-100
1991 Cedar Nook Cottage	Closed		27.90	45-70
1991 Candlelit Cottage	Closed		30.90	50-75
1991 Open Gate Cottage	Closed		30.90	40-70
1991 McKenna's Cottage	Closed		30.90	45-80
1992 Woodsman's Thatch Cottage	Closed		32.90	45-70
1992 Merritt's Cottage	Closed		32.90	60-90
1992 Stonegate Cottage	Closed		32.90	60-90

Thomas Kinkade's Home for the Holidays - T. Kinkade

YEAR ISSUE	EDITION LIMIT	YEAR RETD.	ISSUE PRICE	*QUOTE U.S.$
1991 Sleigh Ride Home	Closed		29.90	50-70
1991 Home to Grandma's	Closed		29.90	45-70
1991 Home Before Christmas	Closed		32.90	50-90
1992 The Warmth of Home	Closed		32.90	60-80
1992 Homespun Holiday	Closed		32.90	55-80
1992 Hometime Yuletide	Closed		34.90	50-80
1992 Home Away From Home	Closed		34.90	75-100
1992 The Journey Home	Closed		34.90	50-70

Thomas Kinkade's Home is Where the Heart Is - T. Kinkade

1992 Home Sweet Home	Closed		29.90	60-120
1992 A Warm Welcome Home	Closed		29.90	60-80
1992 A Carriage Ride Home	Closed		32.90	50-90
1993 Amber Afternoon	Closed		32.90	35-75
1993 Country Memories	Closed		32.90	90-100
1993 The Twilight Cafe	Closed		34.90	50-60
1993 Our Summer Home	Closed		34.90	40-45
1993 Hometown Hospitality	Closed		34.90	40-45

Thomas Kinkade's Thomashire - T. Kinkade

1992 Olde Porterfield Tea Room	Closed		29.90	45-70
1992 Olde Thomashire Mill	Closed		29.90	50-90
1992 Swanbrook Cottage	Closed		32.90	65-125
1992 Pye Corner Cottage	Closed		32.90	60-80
1993 Blossom Hill Church	Closed		32.90	40-70
1993 Olde Garden Cottage	Closed		32.90	65

Thomas Kinkade's Yuletide Memories - T. Kinkade

1992 The Magic of Christmas	Closed		29.90	65-95
1992 A Beacon of Faith	Closed		29.90	50-90
1993 Moonlit Sleighride	Closed		29.90	60-90
1993 Silent Night	Closed		29.90	80
1993 Olde Porterfield Gift Shoppe	Closed		29.90	60-90
1993 The Wonder of the Season	Closed		29.90	65-85
1993 A Winter's Walk	Closed		29.90	40
1993 Skater's Delight	150-day		32.90	45

Tom Sawyer - W. Chambers

1987 Whitewashing the Fence	Closed		27.50	28
1987 Tom and Becky	Closed		27.90	28
1987 Tom Sawyer the Pirate	Closed		27.90	28
1988 First Pipes	Closed		27.90	28

Under Mother's Wing - J. Beaudoin

1992 Arctic Spring: Snowy Owls	Closed		29.90	40
1992 Forest's Edge: Great Gray Owls	Closed		29.90	40
1992 Treetop Trio: Long-Eared Owls	Closed		32.90	45
1992 Woodland Watch: Spotted Owls	Closed		32.90	60
1992 Vast View: Saw Whet Owls	Closed		32.90	50
1992 Lofty-Limb: Great Horned Owl	Closed		34.90	50
1993 Perfect Perch: Barred Owls	Closed		34.90	45
1993 Happy Home: Short-Eared Owl	Closed		34.90	50

Upland Birds of North America - W. Anderson

1986 The Pheasant	Closed		24.50	30
1986 The Grouse	Closed		24.50	30
1987 The Quail	Closed		27.50	32
1987 The Wild Turkey	Closed		27.50	32
1987 The Gray Partridge	Closed		27.50	32
1987 The Woodcock	Closed		27.90	32

Wizard of Oz - J. Auckland

1977 Over the Rainbow	Closed		19.00	40-70
1978 If I Only Had a Brain	Closed		19.00	40
1978 If I Only Had a Heart	Closed		19.00	45
1978 If I Were King of the Forest	Closed		19.00	40-45
1979 Wicked Witch of the West	Closed		19.00	50-65
1979 Follow the Yellow Brick Road	Closed		19.00	50
1979 Wonderful Wizard of Oz	Closed		19.00	50-60
1980 The Grand Finale	Closed		24.00	45-55

Wizard of Oz: A National Treasure - R. Laslo

1991 Yellow Brick Road	Closed		29.90	45
1992 I Haven't Got a Brain	Closed		29.90	45
1992 I'm a Little Rusty Yet	Closed		32.90	45
1992 I Even Scare Myself	Closed		32.90	55
1992 We're Off To See the Wizard	Closed		32.90	65
1992 I'll Never Get Home	Closed		34.90	60
1992 I'm Melting	Closed		34.90	95
1992 There's No Place Like Home	Closed		34.90	70

Yesterday's Innocents - J. Wilcox Smith

1992 My First Book	Closed		29.90	50
1992 Time to Smell the Roses	Closed		29.90	55
1993 Hush, Baby's Sleeping	Closed		32.90	40
1993 Ready and Waiting	Closed		32.90	50

Enchantica

Retired Enchantica Collection - Various

YEAR ISSUE	EDITION LIMIT	YEAR RETD.	ISSUE PRICE	*QUOTE U.S.$
1992 Winter Dragon-Grawlfang-2200 - J. Woodward	15,000	1993	50.00	75
1992 Spring Dragon-Gorgoyle-2201 - J. Woodward	15,000	1993	50.00	75
1993 Summer Dragon-Arangast-2202 - J. Woodward	15,000	1993	50.00	75
1993 Autumn Dragon-Snarlgard-2203 - J. Woodward	15,000	1993	50.00	75

Enesco Corporation

Barbie-Bob Mackie - Enesco

YEAR ISSUE	EDITION LIMIT	YEAR RETD.	ISSUE PRICE	*QUOTE U.S.$
1996 Queen of Hearts Barbie-157678	Open		25.00	25

Barbie-Bob Mackie JC Penney Exclusive - Enesco

1995 Queen of Hearts Barbie-11276	7,500	1995	30.00	30

Barbie-FAO Schwarz Exclusive - Enesco

1994 Silver Screen Barbie-128805	3,600	1995	30.00	30
1995 Circus Star Barbie-150339	3,600	1995	30.00	30

Barbie-Glamour - Enesco

1996 Here Comes The Bride, 1966-170984	Open		30.00	30
1996 Holiday Dance, 1965-188786	10,000		30.00	30

Barbie-Great Eras - Enesco

1996 Gibson Girl Barbie-174769	10,000		30.00	30
1996 1920's Flapper Barbie-174777	10,000		30.00	30

Barbie-Happy Holiday - Enesco

1994 Happy Holidays Barbie, 1994 -115088	5,000	1994	30.00	100-150
1995 Happy Holidays Barbie, 1995 -143154	Yr.Iss.	1995	30.00	30
1995 Happy Holidays Barbie, 1988 -154180	Yr.Iss.	1995	30.00	30
1996 Happy Holidays Barbie, 1989 -188859	Yr.Iss.		30.00	30
1996 Happy Holidays Barbie, 1996 -188816	Yr.Iss.		30.00	30

Barbie-Hollywood Legends - Enesco

1996 Barbie As Scarlett O'Hara in Green Velvet-171085	10,000	1996	30.00	35

Barbie-Nostalgic - Enesco

1994 35th Anniversary Barbie-655112	5,000	1994	30.00	30
1995 Barbie Solo In The Spotlight, 1959-114383	5,000	1995	30.00	45
1996 Barbie Enchanted Evening, 1960-175587	10,000	1995	30.00	30

Cherished Teddies Cherished Seasons - P. Hillman

1997 Spring-"Spring Brings A Season of Beauty"-203386	Open		35.00	35
1997 Summer-"Summer Brings A Season of Warmth"-203394	Open		35.00	35
1997 Autumn-"Autumn Brings A Season of Thanksgiving"-203408	Open		35.00	35
1997 Winter "Winter Brings A Season of Joy"-203416	Open		35.00	35

Cherished Teddies Christmas - P. Hillman

1995 Girl in Green Dress Dtd 95 -141550	Yr.Iss.		35.00	35
1996 Angel w/Birds Dtd 96-176060	Yr.Iss.		35.00	35

Cherished Teddies Easter - P. Hillman

1996 Bear in Bunny Outfit Dtd 96 -156590	Yr.Iss.		35.00	35
1997 Springtime Happiness Dtd 97 -203009	Yr.Iss.		35.00	35

Cherished Teddies Mother's Day - P. Hillman

1996 Mother's Day Dtd 96-156493	Yr.Iss.		35.00	35
1997 Our Love Is Ever Blooming Dtd 97-203025	Yr.Iss.		35.00	35

Cherished Teddies Nursery Rhymes - P. Hillman

1995 Jack/ Jill-114901	Open		35.00	35
1995 Mary/ Lamb-128902	Open		35.00	35
1995 Old King Cole-135437	Open		35.00	35
1996 Mother Goose & Friends-170968	Open		35.00	35
1996 Little Miss Muffet-145033	Open		35.00	35
1996 Little Jack Horner-151998	Open		35.00	35
1996 Wee Willie Winkie-170941	Open		35.00	35
1996 Little Bo Peep-164658	Open		35.00	35

Memories of Yesterday Dated Plate Series - Various

1993 Look Out-Something Good Is Coming Your Way! -530298 - S. Butcher	Yr.Iss.		50.00	50
1994 Pleasant Dreams and Sweet Repose-528102 - M. Atwell	Yr.Iss.		50.00	50
1995 Join Me For a Little Song-134880 - M. Attwell	Yr.Iss.		50.00	50

Precious Moments Beauty of Christmas Collection - S. Butcher

1994 You're as Pretty as a Christmas Tree-530409	Yr.Iss.		50.00	50
1995 He Covers the Earth With His Beauty-142670	Yr.Iss.		50.00	50

Precious Moments Christmas Blessings - S. Butcher

1990 Wishing You A Yummy Christmas-523861	Yr.Iss.		50.00	50
1991 Blessings From Me To Thee -523860	Yr.Iss.		50.00	55
1992 But The Greatest of These Is Love-527742	Yr.Iss.		50.00	50
1993 Wishing You the Sweetest Christmas-530204	Yr.Iss.		50.00	50

YEAR ISSUE		EDITION LIMIT	YEAR RETRD.	ISSUE PRICE	*QUOTE U.S.$

Precious Moments Christmas Collection - S. Butcher

1981	Come Let Us Adore Him-E-5646	15,000		40.00	48-60
1982	Let Heaven and Nature Sing-E-2347	15,000		40.00	40
1983	Wee Three Kings-E-0538	15,000		40.00	40
1984	Unto Us a Child Is Born-E-5395	15,000		40.00	40

Precious Moments Christmas Love Series - S. Butcher

1986	I'm Sending You a White Christmas-101834	Yr.Iss.		45.00	55
1987	My Peace I Give Unto Thee-102954	Yr.Iss.		45.00	90
1988	Merry Christmas Deer-520284	Yr.Iss.		50.00	55
1989	May Your Christmas Be A Happy Home-523003	Yr.Iss.		50.00	55

Precious Moments Inspired Thoughts Series - S. Butcher

1985	Love One Another-E-5215	15,000		40.00	66
1982	Make a Joyful Noise-E-7174	15,000		40.00	40
1983	I Believe In Miracles-E-9257	15,000		40.00	40
1984	Love is Kind-E-2847	15,000		40.00	40

Precious Moments Joy of Christmas Series - S. Butcher

1982	I'll Play My Drum For Him -E-2357	Yr.Iss.		40.00	90-93
1983	Christmastime is for Sharing -E-0505	Yr.Iss.		40.00	60-75
1984	The Wonder of Christmas -E-5396	Yr.Iss.		40.00	45
1985	Tell Me the Story of Jesus-15237	Yr.Iss.		40.00	90-115

Precious Moments Mother's Day Series - S. Butcher

1994	Thinking of You Is What I Really Like to Do-531766	Yr.Iss.		50.00	50
1995	He Hath Made Everything Beautiful In His Time-129151	Yr.Iss.		50.00	50
1996	Of All The Mothers I Have Known There's None As Precious As My Own-163716	Yr.Iss.		50.00	50

Precious Moments Mother's Love Series - S. Butcher

1981	Mother Sew Dear-E-5217	15,000		40.00	50
1982	The Purr-fect Grandma-E-7173	15,000		40.00	40
1983	The Hand that Rocks the Future-E-9256	15,000		40.00	40
1984	Loving Thy Neighbor-E-2848	15,000		40.00	40

Precious Moments Open Editions - S. Butcher

1982	Our First Christmas Together-E-2378	Suspd.		30.00	45-55
1981	The Lord Bless You and Keep You-E-5216	Suspd.		30.00	40-45
1982	Rejoicing with You-E-7172	Suspd.		30.00	40
1983	Jesus Loves Me-E-9275	Suspd.		30.00	45-48
1983	Jesus Loves Me-E-9276	Suspd.		30.00	45-48
1994	Bring The Little Ones To Jesus-531359	Yr.Iss.		50.00	50
1996	You Have Touched So Many Hearts-151114	Yr.Iss.		35.00	35
1996	Peace On Earth...Anyway-183377	Yr.Iss.		50.00	50

Precious Moments The Four Seasons Series - S. Butcher

1985	The Voice of Spring-12106	Yr.Iss.		40.00	110-120
1985	Summer's Joy-12114	Yr.Iss.		40.00	85-100
1986	Autumn's Praise-12122	Yr.Iss.		40.00	53
1986	Winter's Song-12130	Yr.Iss.		40.00	58

Ernst Enterprises/Porter & Price, Inc.

A Beautiful World - S. Morton

1981	Tahitian Dreamer	Retrd.	1987	27.50	30
1982	Flirtation	Retrd.	1987	27.50	30
1984	Elke of Oslo	Retrd.	1987	27.50	30

Classy Cars - S. Kuhnly

1982	The 26T	Retrd.	1990	24.50	25
1982	The 31A	Retrd.	1990	24.50	25
1983	The Pickup	Retrd.	1990	24.50	25
1984	Panel Van	Retrd.	1990	24.50	25

Commemoratives - S. Morton

1981	John Lennon	Retrd.	1988	39.50	100-150
1982	Elvis Presley	Retrd.	1988	39.50	75-125
1982	Marilyn Monroe	Retrd.	1988	39.50	100
1983	Judy Garland	Retrd.	1988	39.50	70
1984	John Wayne	Retrd.	1988	39.50	95

Elvira - S. Morton

1988	Night Rose	90-day		29.50	45
1988	Red Velvet	90-day		29.50	35
1988	Mistress of the Dark	90-day		29.50	35

Elvis Presley - S. Morton

1987	The King	Retrd.	1991	39.50	90
1987	Loving You	Retrd.	1991	39.50	90
1987	Early Years	Retrd.	1991	39.50	90
1987	Tenderly	Retrd.	1991	39.50	90
1988	Forever Yours	Retrd.	1991	39.50	90
1988	Rockin in the Moonlight	Retrd.	1991	39.50	90
1988	Moody Blues	Retrd.	1991	39.50	60-85
1988	Elvis Presley	Retrd.	1991	39.50	75
1989	Elvis Presley-Special Request	Retrd.	1991	150.00	250-300

Hollywood Greats - S. Morton

1981	Henry Fonda	Retrd.	1988	29.95	60
1981	John Wayne	Retrd.	1988	29.95	100
1981	Gary Cooper	Retrd.	1988	29.95	30
1982	Clark Gable	Retrd.	1988	29.95	65
1984	Alan Ladd	Retrd.	1988	29.95	40-60

Hollywood Walk of Fame - S. Morton

1989	Jimmy Stewart	Retrd.	1992	39.50	45
1989	Elizabeth Taylor	Retrd.	1992	39.50	45
1989	Tom Selleck	Retrd.	1992	39.50	45
1989	Joan Collins	Retrd.	1992	39.50	45
1990	Burt Reynolds	Retrd.	1992	39.50	50
1990	Sylvester Stallone	Retrd.	1992	39.50	45

The Republic Pictures Library - S. Morton

1991	Showdown With Laredo	28-day		37.50	38
1991	The Ride Home	28-day		37.50	38
1991	Attack at Tarawa	28-day		37.50	38
1991	Thoughts of Angelique	28-day		37.50	38
1992	War of the Wildcats	28-day		37.50	38
1992	The Fighting Seabees	28-day		37.50	38
1992	The Quiet Man	28-day		37.50	38
1992	Angel and the Badman	28-day		37.50	38
1993	Sands of Iwo Jima	28-day		37.50	38
1993	Flying Tigers	28-day		37.50	38
1993	The Tribute (12")	28-day		97.50	98
1994	The Tribute (8 1/4") AP	9,500		35.00	35

Seems Like Yesterday - R. Money

1981	Stop & Smell the Roses	Retrd.	1988	24.50	30
1982	Home by Lunch	Retrd.	1988	24.50	35
1982	Lisa's Creek	Retrd.	1988	24.50	25
1983	It's Got My Name on It	Retrd.	1988	24.50	30
1983	My Magic Hat	Retrd.	1988	24.50	25
1984	Little Prince	Retrd.	1988	24.50	25

Star Trek - S. Morton

1984	Mr. Spock	Retrd.	1989	29.50	100-200
1985	Dr. McCoy	Retrd.	1989	29.50	75-125
1985	Sulu	Retrd.	1989	29.50	75-100
1985	Scotty	Retrd.	1989	29.50	75-100
1985	Uhura	Retrd.	1989	29.50	60-100
1985	Chekov	Retrd.	1989	29.50	75-150
1985	Captain Kirk	Retrd.	1989	29.50	75-150
1985	Beam Us Down Scotty	Retrd.	1989	29.50	135-150
1985	The Enterprise	Retrd.	1989	39.50	80-150

Star Trek: Commemorative Collection - S. Morton

1987	The Trouble With Tribbles	Retrd.	1989	29.50	150-200
1987	Mirror, Mirror	Retrd.	1989	29.50	150
1987	A Piece of the Action	Retrd.	1989	29.50	75-150
1987	The Devil in the Dark	Retrd.	1989	29.50	100-150
1987	Amok Time	Retrd.	1989	29.50	100-150
1987	The City on the Edge of Forever	Retrd.	1989	29.50	100-175
1987	Journey to Babel	Retrd.	1989	29.50	80-160
1987	The Menagerie	Retrd.	1989	29.50	80-175

Turn of The Century - R. Money

1981	Riverboat Honeymoon	Retrd.	1987	35.00	40
1982	Children's Carousel	Retrd.	1987	35.00	40
1984	Flower Market	Retrd.	1987	35.00	35
1985	Balloon Race	Retrd.	1987	35.00	35

Women of the West - D. Putnam

1979	Expectations	Retrd.	1986	39.50	40
1981	Silver Dollar Sal	Retrd.	1986	39.50	40
1982	School Marm	Retrd.	1986	39.50	40
1983	Dolly	Retrd.	1986	39.50	40

Fairmont

Famous Clowns - R. Skelton

1976	Freddie the Freeloader	10,000		55.00	400
1977	W. C. Fields	10,000		55.00	100
1978	Happy	10,000		55.00	80
1979	The Pledge	10,000		55.00	65

Spencer Special - I. Spencer

| 1978 | Hug Me | 10,000 | | 55.00 | 100 |
| 1978 | Sleep Little Baby | 10,000 | | 65.00 | 65-85 |

Fenton Art Glass Company

American Classic Series - M. Dickinson

| 1986 | Jupiter Train on Opal Satin | 5,000 | 1986 | 75.00 | 75 |
| 1986 | Studebaker-Garford Car on Opal Satin | 5,000 | 1986 | 75.00 | 75 |

American Craftsman Carnival - Fenton

1970	Glassmaker	Closed	1970	10.00	50-60
1971	Printer	Closed	1971	10.00	50-60
1972	Blacksmith	Closed	1972	10.00	50-60
1973	Shoemaker	Closed	1973	10.00	50-60
1974	Pioneer Cooper	Closed	1974	11.00	50-60
1975	Paul Revere (Patriot & Silversmith)	Closed	1975	12.50	50-60
1976	Gunsmith	Closed	1976	13.50	50-60
1977	Potter	Closed	1977	15.00	50-60
1978	Wheelwright	Closed	1978	15.00	50-60
1979	Cabinetmaker	Closed	1979	15.00	50-60
1980	Tanner	Closed	1980	16.50	50-60
1981	Housewright	Closed	1981	17.50	50-60

Artist Series - Various

1982	After The Snow (3 1/4") - D. Johnson	15,000	1982	14.50	15
1983	Winter Chapel (3 1/4") - D. Johnson	15,000	1984	15.00	15
1985	Flying Geese (3 1/4") - D. Johnson	15,000	1985	15.00	15
1986	The Hummingbird (3 1/4") - D. Johnson	15,000	1986	15.00	15
1987	Out in the Country (3 1/4") - L. Everson	15,000	1987	15.00	15
1988	Serenity (3 1/4") - F. Burton	5,000	1988	16.50	17
1989	Househunting (3 1/4") - D. Barbour	5,000	1989	16.50	17

Childhood Treasurers Series - Various

1983	Teddy Bear (3 1/4") - D. Johnson	15,000	1983	15.00	15
1984	Hobby Horse (3 1/4") - L. Everson	15,000	1984	15.00	15
1985	Clown (3 1/4") - L. Everson	15,000	1985	17.50	18
1986	Playful Kitten (3 1/4") - L. Everson	15,000	1986	15.00	15
1987	Frisky Pup (3 1/4") - D. Barbour	15,000	1987	15.00	15
1988	Castles in the Air (3 1/4") - D. Barbour	5,000	1988	16.50	17
1989	A Child's Cuddly Friend (3 1/4") - D. Johnson	5,000	1989	16.50	17

Christmas - Various

1979	Nature's Christmas - K. Cunningham	Yr.Iss.	1979	35.00	35
1980	Going Home - D. Johnson	Yr.Iss.	1980	38.50	39
1981	All Is Calm - D. Johnson	Yr.Iss.	1981	42.50	43
1982	Country Christmas - R. Spindler	Yr.Iss.	1982	42.50	43
1983	Anticipation - D. Johnson	7,500	1983	45.00	45
1984	Expectation - D. Johnson	7,500	1984	50.00	50
1985	Heart's Desire - D. Johnson	7,500	1986	50.00	50
1987	Sharing The Spirit - L. Everson	Yr.Iss.	1987	50.00	50
1987	Cardinal in the Churchyard - D. Johnson	4,500	1987	39.50	40
1988	A Chickadee Ballet - D. Johnson	4,500	1988	39.50	40
1989	Downy Pecker - Chisled Song - D. Johnson	4,500	1989	39.50	40
1990	A Blue Bird in Snowfall - D. Johnson	4,500	1990	39.50	40
1990	Sleigh Ride - F. Burton	3,500	1990	45.00	45
1991	Christmas Eve - F. Burton	3,500	1991	45.00	45
1992	Family Tradition - F. Burton	3,500	1992	49.00	49
1993	Family Holiday - F. Burton	3,500	1993	49.00	49
1994	Silent Night - F. Burton	1,500	1994	65.00	65
1995	Our Home Is Blessed - F. Burton	1,500	1995	65.00	65
1996	Star of Wonder - F. Burton	1,750		65.00	65

Christmas In America - Fenton

1970	Little Brown Church in the Vale, Bradford, IA, Blue Satin	Closed	1970	12.50	15
1970	Little Brown Church in the Vale, Bradford, IA, Carnival	Closed	1970	12.50	15
1970	Little Brown Church in the Vale, Bradford, IA, White Satin	Closed	1970	12.50	15
1971	The Old Brick Church, Isle of Wight County, VA, Blue Satin	Closed	1971	12.50	15
1971	The Old Brick Church, Isle of Wight County, VA, Carnival	Closed	1971	12.50	15
1971	The Old Brick Church, Isle of Wight County, VA, White Satin	Closed	1971	12.50	15
1972	The Two Horned Church, Marietta, OH, Blue Satin	Closed	1972	12.50	15
1972	The Two Horned Church, Marietta, OH, Carnival	Closed	1972	12.50	15
1972	The Two Horned Church, Marietta, OH, White Satin	Closed	1972	12.50	15
1973	St. Mary's in the Mountain, Virginia City, NV, Blue Satin	Closed	1973	12.50	15
1973	St. Mary's in the Mountain, Virginia City, NV, Carnival	Closed	1973	12.50	15
1973	St. Mary's in the Mountain, Virginia City, NV, White Satin	Closed	1973	12.50	15
1974	The Nation's Church, Philadelphia, PA, Blue Satin	Closed	1974	13.50	15
1974	The Nation's Church, Philadelphia, PA, Carnival	Closed	1974	13.50	15
1974	The Nation's Church, Philadelphia, PA, White Satin	Closed	1974	13.50	15
1975	Birthplace of Liberty, Richmond, VA, Blue Satin	Closed	1975	13.50	15
1975	Birthplace of Liberty, Richmond, VA, Carnival	Closed	1975	13.50	15
1975	Birthplace of Liberty, Richmond, VA, White Satin	Closed	1975	13.50	15
1976	The Old North Church, Boston, MA, Blue Satin	Closed	1976	15.00	15
1976	The Old North Church, Boston, MA, Carnival	Closed	1976	15.00	15
1976	The Old North Church, Boston, MA, White Satin	Closed	1976	15.00	15
1977	San Carlos Borromeo de Carmelo, Carmel, CA, Blue Satin	Closed	1977	15.00	15
1977	San Carlos Borromeo de Carmelo, Carmel, CA, Carnival	Closed	1977	15.00	15
1977	San Carlos Borromeo de Carmelo, Carmel, CA, White Satin	Closed	1977	15.00	15
1978	The Church of Holy Trinity, Philadelphia, PA, Blue Satin	Closed	1978	15.00	15
1978	The Church of Holy Trinity, Philadelphia, PA, Carnival	Closed	1978	15.00	15

PLATES

YEAR ISSUE	EDITION LIMIT	YEAR RETD.	ISSUE PRICE	*QUOTE U.S.$
1978 The Church of Holy Trinity, Philadelphia, PA, White Satin	Closed	1978	15.00	15
1979 San Jose Y Miguel de Aguayo, San Antonio, TX, Blue Satin	Closed	1979	15.00	15
1979 San Jose Y Miguel de Aguayo, San Antonio, TX, Carnival	Closed	1979	15.00	15
1979 San Jose Y Miguel de Aguayo, San Antonio, TX, White Satin	Closed	1979	15.00	15
1980 Christ Church, Alexandria, VA, Blue Satin	Closed	1980	16.50	17
1980 Christ Church, Alexandria, VA, Carnival	Closed	1980	16.50	17
1980 Christ Church, Alexandria, VA, White Satin	Closed	1980	16.50	17
1981 San Xavier Del Bac, Tucson, AZ, Blue Satin	Closed	1981	18.50	19
1981 San Xavier Del Bac, Tucson, AZ, Carnival	Closed	1981	18.50	19
1981 San Xavier Del Bac, Tucson, AZ, White Satin	Closed	1981	18.50	19
1981 San Xavier Del Bac, Tucson, AZ, Florentine	Closed	1981	25.00	25

Designer Series - Various

YEAR ISSUE	EDITION LIMIT	YEAR RETD.	ISSUE PRICE	*QUOTE U.S.$
1983 Lighthouse Point - M. Dickinson	1,000	1983	65.00	65
1983 Down Home - G. Finn	1,000	1983	65.00	65
1984 Smoke 'N Cinders - M. Dickinson	1,250	1984	65.00	65
1984 Majestic Flight - B. Cumberledge	1,250	1984	65.00	65
1985 In Season - M. Dickinson	1,250	1985	65.00	65
1985 Nature's Grace - B. Cumberland	1,250	1985	65.00	65
1985 Statue of Liberty - S. Bryan	1,250	1985	65.00	65
1986 Statue of Liberty - S. Bryan	1,250	1986	65.00	65

Easter Series - M. Reynolds

YEAR ISSUE	EDITION LIMIT	YEAR RETD.	ISSUE PRICE	*QUOTE U.S.$
1995 Covered Hen & Egg	950	1995	95.00	95

Mary Gregory - M. Reynolds

YEAR ISSUE	EDITION LIMIT	YEAR RETD.	ISSUE PRICE	*QUOTE U.S.$
1994 Plate w/stand, 9"	Closed	1994	65.00	65
1995 Plate w/stand, 9"	Closed	1995	65.00	65

Mother's Day Series - Fenton, unless otherwise noted

YEAR ISSUE	EDITION LIMIT	YEAR RETD.	ISSUE PRICE	*QUOTE U.S.$
1971 Madonna w/Sleeping Child, Carnival	Closed	1971	10.75	15
1971 Madonna w/Sleeping Child, Blue Satin	Closed	1971	10.75	15
1972 Madonna of the Goldfinch, Carnival	Closed	1972	12.50	15
1972 Madonna of the Goldfinch, Blue Satin	Closed	1972	12.50	15
1972 Madonna of the Goldfinch, White Satin	Closed	1972	12.50	15
1973 The Small Cowper Madonna, Carnival	Closed	1973	12.50	15
1973 The Small Cowper Madonna, Blue Satin	Closed	1973	12.50	15
1973 The Small Cowper Madonna, White Satin	Closed	1973	12.50	15
1974 Madonna of the Grotto, Carnival	Closed	1974	13.50	15
1974 Madonna of the Grotto, Blue Satin	Closed	1974	13.50	15
1974 Madonna of the Grotto, White Satin	Closed	1974	13.50	15
1975 Taddei Madonna, Blue Satin	Closed	1975	13.50	15
1975 Taddei Madonna, Carnival	Closed	1975	13.50	15
1975 Taddei Madonna, White Satin	Closed	1975	13.50	15
1976 The Holly Night, Cardinal	Closed	1976	13.50	15
1976 The Holly Night, Blue Satin	Closed	1976	13.50	15
1976 The Holly Night, White Satin	Closed	1976	13.50	15
1977 Madonna & Child w/Pomegrantate, Carnival	Closed	1977	15.00	15
1977 Madonna & Child w/Pomegrantate, Blue Satin	Closed	1977	15.00	15
1977 Madonna & Child w/Pomegrantate, White Satin	Closed	1977	15.00	15
1978 The Madonnina, Cardinal	Closed	1978	15.00	15
1978 The Madonnina, Blue Satin	Closed	1978	15.00	15
1978 The Madonnina, White Satin	Closed	1978	15.00	15
1979 Madonna of the Rose Hedge, Carnival	Closed	1979	15.00	15
1979 Madonna of the Rose Hedge, Blue Satin	Closed	1979	15.00	15
1979 Madonna of the Rose Hedge, White Satin	Closed	1979	15.00	15
1979 Madonna of the Rose Hedge, Ruby Carnival	Closed	1979	35.00	35
1980 New Born - L. Everson	Closed	1980	28.50	29
1981 Gentle Fawn - L. Everson	Closed	1981	32.50	33
1982 Nature's Awakening - L. Everson	Closed	1982	35.00	35
1983 Where's Mom - L. Everson	Closed	1983	35.00	35
1984 Precious Panda - L. Everson	Closed	1984	35.00	35
1985 Mother's Little Lamb - L. Everson	Closed	1985	35.00	35
1990 Mother Swan - L. Everson	Closed	1990	45.00	50
1991 Mother's Watchful Eye - M. Reynolds	Closed	1991	45.00	50
1992 Let's Play With Mom - M. Reynolds	Closed	1992	49.50	50
1993 Mother Deer - M. Reynolds	Closed	1993	49.50	50
1994 Loving Puppy - M. Reynolds	Closed	1994	49.50	50

Flambro Imports

Emmett Kelly Jr. Plates - Various

YEAR ISSUE	EDITION LIMIT	YEAR RETD.	ISSUE PRICE	*QUOTE U.S.$
1983 Why Me? Plate I - C. Kelly	10,000		40.00	450
1984 Balloons For Sale Plate II - C. Kelly	10,000		40.00	350
1985 Big Business Plate III - C. Kelly	10,000		40.00	350
1986 And God Bless America IV - C. Kelly	10,000		40.00	325
1988 Tis the Season - D. Rust	10,000		50.00	125-150

YEAR ISSUE	EDITION LIMIT	YEAR RETD.	ISSUE PRICE	*QUOTE U.S.$
1989 Looking Back- 65th Birthday - D. Rust	6,500		50.00	125-150
1991 Winter - D. Rust	10,000		30.00	30
1992 Spring - D. Rust	10,000		30.00	30
1992 Summer - D. Rust	10,000		30.00	30
1992 Autumn - D. Rust	10,000		30.00	30
1993 Santa's Stowaway - D. Rust	10,000		30.00	30
1994 70th Birthday Commemorative - D. Rust	5,000		30.00	30
1995 All Wrapped Up in Christmas - Undis.	5,000		30.00	30

Fountainhead

As Free As The Wind - M. Fernandez

YEAR ISSUE	EDITION LIMIT	YEAR RETD.	ISSUE PRICE	*QUOTE U.S.$
1989 As Free As The Wind	Unkn.		295.00	300-600

The Wings of Freedom - M. Fernandez

YEAR ISSUE	EDITION LIMIT	YEAR RETD.	ISSUE PRICE	*QUOTE U.S.$
1985 Courtship Flight	2,500		250.00	1300-1500
1986 Wings of Freedom	2,500		250.00	1300-1500

Ganz

Watching Over You Collection - C.Thammavongsa

YEAR ISSUE	EDITION LIMIT	YEAR RETD.	ISSUE PRICE	*QUOTE U.S.$
1996 Wings of the Wind	Open		40.00	40

Gartlan USA

Club Gift

YEAR ISSUE	EDITION LIMIT	YEAR RETD.	ISSUE PRICE	*QUOTE U.S.$
1989 Pete Rose (8 1/2") - B. Forbes	Closed	1990	Gift	125-150
1990 Al Barlick (8 1/2") - M. Taylor	Closed	1991	Gift	110
1991 Joe Montana (8 1/2") - M. Taylor	Closed	1992	Gift	125-175
1992 Ken Griffey Jr. (8 1/2") - M. Taylor	Closed	1993	Gift	70-90
1993 Gordie Howe (8 1/2") - M. Taylor	Closed	1994	Gift	50-70
1994 Shaquille O'Neal (8 1/2") - M. Taylor	Closed	1995	Gift	65-100
1996 Ringo Starr (8 1/2") - M. Taylor	Yr. Iss.		Gift	30

Bob Cousy - M. Taylor

YEAR ISSUE	EDITION LIMIT	YEAR RETD.	ISSUE PRICE	*QUOTE U.S.$
1994 Signed Plate (10 1/4")	950	1995	175.00	200
1994 Plate (8 1/2")	10,000		30.00	30
1994 Plate (3 1/4")	Open		15.00	15

Brett & Bobby Hull - M. Taylor

YEAR ISSUE	EDITION LIMIT	YEAR RETD.	ISSUE PRICE	*QUOTE U.S.$
1992 Hockey's Golden Boys (10 1/4") signed by both	950	1995	250.00	475
1992 Hockey's Golden Boys (10 1/4") A/P, signed by both	300	1995	350.00	400
1992 Hockey's Golden Boys (8 1/2")	10,000		30.00	30
1992 Hockey's Golden Boys (3 1/4")	Open		15.00	15

Carl Yastrzemski - M. Taylor

YEAR ISSUE	EDITION LIMIT	YEAR RETD.	ISSUE PRICE	*QUOTE U.S.$
1993 Signed Plate (10 1/4")	950	1995	175.00	225
1993 Plate (8 1/2")	10,000		30.00	30
1993 Plate (3 1/4")	Open		15.00	15

Carlton Fisk - M. Taylor

YEAR ISSUE	EDITION LIMIT	YEAR RETD.	ISSUE PRICE	*QUOTE U.S.$
1993 Signed Plate (10 1/4")	950	1995	175.00	250
1993 Plate (8 1/2")	5,000		30.00	30
1993 Plate (3 1/4")	Open		15.00	15

Darryl Strawberry - M. Taylor

YEAR ISSUE	EDITION LIMIT	YEAR RETD.	ISSUE PRICE	*QUOTE U.S.$
1991 Signed Plate (10 1/4")	2,500	1995	150.00	150
1991 Plate (8 1/2")	10,000	1995	40.00	40
1991 Plate (3 1/4")	Retrd.	1995	15.00	15

George Brett Gold Crown Collection - J. Martin

YEAR ISSUE	EDITION LIMIT	YEAR RETD.	ISSUE PRICE	*QUOTE U.S.$
1986 George Brett "Baseball's All Star" (3 1/4")	Open		12.95	15-20
1986 George Brett "Baseball's All Star" (10 1/4") signed	2,000	1988	100.00	200
1986 George Brett "Baseball's All Star" (10 1/4"), A/P signed	24	1988	225.00	N/A

Gordie Howe - M. Taylor

YEAR ISSUE	EDITION LIMIT	YEAR RETD.	ISSUE PRICE	*QUOTE U.S.$
1993 Signed Plate (10 1/4")	2,358	1995	150.00	150-200
1993 Signed Plate (8 1/2")	10,000		30.00	30
1993 Signed Plate (3 1/4")	Open		15.00	15

Joe Montana - M. Taylor

YEAR ISSUE	EDITION LIMIT	YEAR RETD.	ISSUE PRICE	*QUOTE U.S.$
1991 Signed Plate (10 1/4")	2,250	1991	125.00	335-395
1991 Signed Plate (10 1/4") A/P	250	1991	195.00	400-450
1991 Plate (8 1/2")	10,000	1995	30.00	40
1991 Plate (3 1/4")	Open		15.00	15

John Wooden - M. Taylor

YEAR ISSUE	EDITION LIMIT	YEAR RETD.	ISSUE PRICE	*QUOTE U.S.$
1990 Signed Plate (10 1/4")	1,975	1995	150.00	150
1990 Plate (8 1/2")	10,000	1995	30.00	30
1990 Plate (3 1/4")	Retrd.	1995	15.00	15

Johnny Bench - M. Taylor

YEAR ISSUE	EDITION LIMIT	YEAR RETD.	ISSUE PRICE	*QUOTE U.S.$
1989 Signed Plate (10 1/4")	1,989	1991	100.00	200
1989 Plate (3 1/4")	Open		15.00	15

Kareem Abdul-Jabbar Sky-Hook Collection - M. Taylor

YEAR ISSUE	EDITION LIMIT	YEAR RETD.	ISSUE PRICE	*QUOTE U.S.$
1989 Kareem Abdul-Jabbar "Path of Glory" (10 1/4"), signed	1,989	1991	100.00	225-295
1989 Plate (3 1/4")	Closed	1993	16.00	30

Ken Griffey Jr. - M. Taylor

YEAR ISSUE	EDITION LIMIT	YEAR RETD.	ISSUE PRICE	*QUOTE U.S.$
1992 Signed Plate (10 1/4")	1,989	1995	150.00	350
1992 Plate (8 1/2")	10,000		30.00	30

YEAR ISSUE	EDITION LIMIT	YEAR RETD.	ISSUE PRICE	*QUOTE U.S.$
1992 Plate (3 1/4")	Open		15.00	15

Kristi Yamaguchi - M. Taylor

YEAR ISSUE	EDITION LIMIT	YEAR RETD.	ISSUE PRICE	*QUOTE U.S.$
1993 Signed Plate (10 1/4")	950	1995	150.00	200
1993 Plate (8 1/2")	5,000		30.00	30
1993 Plate (3 1/4")	Open		15.00	15

Leave It To Beaver - M. Taylor

YEAR ISSUE	EDITION LIMIT	YEAR RETD.	ISSUE PRICE	*QUOTE U.S.$
1995 Jerry Mathers, (10 1/4") signed	1,963		125.00	125
1996 Jerry Mathers, (10 1/4") A/P signed	234		175.00	175
1995 Jerry Mathers, (8 1/4")	10,000		39.95	40
1995 Jerry Mathers, (3 1/4") miniature	Open		14.95	15

Luis Aparicio - M. Taylor

YEAR ISSUE	EDITION LIMIT	YEAR RETD.	ISSUE PRICE	*QUOTE U.S.$
1991 Signed Plate (10 1/4")	1,984	1995	150.00	200
1991 Plate (8 1/2")	10,000		30.00	30
1991 Plate (3 1/4")	Open		15.00	15

Magic Johnson Gold Rim Collection - R. Winslow

YEAR ISSUE	EDITION LIMIT	YEAR RETD.	ISSUE PRICE	*QUOTE U.S.$
1987 Magic Johnson "The Magic Show" (10 1/4"), signed	1,987	1988	100.00	495-595
1987 Magic Johnson "The Magic Show" (3 1/4")	Closed	1993	14.50	25-35

Mike Schmidt "500th" Home Run Edition - C. Paluso

YEAR ISSUE	EDITION LIMIT	YEAR RETD.	ISSUE PRICE	*QUOTE U.S.$
1987 Mike Schmidt "Power at the Plate" (10 1/4"), signed	1,987	1988	100.00	395-495
1987 Mike Schmidt "Power at the Plate" (3 1/4")	Open		14.50	19
1987 Mike Schmidt A/P	56	1988	150.00	150

Pete Rose Diamond Collection - Forbes

YEAR ISSUE	EDITION LIMIT	YEAR RETD.	ISSUE PRICE	*QUOTE U.S.$
1988 Pete Rose "The Reigning Legend" (10 1/4"), signed	950	1989	195.00	250-300
1988 Pete Rose "The Reigning Legend" (10 1/4"), signed A/P	50	1989	300.00	395
1988 Pete Rose "The Reigning Legend" (3 1/4")	Open		14.50	15

Pete Rose Platinum Edition - T. Sizemore

YEAR ISSUE	EDITION LIMIT	YEAR RETD.	ISSUE PRICE	*QUOTE U.S.$
1985 Pete Rose "The Best of Baseball" (3 1/4")	Open		12.95	15-20
1985 Pete Rose "The Best of Baseball" (10 1/4")	4,192	1988	100.00	385

Ringo Starr - M. Taylor

YEAR ISSUE	EDITION LIMIT	YEAR RETD.	ISSUE PRICE	*QUOTE U.S.$
1996 Ringo Starr, (10 1/4") signed	1,000		225.00	225
1996 Ringo Starr, (10 1/4") A/P signed	250		400.00	400
1996 Ringo Starr, (8 1/4")	10,000		29.95	30
1996 Ringo Starr, (3 1/4") miniature	Open		14.95	15

Rod Carew - M. Taylor

YEAR ISSUE	EDITION LIMIT	YEAR RETD.	ISSUE PRICE	*QUOTE U.S.$
1992 Signed Plate (10 1/4")	950	1995	150.00	175
1992 Plate (8 1/2")	10,000		30.00	30
1992 Plate (3 1/4")	Open		15.00	15

Roger Staubach Sterling Collection - C. Soileau

YEAR ISSUE	EDITION LIMIT	YEAR RETD.	ISSUE PRICE	*QUOTE U.S.$
1987 Roger Staubach (3 1/4" diameter)	Open		12.95	15-20
1987 Roger Staubach (10 1/4" diameter) signed	1,979	1990	100.00	125-195

Sam Snead - M. Taylor

YEAR ISSUE	EDITION LIMIT	YEAR RETD.	ISSUE PRICE	*QUOTE U.S.$
1994 Signed Plate (10 1/4")	950	1995	100.00	200
1994 Plate (8 1/2")	5,000		30.00	30
1994 Plate (3 1/4")	Open		15.00	15

Tom Seaver - M. Taylor

YEAR ISSUE	EDITION LIMIT	YEAR RETD.	ISSUE PRICE	*QUOTE U.S.$
1993 Signed Plate (10 1/4")	1,992	1995	150.00	300
1993 Signed Plate (8 1/2")	10,000		30.00	30
1993 Signed Plate (3 1/4")	Open		15.00	15

Troy Aikman - M. Taylor

YEAR ISSUE	EDITION LIMIT	YEAR RETD.	ISSUE PRICE	*QUOTE U.S.$
1994 Signed Plate (10 1/4")	1,993	1995	225.00	225
1994 Plate (8 1/2")	10,000		30.00	30
1994 Plate (3 1/4")	Open		14.95	15

Wayne Gretzky - M. Taylor

YEAR ISSUE	EDITION LIMIT	YEAR RETD.	ISSUE PRICE	*QUOTE U.S.$
1989 Plate (10 1/4"), signed by Gretzky and Howe	1,851	1989	225.00	225-350
1989 Plate (10 1/4") A/P, signed by Gretzky and Howe	300	1989	300.00	450-575
1989 Plate (8 1/2")	10,000		45.00	45-50
1989 Plate (3 1/4")	Open		15.00	15

Whitey Ford - M. Taylor

YEAR ISSUE	EDITION LIMIT	YEAR RETD.	ISSUE PRICE	*QUOTE U.S.$
1991 Signed Plate (10 1/4")	2,360	1995	150.00	150
1991 Plate (8 1/2")	10,000	1995	30.00	30
1991 Plate (3 1/4")	Retrd.	1995	15.00	15

Yogi Berra - M. Taylor

YEAR ISSUE	EDITION LIMIT	YEAR RETD.	ISSUE PRICE	*QUOTE U.S.$
1991 Signed Plate (10 1/4")	2,150	1995	150.00	175
1991 Plate (8 1/2")	10,000		30.00	30
1991 Plate (3 1/4")	Open		15.00	15

Georgetown Collection, Inc.

Children of the Great Spirit - C. Theroux

YEAR ISSUE	EDITION LIMIT	YEAR RETD.	ISSUE PRICE	*QUOTE U.S.$
1993 Buffalo Child	35-day		29.95	30
1993 Winter Baby	35-day		29.95	30

*Quotes have been rounded up to nearest dollar

YEAR ISSUE		EDITION LIMIT	YEAR RETD.	ISSUE PRICE	*QUOTE U.S.$

Goebel/M.I. Hummel

M.I. Hummel Annual Figural Christmas Plates - M.I. Hummel

| 1995 | Festival Harmony w/Flute 693 | Open | | 125.00 | 125 |
| 1996 | Christmas Song 692 | Open | | 130.00 | 130 |

M.I. Hummel Club Exclusive Celebration - M.I. Hummel

1986	Valentine Gift (Hum 738)	Closed		90.00	120-130
1987	Valentine Joy (Hum 737)	Closed		98.00	120-130
1988	Daisies Don't Tell (Hum 736)	Closed		115.00	115-130
1989	It's Cold (Hum 735)	Closed		120.00	120-150

M.I. Hummel Collectibles Anniversary Plates - M.I. Hummel

1975	Stormy Weather 280	Closed		100.00	75-100
1980	Spring Dance 281	Closed		225.00	195
1985	Auf Wiedersehen 282	Closed		225.00	270

M.I. Hummel Collectibles Annual Plates - M.I. Hummel

1971	Heavenly Angel 264	Closed		25.00	500-900
1972	Hear Ye, Hear Ye 265	Closed		30.00	45-110
1973	Glober Trotter 266	Closed		32.50	150-225
1974	Goose Girl 267	Closed		40.00	75-125
1975	Ride into Christmas 268	Closed		50.00	75-125
1976	Apple Tree Girl 269	Closed		50.00	80-125
1977	Apple Tree Boy 270	Closed		52.50	75-125
1978	Happy Pastime 271	Closed		65.00	80-125
1979	Singing Lesson 272	Closed		90.00	75-100
1980	School Girl 273	Closed		100.00	100
1981	Umbrella Boy 274	Closed		100.00	100-125
1982	Umbrella Girl 275	Closed		100.00	175-200
1983	The Postman 276	Closed		108.00	150-250
1984	Little Helper 277	Closed		108.00	108-150
1985	Chick Girl 278	Closed		110.00	110-140
1986	Playmates 279	Closed		125.00	160-225
1987	Feeding Time 283	Closed		135.00	400-570
1988	Little Goat Herder 284	Closed		145.00	145-175
1989	Farm Boy 285	Closed		160.00	160-225
1990	Shepherd's Boy 286	Closed		170.00	175-245
1991	Just Resting 287	Closed		196.00	196-225
1992	Wayside Harmony 288	Closed		210.00	250
1993	Doll Bath 289	Closed		210.00	250-275
1994	Doctor 290	Closed		225.00	225-250
1995	Come Back Soon 291	Yr.Iss.		250.00	250

M.I. Hummel Four Seasons - M.I. Hummel

| 1996 | Winter Melody 296 | Yr.Iss. | | 195.00 | 195 |

M.I. Hummel Friends Forever - M.I. Hummel

1992	Meditation 292	Open		180.00	195
1993	For Father 293	Open		195.00	195
1994	Sweet Greetings 294	Open		205.00	205
1995	Surprise 295	Open		210.00	210

M.I. Hummel Little Music Makers - M.I. Hummel

1984	Little Fiddler 744	Closed		30.00	75-100
1985	Serenade 741	Closed		30.00	75-100
1986	Soloist 743	Closed		35.00	75-100
1987	Band Leader 742	Closed		40.00	75-100

M.I. Hummel The Little Homemakers - M.I. Hummel

1988	Little Sweeper (Hum 745)	Closed		45.00	50-100
1989	Wash Day (Hum 746)	Closed		50.00	50-100
1990	A Stitch in Time (Hum 747)	Closed		50.00	60-100
1991	Chicken Licken (Hum 748)	Closed		70.00	70-100

Gorham

(Four Seasons) A Boy and His Dog Plates - N. Rockwell

1971	Boy Meets His Dog	Annual	1971	50.00	175
1971	Adventures Between Adventures	Annual	1971	Set	Set
1971	The Mysterious Malady	Annual	1971	Set	Set
1971	Pride of Parenthood	Annual	1971	Set	Set

(Four Seasons) A Helping Hand Plates - N. Rockwell

1979	Year End Court	Annual	1979	100.00	125
1979	Closed for Business	Annual	1979	Set	Set
1979	Swatter's Rights	Annual	1979	Set	Set
1979	Coal Season's Coming	Annual	1979	Set	Set

(Four Seasons) Dad's Boys Plates - N. Rockwell

1980	Ski Skills	Annual	1980	135.00	135
1980	In His Spirits	Annual	1980	Set	Set
1980	Trout Dinner	Annual	1980	Set	Set
1980	Careful Aim	Annual	1980	Set	Set

(Four Seasons) Four Ages of Love - N. Rockwell

1973	Gaily Sharing Vintage Time	Annual	1973	60.00	135
1973	Flowers in Tender Bloom	Annual	1973	Set	Set
1973	Sweet Song So Young	Annual	1973	Set	Set
1973	Fondly We Do Remember	Annual	1973	Set	Set

(Four Seasons) Going on Sixteen Plates - N. Rockwell

1977	Chilling Chore	Annual	1977	75.00	100
1977	Sweet Serenade	Annual	1977	Set	Set
1977	Shear Agony	Annual	1977	Set	Set
1977	Pilgrimage	Annual	1977	Set	Set

(Four Seasons) Grand Pals Four Plates - N. Rockwell

| 1976 | Snow Sculpturing | Annual | 1976 | 70.00 | 120 |

YEAR ISSUE		EDITION LIMIT	YEAR RETD.	ISSUE PRICE	*QUOTE U.S.$
1976	Soaring Spirits	Annual	1976	Set	Set
1976	Fish Finders	Annual	1976	Set	Set
1976	Ghostly Gourds	Annual	1976	Set	Set

(Four Seasons) Grandpa and Me Plates - N. Rockwell

1974	Gay Blades	Annual	1974	60.00	90
1974	Day Dreamers	Annual	1974	Set	Set
1974	Goin' Fishing	Annual	1974	Set	Set
1974	Pensive Pals	Annual	1974	Set	Set

(Four Seasons) Life with Father Plates - N. Rockwell

1982	Big Decision	Annual	1982	100.00	100
1982	Blasting Out	Annual	1982	Set	Set
1982	Cheering the Champs	Annual	1982	Set	Set
1982	A Tough One	Annual	1982	Set	Set

(Four Seasons) Me and My Pals Plates - N. Rockwell

1975	A Lickin' Good Bath	Annual	1975	70.00	100
1975	Young Man's Fancy	Annual	1975	Set	Set
1975	Fisherman's Paradise	Annual	1975	Set	Set
1975	Disastrous Daring	Annual	1975	Set	Set

(Four Seasons) Old Buddies Plates - N. Rockwell

1983	Shared Success	Annual	1983	115.00	115
1983	Endless Debate	Annual	1983	Set	Set
1983	Hasty Retreat	Annual	1983	Set	Set
1983	Final Speech	Annual	1983	Set	Set

(Four Seasons) Old Timers Plates - N. Rockwell

1981	Canine Solo	Annual	1981	100.00	100
1981	Sweet Surprise	Annual	1981	Set	Set
1981	Lazy Days	Annual	1981	Set	Set
1981	Fancy Footwork	Annual	1981	Set	Set

(Four Seasons) Tender Years Plates - N. Rockwell

1978	New Year Look	Annual	1978	100.00	100
1978	Spring Tonic	Annual	1978	Set	Set
1978	Cool Aid	Annual	1978	Set	Set
1978	Chilly Reception	Annual	1978	Set	Set

(Four Seasons) Young Love Plates - N. Rockwell

1972	Downhill Daring	Annual	1972	60.00	100
1972	Beguiling Buttercup	Annual	1972	Set	Set
1972	Flying High	Annual	1972	Set	Set
1972	A Scholarly Pace	Annual	1972	Set	Set

American Artist - R. Donnelly

| 1976 | Apache Mother & Child | 9,800 | 1980 | 25.00 | 56 |

American Landscapes - N. Rockwell

1980	Summer Respite	Annual	1980	45.00	80
1981	Autumn Reflection	Annual	1981	45.00	65
1982	Winter Delight	Annual	1982	50.00	70
1983	Spring Recess	Annual	1983	60.00	75

Barrymore - Barrymore

1971	Quiet Waters	15,000	1980	25.00	25
1972	San Pedro Harbor	15,000	1980	25.00	25
1972	Nantucket, Sterling	1,000	1972	100.00	100
1972	Little Boatyard, Sterling	1,000	1972	100.00	145

Bas Relief - N. Rockwell

1981	Sweet Song So Young	Undis.	1984	100.00	100
1981	Beguiling Buttercup	Undis.	1984	62.50	70
1982	Flowers in Tender Bloom	Undis.	1984	100.00	100
1982	Flying High	Undis.	1984	62.50	65

Boy Scout Plates - N. Rockwell

1975	Our Heritage	18,500	1980	19.50	40
1976	A Scout is Loyal	18,500	1990	19.50	55
1977	The Scoutmaster	18,500	1990	19.50	60
1977	A Good Sign	18,500	1990	19.50	50
1978	Pointing the Way	18,500	1990	19.50	50
1978	Campfire Story	18,500	1990	19.50	25
1980	Beyond the Easel	18,500	1990	45.00	45

Charles Russell - C. Russell

1980	In Without Knocking	9,800	1990	38.00	75
1981	Bronc to Breakfast	9,800	1990	38.00	50-75
1982	When Ignorance is Bliss	9,800	1990	45.00	75-115
1983	Cowboy Life	9,800	1990	45.00	100

China Bicentennial - Gorham

| 1972 | 1776 Plate | 18,500 | 1980 | 17.50 | 35 |
| 1976 | 1776 Bicentennial | 8,000 | 1980 | 17.50 | 35 |

Christmas - N. Rockwell

1974	Tiny Tim	Annual	1974	12.50	30
1975	Good Deeds	Annual	1975	17.50	25-50
1976	Christmas Trio	Annual	1976	19.50	30
1977	Yuletide Reckoning	Annual	1977	19.50	45
1978	Planning Christmas Visit	Annual	1978	24.50	30
1979	Santa's Helpers	Annual	1979	24.50	30
1980	Letter to Santa	Annual	1980	27.50	32
1981	Santa Plans His Visit	Annual	1981	29.50	30
1982	Jolly Coachman	Annual	1982	29.50	30
1983	Christmas Dancers	Annual	1983	29.50	35
1984	Christmas Medley	17,500	1984	29.95	30
1985	Home For The Holidays	17,500	1985	29.95	30
1986	Merry Christmas Grandma	17,500	1986	29.95	65
1987	The Homecoming	17,500	1987	35.00	35-45

YEAR ISSUE		EDITION LIMIT	YEAR RETD.	ISSUE PRICE	*QUOTE U.S.$
1988	Discovery	17,500	1988	37.50	45

Christmas/Children's Television Workshop - Unknown

1981	Sesame Street Christmas	Annual	1981	17.50	18
1982	Sesame Street Christmas	Annual	1982	17.50	18
1983	Sesame Street Christmas	Annual	1983	19.50	20

Encounters, Survival and Celebrations - J. Clymer

1982	A Fine Welcome	7,500	1983	50.00	80
1983	Winter Trail	7,500	1984	50.00	80-100
1983	Alouette	7,500	1984	62.50	80
1983	The Trader	7,500	1984	62.50	63
1983	Winter Camp	7,500	1984	62.50	75
1983	The Trapper Takes a Wife	7,500	1984	62.50	63

Gallery of Masters - Various

1971	Man with a Gilt Helmet - Rembrandt	10,000	1975	50.00	50
1972	Self Portrait with Saskia - Rembrandt	10,000	1975	50.00	50
1973	The Honorable Mrs. Graham - Gainsborough	7,500	1975	50.00	50

Gorham Museum Doll Plates - Gorham

1984	Lydia	5,000	1984	29.00	125
1984	Belton Bebe	5,000	1984	29.00	55
1984	Christmas Lady	7,500	1984	32.50	33
1985	Lucille	5,000	1985	29.00	35
1985	Jumeau	5,000	1985	29.00	35

Julian Ritter - J. Ritter

| 1977 | Christmas Visit | 9,800 | 1977 | 24.50 | 29 |
| 1978 | Valentine, Fluttering Heart | 7,500 | 1978 | 45.00 | 45 |

Julian Ritter, Fall In Love - J. Ritter

1977	Enchantment	5,000	1977	100.00	100
1977	Frolic	5,000	1977	set	Set
1977	Gutsy Gal	5,000	1977	set	Set
1977	Lonely Chill	5,000	1977	set	Set

Julian Ritter, To Love a Clown - J. Ritter

1978	Awaited Reunion	5,000	1978	120.00	120
1978	Twosome Time	5,000	1978	120.00	120
1978	Showtime Beckons	5,000	1978	120.00	120
1978	Together in Memories	5,000	1978	120.00	120

Leyendecker Annual Christmas Plates - J. C. Leyendecker

| 1988 | Christmas Hug | 10,000 | 1988 | 37.50 | 50 |

Moppet Plates-Anniversary - Unknown

| 1976 | Anniversary | 20,000 | 1977 | 13.00 | 13 |

Moppet Plates-Christmas - Unknown

1973	Christmas	Annual	1973	10.00	35
1974	Christmas	Annual	1974	12.00	12
1975	Christmas	Annual	1975	13.00	13
1976	Christmas	Annual	1976	13.00	15
1977	Christmas	Annual	1977	13.00	14
1978	Christmas	Annual	1978	10.00	10
1979	Christmas	Annual	1979	12.00	12
1980	Christmas	Annual	1980	12.00	12
1981	Christmas	Annual	1981	12.00	12
1982	Christmas	Annual	1982	12.00	12
1983	Christmas	Annual	1983	12.00	12

Moppet Plates-Mother's Day - Unknown

1973	Mother's Day	Annual	1973	10.00	30
1974	Mother's Day	Annual	1974	12.00	20
1975	Mother's Day	Annual	1975	13.00	15
1976	Mother's Day	Annual	1976	13.00	15
1977	Mother's Day	Annual	1977	13.00	15
1978	Mother's Day	Annual	1978	10.00	10

Pastoral Symphony - B. Felder

1982	When I Was a Child	7,500	1983	42.50	50
1982	Gather the Children	7,500	1983	42.50	50
1984	Sugar and Spice	7,500	1985	42.50	50
XX	He Loves Me	7,500	1985	42.50	50

Pewter Bicentennial - R. Pailthorpe

| 1971 | Burning of the Gaspee | 5,000 | 1971 | 35.00 | 35 |
| 1972 | Boston Tea Party | 5,000 | 1972 | 35.00 | 35 |

Presidential - N. Rockwell

| 1976 | John F. Kennedy | 9,800 | 1976 | 30.00 | 65 |
| 1976 | Dwight D. Eisenhower | 9,800 | 1976 | 30.00 | 35 |

Remington Western - F. Remington

1973	A New Year on the Cimarron	Annual	1973	25.00	35-50
1973	Aiding a Comrade	Annual	1973	25.00	30-125
1973	The Flight	Annual	1973	25.00	30-95
1973	The Fight for the Water Hole	Annual	1973	25.00	30-125
1975	Old Ramond	Annual	1975	20.00	35-60
1975	A Breed	Annual	1975	20.00	35-65
1976	Cavalry Officer	5,000	1976	37.50	60-75
1976	A Trapper	5,000	1976	37.50	60-75

Silver Bicentennial - Various

1972	1776 Plate - Gorham	500	1972	500.00	500
1972	Burning of the Gaspee - R. Pailthorpe	750	1972	500.00	500
1973	Boston Tea Party - R. Pailthorpe	750	1973	550.00	575

YEAR ISSUE	EDITION LIMIT	YEAR RETD.	ISSUE PRICE	*QUOTE U.S.$

Single Release - N. Rockwell

1974 The Golden Rule	Annual	1974	12.50	30
1975 Ben Franklin	Annual	1975	19.50	35

Single Release - F. Quagon

1976 The Black Regiment 1778	7,500	1978	25.00	58

Single Release - N. Rockwell

1974 Weighing In	Annual	1974	12.50	80-99
1976 The Marriage License	Numbrd	1985	37.50	52-95
1978 Triple Self Portrait Memorial	Annual	1978	37.50	50-95
1980 The Annual Visit	Annual	1980	32.50	70
1981 Day in Life of Boy	Annual	1981	50.00	80
1981 Day in Life of Girl	Annual	1981	50.00	80-108

Time Machine Teddies Plates - B. Port

1986 Miss Emily, Bearing Up	5,000	1986	32.50	50
1987 Big Bear, The Toy Collector	5,000	1987	32.50	45
1988 Hunny Munny	5,000	1988	37.50	40

Vermeil Bicentennial - Gorham

1972 1776 Plate	250	1972	750.00	800

Hackett American

Sports - Various

1981 Reggie Jackson h/s - Paluso	Retrd.	N/A	100.00	1065
1983 Steve Garvey h/s - Paluso	Retrd.	N/A	100.00	150-250
1983 Nolan Ryan h/s - Paluso	Retrd.	N/A	100.00	825
1983 Tom Seaver h/s - Paluso	3,272	N/A	100.00	350
1984 Steve Carlton h/s - Paluso	Retrd.	N/A	100.00	275
1985 Willie Mays h/s - Paluso	Retrd.	N/A	125.00	350-445
1985 Whitey Ford h/s - Paluso	Retrd.	N/A	125.00	295
1985 Hank Aaron h/s - Paluso	Retrd.	N/A	125.00	350-445
1985 Sandy Koufax h/s - Paluso	1,000	N/A	125.00	300-500
1985 H. Killebrew d/s - Paluso	Retrd.	N/A	125.00	200-360
1985 E. Mathews d/s - Paluso	Retrd.	N/A	125.00	225-300
1986 T. Seaver 300 d/s - Paluso	1,200	N/A	125.00	250
1986 Roger Clemens d/s - Paluso	Retrd.	N/A	125.00	600-900
1986 Reggie Jackson d/s - Paluso	Retrd.	N/A	125.00	395
1986 Wally Joyner h/s - Paluso	Retrd.	N/A	125.00	295
1986 Don Sutton d/s (great events) - Paluso	300	N/A	125.00	250
XX Gary Carter d/s - Simon	Retrd.	N/A	125.00	175
1985 Dwight Gooden u/s - Simon	Retrd.	N/A	55.00	85
XX Arnold Palmer h/s - Alexander	Retrd.	N/A	125.00	225
XX Gary Player h/s - Alexander	Retrd.	N/A	125.00	350
1983 Reggie Jackson h/s - Alexander	Retrd.	N/A	125.00	695
1983 Reggie Jackson, proof - Alexander	Retrd.	N/A	250.00	1695
1986 Joe Montana d/s - Alexander	Retrd.	N/A	125.00	595

Hadley House

American Memories Series - T. Redlin

1987 Coming Home	9,500		85.00	85
1988 Lights of Home	9,500	1994	85.00	150
1989 Homeward Bound	9,500		85.00	85
1991 Family Traditions	9,500		85.00	85

Annual Christmas Series - T. Redlin

1991 Heading Home	9,500	1994	65.00	225
1992 Pleasures Of Winter	19,500		65.00	125
1993 Winter Wonderland	19,500		65.00	125
1994 Almost Home	19,500		65.00	125
1995 Sharing the Evening	45-day		29.95	30

Country Doctor Collection - T. Redlin

1995 Wednesday Afternoon	45-day		29.95	30
1995 Office Hours	45-day		29.95	30
1995 House Calls	45-day		29.95	30
1995 Morning Rounds	45-day		29.95	30

Glow Series - T. Redlin

1985 Evening Glow	5,000	1986	55.00	325-450
1985 Morning Glow	5,000	1986	55.00	125-150
1985 Twilight Glow	5,000	1986	55.00	85-125
1988 Afternoon Glow	5,000	1989	55.00	85-125

Lovers Collection - O. Franca

1992 Lovers	9,500		50.00	50

Navajo Visions Suite - O. Franca

1993 Navajo Fantasy	9,500		50.00	50
1993 Young Warrior	9,500		50.00	50

Navajo Woman Series - O. Franca

1990 Feathered Hair Ties	5,000	1994	50.00	50
1991 Navajo Summer	5,000		50.00	50
1992 Turquoise Necklace	5,000		50.00	50
1993 Pink Navajo	5,000		50.00	50

Retreat Series - T. Redlin

1987 Morning Retreat	9,500	1988	65.00	100
1987 Evening Retreat	9,500	1989	65.00	100
1988 Golden Retreat	9,500	1989	65.00	120
1989 Moonlight Retreat	9,500	1993	65.00	85

Seasons - T. Redlin

1994 Autumn Evening	45-day		29.95	30

1995 Spring Fever	45-day		29.95	30
1995 Summertime	45-day		29.95	30
1995 Wintertime	45-day		29.95	30

That Special Time - T. Redlin

1991 Evening Solitude	9,500	1994	65.00	95
1991 That Special Time	9,500	1993	65.00	95
1992 Aroma of Fall	9,500	1994	65.00	95
1993 Welcome To Paradise	9,500		65.00	65

Tranquility - O. Franca

1994 Blue Navajo	9,500		50.00	50
1994 Blue Tranquility	9,500		50.00	50
1994 Navajo Meditating	9,500		50.00	50
1995 Navajo Reflection	9,500		50.00	50

Wildlife Memories - T. Redlin

1994 Best Friends	19,500		65.00	65
1994 Comforts of Home	19,500		65.00	65
1994 Pure Contentment	19,500		65.00	65
1994 Sharing in the Solitude	19,500		65.00	65

Windows to the Wild - T. Redlin

1990 Master's Domain	9,500		65.00	65
1991 Winter Windbreak	9,500		65.00	65
1992 Evening Company	9,500		65.00	65
1994 Night Mapling	9,500		65.00	65

Hamilton Collection

All in a Day's Work - J. Lamb

1994 Where's the Fire?	28-day		29.50	30
1994 Lunch Break	28-day		29.50	30
1994 Puppy Patrol	28-day		29.50	30
1994 Decoy Delivery	28-day		29.50	30
1994 Budding Artist	28-day		29.50	30
1994 Garden Guards	28-day		29.50	30
1994 Saddling Up	28-day		29.50	30
1995 Taking the Lead	28-day		29.50	30

All Star Memories - D. Spindel

1995 The Mantle Story	28-day		35.00	35
1996 Momentos of the Mick	28-day		35.00	35
1996 Mantle Appreciation Day	28-day		35.00	35
1996 Life of a Legend	28-day		35.00	35
1996 Yankee Pride	28-day		35.00	35
1996 A World Series Tribute	28-day		35.00	35
1996 The Ultimate All Star	28-day		35.00	35
1997 Triple Crown	28-day		35.00	35

America's Greatest Sailing Ships - T. Freeman

1988 USS Constitution	14-day		29.50	40
1988 Great Republic	14-day		29.50	40
1988 America	14-day		29.50	45
1988 Charles W. Morgan	14-day		29.50	40
1988 Eagle	14-day		29.50	48
1988 Bonhomme Richard	14-day		29.50	40
1988 Gertrude L. Thebaud	14-day		29.50	45
1988 Enterprise	14-day		29.50	36

The American Civil War - D. Prechtel

1990 General Robert E. Lee	14-day		37.50	75
1990 Generals Grant and Lee At Appomattox	14-day		37.50	50
1990 General Thomas "Stonewall" Jackson	14-day		37.50	55
1990 Abraham Lincoln	14-day		37.50	60
1991 General J.E.B. Stuart	14-day		37.50	45
1991 General Philip Sheridan	14-day		37.50	60
1991 A Letter from Home	14-day		37.50	60
1991 Going Home	14-day		37.50	45
1992 Assembling The Troop	14-day		37.50	75
1992 Standing Watch	14-day		37.50	75

The American Wilderness - M. Richter

1995 Gray Wolf	28-day		29.95	30
1995 Silent Watch	28-day		29.95	30
1995 Moon Song	28-day		29.95	30
1995 Silent Pursuit	28-day		29.95	30
1996 Still of the Night	28-day		29.95	30
1996 Nighttime Serenity	28-day		29.95	30
1996 Autumn Solitude	28-day		29.95	30
1996 Arctic Wolf	28-day		29.95	30

Andy Griffith - R. Tanenbaum

1992 Sheriff Andy Taylor	28-day		29.50	45
1992 A Startling Conclusion	28-day		29.50	45
1993 Mayberry Sing-a-long	28-day		29.50	45
1993 Aunt Bee's Kitchen	28-day		29.50	45
1993 Surprise! Surprise!	28-day		29.50	60
1993 An Explosive Situation	28-day		29.50	45
1993 Meeting Aunt Bee	28-day		29.50	30
1993 Opie's Big Catch	28-day		29.50	30

The Angler's Prize - M. Susinno

1991 Trophy Bass	14-day		29.50	36
1991 Blue Ribbon Trout	14-day		29.50	33
1991 Sun Dancers	14-day		29.50	30
1991 Freshwater Barracuda	14-day		29.50	36
1991 Bronzeback Fighter	14-day		29.50	36
1991 Autumn Beauty	14-day		29.50	36

1992 Old Mooneyes	14-day		29.50	36
1992 Silver King	14-day		29.50	33

Beauty Of Winter - N/A

1992 Silent Night	28-day		29.50	30
1993 Moonlight Sleighride	28-day		29.50	30

The Best Of Baseball - R. Tanenbaum

1993 The Legendary Mickey Mantle	28-day		29.50	30
1993 The Immortal Babe Ruth	28-day		29.50	30
1993 The Great Willie Mays	28-day		29.50	30
1993 The Unbeatable Duke Snider	28-day		29.50	30
1993 The Extraordinary Lou Gehrig	28-day		29.50	30
1993 The Phenomenal Roberto Clemente	28-day		29.50	30
1993 The Remarkable Johnny Bench	28-day		29.50	30
1993 The Incredible Nolan Ryan	28-day		29.50	30
1993 The Exceptional Brooks Robinson	28-day		29.50	30
1993 The Unforgettable Phil Rizzuto	28-day		29.50	30
1995 The Incomparable Reggie Jackson	28-day		29.50	30

Bialosky® & Friends - P./A.Bialosky

1992 Family Addition	28-day		29.50	33
1993 Sweetheart	28-day		29.50	36
1993 Let's Go Fishing	28-day		29.50	36
1993 U.S. Mail	28-day		29.50	36
1993 Sleigh Ride	28-day		29.50	36
1993 Honey For Sale	28-day		29.50	36
1993 Breakfast In Bed	28-day		29.50	36
1993 My First Two-Wheeler	28-day		29.50	30

Big Cats of the World - D. Manning

1989 African Shade	14-day		29.50	37
1989 View from Above	14-day		29.50	30
1990 On The Prowl	14-day		29.50	30
1990 Deep In The Jungle	14-day		29.50	30
1990 Spirit Of The Mountain	14-day		29.50	30
1990 Spotted Sentinel	14-day		29.50	30
1990 Above the Treetops	14-day		29.50	30
1990 Mountain Dweller	14-day		29.50	30
1992 Jungle Habitat	14-day		29.50	30
1992 Solitary Sentry	14-day		29.50	30

Bundles of Joy - B. P. Gutmann

1988 Awakening	14-day		24.50	40-75
1988 Happy Dreams	14-day		24.50	50-75
1988 Tasting	14-day		24.50	40-50
1988 Sweet Innocence	14-day		24.50	40
1988 Tommy	14-day		24.50	35
1988 A Little Bit of Heaven	14-day		24.50	75
1988 Billy	14-day		24.50	35
1988 Sun Kissed	14-day		24.50	30

Butterfly Garden - P. Sweany

1987 Spicebush Swallowtail	14-day		29.50	45
1987 Common Blue	14-day		29.50	38
1987 Orange Sulphur	14-day		29.50	35
1987 Monarch	14-day		29.50	45
1987 Tiger Swallowtail	14-day		29.50	30
1987 Crimson Patched Longwing	14-day		29.50	38
1988 Morning Cloak	14-day		29.50	30
1988 Red Admiral	14-day		29.50	38

The Call of the North - J. Tift

1993 Winter's Dawn	28-day		29.50	30
1994 Evening Silence	28-day		29.50	30
1994 Moonlit Wilderness	28-day		29.50	30
1994 Silent Snowfall	28-day		29.50	30
1994 Snowy Watch	28-day		29.50	30
1994 Sentinels of the Summit	28-day		29.50	30
1994 Arctic Seclusion	28-day		29.50	30
1994 Forest Twilight	28-day		29.50	30
1994 Mountain Explorer	28-day		29.50	30
1994 The Cry of Winter	28-day		29.50	30

Call to Adventure - R. Cross

1993 USS Constitution	28-day		29.50	30
1993 The Bounty	28-day		29.50	30
1994 Bonhomme Richard	28-day		29.50	30
1994 Old Nantucket	28-day		29.50	30
1994 Golden West	28-day		29.50	30
1994 Boston	28-day		29.50	30
1994 Hannah	28-day		29.50	30
1994 Improvement	28-day		29.50	30
1995 Anglo-American	28-day		29.50	30
1995 Challenge	28-day		29.50	30

Cameo Kittens - Q. Lemonds

1993 Ginger Snap	28-day		29.50	30
1993 Cat Tails	28-day		29.50	30
1993 Lady Blue	28-day		29.50	30
1993 Tiny Heart Stealer	28-day		29.50	30
1993 Blossom	28-day		29.50	30
1994 Whisker Antics	28-day		29.50	30
1994 Tiger's Temptation	28-day		29.50	30
1994 Scout	28-day		29.50	30
1995 Timid Tabby	28-day		29.50	30

A Child's Best Friend - B. P. Gutmann

1985 In Disgrace	14-day		24.50	60-90
1985 The Reward	14-day		24.50	40-60

PLATES

YEAR ISSUE		EDITION LIMIT	YEAR RETD.	ISSUE PRICE	*QUOTE U.S.$
1985	Who's Sleepy	14-day		24.50	50-90
1985	Good Morning	14-day		24.50	50-75
1985	Sympathy	14-day		24.50	55
1985	On the Up and Up	14-day		24.50	75-100
1985	Mine	14-day		24.50	90
1985	Going to Town	14-day		24.50	90-125

A Child's Christmas - J. Ferrandiz
1995	Asleep in the Hay	28-day		29.95	30
1995	Merry Little Friends	28-day		29.95	30
1995	Love is Warm All Over	28-day		29.95	30
1995	Little Shepard Family	28-day		29.95	30
1995	Life's Little Blessings	28-day		29.95	30
1995	Happiness is Being Loved	28-day		29.95	30
1995	My Heart Belongs to You	28-day		29.95	30
1996	Lil' Dreamers	28-day		29.95	30

Childhood Reflections - B.P. Gutmann
1991	Harmony	14-day		29.50	70
1991	Kitty's Breakfast	14-day		29.50	40
1991	Friendly Enemies	14-day		29.50	40
1991	Smile, Smile, Smile	14-day		29.50	40
1991	Lullaby	14-day		29.50	40
1991	Oh! Oh! A Bunny	14-day		29.50	30
1991	Little Mother	14-day		29.50	35
1991	Thank You, God	14-day		29.50	40

Children of the American Frontier - D. Crook
1986	In Trouble Again	10-day		24.50	35-45
1986	Tubs and Suds	10-day		24.50	28
1986	A Lady Needs a Little Privacy	10-day		24.50	25-38
1986	The Desperadoes	10-day		24.50	38
1986	Riders Wanted	10-day		24.50	30
1987	A Cowboy's Downfall	10-day		24.50	28
1987	Runaway Blues	10-day		24.50	25
1987	A Special Patient	10-day		24.50	38

Civil War Generals - M. Gnatek
1994	Robert E. Lee	28-day		29.50	30
1994	J.E.B. Stewart	28-day		29.50	30
1994	Joshua L. Chamberlain	28-day		29.50	30
1994	George Armstrong Custer	28-day		29.50	30
1994	Nathan Bedford Forrest	28-day		29.50	30
1994	James Longstreet	28-day		29.50	30
1995	Thomas "Stonewall" Jackson	28-day		29.50	30
1995	Confederate Heroes	28-day		29.50	30

Classic American Santas - G. Hinke
1993	A Christmas Eve Visitor	28-day		29.50	30
1994	Up on the Rooftop	28-day		29.50	30
1994	Santa's Candy Kitchen	28-day		29.50	30
1994	A Christmas Chorus	28-day		29.50	30
1994	An Exciting Christmas Eve	28-day		29.50	30
1994	Rest Ye Merry Gentlemen	28-day		29.50	30
1994	Preparing the Sleigh	28-day		29.50	30
1994	The Reindeer's Stable	28-day		29.50	30
1994	He's Checking His List	28-day		29.50	30

Classic Corvettes - M. Lacourciere
1994	1957 Corvette	28-day		29.50	30
1994	1963 Corvette	28-day		29.50	30
1994	1968 Corvette	28-day		29.50	30
1994	1986 Corvette	28-day		29.50	30
1995	1967 Corvette	28-day		29.50	30
1995	1953 Corvette	28-day		29.50	30
1995	1962 Corvette	28-day		29.50	30
1995	1990 Corvette	28-day		29.50	

Classic Sporting Dogs - B. Christie
1989	Golden Retrievers	14-day		24.50	60-70
1989	Labrador Retrievers	14-day		24.50	60
1989	Beagles	14-day		24.50	40-55
1989	Pointers	14-day		24.50	40-55
1989	Springer Spaniels	14-day		24.50	40
1990	German Short-Haired Pointers	14-day		24.50	55
1990	Irish Setters	14-day		24.50	40
1990	Brittany Spaniels	14-day		24.50	48

Classic TV Westerns - K. Milnazik
1990	The Lone Ranger and Tonto	14-day		29.50	50-75
1990	Bonanza Ô	14-day		29.50	70
1990	Roy Rogers and Dale Evans	14-day		29.50	50-60
1991	Rawhide	14-day		29.50	50
1991	Wild Wild West	14-day		29.50	60
1991	Have Gun, Will Travel	14-day		29.50	50
1991	The Virginian	14-day		29.50	40-60
1991	Hopalong Cassidy	14-day		29.50	60

Cloak of Visions - A. Farley
1994	Visions in a Full Moon	28-day		29.50	30
1994	Protector of the Child	28-day		29.50	30
1995	Spirits of the Canyon	28-day		29.50	30
1995	Freedom Soars	28-day		29.50	30
1995	Mystic Reflections	28-day		29.50	30
1995	Staff of Life	28-day		29.50	30
1995	Springtime Hunters	28-day		29.50	30
1996	Moonlit Solace	28-day		29.50	30

Comical Dalmations - Landmark
1996	I Will Not Bark In Class	28-day		29.95	40
1996	The Master	28-day		29.95	30

YEAR ISSUE		EDITION LIMIT	YEAR RETD.	ISSUE PRICE	*QUOTE U.S.$
1996	Spot At Play	28-day		29.95	30
1996	A Dalmation's Dream	28-day		29.95	30
1996	To The Rescue	28-day		29.95	30
1996	Maid For A Day	28-day		29.95	30
1996	Dalmation Celebration	28-day		29.95	30
1996	Concert in D-Minor	28-day		29.95	30

Coral Paradise - H. Bond
1989	The Living Oasis	14-day		29.50	45
1990	Riches of the Coral Sea	14-day		29.50	30
1990	Tropical Pageantry	14-day		29.50	40
1990	Caribbean Spectacle	14-day		29.50	35
1990	Undersea Village	14-day		29.50	36
1990	Shimmering Reef Dwellers	14-day		29.50	36
1990	Mysteries of the Galapagos	14-day		29.50	33
1990	Forest Beneath the Sea	14-day		29.50	30

Cottage Puppies - K. George
1993	Little Gardeners	28-day		29.50	30
1993	Springtime Fancy	28-day		29.50	30
1993	Endearing Innocence	28-day		29.50	30
1994	Picnic Playtime	28-day		29.50	30
1994	Lazy Afternoon	28-day		29.50	30
1994	Summertime Pals	28-day		29.50	30
1994	A Gardening Trio	28-day		29.50	30
1994	Taking a Break	28-day		29.50	30

Council Of Nations - G. Perillo
1991	Strength of the Sioux	28-day		29.50	30
1992	Pride of the Cheyenne	28-day		29.50	30
1992	Dignity of the Nez Parce	28-day		29.50	30
1992	Courage of the Arapaho	28-day		29.50	30
1992	Power of the Blackfoot	28-day		29.50	30
1992	Nobility of the Algonqui	28-day		29.50	30
1992	Wisdom of the Cherokee	28-day		29.50	30
1992	Boldness of the Seneca	28-day		29.50	45

Country Garden Cottages - E. Dertner
1992	Riverbank Cottage	28-day		29.50	36
1992	Sunday Outing	28-day		29.50	30
1992	Shepherd's Cottage	28-day		29.50	30
1992	Daydream Cottage	28-day		29.50	30
1993	Garden Glorious	28-day		29.50	30
1993	This Side of Heaven	28-day		29.50	33
1993	Summer Symphony	28-day		29.50	30
1993	April Cottage	28-day		29.50	30

Country Kitties - G. Gerardi
1989	Mischief Makers	14-day		24.50	45
1989	Table Manners	14-day		24.50	36
1989	Attic Attack	14-day		24.50	40
1989	Rock and Rollers	14-day		24.50	45
1989	Just For the Fern of It	14-day		24.50	45
1989	All Washed Up	14-day		24.50	50
1989	Stroller Derby	14-day		24.50	39
1989	Captive Audience	14-day		24.50	50

A Country Season of Horses - J.M. Vass
1990	First Day of Spring	14-day		29.50	40
1990	Summer Splendor	14-day		29.50	35
1990	A Winter's Walk	14-day		29.50	35
1990	Autumn Grandeur	14-day		29.50	30
1990	Cliffside Beauty	14-day		29.50	30
1990	Frosty Morning	14-day		29.50	30
1990	Crisp Country Morning	14-day		29.50	30
1990	River Retreat	14-day		29.50	30

A Country Summer - N. Noel
1985	Butterfly Beauty	10-day		29.50	36
1985	The Golden Puppy	10-day		29.50	30
1986	The Rocking Chair	10-day		29.50	36
1986	My Bunny	10-day		29.50	33
1988	The Piglet	10-day		29.50	30
1988	Teammates	10-day		29.50	30

Curious Kittens - B. Harrison
1990	Rainy Day Friends	14-day		29.50	36-45
1990	Keeping in Step	14-day		29.50	36
1991	Delightful Discovery	14-day		29.50	36
1991	Chance Meeting	14-day		29.50	36
1991	All Wound Up	14-day		29.50	36
1991	Making Tracks	14-day		29.50	36
1991	Playing Cat and Mouse	14-day		29.50	36
1991	A Paw's in the Action	14-day		29.50	36
1992	Little Scholar	14-day		29.50	36
1992	Cat Burglar	14-day		29.50	36

Dale Earnhardt - Various
1996	The Intimidator - S. Bass	28-day		35.00	35
1996	The Man in Black - R. Tanenbaum	28-day		35.00	35
1996	Silver Select - S. Bass	28-day		35.00	35
1996	Back in Black - R. Tanenbaum	28-day		35.00	35

Daughters Of The Sun - K. Thayer
1993	Sun Dancer	28-day		29.50	30
1993	Shining Feather	28-day		29.50	30
1993	Delighted Dancer	28-day		29.50	30
1993	Evening Dancer	28-day		29.50	30
1993	A Secret Glance	28-day		29.50	30
1993	Chippewa Charmer	28-day		29.50	30
1994	Pride of the Yakima	28-day		29.50	30

YEAR ISSUE		EDITION LIMIT	YEAR RETD.	ISSUE PRICE	*QUOTE U.S.$
1994	Radiant Beauty	28-day		29.50	30

Dear to My Heart - J. Hagara
1990	Cathy	14-day		29.50	30-60
1990	Addie	14-day		29.50	30
1990	Jimmy	14-day		29.50	30
1990	Dacy	14-day		29.50	30
1990	Paul	14-day		29.50	30
1991	Shelly	14-day		29.50	30
1991	Jenny	14-day		29.50	30
1991	Joy	14-day		29.50	30

Dolphin Discovery - D. Queen
1995	Sunrise Reverie	28-day		29.50	30
1995	Dolphin's Paradise	28-day		29.50	30
1995	Coral Cove	28-day		29.50	30
1995	Undersea Journey	28-day		29.50	30
1995	Dolphin Canyon	28-day		29.50	30
1995	Coral Garden	28-day		29.50	30
1996	Dolphin Duo	28-day		29.50	30
1996	Underwater Tranquility	28-day		29.50	30

Dreamsicles - K. Haynes
1994	The Flying Lesson	28-day		19.50	20
1995	By the Light of the Moon	28-day		19.50	20
1995	The Recital	28-day		19.50	20
1995	Heavenly Pirouettes	28-day		19.50	20
1995	Blossoms and Butterflies	28-day		19.50	20
1995	Love's Shy Glance	28-day		19.50	20
1996	Wishing Upon a Star	28-day		19.50	20
1996	Rainy Day Friends	28-day		19.50	20
1996	Starboats Ahoy!	28-day		19.50	20
1996	Teeter Tots	28-day		19.50	20
1996	Star Magic	28-day		19.50	20

Dreamsicles Christmas Annual Scuptural - K. Haynes
1996	The Finishing Touches	Open		39.95	40

Dreamsicles Heaven Sent - N/A
1996	Quiet Blessings	28-day		29.95	30
1996	A Heartfelt Embrace	28-day		29.95	30
1996	Earth's Blessings	28-day		29.95	30
1996	A Moment In Dreamland	28-day		29.95	30
1996	Sew Cuddly	28-day		29.95	30
1996	Homemade With Love	28-day		29.95	30
1996	A Sweet Treat	28-day		29.95	30
1996	Pampered And Pretty	28-day		29.95	30

Dreamsicles Life's Little Blessings - K. Haynes
1995	Happiness	28-day		29.95	30
1996	Peace	28-day		29.95	30
1996	Love	28-day		29.95	30
1996	Creativity	28-day		29.95	30
1996	Friendship	28-day		29.95	30
1996	Knowledge	28-day		29.95	30
1996	Hope	28-day		29.95	30
1996	Faith	28-day		29.95	30

Dreamsicles Sculptural - N/A
1995	The Flying Lesson	Open		37.50	38
1996	By The Light of the Moon	Open		37.50	38
1996	The Recital	Open		37.50	38
1996	Teeter Tots	Open		37.50	38
1996	Poetry In Motion	Open		37.50	38
1996	Rock-A-Bye Dreamsicles	Open		37.50	38
1996	The Birth Certificate	Open		37.50	38

Dreamsicles Special Friends - K. Haynes
1995	A Hug From the Heart	28-day		29.95	30
1995	Heaven's Little Helper	28-day		29.95	30
1995	Bless Us All	28-day		29.95	30
1996	Love's Gentle Touch	28-day		29.95	30
1996	The Best Gift of All	28-day		29.95	30
1996	A Heavenly Hoorah!	28-day		29.95	30
1996	A Love Like No Other	28-day		29.95	30
1996	Cuddle Up	28-day		29.95	30

Dreamsicles Special Friends Sculptural - N/A
1995	Heaven's Little Helper	Open		37.50	38
1996	A Hug From The Heart	Open		37.50	38
1996	Bless Us All	Open		37.50	38
1996	The Best Gift of All	Open		37.50	38
1996	A Heavenly Hoorah!	Open		37.50	38
1996	A Love Like No Other	Open		37.50	38

Dreamsicles Sweethearts - K. Haynes
1996	Stolen Kiss	28-day		35.00	35
1996	Sharing Hearts	28-day		35.00	35
1996	Love Letters	28-day		35.00	35

Drivers of Victory Lane - R. Tanenbaum
1994	Bill Elliott	28-day		29.50	30
1994	Jeff Gordon	28-day		29.50	30
1994	Rusty Wallace	28-day		29.50	30
1995	Geoff Bodine	28-day		29.50	30
1995	Dale Earnhardt	28-day		29.50	30
1996	Sterling Martin	28-day		29.50	30
1996	Terry Labonte	28-day		29.50	30
1996	Ken Scharder	28-day		29.50	30
1996	#94 Bill Elliott	28-day		29.50	30

YEAR ISSUE		EDITION LIMIT	YEAR RETD.	ISSUE PRICE	*QUOTE U.S.$

Easyriders - M. Lacourciere

1995	American Classic	28-day		29.95	30
1995	Symbols of Freedom	28-day		29.95	30
1996	Patriot's Pride	28-day		29.95	30
1996	The Way of the West	28-day		29.95	30
1996	Revival of an Era	28-day		29.95	30
1996	Hollywood Style	28-day		29.95	30
1996	Vietnam Express	28-day		29.95	30
1996	Las Vegas	28-day		29.95	30

Elvis Remembered - S. Morton

1989	Loving You	90-day		37.50	65-100
1989	Early Years	90-day		37.50	65-75
1989	Tenderly	90-day		37.50	65-100
1989	The King	90-day		37.50	100-130
1989	Forever Yours	90-day		37.50	100
1989	Rockin in the Moonlight	90-day		37.50	100-125
1989	Moody Blues	90-day		37.50	100
1989	Elvis Presley	90-day		37.50	130

Enchanted Seascapes - J. Enright

1993	Sanctuary of the Dolphin	28-day		29.50	30
1994	Rhapsody of Hope	28-day		29.50	30
1994	Oasis of the Gods	28-day		29.50	30
1994	Sphere of Life	28-day		29.50	30
1994	Edge of Time	28-day		29.50	30
1994	Sea of Light	28-day		29.50	30
1994	Lost Beneath the Blue	28-day		29.50	30
1994	Blue Paradise	28-day		29.50	30
1995	Morning Odyssey	28-day		29.50	30
1995	Paradise Cove	28-day		29.50	30

English Country Cottages - M. Bell

1990	Periwinkle Tea Room	14-day		29.50	45
1991	Gamekeeper's Cottage	14-day		29.50	75
1991	Ginger Cottage	14-day		29.50	60
1991	Larkspur Cottage	14-day		29.50	45
1991	The Chaplain's Garden	14-day		29.50	33
1991	Lorna Doone Cottage	14-day		29.50	45
1991	Murrle Cottage	14-day		29.50	36
1991	Lullabye Cottage	14-day		29.50	30

Eternal Wishes of Good Fortune - Shuho

1983	Friendship	10-day		34.95	35
1983	Purity and Perfection	10-day		34.95	35
1983	Illustrious Offspring	10-day		34.95	35
1983	Longevity	10-day		34.95	35
1983	Youth	10-day		34.95	35
1983	Immortality	10-day		34.95	35
1983	Marital Bliss	10-day		34.95	35
1983	Love	10-day		34.95	35
1983	Peace	10-day		34.95	35
1983	Beauty	10-day		34.95	35
1983	Fertility	10-day		34.95	35
1983	Fortitude	10-day		34.95	35

Exotic Tigers of Asia - K. Ottinger

1995	Lord of the Rainforest	28-day		29.50	30
1995	Snow King	28-day		29.50	30
1995	Ruler of the Wetlands	28-day		29.50	30
1996	Majestic Vigil	28-day		29.50	30
1996	Keeper of the Jungle	28-day		29.50	30
1996	Eyes of the Jungle	28-day		29.50	30
1996	Sovereign Ruler	28-day		29.50	30
1996	Lord of the Lowlands	28-day		29.50	30

Familiar Spirits - D. Wright

1996	Faithful Guardians	28-day		29.95	30
1996	Sharing Nature's Innocence	28-day		29.95	30
1996	Trusted Friend	28-day		29.95	30
1996	A Friendship Begins	28-day		29.95	30

Farmyard Friends - J. Lamb

1992	Mistaken Identity	28-day		29.50	30
1992	Little Cowhands	28-day		29.50	30
1993	Shreading the Evidence	28-day		29.50	30
1993	Partners in Crime	28-day		29.50	30
1993	Fowl Play	28-day		29.50	30
1993	Follow The Leader	28-day		29.50	36
1993	Pony Tales	28-day		29.50	30
1993	An Apple A Day	28-day		29.50	30

Favorite American Songbirds - D. O'Driscoll

1989	Blue Jays of Spring	14-day		29.50	36
1989	Red Cardinals of Winter	14-day		29.50	36
1989	Robins & Apple Blossoms	14-day		29.50	36
1989	Goldfinches of Summer	14-day		29.50	36
1990	Autumn Chickadees	14-day		29.50	36
1990	Bluebirds and Morning Glories	14-day		29.50	36
1990	Tufted Titmouse and Holly	14-day		29.50	36
1991	Carolina Wrens of Spring	14-day		29.50	30

Favorite Old Testament Stories - S. Butcher

1994	Jacob's Dream	28-day		35.00	35
1995	The Baby Moses	28-day		35.00	35
1995	Esther's Gift To Her People	28-day		35.00	35
1995	A Prayer For Victory	28-day		35.00	35
1995	Where You Go, I Will Go	28-day		35.00	35
1995	A Prayer Answered, A Promise Kept	28-day		35.00	35
1996	Joseph Sold Into Slavery	28-day		35.00	35

| 1996 | Daniel In the Lion's Den | 28-day | | 35.00 | 35 |
| 1996 | Noah And The Ark | 28-day | | 35.00 | 35 |

The Fierce And The Free - F. McCarthy

1992	Big Medicine	28-day		29.50	30
1993	Land of the Winter Hawk	28-day		29.50	30
1993	Warrior of Savage Splendor	28-day		29.50	30
1994	War Party	28-day		29.50	30
1994	The Challenge	28-day		29.50	30
1994	Out of the Rising Mist	28-day		29.50	30
1994	The Ambush	28-day		29.50	35
1994	Dangerous Crossing	28-day		29.50	30

Forging New Frontiers - J. Deneen

1994	The Race is On	28-day		29.50	30
1994	Big Boy	28-day		29.50	30
1994	Cresting the Summit	28-day		29.50	30
1994	Spring Roundup	28-day		29.50	30
1994	Winter in the Rockies	28-day		29.50	30
1994	High Country Logging	28-day		29.50	30
1994	Confrontation	28-day		29.50	30
1994	A Welcome Sight	28-day		29.50	30

A Garden Song - M. Hanson

1994	Winter's Splendor	28-day		29.50	30
1994	In Full Bloom	28-day		29.50	30
1994	Golden Glories	28-day		29.50	30
1995	Autumn's Elegance	28-day		29.50	30
1995	First Snowfall	28-day		29.50	30
1995	Robins in Spring	28-day		29.50	30
1995	Summer's Glow	28-day		29.50	30
1995	Fall's Serenade	28-day		29.50	30
1996	Sounds of Winter	28-day		29.50	30
1996	Springtime Haven	28-day		29.50	30

Glory of Christ - C. Micarelli

1992	The Ascension	48-day		29.50	30
1992	Jesus Teaching	48-day		29.50	30
1993	Last Supper	48-day		29.50	30
1993	The Nativity	48-day		29.50	30
1993	The Baptism of Christ	48-day		29.50	30
1993	Jesus Heals the Sick	48-day		29.50	30
1994	Jesus Walks on Water	48-day		29.50	30
1994	Descent From the Cross	48-day		29.50	30

Glory of the Game - T. Fogarty

1994	"Hank Aaron's Record-Breaking Home Run"	28-day		29.50	30
1994	"Bobby Thomson's Shot Heard 'Round the World"	28-day		29.50	30
1994	1969 Miracle Mets	28-day		29.50	30
1995	Reggie Jackson: Mr. October	28-day		29.50	30
1995	Don Larsen's Perfect World	28-day		29.50	30
1995	Babe Ruth's Called Shot	28-day		29.50	30
1995	Willie Mays: Greatest Catch	28-day		29.50	30
1995	Bill Mazeroski's Series	28-day		29.50	30
1996	Mickey Mantle's Tape Measure Home Run	28-day		29.50	30

The Golden Age of American Railroads - T. Xaras

1991	The Blue Comet	14-day		29.50	45
1991	The Morning Local	14-day		29.50	50-60
1991	The Pennsylvania K-4	14-day		29.50	40-85
1991	Above the Canyon	14-day		29.50	80-90
1991	Portrait in Steam	14-day		29.50	65-75
1991	The Santa Fe Super Chief	14-day		29.50	105
1991	The Big Boy	14-day		29.50	60
1991	The Empire Builder	14-day		29.50	75
1992	An American Classic	14-day		29.50	60
1992	Final Destination	14-day		29.50	60

Golden Discoveries - L. Budge

1995	Boot Bandits	28-day		29.95	30
1995	Hiding the Evidence	28-day		29.95	30
1995	Decoy Dilemma	28-day		29.95	30
1995	Fishing for Dinner	28-day		29.95	30
1996	Lunchtime Companions	28-day		29.95	30
1996	Friend or Foe?	28-day		29.95	30

Golden Puppy Portraits - P. Braun

1994	Do Not Disturb!	28-day		29.50	30
1995	Teething Time	28-day		29.50	30
1995	Table Manners	28-day		29.50	30
1995	A Golden Bouquet	28-day		29.50	30
1995	Time For Bed	28-day		29.50	30
1995	Bathtime Blues	28-day		29.50	30
1996	Spinning a Yarn	28-day		29.50	30
1996	Partytime Puppy	28-day		29.50	30

Good Sports - J. Lamb

1990	Wide Retriever	14-day		29.50	45-54
1990	Double Play	14-day		29.50	36-50
1990	Hole in One	14-day		29.50	45-50
1990	The Bass Masters	14-day		29.50	40
1990	Spotted on the Sideline	14-day		29.50	36
1990	Slap Shot	14-day		29.50	40
1991	Net Play	14-day		29.50	30-45
1991	Bassetball	14-day		29.50	36
1992	Boxer Rebellion	14-day		29.50	40
1992	Great Try	14-day		29.50	39

Great Fighter Planes Of World War II - R. Waddey

1992	Old Crow	14-day		29.50	30
1992	Big Hog	14-day		29.50	30
1992	P-47 Thunderbolt	14-day		29.50	30
1992	P-40 Flying Tiger	14-day		29.50	30
1992	F4F Wildcat	14-day		29.50	30
1992	P-38F Lightning	14-day		29.50	30
1993	F6F Hellcat	14-day		29.50	30
1993	P-39M Airacobra	14-day		29.50	30
1995	Memphis Belle	14-day		29.50	30
1995	The Dragon and His Tail	14-day		29.50	30

Great Mammals of the Sea - Wyland

1991	Orca Trio	14-day		35.00	45
1991	Hawaii Dolphins	14-day		35.00	43
1991	Orca Journey	14-day		35.00	43
1991	Dolphin Paradise	14-day		35.00	45
1991	Children of the Sea	14-day		35.00	60
1991	Kissing Dolphins	14-day		35.00	39
1991	Islands	14-day		35.00	60
1991	Orcas	14-day		35.00	45

The Greatest Show on Earth - F. Moody

1981	Clowns	10-day		30.00	32-45
1981	Elephants	10-day		30.00	30
1981	Aerialists	10-day		30.00	30
1981	Great Parade	10-day		30.00	30
1981	Midway	10-day		30.00	30
1981	Equestrians	10-day		30.00	30
1982	Lion Tamer	10-day		30.00	30
1982	Grande Finale	10-day		30.00	30

Growing Up Together - P. Brooks

1990	My Very Best Friends	14-day		29.50	36
1990	Tea for Two	14-day		29.50	30
1990	Tender Loving Care	14-day		29.50	30
1990	Picnic Pals	14-day		29.50	30
1991	Newfound Friends	14-day		29.50	30
1991	Kitten Caboodle	14-day		29.50	30
1991	Fishing Buddies	14-day		29.50	30
1991	Bedtime Blessings	14-day		29.50	30

The Historic Railways - T. Xaras

1995	Harper's Ferry	28-day		29.95	30
1995	Horseshoe Curve	28-day		29.95	30
1995	Kentucky's Red River	28-day		29.95	30
1995	Sherman Hill Challenger	28-day		29.95	30
1996	New York Central's 4-6-4 Hudson	28-day		29.95	30
1996	Rails By The Seashore	28-day		29.95	30
1996	Steam in the High Sierras	28-day		29.95	30
1996	Evening Departure	28-day		29.95	30

The I Love Lucy Plate Collection - J. Kritz

1989	California, Here We Come	14-day		29.50	95-200
1989	It's Just Like Candy	14-day		29.50	100-200
1990	The Big Squeeze	14-day		29.50	100-200
1990	Eating the Evidence	14-day		29.50	150-250
1990	Two of a Kind	14-day		29.50	175-200
1991	Queen of the Gypsies	14-day		29.50	110-175
1992	Night at the Copa	14-day		29.50	100-175
1992	A Rising Problem	14-day		29.50	125-200

Japanese Floral Calendar - Shuho/Kage

1981	New Year's Day	10-day		32.50	40
1982	Early Spring	10-day		32.50	40
1982	Spring	10-day		32.50	40
1982	Girl's Doll Day Festival	10-day		32.50	40
1982	Buddha's Birthday	10-day		32.50	40
1982	Early Summer	10-day		32.50	40
1982	Boy's Doll Day Festival	10-day		32.50	40
1982	Summer	10-day		32.50	33
1982	Autumn	10-day		32.50	33
1983	Festival of the Full Moon	10-day		32.50	33
1983	Late Autumn	10-day		32.50	33
1983	Winter	10-day		32.50	33

Jeff Gordon - Various

1996	On The Warpath - S. Bass	28-day		35.00	35
1996	Headed to Victory Lane - R. Tanenbaum	28-day		35.00	35
1996	Gordon Takes the Title - S. Bass	28-day		35.00	35
1996	From Winner to Champion - R. Tanenbaum	28-day		35.00	35

The Jeweled Hummingbirds - J. Landenberger

1989	Ruby-throated Hummingbirds	14-day		37.50	45
1989	Great Sapphire Wing Hummingbirds	14-day		37.50	45
1989	Ruby-Topaz Hummingbirds	14-day		37.50	45
1989	Andean Emerald Hummingbirds	14-day		37.50	45
1989	Garnet-throated Hummingbirds	14-day		37.50	45
1989	Blue-Headed Sapphire Hummingbirds	14-day		37.50	45
1989	Pearl Coronet Hummingbirds	14-day		37.50	45
1989	Amethyst-throated Sunangels	14-day		37.50	45

Joe Montana - Various

1996	40,000 Yards - R. Tanenbaum	28-day		35.00	35
1996	Finding a Way to Win - A. Catalano	28-day		35.00	35
1996	Comeback Kid - A. Catalano	28-day		35.00	35

PLATES

YEAR ISSUE		EDITION LIMIT	YEAR RETD.	ISSUE PRICE	*QUOTE U.S.$
1996	Chief on the Field - Petronella	28-day		35.00	35

Kitten Classics - P. Cooper

1985	Cat Nap	14-day		29.50	40
1985	Purrfect Treasure	14-day		29.50	30
1985	Wild Flower	14-day		29.50	30
1985	Birdwatcher	14-day		29.50	30
1985	Tiger's Fancy	14-day		29.50	33
1985	Country Kitty	14-day		29.50	33
1985	Little Rascal	14-day		29.50	30
1985	First Prize	14-day		29.50	30

Knick Knack Kitty Cat Sculptural - L. Yencho

1996	Kittens in the Cupboard	Open		39.95	40

The Last Warriors - C. Ren

1993	Winter of '41	28-day		29.50	30
1993	Morning of Reckoning	28-day		29.50	30
1993	Twilights Last Gleaming	28-day		29.50	30
1993	Lone Winter Journey	28-day		29.50	30
1994	Victory's Reward	28-day		29.50	30
1994	Solitary Hunter	28-day		29.50	30
1994	Solemn Reflection	28-day		29.50	30
1994	Confronting Danger	28-day		29.50	30
1995	Moment of Contemplation	28-day		29.50	30
1995	The Last Sunset	28-day		29.50	30

The Legend of Father Christmas - V. Dezerin

1994	The Return of Father Christmas	28-day		29.50	30
1994	Gifts From Father Christmas	28-day		29.50	30
1994	The Feast of the Holiday	28-day		29.50	30
1995	Christmas Day Visitors	28-day		29.50	30
1995	Decorating the Tree	28-day		29.50	30
1995	The Snow Sculpture	28-day		29.50	30
1995	Skating on the Pond	28-day		29.50	30
1995	Holy Night	28-day		29.50	30

Legendary Warriors - M. Gentry

1995	White Quiver and Scout	28-day		29.95	30
1995	Lakota Rendezvous	28-day		29.95	30
1995	Crazy Horse	28-day		29.95	30
1995	Sitting Bull's Vision	28-day		29.95	30
1996	Crazy Horse	28-day		29.95	30
1996	Sitting Bull's Vision	28-day		29.95	30
1996	Noble Surrender	28-day		29.95	30
1996	Sioux Thunder	28-day		29.95	30
1996	Eagle Dancer	28-day		29.95	30
1996	The Trap	28-day		29.95	30

A Lisi Martin Christmas - L. Martin

1992	Santa's Littlest Reindeer	28-day		29.50	30
1993	Not A Creature Was Stirring	28-day		29.50	30
1993	Christmas Dreams	28-day		29.50	30
1993	The Christmas Story	28-day		29.50	30
1993	Trimming The Tree	28-day		29.50	30
1993	A Taste Of The Holidays	28-day		29.50	30
1993	The Night Before Christmas	28-day		29.50	30
1993	Christmas Watch	28-day		29.50	30
1995	Christmas Presence	28-day		29.50	30
1995	Nose to Nose	28-day		29.50	30

Little Fawns of the Forest - R. Manning

1995	In the Morning Light	28-day		29.95	30
1995	Cool Reflections	28-day		29.95	30
1995	Nature's Lesson	28-day		29.95	30
1996	A Friendship Blossoms	28-day		29.95	30
1996	Innocent Companions	28-day		29.95	30
1996	New Life, New Day	28-day		29.95	30

Little Ladies - M.H. Bogart

1989	Playing Bridesmaid	14-day		29.50	75-100
1990	The Seamstress	14-day		29.50	60-90
1990	Little Captive	14-day		29.50	45
1990	Playing Mama	14-day		29.50	60-90
1990	Susanna	14-day		29.50	30
1990	Kitty's Bath	14-day		29.50	55-75
1990	A Day in the Country	14-day		29.50	45-75
1991	Sarah	14-day		29.50	45
1991	First Party	14-day		29.50	55
1991	The Magic Kitten	14-day		29.50	30

The Little Rascals - Unknown

1985	Three for the Show	10-day		24.50	30
1985	My Gal	10-day		24.50	25
1985	Skeleton Crew	10-day		24.50	25
1985	Roughin' It	10-day		24.50	25
1985	Spanky's Pranks	10-day		24.50	25
1985	Butch's Challenge	10-day		24.50	25
1985	Darla's Debut	10-day		24.50	25
1985	Pete's Pal	10-day		24.50	25

Little Shopkeepers - G. Gerardi

1990	Sew Tired	14-day		29.50	30
1991	Break Time	14-day		29.50	30
1991	Purrfect Fit	14-day		29.50	30
1991	Toying Around	14-day		29.50	36
1991	Chain Reaction	14-day		29.50	45
1991	Interior Decorators	14-day		29.50	36
1991	Tulip Tag	14-day		29.50	36
1991	Candy Capers	14-day		29.50	36

Lore Of The West - L. Danielle

1993	A Mile In His Mocassins	28-day		29.50	30
1993	Path of Honor	28-day		29.50	30
1993	A Chief's Pride	28-day		29.50	30
1994	Pathways of the Pueblo	28-day		29.50	30
1994	In Her Seps	28-day		29.50	30
1994	Growing Up Brave	28-day		29.50	30
1994	Nomads of the Southwest	28-day		29.50	30
1994	Sacred Spirit of the Plains	28-day		29.50	30
1994	We'll Fight No More	28-day		29.50	30
1994	The End of the Trail	28-day		29.50	30

Love's Messengers - J. Grossman

1995	To My Love	28-day		29.50	30
1995	Cupid's Arrow	28-day		29.50	30
1995	Love's Melody	28-day		29.50	30
1995	A Token of Love	28-day		29.50	30
1995	Harmony of Love	28-day		29.50	30
1996	True Love's Offering	28-day		29.95	30
1996	Love's In Bloom	28-day		29.95	30
1996	To My Sweetheart	28-day		29.95	30

The Lucille Ball (Official) Commemorative Plate - M. Weistling

1993	Lucy	28-day		37.50	125-225

Madonna And Child - Various

1992	Madonna Della Sedia - R. Sanzio	28-day		37.50	38
1992	Virgin of the Rocks - L. DaVinci	28-day		37.50	38
1993	Madonna of Rosary - B. E. Murillo	28-day		37.50	38
1993	Sistine Madonna - R. Sanzio	28-day		37.50	38
1993	Virgin Adoring Christ Child - A. Correggio	28-day		37.50	38
1993	Virgin of the Grape - P. Mignard	28-day		37.50	38
1993	Madonna del Magnificat - S. Botticelli	28-day		37.50	38
1993	Madonna col Bambino - S. Botticelli	28-day		37.50	38

The Magical World of Legends & Myths - J. Shalatain

1993	A Mother's Love	28-day		35.00	35
1993	Dreams of Pegasus	28-day		35.00	35
1994	Flight of the Pegasus	28-day		35.00	45
1994	The Awakening	28-day		35.00	45
1994	Once Upon a Dream	28-day		35.00	45
1994	The Dawn of Romance	28-day		35.00	35
1994	The Astral Unicorn	28-day		35.00	45
1994	Flight into Paradise	28-day		35.00	35
1995	Pegasus in the Stars	28-day		35.00	35
1995	Unicorn of the Sea	28-day		35.00	35

Majestic Birds of Prey - C.F. Riley

1983	Golden Eagle	12,500		55.00	60-80
1983	Coopers Hawk	12,500		55.00	60-80
1983	Great Horned Owl	12,500		55.00	60-80
1983	Bald Eagle	12,500		55.00	60-80
1983	Barred Owl	12,500		55.00	60-80
1983	Sparrow Hawk	12,500		55.00	60-80
1983	Peregrine Falcon	12,500		55.00	60-80
1983	Osprey	12,500		55.00	60-80

Majesty of Flight - T. Hirata

1989	The Eagle Soars	14-day		37.50	50
1989	Realm of the Red-Tail	14-day		37.50	50
1989	Coastal Journey	14-day		37.50	45
1989	Sentry of the North	14-day		37.50	35-50
1989	Commanding the Marsh	14-day		37.50	38
1990	The Vantage Point	14-day		29.50	45
1990	Silent Watch	14-day		29.50	48
1990	Fierce and Free	14-day		29.50	45

Man's Best Friend - L. Picken

1992	Special Delivery	28-day		29.50	30
1992	Making Waves	28-day		29.50	30
1992	Good Catch	28-day		29.50	30
1993	Time For a Walk	28-day		29.50	45
1993	Faithful Friend	28-day		29.50	45
1993	Let's Play Ball	28-day		29.50	36
1993	Sitting Pretty	28-day		29.50	30
1993	Bedtime Story	28-day		29.50	30
1993	Trusted Companion	28-day		29.50	30

Mickey Mantle - R. Tanenbaum

1996	The Mick	28-day		35.00	35
1996	536 Home Runs	28-day		35.00	35
1996	2,401 Games	28-day		35.00	35
1996	Switch Hitter	28-day		35.00	35
1996	16 Time All Star	28-day		35.00	35
1996	18 World Series Home Runs	28-day		35.00	35
1997	1956-A Crowning Year	28-day		35.00	35
1997	Remembering a Legendary Yankee	28-day		35.00	35

Mike Schmidt - R. Tanenbaum

1994	The Ultimate Competitor: Mike Schmidt	28-day		29.50	30
1995	A Homerun King	28-day		29.50	30
1995	An All Time, All Star	28-day		29.50	30
1995	A Career Retrospective	28-day		29.50	30

Milestones in Space - D. Dixon

1994	Moon Landing	28-day		29.50	30
1995	Space Lab	28-day		29.50	30

1995	Maiden Flight of Columbia	28-day		29.50	30
1995	Free Walk in Space	28-day		29.50	30
1995	Lunar Rover	28-day		29.50	30
1995	Handshake in Space	28-day		29.50	30
1995	First Landing on Mars	28-day		29.50	30
1995	Voyager's Exploration	28-day		29.50	30

Mixed Company - P. Cooper

1990	Two Against One	14-day		29.50	36
1990	A Sticky Situation	14-day		29.50	36
1990	What's Up	14-day		29.50	36
1990	All Wrapped Up	14-day		29.50	36
1990	Picture Perfect	14-day		29.50	30
1991	A Moment to Unwind	14-day		29.50	33
1991	Ole	14-day		29.50	33
1991	Picnic Prowlers	14-day		29.50	30

Murals From The Precious Moments Chapel - S. Butcher

1995	The Pearl of Great Price	28-day		35.00	35
1995	The Good Samaritan	28-day		35.00	35
1996	The Prodigal Son	28-day		35.00	35
1996	The Good Shepherd	28-day		35.00	35

Mystic Warriors - C. Ren

1992	Deliverance	28-day		29.50	30
1992	Mystic Warrior	28-day		29.50	30
1992	Sun Seeker	28-day		29.50	30
1992	Top Gun	28-day		29.50	30
1992	Man Who Walks Alone	28-day		29.50	30
1992	Windrider	28-day		29.50	30
1992	Spirit of the Plains	28-day		29.50	30
1993	Blue Thunder	28-day		29.50	30
1993	Sun Glow	28-day		29.50	30
1993	Peace Maker	28-day		29.50	30

Native American Legends - A. Biffignandi

1996	Peace Pipe	28-day		29.95	30
1996	Feather-Woman	28-day		29.95	30
1996	Spirit of Serenity	28-day		29.95	30
1996	Enchanted Warrior	28-day		29.95	30
1996	Mystical Serenade	28-day		29.95	30
1996	Legend of Bridal Veil	28-day		29.95	30
1996	Seasons of Love	28-day		29.95	30
1996	A Bashful Courtship	28-day		29.95	30

Nature's Majestic Cats - M. Richter

1993	Siberian Tiger	28-day		29.50	30
1993	Himalayan Snow Leopard	28-day		29.50	30
1993	African Lion	28-day		29.50	30
1994	Asian Clouded Leopard	28-day		29.50	30
1994	American Cougar	28-day		29.50	30
1994	East African Leopard	28-day		29.50	30
1994	African Cheetah	28-day		29.50	30
1994	Canadian Lynx	28-day		29.50	30

Nature's Nighttime Realm - G. Murray

1992	Bobcat	28-day		29.50	30
1992	Cougar	28-day		29.50	30
1993	Jaguar	28-day		29.50	30
1993	White Tiger	28-day		29.50	30
1993	Lynx	28-day		29.50	30
1993	Lion	28-day		29.50	30
1993	Snow Leopard	28-day		29.50	30
1993	Cheetah	28-day		29.50	30

Nature's Quiet Moments - R. Parker

1988	A Curious Pair	14-day		37.50	45
1988	Northern Morning	14-day		37.50	38
1988	Just Resting	14-day		37.50	38
1989	Waiting Out the Storm	14-day		37.50	38
1989	Creekside	14-day		37.50	38
1989	Autumn Foraging	14-day		37.50	38
1989	Old Man of the Mountain	14-day		37.50	38
1989	Mountain Blooms	14-day		37.50	38

Noble American Indian Women - D. Wright

1989	Sacajawea	14-day		29.50	35-65
1990	Pocahontas	14-day		29.50	35-60
1990	Minnehaha	14-day		29.50	35
1990	Pine Leaf	14-day		29.50	60
1990	Lily of the Mohawk	14-day		29.50	50
1990	White Rose	14-day		29.50	50
1991	Lozen	14-day		29.50	30
1991	Falling Star	14-day		29.50	35

Noble Owls of America - J. Seerey-Lester

1986	Morning Mist	15,000		55.00	50-65
1987	Prairie Sundown	15,000		55.00	55
1987	Winter Vigil	15,000		55.00	40-55
1987	Autumn Mist	15,000		75.00	50-75
1987	Dawn in the Willows	15,000		55.00	55
1987	Snowy Watch	15,000		60.00	60
1988	Hiding Place	15,000		55.00	55
1988	Waiting for Dusk	15,000		55.00	55

Nolan Ryan - R. Tanenbaum

1994	The Strikeout Express	28-day		29.50	45
1994	Birth of a Legend	28-day		29.50	30
1994	Mr. Fastball	28-day		29.50	30
1994	Million-Dollar Player	28-day		29.50	30
1994	27 Seasons	28-day		29.50	30

YEAR ISSUE		EDITION LIMIT RETD.	ISSUE PRICE	*QUOTE U.S.$
1994	Farewell	28-day	29.50	30
1994	The Ryan Express	28-day	29.50	30

Norman Rockwell's Saturday Evening Post Baseball - N. Rockwell

1992	100th Year of Baseball	Open	19.50	20
1993	The Rookie	Open	19.50	20
1993	The Dugout	Open	19.50	20
1993	Bottom of the Sixth	Open	19.50	20

North American Ducks - R. Lawrence

1991	Autumn Flight	14-day	29.50	36
1991	The Resting Place	14-day	29.50	30
1991	Twin Flight	14-day	29.50	30
1992	Misty Morning	14-day	29.50	30
1992	Springtime Thaw	14-day	29.50	30
1992	Summer Retreat	14-day	29.50	30
1992	Overcast	14-day	29.50	30
1992	Perfect Pintails	14-day	29.50	30

North American Gamebirds - J. Killen

1990	Ring-necked Pheasant	14-day	37.50	38
1990	Bobwhite Quail	14-day	37.50	45
1990	Ruffed Grouse	14-day	37.50	38
1990	Gambel Quail	14-day	37.50	42
1990	Mourning Dove	14-day	37.50	45
1990	Woodcock	14-day	37.50	45
1991	Chukar Partridge	14-day	37.50	45
1991	Wild Turkey	14-day	37.50	45

North American Waterbirds - R. Lawrence

1988	Wood Ducks	14-day	37.50	50
1988	Hooded Mergansers	14-day	37.50	50
1988	Pintails	14-day	37.50	40
1988	Canada Geese	14-day	37.50	40
1989	American Widgeons	14-day	37.50	54
1989	Canvasbacks	14-day	37.50	55
1989	Mallard Pair	14-day	37.50	60
1989	Snow Geese	14-day	37.50	45

The Nutcracker Ballet - S. Fisher

1978	Clara	28-day	19.50	36
1979	Godfather	28-day	19.50	20
1979	Sugar Plum Fairy	28-day	19.50	45
1979	Snow Queen and King	28-day	19.50	40
1980	Waltz of the Flowers	28-day	19.50	20
1980	Clara and the Prince	28-day	19.50	45

Official Honeymooner's Commemorative Plate - D. Bobnick

1993	The Official Honeymooner's Commemorative Plate	28-day	37.50	150-200

The Official Honeymooners Plate Collection - D. Kilmer

1987	The Honeymooners	14-day	24.50	75-150
1987	The Hucklebuck	14-day	24.50	90-150
1987	Baby, You're the Greatest	14-day	24.50	75-150
1988	The Golfer	14-day	24.50	85-125
1988	The TV Chefs	14-day	24.50	85-125
1988	Bang! Zoom!	14-day	24.50	85-125
1988	The Only Way to Travel	14-day	24.50	90-125
1988	The Honeymoon Express	14-day	24.50	150-250

On Wings of Eagles - J. Pitcher

1994	"By Dawn's Early Light"	28-day	29.50	30
1994	Winter's Majestic Flight	28-day	29.50	30
1994	Over the Land of the Free	28-day	29.50	30
1995	Free Flight	28-day	29.50	30
1995	Morning Majesty	28-day	29.50	30
1995	Soaring Free	28-day	29.50	30

Our Cherished Seas - S. Barlowe

1992	Whale Song	48-day	37.50	38
1992	Lions of the Sea	48-day	37.50	38
1992	Flight of the Dolphins	48-day	37.50	38
1992	Palace of the Seals	48-day	37.50	38
1993	Orca Ballet	48-day	37.50	38
1993	Emperors of the Ice	48-day	37.50	38
1993	Sea Turtles	48-day	37.50	38
1993	Splendor of the Sea	48-day	37.50	38

Petals and Purrs - B. Harrison

1988	Blushing Beauties	14-day	24.50	55
1988	Spring Fever	14-day	24.50	38
1988	Morning Glories	14-day	24.50	45
1988	Forget-Me-Not	14-day	24.50	36
1989	Golden Fancy	14-day	24.50	30
1989	Pink Lillies	14-day	24.50	30
1989	Summer Sunshine	14-day	24.50	55
1989	Siamese Summer	14-day	24.50	55

Pillars of Baseball - A. Hicks

1995	Babe Ruth	28-day	29.95	30
1995	Lou Gehrig	28-day	29.95	30
1995	Ty Cobb	28-day	29.95	30
1996	Cy Young	28-day	29.95	30
1996	Honus Wagner	28-day	29.95	30
1996	Rogers Hornsby	28-day	29.95	30
1996	Dizzy Dean	28-day	29.95	30
1996	Christy Mathewson	28-day	29.95	30

Portraits of Jesus - W. Sallman

1994	Jesus, The Good Shepherd	28-day	29.50	30
1994	Jesus in the Garden	28-day	29.50	30
1994	Jesus, Children's Friend	28-day	29.50	30
1994	The Lord's Supper	28-day	29.50	30
1994	Christ at Dawn	28-day	29.50	30
1994	Christ at Heart's Door	28-day	29.50	30
1994	Portrait of Christ	28-day	29.50	30
1994	Madonna and Christ Child	28-day	29.50	30

Portraits of the Bald Eagle - J. Pitcher

1993	Ruler of the Sky	28-day	37.50	40
1993	In Bold Defiance	28-day	37.50	38
1993	Master Of The Summer Skies	28-day	37.50	38
1993	Spring's Sentinel	28-day	37.50	38

Portraits of the Wild - J. Meger

1994	Interlude	28-day	29.50	30
1994	Winter Solitude	28-day	29.50	30
1994	Devoted Protector	28-day	29.50	30
1994	Call of Autumn	28-day	29.50	30
1994	Watchful Eyes	28-day	29.50	30
1994	Babies of Spring	28-day	29.50	30
1994	Rocky Mountain Grandeur	28-day	29.50	30
1995	Unbridled Power	28-day	29.50	30
1995	Moonlight Vigil	28-day	29.50	30

Precious Moments Bible Story - S. Butcher

1990	Come Let Us Adore Him	28-day	29.50	30
1992	They Followed The Star	28-day	29.50	30
1992	The Flight Into Egypt	28-day	29.50	30
1992	The Carpenter Shop	28-day	29.50	30
1992	Jesus In The Temple	28-day	29.50	30
1992	The Crucifixion	28-day	29.50	30
1993	He Is Not Here	28-day	29.50	30

Precious Moments Classics - S. Butcher

1993	God Loveth A Cheerful Giver	28-day	35.00	35
1993	Make A Joyful Noise	28-day	35.00	35
1994	Love One Another	28-day	35.00	35
1994	You Have Touched So Many Hearts	28-day	35.00	35
1994	Praise the Lord Anyhow	28-day	35.00	35
1994	I Believe in Miracles	28-day	35.00	35
1994	Good Friends Are Forever	28-day	35.00	35
1994	Jesus Loves Me	28-day	35.00	35
1995	Friendship Hits the Spot	28-day	35.00	35
1995	To My Deer Friend	28-day	35.00	35

Precious Moments Plates - T. Utz

1979	Friend in the Sky	28-day	21.50	50
1980	Sand in her Shoe	28-day	21.50	40
1980	Snow Bunny	28-day	21.50	40
1980	Seashells	28-day	21.50	38
1981	Dawn	28-day	21.50	27
1982	My Kitty	28-day	21.50	36

Precious Moments Words of Love - S. Butcher

1995	Your Friendship Is Soda-licious	28-day	35.00	35
1996	Your Love Is So Uplifting	28-day	35.00	35
1996	Love Is From Above	28-day	35.00	35
1996	Love Lifted Me	28-day	35.00	35

Precious Portraits - B. P. Gutmann

1987	Sunbeam	14-day	24.50	40
1987	Mischief	14-day	24.50	36
1987	Peach Blossom	14-day	24.50	36
1987	Goldilocks	14-day	24.50	35
1987	Fairy Gold	14-day	24.50	35
1987	Bunny	14-day	24.50	30

The Prideful Ones - C. DeHaan

1994	Village Markers	28-day	29.50	30
1994	His Pride	28-day	29.50	30
1994	Appeasing the Water People	28-day	29.50	30
1994	Tribal Guardian	28-day	29.50	30
1994	Autumn Passage	28-day	29.50	30
1994	Winter Hunter	28-day	29.50	30
1994	Silent Trail Break	28-day	29.50	30
1994	Water Breaking	28-day	29.50	30
1994	Crossing at the Big Trees	28-day	29.50	30
1995	Winter Songsinger	28-day	29.50	30

Princesses of the Plains - D. Wright

1993	Prairie Flower	28-day	29.50	45
1993	Snow Princess	28-day	29.50	30
1993	Wild Flower	28-day	29.50	45
1993	Noble Beauty	28-day	29.50	30
1993	Winter's Rose	28-day	29.50	30
1993	Gentle Beauty	28-day	29.50	30
1994	Nature's Guardian	28-day	29.50	30
1994	Mountain Princess	28-day	29.50	30
1995	Proud Dreamer	28-day	29.50	30
1995	Spring Maiden	28-day	29.50	30

Proud Indian Families - K. Freeman

1991	The Storyteller	14-day	29.50	50
1991	The Power of the Basket	14-day	29.50	36
1991	The Naming Ceremony	14-day	29.50	30
1992	Playing With Tradition	14-day	29.50	30
1992	Preparing the Berry Harvest	14-day	29.50	30

1992	Ceremonial Dress	14-day	29.50	30
1992	Sounds of the Forest	14-day	29.50	30
1992	The Marriage Ceremony	14-day	29.50	30
1993	The Jewelry Maker	14-day	29.50	30
1993	Beautiful Creations	14-day	29.50	30

Proud Innocence - J. Schmidt

1994	Desert Bloom	28-day	29.50	30
1994	Little Drummer	28-day	29.50	30
1995	Young Archer	28-day	29.50	30
1995	Morning Child	28-day	29.50	30
1995	Wise One	28-day	29.50	30
1995	Sun Blossom	28-day	29.50	30
1995	Laughing Heart	28-day	29.50	30
1995	Gentle Flower	28-day	29.50	30

The Proud Nation - R. Swanson

1989	Navajo Little One	14-day	24.50	35-45
1989	In a Big Land	14-day	24.50	25
1989	Out with Mama's Flock	14-day	24.50	25
1989	Newest Little Sheepherder	14-day	24.50	35
1989	Dressed Up for the Powwow	14-day	24.50	35
1989	Just a Few Days Old	14-day	24.50	30
1989	Autumn Treat	14-day	24.50	30
1989	Up in the Red Rocks	14-day	24.50	25

Puppy Playtime - J. Lamb

1987	Double Take-Cocker Spaniels	14-day	24.50	40-75
1987	Catch of the Day-Golden Retrievers	14-day	24.50	45
1987	Cabin Fever-Black Labradors	14-day	24.50	45
1987	Weekend Gardener-Lhasa Apsos	14-day	24.50	36
1987	Getting Acquainted-Beagles	14-day	24.50	36
1987	Hanging Out-German Shepherd	14-day	24.50	45
1987	New Leash on Life-Mini Schnauzer	14-day	24.50	45
1987	Fun and Games-Poodle	14-day	24.50	36

Quiet Moments Of Childhood - D. Green

1991	Elizabeth's Afternoon Tea	14-day	29.50	45
1991	Christina's Secret Garden	14-day	29.50	36
1991	Eric & Erin's Storytime	14-day	29.50	30
1992	Jessica's Tea Party	14-day	29.50	33
1992	Megan & Monique's Bakery	14-day	29.50	36
1992	Children's Day By The Sea	14-day	29.50	30
1992	Jordan's Playful Pups	14-day	29.50	33
1992	Daniel's Morning Playtime	14-day	29.50	30

The Quilted Countryside: A Signature Collection by Mel Steele - M. Steele

1991	The Old Country Store	14-day	29.50	36
1991	Winter's End	14-day	29.50	36
1991	The Quilter's Cabin	14-day	29.50	45
1991	Spring Cleaning	14-day	29.50	36
1991	Summer Harvest	14-day	29.50	30
1991	The Country Merchant	14-day	29.50	36
1992	Wash Day	14-day	29.50	30
1992	The Antiques Store	14-day	29.50	33

Remembering Norma Jeane - F. Accornero

1994	The Girl Next Door	28-day	29.50	30
1994	Her Day in the Sun	28-day	29.50	30
1994	A Star is Born	28-day	29.50	30
1994	Beauty Secrets	28-day	29.50	30
1995	In the Spotlight	28-day	29.50	30
1995	Bathing Beauty	28-day	29.50	30
1995	Young & Carefree	28-day	29.50	30
1995	Free Spirit	28-day	29.50	30
1995	A Country Girl at Heart	28-day	29.50	30
1995	Hometown Girl	28-day	29.50	30

The Renaissance Angels - L. Bywaters

1994	Doves of Peace	28-day	29.50	30
1994	Angelic Innocence	28-day	29.50	30
1994	Joy to the World	28-day	29.50	30
1995	Angel of Faith	28-day	29.50	30
1995	The Christmas Star	28-day	29.50	30
1995	Trumpeter's Call	28-day	29.50	30
1995	Harmonious Heavens	28-day	29.50	30
1995	The Angels Sing	28-day	29.50	30

Rockwell Home of the Brave - N. Rockwell

1981	Reminiscing	18,000	35.00	53
1981	Hero's Welcome	18,000	35.00	53
1981	Back to his Old Job	18,000	35.00	53
1981	War Hero	18,000	35.00	35
1982	Willie Gillis in Church	18,000	35.00	53
1982	War Bond	18,000	35.00	35
1982	Uncle Sam Takes Wings	18,000	35.00	75
1982	Taking Mother over the Top	18,000	35.00	35

Romance of the Rails - D. Tutwiler

1994	Starlight Limited	28-day	29.50	30
1994	Portland Rose	28-day	29.50	30
1994	Orange Blossom Special	28-day	29.50	30
1994	Morning Star	28-day	29.50	30
1994	Crescent Limited	28-day	29.50	30
1994	Sunset Limited	28-day	29.50	30
1994	Western Star	28-day	29.50	30
1994	Sunrise Limited	28-day	29.50	30
1995	The Blue Bonnet	28-day	29.50	30

YEAR ISSUE		EDITION LIMIT	YEAR RETD.	ISSUE PRICE	*QUOTE U.S.$
1995	The Pine Tree Limited	28-day		29.50	30

Romantic Castles of Europe - D. Sweet
1990	Ludwig's Castle	19,500		55.00	55
1991	Palace of the Moors	19,500		55.00	55
1991	Swiss Isle Fortress	19,500		55.00	55
1991	The Legendary Castle of Leeds	19,500		55.00	55
1991	Davinci's Chambord	19,500		55.00	55
1991	Eilean Donan	19,500		55.00	55
1992	Eltz Castle	19,500		55.00	55
1992	Kylemore Abbey	19,500		55.00	55

Romantic Flights of Fancy - Q. Lemonds
1994	Sunlit Waltz	28-day		29.50	30
1994	Morning Minuet	28-day		29.50	30
1994	Evening Solo	28-day		29.50	30
1994	Summer Sonata	28-day		29.50	30
1995	Twilight Tango	28-day		29.50	30
1995	Sunset Ballet	28-day		29.50	30

Romantic Victorian Keepsake - J. Grossman
1992	Dearest Kiss	28-day		35.00	35
1992	First Love	28-day		35.00	35
1992	As Fair as a Rose	28-day		35.00	35
1992	Springtime Beauty	28-day		35.00	35
1992	Summertime Fancy	28-day		35.00	35
1992	Bonnie Blue Eyes	28-day		35.00	35
1992	Precious Friends	28-day		35.00	35
1994	Bonnets and Bouquets	28-day		35.00	35
1994	My Beloved Teddy	28-day		35.00	35
1994	A Sweet Romance	28-day		35.00	35

A Salute to Mickey Mantle - T. Fogarty
1996	1961 Home Run Duel	28-day		35.00	35
1996	Power at the Plate	28-day		35.00	35
1996	Saluting a Magnificent Yankee	28-day		35.00	35
1996	Triple Crown Achievement	28-day		35.00	35
1996	1953 Grand Slam	28-day		35.00	35
1997	1963's Famous Facade Homer	28-day		35.00	35
1997	Mickey as a Rookie	28-day		35.00	35
1997	A Look Back	28-day		35.00	35

Santa Takes a Break - T. Newsom
1995	Santa's Last Stop	28-day		29.95	30
1995	Santa's Railroad	28-day		29.95	30
1995	A Jolly Good Catch	28-day		29.95	30
1995	Simple Pleasures	28-day		29.95	30
1996	Skating On Penguin Pond	28-day		29.95	30
1996	Santa's Sing Along	28-day		29.95	30

The Saturday Evening Post - N. Rockwell
1989	The Wonders of Radio	14-day		35.00	40
1989	Easter Morning	14-day		35.00	60
1989	The Facts of Life	14-day		35.00	40
1990	The Window Washer	14-day		35.00	45
1990	First Flight	14-day		35.00	54
1990	Traveling Companion	14-day		35.00	35
1990	Jury Room	14-day		35.00	35
1990	Furlough	14-day		35.00	35

Scenes of An American Christmas - B. Perry
1994	I'll Be Home for Christmas	28-day		29.50	30
1994	Christmas Eve Worship	28-day		29.50	30
1994	A Holiday Happening	28-day		29.50	30
1994	A Long Winter's Night	28-day		29.50	30
1994	The Sounds of Christmas	28-day		29.50	30
1994	Dear Santa	28-day		29.50	30
1995	An Afternoon Outing	28-day		29.50	30
1995	Winter Worship	28-day		29.50	30

Seasons of the Bald Eagle - J. Pitcher
1991	Autumn in the Mountains	14-day		37.50	45
1991	Winter in the Valley	14-day		37.50	38
1991	Spring on the River	14-day		37.50	38
1991	Summer on the Seacoast	14-day		37.50	40

Sharing Life's Most Precious Memories - S. Butcher
1995	Thee I Love	28-day		35.00	35
1995	The Joy of the Lord Is My Strength	28-day		35.00	35
1995	May Your Every Wish Come True	28-day		35.00	35
1996	I'm So Glad That God	28-day		35.00	35
1996	Heaven Bless You	28-day		35.00	35

Sharing the Moments - S. Butcher
1995	You Have Touched So Many Hearts	28-day		35.00	35
1996	Friendship Hits The Spot	28-day		35.00	35
1996	Jesus Love Me	28-day		35.00	35

Single Issues - T. Utz
1983	Princess Grace	21-day		39.50	45

Small Wonders of the Wild - C. Frace
1989	Hideaway	14-day		29.50	45
1990	Young Explorers	14-day		29.50	36-45
1990	Three of a Kind	14-day		29.50	45-75
1990	Quiet Morning	14-day		29.50	36-45
1990	Eyes of Wonder	14-day		29.50	35-45
1990	Ready for Adventure	14-day		29.50	30-45
1990	Uno	14-day		29.50	45
1990	Exploring a New World	14-day		29.50	30-45

Space, The Final Frontier - D. Ward
1996	To Boldly Go...	28-day		37.50	38
1996	Second Star From The Right	28-day		37.50	38
1996	Signs of Intelligence	28-day		37.50	38
1996	Preparing To Cloak	28-day		37.50	38

Spanning America's Railways - D. Tutwiler
1996	Royal York	28-day		29.95	30

Spirit of the Mustang - C. DeHaan
1995	Winter's Thunder	28-day		29.95	30
1995	Moonlit Run	28-day		29.95	30
1995	Morning Reverie	28-day		29.95	30
1995	Autumn Respite	28-day		29.95	30
1996	Spring Frolic	28-day		29.95	30
1996	Dueling Mustangs	28-day		29.95	30
1996	Tranquil Waters	28-day		29.95	30
1996	Summer Squall	28-day		29.95	30

Sporting Generation - J. Lamb
1991	Like Father, Like Son	14-day		29.50	45
1991	Golden Moments	14-day		29.50	45
1991	The Lookout	14-day		29.50	30
1992	Picking Up The Scent	14-day		29.50	30
1992	First Time Out	14-day		29.50	36
1992	Who's Tracking Who	14-day		29.50	45
1992	Springing Into Action	14-day		29.50	30
1992	Point of Interest	14-day		29.50	30

STAR TREK®: 25th Anniversary Commemorative - T. Blackshear
1991	STAR TREK 25th Anniversary Commemorative Plate	14-day		37.50	150-200
1991	SPOCK	14-day		35.00	75-125
1991	Kirk	14-day		35.00	100-125
1992	McCoy	14-day		35.00	60-100
1992	Uhura	14-day		35.00	60-100
1992	Scotty	14-day		35.00	60-100
1993	Sulu	14-day		35.00	60-100
1993	Chekov	14-day		35.00	60-100
1994	U.S.S. Enterprise NCC-1701	14-day		35.00	150

STAR TREK®: Deep Space 9 - M. Weistling
1994	Commander Benjamin Sisko	28-day		35.00	35
1994	Security Chief Odo	28-day		35.00	35
1994	Major Kira Nerys	28-day		35.00	35
1994	Space Station	28-day		35.00	35
1994	Proprietor Quark	28-day		35.00	35
1995	Doctor Julian Bashir	28-day		35.00	35
1995	Lieutenant Jadzia Dax	28-day		35.00	35
1995	Chief Miles O'Brien	28-day		35.00	35

STAR TREK®: Generations - K. Birdsong
1996	The Ultimate Confrontation	28-day		35.00	35
1996	Kirk's Final Voyage	28-day		35.00	35
1996	Meeting In The Nexus	28-day		35.00	35
1996	Picard's Christmas In The Nexus	28-day		35.00	35
1996	Worf's Ceremony	28-day		35.00	35

STAR TREK®: The Movies - M. Weistling
1994	STAR TREK IV: The Voyage Home	28-day		35.00	35
1994	STAR TREK II: The Wrath of Khan	28-day		35.00	35
1994	STAR TREK VI: The Undiscovered Country	28-day		35.00	35
1995	STAR TREK III: The Search For Spock	28-day		35.00	35
1995	STAR TREK V: The Final Frontier	28-day		35.00	35
1996	Triumphant Return	28-day		35.00	35
1996	Destruction of the Reliant	28-day		35.00	35
1996	The Motion Picture	28-day		35.00	35

STAR TREK®: The Next Generation - T. Blackshear
1993	Captain Jean-Luc Picard	28-day		35.00	35
1993	Commander William T. Riker	28-day		35.00	35
1994	Lieutenant Commander Data	28-day		35.00	35
1994	Lieutenant Worf	28-day		35.00	35
1994	Counselor Deanna Troi	28-day		35.00	35
1995	Dr. Beverly Crusher	28-day		35.00	35
1995	Lieutenant Commander Laforge	28-day		35.00	35
1996	Ensign W. Crusher	28-day		35.00	35

STAR TREK®: The Next Generation The Episodes - K. Birdsong
1994	The Best of Both Worlds	28-day		35.00	35
1994	Encounter at Far Point	28-day		35.00	35
1995	Unification	28-day		35.00	35
1995	Yesterday's Enterprise	28-day		35.00	35
1995	All Good Things	28-day		35.00	35
1995	Descent	28-day		35.00	35
1996	Relics	28-day		35.00	35
1996	Redemption	28-day		35.00	35
1996	The Big Goodbye	28-day		35.00	35
1996	The Inner Light	28-day		35.00	35

STAR TREK®: The Original Episodes - J. Martin
1996	The Tholian Web	28-day		35.00	35
1996	Space Seed	28-day		35.00	35
1996	The Menagerie	28-day		35.00	35

STAR TREK®: The Power of Command - K. Birdsong
1996	Captain Picard	28-day		35.00	35
1996	Admiral Kirk	28-day		35.00	35
1996	Captain Sisko	28-day		35.00	35
1996	Captain Sulu	28-day		35.00	35
1996	Captain Janeway	28-day		35.00	35

STAR TREK®: The Voyagers - K. Birdsong
1994	U.S.S. Enterprise NCC-1701	28-day		35.00	35
1994	U.S.S. Enterprise NCC-1701-D	28-day		35.00	35
1994	Klingon Battlecruiser	28-day		35.00	35
1994	Romulan Warbird	28-day		35.00	35
1994	U.S.S. Enterprise NCC-1701-A	28-day		35.00	35
1995	Ferengi Marauder	28-day		35.00	35
1995	Klingon Bird of Prey	28-day		35.00	35
1995	Triple Nacelled U.S.S. Enterprise	28-day		35.00	35
1995	Cardassian Galor Warship	28-day		35.00	35
1995	U.S.S. Excelsior	28-day		35.00	35

STAR TREK®: Voyager - D. Curry
1996	The Voyage Begins	28-day		35.00	35
1996	New Beginnings	28-day		35.00	35
1996	Bonds of Friendship	28-day		35.00	35

Star Wars 10th Anniversary Commemorative - T. Blackshear
1990	Star Wars 10th Anniversary Commemorative Plate	14-day		39.50	125-325

Star Wars Plate Collection - T. Blackshear
1987	Hans Solo	14-day		29.50	125-250
1987	R2-D2 and Wicket	14-day		29.50	75-200
1987	Luke Skywalker and Darth Vader	14-day		29.50	75-200
1987	Princess Leia	14-day		29.50	100-200
1987	The Imperial Walkers	14-day		29.50	75-200
1987	Luke and Yoda	14-day		29.50	100-200
1988	Space Battle	14-day		29.50	300-400
1988	Crew in Cockpit	14-day		29.50	150-300

Star Wars Space Vehicles - S. Hillios
1995	Millenium Falcon	28-day		35.00	35
1995	TIE Fighters	28-day		35.00	35
1995	Red Five X-Wing Fighters	28-day		35.00	35
1995	Imperial Shuttle	28-day		35.00	35
1995	STAR Destroyer	28-day		35.00	35
1996	Snow Speeders	28-day		35.00	35
1996	B-Wing Fighter	28-day		35.00	35
1996	The Slave I	28-day		35.00	35

Star Wars Trilogy - M. Weistling
1993	Star Wars	28-day		37.50	80-125
1993	The Empire Strikes Back	28-day		37.50	85-150
1993	Return Of The Jedi	28-day		37.50	80-100

Symphony of the Sea - R. Koni
1995	Fluid Grace	28-day		29.95	30
1995	Dolphin's Dance	28-day		29.95	30
1995	Orca Ballet	28-day		29.95	30
1995	Moonlit Minuet	28-day		29.95	30
1995	Sailfish Serenade	28-day		29.95	30
1995	Starlit Waltz	28-day		29.95	30
1995	Sunset Splendor	28-day		29.95	30
1995	Coral Chorus	28-day		29.95	30

Those Delightful Dalmations - N/A
1995	You Missed a Spot	28-day		29.95	30
1995	Here's a Good Spot	28-day		29.95	30
1996	The Best Spot	28-day		29.95	30
1996	Spotted In the Headlines	28-day		29.95	30
1996	A Spot In My Heart	28-day		29.95	30
1996	Sweet Spots	28-day		29.95	30
1996	Naptime Already?	28-day		29.95	30
1996	He's In My Spot	28-day		29.95	30

Timeless Expressions of the Orient - M. Tsang
1990	Fidelity	15,000		75.00	95
1991	Femininity	15,000		75.00	75
1991	Longevity	15,000		75.00	75
1991	Beauty	15,000		55.00	55
1992	Courage	15,000		55.00	55

Treasured Days - H. Bond
1987	Ashley	14-day		29.50	60
1987	Christopher	14-day		24.50	45
1987	Sara	14-day		24.50	35
1987	Jeremy	14-day		24.50	45
1987	Amanda	14-day		24.50	45
1988	Nicholas	14-day		24.50	45
1988	Lindsay	14-day		24.50	45
1988	Justin	14-day		24.50	45

A Treasury of Cherished Teddies - P. Hillman
1994	Happy Holidays, Friend	28-day		29.50	30
1995	A New Year with Old Friends	28-day		29.50	30
1995	Valentines For You	28-day		29.50	30
1995	Friendship is in the Air	28-day		29.50	30
1995	Showers of Friendship	28-day		29.50	30
1996	Friendship is in Bloom	28-day		29.50	30
1996	Planting the Seeds of Friendship	28-day		29.50	30
1996	A Day in the Park	28-day		29.50	30
1996	Smooth Sailing	28-day		29.50	30
1996	School Days	28-day		29.50	30

YEAR ISSUE		EDITION LIMIT	YEAR RETD.	ISSUE PRICE	*QUOTE U.S.$

Unbridled Spirit - C. DeHaan

1992	Surf Dancer	28-day		29.50	30
1992	Winter Renegade	28-day		29.50	30
1992	Desert Shadows	28-day		29.50	30
1993	Painted Sunrise	28-day		29.50	30
1993	Desert Duel	28-day		29.50	30
1993	Midnight Run	28-day		29.50	30
1993	Moonlight Majesty	28-day		29.50	30
1993	Autumn Reverie	28-day		29.50	30
1993	Blizzard's Peril	28-day		29.50	30
1993	Sunrise Surprise	28-day		29.50	30

Under the Sea - C. Bragg

1993	Tales of Tavarua	28-day		29.50	30
1993	Water's Edge	28-day		29.50	30
1994	Beauty of the Reef	28-day		29.50	30
1994	Rainbow Reef	28-day		29.50	30
1994	Orca Odyssey	28-day		29.50	30
1994	Rescue the Reef	28-day		29.50	30
1994	Underwater Dance	28-day		29.50	30
1994	Gentle Giants	28-day		29.50	30
1995	Undersea Enchantment	28-day		29.50	30
1995	Penguin Paradise	28-day		29.50	30

Undersea Visions - J. Enright

1995	Secret Sanctuary	28-day		29.95	30
1995	Temple of Treasures	28-day		29.95	30
1996	Temple Beneath the Sea	28-day		29.95	30
1996	Lost Kingdom	28-day		29.95	30
1996	Mysterious Ruins	28-day		29.95	30
1996	Last Journey	28-day		29.95	30
1996	Egyptian Dreamscape	28-day		29.95	30
1996	Lost Galleon	28-day		29.95	30

Utz Mother's Day - T. Utz

1983	A Gift of Love	N/A		27.50	38
1983	Mother's Helping Hand	N/A		27.50	28
1983	Mother's Angel	N/A		27.50	28

Vanishing Rural America - J. Harrison

1991	Quiet Reflections	14-day		29.50	45
1991	Autumn's Passage	14-day		29.50	45
1991	Storefront Memories	14-day		29.50	30
1991	Country Path	14-day		29.50	36
1991	When the Circus Came To Town	14-day		29.50	36
1991	Covered in Fall	14-day		29.50	45
1991	America's Heartland	14-day		29.50	33
1991	Rural Delivery	14-day		29.50	33

Victorian Christmas Memories - J. Grossman

1992	A Visit from St. Nicholas	28-day		29.50	30
1993	Christmas Delivery	28-day		29.50	30
1993	Christmas Angels	28-day		29.50	30
1992	With Visions of Sugar Plums	28-day		29.50	30
1993	Merry Olde Kris Kringle	28-day		29.50	30
1993	Grandfather Frost	28-day		29.50	30
1993	Joyous Noel	28-day		29.50	30
1993	Christmas Innocence	28-day		29.50	30
1993	Dreaming of Santa	28-day		29.50	30
1993	Mistletoe & Holly	28-day		29.50	30

Victorian Playtime - M. H. Bogart

1991	A Busy Day	14-day		29.50	30
1992	Little Masterpiece	14-day		29.50	30
1992	Playing Bride	14-day		29.50	60
1992	Waiting for a Nibble	14-day		29.50	30
1992	Tea and Gossip	14-day		29.50	30
1992	Cleaning House	14-day		29.50	30
1992	A Little Persuasion	14-day		29.50	30
1992	Peek-a-Boo	14-day		29.50	30

Warrior's Pride - C. DeHaan

1994	Crow War Pony	28-day		29.50	30
1994	Running Free	28-day		29.50	30
1994	Blackfoot War Pony	28-day		29.50	30
1994	Southern Cheyenne	28-day		29.50	30
1995	Shoshoni War Ponies	28-day		29.50	30
1995	A Champion's Revelry	28-day		29.50	30
1995	Battle Colors	28-day		29.50	30
1995	Call of the Drums	28-day		29.50	30

The West of Frank McCarthy - F. McCarthy

1991	Attacking the Iron Horse	14-day		37.50	50-60
1991	Attempt on the Stage	14-day		37.50	45
1991	The Prayer	14-day		37.50	54
1991	On the Old North Trail	14-day		37.50	48
1991	The Hostile Threat	14-day		37.50	45
1991	Bringing Out the Furs	14-day		37.50	45
1991	Kiowa Raider	14-day		37.50	45
1991	Headed North	14-day		37.50	40

Wilderness Spirits - P. Koni

1994	Eyes of the Night	28-day		29.95	30
1995	Howl of Innocence	28-day		29.95	30
1995	Midnight Call	28-day		29.95	30
1995	Breaking the Silence	28-day		29.95	30
1995	Moonlight Run	28-day		29.95	30
1995	Sunset Vigil	28-day		29.95	30
1995	Sunrise Spirit	28-day		29.95	30
1996	Valley of the Wolf	28-day		29.95	30

YEAR ISSUE		EDITION LIMIT	YEAR RETD.	ISSUE PRICE	*QUOTE U.S.$

Winged Reflections - R. Parker

1989	Following Mama	14-day		37.50	38
1989	Above the Breakers	14-day		37.50	38
1989	Among the Reeds	14-day		37.50	38
1989	Freeze Up	14-day		37.50	38
1989	Wings Above the Water	14-day		37.50	38
1990	Summer Loon	14-day		29.50	30
1990	Early Spring	14-day		29.50	30
1990	At The Water's Edge	14-day		29.50	30

Winter Rails - T. Xaras

1992	Winter Crossing	28-day		29.50	30
1993	Coal Country	28-day		29.50	30
1993	Daylight Run	28-day		29.50	30
1993	By Sea or Rail	28-day		29.50	30
1993	Country Crossroads	28-day		29.50	30
1993	Timber Line	28-day		29.50	30
1993	The Long Haul	28-day		29.50	30
1993	Darby Crossing	28-day		29.50	30
1995	East Broad Top	28-day		29.50	30
1995	Landsdowne Station	28-day		29.50	30

Winter Wildlife - J. Seerey-Lester

1989	Close Encounters	15,000		55.00	55
1989	Among the Cattails	15,000		55.00	55
1989	The Refuge	15,000		55.00	55
1989	Out of the Blizzard	15,000		55.00	55
1989	First Snow	15,000		55.00	55
1989	Lying In Wait	15,000		55.00	55
1989	Winter Hiding	15,000		55.00	55
1989	Early Snow	15,000		55.00	55

Wizard of Oz Commemorative - T. Blackshear

1988	We're Off to See the Wizard	14-day		24.50	100-180
1988	Dorothy Meets the Scarecrow	14-day		24.50	75-125
1989	The Tin Man Speaks	14-day		24.50	75-125
1989	A Glimpse of the Munchkins	14-day		24.50	75-120
1989	The Witch Casts A Spell	14-day		24.50	75-125
1989	If I Were King Of The Forest	14-day		24.50	75-125
1989	The Great and Powerful Oz	14-day		24.50	100-125
1989	There's No Place Like Home	14-day		24.50	75-150

Wizard of Oz-Fifty Years of Oz - T. Blackshear

| 1989 | Fifty Years of Oz | 14-day | | 37.50 | 100-200 |

Wizard of Oz-Portraits From Oz - T. Blackshear

1989	Dorothy	14-day		29.50	125-200
1989	Scarecrow	14-day		29.50	100-200
1989	Tin Man	14-day		29.50	100-200
1990	Cowardly Lion	14-day		29.50	100-200
1990	Glinda	14-day		29.50	100-200
1990	Wizard	14-day		29.50	100-200
1990	Wicked Witch	14-day		29.50	150-200
1990	Toto	14-day		29.50	150-225

The Wonder Of Christmas - J. McClelland

1991	Santa's Secret	28-day		29.50	30
1991	My Favorite Ornament	28-day		29.50	30
1991	Waiting For Santa	28-day		29.50	30
1993	The Caroler	28-day		29.50	30

Woodland Babies - R. Manning

1995	Hollow Hideaway	28-day		29.95	30
1995	A Springtime Adventure	28-day		29.95	30
1995	Amber Eyes	28-day		29.95	30
1996	Peaceful Dreams	28-day		29.95	30
1996	Cozy Nest	28-day		29.95	30
1996	Tree House Trio	28-day		29.95	30

Woodland Encounters - G. Giordano

1991	Want to Play?	14-day		29.50	30
1991	Peek-a-boo!	14-day		29.50	30
1991	Lunchtime Visitor	14-day		29.50	33
1991	Anyone for a Swim?	14-day		29.50	36
1991	Nature Scouts	14-day		29.50	36
1991	Meadow Meeting	14-day		29.50	33
1991	Hi Neighbor	14-day		29.50	36
1992	Field Day	14-day		29.50	36

A World of Puppy Adventures - J. Ren

1995	The Water's Fine	28-day		29.95	30
1996	Swimming Lessons	28-day		29.95	30
1996	Breakfast Is Served	28-day		29.95	30
1996	Laundry Tug O' War	28-day		29.95	30
1996	Did I Do That?	28-day		29.95	30

The World Of Zolan - D. Zolan

1992	First Kiss	28-day		29.50	45-65
1992	Morning Discovery	28-day		29.50	35
1992	The Little Fisherman	28-day		29.50	45
1993	Letter to Grandma	28-day		29.50	50
1993	Twilight Prayer	28-day		29.50	60
1993	Flowers for Mother	28-day		29.50	50

Year Of The Wolf - A. Agnew

1993	Broken Silence	28-day		29.50	30
1993	Leader of the Pack	28-day		29.50	30
1993	Solitude	28-day		29.50	30
1994	Tundra Light	28-day		29.50	30
1994	Guardians of the High Country	28-day		29.50	30
1994	A Second Glance	28-day		29.50	30

YEAR ISSUE		EDITION LIMIT	YEAR RETD.	ISSUE PRICE	*QUOTE U.S.$
1994	Free as the Wind	28-day		29.50	30
1994	Song of the Wolf	28-day		29.50	30
1995	Lords of the Tundra	28-day		29.50	30
1995	Wilderness Companions	28-day		29.50	30

Young Lords of The Wild - M. Richter

1994	Siberian Tiger Club	28-day		29.95	30
1995	Snow Leopard Cub	28-day		29.95	30
1995	Lion Cub	28-day		29.95	30
1995	Clouded Leopard Cub	28-day		29.95	30
1995	Cougar Cub	28-day		29.95	30
1995	Leopard Cub	28-day		29.95	30
1995	Cheetah Cub	28-day		29.95	30
1996	Canadian Lynx Cub	28-day		29.95	30

Hamilton/Boehm

Award Winning Roses - Boehm

1979	Peace Rose	15,000		45.00	100
1979	White Masterpiece Rose	15,000		45.00	75
1979	Tropicana Rose	15,000		45.00	63
1979	Elegance Rose	15,000		45.00	63
1979	Queen Elizabeth Rose	15,000		45.00	63
1979	Royal Highness Rose	15,000		45.00	63
1979	Angel Face Rose	15,000		45.00	63
1979	Mr. Lincoln Rose	15,000		45.00	63

Gamebirds of North America - Boehm

1984	Ring-Necked Pheasant	15,000		62.50	63
1984	Bob White Quail	15,000		62.50	63
1984	American Woodcock	15,000		62.50	63
1984	California Quail	15,000		62.50	63
1984	Ruffed Grouse	15,000		62.50	63
1984	Wild Turkey	15,000		62.50	63
1984	Willow Partridge	15,000		62.50	63
1984	Prairie Grouse	15,000		62.50	63

Hummingbird Collection - Boehm

1980	Calliope	15,000		62.50	80
1980	Broadbilled	15,000		62.50	63
1980	Rufous Flame Bearer	15,000		62.50	63
1980	Broadtail	15,000		62.50	63
1980	Streamertail	15,000		62.50	80
1980	Blue Throated	15,000		62.50	80
1980	Crimson Topaz	15,000		62.50	63
1980	Brazilian Ruby	15,000		62.50	80

Owl Collection - Boehm

1980	Boreal Owl	15,000		45.00	65-75
1980	Snowy Owl	15,000		45.00	75
1980	Barn Owl	15,000		45.00	75
1980	Saw Whet Owl	15,000		45.00	75
1980	Great Horned Owl	15,000		45.00	75
1980	Screech Owl	15,000		45.00	75
1980	Short Eared Owl	15,000		45.00	75
1980	Barred Owl	15,000		45.00	75

Water Birds - Boehm

1981	Canada Geese	15,000		62.50	65
1981	Wood Ducks	15,000		62.50	65
1981	Hooded Merganser	15,000		62.50	65
1981	Ross's Geese	15,000		62.50	65
1981	Common Mallard	15,000		62.50	65
1981	Canvas Back	15,000		62.50	65
1981	Green Winged Teal	15,000		62.50	65
1981	American Pintail	15,000		62.50	65

Haviland

Twelve Days of Christmas - R. Hetreau

1970	Partridge	30,000		25.00	86
1971	Two Turtle Doves	30,000		25.00	25
1972	Three French Hens	30,000		27.50	28
1973	Four Calling Birds	30,000		28.50	30
1974	Five Golden Rings	30,000		30.00	30
1975	Six Geese a'laying	30,000		32.50	33
1976	Seven Swans	30,000		38.00	50
1977	Eight Maids	30,000		40.00	50
1978	Nine Ladies Dancing	30,000		45.00	77
1979	Ten Lord's a'leaping	30,000		50.00	50
1980	Eleven Pipers Piping	30,000		55.00	84
1981	Twelve Drummers	30,000		60.00	94

Haviland & Parlon

Christmas Madonnas - Various

1972	By Raphael - Raphael	5,000		35.00	42
1973	By Feruzzi - Feruzzi	5,000		40.00	78
1974	By Raphael - Raphael	5,000		42.50	43
1975	By Murillo - Murillo	7,500		42.50	43
1976	By Botticelli - Botticelli	7,500		45.00	45
1977	By Bellini - Bellini	7,500		48.00	48
1978	By Lippi - Lippi	7,500		48.00	53
1979	Madonna of The Eucharist - Botticelli	7,500		49.50	112

Hutschenreuther

The Glory of Christmas - W./C. Hallett

| 1982 | The Nativity | 25,000 | | 80.00 | 125 |

YEAR ISSUE		EDITION LIMIT	YEAR RETD.	ISSUE PRICE	*QUOTE U.S.$
1983	The Annunciation	25,000		80.00	115
1984	The Shepherds	25,000		80.00	100
1985	The Wiseman	25,000		80.00	100

Gunther Granget - G. Granget

1972	American Sparrows	5,000		50.00	125
1972	European Sparrows	5,000		30.00	65
1973	American Kildeer	2,250		75.00	90
1973	American Squirrel	2,500		75.00	75
1973	European Squirrel	2,500		35.00	50
1974	American Partridge	2,500		75.00	90
1975	American Rabbits	2,500		90.00	90
1976	Freedom in Flight	5,000		100.00	100
1976	Wrens	2,500		100.00	110
1976	Freedom in Flight, Gold	200		200.00	200
1977	Bears	2,500		100.00	100
1978	Foxes' Spring Journey	1,000		125.00	200

Imperial Ching-te Chen

Beauties of the Red Mansion - Z. HuiMin

1986	Pao-chai	115-day		27.92	35-50
1986	Yuan-chun	115-day		27.92	35-50
1987	Hsi-feng	115-day		30.92	35
1987	Hsi-chun	115-day		30.92	35
1988	Miao-yu	115-day		30.92	35-50
1988	Ying-chun	115-day		30.92	35-50
1988	Tai-yu	115-day		32.92	35-50
1988	Li-wan	115-day		32.92	35
1988	Ko-Ching	115-day		32.92	35
1988	Hsiang-yun	115-day		34.92	35
1989	Tan-Chun	115-day		34.92	35
1989	Chiao-chieh	115-day		34.92	35

Blessings From a Chinese Garden - Z. Song Mao

1988	The Gift of Purity	175-day		39.92	42
1989	The Gift of Grace	175-day		39.92	40
1989	The Gift of Beauty	175-day		42.92	43
1989	The Gift of Happiness	175-day		42.92	43
1990	The Gift of Truth	175-day		42.92	43
1990	The Gift of Joy	175-day		42.92	43

Flower Goddesses of China - Z. HuiMin

1991	The Lotus Goddess	175-day		34.92	35
1991	The Chrysanthemum Goddess	175-day		34.92	35
1991	The Plum Blossom Goddess	175-day		37.92	40
1991	The Peony Goddess	175-day		37.92	55
1991	The Narcissus Goddess	175-day		37.92	62
1991	The Camellia Goddess	175-day		37.92	50

The Forbidden City - S. Fu

1990	Pavilion of 10,000 Springs	150-day		39.92	40
1990	Flying Kites/Spring Day	150-day		39.92	40
1990	Pavilion/Floating Jade Green	150-day		42.92	44
1991	The Lantern Festival	150-day		42.92	46
1991	Nine Dragon Screen	150-day		42.92	55
1991	The Hall of the Cultivating Mind	150-day		42.92	43
1991	Dressing the Empress	150-day		45.92	46
1991	Pavilion of Floating Cups	150-day		45.92	50

Garden of Satin Wings - J. Xue-Bing

1992	A Morning Dream	115-day		29.92	35
1993	An Evening Mist	115-day		29.92	37
1993	A Garden Whisper	115-day		29.92	40
1993	An Enchanting Interlude	115-day		29.92	40

Legends of West Lake - J. Xue-Bing

1989	Lady White	175-day		29.92	33
1990	Lady Silkworm	175-day		29.92	40
1990	Laurel Peak	175-day		29.92	30
1990	Rising Sun Terrace	175-day		32.92	45
1990	The Apricot Fairy	175-day		32.92	40
1990	Bright Pearl	175-day		32.92	33
1990	Thread of Sky	175-day		34.92	35
1991	Phoenix Mountain	175-day		34.92	35-40
1991	Ancestors of Tea	175-day		34.92	45
1991	Three Pools Mirroring/Moon	175-day		36.92	45
1991	Fly-In Peak	175-day		36.92	40
1991	The Case of the Folding Fans	175-day		36.92	50

Maidens of the Folding Sky - J. Xue-Bing

1992	Lady Lu	175-day		29.92	35
1992	Mistress Yang	175-day		29.92	40
1992	Bride Yen Chun	175-day		32.92	60
1993	Parrot Maiden	175-day		32.92	65

Scenes from the Summer Palace - Z. Song Mao

1988	The Marble Boat	175-day		29.92	30
1988	Jade Belt Bridge	175-day		29.92	30
1989	Hall that Dispels the Clouds	175-day		32.92	40
1989	The Long Promenade	175-day		32.92	35
1989	Garden/Harmonious Pleasure	175-day		32.92	35
1989	The Great Stage	175-day		32.92	40
1989	Seventeen Arch Bridge	175-day		34.92	35
1989	Boaters on Kumming Lake	175-day		34.92	35

International Silver

Bicentennial - M. Deoliveira

1972	Signing Declaration	7,500		40.00	310

YEAR ISSUE		EDITION LIMIT	YEAR RETD.	ISSUE PRICE	*QUOTE U.S.$
1973	Paul Revere	7,500		40.00	160
1974	Concord Bridge	7,500		40.00	115
1975	Crossing Delaware	7,500		50.00	80
1976	Valley Forge	7,500		50.00	65
1977	Surrender at Yorktown	7,500		50.00	60

John Hine N.A. Ltd.

David Winter Plate Collection - M. Fisher

1991	A Christmas Carol	10,000	1993	30.00	35-60
1991	Cotswold Village Plate	10,000	1993	30.00	35-60
1992	Chichester Cross Plate	10,000	1993	30.00	35-60
1992	Little Mill Plate	10,000	1993	30.00	35-60
1992	Old Curiosity Shop	10,000	1993	30.00	35-60
1992	Scrooge's Counting House	10,000	1993	30.00	35-60
1993	Dove Cottage	10,000		30.00	35
1993	Little Forge	10,000		30.00	35

Lalique Society of America

Annual - M. Lalique

1965	Deux Oiseaux (Two Birds)	2,000		25.00	1300
1966	Rose de Songerie (Dream Rose)	5,000		25.00	115
1967	Ballet de Poisson (Fish Ballet)	5,000		25.00	100
1968	Gazelle Fantaisie (Gazelle Fantasy)	5,000		25.00	75
1969	Papillon (Butterfly)	5,000		30.00	50
1970	Paon (Peacock)	5,000		30.00	60
1971	Hibou (Owl)	5,000		35.00	70
1972	Coquillage (Shell)	5,000		40.00	75
1973	Petit Geai (Jayling)	5,000		42.50	100
1974	Sous d'Argent (Silver Pennies)	5,000		47.50	95
1975	Duo de Poisson (Fish Duet)	5,000		50.00	140
1976	Aigle (Eagle)	5,000		60.00	90

Lance Corporation

American Expansion (Hudson Pewter) - P.W. Baston

1975	Spirit of '76 (6" Plate)	4,812	1975	27.50	100-120
1975	American Independence	18,462	N/A	Unkn.	100-125
1975	American Expansion	2,250	N/A	Unkn.	50-75
1975	The American War Between the States	825	N/A	Unkn.	150-200

Sebastian Plates - P.W. Baston

1978	Motif No. 1	4,878	1985	75.00	50-75
1979	Grand Canyon	2,492	1985	75.00	50-75
1980	Lone Cypress	718	1985	75.00	150-175
1980	In The Candy Store	9,098	1985	39.50	40
1981	The Doctor	7,547	1985	39.50	40
1983	Little Mother	2,710	1985	39.50	40
1984	Switching The Freight	706	1985	42.50	80-100

Lenox Collections

Adventures of the Deep Plate Collection - Unknown

1994	Let's Play	Open		39.50	40
1994	A New Day	Open		39.50	40
1994	Shining On	Open		39.50	40
1994	Polar Strollers	Open		39.50	40
1994	New Birth	Open		39.50	40
1994	Gratitude	Open		39.50	40
1994	After Hours	Open		39.50	40
1994	Sea of Joy	Open		39.50	40

American Wildlife - N. Adams

1982	Red Foxes	9,500		65.00	65
1982	Ocelots	9,500		65.00	65
1982	Sea Lions	9,500		65.00	65
1982	Raccoons	9,500		65.00	65
1982	Dall Sheep	9,500		65.00	65
1982	Black Bears	9,500		65.00	65
1982	Mountain Lions	9,500		65.00	65
1982	Polar Bears	9,500		65.00	65
1982	Otters	9,500		65.00	65
1982	White Tailed Deer	9,500		65.00	65
1982	Buffalo	9,500		65.00	65
1982	Jack Rabbits	9,500		65.00	65

Amish Life Plates - D. Patterson

1994	Barn Raising	Open		39.50	40
1994	Country Kids	Open		39.50	40

Annual Christmas Plates - Various

1992	Sleigh - Unknown	Yr.Iss.	1992	75.00	75
1993	Midnight Sleighride - L. Bywater	90-day	1993	119.00	119

Arctic Wolves - J. VanZyle

1993	Far Country Crossing	90-day	1994	29.90	30
1993	Cry of the Wild	90-day	1994	29.90	30
1993	Nightwatch	90-day	1994	29.90	30
1993	Midnight Renegade	90-day	1994	29.90	30
1993	On the Edge	90-day	1994	29.90	30
1993	Picking Up the Trail	90-day	1994	29.90	30

Big Cats of the World - Q. Lemonds

1993	Black Panther	Open		39.50	40
1993	Chinese Leopard	Open		39.50	40
1993	Cougar	Open		39.50	40
1993	Bobcat	Open		39.50	40

YEAR ISSUE		EDITION LIMIT	YEAR RETD.	ISSUE PRICE	*QUOTE U.S.$
1993	White Tiger	Open		39.50	40
1993	Tiger	Open		39.50	40
1993	Lion	Open		39.50	40
1993	Snow Leopard	Open		39.50	40

Birds of the Garden - W. Mumm

1992	Spring Glory, Cardinals	Open		39.50	40
1993	Sunbright Songbirds, Goldfinch	Open		39.50	40
1993	Bluebirds Haven, Bluebirds	Open		39.50	40
1993	Blossoming Bough, Chickadees	Open		39.50	40
1993	Jewels of the Garden, Hummingbirds	Open		39.50	40
1993	Indigo Meadow, Indigo Buntings	Open		39.50	40
1993	Scarlet Tanagers	Open		39.50	40

Boehm Birds - E. Boehm

1970	Wood Thrush	Yr.Iss.	1970	35.00	100-150
1971	Goldfinch	Yr.Iss.	1971	35.00	50
1972	Mountain Bluebird	Yr.Iss.	1972	37.50	45
1973	Meadowlark	Yr.Iss.	1973	50.00	50
1974	Rufous Hummingbird	Yr.Iss.	1974	45.00	50
1975	American Redstart	Yr.Iss.	1975	50.00	50
1976	Cardinals	Yr.Iss.	1976	53.00	53
1977	Robins	Yr.Iss.	1977	55.00	55
1978	Mockingbirds	Yr.Iss.	1978	58.00	58
1979	Golden-Crowned Kinglets	Yr.Iss.	1979	65.00	85
1980	Black-Throated Blue Warblers	Yr.Iss.	1980	80.00	95
1981	Eastern Phoebes	Yr.Iss.	1981	92.50	100

Boehm Woodland Wildlife - E. Boehm

1973	Racoons	Yr.Iss.	1973	50.00	75
1974	Red Foxes	Yr.Iss.	1974	52.50	75
1975	Cottontail Rabbits	Yr.Iss.	1975	58.50	75
1976	Eastern Chipmunks	Yr.Iss.	1976	62.50	75
1977	Beaver	Yr.Iss.	1977	67.50	68
1978	Whitetail Deer	Yr.Iss.	1978	70.00	70
1979	Squirrels	Yr.Iss.	1979	76.00	76
1980	Bobcats	Yr.Iss.	1980	82.50	83
1981	Martens	Yr.Iss.	1981	100.00	100
1982	River Otters	Yr.Iss.	1982	100.00	100

Cat Family Portrait - G. Coheleach

1994	Cougars	Open		39.50	40
1994	Lynx	Open		39.50	40
1994	Tigers	Open		39.50	40
1994	Snow Leopard	Open		39.50	40

Children of the Sun & Moon - D. Crowley

1993	Desert Blossom	Open		39.50	40
1993	Shy One	Open		39.50	40
1993	Feathers & Furs	Open		39.50	40
1994	Little Flower	Open		39.90	40
1994	Daughter of the Sun	Open		39.90	40
1994	Red Feathers	Open		39.90	40
1994	Stars in Her Eyes	Open		39.90	40
1994	Indigo Girl	Open		39.90	40

Crystal Hunter - Unknown

1994	Crystal Tiger	Open		39.50	40
1994	Dreamscape	Open		39.50	40
1994	Crystal Domain	Open		39.50	40
1994	Heart of Crystal	Open		39.50	40

Cubs of the Big Cats - Q. Lemonds

1993	Jaquar Cub	90-day	1994	29.90	30

Darling Dalmations - L. Picken

1993	Three Alarm Fire	90-day	1994	29.90	30
1993	All Fired Up	90-day	1994	29.90	30
1993	Fire Brigade	90-day	1994	29.90	30
1993	Pup in Boots	90-day	1994	29.90	30
1993	Caught in the Act	90-day	1994	29.90	30
1993	Please Don't Pick the Flowers	90-day	1994	29.90	30

Dolphins of the Seven Seas - J. Holderby

1993	Bottlenose Dolphins	Open		39.50	40

Eagle Conservation - R. Kelley

1993	Soaring the Peaks	Open		39.50	40
1993	Solo Flight	Open		39.50	40
1993	Northern Heritage	Open		39.50	40
1993	Lone Sentinel	Open		39.50	40
1993	River Scout	Open		39.50	40
1993	Eagles on Mt. McKinley	Open		39.50	40
1993	Daybreak on River's Edge	Open		39.50	40
1993	Northwood's Legend	Open		39.50	40

Enchanted World of the Unicorn - R. Sanderson

1992	Hidden Glade of Unicorn	90-day	1993	29.90	30
1992	Secret Garden of Unicorn	90-day	1993	29.90	30
1993	Joyful Meadow of Unicorn	90-day	1994	29.90	30
1993	Misty Hills of Unicorn	90-day	1994	29.90	30
1993	Tropical Paradise of Unicorn	90-day	1994	29.90	30
1993	Springtime Pasture of Unicorn	90-day	1994	29.90	30

English Country Cats - A. Mortimer

1994	Pepper & Ginger	Open		39.50	40
1994	Bluebell & Sage	Open		39.50	40
1994	Bib & Tucker	Open		39.50	40
1994	Calico & Cosmos	Open		39.50	40
1994	Peaches & Cream	Open		39.50	40

YEAR ISSUE		EDITION LIMIT	YEAR RETD.	ISSUE PRICE	*QUOTE U.S.$
1994	Buttons & Buster	Open		39.50	40
1994	Sweet Prince & Pansy	Open		39.50	40
1994	Felix & Oscar	Open		39.50	40

Garden Bird Plate Collection - Unknown

1988	Chickadee	Open		48.00	48
1988	Bluejay	Open		48.00	48
1989	Hummingbird	Open		48.00	48
1991	Dove	Open		48.00	48
1991	Cardinal	Open		48.00	48
1992	Goldfinch	Open		48.00	48

Great Castles of the World - Unknown

1994	Neuschwanstein	Open		39.50	40
1994	Alcazar de Segovia	Open		39.50	40
1994	Chateau de Chambord	Open		39.50	40
1994	Houses of Parliment	Open		39.50	40
1994	West Minster	Open		39.50	40
1994	Taj Mahal	Open		39.50	40
1994	St. Basil	Open		39.50	40

Great Cats of the World - G. Coheleach

1993	Siberian Tiger	Open		39.50	40
1993	Lion	Open		39.50	40
1993	Lioness	Open		39.50	40
1993	Snow Leopard	Open		39.50	40
1993	White Tiger	Open		39.50	40
1993	Jaguar	Open		39.50	40
1993	Cougar	Open		39.50	40
1993	Chinese Leopard	Open		39.50	40
1994	Puma	Open		39.50	40

Heaven Sent - Lenox

1994	Cherubs in Clouds	Open		39.50	40
1994	Heaven's Messengers	Open		39.50	40
1994	Angel Blues	Open		39.50	40

I Love Labradors - L. Picken

1994	Little Helpers	Open		39.50	40
1994	Rookie of the Year	Open		39.50	40
1994	Catch of the Day	Open		39.50	40
1994	Just Ducky	Open		39.50	40

International Victorian Santas - R. Hoover

1992	Kris Kringle	90-day	1993	39.50	40
1993	Father Christmas	90-day	1994	39.50	40
1994	Grandfather Frost	90-day	1995	39.50	40
1995	American Santa Claus	90-day	1995	39.50	40

Kimble Barnyard - Kimble

1994	Statement Plate 1	Open		39.50	40
1994	Statement Plate 2	Open		39.50	40

Kimble Cats - Kimble

1994	Happy Cat	Open		39.50	40
1994	Welcome Cat	Open		39.50	40
1994	Fat Cat	Open		39.50	40
1994	Taffy Cat	Open		39.50	40
1994	Cool Cat	Open		39.50	40
1994	Proper Cats	Open		39.50	40
1994	Happy Family Cats	Open		39.50	40
1994	Lucky Cat	Open		39.50	40

King of the Plains - S. Combes

1994	Tsava Elephant	Open		39.90	40
1994	Guardian	Open		39.90	40
1994	Rainbow Trail	Open		39.90	40
1994	African Ancients	Open		39.90	40
1994	Protecting the Flanks	Open		39.90	40
1994	The Last Elephant	Open		39.90	40
1994	End of the Line	Open		39.90	40
1994	Sparring Bulls	Open		39.90	40

Land of Buffalo - T. Lovell

1994	Fire in Buffalo Grass	Open		39.50	40
1994	Four Times to the Sun	Open		39.50	40
1994	Listening for the Drums	Open		39.50	40
1994	Finishing Touch	Open		39.50	40
1994	Long Ago Creature	Open		39.50	40
1994	The Wolf Man	Open		39.50	40
1994	War Bonnet Ceremony	Open		39.50	40
1994	The Gift	Open		39.50	40

Larry Chandler Puppy Portraits - L. Chandler

1994	Smoky	Open		39.50	40
1994	Dutch	Open		39.50	40
1994	Custard	Open		39.50	40
1994	Ebony & Ivory	Open		39.50	40

Life of Christ - J. Fuentes DeFalamanca

1994	Holy Family	Open		39.50	40
1994	Baptism	Open		39.50	40
1994	Crucifiction	Open		39.50	40
1994	Last Supper	Open		39.50	40
1994	Jesus the Good Shepherd	Open		39.50	40
1994	Agony in the Garden	Open		39.50	40
1994	Ascension	Open		39.50	40
1994	Resurrection	Open		39.50	40

Loveable Labs - L. Chandler

1994	Photo Labs	Open		39.50	40

YEAR ISSUE		EDITION LIMIT	YEAR RETD.	ISSUE PRICE	*QUOTE U.S.$
1994	Space Labs	Open		39.50	40
1994	Dental Labs	Open		39.50	40
1994	Science Labs	Open		39.50	40

Magic of Christmas - L. Bywaters

1993	Santa of the Northen Forest	Open		39.50	40
1993	Santa's Gift of Peace	Open		39.50	40
1993	Gifts For All	Open		39.50	40
1994	Coming Home	Open		39.50	40
1994	Santa's Sentinels	Open		39.50	40
1994	Wonder of Wonders	Open		39.50	40
1994	A Berry Merry Christmas	Open		39.50	40

Magnificent Dolphins of the 7 Seas - J. Holderby

1994	Bottlenose Dophin	Open		39.50	40
1994	Dolphins in Ruins	Open		39.50	40

Miracles of Christ - M. Weistling

1994	Wedding at Canna	Open		39.50	40
1994	Walking on Water	Open		39.50	40

Moonlight Fantasy - B. Chall

1994	Moonlight Highway	Open		39.50	40
1994	Moonlight Enchantment	Open		39.50	40
1994	Moonlight Voyager	Open		39.50	40
1994	Orca Moon	Open		39.50	40

Mumm-Birds in Snow - W. Mumm

1994	Cardinals in Winter	Open		39.50	40
1994	Chickadees	Open		39.50	40
1994	Juncos	Open		39.50	40

Nature's Collage - C. McClung

1992	Cedar Waxwing, Among The Berries	Open		34.50	35
1992	Gold Finches, Golden Splendor	Open		34.50	35
1993	Bluebirds, Summer Interlude	90-day	1994	39.50	40
1993	Chickadees, Rose Morning	90-day	1994	39.50	40
1993	Bluejays, Winter Song	90-day	1994	39.50	40
1993	Cardinals, Spring Courtship	90-day	1994	39.50	40
1993	Hummingbirds, Jeweled Glory	90-day	1994	39.50	40
1993	Indigo Buntings, Indigo Evening	90-day	1994	39.50	40

Nature's Nestlings - C. McClung

1994	Golden Moments	Open		39.50	40
1994	New Beginnings	Open		39.50	40
1994	Precious Treasures	Open		39.50	40
1994	Morning Song	Open		39.50	40
1994	Goldfinches	Open		39.50	40
1994	Cardinals	Open		39.50	40
1994	Wren Family	Open		39.50	40
1994	Cardinal Family	Open		39.50	40

Owls of North America - L. Laffin

1993	Spirit of the Arctic, Snowy Owl	Open		39.50	40

Pierced Nativity - Unknown

1993	Holy Family	Open		45.00	45
1994	Three Kings	Open		45.00	45
1994	Heralding Angels	Open		45.00	45
1994	Shepherds	Open		45.00	45

Pierced Religious Plates - Unknown

1994	Pierced Pieta	Open		39.50	40

Royal Cats of Guy Coheleach - G. Coheleach

1994	Afternoon Shade	Open		39.50	40
1994	Jungle Jaquar	Open		39.50	40
1994	Rocky Mountain Puma	Open		39.50	40
1994	Rocky Refuge	Open		39.50	40
1994	Siesta	Open		39.50	40
1994	Ambush in the Snow	Open		39.50	40
1994	Lion in Wait	Open		39.50	40
1994	Cat Nap	Open		39.50	40

Spirit of the Navajo - Unknown

1994	Navajo Hug	Open		39.50	40
1994	Six Days Old	Open		39.50	40
1994	Jewel	Open		39.50	40
1994	The Sentinel	Open		39.50	40
1994	Never Alone	Open		39.50	40
1994	Windy but Warm	Open		39.50	40
1994	Ride to the Song	Open		39.50	40
1994	Girl Holding Puppy	Open		39.50	40

Spirits of the Sky - M. Fields

1994	Soul of the Wolf	Open		39.50	40
1994	Spirit Riders	Open		39.50	40
1994	Medicine Woman	Open		39.50	40
1994	Spirit Lovers	Open		39.50	40
1994	Spirit 8	Open		39.50	40

Victorian Santas - D. Morgan

1994	Kris Kringle	Open		39.50	40
1994	Father Christmas	Open		39.50	40
1994	Grandfather Frost	Open		39.50	40
1994	American Santa	Open		39.50	40
1994	Victorian Santa	Open		39.50	40
1994	97 Santa	Open		39.50	40
1994	Belsnickle	Open		39.50	40
1994	The Magic Never Ends	Open		39.50	40

YEAR ISSUE		EDITION LIMIT	YEAR RETD.	ISSUE PRICE	*QUOTE U.S.$
1994	Checking His List	Open		39.50	40
1994	Twas the Night	Open		39.50	40

Whale Conservation - J. Holderby

1993	Orca	Open		39.50	40

Wilderness Solitude - T. Doughty

1994	Snowy Haven	Open		39.50	40
1994	Midnight Lookout	Open		39.50	40
1994	Old Homestead	Open		39.50	40

Wreaths of the Month - Unknown

1994	Winter Greetings-December	Open		39.50	40
1994	Spring Blessings-May	Open		39.50	40

Lightpost Publishing

Kinkade-Thomas Kinkade Signature Collection - T. Kinkade

1991	Chandler's Cottage	2,500		49.95	50-75
1991	Cedar Nook	2,500		49.95	40-75
1991	Sleigh Ride Home	2,500		49.95	55-75
1991	Home To Grandma's	2,500		49.95	52-75

Lilliput Lane Ltd.

American Landmarks Collection - R. Day

1990	Country Church	5,000	1996	35.00	35
1990	Riverside Chapel	5,000	1996	35.00	35

Lladró

Lladró Plate Collection - Lladró

1993	The Great Voyage L5964G	Open		50.00	50
1993	Looking Out L5998G	Open		38.00	38
1993	Swinging L5999G	Open		38.00	38
1993	Duck Plate L6000G	Open		38.00	38
1994	Friends L6158	Open		32.00	32
1994	Apple Picking L6159M	Open		32.00	32
1994	Turtledove L6160	Open		32.00	32
1994	Flamingo L6161M	Open		32.00	32

Lowell Davis Farm Club

Davis Cat Tales Plates. - L. Davis

1982	Right Church, Wrong Pew	12,500	1986	37.50	90
1982	Company's Coming	12,500	1986	37.50	90
1982	On the Move	12,500	1986	37.50	90
1982	Flew the Coop	12,500	1986	37.50	90

Davis Christmas Plates - L. Davis

1983	Hooker at Mailbox With Present	7,500	1984	45.00	130
1984	Country Christmas	7,500	1985	45.00	75
1985	Christmas at Foxfire Farm	7,500	1986	45.00	150
1986	Christmas at Red Oak	7,500	1987	45.00	50-75
1987	Blossom's Gift	7,500	1988	47.50	100
1988	Cutting the Family Christmas Tree	7,500	1989	47.50	65
1989	Peter and the Wren	7,500	1990	47.50	75
1990	Wintering Deer	7,500	1991	47.50	48
1991	Christmas at Red Oak II	7,500	1992	55.00	75
1992	Born On A Starry Night	7,500	1993	55.00	55
1993	Waiting For Mr. Lowell	5,000	1994	55.00	55
1994	Visions of Sugarplums	5,000	1995	55.00	55
1995	Bah Humbug	5,000		55.00	55

Davis Country Pride Plates - L. Davis

1981	Surprise in the Cellar	7,500	1983	35.00	175-225
1981	Plum Tuckered Out	7,500	1983	35.00	70
1981	Duke's Mixture	7,500	1983	35.00	190
1982	Bustin' with Pride	7,500	1983	35.00	75

Davis Red Oak Sampler - L. Davis

1986	General Store	5,000	1987	45.00	175
1987	Country Wedding	5,000	1988	45.00	125
1989	Country School	5,000	1990	45.00	75
1990	Blacksmith Shop	5,000	1991	52.50	53

Davis Special Edition Plates - L. Davis

1983	The Critics	12,500	1985	45.00	60-145
1984	Good Ole Days Privy Set 2	5,000	1986	60.00	80-125
1986	Home From Market	7,500	1988	55.00	145

March of Dimes

Our Children, Our Future - Various

1989	A Time for Peace - D. Zolan	150-day		29.00	36
1989	A Time To Love - S. Kuck	150-day		29.00	45
1989	A Time To Plant - J. McClelland	150-day		29.00	32
1989	A Time To Be Born - G. Perillo	150-day		29.00	35
1990	A Time To Embrace - E. Hibel	150-day		29.00	55
1990	A Time To Laugh - A. Williams	150-day		29.00	32

Marigold

Sport - Carreno

1989	Mickey Mantle-handsigned	Retrd.		100.00	800
1989	Mickey Mantle-unsigned	Retrd.		60.00	100
1989	Joe DiMaggio-handsigned	Retrd.		100.00	1475
1989	Joe DiMaggio f/s (blue sig.)	Retrd.		60.00	195

YEAR ISSUE		EDITION YEAR LIMIT RETRD.	ISSUE PRICE	*QUOTE U.S.$
1990	Joe DiMaggio AP-handsigned	Retrd.	N/A	2695

Maruri USA

Eagle Plate Series - W. Gaither

1984	Free Flight	Closed 1993	150.00	150-198

Museum Collections, Inc.

American Family I - N. Rockwell

1979	Baby's First Step	9,900	28.50	48
1979	Happy Birthday Dear Mother	9,900	28.50	45
1979	Sweet Sixteen	9,900	28.50	35
1979	First Haircut	9,900	28.50	60
1979	First Prom	9,900	28.50	35
1979	Wrapping Christmas Presents	9,900	28.50	35
1979	The Student	9,900	28.50	35
1979	Birthday Party	9,900	28.50	35
1979	Little Mother	9,900	28.50	35
1979	Washing Our Dog	9,900	28.50	35
1979	Mother's Little Helpers	9,900	28.50	35
1979	Bride and Groom	9,900	28.50	35

American Family II - N. Rockwell

1980	New Arrival	22,500	35.00	50-55
1980	Sweet Dreams	22,500	35.00	38
1980	Little Shaver	22,500	35.00	40
1980	We Missed You Daddy	22,500	35.00	38
1980	Home Run Slugger	22,500	35.00	38
1980	Giving Thanks	22,500	35.00	55
1980	Space Pioneers	22,500	35.00	35
1980	Little Salesman	22,500	35.00	38
1980	Almost Grown up	22,500	35.00	38
1980	Courageous Hero	22,500	35.00	38
1981	At the Circus	22,500	35.00	38
1981	Good Food, Good Friends	22,500	35.00	38

Christmas - N. Rockwell

1979	Day After Christmas	Yr.Iss	75.00	75
1980	Checking His List	Yr.Iss	75.00	75
1981	Ringing in Good Cheer	Yr.Iss	75.00	75
1982	Waiting for Santa	Yr.Iss	75.00	75
1983	High Hopes	Yr.Iss	75.00	75
1984	Space Age Santa	Yr.Iss	55.00	55

Norman Rockwell Gallery

Norman Rockwell Centennial - Rockwell Inspired

1993	The Toymaker	Closed	39.90	55
1993	The Cobbler	Closed	39.90	60

Rockwell's Christmas Legacy - Rockwell Inspired

1992	Santa's Workshop	Closed	49.90	75
1993	Making a List	Closed	49.90	65
1993	While Santa Slumbers	Closed	54.90	65
1993	Visions of Santa	Closed	54.90	100

Pemberton & Oakes

Adventures of Childhood Collection - D. Zolan

1989	Almost Home	Retrd.	19.60	45-60
1989	Crystal's Creek	Retrd.	19.60	45
1989	Summer Suds	Retrd.	22.00	40
1990	Snowy Adventure	Retrd.	22.00	40
1991	Forests & Fairy Tales	Retrd.	24.40	35-45

The Best of Zolan in Miniature - D. Zolan

1985	Sabina	Retrd.	12.50	112
1986	Erik and Dandelion	Retrd.	12.50	100
1986	Tender Moment	Retrd.	12.50	85
1986	Touching the Sky	Retrd.	12.50	83
1987	A Gift for Laurie	Retrd.	12.50	80
1987	Small Wonder	Retrd.	12.50	77

Childhood Discoveries (Miniature) - D. Zolan

1990	Colors of Spring	Retrd.	14.40	30-40
1990	Autumn Leaves	Retrd.	14.40	45
1991	Enchanted Forest	Retrd.	16.60	35
1991	Just Ducky	Retrd.	16.60	42
1991	Rainy Day Pals	Retrd.	16.60	30
1992	Double Trouble	Retrd.	16.60	36-50
1990	First Kiss	Retrd.	14.40	55
1993	Peppermint Kiss	Retrd.	16.60	25
1995	Tender Hearts	19-day	16.60	30

Childhood Friendship Collection - D. Zolan

1986	Beach Break	Retrd.	19.00	54
1987	Little Engineers	Retrd.	19.00	40-65
1988	Tiny Treasures	Retrd.	19.00	30-50
1988	Sharing Secrets	Retrd.	19.00	30-45
1988	Dozens of Daisies	Retrd.	19.00	40
1990	Country Walk	Retrd.	19.00	40

Children and Pets - D. Zolan

1984	Tender Moment	Retrd.	19.00	30-65
1984	Golden Moment	Retrd.	19.00	30-50
1985	Making Friends	Retrd.	19.00	30-50
1985	Tender Beginning	Retrd.	19.00	45
1986	Backyard Discovery	Retrd.	19.00	40-50

1986	Waiting to Play	Retrd.	19.00	45

Children at Christmas - D. Zolan

1981	A Gift for Laurie	Retrd.	48.00	75
1982	Christmas Prayer	Retrd.	48.00	50
1983	Erik's Delight	Retrd.	48.00	68
1984	Christmas Secret	Retrd.	48.00	50-66
1985	Christmas Kitten	Retrd.	48.00	60-75
1986	Laurie and the Creche	Retrd.	48.00	75

Christmas (Miniature) - D. Zolan

1993	Snowy Adventure	Retrd.	16.60	30
1994	Candlelight Magic	19-day	16.60	25

Christmas - D. Zolan

1991	Candlelight Magic	Retrd.	24.80	35

Companion to Brotherly Love - D. Zolan

1989	Sisterly Love	Retrd.	22.00	40-50

Easter (Miniature) - D. Zolan

1991	Easter Morning	Retrd.	16.60	45

Father's Day (Miniature) - D. Zolan

1994	Two of a Kind	Retrd.	16.60	36

Father's Day - D. Zolan

1986	Daddy's Home	Retrd.	19.00	55-115

Grandparent's Day - D. Zolan

1990	It's Grandma & Grandpa	Retrd.	24.40	40
1993	Grandpa's Fence	Retrd.	24.40	45

Heirloom Ovals - D. Zolan

1992	My Kitty	Retrd.	18.80	47

March of Dimes: Our Children, Our Future - D. Zolan

1989	A Time for Peace	Retrd.	29.00	40-50

Members Only Single Issue (Miniature) - D. Zolan

1990	By Myself	Retrd.	14.40	62
1993	Summer's Child	Retrd.	16.60	43
1994	Little Slugger	10-day	16.60	37

Membership (Miniature) - D. Zolan

1987	For You	Retrd.	12.50	102
1988	Making Friends	Retrd.	12.50	75
1989	Grandma's Garden	Retrd.	12.50	72
1990	A Christmas Prayer	Retrd.	14.40	54
1991	Golden Moment	Retrd.	15.00	47
1992	Brotherly Love	Retrd.	15.00	60-90
1993	New Shoes	Retrd.	17.00	40
1994	My Kitty	19-day	Gift	34

Moments To Remember (Miniature) - D. Zolan

1992	Just We Two	Retrd.	16.60	55
1992	Almost Home	Retrd.	16.60	25-40
1993	Tiny Treasures	Retrd.	16.60	27
1993	Forest Friends	Retrd.	16.60	27

Mother's Day (Miniature) - D. Zolan

1990	Flowers for Mother	Retrd.	14.40	40
1992	Twilight Prayer	Retrd.	16.60	22-30
1993	Jessica's Field	Retrd.	16.60	22-40
1994	One Summer Day	Retrd.	16.60	55

Mother's Day - D. Zolan

1988	Mother's Angels	Retrd.	19.00	35-60

Nutcracker II - Various

1981	Grand Finale - S. Fisher	Retrd.	24.40	36
1982	Arabian Dancers - S. Fisher	Retrd.	24.40	68
1983	Dew Drop Fairy - S. Fisher	Retrd.	24.40	40
1984	Clara's Delight - S. Fisher	Retrd.	24.40	45
1985	Bedtime for Nutcracker - S. Fisher	Retrd.	24.40	45
1986	The Crowning of Clara - S. Fisher	Retrd.	24.40	36
1987	Dance of the Snowflakes - D. Zolan	Retrd.	24.40	30-75
1988	The Royal Welcome - R. Anderson	Retrd.	24.40	47
1989	The Spanish Dancer - M. Vickers	Retrd.	24.40	45

Plaques - D. Zolan

1991	New Shoes	Retrd.	18.80	40
1992	Grandma's Garden	Retrd.	18.80	30-50
1992	Small Wonder	Retrd.	18.80	36
1992	Easter Morning	Retrd.	18.80	25-35

Plaques-Single Issues - D. Zolan

1991	Flowers for Mother	Retrd.	16.80	30

Single Issue - D. Zolan

1993	Winter Friends	Retrd.	18.80	45

Single Issue Bone China (Miniature) - D. Zolan

1992	Window of Dreams	Retrd.	18.80	35

Single Issue Day to Day Spode - D. Zolan

1991	Daisy Days	Retrd.	48.00	55

Single Issues (Miniature) - D. Zolan

1986	Backyard Discovery	Retrd.	12.50	107
1986	Daddy's Home	Retrd.	12.50	820

1989	Sunny Surprise	Retrd.	12.50	55
1989	My Pumpkin	Retrd.	14.40	45-60
1991	Backyard Buddies	Retrd.	16.60	36
1991	The Thinker	Retrd.	16.60	35-45
1993	Quiet Time	Retrd.	16.60	66
1994	Little Fisherman	19-day	16.60	36

Special Moments of Childhood Collection - D. Zolan

1988	Brotherly Love	Retrd.	19.00	40-75
1988	Sunny Surprise	Retrd.	19.00	40-50
1989	Summer's Child	Retrd.	22.00	45
1990	Meadow Magic	Retrd.	22.00	35
1990	Cone For Two	Retrd.	24.60	36
1990	Rodeo Girl	Retrd.	24.60	35

Tenth Anniversary - D. Zolan

1988	Ribbons and Roses	Retrd.	24.40	30-45

Thanksgiving (Miniature) - D. Zolan

1993	I'm Thankful Too	Retrd.	16.60	37

Thanksgiving - D. Zolan

1981	I'm Thankful Too	Retrd.	19.00	50-75

Times To Treasure Bone China (Miniature) - D. Zolan

1993	Little Traveler	Retrd.	16.60	35
1993	Garden Swing	Retrd.	16.60	29
1994	Summer Garden	19-day	16.60	25
1994	September Girl	19-day	16.60	25

Wonder of Childhood - D. Zolan

1982	Touching the Sky	Retrd.	19.00	20-50
1983	Spring Innocence	Retrd.	19.00	20-40
1984	Winter Angel	Retrd.	22.00	22-45
1985	Small Wonder	Retrd.	22.00	22-45
1986	Grandma's Garden	Retrd.	22.00	27-45
1987	Day Dreamer	Retrd.	22.00	27-40

Yesterday's Children (Miniature) - D. Zolan

1994	Little Friends	19-day	16.60	40
1994	Seaside Treasures	19-day	16.60	30

Zolan's Children - D. Zolan

1978	Erik and Dandelion	Retrd.	19.00	255
1979	Sabina in the Grass	Retrd.	22.00	250
1980	By Myself	Retrd.	24.00	55
1981	For You	Retrd.	24.00	36

Reco International

Amish Traditions - B. Farnsworth

1994	Golden Harvest	95-day	29.50	30
1994	Family Outing	95-day	29.50	30
1994	The Quilting Bee	95-day	29.50	30
1995	Last Day of School	95-day	29.50	30

Barefoot Children - S. Kuck

1987	Night-Time Story	Retrd. 1994	29.50	45
1987	Golden Afternoon	14-day	29.50	30
1988	Little Sweethearts	Retrd. 1995	29.50	40
1988	Carousel Magic	14-day	29.50	30
1988	Under the Apple Tree	Retrd. 1995	29.50	40
1988	The Rehearsal	Retrd. 1995	29.50	60
1988	Pretty as a Picture	Retrd. 1993	29.50	45
1988	Grandma's Trunk	Retrd. 1993	29.50	45

Becky's Day - J. McClelland

1985	Awakening	90-day	24.50	25
1985	Getting Dressed	Retrd. 1988	24.50	29
1986	Breakfast	Retrd. 1987	27.50	35
1986	Learning is Fun	Retrd. 1988	27.50	28
1986	Muffin Making	Retrd. 1989	27.50	28
1986	Tub Time	Retrd. 1989	27.50	35
1986	Evening Prayer	Retrd. 1990	27.50	28

Birds of the Hidden Forest - G. Ratnavira

1994	Macaw Waterfall	96-day	29.50	30
1994	Paradise Valley	96-day	29.50	30
1995	Toucan Treasure	96-day	29.50	30

Bohemian Annuals - Factory Artist

1974	1974	Retrd. 1975	130.00	155
1975	1975	Retrd. 1976	140.00	160
1976	1976	Retrd. 1978	150.00	160

Castles & Dreams - J. Bergsma

1992	The Birth of a Dream	48-day	29.50	30
1992	Dreams Come True	48-day	29.50	30
1993	Believe In Your Dreams	48-day	29.50	30
1994	Follow Your Dreams	48-day	29.50	30

A Childhood Almanac - S. Kuck

1985	Fireside Dreams-January	Retrd. 1991	29.50	49
1985	Be Mine-February	Retrd. 1992	29.50	45
1986	Winds of March-March	Retrd. 1994	29.50	50
1985	Easter Morning-April	Retrd. 1992	29.50	55
1985	For Mom-May	Retrd. 1992	29.50	55
1985	Just Dreaming-June	Retrd. 1992	29.50	30-55
1985	Star Spangled Sky-July	Retrd. 1995	29.50	45
1985	Summer Secrets-August	Retrd. 1991	29.50	53

YEAR ISSUE	ISSUE	EDITION LIMIT	YEAR RETD.	ISSUE PRICE	*QUOTE U.S.$
1985	School Days-September	Retrd.	1991	29.50	35-60
1986	Indian Summer-October	Retrd.	1991	29.50	45
1986	Giving Thanks-November	Retrd.	1995	29.50	50
1985	Christmas Magic-December	Retrd.	1995	35.00	70

A Children's Christmas Pageant - S. Kuck

YEAR ISSUE	ISSUE	EDITION LIMIT	YEAR RETD.	ISSUE PRICE	*QUOTE U.S.$
1986	Silent Night	Retrd.	1987	32.50	35-55
1987	Hark the Herald Angels Sing	Retrd.	1988	32.50	45
1988	While Shepherds Watched...	Retrd.	1990	32.50	33
1989	We Three Kings	Yr.Iss.	N/A	32.50	33

The Children's Garden - J. McClelland

YEAR ISSUE	ISSUE	EDITION LIMIT	ISSUE PRICE	*QUOTE U.S.$
1993	Garden Friends	120-day	29.50	30
1993	Tea for Three	120-day	29.50	30
1993	Puppy Love	120-day	29.50	30

Christening Gift - S. Kuck

YEAR ISSUE	ISSUE	EDITION LIMIT	ISSUE PRICE	*QUOTE U.S.$
1995	God's Gift	Open	29.90	30

The Christmas Series - J. Bergsma

YEAR ISSUE	ISSUE	EDITION LIMIT	ISSUE PRICE	*QUOTE U.S.$
1990	Down The Glistening Lane	14-day	35.00	35
1991	A Child Is Born	14-day	35.00	35
1992	Christmas Day	14-day	35.00	35
1993	I Wish You An Angel	14-day	35.00	35

Christmas Wishes - J. Bergsma

YEAR ISSUE	ISSUE	EDITION LIMIT	ISSUE PRICE	*QUOTE U.S.$
1994	I Wish You Love	75-day	29.50	30
1995	I Wish You Joy	75-day	29.50	30

Days Gone By - S. Kuck

YEAR ISSUE	ISSUE	EDITION LIMIT	YEAR RETD.	ISSUE PRICE	*QUOTE U.S.$
1983	Sunday Best	Retrd.	1984	29.50	30-40
1983	Amy's Magic Horse	Retrd.	1985	29.50	50-70
1984	Little Anglers	Retrd.	1985	29.50	27
1984	Afternoon Recital	Retrd.	1985	29.50	50
1984	Little Tutor	Retrd.	1985	29.50	30
1985	Easter at Grandma's	Retrd.	1985	29.50	30
1985	Morning Song	Retrd.	1986	29.50	30
1985	The Surrey Ride	Retrd.	1987	29.50	75

Dresden Christmas - Factory Artist

YEAR ISSUE	ISSUE	EDITION LIMIT	YEAR RETD.	ISSUE PRICE	*QUOTE U.S.$
1971	Shepherd Scene	Retrd.	1978	15.00	50
1972	Niklas Church	Retrd.	1978	15.00	25
1973	Schwanstein Church	Retrd.	1978	18.00	35
1974	Village Scene	Retrd.	1978	20.00	30
1975	Rothenburg Scene	Retrd.	1978	24.00	30
1976	Village Church	Retrd.	1978	26.00	35
1977	Old Mill	Retrd.	1978	28.00	30

Dresden Mother's Day - Factory Artist

YEAR ISSUE	ISSUE	EDITION LIMIT	YEAR RETD.	ISSUE PRICE	*QUOTE U.S.$
1972	Doe and Fawn	Retrd.	1979	15.00	20
1973	Mare and Colt	Retrd.	1979	16.00	25
1974	Tiger and Cub	Retrd.	1979	20.00	23
1975	Dachshunds	Retrd.	1979	24.00	28
1976	Owl and Offspring	Retrd.	1979	26.00	30
1977	Chamois	Retrd.	1979	28.00	30

Eagle of America - S. Barlowe

YEAR ISSUE	ISSUE	EDITION LIMIT	ISSUE PRICE	*QUOTE U.S.$
1996	Land of The Free	96-day	29.90	30

The Enchanted Norfin Trolls - C. Hopkins

YEAR ISSUE	ISSUE	EDITION LIMIT	ISSUE PRICE	*QUOTE U.S.$
1993	Troll Maiden	75-day	19.50	20
1993	The Wizard Troll	75-day	19.50	20
1993	The Troll and His Dragon	75-day	19.50	20
1994	Troll in Shinning Armor	75-day	19.50	20
1994	Minstrel Troll	75-day	19.50	20
1994	If Trolls Could Fly	75-day	19.50	20
1994	Chef le Troll	75-day	19.50	20
1994	Queen of Trolls	75-day	19.50	20

Everlasing Friends - S. Kuck

YEAR ISSUE	ISSUE	EDITION LIMIT	ISSUE PRICE	*QUOTE U.S.$
1996	Sharing Secrets	95-day	N/A	N/A
1996	Togetherness	95-day	N/A	N/A

The Flower Fairies Year Collection - C.M. Barker

YEAR ISSUE	ISSUE	EDITION LIMIT	ISSUE PRICE	*QUOTE U.S.$
1990	The Red Clover Fairy	14-day	29.50	30
1990	The Wild Cherry Blossom Fairy	14-day	29.50	30
1990	The Pine Tree Fairy	14-day	29.50	30
1990	The Rose Hip Fairy	14-day	29.50	30

Four Seasons - J. Poluszynski

YEAR ISSUE	ISSUE	EDITION LIMIT	YEAR RETD.	ISSUE PRICE	*QUOTE U.S.$
1973	Spring	Retrd.	1975	50.00	75
1973	Summer	Retrd.	1975	50.00	75
1973	Fall	Retrd.	1975	50.00	75
1973	Winter	Retrd.	1975	50.00	75

Friends For Keeps - S. Kuck

YEAR ISSUE	ISSUE	EDITION LIMIT	ISSUE PRICE	*QUOTE U.S.$
1996	Puppy Love	95-day	29.95	30
1996	Gone Fishing	95-day	29.95	30

Furstenberg Christmas - Factory Artist

YEAR ISSUE	ISSUE	EDITION LIMIT	YEAR RETD.	ISSUE PRICE	*QUOTE U.S.$
1971	Rabbits	Retrd.	1977	15.00	30
1972	Snowy Village	Retrd.	1977	15.00	20
1973	Christmas Eve	Retrd.	1977	18.00	35
1974	Sparrows	Retrd.	1977	20.00	30
1975	Deer Family	Retrd.	1977	22.00	30
1976	Winter Birds	Retrd.	1977	25.00	25

Furstenberg Deluxe Christmas - E. Grossberg

YEAR ISSUE	ISSUE	EDITION LIMIT	YEAR RETD.	ISSUE PRICE	*QUOTE U.S.$
1971	Wise Men	Retrd.	1974	45.00	45
1972	Holy Family	Retrd.	1974	45.00	45
1973	Christmas Eve	Retrd.	1974	60.00	65

Furstenberg Easter - Factory Artist

YEAR ISSUE	ISSUE	EDITION LIMIT	YEAR RETD.	ISSUE PRICE	*QUOTE U.S.$
1971	Sheep	Retrd.	1973	15.00	150
1972	Chicks	Retrd.	1975	15.00	60
1973	Bunnies	Retrd.	1976	16.00	80
1974	Pussywillow	Retrd.	1976	20.00	33
1975	Easter Window	Retrd.	1977	22.00	30
1976	Flower Collecting	Retrd.	1977	25.00	25

Furstenberg Mother's Day - Factory Artist

YEAR ISSUE	ISSUE	EDITION LIMIT	YEAR RETD.	ISSUE PRICE	*QUOTE U.S.$
1972	Hummingbirds, Fe	Retrd.	1974	15.00	45
1973	Hedgehogs	Retrd.	1974	16.00	40
1974	Doe and Fawn	Retrd.	1974	20.00	30
1975	Swans	Retrd.	1976	22.00	23
1976	Koala Bears	Retrd.	1976	25.00	30

Furstenberg Olympic - J. Poluszynski

YEAR ISSUE	ISSUE	EDITION LIMIT	YEAR RETD.	ISSUE PRICE	*QUOTE U.S.$
1972	Munich	Retrd.	1972	20.00	75
1976	Montreal	Retrd.	1976	37.50	38

Games Children Play - S. Kuck

YEAR ISSUE	ISSUE	EDITION LIMIT	YEAR RETD.	ISSUE PRICE	*QUOTE U.S.$
1979	Me First	Retrd.	1983	45.00	50
1980	Forever Bubbles	Retrd.	1983	45.00	48
1981	Skating Pals	Retrd.	1983	45.00	48
1982	Join Me	10,000		45.00	45

Gardens of Beauty - D. Barlowe

YEAR ISSUE	ISSUE	EDITION LIMIT	YEAR RETD.	ISSUE PRICE	*QUOTE U.S.$
1988	English Country Garden	14-day		29.50	30
1988	Dutch Country Garden	14-day		29.50	30
1988	New England Garden	14-day		29.50	30
1988	Japanese Garden	14-day		29.50	30
1989	Italian Garden	14-day		29.50	30
1989	Hawaiian Garden	14-day		29.50	30
1989	German Country Garden	14-day		29.50	30
1989	Mexican Garden	14-day		29.50	30
1992	Colonial Splendor	48-day	1994	29.50	30

Gift of Love Mother's Day Collection - S. Kuck

YEAR ISSUE	ISSUE	EDITION LIMIT	YEAR RETD.	ISSUE PRICE	*QUOTE U.S.$
1993	Morning Glory	Retrd.	1994	65.00	65
1994	Memories From The Heart	Retrd.	1994	65.00	65

The Glory Of Christ - C. Micarelli

YEAR ISSUE	ISSUE	EDITION LIMIT	ISSUE PRICE	*QUOTE U.S.$
1992	The Ascension	48-day	29.50	30
1993	Jesus Teaching	48-day	29.50	30
1993	The Last Supper	48-day	29.50	30
1993	The Nativity	48-day	29.50	30
1993	The Baptism Of Christ	48-day	29.50	30
1993	Jesus Heals The Sick	48-day	29.50	30
1994	Jesus Walks On Water	48-day	29.50	30
1994	Descent From The Cross	48-day	29.50	30

God's Own Country - I. Drechsler

YEAR ISSUE	ISSUE	EDITION LIMIT	ISSUE PRICE	*QUOTE U.S.$
1990	Daybreak	14-day	30.00	30
1990	Coming Home	14-day	30.00	30
1990	Peaceful Gathering	14-day	30.00	30
1990	Quiet Waters	14-day	30.00	30

The Grandparent Collector's Plates - S. Kuck

YEAR ISSUE	ISSUE	EDITION LIMIT	ISSUE PRICE	*QUOTE U.S.$
1981	Grandma's Cookie Jar	Yr.Iss.	37.50	38
1981	Grandpa and the Dollhouse	Yr.Iss.	37.50	38

Great Stories from the Bible - G. Katz

YEAR ISSUE	ISSUE	EDITION LIMIT	YEAR RETD.	ISSUE PRICE	*QUOTE U.S.$
1987	Moses in the Bulrushes	14-day	1994	29.50	30
1987	King Saul & David	14-day	1994	29.50	30
1987	Moses and the Ten Commandments	14-day	1994	29.50	30-38
1987	Joseph's Coat of Many Colors	14-day	1994	29.50	30
1988	Rebekah at the Well	14-day	1994	29.50	35
1988	Daniel Reads the Writing on the Wall	14-day	1994	29.50	35
1988	The Story of Ruth	14-day	1994	29.50	35
1988	King Solomon	14-day	1994	29.50	35

Guardians Of The Kingdom - J. Bergsma

YEAR ISSUE	ISSUE	EDITION LIMIT	YEAR RETD.	ISSUE PRICE	*QUOTE U.S.$
1990	Rainbow To Ride On	Retrd.	1993	35.00	37
1990	Special Friends Are Few	17,500		35.00	35
1990	Guardians Of The Innocent Children	17,500		35.00	35
1990	The Miracle Of Love	17,500		35.00	35
1991	The Magic Of Love	17,500		35.00	35
1991	Only With The Heart	17,500		35.00	35
1991	To Fly Without Wings	17,500		35.00	35
1991	In Faith I Am Free	17,500		35.00	35

Guiding Lights - D Hahlbohm

YEAR ISSUE	ISSUE	EDITION LIMIT	ISSUE PRICE	*QUOTE U.S.$
1996	Robbins Reef	96-day	29.90	30
1996	Cape Hateras	96-day	29.90	30

Haven of the Hunters - H. Roe

YEAR ISSUE	ISSUE	EDITION LIMIT	ISSUE PRICE	*QUOTE U.S.$
1994	Eagle's Castle	96-day	29.50	30
1994	Sanctuary of the Hawk	96-day	29.50	30

Hearts And Flowers - S. Kuck

YEAR ISSUE	ISSUE	EDITION LIMIT	ISSUE PRICE	*QUOTE U.S.$
1991	Patience	120-day	29.50	30
1991	Tea Party	120-day	29.50	30
1992	Cat's In The Cradle	120-day	32.50	33
1992	Carousel of Dreams	120-day	32.50	33
1992	Storybook Memories	120-day	32.50	33
1993	Delightful Bundle	120-day	34.50	35
1993	Easter Morning Visitor	120-day	34.50	35
1993	Me and My Pony	120-day	34.50	35

Imaginary Gardens - S. Somerville

YEAR ISSUE	ISSUE	EDITION LIMIT	ISSUE PRICE	*QUOTE U.S.$
1996	Pussywillows	76-day	29.90	30
1996	Dogwood	76-day	29.90	30

In The Eye of The Storm - W. Lowe

YEAR ISSUE	ISSUE	EDITION LIMIT	ISSUE PRICE	*QUOTE U.S.$
1991	First Strike	120-day	29.50	30
1992	Night Force	120-day	29.50	30
1992	Tracks Across The Sand	120-day	29.50	30
1992	The Storm Has Landed	120-day	29.50	30

J. Bergsma Mother's Day Series - J. Bergsma

YEAR ISSUE	ISSUE	EDITION LIMIT	ISSUE PRICE	*QUOTE U.S.$
1990	The Beauty Of Life	14-day	35.00	35
1992	Life's Blessing	14-day	35.00	35
1993	My Greatest Treasures	14-day	35.00	35
1994	Forever In My Heart	14-day	35.00	35

King's Christmas - Merli

YEAR ISSUE	ISSUE	EDITION LIMIT	YEAR RETD.	ISSUE PRICE	*QUOTE U.S.$
1973	Adoration	Retrd.	1974	100.00	265
1974	Madonna	Retrd.	1975	150.00	250
1975	Heavenly Choir	Retrd.	1976	160.00	235
1976	Siblings	Retrd.	1978	200.00	225

King's Flowers - A. Falchi

YEAR ISSUE	ISSUE	EDITION LIMIT	YEAR RETD.	ISSUE PRICE	*QUOTE U.S.$
1973	Carnation	Retrd.	1974	85.00	130
1974	Red Rose	Retrd.	1975	100.00	145
1975	Yellow Dahlia	Retrd.	1976	110.00	162
1976	Bluebells	Retrd.	1977	130.00	165
1977	Anemones	Retrd.	1979	130.00	175

King's Mother's Day - Merli

YEAR ISSUE	ISSUE	EDITION LIMIT	YEAR RETD.	ISSUE PRICE	*QUOTE U.S.$
1973	Dancing Girl	Retrd.	1974	100.00	225
1974	Dancing Boy	Retrd.	1975	115.00	250
1975	Motherly Love	Retrd.	1976	140.00	225
1976	Maiden	Retrd.	1978	180.00	200

Kingdom of the Great Cats - P. Jepson

YEAR ISSUE	ISSUE	EDITION LIMIT	ISSUE PRICE	*QUOTE U.S.$
1995	Out of the Mist	36-day	29.50	30
1995	Summit Sanctuary	36-day	29.50	30

Kittens 'N Hats - S. Somerville

YEAR ISSUE	ISSUE	EDITION LIMIT	ISSUE PRICE	*QUOTE U.S.$
1994	Opening Night	48-day	29.50	30
1994	Sitting Pretty	48-day	29.50	30
1995	Little League	48-day	29.50	30

Little Angel Plate Collection - S. Kuck

YEAR ISSUE	ISSUE	EDITION LIMIT	ISSUE PRICE	*QUOTE U.S.$
1994	Angel of Charity	95-day	29.50	30
1994	Angel of Joy	95-day	29.50	30

Little Professionals - S. Kuck

YEAR ISSUE	ISSUE	EDITION LIMIT	YEAR RETD.	ISSUE PRICE	*QUOTE U.S.$
1982	All is Well	Retrd.	1983	39.50	95
1983	Tender Loving Care	Retrd.	1985	39.50	50-75
1984	Lost and Found	Retrd.	1995	39.50	45
1985	Reading, Writing and...	Retrd.	1989	39.50	45

Magic Companions - J. Bergsma

YEAR ISSUE	ISSUE	EDITION LIMIT	ISSUE PRICE	*QUOTE U.S.$
1994	Believe in Love	48-day	29.50	30
1994	Imagine Peace	48-day	29.50	30
1995	Live in Harmony	48-day	29.50	30
1995	Trust in Magic	48-day	29.50	30

March of Dimes: Our Children, Our Future - Various

YEAR ISSUE	ISSUE	EDITION LIMIT	YEAR RETD.	ISSUE PRICE	*QUOTE U.S.$
1989	A Time to Love (2nd in Series) - S. Kuck	Retrd.	1993	29.00	45
1989	A Time to Plant (3rd in Series) - J. McClelland	150-day	1993	29.00	50

Marmot Christmas - Factory Artist

YEAR ISSUE	ISSUE	EDITION LIMIT	YEAR RETD.	ISSUE PRICE	*QUOTE U.S.$
1970	Polar Bear, Fe	Retrd.	1971	13.00	60
1971	Buffalo Bill	Retrd.	1972	16.00	55
1972	Boy and Grandfather	Retrd.	1973	20.00	50
1971	American Buffalo	Retrd.	1973	14.50	35
1973	Snowman	Retrd.	1974	22.00	45
1974	Dancing	Retrd.	1975	24.00	30
1975	Quail	Retrd.	1976	30.00	40
1976	Windmill	Retrd.	1978	40.00	40

Marmot Father's Day - Factory Artist

YEAR ISSUE	ISSUE	EDITION LIMIT	YEAR RETD.	ISSUE PRICE	*QUOTE U.S.$
1970	Stag	Retrd.	1970	12.00	100
1971	Horse	Retrd.	1972	12.50	40

Marmot Mother's Day - Factory Artist

YEAR ISSUE	ISSUE	EDITION LIMIT	YEAR RETD.	ISSUE PRICE	*QUOTE U.S.$
1972	Seal	Retrd.	1973	16.00	60
1973	Bear with Cub	Retrd.	1974	20.00	140
1974	Penguins	Retrd.	1975	24.00	50
1975	Raccoons	Retrd.	1976	30.00	45
1976	Ducks	Retrd.	1977	40.00	40

The McClelland Children's Circus Collection - J. McClelland

YEAR ISSUE	ISSUE	EDITION LIMIT	YEAR RETD.	ISSUE PRICE	*QUOTE U.S.$
1982	Tommy the Clown	Retrd.	N/A	29.50	49
1982	Katie, the Tightrope Walker	Retrd.	N/A	29.50	49
1983	Johnny the Strongman	Retrd.	N/A	29.50	39
1984	Maggie the Animal Trainer	Retrd.	N/A	29.50	30

Memories of Childhood - C. Getz

YEAR ISSUE	ISSUE	EDITION LIMIT	ISSUE PRICE	*QUOTE U.S.$
1994	Teatime with Teddy	75-day	29.50	30
1995	Bases Loaded	75-day	29.50	30
1996	Mommy's Little Helper	75-day	29.50	30

Memories Of Yesterday - M. Attwell

YEAR ISSUE	ISSUE	EDITION LIMIT	ISSUE PRICE	*QUOTE U.S.$
1993	Hush	Open	29.50	30
1993	Time For Bed	Open	29.50	30

Column headers: YEAR ISSUE | EDITION LIMIT | YEAR RETRD. | ISSUE PRICE | *QUOTE U.S.$

YEAR ISSUE	Title	EDITION LIMIT	YEAR RETRD.	ISSUE PRICE	*QUOTE U.S.$
1993	I'se Been Painting	Open		29.50	30
1993	Just Looking Pretty	Open		29.50	30
1994	Give it Your Best Shot	Open		29.50	30
1994	I Pray The Lord My Soul to Keep	Open		29.50	30
1994	Just Thinking About You	Open		29.50	30
1994	What Will I Grow Up To Be	Open		29.50	30

Moments At Home - S. Kuck

1995	Moments of Caring	95-day		29.90	30
1995	Moments of Tenderness	95-day		29.90	30
1995	Moments of Friendship	95-day		29.90	30
1995	Moments of Sharing	95-day		29.90	30
1995	Moments of Love	95-day		29.90	30
1996	Moments of Reflection	95-day		29.90	30

Moser Christmas - Factory Artist

1970	Hradcany Castle	Retrd.	1971	75.00	170
1971	Karlstein Castle	Retrd.	1972	75.00	80
1972	Old Town Hall	Retrd.	1973	85.00	85
1973	Karlovy Vary Castle	Retrd.	1974	90.00	100

Moser Mother's Day - Factory Artist

1971	Peacocks	Retrd.	1971	75.00	100
1972	Butterflies	Retrd.	1972	85.00	90
1973	Squirrels	Retrd.	1973	90.00	95

Mother Goose - J. McClelland

1979	Mary, Mary	Retrd.	1979	22.50	70-120
1980	Little Boy Blue	Retrd.	1980	22.50	25
1981	Little Miss Muffet	Yr.Iss.		24.50	25
1982	Little Jack Horner	Retrd.	1982	24.50	27
1983	Little Bo Peep	Yr.Iss.		24.50	25
1984	Diddle, Diddle Dumpling	Yr.Iss.		24.50	25
1985	Mary Had a Little Lamb	Yr.Iss.		27.50	28
1986	Jack and Jill	Retrd.	1988	27.50	40

Mother's Day Collection - S. Kuck

1985	Once Upon a Time	Retrd.	1987	29.50	40-50
1986	Times Remembered	Yr.Iss.		29.50	30
1987	A Cherished Time	Yr.Iss.		29.50	30
1988	A Time Together	Yr.Iss.		29.50	30

Noble and Free - Kelly

1994	Gathering Storm	95-day		29.50	30
1994	Protected Journey	95-day		29.50	30
1994	Moonlight Run	95-day		29.50	30

The Nutcracker Ballet - C. Micarelli

1989	Christmas Eve Party	14-day	1994	35.00	35
1990	Clara And Her Prince	14-day		35.00	35
1990	The Dream Begins	14-day		35.00	35
1991	Dance of the Snow Fairies	14-day	1994	35.00	35
1992	The Land of Sweets	14-day		35.00	35
1992	The Sugar Plum Fairy	14-day		35.00	35

Oscar & Bertie's Edwardian Holiday - P.D. Jackson

1991	Snapshot	48-day		29.50	30
1992	Early Rise	48-day		29.50	30
1992	All Aboard	48-day		29.50	30
1992	Learning To Swim	48-day		29.50	30

Our Cherished Seas - S. Barlowe

1991	Whale Song	48-day		37.50	38
1991	Lions of the Sea	48-day		37.50	38
1991	Flight of the Dolphins	48-day		37.50	38
1992	Palace of the Seals	48-day		37.50	38
1992	Orca Ballet	48-day		37.50	38
1993	Emperors of the Ice	48-day		37.50	38
1993	Turtle Treasure	48-day		37.50	38
1993	Splendor of the Sea	48-day		37.50	38

Plate Of The Month Collection - S. Kuck

1990	January	28-day		25.00	25
1990	February	28-day		25.00	25
1990	March	28-day		25.00	25
1990	April	28-day		25.00	25
1990	May	28-day		25.00	25
1990	June	28-day		25.00	25
1990	July	28-day		25.00	25
1990	August	28-day		25.00	25
1990	September	28-day		25.00	25
1990	October	28-day		25.00	25
1990	November	28-day		25.00	25
1990	December	28-day		25.00	25

Precious Angels - S. Kuck

1995	Angel of Grace	95-day		29.90	30
1995	Angel of Happiness	95-day		29.90	30
1995	Angel of Hope	95-day		29.90	30
1995	Angel of Laughter	95-day		29.90	30
1995	Angel of Love	95-day		29.90	30
1995	Angel of Peace	95-day		29.90	30
1995	Angel of Sharing	95-day		29.90	30
1995	Angel of Sunshine	95-day		29.90	30

The Premier Collection - J. McClelland

1991	Love	7,500		75.00	75

Premier Collection - S. Kuck

1991	Puppy	Retrd.	1993	95.00	125-150
1991	Kitten	Retrd.	1992	95.00	150-200

1992	La Belle	7,500		95.00	95
1992	Le Beau	7,500		95.00	95

Royal Mother's Day - Factory Artist

1970	Swan and Young	Retrd.	1971	12.00	80
1971	Doe and Fawn	Retrd.	1972	13.00	55
1972	Rabbits	Retrd.	1973	16.00	40
1973	Owl Family	Retrd.	1974	18.00	40
1974	Duck and Young	Retrd.	1975	22.00	40
1975	Lynx and Cubs	Retrd.	1976	26.00	40
1976	Woodcock and Young	Retrd.	1978	27.50	33
1977	Koala Bear	Retrd.	1978	30.00	30

Royale - Factory Artist

1969	Apollo Moon Landing	Retrd.	1969	30.00	80

Royale Christmas - Factory Artist

1969	Christmas Fair	Retrd.	1970	12.00	125
1970	Vigil Mass	Retrd.	1971	13.00	110
1971	Christmas Night	Retrd.	1972	16.00	50
1972	Elks	Retrd.	1973	16.00	45
1973	Christmas Down	Retrd.	1974	20.00	38
1974	Village Christmas	Retrd.	1975	22.00	60
1975	Feeding Time	Retrd.	1976	26.00	35
1976	Seaport Christmas	Retrd.	1977	27.50	30
1977	Sledding	Retrd.	1978	30.00	30

Royale Father's Day - Factory Artist

1970	Frigate Constitution	Retrd.	1971	13.00	80
1971	Man Fishing	Retrd.	1972	13.00	35
1972	Mountaineer	Retrd.	1973	16.00	35
1973	Camping	Retrd.	1974	18.00	45
1974	Eagle	Retrd.	1975	22.00	35
1975	Regatta	Retrd.	1976	26.00	35
1976	Hunting	Retrd.	1977	27.50	33
1977	Fishing	Retrd.	1978	30.00	30

Royale Game Plates - Various

1972	Setters - J. Poluszynski	Retrd.	1974	180.00	200
1973	Fox - J. Poluszynski	Retrd.	1975	200.00	250
1974	Osprey - W. Schiener	Retrd.	1976	250.00	250
1975	California Quail - W. Schiener	Retrd.	1976	265.00	265

Royale Germania Christmas Annual - Factory Artist

1970	Orchid	Retrd.	1971	200.00	650
1971	Cyclamen	Retrd.	1972	200.00	325
1972	Silver Thistle	Retrd.	1973	250.00	290
1973	Tulips	Retrd.	1974	275.00	310
1974	Sunflowers	Retrd.	1975	300.00	300
1975	Snowdrops	Retrd.	1976	450.00	500

Royale Germania Crystal Mother's Day - Factory Artist

1971	Roses	Retrd.	1971	135.00	650
1972	Elephant and Youngster	Retrd.	1972	180.00	250
1973	Koala Bear and Cub	Retrd.	1973	200.00	225
1974	Squirrels	Retrd.	1974	240.00	250
1975	Swan and Young	Retrd.	1975	350.00	360

Sandra Kuck Mothers' Day - S. Kuck

1995	Home is Where the Heart Is	48-day		35.00	35
1996	Dear To The Heart	48-day		35.00	35

Sculpted Heirlooms - S. Kuck

1996	Best Friends (sculpted plate)	24-mo.		29.95	30
1996	Tea Party (sculpted plate)	24-mo.		29.90	30
1996	Storybook Memories (sculpted plate)	24-mo.		29.90	30
1996	Patience (sculpted plate)	24-mo.		29.90	30

Songs From The Garden - G. Ratnavira

1996	Love Song	76-day		29.95	30
1996	Rhapsody In Blue	76-day		29.90	30

The Sophisticated Ladies Collection - A. Fazio

1985	Felicia	21-day		29.50	30
1985	Samantha	21-day	1994	29.50	33
1985	Phoebe	21-day	1994	29.50	33
1985	Cleo	21-day		29.50	30
1986	Cerissa	21-day	1994	29.50	33
1986	Natasha	21-day	1994	29.50	33
1986	Bianka	21-day	1994	29.50	33
1986	Chelsea	21-day	1994	29.50	33

Special Occasions by Reco - S. Kuck

1988	The Wedding	Open		35.00	35
1989	Wedding Day (6 1/2")	Open		25.00	25
1990	The Special Day	Open		25.00	25

Special Occasions-Wedding - C. Micarelli

1991	From This Day Forward (9 1/2")	Open		35.00	35
1991	From This Day Forward (6 1/2")	Open		25.00	25
1991	To Have And To Hold (9 1/2")	Open		35.00	35
1991	To Have And To Hold (6 1/2")	Open		25.00	25

Sugar and Spice - S. Kuck

1993	Best Friends	95-day		29.90	30
1993	Sisters	95-day		29.90	30
1994	Little One	95-day		32.90	33
1994	Teddy Bear Tales	95-day		32.90	33
1994	Morning Prayers	95-day		32.90	33
1995	First Snow	95-day		34.90	35

1994	Garden of Sunshine	95-day		34.90	35
1995	A Special Day	95-day		34.90	35

Tidings Of Joy - S. Kuck

1992	Peace on Earth		Retrd. 1995	35.00	45
1993	Rejoice	N/A		35.00	35
1994	Noel		Retrd. 1995	35.00	50

Totems of the West - J. Bergsma

1994	The Watchmen	96-day		29.50	30
1995	Peace At Last	96-day		29.50	30
1995	Never Alone	96-day		35.00	35

Town And Country Dogs - S. Barlowe

1990	Fox Hunt	36-day		35.00	35
1991	The Retrieval	36-day		35.00	35
1991	Golden Fields (Golden Retriever)	36-day		35.00	35
1993	Faithful Companions (Cocker Spaniel)	36-day		35.00	35

Trains of the Orient Express - R. Johnson

1993	The Golden Arrow-England	N/A		29.50	30
1994	Austria	N/A		29.50	30
1994	Bavaria	N/A		29.50	30
1994	Rumania	N/A		29.50	30
1994	Greece	N/A		29.50	30
1994	Frankonia	N/A		29.50	30
1994	Turkey	N/A		29.50	30
1994	France	N/A		29.50	30

Treasured Songs of Childhood - J. McClelland

1987	Twinkle, Twinkle, Little Star		Retrd. 1990	29.50	30
1988	A Tisket, A Tasket	150-day	1991	29.50	30
1988	Baa, Baa, Black Sheep	150-day	1991	32.90	33
1989	Round The Mulberry Bush	150-day		32.90	33
1989	Rain, Rain Go Away		Retrd. 1993	32.90	33
1989	I'm A Little Teapot		Retrd. 1993	32.90	33
1989	Pat-A-Cake	150-day		34.90	35
1990	Hush Little Baby	150-day		34.90	35

Up, Up And Away - P. Alexander

1996	Rally At The Grand Canyon	76-day		29.95	30
1996	Gateway To Heaven	76-day		29.90	30

Vanishing Animal Kingdoms - S. Barlowe

1986	Rama the Tiger	21,500		35.00	35
1986	Olepi the Buffalo	21,500		35.00	35
1987	Coolibah the Koala	21,500		35.00	35
1987	Ortwin the Deer	21,500		35.00	35
1987	Yen-Poh the Panda	21,500		35.00	35
1988	Mamakuu the Elephant	21,500		35.00	35

Victorian Christmas - S. Kuck

1995	Dear Santa	72-day		35.00	35
1996	Night Before Christmas	72-day		35.00	35

Victorian Mother's Day - S. Kuck

1989	Mother's Sunshine		Retrd. 1990	35.00	45-85
1990	Reflection Of Love		Retrd. 1991	35.00	50-80
1991	A Precious Time		Retrd. 1992	35.00	45-75
1992	Loving Touch		Retrd. 1993	35.00	45-49

Western - E. Berke

1974	Mountain Man		Retrd.	165.00	165

Women of the Plains - C. Corcilius

1994	Pride of a Maiden	36-day		29.50	30
1995	No Boundaries	36-day		29.50	30
1995	Silent Companions	36-day		35.00	35

The Wonder of Christmas - J. McClelland

1991	Santa's Secret	48-day		29.50	30
1992	My Favorite Ornament	48-day		29.50	30
1992	Waiting For Santa	48-day		29.50	30
1993	Candlelight Christmas		Retrd. 1995	29.50	55

The World of Children - J. McClelland

1977	Rainy Day Fun	10,000	1977	50.00	50
1978	When I Grow Up	15,000	1978	50.00	55
1979	You're Invited	15,000	1979	50.00	55
1980	Kittens for Sale	15,000	1980	50.00	55

River Shore

Baby Animals - R. Brown

1979	Akiku	20,000		50.00	80
1980	Roosevelt	20,000		50.00	90
1981	Clover	20,000		50.00	65
1982	Zuela	20,000		50.00	65

Famous Americans - Rockwell-Brown

1976	Brown's Lincoln	9,500		40.00	40
1977	Rockwell's Triple Self-Portrait	9,500		45.00	45
1978	Peace Corps	9,500		45.00	45
1979	Spirit of Lindbergh	9,500		50.00	50

Little House on the Prairie - E. Christopherson

1985	Founder's Day Picnic	10-day		29.50	50
1985	Women's Harvest	10-day		29.50	45
1985	Medicine Show	10-day		29.50	45
1985	Caroline's Eggs	10-day		29.50	45

YEAR ISSUE		EDITION LIMIT	YEAR RETD.	ISSUE PRICE	*QUOTE U.S.$
1985	Mary's Gift	10-day		29.50	45
1985	A Bell for Walnut Grove	10-day		29.50	45
1985	Ingall's Family	10-day		29.50	45
1985	The Sweetheart Tree	10-day		29.50	45

Norman Rockwell Single Issue - N. Rockwell

YEAR ISSUE		EDITION LIMIT	YEAR RETD.	ISSUE PRICE	*QUOTE U.S.$
1979	Spring Flowers	17,000		75.00	145
1980	Looking Out to Sea	17,000		75.00	195
1982	Grandpa's Guardian	17,000		80.00	80
1982	Grandpa's Treasures	17,000		80.00	80

Puppy Playtime - J. Lamb

1987	Double Take	14-day		24.50	32-35
1988	Catch of the Day	14-day		24.50	25
1988	Cabin Fever	14-day		24.50	25
1988	Weekend Gardener	14-day		24.50	25
1988	Getting Acquainted	14-day		24.50	25
1988	Hanging Out	14-day		24.50	25
1988	A New Leash On Life	14-day		24.50	30
1987	Fun and Games	14-day		24.50	30

Rockwell Four Freedoms - N. Rockwell

1981	Freedom of Speech	17,000		65.00	100
1982	Freedom of Worship	17,000		65.00	80
1982	Freedom from Fear	17,000		65.00	200
1982	Freedom from Want	17,000		65.00	425

Rockwell Society

Christmas - N. Rockwell

1974	Scotty Gets His Tree	Yr.Iss.		24.50	98
1975	Angel with Black Eye	Yr.Iss.		24.50	45
1976	Golden Christmas	Yr.Iss.		24.50	35
1977	Toy Shop Window	Yr.Iss.		24.50	75
1978	Christmas Dream	Yr.Iss.		24.50	25
1979	Somebody's Up There	Yr.Iss.		24.50	50
1980	Scotty Plays Santa	Yr.Iss.		24.50	25
1981	Wrapped Up in Christmas	Yr.Iss.		25.50	25
1982	Christmas Courtship	Yr.Iss.		25.50	35-60
1983	Santa in the Subway	Yr.Iss.		25.50	35
1984	Santa in the Workshop	Yr.Iss.		27.50	28
1985	Grandpa Plays Santa	Yr.Iss.		27.90	28
1986	Dear Santy Claus	Yr.Iss.		27.90	30
1987	Santa's Golden Gift	Yr.Iss.		27.90	32
1988	Santa Claus	Yr.Iss.		29.90	30
1989	Jolly Old St. Nick	Yr.Iss.		29.90	35
1990	A Christmas Prayer	Yr.Iss.		29.90	35
1991	Santa's Helpers	Yr.Iss.		32.90	33
1992	The Christmas Surprise	Yr.Iss.		32.90	35
1993	The Tree Brigade	Yr.Iss.		32.90	44
1994	Christmas Marvel	Yr.Iss.		32.90	50
1995	Filling The Stockings	Yr.Iss.		32.90	64

Colonials-The Rarest Rockwells - N. Rockwell

1985	Unexpected Proposal	150-day		27.90	32
1986	Words of Comfort	150-day		27.90	32
1986	Light for the Winter	150-day		30.90	35
1987	Portrait for a Bridegroom	150-day		30.90	35
1987	The Journey Home	150-day		30.90	35
1987	Clinching the Deal	150-day		30.90	35
1988	Sign of the Times	150-day		32.90	37
1988	Ye Glutton	150-day		32.90	37

Coming Of Age - N. Rockwell

1990	Back To School	150-day		29.90	45
1990	Home From Camp	150-day		29.90	45
1990	Her First Formal	150-day		32.90	45-65
1990	The Muscleman	150-day		32.90	33
1990	A New Look	150-day		32.90	35
1991	A Balcony Seat	150-day		32.90	33
1991	Men About Town	150-day		34.90	35
1991	Paths of Glory	150-day		34.90	35
1991	Doorway to the Past	150-day		34.90	30-40
1991	School's Out!	150-day		34.90	50-60

Heritage - N. Rockwell

1977	Toy Maker	Yr.Iss.		14.50	50-100
1978	Cobbler	Yr.Iss.		19.50	40-50
1979	Lighthouse Keeper's Daughter	Yr.Iss.		19.50	25-35
1980	Ship Builder	Yr.Iss.		19.50	20-45
1981	Music maker	Yr.Iss.		19.50	24-42
1982	Tycoon	Yr.Iss.		19.50	20-35
1983	Painter	Yr.Iss.		19.50	20-28
1984	Storyteller	Yr.Iss.		19.50	20-30
1985	Gourmet	Yr.Iss.		19.50	20-26
1986	Professor	Yr.Iss.		22.90	23
1987	Shadow Artist	Yr.Iss.		22.90	27
1988	The Veteran	Yr.Iss.		22.90	23
1988	The Banjo Player	Yr.Iss.		22.90	25
1990	The Old Scout	Yr.Iss.		24.90	25
1991	The Young Scholar	Yr.Iss.		24.90	30
1991	The Family Doctor	Yr.Iss.		27.90	40-60
1992	The Jeweler	Yr.Iss.		27.90	35-55
1993	Halloween Frolic	Yr.Iss.		27.90	49
1994	The Apprentice	Yr.Iss.		29.90	46

Innocence and Experience - N. Rockwell

1991	The Sea Captain	150-day		29.90	30
1991	The Radio Operator	150-day		29.90	30
1991	The Magician	150-day		32.90	45
1992	The American Heroes	150-day		32.90	35

A Mind of Her Own - N. Rockwell

1986	Sitting Pretty	150-day		24.90	30
1987	Serious Business	150-day		24.90	28
1987	Breaking the Rules	150-day		24.90	30
1987	Good Intentions	150-day		27.90	28
1988	Second Thoughts	150-day		27.90	28
1988	World's Away	150-day		27.90	28
1988	Kiss and Tell	150-day		29.90	30
1988	On My Honor	150-day		29.90	30

Mother's Day - N. Rockwell

1976	A Mother's Love	Yr.Iss.		24.50	60
1977	Faith	Yr.Iss.		24.50	48
1978	Bedtime	Yr.Iss.		24.50	20-35
1979	Reflections	Yr.Iss.		24.50	30
1980	A Mother's Pride	Yr.Iss.		24.50	25-35
1981	After the Party	Yr.Iss.		24.50	25
1982	The Cooking Lesson	Yr.Iss.		24.50	30
1983	Add Two Cups and Love	Yr.Iss.		25.50	28
1984	Grandma's Courting Dress	Yr.Iss.		25.50	26
1985	Mending Time	Yr.Iss.		27.50	28
1986	Pantry Raid	Yr.Iss.		27.90	28
1987	Grandma's Surprise	Yr.Iss.		29.90	32
1988	My Mother	Yr.Iss.		29.90	32
1989	Sunday Dinner	Yr.Iss.		29.90	30
1990	Evening Prayers	Yr.Iss.		29.90	30
1991	Building Our Future	Yr.Iss.		32.90	33
1991	Gentle Reassurance	Yr.Iss.		32.90	33
1992	A Special Delivery	Yr.Iss.		32.90	35

Rockwell Commemorative Stamps - N. Rockwell

1994	Triple Self Portrait	95-day		29.90	30
1994	Freedom From Want	95-day		29.90	30
1994	Freedom From Fear	95-day		29.90	30
1995	Freedom of Speech	95-day		29.90	30
1995	Freedom of Worship	95-day		29.90	30

Rockwell on Tour - N. Rockwell

1983	Walking Through Merrie Englande	150-day		16.00	16
1983	Promenade a Paris	150-day		16.00	16
1983	When in Rome	150-day		16.00	16
1984	Die Walk am Rhein	150-day		16.00	16

Rockwell's American Dream - N. Rockwell

1985	A Young Girl's Dream	150-day		19.90	20
1985	A Couple's Commitment	150-day		19.90	20
1985	A Family's Full Measure	150-day		22.90	30
1986	A Mother's Welcome	150-day		22.90	30
1986	A Young Man's Dream	150-day		22.90	30
1986	The Musician's Magic	150-day		22.90	25
1987	An Orphan's Hope	150-day		24.90	26
1987	Love's Reward	150-day		24.90	30

Rockwell's Golden Moments - N. Rockwell

1987	Grandpa's Gift	150-day		19.90	25
1987	Grandma's Love	150-day		19.90	35
1988	End of day	150-day		22.90	35
1988	Best Friends	150-day		22.90	23
1989	Love Letters	150-day		22.90	23
1989	Newfound Worlds	150-day		22.90	23
1989	Keeping Company	150-day		24.90	25
1989	Evening's Repose	150-day		24.90	25

Rockwell's Light Campaign - N. Rockwell

1983	This is the Room that Light Made	150-day		19.50	20
1984	Grandpa's Treasure Chest	150-day		19.50	20
1984	Father's Help	150-day		19.50	20
1984	Evening's Ease	150-day		19.50	20
1984	Close Harmony	150-day		21.50	22
1984	The Birthday Wish	150-day		21.50	22

Rockwell's Rediscovered Women - N. Rockwell

1984	Dreaming in the Attic	100-day		19.50	30
1984	Waiting on the Shore	100-day		22.50	23
1984	Pondering on the Porch	100-day		22.50	23
1984	Making Believe at the Mirror	100-day		22.50	23-30
1984	Waiting at the Dance	100-day		22.50	23
1984	Gossiping in the Alcove	100-day		22.50	23
1984	Standing in the Doorway	100-day		22.50	25-35
1984	Flirting in the Parlor	100-day		22.50	25-35
1984	Working in the Kitchen	100-day		22.50	33
1984	Meeting on the Path	100-day		22.50	23
1984	Confiding in the Den	100-day		22.50	23
1984	Reminiscing in the Quiet	100-day		22.50	23
XX	Complete Collection	100-day		267.00	267

Rockwell's The Ones We Love - N. Rockwell

1988	Tender Loving Care	150-day		19.90	25
1989	A Time to Keep	150-day		19.90	25
1989	The Inventor And The Judge	150-day		22.90	30
1989	Ready For The World	150-day		22.90	25
1989	Growing Strong	150-day		22.90	35
1990	The Story Hour	150-day		22.90	42
1990	The Country Doctor	150-day		24.90	25
1990	Our Love of Country	150-day		24.90	25
1990	The Homecoming	150-day		24.90	25
1991	A Helping Hand	150-day		24.90	25

Rockwell's Treasured Memories - N. Rockwell

1991	Quiet Reflections	150-day		29.90	30
1991	Romantic Reverie	150-day		29.90	30

1991	Tender Romance	150-day		32.90	33
1991	Evening Passage	150-day		32.90	33
1991	Heavenly Dreams	150-day		32.90	34
1991	Sentimental Shores	150-day		32.90	34

Roman, Inc.

Abbie Williams Collection - A. Williams

1991	Legacy of Love	Open		29.50	30
1991	Bless This Child	Open		29.50	30

Catnippers - I. Spencer

1986	Christmas Mourning	9,500		34.50	35
1992	Happy Holidaze	9,500		34.50	35

A Child's Play - F. Hook

1982	Breezy Day	30-day		29.95	39
1982	Kite Flying	30-day		29.95	39
1984	Bathtub Sailor	30-day		29.95	35
1984	The First Snow	30-day		29.95	35

A Child's World - F. Hook

1980	Little Children, Come to Me	15,000		45.00	49

Fontanini Annual Christmas Plate - E. Simonetti

1986	A King Is Born	Yr.Iss.		60.00	60
1987	O Come, Let Us Adore Him	Yr.Iss.		60.00	65
1988	Adoration of the Magi	Yr.Iss.		70.00	75
1989	Flight Into Egypt	Yr.Iss.		75.00	85

Frances Hook Collection-Set I - F. Hook

1982	I Wish, I Wish	15,000		24.95	50-75
1982	Baby Blossoms	15,000		24.95	35-39
1982	Daisy Dreamer	15,000		24.95	35-39
1982	Trees So Tall	15,000		24.95	35-39

Frances Hook Collection-Set II - F. Hook

1983	Caught It Myself	15,000		24.95	25
1983	Winter Wrappings	15,000		24.95	25
1983	So Cuddly	15,000		24.95	25
1983	Can I Keep Him?	15,000		24.95	25

Frances Hook Legacy - F. Hook

1985	Fascination	100-day		19.50	35-39
1985	Daydreaming	100-day		19.50	35-39
1985	Discovery	100-day		22.50	35-39
1985	Disappointment	100-day		22.50	35-39
1985	Wonderment	100-day		22.50	35-39
1985	Expectation	100-day		22.50	35-39

God Bless You Little One - A. Williams

1991	Baby's First Birthday (Girl)	Open		29.50	30
1991	Baby's First Birthday (Boy)	Open		29.50	30
1991	Baby's First Smile	Open		19.50	20
1991	Baby's First Word	Open		19.50	20
1991	Baby's First Step	Open		19.50	20
1991	Baby's First Tooth	Open		19.50	20

The Ice Capades Clown - G. Petty

1983	Presenting Freddie Trenkler	30-day		24.50	25

The Lord's Prayer - A. Williams

1986	Our Father	10-day		24.50	25
1986	Thy Kingdom Come	10-day		24.50	25
1986	Give Us This Day	10-day		24.50	25
1986	Forgive Our Trespasses	10-day		24.50	34
1986	As We Forgive	10-day		24.50	25
1986	Lead Us Not	10-day		24.50	25
1986	Deliver Us From Evil	10-day		24.50	25
1986	Thine Is The Kingdom	10-day		24.50	25

The Love's Prayer - A. Williams

1988	Love Is Patient and Kind	14-day		29.50	30
1988	Love Is Never Jealous or Boastful	14-day		29.50	30
1988	Love Is Never Arrogant or Rude	14-day		29.50	30
1988	Love Does Not Insist on Its Own Way	14-day		29.50	30
1988	Love Is Never Irritable or Resentful	14-day		29.50	30
1988	Love Rejoices In the Right	14-day		29.50	30
1988	Love Believes All Things	14-day		29.50	30
1988	Love Never Ends	14-day		29.50	30

The Magic of Childhood - A. Williams

1985	Special Friends	10-day		24.50	35
1985	Feeding Time	10-day		24.50	35
1985	Best Buddies	10-day		24.50	35
1985	Getting Acquainted	10-day		24.50	35
1986	Last One In	10-day		24.50	35
1986	A Handful Of Love	10-day		24.50	35
1986	Look Alikes	10-day		24.50	35
1986	No Fair Peeking	10-day		24.50	35

March of Dimes: Our Children, Our Future - A. Williams

1990	A Time To Laugh	150-day		29.00	39-49

The Masterpiece Collection - Various

1979	Adoration - F. Lippe	5,000		65.00	65
1980	Madonna with Grapes - P. Mignard	5,000		87.50	88
1981	The Holy Family - G. Delle Notti	5,000		95.00	95
1982	Madonna of the Streets - R. Ferruzzi	5,000		85.00	85

YEAR ISSUE		EDITION LIMIT	YEAR RETD.	ISSUE PRICE	*QUOTE U.S.$
Millenium™ Series - Various					
1992	Silent Night - Morcaldo/Lucchesi	Closed	1992	49.50	50
1993	The Annunciation - Morcaldo/Lucchesi	5,000	1993	49.50	50
1994	Peace On Earth - Morcaldo/Lucchesi	5,000	1994	49.50	50
1995	Cause of Our Joy - A. Lucchesi	7,500		49.50	50
1996	Prince of Peace - A. Lucchesi	15,000		49.50	50
Precious Children - A. Williams					
1993	Bless Baby Brother	N/A		29.50	30
1993	Blowing Bubbles	N/A		29.50	30
1993	Don't Worry, Mother Duck	N/A		29.50	30
1993	Treetop Discovery	N/A		29.50	30
1993	The Tea Party	N/A		29.50	30
1993	Mother's Little Angel	N/A		29.50	30
1993	Picking Daisies	N/A		29.50	30
1993	Let's Say Grace	N/A		29.50	30
Pretty Girls of the Ice Capades - G. Petty					
1983	Ice Princess	30-day		24.50	25
Promise of a Savior - Unknown					
1993	An Angel's Message	95-day		29.90	30
1993	Gifts to Jesus	95-day		29.90	30
1993	The Heavenly King	95-day		29.90	30
1993	Angels Were Watching	95-day		29.90	30
1993	Holy Mother & Child	95-day		29.90	30
1993	A Child is Born	95-day		29.90	30
The Richard Judson Zolan Collection - R.J. Zolan					
1992	The Butterfly Net	100-day		29.50	30
1994	The Ring	100-day		29.50	30
1994	Terrace Dancing	100-day		29.50	30
Roman Memorial - F. Hook					
1984	The Carpenter	Closed	1984	100.00	135
Sepaphim Collection by Faro - Faro					
1994	Rosalyn - Rarest of Heaven	7,200	1995	65.00	65
1995	Helena - Heaven's Herald	7,200		65.00	65
1996	Flora - Flower of Heaven	7,200		65.00	65
Single Releases - A. Williams					
1987	The Christening	Open		29.50	30
1990	The Dedication	Open		29.50	30
1990	The Baptism	Open		29.50	30
The Sweetest Songs - I. Spencer					
1986	A Baby's Prayer	30-day		39.50	45
1986	This Little Piggie	30-day		39.50	40
1988	Long, Long Ago	30-day		39.50	40
1989	Rockabye	30-day		39.50	40
Tender Expressions - B. Sargent					
1992	Thoughts of You Are In My Heart	100-day		29.50	30

Rosenthal

YEAR ISSUE		EDITION LIMIT	YEAR RETD.	ISSUE PRICE	*QUOTE U.S.$
Christmas - Unknown					
1910	Winter Peace	Annual		Unkn.	550
1911	Three Wise Men	Annual		Unkn.	325
1912	Stardust	Annual		Unkn.	255
1913	Christmas Lights	Annual		Unkn.	235
1914	Christmas Song	Annual		Unkn.	350
1915	Walking to Church	Annual		Unkn.	180
1916	Christmas During War	Annual		Unkn.	240
1917	Angel of Peace	Annual		Unkn.	200
1918	Peace on Earth	Annual		Unkn.	200
1919	St. Christopher with Christ Child	Annual		Unkn.	225
1920	Manger in Bethlehem	Annual		Unkn.	325
1921	Christmas in Mountains	Annual		Unkn.	200
1922	Advent Branch	Annual		Unkn.	200
1923	Children in Winter Woods	Annual		Unkn.	200
1924	Deer in the Woods	Annual		Unkn.	200
1925	Three Wise Men	Annual		Unkn.	200
1926	Christmas in Mountains	Annual		Unkn.	195
1927	Station on the Way	Annual		Unkn.	200
1928	Chalet Christmas	Annual		Unkn.	185
1929	Christmas in Alps	Annual		Unkn.	225
1930	Group of Deer Under Pines	Annual		Unkn.	225
1931	Path of the Magi	Annual		Unkn.	225
1932	Christ Child	Annual		Unkn.	185
1933	Thru the Night to Light	Annual		Unkn.	190
1934	Christmas Peace	Annual		Unkn.	190
1935	Christmas by the Sea	Annual		Unkn.	190
1936	Nurnberg Angel	Annual		Unkn.	195
1937	Berchtesgaden	Annual		Unkn.	195
1938	Christmas in the Alps	Annual		Unkn.	195
1939	Schneekoppe Mountain	Annual		Unkn.	195
1940	Marien Chruch in Danzig	Annual		Unkn.	250
1941	Strassburg Cathedral	Annual		Unkn.	250
1942	Marianburg Castle	Annual		Unkn.	300
1943	Winter Idyll	Annual		Unkn.	300
1944	Wood Scape	Annual		Unkn.	300
1945	Christmas Peace	Annual		Unkn.	400
1946	Christmas in an Alpine Valley	Annual		Unkn.	240
1947	Dillingen Madonna	Annual		Unkn.	985
1948	Message to the Shepherds	Annual		Unkn.	875
1949	The Holy Family	Annual		Unkn.	185
1950	Christmas in the Forest	Annual		Unkn.	185

YEAR ISSUE		EDITION LIMIT	YEAR RETD.	ISSUE PRICE	*QUOTE U.S.$
1951	Star of Bethlehem	Annual		Unkn.	450
1952	Christmas in the Alps	Annual		Unkn.	195
1953	The Holy Light	Annual		Unkn.	195
1954	Christmas Eve	Annual		Unkn.	195
1955	Christmas in a Village	Annual		Unkn.	195
1956	Christmas in the Alps	Annual		Unkn.	195
1957	Christmas by the Sea	Annual		Unkn.	195
1958	Christmas Eve	Annual		Unkn.	195
1959	Midnight Mass	Annual		Unkn.	195
1960	Christmas in a Small Village	Annual		Unkn.	195
1961	Solitary Christmas	Annual		Unkn.	225
1962	Christmas Eve	Annual		Unkn.	195
1963	Silent Night	Annual		Unkn.	195
1964	Christmas Market in Nurnberg	Annual		Unkn.	225
1965	Christmas Munich	Annual		Unkn.	185
1966	Christmas in Ulm	Annual		Unkn.	275
1967	Christmas in Reginburg	Annual		Unkn.	185
1968	Christmas in Bremen	Annual		Unkn.	195
1969	Christmas in Rothenburg	Annual		Unkn.	220
1970	Christmas in Cologne	Annual		Unkn.	175
1971	Christmas in Garmisch	Annual		42.00	100
1972	Christmas in Franconia	Annual		50.00	95
1973	Lubeck-Holstein	Annual		77.00	105
1974	Christmas in Wurzburg	Annual		85.00	100
Nobility of Children - E. Hibel					
1976	La Contessa Isabella	12,750		120.00	120
1977	La Marquis Maurice-Pierre	12,750		120.00	120
1978	Baronesse Johanna	12,750		130.00	140
1979	Chief Red Feather	12,750		140.00	180
Oriental Gold - E. Hibel					
1976	Yasuko	2,000		275.00	650
1977	Mr. Obata	2,000		275.00	500
1978	Sakura	2,000		295.00	400
1979	Michio	2,000		325.00	375
Wiinblad Christmas - B. Wiinblad					
1971	Maria & Child	Undis.		100.00	750
1972	Caspar	Undis.		100.00	290
1973	Melchior	Undis.		125.00	335
1974	Balthazar	Undis.		125.00	300
1975	The Annunciation	Undis.		195.00	195
1976	Angel with Trumpet	Undis.		195.00	195
1977	Adoration of Shepherds	Undis.		225.00	225
1978	Angel with Harp	Undis.		275.00	295
1979	Exodus from Egypt	Undis.		310.00	310
1980	Angel with Glockenspiel	Undis.		360.00	360
1981	Christ Child Visits Temple	Undis.		375.00	375
1982	Christening of Christ	Undis.		375.00	375

Royal Copenhagen

YEAR ISSUE		EDITION LIMIT	YEAR RETD.	ISSUE PRICE	*QUOTE U.S.$
Christmas - Various					
1908	Madonna and Child - C. Thomsen	Annual	1908	1.00	3000-4500
1909	Danish Landscape - S. Ussing	Annual	1909	1.00	180-225
1910	The Magi - C. Thomsen	Annual	1910	1.00	50-145
1911	Danish Landscape - O. Jensen	Annual	1911	1.00	125-165
1912	Christmas Tree - C. Thomsen	Annual	1912	1.00	75-165
1913	Frederik Church Spire - A. Boesen	Annual	1913	1.50	140-165
1914	Holy Spirit Church - A. Boesen	Annual	1914	1.50	160-240
1915	Danish Landscape - A. Krog	Annual	1915	1.50	100-165
1916	Shepherd at Christmas - R. Bocher	Annual	1916	1.50	112-140
1917	Our Savior Church - O. Jensen	Annual	1917	2.00	95-170
1918	Sheep and Shepherds - O. Jensen	Annual	1918	2.00	95-180
1919	In the Park - O. Jensen	Annual	1919	2.00	95-130
1920	Mary and Child Jesus - G. Rode	Annual	1920	2.00	100-170
1921	Aabenraa Marketplace - O. Jensen	Annual	1921	2.00	75-180
1922	Three Singing Angels - E. Selschau	Annual	1922	2.00	70-90
1923	Danish Landscape - O. Jensen	Annual	1923	2.00	90-120
1924	Sailing Ship - B. Olsen	Annual	1924	2.00	135-165
1925	Christianshavn - O. Jensen	Annual	1925	2.00	112-140
1926	Christianshavn Canal - R. Bocher	Annual	1926	2.00	112-150
1927	Ship's Boy at Tiller - B. Olsen	Annual	1927	2.00	135-180
1928	Vicar's Family - G. Rode	Annual	1928	2.00	105-135
1929	Grundtvig Church - O. Jensen	Annual	1929	2.00	105-125
1930	Fishing Boats - B. Olsen	Annual	1930	2.50	135
1931	Mother and Child - G. Rode	Annual	1931	2.50	135-175
1932	Frederiksberg Gardens - O. Jensen	Annual	1932	2.50	112-120
1933	Ferry and the Great Belt - B. Olsen	Annual	1933	2.50	65-165
1934	The Hermitage Castle - O. Jensen	Annual	1934	2.50	175-300
1935	Kronborg Castle - B. Olsen	Annual	1935	2.50	225-400
1936	Roskilde Cathedral - R. Bocher	Annual	1936	2.50	80-180
1937	Main Street Copenhagen - N. Thorsson	Annual	1937	2.50	200-225
1938	Round Church in Osterlars - H. Nielsen	Annual	1938	3.00	135-300
1939	Greenland Pack-Ice - S. Nielsen	Annual	1939	3.00	325-425
1940	The Good Shepherd - K. Lange	Annual	1940	3.00	200-450
1941	Danish Village Church - T. Kjolner	Annual	1941	3.00	300-500
1942	Bell Tower - N. Thorsson	Annual	1942	4.00	200-450
1943	Flight into Egypt - N. Thorsson	Annual	1943	4.00	550-750
1944	Danish Village Scene - V. Olson	Annual	1944	4.00	240-420

YEAR ISSUE		EDITION LIMIT	YEAR RETD.	ISSUE PRICE	*QUOTE U.S.$
1945	A Peaceful Motif - R. Bocher	Annual	1945	4.00	300-450
1946	Zealand Village Church - N. Thorsson	Annual	1946	4.00	240-280
1947	The Good Shepherd - K. Lange	Annual	1947	4.50	175-285
1948	Nodebo Church - T. Kjolner	Annual	1948	4.50	125-300
1949	Our Lady's Cathedral - H. Hansen	Annual	1949	5.00	200-360
1950	Boeslunde Church - V. Olson	Annual	1950	5.00	150-330
1951	Christmas Angel - R. Bocher	Annual	1951	5.00	300-480
1952	Christmas in the Forest - K. Lange	Annual	1952	5.00	160-180
1953	Frederiksberg Castle - T. Kjolner	Annual	1953	6.00	180-260
1954	Amalienborg Palace - K. Lange	Annual	1954	6.00	100-250
1955	Fano Girl - K. Lange	Annual	1955	7.00	100-270
1956	Rosenborg Castle - K. Lange	Annual	1956	7.00	230-255
1957	The Good Shepherd - H. Hansen	Annual	1957	8.00	90-125
1958	Sunshine over Greenland - H. Hansen	Annual	1958	9.00	125-210
1959	Christmas Night - H. Hansen	Annual	1959	9.00	60-165
1960	The Stag - H. Hansen	Annual	1960	10.00	150-185
1961	Training Ship - K. Lange	Annual	1961	10.00	175-250
1962	The Little Mermaid - Unknown	Annual	1962	11.00	185-300
1963	Hojsager Mill - K. Lange	Annual	1963	11.00	50-110
1964	Fetching the Tree - K. Lange	Annual	1964	11.00	50-90
1965	Little Skaters - K. Lange	Annual	1965	12.00	45-85
1966	Blackbird - K. Lange	Annual	1966	12.00	30-60
1967	The Royal Oak - K. Lange	Annual	1967	13.00	30-50
1968	The Last Umiak - K. Lange	Annual	1968	13.00	30-40
1969	The Old Farmyard - K. Lange	Annual	1969	14.00	30-40
1970	Christmas Rose and Cat - K. Lange	Annual	1970	14.00	35-50
1971	Hare In Winter - K. Lange	Annual	1971	15.00	25
1972	In the Desert - K. Lange	Annual	1972	16.00	21-30
1973	Train Homeward Bound - K. Lange	Annual	1973	22.00	20-30
1974	Winter Twilight - K. Lange	Annual	1974	22.00	21-27
1975	Queen's Palace - K. Lange	Annual	1975	27.50	21-35
1976	Danish Watermill - S. Vestergaard	Annual	1976	27.50	25-42
1977	Immervad Bridge - K. Lange	Annual	1977	32.00	20-30
1978	Greenland Scenery - K. Lange	Annual	1978	35.00	30-35
1979	Choosing Christmas Tree - K. Lange	Annual	1979	42.50	43-63
1980	Bringing Home the Tree - K. Lange	Annual	1980	49.50	50
1981	Admiring Christmas Tree - K. Lange	Annual	1981	52.50	55
1982	Waiting for Christmas - K. Lange	Annual	1982	54.50	60-68
1983	Merry Christmas - K. Lange	Annual	1983	54.50	55
1984	Jingle Bells - K. Lange	Annual	1984	54.50	55-66
1985	Snowman - K. Lange	Annual	1985	54.50	80-90
1986	Christmas Vacation - K. Lange	Annual	1986	54.50	55-63
1987	Winter Birds - S. Vestergaard	Annual	1987	59.50	60-78
1988	Christmas Eve in Copenhagen - S. Vestergaard	Annual	1988	59.50	65
1989	The Old Skating Pond - S. Vestergaard	Annual	1989	59.50	90
1990	Christmas at Tivoli - S. Vestergaard	Annual	1990	64.50	120-170
1991	The Festival of Santa Lucia - S. Vestergaard	Annual	1991	69.50	90-120
1992	The Queen's Carriage - S. Vestergaard	Annual	1992	69.50	80
1993	Christmas Guests - S. Vestergaard	Annual	1993	69.50	90-126
1994	Christmas Shopping - S. Vestergaard	Annual	1994	72.50	75
1995	Christmas at the Manor House - S. Vestergaard	Annual	1995	72.50	85-120
1996	Lighting the Street Lamps - S. Vestergaard	12/96		74.50	75
1997	Roskilde Cathedral - S. Vestergaard	Annual		74.50	75

Royal Doulton

YEAR ISSUE		EDITION LIMIT	YEAR RETD.	ISSUE PRICE	*QUOTE U.S.$
Christmas Plates - Various					
1993	Royal Doulton-Together For Christmas - J. James	Closed	N/A	45.00	45
1993	Royal Albert-Sleighride - N/A	Closed	N/A	45.00	45
Family Christmas Plates - N/A					
1991	Dad Plays Santa	Closed	1991	60.00	60

Royal Worcester

YEAR ISSUE		EDITION LIMIT	YEAR RETD.	ISSUE PRICE	*QUOTE U.S.$
Birth Of A Nation - P.W. Baston					
1972	Boston Tea Party	10,000		45.00	140-275
1973	Paul Revere	10,000		45.00	140-250
1974	Concord Bridge	10,000		50.00	140
1975	Signing Declaration	10,000		65.00	140
1976	Crossing Delaware	10,000		65.00	140
1977	Washington's Inauguration	1,250		65.00	140
Currier and Ives Plates - P.W. Baston					
1974	Road in Winter	5,570		59.50	55-100
1975	Old Grist Mill	3,200		59.50	55-100
1976	Winter Pastime	1,500		59.50	55-125
1977	Home to Thanksgiving	546		59.50	200-250
Kitten Classics - P. Cooper					
1985	Cat Nap	14-day		29.50	36
1985	Purrfect Treasure	14-day		29.50	30
1985	Wild Flower	14-day		29.50	30
1985	Birdwatcher	14-day		29.50	30
1985	Tiger's Fancy	14-day		29.50	33

YEAR ISSUE	EDITION LIMIT	YEAR RETD.	ISSUE PRICE	*QUOTE U.S.$
1985 Country Kitty	14-day		29.50	33
1985 Little Rascal	14-day		29.50	30
1986 First Prize	14-day		29.50	30

Kitten Encounters - P. Cooper

YEAR ISSUE	EDITION LIMIT	YEAR RETD.	ISSUE PRICE	*QUOTE U.S.$
1987 Fishful Thinking	14-day		29.50	30-54
1987 Puppy Pal	14-day		29.50	36
1987 Just Ducky	14-day		29.50	36
1987 Bunny Chase	14-day		29.50	30
1987 Flutter By	14-day		29.50	30
1987 Bedtime Buddies	14-day		29.50	30
1988 Cat and Mouse	14-day		29.50	33
1988 Stablemates	14-day		29.50	48

Schmid: See Lowell Davis Farm Club

Seymour Mann, Inc.

Connoisseur Christmas Collection - M. Bernini

YEAR ISSUE	EDITION LIMIT	YEAR RETD.	ISSUE PRICE	*QUOTE U.S.$
1996 Cardinals CLT-310	25,000		50.00	50
1996 Chickadees CLT-300	25,000		50.00	50
1996 Doves CLT-305	25,000		50.00	50

Connoisseur Collection - M. Bernini

YEAR ISSUE	EDITION LIMIT	YEAR RETD.	ISSUE PRICE	*QUOTE U.S.$
1995 Bluebird CLT-13	25,000		50.00	50
1995 Canary CLT-10	25,000		50.00	50
1995 Cardinal CLT-7	25,000		50.00	50
1995 Dove Duo CLT-1	25,000		50.00	50
1995 Hummingbird Duo CLT-4	25,000		50.00	50
1996 Magnolia CLT-76	25,000		50.00	50
1995 Pink Rose CLT-70	25,000		50.00	50
1995 Robin CLT-16	25,000		50.00	50
1995 Swan Duo CLT-50	25,000		50.00	50

Sports Impressions/Enesco

Gold Edition Plates - Various

YEAR ISSUE	EDITION LIMIT	YEAR RETD.	ISSUE PRICE	*QUOTE U.S.$
XX A's Jose Canseco Gold (10 1/4") 1028-04 - J. Canseco	2,500	N/A	125.00	125
1990 Andre Dawson - R. Lewis	Closed		150.00	150
1988 Brooks Robinson - R. Simon	Closed		125.00	225
1987 Carl Yastrzemski - R. Simon	Closed		125.00	175
1992 Chicago Bulls '92 World Champions - C. Hayes	Closed		150.00	150
1993 Chicago Bulls 1993 World Championship Gold (10 1/4") 4062-04 - B. Vann	1,993	1994	150.00	150
1987 Darryl Strawberry #1 - R. Simon	Closed		125.00	125
1989 Darryl Strawberry #2 - T. Fogerty	Closed		125.00	125
1986 Don Mattingly - B. Johnson	Closed		125.00	125
1991 Dream Team (1st Ten Chosen) - L. Salk	Closed		150.00	300
1992 Dream Team - R.Tanenbaum	Closed		150.00	175
1992 Dream Team 1992 (8 1/2") 5507-03 - C. Hayes	7,500	1994	60.00	300-395
1992 Dream Team 1992 Gold (10 1/4") 5509-04 - R. Tanenbaum	1,992	1994	150.00	150
1991 Hawks Dominique Wilkins - J. Catalano	Closed		150.00	195
1990 Joe Montana 49ers - J. Catalano	Closed		150.00	195
1990 Joe Montana 49ers Gold (10 1/4") 3000-04 - J. Catalano	1,990	1991	150.00	150
1986 Keith Hernandez - R. Simon	Closed		125.00	175
1991 Lakers Magic Johnson - W.C. Mundy	Closed		150.00	225
1991 Larry Bird - J. Catalano	Closed		150.00	195
1986 Larry Bird - R. Simon	Closed		125.00	200
1988 Larry Bird - R. Simon	Closed		125.00	275
1990 Living Triple Crown - R. Lewis	Closed		150.00	150-225
1993 Magic Johnson (4042-04) - R.Tanenbaum	Closed		150.00	150
1988 Magic Johnson - R. Simon	Closed		125.00	225
1993 Magic Johnson - T. Fogerty	Closed		150.00	175
1991 Magic Johnson Lakers Gold 4007-04 - C.W. Mundy	1,991	1991	150.00	175
1992 Magic Johnson Lakers Gold (10 1/4") 4042-04 - R. Tanenbaum	1,992	1994	150.00	150
1991 Magic Johnson Lakers Platinum (8 1/2") 4007-03 - M. Petronella	5,000	1992	60.00	60
1989 Mantle Switch Hitter - J. Catalano	Closed		150.00	295-325
1990 Michael Jordan - J. Catalano	Closed		150.00	275-325
1991 Michael Jordan - J. Catalano	Closed		150.00	195
1992 Michael Jordan - R.Tanenbaum	Closed		150.00	175
1993 Michael Jordan - T. Fogerty	Closed		150.00	200
1992 Michael Jordan Bulls (10 1/4") 4032-04 - R. Tanenbaum	1,991	1992	150.00	275-325
1993 Michael Jordan Bulls Gold (10 1/4") 4046-04 - T. Fogerty	2,500	1993	150.00	150
1991 Michael Jordan Gold (10 1/4") 4002-04 - J. Catalano	1,991	1992	150.00	150
1991 Michael Jordan Platinum (8 1/2") 4002-03 - M. Petronella	1,991	1993	60.00	95
1995 Mickey Mantle "My Greatest Year 1956" 1229-04 - B. Vann	1,956		100.00	100
1991 Mickey Mantle 7 - B. Simon	Closed		150.00	195
1986 Mickey Mantle At Night - R. Simon	Closed		125.00	250
1995 Mickey Mantle double plate set 176923 - T. Treadway	2,401		75.00	75
1987 Mickey, Willie, & Duke - R. Simon	Closed		150.00	800-1000
1992 NBA 1st Ten Chosen Gold (10 1/4") 5501-04 - L. Salk	1,992	1992	150.00	295-395
1992 NBA 1st Ten Chosen Platinum (8 1/2") blue) 5502-03 - J. Catalano	7,500	1993	60.00	125
1992 NBA 1st Ten Chosen Platinum (8 1/2") (red) 5503-03 - C.W. Mundy	7,500	1993	60.00	95
1990 Nolan Ryan 300 - J. Catalano	Closed		150.00	175
1990 Nolan Ryan 300 Gold 1091-04 - T. Fogarty	1,990	1992	150.00	150
1995 Profiles in Courage Mickey Mantle 1231-03 - M. Petronella	Open		30.00	30
1990 Rickey Henderson - R. Lewis	Closed		150.00	150
XX Roberto Clemente 1090-03 - R. Lewis	10,000	N/A	75.00	75
1993 Shaquille O'Neal Gold (10 1/4") 4047-04 - T. Fogarty	2,500	1994	150.00	150
1987 Ted Williams (signed) - R. Simon	Closed		125.00	450-550
1990 Tom Seaver - R. Lewis	Closed		150.00	150
1986 Wade Boggs - B. Johnson	Closed		125.00	150
1989 Will Clark - J. Catalano	Closed		125.00	150
1988 Yankee Tradition - J. Catalano	Closed		150.00	175-225

The Tudor Mint Inc.

Collector Plates - J. Mulholland

YEAR ISSUE	EDITION LIMIT	YEAR RETD.	ISSUE PRICE	*QUOTE U.S.$
1992 4401 Meeting of Unicorns	Closed	1993	27.10	79
1992 4402 Cauldron of Light	Closed	1993	27.10	79
1992 4403 The Guardian Dragon	Closed	1993	27.10	79
1992 4404 The Dragon's Nest	Closed	1993	27.10	79

V-Palekh Art Studios

Russian Legends - Various

YEAR ISSUE	EDITION LIMIT	YEAR RETD.	ISSUE PRICE	*QUOTE U.S.$
1988 Ruslan and Ludmilla - G. Lubimov	195-day		29.87	30-45
1988 The Princess/Seven Bogatyrs - A. Kovalev	195-day		29.87	35-45
1988 The Golden Cockerel - V. Vleshko	195-day		32.87	35
1988 Lukomorya - R. Belousov	195-day		32.87	35
1989 Fisherman and the Magic Fish - N. Lopatin	195-day		32.87	35
1989 Tsar Saltan - G. Zhiryakova	195-day		34.87	35
1989 The Priest and His Servant - O. An	195-day		34.87	35
1990 Stone Flower - V. Bolshakova	195-day		34.87	40
1990 Sadko - E. Populor	195-day		34.87	45
1990 The Twelve Months - N. Lopatin	195-day		36.87	45
1990 Silver Hoof - S. Adeyanor	195-day		36.87	55
1990 Morozko - N. Lopatin	195-day		36.87	70

Villeroy & Boch

Flower Fairy - C. Barker

YEAR ISSUE	EDITION LIMIT	YEAR RETD.	ISSUE PRICE	*QUOTE U.S.$
1979 Lavender	21-day		35.00	125
1980 Sweet Pea	21-day		35.00	125
1980 Candytuft	21-day		35.00	89
1981 Heliotrope	21-day		35.00	75
1981 Blackthorn	21-day		35.00	75
1981 Appleblossom	21-day		35.00	95

Russian Fairytales Maria Morevna - B. Zvorykin

YEAR ISSUE	EDITION LIMIT	YEAR RETD.	ISSUE PRICE	*QUOTE U.S.$
1982 Maria Morevna and Tsarevich Ivan	27,500		70.00	75
1982 Koshchey Carries Off Maria Morevna	27,500		70.00	70
1982 Tsarevich Ivan and the Beautiful Castle	27,500		70.00	90

Russian Fairytales The Firebird - B. Zvorykin

YEAR ISSUE	EDITION LIMIT	YEAR RETD.	ISSUE PRICE	*QUOTE U.S.$
1981 In Search of the Firebird	27,500		70.00	75
1981 Ivan and Tsarevna on the Grey Wolf	27,500		70.00	70
1981 The Wedding of Tsarevna Elena the Fair	27,500		70.00	100

Russian Fairytales The Red Knight - B. Zvorykin

YEAR ISSUE	EDITION LIMIT	YEAR RETD.	ISSUE PRICE	*QUOTE U.S.$
1981 The Red Knight	27,500		70.00	40-70
1981 Vassilissa and Her Stepsisters	27,500		70.00	45-77
1981 Vassilissa is Presented to the Tsar	27,500		70.00	56-75

Villeroy & Boch - B. Zvorykin

YEAR ISSUE	EDITION LIMIT	YEAR RETD.	ISSUE PRICE	*QUOTE U.S.$
1980 The Snow Maiden	27,500		70.00	100
1981 Snegurochka at the Court of Tsar Berendei	27,500		70.00	45-70
1981 Snegurochka and Lei, the Shepherd Boy	27,500		70.00	44-70

W.S. George

Alaska: The Last Frontier - H. Lambson

YEAR ISSUE	EDITION LIMIT	YEAR RETD.	ISSUE PRICE	*QUOTE U.S.$
1991 Icy Majesty	Closed		34.50	34
1991 Autumn Grandeur	Closed		34.50	35
1992 Mountain Monarch	Closed		37.50	40
1992 Down the Trail	Closed		37.50	38
1992 Moonlight Lookout	Closed		37.50	60
1992 Graceful Passage	Closed		39.50	60
1992 Arctic Journey	Closed		39.50	65
1992 Summit Domain	Closed		39.50	62

Along an English Lane - M. Harvey

YEAR ISSUE	EDITION LIMIT	YEAR RETD.	ISSUE PRICE	*QUOTE U.S.$
1993 Summer's Bright Welcome	Closed		29.50	50
1993 Greeting the Day	Closed		29.50	60
1993 Friends and Flowers	Closed		29.50	60
1993 Cottage Around the Bend	Closed		29.50	30

America the Beautiful - H. Johnson

YEAR ISSUE	EDITION LIMIT	YEAR RETD.	ISSUE PRICE	*QUOTE U.S.$
1988 Yosemite Falls	Closed		34.50	50
1989 The Grand Canyon	Closed		34.50	30
1989 Yellowstone River	Closed		37.50	41
1989 The Great Smokey Mountains	Closed		37.50	45
1990 The Everglades	Closed		37.50	45
1990 Acadia	Closed		37.50	45
1990 The Grand Tetons	Closed		39.50	55
1990 Crater Lake	Closed		39.50	40-50

America's Pride - R. Richert

YEAR ISSUE	EDITION LIMIT	YEAR RETD.	ISSUE PRICE	*QUOTE U.S.$
1992 Misty Fjords	Closed		29.50	50
1992 Rugged Shores	Closed		29.50	40
1992 Mighty Summit	Closed		32.50	45
1993 Lofty Reflections	Closed		32.50	60
1993 Tranquil Waters	Closed		32.50	50
1993 Mountain Majesty	Closed		34.50	40
1993 Canyon Climb	Closed		34.50	50
1993 Golden Vista	Closed		34.50	35

Art Deco - M. McDonald

YEAR ISSUE	EDITION LIMIT	YEAR RETD.	ISSUE PRICE	*QUOTE U.S.$
1989 A Flapper With Greyhounds	Closed		39.50	45
1990 Tango Dancers	Closed		39.50	60
1990 Arriving in Style	Closed		39.50	60
1990 On the Town	Closed		39.50	65

Bear Tracks - J. Seerey-Lester

YEAR ISSUE	EDITION LIMIT	YEAR RETD.	ISSUE PRICE	*QUOTE U.S.$
1992 Denali Family	Closed		29.50	35
1993 Their First Season	Closed		29.50	45
1993 High Country Champion	Closed		29.50	45
1993 Heavy Going	Closed		29.50	50
1993 Breaking Cover	Closed		29.50	55
1993 Along the Ice Flow	Closed		29.50	30

Beloved Hymns of Childhood - C. Barker

YEAR ISSUE	EDITION LIMIT	YEAR RETD.	ISSUE PRICE	*QUOTE U.S.$
1988 The Lord's My Shepherd	Closed		29.50	40
1988 Away In a Manger	Closed		29.50	35
1989 Now Thank We All Our God	Closed		32.50	33
1989 Love Divine	Closed		32.50	33
1989 I Love to Hear the Story	Closed		32.50	35
1989 All Glory, Laud and Honour	Closed		32.50	35
1990 All People on Earth Do Dwell	Closed		34.50	35
1990 Loving Shepherd of Thy Sheep	Closed		34.50	35

A Black Tie Affair: The Penguin - C. Jagodits

YEAR ISSUE	EDITION LIMIT	YEAR RETD.	ISSUE PRICE	*QUOTE U.S.$
1992 Little Explorer	Closed		29.50	50
1992 Penguin Parade	Closed		29.50	50
1992 Baby-Sitters	Closed		29.50	50
1993 Belly Flopping	Closed		29.50	55

Blessed Are The Children - W. Rane

YEAR ISSUE	EDITION LIMIT	YEAR RETD.	ISSUE PRICE	*QUOTE U.S.$
1990 Let the/Children Come To Me	Closed		29.50	45
1990 I Am the Good Shepherd	Closed		29.50	45
1991 Whoever Welcomes/Child	Closed		32.50	45
1991 Hosanna in the Highest	Closed		32.50	35
1991 Jesus Had Compassion on Them	Closed		32.50	50
1991 Blessed are the Peacemakers	Closed		34.50	55
1991 I am the Vine, You are the Branches	Closed		34.50	50
1991 Seek and You Will Find	Closed		34.50	35

Bonds of Love - B. Burke

YEAR ISSUE	EDITION LIMIT	YEAR RETD.	ISSUE PRICE	*QUOTE U.S.$
1989 Precious Embrace	Closed		29.50	30
1990 Cherished Moment	Closed		29.50	30
1991 Tender Caress	Closed		32.50	35
1992 Loving Touch	Closed		32.50	40
1992 Treasured Kisses	Closed		32.50	40
1994 Endearing Whispers	Closed		32.50	30

The Christmas Story - H. Garrido

YEAR ISSUE	EDITION LIMIT	YEAR RETD.	ISSUE PRICE	*QUOTE U.S.$
1992 Gifts of the Magi	Closed		29.50	45
1993 Rest on the Flight into Egypt	Closed		29.50	50
1993 Journey of the Magi	Closed		29.50	30
1993 The Nativity	Closed		29.50	30
1993 The Annunciation	150-day		29.50	30
1993 Adoration of the Shepherds	Closed		29.50	30

Classic Waterfowl: The Ducks Unlimited - L. Kaatz

YEAR ISSUE	EDITION LIMIT	YEAR RETD.	ISSUE PRICE	*QUOTE U.S.$
1988 Mallards at Sunrise	Closed		36.50	45
1988 Geese in the Autumn Fields	Closed		36.50	50
1989 Green Wings/Morning Marsh	Closed		39.50	40
1989 Canvasbacks, Breaking Away	Closed		39.50	40
1989 Pintails in Indian Summer	Closed		39.50	40
1990 Wood Ducks Taking Flight	Closed		39.50	40
1990 Snow Geese Against November Skies	Closed		41.50	42
1990 Bluebills Coming In	Closed		41.50	42

Columbus Discovers America: The 500th Anniversary - J. Penalva

YEAR ISSUE	EDITION LIMIT	YEAR RETD.	ISSUE PRICE	*QUOTE U.S.$
1991 Under Full Sail	Closed		29.50	30
1992 Ashore at Dawn	Closed		29.50	35
1992 Columbus Raises the Flag	Closed		32.50	35
1992 Bringing Together Two Cultures	Closed		32.50	47
1992 The Queen's Approval	Closed		32.50	33
1992 Treasures From The New World	Closed		32.50	50-55

Country Bouquets - G. Kurz

YEAR ISSUE	EDITION LIMIT	YEAR RETD.	ISSUE PRICE	*QUOTE U.S.$
1991 Morning Sunshine	Closed		29.50	45
1991 Summer Perfume	Closed		29.50	40
1992 Warm Welcome	Closed		32.50	50
1992 Garden's Bounty	Closed		32.50	45

Country Nostalgia - M. Harvey

YEAR ISSUE	EDITION LIMIT	YEAR RETD.	ISSUE PRICE	*QUOTE U.S.$
1989 The Spring Buggy	Closed		29.50	30

PLATES

YEAR ISSUE		EDITION LIMIT	YEAR RETD.	ISSUE PRICE	*QUOTE U.S.$
1989	The Apple Cider Press	Closed		29.50	40
1989	The Vintage Seed Planter	Closed		29.50	40
1989	The Old Hand Pump	Closed		32.50	50
1990	The Wooden Butter Churn	Closed		32.50	40
1990	The Dairy Cans	Closed		32.50	33
1990	The Forgotten Plow	Closed		34.50	35
1990	The Antique Spinning Wheel	Closed		34.50	40

Critic's Choice: Gone With The Wind - P. Jennis

YEAR ISSUE		EDITION LIMIT	YEAR RETD.	ISSUE PRICE	*QUOTE U.S.$
1991	Marry Me, Scarlett	Closed		27.50	35-55
1991	Waiting for Rhett	Closed		27.50	50-60
1991	A Declaration of Love	Closed		30.50	50
1991	The Paris Hat	Closed		30.50	50-60
1991	Scarlett Asks a Favor	Closed		30.50	55
1992	Scarlett Gets Her Way	Closed		32.50	45
1992	The Smitten Suitor	Closed		32.50	45
1992	Scarlett's Shopping Spree	Closed		32.50	45
1992	The Buggy Ride	Closed		32.50	50-75
1992	Scarlett Gets Down to Business	Closed		34.50	45
1993	Scarlett's Heart is with Tara	Closed		34.50	45
1993	At Cross Purposes	Closed		34.50	50

A Delicate Balance: Vanishing Wildlife - G. Beecham

YEAR ISSUE		EDITION LIMIT	YEAR RETD.	ISSUE PRICE	*QUOTE U.S.$
1992	Tomorrow's Hope	Closed		29.50	40
1993	Today's Future	Closed		29.50	45
1993	Present Dreams	Closed		32.50	40
1993	Eyes on the New Day	Closed		32.50	40

Dr. Zhivago - G. Bush

YEAR ISSUE		EDITION LIMIT	YEAR RETD.	ISSUE PRICE	*QUOTE U.S.$
1990	Zhivago and Lara	Closed		39.50	40
1991	Love Poems For Lara	Closed		39.50	45
1991	Zhivago Says Farewell	Closed		39.50	45
1991	Lara's Love	Closed		39.50	50

The Elegant Birds - J. Faulkner

YEAR ISSUE		EDITION LIMIT	YEAR RETD.	ISSUE PRICE	*QUOTE U.S.$
1988	The Swan	Closed		32.50	33
1988	Great Blue Heron	Closed		32.50	33
1989	Snowy Egret	Closed		35.50	36
1989	The Anhinga	Closed		35.50	36
1989	The Flamingo	Closed		35.50	36
1990	Sandhill and Whooping Crane	Closed		35.50	36

Enchanted Garden - E. Antonaccio

YEAR ISSUE		EDITION LIMIT	YEAR RETD.	ISSUE PRICE	*QUOTE U.S.$
1993	A Peaceful Retreat	Closed		24.50	30
1993	Pleasant Pathways	Closed		24.50	40
1993	A Place to Dream	Closed		24.50	25
1993	Tranquil Hideaway	Closed		24.50	25

Eyes of the Wild - D. Pierce

YEAR ISSUE		EDITION LIMIT	YEAR RETD.	ISSUE PRICE	*QUOTE U.S.$
1993	Eyes in the Mist	Closed		29.50	55
1993	Eyes in the Pines	Closed		29.50	40
1993	Eyes on the Sly	Closed		29.50	60
1993	Eyes of Gold	Closed		29.50	50
1993	Eyes of Silence	Closed		29.50	63
1993	Eyes in the Snow	Closed		29.50	60
1993	Eyes of Wonder	95-day		29.50	30
1994	Eyes of Strength	95-day		29.50	30

The Faces of Nature - J. Kramer Cole

YEAR ISSUE		EDITION LIMIT	YEAR RETD.	ISSUE PRICE	*QUOTE U.S.$
1992	Canyon of the Cat	Closed		29.50	50
1992	Wolf Ridge	Closed		29.50	50
1993	Trail of the Talisman	Closed		29.50	50
1993	Wolfpack of the Ancients	Closed		29.50	50
1993	Two Bears Camp	150-day		29.50	30
1993	Wintering With the Wapiti	150-day		29.50	30
1993	Within Sunrise	150-day		29.50	30
1993	Wambli Okiye	150-day		29.50	30

The Federal Duck Stamp Plate Collection - Various

YEAR ISSUE		EDITION LIMIT	YEAR RETD.	ISSUE PRICE	*QUOTE U.S.$
1990	The Lesser Scaup	Closed		27.50	30
1990	The Mallard	Closed		27.50	45
1990	The Ruddy Ducks	Closed		30.50	30
1990	Canvasbacks	Closed		30.50	42
1991	Pintails	Closed		30.50	35
1991	Wigeons	Closed		30.50	30
1991	Cinnamon Teal	Closed		30.50	30
1991	Fulvous Wistling Duck	Closed		32.50	45
1991	The Redheads	Closed		32.50	45
1991	Snow Goose	Closed		32.50	35

Feline Fancy - H. Ronner

YEAR ISSUE		EDITION LIMIT	YEAR RETD.	ISSUE PRICE	*QUOTE U.S.$
1993	Globetrotters	Closed		34.50	40
1993	Little Athletes	Closed		34.50	50
1993	Young Adventurers	Closed		34.50	50
1993	The Geographers	Closed		34.50	75

Field Birds of North America - D. Bush

YEAR ISSUE		EDITION LIMIT	YEAR RETD.	ISSUE PRICE	*QUOTE U.S.$
1991	Winter Colors: Ring-Necked Pheasant	Closed		39.50	40
1991	In Display: Ruffed Grouse	Closed		39.50	45
1991	Morning Light: Bobwhite Quail	Closed		42.50	60
1991	Misty Clearing: Wild Turkey	Closed		42.50	65
1992	Autumn Moment: American Woodcock	Closed		42.50	45
1992	Season's End: Willow Ptarmigan	Closed		42.50	60

Floral Fancies - C. Callog

YEAR ISSUE		EDITION LIMIT	YEAR RETD.	ISSUE PRICE	*QUOTE U.S.$
1993	Sitting Softly	Closed		34.50	45
1993	Sitting Pretty	Closed		34.50	45
1993	Sitting Sunny	Closed		34.50	35
1993	Sitting Pink	95-day		34.50	35

Flowers From Grandma's Garden - G. Kurz

YEAR ISSUE		EDITION LIMIT	YEAR RETD.	ISSUE PRICE	*QUOTE U.S.$
1990	Country Cuttings	Closed		24.50	45
1990	The Morning Bouquet	Closed		24.50	40
1991	Homespun Beauty	Closed		27.50	40
1991	Harvest in the Meadow	Closed		27.50	40
1991	Gardener's Delight	Closed		27.50	50
1991	Nature's Bounty	Closed		27.50	60
1991	A Country Welcome	Closed		29.50	55
1991	The Springtime Arrangement	Closed		29.50	50

Flowers of Your Garden - V. Morley

YEAR ISSUE		EDITION LIMIT	YEAR RETD.	ISSUE PRICE	*QUOTE U.S.$
1988	Roses	Closed		24.50	30
1988	Lilacs	Closed		24.50	65
1988	Daisies	Closed		27.50	35
1988	Peonies	Closed		27.50	28
1988	Chrysanthemums	Closed		27.50	28
1989	Daffodils	Closed		27.50	28
1989	Tulips	Closed		29.50	30
1989	Irises	Closed		29.50	30

Garden of the Lord - C. Gillies

YEAR ISSUE		EDITION LIMIT	YEAR RETD.	ISSUE PRICE	*QUOTE U.S.$
1992	Love One Another	Closed		29.50	30
1992	Perfect Peace	150-day		29.50	30
1992	Trust In the Lord	150-day		32.50	33
1992	The Lord's Love	150-day		32.50	33
1992	The Lord Bless You	150-day		32.50	33
1992	Ask In Prayer	150-day		34.50	35
1993	Peace Be With You	150-day		34.50	35
1993	Give Thanks To The Lord	150-day		34.50	35

Gardens of Paradise - L. Chang

YEAR ISSUE		EDITION LIMIT	YEAR RETD.	ISSUE PRICE	*QUOTE U.S.$
1992	Tranquility	Closed		29.50	40
1992	Serenity	Closed		29.50	50
1993	Splendor	Closed		32.50	40
1993	Harmony	Closed		32.50	60
1993	Beauty	Closed		32.50	40
1993	Elegance	Closed		32.50	40
1993	Grandeur	Closed		32.50	33
1993	Majesty	150-day		32.50	33

Gentle Beginnings - W. Nelson

YEAR ISSUE		EDITION LIMIT	YEAR RETD.	ISSUE PRICE	*QUOTE U.S.$
1991	Tender Loving Care	Closed		34.50	45
1991	A Touch of Love	Closed		34.50	50
1991	Under Watchful Eyes	Closed		37.50	60
1991	Lap of Love	Closed		37.50	75
1992	Happy Together	Closed		37.50	80
1992	First Steps	Closed		37.50	80

Glorious Songbirds - R. Cobane

YEAR ISSUE		EDITION LIMIT	YEAR RETD.	ISSUE PRICE	*QUOTE U.S.$
1991	Cardinals on a Snowy Branch	Closed		29.50	35
1991	Indigo Buntings and/Blossoms	Closed		29.50	30
1991	Chickadees Among The Lilacs	Closed		32.50	33
1991	Goldfinches in/Thistle	Closed		32.50	33
1991	Cedar Waxwing/Winter Berries	Closed		32.50	34
1991	Bluebirds in a Blueberry Bush	Closed		34.50	37
1991	Baltimore Orioles/Autumn Leaves	Closed		34.50	50
1991	Robins with Dogwood in Bloom	Closed		34.50	45

The Golden Age of the Clipper Ships - C. Vickery

YEAR ISSUE		EDITION LIMIT	YEAR RETD.	ISSUE PRICE	*QUOTE U.S.$
1989	The Twilight Under Full Sail	Closed		29.50	30
1989	The Blue Jacket at Sunset	Closed		29.50	30
1989	Young America, Homeward	Closed		32.50	33
1990	Flying Cloud	Closed		32.50	33
1990	Davy Crocket at Daybreak	Closed		32.50	35
1990	Golden Eagle Conquers Wind	Closed		32.50	35
1990	The Lightning in Lifting Fog	Closed		34.50	35
1990	Sea Witch, Mistress/Oceans	Closed		34.50	35

Gone With the Wind: Golden Anniversary - H. Rogers

YEAR ISSUE		EDITION LIMIT	YEAR RETD.	ISSUE PRICE	*QUOTE U.S.$
1988	Scarlett and Her Suitors	Closed		24.50	60-125
1988	The Burning of Atlanta	Closed		24.50	40-70
1988	Scarlett and Ashley After the War	Closed		27.50	50-65
1988	The Proposal	Closed		27.50	65-75
1989	Home to Tara	Closed		27.50	35
1989	Strolling in Atlanta	Closed		27.50	40
1989	A Question of Honor	Closed		29.50	33-55
1989	Scarlett's Resolve	Closed		29.50	45
1989	Frankly My Dear	Closed		29.50	55
1989	Melane and Ashley	Closed		32.50	35-45
1990	A Toast to Bonnie Blue	Closed		32.50	55
1990	Scarlett and Rhett's Honeymoon	Closed		32.50	45

Gone With the Wind: The Passions of Scarlett O'Hara - P. Jennis

YEAR ISSUE		EDITION LIMIT	YEAR RETD.	ISSUE PRICE	*QUOTE U.S.$
1992	Fiery Embrace	Closed		29.50	65
1992	Pride and Passion	Closed		29.50	70
1992	Dreams of Ashley	Closed		32.50	75
1992	The Fond Farewell	Closed		32.50	75
1992	The Waltz	Closed		32.50	65
1992	As God Is My Witness	Closed		34.50	50
1993	Brave Scarlett	Closed		34.50	50
1993	Nightmare	Closed		34.50	50
1993	Evening Prayers	Closed		34.50	40
1993	Naptime	Closed		36.50	40
1993	Dangerous Attraction	Closed		36.50	45
1994	The End of An Era	Closed		36.50	37

Grand Safari: Images of Africa - C. Frace

YEAR ISSUE		EDITION LIMIT	YEAR RETD.	ISSUE PRICE	*QUOTE U.S.$
1992	A Moment's Rest	Closed		34.50	35
1992	Elephant's of Kilimanjaro	Closed		34.50	50
1992	Undivided Attention	Closed		37.50	45
1993	Quiet Time in Samburu	Closed		37.50	50
1993	Lone Hunter	Closed		37.50	38
1993	The Greater Kudo	Closed		37.50	38

Heart of the Wild - G. Beecham

YEAR ISSUE		EDITION LIMIT	YEAR RETD.	ISSUE PRICE	*QUOTE U.S.$
1992	A Gentle Touch	Closed		29.50	35
1992	Mother's Pride	Closed		29.50	50
1992	An Afternoon Together	Closed		32.50	55
1993	Quiet Time?	Closed		32.50	65

Hollywood's Glamour Girls - E. Dzenis

YEAR ISSUE		EDITION LIMIT	YEAR RETD.	ISSUE PRICE	*QUOTE U.S.$
1989	Jean Harlow-Dinner at Eight	Closed		24.50	35
1990	Lana Turner-Postman Ring Twice	Closed		29.50	30
1990	Carol Lombard-The Gay Bride	Closed		29.50	30
1990	Greta Garbo-In Grand Hotel	Closed		29.50	30

Hometown Memories - H.T. Becker

YEAR ISSUE		EDITION LIMIT	YEAR RETD.	ISSUE PRICE	*QUOTE U.S.$
1993	Moonlight Skaters	Closed		29.50	30
1993	Mountain Sleigh Ride	Closed		29.50	40
1993	Heading Home	Closed		29.50	50
1993	A Winter Ride	Closed		29.50	50

Last of Their Kind: The Endangered Species - W. Nelson

YEAR ISSUE		EDITION LIMIT	YEAR RETD.	ISSUE PRICE	*QUOTE U.S.$
1988	The Panda	Closed		27.50	30-55
1989	The Snow Leopard	Closed		27.50	50
1989	The Red Wolf	Closed		30.50	50
1989	The Asian Elephant	Closed		30.50	50
1990	The Slender-Horned Gazelle	Closed		30.50	50
1990	The Bridled Wallaby	Closed		30.50	50
1990	The Black-Footed Ferret	Closed		33.50	50
1990	The Siberian Tiger	Closed		33.50	45-60
1991	The Vicuna	Closed		33.50	50
1991	Przewalski's Horse	Closed		33.50	35-60

Lena Liu's Basket Bouquets - L. Liu

YEAR ISSUE		EDITION LIMIT	YEAR RETD.	ISSUE PRICE	*QUOTE U.S.$
1992	Roses	Closed		29.50	45
1992	Pansies	Closed		29.50	50
1992	Tulips and Lilacs	Closed		32.50	60
1992	Irises	Closed		32.50	50
1992	Lilies	Closed		32.50	35
1992	Parrot Tulips	150-day		32.50	45
1992	Peonies	150-day		32.50	45
1993	Begonias	150-day		32.50	33
1993	Magnolias	150-day		32.50	33
1993	Calla Lilies	150-day		32.50	33
1993	Orchids	150-day		32.50	33
1993	Hydrangeas	150-day		32.50	33

Lena Liu's Flower Fairies - L. Liu

YEAR ISSUE		EDITION LIMIT	YEAR RETD.	ISSUE PRICE	*QUOTE U.S.$
1993	Magic Makers	Closed		29.50	30
1993	Petal Playmates	Closed		29.50	30
1993	Delicate Dancers	Closed		32.50	33
1993	Mischief Masters	Closed		32.50	33
1993	Amorous Angels	Closed		32.50	33
1993	Winged Wonders	Closed		34.50	35
1993	Miniature Mermaids	Closed		34.50	35
1993	Fanciful Fairies	Closed		34.50	35

Lena Liu's Hummingbird Treasury - L. Liu

YEAR ISSUE		EDITION LIMIT	YEAR RETD.	ISSUE PRICE	*QUOTE U.S.$
1992	Ruby-Throated Hummingbird	Closed		29.50	55
1992	Anna's Hummingbird	Closed		29.50	65
1992	Violet-Crowned Hummingbird	Closed		32.50	60
1993	Rufous Hummingbird	Closed		32.50	33
1993	White-Eared Hummingbird	150-day		32.50	35
1993	Broad-Billed Hummingbird	150-day		34.50	35
1993	Calliope Hummingbird	150-day		34.50	35
1993	The Allen's Hummingbird	150-day		34.50	35

Little Angels - B. Burke

YEAR ISSUE		EDITION LIMIT	YEAR RETD.	ISSUE PRICE	*QUOTE U.S.$
1992	Angels We Have Heard on High	Closed		29.50	40
1992	O Tannenbaum	Closed		29.50	55
1993	Joy to the World	Closed		32.50	85
1993	Hark the Herald Angels Sing	Closed		32.50	45
1993	It Came Upon a Midnight Clear	Closed		32.50	55
1993	The First Noel	Closed		32.50	60

A Loving Look: Duck Families - B. Langton

YEAR ISSUE		EDITION LIMIT	YEAR RETD.	ISSUE PRICE	*QUOTE U.S.$
1990	Family Outing	Closed		34.50	35
1991	Sleepy Start	Closed		34.50	35
1991	Quiet Moment	Closed		37.50	40
1991	Safe and Sound	Closed		37.50	40
1991	Spring Arrivals	Closed		37.50	40
1991	The Family Tree	Closed		37.50	50

The Majestic Horse - P. Wildermuth

YEAR ISSUE		EDITION LIMIT	YEAR RETD.	ISSUE PRICE	*QUOTE U.S.$
1992	Classic Beauty: Thoroughbred	Closed		34.50	40
1992	American Gold: The Quarterhorse	Closed		34.50	50
1992	Regal Spirit: The Arabian	Closed		34.50	40
1992	Western Favorite: American Paint Horse	Closed		34.50	50

Melodies in the Mist - A. Sakhavarz

YEAR ISSUE		EDITION LIMIT	YEAR RETD.	ISSUE PRICE	*QUOTE U.S.$
1993	Among the Dewdrops	Closed		34.50	40
1993	Feeding Time	Closed		37.50	38

Memories of a Victorian Childhood - Unknown

YEAR ISSUE		EDITION LIMIT	YEAR RETD.	ISSUE PRICE	*QUOTE U.S.$
1992	You'd Better Not Pout	Closed		29.50	30
1992	Sweet Slumber	Closed		29.50	55
1992	Through Thick and Thin	Closed		32.50	45

Collectors' Information Bureau *Quotes have been rounded up to nearest dollar

YEAR ISSUE	EDITION LIMIT	YEAR RETD.	ISSUE PRICE	*QUOTE U.S.$
1992 An Armful of Treasures	Closed		32.50	65
1993 A Trio of Bookworms	Closed		32.50	60
1993 Pugnacious Playmate	Closed		32.50	60

Nature's Legacy - J. Sias
1990 Blue Snow at Half Dome	Closed		24.50	30
1991 Misty Morning/Mt. McKinley	Closed		24.50	25
1991 Twilight Reflections on Mount Ranier	Closed		27.50	30
1991 Redwalls of Havasu Canyon	Closed		27.50	28
1991 Autumn Splendor in the Smoky Mts.	Closed		27.50	30
1991 Winter Peace in Yellowstone Park	Closed		29.50	30
1991 Golden Majesty/Rocky Mountains	Closed		29.50	35
1991 Radiant Sunset Over the Everglades	Closed		29.50	30

Nature's Lovables - C. Fracé
1990 The Koala Bear	Closed		27.50	50-60
1991 New Arrival	Closed		27.50	50
1991 Chinese Treasure	Closed		27.50	50
1991 Baby Harp Seal	Closed		30.50	40-50
1991 Bobcat: Nature's Dawn	Closed		30.50	50
1991 Clouded Leopard	Closed		32.50	50
1991 Zebra Foal	Closed		32.50	40-50
1991 Bandit	Closed		32.50	50

Nature's Playmates - C. Fracé
1991 Partners	Closed		29.50	35
1991 Secret Heights	Closed		29.50	35
1991 Recess	Closed		32.50	35
1991 Double Trouble	Closed		32.50	40
1991 Pals	Closed		32.50	33
1992 Curious Trio	Closed		34.50	43
1992 Playmates	Closed		34.50	50
1992 Surprise	Closed		34.50	45
1992 Peace On Ice	Closed		36.50	50
1992 Ambassadors	Closed		36.50	50

Nature's Poetry - L. Liu
1989 Morning Serenade	Closed		24.50	45
1989 Song of Promise	Closed		24.50	35
1990 Tender Lullaby	Closed		27.50	40
1990 Nature's Harmony	Closed		27.50	35
1990 Gentle Refrain	Closed		27.50	30
1990 Morning Chorus	Closed		27.50	35
1990 Melody at Daybreak	Closed		29.50	30
1991 Delicate Accord	Closed		29.50	30
1991 Lyrical Beginnings	Closed		29.50	30
1991 Song of Spring	Closed		32.50	35
1991 Mother's Melody	Closed		32.50	33
1991 Cherub Chorale	Closed		32.50	50

On Golden Wings - W. Goebel
1993 Morning Light	Closed		29.50	45
1993 Early Risers	Closed		29.50	45
1993 As Day Breaks	Closed		32.50	48
1993 Daylight Flight	Closed		32.50	40
1993 Winter Dawn	Closed		32.50	33
1994 First Light	95-day		34.50	35

On Gossamer Wings - L. Liu
1988 Monarch Butterflies	Closed		24.50	35
1988 Western Tiger Swallowtails	Closed		24.50	40
1988 Red-Spotted Purple	Closed		27.50	40
1988 Malachites	Closed		27.50	40
1988 White Peacocks	Closed		27.50	40
1989 Eastern Tailed Blues	Closed		27.50	50
1989 Zebra Swallowtails	Closed		29.50	55
1989 Red Admirals	Closed		29.50	55

On the Wing - T. Humphrey
1992 Winged Splendor	Closed		29.50	30
1992 Rising Mallard	Closed		29.50	40
1992 Glorious Ascent	Closed		32.50	50
1992 Taking Wing	Closed		32.50	45
1992 Upward Bound	Closed		32.50	50
1993 Wondrous Motion	Closed		34.50	50
1993 Springing Forth	Closed		34.50	50
1993 On The Wing	Closed		34.50	50

On Wings of Snow - L. Liu
1991 The Swans	Closed		34.50	35
1991 The Doves	Closed		34.50	45
1991 The Peacocks	Closed		37.50	50
1991 The Egrets	Closed		37.50	50
1991 The Cockatoos	Closed		37.50	50
1992 The Herons	Closed		37.50	40

Our Woodland Friends - C. Brenders
1989 Fascination	Closed		29.00	29
1990 Beneath the Pines	Closed		29.50	32
1990 High Adventure	Closed		32.50	33
1990 Shy Explorers	Closed		32.50	35
1991 Golden Season:Gray Squirrel	Closed		32.50	35
1991 Full House Fox Family	Closed		32.50	45
1991 A Jump Into Life: Spring Fawn	Closed		34.50	35
1991 Forest Sentinel:Bobcat	Closed		34.50	35

Paw Prints: Baby Cats of the Wild - C. Fracé
1992 Morning Mischief	Closed		29.50	45
1993 Togetherness	Closed		29.50	50

| 1993 The Buddy System | Closed | | 32.50 | 33 |
| 1993 Nap Time | Closed | | 32.50 | 33 |

Petal Pals - L. Chang
1992 Garden Discovery	Closed		24.50	40
1992 Flowering Fascination	Closed		24.50	25
1993 Alluring Lilies	150-day		24.50	25
1993 Springtime Oasis	150-day		24.50	25
1993 Blossoming Adventure	150-day		24.50	25
1993 Dancing Daffodils	150-day		24.50	25
1993 Summer Surprise	150-day		24.50	25
1993 Morning Melody	150-day		24.50	25

Poetic Cottages - C. Valente
1992 Garden Paths of Oxfordshire	Closed		29.50	50
1992 Twilight at Woodgreen Pond	Closed		29.50	70
1992 Stonewall Brook Blossoms	Closed		32.50	45
1992 Bedfordshire Evening Sky	Closed		32.50	50
1993 Wisteria Summer	Closed		32.50	60
1993 Wiltshire Rose Arbor	Closed		32.50	50
1993 Alderbury Gardens	Closed		32.50	33
1993 Hampshire Spring Splendor	Closed		32.50	33

Portraits of Christ - J. Salamanca
1991 Father, Forgive Them	Closed		29.50	70
1991 Thy Will Be Done	Closed		29.50	50
1991 This is My Beloved Son	Closed		32.50	45
1991 Lo, I Am With You	Closed		32.50	50
1991 Become as Little Children	Closed		32.50	55
1992 Peace I Leave With You	Closed		34.50	50
1992 For God So Loved the World	Closed		34.50	50
1992 I Am the Way, the Truth and the Life	Closed		34.50	50
1992 Weep Not For Me	Closed		34.50	60
1992 Follow Me	Closed		34.50	55

Portraits of Exquisite Birds - C. Brenders
1990 Backyard Treasure/Chickadee	Closed		29.50	30
1990 The Beautiful Bluebird	Closed		29.50	30
1991 Summer Gold: The Robin	Closed		32.50	33
1991 The Meadowlark's Song	Closed		32.50	33
1991 Ivory-Billed Woodpecker	Closed		32.50	33
1991 Red-Winged Blackbird	Closed		32.50	33

Purebred Horses of the Americas - D. Schwartz
1989 The Appaloosa	Closed		34.50	35
1989 The Tenessee Walker	Closed		34.50	35
1990 The Quarterhorse	Closed		37.50	38
1990 The Saddlebred	Closed		37.50	45
1990 The Mustang	Closed		37.50	39
1990 The Morgan	Closed		37.50	65

Rare Encounters - J. Seerey-Lester
1993 Softly, Softly	Closed		29.50	45
1993 Black Magic	Closed		29.50	55
1993 Future Song	Closed		32.50	65
1993 High and Mighty	Closed		32.50	55
1993 Last Sanctuary	Closed		32.50	50
1993 Something Stirred	Closed		34.50	35

Romantic Gardens - C. Smith
1989 The Woodland Garden	Closed		29.50	30
1989 The Plantation Garden	Closed		29.50	30
1990 The Cottage Garden	Closed		32.50	33
1990 The Colonial Garden	Closed		32.50	33

Romantic Harbors - C. Vickery
1993 Advent of the Golden Bough	Closed		34.50	40
1993 Christmas Tree Schooner	Closed		34.50	55
1993 Prelude to the Journey	Closed		37.50	55
1993 Shimmering Light of Dusk	Closed		37.50	100

Romantic Roses - V. Morley
1993 Victorian Beauty	Closed		29.50	30
1993 Old-Fashioned Grace	95-day		29.50	30
1993 Country Charm	95-day		32.50	33
1993 Summer Romance	95-day		32.50	33
1993 Pastoral Delight	95-day		32.50	33
1993 Springtime Elegance	95-day		34.50	35
1993 Vintage Splendor	95-day		34.50	35
1994 Heavenly Perfection	95-day		34.50	35

Scenes of Christmas Past - L. Garrison
1987 Holiday Skaters	Closed		27.50	40
1988 Christmas Eve	Closed		27.50	35
1989 The Homecoming	Closed		30.50	31
1990 The Toy Store	Closed		30.50	40
1991 The Carollers	Closed		30.50	40
1992 Family Traditions	Closed		32.50	50
1993 Holiday Past	Closed		32.50	65
1994 A Gathering of Faith	Closed		32.50	85

The Secret World Of The Panda - J. Bridgett
1990 A Mother's Care	Closed		27.50	30
1991 A Frolic in the Snow	Closed		27.50	28
1991 Lazy Afternoon	Closed		30.50	31
1991 A Day of Exploring	Closed		30.50	31
1991 A Gentle Hug	Closed		32.50	35
1991 A Bamboo Feast	Closed		32.50	70

Soaring Majesty - C. Fracé
1991 Freedom	Closed		29.50	35
1991 The Northern Goshhawk	Closed		29.50	40
1991 Peregrine Falcon	Closed		32.50	33
1991 Red-Tailed Hawk	Closed		32.50	33
1991 The Osprey	Closed		32.50	35
1991 The Gyrfalcon	Closed		34.50	40
1991 The Golden Eagle	Closed		34.50	40
1992 Red-Shouldered Hawk	Closed		34.50	35

Sonnets in Flowers - G. Kurz
1992 Sonnet of Beauty	Closed		29.50	40
1992 Sonnet of Happiness	Closed		34.50	40
1992 Sonnet of Love	Closed		34.50	35
1992 Sonnet of Peace	Closed		34.50	55

The Sound of Music: Silver Anniversary - V. Gadino
1991 The Hills are Alive	Closed		29.50	35
1992 Let's Start at the Very Beginning	Closed		29.50	35
1992 Something Good	Closed		32.50	45
1992 Maria's Wedding Day	Closed		32.50	50

Spirit of Christmas - J. Sias
1990 Silent Night	Closed		29.50	37
1991 Jingle Bells	Closed		29.50	30
1991 Deck The Halls	Closed		32.50	35
1991 I'll Be Home For Christmas	Closed		32.50	45
1991 Winter Wonderland	Closed		32.50	35
1991 O Christmas Tree	Closed		32.50	33

Spirits of the Sky - C. Fisher
1992 Twilight Glow	Closed		29.50	40
1992 First Light	Closed		29.50	60
1992 Evening Glimmer	Closed		32.50	75
1992 Golden Dusk	Closed		32.50	40
1993 Sunset Splendor	Closed		32.50	33
1993 Amber Flight	Closed		34.50	42
1993 Winged Radiance	Closed		34.50	48
1993 Day's End	Closed		34.50	35

A Splash of Cats - J. Seerey-Lester
1992 Moonlight Chase: Cougar	Closed		29.50	30

Symphony of Shimmering Beauties - L. Liu
1991 Iris Quartet	Closed		29.50	50
1991 Tulip Ensemble	Closed		29.50	35
1991 Poppy Pastorale	Closed		32.50	40
1991 Lily Concerto	Closed		32.50	40
1991 Peony Prelude	Closed		32.50	40
1991 Rose Fantasy	Closed		34.50	50
1991 Hibiscus Medley	Closed		34.50	40
1992 Dahlia Melody	Closed		34.50	50
1992 Hollyhock March	Closed		34.50	35
1992 Carnation Serenade	Closed		36.50	40
1992 Gladiolus Romance	Closed		36.50	60
1992 Zinnia Finale	Closed		36.50	50

Tis the Season - J. Sias
1993 World Dressed in Snow	Closed		29.50	35
1993 A Time for Tradition	Closed		29.50	40
1993 We Shall Come Rejoining	Closed		29.50	35
1993 Our Family Tree	Closed		29.50	30

Tomorrow's Promise - W. Nelson
1992 Curiosity: Asian Elephants	Closed		29.50	40
1992 Playtime Pandas	Closed		29.50	40
1992 Innocence: Rhinos	Closed		32.50	60
1992 Friskiness: Kit Foxes	Closed		32.50	45

Touching the Spirit - J. Kramer Cole
1993 Running With the Wind	Closed		29.50	50
1993 Kindred Spirits	Closed		29.50	50
1993 The Marking Tree	Closed		29.50	50
1993 Wakan Tanka	Closed		29.50	70
1993 He Who Watches	Closed		29.50	60
1994 Twice Traveled Trail	Closed		29.50	30
1994 Keeper of the Secret	95-day		29.50	30
1994 Camp of the Sacred Dogs	95-day		29.50	30

A Treasury of Songbirds - R. Stine
1992 Springtime Splendor	Closed		29.50	45
1992 Morning's Glory	Closed		29.50	45
1992 Golden Daybreak	Closed		32.50	45
1992 Afternoon Calm	Closed		32.50	40
1992 Dawn's Radiance	Closed		32.50	55
1993 Scarlet Sunrise	Closed		34.50	75
1993 Sapphire Dawn	Closed		34.50	45
1995 Alluring Daylight	Closed		34.50	35

The Vanishing Gentle Giants - A. Casay
1991 Jumping For Joy	Closed		32.50	35
1991 Song of the Humpback	Closed		32.50	35
1991 Monarch of the Deep	Closed		35.50	40
1991 Travelers of the Sea	Closed		35.50	60
1991 White Whale of the North	Closed		35.50	50
1991 Unicorn of the Sea	Closed		35.50	50

The Victorian Cat - H. Bonner
1990 Mischief With The Hatbox	Closed		24.50	40
1991 String Quartet	Closed		24.50	50

*Quotes have been rounded up to nearest dollar

YEAR ISSUE		EDITION LIMIT RETD.	ISSUE PRICE	*QUOTE U.S.$
1991	Daydreams	Closed	27.50	35
1991	Frisky Felines	Closed	27.50	43
1991	Kittens at Play	Closed	27.50	45
1991	Playing in the Parlor	Closed	29.50	60
1991	Perfectly Poised	Closed	29.50	55
1992	Midday Repose	Closed	29.50	55

Victorian Cat Capers - Various
1992	Who's the Fairest of Them All? - F. Paton	Closed	24.50	50-60
1992	Puss in Boots - Unknown	Closed	24.50	50
1992	My Bowl is Empty - W. Hepple	Closed	27.50	35
1992	A Curious Kitty - W. Hepple	Closed	27.50	30
1992	Vanity Fair - W. Hepple	Closed	27.50	28
1992	Forbidden Fruit - W. Hepple	Closed	29.50	70
1993	The Purr-fect Pen Pal - W. Hepple	Closed	29.50	45
1993	The Kitten Express - W. Hepple	Closed	29.50	95

Wild Innocents - C. Fracé
1993	Reflections	95-day	29.50	40
1993	Spiritual Heir	95-day	29.50	50
1993	Lion Cub	95-day	29.50	50
1993	Sunny Spot	95-day	29.50	55

Wild Spirits - T. Hirata
1992	Solitary Watch	Closed	29.50	35
1992	Timber Ghost	Closed	29.50	70
1992	Mountain Magic	Closed	32.50	33
1993	Silent Guard	Closed	32.50	50
1993	Sly Eyes	Closed	32.50	50
1993	Mighty Presence	Closed	34.50	40
1993	Quiet Vigil	Closed	34.50	35
1993	Lone Vanguard	150-day	34.50	35

Wings of Winter - D. Rust
1992	Moonlight Retreat	Closed	29.50	38
1993	Twilight Serenade	Closed	29.50	30
1993	Silent Sunset	150-day	29.50	30
1993	Night Lights	150-day	29.50	30
1993	Winter Haven	150-day	29.50	30
1993	Full Moon Companions	150-day	29.50	30
1993	White Night	150-day	29.50	30
1993	Winter Reflections	150-day	29.50	30

Winter's Majesty - C. Fracé
1992	The Quest	Closed	34.50	40
1992	The Chase	Closed	34.50	40
1993	Alaskan Friend	Closed	34.50	45
1993	American Cougar	Closed	34.50	35
1993	On Watch	Closed	34.50	45
1993	Solitude	Closed	34.50	35

Wonders Of The Sea - R. Harm
1991	Stand By Me	Closed	34.50	35
1991	Heart to Heart	Closed	34.50	35
1991	Warm Embrace	Closed	34.50	40
1991	A Family Affair	Closed	34.50	35

The World's Most Magnificent Cats - C. Fracé
1991	Fleeting Encounter	Closed	24.50	40-50
1991	Cougar	Closed	24.50	45-60
1991	Royal Bengal	Closed	27.50	40-50
1991	Powerful Presence	Closed	27.50	45-60
1991	Jaguar	Closed	27.50	40-60
1991	The Clouded Leopard	Closed	29.50	45-60
1991	The African Leopard	Closed	29.50	45-60
1991	Mighty Warrior	Closed	29.50	60
1992	The Cheetah	Closed	31.50	40-60
1992	Siberian Tiger	Closed	31.50	50-80

Waterford Wedgwood USA

Bicentennial - Unknown
1972	Boston Tea Party	Annual	40.00	40
1973	Paul Revere's Ride	Annual	40.00	115
1974	Battle of Concord	Annual	40.00	55
1975	Across the Delaware	Annual	40.00	105
1975	Victory at Yorktown	Annual	45.00	53
1976	Declaration Signed	Annual	45.00	45

Wedgwood Christmas - Various
1969	Windsor Castle - T. Harper	Annual	25.00	200
1970	Trafalgar Square - T. Harper	Annual	30.00	45
1971	Picadilly Circus - T. Harper	Annual	30.00	35
1972	St. Paul's Cathedral - T. Harper	Annual	35.00	45
1973	Tower of London - T. Harper	Annual	40.00	90
1974	Houses of Parliament - T. Harper	Annual	40.00	44
1975	Tower Bridge - T. Harper	Annual	45.00	50
1976	Hampton Court - T. Harper	Annual	50.00	50
1977	Westminister Abbey - T. Harper	Annual	55.00	60
1978	Horse Guards - T. Harper	Annual	60.00	60
1979	Buckingham Palace - Unknown	Annual	65.00	65
1980	St. James Palace - Unknown	Annual	70.00	70
1981	Marble Arch - Unknown	Annual	75.00	75
1982	Lambeth Palace - Unknown	Annual	80.00	90
1983	All Souls, Langham Palace - Unknown	Annual	80.00	80
1984	Constitution Hill - Unknown	Annual	80.00	80
1985	The Tate Gallery - Unknown	Annual	80.00	100-150
1986	The Albert Memorial - Unknown	Annual	80.00	150

YEAR ISSUE		EDITION LIMIT RETD.	ISSUE PRICE	*QUOTE U.S.$
1987	Guildhall - Unknown	Annual	80.00	85
1988	The Observatory/Greenwich - Unknown	Annual	80.00	90
1989	Winchester Cathedral - Unknown	Annual	88.00	88

STEINS

Ace Product Management Group, Inc.

Harley-Davidson Decade Series - Ace
1993	Birth Of A Legend-1900's 99282-94Z	3,000 1995	180.00	180
1993	Birth Of A Legend-1900's (Signaure) 99712-94Z	500 1995	275.00	275
1994	Growth Of A Sport-1910's 99283-95Z	3,000 1995	180.00	180
1994	Growth Of A Sport-1910's (Signature) 99285-95Z	500 1995	285.00	285
1995	Roaring Into The 20's-1920's 99295-96Z	3,000	185.00	185
1995	Roaring Into The 20's-1920's (Signature) 99291-96Z	500	285.00	285
1996	Growing Stronger With Time-1930's 99170-97Z	3,000	185.00	185
1996	Growing Stronger With Time-1930's (Signature) 99171-97Z	500	285.00	285
1993	8 Ltr Stein 99716-94Z	100 1993	875.00	875

Holiday Memories Holiday Steins - Ace
1994	Under The Mistletoe 99467-95Z	5,000 1994	85.00	85
1995	Late Arrival 99498-96Z	5,000 1995	90.00	90
1996	After The Pageant 99495-97Z	5,000	95.00	95

Anheuser-Busch, Inc.

Anheuser-Busch Collectors Club - Various
1995	Budweiser Clydesdales at the Bauernhof - A. Leon	Yr.Iss. 1996	Gift	35-60
1995	The Brew House Clock Tower - D. Thompson	Retrd. 1996	150.00	150-200
1996	The World's Largest Brewer - A. Leon	Yr.Iss.	Gift	35-50
1996	King - A Regal Spirit - D. Thompson	4/97	100.00	100

A & Eagle Historical Trademark Series-Giftware Edition - Various
1992	A & Eagle Trademark I (1872) CS201, tin	Retrd. N/A	31.00	50-100
1993	A & Eagle Trademark I (1872) CS191, boxed	Retrd. N/A	22.00	30-40
1993	A & Eagle Trademark II (1890s) CS218, tin	Retrd. N/A	24.00	40-50
1994	A & Eagle Trademark II (1890s) CS219, boxed	Retrd. N/A	24.00	30-40
1994	A & Eagle Trademark III (1900s) CS238, tin	20,000 1994	28.00	35-50
1995	A & Eagle Trademark III (1900s) CS240, boxed	30,000 1995	25.00	25-30
1995	A & Eagle Trademark IV (1930s) CS255, tin	20,000 1996	30.00	30
1996	A & Eagle Trademark IV (1930s) CS271, boxed	30,000	27.00	27

Anheuser-Busch Founder Series-Premier Collection - A-Busch, Inc.
1993	Adophus Busch CS216	10,000	180.00	180
1994	August A. Busch, Sr. CS229	10,000 1996	220.00	165-220
1995	Adolphus Busch III CS265	10,000	220.00	220
1996	August A. Busch, Jr. CS286	10,000	220.00	220

Archives Series-Collector Edition - Various
1992	1893 Columbian Exposition CS169 - D. Langeneckert	75,000 1995	35.00	35-45
1993	Ganymede CS190 - D. Langeneckert	Retrd. 1995	35.00	60-75
1994	Budweiser's Greatest Triumph CS222 - D. Langeneckert	75,000 1996	35.00	35-60
1994	Mirror of Truth Stein CS252 - D. Langeneckert	75,000	35.00	35

Birds of Prey Series-Premier Edition - P. Ford
1991	American Bald Eagle CS164	25,000 1995	125.00	115-155
1992	Peregrine Falcon CS183	25,000	125.00	125
1994	Osprey CS212	Retrd. 1994	135.00	350-550
1995	Great Horned Owl CS264	25,000	135.00	137

Bud Label Series-Giftware Edition - A-Busch, Inc.
1989	Budweiser Label CS101	Retrd. 1995	14.00	15-25
1990	Antique Label II CS127	Retrd. N/A	14.00	15-25
1991	Bottled Beer III CS136	Retrd. 1995	15.00	15-22
1995	Budweiser Label Stein CS282	Open	19.50	20

Budweiser Military Series-Giftware Edition - M. Watts
1994	Army CS224	Retrd. 1995	19.00	30-40
1994	Air Force CS228	Open	19.00	19
1995	Budweiser Salutes the Navy CS243	Open	19.50	20
1995	Marines stein CS256	Open	22.00	22

Budweiser Racing Series - H. Droog
1993	Budweiser Racing Team CS194	Retrd. 1995	19.00	20
1993	Bill Elliott CS196	25,000 1995	150.00	95-150
1993	Bill Elliott, Signature Edition, CS196SE	1,500 1995	295.00	200-295

YEAR ISSUE		EDITION LIMIT RETD.	ISSUE PRICE	*QUOTE U.S.$

Civil War Series-Premier Edition - D. Langeneckert
1992	General Grant CS181	25,000 1995	150.00	130-150
1993	General Robert E. Lee CS188	25,000 1995	150.00	130-150
1993	President Abraham Lincoln CS189	25,000 1995	150.00	130-150

Classic Series - A-Busch, Inc.
1988	1st Edition CS93	Retrd. N/A	34.95	145-175
1989	2nd Edition CS104	Retrd. N/A	54.95	95-110
1990	3rd Edition CS113	Retrd. N/A	65.00	50-95
1991	4th Edition CS130	Retrd. N/A	75.00	40-85

Clydesdales Holiday Series - Various
1980	1st-Budweiser Champion Clydesdales CS19 - A-Busch, Inc.	Retrd. N/A	9.95	105-125
1981	1st-Budweiser Champion Clydesdales CS19A - A-Busch, Inc.	Retrd. N/A	N/A	150-250
1981	2nd-Snowy Woodland CS50 - A-Busch, Inc.	Retrd. N/A	9.95	200-275
1982	3rd-50th Anniversary CS57 - A-Busch, Inc.	Retrd. N/A	9.95	75-95
1983	4th-Cameo Wheatland CS58 - A-Busch, Inc.	Retrd. N/A	9.95	30
1984	5th-Covered Bridge CS62 - A-Busch, Inc.	Retrd. N/A	9.95	15
1985	6th-Snow Capped Mountains CS63 - A-Busch, Inc.	Retrd. N/A	9.95	15-20
1986	7th-Traditional Horses CS66 - A-Busch, Inc.	Retrd. N/A	9.95	30-40
1987	8th-Grant's Farm Gates CS70 - A-Busch, Inc.	Retrd. N/A	9.95	15-25
1988	9th-Cobblestone Passage CS88 - A-Busch, Inc.	Retrd. N/A	9.95	15-20
1989	10th-Winter Evening CS89 - A-Busch, Inc.	Retrd. N/A	12.95	15-20
1990	11th-An American Tradition, CS112, 1990 - S. Sampson	Retrd. N/A	13.50	20
1990	11th-An American Tradition, CS112-SE, 1990 - S. Sampson	Retrd. N/A	50.00	50-75
1991	12th-The Season's Best, CS133, 1991 - S. Sampson	Retrd. N/A	14.50	20
1991	12th-The Season's Best, CS133-SE Signature Edition, 1991 - S. Sampson	Retrd. N/A	50.00	40-45
1992	13th-The Perfect Christmas, CS167, 1992 - S. Sampson	Retrd. N/A	14.50	20
1992	13th-The Perfect Christmas, CS167-SE Signature Edition, 1992 - S. Sampson	Open	50.00	50
1993	14th-Special Delivery, CS192, 1993 - N. Koerber	Retrd. N/A	15.00	20
1993	14th-Special Delivery, CS192-SE Signature Edition, 1993 - N. Koerber	Retrd. N/A	60.00	95-125
1994	15th-Hometown Holiday, CS211, 1994 - B. Kemper	Retrd. 1994	14.00	15-20
1994	15th-Hometown Holiday, CS211-SE Signature Edition, 1994 - B. Kemper	Retrd. 1994	65.00	85-125
1995	16th-Lighting the Way Home, CS263 - T. Jester	Open	17.00	17
1995	16th-Lighting the Way Home, CS263-SE Signature Edition - T. Jester	10,000 1995	75.00	75-110
1996	17th-Budweiser Clydesdales, CS273 - J. Raedeke	Open	17.00	17
1996	17th-Budweiser Clydesdales, CS273-SE Signature Edition - J. Raedeke	10,000	75.00	75

Clydesdales Series-Giftware Edition - A-Busch, Inc.
1987	World Famous Clydesdales CS74	Retrd. N/A	9.95	20-25
1988	Mare & Foal CS90	Retrd. N/A	11.50	20-40
1989	Parade Dress CS99	Retrd. N/A	11.50	50-115
1991	Training Hitch CS131	Retrd. N/A	13.00	20-25
1992	Clydesdales on Parade CS161	Retrd. N/A	16.00	20-25
1994	Proud and Free CS223	Open	17.00	17
1996	Budweiser Clydesdale Hitch CS292	Open	22.50	23

Collector Edition - J. Tull
1994	Budweiser World Cup Stein CS230	25,000 1994	40.00	40-60

Discover America Series-Collector Edition - A-Busch, Inc.
1990	Nina CS107	100,000 1995	40.00	35-50
1991	Pinta CS129	100,000 1995	40.00	35-50
1992	Santa Maria CS138	100,000 1995	40.00	35-50

Endangered Species Series-Collector Edition - B. Kemper
1989	Bald Eagle CS106 (First)	Retrd. N/A	24.95	400-500
1990	Asian Tiger CS126 (Second)	Retrd. N/A	27.50	75-95
1991	African Elephant CS135 (Third)	100,000 1996	29.00	30-35
1992	Giant Panda CS173 (Fourth)	100,000 1995	29.00	30-35
1993	Grizzly CS199 (Fifth)	100,000	29.50	30
1994	Gray Wolf Stein CS226 (Sixth)	100,000	29.50	30
1995	Cougar Stein CS253 (Seventh)	100,000	32.00	32
1996	Gorilla Stein CS283 (Eighth)	100,000	32.00	32

Giftware Edition - A-Busch, Inc.
1992	1992 Rodeo CS184	Retrd. N/A	18.00	20
1993	Bud Man Character Stein CS213	Retrd. 1996	45.00	45
1994	"Forel" Budweiser Golf Bag Stein CS225	Retrd. 1995	16.00	16
1994	"Walking Tall" Budweiser Cowboy Boot Stein CS251	Open	17.50	18
1995	"Play Ball" Baseball Mitt stein CS244	Open	18.00	18
1995	Billiards stein CS278	Open	24.00	24

YEAR ISSUE	EDITION LIMIT	YEAR RETD.	ISSUE PRICE	*QUOTE U.S.$
1996 BUD-WEIS-ER Frog stein CS289	Open		27.95	28
1996 "STRIKE" Bowling stein CS288	Open		24.50	25

Historical Landmark Series - A-Busch, Inc.
1986 Brew House CS67 (First)	Retrd.	N/A	19.95	25-40
1987 Stables CS73 (Second)	Retrd.	N/A	19.95	25-40
1988 Grant Cabin CS83 (Third)	Retrd.	N/A	19.95	55-90
1988 Old School House CS84 (Fourth)	Retrd.	N/A	19.95	25

Horseshoe Series - A-Busch, Inc.
1986 Horseshoe CS68	Retrd.	N/A	14.95	35-45
1987 Horsehead CS76	Retrd.	N/A	16.00	35-40
1987 Horseshoe CS77	Retrd.	N/A	16.00	35-75
1987 Horsehead CS78	Retrd.	N/A	14.95	40-70
1988 Harness CS94	Retrd.	N/A	16.00	65-75

Hunter's Companion Series-Collector Edition - Various
1993 Labrador Retriever CS195 - L. Freeman	50,000	1996	32.50	35-45
1994 The Setter Stein CS205 - S. Ryan	50,000		32.50	33
1995 The Golden Retreiver Stein CS248 - S. Ryan	50,000		34.00	34
1996 Beagle Stein CS272 - S. Ryan	50,000		35.00	35

Limited Edition Series - A-Busch, Inc.
1985 Ltd. Ed. I Brewing & Fermenting CS64	Retrd.	N/A	29.95	175-200
1986 Ltd. Ed. II Aging & Cooperage CS65	Retrd.	N/A	29.95	45-95
1987 Ltd. Ed. III Transportation CS71	Retrd.	N/A	29.95	35-70
1988 Ltd. Ed. IV Taverns & Public Houses CS75	Retrd.	N/A	29.95	35-50
1989 Ltd. Ed.V Festival Scene CS98	Retrd.	N/A	34.95	30-50

Logo Series Steins-Giftware Edition - A-Busch, Inc.
1990 Budweiser CS143	Retrd.	N/A	16.00	16
1990 Bud Light CS144	Retrd.	N/A	16.00	16
1990 Michelob CS145	Retrd.	N/A	16.00	16
1990 Michelob Dry CS146	Retrd.	N/A	16.00	16
1990 Busch CS147	Retrd.	N/A	16.00	16
1990 A&Eagle CS148	Retrd.	N/A	16.00	16
1990 Bud Dry CS156	Open		16.00	16

Marine Conservation Series-Collector Edition - B. Kemper
1994 Manatee Stein CS203	25,000		33.50	30-40
1995 Great White Shark Stein CS247	25,000		39.50	30-40
1996 Dolphin Stein CS284	25,000		39.50	30-40

Octoberfest Series-Giftware Edition - A-Busch, Inc.
1991 1991 Octoberfest N3286	25,000	N/A	19.00	25-35
1992 1992 Octoberfest CS185	35,000		16.00	16
1993 1993 Octoberfest CS202	35,000	N/A	18.00	18

Olympic Centennial Collection - A-Busch, Inc.
1995 1996 U.S. Olympic Team "Gymnastics" Stein CS262	10,000		85.00	85
1995 1996 U.S. Olympic Team "Track & Field" Stein CS246	10,000		85.00	85
1995 Centennial Olympic Games Giftware Stein CS266	Open		25.00	25
1995 Centennial Olympic Games Premier Edition 22" CS267	1,996	1996	500.00	N/A
1995 Collector's Edition Official Centennial Olympics Games Stein CS259	Retrd.	1996	50.00	50-60

Olympic Team Series 1992-Collector Edition - A-Busch, Inc.
1991 1992 Winter Olympic Stein CS162	25,000	N/A	85.00	45-85
1992 1992 Summer Olympic Stein CS163	Retrd.	1994	85.00	45-85
1992 1992 U.S.Olympic Stein CS168	50,000	N/A	16.00	16

Porcelain Heritage Series-Premier Edition - Various
1990 Berninghaus CS105 - Berninghaus	Retrd.	1994	75.00	65-85
1991 After The Hunt CS155 - A-Busch, Inc.	Retrd.	1994	100.00	75-100
1992 Cherub CS182 - D. Langeneckert	25,000	1996	100.00	75-100

Post Convention Series - A-Busch, Inc.
1982 1st Post Convention Olympic CS53	23,000	1982	N/A	175-300
1982 2nd Post Convention Olympic CS54	23,000	1982	N/A	175-195
1982 3rd Post Convention Olympic CS55	23,000	1982	N/A	200-250
1988 1st Post Convention Heritage CS87	25,000	1988	N/A	115-125
1988 2nd Post Convention Heritage CS102	25,000	1988	N/A	75-95
1989 3rd Post Convention Heritage CS114	25,000	1989	N/A	50-65
1990 4th Post Convention Heritage CS141	25,000	1990	N/A	40-50
1991 5th/Final Post Convention CS174	25,000	1991	N/A	20-50
1992 1st Advertising Through the Decades 1879-1912 N3989	29,000	1992	N/A	75
1993 2nd Advertising Through the Decades 1905-1914 N3990	31,106	1993	N/A	65-75
1994 3rd Advertising Through the Decades 1911-1915 SO85203	31,000	1994	N/A	65
1995 4th Advertising Through the Decades 1918-1922 SO95150	31,000	1995	N/A	55-70

YEAR ISSUE	EDITION LIMIT	YEAR RETD.	ISSUE PRICE	*QUOTE U.S.$
1996 5th Advertising Through the Decades 1933-1938 SO95248	31,000	1996	N/A	70

Sea World Series-Collector Edition - A-Busch, Inc.
1992 Killer Whale CS186	25,000	1996	100.00	60-90
1992 Dolphin CS187	22,500	1996	90.00	60-80

Specialty Steins - A-Busch, Inc.
1975 Bud Man CS1	Retrd.	N/A	N/A	350-465
1976 A&Eagle CS2	Retrd.	N/A	N/A	145-250
1976 A&Eagle Lidded CSL2 (Reference CS28)	Retrd.	N/A	N/A	200-350
1976 Katakombe CS3	Retrd.	N/A	N/A	250-300
1976 Katakombe Lidded CSL3	Retrd.	N/A	N/A	275-400
1976 German Tavern Scene Lidded CS4	Retrd.	N/A	N/A	50-100
1975 Senior Grande Lidded CSL4	Retrd.	N/A	N/A	650-750
1975 German Pilique CS5	Retrd.	N/A	N/A	350-450
1976 German Pilique Lidded CSL5	Retrd.	N/A	N/A	450-500
1976 Senior Grande CS6	Retrd.	N/A	N/A	500-650
1975 German Tavern Scene CSL6	Retrd.	N/A	N/A	200-275
1975 Miniature Bavarian CS7	Retrd.	N/A	N/A	225-275
1976 Budweiser Centennial Lidded CSL7	Retrd.	N/A	N/A	375-475
1976 U.S. Bicentennial Lidded CSL8	Retrd.	N/A	N/A	375-475
1976 Natural Light CS9	Retrd.	N/A	N/A	175-225
1976 Clydesdales Hofbrau Lidded CSL9	Retrd.	N/A	N/A	200-325
1976 Blue Delft CS11	Retrd.	N/A	N/A	2100
1976 Clydesdales CS12	Retrd.	N/A	N/A	250
1976 Budweiser Centennial CS13	Retrd.	N/A	N/A	300-450
1976 U.S. Bicentennial CS14	Retrd.	N/A	N/A	295-450
1976 Clydesdales Grants Farm CS15	Retrd.	N/A	N/A	150-275
1976 German Cities (6 assorted) CS16	Retrd.	N/A	N/A	1800-1900
1976 Americana CS17	Retrd.	N/A	N/A	300-400
1976 Budweiser Label CS18	Retrd.	N/A	N/A	300-450
1980 Budweiser Ladies (4 assorted) CS20	Retrd.	N/A	N/A	1500-2000
1977 Budweiser Girl CS21	Retrd.	N/A	N/A	375-425
1976 Budweiser Centennial CS22	Retrd.	N/A	N/A	325-425
1977 A&Eagle CS24	Retrd.	N/A	N/A	325-375
1976 A&Eagle Barrel CS26	Retrd.	N/A	N/A	100-175
1976 Michelob CS27	Retrd.	N/A	N/A	150-175
1976 A&Eagle Lidded CS28 (Reference CSL2)	Retrd.	N/A	N/A	200-350
1976 Clydesdales Lidded CS29	Retrd.	N/A	N/A	250
1976 Coracao Decanter Set (7 piece) CS31	Retrd.	N/A	N/A	500-600
1976 German Wine Set (7 piece) CS32	Retrd.	N/A	N/A	450-500
1976 Clydesdales Decanter CS33	Retrd.	N/A	N/A	1100-1200
1976 Holanda Brown Decanter Set (7 piece) CS34	Retrd.	N/A	N/A	350
1976 Holanda Blue Decanter Set (7 piece) CS35	Retrd.	N/A	N/A	450-500
1976 Canteen Decanter Set (7 piece) CS36	Retrd.	N/A	N/A	N/A
1976 St. Louis Decanter CS37	Retrd.	N/A	N/A	400
1976 St. Louis Decanter Set (7 piece) CS38	Retrd.	N/A	N/A	1100
1980 Wurzburger Hofbrau CS39	Retrd.	N/A	N/A	250-350
1980 Budweiser Chicago Skyline CS40	Retrd.	N/A	N/A	100-150
1978 Busch Gardens CS41	Retrd.	N/A	N/A	225-350
1980 Oktoberfest— "The Old Country" CS42	Retrd.	N/A	N/A	225-350
1980 Natural Light Label CS43	Retrd.	N/A	N/A	175-300
1980 Busch Label CS44	Retrd.	N/A	N/A	175-300
1980 Michelob Label CS45	Retrd.	N/A	N/A	75-125
1980 Budweiser Label CS46	Retrd.	N/A	N/A	75-125
1981 Budweiser Chicagoland CS51	Retrd.	N/A	N/A	40-50
1981 Budweiser Texas CS52	Retrd.	N/A	N/A	55
1981 Budweiser California CS56	Retrd.	N/A	N/A	55
1983 Budweiser San Francisco CS59	Retrd.	N/A	N/A	175
1984 Budweiser 1984 Summer Olympic Games CS60	Retrd.	N/A	N/A	15
1983 Bud Light Baron CS61	Retrd.	N/A	N/A	35-45
1987 Santa Claus CS79	Retrd.	N/A	N/A	75-85
1987 King Cobra CS80	Retrd.	N/A	N/A	225
1987 Winter Olympic Games, Lidded CS81	Retrd.	N/A	49.95	65-75
1988 Budweiser Winter Olympic Games CS85	Retrd.	N/A	24.95	20
1988 Summer Olympic Games, Lidded CS91	Retrd.	N/A	54.95	30-60
1988 Budweiser Summer Olympic Games CS92	Retrd.	N/A	54.95	20
1988 Budweiser/ Field&Stream Set (4 piece) CS95	Retrd.	N/A	69.95	225-325
1989 Bud Man CS100	Retrd.	N/A	29.95	45
1990 Baseball Cardinal Stein CS125	Retrd.	N/A	30.00	30
1991 Bevo Fox Stein CS160	Retrd.	1994	250.00	200-250
1992 Budweiser Racing -Elliot/Johnson N3553 - M. Watts	Retrd.	1995	19.00	25-40

Sports History Series-Giftware Edition - A-Busch, Inc.
1990 Baseball, America's Favorite Pastime CS124	Retrd.	N/A	20.00	25-35
1990 Football, Gridiron Legacy CS128	Retrd.	N/A	20.00	25
1991 Auto Racing, Chasing The Checkered Flag CS132	100,000	1995	22.00	22
1991 Basketball, Heroes of the Hardwood CS134	100,000		22.00	22
1992 Golf, Par For The Course CS165	100,000	1995	22.00	22
1993 Hockey, Center Ice CS209	100,000		22.00	22

YEAR ISSUE	EDITION LIMIT	YEAR RETD.	ISSUE PRICE	*QUOTE U.S.$

Sports Legend Series-Collector Edition - Various
1991 Babe Ruth CS142 - A-Busch	50,000	1995	85.00	75-85
1992 Jim Thorpe CS171 - M. Caito	50,000	1995	85.00	75-85
1993 Joe Louis CS206 - M. Caito	50,000	1994	85.00	75-125

St. Patrick's Day Series-Giftware Edition - A-Busch, Inc.
1991 1991 St. Patrick's Day CS109	Retrd.	N/A	15.00	45-55
1992 1992 St. Patrick's Day CS166	100,000	N/A	15.00	15
1993 1993 St. Patrick's Day CS193	Retrd.	N/A	15.30	25
1994 Luck O' The Irish CS210	Retrd.	1995	18.00	20
1995 1995 St. Patrick's Day Stein CS242	Retrd.	1995	19.00	19
1996 "Horseshoe" 1996 St. Patrick's Day Stein CS269	Open		19.50	20

Anheuser-Busch, Inc./Gerz Meisterwerke

American Heritage Collection - Gerz
1993 John F. Kennedy Stein GM4	10,000		220.00	220

Gerz Collectorwerke - Various
1993 The Dugout GL1 - A-Busch, Inc.	10,000		110.00	110
1994 Winchester Stein GL2 - A-Busch, Inc.	10,000	1995	120.00	120
1995 "Saturday Evening Post" Christmas Stein #1 GL5 - J.C. Leyendecker	5,000		105.00	105
1996 "Saturday Evening Post" Christmas Stein #2 GL6 - A-Busch, Inc.	5,000		105.00	105

Gerz Collectorwerke Call of the Wild - J. Rideout
1996 Wolf Stein GL9	10,000		139.00	139

Gerz Meisterwerke Collection - A-Busch, Inc.
1994 Norman Rockwell-Triple Self Portrait GM6	5,000		250.00	250
1994 Mallard Stein GM7	5,000		220.00	220
1994 Winchester "Model 94" Centennial Stein GM10	5,000		150.00	150
1995 Giant Panda Stein GM8	3,500		210.00	210
1995 Rosie the Riveter Stein GM9	5,000		165.00	165
1996 Winchester Rodeo Stein GM19	5,000		179.00	179
1996 Winchester Pheasant Hunt Stein GM20	3,500		215.00	215

Gerz Meisterwerke First Hunt Series - P. Ford
1992 Golden Retriever GM2	10,000		150.00	150
1994 Springer Spaniel GM5	10,000		170.00	170
1995 Pointer Stein GM16	10,000		190.00	190
1995 Labrador Stein GM17	10,000		190.00	190

Gerz Meisterwerke Holidays Through the Decades - A-Busch, Inc.
1996 Holidays: Decade of the 30's GM18	3,500		169.00	169

Gerz Saturday Evening Post Collection - J.C. Leyendecker
1993 Santa's Mailbag GM1	Retrd.		195.00	250
1993 Santa's Helper GM3	7,500		200.00	200
1994 "All I Want For Christmas" GM13	5,000		220.00	220
1995 Fourth of July Stein GM15	5,000		180.00	180

CUI/Carolina Collection/Dram Tree

Ducks Unlimited - Various
1987 Wood Duck Edition I - K. Bloom	Retrd.		80.00	200
1988 Mallard Edition II - M. Bradford	Retrd.		80.00	125
1989 Canvasbacks Edition III - L. Barnicle	Retrd.		80.00	100
1990 Pintails Edition IV - R. Plasschaert	Retrd.		80.00	90
1991 Canada Geese Edition V - J. Meger	20,000		80.00	80

Ducks Unlimited Classic Decoy Series - D. Boncela
1992 1930's Bert Graves Mallard Decoys Edition I	Retrd.		100.00	100

Great American Achievements - CUI
1986 First Successful Flight Edition I	Retrd.		10.95	75-95
1987 The Model T Edition II	Retrd.		12.95	30-55
1988 First Transcontinental Railway Edition III	Retrd.		15.95	28-55
1989 The First River Steamer Edition IV	Retrd.		25.00	25
1990 Man's First Walk on the Moon Edition V	Retrd.		25.00	25

Stroh Heritage Collection - CUI
1984 Horsedrawn Wagon - Heritage I	Retrd.		11.95	15-25
1985 Kirn Inn Germany - Heritage II	Retrd.		12.95	15-22
1986 Lion Brewing Company - Heritage III	Retrd.		13.95	25-35
1987 Bohemian Beer - Heritage IV	Retrd.		14.95	19-22
1988 Delivery Vehicles - Heritage V	Retrd.		25.00	25
1989 Fire Brewed - Heritage V I	Retrd.		16.95	19

Hamilton Collection

Mickey Mantle - R. Tanenbaum
1996 The Legendary Mickey Mantle	Open		39.95	40

YEAR ISSUE	EDITION LIMIT	YEAR RETD.	ISSUE PRICE	*QUOTE U.S.$

The STAR TREK® Tankard Collection - T. Blackshear

Year	Item	Limit	Retd.	Issue Price	Quote
1994	SPOCK	Open		49.50	50
1995	Kirk	Open		49.50	50
1995	McCoy	Open		49.50	50
1995	Uhura	Open		49.50	50
1995	Scotty	Open		49.50	50
1995	Sulu	Open		49.50	50
1995	Chekov	Open		49.50	50
1995	U.S.S. Enterprise NCC-1701	Open		49.50	50

Warriors of the Plains Tankards - G. Stewart

Year	Item	Limit	Retd.	Issue Price	Quote
1992	Thundering Hooves	Open		125.00	125
1995	Warrior's Choice	Open		125.00	125
1995	Healing Spirits	Open		125.00	125
1995	Battle Grounds	Open		125.00	125

Royal Doulton

Character Jug of the Year - Various

Year	Item	Limit	Retd.	Issue Price	Quote
1991	Fortune Teller D6824 - S. Taylor	Closed	1991	130.00	200
1992	Winston Churchill D6907 - S. Taylor	Closed	1992	195.00	225
1993	Vice-Admiral Lord Nelson D6932 - S. Taylor	Closed	1993	225.00	225
1994	Captain Hook - M. Alcock	Closed	1994	235.00	235
1995	Captain Bligh D6967 - S. Taylor	Closed	1995	200.00	235
1996	Jesse Owens, lg. D7019 - S. Taylor	Yr.Iss.		225.00	225

Character Jugs - Various

Year	Item	Limit	Retd.	Issue Price	Quote
1993	Abraham Lincoln - M. Alcock	2,500	1994	190.00	250
1991	Airman, sm. - W. Harper	Open		75.00	75
1996	Albert Einstein, lg. - S. Taylor	Open		225.00	225
1995	Alfred Hitchcock D6987 - D. Biggs	Open		200.00	225
1990	Angler, sm. - S. Taylor	Retrd.	1995	82.50	83
1947	Beefeater, lg. - H. Fenton	Open		137.50	150
1947	Beefeater, sm. - H. Fenton	Open		75.00	75
1995	Charles Dickens D6939 - W. Harper	2,500		500.00	500
1989	Clown, lg. - S. Taylor	Retrd.	1995	205.00	205
1991	Columbus, lg. - S. Taylor	Open		137.50	138
1995	Cyrano de Bergerac, lg. - D. Biggs	Open		200.00	200
1983	D'Artagnan, lg. - S. Taylor	Retrd.	1995	150.00	150
1983	D'Artagnan, sm. - S. Taylor	Retrd.	1995	82.50	83
1995	Dennis and Gnasher, lg. - S. Ward	Open		212.50	213
1995	Deperate Dan, lg. - S. Ward	Open		212.50	213
1991	Equestrian, sm. - S. Taylor	Retrd.	1995	82.50	83
1995	George Washington - M. Alcock	2,500	1995	200.00	225
1982	George Washington, lg. - S. Taylor	Retrd.	1994	150.00	175
1994	Glenn Miller - M. Alcock	Open		270.00	300
1971	Golfer, lg. - D. Biggs	Retrd.	1995	150.00	150
1993	Graduate-Male, sm. - S. Taylor	Retrd.	1995	85.00	85
1986	Guardsman, lg. - S. Taylor	Open		137.50	150
1986	Gurardsman, sm. - S. Taylor	Open		75.00	83
1990	Guy Fawkes, lg. - W. Harper	Open		137.50	150
1975	Henry VIII, lg. - E. Griffiths	Open		137.50	150
1975	Henry VIII, sm. - E. Griffiths	Open		75.00	83
1991	Jockey, sm. - S. Taylor	Retrd.	1995	82.50	83
1995	Judge and Thief Toby D6988 - S. Taylor	Open		185.00	200
1959	Lawyer, lg. - M. Henk	Open		137.50	150
1959	Lawyer, sm. - M. Henk	Open		75.00	83
1990	Leprechaun, lg. - W. Harper	Open		205.00	225
1990	Leprechaun, sm. - W. Harper	Open		75.00	85
1986	London Bobby, lg. - S. Taylor	Open		137.50	150
1986	London Bobby, sm. - S. Taylor	Open		75.00	83
1952	Long John Silver, lg. - M. Henk	Open		137.50	150
1952	Long John Silver, sm. - M. Henk	Open		75.00	83
1960	Merlin, lg. - G. Sharpe	Open		137.50	150
1960	Merlin, sm. - G. Sharpe	Open		75.00	83
1990	Modern Golfer, sm. - S. Taylor	Open		75.00	83
1961	Old Salt, lg. - G. Sharpe	Open		137.50	138
1961	Old Salt, sm. - G. Sharpe	Open		75.00	75
1955	Rip Van Winkle, lg. - M. Henk	Retrd.	1995	150.00	150
1955	Rip Van Winkle, sm. - M. Henk	Retrd.	1995	82.50	83
1991	Sailor, sm. - W. Harper	Open		75.00	83
1984	Santa Claus, lg. - M. Abberley	Open		137.50	150
1984	Santa Claus, sm. - M. Abberley	Open		75.00	83
1993	Shakespeare, sm. - W. Harper	Open		99.00	107
1973	The Sleuth, lg. - A. Moore	Open		137.50	150
1973	The Sleuth, sm. - A. Moore	Open		75.00	83
1991	Snooker Player, sm. - S. Taylor	Retrd.	1995	82.50	83
1991	Soldier, sm. - W. Harper	Open		75.00	83
1994	Thomas Jefferson - M. Alcock	2,500	1995	200.00	225
1991	Town Crier, lg. - S. Taylor	Retrd.	1994	170.00	170
1993	Winston Churchill, sm. - S. Taylor	Open		99.00	107
1990	Wizard, lg. - S. Taylor - S. Taylor	Open		175.00	188
1990	Wizard, sm. - S. Taylor	Open		75.00	85
1991	Yeoman of the Guard, lg. - S. Taylor	Open		137.50	150

Great Composers - S. Taylor

Year	Item	Limit	Retd.	Issue Price	Quote
1996	Beethoven, lg. D7021	Open		225.00	225
1996	Chopin, lg. D7030	Open		225.00	225
1996	Mozart, lg. D7031	Open		225.00	225
1996	Tchaikovsky, lg. D7022	Open		225.00	225

Limited Edition Character Jugs - Various

Year	Item	Limit	Retd.	Issue Price	Quote
1992	Abraham Lincoln D6936 - S. Taylor	2,500	1994	190.00	190
1994	Aladdin's Genie D6971 - D. Biggs	1,500	1994	335.00	350
1996	Angel Miniature - M. Alcock	2,500		77.50	78
1993	Clown Toby - S. Taylor	3,000		175.00	175
1993	Elf Miniature D6942 - W. Harper	2,500	1994	55.00	75
1993	Father Christmas Toby - W. Harper	3,500		125.00	125
1996	Geoffrey Chaucer, lg. - R. Tabbenor	1,500		800.00	800
1995	George Washington, lg. - M. Alcock	2,500		200.00	200
1990	Henry VIII - N/A	Open		150.00	150
1991	Henry VIII - W. Harper	1,991		395.00	1000-1300
1991	Jester - S. Taylor	2,500		125.00	150
1994	King & Queen of Diamonds D6969 - J. Taylor	2,500	1994	260.00	275
1996	King and Queen of Hearts Toby - S. Taylor	2,500		275.00	275
1992	King Charles I D6917 - W. Harper	2,500		450.00	495
1994	Leprechaun Toby - S. Taylor	2,500		150.00	150
1992	Mrs. Claus Miniature D6922 - S. Taylor	2,500		50.00	55
1993	Napoleon (Large size) D6941 - S. Taylor	2,000	1994	225.00	225
1994	Oliver Cromwell D6968 - W. Harper	2,500	1994	475.00	475
1996	Pharoah Flambe, lg. - R. Tabbenor	1,500		500.00	500
1991	Santa Claus Miniature D6900 - M. Abberley	5,000		50.00	55
1988	Sir Francis Drake D6805 - P .Gee	Open		N/A	100
1992	Snake Charmer - S. Taylor	2,500		210.00	230
1994	Thomas Jefferson - S. Taylor	2,500		200.00	225
1992	Town Crier D6895 - S. Taylor	2,500		175.00	175
1992	William Shakespeare D6933 - W. Harper	2,500	1994	625.00	175

*Quotes have been rounded up to nearest dollar

INDEX

Ace Product Management Group, Inc. 19, 53-55, 346
Adler, Holly, 58, 299
Adler, Kurt S., 56
Alcock, Martyn, 299
All God's Children, see Miss Martha Originals
All God's Children Collector's Club, 247-248, 342
Althoff, Kenneth, 243-244
Amaranth Productions, 20, 21, 59-61, 309, 338, 346
Amazze, 18, 62-64, 314, 321, 346
American Artists, 346
American Artist Portfolio Inc., 346
Andrew D. Darvas, Inc., 347
Andrews, Kim, 192
Angel Academy Alumni Society, 283, 342
Angela Trotta Thomas, 349
Anheuser-Busch Collectors Club, 66-67, 342
Anheuser-Busch, Inc., 36, 39, 65-67, 308, 316, 318, 329, 346
Anna-Perenna, Inc., 346
Annalee Doll Museum, 70
Annalee Doll Society, 69-70, 342
Annalee Mobilitee Dolls, Inc., 22, 30, 68-70, 335, 346
ANRI U.S., 22, 24, 28, 29, 32, 71-73, 302, 346
ANRI Collector's Society, 73, 342
ANRI Woodcarvings Tour, 73
Aphessetche, Danielle, 108-110, 299
Aprile, Paulette, 232
Apsit, Pete, 108-110, 299-300
Arcadian Pewter, Inc., 19, 74-76, 318, 346
Armani, Giuseppe, 77-79, 300
Armani Society and Armani Collection, 48, 49, 77-79, 342, 346
Armke, Ken, 10
Arriagada, Margarita, 229-230
Art of Glynda Turley, The, 18, 21, 80-82, 336, 346
Artists of the World, 346
Ashton-Drake Galleries, The, 26, 50, 51, 83-85, 302, 310, 320, 346
Attic Babies, 50, 52, 86-88, 319, 346
Attic Babies Collectors' Club, 87-88, 342
Attic Babies Doll Hospital, 14
Attic Babies Factory Tour, 88
Attwell, Mabel Lucie, 141, 300
Autom, 89, 346

B & J Co., 346
Baker, Brian, 240-242, 300
Ball, Bette, 178, 300
BAND Creations, 26, 29, 30, 45, 90-92, 327, 346
Barlowe, Dot, 301
Barlowe, Sy, 301
Barnum, Francis, 301
Barry-Hippensteel, Kathy, 84, 301
Baston, Jr., Prescott "Woody", 301

Bejma, Kathi, 296-298, 301-302
Belcari, Auro, 129-131, 302
Belleek Collectors' International Society, 342, 346
Bello, Yolanda, 83-84, 302
Bergsma, Jody, 266-268, 302
Bernardi, Ulrich, 72, 302
Beswick Factory Tours, 274
Bill Vernon Studios, 349
Bing, Harald, 93-94
Bing & Grondahl, 24, 25, 27, 93-95, 311
Birdsong, Keith, 302-303
Boehm Porcelain Society, 342
Boehm Porcelain Studio, 346
Bolinger, Paul, 57, 303
Boyds Collection, Ltd., 25, 37, 96-98, 319, 346
Boyett, Michael, 219-220, 303
Bradford Exchange, 34, 35, 37, 38, 99-101, 303, 308, 310, 314, 346
Bradford Museum of Collector's Plates, 99-101
Bradford, Suzan, 303
Bradley Doll, 346
Brandywine Woodcrafts, 45, 102-104, 338, 346
Brian Baker's Deja Vu Collection, 240-242, 300
Brian Baker's Deja Vu Collectors' Club, 241-242, 342
Briant & Sons, 346
Bristol Township & Waterfront, see Pacific Rim Import Corp.
Brown, Rick, 303
Browning, Tom, 303-304
Buccellati Silver Ltd., 346
Budweiser, see Anheuser-Busch, Inc.
Buonaiuto, Michael, 140, 304
Buonaiuto, Shelley, 140, 304
Burton, Frances, 304
Butcher, Sam, 141-142, 304
Byers, Bob, 105-107, 304
Byers' Choice Christmas Gallery & Emporium, 107
Byers' Choice Ltd., 14, 23, 42, 105-107, 304, 346
Byers, Joyce, 105-107, 304-305
Bywaters, Lynn, 223

Cain Studios, 346
Cairn Studios, 346
Caithness Collectors Club, 342
Caithness Glass Inc., 346
Calabar Creations, 25, 32, 36, 108-110, 299, 300, 321, 346
Calvesbert, Peter, 195-197, 305
Cameo Guild Studios, 346
Cantrell, Kitty, 219-220, 305
Cape Craftsmen, Inc., 346
Cardew, Collectors' Club, The, 113, 342
Cardew Design, 18, 19, 111-113, 305, 346
Cardew, Paul, 111-113, 305
Carlton Cards, 114-116, 346

Cast Art Industries, Inc., 22, 26, 117-119, 311, 312, 346
Cat's Meow, see FJ Designs/ The Cat's Meow
Cat's Meow Collectors Club, 151-152, 342
Cavanagh Group International, 23, 26, 31, 120-122, 346
Cavanagh's Coca-Cola Christmas Collectors Society, 121-122, 342
Cazenovia Abroad, Ltd., 346
Chandok, Pat, 259, 305
Character Collectibles, 108, 346
Charming Tails, see FFSC, Inc.
Cherished Teddies, see Enesco Corporation
Chilmark, see Lance Corporation
Chilmark Polland Collectors Society, The, 212, 342
Chilmark Registry, The, 212, 342
Chimera Studios, 346
Christensen, James C., 183-185, 305-306
Christopher Radko, 13, 22, 24, 25, 123-125, 326, 346
Christopher Radko Starlight Family of Collectors, 124-125, 345
Classic Collectables by Uniquely Yours, 346
Clay Art, 347
Clement, Jim, 181
Cleveland, Joyce, 306
Clinton, Gary & Jeanie, 290, 292
Cobabe, Laura, 306
Coca-Cola, 120-122, 163, 295
Combes, Simon, 183
Constance Collection, The, 347
Corbridge, David, 158, 306
Cornell Importers, 347
Country Artists, 347
Coventry, Helen, 306
Creart, 347
Cross Gallery, Inc., 347
Crystal World, 126-128, 322, 323, 333, 347
Cybis, 347

Daddy's Long Legs, 347
Edna Dali, 306-307
Danko, Matthew, 238
Darnley, Steve, 307
Dave Grossman Creations, 347
David Winter Cottages, 237-239, 312
David Winter Cottages Collectors' Guild, 238-239, 339, 345
Davis, Lowell, 144-146, 307
Day, Ray, 307
Dear Artistic Sculpture, 18, 19, 129-131, 302, 308, 347
deMatteo, Chip, 189-191, 307
Department 56, Inc., 26, 27, 132-134, 347
Department 56 Tour of One Village Place, 134
Derek, Connie Walser, 187
Dickens Village, see Department 56

Disney, see Walt Disney Classics Collection
Dolfi, 89
Dolly Dingle, 178
Donald Zolan Studio, 349
Donjo Studios, Inc., 347
Doolittle, Bev, 183, 184, 307-308
Dram Tree/C.U.I., 347
Dreamsicles, 117-119, 186
Dreamsicles Collectors Club, 119, 343
Duncan, Catherine, 138-139
Duncan Royale, 23, 30, 42, 138-140, 304, 325, 347
Duncan Royale Collectors Club, 140, 343

EKJ Collectors Society, 158, 343
Ebeling & Reuss, 347
Edna Hibel Society, 343
Edna Hibel Studio, 348
Egg Fantasy, 347
eggspressions! inc., 347
Eklund's Ltd., 347
Enchantica Collectors Club, 343
Enesco Cherished Teddies Club, 143, 343
Enesco Corporation, 32, 37, 43, 51, 141-143, 300, 304, 312, 327, 338, 347
Enesco Musical Society, 141
Enesco Precious Moments Birthday Club, 143, 343
Enesco Precious Moments Collectors' Club, 143, 343
Enesco Treasury of Christmas Ornaments Collectors' Club, 142-143, 343
Ertl Collectibles, 144-146, 307, 347

FFSC, Inc., 147-149, 310, 347
FJ Designs, Inc./Cat's Meow, 45, 150-152, 315, 347
FJ Designs/Cat's Meow Factory Tour, 152
Fabergé, 162, 190
Farina, Ermanno, 129, 130, 308
FARO Studios, 270, 271
Fearon, Declan, 308
Federica Doll Company, 347
Fenton Art Glass Collectors of America, Inc. (FAGCA), 154-155, 343
Fenton Art Glass Company, 28, 31, 153-155, 304, 326, 347
Fenton Art Glass Company Museum & Tour, 155
Fenton, Nancy G., 9
Ferrandiz, Juan, 71-72
Figaro Import Corporation, 347
Figi Graphics, 347
Flambro Imports, 35, 156-158, 306, 323, 337, 347
Flamm, Allan, 156
Fontanini, 330
Fontanini Collectors' Club, 271, 343
Ford, Pat, 308

Forma Vitrum, 7, 8, 27, 30, 41, 159-161, 315, 347
Fracé, Charles, 99, 308
Fraley, Tobin, 308-309
Franklin Mint, The, 7, 9, 31, 43, 50, 162-164, 324, 347
Franklin Mint Museum, 164
Fraser International, Inc., 347
Freedman, Eugene, 141
Furlong, Margaret, 165-167, 309

Gaither, W.D., 235, 309
GANZ, 26, 28, 30, 37, 168-170, 335, 347
Gartlan USA, 18, 171-173, 334, 347
Gartlan USA's "New" Collectors' League, 173, 313, 343
Geenty, David, 187
George Z. Lefton Co., 27, 41, 43, 216-218, 308, 333, 348
Georgetown Collection, 28, 50, 174-176, 319-320, 325, 326, 331, 335, 347
Gibbons, Roger, 309
Giorgio, Nate, 309-310
Gill, Linda, 59, 61, 309
Goebel Miniatures, 179, 317, 324
Goebel of North America, 17, 177-179, 300, 316, 347
Good-Kruger Dolls, 347
Good-Kruger, Julie, 85, 310
Great American Collectors' Guild, 181, 182, 343
Great American Doll Co., 347
Great American Taylor Collectibles Corp., The, 25, 180-182, 347
Greenwich Workshop, 46, 183-185, 306, 311, 317, 319, 339, 347
Griff, Dean, 147, 149, 310
Griffin, James, 310
Griffith, Judith Ann, 310
Grossman, John, 187, 310-311
Gund Inc., 347
Gurney, James, 183, 184, 311
Gustafson, Scott, 184, 311

H & G Studios, Inc., 347
Hackett, Stephen and Gigi, 118, 311
Hadley House, 347
Hallett, Charlotte, 72
Hallett, William, 72
Hallmark Cards, Inc., 347
Hallmark Keepsake Ornament Collector's Club, 343
Hamilton Collection, 37, 39, 51, 186-188, 303, 306, 311, 328, 334, 336, 347
Hand & Hammer Collector's Club, 191, 343
Hand & Hammer Silversmiths, 26, 27, 189-191, 307, 347
Hansen, Hans Henrik, 311
Harbour Lights, 41, 192-194, 313, 330, 340, 347
Harbour Lights Collector's Society, 193-194, 343
Harley-Davidson, 53-55, 324
Harmony Kingdom, 18, 195-197, 305, 318, 347
Harold Rigsby Graphics, 349
Hawthorne Village, 198-200, 328, 347

Haynes, Kristin, 117-119, 186, 312
Heirloom Editions Ltd., 347
Heirloom Limited, 347
Helen Sabatte Designs, Inc., 349
Herbert, Jon, 238, 312
Heritage Collections, Ltd., The, 348
Herrick, Peggy, 312
Hillman, Priscilla, 142, 186, 312
Hine, Tori Dawn Younger, 193, 312-313
Hirsch, Gernot, 313
Hirzinger, Anton, 313
Hoffman, Joseph, 313
Holcombe, Martha, 246-248, 313
Hook, Frances, 314
House of Fontanini, 269-271
House of Fontanini Studio Tour in Italy, 271
Hudson Creek, see Lance Corporation
Hudson Pewter, see Lance Corporation
Hughes, Graham, 287, 288
Hummel, see M.I. Hummel
Hummel, Sister Maria Innocentia (Berta), 177-178, 201-203, 314
Hummel Museum, 203

Imperial Graphics, Ltd., 20, 204-206, 348
Incolay Studios, Inc., 348
Innes, George, 62-64, 314
Iris Arc Crystal, 348

Jack Terry Fine Art Publishing, 349
Jackson, Cliff, 314
Jan Hagara Collectables, Inc., 347
Jan Hagara Collectors Club, 343
Janco Studio, 348
Jauquet, Bill, 270-271, 314-315
Jedlinski, Ronald T., 9
Job, Bill, 159-161, 315
Jody Bergsma Galleries, 346
Johannes Zook Originals, 349
John Hine Studios, Inc., 237-238, 312, 331
Johnston, Connie, 187-188
Jonas, Penni Jo, 315
Jones, Faline Fry, 150, 152, 315
June McKenna Collectibles, Inc., 348

Kato, Ru, 315
Katz, Garri, 315-316
Kaiser Porcelain US, 348
Kay, Sarah, 72-73
Kelly, Emmett Jr., 156-158, 316
Kemper, Bud, 316
Kennedy, Karen, 178, 316
Kennicutt, Donna, 316
Kinkade, Thomas, 99-100, 198-200, 237, 239, 316-317
Kissling, Jutta, 176
Kolesar, Pat, 317
Krystonia, see Precious Art/Panton
Krystonia Collector's Club, 259-260, 344
Kuck, Sandra, 7, 99-100, 266-268, 317
Kuhn, Grete, 337-338
Kurt S. Adler, Inc., 23, 25, 56-58, 299, 303, 322, 328-329, 330, 333, 346

Ladie & Friends, Inc., 22, 29, 51, 52, 207-209, 339, 348
Lalique, 348
Lance Corporation, The, 22, 33, 34, 39, 210-212, 301, 303, 320, 325, 331, 332, 348
Landry, Paul, 184, 317
Larsen, Paul, 178, 317
Lawrence, David, 196, 197, 317-318
Lawton Doll Company, 348
Lee, Ron, 213-215
Lefton's Collector Service Bureau, 216
Legacy Works, 348
Legends, 38, 40, 219-221, 303, 318, 321, 324, 338, 348
Lemax, Inc., 348
Lemon, David, 219-220, 318
Lenox Collections, 222-224, 348
Lenox, Walter Scott, 222, 224
Leon, Anthony, 318
Lightpost Publishing, see Media Arts Group, Inc.
Lilliput Lane, 26, 47, 225-227, 307, 331, 334, 348
Lilliput Lane Collectors' Club, 226-227, 344
Lindblade, Neal, 74-76, 318
Little Cheesers, see GANZ
Little Cheesers Collectors' Club, 169-170, 344
Little Emmett Collectors' Society, 158, 344
Liu, Lena, 99-100, 204-206, 318-319
Lizzie High, see Ladie & Friends
Lizzie High Doll Hospital, 14
Lizzie High Museum, 209
Lizzie High Society, 208-209, 344
Lladró, 8, 14, 228-230, 348
Lladró, Jose, Juan and Vicente, 228
Lladró, Rosa Maria, 229
Lladró Museum, 230
Lladró Society, 22, 30, 48, 229-230, 344, 348
Locker, Mark, 319
Lowell Davis Farm Club, 342
Lowenthal, G.M., 96-98, 319
Lyman, Stephen, 184, 319
Lynette Decor Products, 348

MAGI Entertainment Products, 237-239
MCK Gifts, Inc., 348
M.I. Hummel, 177-178, 198-203, 313, 314, 331
M.I. Hummel Club, 26, 32, 201-203, 343, 348
MacMahon, David, 7, 159
Magus Fine Arts & Collectibles, 348
Mann, Eda, 231-232
Mann, Seymour, 231-232
Margaret Furlong Designs, 28, 165-167, 347
Margaret Furlong Designs Studio Tour, 167
Mark Klaus LTD, 348
Mark Hopkins Sculpture, 348
Mark Hopkins Bronze Guild, 343
Marty Bell Fine Art, Inc., 346
Marty Sculpture, Inc., 348

Maruri U.S.A., 31, 41, 234-236, 308, 348
Maschino-Walker, Marty, 86-88, 319
Mason, Linda, 174-175, 319-320
Masterworks, see Shube's Manufacturing
Masterworks Collectors Club, 283, 344
McClelland, John, 266-267, 320
McClung, Catherine, 223
McClure, Cindy M., 84, 320
McGrory, Anne Transue, 320
McKinnon, Jeff, 174-175
McNeill, Gwen, 320
Media Arts Group, Inc., 46, 47, 237-239, 348
Medina, Dan, 320-321
Melody In Motion, see WACO Products Corp.
Melody In Motion Collectors Society, 295, 344
Memoli, Ken, 321
Memories of Yesterday Collection, see Enesco Corporation
Memories of Yesterday Collectors' Society, 143, 344
Merck, Beth, 249, 250
Merck, E.M., 249-251, 321
Merck, Tim, 249, 250
Meyer, Richard, 321
Meyers, S. N., 62-64, 321
Micarelli, Clemente, 321-322
Michael Boyett Studio, 346
Michael Garman Productions, Inc., 347
Michael's Limited, 41, 44, 45, 240-242, 300, 348
Midwest of Cannon Falls, Inc., 24, 27, 34, 42, 44, 45, 243-245, 312, 329, 332, 334, 337, 338, 348
Miller Import Corp., see Armani
Miller, Larry, 322
Miss Martha Originals Inc., 32, 34, 35, 246-248, 313, 348
Miss Martha Originals Inc. Showroom, 248
Montana, Joe, 172
Monteiro, Mary, 322
Moss Portfolio, The, 348
Mostrom, Jocelyn, 57, 322
Mulargia, Nicolo, 322
Munro Enterprises, Inc., 348
Musgrave, Real, 157-158, 322-323
My Friends and Me, 348
Myer, Richard, 110
Myth & Magic, see The Tudor Mint, Inc.
Myth & Magic Collectors Club, 289, 344

Nagel, Allyson, 323
Nakai, Ryuju, 126-128, 323
Nakane, Seiji, 323
Napoleon, 348
National Association of Limited Edition Dealers (NALED), 350-353
National Fenton Glass Society, 154-155, 343
New Masters Publishing Co., Inc., 348
Newburn, Dianna, 323

Nicole, Maryse, 163, 323-324
Nielson, Jorgen, 94, 324
North American Bear Co., 348
Norrgard, Douglas, 178, 179, 324

Oberweger, Gideon, 8, 9, 232
O'Connell, Michael, 240
Official Sebastian Miniatures
　　Museum, 212
Oldenburg Originals, 348
Old World Christmas, 7, 23, 24, 25,
　　249-251, 321, 348
Old World Christmas Collectors'
　　Club, 251, 344
Olszewski Studios, 348
One Village Place Showroom Tour,
　　134
Opa's Haus, Inc., 348
Open Window Club House
　　Collectors Club, 265, 344
Open Window Video Tour, 265
Orr, Mary Ann, 260
Orrefors of Sweden, 348
Otero, Ben, 54, 324

PFC Collectors Curio Club,
　　261-262, 345
Pacific Rim Import Corp.,
　　24, 27, 37, 41, 252-254, 348
Pangaean Society, The, 212, 344
Pardell, Christopher, 219-220, 324
Past Impressions, 348
Patterson, Gary, 238, 324-325
Pedley, Nada, 272
Pemberton, Donna, 139-140, 325
PenDelfin Family Circle Collectors
　　Club, 344
PenDelfin Studios, 348
Penfield, Sandra, 90-92, 327
Penni Jo's Originals Ltd., 348
Pennibears Collectors Club, 344
Perry, Martin, 195-197
Phelps, Michelle, 281, 282, 325
Phillips, Pamela, 175, 325
Pickard Inc., 348
Pike, Valerie, 325
Pleasantville 1893 Historical
　　Preservation Society, 158, 345
Pocket Dragons, see Flambro Imports
Pocket Dragons & Friends Collectors'
　　Club, 158, 345
Polland, Don, 210, 325-326
Polland Studios, 348
Porsgrunds Porsellansfabrik, 348
Porterfield's, 348
Possible Dreams, 7, 8, 22, 23, 36,
　　255-257, 304, 306, 310, 322, 328,
　　337, 348
Potter, Beatrix, 190, 273
Precious Art/Panton, 33, 258-260,
　　305, 348
Precious Moments Collection,
　　see Enesco Corporation
Prusseit, Barbara, 326
Pulaski Furniture Corporation,
　　261-262, 349

R John Wright Dolls, 349
R.R. Creations, Inc.,
　　45, 263-265, 328, 349
Radko, Christopher, 123-125, 326
Randolph, Lynne, 326

Rawcliffe Corporation, 349
Reavey, Joyce, 175, 326
Reco International Corp., 7, 24, 29,
　　31, 36, 39, 266-268, 301, 302, 316,
　　317, 320, 322, 349
Red Mill Collectors Society, 345
Red Mill Mfg., Inc., 349
Reich, Heio, 266, 267
Resnick, Lynda, 164
Reynolds, Martha, 326
Rhyner-Nadig, Mary, 327
Richards, Jeannette, 90-92, 327
Rigg, Lucy, 142, 327
Riley, Sharon, 327
Rios, Susan, 327-328
Rockwell, Norman, 66, 99-101,
　　121-122, 163, 178-179, 198-199,
　　295, 328
Rolfe, Cindy Marschner, 328
Roman, Inc., 8, 9, 24, 28, 29, 269-271,
　　314, 323, 329, 336, 349
Ron Lee's Collectors Club, 215
Ron Lee's World of Clowns,
　　35, 42, 213-215, 348
Ross, Bronwen, 328
Ross, Doreen, 263, 264, 328
Ross, Dave, 263, 264
Rothenberg, Marjorie Grace,
　　328-329
Royal Copenhagen/Bing & Grondahl,
　　24, 25, 27, 94-95, 311, 324, 349
Royal Doulton, 34, 43, 47, 272-274,
　　299, 339-340, 349
Royal Doulton Factory Tours, 274
Royal Doulton International
　　Collectors Club, 274, 345
Royal Watch Society, The, 197, 345
Royal Worcester, 349
Ryan, Susan, 329

Saint-Alexis Santons, 349
Salvino, Inc., 349
Sandicast Collectors Guild, 345
Sandicast, Inc., 349
Sandy Clough Studio, 347
Santa Claus Network, 256-257, 345
Sarah's Attic, 29, 32, 34, 275-277,
　　330, 349
Sarah's Attic Forever Friends
　　Collectors' Club, 276-277, 345
Sargent, Barbi, 329
Scherback, Alexander, 282, 329
Schifferl, Lou, 329
Schifferl, Pam, 329
Schlesinger, Kandy, 329-330
Schultz, Sarah, 275-277, 330
Sculpture Workshop Designs, 349
Sebastian Miniatures,
　　see Lance Corporation
Sebastian Miniatures Collectors'
　　Society, 212, 345
Sebastian Museum, 212
Second Nature Design, 349
Sedlow, Peter, 282, 330
Seymour Mann, Inc., 30, 31, 50,
　　51, 231-233, 307, 317, 320, 325,
　　326, 348
Seymour Mann, Inc. Doll Club,
　　233, 344
Shade Tree Creations, 349
Shelia's Collectibles, 44, 278-280,
　　335, 349

Shelia's Collectibles Tour, 280
Shelia's Collectors' Society, 280, 345
Shenandoah Designs International,
　　Inc., 349
Sherman, Mark, 330
Shube's Manufacturing, 19, 281-283,
　　325, 330, 339, 349
Silver Deer Ltd., 349
Simonetti, Elio, 269, 270, 330
Sirko, Marlene, 175, 330-331
Skille, Sissel, 175-176
Skrobek, Gerhard, 331
Slack, Ted, 238-239, 331
Slockbower, Joseph, 331
Slocombe, Anthony, 331
Smith, Cindy, 331-332
Smith, Lancy, 180
Smith, III, Leo R., 244-245, 332
Snowbabies, see Department 56
Snow Village, see Department 56
Spencer Collin Lighthouses, 349
Spencer, Irene, 332
Stamey, Gabriele, 332
Stamey, Michael, 332
Starlight Family of Collectors,
　　124, 125, 345
Starlite Collector's Society, 221, 345
Starr, Ringo, 171-173
Stearman, Scott, 332-333
Steiff USA, 349
Steinbach, see Kurt. S. Adler, Inc.
Steinbach Collectors Club, 58, 345
Steinbach, Herr Christian, 333
Steinbach, Karla, 333
Stocker, Adi, 333
Stravitz, David, 333
Studio Collection, 349
Susan Wakeen Doll Company, 349
Sundblom, Haddon, 120
Suzuki, Tom, 333
Swarovski, Daniel, 284
Swarovski America Limited, 17,
　　284-286, 313, 332, 333, 340, 349
Swarovski Collectors Society,
　　284-286, 345
Swarovski Crystal Shop & Visitor
　　Center, 286

Taggart, Misty, 282, 283, 333-334
Talsco of Florida, 349
Tannenbaum, Robert, 334
Tate, David J., 225-227, 334
Tate, Randy, 334
Taylor, Jack, 180, 182
Taylor, Michael, 171, 172, 334
Terpning, Howard, 183
Texas Stamps, 349
Thammavongsa, Christine,
　　168-170, 335
Theroux, Carol, 175
Thomas Kinkade Collectors' Society,
　　239, 344
Thompson, Shelia, 278-280, 335
Thorndike, Annalee, 68-70, 335
Thorndike, Chip, 68-69
Thorndike, Chuck, 68-70, 335
Thorndike, Town, 68-69
Thorpe, Philip, 189-191
Timeless Creations, 349
Timmerman, Ann, 175-176, 335-336
Tomescu, Titus, 83, 84, 336
Towle Silversmiths, 349

Treasury of Christmas Ornaments,
　　see Enesco Corporation
Tripi, Angela, 270, 336
Tudor Mint, The, 33, 39, 287-289,
　　306, 307, 309, 319, 327, 331,
　　337, 349
Turley, Glynda, 80-82, 336
Turner, Virginia Ehrlich, 336

Ulbricht, Christian, 244-245, 336-337
United Design, 22, 26, 28, 290-292,
　　303, 315, 316, 321, 322, 323, 349
United Design Gift Shop & Factory
　　Tour, 292

V.F. Fine Arts, 349
Vaillancourt, Judi, 337
Vaillancourt Folk Art, 349
Van, Tony, 108
Van Hygan & Smythe, 13
Vestergaard, Sven, 94, 337
VickiLane, 349
VickiLane Collectors Club, 345
Victor, Joan Berg, 157, 337
Victoria Ashlea Originals,
　　see Goebel of North America
Viking Import House, 349
Viletta China Co., 349
Volpi, Rosemary, 57

W.T. Wilson Limited Editions, 349
WACO Products, 23, 42, 293-295,
　　315, 323, 339, 349
Wallace Silversmiths, 349
Walnut Ridge Collectibles, 18, 19,
　　296-298, 301-302, 349
Walt Disney Classics Collection,
　　135-137
Walt Disney Company, The, 135, 347
Walt Disney Collectors Society,
　　137, 342
Waterford Crystal, 349
Watson, Jessica, 337
Wedgwood, 349
Wendt & Kuhn, 245, 337-338
Wendt, Grete, 337-338
West, Lynn, 59-61, 338
Whiting, Marlene, 102-104, 338
Whitten, Willy, 219-220, 338
Wickl, Klaus, 338
Wild Wings, 349
Willingham, Preston, 338-339
Willitts Designs, 349
Wimberly, Dick, 282, 339
Wimbledon Collection, The, 349
Windstone Editions Inc., 349
Winston Roland, Ltd., 349
Winter, David, 237, 339
Wisber, Barbara, 207-209, 339
Wisber, Peter, 207-209, 339
Wolf, Joyce, 84
Woodard, Dave, 259, 305
Wysocki, Charles, 198-200, 339

Yates, Manuella, 339-340
Yenawine, Peter, 178
Younger, Bill, 192-194, 340

Zendron, Martin, 340

CIB WROTE THE BOOKS

COLLECTIBLES MARKET GUIDE & PRICE INDEX

Novice and experienced collectors alike turn to the pages of this "encyclopedia" of collectibles for the information they need on the fun and fascinating world of collectibles. Arguably the most comprehensive guide to Limited Edition Collectibles, this book features:

- **560 PAGES** of the most authoritative advice and news about the key aspects of collecting

- 200 PAGE **PRICE INDEX** listing over **50,000 values** for secondary market plates, figurines, cottages, ornaments, dolls, graphics, bells and steins

- Complete listing of **COLLECTOR CLUBS**

- **Over 80 feature articles** showcasing top collectible companies

- How to insure your collection

- Directory of collectible manufacturers

- Over 200 artist biographies

- 36 pages of full-color photography

- Glossary of terms and reading suggestions

- Details on collectible museums and tours

DIRECTORY TO SECONDARY MARKET RETAILERS

Here is a comprehensive, up-to-date guide to buying and selling limited edition collectibles that are only available on the secondary market. This fact-filled directory features **150** of today's most respected **secondary market dealers, exchanges and locator services nationwide.**

This handy, paperback directory is filled with "need-to-know" information such as:

- "Specialists" in individual collectible lines and series

- Hours of operation

- Methods of conducting transactions (i.e. buy outright, consignment, etc.)

- Terms and business history

- Fax numbers and "800" phone numbers where available

- Easy-to-use index that helps you find dealers by state or by area of specialization

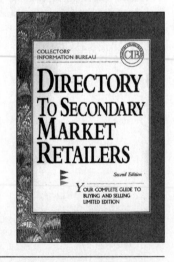

COLLECTIBLES PRICE GUIDE & DIRECTORY TO SECONDARY MARKET DEALERS

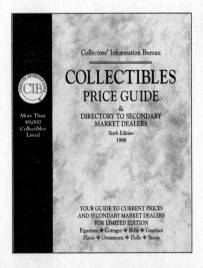

Find out the recent secondary market value of more than 49,000 collectibles in the latest edition of the **COLLECTIBLES PRICE GUIDE**. This book is a "must" for collectors who want to...

- Insure a collection against theft and breakage

- Research the current market value of a piece or collection that you want to buy or sell on the secondary market

- Track the changes in value of your collection for your own enjoyment

- Uncover the history of your collectibles by reading about the...

  ✓ Original Issue Price
  ✓ Issue Date
  ✓ Status (retired, closed, open, etc.)
  ✓ Edition Limit

- Locate dealers who can help you buy and sell on the secondary market

ABOUT LIMITED EDITION COLLECTIBLES

THE CIB COLLECTIBLES REPORT

Read all about the latest news on the ever-changing world of collectibles with The C.I.B. COLLECTIBLES REPORT. This quarterly newsletter keeps you in touch with the fast-paced world of limited edition collectibles.

You'll enjoy page after page of news about...

- **New Product Introductions, some complete with color photography**
- **Collector Club Activities**
- **Artist Signings and Open Houses**
- **Convention News**
- **Feature Columns on the world of collecting**

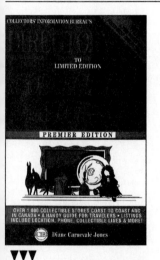

DIRECTORY TO LIMITED EDITION COLLECTIBLE STORES

This directory features over 1,000 collectible stores from coast to coast and in Canada. It's a must for collectors who wish to purchase collectibles by phone, mail or in person. Retailers are listed by state for easy reference, making it an ideal travel companion for collectors. A comprehensive, easy-to-use index lets you find the information you need about individual collectible lines instantly.

COLLECTORS' INFORMATION BUREAU
Publications are filled with information about...

ACE PRODUCT MANAGEMENT GROUP, INC. • ALL GOD'S CHILDREN • AMARATH PRODUCTIONS • AMAZZE GIFTS, INC. • ANHEUSER-BUSCH, INC. • ANNALEE MOBILITEE DOLLS, INC. • ANRI • ARMANI • ASHTON-DRAKE GALLERIES • ATTIC BABIES • AUTOM • BAND CREATIONS • BELLEEK • BING & GRONDAHL • BOYDS COLLECTION LTD. • THE BRADFORD EXCHANGE • BRANDYWINE COLLECTIBLES • BYERS' CHOICE LTD. • CALABAR CREATIONS • CARDEW DESIGN • CAST ART INDUSTRIES • THE CAT'S MEOW • CAVANAGH GROUP INTER-NATIONAL • CHRISTOPHER RADKO • CRYSTAL WORLD • DEPARTMENT 56 • DISNEYANA • DUNCAN ROYALE • EDWIN M. KNOWLES • ENESCO CORPORATION • FENTON ART GLASS COMPANY • FITZ AND FLOYD, INC. • FLAMBRO IMPORTS • FORMA VITRUM • FRANKLIN MINT • FRASER INTERNATIONAL • GANZ • GARTLAN USA • GEO. ZOLTAN LEFTON COMPANY • GEORGETOWN COLLECTION • GLYNDA TURLEY PRINTS • GOEBEL OF NORTH AMERICA • GOEBEL/M.I. HUMMEL • GORHAM • GREEN-WICH WORKSHOP • HALLMARK • HAND & HAMMER • HARBOUR LIGHTS • HARMONY KINGDOM • HAWTHORNE ARCHITECTURAL REGISTER • IMPERIAL GRAPHICS, LTD. • JOHN HINE N.A. LTD. • KIRK STIEFF • KURT S. ADLER, INC. • LADIE AND FRIENDS • LANCE CORP. • LEGENDS • LENOX COLLECTIONS • LIGHTPOST PUBLISHING • LILLIPUT LANE • LLADRÓ • MARGARET FURLONG DESIGNS • MARURI USA • MATTEL • MEDIA ARTS GROUP • MICHAEL'S LIMITED • MIDWEST OF CANNON FALLS • NORMAN ROCKWELL GALLERY • OLD WORLD CHRISTMAS • OLSZEWSKI STUDIOS • PACIFIC RIM IMPORT CORP. • PENDELFIN • POLLAND STUDIOS • POSSIBLE DREAMS • PRECIOUS ART/PANTON • PULASKI FURNITURE, INC. • R.R. CREATIONS, INC. • RECO INTERNATIONAL • REED & BARTON • ROMAN, INC. • RON LEE'S WORLD OF CLOWNS • ROYAL COPENHAGEN • ROYAL DOULTON • SARAH'S ATTIC, INC. • SEYMOUR MANN, INC. • SHELIA'S COLLECT-IBLES • SHUBE'S MANUFACTURING, INC. • SWAROVSKI AMERICA LTD. • THE TUDOR MINT INC. • UNITED DESIGN CORP. • W.S. GEORGE • WACO PRODUCTS CORP. • WALNUT RIDGE COLLECTIBLES • WALT DISNEY • WATERFORD WEDGWOOD USA • WEE FOREST FOLK ...AND MANY MORE!

USE THIS FORM FOR EASY ORDERING!

IN A HURRY? Fax to (847) 842-2205 or Phone (847) 842-2200

Description	Quantity	Price Each	Total
Collectibles Market Guide & Price Index		$23.95	
Collectibles Price Guide		$14.95	
Directory to Secondary Market Retailers		$11.95	
CIB Collectibles Report 1-year Subscription		$15.00	
Directory to Limited Edition Collectible Stores		$14.95	

SHIPPING CHARGES	U.S.	Canada
Up to $14.95	$2.00	$4.00
$15.00 - $22.95	$3.00	$5.00
$23.00 - $61.00	$5.00	$7.00
$62.00 and up	10% of total order	15% of total order

All orders must be prepaid.
Please allow 2 weeks for delivery.

Prices subject to change without notice.

Shipping (see chart at left)	
Handling charge (per order)	$1.00
Illinois residents add 7.75% sales tax Michigan residents add 6% sales tax	
GRAND TOTAL	

Send To:

Name _____
Please print clearly.

Address _____

City _____ State _____ Zip _____

Telephone number (____) _____

❑ My check or money order, payable to the Collectors' Information Bureau, is enclosed.

❑ Please charge my: ❑ VISA ❑ MasterCard ❑ Discover ❑ American Express

Account Number _____

Expiration Date _____

Signature _____

Payable in U.S. funds drawn on U.S. bank.   MG-14

Detach at perforation and mail to: **Order Dept., Collectors' Information Bureau, 5065 Shoreline Road, Suite 200, Barrington, IL 60010.**

NOTES